AMERICAN NATIONAL BIOGRAPHY

AMERICAN NATIONAL BIOGRAPHY

Published under the auspices of the
AMERICAN COUNCIL OF LEARNED SOCIETIES

General Editors

John A. Garraty

Mark C. Carnes

VOLUME 4

OXFORD UNIVERSITY PRESS

New York 1999 Oxford

OXFORD UNIVERSITY PRESS

Oxford New York
Athens Auckland Bangkok Bogotá
Buenos Aires Calcutta Cape Town Chennai
Dar es Salaam Delhi Florence Hong Kong Istanbul
Karachi Kuala Lumpur Madrid Melbourne Mexico City
Mumbai Nairobi Paris São Paulo Singapore
Taipei Tokyo Toronto Warsaw
and associated companies in
Berlin Ibadan

Published by Oxford University Press, Inc.,
198 Madison Avenue, New York, New York 10016
http://www.oup-usa.org

Funding for this publication was provided in part by
the Andrew W. Mellon Foundation, the Rockefeller Foundation,
and the National Endowment for the Humanities,
a federal agency.

Library of Congress Cataloging-in-Publication Data

American national biography / general editors, John A. Garraty, Mark C. Carnes
p. cm.
"Published under the auspices of the American Council of Learned Societies."
Includes bibliographical references and index.
1. United States—Biography—Dictionaries. I. Garraty, John Arthur,
1920– . II. Carnes, Mark C. (Mark Christopher), 1950– .
III. American Council of Learned Societies.
CT213.A68 1998 98-20826 920.073—dc21 CIP
ISBN 0-19-520635-5 (set)
ISBN 0-19-512783-8 (vol. 4)

Printing (last digit): 9 8 7 6 5 4 3 2 1

Printed in the United States of America
on acid-free paper

B

CONTINUED

BURNETT, Alfred (2 Nov. 1824–4 Apr. 1884), entertainer and journalist, was born in Bungay, Suffolk, England. The names of his parents and other facts about his early life are unknown. In 1828 he was sent to live with an aunt in New York City. After four years of schooling in Utica, New York, he moved to Cincinnati, Ohio, in 1836. He later became proprietor of a confectionery business and by 1860 owned three such establishments.

Burnett's success in business gave him the resources and leisure to indulge his interest in the theater. So-called home theatricals or community-based groups, a popular pastime in the United States, may have provided him the opportunity to perfect his skills as a humorist, ventriloquist, and public speaker. In 1845 he traveled with Professor DeBonneville throughout the West in *The Maniac*, then debuted as an actor on the legitimate stage at age twenty-five, playing Hamlet at Wood's Theatre in Cincinnati. In 1850 he joined Enos B. Reed on a European acting tour that had been suggested by Edwin Forrest, one of the preeminent actors of the day.

Burnett also engaged in literary pursuits. He contributed comical verse to local newspapers under the name "Squibs" and in 1847 published a volume titled *Magnetism Made Easy; or, Instructions in Magnetism for the Many*. During the 1850s Burnett tried his hand at two short-lived publishing ventures. He edited a literary magazine called the *Warning Bell* in 1850, and in 1855 he published the *Cincinnati Home Journal*, which billed itself as a "literary, musical, and temperance register." Burnett also wrote the lyrics for several popular songs, including one titled "Mary Vale" (published in 1853, with music by Stewart Macaulay).

At the start of the Civil War, Burnett enlisted in the Sixth Ohio Volunteer Infantry. (He was a longtime opponent of slavery, and in 1843 he had helped protect a fugitive slave from the so-called Scanlon Mob in Cincinnati.) He served in West Virginia and became a correspondent for several Cincinnati newspapers, including the *Cincinnati Commercial*. Some of his reports were collected and published in *Incidents of the War: Humorous, Pathetic and Descriptive* (1863). Burnett rose from the rank of sergeant to captain, serving on the staff of General Granville Moody, the "fighting parson."

After leaving the army in the later years of the war, Burnett returned to the stage. He appeared frequently in New York theaters for nearly two decades, usually as a comic actor or performer in variety shows. According to Dodsworth's *New Theatres and Players* (29 June 1868, p. 368), Burnett performed "humorous entertainment nightly for good, unthinking people." T. Allston Brown's *History of the American Stage* (1870) noted that "as a mimic and ventriloquist, he stands pre-eminent." Often Burnett presented his popular "The Preacher from Hepsidam, a Backwoods Itinerant," with Helen Nash. As was the convention of the day, an evening's bill offered a variety of performers and styles of diversion. Burnett, for example, might deliver a speech or appear with Nash in "Mr. and Mrs. Caudle at Home" or "Our Club; or, The Frolicsome Oyster"; musical acts, carnival-like oddities, and other lecturers or actors performing serious sketches would also appear. Some of Burnett's comical material was published in 1867 as *Alf. Burnett's Comic Faces, Facially Illustrated, Intermingled with Poetic Gems*.

In October 1881 Burnett and F. W. Whittaker assumed management of the Grand Central Theatre for one season. The theater was devoted to "vaudeville entertainments, at cheap prices—making it a first class theatre in all respects," according to the *New York Tribune* (16 Oct. 1881). Burnett continued to perform on the stage himself, and one of his last appearances came in December 1883, only five months before his death.

Although Alfred Burnett's lasting contributions to American theater and journalism were slight, he is a good example of a popular entertainer of the mid- to late nineteenth century. He and performers like him helped expand American theater and its audience at a level below that occupied by the spectacular melodramas of the day, with their simplified plots and famous stars.

• T. Allston Brown, *History of the American Stage* (1870), contains an early citation regarding Burnett. References to his later stage appearances can be found in George C. D. Odell, *Annals of the New York Stage*, vols. 7–12 (1931–1940). A useful secondary source is the sketch of Burnett by Ernest J. Wessen in *Ohio Authors and Their Books, 1796–1950*, ed. William Coyle (1962), pp. 89–90.

KENT NEELY

BURNETT, Charles Henry (28 May 1842–30 Jan. 1902), otologist, was born in Philadelphia, Pennsylvania, the son of Eli Seal Burnett and Hannah Kennedy Mustin. He received his early education in Philadelphia, and in 1860 he entered Yale College, graduating with an A.B. in 1864. While at Yale Burnett was an active participant in undergraduate social and academic organizations.

In 1864 Burnett enrolled in the School of Medicine of the University of Pennsylvania, receiving his M.D. in March 1867. After graduation he was appointed for a one-year term (1867–1868) as resident physician at the Episcopal Hospital. When Burnett completed his residency, he traveled to Europe and spent ten months doing postgraduate studies in Heidelberg, Vienna, and Berlin. He returned to Philadelphia in 1869 and opened a practice in general medicine. After one year his intense desire to become an otologist prompted him to return to Europe to study the functions of the parts of the ear and its diseases.

From 1870 to March 1872 Burnett did research and worked in the laboratories and clinics of three leading physicians who had done important research in the physiology and pathology of the ear. In Vienna he practiced as an otologist in the clinic of Adam Politzer, author of the definitive work on otology of that period. In Berlin he worked in the research laboratories of Rudolph Virchow and Herman von Helmholtz. Virchow was the renowned founder of cellular pathology, an anthropologist and social reformer who augmented Burnett's concepts of the origin, nature, and development of diseases. Helmholtz was a physician, physicist, and physiologist, who applied the principles of physics to biochemistry. In Helmholtz's laboratory in 1871, Burnett conducted important experiments on the physiology of the ear; the results were published in the *Archives of Ophthalmology and Otology* in 1872. Throughout his life Burnett maintained a personal and professional relationship with his European mentors and colleagues.

On his return to Philadelphia in 1872 Burnett decided to confine his practice to diseases and surgery of the ear. He was appointed surgeon and member of the medical board of the Presbyterian Hospital, where he would perform most of his surgeries. He was one of the first surgeons in the United States to perform a mastoid operation. His research efforts and diligence won the recognition of his peers, and he acquired a large and lucrative practice as a surgeon and consulting otologist. From his first article in 1872 until his last, published shortly after his death, Burnett published sixty-six articles and books. His most important works were *The Ear: Its Anatomy, Physiology and Diseases* (1877); *Hearing and How to Keep It* (1879); as editor, *The System of Diseases of the Ear, Nose and Throat* (1893); chapters on otology in Keating's *Encyclopaedia of Diseases of Children* (1889) and in the *American Textbook of Surgery* (1892); and, with E. Fletcher Ingalls and James E. Newcomb, *Textbook of Diseases of the Ear, Nose and Throat* (1901). For many years Burnett edited the section on the progress of otology in the *American Journal of Medical Sciences*.

In 1874 Burnett married Anna Lawrence Davis of Buffalo, New York. They had four children.

On 19 March 1883 Burnett was one of a group of twelve Philadelphia physicians who received a charter to establish the Philadelphia Polyclinic and College for Graduates in Medicine. The institution was created to provide practicing physicians the opportunity to do postgraduate work in medicine and to become medical specialists. A dispensary staffed by the postgraduate students provided free medical service and advice for the poor. Burnett was named professor for diseases of the ear, serving from 1882 until he was named emeritus professor in 1890. At various times in his career in Philadelphia he also served as clinical professor of otology at the Women's Medical College; surgeon at the Presbyterian Hospital; and consulting otologist to the Pennsylvania Institution for the Deaf and Dumb and seven hospitals in the Philadelphia area.

Burnett's desire to test new theories and incorporate the latest surgical and technical developments into the practice of otology, while condemning the rapid acceptance of unproven theories and methods, met with wide approval. Because of his concern for their education, he was held in high esteem by his medical students. He was a fellow of the College of Physicians of Philadelphia; a member of the American Medical Association; a member of the Philadelphia Pathological Society; in 1876, a delegate to the International Medical Congress; president of the American Otological Society, 1884–1885; and a member of the Society of Colonial Wars.

Burnett's long history of poor health and his arduous work schedule was always of concern to his friends. He developed pneumonia and died after a brief illness at his home in Bryn Mawr, Pennsylvania.

• For a biographical sketch and complete list of Burnett's publications, see Francis R. Packard, "Memoirs of Charles Henry Burnett, A.M., M.D., "*Transactions of the College of Physicians of Philadelphia*, 3d ser., 25 (1903): xlvii–1. He is also mentioned by Packard, *History of Medicine in the United States* (1963), pp. 1164–65; W. S. W. Rauschenberger, *An Account of the Institution and Progress of the College of Physicians during a Hundred Years from January 1787* (1887), p. 215; and Burton A. Konkle, *Standard History of the Medical Profession of Philadelphia* (1977).

SAM ALEWITZ

BURNETT, Chester Arthur. *See* Howlin' Wolf.

BURNETT, Frances Hodgson (24 Nov. 1849–29 Oct. 1924), author and playwright, was born Frances Eliza Hodgson at Cheetham Hill, Manchester, England, the daughter of Edwin Hodgson, a shopkeeper and silversmith, and Eliza Boond. After her father's death in 1853, her mother attempted to maintain both his small business and the comfortable middle-class position that the family held, but she finally failed. Frances and her four siblings—she was the third child and first daughter—were soon moved, first to the home of relatives in Seedley Grove and then, in 1855, to Islington Square, a shabbily genteel address deep in industrial Manchester and surrounded on every side by the hovels of impoverished mill workers. Here, where smut rained down from mill smokestacks and pigs rooted in the garbage that lay piled in the streets outside their square, Frances's mother lived in fear of her children's infection not only by the physical diseases of the poor but also by their manner of speech. Some protection against the latter threat was offered by the local dame school, which provided Frances with her only formal education. Finally, however, the school neither quashed her fascination with dialects—which would emerge in her later fiction—nor satisfied her intellectual curiosity. In the slums of Manchester she became the autodidact she would remain, one with a self-sustaining imagination and a marked interest in storytelling.

The economic fortunes of both Manchester and the Hodgsons were soon further devastated by the far-reaching effects of the American Civil War, which threw the city's textile mills into disarray. Eliza Hodgson and her family, however, soon reversed the path of the diminished cotton crop; her brother William Boond had settled prosperously in Tennessee years before, and at his advice the Hodgsons left England for the United States in May 1865. At her new home in New Market, outside of Knoxville, young Frances exulted in the hills and woods of the South; the intense love of nature that she first discovered there would be suggested in the pastoral themes of much of her later work. Although Tennessee provided a welcome change of setting, its postbellum economy did not permit any rapid alleviation of the family's poverty. Frances attempted to help her mother by teaching music and even raising chickens, but she achieved success when she discovered, in an old copybook, a story she had written earlier; she rewrote the piece and sold it to *Godey's Lady's Book* in 1868. At age nineteen she had launched what would be a lifelong literary career.

Burnett would prove herself to be mistress of a variety of genres during her fifty-six years of writing. Her earliest stories, in magazines such as *Godey's* and *Peterson's Ladies' Magazine*, and ultimately in *Scribner's Monthly* and *Harper's*, were popular adult romances. Formulaic and consistently successful, they generally featured a protagonist who, despite an early life characterized by mundane surroundings and hard luck, found both love and an inevitably happy ending. Burnett's own life seemed to be following such a plot when she married Dr. Swan Burnett of Knoxville in 1873; after the couple's first child was born a year later, Burnett accompanied her husband to Paris for a year of medical study. With the birth of a second child in 1876, the Burnetts returned to Tennessee (the writer's life to come would at times seem to be spent crossing the Atlantic).

The return to the United States marked another phase of Burnett's literary career. She had earlier published a number of individual stories of the English working class that, in 1877, were released together as *Surly Tim and Other Stories*; the same year saw the publication of *That Lass o' Lowrie's*, her first full-length novel and great literary success. Both of these works and the novel *Haworth's* (1879) displayed Burnett's mastery of the Lancashire dialect and were largely realistic portrayals of working-class life, not unlike those of Charles Dickens and Charlotte Brontë. Variously described as adult fiction, realist fiction, and even "industrial" fiction, the two novels were written with an eye for critical as well as popular approval and achieved a good measure of each.

Following her husband's medical career, Burnett settled in Washington, D.C., in 1877 and continued to produce popular work. Soon she was ready to make the leap into her final and most enduring fictional genre: children's literature. In *St. Nicholas* magazine she serialized the stories that would become *Little Lord Fauntleroy* (1886), featuring a character based on her son Vivian and surely her most famous individual creation. In this modern Cinderella tale—in some sense an echo of her early adult romances—an American youth inherits an English title and by virtue of his innocent character reconciles his warring relatives. Though roundly mocked by sophisticated critics, it was Burnett's hugest commercial success and assured her of a continuing large income.

In 1887 Burnett attended Queen Victoria's Jubilee in London and renewed her attachment to the country of her birth; for the next twenty-five years she maintained residences in England, and sometimes in Italy, as well as in the United States. She transferred her most recent success to the London stage with an 1889 version of the Fauntleroy story; a decade of playwriting followed, culminating in *The Lady of Quality* (1896), her greatest stage success. During these years she developed a close friendship with her London theatrical manager, Stephen Townesend, even as her distant relationship with her husband deteriorated. In 1898 she divorced Swan Burnett and married Townesend—ten years her junior—two years later in Genoa, Italy. Her fame and the hint of scandal in this series of events attracted the attention of the newspapers, which Burnett attempted to ignore, but in 1902 she was separated from Townesend as well. The realities of married life never quite conformed to her romantic expectations.

In the last quarter century of Burnett's life, she devoted her literary efforts to writing fairy stories for children and long romances of social life for adults. Finally obtaining U.S. citizenship in 1905, she built a home at Plandome, Long Island, in 1909, and lived there for most of her remaining life. There she wrote *The Secret Garden* (1911), which while not particularly praised in its day has proved to be her most enduring work. Richly descriptive and quasimythical in plot, it is Burnett's masterpiece and a classic of children's literature. Inspired by the memory of a rose garden she had planted while leasing "Maytham Hall" in Kent during the 1890s, it also drew on Burnett's lifelong fascination with children and her own youthful experiences of nature in Tennessee. It remains—along with *A Little Princess* (1905) and *The Lost Prince* (1915)—widely read in both England and the United States. Major motion pictures were made of *Little Lord Fauntleroy* in 1921, 1936, and 1980, of *The Secret Garden* in 1993, and of *A Little Princess* in 1939. Tending her own garden while producing her last works, Burnett lived perhaps her happiest years at Plandome until her death there.

Burnett has an undeniable place in any study of the popular literature of the late nineteenth century, and her early realistic novels are minor but representative works of the larger schools of American and British realism. Her masterful rendering of dialect in these pieces more strongly suggest her enduring interest in folk-tale, however, which together with her more generally romantic temperament shaped the children's literature that is her true legacy. Early on she had abandoned any ambition to excel in what she called "the world of actual literature," preferring instead to write stories "in which the most wildly romantic situation is made compatible with perfectly every-day and unromantic people and things" (Burnett, *The Romantick Lady*, pp. 51, 301).

• Princeton University has a large collection of Burnett's professional correspondence in its Scribner Archives. Burnett's memoir, *The One I Knew Best of All: A Memory of the Mind of a Child* (1893; repr. 1980), and her son Vivian Burnett's adulatory *The Romantick Lady (Frances Hodgson Burnett)* (1927) provide interesting, albeit biased, contemporary biographical information. Ann Thwaite, *Waiting for the Party: The Life of Frances Hodgson Burnett 1849–1924* (1974), is an important modern assessment. A thorough critical study is Phyllis Bixler, *Frances Hodgson Burnett* (1984), which contains an extensive selected bibliography of Burnett's fiction, drama, and essays as well as other relevant critical and biographical sources. Francis Molson's article on Burnett in *American Literary Realism* 8 (Winter 1975): 35–41, surveys critical reception of Burnett both during and after her lifetime. An obituary is in the *New York Times*, 30 Oct. 1924.

W. FARRELL O'GORMAN

BURNETT, Leo (21 Oct. 1891–7 June 1971), advertising executive, was born in St. Johns, Michigan, the son of Noble Burnett, a dry goods dealer, and Rose Clark. Leo Burnett got his first exposure to advertising layout and copy by watching his father prepare ads for the local newspaper. His father's connections got Leo his first jobs as a printer's devil at the newspaper and a summer reporter on rural weeklies. After graduating from high school, Burnett served for a time as a rural schoolmaster before graduating from the University of Michigan in 1914. Then he became a police reporter for the *Peoria Journal*. His grand plan at that time was to become the publisher of the *New York Times*. But when a former classmate told him he was making $35 a week in advertising (twice what Burnett was earning), Burnett went to Detroit, where he found a job in the advertising department of the then independent Cadillac Motor Car Company. There he edited the *Cadillac Clearing House*, a company house organ, and later became advertising director. In 1918 he married Naomi Geddes, with whom he had three children.

After a six-month stint in the navy, during which he was stationed at the Great Lakes Naval Station in Chicago in 1918, Burnett joined a group of executives in 1919 who left Cadillac to form the LaFayette Motors Company in Indianapolis, Indiana. He was named advertising manager of the new firm. Shortly thereafter, when LaFayette decided to move its operations to Racine, Wisconsin, Burnett stayed on in Indianapolis, joining Homer McKee Company, a local advertising agency. At Homer McKee, Burnett specialized in automobile advertising, handling the accounts of the Marmon, Stutz, and Peerless companies. Remaining there throughout the 1920s, Burnett seemed to have entered into a safe, comfortable life, one that would bring him moderate success on a local level. As he later noted, he was "very happy there." With his fortieth birthday approaching, however, Burnett began to visualize a larger life for himself in a bigger city. Soon, Erwin, Wasey and Company, a New York ad firm, hired Burnett as creative head for its Chicago office. Burnett spent five successful years in Erwin, Wasey's Chicago office, as vice president and creative head.

Then, in 1935, with eight associates from Erwin, Wasey, Burnett started his own ad firm in Chicago. These were difficult years, but Burnett believed there was a crying need for a truly creative agency in the Chicago area. Launched with meager capital of $50,000, in an "office" that was just a suite in Chicago's Palmer House, with a handful of women's products accounts, Leo Burnett Company, Inc., was successful enough to move to new and larger quarters in the London Guarantee Building a month later. The first year, however, was a struggle: with its largest clients the Hoover Company, Minnesota Valley Canning Company, and Realsilk Hosiery Mills, the firm reported total billing of around $900,000.

For over a decade the Leo Burnett agency muddled along with billings under $10 million. Slowly the firm expanded, taking over floor after floor in the London Guarantee Building. But the real growth came after World War II, with the great burst in postwar prosperity. Billings grew from $10 million in 1946 to $22 million in 1950 and $55 million in 1954. By the mid-fifties, the Burnett agency was becoming a factor to be reckoned with on the national advertising scene. A number of large clients came to the Burnett agency during these years, including Kellogg, Campbell's Soup, and part of Procter and Gamble. The inventiveness of Leo Burnett's advertising was the most important factor in attracting these companies.

The first of the characteristic Leo Burnett advertising touches was his development of the Jolly Green Giant for the Minnesota Valley Canning Company. The campaign exemplified perfectly his principles of advertising and how he used these to create a highly successful agency. Burnett believed that it was the agency's task to find the "inherent drama" in the product itself and then to present it effectively, largely through the use of nonverbal archetypes and symbols. The Jolly Green Giant, one of the most effective symbols in the entire history of advertising, struck a chord in the American public's subconscious and rapidly became part of the national folklore. The tiny Minnesota firm, with just $5 million in sales in 1935, became a giant itself in the years after World War II. Burnett's advertising campaign was so successful that in 1950 the firm changed its name to Green Giant. By the mid-1980s, Green Giant was still a Burnett client, with billings of $50 million a year.

Because of Leo Burnett's success with Green Giant, the Philip Morris Company approached the firm in 1954 to develop a campaign for its Marlboro brand of filter cigarettes. Like other filter cigarettes at the time, Marlboros were marketed as "women's cigarettes," with a delicately designed white package and an ad campaign stressing that they were "Mild as May." Philip Morris wanted to make the cigarette more attractive to men and turned to Burnett to develop this campaign. Leo Burnett himself came up with the winning idea, one that became a classic in American advertising. Deciding to create a "Marlboro Man," Burnett posed the question: "What's the most masculine type of man?" Burnett remembered a dramatic black-and-white photograph of a cowboy on a *Life* magazine cover. Although other occupations were also featured in the first series of ads for Marlboro, the cowboy image soon became dominant. Leo Burnett had captured an image of how Americans liked to think of themselves, encapsulated it in simple pictures of a series of rough-hewn men, and brought Marlboro from a market share of less than 1 percent in 1953 to become the largest-selling cigarette in the world.

Leo Burnett and his agency had found their metiér. Following on the heels of the Marlboro Man and the Jolly Green Giant came Tony the Tiger for Kelloggs' Frosted Flakes, the Pillsbury Doughboy, Charlie the Tuna for Starkist, the phenomenally popular Morris the Cat for 9-Lives, the "lonely" Maytag repairman, and many others. Another highly successful campaign for the Burnett agency was for United Airlines. Applying the same principles that sparked his other campaigns, Burnett added a "human element" to the airline company by talking about the "friendly skies of United" in its campaign. More than twenty years later, "Fly the friendly skies" was still United's theme, and it was recognized by 94 percent of people polled.

As popular as Burnett's ads were with the public, however, they were not universally appreciated by the advertising world, where they were often perceived as corny and unsophisticated. Many in New York felt that much of his work was too similar, too much a "menagerie" of animals. By the 1960s, some felt Burnett and his ads had become an antiquated product of the "Chicago School" of advertising. Stephen Fox, though, in *The Mirror Makers*, summed up Burnett's influence in this manner: "Simplicity, clarity, and peopletalk. Straightforward without being flat-footed. Warm without being mawkish. The lighter the touch, the heavier the wallop."

Leo Burnett was hardly a Hollywood image of an advertising man or the founder of a huge international agency. A short, pear-shaped man, with a perpetually rumpled suit, sloping shoulders, and a comfortable paunch, he had prominent lips, jowly cheeks, and heavy glasses. Further, he had a diffident manner and was almost completely inarticulate, except on paper, where it counted most. As his colleagues in Chicago recognized, Leo Burnett was a simple, hardworking man who created simple, effective advertising. He died at his home in Lake Zurich, Illinois.

• Neither Leo Burnett's personal papers nor his company files were open to researchers as of the early 1990s. Some of Leo Burnett's speeches, memos, and letters are collected in a volume published by the ad firm, *Communications of an Advertising Man* (1961). Some of his letters can also be found in the Fairfax M. Cone Papers, Regenstein Library, University of Chicago, and in the David Ogilvy Papers, Manuscript Division, Library of Congress. Several issues of *Advertising Age* devoted space to Burnett and his agency. The fiftieth anniversary issue (5 Aug. 1985) of *The Burnettwork*, a company organ, has information on the agency's development. Stephen Fox, in *The Mirror Makers: A History of American Advertising and Its Creators* (1984), places Burnett within the creative revolution of the 1950s and 1960s. Obituaries are in *Advertising Age*, 14 June 1971 and 21 June 1971; the *New York Times*, 9 June 1971; and *Time*, 21 June 1971.

JOHN N. INGHAM

BURNETT, Waldo Irving (12 July 1828–1 July 1854), zoologist and physician, was born in Southborough, Massachusetts, the son of Joel Burnett, a physician, and Sarah (maiden name unknown). His early education, obtained at local schools, seems to have been eclectic, and he neither sought nor received a college degree. From his father, who was a skilled physician and a dedicated botanist and entomologist, he acquired an interest and received training in medicine and zoology. In his early boyhood, he embarked on the study of insects and other animals with an intensity that would characterize his life. He was precocious, something of a prodigy, and an autodidact. He developed such ability in mathematics that his teachers were no longer capable of giving him instruction. Almost without assistance he mastered French, Spanish, and German. By the age of sixteen he had dedicated himself to the study of medicine; his decision was stimulated by involvement in his father's professional activities. Equally enthralled by entomology, he collected, studied, and classified insects, demonstrating critical powers of inquiry and observation. A change in the family's finances following his father's death during Burnett's sixteenth year made it necessary for him to begin teaching school as he embarked on the study of medicine. He received his medical education under the direction of Dr. Joseph Sargent of Worcester, Massachusetts, at the Tremont Medical School in Boston and Massachusetts General Hospital and became a skilled microscopist and essayist. For two consecutive years (1847 and 1848) he was awarded the prize for the best essay offered by the Boylston Medical Society. In the first of his prize essays, titled "Cancer," he addressed the subject in terms of microscopic tissue structure, a pioneering insight for the time. His second essay, "The Sexual System," was one of the earliest American contributions to the fields of reproductive biology and embryology. Burnett was awarded the degree of doctor of medicine in 1849 at the age of twenty-one. Shortly thereafter, he embarked for Europe, where he spent four months, mostly in Paris, engaged in microscopic observations and the study of natural history. While in Paris, he discovered that he had tuberculosis, the disease that eventually killed him. Returning to the United States, he became a peripatetic scholar for reasons of health. Based in Boston, he passed the winters in South Carolina, Georgia, or Florida. In spite of his constant travels, he was incessantly occupied with microscopic observations and accomplished an almost incredible amount of intellectual labor.

Burnett became an active member of the Boston Society of Natural History whilst still a medical student. He was elected curator of entomology in 1848, and beginning in 1845 he published extensively. At the close of his short life, he had produced about fifty papers and other scholarly contributions. The quality and diversity of his research and his productivity were soon recognized. In 1851 he was elected to membership in the American Academy of Arts and Sciences. At age twenty-three he was one of the youngest members ever admitted into that body. At about the same time, he became an associate editor of the *American Journal of Science and Arts*. Most of Burnett's publications were concerned with six areas of activity, namely, microscopic anatomy, e.g., kidney, spleen, bioluminescent organs; embryology, e.g., parthenogenesis and the development of viviparous aphids and philosophical speculations; entomology, e.g., insect metamorphosis and hibernation; cytology, e.g., nature of the cell, cell division, the role of the nucleus, and gametogenesis; human pathology, especially changes in microscopic structure of cells and tissues; and critical reviews of recent scientific publications, mostly European. His papers appeared in *Proceedings and Journal of the Boston Society of Natural History*, *Proceedings and Memoirs of the American Academy of Arts and Sciences*, *American Journal of Sciences*, *Boston Medical and Surgical Journal*, *Proceedings of the Boston Society for Medical Improvement*, and the *American Journal of Medical Science*. His major work, "The Cell, Its Physiology, Pathology, and Philosophy, as Deduced from Original Observations: To which Is Added Its History and Criticism," was published in 1853 in the *Transactions of the American Medical Association*. This prize essay, at 187 pages and forty-seven figures, is almost book-length. As the title implies, the work contains both the results of his own original research as well as a synthetic overview of the subject. The topic is discussed under four headings: Cell Genesis, i.e., the origin of cells; Cell Physiology, i.e., normal cell function; Cell Pathology, i.e., the function of diseased cells; and Cell Philosophy, i.e., the relationship between cellular organization and teleology and the cellular basis of neural function, behavior, and the intellect. It is possible that this book had its origins in a course of lectures on microscopic anatomy that he delivered at the Medical College in Augusta, Georgia, in the winter of 1851. Burnett's *The Cell* is of significance because it can be regarded as the first book in English devoted specifically to cells. It is also important in the field of pathology. Burnett's concept that cancerous tissue is derived from normal cell types that have become neoplastic and his approach to pathological anatomy invite a favorable comparison with the views of Rudolf Virchow in his 1858 *Cellular Pathology, as Based upon Physiological and Pathological Histology*. Burnett's last major work was his translation from the German and extensive annotation of Carl Theodor von Siebold's *Anatomy of the Invertebrata*, which appeared in 1854.

Plagued with ill health throughout his life, Burnett died at his boyhood home of Southborough, Massachusetts. He was highly regarded by his contemporaries, and his death was considered by Jeffries Wyman, the Sillimans, James Dana, Louis Agassiz, Asa Gray, and Wolcott Gibbs to be a major setback to the progress of science in the United States.

• An obituary is Jeffries Wyman, "Notice of the Life and Writings of the Late Dr. Waldo Irving Burnett," *American Journal of Science and Arts* 18 (1854): 255–64.

JOHN P. WOURMS

BURNETT, Whit (14 Aug. 1899–22 Apr. 1973), anthologist, editor, and short story writer, was born Whitney Ewing Burnett in Salt Lake City, Utah, the son of Benjamin James Burnett, a contractor, and Anna Marian Christensen. He began his career in 1916 working as a reporter for a newspaper in Salt Lake City. His other early positions included reporter for the *Los Angeles Evening Express* (1918), editor for the Associated Press in Los Angeles (1919–1920) and in San Francisco (1921), copy desk editor for the *New York Times* (1924–1925), and assistant city editor for the Associated Press in New York City (1926–1927). He attended the University of Southern California (1918), the University of Utah (1920), and the University of California (1921). Two of his novelettes, "Smooth" (Aug. 1922) and "Growth" (Feb. 1923), appeared in *Smart Set*, then one of the most coveted markets for young creative writers. According to Martha Foley, Burnett found himself unemployed in Los Angeles and at her suggestion and with a loan from her went to New York City. When she traveled to the East Coast, he intercepted her while she waited for a train in New York City, and they began sharing an apartment. He and Foley then lived in Paris, where Burnett was city editor for the Paris edition of the *New York Herald* (1927–1928). They next moved to Vienna, where Burnett was an organizer for the Balkan news service for the *New York Sun and Consolidated Press* (1929–1931). They married in 1930, and their son was born a year later.

Foley and Burnett had long been troubled by the declining market for good short stories. H. L. Mencken had abandoned his *Smart Set* for the *American Mercury*, where he intended to publish very little fiction. In general, serious magazines were publishing less fiction than formerly. The catalyst that resulted in *Story* came when Burnett's "Two Men Free" was selected for Edward J. O'Brien's *The Best American Short Stories of 1930*. Despite such a literary honor, Foley realized Burnett would still have few places to publish. The two collaborated on *Story*, a magazine devoted entirely to the publication of good short fiction.

Story began on a very limited budget with a first issue of 167 copies (Apr.–May 1931), and its financial condition remained precarious for its first two years, although the *Sunday London Times Literary Supplement* and the *New York Herald Tribune* praised the first issue, and both circulation and submissions rapidly increased. Among the early contributors were Kay Boyle, Conrad Aiken, William Carlos Williams, and Eugene Jolas. By its third issue, work by the previously unpublished James T. Farrell appeared. Farrell was the first of a long list of *Story* discoveries that would eventually include William Saroyan, Richard Wright, and Joseph Heller. After publishing in Europe, Foley and Burnett were invited to New York City by Bennett Cerf and Don Klopfer of Random House and Harry Scherman, president of the Book-of-the-Month Club. By this time, they had lost their jobs in Vienna and were living as freelancers in Majorca, so poor that only the settlement of a long-disputed legacy in the Foley family enabled them to make the trip. On their return to New York, *Story* became an American publication controlled by a corporation of Cerf, Klopfer, Scherman, Foley, and Burnett under the auspices of Random House, with Foley and Burnett as editors.

From its first American issue in April 1933, *Story* was phenomenally successful. Circulation rose until it peaked at nearly 25,000 in 1936. The list of contributors was a dizzyingly impressive roll call of American authors, many of whom, although already established, were glad to publish work unsuited to the slick magazines. In his *The Literary Life and the Hell with It* (1939), Burnett published the following from a grateful William Saroyan, "Much of the credit for the healthy growth in recent years of the American story is due to *Story*. Before *Story*'s appearance in America any honest writer whose form seemed to be the short prose form could not help feeling the futility of writing anything, inasmuch as there was no place to send it" (p. 201). Saroyan's first major publication, "The Daring Young Man on the Flying Trapeze," had appeared in the February 1934 issue of *Story*.

Story began to lose circulation in the late 1930s, dropping to 8,000 by 1940. The November–December issue of 1941 marked the departure of Martha Foley, who had separated from Burnett. Following his divorce, Burnett married Hallie Southgate Abbett in 1942. The couple had two children. With her assistance, he continued to edit the magazine, but publication became irregular. Between 1948 and 1951 it appeared as a book twice a year and then did not appear again until 1960, surviving until 1964. The magazine was revived as a quarterly in the autumn of 1989.

Burnett's career included editorial connections with J. B. Lippincott from 1939 to 1949, E. P. Dutton from 1949 to 1973, and Hawthorn Books from 1953 to 1961. He also taught a course in the short story at Columbia University from 1936 to 1943, Queens College in 1940, and Hunter College from 1957 to 1958. He edited more than thirty anthologies on subjects as varied as philosophy, religion, and personal anecdotes. Yet Burnett's interest in the short story remained paramount. In their foreword to *Story Jubilee* (1965), Whit and Hallie Burnett wrote:

> We are in a period of an enormous variety of tensions, individual, collective and cultural, and many are being released in the short and apposite form of stories. The short story is the perfect medium for the fictional evaluation of our less than serene days and our volatile, changing natures. . . . And . . . in short stories we will see the most effective world-in-miniature dramatizations of the conflicts of our time. (p. xiv)

Burnett died in Norwalk, Connecticut. Because his creative energy was dissipated in his editorial work, he is remembered primarily as a formative influence on American literature, as a crucial force in maintaining the short story as a means of serious literary expression. Although he edited anthologies on numerous subjects, also writing both fiction and essays, he is forever linked to *Story*, a magazine of vital importance to the development of American literature in the third and fourth decades of the twentieth century.

• Additional information concerning Burnett may be found in Martha Foley's papers in the American Heritage Center of the University of Wyoming. The best account of Burnett's early career is found in Martha Foley, *The Story of "Story": A Memoir* (1980). This memoir, left uncompleted at Foley's death, was edited by Jay Neugeboren. Burnett, *The Literary Life and the Hell with It* (1939), is a collection of his informal literary essays from *Story*, one of which, "The First Five Years . . . ," is an early history of the magazine. Several of his stories are collected in *The Maker of Signs: A Variety* (1934). An obituary is in the *New York Times*, 24 Apr. 1973.

DALTON GROSS
MARYJEAN GROSS

BURNETT, W. R. (25 Nov. 1899–25 Apr. 1982), novelist and screenwriter, was born William Riley Burnett in Springfield, Ohio, the son of Theodore Addison Burnett, an aide to the governor, and Emily Upson Colwell Morgan. Burnett attended the Miami Military Institute at Germantown, Ohio, graduating in 1919. That same year he attended Ohio State University for one semester in the School of Journalism. In 1921 Burnett married Marjorie Louise Bartow and worked as a factory shop steward and insurance salesman. The couple had no children. Later that year he became a statistician for Ohio's Department of Industrial Relations. During the next six years he wrote short stories, plays, and novels. Overcoming nervous exhaustion caused by rejection of his work and the monotony of his job, he quit in 1927, moved to Chicago, and began writing full time.

Both attracted to and repulsed by 1920s Chicago, Burnett worked as a hotel desk clerk and wrote about the gangsters and underworld that ruled during the Prohibition era. His first novel, *Little Caesar* (1929), was returned for rewriting by Scribner's. But another publishing house, Dial, accepted it, and it became an immediate bestseller and a Literary Guild selection. Adapted for cinema, it established the tough-guy image portrayed in numerous motion pictures and novels. The movie made Edgar G. Robinson (who starred as Caesar "Rico" Bandello) a star and Burnett one of the best-paid screenwriters and consultants in Hollywood. He went on to help write the screenplays for *The Finger Points* (1931), *Scarface* (1932), *The Beast of the City* (1932), *The Whole Town's Talking* (1935), and *Dr. Socrates* (1935).

Burnett's next novel, *Iron Man* (1930), proved equally successful; it became both a Book-of-the-Month Club selection and a motion picture of the same name by Universal in 1931. A story released that same year, "Dressing Up," won the O. Henry Memorial Award for best short story. In the 1930s Burnett published about one novel a year. The list includes *Saint Johnson* (1930); *The Silver Eagle* (1931); *The Giant Swing* (1932); *Dark Hazard* (1933), another Book-of-the-Month Club selection; *Goodbye to the Past: Scenes from the Life of William Meadows* (1934); *The Goodhues of Sinking Creek* (1934); *King Cole* (1936), which was published in England as *Six Days' Grace* (1937); and *The Dark Command: A Kansas Iliad* (1938). Although his first novels tagged Burnett as a tough-guy writer, only one-third of his work fits this category. In addition to gangster novels, his fiction includes stories about prizefighters and professional sportsmen, an exposé of American politics, Civil War tales, and westerns.

Burnett married a second time, in 1941 to Whitney Forbes Johnstone; they had no children. His next novel, *High Sierra* (1940), signaled a new approach to his earlier gangster novels. This novel depicts an aging gangster, Roy Earle, who after leaving prison confronts a transformation in the traditional values of right and wrong held by society. When he commits his final robbery, he retreats to the mountains of California, where he hides from the police and is eventually killed. Burnett worked with John Huston in 1941 to write the screenplay for *High Sierra*, which starred Humphrey Bogart. The National Board of Review named the film one of the ten best of 1941.

Throughout the 1940s Burnett continued to write novels and screenplays about gangsters and crime, among them *The Quick Brown Fox* (1942), *Nobody Lives Forever* (1943), *Tomorrow's Another Day* (1945), *Romelle* (1946), and *The Asphalt Jungle* (1949). *The Asphalt Jungle* was part of a trilogy, which included *Little Men, Big World* (1951) and *Vanity Row* (1952). In 1950 *The Asphalt Jungle* was adapted for cinema and has since been recognized as a classic. Other screenplays include *This Gun for Hire* (1942), a film that introduced Alan Ladd; *Wake Island* (1943); and *The Great Escape* (1963). The latter two received Academy Award nominations for best screenplay. Despite his success in Hollywood, Burnett claimed that he never wrote novels with movies in mind but that his screenwriting career allowed him to continue doing what he liked best—writing novels. Although he wrote less in his later years, he continued to write short stories and novels. He died in Santa Monica, California, leaving five novels in various stages of completion.

Burnett received the Grand Masters Award in 1980 from the Mystery Writers of America for his contribution to crime writing and the gangster novel. He also received two Writers Guild awards for best screenplay. Burnett achieved popularity both in the United States and in England. All his books have been translated into foreign languages, and *The Asphalt Jungle* has been published in twelve, including Serbo-Croat and Chinese. The influence Burnett had on American culture can be witnessed in the never-ending gangster and crime images that endure in movies and novels. *Little Caesar*, *High Sierra*, and *The Asphalt Jungle* were firsts in dealing with criminals. Because of this, Burnett has been a major influence on others who would try to imitate his style.

• Other Burnett books include *Adobe Walls: A Novel of the Last Apache Rising* (1953); *Pale Moon* (1956); *Bitter Ground* (1958); *Mi Amigo: A Novel of the Southwest* (1959); and *The Cool Man* (1968). *Little Caesar*, *The Asphalt Jungle*, *High Sierra*, and *Vanity Row* were released again in 1984. He wrote and coauthored plays for screen and television, including "The Untouchables" and "Bonanza," and contributed short stories to magazines such as *Esquire*, *Harper's*, *Scribner's*, and *Collier's*. See also David Madden, *Tough Guy Writers of the Thirties* (1968), and the *New York Times*, 29 Apr. 1982, and *Newsweek* and *Time*, both 10 May 1982, for obituaries.

SUSAN GUNTER
ELIZABETH ARCHULETA

BURNETTE, Dorsey (28 Dec. 1932–19 Aug. 1979), country-rock musician, was born in Memphis, Tennessee, the son of Dorsey Burnette, Sr., and Willy May (maiden name unknown). He grew up in the Lauderdale Courts area of the city, a public housing project that from 1948 until 1954 was the home of Gladys, Vernon, and Elvis Presley. Burnette, two years older than Elvis Presley, made friends among an older crowd that included Jesse Lee Denson, who later recorded for the Vik subsidiary of RCA Victor as Lee Denson. Initially, both Burnette and Denson chose boxing as their career. At a 1949 Golden Gloves championship in Memphis, Burnette met Paul Burlison, another would-be fighter. They had a mutual interest in music but did not explore it until 1951, because Burlison went into the army shortly after they met. While Burlison was in the service, Burnette and his younger brother Johnny began working as a musical duet. An appliance store sponsored them on KWDI, West Memphis, in the late 1940s, and they played at basement parties in Lauderdale Courts with Denson and Johnny Black, older brother of Bill Black (later the bass player in Presley's original backup group).

Burnette also worked as a cotton picker, riverboat deckhand, fisherman, carpet layer, and electrician. Then, beginning in 1951, Dorsey and Johnny Burnette and Burlison began playing together, both as a trio and as part of other groups. In 1954 they went to Corinth, Mississippi, to cut their first record, "You're Undecided" / "Go Mule, Go," for the Von label in Booneville.

By late 1955 Dorsey Burnette was working at Crown Electric in Memphis as an apprentice electrician, where Burlison also worked, as a journeyman electrician. Presley had been a delivery boy at the same firm but had quit early in 1955 to join the group Louisiana Hayride. The Burnettes took his example to heart, quit their day jobs as well as their job with Doc

McQueen's western swing band at the Hideaway Club, and formed the Rock 'n' Roll Trio with Burlison.

In March 1956 the trio decided to bypass local record labels, local radio, and local television and go to New York. Johnny Burnette worked in the garment district, and Dorsey Burnette and Burlison worked as electricians. They found out about the Wednesday night auditions for the "Ted Mack Amateur Hour" and were given the fast track onto the show, networked nationally by ABC. They won three straight appearances in April and May 1956, which gained them a slot on the finalists' tour in September. Between the second and third appearances, they were signed to a management contract by bandleader Henry Jerome, who got them a deal with the Coral division of Decca Records.

Signed as the Rock 'n' Roll Trio, the Burnettes and Burlison recorded what is now some of the most critically acclaimed rockabilly music, but they found no chart success during the 1950s. Dorsey Burnette, upset by the new billing of "Johnny Burnette and the Rock 'n' Roll Trio," quit in December 1957. He went back to Memphis, recruited a band, and toured briefly as Dorsey Burnette and the Rock & Roll Trio.

During or after his stint with his own trio, Dorsey recorded a demo session at Sun Records with Fabor Robison (owner of Fabor Records and sometime manager of Johnny Horton and Jim Reeves, among others). "He told me I could go to the 'Louisiana Hayride' or come out to California to do 'Town Hall Party,'" Burnette told Sanford Brokaw. "I had boxed in Shreveport, but I had never been to California, so I decided to come out to L.A."

Burnette relocated to California in 1958. By then the Rock 'n' Roll Trio had disbanded, and Johnny Burnette joined his older brother. They found out where Rick Nelson lived and drove out to his house to pitch him songs. Nelson remembered the Burnettes' recordings and invited them to audition their songs for him. Among the Burnettes' songs Nelson subsequently recorded were "Waitin' in School," "Believe What You Say," "It's Late," and "Just a Little Too Much," all major hits. Their success as songwriters got the Burnettes an Imperial Records contract. While affiliated with Imperial and its publishing arm, Commodore Music, they also wrote songs for other artists on the roster.

In 1959 Burnette pitched "Tall Oak Tree" to Nelson, who turned it down, saying it was too religious. Burnette recorded it himself for Era Records, and it became a big pop hit. He continued to record for Era, but without further success. Herb Newman, the owner of Era Records, sold Burnette's contract and the masters of his last two Era sessions to Dot Records in May 1961. Burnette recorded prolifically for Dot—three singles and an album during a six-month contract—but nothing charted.

The Dot contract witnessed the beginning of a personal and professional downslide for Burnette, probably exacerbated by his brother's death from drowning in 1964. He was affiliated with over a dozen labels between the end of his Dot contract and his death in 1979; the most successful was with Capitol Records between 1972 and 1974. By the time Burnette signed with Capitol, he had decided to record country music. After Capitol, he signed with Tamla-Motown's short-lived country division, Melodyland, then moved to Calliope Records before being signed to Elektra Records.

His first Elektra single had barely hit the market when Burnette died of a heart attack at his home in Canoga Park, California. Delaney Bramlett (of Delaney and Bonnie) organized a benefit concert for Dorsey's widow. Kris Kristofferson, Tanya Tucker, Glen Campbell, and Roger Miller were among those who appeared.

Despite the 376 published compositions, several of which were major pop hits for Rick Nelson, Burnette seems to be chiefly remembered for his work with the Rock 'n' Roll Trio. He was approached shortly before his death by Led Zeppelin and other rock bands, all of which knew him from his work with the Trio. The Rock 'n' Roll Trio had a spectacularly untamed quality that epitomized the rawness and unsophistication of early rock 'n' roll.

• Among the articles that touch on Burnette's career are Helen Bolstad, "Johnny Burnette," *TV Radio Mirror*, June 1961, p. 13; Sanford Brokaw, "Dorsey Burnette: Early Days in Memphis," *Country Song Roundup*, June 1978, p. 4; Dan Nooger, "Tear It Up," *New York Rocker*, Nov. 1979; John Blair and Tom Henneberry, "The Johnny Burnette Trio," *Time Barrier Express*, Apr.–May 1980; Robert Palmer, "Billy Burnette Rekindles Family Magic," *Rolling Stone*, 27 Nov. 1980; and Aaron Fuchs, "Johnny Burnette & the Rock and Roll Trio," *Goldmine*, Sept. 1982.

COLIN ESCOTT

BURNHAM, Clara Louise Root (26 May 1854–20 June 1927), author, was born in Newton, Massachusetts, the daughter of Dr. George Frederick Root, a composer, and Mary Olive Woodman, a musician. Burnham intended to become a musician like her parents. During her early years in Newton and Reading, Massachusetts, and after she moved to Chicago with her parents at the age of nine, Burnham studied all aspects of music, particularly the piano. After attending public and private schools in Chicago, she studied at the Chicago Musical College. Two circumstances interfered with her desire for a musical profession, however. These included her marriage to lawyer Walter Burnham at the age of nineteen and a challenge from her brother Fred. The latter, enthralled by Burnham's absorbing and amusing letters, encouraged her to write her first story. According to Burnham, Fred "shut me into a room with him one day, and opening a very business-like looking knife, declared with a fearful scowl that I should not leave that room alive unless I promised to try faithfully to write a story." Burnham's first efforts did not meet with success; in fact, one critic told her to give up writing if she were already middle-aged. She persevered, however, and finally published a poem in the magazine *Wide Awake*. In the late 1870s Burnham's stories and poems appeared in other magazines, including the *Youth's Companion* and *St. Nicholas*. Occasionally she submitted her work under the pseudonym Edith Douglas.

Burnham published her first novel, *No Gentlemen*, in 1881. *A Sane Lunatic* (1882) quickly followed, then *Dearly Bought* (1884). During her next forty-three years Burnham wrote almost thirty novels. A clear, direct writing style, fluid narrative, vivid descriptions of natural surroundings, clever plot structures, well-developed characters, realistic dialogue, and frequent infusions of humor characterized her uplifting romance novels. Many were set in New England, where Burnham had spent her early childhood and her summers.

In 1900 Burnham's husband Walter died, leaving her a childless widow, and her health began to deteriorate. At that point she turned to Christian Science and found solace and healing. In her book *A View of Christian Science* (1912), Burnham described her early antagonism toward the religion, how she overcame it, and how through Christian Science, "One after another of the conditions which hampered my life slipped away." Beginning with *The Right Princess* (1902), all of Burnham's novels had a Christian Science agenda. *Jewel* (1903), which she later proclaimed to be her favorite, was dominated by Christian Science doctrine and accounts of her characters' conversions. Her subsequent romance novels were not so doctrinaire but still stressed thinking and acting "right." Interestingly enough, the Christian Science messages were so cleverly woven into the fabric of her stories that old readers remained faithful to Burnham's work, while new readers became attracted to it. Burnham's narrative style continued to be absorbing, amusing, and uplifting.

In addition to her writing, Burnham led an active, engaging life. Working on her novels only three hours per day, she also wrote librettos for her father's cantatas and operettas and maintained her skill as a pianist. Described as a vivacious and engaging conversationalist, Burnham enjoyed her social contacts and activities in Chicago, her summers in the family bungalow, "The Mooring," on Bailey Island in Casco Bay, Maine, and her travels to various parts of the United States. With Robert A. Dempster, Burnham dramatized her novel *The Right Princess* and produced it as *The Moon Calf* in 1912. She also sold the motion picture rights to her last romance novel, *The Lavarons* (1925). Burnham's very last novel, *Tobey's First Case* (1926), marked her first attempt to write a mystery. For someone who had begun life assuming she would be a musician, Burnham strayed far afield—much to the benefit of her adoring readers. Burnham died at her summer home in Maine.

• Biographical sketches of Clara Louise Burnham appear in various sources. For example, Lydia Avery Coonley wrote one in *The Writer* (Sept. 1895). Grant Overton devoted a chapter to Burnham in *The Women Who Make Our Novels* (1918). Other references occur in Frances E. Willard and Mary A. Livermore, eds., *American Women* (1897; repr. 1973); *The National Cyclopaedia of American Biography* (1931), a substantial account, which includes a full-page picture of Clara Louise Burnham; and Lina Mainiero, ed., *American Women Writers* (1979). Obituaries are in the *New York Times*, *Boston Transcript*, and *Boston Herald*, 22 June 1927.

DOROTHY MCLEOD MACINERNEY

BURNHAM, Daniel Hudson (4 Sept. 1846–1 June 1912), architect and urban planner, was born in Henderson, New York, the son of Edwin Burnham, a wholesale drug merchant, and Elizabeth Keith Weeks. In 1855 the Burnham family moved to Chicago, where Burnham's father achieved significant commercial success and served as president of the Chicago Mercantile Association. Daniel Burnham was sent back east in 1863 after high school in Chicago, where he had excelled at drawing but not at academic work. For several years he studied to prepare for Harvard or Yale, but suffering from what he later termed "stage fright," he failed the college entrance examinations. Burnham returned to Chicago in 1867, worked for four months as a sales clerk, tried a stint as a draftsman apprentice in the office of the noted Chicago architect William LeBaron Jenney, and then headed to Nevada, where he engaged in prospecting and unsuccessfully ran for political office in 1869. He returned to Chicago in 1870 to resume a career in architecture. While working for Peter B. Wight in one of several architectural firms with which he was associated after his return, Burnham met a fellow draftsman, John Wellborn Root, and together they established their own office in 1873.

The firm of Burnham and Root started modestly but quickly flourished with the opportunities for reconstruction and expansion created by the devastating Chicago fire of 1871 and the growing economic dynamism of the city. Their first major commission was a house for John B. Sherman, the manager of the stockyards. The Sherman commission led both to recognition of the firm by Chicago's business and social elite and to Burnham's marriage to Sherman's daughter, Margaret, with whom he had five children. Burnham proved an effective administrator of the firm and was successful in securing and maintaining client relationships, while Root was the firm's principal designer. Their designs, however, were collaborations with Burnham taking the lead in laying out the plan and Root taking the lead in designing the exterior. The products of the firm were wide-ranging, including houses, churches, hospitals, railroad stations, office buildings, and ceremonial structures. Burnham and Root achieved greatest renown for highrise buildings, which were precursors to the skyscrapers that have come to dominate urban business districts since the last two decades of the nineteenth century.

Three highrises built by the firm in Chicago are considered prototypes of the modern skyscraper. The Montauk Block (1882), since demolished, embodied the emphasis on function at the core of what became the modernist movement in architecture. The developer, Peter Brooks, in instructions for Burnham and Root directed: "The building throughout is to be for use and not for ornament. Its beauty will be in its all-adaptation to its use" (Hines, p. 52). The rigorous austerity of the Montauk Block, which integrated form and function, prompted the architectural historian Thomas Tallmadge to conclude in his architectural history, *Architecture in Old Chicago* (1941), that "what Chartres was to the Gothic Cathedral the Montauk Block was to the high commercial building" (p. 142). The Rookery (1888), while designed by Root with a more elaborate Romanesque exterior detail, evidenced Burnham's rigorous planning in a scheme of four wings surrounding a central light well. Modernist design and skillful planning to maximize the availability of light for the newly emergent class of white-collar workers who would occupy the highrise structures were demonstrated again in the undulating bay windows of the severe facade created for the Monadnock Building (1892). Chicago architect Louis Sullivan, in his memoir *The Autobiography of an Idea* (1924), characterized the sixteen-story structure as "an amazing cliff of brickwork, rising sheer and stark, with a subtlety of line and surface, a direct singleness of purpose, that gave one the thrill of romance" (p. 309).

Burnham was active in professional organizations and as a booster of Chicago. Concerned that the American Institute of Architects was insufficiently responsive to the interests of architects practicing outside the East Coast, he was instrumental in the creation of the Western Association of Architects in 1884. The World's Columbian Exposition was organized to celebrate the 400th anniversary of the discovery of America. Congress determined (after intensive competition among several cities) that the exposition would be held in Chicago, providing a further means to demonstrate the growth, vitality, and vision of Chicago and the maturity of its architectural aesthetic. Working with the landscape architect Frederick Law Olmstead, Sr., Burnham and Root became deeply involved in the project; in 1890 Burnham was designated chief of construction for the Exposition, and Root was designated consulting architect. Root, however, died prematurely in 1891. Burnham labored on to make the exposition a national enterprise, securing the effective involvement not only of Chicago architects such as Adler and Sullivan, Burling and Whitehouse, Jenney and Mundie, Henry Ives Cobb, and Solon S. Beman but also of Richard Morris Hunt; McKim, Mead, and White; and George B. Post of New York; Peabody and Stearns of Boston; and Van Brunt and Howe of Kansas City to design the several buildings.

In consultation with the collaborating architects involved, Burnham presided over a program in which the design of the buildings for the exposition was neoclassical in style with a beaux-arts regularity of plan and detail. The architects also sought to bring the arts of sculpture and painting into the planning of the exposition. To that end Burnham designated the sculptor Augustus Saint-Gaudens as arts consultant. After one planning meeting an exuberant Saint-Gaudens took Burnham aside and said, "Look here, old fellow, do you realize that this is the greatest meeting of artists since the fifteenth century!" (Moore, vol. 1, p. 47).

By force of personality, attention to detail, and diplomatic ability to administer the diverse colleagues and interests smoothly and efficiently, Burnham delivered the Columbian Exposition buildings and grounds with great success. The exhibition grounds were known as the "White City," reflecting the dreamlike uniformity of coloration. The integration of architecture with other arts in the Columbian Exposition became the apotheosis of what was termed the American Renaissance. Henry Adams, visiting the exposition, speculated in his *Autobiography* (1905) that "Chicago was the first expression of American thought as a unity" (p. 343) and expressed the hope that in the future Americans "would some day talk about Hunt and Richardson, La Farge and St. Gaudens, Burnham and McKim, and Stanford White when their politicians and millionaires were otherwise forgotten" (p. 341). As years passed, however, the Columbian Exposition and the American Renaissance it embodied and expressed came to be viewed as a passing moment of cultural consensus when a shared sense of developing neoclassical tradition had captured the nation's sensibilities. That consensus would break down in the face of conflicting social, economic, and aesthetic trends ascendant following World War I. One of the participating architects, Louis Sullivan, even published a vigorous attack in his 1924 *The Autobiography of an Idea* asserting that the exposition had set American architecture back fifty years with a retrograde emphasis on an antique revival.

The immediate success of the Columbian Exposition, however, brought Burnham substantial national recognition, including honorary degrees in 1894 from Harvard and Yale, whose entrance exams he had failed, and election in 1893 and 1894 to the presidency of the American Institute of Architects. Meanwhile, devastated by the loss of his partner Root during the planning stages of the exposition, Burnham faced the need to reconstitute his architectural practice. He continued a practice in commercial buildings as D. H. Burnham and Company, where he was joined by his sons Hubert and Daniel, Jr., and such other talented younger professionals as Charles Atwood, Frederick P. Dinkelberg, and Ernest Graham, thereby extending his influence directly to the next generation of Chicago-trained architects. The firm's buildings marked the transition from the final flowering of what Ada Louise Huxtable in *The Tall Building Reconsidered* (1992) identified as the "First Skyscraper Age" of functional highrise buildings exemplified by structures such as the Reliance Building in Chicago (1894) designed by Burnham and Atwood. Commenced before the Columbian Exposition, the Reliance Building employed as a substitute for elaborate ornamentation the generous use of glass and skillful window construction permitted by manipulating a steel frame. By contrast, the firm's Flatiron Building in New York (1902), for which Dinkelberg was chief designer, reflected Huxtable's "Second Skyscraper Age" of eclectic high-rise design with Gothic and Renaissance detailing in the beaux-arts style the Columbian Exposition had popularized.

After the exposition Burnham's professional focus increasingly emphasized public work and city planning. In 1901 he became chairman of the McMillan Commission, which was established by Congress on a resolution offered by Senator James McMillan of Michigan and was directed to develop a plan for the development of Washington, D.C. The commission initially consisted of Burnham and Frederick Law Olmstead, Jr., whose father had worked closely with Burnham on the Columbian Exposition. Burnham and Olmstead in turn arranged appointment of Charles McKim and Augustus Saint-Gaudens as commissioners; both men had worked with Burnham in creating the Columbian Exposition.

The commission undertook a study of the European capitals that had provided inspiration for the original plan for Washington, D.C., drawn by the French engineer Pierre Charles L'Enfant. The commission's proposals in 1902 were designed to enhance the L'Enfant plan by restoring clear vistas to the Mall, which had become cluttered as the nineteenth century progressed, and extending the Mall beyond the Washington Monument to the Potomac River. The plan also proposed completing the L'Enfant vistas with architectural compositions. In implementing the McMillan Commission's plan, Burnham was able to coordinate a private engagement he had received from the Pennsylvania Railroad to design a new station in Washington, D.C. The railroad agreed to move the location for the new Union Station from the Mall to a new site north of the U.S. Capitol. This move cleared the Mall of a discordant structure and created a new vista from the Capitol building to the confluence of several of L'Enfant's radiating grand avenues, where Burnham's massive neoclassical Union Station (1907) provided an impressive gateway to the nation's capital city.

Following his service on the McMillan Commission, Burnham continued his work as a city planner and became a principal exponent of the "City Beautiful Movement." He crafted plans for Cleveland (1903) and San Francisco (1905). On the appointment of the then secretary of war, William Howard Taft, he prepared a city plan for Manila and a summer capitol at Baguio (1905) in the newly acquired American possessions in the Philippines. Ultimately, Burnham developed an elaborate plan for the city of Chicago (1909), which led to an ambitious program of parks and thoroughfares by the city. Burnham's bold visions were the crystallization of his ambitious credo: "Make no little plans; they have no magic to stir men's blood and probably themselves will not be realized. Make big plans; aim high in hope and work, remembering that a noble, logical diagram once recorded will never die, but long after we are gone will be a living thing, asserting itself with ever-growing insistency" (Hines, p. xxiii, n. 8).

Burnham demonstrated the durability of broadly conceived plans in the selection of site and architect for the Lincoln Memorial in Washington, D.C. In 1910 President William Howard Taft appointed Burnham chairman of the National Commission of Fine Arts, which was created to give advice to the federal government on artistic issues. With Burnham's leadership, the Commission of Fine Arts skillfully undertook to encourage the Lincoln Memorial Commission to locate the memorial at the end of the Mall as envisioned by the McMillan Commission plan and to appoint Henry Bacon, who had executed the designs of McKim, Mead and White at the Chicago Exposition, as the architect.

Burnham fused the entrepreneurial success of an architect skilled in satisfying wealthy clients with a personal commitment to contribute his services generously to his community, his profession, and the arts in general. He undertook his public planning exercises without compensation. He sought to bring sculptors and painters into the process of shaping and realizing the projects with which he was involved. As an outgrowth of the Columbian Exposition, Burnham joined Charles McKim, Augustus Saint-Gaudens, and the painters Edwin Blashfield and Francis Millet in organizing the American School for Architecture in Rome, ultimately known as the American Academy in Rome, to provide developing American architects opportunities to study classical and neoclassical architecture in Europe in the company of painters and sculptors. Burnham died in Germany in 1912 while on his seventh tour to Europe.

• Burnham's papers are in the Chicago Art Institute Library. Thomas S. Hines, *Burnham of Chicago: Architect and Planner*, 2d ed. (1979), is an excellent biography that contains an extensive appendix discussing sources of material about Burnham and his work. An earlier two-volume biography was written by a member of his staff and later a successor as chairman of the Commission of Fine Arts, Charles Moore, *Daniel H. Burnham: Architect, Planner of Cities* (1921). Burnham's position in the evolution of Chicago's architecture and city planning is placed in larger context by Daniel Bluestone, *Constructing Chicago* (1991). The seminal role of buildings by Burnham and Root in the development of the highrise building is discussed by Paul Goldberger, *The Skyscraper* (1981). Burnham's approach to city planning is discussed in Thomas S. Hines, "The Imperial Mall: The City Beautiful Movement and the Washington Plan of 1901–1902," in *The Mall in Washington, 1791–1991*, ed. Richard Longstreth (1991), and in Joan Draper, "Paris by the Lake: Sources of Burnham's Plan of Chicago" in *Chicago Architecture: 1877–1922*, ed. Joan Zukowsky (1987).

DOUGLAS P. WOODLOCK

BURNHAM, Frederick Russell (11 May 1861–1 Sept. 1947), explorer, scout, and miner, was born in Tivoli, Minnesota, the son of Reverend Otway Burnham, a Congregational minister and missionary, and Rebecca Russell. One family story has it that his mother left him among corn stalks for an entire day while their settlement was under an Indian attack during the 1862 war with the Sioux. Certainly not proven, this story has an interesting ring to it, since Burnham was to spend much of his life hiding or escaping from American Indians or South African peoples during his career as a scout.

In 1871 the Burnham family moved to Los Angeles, California, after Burnham's father suffered a lung injury. Two years later the senior Burnham died, and Frederick Burnham made the first of a number of fateful decisions; he chose to remain in California rather than return with his mother and brother to the Midwest. He worked as a mounted messenger for the Western Union company at the age of thirteen. Later he underwent two rigorous apprenticeships in scouting from two men who were veterans of the Indian campaigns of General George Crook. Thus, by his early twenties, Burnham knew and understood frontier life better than many persons twice his age. He served as a civilian scout in Arizona, struck gold himself on Christmas Day 1883, and returned to the Midwest, where he married Blanche Blick of Clinton, Iowa, in 1884. The couple had two children during the course of a long and fruitful partnership. Although the Burnhams bought an orange grove and homestead in Pasadena, California, they were destined to be wanderers rather than settlers.

Africa held a permanent fascination for Burnham. In 1893 he, his wife, and their child Roderick left California, made their way north to Vancouver, traversed Canada, and then left the East Coast for England and France before they shipped to Durban, Natal, in present-day South Africa. Entranced by the colorful career of Cecil Rhodes, Burnham and his family went north from Durban into Mashonaland (in modern Zimbabwe). They arrived at the outpost of the British South Africa company to find that war had broken out between Lobengula, the king of the Matabele, and the British traders and miners. Originally, Burnham intended to stay out of the affair, but he joined the British (14 Aug. 1893) after being offered 6,000 acres of land in return. As the British proceeded to win the fighting, Burnham and two companions held the distinction of being the first white persons to enter Bulawayo, the capital of the Matabele people. The Burnhams' second child, Nada, was probably the first white child born in that city.

Burnham turned to mining in Rhodesia, as the area soon came to be called. Members of his wife's family came from the United States and joined them in Bulawayo. After a trip to London in 1895–1896, the Burnhams returned and became embroiled in what was called the Matabele rebellion. Burnham scouted effectively, and when the rebellion was over, the Burnham family returned to America. They again went back to Africa in 1898 but soon after left to participate in the Alaskan gold rush. Burnham built a family home in Skagway, Alaska, but then Field Marshal Frederick Lord Roberts asked him to serve as chief of scouts for the British army in the Boer War. Burnham agreed and left at once for Africa.

Burnham's participation in the war has become the stuff of legend for scouts. He floated down a river concealed in an oxhide, operated behind Boer lines, and was captured by the Boers twice, escaping both times. After suffering a wound, he was invalided to England in June 1900. He received the rank of major in the British army and was honored by Queen Victoria; he was awarded both the distinguished service order and the South African medal. He returned to Africa in 1901 and explored the Volta River in West Africa.

Burnham and his family returned to the United States in 1904. He entered the employ of the Guggenheim syndicate, directed an American colony in Mexico (1908–1914), and meddled to some extent in that country's revolution in 1911. When the Burnhams returned to the United States in 1914, they had exhausted their financial resources. In 1918 Burnham was prepared to enter the intended "Roosevelt brigade" but was disappointed when the mobilization did not take place. Before U.S. entry into World War I, he worked with pro-British groups in the United States and sought to mobilize support for the Allied cause.

Burnham found oil in Dominguez Hills, California, after World War I, land over which he had herded cattle some fifty years earlier. He was able to retire to a life of wealth, and he and his wife were prominent citizens of southern California during the 1930s. He died in Santa Barbara. In 1952 the U.S. Department of the Interior named an 8,853-foot peak in the mountains east of Pasadena for the intrepid explorer and scout.

Burnham led a remarkable life and career. Always on the move, usually on the frontier (whether in North America or South Africa), he embodied to many persons the frontier spirit of Americans in the late nineteenth century. His friendship with leading British imperialists such as Cecil Rhodes was noteworthy; they appear to have regarded him as virtually one of a kind. In his devotion to family life (he brought his wife and children with him on almost all of his travels) he was nearly unique among the scouts of his day. Throughout his life and career ran a distinct thread of Victorian romanticism. Though raised on the American frontier, he took readily to the ideas and visions of British imperialists. It is possible that in Frederick Russell Burnham, Cecil Rhodes found the closest that he ever came to his vision of a British-American union of peoples that he believed would dominate the globe. For his own part, Burnham appears to have embraced travel, adventure, and warfare as means toward the fulfillment of his own beliefs in a world that would combine American adventure, British order, and a new socialism (he was at one time a follower of Edward Bellamy).

• Burnham's papers are in the Sterling Library of Yale University. He wrote two autobiographies, *Scouting on Two Continents* (1926) and *Taking Chances* (1944). Many of his letters are published in *An American Family on the African Frontier: The Burnham Family Letters, 1893–1896*, ed. Mary Bradford and Richard Bradford (1993). See also James E. West and Peter O. Lamb, *He-Who-Sees-in-the-Dark: The Boys' Story of Frederick Burnham, the American Scout* (1932); R. R. Money,

"The Greatest Scout," *Blackwoods Magazine*, Jan. 1963, pp. 42–52; and Byron Farwell, "Taking Sides in the Boer War," *American Heritage* 27, no. 3 (Apr. 1976): 20–25, 92–97.

SAMUEL WILLARD CROMPTON

BURNHAM, James (22 Nov. 1905–28 July 1987), political writer and editor, was born in Chicago, Illinois, the son of Claude George Burnham and Mary May Gillis. Burnham's father was vice president of the Burlington Railroad and provided his son with a comfortable home life and excellent educational opportunities. Burnham entered Princeton University in 1923 and graduated in 1927 with a bachelor's degree in philosophy. In his senior year he was named the "first scholar" of his class. From there he went to Oxford University in England, earning his M.A. in philosophy at Balliol in 1929. In 1930 he returned to the United States and accepted a teaching position at the Washington Square College of New York University. He taught philosophy there until 1954. In 1935 Burnham married Marcia Lightner; they had three children.

Despite Burnham's middle-class upbringing, by the early 1930s his thinking moved leftward. During an automobile tour of the Midwest in 1932 he saw the poverty and suffering of the Great Depression. He also read the writings of Leon Trotsky and Karl Marx and became convinced that capitalism was ending and must be replaced with a socialist society. By 1935 he had joined the Trotskyite Fourth International party, becoming co-editor of its organ the *New International*. He stayed in near-constant contact with Trotsky by telegram and wrote for militant intellectual journals, such as *Partisan Review*. Throughout the 1930s Burnham was a member in good standing of New York City's radical intelligentsia.

By 1940, however, Burnham began to have another change of heart. He was angered by the Nazi-Soviet pact of 1939 and the accompanying Soviet invasion of Poland. Burnham believed that the Union of Soviet Socialist Republics (USSR) had come to be dominated by a totalitarian dictator, Joseph Stalin, and by a cadre of faceless bureaucrats. He differed strongly with Trotsky's view that the country remained at root a "workers' state." He was further disillusioned when, in reply to his protests against this party stance, he was personally attacked by Trotsky and other party members. Burnham began to see Trotskyites and all Marxists as totalitarian. "I am a little tired, I confess," Burnham wrote, "of the habit of settling accounts with opponents and critics . . . by smug references to 'rationalizations' and the 'pressure of alien classes and influences.'" He formally resigned from the party in March 1940.

Burnham remained prominent on the intellectual scene. In 1941 he authored a response to Trotskyism in what was to be one of his most important books. Titled *The Managerial Revolution*, it argued that, instead of the working class, the most powerful influence on the world was a "new class" of managers, bureaucrats, and technicians. Managers were the engines of government, finance, and heavy industry, and the most powerful nation-states harnessed these managers in their service. Adolf Hitler's Germany had very effectively mastered this new social force, and Burnham gloomily predicted that Germany likely would emerge victorious in the Second World War. Burnham's prediction did not prove accurate, but most social scientists believe that his diagnosis of a "managerial revolution" was original and prescient.

After World War II Burnham's interests turned increasingly to foreign affairs. He became convinced that Stalin's Soviet Union was an aggressive, expansionist power threatening the existence of the West. Burnham was now an anti-Communist. As early as 1944 he wrote a lengthy internal memorandum for the Office of Strategic Services, outlining his view of the coming postwar threat from the Soviet Union. Between 1947 and 1953 he expanded on this conclusion and wrote three powerful books urging that the United States take action against international Communism: *The Struggle for the World* (1947), *The Coming Defeat of Communism* (1950), and *Containment or Liberation?* (1953). In all of these Burnham argued that "what the Soviets want is the world," and he called for a U.S. offensive against Communism. "The summons is for nothing less than the leadership of the world, for that or nothing," Burnham wrote. "If it is reasonable to expect failure, that is only a measure of how great the triumph could be." Burnham was an activist for his cause. He lectured at the National War College, joined numerous anti-Communist organizations, testified before the House Un-American Activities Committee, and consulted with the Central Intelligence Agency (CIA). His writings gained notice in diplomatic and governmental circles, and they are credited by most historians of the period with helping to move U.S. policy toward the doctrine of "containment" of Soviet Communism, despite the fact that by the early 1950s Burnham believed that containing the Soviet Union was no longer sufficient.

By the mid-1950s Burnham had moved decisively to the right. He castigated liberals as "mistaken in their predictions, false in their analyses, wrong in their advice, and through the results of their actions injurious to the interests of the nation." He labeled the containment policy as "simply the bureaucratic verbalization of a policy of drift." He refused to publicly denounce the activities of Senator Joseph McCarthy and supported the idea that Communists had penetrated the federal government. In 1955 he became a senior editor for the new magazine of William F. Buckley, Jr., the *National Review*, which became the nation's first and most important journal of conservative opinion and ideas.

Burnham spent the rest of his career at the *National Review* and was one of the most important members of the circle of intellectuals associated with it. For nearly every issue of the magazine, he wrote a column, "The Third World War," on the progress of the Cold War. He continued to urge stronger U.S. measures against the Soviets. "Whether [the Soviets] are strong or weak, we are bound to lose in the end if we refuse to try to win," said a typical Burnham piece. Even more important, he became a close friend and mentor to Buckley, the magazine's editor in chief. "I value [our relationship] second to none with any other man," Buckley once told him. Burnham urged Buckley to move the *National Review* away from extremism and the "radical right" so that it might be explicitly conservative yet also pragmatic and relevant. Thus Burnham campaigned vigorously for the *National Review* to repudiate the John Birch Society, told conservatives that Medicare was an important and necessary governmental initiative, and gave reluctant support to the Panama Canal Treaty. "I am, you might say, *National Review*'s left wing," Burnham once told a friend. In almost all of these cases, Buckley took Burnham's advice, and as the years passed Buckley unmistakably guided the *National Review* in a direction that Burnham approved. Burnham was an important influence on the magazine.

Burnham continued to write books. In 1964 he wrote *Suicide of the West*, which was perhaps his most important book and his most popular work among contemporary conservatives. In it Burnham argued that the West was in decline and that liberalism accompanied, justified, and provided a verbal rationalization for it. Liberalism justified ruinous welfare policies and seemed to give its blessing to Western withdrawal from the Third World and to retreat versus Communism. Only by removing liberalism from the circles of power could the West begin to reverse its fall. Burnham applied this model within much of his commentary on the Cold War for the rest of his career, using it especially in his analysis of the U.S. defeat in Vietnam.

Burnham was forced to retire from the *National Review* in 1978 after suffering a debilitating stroke. In 1983, in recognition of Burnham's many years of service to the conservative and anti-Communist cause, President Ronald Reagan awarded him the Presidential Medal of Freedom. Burnham died in Kent, Connecticut. He is remembered as a penetrating analyst of social trends, a fervent anti-Communist, and a crucial figure in the growth of postwar American conservatism.

• The most important primary sources for a study of Burnham are the William F. Buckley, Jr., Papers at Yale University and the James Burnham Collection in the archives of the Hoover Institution on War, Revolution, and Peace at Stanford University. See also Burnham's "The Third World War" columns in nearly every issue of the *National Review* from 1955 through 1978. The best secondary literature on Burnham includes John P. Diggins, *Up from Communism: Conservative Odysseys in American Intellectual History* (1975); Samuel T. Francis, *Power and History: The Political Thought of James Burnham* (1984); George Nash, *The Conservative Intellectual Movement in America since 1945* (1976); and Kevin J. Smant, *How Great the Triumph: James Burnham, Anticommunism, and the Conservative Movement* (1992).

KEVIN SMANT

BURNHAM, Sherburne Wesley (12 Dec. 1838–11 Mar. 1921), astronomer, was born in Thetford, Vermont, the son of Roswell O. Burnham and Miranda Foote, farmers. He attended the local Thetford Academy, graduated in 1857, and taught himself shorthand and stenography. The following year he went to New York and began working as a secretary with a publishing firm. In 1861, soon after the Civil War broke out, Burnham got a job as a civilian court reporter in the army court martial, which dealt with civilians in occupied New Orleans. After the war ended he moved to Chicago, where by 1867 he and two friends succeeded in getting the contract for recording trials in the Chicago and Cook County courts. In 1868 Burnham married Mary Cleland; they had six children who survived to adulthood.

Burnham had become interested in astronomy at the Thetford Academy through reading *The Geography of the Heavens* by Elijah H. Burritt. On a business trip to London in 1861 he bought his first telescope, a small terrestrial spyglass mounted on a tripod. He soon decided he needed a better instrument and acquired a professional-quality four-inch refractor made by Henry Fitz, the best early American telescope maker. Burnham probably bought this from a Union soldier who had "liberated" it from a Louisiana plantation, academy, or college. In Chicago after the war he quickly became a dedicated observer. Almost immediately he started observing double stars, which became his sole interest in astronomy. In 1869 he ordered a six-inch visual refractor that would "do on double stars all that it was possible for any instrument of that aperture to do" from Alvan Clark & Sons, the great telescope makers. Burnham built a small wooden shelter for it in the back yard of his home, where he observed by night after working in the courthouse all day. In 1873 he sent his first list of newly discovered double stars to the Royal Astronomical Society in London, which published it. Within two years he had published five papers reporting a total of three hundred new doubles. His success was based not only on his excellent telescope but also on his very keen eyesight, powers of concentration, tremendous drive, self-confidence, and stenographic skill and experience, necessary for recording measurements and drawing up lists of stars.

In libraries in Chicago and in eastern cities and colleges on his vacations, Burnham compiled a manuscript catalog from observatory publications, in which he intended to include all "good published measurements of double stars." By 1873 he was in correspondence with Simon Newcomb and Edward S. Holden at the Naval Observatory. Newcomb, the most famous American astronomer of the time, was the chief adviser of the James Lick Trust, charged in 1876 with building "a telescope second to none" at a western mountaintop observatory. He and Holden, his assistant, recommended that Burnham test the Mount Hamilton, California, site that Lick himself had chosen for the observatory before his death. In 1879 Burnham brought his six-inch telescope there and observed with it nearly every night from the end of August until mid-October. He pronounced Mount Hamilton excellent, and Lick Observatory was built there.

Back in Chicago, Burnham continued observing with the 18½-inch Clark refractor of Dearborn Observatory, close to the Lake Michigan shore near his home. He made many more double-star discoveries and measurements there, as he did as a guest observer on short visits to Dartmouth, Rochester, and the Naval Observatory. In 1881 Holden became director of the recently built Washburn Observatory of the University of Wisconsin; Burnham worked there as a professional for a year but then returned to his court reporting in Chicago. Before he left Madison, he sold his six-inch refractor to Washburn Observatory, afterward observing with the Dearborn refractor. He returned to Mount Hamilton twice while Lick Observatory was under construction, observing with its 12-inch Clark refractor, and in 1888, when Lick's 36-inch "monster" refractor was completed, he resigned his job in Chicago and went west to join its staff. He discovered still more binary stars and measured accurately the separations and position angles of many more. However, he clashed with Holden, who had left Wisconsin to become director of the new observatory. In the summer of 1892 Burnham resigned his Lick position with an angry, well-publicized blast and returned to Chicago, where he was appointed the reporter for the U.S. District Court.

Soon afterward, University of Chicago president William Rainey Harper and George Ellery Hale, who as a boy growing up in Chicago had learned about telescopes from Burnham, secured the funds to build a new, even larger refractor to "lick the Lick"—the giant 40-inch Yerkes Observatory telescope at Williams Bay, Wisconsin. As soon as it went into operation in 1897, Burnham began observing regularly with it two nights a week, keeping his courtroom job in Chicago and commuting to Williams Bay by train each weekend. Finally in 1902, at the age of sixty-three, he retired from the court and went on the University of Chicago payroll as a part-time astronomer, still observing two nights a week and living in the city with his family the rest of the time. Burnham retired from that position in 1914, at age seventy-five, and published his last astronomical paper in 1918. He died at his home in Chicago, after a long life of working hard, staying up all night, smoking cigars, and drinking wine.

Burnham was the outstanding double-star astronomer of the days of visual observing. With no academic training in astronomy, he discovered 1,336 previously unknown binaries, made tens of thousands of highly accurate measurements of known double stars, published more than one hundred papers, and left as his legacy the four-volume *A General Catalogue of Double Stars within 121 Degrees of the North Pole* (1906). Burnham's double-star measurements were vitally important in establishing quantitatively that Newton's laws of motion and his law of gravitation do work for stars far from the solar system in which these laws were discovered and established; in providing measurements of the masses of stars (which cannot be found in any other way); and in establishing the large number of stars which, unlike our sun, have close stellar companions. He was the outstanding American pioneer in the double-star field, in which many trained professional astronomers followed his lead, beginning with Robert G. Aitken at Lick Observatory, William J. Hussey there and at the University of Michigan, and George Van Biesbroeck at Yerkes Observatory, all of them his initial successors in this field.

• The main collection of Burnham's letters is in the Mary Lea Shane Archives of the Lick Observatory, Santa Cruz, Calif. It includes a two-page chronology of his life, apparently drawn up by him and completed by one of his children soon after his death. There are smaller collections of his correspondence, mostly with astronomers, in the Yerkes Observatory Archives, Williams Bay, Wis.; the Richard S. Floyd Papers and the George Davidson Papers in the Bancroft Library, University of California, Berkeley; and the Simon Newcomb Papers, in the Library of Congress. Two excellent memorial biographies are E. E. Barnard, "Sherburne Wesley Burnham," *Popular Astronomy* 29 (1921): 309–24, and Edwin B. Frost, "Sherburne Wesley Burnham 1838–1921," *Astrophysical Journal* 54 (1921): 1–8. Obituaries are in the *Chicago Tribune*, 12 Mar. 1921, and the *New York Tribune*, 11 Mar. 1921. The introduction to Burnham's "A General Catalogue of 1290 Double Stars Discovered from 1871 to 1899," *Publications of the Yerkes Observatory* 1 (1900): 1–296, relates his career up to that time. Most of his papers on double-star discoveries are listed as references in his *General Catalogue* (1906). Two other interesting papers are "Small vs. Large Telescopes," *Sidereal Messenger* 4 (1885): 193–99, and "Report of Mr. S. W. Burnham" (on his site test of Mount Hamilton), *Publications of the Lick Observatory* 1 (1887): 13–23. The mounting of Burnham's six-inch refractor is on display at the Adler Planetarium, Chicago; its lens is in use in a newer telescope on the campus of the University of Wisconsin–Madison.

DONALD E. OSTERBROCK

BURNHAM, William Henry (3 Dec. 1855–25 June 1941), professor of psychology, was born in Dunbarton, New Hampshire, the son of Samuel Burnham, a farmer and proprietor of the general store, and Hannah Dane. He entered Harvard in 1878, following three years of teaching while he prepared for the university; he graduated with honors in 1882. He taught at Wittenberg College (Springfield, Ohio) and at the Potsdam (N.Y.) Normal School before enrolling in graduate studies in psychology at Johns Hopkins University in 1886. At Hopkins he was part of a group of students of G. Stanley Hall that included Joseph Jastrow, E. C. Sanford, G. T. W. Patrick, and John Dewey. Burnham completed his Ph.D. under Hall in 1889.

In 1888 Hall became president of the newly created Clark University in Worcester, Massachusetts, and drew heavily on the Hopkins group for his new faculty. His choices included Sanford, H. H. Donaldson in psychology and physiology, and, in 1890, Burnham as docent in pedagogy and school hygiene (the practice of hygiene in school settings. Soon Franz Boas was added in anthropology, creating an influential group of young faculty in the social sciences. Burnham was promoted to instructor in 1892, assistant professor in 1900, and professor in 1906. Hall controlled Burnham's professional development and career, as he routinely did with others at Clark.

Burnham's initial work involved research on memory and, following Hall's influence, child study. Like Hall, Burnham espoused but did not really practice the new experimentalism. Although he published more than 200 papers and articles, they typically encompassed a consolidation of existing information and new findings, often with an emphasis on application. A former student recalled him as "a careful teacher of subjects largely secondary in the training of a psychologist-education, learning and school hygiene. In these fields he often left his students bewildered by his many references and obvious mastery of a complex and voluminous literature" (*American Journal of Psychology*, p. 611). Throughout his career Burnham was broadly read in the worldwide literature in these areas as well as in psychology.

By the early 1900s Burnham had developed areas of interest that were to intertwine and ultimately be fully developed in the 1920s. He viewed education from a practical as well as theoretical perspective, contributing articles on developments in other countries as well as in the history of education. In *The History of Education as a Professional Subject* (1908) he provided the overview and Henry Suzzallo of Teachers' College the syllabus for an alternative approach to understanding the history of education. Burnham argued that such a history cannot be presented as the ideas of a few men but rather must examine the work of teachers as well as the cultural and social influences on education. He noted, for example, that historians had basically ignored the education of women and girls and that even textbooks designed to be used primarily by girls failed to include accounts of great women teachers or to mention modern theories related to the education of women. Burnham tended to argue that an eclectic perspective was needed to understand the subject of education.

Originally school hygiene was concerned with the effects of physical factors on school performance, a wide range of factors from posture to the design and construction of the school building; to those factors Burnham incorporated mental functions as well. Soon after 1900 his thinking in this regard influenced several graduate students at Clark, notably H. H. Goddard and Lewis Terman. By 1912 the new field of mental testing was rapidly developing as a mechanism for measuring mental hygiene, that is, one's mental functioning in the world, with a practical emphasis on detecting defectives, that is, the "feebleminded." Burnham retained a broader perspective than mere testing, as evidenced in his paper describing the social influences on mental productivity that was published in the journal *Science* in 1910. The mental hygiene movement, begun around 1910, involved applied psychologists, psychiatrists, physicians, social workers, educators, and lay people. Burnham helped to found the Massachusetts State Society for Mental Hygiene and served as its president (1916–1920) and in 1917 became a board member of the National Committee for Mental Hygiene (later the National Association for Mental Health), serving until his death. He contributed articles to the society's journal, *Mental Hygiene*, typically emphasizing factors that contributed to normal, rather than abnormal, mental functioning.

In 1924 Burnham published *The Normal Mind*, in many ways a compilation of his thinking in psychology. In it he presented a model of the development of mental functioning, describing how various influences can produce abnormal conditions, whether mental, social, moral, or motor retardation, and suggesting ways of alleviating malfunctions. His starting point was that healthy mental development is affected by a number of processes other than just one's mental state; in assessing a person's mental health, genetic, physiological, and anatomical influences must be considered but also social and moral development. The incorporation of these factors was a function of Burnham's longstanding concern for interacting physical and social effects on mental performance.

Burnham's perspective on mental development was strongly influenced by the work of Pavlov, whose principles he began to summarize and apply in 1917, a decade before they were available in English. Burnham posited that the mind develops as a series of internal and external events become associated; these associations often are formed without the person being aware of them; the basis for the association is the conditioned response to the event. Burnham viewed individual differences in development as arising from different conditioned responses produced by different experiences. Emotions, especially potentially debilitating ones such as fear, were viewed as conditioned responses. This was consistent with the research and developing behaviorist perspective of John B. Watson and others. In contrast to Watson, however, Burnham made extensive use of Pavlov's concept of inhibitory conditioned responses, emphasizing, for example, how easy it is for a child to learn to be fearful and inhibited in school situations. In addition, Burnham believed that psychological development involved more mechanisms than conditioned responses, as emphasized by the behaviorists, and intelligence, as emphasized by mental testers. He stressed the importance of volition, emotion, and special abilities (for example, talent in painting or music) in the evaluation of the normal (that is, healthy) mind. Arrested mental development can result from a problem in any of these areas of functioning. Thus any attempt to alleviate an abnormal mental condition might help, whether or not the philosophy behind the particular method is itself sound.

After Burnham retired in 1926, he continued to live in the Worcester area and was professionally active, publishing a number of papers and two books. *Great Teachers and Mental Health* (1926) described the practices of outstanding teachers in promoting mental health, and *The Wholesome Personality* (1932) expanded on themes introduced earlier in *The Normal Mind*.

He also continued his involvement in editing *Pedagogical Seminary*, which had begun in 1900, until his death in Dunbarton, New Hampshire.

Burnham was one of fifteen editors of Paul Monroe's *Cyclopedia of Education*, a member of the American Psychological Association, and a fellow of the American Association for the Advancement of Science. He was influential through his teaching, his writing, and his students, though his influence during his lifetime was diminished by a number of factors. One was that Hall, though a close friend and mentor, was resistant to sharing professional prestige. For example, Burnham had taken on extensive editorial responsibilities for *Pedagogical Seminary* for at least five years before his name appeared on the masthead, and he was de facto editor for years while still listed as assistant or associate. In addition, Burnham was not an experimentalist at a time when it was becoming the dominant orientation in psychology. Theoretically his perspectives did not fit well with either the developing behaviorist view or the emphasis on mental testing as the measurement of genetically controlled traits. He did not share the genetic—often eugenic—orientation of the mental testers, and he devoted a chapter of *The Normal Mind* to examples of "feeblemindedness" caused by social, physical, and emotional factors that could be remedied.

Burnham's wholistic view on mental health was well received in his day, but it was not until the late 1950s that therapies were developed that demonstrated the validity of such models. Similarly, his call to study the history of teachers, women, physical education, and other allied subjects stood in marked contrast to the traditional view that the history of education comprised only the thoughts of a few great men. In short, Burnham's views were more compatible with and in many ways anticipated those of later eras.

• Some of Burnham's correspondence can be found in the G. Stanley Hall Papers at Clark and the Lewis Terman Papers at Stanford. A list of his more important papers can be found in R. I. Watson, *Eminent Contributors to Psychology*, vol. 1 (1974). Obituaries are in the *American Journal of Psychology* 54 (1941): 611–12, and *Mental Hygiene* 25 (1941): 647–49.

HORACE G. MARCHANT III

BURNS, Anthony (31 May 1829?–27 July 1862), fugitive slave and pastor, was born in Stafford County, Virginia; his parents (names unknown) were slaves of the Suttle family. Burns's father had died during his infancy. Influenced by his devout mother, he converted to the Baptist faith and later became an unofficial preacher to other slaves. Burns's owner, Charles F. Suttle, farmed in Stafford until 1852, when he moved to Alexandria to become a commission merchant. Suttle prospered and sufficiently distinguished himself that both communities elected him to various offices.

Intelligent and sensitive, Burns taught himself to read and write with the help of two sympathetic young white women, who dared ignore Virginia's law against teaching blacks, and some white schoolchildren in return for amusing them and doing them small favors. From age seven he was hired out annually to employers in Stafford County as well as nearby Culpeper and Fredericksburg and thereafter usually saw his owner only once a year between hires. As a hireling, Burns became quasi-free when he was paid for his work, was allowed to refuse some hires, self-hired, and arranged for the hiring of other slaves. He became more mobile in traveling to and from work sites and, in the urban setting of his later hires, was less supervised and could more easily associate with free blacks, many of whom were city based. He worked a variety of hires, including druggist's assistant, sawmill operator, and stevedore, and was sufficiently skilled and reliable to be fairly well treated as a slave, but, as Frederick Douglass concluded of his own bondage, "give him a bad master, and he aspires to a good master, give him a good master and he wishes to become his own master."

During one of his hires, Burns accidentally broke his right hand; the wound was not properly doctored, and thereafter a large piece of broken bone protruded from the back of his hand. Although he could still use the hand, he feared he would be sold south (as he claimed Suttle had once tried to do) and put to some new kind of work that he would perform so poorly as to be mistreated; so he decided to escape. While hired as a stevedore on the Richmond docks, he enlisted the aid of a sailor who stowed Burns aboard his Boston-bound ship in February 1854.

From an intercepted letter Suttle learned of Burns's whereabouts, went to Boston to reclaim his leading wage earner, and obtained a warrant for his arrest from U.S. Commissioner Edward G. Loring under the Fugitive Slave Law. Though the warrant contained two defects, Burns was arrested on 24 May on a false charge of theft (to lull his suspicions). Learning of the arrest, Boston's Vigilance Committee staged a mass protest meeting in Faneuil Hall on the evening of 26 May that abolitionists Wendell Phillips and Theodore Parker addressed. At its midpoint a militant faction, headed by Thomas W. Higginson, interrupted the proceedings to lead an armed attack on the Boston Court House to rescue the prisoner. The attack was repulsed, but a guard, specially deputized into federal service, was killed. To counter any more rescue attempts, the federal officials promptly assembled a posse; it consisted of approximately 180 soldiers and marines and 120 armed civilians known as the "marshal's guard."

On Saturday morning, 27 May, Suttle announced his willingness to sell Burns for $1,200, and the black minister Leonard A. Grimes raised this sum from Bostonians, mostly Whig businessmen. But U.S. District Attorney Benjamin F. Hallett delayed the sale until after midnight, and no sale could take place on Sunday. He cited the killing of the guard as his justification for insisting on the fugitive's return to Virginia (when he could be sold). However, on Sunday, Suttle decided not to sell—apparently because of political pressure from the administration and his home state. He also was incensed by the legal harassment and physical intimidation he had suffered from the Vigilance Committee and the black community. He referred to both the political pressure and the harassment in a letter to Bostonians written after his return to Virginia when he increased his sale price to $1,500 (a sum Grimes could not raise). He also castigated Boston's mayor for refusing his request for police protection in a letter to his local newspaper.

Though defense counsel Richard Henry Dana, Jr., emphasized the defects in the record, Commissioner Loring used Burns's replies to his master on the night of his arrest, ruling that the replies were "admissions" rather than testimony, which was inadmissible under the law. Anticipating the decision, Hallett had asked the mayor to muster the militia and the police to keep the peace while the federal force would execute the law. The mayor agreed as long as the government reimbursed the city for its expenses. President Franklin Pierce approved Hallett's request while also ordering his adjutant general to Boston to supervise the military arrangements. Hallett assembled almost 2,000 armed men, the largest posse ever assembled in American history, to march the prisoner one-third mile to the wharf where a U.S. revenue cutter shipped him back to Richmond. Total costs of the nine-day affair have been estimated at $40,000. About 50,000 persons, some in town attending anniversary conventions, turned out to witness the rendition, and Burns later noted wryly that "there was lots of folks to see a colored man walk through the streets."

As in many prosecutions against slave rescuers, the government did not convict the courthouse rioters for obstructing federal officers executing process. The indictment included the Faneuil Hall speakers, Phillips and Parker, who did not know of the plan to attack the courthouse. U.S. Supreme Court Justice Benjamin R. Curtis quashed the case in circuit court because of a defect in the indictment that Hallett unknowingly had based on Loring's defective warrant for Burns's arrest. Hallett exculpated himself to the president and blamed Loring, who had not sufficiently described his authority as commissioner to return runaways. Later Governor John A. Andrew referred to the warrant against Burns, saying that it "did not appear on its face to have been issued by any magistrate authorized by the Act of Congress."

In Virginia, Burns was punished and sold to a David McDaniel for $905, or $295 less than Bostonians had offered Suttle. By chance Bostonians learned of his whereabouts, and Grimes raised McDaniel's price of $1,300. En route to Baltimore, where the exchange would occur, the owner was threatened by passengers aboard the steamboat who would keep the notorious runaway enslaved. But McDaniel sent the terrified Burns below deck, drew his revolver, and told them that he would deliver his slave to Grimes as promised, even if it cost him his life, whereupon they backed down.

The new freedman refused to cash in on his fame and indignantly rejected P. T. Barnum's offer of $500 to show himself in his museum, although he told his story on abolitionist platforms and sold copies of his "slave narrative," as told to Charles E. Stevens, to help finance his education. A Boston benefactress helped him obtain an education at Oberlin College's preparatory department in 1855–1856, 1857–1858, 1860–1861, and a shorter course in 1861–1862. He briefly became pastor of a black Baptist church in Indianapolis in 1860 but reportedly was threatened by the enforcement of Indiana's Black Laws that would fine and imprison him. So he had to leave his own country to found his church among the fugitive slave community at St. Catharines, Ontario, Canada. He never married and died of tuberculosis in St. Catharines, shortly before Abraham Lincoln issued his preliminary Emancipation Proclamation.

The Burns affair was the most important and publicized fugitive slave case in the history of American slavery because of its unique set of circumstances. It coincided with the passage of the Kansas–Nebraska Act and with the Sherman M. Booth fugitive slave rescue case earlier that year, all of which contributed to national political realignment over the slavery issue. In Massachusetts, antislavery parties succeeded Whiggery. Eight states now enacted new personal liberty laws to counter the 1850 Fugitive Slave Law. An 1855 Massachusetts statute protected alleged fugitives with due process of law while punishing state officials and militiamen involved in recaption. Two Know Nothing legislatures resolved to remove Loring from his state probate office under this statute, but the governor refused to comply. In 1858 a Republican governor and legislature did remove him, occasioning a dramatic debate in the house between John Andrew, defender of the courthouse rioters who argued for removal, and Caleb Cushing, the attorney general who had ensured the fugitive's return and prosecuted the rioters. After Burns's rendition, no owner chanced recovery in the city.

Throughout his ordeal Anthony Burns demonstrated his intelligence and resourcefulness, courage and humor, honesty and integrity. As the victimized protagonist of the affair, he became "the fugitive." He originally had discouraged the legal defense that Bostonians urged on his behalf, telling his lawyer that "I shall fare worse if I resist," for his master was "a malicious man if he was crossed." And so he was returned, punished, sold, and celebrated as the "Boston Lion."

• The Massachusetts Historical Society holds several letters of Burns and R. H. Dana's manuscript journal, most of which Robert F. Lucid has edited as *The Journal of Richard Henry Dana, Jr.* (3 vols., 1968). Manuscript and newspaper collections in Boston area depositories contain numerous references to the case. Contemporary newspaper reports of the events in Boston are reprinted in *The Boston Slave Riot, and Trial of Anthony Burns* (1854; repr. 1972). The main source for Burns's slave life is his narrative, as told to Charles E. Stevens, *Anthony Burns: A History* (1856; repr. 1969). Jane H. Pease and William H. Pease's booklet, *The Fugitive Slave Law and Anthony Burns* (1975), analyzes possible alternatives to the law's enforcement through the format of an introductory essay followed by source documents. Four authors investigate specific aspects of the case: Fred Landon, "Anthony Burns in Canada," Ontario Historical Society *Papers and Records* 22 (1925): 162–66; David R. Maginnes, "The Case of the Court House Rioters in the Rendition of the Fugitive Slave Anthony Burns, 1854," *Journal of Negro History* 56 (1971): 31–42; Harold Schwartz describes cases from 1850 to 1854 in "Fugitive Slave Days in Boston," *New England Quarterly* 27 (1954): 191–212; and Samuel Shapiro focuses on Dana's role in "The Rendition of Anthony Burns," *Journal of Negro History* 44 (1959): 34–51, and in *Richard Henry Dana, Jr., 1815–1882* (1961). Francis Jackson's manuscript ledger of the Vigilance Committee's activities during its existence from 1850 to 1861, deposited in the Bostonian Society, calculates the cost of assisting fugitives during this period. The society has copy bound this record as the *Account Book of Francis Jackson, Treasurer, the Vigilance Committee of Boston*. Wilbur H. Siebert fleshes out these numbers in his pamphlet, *The Vigilance Committee of Boston* (1953), and in his article, "The Underground Railroad in Massachusetts," published in American Antiquarian Society *Proceedings*, n.s., 45 (1935): 25–100, and as an offprint the following year. Stanley W. Campbell discusses the enforcement of the Fugitive Slave Law from 1850 to 1860 in *The Slave Catchers* (1970), and Maginnes provides the most detailed account of the case in "The Point of Honor: The Rendition of the Fugitive Slave Anthony Burns, Boston, 1854" (Ph.D. diss., Columbia Univ., 1973).

DAVID R. MAGINNES

BURNS, Arthur Frank (27 Apr. 1904–26 June 1987), economist and government official, was born in the Jewish ghetto of Stanislau, Austria, the son of Nathan Burns, a housepainter, and Sarah Juran. Burns immigrated to the United States with his family in 1914, settling in Bayonne, New Jersey. He worked his way through Columbia University, earning an A.B. and an A.M. in 1925 and a Ph.D. in economics in 1934.

Though he taught at Rutgers (1927–1944) and Columbia (1941–1967), Burns's reputation as an economist rests on his work at the National Bureau of Economic Research (NBER), which Burns's mentor, Welsey Clair Mitchell, organized in 1920 to establish reliable measures of economic activity and to construct a verifiable model of the business cycle. Burns joined the bureau as a researcher in 1930, advanced through the ranks, and in 1944 succeeded Mitchell as the NBER's research director. His personal life moved apace. In 1930 he married Helen Berstein, forming a happy union that produced two children and lasted until his death.

In 1938 Burns helped create the Index of Leading Economic Indicators, whose movements presage those of the economy as a whole. In 1946 he and Mitchell published *Measuring Business Cycles*, a massive study detailing the ups and downs of the American economy over the previous century. Though the definitive work on the subject, this book offered no theory of the business cycle, and neither Burns nor Mitchell ever developed one. They were both suspicious of economic theory, preferring statistical research and inductive reasoning. Along these lines, in 1946 and 1947 Burns published attacks on the theories of John Maynard Keynes, which were gaining ground among economists, arguing that Keynes's techniques for estimating consumption and investment did not accord with observed behavior.

In 1953 the recently elected president, Dwight D. Eisenhower, appointed Burns chairman of the Council of Economic Advisors (CEA), largely on Burns's reputation as an expert on the business cycle and as an anti-Keynesian. Because of the political ineptness of his predecessor and internal squabbling, the new chairman inherited an institution that had lost the confidence of the president and Congress and seemed destined for extinction. Burns reorganized the CEA, asserting control over its operations and directing its work toward providing the president with professional advice about economics. He also contributed to policy. Burns helped persuade Eisenhower to cut taxes and accelerate spending to deal with the 1953–1954 recession and influenced his decisions, for example, on business taxation and highway construction. In doing so Burns demonstrated the CEA's utility, rescuing it from oblivion and recasting it in the form it would retain for at least forty years.

In 1957 Burns returned to the faculty of Columbia. He continued his contacts in Washington, however, including those with Vice President Richard M. Nixon. In early 1960 he advised Nixon that a recession was probable later in the year, during the presidential election, and that the administration needed to cut taxes and interest rates to prevent it. President Eisenhower refused to act, and the recession materialized as Burns had predicted, just before the election, which Nixon (who had won the Republican presidential nomination) lost by a narrow margin.

When Nixon became president in 1969, he took Burns to Washington with him, giving the economist a place on the White House staff before appointing him in early 1970 chairman of the Federal Reserve Board, the nation's central bank.

During Burns's eight-year tenure at the Fed, stagflation—simultaneous inflation and recession—constituted the nation's chief economic problem. Burns initially attributed it to "economic rigidities," particularly labor unions' ability to force wages higher regardless of the level of unemployment. In response, Burns urged a system of wage-price controls, which Nixon imposed in August 1971. At first this policy worked well, producing low inflation and high growth in 1972. Burns, however, believed that the political survival of controls required stable interest rates, and during 1972 and early 1973 the Fed expanded the money supply rapidly to keep the cost of money down. This policy, coupled with bad harvests around the world, an international economic boom, and the Arab oil embargo, created runaway inflation in 1973 and 1974 that, in turn, wrecked controls.

This disaster led Burns to rethink his ideas. He decided that heavy government spending, taxes, and regulation were retarding economic activity and pushing prices higher and that to restore prosperity all three had to be reduced and monetary growth restricted. Accordingly, the Fed pushed interest rates to record highs in 1973 and 1974—an action that probably intensified the severe 1974–1975 recession—and allowed only modest monetary expansion during the subsequent recovery. This policy created hostility toward the Fed, particularly in Congress, but Burns's political skills and a robust recovery deflected attacks on the institution. Nevertheless, when Burns left the Fed in 1978, unemployment and inflation were somewhat higher than in 1970. His thinking did, however, influence the economic reforms of the late 1970s and early 1980s.

As Fed chairman, Burns also had to deal with the collapse of the international system of fixed exchange rates that had been established after World War II. Burns fought hard to defend fixed rates, and though he eventually had to acquiesce to a system of floating currencies he played an important role in establishing the framework of international cooperation that allowed this new order to function.

President Jimmy Carter, unhappy with high interest rates and preferring to pick his own chairman, did not reappoint Burns. In 1981, however, President Ronald Reagan made Burns ambassador to West Germany. Burns spent the next four years in Bonn, effectively smoothing over disputes arising from intensified Cold War tensions, which the Germans found particularly alarming. The ambassador retired to Washington in 1985 and died two years later in Baltimore, Maryland.

Despite an intimidating professional manner, Burns had considerable personal charm that won him a vast number of friends, and these contacts often had far-reaching implications. He helped train many of the nation's preeminent economists, including Milton Friedman, Alan Greenspan, Geoffrey Moore, and Julius Shiskin. Burns advanced the careers of numerous government officials, most notably Greenspan and George Shultz.

• Burns's papers from his years at the NBER and the CEA are at the Dwight D. Eisenhower Library in Abilene, Kans., and those from his years in the Nixon administration and at the Federal Reserve Board are in the Gerald R. Ford Library in Ann Arbor, Mich. Burns published his dissertation as *Production Trends in the United States since 1870* (1934). *The Frontiers of Economic Knowledge* (1954) contains Burns's scholarly writings between 1945 and 1953 and includes his critiques of Keynes, while *The Business Cycle in a Changing World* (1969) includes the same for the years from 1957 to 1969. *The Reflections of an Economic Policymaker* (1978) makes available many of Burns's statements as Federal Reserve chairman, and *The Anguish of Central Banking* (1979) is a reflection on these years. Burns outlined his thinking about relations between the United States and Germany in *The United States and Germany: A Vital Partnership* (1986). His last book, *The Ongoing Revolution in American Banking* (1988), constituted the first installment of what Burns intended to be a larger study of the changing American financial system, but he died before he could proceed further.

Wyatt Wells, *Economist in an Uncertain World: Arthur F. Burns and the Federal Reserve, 1970–1978* (1994), which concentrates on Burns's years at the central bank but covers the rest of his life as well, provides probably the most complete account of Burns's life. Edward S. Flash, Jr., *Economic Advice and Presidential Leadership: The Council of Economic Advisers* (1965), examines Burns's work at the council. Donald Kettl, *Leadership at the Fed* (1986), gives a good account of Burns as a political operator. Robert Solomon, *The International Monetary System, 1945–81* (1981), contains a thorough account of Burns's international dealings. John T. Wooley, *Monetary Politics: The Federal Reserve and the Politics of Monetary Policy* (1984), examines important aspects of monetary policy during Burns's tenure at the Fed.

WYATT C. WELLS

BURNS, David (22 June 1901–12 Mar. 1971), actor, was born in New York City's legendary immigrant community on Mott Street, the son of Harry Burns, a policeman in Chinatown, and Dora (maiden name unknown). Burns had planned to follow his father into a career in law enforcement until he saw a notice on his high school's bulletin board seeking theatrical extras to work for twenty dollars a week. His experience as an extra changed his career plans completely. He began searching in earnest for theatrical work in the early 1920s, making his Broadway debut in *Polly Preferred* (1923). Work was difficult to find, so he went to London to appear in the West End productions of such popular plays as George S. Kaufman and Moss Hart's *Dinner at Eight* (1932); Cole Porter's *Nymph Errant* (1933), starring Gertrude Lawrence; and George Abbott and John Cecil Holm's *Three Men on a Horse* (1935). Burns also tried Hollywood, although he was only given small supporting roles in such films as *Rendezvous* (1935), *Strangers on Honeymoon* (1936), *The Great Ziegfeld* (1936), and *The Gang's All Here* (1939), as well as the English movie *Sidewalks of London* (1938), also known as *St. Martin's Lane*, with Charles Laughton and Vivien Leigh.

Burns had a long run as Banjo (a character based on Harpo Marx) in the Broadway production of Kaufman and Hart's *The Man Who Came to Dinner* (1939). He also appeared in London for several years in the late 1930s and early 1940s (he had first appeared there in *Nymph Errant* in 1933), where his comic gifts were particularly appreciated. He worked consistently as an actor, but usually with little significant recognition despite the fact that he was as well liked by audiences as he was by his colleagues. In fact, he is best remembered for roles that he played later in life, perhaps as a result of the fact that he had finally attained the age at which most character actors thrive. From the late 1940s on, Burns's roles got better and larger. He scored personal successes in *Make Mine Manhattan* (1948) and Cole Porter's *Out of This World* (1950) and won his first Tony Award for supporting actor as the blustery small-town mayor in Meredith Willson's *The Music Man* (1957), starring Robert Preston. Burns also appeared in some flops, such as 1947's *I Gotta Get Out*. It only ran for four performances, but Burns, typically, received outstanding reviews for his performance. Another Tony Award came his way for his role as Senex, the doddering and lecherous father, in Stephen Sondheim's *A Funny Thing Happened on the Way to the Forum* (1962), starring Zero Mostel. Burns was quoted in his *New York Times* obituary as stating during this time of his supporting actor success that "I'm the best unknown actor around."

In 1964 Burns received some of the greatest accolades of his career for creating the role of Horace Vandergelder in Jerry Herman's *Hello, Dolly!* starring Carol Channing. As the garrulous "half-a-millionaire" in this musical adaptation of Thornton Wilder's *The Matchmaker*, Burns's comic gifts were seen to full advantage. He remained in the cast of the long-running musical for over three years, and Herman, the show's composer-lyricist, recalled in his memoirs that Burns "was amazing because he was able to make Mr. Vandergelder irascible and grumpy and endearing and lovable all at the same time. I've seen a lot of Vandergelders who were simply grumpy, but Davey Burns could growl and make you love him because he was harmless, like a little pet tiger." Burns was next cast as the elderly secondhand furniture dealer in Arthur Miller's drama *The Price* (1968), but illness forced him to leave the cast four days before opening. However, he rejoined the production a few weeks later, and his expert performance received considerable critical acclaim.

In February 1970 Burns played the lead in Art Buchwald's *Sheep on a Runway*, leading critic Clive Barnes to write in the *New York Times* (2 Feb. 1970) that "David Burns is one of the few men who can make a flat line sound like Mount Everest. He is quite wonderful in this, with his growling, insecure pompousness beautifully displayed." Later that year, Burns played the role of the "dunderheaded colonel" in *Lovely Ladies, Kind Gentlemen*, a musical adaptation of the John Patrick play *Teahouse of the August Moon*. Again, Burns received kudos from the critics, although the musical itself was panned and closed after a short run. Of his performance in *Lovely Ladies, Kind Gentlemen*, a *New York Times* (29 Dec. 1970) reviewer noted that Burns "stopped the show. Whatever you think of the show, I challenge you not to adore Mr. Burns." Burns was nominated for a Tony Award for best actor in a musical.

Burns occasionally appeared in supporting roles in films, most notably in *Deep in My Heart* (1954), *It's Always Fair Weather* (1955), *Let's Make Love* (1960), and *Who Is Harry Kellerman and Why Is He Saying Those Terrible Things about Me?* (1971). He was also a frequent guest star on television and appeared in the series "The Trials of O'Brien."

Although he was a New Yorker, Burns favored the country and bought a "get-away" farm in Middle Smithfield, Pennsylvania, where he cultivated flowers and relaxed between lengthy theater runs and television and film appearances. While appearing in the out-of-town tryout performances at Philadelphia's Forest Theatre of the John Kander–Fred Ebb musical, *70 Girls 70*, Burns was stricken with a heart attack during a performance and died shortly thereafter at Jefferson Hospital. His wife, Mildred, was in the audience when he was stricken.

Although he appeared in all genres and in all of the entertainment media of the twentieth century (stage, radio, film, and television), audiences appreciated Burns most in comedies, and his greatest successes were on the stage. Short, pudgy, and gravelly voiced, Burns specialized in playing comic versions of authority figures (lawyers, executives, and military men) and occasional villains, usually of the most endearing, and ultimately reformable, sort.

• For information on Burns, see Gerald Bordman, *American Musical Theatre: A Chronicle* (1992); Gerald Bordman, *American Theatre: A Chronicle of Comedy and Drama, 1930 to 1969* (1996); Jerry Herman, with Marilyn Stasio, *Showtune: A Memoir* (1996); and Lee Alan Morrow, *The Tony Award Book* (1987). An obituary is in the *New York Times*, 13 Mar. 1971.

JAMES FISHER

BURNS, James Aloysius (13 Feb. 1867–9 Sept. 1940), educator, was born in Michigan City, Indiana, the son of Patrick Burns and Bridget Connolly. Burns attended elementary school in Michigan City, Indiana, at the St. Ambrose Academy, which provided his first contact with the Congregation of Holy Cross. At age thirteen he enrolled in the printing apprenticeship program of the Manual Labor School, located on the campus of the University of Notre Dame and run by the brothers of the Holy Cross Congregation. While there he also completed his high school degree in the commercial course, and at age seventeen he entered the collegiate department of the University of Notre Dame. During his first two and a half years there he continued to work at the university print shop. In his third year he entered the classical program as a full-time student. In 1888 he received an A.B. in chemistry from the University of Notre Dame and entered the Congregation of Holy Cross. He taught chemistry at Sacred Heart College, Watertown, Wisconsin, and studied theology, 1889–1891. He taught chemistry at the University of Notre Dame from 1891 to 1900. Burns also studied for the priesthood from 1891 to 1893 and was ordained a Roman Catholic priest in 1893. He received an M.A. in chemistry from the University of Notre Dame in 1895.

Burns's education views allied him with the progressive wing of the congregation led by Father John A. Zahm. When Zahm became provincial of the Indiana Province, it marked a significant change in Burns's life as well as the direction that the congregation and Notre Dame would take. In 1900 Zahm appointed Burns president of Holy Cross College, the congregation's Washington, D.C., House of Studies for seminarians and a place of residence for priests pursuing graduate studies at the Catholic University of America. From 1904 to 1919 Burns turned out a generation of "well-educated priests, men who came back to Notre Dame and served as a leaven for a new intellectualism" (Doll, p. 35). Among those Burns influenced in this period were three presidents of Notre Dame: Charles O'Donnell, Matthew Walsh, and John A. O'Hara, later cardinal archbishop of Philadelphia.

During his time as president of Holy Cross Burns also completed studies for his doctorate in education, receiving a Ph.D. from Catholic University in 1907.

For his dissertation he wrote a history of Catholic education to 1840 that was published in 1908 as *The Catholic School System in the United States: Its Principles, Origin, and Establishment.* A second volume published in 1912 completed the history to 1910, *The Growth and Development of the Catholic School System in the United States.* These two volumes remained the definitive histories of Catholic education for the next fifty years.

The subject matter of Burns's dissertation admirably shows one of his contributions to educational thought: Catholic education must be viewed as a whole from the elementary level to the college level, with each level feeding into the next. To understand this whole, one must understand its foundations at the elementary or parish school level. This study also fit in with the work he was doing in the Catholic Educational Association (CEA), which he cofounded in 1904 and through which he was intimately involved in the Central Catholic High School movement. Since few individual parishes could afford to provide education beyond the eighth grade level, Catholic students went to public high schools and then often on to public colleges rather than Catholic ones. The Central Catholic High School movement was an attempt to correct this leakage by having parishes join together to support one high school that would provide both terminal and college preparatory courses. This would unite the entire Catholic educational system and do for it what central high schools were doing for the public school system. Without such a connecting link parish schools and Catholic colleges stood as separate and often isolated institutions. The emergence of central Catholic high schools would also ensure that Catholic colleges could disband their preparatory departments and concentrate on the collegiate level.

In 1919 Burns was appointed president of Notre Dame and changed forever the nature of the institution. In the three short years of his tenure, Burns reorganized the university's management structure, finances, and curricula and raised the educational standards. As president emeritus he completed a campaign that raised $1 million for the first cash endowment in the university's history. The student weekly, the *Scholastic* (53, 1919), aptly commented that "In Father Burns, . . . we have a man who knows and appreciates [Notre Dame's] . . . past, understands her present, and is capable of directing her future to the highest development."

Burns's appointment as president of Notre Dame in 1919 coincided with his concentration on the improvement of the college level of instruction using his successive offices as president of Notre Dame, 1919–1922, and provincial of the Indiana Province, 1927–1938, to work for changes. Burns emphasized the need for faculty to strive for intellectual excellence by intensifying their research and scholarly production. As provincial Burns applied these standards to those priests who were to become faculty members at Notre Dame by sending them for graduate work in the United States and abroad. When Burns was able to appoint his old protégé John A. O'Hara president of Notre Dame, many of the plans that Burns had begun in his 1919–1922 presidency were brought to fruition, especially the development of a graduate school and the construction of needed buildings. As Trevor Arnett of the General Education Board wrote to Burns in 1935 after he and his wife visited Notre Dame, "We are glad to see the great progress which the University is making and the wonderful growth that it has had since the visit which Dr. Buttrick and I made some years ago." Burns's last two years were spent at Notre Dame serving the congregation as first assistant superior general. He died in South Bend, Indiana.

Throughout his life Burns showed a high degree of consistency in his educational views. His main interest was the development of Notre Dame and other Catholic colleges into first-rate educational institutions. While many Catholic educator-priests have made contributions on one level of education, Burns is the only Catholic educator to have made contributions on many levels: the study of the history of the Catholic school system, the push for central Catholic high schools, and the upgrading of one of the preeminent Catholic institutions of the twentieth century, the University of Notre Dame.

• Burns's presidential papers are in the Archives of the University of Notre Dame. Information on Burns is also found in the presidential papers of Fathers Cavanaugh, Walsh, and O'Hara, as well as in the Endowment Drive Papers, Alumni Office Papers, and the Howard papers (available as photostatic copies), all at Notre Dame. The Archives of the Indiana Province of the Priests of Holy Cross, Notre Dame, Ind., contain additional information on Burns in the administrative correspondence of Zahm, Morrissey, O'Donnell, and Burns as well as in Burns's general correspondence, Private Papers of James A. Burns, Private Papers of Father Patrick J. Carroll, and the papers of Paul J. Foik on microfilm. For a biography of Burns and the most complete listing of articles and books by Burns and articles about Burns, see Anna Rose Kearney, "James A. Burns, C.S.C.—Educator" (Ph.D. diss., Univ. of Notre Dame, 1975). For Burns's influence on the education of Holy Cross priests, see James P. Doll, C.S.C., "The History of Graduate Training for Holy Cross Priests," *Educational Conference Bulletin of the Priests of Holy Cross* 25 (Dec. 1957): 24–42. Burns's efforts at Notre Dame are covered in Thomas T. McAvoy, C.S.C., "Notre Dame 1919–1922: The Burns Revolution," *Review of Politics* 25, no. 4 (Oct. 1963): 431–50. Obituaries are in the *Notre Dame Alumnus* 7 (1940): 24–25, and the *South Bend (Ind.) Tribune*, 10 Sept. 1940.

ANNA ROSE KEARNEY

BURNS, John Anthony (30 Mar. 1909–5 Apr. 1975), political leader, was born in Fort Assinneboine, Montana, the son of Harry Jacob Burns, a noncommissioned officer in the U.S. Army, and Anne F. Scally. When Burns was four years old, his father was transferred with the family to Fort Shafter in Honolulu, Hawaii. Shortly thereafter, his father abandoned the family, and Burns grew up in Kalihi, a poor neighborhood near Fort Shafter. His early life among nonwhite and racially diverse neighbors helped to shape his egalitarian views and his ability to work with various ethnic groups. Burns graduated from St. Louis High School and attended the University of Hawaii. He married Beatrice Majors Van Fleet, an army nurse, in 1931, and they had three children. Burns joined the Honolulu Police Department in 1934 and with the rank of captain served as its Espionage Bureau chief during World War II. After the war, Burns resigned from the police department and, while engaging in a number of private businesses, actively became involved in building the Democratic party of Hawaii.

The Republican party had dominated the government and politics of Hawaii since 1900, when Hawaii became a territory of the United States. The Hawaii economy was heavily dependent on sugar and pineapple cultivation, which required a large base of agricultural workers, mainly imported from China, Japan, and the Philippines. They became the nucleus of Hawaii's multiethnic society. The aftermath of World War II saw the rise of labor unions and a greater participation of nonwhites in political and economic arenas. Especially active were the Americans of Japanese ancestry, whose distinguished military service in the European theater provided them with the confidence to challenge the status quo, which was largely controlled by the Republican party led by conservative white businessmen.

In this postwar era of change, Burns stepped in to develop the Democratic party as a vehicle for political reform. He was not a charismatic leader; stern in public appearance, he was comfortable in small groups and spent much of his early efforts fostering grassroots party organization. The Japanese-American veterans were especially drawn to him; many had law and other professional degrees from prestigious mainland universities made possible by the GI Bill of Rights, and they would serve faithfully with Burns as stalwarts of the Democratic party.

The election of 1954 was the watershed. To the surprise of even the victors, the Democratic party slate, largely fashioned under the leadership of Burns, won a majority of seats in the territorial legislature to end over fifty years of rule by the Republicans. However, Burns himself, who ran at the head of the ticket for delegate to Congress, was defeated. He eventually won that seat in 1956 and was reelected in 1958. His skillful maneuvering in the U.S. Congress contributed to efforts to make Hawaii the fiftieth state of the United States, achieved in 1959. Statehood, while favored by the vast majority of Hawaii's citizens, was especially important to Burns and the Democrats, for it meant self-government and full citizenship rights. Hawaii could now elect its governor and send its share of voting members to the U.S. Congress.

Burns ran for governor of the new state in 1959 and lost, but he won the governorship in 1962 and was reelected in 1966 and 1970. Ill health prevented him from actively finishing his term in 1974, and he died in Honolulu.

Burns's stature has grown since his death. The Democratic party that he helped to rejuvenate in the 1950s continued to dominate Hawaii politics through the early 1990s. Besides gaining statehood for Hawaii, he influenced Congress to establish in 1960 the East-West Center in Hawaii, which serves as an educational and cultural bridge between Asia/Pacific nations and the United States. Under his leadership, the state of Hawaii enacted progressive social and labor legislation, including an abortion bill that he, as a Catholic, personally opposed but permitted to become law without his signature. He valued education and established a statewide system of community colleges. He helped to develop the University of Hawaii into a full-fledged state university with graduate and research programs; the medical school is named after him as well as the administration building at the East-West Center. There were major capital improvements; notable were the new state capitol, major highways, and an enlarged Honolulu International Airport.

Viewed as a radical by the press and the business community when first elected to office, Burns is fondly remembered for his personal conservative ways and for his egalitarianism. As governor, he received an invitation to join the most exclusive club in Honolulu, which did not then accept nonwhite members. His response in declining the invitation reflects the character of the man and of the Hawaii he espoused: "I do not, of course, presume to pass judgment or to quarrel with the privilege of members to make such rules as they wish. It is, however, a deep and sincere conviction with me that Hawaii—the land of Aloha—must strive, in every deed and word, to exemplify the high ideals to which she publicly subscribes, and that as governor I must exercise even greater discipline than as a private citizen in the effort to attain such goals." Burns was the leading figure in Hawaii politics when and since Hawaii became the fiftieth state.

• Besides the governor's official papers in the Hawaii State Archives, Honolulu, extensive interviews with key associates are recorded in the John A. Burns Oral History Project at the University of Hawaii. Samuel Crowningburg-Amalu, *Jack Burns: A Portrait in Transition* (1974), is a commissioned biography. The politics of the Burns era are described in Paul C. Phillips, *Hawaii's Democrats: Chasing the American Dream* (1982). Tom Coffman, *Catch a Wave: A Case Study of Hawaii's New Politics* (1973), is a vivid account of the 1970 election.

RICHARD H. KOSAKI

BURNS, John Horne (7 Oct. 1916–10 Aug. 1953), novelist, was born in Andover, Massachusetts, the son of Joseph L. Burns, a patrician Irish Catholic lawyer educated at Harvard, and Catherine J. (maiden name unknown), the "hard-nosed" daughter of a wealthy accountant. In his family, Burns wrote, "each individual was permitted to develop along his own lines of genius or mania, but was never allowed to conflict with the interests of the group or with the others" (Warfel, p. 65). He attended St. Augustine's School for eight years, then Phillips Andover Academy and Harvard College, where he played squash and sang in the glee club, graduating in 1937 Phi Beta Kappa in English.

In 1937 Burns joined the Loomis School in Windsor, Connecticut, where he taught English until he was drafted in 1942. After a year as an infantry private, he went into officer's training, reportedly because he had learned Italian at Harvard. "Instead of being sent to the slaughter at Salerno," he wrote, "[I] sat out the war reading prisoner of war mail in Africa and Italy" (Kunitz, p. 151). This service in military intelligence provided the raw material of his first book. *The Gallery* (1947) contains nine fictional "portraits" of Americans and Italians in occupied Naples interspersed with journalistic "promenades" into Casablanca, Fedhala, Algiers, and Naples. Burns captured the arrogance, compassion, and lust of Americans overseas with such insight and detail that, though this is a young writer's book, dominated by "sensitivity," it remains a premiere American novel of World War II.

Burns returned to the Loomis School in 1946, but when *The Gallery* became a bestseller and was chosen "best war book of the year" by the *Saturday Review*, he moved to Boston to write full time. With Norman Mailer and James Jones, Burns was thought to be among the best young writers to emerge from the war.

Burns's heightened sensitivity to sexuality and power, revealed so humorously in the "Father Donovan" and "Momma" chapters of *The Gallery*, took a bitter, satiric turn in *Lucifer with a Book* (1949), an intimate but disconcerting portrait of an exclusive boys' school, obviously Loomis. Critics savaged this novel for its self-righteousness, arch dialogue, and clichéd romance between Betty Blanchard and hero Guy Hudson, whose interest in student Ralph DuBouchet smoulders and flares. This was hardly what readers or critics expected, and despite patches of good writing, *Lucifer* met with what Burns termed "raucous opposition." "I can be as nasty with myself as I can be with others," Burns wrote about this time (Mitzel, p. 8). Yet his cynicism was balanced by a Whitmanesque optimism: "Nothing is worth writing about except America, for we have the power to *be* the future, whereas everything else in the world is either standing still or looking into the past" (Warfel, p. 65).

Supporting himself by writing eleven travel articles for *Holiday* magazine, Burns moved to Italy around 1950, reportedly to live with a male Italian lover. However, his third novel, *A Cry of Children* (1952), is set in Boston and deals with pianist David Murray, his tumultuous love life with lower-class Isobel Joy, and his eventual marriage to singer and former nun Mary Desmond. With its scathing social satire, homosexual beatings, alcoholic benders, and back-alley abortions, *A Cry* is tough naturalism in the vein of John O'Hara but is redeemed by Burns's insights into music, Catholicism, and ritual. Probably his best book, it employs multiple points of view skillfully and shows a fine ear for dialogue but was "admired by practically no one," Burns wrote (Kunitz, p. 151). Critics panned him again.

His failure to win an audience depressed Burns, who by 1953 was living in "a chilly villa outside Florence" working on his fourth novel, which dealt with St. Francis of Assisi in modern life ("The Stranger's Guise," unpublished). Of this period, Gore Vidal wrote, "He seemed to have lost some inner sense of self, gained in the war. . . . Night after night, he would stand at the Excelsior Hotel bar in Florence, drinking brandy[,] . . . insulting imagined enemies and imagined friends, and all the while complaining of what had been done to him by book reviewers" (Zinsser, p. 109). Burns died in Livorno of a cerebral hemorrhage, probably the result of alcoholism.

A general reassessment of the 1950s has led to reappraisal of Burns's work, particularly *The Gallery*, which was published in four languages. Critic William Zinsser has written,

> What elevated his novel to literature was its mixture of disillusionment and hope. Burns fell in love with the despised and exploited "Eyeties" and "ginsos" [Italians] and brought that love back with him. But he also brought back a deep despair over the arrogance of American power and privilege—and thereby wrote the proto-Vietnam novel of war. (p. 108)

"The Leaf" chapter anticipated Joseph Heller's *Catch 22*, and motifs in *Lucifer* and *Cry* look forward to J. D. Salinger's *The Catcher in the Rye*.

The homosexual themes of Burns's work have also attracted attention. As John Aldridge early recognized, Burns had "no choice but to let the real meaning of his material carry him where it would even if it meant a serious and inevitable weakening of his total [artistic] achievement" (Kunitz, p. 152). John Mitzel has written a short "appreciative biography" on the gay Burns. While Burns never wrote an explicit novel, his male characters practice an "erotics of the closet" with each other and the reader. Though Burns did not hide his homosexuality, his novels were not quite so open, but his skill in depicting, often humorously, the discourses of this ambiguity and fluidity of sexuality in general continues to attract attention.

• There is no collection of Burns's journalism or of his papers, but his correspondence with Harper & Row is at Princeton University. Many letters are privately held. A 1955 essay, "The Creative Writer in the 20th Century," was reprinted in 1979. John Mitzel, *John Horne Burns: An Appreciative Biography* (1974), gives a gay-oriented overview of Burns's life, while Mark T. Bassett has written in detail on Burns in New York in the late 1940s in "Popular Success and the Writer: The Case of John Horne Burns," *Publications of the Missouri Philological Association* 9 (1984): 52–57. Bassett also reviewed in *Biography: An Interdisciplinary Quarterly* 11, no. 2 (1988): 151–58, an earlier essay by Indro Montanelli, "John Horne Burns: A Portrait." Burns is mentioned in memoirs by Gore Vidal, *Homage to Daniel Shays* (1972), and William Zinsser, "*The Gallery* Revisited," *Sewanee Review* (Winter 1992): 100, 105–12. An autobiographical sketch written by Burns just before his death appears in Stanley J. Kunitz, ed., *Twentieth Century Authors*, supp. 1 (1955). Another for Harper & Row is entirely quoted in Mitzel, pp. 5–8. Harry R. Warfel, *American Novelists of Today* (1951), has a brief biography. See also Robert E. Spiller et al., *A Literary*

History of the United States (1974), and Martin Tucker, *Literary Exile in the 20th Century* (1991). An obituary is in the *New York Times*, 14 Aug. 1953.

WILLIAM H. MARLING

BURNS, Otway, Jr. (1775–25 Oct. 1850), privateer, shipbuilder, and state legislator, was born on Queen's Creek, Onslow County, North Carolina, the son of Otway Burns and Lisanah (maiden name unknown), farmers. Little is known of Burns's education or youth. Apparently he went to sea at an early age and became a skilled seaman. In 1806 the Onslow County Court apprenticed an orphan lad to Burns to learn navigation. Prior to the War of 1812, Burns was master of a merchantman engaged in the coastwise trade between North Carolina and New England.

The War of 1812 provided Burns the opportunity to gain fame and fortune. His interest in privateering led him to New York, where he purchased the fast schooner *Zephyr*, which he armed and renamed the *Snap Dragon*. Backed by shareholders in New Bern and Tarboro, Burns took the *Snap Dragon*, six guns, and eighty crewmen to sea to harass British commerce. His exploits became legend; indeed it is difficult to separate fact from fiction. Burns commanded the *Snap Dragon* on three successful voyages raiding British shipping from Nova Scotia to Brazil. On the first voyage to the Spanish Main, Burns captured eight ships and returned a prize ship to New Bern with a cargo of hides, yams, and eighteen slaves. The second cruise proved to be the most profitable. Preying on British ships sailing to Canada, the *Snap Dragon* took cargo valued at about $.5 million. On Burns's third voyage, again to the Spanish Main, only one prize was taken. Rheumatism caused Burns to relinquish the *Snap Dragon* to another captain, and on its fourth voyage the ship was captured by the British.

Burns had become one of the most storied privateers of the War of 1812. Described by his biographer Walter Francis Burns as a man of "Herculean strength and tireless endurance," he was a stern disciplinarian and a bold, skillful seaman. He possessed "a mind active and acute, a courage which knew no shrinking, a steady nerve, quick temper but serene self-confidence, and iron will" (pp. 73–74). Two stories suffice to demonstrate Captain Burns's pugnacious demeanor. Early on his first privateering voyage, several crewmen went ashore in the West Indies and were delayed by drunkenness. A brawl ensued, and Burns went to fetch them. Allegedly he "cut them down with a cutlass, not mortally wounding any but slashing until blood ran in streams" (Burns, pp. 86–87). On another occasion, as the *Snap Dragon* lay in port at New Bern, a crowd gathered on the wharf. A prominent antiwar man, François-Xavier Martin, later a supreme court judge in Louisiana, characterized Burns's crew as "licensed robbers." Burns took umbrage and promptly caught "the word-slinger by the seat of his breeches and collar of his coat, [and] flung him into the Neuse River" (Burns, p. 81; Lemmon, p. 24).

Using wealth gained by privateering, Burns entered business with the same vigor and ability he had shown on the high seas. He built ships and engaged in various other pursuits, including a partnership in a saltworks and a brickkiln. In 1818 he built North Carolina's first steamship, the *Prometheus*, for use on the Cape Fear River. Other ships built by him were the *Warrior* in 1823 and the *Henry* in 1831. He also owned a store and operated both merchant and fishing ships. In time Burns lost most of his fortune but not his fame.

Burns's popularity led to a substantial political career. Between 1821 and 1835 he represented Carteret County in eleven legislative assemblies, seven as a commoner and four as a senator. He voted regularly but rarely sponsored bills or motions. Sometimes his votes seemed inconsistent, but it is clear that he supported internal improvements, especially canals and railroads, and favored state action to boost the economy. He also supported the free election of sheriffs, local banks, and the suppression of election day "treating." He opposed the state bank with Jacksonian vigor.

Burns took a liberal position regarding blacks. He favored emancipation upon request of owners and opposed measures to prevent free blacks from entering North Carolina (*North Carolina House Journal*, 1826–1827, p. 180). In 1834 he voted against a bill denying the general assembly the power to abolish slavery (*North Carolina Senate Journal*, 1833–1834, pp. 114–15). He also joined efforts to repeal all acts prohibiting literary instruction of slaves and those prohibiting all persons of color, bond or free, from preaching in their respective religious societies or congregations (*North Carolina Senate Journal*, 1834–1835, p. 44).

A Jacksonian Democrat who opposed nullification and the Bank of the United States, Burns was particularly popular with the people of western North Carolina because of his democratic principles and his support of state-sponsored internal improvements, a position that deviated from other Jacksonian Democrats of his time. He advocated the addition of new counties and a state constitutional convention to redistrict the state. He voted with the one-vote majority to call the constitutional convention of 1835. His eastern constituents never forgave him, and he was defeated in the next election. When Yancey County was organized in 1833, grateful westerners there named their county seat "Burnsville" in his honor.

Because of Burns's worsening economic plight, in 1835 or 1836 President Andrew Jackson appointed him keeper of the Brant Shoals Lighthouse at Portsmouth Island. He remained on the Outer Banks until his death there. In his last years he retained his reputation for independence and cussedness. To the end, he gloried in his maritime past, fine whiskey, and a good fight. Burns married three times: in 1809 to Joanna Grant, with whom he had his only child and from whom he was separated prior to her death in 1814; in 1814 to Jane Hall, who died in 1839; and in 1842 to Jane Smith, who also predeceased him.

In his long life Burns experienced both success and failure. His reputation as North Carolina's most famous privateer is secure, and his appeal to the electorate probably lay in his maritime legend.

• Primary sources on Burns are scarce, but valuable information can be gleaned from the records of Onslow, Craven, and Cartaret counties and from North Carolina legislative journals and papers. Two notable secondary accounts are Walter Francis Burns, *Captain Otway Burns* (1905), and Sarah McCulloch Lemmon, *Frustrated Patriots: North Carolina and the War of 1812* (1973). See also Harold J. Counihan, "The North Carolina Constitutional Convention of 1835: A Study in Jacksonian Democracy," *North Carolina Historical Review* 46 (Oct. 1969): 335–64.

MAX R. WILLIAMS

BURNS, William John (19 Oct. 1861–14 Apr. 1932), detective, was born in Baltimore, Maryland, the son of Michael Burns, a merchant tailor, and Bridget Trahey. The family moved to Columbus, Ohio, where William attended parochial schools and business college. In 1880 Burns married Annie Maria Ressler; the couple had six children. When his father won election as police commissioner of Columbus, Burns first developed his detective skills by assisting in a number of important cases, including discovery of fraudulent voter tally sheets in an 1885 election and conviction of a gang of arsonists who had extorted thousands of dollars from insurance companies.

In 1889 Burns joined the U.S. Secret Service. In his first major case he broke up a notorious counterfeit ring that had printed millions of dollars' worth of fake gold certificates. In another instance Burns exposed the activities of a group of Costa Rican revolutionaries who had manufactured counterfeit money in New York City to fund their political agitation. Burns also uncovered a plot that involved two highly skilled counterfeiters who had printed and distributed fraudulent bills from a prison cell. In addition the detective determined how some $30,000 worth of double-eagle gold pieces had disappeared from a tightly secured vault within the U.S. Mint in San Francisco.

In 1903 the Department of Interior requested Burns to investigate land frauds in Oregon, Washington, and California. Working in close harmony with special prosecutor Francis J. Heney, Burns discovered extensive corruption that included filing false land claims and false affidavits and bribery of officials at every level of government. Burns's and Heney's efforts led to the laying of more than one hundred indictments, thirty-four cases, and thirty-three convictions, including that of veteran U.S. senator John H. Mitchell of Oregon.

In 1905 Fremont Older, editor of the *San Francisco Bulletin*, and Rudolph Spreckels, millionaire businessman, persuaded Burns and Heney to conduct a thorough examination of city government in San Francisco. During the next three years, the two men laid bare a trail of corruption that reached into the highest echelons of the city's business and political elite, including utility officials, realty promoters, and railroad magnates. After a dramatic trial, the court sentenced Abraham Ruef, political boss of San Francisco, to fourteen years in the penitentiary.

In 1910 Burns participated in his most sensational case. A huge explosion had destroyed the building of the vehemently anti-union *Los Angeles Times* and claimed the lives of twenty people. Based on evidence found in Los Angeles, Burns surmised that the crime was linked to a series of bombings perpetrated by the International Association of Bridge and Structural Ironworkers (BSIW) in Indiana as part of their war against "open shop" employers. For the next several months the detective and his agents carried on a nationwide manhunt until Burns felt confident that he had accumulated sufficient evidence to arrest John J. McNamara, secretary of the BSIW, and his brother, James. Employing subterfuge, Burns's operatives spirited both McNamaras out of Indiana and took them to Los Angeles to await trial. A detailed description of the dynamite plot by Ortie E. McManigal, a union member, strengthened Burns's case. Organized labor and others vociferously denounced Burns, who they claimed had kidnapped and framed two innocent men. When the McNamaras, who had previously denied all charges, unexpectedly changed their plea to "guilty" in the hope of securing lighter sentences, their confessions produced repercussions that affected organized labor, the Socialist party, reform politics, and industrial relations in America.

Burns had left government service in 1909 to establish, with his son Raymond, the William J. Burns National Detective Agency, with headquarters in New York City and branches throughout the country. He won a contract for protection of the American Bankers' Association with its 12,000 member banks and also numbered the National Retail Dry Goods Association and several hotel chains among his clients. In 1913 assassins gunned down prominent New York City gambler Herman Rosenthal. Burns's agency played a role in this case, which led to the execution of police lieutenant Charles L. Becker and four professional gunmen as well as imprisonment of several police inspectors. Burns also became involved in the sensational Leo Frank case in Atlanta, Georgia. After an emotional trial rife with anti-Semitic overtones, the jury found Frank, a Jew, guilty of the murder of a fourteen-year-old girl. In March 1914 Burns unearthed a massive amount of evidence that indicated that Frank was innocent and that another man, James Conley, had committed the crime. At one point a furious lynch mob tried to hang Burns as a "Jew lover." Based on Burns's findings, however, the governor of Georgia commuted Frank's death sentence. (Frank was then lynched, nevertheless.) During World War I J. P. Morgan hired Burns's firm to provide security for manufacturers who shipped munitions to the allies. Burns's agency handled thousands of cases and evolved into an institution of international stature.

In 1921 Attorney General Harry M. Daugherty induced Burns to serve as director of the Federal Bureau of Investigation. In his new post Burns waged a relentless battle against the Ku Klux Klan, which he believed represented a sinister force in America. Critics, however, blasted Burns's administration of the bureau because of his use of ruthless methods such as illegal searches and seizures, employment of people of dubious reputation, and political favoritism. Burns retired from the FBI in 1924 with a tarnished image.

In 1927 Harry Sinclair, one of those accused of bribery in the Teapot Dome scandal, hired the Burns agency to maintain surveillance over the jury that was trying his case. When Sinclair was acquitted, the presiding judge denounced Burns's "shadowing" as tantamount to jury tampering and levied a fine of $1,000 on the firm. Burns retorted with such vehemence that the judge charged him with contempt of court and sentenced him to fifteen days in jail. On appeal Burns won a reversal of this judgment.

Publications by Burns include a detective novel, *The Crevice* (1915), written with Isabel Ostrander. In it the hero, who closely resembles Burns, reveals some of his sleuthing techniques and his understanding of the criminal mind. In *The Masked War* (1913) Burns describes his lengthy investigation of the Bridge and Structural Ironworkers union, which culminated in the McNamara–*Los Angeles Times* bombing case. *Stories of Check Raisers and How to Protect Yourself* (1925) served as a guidebook to prevent banking frauds.

William Burns died at his home in Sarasota, Florida. Controversial all of his life, Burns still ranks as America's most outstanding detective. In commenting on his career, the *New York Times* (16 Apr. 1932), after noting that Burns "was not always scrupulous or even subtle" in his methods, attributed his success to "native shrewdness, exceptional courage, direct methods and a bluff honesty not usually associated with private detectives."

• Gene Caesar, *Incredible Detective* (1968), is a full-length biography of Burns. For studies of his land fraud cases see Lincoln Steffens, "The Taming of the West: Discovery of the Land Fraud System, a Detective Story," *McClure's*, Sept. 1907, pp. 489–505, and "The Taming of the West: Heney Grapples the Oregon Land-Graft," *McClure's*, Oct. 1907, pp. 585–602. San Francisco's graft scandals as exposed by Burns are examined in Walton Bean, *Boss Ruef's San Francisco* (1952); *Current Literature*, June 1911, pp. 602–7; "Exploits of Detective Burns," *Literary Digest*, 6 May 1911, pp. 912–13; and Steffens, "William J. Burns, Intriguer," *McClure's*, Apr. 1908, pp. 614–25. Some studies that highlight Burns's part in the McNamara case are Graham Adams, Jr., *Age of Industrial Violence, 1910–1915* (1966); Geoffrey Cowan, *The People v. Clarence Darrow* (1993); Harvey J. O'Higgins, "The Dynamiters: A Great Case of Detective William J. Burns," *McClure's*, Aug. 1911, pp. 347–64; "Burns' Story on the Trail of the Men Higher Up," *McClure's*, Jan. 1912, pp. 363–71; Herbert Shapiro, "The McNamara Case: A Crisis of the Progressive Era," *Southern California Quarterly*, Feb. 1977, pp. 271–87; and Grace Heilman Stimson, *Rise of the Labor Movement in Los Angeles* (1955). For Burns's career as director of the FBI, see Samuel Hopkins Adams, *Incredible Era* (1939); "The History of William J. Burns," *Nation*, 23 Nov. 1927, p. 561; and Francis Russell, *The Shadow of Blooming Grove* (1968). Obituaries are in the *New York Times*, the *Washington Evening Star*, and the *Cleveland Press*, all 15 Apr. 1932.

GRAHAM ADAMS, JR.

BURNSIDE, Ambrose Everett (23 May 1824–13 Sept. 1881), soldier and businessman, was born in Liberty, Indiana, the son of Pamelia Brown and Edghill Burnside, a law clerk and farmer. The Burnsides had nine children and only a modest income, so Ambrose received no more than a rudimentary education before starting work as an apprentice tailor in 1840. His father took advantage of a term in the state legislature to have the boy appointed to the United States Military Academy at West Point, which he entered on 1 July 1843. He graduated eighteenth out of thirty-eight cadets in the class of 1847 and was commissioned second lieutenant in the Third U.S. Artillery. His battery was serving in the Mexican War, and he joined it in Mexico City, too late to see action. Bored, he gambled away six months' pay. Further embarrassment was prevented by a posting, in spring 1848, to Fort Adams, Rhode Island.

In 1849, Burnside was transferred to Las Vegas, Nevada, guarding the Santa Fe Trail. Skirmishing with Apaches convinced him that mounted troops needed a better weapon than the cumbersome muzzle-loading carbine then in service, and he began devising a breechloader. In 1852, he returned to Fort Adams, where he married Mary Richmond Bishop. They were childless. In 1853, he resigned his commission in order to manufacture carbines, establishing a works at Bristol, Rhode Island. Congenial, and liked in political circles for his moderate views, Burnside was appointed major general of Rhode Island militia in 1855. Believing that he was to receive a substantial army contract, Burnside went deep into debt manufacturing guns. But he received only token orders and had to turn over both plant and patent to his creditors in 1858. His old classmate and friend George B. McClellan (1826–1885) came to the rescue, securing him a position with the Illinois Central Railroad. In 1860, he became treasurer of the company and was able to free himself from debt.

On 15 April 1861, at the onset of civil war, Burnside was appointed colonel of the First Rhode Island Regiment, which quickly advanced to defend Washington. In the capital, Burnside became friendly with President Abraham Lincoln, a connection that enhanced his career. At the first battle of Manassas (21 July 1861), Burnside commanded a brigade that saw severe fighting and did as well as other green troops. On 6 August, he was commissioned brigadier general of volunteers.

In October, Burnside was given an independent command and began concentrating regiments at Annapolis, Maryland, for amphibious operations against the North Carolina coast. In conjunction with the navy, he was to liberate the towns along the North Carolina sounds. Regiments would then be raised from the thousands of citizens who allegedly had remained loyal to the Union, and the region would be returned to normal relations with the national government.

Despite poor weather and supply problems, the expedition was successful in achieving its initial goals. In January 1862, the fleet sailed to Hatteras Inlet, destroying the small Confederate naval flotillas in Albemarle and Pamlico sounds. Roanoke Island fell in February, with a haul of twenty-six hundred prisoners and thirty-two artillery pieces. In March, the Federals fought a severe engagement at New Bern, which gave them possession of this town and then Beaufort. Burnside was aided in the campaign by able subordinates, whom he always relied on to exercise initiative once battle was joined. Also, many Confederates were poorly equipped, second-line troops of indifferent quality. The expedition failed, however, in its larger mission of recruiting North Carolinians for the Federal forces and creating a pocket of Union sentiment in the South, as national feeling in the area had been overstated.

Burnside was commissioned major general on 18 March 1862. In July, he was sent to reinforce the Army of the Potomac, fighting under McClellan on the Virginia Peninsula. McClellan's failure in the Peninsula campaign cost him the administration's confidence, and Lincoln offered command of the Army of the Potomac to Burnside, who declined. Following the defeat of John Pope's Army of Virginia at the second battle of Manassas in August, the command was again offered to Burnside and again refused, but this soured Burnside's relations with McClellan's circle.

In September Confederate general Robert E. Lee invaded Maryland. In the campaign that followed, Burnside commanded the right wing of McClellan's army, comprising his own Ninth Corps and Joseph G. Hooker's First Corps. Lee courted disaster by dividing his army on enemy soil, sending a third of it under Thomas J. ("Stonewall") Jackson to capture the Union garrison at Harpers Ferry, Virginia. McClellan had the opportunity to destroy Lee's army piecemeal but was slow in moving. Burnside shares the blame for not pushing harder against the rebel defenses at South Mountain, allowing the Confederates time to reunite at Antietam Creek.

During the battle there on 17 September, Burnside was unfairly accused of being slow in attacking the Rohrbach Bridge across Antietam Creek. He was also unjustly charged with sulking and refusing to take command of the Ninth Corps, which McClellan, with great impropriety, had taken from Burnside's wing on the left and placed on the extreme right of the line. However, it can be said that Burnside probably should have given more direction to Jacob Dolson Cox, who was new to command of the Ninth Corps, having taken over after Jesse L. Reno's death at South Mountain. Also, Burnside's men failed to find a lightly guarded ford across the creek that would have allowed them to flank the bridge and save much of the slaughter there.

Burnside was made commander of the Army of the Potomac when McClellan was dismissed on 7 November. He developed a plan to avoid a head-on encounter with Lee by sidestepping the rebels, bridging the Rappahannock River at Fredericksburg, and making a dash for Richmond. Lee would then have to fight for his capital at a disadvantage. Lincoln was skeptical of the plan, which relied on surprise and speed, neither of which, as it turned out, was achieved. Pontoons to bridge the Rappahannock were late in arriving. A limited crossing became possible on 17 November, but Burnside refused to sanction the advance, fearing his army would be caught straddling the river. Consequently, the heights commanding the town were seized by Lee, and when Burnside finally launched a full frontal assault on 13 December, the entrenched rebels cost him over twelve thousand casualties. Burnside was poorly served by lackluster subordinates, but he failed to develop a clear plan of battle or to ensure that his generals acted with energy and understanding. Following a further abortive movement in January 1863, the infamous Mud March, Burnside resigned as army commander.

On 25 March, Burnside was assigned to command the Department of the Ohio, comprising Ohio, Indiana, Illinois, Michigan, and Kentucky. His appointment was welcomed by Republicans, but many Democrats hated him because of his General Order No. 38, which included mere criticism of the government in its list of treasonous acts. Under this order, two newspapers were suppressed, several rebel sympathizers were executed, and the Copperhead politician Clement L. Vallandigham was put beyond the Union lines and forced to enter the Confederacy in May 1863. On the battlefield, Burnside was victorious during this period. He destroyed John Hunt Morgan's cavalry raid into Indiana and Ohio in the summer of 1863. In September, he took Knoxville, liberating East Tennessee from the Confederates, and he successfully defended the city against James Longstreet's siege in November and December.

Burnside was recalled to command his old Ninth Corps in Ulysses S. Grant's 1864 Virginia campaign. He fought in the Wilderness, at Spotsylvania, at Cold Harbor, and in the operations around Petersburg. Again he was accused of lacking finesse and letting opportunities slip, and his relations with his immediate superior, George Gordon Meade, deteriorated steadily. The end came for Burnside with the Crater debacle on 30 July. In this episode, Union engineers exploded a mine under a section of the Confederates' line outside Petersburg. Burnside's corps led the attack into the resulting breach, but the assault failed with huge losses—four thousand to the Ninth Corps alone. A Court of Inquiry convened by Meade found Burnside responsible. This was only partially true, however, because late in the planning, Meade stopped Burnside from using fresh black regiments in the vanguard, with the result that exhausted white troops had to take the lead, and because Burnside was poorly supported by other corps generals.

Burnside did not serve again during the war. He continued to prosper as a railroad executive and also branched out successfully into engineering. Recognized as a leading citizen in his adopted state of Rhode Island, he served three terms as governor (1866–1868) and concluded his political career as a state senator. Originally a conservative Democrat who supported slavery, he came during the war to see the need for emancipation. He championed the use of black troops and was a moderate defender of the rights of the freedmen after 1865. He traveled abroad, observing the Franco-Prussian War of 1870–1871. Burnside was an able manager and soldier who was perhaps at times thrust into situations beyond the limits of his military capacities. He died of heart failure at "Edghill," his country estate near Bristol, Rhode Island.

• Burnside's surviving correspondence is limited. It is housed mainly in the Ambrose E. Burnside Collection, Generals' Papers, and the Ambrose E. Burnside Papers, Generals' Reports and Books, both in the National Archives, Washington, D.C., and in the Ambrose E. Burnside Papers at the Rhode Island Historical Society, Providence. Daniel Reed Larned, one of Burnside's staff officers, commented extensively on his chief in wartime; see his papers in the Library of Congress Manuscript Division, Washington, D.C. Official reports are in *War of the Rebellion: A Compilation of the Official Records of the Union and Confederate Armies* (128 vols., 1880–1901). See also *Senate Report No. 108*, 37th Cong., 3d sess., and *Senate Report No. 142*, 38th Cong., 2d sess., for congressional investigations of events at Fredericksburg and Petersburg.

There is only one modern biography: William Marvel, *Burnside* (1991). Earlier volumes lacked objectivity but can be useful. They include Daniel Ross Ballou, *The Military Services of Maj.-Gen. Ambrose Everett Burnside in the Civil War* (1914); Ben Perley Poore, *The Life and Public Services of Ambrose E. Burnside* (1882); and Augustus Woodbury, *Ambrose Everett Burnside* (1882). Civil War studies that consider Burnside's generalship include Edward J. Stackpole, *Drama on the Rappahannock* (1957), and T. Harry Williams, *Lincoln and His Generals* (1952).

MICHAEL C. C. ADAMS

BURNSIDE, R. H. (13 Aug. 1870–14 Sept. 1952), director, producer, and playwright, was born Robert Hubber Thorne Burnside in Glasgow, Scotland. His father, unnamed in biographical sources, was the manager of Glasgow's Gaiety Theatre; his mother was Margaret or Marguerite (maiden name unknown), an actress. Burnside's first name is sometimes given in biographical sources as "Richard," a mistake that arose because he invariably went by his initials "R. H." (or his nicknames "Burny" and "Zipp") and made a point of keeping his given names secret. As a child, Burnside traveled on theatrical tours with his mother. His formal education was sketchy and ended early after he performed, costumed as a dog, in the musical burlesque *The Bohemian Girl* at a seaside resort. It was a command performance for the Prince of Wales. Burnside's story was that the prince came backstage after the performance and tipped him half a gold sovereign. From the age of ten, Burnside began running away to go with theatrical troupes to London. Once he worked as a call boy at the Gaiety Theatre in London for three months before being brought back to his family.

In early adolescence, Burnside left home altogether for backstage work in London. He became a call boy at the Savoy Theatre, home of the Gilbert and Sullivan operettas, under its famous stage manager, Richard Barker. By age eighteen he had progressed to assistant stage manager at London's Alhambra Theatre, then was employed at other theaters, and was stage manager for touring productions. In 1894 he was engaged by American soprano beauty Lillian Russell as stage manager for her English tour of *The Queen of Brilliants*. Burnside came to the United States that year with Russell's company and remained with it for three seasons.

Following his time with Russell, Burnside spent two seasons as stage manager of the Bostonians, America's first troupe to present Gilbert and Sullivan's works. By the turn of the century, he had gone beyond stage managing to make a name for himself as cowriter and director of frothy musical entertainments such as were staples of the popular theater of the time. Burnside himself lost count of how many of these productions he helped to create. During a career of fifty years, he was involved with more than 200 productions, and perhaps the number was nearer 300. The standard pattern was to base the show around some well-known entertainer; Burnside did so for Eddie Foy, Montgomery and Stone, DeWolfe Hopper, Elsie Janis, and Vernon and Irene Castle. The musical's plot told a slight, predictable story with plenty of opportunities for "star turns" by the headliners, plus jokes, songs and dances, and some eye-popping production numbers with many good-looking chorus girls. Ephemeral and derivative as such shows were, they were public favorites. At times Burnside collaborated on songs for these shows; of them, only "Poor Butterfly" (1915), is remembered.

Burnside had two major employers among producers during this period of his life. One was the Shubert organization, for whom he began as manager of a touring show. The other was Charles Dillingham, who first hired him as a play doctor for *The Red Mill* (1906). For both these employers in turn, Burnside created the shows for which he was most widely known: the enormous extravaganzas, half musical show and half circus, staged annually at the Hippodrome Theatre. The theater was an extravaganza in itself: the width of a city block, with a seating capacity of 5,200, a stage apron sixty feet across, a water tank that could mount diving exhibitions or be used as an ice rink, and shows with elephants and animal acts that used hundreds of performers in the cast, and hundreds more backstage. It was a New York tourist attraction in its day, drawing patrons from across the nation.

Burnside's first show at the Hippodrome was mounted in 1908, when the theater was under Shubert management. According to the review in the *New York Evening Journal* (11 Sept. 1908), it was a knockout. "It starts at eight with a baseball game . . . It closes on the road to midnight with a midair bombardment by flying machines and a deep-sea upheaval by mermaidens. Between these extremes . . . lie a circus that ranges from pet polar bears to the untamed clowning of Marceline, a horse race on a treadmill track . . . and a ballet, 'The Land of Birds,' that . . . is the most gorgeous girl picture I have ever seen." This was an aerial ballet. "It was the whole aviary on dress parade—160×110 feet of fluttering, feathery girl, running the whole rainbow of color, flying and flocking and counterflocking into new combinations of color at every pulse of the [music]." The reviewer had never seen such audience reaction: "It went to the lungs of an audience of five thousand last night. When the live wire girls of the aerial ballet came soaring over our heads almost into the balcony, dropping roses as they flew, a shout went up to greet them. The Hippodrome had never housed such a shout."

Burnside introduced his most famous innovation in the 1909 show: a secret device that allowed sixty chorus girls to march down into the water tank—and never come up again. Not for many years did the director reveal the air-lock mechanism that made the illusion possible. In 1910 Burnside was married to Kathryne Hyland. The couple established a home in Ridgewood, New Jersey, and there raised three children. Meantime, he continued with his Hippodrome shows, which demanded multiple talents, both creative and managerial. Burnside created a series of Hippodrome shows for the Shuberts. Then, following a fistfight with J. J. Shubert, he left and refused to come back. He returned only when Charles Dillingham assumed management of the Hippodrome in 1915. He continued with the shows into the 1920s, when rising production costs ruled out any more of the extravaganzas.

In the 1920s Burnside continued to create musical comedies for Broadway in the same style as the past. Privately, also, he staged a number of the Lambs Club entertainments, called "Gambols," and served as club shepherd during 1918–1921. He had been a member of the club since 1897. He further founded a production jobbing firm that offered all the elements, from costumes to cue sheets, necessary for a local theater to stage a musical production. The depression years and competition from Hollywood musicals effectively killed off Burnside's kind of Broadway show in the 1930s. In the seven years between his staging of the musicals *Hold Your Horses* (1933) and *Walk with Music* (1940), his only Broadway stage work was a summer season of Gilbert and Sullivan for the Civic Light Opera Company in 1935.

Burnside liked to complain to interviewers in later years that his Hippodrome reputation for big effects kept him from being chosen for more modest productions. In truth, it led him instead to jobs staging spectacles outside the theater. The biggest of these, the "Freedom" pageant at the 1926 Philadelphia Sesquicentennial, had a cast of 2,700. At other times he "staged great spectacles at Madison Sq[uare] Garden, Grand Central Palace, Buffalo Bill & Pawnee Bill's Circus, also . . . the Barnum and Bailey Circus" and a "cowboy spectacle" at the 1939 New York World's Fair (*Variety*, 17 Sept. 1952).

In 1942 Burnside organized the Boston Comic Opera Company, a Gilbert and Sullivan troupe that toured eastern cities including Boston and New York. His last work on Broadway came fifty years after he had arrived with Lillian Russell. He staged for the Shuberts a revival of a turn-of-the-century operetta, *Robin Hood* (1944). The *New York Times* reviewer called him "a sort of one-man campaign to keep the operettic classics alive . . ." (8 Nov. 1944).

In declining health and with his wife dead since 1940, Burnside moved into quarters in the Lambs Club. An interviewer in 1942 described Burnside in his seventies as "a courtly gentleman of the old school," and Lambs Club member Joe Laurie, Jr., said in a *Variety* tribute: "He was loved by his fellow Lambs, who sat around with him, his daily glass of sherry in his hand, as he would [open] his golden store of theatrical memories."

Burnside's Ridgewood home, unoccupied for years, became rundown and was vandalized. The house contained an enormous cache of theatrical materials from Burnside's long career. Acquired by the New York Public Library, the Burnside papers became a significant source for theater history. After suffering a stroke, Burnside died in a Metuchen, New Jersey, nursing home.

• Materials on the life and career of Burnside are in the Billy Rose Theatre Collection at the New York Public Library for the Performing Arts, Lincoln Center. A discussion of Burnside's papers and the questions surrounding their origins is by Avi Wortis, "The Burnside Mystery: The R. H. Burnside Collection and the New York Public Library," *New York Public Library Bulletin*, Oct. 1971. A partial list of his productions is in *Who Was Who in the Theatre: 1912–1976*. A sketch of Burnside as creator of the Hippodrome shows is by Frank Ward O'Malley, "'Zipp'—A Remarkable Judge of Human Nature," *American Magazine*, Mar. 1920. Helpful journalistic reviews of his career include: Helen Ormsbee, "A Many-Sided Veteran," *New York Herald Tribune*, 11 June 1940, with portrait; Sheilah Graham, "Broadway," *Newark (N.J.) Evening News*, 30 Mar. 1942; Lucius Beebe, "Stage Asides: Good Old Days Find a Champ," *New York Herald Tribune*, 5 Nov. 1944; Joe Laurie, Jr., "Salute to 'Burny'," *Variety*, 17 Sept. 1952. Obituaries are in the *New York Times* and *New York Herald Tribune*, both 15 Sept. 1952, and in *Variety*, 17 Sept. 1952.

WILLIAM STEPHENSON

BURPEE, David (5 Apr. 1893–24 June 1980), businessman and horticulturist, was born in Philadelphia, Pennsylvania, the son of W. Atlee Burpee, the founder of the W. Atlee Burpee Seed Company, and Blanche Simons. His father founded the company in Philadelphia in 1878 as a catalog and mail-order retailer of poultry and livestock. The company met with success when it shifted its emphasis from animals and fowl to seeds. Burpee's father actively encouraged his sons to follow him in the seed business. When his father became ill with a liver ailment, Burpee ended his studies in agriculture at Cornell University and served as his assistant until the elder Burpee's death in 1915.

Burpee assumed the directorship of the seed company at the age of twenty-two and began to display an impressive business acumen. Under his leadership for fifty-five years, the company continued his father's emphasis on quality and integrity while seeking to find ever more varieties of plants. To this end, Burpee used two principal methods: discovery of plants through travel and scientific development conducted on the Burpee estates. Burpee made frequent trips to Europe and managed to gain exclusive rights to some varieties of flowers and vegetables while being the first American distributor of others. The company maintained large farms in Pennsylvania, California, and New Jersey for producing seed and for the breeding and development of new varieties. One of these estates, "Fordhook," near Doylestown, Pennsylvania, served as both home, farm, and laboratory for Burpee and his wife Lois Torrance, also a horticulturist, whom he married in 1938. They had two children.

Under Burpee's leadership, the company marketed the first commercial hybrid seeds, for a red and gold marigold, in 1939. Burpee held marigolds in particularly high esteem, and throughout his presidency the company produced spectacular hybrid marigolds that won a number of awards. His love of the marigold led him in 1959 to lead an effort to have it named the national flower. This effort ultimately led to the founding of the Marigold Society of America in 1978.

Near the end of World War II, Burpee aided victory gardens with new seeds for cucumber and tomatoes, the first hybrids to be marketed of these plants. In addition, the company sent thousands of pounds of seeds to Allied countries under the Lend-Lease Act. Shortly after the conclusion of World War II, Burpee scientists discovered a method for multiplying the chromosome structure of a flower. This method resulted in common flowers such as the black-eyed Susan being built into the more spectacular Gloriosa daisy.

During Burpee's tenure as head of the company, he recognized and dramatically pursued successful marketing methods. As the ability of the average American to consume goods increased, so did the interest in new and interesting products. In the seed business this translated into the need for more and new varieties and types of plants. Thus Burpee and the company's horticulturists constantly worked to breed new colors, textures, and other qualities into plant species. Experimentation in plant breeding at Fordhook and the "Floradale" farms in California produced the Big Boy hybrid tomato that was the industry standard for years. In addition to aesthetics, Burpee noted the value of a plant's name in marketing. For example, few zinnias enjoy such a name as Burpee's "Firecracker Zenith" variety. By the 1950s the company had grown so large that it had research centers on both coasts and a nationwide distribution. Burpee's Floradale farm shipped products from a mail-order house in Riverside, California, while Fordhook seeds traveled outward from a house in Philadelphia. The mail-order house in Clinton, Iowa, served the Midwest.

Burpee succeeded in business as the president of the nation's largest seed company, but his impact extends today into the entire realm of American horticulture and agriculture. Moreover, through his choice to maintain an entertaining catalog, his company, like Sears and Roebuck, became a cultural icon in homes throughout the United States. His father filled the catalog with witticisms and narratives of his sojourns in the nation and Europe looking for new plants. Wisely, Burpee continued this tradition of producing a catalog that both entertained and advertised.

Burpee involved himself in a great many clubs and associations. Many of these groups served to promote the seed trade or particular breeds of plant, such as the Sweet Pea Society. Burpee also maintained membership in several gentlemen's clubs, including the Poor Richard and the Sphinx. In addition, he worked on the boards of banks, businesses, and a hospital.

Burpee died in Doylestown, Pennsylvania. His career in business and horticulture spanned the greatest change in that arena in a century: the advent of hybridization. His legacy is his strong, well-known mail-order company. Equally important, though, are the many varieties of vegetables and flowers that he helped to develop.

• For more information on Burpee, see Ken Kraft, *Garden to Order* (1963), which often quotes him. Also see Joseph J. Fucini and Suzy Fucini, *Entrepreneurs: The Men and Women behind Famous Brand Names and How They Made It* (1985). The company at the time Burpee became its president is described in the company-published *Forty Years of Burpee Service, 1876–1916* (1916), and the seed catalogs themselves also document the company under his management. An obituary is in the *New York Times*, 26 June 1980.

JAMES H. TUTEN

BURR, Aaron (4 Jan. 1716–24 Sept. 1757), Presbyterian minister and college founder, was born in Upper Meadows, Fairfield, Connecticut, the son of Daniel Burr, a prosperous farmer, and his wife Elizabeth. (By the Old Style form of dating, his year of birth was 1715.) After graduating from Yale College in 1735, he remained in New Haven to study theology, during which time he was caught up in the colonial revival of religion known as the Great Awakening. With several other Yale classmates, Burr underwent a moving personal conversion and also came under the influence of the most capable defender of the Awakening, Jonathan Edwards of Northampton, Massachusetts. Shortly after Burr was, as he put it, "brought to the footstool of sovereign grace," he was licensed to preach. On 21 December 1736 the Presbyterian Church of Newark, New Jersey, invited him to serve for a probationary year, at the conclusion of which he was ordained and installed as the regular minister.

In his Newark charge, Burr immediately aligned himself with other friends of revival, some like himself former Congregationalists from New England, others Scots-Irish pietists who had also recently immigrated to the region. Though usually moderate in his opinions, carefully spoken in the pulpit, and reasonable rather than enthusiastic, Burr nonetheless practiced what he preached by leading revivals in the Newark church in August 1739 and the winter of 1740–1741.

From the start of his Newark ministry Burr had tutored a few local boys in Greek, Latin, and other liberal arts. He also cooperated with Robert Ross in producing a much-reprinted *Introduction to the Latin Tongue*. These educational interests, along with his pro-revival (or New Side) connections, led him to an active part in promoting higher education. With three other New Side ministers, Burr made plans from as early as 1741 for a college to prepare young men for the Presbyterian ministry and also to train leaders for society at large. In 1746 these plans bore fruit in the founding of the College of New Jersey. Jonathan Dickinson was called as its first president, and the new institution met in Dickinson's Elizabeth-Town manse. When Dickinson died in early 1747, Burr was asked to take over instruction, which he did from his home in Newark. On 9 November 1748, after securing a more stable charter from Jonathan Belcher, a new governor kindly disposed to New Side piety, Burr was formally appointed as president and then presided over the first commencement of the institution that later became Princeton University.

Burr's Congregational connections ensured that the new college would have a healthy number of students from New England along with a majority from New York, New Jersey, and Pennsylvania. In 1751 he wrote to his friend Joseph Sterrett that the college was then instructing forty to fifty students, up considerably from the eight he had inherited from Dickinson.

Burr's effective management of the new enterprise put the college solidly on its feet. But it was exhausting labor. While taking the leading role in day-to-day instruction and continuing to serve his Newark church, he was ever active in raising funds. For his first three years as president he served without salary. When the trustees determined to seek a new permanent location, Burr superintended the construction of a president's house and a spacious main building (Nassau Hall) in Princeton. Burr made sure there were no "superfluous ornaments" in the building, but once it was built he did have an organ installed, the first to grace a Presbyterian place of worship in the British colonies. Finally, in December 1756, the structures were finished enough so that the students, Burr, and the president's young family could move in.

This family was the result of what was by all account's Burr's singularly felicitous marriage on 29 June 1752. The bride was Esther Edwards, daughter of Burr's theological mentor. He was thirty-six, she was twenty, a disparity in age that set a few tongues to wagging in Newark. But Esther, who possessed a full measure of her father's intelligence, the same kind of piety as her husband and father, and more wit than either of them, made a good match. In an epistolary diary kept from October 1754 to September 1757, Esther Burr left one of the earliest and most revealing records of the life of a well-bred colonial woman. It catalogs an unceasing round of domestic duties for herself as well as never-ending public activities for her husband. To this union were born two children, Sarah (called Sally) who would marry the noted Connecticut jurist, Tapping Reeve, and Aaron, Junior, the future soldier, vice president, duelist, and political conniver.

From Newark and then Princeton, Burr carefully monitored the growing imperial tension between Britain and France. After the French and Indian War broke out in 1754 and fighting menaced Esther's family in western Massachusetts, Burr regularly commented on the conflict. A notable discourse on New Year's Day, 1755, was one of the first American statements to combine evangelical convictions about providence and contemporary principles of republican liberty that were only then beginning to make their way in the colonies. In September 1756, shortly before the move to Princeton, he publicly contrasted "the Horrors of *Popery, Slavery* and *Death*" promoted by France and "all the incalculable *Privilege* of unadulterated *Christianity; British Liberty and Property*," enjoyed by the colonists. In portraying the colonial wars in this fashion, Burr became an articulate exponent of that singular combination of secular and religious rhetoric that, when turned from France to Britain, would soon justify the American Revolution.

Burr did not, however, live to develop such thoughts. Worn out by unstinting activity that included a flying trip to western Massachusetts and the funeral sermon for his friend Governor Belcher, preached while he was suffering a fever, Burr died before his first year in Princeton was over.

For the sake of his own reputation, Burr had the misfortune of belonging to a family of remarkable renown: as son-in-law of America's greatest early theologian, husband of one of America's earliest women diarists, father of a fascinating reprobate. Yet he too was a notable person who balanced ardent religion, cool reasoning, and administrative savvy as well as anyone in his generation and, in his pronouncements on the colonial crisis of the 1750s, anticipated the ideology that, less than a generation later, created the United States of America.

• Burr left a detailed account book for his time as president of the College of New Jersey, which may be consulted at Princeton University. A few other manuscripts are located there as well as at the Presbyterian Historical Society and the Historical Society of Pennsylvania in Philadelphia. The best short accounts of his life are from nineteenth-century sources: William B. Sprague, *Annals of the American Pulpit*, vol. 3: *Presbyterians* (1868), and Franklin Bowditch Dexter, *Biographical Sketches of the Graduates of Yale College* (1885), the latter containing full bibliographical information for his six published works. For Burr's activities as an educator, see Thomas Jefferson Wertenbaker, *Princeton, 1746–1896* (1946), and James McLachlan, ed., *Princetonians, 1748–1768* (1976); for the contexts of his church activities, Leonard J. Trinterud, *The Forming of an American Tradition: A Re-examination of Colonial Presbyterianism* (1949); and for an interpretation from the perspective of his famous son's biography, Milton Lomask, *Aaron Burr: The Years from Princeton to Vice President, 1756–1805* (1979). The extraordinarily interesting *Journal of Esther*

Edwards Burr, 1754–1757 was published in 1984 with a helpful introduction by Carol F. Karlsen and Laurie Crumpacker.

MARK A. NOLL

BURR, Aaron (6 Feb. 1756–14 Sept. 1836), revolutionary soldier, U.S. senator, and vice president of the United States, was born in Newark, New Jersey, the son of Aaron Burr, a theologian and the second president of the College of New Jersey (later Princeton University), and Esther Edwards, the daughter of Jonathan Edwards. Burr's parents died before he was three years old, and his maternal uncle, Timothy Edwards, raised him. Tapping Reeve, who became a judge of the Connecticut Supreme Court and was the founder of one of the first law schools in the United States, served as Burr's tutor and later married Burr's sister Sally. Burr entered the College of New Jersey at age thirteen and graduated with distinction in 1772. He subsequently began the private study of theology, but in 1774 he changed to law.

The Revolution interrupted Burr's studies in 1775, and he joined the American army besieging Boston. Although he disliked Benedict Arnold, he served as a captain on Arnold's staff during the Quebec campaign of 1775–1776. On account of his valor during the failed effort to seize the city, the Continental Congress promoted Burr to the rank of major and appointed him to George Washington's secretarial staff. But within days of Burr's arrival at Washington's headquarters, an ongoing conflict developed between the two men.

On 22 June Burr transferred to the staff of Major General Israel Putnam, who was Washington's second in command in New York City. As Putnam's aide-de-camp, Burr was sent into New Jersey and elsewhere on recruiting trips. He inspected the American defenses on Long Island and accurately reported that they could not hold against an invading army. Following the initially successful operations of the British forces under the command of General William Howe, Burr played a central role in rescuing many of the American troops trapped at Brooklyn Heights. As American forces subsequently fled from New York City, Burr assisted Putnam in rescuing a brigade that faced entrapment by British forces that landed north of the city on 15 September.

In July 1777 the Continental Congress commissioned Burr as a lieutenant colonel with a regimental command in the Continental army, which spent the winter of 1777–1778 at Valley Forge, Pennsylvania. Because of his reputation for courage and instilling discipline in his troops, Burr was soon placed in command of the forces in defense of the "Gulph," a vulnerable area between mountains about six miles south of the American encampment where the British might attack. During this period Burr probably sympathized with those officers who attempted to replace Washington with another commander in chief. But Burr did not take an active role in this failed effort, known as the "Conway Cabal."

On 28 June 1778 Burr participated in the battle of Monmouth Courthouse in New Jersey. For a lengthy period his regiment was forced to remain in a dangerously exposed area. Burr's second in command fell to a British cannonball, and his horse was killed beneath him. Extreme humidity and a temperature that reached 96 degrees killed almost as many men as did the soldiers' weapons. Of the 106 American dead, 37 had died of sunstroke. Burr's health, which had been poor for several months, became worse. For years afterward he would suffer from bouts of nausea and prolonged headaches.

After a winter of conducting patrol activities, Burr informed Washington on 10 March 1779 that he was resigning from the army on account of his poor health. Although Washington expressed his regret at the "loss of a good officer," he was relieved to be rid of a troublesome subordinate. For his part, Burr was glad to end an assignment that offered no significant military advancement.

Burr's health problems prevented him from resuming his legal studies until 1780. Two years later he was admitted to the New York bar and married Theodosia Bartow Prevost, who was ten years his senior. They would have one child, but Theodosia Burr was frequently in poor health and died in 1794. In 1783 he moved to New York City, where he soon competed with Alexander Hamilton to be the city's most prominent lawyer. But his generosity and his poor speculative investments greatly diminished his large earnings.

In April 1784 Burr's political career began when the voters of New York City selected him to one of the nine seats in the state assembly that were allotted to the city and county of New York. By the late 1780s in New York, Hamilton and George Clinton were leading two competing groups that dominated the state's politics. In September 1789 Clinton appointed Burr as New York's attorney general. Two years later, despite Burr's involvement in a controversial public land deal, the Clinton-dominated legislature selected Burr for the U.S. Senate over Hamilton's father-in-law, Philip Schuyler, and thus created Hamilton's hostility toward Burr. Burr served one term in the Senate, during which he initially adhered to a position between the two national parties that were coalescing around Thomas Jefferson and Alexander Hamilton. But later Burr staunchly supported the Republican party on important issues, as when he opposed Jay's Treaty and defended the Democratic-Republican societies against criticism by President Washington. In 1796 the Republicans selected Burr to run with Jefferson on the party's national ticket, and in defeat the New Yorker received thirty electoral votes.

Burr also failed to win reelection to the U.S. Senate in 1797 on account of the changing politics in New York State. The following year, however, Burr won a seat in the state senate. He subsequently sponsored a bill that provided for separate districts from which presidential electors would be selected. Moreover, Burr successfully supported bills that benefited companies in which he had invested his own money. His subsequent defeat at the polls in 1799 can be attributed to the legislation that enhanced his investments.

Nevertheless, Burr had been building a strong political organization around the General Republican Committee. The nucleus of this organization was a small group known as the Burrites, who mobilized the voters of New York City and in April 1800 won a majority of the seats in the state legislature. This victory guaranteed the Republicans the Empire State's entire electoral vote in the presidential election. Burr then engineered his selection as vice president on the ticket with Jefferson.

Jefferson and Burr subsequently defeated the Federalist party's candidates in the presidential election of 1800. But under the election system of that time, before the passage of the Twelfth Amendment, the presidential electors did not vote for president and vice president separately. Each elector cast two ballots, and the candidate who received the greatest number of votes, if that number was a majority of the whole number of electors selected, was elected president, and the candidate who received the second highest number was elected vice president. All the Republican electors cast their votes for Jefferson and Burr. The two were thus tied, and the contest went to the House of Representatives, where the Federalists controlled the votes of enough states to prevent the election of Jefferson.

Burr published a letter asserting that he would not compete with Jefferson for the presidency, and the New Yorker refused to negotiate with the Federalists for their support. Nevertheless, a deadlock developed, and for thirty-five ballots neither Jefferson nor Burr received a majority of the votes of the states. But on the thirty-sixth ballot, partly because of Hamilton's opposition to Burr, the Federalists in the Maryland and Vermont delegations did not vote, which led to Jefferson's election.

Yet Jefferson had doubts about Burr's actions during the deadlock in the House of Representatives, and the Virginian wanted James Madison to be his successor as president. Jefferson thus did not confer with Burr in filling cabinet posts, and the president greatly limited the number of Burrites appointed to lesser positions. The New Yorker's political situation then worsened owing to the controversy that developed over the effort to repeal the Judiciary Act of 1801. Noting the clause in the Constitution that allowed federal judges to hold their positions during good behavior, Burr questioned whether it was constitutional to rescind the Judiciary Act and deprive twenty-six judges of their offices. But most of the leading Jeffersonians were convinced that the Judiciary Act was simply an attempt by the outgoing John Adams administration to establish a Federalist stronghold in the national government that would prevent the Republicans from enacting their program of reform. Thus the ruling Jeffersonians denounced Burr's viewpoint and repealed the Judiciary Act.

Burr also antagonized and alienated Republican leaders by participating in an 1802 Federalist celebration honoring George Washington's birthday, and Burr also denounced a vituperative pamphlet that attacked the Adams administration. Sensing that the pamphlet would do the Republican party more harm than good, he proposed to suppress it by purchasing all 1,250 copies. This action triggered the so-called Pamphlet War between the Burrites and the anti-Burrites. Leading the latter faction was James Cheetham, who made the unsubstantiated charge that Burr had schemed with the Federalists in 1801 to steal the presidency from Jefferson. By March 1802 Burr had decided to leave the Republican party, whose reigning leaders had abandoned him.

In 1804 the Republican leaders replaced Burr as the party's vice presidential candidate. That same year he ran for governor of New York against Morgan Lewis, the regular Jeffersonian candidate. During the campaign, Burr refused to accept assistance from New England Federalists in exchange for a promise to combine New York with New England in a secessionist scheme. In addition, Hamilton continued his opposition to the vice president by circulating letters that contained disparaging remarks about Burr. Although most Federalists voted for the vice president despite Hamilton's remarks and Burr's opposition to disunion plans, Lewis easily won the election with help from the Clinton and Livingston factions.

Following the election, Burr became increasingly angry at those he held responsible for his political downfall. But his libel suit against Cheetham brought him no satisfaction since he considered Cheetham a mere hired hand of powerful anti-Burr leaders. Thus Burr felt that the most effective response would be through the code duello. In June the vice president issued a challenge to Hamilton, after Hamilton refused to make a comprehensive disclaimer of his derogatory comments of Burr uttered during the gubernatorial campaign.

Hamilton accepted Burr's challenge, and the two men met in Weehawken, New Jersey, on 11 July 1804. As a result, Hamilton suffered a fatal wound as a ball lodged in his spine. As Hamilton fell, he fired his pistol wildly and, according to his second, involuntarily. Burr was not wounded. After Hamilton died the next day, an outpouring of mourning occurred. Overnight, in the minds of many in the northern and middle states, Burr became a cold-blooded murderer.

With warrants out for his arrest in New York and New Jersey, Burr traveled to Philadelphia and then to the South to escape capture. During his last days as vice president, he had begun to envision the creation of a new nation by seizing Spanish territory in the Trans-Mississippi West and perhaps by separating much of the Trans-Appalachian area from the rest of the United States. Burr enlisted the support of those Americans who might be of help, including wealthy Harman Blennerhassett, though he never disclosed his full intentions to any individual.

One of Burr's allies was General James Wilkinson, the ranking general of the U.S. Army and a secret pensioner of the Spanish government. Burr and Wilkinson discussed a plan for an expedition into Mexico. Indeed, Zebulon Pike's famous expedition that led to the discovery of Pike's Peak was actually a military reconnaissance for an invasion of Mexican territory.

In April 1805 Burr traveled to the West, then down the Mississippi River to New Orleans. Despite a warm welcome from a number of leaders, Burr was disappointed that there did not appear to be an immediate prospect of a clash between U.S. and Spanish troops on the Louisiana-Texas frontier. Without this fighting and a subsequent American invasion of Mexican territory, Burr did not believe he could implement his plan.

Returning to Washington, Burr did not gain British interest in his plan, but the Spanish government did provide him with $10,000 ostensibly to defend Spanish America against U.S. filibustering expeditions. Then in the summer of 1806 Burr led sixty followers and a half dozen flatboats down the Mississippi River. But Wilkinson, concerned about his own safety, refused to be further involved. Instead, he informed President Jefferson of "a deep, dark, wicked, and widespread conspiracy" and ordered the arrest of Burr and his followers when they reached the lower Mississippi for allegedly seeking the secession of the Louisiana Territory. After being paroled, Burr attempted to flee to Spanish territory but was again captured and sent to Virginia. In 1807 he was indicted for treason and brought to trial in the U.S. Circuit Court in Richmond, Virginia, with Chief Justice John Marshall as the presiding judge.

Personal and political conflict between Jefferson and Marshall carried over into the trial. Regarding the law of treason, Marshall gave a very restricting interpretation of the meaning of the Constitution's words "levying war." Under Marshall's interpretation, Burr's absentee connection with the gathering of Burr's followers at Blennerhassett Island was insufficient to make him guilty of treason. Despite Jefferson's strenuous efforts to obtain a conviction, Marshall's definition of the law resulted in Burr's acquittal.

During the years 1808–1812 Burr lived in Europe, where he unsuccessfully attempted to interest Great Britain and France in his plan for creating a new nation in the Southwest. In May 1812 he returned to the United States and again began to practice law in New York. But within two months he received word of the death of his only grandchild, Aaron Burr Alston, and in December his beloved daughter, Theodosia, was lost at sea. In July 1833, at age seventy-seven, Burr married Elizabeth Brown Jumel, a well-to-do widow in her fifties. But within a year he had squandered much of her fortune, and she sued for divorce alleging that Burr had recently committed matrimonial offenses "at divers times with divers females." The divorce was granted on the day Burr died in Port Richmond, Staten Island.

• Most of Burr's manuscripts are in the New-York Historical Society. Additional correspondence is in the Yale University Library; the Library of Congress; and the Henry E. Huntington Library, San Marino, Calif. Also see *Political Correspondence and Public Papers of Aaron Burr*, ed. Mary-Jo Kline et al. (2 vols., 1983), and *Memoirs of Aaron Burr with Miscellaneous Selections from His Correspondence*, ed. Matthew L. Davis (2 vols., 1836–1837). The best biography is Milton Lomask, *Aaron Burr* (2 vols., 1979, 1982). Also useful are Nathan Schachner, *Aaron Burr* (1937), and Herbert Parmet and M. B. Hecht, *Aaron Burr* (1967).

STEVEN E. SIRY

BURR, Esther Edwards (13 Feb. 1732–7 Apr. 1758), diarist, was born in Northampton, Massachusetts, the daughter of Jonathan Edwards, a minister and author, and Sarah Pierrepont. Burr was the third in a family of eleven children. She was educated at home. As the child of the minister in a large town, she enjoyed a comfortable lifestyle and social prominence. The years of her childhood fell in the period of religious revivals known as the Great Awakening. In 1750 her father was dismissed from his Northampton pastorate because of conflicts with his congregation. After a period of uncertainty and hardship for the Edwardses while her father contemplated job offers from as far away from Northampton as the American South and even Scotland, the family finally relocated in 1751 to frontier Stockbridge, Massachusetts, a town on the New York border where Edwards would serve as missionary to the Indians.

In 1752, after a romantic five-day courtship, Esther Edwards married Aaron Burr, who was sixteen years her elder. Son of a prosperous Connecticut landowner, Aaron Burr was both the Presbyterian minister of Newark, New Jersey, and the founding president of the newly formed College of New Jersey (later known as Princeton). In marrying Burr, Esther assumed a high social station with heavy responsibilities. She bore a daughter in 1754 and in 1756 a son who would later become the infamous slayer of Alexander Hamilton. In 1757 she was widowed when Aaron Burr succumbed to a fatal attack of malaria after a journey. Esther Burr died after a brief illness of unknown causes in Princeton, New Jersey, less than a month after the death of her father, who had arrived in Princeton just two months previously to assume the college presidency left vacant by the death of his son-in-law.

In October 1754 Burr had commenced the personal journal on which her historical interest rests; she suspended it with an entry on 2 September 1757, describing the departure of Aaron, Sr., on a journey to preach the funeral sermon of New Jersey's late governor. What history calls her journal could actually be considered one-half of an interactive work in which she and a girlhood friend living in Boston, Sarah Prince (whom Burr called "Fidelia," while Prince called Burr "Burrissa"), maintained an exchange of personal reports and comments on each other's dispatches. Prince was the daughter of Thomas Prince, a Boston minister and author, in status comparable to and in theology congenial with Jonathan Edwards. Sarah Prince had visited Burr in Newark during Burr's pregnancy earlier in 1754. The journal consists of dated and numbered installments that were exchanged with Prince in packets carried between Newark and Boston by private individuals, sometimes supplemented by other letters on more personal topics that the two young women would burn after reading.

In the words of her modern editors, Burr's journal "is an excellent example of women's literary efforts as they appeared in the mid-eighteenth century. . . . [Burr] participated in the emergence of private documents as a female literary genre." At a minimum, according to Carol F. Karlsen and Laurie Crumpacker, Burr's journal places her in "a tradition of American women writers from Anne Bradstreet to Harriet Beecher Stowe" ("Introduction," p. 23) Much of especially the early part of the journal is occupied with Burr's critical reflections not only on her literary and religious reading (both American and English and in both prose and verse), but also on the sermons she heard and on the manners of her neighbors and visitors in New Jersey. Her necessarily hurried prose does not, as it hardly could, rival the artistic distinction achievable in the far more favorable writing conditions enjoyed, for instance, by her father; nor can her subjects compete with the range his finer education made possible among philosophy, history, and theology; but on her own subjects—devotional religion, religion, family, romantic love, popular literature, friendship, and nature—her writing displays a liveliness and wit her father could not match. As a humorous commentator on the manners and mores of her time, Burr begs comparison with Madam Sarah Knight, earlier in the eighteenth century, and Alice James, in the later nineteenth. In subject matter and tone, if not in form, Burr is arguably a worthy forerunner of Emily Dickinson.

Burr's journal is obviously of the keenest interest to students and lovers of women's history, American history, and religious history. But it has equal claim on the student of literary history, both the political-cultural history of American literature and the generic history of personal writing. And unlike many documents that could claim the latter, Burr's journal also displays significant literary (aesthetic, linguistic, dramatic) aspirations as well. Jonathan Edwards's friend and student Samuel Hopkins described Burr as a child in his biography of her father as having "a lively, sprightly imagination, a quick and penetrating thought [and] . . . a peculiar smartness in her make and temper. . . . She knew how to be pleasant and facetious." Her sister Lucy reminded a third sister, Mary, in a private letter, that Burr "never could bear pestering very well." Composed and, whenever possible, corrected, in odd moments snatched from a crushing double shift of domestic labor and social duties, to the demanding literary standards that Sarah Prince and other literary young women of their circle expected of "Burrissa," the journal of Esther Edwards Burr bears out both Hopkins's and Lucy Edwards's assessments of her character, making it a highly readable, sometimes poignantly beguiling document.

• Esther Edwards Burr's letter-journal is held in Beinecke Rare Book and Manuscript Library at Yale University. Various letters are held in the Manuscript Collections, Franklin Trask Library, Andover Newton Theological School, Newton Center, Mass. The most substantial biographical treatment is the introduction to Carol F. Karlsen and Laurie Crumpacker, eds., *The Journal of Esther Edwards Burr, 1754–57* (1984). The most sustained discussion of the text is Crumpacker's earlier dissertation, "Esther Burr's Journal, 1754–1757: A Document of Evangelical Sisterhood" (Ph.D. diss., Boston Univ., 1978). Ruth Barnes Moynihan, Cynthia Russett, and Crumpacker provide a thoughtful assessment in the headnotes to their selections from Burr's journal in their anthology *Second to None: A Documentary History of American Women*, vol. 1 (1993).

CAROL M. BENSICK

BURR, George Lincoln (30 Jan. 1857–27 June 1938), librarian, historian, and educator, was born in Oramel, New York, the son of William Josiah Burr, a physician, and Jane Lincoln. Educated in the public schools of Newark Valley and the Cortland Academy, Burr worked as a printer to pay for his schooling. In 1877 he entered Cornell University, where he received his A.B. four years later. Upon graduation, thanks to the friendship shown by Cornell president Andrew Dickson White, Burr was named an instructor in history as well as White's personal secretary and librarian.

White arranged for Burr to spend the years 1884–1886 and 1887–1888 traveling in Europe. There he studied at the Universities of Leipzig and Paris, as well as at the École des Chartes and later at the University of Zurich. Burr also tracked down and purchased numerous rare books and manuscripts for his patron. (In 1902 he published "A Witch-Hunter in the Book-Shops," recounting his many discoveries.)

After returning to Cornell in 1888 Burr prepared three carefully annotated catalogs of White's library, one on the Protestant Reformation (1889), a second on the French Revolution (1894), and a third on miscellaneous subjects (1897). He tirelessly built up the White library and amassed a valuable collection of works on the Reformation and witchcraft even as he continued his teaching.

Although Burr never obtained a doctorate in history, he gradually established himself as a leading authority on witchcraft. In 1886 he presented a paper to the History and Political Science Association on a sixteenth-century manuscript of a book written against the persecution of witches, a document he had found in a German library. Burr published a series of scholarly articles dealing with the subject, notably "The Fate of Dietrich Flade" (1891), on a German victim of witchcraft hysteria, and "New England's Place in the History of Witchcraft" (1911), dealing with persecution in America. In 1914 his collection of primary sources on the craze in colonial America, *Narratives of the Witchcraft Cases, 1648–1706*, appeared. It was his final word on the subject.

Burr could also turn his hand to practical matters. In 1895, when a long-standing boundary dispute between Venezuela and Great Britain came to a head,

President Grover Cleveland was requested to appoint a neutral commission to resolve the issue. One of the five commissioners named was White, who called on his friend Burr to help settle tangled historical questions because of his "fidelity to truth and justice." Burr explored the sources available in the Netherlands, learning Dutch so as to read the original documents. He worked feverishly between March and October 1896, when he returned home with his discoveries. By 1899, thanks in part to Burr's work, the dispute was resolved in Britain's favor. He summarized his efforts in "The Guiana Boundary" (1900).

Burr's work for the commission only briefly interrupted his teaching and historical scholarship. At Cornell he gained a reputation as a popular but demanding instructor. His classroom lectures were rather informal, marked by a rapid-fire delivery and frequent bibliographical references. (Burr would always enter the lecture hall carrying an armful of books.) He sought to re-create the atmosphere of a particular period, as well as paint vivid word portraits of figures such as Erasmus and Luther. In his graduate seminars, Burr focused on problems of methodology, emphasizing paleography, diplomatics, and historical geography. During his lengthy teaching career—he held the chair of medieval history from 1892 until he retired in 1922—Burr trained future prominent historians such as Roland H. Bainton, Leo Gershoy, and Louis R. Gottschalk. In 1931 twenty-one of his former students published a festschrift, *Persecution and Liberty*, in his honor.

Two deep personal losses marred the long happiness that Burr enjoyed at Cornell. In 1907 he had married Martha A. Martin, but she died in 1909 after giving birth to a stillborn child. In 1918 Burr's patron and friend, Andrew D. White, died at age eighty-six. Burr honored his memory with an eloquent eulogy given at a campus memorial service and a fond reminiscence published in the *Dictionary of American Biography* (1936).

Despite his extensive knowledge of witchcraft, religious liberty, and toleration, Burr never completed a substantial original work on these subjects. A meticulous scholar, he continually gathered fresh material both at home and abroad. A perfectionist when it came to writing, he composed slowly and laboriously. Burr did edit for publication and prepare an introduction to the lengthy manuscript *Materials toward a History of Witchcraft*, left unfinished by Henry Charles Lea at his death in 1909, but he did not live to see it appear in print. Always a voracious reader, Burr served as associate editor of the *American Historical Review* from 1905 to 1916, preparing numerous reviews of books written not only in English, but also in German, French, and Dutch.

In a tribute to his scholarship and service, the American Historical Association elected Burr as its president in 1916. He used his presidential address "The Freedom of History" to trace the development of liberty in the historical profession from ancient Greece to modern times. He stressed the limitations that political and religious forces had attempted to place on historians and declared that their discipline had eventually liberated itself. Burr declared his firm belief that "on the freedom of history . . . all our other freedom rests."

Burr spent the remainder of his life at Cornell, devoting himself to the personal well being of all students and becoming known affectionately as "Poppy Burr." In poor health from 1935, he died in Ithaca. Burr's importance as a historian was diminished because he produced no full-length book on either witchcraft or the history of liberty. But his efforts to discover and publish original documents, combined with his stewardship of the White library, earned Burr a reputation as an eminent scholar.

• A collection of Burr's papers is in the Cornell University library. The biography by Roland H. Bainton, *George Lincoln Burr: His Life* (1943), contains numerous selections from his writings (ed. Lois Oliphant Gibbons) and a complete bibliography. Appreciations are in J. Franklin Jameson, *Persecution and Liberty: Essays in Honor of George Lincoln Burr* (1931), and F. M. Powicke, *Ways of Medieval Life and Thought* (1951). Obituaries are in the *New York Times*, 28 June 1938, *American Historical Review* 44 (Oct. 1938), *Proceedings of the American Antiquarian Society*, n.s., 48 (Oct. 1938), and *Speculum* 14 (July 1939).

JAMES FRIGUGLIETTI

BURR, Raymond (21 May 1917–12 Sept. 1993), actor, was born Raymond William Stacy Burr in New Westminster, British Columbia, Canada, the son of William Johnston Burr, a Canadian hardware dealer, and Minerva Smith, an American pianist and music teacher. Burr's early years were spent in an unusual mixture of privilege and privation. Traveling at a young age with his parents and later with his maternal grandfather, he was exposed to other cultures and languages, notably Chinese. At the same time, Burr suffered emotionally from the separation of his parents when he was five or six years old. His mother brought Burr and his two younger siblings to Vallejo, California, while his father remained in British Columbia.

Burr briefly attended San Rafael Military Academy, but he was fated never to complete high school, due to the financial pressures wrought by the Great Depression. During his adolescent years, Burr worked at a number of different jobs; he ran a store, worked for a weather station, and enrolled in the Civilian Conservation Corps. He found his true vocation through an acting part in Vancouver when he was twelve and a singing performance on Benny Walker's KGO radio show in San Francisco, at fifteen. His early years of varied employment had fashioned him into a self-reliant young man with a great capacity for work.

At age nineteen Burr toured with the Toronto summer theater. He sang in a café in Paris, and in February 1941 he made his first appearance on Broadway in *Crazy with the Heat*. By this time his talent and drive were making him known to a larger audience, and he moved on to direct the Pasadena Community Playhouse in 1943. In the following year Burr joined the

U.S. Navy and served in counterintelligence. The ship that he was on was hit by Japanese kamikaze planes, and Burr suffered a shrapnel wound in his spine. He later received the Purple Heart for the injuries that he had sustained. Following the conclusion of World War II and his recovery from the injury, Burr was ready to give his all to acting.

He worked in film and radio for the next ten years. Generally assigned to "bad-guy" roles because of his size and weight (he stood 6′2″ and his weight varied between 200 and more than 300 pounds), Burr worked his way up the ladder of the film industry during the early 1950s. He won favorable attention as the district attorney in *A Place in the Sun* (1951) and became known to many filmgoers through his role as the murderous Lars Thorwald in Alfred Hitchcock's *Rear Window* (1954). Despite his love for both film and radio, Burr eventually found that the new medium of television was his strongest suit. In 1957 he was chosen over 200 competitors to star as the district attorney "Perry Mason" on the Columbia Broadcasting System (CBS).

The show aired on 21 September 1957, opposite a strong rival, the Perry Como show on NBC. Although critics were unimpressed by "Perry Mason," the public responded with enthusiasm that eventually grew into devotion. In many American households, Saturday evenings were reserved for watching the program, and by late 1959 "Perry Mason" recorded an audience of more than 30 million viewers. Burr won the *TV Guide* award for most popular male television personality in 1960, and the program won two Emmy awards, for best leading actor in a dramatic series. The success of the show was attributed to Burr's ability to convey a sense of Mason's thoughtful but relentless pursuit of the truth. More than any other television program of the era, "Perry Mason" brought about an increased, albeit amateur, interest in the law and in criminal justice on the part of the American public.

After filming the last episode of "Perry Mason" in 1966, Burr began a new program, "Ironside" (1967–1975), in which he portrayed a wheelchair-bound chief of detectives. The show enjoyed considerable success, and Burr also turned his hand to made-for-television movies and miniseries, such as *A Man Whose Name Was John* (1973), *Seventy-Nine Park Avenue* (1978), and *Centennial* (1978). Burr also enjoyed the rare pleasure of being asked to return to his original and most successful genre in 1985. He filmed Perry Mason specials for the rest of his life, thereby becoming well known to a generation of television viewers who had not even been born when he had commenced the original "Perry Mason" in 1957. In this he joined a select group of television stars, such as Dinah Shore and Dick Van Dyke, who were renowned for their longevity on the television screen.

Burr experienced considerable tragedy in his personal life. He married three times: to Annette Sutherland in 1942 or 1943, to Isabella Ward in 1948, and to Andrina Morgan in 1954. His first wife died in a plane crash in 1943, and Burr gave custody of their son to her parents (the boy died of leukemia in 1953). Burr and his second wife divorced in 1952, and his third wife died of cancer within a year of their marriage. Following these disasters, Burr lived a quiet personal life on a remote Pacific island that he purchased and his ranch near Healdsburg, California, where he raised sheep and cultivated grapes for wine. He died on his ranch.

Burr's career branched through the three fields of radio, film, and television, but it was as "Perry Mason" and "Ironside" that he became known to millions of Americans. Burr was one of the most prolific and long-lasting of the early actors of American television. In his best-known television role, Burr appears to have stood for a curiously magnetic American archetype: the stern and sober attorney who acted as a champion of justice for the falsely accused. In the formation of the formidable and even grim character that he portrayed, there was personal experience as well as talent. Burr had known heartache from an early age, had made his own way in the world, and had experienced great tragedy in his personal life. He was well suited to play the intense, brooding attorney who always got to the bottom of the matter. It is also true that Burr was fortunate in the timing of his entrance into television. He benefited from the fact that there were only three major television networks during the 1950s and 1960s. In the decades that followed, the proliferation of cable television and dozens of networks would work to lessen the chance that any television actor, even one as dynamic and forceful as Burr, could enjoy such popularity and longevity on the screen. Thus, the success of "Perry Mason" stands both as a testament to Burr's acting skill and as an icon of the era of early American television.

• The most important source for Burr's life and career is Ona Hill, *Raymond Burr: A Film, Radio and Television Biography* (1994). In addition there are numerous pieces on Burr in *TV Guide* and *People Weekly*, both at the time of his success with the original Perry Mason show (1957–1966) and during the return of the program (1985–1993). Obituaries are in the *New York Times*, 14 Sept. 1993; *TV Guide*, 25 September 1993; and *Time*, 27 Sept. 1993.

SAMUEL WILLARD CROMPTON

BURR, Theodosia (21 June 1783–Jan. 1813), society belle and political heroine, was born in Albany, New York, the daughter of Aaron Burr, a lawyer, politician, and later vice president of the United States, and Theodosia Prevost. Steeped in the educational philosophy of Jean Jacques Rousseau, author of *Émile*, and of Mary Wollstonecraft, the author of *A Vindication of the Rights of Women*, Aaron Burr took great interest in the care and education of Theodosia, determined that she have an education as good as any boy's. He made certain that in addition to the customary French, music, and dancing she take arithmetic, Latin, Greek, and English composition—the last in the form of letters to him, which he promptly returned with detailed criticisms. His wife's health had been in decline from the first years of their marriage. When she died in May

1794 ten-year-old Theodosia became, in effect, the mistress of "Richmond Hill," her father's magnificent country estate on the outskirts of New York City.

Young Theodosia proved equal to the task in large part because of the meticulous social education her father had given her. At Richmond Hill she served as hostess to a stream of distinguished guests, both foreign and American, such as Talleyrand, the French foreign minister in the 1790s and early 1800s, Louis Philippe, the future king of France (1830–1848), and the Mohawk chief Joseph Brant. Theodosia acquired fame as one of the belles of New York society and became one of the best educated American women of her time.

On 2 February 1801 Theodosia married Joseph Alston, a member of one of the greatest planting families of South Carolina, whom she had met on his travels in New York. The marriage left her women friends aghast. Why, they wondered, would one of such great beauty and personality marry a southerner they considered so devoid of any attractive character or personality traits? He was described as "rich, but a great dasher, dissipated, ill-tempered, vain, silly, ugly, and of unprepossessing manners" (Maria Nicholson to Mrs. Gallatin; Henry Adams, *Life of Albert Gallatin* [1879], pp. 244–45). The marriage produced, however, an affectionate union and a southern base of support for Aaron Burr's politics. In 1802 the birth of their only child weakened Theodosia's frail constitution, forcing her into a continuous succession of visits to spas and doctors to no avail. Nor did any of the things Alston's great wealth could provide—social status, servants, and the cushioned ease of four lavishly furnished homes (their principal home was "The Oaks" on the Waccamaw River)—bring relief.

Added to these personal difficulties for Theodosia was the great weight of the political demise of her father after 1800. First, there was the loss of the presidency to Thomas Jefferson in 1800. Then came the duel with Alexander Hamilton in 1804. Hamilton had thrown his great political strength against Burr in the runoff election between Jefferson and Burr for president in the House of Representatives. He felt that Burr was dangerous and should not be trusted with the reins of government. Hamilton voiced dissatisfaction with Burr as a candidate for governor of New York in 1804, feeling that if Burr were elected, he just might join with the political malcontents of New England in trying to bring about the secession of New York and New England from the Union. Burr lost the election, for which he blamed Hamilton. But what angered Burr the most was Hamilton's charge (without hard evidence) that Burr had had sexual relations with Theodosia. The duel followed, in which Hamilton was killed. The death of Hamilton—he made no effort to harm Burr, instead firing in the air—led to Burr's being ostracized from polite American society.

Following this, Burr developed the "western conspiracy" of 1806. What he intended to do is not altogether clear. It appears, however, that he planned an expedition down the Ohio and Mississippi rivers to New Orleans, where he hoped to get the Spanish territory in what is now the United States to secede and join up with the western American territory in a separate western state. Before Burr's expedition down the Ohio, Theodosia had visited Harman Blennerhassett and his wife, who had actively supported the conspiracy, at their river island home from which the expedition began. She was later joined there by Alston for several weeks before their return to South Carolina. Theodosia was with Burr during his conspiracy trial in Richmond, giving him aid and sustenance. After his acquittal, she took possession of his personal papers in New York when he departed for a four-year exile in Europe. All during this time she raised money to send to Burr and sought the aid of people such as Dolley Madison and Secretary of the Treasury Albert Gallatin in smoothing his return.

When in July 1812 Burr was reestablished in New York, Theodosia was not able to join him immediately. The death of her son in June had weakened her to the point that she was not able to depart from New York until December. She sailed on the *Patriot* from Georgetown (Alston had just been elected governor, thus preventing him from accompanying her) never to reach her destination. As to what may have happened to her ship, there are three distinct possibilities—it may have been lost in a severe storm in early January off the Outer Banks of North Carolina, it may have been captured by pirates and the passengers killed, or it may have run aground with the passengers murdered by the notorious Carolina "bankers" (outlaws who preyed on shipping along the Outer Banks). A story in a New York newspaper, *The Advertiser*, on 23 June 1820 gives plausible support to the ship having been captured by pirates. Two pirates about to be executed in New Orleans stated that they had posed as crew members of the *Patriot*, then risen up and seized the ship after two or three days at sea, taking a sizable amount of money and plate (belonging mainly to Mrs. Alston), putting all the passengers in the hold, and scuttling the ship before departing for land in a boat. A major loss with the *Patriot* was the papers of Aaron Burr, which should have shed considerable light on his politics and what he was really up to in the West.

Theodosia Burr is one of the most interesting women in American history. Superbly educated for her time, she joined through marriage the highest level of American polite society. She was a strong political support to both her father, Aaron Burr, and her husband, Joseph Alston. Her mysterious death has, however, largely relegated her to the world of shadowy romance.

• The Harman Blennerhassett Papers in the Library of Congress contain much material on the involvement of Theodosia and Joseph Alston in Aaron Burr's western conspiracy. Two good short accounts of Theodosia Burr are Meade Minnigerode, "Theodosia Burr, Prodigy, an Informal Biography," *Saturday Evening Post*, 6 Sept. 1924, and Ronald Ray Swick, "Theodosia Burr Alston," *South Atlantic Quarterly* 74 (1975): 495–506. See also James Parton, *The Life and Times of Aaron Burr* (1892); H. Wandell and Meade Minnigerode,

Aaron Burr (1925); Milton Lomask, *Aaron Burr* (1979); and Charles F. Pidgin, *Theodosia, the First Gentle Woman of Her Time: The Story of Her Life, and a History of Persons and Events Connected Therewith* (1907). For the ghostly legends of Theodosia Burr, see Julian Stevenson Bolick, *The Return of the Gray Man* (1961).

JAMES M. CLIFTON

BURR, William Hubert (14 July 1851–13 Dec. 1934), engineer, was born in Watertown, Connecticut, the son of George William Burr, a railroad employee, and Marion Foote Scoville. Burr was educated by private tutor before attending Watertown Academy and Rensselaer Polytechnic Institute (RPI), from which he graduated with a degree of civil engineer in 1872.

Burr's first job after graduation was with the Phillipsburg Manufacturing Company, a builder of wrought iron bridges. After two years he transferred to a position with the Newark, New Jersey, waterworks. After a year in that post, he accepted an invitation from RPI to become a temporary instructor in the Department of Mechanics. In 1876 he assumed the title of William Howard Taft Professor of Rational and Technical Mechanics. That same year Burr married Caroline Kent Seelye; they had three children before she died in 1894. Burr married Gertrude Gold Shipman in 1900; they had one daughter.

The mid-1870s were an interesting time for engineering education, as the field was just entering a crucial transition. Before 1870, although engineering schools existed in the United States, most engineers entered the profession by learning through experience in the field. By 1900, however, most engineers were educated through formal classroom instruction at a college or university. Burr firmly endorsed this shift, arguing that students needed to know why things worked as much as how they worked. He authored two textbooks while teaching at RPI: *A Course on the Stresses in Bridge and Roof Trusses, Arched Ribs, and Suspension Bridges* (1880) and *The Elasticity and Resistance of the Materials of Engineering* (1883). Both books provided students with an understanding of the basic principles underlying their subjects; both, in revised editions, remained in print for many years. While Burr advocated a mathematical basis for structural analysis, he made it clear that the goal of his work was the construction of better bridges, not abstract theorizing. In this regard Burr was firmly within the practical tradition of American engineering education.

In 1884 Burr accepted a position as an assistant to the chief engineer of the Phoenix Bridge Company in Phoenixville, Pennsylvania. (This decision, too, was typical of members of engineering faculties of his generation, who often spent summers or even longer periods of time working in industry to stay abreast of developments in their fields.) Burr remained with Phoenix Bridge, one of the nation's leading bridge-building firms, until 1891. Phoenix pioneered the development of standardized designs for truss bridges, especially for the railroads, and Burr became the general manager of the firm. He played an important role as the firm struggled with the transition to steel, which was much stronger than iron as a structural material, and he helped develop standards for modern steel design. He also superintended the design and construction of a number of leading bridges, including a three-span railroad truss across the Ohio River at Cincinnati in 1888 that included a record-length center span of 550 feet.

In 1891 Burr accepted an offer to become the vice president of Sooysmith and Company, a New York engineering consulting firm that specialized in foundations and construction. But he remained there only a year before returning to education when Harvard appointed him a professor of civil engineering in 1892. This stay, too, was short, for in 1893 Burr moved to Columbia University in order to build and improve that school's civil engineering program. Until he retired as emeritus professor in 1916, Burr devoted himself to this task. According to one of his students, James Kip Finch, a future dean of engineering at Columbia, Burr required students to find out for themselves in order to really learn. His classes did not offer "predigested, easily assimilated information; neither was his teaching of the inspirational type" (Finch, p. 1619). But he was a leader in engineering education of this time, stressing that engineering students required a broad and liberal base in order to earn professional parity with doctors and lawyers. He considered himself the first American engineering professor to teach practical design work in iron and steel construction, to offer analytic designs of drawbridges, and to introduce a rational theory of earth pressure in design of masonry arches. Burr also took great pride in stressing the combination of theoretical understanding and practice. Although he acknowledged that he was occasionally accused of being too theoretical, Burr himself was never far removed from practical engineering work.

Burr also continued to revise his engineering textbooks and to write new ones. The eighth edition of the volume on bridge and roof trusses appeared in 1893; a revised and enlarged ninth edition was published in 1900. The book on engineering materials appeared in a fourth enlarged edition in 1894 and a further enlarged sixth edition in 1903. With Columbia colleague Myron S. Falk, he published *Graphic Methods by Influence Lines for Bridges and Roof Computations* (1905), a book outlining an advanced method of calculating the stress in trusses. In 1912 *Design and Construction of Metallic Bridges* appeared, a completely rewritten version of his book on bridge and roof design. The next year *Suspension Bridges, Arch Ribs, and Cantilevers* (again coauthored with Falk) was published, providing students with more advanced treatments of this subject.

During his entire career at Columbia, Burr also retained an active engineering consulting practice that led to his involvement with many of the largest and most exciting engineering projects of the day. In 1893 he was appointed to a presidential board that investigated possible canal routes across Central America. The board initially favored a route through Nicaragua because of difficulties in obtaining rights in Panama, but after the French company that had begun the canal made a new offer to the United States in 1902, the board was reassembled. This time it supported a canal across Panama. In 1904 Burr was appointed by President Theodore Roosevelt to a new commission to study the merits of locks rather than a sea-level canal.

Burr also acted as a consultant for a number of other government bodies. In 1893 he was a consulting engineer for the New York City Department of Public Works on the Harlem River Ship and Barge Canal, and from 1895 to 1898 he worked with the same organization on the Harlem River Drive. In 1894 he was named to another presidential commission that studied building a suspension bridge across the Hudson River at Manhattan; a similar commission in 1896 involved a study of a proposed deep harbor project at San Pedro, California. In 1902 Burr chaired a committee for studying New York City's water supply, examining the possibilities of drawing water from the Catskill Mountains. The committee, which Burr chaired, produced a massive document that examined ways to reduce waste, improve quality, and plan for the future, as well as preliminary estimates on the costs of developing reservoirs in the Catskills and aqueducts into New York City. In 1911 Burr was appointed by the governor to consider the design of the New York State Barge Canal, a major expansion of the Erie Canal system.

So extensive was Burr's consulting work that some students (and Presidents Seth Low and Nicholas Murray Butler of Columbia) occasionally worried that Burr was spending too little time on campus. Throughout his career, however, he balanced these commitments in a professional manner. After he retired, Burr continued to work as a consulting engineer. From 1916 to 1918 he took part in the preliminary studies of what became the Holland Tunnel, helping to conduct surface and subsurface examinations and ventilation research, and helping to develop costs and estimates. Burr was for many years a consultant for New York's Port Authority on various bridges, including the George Washington Bridge over the Hudson River, and in 1930 he became the Port Authority's consulting engineer on all construction work, including the Lincoln Tunnel.

Burr's work was considered first-rate by his peers, and he received a number of awards and recognitions. In 1900 his design for a bridge over the Potomac River at Washington, D.C. (completed in 1931) won first prize in a competition. In 1891 he won the American Society of Civil Engineers (ASCE) Thomas Fitch Rowland Prize for his paper, "The River Spans of the Cincinnati and Covington Elevated Railway, Transfer and Bridge Company." The British Institution of Civil Engineers presented Burr with its gold medal in 1912 for a paper on "Composite Columns of Concrete and Steel." A long-time member of the ASCE, which he joined in 1874, Burr served as the director of the society from 1894 to 1896. Burr also had professional ties to both England and Japan.

With his varied interests in all facets of civil engineering and his careers in both industry and academia, Burr was typical of the leaders of his generation who advanced engineering from the status of a craft activity to that of a profession. He assisted that transition through his engineering practice, his teaching, and his writing.

• Archival records about Burr are in the William H. Burr Ephemera File in the Columbiana Collection at Columbia University. This includes a biographical file. Additional correspondence concerning Burr's activities as a faculty member at Columbia can be found in the Central File, Burr subseries, in the Columbia University Archives. Both collections are in Low Memorial Library. Other works by Burr include "Forty-one Years a Builder," *Columbia Alumni News* 7 (5 May 1916): 905–08; "The Technical School and the University," *Columbia University Quarterly* (Dec. 1906); *Ancient and Modern Engineering and the Isthmian Canal* (1902); and *Report of the Commission on Additional Water Supply for the City of New York* (1904). General information on Burr can be found in *Who's Who in Engineering* (1931); James Kip Finch, "William Hubert Burr," *Transactions of the American Society of Civil Engineers* 100 (1935): 1617–21. An obituary is in the *New York Times*, 14 Dec. 1934.

BRUCE E. SEELY

BURRELL, Berkeley Graham (12 June 1919–30 Aug. 1979), business executive and civic leader, was born in Washington, D.C., the son of Hayward G. Burrell and Fannie Miles. Although his parents' occupations are unknown, both his father and mother were natives of the District of Columbia, and Burrell's roots in the area ran deep. After graduating from Dunbar High School at the age of fifteen, he worked as a driver for a local pharmacy and apparently also drove a cab for a while. He married at age sixteen (wife's name unknown), and the marriage produced a son before ending in divorce seven years later.

In 1941 Burrell gained a position at the federal Bureau of Standards, where he worked in the glass section producing prisms and bombsights. He also attended nearby Howard University between 1941 and 1943 but did not graduate. He entered the U.S. Army in 1945 and rose to the rank of first sergeant before receiving his discharge from active duty in 1946. Determined to go into business for himself, he returned to his hometown and opened a dry cleaning store with $100 in capital. Having chosen his first location wisely, he was soon able to open three additional stores, only to struggle to meet payments when the other locations proved less successful. Burrell's early struggles to achieve business success shaped his later views on minority-owned businesses. He also took an interest in local civil rights activities, becoming a member of both the Urban League and the National Association for the Advancement of Colored People (NAACP).

By 1951 Burrell's resources were sufficient enough for him to consider expansion, and with $30,000 in borrowed funds he purchased a large dry cleaning facility that came with nineteen retail outlets. Although he was soon recalled to active duty in the army with the advent of the Korean War, he managed to maintain the business with the help of a new partner, A. Parthenia "Pat" Robinson, the daughter of a North Carolina barber. Burrell married her in 1951; although the marriage produced no children, it did provide him with a strong partner in all of his business affairs.

As Burrell's Superb Cleaners continued to grow, its owner sought to communicate his hard-earned business experience to other African-American entrepreneurs. Long active in the National Business League (NBL)—an organization founded by Booker T. Washington in 1900 with the goal of empowering African-American businessmen—Burrell became the organization's president in 1962. By this time a prominent figure in local business circles (he served on three occasions as president of the District of Columbia's Chamber of Commerce), Burrell admired the philosophy of the NBL's founder and deplored its then-moribund condition. Possessing a "burning desire to rebuild it" (oral history, p. 18), he initially ran the organization's affairs out of the back of his own office. With hard work and a little luck, he succeeded in his goal; by 1970 the organization had grown from thirteen to seventy-six chapters with a staff of sixteen (none when Burrell took over) and more than 10,000 members nationwide. Ironically, this revitalization occurred at a time when Washington's reputation was coming under increasing criticism from the younger, more militant members of the growing civil rights movement, many of whom viewed Burrell's hero as an "Uncle Tom."

Much of the growth enjoyed by the NBL was due to Burrell's success in involving the federal government in its operations. He sought funding for minority businessmen as early as 1963 from the Small Business Administration, and in 1967 he achieved his greatest success with Project Outreach, a Department of Commerce–funded program meant to promote African-American businesses in selected cities. By 1972 NBL–sponsored projects in sixteen cities were receiving $1 million annually, and although overall results proved disappointing (owing in large part to the inexperience of the program beneficiaries), Burrell retained both his guarded optimism and his pragmatism. Anticipating that large-scale federal promotion of minority business startups might be a thing of the past, he shifted the NBL's focus in the later years of his presidency toward assisting existing business.

Although honored for his efforts—he received the SBA's Small Businessman of the Year Award in 1965 and was listed as one of *Ebony* magazine's "100 Most Influential Blacks in America" during the 1970s—Burrell often felt frustrated by what he perceived to be a lack of understanding of basic business principles and practices on the part of many African Americans. In an effort to educate African Americans about the business achievements of their predecessors, he coauthored (with John Seder) *Getting It Together: Black Businessmen in America* (1971), which contained inspiring success stories. During the 1970s he also wrote a nationally syndicated column, "Down to Business," which ran in several African-American newspapers. A longtime Republican, he advised several presidents on business matters and was particularly close to Richard Nixon, serving as vice president on his Advisory Council for Minority Enterprises.

In addition to his dry cleaning enterprise, Burrell also operated the Merchant Prince Corporation, which produced African-American greeting cards. He lectured on business topics at a number of universities, including Morgan State, Vanderbilt, Fisk, and Howard, and served as a board member of the Joint Council on Economic Education and the Corporation for Blacks in Public Broadcasting. Burrell was also a longtime civic booster of his hometown, serving on its Citizens Traffic Board, the D.C. Apprenticeship Council, and the Police Chief's Advisory Committee on Community Relations; he was also a senior warden of St. Mary's Episcopal Church. He died in Washington after being stricken by a heart attack at a church meeting.

Realistic in his expectations and flexible in his approach to problem-solving, Berkeley Burrell played a major role in the revitalization of the National Business League. An admirer of both Richard Nixon and Booker T. Washington at a time when neither was popular with many African Americans, he could point to his own success in business as perhaps the greatest testimony to the wisdom of his efforts.

• While there is no known collection of Burrell's papers, he was the subject of a 1970 oral history interview held as part of the Ralph J. Bunche Oral History Collection at the Moorland-Spingarn Research Center at Howard University, Washington, D.C. He was the subject of Joel Dreyfus's "Rowboating in the Economic Mainstream: The NBL Keeps Moving Despite Rough Waters," *Black Enterprise*, Jan. 1975, pp. 43–45, and "Nixon Invites First Black Businessman to Wage-Price Briefings," *Jet*, 14 Oct. 1971, p. 22; he was also featured in a lengthy article in the *New York Times*, 3 Nov. 1974. Obituaries are in the *Washington Post*, 31 Aug. 1979; *New York Times*, 2 Sept. 1979; and *New York Amsterdam News*, 8 Sept. 1979.

EDWARD L. LACH, JR.

BURRILL, Thomas Jonathan (25 Apr. 1839–14 Apr. 1916), plant pathologist, was born in Pittsfield, Massachusetts, the son of British immigrants John Burrill and Mary Francis, farmers. The family moved to Stephenson County, Illinois, when he was nine years old. A shy and somewhat reclusive young boy, he entered the state university at Normal in 1862, where he developed an interest in natural history as a result of close association with such members of the Illinois Natural History Society as the curator of the society, Joseph A. Sewall, who was his botany teacher; the first state entomologist, Benjamin D. Walsh; and George W. Vasey, who eventually became botanist with the U.S. Department of Agriculture. After graduating in 1865, Burrill was superintendent of schools in Urbana until 1868. During this time he continued to pursue botany and natural history. He served as botanist on John Wesley Powell's Rocky Mountain Expedition in

1867, which took him to the Grand Canyon of Colorado, where he collected specimens that he later donated to the University of Illinois Herbarium. In 1868 he married Sara H. Alexander from Seneca Falls, New York. They had two children.

In 1868 he was appointed to teach algebra at the newly opened Illinois Industrial University in Urbana (now University of Illinois). In addition, he was soon named assistant professor of natural history and botany, an appointment he eagerly took up. He helped plant most of the trees on the campus, collected specimens across the state, and became one of the more revered teachers and active administrators at the university. In 1869 he led an expedition through the state from Chicago to Cairo, collecting numerous specimens for preservation and study. Shortly thereafter he allied himself with the Illinois Horticultural Society and published voluminously in its *Transactions of the Illinois State Horticultural Society*. He was also instrumental in developing the Agricultural College of the University of Illinois.

Despite a lack of foreign graduate work, Burrill became one of the American pioneers of the "New Botany," whose methods and aims, imported from Germany, included the use of such new instruments as the microscope and involved close anatomical, cytological, and experimental investigations of plants in the laboratory as well as in the field. Burrill examined the activity of pathogenic microbes on important horticultural and agricultural varieties of plants. He distinguished himself with both studies of economically important fungal diseases, such as various rusts and mildews, and a survey of the cryptogamic flora (spore-bearing plants, including ferns and mosses) of Illinois. But it was in the area of bacterially induced plant diseases that Burrill became one of the premier American scientists of his day.

In 1877, just two years after Robert Koch, in Berlin, demonstrated that bacteria could cause animal disease, Burrill began a series of investigations that would point to bacteria as a cause of plant disease. Although his initial suggestion that "numbers of minute, moving things" were the cause of fire-blight of pears (a disease ravaging midwestern orchards) was met with disbelief, Burrill soon convinced the increasing number of Americans entering the new field of plant pathology that the small moving things were disease-causing bacteria by designing an elegant series of experiments involving isolation of the causal agent, inoculation of healthy plants, and close descriptions of the disease. The microscopic causal organism was named *Micrococcus amylovorus* (now renamed *Erwinia amylovora*) and was reported in a classic paper published in the *American Naturalist* in 1881. For this work, Burrill is often cited as one of the founding fathers of bacterial plant pathology. Burrill continued research on such important plant diseases as ear-rots of corn, peach yellows, potato scab, rusts of blackberry and raspberry, and, later on, the bitter-rot of apples. He also explored the toxic effects of certain plants such as poison ivy, undertook temperature and nutritional studies of plants, examined weed control, and pioneered in the study of soil bacteria that form symbiotic relationships with leguminous plants.

Burrill's work as an administrator was equally distinguished. During his long career at the University of Illinois, he served as dean of the graduate school (1894–1905), acting president (1891–1894, 1904), and, for a long time, vice president (1879–1912). He held the post of president of the American Microscopical Society (1885–1886), and at the time of his death was president of the Society of American Bacteriologists.

To the end Burrill appears to have maintained his diffident demeanor and enjoyed a stable and quiet private life. He died in Urbana, Illinois.

• Burrill's papers are located in the university archives of the University of Illinois at Urbana-Champaign. His influence on the development of American plant pathology is discussed in Andrew Denny Rodgers, *Erwin Frink Smith: A Story of American Plant Pathology* (1952), and his influence on American botany is briefly discussed in Rodgers, *American Botany 1873–1892, Decades of Transition* (1944). The most recent biographical sketch is Halbert H. Thornberry, "Thomas Jonathon Burrill's Contributions to the History of Microbiology and Plant Pathology," *Transactions of the Illinois State Horticultural Society* 100 (1966): 19–42. A longer biographical essay containing a complete bibliography of Burrill's work is Eugene Davenport, "Dr. Thomas Jonathon Burrill Memorial Address," *Transactions of the Illinois State Horticultural Society* 50 (1916): 67–97. See also S. A. Forbes, "Thomas J. Burrill," *Alumni Quarterly and Fortnightly Notes of the University of Illinois* 1, no. 1 (1916): 407–17. For obituary notices see *Botanical Gazette* 62 (1916): 153–54, *Acta Berg* 3 (2): 178, *Torreya* 16: 149–50, *Phytopathology* 8: 1–4, and *Transactions of the American Microscopical Society* 35: 269–70.

VASSILIKI BETTY SMOCOVITIS

BURRINGTON, George (c. 1680–22 Feb. 1759), twice governor of North Carolina, was born in Devonshire, England, of untraced ancestry. Little is known about Burrington's personal life, education, or experiences before becoming governor. He was married, possibly more than once, but records do not substantiate that any wife was ever in North Carolina. His sole heir was a son born in 1738, long after Burrington had left the colony. He once boasted that his prominent family was the first to rally to William of Orange. It is likely that his political connections secured an appointment as captain in the British army in 1715 and influenced the Carolina proprietors to choose him to succeed the deceased Charles Eden in 1723. Burrington took the oath in North Carolina on 15 January 1724.

Almost from his first days as governor he exhibited the contradictory personality traits that mark his colonial career. On one hand, he demonstrated energy, initiative, and sometimes vision. He promoted vigorously the settlement of the Cape Fear region, a project commenced under Governor Eden. He advocated a simplified landgranting system and then took advantage of the eased rules to claim thousands of acres for himself. On the other hand, he seldom maintained civil relationships with anyone, believing that any opposition sprang from base motives. A debate with Burrington often ended with the governor delivering a physical threat in coarse, abusive, and profane language. He found some support by allying himself to the "popular party," settlers who opposed the proprietors' arbitrary use of their powers. This put Burrington at odds with Chief Justice Christopher Gale, a respected man in the colony and a leader of the proprietary party. The governor even attempted to break into Gale's home to accost him. Gale, with the support of other councilors, responded by sailing to England to complain to the proprietors. While the report of chaos in the colony may have had influence, Burrington's ties to proprietary opponents may have been more crucial in the decision to remove him. In July 1725 Sir Richard Everard arrived in North Carolina to take over the governorship, which Burrington reluctantly surrendered.

Although he spent much of the next several years at his plantation, Burrington continued to cause political storms. He led the antiproprietary forces, men who opposed the new governor in any way possible. Burrington, as was his style, leveled capricious and unsubstantiated charges of misbehavior in office against Sir Richard. At one point he challenged the governor to a duel. Though indicted, Burrington was never tried and charges were eventually dropped. When he learned in 1729 that the proprietors were preparing to return the colony to the Crown, Burrington departed for England intent on regaining the governorship. In London he rekindled an old friendship with the duke of Newcastle, dispenser of patronage. Although opposed by some members of the board of trade, Burrington received reappointment, being sworn into office at Edenton on 25 February 1731.

Burrington's second term was as disastrous as the first. Once more, he had a program, and he tried to implement it. More roads were built, including major links between the Virginia boundary and Cape Fear and another between New Bern and settlements to the south. Burrington visited every hamlet; he explored unmapped wilderness; he participated in charting shipping channels; he expended personal funds for poor relief.

Unfortunately, Burrington's program soon became secondary to his political battling. As intransigent as ever, Burrington now felt as royal governor that he had broad powers to enforce his will. He purged the council of old enemies to pack it with supporters, exceeding the rights of any governor in the process. Following his instructions from the Board of Trade, he urged the assembly to require registration of previously claimed lands and payment of quitrents in money of proved worth. When the assembly balked, he threatened to impose more stringent rules for obtaining land, thus alienating all settlers who believed easy access to unclaimed acreage to be a right. Complaints against Burrington multiplied as officials tried to have Burrington removed from office. By early 1733 North Carolina government barely functioned. Burrington countered the charges by claiming that plots and conspiracies against him had caused the political crisis. But few believed him, and by the spring of 1733 he had lost the support of the duke of Newcastle. Gabriel Johnston was appointed governor as successor, though he did not reach North Carolina until November 1734.

Possibly in real danger from a formidable number of foes, Burrington was probably eager to leave the colony shortly after Johnston's arrival. While his two terms produced some accomplishments, his tempestuous temperament guaranteed failure in a position requiring tact and skill in dealing with officials and settlers. One wonders why either proprietors or Crown considered Burrington suited for political leadership. If Burrington arrived in North Carolina from a shadowy background, he slipped back into obscurity in England after 1734. Income from his North Carolina lands allowed him to lead a comfortable existence. He is credited with publishing two books. Ironically, Burrington, a man noted for violent threats and behavior, lost his life to a robber in St. James Park, London.

Burrington holds a unique niche in colonial North Carolina history, having served as governor under the moribund proprietary and as the first Crown appointee. He also earned the distinction of being so controversial and ineffective that he was dismissed twice.

• Some of Burrington's official correspondence are in William L. Saunders, ed., *The Colonial Records of North Carolina*, vols. 2 and 3 (1886). In the absence of extensive collections of personal papers from the era, it is almost impossible to gain any deep understanding of Burrington's personality or the nuances of political controversies that swirled around him.

Most extant biographies focus on Burrington as royal governor, but a sketch of his life is in Marshall DeLancey Haywood, *Governor George Burrington, with an Account of His Official Administrations in the Colony of North Carolina, 1724–1725, 1731–1734* (1896). A shorter version of this account by Haywood is in Samuel A. Ashe, ed., *Biographical History of North Carolina: From Colonial Times to the Present*, vol. 1 (1905), pp. 203–6.

For appraisals of various facets of Burrington's years as royal governor, see Blackwell P. Robinson, *The Five Royal Governors of North Carolina, 1729–1775* (1963), pp. 1–11. William S. Price, Jr., "A Strange Incident in George Burrington's Royal Governorship," *North Carolina Historical Review* 51, no. 2 (Apr. 1974): 149–58, explores the man's relationship to the duke of Newcastle. A. Roger Ekirch, *"Poor Carolina": Politics and Society in Colonial North Carolina, 1729–1776* (1981), pp. 53–66, concludes that too much attention has been paid to Burrington's personality flaws and not enough emphasis given to the fact that he destroyed his ability to govern by threatening the land tenure system. Hugh T. Lefler and William S. Powell, *Colonial North Carolina: A History* (1973), pp. 89–92, emphasize that both Burrington's personal style and his attempted reform of the land system caused the assembly to oppose him as a threat to colonial liberties.

CONVERSE D. CLOWSE

BURRITT, Elihu (8 Dec. 1810–6 Mar. 1879), reformer, was born in New Britain, Connecticut, the son of Elihu Burritt, a farmer and cobbler, and Elizabeth Hinsdale. Burritt's mother made the Bible and the religion of John Calvin the basis of the Christian nurture of her ten children. Elihu attended the local district school and showed a marked aptitude for scholarship. After his father's death in 1827, he apprenticed himself to a local blacksmith and independently continued his studies, particularly in languages.

Burritt moved to Worcester in 1837 because he had learned of the extensive collection of rare language books at the American Antiquarian Society. He studied these books assiduously while he supported himself as a journeyman blacksmith. Within a year's time he claimed that he could read up to fifty languages "with more or less facility" (Tolis, p. 16). The actual number was closer to thirty, and his proficiency varied from language to language, but it was a remarkable achievement nevertheless. Governor Edward Everett heard about Burritt's attainments and glowingly referred to them at an educational convention in 1838. Thus Burritt became known as "the learned blacksmith," a sobriquet he would have for the rest of his life.

After failing in the publication of *Literary Geminae*, a dull literary magazine, Burritt enjoyed considerable success as a lyceum lecturer from 1841 to 1843, speaking from Maine to Virginia on the theme of self-cultivation. At first he drew large audiences and received handsome fees, but by mid-1843 audience curiosity had worn thin, and fees had declined sharply. Burritt then became determined to fill "a useful place in society" and be of "benefit to mankind" (Tolis, p. 63).

The wave of revivalism that had peaked between 1825 and 1835 was still being felt throughout the nation, and Burritt, an active member of the First Congregational Church of Worcester, became an itinerant evangelist and earnest temperance lecturer. He also aligned himself with the antislavery Liberty party and became one of its most ardent spokesmen. In 1844 he began publishing the *Christian Citizen* (1844–1851), a weekly newspaper unabashedly devoted to temperance, political abolition, peace, and many other evangelical enterprises. Burritt wrote practically all the articles, which in the main were well-reasoned and forcefully expressed.

In 1843 Burritt delivered his first peace lecture. Although he had not met William Ladd, the venerated founder of the American Peace Society (1828) and its greatest leader until his death in 1841, he was familiar with his writings. Other influential peace reformers, after they came to know Burritt, saw in him William Ladd redivivus. They admired his forthright opposition to all war, defensive as well as offensive. The American Peace Society had amended its constitution in 1837 to condemn defensive war but had begun to hedge not long after Ladd's death. In 1845 Burritt assumed editorial duties of the society's periodical, the *Advocate of Peace*, and filled it with articles and anecdotes decrying the principle of defensive war as sophistical and un-Christian. The following year, however, the supporters of defensive war deftly outmaneuvered Burritt's faction and steered the organization along an equivocal middle course on the vexed question. Burritt resigned as editor and with his friends Samuel E. Coues, Amasa Walker, and Joshua P. Blanchard withdrew from the executive committee of the society.

Burritt sailed to England in June 1846 and founded the ambitious and somewhat grandiose League of Universal Brotherhood, whose goal was to initiate reforms conducive to world peace, universal brotherhood, and mutual respect among nations and individuals. Founded in Pershore in July 1846, the league eventually numbered thousands of members in Great Britain (where it was most active), the United States, and Continental Europe. Members were required to sign a somewhat controversial pledge vowing to abstain from all war and military involvement and coming close in principle to promising nonresistance. British Quakers were far and away the most loyal and energetic supporters of the league.

Burritt's greatest collective contribution to the peace movement was organizing a series of international peace conventions in Europe from 1848 to 1851. Their chief end was to publicize William Ladd's lofty vision of and plan for a Congress and a Supreme Court of Nations—the former to frame a body of international law, the latter to adjudicate all international disputes on the basis of that law. It was known as the "American Plan" in deference to Ladd. Four international peace conventions were held: in Brussels (1848), Paris (1849), Frankfort (1850), and London (1851). The Paris convention, which lasted three days, was an unqualified success, with more than 1,500 distinguished delegates and spectators attending. Victor Hugo presided and delivered a magnificent opening address. Although the London Peace Society assisted in the organizational work, the four conventions clearly owed their success to Burritt's unflagging efforts.

Believing that reducing prohibitive overseas postage rates was essential to realizing world peace, Burritt almost single-handedly organized and directed movements in England and the United States to try to convince both governments to lower overseas postage rates for letters to one penny, or two cents. In the United States he entreated the crusading senator Charles Sumner "to nail the flag of (one) penny ocean postage to your masthead, and never strike or lower it. There is power in the very word *penny*" (Tolis, pp. 218–19). Although he did not live to see penny postage for letters, ocean penny postage for postcards was instituted in 1875. Nonetheless, he was one of the two major postal reformers of the nineteenth century; the other was Rowland Hill of England (whose aid Burritt enlisted), the father of domestic penny postage instituted in that country in 1840.

The gathering storm over the issue of slavery rekindled Burritt's interest in the subject in the 1850s. In 1853 he revived the old antislavery idea of Free Labor Produce Associations that would sell or use raw materials and manufactured goods that were grown or produced only by free labor. At the same time, he established the National Compensated Emancipation Society, which advocated that slaveholders be compensated for manumitting their slaves; money for this purpose was to come from the sale of public lands west of the Mississippi. The outbreak of the Civil War rendered both schemes irrelevant.

Burritt returned to England in 1863 and two years later was appointed the consular agent at Birmingham. His main duty was to send detailed annual reports concerning the industrial and agricultural productions of Birmingham. As Burritt wrote to a former reform associate, Gerrit Smith, "the business is simple, merely commercial" (Tolis, p. 274). Because he never married, two of his nieces came to England to keep house for him. It was the most comfortable, enjoyable, and best-paying job he had ever held, but in 1869 the incoming administration of President Ulysses S. Grant removed him for reasons of patronage. Burritt returned to his native New Britain, where he lived out the last nine years of his life and died as the town's favorite son.

• Burritt's manuscripts and correspondence are voluminous. The best single collection is at the New Britain Public Institute, which also houses his invaluable manuscript, "Journals" (21 vols., 1841–1859). These "Journals" have gone largely unnoticed by social historians. Other significant Burritt papers are at Central Connecticut State University, the American Antiquarian Society, the Boston Public Library, the Massachusetts Historical Society, and the Friends House Library in London, England. Merle Curti, *American Peace Crusade* (1929), deals admirably with Burritt, and Curti's *The Learned Blacksmith: The Letters and Journals of Elihu Burritt* (1937) is excellent. The only modern biography is Peter Tolis, *Elihu Burritt: Crusader for Brotherhood* (1968); a merit of this study is its comprehensive and detailed bibliography, which includes Burritt letters privately held. Charles Northend, *Elihu Burritt: A Memorial Volume* (1879), though based on little research, is still interesting.

PETER TOLIS

BURROUGHS, Edgar Rice (1 Sept. 1875–19 Mar. 1950), author, was born in Chicago, the fifth of six sons of businessman George Tyler Burroughs and Mary Evaline Zieger. He was the creator of Tarzan, a unique icon of twentieth-century literature whose name is recognized around the world. Burroughs's early struggles against poverty and failure and his ultimate celebrity have been cited as the quintessential American success story.

Burroughs received his primary education in Chicago, where he studied Greek and Latin before learning English composition. Early in 1891, when an epidemic of influenza broke out in Chicago, his parents sent him to Idaho where his two older brothers, Harry and George, with a Yale University classmate named Lew Sweetser, owned a ranch in Cassia County. For a fifteen-year-old city boy, the change was dramatic and exciting. Burroughs's lifelong love of horses and cowboys dates from this period. He became an expert broncobuster and met such characters as "Texas Pete," whom he wrote into his western novel *The Bandit of Hell's Bend* (1925).

In fall 1891 he was sent to Phillips Academy in Andover, Massachusetts, where he was elected class president, but he rebelled against the formal curriculum and was expelled after one semester. His father, a Union cavalry officer during the Civil War, was convinced that his son needed the discipline of military training and sent him to the Michigan Military Academy at Orchard Lake (near Pontiac) in autumn 1892. The commandant was Captain Charles King, whom Burroughs greatly admired as a stern but fair disciplinarian as well as "the writer of the best army stories that ever were written." It is no accident that four fictional characters in Burroughs's later works were named "King."

After graduation from the academy in 1896, Burroughs remained briefly as assistant commandant with the rank of professor of geology, cavalry, and Gatling gun. He had set his sights on West Point but failed the entrance examinations (14 of 118 applicants were accepted), so he enlisted in the regular army, requesting the most difficult assignment possible. He soon was at Fort Grant, Arizona, attached to "B" Troop of the Seventh U.S. Cavalry. He described his duties as "digging boulevards in the desert where no boulevards were needed" and riding after Indian outlaws such as the "Apache Kid" without strategy or success. He developed a powerful sympathy for Geronimo and his band of renegade Apaches, whose history he later wrote in two acclaimed novels: *The War Chief* (1927) and *Apache Devil* (1933).

To allay the drudgery of camp life, he and a few close friends formed "The May Have Seen Better Days Club," one of whose members was a former British army officer, Carson Napier, who became the model for the hero of Burroughs's popular Venus stories, written between 1931 and 1941. Burroughs suffered severe dysentery and was sent to the post infirmary where, to his dismay, it was discovered that he had a heart murmur that would disqualify him for an army commission. He obtained an honorable discharge and returned to his brothers' cattle ranch in Idaho.

Always restless and eager to start his own business, Burroughs bought a stationery store in Pocatello in early 1898, but by the end of the year he was glad to sell it back to its original owner and rejoin his brothers at the Snake River ranch. By 1899 he had decided that the cattle business was not for him either, so he returned to Chicago to work for his father, who owned and operated the American Battery Company. At the World's Columbian Exposition in Chicago in 1893, Burroughs created a sensation by driving the world's first electric car through the fairgrounds as an advertisement for his father's company. His preoccupation with cars probably stemmed from this experience.

Encouraged by a regular salary of $15 per week, he married his childhood sweetheart, Emma Centennia Hulbert, in 1900. After three years of hand-to-mouth living, the couple yielded to the lure of gold and joined brother George in Idaho where they operated a gold dredge in the heart of the Sawtooth Mountains, a region that Burroughs later recalled as "the most beautiful spot on earth." But the gold business soon failed, and he and Emma moved to Salt Lake City, where he took a job as a railroad policeman. When this work palled, the couple returned to Chicago.

From 1904 to 1910 Burroughs held a succession of temporary jobs: he was a timekeeper for a construction company, sold light bulbs to janitors and candy to drugstores, peddled Stoddard's lectures from door to door, and worked as an accountant for the E. S. Winslow Company. Finally, at a low point, he offered his services as a commissioned officer in the Chinese army, a venture mercifully aborted. Early in 1908 he landed an excellent job as manager of the clerical department at Sears, Roebuck & Company, but he felt that his destiny lay elsewhere and resigned in August, determined to go into business for himself.

An even bleaker period followed, during which he pawned his wife's jewelry to buy food, lunching daily on three cents' worth of ginger snaps. The couple were living in Oak Park, a suburb, when their first child was born in 1908. In 1909 a second child was born, by which time Burroughs was working as an office manager for Physicians Co-Operative Association, which sold a nostrum called "Alcola," advertising it as a cure for alcoholism. The Food and Drug Administration closed down the business within a year, after which Burroughs and his Alcola partner formed the Stace-Burroughs Company, which sold booklets (written by Burroughs) on expert salesmanship. This experience was amusingly parodied in Burroughs's *The Efficiency Expert*, written in 1919 but not published in book form until 1966.

When this company sank without a trace, Burroughs formed a business that sold pencil sharpeners. Checking through various pulp fiction magazines to see if his ads were correct, he began reading some of the stories and decided, "If people are paid for writing such rot, I can write something just as rotten."

Thus, early in 1911 he began to write his first story, influenced by the currently popular theories of astronomer Percival Lowell regarding the canals of Mars. It was a Martian romance, replete with dried riverbeds, the atmosphere plant, incredible flora and fauna, a beautiful princess, and a swashbuckling hero from Virginia named Captain John Carter. It ended in a cliffhanger that promised an exciting sequel (a Burroughs trademark). He sent it to Thomas Newell Metcalf, editor of *All-Story*, a pulp fiction magazine owned by the Frank A. Munsey Company. Metcalf accepted the story immediately, changed its title to "Under the Moons of Mars," and published it in six installments from February to July 1912. Burroughs received $400 for the story, a staggering sum for him at that time.

Metcalf suggested that Burroughs write a second story along the lines of Arthurian legend. Burroughs obliged with a carefully researched Gothic romance of the Plantagenet kings of England, entitled "The Outlaw of Torn." The manuscript was rejected by *All-Story*, but Burroughs eventually sold it to Street & Smith's *New Story Magazine* where it was published in five installments in 1914. In the meantime, he had begun writing his third story, "Tarzan of the Apes," in December 1911, finishing it the following May. It was a compelling study of the interplay between heredity and environment, which had occupied him for some time. Metcalf liked it so well that he published it complete in one issue of *All-Story* in October 1912. It was immediately popular. Burroughs received $700 and decided to devote full time to writing.

The floodgates were down: during the next twelve years he wrote eight novels and sold all of them. In true business fashion, he kept a daily ledger of the number of words written and the dates on which he began and ended each story. Although he protested that writing was a business like any other, merely to keep food on the table, he found himself expressing pent-up ideals in a way that captivated his reading public.

J. H. Tennant, editor of the *New York Evening News*, published "Tarzan of the Apes" as a serial, and other newspapers followed suit, so that a demand was created for the story in book form. After many rejection slips from major publishing houses, Burroughs received an offer from A. C. McClurg & Company, Chicago, which had previously rejected it. A contract was signed, and *Tarzan and the Apes* was published on 17 June 1914. It became a national bestseller. McClurg went on to publish twenty-nine of Burroughs's books between 1914 and 1929, subcontracting with the A. L. Burt Company for reprints of the first five Tarzan novels and with Grosset & Dunlap for reprints of all other titles. The majority of them were illustrated by J. Allen St. John, a Chicago artist who became identified with Burroughs.

For the rest of his writing career, Burroughs adopted the practice of selling first serial rights to the pulp magazines while retaining reprint and book rights for himself. Thus, with few exceptions, his works were serialized in magazines before appearing in book form. His first story, retitled *A Princess of Mars*, was published as a novel by McClurg in 1917. It was dedicated to his third child, John Coleman Burroughs, who eventually illustrated the first editions of twelve of his father's books.

Tarzan of the Apes was adapted for the silent screen in 1916 with Elmo Lincoln in the title role and Enid Markey as Jane. A huge success when it premiered two years later, it was one of the first six films ever made that grossed more than $1 million. Two more Elmo Lincoln films followed, as well as five additional silent films featuring, in succession, Gene Pollar, P. Dempsey Tabler, James H. Pierce (who married Burroughs's daughter), and Frank Merrill, a professional gymnast. In 1932 Olympic swimming champion Johnny Weissmuller made his debut as Tarzan with Irish actress Maureen O'Sullivan as Jane. The muscle-bound Weissmuller was advertised as "the world's most perfect man." He made twelve Tarzan movies from 1932 through 1948, during which time three other Olympic champions were given their chance at the role: Buster Crabbe (1933), Herman Brix (1935 and 1938), and Glenn Morris (1937). The film characterizations of Tarzan, which included both full-length features and serials, were entirely unlike the literary Tarzan, much to the disappointment of his creator.

After Weissmuller's retirement in 1948, and continuing through 1991, the successive actors to play Tarzan were Lex Barker, Gordon Scott, Denny Miller, Jock Mahoney, Mike Henry, Ron Ely, Miles O'Keeffe, Christopher Lambert, Joe Lara, and Wolf Larson.

In 1919 Burroughs purchased a 540-acre ranch in the San Fernando Valley of California. Here, he played at being a gentleman farmer while solidifying his multimillion-dollar industry. He named the ranch "Tarzana," and the city that inevitably sprang up around him was so named on 11 December 1930 with the official installation of the Tarzana Post Office.

Burroughs incorporated himself on 26 March 1923 and by 1931 decided to publish his own books without the intervention of a "middle man." One of the most enduring enterprises initiated by Edgar Rice Burroughs, Inc., was the syndication of Tarzan in daily and Sunday newspapers, beginning in 1931 with Rex Maxon as artist; later artists included Hal Foster and Burne Hogarth. The first Tarzan radio shows were produced in 1932 featuring Burroughs's daughter, Joan, and her husband James H. Pierce (star of *Tarzan and the Golden Lion*, 1927). These shows were the first to be prerecorded for shipment to foreign markets. In 1934, when the Pierces left the show, Carlton Kadell assumed the title role, playing two 39-episode serials until 1935. In 1951 a new series started with Lamont Johnson as Tarzan. These half-hour features aired every Saturday night for a year. A Tarzan television series began in 1966, featuring Ron Ely, and ran for four years. A second series with Wolf Larson began in 1991 but was discontinued after two years. Meanwhile, Tarzan had become a staple for the comic book industry worldwide, while the novels were translated into thirty-four languages, including Russian, Esperanto, and Hebrew.

In 1934 Burroughs and his wife divorced. Four months later he married Florence Gilbert Dearholt, a former actress and divorcée with two small children. They divorced in 1942.

During World War II Burroughs, who in 1919 had held the rank of major in the Illinois State Militia, became the country's oldest war correspondent, serving until 1945. His "Laugh It Off" column was published regularly in the *Honolulu Advertiser*. He visited Australia and several Pacific atolls as a reporter, and he went on several bombing missions.

After the war, Burroughs retired to a modest home in Encino, California, where he died. His ashes were buried beneath a black walnut tree in the front yard of his corporation headquarters on Ventura Boulevard. In the last year of his life he reread all of his books "to see what I had said and how I'd said it." His published legacy was enormous, with a total of twenty-six Tarzan books, eleven Martian stories, seven Pellucidar ("Earth's Core") books, five Venus stories, and eighteen miscellaneous novels including four westerns, four social satires, a moon saga, and an incomparable prehistoric trilogy, *The Land That Time Forgot*. He was planning a new series of stories on Jupiter at his death. An unpublished novel written in 1941, *I Am a Barbarian*, was found in his safe in 1965. It was a historical romance of imperial Rome during the reign of Caligula and was the last book to be published by Edgar Rice Burroughs, Inc.

Burroughs did not write for children. His style was lucid and poetic; his words chosen intuitively to stimulate emotion and intellect simultaneously, resulting in a basic appeal to readers of all ages. For this reason he cannot be compared with other writers, nor did he seek or desire comparisons. He rarely read fiction, preferring documentary accounts and biographies. His favorite poets were Robert Service, Henry Herbert Knibbs, and Rudyard Kipling. He greatly admired Jack London and once offered to write his biography, but he gave it up when he learned that a London biography was already in progress. Burroughs predicted the invention of radar, sonar, television, teletype, radio compass, the automatic pilot, homing devices on bombs and torpedoes, genetic cloning, living organ transplants, antigravity propulsion, and many other concepts deemed totally fantastic in his time. His soaring imagination, coupled with the sure instinct of a master storyteller, assures him a position of honor among American writers of the twentieth century.

• An unpublished, untitled autobiography written in 1931 is the source for several passages in this essay. The definitive biography of Burroughs is Irwin Porges, *Edgar Rice Burroughs: The Man Who Created Tarzan* (1975). George T. McWhorter, *Burroughs Dictionary* (1987), is a concordance to Burroughs's complete published works. For bibliographical references, see McWhorter, *Catalog of the Edgar Rice Burroughs Memorial Collection* (1991). The standard bibliography is Henry Hardy Heins, *A Golden Anniversary Bibliography of Edgar Rice Burroughs* (1964). Erling B. Holtsmark, *Tarzan and Tradition* (1981), provides stylistic analyses of Burroughs's works. For information on the Tarzan films, consult Gabe Essoe, *Tarzan of the Movies* (1968).

GEORGE T. MCWHORTER

BURROUGHS, John (3 Apr. 1837–29 Mar. 1921), naturalist and author, was born in Roxbury, New York, the son of Chauncey A. Burroughs and Amy Kelly, farmers. He attended district schools in Roxbury and later studied briefly at two academies in Upstate New York. He became a teacher in 1854, at the age of seventeen, and for the next decade he taught in rural schools in New York, New Jersey, and Illinois. He studied medicine for a few months with a physician in Tangore, New York, where he met Ursula North, a farmer's daughter. The two married in 1857; they adopted one child, born in 1878 to a woman with whom Burroughs had an extramarital affair (his wife did not learn of the child's paternity until several years later). During the 1850s Burroughs discovered the Transcendentalist writings of Ralph Waldo Emerson. As Burroughs put it, he became Emerson's "captive" and his "whole intellectual outlook was colored by him." He also came upon the works of John James Audubon, whose writing he described as "bringing together fire and powder" in a way that propelled him into a career as a naturalist.

Burroughs began writing in 1857. In 1860 he contributed a number of essays to the New York *Saturday Press* and an essay entitled "Expression" to the *Atlantic Monthly*. In 1861–1862 the New York *Leader* published a series of brief pieces under the title "From the Back Country," his first writings on nature. Emerson's influence was evident in much of Burroughs's early writing; in "Expression" it was so strong that editor James Russell Lowell carefully checked it for plagiarism.

In 1863 Burroughs moved to Washington, D.C., where he worked at the Currency Bureau of the Treasury Department. He became a close friend and ardent admirer of Walt Whitman. The two walked in the woods near the city, and Burroughs taught the poet much about nature, especially birds. One example of his influence is the knowledge Whitman displays about the hermit thrush and its song in "When Lilacs Last in the Dooryard Bloom'd." At the time, Whitman was widely disparaged as a poet, and Burroughs was one of a small group that came to his defense. In 1867 *Notes on Walt Whitman as Poet and Person* appeared; Burroughs is listed as the author on the title page, but the style and content suggest that Whitman was a close collaborator, if not a coauthor. In 1871 he published his first major literary success, a volume of essays on nature entitled *Wake-Robin*, perhaps his best-known work.

In 1872 Burroughs resigned from the Treasury Department and moved to southern New York, where he served briefly as a bank examiner. He built a stone house, "Riverby," at West Park on the Hudson River, where he planted fruit trees and a vineyard and grew berries as a source of additional income. There and at "Slabsides," a cabin he built in the woods several miles from the river, he devoted himself to writing. Houghton Mifflin regularly published his books, and he contributed routinely to the most prestigious periodicals of the day. As early as 1877 some of his essays were adapted for use as school texts. During this period he produced a number of volumes on nature, notably *Winter Sunshine* (1875); *Locusts and Wild Honey* (1879); *Pepacton* (1881), a narrative of a rowboat trip down the East Branch of the Delaware River; *Signs and Seasons* (1886); and *Riverby* (1894).

All of Burroughs's writings convey the author's enthusiasm for the subject. As a naturalist, he was an accurate observer, reporting his findings in simple, graceful, concrete prose. He scorned such nature writers as Ernest Thompson Seton and the Reverend William Long, who endowed animals with human abilities and other improbable traits. He expressed his contempt in an article titled "Real and Sham Natural History" (*Atlantic Monthly*, March 1903). President Theodore Roosevelt (1858–1919), who described writers of that genre as "nature fakers," congratulated him on the essay, and the two developed a close friendship. Burroughs accompanied the president on a journey to Yellowstone Park in 1903 and later visited him at the White House and at his home on Long Island. In 1906 he published *Camping with Roosevelt*. His friends also included Thomas Edison, Harvey Firestone, and Henry Ford.

Meanwhile, in 1901 Burroughs met Dr. Clara Barrus, a psychiatrist who admired his writings. She became his companion at home and on his travels, serving as his physician, typist, and literary assistant. She lived in a house on the grounds of Riverby, and as Burroughs grew older and his wife's health declined, the couple eventually moved in with her. Thanks in part to Barrus's assistance, Burroughs's literary output increased. Among his writings was a biography, *John James Audubon* (1902), but most of his later work dealt with questions of philosophy and theology in light of scientific theory of the last one hundred years. Science, he had argued in *The Light of Day* (1900), invalidates orthodox religion. Emerson's and Whitman's Transcendentalism continued to influence his thinking, but in a form increasingly modified by his study of such scientists as Charles Darwin, John Tyndall, and Thomas Huxley. He was also especially interested in the French philosopher Henri Bergson, whose theory of creative energy he found to be in harmony with Transcendentalism. Typical of these later philosophical volumes are *Time and Change* (1912) and *Accepting the Universe* (1915). In 1915 the American Institute of Arts and Letters awarded him its Gold Medal.

Burroughs's wife died in 1917. Four years later he died in a railroad car while returning from California to New York. As his literary executor, Barrus edited *Under the Maples* (1921), *The Last Harvest* (1922), and *The Heart of Burroughs's Journals* (1928). She also wrote his principal biography.

Burroughs died at the height of his reputation. Although his place as a naturalist and nature writer remains secure, interest in his philosophical writings and literary criticism declined soon after his death, as the subjectivism of Transcendentalist thought gave way in the twentieth century to more materialistic and objective philosophies such as pragmatism and positivism. Since the mid-nineteenth century, however, there has been increased interest in all aspects of nature. Activities such as camping, mountain-climbing, bird-watching, and botanizing have become popular pastimes, and environmentalism, conservation of natural resources, and protection of endangered species are now important political issues. To those who enjoy and wish to preserve the natural environment, Burroughs's writings on nature continue to fuel their enthusiasms and support their convictions.

• The Library of Congress, Manuscript Division, contains much Burroughs material, including letters to Walt Whitman and Richard Maurice Bucke, a biographer of Whitman. Extensive correspondence between Burroughs and his friend Myron Benton is in the Henry W. and Albert A. Berg Collection of English and American Literature in the New York

Public Library. A large collection of papers and letters is in the Clifton Waller Barrett Library at the University of Virginia. His journal manuscripts are in the Vassar College Library. Other important Burroughs papers are in the Henry E. Huntingon Library, San Marino, Calif.; the Houghton Library at Harvard University; the Library of the American Academy of Arts and Letters; the University of Texas Library; and the Beinecke Rare Books and Manuscript Library at Yale University. The best biography is Clara Barrus, *The Life and Letters of John Burroughs* (2 vols., 1925). Also see Barrus, *Whitman and Barrus, Comrades* (1935). For a discussion of Burroughs's thought and literary significance see Perry D. Westbrook, *John Burroughs* (1974).

PERRY D. WESTBROOK

BURROUGHS, Nannie Helen (2 May 1879–20 May 1961), school founder, was born in Orange, Virginia, the daughter of John Burroughs, a farmer and itinerant Baptist preacher, and Jennie Poindexter, a cook. After moving to Washington, D.C., with her mother in 1883, Burroughs graduated in 1896 with honors in business and domestic science from the Colored High School on M Street. When racial discrimination barred her from obtaining a position either in the Washington, D.C., public schools or the federal civil service, Burroughs worked as a secretary, first for the Baptist *Christian Banner* in Philadelphia and then for the National Baptist Convention's Foreign Mission Board. She moved to Louisville, Kentucky, from 1900 to 1909 when its headquarters relocated there. Studying business education, she organized a Women's Industrial Club for black women, which evolved into a vocational school.

In 1900 Burroughs helped found the separate Woman's Convention, an auxiliary to the National Baptist Convention, and she served for forty-eight years as its corresponding secretary. Recruiting about 1.5 million black women—more than 60 percent of the entire convention's membership—the Woman's Convention was a congress of delegates from local churches, district associations, and states. It promoted charity work and home and foreign missions. Burroughs, who had spoken eloquently on "Women's Part in the World's Work" to the First Baptist World Alliance in London in 1905, also edited the *Worker*, a quarterly missionary magazine, which she began in 1912 and then revived in 1934, with the support of the white Woman's Missionary Union of the Southern Baptist Convention.

Burroughs also convinced the Woman's Convention to found the National Training School for Women and Girls, Incorporated (NTS), which opened on 19 October 1909, in Lincoln Heights, Washington, D.C. Serving as school president until her death, Burroughs raised money, primarily among black women, to pay off the $6,000 purchase price. By 1960 its physical plant had expanded from one to nine buildings and from six to thirteen acres; NTS also received some support from the white Woman's American Baptist Home Mission Society. The school's title did not include the word "Baptist," since it admitted young women and girls of all religious denominations. Enrollment rose to between 100 and 150 students, who could choose either the trade school or the seminary; the latter offered four divisions: seventh and eighth grades, a four-year high school, a two-year normal school, and a two-year junior college. By 1934 more than 2,000 girls and women from the United States, the Caribbean, and Africa had taken academic, domestic science, trade, social service, and missionary training courses. To pay for their education, some students worked on campus, while others were domestic servants during the summer.

Keenly aware of the limited employment opportunities for black women, Burroughs emphasized preparing students for employment as ladies' maids and laundresses. Domestic work, she believed, should be professionalized and even unionized. Burroughs inculcated a creed of racial self-help through her "three Bs—the Bible, the bath, and the broom: clean life, clean body, clean house." Students were trained to become respectable workers by being pious, pure, and domestic. But instead of being submissive, they were to become proud black women, inspired by a required course in African-American history and culture. In 1927 Burroughs presented a paper to the Association for the Study of Negro Life and History on "The Social Value of Negro History." Under her leadership, NTS served as a center for African-American community organizations and hosted the 1923 convention of the International Council of Women of the Darker Races. Burroughs, who participated with black clubwomen in memorializing the Anacostia home of Frederick Douglass, was active in the National Association for the Advancement of Colored People (NAACP) and served in the 1940s, along with Mary McLeod Bethune, as one of two black women vice presidents on its national board.

Burroughs fought for thirty years for NTS's independence. When the National Baptist Convention of the United States of America, Inc. (NBC, U.S.A. Inc.), its new name after an internal division in 1915, charged that the school lacked a valid charter, Burroughs proclaimed, "This is God's hill," entrusted to her "and to the Negro Baptist women of America" for the black women of the world. The NBC, U.S.A. Inc. withdrew support from the school in June 1938 and urged that the Woman's Convention also sever its connections. Although the NBC, U.S.A. Inc. voted in 1939 to dismiss Burroughs from the Woman's Convention, the women rallied behind her. She continued to serve as corresponding secretary during the years when the school had no official financial support. In 1939 its charter legally incorporated several changes adopted earlier: the self-perpetuating board of trustees changed its name to the National Trade and Professional School for Girls, the board was streamlined, and the property was conferred to the Woman's Convention. The school began a fundraising campaign since insufficient funds had caused it to close from 1935 to 1938. In 1947 new leaders of the NBC, U.S.A. Inc. formally endorsed the school, and in 1948 the Woman's Convention elected Burroughs president.

Renamed in her honor in 1964, the school was designated a National Historic Landmark in 1991.

Burroughs spoke out on many contemporary political and social issues and was put under surveillance by the federal government in 1917. She argued that until black men and women freely exercised their Fifteenth Amendment voting rights they could not stop lynching and racial discrimination. Forming networks with other women, she chaired the National Association of Colored Women's (NACW) Anti-Lynching Committee, was a charter member of the Anti-Lynching Crusaders, and belonged to the Commission on Interracial Cooperation's Women's Division. A regional president of the NACW, Burroughs chaired its Citizenship Department, which encouraged women to organize citizenship groups. She founded and became president of the short-lived National Association of Wage Earners, whose purpose was to affiliate working women with the NACW clubwomen. Burroughs, president of the National League of Republican Colored Women, was appointed in 1932 by President Herbert Hoover to chair a committee reporting on Negro housing at the President's Conference on Home Building and Home Ownership. During the depression she assisted Washington families by helping to set up a medical clinic, convenience store, and the farming, canning, and hair-dressing operations of the self-help Cooperative Industries, Inc.

In 1944 Shaw University in Raleigh, North Carolina, conferred on Burroughs an LL.D., and in 1958 the Washington chapter of the Lincoln University Alumni Association honored her at its annual Founders Day Banquet. She never married. Burroughs died in Washington, D.C. The District of Columbia honored her by naming 10 May 1975 the first Nannie Helen Burroughs Day.

Although contemporaries compared her to Booker T. Washington because of her advocacy of industrial education, she accepted neither black subservience to whites nor female subordination to male authority. Indeed, she told Negro men to "glorify" black women for their many family and community contributions and not treat them as "slaves and servants" (*Pittsburgh Courier*, 23 Dec. 1933). Fighting brilliantly and stubbornly for the Woman's Convention, the National Training School, and for racial pride, Burroughs became a powerful role model for future generations.

• Burroughs's papers, with a finding aid, are in the Library of Congress. They consist of correspondence, reports, student and financial records, newspaper clippings, and other memorabilia of her career and of the history of the National Training School for Women and Girls, Incorporated. Burroughs's notable writings include the fundraising, satirical *The Slabtown District Convention: The Most Popular Church Play in the Country: A Comedy in One Act, Full of Wit, Good Sense, Practical Lessons*, 17th ed. (1961), and *Think on These Things* (1982), a collection of short religious and secular sayings, among them her "Twelve Things the Negro Must Do for Himself." Earl L. Harrison's biography, *The Dream and the Dreamer* (1956; 1972), provides a contemporary's personal and anecdotal assessment. More scholarly is Opal V. Easter, *Nannie Helen Burroughs* (1995), which discusses the Woman's Convention and the National Training School and her role as a clubwoman and political activist. Other essential sources are Evelyn Brooks Barnett, "Nannie Burroughs and the Education of Black Women," in *The Afro-American Woman: Struggles and Images*, ed. Sharon Harley and Rosalyn Terborg-Penn (1978); and Evelyn Brooks Higginbotham, *Righteous Discontent: The Women's Movement in the Black Baptist Church 1880–1920* (1993). Higginbotham explains how the Woman's Convention—and Burroughs—employed "the politics of respectability" and "self-help strategies" to reform society and "to demand full equality with white America" (p. 221). Also useful on Burroughs is Marcia G. Synnott's essay "Nannie Helen Burroughs," in *Women Educators in the United States, 1820–1993*, ed. Maxine Schwartz Seller (1994).

MARCIA G. SYNNOTT

BURROUGHS, William Seward (28 Jan. 1857?–14 Sept. 1898), inventor, was probably born in Rochester, New York, the son of Edmund Burroughs, a mechanic, and Ellen Julia Whipple. (Birth records are not extant; various sources place his birth in Rochester or Auburn, New York, on 28 January, in 1851, 1853, 1855, 1857, or 1858.) Burroughs's family moved to Lowell, Michigan, when he was three years old in an attempt to improve their uncertain financial situation. They moved to Auburn, New York, a few years later. His father's unsuccessful attempts to succeed through invention led him to discourage his son from the life of a mechanic and inventor. Instead, after Burroughs's primary and secondary schooling, his father encouraged him to take a job at the Cayuga County National Bank in Auburn. The bank promoted him in 1878 to an important clerical job. Shortly thereafter, he married Ida Selover; they had four children.

Burroughs's experience as a bank clerk was critical to his future career as an inventor. As a clerk, he learned firsthand the drudgery of financial transactions. He observed that he spent three-quarters of his time either trying to prevent errors or to find errors already made. Having already become acquainted with mathematical shortcuts from a lecture when he was fourteen years old, Burroughs began to consider the advantages of a machine to perform arithmetic for bank accounting. In 1882 his doctor diagnosed him with early stages of tuberculosis and told him to find a career that did not confine him indoors. Burroughs and his family left that fall to join his father in St. Louis, Missouri.

With his father's help, Burroughs found a job at the Hall and Brown Machine Company, where he soon became their all-purpose mechanic. After work, he drew sketches of his ideas for an adding machine. In 1884, while working on a job for the Scruggs, Vandervoort, and Barney retail dry-goods store, conversation turned to Burroughs's machine. Thomas Metcalfe, an attorney for the store, and Richard Scruggs, the senior partner, took great interest in the idea and gave Burroughs $700 to make a model of his machine in exchange for shares of stock in a future company. With the money in hand, Burroughs quit his job to look for a small machine shop where he could rent space and use their equipment. Joseph Boyer of the Boyer Machine Shop, and an inventor in his own right, rented him the space and lent him an assistant.

For the next several years, Burroughs spent the majority of his time experimenting on and raising money for his machine. To avoid problems with humidity, he made his drawings on polished zinc. He developed two important technical breakthroughs. One was a pivoting bar connecting the adding and printing mechanisms. This allowed Burroughs to add and print simultaneously with virtually no friction. Earlier machines had sliding or rotating mechanisms that wore out. Burroughs's pivot avoided wear altogether. Another key invention was to separate the functions of pressing the keyboard from performing the arithmetic. Only after the operator keyed in a number was the calculation effected by pulling a lever. This allowed operators to make corrections before calculating. He submitted his first of several patent applications in January 1885.

Burroughs's third model worked well enough for the partners, now joined by William Pye, to organize the American Arithmometer Company in January 1886, capitalized at $100,000. Burroughs spent the entire sum by 1888, when the partners reluctantly increased the stock to $200,000. By 1889 the impatient investors pushed Burroughs into manufacturing fifty machines for sale. He contracted with Joseph Boyer to build the machines, which were delivered in 1890. With the company once more out of money, Burroughs unsuccessfully attempted to raise money for overseas manufacture of the machines by traveling to Britain. Upon his return to St. Louis, Burroughs found that the original fifty machines were worthless, because they broke down and gave incorrect results. The problem was that operators varied in the speed with which they pulled the calculating lever, causing the oversensitive adding mechanisms to overshoot. Eventually convincing the investors to fund one more effort to fix the design, Burroughs in 1890 invented a mechanical dashpot to ensure that the calculating lever could be pulled at only one speed. This invention did the trick, and the new model machines were a great success. From this point on, the company grew rapidly, with Burroughs continuing to improve his machine. Then, in 1894, his wife died.

Burroughs's success came at great cost to his health, which began to fail. Heeding doctors' orders, he retired to Citronelle, Alabama, in 1896, where he soon died from tuberculosis. He was survived by a second wife, Nina, whose maiden name is unknown.

His company went on to become the Burroughs Adding Machine Company, the world's largest manufacturer of adding and accounting machines, and later, as the Burroughs Corporation, an important computer vendor. The success of the company was due largely to Burroughs's painstaking attention to detail. His machines were well known for their robustness and reliability, and his company continued that tradition. Burroughs was an important figure in the "heroic age of invention" at the turn of the century. His success, like that of many other inventors, came from a deep understanding of the problem to which he applied mechanical skills. He knew what his machine had to do from his years of working as a bank clerk. Because it successfully did these things, the banking industry became and remained the primary client of Burroughs's company. The Burroughs Corporation became one of the mainstays of the office machine industry, which itself rose upon the tide of increasing bureaucratization during the "information age."

• Biographical materials can be found in the Burroughs Collection at the Charles Babbage Institute (CBI) of the University of Minnesota. Virtually all the material on Burroughs was written a number of years after his death by the Burroughs Adding Machine Company, based on reminiscences of his contemporaries. The best later source is Ray Abele's unpublished manuscript "The Burroughs Story" (1975). The best early source is J. W. Speare, "Development of Mechanical Accounting," a five-part article in the company magazine *The Burroughs* 3, nos. 1–5 (1909). These, along with a number of unpublished company biographies, exist at CBI. The few primary sources are newspaper clippings and letters from the mid-1890s. See also William Hyde and Howard L. Conrad, *Encyclopedia of the History of St. Louis* (1899); and the obituary in the *St. Louis Daily Globe-Democrat*, 18 Sept. 1898.

STEPHEN B. JOHNSON

BURROW, Trigant (7 Sept. 1875–24 May 1950), psychiatrist, psychoanalyst, and phylobiologist, was born in Norfolk, Virginia, the son of John W. Burrow, a wholesale pharmacist, and Anastasia Devereux. His Protestant father was widely read in science and a freethinker. His devoutly Roman Catholic mother was intelligent, cultured, and moody. A painful rift between the parents exposed the son to human conflict and may have been an important background factor to his lifelong sensitive study of human interrelationships. The youngest of four children, Burrow was painfully affected by the death of his sister when he was twelve years old.

Burrow, an excellent student, was educated in local private schools. In 1888 he was sent to St. Francis Xavier Academy in New York City. He obtained a classical education at Fordham University, graduating in 1895. After a year of premedical studies he entered the University of Virginia, obtaining his M.D. in 1899. Burrow remained another year as demonstrator in biology; then he spent a year in Europe with his roommate and lifelong friend Cornelius C. Wholey. Burrow served briefly at the University Frauenklinik in Munich. They attended courses with Wagner von Jauregg and Richard von Krafft-Ebing, renowned professors of neuropsychiatry at the University of Vienna. They also visited briefly important medical centers in Berlin.

Further postgraduate education in Baltimore at the Johns Hopkins University included courses in bacteriology and pathology, rounds with the famous Canadian-born physician and medical historian Sir William Osler, and work in the neurological dispensary. Concurrently, Burrow studied English literature and served as assistant in experimental psychology. In 1909 Burrow earned his doctorate in psychology with a dissertation on problems of attention. He briefly met Freud and Jung during their Clark University trip in September 1909.

Burrow married Emily Sherwood Bryan in 1904; they had two children. Many letters reveal Burrow as an attentive and affectionate husband and father. The family spent the year 1909–1910 in Zurich in order for Burrow to study with Jung. He attended Jung's seminars and was in daily psychoanalysis with him. Burrow found his work with Jung rewarding. However, when Freud broke with Jung, he sided with Freud. World War I prevented his planned psychoanalysis with Freud.

Returning to Baltimore, Burrow was the first American-born psychoanalyst to open an office for the practice of psychoanalysis. Adolf Meyer, chair of the Department of Psychiatry, appointed him to the clinical psychiatry faculty at Johns Hopkins. A strict Freudian then, he joined in the founding of the American Psychoanalytic Association in 1911 and served as its president in 1925. Papers on the "primary identification" of the infant with its mother (1913 on) and on homosexuality were significant original psychoanalytic contributions. The Burrow family spent summers at Lake Chateaugay in the Adirondacks, first at Alys Bentley's camp. She was one of the first American exponents of rhythmic dancing as a means of self-expression. Later Burrow developed his own Lifwynn Camp ("Lifwynn," the Anglo-Saxon word meaning "joy of life").

Gradually Burrow became disillusioned with the inadequacy of the individual approach to mental disorders. The focus of his interest shifted to the discord, equivocations, and illusions of society. His theoretical speculations were concretized in his analysis of Clarence Shields, whose alien personality intrigued him. In 1918, at the instigation of Shields, they switched analytic roles, leading to a shared and a mutual recognition of the authoritarianism of the analyst and a mutual egalitarian analysis of each other. Appalled by his newly gained insights into his own authoritarian and restricted personality, Burrow withdrew from standard individual psychoanalytic practice in 1921 and henceforth devoted himself to group analytic work. With Shields he expanded their inquiry in 1923 by including students and patients. Conceiving of intrapsychic and interpersonal phenomena as social manifestations, the experimental groups focused on group interaction. He published this work in journals such as the *Journal of Abnormal Psychology and Social Psychology* and the *American Journal of Psychiatry* and in his book *The Social Basis of Consciousness* (1927).

In 1926 Burrow moved his practice to New York City and in 1927 cofounded the Lifwynn Foundation for Laboratory Research in Analytic and Social Psychiatry. Freud reacted negatively to his writings, complaining of his failure to provide details of methods and results. These involved deep probing of underlying motivations and feelings as experienced and expressed in the immediate moment in and by the group, including Burrow and Shields. Burrow regarded his research as a public health investigation and aimed at results in terms of group transformation rather than individual improvement. Relations with psychoanalytic colleagues became strained. In 1933 Burrow was excluded by the American Psychoanalytic Association through its change into a confederation of local societies and the denial of membership to him by the New York society.

In his 1932 *The Structure of Insanity*, Burrow returned to the problem area of his doctoral dissertation, the role of attention as the physiological process mediating the relationship of organism to environment. He contrasted the mode of *ditention*, of separation, of private self-interest, from that of *cotention*, or the common, undifferentiated concerns of the human species. He increasingly focused on the physiological correlates of these contrasting attentional modes. Instrumental studies in the 1940s showed clear differences in brainwaves, respiration, and eye movements as subjects shifted from *ditention* to *cotention*. In 1945 the Lifwynn Foundation moved from New York City to Westport, Connecticut, to be nearer to Burrow's home in Greens Farms, Connecticut. He died there of malignant lymphoma. The Lifwynn Foundation existed decades after his death.

In the philosophical tradition of La Rochefoucauld and Nietzsche, Burrow targeted in phyloanalysis mankind as diseased through the misuse of symbols. The individual learns to create an egocentric false "I"-persona and defensively uses individual, self-regarding, and isolating *ditention* rather than the unifying phylic *cotention*. He antagonized the orthodox Freudians but criticized the anti-Freudians even more strenuously. Increasingly isolated, Burrow's direct influence was confined to the small group of collaborators at the Lifwynn Foundation and to general scientific forums. His indirect influence, however, often unacknowledged, can be seen on such innovators as Karen Horney and Harry Stack Sullivan.

Burrow was described as original, witty, and most entertaining. He was a warm, clear, and prolific letter writer. In his letters with friends (such as Sherwood Anderson and D. H. Lawrence), with colleagues (Adolf Meyer, Freud, and Abraham A. Brill), and with patients he was formal but friendly. His scientific writings were often clumsy and difficult, as he himself complained.

Burrow anticipated many conceptual and professional developments of the second half of the century. His genetic and developmental approach foresaw some newer conceptions of consciousness in neuroscience and evolutionary psychology. Burrow's group analysis foreshadowed later group relations approaches. He questioned the concepts of normalcy and the "image" of oneself as isolated and discrete. He recognized man's neurodynamic dislocation in relation to the environment and attempted to relate individual behavior to the motivation and function of man as a phylum. Burrow marched to a different drummer in the tradition of the great American originals in seeing the significance of nonverbal behavior, of the pathogenic potential of the person's concept of self, and of interdisciplinary approaches to neurosis.

Burrow did not found a school. He was no proselytizer nor reformer and did not believe that his secular type of conversion could come from above. It had to evolve in those with an open mind. Man could achieve wholeness with his fellows only by moving through fragmentation to a transpersonal mode, only by cotentive changes in his consciousness.

• The cataloged Burrow papers are in the Department of Manuscripts and Archives, Yale University Library, New Haven, Conn. (A microfilmed set is in the Library of Congress.) Correspondence with Freud is in the Papers of S. Freud, Series B, Box 6, Manuscript Division, Library of Congress. The best introductions to Burrow's thought are Trigant Burrow, *Preconscious Foundations of Human Experience*, ed. William E. Galt (1964); *Toward Social Sanity and Human Survival: Selections from His Writings*, ed. Alfreda S. Galt (1984); and *A Search for Man's Sanity: The Selected Letters of Trigant Burrow with Biographical Notes*, prepared by the Editorial Committee of the Lifwynn Foundation, William E. Galt, chairman (1958). Burrow published during his lifetime *The Structure of Insanity: A Study in Phylopathology* (1932), *The Biology of Human Conflict: An Anatomy of Behavior, Individual and Social* (1937), and *The Neurosis of Man: An Introduction to a Science of Human Behavior* (1949). He also published sixty-seven papers in various medical, psychiatric, psychoanalytic, and sociological journals with some translated into German and French and listed in *A Search for Man's Sanity*. *Who's Who in America* recorded Burrow first in 1928–1929 and continued annually until his death. Recent retrospectives include John R. Neill, "Trigant Burrow Remembered," *Psychotherapy* 4 (1990); Alfreda S. Galt, "Trigant Burrow and the Laboratory of the 'I,'" *Humanistic Psychologist* (1995); Hans Syz, "Summary Note on the Work of Trigant Burrow," *International Journal of Social Psychiatry* 4 (1961); and Walther Riese, "The Brain of Dr. Trigant Burrow . . . Scope and Limitations of Anatomic Investigations in Relation to Mental Ability," *Journal of Comparative Neurology* (1954). An obituary is in the *New York Times*, 26 May 1950.

CHRISTOPHER T. BEVER

BURROWS, Julius Caesar (9 Jan. 1837–16 Nov. 1915), U.S. representative and U.S. senator, was born in Grahamville, North East Township, Erie County, Pennsylvania, the son of William Burrows and Maria B. Smith, farmers. Julius's mother, a student of history with a "fervid imagination," named his brothers Christopher Columbus, Jerome Bonaparte, and Hannibal. Burrows never appreciated his own and his siblings' names, explaining, "I have detested 'highfaluting' names and titles all my life. I have invariably parted my hair on the side, and have been plain Mr. Burrows ever since coming to the Senate. It was a mistake to tag my brothers and me the way they did."

In 1850 Julius moved with his family to a farm near Kingsville, Ashtabula County, Ohio, where he attended a district school, Kingsville Academy, and then the Grand River Institute, Austinburg, Ohio. Before the age of nineteen he became principal of Madison Seminary in Lake County, Ohio, where he met Jennie S. Hibbard, the assistant principal. He married her in 1856, and they had one child. Jennie died in August 1864. On 25 December 1867 he married Frances S. Peck; they had no children together.

In 1858 Burrows moved to Jefferson, Ashtabula County, Ohio, where he became principal of the Union School. While Burrows was principal, he also studied law in the firm of Cadwell and Simonds and was admitted to the bar in 1859. That same year he moved to Kalamazoo, Michigan, where he assumed the principalship of Gull Prairie Seminary in Richland, Kalamazoo County, and began a legal practice with A. A. Knappen.

On 17 June 1862 Burrows, "inflamed with patriotism," accepted an officer's commission offered by Michigan's governor, Austin Blair, and became captain of Company D in the Seventeenth Regiment, Michigan Volunteer Infantry. During the Civil War he participated in a number of battles, including those at Antietam, Fredericksburg, and Vicksburg. Burrows fought his last Civil War battle at Blue Springs, Tennessee, on 10 October 1863. Even though he escaped "without a scratch," this engagement proved quite conclusively that he was physically unfit for further military service. Friends of his both at home and in military service believed that he could better serve in Abraham Lincoln's campaign for reelection than in the Union army. Thus, he was honorably discharged on 19 October 1863. After John Wilkes Booth assassinated Lincoln, in 1865, Burrows, who once said that the fallen president was the greatest person he ever knew, was chosen by the people of Kalamazoo to present a public eulogy of Lincoln.

Burrows was first elected to public office in 1864, when he became circuit court commissioner for Kalamazoo County. In 1866 he was elected the county's prosecuting attorney and was reelected in 1868. Returning to private practice, he formed a law partnership with Henry F. Severens that lasted until Burrows went to Washington and the House of Representatives.

Elected to the U.S. House of Representatives in 1872, Burrows became a fixture in that body from 1873 until 1895 except for 1875–1879 and 1883–1885. He proved to be an excellent parliamentarian and a gifted orator, and his peers and constituents thought of him as an honest, well-informed legislator.

Although generally considered to be a conservative Republican, Burrows was ever his own man. Thus, in an age where laissez faire seemed to be the watchword, he favored federal legislation that safeguarded voting rights for the recently freed black men. Burrows supported federal regulation of commerce involving railroad interests, even though railroad magnates opposed such supervision. He argued that the power of the Congress to regulate "was ample, absolute, exclusive and supreme." To Burrows, it was clear that "the authority of Congress could not be construed" to be "limited to navigation, as the railroad interest, had proposed." James A. Garfield said of Burrows's argument, "It is a white light that will clearly guide and mark this course of railroad legislation for all time to come." As time progressed, Burrows gained recognition within the Republican party and served on the powerful House Ways and Means Committee. In 1884 he was a delegate-at-large to the Republican National Convention, and in 1889 he was a candidate for Speaker of the House.

Usually supporting Republican conservatism, Burrows advocated protection of American industry and, thus, consistently backed high tariffs. After the McKinley Tariff of 1890 passed in the House, William McKinley acknowledged Burrows's efforts saying, "No man's thought and labor did more for the Tariff Bill of 1890 than did that of Mr. Burrows. For months he gave it his almost undivided time and attention. He is the member most valued and appreciated by the Committee." In the 1890s Burrows opposed the purchase and unlimited coinage of silver.

Elected to the Senate in 1895, Burrows sat on the Finance Committee. A close friend of President McKinley, he supported McKinley's call for war against Spain in 1898 and the acquisition of the Philippines after the war. Burrows backed the Seventeenth Amendment, which called for the popular election of senators. He favored progressive legislation that established a postal savings bank system and helped lead the fight against reseating Republican Matthew Quay in the Senate, because Quay had been appointed by Pennsylvania's governor and not selected by the state legislature. Burrows did not always side with the winners. For example, he opposed the admission of New Mexico and Arizona into the Union as states. As chair of the Committee on Privileges and Elections, he fought unsuccessfully to oust Senator Reed Smoot, a Mormon from Utah who, Burrows charged, favored polygamy. He fought in vain against the Wilson-Gorman Act, which lowered tariffs. In 1908 the Republican National Committee named him temporary chair of the Republican National Convention held in Chicago.

In 1910 the Republican party sustained significant losses as the Progressive movement advanced. Burrows seemed too conservative to many of his constituents, and he was defeated for reelection by Charles E. Townsend of Jackson.

In 1908 Burrows was named to the National Monetary Commission, which was empowered "to enquire into and report to Congress . . . what changes are necessary or desirable in the monetary system of the United States, or in the laws relating to banking and currency." He served as vice chair of this commission until 31 March 1912. He then returned to Kalamazoo, where he lived until his death there.

Burrows served much of his adult life in Congress. As a representative and later a senator, he was able to shape policy and legislation because of his political skills, his length of service, and his close ties with influential Republicans, who often controlled Congress and the White House. By the end of his political career, however, Republican dominance along with his own influence was waning. By that time the Progressive movement was in full flower.

• The only major biography of Burrows is William Dana Orcott, *Burrows of Michigan and the Republican Party* (1917). A shorter sketch is in Charles Moore, *History of Michigan*, vol. 4 (1915), and another is included in the *Biographical Directory of the American Congress, 1774–1971* (1971). Obituaries are in the *Grand Rapids Press* and the *Detroit Journal*, both 17 Nov. 1915.

ROBERT BOLT

BURROWS, Millar (26 Oct. 1889–29 Apr. 1980), biblical scholar and Dead Sea Scrolls expert, was born in Wyoming (now a part of Cincinnati), Ohio, the son of Edwin Jones Burrows, a carriage manufacturer, and Katharine Douglas Millar, an amateur musician and painter. After graduating from Cornell (B.A., 1908–1912) and Union Theological Seminary in New York City (B.D., 1912–1915), he was ordained in June 1915 a minister in the Presbyterian church. He married Irene Belle Gladding one month later, and they had one son. After a stint as pastor of a rural church in Wallace, Texas (1915–1919), Burrows supervised a rural church survey in Texas under the auspices of the Interchurch World Movement. The charismatic preaching and fundamentalist doctrine he encountered was foreign to his ecumenical, even skeptical, approach to religion. In the fall of 1920 he was appointed college pastor and professor of Bible at Tusculum College in Greeneville, Tennessee, and his journey from active ministry to scholarship began. He attended Yale (1923–1925) and received his Ph.D. with a thesis on "The Literary Relations of Ezekiel," under the direction of Charles C. Torrey.

Following doctoral studies, Burrows had academic appointments that included professor of biblical literature and history of religions at Brown University (assistant, 1925–1928; associate, 1928–1932; full professor and department chairman, 1932–1934), Winkley Professor of Biblical Theology at Yale Divinity School (1934–1958), and eventually chairman of the department of Near Eastern languages and literatures at Yale Graduate School (1950–1958). He served as visiting professor of religion at the American University of Beirut in 1930–1931.

His professional service positions included editor, with E. A. Speiser, of *The Annual of the American Schools of Oriental Research* (1931–1945); a directorship, American School of Oriental Research in Jerusalem (1931–1932); president, American Schools of Oriental Research in Jerusalem and Baghdad (1934–1948); trustee, American Schools of Oriental Research (1934–1953); and president, Society of Biblical Literature and Exegesis (1954). He also served several years on editorial committees for the *Journal of Biblical Literature* and *Vetus Testamentum*.

Respected by his peers for his scholarship on the Dead Sea Scrolls, Burrows became known to the wider public through his role in the discovery (in 1947) and publication of some of these texts. These ancient scrolls, written by a Jewish sect at the time of Christ, were found at Qumran, on the northwest coast of the Dead Sea in Israel. His significant involvement with the texts partly resulted from his work at the American School of Oriental Research at Jerusalem when the manuscripts were discovered. He was one of the first scholars to see and work on the scrolls and recognize their importance. It was his decision to call the texts "Dead Sea Scrolls," a name that caught the popular fancy. Through two widely read books, *The Dead Sea Scrolls* (1955), which included his translations of some of the texts and an introduction, and *More Light on the Dead Sea Scrolls: New Scrolls and New Interpretations* (1958), he interpreted for the general reader the scholarly discussions of this important discovery. Soon after the find, some writers made highly speculative, even sensationalistic, claims about it. It was suggested, for example, that Jesus and/or John the Baptist were at one time a part of the Qumran community and that the scrolls are Christian documents. Burrows charted a cautious course, pointing out both similarities and differences between early Christianity and the Jewish sect that wrote the scrolls. His moderate approach has generally stood the test of time.

Burrows's personal experience with excavation was limited; he was, however, a scholar of the Bible whose acquaintance with archaeologists and their work made him an important interpreter of archaeological findings.

In the second major effort of his scholarly career, he was a leading member (beginning in 1938; vice chairman, 1958–1963) of the Standard Bible Committee, the team of biblical scholars commissioned by the National Council of Churches, which produced the Revised Standard Version of the Bible. With expertise in both the Old and the New Testament, an increasingly rare qualification among biblical scholars, he worked on translating both. Until his death he continued to work as a corresponding member on the translation committee, while also serving as an advisory member of the translation team for the Apocrypha, ancient Jewish books that are not included in the Protestant canon of Scripture. Among his fellow members, he was known for the meticulous concern for detail that he brought to his work.

From 1954 to 1957 he served as president of American Middle East Relief, Inc., a national organization providing relief to Palestinian Arab refugees. In addition to his lifelong fondness for performing magic tricks, he loved photography, playing the piano, singing, and composing songs. He died in Ann Arbor, Michigan.

• Burrows wrote eleven books, most of them aimed at scholarly audiences, including *The Basis of Israelite Marriage* (1938), *Bible Religion: Its Growth in the Scriptures* (1938), *What Mean These Stones? The Significance of Archaeology for Biblical Studies* (1941), *An Outline of Biblical Theology* (1946), *Palestine Is Our Business* (1949), and *Diligently Compared: The Revised Standard Version and the King James Version of the Old Testament* (1964). He edited *The Dead Sea Scrolls of St. Mark's Monastery* (vol. 1, *The Isaiah Manuscript and the Habakkuk Commentary*, 1950; vol. 2, *Plates and Transcription of the Manual of Discipline*, 1951). He contributed nearly one hundred articles to journals and books in biblical studies, especially in archaeology, biblical theology, and Old Testament studies. A festschrift, *Essays in Honor of Millar Burrows* (1959), contains a complete bibliography to 1958. *The Cup and the Unicorn: Episodes from a Life: Millar Burrows, 1889–1980*, by his son Edwin Gladding Burrows, published in 1981, is a memorial booklet containing photographs, diary entries, and "fleeting impressions" of Burrows. A small collection of his personal papers is in the Yale Divinity School Library.

CALVIN MERCER

BURROWS, William W. (6 Oct. 1785–5 Sept. 1813), naval officer, was born in Kensington, Pennsylvania, near Philadelphia, the son of W. W. Burrows, a former commandant of the marine corps. William received an early education based on the classics and modern languages, especially German. He displayed a talent for art, frequently drawing naval vessels. His father, upon seeing this interest in the sea, arranged for his son to be instructed in various aspects of the navy. After William made satisfactory progress in this field, his father procured an appointment for him as a midshipman in the U.S. Navy. On 10 November 1799 William joined the crew of the 24-gun *Portsmouth* bound for France. His next assignment was to the Mediterranean aboard the 38-gun *Philadelphia* in 1800. Two years later he joined the *Constitution* and served throughout the Tripolitan War. Besides the *Constitution*, Burrows served on the schooner *Vixen*, the 16-gun *Siren*, and the 32-gun *Essex* while in the Mediterranean. He earned the rank of lieutenant on 19 March 1807 and returned to the United States that same year.

In 1808 Burrows commanded *Gunboat 119* on the Delaware River enforcing Thomas Jefferson's embargo. In 1809 he served as third lieutenant on the 44-gun *President* and later that year became first lieutenant on the 18-gun *Hornet*. Upon discovering that some of his former subordinates outranked him, Burrows resigned his commission. However, Secretary of the Navy Paul Hamilton refused to accept the resignation and instead offered Burrows a temporary furlough, which the lieutenant accepted. While on furlough, Burrows served on the merchant ship *Thomas Penrose* bound for India and China. On the return voyage, a British ship captured the vessel and took it to Barbados before releasing the crew. Upon his return to the United States, Burrows received command of the *Enterprise*.

The *Enterprise*, with a crew of 102 men, fourteen eighteen-pound carronades, and two long nine-pounders, left Portsmouth, New Hampshire, on 1 September 1813 to guard against privateers between Cape Ann and the Bay of Fundy. On 5 September, near Pemaquid (Penguin) Point off the coast of Maine, the crew sighted an enemy vessel, HMS *Boxer*. The *Boxer* was under the command of Captain Samuel Blythe and mounted twelve eighteen-pound carronades and two long six-pounders. Accounts differ as to the size of the *Boxer*'s crew: British sources maintain 66, American sources report 104.

At 3:20 that afternoon the two vessels moved within half a pistol shot of each other and opened fire. Early in the engagement, an eighteen-pound shot struck Captain Blythe, killing the British officer instantly on the deck of his vessel. Command of the *Boxer* fell to Lieutenant David McCreery. Almost simultaneously, Lieutenant Burrows also fell to enemy shot. While helping his crew run out a carronade, Burrows had raised a leg against a bulwark, and the shot hit his thigh, passed through, and entered his torso. He refused to be carried below and continued to lie on the deck shouting that the colors not be struck. Lieutenant Edward McCall assumed command of the *Enterprise*.

At 3:30 the *Enterprise* moved along the starboard tack, and its guns continued to fire upon the *Boxer*. Before the battle, for some unknown reason, either forethought of a possible tactical advantage or simply to improve the ship's trim, Burrows had repositioned a nine-pounder from the bow to the stern, aiming the weapon through his cabin window. This move proved brilliant as the battle unfolded. The *Enterprise* proceeded to move off the *Boxer*'s starboard bow and continued to rake the British vessel with fire. Within five minutes the *Boxer*'s main topmast and topsail yardarm fell. As the *Enterprise* moved ahead on the starboard tack, the repositioned weapon inflicted heavy damage on the British vessel. By 4:00 the *Boxer* lay defeated, but its flags still flew as Captain Blythe had nailed them to the mast before the battle. Unable to lower their colors, the crew eventually managed to hail the *Enterprise* and shout their surrender. With the battle won, Burrows allowed himself to be carried below, where he died soon thereafter. The indomitable courage and sailing skill Burrows demonstrated in the fight suggest that he might have enjoyed a distinguished career in the navy.

Following the battle, Lieutenant McCall took the *Enterprise* and its capture into Portland, Maine, where Lieutenant Burrows and Captain Blythe were buried side by side. Local military and the city of Portland provided all the ceremony that could be mustered on such short notice. The U.S. Congress honored Burrows by approving a measure to grant his nearest male relative a gold medal. Burrows never married.

• No collection of William W. Burrows's papers exists. Most literature on Burrows focuses on the battle between the *Enterprise* and the *Boxer*. Early accounts of this battle are in James Fenimore Cooper, *The History of the Navy of the United States of America* (1839); Theodore Roosevelt, *The Naval War of 1812* (1882); and A. T. Mahan, *Sea Power in Its Relations to the War of 1812* (1905). Later accounts include sections in Francis F. Beirne, *The War of 1812* (1949), and C. S. Forester, *The Age of Fighting Sail* (1956). For a listing of Burrows's early service consult *Register of Officer Personnel: United States Navy and Marine Corps and Ships' Data 1801–1807* (1945). Fletcher Pratt, *Preble's Boys: Commodore Preble and the Birth of American Sea Power* (1950), provides one of the most complete accounts of Burrows's career. Contemporary appraisals of Burrows's character and career are given in *Analectic Magazine* 1 (Nov. 1813) and *Niles's Weekly Register* 5, supp. (Sept. 1813–Mar. 1814). William Dudley, ed., *The Naval War of 1812: A Documentary History* (1992), provides copies of contemporary reports from officers and the battle's casualty and damage lists from both the *Enterprise* and the *Boxer*.

RICHARD P. HAYDEL

BURROWS, William Ward (16 Jan. 1758–6 Mar. 1805), first commandant of the U.S. Marine Corps, was born in Charleston, South Carolina, the son of William Burrows, a lawyer, and Mary Ward. He studied law in both Charleston and London, England. Returning to America in 1775, he fought in the revolutionary war as part of the South Carolina militia. After the peace he relocated to Philadelphia and established a successful law practice. In 1783 he married Mary Bond; they had three children. Burrows was a Federalist by persuasion and well liked in social circles because of his pleasant, diplomatic demeanor. More importantly, he cultivated close personal ties with leading party figures such as Robert Morris, Alexander Hamilton, and President John Adams. The prospects of war with France were then looming, and on 11 July 1798 Congress established the U.S. Marine Corps as a branch of the navy. Burrows's political standing manifested on the following day when President Adams appointed him major commandant of the nacsent corps. On 23 August 1798 Burrows officially opened his headquarters in Philadelphia, then the nation's capital, and commenced recruiting marines for sea duty.

The task confronting Burrows was a daunting one. In 1798 the marines consisted of only four officers and one hundred rank and file. Nonetheless, the new commandant energetically threw himself into recruiting, equipping, and training his charge. Within one year the marines achieved their authorized strength of 32 officers and 848 men, who were deployed on 25 naval vessels. Though numerically small, Burrows's marines were actively engaged and fought with distinction throughout the Quasi-War with France. On 9 February 1799 a detachment serving aboard the frigate *Constellation* under Lieutenant Bartholomew Clinch assisted in capturing the French frigate *Vengeance*. Clinch also directed marines the following year when the *Constellation* met and defeated the *L'Insurgente* on 7 February 1800. Another detachment under navy lieutenant Isaac Hull and marine captain Daniel Carmick staged a daring, daylight sortie that captured the privateer *Sandwich* at Puerto Plata, Santo Domingo. Burrows's insistence on training and discipline clearly paid dividends. In two years of warfare his marines had demonstrated their worth to the nation and established traditions of élan and resourcefulness as hallmarks of the corps.

Though Burrows was successful in rendering the marines a combat arm, he encountered difficulty in drawing up administrative procedures for personnel at sea. The act establishing the corps had unfortunately omitted the revolutionary war practice, inherited from the British, that marines were governed on land by the

Articles of War (military rules of conduct) and by the *Naval Regulations* while afloat. The resulting ambiguities enabled ship captains to send marines on personal errands, order them aloft into sails, and otherwise treat them as common naval personnel. This practice resulted in ongoing friction between the two services and several duels. Disputes over rank and assignments became so rancorous that navy captain Thomas Truxtun threatened to campaign to have the Marine Corps abolished. Burrows and acting secretary of the navy Henry Dearborn moved swiftly to promulgate new, more precise regulations. They reaffirmed the corps's subordination to naval authority but hereafter forbade ship captains from assigning marines to common shipboard duties. The new rules were well received, and the controversy over the duties of marines at sea subsided.

Burrows's leadership continued to give a permanent shape to the corps. Following his promotion to lieutenant colonel commandant in May 1800, he was instructed to relocate his headquarters from Philadelphia to the new national capital at Washington, D.C. He performed his tasks with the usual alacrity and, in concert with President Thomas Jefferson and Secretary of the Navy Robert Smith, arranged the location for a barracks and headquarters. The site chosen, at the corner of Eighth and I streets ("8th and Eye") has remained in use, while the headquarters and White House remain the oldest public buildings in Washington. Burrows was also cognizant of the need for the Marine Corps to maintain a visible public profile despite its small size. When the Peace Establishment Act of 1800 cut his command in half, he managed to have provisions inserted creating a Marine Corps Band. The band gave its first open air performance on 21 August 1800 and subsequently played at the inauguration of Jefferson in March 1801. The band has since functioned as the "President's Own" and has played at every succeeding inauguration to date as well as many other national ceremonies.

The onset of war with the Barbary States in 1801 necessitated immediate expansion of the corps, and Burrows oversaw acquisition and training of five hundred additional marines. Like their predecessors, these marines distinguished themselves in numerous engagements and garnered additional luster. Burrows managed their affairs stateside throughout most of the conflict until 6 March 1804, when ill health forced his resignation. He was replaced by Major Franklin Wharton. Burrows died in Washington.

Despite his lack of formal military training, Burrows displayed leadership and administrative abilities of a high order. Through his considerable social skills and political contacts, he influenced politics and legislation on behalf of the Marine Corps. He guided and nurtured the corps during his six-year tenure as commandant, laying the foundations of excellence and *esprit de corps* essential to military identity, and was also the only commandant to lead the marines in two major conflicts. Burrows's insistence on efficiency, economy, and concern for the well being of his men brought to his office a style and tone that has influenced subsequent commandants.

• Burrows's official correspondence is in RG 127, Records of the U.S. Marine Corps, and RG 80, Record of the Navy Department, National Archives. A small collection of personal letters is in the Ralph Izard Papers, South Caroliniana Library, University of South Carolina. See also Dudley W. Knox, ed. *Naval Documents Related to the Quasi-War between the United States and France* (7 vols., 1935–1938); and Knox, ed., *Naval Documents Related to the United States's Wars with the Barbary Powers* (6 vols., 1939–1944). For detailed overviews of Burrows and his endeavors consult Allan R. Millett, *"Semper Fidelis": The History of the United States Marine Corps* (1980), and Alfred J. Marini, "The British Corps of Marines, 1746–1771, and the United States Marine Corps, 1798–1818." (Ph.D. diss., Univ. of Maine, 1979). Less erudite but still informative are Karl Schuon, *Home of the Commandants* (1966), and two articles by Edwin N. McClellan, "First Commandant of the Marine Corps, William Ward Burrows," *Daughters of the American Revolution Magazine* 59 (Mar. 1925): 155–59, and "How the Marine Corps Band Started," *U.S. Naval Institute Proceedings* 49 (Apr. 1923): 581–86.

JOHN C. FREDRIKSEN

BURT, Struthers (18 Oct. 1882–29 Aug. 1954), poet, prose writer, and rancher, was born Maxwell Struthers Burt in Baltimore, Maryland, the son of Horace Brooke Burt, a Philadelphia lawyer then in Baltimore on business, and Hester Ann Jones. From the age of six months, Burt grew up in Philadelphia, attended private schools there, and became the youngest reporter in Philadelphia, working on the *Times* (1898–1900) under Philip Keats Speed, the great-grandnephew of John Keats. Burt enrolled at Princeton University, where he was an editor of the *Nassau* and *Bric-A-Brac* and the editor in chief of the *Tiger*. He also wrote two librettos for the Triangle Club. After graduating in 1904, he studied at the University of Munich (1904–1905) and at Merton College, Oxford University (1905–1906). He left Merton without a degree to teach English at Princeton (1906–1908).

The West, his ultimate home, beckoned Burt from his teenage years. A paternal great-grandfather, Nathaniel Burt, had migrated from Ireland, became a fur trader in the Northwest, and later was a merchant in Philadelphia. Burt occasionally worked for an uncle in California, obtained property at Jackson Hole, Wyoming, in 1908, and started the Bar BC Ranch with a partner at nearby Moran in 1912. But always tugging against this lure of western freedom was an imbedded awareness that there were six generations of conservative American-Welsh Baptist clergymen among his mother's forebears.

Burt married Katharine Newlin in 1913. She was from Fish-kill-on-Hudson, New York, attended a private school in nearby Newburgh, New York, and went abroad to study kindergarten work in Munich. She wrote and published children's stories in England, where she had met Burt, at Oxford. She gave birth to their son, Nathaniel, at their snowbound Wyoming ranch and later had their daughter, Julia, there too.

Burt's duty with the U.S. Air Service for a few months in 1918 hardly interrupted his progress in developing the family's ranching concerns, which included attracting visitors to their dude ranch and boys' ranch. (*The Diary of a Dude-Wrangler* [1924] details Burt's efforts.) Meanwhile, Katharine Newlin Burt became a respected writer, publishing many novels and books for children and coauthoring two screenplays. She was also fiction editor for the *Ladies' Home Journal* (1928–1930). Nat Burt, the couple's son, became a novelist, poet, and historian and lectured on music at Princeton.

Struthers Burt contended that ranching eight months a year until after World War I delayed his establishing himself as a writer. Thirty-one when his first short story was accepted, he soon became a successful poet and fiction writer. *In the High Hills* (1914) and *Songs and Portraits* (1920) are early books of poems, while *John O'May, and Other Stories* (1918) and *Chance Encounters* (1921) contain some of his best early stories.

The Burts developed an annual pattern of ranching in Wyoming until fierce weather pushed them back to the East, notably to a winter home in Southern Pines, North Carolina. This sense of being between two worlds finds expression in many ways in Burt's writings, which combine eastern romantic gentility and western ruggedness. Poems collected in *When I Grew Up to Middle Age* (1925) and dedicated to his mother praise friendship, love, and nature romantically and also comment on weather, the seasons, and death realistically. The poems are observant, imagistic, and wordy and alternately display odd, surprising, clever, and forced elements of prosody. Some read like lyrics to be set to music. Others are didactic, as his nonfiction prose can often be.

The best of his many novels include his first, *The Interpreter's House* (1924), which features a middle-aged hero who, after tumultuous early experiences, hopes to find peace in a search for beauty and wisdom. *The Delectable Mountains* (1927), which has autobiographical overtones, tells of the marriage, separation, and then reunion of a proper Philadelphian and a Broadway chorus girl who goes ranching with him in Wyoming. *Along These Streets* (1941) depicts Philadelphia as a challenging but often dreary place and features a hero condemned by an uncle's bequest to stay some months a year in the city, against his own desire. Selling well, these novels were described by reviewers as well written and mature, but in spots didactic and slow moving. Other novels by Burt, both earlier and later, now seem like tired efforts to be melodramatic or innovative.

Burt's short stories are better than his long fiction. Three of them, first appearing in *Scribner's Magazine*, were republished in the annual *The Best Short Stories* series. They are "Water-Hole" (1915), "A Cup of Tea" (1917), and "The Blood-red One" (1919). But his best story is probably "Each in His Generation" (1920), which won the 1920 O. Henry Memorial Prize and skillfully contrasts a pre-1900 uncle, of Victorian mores, and his nephew, a product of the Roaring Twenties. Collections of Burt's various stories ended with *They Could Not Sleep* (1928).

Burt may be remembered, if at all, not for his poetry or very much of his fiction but for his nonfiction prose. He gradually became a belligerent idealist fighting for good causes. An early work is *The Other Side* (1928), a now dated, sometimes pompous effort in which he forcefully defends the United States against any and all European criticism. When totalitarianism seemed to be on the verge of becoming a worldwide threat, he opposed efforts of American politicians to censor and appease by writing *American Writers' Manifesto* (1941); he circulated it widely, obtained the signed support of a hundred or so fellow authors, including Floyd Dell, Frank Waters, E. B. White, and Max Lerner, and published the results. He even favored arming Finland against the Soviet Union.

Two other of Burt's nonfiction books still have value and considerable charm. They are *Powder River: Let 'er Buck* (1938), which was part of the Rivers of America Series and in which Burt presents the history of American Indians, white soldiers, outlaws, lawmen, and settlers along the glorious Wyoming River; and *Philadelphia, Holy Experiment* (1945), which is Burt's puzzled explanation of his "passion, often against my better judgment, for the city I am going to berate, compliment, despise and hold up to admiration."

In poor health from about 1950, Burt attended the fiftieth anniversary of his Princeton class, returned to his home in Wyoming, and died two months later in a hospital at Jackson Hole. It must be concluded that, although he was a vigorous man and a feisty crusader, he is properly defined as a versatile, once-admired, but now almost forgotten author.

• Most of Burt's papers and manuscripts are in the Princeton University Library. Alexander D. Wainwright, "A Check List of the Writings of Struthers Burt '04," *Princeton University Library Chronicle* 19 (Spring 1959): 123, is a standard bibliography. Raymond C. Phillips, Jr., *Struthers Burt* (1983), part of the Boise State University Western Writers Series, naturally stresses Burt's western writings. Charles C. Baldwin, *The Men Who Make Our Novels* (1925), and Harry R. Warfel, *American Novelists of Today* (1951), contain informative comments on Burt. Burt's professional relationship with Maxwell Perkins, his favorite editor, is suggested here and there throughout *Editor to Author: The Letters of Maxwell Perkins*, ed. John Hall Wheelock (1950); in addition, Burt's own essay, "Catalyst for Genius," *Saturday Review* 34 (9 June 1951): 6–8, 36–39, though nominally about Perkins, reveals much about Burt as observer and amateur psychoanalyst of other writers. More modern surveys of American poetry and fiction uniformly lack any consideration of Burt. Obituaries are in the *New York Times*, 30 Aug. 1954, and *Time*, 13 Sept. 1954.

ROBERT L. GALE

BURT, William Austin (13 June 1792–18 Aug. 1858), surveyor and inventor, was born in Petersham, Massachusetts, the son of Alvin Burt and Wealthy Austin, farmers. In 1802 Burt's father, in financial difficulties, moved his family to Freehold, New York, and a year later to Broadalbin, New York. In 1810 the family moved again, this time to Wales Center, near Buffalo, New York. Because his labor was needed on the family's farm, Burt's formal education effectively ended at the age of nine, save for three-week stints at the ages of fourteen and sixteen. Burt, however, avidly pursued self-education, largely teaching himself the principles of astronomy, mathematics, and navigation and inventing a shorthand system for his own use. He also developed an aptitude for mechanics. By the age of twenty he was surveying lands in western New York and erecting flour and saw mills.

During the War of 1812 Burt twice served briefly with the New York militia. In 1813 he married Phoebe Cole, the daughter of a local merchant and an old family friend. They had five children, all of whom later worked with their father surveying public lands. After a brief and apparently unsuccessful period in a mercantile partnership with his father-in-law, Burt returned to survey and millwright work in Erie County, New York. By the mid-1810s Burt was a respected member of his community, serving as justice of the peace, school inspector, and postmaster.

After several trips westward (1817, 1822, 1823), Burt moved his family to Michigan in 1824 and settled at Mount Vernon, north of Detroit. There he engaged in a variety of occupations, including surveying, farming, carpentry, and millwrighting. He quickly achieved local prominence. In 1826 and 1827 he was a member of Michigan's Territorial Council. He served as Macomb County surveyor from 1831 to 1834, and in 1832 George B. Porter, Michigan's territorial governor, appointed Burt a state district surveyor. From 1833 to the 1850s he served as associate judge of the local circuit court and as postmaster of Mount Vernon. In 1829 Burt invented and patented a "typographer," a forerunner of the modern typewriter. Although never produced commercially, the device was the first of its type patented in the United States.

During the 1830s pressure from settlers led the U.S. government to begin surveys of public lands in the frontier area that would become the states of Michigan, Wisconsin, Illinois, Iowa, and Minnesota. Burt, who had sought for several years an appointment as a federal deputy surveyor in order to secure contracts for surveying public lands, finally received that appointment on 25 November 1833. His first surveying contract involved public lands in northeastern Michigan. He completed the work at a financial loss, but Micajah T. Williams, surveyor-general for the Northwest Territory, commented: "For a first contract, he has returned the most satisfactory work I have yet met with" (Brown, p. 267). Other contracts quickly came his way, and from 1833 on Burt largely abandoned his other pursuits and devoted the remainder of his career to surveying public lands.

In May 1835, while surveying public lands in Wisconsin Territory with several of his sons, Burt observed that heavy local mineral deposits acted so strongly on the ordinary magnetic compass that accurate surveying was impossible. Recognizing that only a nonmagnetic compass could operate accurately in regions with iron concentrations, Burt invented a solar compass that summer. Burt recognized that measurements of the sun's position in the sky, coupled with existing astronomical tables, would allow him to determine local apparent time, latitude, and solar declination (the angle between true north and magnetic north). The instrument he designed incorporated adjustments for these three factors. Burt took a prototype of his invention to Philadelphia later in 1835. He had William J. Young, a prominent mathematical instrument maker, begin manufacturing the device, patented on 25 February 1836. In the early 1840s the U.S. surveyor-general's office began recommending that its surveyors use Burt's solar compass. To assist these users, Burt published *Description of the Solar Compass Together with Directions for Its Adjustment and Use* (1844).

From 1840 to 1847 Burt worked on contracts that involved surveying most of Michigan's Upper Peninsula. On 19 September 1844, while running township lines in Marquette County, he observed very strong irregularities and variations in readings from a traditional magnetic needle compass being used alongside his solar compass. Recognizing that the unprecedented irregularities he was observing were probably due to massive mineral deposits, he had his associates search the area. They quickly returned with specimens of high-grade iron ore. Burt's discovery prepared the way for the opening of the Marquette Range, the first of the great Lake Superior ore ranges that were to supply the bulk of American-produced iron ore in the late nineteenth century and through the twentieth century.

Burt continued to survey public lands until he retired in 1851. His reputation for honesty, reliability, and accuracy kept him in heavy demand. He was often engaged to resurvey areas that had been poorly or fraudulently surveyed. The year he retired Burt traveled to the Crystal Palace Exposition in London to exhibit an improved version of his solar compass. The instrument received a premium award, supplementing the Scott Medal that the earlier version had received from the Franklin Institute (1840). Moreover, by the 1850s the U.S. government's survey office considered Burt's solar compass to be nearly indispensable for surveying in mineral districts and had made it required equipment on all public land surveys. To assist surveyors in using his improved instrument, Burt wrote *A Key to the Solar Compass and Surveyor's Companion* (1855, 2d ed., 1858). At the end of the twentieth century the solar compass was still being used, although the increased use of satellites for position location data was making it less common.

On his voyage back to the United States from London in 1851, Burt invented an equatorial sextant, designed along the lines of the solar compass but intended as an aid to navigation at sea. He patented this device in 1856, but it did not become popular because of its high cost.

Burt was elected to the state legislature in 1852 on his return to Michigan. In the 1852–1853 session he played a central role in designing the legislation that led to the construction of the Sault Ste. Marie Ship Canal, which created a navigable waterway linking Lake Superior and Lake Huron. In 1857 Burt moved to Detroit, where he began training seamen in the use of his equatorial sextant. He suffered a severe heart attack and died in Detroit.

• Burt's papers are at the Longyear Research Library of the Marquette County (Mich.) Historical Society. Burt prepared a very short autobiographical sketch of his youth, published in *Michigan Pioneer and Historical Society Collections* 28 (1897–1898): 646–47. The most complete account of Burt's career is John S. Burt, *They Left Their Mark: A Biography of William Austin Burt and His Sons* (1985). Supplementary material may be found in Silas Farmer, *The History of Detroit and Michigan*, vol. 2 (1889); Henry M. Burt and Silas W. Burt, *Early Days in New England: Life and Times of Henry Burt of Springfield and Some of His Descendants . . .* (1893); and Horace E. Burt, *William Austin Burt* (1920). Useful articles on Burt include George H. Cannon, "The Life and Times of William A. Burt, of Mt. Vernon, Michigan," *Michigan Pioneer and Historical Society Collections* 5 (1882): 114–23; Horace E. Burt, "William Austin Burt: Inventor," *Michigan History* 6 (1922): 175–93; and Alan S. Brown, "William Austin Burt: Michigan's Master Surveyor," *Papers of the Michigan Academy of Science, Arts, and Letters* 47 (1962): 263–74. An account focusing specifically on Burt's solar compass is John Burt, *History of the Solar Compass, Invented by William A. Burt* (1878). An obituary is in the *Detroit Free Press*, 20 Aug. 1858.

TERRY S. REYNOLDS
BARRY C. JAMES

BURTON, Asa (25 Aug. 1752–1 May 1836), Congregational pastor, was born in Stonington, Connecticut, the sixth child of Jacob Burton and Rachel Benton, farmers. In spite of his family's poverty, the encouragements of a visiting minister determined Burton to enter the Congregational ministry and "to make religion the great object of my attention." At the comparatively late age of twenty, he was admitted to Dartmouth College, where he came under the personal eye of the president, Eleazar Wheelock. Because of his lack of preparation, Burton found the study of "such authors as Locke and Edwards" challenging, but he eventually found "metaphysics" of the Edwardean sort "more and more pleasing the longer I attended to it." Despite the disruptions caused by the outbreak of the American Revolution, he graduated from Dartmouth in 1777 and was licensed to preach that fall. While awaiting a permanent call to a parish, he studied theology with Levi Hart of Preston, Connecticut, who taught him the theology known as the New Divinity, which developed and systematized the Calvinism of Edwards. In 1778 Burton served congregations in Topsfield, Connecticut, and in Windsor and Royalton, Vermont. In January 1779 he was ordained pastor of the Congregational church in Thetford, Vermont.

Burton found that the Thetford church and its congregation consisted of no more than a barn and fifty-seven "rough, uncivilised, and uncultivated" families. Believing in the importance of maintaining a strict discipline in the church, he at once began to "preach against every evil practice prevalent, and, if any found fault, to preach more plainly and pointedly." This provoked resistance, which Burton often silenced by suspending communion. A general evangelical revival broke out in Thetford, which lasted until 1802 and added eighty members to the church. Another revival broke out in 1821, in which a further 150 people were converted. Yet, despite these successes, Burton was frequently depressed by his own "stupidity, coldness, and barrenness" in religion, and even at the end of his life, he was assailed by the fear that "this awful stupidity" would show "that I am deceived, and may yet perish forever."

In addition to his usual round of parish duties, Burton conducted preaching missions throughout northern Vermont, served as chaplain to the state assembly, and sat as a trustee for Middlebury College and for the University of Vermont at its founding in 1791. But the work for which he became known was the training of ministerial candidates. From 1787 to 1817, Burton personally trained "nearly sixty" candidates, relying mostly on his theological essays, which he published in 1824 as *Essays on Some of the First Principles of Metaphysics, Ethics, and Theology*. As the pupil of Levi Hart, Burton preached and taught the "consistent Calvinism" of the New Divinity. But in the twenty years that separated Burton's ordination from the death of Jonathan Edwards, Edwards's New Divinity disciples had divided into a number of vigorous sub-schools over precisely the "metaphysical" questions Burton had come to relish as a student.

The mainstream of Edwardean divinity analyzed human volition as a series of moral activities that was governed by the spiritual orientation (or "taste") of the soul. But a minority party of Edwardeans, with Nathanael Emmons of Franklin, Massachusetts, as their head, insisted that no evidence for the existence of such a "taste" existed, and that human volition was entirely a series of "exercises" directly caused by "the immediate agency of God." Burton's *Essays* became one of the principal statements of the "taste scheme," since he insisted that, between perception and volition, there must intervene "feeling" or desire; and just as thought indicates the existence of a thinking faculty, and willing the existence of a volitional faculty, the experience of desire of "feeling" must indicate the existence of a faculty of "feeling" or "taste," which mediates between human action and God's supernatural control. "Taste, or the heart" is the real "spring of action," and it is in the "taste" rather than the "exercise" of the will that "every moral agent is sinful, or holy, according to his character." Burton represents a serious attempt on the part of American thinkers to break free from the influence of Locke's *Essay on Human Understanding*, as well as to render Calvinist determinism palatable by making its influence indirect (on the "taste") rather than immediate (through the "exercise" of the will).

Burton remained pastor of the Thetford church until his death. He was married three times, first in 1778 to his half cousin, Mercy Burton (d. 1800); then, in 1801 to Mary Child (d. 1806); and lastly to Rhoda Braman White in 1809 (d. 1818). Of his three children, only one survived into adulthood. He died in Thetford.

• Before his death, Burton composed a short autobiography for his daughter, which became the basis for the biographical sketches that appeared in the *American Quarterly Register*, vol. 10 (May 1838), and in William B. Sprague's *Annals of the American Pulpit*, vol. 2 (1857). The manuscript was subsequently divided, and the two parts deposited at Yale and Vassar. The First Congregational Church of Thetford published portions of the manuscript for their bicentennial as *The Life of Asa Burton Written by Himself*, ed. Charles Latham, Jr. (1973). Burton published only fifteen sermons during his lifetime, and modern scholarly attention to Burton has concentrated almost entirely on his *Essays*. See Allen C. Guelzo, *Edwards on the Will: A Century of American Theological Debate, 1750–1850* (1989); James Hoopes, *Consciousness in New England: From Puritanism and Ideas to Psychoanalysis and Semiotic* (1989); and Bruce Kuklick, *Churchmen and Philosophers: From Jonathan Edwards to John Dewey* (1985).

ALLEN C. GUELZO

BURTON, Harold Hitz (22 June 1888–28 Oct. 1964), U.S. Supreme Court justice, was born in Jamaica Plain, Massachusetts, the son of Alfred Edgar Burton, a civil engineering professor, and Gertrude Hitz. His father taught at the Massachusetts Institute of Technology and was dean of the faculty. Burton and his brother lived with their mother in Leysin, Switzerland, until she died when Burton was seven; the remainder of his early years were spent in Massachusetts. Burton then attended Bowdoin College, from which he received the A.B. summa cum laude in 1909. He matriculated that fall at Harvard Law School and graduated with the LL.B in 1912.

On Burton's graduation from law school he married a childhood friend, Selma Florence Smith, on 15 June 1912; they were to have four children. Soon after marrying they moved to Cleveland, Ohio; Burton admired that city's reform mayor, Tom L. Johnson, and Selma Burton had an uncle with whom Burton could begin practice. After two years of practice in Cleveland, Burton followed his wife's uncle to Salt Lake City, Utah, to practice law in the legal department of Utah Power and Light Company, and later of Utah Light and Traction Company. He subsequently practiced with the Idaho Power Company and Boise Valley Traction Company, both in Boise.

When the United States entered World War I, Burton joined the infantry. He was commissioned a first lieutenant and sent to France, where he saw battle and was later the operations officer of his regiment. Finishing the war as a captain, he resigned his commission in 1919 and returned to Cleveland, where he resumed practicing corporate law with Day, Day, and Wilkin.

In 1925 Burton became a partner in his own firm, Cull, Burton & Laughlin. He combined his general business practice with a spate of civic activities and a stint as a part-time lecturer in corporation law at Western Reserve University Law School. Burton, a Republican, designed all these activities to prepare himself for political office. In 1927 he was elected to the East Cleveland Board of Education. He won a seat in the Ohio House of Representatives in 1928 and served from January until October 1929. Then he became the Cleveland director of law, serving until 1932. During that tenure, he also served for brief periods as acting city manager and acting mayor.

From 1932 to 1935 Burton practiced law with Andrews, Hadden, and Burton in Cleveland, while engaging himself with current political issues. In 1935 he was elected mayor of Cleveland, the office he held until his election to the U.S. Senate in November 1940. President Harry S. Truman got the chance to make his first Supreme Court appointment when Justice Owen Roberts resigned at the close of the Court's term in July 1945. President Franklin D. Roosevelt had appointed no Republicans to the Supreme Court (although he did elevate one to Chief Justice), and Truman was eager to appear conciliatory. Burton had come to know Truman well in the Senate, serving on Truman's Special Committee to Investigate the National Defense. A further political benefit was that the Democratic governor of Ohio was sure to appoint a Democrat to replace Burton in the Senate. On 18 September 1945, Truman submitted Burton's name to the Senate, which confirmed him unanimously the next day without holding hearings.

In thirteen full terms on the Court, Burton was unfailingly polite, though perhaps a bit distant, in his dealings with his fellow justices. His Supreme Court colleagues held him in the highest personal regard, as had his Senate colleagues. Unlike many of the justices, particularly Felix Frankfurter, Burton never lobbied his colleagues about opinions, except through the formal channels of the weekly Court conferences and by circulating drafts among their chambers. In part, this reluctance may have come from the realization that his own intellect was not so high that he could hope to influence orally justices of the caliber of Frankfurter, William O. Douglas, Hugo Black, or Earl Warren.

In part, too, Burton's decision not to enter into informal give-and-take with the other justices was a byproduct of his nearly compulsive work habits on the Court. During term time he worked from eight to five, six or seven days a week, lunching either with his colleagues on argument days or, more usually, alone at his desk. The early evenings were often spent at Washington social functions, but Burton invariably returned to his chambers, where he worked until eleven at night. He showed a similar consistency in the way in which he organized his opinions. Each Burton opinion, from almost his first days on the Court, flowed in an inflexible format from beginning to end.

Ideologically, Burton came to the Court with rather mature views in most areas, and he did not shift his position on major issues over the course of his tenure. As the personnel on the Court changed, he found himself first more influential, and then less so. During his first four terms he tended to agree with a loose coalition of five or six justices. The remaining justices, though, especially Douglas and Black, formed a more consistent core with a more unified view of the judicial process. Several personnel changes during Burton's first four terms resulted in an increase in his influence. By the October 1949 term he was a member of a solid four-vote group of centrists (with justices Tom Clark, Stanley Reed, and Sherman Minton), with the remaining five justices split on either side. This situation continued for four terms until Earl Warren's appointment as chief justice in 1953. From then on, Burton's influence waned; Justice William Brennan, who joined the Court in 1956, tended to align himself with Warren, Douglas, and Black, creating a dominant four-vote bloc that increasingly controlled the outcomes of cases.

In public law areas such as criminal law, race discrimination, and national security, Burton tended to defer to the actions of government, whether on the state or federal level. Thus his votes and opinions can be seen as either liberal or conservative, depending on whether the state action involved was liberal or conservative. In no area, though, were his votes utterly predictable. In some instances throughout all the public law areas, Burton voted against the government's position. In the criminal law field, he generally voted to permit police and prosecutors freer reign over suspects and defendants than the Court would tolerate under Chief Justice Warren. By contrast, in racial discrimination cases the government action was primarily by the federal government, which moved toward integration and more equal treatment of Caucasians and African Americans. Burton again voted to defer to the decisions of government and in general voted to uphold the federal government's power over the states. In national security cases, he almost always voted to sustain the federal government's power.

In commercial law cases involving federal action, Burton occasionally supported the government's position but usually voted against any expansion of government's powers. In purely private-law areas, he often voted to circumscribe the rights of labor unions and took a narrow view of the antitrust laws' reach.

By June 1957 Burton had begun to exhibit the symptoms of Parkinson's disease. During the October 1957 term (which ran through June 1958) his physical condition became progressively worse, and after the term his physician advised him to resign. Because of the case involving desegregation of schools in Little Rock, Arkansas, Burton felt unwilling to resign immediately. He stayed on the Court into the beginning of the October 1958 term, although he had privately advised President Dwight D. Eisenhower during the summer that he would resign as soon as the Court's business permitted. He finally submitted his resignation effective 13 October 1958. Potter Stewart was nominated and quickly confirmed to replace him.

In retirement Burton sat by designation in the U.S. Court of Appeals for the District of Columbia Circuit through four years. Finally he succumbed to Parkinson's disease and died in George Washington Hospital in Washington, D.C.

Although Burton can in no way be considered a judge of major influence, he nonetheless played an important role in moving the Court from its New Deal emphasis on upholding federal powers at the expense of the states and individuals, to the Warren Court's focus on a more tempered federal reach and a larger sphere of individual rights. He was consistent without being doctrinaire, meticulous, and an indefatigable worker.

• Burton's papers are in the Manuscript Division of the Library of Congress in Washington, D.C. A book-length biography is Mary Frances Berry, *Stability, Security, and Continuity: Mr. Justice Burton and Decision-Making in the Supreme Court, 1945–1958* (1978), which includes a complete bibliography of works by and about Burton as well as a list of his law clerks. See also David N. Atkinson, "Justice Harold H. Burton and the Work of the Supreme Court," Cleveland State Law Review 27 (1978): 69–83; and Richard Kirkendall, "Harold Burton" in *Justices of the United States Supreme Court*, ed. Leon Friedman and Fred L. Israel (1997), pp. 2617–27. An obituary is in the *New York Times*, 29 Oct. 1964.

ERIC A. CHIAPPINELLI

BURTON, Hutchins Gordon (1782–21 Apr. 1836), North Carolina governor and congressman, was born in Mecklenburg County, Virginia, the son of John Burton and Mary Gordon. After the death of John Burton, his widow and her three-year-old son took up residence in the home of Colonel Robert Burton, a paternal uncle, at Williamsboro in Granville (now Vance) County, North Carolina. The uncle, a revolutionary leader and soldier, became Burton's guardian and mentor. Burton attended the University of North Carolina in 1795 but did not graduate. He read law with Judge Leonard Henderson at a school the judge operated in his Williamsboro home. About 1803 Burton relocated to Mecklenburg County, North Carolina, and in 1806 he was admitted to the state bar and opened a Charlotte practice.

Burton was a capable attorney and in time became a leader of the North Carolina bar. Like many of his legal contemporaries, he moved easily into politics. In 1809 and 1810 he represented Mecklenburg County in the North Carolina House of Commons. He resigned soon after the beginning of his second term, after his election as attorney general, an office he held from 28 November 1810 to 16 November 1816.

In 1812 Burton married Sarah Wales Jones, daughter of the revolutionary war and state political leader Willie Jones, and moved to her home in Halifax. He represented the borough of Halifax in the 1817 general assembly, and in 1819 he entered the U.S. House of Representatives as an "anti-Democrat" in keeping with his Federalist predilections. He, however, joined the Old Republicans in opposing the expansion of the federal government. He served in the Sixteenth, Seventeenth, and Eighteenth Congresses with no particular distinction.

Burton was somewhat overawed by contemporaries such as Henry Clay, John C. Calhoun, Daniel Webster, and Thomas Hart Benton and was reluctant to venture often into debate. When he did rise to protest the tariff or to complain about the laws governing smallpox vaccinations, he was apologetic and unctuously humble in demeanor. At the same time, he employed a rhetorical style that built to a rather forceful and witty conclusion. For example, when supporting a cut in the army's size, Burton dealt satirically with the claim that downsizing would prostrate an essential establishment by alienating officers. He lamented that "when we get to war, some fifteen or twenty years hence, perhaps with the inhabitants of the moon, . . . we cannot expect the services of these men" (*Annals of Congress*, 16th Cong., 2d sess., p. 926).

One interesting aspect of Burton's congressional career is his participation in a mess in Alfred R. Dowson's rooming house. During his tenure, a number of prominent Old Republicans took their meals there, including John Randolph of Roanoke, Nathaniel Macon, Welden Edwards, John Branch, and Willie P. Mangum.

Burton resigned from Congress and on 4 December 1824 assumed the governorship of North Carolina. He held that office for three terms, from December 1824 to December 1827. He endorsed both internal improvements and education but held education to be more important. He advocated state support for public schools. In 1825 the legislature enacted a measure establishing a literary fund "for the establishment of common schools" much to Burton's satisfaction. As president of the Literary Board, he was associated with the first efforts to create a common school system, but the process was painfully slow. Little had been accomplished before Burton's governorship ended.

The other highlight of Burton's tenure was the visit to North Carolina by the marquis de Lafayette, a man much beloved for his service in the American Revolution. Burton was his Raleigh host. He noted that North Carolina could not honor Lafayette with the wealthy displays of her sister states, but that she would yield to none in her devotion to liberty. Lafayette, with a military escort, proceeded to Fayetteville, the county seat of Cumberland County named in his honor, before exiting for South Carolina. The visit inspired Burton's oratory and excited the state.

In 1826 President John Quincy Adams nominated Burton to serve as territorial governor of Arkansas. This nomination was frustrated in the Senate by Andrew Jackson's supporters. Burton returned to private activities in Halifax and undertook the life of an attorney and planter. He lived in town but had a summer home named "Rocky Hill" near Ringwood in southwestern Halifax County. It was his intention to move to either Rocky Hill or Texas, where he had acquired significant holdings. However, death overtook Burton on a trip from Salisbury to visit his cousin, Robert H. Burton, in Lincoln County, North Carolina. He died either in Iredell or Lincoln county at a wayside inn. Relatives buried him at Unity Church, near Beattie's Ford, in Lincoln County. His wife learned of his death three weeks later. Burton had several children, although the number is elusive. The 1830 census indicates that five children were at home and that the family owned forty-six slaves.

Burton was active in public affairs during a period of political realignment. A member of the plantation aristocracy, he was first a Federalist, then an Old Republican (or Democratic Republican), and then a National Republican. In 1824 he supported the presidential candidacy of William H. Crawford, the caucus nominee, prior to Crawford's stroke, when he threw his support to John Quincy Adams. A popular figure who easily attracted friends and political supporters, Burton held important public positions and acted effectively. His legacy is that of a useful citizen of good humor and character. Perhaps his most important contribution was to the public school movement in North Carolina.

• Primary materials regarding Burton include the Governor's Letter Books, North Carolina State Archives, Raleigh; the *Annals of Congress*; and periodic references in the *Raleigh Register*. His messages on education may be found in C. L. Coon, *The Beginnings of Public Education in North Carolina* (1908). See also W. C. Allen, *History of Halifax County* (1918), and Daniel Lindsey Grant, *Alumni History of the University of North Carolina*, 2d ed. (1924).

MAX R. WILLIAMS

BURTON, Marion LeRoy (30 Aug. 1874–18 Feb. 1925), college and university president, was born near Brooklyn, Iowa, the son of Ira John Henry Burton and Jane Adeliza Simmons, farmers. The Burtons moved to Sioux City, Iowa, in 1881 and then to Minneapolis, Minnesota, in 1882 to improve the family's economic condition. The next year his father died, and he and his siblings worked at odd jobs to help support the family. After one year of high school Burton found work at a pharmacy, and after four years of independent study he passed the state licensing exam to become a pharmacist. He was offered a position as a pharmacist but turned it down to go back to school.

Burton entered the academy of Carleton College in Northfield, Minnesota, in 1893. Three years later he became a Carleton freshman and graduated with honors in 1900. Shortly after graduation he married Nina Leona Moses; they had three children. For three years (1900–1903) Burton was a high school principal in Montevideo, Minnesota, until he obtained a scholarship to attend Yale Divinity School in 1903. He graduated summa cum laude in 1906 and, in one year, earned his doctorate there. Yale published his dissertation, *The Problem of Evil*, in 1909 and appointed him as an assistant professor in systematic theology, a position he held for one year before accepting a call to the ministry at the Church of the Pilgrims in Brooklyn, New York. He resigned in 1909 to accept the presidency of Smith College in 1910; the intervening period was spent abroad, where he studied European models of higher education.

Since its opening as a women's college in 1875, Smith College had set a high standard for scholarship. Enrollment was growing and finances were sound, but the physical plant and the faculty-student ratio were inadequate to meet the needs of the students. Burton was equally committed to higher education for both men and women, and he believed that the intelligence of both sexes was equal. His experience at coeducational Carleton gave him an appreciation for the educational needs of women, and he set a goal to improve Smith College. Burton announced that he intended to raise $1 million to support the faculty. In three years he successfully raised the money, and in 1915 he was able to hire additional faculty and to raise the salaries of the existing staff. As immediate needs were met the trustees decided that a portion of the money would be used to build a biological laboratory, which they named for Burton. Although Smith's curriculum needed updating when he arrived, Burton was unable to give it his attention until 1915. He streamlined the curriculum, establishing a structured path leading to graduation with well-defined standards of scholarship. Burton also established a grading system and encouraged faculty research by listing their publications in his annual reports.

On 31 January 1917 Burton accepted the presidency of the University of Minnesota. Three months later the United States entered World War I. In addition to problems caused by the departure of students and faculty to support the war effort, Burton was forced to deal with accusations of disloyalty against several faculty members who either were German or had expressed antiwar sentiments. He was too willing to give credence to these claims; most proved to be due to malice or misunderstandings.

Burton was adept at persuading the Minnesota legislature to provide funding to meet his goals, and in 1919 he acquired a $5 million appropriation for a ten-year building program and faculty improvement. He also obtained a Rockefeller Foundation endowment of $1 million for hospital expansion. Because of Burton's foresight the university coped well with the influx of students after the war. Enrollment in 1919 rose to 8,000, a growth of 2,000 students over the prewar high. The legislature's promise of tuition for veterans permitted a larger proportion of students from modest financial backgrounds to attend college. In spite of his achievements, Burton was discouraged. The library was inadequately housed. Financial problems were growing, and he was frustrated because he could not meet with the student body because of the lack of an adequate meeting hall. After only two and a half years at Minnesota, Burton received overtures from the University of Michigan. On 29 December 1919 he announced that he had accepted the presidency of the University of Michigan.

Although Michigan's attractions included many of the amenities that Burton perceived as essential elements in higher education, he followed the same administrative pattern at Michigan as he had at Smith and at Minnesota. In the five years of his administration he persuaded the legislature to appropriate more than $9 million for campus improvements. He accomplished this in the face of health problems that had begun in Minnesota. After collapsing in late 1924 Burton died a few months later in Ann Arbor of complications from heart disease and pneumonia.

Burton's contributions to higher education were as a fundraiser. He was responsible for revitalization of the physical plants and faculty enhancement at the three institutions he served as president. He was a noted orator, and the highlight of his speaking career was delivering the speech nominating Calvin Coolidge for president at the Republican Convention in Cleveland in 1924. Burton did not separate himself from the concerns of the student body. He enjoyed student contact and was interested in their concerns and interests.

• Burton's personal papers are located in the Michigan Historical Collection, University of Michigan. Archival records at Smith College, University of Minnesota, and University of Michigan reflect Burton's administrative activities. Aside from his dissertation, Burton's other publication is *Our Intellectual Attitude in an Age of Criticism* (1913). Memorials to Burton are in *Carleton College News Bulletin*, Apr. 1925, and *Minnesota Alumni Weekly*, 26 Feb. 1925. The University of Michigan published a pamphlet, *Marion LeRoy Burton, 1874–1925* (1925). Obituaries are in the *New York Times* and the *Detroit Free Press*, 19 Feb. 1925.

PENELOPE KROSCH

BURTON, Phillip (1 June 1926–10 Apr. 1983), congressman, was born in Cincinnati, Ohio, the son of Thomas Burton, a salesman and physician, and Mildred Leonard. He spent his boyhood in the Midwest, living in Cincinnati, Detroit, and Milwaukee before the family moved to San Francisco during his high school years. Burton graduated from the University of Southern California in 1947 and from Golden Gate Law School in 1952. He served in the navy's V-12 program while attending USC during World War II and enlisted as a lawyer in the air force during the Korean War; in neither war did his military obligations take him outside California. In 1953 he married Sala Galant Lipschultz; they had one child. He immediately became active in Democratic politics in San Francisco and in 1954 challenged incumbent William "Cliff" Berry for a seat in the California assembly. Berry died during the primary campaign, but Burton had alienated San Francisco boss William Malone, who exacted revenge by insuring Burton's defeat. Two years later Burton challenged another incumbent assemblyman, Republican Tommy Maloney, and defeated him by appealing to the neglected voting potential of African-American and Chinese communities.

During his eight years in the California assembly, Burton became an advocate for the underprivileged. He assisted Mexican-American farm workers and welfare recipients and gained notoriety in 1960 by defending student protests against the House Committee on Un-American Activities (HUAC) in San Francisco. The capstone of his career in Sacramento was AB 59, a 1963 bill that revamped the California welfare system, creating an expensive program of unprecedented scope. Its passage revealed Burton's extraordinary talents, for it came in spite of strong opposition. His manipulation of the legislative process was so shrewd that his biographer considered it "one of the most astonishing legislative feats of his career" (Jacobs, p. 100). By the time he left the assembly, Burton had amassed power in the assembly second only to that of Speaker Jesse Unruh. When the federal courts mandated reapportionment of California's congressional districts, Unruh assigned the Bay Area to Burton. Burton, who soon became one of the masters of the art of gerrymandering, designed a district in San Francisco that assured his own election to Congress in 1964.

Emerging as one of the most liberal members of Congress, Burton supported seating the antisegregationist Mississippi Freedom Democratic party at the Democratic National Convention in 1964 and in 1965 voted with only two other members of Congress against funding for the war in Vietnam. He built a liberal coalition in the House that enacted legislation to protect miners against black lung disease, improve health and safety standards in mines, and guarantee that payments to miners would increase by linking them to civil service pay.

By the late 1960s and early 1970s, assured that his district was safe, Burton promoted controversial social legislation. His efforts rescued Supplemental Security Income (SSI) from President Richard Nixon's moribund Family Assistance Plan and extended food stamp benefits to striking farm workers. With the support of environmental groups, he fashioned federal land in the San Francisco Bay Area into Golden Gate National Recreation Area, fending off efforts from the armed services to preserve key property. In 1975 he succeeded in eliminating the notorious anti-Communist House Internal Security Committee (formerly HUAC) by lining up new assignments for its members and then striking it as a standing committee.

As Burton's influence increased, he laid plans to bid for a senior leadership position among House Democrats. As chair of the liberal Democratic Study Group in 1971, he used campaign funds to build political debts among newly elected representatives. He worked with freshmen members of the 1974 post-Watergate Congress to limit the seniority system and change how members were assigned to committees. Burton's power grew, but his acerbic personality, aggressive tactics, and willingness to defy House customs alienated some of his colleagues. Nonetheless, in 1974 he won election as the chair of the Democratic caucus, making him the fourth-ranking Democrat in the House. When Speaker Carl Albert retired in 1976 and Thomas P. "Tip" O'Neill took his place, Burton sought election as majority leader. In a four-way contest between Burton, Richard Bolling of Missouri, John McFall of California, and Jim Wright of Texas, Burton lost to Wright on the third ballot by a single vote, 148–147.

Shunted aside by House leadership as the Democrats reorganized after his defeat, Burton established a new power base from the unlikely platform of his chairmanship of the Subcommittee on National Parks and Insular Affairs. Although he had little personal interest in the outdoors, he appreciated the growing influence of the environmental movement and soon became one of its most effective advocates. Between 1977 and 1980 he successfully increased appropriations to ensure a broad expansion of the national park system, employing tactics that his biographer called "park barrel" politics to win support for the creation of thirty-nine new units in the system and the addition of nearly two million acres to existing parks. Against strong opposition he prevented the Disney corporation from developing Mineral King and expanded the Santa Monica National Recreation Area, both in his home state of California.

Burton continued to exercise influence in California politics by nurturing protégés and mastering the reapportionment process. His promotion of his brother John Burton, Henry Waxman, and Howard Berman in California politics and in Congress and of Willie Brown, whose tenure as Speaker of the California assembly was at the time the longest in history, led pundits to describe a "Burton machine." Burton at first won Republican support for his reapportionment plans by protecting incumbents, but after the 1980 census he designed a plan that enhanced Democratic control of the California congressional delegation from a ratio of 22 to 21 to a ratio of 28 to 17. While Republicans used new computer programs to devise counterproposals, Burton relied on his own archaic methods to develop a plan that withstood court challenges and maintained the sizable Democratic advantage.

The Republican resurgence of the early 1980s, Burton's long absences from his district, and the changing composition of the district made Burton vulnerable in the 1982 election campaign. He established support among new constituencies, including gays, environmentalists, and the police, and won convincingly. Plagued by health problems exacerbated by poor diet and a lifelong habit of heavy smoking, Burton died in San Francisco the following spring of a ruptured artery in his abdomen, complicated by heart disease.

Burton's career spanned the heights of postwar liberalism during the 1960s and the rise of Ronald Reagan conservatism during the 1980s. Few politicians in the late twentieth century matched his ability to manipulate the political system, an art he practiced with tools that ranged from forming coalitions of unlikely allies to gerrymandering California's political districts. His legacy includes legislation protecting the environment and providing financial assistance to people outside of the mainstream of American politics. In the 1970s he led the movement to reform congressional rules, diminishing the value of seniority and reducing the power of committee chairs. Although he fell one vote short of Democratic party leadership, Burton was one of the most influential liberals in Congress in the postwar era.

• Burton's personal papers are in the Bancroft Library at the University of California, Berkeley. John Jacobs, *A Rage for Justice: The Passion and Politics of Phillip Burton* (1995), is an excellent biography that is especially strong on Burton's role in California politics. An obituary is in the *New York Times*, 11 Apr. 1983.

ANDREW J. DUNAR

BURTON, Theodore Elijah (20 Dec. 1851–28 Oct. 1929), senator and congressman, was born in Jefferson, Ohio, the son of the Reverend William Burton, a Presbyterian minister, and Elizabeth Grant. After attending Grand River Institute in Austinburg, Ohio, Burton entered Grinnell College (Iowa) as a sophomore and graduated from Oberlin College in 1872. He received legal training in the office of Judge Lyman Trumbull of Chicago before being admitted to the Ohio bar in 1875. He practiced law in Cleveland, Ohio, served on the city council from 1886 to 1888, and then was elected as a Republican to the U.S. House of Representatives in 1888. After completing one term, he lost to Tom L. Johnson before regaining his seat in 1894.

The tall, slight, and quiet-mannered Burton looked more like a college professor than a politician, yet he battled for forty-one years in the Congress. He rose to the chairmanship (1898–1908) of the House Committee on Rivers and Harbors, inspiring the renovation of the harbors of key port cities and effecting other maritime improvements. Recognized as a navigational and financial expert, he also became known for his opposition to pork-barrel legislation and his occasional political independence. In 1907, encouraged by President Theodore Roosevelt, he unsuccessfully challenged progressive Democratic incumbent Tom Johnson in the Cleveland mayoralty contest. He also opposed Senator Marcus Hanna's domination of Ohio Republican politics and briefly acted as a progressive insurgent. In January 1909 he replaced conservative Joseph Foraker in the Senate. Thereafter his reform zeal cooled considerably, as he became a strong defender of President William Howard Taft and the Republican old guard. He played a key role in Taft's renomination in 1912, thereby antagonizing progressive elements in Ohio. Burton was especially sensitive about his unpopular stand on legislative measures. He had voted for the controversial Payne-Aldrich Tariff of 1909 and had supported President Woodrow Wilson's desire to repeal the Panama Canal Toll Exemption Act of 1912, which had exempted U.S. vessels from canal levies. With deep conviction, he favored the neutralization of the Panama Canal—an unpopular stand among Republicans. As a result, in 1914 Burton declined to seek reelection, and Warren G. Harding became Burton's Republican successor.

In the following years Burton practiced law, presided over a Wall Street bank, and became Ohio's favorite-son candidate for the presidency in 1916. In 1920 he again was elected to the House of Representatives, serving until 1928. In 1924 he was the keynote speaker at the Republican National Convention. During the 1920s he played an active part in arms limitation movements, labored on the World War Debt Funding Commission, and advocated American participation on the World Court. On domestic issues, Burton usually remained a conservative, opposing the veterans' bonus and the McNary-Haugen farm bill. He was politically close to Presidents Calvin Coolidge and Herbert Hoover. In 1928 he again was elevated to the Senate, where he remained until his death in Washington, D.C.

A bachelor, Burton devoted himself completely to his work, which also involved the writing of several books, including *Financial Crises and Periods of Industrial and Commercial Depression* (1902) and *The Life of John Sherman* (1906).

Burton's legacy includes an aversion to pork-barrel legislation, a commitment to world peace, and a longtime devotion to congressional service. No other person had ever returned to serve in both the House and the Senate after having completed earlier successive stints in those bodies. His conservative career bridged the McKinley and the Harding-Coolidge eras. Even Burton's critics admired him for his integrity and resourcefulness.

• The Burton papers are located at the Western Reserve Historical Society, Cleveland. A biography, although less than adequate, is Forrest Crissey, *Theodore E. Burton, American Statesman* (1956). See also Hoyt Landon Warner, *Progressivism in Ohio, 1897–1917* (1964), and James N. Giglio, *H. M. Daugherty and the Politics of Expediency* (1978). An obituary is in the *New York Times*, 29 Oct. 1929.

JAMES N. GIGLIO

BURTON, William Evans (24 Sept. 1802–10 Feb. 1860), actor and editor, was born in London, England, the son of William George Burton, a printer (maiden name unknown). Hoping his child would become a clergyman, the elder Burton enrolled him at St. Paul's School, but at the age of eighteen Burton had to withdraw and take charge of his family's printing business when his father died.

While still a teenager Burton grew interested in publishing his own monthly magazine and in a career on the stage. Although his first attempt at founding a literary journal failed, his theatrical career grew increasingly more promising. He married Elizabeth Loft, an English actress, in 1823; they had one son. Little is known of his first wife, and the marriage apparently ended in divorce. After performing in amateur productions, Burton joined a professional company in 1825. Six years later Burton played Hamlet at London's Pavilion Theatre. Although longing to portray all the leading figures in Shakespearean tragedy, he soon realized that his true talents lay in comic theater. In 1832 Burton became a comedian at the Haymarket when John Liston resigned, but he was later forced to seek other work when Liston decided to return.

Hoping to find steady employment, Burton accepted an offer in 1834 from the Arch Street Theatre in Philadelphia and left for the United States. On 18 July 1834 he married his second wife, London actress Caroline Glessing. In September 1834 Burton made his theatrical debut in the United States by playing

Wormwood in *The Lottery Ticket* and Dr. Ollapod in *The Poor Gentleman*. The Arch Street Theatre allowed Burton to showcase his talents for American audiences. Burton played Goldfinch in *The Road to Ruin*, Sir Peter Teazle, Dogberry, and Bob Acres. A born comedian, Burton endeared himself to the public.

Three years after arriving in Philadelphia, Burton fulfilled his dream of founding and editing a literary magazine, the *Gentleman's Magazine*, a monthly. The periodical, published from 1837 to 1840, contained beautiful illustrations, original stories, articles, poems, and reviews. Frequently resorting to lighthearted humor and satire, Burton also included a series dealing with a French policeman named Vidocq. Burton's magazine might have been the first to deal with the adventures of a detective.

Burton's most famous collaborator on the *Gentleman's Magazine* was Edgar Allan Poe. Poe's name first appeared as co-editor on the July 1839 issue. The Burton-Poe relationship lasted only a year and was stormy. Poe felt that Burton was not truly devoted to the literary arts, and Burton believed that Poe devoted too much space to literary analysis. Poe's association with the *Gentleman's Magazine* ended with the June 1840 issue, and in October Burton sold the magazine and again focused his creative energies on the theater.

After a failed attempt in 1841 to manage a theater in New York, Burton returned to Philadelphia. He not only managed two theaters in Philadelphia but also the Front Street Theatre in Baltimore and a playhouse in Washington, D.C. In July 1848, he again returned to New York. Opening a small house on Chambers Street, Burton managed Burton's Theatre (originally named the Chambers Street Theatre) until it closed in September 1856, when he then opened the Metropolitan Theatre under the name Burton's New Theatre. During its eight-year existence, Burton's New Theatre became New York's leading theatrical venue. Burton's alternating serious, classic plays with boisterous, raucous comedies proved very popular with the New York audience, which also found Burton's own portrayals of such characters as Falstaff, Bottom, Sir Toby, and Caliban delightful and thoroughly entertaining.

Burton gave his final performance at Mechanics Hall in Hamilton, Canada, in December 1859. Returning to New York, he died of heart disease and was survived by three daughters. He left a considerable library, including a large collection of Shakespeareana. Burton's jovial nature and his reputation as a scholar and a gentleman helped attract thousands of Americans to the various playhouses he managed.

• Burton's diary and a list of the plays in his library can be found at Harvard University. Some of his principal works include *Ellen Wareham* (1833); *The Ladies' Man* (1835); *Burton's Comic Songster* (1837); *The Yankee among the Mermaids, and Other Waggeries and Vagaries* (1843); *The Baronet's Daughter, and The Secret Cell!* (1845); *St. Vallier's Curse* (1852); and *The Cyclopaedia of Wit and Humor* (1858). Biographical information appears in William L. Keese, *William E. Burton, Actor, Author and Manager* (1885), and "William E. Burton," *Publications of the Dunlap Society* 14 (1891). See also Robert D. Jacobs, *Poe: Journalist and Critic* (1969), and Frank Luther Mott, *A History of American Magazines* (1938–1968).

MICHAEL L. BURDUCK

BUSCH, Adolphus (10 July 1839–10 Oct. 1913), company executive, was born at Mayence-on-the-Rhine, Hesse (in what is now Germany), the twenty-first child of Ulrich Busch, a wealthy land and vineyard owner and merchant; his mother, Barbara Pfeiffer, was Ulrich Busch's second wife. Educated at the Gymnasium in Mainz, the Academy of Darmstadt, and the pre-university school of Brussels, Busch spoke fluent French, German, and English and had some facility with Spanish and Italian. He briefly worked for his father and then for a mercantile house in Cologne. In 1857 he followed several older brothers to America, going directly to St. Louis, Missouri, where his first job was as a clerk on a river steamer.

In 1859 Adolphus used inherited funds to start a malt house with Ernst Wattenberg and also a brewery supply business, in partnership with his brother Ulrich. Among his customers was the brewery of Eberhard Anheuser. The Busch brothers became acquainted with Anheuser's daughters, and in 1861, in a double wedding, Ulrich married Anna while Adolphus married Lilly. The couple had fourteen children, of whom nine survived to adulthood.

Adolphus was drawn to the northern side in the Civil War and served a few months in 1861 under General John McNeil in northern Missouri before returning to business. Father-in-law Anheuser was not a good salesman, and his brewery was soon in debt to Adolphus's supply company. In 1865 Adolphus became part owner of the business—the beginning of his lifelong association with the brewery.

The brewery was growing steadily during the 1860s, expanding from 8,000 barrels sold in 1865 to 18,000 in 1870. During this decade the business began several initiatives that started it on the road to becoming the world's largest brewing company. Adolphus was a visionary who detected a vast, untapped market southwest of St. Louis. In 1872 he began shipping beer to Texas by icing down the shipments and building a series of icehouses by the railroads to provide reicing service. The highly perishable nature of beer made cold storage necessary. Another improvement was the development of techniques to employ the newly discovered process of pasteurization to beer. In 1873 their brewing technicians developed a method to pasteurize bottled beer by immersing the bottles in a hot water bath. Thus equipped with a new technology and the experience of marketing in Texas, the company easily slipped the bounds of St. Louis and the tough local competition provided by many small breweries and the giant Lemp Brewery, and began selling beer all over the far western frontier. Bottling beer was not novel, but the expanded scale generated a whole new industry in bottles, labels, corks, wire, and so on. Also in 1873 Busch became a full partner with his father-in-law, and the company became known as the E. Anheuser and Co. Brewing Association.

By 1875 sales were up to 34,797 barrels per year. In 1879 the company incorporated with $240,000 in capital and became the Anheuser-Busch Brewing Association. Busch was the secretary and treasurer of the company. The following year Busch and his friend Carl Conrad developed a lighter style of beer, of the kind popular in eastern Europe. At first the beer was sold exclusively in kegs to a local bottler. Named for the town of Budweis, Czechoslovakia, this new "Budweiser" beer proved so popular that the trademark was reassigned to the brewery in 1883 when the bottler went bankrupt. Budweiser became the flagship brand that led the company's unprecedented sales climb.

Adolphus also became a pioneer in refrigerated railway cars, which were introduced at the 1876 Centennial Exhibition in Philadelphia. Budweiser, pasteurization, and artificial cooling were the three props that spurred the company's growth. By 1877 Anheuser-Busch had become the 32d-largest brewery in the United States. Following the death of Eberhard Anheuser in 1880, Adolphus became the sole leader of the brewery, and his genius for technical innovation and marketing was given free reign. Busch's philosophy was to hold the stock in the corporation tightly and finance expansion from profit rather than borrowing. He believed it was best to control as many aspects of the total beer distribution business as possible and to embrace promising new technology faster and more completely than his competitors. In 1883 artificial refrigeration was installed in the St. Louis brewing plant to supplant the ice-cooled cellars that were the previous standard for the industry. Bottled beer sales grew until Busch saw a need to acquire glass companies in the area to assure his supply of bottles. Sales during this decade mushroomed from 318,082 barrels in 1885 to 702,075 barrels in 1890. During 1890 the American Federation of Labor boycotted Anheuser-Busch beer as "scab" beer, but in 1891 Adolphus signed his first contract with the Knights of Labor to allow his brewery workers to unionize and thus ended his labor difficulties.

Despite the success of Anheuser-Busch beers, Busch invested in local breweries in Texas and Louisiana to diversify his interests. In 1891 Busch rejected a $10 million offer from a British syndicate for his St. Louis brewery. Throughout the 1890s Adolphus continued to expand and diversify. Perhaps his most significant purchase was the American rights to the diesel engine from the German inventor Rudolph Diesel for $1 million cash. During World War I Busch Corporation engines powered America's submarines.

During this decade Adolphus also acquired a little-known painting, *Custer's Last Fight*, by Cassilly Adams. He then had it lithographed and used it in one of the first nationwide advertising campaigns. As a result, the scene became the most popular historical image in the United States, and its advertising message was seen in nearly every barroom in America.

By 1900 Anheuser-Busch had clearly passed rival Pabst as the largest brewery in the world, and the following year sales passed the one-million-barrel mark. Adolphus increased his philanthropy and civic involvement during these years. Each winter in particular he donated cash to individuals and committees representing charities on behalf of the poor people of St. Louis. Busch served as foreign relations chairman for the 1904 St. Louis World's Fair, the Louisiana Purchase Exposition. Among other honors, his work in this project won him the Order of the Crown, second class, from the German emperor Wilhelm II in 1905.

In 1906 Adolphus was visiting San Francisco when the great earthquake hit. He immediately wired for $100,000 for relief work. Later that year his health began a downward spiral; he was suffering from dropsy and heart disease.

In 1907 the brewery's pre-Prohibition sales peaked at 1.6 million barrels. That same year Busch prevented a run on the LaFayette South Side Bank in St. Louis, another of his businesses, when he personally guaranteed every deposit. In 1908 Busch gave $100,000 to the victims of the Reggio and Messina earthquake in Italy. He also made a $50,000 donation to the Germanic Museum at Harvard the same year, followed by another $150,000 the next year. In 1910 Busch bought 90 percent of the corporate shares for the building of his namesake hotel, the Adolphus, in Dallas, Texas.

In 1911, the fiftieth wedding anniversary of Adolphus and Lilly Busch was one of the grandest social events of the year. The main celebration was held at the family's winter home in Pasadena, California, while in St. Louis another was held for the thousands of Busch employees. Gifts were received from the German emperor, President William Howard Taft, and former president Theodore Roosevelt (1858–1919) among other dignitaries. In honor of the event, Adolphus and Lilly gave each of their children a new home in America or Germany.

In 1913 Adolphus and many of his friends went to Villa Lilly, the Busch estate near Langenschwalbach in the Wiesbaden area of Germany, for the fall hunting season, hoping that the philanthropist's health might improve. Adolphus died there, surrounded by family and friends. His funeral in St. Louis was the largest and most widely attended in the city's history. He left between $50 and $60 million, about $200,000 to various charities, and was highly regarded in the St. Louis area.

• The business correspondence of Adolphus Busch (1880–1910) and the minutes of the board of directors of the corporation are held by the archives of Anheuser-Busch Inc. in St. Louis. The corporate archives also has on file the "Life of Adolphus Busch," prepared by a company employee, G. A. H. Mills. Business aspects of Adolphus's life are well covered in Ronald J. Plavchan, "A History of Anheuser-Busch, 1852–1933" (Ph.D. diss., St. Louis Univ., 1969). Maxine S. Sandberg, "Life and Career of Adolphus Busch" (M.A. thesis, Univ. of Texas, 1952), covers family and social matters. Alice Busch Tilton's privately printed *Remembering* (1947) is a nostalgic history by a family member. Roland

Krebs's corporate publication, *Making Friends Is Our Business: 100 years of Anheuser-Busch* (1953), has many anecdotal memories from former employees and business associates. The life of Adolphus and the early history of the brewery are covered in Peter Hernon and Terry Ganey, *Under the Influence: The Unauthorized Story of the Anheuser-Busch Dynasty* (1991). Significant articles include Gerald Holland, "Adolphus Busch: The King of Beers," *American Mercury*, Oct. 1929, pp. 171–78; and (no author cited) "King of Bottled Beer," *Fortune*, July 1935, pp. 42–49. The *St. Louis Globe-Democrat* and the *St. Louis Post-Dispatch* both had long, detailed obituaries, tributes, and editorials of praise on 11, 12, 25, and 30 Oct. 1913.

HERMAN W. RONNENBERG

BUSCH, August Anheuser, Jr. (28 Mar. 1899–29 Sept. 1989), corporate executive and philanthropist, was born in St. Louis, Missouri, the son of brewmaster August Anheuser Busch, Sr., and Alice Zisemann. Busch, known as "Gussie," was accustomed to wealth and was steeped in a rich family tradition from his grandfather, Adolphus Busch, who had founded Anheuser-Busch in 1876. Without much formal education—"I never graduated from anything"—he began at the bottom as a vat scrubber, determined to learn the brewing business. With his relentless drive he rose to general superintendent in just two years during Prohibition. Then on 7 April 1933 came repeal. The "greatest moment of my life," said Busch, who became a dedicated Democrat. A bright red and yellow beer wagon drawn by eight Clydesdales paraded up Pennsylvania Avenue in Washington, D.C., with beer for the new president, Franklin D. Roosevelt.

After their father's tragic suicide in 1934, Busch's brother Adolphus Busch III assumed the presidency of the number one brewery, but under his administration national sales slipped to fourth. Assuming that position in 1946, following his brother's death, Busch used his bulldog determination to force radical changes on the company. He totally renovated the St. Louis plant and built four new branches in other cities to eliminate wasteful shipping costs. Total expenses reached $134 million by 1953, but that year saw Anheuser-Busch vault again to first in national sales, reaching $400 million. "Being first is everything," he bellowed to his workers as he demanded "quality" of product. Visiting all branch plants personally, he often inspected washrooms first as barometers of efficiency. When a production miscalculation altered the taste of the product at one plant, Busch ordered all beer on hand to be dumped down the sewers. He stuck to traditional and painstaking methods, refusing to imitate cheaper competitors. Through it all, he proved resolute, determined, and persistent. He ran the business "in a way that would make my grandfather, my father, and my brother proud of me."

Busch had no patience with incompetence. In a voice like "a hoarse lion," he roared at board members—"dammit, because I said so!"—bludgeoning his way through every issue or problem. Few doubted his business genius. Alfred Fleishman, who handled brewery publicity for many years, was "fired every Monday, Wednesday, and Friday," then just as quickly rehired. He crafted Busch's public image as "the soft heart with the hard nose," the capable business executive and community philanthropist. The media creation fitted reality, however, for Busch's personality fluctuated between the tyrannical and the sociably good-natured. Always loyal to St. Louis, he served on boards for the symphony, the St. Louis Municipal Opera, and various banks. He led an $18 million drive for St. Louis University's Busch Memorial Center in 1960.

Busch's "outsized zest for life" reached fulfillment when Anheuser-Busch purchased the St. Louis Cardinals National League baseball club in February 1953, blocking its imminent move to Milwaukee. For $3.75 million the brewery presented Busch with his "personal toy," in the words of sportswriter Bob Broeg. Stan Musial and Red Schoendienst, Cardinal players and hunting companions, had first broached the subject to him, and business advantages, such as identifying beer with baseball at the games and gaining media exposure, and civic duty proved decisive. His attempt to rename the ballpark "Budweiser Stadium," however, provoked objections from Ford Frick, National League president, and Mrs. D. Leigh Colvin, head of the Woman's Christian Temperance Union, who criticized the proposal as "part of the grand strategy of the brewing industry to use major sports to promote drinking." The field instead became "Busch Stadium," a name carried over to the new facility in 1966. Busch harangued the brewery executives to contribute $5 million to that project.

Busch's new baseball affiliation had its frustrations, however, especially when the Major League Players' Association was headed by labor leader Marvin Miller. When the players struck in 1972, Busch was furious, for he had granted the first $1 million payroll to his club in 1969: "We won't give them another [blank] cent." Vindictively, he forced Cardinal players to use commercial flights and to double up in hotel rooms, while canceling the free beer customarily sent to their homes.

Another labor dispute erupted in 1976. Busch favored an owners' lockout, but Commissioner Bowie Kuhn ordered spring training to reopen, leaving Busch livid. After Kuhn upbraided him for his salty language in meetings, Busch successfully effected Kuhn's ouster. A triumphant Busch pounded the council table with his cane: "He should clean out his desk tomorrow!" Kuhn later wrote that he had been trampled by the "power of Anheuser-Busch."

By the time of Busch's retirement as president of Anheuser-Busch in 1975, the company had become the largest brewery internationally, with a full 25 percent of the American market. Budweiser alone was the world's most popular beer. Busch retained his headship of the Cardinals and rooted for them as enthusiastically as a bleacher fan. They won six pennants (1964, 1967, 1968, 1982, 1985, and 1987) and three world championships (1964, 1967, and 1982) during his tenure. Someone estimated that just one year's beer production would fill 50,000-capacity Busch Stadium two and one-half times. The "king of beer" found that baseball truly helped sell his product.

Busch was married four times. In 1918 he married Marie Christy Church, with whom he had two children before her death in 1930. In 1933 he married Elizabeth Overton Dozier. They had two children and were divorced in 1952. His third marriage, in 1952 to Gertrude Josephine "Trudy" Buholzer, to whom he proposed on their first date, produced seven children and ended in a bitter divorce in 1978. Three years later Busch married his secretary, Margaret Snyder, who died in 1988. They had no children. The Busch family suffered its share of tragedy. A nephew was kidnapped in 1930, a daughter was killed in an auto accident in 1974, and one of Busch's sons accidentally shot a close friend a year later.

Like a feudal lord, Busch presided over his 281-acre "Grant's Farm" in St. Louis County. He loved his horses, hunting, boxing, and poker. He drove a coach-and-four for privileged visitors to his estate, such as fellow Missourian Harry Truman. In 1975 Busch was named to the Missouri Sports Hall of Fame. Rated the seventh wealthiest man in the United States in his last years, he was reputedly worth $1.3 billion. He died at Grant's Farm. President George Bush eulogized Gussie as "a man who cared deeply about individual spirit and accomplishment."

• Files on Busch are in the Baseball Hall of Fame Library at Cooperstown, N.Y., and in the archives of the *Sporting News* in St. Louis, Mo. A negatively slanted account of the Busch family is Peter Hernon and Terry Ganey, *Under the Influence: The Unauthorized Story of the Anheuser-Busch Dynasty* (1991). In contrast see the laudatory newspaper accounts at the time of Busch's retirement from the company presidency by Roy Malone, William H. Kester, and Bob Broeg, "Gussie Busch," *St. Louis Post-Dispatch*, 25–29 Aug. 1975; see also Roger Thurow, "The King of Beers and Beer of Kings Are at Lagerheads," *Wall Street Journal*, 3 Apr. 1992; Leonard Koppett, "Beer, Busch, and Baseball," *New York Times Magazine*, 11 Apr. 1965; and William Leggett, "A Bird in Hand and a Burning Busch," *Sports Illustrated*, 23 Mar. 1970. For Busch's stormy yet successful career as a baseball figure, consult Bowie Kuhn, *Hardball: The Education of a Baseball Commissioner* (1987), Marvin Miller, *A Whole Different Ball Game: The Sport and Business of Baseball* (1991), and especially Broeg, *Redbirds: A Century of Cardinal Baseball* (1992), noteworthy for a colorful and informative section titled "Gussie." Obituaries are in the *New York Times* and the *St. Louis Post-Dispatch*, both 30 Sept. 1989.

WILLIAM J. MILLER

BUSEMANN, Adolf (20 Apr. 1901–7 Nov. 1986), aeronautical engineer, was born in Lübeck, Germany, the son of Cornelius Buzeman. Busemann's father changed his name to Busemann in 1908. After earning his Ph.D. in engineering in 1924 from Brunswick Technical University, Busemann worked as an aeronautical research scientist at the Kaiser Wilhelm Institute for Flow Research from 1925 to 1931 under the leadership of Ludwig Prandtl. While there he married Magdalene Krage in 1927; they had three daughters.

In 1931 Busemann became Privatdozent at the University of Dresden, where he worked until 1935. During that time he was also involved in aerodynamic testing at the Göttingen wind tunnel laboratory, where he made substantial contributions to the field of aerodynamics. In 1933, for example, he showed that thin aerofoils delay and reduce sharp increases in drag (or air resistance). Drag increases sharply as an aircraft approaches the speed of sound (Mach 1 or 660 to 760 miles per hour depending on temperature). Busemann's solution was novel not only for showing that wave drag is proportional to the square of the thickness ratio of the wing, but also for proposing to build such foils into a biplane designed in such a manner as to ensure that the waves caused by the upper wing would be compensated for or even cancelled by the lower wing. Wave interference in effect reduced wave drag. An improved solution was devised two years later when Busemann pointed out that swept-back wings might provide a solution to the problem of vibrations, since wave drag might be completely canceled out by sufficient sweepback. As the speed of an aircraft increased and approached 1,000 to 1,200 kilometers per hour, serious buffeting would occur and threaten to tear the aircraft apart at the seams. Swept wings, Busemann theorized, delayed the buffeting until a higher speed was attained and might allow stable flight in the vicinity of Mach 1. His presentation of such findings at the 1935 aerodynamic conference in Volta, Italy, met with skepticism. Participants in the conference such as Theodore von Kármán played for a while with the idea and then set it aside. Soon, however, Albert Betz, Woldemar Voigt, and Alexander Lippisch echoed Busemann's approach, advocating a delta-shaped aeroplane wing and deserve a share of the credit for solving the sound barrier problem.

In 1936 Busemann took over the direction of the Institute for Gas Dynamics at the Hermann Göring Aeronautical Research Center in Völkenrode. In 1937 he joined the Nazi party, but he does not appear to have been an active member, instead incurring trouble with Nazi bureaucracy as he moved to protect colleagues from denunciation and publicly criticized the party. His motives for joining remained unclear to his friends, although one motive may have been the wish to ensure his appointment as professor at the Technical University at Charlottenburg.

During World War II Busemann carried on his research, and afterward he spent two years in England as lecturer under contract to the British Ministry of Supply. In 1947 he came to the United States through Project Paperclip, which selected scientists who had worked in Nazi Germany to further their research on U.S. soil. During the war several U.S. scientists had come to conclusions about shock waves similar to those to which Busemann had come, and when he arrived he was able to corroborate their findings on compressibility at transonic speeds. Busemann first worked as a consultant to the British National Physical Laboratory before moving on to work at the National Advisory Committee on Aeronautics (NACA) as chief scientist at Langley Field, Virginia. While there he taught a variety of classes, such as kinetic theory and applied mechanics. He also perfected the famous Busemann "apple curve," a mathematical construct for calibrating isentropic flows through parameter space. The successful application of his expertise was demonstrated early on with the design and production of the F-86 Sabre, the frontline American jet fighter used in the Korean war.

Busemann remained with NACA (later NASA) until 1964, as the creative mind behind the Gas Dynamics Laboratory. During that time, he became interested in magnetoplasmadynamics, a field that seemed quite promising and indeed helped solve such problems as atmospheric reentry of missiles. Busemann was also involved in the early planning stages for sending a human being to the moon, although he was in a minority group that advocated building a rocket that could reach the moon directly, instead of first developing an orbital space station from which scientific and technical knowledge could be gathered. In Busemann's opinion, there was little to be derived from orbital science that could not be obtained on earth. He taught aeronautical engineering at the University of Colorado from 1964 until 1971, when he retired. During his tenure there, he continued his research and advised NASA on the use of tiles on the space shuttle that could withstand greater temperatures than aluminum alloys could.

Called "a giant in the field of aerodynamics" and "the father of supersonic flight," Busemann pursued research interests that spanned a great many fields and subfields of aeronautics, including aerodynamics, heat and matter exchange, magnetohydrodynamics, sonic boom reduction, airport safety, and orbital transfer. Many designs he proposed were ahead of their time, such as a pump system devised in 1930 that was not built till 1962. Other patents expired before practical inventions could be constructed. His methods to calculate pressure and force coefficient for various wing shapes produced quicker results than did the more sophisticated theories that NASA later applied. His capacity for simple approaches to complex problems, according to some, epitomizes the Riemannian tradition, which gives the broader sense of method an importance equal to the specific mathematical results. Busemann's "geometric intuition" served as an inspiration to many scientists and engineers, and the solutions he derived using such intuition have become standards in aerodynamics.

• The National Air and Space Museum of the Smithsonian Institution has a biographical file with clippings on Busemann. The National Archives, College Park Branch, has the "Paperclip" file on Busemann, which summarizes his activities between 1933 and 1945 as well as his path to the United States (in RG 319). He collaborated on his last work, *Hypersonic and Planetary Flight Entry Mechanics*, with Nguyen X. Vinh and Robert D. Culp (1980). Elizabeth A. Muenger, *Searching the Horizon* (1985), and James R. Hansen, *Spaceflight Revolution* (1995), clarify the environment in which Busemann worked until he left NASA. Richard Hallion, *Supersonic Flight: The Story of the Bell X-1 and Douglas D-558* (1972), contains some information on the background to early supersonic flight.

GUILLAUME DE SYON

BUSH, Benjamin Franklin (5 July 1860–29 July 1927), railroad president, was born in Wellsboro, Pennsylvania, the son of James Bush and Rosella Henry, occupations unknown. After studying surveying at the state normal school in Mansfield, Pennsylvania, he took his first railroad job as a rodman with the Northern Pacific railroad in 1882. An avid fisherman and enthusiastic follower of the precepts of Izaak Walton, Bush originally pursued railroad work as a means to continue his outdoor activities. He rose to the position of division engineer and then in 1887 assumed the same job with the Union Pacific railroad in Idaho and Oregon. Three years later he ascended to chief engineer and general superintendent of the Oregon Improvement Company, which later became the Pacific Coast Steamship Company of Seattle.

In 1896 Bush became general manager of the Northwestern Improvement Company, which coordinated coal operations for the Northern Pacific railroad. In 1903 he was named vice president and general manager of the Consolidated Coal Company of St. Louis, Missouri. In that capacity he served as fuel agent for the Missouri Pacific railroad. (The Missouri Pacific was the centerpiece of the network established by railroad magnate and speculator Jay Gould; after his death in 1892, the operations passed to his son, George J. Gould, and other investors.) As fuel agent for the Missouri Pacific, Bush oversaw the coal operations of the Gould companies in the Southwest and the West. Through his work with coal producers, steamship lines, and railroads, Bush became an authority on coal and fuel issues. Bush was a recognized expert on the mining and transportation of coal. He was a consulting engineer to the U.S. Geological Survey with regard to mining matters in 1900, and in 1907 President Theodore Roosevelt appointed him to an advisory board on fuel issues.

When the Gould interests gained control of the beleaguered Western Maryland railroad in 1907, Bush was made president. He led the line through receivership and returned it to economic health, and in 1911 he was rewarded by his election as president of the Missouri Pacific & Iron Mountain railroad, also controlled by the Gould interests. In 1913 he was named president of the Denver & Rio Grande and the Western Pacific railroads. He resigned from those railroads in 1915, however, to devote his full attention to the troubled Missouri Pacific & Iron Mountain. That line entered receivership in 1915, with Bush as sole receiver. Within two years Bush had reorganized the company and returned it to a position of economic viability. In 1917 the line emerged from receivership with its name shortened to the Missouri Pacific, and Bush again was installed as president.

Typically Bush worked to improve the position of his lines by upgrading and restoring real estate and rolling stock, by engaging in public relations to improve the popular perception of the line, and by finding ways to increase the efficiency of the operations (including altering schedules, changing fee structures, and transporting coal more economically). From 1918 until 1920 during the war emergency, the government assumed control of the railroads. Bush served the government as regional director of the railroads in the Southwest region. After the war, when the railroads were returned to corporate control in 1920, Bush resumed the president's chair. In 1923 he was elected chairman of the board of directors of the Missouri Pacific, and he remained on the board after his retirement a year later.

After retirement Bush pursued banking and farming interests in the St. Louis area. He became vice president of the Boatmen's Bank of St. Louis in 1924. He took pleasure in farming, and he put that interest to practice by managing the operation of a model farm near St. Louis. A robust man, Bush enjoyed outdoor pastimes, including hunting and fishing. He was a member of numerous professional organizations including the American Railway Association, the American Railway Guild, the American Society of Mining Engineers, and the American Mining Congress. He served as president of the Missouri, Kansas, and Arkansas Coal Operators Association. He was also a member of the Presbyterian church. Bush had married Catherine Idelia Hawkins in 1883; they had one daughter. Bush died in his adopted city of St. Louis.

Bush was neither one of the great railroad builders of the nineteenth century nor one of the giants of the industry in the twentieth century. He was, however, one of a handful of prominent executives during a difficult period of competition and consolidation among the numerous rail lines. He brought more technical skills to his job than most railroad executives, and he enjoyed a reputation as an intelligent and able leader whose positive and dynamic personality could improve difficult situations.

• The most extensive biographical sketch is in the *National Cyclopedia of American Biography*, vol. 23, pp. 203–4. Obituaries are in the *New York Times* and the *St. Louis Globe Democrat*, both 30 July 1927.

ROGER A. HALL

BUSH, George Washington (1790?–5 Apr. 1863), pioneer, farmer, and cattleman, was born probably in Pennsylvania or Louisiana. His mother was Scotch-Irish, his father perhaps East Indian; little is known of Bush's birth and ancestry. He may have been born as early as 1770. However, that would have made him seventy-four by the time he came to Oregon in 1844. Oral tradition among the family gives the date as 1779.

Bush was a successful cattle trader in Missouri beginning around 1820 and became quite wealthy. In 1831 he married Isabella James, a German woman; they had five children. Because Missouri was not well disposed toward people of color, Bush took the opportunity to travel west in a wagon train led by Michael T. Simmons of Kentucky.

Bush found Oregon only a little more tolerant than Missouri. The provisional government voted to exclude blacks and to whip those who would not leave, but the legislation apparently was never enforced. The land north of the Columbia River, which, it was thought, would become British, beckoned the Simmons party. On high open ground south of what is now Olympia, Bush staked a claim that has since been known as Bush Prairie. It was the first American settlement on Puget Sound. Bush is thought to have brought a considerable sum of money with him. With the food and supplies this money afforded, the little colony was able to survive the first cold winter. The Bush home soon became a haven for the exhausted pioneers who came into the area.

When the treaty of 1846 set the boundary between British and American claims at the 49th parallel, Bush found himself in American territory. He continued to raise wheat and cattle. Although he pioneered settlement on Puget Sound, his property was at risk, as the census of 1850 had listed him as Negro, and, as such, he could not own property. By the time Washington Territory was formed in 1853, the Bush claim was one of its most valuable properties. It consisted of 640 acres, which under the Donation Land Law every married man could claim.

Bush had made many friends by this time because of his willingness to share what he had with those less fortunate than himself. It is not surprising, therefore, that these friends banded together under the leadership of Simmons and put through the Washington territorial legislature in 1853 an act specifically exempting Bush from the prohibition of ownership.

In 1854 Congress was memorialized to help Bush perfect his claim, under the Donation Land Law. The memorial stated that Bush:

> has resided upon and cultivated said tract of land continuously from said year 1845 to the present time, and that his habits of life during said time have been exemplary and industrious; and that by a constant and laborious cultivation of his said claim, and by an accommodating and charitable disposal of his produce to emigrants, he has contributed much towards the settlement of this Territory.

Although he was allowed to keep his land, Bush was denied citizenship. Even though he was one of the leading citizens of his community he never had the right to vote.

Bush lived just long enough to hear of the Emancipation Proclamation issued in January 1863. After his passing at his home, residents of the area continued to speak of him with respect as one who overcame the difficulties of pioneer life, not only for his family, but for many other settlers as well. Ezra Meeker, a pioneer of 1852 who later went on to prominence, spoke of

Bush's generosity when the large number of immigrants in 1852–1853 caused a food shortage:

The man divided out nearly his whole crop to new settlers who came with or without money. . . . "Pay me in kind next year," he would say to those in need; and to those who had money he would say, "don't take too much . . . just enough to do you"; and in this wise divided his large crop and became a benefactor to the community.

If success can be measured by material possessions, financial security, and the love and respect of one's family and friends, Bush was a very successful man.

• The Afro-American Collection at the Washington State Historical Society contains many short items on Bush. The most reliable work on Bush is Paul Thomas, "George Bush" (M.A. thesis, Univ. of Washington, 1965). A shorter assessment of his accomplishments is in Murray Morgan, *Puget's Sound: A Narrative of Early Tacoma and the Southern Sound* (1979). On Bush's ethnicity, see Bureau of the Census, *Compendium of the Seventh Census: Negro Population, 1790–1915*.

FRANK L. GREEN

BUSH, John Edward (15 Nov. 1856–11 Dec. 1916), businessman and politician, was born a slave in Moscow, Tennessee. In 1862 his master moved him and his mother to Arkansas to keep them from being freed when the Union army moved into western Tennessee. His mother died when Bush was only seven years old. He was educated in the freedmen's and public schools of Little Rock and was considered a good student by his teachers. He paid his school tuition by molding bricks. In 1876 he graduated from high school with honors and was immediately appointed principal of Capital Hill School, a public institution for African Americans in Little Rock. In 1878 he moved to Hot Springs, where he was named to head that city's African-American high school.

In 1879 Bush returned to Little Rock, where he married Cora Winfrey, the daughter of a wealthy African-American contractor, Solomon Winfrey. The couple had four children. Bush was a member of the Missionary Baptist church. He obtained a job as a clerk in the city post office's railway service, rising to the position of district supervisor. He held this position until 1892. Bush also invested in Little Rock real estate and dealt in city properties for the rest of his life. In 1889 he began publishing a newspaper for African Americans, the *American Guide*.

In 1882 Bush, according to his own account, decided to organize an African-American insurance company in response to criticism of his race by a white man who had been approached by a black woman for assistance in burying her husband. With another postal employee, Chester W. Keatts, Bush founded the Mosaic Templars of America, an African-American fraternal organization that provided burial and life insurance for its members and was also a loan association and a hospital. The association bought Bush's newspaper and renamed it the *Mosaic Guide*. By 1913 the group claimed some eighty thousand members.

In the 1880s Bush became involved in Republican politics in Arkansas, an activity that may have secured him his job with the post office. His early role is obscure, although by 1883 he was busy in the party's Sixth Ward organization in Little Rock. By 1884 he won election as a delegate to the Pulaski County Republican Convention; a delegate to the state convention, where he served as secretary; and a member, by proxy, of the state executive committee. In the 1884 county convention he unsuccessfully pushed for more nominations for county offices to be allotted to African Americans. In subsequent years he filled a variety of jobs and positions in city and county party organizations. By 1892 he had become important enough to serve as a delegate to the Republican National Convention, a position he held again in 1912.

In politics Bush was associated with Powell Clayton, a former governor and U.S. senator who was the state's party boss, and Mifflin W. Gibbs, a prominent African-American attorney and party leader. In 1898, with the backing of Clayton, Bush secured the position of U.S. receiver of public lands from President William McKinley. Bush survived repeated efforts to remove him over the next fourteen years. His chief opposition came from "Lily-White" Republicans in Arkansas who sought to purge blacks from the party. Ultimately the patronage of Clayton and white businessmen in Little Rock along with support from Booker T. Washington allowed him to continue in the position until the Republicans lost the White House in 1912.

Bush, a successful businessman and politician, became an early supporter of the policies of Washington. He joined Washington's National Negro Business League in 1900 and served on its national executive committee, and in 1905 he convinced Washington to visit Little Rock. Bush openly embraced Washington's policy of black self-help and nonconfrontation. Even so, he refused to accept the idea that African Americans should be second-class citizens. As early as 1891 he led protests in an unsuccessful effort to block Democratic legislative efforts to segregate railroad coaches. He continued to oppose infringements on African-American civil rights thereafter, leading protests against efforts in 1903 to segregate streetcars in Arkansas and supporting black boycotts of several streetcar lines within the state. Bush died in Little Rock.

• A full biography of Bush is in A. E. Bush and P. L. Dorman, *History of the Mosaic Templars of America—Its Founders and Officials* (1924). A recent academic treatment of his life is C. Calvin Smith, "John E. Bush of Arkansas, 1890–1910," *Ozark Historical Review* 2 (Spring 1973): 48–59. A short obituary is in the (Little Rock) *Arkansas Gazette*, 15 Dec. 1916.

CARL MONEYHON

BUSH, Prescott Sheldon (15 May 1895–8 Oct. 1972), banker and U.S. senator, was born in Columbus, Ohio, the son of Samuel Prescott Bush, a manufacturer of railway equipment, and Flora Sheldon. Raised in comfortable circumstances, Bush attended Columbus public schools, St. George's School in Newport,

Rhode Island, and Yale College, where he earned a B.A. in 1917. At Yale, he was a three-sport athlete (baseball, football, golf), president of the glee club, and a member of the prestigious secret society, Skull and Bones. The quintessential "big man on campus," he seemed headed for a career in law and politics.

Bush's postgraduate plans were altered by World War I. Having enlisted as a private in the Connecticut National Guard in 1916, he attended the U.S. Army's officer training school and was commissioned a captain of field artillery in 1917. Bush saw considerable action in France and remained with Allied occupation forces in Germany until his discharge in 1919. Eager to get on with life after the war, he passed up law school to seek his fortune in the business world. In his first job, Bush sold wholesale hardware for a company based in St. Louis. He then became involved in sales and management in the floor covering business in Columbus and in Braintree, Massachusetts, before the U.S. Rubber Company hired him to head its flooring department in New York in 1924. He had married Dorothy Walker of St. Louis, the daughter of banker G. H. Walker, in 1921. They had five children, one of whom, George Herbert Walker Bush, would become the forty-first president of the United States.

In 1926 Prescott Bush joined the Wall Street banking firm of W. A. Harriman and Company at the urging of his father-in-law, who was then the Harriman president. He fit easily into the elite investment operation owned by W. Averell Harriman and his brother, E. Roland, and presided over by Walker. When the comparatively young Harriman and Company merged with Brown Brothers, an old and respected New York banking concern, in 1930, Walker retired and Bush was made a partner in the newly constituted Brown Brothers, Harriman and Company. He proved expert at recruiting new clients and building up deposits during the difficult depression years. As a key player in the arrangement of financing for William S. Paley's purchase of the Columbia Broadcasting System in 1931, Bush won the business of that fledgling enterprise. In addition, he secured the accounts of Dresser Industries, Prudential Insurance, and other developing companies for Brown Brothers, Harriman and made a number of lucrative corporate connections for himself along the way.

Having achieved success and financial security, Bush devoted more time to interests outside of business. He served on the Executive Committee of the U.S. Golf Association, the principal rule-making body for his favorite pastime, for eight years, and was USGA president in 1935. Also in 1935, Bush succeeded General Foods president Colby Chester as moderator of the Representative Town Meeting in Greenwich, Connecticut, where he had made his home since 1924; he held the post for seventeen years. His charitable work included participation in an effort to assist displaced Wall Street workers in 1938 and the chairmanship of successful fundraising campaigns during World War II for the United Services Organization (USO) and the National War Fund, which contributed to 600 relief agencies. He also served two terms as a Yale trustee between 1944 and 1958 and was Connecticut chairman for the United Negro College Fund in 1951.

Bush's postwar fundraising for the Republican party led ultimately to his candidacy for high office. While acting as chairman of the Connecticut Republican Finance Committee in 1950, he was given his party's nomination for U.S. senator to oppose appointed incumbent Democrat William Benton in a special election. Despite a colorful campaign that made effective use of the new medium of television, he lost to Benton by 1,102 votes of the over 850,000 cast. Bush sought a rematch with Benton for a full six-year term in 1952 but was denied the Republican nomination at the state party convention. He got another chance in another special election when Connecticut's senior senator, Brien McMahon, died later that year. Bush trounced former congresswoman Clare Boothe Luce and six others to win a convention endorsement and went on to defeat Democratic congressman Abraham Ribicoff by 28,960 votes, aided by Republican presidential candidate Dwight D. Eisenhower's 130,000-vote landslide in Connecticut. In 1956 he was reelected by 131,369 votes over another Democratic congressman, Thomas J. Dodd, and Eisenhower more than doubled his 1952 victory margin in the state.

Bush was well respected but never emerged as a leader in the Senate. Like his friend and occasional golf partner President Eisenhower, he favored cuts in federal expenditures and taxes, balanced budgets, less government intrusion in the economy, a modest dose of social legislation, and an internationalist, anticommunist foreign policy. As an influential member of the committees on Banking and Currency, Public Works, and Armed Services, Bush generally advanced the interests of the financial community and his home state and promoted a Cold War military buildup designed to counter Soviet power. Specifically, he assisted in the revision of the Securities Exchange Act, which simplified regulations governing the sale of securities in 1954; helped to draft the 1956 act establishing the interstate highway system; pushed successfully for flood control and urban renewal legislation beneficial to Connecticut; and backed the development of long-range missiles and the Polaris submarine. He was also an early advocate of giving the president a line-item veto (the power to veto individual amendments to a bill).

Bush's basic conservatism was leavened somewhat by his staunch support of civil rights legislation and opposition to the dilatory maneuvers of southern Democrats. He also sided with those who attempted to curb the reckless investigations of Senator Joseph R. McCarthy. Expressing a "sense of shame" at the Wisconsin Republican's behavior during the U.S. Army–McCarthy hearings, Bush introduced a resolution calling for a uniform code of conduct at committee proceedings and voted with the majority for McCarthy's censure in 1954. After Democrat John F. Kennedy replaced Eisenhower in the White House, Bush was generally in opposition to presidential initiatives. A notable exception was the legislation creating the Peace Corps, which Bush cosponsored in 1961.

Bush declined to run for reelection in 1962 for health reasons and returned to Brown Brothers, Harriman as a dispenser of sage advice. Blessed with the look and manner of a statesman, he thoroughly enjoyed public life and often regretted he had not entered it earlier. In his last years, Bush found satisfaction in the career of his son George, who had succeeded in the oil business, had won two terms in the U.S. House, and was serving as the U.S. permanent representative to the United Nations at the time of his father's death in New York City.

• The Prescott S. Bush Papers are in the Department of Historical Manuscripts and Archives in the University of Connecticut Library in Storrs and consist largely of speeches, press releases, scrapbooks, and other materials relating to Bush's senatorial career. An interview with Bush, conducted by John T. Mason, Jr., in 1966, is in the Columbia Oral History Collection. George Bush (with Victor Gold), *Looking Forward* (1987), and Fitzhugh Green, *George Bush* (1989), contain useful information on the president's father. Articles on Bush can be found in *Current Biography* (1942 and 1954); Eleanora Schoenebaum, ed., *Political Profiles: The Eisenhower Years* (1977); and Nelson Lichtenstein, ed., *Political Profiles: The Kennedy Years* (1976). See also Sidney Hyman, *The Lives of William Benton* (1969); Gary W. Reichard, *The Reaffirmation of Republicanism* (1975); Richard M. Fried, *Men against McCarthy* (1976); Joseph I. Lieberman, *The Legacy: Connecticut Politics 1930–1980* (1981); and Timothy Noah, "Old Bland-Dad," *New Republic*, 3 Apr. 1989. An obituary is in the *New York Times*, 9 Oct. 1972.

RICHARD H. GENTILE

BUSH, Vannevar (11 Mar. 1890–28 June 1974), science administrator and engineer, was born in Everett, Massachusetts, the son of Richard Perry Bush, a Universalist minister, and Emma Linwood Paine. Bush grew up in modest circumstances in Chelsea, Massachusetts, and attended Tufts University, graduating in 1913 with a B.S. and an M.S. At Tufts he first encountered electrical engineering and an ideology of engineering; he also developed there his lifelong interests in invention and the patent system. With the idea of improving his career prospects, Bush first enrolled in 1915 in the graduate program in mathematical physics at Clark University but left shortly afterward. He then enrolled in a graduate doctoral engineering program jointly offered by MIT and Harvard and received a doctorate of engineering after one year of heroic efforts with a thesis on the oscillatory behavior of currents in power lines. The joint degree was rare; the doctorate was only the fifth awarded by MIT. Bush, who was a mathematics instructor at Tufts in 1914–1915, rejoined the Tufts faculty in the fall of 1916 as an assistant professor of electrical engineering. At this time, he became a technical consultant to the Morgan-financed American Research and Development Corporation (AMRAD), which was seeking promising radio inventions. During World War I he invented an electromagnetic device for determining the location of submarines; frustrating experiences with the navy influenced his later views. In 1916 he married Phoebe Davis; they had two sons.

Bush joined the MIT faculty in 1919 as an associate professor of electrical power in the electrical engineering department. At MIT, as in the world of defense research and development, a basic problem was to keep the highly different worlds of abstruse knowledge and of concrete practical applications functioning effectively while coordinating the necessary flow of information, people, devices, and funds between them. Bush's correspondence and publications, even as late as the autobiographical *Pieces of Action* (1970), are filled with observations and thoughts on this problem. In the electrical engineering department, the mathematically talented Bush upgraded the sophistication of the courses and encouraged research among the faculty and students. In 1923 he became a full professor. By that date Bush was director of graduate study in the department and of the department's research division. The calculation of power circuits, a speciality of his, was complex and arduous. Given his mathematical bent and talent for tinkering, he was led by this problem to a concern for new methods of semi-automatic and automatic computing. Bush aimed for devices capable of more than numerical manipulations; he foresaw them as analytic aids to the human intellect.

The MIT tradition stressed service to industry, and maintaining close relations with the corporate world was no problem to Bush. As a private consultant, he became involved in manufacturing ventures with important consequences in the business world (and for him personally as an investor). With his former college roommate, Lawrence K. Marshall, he worked on a thermostat device, which resulted in the development of a concern, Metals and Controls, later part of Texas Instruments. Another venture of his started with a gas rectifier eliminating the batteries then needed for radios. The resulting manufacturing concern, the Raytheon Corporation, eventually turned into a large conglomerate.

Change came to MIT in 1930 with the arrival of Karl T. Compton, previously the chair of the physics department at Princeton, as the Institute's new president. Compton had no intention of severing ties with industry; on the contrary, given the onset of the Great Depression, he was for expanding such relations, even for a greater involvement with the federal government, something not uppermost in the mind of the conservative Bush. But both men wanted an increased concentration on the basic sciences and their deliberate application to practical problems. When Bush became vice president and dean of engineering at the Institute in 1931, mathematics loomed large in his actions. Later, in private correspondence in 1938, he stated that besides strengthening "pure or formal analysis" in the mathematics department, he recruited and supported "men of mathematical power" in all the science and engineering departments.

At the same time Bush was much concerned with relations with industry, particularly in regard to patent rights. In 1935 he served on the Science Advisory Board's Committee on the Relation of the Patent System to the Stimulation of New Industries. At the Institute he fashioned a patent policy encouraging an amicable division of any patent income between the faculty, MIT, and industry. While he carefully supervised the Office of Industrial Cooperation's dealings with the corporate world to make sure that the roles of the university and of business were scrupulously separated, he zealously advocated the intrinsic value of university research.

Visibility as an administrator did not hinder Bush's election to the National Academy of Sciences in 1934, but his achievements as an inventor and developer were undoubtedly considered of more consequence. In the 1920s he had encouraged his students to devise means for mechanizing the integration of equations; by 1931 he had produced with his students the differential analyzer for the solution of integral equations. An analog computer that worked electromagnetically, the differential analyzer was cumbersome. Nevertheless, it was duplicated and used on many engineering and scientific problems before World War II. Bush and his associates pushed the development of more advanced devices, aiming eventually for a fully automatic electronic machine. Punched tape was used for control, and Bush explored the applicability of microfilm. With the aid of a grant from the Rockefeller Foundation, the MIT group produced the 100-ton Rockefeller Differential Analyzer, which was operated continuously for the navy during the war. Bush was also involved with Navy Department efforts to produce codebreaking machines.

In 1938 Bush became president of the Carnegie Institution of Washington (CIW), an assemblage of research institutes with an endowment, modest by today's standards, only surpassed by that of the Rockefeller Institute (now Rockefeller University). One oral tradition has it that Bush took the position because he saw the coming of World War II and wanted to position himself to take control of the mobilization of science and technology. Although this recurring story reflects the awe in which some held Bush, it appears to be baseless. According to a second oral tradition, Bush left Cambridge because he saw his chances of succeeding Compton as president as rather slim. Such oral traditions overlook the prestige of CIW in the American research community at the time and a possible desire on Bush's part to try something new. Because the range of interests represented by CIW did not match any of Bush's specialities, his appointment surprised many. Bush plunged enthusiastically into intellectual areas new to him, such as genetics and evolution; perhaps his most significant move before becoming immersed in war-related activities was the hiring of the geneticist Barbara McClintock for the Cold Spring Harbor Laboratory. CIW also introduced Bush to centers of influence in Washington and New York that would prove useful to him in wartime; the Institution reinforced his respect for basic research and his belief in the need to nurture small, interacting basic research groups.

Three other activities of the late 1930s further prepared Bush for his wartime tasks. In 1938 he was appointed chair of the National Advisory Committee for Aeronautics (NACA), which governed a research establishment largely devoted to engineering and included both representatives of the federal government and qualified private citizens. Even more important for Bush's actions and policies was the constellation of specialized advisory committees overseeing particular parts of NACA's program. Bush, who resigned as chair of NACA early in the war, was so confident of that program's effectiveness that he specifically exempted aeronautics from the oversight of the new wartime agencies. The National Research Council (NRC), the operating arm of the National Academy of Sciences (NAS), similarly influenced Bush's later thoughts and actions. From July 1936 to January 1940 he served as chair of the Council's Division of Engineering and Industrial Research, still another widely representative committee engaged in planning and reviewing programs. Although the chairmanship helped to expand Bush's range of contacts and experiences even more, it had the ambiguous effect of enhancing his respect for the National Academy of Sciences and what it stood for while spurring his doubts about its suitability as the lead agency in wartime mobilization. When the NRC formed the Committee on Scientific Aids to Learning, chaired by James B. Conant, Bush was an obvious choice for membership on it because of his exploits in automating computing and his growing interest in applying new technology to information retrieval. In *Pieces of the Action*, he recalled how discussions at the Committee on the problems of scientific mobilization in the impending war involved several individuals who would play important roles in the Office of Scientific Research and Development: in addition to Conant, Frank B. Jewett, head of Bell Telephone Laboratories and later president of NAS; Karl T. Compton; Richard Tolman, graduate dean at the California Institute of Technology; and the staff director, Irwin Stewart, who would serve as the executive secretary of OSRD.

Bush acted on his concerns in 1940 by having Frederick Delano, a nephew of President Roosevelt and the head of the National Resources Planning Board (as well as a trustee of CIW), introduce him to Harry Hopkins, a close aide to the president who was coordinator of special projects for the administration. Given entré to the president by Hopkins, Bush found that his ideas were accepted, and Roosevelt appointed him head of the National Defense Research Committee (NDRC), which had come into existence under the authority of World War I legislation forming a Council of National Defense for a future emergency. Throughout the war Bush retained direct access to the president and a separate budget. In 1941 his role was enlarged by his becoming director of a new agency, the Office of Scientific Research and Development (OSRD), which encompassed NDRC, with Conant as its chair, and a new body, the Committee on Medical Research (CMR). NDRC/OSRD had notable triumphs related to the development of radar, the proximity fuse, fire control, military medicine, nuclear weaponry in its early stages, metallurgy, and many other areas. Besides aeronautics, OSRD kept out of only one other significant area of wartime development, synthetic rubber production.

Writing years later, Bush candidly admitted that NDRC "was an end run, a grab by which a small company of scientists and engineers acting outside established channels got hold of the authority and money for the program for developing new weapons." Bush believed that wartime needs could not wait on the slow procedures of existing agencies. Although in 1936 he had been a supporter of the Liberty League's campaign for the Republican presidential nominee, Alf Landon, the conservative Bush maintained a successful relationship with Roosevelt, whose leadership and style of operating he came to admire. Given his budget and relations with the White House, Bush possessed freedom of action—often to the dismay of the armed services and civilian executive agencies. He skillfully cultivated key individuals in the executive and legislative branches and coopted some potential adversaries by involving them in the mesh of committees that he commanded. Bush publicly insisted that his agency's proper scope was limited to the research and development of devices and systems for actual military operations. Pilot projects, production, procurement, and actual war operations belonged elsewhere. His administrative style was to keep program decisions and their execution in the hands of the network of committees—that is, in the hands of the technically competent. His role as director was to fix general policy and to settle disputes at lower levels.

Looking back after the war, Bush regarded the OSRD contract as one of the agency's greatest innovations. For the first time in U.S. history the federal government could procure not only tangible objects but also intellectual products, in the form of texts, mathematical equations, and scientific symbols. Using the flexible contract, OSRD placed commitments with universities and industrial organizations that it rated as best qualified for specific tasks. As a result, certain already strong universities (MIT, Caltech, Johns Hopkins, Chicago, Columbia, and Harvard) and industrial concerns (such as AT&T) were by and large the beneficiaries of OSRD contracts, attracting the attention of antimonopoly-minded New Dealers and the ire of similar institutions not so favored.

Bush and others involved in the wartime mobilization of science consciously attempted to minimize disruptions of the existing order of production. By concentrating on the stages of research and development anterior to production, Bush was able to keep out of the often delicate economic and social issues accompanying the actual procurement of arms and supplies. This approach also helped minimize intrusion into issues of military strategy, tactics, and combat doctrines. Not that establishing new organizations and facilities could be completely avoided, most notably in connection to the proximity fuse and radar. In the case of the proximity fuse, the entire spectrum from research to production and combat utilization was put under Section T headed by Mere Tuve of CIW, which reported directly to Bush rather than NDRC; Section T operated through the Applied Physics Laboratory at Johns Hopkins University using navy procurement contracts.

In the case of radar, the Radiation Laboratory at MIT was created; although initially limited to research and development, the Rad Lab found it necessary to expand its functions. Nuclear weapons presented another, if partial, exception to Bush's reluctance to form new entities and facilities; NDRC absorbed a committee, S-1, already set up to pursue development in this area. Spurred by fear of Nazi progress in the development of nuclear devices, Bush advanced the American program to the point where its prospective gargantuan size threatened to overwhelm OSRD. Although he arranged to spin off the program to the Army Corps of Engineers, he and Conant remained intimately involved in it as advisers and overseers.

Acting unofficially as science adviser to President Roosevelt, Bush steered away from involving OSRD in social policies and postwar planning, but he made a point of personally responding to presidential queries to maintain good relations with the White House. Some in Congress and executive agencies were concerned, however, about OSRD's concentration of contracts and the implications of its emphasis on weaponry and the physical sciences for the postwar period. To have a basic research ideology applied by a ministry of the best science and engineering minds largely insulated from the political process was not the critics' idea of good public policy.

Responding to such concerns, Bush arranged in 1944 for Roosevelt to send him a letter asking for proposals on federal policies for the sciences in peacetime. True to form, Bush set up committees to advise him on particular areas; he then published the reports of the committees as appendixes in the finished document, *Science, the Endless Frontier*, in 1945. The overall proposal was Bush's, departing in significant ways from the recommendations of his advisers. At the time of its release, it was widely acclaimed as an important plan for postwar scientific research in the United States. Bush called for the formation of a National Research Foundation (renamed the National Science Foundation) to aid basic research in general. He also strongly advocated federal support of targeted basic and applied research in two areas, health and national security. To help bright young people to go into the sciences, Bush favored a program of financial aid, large by the standards of the day, at the undergraduate and graduate levels. (The educational provisions of his plan were never fully implemented, however, when NSF came into existence.) The new agency was to be governed by a National Science Board composed of qualified individuals with the authority to name and supervise the director of the Foundation. Outside committees would help direct the operating divisions. *Science, the Endless Frontier* sidestepped the ticklish question of aid to industry and downplayed any role the Foundation might have in advising the president or Congress.

The report was released by the new president, Harry S. Truman. During its gestation, the director of the Bureau of the Budget, Harold D. Smith, had become concerned about the proposed organizational arrangement of the Foundation, which ran counter to his beliefs about accountability and efficiency. Several important aspects of that arrangement convinced Smith to oppose legislation that closely followed Bush's recommendations: the insulation of the head of the Foundation from the political process; disregard of federal research and development agencies; the omission of the social sciences and biology (other than medical fields); and the tilt toward the physical sciences and war-related matters. Smith convinced Truman to defer the liquidation of OSRD to smooth the transition to peacetime while alternatives to Bush's proposals could be studied. Bush, on the other hand, strongly supported the liquidation of OSRD at war's end because its successes had resulted in large measure from the exercise of federal powers appropriate for an emergency, not peacetime. Greatly fearing the aggrandizement of the national government, he wanted simply to advance scientific knowledge and help apply it in the areas of national security and health, which he deemed appropriate for federal involvement. As always, he aimed to minimize linkages with social and economic policies. Both he and Smith apparently assumed the new agency would come into existence fairly soon, but the two competing legislative proposals (one roughly representing Bush's position, the other roughly the administration's) produced a stalemate in Congress. Bush was able to liquidate OSRD.

The coming of the Republican-dominated Eightieth Congress encouraged Bush to continue his opposition. He kept reminding everyone that the new agency had to get its funds through the established budgetary process involving both the White House and Congress. Recalling his experience with NACA, Bush considered having federal representatives on both the proposed National Science Board and the divisional committees. Nevertheless, Truman vetoed the first NSF bill, arguing that the director should be a presidential appointee and responsible to him, not the Board. The next Congress, controlled by the Democrats, passed legislation meeting the president's objections, which Truman signed in 1950; it no longer contained the provisions for medical and national defense programs. The new agency started life with a minuscule budget that severely limited its effectiveness, and it could not compete with the research interests of the military and the burgeoning grant program of the National Institutes of Health. (Only after the Soviet Union's scientific coup of putting the first satellite, Sputnik, into orbit in outer space did NSF's budget begin to grow significantly, and then the agency had some of the impact Bush desired.)

By late 1945 the Truman administration had largely frozen Bush out of the policy-making process for the sciences. While he was seen as a great expert on research and development related to national security, his general stance departed considerably from the administration's views. The civilian agencies resented his implicit downgrading of their roles, and many in the armed services saw him as a menace to their missions. In congressional testimony Bush had suggested that the military limit its work in technological development to improvements in existing weapons and equipment. Not only was this taken to be an affront to the professionalism of the officer class; it implied further drastic diminutions of their missions in the preparation for and conduct of warfare. But during the years 1946–1949 (before and after the unification of the armed services), Bush headed the Research and Development Board (originally the Joint Research and Development Board), charged with sorting out technological rivalries among the services and fashioning a planning and operating procedure for defense research and development that would be both rational and economical. In retrospect, we can see that Bush underestimated the tenacity and bureaucratic skills of the officer class. Frustrated in his efforts and in ill health, Bush resigned in 1949, the year he published the best-selling *Modern Arms and Free Men: A Discussion of the Role of Science in Preserving Democracy*. Later, he participated in the unsuccessful attempt to halt the first hydrogen bomb test; and, at hearings concerning allegations that J. Robert Oppenheimer had betrayed secret U.S. nuclear research to the Soviet Union, Bush scathingly attacked the investigating committee, the Personal Security Board.

Bush returned to CIW, retiring in 1955. Remaining active, as well as being highly honored for his achievements, he renewed his activities in the information area, working for the automation of libraries and the further development of aids in learning, including what would come to be called hypertext. He also served as a trustee of various nonprofit organizations. Perhaps the most satisfying stint of this kind was his life membership (1947–1971) in the MIT Corporation, of which he was chair from 1957 to 1959; he was a director of American Telephone and Telegraph (1947–1962) and Merck & Co. (1949–1962) and chaired Merck's board from 1957 to 1962. Bush died in Belmont, Massachusetts.

As a leading pioneer in creating the role of science adviser to the federal government, Bush had a profound influence on the policy-making environment in which basic and applied science could be seen to meet national needs. Adept at taking advantage of the opportunities presented to him, he also succeeded by the force of his personality—a shrewd toughness laced with dry humor. His great skills fostered a great self-assurance not always to everyone's liking. Bush attracted both warm adherents and strong detractors.

• A collection of Bush papers is in the Library of Congress, roughly covering his years in Washington; a smaller one in the MIT archives covers the period from his retirement from CIW until his death. Many collections in the MIT archives bear on his pre-Washington career. The records of OSRD are in RG 227 in the National Archives, as are many related record groups. The CIW archives have Bush files of the CIW years. The two collections of Bush's essays are *Endless Horizons* (1946) and *Science Is Not Enough* (1967); both include "The Builders" (1945), an important parable of his conservative vision. The best general introduction to Bush's career is Daniel K. Kevles, *The Physicists: The History of a Scientific Community in America* (1977; repr., with new preface, 1995). For the MIT background, see Karl L. Wildes and Nilo A. Lindgren, *A Century of Electrical Engineering and Computer Science at MIT, 1882–1982* (1985). Two useful articles on Bush are Larry Owens, "Vannevar Bush and the Differential Analyzer," *Technology and Culture* 5, no. 3 (1986), and Nathan Reingold, "Vannevar Bush's New Deal for Research," *Historical Studies in the Physical and Biological Sciences* 17, pt. 2 (1987). Perspectives on Bush's activities in the information field are in James Nyce and Paul Kahn, eds., *From Memex to Hypertext: Vannevar Bush and the Mind's Machine* (1991), and Colin Burke, *Information and Secrecy: Vannevar Bush, Ultra, and the Other Memex* (1994). Jerome Wiesner's account in the *Biographical Memoir* series of the National Academy of Sciences, 50 (1979): 89–117, is a useful if hagiographic essay, with a good bibliography of Bush's writings and lists of his offices and honors.

NATHAN REINGOLD

BUSH-BANKS, Olivia Ward (27 Feb. 1869–8 Apr. 1944), writer, was born in Sag Harbor, New York, the daughter of Abraham Ward, probably a fisherman, and Eliza Draper, both members of the Montauk Indian tribe of Long Island and both also of African descent. When Olivia was nine months old her mother's death forced the family to move to Providence, Rhode Island. Shortly after her father's remarriage, Olivia came under the guardianship of her maternal aunt Maria Draper, whom she credited with having given her an education and a preparedness for life. Her aunt's determination and endurance, Bush-Banks believed, was a result of her Native American upbringing. Olivia graduated from Providence High School, where she was trained as a nurse and developed strong interests in drama and literature.

In 1889 Olivia married Frank Bush in Providence and soon gave birth to two daughters. The marriage was ill-fated, however, and the couple divorced by 1895. From the end of the century to about 1915 Olivia Bush shuttled between Boston and Providence, taking any available job to support her family. In part to earn income she wrote poetry and in 1899 published her first volume of verse, *Original Poems*, which yielded some small financial rewards. The collection consisted of ten poems, including elegies extolling African-American courage and virtue ("Crispus Attucks," "The Hero of San Juan Hill"), imaginative odes to faith and perseverance ("My Dream of the New Year"), and verses celebrating the ecstasies of religion ("Treasured Moments," "The Walk to Emmaus"). Several works from *Original Poems* were reprinted in the *Voice of the Negro*, one of the premier African-American periodicals of the first decade of the twentieth century. Bush shared publication in the *Voice* with other notable African-American poets such as James David Corrothers, Georgia Douglas Johnson, and Daniel Webster Davis.

Caring for her children and her Aunt Maria made writing difficult as a full-time career. In about 1900 Bush became assistant drama director of the Robert Gould Shaw Community House in Boston. From 1900 to 1904 she also contributed to the *Colored American Magazine*, and thus she had poems published in the two journals that had the largest circulation among African Americans in the decade before 1910.

Bush's second collection, *Driftwood* (1914), expanded the themes set forth in *Original Poems*. *Driftwood* included poems, short prose pieces, and several elegies addressed to Abraham Lincoln, Frederick Douglass, William Lloyd Garrison, Wendell Phillips, and Paul Laurence Dunbar, who praised the volume in his preface. Bush would soon depart from the pious sensibility shown in both volumes: her only published play, *Memories of Calvary: An Easter Sketch* (c. 1917), was also her last effort at purely religious pastoralism.

After about 1916 Olivia Bush married Anthony Banks, a Pullman porter. They lived in Chicago, where she founded the Bush-Banks School of Expression and became a drama instructor in the public schools. While at the Shaw Community House, she had decided that drama was indeed her creative strength. It is perhaps during this period (c. 1920) that Bush-Banks's unpublished play, "Indian Trails; or Trail of the Montauk," was written. This play, whose characters closely depict the society of the Algonquians, demonstrates Bush-Bank's knowledge of and facility with the nuances of the Algonquian language and material culture. Only small fragments of the play today survive, but it was probably written in response to a 1918 New York State Supreme Court case, *Wyandank Pharoah v. Jane Ann Benson et al.*, which declared the extinction of the Montauk tribe. The play is a romantic idyll with political and cultural undertones; while it mourns a dissolving Montauk unity, it also reaffirms that unity when O-ne-ne ("Wild Pigeon") brings word that whites have agreed to return land to the tribe.

The fragmentation of the Montauks as a result of the *Benson* case caused Bush-Banks to redirect her creative energies and pursue the African-American experience as a principal form of expression. During the early years of the Great Depression she furthered her artistic interests and also began her journalistic efforts in African-American culture. She championed the artists, musicians, and writers of the Harlem Renaissance and was associated with Langston Hughes, Countee Cullen, Julia Ward Howe, A. Philip Randolph, Paul Robeson, W. E. B. Du Bois, and many other leading lights of the period. She also participated in the Federal Theater Project of the Works Progress Administration in 1936, coaching drama for three years in Harlem at the Abyssinia Community Center run by the Reverend Adam Clayton Powell, Sr. The 1930s seemed also to bring about a change in the tone of Bush-Banks's works. Perhaps the class consciousness that typified the Harlem Renaissance clashed with Bush-Banks's earlier coming-to-terms with her Afro-Indian heritage. Several unpublished short sketches, including "Greenwich Village Highlights" (c. 1929), "New Year Musings" (1932), and "Black Communism" (1933), as well as the unpublished one-act play, "A Shantytown Scandal" (c. 1935), indicate Bush-Banks's growing disaffection with the Harlem Renaissance, which seemed to suffer a sharp decline in spirit at the onset of the Great Depression.

Perhaps Bush-Banks's lasting contribution to the literature of the Harlem Renaissance is her "Aunt Viney's Sketches," a cycle of stories that themselves are folk pronouncements on the depression and on the Harlem scene. (In 1937 Bush-Banks sent six Aunt Viney stories to the Library of Congress, but the copyright application was left unfinished.) She may have intended the title character as a contrast to the young slave woman created by Dunbar in his short story "Viney's Free Papers"; Dunbar's Viney uses her newly found freedom as a weapon against her community. Bush-Banks's Aunt Viney is a mature, lively, sagacious African-American woman whose hard-won folk wisdom, conveyed through the richness and power of vernacular speech, renders both racial pride and deft cultural criticism. In this Bush-Banks strongly echoes the efforts of her predecessors, notably Dunbar and Charles Chesnutt, and she precedes Langston Hughes's famous "Simple" tales, which first appeared in 1943.

Although only two books of poetry, a play, two poems ("A Picture" [1900] and "On the Long Island Indian" [1916]), and three essays in magazines ("Undercurrents of Social Life" [1900] and "Echoes from the Cabin Song" and "Essay on John Greene" [both 1932]) represent Bush-Banks's published works, her total output reveals a creative life that touched other lives. Not only did she provide documentation and social criticism of the Harlem Renaissance, an important era in American life and letters, but her literary contributions to that period and the one immediately preceding it are considerable. While the spirit of her Native American ancestry informs her earlier writing, African-American folk expression and culture is a feature of her mature work. These inseparable constituents formed her unique vision, which contributed to the broadening of American culture. Bush-Banks died in New York City.

• Bush-Banks's great-granddaughter, Bernice F. Guillaume, edited *The Collected Works of Olivia Ward Bush-Banks* (1991). See also Guillaume's articles on Bush-Banks, notably "Character Names in *Indian Trails* by Olivia Ward Bush (Banks): Clues to Afro Assimilation in Long Island's Native Americans," *Afro-Americans in New York Life and History* 10, no. 2 (1986): 45–53; "The Female as Harlem Sage: The 'Aunt Viney's Sketches' of Olivia Ward Bush-Banks," *Langston Hughes Review* 6, no. 2 (1987): 1–10; and "Olivia Ward Bush: Factors Shaping the Social and Cultural Outlook of a Nineteenth-century Writer," *Negro History Bulletin* 43 (Apr.–June 1980): 32–34.

NATHAN L. GRANT

BUSH-BROWN, Henry Kirke (21 Apr. 1857–1 Mar. 1935), sculptor, was born Henry Kirke Bush in Ogdensburg, New York, the son of Robert W. Bush and Caroline Udall. At an early age he was adopted by his aunt Lydia Udall Brown, wife of the sculptor Henry Kirke Brown, and raised at their farm near Newburgh, New York. After completing his education at the Siglar School, Henry began to study sculpture with his uncle. Taking the name Bush-Brown, he went to New York City and studied at the National Academy of Design. In 1886 he married Margaret W. Lesley, a painter from Philadelphia; the couple had four children. Later that year, on the advice of his uncle's pupil and assistant, the sculptor John Quincy Adams Ward, Bush-Brown went to Paris, where he studied at the Académie Julian under Antonin Mercie. Then he went to Florence, where he completed a statue of Richard Stockton that Brown had left unfinished at his death.

Bush-Brown returned from Europe in 1890 and first achieved national recognition when his dramatic *Buffalo Hunt* was exhibited at the 1893 Chicago Columbian Exposition. The state of Pennsylvania commissioned bronze equestrian statues of General George C. Meade (1896) and General John F. Reynolds (1898) for Gettysburg Memorial Park. Late in the 1890s Bush-Brown designed a statue of Justinian for the Appellate Court Building in New York City. At the 1901 Pan-American Exposition in Buffalo he exhibited the group *Truth*, and in 1902 he designed an imposing memorial relief tablet for the Union League of Philadelphia commemorating the regiments that institution raised during the Civil War. At the 1904 St. Louis Exposition he showed a piece titled *Infant Conversation*. He also executed two important equestrian statues: *General Anthony Wayne* was erected at Valley Forge in 1908, and *General John Sedgwick* was unveiled at Gettysburg in 1913.

In 1910 Bush-Brown relocated to Washington, D.C., occupying himself with portrait busts and a number of public memorials such as the *Lincoln Memorial* at Gettysburg. He spent the last years of his life organizing his uncle's papers, which he donated to the Library of Congress. He was a member of the National Sculpture Society and the Architectural League of New York. Never a major figure, Bush-Brown was a competent sculptor of portrait busts and public memorials whose simple, direct, and naturalistic style appealed to conservative American taste. Although he was fairly well known during his lifetime, his work is now known only to specialists. He died in Washington, D.C.

• Brief summaries of Bush-Brown's career are in Lorado Taft, *The History of American Sculpture* (1903), and Wayne

Craven, *Sculpture in America* (1968; rev. ed., 1984). See also *Art Digest*, 15 Mar. 1935. Obituaries are in the (Washington, D.C.) *Evening Star* and the *New York Times*, both 2 Mar. 1935.

ROBERT WILSON TORCHIA

BUSHMAN, Francis X. (10 Jan. 1883–23 Aug. 1966), silent film star, was born Francis Xavier Bushman in Baltimore, Maryland, the son of John Bushman, a traveling salesman, and Mary Norbeck. Bushman abandoned his Catholic parochial school education at the age of fifteen and began working in a dry-goods store by day while appearing as a "bit" player with various stock companies that performed in Baltimore. In 1902 Bushman married Josephine Fladune; the couple had five children, including Ralph, who appeared as a minor film actor in the 1920s and 1930s under the name Francis X. Bushman, Jr. To support his family, a year after the marriage Bushman began working as a model at the Maryland Art Institute; he posed for the statue of Lord Baltimore in front of the Baltimore Courthouse and for the statue of Nathan Hale at Harvard, and he also appeared in a number of song slides (which featured actors illustrating the printed lyrics of popular numbers, projected onto the theater screens). Bushman turned to acting in 1908, and in 1911 he began his film career as a member of the Essanay Company in Chicago. His first film, *His Wife's Friend*, was released on 1 June 1911; the actor subsequently appeared in more than 100 short subjects for the company.

By 1912 Bushman had become Essanay's most prominent male star, and a year later he was given artistic control of his films and a new leading lady named Beverly Bayne. Bushman possessed a classic, granite-jawed profile and a muscular body that gained for him the title "Apollo of the Movies." His image was leonine majesty, and Bushman's reputation as the most popular male screen actor in the United States was confirmed when the readers of *Ladies World* in July 1914 named him the "Typical American Hero." The actor received more than 1 million votes in a competition designed to promote the magazine's circulation, to encourage film companies to take out advertising boosting their contract players, and, ultimately, to find the leading man for a 1914 feature film, *One Wonderful Night*.

Bushman was at the height of his fame in 1915 when he and Bayne joined the Metro Company. In 1916 they starred in a widely acclaimed production of *Romeo and Juliet*. Columnist Arthur Brisbane wrote, "His is the best-known name and face in the world." It was Bushman's face and body that appealed to the public rather than his acting style, which by modern standards appears wooden and overly melodramatic. Five secretaries worked full-time for Bushman answering an average of 30,000 fan letters a week. "He was a god; a world worshipped hero," Ruth Biery wrote in *Photoplay* (Jan. 1928).

Bushman's world collapsed in 1917 when his wife sued for divorce. The marriage had been kept secret because it was rightly feared that female fans would not accept a married man as their hero. The fact that Josephine Bushman was now unattractive and overweight did not help the situation, and Bushman's marriage in 1918 to Bayne did nothing to salvage the actor's career. In an effort to escape negative publicity, Bushman and Bayne sailed for Europe in 1919, but on their return found little work. Before 1918 Bushman had appeared in more than 130 films; between 1920 and 1925 he appeared in only three. Bushman and Bayne subsequently divorced in 1925, and Bushman was later married for a third and fourth time.

A comeback seemed possible in 1926, when Bushman was seen as Messala in MGM's production of *Ben-Hur*, but a supposed snub by Bushman's butler of company boss Louis B. Mayer led to the actor's blacklisting by the major Hollywood studios. In the 1930s and 1940s Bushman appeared in fewer than a dozen films, the majority produced by "poverty-row" companies, and always in minor character roles. In the 1950s he began appearing as a character actor on television and also played himself on a 1956 episode of "The George Burns and Gracie Allen Show." With his fifth wife, Iva Millicent Richardson, Bushman appeared on the television quiz show "The Big Surprise" and won $30,000, leading him to boast that his career now ran "from lantern slides in 1906 to TV quiz shows."

Bushman made cameo appearances in a few major feature films of the 1940s and 1950s, playing Bernard Baruch in *Wilson* (1944) and King Saul in *David and Bathsheba* (1951). His last film was *The Ghost in the Invisible Bikini* (1966). Bushman died at his home in the Pacific Palisades district of Los Angeles, shortly after completing a role in the television series "Voyage to the Bottom of the Sea."

• There are no extant papers of Bushman. He wrote two articles in fan magazines, "From the Inside of the Studio," *Picture-Play Weekly*, 10 Apr. 1915, pp. 1–4, and "How I Keep My Strength," *Photoplay*, June 1915, pp. 59–62. See also Katherine A. Synon, "Francis X. Bushman, Romanticist," *Photoplay*, July 1914, pp. 55–60; Wycliffe A. Hill, "Most Handsome Man in the Movies," *Movie Magazine*, Aug. 1915, p. 12; and Ruth Biery, "What Killed Francis X. Bushman," *Photoplay*, Jan. 1928, pp. 34–35, 88. An excellent modern source of information on Bushman is a career article by Larry Lee Holland, "Francis X. Bushman," *Films in Review*, Mar. 1978, pp. 157–73.

ANTHONY SLIDE

BUSHMILLER, Ernie (23 Aug. 1905–15 Aug. 1982), cartoonist, was born Ernest Paul Bushmiller in the South Bronx, New York, the son of Ernest George Bushmiller, an artist, vaudevillian, and bartender, and Elizabeth Hall. Young Ernie quit school after completing the eighth grade and went to work as a copy boy at the *New York World*; evenings, he attended classes at the National Academy of Design. Running errands for the staff cartoonists, he inveigled occasional drawing assignments, one of which was illustrating a Sunday feature about magic by Harry Houdini. Early in 1925 he was asked to ghost a comic strip called *Fritzi Ritz* when its originator, Larry Whittington, left to work for William R. Hearst's rival paper. Cast in the mold of Cliff Sterrett's *Polly and Her Pals* and launched on 9 October 1922, *Fritzi Ritz* was a "pretty girl strip" the comedy of which is generated by a beautiful flapper who wins a beauty contest and becomes a movie actress in the New York film colony.

In 1930 Bushmiller married Abby Bohnet, the daughter of a train conductor, and the next year they went to Hollywood, where Bushmiller wrote gags for Harold Lloyd, continuing *Fritzi Ritz* at the same time. The couple had no children. The Bushmillers returned to the Bronx after about a year, but Ernie, recognizing that Hollywood, not New York, was the film capital, shifted the venue of his strip to the West Coast. This change, however, was not to produce as profound an effect on the feature as the introduction in the spring of 1933 of Fritzi's niece, a fuzzy-haired, slot-nosed, seven-year-old named Nancy.

Fritzi in the 1930s was a shapely, sexy glamour girl, and Bushmiller exploited his ability to draw a pretty girl; virtually every time Fritzi sat down, she assumed a pinup pose, and she was frequently seen at her dressing table in her underwear or a negligee. Despite this high-voltage sex appeal, Fritzi's fireplug-shaped niece stole the show. The strip told continuing stories in those years, and in 1935 Bushmiller did a continuity about Nancy running away. Although scarcely a tear-jerking sequence, it apparently tugged enough at readers' heartstrings to yank Nancy to their bosoms. Bushmiller had unwittingly permitted his title character to be upstaged. Then, on 24 January 1938, Bushmiller introduced Sluggo, the stubbly-headed tough kid who becomes Nancy's constant companion, and before too many more months the cartoonist capitulated to what was now obvious: Nancy was clearly his star. Bushmiller struck Fritzi's name from the strip's marquee and put Nancy's in its stead. From that point on, the strip ran few continuities. It became a gag-a-day strip, and Bushmiller refined his art, honed it to its barest essentials, and thereby produced a comic strip that in many respects was the very apotheosis of a comic strip.

In simplifying his style, reducing it to the absolute minimum graphic representation necessary for its narrative purpose, Bushmiller transformed his visuals into virtual pictographs, and his strip became a kind of hieroglyphic. As one critic said, "A Bushmiller house is not a drawing of an individual house that could or does exist in reality but a symbol of all houses, of Houseness itself" (Dwight Decker, *Amazing Heroes*, 1 Feb. 1989, p. 72). This distillation of his style to iconography aimed at a single purpose—to deliver the day's joke in as economical a manner as possible.

In conjuring up jokes, Bushmiller came to rely to a great extent on props, and in so doing, he gave the strip its unique flavor. Describing his method, Bushmiller said, "I jot down items such as toaster, leaky roof, folding chair, mail box, windy day—anything that comes to mind. Looking at the advertising in a magazine also helps, or a Sears Roebuck catalog. When I find an item that seems likely, I start to kick it around in my mind to see if I can work out a funny situation."

As a result of Bushmiller's way of working perhaps, *Nancy*'s humor is more consistently visual than is that in many gag strips; an understanding of the gag depends on comprehending the picture in the last panel, a picture in which the prop plays a vital part. In nearly every installment of the strip during its vintage years (1944–1959), the preceding panels are a verbal build-up to a visual punch line. In this, Bushmiller blends word and picture in such a way that each contributes meaning to the other, both together creating a meaning that neither has by itself, the very definition of the medium.

But Bushmiller's strip was resolutely one-dimensional. Our interest in it as well as our appreciation of its humor stems almost entirely from a kind of admiration for Bushmiller's ingenuity in using physical objects as the bases for his jokes. Virtually every strip is an exercise in problem solving. Nancy is Bushmiller's alter ego. Her everlasting role is the same as the cartoonist's—to figure out how to use some prop to get a laugh. She reads about a man who believes Martians are living on Earth and two panels later finds spectacles with three lenses. She feeds plant food to her plant, wonders if she's given it too much, and then it burps at her. She wanders through a funhouse of trick mirrors, and after seeing herself distorted in a dozen ways, she leaves and stops to look at herself in a regular mirror so she can rejoice in how gorgeous she feels when she comes out. Every day, her raison d'être is to set up a situation that will lead to the visual punch line of the last panel in which the prop gets the laugh. She has no personality; she is a simple plot device. Mark Newgarden and Paul Karasik observe that Bushmiller sacrificed everything to his punch line: "Characterization, atmosphere, emotional depth, social comment, plot, internal consistency, and common sense are all merrily surrendered in Bushmiller's universe to the true function of a comic strip—to provoke the 'gag reflex' of his readership on a daily basis" (Walker, p. 98).

Bushmiller created an autobiographical character named Phil Fumble for the "topper" strip that appeared at the top of the *Fritzi Ritz* Sunday page (which debuted 6 Oct. 1929). Phil eventually became Fritzi's permanent beau, creating perhaps the only poetry in Bushmiller's oeuvre; in delineating Fritzi, the cartoonist had been inspired by his wife, so it was appropriate that his look-alike should be a devotee at the same shrine.

Bushmiller was one of the founders of the National Cartoonists Society and received its Reuben trophy as Cartoonist of the Year in 1976. He continued drawing *Nancy* until the late 1970s, when Parkinson's disease rendered him incapable of drawing any longer, but he supervised the strip's production until his death at

Stamford, Connecticut. In its simplicity of graphic design, in its single-minded purpose, in its steady reliance upon verbal-visual blending, *Nancy* is in some respects the quintessential comic strip even though its title character has almost no individual personality.

• Although *Nancy* was one of the most popular comic strips of the 1940s and 1950s, almost nothing has been written about its creator. Most of the biographical information contained herein can be found as chapter notations in *The Best of Ernie Bushmiller's Nancy*, written and edited by Brian Walker (1988), a volume that reprints a thoughtful sampling of the strip from throughout its run. An obituary is in the *New York Times*, 17 Aug. 1982.

ROBERT C. HARVEY

BUSHNELL, David (30 Aug. 1740–1826), inventor, was born in Saybrook, Connecticut, the son of Nehemiah Bushnell and Sarah Ingham, farmers. By the time Bushnell entered Yale, he had developed concepts for both a submarine and an underwater explosive. At college, he experimented with gunpowder and proved that it could explode underwater. During the summer of 1775, the year he graduated, the thirteen colonies were in the throes of revolt against Great Britain, and Bushnell felt that an offensive weapon would be a useful tool against the Royal Navy in the ensuing conflict. With that in mind, he constructed his submarine in Saybrook during the spring and summer of 1775. Although he was secretive about his work, several colonial notables knew of it, including Ben Franklin.

The rudimentary wooden submarine, which was six feet high and seven and one-half feet long, resembled a tortoise with its two external shells joined together, hence the name *American Turtle*. A one-man operation, it held enough air to sustain the occupant for thirty minutes. The entrance to the vessel was elliptical and had a brass watertight cover that was screwed shut by the operator. Inside a brass crown atop the cover were three round doors that could be opened to admit air. There were several small windows for light and two air pipes, one for admitting air and the other for expelling air via a ventilator. The pipes automatically shut when the vessel was below water and opened when it surfaced. The vessel was ballasted with lead, which could be discarded if the operator needed to surface quickly. Inside, there was an oar for rowing, a rudder for steering, an oar for ascending and descending, an aperture with a valve for admitting water for descending, and two brass pumps to eject the water when ascending. A compass determined the course, and a barometer measured descent. The purpose of the submarine was to carry and deliver a powder magazine that could destroy a ship. A woodscrew would be fastened to the hull of a ship, and a rope would connect the magazine to the screw. The magazine contained a timing mechanism that sprung a lock that fired the powder.

By the summer of 1776 the *Turtle* was ready to go into action. A massive British fleet had assembled off New York City under Admiral Richard Howe in his flagship HMS *Eagle*. At this crucial time, Bushnell put the *Turtle* on a sloop and headed for Manhattan with its operator, Sergeant Ezra Lee of Lyme, Connecticut, to test the sub against the British fleet. On the night of 6 September 1776 the *Turtle* was towed out to HMS *Eagle*, just above Staten Island. Sergeant Lee attempted to affix the explosive to the ship's hull, but the auger hit an iron bar and he was forced to give up. Before he was rescued by the Americans, he detonated the mine. The mission was not a success, but it proved that the submarine and the mine were operable.

Not easily defeated, Bushnell's operator made two other futile attempts on British ships anchored off Fort Lee, New Jersey. Each time the sub was detected by alert seamen, and the attack was foiled. Bushnell gave up on this enterprise because, as he explained in a letter to Thomas Jefferson in October 1787, "the situation of public affairs was such, that I despaired of obtaining the public attention, and the assistance necessary. I was unable to support myself, . . . Beside I found it absolutely necessary, that the operators should acquire more skill in the management of the Vessel, before I could expect success" (Morgan, vol. 6, pp. 1506–7).

Bushnell next turned to naval mines as a way to harass the British. He constructed two mines for the attack on the HMS *Cerberus* anchored in Black Point Bay, between New London and Saybrook, on 13 August 1777. Each mine consisted of two twenty-inch-long, twelve-inch-wide iron vessels connected by two wheel-like iron bars at each end. An iron tube lay between the bars. The upper vessel projected above the water, while the lower one, below the water, contained the powder. The two mines were connected by a line 600 yards long. The mines were set adrift, and one landed near the *Cerberus*, but the ship's captain cut the line and averted an explosion. Instead, the mine demolished a schooner astern of the frigate, killing three men and injuring one.

In December 1777 Bushnell was in Bordentown, New Jersey, where he devised plans to harass the British who occupied Philadelphia. He designed a mine that exploded on contact using a springlock device as a detonator. The mines were suspended below kegs tied together by rope and then set afloat. In late December the floating mines were sent down the Delaware River toward the British ships at anchor near Philadelphia, but by then some of the ships had left. Despite the fact that the mines did not reach their intended targets, they exploded and scared the British into firing at any floating object they saw in the Delaware. This encounter, known as the Battle of the Kegs, was immortalized in a poem by Francis Hopkinson.

After serving as commander of the Corps of Sappers and Miners during the Revolution, Bushnell returned to Saybrook in 1783 and abruptly left in 1787. He surfaced in the 1790s in Columbia County, Georgia, where he taught school; he then moved to Warren County, where he practiced medicine under the name of Dr. Bush. It is not known where he died. Found among his belongings after his death was a machine that may have been a model for a submarine torpedo. Bushnell never married.

An example of Yankee ingenuity at its best, Bushnell received the epithet "Father of Submarine Warfare" because he constructed the first practical, functioning underwater vessel that met the criteria of a modern submarine. It was maneuverable and submersible, had a sufficient air supply, and carried an offensive weapon. Coupled with his naval mines and rudimentary torpedoes, Bushnell's vessel showed him to be a true pioneer in the development of undersea warfare.

• Bushnell's papers are in the Manuscripts and Archive Division, Sterling Memorial Library, Yale University. The most complete biography is Frederick Wagner, *Submarine Fighter of the American Revolution: The Story of David Bushnell* (1966). Another useful biography is Marion Hepburn Grant, *The Infernal Machines of Saybrook's David Bushnell: Patriot Inventor of the American Revolution* (1976). Henry L. Abbot, comp., *Beginning of Modern Submarine Warfare under Captain Lieutenant David Bushnell* (1966), contains copies of period documents treating the life and inventions of Bushnell. Alex Roland, *Underwater Warfare in the Age of Sail* (1978), assesses Bushnell's contribution to undersea warfare in the light of its historic development. William J. Morgan, ed., *Naval Documents of the American Revolution* (1972), contains the correspondence of Thomas Jefferson, George Washington, Bushnell, and others regarding Bushnell's experiments with submarines, torpedoes, and mines. See also David W. Thomson, "David Bushnell and the First American Submarine," United States Naval Institute *Proceedings* 68, no. 2 (1942): 176–86, for a brief history of submarine development and Bushnell's inventions and experiments. Henry P. Johnston, "Sergeant Lee's Experience with Bushnell's Submarine Torpedo in 1776," *Magazine of American History* 29 (Mar. 1893): 262–66, contains Lee's version of the first sea trial of the *Turtle* and its use as an offensive weapon.

EVELYN M. CHERPAK

BUSHNELL, Horace (14 Apr. 1802–17 Feb. 1876), Congregationalist minister and theologian, was born in Litchfield, Connecticut, the son of Ensign Bushnell, a farmer and owner of a small textile mill, and Dotha Bishop, a farmer and director of a cloth-dressing shop. In 1805 the family moved from their modest farm in Litchfield to nearby New Preston, where Horace eventually worked in his father's textile mill until he entered Yale College in 1823. He graduated four years later and became a schoolteacher in Norwich, Connecticut, before spending ten months as the associate editor of the *Journal of Commerce* in New York City. Dissatisfied with both teaching and journalism, he returned to Yale in 1829 to enter law school and completed his studies in 1831.

A religious conversion later that year ended months of troubling doubts about faith, and in the autumn he entered Yale Divinity School, where he studied under Nathaniel William Taylor, who was defending Calvinism against the Unitarians and adapting it to revivalist piety. Bushnell found Taylor unconvincing, and in his first theological essay, "On Moral Agency" (1832), he criticized Taylor for ignoring the disharmony and contradiction in moral experience and trying to formulate moral philosophy as a systematic science. After receiving a call in 1833 from North Church (Congregational) in Hartford, Bushnell left Yale and assumed the duties of a pastor. In September he married Mary Apthorp of New Haven, with whom he had five children.

In Hartford Bushnell grew to dislike both the revivalism of the flourishing First Congregational Church and the liturgical piety of the Episcopalians at St. John's Parish. Finding it difficult to attract new members, he felt tempted to return to the academy, especially when Middlebury College in Vermont offered him its presidency in 1840, but he declined the offer and began to devote more of his energies to lecturing and writing. Although he had begun in 1835 to suffer from the tuberculosis that would plague him throughout his life, he undertook lecture tours in 1842 in Connecticut, New York, and Ohio. He wrote on political and social issues, opposing both woman suffrage and the Democrats' policy of distributing offices as political rewards. In the presidential campaign of 1844, however, he turned on the Whigs and their leader Henry Clay, criticizing them in his sermon, "Politics under the Law of God," for supporting the compromise of 1820 that allowed slavery to expand into Missouri.

A zealous anti-Catholic, Bushnell joined in 1843 in the formation of the Protestant League, which soon reorganized itself as the Christian Alliance, to oppose the papacy and support religious liberty in Catholic countries. In 1846 he represented the Christian Alliance at the founding of an international Evangelical Alliance in London, but he balked at its requirement that member denominations conform to an orthodox creed, and he fretted that the organization lacked sufficient zeal for Protestant liberty in Catholic countries. When he returned to the United States, his 1847 address to the American Home Missionary Society, "Barbarism the First Danger," alerted Protestants to the need to redeem the American West from both Catholicism and infidelity. Throughout his life he displayed an Anglo-Saxon chauvinism, expressing animosity toward the Catholic church and revealing his incomprehension of the problems of Catholic immigrants.

In his *Discourses on Christian Nurture* (1847), Bushnell argued that the family should become a nursery of piety—and the congregation a family—in which children would grow into faith without needing to undergo a dramatic conversion experience. He believed that the "artificial fireworks" of revivalism undermined both the ideal of the gradual nurturing of religious faith and a proper view of the baptismal covenant. When critics charged that his denial of the necessity of a conversion experience entailed a false view of original sin and cast doubt on the need for special grace, the publisher—the Massachusetts Sunday School Society—repressed the book, but Bushnell arranged for its continued publication. In 1861 he issued a second edition under the title *Christian Nurture*.

The year 1848 was a turning point. He told friends of a private religious experience that gave him new insight into the Christian faith. He expressed this insight in his essay on "Christian Comprehensiveness" in the 1848 *New Englander*, which drew on the eclectic philosophy of Victor Cousin in France to argue that the historical analysis of conflicting doctrines would allow theologians to attain an outlook that recognized the truths in opposing positions. *God in Christ* (1849) represented his effort to apply Christian comprehensiveness to the various doctrines dividing New England Protestants. The book redefined the doctrine of the Trinity as an assertion of the paradoxical presence and elusiveness of God, restated the doctrine of Atonement as a sacrifice designed to renovate human character, and appealed for a religion of spirit rather than of dogma. He hoped that the book might both answer Unitarian criticisms and convince orthodox Calvinists to modify their views. The book's opening essay, a "Dissertation on the Nature of Language," argued that the language of philosophy and theology consisted of figures and metaphors that pointed toward the truth but never literally represented it. This meant that religion had "a profound alliance with poetry" and that the quest for a scientific theological system could only fail.

The book drew baffled and irritated reviews and prompted calls that he be tried for heresy by the Hartford North Consociation, to which his church belonged. Though weakened by his illness, Bushnell defended himself before the Hartford Central Association of ministers, publishing his answer in 1851 as *Christ in Theology*, in which he insisted that he was closer to the historic doctrine of the Church than were his accusers. When a trial seemed imminent in 1852, North Church withdrew from the consociation, and Bushnell, now coughing blood, recovered from the emotional stress with a strenuous western trip to Minnesota.

Continued poor health prompted Bushnell to take trips to Cuba in 1855 and California in 1856. During his stay in San Francisco he helped select the location of the new College of California, and though he returned to Connecticut in 1857 the trustees offered him the presidency, an offer he officially declined in 1861. He continued to raise funds for the school.

Before leaving for California he had begun work on the book that he had hoped would reconcile faith and reason, revelation and science, the natural and the supernatural. He published it in 1858 under the title *Nature and the Supernatural*, believing that it would challenge the rationalistic naturalism of both the German Hegelians and materialists and the American Transcendentalists. Bushnell aspired to preserve a place for the supernatural in Christianity while conceding that everything in the visible world observed fixed laws. Expanding a distinction that he had discovered in Samuel Taylor Coleridge's *Aids to Reflection*, he defined nature (the realm of "things") as a chain of causes and effects and the supernatural (the realm of "powers") as anything that acted on the chain from outside it. In this sense, he argued, human persons were themselves supernatural, able freely to intervene in nature, so that the concept of a supernatural God should offer no offense to reason. Bushnell then proceeded to argue that disorder and deformity in the world disproved the rationalist confidence in progress and development, whether in nature or in history, and that only a conception of God as a power above nature could offer an alternative to despair or resignation.

Bushnell's *Sermons for the New Life*, also published in 1858, revealed that he remained critical of the pervasive rational orthodoxy that amassed "evidences of Christianity" to prove the truth of Christian doctrine and the authenticity of the biblical revelation. He believed that faith had nothing to do with propositions, that no metaphysical system could demonstrate the credibility of Christianity, and that faithfulness often required an assent that could never rest in the security of rational evidence.

Once again, the reviews disappointed him, and his continued poor health brought further discouragement. In 1859 he resigned his pulpit and traveled with his wife to Wisconsin and then to the water cure at Clifton Springs, New York. Increasingly the sectional crisis occupied Bushnell's attention as he became convinced that the deepest cause of the conflict was the absence of moral authority in American government. Although he had opposed the abolitionist movement, he deplored the Fugitive Slave Law, urged a gradual elimination of slavery, supported Abraham Lincoln, and vigorously promoted the northern cause in the Civil War, delivering orations that used Christian categories of sin and atonement to interpret the war as a sacrificial event that was turning an artificial national compact into a providential unity.

In 1864 he collected earlier essays into a book entitled *Work and Play*, in which he described religion as the highest form of play—an activity that was its own end. The essays also displayed again his Anglo-Saxon chauvinism, and in 1869 his social conservatism found still further expression in his booklet *Women's Suffrage: The Reform against Nature*, a celebration of motherhood and domesticity as the only options for responsible women.

Despite his ventures into politics and social issues, his heart belonged to theology. In 1866 he published *The Vicarious Sacrifice*, in which he presented a "moral view" of the atonement as a divine work designed to reconcile sinful men and women to God. He contended that the doctrine of propitiation, which traditionally had designated the change wrought in God by Christ's death on the cross, referred instead to the change in the believer's conception of God that accompanied the experience of inward reconciliation.

After further reflection on the conclusions he had reached in *The Vicarious Sacrifice*, Bushnell decided that he had described atonement too simply as a change in human orientation. In his *Forgiveness and Law* (1874) he observed that true inward forgiveness required a difficult identification with the wrongdoer, a painful inward change on the part of the wronged party. By analogy, the forgiveness represented by the doctrine of atonement must also have required an inward change in God, a costly sacrifice in which God's love overcame God's rightful offense at human sinfulness. Bushnell's willingness to elaborate such analogies contributed to a growing tendency among American liberal theologians to revise earlier conceptions of God as a sovereign Judge or Governor, while his confidence in an immediate and intuitive knowledge of God (a "new inner sense"), derived in part from his reading of Jonathan Edwards (1703–1758), helped to overcome the reliance on rational proofs and evidences that preoccupied many of his contemporaries.

Acquaintances described Bushnell as nervous and energetic in manner. He was a vigorous orator, given to sweeping gestures, though only after many years of preaching did he venture into the pulpit without a manuscript. He called for "manly" ministers with "power to contrive and lead" and a capacity for "tough" thinking, and he strove to embody those ideals himself. Young admirers sometimes found him initially unapproachable; some theological opponents thought him unduly satirical and ironic in his polemics. He was wont to describe some of them, in return, as "theological hunkers," though he carried on a lively and genial correspondence with his Unitarian friend Cyrus Bartol, and he went out of his way to seek reconciliation with Joel Hawes, the minister at First Church in Hartford, who persisted for years in trying to bring Bushnell to trial for heresy.

Although Bushnell was neither an academic theologian nor a learned historian of doctrine, liberal theologians of the late-nineteenth century saw him as the chief American precursor of what they called the New Theology, a theologian whose view of Christianity as a "life" rather than a set of propositions foreshadowed their own views, whose organic conception of family and society prepared the way for the Social Gospel, and whose thoughts on language anticipated later discontent with theological dogmatism. In the early twentieth century the Religious Education Movement, an effort within mainstream Protestantism to revamp the traditional Sunday school, found its charter document in Bushnell's *Christian Nurture*.

When he was fifty-two he complained to a friend that his day had "not yet come," and it is true that he was more influential after his death than before it, not because later theologians studied his works carefully, but because such successors as Theodore Munger, Arthur C. McGiffert, Williston Walker, and John Wright Buckham found in him germinal ideas that fit the liberal theological temper of their own times. He died in Hartford.

• The Bushnell papers are located in the Yale Divinity School Library, the Beinecke Library, and the Sterling Library at Yale University. Additional papers are available in the Houghton Library, Harvard University. A thorough bibliography can be found in James O. Duke, *Horace Bushnell: On the Vitality of Biblical Language* (1984). Bushnell's daughter Mary Bushnell Cheney wrote the standard nineteenth-century biography, *Life and Letters of Horace Bushnell* (1880). Later biographical and critical accounts include Noah Porter, "Horace Bushnell," *New Englander* 36 (Jan. 1877): 152–69; Theodore Munger, *Horace Bushnell: Preacher and Theologian* (1899); Frank Hugh Foster, "Horace Bushnell as a Theologian," *Bibliotheca Sacra* 19 (Oct. 1902): 601–22; Barbara M. Cross, *Horace Bushnell: Minister to a Changing America* (1958); H. Shelton Smith, ed., *Horace Bushnell* (1965); Donald A. Crosby, *Horace Bushnell's Theory of Language* (1975); Conrad Cherry, *Nature and Religious Imagination* (1980); David L. Smith, *Symbolism and Growth: The Religious Thought of Horace Bushnell* (1981); Conrad Cherry, ed., *Horace Bushnell, Sermons* (1985); and Robert L. Edwards, *Genius of Singular Grace: A Biography of Horace Bushnell* (1992).

E. Brooks Holifield

BUTLER, Andrew Pickens (18 Nov. 1796–25 May 1857), judge and senator, was born in Edgefield, South Carolina, the son of William Butler, a soldier and politician, and Behethland Foote Moore. Butler attended the well-known Dr. Moses Waddell's Academy at Willington in neighboring Abbeville County, which also produced Senators John C. Calhoun and George McDuffie and other well-known South Carolinians. Butler then attended South Carolina College in Columbia (now the University of South Carolina), graduating in 1817. After a year of reading law, he was admitted to the bar in December 1819. By 1850 Butler was a very wealthy planter who owned a thousand acres, valued at $20,000, and sixty-four slaves, who produced 112 bales of cotton that census year.

Butler was uncle to South Carolinian Matthew Calbraith Butler, a Confederate general and U.S. senator. Several historians have mistakenly identified Congressman Preston Smith Brooks as the nephew of Senator A. P. Butler. Actually he was Butler's first cousin once removed. Brooks's grandmother was Butler's aunt, and Brooks's father, Whitfield Brooks, was Butler's first cousin. In Edgefield, patrician clans formed interlocking relationships through marriage. Butler was named for the revolutionary war general Andrew Pickens. Pickens's grandson, Francis Pickens, married the eldest daughter of Eldred Simkins. Simkins's second oldest daughter, Susan Ann Simkins, married Butler; they had no children. Four distinguished families, the Brookses, Butlers, Simkinses, and Pickenses, were interlinked in the Edgefield and South Carolina elite. Butler's first wife died shortly after their marriage, and in 1832 he married Harriet Hayne. Harriet died in 1834, soon after the birth of their only child, Eloise Breverd Butler. Eloise Butler married Johnson Hagood, who was elected governor of South Carolina in 1880.

After admission to the bar in 1818, Butler started a law practice in Columbia, but upon the death of his brother, Major George Butler, he moved back to his hometown of Edgefield. There he established a successful practice, expanding into the districts of Lexington, Barnwell, and Newberry. Initially Butler was associated in his law practice with General Waddy Thompson and later with Nathan L. Griffin. While some of his contemporaries believed that he "was not a very learned or profound lawyer," many felt that Butler distinguished himself with his impassioned speech, power of illustration, and scathing wit and humor.

By 1824 Butler's congenial nature and success as a lawyer earned him a place as an aide to Governor Richard Manning. In the same year Butler was elected to the state legislature as a representative from Edgefield. During the next decade he alternated service between the state house and senate. In the legislature Butler, as a leader of the Calhoun faction, favored calling the convention that ended in nullification. In addition to his actions in the state legislature, Butler in 1833 founded and commanded a company of cavalry in the state militia, the famed Edgefield Hussars, when President Andrew Jackson threatened military intervention in South Carolina.

As the nullification crisis passed, Butler's loyalty was rewarded in 1833 with an appointment as a judge on the sessions court, holding his first term in Charleston in January 1834. In 1835 Butler became the judge of the state court of common pleas, a post he held for eleven years. While some of his contemporaries believed that "he was impetuous and sour on the bench without knowing it," most who appeared before him felt that "his charges and opinions were clear and lucid, not dealing in many words, not writing an essay to show his learning and research, but delivering a judgement" (O'Neall). When Butler was appointed to the U.S. Senate to fill the vacancy left by McDuffie's resignation in 1846, a fellow judge, John Belton O'Neall, commented that "he left the bench with regret, and that he often looked back to it with a wish to return."

Butler spent the rest of his life as a senator, winning reelection in 1848 and 1854. While Calhoun was alive, Butler was the junior senator from South Carolina and used the elder senator's pull to gain the chair of the Judiciary Committee over rivals such as William Seward and Salmon P. Chase. Butler faithfully represented the slaveholding interests of his state, especially South Carolina's upcountry elite. Initially, Butler followed Calhoun's lead in the political crisis of 1849–1850, opposing California's request for admission as a free state and calling for a stringent fugitive slave law. However, the death of Calhoun in July, in the midst of the California crisis, enabled Butler to take a more moderate course. He then supported the Compromise of 1850, receiving much criticism at home for this position.

For the rest of his career, Butler attempted to steer a middle course between the fire-eaters' secessionist impulses and unwavering support for the institution of slavery and his own strong desire to preserve the Union and penchant for compromise. Butler's advocacy of the South necessarily brought about conflict with Massachusetts senator Charles Sumner over the issue of slavery in the Kansas-Nebraska territory. In a series of speeches and debates on the Senate floor extending from 1854 to 1856, Butler and Sumner exchanged quips designed to gain the upper hand in the debate and please audiences back home. Butler argued that the Missouri Compromise was a failure and unconstitutional, Congress having no right to prevent the spread of slavery into any territorial region. Furthermore, Butler criticized northerners, such as Sumner, for abrogating their duty to faithfully uphold the Fugitive Slave Law. Finally, Butler vehemently defended slavery and charged northern abolitionists with fanaticism, which fanned smoldering sectional fires.

Known for his fiery invective, Sumner responded to Butler's consistent defense of slavery and his attacks on northern radicals in a speech, "The Crime of Kansas," on 19 May 1856, which was considered particularly vituperative. Sumner charged that Butler "has chosen a mistress to whom he has made his vows; and who, though ugly to others, is always lovely to him; though polluted in the sight of the world, is chaste in his sight—I mean the harlot slavery." Sumner stated further that "Butler shows his incapacity for accuracy, whether in stating the Constitution, or in stating the law. . . . He cannot open his mouth, but out there flies a blunder." Butler was absent from the Senate at this time, but his young Edgefield cousin, Congressman Preston Smith Brooks, heard the remarks and took exception to them. Feeling the honor of his kinsman, state, and region had been slighted, Brooks sought to chastise Sumner. On 22 May Brooks marched into the Senate chamber and, finding Sumner at his desk, struck him several times about the head with his cane, beating the senator insensible. An attempt to expel Brooks for his actions failed because the House of Representatives could not get the required two-thirds vote. Brooks resigned and then ran for his vacated seat; he was overwhelmingly reelected. Butler staunchly defended the actions of his young relative, explaining that Brooks "felt that if something was not done he could not face his constituents without losing his usefulness, and without there being a taint on his honor and his courage."

This incident symbolized the increasingly diverging cultures of northern and southern societies in the late antebellum period. Butler died in Edgefield shortly after the caning. He preached a fiery defense of slavery but consistently voted for compromise, accepting a free California and popular sovereignty in Kansas and Nebraska. Butler prophetically cautioned that continuing regional fanaticism would result in "sectional alienation, local disunion, injustice, civil strife, and, perhaps, servile insurrection."

• Only a few items are in the A. P. Butler Papers at the South Caroliniana Library, University of South Carolina, Columbia. Detailed biographical sketches are Judge Belton O'Neall, *Biographical Sketches of the Bench and Bar of South Carolina*, vol. 1 (1859; repr. 1975), and N. Louise Bailey et al., *Biographical Directory of the South Carolina Senate, 1776–1985*, vol. 1 (1986). The speeches and events leading up to the Brooks-Sumner affair are covered in a number of books, especially David Donald, *Charles Sumner and the Coming of the Civil War* (1960). Harlan Joel Gradin, "Losing Control: The Caning of Charles Sumner and the Breakdown of Antebellum Political Culture" (Ph.D. diss., Univ. of North Carolina at Chapel Hill, 1991), does an excellent job of analyzing the cultural meanings of the speeches of Sumner and Butler.

Orville Vernon Burton, *In My Father's House Are Many Mansions: Family and Community in Edgefield, South Carolina* (1985), places Butler in the context of his community.

ORVILLE VERNON BURTON

BUTLER, Benjamin Franklin (14 Dec. 1795–8 Nov. 1858), attorney general of the United States, was born in Columbia County, New York, the son of Medad Butler, a judge and state legislator, and Hannah Tylee. At age sixteen he began to study the law under future president Martin Van Buren, commencing a lifelong personal and political friendship. Butler was admitted to the bar and became Van Buren's law partner in 1817. He married Harriet Allen the following year. The couple would have one child.

Butler played a key role on a panel appointed in 1824 to codify and revise the Empire State's laws. An important legal reform, the project was New York's first systematic assemblage of common law, colonial law, and state law. It was completed in 1827 and published the following year as *The Revised Statutes of the State of New York*, and as an outgrowth of that Butler was elected to the state legislature, where he served from 1827 to 1833.

His partnership with Van Buren placed Butler in the inner councils of the Albany Regency, the vehicle through which Van Buren controlled party affairs in the state. Regency chiefs, like Butler, came from the Bucktails, a faction of young officeholders who had battled against DeWitt Clinton for control of the Democratic-Republicans in the 1820s. Butler shared much of the outlook of Regency leaders who pioneered aspects of the modern American political party. Their most important contribution was redefining the political party as a positive, democratic entity that facilitated the participation of masses of people in public life and checked the ambitions of individual politicians. Also typical of the Regency, Butler accepted the necessity of a patronage-based party.

However, Butler was an unusual Regency lieutenant. He had a puritanical streak and an intellectual orientation; he was more comfortable reading law in his private study than bargaining in the world of practical politics. This inclination was one reason Butler never achieved a top leadership post in government. He was active in the temperance movement and also favored Sabbatarian restrictions, uncommon positions for a leading Democrat.

Butler was district attorney of Albany County from 1821 to 1824 and a member of the Board of Regents of the State University of New York from 1829 to 1832. He tried unsuccessfully to win the Democratic caucus's support for state attorney general. His unwillingness to leave his Albany law practice and his wife's opposition to living in Washington prevented Butler from pursuing election to the Senate in 1832.

When Van Buren became vice president in 1833, he lobbied for Butler's appointment as attorney general to replace Roger B. Taney. While still reluctant to leave Albany, Butler succumbed to Van Buren's persuasions that a cabinet post would broaden his professional horizons. For President Andrew Jackson, the key criterion for the post was support of the administration's positions on dismantling the Bank of the United States and on American Indian removal. Butler backed these policies, and "Old Hickory," impressed with Butler's diligence and legal talent, nominated him. Senatorial anger over Jackson's withdrawal of federal funds from the bank delayed Butler's confirmation until June 1834, but he assumed the duties of attorney general in the fall of 1833. As attorney general he wrote Jackson's Protest against the Senate's censure of the removal of federal deposits from the bank, defending the action on both legal and Constitutional grounds. Butler also served as acting secretary of war in the final months of the Jackson presidency.

Butler remained attorney general in the Van Buren administration, achieving greater influence than under Jackson. In the first year, Butler was one of the president's top advisers, significantly influencing the development of the independent treasury. He resigned in January 1838, mostly because he and his wife disliked Washington. Butler then settled in New York City, where he served as U.S. attorney for the Southern District of New York.

Over the next two decades, Butler's political activities increasingly revolved around free soil and slavery. He was representative of public figures whose careers began in the party battles of the Jacksonian era and ended in the sectional disputes of the Civil War era.

Having witnessed the suicide of a slave woman sold apart from her family, Butler detested slavery, but he worked to limit discussion of bondage and other divisive sectional issues in order to maintain party unity. In the election of 1836, Butler defended Van Buren against charges that the candidate did not support the South. Along with Van Buren, he maneuvered to stifle the emergence of abolitionism as a political issue in the campaign of 1840.

The election of 1844 showed the growing importance of free soil to Butler but also his continued commitment to Democratic unity. His arguments against the extension of slavery influenced Van Buren's decision to oppose the annexation of Texas, the major issue in the jockeying for the presidential nomination. At the Democratic convention, Butler headed the New York delegation, which supported Van Buren, but he accepted the nomination of James Polk in the spirit of party unity.

Following Polk's victory, Van Buren urged him to name Butler either secretary of state or secretary of the treasury, claiming New York deserved a major portfolio for supporting the Democrat. During the transition, southerners lobbied against Butler's inclusion in the cabinet because of his antislavery outlook. Polk offered Butler the post of secretary of war, which the New Yorker promptly rejected. A day later, Butler received a letter from Van Buren urging acceptance of the position since it provided some cabinet voice for the Regency; but by then the president had named conservative New York Democrat William L. Marcy. In an effort to satisfy the Regency, Polk appointed

Butler to his old job as federal attorney for southern New York.

Butler played an important role in the Free Soil campaign of 1848 and was briefly considered as the party's nominee. He was a prominent figure at the New York Free Soil Convention in Utica in June and wrote and delivered the platform at the national convention in Buffalo in August. Moreover, Butler convinced Van Buren, the party's candidate for president, to embrace the movement, positioning it as a northern Democratic party and forcing southerners to cooperate in the future. While opposed to the extension of slavery, Butler saw the Free Soilers more as a political tool than did other New York Democrats, who stressed the antislavery component. Butler was dismissed by Polk as federal attorney, punishment for leading the revolt against the regular Democratic organization.

Over the next decade, Butler largely withdrew from political affairs and operated a lucrative law practice in New York City. His occasional participation in public life demonstrated the growing importance of the sectional conflict. In his first public appearance since 1848, he strongly denounced the Kansas-Nebraska Act at a rally in May 1854. Completing the transition from Jacksonian Democrat to Republican, he cast his last presidential ballot for John Frémont in 1856. Butler died in Paris, France.

Often confused with the Civil War general and Massachusetts governor of the same name, Butler was part of the development of the American political party. As a Regency lieutenant, he helped change the understanding of a faction, or party, from something to be feared to an institution performing positive functions. Butler is also symbolic of second-level figures who achieved important positions through attachment to major politicians. If not for the apprenticeship with Van Buren, Butler might have led a quiet, if successful, life focused on the law and scholarship. Finally, Butler's political career showed the growing influence of slavery in the antebellum United States. Hardly a proactive antislavery figure, Butler, like many northerners, tried to keep slavery out of public life but gradually shaped much of his political outlook on opposition to the extension of slavery.

• The major manuscript collection is the Benjamin F. Butler Papers at the New York State Library in Albany. There are also Butler papers at the Columbia Historical Society in Kinderhook, N.Y. The best secondary work is William D. Driscoll, *Benjamin F. Butler: Lawyer & Regency Politician* (1987). Also see Arthur A. Ekirch, Jr., "Benjamin F. Butler of New York: A Personal Portrait," *New York History* 58 (1977): 47–68. Many fine works on the Democratic party of the Jacksonian era contain significant mention of Butler. Some of the better ones are Donald B. Cole, *Martin Van Buren and the American Political System* (1984); Robert V. Remini, *Martin Van Buren and the Making of the Democratic Party* (1959); Arthur M. Schlesinger, Jr., *The Age of Jackson* (1945); and Major L. Wilson, *The Presidency of Martin Van Buren* (1984).

DAVID OSBORN

BUTLER, Benjamin Franklin (5 Nov. 1818–11 Jan. 1893), governor of Massachusetts and Civil War general, was born in Deerfield, New Hampshire, the son of John Butler, a seaman, and Charlotte Ellison, both of Scots-Irish descent. John Butler died while his son was still an infant, and in 1828 Charlotte moved to Lowell, Massachusetts, to keep a boardinghouse for female factory workers. Butler was educated at Waterville (now Colby) College, which he attended from 1834 to 1838. He studied law while clerking for the Lowell attorney William Smith and was admitted to the bar in 1840. In 1844 he married the actress Sarah Hildreth, with whom he had four children, three of whom survived to adulthood.

Butler established a reputation as an adroit attorney willing to use spectacular tricks to win cases. Never afraid of offending the establishment, he often took unpopular cases, particularly those involving the rights of labor. Building up a flourishing practice in both Lowell and Boston, he also engaged in real estate operations and accumulated a considerable fortune.

Butler was enamored of politics. Active in the Democratic party, he supported the Democratic–Free Soil coalition of 1850, advocated a ten-hour law for labor, and appealed to Irish Catholics. He was defeated when he ran for the state assembly in 1851 and for Congress in 1852, but in 1853 he served one term in the Massachusetts legislature and in the state constitutional convention. A supporter of the Buchanan administration, he was elected to the state senate in 1858 and ran unsuccessfully for governor in 1859. The next year he served as a delegate to the Democratic convention in Charleston, where he submitted a one-man minority platform report calling for reendorsement of the Kansas-Nebraska Act and voted over fifty times for Jefferson Davis as the party's candidate for president. When the convention broke up to meet again in Baltimore, he sided with the prosouthern faction of the party supporting John C. Breckinridge and became its candidate for governor of Massachusetts.

In the meantime, Butler had attained the rank of general in the state militia. He had also acquired an interest in the failed Middlesex Mills, which he helped to rehabilitate. During the secession crisis he prevailed upon Governor John A. Andrew to buy the overcoats made at the mill for the militia troops, and when war broke out he offered his services to Andrew, who commissioned him brigadier commanding general of the Massachusetts militia. By his willingness to put aside his anti-Republican prejudices and rally to the flag, he served as an inspiration for many of his party associates, including the Breckinridge Democrats, performing a valuable service for the Union.

Butler was soon to be engaged in a series of highly sensational operations. First, he succeeded in ending the isolation of the capital. Prevented from taking the direct route to Washington by the destruction of the railroad tracks north of the city, he transported his troops by rail to Perryville, Maryland, where he seized a ferryboat and shipped the troops to Annapolis, enabling them to reach the capital via Annapolis Junction.

After a quarrel with Governor Andrew about the general's expressed willingness to suppress slave insurrections, Butler marched into Baltimore, captured the city without General Winfield Scott's specific approval, and cowed insurgent citizens. Upon Scott's insistence that the flamboyant general be curbed, Abraham Lincoln assented to his transfer to Fortress Monroe, while at the same time promoting him to major general.

At his new post Butler again made headlines. Confronted with three runaway slaves who had been employed on Confederate fortifications, he refused an enemy demand for their return. Declaring them to be "contraband of war," he seized the fugitive slaves and employed them himself. Butler's expression captured the imagination of the country; the secretary of war upheld his action, and in August 1861 Congress passed the first Confiscation Act, in effect accepting Butler's solution and making it the policy of the country. On 10 June, however, he had suffered a setback by losing the battle of Big Bethel near Yorktown, Virginia.

Late in August Butler was in command of troops accompanying Commodore Silas H. Stringham on an expedition against the forts guarding Hatteras Inlet in North Carolina. Assisting in the capture and investing of the forts, he earned the gratitude of the president, who was much in need of a military victory. Butler then went on a recruiting mission to New England, only to become involved in another quarrel with Governor Andrew, who refused to commission several Democrats Butler had appointed.

Butler was next assigned to Ship Island near the estuary of the Mississippi River. There he was well placed to seek, and to secure, command of the land forces that would accompany the fleet of Commodore David Glasgow Farragut in the War Department's developing plan for the capture of New Orleans. As the plan was realized, Farragut ran past the forts guarding the approach to the city and seized it on 25 April 1862, while Butler took the forts from the rear and occupied the city.

Butler's administration of New Orleans was one of the most sensational episodes of his career. Vigorously taking command of the insurgent city, he established order by dealing forcefully with enemy sympathizers. He executed a rebel who had torn down the American flag, arrested the mayor and other obstreperous Confederate supporters, and issued his famous General Order No. 28, threatening to treat all females who misbehaved toward his troops as "women of the town plying their avocation." An outcry resulted, but the harassment of Federals by local ladies, who had been molesting them in a variety of ways, including emptying slop on them, ceased. When bankers tried to conceal Confederate specie, Butler pursued them and seized the gold; when foreign consuls hid silver taken from the vaults of the Bank of Louisiana or showed excessive sympathy for the Confederacy, he declined to recognize their special status and confiscated the silver. However, he also cleaned up the streets, prevented yellow fever, aided the poor, and kept order in a city totally isolated and weakly held. In addition, he took over and utilized a black force previously organized by the Confederates. Southerners were so incensed by his actions that they declared him an outlaw and called him "Beast Butler."

Confederates and consuls were not, however, the only people who criticized Butler's regime, and there were constant rumors of corruption involving either the general himself or his brother, subordinates, and henchmen. It was even asserted that he stole silver spoons. While this specific charge was spurious, it was true that he was surrounded by northerners who profited from the occupation while he looked the other way. By this means, he built up a loyal following that was useful for political endeavors later on, but at the time his actions subjected him to severe censure.

Yielding to this sentiment against Butler, Lincoln recalled him in December 1862. The general's numerous supporters, particularly the radicals whose ideas he was beginning to share, were outraged and demanded his restoration. He was even mentioned as a possible presidential candidate, and a laudatory biography, *General Butler in New Orleans*, was published by James Parton. Constant pressure was exerted on the president to send Butler back to New Orleans or give him another command; after weighing several options, Lincoln placed him in charge of the Department of Virginia and North Carolina.

In his new command Butler employed the same methods he had used in New Orleans. He cleaned up the city of Norfolk, but not without awarding lucrative positions to relatives and followers. He quarreled with Governor Francis H. Pierpont of Restored Virginia, and rumors of corruption in his command were rife. Although Ulysses S. Grant utilized Butler as a commissioner for prisoner exchanges, the Confederates were reluctant to deal with him, and he accomplished little.

The spring campaign of 1864 severely damaged Butler's military reputation. Ordered to cooperate with General Grant's campaign against Richmond by moving his Army of the James upriver from the coast, he was unable to seize Petersburg, even though the city was only weakly defended. After a repulse at Drewry's Bluff, he found himself "bottled up" at Bermuda Hundred. Thereafter Grant attempted to remove him from tactical command altogether, but Lincoln could not afford to offend so politically powerful a general, now a Republican, and in the fall of 1864 sent him to New York City to keep order during the elections.

After the president's reelection, however, Butler's military career came to an end. Commanding the troops in a naval expedition against Fort Fisher in North Carolina, he vainly tried to reduce the Confederate stronghold by exploding a powder boat but was unable to take his objective by assault and withdrew his forces. His recall followed. His appeal to a wide group of admirers remained undiminished nonetheless.

When Andrew Johnson became president Butler hoped to join the cabinet. Failing in this endeavor and unable to establish close relations with Johnson, he became one of the most bitter opponents of the new president and his Reconstruction policy. Elected from Essex County to the House of Representatives in November 1866, he entered Congress as a spokesman for the radical Republicans, demanding not only a reversal of the president's policies, but his impeachment as well. When the House finally impeached Johnson, Butler was chosen one of the managers in presenting the case against the president in the ensuing Senate trial. He drew up an article accusing the president of delivering speeches denying the legality of Congress and made the opening speech against the president, but ultimately his undignified methods contributed to the failure to convict.

The nomination of Grant as the Republican presidential candidate in 1868 confronted Butler with new difficulties. Because of negative reflections on his military prowess in Grant's final report, Butler had broken completely with his former commander. In the fall of 1868 he was reelected to Congress despite Grant-supported Republican opposition. Nevertheless, he managed to reestablish good relations with the incoming president. In fact, during Grant's administration Butler emerged as one of the president's principal supporters, heading one of the great machines upon which Grant increasingly relied. As chairman of the House Committee on Reconstruction, Butler introduced various radical measures, such as additional requirements for states not yet reconstructed, force bills, and the 1875 Civil Rights Act. He differed with the administration only in his insistence on payment of federal bonds in greenbacks and in his advocacy of woman suffrage. His position on these two issues also scandalized the Brahmins at home, who thwarted his bids for governor in 1871 and 1873.

In Congress, as elsewhere, Butler was involved in scandal. He defended Oakes Ames (1804–1873), the perpetrator of the Crédit Mobilier affair and was also the author of the "salary grab" raising congressmen's remuneration. In addition, he was tarred by the moieties scandal involving his henchman John D. Sanborn as well as by the appointment of yet another dubious supporter, William A. Simmons, as collector of the Port of Boston. These and other embarrassments, as well as the panic of 1873, led to Butler's defeat in 1874.

Butler was not finished with politics, however. Making a comeback as a congressman from Middlesex County in 1876, he soon broke with the Republican administration of Rutherford B. Hayes and, with the help of the Democrats, in 1878 and 1879 again sought the governorship of Massachusetts. In 1880 he openly rejoined his old party, and in 1882 he was finally elected governor of Massachusetts on the Democratic ticket.

As governor he continued to be provocative—investigating the poorhouse in Tewkesbury, issuing a controversial Thanksgiving Proclamation attacking the clergy's meddling with politics, and dramatically appearing at the Harvard commencement in spite of the university's refusal to give him the honorary degree customarily bestowed upon the governor. He also appointed the state's first Irish and black judges. These accomplishments so upset the Brahmin elite that his enemies succeeded in defeating him for reelection. Attempting once more to return to politics, Butler accepted the nomination of the People's party for president in 1884. Even though the Republicans secretly financed his campaign to undercut the Democratic vote for Grover Cleveland, Butler failed to carry a single state.

In his last years Butler remained a radical, defending the Haymarket rioters and supporting the Populist candidate for president in 1892. His memoirs, *Butler's Book*, appeared in 1891. As flamboyant as its author, the book was a great success. Butler died in Washington.

Always outspoken and controversial, the bulky balding Butler with his drooping eyelid was never able to shake off rumors of corruption, which, rightly or wrongly, followed him wherever he went. Yet he deserves credit for his successful advocacy of the rights of labor, blacks, and women and for rallying Democrats to the national cause during the Civil War.

• There is a vast collection of Butler papers in the Library of Congress. Other Butler material may be found at the Massachusetts Historical Society, Boston, and many of Butler's letters have been published in Jesse Ames Marshall, ed., *Private and Official Correspondence of Gen. Benjamin F. Butler during the Period of the Civil War* (5 vols., 1917). The leading biographies are Hans L. Trefousse, *Ben Butler: The South Called Him Beast* (1957), and Richard S. West, Jr., *Lincoln's Scapegoat General: A Life of Benjamin F. Butler, 1818–1893* (1965). Other biographies include Robert S. Holzman, *Stormy Ben Butler* (1954); Howard P. Nash, Jr., *Stormy Petrel: The Life and Times of General Benjamin F. Butler, 1818–1893* (1969); and, for an anti-Butler perspective, Robert Werlich, *"Beast Butler": The Incredible Career of Union Major General Benjamin F. Butler* (1962).

HANS L. TREFOUSSE

BUTLER, Charles Wilfred (10 Aug. 1911–3 Dec. 1973), designer for the aerospace industry, was born in Perth Amboy, New Jersey, the son of Wilfred Butler and Letitia Powell. Virtually nothing is known about his early life, and even retracing his professional career and personal life is somewhat difficult. He attended classes in architecture and design at various times in Philadelphia, particularly at the Pennsylvania Museum School of Industrial Design (later Philadelphia College of Art), where he studied in the mid-1930s with well-known designer Alexey Brodovitch. Butler worked briefly for the Jentner Exhibits Corporation and was a consultant to the Board of Design of the 1939 World's Fair in New York. After brief service in the navy during the earlier part of World War II, he worked for the transportation division of Raymond Loewy's New York office from June 1944 to January 1948. Leaving Loewy's firm to establish an independent practice specializing in airline corporate imagery and aircraft interiors, he devoted himself to this line of work for the rest of his life. His practice, based in New York, was the partnership of Butler & Zimmerman from 1948 to 1959, at which time he established the firm of Charles Butler Associates. His first large airline commission was as a consultant on the redesign of Northwest Airlines's Boeing Stratocruisers in the late 1940s. Although the bread and butter of Butler's design practice then and later was in the field of corporate aviation, creating executive aircraft interiors for clients such as General Motors, King Farouk, and Chiang Kai-shek, he made his real mark on commercial aviation by designing a series of interiors for British-built airliners in the fifties and sixties. The first of these was for Trans Canada Airlines (TCA) when that company purchased the English-made Vickers Viscount in 1953.

TCA hired Butler to "Americanize" the interiors of their new turboprop Viscounts. He provided them with squared-off seats that contained folding trays, curvilinear cabin, and an overhead luggage rack of vinyl-covered fiberglass that replaced the old-fashioned netting of the original Vickers hatrack. His introduction of light colors, warm tones, and new interior materials, particularly plastics, became a trademark of his fifties work. Regionalizing the palette of airline color schemes, he used greens, browns, and reds for northern airlines and blues, aquas, and soft greens for southern carriers, blending the sets when airlines had routes in both areas of the country. With the success of the aircraft Butler designed for TCA, Capital Airlines, based in Washington, D.C., hired him to do a comparable redesign of its new Viscounts in 1954. For these interiors Butler used a fabric he called "Mt. Vernon Plaid," which combined watermelon, beige, and light green. After his work on the Viscount, he was commissioned by TCA to create the interiors of the Vickers Vanguard in 1957–1960 and by Continental Airlines to design the interiors of the new Vickers 800 series Viscounts in 1957–1960. Along with the latter job, he developed the styles in ticket offices and the corporate imagery of Continental in the late fifties and early sixties. He also designed the logo, corporate imagery, and flight attendant uniforms for Canadian Pacific Airlines as it entered the jet age in 1960–1961 with the new Douglas DC-8s. The success of his work on the Viscount brought him a number of commissions in the early sixties from British aircraft manufacturers, who saw Butler as their entrée to airplane sales in the lucrative North American market with its diverse array of airlines.

The most important British jet planes for which Butler designed the interior spaces were the Vickers VC-10 (1962), the BAC-111 (1962–1963), the Hawker-Siddeley Trident (1958–1964), and the British Aerospace Concorde, designed in 1966 and put into service in 1976. In this boom time of the late fifties and early sixties, Butler established Charles Butler Design for Industry in London and expanded his New York office to fifteen people, who worked under his vice president Robert J. Price. His last job for a British aircraft manufacturer was the design of the interior of the BAC-311 (1968). This was a large aircraft intended to compete with American jumbo jets and other wide-body planes introduced in the late sixties and early seventies, such as the Boeing 747, Lockheed L-1011, and Douglas DC-10. The BAC-311 never went into production because of Britain's participation in the establishment of the European Airbus consortium in 1969–1970.

In addition to his contributions to Britain's aviation industry in the postwar jet age, Butler also worked on the complete redesign of the Bell OH-4A prototype military helicopter of 1961, transforming it into the Bell 206 Jet Ranger of 1965, one of the most successful helicopters to date. Butler's office planned the machine as if it were an automobile, designing it from the inside out and using plasticine models to style the exterior. The result was so popular that it may well have catalyzed the Hughes Aircraft Co. to hire Henry Dreyfuss Associates in the mid-1960s to design the interior of their conversion of the army OH-6 helicopter into the Hughes (now McDonnell Douglas) Model 500. Moreover, the popularity of Bell's Jet Ranger most probably influenced Fairchild-Hiller to hire Butler's former employer Loewy in 1967–1968 to redesign their OH-5 military helicopter into the civil FH-1100.

Butler's firm continued to receive corporate imagery jobs from airlines. In 1970 Trans World Airlines hired him to redesign its logo, signage, terminal ticket counters at New York's Kennedy Airport, and airplane interiors, a design image originally established by Loewy in the early 1960s. The implementation of this corporate identity program was under way when Butler died. His office, working under Price, finished the project and other pending jobs before closing completely in 1975.

The date of Butler's marriage to Leta Counihan is unknown. They had a son and two daughters and lived in Greenwich, Connecticut, where Butler died. A gregarious person, Butler was adept at socializing with aerospace executives, a trait that helped him secure prominent commissions. He was socially active in the Greenwich Country Club and the Union League Club in New York and was professionally active in his own field of aircraft interior design. Butler had a much greater impact than many better-known industrial designers in determining how people have flown in the jet age. His greatest contributions were in helping to make British airliners successful in North America and a viable commercial product throughout the world. He was also the first freelance industrial designer, as opposed to an aeronautical engineer working for the helicopter company, to completely design one of America's most important helicopters.

• Robert J. Price, Peterborough, N.H., has archival records and information on Butler's work. The Raymond Loewy Papers in the Library of Congress contain records of Butler's employment with Loewy as well as Loewy's work on the FH-1100. Additional information on Butler's work in commercial aviation is in John Zukowsky, ed., *Building for Air Travel:*

Architecture and Design for Commercial Aviation (1996), and George Christian, "Comfort in Airline Cabin Design Makes Dollar Sense," *Aviation Week*, 14 May 1956, pp. 92–93, 95, 97, 99, 101. Richard Weeghman, "For Whom Doth Bell Toil," *Flying*, May 1966, pp. 102–7, and Zukowsky, "Design for the Jet Age: Charles Butler and Uwe Schneider," *Design Issues* (Autumn 1997): 66–81, contain information on Butler's work on the Bell 206 helicopter. Butler's obituary is in the *Greenwich Time*, 4 Dec. 1973.

JOHN ZUKOWSKY

BUTLER, Elizabeth Beardsley (1 Dec. 1884–2 Aug. 1911), social reformer, was born possibly in Brooklyn, New York, the daughter of Frederic(k?) Butler. Her mother's name is not known. She attended Packer Collegiate Institute in Brooklyn from 1898 to 1903 and Adelphi College in 1904. She then enrolled at Barnard College, where she studied political and social ethics, sociological principles, and liberal and socialist theories of social change. After graduating in 1905, she took courses at the New York School of Philanthropy.

A pioneer in empirical social investigation, Butler earned her living and reputation researching women and children wage earners in several northern urban communities, including Jersey City, Pittsburgh, and Baltimore. Like other college-educated social reformers of the early twentieth century, she believed that well-publicized research would galvanize American businessmen, civic leaders, and legislators to improve the living and working conditions of the working class. Butler held executive positions in several of the most important social reform organizations of the early twentieth century. Between 1905 and 1911 she worked for the Consumers' League of New Jersey, the New Jersey Child Labor Committee, the Rand School of Social Science, and the Bureau of Social Research of the New York School of Philanthropy. Her first social investigations examined industrial homework (the production of commercial goods in the home) and child labor and were featured in 1907–1908 in *Charities and the Commons*, a major social reform journal.

Butler earned a national reputation as a social investigator in 1909 with the publication of *Women and the Trades: Pittsburgh, 1907–1908*, the first general survey of wage-earning women in an American city and the first volume of the famous Pittsburgh Survey. Funded and published by the Russell Sage Foundation, the Pittsburgh Survey holds landmark status in the history of empirical social investigation for its comprehensive study of life and labor in an American city. Part of the social survey movement of 1906–1930, the Pittsburgh project was the first of 2,500 surveys of local communities engaging in self-study of economic and social conditions to promote social reform. The survey resembled English social investigations associated with Charles Booth and Seebohm Rowntree but was closer to investigative reporting than academic social science. Butler worked with a research team that included the most notable social scientists and liberal reformers of the early twentieth century, including Paul Underwood Kellogg, John R. Commons, Lewis Wickes Hine, Edward T. Devine, and Florence Kelley. The completed survey included four books and two collections of articles, published between 1909 and 1914, on living and working conditions, health care, civic agencies, and economic and social problems in Pittsburgh and adjoining Homestead. It launched an intensive publicity campaign and a traveling exhibit to mobilize public support for social change.

Kellogg, the survey's editor, praised Butler's mapping of women's work in Pittsburgh for its "epic quality." Based on visits to over 400 shops and factories, *Women and the Trades* became a model of social investigation of women's wage earning for its ambitious accounts of wages and hours, work environments, production processes, technological innovations, work pace, job training and mobility, co-worker relations, labor-management relations, and unionization. *Women and the Trades* featured factory operatives, sales clerks, commercial laundresses, and telephone operators who worked long hours under strict male supervision for low pay. Although Butler surveyed many women's occupations, she consciously omitted domestic and personal service and clerical work; neither fit her concerns for industrial and commercial conditions. Butler portrayed Pittsburgh's wage-earning women as passive victims of an uncaring economic order that exploited workers and retarded trade unionism. According to this view, women could not protect themselves from deleterious working conditions and needed state and federal labor laws to limit hours and guarantee minimum wages. *Women and the Trades* has become a classic in the genre of the social survey and liberal reform of the early twentieth century.

After Butler completed *Women and the Trades*, she researched the wages and working conditions of sales clerks in Baltimore for the Consumers' League of Maryland. The product of her several-month-long investigation, *Saleswomen in Mercantile Stores: Baltimore, 1909*, was published by the Russell Sage Foundation in 1912, a year after Butler died of tuberculosis.

Butler's sudden death at the age of twenty-six at Saranac Lake, New York, stunned and saddened her colleagues in liberal social reform. Kellogg considered her an "interpreter of rare gifts" who was "venturesome, incisive, quick to pare away the husk of a thing and lay bare the truth back of it." John M. Glenn, director of the Russell Sage Foundation in the early twentieth century, characterized Butler as "quiet," "thoughtful," "thorough," and "sympathetic," a person who made friends with people from all walks of life. "A convinced socialist," Butler was passionately committed to the principles of social justice and feminism. She wanted working-class women to have more choices in their lives. Her social investigations had revealed women imprisoned in unskilled, dead-end, low-wage work from which they were eager to escape. If women could train for skilled jobs, Butler believed they could then envision wage work as a career and an attractive alternative to housewifery. In her closing comment in *Women and the Trades*, she wrote: "Pending such adjustment, we shall do well to remember that inferior and monotonous work processes are no preparation for intelligent home making. Higher earnings and increased industrial efficiency go far toward developing in working women a sense of responsibility, personal and social, toward whichever group they choose to become a part."

• No collection of Butler's papers exists. The only assessment of Butler's life and work is to be found in Maurine Weiner Greenwald, "Women at Work through the Eyes of Elizabeth Beardsley Butler and Lewis Wickes Hine," in Butler, *Women and the Trades: Pittsburgh, 1907–1908* (1909; repr. 1984). An obituary is in *Survey*, 19 Aug. 1911.

MAURINE WEINER GREENWALD

BUTLER, Hugh Alfred (28 Feb. 1878–1 July 1954), U.S. senator, was born in Calhoun, Iowa, the son of Harvey Gibson Butler and Ida Wills, farmers. In 1884 the family moved to a homestead south of Cambridge, Nebraska. In 1895 Butler entered Doane Academy in Crete, Nebraska, and the next year he enrolled in Doane College, a Congregational school. Graduating in 1900 with a bachelor of science degree, he considered studying law but instead took a job with the Burlington Railroad. In 1903 Butler married his college sweetheart, Fay Johnson; they had two sons, both of whom died early in life.

In 1908 Butler invested some of his money in the milling industry and quickly became involved in the grain trade. After holding executive positions with several mills, he put up all of the financing for a partnership with J. LeRoy Welsh and in 1918 founded the Butler-Welsh Grain Company in Omaha, an operation that provided the financial and political base critical to Butler's later senatorial campaigns. Butler steadily rose to prominence in the grain trade, serving as president of the Grain and Feed Dealers' National Association for 1931–1932.

During the farm depression of the 1920s, Butler also invested heavily in farm mortgages, and the foreclosures of two farms brought him ownership of over 550 acres of land near his family's old homestead. Under the able leadership of his brother and two partners, the operation became a very successful ranch of 1,800 acres, allowing Butler to campaign as "a farmer" when it was politically helpful to do so.

In addition to farming and the grain business, Butler became active in and held high offices in Rotary International and in numerous other civic clubs and organizations. He served on the Omaha Board of Education from 1929 to 1932, a term as chairman of the board of trustees of First Central Congregational Church in Omaha, and a year as moderator of the state Congregational conference. For thirty-seven years (1917–1954) he was a member of the board of trustees of Doane College, and for many of those years he was president of that board. He became the college's major benefactor and almost single-handedly kept it solvent during some very difficult years.

Working his way up in the Republican party, Butler served as chairman of the Douglas County (Omaha) Republican party and in 1936 was elected national committeeman for Nebraska at a time when the Republican party in that state was in a shambles. His help in rebuilding the party further added to his name recognition and support across the state. Butler was elected to the Senate in his first try for elective office in 1940, defeating pro–New Deal governor Robert L. Cochran. An automobile accident just after his successful senatorial campaign in 1940 resulted in his wife's death in February 1941 and left Butler without any family as he began his senatorial career. The sense of personal emptiness he felt explains much of his interest in providing for the college educations of others and his full-time commitment to work for Doane College and the U.S. Senate. He immersed himself in the work of the Senate, in Republican politics, and in his continuing efforts on behalf of Doane.

As a first-term senator, Butler quickly laid out his conservative position on nearly every issue before the Senate. His election at a time when there were few Republicans in the Senate ensured him seniority and prominence when the Republican party regained control of the Senate in 1947. During the Eightieth Congress (1947–1949) and the Eighty-third Congress (1953 until his death), he chaired the Senate Committee on Interior and Insular Affairs, where he successfully thwarted the efforts of those seeking statehood for Alaska and Hawaii.

Sensing clearly the conservative mood of Nebraskans, Butler was easily reelected in 1946 and in 1952, both times handily defeating popular, moderate Republican governors in primaries, Dwight Griswold in 1946 and F. Valdemar "Val" Peterson in 1952. Nebraska's Democrats put up only token opposition to Butler in both of these elections. Butler's success as a politician lay not in what he accomplished in Washington, but in his mastery of the Nebraska Republican party. There are no monuments to Butler in Washington, but his name was known in nearly every household in Nebraska. By using political liaisons in every county, he ensured his hold on the seat in the Senate and controlled the state party apparatus. With agents in nearly every community reading and clipping local newspapers, he kept in close touch with the people, often sending personal, handwritten notes of congratulations or condolences as the occasion warranted.

A fiscal conservative throughout his senatorial career, Butler blamed most of the nation's ills on the New Deal and worked toward its eradication. He eagerly supported such legislative initiatives as the Taft-Hartley Act, which strengthened employers' rights in relation to labor unions, and consistently urged the reduction of government spending and an end to welfare programs.

In foreign policy, Butler was an isolationist. He opposed pre–Pearl Harbor efforts to aid England in World War II and was wary of membership in the proposed United Nations, although he reluctantly voted for the charter creating that organization in 1945. During the Cold War years, he consistently opposed all programs of foreign aid and "entangling alliances," such as the North Atlantic Treaty Organization (NATO). At the same time, Butler became one of the more ardent anti-Communists in the Senate. At the time of his death, he was wrestling with how to vote in the Senate's upcoming censure of Republican senator Joseph R. McCarthy of Wisconsin.

A supporter of Senator Robert A. Taft's presidential candidacy in 1944, 1948, and 1952, Butler was deeply disappointed in the Ohioan's failure to win the Republican nomination. Although he publicly supported the 1944 and 1948 tickets led by Thomas Dewey and the 1952 ticket led by Dwight Eisenhower, privately he expressed dismay over the defeat of more conservative leaders within the party. Butler's popularity among Nebraska's voting populace remained strong until his death in Bethesda, Maryland. With his leadership, the Republican party in the state had revived from its doldrums to become almost invincible.

• Butler's papers are in the Nebraska State Historical Society in Lincoln. The most complete biography is Justus F. Paul, *Senator Hugh Butler and Nebraska Republicanism* (1976). An earlier study, devoted primarily to Butler's work for Doane, is Ben F. and Ruth M. Sylvester, *A Man and His College: The Butler-Doane Story* (1954). Donald Ziegler, *A College on a Hill: Doane* (1990), contains information concerning Butler's relationship with the college. Articles by Paul, including "The Making of a Senator: The Early Life of Hugh Butler," *Nebraska History* 47 (Autumn 1968): 247–67; "Butler, Griswold, Wherry: The Struggle for Dominance of Nebraska Republicanism, 1941–1946," *North Dakota Quarterly* 43 (Autumn 1975): 51–61; and "Isolationism versus Internationalism? The Republican Senatorial Primary in Nebraska, 1946," *Nebraska History* 56 (Spring 1975): 145–56, provide insights into Butler's early life and political views. Three books by Ernest Gruening, which put Butler's antistatehood views in a negative light, are *The State of Alaska* (1954), *The Battle for Alaska Statehood* (1967), and *Many Battles: The Autobiography of Ernest Gruening* (1973). Two articles by Paul, "The Power of Seniority: Senator Hugh Butler and Statehood for Hawaii," *Hawaiian Journal of History* 9 (1975): 140–47, and "Political Partisanship and the Alaskan Territorial Governorship, 1947–1953," *Northern Review* 1 (Fall 1987): 21–24, 38, provide additional information about Butler's role on the statehood issue. Butler's opposition to foreign involvements is illustrated in Paul, "Senator Hugh Butler and Aid to Latin America, 1943–1944," *South Dakota History* 8 (Winter 1977): 34–45. Obituaries of some length are in the *Omaha World-Herald* and the *New York Times*, 2 July 1954.

JUSTUS F. PAUL

BUTLER, James (1755–1842), itinerant schoolmaster and author, was born in England and emigrated to Pennsylvania. Nothing is known of Butler's early life, including the period when he published his novel, *Fortune's Foot-ball; or, The Adventures of Mercutio* (1797–1798), and very little thereafter. Local records place him in various parts of Mifflin and Indiana counties from 1804 to 1842, identifying the township or the schoolhouse in which he taught: near McCoysville in 1807; in Mifflintown in 1813–1814 and 1817; in Milford in 1816 and from 1824 to 1829; and in or near McVeytown, Aaronsburg, Lack, and Turbett during unspecified years. He was probably married, for he is known to have had a grandson. From census records, it is probable that he was living in Fermanagh Township in 1830 in a household that also included a woman between the ages of thirty and thirty-nine. Until his death in Mifflintown he served as an unofficial archivist, recording births and deaths in the surrounding area, but these records have not survived.

More is known about his writings than his life. In addition to *Fortune's Foot-ball,* Butler published *American Bravery Displayed* (1816), a record of the naval engagements of the War of 1812, and a piece on the defeat of General Arthur St. Clair, which has not survived. A contemporary account calls Butler "[t]he only author, which [Mifflin] county has at any time produced" and says that he "used to indulge himself in framing a kind of doggerel, mostly satiric, not withstanding which, they [*sic*] possessed some degree of merit" (Ellis, p. 790). Additionally, he compiled a school reader composed of patriotic writings, which also has not survived. His place in American history rests upon his novel and *American Bravery.*

Butler's title, *Fortune's Foot-ball,* is unfortunately more intriguing than his novel, which is a pastiche of characters and narrative techniques from picaresque and sentimental fiction. In his preface, Butler says that his purpose is "to propagate the sentiments of virtue—to stimulate youth to an humble resignation to the dispensations of providence—and to discountenance vice" (1:5). But his novel—which is filled with love affairs, storms, pirates, war, impressment, and exotic settings—does not live up to this purpose. Its plot intersperses accounts of Mercutio's travels and adventures throughout the narrative of his three love affairs: with the virtuous Lucinda, who dies on the day they are to marry; with Leonora, the daughter of the doge of Venice, who bears him an illegitimate son before also dying; and with Isabella, who provides the traditional happily-ever-after conclusion. Propelling this plot are "Fortune, that fickle Goddess" (2:2) and "all bounteous Providence" (2:184), whose workings are invariably just. For the vicissitudes and uncertainties that result, Butler advocates resignation, and, thus, his hero Mercutio matures when—having suffered "a long series of misfortunes, disappointments, and dangers"—he acquires "a uniformity of temper and a serenity of countenance" (2:5).

Describing the purpose of *American Bravery Displayed,* Butler writes: "The design was to present to the citizens of the United States, and others, a faithful narrative of the ardent and convulsive struggles of our infant marine force . . . in resisting the arrogant, and no less villanous [*sic*] depredations and murders of the most formidable naval power (in numbers, discipline and pecuniary resource) that ever unfurled a sail or explored the Antipodal seas" (pp. ix–x). *American Bravery* is more a chronicle than a narrative, giving the facts of the naval engagements of the War of 1812 and including verbatim excerpts from the captains' official records for the most famous battles (for example, Stephen Decatur's (1779–1820) account of the *United States*'s capture of the *Macedonia* and Isaac Hull's of the *Constitution*'s capture of the *Guerriere*). The typical entry records the name of the ship captured, its cargo, and disposition of the ship and crew. Butler identifies his source as *The Weekly Register* by H. Niles of Baltimore, Maryland.

Scanty historical records for his area of Pennsylvania and the relative insignificance of his writings make it unlikely that much will ever be known about James Butler. However, the few facts available about him and the portrait that emerges from his writing suggest that he was an ardent patriot and an active citizen.

• The sole source for biographical information about Butler is Franklin Ellis, *History of That Part of the Susquehanna and Juniata Valleys Embraced in the Counties of Mifflin, Juniata, Perry, Union, and Snyder* (1886). For examinations of his novel see Herbert Ross Brown, *The Sentimental Novel in America* (1940); Cathy N. Davidson, *Revolution and the Word* (1986); Tremaine McDowell, "Sensibility in the Eighteenth-Century Novel" *Studies in Philology* 24 (1927): 383–402; and Henri Petter, *The Early American Novel* (1971).

DAVID M. CRAIG

BUTLER, Lee Pierce (19 Dec. 1884–29 Mar. 1953), professor and rare book curator, was born in Clarendon Hills, Illinois, the son of John Pierce Butler (a.k.a. Wallace due his desire to serve twice in the Civil War), a real estate agent, farm manager, and railroad employee, and Evaline ("Eva") Content Whipple, an occasional U.S. postal mistress. Butler spent his early childhood on "Blythewood," a 460-acre farm outside Pittsfield, Massachusetts, that was designed by F. L. Olmsted & Company and owned by Wirt D. Walker, a Chicago attorney. Infantile paralysis left Butler with scoliosis and a slight lameness, which was still apparent in his adult life; his early childhood was also marked by a serious case of scarlet fever and catarrh that left him almost completely deaf. He nevertheless earned a Ph.B. in 1906 and an M.A. in Latin in 1910 from Dickinson College. Butler taught science and mathematics briefly at Locust Dale Academy in Virginia during the fall of 1906. He started at Union Theological Seminary but then transferred to divinity school at Hartford Theological Seminary to study early medieval church history, and he received a B.D. in 1910 and a Ph.D. in 1912. After difficult pastorates as a deacon in the Episcopal church in Indianapolis, Indiana, as well as DeSoto and Ironton, Missouri, he moved back to his parents' home in Clarendon Hills in late 1912.

In Chicago he worked first as a day laborer, then in his father's railroad freight office, and occasionally as a supply deacon for the Episcopal church, before a chance meeting with Dr. W. N. C. Carlton, the librarian at the Newberry Library. Carlton offered Butler a post at the Newberry in 1916, which he accepted with alacrity. Butler rose rapidly and in late 1919 became the custodian of the John M. Wing Foundation on the History of Printing. Fluent in seven languages, Butler traveled abroad, where he collected extensively and became exceedingly well known to the English and Continental booksellers. Although his hearing never improved, newly designed hearing aids allowed him to communicate with others. During his tenure, the Wing Foundation bought 1,850 incunabula (books printed before 1501) that represented eleven countries, 95 cities, and 516 printers. He is also partially credited with assuring that the massive Vollbehr Collection of incunables went to the U.S. Congressional Library: his testimony helped convince congressmen to appropriate the requisite funds for its purchase. Butler's achievements at the Newberry enabled scholars to adopt a geographical perspective in studying the nature of civilization and the spread of culture because he had provided geographical access to the newly acquired materials. They could also now find textually significant works at the Newberry rather than having to depend on the British Museum or the Bibliothèque Nationale. Even foreign scholars began to visit the Newberry Library. In 1926 he married Ruth Lapham, curator of the Edward A. Ayer Collection of Americana at the Newberry; they had no children.

In 1931 Butler joined the University of Chicago faculty in the graduate library school as a professor of bibliographical history. His years of academic and theological work had prepared him to recognize and sympathize with the new scientific approach to librarianship, such as the use of new social science techniques. The fullest articulation of his advocacy of social scientific ideas, notably quantification and its concomitant precision, can be found in his now classic *Introduction to Library Science* (1933). Recanting this position late in his life, Butler found himself in an ideological conflict, with the social scientist Douglas Waples, that became legendary in the 1940s. In simplistic terms, their conflict was the start of the qualitative versus quantitative debate in librarianship. Ultimately, Butler referred to many of the developments within librarianship as scientistic and began to argue for something more—a deeper, more spiritual librarianship ("Librarianship as a Profession" and "The Cultural Function of the Library," *Library Quarterly* 21 [Oct. 1951] and 22 [Apr. 1952], respectively). His lasting impact can be seen in the work of his graduate students, such as Rudolph Hirsch, Arna Bontemps, Jesse H. Shera, Lester Asheim, and Haynes McMullen.

Butler liked to travel and read, and he was especially fond of detective stories. His memberships included the Masons (3d degree), the Cliff-Dweller's, the American Library Association, the American Institute for the Graphic Arts, the Caxton Club, Society for Typographic Arts, and the Chicago Literary Club. While a visiting professor at the University of North Carolina at Chapel Hill, Butler died as a result of an automobile accident outside Burlington, North Carolina.

An authority on the history of books and printing, Butler challenged the older humanistic world view in librarianship while defending the new scientific outlook being developed at Chicago. The intellectual crisis and conflict made his classroom and office an exciting place to be. He is viewed as one of the finest minds in library science.

• Few of Butler's papers are extant at the Newberry Library and in the Department of Special Collections at the University of Chicago's Regenstein Library. The standard work assessment of his life and contributions is John V. Richardson, Jr., *The Gospel of Scholarship: Pierce Butler and a Critique of American Librarianship* (1922), which reprints Butler's *Introduction to Library Science* and two of his sermons. See also Richardson's *The Spirit of Inquiry: The Graduate Library School at Chicago, 1921–1951* (1982) and Charles I. Terbille, "Competing Models of Library Science: Waples-Berelson and Butler," *Libraries & Culture* 27 (Summer 1992): 296–319. An obituary is in the *New York Times*, 29 Mar. 1953.

JOHN V. RICHARDSON JR.

BUTLER, Marion (20 May 1863–3 June 1938), U.S. senator, was born in Sampson County, North Carolina, the son of Wiley Butler and Romelia Ferrell, prosperous farmers. After a comfortable if not privileged childhood, Butler graduated in 1885 from the University of North Carolina, where he had been active in literary societies and oratorical contests but only an average student. He returned home to run the family farm, to serve as principal of Salem High School, and, in 1893, to marry Florence Faison, with whom he had five children by 1900. During these years Butler vigorously championed educational reform, especially through the North Carolina Teachers' Assembly, which lobbied for better schools and improved teacher training, and as a trustee of the University of North Carolina from 1891 to 1899. In the latter year he also studied law at the university and was licensed to practice.

Butler's real talents and ambitions, however, were in politics. His early triumphs stemmed from his prominent involvement in the efforts of the Farmers' Alliance to secure economic and political reform. He was elected the Alliance's county president in 1888, state president in 1891 and 1892, and national president in 1894. He promoted both the Alliance and his own political career through the *Clinton Caucasian*, a local newspaper he purchased in 1888 and later moved to Raleigh. Butler was elected to the state senate in 1890 as an Alliance Democrat but in 1892 joined the new People's party, becoming the party's state chairman in 1894. He organized a successful fusion with North Carolina's Republicans in the campaign of that year and secured the defeat of the long-dominant Democrats. Controlling the state legislature, the fusionists then elected Butler to the U.S. Senate.

In the Senate (1895–1901), Butler earned a reputation for having a sharp tongue as he vociferously advocated an expansion of governmental activity and responsibility and championed Populist reform proposals, especially antimonopoly and referendum measures, constitutional amendments for popular election of senators and judges, and tax and monetary legislation. He had little tangible success, however, beyond playing an instrumental role in helping establish the system of rural free delivery of mail.

More conspicuous were Butler's activities in political management. For eight years (1896–1904), he served as the national chairman of the People's party while continuing as the party's state chair in North Carolina. A champion and beneficiary of fusion politics, Butler in 1896 helped direct the Populists' national fusion with the Democrats on the presidential candidacy of William Jennings Bryan even as he maintained the coalition with Republicans in North Carolina. Often autocratic in his methods and imperious in his attitudes, Butler was soon embroiled in the factional dispute between fusion and antifusion Populists that disrupted his party. Butler managed to retain control of the party's official machinery, at times cooperating with conservative Democrats and Republicans to weaken rivals in his own party. In 1900 he again successfully promoted the Populist presidential nomination of the Democratic Bryan while arranging Populist-Republican fusion in North Carolina in an attempt to gain reelection to the Senate. His reelection hopes failed, however, owing to the enactment of new election laws by the 1899 Democratic legislature that, by disrupting fusion and disfranchising many of its political voters, helped assure Democratic political success.

After 1901 Butler increasingly moved closer to the Republicans, even privately supporting the 1904 election of Theodore Roosevelt (1858–1919) while remaining Populist national chairman. Butler then joined the Republican party and thereafter attempted both to play an influential role in state and national politics and to gain appointments to numerous important federal positions, from secretary of agriculture to ambassador to Mexico. To his dismay, however, Butler was relegated to little more than serving as a consultant on patronage questions and as a delegate to each Republican National Convention from 1908 through 1932. Butler regarded himself as a progressive Republican, but as before, his ambition often distorted his reform ideas, and he always accommodated himself to the rightward drift of Republicans in both state and national politics, narrowing his views in an attempt to maintain his political relevance. He campaigned harshly against Bryan in 1908, helped nominate Warren G. Harding in 1920, supported Calvin Coolidge for reelection in 1928 and Herbert Hoover (1874–1964) in 1932, and favored Alfred M. Landon in 1936.

Butler was more successful in his business ventures, including a number of entrepreneurial and speculative projects, such as cotton mills, western mining and oil leases, and foreign development schemes, in which he drew upon his political experiences and contacts. He also became a successful lawyer, with offices in both North Carolina and Washington, D.C., specializing as a lobbyist for private legislation and for corporations seeking federal contracts. He died in Takoma Park, Maryland, a Washington suburb.

• The political and personal papers of Butler are in the Southern Historical Collection of the University of North Carolina Library. A sympathetic biography is James L. Hunt, "Marion Butler and the Populist Ideal, 1863–1938" (Ph.D. diss., Univ. of Wisconsin, 1990). Butler's early career is treated in Hunt, "The Making of a Populist: Marion Butler, 1863–1895," *North Carolina Historical Review* 62 (1985): 53–77, 179–202, 317–43. His role in the 1896 election is favorably described in Robert F. Durden, *The Climax of Populism: The Election of 1896* (1965), while the limits of Butler's reform politics are cataloged in Peter H. Argersinger, *Populism and Politics: William A. Peffer and the People's Party* (1974); Bruce Palmer, *"Man over Money": The Southern Populist Critique of American Capitalism* (1980); and C. Vann Woodward, *Tom Watson: Agrarian Rebel* (1938). A useful contemporary assessment is Carl Snyder, "Marion Butler," *Review of Reviews* 14 (1896): 429–33. An obituary is in the *New York Times*, 4 June 1938.

PETER H. ARGERSINGER

BUTLER, Matthew Calbraith (8 Mar. 1836–14 Apr. 1909), Confederate general and U.S. senator, was born in Greenville, South Carolina, the son of William Butler (1790–1850), a U.S. naval surgeon, and Jane Tweedy Perry. The eleventh of sixteen children, Butler spent his early youth in the South Carolina upcountry and attended Greenville Academy. In 1848 he accompanied his father, who had been appointed an agent to the Cherokee Indians, to Fort Gibson in the Indian Territory. His father died in 1850, and in 1851 Butler returned to South Carolina, settling in Edgefield, where he lived with U.S. senator Andrew P. Butler, his uncle. He entered South Carolina College in 1854 but left in 1857 before graduating. After studying law with his uncle and beginning a law practice in Edgefield, he married Maria Simkins Pickens in 1858. They had five children. This marriage connected Butler with one of the wealthiest and politically most influential families in the state, and in 1860 he was a rising young lawyer-planter with a seat in the South Carolina legislature. Like his father-in-law, Francis W. Pickens, the governor in 1860, Butler was a secessionist Democrat.

Soon after the outbreak of the Civil War Butler resigned from the legislature to accept a captain's commission in an Edgefield company of cavalry that was part of Hampton's Legion. He saw extensive service in the Virginia theater. His actions at First Manassas in July 1861 earned him a promotion to major, and in August 1862 he was made colonel of the Second Regiment, South Carolina Cavalry. After participating in Second Manassas, the Antietam campaign, and the Chambersburg raid of 1862, he lost his right leg (below the knee) from a wound received at the battle of Brandy Station in June 1863. On 1 September 1863 he was promoted to brigadier general and on 17 September 1864 attained the rank of major general. He commanded brigades and divisions under Generals Jeb Stuart and Wade Hampton in the heavy Virginia fighting of 1864. At the end of the war he was in South Carolina attempting to block William T. Sherman's advance.

Butler was financially ruined by the war. His seventy slaves had been set free, and he was in debt for $15,000. He resumed his law practice and briefly held political office as a state representative from Edgefield District before the Republicans gained power in South Carolina under the terms of Congressional Reconstruction in 1867. Butler first opposed Republican rule through a fusion strategy. He and other conservative white Democrats tried to align with dissident elements detached from the Republican party. Included in this strategy was an appeal to black voters to abandon the Republicans. The strategy failed, largely because the Democrats had little of substance to offer to the freedmen. After being defeated in his bid for lieutenant governor in 1870 and seeing the Republicans win handily in the state and national elections of 1872, Butler abandoned fusion for the straight-out strategy of rebuilding the Democratic party through direct appeals to the racial pride of whites.

The straight-out strategy carried the state for the Democrats in 1876 and ended Reconstruction in South Carolina. Butler played a major role in the Democratic success through his participation in the notorious Hamburg riot on 8 July 1876. Touched off by the refusal of black militia to make way for two whites, the riot resulted in the deaths of six blacks and one white. In September Butler, who was active in the rifle and saber clubs of nearby Edgefield, organized and helped arm the white militia that attacked the town and killed captured blacks who were trying to escape. This brutal use of force by whites set the tone for a Democratic campaign of intimidation against black voters.

In December 1876 the Democratic legislature elected Butler to the U.S. Senate. He served three terms in the Senate as the loyal lieutenant of Hampton, the state's most powerful Democrat. Like Hampton, Butler was not an active legislator. Aside from securing some federal funds for internal improvements in Charleston, he was best known for his support of black emigration. Citing "an unrelenting, unforgiving, incurable race prejudice" among whites, he sponsored a bill in 1890 that provided federal aid to blacks wishing to emigrate to Africa. The bill, which had no chance of passage, was an attempt on Butler's part to counteract the rising antiblack virulence of the insurgent agrarian movement in South Carolina led by Benjamin Tillman. Conservative Democrats such as Hampton and Butler, men whose leadership rested on their stature as Confederate war heroes, were out of touch with a new generation of white voters in South Carolina caught up in an agricultural depression. By playing upon their racial phobias and using blacks as a scapegoat, Tillman forged these voters into a political movement that swept Hampton from power in 1890 and defeated Butler in his bid for reelection to the Senate in 1894.

After his Senate defeat, Butler retired from politics and practiced law in Washington, D.C. Appointed by President William McKinley as a major general of volunteers in the Spanish-American War, he took part in the Spanish evacuation of Cuba. He was president of a Mexican mining company in 1906, when he married Nannie Whitman; they had no children (his first wife had died at an unknown earlier date). He died in Washington.

• Collections of Butler's papers can be found in the Dalton collection at the Duke University library, the Southern Historical Collection at the University of North Carolina at

Chapel Hill, and the South Caroliniana Library at the University of South Carolina. E. L. Wells, *Hampton and His Cavalry in '64* (1899), and U. R. Brooks, *Butler and His Cavalry in the War of Secession* (1909), cover his war record. There is no biography, but Benjamin F. Perry, *Reminiscences of Public Men* (1899), and J. C. Hamphill, *Men of Mark in South Carolina*, vol. 4 (4 vols., 1907–1909), provide useful sketches. The political setting in which Butler served as a senator can be traced in William J. Cooper, *The Conservative Regime: South Carolina, 1877–1890* (1968). A balanced account of his role in the Hamburg riot can be found in Joel Williamson, *After Slavery: The Negro in South Carolina during Reconstruction, 1861–1877* (1965). An obituary is in the Charleston *News and Courier*, 15 Apr. 1909.

WILLIAM L. BARNEY

BUTLER, Mother Marie Joseph (22 July 1860–23 Apr. 1940), Roman Catholic nun and founder of schools and colleges, was born Johanna Butler in Ballynunnery, County Kilkenny, Ireland, the daughter of John Butler and Ellen Forrestal, prosperous farmers. Johanna initially attended a secular Irish national school, but her secondary education was under the direction of the Sisters of Mercy in the town of New Ross. As her interest in religious life developed, she was influenced by a friend whose sister had joined the congregation of the Sacred Heart of Mary. Founded in France in 1849 by Père Jean Gailhac and a wealthy widow, Mme Apollonie Cure, the congregation devoted itself to providing quality Catholic education for girls.

At the age of sixteen Johanna Butler set sail for the congregation's headquarters in Béziers, France. Under her new name of Marie Joseph, the novice was assigned in 1879 to the congregation's school in Oporto, Portugal; soon after she was transferred to the school in Braga, Portugal, where she headed the English and French departments and eventually became superior of the local community.

In 1903 Mother Butler came to the United States to direct and invigorate the congregation's school in Sag Harbor, Long Island, New York. As the congregation's educational endeavors expanded, she was called upon to work at its schools in Brooklyn and the Bronx.

The establishment of Marymount College realized the congregation's goal of providing higher education for Catholic women. Mother Butler's reputation as an excellent teacher, administrator, and superior, coupled with her commitment to quality education, made her the obvious choice for establishing and heading the new school. On 9 December 1907, with seven other sisters, she took up residence at Reynard Mansion in Tarrytown, New York, on a hill overlooking the Hudson River. The site was a gift of Mother Butler's cousin, James Butler, in memory of his wife, Mary Anne, who believed in the importance of higher education for Catholic women. Mother Butler named Marymount in honor of the Sacred Heart of Mary and in memory of Mary Anne O'Rourke Butler. Under her direction the school opened as a junior school and academy in 1908 with one student. Soon, even though the student body consisted of only a handful of students, she was making plans to expand the campus.

Marymount was chartered as a college in 1919, and Mother Butler was named the first president. Her goal was to create a college comparable to the best secular institutions of higher learning. Convinced that women's sphere included, but extended beyond, the home, she created a curriculum blending traditional values with progressive thought. Courses in law and political economy helped to enlarge the traditional curriculum; religious training included four years of study in Christian apologetics, coupled with charitable work and involvement in social causes. While fostering what she called "the three C's" of catholicity, charity, and courtesy, Mother Butler also prepared Marymount students to take an active role in public affairs. She hoped to produce politically astute, intellectually keen, socially active, and religiously motivated graduates.

Mother Butler's keen business sense allowed her to expand the campus at Tarrytown to meet the needs of a growing student body and to establish the congregation's American novitiate and a lay retreat movement. Though associated most closely with Marymount at Tarrytown, Mother Butler helped establish nine other Marymount high schools and colleges in California, New York City, France, and Italy. The international campuses (Mariemont in Neuilly, France, opened in 1923; Mariamonte in Rome opened in 1930) allowed Mother Butler to develop one of the first study abroad programs. Since her death, Marymount schools and colleges have multiplied in the United States and Europe and have spread to Africa and South America.

In recognizing her leadership, devotion to her sisters, and rich spiritual life, the congregations unanimously elected her to the first of three terms as superior general in 1926, a position she held for the rest of her life. Having become a U.S. citizen in 1927, she was the first American to head a major religious community headquartered in Europe. Although she maintained her principal residence at Marymount in Tarrytown, she traveled extensively as superior general, visiting the congregation's institutes and establishing new ones.

The establishment, expansion, and reputation of Marymount schools and colleges testify to a successful and ambitious national and international educational leader; the reminiscences of colleagues and friends reveal a respected, witty, well-liked, and deeply religious woman.

• Archival matter on Mother Butler is located at Marymount Convent in Tarrytown, N.Y. An anonymous editor collected her writings, which were published under the title *As the Eagle: The Spiritual Writings of Mother Butler* (1954). For a eulogistic biography, see Katherine Burton, *Mother Butler of Marymount* (1944).

KATHLEEN A. MAHONEY

BUTLER, Nicholas Murray (2 Apr. 1862–7 Dec. 1947), educator, politician, and president of Columbia University, was the son of Henry Leny Butler, an importer and textile manufacturer, and Mary Jones Murray. From early childhood Butler was an enthusiastic, self-motivated student. He attended public high School in Paterson, New Jersey, graduating at age thirteen after passing a series of rigorous examinations. He continued his education privately from age fourteen to seventeen, learning Latin and Greek and doing further work in mathematics.

Butler entered Columbia College in the fall of 1878. He devoted himself to his studies, attending extra lectures and earning excellent grades. Despite his commitment to academics, Butler found the time to involve himself in student life and to support himself financially. He helped to run the student journal and worked on the yearbook staff. By living with his uncle in Brooklyn, working for the *New York Tribune*, and teaching at two private schools, Butler paid for almost all his college expenses. He graduated in 1882 with many honors: Class Day Orator, Greek salutatorian, winner of the Chandler Historical Prize, and the recipient of a three-year fellowship in letters, a grant of $500 per year. He was also voted "Height of Piety" by his senior class. Butler earned his master's degree in 1883 and his doctorate in philosophy in June 1884, both from Columbia. Unfortunately, both his master's and doctoral theses have been lost. Butler traveled to Europe for a year, studying in Paris and Berlin, where he was deeply impressed by both the country of Germany and the German philosophic and pedagogic tradition.

Butler returned to Columbia, and with the help of President Frederick A. P. Barnard, who had noticed Butler as an undergraduate, was appointed an assistant professor (1885) and later an adjunct professor (1889) in the philosophy department. Butler became interested in educational theory, publishing articles in the magazine *Science* (Dec. 1885–Nov. 1887) on the scientific study of learning and educational methodology. His essays and lectures were collected in *The Meaning of Education* (1915).

Butler shared with President Barnard a concern about the lack of formal teacher training, and together they attempted to convince the trustees of Columbia to create a graduate school of education affiliated with the undergraduate college. Toward this end, Butler gave a series of free lectures titled "Pedagogy or the Science of Education." The series was immensely popular with New York City teachers, and the auditorium in which he spoke was often packed to capacity.

In February 1887 Butler was offered the presidency of the Industrial Education Society of New York, an organization interested in the promotion of industrial education—drawing, woodworking, and steel-working—in the schools. Though not primarily interested in vocational education, Butler accepted the position and used it to organize Teachers College in September 1887. Butler also married Susanna Edwards Schulyer in 1887; they had one child.

In 1890 Butler was appointed dean of the Department of Philosophy. Under the new college president, Seth Low, a charter to affiliate the Teachers College with Columbia College was signed in December 1892 and went into effect on 1 July of the following year. Butler also founded the magazine *Educational Review*, serving as its editor from 1891 to 1919.

After these successes, Butler turned his attention to the public school systems. As a member of the New Jersey State Board of Education from 1887 to 1895, including a term as president in 1892, he fought against the partisan politics and political favoritism rampant in local boards of education. To combat unfair hiring processes, Butler followed a practice favored by the so-called "administrative Progressives" of the era and both centralized control of the school system and instituted a statewide teacher certification examination. Butler was heavily involved in the politics surrounding the New York public school system and in writing or editing every important reform movement in its reform documents between 1889 and 1896. His greatest success was in the lobbying for the passage of the Unification Act of 1904, which gave control of the educational system to a board of eleven regents, elected every eleven years, and one commissioner, elected every six years. He was president of the National Education Association from 1894 to 1895 and a member of its influential Joint Committee on College Entrance Requirements. The joint committee's report in 1899, which was strongly supported by Butler, prompted the creation in 1901 of the College Entrance Examination Board (CEEB), soon widely required for college admissions. Butler was its chairman for thirteen years.

Butler was appointed president of Columbia University in 1902, a position he would hold for forty-three years. A notably strong and visionary leader, he was often criticized as dictatorial. Under his leadership the university grew substantially in size and prestige. Five divisions were added, including a summer school, an extension division, and a school of journalism. Butler envisioned the university in two very different ways: both as a corporation and as a central institution in a civilized society. As a corporation, Butler believed Columbia should be managed and marketed like any other business. As he explained to a Columbia trustee, "the management of a university such as ours is merely like the task of running a railroad." He always insisted on tight internal control of Columbia's finances; for example, university donors were not allowed to influence appointments for the chairs they endowed. Butler refused more than $9 million of grant money offered under conditions he termed "dishonorable and humiliating." Yet he also saw himself as shaping a generation of thinkers, with a responsibility to society for the nature of the instruction Columbia offered. A liberal arts education was Butler's ideal; he believed that overspecialization and overly technical knowledge was rooted in, and perpetuated, materialism and greed.

This dual conception of the university as a business and as a societal center for liberal thought expressed itself in Butler's handling of the many controversies over academic freedom that arose during his presidency. For the most part, Butler strongly supported his faculty's freedom of thought. To a woman's complaint that sociologist Franklin Giddings was teaching atheism, Butler replied, "I'm glad you told me, madam, we aim to teach everything at the University." Yet his liberal position was tempered by a keen desire to maintain Columbia's prestige. When judges unanimously awarded the Pulitzer Prize for fiction to *For Whom the Bell Tolls*, Butler's objections to the moral content of Hemingway's novel prompted him to warn the Pulitzer advisory board, "I hope that you will reconsider before you ask the university to be associated with a work of this nature." Butler has also often been criticized for firing members of the faculty when personal scandal touching their lives threatened to reflect badly on the university.

After his first wife's death, he married Kate La Montaigne in 1907. The new Mrs. Butler had enormous influence over her husband. Tyrannical and intensely possessive, she refused to allow Butler to see any member of his family, including, in later years, his daughter.

In 1925 Butler became president of the Carnegie Endowment for Peace, a position he held until December 1945. He chaired the Lake Mohank Conferences on International Arbitration and was a sponsor of the Kellogg-Briand treaty (1929), signed by the United States, France, Great Britain, Japan, Italy, Belgium, Poland, and Czechoslovakia, which condemned use of the threat of war as an instrument of international policy. For these efforts he shared the Nobel Peace Prize with Jane Addams in 1931.

Although he engaged in statesmanship, Butler was also heavily involved in politics. Staunchly Republican, even reactionary, he visited Kaiser Wilhelm in 1905 and Benito Mussolini in 1924; yet he backed U.S. support of the Allies in both World Wars. His vigorous opposition to Prohibition gained attention as well. Though not politically ambitious for himself, Butler served as an adviser and friend to several presidents. His actual political involvement was limited to a 1912 Republican nomination as vice presidential candidate, following the death of Vice President James Sherman, and an unsuccessful attempt at the Republican presidential nomination in 1920. At different times, however, Butler was offered a wide range of political posts: assured seats in the New York state assembly, the nominations for mayor of New York City and governor of New York, appointment as secretary of state, and ambassadorships. President Warren Harding offered Butler the choice of any post in his administration, but he refused them all.

What Butler craved were behind-the-scenes political influence and close friendships with men of power. He boasted of having known thirteen presidents, seven of them "very intimately." Theodore Roosevelt called Butler his "closest friend," although the friendship finally disintegrated in a bitter political disagreement over Roosevelt's handling of labor and union issues. William McKinley said of Butler, "In my opinion, the ablest politician in the United States, with a single exception, is Nicholas Murray Butler." Butler wrote many collections of political commentary, including *True and False Democracy* (1907), *Why Should We Change Our Form of Government? Studies in Practical Politics* (1912), *Scholarship and Service: The Policies and Ideals of a National University in a Modern Democracy* (1921), and *Why War? Essays and Addresses on War and Peace* (1940). For years, Butler was a fixture at the Republican National Convention, a constant visitor to the White House, and one of the most powerful yet least-known forces in American politics.

Butler's political influence waned after Harding's administration. He remained president of Columbia until October 1945, when his blindness, deafness, and old age compelled the trustees to request his resignation. Butler died at Columbia Presbyterian Hospital in New York City.

Butler is a key figure in the history of American education, a man whose legacy still exerts the hidden but far-reaching influence he always craved, chiefly in his shaping of Columbia and the university ideal, in his efforts at public school reform, and his support of college preparation through the CEEB. At Columbia he was called affectionately, but with an undertone of criticism, "Czar Nicholas." For his achievements in education, Theodore Roosevelt dubbed him "Nicholas Miraculous Butler." Undeniably, Butler loved his association with the powerful in society. On the senate floor, Robert M. La Follette lampooned him as a "bootlicker of men of fortune." Yet even if he did play the sycophant in certain circumstances, he commanded a degree of practical and moral power that few American university administrators have had the strength of character to wield.

• Butler's papers are housed in the Rare Book Room of Columbia University's Butler Library. The best and most complete biography of Butler is Albert Marrin, *Nicholas Murray Butler* (1976). For a discussion of Butler's contributions to education, especially the founding of Teachers College and his work in the public school systems, see Richard Whittemore, *Nicholas Murray Butler and Public Education* (1970). Butler's own recollections can be found in *Across the Busy Years: Recollections and Reflections* (1939–1940). An obituary is in the *New York Times*, 8 Dec. 1947.

ELIZABETH ZOE VICARY

BUTLER, Pierce (11 July 1744–15 Feb. 1822), U.S. senator and member of the Constitutional Convention of 1787, was born in County Carlow, Ireland, the son of Sir Richard Butler, a baronet and member of the Irish Parliament, and Henrietta Percy. Because Butler was third in line to inherit his father's lands and title, his parents purchased a commission in the army for him when he was eleven. By the age of fourteen he was on active duty with the Twenty-second Regiment of Foot in Canada, where in 1758 he took part in the capture of the French fortress of Louisbourg. In 1762 he transferred to the Twenty-ninth Regiment, in which he held the rank of major by 1766. Two years later, while stationed in South Carolina, he tried to elope with a fifteen-year-old heiress, but her stepfather forestalled the marriage. In 1771 Butler married Mary

Middleton, the daughter of Thomas Middleton and Mary Bull. Also an heiress, she brought extensive landholdings in the southern part of the colony near Beaufort as well as a connection with some of the leading local families. Butler and his wife had eight children, five of whom survived to adulthood.

When his regiment returned to England in 1773, Butler sold his commission and used the proceeds to buy lands in Georgia. Further purchases and grants soon made him one of the largest landholders in South Carolina, where he owned tracts in the western part of the state as well as in the coastal regions. In the 1790s he transferred most of his slaves to St. Simons Island and adjacent areas in Georgia. Naming one of his plantations "Experiment," he proved to be an innovative planter fortunate enough to have a skillful and reliable overseer. As a result, Butler's rice and long-staple cotton crops were sufficiently profitable for him to be an absentee owner. At his death, Butler's extensive holdings, which included approximately 1,000 slaves as well as properties in Pennsylvania, Tennessee, Georgia, and South Carolina, were worth well over $1 million.

Butler's public career was that of a South Carolinian. During the Revolution, he served mainly as the governor's adjutant general (1779) and in other staff positions. At the time, he maintained that illness precluded a more active role; later, at the Constitutional Convention, James Madison recorded that Butler admitted that "if he himself had been called into public life within a short time after his coming to America, his foreign habits opinions & attachments would have rendered him an improper agent in public affairs" (Farrand, vol. 2, p. 236). Evidently, the voters of South Carolina did not believe that he was too recent an arrival, for they elected him to the state legislature in 1776, and with minor intermissions he continued to serve in the general assembly until 1799. By the end of the 1780s he identified with the interests of the backcountry and favored moving the capital from Charleston to a more central location at Columbia; he also advocated more equitable representation for western districts.

In 1787 the legislature chose him as one of its delegates to the Constitutional Convention in Philadelphia. His colleagues from South Carolina, Charles Pinckney, Charles Cotesworth Pinckney, and John Rutledge, were more conspicuous and probably more influential there than Butler, but he spoke approximately seventy times. He was responsible for the suggestion that the convention keep its proceedings secret and for proposing the clause requiring states to return fugitive slaves that became Article IV, Section 3 of the Constitution. Butler also served on the committee that devised—and he claimed to have proposed—the electoral college system for electing the president. Committed to protecting the rights of states and slavery, Butler wanted wealth as well as population to serve as a basis for apportioning representation in Congress. But he also wished to avoid a "rank aristocracy" (Farrand, vol. 2, p. 202) and, after some hesitation, maintained that the government should be grounded on a broad, popular franchise. Moreover, he was willing to compromise peripheral issues for the sake of unity. After the convention had completed its work, he observed that the Constitution reflected "a pretty General Spirit of Accomodation," because members recognized that the United States was "Slighted from abroad and totering on the brink of Confusion at home" (Bell, p. 79).

Butler expected to be, and was, chosen to the Senate by the state legislature. During the first session of Congress, he supported Alexander Hamilton's proposals for the assumption of state debts and the establishment of a bank by the federal government. However, Butler objected to the Judiciary Act of 1789, which he believed infringed upon the prerogatives of the state courts by creating federal district and circuit courts. After his reelection to the Senate (5 Dec. 1792), he openly broke with the administration and vehemently opposed the Jay Treaty of 1795, which presaged better relations with England. Butler, who was pro-French, undoubtedly found the agrarian orientation of the emerging Republican party to be congenial; he may also have been reacting against his Federalist in-laws, with whom he was having personal difficulties, and may have been offended because he did not receive a diplomatic appointment for which he had hoped. Considered, but not chosen, as the Republican vice presidential running mate for Thomas Jefferson in the election of 1796, Butler resigned from the Senate on 25 October 1796. Popular approval of his opposition to the Jay Treaty encouraged him to run for the House of Representatives in 1796 and 1798, but both times he lost to Federalist party candidates. Reelected to the Senate to fill the term of a deceased colleague, Butler assumed his seat in November 1802 in time to support the Louisiana Purchase. But he opposed the Twelfth Amendment to the Constitution, which modified the electoral college system for electing the president and vice president, because, he maintained, the alterations would dilute the influence of the smaller states. He also allowed Aaron Burr, who had killed Hamilton in a duel, to spend several weeks as a fugitive on one of his plantations in Georgia. And on 21 November 1804, with less than half his term elapsed, Butler once again resigned from the Senate, ostensibly because he was disenchanted with the tenor of politics in general and the Republican party in particular, which he believed was adopting Federalist principles. Thereafter, his chief public service was as a director of the Second Bank of the United States (1816–1819). During the later part of his life, Butler resided in Philadelphia, where he died.

An irascible and impatient man, Butler alienated many individuals. His relationship with two of his children was seriously strained, and Senator William Maclay of Pennsylvania, who did not share Butler's opinions about slavery, observed in regard to the first two senators from South Carolina (Butler and Ralph

Izard), that "Pride makes Fools of them. or rather compleats What nature began" (Bowling and Veit, p. 227). Despite Butler's erratic course as a politician, he was a conspicuous figure among the postrevolutionary South Carolina elite, an active defender of slavery, and a contributing member of the Constitutional Convention.

• The South Caroliniana Library, Columbia, S.C., the Historical Society of Pennsylvania, the Library of Congress, and the British Library, London, have important collections of Butler manuscripts. Max Farrand, ed., *The Records of the Federal Convention of 1787*, rev. ed. (1966), and James H. Hutson, ed., *Supplement to Max Farrand's "The Records of the Federal Convention of 1787"* (1987), document his most significant public service. Kenneth R. Bowling and Helen E. Veit, eds., *The Diary of William Maclay and Other Notes on Senate Debates* (1988), also mentions him frequently. Useful secondary accounts include Malcolm Bell, Jr., *Major Butler's Legacy, Five Generations of a Slaveholding Family* (1987); Francis Coghlan, "Pierce Butler, 1744–1822, First Senator from South Carolina," *South Carolina Historical Magazine* 78 (1977): 104–19; Lewright B. Sikes, *The Public Life of Pierce Butler, South Carolina Statesman* (1979); and S. Sidney Ulmer, "The Role of Pierce Butler in the Constitutional Convention," *Review of Politics* 22 (1960): 361–74.

ROBERT M. WEIR

BUTLER, Pierce (17 Mar. 1866–16 Nov. 1939), lawyer and U.S. Supreme Court justice, was born in Dakota County, Minnesota, the son of Patrick Butler and Mary Gaffney, farmers. His parents were Irish immigrants who came to the United States in 1848 because of the potato famine. Butler worked during his youth on the family farm and delighted in his parents' tales of Ireland and their supposed acquaintance with General Ulysses S. Grant. He initially attended a humble one-room country school, but at the age of fifteen he enrolled in the college preparatory division of Carleton College in nearby Northfield, Minnesota.

After completing the two-year preparatory course at Carleton, Butler narrowly missed gaining admission to the U.S. Military Academy. He remained instead at Carleton, a Congregationalist school, but he did not abandon his Catholic faith. During his college years he developed a conservative political philosophy that would remain with him throughout his life. He admired individual assertiveness and the business community, and he thought government intervention caused more harm than good. Ironically, given his future accomplishments, he did poorly in logic and constitutional law.

Following his graduation from Carleton in 1887, Butler moved to St. Paul, where he clerked and read law in the firm of Pinch and Twohy. John Twohy, a partner in the firm, was especially fond of the raw, six-foot, 200-pound country boy, and he not only trained Butler in the law but also brought him into the Twohy home. At a Sunday evening dinner at the Twohys, Butler met Annie M. Cronin, the half-sister of Twohy's wife. Butler and Cronin married in 1891. They had eight children.

In 1888 Butler was admitted to the Minnesota bar and voted in his first presidential election. He backed Democrat Grover Cleveland, and despite the support he received in subsequent years from Republicans, Butler remained a Democrat throughout his life. He worked briefly (1891–1892) as an assistant county attorney and in 1892 was elected county attorney for Ramsey County. He aggressively prosecuted Ed Murphy, St. Paul's most notorious saloonkeeper. While some were surprised to see Butler take on a fellow Irishman, Catholic, and Democrat, the local Women's Christian Temperance Union praised Butler lavishly.

Butler easily won reelection as county attorney in 1894, but he decided he would rather build a career in civil practice. Over the next twenty years he worked with various partners and law firms in the St. Paul area. His best and most lucrative clients were utilities and railroads, both in the United States and in Canada. However, he resisted thinking of himself as a corporate lawyer. He loved litigation, and in the courtroom he was witty, animated, and adept at undermining hostile witnesses. While those who experienced Butler's bullying and sarcasm on the witness stand no doubt disliked him, members of Butler's chosen profession regarded his work highly and chose him to be president of the Minnesota State Bar Association in 1908. Butler, in the words of one contemporary, "was a man easy to meet, but dangerous to oppose."

In 1906 Butler ran unsuccessfully for the state senate in an overwhelmingly Republican district, losing by only twenty-three votes. The defeat seemed to sap once and for all his interest in electoral politics, but he continued to work closely with prominent political figures in both parties. He advised Minnesota governors John A. Johnson and Winfield S. Hammond, both Democrats, and in 1909 he accommodated a request from George W. Wickersham, President William H. Taft's attorney general, to bring actions against flour millers and meat packers for alleged violations, respectively, of the Pure Food and Drug Act and the Sherman Anti-Trust Act.

Beginning in 1907 and continuing until 1924, Butler also served on the Board of Regents of the University of Minnesota. In this role he was at the center of several heated controversies involving the dismissal of professors for either Socialist sympathies or pacifism during World War I. The most notable of the fired academics was professor of political science William Schaper, who considered Butler more disrespectful of academic freedom than anyone else on the board of regents.

In 1922 former president and now Chief Justice Taft recommended to President Warren Harding that Butler be nominated to fill a U.S. Supreme Court seat being vacated by Justice William R. Day. Butler had strong support from midwestern business interests as well as from Democrats, and many Catholics saw Butler as a worthy nominee for the "Catholic seat," which had been unfilled since the earlier retirement of Justice Edward White. Opposed to Butler were Senate progressives, who recalled his attacks on Professor Schaper and wondered if he possessed the proverbial "judicial temperament." Labor interests worried about Butler's frequent representation of railroads and utility companies, and even Senator-elect Henrik Shipstead opposed his fellow Minnesotan. The appointment of Judge Elbert Gary, chief of the United States Steel Corporation, Shipstead said, "would not, in our opinion, be more unfitting or improper than the appointment of Mr. Butler."

On 21 December 1922 a threatened filibuster against Butler failed to materialize, and a last-minute burst of Ku Klux Klan anti-Catholicism fell on deaf ears. The Senate, after a 3.5-hour debate in executive session, confirmed Butler as associate justice by a vote of 61 to 8, with a whopping 27 abstentions.

Butler's work on the U.S. Supreme Court was industrious and even dogged. He wrote 323 majority opinions during his seventeen years on the Court. His goal, it seems, was to speak in a neutral, objective voice. One of Butler's sons later reported that his father went over each of his opinions with a blue pencil and scratched out any statement that might be quotable. He believed strongly in precedent, observing in *Pacific Railroad Commission v. Pacific Gas & Electric* (1938), "Our decisions ought to be sufficiently definite and permanent to enable counsel usefully to advise clients. Generally speaking, at least, our decision of yesterday ought to be the law of today."

Beyond their craftsmanship, Butler's opinions were noteworthy for their conservatism, particularly but not exclusively with regard to the protection of business interests. The laissez faire philosophy he had developed at Carleton became central in his worldview, and he feared the expansion of government programs. Such programs, Butler said, would "weaken character and leave the individual man and woman without the motive or hope or inspiration necessary to freedom and morality."

Butler never wavered. He tried to slow government fixing of rates and prices in *Michigan v. Duke* (1925), interpreted the taxing power narrowly in *Panhandle Oil v. Mississippi* (1928), and deplored the impairment of contract rights in *Coolidge v. Long* (1937). A string of decisions in the 1920s supporting the "reproduction theory" for valuation of utility property exemplifies Butler's distinctive guardianship of the property rights of business interests. Unlike the competing "prudent investment theory," Butler's preferred approach allowed public utilities to invoke the current worth of their enterprises in squabbles over rates and public takings.

In the 1930s, when President Franklin Roosevelt locked horns with the conservative "Four Horsemen" of the U.S. Supreme Court, Butler clearly counted among the latter. He is credited with playing an especially important role in holding the conservative block together in the face of growing public criticism, an accomplishment that may be more significant than his judicial thought in and of itself. In constitutional cases coming before the Court, he voted against virtually every major aspect of Roosevelt's New Deal: the National Industrial Recovery Act, the Wagner Act, the Social Security Act, the Agricultural Adjustment Act, the Frazier-Lemke Act, and the Tennessee Valley Authority.

Although not as important in the overall body of his judicial work as his property decisions, Butler's opinions in other areas were also conservative. The rock-ribbed commitment to Americanism that had contributed to the Schaper witch hunt at the University of Minnesota remained strong, and Butler believed every citizen owed the nation unflinching loyalty. "Allegiance to government and protection by it are reciprocal obligations," he said, "and, stripped of all sentiment, the one is the consideration for the other; that is, allegiance for protection and protection for allegiance." Thus, while Butler opposed state sterilization of mental "defectives" and wiretapping in his dissents in *Buck v. Bell* (1927) and *Olmstead v. United States* (1928) respectively, in such cases as *Stromberg v. California* (1931) and *Near v. Minnesota* (1931) he supported government intrusion upon the civil liberties of dissenters.

This brand of patriotism was also evident in assorted citizenship and naturalization cases, most notably *Schwimmer v. United States* (1929). Rosika Schwimmer was a 49-year-old pacifist who could not in good conscience swear to bear arms for the nation. This stance, Butler said in writing for the Court's majority, made her ineligible for naturalized citizenship. In every case involving aliens, radicals, or pacifists who refused to swear unqualified allegiance, he voted against granting citizenship.

Even in the area of civil rights for African Americans Butler emerged as a voice of caution and conservatism. In 1932 he dissented from an opinion overturning the notorious conviction of seven African-American men known as the "Scottsboro Boys." He also dissented in the same year when a majority of the Court declared unconstitutional the Texas Democratic party's exclusion of African Americans from the party's primaries. The party, in Butler's opinion, functioned as a private agency and therefore was not bound by the constitutional guarantee of equal protection of the laws.

Toward the end of the 1930s, illness plagued Butler, and he was unable to participate in the 1939 session of the Court. He died in Washington, D.C. Eulogists remembered him as a self-made man, a skillful and aggressive litigator, and a meticulous, highly principled member of the nation's highest Court for more than seventeen years.

• The Butler papers have not been formally collected. However, selected papers concerning his early career are at the Minnesota Historical Society, and materials relating to his U.S. Supreme Court nomination are at the University of Washington. Francis Joseph Brown, *The Social and Economic Philosophy of Pierce Butler* (1945), examines different aspects of Butler's opinions. David J. Danelski, *A Supreme Court Justice Is Appointed* (1964), analyze his nomination and confirmation. Fred Rodell, *Nine Men: A Political History of the Supreme Court from 1790 to 1955* (1955), offers a lively commentary on Butler and the "Four Horsemen."

DAVID RAY PAPKE

BUTLER, Pierce Mason (11 Apr. 1798–20 Aug. 1847), governor of South Carolina, was born at Mount Willing in Edgefield District, South Carolina, the son of William Butler, a planter and U.S. congressman, and Behethland Foote Moore. In 1810 William Butler retired from Congress "in favor of John C. Calhoun" (Jervey, pp. 297–98), thereby helping to establish a supportive relationship between young Pierce and Calhoun. Pierce Butler was educated at Moses Waddell's academy in Abbeville and commissioned a lieutenant in the U.S. Army in 1818. He rose to the rank of captain and served at Fort Gibson in Oklahoma until 1829, when he resigned his commission and settled in Columbia with his new wife, Miranda Julia Duval of Maryland; the couple would have six children.

Butler pursued a career in banking and public affairs, eventually becoming president of the State Bank of South Carolina. Having early on been encouraged by Calhoun, Butler signed the 1832 state ordinance of nullification. Also interested in education, he served as a trustee of South Carolina College. After fighting in the Seminole War he returned to Columbia and was elected governor of the state in 1836. As governor he attempted to move away from the controversial issue of nullification and promoted social and economic measures beneficial to his state. These included public education and support for the newly proposed Louisville, Cincinnati and Charleston Railroad. Both Butler and his successor, Patrick Noble, made significant efforts to improve the free school system in South Carolina. The upshot of this was a report issued by the Reverends Stephen Elliot and James Thornwell that criticized the state public school system on the grounds that few regular reports had been issued during its almost three decades of existence and that state money spent on the system could not be correlated to the number of needy students attending free schools. The report recommended that the system be supervised by one or more salaried public officials. Unfortunately the efforts of Butler and Noble did not produce changes.

After completing his term as governor in 1838, Butler returned to Fort Gibson and served as an agent to the Cherokees until 1846, when he was forced to resign because of ill health. He was fair and just in his dealings with the Indians and harbored strong sympathies for their plight. He resumed his army service as colonel of the Palmetto regiment when the Mexican War began. Although in poor health, he traveled with his regiment from Charleston to Veracruz, where he served under General Winfield Scott in the most famous campaign of the war, the march from the coast to Mexico City. When unable to walk or ride, Butler was carried by ambulance at the head of his regiment. He continually reminded his men that "South Carolina had always claimed a character for spirit, which her enemies had denied . . . and must perish man by man sooner than justify the taunts that had been cast upon her" (Snowden, p. 625).

On 20 August at Churubusco, Butler and his regiment came under intense fire from enemy troops. Although wounded twice, he insisted on leading the assault. He was killed when a musket ball pierced his brain. A popular soldier and commander, he was mourned and eulogized by many, including his commanding officer General James Shields and the editor of the Charleston *Mercury*. The latter wrote, "[t]he death of this gallant South Carolinian will create a profound and extended sorrow in this country" (*Mercury*, 15 Sept. 1847).

Although not handsome, Butler was distinguished in appearance and made his mark in public affairs as a statesman and military hero. While his professed honor and valor can be seen as stereotypically "southern," his support for broad social and economic changes in the palmetto state made him unique among the leaders of his generation.

• There are no major collections of papers or published biographies of Pierce Mason Butler. The "Extracts from Reports . . . " that Butler wrote in 1843 and 1845 while agent to the Cherokees are located in the Yale University Library at New Haven. The Charleston *Mercury* is replete with materials on Butler, especially in September 1847. Particularly important is an obituary published on 15 Sept. 1847. For good summary accounts see Theodore Jervey, "The Butlers of South Carolina," *South Carolina Historical and Genealogical Magazine* 4 (1903): 296–311; Yates Snowden, *History of South Carolina*, vol. 2 (1920), pp. 605 and 624–27; and Miles S. Richards, "Pierce Mason Butler: The South Carolina Years 1830–1841," *Proceedings of the South Carolina Historical Association* (1985), pp. 40–56.

LEWRIGHT B. SIKES

BUTLER, Richard (1 Apr. 1743–4 Nov. 1791), soldier and government official, was born in St. Bridget's Parish, Dublin, Ireland, the son of Thomas Butler, the younger son of a baron, and Eleanor Parker. In 1748 the family immigrated to Pennsylvania and subsequently farmed in Cumberland County. During Henry Bouquet's 1764 march against the Delaware and Shawnee Indians in the Ohio country, Butler served as an ensign with the Pennsylvania troops. Some sources say that he studied law and some that he farmed as a young man, but by the beginning of the 1770s he and his brother had set themselves up in the Indian trade in western Pennsylvania and what is now southern Ohio. By middecade Richard Butler was one of the most important traders at Fort Pitt. At some point he married Mary Smith; the couple had at least three children.

After America's revolutionary government appointed commissioners to treat with the Indian nations in 1775, Butler was appointed agent for the central Indian department. In this capacity, he traveled to Delaware, Shawnee, and other settlements north and west of the Ohio River in an effort to secure their neutrality in America's conflict with Britain. The following year he entered the Continental army, appointed by Congress as a major in a Pennsylvania unit. He participated in a number of the most noted engagements of the revolutionary war and served under several famous commanders. As a lieutenant colonel in Daniel Morgan's rifle corps, he fought at the battles of Saratoga in 1777. He then rejoined George Washington's army as colonel of the Ninth Pennsylvania Regiment. With Anthony Wayne as his immediate superior, Butler led troops at Monmouth Courthouse in 1778. The following year he played a key role in Wayne's overwhelming of the British position at Stony Point, New York, commanding the column that attacked the northern flank of the Hudson River stronghold. He aided his friend Wayne in a very different way in January 1781, when he helped contain and defuse a mutiny among the Pennsylvania line. Later that year Butler's was among the units transferred to the marquis de Lafayette's army in Virginia. In June troops under Butler's command surprised British units at Spencer's Ordinary (or Spencer's Tavern). This seesaw engagement was the first clash between significant portions of Lafayette's and Charles Cornwallis's forces. Present at Yorktown, Butler then proceeded with Wayne to South Carolina to support General Nathanael Greene. He was brevetted brigadier general in 1783.

In March 1784 Congress appointed Butler as an Indian commissioner. By the treaty of peace, Britain recognized U.S. sovereignty over the Old Northwest, but no mention was made of the native peoples, whose occupancy rights to the territory north and west of the Ohio River had long been affirmed. It fell to Butler and his fellow commissioners to clarify U.S. claims with respect to the Indians. They did so aggressively, dictating terms on the assumption that, like their British allies, the Indians had been conquered. At Fort Stanwix in western New York in October 1784, Butler, Arthur Lee, and Oliver Wolcott, backed by troops, extracted from an Iroquois delegation the concession of their people's claims to territory west of Pennsylvania. At a conference at Fort McIntosh in western Pennsylvania the following January, Butler, Lee, and George Rogers Clark imposed upon Wyandot, Delaware, Ottawa, and Chippewa representatives a boundary that, in effect, excluded their people from all but the northern reaches of present-day Ohio. In 1786, in the company of Clark and Samuel H. Parsons, Butler played a crucial role in negotiations with a delegation of Shawnee at the mouth of the Great Miami River. When Shawnee leaders balked at the terms—that they acknowledge the United States as the "sole and absolute sovereign" of the territory yielded by Britain, that the Shawnee confine themselves to land allotted to them west of the Miami, and that they deliver hostages to be held until all the Americans they had taken captive were released—Butler declared that to refuse meant war and "the destruction of your women and children." The terms, he insisted, were "liberal and just; and you . . . should be thankful for the forgiveness and offers of kindness of the United States" (*Olden Time* 2, p. 524). The browbeaten Shawnee delegation acquiesced. Later in 1786 Congress appointed Butler superintendent of Indian affairs for the Northern District. Two years afterward he became a justice of the court of common pleas for Allegheny County, Pennsylvania. Resident in Pittsburgh, he was elected in 1790 to the state senate.

By the treaties Butler helped impose, Indian tribes formally ceded their claims to the portion of the northwestern frontier of most immediate interest to an expanding nation. Yet many Indians did not feel compelled to abide by agreements coerced out of delegations not entirely representative of tribal sentiment, nor did they feel obliged to tolerate white settlement beyond the Ohio. Neither was the United States necessarily well equipped to make good on its aggressive claims to the Northwest. Nothing better illustrates this than the ironic final chapter of Butler's life. In 1791, shortly after chairing a court of inquiry that cleared Josiah Harmar of responsibility for the misfortunes that had attended his expedition against Ohio Indians, Butler, now a major general, departed on another such expedition as second in command to an ailing Major General Arthur St. Clair. Charged with establishing a string of forts along what is now the Ohio-Indiana border, the operation was slow to start and plagued by inadequate supplies, poor weather, and desertion. Moreover, Butler and St. Clair quickly fell to quarreling over the method and pace of advance. On 3 November the expedition was encamped at a site about 100 miles north of the Ohio in present-day Mercer County, Ohio. When sentries reported growing numbers of Indians in the vicinity, Butler did not even pass word on to St. Clair. The next morning a force led by the Miami warrior Little Turtle that included Shawnee, Delaware, Potawatomi, Chippewa, and Ottawa surprised and overwhelmed Butler and St. Clair's troops. Badly wounded in the close fighting, Butler insisted on being left behind as the troops were put to flight. He died from a tomahawk blow to the head, one of some six hundred white soldiers killed in this greatest single defeat suffered by a U.S. military force at the hands of Native Americans. According to at least one account, Butler's heart was subsequently cut out, cut up, and eaten by the victors.

• A collection of Butler papers is in the Burton Historical Collection at the Detroit Public Library. Portions of a journal Butler kept in 1785–1786, including an account of his negotiations with the Shawnee, were printed in a nineteenth-century historical magazine edited by Neville Craig, *Olden Time* 2 (1847): pp. 433–64, 481–525, 529–31. This volume has been reprinted in book form several times. Material on Butler's treaties and on the St. Clair expedition is in *American State Papers: Military Affairs*, vol. 1 (1832) and *American State Papers: Indian Affairs*, vol. 1 (1832). For a brief sketch, see Simon Gratz, "Biography of General Richard Butler," *Pennsylvania Magazine of History and Biography* 7 (1883): pp. 7–10. For more complete discussions of various aspects of Butler's career, see Edward G. Williams, *Fort Pitt and the Revolution on the Western Frontier* (1978); Charles Stillé, *Major-General Anthony Wayne and the Pennsylvania Line in the Continental Army* (1893); Colin G. Calloway, *The American Revolution in*

Indian Country (1995); and Wiley Sword, *President Washington's Indian War: The Struggle for the Old Northwest, 1790–1795* (1985).

PATRICK G. WILLIAMS

BUTLER, Selena Sloan (4 Jan. 1872?–7 Oct. 1964), community leader and child-welfare activist, was born in Thomasville, Georgia, the daughter of Winnie Williams, a woman of African- and Native-American descent, and William Sloan, a Caucasian man who reportedly supported her and her older sister but lived apart from the family. Even after her mother died, presumably at a fairly young age, she kept quiet about her father's identity. Communication between them was minimal. At age ten, having been schooled by missionaries in Thomas County, she was admitted, on scholarship, to the Atlanta Baptist Female Seminary (now Spelman College) in Atlanta and received her high school diploma in 1888 as a member of the school's second graduating class. After graduation she taught English and elocution in the public schools in Atlanta until around 1891, when she took a position at the State Normal School in Tallahassee, Florida (now Florida Agricultural and Mechanical State University).

In 1893 she married Henry Rutherford Butler, a pediatrician from North Carolina and one of the first black physicians to establish a practice in Atlanta. Later he became a partner in one of the nation's first black-owned drugstores and the first such drugstore in Georgia. The couple had one child together. Throughout their marriage the Butlers traveled extensively within the United States and abroad. In 1894, while he took continuing medical coursework at Harvard Medical School in Cambridge, Massachusetts, she attended the Emerson School of Oratory at Martha's Vineyard in order to further her elocution skills. At the same time, she continued her work with the Atlanta Women's Club (she was a charter member) and represented it at the organizational meeting of the National Federation of Colored Women's Clubs in Boston in the late 1890s.

After returning to Atlanta in 1895, the Butlers established residence in the Old Fourth Ward, a fashionable black neighborhood near the campus of Morris Brown University (now Morris Brown College). That same year the board of education asked Butler to run a pioneering night school for black adults held at the Yonge Street School. She also established, edited, and published the *Woman's Advocate*, a monthly newspaper focused on the interests of black American women. In the early 1900s, unable to find a kindergarten class that would admit her son, Henry Jr., because of his race, Butler established a kindergarten in the basement of her home that the neighborhood children also attended. In 1911, after these youngsters were in elementary school, Butler founded the nation's first black parent-teacher association. About eight years later it developed into the statewide Georgia Colored Parent-Teacher Association (GCPTA), later named the Georgia Conference of Colored Parents and Teachers. Continuing her efforts on behalf of the education of black children, in 1926 Butler established and became founding president of the National Congress of Colored Parents and Teachers, which would merge with the white national PTA in 1970. At that time she was designated as a national founder, along with Alice McLellan Birney and Phoebe Hearst, who had founded the previously all-white national PTA.

Butler's role in black community affairs extended well beyond education. An active clubwoman, she served as a delegate to the founding convention of the National Association of Colored Women in Boston in 1896 and as the first president of the Georgia Federation of Colored Women's Clubs. Interested in promoting better relations between blacks and whites, she as well as her husband was a member of the Georgia Commission on Interracial Cooperation, founded in Atlanta in 1919. At the end of World War I, Butler was honored by the American Red Cross for her help in entertaining black enlistees at Camp Gordon near Atlanta and for leading the Atlanta office's sale and distribution of war savings stamps and certificates. Butler became an organizer of the Ruth Chapter of the Order of the Eastern Star in Atlanta and was grand lecturer of the lodge in Georgia. In 1930 she joined a group of white and black southern women in forming the Southern Women for the Prevention of Lynching. In 1943 this group was absorbed into the Southern Regional Council along with the Georgia Commission on Interracial Cooperation. Butler's influence was also felt nationally. Sometime in 1930–1931 President Herbert Hoover asked her to serve on his White House Conference on Child Welfare and Protection as a representative of the National Congress of Colored Parents and Teachers. In this capacity she served on the Infant and Pre-school Child Committee, whose work contributed to the writing of the memorable "Children's Charter."

A few years after her husband's death in 1931, Butler sojourned in Europe with her son, by then a graduate of Harvard Medical School. During her stay in London, Butler worked with the Nursery School Association headed by the duke of Gloucester and also assisted Lady Astor Washead's cancer association campaign. After U.S. entry into World War II, Butler followed her son to Fort Huachuca in Arizona, where he underwent officer training. While there she organized a Gray Lady Corps and again worked with the American Red Cross. She returned to Atlanta in 1947 and later followed her son and daughter-in-law to Los Angeles, where Henry Butler, Jr., was working as the first black physician on the staff of Good Samaritan Hospital. Active in the Congregational church, Butler served on the boards of the Sojourner Truth Home and of Las Madrinas, the mothers' organization of Alpha Kappa Alpha sorority. She died in Los Angeles and was buried next to her husband in Oakland Cemetery in Atlanta.

Butler played an important role in the development of interracial efforts on behalf of the welfare and education of children and as a leader and mentor within the black community. Her work with the Georgia Colored PTA forged a successful link with its white national counterpart, and she was unusually successful at achieving communication between the two groups at the local level. Her efforts to improve civic mindedness within the black community made her an important figure in national as well as African-American history.

• Biographical files and two important historical booklets are kept in the archives at the Robert W. Woodruff Library within Atlanta University Center: Narvie J. Harris, *Golden Anniversary History: Pioneering, Programming, Planning & Projecting* (1970) and *Founder: Georgia Congress Colored Parents and Teachers* (1971), the latter of which contains copies of letters to and from Butler. Butler's speech, "The Chain-Gang System," read before the National Association of Colored Women at Nashville, Tenn., on 16 Sept. 1897, is also an important source. Useful secondary sources include Florence Matilda Read, *The Story of Spelman College* (1961); GCCPT, *History of the Georgia Congress of Colored Parents and Teachers* (1970); and Charles Harris Wesley, *The History of the National Association of Colored Women's Clubs* (1984). Obituaries and memorial articles are in the *Atlanta Daily World*, 8 Oct. 1964, and the *Atlanta Journal and Constitution*, 7–9 Oct. 1964.

MICHELLE M. STRAZER

BUTLER, Smedley Darlington (30 July 1881–21 June 1940), U.S. Marine Corps major general, was born in West Chester, Pennsylvania, the son of Thomas Butler and Maud Darlington, both respected Quakers. His father was a lawyer, judge, and later a powerful member of Congress who served as chairman of the House Naval Affairs Committee in the 1920s. Educated in local Quaker schools, Smedley Butler dropped out when the United States went to war with Spain in 1898. As he was only sixteen years old, Butler lied about his age to secure a second lieutenant's commission in the marines. He thus began a storied career of more than thirty years, during which he would win two Congressional Medals of Honor and earn the sobriquet "Old Gimlet Eye" for his steely eyed glare.

Although Butler always paid dues to his Quaker sect, he never abided by its pacifist tenets. At five feet, four inches tall, weighing approximately 140 pounds, he was a fighting marine and proud of it. In the Boxer Relief Expedition to China in 1900, he was wounded twice, cited for bravery, and promoted to the brevet rank of captain. In 1905 he married Ethel Conway Peters; they had three children. In an era when the marines could be compared to an elite light infantry force, he subsequently participated in interventions in Honduras (1903), the Philippines (1905–1907), Nicaragua (1912), Panama (1913), and Mexico (1914). In 1915 Major Butler fought in Haiti to suppress the elusive "cacos," who were, depending on one's point of view, either bandits or insurrectionists. It was Butler who reduced the supposedly impregnable caco fortress of Fort Rivière. When the smoke of battle cleared, fifty-one cacos lay dead, and the back of the Haitian resistance was broken. In 1916 Butler created and led a national police force, the Gendarmerie d'Haiti, at the rank of a Haitian major general.

Butler was an aggressive troop commander and a stern disciplinarian, but as he always led from the front, his men loved him. Over and over again his offensive élan won the day. He and his marines fought wherever they were sent by the State Department to protect American citizens and property. While Butler was always wise enough to understand that this often amounted to protecting American business interests, he loved the campaigning, often working himself to near collapse.

For his excellent command of a giant American camp in Brest, France, during the First World War, Butler was awarded the Distinguished Service Medal of both the army and the navy and was promoted to the rank of brigadier general at the age of thirty-seven. He always regretted, however, that he had not been given a combat command, which he blamed on the army's prejudice against the Marine Corps and on personal enemies within the marine bureaucracy.

Butler commanded the marine base at Quantico, Virginia, between 1920 and 1924 before securing a leave of absence from the corps to become the director of public safety for the city of Philadelphia. In that capacity he waged a very colorful war against crime, corruption, and bootlegging, and his national popularity grew apace. He soon realized these scourges could never be fully eradicated, and as his frustrations accumulated, so too did his critics. At the end of 1925 Butler's vigorous and honest enforcement of laws had become too much for the city's politicians and police, and Philadelphia's mayor forced Butler to resign and return to active duty.

Commanding the Marine Expeditionary Force in China between 1927 and 1929, Butler demonstrated the sensitive skills of a diplomat. He cleverly parlayed among various nationalist generals and war lords in order to protect American lives and property and ultimately won the public acclaim of contending Chinese leaders. He battled simultaneously to keep his marines fit and ready against the twin enemies of prostitution and alcoholism. In the end he succeeded at both tasks. In formal competition marching and marksmanship, his men bested the vaunted British Coldstream Guards.

Butler returned to Quantico in 1929. In this two stints as base commander, Butler might very well have won his most important battle, helping to preserve the Marine Corps' existence against critics in the army and the Congress who during postwar budget fights argued that the army could do the work of the marines. He directed the camp's growth until it became the "showplace" of the corps. He also set about vigorously to keep the marines in the public limelight. His Quantico Marines football team in four years amassed a record of 38–2–2 against powerful service teams as well as civilian schools, and bulldog mascot "Sergeant Major Jiggs" became a national symbol of marine tenacity and aggressiveness. Butler also won national attention by taking thousands of his men on long field marches, many of which he led from the front, to Gettysburg and other Civil War battle sites, where they conducted large-scale reenactments before crowds of often distinguished spectators.

For all his good works, Butler's last years as a marine were not happy ones. Throughout his career he had always been critical, often harshly, of the "bookish" officers who won promotion through staff work and "politicking" at the expense of the marines in far-off places who, like Butler, were too busy fighting to go to service schools and war colleges. He bitterly resented the elitism of the "Annapolis crowd," who in turn disliked his outspokenness. Despite Butler's seniority, the "admirals without ships" blocked his appointment as Marine Corps commandant. Major General Butler resigned his commission on 1 October 1931.

In his remaining years, Butler became a popular lecturer who, protesting the possibility that he was fighting for American oil interests in China and the fruit industry and bankers in Central America, damned capitalist profiteers and warmongers while advocating American isolationism and prohibition. He caused a stir by claiming that a businessman had tried to get him to lead a Fascist group, an offer he stoutly refused. In 1935 Butler published what he hoped would be an embarrassing memoir, *War Is a Racket*. His activities did not endear him to his many former colleagues, but none ever questioned his sincerity or his patriotism. Butler died of cancer in Philadelphia. Always colorful and perhaps eccentric, Butler was a marine's marine.

• Butler's personal papers and other memorabilia are in Newton Square, Pa., and the Marine Corps Oral History Collection at the U.S. Marine Corps Historical Center in Washington, D.C. Lowell Thomas wrote the first study of General Butler, *Old Gimlet Eye*, in 1933. While still interesting, it is neither scholarly nor unbiased. Many valuable references are in Allen R. Millett, *Semper Fidelis: The History of the United States Marine Corps* (1980). Also Hans Schmidt, *Maverick Marine, General Smedley D. Butler and the Contradictions of American Military History* (1987), is valuable even if too speculative.

J. DAVID VALAIK

BUTLER, Walter (1752–30 Oct. 1781), Loyalist officer, was born in Butlersbury (now Fonda, N.Y.), the son of John Butler, a British Indian Department officer and interpreter, Catharine Bratt. Butler's childhood years were spent in the Mohawk Valley of Upper New York. As a member of a prominent family in an age of profit and preferment during the Johnson regime, he enjoyed status and privilege. His father was closely connected to the omnipotent Sir William Johnson, both as an officer among the Indians and as an interpreter at councils. Butler was sent to Albany to study law, being admitted to the bar in 1775, but his true interest was the military. As early as 1768, he was appointed ensign in the county militia; he seemed to thrive in a regimental environment. With the outbreak of the rebellion and civil war in colonial America, both Butler and his father, loyal to the king, fled to Montreal, while the remainder of the Butler family were interned at Albany.

In the early autumn of 1775 Butler assisted in the capture of the rebel Ethan Allen, who was on a mission to seek the neutrality of the Seven Nations of Canada, at Longue-Pointe, near Montreal. He then visited England, returning as an ensign in the Eighth Regiment of Foot (the King's Liverpool Regiment) to participate in the British-Indian victory over the colonial rebels at the battle of Les Cèdres in May 1776. The battle hastened the American retreat from Montreal and ended any further invasion threats to Canada from the forces of the Continental Congress.

In the summer of 1777 Butler, now a lieutenant in the Eighth Regiment of Foot, accompanied a strong contingent of British regulars, refugee Loyalists, and about 800 Indian allies, mostly Seneca, Mohawk, and others from the lower lakes, to the rebel stronghold at Fort Stanwix (now Rome, N.Y). This return to the Mohawk Valley, where most of these loyal Americans had recently lived and farmed, was intended to expel the colonial rebels from their dominant position in the region and restore the authority of the king. The expeditionary force besieged the fort, but news was soon received that a rebel column was advancing to relieve the place. At Oriskany on 6 August, about six miles to the east of the fort, the rebel column was surprised and severely mauled as it attempted to cross a thick marsh in the bottom of a deep ravine. The battle continued for a considerable time after the first shock of volley fire from the Crown forces hidden in the surrounding thickets. Only a heavy rainstorm forced the combatants to discontinue for a time the fierce and bloody fighting, much of it hand-to-hand and of an internecine nature and between former friends and neighbors. The rebel casualties were staggeringly high, with estimates of between 200 and 500 killed. Yet the victory was bittersweet for the king's forces and especially for the Indian allies, who lost thirty-three men—many of them prominent Seneca chiefs or warriors, which left their people in a seething rage and vowing revenge. Following the battle, the expeditionary force lifted the siege and returned to Canada.

The battle of Oriskany was one of the most bloody and intense engagements of the entire war, and it resulted in a mutual desire between Loyalists and rebels to fight with a determined passion for control of the Mohawk Valley. This bitter civil war would last for the next four years and more.

Immediately after Oriskany, Butler and a small party under a flag of truce foolishly attempted to recruit in the area for the Crown. He was soon captured, tried by court-martial, and sentenced to be hanged as a spy. Through the help of some of his old friends from his law school days, who were now serving in the Continental army, Butler managed an escape and eventually made his way safely to the British and Loyalist base of Fort Niagara. In September 1777, while Butler was still imprisoned, "beating orders" were given to his father to raise and command a Loyalist provincial corps to consist of eight companies (eventually expanded to ten), of which two companies would be composed of men speaking "the Indian language and acquainted with their customs and manners of making war." The ranks of the other companies were to be filled with men familiar with the forest and able to endure excessive fatigue. This corps—Butler's Rangers—was a highly paid, well-trained, and special unit. Although initially ordered to arm and clothe themselves at their own expense, the corps eventually adopted a standard uniform of dark green coats faced red and small black leather caps. Many of the Rangers retained buckskin leggings and moccasins. The Rangers fought in the Indian manner and often charged while giving the "Indian yell." The strategic military call of Butler's Rangers was to act in concert with the Indian allies in conformity with British Indian policy for the war, which was fixed firmly on the objective "to worry the enemy" and to destroy "their Fields of Corn and Cattle; all their Bridges, ferry Boats or others and Mills . . . rendering the Fordable places impassable . . . [through] incessant incursions into all frontiers."

From the autumn of 1778 until his death, Walter Butler served as captain in Butler's Rangers. During the summer of 1778, while Butler was in Quebec City to regain his health and to apply for arms and clothing for the Rangers, his father led a mixed force of Rangers and Indians to Wyoming Valley (near Wilkes-Barre, Pa.). There they won a smashing victory on 3 July over the colonial rebels at Forty Fort, following which several forts were burned, crop fields destroyed, and the livestock removed to feed the expedition. In early November Walter Butler, now back at Fort Niagara, was given his first major command with instructions to harass the rebel back settlements. At Cherry Valley, New York, south of the Mohawk River, on 11 November, 200 Rangers and a detachment of British regulars complemented by about 600 Indian allies, mostly Seneca, struck the fort and the village. As the Rangers and Regulars besieged the fort, the Seneca and some others drifted away and attacked the village and nearby farms, burning houses and slaughtering thirty-one civilians, mostly women and children. The Seneca were apparently motivated by revenge for the losses they had suffered the previous year at Oriskany. Young Butler had clearly lost control of his command. His authority was ignored by the Indian allies, who had little respect for the inexperienced and rather too self-confident Loyalist officer. At the same time, Butler was helpless in attempting initially to stop the killings, as he was faced with some formidable and stubborn defenders—who no doubt would have made a sortie from the fort if the Rangers had withdrawn at that moment to restore order in the village.

The events of 11 November haunted Butler, who nonetheless vigorously and indignantly insisted in written reports that the human tragedy of that day was not his fault and went well beyond his personal control. After spending the winter at Fort Niagara, Butler participated throughout the summer of 1779 in combating the rebel expedition under John Sullivan, which ravaged and destroyed the "castles" and cornfields throughout Iroquoia and disrupted the unity of the Confederacy. This campaign left Butler quite unwell, and he was sent to Montreal to recuperate. He spent several months there, enjoying the social life and rejoicing at the arranged release and reunion of the Butler family in 1780. Upon returning to Fort Niagara, he was ordered to lead a detachment of Rangers and Indians to Oswego and link with the Ross Expedition, which was destined to attack throughout the Mohawk Valley. This October 1781 raiding excursion was only a partial success, as some farms were destroyed, a village was burned, and a hard fought but indecisive battle was waged near Johnston, New York. Following this latter engagement, Ross began a retreat to the British base at Carleton Island on the southeast shore of Lake Ontario. At West Canada Creek, a small tributary running north from the Mohawk River, while covering the retreat, Butler was mortally wounded on 30 October, being struck in the head by a musket ball. Either dead or dying, he was purportedly scalped by an Oneida serving with the colonial rebels.

In the United States, Butler has been vilified in several books and novels, with particular attention being paid to his role in the Cherry Valley massacre. This character assassination was even developed in a Hollywood movie, *Drums along the Mohawk* (1939), in which he was portrayed as practically the devil incarnate. Yet in Canada, Butler is viewed as a dedicated and active young Loyalist officer who served and died in the defense of the Crown and the unity of the empire. These contrasting views or interpretations symbolize the stark differences in the nature and development of the national characteristics and evolution of these two separate and sovereign nations in North America.

• The Public Record Office (London) contains the War Office Papers 28, vols. 1–10, which provide detailed correspondence of the activities and campaigns of Butler's Rangers. Other published works include E. A. Cruikshank, *Butler's Rangers* (1893; repr. 1975); Mary Beacock Fryer, *King's Men* (1980); and Barbara Graymont, *The Iroquois in the American Revolution* (1972), which offers a solid scholarly analysis of the Six Nations Confederacy of Iroquois, who were closely associated with Butler's Rangers during the American colonial rebellion. A muster roll with comments of all ten companies of the Rangers has been compiled by M. R. Fryer and William A. Smy, *Rolls of the Provincial (Loyalist) Corps, Canadian Command: American Revolutionary Period* (1981). Other sources include H. C. Mathews, *The Mark of Honour* (1965); Howard Swiggett, *War out of Niagara: Walter Butler and the Tory Rangers* (1933); and William Kinby, *Annals of Niagara* (1896). Both of the latter should be read with caution.

ROBERT ALLEN

BUTLER, William (17 Dec. 1759–23 Sept. 1821), revolutionary war soldier and congressman, was born in Prince William County, Virginia, the son of James Butler and Mary Simpson, farmers. He attended grammar schools in his early years, and when he was about twelve years old his family moved to Ninety Six

District, in western South Carolina. At the outbreak of the American Revolution in 1775, although he was only fifteen, he declared for the rebels and joined the South Carolina militia. Late that fall he accompanied Colonel Richard Richardson on a campaign into the backcountry of South Carolina to disperse a powerful concentration of Loyalists under the leadership of Patrick Cuningham. On 22 December he took part in a battle against Cuningham's forces at Great Canebrake on Reedy Creek, in which the Loyalists were dispersed. Because heavy snow fell during the last days of this operation, it came to be known as the "Snow Campaign." From July to September 1776 he served in Major Andrew Williamson's campaign against the Cherokee Indians in the uplands of North Carolina and South Carolina. Primarily, his orders were the same as the rest of Williamson's army: to march through difficult terrain and to destroy Cherokee towns and crops.

In 1779 Butler joined the cavalry forces of Count Casimir Pulaski, commonly known as Pulaski's Legion, with the rank of lieutenant. On 20 June he fought in the savage battle of Stono, where Major General Benjamin Lincoln's army attacked a British rear guard protecting General Augustine Prevost's retreat toward Charleston. In the battle, Butler was with the legion as it charged the enemy's position in order to cover a tactical retreat by Lincoln; it finally forced the British to abandon the field. He also was with Pulaski at the siege of Savannah, Georgia, in the fall of 1779, and he saw Pulaski fall to British gunfire on 9 October, when Pulaski valiantly but vainly led a cavalry charge on enemy positions. Butler joined the command of Brigadier General Andrew Pickens in the spring of 1780 and took part in the successful siege of Augusta, Georgia, from 19 May to 5 June of that year. In 1781 he served for a time under General William Henderson with the rank of captain, and in 1782 he rejoined General Pickens as a captain of Mounted Rangers. By that time he nursed a towering hatred for William "Bloody Bill" Cuningham and his Loyalist followers; in 1781 Butler's father and a younger brother James had been killed by these troops after they had surrendered in the battle of Cloud's Creek. Therefore, Butler was delighted when in May 1782 he caught Cuningham's force unawares near Lorick's Ferry on the lower Saluda River and destroyed it as a fighting unit. During the fight Butler chased Cuningham on horseback, ineffectually firing two pistols at him. Cuningham lost an expensive sword, which was ripped from his side by underbrush. Butler retrieved the sword and wore it for the remainder of his military career, but he was distressed that Cuningham escaped to Florida. Cuningham was later rewarded by the British with a military pension.

At the war's end in 1783, Butler returned to his home in Edgefield County, South Carolina, on the Saluda River near Mount Willing and indulged his fondness for fine horses. In 1784 he married Behethland Foote Moore, with whom he had eight children. An imposing and handsome man possessed of an impressive war record, he soon became active in politics. In 1787 he was elected to the state house of representatives and served there until 1795, ardently arguing against any suggestion of leniency for former Loyalists. He was a member of the state convention that adopted the Federal Constitution in 1788, although he opposed it from the start and voted against it. In 1791 he was chosen by his neighbors to serve as sheriff of the Ninety Six District. Continuing his interest in things military, he was elected brigadier general of the state militia in 1794, and two years later he was promoted to major general. He ran for Congress in 1796 as an Antifederalist but was overwhelmingly defeated by the Federalist candidate, R. G. Harper. Four years later, when Harper chose not to run again, Butler was elected to Congress and served six terms. As a congressman, he consistently supported all proslavery measures and the embargo of President Thomas Jefferson. During the War of 1812, as major general of South Carolina militia, Butler commanded all troops raised for the state's defense but was never compelled to take the field. Retiring from Congress on 3 March 1813, he lived quietly for the remainder of his days on his Saluda River plantation, where he died.

• The best source on Butler's life is written largely by his son, Andrew P. Butler: *Memoirs of General William Butler: Including a Brief Sketch of His Father and Brother, Who Fell in the Revolution, at Cloud's Creek, Lexington District, S.C.*, ed. Thomas P. Slider (1885). His military ranks in the revolutionary war are outlined in Francis B. Heitman, *Historical Register of Officers of the Continental Army during the War of the Revolution, April, 1775, to December, 1783* (1914). Sketches of his life are in Alexander Garden, *Anecdotes of the Revolutionary War in America, with Sketches of Character of Persons the Most Distinguished in the Southern States . . .* (1822); and Joseph Johnson, *Traditions and Reminiscences Chiefly of the American Revolution in the South* (1851). Useful background on the war in the South is in Edward McCrady, *The History of South Carolina in the Revolution, 1775–1780* (1901); Henry Lumpkin, *From Savannah to Yorktown: The American Revolution in the South* (1981); and John S. Pancake, *This Destructive War: The British Campaign in the Carolinas, 1780–1782* (1985).

PAUL DAVID NELSON

BUTTERFIELD, Billy (14 Jan. 1917–18 Mar. 1988), jazz trumpeter, was born Charles William Butterfield in Middleton, Ohio. His parents' names are unknown. He studied privately with cornetist Frank Simons in his youth. At Transylvania College in Lexington, Kentucky, his intended medical studies gave way to work with dance bands. He soon quit school to join Andy Anderson's local band. While playing with Anderson's band in 1936, he was heard by bandleader Bob Crosby and his bassist, Bob Haggart. Butterfield was playing in Pittsburgh, Pennsylvania, in September 1937 with Austin Wylie's band when he was hired to join Crosby's big band. With Crosby's band he toured coast to coast, but also held a long residency (beginning in March 1938) at the Blackhawk restaurant in Chicago, Illinois, and made recordings, most notably of Haggart's ballad "I'm Free" (Oct. 1938), which was subsequently retitled and popularized as "What's New."

Butterfield grew tired of being away from his wife, Dorothy ("Dottie"), and their new child. (Butterfield eventually had three more children.) He left Crosby's band in June 1940 to stay in Chicago. But the little-known band of Bob Strong ended up touring anyway, and by September 1940 Butterfield had joined Artie Shaw. On recordings from that month he was featured with the big band on "Stardust," a popular hit, and with Shaw's Gramercy Five on "Special Delivery Stomp."

Butterfield left Shaw in March 1941 to join Benny Goodman's big band, with which he recorded "Something New" in May. He remained with Goodman until late November. Although he would work with Goodman occasionally over the next twenty-six years, none of these reunions were significant, apart from a fine little studio session with Goodman as a fellow sideman under the leadership of pianist Mel Powell in February 1942 and a performance at the Newport Jazz Festival in 1958.

Early in 1942 Butterfield joined the big band of Les Brown, to which he contributed solos on "Sunday" and "Out of Nowhere." This affiliation overlapped with work in television studio bands, initially for NBC and CBS, from 1942 until 1944. In 1944 he was drafted into the U.S. Army. After infantry training, he served until 1945 in what was, by his own account, a mediocre military band.

From 1946 to 1947 Butterfield led his own big band, which was unsuccessful and left him deeply in debt. He began working in the ABC television studios, playing for part of this time in an orchestra under Paul Whiteman's direction. To help recover his losses and for enjoyment's sake, he concurrently played jazz in New York City nightclubs, mainly at Nick's, but also at Eddie Condon's and Jimmy Ryan's. During these years he arrived at an informal agreement with cornetist Bobby Hackett, whereby one could be temporarily away from ABC for jazz jobs as long as the other stayed available for the studio. Among Butterfield's recordings from this decade of studio work are the trumpet background to Louis Armstrong's vocal on "Blueberry Hill" (1949); several sessions with Condon's groups, including *Jammin' at Condon's* (1954) and *The Roaring Twenties* (1957); and an ad hoc all-star album released as *Session at Riverside* (1956).

By the late 1950s, opportunities for work in New York City had diminished significantly for a musician of Butterfield's ilk. He led bands in Maryland, in Richmond, Virginia, and in Atlanta, Georgia, where he founded a touring band in which his wife sang. In the mid-1960s he and his family settled permanently in Fort Lauderdale. He was reunited with some of Crosby's sidemen in the World's Greatest Jazz Band of Yank Lawson and Bob Haggart, in which he played trumpet and flugelhorn steadily from 1968 to 1972 and thereafter a few times annually for tours, including 1974 performances in Europe. The band's recordings included the album *Live at the Roosevelt Grill* (1970). Butterfield often worked with tenor saxophonist Flip Phillips in the 1970s. As international jazz festivals grew in popularity, he regularly toured Europe during the 1970s and into the 1980s, also performing in South Africa. He died in North Palm Beach, Florida.

In the typically energetic context of hybrid swing-and-dixie jazz bands, Butterfield was a perfectly accomplished but unexceptional trumpeter. When paired with a fiery cornetist or trumpeter such as Wild Bill Davison (with Condon) or Lawson, the other musician would take the lead, and Butterfield would serve in a subsidiary role. His high reputation rests on the uncommon beauty of his ballad playing, of which Shaw's "Stardust" is probably the finest example.

• The principal biographical essay on Butterfield is in John Chilton, *Stomp Off, Let's Go!: The Story of Bob Crosby's Bob Cats & Big Band* (1983). Interviews are by Les Tomkins, "The Billy Butterfield Story," *Crescendo International* 13 (Dec. 1974): 6–7; Steve Voce, "I Can Hit as High as I Ever Did," *Melody Maker* 49 (2 Nov. 1974): 60; and Alan Littlejohn, "Billy Butterfield," *Jazz Journal International* 38 (Feb. 1985): 16–18. Information about Butterfield also appears in Albert McCarthy, *Big Band Jazz* (1974); George T. Simon, *The Big Bands*, 4th ed. (1981), p. 468; D. Russell Connor, *Benny Goodman: Listen to His Legacy* (1988); and Gunther Schuller, *The Swing Era: The Development of Jazz, 1930–1945* (1989). An obituary is in the *New York Times*, 19 Mar. 1988.

BARRY KERNFELD

BUTTERFIELD, Daniel (31 Oct. 1831–17 July 1901), soldier and businessman, was born in Utica, New York, the son of John Butterfield, a businessman, and Malinda Harriet Baker. From his father, president of the Overland Mail and partner in the American Express Company, Butterfield acquired an interest in organizing and administering business corporations. He attended private academies before graduating at eighteen from Union College. Following a brief attempt to study law, he traveled extensively in the South, where he foresaw sectional conflict. In 1857 he married Elizabeth (full name unknown); they had no children. She died in 1877.

Moving to New York City in 1850 or 1851, Butterfield entered the family business as superintendent of the eastern division of American Express. In his spare hours, he became involved in New York militia affairs; by the outbreak of the Civil War he was colonel of the Twelfth New York State National Guard. In April 1861 he offered his regiment to Republican governor Edwin D. Morgan, but Morgan declined to accept it until Secretary of State William H. Seward, father of one of Butterfield's classmates, intervened in the colonel's behalf.

Butterfield recruited the Twelfth New York to proper strength in a matter of days. Late in April he led the outfit to the defense of the U.S. capital, where it was mustered into Federal service for a term of ninety days. On 24 May, only hours after a state referendum ratified Virginia's ordinance of secession, the

Twelfth became the first regiment to cross the Potomac, spearheading a column that occupied Alexandria.

Shortly after his regiment's term of service ended in early August, Butterfield was nominated brigadier general of volunteers and received command of a V Corps brigade in Major General George B. McClellan's Army of the Potomac. Despite his lack of field experience, the new brigadier performed gallantly during the Peninsula campaign. On 27 June 1862, at Gaines's Mill, Butterfield rescued the colors of an embattled regiment and led the outfit in a counterattack. His heroics gained him a painful wound but also a Medal of Honor, awarded thirty years after the deed. At Malvern Hill, 1 July, Butterfield's brigade guarded McClellan's rear during his retreat to the James River.

While the army nursed its wounds at Harrison's Landing, Butterfield spent his off-hours composing bugle calls. His most famous effort occurred when he revised a lights out call that had appeared in military manuals as early as 1835, lengthening and reemphasizing some of its notes. When his brigade bugler substituted the revised call, it became an immediate favorite in the army; later it was adopted by other Union and Confederate commands as well. Although not an original composition, "Butterfield's Lullaby" has come down through history as "Taps," the haunting melody that beckons soldiers, living and dead, to their rest.

From the James, Butterfield's brigade was transferred to northern Virginia, where, on 30 August, it launched a costly and ineffective attack against the Confederate left flank at Second Manassas (Bull Run). Illness kept Butterfield out of action at Antietam, although he recovered to lead a V Corps division, then the corps itself. By November he was a major general of volunteers. One headquarters observer declared that staunch Republican Butterfield had been promoted "faster than almost any other civilian who has not been an avowed political appointment."

At Fredericksburg, 13 December, Butterfield's corps suffered 2,440 casualties attacking impregnable enemy positions. In the aftermath of the fiasco, he reverted to divisional command, a demotion he ascribed to army politics. Partly as a result, in January 1863 he left the field to serve as chief of staff to Major General Joseph Hooker, the new army leader. Butterfield forged an uneven record as a staff officer. He handled paperwork efficiently and devised a system of corps badges (based on an idea by Major General Philip Kearny) that helped raise morale throughout the army. On many occasions he also made himself obnoxious to Hooker's subordinates, winning the nickname "Little Napoleon." Some observers considered him a bad influence on Hooker, who had a weakness for women and alcohol. The commander of Hooker's escort claimed that, owing partly to Butterfield, "the headquarters of the Army of the Potomac was a place to which no self respecting man liked to go and no decent woman could. It was a combination of bar-room and brothel."

During the Chancellorsville campaign, Butterfield tried with limited success to coordinate operations between two wings of Hooker's army. After the Union defeat cost Hooker his job, Butterfield stayed on to serve Major General George Gordon Meade during the battle of Gettysburg. Butterfield played a prominent role in framing the agenda of a council of war at Meade's headquarters on 2 July, at which the army's senior leaders voted to fight at Gettysburg for a crucial third day.

In later months, Butterfield precipitated a long-lived controversy by claiming that Meade had ordered him to draw up a plan to retreat from Gettysburg, which the army leader intended to implement even after the battle began. While conceding that he may have empowered the staff officer to plan a fallback as a contingency option, Meade denied to a congressional committee that he had intended to quit the field once the fighting started. Most historians have accepted Meade's word, regarding Butterfield's accusation as the result of a genuine misunderstanding or as a deliberate falsehood prompted by personal animosity (Meade had deposed Butterfield in command of the V Corps after Fredericksburg). In any case, when the chief of staff left the army on 3 July after taking a minor wound, Meade replaced him, quickly and permanently.

When Hooker was reinstated to field command and sent west in September 1863, the recently recovered Butterfield accompanied him to his new station. Butterfield's experience in transportation management enabled him to plan the transfer of Hooker's XI and XII Corps from Virginia to Tennessee, one of the most complex logistical undertakings of the war. In the West, Butterfield served as Hooker's chief of staff throughout the Chattanooga campaign before returning to field service in April 1864 as commander of the Third Division, XX Corps, Army of the Cumberland. Butterfield saw action during much of the Atlanta campaign before dysentery forced him to take sick leave. After recovering at his summer home at Cold Spring, New York, he was limited to court-martial duty and special assignments for the War Department.

In July 1863 Butterfield had gained a plum appointment as colonel of the Fifth U.S. Infantry. In January 1866 he was tendered command of installations in New York Harbor as well as the superintendency of the General Recruiting Service of the U.S. Army. In March 1870 Butterfield resigned his commission to become director of the U.S. Subtreasury in New York City. In later years he was involved in railroad construction, real estate, and banking. He ran unsuccessfully for Congress in 1892, traveled, wrote articles on history, and helped plan and supervise numerous military and civilian celebrations. He died at Cold Spring, survived by his second wife, Julia Lorrilard James, but no children.

Butterfield's rapid rise in the volunteer service and his regular army appointments cannot be reconciled with his limited talent as a field commander. Family prominence, high rank in the militia, and political connections appear to have been responsible. His managerial and organizational talents served him well as a staff officer, although his officiousness and his sometimes abrasive personality weakened his usefulness as a liaison between army headquarters and subordinate commanders. Despite his prominent position in the Union hierarchy, despite serving in important campaigns in the two major theaters of operations, and despite winning a Medal of Honor, he is remembered chiefly—but inaccurately—as the composer of "Taps."

• Some of Butterfield's wartime and postwar correspondence can be found in the Lucia Chauncey Porter Papers in the U.S. Military Academy Library. His campaign reports form part of *The War of the Rebellion: A Compilation of the Official Records of the Union and Confederate Armies* (128 vols., 1880–1901). The most comprehensive source of biographical information is Julia Lorrilard Butterfield, ed., *A Biographical Memorial of General Daniel Butterfield* (1904). His role as chief of staff to Generals Hooker and Meade is covered in Joseph Hebert, *"Fighting Joe" Hooker* (1944), and Freeman Cleaves, *Meade of Gettysburg* (1960). The Meade-Butterfield controversy is examined in Edwin B. Coddington, *The Gettysburg Campaign: A Study in Command* (1968), and Harry W. Pfanz, *Gettysburg: The Second Day* (1987). Contemporary assessments of Butterfield appear in Allan Nevins, ed., *A Diary of Battle: The Personal Journals of Colonel Charles S. Wainwright, 1861–1865* (1962), and David S. Sparks, ed., *Inside Lincoln's Army: The Diary of Marsena Rudolph Patrick, Provost Marshal General, Army of the Potomac* (1964). A more sympathetic portrait emerges in the wartime correspondence of Butterfield's brigade bugler, Oliver Willcox Norton, *War Letters, 1861–1865* (1903). A good account of what occurred at Berkeley Hundred in the summer of 1862 is Russell Booth, "Butterfield and 'Taps'," *Civil War Times Illustrated* 16 (Dec. 1977): 35–39. An obituary is in the *New York Times*, 18 July 1901.

EDWARD G. LONGACRE

BUTTERFIELD, John (18 Nov. 1801–14 Nov. 1869), western pioneer, express company operator, and investor, was born in Berne, near Albany, New York, the son of Daniel Butterfield (his mother's name is unknown). His formal education consisted of intermittent attendance at local public schools. As a young man he became a stagecoach driver in New York State and later an investor in barges plying the Erie Canal.

In 1822 Butterfield moved to Utica, New York, where he lived most of his life. That same year he married Malinda Harriet Baker; they had nine children. In Utica, Butterfield founded the street railway company, built a grand hotel and business block, and in the mid-1840s took a leading part in the establishment of the New York, Albany and Buffalo Telegraph system. He became Utica's mayor in 1865.

Because the railroads built in the 1830s were shortlines, much freight required transshipment from one line to another or from railroads to stagecoaches to canal boats. This fragmentation led to the rise of express companies that organized the delivery of high-value merchandise by arranging through-shipment for it on the various railroads, stagecoaches, canal boats, and steamboats. In 1849 Butterfield formed an express company of Butterfield, Wasson & Company. In 1850 he joined Henry Wells and William Fargo to found the American Express Company. By 1860 this enterprise had become one of five giant long-distance express firms in the United States. By 1864 the American Express Company moved more than thirty railroad cars daily from the East to the Midwest and West and conveyed freight over routes totaling 8,000 miles. Its messengers traveled daily more than 30,000 miles.

Butterfield's most memorable involvement in the transcontinental express business was the establishment of the Overland Mail Company. In the late 1850s the United States was struggling to provide adequate communication between its westernmost rail terminals in Missouri and Iowa and the burgeoning California goldfields and cities. Government efforts to establish a mail service between East and West were clouded by sectional fighting between North and South. In 1857 Congress established a $600,000-a-year subsidy for the southern route between Missouri and San Francisco. Butterfield won the contract, which the *Chicago Tribune* called "one of the greatest swindles ever perpetrated upon the country by the slave-holders."

Butterfield's new venture began regular service in September 1858. For its day it was a truly giant enterprise that required extensive organizational skills. The route, 2,795 miles, was the longest stagecoach line in the United States. It provided service twice a week from the railhead at Tipton, Missouri, along roads that headed south to Fort Smith, Arkansas, and then west across Indian Territory and Texas to El Paso, to Tucson and Fort Yuma in Arizona, then across the Imperial Valley to Los Angeles, and finally north via the San Joaquin Valley to San Francisco. A branch line ran from the Imperial Valley to the California port of San Diego. The ride from Missouri to San Francisco took twenty-five days.

The Butterfield Stage system required an investment of nearly $1 million, 1,000 horses, 500 mules, 800 sets of harnesses, and nearly 500 vehicles. Eventually there were 200 way stations and relay posts. It took a labor force of more than 800 employees to service the stations and drive the coaches. Butterfield's operation became part of the American Express Company. Its major business was the transportation of mail. Passengers were relatively few since fares were high at $200 westbound from Memphis to San Francisco and $100 eastbound. In addition, passengers had to buy their own meals at way stations and were limited to a baggage allowance of forty pounds.

Butterfield's superb organizational and administrative skills assured that the line operated successfully and was profitable. Soon competitors emerged, including stagecoach operator Russell, Majors and Waddell. The outbreak of the Civil War and the secession of Texas from the Union in March 1861, however, destroyed the original Butterfield route. In March 1862 the federal government shifted the transcontinental mail to a central route and provided a $1 million annual subsidy to the Butterfield firm to manage it. Soon Butterfield's coaches operated daily service between

St. Joseph, Missouri, and Placerville, California. The stages did not have long to run. On 10 May 1869 the Union pacific and the Central Pacific completed a transcontinental railroad line with the driving of the golden spike at Promontory, Utah. The American Express Company lived on, transferring its operations from road to rail.

Butterfield died in Utica.

• For more information on Butterfield's role in the development of transcontinental transport systems, see Ray Allen Billington, *Westward Expansion: A History of the American Frontier* (1960), pp. 635–42; Roscoe P. Conkling and Margaret B. Conkling, *The Butterfield Overland Mail, 1857–1869* (1967); Le Roy Hafen, *The Overland Mail* (1926); Ralph Moody, *Stagecoach West* (1967); and George Rogers Taylor, *The Transportation Revolution, 1815–1860* (1951).

STEPHEN SALSBURY

BUTTERFIELD, Kenyon Leech (11 June 1868–26 Nov. 1935), college president and rural sociologist, was born in Lapeer, Michigan, the son of Ira Howard Butterfield, Jr., and Olive F. Davison, farmers. He spent part of his boyhood on the family's dairy farm and studied at the Michigan Agricultural College (now Michigan State University), which his grandfather Ira H. Butterfield had helped to found. There Butterfield took courses with the eminent horticulturist Liberty Hyde Bailey and, as friend Ray Stannard Baker later recalled, "was inevitably elected president!" of student societies, the college journal *Speculum*, his class, and the campus YMCA. Deeply committed to Congregationalism, Butterfield considered his religious calling before graduating with a B.A. in 1891; Harriet E. Millard, whom he married in 1895 and with whom he had two children, promised to follow him, if sent, into religious mission fields. He participated in missions through much of his life, but they did not become his principal vocation.

Butterfield became secretary to the Michigan Agricultural College president immediately after his graduation. He also edited Michigan's *Grange Visitor* magazine from 1892 to 1896, after which he edited the *Michigan Farmer* department that covered Grange activities. Convinced that farmers needed more education and social organization, Butterfield persuaded Michigan's legislature to fund farmers' institutes (programs about agriculture conducted in various locations around the state). He superintended institutes from 1895 to 1900 and urged his alma mater to create an extension department in 1898. Eager to improve his understanding of the rural world, and especially of the churches on which he wrote a thesis, Butterfield began the study of sociology with Charles Horton Cooley at the University of Michigan in 1900. In 1902 Butterfield earned an M.A. in sociology. Later that same year he organized a conference on rural life at Michigan Agricultural College and conducted the second course ever offered on rural sociology, at the University of Michigan (the University of Chicago had offered the first course on that specialty in 1897). The following year he became president of Rhode Island's State College of Agriculture and Mechanic Arts (now the University of Rhode Island). A tour of his new region in 1904 convinced him that the Massachusetts Agricultural College had the best chance of any school in New England for "leadership in agricultural education," and in 1906 he became its president.

Butterfield brought an established reputation and a clear direction to his new post. Having pressed for an ambitious extension program both in Rhode Island and in Michigan, he advocated extension work in a 1904 speech to the Association of American Agricultural Colleges and a year later became chairman of the association's new Committee on Extension. He also pursued rural intellectual and social improvement by organizing conferences at his Rhode Island school in 1904 and at the Massachusetts Agricultural College in 1907; the Rhode Island League for Rural Progress, and the Massachusetts and New England Federations for Rural Progress all grew out of these meetings of church leaders, Grangers, educators, and other reformers.

Appointed to Theodore Roosevelt's Commission on Country Life in 1908, he worked closely with other rural progressives who had grown up in farming and left it for other careers. His former teacher Liberty Hyde Bailey, who had become dean of the New York College of Agriculture at Cornell, chaired the commission and directed its ambitious research; Butterfield worked on the improvements that he hoped churches could bring to often dull and isolated rural lives. The commission, however, emphasized churches less than Butterfield wanted and instead considered the possible achievements of rural social institutions generally. Reporting to Roosevelt in January 1909, it then faded out of existence largely because congressional opposition to Roosevelt's several novel commissions thwarted its funding. Nevertheless, a network of church and YMCA leaders, Grangers, sociologists, and educators, with all of whom Butterfield had frequent contact, continued to advocate rural social and educational improvement. In 1917 Butterfield tried to form a permanent organization of rural reformers, and in 1919 a National Country Life Conference created the American Country Life Association and made Butterfield its president. News of the honor reached him in Europe.

Always intrigued by world affairs, Butterfield had traveled to Europe in 1913 as a member of the American Commission to Study Rural Credits and Agricultural Cooperation and had returned to France in 1918 with the YMCA's educational commission. He stayed through much of 1919 to help the U.S. Army develop courses on rural life for soldiers who were waiting to go home. After returning to Massachusetts, he helped in 1920 to organize the World Agriculture Society, which he hoped would promote rural progress around the globe. As a member of the Burton Commission on Christian Education in China from 1920 to 1922, Butterfield visited Japan, Korea, and China with his wife in the first of a long series of mission studies and travels in which he urged particular attention to the social and educational needs of rural communities.

Butterfield left the Massachusetts Agricultural College in May 1924 because he was distressed by the state's legislative supervision of the school's finances. He then served as president of Michigan Agricultural College (as of 1925, Michigan State College) from September 1924 until May 1928, when he returned from the International Missionary Conference in Jerusalem to discover that the college's board, troubled by what it saw as excessive spending that resulted from his ambitious expansions of the school, had extended his leave and wanted his resignation. He immediately resigned and devoted much of his remaining life to travels, which began with a 1929 observation of South African rural conditions that was sponsored by the Carnegie Corporation; and to advising the International Missionary Council on rural missions. A resident of Asbury, New Jersey, through most of his life after leaving Michigan State College, he moved back to Amherst, Massachusetts, several months before his death there.

A pioneer of extension education, early teacher of rural sociology, disappointed administrator of agricultural education, and prolific writer on the social improvement of rural communities, Butterfield compiled a long bibliography that included, among its best-known titles, *Chapters in Rural Progress* (1907), *The Country Church and the Rural Problem* (1911), *The Farmer and the New Day* (1919), and *A Christian Program for the Rural Community* (1923).

• The Library of Congress and the Archives and Manuscripts Department of the University of Massachusetts library both hold extensive collections of Butterfield's papers, and the archives at Michigan State University and the University of Rhode Island have other materials about his education and career. More than thirty of Butterfield's sociological and reformist books and essays are listed in *The National Union Catalog Pre-1956 Imprints*. Butterfield's ideas and activities are discussed in Merwin Robert Swanson, "The Country Life Movement in America, 1900–1920" (Ph.D. diss., Univ. of Minnesota, 1972); Swanson, "The Country Life Movement and the Churches," *Church History* 46 (Sept. 1977): 358–73; Wayne D. Rasmussen, *Taking the University to the People: Seventy-Five Years of Cooperative Extension* (1989); William L. Bowers, *The Country Life Movement in America, 1900–1920* (1974); Madison Kuhn, *Michigan State: The First Hundred Years* (1955); Herman F. Eschenbacher, *The University of Rhode Island: A History of Land-Grant Education in Rhode Island* (1967); and Harold Whiting Cary, *The University of Massachusetts: A History of One Hundred Years* (1962). An obituary is in the *New York Times*, 27 Nov. 1935.

DONALD B. MARTI

BUTTERFIELD, Paul (17 Dec. 1942–3 May 1987), blues harmonica player and bandleader, was born in Chicago, Illinois, the son of middle-class parents whose names and occupations are unknown. Butterfield was raised in Chicago, where blues music was regularly performed in small clubs on the city's South Side, catering primarily to a black audience who had migrated to the city in the 1930s, 1940s, and 1950s looking for better employment opportunities. Butterfield was one of the few young white musicians to befriend the older bluesmen and was soon sitting in with band members as a harmonica player.

After graduating from high school, Butterfield enrolled in the University of Chicago, where he met another young blues fan, guitarist Elvin Bishop. The duo began playing together, and eventually they began performing in local clubs, often accompanied by bassist Jerome Arnold and drummer Sam Lay, who were then working as accompanists for the urban bluesman Howlin' Wolf (born Chester Burnett). When the band was discovered by record producer Paul Rothschild, he signed them to the Elektra label but insisted that they add another guitarist to the lineup. Michael Bloomfield, another local virtuoso, was brought on board and the original band was born.

The Paul Butterfield Blues Band was important for a number of reasons. Unlike other white blues revivalists who specialized in re-creating the rural, acoustic blues sounds of the 1920s and 1930s, Butterfield's band specialized in the more raucous, contemporary, electrified blues sound that was played in Chicago by elder musicians like Howlin' Wolf and Muddy Waters (born McKinley Morganfield). Butterfield's band was also racially mixed, with the lead players white and the rhythm section black—also unusual for a revival band. Butterfield placed his harmonica directly next to the microphone, cupping his hands over both, producing a powerful, often distorted sound. His lead vocals intentionally imitated the accent and tonality of traditional blues performers, a sound that was highly unusual in popular music of the day.

Although Butterfield's first album was made up primarily of blues covers, his second and most famous recording, *East-West* (1971), featured a prolonged, thirteen-minute jam melding diverse influences, including jazz, twentieth-century atonal music, rock, and Indian music—leading the way to the sometimes excessive rock instrumentals of groups like Cream. This album also introduced keyboardist Mark Naftalin. The band accompanied folk rocker Bob Dylan at his infamous 1965 appearance at the Newport Folk Festival, when the traditional folk audience was so enraged by Dylan's performance on electric guitar that they booed him off of the stage.

Bloomfield left the band in 1967 to form another rock-blues outfit, Electric Flag, and Butterfield expanded the band to include a rhythm and blues–flavored horn section—including future light-jazz artist David Sanborn on alto saxophone. With this band, Butterfield recorded his last notable album, *The Resurrection of Pigboy Crabshaw* (1968). The band produced two more albums and then finally broke up in the early 1970s after appearing at the famous 1969 Woodstock Rock Festival in New York.

Butterfield settled in Woodstock, where in 1972 he formed a more acoustic blues–oriented group called Better Days, featuring whiz guitarist Amos Garrett, keyboard player Ronnie Barron, bass player Billy Rich, drummer Chris Parker, and vocalist Geoff Muldaur. Despite this superstar lineup, the band's two albums were fairly low-key affairs, and Butterfield soon descended into a growing dependency on alcohol and drugs. He managed to record a solo album in the mid-1970s, featuring a lackluster collection of pop-funk numbers on which he played very little harmonica, limiting himself to doodling on the synthesizer. He also appeared in the 1976 farewell concert/movie *The Last Waltz* as one of the "living legends" who influenced the rock group the Band; he later toured with the Band's former bassist Rick Danko and drummer Levon Helm.

Butterfield was almost totally inactive in the 1980s following the failure of his 1981 comeback album, another unappealing mixture of white soul backed by mechanical, synthesized accompaniments. He made one final comeback attempt in 1987, shortly before his death in Los Angeles, California, from a heart attack that was related to his continuing drug addiction.

In his most creative years in the mid-1960s, Butterfield was an authentically exciting performer, whose raspy vocals and energetic harp playing defined the sound of his band. He was also a talented bandleader, who brought together a unique group of musicians to form an ensemble that looked both back toward the blues tradition and forward to the coming sounds of hard rock. Butterfield's covers of traditional blues songs helped introduce them to a white, well-educated audience, many of whom went on to become fans of the original musicians from whom he took his inspiration; in this way, he helped popularize the music and sound of traditional performers like Muddy Waters, leading directly to the renaissance of interest in the urban blues in the 1970s.

• For more information about Butterfield's career, consult James R. McDonald, "White Bluesman: The Influence and Career of Paul Butterfield," *Popular Music and Society* 13 (1989): 39–45. See also Don DeMichael, "Father and Son: An Interview with Muddy Waters and Paul Butterfield," *Down Beat* 56 (Sept. 1989): 68–71. Obituaries are in the *New York Times* and the *Los Angeles Times*, both 6 May 1987.

RICHARD CARLIN

BUTTERWORTH, Benjamin (22 Oct. 1837–16 Jan. 1898), lawyer and congressman, was born in Hamilton, Butler County, Ohio, the son of William Butterworth, a farmer and schoolteacher, and Elizabeth Linton. After completing preparatory training at local public schools and the Lebanon Academy in Maineville, Butterworth attended Ohio University. He studied law with Durbin Ward and William M. Ramsey in Cincinnati and graduated from the Cincinnati Law School in 1861. A Quaker who fought in the Civil War with the rank of major, Butterworth in 1863 married Mary E. Seiler. They had four children. Butterworth was appointed assistant U.S. district attorney for southern Ohio in 1868, serving under Warner Bateman. Although he was appointed district attorney in 1870, he resigned the position shortly thereafter to resume his law practice with a cousin, George S. Bailey. Living in a strongly Democratic district, Butterworth in 1871 was nominated by local Republicans for the Ohio Senate, and he came within 126 votes of winning the election. Two years after this narrow defeat, he carried the same district by a majority of eighty-six votes and represented Warren and Butler counties in the state senate from 1873 to 1875.

Butterworth relocated to Cincinnati in 1875 to practice law in a larger city with greater economic and political opportunities. There he won election to the U.S. House of Representatives in 1878 and 1880. Butterworth suffered defeat in 1882 at the hands of his Democratic opponent, John F. Follett, losing primarily because of the defection of German-American voters on the temperance question. President Chester A. Arthur wanted to appoint the former congressman to his cabinet as postmaster general, but the chief executive ultimately succumbed to greater political pressure from Indiana politicians and selected Judge Walter Q. Gresham for that portfolio. In June 1883 Butterworth accepted the position of commissioner of patents, which he held for two years. At the president's request, he also served as special commissioner to investigate certain portions of the Northern Pacific Railroad lines.

Butterworth's interest in national politics continued after he left the House. He was one of the custodians of President Arthur's unsuccessful endeavor at the Republican National Convention at Chicago in 1884 to win renomination. In that same year, Butterworth succeeded in reclaiming his House seat, defeating Follett by over 1,600 votes. He served in Congress from 1885 to 1891, representing the First Congressional District. His integrity, sense of humor, and good fellowship endeared him to his colleagues. Some of his major speeches were on political contributions (1880), pensions and appropriations (1886), support for the eight-hour law (1890), protective tariffs (1888 and 1890), and commercial trade with Canada (1890). In keeping with Republican doctrine, Butterworth sponsored bills to punish bribery at elections and preserve the purity of electoral contests. He favored a federal elections law to protect African-American suffrage in the South. Butterworth also enthusiastically championed the reciprocity doctrine advanced by Secretary of State James G. Blaine, who sought a mutual and beneficial exchange of special privileges between nations.

Butterworth maintained a close relationship with Benjamin Harrison (1833–1901), an Indiana Republican who had served in the Senate prior to becoming president of the United States. During the presidential campaigns of 1888 and 1892, Butterworth dispatched letters to Harrison, the party's nominee for the presidency, in which he freely offered his advice on various matters. He suggested in 1888 that Harrison mention the fruits of labor for the working man and the issue of tariff revision in his letter accepting the nomination. He also encouraged Harrison to use such "catch-words and phrases" in the campaign that mothers and fathers would want "to repeat to their children" as "containing the law and the prophets touching the opportunities, duties and responsibilities that attach to citizenship in the United States." After reading Harrison's letter of acceptance in 1892, Butterworth praised the content: "There is not a superfluous word or suggestion from beginning to end. We are made stronger for the fight by reason of what you have written. You are daily growing in strength and your election seems assured." Near the end of the contest in 1892, Butterworth predicted that the president, if reelected, would possess the opportunity "to pitch the tone of American politics above the rattle and brawl of dance houses." Moreover, he reminded Republicans that politics was not a game; rather, it had a "relation to the peace, prosperity & happiness of the American people." Although holding similar positions on most issues with Harrison, Butterworth, a champion of tariff revision without endangering the principle of protectionism, expressed reservations with some of the high protectionist features in the McKinley Tariff of 1890.

Upon his voluntary retirement from the House of Representatives in 1891, Butterworth opened a law office in the nation's capital, specializing in patent law. His interest in politics, however, never ceased during this interlude. President Harrison in 1892 appointed Butterworth, a former regent of the Smithsonian Institution, president of the World's Fair Commission to the European governments to plan for the exposition at Chicago in 1893. In 1897 the new Republican president, William McKinley, appointed Butterworth commissioner of patents, the job he had held previously under Arthur. Although he accepted this position, Butterworth would have preferred to be solicitor general. He died the next year in Thomasville, Georgia.

A kindhearted man known for his absolute integrity and exceptional debating skills, Butterworth, a star stump speaker, was a Republican stalwart. Although he maintained a streak of independence and demonstrated sympathetic concern for labor and tariff revision, he was above everything else loyal to his party. He was a trusted adviser to Presidents James A. Garfield and Benjamin Harrison. Butterworth also benefited from his close personal and professional associations with several Ohio leaders who gained national attention during the late nineteenth century. Like many others of his generation, he retained his principles against all arguments that sought to turn him from his idea of right and justice.

• Butterworth left no personal papers. Some of his letters may be mined from the manuscript collections of his contemporaries, including Harrison. The Ohio Historical Society Library in Columbus has valuable collections pertaining to this period. Butterworth's speeches are in the *Congressional Record* (1879–1883; 1885–1891). The only substantial article on Butterworth is Leonard Schlup, "Rejuvenated Republican: Benjamin Butterworth of Ohio and His Letters to Benjamin Harrison in 1888," *Research Journal of Philosophy and Social Sciences* (1996): 29–36. Brief sketches of his life are in W. A. Taylor, *Ohio in Congress from 1803 to 1901* (1900); and Fred Starek's piece in *Twenty Years in the Press Gallery*, ed. O. O. Stealey (1906). Obituaries are in the *Cincinnati Times-Star*, *Cincinnati Commercial Tribune*, *Cincinnati Enquirer*, *Cincinnati Post*, *Washington Post*, and *New York Times*, 17 Jan. 1898.

LEONARD SCHLUP

BUTTERWORTH, Charles (26 July 1896–13 June 1946), character actor, was born in South Bend, Indiana, the son of Charles M. Butterworth, a doctor, and Frances E. Slattery. He grew up in South Bend and attended public schools. By high school, he had developed a few comic routines and was in demand at local charity shows. After graduating from South Bend High School, he worked various odd jobs, one of which was as a reporter for the *South Bend News-Times*.

After he entered Notre Dame University in 1918, he continued to work for the *News-Times* after school and on vacations. He later attributed the bulk of his success as a performer to his newspaper background, since it was while covering the tedious luncheon circuit for the *News-Times* that he got the inspiration for his signature monologues: "The Rotary Speech" and "The After-Dinner Speaker."

He graduated from Notre Dame in 1924 with a bachelor of laws degree; then he moved to Chicago, where he worked for the *Chicago American* and entered small-time vaudeville as a monologist. He made his professional stage debut in 1924 at the Orpheum Theater in Waukegan, Illinois. His loony and sophisticated monologues did not go over well on the vaudeville circuit, so he moved to New York City, where he worked briefly at the *New York Times* as a circulation department canvasser, and then landed a reporting job on the *Mount Vernon (N.Y.) Argus*. He spent his spare time working on vaudeville sketches.

Butterworth left the *Argus* to take a job as secretary to fellow Notre Dame alumnus J. P. McEvoy, who was writing the book for the Broadway revue *Americana*. Butterworth used his secretarial job to wheedle an audition from the show's producer, Richard Herndon, and Herndon added Butterworth to the show doing an expanded version of his vaudeville centerpiece, "The Rotary Speech." Before the show's opening, its star, Willie Collier, feeling that *Americana* was too amateurish, quit. Butterworth was assigned to several of Collier's skits. When the show opened 26 July 1926, Butterworth received rave reviews, and his "Rotary Speech" was singled out for special praise.

Butterworth followed up that success with appearances in several Broadway musicals: *Allez Oop* (1927), *Good Boy* (1928), *Sweet Adeline* (1929), and *Flying Colors* (1932), establishing himself, in the words of the *New Yorker* (27 July 1935), as "a master of anticlimaxes, nonsequiturs, of bashful effrontery and vaingloriousness."

In February 1930 *Vanity Fair* offered its readers an explanation of Butterworth's unique stage appeal: "He is a melancholy fugitive wraith among our more robust American comics; there is no one remotely like him, no one remotely as funny. For he is a very master of understatement; his extraordinary features seem to ponder a fact interminably before he dismisses it with three words that are thus inevitably the three funniest words possible."

Butterworth made his film debut in 1930 in *The Life of the Party* and quickly developed a distinct screen persona as a vacillating, indecisive nonentity with a deadpan expression. He tended to be cast as shy, sad-looking everymen or elegant fools. His more memorable screen characters included ineffectual millionaires Count de Savinnac and George Vane Bassingwell in *Love Me Tonight* (1932) and *Ruggles of Red Gap* (1935), respectively; Willis, the timid clerk who finds himself mistaken for Public Enemy No. 2 in *Baby Face Harrington* (1935); and Graves, the butler who becomes involved with Mae West in *Every Day's a Holiday* (1937). "His peculiar talent makes it difficult to create a star role for him, but he stands first in the he-stole-the-picture class," said the *New Yorker* (27 July 1935). In 1932 Butterworth married Ethel Kenyon Sutherland, who had previously been married to director Eddie Sutherland. They had no children, and their marriage ended in divorce in 1939.

Butterworth appeared as Fred Astaire's costar on the radio program "The Packard Show," which debuted 8 September 1936. Astaire left the series after its first season, and in its second and final season Butterworth's costar was Lanny Ross.

Butterworth's other notable movies included *The Cat and the Fiddle* (1934); *Bulldog Drummond Strikes Back* (1934); *Forsaking All Others* (1934); *Magnificent Obsession* (1935); *Swing High, Swing Low* (1937); *Second Chorus* (1940), in which he uttered a memorable line: "I said music, and Father said bottlecaps. Father won"; *The Boys from Syracuse* (1940); *This Is the Army* (1943); and *Follow the Boys* (1944).

Offscreen, Butterworth was a drinking buddy of such notable wits as Robert Benchley and Corey Ford, and he was reputed to have written many of his better onscreen lines himself. "I'm selling a personality," he told the *Newark News* in 1937. "And to do this, I have to be careful it doesn't go out of character."

In the 1940s, as screwball comedies began to fade, Butterworth was offered fewer film roles, and he began directing his career back to the stage. He returned to Broadway in the 1942 musical comedy *Count Me In*. Toward the end of World War II, he did an eight-month United Service Organizations tour of Pacific army bases, and on his return he was featured in the Broadway show *Brighten the Corner* (1945), which ran for only twenty-nine performances. He made no movies at all in the final two years of his life. He died in Los Angeles when his car skidded off the road and hit a lamp post.

• Clippings files on Butterworth are maintained by the Billy Rose Theatre Collection at the New York Public Library for the Performing Arts, Lincoln Center, and the Margaret Herrick Library of the Academy of Motion Picture Arts and Sciences, Beverly Hills, Calif. Bare-bones biographical information on Butterworth can be found in several reference books, the most valuable of which are David Quinlan, *Quinlan's Illustrated Directory of Film Comedy Actors* (1992), *The Videohound & All-Movie Guide Stargazer* (1996), and *Who Was Who in the Theatre, 1912–1976* (1978). Two of the more valuable individual articles on Butterworth are Alva Johnson, "Profiles: The Mad Hatter of Hollywood," *New Yorker*, 27 July 1935, and Ward Morehouse, "Butterworth Star of New Comedy," *Baltimore Sun*, 16 Dec. 1945. An obituary is in the *New York Times*, 14 June 1946.

LYNN HOOGENBOOM

BUTTON, Stephen Decatur (8 June 1813–17 Jan. 1897), architect, was born in Preston, Connecticut, the son of Roswell Button and Lydia (maiden name unknown), farmers. He served an apprenticeship with his father's brother, Samuel Button, a carpenter. At age twenty-one he became an assistant to an architect in New York City, George Purvis. Before 1840 he struck out on his own and moved to Hoboken, New Jersey. Although he is assumed to have engaged in the design and perhaps the construction of buildings, nothing is known of his work there. His association with Joseph C. Hoxie, his brother-in-law and later partner, appears to date from the Hoboken years.

In 1843 he relocated to Florida and subsequently to Georgia. He moved to Montgomery, Alabama, after winning the competition to design the state capitol (1845–1847) with a design in Greek revival style. During this period he received commissions for a theater and several residences in Montgomery, as well as the Agricultural College at Auburn, Alabama. Although he moved to the Philadelphia area in 1848, he executed at least one later commission in Montgomery, the Central Bank of Alabama (1856).

In Philadelphia Button formed a partnership with Hoxie, which lasted until 1852. The partnership's earliest design was the Egyptian revival Odd Fellows' Cemetery entrance gate (c. 1849, demolished). A later gate, for Mount Moriah Cemetery (1855), by Button alone, is a picturesque composition, eclectically combining a triumphal arch, battlemented towers, and Flemish gables. It was, however, the Italianate that was Button's favored style. As an article written by one of his pupils for *American Architect and Building News* in 1892 noted, "Mr. Button's design in his best public buildings is always more largely influenced by the architecture of the Italian Renaissance than by the gothic style." Button's first marriage, to Maria Pierta, was childless. In 1852 he married Hannah Maria Goodhill; they had two children who survived to adulthood.

During the boom years of the 1850s, until the panic of 1857 virtually halted building activity in Philadelphia, Button, in partnership with Hoxie and then individually, designed numerous houses, a hotel, a firehouse, the Spring Garden Institute, the Kensington Home for Widows and Orphans, and four churches. As Philadelphia expanded westward, Button responded to the demand for commercial buildings, designing at least a dozen for that city, as well as a block of stores in New Orleans. A major commission was the main office of the Pennsylvania Railroad (1856–1858, demolished). Button's surviving commercial buildings are prime examples of what has been described as "Philadelphia functionalism," a system that emphasized the height and utilitarian purposes of these five-story structures. His Lewis Building (1852) stressed verticality through the thinness and continuity of slender cast-iron piers, which allowed for broad expanses of glass. The slightly later Leland Building (1855) is granite, with unornamented piers rising four stories above the first floor arcade. Its base, shaft, and capital system prefigures the work of Louis Sullivan and the development of the American skyscraper.

Although he is considered a Philadelphia architect and maintained offices in that city, Button actually lived across the Delaware River in Camden, New Jersey. His practice in that growing city was almost as extensive as in its larger neighbor. One of his earliest works there, during his partnership with Hoxie, was the Camden County Building (1852, demolished). Although his practice in Philadelphia declined after the 1850s, it remained strong in Camden. There he designed seventeen churches, two ferry houses, and a bank, as well as thirteen public schools, of which one, the Richard Fetters School (1875) survives. He also designed Camden's city hall (1874–1875, demolished). The building was fitted with a mansard roof in the by-then fashionable Second Empire style, although the tower was still unabashedly Italianate. His Second Presbyterian Church (1865) is a polychromed, eclectic combination of Italianate and high Victorian gothic elements.

Another major locus for Button's later work was Cape May, New Jersey, where he was responsible for some forty buildings over three decades. His first commission was for a summer house in 1863; his last, near the end of his long life, was for the five houses known as Atlantic Terrace, completed in 1892. The largest was the Stockton Hotel (1868–1869), a colonnaded and pedimented behemoth planned to accommodate 1,000 vacationers. Never a financial success, it was demolished in 1911. More lasting was the smaller Windsor Hotel (1879), which, with its dormered French roof and two-story arcaded porches, almost looks like a line of summer cottages strung together. Jackson's Clubhouse (1872), despite its original function as a gambling hall, is the best example of Button's typical large resort cottage. A simple cubical form, with rear wing, it achieves interest through Italianate detailing, which includes a square tower, heavy bracketed cornice, and arcuated porch. Another large dwelling, the John B. McCreary house (1869–1870), is somewhat unusual in Button's oeuvre, its massing and pointed and Tudor-arched openings relating it to the Gothic revival. Button also designed smaller cottages for Cape May, including Stockton Place (1871–1872), a row of eight houses, some now intact and others heavily altered. Narrow, with gable ends toward the street and a plethora of jigsawn ornament, they represent the type of relatively modest cottages popular in seaside resorts in the second half of the nineteenth century.

Button died in Camden, where he had lived for almost fifty years. The styles of architecture he had espoused were no longer fashionable in major centers, although he had continued to find work in small towns in New Jersey until the 1890s. His urban buildings have not fared well. The Alabama capitol burned in 1849; Button was not retained to design its replacement, although some of the foundations of his building were reused and its plan followed in part. Most of his Philadelphia and Camden buildings fell victim to the growth and redevelopment of those cities in the late nineteenth and early twentieth centuries. His most enduring legacy has been the seemingly more ephemeral resort architecture he created in Cape May, where designs he introduced, such as the cubical Italianate villa, were reproduced by others, helping to give the town a remarkably cohesive appearance. Several of his larger houses, including Jackson's Clubhouse and the McCreary house, have been converted into successful bed-and-breakfast inns, and many of the smaller cottages continue to serve as residences.

• Most information about Button's life and works is scattered in local architectural histories. An overview, with emphasis on his career in Philadelphia, appears in Richard J. Webster's 1963 master's thesis at the University of Delaware, "Stephen D. Button: Italianate Stylist." Another brief biography and partial list of his commissions is in Sandra L. Tatman and Roger W. Moss, *Biographical Dictionary of Philadelphia Architects, 1700–1930* (1985). Further references to his Philadelphia work may be found in Richard J. Webster, *Philadelphia Preserved* (1976), and James F. O'Gorman et al., *Drawing toward Building* (1986), while his output in Cape May, New Jersey, is covered in George E. Thomas and Carl Doebley, *Cape May* (1976). For an assessment of his contributions to the development of American commercial architecture, see Winston J. Weisman, "Philadelphia Functionalism and Sullivan," *Journal of the Society of Architectural Historians* 20 (Mar. 1961): 3–19.

CONSTANCE M. GREIFF

BUTTRICK, Wallace (23 Oct. 1853–27 May 1926), Baptist minister and philanthropy executive, was born in Potsdam, New York, the son of Charles Henry Buttrick and Polly Dodge Warren. Young Buttrick studied at the Ogdensburg Academy and Potsdam Normal School between 1868 and 1872. He married Isabella Allen of Saginaw, Michigan, in 1875; the couple had three children. Buttrick worked as a railway mail clerk for five years. He then entered Rochester Theological Seminary in Rochester, New York, and graduated in 1883. Ordained in the Baptist ministry, Buttrick initially served at First Baptist Church in New Haven, Connecticut, where he was the pastor for six years. From 1889 to 1892 he was the pastor of First Baptist Church in St. Paul, Minnesota, and from 1892 to 1902 he was the pastor of Emmanuel Baptist Church in Albany, New York. There Buttrick met with other Baptist ministers such as Samuel Zane Batten, William Newton Clarke, and Walter Rauschenbusch in the Marlboro Brotherhood of the Kingdom Conference to study the application of the gospel to contemporary social issues.

During his ministry, Buttrick was a trustee of the University of Rochester and Rochester Theological Seminary and a member of the executive board of the American Baptist Home Mission Society and chair of its committee on education. In those capacities, he worked closely with Frederick T. Gates, a fellow alumnus of Rochester Theological Seminary and Baptist pastor in Minnesota and New York. In 1888 Gates had become a confidential adviser to John D. Rockefeller on philanthropy. In 1900 he asked Buttrick to study American Baptist Home Mission Society schools for black youth in the South. When Rockefeller created the General Education Board with a $1 million gift two years later, Gates became its president. Buttrick's report on Baptist schools in the South led to his appointment as the board's secretary and executive director. Buttrick continued to be motivated by a vision of the social application of the gospel that was nourished by his participation in Rauschenbusch's Marlboro Brotherhood of the Kingdom conferences. "I am more and more impressed with the idea that the teaching of Jesus has never had a fair show," Buttrick wrote to Robert C. Ogden in 1907. "Lately I have come to see that the teachings of Jesus abound in helpful social teachings not only for his day but for all times and for all peoples."

Buttrick became a key member of a bureaucratic elite who managed a new "benevolent empire." Built on contributions from Rockefeller, Ogden, Andrew Carnegie, George Foster Peabody, and others, it included the General Education Board, the Southern Education Board, and the Anna T. Jeanes, George Peabody, and John F. Slater funds. These philanthropic agencies had interlocking trustees, officers, and programs. Buttrick, for example, was a member and officer of the Southern Education Board from 1901 to 1914, a trustee and agent of the Slater fund for several years, and a special adviser to the trustees of the Peabody fund. As secretary and executive director of the General Education Board, his initial work was to survey public and private education throughout the country with an eye to assessing how private philanthropy might most effectively encourage state and local agencies to increase their support of education. By 1909 Rockefeller's endowment of the General Education Board had risen to $54 million.

The early work of the General Education Board moved in two directions. First, it sought to identify private colleges and universities across the country that showed evidence of having long-term merit. The criteria of selection included a strategic location, a constituency likely to sustain the institution, and other signs of vitality. The board then sought to strengthen the endowments of those institutions. It enabled Teachers College of Columbia University, for example, to establish the Lincoln School, which explored progressive methods of education. Second, the General Education Board sought to encourage the extension, maintenance, and strengthening of primary and secondary public education. It conducted an exhaustive study of schools conducted on the model of the Gary, Indiana, system, which expanded extracurricular activities, grouped students according to ability, and sought efficient utilization of school facilities. While the Southern Education Board, staffed and led by regional educators, led the public education campaigns in the South, the General Education Board provided private philanthropic encouragement to state and local efforts. In an era of racial segregation, those efforts did far more to improve the quality of education for white than for black people, but African Americans also benefited. Recognizing the necessity of economic development to sustain public education in the region, the board also cooperated with Seaman A. Knapp of the Department of Agriculture to underwrite the work of farm demonstration agents to improve farm productivity in rural areas.

In 1914 the General Education Board awarded $1.5 million to the medical school at Johns Hopkins University, enabling it to begin full-time clinical training in certain medical fields. The grant reflected Buttrick's increasing interest in medical education. After a visit to China in 1914, he organized and became director of the China Medical Board, which was created by the Rockefeller Foundation to introduce western medical science and hygiene to China. In May 1917 Buttrick succeeded Gates as president of the General Education Board, and six years later he became its chair. During Buttrick's 23-year tenure with the board, it awarded $1 million in grants for agricultural education, $1.7 million to state education departments, $12 million for African-American education, $35 million for medical education, and $66.4 million to endow, equip, and maintain 291 colleges and universities. Buttrick died in Baltimore, Maryland.

• The largest collection of Buttrick papers is in the archives of the General Education Board at Rockefeller University in Tarrytown, N.Y., but there is also Buttrick material in the American Baptist Home Mission Society Papers at the American Baptist Historical Society in Rochester, N.Y., and in the Robert C. Ogden, Southern Education Board, and Booker T. Washington Papers at the Library of Congress. For more information, see Robert Andrew Baker, "The American Baptist Home Mission Society and the South, 1832–1894" (Ph.D. diss., Yale Univ., 1947), Charles L. White, *A Century of Faith* (1952), Sandy Dwayne Martin, "The American Baptist Home Mission Society and Black Higher Education in the South, 1865–1910," *Foundations* 24 (Oct.–Dec. 1981): 310–27, Louis R. Harlan, *Separate and Unequal: Public School Campaigns and Racism in the Southern Seaboard States, 1901–1915* (1958), and Raymond Blaine Fosdick, *Adventure in Giving: The Story of the General Education Board* (1962). An obituary is in the *New York Times*, 28 May 1926.

RALPH E. LUKER

BUZHARDT, Joseph Fred (21 Feb. 1924–16 Dec. 1978), lawyer, was born in Greenwood, South Carolina, the son of Joseph Fred Buzhardt, Sr., a lawyer, and Edna Hardin. Buzhardt enrolled at Wofford College in 1941, volunteered for the air corps one year later, and was called to active duty in February 1943. He also received an appointment to the U.S. Military Academy at West Point in 1943, earned his B.S. and commission in 1946, and served in the air force until 1950. Buzhardt received his LL.B., magna cum laude, in 1952 from the University of South Carolina, where he was editor of the *University of South Carolina Law Quarterly* and first honor graduate. After being admitted to the South Carolina bar in 1952, he went into practice with his father and was active in civic and professional organizations.

In 1958 Buzhardt became a legislative assistant to Senator Strom Thurmond (then a South Carolina Democrat, who became a Republican in 1964), a friend and former law partner of Buzhardt's father. Buzhardt worked extensively on issues relating to the military and was involved in the controversy surrounding Thurmond's allegation that members of the John F. Kennedy administration had restricted military leaders in their attempts to speak out against communism. Buzhardt became Thurmond's administrative assistant in 1965. In 1966 Buzhardt returned to legal practice with his father in McCormick, South Carolina.

When President Richard M. Nixon put together his new administration in 1969, Buzhardt was slated to be legal counsel to the Defense Department. However, opposition by civil rights advocates blocked his appointment; opponents claimed that his close ties to Thurmond's segregationist policies made Buzhardt unfit to oversee the Pentagon's program to end discrimination. Nixon instead appointed Buzhardt a special assistant to the secretary of defense and staff director of a special commission to study the Defense Department. The report of the special commission, largely Buzhardt's work, won universal praise, including a laudatory column by Carl Rowan, who had been one of his most vocal critics.

The secretary of defense, Melvin Laird, was among those impressed by Buzhardt's work on the commission, and in 1970 Nixon appointed Buzhardt general counsel of the Defense Department. The Senate easily confirmed the nomination, and Buzhardt took office on 20 August 1970. As general counsel to the Defense Department, Buzhardt handled many of the difficult situations the military faced in the early 1970s, including scandals involving the misuse of United Service Organizations funds, the use of army intelligence to spy on civilians, unauthorized bombing in Southeast Asia, and cost overruns by defense contractors. Perhaps most notably, from 1971 to 1973 he represented the Department of the Army in the prosecution of Daniel J. Ellsberg and Anthony J. Russo, two Rand Corporation consultants accused of leaking to the press the Pentagon Papers (a classified collection of documents, compiled by the Defense Department, that traced U.S. involvement in Vietnam). The proceedings against Ellsberg and Russo ended in a mistrial on 11 May 1973 after it became known that administration officials had participated in a burglary of the office of Lewis Fielding, Ellsberg's former psychiatrist.

As the legal problems arising from the Watergate break-in mounted, Nixon announced on 10 May 1973 that Buzhardt would move to the White House on a temporary basis as special counsel on Watergate matters. Defending Nixon proved to be a professionally trying and personally painful experience. Buzhardt played a major role in the preparation of the presidential statement on Watergate, released on 22 May 1973, in which Nixon denied knowledge of the Watergate burglary or the ensuing cover-up and explained an initial restriction of the investigation by citing reasons of national security. In late June, John Dean, Nixon's fired White House counsel, testified before the Senate Watergate Committee that Nixon had been deeply involved in the cover-up. Buzhardt prepared a response that contended that Dean was the "principal actor in the Watergate cover-up."

Alexander Butterfield, aide to former White House chief of staff H. R. Haldeman, gave testimony before the Senate Watergate Committee on 16 July 1973 that revealed the existence of an elaborate voice-activated taping system in the White House. Nixon initially refused to allow even his own legal team access to the tapes. When the special prosecutor subpoenaed the tapes, the president refused to comply, citing executive privilege. Judge John Sirica ruled that the president had to turn over the tapes, and the Supreme Court upheld that ruling on 12 October.

Even as Watergate engulfed the Nixon White House, another legal problem claimed Buzhardt's attention. In October 1973 Buzhardt played an important role in the negotiations that led to the resignation of Vice President Spiro Agnew, who had accepted illegal cash payments both as governor of Maryland and as vice president.

After the Supreme Court's October ruling, Nixon finally relented and allowed Buzhardt, and only Buzhardt, to listen to the tapes. In this capacity it fell to Buzhardt to make known to Sirica an 18½-minute gap in a key conversation with Haldeman. Haldeman's notes on the meeting revealed that the missing portion of the conversation pertained to Watergate.

Nixon's relations with his own legal team became increasingly adversarial. On 29 November the president's press secretary, Ronald Ziegler, announced that the legal team had made "some mistakes" and was therefore being reorganized. On 4 January 1974 James D. St. Clair was named special counsel to the president to handle the Watergate defense. Buzhardt became counsel to the president, a position that had remained vacant since Dean had been fired. Buzhardt continued to play a major role in Nixon's Watergate defense. On 11 April 1974 the House Judiciary Committee subpoenaed forty-two tapes; Buzhardt oversaw preparation of edited transcripts of the tapes.

In the early hours of 13 June Buzhardt, who had been working seven days a week, sixteen to eighteen hours a day, suffered a heart attack. He was back at work by July. When the special prosecutor sought further tapes, Nixon refused; on 24 July the Supreme Court ruled that Nixon had to surrender the tapes. Nixon informed Buzhardt that there might be a problem with one of the tapes. When Buzhardt listened to the tape of 23 June 1972, he became convinced that the president had participated in an initial step in the cover-up. Buzhardt was concerned that the brief submitted to the House Judiciary Committee had misrepresented the events of 23 June. As a lawyer, he believed that he had a duty to convince his client to change his plea or to correct the misrepresentation himself. Buzhardt argued with Ziegler and White House chief of staff Alexander M. Haig that the president must resign. Facing certain impeachment, Nixon announced his resignation on 8 August, effective the following day.

Buzhardt resigned as presidential counsel on 15 August 1974, although he continued to serve in the office as Gerald Ford's presidential counsel until 5 October. He returned to South Carolina and private legal practice with the firm of Dowling, Sanders, Dukes, Novit and Svalina. He died of a heart attack in Hilton Head, South Carolina.

Buzhardt was a quiet, withdrawn man, devoted to conservative politics. Friends knew him as a humble, decent man and a devout Baptist. He had married Imogene Sanders of McCormick, South Carolina, in 1946; the couple had four children.

Buzhardt remains best known as Nixon's lawyer during Watergate. In that capacity he attempted to preserve a proper attorney-client relationship with the president while balancing that relationship against his own ethical standards and his duties as an officer of the court. Buzhardt's ability to keep all of these obligations in sight distinguished his role.

• Buzhardt's papers are at Clemson University. The best information regarding his life and career is in the clipping file in his papers, which mostly pertain to Watergate. Buzhardt did not write much for publication, but he did contribute a brief essay on "Damages" to a "Survey of South Carolina Law: May 1955–April 1956," *South Carolina Law Quarterly* 9 (1956): 48–49. Buzhardt was a source for Bob Woodward and Carl Bernstein, *The Final Days* (1976), which details his role as Nixon's lawyer during Watergate. Other accounts of Buzhardt's activities relating to his defense of Nixon appear in Theodore H. White, *Breach of Faith: The Fall of Richard Nixon* (1975); Richard Nixon, *RN: The Memoirs of Richard Nixon*, vol. 2 (1978); Stanley I. Kutler, *The Wars of Watergate: The Last Crisis of Richard Nixon* (1990); Leon Jaworski, *The Right and the Power: The Prosecution of Watergate* (1976); and John J. Sirica, *To Set the Record Straight* (1979). Obituaries are in the *New York Times* and *Washington Post*, 17 Dec. 1978.

MICHAEL S. MAYER

BYAS, Don (21 Oct. 1912–24 Aug. 1972), tenor saxophonist, was born Carlos Wesley Byas in Muskogee, Oklahoma. The names and occupations of his parents are unknown, and little is known of Byas's early life or musical training. As a teenager he played alto saxophone with Bennie Moten and Walter Page in the late 1920s and then with his own group in the early 1930s; he switched to tenor in 1933 and settled in California. Over the next few years he played with Lionel Hampton (1935); Eddie Barefield and Buck Clayton (both 1936); Don Redman, Lucky Millinder, and Andy Kirk (1939–1940); and Benny Carter (Sept. 1940). He recorded with Timme Rosenkrantz in 1938, and in September 1940 he cut two tunes with Billie Holiday and Her Orchestra.

Byas's career reached its turning point when he joined the Count Basie Band. On "Harvard Blues," made in May 1940 with the Basie group, he played a solo that typifies his style at the time. It has been vividly described by musician and jazz historian Gunther Schuller:

> Perfectly constructed, it is simple and affecting, poignant and languorous. Playing softly with a sense of intimacy not often encountered in jazz, Byas places each of his notes as if they were a series of incontrovertible truths. . . . Listen especially . . . for Byas's anguished moan, followed by a simple downward scale. (p. 255)

Already Byas had the huge tone that became his trademark; he was technically flawless even at breathtaking speeds, playing in a style influenced by Art Tatum. Harmonically, at least, he was more advanced than Coleman Hawkins.

In 1941 Byas took over the chair formerly held by Lester Young in Basie's band. In addition to his work with Basie and with smaller, Basie-led groups, he recorded prolifically throughout the 1940s with a variety of groups as a sideman and, increasingly, under his own name. In 1944 he seemed to be everywhere. In late May he recorded several tunes with Coleman Hawkins and His Sax Ensemble, appearing as a costar in this illustrious group. In early June he cut three tunes on Folkways with Mary Lou Williams and Her Orchestra, contributing a particularly noteworthy collaboration with Williams on "Man o' Mine." In September he recorded four tunes with Hot Lips Page and His Orchestra, showcasing his massive tone on "These Foolish Things," and in November he recorded again with Hawkins. Finally, he was a member of Dizzy Gillespie's first small group on Fifty-second Street, and he briefly replaced Gillespie in Charlie Parker's quintet the following year.

In addition to playing with Parker, Byas continued to perform and record prolifically in 1945, leading his own quartet and quintet in a variety of venues and sessions. In January he recorded four tunes with the Don Byas All-Stars and, in October, four more with a quartet (both sessions were for the Black and Blue label). Byas's unique mix of boppish harmonies and swing rhythms is clearly in evidence in a Townhall concert with Slam Stewart, Teddy Wilson, and others, particularly in the group's rendition of the bop standard "I Got Rhythm." During that summer he would often play with Parker at the Downbeat Club on Fifty-second Street, then move to an adjoining club during intermissions to play duets with Hawkins.

Byas did not slow down at all in 1946. He won the Esquire Silver Award, performed in January with Leonard Feather's Esquire All-Americans (the group included Duke Ellington, Johnny Hodges, and Louis Armstrong), and in February recorded with Gillespie. He also waxed his second version of "Body and Soul" that year; it remains one of the few to rival the legendary Hawkins effort and has been described as "yet another ravishing tenor seduction of the melody, virtuosic and ardent" (Giddins, p. 50). That summer Byas traveled to Europe with Don Redman's band and, attracted by the enthusiastic reception, decided to move there permanently, first to France and subsequently to the Netherlands and then Denmark.

Despite his physical absence from the American scene, Byas continued to tour and record prolifically over the next decade. He worked frequently as a soloist throughout Europe and performed regularly at festivals like the Paris Jazz Fair. In 1950 he toured the Continent with Ellington, and in the early 1950s he recorded some extraordinary sessions for Vogue with Roy Eldridge. He cut a number of sides for Blue Star records between 1946 and 1952. The later 1950s were somewhat quieter, but he become more visible again beginning in 1960. He returned to the United States for the first time since his move to Europe to appear at the 1960 Newport Jazz Festival, and he shared the stage with Hawkins and Benny Carter for a 1960 Jazz at the Philharmonic tour. He appeared on a 1961 tribute to Cannonball Adderly on Columbia Records and played strongly on a January 1964 live session recorded for Black Lion records in Copenhagen. He ended the decade with a 1968 recorded meeting with Ben Webster. In 1970 he played with Art Blakey in the United States and toured Japan with the drummer. He recorded a 1971 session with strings and made his final recording in 1972, a quartet date in Holland that included the Spanish pianist Tete Montelieu. In the last years before his death, Byas also continued to play in jazz and dance bands throughout Europe. He died of lung cancer in Amsterdam.

Byas was the most brilliant of Hawkins's followers. Though he never varied his phrasing as much as Hawkins, his playing was almost as evocative, with its huge tone and plangent emotionalism on ballads and his technical perfection on up-tempo pieces. And though his rhythmic conception remained rooted in swing, he was a crucial transitional player between the swing and bop eras, a highly influential precursor of bop in his extensive use of substitute chords. In the end, his unique combination of bop harmonies, swing rhythms, and lyric intensity guarantees Byas's place in jazz history.

• The most concise discussion of Byas's music is in Tom Piazza, *The Guide to Classic Recorded Jazz* (1995). Also valuable are Max Harrison et al., *The Essential Jazz Records*, vol. 1: *Ragtime to Swing* (1984); John Chilton, *The Song of the Hawk: The Life and Recordings of Coleman Hawkins* (1990); and Martin Williams, *The Jazz Tradition* (1970; rev. ed., 1983). Discographies include D. B. Wilke, "A Don Byas Discography, 1938–1972 (Part I: 1938–1943)," *Micrography*, no. 46 (1978): 17. A good capsule overview is in Ian Carr et al., *Jazz: The Rough Guide* (1995). Finally, there are many brief articles and discussions readily available. See, for example, Gunther Schuller, *The Swing Era: The Development of Jazz, 1930–1945* (1989); Gary Giddins, *Rhythm-a-Ning: Jazz Tradition and Innovation in the 80s* (1985); J. Burns, "Don Byas," *Jazz Journal* 18, no. 1 (1965): 5; and M. Hennessey, "Don Byas: Emphatic Expatriate," *Down Beat* 34, no. 15 (1967): 23. An obituary is in the *New York Times*, 29 Aug. 1972.

RONALD P. DUFOUR

BYERLY, Perry (28 May 1897–26 Sept. 1978), geophysicist and seismologist, was born in Clarinda, Iowa, the son of Perry Byerly, a businessman, and Pauline Watson. Byerly was a sickly child, and on the advice of his doctor, the family moved to the dry climate of California in 1905. They settled in the Los Angeles area but moved often as his parents searched for the best area for their son. As a result, Byerly attended more than a dozen high schools before graduating from the High School in Redlands, California, in 1916.

Partly because of his uncertain physical condition, Byerly was an avid reader as a boy. He was especially fond of poetry, an attraction he maintained throughout his life. Although his parents were not highly educated, Byerly was encouraged by his teachers to attend college. In 1917 he matriculated at the University of Redlands, where he spent one year before transferring first to the University of Southern California and finally in 1920 to the University of California at Berkeley. He first majored in mathematics, but as a condition of his transfer to Berkeley, he switched his major to physics in order to hold an assistantship in that department. At Berkeley Byerly earned an A.B. in 1921, an M.A. in 1922, and a Ph.D. in physics in 1924.

Although Byerly's degree was in physics, his doctoral research focused on the fledgling area of geophysics. Byerly's dissertation was a study of the thermal resistance of plane surface joints in graphite. Following completion of his degree, Byerly spent a year teaching physics at the University of Nevada at Reno. When a position at Berkeley's seismographic station was vacated by Byerly's friend the Reverend James B. Macelwane, S.J., Byerly replaced him on the staff. Byerly spent the remainder of his career at Berkeley.

At the time that Byerly joined the field, geophysics and seismology were just beginning to develop into recognized specialties. During the early part of Byerly's career, the development of new seismographic instruments and advances in the theoretical understanding of the nature of the earth's crust and core transformed these studies into exciting and important fields of research. Byerly's own work both drew upon and contributed to these developments. His earliest geophysical papers addressed the various aspects of the way that the seismic waves generated in earthquakes travel through the earth. In particular, Byerly focused on the travel times of P (longitudinal) waves, and the ways in which the detection of these could be used to discover information about the structure of the earth's crust. He was also instrumental in the expansion of the network of seismographic stations in northern California. Through his leadership in promoting earthquake research, Berkeley's network grew over the course of his career from just two stations to a total of sixteen, a growth that allowed for greater accuracy in pinpointing the location and size of earthquakes in the region.

Byerly was also a leader in the description and analysis of earthquakes, including the study of ground motion, the character of surface breaks, and the expected frequency of earthquakes along a given fault. Much of this information could be gleaned from the careful study of the wave packets recorded on seismographs. One of Byerly's most significant discoveries resulted from his analysis in 1926 of the compression or dilation of P waves that could be used to infer the fault plane from which a given earthquake originated. Using a similar analysis of S (transverse or shear) waves generated in earthquakes, Byerly was able to determine the actual direction of the initial displacement. When this analysis was applied to the problem of the Atlantic Ridge in the early 1960s, Byerly found that the displacement direction of this ridge was exactly the opposite of that which had long been expected. This turned out to be convincing evidence of the spreading of the sea floor in this region. The discovery contributed to the acceptance of the hypothesis of plate tectonics, the theory that the earth's crust is composed of discrete, mobile, geological plates. He was also well known for his analysis of what he termed "False S" waves—P waves that could often be misinterpreted as high-frequency primary S waves—and was noted for work on determining the amount of energy released when a fault breaks.

In addition to his work in the experimental and theoretical aspects of seismology, Byerly was a leader in the emerging fields of earthquake engineering and the analysis of seismic hazard. He consulted on many occasions with leaders in both business and government regarding the seismic safety of buildings and nuclear reactors. A leader in the growth of the Seismological Society of America and its secretary from 1931 to 1956, he also served on the National Research Council, as president of the International Association of Seismology and Physics of the Earth's Interior from 1960 to 1963, and was instrumental in the founding in 1965 of the International Seismological Center in Edinburgh, Scotland. As one of the world's leading seismologists, Byerly had close ties with other internationally recognized geoscientists, including Hugo Benioff, Beno Gutenberg, and Charles Ritcher at Caltech; Harold Jeffreys in England; and Victor Conrad on the Continent. Byerly was also an effective teacher who helped to launch the careers of a whole generation of seismologists, many of whom went on to successful academic careers.

In 1925 Byerly married Ardis Gehring; they had one child. After her death in 1929, he married Elsie Gillmor in 1932, they had two children before they were divorced in 1940. He married Lillian Nuckolls in 1941. At the time of his death in Oakland, California, Byerly was an elder statesman of seismology, a discipline he had helped to create. Byerly's experimental and theoretical insights and his contributions to the disciplinary structure of the field of seismology made him one of the most significant geophysicists of the century.

• A collection of Byerly's papers is in the Bancroft Library at the University of California at Berkeley. A lengthy biographical tribute to Byerly by Bruce A. Bolt is in the *Bulletin of the Seismological Society of America* 69 (1979): 928–45. Byerly was also the subject of a memorial essay by John Verhoogen in the National Academy of Sciences, *Biographical Memoirs* 55 (1974): 95–105. For historical work on the development of geophysics and seismology, see K. E. Bullen and Bruce A. Bolt, *Introduction to the Theory of Seismology*, 4th ed. (1985); Judith R. Goodstein, "Waves in the Earth: Seismology Comes to Southern California," *Historical Studies in the Physical Sciences* 14 (1984): 201–30; and Lewis Pyenson, *Cultural Imperialism and Exact Sciences: German Expansion Overseas 1900–1930* (1985).

DAVID A. VALONE

BYERLY, William Elwood (13 Dec. 1849–20 Dec. 1935), mathematician and educator, was born in Philadelphia, Pennsylvania, the son of Elwood Byerly, a merchant, and Rebecca Potts Wayne. Byerly grew up in New Jersey, where he was privately tutored until he entered Harvard University in the fall of 1867. He received his A.B. in 1871 at the top of his class, which included Henry Cabot Lodge and the mathematician William E. Story. Remaining at Harvard for graduate studies, in 1873 he received one of the first two Ph.D. degrees awarded by that institution. His dissertation, "The Heat of the Sun," was directed by Benjamin Peirce but was not subsequently published; however, he had the distinction of being the recipient of the first doctorate in mathematics to be awarded in the United States.

Byerly accepted an assistant professorship at Cornell University (1873–1876) and then returned to a similar position at Harvard (1876–1881). In 1881 he was promoted to full professor, and in 1905 he became Perkins Professor of Mathematics after the death of James M. Peirce. He held this position until 1913, when an oculist advised that unless he relinquished his professional duties he would become blind within two years. Byerly reluctantly accepted this prognosis and lived another twenty-two years in retirement in reasonable health.

Byerly's academic career was unusual. Although serving as an editor of *Annals of Mathematics* (1899–1911), he did little creative research of his own—indeed, the dozen or so papers he wrote were almost exclusively devoted to what are clearly pedagogical topics, i.e., elaborations of textbook-level problems. Hence, Byerly's primary scholarly activity was his teaching and the first-rate textbooks that he produced based on his classroom experience. He loved to teach and was truly devoted to his subject and to his students. As one of his colleagues observed, "While others teach the subject, Byerly teaches the class." As a measure of the respect in which he was held at Harvard, when the prestigious Perkins professorship became vacant, although more active research-oriented candidates were available, Byerly was chosen for the position.

The most famous of Byerly's texts were *Elements of Differential Calculus* (1879), *Elements of Integral Calculus* (1881), *Elementary Treatise on Fourier's Series, and Spherical, Cylindrical, and Ellipsoidal Harmonics* (1893), *Introduction to the Use of Generalized Coordinates in Mechanics and Physics* (1916), and *Introduction to the Calculus of Variations* (1917). Each book ran into several editions that presented the material with a modicum of theory and with a heavy reliance on illustrative examples. The first two were essentially elementary and successfully rivaled their British competitors, such as the works of Joseph Edwards and Isaac Todhunter, while, strictly speaking, the others had no competition in the English language. All were deservedly popular, but, due to the scarcity of examples to completely illustrate the scope of the material, the latter three books were less satisfactory. Stated bluntly, some of Byerly's theoretical asides and comments in these books simply were wrong. However, notwithstanding such defects—because students were not reading them for theory but for computational techniques—they are still useful.

In addition to his purely pedagogical contributions, Byerly played a highly respected and visible role in the life of his university. He was one of the first Harvard professors to agree to give private instruction to women, which he did actively from 1879 to 1889. In 1882, when the Cambridge Society for the Collegiate Instruction of Women was formally incorporated and became Radcliffe College, he was one of the original incorporators, a member of the corporation, and a member until 1924 of its executive board (the Council). For many years he was chairman of the academic board and often functioned as the official spokesman for Radcliffe before the Harvard faculty. After his retirement in 1913, university president Charles Eliot described Byerly as "the most indispensable person connected with the growth and development of Radcliffe College." In 1933 the new physics and chemistry laboratory building at Radcliffe was named the William Elwood Byerly Hall. He was also active in the work of the National Education Association and in 1893 was a member of a committee of ten charged with the investigation of teaching in secondary schools. The report the committee issued was long highly regarded in the educational community for its significance.

Byerly married Alice Worcester Parsons of Boston in 1885; they had two children. She died in 1918. In 1921 he wed Anne Carter Wickham Renshaw of Virginia. Byerly died in Swarthmore, Pennsylvania.

• A detailed biographical article on Byerly by Julian L. Coolidge is in the *Bulletin of the American Mathematical Society* 42 (May 1936): 295–98. An article by Byerly that contains his reminiscences about his student days at Harvard College and his relationship with Benjamin Peirce is in the *American Mathematical Monthly* 32 (Jan. 1925): 5–7. An obituary is in the *New York Times*, 21 Dec. 1935.

JOSEPH D. ZUND

BYFORD, William Heath (20 Mar. 1817–21 May 1890), gynecologist and advocate of medical education for women, was born in Eaton, Ohio, the son of Henry Byford, a mechanic, and Hannah Swain. Henry Byford moved his family to southwestern Indiana shortly after William's birth and died there nine years later. Young William did odd jobs to help out, but about 1830 Hannah Byford had to move the family to her father's farm in Crawford County, Illinois. During the next few years William often asked to be allowed to learn a trade to help support the family and improve his own prospects. He finally became apprenticed to a tailor, who moved away two years later. At this time William decided on medicine for his career, although he never mentioned the reason. His reading and studies in chemistry, physiology, and natural history may have steered him in this direction.

In 1837 Dr. Joseph Maddox of Vincennes, Indiana, took Byford into his office as a pupil. After eighteen months Maddox, impressed by Byford's progress, suggested he appear before the state's three-man examining board. When the board approved Byford's qualifications, he chose Owensville, a small town south of Vincennes, in which to begin his practice.

After two years in Owensville, Byford moved to nearby Mount Vernon, where he associated with Dr. Hezekiah Holland. In 1840 he married Mary Anne Holland, the daughter of his associate. During the following decade with Holland, Byford acquired valuable experience. He received an M.D. degree from the Ohio Medical College in Cincinnati in 1845.

In 1849 the Evansville (Indiana) Medical College, admitting its first class that fall, invited Byford to take its chair of anatomy. Three years later he moved to the chair of the theory and practice of medicine. Late in 1854 the college had to suspend operations, but Byford remained in Evansville, in general practice, until 1857.

Rush Medical College in Chicago asked Byford that year to join its faculty as professor of obstetrics and diseases of women and children. Byford thus succeeded John Evans, later the second territorial governor of Colorado, who was then leaning more toward business and politics than medicine.

The administration at Rush had probably become aware of Byford because of his publications. Among the more important were a major review of scrofula (*Transactions of the American Medical Association* 8 [1855]: 493–534), in which he stressed the importance of physical and mental exercise, an epidemiological study of typhoid and its complications in Mount Vernon (*American Journal of Medical Science* 41 [Jan. 1851]: 61–70), and a comprehensive account of milk sickness (*Nashville Journal of Medicine and Surgery* 9 [1855]: 460–73).

In 1858 Byford first declared his longtime interest in physical examination with a paper titled "Advantages of the Prone Position in Examining the Foetal Circulation as a Diagnostic Sign of Pregnancy." He also designed and used an ingenious examination table. The following year he reported at length on a group of cases he had gathered from around Illinois as chairman of the Illinois State Medical Society's Committee on Obstetrics and Diseases of Women. Byford performed the first ovariotomy in Chicago in 1860, a major surgical contribution. Over the next thirty years he wrote extensively on the medical and surgical conditions of the ovaries.

His writing and teaching also included much on the uterus. In 1875 his review "Treatment of Fibrous Tumors of the Uterus by Ergot" for the American Medical Association aroused interest not only because it included apparently the first successful case of such treatment but also because it summarized 100 additional cases.

Surgical technique, Byford believed, was of great importance. In the 1 September 1883 issue of the *Journal of the American Medical Association* he stressed the need for careful and minimal handling of tissues: "Sometimes . . . injudicious thoroughness and earnestness in an examination to ascertain the exact condition of the patient develops an acute inflammation that inflicts fearful suffering, and perhaps cripples the patient for life" (p. 226).

Byford's interests ran beyond the strictly medical. In his 1877 presidential address before the Tri-State Medical Society at Vincennes he spoke on "The Second Decade of Life." In this he drew attention to the importance of character formation, the provision of healthful surroundings for school and play, and the role of the doctor in these and other aspects of growth and development.

He played substantial roles in the founding and support of two institutions important for the medical education of women. When Dr. Mary H. Thompson decided to establish a hospital for women and children in Chicago near the end of the Civil War, she received Byford's financial, professional, and psychological support. This was of such value that her Chicago Hospital for Women and Children, opened in 1865, was popularly known for many years as "Dr. Byford's Hospital." Renamed the Mary Thompson Hospital after her sudden death in 1895, this institution continued until 1988.

In 1859 Byford had left Rush because of its refusal to improve its curriculum. He and his colleagues then founded the Chicago Medical College (later the Northwestern University Medical School). Byford received the chair of obstetrics. Ten years later when Thompson, feeling the need for more medical education, applied to Rush, the college rejected her because of her sex. Shortly thereafter, and at Byford's urging, the Chicago Medical College admitted Thompson and three other women in the fall of 1869. Although Thompson received her second M.D. degree in 1870, the college bowed to its male students' demands and refused that fall to allow the other three women to attend their second year.

Next Byford led a group to establish and fund the Woman's Hospital Medical College of Chicago, which admitted its first seventeen students in the fall of 1870. This college, which later ran into financial difficulties, was purchased by Northwestern University in 1892 but was closed in 1902.

When Rush created a chair of gynecology in 1879 specifically for Byford, he returned and held that position until his death. Another point in Rush's favor was that it was closer to the Woman's Medical College than was the Chicago Medical College.

Byford wrote four books: *A Treatise on the Chronic Inflammation and Displacements of the Unimpregnated Uterus* (1864), *The Practice of Medicine and Surgery Applied to the Diseases and Accidents Incident to Women* (1865; 4th ed., coauthored by his son Henry T. Byford, 1888), *The Philosophy of Domestic Life* (1869), and *A Treatise on the Theory and Practice of Obstetrics* (1870; 2d ed., 1873).

Byford served as editor or coeditor of several medical journals. One, the *Chicago Medical Journal and Examiner*, not only achieved national status but also encouraged the use of the metric system.

Playing substantial roles in several medical organizations, Byford was a founder of the American Gynecological Society in 1876 and served as its president in 1881. He also helped found the Chicago Gynecological Society and became its first president in 1878. The British Gynaecological Society elected him a life member. Byford, who had joined the American Medical Association in 1854, urged the admission of women to the association. In 1876 he nominated Sarah Hackett Stevenson, who was then elected the first woman member.

Five children were born to William and Anne Holland Byford before her death in 1864. The youngest, Henry Turman Byford, became well known as both a gynecologist and an artist. In 1873 Byford married Lina W. Flershem of Buffalo, New York. Their only child died in infancy. Byford died in Chicago.

A religious man and a nondrinker, Byford was devoted to his family and his work. Short and solidly built, the kindly and curious physician quickly made a favorable impression. He contributed substantially to the development of the specialty of gynecology by his operations and treatments, his articles and books, and his work with organizations. He pioneered in and supported both undergraduate and postgraduate medical education for women.

• The major biographical source for Byford is William K. Beatty, "William Heath Byford: Physician and Advocate for Women," *Proceedings of the Institute of Medicine of Chicago* 39 (Jan.–Mar. 1986): 6–23, which includes a list of many of his writings and a portrait. Contemporary accounts include Howard Conard, "Dr. William Heath Byford," *Magazine of Western History*, Jan. 1890, pp. 320–24, which was written a few months before Byford's death. Although delivered five years later, Delaskie Miller's address at the presentation of a bust of Byford to Rush Medical College contains a valuable picture of the man by a friend and colleague, in *Chicago Clinical Review* 4 (June 1895): pp. 440–51. Edward W. Jenks, also a longtime friend and colleague, wrote the obituary of Byford for the American Gynecological Society in its *Transactions* 15 (1890): 401–6. A committee of the Chicago Gynecological Society wrote its memorial to Byford, which appeared in the first volume of its *Transactions* (1892–1893): iii–vii (includes a partial list of his publications). Also helpful is that society's memorial meeting for Byford, held on 13 June 1890; a three-page obituary by H. P. Merriman is followed by comments from other colleagues, in *North American Practitioner* 2 (July 1890): 328–33.

WILLIAM K. BEATTY

BYLES, Mather (15 Mar. 1707–5 July 1788), Congregationalist clergyman and poet, was born in Boston, Massachusetts, the son of Josiah (Josias) Byles, a saddler, and Elizabeth Mather, the widow of William Greenough and a daughter of Increase Mather. His father died when he was a year old, and he was brought up by his mother, his grandfather, and his formidable uncle Cotton Mather. Destined for the ministry since birth, he received his Harvard A.B. in 1725 and his A.M. in 1728. In 1732 he became the first minister of the Hollis Street (Congregational) Church in Boston and remained in that charge for forty-five years. Byles, a Loyalist, supported Governors Francis Bernard and Thomas Hutchinson and lost his pulpit when Massachusetts rebelled. His first wife, Anna Noyes Gale, whom he married in 1733, was the daughter of Oliver Noyes, a physician and merchant of Boston, and the widow of Azor Gale, Jr. She was a niece of Jonathan Belcher, the royal governor and chief benefactor of Byles's church. After her death in 1744, he married in 1747 Rebecca Tailer, daughter of William Tailer, a former lieutenant governor. With his first wife he had six children, but only one son, Mather Byles, Jr., survived him. With his second wife he had three children, but was survived only by two daughters.

Byles, who inherited the Mather name and library, never matched the high seriousness of his forebears. He was admired in his lifetime, but although he remained true to orthodox Calvinism in theology, he treated his intellectual inheritance as a trellis on which to grow carefully cultivated flowers of wit and punning language. His sermons were praised for their sonorous language and elaborate descriptive passages, not for their probing ethical, moral, or theological content. During his years in the pulpit, he was often chosen to deliver sermons on state occasions such as the funerals of royal governors or their wives. Twice he spoke for the Establishment at the executions of persons guilty of infanticide.

Byles's first heroes were poets: he preserved copies of the admiring letters that he wrote in the 1720s and 1730s to Alexander Pope, Isaac Watts, and James Thomson. Pope and Watts, who were touched by the enthusiasm of the youth "from the remote shores," replied. He had a gift for fluent poetry, as great as any of his American contemporaries, and published considerable amounts in the 1740s in the *New England Weekly Journal*. In style, Mather's official poetry, which followed the example of Isaac Watts, can be characterized as "the religious sublime," full of hyper-emotive language that was intended to inspire exalted emotion in the reader. In private, he and his friends amused themselves by writing anonymous verse parodies of ballads about famous heroes. "Some Excellent Verses on Admiral Vernon's Taking the Forts and Castles of Carthagena," first published in 1741 and reprinted in *A Collection of Poems. By Several Hands* (1744), by Joseph Green or by Byles himself, makes fun of a British military disaster by casting it into mock-heroics.

As in his sermons, Byles was often the spokesman for decorous Establishment views. His poems on the deaths of George II and Queen Caroline were published in Boston and no doubt sent to London as demonstrations of provincial loyalty. His best early work was collected in his *Poems on Several Occasions* (1744). A characteristic title is *Poems. The Conflagration Applied to That Grand Period or Catastrophe of Our World, When the Face of Nature Is to be Changed by a Deluge of Fire, As Formerly It Was by That of Water. The God of Tempest and Earthquake*, published in reaction to the great New England earthquake of 1755. Some of his hymns were published in collections by Watts. He was a lifelong friend of Benjamin Franklin, who admired his conviviality and his facility with words, but Byles had none of Franklin's intellectual depth.

Byles came to grief during the Revolution. When the British occupied Boston he stayed behind when the patriots fled, preached in the First Church, and cultivated public friendships with the British. When the British evacuated the city in March 1776, his son, who had become an Anglican clergyman, left with them for Halifax. The father remained, and professed astonishment when patriots in his returning congregation preferred charges and dismissed him in 1777. He was put on public trial and sentenced to banishment, which was commuted to house arrest. Throughout, Byles preserved his good humor and capacity for making puns, referring to the sentry stationed outside his house as his "Observe-a-Tory." For the rest of his life he and his maiden daughters, who devoted themselves to his well-being, lived quietly, dependent on the charity of his friends. He died in Boston. His daughters, who lived into the nineteenth century, continued to behave as if they were members of the genteel, Anglophile pre-Revolutionary society that their father had exemplified.

• Most of Byles's papers are at the Massachusetts Historical Society. They consist of original letters and copies of material held in Halifax, Nova Scotia, and Derby, England. The New England Historic Genealogical Society has one of Byles's letterbooks, which also includes letters by his daughters. It contains many of the answers to letters held by the Massachusetts Historical Society. Byles's *Works*, first published in eighteen separate volumes during his lifetime, was republished in facsimile by Benjamin Franklin V (1978). The Harvard library catalog lists forty-eight works with material by, or dedications to, Byles. Yet his bibliographical listings are somewhat confused; works are attributed to him that were obviously written by his son. Many of Byles's amusing poems have only survived in manuscript commonplace books and diaries. Nathan Fisk's notebook, begun when he was a student at Harvard in the 1750s and kept through the 1780s, contains pieces by Byles and Nathaniel Gardner, Jr.; it is preserved at the American Antiquarian Society. By far the best brief sketch of his life is in Clifford K. Shipton, *Sibley's Harvard Graduates*, vol. 7: *Biographical Sketches of Those Who Attended Harvard College in the Classes 1722–1725* (1945). David S. Shields, *Oracles of Empire: Poetry, Politics, and Commerce in British America, 1690–1750* (1990), puts Byles's poetry into context. The only full-scale study of his life is Arthur W. H. Eaton, *The Famous Mather Byles: The Noted Boston Tory Preacher, Poet and Wit (1707–1788)* (1914).

MARY RHINELANDER McCARL

BYNNER, Witter (10 Aug. 1881–1 June 1968), poet and playwright, was born in Brooklyn, New York, the son of Thomas Edgarton Bynner and Annie Louise Brewer. His parents separated when he was seven as a consequence of his father's alcoholism, and he and his younger brother lived for three years with his mother and her family in Norwich, Connecticut. After his father's death in 1891, the family moved to Brookline, Massachusetts, to live with his father's sisters.

Bynner was a diligent but not especially distinguished student, and his major accomplishment in high school was editing the school literary magazine during his senior year. That role proved decisive in his choice of a career: when he found that he had no poetry for one issue of the magazine, he quickly wrote a poem himself and enjoyed the activity so much that he decided to make it his life's work. He attended Harvard, where he served on the editorial board of the *Harvard Advocate* for two years prior to his graduation with an A.B. in 1902. After traveling in Europe that summer, he joined the staff of *McClure's* magazine and remained there for four years. He secured for publication manuscripts by several noted writers, including O. Henry and the English poet A. E. Housman, whose first U.S. publication was in the pages of *McClure's*.

Bynner left *McClure's* in December 1906 to devote himself to his own writing, and a month later he moved to Cornish, New Hampshire, where he rented rooms in the home of a Harvard classmate, the sculptor Homer Saint-Gaudens. Cornish became Bynner's base for the next nine years as he wrote poetry while supporting himself as a freelance manuscript reader for the Boston publisher Small, Maynard and Company. Bynner's first book, *An Ode to Harvard, and Other Poems*, was published by the company in June 1907. Two one-act plays followed: *Tiger* (1913) and *The Little King* (1914). Bynner's next book, *The New World* (1915), was a revision of a Whitmanesque poem extolling the virtues of America, originally titled "The Immigrant," that he had delivered as the Phi Beta Kappa poem at Harvard in 1911. Bynner championed the American experience as a suitable literary subject and, like Whitman and Emerson, called for a national literature that freed itself from European dominance.

Bynner left Cornish in 1915 and for the next seven years became a supporter of liberal causes, traveling around the country to give speeches and demonstrate on behalf of pacifism, woman suffrage, and civil rights; these sympathies often found their way into his verse. During this period, Bynner also launched the so-called Spectra Hoax, for which he became widely known. The hoax was concocted by Bynner and his friend and fellow poet Arthur Davison Ficke to prove that the reading public paid more attention to schools of poetry than to poetry itself. Each of them assumed a fictitious identity as a European émigré poet living in Pittsburgh—Bynner was "Emanuel Morgan" and Ficke was "Anne Knish"—and in late 1916 published *Spectra: A Book of Poetic Experiments*. The "Spectric School," as the pseudonymous poets explained in their intentionally pompous preface, was devoted to poetry of the mind, a "process of diffraction by which are disarticulated the several colored and other rays of which light is composed." Bynner and Ficke favorably reviewed the book under their own names.

Many critics dismissed the book as insubstantial, but an influential few, like the writers Edgar Lee Masters, John Gould Fletcher, and Eunice Tietjens, praised it as a more profound alternative to the then-fashionable school of imagism. For several years "Morgan" and "Knish" published Spectric verse in such leading magazines as *Poetry* and *The Little Review* while Bynner and Ficke debated its merits in public lectures before enthusiastic audiences. Bynner also published a book of verse, *Pins for Wings* (1920), as Morgan. Finally, in the early 1920s, Bynner apparently grew tired of the game and began acknowledging that he and Ficke had invented Spectrism. Many heretofore sympathetic critics felt duped and said so. Meanwhile, Bynner had grown rather fond of his alter ego and continued to write and publish some of his subsequent work under the name Emanuel Morgan.

Bynner had developed an interest in Chinese T'ang poetry as a consequence of a trip to the Orient that he and Ficke had taken in the spring of 1917. That interest intensified in the fall of 1918, when Bynner taught for a semester at the University of California, Berkeley. There he met the Chinese scholar Kiang Kang-hu, who had fled to the United States after denouncing a plot to overthrow the emperor. Kiang had translated many poems from the T'ang dynasty (618–906 A.D.), and Bynner came to appreciate them even more through long discussions with Kiang. The essence of T'ang poetry, in Bynner's view, was its expression of an "intuitional sense of oneness in man, nature and eternity," as he described it many years later in a tribute to Kiang. This sense of oneness, together with the Whitmanesque sentiment of the primacy of universal over individual love, became the overriding themes of Bynner's own poetry.

Bynner and Kiang worked on a translation of T'ang dynasty poems that had never been rendered in English. *The Jade Mountain* (1929) was the result of eleven years of effort, including a ten-month stay in China. Their cooperative effort was aided by a mutual commitment to preserving the syntactical simplicity of classical Chinese. Although Bynner had no prior knowledge of written Chinese, he became familiar with the ideograms and learned to speak the language during his years of work on the manuscript. *The Jade*

Mountain was well received by both scholars and poets, and it is recognized as a major contribution to North American literature in the twentieth century.

In 1922, while working on *The Jade Mountain*, Bynner visited Santa Fe, New Mexico, and decided to remain there. When D. H. Lawrence and his wife visited in 1923, Bynner accompanied them on an extended trip through Mexico. There he became attached to the town of Chapala, near Guadalajara; he returned there regularly in the following years and bought a house there in 1940. For the remainder of his life he divided his time between Santa Fe and Chapala.

Bynner was a prolific author. He published a collection of his plays, *A Book of Plays* (1922); *A Book of Love* (1923), a translation of poetry by Charles Vildrac; the poetry collections *Caravan* (1925) and *Indian Earth* (1929); his best-known play, *Cake* (1926); and an extended essay, *The Persistence of Poetry* (1929). His later poetic works included *Eden Tree* (1931), a sequel to *The New World*; *Guest Book* (1935), a series of witty and often satirical portraits of his friends; *Selected Poems* (1935); *Against the Cold* (1940), a series of poems about death written as his health began to decline; *The Way of Life According to Laotzu* (1944), his own retelling of the *Tao te Ching*; *Take Away the Darkness* (1947); *Book of Lyrics* (1955); and *New Poems* (1960). He also published a memoir of his friendship with D. H. Lawrence titled *Journey with Genius* (1951).

Bynner, who never married, was briefly engaged to Edna St. Vincent Millay in 1921. In 1930, apparently comfortable with public acknowledgment of his homosexuality, he began a lifelong relationship with an admirer, Robert Hunt, who became not only his lover but his personal assistant, editor, household manager, and nurse as Bynner grew increasingly blind. Hunt was also an alcoholic who could be belligerent and abusive—more than an echo of Bynner's long-dead father—but Bynner put up with him. When Hunt died suddenly in 1964, Bynner was devastated and shortly afterward suffered a stroke that left him disabled. He died in a sanatorium in Santa Fe.

• Many of Bynner's papers are at the Humanities Research Center of the University of Texas in Austin and the library of Mills College in Oakland, Calif. A five-volume collection of Bynner's poems, plays, and letters, *The Works of Witter Bynner*, was edited by James Kraft and published posthumously between 1978 and 1981. Biographical information on Bynner is in James Kraft, *Who Is Witter Bynner?* (1995). Anne H. Tayler's essay "Witter Bynner" in the *Dictionary of Literary Biography*, vol. 54, is also helpful. In addition see William Jay Smith, *The Spectra Hoax* (1961), and Robert O. Lindsay, *Witter Bynner: A Bibliography* (1967). An obituary is in the *New York Times*, 3 June 1968.

ANN T. KEENE

BYRD, Harry Flood (10 June 1887–20 Oct. 1966), governor of Virginia and U.S. senator, was born in Martinsburg, West Virginia, the son of Richard Evelyn Byrd, a lawyer, and Eleanor Bolling Flood. A direct descendant of the colonial William Byrds, Harry Byrd grew up in Winchester, Virginia, in modest circumstances. At age fifteen he left school to take over the failing family newspaper, the Winchester *Evening Star*, and through hard work and thrift turned it into a profitable venture. Moving into the apple orchard business, he created a multimillion dollar operation that brought him financial security and a national reputation as one of the largest apple growers in the country. In 1913 he married Anne Douglas Beverley; they had four children, one of whom, Harry Byrd, Jr., succeeded his father in the U.S. Senate.

Byrd was elected to the Virginia Senate in 1915. Rarely involved in legislative debates, he quietly but effectively pursued interests in highways and finance. He also served as state fuel administrator during World War I. Chosen Virginia Democratic party chairman in 1922, he led the successful fight against a highway bond issue in 1923 that confirmed pay-as-you-go as the fiscal policy of the Old Dominion and solidified his control of the political organization that he soon reshaped into his own machine.

Elected governor in 1925, Byrd modernized Virginia government by streamlining the bureaucracy and expanding the authority of the executive. His major reorganization proposals reduced the number of elected state officers from eight to three (governor, lieutenant governor, and attorney general), abolished many state agencies and consolidated all others into eleven departments, and instituted a new system of tax segregation that separated state and local sources of taxation for greater equity and efficiency. Byrd's enthusiasm, energy, and political skills were primarily responsible for the ease with which all that he proposed won the approval of the general assembly and the electorate.

Governor Byrd furthered his record of progressive leadership with his "program of progress" that attracted new industries and residents through tax cuts and recruiting, increased tourism, and left a state surplus of over $4 million when he departed office. He was the Commonwealth's number one "booster," supporting creation of the Shenandoah National Park and traveling across the state to promote roads, tourism, and airport development, the latter encouraged by the exploits of his brother, polar explorer Richard Evelyn Byrd, Jr. (1888–1957). A notable achievement was his advocacy of a strong antilynching bill passed by the legislature in 1928. Byrd's governorship reflected the business progressivism of the 1920s that emphasized economy, efficiency, and industrial growth, but paid little attention to the problems of agriculture, poverty, and labor relations.

When Byrd "retired" to his orchards in 1930, he was still an energetic young man who had a long political career ahead of him. Although the apple business consumed much of his time, he remained highly involved in state affairs. He also undertook a modest presidential campaign in 1932 that ended with the fourth-ballot convention victory of Franklin Roosevelt. While this was as close as he ever came to the presidency, Byrd flirted with a token protest candidacy against Roosevelt in 1944 and in 1960 won fifteen electoral votes when disaffected southern electors chose not to support the nominees of their parties.

When Virginia senator Claude Swanson was appointed secretary of the navy in 1933, Byrd was appointed to fill his seat in the Senate, where for more than thirty years he argued on behalf of balanced budgets, reduced federal spending, and states' rights. Reelected for six terms by overwhelming margins, Byrd adhered to a nineteenth-century Jeffersonian philosophy that favored a laissez-faire economic and political order in which government activity was minimal and rugged individualism reigned supreme. He became a vociferous critic of the New Deal, joining a conservative coalition of congressmen who opposed the growth of government. For twenty years he chaired the Joint Committee on Reduction of Non-essential Federal Expenditures, whose reports derided the bloated federal bureaucracy. Predictably, his Senate record was remarkably negative. He voted against aid to education, public housing, prolabor legislation, antipoverty programs, and minimum wage increases. Although he was not an isolationist and supported major defense appropriations, he opposed most foreign aid programs, such as the Marshall Plan and the Truman Doctrine, because of their cost.

By the 1950s Byrd had assumed the role of an elder statesman. He had achieved national prominence as the conservative spokesman for an older order, but his positions alienated him from a more liberal national Democratic party, particularly on civil rights. After 1944 he pursued a "golden silence" during presidential campaigns. Chairman of the important Senate Finance Committee from 1955 to 1965, Byrd was respected for his independence and fairness. Although he frequently delayed social and fiscal legislation that he found philosophically offensive, he never totally obstructed it.

During his Senate years, Byrd continued to control Virginia politics, helping to select gubernatorial candidates, advising them on legislation, and keeping the Old Dominion committed to honest but parsimonious government. As depression and war changed the nature of the Commonwealth and the nation, Byrd was hard-pressed to maintain his authority. Faced with the Supreme Court's desegregation decision of 1954, he orchestrated a policy of massive resistance to thwart its implementation in Virginia, but doctrines of interposition, school-closing laws, and political demagoguery ended in ignominious defeat in 1959. He spent his final years unsuccessfully combating the budget deficits, civil rights legislation, and social programs of President John F. Kennedy and Lyndon B. Johnson. Byrd retired from the Senate on 11 November 1965, undoubtedly feeling the effects of a brain tumor that took his life eleven months later at his beloved "Rosemont" in Berryville, Virginia.

Byrd was the most prominent Virginian of the twentieth century. Although his influence at the national level was limited by his increasingly unfashionable view of government and balanced budgets, his leadership of Virginia was practically unchallenged for over forty years. That legacy, however, was mixed. After a dynamic governorship, Byrd settled into a conservatism that obstructed economic and social progress in the state. He could not adapt his individualistic ethic to the demands of modern society. As V. O. Key said of Virginia's leaders in his *Southern Politics in State and Nation* (1949), "Men with the minds of tradesmen do not become statesmen."

• Byrd's papers are at the University of Virginia Library. Other important collections that include extensive correspondence with and about Byrd are those of Senator Carter Glass, Representative Howard Smith, and Everett R. Combs at the University of Virginia Library; Representative William Tuck and Senator A. Willis Robertson at the College of William and Mary Library; the executive papers of Virginia governors at the Virginia State Library; and the papers of William T. Reed at the Virginia Historical Society. Ronald L. Heinemann, *Harry Byrd of Virginia* (1996), is a full-length biography. Alden Hatch, *The Byrds of Virginia* (1969), offers anecdotal information. A formidable number of articles, monographs, and biographies on twentieth-century Virginia political history address Byrd's leadership of the machine. The best of these is J. Harvie Wilkinson, *Harry Byrd and the Changing Face of Virginia Politics, 1945–1966* (1968). Allen Moger, *Virginia: Bourbonism to Byrd, 1870–1925* (1968), is good on the origins of the Byrd organization. The most thorough treatment of Byrd's governorship is Robert T. Hawkes, Jr., "The Career of Harry Flood Byrd, Sr., to 1933" (Ph.D. diss., Univ. of Virginia, 1975). A brief but complete history of Virginia politics since the Civil War can be found in Edward Younger and James T. Moore, eds., *The Governors of Virginia, 1860–1978* (1982). James R. Sweeney offers an assessment of Byrd's political philosophy in "Harry Byrd: Vanished Policies and Enduring Principles," *Virginia Quarterly Review* 52 (Autumn 1976): 596–612. Helpful biographies include William B. Crawley, Jr., *Bill Tuck: A Political Life in Harry Byrd's Virginia* (1978), Bruce J. Dierenfield, *Keeper of the Rules: Congressman Howard W. Smith of Virginia* (1987), and Henry C. Ferrell, Jr., *Claude A. Swanson of Virginia: A Political Biography* (1985). The best analysis of massive resistance is James Ely, *The Crisis of Conservative Virginia: The Byrd Organization and the Politics of Massive Resistance* (1976). An extensive obituary is in the Richmond *Times-Dispatch*, 21 Oct. 1966.

RONALD L. HEINEMANN

BYRD, Richard Evelyn (25 Oct. 1888–11 Mar. 1957), naval aviator and explorer, was born in Winchester, Virginia, the son of Richard Evelyn Byrd, an attorney, and Eleanor Bolling Flood. The family had long been prominent in Virginia; Byrd's brother Harry served as governor and several terms as a U.S. senator. After traveling alone around the world at the age of twelve, Byrd attended the Shenandoah Valley Military Academy, Virginia Military Institute (1904–1907), the University of Virginia (1907–1908), and the U.S. Naval Academy, receiving his ensign's commission in 1912.

Byrd served on several battleships; while on USS *Washington* he twice saved drowning men, for which he received a letter of commendation from the secretary of the navy and the Congressional Life Saving Medal. In 1915 he married Marie Donaldson Ames; they had four children.

Byrd was retired in March 1916 because a foot he had injured practicing gymnastics at the academy had not healed properly. He was soon returned to duty and in 1917 was sent to Pensacola for flight training, becoming naval aviator 608 in April 1918. He then became commander of two naval air stations in Nova Scotia, conducting antisubmarine patrols. Pioneering aerial overwater navigation and inventing a bubble sextant for that purpose, Byrd proposed that the navy fly large aircraft across the Atlantic for delivery to Europe. As the war drew to a close, he conducted the navigational preparations for the first successful transatlantic flight when the NC-4 flew from Rockaway, Long Island, to Lisbon, Portugal, and on to Plymouth, England, in 1919. Circumstances, however, permitted Byrd to accompany the flight only as far as Nova Scotia.

As assistant to the director of naval aviation, serving as the navy's liaison officer to Congress from 1919 to 1921, Byrd was an ardent and eloquent spokesman for the importance of aviation to the navy and the nation. He was responsible for the legislation that created the navy's Bureau of Aeronautics.

In 1925 Byrd led a naval party that accompanied the Donald B. MacMillan expedition to Greenland. Using aircraft, they explored 30,000 square miles of northern Greenland and neighboring Ellesmere Island.

Released from active duty in 1925, Byrd began planning a flight to the North Pole. He obtained $15,000 from Edsel Ford (and named the expedition's Fokker Trimotor *Josephine Ford*, for Edsel's young daughter) and a similar amount from John D. Rockefeller, Jr. The expedition departed Brooklyn Navy Yard on 5 April 1926 and arrived at Kings Bay, Spitzbergen, on 29 April to find the Amundsen-Ellsworth-Nobile expedition already there, preparing to fly over the Pole in the airship *Norge*.

Taking off just after midnight on 9 May 1926, with Floyd Bennett at the controls while Byrd navigated, Byrd reached the Pole at 9:02 A.M.; and circling it, made "a nonstop flight around the world in a very few minutes."

Not surprisingly, protests arose in Europe regarding the legitimacy of Byrd's claim to have reached the Pole two days before the *Norge* departed Spitzbergen for its transpolar flight to Alaska. It was claimed Byrd could not have completed a round trip to the Pole, 1,360 miles, in 15½ hours. The National Geographic Society investigated and confirmed Byrd's navigational calculations; however, not all critics were convinced. In May 1996 the Ohio State University's Byrd Polar Research Institute revealed that a long-lost diary of the flight contains entries that suggest Byrd turned back toward Spitzbergen just short of the 88th degree of latitude, more than a hundred miles short of the Pole. Byrd was promoted to commander and awarded the Medal of Honor, the Distinguished Service Medal, and the National Geographic Society's Hubbard Medal.

Byrd soon began planning a nonstop transatlantic flight, using an enlarged Fokker Trimotor, *America*, with his trusted companion Floyd Bennett piloting. He was not in the race with Lindbergh to win the Orteig Prize; he wished to demonstrate the feasibility of commercial transatlantic flight by multiengine aircraft.

On a test flight flown by Anthony Fokker, the nose-heavy aircraft overturned on landing. Byrd suffered a broken arm, but Bennett was so seriously injured he was unable to make the transatlantic flight, which departed Roosevelt Field at 5:27 A.M. on 29 June 1927, with Bernt Balchen, Bert Acosta, and George Noville accompanying Byrd. After crossing the Atlantic and finding Paris weathered in, they returned to the French coast and ditched safely just offshore at Versur-Mer, having flown 4,200 miles.

Byrd next obtained funding from the American and National Geographic societies, wealthy businessmen, and a number of smaller contributors for an expedition to explore Antarctica.

Two ships carrying forty-two men, equipped with four aircraft, ninety-four dogs, and two years' worth of scientific and medical supplies arrived at the Bay of Whales in December 1928. A camp called Little America was built on the Ross Ice Shelf, where the party overwintered and conducted several expeditions discovering mineral deposits and mapping 150,000 miles of hitherto unknown territory. On 28 November 1929, accompanied by Balchen, Ashley McKinley, and Harold June, Byrd flew to the South Pole, arriving at 1:14 A.M. Greenwich time on November 29. Awarded the Navy Cross and promoted to rear admiral, Byrd was soon at work on a second, larger antarctic expedition, which arrived at Little America on 17 January 1934.

While fifty-six men developed Little America, adding shops and laboratories and conducting research in a variety of scientific fields, including auroral phenomena, geology, and the collection of plant fossils and minerals, Byrd spent the winter alone in a hut 123 miles closer to the Pole, conducting weather observations. He nearly succumbed to carbon monoxide escaping from a defective stove. Unwilling to risk other men's safety in the −70°F temperatures of the antarctic winter night, he remained at his post for several months until his companions at Little America, their suspicions aroused by his garbled radio messages, dispatched a rescue party.

President Franklin D. Roosevelt met Byrd's ship on its return in May 1935 and in 1939 recalled him to active duty as the commanding officer of the U.S. Antarctic Service, intended to further explore and establish a permanent base on the continent. The expedition, unlike the first two, was partly funded by the government, with Byrd obtaining the remainder. After discovering new islands and mountain ranges and mapping 700 miles of coastline, the expedition was recalled in 1941 as war threatened.

During World War II Byrd visited the Pacific theater several times, planning a series of air bases to support the island-hopping campaigns. He also studied the use of aerial ground support in the European theater. He witnessed the Japanese surrender aboard USS *Missouri* and inspected the atomic bombs' effects at Hiroshima and Nagasaki. For his services to the nation during World War II, he received the Legion of Merit in January 1945.

In 1946 Byrd became commander of the navy's Operation Highjump, an expedition of 4,000 men to Antarctica that mapped, by aerial photography, more than 1.5 million square miles of the continent.

Byrd was instrumental in arranging for the U.S. antarctic crew to participate in the International Geophysical Year, which began in July 1957. As officer in charge of the U.S. Antarctic Programs, Byrd supervised the planning of Operation Deep Freeze I, to conduct further exploration of the antarctic, including construction of an observation station at the Pole. He returned to the continent for the last time from December 1955 to February 1956, flying over the Pole to determine the feasibility of landing aircraft there.

During his solitary winter in Antarctica, Byrd had spent much of his time contemplating the prospects for world peace. As the threat of war in Europe grew after his return to the United States, he joined other prominent Americans in seeking to prevent it or, failing that, to avoid American involvement. As honorary chairman of the No-Foreign-War Crusade, he broadcast an appeal to Europe in 1938 urging peace; but as war approached he publicly supported President Roosevelt's policies. After the war he founded the Iron Curtain Refugee Campaign of the International Rescue Committee and served from 1950 until his death as honorary chairman of the IRC's board of directors. Shortly before his death at his home in Boston, he received the Department of Defense Medal of Freedom.

Meticulous in planning and organizing his expeditions, Byrd could be short-tempered and abrasive, but he was generous with praise for his colleagues; he excelled as a leader and inspired intense loyalty.

On 25 October 1965 a bust of Byrd was dedicated at McMurdo Station, Antarctica, bearing his wish: "I am hopeful that Antarctica in its symbolic robe of white will shine forth as a continent of peace as nations working together there in the cause of science set an example of international cooperation."

• Byrd's private papers are held by his family. The Columbia University Oral History Collection contains personal recollections by some of Byrd's colleagues. His published accounts of his explorations are in *Into the Home of the Blizzard* (1928), *Skyward* (1928), *Little America* (1930), *Discovery* (1935), *Exploring with Byrd* (1937), *Alone* (1938), and a large number of articles in *National Geographic* and other magazines. A highly readable biography is Edwin P. Hoyt, *The Last Explorer: The Adventures of Admiral Byrd* (1968).

For more technical information, see John M. McClellan, "Some Scientific and Engineering Techniques Pioneered by Rear Admiral Richard E. Byrd in Oceanic and Polar Explorations" (M.A. thesis, Pennsylvania State Univ., 1970). A man of Byrd's extraordinary achievements is not without his critics; for an example, see Richard Montague, *Oceans, Poles and Airmen* (1971). See also John Noble Wilford, "Did Byrd Reach Pole? His Diary Hints 'No,'" *New York Times*, 9 May 1996. An obituary is in the *New York Times*, 12 Mar. 1957.

VINCENT P. NORRIS

BYRD, Roy. *See* Professor Longhair.

BYRD, William (1652–4 Dec. 1704), Virginia colonial officer and planter, was born in London, England, the son of John Bird, a goldsmith, and Grace Stegge. Because his father was a member of a powerful labor guild, Byrd (who later changed the spelling of his name, probably because it sounded more "elegant") grew up aspiring to a comfortable but lower-middle-class position in caste-bound London. However, when he was eighteen he received a letter from his uncle, Thomas Stegge, a plantation owner in Virginia, asking Byrd to join him and become his heir. Accepting the opportunity to secure position and wealth as a landed gentleman in the new world, Byrd sailed to Virginia in the autumn of 1670 and joined his kinsman on his plantation of 1,800 acres near the fall line of the James River. A year later Stegge died, and Byrd inherited his entire estate. In that same year Byrd accompanied a party that crossed the Blue Ridge Mountains and explored the western wilderness. Quickly, the young man proved himself an able husbandman, caring for his tobacco plantations and improving the Indian trade that his uncle had begun. Soon he was recognized throughout the colony as a rising man of property and influence. In fact, he was typical of that group of Virginia leaders that arrived in the colony in the last half of the seventeenth century and established powerful families that would dominate Virginia in the next century. Needing a wife with experience in managing slaves and handling the domestic duties of a plantation, he married Mary Horsmanden, a well-connected widow, in 1673. They had five children before her death in 1699.

In 1676 Byrd became involved in a conflict with Virginia governor Sir William Berkeley, on the side of his neighbor, Nathaniel Bacon. The powerful Susquehanna Indians had raided Bacon's place and slain his overseer; they also had killed three of Byrd's servants. The governor, thinking these matters not important enough to start a general Indian war, had refused to allow the Virginia frontiersmen to retaliate. Byrd, sensing that Indian war was imminent near his homestead, sent his wife and young son, William Byrd II, to England, then joined Bacon in attacking the natives without the governor's permission. A short time afterward, when Bacon became a full-blown rebel against the governor, Byrd distanced himself from his erstwhile friend and sided with Berkeley, who pardoned him for his earlier indiscretion. When the rebellion collapsed in 1677, Byrd's wife and child returned, and he was elected to the House of Burgesses, where he served until 1682. A year later he was appointed by the governor, Thomas, Lord Culpeper, to the Council, retaining the position for the rest of his life and achieving the presidency in 1703. As a councilman, Byrd associated with a middle group of like-minded colleagues who strove to resist some imperial demands of royal governors while attempting to remain as cooperative as possible. He did, however, stand forcefully against Governor Francis Nicholson when that gentleman became "despotic, cantankerous, and inconsistent" (Hatch, p. 44). In 1687 he visited England to secure the position of auditor and receiver general of the royal revenues in Virginia, with a salary of £500 per year. Accomplishing his purpose in 1688, King James II also gave him the title "armiger," or "armorbearer to the king." When William and Mary ascended the throne in 1688, he was confirmed in both position and title.

By the 1690s Byrd was firmly established as a prominent planter, trader, and man of political influence in Virginia. He took possession in 1688 of a splendid new property, "Westover," on the James River, in a location more central to business and politics than had been his old place at the fall line. Purchased from Theodorick and Richard Bland, Westover was for many years the county seat of Charles City County, with the courthouse and Westover Parish Church located nearby. In 1690 Byrd erected a large wood frame house on the site and lived there comfortably during his remaining years. His son, William Byrd II, later obliterated the house and replaced it with the superb brick mansion that still stands. Also, Byrd started a collection of books and manuscripts that his son vastly expanded; much later, when this library was liquidated by his grandson, William Byrd III, it may have been purchased by Thomas Jefferson. Appointed commandant of the Henrico County militia, Byrd was responsible for the protection of his part of the Virginia frontier from Indian depredations. In the early 1690s he helped establish the College of William and Mary, and he served as a trustee until his death. When 500 Huguenots fled to Virginia from France in 1699 and 1700, Byrd helped them to settle at Manakin on the James River, twenty miles above Westover. Wrote historian Robert Beverley in 1705, Byrd "receiv'd them with all the tenderness of a Father; and ever since has constantly given them the utmost Assistance" (p. 283).

Over the years, Byrd continued to make large profits from the cultivation of tobacco, using his extensive trade connections with Barbados to import many slaves for his own labor. Also, he became deeply involved in the profitable slave trade, supplying his neighbors' needs as well. Although he mostly acted as a middleman, receiving slaves on consignment and selling them for huge profits, in 1697 he became principal owner of a slave ship, the *William and Jane*, which later was captured by a French privateer. Meantime, his factors in England provided him and his family with sumptuous furniture, clothing, foodstuffs, and farm implements, and he sent his son and a daughter to London to be educated. Speculating in land, he came to possess thousands of acres, some of which he sold, most of which he kept. He drew upon the Indian trade of the Virginia hinterland for furs, beaver pelts, and deer skins, shipping these goods to Europe and the West Indies, along with agricultural products such as maize and flour, in his own merchant vessels. He became an expert in Indian affairs and often was called upon by government officials to deal with the natives. In 1685 he attended a conference at Albany, New York, to sign a treaty with the Iroquois. He died at Westover, rich in accomplishments and material possessions.

• Byrd's "Letter Book," in the Virginia Historical Society Library, is the most valuable primary source. Printed materials are *The Writings of Colonel William Byrd of Westover in Virginia, Esq.*, ed. John Spencer Basset (1901), containing an excellent biographical sketch of Byrd; *The Correspondence of the Three William Byrds of Westover, Virginia, 1684–1776*, ed. Marian Tinling, vol. 1 (1977), with an excellent biographical sketch by Louis B. Wright; and *Virginia Magazine of History and Biography* 35 (1927): 224–30. Also see Henry R. McIlwaine and W. L. Hall, eds., *Executive Journals of the Council of Colonial Virginia, 1680–1754*, vol. 1 (1925); Robert Beverley, *The History and Present State of Virginia*, ed. Wright (1947); and Warren M. Billings, ed., *The Old Dominion in the Seventeenth Century: A Documentary History of Virginia, 1606–1689* (1975). Other sources are Richard Croom Beatty, *William Byrd of Westover* (1932); William D. Houlette, "William Byrd and Some of His American Descendants," *Tyler's Quarterly Historical and Genealogical Magazine* 16 (1934): 36–42, 93–100; Wright, "The Byrds' Progress from Trade to Genteel Elegance," in his *The First Gentlemen of Virginia: Intellectual Qualities of the Early Colonial Ruling Class* (1940): 312–48; Alden Hatch, *The Byrds of Virginia* (1969); and Pierre Marambaud, "Colonel William Byrd I: A Fortune Founded on Smoke," *Virginia Magazine of History and Biography* 82 (1974): 430–57. Byrd's book collection is discussed in William D. Houlette, "The Byrd Library," *Tyler's Quarterly Historical and Genealogical Magazine* 16 (1934): 100–09. His politics are explained in Wright, "William Byrd's Defense of Sir Edmund Andros," *William and Mary Quarterly* 2 (1945): 47–62; and Wright, "William Byrd's Opposition to Governor Francis Nicholson," *Journal of Southern History* 11 (1945): 68–79. Clarence W. Alvord and Lee Bidgood, *The First Explorations of the Trans-Allegheny Region by the Virginians, 1650–1674* (1912), describe his Blue Ridge explorations.

PAUL DAVID NELSON

BYRD, William (28 Mar. 1674–26 Aug. 1744), author, planter, and Virginia councilor, was born on his father's plantation in Charles City County near Richmond, Virginia, the son of William Byrd, a planter and trader, and Mary Horsmanden Filmer. Byrd was sent at age seven to England to live with his maternal uncle, Daniel Horsmanden, and to attend Felsted Grammar School in Essex under the tutelage of its headmaster, Christopher Glasscock. Byrd became well grounded in the classics, and throughout his life he read Hebrew, Greek, or Latin almost daily. In 1690 Byrd's father sent him to the Rotterdam, the Netherlands, to learn business methods with merchants Jacob Senserff and Johannes Texelius. Not liking this situation, Byrd persuaded his father to apprentice him to the mercantile firm of Perry and Lane in London.

In 1692 Byrd entered the Middle Temple to study law and in April 1695 became a licensed attorney in England.

In 1696 Byrd returned to Virginia, where he was elected to the House of Burgesses from Henrico County. The next year he left again for England. On 29 April 1696, through the influence of a friend, Sir Robert Southwell, Byrd was elected a fellow of the Royal Society, only one of two Virginians to achieve that honor during the colonial period. In 1697 he was chosen to the council of the Royal Society. The first paper he prepared for the society in 1697 was "An Account of a Negro Boy That Is Dappled in Several Places of His Body with White Spots." Over the years he kept in touch with the British scientific community, especially Dr. Hans Sloane and Charles Boyle, the earl of Orrery. When he was in America, Byrd sent his correspondents specimens of flora, fauna, and minerals. The society members were thrilled in 1697, when he presented them with "a live Rattlesnake in a Box, wherein he had lain 7 months without food" (*Journal Book of the Royal Society*, 20 July 1697) and also a live opossum.

On his return to England in 1697, Byrd presented an address of the Virginia Assembly to the Board of Trade and acted as an attorney on behalf of Governor Sir Edmund Andros regarding charges brought by the Reverend James Blair, commissary of the Anglican church in Virginia. In appearing before the archbishop of Canterbury and the bishop of London at Lambeth Palace, Byrd discovered that he was not a very good practicing attorney; he failed to attach culpability to Blair, who was completely exonerated in the dispute. In October 1698 Byrd was appointed Virginia's agent in London, and as such he protested the use of tax money from Virginia to assist military operations in the northern colonies. His agency came to an end when he alienated the Board of Trade by going over the head of Governor Francis Nicholson in presenting an address to the king from the Virginia Council and House of Burgesses.

A gentleman of leisure, Byrd moved in fashionable society, regularly attending the theater and balls, visiting with London's notables, and all the while vainly seeking a prospect for marriage. He is reputed to have been one of the four collaborators who wrote the play *The Careless Husband* (1704). In Williamsburg, Virginia, in later years, he was a producer and sometimes an actor and songwriter for amateur theatricals. During his second stay in England, Byrd wrote out most of a brief history of Virginia, the text of which was used by John Oldmixon for *The British Empire in America* (1708) and probably by Robert Beverley for his *The History and Present State of Virginia* (1705). Byrd probably intended to publish his own history, but the manuscript is not extant. The first part of Byrd's later *History of the Dividing Line* (1841) is possibly an abridgment of it.

Learning of his father's death, Byrd returned to Virginia in 1705. He was the sole heir of his father's estates, and he also inherited the posts of receiver general, from which he received 3 to 5 percent of the colony's tax receipts as a commission, and auditor. In 1706 this latter post was separated from the receiver generalship, which Byrd retained. In 1709 he took his father's place in the Virginia Council, a position he held until his death. He was one of the governors of the College of William and Mary and was colonel of the militia, in which capacity, in 1710, he was appointed the chief military commander for the counties of Henrico and Charles City.

In 1706 Byrd married Lucy Parke, daughter of Colonel Daniel Parke. They had four children, two of whom survived infancy. Byrd's diary for 1709–1712 tells of his sexual encounters and spats with his wife, with Byrd struggling to exact submission from Lucy. After the murder of his father-in-law, who had served as governor of the Leeward Islands, Byrd agreed to an arrangement whereby all of Parke's Virginia estates would be given to him in return for his assuming all of Parke's debts. The debts proved more substantial than Byrd had expected, and he had great difficulty for the remainder of his life paying off the creditors.

Byrd returned to England in 1715. His wife joined him the following year but died of smallpox in November 1716. On behalf of the Virginia Council, he challenged before the Board of Trade certain policies of Governor Alexander Spotswood. Especially offensive was Spotswood's practice of creating courts of oyer and terminer, which diminished the authority of the council as the General Court, the highest tribunal in the colony. In danger of being dismissed as a councilor, Byrd complied with orders from the Board of Trade to return to Virginia to effect a reconciliation with Spotswood. After a brief stay in Virginia, Byrd went back to London in fall 1721 for his final sojourn in England. Again he was rebuffed in his efforts to establish courtships with several of England's eligible heiresses, expressing himself through flowery letters. In 1724 he married Maria Taylor, who was twenty-five years younger than he. They had four children. About 1725 he produced a pamphlet, *The Female Creed*, a satire on women's superstitions.

Byrd was a physical culturist and regarded himself as an amateur physician, attending to the medical needs of his family and slaves. He "danced" his "dance" every morning; had only warm milk for breakfast; called attention to the dangers of eating meat, although he indulged in bear meat as a source of virility; and drank ginseng tea to promote a long life. While in England he published *A Discourse Concerning the Plague with Some Preservatives against It* (1721), in which he extolled "the singular virtue of Tobacco, in checking the contagion of the Plague." Tobacco "is a powerful resister of poison in every degree."

Returning to Virginia for good in 1726, Byrd resumed his seat in the council. Upon the death of Lieutenant Governor Hugh Drysdale in that year, Byrd again unsuccessfully sought the governor's office. In spring and fall 1728 he was one of the seven members of a joint commission to survey the Virginia–North Carolina boundary line. On 5 March 1728 the commissioners, accompanied by four surveyors, forty laborers, and a chaplain, started from Currituck Inlet on the Atlantic Coast and proceeded westward through the Dismal Swamp. In six weeks they reached the Meherrin River. The North Carolina commissioners dropped out, but the survey continued to Peters Creek (now in Patrick County, Va.), 242 miles from the Atlantic Ocean. In *The History of the Dividing Line Run in the Year 1728* Byrd described the flora and fauna and humorously commented on back country farmers; in *The Secret History of the Dividing Line* (1929) he included satirical pen portraits of the participants in the expedition. He also wrote *A Description of the Dismal Swamp and a Proposal to Drain the Swamp* (1789).

In 1732 Byrd visited Spotswood's plantation and iron foundry at Germanna to learn about iron mining, recording his trip and a portrayal of back country life in the amusing *A Progress to the Mines* (1841). Three years later he described his exploration of the 105,000-acre tract along the Roanoke River that the Virginia government had granted him in *A Journey to the Land of Eden* (1841). Byrd provided notes for the promotional pamphlet *Neu-gefundenes Eden* (Newly found Eden), published in 1737 by Samuel Jenner in an unsuccessful effort to enlist Swiss-German settlers for Byrd's Roanoke lands. Byrd founded the Virginia cities of Petersburg and Richmond. In 1736 he was one of three royal commissioners that set the bounds of the Fairfax grant, located between the Rappahannock and Potomac rivers.

Raising mainly tobacco, Byrd experimented with crop diversity, vineyards, and production of naval stores. He engaged in American Indian trade and prospected for coal, iron, and copper. He kept a close watch on plantation details, frequently visiting the far fields and interesting himself in the day-to-day lives of his slaves. "Like one of the patriarchs, I have my flocks and my herds, my bondmen and bondwomen," he wrote to the earl of Orrery, 5 July 1726, "so that I live in a kind of independence of everyone but Providence. . . . I must take care to keep all my people to their duty, to set all the springs in motion, and to make everyone draw his equal share to carry the machine forward." Byrd detested slavery, and on occasion intervened to prevent his first wife from whipping servants. Although he trafficked in slaves himself, he blamed the excrable commerce on "the saints of New England." Calling slavery debasing and dangerous, he wrote to John Perceval, earl of Egmont, on 12 July 1736: "I am sensible of many bad consequences of multiplying these Ethiopians among us. They blow up the pride, & ruin the industry of our white people."

One of the foremost landmarks in Virginia is Byrd's mansion, "Westover," located on the James River, twenty-five miles east of Richmond. Byrd went to great expense in building this brick Georgian structure in 1730–1734, replacing the wooden home erected by his father. Some architectural historians in the twentieth century speculated that Byrd's son William Byrd III was the actual builder. The mansion has magnificent interior and exterior accessories, and the facade resembles the "Governor's Palace" in Williamsburg. While Byrd lived there, Westover boasted great entrance gates, beautiful walled gardens, a library of 3,600 volumes, and important portrait, print, and engraving collections.

In 1743 Byrd served as president of the Virginia Council. He died at his home in Charles City County. At the time of his death he owned over 179,400 acres of land. Although not successful at land speculation, he had managed to pay off his debts.

Byrd exercised enormous social and political influence in Virginia. With the publication of his writings, he has emerged as one of the most prominent authors in early America of belles-lettres and journals/diaries. He achieved considerable skill as a satirist and in general displayed a refreshing sense of humor and worldliness, unpretentious and yet sophisticated. The apotheosis of a Virginia gentleman, embodying the correct virtues and vices, Byrd considered himself equal in status to an English nobleman.

• Many of Byrd's manuscripts are at the Virginia Historical Society. Most of his writings were first published long after his death, including Marion Tinling, ed., *The Correspondence of the Three William Byrds of Westover, Virginia, 1684–1776* (2 vols., 1977); Louis B. Wright, ed., *The Prose Works of William Byrd of Westover* (1966); Wright and Tinling, eds., *The Secret Diary of William Byrd of Westover, 1709–1712* (1941); Wright and Tinling, eds., *The London Diary (1717–1721) and Other Writings* (1958); and Maude H. Woodfin, ed., *Another Secret Diary of William Byrd of Westover 1739–41 with Letters & Literary Exercises 1696–1726* (1942). Material supplied by Byrd is in Richard C. Beatty and William J. Mulloy, eds. and trans., *William Byrd's Natural History of Virginia; or, The Newly Discovered Eden* (1940), containing both the original German version by Samuel Jenner and the English translation. Margaret B. Pritchard and Virginia S. Sites, *William Byrd II and His Lost History: Engravings of the Americas* (1993), analyzes copperplate engravings at the Bodleian Library, Oxford University, and prints at Holkham Hall, Norfolk, England, that Byrd allegedly intended to include in his history of Va. A full biography of Byrd is Pierre Marambaud, *William Byrd of Westover 1674–1744* (1971). Less comprehensive are Beatty, *William Byrd of Westover* (1932), and more in the form of an essay, Kenneth A. Lockridge, *The Diary, and Life, of William Byrd II of Virginia, 1674–1744* (1987). Insight into Byrd's relationship to culture in a broad sense is in Richard B. Davis, *Intellectual Life in the Colonial South, 1585–1763* (3 vols., 1978), and Wright, *The First Gentlemen of Virginia*, chap. 11 (1940, repr. 1964). Byrd's plantation house is discussed in Thomas T. Waterman, *The Mansions of Virginia* (1945), and family life at Westover is in Daniel B. Smith, *Inside the Great House: Planter Family Life in Eighteenth-Century Chesapeake Society* (1980). Byrd's view of women is the theme of Lockridge, *On the Sources of Patriarchal Rage: The Commonplace Books of William Byrd and Thomas Jefferson and the Gendering of Power in the Eighteenth Century* (1992). Particular aspects of Byrd as author, scientist, and lawyer are examined in Willie T. Weathers, "William Byrd: Satirist," *William and Mary Quarterly*, 3d ser., 4 (1941): 26–41; Woodfin, "William Byrd and the Royal Society," *Virginia Magazine of History and Biography* 40 (1932): 23–34, 111–23; James R. Masterson, "William Byrd in Lubberland," *American Literature* 9 (1937–1938): 153–70; and Wright, "William Byrd's Defense of Sir Edmund Andros," *William and Mary Quarterly*, 3d ser., 2 (1945): 47–62.

HARRY M. WARD

BYRNE, Andrew (30? Nov. 1802–10 June 1862), Roman Catholic bishop, was born in the town of Navan, about forty miles northwest of Dublin, Ireland, the son of Robert Byrne and Margery Moore. There is no record of his actual date of birth, yet according to parish records in Ireland, he was baptized on 3 December 1802. Since his given name was Andrew, he may have been born on 30 November, the feastday of St. Andrew the apostle. Little is known of his early life or education except that, while a seminarian in Navan, Byrne heard Bishop John England of Charleston, South Carolina, recruiting prospective priests. Answering the call, Byrne arrived in Charleston in the early 1820s and completed his priestly formation under Bishop England, who ordained him on 11 November 1827.

The Charleston diocese then included both of the Carolinas and Georgia, and Byrne's first assignment was that of a missionary in North Carolina. He returned to Charleston in 1830 as pastor of St. Mary's Church. In 1833 he accompanied Bishop England to the Second Provincial Council in Baltimore as vicar general. Byrne's relationship with England apparently deteriorated, however, and he left the diocese in April 1836, transferring to the diocese of New York, where he quickly made a name for himself as a preacher-pastor at three different churches in New York City.

Byrne's proven abilities as pastor and his connection with New York bishop John Hughes, plus his prior southern experience, all made him a natural choice for a diocese on the southwestern frontier. After Pope Gregory XVI created the diocese of Little Rock in 1843, Byrne was consecrated as its bishop. He arrived in Little Rock in June 1844 with just two priests to minister to the entire state of Arkansas. Throughout his eighteen years as prelate, Byrne never had more than ten priests at any one time. He maintained the diocese with funds from the Austrian Leopoldine Society and the French society for the Propogation of the Faith. With this help, Byrne purchased land, sustained his clergy, and built schools. Profits from land sales allowed him to open the College of St. Andrew at Fort Smith in 1849. He traveled to Naas in County Kildare, Ireland, to persuade the Sisters of Mercy to locate a convent in Little Rock. By the Civil War, the Mercy Sisters had established convent schools in Little Rock, Fort Smith, and Helena.

During the nativistic, anti-Catholic, Know-Nothing uproar of the 1850s, Byrne studiously avoided political disputes, particularly those involving slavery. There is no evidence that he ever owned slaves, and his correspondence yields no opinion on the subject. Like many Catholic prelates of the period, Byrne probably did not see the issue as one of moral or religious concern. Never content with his position, in 1846 he persuaded his fellow bishops at the Sixth Provincial Council in Baltimore to petition the Vatican to abolish the Arkansas diocese so that Byrne could be sent as bishop to the newly created diocese of Buffalo, New York. Rome dismissed this recommendation and refused Byrne's later request for a transfer in 1853. In 1850 the Arkansas diocese was attached to a newly created ecclesiastical province of New Orleans with that see now raised to an archbishopric. Together with bishops from Mississippi, Alabama, Texas, and northern Louisiana, Byrne attended provincial councils in 1856 and 1860.

In spite of Byrne's attempts to attract both clergy and laity to Arkansas from Ireland during the 1850s, Catholics numbered only 1 percent of the state's population by 1860. His last trip to Ireland in 1858–1859 yielded few recruits for his missionary diocese. The Civil War closed the College of St. Andrew in 1861, when most of his male students were drafted into the Confederate army. Though the war disrupted international communications, making it more difficult for him to secure funding from Europe, Byrne persevered against great odds and laid sound foundations for a diocese that would survive the Civil War. Byrne died in Helena, Arkansas, at St. Catherine's Mercy Convent.

• Letters and documents pertaining to Bishop Byrne's life, and his personal register from 1844 to 1850, can be found in the Archives of the Diocese of Little Rock, St. John's Catholic Center, Little Rock, Ark. Other letters of Bishop Byrne are in the Archives of the Archdiocese of New Orleans, Old Ursuline Convent, New Orleans, La.; some material is also in the Archives of the University of Notre Dame. Earlier works on Bishop Byrne have often used Fr. Richard N. Clarke, *Lives of the Deceased Bishops of the Catholic Church in the United States* (2 vols., 1872), and the Diocesan Historical Commission, *A History of Catholicity in Arkansas* (1925). There is also a typescript history of Arkansas Catholicism up to 1843 by Francis S. Guy, "The Catholic Church in Arkansas, 1541–1843" (M.A. thesis, Catholic Univ. of America, 1935). An obituary is in the Little Rock *Arkansas Gazette*, 28 June 1862.

JAMES M. WOODS

BYRNES, James Francis (2 May 1882–9 Apr. 1972), U.S. senator and secretary of state, was born in Charleston, South Carolina, the son of James Francis Byrnes, a Charleston city clerk, and Elizabeth McSweeney, a dressmaker. His father died before Byrnes was born, and at age fourteen Byrnes left school to help support his family. While working as a messenger in a law office, he took shorthand lessons and qualified as a court stenographer. To obtain the court position he had to misrepresent his year of birth as 1879, and he used that date the rest of his life. Under the tutelage and surrogate fatherhood of two judges, he was schooled in literature and history and read law. He passed the South Carolina bar exam in 1903 and began practice in Aiken, but he also continued to work as court stenographer. Born an Irish Catholic, Byrnes formally converted to the Episcopal church upon his 1906 marriage to Maude Busch. They had no children.

Byrnes entered politics in 1908 with a successful campaign for local prosecutor. Known to voters as

Jimmy Byrnes, he retained that form of his name throughout his public life. In 1910 he won the Democratic nomination for South Carolina's Second Congressional District and served in the House of Representatives from 1911 to 1924. Well liked by members of both parties, he developed a talent for forging compromises. He later remarked that political issues are "really a matter of policy, not principle." He became a member of the Appropriations Committee in 1917 and worked regularly with Assistant Secretary of the Navy Franklin D. Roosevelt on naval funding. The two rising political stars formed a permanent friendship. Byrnes admired Woodrow Wilson and became one of the president's valued congressional lieutenants. He urged ratification of the Treaty of Versailles and continued after the treaty's defeat to extol the League of Nations concept.

In 1924 Byrnes suffered his only electoral defeat. A ruthless opponent, Coleman L. Blease, exploited issues of race and religion to deny Byrnes's bid for a U.S. Senate seat. Although an avowed segregationist like most southern political leaders, Byrnes had rejected any association with his state's extensive Ku Klux Klan organization. He abhorred Klan violence and, moreover, would not align against the Catholic religion of his birth. Klan members colluded with Blease to identify Byrnes as a Catholic, which was politically fatal in overwhelmingly Protestant South Carolina. Byrnes moved to Spartanburg and became a partner in a prominent law firm.

Byrnes won his coveted place in the Senate in 1930. Armed with the endorsement of his Episcopal minister, he challenged Blease, who had proved incapable of assisting South Carolinians suffering from the Great Depression. Byrnes also obtained the financial backing of wealthy South Carolina native Bernard M. Baruch, and they began a political alliance and friendship that endured for thirty-five years. Byrnes espoused Baruch's philosophy of fiscal conservatism in the U.S. Senate, and he also became the conduit of Baruch's enormous wealth to other Senate Democrats, including Harry S. Truman of Missouri. His ability to dispense Baruch's campaign money made Byrnes one of the most powerful politicians in Washington.

Senator Byrnes was a fixer, a Washington insider who accomplished things. His economic conservatism led him to vote against some extreme measures of Roosevelt's New Deal, such as authority for sit-down strikes, but he actively shepherded the passage of most major New Deal legislation. In the process, he secured significant relief funds for his home state, including the huge Santee-Cooper Dam project. By 1937 he decided that the worst of the depression was over, and he became a key figure in a conservative coalition of southern and western legislators from both parties who began to distance themselves from the New Deal. He backed Roosevelt's 1937 plan to enlarge the Supreme Court, but he opposed the president's moves in 1938 to purge some conservative Democrats in Congress. With the 1939 outbreak of war in Europe, the growing Byrnes-Roosevelt tension dissipated, and Byrnes worked his legislative magic to help the White House gain repeal of the Neutrality Acts and passage of the Lend-Lease Bill to send aid to Britain. Despite their occasional differences, Roosevelt paid his debt to the senator in June 1941 by naming Byrnes an associate justice of the U.S. Supreme Court.

Byrnes sat on the Supreme Court for one term, 1941–1942, before Roosevelt asked him to undertake an urgent wartime assignment. In October 1942 Roosevelt made Byrnes the head of the Office of Economic Stabilization, and in May 1943 the president issued an executive order creating a superagency, the Office of War Mobilization (OWM), which later became the Office of War Mobilization and Reconversion (OWMR). As OWM/OWMR director with his office in the White House, Byrnes was essentially "assistant president" for domestic affairs for the war's duration. Roosevelt delegated sweeping executive powers to Byrnes to initiate policies, plan programs, and coordinate all federal agencies in production, procurement, and distribution of all war materials—military and civilian. This arrangement relieved Roosevelt of managing the home front and allowed him to concentrate on the military and diplomatic conduct of the war. Eclipsing the influence of Vice President Henry Wallace and War Production Board chairman Donald Nelson, Byrnes directed such diverse aspects of American life as food rationing, sports scheduling, closing time for bars, and absentee voting for soldiers.

In 1944 Byrnes expected the vice presidential nomination and subsequently a chance for the presidency in 1948 or earlier because of Roosevelt's declining health. The president seemed to prefer Byrnes on the ticket, but strategists within the party raised objections. Labor leaders disliked Byrnes's "hold the line" orders on wages in war industries, and the powerful New York State party boss calculated that Byrnes's segregationist record would cost 200,000 black votes in his state. The nomination went to Harry Truman. Roosevelt disappointed Byrnes a second time in 1944, when he selected Edward R. Stettinius, Jr., to succeed Cordell Hull as secretary of state. The president surprised the OWMR director, however, with an invitation to accompany him to Yalta in February 1945 for the summit meeting with Joseph Stalin and Winston Churchill. Byrnes provided Roosevelt one last service by reassuring Senate conservatives that the president had made the best bargain possible with Stalin on such issues as the proposed United Nations (UN).

When Roosevelt's sudden death thrust Truman into the White House in April 1945, the new president immediately asked Byrnes to be his secretary of state. The president waited until Stettinius completed the signing of the UN Charter before revealing the change, and Byrnes joined the cabinet in July. In May and June Byrnes served as the president's personal representative on the top-secret Interim Committee to decide on the use of the atomic bomb. As director of OWMR, Byrnes had advocated "hard war," that is, making maximum use of U.S. resources to end the war as quickly and efficiently as possible. His political experience convinced him that Congress and the public expected nothing less. Consequently, he maintained that, after expenditures of $2 billion on development of the atomic bomb, it had to be used as soon as it was available to secure unconditional surrender from Japan and spare additional U.S. casualties. His privileged access to the president gave Byrnes's opinion pivotal influence.

Byrnes's obvious intent to use the bomb against a nearly exhausted Japan has led some historians to argue that he wanted to demonstrate U.S. power to the Kremlin. The argument derives largely from circumstantial evidence. Frustrated by Soviet recalcitrance in Eastern Europe, Byrnes and other U.S. strategists were well aware that the United States possessed a weapon as yet unavailable to the Soviet Union. As secretary of state from 1945 to January 1947, Byrnes met with Stalin and Soviet foreign minister V. M. Molotov at Potsdam, London, Paris, New York, and Moscow. At none of these sessions did Byrnes overtly threaten the Soviets with the bomb, and in fact he often employed his well-practiced skills of legislative compromise and tried to strike bargains with Soviet leaders. In a major speech at Stuttgart in September 1946, he issued a tough warning to Moscow about the future of Germany, but criticism grew in Congress and within the administration that Byrnes was an appeaser of the Russians. Ever since Byrnes's direct talks with Stalin in December 1945, the president himself had thought that the secretary of state was "babying the Soviets," and Truman was also convinced that Byrnes continued to resent him because of the 1944 vice presidential selection. When Truman failed to defend Byrnes against his critics, the secretary of state resigned in January 1947.

The former secretary of state became increasingly critical of the president's domestic Fair Deal and eventually broke politically with Truman. On a platform disparaging federal encroachment in local and individual affairs, Byrnes ran successfully for governor of South Carolina and served in that post from 1951 to 1955. In 1952 he led an Independents for Eisenhower movement in the South. Although a moderate on racial issues by southern standards, he defended his state's segregated school system, and after the 1954 Supreme Court decision outlawed such segregation, he helped organize the call for massive resistance to its implementation. He refused to support either major party in 1956, and in 1960 he broke completely with the Democratic party. He endorsed Richard Nixon that year and Barry Goldwater in 1964. With the octogenarian Byrnes actively assisting, Nixon carried South Carolina and nine other states of the old Confederacy in 1968. Nixon's victory marked a historic shift in presidential voting in the South to the Republican party, and the new president thanked Byrnes for helping make his "southern strategy" successful. Byrnes died at his home in Columbia, South Carolina.

Byrnes was one of the most powerful politicians in the United States in the 1930s and 1940s. His former Senate colleagues approved his appointments to the Supreme Court and as secretary of state unanimously without even conducting hearings. He was the first American ever to be a congressman, senator, Supreme Court justice, secretary of state, and governor. Byrnes's strength was as a political pragmatist, but that pragmatism failed him after 1945 as principles began to loom larger in international and domestic politics. Ideological definitions of the Soviet threat to American interests ran counter to his horse-trading approach to diplomacy. The undeniable justice of desegregation overrode his notion of what was practical in the South. Yet through more than five decades he remained a remarkable political strategist and dedicated public official.

• The Byrnes papers are in Cooper Memorial Library, Clemson University, Clemson, S.C. Byrnes wrote two memoirs: *Speaking Frankly* (1947), on his years as secretary of state; and *All in One Lifetime* (1958), on his various positions. A full biography of Byrnes that includes a good bibliography of his multifaceted career is David Robertson, *Sly and Able: A Political Biography of James F. Byrnes* (1994). Because of intense scholarly interest in the atomic bomb decisions and the origins of the Cold War, most specialized monographs on Byrnes concentrate on his work on the Interim Committee and as secretary of state. See Robert L. Messer, *The End of an Alliance: James F. Byrnes, Roosevelt, Truman, and the Origins of the Cold War* (1982); Gar Alperovitz, *Atomic Diplomacy: Hiroshima and Potsdam: The Use of the Atomic Bomb and the American Confrontation with Soviet Power*, expanded and updated ed. (1985); Kendrick A. Clements, ed., *James F. Byrnes and the Origins of the Cold War* (1982); Patricia Dawson Ward, *The Threat of Peace: James F. Byrnes and the Council of Foreign Ministers, 1945–1946* (1979); Richard D. Burns, "James F. Byrnes (1945–1947)," in *An Uncertain Tradition: American Secretaries of State in the Twentieth Century*, ed. Norman A. Graebner (1961); and George Curry, *James F. Byrnes, 1945–1947* (1965). On the OWMR, see John William Partin, "'Assistant President' for the Home Front: James F. Byrnes and World War II" (Ph.D. diss., Univ. of Florida, 1977). An obituary is in the *New York Times*, 10 Apr. 1972.

DAVID L. ANDERSON

BYRNES, John William (12 June 1913–12 Jan. 1985), statesman, was born in Green Bay, Wisconsin, the son of Charles W. Byrnes, a school superintendent, and Harriet Schumaker. He attended the local parochial and public schools in Green Bay and the University of Wisconsin at Madison, from which he graduated with a B.A. in 1936 and an LL.B. in 1938. Specializing in banking and financial regulation, Byrnes accepted an appointment as special deputy commissioner with the state of Wisconsin, a post he held until 1941, when he opened his law practice in Green Bay. Joining the state senate in 1940 as its youngest member, Byrnes was the first Republican to be elected from his district in many years. In a short period of time, the freshman Republican became the majority floor leader and later the chairman of the Judiciary Committee. He wrote several important laws, among them the act that created the Veteran's Recognition Board and the Wisconsin Soldier's Voting Law.

In November 1944 Byrnes successfully ran for election to the U.S. House of Representatives from the Eighth District, defeating an incumbent Democrat, and he held that seat until his retirement in 1972. Taking office in January 1945, he sat on the House Civil Service Claims and War Claims Committees. When the Republicans swept the House and the Senate in the 1946 elections, Byrnes received appointment to the tax-writing Ways and Means Committee. In time, he became the second-ranking Republican representative on that committee, behind Noah Mason (R.-Ill.). In 1947 Byrnes married Barbara Preston; they had six children.

Byrnes also sat on the House Un-American Activities Committee and was a primary supporter of the Mundt-Nixon Subversive Activities Control Bill (1948). Among his other important votes, he favored the Taft-Hartley Labor Law of 1947, the construction of the St. Lawrence Seaway, and the Landrum-Griffin Labor Bill of 1959. In the field of foreign policy, Byrnes voted in favor of assisting those nations in great need of humanitarian aid while attempting to scale back the amount of the aid requested. Though not an isolationist, he supported attempts in both 1947 and again in 1951 to reduce the amount of arms and financial assistance going to Europe. The Wisconsin congressman likewise voted in favor of President Dwight D. Eisenhower's Mideast doctrine (1957).

Active in Republican party politics, Byrnes gave keynote addresses at the national convention of the Young Republican Federation in 1947 and at the Wisconsin State Republican Convention in 1948. The following year, he was among the small group who formed the Chowder and Marching Club, an influential semisocial, semipolitical group of Republican politicians that included California representative Richard M. Nixon.

In 1963 Byrnes became the ranking Republican member of the House Ways and Means Committee, then chaired by Representative Wilbur D. Mills (D.-Ark.). Though Byrnes and Mills disagreed about such issues as welfare and Medicare, they formed an effective working relationship that sought compromise rather than confrontation. Many bills that passed the Ways and Means Committee were "shepherded" by both men as they went to the floor of Congress. Byrnes was a strong advocate of eliminating laws that favored specific industries, and he lobbied for legislation granting parents an income tax deduction for the cost of child care.

In 1963 Byrnes successfully defended himself against charges that he accepted preferential prices in a Mortgage Guaranty Insurance Corporation stock purchase. Denying before his House colleagues that he received any preferential treatment, Byrnes transferred the stocks to scholarship funds for his children. In addition to serving on the Ways and Means Committee, he was chairman of the House Republican Policy Committee from 1959 until 1965, when a change in party rules barred him from holding two ranking offices simultaneously.

Through the efforts of both Byrnes and Mills, the Tax Reform Act of 1969 passed the House and became law the following year. Despite being a loyal Republican, Byrnes unsuccessfully opposed the Nixon administration's Revenue Sharing Plan of 1972, which provided federal grants to state and local governments and allowed them to determine the use of the funds. (Years before, Byrnes had similarly criticized a Republican administration's budget requests, deeming President Eisenhower's planned expenditures for housing and education to be too costly.) Byrnes labeled himself a fiscal conservative, opposed to raising the debt ceiling and favoring among other things voluntary health insurance for senior citizens and a balanced federal budget, his main reason for disagreeing with the 1972 Revenue Sharing Plan. He ended his career in Congress that year, having chosen not to run for reelection.

Byrnes, who resided in Arlington, Virginia, until his death, then resumed his law practice with the firm of Foley, Lardner, Hollabaugh & Jacobs. A devoted family man, he found diversion in photography, golf, and swimming. He died in Marshfield, Wisconsin.

Byrnes's fiscal conservatism often put him at odds with the political currents of his time, even during Republican administrations, but a quarter century after he left the House of Representatives his views were to be widely shared. It then became common for members of Congress to advocate the sorts of tax cuts he had wished to see, to champion a balanced federal budget, and to oppose federally mandated health care programs. Nevertheless, Byrnes in his own day was by no means isolated at the political fringe; he enjoyed considerable success within the Republican party and within the legislative body where he served for twenty-eight years.

• The John W. Byrnes Papers at the University of Wisconsin–Green Bay Area Research Center contain legislative papers, political correspondence, photographs, films, video tapes, and audio recordings. Most of the collection is closed to researchers until 2005. An oral history entitled "Reminiscences of John W. Byrnes" (1967) is in the Social Security Project, Oral History Research Project, Columbia University.

Byrnes's career in Congress is discussed in Charles O. Jones, *Party and Policy-Making: The House Republican Policy Committee* (1964), and John F. Manley, *The Politics of Finance: The House Committee on Ways and Means* (1970). An obituary is in the *New York Times*, 14 Jan. 1985.

LEO J. DAUGHERTY III

BYRNES, Thomas F. (15 June 1842–7 May 1910), New York City police official, was born in Ireland, the son of William Byrnes and Rose Doyle. The family immigrated to New York City when Thomas was an infant. After a limited formal education and training as a gas fitter, he joined the Union army in 1861. When his term of enlistment ended in 1863, Byrnes joined the New York Metropolitan Police Department. He rose rapidly through the ranks: he became a roundsman (a title then used for a first-level supervisor) in 1868, a sergeant in 1869, a captain in 1870, and the head of the detective bureau with the rank of inspector in 1880. Byrnes made his reputation by arresting members of the gang that in 1878 robbed the Manhattan Bank that was located in the precinct he commanded.

As head of the detective bureau, Byrnes gave protection of the financial district top priority. He established a Wall Street office and announced that all known criminals found south of Fulton Street would be immediately arrested. The special care and attention Byrnes provided to Wall Street was acknowledged by financier Jay Gould and others who tendered a dinner in his honor in 1886. Byrnes became a wealthy man, perhaps because of the counsel provided by his Wall Street admirers. In 1890 he bought a Fifth Avenue building for $250,000, which doubled in value over the next twenty years.

Byrnes was an authoritarian head of the detective bureau, replacing twenty-one of twenty-eight detectives upon taking command. He made extensive use of stool pigeons, often petty criminals who were allowed to continue their illegal activities as long as they provided information to the police. A ferocious and imaginative interrogator, Byrnes was prepared to do anything necessary to make suspects confess. In his view, "It is not remorse that makes the hardened criminal confess; it is anxiety and mental strain" (*New York Times*, 8 May 1895). Journalist Lincoln Steffens described Byrnes as "simple, no complications at all—a man who would buy you or beat you, as you might choose, but get you he would" (quoted in Richardson, p. 211). He instructed his detectives to keep "incessant watch" upon anarchists, and he wanted police officers to maintain absolute secrecy about their operations.

Byrnes's power and fame grew throughout the 1880s. The New York legislature reorganized the detective bureau to his specifications in 1882; he published a book of sketches of career criminals entitled *Professional Criminals of America* in 1886; Julian Hawthorne published five short novels supposedly based upon "the files of Inspector Byrnes" in 1886–1887; and in 1888 he was promoted to the newly created rank of chief inspector.

In 1892 Byrnes became superintendent of police, the ranking officer in the department. The autocratic methods that had served him well in the detective bureau created constant friction with the politically appointed board of commissioners. In 1894 he was called to testify before the Lexow Committee's inquiry into systematic police corruption. He admitted to a net worth of $350,000, but the committee did not press him about the sources of his wealth beyond his comments about the investment advice he received from Jay Gould. The committee's presentation of ample testimony of systematic corruption and brutality in the police department led to the creation of a reform police board presided over by Theodore Roosevelt. The new board's distrust of Byrnes led to his forced retirement in May 1895.

Byrnes had married Ophelia Jennings in 1875; they had five children. Following his retirement he spent his remaining years looking after his extensive real estate investments and participating in numerous clubs. He died at his home in New York.

• Byrnes published two articles in the *North American Review* that give his views of crime and police: "Nurseries of Crime," 149 (Sept. 1889): 355–62, and "How to Protect a City from Crime," 159 (July 1894): 100–107. James F. Richardson, *The New York Police: Colonial Times to 1901* (1970), places Byrnes's career in the context of police history. Maurice Bassan, *Hawthorne's Son: The Life and Literary Career of Julian Hawthorne* (1970), details the literary collaboration between Byrnes and Hawthorne. New York newspapers devoted considerable attention to Byrnes's career upon his retirement. See the *New York Times*, the *New York Tribune*, and the *New York Herald*, 28 May 1895. Obituaries are in the *Times* and *Tribune*, 8 May 1910.

JAMES F. RICHARDSON

BYRNS, Joseph Wellington (20 July 1869–4 June 1936), Speaker of the U.S. House of Representatives, was born near Cedar Hill, Robertson County, Tennessee, the son of James H. Byrns and Mary Jackson, farmers. He received an LL.B. from Vanderbilt University in 1890; the following year Byrns entered the practice of law in Nashville. He married Julia Woodard in 1898, with whom he had a son.

Byrns began his political career in 1894 with a successful campaign for election as a Democrat to the lower chamber of the Tennessee legislature. Reelected in 1896 and 1898, he served as speaker in 1899. Byrns was elected to the state senate in 1900, but he was defeated in a contest for district attorney general of Davidson County in 1902. In 1904 Byrns served as a Democratic presidential elector. In 1908 he upset the incumbent congressman from the Nashville area, campaigning intensively on the issue of securing a dam and lock on the Cumberland River. After entering Congress, Byrns gained the promised appropriation, and he continued to cultivate his constituents over the years, working hard for their interests and impressing them with his gentleness, geniality, and folksiness. "Call me Joe," he often said. "I don't like that 'Mister' stuff." Byrns benefited politically from his imposing looks; he stood more than six feet tall and was beetle-browed. Not until 1932 would he be challenged for his congressional seat, and he was reelected then by a margin of five to one.

Byrns initially served on the House Indian Affairs Committee but was reassigned to the powerful Appropriations Committee two years later. On the Appropriations Committee, he gradually developed influence in Congress and became known as "Work Horse Joe" for his diligence and budgetary knowledge. Byrns also established a reputation as a staunch Democrat. This led him occasionally to compromise his commitment to economy in government and prohibition of alcoholic beverages. For example, as an appropriations subcommittee chairman during World War I, he became central to securing large outlays to finance U.S. war efforts at President Woodrow Wilson's urging. In 1928

Byrns supported the Democratic party's antiprohibition plank.

During the 1920s Byrns's reputation continued to grow, chiefly as a critic of Republican high-tariff policies and claims regarding government economy. By 1928 he was ready to assume additional responsibilities and became chairman of the Democratic National Congressional Committee. He was a leading candidate for the Democratic nomination for U.S. senator from Tennessee in 1930, but he withdrew because of emerging cardiac problems. Nevertheless, in 1931 Byrns became a significant legislative leader upon his succession to the chairmanship of the House Appropriations Committee. He attracted attention through his proposal, as an economy measure, to unify the army and the navy. Byrns was also instrumental in defeating a federal sales tax measure sponsored by other Democratic congressional leaders. He commented, "Mah party had always stood for taxing those who best kin pay."

His concern for his health led Byrns to forsake his roles as chairman of the Appropriations Committee and the new Economy Committee after the Democratic landslide of 1932. He accepted instead the then less burdensome job of House majority leader. Except for his refusal to sponsor the 1933 Economy Bill, even though he voted for it, Byrns was a loyal champion of Franklin D. Roosevelt's legislative program, even supporting the administration's later big-spending program. The only administration measure that Byrns personally sponsored was that which established the Civilian Conservation Corps. He considered his chief responsibility to be the promotion of the administration's entire legislative program.

After Speaker Henry T. Rainey died, Byrns became a candidate for the speakership in January 1935. Roosevelt preferred either William Bankhead or Sam Rayburn for the job, seeing them as more forceful leaders, but the Democratic caucus chose the popular Byrns instead. Byrns proved to be an able tactician, and his powers of persuasion were low-key but effective. Especially notable as a leadership device was his appointment of fifteen deputy whips who kept him in close touch with Democratic congressmen. Charming, well informed, and honorable, Byrns was held in high regard by virtually all members of the House. He was mortally stricken after presiding over a meeting of the House, and he died in Washington, D.C.

• Fire destroyed Byrns's papers, but the Herbert Hoover Papers in the Herbert Hoover Library, West Branch, Iowa, contain forty-five pages of Byrns's manuscripts. The Springfield Public Library, Springfield, Tenn., has his scrapbooks and other pertinent items. The essential works on Byrns are two by J. M. Galloway, "The Public Life of Joseph W. Byrns" (M.A. thesis, Univ. of Tenn., 1962), and "Speaker Joseph W. Byrns: Party Leader in the New Deal," *Tennessee Historical Quarterly* 25 (Spring 1966): 63–76. See also John Dean Minton, *The New Deal in Tennessee, 1932–1938* (1979). Significant biographical materials are in the *Nashville Tennessean* and the *New York Times*, 4 and 5 June 1936.

DONALD R. MCCOY

BYRON, Arthur (3 Apr. 1872–16 July 1943), actor, was born Arthur William Byron in Brooklyn, New York, the son of Oliver Doud Byron, an actor-manager, and Mary Kate Crehan, an actress. His stage experience began at three months, when his mother carried him onstage in *Across the Continent*. Following education at St. Paul's School, Garden City, Long Island, he joined his parents' touring company at sixteen. After two seasons with them, he joined the company of Sol Smith Russell, then played in a San Francisco stock company. In 1894 he became a member of John Drew's company for six seasons and was given increasingly important supporting roles. He married Lillian Hall, an actress and dancer, in 1898; they had no children.

By 1902 Byron had begun to get leading roles, and he was starred for the first time in *Major André* (1903). In a curtain speech, the play's author, Clyde Fitch, praised Byron's "conscientiousness as an artist, his sincerity and his power, his true American quality; and . . . assigned him to a place among the very best of our native actors" (*New York Times*, 11 Nov. 1903). In demand as a capable and versatile performer, Byron went from one engagement to another during the next decade. He was leading man to a series of female stars: Amelia Bingham (*The Climbers*, 1902), Mary Mannering (*The Stubbornness of Geraldine*, 1902), Maxine Elliott (*Her Own Way*, 1903; *The Inferior Sex*, 1910), Maude Adams (*The Little Minister*, 1904; *'Op o' Me Thumb*, 1904; *Chantecler*, 1911; *What Every Woman Knows*, 1911), Ethel Barrymore (*Her Sister*, 1907), and Minnie Maddern Fiske (*The High Road*, 1912). After a divorce from Hall, in 1905 he married actress Kathryn Keys, with whom he had appeared in the farce-comedy *Jack's Little Surprise* (1903); they would have three children.

The model of a theater professional, Byron was continuously employed in tours, regional productions, and stock companies nationwide between New York appearances. He also appeared in summer stock in Skowhegan, Maine, where his family had a vacation home. One of his longest runs in a single play began in 1906, when for 880 performances he starred as millionaire John Burkett Ryder in the Chicago company of *The Lion and the Mouse*. His all-time record for performances in a single play was in *The Boomerang* (1915–1918) as Dr. Gerald Sumner, who thinks he can cure another man's lovesick jealousy only to find the same malady in himself. By the time the play closed on the road, Byron had played the role 1,232 times and was the only remaining original cast member. He followed this success with a run of 800 performances, in New York and on tour, as The Friend in the light comedy *Tea for Three* (1918–1920).

These two long runs identified Byron in public consciousness as a player of sophisticated comedy. Critics commented especially on his mastery of voice and delivery. The *New York Telegraph*'s critic wrote of his performance in *Tea for Three*: "Speeches that would look lengthy in type and sound monotonous with less vivacity or suitability of utterance become engaging, sparkling and memorable in Mr. Byron's engaging manner of speaking them" (20 Sept. 1918). Though not the only kind of role he played, comedy defined his successes in the following decade. In *The Ghost Between* (1921), he was a doctor who prescribed himself for a grieving widow; in *Spring Cleaning* (1923), he was a husband who halts his wife's heedless drift into dalliance; in *A Kiss in a Taxi* (1925), he was an aging Parisian boulevardier who finds himself identified as his paramour's "father"; in *The Marquise* (1927), he was a sardonic French aristocrat. In March 1928 he ventured into vaudeville at the Palace in New York, appearing in a short play with his wife and two daughters.

The year 1929 brought Byron success in a serious role, that of state's attorney Martin Brady, who cannot halt a young convict's step-by-step downfall in prison, in *The Criminal Code*. The *New York Times* wrote, "Always an uncommonly good actor, Mr. Byron here reveals himself as one of the leaders of his profession" (3 Oct. 1929). Another success followed, in *Five-Star Final* (1930), in which Byron portrayed a newspaper editor heartsick at the tragedy his tabloid's sensationalizing has brought to innocent members of a family. Worsening conditions for depression-era Broadway led Byron to Hollywood. There in four years he appeared in twenty-five films, usually playing older men of public stature and authority. He was the warden in *20,000 Years in Sing Sing* (1933), the banker Baring in *The House of Rothschild* (1934), president of the United States in *The President Vanishes* (1934), and in others a judge, a district attorney, a governor, a general, and a secretary of state. His final film was *The Prisoner of Shark Island* (1936).

Byron returned to the stage in 1936 as the Grand Inquisitor opposite Katherine Cornell in *Saint Joan*. To one critic, his performance "wrapped a cloak of magnificence around his shoulders as an actor." The same year he appeared as Polonius opposite John Gielgud in *Hamlet*. His final appearance was as King Zedekiah in *Jeremiah* (1939). During its run, he celebrated his fiftieth year as a professional actor, having started with his father's company in 1889. He could look back at having played more than 300 characters in more than 10,000 performances.

Long concerned about working conditions for others in his profession, Byron had been a founding member of the Actors' Equity Association in 1913. An article he wrote for the *Drama* (Oct. 1920) deplored the changing conditions for actors in his lifetime with the result that "the calling is now a gamble—not a profession." In 1938, after holding lesser offices over the years, he was elected president of Actors' Equity, though declining health led him to withdraw from the office in 1939. Inactive the last few years of his life, he died in Studio City, California, which was the home of a daughter.

• Clippings, playbills, photographs, and uncollated materials on the life and career of Byron are in the Billy Rose Theatre Collection at the New York Public Library for the Performing Arts, Lincoln Center. He is profiled, with numerous personal reminiscences, in J. B. Kennedy, "Leading Man," *Collier's*, 21 Jan. 1933. For a list of his stage appearances, see *Who Was Who in the Theatre, 1912–1976* (1978). For his screen appearances, see James R. Parish, *Hollywood Character Actors* (1978). Portraits and photographed scenes from productions are in Daniel C. Blum, *A Pictorial History of the American Theatre* (1960) and *A New Pictorial History of the Talkies* (1968). An obituary appears in the *New York Times*, 18 July 1943.

WILLIAM STEPHENSON

BYRON, Oliver Doud (14 Nov. 1842–22 Oct. 1920), actor and manager, was born in Frederick, Maryland. His parents' names are unknown. His theatrical career began in January 1856, when at the age of thirteen he was hired by the Holliday Street Theatre in Baltimore to play one of the schoolboys dosed with sulphur and molasses in *Nicholas Nickleby*, which starred Joseph Jefferson. He continued to work at that theater for the next three years, playing youthful parts.

In 1859 Byron went to Virginia to become a member of the Richmond Theatre Company, working with John Wilkes Booth among others. At the outbreak of the Civil War, he returned to the Holliday Street Theatre and remained there through the 1862 season, acting with touring stars E. L. Davenport and James Wallack. In the 1862–1863 season, Byron joined Lucille Western's acting company in Brooklyn, New York. He is believed to have originated the role of "Richard Hare" in Western's great hit *East Lynne*, which was introduced that year. The next season he joined Laura Keene's company, also located in Brooklyn. At this time, his name was given on playbills as Oliver B. Doud.

During the next four years, Byron worked with resident companies at theaters in Louisville, Mobile, Pittsburgh, and Cincinnati. In Mobile he alternated playing Othello and Iago with Edwin Booth. During the 1868–1869 season at the Varieties Theatre in New Orleans, he played leads for the first time. In November 1868 he married actress Mary Kate Crehan; they had one son. In 1869 he advanced to playing leads in popular favorites such as *Don Cesar de Bazan* and *Lost in London* at the Bowery Theater in New York City. Byron played more leading roles at the Bowery in 1870 in plays such as *Metamora* and *The Corsican Brothers*. That year for the first time his name was listed as Oliver Doud Byron.

Concurrently, Byron bought the rights to a failed play, James J. McCloskey's *New York in 1837; or, The Overland Route*. With two new scenes added and the new title *Across the Continent*, this sensational melodrama captivated the public upon its opening in New York in March 1871. Plot elements played on the current interest in the use of the telegraph and the opening of the transcontinental railroad across the West. It also allowed Byron to be a stalwart, action-oriented hero. The review in the *New York Times* (14 Mar. 1871) spoke of an audience "which crowded the house" and greeted with "applause from below and cheers from above" the play's flag-waving conclusion, in which attacking Indians were overcome and virtue triumphed over villainy.

Byron was able to tour as the actor-manager of his own company all across America for the next twenty-five years, with *Across the Continent* as the staple of his repertoire. Audiences ranged, Byron said, from "the kid-gloved" to "the woolen mittened." His wife, known professionally as Kate Byron, toured with him. Their son, actor Arthur Byron, also became part of the troupe. In 1874 his wife's fourteen-year-old sister—later, as Ada Rehan, becoming one of the era's famous actresses—first appeared on the stage in this play. It also provided early engagements for Maude Adams, William Gillette, and Minnie Maddern Fiske. The Broadway star Henry Miller said his youthful inspiration to become an actor was seeing Byron in *Across the Continent*.

His niche in the popular theater established, Byron produced other plays that followed the same pattern: black-and-white characters, fights, gunplay, far-flung settings, and sensational scenic effects. Other plays he introduced were *Ben McCullough; or, the Wanderer's Divorce* (1873); *Donald McKay, the Hero of the Modoc War* (1874), in which he played three roles; *Thoroughbred* and *Rebel to the Core* (both 1876); *The Inside Track* (1885); *The Upper Hand* (1888); and *The Plunger* (1890). Reviewers were condescending toward these entertainments but maintained that Byron offered the public good performers and a high standard of production.

By the early 1890s, however, *Across the Continent* had grown familiar to all. Public taste was turning away from such escapism, and Byron, entering his fifties, was no longer the "young actor with plenty of crude vigor" described in 1871 reviews. His last offerings, *The Heart of Africa* (1894), *Ups and Downs of Life* (1895), and *Turn of the Tide* (1896), did not succeed. He lapsed into inactivity for several years, his career as a star over.

Byron returned to the stage in 1904 in support of his sister-in-law during her final Broadway season of plays. In 1905 he played a supporting role in *The Man on the Box*, starring Henry E. Dixey. Between 1906 and 1908, he toured again in one of the road companies of a Broadway hit, *The Lion and the Mouse*. He took a last small role in *General John Regan* (1913), closing a career that had begun fifty-seven years earlier. He died at his home in Long Branch, New Jersey.

Byron's career encompassed the change in the American theater in which mounting of productions shifted from local stock companies, which imported touring stars, to complete touring companies of a production that the stars brought with them. He was able to give a generation of playgoers across the nation the kind of exciting, sensational plays they craved. As with other actors of the time, Byron was largely accepted and remembered for one role. Reviewers of his early work describe him as "an actor of very fair capacity . . . especially forcible in his method of delivery when strong passion . . . is to be expressed" (*New York Times*, 28 Apr. 1874), and one "who possesses many natural advantages for a player, such as a good voice, a not ungraceful figure, and considerable ease of deportment, but . . . who has a habit of . . . addressing many of his speeches to [the audience] instead of to the actors upon the stage" (quoted in Bordman, p. 31). He was left behind when the American theater changed to more sophisticated, character-based drama.

• Various materials on Byron's life and career are found in the Billy Rose Theatre Collection of the New York Public Library for the Performing Arts, Lincoln Center. Contemporary biographical sketches are in John B. Clapp, *Players of the Present* (1899), and Walter Browne and E. De Roy Koch, *Who's Who on the Stage* (1908). Portraits of Byron and his wife are in George Odell, *Annals of the New York Stage*, vols. 9 (1937) and 10 (1938). See also Gerald Bordman, *The American Theatre: A Chronicle of Comedy and Drama, 1869–1914* (1994). An obituary is in the *New York Times*, 23 Oct. 1920.

WILLIAM STEPHENSON

C

CABELL, James Branch (14 Apr. 1879–5 May 1958), author, was born in Richmond, Virginia, the son of Robert Gamble Cabell II, a physician, and Anne Branch. He traced his roots on his mother's side to seventeenth-century Jamestown, Virginia, to which his ancestors came from England. In time, the Cabells became one of the most prominent families in the commonwealth. Cabell's great-grandfather was a governor of Virginia, and his grandfather was a personal physician to Confederate general Robert E. Lee. Cabell's parents divorced in 1907, an uncommon event in their stratum of Richmond society of the era.

Cabell grew up immersed in the history of Virginia and in a city that lived deeply in the shadow of the recent Confederate cause, themes that he personally took seriously and that appear in a number of his books. He attended private schools in Richmond and was graduated with high honors in 1898 from the College of William and Mary. He was a precocious student, having taught French and Greek at the college before he took his undergraduate degree. He was also encouraged by the faculty to publish work that he had written to fulfill class assignments.

On the eve of his graduation, Cabell became embroiled in a controversy that may have precipitated in part the ironic worldview that permeates many of his fifty-two books and that was a lifelong part of his personality. He was a member of a small group of students who had come under the literary and social influence of the college librarian, Charles Washington Coleman. No records exist regarding the matter, but the faculty was known to have discussed the group and apparently suspected that some impropriety, perhaps ongoing, had been committed. Although no specifics were ever mentioned, the rumors revolved around homosexuality. Indignant, and believing his honor to have been impugned, Cabell briefly withdrew from school but soon returned. The damage had been done, however, and what may have been no more than vicious rumor caused the young and impressionable Cabell to live in virtual isolation in the weeks preceding his graduation.

After graduation Cabell returned to Richmond, where he was briefly engaged in newspaper work in the pressroom of the *Richmond Times*. In 1899 he moved to New York to accept employment as a reporter on the staff of the *New York Herald,* and in 1901 he became a reporter for the *Richmond News*. In the same year, however, another event occurred that probably helped shape his worldview: he was accused of involvement in the murder (which was never publicly resolved) of one of his mother's cousins in Richmond. Cabell denied complicity in the crime throughout his lifetime, but because the cousin in question enjoyed an unfavorable reputation in Richmond, Cabell conceded that he had needed killing.

With the exception of the years 1911 through 1913, when he worked in the office of a coal mining business owned by an uncle in West Virginia, Cabell devoted the remainder of his life to writing. He first worked as a subsidized genealogist researching the Branch family, out of which came *Branchiana: A Record of the Branch Family in Virginia* (1907) and *Branch of Abingdon: A Record of the Branch Family in England* (1911). Cabell had also published short fiction in a number of national magazines, as well as *The Eagle's Shadow* (1904), *The Line of Love* (1905), *The Cords of Vanity* (1909), and *Chivalry* (1909).

Cabell married the widow Priscilla Bradley Shepherd in 1913; they had one child. By this time Cabell was settled into the daily routine of a professional writer, his career soon receiving a boost from the Chicago newspaper critic Burton Rascoe, who discovered the new author following the 1917 publication of *The Cream of the Jest*. So enamored of Cabell's work was Rascoe that he compared him favorably to Anatole France, a writer who at the time was enjoying enormous popularity throughout Europe. Cabell also continued his genealogical work, with the Virginia War History Commission, the Virginia chapter of the Sons of the Revolution, and other state historical groups. He also served briefly as guest editor of the *Reviewer,* a Richmond-based little magazine. It was here that he met Margaret Waller Freeman, one of the magazine's staff of four and the woman who would years later become his second wife. From 1932 to 1935 he was one of the editors of the *American Spectator*.

The watershed year of Cabell's career was 1919, when, with the publication of *Jurgen,* his name became a household word. *Jurgen* is a fantasy based on real and fabricated myths, interlaced with delicate but obvious threads of sexual innuendo. The book was seized in 1920, when John S. Sumner, executive secretary for the New York Society for the Suppression of Vice, arrived at Cabell's publisher and, armed with a warrant, demanded the plates and all copies of *Jurgen*. Sumner charged that the book was "lewd, lascivious, indecent, obscene and disgusting." This action set in motion one of the major literary trials of the century. The ensuing suppression of the novel and the trial that followed were the talk of the literary world, and the book's exoneration by a New York court in 1922 served to heighten interest in the Cabell canon. The generally shy and retiring Cabell, whose name was often mispronounced, commented during the ordeal that the name "rhymes with rabble."

As early as 1915 Cabell had undertaken an ambitious plan to create a major literary saga, which ultimately saw fruition as the eighteen-volume series "The

Biography of the Life of Manuel," comprising twenty-one titles. Called the Storisende Edition, the series is set in the fictional realm of Poictesme and traces Manuel, its protagonist, from medieval Europe to twentieth-century America. Published between 1927 and 1930, it includes *Beyond Life, Figures of Earth, The Silver Stallion, Domnei* and *The Music from Behind the Moon, Chivalry, Jurgen, The Line of Love, The High Place, Gallantry, Something about Eve, The Certain Hour, The Cords of Vanity, From the Hidden Way* and *The Jewel Merchants, The Rivet in Grandfather's Neck, The Eagle's Shadow, The Cream of the Jest* and *The Lineage of Lichfield, Straws and Prayer-Books,* and *Townsend of Lichfield.*

One of the most ambitious cycles in American literature, "The Biography" revolves around history, myth, religion, and folklore, placing real and imaginary stories side by side and exploiting the western philosophical tradition from the time of ancient Greece to the modern era. Whimsy, irony, satire, allegory, double entendre, time distortions, and the inversions of traditional myths—all are used by Cabell as fictional devices in this series, which includes novels, short stories, poems, and essays. His work prompted critic H. L. Mencken to comment that Cabell was "a scarlet dragonfly imbedded in opaque amber."

In the Storisende Edition Cabell sets out to explore what he considers the three dominant attitudes that Manuel and his descendants, and by extension Western civilization, have possessed over the centuries: the chivalric attitude, the gallant attitude, and the poetic attitude. In the preface to the first volume Cabell writes that "the descendants of Manuel have at various times very variously viewed life as a testing; as a toy; and as raw material. They have variously sought during their existence upon earth to become . . . admirable; or to enjoy life; or to create something more durable than life."

Following the publication of the Storisende Edition, Cabell's reputation declined. The decade of the 1930s had little use for a romancer and mythmaker as the economic turmoil caused by the stock market crash and the Great Depression took its toll. Accordingly, Cabell shortened his public name to Branch Cabell, making a pun on the idea of being a branch of the former author, and entered the world of the nonfiction writer.

In *Some of Us* (1930) Cabell offers a defense of his works and that of several of his contemporaries, while in *These Restless Heads* (1932), *Special Delivery* (1933), and *Ladies and Gentlemen* (1934) he deals with aesthetics, autobiography, his reading public, and famous authors who have preceded him. *Let Me Lie* (1947), *Quiet Please* (1952), and *As I Remember It* (1955) are autobiographical and historical, dealing with Virginia's past.

In the trilogy "The Nightmare Has Triplets" (*Smirt* [1934], *Smith* [1935], and *Smire* [1937]) Cabell returned to fiction and produced a work that critics have compared to Joyce's *Finnegans Wake*. In these three novels Cabell creates a nonsense world, but unlike Joyce's work the books are not linguistically inaccessible to most readers.

Another fictional trilogy is "Heirs and Assigns," comprised of *Hamlet Had an Uncle* (1940), *The King Was in His Counting House* (1938), and *The First Gentleman of America* (1942). These novels are based on historical research, the first treating the source for Shakespeare's play, the second the Medici family, and the third the story of an influential Native American from the early colonial era. As a whole, the trilogy centers on political and ethical considerations.

Toward the end of his life Cabell began to suffer from the Virginia winters. Although short and generally mild, they caused difficulties for him because of his worsening respiratory problems. He saw as a solution an annual winter removal, beginning in the 1930s, to St. Augustine, Florida, where he soon became interested in local history.

Cabell's final trilogy was appropriately titled "It Happened in Florida" and consisted of *The St. Johns* (1943), written in collaboration with historian A. J. Hanna, *There Were Two Pirates* (1946), and *The Devil's Own Dear Son* (1949). The first of these works is nonfictional, written for the Rivers of America series. Although the second two books have as their bases the early Spanish history of Florida, they are reminiscent of the Cabellian theme expressed in *Jurgen:* the search for youth and the ultimate grappling with approaching old age, and finally resignation.

Cabell created one of the great mythic sagas in modern literature. In his most ambitious work, the Storisende Edition, he grapples with the central question of identity in the modern world. In such later works as "The Nightmare Has Triplets" trilogy one finds him working on the forefront of fiction in the first half of the twentieth century.

Priscilla Bradley Cabell died in St. Augustine in 1949, and the following year Cabell married Margaret Freeman. The couple, along with Cabell's only child, lived at the family's Richmond residence, 3201 Monument Avenue, the place of Cabell's death.

• The bulk of Cabell's papers and personal library are held in the Alderman Library of the University of Virginia and at the James Branch Cabell Library at Virginia Commonwealth University of Richmond. Biographies include Joe Lee Davis, *James Branch Cabell* (1962), and Edgar MacDonald, *James Branch Cabell and Richmond-in-Virginia* (1993), the definitive biography. Critical appraisals appear in Arvin R. Wells, *Jesting Moses* (1962); Desmond Tarrant, *James Branch Cabell* (1967); Oscar Cargill, *Intellectual America* (1941); Carol Van Doren, *James Branch Cabell* (1932); Harlan Hatcher, *Creating the Modern American Novel* (1935); Louis D. Rubin, Jr., and Robert D. Jacobs, eds., *South: Modern Southern Literature and Its Cultural Setting* (1961); and Louis D. Rubin, Jr., *No Place on Earth: Ellen Glasgow, James Branch Cabell and Richmond-in-Virginia* (1959). Two periodicals devoted entirely to Cabell are *Kalki* and the *Cabellian*. Two informative articles are Leon Howard, "Figures of Allegory," *Sewanee Review* 42 (Jan.–Mar. 1934): 54–66, and Edmund Wilson, "The James Branch Cabell Case Reopened," *New Yorker,* 21 Apr. 1956, pp. 129–56.

MAURICE DUKE

CABELL, James Lawrence (26 Aug. 1813–13 Aug. 1889), teacher of medicine and sanitarian, was born in Nelson County, Virginia, the son of George Cabell, a physician, and Susanna Wyatt. George Cabell's brother Joseph was a founder of the University of Virginia. In 1839 James Cabell married Margaret Gibbons. They had no children of their own but did adopt two nieces.

After receiving his M.A. in literature from the University of Virginia (1829–1833), Cabell attended one course of lectures in medicine at the University of Maryland in 1834 and was awarded an M.D. He pursued postgraduate training in the hospitals of Baltimore, Philadelphia, and Paris. From France he was called home to be professor of anatomy, surgery, and physiology at Virginia in 1837. While his uncle's position in the university no doubt influenced the choice, Cabell's extensive training qualified him for a place among the elite of American medicine in spite of his youth. For more than fifty years he was a central figure of the medical school's faculty, acquiring a reputation as a distinguished teacher, scholar, and clinician.

In addition to medical articles on topics as diverse as gunshot wounds, municipal sanitation, pneumonia, and international quarantine, Cabell published *Testimony of Modern Science to the Unity of Mankind* in 1858. The previous decades had seen an active debate on the question of whether there is one human species literally descended from Adam or several. This tied into the larger discussion of speciation that would culminate in Charles Darwin's *Origin of Species* in 1859. Southerners were divided between the realization that a separate species for blacks helped justify slavery and adherence to a literal interpretation of the Old Testament. Cabell argued that blacks were one of the fixed varieties of humankind, but that there was only one human species. His work was prefaced by a cleric and explicitly supported the biblical account. He also made it clear, however, that he was not antislavery; rather, he believed that the black variety was inferior to the Anglo-Saxon and that slaves had become more civilized through contact with their white masters. The impact of Cabell's essay was lost amid the turmoil of the Civil War and the major redirection of ethnology caused by Darwin's work.

During the Civil War Cabell ran the Confederate military hospital at Charlottesville, Virginia. In the 1870s he achieved national prominence as an advocate of public health reform when he became president of both the American Public Health Association and the Medical Society of Virginia. The American Public Health Association, composed of sanitarians who promoted public health reform, held its first meeting in 1872. The members of the APHA maintained that a filthy environment caused disease, and they argued for the provision of pure air, pure water, adequate drainage and sewerage, and the collection of vital statistics. Cabell actively promoted this cause and lobbied for governmental action before state medical societies and through his state and national congressional representatives.

Although the board of health founded in Virginia in 1872 was ineffective because of lack of funding, Cabell did see one realization of his vision in the creation of the National Board of Health, established by Congress in the wake of the devastating yellow fever epidemic of 1878. Although this board's main duty was to fight yellow fever, while Cabell and his colleagues had been pushing for a broader national department of sanitation, the public health reformers saw the board as a step forward. Cabell became its first president in 1879.

The National Board of Health was the first federal public health agency. Its principal tools in fighting yellow fever were quarantine and disinfection, pursued under the assumption that a yellow fever germ existed and that it could be killed by heat and known antimicrobial substances. Cabell directed the board's activities in setting up quarantine stations along the Gulf Coast, maintaining inland railroad inspection stations, and urging southern towns to increase the cleanliness of their streets and privies. The board had only limited powers and funds to enforce its recommendations and met considerable resistance from local officials. Cabell and his colleagues on the board were unable to pursue their principal goal of sanitation because so much of their effort was devoted to quarantine. When yellow fever did not return in the years following 1879, Congress felt less impelled to support a national health agency. It voted no further funds to the National Board after 1883, and the board subsequently ceased operations.

The demise of the National Board of Health was due to multiple causes, including opposition by some state boards of health, adept lobbying by another federal agency for the same powers, and controversies around the ways in which board funds had been spent. Cabell himself might have been a stronger advocate for the board, but financial reasons kept him from moving to Washington on a full-time basis. He could not afford to leave his lucrative practice and teaching position for the unpaid job of National Board president. Ill health and age also contributed to the weakening of his voice. Although he was bitter about the inconstancy of Congress, Cabell did believe that the National Board had demonstrated the potential for federal action to promote public health research and reform.

Cabell died at a friend's house in Albemarle County, Virginia.

• Cabell's letters are found in the Cabell papers of the University of Virginia as well as in the National Archives (Records of the National Board of Health). His public health views are well summarized in "Address in State Medicine and Public Hygiene," *Transactions of the American Medical Association* 29 (1876): 551–83. A brief biography and a bibliography are in Paul Addis's entry in the *Dictionary of American Medical Biography*, ed. Martin Kaufman et al. (1984). On the National Board of Health see Margaret Humphreys, *Yellow Fever and the South* (1992). An obituary is in *Transactions of the Medical Society of Virginia* 20 (1889): 292–96.

MARGARET HUMPHREYS

CABELL, Nathaniel Francis (23 July 1807–1 Sept. 1891), author, was born at "Warminster," his family's plantation in Nelson County, Virginia, the son of Nicholas Cabell, Jr., and Margaret Read Venable, merchant planters. Cabell was left fatherless at the age of two and was raised by his mother as a conservative Presbyterian. He graduated from Hampden-Sydney College in 1825 and earned a degree in law from Harvard College in 1827. Following graduation he moved to Prince Edward County, Virginia, where he practiced law for four years.

In 1831 Cabell married Anne Blaws Cocke, with whom he had six children. He returned to Warminster in 1832 and shortly thereafter moved to "Liberty Hall," which he had inherited, also in Nelson County. He remained there until shortly before his death. After the death of his first wife, Cabell married Mary M. Keller of Baltimore in 1867. The union produced no offspring. Although an ardent and lifelong Presbyterian, Cabell gradually came under the influence of Emanuel Swedenborg, the Swedish scientist, philosopher, and interpreter of the scriptures, whose followers founded the Church of the New Jerusalem, or New Church. In 1837 Cabell withdrew from the Presbyterian church, and in 1842 he was baptized into the New Church, his family soon following him. Swedenborg's interpretation of the Bible exerted a particularly strong influence on Cabell.

Cabell wrote primarily on religion and the history of Virginia agriculture, tracing it to its origins in 1607. His editing projects, however, were eclectic. Between 1840 and 1842, he published a series of essays in the *New Jerusalem Magazine* under the title "Excerpts, or Readings with My Pencil"; he also wrote for the *New-Churchman.* His article on the New Church was included in Israel D. Rupp's *An Original History of the Religious Denominations at Present Existing in the United States* (1844). Other works by Cabell include *Reply to Rev. Dr. Pond's "Swedenborgianism Reviewed"* (1848), *A Letter on the Trinal Order for the Ministry of the New Church* (1848), and the single published chapter of *The Progress of Literature during the Preceding Century when Viewed from a Religious Standpoint* (1868). In 1873 and 1874 he published articles on the Apostle Paul under the title "Horae Paulinae" in the *New Jerusalem Messenger.*

During these years Cabell was also working in areas other than theology. His studies on agriculture appeared in the *Farmers' Register* and elsewhere; he edited the letters between a distant relative and the founder of the University of Virginia in *Early History of the University of Virginia as Contained in the Letters of Thomas Jefferson and Joseph C. Cabell* (1856); edited part of the Lee Papers, which appeared in the *Southern Literary Messenger* from 1858 to 1860; and contributed to the *Memoirs of Professor George Bush* (1860). Cabell was also an active genealogist, preparing works on the Cabell and Carrington families of Virginia.

Cherishing a lifelong ambition to write a comprehensive agricultural history of Virginia, Cabell collected and annotated an extensive variety of manuscripts and letters for the purpose. Although the project was unfinished at the time of his death, his extensive assemblage of materials remains intact. A scholarly and affable man who numbered among his friends many with divergent views on religion, Cabell was always ready to share his personal library and the results of his research with close colleagues.

Late in life Cabell took up residence at the home of a daughter and son-in-law in Bedford City, Virginia, where he remained until his death. Cabell's chief contributions lay in his apologies for Swedenborgianism and his accounts of agriculture, particularly its history, in Virginia. His edited projects provide information about Virginia in the nineteenth century.

• Cabell's collection of agricultural papers is in the Virginia State Library in Richmond. Those interested in this collection should consult the *Virginia State Library Bulletin* (Jan. 1913, July–Oct. 1918) for a more complete description. The Alderman Library at the University of Virginia and the Virginia Historical Society in Richmond hold collections of Cabell materials. The most authoritative biographical account may be found in Alexander Brown, *The Cabells and Their Kin* (1895; repr. 1939, 1978).

MAURICE DUKE

CABELL, Samuel Jordan (15 Dec. 1756–4 Aug. 1818), revolutionary soldier and congressman, was born at "Union Hill" in Amherst County, Virginia, the son of Margaret Jordan and William Cabell, a prominent planter who served on the colony's important revolutionary committee of safety and was chairman of the Amherst Committee. With the approach of the Revolution, Colonel William Cabell dropped plans to send Samuel to college in England and enrolled him instead at the College of William and Mary. Samuel attended from 1772 until December 1775, when Virginia militia clashed with British regulars at Great Bridge near Norfolk. Colonel Cabell, who was meeting in Williamsburg with the Virginia Committee of Safety when the battle occurred, sent Samuel home to raise a company of riflemen for Virginia's defense.

Samuel's task was made easier by the intensity of revolutionary sentiment in frontier Amherst. Within two months the full complement of seventy-eight enlisted men and officers, headed by Cabell, who was commissioned captain, was ready to march. Armed with tomahawk and long rifle and dressed in the frontier garb of buckskin and linsey-woolsey, they proceeded to Williamsburg in March 1776. There they were attached as light infantry to General Andrew Lewis's Sixth Virginia Regiment. In September they marched northward to join General George Washington's army in retreat across New Jersey.

The Sixth Virginia joined the Continental army in time to participate in two important battles in the winter of 1776–1777. On Christmas night they crossed the Delaware River with Washington and helped to capture 1,400 Hessian mercenaries still groggy from holiday celebrations. Several weeks later they fought again at Princeton, where their victory compelled the British to evacuate most of New Jersey.

Over the summer of 1777 Cabell's rifle company was reassigned to Colonel Daniel Morgan's Rangers, becoming part of a select corps of 500 expert riflemen whose skills as marksmen and woodsmen became legendary. Washington sent Morgan's riflemen to New York to aid General Horatio Gates, whose forces opposed the British army under General John Burgoyne advancing toward Albany. During September and October the two armies engaged in skirmishes and several pitched battles. The first of these at Freeman's Farm on 19 September ended inconclusively with the Americans retaining control of the high ground at Bemis Heights. On 7 October Burgoyne opened the second battle of Freeman's Farm with a flanking movement, which Morgan's Rangers, led by the Amherst Rifles, counteracted. Having blocked the British flanking movement, the Americans charged the British earthworks and forced Burgoyne to retreat. Soon thereafter at Saratoga he surrendered his entire army. Morgan's riflemen drew special praise from Gates for their important role in the victory. One of Burgoyne's ablest officers, General Simon Fraser, fell during the battle to the fire of a sharpshooter from Cabell's company. For the courage he showed under fire at the head of the Amherst riflemen, Cabell was promoted to the rank of major.

After Burgoyne's surrender Cabell and his company rejoined Washington's army. Cabell spent the winter of 1777–1778 at Valley Forge as brigade inspector. He fought in Washington's 1778 and 1779 campaigns and was promoted in November 1779 to lieutenant colonel. Soon afterward he was assigned to General Benjamin Lincoln's army in South Carolina. In April 1780, after a forced march of 500 miles in thirty days, Cabell and his men arrived in Charleston only to be part of America's greatest defeat of the war. In May General Lincoln surrendered Charleston, and Cabell became a prisoner of war along with 5,400 other American soldiers. Cabell was held for fourteen months at Haddrell's Point, South Carolina. Paroled in August 1781, he returned to Amherst, from which he had been absent, with the exception of two brief furloughs, for over five years. Never exchanged, he was still on parole when the war ended.

In 1781 Cabell married Sarah "Sally" Syme, the daughter of Colonel John Syme, a wealthy planter and half brother of Patrick Henry. For the next few years they resided at Union Hill while their country home was being completed. In 1785 they moved into "Soldier's Joy" in what became Nelson County. They had nine children.

The courage he repeatedly exhibited during the Revolution while leading the Amherst Rifles made Cabell a local hero, respected by his men and idolized by Amherst's citizens, who reportedly revered him next to Washington. His military reputation, together with exceptional oratorical and electioneering skills, gave Cabell a decided advantage in any local political contest. Appointed a justice of the peace upon his return from the war, he became county lieutenant in 1784 and was elected to the Virginia House of Delegates in 1785, where he served until 1792. Both he and his father were overwhelmingly elected to represent Amherst at the Virginia Convention of 1788. They stood solidly with Henry in opposing the Constitution, but the adoption of the Bill of Rights appeased Samuel Cabell. In 1794 he was elected to the Fourth Congress and was reelected to the three succeeding Congresses, serving from 4 March 1795 to 3 March 1803. His congressional career was undistinguished. He performed committee assignments faithfully but rarely participated in House debates. An ardent Democratic Republican, he strongly endorsed Thomas Jefferson's views on the need for economy in government. Declining to stand for reelection in 1802, he retired from public life upon the adjournment of the Seventh Congress. For the next fifteen years he managed his tobacco plantation and pursued the life of a gentleman farmer at Soldier's Joy, where he died.

• No personal or business papers, diaries, or journals of Cabell are known to exist. The Cabell Family Papers, 1774–1941, Virginia Historical Society, Richmond, contain a few scattered letters to and from Cabell, but the bulk of that collection concerns other members of the large and important Cabell family. The Massie Family Papers, 1696–1856, and the Preston Family Papers, 1727–1896, both located at the Virginia Historical Society, contain a few miscellaneous Cabell items. Alexander Brown, *The Cabells and Their Kin* (1895), though dated, is the best published source about Cabell's life.

CHARLES D. LOWERY

CABELL, William (13 Mar. 1730–23 Mar. 1798), revolutionary political figure, antifederalist, and tobacco planter, was born in the James River valley, north of Richmond, Virginia, the son of William Cabell and Elizabeth Burks. His father was a surgeon of the Royal Navy, who was born in Wiltshire, England, migrated to Virginia in the early 1720s, and married into a wealthy planter family in 1726. As his family grew, Cabell's father took up extensive lands in the upper James River valley. As a leading planter on a frontier, he served as vestryman, deputy sheriff, justice of the peace, and militia officer, as well as practicing medicine.

William Cabell and his brothers shared and then inherited their father's role and prestige in the southwestern Piedmont. Perhaps educated at the College of William and Mary, Cabell was a vestryman in 1750 and deputy sheriff by 1753. That year he received 2,700 acres from the Crown. In 1756 he married Margaret Jordan, the daughter of Colonel Samuel Jordan, the leading planter of neighboring Buckingham County. The couple had seven children who survived to adulthood.

In 1761 the Cabells engineered the separation of Amherst County from Albemarle, which opened more and higher offices to their interest. Cabell immediately became a justice of the peace, a lieutenant of the county militia under his father who was colonel, church warden of the new parish, county surveyor, and coroner. He and his family also invested in the local iron industry and the nascent James River Canal Company. Always assiduous in accumulating land and slaves, the family held over 25,000 acres, mostly alluvial, at the time of the father's death in 1774. William Cabell developed a portion of that land into his estate, "Union Hill," where he cultivated a reputation for horsemanship, hospitality, and careful plantation management. Besides tobacco farming, Cabell also had his own smithy, tannery, and wool cloth industry prior to 1770.

Elected to the House of Burgesses from Amherst in the early 1760s, Cabell played no conspicuous role in the Stamp Act crisis. In 1769 and 1770, however, he became a strong supporter of the nonimportation agreements against the Townshend Duties. In 1774, after the governor, Lord Dunmore, dissolved the House of Burgesses, Cabell was among those who met at Raleigh Tavern, Williamsburg, to call for renewed boycotts and a continental congress. As the revolutionary crisis deepened, he was elected in 1775 and 1776 to the Virginia Committee of Safety, which was responsible for political and military mobilization.

As a member of the Virginia Conventions of 1775 and 1776, Cabell supported the call for independence. Along with George Mason, he served on the committees that drafted the famed Virginia Declaration of Rights and the Constitution of 1776. Under the new constitution, he was the first state senator from his district comprising Amherst, Buckingham, and Albemarle, Thomas Jefferson's home county. On completion of his term in 1781, he was elected to the House of Delegates for three annual terms (1781–1783, 1787–1788). During the 1783 session, as chairman of the Committee on Religion, he played an early role in the gradual disestablishment of the church by presenting Baptist petitions for liberalizing the vestry and marriage laws in the interests of dissenters. Both failed in that session but were harbingers of the future.

While still a member of the House of Delegates in 1787, Cabell made clear his opposition to the proposed U.S. Constitution. Unanimously elected from Amherst to Virginia's ratifying convention, he supported the moderate antifederalist position that sought to delay ratification until there were amendments, including what became the Bill of Rights. Cabell was essentially aligned with his old friend George Mason against James Madison, whose family, incidentally, had been rivals of the Cabells in the western Piedmont for decades. During the subsequent national elections the Cabell interest was part of the coalition that prevented Madison from being elected a U.S. senator. Cabell and his local allies also supported James Monroe in his unsuccessful effort to win election to the U.S. House of Representatives over Madison. Here the Cabells, while carrying Amherst nearly unanimously for Monroe, failed in their bid to thwart Madison and the federalist faction. Nonetheless, he accepted election to the new electoral college and cast a vote for George Washington.

After 1789 Cabell withdrew from state and national politics. He remained active in his county and region, continuing to serve, for instance, as a trustee of Hampden Sydney College, which he had helped found in 1776. Two of his sons inherited the leadership of the Cabell interest and became rather prominent political figures—Samuel Jordan Cabell, served in the Continental army, the House of Delegates, and the U.S. Congress, while William Cabell served in the Virginia legislature and with his father the ratifying convention.

Cabell died at Union Hill, Amherst County, Virginia, leaving to his sons and sons-in-law more than 30,000 acres, divided into several large plantations in three counties of the upper James River valley, and many slaves. He was a notable member of the Virginia gentry and helped guide the Commonwealth into and through the American Revolution.

• The Cabell Family Papers are at the Virginia State Library. Valuable biographical information is available in some older sources. For the family as a whole, see Alexander Brown, *The Cabells and Their Kin* (1895). There are interesting antebellum sketches of William Cabell in Hugh Blair Grigsby, *The Virginia Convention of 1776* (1855; repr. 1969), and William Meade, *Old Churches, Ministers, and Families of Virginia* (1857). The most convenient source for understanding the political context of Cabell's career is Norman Risjord, *Chesapeake Politics, 1781–1800* (1978).

RICHARD P. GILDRIE

CABELL, William H. (16 Dec. 1772–12 Jan. 1853), judge and governor of Virginia, was born in Cumberland County, Virginia, the son of Colonel Nicholas Cabell and Hannah Carrington. In 1785 Cabell entered Hampden Sydney College, and in 1790 he attended the College of William and Mary, where he studied law under George Wythe. After Wythe moved to Richmond, Cabell followed him in 1793 and completed his study of the law. He was licensed to practice the following year. He married Elizabeth Cabell, a cousin, in 1795. She died in 1801, and in 1805 he married Agnes Gamble of Richmond. It is not known whether he had children from either marriage.

Cabell represented Amherst County in the Virginia House of Delegates during the 1796 session, again in the 1798–1799 session, and from 1802 to 1805. Later, looking back on his political career, he was proud of his having voted in the legislature for the Virginia Resolutions of 1798, which declared the Alien and Sedition Acts to be unconstitutional; and, as an elector in the Electoral College, having voted for Thomas Jefferson in 1800.

In 1805 the General Assembly elected Cabell governor. He was reelected twice, serving the maximum three one-year terms. Several times his supporters urged him to run for Congress, but he refused; he was committed to a career in the law. Even when he was governor, he watched for judicial retirements and hoped he could become a judge in the General Court. In this ambition he succeeded. In 1808 the legislature appointed him to the General Court and gave him the circuit, or superior, courts he wanted; the circuit ran above Richmond through counties along the James River. In 1811, when the General Assembly expanded the state's highest court, the Virginia Supreme Court of Appeals, from three to five members, he was appointed to fill one of the seats. He also took a seat on the governor's council that year.

Like his brother, Joseph Carrington Cabell, William Cabell was interested in promoting education. He was on the board of commissioners chosen by the legislature in 1818 to determine the site and formulate a plan for founding the University of Virginia. He was also a trustee of Hampden Sydney College (1809–1830).

Cabell's plantation, Montevideo, was in Buckingham County on the James River. He resided there when he traveled his General Court circuit; later, he returned to Montevideo when the Court of Appeals in Richmond was not in session. He enjoyed country life, and his friends in the legal profession, such as William Wirt, enjoyed visits to his estate. He was known for being a practical, down-to-earth country gentleman. Lawyers who argued before him knew he gave little credence to flowery rhetoric and courtroom showmanship, but took a common-sense approach in writing his opinions. In 1842 the legislature elevated him to president of the court. He retired from the bench in 1851 and died in Richmond.

• Cabell's autobiographical "Memo of Periods in the Life" is held at the Virginia Historical Society; the Cabell Family Papers are in the library of the University of Virginia. Cabell's court opinions were published in the court reports of the Virginia Supreme Court of Appeals. For his terms as governor, see the *Calendar of Virginia State Papers*, and his messages to the legislature in the *Journal of the House of Delegates*. His life and career are discussed in Alexander Brown, *The Cabells and Their Kin* (1895).

F. THORNTON MILLER

CABELL, William Lewis (1 Jan. 1827–22 Feb. 1911), Confederate general, was born in Danville, Virginia, the son of Benjamin W. S. Cabell and Sarah Epes Doswell. His father, who descended from a distinguished Virginia family, was a veteran of the War of 1812, a member of the Virginia Assembly, a delegate to the Virginia Constitutional Convention of 1829–1830, and a newspaper editor. In 1850 Cabell graduated from West Point, thirty-third in a class of forty-four, and during the next eleven years served as a line officer, quartermaster, and the Utah expedition of 1858, in which year he attained the rank of captain. He married Harriet A. Rector in 1856; they had six children.

Believing that civil war was inevitable, in the spring of 1861 Cabell resigned from the U.S. Army and went to Little Rock, Arkansas, where he offered his services to Governor Henry Rector, to whom he was related by marriage. In April 1861 President Jefferson Davis commissioned him a major and sent him to Richmond, Virginia, to organize the Confederacy's quartermaster, commissary, and ordnance departments. During the summer and fall of 1861 he served first as chief quartermaster to General P. G. T. Beauregard and then on the staff of General Joseph E. Johnston. While thus employed, he joined with those two generals in designing the Confederate battle flag, an action prompted by a desire to provide the southern troops with a banner that could be more easily distinguished from the North's "stars and stripes" than the Confederacy's original national flag, the "stars and bars."

In January 1862 Cabell was ordered to report to General Albert Sidney Johnston, Confederate commander in the West, who in turn assigned him to Major General Earl Van Dorn's army in Arkansas. Having been promoted to brigadier general, Cabell commanded the White River District and, following Van Dorn's defeat at the battle of Pea Ridge (7–8 Mar. 1862), organized the ferrying of his army across the Mississippi to Memphis, Tennessee. During the summer and fall of 1862 he headed a Texas brigade and then an Arkansas brigade in Brigadier General Dabney H. Maury's division. On 3–4 October 1862 he led the latter unit in Van Dorn's bloody and futile assault on Corinth, Mississippi, and the following day participated in a desperate rearguard action at Davis's Bridge on the Hatchie River, suffering wounds that temporarily disabled him for field service. While recuperating, he conducted an inspection of the staff department of the Trans-Mississippi Army, returning to duty in February 1863 as commander of the District of Northwest Arkansas. He recruited and organized a cavalry brigade that, as part of Major General James F. Fagan's division, helped turn back a Union thrust into southern Arkansas at Mark's Mill on 25 April 1864 by capturing a large wagon train and killing or capturing its entire escort.

Cabell's military career came to a climax and conclusion with Major General Sterling Price's invasion of Missouri in the fall of 1864. At Pilot Knob, Missouri, on 27 September 1864, in an assault to which he was opposed, Cabell's brigade was the only Confederate unit to reach the parapet of a Union fort before being repulsed with heavy losses. During the battle of Westport, near Kansas City, Missouri, 23 October 1864, his brigade was badly mauled while vainly resisting the attack of a superior enemy force but did succeed, thanks to his initiative, in saving Price's wagon train from capture by setting fire to the prairie grass, thereby compelling the Federals to fall back. Finally, on 25 October 1864, Price having ignored his warnings that the enemy was pressing the Confederate rear in heavy strength, the remnants of Cabell's brigade were overwhelmed, and he was taken prisoner along with Major General James S. Marmaduke, a division commander in Price's now thoroughly routed army. Sent first to a prison on Johnson's Island in Lake Erie, Cabell subsequently was transferred to Fort Warren in Boston Harbor, where he remained until released on 28 August 1865.

Going to Fort Smith, Arkansas, he studied then practiced law until 1872, when he moved to Dallas, Texas. He became vice president and manager of the Texas Trunk Railway, was elected mayor in 1874, 1875, 1876, and 1882, and was U.S. marshal for the Northern District of Texas from 1885 to 1889, having been appointed to that post by President Grover

Cleveland. From 1893 to 1907 he was a supervisor for the Louisiana State Lottery and then for the Honduras National Lottery. He died at his home in Dallas.

Known to his friends and troops as "Tige," and described by another Confederate general as possessing an "élan and chivalrous bearing" that was "inspiring [to] all who looked upon him," Cabell was an able staff officer who displayed exceptional courage and skill commanding both infantry and cavalry. He spent most of his Civil War career in the Trans-Mississippi, but had he served instead, as he briefly did at the outset of the war, in his native Virginia, it is possible that he would have attained higher rank, for which he seems to have been qualified, and greater fame. As it was, he experienced the gratification of being elected unanimously in 1890 lieutenant general of the Trans-Mississippi Department of the United Confederate Veterans and, upon completing his tenure in that post, of becoming the honorary commanding general of all United Confederate Veterans, remaining so until he died.

• For Cabell's Civil War career, the best sources are the pertinent volumes of *The War of the Rebellion: A Compilation of the Official Records of the Union and Confederate Armies* (128 vols., 1880–1901) and his own postwar writings, the most important of which are "The Confederate States Flag," *Southern Historical Society Papers* 31 (Feb. 1923): 68–70, and *Report of Gen. W. L. Cabell's Brigade in Price's Raid in Missouri and Kansas in 1864* (1900); an extract from the latter, describing his capture at Mine Creek, was published in the *Confederate Veteran* 8 (Apr. 1900): 153–54. Despite errors and contradictions between them and other sources, the best overall accounts of Cabell's life are in Clement A. Evans, ed., *Confederate Military History: Louisiana and Arkansas* (1899), pp. 391–94, and an obituary in *Confederate Veteran* 19 (Apr. 1911): 179–80. The details concerning his family background and connections are presented in Alexander Brown, *The Cabells and Their Kin* (1895). For Cabell's role in military operations in Mississippi, Arkansas, and Price's Missouri expedition, see Albert Castel, *General Sterling Price and the Civil War in the West* (1968; paperback ed., 1993).

ALBERT CASTEL

CABEZA DE VACA, Alvar Núñez. *See* Núñez Cabeza de Vaca, Alvar.

CABLE, George Washington (12 Oct. 1844–31 Jan. 1925), author, was born in New Orleans, Louisiana, the son of businessman George Washington Cable, Sr., and Rebecca Boardman. His parents were originally northerners, and this fact contributed ultimately to accusations in the southern press that Cable did not present the South accurately in his writings. In fact, Cable was deeply immersed in both the contemporary life and the rich history of Louisiana, and he was particularly sensitive to the complex interactions of race, gender, and economics in the Deep South.

Part of that sensitivity may be traced to firsthand experience. At the time of Cable's birth, his father was a prosperous entrepreneur whose varied business dealings were tied to the riverboat trade. But when the national economy wavered, so did the family's economic standing—and the father's health. Ruined by business reverses, the elder Cable died in 1859, and fourteen-year-old George was left to support the family.

Initially he worked as a marker in a customhouse, and with the outbreak of the Civil War shortly thereafter his future seemed even less promising, as he did not want to take the oath of allegiance to the United States and be forced to enlist in the Union army. But in fact the war led to positive changes in Cable's life. Unlike most young males in the city, Cable—just five feet five inches tall and barely 100 pounds—was able to escape occupied New Orleans in the spring of 1863 by posing as a child. That October he enlisted in the Fourth Mississippi Cavalry, served until the end of the war, and was wounded twice in battle. While in the Confederate army he was a clerk for General Nathan Bedford Forrest, and he also found time to indulge his lifelong passion for self-education. At the end of the war Cable returned to New Orleans and worked as grocery clerk, errand boy, rodman with a surveying crew, and accountant. In December 1869 he married Louise Stewart Bartlett, a neighbor of northern ancestry. They had seven children.

At about this time, Cable began writing a column for the popular New Orleans newspaper, the *Picayune*. Nearly one hundred columns were published under his pen name of "Drop Shot," and many reflected Cable's wide and growing knowledge of American and English writers, including Edgar Allan Poe, Nathaniel Hawthorne, Charles Dickens, and William Shakespeare. Still other columns featured his own poems, while an increasing number addressed civic affairs and social problems in the South. Through the "Drop Shot" columns, Cable was finding his literary voice, polishing his craft as a writer, and determining his own often liberal positions on matters of local and regional concern.

By 1871 the *Picayune* was using its popular columnist in other capacities. Much has been made of Cable's alleged dismissal from the *Picayune* later that year on the grounds that he refused to review a local play because of a puritanical dislike of theater. However, although his wife and mother opposed drama on religious grounds, Cable himself seems to have been responsive to the theater from an early age. Indeed, his keen ear for local dialect, the striking use of lighting and setting, and the heavy reliance on physical gesture that are characteristic of his best stories and novels may be attributed to his deep interest in Shakespeare (and, evidently, Molière). Always something of a didactic writer, Cable perceived drama as a potential tool for social reform among the illiterate—a stance that helps explain his willingness, at the end of his life, to see his stories produced as motion pictures.

The *Picayune* also had attempted to use Cable as a reporter, and although he was temperamentally ill suited to this sort of activity he did enjoy doing the research involved in preparing journalistic essays. In February 1872 Cable wrote a series of articles on the churches and charities of New Orleans, based on his research in municipal archives, and at about this time he began to write fiction, basing many of his stories on anecdotes he discovered in historical records. His efforts quickly bore fruit. In early 1873 Edward S. King, accompanied by illustrator J. Wells Champney, arrived in New Orleans to begin work on a series of essays entitled "The Great South" for *Scribner's Monthly*, a New York–based magazine. At King's urging, Cable submitted his tale "'Sieur George" to his editors. This story of an American army officer's moral degeneration in the enervating, exotic environment of New Orleans, which deeply impressed the staff at *Scribner's*, was published in the October 1873 issue of the magazine. Cable enjoyed immediate national acclaim, his success attributable in part to the extreme popularity of regional, or "local color," fiction after the Civil War. Readers in the northern United States and in Europe were eager to read fiction set in the less familiar areas of America, and Cable was the first writer to exploit the Deep South and, in particular, New Orleans—a city perceived as quaintly foreign and vaguely disreputable. Cable produced historically accurate, lushly evocative tales of Louisiana in rapid succession, including the much-anthologized "Belles Demoiselles Plantation" (published in *Scribner's* in 1874), which records the collapse of a magnificent plantation house into the Mississippi River and the attendant drownings of the seven girls who lived in it, plus *Madame Delphine*, a controversial 1881 novella that traces the effects of miscegenation on an unmarried black woman and her beautiful mulatto daughter. In 1879 Scribner's publishing house brought out Cable's first collection of short stories, *Old Creole Days*, which uses both comedy and tragedy to present the history of New Orleans from the Louisiana Purchase to Cable's own day. Also in 1879, serialization began of his violent and technically sophisticated novel *The Grandissimes*, which examines the personal and societal costs of the sexual and economic exploitation engendered by slavery. The novel was released in book form in 1880. Largely on the strength of *Old Creole Days*, *Madame Delphine*, and *The Grandissimes*, Cable came to be perceived not simply as a regional writer, but as one of the most important authors in the United States. In his day he was compared frequently with Turgenev, Flaubert, Hugo, and Hawthorne, while a list of "Forty Immortals" published in *The Critic* in 1884 ranked Cable ahead of Mark Twain.

Various explanations have been offered for the subsequent decline in Cable's reputation and literary output. For one thing, the financial problems that had been dogging him since his father died were only exacerbated by his ever-growing family. He thus felt compelled to obtain funds as a traveling lecturer, often in the company of Mark Twain. Billing themselves as the "Twins of Genius," the unusually tall Twain and the unusually short Cable made a great deal of money on the lecture circuit, but both found that the difficulties of life on the road sapped energies that might have been directed toward writing.

Another problem was that Cable's didactic impulse became an insistent feature of his life and work. Beginning in the early 1880s, Cable devoted much time to preparing public lectures and essays calling overtly for social reform, particularly in the areas of black rights and prison conditions. However commendable, such activity only hurt Cable's work as a creative writer. For example, in *Dr. Sevier* (1884), a potentially powerful novel, Cable too obviously uses his characters simply to illustrate the evils he was challenging in his personal life as a member of the Prisons and Asylums Aid Association. Indeed, his fiction after the mid-1880s became so stridently moralistic and pedantic that eventually Richard Watson Gilder, the *Century* magazine editor who had deeply admired Cable's early work, urged him to reread Hawthorne to see how didactic material could still be presented with artistic grace.

Another factor in Cable's sudden loss of power as a writer of fiction was his removal from New Orleans. Several trips to New York and Hartford, beginning in 1875, confirmed that the North offered the intellectual and cultural stimulation that Cable craved. The North also came to seem more hospitable than his hometown: his fellow New Orleanians had grown increasingly antagonistic toward Cable over what they perceived as his derogatory portraits of southerners—and his alleged suggestion that Creoles had Negro blood. As New Orleans writer Grace King, his contemporary, expressed the matter, Cable had "stabbed the city in the back . . . in a dastardly way to please the Northern press"—an attitude hardly mitigated by Cable's lecturing throughout the South on the evils of segregation and the implied moral superiority of the North. By 1885 he had relocated permanently to Northampton, Massachusetts, where his energies were further dispersed by his work with local Bible study classes and the "Home Culture Clubs." The latter were designed to introduce the working classes to the arts, a project dear to the self-educated Cable, who harbored the hope, never realized, that these clubs would evolve into a kind of people's university.

Cable's publication record after his move to Northampton reflects the dispersal of his talents. The long works of fiction, such as *John March, Southerner* (1894), *Bonaventure* (1888), and *The Cavalier* (1901), lack the power and clarity of vision of *The Grandissimes.* Even his short fiction suffered. His *Strange True Stories of Louisiana* (1889), based on research by hired staff members, offers fact-packed but lifeless anecdotes rather than the polished, moving tales of *Old Creole Days*. Tellingly, his best-known writings from this period are *The Silent South* (1885) and *The Negro Question* (1890), which served only to alienate further the southerners who had once been his most ardent supporters, and *The Busy Man's Bible* (1891) and *The Amateur Garden* (1914), works not of a creative writer but rather a moralist and philanthropist. Far removed from the city whose charms had served as ballast for his reformist impulses, Cable in Northampton became a different kind of writer, one whose calls for social improvement had effectively silenced his voice as a creator of fiction.

Significantly, Cable himself seems to have been unconcerned with the decline in his reputation as a fiction writer. After 1885 he concentrated on social reform, cultivated friendships with fellow writers and philanthropist Andrew Carnegie, visited England (1898, 1905), and attended to family matters. After his first wife died, in 1904, Cable married Eva Colgate Stevenson in 1906; six months after her death in 1923, he married Hanna Cowing. He had no children by either wife. Cable himself died in St. Petersburg, Florida, two years later.

In recent years interest in Cable has been on the increase. The centennial of the publication of *The Grandissimes* in 1980 led to that novel's being recognized as a major achievement in nineteenth-century American fiction and an important precursor of the modern novel. The stories of *Old Creole Days* likewise have enjoyed renewed interest by students and scholars of southern literature.

• Most of Cable's letters and manuscripts are at Tulane University in New Orleans; his correspondence with his editors is included in the archives of Scribners Publishers, in New York. Cable is the subject of four biographies: Lucy Leffingwell Cable Biklé, *George W. Cable: His Life and Letters* (1928); Philip Butcher, *George W. Cable* (1962); Arlin Turner, *George W. Cable: A Biography* (1966); and Louis D. Rubin, Jr., *George W. Cable: The Life and Times of a Southern Heretic* (1969). Philip Butcher, *George W. Cable: The Northampton Years* (1959), explores Cable's later life. An excellent collection of reviews and critical commentaries is Arlin Turner, *Critical Essays on George W. Cable* (1980), while Alice Hall Petry examines his first story collection in *A Genius in His Way: The Art of Cable's Old Creole Days* (1988).

ALICE HALL PETRY

CABOT, Godfrey Lowell (26 Feb. 1861–2 Nov. 1962), manufacturer, was born in Boston, Massachusetts, the son of Samuel Cabot, a physician and prominent member of the unofficial first family of Boston, and Hannah Lowell Jackson. In 1882 Cabot graduated from Harvard, where he studied chemistry. Following graduation, he studied at Zurich Polytechnicum and University in Switzerland and again at Harvard in 1891 and 1892. In 1890 he married Maria Buckminster Moors, with whom he had five children.

With money he inherited from his father, Cabot started a business manufacturing carbon black, first in Pennsylvania but chiefly, during his active years, at the hamlet of Grantsville, West Virginia. Carbon black, the fine black residue powder of incompletely burned hydrocarbons such as flare gas (gas otherwise wasted in exploring for oil and the gas Cabot used in his manufacturing business) and heavy distillates of crude oil, had long been used as a pigment in printing inks, paints, and many other applications. Early in the twentieth century, however, carbon black's superior properties in compounding rubber for motor vehicle tires were discovered, greatly increasing demand for it. At that point Cabot's manufacturing business was well established.

After World War I Cabot began to lose interest in the carbon black business, which he had always run as a single proprietorship with, he claimed, no records other than his checkbook. The gas fields he employed were becoming increasingly connected with industrial and domestic consumers and could no longer supply his plants. He did not shut down his business, however, but closely supervised his second son Thomas, as the younger Cabot scouted new, more abundant sources of flare gas in the Texas oil fields. Cabot rather grudgingly approved of his son's success in turning the company into a multimillion-dollar corporation. Godfrey Cabot lived to see the entire technical and geographic basis of the oil industry revolutionized with a furnace that successfully burned a transportable, low-end, heavy residue from the refining of gasoline. Such triumphs were undeniably the results of the hard work of Thomas and his few close associates; nevertheless, Cabot refused to turn over formal leadership of the company to his son until very late in his long life. By that time he was the chief factor in carbon black manufacture throughout the world.

Cabot was gregarious, a true cosmopolite, and was interested in a wide range of human concerns. Yet he was also a pillar of the Watch and Ward Society, a group dedicated to enforcing public morals, and his son Thomas later described a boyhood of stern discipline, including absention from tobacco, alcohol, and even coffee, and his share of painful spankings. Cabot succeeded, for a generation at least, in helping to make Boston the most moral of great American cities, at least on the surface.

Although Cabot never learned to drive an automobile, at age fifty-five he piloted an airplane in World War I (a Burgess-Dunn seaplane), and as an officer in the U.S. Naval Reserve he patroled Boston Harbor for German submarines. He patented a device for picking up objects from the ground while in flight and a method for refueling in flight; subsequent developments in aviation quickly made his inventions obsolete. He later endowed a chair in aeronautical engineering at Norwich University. He made many philanthropic bequests, primarily to promote American journalism, scientific research, and inter-American relations. His mind remained lucid until he was almost a century old, and he wrote frequently to newspapers about public affairs. He joked at the very idea of such a thing as a "Boston Brahmin" and claimed to have the world's largest collection of versions of the old toast,

Here's to good old Boston,
The home of the bean and the cod,
Where the Lowells speak only to Cabots
And the Cabots speak only to God.

• The letterbooks of Godfrey Lowell Cabot and his son Thomas relating to affairs of the Cabots' carbon black enterprises are in the possession of the Cabot Corporation, but they terminate in the mid-1920s, when the old letterpress system was abandoned. Albro Martin, "The Blacker the Better—A History of the Cabot Corporation" (1983), an unpublished manuscript, is also the property of the company. Leon Harris, *Only to God: The Extraordinary Life of Godfrey Lowell Cabot* (1967), contains much interesting information but leans heavily on the sensational. Thomas Dudley Cabot, *Beggar on Horseback* (1979), is also informative, but discussion of Godfrey Cabot is limited to the first several pages. Obituaries are in the *New York Times* and the *Boston Globe*, 3 Nov. 1962.

ALBRO MARTIN

CABOT, Hugh (11 Aug. 1872–14 Aug. 1945), surgeon, educator, and medical reformer, was born in Beverly Farms, Massachusetts, the son of James Elliot Cabot, an architect, naturalist, and graduate of Harvard Law School, and Elizabeth Dwight. The youngest of seven boys, Cabot was an active child, exposed to music, the Unitarian religion, the challenge of the outdoors, and his parents' philanthropic ideals. His privileged yet altruistic upbringing underlay his future productive life.

Frequently exploring the Brookline area with his father, Cabot embarked on a trip in the Adirondacks at age thirteen. Thereafter he explored much of North America, including Canada. His favored pursuit was to seek unmapped territory with his Native-American companion, Tommy. Cabot sailed as extensively as he trekked, learning the fishing trade and befriending fishermen along the New England and Canadian coasts.

While taking on such challenges, Cabot thrived professionally. He earned an A.B., cum laude, from Harvard University in 1894. Four years later he earned an M.D. from Harvard Medical School. He completed his internship at Massachusetts General Hospital and entered private practice in 1900 as a surgeon. In 1902 he married Mary Anderson Boit, with whom he would have four children. That same year he became assistant surgeon at Massachusetts General Hospital, where he served as surgeon from 1912 to 1919. He simultaneously served as surgeon at Baptist Hospital from 1900 to 1919. Cabot additionally took on the role of professor of surgery from 1910 to 1918 and clinical professor in 1919 at Harvard Medical School. Focused on urology, he organized a Department of Genitourinary Surgery at Massachusetts General, founded the American Board of Urology, and served as president of the American Urological Association in 1911 and as president of the American Association of Genito-Urinary Surgeons in 1914.

During this time Cabot's conviction that the United States should enter World War I brought him into opposition with German influences at home and even the president of the United States. He left for England in 1916 and served with the Harvard Unit in the Royal Army Medical Corps. In 1917 he went to France with the British Expeditionary Force, served as commander of General Hospital No. 22 until 1918, and held the rank of lieutenant colonel in the Royal Army Medical Corps until January 1919. Meanwhile, Cabot remained academically active by editing *Modern Urology* (1918; 3d ed., 1936).

With the end of the war Cabot in 1919 assumed the posts of professor and director of surgery at the University of Michigan Medical School. Although other faculty members were in line for the position of dean, Cabot was appointed dean as early as 1921 and proved a catalyst within the university. Cabot enacted change in the medical curriculum, reducing the number of required lecture and laboratory hours and implementing comprehensive examinations. He forbade private practice by the faculty, paid them proportionately to their care of patients at University Hospital, and adjusted them to a limited full-time basis. The hospital was opened by the state in 1925 and allowed patients to pay what they could afford, an ideal Cabot espoused and advocated throughout his life. To safeguard academic autonomy he subdivided the department by specialties, such as genitourology and neurosurgery, and then promoted their cooperation. Although Cabot was highly successful in achieving his goals, he did not go about them gracefully. Many of the faculty and other medical professionals were unhappy with him and thought him tyrannical.

Regardless of the opposition, Cabot pursued educational reform nationwide. As president of the American Association of Medical Colleges from 1925 to 1926 and as a member of the Commission of Medical Education, he advanced the inclusion of disciplines such as anthropology and psychology in the medical curriculum. He also endorsed early clinical practice for the students, which he believed more necessary than research.

Cabot's strong personality and resolute commitment to a teaching-only faculty at Michigan led him into conflict with the faculty and university regents, who in 1930 asked Cabot to resign as dean and professor of surgery. Cabot adamantly refused, and the regents ousted him later that year. Proudly advising his colleagues to "stick to your principles and don't worry too much about the cost" (*Lancet*, 15 Sept. 1945), Cabot left the university.

Within two weeks William James Mayo invited Cabot to join the Mayo Clinic and the faculty at the University of Minnesota Graduate School of Medicine. There Cabot became recognized as a stimulating teacher who asserted the psychological factors of illness. His progressive thinking was valued, and he established his plan for a complete, full-time teaching faculty. He also advocated sex education and the expansion of nursing education, promoting his ideas through publications such as *Surgical Nursing* (1931).

Cabot also focused on medicine outside of academia. As early as 1915 he voiced his vision for group medical practice rather than competition among physicians. By 1920 he had studied health insurance in countries that guaranteed it and promoted it nationally. In *The Doctor's Bill* (1936), written for the lay public, he expounded on the benefits of prepaid group health care for both doctors and patients. Cabot argued that it would lower costs while providing cooperative service through diverse experts. He urged the government to undertake unpaid costs of medical schools, hospitals, and appropriate care for the indigent. In 1937 Cabot joined physicians from the Medical Advisory Committee of the American Foundation and formed a committee that drafted "Principles and Proposals," which drew substantial support and a hearing from President Franklin Delano Roosevelt. These rebellious yet popular ideas contributed to tension at the 1938 National Health Conference, where Cabot vehemently led the argument for the need of group practice at prepaid rates. Cabot's pre–World War II speech before the Group Health Association of Washington, D.C., in which he stated that the current practice of medicine is "pure fascism of the Italian type," appeared in the *New York Times* (5 May 1938). His first wife having died in 1936, he married Elizabeth Cole Armory in 1938. They had no children.

In October 1938 Cabot testified as a witness against the American Medical Association and the District of Columbia Medical Society for illegally discouraging the practice of prepaid group health care. The physicians involved were found guilty, barred from medical society membership, and forbidden to provide hospital care. The U.S. Supreme Court upheld this verdict, which stimulated the establishment of other prepayment health groups. Cabot further showed his allegiance by organizing such practices despite strong opposition from other professionals.

Cabot retired in 1939 from the university, reentered private practice, and applied his energy to reform. The enterprising surgeon organized the Association of Hospital Service Corp. in Boston, known as the Blue Cross, and a nonprofit organization, the White Cross, which ended with U.S. entry into World War II.

Cabot's focus on health care reform is evident in numerous activities, including his advocacy of the freedom of all licensed physicians to practice in hospitals and the approval of the sale of drugs under generic names. He published on the costs of medical care and the benefits of group practice until 1943 and, despite local hostility, became the Massachusetts chair of the Committee for Russian War Relief. Cabot was a fellow of the American College of Surgeons and an honorary fellow of the Royal Society of Medicine, London.

Never giving up challenges, not even those of nature, Cabot died while sailing with his wife on Frenchman's Bay, Ellsworth, Maine.

• The Michigan Historical Collections at the University of Michigan holds information about Cabot's life while at Michigan. *Physicians of the Mayo Clinic and the Mayo Foundation* (1937) contains an almost complete listing of Cabot's publications up to 1937. There is extensive information on Cabot's life at Michigan in Horace Davenport, *Fifty Years of Medicine at the University of Michigan 1891–1941* (1986). His ousting by the regents of the University of Michigan is discussed in the *New York Times*, 9 and 11 Feb. 1930. The American Foundation's promotion of public funds to supplement the costs of health care, medical schools, and research laboratories is covered in the *New York Times*, 25 Oct. 1937. Coverage of Cabot's "rebellious" speeches at the National Health Conference is in the *New York Times*, 19 and 24 July 1938. The *Times* also carried a letter to the editor from Cabot explicating the need for group health service (25 July 1938) and an opponent's response (4 Aug. 1938) and also covered Cabot's appearance as witness against the American Medical Association (18 Oct. 1938). Obituaries are in the *New England Journal of Medicine* 233 (1945): 706–7; *Lancet* (8 Sept. 1945): 322; *Survey Graphic* (Sept. 1945); and the *New York Times*, 16 Aug. 1945.

KIMBERLY A. HALL

CABOT, John (1450?–1498?), navigator and explorer, may have been born in Genoa, Italy. His parents are unknown. In 1498 the Spanish ambassador in London referred to him as "another Genoese like Colon (Columbus)," and most scholars accept Genoa as John Cabot's place of birth, although no documents have been found to confirm this. Records in Venetian archives, however, document the granting of citizenship in that republic to John Cabot sometime during the period between 9 November 1471 and 28 July 1473. The 28 March 1476 senatorial confirmation of the grant mentions that he had been a resident of Venice for fifteen years. In the letters patent from England's King Henry VII granting him permission "to sail to all parts, regions and coasts of the eastern, western and northern sea," Cabot is identified as a citizen of Venice. Like his contemporary Christopher Columbus, however, Cabot has been claimed by several places, including the Channel Islands, the Venetian Lagoon Island, Chioggia, and Gaeta in the kingdom of Naples. In 1988 Robert Fuson pointed out that the name Cabot is "pure Catalan" and suggested that the discoverer was a Catalonian from the town of Bonavista. Unless new documents are found to the contrary, Genoa and Venice seem secure in their claims on John Cabot's nativity and citizenship.

During the period 1490–1493, a Venetian named "John Cabot Montecalunya" was active building harbor works in Barcelona and Valencia. Whether he was the explorer/discoverer of the same name is a matter of debate. The historical John Cabot appears to have been in England by 1495 and to have made his way to Bristol, where a profitable long-range trade based on the carriage of Icelandic codfish to the Iberian Peninsula was centered. It has been suggested that shrinking stocks in the traditional fishing grounds encouraged Bristol magnates to invest in occasional explorations aimed at finding the mythical "Isle of Brasil" and the "Island of the Seven Cities" or "Antilia," which were believed to lie in the ocean somewhere between westernmost Europe and the eastern shores of Asia.

In its broad outlines the plan of discovery that Cabot proposed to England's monarch probably resembled the one Columbus had earlier persuaded Ferdinand and Isabella to back. Cabot, however, planned to sail west to Asia on a more northerly track, calling at the Isle of Brasil, whereas Columbus had expected Antilia to serve as his way station to the Indies. Although refusing to back Cabot's scheme directly, England's Henry VII granted him and his three sons, Lewis (Ludovico), Sebastian, and Sancio, permission to sail "to discover and find whatsoever isles, countries, regions or provinces of heathens and infidels, in whatsoever part of the world they be, which before this time were unknown to all Christians." According to the report of a Bristol chronicler, Cabot made a landfall in the West on 24 June 1497 with the ship *Mathew*, the first documented post-Viking European landfall in North America. In part because crucial cartographic evidence was not found until 1843, the location of Cabot's landfall, the subject of lengthy debate, was variously placed at literally dozens of venues from Greenland to Florida. Scholarly consensus has since placed Cabot's landfall in the island-strewn region between the Gulf of St. Lawrence and the Atlantic Ocean.

One of the five extant contemporary discussions of Cabot's voyage is included in a letter dated 23 August 1497 that Lorenzo Pasqualigo wrote from England to his brothers in Venice. In it, Pasqualigo reported the return in a small ship of "that Venetian of ours" who said he had discovered terra firma 700 leagues across the sea. Pasqualigo, and doubtless most others, believed the discovery to have been "the country of the Grand Khan," although, upon landing, Cabot had failed to encounter any people. He did, however, find and present to the king "certain snares which were spread to take game and a needle for making nets." Notched and felled trees also were evidence of unseen inhabitants. Described as "being in doubt" or uneasy, Cabot returned to his ship and set sail for Bristol. Two islands were sighted, but to hasten his return, Cabot did not land on them.

Pasqualigo went on to tell that a delighted King Henry VII promised Cabot ten armed ships with prisoners to crew them for a return voyage in the coming spring. Cabot and his wife and family were reported to be enjoying the king's largess, and the English people were described as "running after him like mad" in eagerness to enlist in his adventure. The Venetian Pasqualigo was particularly pleased to report that the large cross Cabot had erected to mark his landing bore the banner of Venice's St. Mark as well as that of England.

The geopolitical import of Cabot's accomplishment was stressed by Raimondo de Soncino, London agent of the duke of Milan, in a report dated 18 December 1497. Soncino wrote that England's king "gained a part of Asia without a stroke of the sword" through Cabot's discovery in the western ocean. Soncino styled Cabot a man "of kindly wit and a most expert mariner" who had achieved this feat "in a little ship with eighteen persons." Starting from Bristol, Cabot "passed Ireland which is still farther west, and then bore towards the north, in order to sail to the east [of Asia], leaving the north on his right hand after some days." "After having wandered for some time he at length arrived at the mainland," Soncino continued, "where he hoisted the royal standard, and took possession for the king here; and after taking certain tokens he returned." Cabot employed a world map and globe of his own construction to demonstrate where his discovery was located, and his English crewmen verified his description of the excellence of the land and its temperate climate. In addition to believing that Brazil wood and silk were native to the new land, Cabot and his crew asserted "that the sea there is swarming with fish, which can be taken not only with the net, but in baskets let down with a stone, so that it sinks in the water."

As previously mentioned, however, no maps or documents by John Cabot have survived. A marginal inscription on a 1544 world map, found in 1843 and attributed to Sebastian Cabot, memorializes his father's discovery. Although incorrect in its chronology, the caption states in Latin and Spanish:

> This land was discovered by John Cabot the Venetian, and Sebastian Cabot his son, in the year . . . 1494 [1497] on the 24th of June in the morning, to which they gave the name Land First Seen (prima Terra Vista), and to a large island which is near the said land they gave the name Saint John, because it had been discovered the same day. The people of it are dressed in the skins of animals; they use in their wars bows and arrows, lances and darts, and certain clubs of wood, and slings. It is a very sterile land. There are in it many white bears, and very large staglike horses, and many other animals; and likewise there is infinite fish, sturgeons, salmon, very large soles a yard in length, and many other kinds of fish, and the greatest of them are called Baccallaos (codfish); and likewise there are in the same land hawks black as crows, eagles, partridges, linnets, and many other kinds of birds of different species.

The placement of the words "prima terra vista" across the entrance to the Gulf of St. Lawrence on Sebastian's map leaves little doubt as to the general area of his father's discovery. The exact locations of Cabot's landfall and the coast he sailed along are far more difficult to determine and have become matters for an ongoing and lively scholarly debate. The most important Cabot document published in the twentieth century is known as the "John Day Letter." The undated letter, from an English merchant named John Day (alias Hugh Say) to an "El Almirante Mayor" in Spain, does not refer to John Cabot by name, but it discusses the Cabot voyage of 1497. The strongest body of scholarly opinion identifies the grand admiral to whom the letter is addressed as none other than Christopher Columbus. In his letter Day corroborates much of what was already known about the 1497 Cabot voyage and also provides, for the first time, a contemporary statement of new information and exciting possibilities for interpretation. Day wrote that the expedition left Bristol at the end of May and took thirty-five days to reach the "tierra de primera vista." The wind was from the east and northeast, and the sea was calm both going and returning. They spent about a month exploring the coast between the latitude of Dursey Head in Ireland (51°34′N) and the mouth of the Bordeaux (Gironde) River (45°35′N), roughly the area from the northern tip of Newfoundland south to Nova Scotia. According to Day most of the land sighted was discovered after Cabot had begun his return to England.

The Day letter was made known in 1956 by Louis A. Vigneras, an American expert on early voyages of discovery, who encountered it in the Archivo de Simancas. Until its appearance, many historians accepted W. F. Ganong's meticulous 1929 reconstruction of Cabot's route as authoritative if not definitive. In that reconstruction Cabot's landfall was on Cape Breton Island, in northern Nova Scotia. From there Ganong had the explorer turning to follow the south coast of Newfoundland to Placentia Bay, "whence, sighting the Avalon Peninsula, he passed direct to England." Armed with the new Day letter data on the voyage and landfall, scholars formulated heretofore untested Cabot route hypotheses. They were what one Cabot expert likened to "a restorative tonic," reviving and adding new zest to an age-old debate.

In late spring 1498, Cabot departed Bristol with a small fleet to return to his newfound land. One contemporary reported that Cabot planned to sail south along that coast until he reached Cipangu, as Japan was then known, where he believed the jewels and spices of world trade originated. Once established there, Cabot intended to set up a trading factory that would make London "a more important mart than Alexandria." How close he came to his goal is a matter for speculation because his expedition never returned. At least some of his party may have made a successful landing in North America and thereby become the source of the broken Italian gilt sword and silver earrings possessed by the Indians whom Gaspar Côrte-Real encountered in Newfoundland a few years later. Of course it is equally possible that those artifacts were left during Cabot's first voyage the year before.

• The best place to begin a study of the enigmatic discoverer John Cabot is the cautionary essay "The John Cabot Mystique," written by Robert H. Fuson, a longtime student of the history of discovery. It is included in Stanley H. Palmer and Dennis Reinhartz, eds., *Essays on the History of North American Discovery and Exploration* (1988). A comprehensive though dated Cabot bibliography was prepared by George Parker Winship to mark the four-hundredth anniversary of the discoverer's first visit to North America; it appeared under the title *Cabot Bibliography, with an Introductory Essay on the Careers of the Cabots Based upon an Independent Examination of the Sources of Information* (1900). For English language translations and bibliographic citations of the key Cabot documents, none is more convenient than the first volume of David B. Quinn, *New American World: A Documentary History of North America to 1612* (1979). Most of the quotations in this sketch are from this source. Those interested in the Cabot landfall debate should consult W. F. Ganong's 1929 reconstruction, "John Cabot—The Cosa Map and the Cape Breton Landfall," reprinted in his *Crucial Maps in the Early Cartography and Place-Nomenclature of the Atlantic Coast of Canada* (1964). Two of the best post–John Day Letter reconstructions of Cabot's route and landfall are Melvin H. Jackson, "The Labrador Landfall of John Cabot: The 1497 Voyage Reconsidered," *Canadian Historical Review* 44 (1963): 122–41, and John T. Juricek, "John Cabot's First Voyage," *Smithsonian Journal of History* 2 (1967–1968): 1–21. Every student of Cabot should consult James A. Williamson, *The Cabot Voyages and Bristol Discovery under Henry VII* (1962); prepared for the Hakluyt Society, it contains all the relevant Cabot documents plus an essay by R. A. Skelton on the cartography of the voyages.

LOUIS DE VORSEY, JR.

CABOT, John Moors (11 Dec. 1901–23 Feb. 1981), diplomat and author, was born in Cambridge, Massachusetts, the son of Godfrey Lowell Cabot, an industrialist and philanthropist, and Maria Buchminster Moors. Reared in the elitist tradition of this famous Boston family he, like his father, studied at Harvard, where he received his bachelor of arts degree in 1923. Two years later Cabot earned a bachelor of letters in modern history from Brasenose College, Oxford University, where his research examined the subject of the Hungarian-Rumanian boundary. Cabot married Elizabeth Lewis in 1932, a union that subsequently yielded four children.

Cabot began a career in the Foreign Service in 1926 that would span four decades and touch seven presidential administrations. His first post, vice consul to Peru from 1927 to 1928, initiated an association with Latin America that would attach him to the U.S. legations in the Dominican Republic, Mexico, Brazil, Guatemala, and Argentina and establish him as an authority on the region. His expertise was acknowledged by his appointment in Washington, D.C., in 1942 as assistant chief of the State Department's Division of American Republics and as chief of the Division of Caribbean and Central American Affairs two years later. While serving in the latter post in 1944 he was made Latin American area adviser to the pivotal Dumbarton Oaks Conference, contributed to the Mexico City Conference, which designed a framework for postwar relations among the American republics, helped draft the charter of the Organization of American States, and attended the 1945 United Nations inaugural session in San Francisco.

During the early years of the Cold War, Cabot served in strategic and problematic posts in both hemispheres. As chargé d'affaires in Buenos Aires in 1945, despite his participation in a campaign against fascism designed to expose Nazi sympathizers, he worked to soften U.S. policy toward the Peron government, hoping to discourage Argentine alignment with the Soviet Union. As chargé to Belgrade in 1947, perhaps his most significant assignment, his communiqués to Washington anticipated the drift in Soviet-Yugoslav relations and spurred the State Department to exploit the split. In 1948 he joined the legation in Shanghai where, as consul general, he observed the defeat of U.S. protégé Chiang Kai-shek in 1949 and coordinated the withdrawal of U.S. citizens from the area. While in Asia he noted that the Chinese Communists were not subservient to Moscow, and he argued that some accommodation should be made toward possible relations with Mao's government. Upon his return to Washington in 1949 Cabot pressed with impunity for a Titoist approach to Communist China that would exploit differences between the Chinese and Soviet Communists and encourage a breech similar to that which had occurred between Marshall Tito's Belgrade government and the Kremlin. Such an approach would have replaced the United States's insistence on supporting Chiang with a pragmatic acceptance of the geopolitical realities of Asia.

Cabot, having been elevated to the rank of career minister in 1948 while still attached to Shanghai, was appointed minister to Finland in 1950. Occupying that post at the height of the Cold War, he worked through a relatively uneventful two years to sustain a balanced U.S. relationship with Helsinki while that government labored to maintain a precarious independence while appeasing Moscow. In 1953 he joined the U.S. delegation to the Inter-American Economic and Social Conference in Caracas, Venezuela, where he intimated that the United States would be responsive to the needs of the Latin American republics. As assistant secretary of state for Inter-American affairs in 1953–1954, he affirmed a belief that the United States should not withhold support from Latin America and cautioned the Eisenhower administration to seize the social reform initiative from the Communists in Latin America. He contended publicly that the lack of a Marshall Plan (financial aid) for the region was a major source of resentment toward the United States, and he expressed his frustration that Secretary of State John Foster Dulles failed to appreciate this fact.

In 1954 Cabot made a valiant, although futile, effort to persuade the Eisenhower administration to address Latin America through economic rather than political policy. He was consistent in his opposition to the leftist regimes of Latin America, as evidenced by his acceptance of the Central Intelligence Agency–organized coup to remove the Arbenz government in Guatemala in 1954. Unlike many in the Eisenhower administration, however, he was convinced that the Communists in Latin America were indigenous and were not merely proxies of the Soviet Union and that the major threat to hemispheric harmony was not ideology but economics.

After serving as ambassador to Sweden from 1954 to 1957, where the Swedes lauded him for his public relations efforts, Cabot returned to Latin America as ambassador to Colombia from 1957 to 1959 and to Brazil from 1959 to 1961; he continued to advocate a shift in U.S. policy toward economic intervention in Latin America. In Bogota he became frustrated with the inability of the Colombian leaders to respond to the grassroots agitation for change. After the move to Brazil, Cabot worked to sort out U.S.-Brazilian commercial difficulties that had been aggravated by a stubborn Brazilian nationalism and to resolve a boundary dispute between Peru and Ecuador. While in Washington on leave in 1960 he learned that aid for Latin America was finally going forward, albeit as a reaction to the aggressive behavior of Fidel Castro's Cuba.

Although Cabot was one of the few ambassadors continued at their posts by the Kennedy administration, his tenure in Brazil was quickly terminated. When, at the behest of Kennedy adviser Adolf Berle, Jr., Cabot tried to persuade Brazilian president and ardent nationalist Janio Quadros to support U.S. opposition to Cuba, he was rebuffed as a meddler in Brazilian politics, recalled by Kennedy, and subsequently reassigned to Warsaw. The assignment in Poland was important because the State Department used the Warsaw embassy as its only conduit for communication with Communist China. From 1962 to 1965 Cabot led discussions with Chinese Communists on subjects ranging from arms control to Vietnam, and he helped establish the foundation on which normalized relations would later be built. When President Lyndon Johnson replaced him at Warsaw in 1965, Cabot chose to spend his last year in the Foreign Service as deputy commandant of the National War College in Washington, D.C. After retiring in 1966 he served for one year as a lecturer at the Fletcher School of Law and Diplomacy at Tufts University and also as a consultant for the School of Foreign Service at Georgetown University.

Cabot's contribution to U.S. diplomacy was noteworthy. He presented perceptive advice from the field that provided practical insight to those in Washington at work developing U.S. Cold War policy. Although rarely heeded, he offered persistent support for U.S. initiatives to preempt Soviet influence in Latin America. He died in Washington, D.C.

• Cabot's papers, including his diaries, are available on microfilm under the title *Diplomatic Papers of John Moors Cabot, 1929–1978* (1985), from University Publications of America. He shared his expertise and experience in three books: *The Racial Conflict in Transylvania* (1926), *Toward Our Common American Destiny* (1955), and *The First Line of Defense* (1979). To place Cabot's work in context it is useful to examine the *Foreign Relations of the United States* volumes for the appropriate years and nations as well as the biographies and memoirs of the presidents and secretaries of state under whom he worked. For details on Cabot's involvement in Latin America in the 1950s, see Stephen G. Rabe, *Eisenhower and Latin America* (1988). To place Cabot's involvement in Sino-American relations in context, see Nancy Bernkopf Tucker, *Patterns in the Dust: Chinese-American Relations and the Recognition Controversy, 1949–1950* (1983). An obituary is in the *New York Times*, 25 Feb. 1981.

DONALD A. RAKESTRAW

CABOT, Sebastian (c. 1476–c. 1557), explorer, was born either in Venice, Italy, or Bristol, England, the son of John Cabot, a merchant and explorer, and Mattea (maiden name unknown). The precise date of his birth is unknown, but documents indicate that it was before 1486. In one account Cabot stated that his father brought him from Venice to England when he was very young. In a second record he claims being born in England, taken to Venice by his father, and returned to England when he was four years old. His father sailed the northern seas between 1491 and 1498 searching for new countries. There are no records other than Sebastian Cabot's own claims that he accompanied his father's expeditions.

The date of the Cabot discovery of North America is controversial. An explanatory note on a map made by Cabot in 1544, about fifty years after the discovery, credits John and Sebastian Cabot with discovering land, which they named "First Land Seen," on 24 June 1494. The first patent (a royal document granting permission to explore and conferring rights to territory discovered and to trade) granted by the English Crown to the Cabots, however, is dated almost two years later, 5 March 1496. Carrying this patent, Cabot's father and, perhaps, Cabot himself sailed from Bristol to North America on the *Matthew* in 1497. This voyage and discovery is documented by Henry VII's privy purse records that note payment of £10 on 10 August 1497 to "Him who found the New Isle." All records of the 1494 voyage and discovery appear rooted in Sebastian Cabot's notation on his 1544 map and thus are discounted. Further, the 1494 date on the map may be a copying error. The Roman numeral seven, VII, would, if the first two strokes were made carelessly, appear as IIII, which is the style in which the Roman four then was written.

John Cabot's description of his 1497 discovery and subsequent itinerary also is controversial. Newfoundland probably was his landfall, but arguments have been made for Cape Breton, Nova Scotia, and other places as far south as Maine. Historian Samuel Eliot Morison locates his single landing near Griquet, Newfoundland, after his landfall at nearby Cape Delgado, the northeasternmost point of Newfoundland. Morison also does not believe that Cabot's father sighted the North American mainland on his 1497 voyage, but others do.

In 1505 Sebastian Cabot received an annual pension of £10 from King Henry VII to be paid from customs receipts at Bristol. The grant's wording suggests that it was for services rendered in Bristol, but it may have been for participation in voyages subsequent to John Cabot's last voyage of 1498. According to Peter Martyr in *De Orbo Nove Decades* (1516), an Italian humanist at the court of Spain who collected records of the earliest voyages to the New World, Sebastian Cabot personally told him of outfitting an expedition of two ships and 300 (a logistically unlikely number) men at his own expense that sailed around 1508 to explore northwestern seas and the North American coast. According to some accounts, Cabot may have reached Cape Chidley; the northernmost point of Labrador. Here pack ice and icebergs forced him to retreat. Thereafter he sailed south along the coast to, according to contemporary accounts, some point between Delaware Bay and the south end of Florida. Thus, if he may be believed, he explored the East Coast of North America from Labrador to Florida. Martyr's account and those of Francisco López de Gomara in his *Historia General* (1552) and of Giovanni Baptista Ramusio in his *Viaggi I* (1550) and *Viaggi III* (1556) are supported only by Cabot's assertions. Thus there is no independent documentary evidence of Cabot's purported voyage in search of the Northwest Passage.

In 1512 Cabot entered Spanish service, where he was employed in making charts and training pilots. From 1526 to 1530 he commanded a well-documented expedition to follow Magellan's route around the world and to find a less hazardous route to the Pacific. After discovering and exploring the River Plate estuary in 1527, he abandoned the search for a westward passage. He sent one ship back for reinforcements in 1528, and, receiving none, he returned to Spain in 1530. He then faced judicial inquiry for seven years but was allowed to resume his position as master pilot in 1532. After further difficulty he returned to England in 1548.

On his return, Cabot engaged in trading, chart making, and promoting voyages, but he did not go to sea. He became governor for life of the Muscovy Company in 1555 and was granted a life pension of 250 marks per annum by Queen Mary on 27 December 1555. Around 1510 Cabot had married an Englishwoman named Joanna (maiden name unknown), who soon died during his early days in Bristol. They had one daughter. His second wife, a Spanish woman named Catalina de Medrano, died in 1547. In the late autumn of 1557 Cabot's pension payments stopped. His actual date of death and burial place are unknown.

Cabot's reputation as an important navigator and as a participant in the discovery and exploration of North America appears mainly to rest on self-advertisement and ambiguous references to the discovery of Newfoundland by his father. Morison concluded that Cabot may or may not have participated in his father's voyages to Newfoundland. Cabot's claim of making a voyage to seek the Northwest Passage and outlining the East Coast of North America is widely disbelieved. Although several writers credit his tale, their accounts are wildly contradictory. His trip to the River Plate, however, is a well-documented, substantial exploratory effort, though Spanish authorities considered it a failure. On the other hand, Cabot retained support and a pension from the English Crown until his death, and his reputation as a chart maker and as pilot major of Spain remains high. Cabot was an important chart maker, trainer of pilots, and promoter of trading voyages.

• Cabot's diverse original documents are widely scattered in English, Spanish, and French depositories. Henry Harisse, *John Cabot, Discoverer of North America and Sebastian His Son* (1896; repr. 1968), is the first comprehensive, critical reevaluation of Sebastian Cabot's place in history and contains the largest number of citations of the original sources. Richard Hakluyt, *Divers Voyages Touching the Discoverie of America* (1582; repr. 1966), is an early account of Cabot's voyages; Samuel Eliot Morison, *The European Discovery of America: The Northern Voyages* (1971), critically evaluates the Cabots' history; David B. Quinn, *Sebastian Cabot and Bristol Exploration* (1968), is a short biography sympathetic to Cabot's claims; James A. Williamson, *The Cabot Voyages and Bristol Discovery under Henry VII* (1962), summarizes the Cabot biographies through 1470 and reprints many pertinent documents.

RALPH L. LANGENHEIM, JR.

CABRINI, Frances Xavier (15 July 1850–22 Dec. 1917), educator and founder, was born Maria Francesca Cabrini in Saint' Angelo Lodigiano, Italy, the daughter of Agostino Cabrini and Stella Oldini, farmers. Cabrini's early life was greatly influenced by the political and religious disputes of her day. The drive for Italian unification, *risorgimento*, under the leadership of Garibaldi, was sweeping the country. The opposing religious perspectives of Gallicanism and Ultramontanism led Pope Pius IX to call the First Vatican Council (1869–1870), where the doctrine of papal infallibility was proclaimed. These forces created in Cabrini a personality open to the broad social and religious currents she encountered in life.

Cabrini received an excellent education for her day and position in society from the Daughters of the Sacred Heart between 1863 and 1868. Trained to be a teacher, she taught in elementary schools for several years before accepting an invitation to join the staff at an orphanage, the House of Providence, in Codogno. In 1877 Cabrini joined the religious community administering the House, the Sisters of Providence, and was promptly named superior as a novice. However, Cabrini withdrew from the sponsoring order because of internal dissension at the orphanage and with seven other sisters from the House founded the Institute of Salesian Missionaries of the Sacred Heart (also known simply as Missionaries of the Sacred Heart) in November 1880.

Cabrini started schools in Grumello and Milan as community apostolates while she worked to achieve pontifical approbation for her community. In 1888 she met Bishop Giovanni Scalabrini, who invited her to send sisters to the United States to join his fledgling community in its work with Italian immigrants. On 31 March 1889 Cabrini and six other sisters from her order arrived in New York City to begin work in the United States. Initially Cabrini's sisters settled at New York's St. Joachim's parish, which was administered by Scalabrini's priests. Dissatisfied, however, with her reception and the work given the sisters by Scalabrini, Cabrini broke with her Italian compatriot and started her own ministry.

Over the next twenty-eight years Mother Cabrini, as she was known, made nine separate visits to the United States, interspersed by foundations of her community in Nicaragua, Panama, Argentina, Brazil, France, Spain, and England. During these years Cabrini's institute grew in number and expanded throughout the country with the founding of schools, orphanages, and hospitals. The work of the Missionaries of the Sacred Heart was directed primarily toward poor and less-educated southern Italians. Cabrini believed in the preservation of Italian cultural identity but was opposed to nationalistic institutions that alienated immigrants and did not allow them to assimilate into American life. This general philosophy became the ideological foundation on which the Missionaries of the Sacred Heart conducted their apostolates.

First and foremost Cabrini was an educator. Her philosophy of education has been called a "pedagogy of love." She adopted a holistic approach to education, promoting the study of science, mathematics, history, and language, as well as music, drama, needlework, and physical education. She sponsored no separate intellectual development from what she called "education of the heart." Cabrini was one of the first promoters of bilingual education. The student was the objective of a Cabrinian education; she personalized education before it became fashionable. She believed teaching to be a vocation where zeal for the work and love for the student were essential.

Cabrini was responsible for the founding of many schools and orphanages. Her first schools were established in Brooklyn (1892) and New York (1899). She revived demoralized Italian communities in New Orleans (1892) and Newark (1899) through the establishment of schools. The institute moved west, founding schools in Chicago (1899), Denver and Seattle (1903), and Los Angeles (1905). Often schools were affiliated with orphanages. The first orphanage, Holy Angels, was founded in New York City in 1899 but within a year relocated to West Park, New York, a former Jesuit novitiate overlooking the Hudson River near Poughkeepsie. Subsequent orphanages were established in New Orleans (1896); Arlington, New Jersey, and Seattle (1903); and Denver and Los Angeles (1905). Cabrini stipulated that children be kept in orphanages until they were placed in good homes or were able to look after themselves and earn a decent living. To this latter end Cabrini introduced industrial schools and practical arts into her orphanages. Separate industrial schools, such as St. Lucy's in Scranton, Pennsylvania, were also established to facilitate the development of youth.

Cabrini's Missionaries of the Sacred Heart operated hospitals that catered to Italians but served all in need. At the request in 1891 of Archbishop Michael Corrigan of New York, Cabrini agreed to staff the Cristofero Colombo Hospital in New York City, founded in 1890 and affiliated with Scalabrini's parish. The deteriorating relationship between Scalabrini and Cabrini led the latter to found Columbus Hospital in New York City in 1892. The hospital later changed to another New York location and added a free dispensary for the indigent and poor. Chicago's Columbus Hospital, designed for the affluent and equipped with the latest advances in modern medicine, opened in February 1905. Cabrini's hope was that paying patients could help underwrite the costs of maintaining facilities for the poor. In 1911 Columbus Extension Hospital opened in Chicago to aid the indigent.

During her life Cabrini founded sixty-seven establishments in the United States, Europe, and Latin America. She was described as the "saint of the immigrants" and a "noble heroine of charity." A modern woman who was keenly aware of the currents of the world, she foresaw the twentieth century as one of revolution and thus tailored her philosophy of education, health care, and social service to accentuate the intrinsic value and dignity of each individual, an emphasis that characterized the age. She developed a philosophy of education that combined the need for Americanization with the preservation of Italian cultural heritage. She died in Chicago and was canonized in 1946 by Pope Pius XII.

• The single greatest depository of Cabrini's papers is the archives of the Missionary Sisters of the Sacred Heart in Rome. Manuscript letters, annals of the Institute of the Missionary Sisters of the Sacred Heart, and reports to ecclesiastical and civil officials are extant. The Scalabrinian Archives in Rome contains correspondence between Scalabrini and Cabrini. Comprehensive investigative reports preliminary to the beatification and canonization of Cabrini are held in the Vatican Archives. Many biographies of Cabrini are available, including Mary Louise Sullivan, *Mother Cabrini—"Italian Immigrant of the Century"* (1992); Pietro Di Donato, *Immigrant Saint* (1960); Achille Mascheroni, *Madre Cabrini: La Santa che scoprì gli italiani in America* (1983); Giuseppe dall' Ongaro, *Francesca Cabrini: La Suora che conquistò L'America* (1982); and Theodore Maynard, *Too Small a World* (1945). Several learned treatises that analyze Cabrini's theory of education have been completed, the best of which are M. Caritas Elizalde, "Mother Cabrini's Educational Ideals" (M.A. thesis, Univ. of Santo Tomas, Manila, 1949), and Stella Maris Roniger, "Contributions of the Missionary Sisters of the Sacred Heart to Education in Italy and the United States" (M.A. thesis, Fordham Univ., 1938).

RICHARD GRIBBLE

CACERES, Ernie (22 Nov. 1911–10 Jan. 1971), jazz saxophonist and clarinetist, was born Ernesto Caceres in Rockport, Texas. Caceres took up the clarinet, saxophone, and guitar in his youth. In the 1930s he began playing music professionally in a trio with his brothers, Emilio, a violinist and the leader of the group, and Pinero, who played trumpet and piano. The Emilio Caceres Trio first played in San Antonio and later in the 1930s performed in Detroit and New York City. In 1937 the group played on Benny Goodman's "Camel Caravan" radio show. Caceres then left his brothers' trio and established a career as a sideman in big bands through the late 1930s and 1940s. Along with Harry Carney, Caceres was the first baritone sax player to gain a reputation as a soloist. Caceres's sound was more biting and his playing perhaps more versatile than Carney's; while Carney's lush baritone was a fixture in the Duke Ellington band for several decades, Caceres played with virtually every major big band of the swing era.

In 1938 Caceres joined the Bobby Hackett band, with which he performed intermittently for thirty years. In 1939 and 1940 he toured with the Jack Teagarden band, then joined Glenn Miller's group in 1940. He stayed with the Miller big band through 1942, then played with Tommy Dorsey in 1943, Goodman in 1943 and 1944, Woody Herman in 1944, and Billy Butterfield in 1944 and 1945. Caceres also appeared with the Eddie Condon band in nightclubs from 1942 to 1948, and in 1945 and 1946 he served in a U.S. Army band. Through this period Caceres was featured mainly on alto or baritone saxophone but sometimes played solo clarinet. On baritone saxophone he was known for a uniquely raspy, hard-edged sound and ebullient style. Caceres's clarinet work was distinguished by a dynamic, fervent approach and reedy but full sound.

In the 1940s Caceres was also one of the most sought-after studio musicians. He was featured on recordings with Goodman, Sidney Bechet, Muggsy Spanier, Roy Eldridge, Coleman Hawkins, Billie Holiday, and Louis Armstrong. In 1948 and 1949 Caceres won polls conducted by *Metronome* magazine, an especially impressive achievement because he was a swing and Dixieland performer competing against increasingly popular bebop players. In 1949 he performed for a *Metronome* All-Stars recording, incorporating some bebop elements into his playing.

Caceres briefly led his own quartet in 1949 and the next year joined the studio orchestra on Garry Moore's television show. For six years Caceres appeared as a featured performer on the Moore show. In 1956 and 1957 he joined Bobby Hackett's band as a soloist on baritone saxophone, reuniting with his brother Pinero, who also appeared with Hackett's band.

In the early 1960s Caceres rejoined Butterfield's band for several performances in Newport News, Virginia, and returned to San Antonio with Jim Cullum's Happy Jazz Band and Chuck Reilly's Alamo City Jazz Band. In 1969 he and his brother recorded an LP, *Ernie and Emilio Caceres* (Audiophile). Two years later Caceres died in San Antonio after a long illness.

Caceres was one of the first jazz musicians to achieve recognition as a virtuoso soloist on the baritone saxophone, but he was also known for his skillful alto and clarinet work and for his versatility in a variety of musical formats. He was one of the leading sidemen in the heyday of the big band era.

• Brief but useful summaries of Caceres's career can be found in Barry Kernfeld, ed., *New Grove Dictionary of Jazz* (1988), and John Chilton, *Who's Who of Jazz: Storyville to Swing Street* (1985). See also "Virtuoso: A Guy Named Ernie Caceres," *Second Line* 24 (1970): 417; and Gunther Schuller, *The Swing Era: The Development of Jazz, 1930–1945* (1989). An obituary is in the *New York Times*, 11 Jan. 1971.

THADDEUS RUSSELL

CADBURY, Henry Joel (1 Dec. 1883–7 Oct. 1974), New Testament scholar and pacifist, was born in Philadelphia, Pennsylvania, the son of Joel Cadbury, Jr., a partner in a successful plumbing business, and Anna Kaighn Lowry. The Cadburys were members of a large transatlantic Quaker family, and Henry Cadbury grew up attending Quaker schools. In 1899 he graduated from Penn Charter, in 1903 from Haverford College, and 1904 from Harvard University with a master's degree in Greek.

After Harvard, Cadbury taught classics and history for a year in the University Latin School in Chicago, then three years at Westtown School, in Chester County, Pennsylvania. His interest in Bible study grew during this period and he returned to Harvard in 1908. In 1914 he earned a Ph.D. in ancient languages with a specialty in biblical and patristic Greek. While working on his degree at Harvard, Cadbury returned to Haverford in 1910 as an instructor in Greek and remained on the faculty until 1919. In 1916 he married Lydia Caroline Brown, and in 1917 the first of their four children was born.

In fall 1918, Cadbury wrote a letter to the *Philadelphia Public Ledger* denouncing the vengeful spirit of the American public toward the Germans. The public outcry that ensued led Haverford to suspend Cadbury for a year, with the understanding that the board would make a final decision about his position in the spring. Cadbury spent a portion of the year working for the newly formed American Friends Service Committee in Philadelphia. Realizing that his return to the Haverford faculty was in question, he decided to save Haverford the embarrassment of firing him by accepting a position in 1919 at Andover Theological Seminary in Cambridge teaching New Testament studies. He remained at Andover until 1926, when he went to Bryn Mawr College to teach Bible. In 1934 he accepted the Hollis Chair of Divinity at Harvard and remained there until 1954. He was also director of the Andover-Harvard Theological Library from 1938 to 1954.

Cadbury had meanwhile begun a prolific career as a writer, both on biblical literature and on Quaker history, regarding the latter as his avocation. In 1920 his Harvard thesis, *The Style and Literary Method of Luke*, was published and brought him to the attention of biblical scholars worldwide for his interpretation of Luke in terms of the culture and language of the time. He was able to prove definitively that Luke was not a physician, as had been thought, and Cadbury was known throughout his lifetime as the foremost living Luke scholar. *National Ideals in the Old Testament* was also published to acclaim. This was followed by *The Making of Luke-Acts* (1927); *The Acts of the Apostles*, with Kirsopp Lake (in *The Beginnings of Christianity*, 1934); *The Peril of Modernizing Jesus* (1937); *Jesus: What Manner of Man* (1947); and *The Book of Acts in History* (1955) among many others. His writing style was simple and lucid, and his pioneer work in introducing the methods of form criticism to biblical scholarship won him the respect of biblical scholars worldwide, while his approach to Jesus as a man of his times was eagerly received by scholars and lay persons alike.

In 1930 Cadbury was appointed by the American Standard Bible Committee to produce a revision of the New Testament. The committee met for seventeen years, finally producing the Revised Standard Version in 1946. Cadbury relished this work, comparing it to the writing of detective stories. He was by this time internationally recognized and became president of the Society of Biblical Literature, as well as of the Studiorum Novi Testamenti Societas. He was a member of many other learned societies, and received six honorary degrees.

An outspoken pacifist, Cadbury opposed peacetime conscription, often appearing as a character witness for young men who refused to register. His opposition to loyalty oaths led him to support Jehovah's Witnesses and others who refused to swear, and his conviction presented him with a crisis of conscience when he was asked to sign such an oath himself as a teacher in Massachusetts while at Harvard. Ultimately he was allowed to sign a special statement. He supported the American Civil Liberties Union, often doing research in its behalf, and he served for twenty-two years as chair of the board of the American Friends Service Committee, from 1928 to 1934 and again from 1944 to 1960. In this capacity he traveled to Oslo in 1947 in a borrowed tuxedo with tails to receive the Nobel Peace Prize given to the American Friends Service Committee and the Friends Service Council of London for their work during World War II.

Retiring from Harvard in 1954, Cadbury remained very active, lecturing widely and traveling for the American Friends Service Committee, as well as spending time in research in England. He continued to write and publish, three of his books appearing as he neared ninety: *John Woolman in England: A Documentary Supplement* (1971), *Narrative Papers of George Fox* (1972), and *Friendly Heritage; Letters from the Quaker Past* (1972). He died in Haverford after a fall.

A quiet, unassuming man, Cadbury was known for his capacity to draw out the opinions of his students, for his reluctance to state his own, for his willingness to assist younger scholars, and for his keen wit. Opposed to trying to read the present into the past, he was equally clear that the past should not rule the present and therefore was always ready for innovation in the organizations and institutions he served. In New Testament scholarship he was recognized for his rigor in applying the methods of philology rather than theology to an understanding of the texts and his insistence that the life of Jesus must be understood in terms of his culture and environment. He believed action rather than belief was the true mark of religious life. While he caused many to question their unexamined faith, his own life was seen as based on the teachings of Jesus. After the major work on the Revised Standard Version of the New Testament was finished, he again became chair of the AFSC board and devoted many hours to this work. When someone asked him if this had been an abrupt transition, he answered, "No, I am still trying to translate the New Testament."

• The largest collection of Henry J. Cadbury's papers is in the Quaker Collection, Haverford College Library. Other repositories are Bryn Mawr College Library; Lilly Library, Earlham College Archives (Richmond, Ind.); Friends Historical Library, Swarthmore College; Friends Historical Collection, Guilford College (Greensboro, N.C.); Harvard University Archives; and American Friends Service Committee Archives (Philadelphia, Pa.). A complete bibliography of Cadbury's writings has recently been compiled and is at the Quaker Collection, Haverford College. Major publications in addition to those already cited include *Annual Catalogue of George Fox's Papers, Compiled in 1694–1697* (1939); an edition of *George Fox's Book of Miracles* (1948); his transcription of *Letters to William Dewsbury and Others* (1948); "Negro Membership in the Society of Friends," *Journal of Negro History* 2 (1936): 151–213; "Two Worlds," William Penn Lecture, Philadelphia Yearly Meeting (1945); "A Quaker Approach to the Bible," Ward Lecture, Guilford College (1953); *The Eclipse of the Historical Jesus*, Pendle Hill pamphlet 133 (1964); "Quakers and Peace," *Nobel Lectures*, vol. 2 (1926–1950), ed. Frederick W. Haberman (1972); "Between Jesus and the Gospels," *Harvard Theological Review* 16 (1923): 81–92; and "The Dilemma of the Ephesians," *New Testament Studies* 5 (1958): 91–102. Books and articles about Cadbury include Margaret Hope Bacon, *Let This Life Speak: The Legacy of Henry Joel Cadbury* (1987); Mary Hoxie Jones, "Henry

Joel Cadbury; A Biographical Sketch," in *Then and Now: Quaker Essays, Historical and Contemporary*, ed. Anna Cox Brinton (1960); S. Garlin Hall, "The Contribution of Henry J. Cadbury to the Study of the Historical Jesus" (Ph.D. diss., Boston Univ., 1961); Amos Wilder, "A Grammarian with a Difference," *Harvard Magazine*, May 1975, pp. 46–52; "In Memoriam," *New Testament Studies* 21 (1974–1975): 313–17; George W. MacRae, "Henry Joel Cadbury," in *Profiles from the Beloved Community* (1976); and Henry C. Niles, "The Wit and Wisdom of Henry Cadbury," *Harvard Divinity Bulletin* 29, no. 2 (1965): 35–48.

MARGARET HOPE BACON

CADILLAC, Sieur de. *See* Lamothe Cadillac, Antoine Laumet de.

CADMAN, Charles Wakefield (24 Dec. 1881–30 Dec. 1946), composer, was born in Johnstown, Pennsylvania, the son of William Charles Cadman, a chemist, and Caroline Wakefield. Cadman began piano lessons at thirteen and soon afterward composed simple melodies; he abandoned his formal education the following year. To finance his future musical education, he played the organ at various Pittsburgh churches and became an errand boy at twenty dollars a month to Joseph Schwab (brother of Charles) at the Carnegie Steel Mill in 1895. At the age of seventeen, Cadman self-published "The Carnegie Library March" (1898) and eventually sold some six thousand copies door to door. In Pittsburgh he briefly studied harmony and theory with Leo Oehmler (1902) and orchestration with Luigi von Kunits (1908), concertmaster of the Pittsburgh Symphony Orchestra, and with Emil Paur, its conductor. From 1907 to 1910 he was the organist at the East Liberty Presbyterian Church, Pittsburgh, and in 1908 he became the accompanist to the Pittsburgh Male Chorus. That year he was appointed music editor and critic of the *Pittsburgh Dispatch*. He also was the Pittsburgh correspondent for the *Musical Courier* (1908–1910).

Although Cadman was exposed to Indian legend and lore as a youth, it was not until 1907, after reading *Indian Story and Song* (1900), by the Washington, D.C., ethnologist Alice C. Fletcher, that he was inspired to compose solo songs and piano works based on Indian melodies. Through correspondence, Fletcher urged Cadman to live among and research the Omaha Indians in Nebraska. He followed her advice and soon met Francis La Flesche, an Omaha Indian working in the Office of Indian Affairs. Together, Cadman and La Flesche were pioneers in making early cylinder recordings and transcriptions of Omaha Indian tribal melodies for the Smithsonian Institution (Aug. 1910). Cadman learned to play their instruments and later arranged or "idealized" (adapting the melody into a nineteenth-century harmonic idiom) their music for concert audiences. He described his work in an article in the *Musical Quarterly* (July 1915), "The 'Idealization' of Indian Music."

Cadman's early "Indian" works did not enjoy wide popularity until "From the Land of the Sky-blue Water" was included as an encore by the American soprano Lillian Nordica at a Cleveland, Ohio, recital on 8 February 1909. The work was written six months before Cadman had ever visited an Indian reservation and was rejected by five publishers before the White-Smith Music Publishing Company accepted it for publication in 1909. The most beloved of all "Indianist" songs, the original pencil manuscript was donated by Cadman to the Library of Congress in 1915. His most successful song, the ballad "At Dawning" (1906), was not based on Indian melodies but had a similar story being popularized by tenors John McCormack and Alessandro Bonci. Although the Oliver Ditson Company purchased the work outright for fifteen dollars several years before its success, they generously rewrote the contract and paid Cadman on a royalty basis. The song ultimately surpassed one million copies sold before the composer's death. The lyrics to these songs were written by Cadman's longtime friend, confidante, and principal lyricist, Nelle Richmond Eberhart.

With the commercial success of his songs, Cadman lived comfortably and devoted much of his time to serious composition, including the Trio in D Major (1913), which was hailed as the first use of ragtime elements in an American chamber work. His American Indian opera, *Shanewis* (The Robin Woman), based on authentic Indian melodies, was premiered by the Metropolitan Opera on 23 March 1918. Receiving twenty-two curtain calls after its first performance, it was the first American opera with a contemporary American setting staged at the Met, the first American opera with a libretto by a woman (Eberhart) at the Met, and the first American opera to be performed a second season.

By the early 1920s Cadman had become a self-proclaimed expert on American Indian music, and from 1909 to 1940 he toured North America and Europe, delivering his celebrated "Indian Talk." Demonstrating Indian melodies on the piano and with an Indian flageolet, he was often supported by the Cherokee-Creek mezzo-soprano "Princess" Tsianina Redfeather.

When not on tour, Cadman returned to Los Angeles, where he had resided since 1916. He gave freely of his time to further culture in the southern California vicinity and was a charter member of the Theater Arts Alliance (1919), the founding organization of the Hollywood Bowl. Cadman was a featured Bowl soloist no fewer than seven times in his career, and entire evenings were declared "Cadman Nights" during the seasons of 1922, 1923, and 1924. He also donated much time to the field of musical education and was director of education for the California Federation of Music Clubs (1921) and a lecturer on music at the University of Southern California.

With Hollywood close by, it was natural for Cadman to gravitate toward the motion picture studios. Assembling scores for several silent films, including *The Vanishing American* (1925), in 1929 Cadman eventually was contracted by the Fox Film Corporation to compose music for talking pictures. His scores included *The Sky Hawk* (1929), *Captain of the Guard* (1930),

Women Everywhere (1930), and *Harmony at Home* (1930). Before leaving Fox in 1930, Cadman became embroiled in a public dispute with the Metro-Goldwyn-Mayer composer Dmitri Tiomkin over the future direction of music for motion pictures. Cadman felt that music for motion pictures should be based on classical or traditional styles and was opposed to Tiomkin's "popular jazz" approach. Eventually Cadman relented in his position, but only after his severance from the studios was complete.

By the early 1930s public interest in the Indianist movement had waned, and Cadman recognized that his base of support was eroding. Though he was voted the most popular American composer of 1930 by the National Federation of Music Clubs, Cadman sensed that the public was no longer content with simple, idealized melodies and maudlin lyrics. As late as 1935 the California Pacific International Exposition at San Diego declared 4 September "Cadman Day." The event was based entirely on Cadman's past association with American Indian music and included a ceremony making him an honorary Indian chief. The following year Cadman again received national attention when he was the only member to resign from the American Music Committee of the Berlin Olympic Games Festival. He declared the Nazi regime "repugnant."

Cadman spent the last decade of his life promoting his serious works, which he held in high regard. These attained little acceptance beyond southern California, his major base of support. The only major exception was in March 1940, when the premiere of his *Pennsylvania* Symphony was broadcast nationally from the Pantages Theater in Hollywood, with Albert Coates conducting the Los Angeles Philharmonic Orchestra. The symphony received enthusiastic acclaim, but Cadman could not interest the major eastern orchestras in a performance. In fact, Cadman had difficulty getting any of his symphonic works, old or new, performed by American orchestras during his last years.

The difficulty was twofold. First, Cadman handled his own public relations, which had become ineffective, and second, deteriorating political conditions in Europe during the mid-1930s brought many talented European composers and conductors to American shores. Competition for performances and publicity was intense.

Living the last three years of his bachelor life in semifrugality at a modest hotel in Los Angeles, Cadman tried to maintain his old stature, though he was in poor health. He died in Los Angeles.

• Cadman's manuscripts, letters, and memorabilia were presented to Pennsylvania State University by the Cadman estate in 1970. The New York Public Library for the Performing Arts also has a collection of Cadman's holographic scores. In 1937 Cadman published *Catalog: Complete Musical Works of Charles Wakefield Cadman* under the pseudonym Charles William Wakefield. Another catalog using the same title edited by Charles N. Fielder, Cadman's principal music copyist, was published in 1951 by the Cadman estate. The most authoritative source is Harry Perison, "Charles Wakefield Cadman: His Life and Works" (Ph.D. diss., Eastman School of Music, 1978). An obituary is in the *New York Times*, 31 Dec. 1946.

LANCE C. BOWLING

CADMAN, S. Parkes (18 Dec. 1864–12 July 1936), minister, was born Samuel Parkes Cadman in Wellington, Shropshire, England, the son of Samuel Cadman, a coal-mine charter master and lay Methodist minister, and Betsy Parkes. After he reached age eleven Cadman attended school for only "a few slim months" each year; otherwise he worked from six in the morning until three in the afternoon loading coal into pony carts and hauling them to the mine shaft. He found "a new direction" for his life when he experienced a religious conversion at age sixteen. He preached his first sermon a year later and at age twenty earned his license as a lay preacher. The next year, when he was proposed as a candidate for the ministry, he joyfully exclaimed, "I will never go into the mines again!" (Hamlin, p. 46). He subsequently won a three-year theological scholarship at Richmond College of the University of London.

In 1888, the year before he graduated, Cadman married Lillian Esther Wooding; they had three children. Two years after their marriage they moved to the United States, which had early attracted Cadman and where he had been promised a church. First located in Duchess County, New York, Cadman served Methodist churches in Milbrook and Verbank and began his practice of holding question-and-answer sessions on topics of current interest. In 1891 he started writing articles for the *New York Ledger*, and two years later he became pastor of the Central Methodist Episcopal Church of Yonkers. In 1895 he moved to the Metropolitan Temple (Methodist) in Manhattan, where the congregation increased by sixteen hundred members during his stay. In late 1900, Cadman, who refused to believe in a literal hell, frowned on Protestant division, and considered science and philosophy friends of religion, accepted the pulpit of the Central Congregational Church of Brooklyn, where he remained the rest of his life. A man of tremendous energy who delivered his sermons with "rejoicing urgency," Cadman often supervised as many as seven assistant ministers.

For more than twenty years Cadman gave a half-hour Sunday afternoon lecture for men only at the Bedford Avenue YMCA in Brooklyn, followed by an hour-long question-and-answer session. A rapid reader, he quickly grasped ideas and was able to convey both the spirit and the style of the books he read as well as their contents. Beginning in 1923 his crowded sessions were broadcast to a national radio audience, sometimes generating as many as two thousand letters per week. Called the first radio pastor, Cadman gained renown as "one of the few popular preachers who really cares for learning." Contemporaries described his knowledge as "encyclopediacal in its accuracy and range" (Newton, p. 176). In 1924, after he began his four-year tenure as the president of the Federal Council of the Churches of Christ in America, he moved his broadcasts to the National Broadcasting Company's Cathedral Studio on Fifth Avenue, where he continued to delight his huge audience (estimated at five to seven million listeners) by answering diverse questions with "Gatling-gun rapidity" (Pringle, p. 64). He added more than ten million readers to his audience after 1926, when his syndicated question-and-answer column began appearing in the *New York Herald Tribune* and ultimately in more than one hundred other newspapers. Cadman also was a prolific writer who turned out six books in one twelve-year period.

For the most part, members of Cadman's audience found his common sense answers to their questions accurate and witty. When asked by a parent to suggest an appropriate book on sex education for a ten-year-old, Cadman shot back six titles. Although he told a reader who longed to call God "Mother" that "no law of logic or of religion known to me prevents you" from doing so and encouraged her to "go forward" in her thinking, he also proposed a "compromise": she could call God our "Parent" (*Answers to Everyday Questions*, p. 179). Responding to a question on evolution, Cadman suggested that humans had a whole menagerie of animals as forebears. "Sometimes the ape is uppermost, and sometimes the ass," he explained, adding: "I am inclined to believe in it: it explains a lot" (Newton, p. 181).

Cadman had flirted with pacifism, but with the outbreak of World War I he became an ardent supporter of the Allied cause. He described the acts of the kaiser as those of "a devil incarnate" and declared: "This war is purging the nations. . . . It is sweeping away the trivial and frivolous and revealing the deep and serious." He urged Americans to "Prepare! Prepare! Prepare!" Taking his own advice, he became the chaplain of the Twenty-third Infantry Regiment of the New York National Guard and in 1916 lost fifteen pounds serving on the Mexican border. After the United States joined the Allies in 1917, Cadman blessed its crusade as "that of Christ" (Pringle, pp. 66–67), but following the armistice in 1918 he ceased to romanticize war and worked instead for peace. He bitterly opposed those senators who kept the United States out of the League of Nations, calling them "bloated specimens blocking world progress" (*New York Times*, 13 July 1936). No longer an advocate of preparedness, by 1926 he opposed military training in schools.

Calling himself a liberal-conservative, Cadman worked to make the social system more caring, insisting that "capitalism must be constantly setting its house in order" (McConnell, p. 488). He opposed the compulsory loyalty oaths for teachers that half the states had adopted in the 1920s; urged the adoption of the Child Labor Amendment to the Constitution, which was submitted to the states in 1924; and lobbied to outlaw company unions, which had grown enormously following passage of the National Industrial Recovery Act of 1933.

Considered "the foremost preacher in all the world" by many of his contemporaries, Cadman received twelve honorary doctorates and lectured at many universities. Despite his travels and the fact that his popularity on the lecture circuit was surpassed only by that of William Jennings Bryan, Cadman seldom missed a Sunday in his own church from early fall to late spring. He crossed the Atlantic more than sixty times, often spending summers in England, where he preached, lectured, and tended to the business of international church organizations. Active in world affairs, he chaired, in 1934, the American Christian Committee for German Refugees, which aided Jews and Christians alike, publicly denounced Hitler the next year, and campaigned unsuccessfully for his country's nonparticipation in the 1936 Olympic games, held in Germany.

Cadman was counting on another active decade in his Brooklyn church when he collapsed from acute appendicitis while preaching in a Methodist church in Plattsburg, New York. He died there a week later of peritonitis. Cadman Plaza in downtown Brooklyn bears his name.

• A search failed to turn up any Cadman papers, but his career in Brooklyn can be followed in the morgue of the *Brooklyn Eagle*, located in the Brooklyn Public Library. Cadman's numerous books include *Charles Darwin and Other English Thinkers: With Reference to Their Religious and Ethical Value* (1911; repr. 1971), *William Owen . . .* (1912), *The Three Religious Leaders of Oxford* (1916), *Ambassadors of God* (1920), *Christianity and the State* (1924), *The Lure of London* (1925), *Imagination and Religion* (1926), *The Christ of God* (1929), *Answers to EveryDay Questions* (1930), *The Parables of Jesus* (1931), *The Prophets of Israel* (1933), and *Adventure for Happiness* (1935). Among his many articles are "English-Speaking Men and the War," in *Kaiser or Christ?: The War and Its Issues* (191?), and "God and Evolution: Darwin's Theory of National Selection," in William M. Goldsmith, *Evolution or Christianity: God or Darwin?* (1924). A full-length biography is Fred Hamlin, *S. Parkes Cadman: Pioneer Radio Minister* (1930). For a lively written short biography, see Henry F. Pringle, *Big Frogs* (1928), pp. 58–71. Other short biographies are in William G. Shepherd, *Great Preachers: As Seen by a Journalist* (1924), pp. 84–97, and Joseph Fort Newton, *Some Living Masters of the Pulpit: Studies in Religious Personality* (1923), pp. 168–84. Obituaries are in the *New York Times*, 13 July 1936, and *Religion in Life: A Christian Quarterly* 5 (1936): 483–93.

OLIVE HOOGENBOOM

CADMUS. *See* Zachos, John Celivergos.

CADWALADER, John (10 Jan. 1742–10 Feb. 1786), revolutionary war soldier, was born in Philadelphia, Pennsylvania, the son of Thomas Cadwalader, a physician, and Hannah Lambert. Cadwalader received his education in the College of Philadelphia (now the University of Pennsylvania), then organized a prosperous mercantile business with his brother Lambert Cadwalader in his native city. In 1768 he married Elizabeth Lloyd. By the time of the Revolution, Cadwalader had become a leading entrepreneur in the province of Pennsylvania. From the outset of difficulties with Great Britain he used his social status and wealth to influence his fellow citizens in favor of protest against violations of colonial liberties. He was made a member of the Philadelphia committee of safety and made captain of the City Troop, or "Silk-Stocking Company." His vigor in organizing and drilling his troops brought him military recognition in Pennsylvania, and he was appointed colonel of a Philadelphia battalion and later brigadier general of the Pennsylvania militia.

In late 1776 Cadwalader was ordered by General George Washington to cross the Delaware River at Bristol, Pennsylvania, with 1,500 militiamen and support the commander in chief's operations against Trenton. Due to ice in the river, Cadwalader did not get his troops into New Jersey until after Washington had successfully concluded the battle of Trenton. Nevertheless, Cadwalader and his men fought in the battle of Princeton on 3 January 1777, for which service Washington recommended that Congress promote Cadwalader to brigadier general in the Continental army. When offered this rank, Cadwalader declined, expressing a desire to remain with his Pennsylvania militiamen. Later he regretted his decision. On 30 September 1780 he declared to Washington, "I have now reason to wish I had accepted the command given me by Congress; but at that time I conceived that the war was near a conclusion" (Heathcote, p. 7). Washington, retaining his confidence in Cadwalader, in September 1777 asked him to mobilize militiamen on Maryland's eastern shore against General William Howe's invasion from Chesapeake Bay toward Philadelphia. Successful in this task, Cadwalader joined Washington as a volunteer in the battles of Brandywine and Germantown and in the following winter conducted successful irregular guerrilla warfare against British foraging parties around Philadelphia.

When the British evacuated Philadelphia on 18 June 1778, Cadwalader entered the city, organized a troop of volunteer soldiers, and joined Washington in harassing Sir Henry Clinton's march across New Jersey toward New York. Taking no part in the battle of Monmouth on 28 June he returned to Philadelphia in early July. On the fourth of that month, Cadwalader fought a duel with General Thomas Conway. Conway had been accused of plotting to remove Washington from command of the Continental army in the previous winter, and his present conduct toward American officers, Cadwalader included, was considered "offensive." In the duel, Cadwalader fired his pistol and wounded Conway in the mouth and neck. Although Conway appeared mortally stricken, he slowly recovered and on 23 July wrote Washington a letter of apology.

The revolutionary war shifted to other theaters, and Cadwalader's role was now at an end, despite the fact that he stood high in the estimation of Washington and the other Continental army officers as a gentleman and a good soldier. In 1779 he married Williamina Bond. After American independence was secured he moved to Maryland and served in the state legislature. His last years were vexed by a dispute with a fellow Pennsylvanian, Joseph Reed. In 1782 a letter was published containing derogatory remarks about Reed's conduct in the Trenton campaign; Reed was convinced it came from the pen of Cadwalader. Reed accused Cadwalader publicly, and in 1783 Cadwalader angrily wrote *A Reply to General Joseph Reed's Remarks . . .*, denying his suggestions. In 1785 Cadwalader joined with John Beale Bordley and Samuel Powel in organizing the Philadelphia Society for the Promotion of Agriculture, in order to encourage intensive farming based upon English practices instead of the extensive farming that was employed by most American farmers. Cadwalader died in Shrewsbury, Kent County, Maryland. He had at least one child, but with which wife is unclear.

• Cadwalader's correspondence with George Washington is in the Washington Papers, Library of Congress. His published correspondence includes "Selections from the Military Papers of General John Cadwalader (1776–1780)," *Pennsylvania Magazine of History and Biography* 32 (1908): 149–74; and "Prelude to Valley Forge (Cadwalader to Washington, Dec. 3, 1777)," *Pennsylvania Magazine of History and Biography* 82 (1958): 466–71. Charles W. Heathcote, "General John Cadwalader: A Sturdy Pennsylvania Military Officer and Devoted to General Washington," *Picket Post* 70 (1960): 4–9, 28, assesses Cadwalader's military career. His interest in agricultural reform is discussed in Lucius F. Ellsworth, "The Philadelphia Society for the Promotion of Agriculture and Agricultural Reform, 1785–1793," *Agricultural History* 42 (1968): 189–99. Cadwalader's domestic establishment is described in Nicholas B. Wainwright, *Colonial Grandeur in Philadelphia: The House and Furniture of General John Cadwalader* (1964).

PAUL DAVID NELSON

CADWALADER, Lambert (1743–13 Sept. 1823), revolutionary war soldier, was born in Trenton, New Jersey, the son of Thomas Cadwalader, a physician, and Hannah Lambert. He received a fine literary and classical education at the College of Philadelphia (now University of Pennsylvania) then went into business with his brother, John Cadwalader, in Philadelphia. Their business flourished, and by the mid-1770s he and John Cadwalader were leading citizens in the province of Pennsylvania. As tensions arose with Great Britain, he sided with his American neighbors. In 1765, responding to the Stamp Act, he signed a merchants' agreement to boycott English goods. A year later he belligerently declared, "Let us only enjoy liberty but half a century longer, and we will defy the power of England to enslave us" (Rawle, "Col. Lambert Cadwalader, a Sketch," p. 3). In 1774 he was appointed a member of the Philadelphia Committee of Superintendence and Correspondence. A year later he was elected a member of the Pennsylvania Provincial Assembly, serving on that body's Committee of Correspondence, and in 1776 he attended the Pennsylvania state constitutional convention.

Meanwhile, Cadwalader also served as a soldier. In 1775 he was appointed captain of one of four Philadelphia blueblood companies called "the Greens." On 4 January 1776 he was promoted to lieutenant colonel of the Third Pennsylvania Battalion, commanded by Colonel John Shee. In late June he marched with his battalion to Kingsbridge on Manhattan and assisted in the construction of Fort Washington, which, with Fort Constitution (later Fort Lee) on the opposite bank of the Hudson River, was intended to thwart enemy shipping on that stream. He rushed with his men on 27 August to assist General George Washington in the battle of Long Island but arrived after the battle had been lost to the British. However, his battalion was quickly emplaced on the left flank of American entrenchments on Brooklyn Heights, where it was engaged in constant skirmishing for the next two days. On the evening of the 29th, his Pennsylvanians were extricated from Long Island by John Glover's regiment of Marblehead boatmen and posted in defensive lines south of Fort Washington. Upon Colonel Shee's resignation from the army on 25 September, Cadwalader took command of the Third Pennsylvania Battalion and was promoted to colonel. In early November British troops threatened Fort Washington, but Congress and General Nathanael Greene determined that the fort could be held. Therefore, Cadwalader and his Pennsylvanians were among the patriot troops defending Fort Washington when it was assaulted on 16 November by General William Howe. Although Cadwalader, according to an eyewitness, in "gallant style . . . with an inferior force, maintained his position" for a time, he was overwhelmed, along with the entire garrison of almost three thousand men, and taken prisoner (Rawle, p. 11).

Cadwalader was quickly released from captivity, for General Howe remembered the kindness that Cadwalader's father had earlier shown British prisoners in Philadelphia and returned the favor. In early 1777 Cadwalader was appointed commander of the newly formed Fourth Pennsylvania Regiment. However, as he had only been paroled by Howe and not exchanged for an officer of equal rank, he felt obliged not to take up his command. Some of his friends insisted that he was under no such constraint, but high-ranking American officers whom he consulted disagreed. Finally, he laid the matter before General Washington, who tried to effect an exchange. However, Washington himself indirectly ended Cadwalader's chances by issuing a general order, in retaliation for supposed unfair treatment of General Charles Lee, that no enemy officers of field grade were to be released. Thus unable to return to active service, Cadwalader resigned his commission on 29 January 1779 and allowed the regiment's actual commander, Lieutenant Colonel William Butler, to be designated lieutenant colonel commandant.

Reentering politics, Cadwalader joined forces with Pennsylvanians who wished to amend or replace the state's constitution of 1776, which they thought too democratic, but he and they were not successful. In 1784 he was elected a delegate to the Continental Congress and held this office for two one-year terms. He spoke little but worked assiduously on committees, including the Grand Committee, which received the report of the Annapolis Convention, calling for a federal convention to rewrite the Articles of Confederation. He served two terms as a Federalist in the House of Representatives, 1789–1791 and 1793–1795, then retired from public life. In 1793 he married Mary McCall, with whom he had two children. In his later years he lived near Trenton, New Jersey, on an estate named "Greenwood," dispensing hospitality to numerous visitors, particularly Washington. Dying there, he was widely remembered for his "good breeding, courtesy and elegance" and his "enlarged and cultivated understanding, regulated by classical taste and improved by habits of general reading" (Rawle, p. 14).

• Cadwalader's correspondence with Washington is in the George Washington Papers, Library of Congress, and John C. Fitzpatrick, ed., *The Writings of George Washington from the Original Manuscript Sources, 1745–1799*, vols. 6, 12–13, 15, 31 (1932–1939). William Henry Rawle has two biographical essays: *Colonel Lambert Cadwalader, of Trenton, New Jersey* (1878) and "Col. Lambert Cadwalader, a Sketch," *Pennsylvania Magazine of History and Biography* 10 (1886): 1–14. Useful background information on Cadwalader and his Third Pennsylvania Battalion is John B. B. Trussell, Jr., *The Pennsylvania Line: Regimental Organization and Operations, 1776–1783* (1977); and Douglas Southall Freeman, *George Washington: A Biography*, vol. 4 (1951).

PAUL DAVID NELSON

CADWALADER, Thomas (1708–14 Nov. 1779), physician, was born in Philadelphia, Pennsylvania, the son of John Cadwalader and Martha Jones. His parents were among the early Welsh Quaker settlers of Pennsylvania. His father, who had been a schoolmaster in Wales, was a merchant in Philadelphia; his mother was the daughter and granddaughter of physicians.

Thomas Cadwalader studied medicine with his uncle Dr. Evan Jones. Drawn into Benjamin Franklin's circle, he became one of the founders and first directors of the Library Company of Philadelphia in 1731. The same year Cadwalader went to London, where he is said to have attended the lectures of William Cheselden at St. Thomas's Hospital. He is also said to have received an M.D. from the University of Rheims. While in London, together with his fellow director Thomas Hopkinson, he made the first purchase of books for the Library Company. On his return home he was reelected to the Library's board in 1733.

In Philadelphia Cadwalader joined other physicians in inoculating for smallpox and in publicly recommending a course of treatment during the smallpox epidemic of 1737–1738. As opportunity offered, he performed anatomical dissections, principally for the benefit of colleagues. In 1745 he published the work for which he is best known, *An Essay on the West-India Dry-Gripes*. The work described lead poisoning, a condition that the author ascribed to the consumption of Jamaica rum distilled through lead pipes. He recommended a mild diet, moderate exercise, and gentle laxatives. The pamphlet contained three case studies from his practice, the report of a postmortem he had performed in London, and a clinico-pathological report of a case of osteomalacia in 1742 that, in William S. Middleton's judgment, "in several details . . . outweighs the Essay in importance" (*Annals of Medical History*, p. 108).

In 1738 Cadwalader married Hannah Lambert of Burlington, New Jersey, daughter of a well-to-do landowner, and the next year they moved to Trenton, New Jersey. They had nine children. He became Trenton's chief burgess in 1745. But he returned to Philadelphia in 1750, leaving Trenton £500 to establish a subscription library like Philadelphia's. He was elected to the Philadelphia Common Council in 1751 and named to the Provincial Council in 1755. He also became a trustee of the Academy and College of Philadelphia (now University of Pennsylvania) in 1751, one of the first staff of attending physicians of the Pennsylvania Hospital in 1752, and a director once more of the Library Company in 1752. He was elected a member of the short-lived Philadelphia Medical Society in 1766 or 1767 and a member of the American Philosophical Society in 1768, becoming one of its vice presidents the next year.

Disowned by the Friends in 1745 for involvement in a privateering venture, he vigorously supported military defense in the French and Indian War, even making a voluntary contribution to provide funds the Quaker-dominated assembly would not allocate. Cadwalader opposed the Stamp Act and other measures of British imperial control, and he signed the Non-Importation Agreement in 1765. In 1773 he presided over the "Great Tea Meeting" at the Pennsylvania State House, which Benjamin Rush called "the first throe of that convulsion" that separated the American colonies from Great Britain. After the outbreak of hostilities, Cadwalader was sometimes asked to examine candidates for appointment as military surgeons or to inspect the conditions of prisons. As the British army approached Philadelphia in 1777, he retired to a son's house in Delaware. In 1779 he went to another son's home near Trenton, where he died a few months later.

• See Charles W. Dulles, "Sketch of the Life of Dr. Thomas Cadwalader," *Pennsylvania Magazine of History and Biography* 27 (1903): 262–78; Charles P. Keith, *The Provincial Councillors of Pennsylvania . . . 1733–1776* (1883), pp. 370–74; William S. Middleton, "Thomas Cadwalader and His Essay," *Annals of Medical History*, 3d ser., 3 (1941): 101–13. Cadwalader's prescription book, 1767–1768, is in the Historical Society of Pennsylvania in Philadelphia. Rush's judgment on the tea protest is in *Letters of Benjamin Rush*, ed. L. H. Butterfield, vol. 2 (1951), p. 1014.

WHITFIELD J. BELL, JR.

CADY, Daniel (29 Apr. 1773–31 Oct. 1859), lawyer and judge, was born in Chatham (now Canaan), New York, the son of Eleazer Cady and Tryphena Beebe, farmers. All his life, in work, family, religion, and personal character, Cady reflected the conservative tradition of his Connecticut-born parents. Several sources suggest that as a young man Cady worked as a shoemaker. His oldest daughter, Tryphena Cady Bayard, discounted this story, however, as the fabrication of Cady's political opponents during his race for Congress in 1814. A story that he early lost the sight in one eye may also be apocryphal. When he was about sixteen years old he became a teacher to support himself while he studied law. He completed his legal studies in Troy, New York, with John Woodworth, who later became an attorney general and justice of the supreme court in New York, and was admitted to the bar in 1795. He practiced in Florida, New York, for a brief period before he moved to Johnstown, New York, the county seat of Montgomery County, about 1799. Except for 1843–1847, when he resided in Albany, Cady remained in Johnstown for the rest of his life. In 1801 he married Margaret Chinn Livingston, the daughter of Elizabeth Simpson and revolutionary war colonel James Livingston. They had ten children, five of whom lived to adulthood.

From the beginning of his law practice in the late 1790s until 1847, Cady practiced law actively and widely. In 1812, in one of his most famous cases, he worked on a team with Aaron Burr and Ebenezer Foote in the successful defense of Solomon Southwick against charges of bribing the Speaker of the assembly.

As a lawyer, Cady specialized in real property law and did much of his work for land speculators, including his brother-in-law Peter Smith and his nephew Gerrit Smith. He also represented the heirs of Sir William Johnson in their attempt to reclaim land confiscated by the state of New York because of Johnson's Loyalist connections. Cady became a land speculator in central New York, buying land in both Montgomery County and Seneca County. He thought of himself as "much of a financier," and although he tried very hard "to keep down my passion for purchasing wild lands," he continued to buy undeveloped tracts at least through the 1830s. He "took great pleasure," reported one local historian, "in agricultural operations, especially the reclaiming of waste lands."

In 1808 Cady began almost a decade of political service. He was a member of the New York Assembly from 1808 to 1813, a village trustee in 1808, a town supervisor in 1809 and 1810, district attorney in 1813, and a Federalist member of Congress from 1815 to 1817. Even as he began his term in Congress, however, he was disillusioned with politics. The "Great City of Washington," he wrote in the fall of 1816, "has nothing in its favor but its name . . . I go there with reluctance. I consider it a political *Golgatha*." With the demise of the Federalist party, Cady returned to private law practice in 1817.

On 7 June 1847 Cady, a Whig in a Democratic district, was elected by a large majority as justice of the Fourth District of the New York State Supreme Court. He served in this position until his resignation on 1 January 1855. He also served as judge of the court of appeals in 1853 and as a Republican presidential elector and president of the state electoral college in 1856.

Along with work, Cady made family the focus of his life. He was extremely shy, and according to his daughter Elizabeth Cady Stanton, the women's rights activist, "there were but two places in which he felt at ease, in the courthouse and at his own fireside." Devastated at the loss of all of his sons, Cady found an eager law student in Elizabeth. In his office, she first learned about the legal disabilities of women under New York state law. Stanton recalled that her father prevented her from cutting offending laws out of his law books and told her, "When you are grown up, and able to prepare a speech, you must go down to Albany and talk to the legislators." In 1854 she took his advice and became the first woman to speak to the New York state legislature.

Cady was a committed churchgoer. "Perhaps no member of the church was more regular and punctual than he—certainly no male member," noted one minister. Although he did not formally join the Presbyterian church in Johnstown until 1839, he was profoundly influenced all of his life by the New England Congregational tradition of his youth.

In March 1859 Cady became totally blind. He died at his home in Johnstown. He was best known as an influential and distinguished lawyer and a man of exceptional integrity. Contemporaries noted that he was reserved, even taciturn in manner, but his moral uprightness, intellectual brilliance, courtesy, concern for others, and conscientious attention to duty earned him universal respect. He was "always the peer of the giants of the bar in all parts of the State" (Ellis, p. 104). At his death, his professional colleagues hailed him as "the very image and personification of justice," "a model lawyer and a model man," trusted for his "purity, honesty, and Roman firmness." As one young colleague later wrote, "Although Daniel Cady had a giant intellect, a commanding presence, with great book-learning, yet his greatest power with the people and before juries was his purity, truthfulness and integrity. That reputation . . . gave a magic to his every act and word."

• Letters from Cady are in the Gerrit Smith Papers, Syracuse University, and the Elizabeth Cady Stanton Papers, Library of Congress. Other manuscript sources include the Weed papers, University of Rochester, and the Index to First Presbyterian Church Records, Johnstown (N.Y.) Public Library. Information about Cady is in Orrin Peer Allen, *Descendants of Nicholas Cady of Watertown, Massachusetts* (1910); Irving Browne, "The New York Court of Appeals, Part I," *Green Bag* 2, no. 7 (July 1890): 277–91; Edward Finch Bullard, "Daniel Cady," *Green Bag* 9, no. 3 (Mar. 1897): 93–96; Alden Chester, *Courts and Lawyers of New York* (1925); Franklin Ellis, *History of Columbia County, New York* (1878); Peyton F. Miller, *A Group of Great Lawyers of Columbia County, New York* (1904); William Raymond, *Biographical Sketches of the Distinguished Men of Columbia County* (1851); and Elizabeth Cady Stanton, *Eighty Years and More* (1898; repr. 1993). Obituaries are in the *Johnstown Independent*, 25 Nov. 1859, and James P. Fisher, *A Discourse Delivered in the Presbyterian Church, Johnstown, November 6, 1859, the Sabbath Immediately following the Funeral of the Hon. Daniel Cady* (1859).

JUDITH WELLMAN

CAESAR, Doris (11 Nov. 1892–1971), sculptor and painter, was born Doris Porter in Brooklyn, New York, the daughter of Alfred Hayes Porter, a lawyer and later the president of Royal Baking Powder Co., and Lillian Dean. Her early childhood was typical of upper-middle class European-American children of the time until her mother died in 1903. Caesar grew closer to her father after her mother's death, and their relationship was instrumental in developing her interest in art. In 1909 she was studying at the prestigious Spence Academy in the morning, then running off to study painting and drawing at the Art Students League in the afternoon. At the Art Students League she met with friends and talked about "painting, people and politics" (Goodrich and Baur, p. 25). She later described herself at sixteen years old as "practically a bohemian." Her studies continued until late in 1913, when she met and married Harry Caesar. Doris Caesar spent the next twelve years in a fairly conventional lifestyle, giving birth to two children in 1914 and 1916 and devoting her time to her new family. At the onset of World War I Caesar was left to care for the household alone. If these domestic aspects of Caesar's life were all-consuming at the time, they did not diminish her desire to pursue her artistic career.

Caesar gave birth to her third child in 1923. Shortly thereafter, in 1924, Caesar's father died, and she describes it as an "incredible loss" (Bush, p. 37). In spite of these two life-altering events, or perhaps because of them, Caesar again sought formal art education. In 1925 she enrolled in Alexander Archipenko's Art School, where she studied sculpture for the first time. This was an important decision in Caesar's life, one that marks a turning point in both her personal life and her career.

Eventually, Caesar rented a studio space with two other women, Sybil Kennedy and Barbara Dunbar, who studied sculpture with her at Archipenko's school. At their loft on Lexington Avenue they worked almost obsessively on their art. Caesar's art was heavily influenced by Archipenko, and she distinguished herself as an expressionist at this time. Little of the art that Caesar produced from this period (mid-1920s to early 1930s) is intact today. After casting her first bronze, *Hookey* (1927), a sculpture of a ten-year-old African-American boy, Caesar carried it herself to E. Wehye's gallery on Lexington Avenue. Thus began a long, fruitful relationship with Wehye.

Four years later Caesar had her first one-artist show at the Montross Gallery in New York City. This first exhibition was criticized severely for "over-emphasizing portrait heads" (Bush, p. 41), but Caesar continued to work relentlessly. This early criticism must have had a great effect on her, however, because as her work progressed the heads became continually smaller, eventually becoming "mask-like with a generalized suggestion of primitive African art" (Goodrich and Baur, p. 34).

Caesar held her next solo show at the Wehye gallery in 1937 and received attention from the *New York Times* for her radical interpretations of the human form, her subjects having "dislocated, attenuated limbs that warp and flow in serpentine fashion" (*New York Times*, 22 Feb. 1964). In 1939 her piece *Thinking Woman* won the Anna Hyatt Huntington first prize at the National Association of Women Painters and Sculptors Exhibition. By 1940 Caesar was nationally known and enjoyed her sixth one-artist exhibition, Doris Caesar's Sixth.

Around this time, Caesar wrote two volumes of poetry, both published by G. P. Putnam's Sons. *Phantom Thoughts* (1934) and *Certain Paths* (1937) were not critically well received, but they emphasized Caesar's diversity and commitment to artistic production. Her poetry was free-form and highly personal; several poems in *Certain Paths*, such as "A Statue Stood" and "In Space One Finds," speak directly about the physical features and nature of sculpted work.

Caesar participated in such enriching activities in the art world as Sunday forums, Greenwich Village, and the New School for Social Research, among others. She was the vice president of the Board of the National Association of Women Artists, a board member of the New York Society of Women Artists, and part of the "New York 6," who showed in Paris in 1950. Certainly these activities show concern for the promotion of women's art within the New York Scene.

The most compelling shift in Caesar's art came about during the late 1940s and early 1950s, when she moved north of New York City to Salem Center, New York, giving up her home and studio in town. At that time she abandoned the male form entirely and began a long fascination and commitment to depicting the female form. In her female nudes she created expressionist interpretations of women's experiences through the tension of muscles and smooth and rough areas of surface "skin."

Caesar often worked from fifteen to twenty hours a day as her sculptures moved toward abstraction without losing the polish of her earlier work. She developed the ability to convey emotion without relying on facial expressions, which had all but disappeared from her figures. During the 1950s Caesar held ten successful one-artist shows, and she participated in a much-acclaimed group exhibition at the Whitney Museum in 1959. This exhibition, titled Four American Expressionists, featured Chaim Gross, Karl Knaths, and Abraham Rattner along with Caesar.

In 1957 the Caesars moved from Salem Center to Litchfield, Connecticut, where Caesar lived for the rest of her life. Here she worked in a quaint studio, continuing to produce sculpture diligently well into the late 1960s. As Caesar grew older, her focus shifted again from the "sorrows and difficulties" of life to strength. "My thinking runs now in the direction of strength. It is the strength in people that moves me. The wonderful power to handle and accept, or if not to accept, to beat" (quoted in Bush, p. 59). Caesar's final show was at the Weyhe Gallery in 1967. She died in Connecticut.

Doris Caesar's contributions to the art world were many. She left the legacy of her timeless sculptures of women and her volumes of poetry. She had an enduring spirit that enabled her to continue her work well into her seventies. She embraced the idea of the "New Woman," entering the male-dominated discipline of sculpture and applying herself with vigor and a relentless desire to improve as an artist. She did so and excelled at it even under the constraints of motherhood and marriage.

• The most complete records of Doris Caesar's life and works are at Syracuse University in the Doris Caesar Manuscript Collection. Martin Bush's biography, *Doris Caesar* (1970), makes thorough use of the manuscript collection and offers a complete listing of all of Caesar's shows and an extensive bibliography, including reviews of these shows. Exhibition catalogs from Caesar's shows are also useful. Lloyd Goodrich and John I. H. Baur, *Four American Expressionists: Doris Caesar, Chaim Gross, Karl Knaths, Abraham Rattner* (1959), offers extensive photographs of Caesar's work and an evaluation of her style and technique. Caesar is also mentioned in Sherry Piland, *Women Artists: An Historical, Contemporary and Feminist Bibliography, 2d ed.* (1994), and Jules Heller and Nancy G. Heller, *North American Women Artists of the Twentieth Century* (1995).

DAWN M. CICERO

CAFFERY, Donelson (10 Sept. 1835–30 Dec. 1906), U.S. senator, was born in Franklin, Louisiana, the son of Donelson Caffery and Lydia Murphy, who migrated to Louisiana as children. The younger Donelson Caffery, son of a local jurist and grandson of an influential former parish sheriff, was educated in a Franklin private school before attending St. Mary's College in Baltimore, Maryland. Upon his return from college, Caffery studied law under Franklin attorney Joseph W. Walker and then attended the University of Louisiana (present-day Tulane University) Law School. Caffery subsequently acquired "Ivanhoe Plantation" along Bayou Cypremort, near the Gulf of Mexico, and engaged in sugar production. According to the 1860 census, Ivanhoe Plantation, then valued at $15,000, consisted of 1,540 acres, 240 of which were improved, and was worked by thirty-three slaves. Although opposed to secession, Caffery volunteered for service in the Crescent Rifles after Louisiana seceded in January 1862. The unit was subsequently mustered into Confederate service as the Thirteenth Louisiana Regiment. After distinguished service at the battle of Shiloh (1862), Caffery was transferred to the staff of General W. W. Walker, commander of the First Louisiana Regulars. Caffery served on Walker's staff until the end of the Civil War.

Following the war's conclusion, Caffery returned to his native St. Mary Parish and entered local politics, serving as the local clerk of court for a six-month period. He utilized savings from his clerk's salary to complete his legal training. In 1866 he passed the state bar examination and entered private practice. As an attorney, Caffery gained considerable regional notoriety for superb oratorical abilities as well as his effort to drive South Louisiana Republicans from local office. This political agitation resulted in his indictment for threatening use of force against Republican J. Hale Syper. During the ensuing trial, Caffery was acquitted, largely on the basis of his moving defense before the jury.

In 1869 Caffery married Bethia Richardson; they had nine children. Shortly after his marriage, Caffery resumed his long-suspended sugar operation in St. Mary Parish, but because of the expenses of restoring formerly neglected Ivanhoe Plantation to productivity, his legal practice would remain his primary source of income. His vast courtroom experience served him well on the stump when he resumed his political career in the 1870s. After a failed bid for the Louisiana Senate, he engaged in unsuccessful electioneering for the Democratic party in St. Mary Parish, a bastion of Republican support in the Pelican State's sugar belt. Caffery was elected as a delegate to the 1879 state constitutional convention, convened by Democrats for the expressed purpose of purging many "radical" provisions of the 1868 constitution from Louisiana's fundamental law. He figured prominently at the convention, arguing persuasively against the proposed repudiation of Louisiana's Reconstruction debts. Following the convention, he campaigned vigorously for the proposed state constitution, which the state's electorate eventually ratified.

Retiring from politics in the early 1890s, Caffery then became embroiled in the bitter controversy over Louisiana's lottery. In 1891–1892 he actively supported the successful gubernatorial campaign of his cousin, antilottery candidate Murphy J. Foster. Caffery also campaigned successfully in 1892 for a seat in the Louisiana Senate. Later in 1892 Foster appointed Caffery to fill the unexpired term of the recently deceased U.S. senator R. L. Gibson. The Louisiana legislature, in 1894, elected Caffery to a full term in the U.S. Senate. As U.S. senator, Caffery, a faithful supporter of President Grover Cleveland, opposed "free silver, protective tariffs, war with Spain, Hawaiian annexation, and acquisition of the Philippines" (Carleton, p. 140). His unpopular positions regarding American monetary matters and the protective tariffs essential to the Louisiana sugar industry cost him the support of the Louisiana Democratic party. Caffery played a prominent role, in 1896, in the formation of the National Democratic party, a splinter group that withdrew from the parent organization in opposition to the regular Democratic party platform plank on federal monetary policy. In the face of overwhelming opposition to his reelection, Caffery retired from politics at the end of his senatorial term in 1900 and declined the presidential nomination of the then rapidly disintegrating National Democratic party. He subsequently made his home in Franklin, Louisiana, and resumed the practice of law and the operation of his sugar plantation. Caffery died during a visit to New Orleans.

Caffery's life, political career, and political philosophy were profoundly shaped by the sense of noblesse oblige that impelled into the political arena persons of his generation and high social station. He gained fleeting national recognition only when he deviated from conventional patterns of political behavior by abandoning the interests of the sugar industry, from which he derived a large portion of his income, in favor of what he believed to be the best interest of the nation as a whole. While Caffery gained considerable respect for following his beliefs, his conviction to principle cost him his political career.

• Caffery's extant records are in the Caffery Family Papers, Southern Historical Collection, University of North Carolina at Chapel Hill. The most comprehensive account of Caffery's career remains the now dated, expository career biography by Lucile Roy Caffery, "The Political Career of Senator Donelson Caffery," *Louisiana Historical Quarterly* 27 (1944): 783–853. See also Mark T. Carleton, "Caffery, Donelson [II]," *Dictionary of Louisiana Biography*, vol. 1 (2 vols., 1988). The following secondary works provide excellent overviews of Louisiana politics during the Reconstruction and Bourbonism eras: Joe Gray Taylor, *Louisiana Reconstructed* (1974); and William Ivy Hair, *Bourbonism and Agrarian Protest: Louisiana Politics, 1877–1900* (1971). Caffery's obituary is in the New Orleans *Daily Picayune*, 31 Dec. 1906.

CARL A. BRASSEAUX

CAFFERY, Jefferson (1 Dec. 1886–13 Apr. 1974), professional diplomat, was born Thomas Jefferson Caffery in Lafayette, Louisiana, the son of Charles Duval Caffery, a prominent lawyer and the mayor of Lafayette, and Mary Catherine Parkerson. After a comfortable childhood, Caffery attended Louisiana State University for a year before transferring to Tulane University, where he graduated in 1906. He then returned to Lafayette, where he studied and practiced law for the next four years. He grew restless at home and found law not congenial, so in 1910 he applied for a position in the newly established career diplomatic service. After studying at the Catholic University in Washington, Caffery passed the qualifying exam for the diplomatic corps. In March 1911 he received his first assignment as the second secretary at the U.S. embassy in Caracas, Venezuela. Over the next fifteen years he held a variety of diplomatic posts in Latin America, Europe, and Asia. He served at the Paris Peace Conference in 1919, and he was the counselor of the embassy in Tokyo in 1923, where he coordinated U.S. relief for the earthquake that devastated the city.

In 1926 Caffery received his first assignment as chief of a U.S. diplomatic mission, when he became minister to El Salvador. Caffery served as ambassador in other Latin American capitals in the remainder of the 1920s and the 1930s. He was ambassador to Cuba during the period when Fulgencio Batista rose to power. Anti-American sentiment intensified during this period, and Caffery narrowly escaped assassination in 1934.

Caffery left Cuba in 1937 to take up what became the longest assignment of his career, as ambassador to Brazil. In Rio de Janeiro Caffery helped expand Franklin D. Roosevelt's Good Neighbor policy by increasing trade between the two nations. Soon after he arrived in Brazil, Caffery married Gertrude McCarthy; the couple had no children. During his first year in Brazil, Caffery clashed with his German counterpart, whom he characterized as a "Nazi go-getter." Before the outbreak of World War II, Caffery had only limited success in convincing Brazilian dictator Getúlio Vargas that his country's interests lay in resisting the blandishments of Germany and aligning itself with the United States. Once war broke out Caffery often was less assertive than his superiors in Washington in encouraging Brazil to break with Germany. Concerned that overt pressure on Brazil might backfire, Caffery advised Washington to treat the Vargas government gently. The State Department concurred, but the United States had little influence with Vargas.

Caffery's cautious professionalism helped win him the most important diplomatic assignment of his career—ambassador to France from 1944 to 1949. When President Roosevelt appointed him to the Paris embassy, Caffery was the first career Foreign Service officer to occupy this important position. As he had done in Brazil, Caffery served as an intermediary between officials in Washington, D.C., and those in the country to which he was assigned. Immediately upon taking up the Paris post, Caffery became convinced that the political stability of France depended upon its economic recovery. He argued that the persistence of economic hardship fostered the interests of the French Communist party and the Soviet Union. He advocated economic assistance, and his superiors in Washington included his views in the construction of the Marshall Plan in 1947 and 1948.

Caffery also became involved in the growing conflict between France and the Vietminh in Vietnam from 1947 to 1949. The U.S. ambassador believed that France's dependability as an ally of the United States in Europe rested on the ability of the French government to defeat the Vietminh, so he urged the U.S. government to support France in its war. Officials in Washington expressed doubts that France, given its colonial history, could gain the support of the Vietnamese population. Caffery was instrumental in persuading his superiors that France could gain the support of a significant segment of the local Vietnamese population by offering quasi independence to Vietnam under the leadership of the former emperor Bao Dai. Events proved him wrong, however; Bao Dai had no support among ordinary Vietnamese.

Caffery's last ambassadorial assignment was to Egypt, where he served from 1949 to 1954. After a group of Egyptian army officers led by Colonels Mohammed Naquib and Gamal Abdel Nasser overthrew King Farouk in July 1952, Caffery acted as an intermediary between the new Egyptian authorities and the British government. Caffery arranged for a gradual departure of British forces rather than the immediate withdrawal demanded by the Egyptians.

When Caffery retired from the Foreign Service in 1955, he had served as chief of mission longer than any previous ambassador. He returned to Louisiana, where he practiced law and arranged his private papers. He died in Lafayette. He was a dedicated public servant, but he had a narrow vision. He suffered from what critics of the Foreign Service call "localitis," that is, a tendency to see issues through the prism of the country to which he was assigned. His achievements were overshadowed by those of other career diplomats like George Kennan or Charles Bohlen or politician/diplomats like Averell Harriman.

• Caffery's personal papers are at the University of Southwestern Louisiana, Lafayette. A chronology of Caffery's career appears in Philip F. Dur et al., *Jefferson Caffery, Ambassador Extraordinary: An Outline of His Career* (1974). Biographical studies appear in Dur, "Jefferson Caffery of Louisiana: Highlights of His Career," pt. 1, *Louisiana History* 15 (1974): 5–34, and pt. 2: 367–402; Steven C. Sapp, "Jefferson Caffery, Cold War Diplomat: American-French Relations, 1944–1949," *Louisiana History* 23 (1982): 179–92; and Dur, "Ambassador Caffery and the French Alliance," *Louisiana History* 27 (1986): 249–60.

ROBERT D. SCHULZINGER

CAFFIN, Charles Henry (4 June 1854–15 Jan. 1918), art critic and author, was born in Sittingbourne, Kent, England, the son of the Reverend Charles Smart Caffin, a Church of England minister, and Harriet (maiden name unknown). Both parents were talented amateur artists. In 1873 Caffin received a scholarship to attend Pembroke College at Oxford University, where he received his B.A. in 1877. Following graduation, he worked as a teacher for several years before joining an itinerant theater troupe, Ben Greet and His Shakespearean Players, as an actor and stage manager. In 1888 he married fellow player Caroline Scurfield; they had two daughters. Caffin and his family immigrated to the United States in 1892. He first worked in the decorations department of the World's Columbian Exposition in Chicago, which led to his next job making cartoons for mural paintings in the new Library of Congress in Washington, D.C. His first essay on art and architecture was published in Herbert Small's *Handbook of the New Library of Congress* (1897).

In 1897 Caffin moved to New York, first living in Mamaroneck on Long Island Sound before settling permanently in New York City by 1908. Caffin's affiliation with several major magazines and newspapers span this period: art editor for *Harper's Weekly* (1897–1901) and the American supplement for *International Studio* (1901–1905); art critic for the *New York Post* (1897–1900), *New York Sun* (1901–1904), and *New York American* (1913–1918); and contributor to *Harper's Monthly*, *Century*, *Art and Progress*, *Craftsman*, *Putnam's Monthly*, and other influential periodicals. In these various capacities, Caffin joined a small, often embattled group of progressive critics who sought to inform the broad public during a turbulent period of transition from Victorian artistic standards to fundamentally different modern methods and ideals. He also authored more than a dozen books on art appreciation, art history, and contemporary art. Especially important were *Photography as a Fine Art* (1901), which posited the medium's independence and argued for a factual or "straight" approach to photography that would free painting to explore more abstract modes of expression, and two pioneering books on the relatively neglected subject of American art: *American Masters of Painting* (1902) and *American Masters of Sculpture* (1903). Rather than topical surveys, each of these volumes consisted of thirteen focused monographs on key artists such as Inness, Homer, French, and Saint-Gaudens and demonstrated Caffin's strong commitment to defining a distinct national artistic identity.

Caffin's writings on art are based on a set of theories about art and its essential relationship to life that made him particularly receptive to early modernism. The principal elements in Caffin's theory, which he summarized in *Art for Life's Sake* (1913), included faith in evolution as a means of meeting the challenges of a new historical era; the necessity of art as a moral paradigm and spiritual agent; supremacy of individual expression over academic order; familiarity with the arts and crafts movement and synesthetic concepts that recognized the inherent formal qualities of each medium while remaining open to the possibilities of higher cross-fertilization; and reverence for nature as a prime source of artistic inspiration and ultimate truth. In *Art for Life's Sake*, Caffin insisted, "Religion, Morality and Art should be inseparable in the Wholeness of Life. For Religion represents man's attitude toward the universal; Morality, the code of conduct which he shapes thereto, while Art is inevitably the symbol of expression of what he has made his code of conduct and of his attitude toward the universal" (p. 137).

Caffin's critical advocacy of modern art was especially evident in his close association with pioneering dealer and photographer Alfred Stieglitz. His *Photography as a Fine Art* featured Stieglitz, and his many contributions to the journal *Camera Notes*, which Stieglitz edited, reflected their shared commitment to "straight" photography, which emphasized the inherent properties of the medium by means of a direct, through-the-lens method without cropping, retouching, or other strategies used to simulate painting. Caffin was also allied with Stieglitz's vanguard 291 group and gallery between 1908 and 1917. During this period he wrote regularly for *Camera Work*, the "voice of 291," and offered insightful reviews of work by Paul Cézanne, Henri Matisse, and other advanced European artists as well as works by emerging American modernists such as John Marin and Marsden Hartley. Throughout the mid-1910s, Caffin also used his position as art critic for the *New York American* to heighten public awareness of modern art, asserting in 1913,

> The Little Gallery, No. 291 Fifth Avenue, has become the incubator for artistic ideas. Some regard it as a hothouse of artistic anarchy. Possibly it is, and thereby the more desirable and needful. For the average American, despite his boast of progressiveness, is apt, in matters intellectual and esthetic, to be as narrow and smugly complacent as our Puritan forebearers. ("Drawings by Walkowitz on view at 'Little Gallery,' 6 Jan., p. 8)

Caffin died in New York City. Estimates of his contributions as a critic and historian vary. Among his contemporaries, Stieglitz clearly appreciated his views, but others, such as fellow critic Willard Huntington Wright, discounted his approach for being "broad enough to tolerate all opinion," a complaint that failed to recognize Caffin's overriding priority of broadening the audience for early modern art in the United States.

• Caffin's papers, including a biographically informative interview with his daughter Mrs. Donna Layton, are in the Archives of American Art, Washington, D.C. Fifteen letters to Alfred Stieglitz, written between 1901 and 1915, are in the Stieglitz Archive, Beinecke Library, Yale University. Besides those cited in the text, Caffin's books include *How to Study Pictures* (1905), *The Story of American Painting* (1907), *A Child's Guide to Pictures* (1908), *A Guide to Pictures for Beginners and Students* (1908), *The Art of Dwight W. Tryon* (1909), *The Story of Dutch Painting* (1909), *The Story of Spanish Painting* (1910), *The Story of French Painting* (1911), *How to Study the Modern Painters* (1914), and *How to Study Architecture* (1917). Among his many important essays for *Camera Work* are "Of Verities and Illusions" (Oct. 1905, Jan. 1906, Apr. 1906), "Henri Matisse and Isadora Duncan" (Jan. 1909), "A Note on Paul Cézanne" (Apr.–July 1911), and "What 291 Means to Me" (July 1915). For a full biographical and critical study, see Sandra Lee Underwood, *Charles H. Caffin: A Voice for Modernism, 1897–1918* (1983).

JEFFREY HAYES

CAGE, John (5 Sept. 1912–12 Aug. 1992), composer and philosopher, was born John Milton Cage, Jr., in Los Angeles, California, the son of John Milton Cage, Sr., an inventor, and Lucretia Harvey, a reporter for the *Los Angeles Times*. Cage had early aspirations to be either a minister or a writer. In 1930, after two years at Pomona College, he went to Europe, where he studied architecture with Ernö Goldfinger and piano with Lazare Lévy in Paris. There he also began painting, writing poetry, and composing music. On his return to California in 1931, he studied composition with Richard Buhlig, developing a method employing two 25-tone ranges. He then moved to New York to learn more about harmony and music theory under the tutelage of Adolph Weiss; at the New School for Social Research in 1933, he also studied modern harmony, contemporary music, and Oriental and folk music with Henry Cowell. Cage's training culminated in 1934 with counterpoint lessons from Arnold Schoenberg, both privately and at the University of Southern California; he also attended Schoenberg's classes in counterpoint and analysis at the University of California, Los Angeles. In June 1935, after a brief courtship, Cage married Xenia Andreyevna Kashevaroff; they had no children and were divorced in 1945.

In 1937 Cage became composer-accompanist for Bonnie Bird's modern dance classes at the Cornish School in Seattle, where he met Merce Cunningham. He organized a percussion orchestra, collected musical instruments, and made tours throughout the Northwest. There he also met the painter Morris Graves and arranged for an exhibition of his work. While in Seattle, Cage composed his *First Construction (in Metal)* for 6 Percussionists (1939).

Cage's early interest in noise led him to develop methods of writing complex rhythmic structures for percussion instruments. Drawing on Cowell's extended piano techniques, he came to invent the "prepared piano," thus transforming the traditional instrument into a new "percussion" orchestra by placing objects—such as screws, coins, and erasers—on and between the strings. *Bacchanale* (1938), Cage's first prepared piano piece, was written for a dance by Syvilla Fort (1938); a revised version was performed in Seattle in April 1940. In 1941 Cage traveled to Chicago, where he taught a class in experimental music at the School of Design. On a commission from CBS's "Columbia Workshop," he composed *The City Wears a Slouch Hat* for 4 Percussion and Sound Effects (1942), to a text by the poet Kenneth Patchen. In 1942 Cage settled in New York and there began a lengthy professional and personal association with Cunningham, then a dancer with the Martha Graham Company. In February 1943 Cage gave a concert of percussion music at the Museum of Modern Art, a widely reported event that established his reputation as an experimental composer.

In 1945, newly divorced and experiencing a "crisis of faith" about composition, Cage began a study of Eastern philosophies, first Indian philosophy and music with Gita Sarabhai and then Zen Buddhism with D. T. Suzuki at Columbia University. During this period, Cage composed *The Seasons* (1947), written on commission for the dance impresario Lincoln Kirstein, and his most important work for the prepared piano, the Sonatas and Interludes (1946–1948). The latter, performed by Maro Ajemian at Carnegie Hall in January 1949, won attention as a major event and earned the composer citations from the Guggenheim Foundation and the National Academy of Arts and Letters, which credited him with having "extended the boundaries of music."

Cage continued to have an active involvement in the avant-garde. He became friends, for example, with Marcel Duchamp, a kindred spirit whose "readymades"—objects such as a urinal or a bicycle wheel—made sculpture and painting a medium for serendipity and were aimed at subverting conventional notions of fine art. Cage's *Music for Marcel Duchamp* (1947) is another exercise in creating a highly patterned sequence of indeterminate sounds based on an arbitrary number scheme. In 1948 he taught at Black Mountain College in North Carolina, where he spent time with the visionary engineer and thinker R. Buckminster Fuller, the abstract expressionist painter Willem de Kooning, and the formal abstractionist painter and art teacher Joseph Albers, among others. In 1949 Cage was again in Europe, on tour with Cunningham; on that trip he met the *enfant terrible* of contemporary French music, Pierre Boulez. When he returned to New York, Cage helped to form, with the painter Robert Motherwell and others, the Artists Club. Dating from this period are two early text pieces, "Lecture on Nothing" and "Lecture on Something"; his String Quartet in Four Parts was written in 1949–1950.

In 1950 Cage began developing means for composition with chance operations, using as his primary director the *I Ching* or "Book of Changes," one of the most influential books in the Chinese Confucian canon. Then he happened to meet a worthy collaborator, pianist David Tudor, who realized many of Cage's early chance compositions, including the seminal *Music of Changes* (1952), in which the performer shares the composer's creative role. In 1950 Cage completed a score, using prepared piano and tape, for Herbert Matter's award-winning film *Works of Calder* (1945–1950). He also composed *Imaginary Landscape no. 4* for 24 Performers on 12 Radios (1951), the Concerto for Prepared Piano and Chamber Orchestra (1952), and his first piece for tape, *Imaginary Landscape No. 5* (1952), for a dance by Jean Erdman. Influenced by Rauschenberg's monochromatic paintings, Cage created the notoriously tacet *4′ 30″*, during which no sounds are intentionally produced; Tudor first performed it in Woodstock, New York, in August 1952. A decade later, Cage would produce a second "silent" piece, *0′ 00″*, "to be played in any way by anyone" (1962).

When the Merce Cunningham Dance Company was formed in 1953, Cage became its first music director, a position he maintained for more than thirty years. In 1954 he moved to a cooperative community established by Paul and Vera Williams in Rockland County, New York. After a concert tour in Europe with Tudor, Cage became acquainted with the painter Jasper Johns, whose pop-oriented work helped to supplant abstract expressionism as the dominant American art movement of the period. Cage continued with his *Music for Piano* series (1952 onward), using imperfections in manuscript paper to guide his composition. From 1956 to 1960 he occasionally taught classes at the New School for Social Research attended by George Brecht, Al Hansen, Dick Higgins, and Allan Kaprow, among others. In 1958 a 25-year retrospective concert of Cage's music was given at Town Hall in New York.

A year later Cage spent a summer teaching experimental music at Darmstadt, Germany, and presented his "Indeterminacy, New Aspects of Form in Instrumental and Electronic Music" at the Brussels World Fair. In Milan, where he was able to work in a radio station, he put together the tape of *Fontana Mix* for Any Sound Sources or Actions (1958). After another stint at the New School, he was a fellow at Wesleyan University, where he completed his first monograph, *Silence: Selected Lectures and Writings* (1961), which became a classic in twentieth-century musical aesthetics. In 1961 he completed *Atlas Eclipticalis* for 1 to 86 Specified Instruments, commissioned by the Montreal Festivals Society.

While in Italy in 1958, Cage had enjoyed success as a contestant on a radio quiz show called "Lascia o Raddoppia" (roughly meaning "Double or Nothing"), winning $6,000 by answering correctly a host of questions about mushrooms. At the New School the following year, he conducted courses not only on music but also on mushroom identification. In 1962, as an outgrowth of this avocation, he helped found the New York Mycological Society.

After an extensive concert tour of Japan with Tudor, Cage directed, in 1963, the first New York performance of Erik Satie's marathon *Vexations* (c. 1893). During the 1960s Cage went on his first world tour with the Cunningham Dance Company and joined with Jasper Johns in forming the philanthropic Foundation for Contemporary Performance Arts in New York. At this time he encountered the controversial ideas of two lasting influences, Marshall McLuhan, the Canadian cultural critic best known for the concept "the medium is the message," and Henry David Thoreau, the advocate of passive civil disobedience and of oneness with nature whose *Journals* Cage read avidly. Yet another pairing of Cage's enthusiasms was realized when he played with Marcel Duchamp demonstration chess games on a board designed to operate on computer-assisted "aleatory principles" (*Reunion*; Toronto, Mar. 1968). In 1969, at the University of Illinois at Urbana–Champaign, Cage created (with Lejaren Hiller) *HPSCHD* for 1 to 7 Amplified Harpsichords and 1 to 51 Tapes, a complex work of auditory and visual stimuli. That year he also published *Notations*, a valuable compilation of manuscripts by contemporary composers, and executed his first visual work (with Calvin Sumsion), *Not Wanting to Say Anything about Marcel*, at Hollander's Workshop in New York.

Throughout the 1970s, Cage traveled extensively while producing works in a variety of media. Using star charts as his guide, he composed in 1974–1975 *Etudes Australes*, and in 1975–1976 *Child of Tree* and *branches*, both scored for Percussion and Amplified Plant Materials. Commissioned by the Canadian Broadcasting Company on the occasion of the bicentennial of the United States, Cage's *Lecture on the Weather* (1976) combined spoken texts by Thoreau, a film by Luis Frangella, and weather recordings by Marianne Amacher; two other works from 1976 are *Renga* for 78 Instruments or Voices and *Apartment House 1776* for 4 Voices and Any Number of Instruments. In 1977 Cage began work on his mammoth violin work, *Freeman Etudes*, left incomplete until 1991, and wrote *Inlets* for 3 Performers on Conch Shells.

The multifaceted nature of Cage's involvement in the arts was particularly evident in 1978. He created a set of color etchings, *Score without Parts (40 Drawings by Thoreau): Twelve Haiku*, incorporating drawings by Thoreau; Cage began making prints at Crown Point in Oakland (later San Francisco), California, where he returned annually to produce such series as *Seven Day Diary* (1978), *Dereau* (1982), *Dramatic Fire* (1989), and *Smoke Weather Stone Weather* (1991). Also in 1978, he published the first volume of his *Writing through Finnegans Wake* and realized—in and around Bologna, Italy—his lively *Alla Ricerca del Silenzio Perduto* for Prepared Train.

In 1979 Cage went to Paris to work at IRCAM (Institut de Recherche et de Coordination Acoustique/Musique, under the direction of Pierre Boulez) in order to complete work on *Roaratorio, an Irish Circus on Finnegans Wake* for Voice, Tape, and Any Number of Musicians, which had been commissioned by the German radio network Westdeutscher Rundfunk (WDR) in Cologne. In 1981–1982 Cage created his fanciful *hörspiel* (radio play) *James Joyce, Marcel Duchamp, Erik Satie: Ein Alphabet*, also for WDR. In 1981 he wrote *Composition in Retrospect* (pub. 1993), composed *Thirty Pieces for Five Orchestras* and *Dance/4 Orchestras*, and on National Public Radio gave a night-long reading of his *Empty Words: Writings '73–'78* (1979). In 1982 his scores and prints were exhibited for the first time, at both the Whitney Museum of American Art in New York and the Philadelphia Museum of Art; in 1983 he began producing pencil rock tracings on handmade paper, *Where R = Ryoanji* (1983–1992).

In 1984 Cage began working on computer, employing specially made programs. By 1987 several large-scale computer-assisted works were completed and premiered, including his only sound installation, *Essay*, with manipulated texts from Thoreau's *Essay on Civil Disobedience*, and his first opera, *Europeras 1 & 2*, a chance-determined, musico-dramatic stage collage put on in Frankfurt, Germany. Also from this year was his *Two* for Flute and Piano, the first in a series of "number pieces" utilizing a radically flexible system of "time-bracket notation," which became his compositional method of choice. In 1988–1989 he held the prestigious Charles Eliot Norton Chair at Harvard University, for which he wrote and delivered six mesostic "lectures" incorporating the writings of Thoreau, McLuhan, and other authors, published as *I–VI* (1990); a highly original poetic form developed by Cage, mesostics use a composed "source text" and a generating string of letters down the center of a page that spell a name, word, or line of text relating (or not) to the subject of the poem. In 1989 a joint exhibition titled Dancers on a Plane: John Cage, Merce Cunningham, Jasper Johns was mounted in London and Liverpool, and in 1990 Cage's watercolors were exhibited as New River Watercolors at the Phillips Collection in Washington, D.C. Cage attended in 1990 the premiere of his *Fourteen* for Piano and Small Orchestra in Zürich, Switzerland, and his *Europeras 3 & 4* at London's Almeida Festival; in 1991 his *Europera 5* followed, a diminutive version in the *Europeras* series, staged in Buffalo, New York. Cage also began designing his evolving work for museum, *Rolywholyover: A Circus*, seen successively, after his death, in Los Angeles, Houston, New York, Mito (Japan), and Philadelphia. In 1991 Cage was in Zürich for another performance of his *Europeras 1 & 2* and the premiere of *Beach Birds*, his final dance collaboration with Cunningham. During this period, Cage made suites of handmade paper and edible drawings at Rugg Road Papers in Boston.

In 1992, the last year of his life, Cage attended innumerable eightieth birthday celebrations. He composed orchestral works for the Hessischer Rundfunk (Frankfurt), WDR (Cologne), and the American Composers Orchestra (N.Y.), and some twenty "number pieces" for various smaller ensembles. He also completed his only film, the strikingly minimalist *One*^{11}. His death in New York, which took place just weeks before his eightieth birthday, circumvented his attendance at two extensive Cage festivals; he also did not live to see, in 1993, an exhibition of his visual works at the Venice Biennale.

Cage's influence has been widespread and profound. With the passing years, he departed from the pragmatism of precise musical notation and circumscribed performance, electing instead to mark his creative intentions in graphic symbols, generalized, poetic instructions, and flexible time relationships. His primary contribution was his establishment of the principle of indeterminacy in music. By adapting Zen Buddhist practices to composition, Cage succeeded in bringing both authentic spiritual ideas and a liberating attitude of play to the enterprise of Western art. His chance procedures, guided first by the throwing of coins or dice and later by random number generators, led to a highly imaginative system of total serialism, resulting in a body of "once-only" works, any two performances of which can never be the same. Cage's mature works are often said to be "just" sounds—free of judgments about whether they are musical or not, free of fixed relations, and free of memory and taste.

Cage was also a brilliant writer, much influenced by the manner, grammar, syntax, and glorious illogic of Gertrude Stein. Although his more characteristic books did not appear until the 1960s—he had previously coauthored, with K. Hoover, *Virgil Thomson: His Life in Music* in 1959—early in his career he was a contributor to such periodicals as *Perspectives of New Music* and *Modern Music* and edited the short-lived magazine *Possibilities*. Of singular importance was his development of mesostics, analogous to the indeterminacy of his musical works; eventually they too were composed via computer, the "source text" being machine-pulverized and then enhanced by Cage into varyingly coherent, highly evocative poetic texts. While the most ambitious example of mesostics can be seen in his Harvard lectures, they appear elsewhere in his late writings, such as *Anarchy* (1988) and *Overpopulation and Art* (1992).

Until the late 1960s Cage was frequently denounced by critics and audiences imbued with the traditions of classical music. To many he seemed to be either a jester, making a mockery of fine art, or an earnest fool, unable to fathom how far he had gone off the deep end. Among artists and devotees of the experimental school, however, he was seen as a genius who was taking the possibilities of sound—be it musical in the conventional sense or seemingly just noise—further than any other composer had dared to venture. Complementing his use of sound was his sensitivity to the effects of silence, which in turn opened up the potential for indeterminacy in rhythm and introduced an awareness of musical performance as an environment. Cage thereby managed to break away from the concept of "art" music as inviolate, sealed off from events of the everyday world. When the American counterculture of the 1960s began to attract enthusiastic adherents on university campuses across the country—coinciding with the appeal of consciousness-altering drugs, the popularity of psychedelic music, and revulsion at American military involvement in Southeast Asia—Cage came to be considered a visionary. His worldview, rooted in Zen principles of openness to everything and of not making value judgments, was idealized. But within the realm of concert halls and music-making in the classical vein, Cage had also attained a new prominence and respect, as indicated by his election to the American Academy and Institute of Arts and Letters in 1968. Recognition from the establishment continued to the time of his death. He was made a member of the American Academy of Arts and Sciences in 1978 and inducted into the American Academy of Arts and Letters in 1989. The Mayor's Award of Honor was bestowed on him in New York City in 1981. He was named a commander of the Order of Arts and Letters by the French minister of culture in 1982. In the summer of 1989 he was guest artist at international festivals in Leningrad and Moscow. In late 1989 he traveled to Japan where, in formal dress, he received the prestigious Kyoto Prize.

• In 1993 Cage's music manuscripts, numbering some 27,000 pages, were acquired by the New York Public Library for the Performing Arts, at Lincoln Center. His correspondence, spanning some fifty years, is housed at Northwestern University; materials relating to his published writings are housed at Wesleyan University. Other materials, including many original text manuscripts, a permanent art collection, and ephemera of various kinds, are housed at the John Cage Trust in New York. In addition to those already cited, Cage's own writings include *A Year from Monday: New Lectures and Writings* (1967), *To Describe the Process of Composition Used in Not Wanting to Say Anything about Marcel* (1969), *M: Writings '67–'72* (1973), (with D. Charles) *For the Birds* (1981), (with S. Barron) *Another Song* (1981), *Themes and Variations* (1982), and *X: Writings '79–'82* (1983). Anthologies of writings by Cage include three volumes edited by R. Kostelanetz: *John Cage* (1970), *Conversing with Cage* (1987), and *John Cage, Writer: Previously Uncollected Pieces* (1993); see also J. Retallack, *MUSICAGE: Cage Muses on Words, Art, and Music* (1995). For a study of Cage's music as a whole, see J. Pritchett, *The Music of John Cage* (1993), which has become a standard reference. See also H. -K. Metzger and R. Riehn, eds., special issue of *Musik-Konzept* (2 vols., 1990), which includes a list of works, discography, and extensive bibliography.

For biographical information, see D. Revill, *The Roaring Silence John Cage: A Life* (1992). Anthologies of writings about Cage include P. Gena and J. Brent, eds., *A John Cage Reader: In Celebration of His 70th Birthday* (1982); R. Fleming and W. Duckworth, eds., *John Cage at Seventy-five* (1989); R. Kostelanetz, ed., *Writings about John Cage* (1993); and M. Perloff and C. Junkerman, *John Cage: Composed in America* (1994). Cage's visual works are the subject of K. Brown, "Changing Art: A Chronicle Centered on John Cage," in *John Cage: Etchings 1978–1982*, ed. W. Diamond and C. Hicks (1982).

LAURA KUHN

CAGNEY, James (17 July 1899–30 Mar. 1986), actor, was born James Francis Cagney, Jr., on the Lower East Side of New York City, the son of James Francis Cagney, a bartender, and Carolyn Nelson. Cagney was raised in New York's multicultural Yorkville neighborhood, and by age fourteen he was working to help support his mother, three brothers, and sister. He graduated from Stuyvesant High School and attended Columbia University for a year until his father died in 1918.

Cagney's performing career began at age nineteen when he appeared in theatricals and a vaudeville revue; these led in 1920 to a major role in the Broadway show *Pitter Patter*. In 1922 he married a dancer in the show, Frances Willard "Billie" Vernon. That same year they both went to Hollywood, but neither could find work in the movies. Returning to New York, they danced on the vaudeville circuit, and Cagney earned critical attention for several stage roles. By 1929 he had played eight leading roles on Broadway, and he reprised his stage role in the musical *Penny Arcade* for the Warner Bros. film *Sinner's Holiday* (1930).

The lithe, handsome, redheaded Cagney quickly rose to stardom at Warner Bros. by playing a cocky Irish gangster in *Public Enemy* and *Smart Money* (both 1931), but the versatility of the fast-talking New Yorker who had begun his theatrical career as a dancer went far beyond the portrayal of gangsters. His ironic wit and subtle talent for playing comedy, for example, was first revealed in *Blonde Crazy* (1931).

Despite early success at Warner Bros., Cagney was one of the first talking picture stars who was determined to be independent of the restrictive Hollywood studio system. In 1931 he rebelled by spending six months in New York while renegotiating his contract. It was an unusual and bold step but proved successful when his salary doubled. He returned to Hollywood and starred in a series of rapidly produced (nineteen in four years) popular movies, with his brother William as his astute business manager. Among his early hits as a quick-fisted feisty rogue were *Taxi* and *Winner Take All* (both 1932), *Hard to Handle* and *Lady Killer* (both 1933), and *Jimmy the Gent* (1934). All of these films were mass produced by the dream factory system, yet Cagney brought his own personality, inventiveness, and irrepressible high spirits to each role.

In *Footlight Parade* (1933) Cagney again starred as a light-footed wise guy, a stage director facing the impact of talking movies on Broadway musicals. This time, however, he was a razzle-dazzle leading man who could dance and sing; his "Shanghai Lil" number, which topped the three Busby Berkeley productions, made the film a gem in the Cagney oeuvre. Depression-era audiences responded to Cagney's confident wit and vitality, and even the film's tributes to Franklin D. Roosevelt and the National Recovery Administration are not heavy-handed. *Footlight Parade* is one of Cagney's best movies, distinguished from most films he made in the 1930s by a lavish budget and a talented supporting cast.

Although he was typecast as a big city gangster, Cagney more often played a lovable tough guy, notably in *Here Comes the Navy* (1934), which was nominated for an Academy Award as best picture, and *Devil Dogs of the Air* and *G-Men* (both 1935). In nine films he was teamed with his close friend Pat O'Brien, and their screen chemistry and Irish-American wit coupled with gritty energy delighted audiences.

Unhappy with the roles assigned to him in *A Midsummer Night's Dream*, *The Irish in Us*, and *Ceiling Zero* (all 1935), Cagney broke his lucrative contract with Warner Bros. to work for a new independent film company, but he later returned to the Warners studio to make *Boy Meets Girl* and *Angels with Dirty Faces* (both 1938); for the latter he received his first Oscar nomination as best actor. *Each Dawn I Die* and *The Roaring Twenties* (both 1939) and *The Strawberry Blonde* (1941) were Cagney's other memorable films among the dozen he made at Warner Bros. from 1938 to 1942.

In 1940 Cagney appeared before the House Un-American Activities Committee in response to allegations that in 1934 he had associated with political subversives and contributed to left-wing organizations. Repeating his claim that he had always been a loyal citizen, Cagney was cleared by the committee. His appearance in no way diminished his popularity. The public continued to appreciate Cagney's performances, thronging to see him in *City for Conquest* (1941), *Johnny Come Lately* (1943), *Mister Roberts* (1955), *Man of a Thousand Faces* (1957), *Shake Hands with the Devil* (1959), and his last film before retiring, *One, Two, Three* (1961).

Despite his below-average stature and unprepossessing features, Cagney was dynamic on stage or screen, exuding an irrepressible energy and confidence that came to personify the classic street-smart movie tough guy. He was the most-impersonated star in show business, his wise guy persona and staccato delivery creating a new image of the cocksure Irish-American Catholic hero, especially in *The Fighting 69th* (1940) and *Captain of the Clouds* (1942). For some Irish Americans, however, Cagney's success in hoodlum roles created an unfortunate stereotype of the fictitious "fighting Irish," which diminished only as Irish Americans assimilated into mainstream society. In private life, Cagney was rather shy, soft-spoken, gentle, and drank little. His sister, Jeanne Cagney, was also a film actress, and his brother William Cagney was an actor and producer in Hollywood. He and Billie had no children but adopted a son, James, and a daughter, Cathleen.

Cagney was nominated for nine Academy Awards and won one, for his portrayal of the patriotic Broadway song-and-dance man George M. Cohan in *Yankee Doodle Dandy* (1942). Cagney sought the role in order to forestall rumors about his left-wing associations, but its perfect blend of acting, singing, and dancing has seldom been seen on the big screen. Cagney was the first actor to receive the Life Achievement Award of the American Film Institute (1974) and was also a recipient of the Kennedy Center Honors (1980) and the Medal of Freedom (1984). After performances in sixty-two movies, he retired in 1961 as a gentleman farmer in Dutchess County, New York, where he bred Morgan horses and Scottish Highlander cattle. Late in life Cagney also became a talented painter.

Despite chronic health problems, at age eighty-two Cagney emerged from twenty years of retirement to critical acclaim in the turn-of-the-century epic *Ragtime* (1981). Cagney also made a few television appearances, most notably as an elderly ex-boxer in *Terrible Joe Moran* (1984), his last film. At his death at his farm in Stanfordville, New York, Cagney was eulogized by his friend, then president Ronald Reagan, as one of America's "finest artists." More precisely, Cagney had risen from obscurity to become a movie legend personifying independence, courage, resourcefulness, and self-esteem in the context of modern urban culture.

• For more biographical information see Andrew Bergman, *James Cagney* (1973), and Cagney's two autobiographies, *Cagney by Cagney* (1976) and, with Doug Warren, *James Cagney: The Authorized Biography* (1983). Also see Richard Schickel, *James Cagney: A Celebration* (1985), and Robert Sklar, *City Boys: Cagney, Bogart, Garfield* (1992). An obituary is in the *New York Times*, 1 Apr. 1986.

PETER C. HOLLORAN

CAHAN, Abraham (7 July 1860–31 Aug. 1951), editor and author, was born in Podberezy, Lithuania, the son of Shakhne Cahan and Sheyne Sarah Goldarbeter, both teachers. Cahan was five when his family moved to nearby Vilna, where he graduated from the Vilna Teachers' Institute for Jewish students in June 1881. Assigned to a public school in Velizh, he fled less than a year later under threat of political persecution for suspected radical activities, emigrating to the United States in June 1882.

Cahan settled on New York's Lower East Side. In 1885 he married Aniuta "Anna" Bronstein; they had no children. Learning English quickly, Cahan soon began to write articles for the New York dailies and Yiddish columns for the Jewish socialist press. He became a major voice in socialism and labor, the first advocate to deliver speeches in Yiddish—the native tongue of most Eastern European Jewish immigrants. In 1891 he began editing the *Arbayter tsaytung* (Worker's paper), and from 1894 to 1897 he edited the more literary *Tsukunft* (Future) as well. After a factional dispute, Cahan and a few associates left both papers and founded the Yiddish daily *Forward*.

Policy arguments, however, led Cahan to resign within the year, and he soon joined the staff of the *New York Commercial Advertiser* as a full-time reporter under Lincoln Steffens, its city editor. There he gained invaluable experience in English journalism. Counseled by Steffens, Cahan learned to seek "the story behind the story" for insight into his assigned subjects. He interviewed an astonishing variety of people, from immigrants of diverse ethnic heritage to President William McKinley and Buffalo Bill. Upon leaving the *Advertiser* in 1901, Cahan returned briefly to the *Forward* in 1902 but left again when his authority was challenged. In the summer of 1903, however, he accepted the editor's chair once more and retained it for nearly fifty years.

On taking over the daily, Cahan transformed it from a stodgy socialist vehicle for doctrinaire polemics into a broad-ranging newspaper for workers and their families. It soon became the leading Yiddish newspaper in the world, with a circulation of approximately 250,000 during its heyday in the mid-1920s.

As Ronald Sanders writes in *The Downtown Jews*, under Cahan's leadership, the *Forward* became "the immigrants' friend and confidant—nay more, it was a patient and omniscient father, wise in the ways of America" (p. 263). The *Forward* vigorously supported organized labor, especially the garment workers, mostly Russian Jews, who dominated the ready-made clothing industry. Cahan also highlighted cultural development, entertainment, and mundane concerns, using the daily to educate and Americanize the immigrants. Seeking new ways to attract readers, women as well as men, Cahan introduced the "*Bintl briv*" ("Bundle of letters"), a personal-advice column that gained immediate popularity in January 1906 and was widely read for decades. Readers wrote letters describing their problems, and Cahan answered them himself in the early years of the feature. To gain subscribers the *Forward* offered premiums, including the first two volumes of a Yiddish history of the United States that Cahan wrote for this purpose.

By 1923 the *Forward* was published nationally in eleven cities, but with the decline of spoken Yiddish in the home, it lost readers, retaining mostly the fading older generations. After a stroke in 1946, Cahan relinquished most of his editorial control. He died in New York.

By 1923 Cahan's 22-year career as an author of fiction in English had ended, having culminated in 1917 with the publication of *The Rise of David Levinsky*. With help from W. D. Howells in the 1890s, Cahan had rapidly acquired the reputation of a "new star of Realism," as Howells praised him when reviewing his first novel, *Yekl, a Tale of the New York Ghetto* (1896). Before 1896 Cahan had published only two English stories, both in 1895. In 1898 he gathered those two stories, along with two others and an unpublished novelette, compiling them in *The Imported Bridegroom and Other Stories of the New York Ghetto*. During the next few years Cahan published six additional stories in leading monthlies, all written during his tenure with the *Commercial Advertiser*.

Cahan's early stories largely established the basic methods, materials, and ideas that reappear in his later fiction. Alienation, tenuously resolved or not, is a principal theme, the Jewish district of New York his typical setting, realism subject to irony the dominant mode, and melancholy tempered with humor his prevailing tone. His characters, with occasional exception in his later stories and most notably in *The White Terror and the Red: A Novel of Revolutionary Russia* (1905), are Eastern European Jewish immigrants trying to adapt to the New World. Even the two exceptional stories, however, deal with Gentile immigrants, and *The White Terror and the Red* is Cahan's only example of English fiction set exclusively outside of the United States.

Cahan was "the first to introduce . . . all the new Russian writers" to American readers and among the first to translate important fiction by Anton Chekhov (Rischin, p. xxxix), whom he regarded, along with Tolstoi, as Russia's preeminent literary realist. "In literary matters Cahan was from first to last a Realist," Jules Chametzky asserts; concern with authenticity and the increasing awareness of science, technology, and fact subordinated his limited interest in romance and ideality (Chametzky, pp. 29, 30). In the July 1898 *Atlantic Monthly*, Cahan wrote:

> Hidden under an uncouth surface [in the ghetto] would be found a great deal of what constitutes the true poetry of modern life,—tragedy more heart-rending, examples of a heroism more touching, more noble, and more thrilling, than anything that the richest imagination of the romanticist can invent. While to the outside observer the [immigrants'] struggles may appear a fruitless repetition of meaningless conflicts, they are, like the great labor movement of which they are a part, ever marching onward, ever advancing. ("Russian Jew in America," p. 135)

This statement testifies that Cahan's literary values and socialist ethic were integrally related during his first few decades in the United States, although the link is more apparent in his tendentious Yiddish novels than his English fiction.

Cahan's thematic realism extends from motivation and portraiture to details of physical setting. In places it is so honest and graphic that he was criticized by Gentile reviewers and Jewish readers alike for depicting vulgar, egocentric characters that verge on anti-Semitic stereotypes. Cahan repulsed such attacks by observing that his aim was to represent reality, that literature should reflect life, and that truth is not always attractive on the surface. "Will it not be well for this Nation," he asked some years later, "if strong, new, American writers arise who will dare to give us life—*real life*, with its comedy and its tragedy mingled—giving us what in my Russian day we called *the thrill of truth*?" (Ernest Poole, "Abraham Cahan," *Outlook*, Oct. 1911, p. 478). This *truth* informs Cahan's own fiction.

In *Yekl* Cahan shows how American freedom can corrupt an egoistic immigrant of weak character, such as Yekl, but can elevate a woman of virtue and inner strength, such as his wife Gitl, whose steadfastness enables her to transform the woe of desertion into a new life of love and opportunity. Likewise, Asriel Stroon in "The Imported Bridegroom" is a secularized Polish Jew who has lived in New York for twenty years when he suddenly craves to return to his Hebrew faith. Having no son of his own, Stroon imports a Talmudic prodigy from Poland as a prospective groom for his Americanized daughter, Flora, who rejects so anachronistic and unsophisticated a match. When the prodigy turns from the Talmud to secular knowledge, however, Flora marries him only to discover on their wedding day that he has fallen more in love with ideas than with her, leaving her completely desolate as the story closes.

Cahan's second novel, *The White Terror and the Red*, focuses on the radical underground in Russia during the early 1880s. More important than its contrived love story is Cahan's realistic depiction of radicalism and life in prerevolutionary Russia. Especially vivid is his representation of anti-Semitic rioting tacitly supported by the government. Although the social idealism of the radicals seems exaggerated, Cahan wrote elsewhere of the noble aims and spiritual investment that existed among the young revolutionaries, so in his view the portraits are not as romanticized as they may now appear.

After completing *The White Terror and the Red*, Cahan turned his attention to the *Forward*, not expecting to publish more fiction in English. But in 1912 he agreed to write a series of two articles on the successful Jewish businessman in America for *McClure's Magazine*; the two articles became instead a serialized novel in four installments, "The Autobiography of an American Jew: The Rise of David Levinsky" (Apr.–July 1913). Four years later an enlarged version was published as *The Rise of David Levinsky* (1917). It became Cahan's chef d'oeuvre, a work often considered the best novel written on the period of mass immigration to America from 1880 to 1924.

Cahan's last novel has the format of an autobiography narrated by a millionaire industrialist at the age of fifty-two. Though wealthy and influential, he is alienated because his life has been devoted to acquisition and conquest, to money, sex, and power. Consumed by self-pity Levinsky wants what he cannot gain: love and meaning. His ego, inflated to quell his basic insecurity, makes it impossible for him to realize such an aim; as he confesses in commencing his autobiography, his "inner identity" remains the same as before he emigrated from Russia decades earlier, and his life seems "devoid of significance."

Levinsky's narrative describes the growth of the ready-made clothing industry, from sweatshops and contractors to manufacturers, exposing the exploitation and chicanery rife at the time. Cahan's massive novel compares with Dreiser's Cowperwood trilogy and illustrates Social Darwinism in action, a philosophy to which Levinsky himself subscribes. It emphasizes alienation in a capitalistic, technological arena where money alone cannot bring fulfillment.

Cahan was an ardent, effective spokesman for his time. In journalism he advocated rapid acculturation and democratic socialism for Jewish immigrants so that they could gain social and economic stability in the New World. In literary criticism he promoted realism, essential and literal truth; and in English fiction, he represented that truth from his earliest stories through *The Rise of David Levinsky*. As H. L. Mencken said of Cahan: "It is a fine feat to write a first-rate novel, but it is also a fine feat to steer a great newspaper from success to success in difficult times. He has done both" (*Forward*, 23 Apr. 1993, p. 9).

• Cahan's papers are at the YIVO Institute for Jewish Research in New York City. His most important uncollected stories are listed in the Marovitz and Fried bibliography mentioned below; these include "The Apostate of Chego-Chegg," "Rabbi Eliezer's Christmas," "The Daughter of Reb Avrom Leib," "A Marriage by Proxy," "Dumitru and Sigrid," and "Tzinchadzi of the Catskills." In *Grandma Never Lived in America: The New Journalism of Abraham Cahan*, ed. Moses Rischin (1985), the anthology of ephemeral writings and Rischin's comprehensive introduction are superb. The first two volumes of Cahan's five-volume Yiddish autobiography, *Bleter fun mayn lebn* (1926–1931), are available in English as *The Education of Abraham Cahan*, trans. Leon Stein et al. (1969). Two critical books published exclusively on Cahan are Jules Chametzky, *From the Ghetto: The Fiction of Abraham Cahan* (1977); and Sanford E. Marovitz, *Abraham Cahan* (1996). Also essential are Theodore Marvin Pollock, "The Solitary Clarinetist: A Critical Biography of Abraham Cahan, 1860–1917" (Ph.D. diss., Columbia Univ., 1959); and Ronald Sanders, *The Downtown Jews: Portraits of an Immigrant Generation* (1969). Useful bibliographies are Ephim H. Jeshurin, *Abraham Cahan Bibliography* (1941); Marovitz and Lewis Fried, "Abraham Cahan (1860–1951): An Annotated Bibliography," *American Literary Realism, 1870–1910* 3 (1970): 196–243; and "Abraham Cahan: 1860–1951," in *Jewish American Fiction Writers: An Annotated Bibliography*, comp. and ed. Gloria L. Cronin, Blaine H. Hall, and Connie Lamb (1991).

SANFORD E. MAROVITZ

CAHILL, Holger (13 Jan. 1887–8 July 1960), author and curator, was born Sveinn Kristjan Bjarnarson, in Snifellsnessyslu, Iceland, the son of Björn Bjarnarson, a laborer, and Vigdis Bjarnadóttir. Cahill, however, later claimed he was born in St. Paul, Minnesota, in 1893. In the 1890s the Bjarnarsons emigrated to North Dakota, where they hoped to obtain land. Unable to purchase property, Björn worked as a hired hand. Vigdis, whom Cahill later described as a stern "peasant woman" with a poetic streak, and Björn, "a failure in almost everything he did," quarreled frequently, separating when Cahill was eleven. Struggling to support her son and his younger sister after Björn departed, Vigdis sent the boy to live with an Icelandic family on a nearby farm. After the family removed him from school, put him to work in the fields, and pressured him to be confirmed in the Lutheran church, he ran away. Settled with another family, Cahill finished high school and then set off for Canada, where he worked as a farm laborer and cowherder. By 1907 he was back in the United States, holding a job as a railroad clerk in St. Paul. While there, he later recalled that he read "Tolstoi by the acre" and took a correspondence course in journalism. This was followed by short stints as a watchman on a Great Lakes steamer and as an insurance salesman in Cleveland.

Anxious to pursue a career in writing, Cahill left for New York City on a freight train, his entire savings sewn into his underclothing. There he found a night job as a short-order cook and, in 1913, enrolled in writing classes at New York University. In one class, he met novelist Michael Gold, who hired Cahill as a reporter for the newspaper Gold was editing, the *Bronxville Review*. Having changed his Icelandic name, Cahill wrote and edited for several more small newspapers before concluding that he was not meant to be a journalist.

Cahill took a room in Greenwich Village, which was inhabited at that time by artists, writers, and radicals. He frequented local bars like the Hell Hole and the Working Girls' Home, where he and his friends gathered to drink and discuss art and socialism. Also, between 1915 and 1919 he took courses at Columbia University and between 1921 and 1924 at the New School for Social Research. He did not seek a degree and studied whatever interested him, mostly philosophy, economics, and other social sciences. During this time he encountered two professors—John Dewey and Thorstein Veblen—who helped mold his ideas about art. Like Dewey, Cahill came to believe that art must hold a significant place among "the activities, the objects, and the scenes of everyday life." Veblen's influence as well as a 1922 visit to some of the great folk art museums of Europe, such as the Nordiske in Sweden, opened his eyes to the perception of handicrafts as art.

In 1919 Cahill began to study art seriously on his own, although he also learned from artist friends. That same year he married Katherine Gridley, an art student from Detroit; they had one child. The couple lived in the same Greenwich Village building as John Sloan, who befriended Cahill. *Shadowland Magazine* offered to pay Cahill, by then a freelance writer, five cents a word to write on art. After Cahill wrote an article on Sloan, the painter hired him to publicize an exhibit of the Society of Independent Artists, of which Sloan was president. The inventive Cahill planted news stories about the ghost of a dead female artist who haunted the show and mysteriously placed one of her paintings in it, thus causing attendance to triple.

Impressed with his results, John Cotton Dana, director of the Newark Museum, commissioned Cahill to publicize one of the museum's exhibits and, in 1922, named him assistant director. Cahill built the museum's collection of contemporary American art, buying paintings by Max Weber, John Sloan, Robert Henri, and others. He organized the first major shows of American folk painting and sculpture: "American Primitives" (1930) and "American Folk Sculpture" (1931). He also found time to write a novel, *Profane Earth* (1927), and three biographies—*George O. "Pop" Hart* (1928), *Max Weber* (1930), and *A Yankee Adventurer: Frederick Townsend Ward* (1930).

Cahill's first marriage ended in divorce in 1927. At the Newark Museum, he met Dorothy Canning Miller, an apprentice at the museum, whom he married in 1938. She later recalled that he was "very gay and debonair," had "a wonderful sense of humor," and knew all the modern artists personally.

In 1931 Cahill left the Newark Museum to become director of exhibitions at the New York Museum of Modern Art, serving also as acting director in 1932 while Alfred H. Barr, Jr., was on leave. There he produced precedent-setting exhibitions and accompanying catalogs: "American Painting and Sculpture, 1862–1932," "American Folk Art" (based on the Abby Aldrich Rockefeller Collection, which he helped create and later installed at Colonial Williamsburg), and "American Sources of Modern Art" (Mayan, Aztec, and Incan). He also authored and/or edited other art books. In 1934 Cahill organized New York's First Municipal Art Exhibition at Rockefeller Center, and in 1939 he arranged the exhibit "American Art Today" at the New York World's Fair.

In 1935, Works Progress Administration director Harry Hopkins appointed Cahill to head the Federal Art Project, a work relief program designed to employ some 40,000 creative artists. From August of that year to the program's demise in 1943, Cahill's vision and administrative abilities shaped the FAP. While aiding destitute artists, he also encouraged new talents (including many African Americans and women) and increased awareness of and participation in art by groups of people who had barely been touched by it before. By 1943, more than 5,000 artists had been employed, including most of the painters who came to prominence in the 1940s, 1950s, and 1960s—Willem de Kooning, Jackson Pollock, Jacob Lawrence, Raphael Soyer, and Stuart Davis, to name but a few. As a result of their work, 2,500 murals adorned public buildings from Maine to California. Also, FAP artists produced 8,000 easel paintings, 11,000 prints, and numerous sculptures, many of which were included in traveling exhibits that circulated among the 103 Community Art Centers the WPA established, allowing people from Greenville, Mississippi, to Casper, Wyoming, to view the works of living Americans. At those community centers, as well as at settlement houses and schools, WPA art teachers instructed adults and children in painting, sculpting, potting, and print making. In keeping with Cahill's desire to explore the country's folk art traditions, the WPA hired former illustrators and commercial artists to create 22,000 plates for a massive *Index of American Design*.

Despite these successes, Cahill encountered frustrations that made him vow he would never again be involved with big government projects. In some states, politicians forced him to accept unsuitable and incompetent persons as FAP administrators. Conservative congressmen accused left-wing project artists of spreading Communist and/or New Deal propaganda through their art. Short-term and inadequate appropriations resulted in repeated layoffs of project personnel. When Cahill loyally followed orders from President Franklin D. Roosevelt and Hopkins to cut back on hiring, desperate artists denounced him.

Released from these burdens in 1943, Cahill turned his full attention to writing. In 1947 his novel about wartime Shanghai, *Look South to the Polar Star*, appeared; in 1950 he wrote the introduction to *The Index of American Design*; and in 1956 he published *The Shadow of My Hand*, a novel set on the Dakota prairie of his childhood. In 1957 Cahill received a Guggenheim Fellowship for creative writing. When he died at his summer home in Stockbridge, Massachusetts, he left an unfinished novel.

• "The Reminiscences of Holger Cahill," including an interview with his second wife, Dorothy Miller, are located in the Columbia University Oral History Collection. Some of his papers pertaining to the FAP are in "Federal Support of the Visual Arts: The New Deal and Now" at the Library of the National Collection of Fine Arts, Smithsonian Institution, Washington, D.C. Other works by Cahill besides those mentioned in the text include "Introduction," in *New Horizons in American Art*, ed. Cahill (1936); Alfred H. Barr, Jr., and Cahill, eds., *Art in America in Modern Times* (1934) and *Art in America: A Complete Survey* (1935); and "American Resources in the Arts," in *Art for the Millions*, ed. Francis V. O'Connor (1973), which also includes a brief biographical account. There is no biography, but a short biographical sketch can be found in Richard D. McKinzie, *The New Deal for Artists* (1973). See also William F. McDonald, *Federal Relief Administration and the Arts* (1969); Barbara Blumberg, *The New Deal and the Unemployed: The View from New York City* (1979); and Barbara Rose, *American Art since 1900: A Critical History* (1968). An obituary is in the *New York Times*, 9 July 1960.

BARBARA BLUMBERG

CAHILL, Marie (20 Dec. 1870–23 Aug. 1933), actress, was born in Brooklyn, New York, the daughter of Irish natives Richard Cahill, a brush manufacturer, and Marie Grogean. While the completeness of her education is uncertain, Cahill spent her childhood in parochial schools. Her Catholic upbringing shaped her career and her reputation as a reformer of show business morals.

At the age of sixteen Cahill made her theatrical debut at Harley Merry's Stock Company in *Kathleen Mavourean*. By age eighteen Cahill had made it to New York City playing in *C.O.D.* at the Eighth Street Theatre. She began playing in musical comedy that year in *The Tin Soldier* by Charles Hoyt. In the following years Cahill continued to play in New York, toured Europe, and appeared in popular favorites such as *Morocco Bound* (1894), *The Sporting Life* (1898), *Monte Carlo* (1898), *Three Little Lambs* (1899), and *Star and Garter* (1900). The theater at this time, largely dominated by the Syndicate, a producing organization that held a virtual monopoly of the roadhouses, did not invite innovation. The touring system encouraged stock character types and a stagnant repertoire.

Cahill's career took a dramatic turn in her favor when she sang "Nancy Brown" in *The Wild Rose* in 1902. The author of the song disliked her interpolations, but the audiences loved the rendition, and subsequently an entire musical was written around it. Along with another song, "Under the Bamboo Tree" from *Sally in Our Alley* (1902), Cahill performed "Nancy Brown" in her vaudeville act for years. Cahill opened *Nancy Brown* in 1903 and that same year married her business manager, Daniel V. Arthur. There is no record that the couple had any children. From this time on Cahill limited her roles to those comedy types similar to Nancy Brown, playing in *Moonshine* (1905), *Marrying Mary* (1906), *The Boys and Betty* (1908),

Judy Forgot (1910), *The Opera Ball* (1912), and *Ninety in the Shade* (1915). When asked why she wasted herself in musical comedy, Cahill replied that "comedy is the most difficult form of dramatic art. . . . Some players are funniest when they try to be serious. I succeed in being funny chiefly by studying people in real life and reproducing natural humor" ("A Serious Talk with a Funny Woman," p. 333). In this Cahill differed from other popular comediennes, who relied on exaggerated facial expressions and gestures. After 1915, although still popular in vaudeville, Cahill's musical comedy career waned as the popularity of theater as a whole declined. Competition with sports and the growing motion picture industry led to a commercialization of the theater. Cahill performed in a musical review, *Merry-Go-Round*, in 1927 and made her last appearance in 1930 as Mrs. Wentworth in *The New Yorkers*. She died in New York City.

Cahill had a specific agenda for the musical theater. In a 1906 interview she said:

> I have always wanted to make musical comedy something human. I wanted choruses that resembled ladies and gentlemen instead of imbeciles or automatons. I wanted to remove all suggestiveness from musical comedy. And I wanted the star, whether male or female, to be able to come out on the stage and sing a song without the need of gyrations and sounds from a chorus. Choruses look pretty and give motion to the piece, but a man singer worth while doesn't need them for a support when he comes on to sing. These are my ideals, and I hope to come nearer and nearer to them. ("A Serious Talk with a Funny Woman," p. x)

Cahill lost roles and sometimes seemed hard to work with because she clung to her moral values. When she was a young actress, a show that required her to wear tights proved a moral dilemma for Cahill. She consulted her family, and her mother told her to "wear them and put modesty into them." She often succeeded in making certain changes, however, for the chorus in her own shows always dressed conservatively. Cahill also wanted to establish a school for chorus girls to teach them how to get out of the chorus and into principal roles while simultaneously attempting to make the function of the chorus more decorous. Cahill's own popularity proved that suggestive costumes and gestures were not needed to win over the public. The theater in Cahill's time had acquired a limited repertoire intended to appeal to a mass audience. While new theater groups, such as the Provincetown Players, grew up to battle this commercialization from without, Cahill attempted her reform from within the genre of musical comedy itself.

• The Harvard Theatre Collection and the Frank Lenthall Collection contain a great deal of production information concerning Cahill. A number of contemporary articles chronicle parts of her life and career: in "If I Had Aladdin's Lamp" in the *Green Book Album*, vol. 1 (1909), she expresses her desire for better musical comedies; Ada Patterson, "Three Funny Women of the Stage," *Theatre Magazine*, May 1904, and "A Serious Talk with a Funny Woman," *Theatre Magazine*, Dec. 1906, look candidly at her concerns for the theater and her style of acting. Significant reviews of her performances and career can be found in *Cosmopolitan*, Jan. 1915; *Boston American*, 26 Jan. 1906; the *New York Dramatic Mirror*, 17 Feb. 1906; the *New York Times*, 24 Aug. 1933; William Winter, *American Stage of Today* (1916); and George Melborne, *Famous Players of Today* (1904). A collage of pictures of Cahill in various roles can be found in Daniel Blum, *Great Stars of the American Stage: A Pictorial Record* (1952). Her obituary is in the *New York Times*, 24 Aug. 1933.

MELISSA VICKERY-BAREFORD

CAHN, Edmond Nathaniel (17 Jan. 1906–9 Aug. 1964), lawyer, law teacher, and legal philosopher, was born in New Orleans, Louisiana, the son of Edgar Mayer Cahn, a prominent lawyer, and Minnie Sarah Cohen. He attended public schools and then Tulane University, from which he received a B.A. in 1925 and a J.D. in 1927.

After graduating from law school first in his class, Cahn moved to New York City, where he practiced law for the next twenty-three years. He specialized very successfully in trusts and estates and later in tax law. In 1930 he married Lenore Lebach; they had two children.

While in practice, Cahn regularly published articles on trusts, wills, and taxation and lectured in programs for practicing lawyers. In 1945 he agreed to become the first editor in chief of the *Tax Law Review*, sponsored by the New York University School of Law, which during his seven years as editor became the leading scholarly publication in the tax field. He accepted the post on the condition that NYU would allow him to teach jurisprudence and would not ask him to teach tax courses.

He became an assistant professor at NYU in 1946, associate professor in 1947, and full professor in 1948. He began writing on jurisprudence in 1945, and for the next nineteen years he produced, in addition to other publications, a yearly article on jurisprudence (later on constitutional theory) for NYU's *Annual Survey of American Law*.

His first and perhaps best book, *The Sense of Injustice*, appeared in 1949. Judge Jerome Frank, who later became his closest friend, hailed it in the *New York Times Book Review* (18 Dec. 1949) as "the most impelling discussion since Aristotle on the subject of justice." Cahn opposed the age-old tendency of lawyers and legal philosophers to overemphasize concepts and abstractions; he insisted that the purpose of law was to satisfy the needs of actual human beings, that a chief end of law was to promote justice, that justice was not a vague ideal but the concrete process of remedying injustice, and that the sense of injustice was an active force in the shaping of law.

In 1950 Cahn abandoned law practice completely in order to devote full time to scholarship. He was commissioned by the American Law Institute to write a survey of the interplay between law and morals in American court opinions. When a draft of the first section was condemned as "controversial," Cahn opted to complete the project on his own. This resulted in his second book, *The Moral Decision* (1955). It was aimed largely at a lay audience and sought to identify the ethical insights that American courts had developed through an examination of the moral drama and implications of actual judicial decisions. The poignant section of the book on "death" was written in 1954, when Cahn was ill with tuberculosis, facing a risky lung operation, and unsure of his own survival.

In 1955, on the strength of his first two books, Cahn was awarded the American Philosophical Society's Phillips Prize in Jurisprudence, which had been bestowed only eight times since the prize's inception in 1888.

At NYU Cahn was a notable teacher and, in effect, the school's master of ceremonies; he originated, planned, and moderated series after series of major public events. During the years 1948 to 1952 he arranged five annual conferences on the "Social Meaning of Legal Concepts." In 1950 he started a series called "Books for the Bar," which several times a year brought authors to the school for a panel discussion of their work. In 1953 he organized a conference on judicial review; the proceedings, edited by Cahn, were published as *Supreme Court and Supreme Law* (1954). He organized an "International Seminar on Constitutional Review" (1960) and the first four James Madison Lectures (1960–1963), delivered by Chief Justice Warren and Justices Black, Douglas, and Brennan, which were published in a volume Cahn edited, entitled *The Great Rights* (1963).

Cahn turned to writing on constitutional law in the early 1950s. He had been a staunch proponent of civil rights and became the leading academic supporter of the "liberal" decisions of the U.S. Supreme Court under Chief Justice Warren; they accorded with his own deeply held views about the importance of remembering the moral ends of law and not letting abstract concepts prevail over the needs of actual human beings. He became a close personal friend of half the members of the Court, especially Hugo Black, with whom he frequently corresponded.

Although uncomfortable joining groups, Cahn was for a time a member of the board of the Union for Democratic Action, the predecessor of Americans for Democratic Action. He later was active in the New York League to Abolish Capital Punishment and, shortly before his death, was elected to the national board of the American Civil Liberties Union.

Cahn was a Reform Jew who quoted from the Bible and Talmud, which he knew thoroughly (if only in translation), as readily as he quoted from Greek and Latin classics. He took a deep interest in legal developments in Israel and engaged in public correspondence with Prime Minister David Ben-Gurion about freedom of the press in Israel. The relationship between religion and the state, both in Israel and the United States, and the relationship between law and religion were predominant themes in his later writing. From 1960 on, he offered a course on "adjudicative ethics" at the Jewish Theological Seminary.

The last book he published during his lifetime was *The Predicament of Democratic Man* (1961). It explored the question of the extent to which citizens, who are supposed to be the source of political authority in a democracy, are therefore morally responsible for the misdeeds of their government.

Cahn died of a sudden heart attack in New York on the day he was to leave for a conference in Israel. He was working at the time of his death on a book to be called "The Meaning of Justice." Like his other work, it was intended to reach out beyond lawyers.

Cahn was an elegant prose stylist, a witty conversationalist, and a man of broad culture, humanity, and integrity. He combined a sharp complex mind with an intense passionate spirit and concern for the human consequences and repercussions of law. He was not a system-builder; he kept his distance from the dominant schools of legal philosophy such as positivism and natural law. His work has been largely eclipsed by more systematic and philosophically sophisticated theories about the relationship between morals and law that have been developed since his death. Nonetheless, it is a body of work of great beauty and insight and retains the power to inspire those who believe that law is and must be concerned with eliminating injustice.

• Cahn's papers are in the New York University law library; his extensive correspondence with Jerome Frank is in the Yale University Library; correspondence with Hugo Black and Irving Brant is in the Library of Congress. For memorial tributes and appreciations, see *New York University Law Review* 40 (1965): 207–84; this issue also contains a bibliography of Cahn's publications, as does Lenore L. Cahn, ed., *Confronting Injustice: The Edmond Cahn Reader* (1966), a collection of his articles and unpublished papers. An informative profile, "Edmond Cahn," is in *New York University Law Center Bulletin* (Winter 1960): 11–12. Extended appraisals appear in Paul Ramsey, *Nine Modern Moralists* (1962); Jay A. Sigler, "Edmond Cahn and the Search for Empirical Justice," *Villanova Law Review* 12 (1967): 235–50; Daniel Day Williams, "Law and Disorder: Some Reflections on the Political Philosophy of Edmond Cahn," in *Social Responsibility in an Age of Revolution*, ed. Louis Finkelstein (1971); and Bruce S. Ledewitz, "Edmond Cahn's Sense of Injustice: A Contemporary Reintroduction," *Journal of Law and Religion* 3 (1985): 277–330. For brief accounts of Cahn's place as a legal philosopher, see Thomas A. Cowan, "A Report on the Status of the Philosophy of Law in the United States," *Columbia Law Review* 50 (1950): 1097–98, and James Herget, *American Jurisprudence 1870–1970: A History* (1990).

EDWARD M. WISE

CAIN, James M. (1 July 1892–27 Oct. 1977), novelist and journalist, was born James Mallahan Cain in Annapolis, Maryland, the son of James William Cain, an English professor and college president, and Rose Mallahan, an opera singer. He graduated from Washington College in Chesterton, Maryland, at age seventeen in 1910. Cain held odd jobs and studied singing briefly in hopes of pursuing an opera career before he decided to become a writer in 1914. He returned to Washington College to teach English and math and earn a master's degree in drama (1917), while he tried unsuccessfully to publish short stories in magazines. He began his journalism career, which was to span six decades, in 1918 at the *Baltimore American* and the *Baltimore Sun*. At the *Sun* Cain became acquainted with his lifelong friend and mentor, H. L. Mencken, who later published many of Cain's short stories, sketches, and satiric dialogues in *American Mercury*. Mencken called Cain "the only author I ever knew who never wrote a bad article" (*Baltimore Sun*, 5 June 1946).

Cain interrupted his career at the *Sun* to serve in the U.S. Army during World War I, where he edited his company's newspaper and saw action in France. He returned to the *Sun* in 1919 and married Mary Rebekah Clough, a teacher, in 1920. They had no children. In 1923 Cain left the *Sun* to teach English and journalism at St. John's College in Annapolis, Maryland. He separated from Clough in 1923. Cain wrote editorials for Walter Lippmann at the *New York World* from 1924 to 1931. These editorials and the other pieces he was publishing in periodicals such as *Nation*, *Atlantic Monthly*, *American Mercury*, and *Saturday Evening Post* during this period consolidated his reputation as a witty commentator and biting social satirist. Many of these essays and dialogues were collected and published as *Our Government* (1930). In 1927 Cain divorced Clough, and that same year he married Elina Sjösted Tyszecka. They had no children. He was briefly managing editor of the *New Yorker* in 1931 before moving to Hollywood, where he was employed off and on as a screenwriter for various studios until 1948. Although largely a failure at screenwriting, he continued to write articles, syndicated columns, short stories, and the novels for which he is most famous.

Cain published his first novel, *The Postman Always Rings Twice* (1934), when he was forty-two years old. A popular—if controversial—success, it tells the story of California drifter Frank Chambers and Cora Papadakis, whose torrid and often violent love affair leads them to murder Cora's husband before turning against each other. It was successful in every imaginable medium—hardcover and paperback bestseller, syndication, play (which Cain wrote), and movie—although the book was banned in Canada and the film was delayed by difficulties with the Hays Office censors. Cain followed up with a serial in *Liberty*, "Double Indemnity" (1936), the story of an insurance salesman and his lover who kill her husband so they can collect the insurance money but find they no longer love each other after the murder is done. Ross Macdonald called *Postman* and "Double Indemnity" "a pair of native American masterpieces" (*New York Times*, 2 Mar. 1969). *Serenade* (1937), which recounts an affair between a Mexican prostitute and an opera singer, was similarly controversial not only for sex and violence but also for its representation of homosexuality. *Mildred Pierce* (1941), the story of a depression-era housewife turned restaurateur, recounts how one woman who makes it in a man's world is ultimately ruined by the machinations of her greedy daughter.

Although Cain was never a successful playwright or screenwriter, thirteen films were made from his novels and short stories. Among the best-known are Billy Wilder's *Double Indemnity* (1943), with Fred MacMurray, Barbara Stanwyck, and Edward G. Robinson; *Mildred Pierce* (1945), which won Joan Crawford an Academy Award; and *The Postman Always Rings Twice* (1946), with Lana Turner and John Garfield.

Cain divorced his second wife in 1942 and was married to his third, actress Aileen Pringle, from 1944 to 1947. In 1946–1947 Cain dedicated his energies to an ambitious plan to organize all writers who owned copyrights into what he called the American Authors' Authority. The authority would have been a central repository and trustee for its members' copyrights and a lobbying organization for their interests. The plan called for using collective action to enable writers to maintain control of their copyrights and subsidiary rights to reprints, film adaptations, and translations when negotiating with producers and publishers. The proposal for the authority was defeated by opposition from producers and publishers, by frictions between various professional organizations for writers, by the anti-Communist hysteria of the period, and by the conservatism of American authors, who preferred to see themselves as gentlemen of letters rather than as producers of a product that was both creative and commercial. Always an apolitical man, Cain was particularly mystified by repeated charges allying the Authors' Authority with the Communist party, explaining the very capitalist origins of the authority as follows: "It's simply a plan to enforce our own rights. It's not the principle we're interested in, it's the money" (Hoopes, *Cain*, p. 399).

In 1947 Cain married his fourth wife, opera singer Florence Macbeth Whitwell; they had no children. In 1948 they returned to Hyattsville, Maryland, where he remained, continuing to publish, until his death. Critics position Cain as one of the foremost exponents of the "hard-boiled" fiction of the 1930s and 1940s, a school of writing including works by Dashiell Hammett, Horace McCoy, and Raymond Chandler, which is characterized by terse, colloquial dialogue, minimalist prose, violent action, fast plotting, and a cynical, ironic, or even existential tone. Cain is particularly known for his first-person "low-life" narrators, for his use of the fictional confession as a form, and for the quality of his dialogue and the tightness of his prose.

Cain published eighteen novels, six magazine serials, and seventeen short stories. His books are translated into more than seventeen languages and have sold steadily for more than fifty years. Although undeniably popular, Cain's literary reputation has been the topic of much debate. His American contemporaries focused on the "trashy" nature of his writing. Edmund Wilson called Cain one of "the poets of the tabloid murder" (*New Republic*, 11 Nov. 1940), and James T. Farrell excoriated Cain for his "movietone realism," claiming that Cain's work was as shallow, commercial, and without redeeming social value as the films coming out of Hollywood at the time (*Literature and Moral-*

ity [1947]). The French, on the other hand, considered Cain the literary equal of William Faulkner, Ernest Hemingway, John Steinbeck, and John Dos Passos. He was read with respect by André Gide, Jean-Paul Sartre, and Albert Camus, who modeled his *The Stranger* on Cain's *Postman*. Cain, who had a horror of becoming "a writer with a message," did very little worrying about his reputation, preferring to describe himself as merely "a newspaperman who writes yarns on the side" (Hoopes, *Cain*, p. 549).

• Cain's papers are at the Library of Congress. His works not mentioned above include *Love's Lovely Counterfeit* (1942), *Three of a Kind* (1943), *Past All Dishonor* (1946), *Sinful Woman* (1947), *The Butterfly* (1947), *The Moth* (1948), *Jealous Woman* (1950), *Root of His Evil* (1951), *Galatea* (1953), *Mignon* (1962), *The Magician's Wife* (1965), *Rainbow's End* (1975), and *The Institute* (1976). For collections of Cain's journalism and short fiction, see Roy Hoopes, ed., *Sixty Years of Journalism by James M. Cain* (1985) and *The Baby in the Icebox and Other Short Fiction by James M. Cain* (1981). See Hoopes, *Cain: The Biography of James M. Cain* (1982; 2d ed., 1987), for a detailed account of Cain's life. Book-length studies are David Madden, *James M. Cain* (1970) and *Cain's Craft* (1985). See also Joyce Carol Oates, "Man under Sentence of Death: The Novels of James M. Cain," in *Tough Guy Writers of the Thirties*, ed. David Madden (1968). For information on the American Authors' Authority, see Richard Fine, *James M. Cain and the American Authors' Authority* (1992).

ERIN A. SMITH

CAIN, Richard Harvey (12 Apr. 1825–18 Jan. 1887), clergyman and politician, was born to free parents in Greenbriar County, Virginia (now West Virginia). In 1831 his family moved to Gallipolis, Ohio. Cain was educated at local schools and worked on an Ohio River steamboat before being licensed to preach in the Methodist Episcopal church in 1844. Complaining of racial discrimination in the church, he resigned and joined the African Methodist Episcopal church. Assigned a pulpit in Muscatine, Iowa, he was ordained a deacon in 1859. He returned to Ohio and in 1860 attended Wilberforce University. From 1861 to 1865 he served as pastor at Bridge Street Church in Brooklyn, New York, and was elevated to elder in 1862. He participated in the 1864 national black convention in Syracuse, New York, that advocated abolition, equality before the law, and universal manhood suffrage. He married Laura (maiden name unknown), and they adopted a daughter.

In 1865, following the Civil War, church leaders sent Cain to Charleston, South Carolina. He reorganized the Emanuel AME Church, which had been disbanded by white leaders in 1822 in the hysteria that accompanied the Denmark Vesey slave conspiracy. Under Cain's leadership it became the state's largest AME congregation by 1871. In 1866 he was appointed superintendent of the southern division of the AME Conference. He successively edited two Republican newspapers, the *South Carolina Leader* from 1866 to 1868 and the *Missionary Record* from 1868 to 1878. The *Missionary Record* was sponsored by the AME church and was influential in the state's black community. In 1865 he attended the Colored Peoples' Convention in Charleston where he wrote one of the documents published by the convention, "Address to the People of South Carolina." In the "Address" Cain called for "even-handed justice," the right of black men to vote, to have trials by jury, and to acquire homesteads. The "Address" also advocated abolition of the recently adopted black code, a series of measures designed to restrict blacks to menial and agricultural labor while sanctioning corporal punishment and imposing vagrancy and curfew laws that did not apply to whites.

Cain became one of South Carolina's leading political figures after Congress enacted Reconstruction legislation in 1867 that reestablished military authority over the southern states, granted black men the right to vote and hold political office, and disfranchised those who had supported the Confederacy. Active in the Republican party, he represented Charleston in the 1868 state constitutional convention. He was elected to the state senate in 1868. Although he was defeated for reelection in 1870, he was selected chair of the Republican party in Charleston from 1870 to 1871, and in 1872 he was elected to Congress as South Carolina's at-large representative, serving from 1873 to 1875. He did not run for reelection immediately but was elected again in 1876, serving from 1877 to 1879. He also served as president of the Enterprise Railroad Company, a corporation formed by black leaders in Charleston in 1870 to operate a horse-drawn streetcar line to haul freight between the South Carolina Railroad terminal and the wharves on the Cooper River. The railway did not prosper, and white businessmen took it over by 1873.

Cain was blunt, assertive, and sometimes inconsistent on issues that affected the destiny of black people. He persistently supported proposals to make land available to freedmen. At the 1868 constitutional convention he introduced a resolution to petition Congress for a $1 million loan to aid in the purchase of land, but Congress failed to act on it. In 1869 he supported the establishment of a state land commission and served as one of its agents. The commission, authorized to purchase land and redistribute it to landless blacks and whites, proved to be corrupt and ineffective. In 1871 Cain purchased 2,000 acres near Charleston, which were subdivided, named Lincolnville, and sold in 25-acre parcels. When Cain failed to make payments on the mortgage, and foreclosure proceedings were initiated, he was indicted for obtaining money under false pretenses. Because of a legal technicality he never came to trial. Though he promised to return money he had taken as payments for land, little was ever repaid.

His support for civil rights measures was more equivocal than his advocacy for land. In 1868 he opposed a civil rights bill in the state senate designed to prohibit discrimination in public facilities but strongly supported a similar measure in 1874 in the U.S. House saying, "We do not want any discrimination to be made. I do not ask for any legislation for the colored people of this country that is not applied to the white people of this country. All that we seek is equal laws, equal legislation, and equal rights throughout the length and breadth of this land."

Considered a political maverick, he alienated some Republicans and fellow blacks through his sharp attacks on northern white Republicans. In 1870 he joined other black leaders, including Robert De Large, Alonzo Ransier, and Martin R. Delany, in successfully demanding that white Republicans concede to black men a greater portion of major political offices. In 1871 he shocked and enraged Republicans when he supported the Democrats in the municipal election, arguing in the *Missionary Record* that black men should cooperate with whites. He also supported Martin Delany in 1871 in criticizing white Republican leaders who patronized light-skinned black leaders, and they condemned the brown men who acquiesced in the arrangement, thereby excluding darker black men from positions of power. He excoriated Republicans of both races for their constant conflicts over political patronage, which Cain insisted were destroying the Republican party.

In 1880 he was ordained a bishop in the AME church and presided over a district comprising Louisiana and Texas. He helped found and served as president of Paul Quinn College, an AME institution in Waco, Texas. Later he served as bishop of a district composed of New York, New Jersey, and Pennsylvania. He died at his residence in Washington, D.C.

Richard H. Cain was one of South Carolina's foremost Reconstruction leaders. As an AME minister, a newspaper editor, and a Republican politician, Cain was forceful and controversial in insisting that black people share in traditional American values through the right to participate in the political system and the opportunity to acquire land.

• Several letters from Cain are in the Governors' Papers in the South Carolina Department of Archives and History. Scattered issues of the *Missionary Record* are in the South Caroliniana Library at the University of South Carolina and the Harvard University Library. There is no biography. Pertinent information on his life and career is in Kenneth Mann, "Richard Harvey Cain, Congressman, Minister and Champion for Civil Rights," *Negro History Bulletin* 35 (Mar. 1972): 64–66; Joel Williamson, *After Slavery: The Negro in South Carolina during Reconstruction, 1861–1877* (1965); Maurine Christopher, *America's Black Congressmen* (1971); William J. Simmons, *Men of Mark: Eminent, Progressive and Rising* (1887); and Thomas Holt, *Black over White: Negro Political Leadership in South Carolina during Reconstruction* (1977).

WILLIAM C. HINE

CAIN, Stanley Adair (19 June 1902–1 Apr. 1995), educator, botanist, and ecologist, was born in Jefferson County, Indiana, the son of Oliver Ezra Cain and Lillian Whitsitt, farmers. He received his B.A. degree from Butler University in 1924, his M.A. from the University of Chicago in 1927, and his Ph.D. in botany from Chicago in 1930.

As early as 1927 Cain published a paper, "Airplane Photography and Ecological Mapping," in the *Proceedings of the Indiana Academy of Science*. This article described one of the earliest American uses of aerial photography to prepare a base map of natural vegetation. Cain himself took the photographs from a biplane and pieced them together to create a mosaic that was then verified by observation on the ground.

During the 1930s and 1940s Cain maintained his ecological approach, publishing papers on the vegetation of Indiana, the Great Smoky Mountains, Wyoming, Michigan, and New York. These botanically technical papers on plant ecology and geography established his reputation in the scientific community.

In 1940 Cain married Louise Gilbert. They had one son.

After World War II Cain's ecological interests broadened. In 1948 he participated in a panel on natural resources at the centennial meeting of the American Association for the Advancement of Science. In his talk, which was quoted on the front page of the *New York Times* (15 Sept. 1948), Cain warned that the natural resources on which life depended were "not quantitatively adequate to permit a continuing consumption at present world rates," so that humankind faced the dual problems "of the conservation of natural resources and the limitation of population or continuing along the path, with an accelerating rate, toward self-destruction." Thereafter, although Cain continued for some years to publish papers in the field of botany, he increasingly focused on the application of ecological thinking to the problems of humanity and human impact on the environment.

In 1950 Cain accepted a newly endowed chair at the University of Michigan. Previously, he had taught at Butler University (1924–1930), Indiana University (1933–1935), and the University of Tennessee (1935–1945) and had served as chief of the science section of the American Army University in Biarritz, France. He had also been a researcher at the Cranbrook Institute of Science, Bloomington Hills, Michigan (1946–1950). At the University of Michigan he founded the Department of Conservation—the first academic unit devoted to the study of the interrelationship between humans and the environment.

Cain adopted an interdisciplinary approach to environmental matters in his development of the Department of Conservation, of which he was chairman between 1950 and 1961. He wished to provide intellectual leadership for environmental reform by producing managers capable of integrating diverse competencies and resources to obtain solid solutions. Cain's outstanding reputation as a scholar attracted talented students to the program. His graduate students, numbering more than fifty, represented a significant contribution to the field of ecology; many went on to hold positions of leadership in government, industry, and higher education.

While at Michigan Cain became involved in wider public service. He was among those who saw the need for ecologists to transfer their expertise from the academy to government in order to incorporate the principles of ecology into public policies. In 1959 he accepted an appointment from Governor G. Mennen Williams of Michigan to the State Conservation Commission and served on that body for six years, two as chairman. During his tenure, the commission developed the first comprehensive natural resources department in any state.

In 1965 Cain left the Conservation Commission when he was appointed assistant secretary in the U.S. Department of Interior. He was responsible for the National Park Service, Bureau of Sport Fisheries and Wildlife, and Bureau of Commercial Fisheries. The first ecologist to hold a secretarial post in the federal government, he was credited with helping to reorient the Interior Department toward acting as the custodian of all the nation's resources, not merely those in the West, as had been traditional.

While assistant secretary, Cain delivered more than sixty major speeches throughout the United States and abroad, dealing with environmental issues. Because he believed it important to educate the public about conservation and the environment, Cain welcomed the opportunity to communicate with a wider audience.

Despite his many responsibilities as assistant secretary, Cain also served from 1966 to 1968 as chairman of the Committee on Multiple Use of the Coastal Zone, a section of the President's Marine Science Council. Dedicated to finding ways of securing a balance between preservation and development of the coastal zone, Cain guided the committee's analysis of the conflicting interests involved in this important segment of the environment. After stepping down as assistant secretary in 1968, he returned to Michigan, where he was director of the Institute for Environmental Quality from 1970 to 1972.

Cain retired from the University of Michigan in 1972 and was appointed to a planning commission that established the University of California, Santa Cruz's College VIII, which emphasized environmental studies. He also taught at Santa Cruz for the rest of the decade and contributed to the development of the school's undergraduate program in environmental studies.

Cain's environmental interests were not confined to the United States. In 1955, under contract to UNESCO, he spent a year in Brazil studying rainforest vegetation, with the objective of assisting the Brazilian Malarial Service in localizing mosquito control. He was also one of the five vice presidents of the International Biological Program between 1966 and 1968. He took part in numerous international conferences.

Over the course of a long career, Cain authored more than 130 articles. He also wrote two books: *Foundations of Plant Geography* (1944), which, when reissued in 1971, was judged by a reviewer in *Choice* (Dec. 1971) as a book that "should be on the personal bookshelf of every botanist"; and *Manual of Vegetation Analysis* (1959), written with G. M. de Oliveira Castro.

Cain received numerous honors. He was president of the Ecological Society of America (1958); vice president of the IX International Botanical Congress (1959); Conservationist of the Year, State of Michigan (1965); recipient of the Eminent Ecologist Award, Ecological Society of America (1969); a member of the National Academy of Sciences (1970–1975); and Benjamin Franklin Fellow of the Royal Society of Arts, London (1970–1975). He was given the Conservation Service Award of the Department of Interior (1976), and the Aldo Leopold Medal for Service to Wildlife Conservation, from the Wildlife Society (1975). Known among associates for his modesty and politeness, Cain died in Santa Cruz, California.

• Cain's correspondence and other materials are at the University of California, Santa Cruz. Useful obituaries are in the *Ann Arbor News* and the *Santa Cruz Sentinel*, both 2 Apr. 1995.

RICHARD HARMOND

CAJORI, Florian (28 Feb. 1859–14 Aug. 1930), mathematical historian, was born in St. Aignan (near Thusis), in the canton of Graubünden, Switzerland, the son of Georg Cajori, a well-known Swiss engineer and contractor who built bridges and highways, and Catherine Camenisch. The young Cajori attended school in Zillis and Chur, Switzerland, before coming to the United States in 1875. During 1876–1878 he attended the State Normal School in Whitewater, Wisconsin, and after graduation he taught in a country school before entering the University of Wisconsin. There Cajori received his B.S. in 1883 and then studied at the Johns Hopkins University (Jan. 1884–June 1985) before obtaining his M.S. in 1886 from the University of Wisconsin.

Cajori was an assistant professor of mathematics (1885–1887) and professor of applied mathematics (1887–1888) at Tulane University, and in 1894 that institution awarded him a Ph.D. Leaving New Orleans, Cajori settled in Colorado Springs, Colorado, where he served at Colorado College as professor of physics (1889–1898), professor of mathematics (1898–1918), and dean of the Department of Engineering (1903–1918). In 1918 he became professor of the history of mathematics at the University of California at Berkeley. The first such professorship in the United States, it was expressly created for him. Cajori held this position until his retirement in July 1929.

Cajori was a pioneer in the history of mathematics, and during his lifetime his research and scholarship was highly respected, as evidenced by the D.Sc. and three LL.D. honorary degrees awarded to him. During 1917–1918 he served as president of the Mathematical Association of America, and he was elected vice president of the American Association for the Advancement of Science (1923), the History of Science Society (1924–1925), and the Comité International d'Histoire des Sciences (1929–1930). Although he was not a research mathematician, in a 1903 poll conducted by *American Men of Science* of science leaders in America, he was rated thirty-first (out of eighty) in mathematics.

Cajori was a prolific writer, publishing papers, reviews, and a dozen or so books. The books were the most influential, and, apart from the textbooks *An Introduction to the Modern Theory of Equations* (1904) and *Elementary Algebra: First Year Course* (1915), written in collaboration with Letitia R. Odell, they were devoted to historical matters. Three of his books were especially noteworthy and enjoyed great popularity. *A History of Mathematics* (1894) was the first American book of its kind, and it literally pioneered the idea of a popular presentation of the subject in the nineteenth century. A revised edition appeared in 1919, and it is still of value in checking dates and sources. His *History of Mathematical Notations* (2 vols., 1928–1929) is simply monumental and remains unsurpassed in its detail and meticulous scholarship; it is generally regarded as Cajori's greatest contribution to the history of mathematics. Finally, his edition of Newton's *Principia* (published posthumously as *Sir Isaac Newton's "Mathematical Principles" of Natural Philosophy and His System of the World* [1934]) is unquestionably the most readily available rendition of this great work in the English language. Cajori intended to simplify the language and to replace obsolete expressions such as "reciprocally in the subduplicate ratio" with "inversely as the square root" in order to make this work more accessible to contemporary readers. Unfortunately, he did neither in an accurate and consistent manner. His "improved" language was based on a modernization of the 1729 Motte translation—without reference to Newton's Latin edition—and contains numerous errors and deviations from the original meaning. Likewise, his modernization of the technical language was incomplete and not entirely consistent. Hence, his presentation of Newton neither faithfully serves the modern reader nor the historian of science with regard to Newton's original thoughts. The edition was accompanied by a fifty-page appendix of critical and historical notes that is useful but hardly excuses Cajori's license with the book.

Throughout his lifetime Cajori's name was synonymous with the history of mathematics, and he was deservedly the American pioneer in the subject. This was due not only to his modest bearing but also to his kindness and personal charm. Largely because of the development of the subject and his edition of Newton's book, Cajori's reputation has somewhat faded among professionals. Yet notwithstanding this fact, it should not be forgotten that—particularly in the United States—he literally created the history of mathematics as an academic discipline worthy of study.

In 1890 Cajori had married Elizabeth G. Edwards of St. Louis; they had one son. In his later years Cajori's health began to fail, and in February 1930 he had a serious operation from which he did not fully recover. He died at his home in Berkeley.

• Cajori's books not mentioned above include *The Teaching and History of Mathematics in the United States* (1890), *A History of Elementary Mathematics with Hints on Methods of Teaching* (1896), *A History of Physics in Its Elementary Branches Including the Evolution of Physical Laboratories* (1899), *A History of the Logarithmic Slide Rule and Allied Instruments* (1909), *William Oughtred, a Great Seventeenth Century Teacher of Mathematics* (1916), *History of the Conception of Limits and Fluxions in Great Britain from Newton to Woodhouse* (1918), *Mathematics in Liberal Education: A Critical Examination of the Judgments of Prominent Men of the Ages* (1928), *Early Mathematical Sciences in North and South America* (1928), and *Checquered Career of Ferdinand Rudolph Hassler* (1929). The definitive obituary on Cajori appears in *Isis* 17 (Apr. 1932), and it contains a complete list of his almost 300 publications. Obituary notices are also in the *American Mathematical Monthly* 37 (Nov. 1930); the *Bulletin of the American Mathematical Society* 36 (Nov. 1930); and *Science* 72 (19 Sept. 1930).

JOSEPH D. ZUND

CALAMITY JANE (1 May 1852–1 Aug. 1903), legendary western woman, was born Martha Cannary in Princeton, Missouri, the daughter of Robert Cannary (also spelled Canary). Her mother's identity is unknown. In 1865, enticed by news from the Montana gold fields, her father moved the family to Virginia City, Montana. After her mother died in 1866, the family settled in Salt Lake City. Following her father's death in 1867, an adolescent but determined Calamity Jane traveled to Fort Bridger, Wyoming. From there she embarked upon the transient existence that would characterize her life in the West, especially in the Black Hills mining camps of South Dakota and Wyoming.

Although stories differ, some event resulting from her adventurous spirit earned her the nickname "Calamity Jane." It became an appropriate one because she seldom went unnoticed in public. Physically unattractive, stocky, independent-minded, and unrefined in the social graces, she did not fit the mold of Victorian womanhood. Most comfortable living in or near railroad camps, military forts, and mining towns, she liked to socialize with railroad workers, soldiers, miners, and cowboys. Menial jobs and prostitution probably kept her economic status just short of abject poverty. Wearing men's clothes, swearing, drinking, and shooting earned her a colorful reputation. What made her an endearing figure to some people was her extroverted personality, which, when heightened by her insatiable appetite for alcohol, could range from comic to riotous. Her revelries often were capped by some altercation with the law, usually on charges of drunkenness or public disturbance.

Calamity Jane was not devoid of virtue, however. In Deadwood, South Dakota, her favorite residence, the poor and sick occasionally received her unconditional sympathy and generosity. During the smallpox epidemic in 1878, at great risk to herself she consoled many people afflicted with the disease. Secondhand stories abound about other charitable actions, but to some newspaper editors and prominent citizens a long, dark shadow had been indelibly cast over her character.

Calamity Jane attempted several times to lead a settled life but found the regimen too confining. She reportedly had numerous common-law and two legitimate marriages. A popular allegation is that she married James "Wild Bill" Butler Hickok in 1876. That summer, during the Black Hills gold rush, she met Hickok at Fort Laramie, Wyoming, and accompanied him and three other people to Deadwood. From the time of their arrival to his death on 2 August 1876, she was frequently seen with him in town. Follow-up stories about an amorous affair coupled with a fraudulent diary have alleged that she gave birth to a daughter, whom she later left at a Catholic academy in Sturgis, South Dakota. These stories, which have been proven to be false, were an attempt to give Calamity Jane a flesh and blood legacy. According to her autobiography, she married Clinton Burk, a Black Hills hack driver, in 1885. The inscription "Mrs. M. E. Burke [*sic*]" beneath the words "Calamity Jane" on her headstone would seem to support her claim, but no official documentation has confirmed their union.

Calamity Jane achieved national renown when she was featured in Edward L. Wheeler's popular dime novels *Deadwood Dick, the Prince of the Road; or, The Black River of the Black Hills* (1877) and *Deadwood Dick on Deck; or, Calamity Jane, the Heroine of Whoop-Up* (1878) and in Mrs. William Loring's novel *Calamity Jane: A Story of the Black Hills* (1887). As a result of the popularity of these stories, the real and the fictional Calamity Jane became one in the public eye; in turn, she was credited with her fictional counterpart's extraordinary escapades, which included being an army scout, a teamster, a Pony Express rider, and a law officer. Calamity Jane perpetuated and profited from these tall stories in her autobiography, *Life and Adventures of Calamity Jane by Herself* (1896). She further developed her public image by performing as an unbridled western woman in 1896 with Kohl and Middleton, a Minneapolis amusement firm that operated dime museums, and in 1901 at the Pan-American Exposition in Buffalo, New York. She died two years later in Terry, South Dakota, from either "inflammation of the bowels" or alcoholism. She is buried next to Wild Bill Hickok in Mount Moriah Cemetery in Deadwood.

From the 1920s through the 1950s Calamity Jane's legend continued to be glamorized and romanticized in books and movies. In actuality, the bawdy atmosphere of saloons and the seamier sides of life appealed to her character. Her supporters either enjoyed her raucous nature or welcomed her caring and sympathetic spirit, regardless of her past. Her detractors wished she had exercised a modicum of self-respect and exhibited a more acceptable form of public behavior for a woman of her time.

• The best source of information about Calamity Jane is Roberta Beed Sollid, *Calamity Jane: A Study in Historical Criticism* (1958); the 1995 reprint contains a critique of books and motion pictures by Richard W. Etulain. Two good historiographical articles have been written by James D. McLaird, one as an introduction to the 1995 edition of Sollid's book, the other, "Calamity Jane: The Life and the Legend," *South Dakota History* 24 (Spring 1994): 1–18. McLaird examines the alleged diary in "Calamity Jane's Diary and Letters: Story of a Fraud," *Montana: Magazine of Western History* 45 (Autumn/Winter 1995): 20–35. For a copy of the diary, see Nolie Mumey, *Calamity Jane, 1852–1903: History of Her Life and Adventures in the West* (1950), pp. 84–126. An obituary is in the *Deadwood Pioneer-Times*, 2 Aug. 1903.

CARL V. HALLBERG

CALDER, Alexander (22 July 1898–11 Nov. 1976), sculptor, was born in Philadelphia, Pennsylvania, the son of Alexander Stirling Calder, a sculptor, and Nanette Lederer, a painter. Alexander "Sandy" Calder was the grandson of Alexander Milne Calder, who was known for his sculptural decoration of Philadelphia's City Hall, completed in 1886. Both of his parents attended the Pennsylvania Academy of the Fine Arts. His father was chief of sculpture for the last great Beaux-Arts sculptural exhibition, the Panama-Pacific Exposition held in San Francisco in 1915, and his mother continued to work as a portrait painter throughout her life.

Despite the influence of a family of artists who were reasonably successful at obtaining public commissions, young Calder was fascinated with science and technology rather than art. He attended Stevens Institute of Technology in Hoboken, New Jersey, from 1915 to 1919, earning a bachelor's degree in mechanical engineering. After holding a number of unsatisfactory positions in engineering, he enrolled at the Art Students League in New York City in 1923. The painter John Sloan was the greatest influence on Calder at the league, and he produced oil paintings of city scenes inspired by Sloan's work. Calder's drawings of this period show his quick mastery of illustration, the forte of many of his teachers, particularly Boardman Robinson. With a penchant for direct observation and a facility with pencil and pen, Calder gained a reputation among his fellow students. Classmate Clay Spohn recalled in his memoirs (Archives of American Art):

> [Calder] was one of the real characters there—very humorous, very funny—always joking and kidding around, never seeming to take anything seriously. He was always (or so it seemed) drawing pictures of circus animals. . . . Calder was one of the few persons at the League who was a threat to the dangerous over-seriousness of the academic group and instructors who were there at that time.

In 1924 Calder became a freelance artist for the *National Police Gazette*, contributing humorous sketches of sporting events and circus performances. His first illustrated book, *Animal Sketching*, published in 1926, was based on studies at the Bronx and Central Park zoos in New York City. In this small volume, Calder explained how to draw animals in motion. That year Calder also made his first trip to Paris, where he attended sketching classes at the Académie de la Grande Chaumière. While in Paris he made wood and wire animals with movable parts and also the first pieces of his miniature *Circus* (Whitney Museum of American Art, New York City). Performances of this magical, hand-operated circus helped to introduce Calder to the Parisian avant-garde and to potential patrons. Fun-loving, even hilarious in his mimicking of animal sounds, Calder became famous for his amusing parlor performances of the circus, which were later immortalized in a 1961 film, *Cirque Calder*. From 1926 to 1930 Calder continued to construct human figures, animals, and portrait heads in wire and carved similar subjects in wood. These amusing works, exhibited in New York City, Paris, and Berlin, gave him the reputation of a humorist.

After a visit to Piet Mondrian's studio in 1930, Calder began to experiment with abstract constructions. He was encouraged to join Abstraction-Création and became one of the few Americans to be actively involved with the artists' group. Although Calder claimed that his first visit to Mondrian's studio moved him to become an abstract artist, it was his friendship with Joan Miró and his involvement with artists of Abstraction-Création that helped sustain his initial creation of metal and wood constructions. Fashioning his first abstract sculptures in a city charged with artistic tensions between surrealists and constructivists, Calder synthesized the biomorphic panels of Miró and the fantastic biomorphs and personages of Jean Arp, Alberto Giacometti, and others. To these many artistic influences Calder added his mechanical ingenuity, his training as an engineer, and his fascination with popular science.

In 1931 Calder exhibited his first abstract constructions, which he called "universes," at the Galerie Percier in Paris. Because of his awareness of cosmic forms in the works of his contemporaries, such as Wassily Kandinsky and László Moholy-Nagy, at a time when astronomical discoveries continued to make headlines, it is not surprising to learn of his preoccupation with the cosmos. In 1930 the identification of the ninth planet, Pluto, was hailed as the major astronomical discovery of the century. Concurrently, new theories about the solar system continued to interest a worldwide audience. Although Calder does not specifically mention the exciting astronomical discoveries of the early 1930s, his drawings and constructions suggest a connection with them. A statement he later prepared concerning the basis of his abstract forms describes these works:

> I think at that time [1930] and practically ever since, the underlying sense of form in my work has been the system of the Universe, or part thereof. For that is a rather large model to work from. What I mean is the idea of detached bodies floating in space, of different sizes and densities, perhaps of different colors and temperatures, and surrounded and interlarded with wisps of gaseous condition, and some at rest, while others move in peculiar manners, seems to me the ideal source of form. I would have them deployed, some nearer together and some at immense distances. And great disparity among all of the qualities of these bodies, and their motions as well. ("What Abstract Art Means to Me," p. 8)

As the creator of the mobile, a sculptural composition of painted metal sheets cut into irregular shapes and suspended from wire rods, Calder was among a number of twentieth-century artists who explored kineticism in sculpture. For his first series of abstract constructions incorporating motion, Calder turned to a formula for moving elements he had used earlier. *Crank-Driven Mobile*, for example, is a variation on a system for kinetic sculpture he had developed as early as 1929; within a wire frame, he positioned two rotating abstract elements. The term "mobile" was offered by the celebrated Dada artist Marcel Duchamp in 1932 on his first visit to Calder's Paris studio. Thereafter, Calder's early kinetic constructions were referred to as mobiles or simply as "objects." After 1931 he exhibited kinetic constructions frequently in both Paris and New York City. In 1934 *A Universe* was acquired by the Museum of Modern Art in New York City. This work features an open sphere, which corresponds to the universe, supporting small wooden balls, which represent the planets. With such constructions Calder demonstrated his indebtedness to astronomical instruments of the past, including the armillary sphere and the eighteenth-century orrery. The mechanized orrery, which demonstrated the planets in orbit around the sun, was operated by hand or by clockwork. In addition, Calder used his knowledge of laboratory instruments from his training in kinetics at the Stevens Institute of Technology. In such works as *The White Frame* (Moderna Museet, Stockholm), 1934, he incorporates various types of motion: simple rotary motion, vertical motion, and periodic oscillation. The composition features the primary colors, geometric shapes, and basic categories of motion presented in elementary physics textbooks, all set within the boundaries of a white wooden frame.

Geometric forms dominated Calder's first mobiles, but biomorphic elements assumed greater importance after 1934. The sculptor refined his wind-driven mobiles in subsequent years to produce elegant, space-encompassing abstractions of gracefully bending wires. Calder remained fully committed to abstraction during the 1930s and was encouraged by European modernists, including Miró, Duchamp, Arp, and Fernand Léger. While his American contemporaries were only beginning to discover constructivism, Calder was holding solo exhibitions of his abstract constructions and drawings, both in the United States and in Europe.

In 1931 Calder married Louisa James, a grandniece of author Henry James; they had two children. In 1933 he bought a farm in Roxbury, Connecticut, and thereafter divided his time between visits to Europe and longer periods of residence in the United States.

Calder's artistic production of the 1930s included set designs and decor for modern dance performances. His "plastic interludes" were circles and spirals performing on an empty stage during the intermissions of Martha Graham's ballet *Horizons*. Calder also designed a mobile set for Erik Satie's symphonic drama, *Socrate*, performed in Hartford, Connecticut, in 1936. In his later years he created costumes and set designs for various ballets and theatrical productions.

In 1937 Calder constructed *Whale* (Museum of Modern Art), his first stabile, as he called his abstract constructions that did not move. That year he was also commissioned to design a mercury fountain for the Spanish Pavilion of the Paris Exposition. The result was an artistic and technical triumph. Positioned next to Pablo Picasso's *Guernica*, it successfully combined Calder's engineering skills with the inventive mobile and stabile forms to produce a compelling work with unique materials. Using mercury as part of a kinetic composition, the work was the first of several remarkable fountain sculptures by Calder. For the New York World's Fair of 1939, he designed an aquatic "ballet" as a fountain to be located outside the Consolidated Edison Company pavilion. The ballet was made up of five precisely timed "scenes" "performed" by fourteen jets of water that surged as high as forty feet. Bursts of water were to accent the ballet by falling back into the basin with an explosive sound. Although the ballet did not function properly, the project was the basis for a fountain commissioned in 1954 by Eero Saarinen for the General Motors Technical Center in Warren, Michigan, entitled *Ballet of the Seven Sisters*. This complex aquatic mobile was made up of jets of water that varied from slender vertical jets to rotating patterns and forceful streams.

Lobster Trap and Fish Tail, 1939, commissioned by the Museum of Modern Art for its new building designed by Edward Durell Stone, is an example of the delicate balance Calder achieved in his wind-driven mobiles, deploying various forms constructed of painted sheetmetal and wire.

The Museum of Modern Art held a major retrospective of Calder's work in 1943. Calder exhibited mobiles and stabiles as well as jewelry and toys. Later retrospective exhibitions included paintings, drawings, prints, book illustrations, and tapestries, all created with Calder's bold, abstract element in primary colors. During the 1940s he exhibited mobiles in Paris, Berne, Rio de Janeiro, and San Francisco. His mobiles were used in the ballet *Symphonic Variations*, produced in 1949 in Rio de Janeiro. During the 1950s Calder developed new forms of mobiles, including "Towers," wire constructions with moving elements attached to a wall, and "Gongs," sound mobiles. In 1952 Calder's work was selected for exhibition at the Venice Biennale, where it received first prize for sculpture.

Calder established a new studio in Saché, France, in 1954 and moved there with his family. He completed three major public commissions in 1958, including *Whirling Ear* for the Brussels World's Fair, *Spirale* for the UNESCO building in Paris, and *.125* for Idlewild (now Kennedy) International Airport in New York City. Large stabiles were exhibited at the Galerie Maeght, Paris, in 1959, and another stabile, *The City*, was purchased by the Museo de Bellas Artes, Caracas, in the following year.

After 1960 Calder received many commissions for public sculpture, both in the United States and Europe, most of which were for stabiles measuring forty to fifty feet in elevation. Calder's arching forms, dynamic surfaces, and biomorphic imagery were the appropriate complement to the geometric regularity and severity of modern architectural complexes. They encouraged pedestrian traffic beneath their curving elements and presented changing appearances from different vantage points. Calder's stabiles became something of a status symbol, indicating the substantial commitment of their patrons to public art.

Teodelapio, a stabile originally fabricated for an exhibition in Spoleto, Italy, in 1962, served as a monumental gateway to the city. Calder designed *Man* for the Montreal World's Fair in 1967 and *La Grande Vitesse* for Grand Rapids, Michigan, in 1969, the first work to be funded under the Works of Art in Public Places Program of the National Endowment for the Arts. The red *La Grande Vitesse* became a trademark of Grand Rapids and stimulated local interest in modern art, particularly in abstract sculpture. Stabiles of forty feet or more were installed in many cities and outside corporate headquarters. One of the finest examples is *Flamingo*, 1974, which was commissioned by the General Services Administration. Located outside federal office buildings designed by Mies van der Rohe at Federal Center Plaza in Chicago, the scarlet stabile provides a visual transition between human scale and the massive dimensions of the nearby skyscrapers. At the time of his death in New York City in 1976, Calder had recently completed a colossal stabile, *L'Araignée Rouge*, at the Rond Point de la Défense metro station in Paris. Two public commissions not completed until after his death are now located in Washington, D.C. An untitled mobile was installed in 1977 in the East Building of the National Gallery of Art. This mobile, measuring almost seventy-six feet across, fails to satisfy Calder's original intention for a composition of motions. Engineered with air vents in the vast atrium designed by I. M. Pei, the mobile describes a limited motion. Calder's other posthumous work is *Mountains and Clouds*, installed in 1985 in the recently completed Hart Senate Office Building at the U.S. Capitol. This work was unique in that it combined a motorized mobile with a large stabile. The ominous design, featuring a motif of black clouds descending upon massive, almost impenetrable "mountains," is in notable contrast to the buoyancy of his earlier stabiles.

As the first American artist to achieve international success for his constructivist/surrealist sculpture, Calder exerted a strong influence on younger artists committed to abstraction. Besides introducing the mobile and the stabile, Calder was one of the first American artists, along with David Smith, to explore the potential of the use of industrial materials in creating a personal aesthetic. His allusions to fantastic animal forms in brightly painted sheets of metal attracted the attention of sculptors interested in whimsical creatures in polychrome.

Calder holds art historical significance as the first American modernist to receive international acclaim and the first to create a major, wholly original mode of modern art. His legacy includes the use of kineticism by sculptors in Europe and the United States and the fascination with organic imagery in an abstract mode. Jean Tinguely, Harry Kramer, George Rickey, and others owed much to these early experiments. Calder also extended his creative expression to include not only the fine arts, but also household items, textile design, and stage designs and decor. His achievements are based not only on his mechanical ingenuity, but also on his brilliant fusion of the aesthetics of modernism with popular culture. His use of "found" materials and imagery derived from commercial products such as coffee cans and cigar boxes reveals his commitment to freedom of expression and his refusal to submit his creative spirit to the orthodoxy of any group.

As an American pioneer in monumental sculpture, Calder helped to revitalize the appearance of public commissions in the 1960s and 1970s. Playful but imposing, static but stimulating "street traffic" beneath their arches, Calder's stabiles are unprecedented works. Many sculptors have followed Calder's example, both in imagery and manner of execution. Colossal abstractions of industrial metals are now routinely produced by fabricators with the supervision of artists. Calder fused figuration and abstraction to create new forms, joining his knowledge of industrial materials with a vivid imagination for fantastic imagery. Calder will remain among the most creative and admired American sculptors of the twentieth century.

• The papers of Alexander Calder (including photographs, early catalogs, newspaper clippings, and articles) are in the Archives of American Art, Washington, D.C. His autobiography is *Calder: An Autobiography with Pictures* (1966). The artist's most useful statement about his work is "What Abstract Art Means to Me," *Museum of Modern Art Bulletin* 18 (Spring 1951): 8. A biography of the Calder family written by the sister of the sculptor is Margaret Calder Hayes, *Three Alexander Calders: A Family Memoir* (1977). See also the critical monograph, Joan M. Marter, *Alexander Calder* (1991), and Jean Lipman, *Calder's Universe* (1976). Amy Golden published a noteworthy obituary in *Art in America* 65 (Mar. 1977): 70–73.

JOAN MARTER

CALDER, Alexander Milne (23 Aug. 1846–14 June 1923), sculptor, was born in Aberdeen, Scotland, the son of Alexander Calder, a sculptor, and Margaret Milne. Calder moved to Edinburgh in 1864, and there he received his earliest training as a stonecutter under John Rhind. In 1867 Calder left for Paris and London. In Paris he was inspired by the ambitious public architecture of the Second Empire that was being erected everywhere. He found these buildings and their accompanying decorative programs to be instructional as well as aesthetically pleasing, a combination he would eventually strive for in his own work. In London he obtained a job working on the Albert Memorial, for which he portrayed in stone Queen Victoria's husband Albert lamenting. With a small amount of cash, Calder set sail from London in 1868 and immigrated to the United States. Although he landed in New York, it was during a visit to Philadelphia that he met the daughters of John Stirling, who had recently arrived from Glasgow. After a brief courtship he married Margaret Stirling in November 1869. During this period Calder became aware that sculptors were needed in Philadelphia, so the newly married couple decided to settle there. The next year they celebrated the birth of Alexander Stirling, the first of six children, who would himself pursue a successful career as a sculptor. In 1871 Alexander Milne Calder became an American citizen.

Calder had enrolled as a student of the Pennsylvania Academy of Fine Arts in 1868. At the academy he received instruction from the woodcarver and sculptor Joseph A. Bailly and the realist painter Thomas Eakins. In 1872 Calder was chosen by the architect John MacArthur to design and model the decorative groups planned for both the inside and the outside of Philadelphia's new city hall. Among more than 250 relief statues and group sculptures he completed for the project were four realistically depicted menacing eagles with hooked beaks and sharp talons that were to be placed over the entrances. Calder's works were highly acclaimed, and he was well represented at the Centennial Exhibition in 1876. Throughout his career he continued to make numerous historical, allegorical, and emblematic designs, often using wildlife such as otters, fish, snakes, bison, squirrels, and eagles in his compositions. In 1881 Calder entered the competition for the equestrian statue of *General George Meade* in Fairmount Park in Philadelphia, which he won and completed in 1887. Perhaps his best-known work is that of the colossal, 37-foot-high bronze statue of *William Penn* (1894), which rests on the dome of Philadelphia's city hall. When the statue was erected Calder watched helplessly from the ground as it was mounted in the wrong direction. Among his other works are portrait busts and figures, all rendered in a realistic style that emphasizes factual likeness.

Calder's career as a sculptor influenced both his son Alexander Stirling, who established a solid reputation as a sculptor whose works were executed in the romantic style, and his grandson Alexander, who became one of the most important sculptors of twentieth-century modernism and the inventor of the mobile. The three Calders represent 125 years of sculptural innovation and challenge in both the nineteenth and twentieth centuries. Alexander Milne's works were noted for their realism and symbolic language, while his son's romantic works emphasized mood and character, and his grandson led the vanguard movement toward abstraction in sculpture. The legacy that Alexander Milne Calder left to his progeny was the desire to create with passion uplifting works based on truth and beauty.

Calder's career flourished during the post–Civil War era, in which the demand for grand public sculpture grew. His mature style was noted for its monumental and rough-hewn realism, which was consistent with the prevailing taste for factual likeness. He remained in Philadelphia, where he continued to work for approximately twenty years on the decoration of the city hall and produced numerous allegorical figures for various locations. Calder died in Philadelphia.

• Information on Calder is limited and is confined to brief references in works on his son Alexander Stirling Calder and his grandson Alexander Calder. See also a brief summary in Jean Davidson, "Four Calders," *Art in America* 50 (Winter 1962): 69–73. The most comprehensive look at Calder's life and career is in Margaret Calder Hayes, *Three Alexander Calders: A Family Memoir* (1977), written by Alexander Calder's sister. The best source for images is F. Faust, *The City Hall, Philadelphia* (1879), which contains approximately 200 plates of both the interior and exterior of the building.

BRITT STEEN ZUÑIGA

CALDER, A. Stirling (11 Jan. 1870–6 Jan. 1945), sculptor, was born Alexander Stirling Calder in Philadelphia, Pennsylvania, the son of Alexander Milne Calder, a stonecutter who became a sculptor, and Margaret Stirling. Natives of Scotland, Calder's parents immigrated in 1868 to the United States, where the elder Calder found much success in Philadelphia, working on commemorative statues (he had worked on the Albert Memorial in London). As a boy Calder dreamed of a military career. After he was rejected by the U.S. Military Academy at West Point, however, he turned his attention to art. In 1885 he entered the Pennsylvania Academy of the Fine Arts, as his father had done, and studied under the realist painter and portraitist Thomas Eakins and his student Thomas Anshutz. In 1890 he left for Paris and studied for a year under Henri Chapu at the Académie Julian and then at the École des Beaux-Arts under Alexandre Falguière. Chapu and Falguière were two of France's most gifted sculptors and were talented portraitists in the naturalistic style. Calder eventually gained a reputation for grand architectural sculpture, yet he remained interested in portraiture that was realistic and informal, reflecting the combined influences of his French and American teachers.

In 1892 Calder returned to Philadelphia, where he began to model portrait busts and nudes. Recognition soon followed as he received the gold medal of the Philadelphia Art Club in 1893. In 1894 Calder won a commission to sculpt a portrait bust of Samuel Gross, the prominent Philadelphia surgeon, which immediately boosted Calder's financial situation. In February 1895 he married the painter Nanette Lederer, with whom he had studied at the Pennsylvania Academy of the Fine Arts. They had two children, one of whom, Alexander, became one of the foremost sculptors of the twentieth century. The couple left for Paris in 1895 and stayed for two years. When they returned to Philadelphia, portraits and figure studies occupied Calder for many years, during which time he also taught at the Pennsylvania Academy. Calder's appointment in 1904 to the St. Louis Exposition's advisory committee was instrumental in energizing his career as a sculptor, as was his receipt of a silver medal at the exposition. During this period he sculpted *The Man Club* (1901, Pennsylvania Academy of the Fine Arts), a portrait of his son that was a romantic interpretation of America's cultural roots. Other major works of this period are the *Sun Dial* in Fairmount Park, Philadelphia (1903), and the *Sewell Cross* (1905), a funerary monument for General William Joyce Sewell in Camden, New Jersey.

In 1905 Calder's health began to fail, causing him to move to a ranch sanatorium at Oracle, Arizona. He ceased work for more than a year. The family's subsequent move to Pasadena, California, was followed by a brief residence in New York from 1910 to 1913, during which time Calder taught at the National Academy of Design and later at the Art Students' League. While in New York he completed the bronze and marble architecture-sculpture *Henry Charles Lea Memorial* (1912; Laurel Hill Cemetery, Philadelphia), which proved to be one of Calder's most important works. By 1913, the year he was elected as academian at the National Academy, he had already begun work on a number of sculptures, including *Fountain of Energy* for San Francisco's Panama–Pacific Exposition in 1915; he eventually became head of its sculptural program. *Fountain of Energy*, which won the exposition's Designer's Medal, depicted the four oceans of the Earth, surmounted by a horseman, bearing Fame and Glory on his shoulders.

After Calder returned to New York in 1916, he received a number of commissions for monumental sculptures, among them the *Depew Memorial Fountain* (1917, Indianapolis, Ind.); the *Swann Memorial Fountain* (1924, Philadelphia); the *Leif Ericsson Memorial* (1932, donated to Reykjavík, Iceland), which won the gold medal of the Architectural League of New York; and *Tragedy and Comedy*, a monument to Shakespeare (1932, Philadelphia).

Although thoroughly wedded to the Beaux-Arts tradition in his devotion to classicism in art, Calder was one of the few sculptors of his day to combine aspects of the new modernism, which had been revealed to the American public at the Armory Show in 1913, with his later work. The full-length statue of *George Washington*, with the figures of Wisdom and Justice on each side of him, for New York City's Washington Square Arch (1918), for example, is modeled on the statue in the Virginia state capital by Jean-Antoine Houdon, characterized by a classicizing realism, but the somewhat flat and less realistic allegorical figures suggest a pseudomodern style through their references to cubism.

Calder also created informal nude studies that combine classicism with realism. He sculpted fine portraits of his friends and children and portraits of the social realist painters Robert Henri and George Bellows in addition to a study made for the planned monument to Walt Whitman. These works reveal Calder's technical mastery as well as his ability to achieve insightful portrayals of his sitters.

Deeply devoted to his work, Calder was described as introspective and moody. He preferred discussion of psychology and philosophy over social life and public appearances. He worked almost up until he died, continuing to sculpt in addition to serving on numerous art committees and organizations. Calder's last completed work was a bust of British prime minister Winston Churchill that was exhibited at Grand Central Galleries in New York in 1944. Calder died in New York City.

• Published biographical material is limited; some information is in *Who Was Who in America*, vol. 2 (1950). Nanette Calder edited a privately printed volume on her husband, *Thoughts of A. Stirling Calder on Art and Life* (1947). Other references are included in Alexander Calder (Calder's son), *Calder: An Autobiography with Pictures* (1966), and Wayne Craven, *Sculpture in America* (1968).

BRITT STEEN ZUÑIGA

CALDWELL, Anne (1867–23 Oct. 1936), librettist, lyricist, and playwright, was born in Boston, Massachusetts. Her father was a master of a Latin school in Boston, and her mother was a pianist (their names are not known). As a small child, Caldwell improvised words to the opera scores her mother played on the piano. She attended Friends Academy in New Bedford and public school in Fairhaven, Massachusetts. Her hope of a career as an opera singer was squelched by the toll taken on her voice when she toured with a juvenile opera company from the age of fourteen. She turned then to musical comedy and frequently performed in New York in shows like *The Tar and the Tartar* (1891). She left the stage in 1904 when she married James O'Dea, a writer of popular songs.

In those days, when Broadway musicals incorporated songs by many different composers, the O'Dea-Caldwell husband-and-wife songwriting team established a record of well-received numbers written for various musicals, for example, "Old Man Manhattan" for *The Social Whirl* (1906). Caldwell composed the music (with Manuel Klein) to her husband's lyrics for *Top o' the World* (1907) but then turned from composing to writing lyrics and librettos. With their royalties they built a mansion in Rockville Centre, Long Island. She later opened a taxicab garage called Acco across from the railway station there, because she was tired of "the verminy vehicles of incalculable age that transported her from the station to the handsome O'Dea Home" (*New York Star*, 6 Oct. 1916). O'Dea and Caldwell had two children.

In 1910 Caldwell wrote *The Nest Egg*, her first nonmusical play. The role of the lovable spinster Hetty Gandy was played by comedienne Zelda Sears, whose talent had originally inspired Caldwell's effort. According to the *New York Times* review (23 Nov. 1910), "[T]he little drama of misunderstandings . . . had the Bijou audience laughing almost steadily for two hours or more last night. [The play] is written quite frankly for laughs, and it certainly does get them. But there is a deal of shrewd philosophy and observation in the chief character, and in its essentials it is certainly American and real." However, Caldwell's next straight play, an Irish comedy, *Top o' the Mornin'* (1912), did not make it beyond out-of-town tryouts. She achieved success again with *When Claudia Smiles* (1914), a farce with songs, starring Blanche Ring.

Caldwell and O'Dea together wrote a farce, *Uncle Sam* (1911), and collaborated with others on *The Lady of the Slipper* (1912) and on *Chin Chin* (1914). O'Dea died suddenly of pneumonia before *Chin Chin* reached the stage; it was a project dear to his heart, for he had long wished to write songs for Montgomery and Stone, so Caldwell (who also wrote the book) saw it through to completion. The musical comedy extravaganza, combining circus elements, ragtime, and a Chinese setting, was the biggest hit of the season. Among the other musicals for which Caldwell wrote the book were *Go to It* (1916, with John E. Hazzard), *Jack O'Lantern* (1917, also lyrics, with Robert Hubber Thorne Burnside), *The Lady in Red* (1919, also lyrics), *The Sweetheart Shop* (1920, also lyrics), *Tip Top* (1920, also lyrics, with Burnside), *The Magnolia Lady* (1924, also lyrics), *Oh Please!* (1926, with Otto Harbach), *Take the Air* (1927, also lyrics, with Gene Buck), and *Three Cheers* (1928, also lyrics, with Burnside).

Some of her most popular work was done in collaboration with Jerome Kern: *She's a Good Fellow* (1919), *The Night Boat* (1920), *Hitchy-Koo, 1920* (1920), *Good Morning, Dearie* (1921), *The Bunch and Judy* (1922), *Stepping Stones* (1923), *The City Chap* (1925), and *Criss Cross* (1926). Perhaps her best-loved songs were "Ka-lu-a," "Blue Danube Blues," and "Every Girl" from *Good Morning, Dearie*; "Wait Till the Cows Come Home" from *Jack O'Lantern*; and "I Know That You Know" from *Oh, Please!*

Caldwell moved to Hollywood in 1931. Among the motion pictures she worked on were *Dixiana* (1932), *Babes in Toyland* (1933), and *Flying Down to Rio* (1934). She served as secretary of the World's Service Council of the Young Women's Christian Association. In 1920 she adopted Patrick, an orphan of whom her husband had been fond. She died at her home in Beverly Hills. Her *New York Times* obituary (24 Oct. 1936) quoted Gene Buck, the president of the American Society of Composers, Authors, and Publishers (ASCAP), who called her "America's leading woman librettist." Her work was described as "notable for its humor and tender sentiment."

• The Billy Rose Theatre Collection of the New York Public Library for the Performing Arts at Lincoln Center has a clippings file on Caldwell. She was the subject of two profiles by Ada Patterson in *The Theatre* (Mar. 1911, p. 90; June 1915, pp. 305–6). Besides reviews of her plays in the *New York Times*, there are assessments of her work in Gerald Bordman, *American Musical Theatre* (1978), and Samuel L. Leiter, *The Encyclopedia of the New York Stage, 1920–1930*, vol. 1 (1985).

FELICIA HARDISON LONDRÉ

CALDWELL, Captain Billy (17 Mar. 1780?–28 Sept. 1841), British Indian Department officer and business manager of Illinois Potawatomi Indian bands, was born near Fort Niagara, the son of William Caldwell, an officer in the British service, and a daughter of Rising Sun, a Mohawk.

In the decades following his death, Captain Billy Caldwell's life story was misrepresented by successive Chicago-area legend-makers. They converted him into a great "half-breed Potawatomi" chief and Tecumseh's personal secretary whose true Indian name was supposedly "Sagaunash" (in Potawatomi, *Sokonosh*). Actually, *Sokonosh* is the Potawatomi-Ojibwa word for an ethnic category, the English-speaking Canadians, and Caldwell identified himself as an Anglo-Irishman. His successive identities and career were products of and formed on several intercultural frontiers.

His birth resulted from a casual liaison between his father, Captain William Caldwell of Walter N. Butler's Loyalist ranger battalion, and a Mohawk woman at Butler's base near Niagara. When William was transferred to Detroit to help counter U.S. incursions, he deserted his firstborn son. As a result, Billy spent his early years among the refugee Mohawk, who after 1783 resettled on the Grand River at the head of Lake Ontario. There he came under the enduring patronage of the genial Daniel Claus and his son William, successive British deputy superintendents of Indian Affairs.

After the revolutionary war, William Caldwell settled in Detroit, married a prominent Métis woman, Suzanne Baby, and started building a family and estate. About 1789, William took Billy from his mother's village and incorporated him into his growing family as a bastard son who was a potential threat to his legitimate children's patrimony. Billy was given a "fair plain education" aimed at grooming him for a suitably dependent position as manager of the family's farm near Amherstburg, Canada West (in present-day Ontario). In 1797, Billy rebelled, immigrating into a third borderland, the Michigan-Illinois fur-trade frontier. There he became a clerk in the Thomas Forsyth–John Kinzie fur-trading partnership, began a lasting association with the Potawatomi, and married La Nanette, a Catholic woman from this tribe's powerful Fish Clan, the daughter of Wabinema (White Sturgeon) and the niece of Neshkotnemek (Mad Sturgeon). She soon died.

In 1811, Billy Caldwell had become chief clerk at the Forsyth-Kinzie post near Fort Dearborn. By then his second wife, local Indian trader Robert Forsyth's daughter from an Ojibwa woman, had also died, and he had remarried an unidentified Métis woman. He and his three wives produced some eight to ten children, none of whom survived him.

Because Caldwell had developed much influence among the fractious tribes around Lake Michigan, both U.S. and British authorities sought to enlist his loyalty for the coming War of 1812. Rejecting a lucrative offer from Governor William H. Harrison of the Indian Territory, he declared himself a "true Briton" and made his way to Fort Malden in Amherstburg seeking an army commission. By then a colonel of the militia, his father arranged commissions for his legitimate sons but spurned Billy's overtures for one. Billy eventually obtained a place as captain in the paramilitary Indian Service, serving throughout the war as liaison to and leader of detachments of Indian warriors, mainly Potawatomi. At the 1813 River Raisin fight, he suffered a near-fatal wound (his throat was cut by a wounded Kentucky officer whose life he was trying to save), and that same year he fought at Fort Stephenson and Moravian Town, among other battles.

As the War of 1812 drew to a close, Captain Billy Caldwell sought a permanent post for himself as superintendent of Indian Affairs for the Western (Detroit River) District, which made him a competitor with his father, who also wanted this important office. Billy initially failed in this endeavor, however, and William Caldwell was granted the appointment, with Billy as his assistant. He then successfully conspired to have his father deposed, with himself as replacement. But Billy proved inept at peacetime administrative duties and was himself discharged in 1816. Over the next four years, Caldwell hewed to his British loyalties, trying unsuccessfully to establish himself as a merchant. Only after his father's death in 1820, when he learned he had been disinherited, did he abandon his Canadian residence and British affiliation.

Caldwell then returned to the Chicago area, where he worked to gain acceptance as a loyal American "in trade" and a booster of postwar Chicago. Until then he had studiously avoided his Indian (i.e., Mohawk) heritage, identifying himself as Anglo-Irish and British or American. But inexorably he was drawn back into the "Indian business" through political-economic relationships with the Forsyths, Kinzies, and other influential Americans. They exploited his services and Indianness, securing his appointment in 1832 as an American-appointed Potawatomi "Indian chief" to aid them in negotiating treaties containing terms favorable to themselves. Caldwell played a more complex role, however, working also to serve the interests of the Potawatomi as well as his own. About his identification as an "Indian chief" he protested, writing his half brother William, "I will be a political Indian only insofar as it is of benefit to my Red brethren."

His relationships with the Chicago elite ended in 1833, when the last Potawatomi treaty ceded their remaining lands to the United States and obligated them to leave the Great Lakes area and resettle in western Iowa. There, on the Upper Missouri River "Indian barrier" frontier near Council Bluffs, Iowa, Captain Billy Caldwell died, ending his new career as business manager for the Potawatomi. Buried near his home, he was later reinterred (under a cold American racial stereotype) beneath a headstone reading simply "Indian Chief." Soon after his death, real Potawatomi chiefs left a memorial epitomizing what they thought of him by petitioning American authorities to have their official tribal name changed to the "Billy Caldwell Band of Potawatomi Indians." Using his name as a powerful symbol, they were signaling their continuing resistance to further land cessions and displacements.

• Most documentation concerning Caldwell's life is in the James A. Clifton Great Lakes–Ohio Valley Ethnohistory Archive, Waldo Library, Western Michigan University. Extensive bibliographies are in James A. Clifton, "Merchant, Soldier, Broker, Chief," *Illinois State Historical Society Journal* 71 (1978): 185–210, and "Personal and Ethnic Identity on the Great Lakes Frontier," *Ethnohistory* 25 (1978): 69–94. The most important manuscript sources are BL, Add. Mss 21885: 121; RG 10, A1, 4, and A2, 28, 30–34; and, the Caldwell Papers, MG 24, B147, Public Archives of Canada; Chicago Historical Society; and the Lyman Draper Collections, State Historical Society of Wisconsin. Much additional documentation is contained in the Chicago-area Potawatomi files of RG 75, National Archives.

JAMES A. CLIFTON

CALDWELL, Charles (14 May 1772–9 July 1853), physician, author, and teacher, was born in Caswell County, North Carolina, the son of Charles Caldwell, a farmer. His mother's maiden name was Murray, although her given name is unknown. Caldwell's father was an elder in the Presbyterian church and wanted Charles to become a minister. Accordingly, from the age of eleven to fourteen, Caldwell studied Latin and classical literature at a Latin school operated by Dominie Harris in Mecklenburg County. By the time Caldwell left Harris's school, however, he had decided against a religious career.

Having lost his parents by age fifteen, Caldwell could not afford to attend a college in the North as he had intended. Accepting an offer around 1786 to take charge of the Snow Creek Seminary grammar school near Bushy Mountains, North Carolina, he taught many pupils older than himself. After two years, Caldwell moved to another school, the Center Institute, near Salisbury, North Carolina, where he taught and read extensively in history, biography, travel, poetry, anthropology, and religion. Two years later, he picked medicine as a career, primarily because his father had adamantly opposed Caldwell's first two choices, the military and the law.

In 1791 Caldwell studied medicine as an apprentice under Dr. Harris, a brother of his schoolteacher, in Salisbury. Disappointed in his preceptor, Caldwell traveled to Philadelphia and in 1792 matriculated in the Medical Department of the University of Pennsylvania. In 1793, while he was a student at the university, a deadly yellow fever epidemic broke out in the city. Caldwell, who volunteered his services at the Bush Hill Hospital during the epidemic, supported Benjamin Rush's heroic regimen of bleeding and purging yellow fever patients. Caldwell and Rush became close friends, and at the latter's behest Caldwell translated and edited J. Frederick Blumenbach's *Elements of Physiology* (1795) from the original Latin.

Mentally and physically exhausted by his medical studies, yellow fever experience, and translation efforts, Caldwell in 1794 accepted the post of surgeon in a brigade of volunteers that joined President George Washington's expedition to put an end to the Whiskey Rebellion. Two years later, he received an M.D. from the University of Pennsylvania. In the defense of his thesis on *An Attempt to Establish the Original Sameness of Three Phenomena of Fever* (1796), which, according to his autobiography, was partly suppressed by the medical faculty, Caldwell attacked Rush and some of his teachings. This incident severed temporarily the close relationship that had developed between the two men. The two men renewed their friendship near the end of Rush's life, and Caldwell wrote a memoir of Rush for *Port Folio* after the latter's death in 1813.

An excellent horseman and a skilled fencer, the 6′2″ Caldwell presented an imposing figure. He was most proud of his oratorical skills, which he practiced continuously in front of a mirror. Enjoying the sound of his own voice and convinced of the righteousness of his own views, Caldwell relished debate and controversy. Extremely ambitious, pompous, vain, and possessing a colossal ego, Caldwell had few close friends. Reclusive when not engaged in debate or argument, Caldwell alienated many of his professional colleagues. Anyone who questioned his views became a recipient of vitriolic attacks. Caldwell believed that his vicious review—of which he was quite proud—of the second edition of Samuel Stanhope Smith's *Essay on the Causes of the Variety of Complexion and the Figure in the Human Species* (1810) was instrumental in causing the Presbyterian clergyman's death.

Although Caldwell's personality and his personal attacks on Rush ensured that he would never realize his dream of teaching medicine at the University of Pennsylvania, Caldwell remained in Philadelphia until 1819, waiting for an offer that would never be made. After graduating from medical school, he commenced private practice. When a yellow fever epidemic broke out in the city in 1797, Caldwell again supported Rush's therapeutics and sided with his enemy in espousing the fever's domestic origin and its noncontagiousness. Accordingly, Caldwell joined the Academy of Medicine (formed in 1798 to oppose the College of Physicians of Philadelphia, which stood against the views espoused by Rush and his followers). A member of the city board of health, the Philadelphia Medical Society, and the American Philosophical Society, Caldwell was also a member of the College of Physicians of Philadelphia but was stripped of his fellowship in 1803 because of nonpayment of dues. From 1805 to 1811 Caldwell delivered clinical lectures at the Philadelphia Almshouse, and in 1810 and 1811 he offered one of the country's first private courses on medical jurisprudence. In 1799 Caldwell married Elizabeth Leaming; they had one child.

In 1815 the University of Pennsylvania created a new department called the Faculty of Natural Sciences. Having sought and been offered the appointment as professor of geology and philosophy of natural history, Caldwell delivered three courses from 1816 through 1819. This was the only appointment he ever received from the university. Embittered by what he considered unfair treatment by the school's medical faculty, Caldwell looked elsewhere for teaching opportunities and in 1819 accepted the chair of the institutes of medicine at Transylvania University in Lexington, Kentucky.

Caldwell gave up private practice and devoted all his efforts to reorganizing the moribund program at Transylvania. Appalled at the university's lack of books and facilities, Caldwell successfully lobbied the state legislature for funding. He not only toured the country to promote the school, but in 1821 he traveled to Europe to purchase books and instruments for the faculty and students. In 1821 he met Franz Joseph Gall in Paris and became a convert to phrenology. Through Caldwell's efforts Transylvania University soon had one of the leading medical schools in the West and owned one of the finest libraries in the country. Caldwell was dismissed from Transylvania in 1837, however, after leading an unsuccessful effort to have the school moved from Lexington to Louisville.

Joining the faculty of the Medical Institute of the City of Louisville in 1837, Caldwell worked tirelessly to build up the program. Besides teaching at the institute and offering clinical lectures, he raised funds from the state and the city council, recruited students, established an affiliation with a local hospital, and traveled to Europe to acquire books for a library and artifacts for a museum. As he had done in Lexington, Caldwell built up within a few years a strong program in Louisville. In 1849 the board of managers, citing Caldwell's advanced age, discharged the 77-year-old professor. Naturally, the indignant Caldwell suspected a conspiracy.

Caldwell was a prolific author. According to one of his biographers, Caldwell's many works amounted to more than 10,000 printed pages. Besides his translation of Blumenbach, Caldwell translated American editions of Jean Senac's *Treatise on the Hidden Nature, and the Treatment of Intermitting and Remitting Fevers* (1805), J. L. Alibert's *Treatise on Malignant Intermittents* (1807), and Pierre-Joseph Desault's *Treatise on Fractures, Luxations, and Other Affections of the Bones* (1811), and he edited an 1816 American issue of William Cullen's *First Lines in the Practice of Physic*, which included a critical review of Rush's theories. While his publications on febrile miasms and quarantine won for him two Boylston Prizes (awarded annually by Harvard's medical school) in 1830 and 1835, the medical profession tended to ignore the scores of verbose and self-serving works he produced.

A strong proponent of phrenology, Caldwell's *Elements of Phrenology*, published in 1824, became the first American work on the subject. His *Facts in Mesmerism* (1842) defended mesmerism and its value to medicine. Caldwell's *Essays on Malaria and Temperament* (1831), *A Discourse on the Vice of Gambling* (1835), and *Thoughts on the Original Unity of the Human Race* (1830) reflected his diverse interests as well as the variety of his publications. Besides medicine, Caldwell wrote on belles lettres, fine arts, biography, history, ethnology, and religion. In 1814 he succeeded Nicholas Biddle as editor of *Port Folio* and was a frequent contributor to that literary magazine. After divorcing his wife, who died in 1834, Caldwell married in 1842 Mary Warner Barton; they had no children.

Caldwell is best remembered for his *Autobiography*, which was edited by his sister-in-law Harriet W. Warner and published two years after his death. A chronicle of the many battles he claimed to have fought on the side of truth, the work is full of defamatory remarks about his enemies, both real and imagined, and unsubstantiated assertions concerning his own career. Caldwell's personality, though controversial, should not detract from the recognition of his indefatigable efforts to establish strong educational programs at the medical schools of Transylvania University and Louisville. He died in Louisville.

• No sizable collection of Caldwell's personal papers has been located. His account and ledger books from 1798 to 1816 are owned by the Historical Society of Pennsylvania. Besides those mentioned in the text, Caldwell's important publications include *Semi-annual Oration, on the Origin of Pestilential Diseases, Delivered before the Academy of Medicine of Philadelphia, on the 17th Day of December 1798* (1799); *An Anniversary Oration on the Subject of Quarantines, Delivered to the Philadelphia Medical Society on the 21st of January, 1807* (1807); *Outlines of a Course of Lectures on the Institutes of Medicine* (1823); *Medical and Physical Memoirs*, 2 vols. (1826; 1827); "Thoughts on Febrile Miasms, Intended as an Answer to the Boylston Medical Prize Question, for the Year 1830, 'Whether Fever Is Produced by Decomposition of Animal or Vegetable Substances, and If by Both, Their Comparative Influence?'" *Transylvania Journal of Medicine and the Associated Sciences* 3 (1830): 457–519; and *Thoughts on Quarantine and Other Sanitary Systems, Being an Essay Which Received the Prize of the Boylston Medical Committee, of Harvard University, in August 1834* (1834). B. H. Coates, *Biographical Notice of Charles Caldwell, M.D.* (1855); *Medical Examiner*, n.s., 11 (1855): 211–26; *American Medical Monthly* 5 (1856): 241–84; Lunsford P. Yandell, "Medical Literature of Kentucky," *Transactions of the Kentucky State Medical Society* (1876): 38–66; and Caldwell's *Autobiography* (1855), are the best contemporary sources for information on Caldwell's life and career. Also useful are William Shainline Middleton, "Charles Caldwell, A Biographical Sketch," *Annals of Medical History* 3 (1921): 156–78; Emmet F. Horine, *Biographical Sketch and Guide to the Writings of Charles Caldwell, M.D. (1772–1853)* (1960); and Lloyd G. Stevenson's introduction to the *Autobiography of Charles Caldwell, M.D.* (1968), pp. v–xxvi.

THOMAS A. HORROCKS

CALDWELL, David (22 Mar. 1725–25 Aug. 1824), Presbyterian minister, self-trained physician, and schoolmaster, was born in Lancaster County, Pennsylvania, the son of Andrew Caldwell and Ann Stewart, farmers. At the age of seventeen Caldwell became a carpenter's apprentice and four years later a journeyman carpenter. At age twenty-five he experienced a religious conversion and a call to the ministry. He studied at the Reverend Robert Smith's academy from 1750 to around 1756 and then taught at the school. The date of his enrollment in the College of New Jersey (now Princeton University) is not known, but he graduated in 1761.

After graduation Caldwell taught school in Cape May, New Jersey, for a year and then studied theology with Princeton president Samuel Finley. The New Brunswick Presytery licensed him on 8 June 1763 and assigned him as a missionary in North Carolina for a year of probationary preaching. The New Brunswick Presbytery ordained Caldwell on 6 July 1765. The next year he married Rachel Craighead; they had nine children. In 1767 he accepted calls from two North Carolina Presbyterian congregations, Buffalo (a New Side congregation) and Alamance (Old Side). To augment his income, he opened an academy and studied and practiced medicine.

During the Regulator uprising, a frontier rebellion against oppressive low-country North Carolina officialdom, Caldwell assured Governor William Tryon of Presbyterian loyalty and admonished his parishioners to rely on peaceful remonstrance. Prior to the battle of Alamance between provincial troops under Tryon's command and two thousand armed Regulators, Caldwell tried, without success, to mediate the dispute. As a regional correspondent for the Wilmington, North Carolina, newspaper, the *Cape Fear Mercury*, he followed closely the events of the prerevolutionary controversy. In the spring of 1776 he repeatedly preached a sermon, "The Character and Doom of the Sluggard," which made a comprehensive moral and psychological case for American resistance.

Throughout the war Caldwell was a leader of the patriot community in Guilford County. His neighbors elected him a delegate to the Fifth Provincial Convention, which met in November 1776 to draft North Carolina's first state constitution. He served on the committee and probably helped frame provisions that barred clergymen from the legislature and required state-level officeholders to affirm the truths of the Protestant religion.

When General Charles Cornwallis invaded the state in the spring of 1781 and spawned partisan war between patriot and Loyalist civilians, Caldwell became a marked man and went into hiding. At one point Rachel Caldwell whisked a patriot courier out the back door of the Caldwell house and hid him in the branches of a nearby locust tree just as British troops came in the front door. Loyalist forces later burned the house after making a bonfire of Caldwell's books and papers. Caldwell's amateur work as a country doctor was widely respected, and during 16–18 March 1781, following the battle of Guilford Courthouse, he worked around the clock caring for Nathanael Greene's wounded troops and performing numerous amputations.

A staunch Antifederalist in 1788, Caldwell was a delegate to the convention in Hillsborough that voted not to ratify the federal Constitution. He insisted that the proposed Constitution be judged solely according to six "maxims" or "fundamental principles of every free government," a mix of Lockean and republican notions. This stance threw the Federalists in the convention on the defensive and contributed to their defeat in Hillsborough, although Caldwell played no further prominent role in the convention's debates.

Throughout his ministry in North Carolina, Caldwell taught young men who came to him for instruction. After the Revolution, he built a log school near his house, where as many as twenty students at a time may have been in residence. His wife and his four oldest sons served as tutors. Modeled on the College of New Jersey and preparatory schools operated by Presbyterians in the middle colonies, Caldwell's school taught Latin, Greek, Hebrew, mathematics, and moral philosophy, using John Witherspoon's Princeton lectures as a text.

Like Witherspoon, Caldwell was a theological moderate, not in the sense that he shunned controversy but in the sense that he maintained allegiance to diverging theological and philosophical positions. Influenced by the pioneer North Carolina Presbyterian minister Hugh McAden, who preached at Caldwell's installation service at the Buffalo Church, Caldwell sought to reconcile Old Side and New Side Presbyterians. He acknowledged the New Side belief that a mutual compact between the pastor and parishioners should govern a church while at the same time adhering in practice to the Old Side way of a minister ruling his flock. During the Great Revival of 1801, Caldwell characteristically appreciated but also sought to restrain camp meeting enthusiasm.

Typical of Caldwell's moderation was his role in a theological dispute sometime during the 1790s over the doctrine of universal salvation, which had been preached in the bounds of the presbytery by the Reverend Robert Alexander, an articulate young Princeton graduate. Caldwell's gentle rejoinder to Alexander appealed to Scripture, the classics, and the laity's own common sense in maintaining that salvation could not be an indiscriminate divine act nor could it be unrelated to personal character and religious commitment.

Three of Caldwell's children suffered in adulthood from debilitating mental illness, draining his energy and deepening his insight into human nature during his later years. Actively involved in teaching well into his eighties, Caldwell died in Guilford County, North Carolina.

• Papers relating to Caldwell are in the records of the Buffalo Presbyterian Church, Greensboro, N.C., and in the Eli Caruthers Papers at Duke University. The major source on Caldwell is Eli Caruthers, *A Sketch of the Life and Character of the Reverend David Caldwell* (1842). Mark F. Miller, "David Caldwell: The Forming of a Southern Educator" (Ph.D. diss., Univ. of North Carolina at Chapel Hill, 1979), tracks down nearly all of the additional surviving data and demonstrates where Caruthers can be accepted and where he must be used with caution. Robert M. Calhoon, *Evangelicals and Conservatives in the Early South, 1740–1861* (1988), and Alice M. Baldwin, "Sowers of Sedition," *William and Mary Quarterly* 5 (1948): 52–76, discuss Caldwell's contribution to revolutionary ideology.

ROBERT M. CALHOON

CALDWELL, Erskine (17 Dec. 1903–11 Apr. 1987), writer, was born Erskine Preston Caldwell in White Oak, Coweta County, Georgia, the son of Ira Sylvester Caldwell, a minister, and Caroline Bell, a teacher. Caldwell much later believed that being brought up as a minister's son in the Deep South was "my good fortune in life," for his family's frequent moves to different congregations in the region gave him an intimate knowledge of the people, localities, and ways of life that would inform his fiction and documentary writing. As a youth he observed, with his father's active encouragement, the "antics and motivations" of the southern poor in their pursuit of material and spiritual satisfaction. He noted the quirks of sexual, social, and race relationships in the world around him and listened avidly to stories told in his family and community. Eventually he decided that his main goal in life was to become a storyteller himself.

Caldwell attended Erskine College, in South Carolina, and also took courses at the University of Virginia and the University of Pennsylvania between 1920 and 1925. He served a more practical apprenticeship to writing as a newspaper reporter for the *Atlanta Journal*; as a book reviewer for the *Journal*, the *Houston Post*, and the Charlotte (N.C.) *Observer*; and by practicing his craft in scores of essays, poems, jokes, stories, and novels, which he submitted, largely unsuccessfully, for publication during the late 1920s. In 1925 he married Helen Lannigan, with whom he later had two sons and a daughter. His first novel, *The Bastard*, was published in 1929, followed by a second, *Poor Fool*, in 1930; but later he preferred to acknowledge the short story collection *American Earth* (1931) as his first book. The stories in this collection, many of which first appeared in little experimental magazines, revealed many of the qualities and preoccupations that would characterize Caldwell's later writing: a grimly deterministic view of human existence qualified by a burlesque sense of its absurdity; a keen interest in the manipulation of power between men and women, whites and blacks, rich and poor; a considerable disposition toward vulgar comedy and gothic violence; and a starkly simple prose style that depended for its impact on startling patterns of imagery and choral repetitions.

With his next two novels, *Tobacco Road* (1932) and *God's Little Acre* (1933), Caldwell achieved not only critical and popular success, but also some notoriety. Both books were set among the poor whites of his southern childhood, and both displayed a mixture of muckraking anger and grotesque sexual behavior that upset southern loyalists and northern moralists alike. Despite or because of this, *Tobacco Road*, adapted for the stage by Jack Kirkland, ran on Broadway for over seven and a half years, and *God's Little Acre*, after a highly publicized obscenity trial, became one of Caldwell's perennial bestsellers. The financial rewards of these successes, however, did not come for some time, and in 1933 Caldwell went west to try his luck as a screenwriter in Hollywood. He later described his intermittent, twenty-year association with film writing as a "toilsome and far-from-happy career," saying that in terms of his ability to write fiction it was "just a waste of time" but that it gave him a comfortable income when he dearly needed it.

During the early years of the Great Depression, Caldwell's novels and stories provided complex literary images of poor people as his political sympathies moved leftward, culminating in his most distinctly proletarian collection of stories, *Kneel to the Rising Sun* (1935). In that same year Caldwell, like many other authors, turned to documentary writing, recording in *Some American People* a personal journey through an economically ravaged nation. The following year he arranged to collaborate with the photographer Margaret Bourke-White on a photo-text on his native South, *You Have Seen Their Faces* (1937). This was the first of four joint projects with Bourke-White, whom Caldwell married in 1939 after his divorce from Helen the previous year. The two traveled to Czechoslovakia for *North of the Danube* (1939), across the United States for *Say, Is This the U.S.A.* (1941), and to the Soviet Union for *Russia at War* (1942). They were divorced in 1942. Caldwell's documentary work, especially the books on American subjects, represented a novel development in the genre, for he brought to it much of the anecdotal inventiveness of his fiction. Thus his nonfiction, too, was characterized not simply by exposés of the social inequities and suffering of the age, but also by a sense of the foolish, the outrageous, and the whimsical in human nature.

After returning to the United States in 1942, Caldwell resumed writing fiction with *Georgia Boy* (1943), a collection of linked comic short stories about a southern family. It was well received critically but was one of the last pieces of his fiction to gain such approval. Margaret Bourke-White reported in her autobiography that one of Caldwell's favorite sayings was "The life of a writer is just ten years," and indeed there is a general consensus that the period spanning *Tobacco Road* (1932) and *Georgia Boy* (1943)—a period that also included the short stories in *We Are the Living* (1933), the four documentary works with Bourke-White, and the novels *Journeyman* (1935) and *Trouble in July* (1940)—was Caldwell's decade of greatest achievement. Thereafter he abandoned documentary writing for over twenty years, and his fiction grew more formulaic, despite his efforts to find new subjects.

During the 1940s Caldwell completed a ten-novel cyclorama of southern life (begun with *Tobacco Road* and *God's Little Acre*) in which he attempted to move beyond depictions of the isolated lives of rural poor whites into portrayals of more urbane middle- and upper-class southerners. However, reviewers and critics tended to agree that the unique combination of comic zest, crusading zeal, and spiritual enquiry that had characterized his earlier work was seriously diminished in such novels as *A House in the Uplands* (1946), *This Very Earth* (1948), and *Place Called Estherville* (1949). The deterioration in Caldwell's work has been variously attributed to exhaustion, to his estrangement, after years of travel, from his native southern material, to his marital problems, and to his desire for financial success, which led him to exploit and parody his earlier work. Certainly the decline in his critical status did not seem to affect sales, especially when his books were produced in cheap paperback editions with lurid covers. Between 1946 and 1950 over five million copies of the Signet edition of *God's Little Acre* were sold, and Caldwell was hailed as "The World's Most Popular Novelist."

Caldwell's third marriage was to June Johnson, in 1942. A son was born, but by 1945 the marriage was faltering, although the divorce did not come until 1955. Caldwell once described himself as a "morosely lonely" man, and Helen, his first wife, noted an ominous tendency to cut himself off from people. Margaret Bourke-White wrote of his "unfathomable silences" and "frozen moods," and June was distressed by his reclusive unsociability. Solitariness had been one of the most salient features of his childhood, enhanced by his family's frequent moves, his mother's decision to educate him at home for many years, and later by his need for isolation to write. He tended to look to his wives for cheer and support, yet they found his moodiness difficult to endure. In 1957 Caldwell married Virginia Fletcher, a woman who was able and willing to provide the congeniality on which he depended while helping him guard his solitude; this marriage endured until his death.

The novels and stories that Caldwell wrote during the 1950s—*Gretta* (1955), *Gulf Coast Stories* (1956), *Certain Women* (1957), and *Claudelle Inglish* (1958)—all showed an interest in the psychology and particularly the sexual behavior of neurotic women. Caldwell attributed this emphasis partly to his unhappy personal relationships, although more skeptical critics suspected his willingness to trade profitably on a reputation as "America's Most Censored Author." At the end of the decade, however, Caldwell renewed his interest in one of his earlier literary subjects that was neither notably saleable nor salacious: his concern for the lives of black people and all the intricacies of their relationships to whites. This theme formed the basis of many of his novels in the 1960s, such as *Jenny by Nature* (1961), *Close to Home* (1962), *Summertime Island* (1968), and *The Weather Shelter* (1969). At the same time, Caldwell's interest in nonfiction revived in two autobiographical excursions into his southern past, *In Search of Bisco* (1965) and *Deep South* (1968), both again centrally concerned with race. He also resumed his travel reportage, although the political radicalism and the eccentric details that had enlivened his earlier documentaries were no longer in evidence.

Although Caldwell published well over fifty books of short stories, novels, and nonfiction in his long career, his reputation will probably rest on the work he did in the 1930s and early 1940s, when he was most engaged with the literary experiments and political spirit of the age. His later and more formulaic work, his candid concern with sales, and his increasing disregard for the opinions of other writers and critics isolated him from literary recognition in his own country. By contrast, his status remained high abroad, notably in the Soviet Union and in France, where he was considered one of "les cinq grands" along with Ernest Hemingway, William Faulkner, John Dos Passos, and John Steinbeck. It was not until 1984 that he finally was elected to the American Academy of Arts and Letters, fifty years after the publication of his most acclaimed work. Much earlier, Faulkner had commented that "the first books, *God's Little Acre* and the short stories, that's enough for any man"; but for Caldwell, who continued to write virtually until his last days, there was no such sense of sufficiency. Writing was in every way the business of his life, and he chose, perhaps wrongly, not to rest on his remarkable early achievements. Had he done so, he might better have assured his standing as one of the most innovative American writers, whose comic vision of the grotesque absurdity of his characters' antics was carefully balanced by his insistence on the inequity and deprivation of their lives.

• Caldwell's papers are in the Erskine Caldwell Collection of the Baker Library of Dartmouth College. Other books written by Caldwell include *The Sacrilege of Alan Kent* (1936); *Southways* (1938); *The Sure Hand of God* (1947); *Episode in Palmetto* (1950); *Love and Money* (1954); *Miss Mamma Aimee* (1967); *Writing in America* (1967); and *Annette* (1973). He was editor of *The American Folkways Series* (25 vols. 1941–1954). He wrote two formal autobiographies, *Call It Experience* (1951) and *With All My Might* (1987). Biographical and critical material may be found in the following: *Pembroke Magazine* 11 (1979), which contains thirty essays and tributes to Caldwell by scholars and his associates; Scott MacDonald, ed., *Critical Essays on Erskine Caldwell* (1981); James E. Devlin, *Erskine Caldwell* (1984); Edwin T. Arnold, ed., *Conversations with Erskine Caldwell* (1988); Edwin T. Arnold, ed., *Erskine Caldwell Reconsidered* (1990); and Sylvia J. Cook, *Erskine Caldwell and the Fiction of Poverty: The Flesh and the Spirit* (1991). An obituary is in the *New York Times*, 13 Apr. 1987.

SYLVIA JENKINS COOK

CALDWELL, Eugene Wilson (3 Dec. 1870–20 June 1918), radiologist, was born in Savannah, Missouri, the son of William W. Caldwell, a prominent lawyer, and Camilla Kellogg. After Caldwell graduated from high school, the family moved to Concordia, Kansas, and at seventeen he enrolled at the University of Kansas in Lawrence to study electrical engineering. Beginning in his sophomore year, Caldwell worked as an assistant to physicist Lucien I. Blake, who requested Caldwell's assistance for extended experiments in submarine telephony off the coast of Taunton, Massachusetts, during the summers.

After his graduation in 1892 with a baccalaureate in engineering, Caldwell chose to remain in the East. His first job, at the Bell Telephone Laboratory in Boston, appears to have been unfulfilling; by September 1892 he had accepted a position as an electrical engineer with the J. G. White Company in Baltimore, Maryland. After completion of his project—installing an electrical railway between Baltimore and Fort McHenry—he was given a job at the National Iron Works in Linwood, Pennsylvania. Unbearably bored by the lack of work there, in the summer of 1893 Caldwell once again traveled to Massachusetts to assist Blake. After a brief return to Lawrence, Caldwell was needed to oversee Blake's governmental work in New York, where by October 1895 he had secured a job at the Metropolitan Telephone and Telegraph Company. Also by this time Caldwell had been elected to membership in Sigma Xi, an honorary scientific society;

this likely had a great influence on his future, as it broadened his scope of scientific contacts and allowed in-depth discussions with prominent scientists.

German physicist Wilhelm K. Roentgen's discovery of X-rays took place in late 1895, and Caldwell's growing interest in the developing field propelled him to purchase X-ray apparatus from a commercial photographer in fall 1897. He worked on the apparatus, and by Christmas 1897 the equipment was in "good shape," and he was shortly anticipating having "the very best outfit in the country" (Brown, p. 170). Despite an arrangement with Ford, a surgical instruments company, Caldwell's fledgling consulting business—his business card said that he did "X-ray work for physicians"—was not doing well. In 1898 he wrote to his parents that he was attempting to sell the equipment and find a permanent job, had offered his skills in the event of war, and was considering joining Blake again. However, by March 1899 Caldwell was beginning to receive recognition for his electrical work with X-ray equipment, and May of that year marked the first of Caldwell's contributions to roentgenology, taking the form of an improved electrical current interrupter, which he presented and demonstrated at the 1899 New York Electrical Exposition. At this point he demonstrated that, with the improved induction coil, it was possible to obtain clear X-ray images in a fraction of the standard exposure times. Unfortunately, this discovery was too late to benefit Caldwell, as even by 1897 he was painfully aware of the radiation dermatitis on his left hand, and the protective measures he subsequently undertook were insufficient to prevent his eventual death from complications of these injuries.

In 1901 Caldwell was asked to set up and operate a new X-ray laboratory (the Edward N. Gibbs Laboratory) at the University and Bellevue Hospital Medical College in New York City. In 1902 he enrolled in medical school there, maintaining his operation of the Gibbs Laboratory and his half interest (established in Dec. 1899) with Ford surgical instruments, now W. F. Ford Electric Company. By 1903, time constraints had forced him to sever his ties with Ford and focus solely on roentgenology. Also in 1903 he and William Allen Pusey published a textbook, *The Practical Application of the Roentgen Ray in Therapeutics and Diagnosis*, which was so well received that a second edition was published in 1904. He received his medical degree in 1905 and in 1907 was elected president of the American Roentgen Ray Society (ARRS). The quality of his work was well known, and he was frequently called upon by other physicians for his interpretations of their X-ray films of patients. In addition, he was chosen to X-ray the mayor of New York City after the latter was shot in 1910 and to interpret the images for the surgeons. He was appointed visiting physician at Presbyterian Hospital in New York the same year. In 1913 he married Elizabeth Perkins.

Caldwell was one of many early radiologists to fall victim to the object of their study. By 1907 his radiation dermatitis had progressed to the point that a surgeon friend excised the lesions and performed skin grafts to alleviate his pain. Although he would attain the rank of major, his involvement in World War I (1917–1918) was limited by a skin abrasion on his left hand, which rapidly developed into malignancy. His surgeon friend recommended amputation of the affected finger but was unavailable in New York to perform the surgery. Following amputation by another surgeon, Caldwell required the attention of his friend, who reamputated that finger and a second, and determined the existence of axillary metastases, eventually requiring amputation at the shoulder. Caldwell died a few days after the surgery in New York. An autopsy indicated that his death was from septic complications of his dermatitis and amputations rather than from the invasive carcinoma itself.

Over the two decades of his work in roentgenology, Caldwell provided numerous advances in many aspects of the field. His electrical and mechanical improvements included the inventions of a portable X-ray machine; two stereoscopic X-ray apparati (known as fluoroscopes), the latter of which was tested and used in the final months of World War I; and controlled movement for Bucky's grid (a device that blocked secondary blurring radiation from reaching the radiograph but left the imprint of the grid on the plate). In 1907 he reported a method of viewing the paranasal sinuses by X-ray, a technique that bears his name. Perhaps his most significant contributions, however, lie in the foundations he built for the eventual evolution of radiology as a separate medical specialty. Historian Robert N. Berk observed that Caldwell managed to elevate X-ray technology above the "realm of photographers, electrologists, entrepreneurs, and charlatans" by his own example. Despite the fact that he possessed all of the equipment and possibly knew more about the technology than anyone else, Caldwell was firm in his belief that a specific medical education was required for its appropriate use. He was very concerned about the use of X-rays and radiographs by nonspecialists, warning in the preface to the first edition of his textbook that "there is a tendency among medical men either to underestimate the value of the X-Ray as an aid to diagnosis or to fail to appreciate its limitations." In 1920 the ARRS established the annual Eugene Wilson Caldwell Award and Lecture.

• The earliest biography of Caldwell, delivered by Preston W. Hickey in The 1928 Caldwell Lecture, appeared in the *American Journal of Roentgenology* 25 (1931): 177–95, and was subsequently expanded in Percy Brown, *American Martyrs to Science through the Roentgen Rays* (1936). Both contain complete bibliographies, and Hickey's report includes drawings of many of Caldwell's inventions. Brown's chapter concerning Caldwell was reprinted in the *American Journal of Roentgenology* 165 (1995): 1051–59. A useful account of Caldwell's experiences can be found in Ruth Brecher and Edward Brecher, *The Rays: A History of Radiology in the United States and Canada* (1969). As a retrospective evaluation of Caldwell's contributions to the early era of roentgenology, Robert

N. Berk comments on "Why Caldwell?" in the *American Journal of Roentgenology* 164 (1995): 1321–22. Caldwell's will is reported in the *New York Times*, 23 July 1918.

JOANNA B. DOWNER

CALDWELL, Henry Clay (4 Sept. 1832–15 Feb. 1915), jurist, was born in Marshall County, Virginia (now W.Va.), the son of Van Caldwell and Susan M. (maiden name unknown), farmers. In 1836 the Caldwell family moved to Davis County in the section of the Wisconsin Territory that later became the state of Iowa, living as close neighbors to the Sac and Fox Indians and the Sac leader, Black Hawk. The young Caldwell worked on his father's farm and attended public schools until, while still in his teens, he began to read law at the firm of Wright & Knapp in Keosauqua, Iowa. Caldwell was admitted to the Iowa bar in 1852 and became a junior partner at Wright & Knapp. In 1854 he married Harriet Jane Benton, with whom he had three children. Continuing his early success, in 1856 Caldwell was elected prosecuting attorney of Van Buren County. Two years later he ran as a Republican for state representative from Van Buren County and was elected to the Eighth Iowa General Assembly. He was appointed chair of the Judiciary Committee and served most of two terms from 1859 until joining the Union army in 1861.

Caldwell was commissioned a major in the famed Third Iowa Cavalry, leading important battles in Missouri and Arkansas. His success as an officer during the war was rewarded with promotions to lieutenant colonel and colonel. General Davidson wrote in his official report on the capture of Little Rock that Caldwell, "whose untiring devotion and energy never fags, during night or day, deserves for his gallantry and varied accomplishments as a cavalry officer, promotion to the rank of a general officer" (Scott, p. 115).

While being considered for promotion to brigadier general, Caldwell was appointed U.S. district judge for the Eastern District of Arkansas by President Abraham Lincoln in June 1864. Coming to Arkansas from the North, Caldwell faced initial hostility and suspicion from the Arkansans he had once fought and was now to serve. Caldwell showed no postwar biases, however, often supporting requests for clemency for ex-Confederate Arkansas legislators, for example, and he soon earned a reputation as a fair, impartial, honest judge handling a wide range of difficult Reconstruction issues.

Caldwell served as district judge in Little Rock until early 1890, when President Benjamin Harrison appointed him circuit judge for the Eighth U.S. Circuit, the largest circuit in the United States, at the time comprising one-fourth of the country's possessions, excluding Alaska.

During his judicial career, Caldwell made noteworthy rulings in the areas of debtor and creditor, railroad receiverships, and the property rights of married women. His rulings and public addresses denouncing so-called anaconda mortgages—flagrantly usurious relationships between lenders and tenants—inspired the organizing of the influential farmers' "Wheel" societies in Arkansas. He was also known as a supporter of free silver, temperance, and woman suffrage. His reputation was as a judge who protected the rights of the worker against abuse by the corporation and who believed the courts were where, in his own words from an 1894 courthouse dedication, "the person, the liberty, the reputation and the property of every citizen shall find ready and effectual protection."

In 1896 Caldwell was considered a possible candidate for the presidency, and in 1900 he was deemed a potential running mate for William Jennings Bryan owing to his strong stand on the "silver question," but he declined to run in either election.

Caldwell served as a federal judge for thirty-nine years, longer than any other jurist until that time. When he retired in 1903 Caldwell received accolades from government officials and former colleagues. President Theodore Roosevelt commended his "long and faithful service" and the "ability and integrity . . . [of his] impartial administration of law and justice" (Stiles, p. 237). Attorney and former Secretary of the Interior John W. Noble expressed the consensus opinion of Caldwell, in writing: "From the forum to the field, and from the field to the court, your course has been marked by a single purpose to do your duty; and this you have done with marked fidelity to every trust and with usefulness to all" (Stiles, p. 237).

Caldwell moved west after he left the court, occasionally visiting family and friends in Arkansas and Iowa in his later years. He died in Los Angeles, California.

Though little remembered today, Henry Clay Caldwell during his lifetime seems to have been almost universally respected by members of all political persuasions, by the common man as well as the legal authority, for his integrity, common sense, and dedication to justice. His judicial rulings, only one of which was ever overturned by the U.S. Supreme Court, helped heal the wounds of the Civil War and forged the beginnings of a more modern legal system during the westward expansion of the United States.

• The most detailed biographical treatments of Caldwell's life may be found in Edward H. Stiles, *Recollections and Sketches of Notable Lawyers and Public Men of Early Iowa* (1916), and in Henry W. Scott, *Distinguished American Lawyers, with Their Struggles and Triumphs in the Forum* (1891). Caldwell's Civil War service with the Third Iowa Cavalry is summarized in Benjamin F. Gue, *History of Iowa: From the Earliest Times to the Beginning of the Twentieth Century*, vol. 2 (1903). Selective bibliographies of his essays and speeches appear in Alice Marple, *Iowa Authors and Their Works: A Contribution Toward a Bibliography* (1918), and in Stiles. An obituary is in the *New York Times*, 17 Feb. 1915.

JULIE A. THOMAS

CALDWELL, Joseph (21 Apr. 1773–27 Jan. 1835), astronomer, mathematician, and educator, was born in Lamington, New Jersey, the son of Joseph Caldwell and Rachel Harker. The death of her husband just two days before Joseph's birth left Rachel Caldwell nearly destitute. In 1784 she moved the family to Princeton, where the court ordered eleven-year-old Joseph to be bound out to a printer. His mother immediately took steps to place him in a local grammar school; her intervention brought Joseph under the guidance of the eminent John Witherspoon, president of the College of New Jersey (now Princeton University). The family moved, however, to Newark and then Elizabethtown (now Elizabeth), which kept Joseph from continuing with his schooling until 1787, when he was able to go back to the grammar school in Princeton. He subsequently entered the college there and graduated with the class of 1791. He became a mathematics tutor at Princeton in 1795 but left that position the following year to accept the professorship of mathematics at the recently established University of North Carolina. In 1804 Caldwell married Susan Rowan of Fayetteville, North Carolina; she died in 1807.

Elected president of the university in 1804, Caldwell added training in mathematics and sciences to the standard curriculum of Greek and Latin classics. He initiated innovative methods such as the use of textbooks in classrooms, including his *A New System of Geometry*, which was published in 1806. In 1809 he married a widow, Helen Hogg Hooper, whose father was one of the founders of the University of North Carolina. In 1812 Caldwell retired from the presidency to take up again the more active study and teaching of mathematics. But in 1817 he accepted reappointment as president.

Caldwell emerged during his second presidency as the leading mathematician and astronomer in the South; his important *A Compendious System of Elementary Geometry* was published in 1822. Two years later he traveled to Europe to purchase books for the university library and scientific equipment. On his return in 1825 he initiated what one historian termed "the first systematic observations upon the heavens" in the nation, and between 1827 and 1830 he used his own money to build an observatory (the trustees repaid him shortly before his death). In 1829 Caldwell inaugurated the study of physics at the university, reportedly providing the "first equipment for the teaching of electricity ever used in the United States."

Caldwell's European travels convinced him that North Carolina was in need of modernization. Two years after the first American railroad was built, he wrote a series of newspaper articles, published in book form as *The Numbers of Carlton* (1828), in which he advocated the construction of a major railway across the state. In 1829 he charged that North Carolina was "three centuries behind in public improvements and education." His *Letters on Popular Education Addressed to the People of North Carolina* (1832) criticized the failure of state government to provide schools and train teachers; the eleven letters proposed plans for a modern school system from the elementary level through college. Another instance of Caldwell's enlightened, progressive outlook was his involvement in the founding, in 1827, of the North Carolina Institution for the Instruction of the Deaf and Dumb. In seeking to persuade the state legislature to allocate funds for improvements in infrastructure and education, Caldwell was the first prominent advocate of a pragmatic progressivism that would be a salient feature of North Carolina politics in later times. It should be noted, however, that despite his northern birth and progressive outlook, Caldwell was a slave owner. According to the autobiography of noted abolitionist Levi Coffin, Caldwell did not believe in separating slave families. Nevertheless, he was apparently not opposed to the South's "peculiar institution."

Caldwell, who regarded the "world of men as a laboratory for the working of providence," held unshakable views about the way things should be done. Although he exhibited extraordinary energy, he was nevertheless stern in manner, highly disciplined, and devoted to his faith as a Presbyterian minister. In later life, he became chronically ill, yet he maintained the vigor of his thinking. Unable to carry out many of the duties he had formerly taken upon himself, he stayed head of the university that he always staunchly defended against any critics. Caldwell died in Chapel Hill.

• Caldwell's papers, 1791–1835, are in the Manuscripts Department of the Southern Historical Collection, Wilson Library, University of North Carolina at Chapel Hill. His *Letters on Popular Education* were reprinted in Charles L. Coon, *The Beginnings of Public Education in North Carolina*, vol. 2 (1908), and some of his sermons were printed in Colin McIver, *The Southern Preacher* (1824). Biographical sources include *The Autobiography and Biography of Rev. Joseph Caldwell* (1860); Walker Anderson, *Oration on the Life and Character of the Rev. Jos. Caldwell* (1835); Kemp P. Battle, *History of the University of North Carolina* (2 vols., 1907–1912); Hope Summerell Chamberlain, *Old Days in Chapel Hill* (1926); Guion Griffis Johnson, *Antebellum North Carolina: A Social History* (1937); *University of North Carolina Record*, Apr. 1900; *North Carolina University Magazine*, May 1844 and Mar. 1860; F. P. Venable, "A College President of a Hundred Years Ago," *University of North Carolina Record*, Apr. 1911; and C. A. Smith, "Presbyterians in Educational Work in North Carolina since 1813," *Union Seminary Review*, Dec. 1913 and Jan. 1914. See also Levi Coffin, *The Reminiscences of Levi Coffin* (1876), pp. 15, 23–28.

JAMES M. PRICHARD

CALDWELL, Mary Gwendolin Byrd (21 Oct. 1863–5 Oct. 1909), philanthropist and socialite, was born in Louisville, Kentucky, the daughter of William Shakespeare Caldwell, a plant operator, and Mary Eliza Breckenridge. Soon after the death of Caldwell's mother, her father, who had made a fortune constructing and operating gas plants in the Midwest, moved the family to New York City where, shortly before his death in 1874, he converted to Roman Catholicism and enrolled his two daughters in the Academy of the Sacred Heart, their primary source of education. Under the terms of his will, Caldwell and her sister, Mary Elizabeth, were made wards of Catholic friends and, on their twenty-first birthdays, were to donate a third of their vast inheritance to the Catholic church.

It is not clear whether the $300,000 that she donated to the Catholic church in 1884 to found a national school to advance Catholic philosophy and theology established Caldwell as the founder of the institution. According to the *New York Times* (16 Nov. 1904), the donation was made to "endow the College of Theology in the university." Now known as the Catholic University of America, the *Times* referred to it then as the Catholic University of the United States and as the Roman Catholic University at Washington. It also is not clear whether the gift was motivated by her lengthy and strong friendship with fellow Kentuckian John Lancaster Spalding, first bishop of Peoria, Illinois, or by the clause in her father's will. Later Caldwell added $80,000 to her gift ($60,000 to endow the Chair of Theology and $10,000 each for two scholarships).

As young adults, Caldwell and her sister traveled together extensively in Europe and ultimately became part of international society. This led to Caldwell's engagement in 1889 to Prince Joachim Joseph Napoleon Murat, the invalid grandson of the king of Naples, who was twice her age. She called off the engagement, however, after the prince insisted that Caldwell split her fortune with him. One of her guardians, Eugene Kelly, was quoted as saying that Caldwell was too intelligent and too aware of the value of money to let hers ever get out of her control. In Paris in 1896 she married a middle-aged nobleman, Françoise Jean Louis, Marquis des Monstiers-Mérinville.

Mary Elizabeth, who had become Baroness von Zedtwitz and who also lived abroad, had embraced the Lutheran faith. After her husband died in 1896, the sisters became very close, and many of Caldwell's contemporaries believed that her sister influenced her ultimate decision to renounce Catholicism. In the fall of 1904 Caldwell formally announced that she wished to rid herself of the "subtle, yet overwhelming, influence" of the Catholic church, claiming that, while living in Europe, "her honest Protestant blood" had "asserted itself." Her statement stunned the Catholic church, and church officials in Washington removed her portrait from Catholic University. One of its larger buildings, however, still carries her name. Bishop Spalding could not account for Caldwell's decision, as he had always known her to be a good Catholic, whereas Father Dennis Stafford of St. Patrick's Church in Washington, D.C., felt that her ill health had played a part in her change of faith. In 1902 Caldwell had suffered a paralyzing stroke, which had left her speech so impaired that she had to communicate by writing. But among the friends who knew her well, Caldwell's renunciation did not come as a great surprise because she had a reputation for being very impulsive and somewhat eccentric.

In 1905 Caldwell and the marquis separated. In order to retain her title and to prevent a divorce, she agreed to pay him $8,000 a year. Four years later, Caldwell died on board an ocean liner waiting to dock at New York harbor. Bright's disease was listed as the immediate cause of death. Some of her friends believed she had made the very taxing voyage to consult medical specialists in the United States, but others thought she had returned in order to die on American soil. Caldwell was buried in Louisville, Kentucky.

• Information on Caldwell and her family is available at the Filson Club in Louisville, Ky. Highlights of Caldwell's life as well as notices of her benefactions to the Catholic church are recorded in the *New York Times*: 10 Dec. 1884; 15 June 1885; 23 July and 1 Nov. 1889; and 14 Oct. 1896. Caldwell's controversial decision to leave the church is covered in the *New York Times*, 30 Oct. and 16 Nov. 1904, which include interviews with Caldwell as well as reaction to her action. For information on her association with Catholic University, see *Profiles of American Colleges*, 19th ed. (1992). An obituary is in the *New York Times*, 6 Oct. 1909.

PATRICIA FOX-SHEINWOLD

CALDWELL, Otis William (18 Dec. 1869–5 July 1947), botanist and science educator, was born in Lebanon, Indiana, the son of Theodore Robert Caldwell and Belle Brenton, farmers. When Caldwell's mother died in 1877, he and his siblings were placed under the care of Jane Love, a commiserating neighbor who would eventually become their stepmother.

Caldwell graduated from Franklin College in 1894. After spending a year as a high school principal, he entered the University of Chicago as one of the first graduate students in the newly formed Division of Botanical Sciences, headed by the eminent botanist John Merle Coulter. In 1897 he married Cora Burke Caldwell. They had two children, one of whom died in childhood.

In 1898 Caldwell received his doctoral degree with a dissertation titled "Morphology of Lemma Minor, with Ecological Notes." Originally a study of the form and arrangement of plant parts—their roots, stems, leaves, and flowers—morphology, partly under the influence of ecology, had become a study of plant associations, the conditions that determine them, and the adaptation of the parts. With its interest in the ecological as well as the broader social relations of plants and their environment, the new morphology of Coulter and his graduate students blurred the traditional distinctions between theoretical and applied botany, botany and biology, biology and the physical sciences, and to a certain extent science and the social milieu.

For this new generation of botanists, real biology was inseparable from the clustering and reproduction not only of the great groups of plants, but from those of human society as well—the larger forces of church, school, home, community, and work. Secure in the morphological minutiae of nonadaptive evolution yet committed to the broad social goals of popular education, Coulter and his students searched for a common link between the life history of plants, the reproductive cycles of the great groups, and the life adjustment problems of America's school children. Their reduction of evolutionary theory to simple stimulus and response mechanisms together with their effort to identify in plants an ecological anatomy of health and disease gave them the basis for a "biological conception of education"—Caldwell's prescription for how an "appreciation of the aesthetic aspects of plant life" could lead to "a general understanding of life's problems," provide a scientific basis for "good citizenship," and make students "civically and socially intelligent."

In 1898 Caldwell became head of the Department of Biology at the Eastern Illinois State Teachers College at Charleston. He held this position until 1907 when he became associate professor and later professor of botany and head of the Department of Natural Sciences in the School of Education at the University of Chicago. In 1917 he left the University of Chicago for Columbia University, where he was professor of education and director of the Lincoln School until 1927, at which time he became the director and a professor of the Institute of School Experimentation. He remained at Columbia until his retirement in 1935.

Caldwell's academic and professional accomplishments are extensive. In 1902 he helped to establish the Central Association of Science and Mathematics Teachers (CASMT), serving as its president in 1905 and 1906. Agitating for the reform of science teaching, the CASMT soon became a powerful voice. Caldwell participated in the founding of the American Council of Science Teachers, the National Council of Elementary Science, the National Association for Research in Science Teaching, and the National Society for the Study of Education.

Caldwell developed plans for the first high school general science course between 1908 and 1914, culminating in the publication of the first general science textbook, *Elements of General Science* (1914). Coauthored with William Eikenberry, the textbook was compiled from course notes and outlines. Caldwell hoped that the broad, biological knowledge provided by the general science course would bring about a reconstruction of the individual. He believed that social peace, industrial harmony, economic prosperity, and health and happiness would follow. If it were to become an organic part of general education, science would have to provide as much for the development of "desirable attitudes and ideals as for instruction in general knowledge." "What science may *do for men* must become subordinate," Caldwell said, "to what science may *do to men*." It would also have to provide "a substitute for rural life," drawing its lessons from the small farm and village since they, unlike the shifting sands of a desolate urban landscape, "had something on which to build." That something—a quasi-religious attachment to the soil, keen observational skills born of the daily contact with nature, and a belief in the character-building value of manual labor—preoccupied educational leaders in general, many of whom feared the corrosive effects of urban industrialism.

The benefits of modernity, Caldwell believed, would go to those who had learned "the types of reorganization and reconstruction of themselves" that only science could offer. What students needed most was "a general foundational training . . . using as the basis the science topics of the home, community, and common industries, of personal health and of civic relationships." What Caldwell termed "cultural botany"—a science in which plants, animals, and human beings were all bound together by a common vegetable or nutritive dependency—would impart such important social values as cooperation, self-help, and diversity.

Caldwell first came to national prominence in 1918 as chairman of the National Education Association's Committee on the Reorganization of Secondary School Science, which set the standards for science teaching in the country. Later, as general secretary of the American Association for the Advancement of Science Committee on the Place of Science in Education, he helped create the American Science Teachers Association, a forerunner of the National Science Teachers Association.

In a festschrift honoring him on his seventieth birthday, Helen Keller, acquainted with Caldwell through his work for the American Foundation for the Blind, praised him for placing science within the realm of traditional American values. "In you," she wrote, "shines truly the spirit of America. It is because of the American heritage—to think and experience for oneself, to apply science freely for the benefit of the people—that teachers like you in the sense of creators arise among us." On the occasion of Caldwell's death, Morris Meister, president of the National Science Teachers Association and founder of the Bronx High School of Science, remarked: "Every great advance in science teaching during the past five years is intimately associated with his name." According to the editor of *Science Education*, Caldwell did "more to place science teaching on the pedestal it occupies today than any other man."

Caldwell died at his farm in New Milford, Connecticut. Caldwell testifies in his life and work to the ongoing connection of science, technology, and society that has taken up so much educational interest in the United States. His interest in the relations of water, air, and soil to a sustainable human habitat, although often turned to conservative social purposes, contained an ecological perspective far in advance of his age.

• Caldwell's private papers and correspondence are in the possession of his daughter, Esther Harrop of Princeton, New Jersey, and may be accessed through John M. Heffron, Department of Educational Foundations, University of Hawaii. His most popular books include *Plant Morphology* (1904), *Practical Botany* (1911), *Elements of General Science* (1914), *Then and Now in Education* (1923), *Biology in the Public Press* (1923), *Open Doors to Science* (1925), and *Biological Foundations of Education* (1931). No book-length biography of Caldwell has yet been published. Two chapters on Caldwell and his career in science education appear in John M. Heffron, "Science, Southernness, and Vocationalism: Rockefeller's 'Comprehensive System' and the Reorganization of Secondary School Science Education, 1900–1919," (Ph.D. diss., Univ. of Rochester, 1988). Heffron's bibliography contains a complete listing of Caldwell's publications. For a list of the national organizations in which Caldwell was active and an assessment of his influence in science education, see the obituaries in *School Science and Mathematics* 67 (Oct. 1947): 598; *The Science Teacher* 14 (1947): 114; and *Science Education* 21 (December 1947): 286.

JOHN M. HEFFRON

CALDWELL, Taylor (7 Sept. 1900–30 Aug. 1985), novelist, was born Janet Miriam Holland Caldwell in Manchester, England, the daughter of Arthur F. Caldwell, a commercial artist, and Anna Markham. Dismayed at all the Germans working in his trade in England, the intolerant Arthur Caldwell bundled his family off to America when his daughter was six. In later years she recalled an unhappy childhood with a stern father. She retreated to a world of the imagination from an early age.

Caldwell's father did not approve of women's education so his daughter went to work at fifteen. She served as a yeomanette (i.e., a female yeoman) in World War I, then married William Fairfax Combs in 1919. The couple had a daughter, but the marriage did not last. She later described her first husband as "shiftless." In 1923–1924 Caldwell was employed by the U.S. Department of Labor, and between 1924 and 1931 she worked for the U.S. Immigration and Naturalization Service in Buffalo, New York. In 1931 she obtained a divorce from Combs, received her bachelor's degree from the University of Buffalo, and married her boss, J. Marcus Reback, with whom she also had a daughter.

Once wed to Reback, Caldwell stayed home, caring for her two daughters and pursuing her childhood dream of writing. Her first published works were articles for confession magazines, but she worked on novels as well. In 1938 Maxwell Perkins at Scribner's accepted one, *Dynasty of Death.* According to the Caldwell legend, it was he who suggested that the book would sell better if she dropped the "feminine" Janet and used "Taylor Caldwell" as her pen name. The book, a lengthy saga about a family of munitions merchants, garnered respectable if not entirely enthusiastic reviews and sold well.

From that time until the very end of her life, Caldwell produced more than thirty bestselling novels, which also appeared under the names Max Reiner and Marcus Holland. Many of these were family melodramas, including *The Eagles Gather* (1940), *This Side of Innocence* (1946), and *Ceremony of the Innocent* (1976). Others employed a religious theme, like her *Dear and Glorious Physician* (1959), a biography of St. Luke. Reback helped her with research and frequently represented her. Much was made in the popular press of her habit of writing through the night—and of her refusal to read (let alone revise) her manuscripts once a draft was typed.

Caldwell's books sold millions of copies. Her sense of melodrama, her interest in characters with power and money, and her gift for colorful (especially historical) detail attracted a wide readership. She once explained, "My most lyrical prose has resulted from the anticipation of big checks. . . . The profit motive cannot be removed from an artist." Reviewers, however, generally disagreed with the reading public's assessment of her talents. *Time* magazine's review (19 May 1947) of *There Was a Time* (1947) jeered that the book had "the color-blind prose and inability to distinguish real emotions from salable affections that were written all over earlier Caldwell works," and Anthony Boucher wrote of *The Late Clara Beame* (1964) in the *New York Times*, "It appears that the author simply jots down a mass of words, in such order as to make the average unpublished amateur manuscript seem a masterpiece."

Caldwell had particular scorn for reviewers and suggested that much of the criticism of her books stemmed from the liberal character of the literary establishment. A lifelong conservative and a virulent anticommunist, she wrote in her autobiography, *On Growing Up Tough* (1971), "If you are an anti-communist, you are, per se, *not* a serious writer." Her politics encroached to some extent on her books. Cynthia Walker notes in Lina Mainiero's *American Women Writers* (1979) that "many of [Caldwell's] protagonists possess a Coriolanian contempt for the lower classes, regarded as destructive rabble, incapable of thought or feelings. Her American protagonists assert an almost paranoiac conviction that freedom has steadily decreased since Teddy Roosevelt was president."

The recipient of a John Birch Society plaque as a "Great American Patriot and Scholar," Caldwell remained controversial throughout her life. A September 1978 article in *Crawdaddy* by William M. Kunstler suggested that she had confounded the FBI with accusations about political assassinations of the 1960s. In 1972 she cooperated with psychic/hypnotist Jess Stearn on *The Search for a Soul*, in which the pair explored a number of the novelist's past incarnations. Her controversy was private as well as public. Reback died in 1970, and Caldwell briefly married William E. Stancell in 1972, divorcing him in 1973. In 1978 she married her manager, Robert Prestie. When Caldwell had a stroke two years later and moved with Prestie to Greenwich, Connecticut, her daughter Mary Fried sued the pair for $5 million, claiming that her mother had been moved against her wishes and asking to be named conservator of the estate. After her mother and stepfather filed a countersuit, all charges were dropped, but the family remained estranged until Caldwell's death in Greenwich.

• In addition to the sources named above, see John K. Hutchen, "People Who Read and Write," *New York Times*, 28 Apr. 1946, and Edwin McDowell, "Behind the Best Sellers," *New York Times*, 11 Jan. 1981. An obituary is in the *New York Times*, 2 Sept. 1985.

TINKY "DAKOTA" WEISBLAT

CALEF, Robert (?1648–13 Apr. 1719), strident critic of the Boston clergy's views concerning witchcraft, was apparently born in England; his parents' names are unknown. By the late 1680s Calef was settled in the Boston area as a cloth merchant; little is known, however, of his personal life or family. Outraged by the witchcraft episode of 1692 and by what he perceived as the blind zealotry of the participating clergy, Calef was the most outspoken, persistent, and vocal critic of the prolonged affair. Although he believed that blame for the hysteria and its excesses was widely shared, he directed his sharpest barbs at Cotton Mather, then a young minister in his late twenties. In the wake of the infamous trials, during which nineteen men and women were put to death and dozens more were accused, Mather had written an elaborate account of these and other episodes of apparent demonic possession. Titled *Wonders of the Invisible World*, it contained a defense of the Salem judges' methods and behavior, including their controversial use of "spectral evidence," that is, testimony about "invisible things" seen only by the purported victims of witchcraft. After the formal trials had ended, Mather had also become personally involved in the cases of two "possessed" women, Sarah Good and Margaret Rule, and he wrote about both in a pair of unpublished manuscripts, "A Brand Plucked from the Burning" and "Another Brand Plucked from the Burning." Calef, who was present during one of Mather's attempts to exorcise Margaret Rule, obtained a copy of the minister's account and then circulated his own version of the event. He accused both Cotton and his father, Rev. Increase Mather, of exerting pressure on the victim to provide the responses they wanted to hear; even more damning, he accused the younger minister of blatantly sexual behavior, rubbing Rule's uncovered stomach and breasts to bring her "relief." Mather responded by denouncing Calef from the pulpit and filing a lawsuit against him. This was subsequently dropped, but both men energetically pursued an extended epistolary debate that provided ample material for Calef's only published work, *More Wonders of the Invisible World*, completed in 1697. Unable to find a local publisher—the Mathers were a powerful clerical dynasty in New England, and the merchant was a relative unknown—Calef offered his manuscript in London, and the book was finally printed in 1700. A copy of it was burned in Harvard Yard at the order of Increase Mather, president of Harvard College, and a year later Cotton Mather's congregation came to the defense of their pastor in a pamphlet (*Some Few Remarks upon a Scandalous Book*). But the damage to Mather's reputation had already been done. Not insignificantly, Mather himself never responded publicly in print to Calef's allegations.

Although Calef was accused of political machinations by his contemporaries and by some later historians, there is little reason to suspect clandestine motives; in fact, as a businessman Calef stood to lose more than to gain by prolonged dispute with one of New England's most celebrated families. By most accounts, however, *More Wonders of the Invisible World* was a literary milestone that helped to shift prevailing views about witchcraft. No unbeliever himself, Calef grounded his own arguments and convictions, like those of his opponents, firmly in the Bible. That witches existed, he was absolutely certain. But, he insisted, the scriptures "have not sufficiently, nor at all described the crime . . . whereby the culpable might be detected. Hence periodically the world has discovered "an imaginary crime . . . which has produced a deluge of blood." Worse still—here he took particular aim at Cotton Mather, who often wrote and spoke as if Satan's authority was virtually unchecked—current ideas about the extraordinary abilities of witches render, for all practical purposes, "the power of God, and his providence, of none effect." Thus for Calef the issues at stake were both practical and theological. The Bible he believed, did not provide adequate information by which real witches might reliably be identified and convicted. But even more, an overriding fear of witches and witchcraft represented a failure to rely on God's own powerful oversight of human affairs.

Despite his years as a disputant Calef apparently kept his own reputation intact, for by tradition he held several town offices in Boston prior to his death in that city.

• Calef's *More Wonders of the Invisible World* has been printed numerous times, most recently in a reprint of George Lincoln Burr, ed., *Narratives of the Witchcraft Cases: 1648–1706* (1975).

ELIZABETH NORDBECK

CALHERN, Louis (19 Feb. 1895–12 May 1956), stage and screen actor, was born Carl Henry Vogt in Brooklyn, New York, the son of Eugene Adolph Vogt, a tobacconist, and Hubertina Friese. When Carl was six, the family moved to St. Louis, where he and his sister, Emmy, grew up in a comfortable middle-class household. The seeds of his future life on the stage sprouted early: a favorite pastime of the Vogt children was putting on plays with their friends. His first professional theatrical engagement, however, was pure luck.

When Carl Vogt was seventeen and a high school football player, the entire team was hired to appear as supers in a traveling theatrical troupe's production of *Much Ado about Nothing*. That experience set Carl on the course he was to follow for the rest of his life. He couldn't even wait to finish school. Persuading his father to advance him $100, he set his sights on New York and an acting career. Carl's uncle Henry Vogt, who considered acting a less than exemplary profession, insisted that his nephew change his name so as not to disgrace the family. Young Carl acquiesced and chose a stage name: Louis, for the city of St. Louis; Calhern, a contraction of Carl Henry.

After months of making the rounds of New York repertory companies, Calhern got his first break playing an office boy in *The Fourth Estate*, produced by the Prospect Theatre stock company in the Bronx. The year was 1912; his salary was $9 a week. Over the next few years Calhern gained experience in virtually all forms of live entertainment: burlesque, vaudeville, stock, carnivals, and a Shakespearean company. In 1914 he joined the Park Theatre stock company in St. Louis, where he also acquired offstage skills. He was a stage manager, a prop man, and a set designer as well as a performer, all of which laid the groundwork for his subsequent reputation for extraordinary versatility in the profession. In 1917 Calhern joined the army and served in World War I as a sergeant with the 143d Field Artillery in France. He was discharged on the West Coast in 1919.

Jobs were scarce, but Calhern was able to win a role in *Lombardi, Ltd.* on tour; he then played a leading man with the Morosco Stock Company in Los Angeles. At this point Hollywood scouts, looking for a new romantic lead, "discovered" Calhern, and during 1920–1921 he appeared in three silent films. The next year he was back in New York in *The White Peacock*. Broadway audiences began to notice Calhern in 1923, when he played in George M. Cohan's *Song and Dance Man*. The next year, on Cohan's recommendation, Calhern was the juvenile lead opposite Judith Anderson in *Cobra*, a part that established his reputation as a Broadway romantic lead. Subsequently, roles opposite such stars as Laurette Taylor in *In the Garden* (1925) and Ethel Barrymore in *The Love Duel* (1929) further burnished his growing reputation as a matinee idol. Critic Alexander Woollcott described him as "excellent, unsparing, true and vivid" in *The Dark* (1927). With fame, however, came irresistible opportunities to live the frenetic life of the rich and famous in the 1920s. Calhern embarked on a period as a hard-drinking, debonair playboy who, with such cronies as John Barrymore, loved a good time.

In the 1930s Hollywood beckoned, and Calhern played a series of gangsters, crooked lawmen, and suave scoundrels in a variety of mostly inferior films. By 1940, however, after overhearing a producer remark that a certain role needed a young Louis Calhern, he decided to focus his talents on character parts. The decision marked a turning point in Calhern's career. He took roles in two plays: opposite Dorothy Gish in *Life with Father* (1940) and later a lead in *Jacobowsky and the Colonel* (1944), which critic John Mason Brown described as "a brilliant job carried off with great flourish and style." The year 1946 brought Calhern his greatest Broadway triumph. Despite the incredulity of a theater community familiar with Calhern's flamboyant, bon vivant lifestyle, he was cast as the respectable and revered Supreme Court Justice Oliver Wendell Holmes in *The Magnificent Yankee*. Critically acclaimed—Burns Mantle wrote that it seemed "as though Calhern had been in training for this success most of the years of his professional life"—he won the Donaldson Award, the Delia Austrian Medal of the Drama League of New York, and the Barter Theater Award for best performance of the season. Calhern repeated this remarkable stage success in subsequent movie, radio, and television versions.

In the 1940s and early 1950s Calhern made such memorable films as *Notorious* (1946) *Arch of Triumph* (1948), *The Red Pony* (1949), and *The Asphalt Jungle* (1950) as well as many forgettable ones. On Broadway again in 1948, he received the first Monarch Award for his performance in *The Play's the Thing* and then set his sights on a part that has been called the toughest of all dramatic roles, King Lear. The play had obsessed him for thirty-five years. He had read it in all its editions, including first folio, and had memorized it in its entirety.

Calhern's *Lear*, which opened in December 1950, brought praise from Brooks Atkinson, who wrote that the king was "intelligible, human and dramatic," and from John Mason Brown, who stated, "No career in the contemporary theater has taken a more encouraging turn than Calhern's . . . he has mastered the all-round job of being an exceptionally good actor."

Serious recognition came late to Calhern. He, perhaps, explained the reasons himself in an interview by critic Ward Morehouse in 1951, during the run of *King Lear*: "I was drunk for about 15 years. I kept on acting . . . but I wasn't any good. During the last 10 years I've taken my career seriously; I've tried to become a better actor. Perhaps I am. I changed over from romantic leads to character parts because I was getting a little old." He continued making films over the next five years, including *Julius Caesar* (1953), *Executive Suite* (1954), *Blackboard Jungle* (1955), and *High Society* (1956), until his sudden death from a heart attack in Nara, Japan, while on location for his sixty-ninth motion picture, *Teahouse of the August Moon* (1956).

Louis Calhern was married and divorced four times. All of his wives were actresses. The first was actress and author Ilka Chase (married 1926, divorced 1927), followed by Julia Hoyt (married 1927, divorced 1932), Natalie Schafer (married 1933, divorced 1942), and Marianne Stewart (married 1946, divorced 1955). He had no children.

• The Players Collection of the New York Public Library for the Performing Arts is an important source of information on Calhern's career. There is a detailed description of the biographical facts of his life in *Current Biography* (1951), pp. 87–90. See also *Who Was Who in the Theatre, 1912–1976* (1978) and Dickson Hartwell, "The Man Who Startled Hollywood," *Saturday Evening Post*, 26 May 1951. An extensive obituary is in the *New York Times*, 13 May 1956.

ADELE S. PARONI

CALHOUN, George Miller (29 Jan. 1886–15 June 1942), classical scholar, was born in Lincoln, Nebraska, the son of James Duncan Calhoun, a newspaper editor and publisher, and Odus Marcella Alderman. The family's southern roots led Calhoun to J. B. Stetson University in Florida, from which he graduated in 1906. He then went to the University of Chicago to work with R. J. Bonner and obtained his Ph.D. in Greek in 1911. Calhoun taught for six years at the University of Texas. In 1913 he married Ellinor McKay Miller, with whom he had two children. In 1917 he moved to the University of California at Berkeley, where he remained as assistant professor, then associate professor (1920), and finally professor (1926), as well as chair of the Greek department (1923–1924) and the classics department (1939–1942). He was a formidable teacher and for twenty-five years a mainstay of classics at Berkeley; with his colleague Ivan Linforth he founded the Sather Classical Lectures series, the most distinguished lectures in the field of classics. In addition he was a Visiting Carnegie Professor in Copenhagen, Oslo, and Stockholm (1928), served as president of the American Philological Association (1940–1941), and managed the University of California Press (1924–1933).

Calhoun's scholarship was concentrated in two areas: ancient Greek law and Homer. The first interest led to a dissertation under Bonner's direction on *Athenian Clubs in Politics and Litigation*, published in Austin in 1913. This was followed by many articles and books, among them *The Business Life of Ancient Athens* (1926); with Catherine Delamere, *A Working Bibliography of Greek Law* (1927); and *The Growth of Criminal Law in Ancient Greece* (1927). The last of these is his most important and influential book: Calhoun shows how in early Greece crimes against individuals (such as assault and homicide) were treated much like modern torts. He argues that the decisive step to "true criminal law" came in the sixth century B.C. with the legislation of Solon that allowed every citizen to prosecute certain offenses, including attacks on individuals. Despite modifications of detail, Calhoun's thesis is widely accepted, and the book is still important and useful for the clarity and insight with which it sets out a broad theoretical background for understanding this aspect of Greek law. Calhoun later was asked to contribute a chapter on Greek law to a volume on the history of legal science. When the comprehensive project was abandoned, Calhoun agreed to the separate publication of his chapter, and although his untimely death from a heart attack in Berkeley prevented any revision, the brief sketch was published as *Introduction to Greek Legal Science* (1944).

After 1930 Calhoun turned his attention largely to the study of Homer. He "read Homer again and again with ever-growing admiration" (Linforth, p. 58) and, as in his work on law, focused his attention on basic issues. In this case it was the "Homeric question" concerning the nature of Homeric composition and its implications for Homeric criticism. In 1928 the debate was radically altered when Milman Parry, a former student of Calhoun's, argued that Homer composed orally using set verses and expressions drawn from a centuries-old oral tradition. To some this suggested a mechanistic composition inconsistent with the evident quality of the poems. Calhoun took issue with Parry in "The Art of Formula in Homer," a famous article on the meaning of the expression "winged words" (1935), and this paper, with Parry's response, has long exemplified the debate between Parry's purely functional understanding of Homeric "formulas" and a more aesthetic appreciation of the formulas as having their own specific effect. Despite this disagreement, Calhoun accepted much of Parry's work and built on his insights. Parry himself had high regard for Calhoun, as did Parry's son Adam, who in a review of his father's work (1971) praises Calhoun as one of the few scholars who "can use Parry's insights into Homeric style to understand more of how the Homeric poems are put together." Because of his untimely death, Calhoun published fewer than a dozen articles on Homer, but his understanding of the text has endured, while much other work in this rapidly changing field is transitory. Calhoun, "a gentleman and a scholar" (Linforth, p. 58), made lasting contributions to scholarship on Homer and Greek law and put his stamp on a quarter-century of classics at Berkeley.

• There is no known archive of Calhoun's papers. There is information on Calhoun in Sterling Dow, *Fifty Years of Sathers* (1965), and Joseph Fontenrose, *Classics at Berkeley: The First Century 1869–1970* (1982). There is a full bibliography on Calhoun in the entry Fontenrose in *The Biographical Dictionary of North American Classicists*, ed. Ward Briggs (1994). An obituary by Ivan Linforth is in the *Classical Journal* 38 (1942–1943): 57–59.

MICHAEL GAGARIN

CALHOUN, John (14 Oct. 1806–13 Oct. 1859), politician and territorial officeholder, was born in Boston, Massachusetts, the son of Andrew Calhoun, a successful merchant, and Martha Chamberlain. He spent his youth on a farm in Montgomery County, New York, to which his family had moved following his father's retirement. After completing his studies at Canajoharie Academy, Calhoun turned to the study of law. Restless and looking for opportunity, he left home and family in 1830 and settled in Springfield, Illinois, where he continued his law study and taught school. He married Sarah Cutter the following year; they had nine children, seven of whom grew to adulthood.

Captivated by the image of Andrew Jackson, Calhoun quickly found the excitement he sought in politics. He developed a close friendship with Stephen A. Douglas and participated in Douglas's efforts to organize the Democratic party in Illinois. Within a short time, Calhoun was widely recognized as a party leader. Following brief service in the Black Hawk War in 1832, he was appointed Sangamon County surveyor, an important position on this fast-growing frontier. His friends included Abraham Lincoln, whom he had first met during the Black Hawk War, and as the demand for survey work increased, Calhoun offered Lincoln the post of deputy surveyor. Lincoln hesitated at first, aware of the political differences between them, but finally accepted the offer and with Calhoun's help developed his own surveying skills. While they often opposed one another in political contests, Calhoun and Lincoln remained good friends.

Although he was one of the ablest stump speakers in the state, Calhoun's political career never prospered, partly because he sought elective office as a Democrat in the state's only Whig stronghold. After his defeat in 1836 for the state legislature, Calhoun won election in 1838 as the only Democrat in the county's delegation, but it was the last time he held an elective office on the state level. As a legislator, Calhoun took a strong public stand on the slavery question, insisting in a series of resolutions that Congress had no constitutional power to interfere with slavery in the District of Columbia or in the territories. Following his term in the legislature, he served briefly as clerk of the lower house and as clerk of the county circuit court. In 1846 he was defeated for the Democratic nomination for governor, and in 1852 he ran unsuccessfully for Congress against

Richard Yates, the Whig candidate. In 1849 Calhoun was elected to the first of three one-year terms as mayor of Springfield. In the meantime, he continued to serve his party, stumping the state on behalf of Democratic candidates, debating the issues with Whig candidates, including Lincoln, and twice serving as a Democratic presidential elector, in 1844 and 1852.

The passage by Congress of Douglas's Kansas-Nebraska Act in 1854 marked a turning point in Calhoun's life. At Douglas's request, Calhoun was appointed surveyor general of the two new territories by President Franklin Pierce and promptly left Illinois to take up his residence in Kansas. It was inevitable that Calhoun should become a controversial figure in territorial Kansas, for the land situation was extremely confused. American Indian title to much of the region had not been extinguished before the settlers moved in, and the first federal land office did not open until 1856. Furthermore, the territory became the scene of bitter and sometimes bloody rivalry between proslavery Missourians and antislavery emigrants from the free states for control of the territorial government. Calhoun fulfilled the responsibilities of his office despite the breakdown of law and order. As a follower of Douglas, he believed slavery was a local institution to be decided by the people of the territory, and he hoped to organize a viable Democratic party on the basis of this doctrine of popular sovereignty. He soon discovered that there was little room for his position between the proslavery and antislavery extremes.

In 1857 Calhoun was elected to the convention that met in Lecompton, the territorial capital, to draft a constitution for a proposed state of Kansas and was chosen its president. He fought hard for the full submission of the constitution to the voters for ratification, but the convention, dominated by proslavery advocates, defeated his efforts. Instead a partial submission on the slavery question only was adopted, so worded as to be no referendum at all. The Lecompton constitution ignited a national crisis when it was forwarded to Congress. Douglas attacked it as a travesty on popular sovereignty, and the Republicans denounced it as a fraud. Much of the abuse was heaped on Calhoun, who was portrayed not only as a blundering politician but also as a malevolent conspirator. He left Kansas to plead his case in Washington, D.C., but he received little satisfaction. In the heated atmosphere of the time, Calhoun was held responsible for the effort to foist slavery on a population that did not want it. When he returned, it was not to Kansas, for he had persuaded the Buchanan administration to shift his office to Nebraska City. His commission expired shortly afterward.

Calhoun died from accidental poisoning in St. Joseph, Missouri, disgraced and reviled. Only after his death was he remembered, especially in Illinois, as a man of amiable disposition and fine mind who, by some mystery, had become involved in the "Lecompton fraud" (*Chicago Times*, 18 Oct. 1859).

• Some Calhoun letters are in the Stephen A. Douglas Papers, Regenstern Library, University of Chicago; there are fragmentary references in Roy P. Basler et al., eds., *The Collected Works of Abraham Lincoln* (1953). The most complete account of Calhoun's life and career is in Robert W. Johannsen, "John Calhoun: The Villain of Territorial Kansas?" *Trail Guide* 3, no. 3 (1958): 1–19. A shorter notice, with information on his family, is in John Carroll Power, *History of the Early Settlers of Sangamon County, Ill.* (1876). Brief mentions are in Benjamin P. Thomas, *Lincoln's New Salem* (1934; rev. ed., 1988), and Albert J. Beveridge, *Abraham Lincoln, 1809–1858* (1928). For an overview of the times, see Kenneth M. Stampp, *America in 1857: A Nation on the Brink* (1990). An obituary is in the *Chicago Times*, 18 Oct. 1859.

ROBERT W. JOHANNSEN

CALHOUN, John C. (18 Mar. 1782–31 Mar. 1850), vice president, U.S. senator, and secretary of state, was born John Caldwell Calhoun at what was then known as the District of Ninety-six, later known as Abbeville, on the frontier of southwestern South Carolina, the son of Patrick Calhoun, a prosperous Scotch-Irish farmer and one of the largest slave owners in the backcountry, and Martha Caldwell, also of Scotch-Irish descent. John Calhoun was the couple's third son, and though like his older brothers and sister he did his share of farm work, the family considered him to have such promise that he deserved a better education than the local field schools afforded. Calhoun attended Moses Waddel's school in Appling, Georgia, where he studied Latin, Greek, and mathematics and read widely in history and philosophy, especially the works of John Locke. In October 1802 he was admitted to the junior class of Yale College. He graduated with distinction in 1804. Some months later he began the study of law in Charleston under Henry William DeSaussure, a Federalist in politics and one of the most prestigious lawyers in the city. Calhoun soon decided that he needed more formal training in the law and enrolled in Tapping Reeve's noted law school at Litchfield, Connecticut.

Calhoun was again exposed to Federalist politics from Reeve and other notables in Litchfield, but he rejected their explanations of public policy and was outspoken in his defense of Jeffersonian-Republicanism. He completed his studies at Reeve's law school in the fall of 1806. Returning to South Carolina he was admitted to the bar in December 1807. He practiced law briefly but soon decided that he would make his career and his living as a planter and in public service. He was elected to the South Carolina legislature the following year, but after only one term he was elected to the U.S. House of Representatives as a Jeffersonian-Republican. He served three terms in the Twelfth through the Fourteenth Congresses from 4 March 1811 to 3 November 1817. Just before his first election to the House of Representatives, Calhoun married his cousin Floride Bonneau Colhoun in 1811. The couple had ten children, seven of whom lived to maturity.

In early April 1812 Calhoun became chairman of the House Foreign Relations Committee, and in June of that year the Congress passed President James Madison's war message in a declaration that followed Calhoun's report on the message. One of the small group of congressmen who had pushed for war with Great Britain, Calhoun was considered a preeminent "War Hawk." On the conclusion of the war in 1815, he emerged as a leading nationalist. He drafted the bill that created the Second Bank of the United States. Relying on the cash put up by incorporators of the bank, or the "bonus," Calhoun framed a bill that would have provided federal funds for a national scheme of internal improvements, and he supported the protective tariff of 1816 to ward off a postwar flood of foreign goods that threatened American economic development. Madison approved all of this legislation except the Bonus Bill. Congress was unable to override his veto.

Calhoun resigned his seat in the House to accept the post of secretary of war in the new Monroe administration. He inherited a department that had been grossly mismanaged during the war by a succession of incompetent secretaries. The able secretary of the treasury, William H. Crawford, who was also acting as War Department head, had begun a process of reorganization. Calhoun pushed Crawford's plan to completion and managed to keep the small professional army intact in the face of an economy-minded Congress. In addition, as secretary he encouraged the migration of Georgia Cherokee Indians west and reformed the factory system of trade with the Indian tribes so that white traders' activities were more carefully monitored. Calhoun also sponsored several important surveying expeditions into the far northwest. His reports to Congress were competent state papers that gained him political reputation but also excited the opposition of formidable rivals.

In cabinet council, Calhoun sought to discipline his southwestern commander, Andrew Jackson, who had made an unauthorized foray into Spanish-held Florida. But the president, backed up by his secretary of state John Quincy Adams, quashed Calhoun's proposed censure of Jackson for insubordination.

In 1824, on the expiration of Monroe's second term, Calhoun was a candidate for the Republican congressional caucus nomination, which had been tantamount to election to the presidency. But he was unable to cope with the political capacity and popularity of his competitors, Jackson, John Quincy Adams, Henry Clay, and Crawford. Calhoun settled for the vice presidency. In the election that followed, none of the presidential candidates received a majority. As the Constitution prescribed, the issue was settled in the House of Representatives, each state casting one vote. With the support of Clay, Adams was elected on the first ballot even though Jackson had the most popular votes.

Calhoun joined with Martin Van Buren, then a senator from New York, in opposing the Adams administration. His followers joined in a pro-Jackson coalition that provided essential support for Jackson's nomination by state legislatures and "spontaneous" conventions and his subsequent election to the presidency in 1828. As vice president, Calhoun engaged in a public exposition of the role of that office in a series of published essays he signed as "Onslow," a noted speaker of the British Parliament. An adversary who signed himself "Patrick Henry" was thought to be the president himself. The debate veered away from the functions of the vice presidency to the broader context of power and liberty. The exchange marked Calhoun as a powerful debater and a close student of political theory.

Meanwhile, Calhoun had been caught up in the debates over the Tariff of 1824, which he had indirectly opposed, and the Tariff Bill of 1828, which he had supported when it was thought that the protectionist demands of northern manufacturers would lead to its defeat in Congress. But under the leadership of Clay, the tariff bill passed; President Adams signed it into law.

A tariff with such strong protectionist features was seen to be so harmful to southern planter interests that it was denounced, especially in South Carolina, as "the Tariff of Abominations." At the request of the South Carolina legislature Calhoun drafted papers entitled "Exposition" and "Sundry Resolutions" that threatened nullification of a federal law such as the tariff if found to be inimical to a given state or states' vital interests. In making his case, Calhoun claimed original sovereignty for the states. The Constitution, he argued, was a compact or contract between the federal government and the states, with the federal government limited to enumerated powers spelled out in the Constitution. The federal government was merely the agent for the states. If a state deemed the federal government to have broken the contract by enacting a given law, it was the duty of the state through a convention or referendum to nullify that law.

Calhoun's authorship of the "Exposition" was supposed to be secret, but it soon became public knowledge, particularly when it served as the theoretical basis for a direct challenge to the new Jackson administration, in which Calhoun served as vice president. Van Buren, who had become secretary of state, was determined to root out Calhoun's influence in the administration. He utilized the adverse impact of the "Exposition" on Jackson's nationalist views to Calhoun's disadvantage. Through intermediaries Van Buren also raked up Calhoun's attempt to censure Jackson for his Florida foray. The president was extremely sensitive on that topic, which Clay had made the subject of an embarrassing congressional investigation.

The Peggy Eaton affair further damaged Calhoun's relationship with the administration. Calhoun's wife and the wives of his followers in the cabinet had refused to accept socially Peggy Eaton, the wife of the secretary of war, because of her alleged infidelities. Jackson defended what he saw as the honor of a wronged woman and insisted on proof. When nothing specific was forthcoming, Jackson blamed Calhoun and his associates in the cabinet.

At this point Van Buren decided the cabinet should be reconstituted, his own position included, to purge the administration of Calhoun's influence. All cabinet members either resigned or were forced to resign, and politicians who favored Van Buren replaced them. Congress was not in session so the replacements were made on an interim basis. Van Buren was appointed minister to Great Britain, but when Congress convened on 5 December 1831, in a tie vote, broken by Vice President Calhoun, the Senate refused to confirm his appointment. This contrived humiliation of Van Buren moved Jackson to select him as his running mate in 1832 and presumably his successor in 1836. Calhoun was effectively ruled out of the Democratic party. Accordingly, he resigned the vice presidency and was elected a U.S. Senator from South Carolina. In 1832 Congress passed another protective tariff.

The Nullification party had now gained the upper hand in South Carolina. Extremists demanded separation from the Union if the new tariff of 1832 was not rescinded, and the South Carolina legislature enacted an ordinance of nullification. Although Calhoun's "Exposition" was utilized to justify nullification, he sought to avoid what might lead to armed conflict between Nullifiers and the Unionists. The Jackson administration threatened military intervention if nullification was undertaken but was willing to compromise on the tariff. Calhoun, seeking to head off such a confrontation, met with Clay and they worked out the Compromise Tariff of 1833, which scaled rates on commodities deemed essential to the southern planters down to the approximate level of the 1816 tariff. A national crisis was thus avoided.

Complicating these political maneuvers was the issue of slavery, which had been given much publicity by northern abolitionists and Adams, now a congressman from Massachusetts, who presented their petitions in the House. Calhoun had been concerned about the growth of antislavery sentiment not just in the free states but in western Europe since the Missouri Compromise debates of 1819–1821. The Nat Turner slave uprising in 1831 had contributed an emotional outburst to the already heated rhetoric in South Carolina over nullification. Calhoun then stated in more direct terms than he had used in the "Exposition" his views on minority rights within a federal republic. In what came to be known as the Fort Hill Address he proposed what he called a "concurrent majority," which would give a proportional weight to all the diverse economic and social interests of the nation. Slavery, he believed, was the principal minority institution that must be protected in an industrializing economy.

For the next twenty years, most of which he served in the U.S. Senate, Calhoun constantly fought for an accommodation of slavery in the Union. Briefly he held the cabinet post of secretary of state in the Tyler administration, where he vigorously supported the annexation of Texas in part because it would constitute additional slave territory and in part to act as a buffer against British interests in Mexico.

Returning to the Senate in 1845, Calhoun strongly opposed the Mexican-American War because he feared the addition of vast additional new territories to be gained from Mexico would make the divisive issue of slavery much more dangerous. Calhoun's fears were borne out when Congressman David Wilmot in August 1846 introduced an antislavery rider to an appropriation bill, declaring any territory that might be gained from Mexico free soil. For the remaining four years of his life Calhoun dedicated himself to defending slavery and to raising the specter of disunion if southern interests were not adequately protected. He opposed the admission of Oregon as a free state in 1848 and the admission of California in 1849 under a free soil constitution. He saw in these moves a drastic shift in the sectional balance, against the South, that seemed to justify his fears for the maintenance of the Union.

The "Southern Address" that he prepared in February 1849 charged that a conspiracy existed in the free states that sought to emancipate the slaves. It was an incendiary document aimed at rallying public opinion in the South.

Later that year, Calhoun supported the Nashville convention of representatives from the slave states to protest the admission of California as a free state and to insist that the remainder of the Mexican cession be thrown open to slavery. He hoped that the convention would propose demands that the federal government explicitly protect slavery and utilize its military power if necessary to defend slave interests in the new territories. Under this pressure the free states would be compelled to make a satisfactory adjustment. California petitioned for admittance to the Union as a free state in September 1849. Congress now took seriously the threat of disunion.

Leaders of both parties, headed by Clay and Daniel Webster for the Whigs and Stephen A. Douglas of Illinois for the Democrats, sought to compromise the issue before the Nashville Convention met. Calhoun made his last speech against the compromise measures on 4 March 1850. He still held out hope for the Union if the North would ensure what amounted to autonomy for the South and its institutions. He died in Washington before the Compromise of 1850 eased tensions between the sections sufficiently to defuse any concerted move for disunion by the Nashville Convention.

In Calhoun's last years he drafted two essays that set forth his ideas on political theory. The first and shorter essay, "The Disquisition on Government," is the more significant in that Calhoun sought to develop a consistent theory on minority rights within the context of majority rule. He urged universal recognition of the inequality of mankind and the differentiation of social and economic concerns. For an organized society to work in a harmonious and practical sense, these differences, Calhoun contended, had to be recognized and then institutionalized. He was of course arguing for his section and its "peculiar institution," but nowhere does he mention slavery in the essay. Calhoun's thought as developed in the "Disquisition," and to a lesser extent in his "Discourse on the Constitution," remains an original contribution to the history of political theory. His assertion of pluralism in political representation has influenced diverse critics of society, including liberal supporters of civil rights and conservative defenders of special social and economic interests.

• The major source for Calhoun material is the monumental, multivolume *Papers of John C. Calhoun*, ed. W. Edwin Hemphill et al. (1959–). In addition to his personal correspondence and state papers, most of Calhoun's speeches are reprinted in these volumes, as is his participation in congressional debates. For biographical treatment of Calhoun, see Charles M. Wiltse, *John C. Calhoun* (3 vols., 1944–1951); Margaret Coit, *John C. Calhoun: An American Portrait* (1950); Gerald M. Capers, *John C. Calhoun, Opportunist: A Reappraisal* (1960); Richard N. Current, *John C. Calhoun* (1963); John Niven, *John C. Calhoun and the Price of Union* (1988); and Irving H. Bartlett, *John C. Calhoun, a Biography* (1993). Calhoun's role in politics and antebellum American society is considered in Richard Hofstadter, *American Political Tradition* (1949); Vernon Parrington, *Main Currents in American Thought*, vol. 2 (1926); Arthur Schlesinger, Jr., *The Age of Jackson* (1945); William W. Freehling, "Spoilsmen and Interest in the Thought and Career of John C. Calhoun," *Journal of American History* 52, no. 1 (June 1965); and Robert V. Remini, *Andrew Jackson* (3 vols., 1977–1984) and *Henry Clay: Statesman for the Union* (1991). On the nullification crisis, three books deserve consideration: Freehling, *Prelude to Civil War: The Nullification Controversy in South Carolina* (1968); Merrill D. Peterson, *Olive Branch and Sword: The Compromise of 1933* (1982); and Richard Ellis, *The Union at Risk: Jacksonian Democracy, States' Rights and the Nullification Crisis* (1987). For eulogies of Calhoun that contain some valuable factual material, see J. P. Thomas, ed., *The Carolina Tribute to Calhoun* (1857); and *The Death and Funeral Ceremonies of John Caldwell Calhoun* (1850).

JOHN NIVEN

CALHOUN, Patrick (21 Mar. 1856–16 June 1943), railroad attorney and streetcar syndicator, was born on the family plantation, "Fort Hill," near Pendleton, South Carolina, the son of Andrew Pickens Calhoun, a prosperous antebellum plantation owner who was later ruined by the war, and Margaret Maria Green. He was a grandson of U.S. vice president John C. Calhoun. In 1871 Patrick apprenticed himself to his maternal grandfather, Duff Green, in Dalton, and was admitted to the Georgia bar in 1875. He moved to St. Louis the following year and was admitted to the Missouri bar, but ill health forced his retirement to his brother John Calhoun's Arkansas plantation. Settling in Atlanta, he resumed his legal practice and in 1885 married Sarah Porter Williams, daughter of Charleston banker George W. Williams. They had eight children.

In 1887 Calhoun became the senior partner in the firm of Calhoun, King and Spalding and entered a career consolidating rail companies. His famous grandfather had believed that the economic future of the South depended on developing rail lines to the Midwest in order for southern ports to successfully compete with Boston, New York, and Philadelphia. This became Calhoun's cause as well, and he worked to unify southern railroads under the auspices of the Richmond Terminal Company, a holding company. Working closely with his brother John, Calhoun played an important role in the creation of the southern railway system in 1894.

While in Richmond Calhoun undoubtedly observed the important pioneering work being done by Frank J. Sprague in creating a viable network of streetcar lines in the Richmond area, for he became a syndicator of traction companies in major cities nationwide, drawing on the valuable connections he had made in New York financial circles during the Richmond Terminal work. During the 1890s Calhoun's involvement with steam railroads declined, he resigned his law partnership in Atlanta, and he reputedly began seeking traction franchises in cities such as Philadelphia, Pittsburgh, and Baltimore. He directed the attention of the Brown brothers of New York to the St. Louis traction company and helped engineer its sale for about $4.5 million in 1899.

In Cleveland Calhoun added a new element to his speculations when he founded a luxury residential subdivision in the eastern heights, overlooking what is now the University Circle center of cultural and educational institutions. He was perhaps lured there by the pioneering electric traction work done in East Cleveland in 1884, or by his ties to East Cleveland resident John D. Rockefeller (who had invested in the terminal); the development was his only known venture into the real estate end of streetcar suburbs.

The Euclid Heights Allotment was a restricted subdivision of curving streets, scenic views, installed utilities, and grand homes, all nestled in the midst of Cleveland's new park system and linked by electric streetcar to downtown. Calhoun even proposed, as early as 1895, that a fleet of motor coaches would drive Euclid Heights residents to the center city, a plan that never materialized. He moved his family from Atlanta to the first of his two Euclid Heights homes in 1896. The allotment was built around the Euclid Club and its eighteen-hole golf course—built with Rockefeller's help—which hosted the first National Amateur Championship in 1907. The venture went bankrupt in 1914 as the automobile changed the investment dynamics of Cleveland real estate.

Calhoun, however, spent little time with his family in Cleveland as his business carried him further west. In 1902 he headed a syndicate, United Railroads, which purchased San Francisco's traction franchise. Calhoun was indicted in 1908 on charges that United Railroads had obtained an advantageous contract by bribery. His first trial ended with a hung jury, and a motion was made to dismiss charges for lack of evidence, but the case dragged on until the court of appeals ordered the charges dismissed in 1911. When it was discovered that he had lost $890,000 of United Railroads funds in his Solano Irrigated Farms venture and that another $207,000 was unaccounted for, he was forced to resign as president of the firm in 1913.

After his reversals in California and Ohio, Calhoun faded from public view. He claimed he had personally lost $2.5 million in the San Francisco earthquake and that his enemies forced him to stay in the court's jurisdiction during the entire time of his trial, which prevented him from attending to his many investments around the country. His fortunes declined to the point that in 1916 he was sued for back rent on his New York City office. He attempted to maintain his interests in Kentucky coalfields, plantation properties in South Carolina, and his wife's family home in Charleston but lost each under the pressure of creditors.

In 1935 Calhoun's fortunes were revived when he was able to negotiate a drilling lease for the Barnstable Oil Company with the Newhall Land and Farming Company near Los Angeles, California. A major oil strike was made there the following year, and at the age of eighty he was again financially comfortable. Calhoun was struck and killed by a speeding car in Pasadena, California. He is buried at his Fort Hill birthplace.

• Information on Calhoun is scattered, and no archives of his papers are known to exist. Genealogical information is in L. D. McPherson, *Calhoun, Hamilton, Baskin and Related Families* (1957), and Margaret H. Cannon, *South Carolina Genealogies*, vol. 1 (1983). His years with Calhoun, King and Spalding are in Della Wager Wells, *The First Hundred Years: A Centennial History of King and Spalding* (1985). Also see Maury Klein, *The Great Richmond Terminal: A Study in Businessmen and Business Strategy* (1970), and William C. Barrow, "The Euclid Heights Allotment: A Palimpsest of the Nineteenth-century Search for Value in Cleveland's East End," (master's thesis, Cleveland State Univ., 1995). Mention of Calhoun's work in St. Louis is in a *St. Louis Star* article on 7 Mar. 1899. The San Francisco trials are in Walton Bean, *Boss Ruef's San Francisco* (1952), and Lately Thomas, *A Debonair Scoundrel* (1962). His role in securing the oil lease is in Ruth Waldo Newhall, *The Newhall Ranch: The Story of the Newhall Land and Farming Company* (1958). Calhoun is affectionately described by his daughter and son-in-law in Mildred Calhoun Wick, *Living with Love* (1986), and Warren Corning Wick, *My Recollections of Old Cleveland* (1979). Obituaries are in the *Atlanta Journal*, 17 June 1943, and the *New York Times*, 18 June 1943.

WILLIAM C. BARROW

CALHOUN, William Barron (29 Dec. 1796–8 Nov. 1865), lawyer, writer, and politician, was born in Boston, Massachusetts, the son of Andrew Calhoun, a merchant, and Martha Chamberlain. His father was one of the founders of Boston's Park Street Church. Calhoun was prepared for college by Harvard graduate William Wells, then he attended Yale, graduating in 1814. While a senior at Yale, Calhoun was one of the editors of a student publication, the *Athenaeum*, and writing articles became an important part of his life's work. After college Calhoun studied law, first in Concord, New Hampshire, where his father was living, and then for three years in Springfield, Massachusetts, with George Bliss, a prominent lawyer. In 1818 Calhoun was admitted to the bar in Springfield, the city where, four years later, he opened his law office. He was not enthusiastic about practicing law and was said to be "lacking in the qualities that shine in a court of law" (Green, p. 381). However, his law education provided a foundation for his public service and for his future writing, which expressed his concerns for social and economic welfare and political justice.

Early in life Calhoun took an interest in public affairs, and he served in various positions over many years. Although he did not actively seek public office, he was chosen in 1825 to represent Springfield in the Massachusetts House of Representatives, and he held his seat for ten years. In 1828, 1829, 1830, 1832, and 1833 Calhoun was Speaker of the House. His election to that position in 1828, by an unprecedented unanimous vote, caused the *Boston Courier* to comment that the Connecticut Valley "may feel proud of its present distinction" (Green, p. 398). In the troublesome sessions of the legislature, when national issues became contentious subjects of state debate, Speaker Calhoun's tall, distinguished figure brought dignity to the floor. He put forth the resolution of the house that condemned nullification and declared the "right claimed by the convention of South Carolina for that State of annulling any law of the United States which it may deem unconstitutional, is unauthorized by the letter or spirit of the Constitution" (Green, p. 426).

Local concerns of Springfield's citizens included the lack of funding for education and the failure of their schools to keep up with improvements in methods of instruction. After an 1825 study reported on the seriousness of the situation, a school committee was appointed, headed by Calhoun. He became involved with the reform movement in education in Massachusetts and in 1830 was chairman of the meeting in Boston that organized the American Institute of Instruction, which became a national leader in improvement of systems of education. He served as its vice president for three years and then as president from 1833 to 1839.

In 1834 Calhoun was elected as a Whig to the Twenty-fourth Congress, and he was reelected to the three succeeding Congresses. In the Twenty-sixth Congress he was chairman of the Committee on Private Land Claims. His elections to Congress occurred during years of increasing tension over slavery. Calhoun specifically stated that he had voted against the admission of Arkansas because its constitution recognized slavery. He then referred to slavery as "this infernal traffic . . . so abhorrent to us all" and stated that Congress should, within its appropriate authority, "bring this moral, social, and political evil, in all its forms, . . . to an end" (Green, p. 443). In 1837 he married Margaret Howard Kingsbury; they had three children.

Although Calhoun had been unopposed in two of his congressional elections, he declined nomination for a fifth term because health problems curtailed his strength. Apparently suffering from tubercular and respiratory symptoms, he retired from Congress in 1843. The Calhouns purchased a large lot on Chestnut Street in Springfield and built a spacious home. Calhoun continued his public service and was a presidential elector for Henry Clay in 1844. As the Mexican War became an issue in Massachusetts politics, Calhoun was elected in 1846 to the state senate as an antiwar Whig. He served as president of the senate during his two years there. Calhoun then moved from the legislative to the executive branch of state government to become secretary of the commonwealth from 1848 to 1851 and bank commissioner from 1853 to 1855. Calhoun had written, in 1849, a study of the condition of Massachusetts banks. In 1859 the now venerable Calhoun was called upon to serve in municipal government as mayor of Springfield. His final public role was to represent Springfield, for one more year, in the state house of representatives in 1861.

Calhoun was a trustee of Amherst College from 1829 until his death; during 1850 he lectured in political economy at the college. In 1858 he became a member of the First Congregational Church in Springfield, and in his last years he was elected a deacon. Throughout his life he wrote articles and editorials on education and good government for the *Springfield Republican*. Like his speeches, Calhoun's articles were neither brilliant nor sensational, but they were factual and carefully reasoned. His retirement was marked by struggle with disease. He died in Springfield, having held many offices of public trust and having contributed to the improvement of that city.

• Brief biographies of Calhoun are in Charles Wells Chapin, *Sketches of the Old Inhabitants and Other Citizens of Old Springfield* (1893), and Franklin Bowditch Dexter, *Biographical Sketches of the Graduates of Yale College with Annals of the College History*, vol. 6, *September, 1805–September, 1815* (1912). Chapin and Dexter provide details on Calhoun's career and some feeling for his personal life, and Dexter also has a bibliography that includes a few of Calhoun's writings. Mason A. Green, *Springfield, 1636–1886: History of Town and City Including an Account of the Quarter-Millenial Celebration at Springfield, Mass., May 25 and 26, 1886* (1888), describes Calhoun within the scene of political developments in Massachusetts. A lengthy obituary is in the *New York Times*, 10 Nov. 1865.

SYLVIA B. LARSON

CALIFORNIA JOE (8 May 1829–29 Oct. 1876), plainsman and army scout, was born Moses Embree Milner in Standford, Kentucky, the son of Sarah Ann and Embree Armstead Milner, planters. Plantation life in the Kentucky wilderness was hardly genteel; the Milner home was a log cabin, as was the schoolhouse where the young Milner was an able student. Along with "book learning," Milner excelled in tracking and hunting, which meant his family always had fresh meat to eat. Even as a boy he was known for his skill in shooting his father's long-barreled rifle, a talent his family regarded as wholly in keeping with his father's past military experiences in George Washington's revolutionary army and in the War of 1812. Like Daniel Boone, another woodland-wise Kentuckian, Milner honed his natural abilities with patient practice until, at age fourteen, he and his muzzle-loading rifle were a nearly unbeatable pair. The precision of his shooting, especially, would come to be legendary and, if true, could be matched today only by experts using high-powered rifles. In any event, he was a crack shot and a stealthy hunter well at home in the wilderness.

Milner found the wilderness surrounding his family's home was becoming less wild, so, to his parents' distress, he quit school and one August morning in 1843 headed out for a few days' hunting that became five years. Milner may not have intended to leave home, but once into the forest he just kept going west until in September he found himself in St. Louis, the center of fur trade in America. Milner latched on to a party of fur trappers heading for Independence, Missouri, and a hunting trip up in the Platte River valley. He learned how to trap well, and his rifle skills were appreciated by the other trappers. During that long autumn and winter of trapping, the boy shared and survived hardships with the older trappers, listened to their tall tales of adventure, and gained knowledge and experience that he would soon parlay into a colorful and peripatetic career.

In the spring of 1844 the trappers met an agent from the American Fur Company in Fort Laramie who convinced them to sell their furskins there instead of traveling back to Independence. Located in Oglala Sioux country near the Platte River of the Wyoming Territory, Fort Laramie was the most famous and notorious of the fur trading posts, "home" to famous and infamous trappers, frontiersmen, and mountain men. A few days after arriving in Fort Laramie, Milner joined another group of trappers, led by Jim Baker, heading for the Yellowstone River to trade with the Indians there and to provide escort back to Fort Laramie for other trappers coming in with their winter catches. When they reached the Powder River, they discovered a band of Blackfoot, who were considered "hostiles." There were more Blackfoot than trappers, and Baker, who had had many such encounters before, ordered a surprise attack on the Indians. It was a rout, and a bloody one. The trappers killed eighteen Blackfoot warriors and destroyed their nearby village, though the women and children managed to escape to the hills. The fifteen-year-old Milner killed three of the warriors. One of those men he shot from a distance of 400 yards, a phenomenal shot that won him the admiration of his comrades and the beginnings of a reputation as an Indian fighter.

The rest of the journey was uneventful, with successful trading among the Indians of the Yellowstone Valley. Upon the trappers' return to Fort Laramie in the spring of 1846, Milner parted with them and signed on as a hunter for the American Fur Company. Yet again his skill with a rifle added to his reputation, this time as a buffalo hunter. On his hunting trips he would often camp nights at Sioux villages, and over the course of two years he learned to speak the Sioux language. Milner eventually moved from Fort Laramie to Fort Bridger and came under the employ and tutelage of Jim Bridger himself, working as a livestock herder and muleskinner. It was also at Fort Bridger that Milner, still a teenager, acquired his reputation as a very hard drinker—he shot the man who drank his shot of whiskey, or so the story goes. Further exploits and adventures followed—including service as an army guide during the Mexican War. Some may be true, some garnished, but what was becoming clear was that Milner was making a name for himself in the Wild West.

While young Milner had been gone, the Milner family had moved from Kentucky to Warren County, Missouri. Being an expert tracker, Milner found them and in 1848 just suddenly reappeared, ending his five-year absence. One other skill he had developed while away from home was how to tell a whopping story. He had also begun to develop into a rather eccentric character, with his flyaway hair and charming loquaciousness. Whether he had yet acquired his ever-present briar pipe is unknown, but he was already good at attracting attention. One person who attracted *his* attention was Nancy Emma Watts, and in 1850 they married. Their honeymoon trip was a covered wagon journey across the Great Plains to California. For the next twenty-six years there would be years at a spread when Nancy would not see him. Nevertheless, she adored Milner, and they had four sons, who also adored him. When he was home he told wonderful and exciting stories. And when he was away he wrote thrilling letters, sporadically. During one of his trips back to California, he moved his family to Corvallis, Oregon, where he had built them a new home. Sometimes, later on, he took his older sons with him on his wanderings.

It may have been after his move to California with his new bride and his subsequent return to the western frontiers of Idaho and Montana and the Indian territories that his name became California Joe. How he acquired the name is unclear, but a logical story holds that, upon being asked his identity by some less than trustworthy characters, Milner circumspectly said he was called "Joe" and came from California. At any rate, few if any of his contemporaries ever knew him by any other name. And he was certainly known throughout the West—as an incredible rifle shot, a superb guide, a clever Indian fighter, and a roustabout and very hearty drinker. His skills as a scout were often sought by the army, and when he was not scouting he tried his hand at ranching and mining, the latter endeavor gaining him some unhappy enemies.

One of Joe's closest friends was another army scout with a reputation, Wild Bill Hickok. Joe and Hickok probably met at Fort Riley, Kansas, in 1866, in the course of their scouting duties. The men held each other in high regard, with Hickok perhaps the more coolly dangerous of the two. They were not often together (contrary to what has become popular myth), and when Hickok was backshot by John McCall in a Deadwood, South Dakota, saloon on 2 August 1876, Joe was not there to save his friend. When he did return to Deadwood and found out not only that Hickok was dead but that a rigged jury and court had let his killer go, Joe turned murderously mad and went after McCall to challenge him to a gunfight. McCall, being a coward but not stupid, fled, only to be later arrested, tried, and hanged for Hickok's murder. But that was in March 1877, after Joe's own death.

In 1868, two years after California Joe and Wild Bill met, the U.S. Army, in the person of Colonel George Armstrong Custer and the Seventh Cavalry, again required Joe's services, this time for the winter campaign along Oklahoma's Washita River. Joe made quite a first impression on Custer. In *My Life on the Plains*, Custer gives a wonderfully full physical description of Joe: "[He was] over six feet in height, and possessing a well-proportioned frame. His head was covered with a luxuriant crop of long, almost black hair (Custer, pp. 234–36). Custer also noted that Joe was an "inveterate smoker. . . . The endurance of his smoking powers was only surpassed by his loquacity," and there "was but little of the western country from the Pacific to the Missouri River with which California Joe was not intimately acquainted" (Custer, pp. 237–38).

This was the man Custer chose to be chief scout. On his first night in his new job, Joe led a column of soldiers out to search for Indians. To celebrate his promotion, Joe had filled his canteen with rotgut whiskey and was imbibing steadily as in the dark his mule led him away from his column. Suddenly the soldiers heard violent screams ahead of them. Thinking they were about to engage a frenzied enemy, they instead discovered their scout, roaring drunk and so frantic to fight Indians that the soldiers had to hog-tie him to his mule to get him back to camp. Custer removed Joe as chief scout, but he kept him as a regular scout and as one of his favorite companions. At every opportunity Joe would entertain Custer with "peculiar but generally correct" ideas about how to conduct an Indian campaign (Wheeler, p. 97). Around January 1869 Joe wandered off yet again, but he kept up a lively and erratic correspondence with Custer and his wife Libbie for the rest of his life.

In the summer of 1876 Joe was in the Black Hills—ostensibly to chase out prospectors, but also doing some clandestine prospecting of his own—when Custer engaged in his last Indian campaign, but without his rowdy scout. Joe lost two great friends that summer, Custer and Hickok. On 26 October, drunk and angry, Joe beat up several unarmed agency Indians at Fort Robinson, Nebraska, shouting, "I'll show you how you killed Custer!" (Wheeler, p. 97). Three days later and sober, Joe had an argument with Thomas Newcomb, one of the quartermaster's employees. The reason for the argument is unclear, but it was serious enough that both men drew their pistols. Joe, however, managed to convince Newcomb "to put up your dam' gun and have a drink" (Milner, p. 279). Folks in the vicinity thought that that was the end of the matter, but Newcomb returned later with a Winchester rifle and shot Joe in the back and killed him as he was talking to some friends. Newcomb was arrested and set free when no civil charges were made against him, and then disappeared. Joe's true name was discovered when the fort's doctor, V. T. McGillycuddy, emptied Joe's pockets and found a packet of letters addressed to Moses Milner of Kentucky, "and under that name I buried him the next day on the banks of the White

River" (Milner, p. 281). Joe's headstone in the fort's cemetery identified him simply as "Moses Milner, Scout."

California Joe was a singular and extraordinary example of the kind of man who both tamed the West and made it wild. He did not go down in legend the way others did, but in his own time he was as famous. What makes his story worth preserving is not merely his real and elaborated exploits—some of which are abhorrent while others are hilarious—but his voice. That someone as unrooted as he would leave behind any trace, would maintain a relationship of reciprocal love with a wife and children, would maintain a substantial correspondence with them and with the Custers over a period of many years (indeed, Joe's letter-writing and letter-saving is remarkable) and from many places, *and* would make such a vivid impression on a man who was only briefly his commanding officer bespeaks someone extraordinary and worth remembering. California Joe's voice offers a unique and genuine look at a time both vibrant and deadly. For better and for worse, California Joe was America's West.

• Some of California Joe's correspondence survives with the Milner family and some is collected in the Custer correspondence. Milner Family Papers, including the manuscript and letters relating to Joe's biography by his grandson Joe E. Milner, are in the archives of the Washington State University Library. Information is also contained in the Ricker papers at the Kansas State Historical Society. Photographs of California Joe, with his ever-present briar pipe, gun, and dog, are in the collection of the Kansas State Historical Society, as are contemporary newspaper articles. A full-length biography is Joe E. Milner and Earle R. Forrest, *California Joe: Noted Scout and Indian Fighter; With an Authentic Account of Custer's Last Fight by Colonel William H. Bowen* (1935; rev. ed., 1987); the 1987 foreword by Joseph G. Rosa is useful in correcting some of the hearsay and fiction that the subject's grandson let slip into the narrative. For contemporary accounts of California Joe, the most interesting is General George A. Custer, *My Life on the Plains* (1876; 1952, 1966 versions edited by Milo Milton Quaife). Julia B. McGillycuddy, *McGillycuddy Agent: A Biography of Dr. Valentine T. McGillycuddy* (1941), is useful because Dr. McGillycuddy knew California Joe at Fort Robinson. Almost wholly unreliable is J. W. Buel, *Heroes of the Plains* (1882), in which Moses Embree Milner/California Joe is confused with Truman Head, the "California Joe" of Colonel Hiram Berdan's Civil War sharpshooters; Buel also gets things wrong about Wild Bill Hickok and Buffalo Bill Cody. Among modern references, besides his foreword, see Rosa's *Wild Bill Hickok: The Man and His Myth* (1996); Arthur Woodward, "Historical Sidelights on California Joe," *The Westerners, Los Angeles Corral, Eighth Brand Book* (1959), pp. 208–9; and Edward S. Godfrey, "Some Reminiscences, Including the Washita Battle, November 27, 1868," *The Custer Reader*, ed. Paul Andrew Hutton (1992), pp. 159–79. See also Dee Brown, *The American West* (1994); Evan S. Connell, *Son of the Morning Star* (1984); Jay Monaghan, ed., *The Book of the American West* (1963); Paul Trachtman, *The Old West: The Gunfighters* (1974); and Keith Wheeler, *The Old West: The Scouts* (1978). Hollywood film renditions of the Wild Bill Hickok story often erroneously include California Joe as being present at the poker game during which Hickok was shot.

E. D. LLOYD-KIMBREL

CALKINS, Clinch (15 July 1895–26 Dec. 1968), poet, polemicist, and novelist, was born Marion Clinch Calkins in Evansville, Wisconsin, the daughter of Judson Wells Calkins, a politically liberal owner of a general store, and Julia Clinch, a lover of music and literature. Calkins graduated from the University of Wisconsin in 1918, packed artillery shells in a Milwaukee plant, and then returned to Madison to teach in the university's English and art history departments and to do social work. She submitted a poem, "I Was a Maiden," to an annual competition in the *Nation*, a favorite magazine in her parents' house. Wanting a "neutral" name that was neither masculine nor feminine, she dropped her first name and entered the contest using "Clinch Calkins." Shortly thereafter the magazine's editor, Oswald Garrison Villard, traveled to Wisconsin to tell Calkins her poem had won first prize but couldn't be published, because it was so "advanced" it would cost the magazine its mailing privileges. Instead the poem was given third prize and was not printed. Calkins recalled that the magazine "after that, discontinued its poetry contest." "I Was a Maiden" was published in Calkins's *Poems* (1928). The lines that were too "advanced" for the *Nation* were: "My lover holds me in his close embrace / And all his members with mine tightly lace / And he has died and I will bear his son. / I'll name him after love, Corruption!"

In the mid-1920s Calkins moved to New York City and was a vocational counselor in the school system and a social worker at Lillian Wald's Henry Street Settlement. Her father, alarmed at her moving to the dangerous city, insisted that she take a revolver with her. Soon comfortable in New York, Calkins buried the pistol in the graveyard of Trinity Church. One of the immigrant boys she was teaching scolded her, "My God, Miss Calkins, I coulda used that gat!"

In 1927 Calkins worked as a bibliographer in Florence, Italy, for art historian Richard Offner. She wrote poems and (under the name "Majollica Wattles") humorous columns for the *New Yorker* in its first years. Her *Poems* was published by Alfred A. Knopf to enthusiastic praise. In his review Lionel Trilling wrote that Calkins was "producing one of the finest bodies of American poetry today."

Calkins's greatest success, however, came in a work of social criticism. With funding and 300 case histories from the National Federation of Settlements, she wrote *Some Folks Won't Work* (1930), a book documenting what happens to people who lose their jobs. The book appeared less than a year after the 1929 crash and was reviewed on the front page of the *New York Times Book Review*. It became both a bestseller and, in a real sense, the first book of the depression. Marquis Childs said the book would touch the heart of the most complacent Babbitt. Paul Douglas wrote, "I am a statistician and I pride myself on being tough-minded, but these stories left me weak with the anguish which always comes from seeing brave souls struggling with impersonal fate. . . . I can only wish that every comfortable family may take the occasion to read this book."

Calkins's book brought her to the attention of Harry Hopkins, Franklin Roosevelt's right-hand man. When the New Deal began in 1933, Hopkins invited her to to join his Federal Emergency Relief Administration (FERA). Calkins traveled the country reporting on economic conditions and sometimes ghostwrote for Hopkins; his *Spending to Save: The Complete Story of Relief* (1936) has many echoes of *Some Folks Won't Work* because they come from the same author.

Calkins and her husband, Mark Merrell, whom she had married in 1929 and who headed the drug industry division of the National Recovery Administration (NRA), socialized with many important New Dealers. One of them, A. A. Berle, later wrote, "I think she kept many of us healthy and sane through those years. . . . For her, there were neither high nor humble—merely men and women appreciated and esteemed for their qualities, the best of which she evoked." The couple had one daughter. Calkins was especially close to Henry Alsberg, the director of the Federal Writers' Project, and his second-in-command, her fellow Wisconsin alumnus Clair Laning; the night Alsberg was ignominiously fired he sought refuge in a party thrown by Calkins and her husband.

In 1936 the Senate voted to investigate whether workers trying to organize labor unions were being denied their constitutional rights of free speech and assembly. The investigation by Senator Robert La Follette's Civil Liberties Committee drew more media attention than any congressional inquiry since the one organized to look into the Teapot Dome scandal. Calkins, seconded to the committee's staff, reported what she heard and saw in *Spy Overhead* (1937; repr. 1971), the first book to examine industrial espionage.

In 1939, while caring for her young daughter, Calkins wrote a verse drama, "State Occasion," about the rise of an American fascist. In 1943 Broadway producer Lee Simonson complained in print that he hadn't anything he wanted to produce. Calkins sent him her play, and Simonson optioned it. He finally decided the play's time had passed, and "State Occasion" was instead produced at Catholic University, with Alan Schneider directing and Ed McMahon in a small role.

After World War II Calkins devoted many years to preparing a biography of inventor Marchese Guglielmo Marconi with his daughter, Degna. The biography appeared in 1962, but by that time Calkins had withdrawn from the project. While continuing to write poetry, some of which appeared in the intellectual review journal *Botteghe Oscure* and her second book of poems, *Strife of Love in a Dream* (1965), she turned to fiction. *Lady on the Hunt*, a satire on the fox-hunting set, appeared to mixed reviews in 1950. Two years later she published *Calendar of Love*, a portrait of two Washington couples' lives against the public turmoil of the previous thirty years. The reviews this time were more positive; Paul Pickrel in the *Yale Review* commended the book for its "sense of life responsibly lived." Particularly praised was Calkins's journalistic rendering of little-known aspects of the New Deal, notably, as one reviewer put it, "the borning and squalling days of the NRA." Calkins died in McLean, Virginia.

• Calkins's archive is still in her family's possession. Profiles on her appeared in the *Milwaukee Journal*, 5 Oct. 1952, and the *Washington Sunday Star*, 14 Dec. 1952. Her most important book, *Some Folks Won't Work*, is discussed in William Stott, *Documentary Expression and Thirties America* (1973; repr. 1986). Obituaries are in the *New York Times*, the *Washington Post*, and the *St. Louis Post-Dispatch*, all 28 Dec. 1968.

WILLIAM STOTT

CALKINS, Earnest Elmo (25 Mar. 1868–4 Oct. 1964), advertising agent and writer, was born in Geneseo, Illinois, the son of William Clinton Calkins and Mary Harriet Manville. When Earnest was three months old, the family moved to nearby Galesburg, where his father became a self-taught lawyer, elected city attorney. Except for a brief period of private schooling, Calkins was educated in the public schools. When he was six, measles aggravated an inherited tendency and made him somewhat deaf. His hearing continued to weaken gradually until, in middle age, he became completely deaf. Overcoming this handicap became a central concern of Calkins's life.

In grade school Calkins became a ravenous reader and developed an admiration for beautifully printed books. In Baptist Sunday school he read the Bible through three times. Calkins acquired a foot-treadle press, bought some used type, and briefly wrote and printed a small magazine. While in high school, he got a Saturday and summer job in a newspaper office, setting patent medicine and display ads, personals, and high school and college news, which he also wrote. Calkins kept this job, joining the typographical union, while attending Knox College.

Deafness made Calkins's college experience difficult because he could not hear classroom lectures or participate in most extracurricular events. He wrote for and eventually edited the school magazine, *Coup d'Etat*, in which he published an article about the trade periodical *Printers' Ink*, which secured him a free subscription and turned his attention toward advertising as a possible career. Calkins received his A.B. from Knox in 1891 when the trustees overruled the faculty decision not to award him a degree because of a conditioned course in geology.

After another summer as reporter and printer on the *Galesburg Evening Mail*, Calkins went to New York City to seek his fortune. He prepared a newsletter for a cotton broker, then edited the *Butchers' Gazette and Sausage Journal* for an irascible publisher before returning to Galesburg in 1883, burdened with debt. Calkins rejoined the *Mail* as reporter and columnist while launching a copywriting service for local advertisers. For a hardware store he entered an ad-writing contest sponsored by a national carpet-sweeper company. There were 1,433 entries, and Calkins won.

In 1894 he left Galesburg again, becoming advertising manager for a Peoria department store and also writing a column for a morning paper. Ambitious to return to New York, Calkins sent samples of his copy to Charles Austin Bates, whose agency was one of the first to provide clients with copy as well as to secure space in magazines and newspapers. Bates offered Calkins a job, and in four years he advanced to become head of the copy department. He studied at the Pratt School of Design and set up an art department at the Bates agency to provide advertisers with illustrations as well as text for ads.

With Ralph Holden, a fellow employee at Bates, Calkins launched in 1902 the prototype of the modern advertising agency. Holden managed business aspects of the firm and made the most of face-to-face contacts, while Calkins contributed the creative advertising ideas. Calkins and Holden prepared campaigns for their clients that were directed at influencing consumer attitudes and behavior. The appearance of advertisements was transformed, with careful attention to typography and to illustration, including the introduction of photography. In 1908 Calkins arranged the first exhibition of advertising art at the National Arts Club. Before advertising appeared, campaigns were presented to salesmen and dealers to win their approval. The firm engaged in market and motivational research by ringing doorbells and talking with housewives. They began to counsel clients on the design of packaging and products. Calkins persistently strove to elevate the ethical standards of advertising, seeking to have its practitioners ranked as professionals alongside clergymen, physicians, and lawyers. "Advertising," he asserted, "is the supreme flowering of a sophisticated civilization" (*Louder, Please!* p. 4). In 1905 Calkins and Holden published *Modern Advertising*, the first textbook to present the pattern of innovative procedures practiced by their firm. In 1925 Calkins was the first individual presented by the Harvard Business School with the Edward W. Bok medal for distinguished service "for his pioneering efforts in raising the standards, both of the planning and execution of advertising, for the integrity in the profession and for his unselfish devotion to the young men with whom he came in contact" (*New York Times*, 23 Feb. 1926).

In 1904 Calkins married Angie Cushman Higgins; they had no children. Angie Higgins had worked on the *Ladies' Home Journal* and thus knew Bok. This gave Calkins and Holden an entry with the Cyrus Curtis publications. The firm also had ties to S. S. McClure, a Knox graduate who had founded the college magazine that Calkins later edited. For years Calkins and Holden managed the advertising for *McClure's Magazine* and McClure's Books. Magazines generally were a staple of the firm's business. Among the firm's other major clients were J. B. Williams Shaving Soap, Sherwin-Williams Paint, Pierce-Arrow Motor Cars, H. J. Heinz, Ingersoll Watches, and Welch's Grape Juice. Calkins made national figures of Sunny Jim in advertising for the cereal Force, and of Phoebe Snow in advertising for the Lackawanna Railroad. In 1927—the year after Holden's death—the Calkins and Holden agency ranked fourteenth in total bookings among American advertising agencies. Calkins retired from the profession in 1931, and his agency was merged into the Interpublic Group of Companies.

In retirement Calkins expanded an activity in which he had been long engaged, that of freelance writer. His main themes were advertising and his deafness. He contributed articles to every advertising journal and was a contributing editor of *Advertising and Selling*. Calkins followed the textbook with several other books about advertising. While condemning advertising's faults, such as paid testimonials, pseudoscientific jargon, unwarranted superlatives, and emphasis on fear and sex, Calkins in *Business the Civilizer* (1927, pp. 12, 24) credited advertising not only with "the amelioration of the housewife's lot" but more broadly with the creation of economic "good times." Of some fifty articles he wrote for the *Atlantic Monthly*, the first was "On the Technique of Being Deaf" (Jan. 1923); his deafness formed a central strand in two autobiographies, *Louder, Please!* (1924) and *And Hearing Not* (1946). Calkins published on a wide range of other topics, and some of his articles were based on lectures he had delivered. Main themes included the history of elegant printing, his European travels, and the making of ship models. He boasted that he had never received a rejection slip.

Knox College awarded alumnus Calkins membership in Phi Beta Kappa. For the college's centennial he published *They Broke the Prairie* (1937), the intertwined history of Knox and Galesburg; made a model of the original campus; and wrote a pageant that was performed, "The Masque of Prairie Pioneers."

After his wife's death in 1950, Calkins lived on in his Park Avenue apartment in New York, writing and giving interviews on the state of advertising and of the business world. He died in New York City.

Calkins was recognized by his peers not only as a creative pioneer in advertising agency practice but also for playing a key role in changing advertising from a generally disreputable business into a respectable profession. He emerged as the primary spokesman for the ethics and aesthetics of advertising and helped to define its special place within the broader realm of business.

• Calkins's papers are in the Henry W. Seymour Library of Knox College, Galesburg; Carley Robison, archivist, provided helpful aid. Of the two autobiographies, *And Hearing Not* (1946) is the more inclusive. Other Calkins books include *The Business of Advertising* (1915), *The Advertising Man* (1922), and *Care and Feeding of Hobby Horses* (1935). An important article by Calkins is "Mr. Calkins Looks Back Twenty-five Years at Advertising," *Printers' Ink*, 9 Jan. 1930, pp. 3–6, 156–70. Evaluations of Calkins's contributions appear in Otis Pease, *The Responsibilities of American Advertising* (1958); James P. Wood, *The Story of Advertising* (1958); Daniel Pope, *The Making of Modern Advertising* (1983); and Roland Marchand, *Advertising the American Dream* (1985). Obituaries are in the *New York Times*, 6 Oct. 1964; *Galesburg Labor News*, 8 Oct. 1964; *Printers' Ink*, 9 Oct. 1964; and *Advertising Age*, 12 Oct. 1964.

JAMES HARVEY YOUNG

CALKINS, Gary Nathan (18 Jan. 1869–4 Jan. 1943), zoologist, was born in Valparaiso, Indiana, the son of John Wesley Calkins, a retail merchant, and Emma Frisbie Smith. In 1886 he entered the Massachusetts Institute of Technology, where he became keenly interested in biology through William Thompson Sedgwick, a professor in bacteriology and public health. After receiving a B.S. in 1890, Calkins was appointed lecturer in biology at MIT and assistant biologist and microscopist for the Massachusetts State Board of Health until 1893. From 1891 to 1893 he published several papers on microscopic examinations of water supplies and the impact of Protozoa in them. After spending the summer of 1893 at the Marine Biological Laboratory (MBL) in Woods Hole, Massachusetts, he entered graduate school at Columbia University and in 1898 received a Ph.D. in zoology, under the direction of Edmund Beecher Wilson, whose expertise was in embryology and cell structure. While in graduate school, Calkins was appointed tutor in zoology at Columbia in 1894. In 1894–1895 he offered a course in the special morphology of the Protozoa, described as "the first course in protozoology in the country" (Wenrich, p. 4). He married Anne Marshall Smith in 1894; they had no children. Calkins advanced to instructor at Columbia in 1899, adjunct professor in 1903, and professor of invertebrate zoology in 1904. From 1898 to 1901 he published on parasites in brook trout and on one-celled organisms potentially related to illness in humans. From 1902 to 1908 Calkins was consulting biologist to the state cancer laboratory in Buffalo, New York, and for a time he thought that cancer might be somehow related to one-celled organisms.

From 1901 Calkins's special interest was the protozoans, generally considered the most primitive animals. Earlier work by researchers in this field had been especially on those involved in human and animal illnesses, but many species had been described by zoologists, including David Simons Kellicott and Alfred Cheatum Stokes in the late 1800s. In 1901 Calkins published *The Protozoa*, the first U.S. book solely on this group of animals. His position at Columbia became in 1907 professor of protozoology, the first appointment with that title in any U.S. college. He wrote *Protozoology* in 1908. After his wife's death, Calkins married Helen Richards Williston (Colton) in 1909; they had two sons and raised a son by her first marriage.

Throughout his career Calkins carried out studies on the ciliate protozoans, free-living single-celled animals characterized by short hair-like processes (cilia) used chiefly for locomotion. Many species have occasional union (conjugation) between individuals that include an exchange of protoplasm. Calkins was interested in the significance of this exchange on the longevity of the individual. His preferred subject was *Uroleptus mobilis*, a ciliate protozoan found among freshwater plants. With live specimens in the laboratory, which were isolated daily for study, he determined their reaction to various chemicals and to changes introduced into their environment. For one study, Calkins continued a series of cultures from an individual through 742 generations. He concluded that a protozoan advances from youth to maturity to old age, but it is renewed by conjugation. At that time the macronucleus disintegrates, and its products are reorganized into a new one, so that a new generation begins. He believed that conjugation was vital to the survival of ciliate protozoans, and that they could not continue indefinitely solely by division (1934). After some years of debate by zoologists, Calkins's belief that conjugation rejuvenates the organism became generally accepted. He pioneered in techniques of microscopic dissection and described the physiology and cell structure of protozoans in careful detail. Not a taxonomist, he described very few new species. He considered the free-living Protozoa readily obtainable subjects for providing information on the single living cell, which he believed could be useful in studying biological problems in more complex organisms.

In 1914 Calkins published the textbook *Biology*, and his most widely known book, *The Biology of the Protozoa*, came out in 1926 (2d ed., 1933). This was followed by *Smallest Living Things* in 1932. With Frank M. Summers he edited *Protozoa in Biological Research* (1941), a collection of articles by more than twenty authors, indicating how his field had expanded in his lifetime. Calkins had contributed to that expansion; his courses at Columbia University and at MBL were well attended and led to further studies in the field of protozoology. His student Lorande Loss Woodruff, later an expert in the same field, called Calkins "a brilliant lecturer" with "unfailing enthusiasm" (p. 16).

After his first visit to MBL in 1893, Calkins continued to spend most summers there for research. In 1902 he compiled a catalog of marine protozoans in the vicinity of Woods Hole. He served as clerk of the MBL corporation from 1912 to 1924, secretary of the board from 1925 to 1931, and trustee from 1938 to 1940.

During 1926–1927 Calkins was director of the American University Union in Paris, France, and he visited many European universities to interview students of zoology for fellowships provided by the Rockefeller Foundation. On sabbatical leave in 1935 he presented lectures at the School of Tropical Medicine of Puerto Rico University.

Calkins became professor emeritus at Columbia University in 1939. From 1937 to his death he was a member of a consulting board on cancer research for that university. A member of many scientific societies, he was president of the American Society for Cancer Research (1913–1914) and of the Society of Experimental Biology and Medicine (1919–1921). He was elected to the National Academy of Sciences in 1919. He died in Scarsdale, New York.

A pioneer and leader in the young field of protozoology, Calkins contributed careful research and influenced many students through his classes and books.

• Some administrative correspondence by Calkins from 1928 to 1930 is in the archives of Columbia University. A tribute to

Calkins is L. L. Woodruff, "Memorial to Dr. G. N. Calkins," *Biological Bulletin* 87 (1944): 15–16. Biographical material that relates Calkins to his profession is David Henry Wenrich, "Some American Pioneers in Protozoology," *Journal of Protozoology* 3 (1956): 1–7, and Reginald D. Manwell, *Introduction to Protozoology* (1968), pp. 596–602. An obituary is in the *New York Times* and the *New York Herald Tribune*, 5 Jan. 1943.

ELIZABETH NOBLE SHOR

CALKINS, Mary Whiton (30 Mar. 1863–26 Feb. 1930), psychologist and philosopher, was born in Hartford, Connecticut, the daughter of Wolcott Calkins, a Protestant clergyman, and Charlotte Whiton, a social activist. The close-knit family included two daughters and three sons, and Mary remained devoted to her family and its Christian values her entire life.

Calkins received her early education in Buffalo, New York, where her father served as pastor of the North Presbyterian Church from 1866 to 1880. A graduate of Yale University and Union Theological Seminary, Calkins's father made sure that his children were well educated. As a child, Calkins learned easily and eagerly and displayed broad and unusual intellectual interests. In 1880, when her father assumed a Congregational pastorate in Newton, Massachusetts, Calkins entered Newton High School. Her graduation essay, "The Apology Which Plato Should Have Written," a vindication of the character of Xanthippe, displayed the singular character of her interests.

In 1882 Calkins entered Smith College as a sophomore. Her undergraduate studies were interrupted when her younger sister Maud became critically ill and died that spring. Grief-stricken, Calkins remained at home during the 1883–1884 academic year, studying Greek and tutoring two of her younger brothers. She returned to Smith in 1884 with senior standing and graduated in 1885 with a concentration in classics and philosophy. The following year she spent studying on her own and exploring social and economic issues with a group of women who formed the Newton Social Science Club. Research for her first publication, *Sharing the Profits* (1888), a work that reveals her strong sense of social justice and her commitment to progressive social policies, was undertaken that year.

In May 1886 Calkins traveled to Europe with her family and spent time in Paris and Leipzig and several months in Greece, where she visited historical sites and studied modern Greek. When she returned to the United States, she was offered and accepted a position teaching Greek at Wellesley College, near her family's home, a position she held for three years. Calkins proved to be an enthusiastic and engaging teacher, but her deep and abiding interest in philosophy drew her away from classics. A colleague in the philosophy department learned of Calkins's desire to study philosophy further and recommended her as the appropriate person to offer courses in the new science of psychology. Wellesley's president made the appointment on the condition that Calkins study the subject for a year. Calkins experienced some difficulty locating a graduate school that would welcome a woman, but, assisted by a petition from her father and a letter from the president of Wellesley, she was finally permitted to attend classes at Harvard University.

In October 1890 Calkins began attending seminars with William James, who had just published his monumental text *Principles of Psychology* (1890), and with Josiah Royce, who was formulating his own variant of absolute idealism. During that year she also carried out experimental investigations with Edmund C. Sanford from Clark University. In addition to preparing her for a new position at Wellesley, her studies laid the groundwork for her lifelong work in experimental psychology, theoretical psychology, and philosophy.

Calkins returned to Wellesley in 1891 as instructor in psychology, and she opened the first psychological laboratory at an American women's college. She incorporated experimental work into the undergraduate curriculum; a number of the studies completed in the laboratory were published in psychological journals during the 1890s. Eager to pursue further study of the new science, Calkins sought advice from Royce, James, and Sanford about the most appropriate places for a woman to study. She seriously considered going abroad to study with Hugo Münsterberg at the University of Freiburg, but she shifted her plans when Münsterberg was imported to teach experimental psychology at Harvard in 1892. Calkins once again petitioned Harvard for permission to attend classes, and for the next three years she worked with Münsterberg, James, and Royce at Harvard while continuing to teach at Wellesley.

Calkins had become interested in the association of ideas while studying with James and chose to investigate the influence of frequency, recency, and vividness on the durability of associations in Münsterberg's laboratory. While conducting this research, she invented a technical memorizing method still widely employed in memory research—the method of paired associates. In 1895 she presented her theoretical and experimental work on association at an unofficial doctoral defense. Her committee, comprised of the members of Harvard's philosophy department, unanimously recommended her for the Ph.D., but Harvard refused to award the degree because Calkins was a woman.

Although Calkins never lost her interest in experimental psychology, she turned the laboratory work over to a younger colleague, Eleanor Gamble, in 1898. That same year she was promoted to professor of philosophy and psychology, and for her remaining thirty-one years at Wellesley she taught courses in philosophy and seminars in psychological theory and supervised research in both disciplines. Most of her books, including *An Introduction to Psychology* (1901), *The Persistent Problems in Philosophy* (1907), *A First Book in Psychology* (1909), and *The Good Man and the Good* (1918), were written with her students' needs in mind.

Calkins made significant theoretical contributions to psychology. Philosophically astute, she noticed the tension between the deterministic view of human functioning provided by scientific psychology and the freedom, individuality, and moral worth of the individuals she encountered in her daily life. The dilemma was particularly acute for Calkins, who was a deeply religious person. Münsterberg's distinction between the "objectifying sciences" and the "subjectifying sciences" was the key that helped Calkins reconcile her work in atomistic psychology with her commitment to the value of the individual person. She argued that consciousness needed to be examined both from the objective standpoint, as a science of ideas, and from the subjective standpoint, as a science of selves. This "double entry" bookkeeping approach was presented systematically in her first textbook *An Introduction to Psychology*, and it was explored more fully in her *Der doppelte Standpunkt in der Psychologie* (1905). By 1909 she had shifted to a "single entry" approach, stating that although she did not deny the validity of the objective standpoint, she had come to "question the significance and the adequacy, and deprecate the abstractness of the atomistic science of ideas" (preface to *A First Book in Psychology*). She later wrote, "With each year I live . . . I am more deeply convinced that psychology should be conceived as the science of the self, or person, as related to its environment, physical and social" (Murchison, pp. 41–42).

Calkins's most enduring work, *The Persistent Problems in Philosophy*, combined a clear exposition of leading philosophical positions with a critical evaluation of their merits. Her careful examination of the texts of great philosophers served to persuade Calkins of the merits of Royce's personal idealism. In subsequent works she developed her own doctrine of "personalistic absolutism," based on her study of G. W. F. Hegel, F. H. Bradley, and Royce. This position was a form of idealism because, she argued, the universe is completely mental in nature; it was personalistic because every mental existent is a self or "a part, phase, aspect or process of a self"; and it was absolutistic because the universe "literally is one all-including . . . self of which all the lesser selves are genuine and identical parts" (Adams, pp. 202, 209).

Calkins's contributions to psychology and philosophy earned her many honors. In James McKeen Cattell's *American Men of Science* (1903), Calkins was ranked twelfth among fifty top psychologists. She was the first woman elected president of the American Psychological Association (1905) and president of the American Philosophical Association (1918). Having been denied the doctorate by Harvard in 1895, she was given honorary doctorates by Columbia University in 1909 and by Smith College in 1910. Calkins's work was recognized internationally, and in 1928 she was made an honorary member of the British Psychological Association.

In addition to her intellectual work, Calkins found time to support progressive social causes like the Consumers' League and the American Civil Liberties Union. She was a pacifist and a devout Christian who frequently voted the Socialist party ticket. One of Calkins's students described her as "the most perfectly integrated personality I have ever known. . . . Her philosophy, ethics, religion, psychology, and daily life were harmonious" (*In Memoriam*, p. 24). Calkins retired from Wellesley College in 1929, planning to devote herself to writing and hoping to spend more time with her mother. Inoperable cancer was discovered in the fall of that year and she died in Newton, Massachusetts.

Equally eminent as a psychologist and a philosopher, Calkins advocated a personalistic approach to psychology and philosophy. Although her personalist position was never widely accepted in either discipline, she provided a counter voice that forced her opponents to rethink their own positions. Later in her career, she was comforted by signs of renewed opposition to atomistic psychology and increased interest in the study of the whole person. As one of the clearest expounders of Hegelian idealism, she would have derived satisfaction from her contribution to the dialectical development of thought in philosophy and psychology.

• A small collection of Calkins's papers are held at the Wellesley College Archives. Her autobiographical sketch in Carl Murchison, ed., *A History of Psychology in Autobiography*, vol. 1 (1930), provides her account of the development of her psychological career as well as a clear statement of her self psychology. For a detailed account of Calkins's philosophical position, consult her chapter, "The Philosophical Credo of an Absolutistic Personalist," in *Contemporary American Philosophy*, vol. 1, ed. George P. Adams (1930). For accounts of Calkins's life and contributions to psychology, see Laurel Furumoto, "Mary Whiton Calkins (1863–1930)," in *Women in Psychology: A BioBibliographic Sourcebook*, ed. A. O'Connell and N. F. Russo (1990); and Furumoto, "Mary Whiton Calkins (1863–1930): Fourteenth President of the American Psychological Association," *Journal of the History of the Behavioral Sciences* 15 (1979): 346–56. *In Memoriam: Mary Whiton Calkins, 1863–1930* (1931) contains a biographical sketch by her brother Raymond Calkins and a tribute to her work in philosophy by Edgar Sheffield Brightman. Obituaries are in the *Boston Transcript* and the *Boston Globe*, 27 Feb. 1930.

DEBORAH JOHNSON

CALKINS, Norman Allison (9 Sept. 1822–22 Dec. 1895), educator, administrator, and author, was born in Gainesville, New York, the son of Elisha Deming Calkins, a pioneer settler and farmer, and Abigail Lockwood. From four years of age, Calkins attended the local schools, later also attending a classical academy.

At eighteen Calkins began to teach school in Castile, New York, during the winter months. He then moved to the school at Gainesville, eventually being appointed its principal. He left in 1845 when he was elected county superintendent of schools. He was reelected for the 1846–1847 school year but resigned in the fall in order to move to New York City and assume the editorship of the *Student*.

This monthly magazine was intended both for family amusement and as a school reader. It fostered Calkins's belief that learning was augmented by the frequent introduction of new reading materials. The magazine was popular and eventually merged with its main competitor, the *Schoolmate*, becoming *Student and Schoolmate*. During his time as editor Calkins also conducted teachers' institutes throughout New York, New Jersey, Connecticut, and Pennsylvania. In 1854 he married Mary Hoosier; they had two children.

Calkins left the magazine shortly before the publication of his first book, *Primary Object Lessons*, in 1861. A year later, at the age of forty, he was elected assistant superintendent of schools in New York City in charge of primary grades, assuming the post in January 1863. He held this position through consecutive elections until his death thirty-three years later. In 1864 he also became instructor in methods and principles of education at the Saturday Normal School, holding the same position at its successor, the Normal College of the City of New York, until the Saturday sessions were discontinued in 1882. Through this forum he was able to spread his educational theories to a wide audience for nearly twenty years.

Calkins's main original contribution and legacy lay in his books on educational theory and his teachers' guides. He had studied Robert Owen's experimental utopia at New Harmony, Indiana, and through it had been exposed to the Pestalozzian principles of object teaching. Pestalozzi, a Swiss educator working at the close of the eighteenth century, focused on the need for observation as the basis for learning. The role of the teacher was to help children observe accurately and report their findings correctly and astutely. Calkins expressed the aim of his first and most popular book, *Primary Object Lessons for a Graduated Course of Development: A Manual for Teachers and Parents* (1861), in the book's preface: "an earnest desire to contribute something toward a general radical change in the system of primary education in this country—a change from the plan of exercising the memory chiefly to that of developing the observing powers—a change from an artificial to a natural plan—one in accordance with the philosophy of mind and its natural laws of development."

This method represented a significant change in the orientation of primary education. The focus was beginning to move from learning facts to the development of a child's ability to obtain and use knowledge; the acquisition of a skill, rather than of information, was the goal. Calkins's books proved very successful, especially his first, which went through forty editions in twenty years and was translated into a number of languages, including Spanish and Russian. The book was used extensively in Europe and South America as well as in the United States.

In addition to his writing, teaching, and administrative duties, Calkins was active in the National Educational Association. A member throughout his career, he served as its vice president in 1876, vice president of the department of superintendence in 1882, and president of that department in 1882–1883. He was elected treasurer for three consecutive years and served as president in 1886. In addition, he was chairman of the board of trustees from the time the association was established in 1886 until his death. During this time he was able to raise funds totaling $50,000.

A religious man, Calkins spent twenty-six years (1857–1883) as treasurer of the American Congregational Union. During this time the organization focused on erecting churches in the West, and Calkins's able management facilitated this. He died in New York City.

• Information on Calkins's educational philosophy can best be obtained from his own works: *Primary Object Lessons* (1861); *Phonic Charts* (1869); *How to Teach: A Graded Course of Instruction and Manual of Methods*, written with Henry Kiddle and Thomas F. Harrison (1873); *Aids for Object Teaching, Trades and Occupations* (1877); *Natural History Series for Children* (1877); *Manual of Object-Teaching* (1881); *From Blackboard to Books* (1883); and *Ear and Voice Training* (1886). For information on his life see *Journal of Proceedings and Addresses of the Thirty-Fifth Annual Meeting*, National Educational Association (1896): 218–26, and obituaries in the *New York Times*, 23 Dec. 1895, and the *New York Tribune*, 24 Dec. 1895.

CLAIRE STROM

CALL, Richard Keith (24 Oct. 1792–14 Sept. 1862), territorial governor of Florida (1836–1839, 1841–1844), was born in Prince George County, Virginia, the son of William Call and Helen Meade Walker, farmers. Upon the death of William, Helen moved her family to Kentucky. For two years Richard Call attended Mount Pleasant Academy near Clarksville, Tennessee.

In 1813 Call became a third lieutenant in a volunteer company that served under militia general Andrew Jackson in the Creek campaigns. Commissioned a first lieutenant in the United States Forty-fourth Infantry in 1814, he served with Jackson's forces at Pensacola and New Orleans. He was brevetted captain for bravery and in 1818 took part in Jackson's invasion of Florida, where Jackson made him an aide-de-camp. He was promoted to full captain in August 1820.

After ratification of the Adams-Onis treaty (1821) Call conducted the preliminary transfer negotiations for Florida with the Spanish governor at Pensacola. He resigned from the army in 1821 and served two terms in the territorial legislature (1822, 1823). Possessing little legal training, he nonetheless built a fruitful law practice in Florida based upon land litigation.

President James Monroe named Call brigadier general of militia in 1823, and in the same year Call was elected territorial delegate to the Eighteenth Congress. At the end of the session in 1824 he married Mary Letitia Kirkman in Nashville, Tennessee. Call was described by his friends at this time as a tall, erect man of fair personal appearance, noted for his melodious voice and dynamic and ostentatious manner. Critics saw him as a man of selfish ambition, lofty and arrogant pride, and "vanity beyond conception."

In Florida Call came under fire for his association with land speculators. His pride offended, he refused to stand for reelection but arranged his appointment in 1825 as receiver of public monies in the federal land office in Tallahassee. His friends were derided as the "Call party" or, more often, the "Nucleus," but by 1829 the group even included the governor, William P. DuVal. President Jackson made Call assistant legal counsel for all Spanish land cases arising in Florida. The influence of Call's Nucleus waned as Martin Van Buren's influence in the Jackson administration increased, but in 1836, undoubtedly because of his long personal friendship with Jackson, Call was named governor of Florida.

On the eve of her husband's governorship Mary Call died. Saddened and ill, Call turned to the great challenge of his first term, the Second Seminole War (1835–1842). Earlier, as militia general, he had engaged in an unsuccessful battle supporting General Duncan L. Clinch's regulars, in which the performance of the militia had been bitterly criticized. Jackson nevertheless gave Governor Call command of all the forces in Florida until the arrival of General Thomas S. Jesup. In the interim Call executed an attack upon the Seminoles that failed largely because of badly coordinated logistics. Furious, Jackson then relieved Call of command. Relations between the two were never close again.

The financial panic of 1837 posed another challenge for Call. The banks of the territory, which Call favored, raised capital by selling bonds endorsed by the territorial government. When they failed and the bondholders sought redress, blame was heaped on Call and on the bankers, many of whom were Call's Nucleus associates. With this controversy at white heat a convention was elected to write a constitution for the proposed state of Florida (1838). Its antibank majority, which soon organized as Florida's Democratic party, wrote a document severely restrictive of banks. Call and his Florida cronies were left in the cold, and by 1840 they were being identified with the Whigs.

Call persistently criticized the Van Buren administration's conduct of the Seminole War. Democrats just as persistently lobbied for his removal, and in late 1839 he was dismissed. Call then made a national speaking tour on behalf of William Henry Harrison, and the victorious Harrison reappointed Call governor in 1841. Financial problems dominated his term. He rejected demands that the bank bonds be repudiated, but the legislature repudiated them over his veto. Call was not reappointed in 1844. When Florida became a state in 1845, the Whigs nominated Call for governor, but he was defeated. Thereafter he took up the life of a planter, growing cotton.

Call was devoted to both slavery and the Union, and from his plantation he viewed growing sectional tensions with alarm. He saw the Mexican War, "wantonly provoked," as inflaming the tensions. A strong supporter of the Compromise of 1850, he threw his influence behind Whig candidates in 1852. When the party disintegrated, he clutched at the American party of 1856 as a conservative pro-Union movement. He was a delegate to its national convention but declined its vice-presidential nomination. In 1859, fearing the rapid growth of the Republicans, Call supported Stephen A. Douglas for the Democratic presidential nomination. After the Democrats split at their Charleston convention in 1860, he turned in despair to the Constitutional Union party and was a member of its state convention. After Abraham Lincoln's election he argued that it was not cause for secession, which he termed "high treason." He denounced the convention that voted the secession of Florida as having "opened the gates of Hell." Call was skilled in the emotional language of romanticism and likened the glory of the Union and Constitution to that of the Bible and Cross. Reluctantly Call accepted the Confederacy but as early as 1862 foresaw its defeat and wrote, "It will be terrible and fatal."

He died at his townhouse, "The Grove," in Tallahassee.

• Two collections of Call papers exist: one is in the Florida Historical Society Library in the University of South Florida, Tampa; the other is in the Southern Historical Collection in the University of North Carolina, Chapel Hill. Use of the latter is restricted. Many Call letters in the Andrew Jackson papers, Library of Congress, are reproduced in John Spencer Bassett ed., *Correspondence of Andrew Jackson* (6 vols., 1926–1933), and in the new edition of papers being prepared at the University of Tennessee Press under the editorship of Sam B. Smith and Harriet C. Owsley. Also important is Clarence Edwin Carter ed., *Territorial Papers of the United States*, vols. 22 through 26, *The Territory of Florida* (1956–1962). The only biography is Herbert J. Doherty, Jr., *Richard Keith Call: Southern Unionist* (1961). See also Herbert J. Doherty, Jr., *The Whigs of Florida, 1845–1854* (1959), and Caroline Mays Brevard, "Richard Keith Call," *Florida Historical Quarterly* 1 (July, Oct. 1908): 3–12, 8–20. An obituary is in the Tallahassee *Florida Sentinel*, 16 Sept. 1862.

HERBERT J. DOHERTY, JR.

CALLAHAN, Joe. *See* Callahan, Walter.

CALLAHAN, Patrick Henry (15 Oct. 1866–4 Feb. 1940), businessman and Catholic layman, was born in Cleveland, Ohio, the son of Cormac John Callahan, a livestock dealer, and Mary Frances Connolly. The son of immigrants, Callahan grew up in an Irish-Catholic parish in Cleveland. His father's business brought him into contact with the city's diverse population. He attended parish schools and a business college for one year and served briefly as one of industrialist Marcus Hanna's personal secretaries.

A talented athlete standing over six feet in height, Callahan tried professional baseball for a brief spell but then turned to business. He went to work as a salesman for the Glidden Varnish Company in Chicago from 1889 until 1892, when he joined the Peaslee-Gaulbert Paint Company of Louisville, Kentucky. In the meantime he had married Julia Laure Cahill in 1891; they had three children.

Callahan's business career began to flourish in the mid-nineties. In late 1894 a group of investors organized the Louisville Varnish Company (LVC) with Callahan as manager; five years later he was elected president, a position he held until his death. LVC specialized in supplying varnish and lacquer to furniture and appliance manufacturers in the East, the Chicago area, and North Carolina. Throughout his presidency Callahan adjusted to changing markets. For example, when industrial sales dropped precipitously during the Great Depression, LVC entered the consumer market with small cans. The "Varnall" and "Fixall" brand names became well known as the company grew into a medium-sized supplier.

Callahan's antiunion paternalism and application of his religious beliefs led him to be concerned about the workers in his plant and labor in general. With the help of Monsignor John A. Ryan of the Catholic University of America, Callahan designed a profit-sharing plan that became an industry standard. "Man was not made for Business," Callahan maintained, "but Business was made for Man." Every man deserved a "living wage" for a day's work. The LVC profit-sharing plan weathered even the Great Depression after a brief hiatus.

Business success and organizational acumen allowed Callahan to delve into other interests, or "hobbies," as he often called them. He enjoyed debate, conversation, and political discourse, and soon joined progressives in their war with the Whallen brothers' Democratic party machine in Louisville. After allying himself with the administration of progressive governor James B. McCreary, Callahan was given the honorary title of "Colonel," which he used the rest of his life as an informal entree into southern circles.

Nominally a Democrat, Callahan became an avid supporter of Woodrow Wilson. Although he supported most progressive reforms, Prohibition became his focal point. This decision came from his own bout with alcoholism as a young man and that of two of his children. He became convinced that the Irish-American male, in particular, could not tolerate the "creature," an old country nickname for alcohol.

The *Callahan Correspondence*, a mimeographed circular of letters with religious, business, political, and other notable figures, came from his work during World War I with the Commission on Religious Prejudices of the Knights of Columbus (K of C). He used his organizational skills to found K of C activities in military training camps. With Callahan at its head as chairman, the commission studied anti-Catholicism in the war period, published pamphlets, and confronted sources of prejudice such as the Ku Klux Klan.

Callahan's first report for the commission in 1915 echoed a sentiment he would often restate: "Each camp must muzzle its own fools." He scolded Protestants and Catholics alike for inserting religion into politics and became as much an opponent of Catholic politicians such as Boston mayor James Curley as he was of Protestant demagogue Tom Watson of Georgia. His views, along with his Prohibitionism, put Callahan outside the mainstream of Catholicism in America. Thus began Callahan's career as an autonomous Catholic, for he soon ran into opposition from the K of C hierarchy.

In the 1920s Callahan's independence became even more pronounced as he developed friendships with such diverse personalities as William Jennings Bryan and H. L. Mencken. He first met Mencken in 1925 in Dayton, Tennessee, during the Scopes Trial. Throughout his life Callahan's engaging personality enabled him to meet with people of opposing views and aided his efforts in behalf of religious toleration.

Long before Al Smith's nomination for president in 1928, Callahan worked hard against the New Yorker, whom he dismissed as "nothing more or less than a landlord's agent" (a scathing Irish critique). This campaign brought Callahan into uneasy alliances with other anti-Smith forces, but he took it as an opportunity to open dialogues with people who held anti-Catholic prejudices. For the only time in his life Callahan fully supported a Republican, Herbert Hoover, for president. After the election he argued that Smith had probably gained as many votes from being Catholic as he lost.

With the onset of the Great Depression Callahan happily returned to the Democratic fold and became an early supporter of Franklin D. Roosevelt. Although he lamented the fall of national Prohibition, Callahan never wavered in his faith in the New Deal. He acted as a buffer between Roosevelt and some of the president's severest Catholic critics, particularly Father Charles E. Coughlin.

Callahan played out many roles during his life: transplanted southerner, businessman, champion of religious and racial toleration, codesigner of a profit-sharing plan, lifelong progressive, and staunch prohibitionist. He made hard-and-fast enemies as well as friends. He was always a maverick Catholic and rarely followed the dictates of the hierarchy and laity. Writing incessantly to friend and foe, he encouraged much-needed dialogue on a wide range of subjects. Perhaps Monsignor Ryan, who often clashed with Callahan over social and political questions, best summed up his life: "He was a genuine man, a sincere Christian and a profound lover of justice. We shall not soon see his like again." Callahan died in Louisville.

• Callahan's papers are in numerous places, including Catholic University of America, Notre Dame University, and the Filson Club in Louisville, and in the papers of his correspondents, ranging from Franklin D. Roosevelt to H. L. Mencken. Copies of the *Callahan Correspondence* (covering the years 1920–1939) are in numerous libraries. Callahan published articles in journals and magazines such as *Fortnightly Review* and *Commonweal*. Studies of Callahan include Joseph G. Green, Jr., "Patrick Henry Callahan: The Social Role of an American Catholic Lay Leader" (Ph.D. diss., Catholic Univ. of America, 1963), and Edward Cuddy, "Colonel Patrick Henry Callahan, Proponent of Cooperative Citizenship" (M.A. thesis, Catholic Univ. of America, 1959).

See also studies by William E. Ellis, including "Patrick Henry Callahan: A Kentucky Democrat in National Party Politics," *Filson Club History Quarterly* 51 (Jan. 1977): 17–30; "Patrick Henry Callahan: The Fight for Religious Toleration," in *An American Church: Essays on the Americanization of the Catholic Church*, ed. David J. Alvarez (1979); "Labor-Management Relations in the Progressive Era: A Profit-Sharing Experience in Louisville," *Register of the Kentucky Historical Society* 78 (Spring 1980): 140–56; "Catholicism and the Southern Ethos: The Role of Patrick Henry Callahan," *Catholic Historical Review* 69 (Jan. 1983): 41–50; "Kentucky Catholic and Maryland Skeptic: The Correspondence of Colonel Patrick Henry Callahan and H. L. Mencken," *Filson Club History Quarterly* 58 (July 1984): 336–48; *Patrick Henry Callahan (1866–1940): Progressive Catholic Layman in the American South* (1989); and "Patrick Henry Callahan: A Maverick Catholic and the Prohibition Issue," *Register of the Kentucky Historical Society* 92 (Spring 1994): 175–99. An obituary is in the *Courier-Journal*, 6 Feb. 1940.

WILLIAM E. ELLIS

CALLAHAN, Walter (27 Jan. 1910–10 Sept. 1971), country musician who, with his brother Homer Callahan, formed the duet the Callahan Brothers, was born in Asheville, North Carolina, the son of Bert Callahan, the postmaster of Laurel, North Carolina, and Martha Jane (maiden name unknown). Bert Callahan played organ and taught singing, and Martha Jane Callahan also played the organ and was an accomplished singer. Walter and Homer Callahan began as one of the brother acts of the 1930s, along with the Monroe Brothers and the Allen Brothers. They were both good vocalists as well as multi-instrumentalists: Walter played guitar and string bass, while Homer played guitar, string bass, mandolin, ukelele, violin, and five-string banjo. Along with a penchant for duet yodeling, they were adept blues artists, relying on flat-pick guitars or mandolin and guitar to achieve the "white" blues sound.

The Callahans were influenced by the Georgia string band the Skillet Lickers, with fiddler Gid Tanner and guitarist Riley Puckett; Pop Stoneman; and Jimmie Rodgers, and their tunes included gospel numbers, ballads, as well as the blues. They were among the earliest white musicians to produce versions of black popular songs and so make them palatable to white audiences. The Callahans recorded ninety-one selections for the American Recording Company and Columbia beginning in 1934 until 1951. Among their most well-known are "St. Louis Blues," "Asheville Blues," "Rattle Snake Daddy," and "Freight Train Blues." Other releases included "Little Poplar Log House," "Gonna Quit My Rowdy Ways," and "She's My Curly Headed Baby." Homer also recorded as a solo performer.

The Callahan Brothers learned the hill songs and ballads in the western highlands of North Carolina. According to Dean Tudor and Nancy Tudor, in *Grass Roots Music* (1979), North Carolina was one of the regional centers of old-time music, the third of four to be developed. The others were Atlanta, Georgia; Galax, Virginia; and lastly, Texas. North Carolina had a strong contingent of the string-band style, as well as finger-picking banjo, a style apart from the frailing method. Fiddle playing was emphasized in the Union Grove, North Carolina, competitions, but the Callahans' proficiency at yodeling at the 1933 Rhododendron Festival in Asheville brought them their first national recognition.

After traveling to New York City to record in 1934, the Callahans gradually began to do radio performances in addition to their shows at the burgeoning folk festivals in their region of the state. The Callahans first made their home on radio station WWNC in Asheville in 1934. In 1935 they moved to WHAS (Louisville, Ky.), then in 1936, WWVA (Wheeling, W.Va.). Later they worked at WLW (Cincinnati, Ohio), and in 1940 the Callahans worked at KWTO (Springfield, Mo.), KVOO (Tulsa, Okla.), followed by KRLD (Dallas, Tex.), and KWFT (Wichita Falls, Tex.) during World War II.

To further bring themselves into the homes of their listening audience, the Callahans sold illustrated songbooks in which their radio performances were transcribed, which lent a permanence to their songs, similar to their recordings. Some 150 titles were marketed.

During much of the 1940s the Callahans played on radio stations in Dallas or Wichita Falls, Texas. Having been preceded by a brother act known as Bob and Joe, Walter and Homer decided to adopt Joe and Bill, respectively, as their stage names in 1941. They were known by these names for the rest of their professional lives.

In 1945 the Callahans appeared in a film with Jimmy Wakely, *Springtime in Texas*. They also went on tours with other musicians. In 1951 the Callahans became the opening act for Lefty Frizzell, then a new force in country music and one of the mainstays of the honky-tonk style. As the new style was giving the music an invigorating modernity, the older type of country songs played by the Callahans were lessening in popularity. The brothers recorded a final eight titles for Columbia in 1951, but the two retired from full-time performing at the end of the 1950s.

The Callahan Brothers performed a mix of blues, hillbilly, and western music. In 1935 the duo was one of the first acts to record "The House of the Rising Sun" (their title: "Rounder's Luck"), a piece that made the folk rounds in the 1960s and ended up as a rock piece by the British group the Animals. Given their extensive recordings, it seems obvious that the Callahans were synthesists who saw material in these three different types of American music.

Their lively approach to the mountain music, along with mournful harmonies and Homer's instrumental versatility, foreshadowed bluegrass, their foray into a more typical late 1940s country band with electric steel and standard guitars notwithstanding.

In the 1960s Joe moved to Asheville and worked in the grocery business. Bill worked for an auto parts company, playing music as a sideline. Joe died of cancer.

• The Country Music Foundation's archives in Nashville, Tenn., is a source for material on Callahan. The Callahan Brothers' recordings appear in a few old-time and white-country blues anthologies. In 1975 Old Homestead issued *The Callahan Brothers*, an album that collected several of their tunes. Douglas B. Green, *Country Roots: The Origins of Country Music* (1976), has a little information on the Callahans, as does Dean Tudor and Nancy Tudor, *Grass Roots Music* (1979).

PATRICK J. O'CONNOR

CALLAS, Maria (2 Dec. 1923–16 Sept. 1977), legendary operatic singing actress, was born Cecilia Sophia Anna Kalogeropoulos in New York City, the daughter of Georges Kalogeropoulos, a pharmacist, and Elmina Evangelia Dimitroadis. The family had arrived in the United States from Greece a few months earlier. The family surname was legally changed to Callas in 1926 shortly before Maria was christened in the Greek Orthodox Cathedral in Manhattan. In 1927 Georges opened his own pharmacy. After her father lost this business in 1929 during the stock market crash, the family moved to Washington Heights, where Callas attended public school. Her parents' marriage was not a happy one, and, when it became evident that Callas had unusual vocal potential, her mother decided to seek a new life apart from her husband. Evangelia and Georges mutually agreed to separate. Obsessed with turning at least one of her daughters into a famous artist, she made plans to return to her own family. Shortly after Callas graduated from the eighth grade in January 1937, she returned to Greece with her mother.

Callas began her vocal studies with Maria Trivella at the National Conservatory in Athens (1937–1939) after her mother falsified her age to comply with the entrance requirements. The famous Spanish soprano, Elvira de Hidalgo, had joined the faculty at the Athens Conservatory and accepted Callas as a scholarship student in 1939. Thus began a professional association that lasted five years. Callas made her formal operatic debut on 27 November 1940, with the National Lyric Theater in Athens, as Beatrice in Franz von Suppé's operetta *Boccaccio*; she was listed in the program as M. Kalogeropoulos. Shortly after the Nazi occupation of Athens, the illness of a colleague allowed her to debut as Tosca (4 July 1941) with the National Opera, a role she sang with great success the following season. She continued to sing sporadically in Greece throughout the occupation. After the war Callas found the terms of her new contract with the company unacceptable, and she returned to New York in September 1945. Edward Johnson offered her a Metropolitan Opera contract to do *Madama Butterfly* and *Fidelio,* which she turned down. Callas had no professional engagements for two years, but then she was "discovered" by the tenor Giovanni Zenatello. He cast her in the lead of Ponchielli's *La Gioconda* at the Arena in Verona (3 Aug. 1947) with Tullio Serafin conducting.

During rehearsals she met the businessman and industrialist Giovanni Battista Meneghini, and they were married in 1949. At that point Meneghini took over the management of her career, and she became Maria Meneghini Callas. The five performances at Verona represented a modest new beginning, and Serafin was impressed enough to arrange most of her subsequent early engagements. He conducted her next appearance as Isolde at the Teatro la Fenice (30 Dec. 1947) as well as her debuts in Genoa (Isolde on 12 May 1948), Turin (Aida on 18 Sept. 1948), Florence (Norma on 30 Nov. 1948), Rome (Kundry on 26 Feb. 1949), and the Teatro Colón in Buenos Aires (Turandot on 20 May 1949).

The next major turning point in her career was at Venice's Teatro la Fenice, where she sang both Brünnhilde in *Die Walküre* and Elvira in *I Puritani* within two weeks (8 and 19 Jan. 1949). This was the first time in decades that a dramatic soprano had successfully negotiated the florid passages of Bellini's opera, and she followed this tour de force with her Kundry in *Parsifal* at the Teatro dell'Opera in Rome. Callas had a big voice with a range of almost three octaves, a unique tonal quality, and dazzling technical skills. The range of roles that she undertook in the space of less than two years is astounding and gives an indication of the new vocal dimension that she brought to the bel canto repertoire. De Hidalgo had studiously prepared Callas as the heir to a lost tradition, a tradition that demanded the seamless fusion of very difficult melodic lines with highly ornate and expressive ornamentation. Her musical instincts were never in doubt. Now she had acquired the technique to allow them to flourish. She was largely responsible for introducing this repertoire to a new and enthusiastic public.

After her success as Elvira, Callas began to concentrate on interpreting the Bellini-Donizetti-Rossini bel canto operas, in which she made highly personal and lasting contributions to the operatic world. The two primary musical influences on Callas were de Hidalgo and Serafin, both masters of the bel canto style who understood the sense behind the seemingly unpretentious music with its daunting fioriture and inner elasticity. De Hidalgo was a specialist in the bel canto repertory, and with her training and Serafin's refinements, Callas became a master of fioriture; her renditions were a unique combination of drama, innate musicality, and fluidity. Artistically Callas was related to a long line of famous singing actresses: Angelica Catalani, Maria Malibran, Giuditta Pasta, and Wilhelmine Schroeder-Devrient, who, interestingly enough, were faulted for the same weaknesses—uneven vocal registers, roughness, and excessive tremolo, as well as a preoccupation with a dramatic portrayal of the character that sometimes diminished their vocal purity and beauty. These artists were, however, vocal types long since forgotten by the 1940s, and Callas burst upon the operatic world like a new phenomenon.

Callas made her La Scala debut as a last-minute substitute for Renata Tebaldi in *Aida* (12 Apr. 1950) and during the next decade was honored with several important opening nights. It was in Italy that her historic collaborations with Luchino Visconti (*La Vestale,* 1954), Herbert von Karajan (*Lucia di Lammermoor,* 1954), and Franco Zeffirelli (*Il Turco in Italia,* 1955) began. Rudolf Bing had discussed an engagement with the Metropolitan Opera, but Callas and her husband decided she would make her long-awaited American debut as Norma with the Lyric Theater of Chicago (1 Nov. 1954). She became an immediate celebrity and followed this success with *La Traviata* and *Lucia.* At the same time EMI had started Angel Records, and Callas's recordings of *Tosca, Lucia di Lammermoor,* and *I Puritani* became immediate bestsellers. Shortly before finishing the 1955 Chicago season, Callas signed a contract with the Metropolitan Opera to open the 1956 season, making her debut in the title role of Bellini's *Norma* (29 Oct. 1956). This performance was an excellent example of her uncanny ability to realize the composer's genius while creating a character that was singularly her own. She presented the New York critics with an exciting new theatrical experience. In her two seasons with the Met (1956 and 1958) she only sang a total of twenty-one performances of Norma, Tosca, Lucia, and Violetta before falling out with General Manager Rudolf Bing. After months of sparring on both sides regarding details of repertoire and dates, on 6 November 1958 Bing sent a telegram canceling Callas's contract, accusing her of breaking its terms. This rift between two of the opera world's superstars was never healed. She did return for two performances of *Tosca* (19 and 25 Mar. 1965) in partnership with Tito Gobbi, and this incomparable pair brought Scarpia and Tosca to life as had rarely been done before. Gobbi wrote in his memoirs that Callas "was set apart: not just in the top rank but beyond even that—something unique."

The so-called Callas-Tebaldi feud of the 1950s pitted a bel canto singer against a leading exponent of verismo singing. This was a nonsensical "apples and oranges" brouhaha fueled by the press, exploited by agents and impresarios, and raised to a fever pitch by the respective fans. Both artists, however, were at the right place at the right time since the LP era allowed them to benefit from massive record sales, Callas with EMI/Angel under the sponsorship of the legendary Walter Legge and Dario Soria, and Tebaldi with the equally formidable Decca/London. The strained relations with Rudolf Bing at the Metropolitan, with Antonio Ghiringhelli at La Scala, as well as with other companies, including those at Chicago and Rome, often were blown out of proportion by the press. Her professional standards coupled with a self-critical temperament and increasing vocal problems almost guaranteed conflicts with management and colleagues. She was, however, always highly respected for her intelligence, musicality, and dramatic magnetism.

Her meeting with the flamboyant Greek shipping tycoon Aristotle Onassis in 1959 was both a blessing and a tragedy for Callas. It marked the beginning of the end of her artistic career for, although Onassis was impressed with her celebrity status, he was not interested in her artistry and musicianship. Meneghini filed for a legal separation from Callas in September, and the couple mutually agreed on a property settlement. Callas's carefully wrought career began to disintegrate slowly as the change in her personal life had disastrous affects on her ability to perform. Occasional flaws blossomed into critical faults. Her concentration and total commitment to singing and acting perfection were replaced by new emotions and priorities. The relationship with Onassis damaged her career, and her final opera performance was as Tosca at the Royal Opera House, London (5 July 1965). In 1966 she renounced her United States citizenship, a right she had by virtue of birth, reverting to Greek citizenship and paving the way for her divorce from Meneghini, in the hope that Onassis would marry her. Their relationship ended in 1968 prior to his marriage to Jacqueline Kennedy, but it resurfaced intermittently after Callas moved to Paris.

The release of Pier Paolo Pasolini's 1971 film *Medea,* based on Euripides' play, demonstrated that acting without singing was a step backward artistically for Callas. Fortunately, her master classes at the Juilliard School of Music in New York, organized by Peter Mennin (twenty-four videotaped classes between Oct. 1971 and Mar. 1972) provided a far more congenial framework for her talents. Adherence to the highest musical standards made Callas the incomparable artist she was, but they were also her downfall, as she had to work with many lesser talents, including general managers of famous opera houses. Eventually, when no one was there to support, encourage, and defend her, she attempted to make a comeback, but it compromised all that she had stood for artistically. As she attempted to salvage herself, she elected to do it in a way guaranteed to ruin her. The collaboration with Giuseppe di Stefano on the Turin production of Verdi's *I Vespri Siciliani* (10 Apr. 1973) was by all accounts horrendous. Several months later the two undertook an ill-advised worldwide tour that began in Hamburg, West Germany (25 Oct. 1973). Their 1974 North American tour of nineteen concerts was a success in sentimental terms only, as was the nine-concert Far East tour that October and November. Callas died of a heart attack in her apartment in Paris.

Callas was a profound artist who lived her roles; singing them was not enough. A perfectionist, she encountered her most obdurate resistance when she faced an entrenched system such as that in Milan, Rome, or New York. On the other hand, she was at her best when directed by such artists as Visconti and Zeffirelli or performing in such places as Chicago and Dallas, where every effort was made to produce music theater in its most complex and overpowering dimensions. She performed the forty-three roles in her repertoire over 500 times; eighteen were recorded commercially, and ten, perhaps more, are available on private disks; in addition she recorded Carmen, Manon Lescaut, Mimi, and Nedda. She was certainly the most fascinating operatic personality of her age. In common with all great performers, she had an immediately recognizable individual sound. Added to this was her exquisite taste in all subtleties of bel canto singing: elegant ornamentation, accurate and tasteful trills, sensitive timing of portamentos, and wonderful changes of color and intensity so that every phrase was active and alive. Basically intuitive, she always had a sense of communication with her audience. The voice and musicianship were hers at birth; her artistic achievements were the result of focused and unceasing hard work. Her place in operatic history is unquestioned as one of the greatest singing actresses; in her prime Callas was the *prima donna assoluta del bel canto* and a box office sensation who rivaled the fame of Enrico Caruso and Feodor Chaliapin.

• The most comprehensive bibliography can be found in Robert H. Cowden, *Concert and Opera Singers: A Bibliography of Biographical Materials* (1985; rev. and expanded as *Singers of the World,* 1994). Autobiographical materials appearing in *Oggi* (Jan. and Feb. 1957), edited by Anita Pensotti, give her view of events up to 1956. Biographical information can be found in John Ardoin, *Callas at Juilliard: The Master Classes* (1987); John Ardoin, *The Callas Legacy: The Complete Guide to Her Recordings,* 3d rev. ed. (1991); Evangelia Callas, *My Daughter Maria Callas* (1960; enlarged 1967); Jackie Callas, *Sisters* (1990); Gina Guandalini, *Callas, l'ultima diva: analisi di un fenomno* (1987); George Jellinek, *Callas: Portrait of a Prima Donna* (1960); Réal La Rochelle, *Callas, la diva et la vinyle* (1987); David A. Lowe, ed., *Callas as They Saw Her* (1986); Giovanni Battista Meneghini, *My Wife Maria Callas* (1982); Pierre-Jean Rémy, *Maria Callas: A Tribute* (1978); Michael Scott, *Maria Meneghini Callas* (1991); Nadia Stancioff, *Maria: Callas Remembered* (1988); and Henry Wisneski, *Maria Callas: The Art behind the Legend,* with performance annals 1947–1974 and a discography of private recordings by Arthur Germond (1975). See also *Current Biography Yearbook 1956*; Rodolfo Celletti, *Le Grandi Voci,* with discography by Raffaele Vegeto (1964); Alan Jefferson, *International Dictionary of Opera* (1993); Jürgen Kesting, *Die Grossen Sänger* (1986); Elisabeth Schwarzkopf, *On and Off the Record: A Memoir of Walter Legge* (1982); Desmond Shawe-Taylor, *The New Grove Dictionary of Opera* (1992); and Franco Zeffirelli, *Zeffirelli: An Autobiography* (1986). Important articles include the issue titled "Maria Callas: ses récitals 1954–1969," *L'Avant-Scène Opéra* 44 (1982). An obituary by Raymond Ericson is in the *New York Times,* 17 Sept. 1977.

ROBERT H. COWDEN

CALLAWAY, Cason Jewell (6 Nov. 1894–12 Apr. 1961), business executive, agriculturist, and developer, was born in LaGrange, Georgia, the son of Fuller Earle Callaway and Ida Jane Cason. His father was the founder of Callaway Mills, Inc., a highly successful cotton processing firm. He attended Bingham Military School in Asheville, North Carolina, followed by one year at the University of Virginia. He enjoyed a successful year at Charlottesville, but his father decided that he needed skills training. Therefore, he enrolled at Eastman School of Business in Poughkeepsie, New York. Young Callaway was given responsibility for Valley Waste Mills, a division of his father's Callaway Mills. At age twenty he organized Valley Waste Mills into a great commercial success as a pioneering recycling operation. His achievements gained his father's attention as well as that of other top managers in the firm, since the waste division netted more than $1 million in profits during the three-year period just before U.S. entry into World War I.

Callaway's career was interrupted for a stint as a naval officer during World War I. Owing to his connections in the textile industry, he was posted to duty at the Navy Supply Corps' Bureau of Supplies and Accounts in Navy Department Headquarters in Washington, D.C. It was here that Callaway first met Franklin D. Roosevelt, then assistant secretary of the navy, whose offices were just down the hall from the Supply Corps.

At twenty-five years of age Callaway returned to LaGrange as a more sophisticated and worldly person. His father, though still short of his fiftieth birthday, was exhausted from managing an increasingly larger and more complex organization and welcomed him home by putting him in charge of two large mills, Manchester and Milstead. In 1920 Cason Callaway had married Virginia Hollis Hand, with whom he had three children.

During the 1920s Callaway's father passed on more duties to him. With the death of Fuller Callaway in 1928, the full responsibility for all operations, sales, and finances fell directly on Cason Callaway, now thirty-four years old. He immediately set about repurchasing company stock for the family and expanding the scope of the firm's textile empire. He became a supersalesman, equally at home in New York or Detroit, closing multimillion dollar sales contracts with firms like General Motors, or near LaGrange, making arrangements with the local railroad for shipments. He had developed an uncanny ability to select successful managers and staff personnel, which paid off many times over in efficiency. Constantly looking for new products, he successfully entered the rug and tire cord businesses.

In 1935 Callaway became chairman of the board of Callaway Enterprises, with the presidency going to his younger brother Fuller Earle Callaway, Jr. Cason Callaway had successfully weathered the worst parts of the Great Depression and was now free to accept leadership positions, such as president of the American Cotton Manufacturers Association, regent of the University System of Georgia, and ad hoc posts with the new Roosevelt administration in Washington. During this time Callaway made good on his statement, "Profits are essential, but they are not the sole aim of this business. We assure them by dividing them with employees through wage increases and a regular system of profit sharing; and with the consumer through price reductions whenever that becomes possible" ("He Took an Idea to Market," *Nation's Business*, Oct. 1930, pp. 44–46). The great Callaway philanthropies were ahead.

Callaway was very aware of the decline and erosion of the soil in Georgia and especially in Middle Georgia, where LaGrange was located. With his boundless energy, he set about becoming a farmer—but not a for-profit farmer. He set up a 40,000-acre showplace and experimental operation near Hamilton, Georgia, which he named Blue Springs Farms and which became his love for more than a decade. Here the very finest in every variety of row crops, vegetables, and trees was propagated and shown to the public. He espoused mechanization and efficiency in agronomy and then moved to developing the best in swine, beef, dairy, and wool production. Through his leadership, more than 100 Georgia counties developed showplace farms, called "Georgia Better Farms," to lead the way for farmers on the local level.

During the 1930s Roosevelt and Callaway developed a close friendship. The president spent many days relaxing with the Callaway family during his trips to the "Little White House," which is near LaGrange and Blue Springs Farms.

In 1937 Callaway left active management of the textile firm to his brother and others and devoted himself fully to Blue Springs Farms, his duties with the university system regents, and, later, as a board member of U.S. Steel, Shell Oil, Trust Company of Georgia, and Chemical Bank. Further, he actively served on the Warm Springs Foundation Board and headed up several statewide fund drives during the war, while still serving as a leader in the American Cotton Manufacturers Association.

Callaway was a complex man. He would succeed in one area and then go on to a new and entirely different challenge. In 1947 he had a mild heart attack and was ordered by his doctors to "take it easy," which he did until late 1948, when his final, climactic dream took form in what has become well known as a southern showplace, the Callaway Gardens. For twenty years he had been a highly successful industrialist, and for ten years he had been a showplace agriculturist. Integrated into those years had been unprecedented service, association with great political and industrial leaders, and much travel. For another ten or more years he developed his gardens.

For years, Callaway's gardens grew, and his dream for a place of beauty materialized. He brought in many compatible varieties of flowering trees and shrubs, but, in his own evaluation, his biggest contribution was his insistence on the use of native plants and flowers. Also, he developed a large vegetable garden with every imaginable variety growable in Georgia. The vegetables were for viewing and beauty but also provided fresh produce for the gardens' restaurants and hotel.

Along the way Callaway had turned over more and more of his empire to the Callaway Foundations, which he lived to see benefit every aspect of life in Georgia. Especially helpful were the funds that provided salary increments to attract and keep top national scholars in the state's public and private colleges and universities. He died at Blue Springs Farms.

Callaway's life is an example for all who aspire to great success and a useful life. Born into a wealthy family, he increased that wealth manyfold and through his dedication and leadership made his state and nation more prosperous and pleasant.

• The main repository for primary information related to Callaway is the Troup County Historical Society and Archives in LaGrange, Ga. The vast amount of letters, documents, and clippings provide insight and details into the lives and accomplishments of Callaway family members as well as nonfamily executives of Callaway Mills, Inc. Certain Callaway correspondence, especially from 1947 forward, remains in the private vaults and repositories of the Callaway Foundation. Callaway wrote one book, *What Is an Executive?* (1961). A privately published biography is Paul Schubert, *Cason Callaway of Blue Springs* (1964). Howard H. Callaway, "The Story of a Man and a Garden" (1965), provides special insight into the development of Callaway Gardens. An obituary is in the *LaGrange (Ga.) Daily News*, 13 Apr. 1961.

GENE MURKISON

CALLAWAY, Fuller Earle (15 July 1870–12 Feb. 1928), textile manufacturer, was born in LaGrange, Georgia, the son of Abner Reeves Callaway, a planter, teacher, and Baptist minister, and Sarah June Howard. His father had a turbulent economic life because of the disasters associated with the Civil War. The young Fuller Callaway had very little formal education and dropped out after only one year of elementary school. Teachers of the day saw little hope for young Callaway, especially after his mother's death when he was only eight years of age.

A story that appears in nearly all of the various papers and materials concerning the Callaways has to do with young Fuller's initiation into business and the whole area of investments. He received a nickel in payment for providing fresh water to a barn building crew. Even though he had walked barefoot several miles to LaGrange from the farm to which his family had moved and had his heart set on a pair of boots, it was discovered that five cents would not be enough to make such a purchase. For whatever reasons, he then passed up all the tempting treats and candy in order to purchase three spools of sewing thread. After walking back to the farm, he arose early the next morning and for a few days walked the country roads until he found three farm wives willing to pay a nickel for each of the spools. This energized the young boy who then returned to town and bought even more thread. Within a few weeks, he was a full-fledged peddler with a supply of needles, thread, thimbles, scissors, and measuring tapes. This life continued for four years and at the youngish age of twelve, Fuller took his savings of $60 and bought an old mule, a ramshackle wagon, a secondhand harness, and a few tools and proceeded to farm for two years. At the end of those two years, he had $500 in savings and was enticed by an older brother to move to LaGrange and go to work in a general clothing store, where he learned retailing. He quit to start his own business in 1888 when he was only eighteen years of age.

At age twenty Fuller made what he often called the best deal in his lifetime when he met his future wife, Ida Cason. She was from a small town called Jewell, which was over 135 miles away near Augusta, Georgia, and she was attending one of the female institutes in LaGrange at the time. This 18-year-old young woman was to make a major impact on the direction and philosophies of future Callaway generations, and she is memorialized in the famous Callaway Gardens near Pine Mountain, developed by one of Fuller's sons.

The couple married in 1891, and they had two children.

Although Fuller Callaway had just one year of formal schooling, he read and studied for one hour every night of his life. He placed great value on applied studies, later sending both of his sons to the Eastman Business School in New York, an applied, pragmatic type of institution.

During the 1890s Callaway became a highly successful young merchant, and his fame spread. A group of Atlanta investors offered to build a huge, block square, multi-storied store in Atlanta, give Fuller 49 percent ownership, and pay him $25,000 a year to manage it. Even though tempted, young Fuller stuck to his ownership dreams and remained in LaGrange.

A major turning point occurred in Fuller Callaway's life in 1895. A group of investors had built the Dixie mills earlier, but the machinery was ancient and obsolete, having been removed from mills being updated in the north. In 1895 the investors asked Fuller to reorganize and redesign the mill. This he did in an aggressive manner by traveling to New England, purchasing new equipment, and returning to discard all the old machines, thus modernizing the plant. The following few years were highly successful under the supervision of Fuller and the direct superintendency of his then colleague, O. A. Dunson, who was later to manage and run large operations alongside and in competition with the Callaways. A new group of investors soon arrived and persuaded Fuller to take charge and set up a new mill.

The period between 1900 and 1910 saw Callaway at full pitch. He engineered new cotton mills and related industries in and around LaGrange. His stores continued to grow and prosper. When the Dunsons challenged his leadership, he simply left them, whereupon the Callaways became true adversaries of what became the Truitt-Dunson Mill Groups. Callaway not only was a top mill developer and operator but stood out as a master salesman. His many forays into the New York buying centers resulted in much needed sales and led to many increases in mill sizes as well as jumps in employment.

By 1920 the Callaway empire had expanded to include several large cotton mills in and around LaGrange, warehouses, banks, and department stores. While the empire was growing, Callaway constructed schools, recreation centers, hospitals, libraries, and theaters. When told by a journalist from the *American Magazine* that he was a great philanthropist, he replied, "Philanthropist—Nothing! It's business." Callaway pointed out that his employees stayed with the mills because they were satisfied, happy, and made fair wages. This typified the philosophy of Fuller Callaway, Sr. He did not think at the level of the esoteric, the do-gooder, or the philanthropist. He thought pure business, but it is interesting that his methods and his thoughts on motivation were decades ahead of the emergence of the now classic human resource management research.

After 1920, with his elder son Cason home from World War I, Callaway started to detach himself from operations of the empire and took a flier into politics, serving as railroad commissioner for Georgia. President Woodrow Wilson offered him the cabinet post of Secretary of the Interior. The offer was debated in the Callaway household, but it was decided that obligations in Georgia prohibited acceptance of the offer.

As the 1920s progressed, Callaway mellowed into old age, yet only as far as his fifties. His doctors convinced him to "slow down" and pass responsibilities to his sons and other trusted managers. He read innumerable books and thought about his life and accomplishments. His amazing mind retained facts and memories to the end. He died relatively young of heart disease in LaGrange, and the Baptist minister at his funeral said, "Fuller Earle Callaway had the most all-encompassing mind of any man I ever knew."

• The main public repository for primary information related to the life of Fuller E. Callaway, Sr. is the Troup County Historical Society and Archives in private vaults and repositories of the late Fuller E. Callaway, Jr. Many anecdotes appear in Arthur B. Edge, *Fuller E. Callaway, 1870–1928, Founder of Callaway Mills* (1954), which includes a speech honoring Fuller Callaway, Sr. by Arthur B. Edge, a Callaway Executive, who had access to private material. Donna Jean Whitley, *Fuller E. Callaway and Textile Development in LaGrange, 1895–1920* (1989), provides information focused on Callaway's involvement in textile mill development to 1920.

GENE MURKISON

CALLENDER, Guy Stevens (9 Nov. 1865–8 Aug. 1915), economist and historian, was born in Hartsgrove, Ohio, the son of Robert Foster Callender and Lois Winslow. The family moved to the Western Reserve (in present-day northeastern Ohio) when Callender was a child. At an early age he demonstrated that he had an active mind, intellectual curiosity, and a strong physical constitution; these attributes, along with his being an avid reader of books, led him at the age of fifteen to teach in the district schools of Ashtabula County. Using his savings from several winters of teaching and his summer earnings made working on the family farm, Callender succeeded in paying for college preparatory courses at New Lyme Institute, South New Lyme, Ohio.

In 1886, at the age of twenty-one, Callender enrolled at Oberlin College in Oberlin, Ohio, where he took the classical course. There he was influenced by James Monroe, professor of political science and modern history, who taught courses in political economy and sponsored Callender's volunteer work in the Political Economy Club. In this elective club work Callender participated in daily recitations and learned how to produce research papers in which one argued a single position. Aside from excelling academically, Callender also was an active participant in extracurricular organizations, including the Oberlin Glee Club, the Oratorical Association, the Phi Delta Society, the *Review* (the student newspaper), and the Traveling Men's Association. In these groups some of Callender's affinity for leadership and exactness became evident. He graduated with a B.A. in 1891, counting among his classmates John R. Commons and Robert A. Millikan.

After a year spent traveling and working in the business departments of newspapers in Cincinnati, Indianapolis, and Chicago, Callender sought "to take on the 'wise aspect of a student' again." In 1892 he enrolled for graduate study in political science at Harvard University, from which he received a B.A. (1893), an M.A. (1894), and a Ph.D. (1897). During his graduate studies at Harvard he served for some time as instructor in economics at Wellesley College, and he was considered an "outstanding man among our graduate students" by Frank W. Taussig and other members of the teaching faculty. Following the award of his Ph.D., Callender held an appointment as instructor in economics at Harvard from 1897 to 1900. There he conducted a course in American economic history, which he personally created. In 1900 he was appointed professor of political economy at Bowdoin College; in 1903 he accepted an appointment as professor in the Sheffield Scientific School of Yale University, where he continued to teach and engage in scholarly research until 1915. He also served as a member of the Governing Board of the Sheffield Scientific School. In 1904 Callender married Harriet Belle Rice; they had one son.

Callender published his only book, *Selections from the Economic History of the United States, 1765–1860*, in 1909. In it he revealed his entire theory of the progress of the United States from the beginning of colonization until the Civil War. Callender's most important contributions are to be found in the condensed, precisely written introductory essays that precede each chapter. His article "The Early Transportation and Banking Enterprises of the States in Relation to the Growth of Corporations" in the *Quarterly Journal of Economics* (Nov. 1902) was also well recognized and consulted by scholars.

Callender was well respected by his colleagues and his students. As a member of the American Historical Association and the American Economic Association, he was a frequent contributor as a book reviewer, essayist, and speaker. Callender's contribution to scholarship is probably best summarized in his article "The Position of American Economic History," published in the *American Historical Review* (Oct. 1913). He argued that American economic history should "be pursued as a separate subject of study" and that economic historians must be prepared to interpret facts. For Callender, economic history was more than the chronological recital of events of commercial and industrial significance. He sought historical explanations by applying the principles of economic science to the economic and social development of communities. His published studies included an analysis of the part played by economic factors in the adoption of the federal Constitution and in the debate over the economic basis of slavery in the South.

Prior to his death, Callender worked on several writing projects, including a comprehensive, multivolume economic history of the United States. This major study was never completed because of his poor health; he had never fully recovered from an earlier nervous breakdown, in 1905–1906. Another work in progress was a critical essay of Arthur Young's *Political Essays Concerning the British Empire* (1772), which focused on the history of British colonies in America. Until then, Young's essays had not been generally appreciated or known by American scholars. Callender was also at work on an introduction for a new edition in two volumes of *American Husbandry*, which was first published in London in 1775. Callender's review of *Cyclopedia of American Government* (edited by A. S. McLaughlin and Albert Bushnell Hart) appeared in the *Yale Review* shortly after his death. According to commentator C. W. Mixter, this highly critical review showed "in a marked degree the range, vitality and acuteness of his thinking" (*Yale Alumni Weekly*, Oct. 1915).

Callender was the recipient of numerous awards and honors. Two months before his death the Oberlin College chapter of Phi Beta Kappa elected him to membership. Upon Callender's death from a cerebral hemorrhage in Branford, Connecticut, members of the Oberlin College class of 1891 purchased from his widow his library of some 2,500 volumes and gave it to the institution in his memory. The class raised additional funds to purchase other titles on economic history, thus rounding out and completing the collection. A small amount of money was also set aside as an ongoing fund to keep the collection up-to-date. Callender's gift to the College Library, established by his graduating class, set an Oberlin precedent.

• A manuscript group bearing Callender's name contains some personal manuscript research notes. These historical materials largely relate to the economic history of the Upper Midwest. Also held there are notes on "Internal Improvements in Ohio," the "early History of the Canal," and economic developments in the state of Illinois (six folders). These notes may have been part of the 1915 book purchase. The book purchase itself is documented in the records of the Oberlin College Library and in the personal papers of director Azariah Smith Root. Callender's "Class Letters" for 1891 and his alumni records folder deposited at the archives offer considerable information on his life. An obituary is in the *Oberlin Alumni Magazine*, Dec. 1915, pp. 86–88.

ROLAND M. BAUMANN

CALLENDER, James Thomson (1758–17 July 1803), political writer and newspaper editor, was born in Scotland, the son of a tobacconist. Of his childhood and youth little is known, except that he was raised as a Presbyterian and received a classical education. He first came to prominence in 1782 when he published a work critical of Dr. Samuel Johnson. A supplementary volume published in 1783 was less successful, and for the next seven years he worked as a clerk. During this period he married (wife's name unknown), eventually having four children. Displaying early a strong sense of self-righteousness and a Calvinist contempt for human depravity, Callender destroyed his career as a clerk by agitating for the dismissal of a superior, whom he accused of corruption. Thereafter, from about 1790, he moved toward radicalism, writing a number of anonymous pamphlets critical of British politics and extolling Scottish nationalism. In 1792 he became a member of the Scottish Friends of the People, attending the Edinburgh Convention in December 1792 as a militant radical. Later that month, Lord Gardenstone, his patron, admitted to the authorities Callender's authorship of *The Political Progress of Britain,* a seditious pamphlet. Outlawed in January 1793, Callender was forced to flee to the United States. He took with him a bitter resentment of his treatment and a paradoxical commitment to democracy combined with a Swiftian hatred of humanity in the round.

Callender arrived alone in Philadelphia from Dublin in May 1793. In December 1793 Andrew Brown offered him a job as reporter of congressional debates for the *Philadelphia Gazette.* He quickly gained notoriety for what Federalists regarded as his partisan reports. In February 1796, Brown dismissed him for having written anonymously for Benjamin Franklin Bache's newspaper, the strongly Republican *Aurora.*

By this time his family had joined him, and Callender was striving to make ends meet by writing pamphlets supportive of the Jeffersonians. For more than two years he acted with Bache, John Beckley, James Carey and others as propagandists, with connections to the highest levels of the Republican party. Callender's contributions included virulent attacks on President George Washington and other Federalists, but also a fervent commitment to democracy and economic nationalism. Drawing on Antifederalist arguments of 1787–1788, he criticized the undemocratic features of the Constitution, rejecting the need for a senate and for an executive with significant powers. He thereby gained the hostility of moderate Republicans, both for his militancy and for his personal virulence.

In July 1797 Callender published an exposé of Alexander Hamilton's (1757–1804) affair with Maria Reynolds, a married woman, which shattered Hamilton's career. It also led to Federalist harassment. Although openly assisted by Thomas Leiper, and more circumspectly by Thomas Jefferson—both of whom were to become his father figures—by early 1798, demoralized by the death of his wife, Callender was destitute and drinking heavily. In March, temporarily replacing Bache as editor of the *Aurora,* he led the Republican campaign for the publication of the XYZ dispatches, reports from three commissioners in Paris who were trying to reach an American-French agreement to prevent war. The dispatches showed that the French representatives (X, Y, and Z) were soliciting bribes. The result was disastrous for his party, which plummeted in popularity with the news of "French perfidy." When the Alien and Sedition Acts were passed, Callender, fearing arrest, fled to Virginia, leaving his children with Leiper.

After several months recuperating on Senator Stevens Thomson Mason's (1760–1803) plantation, Callender—repeatedly encouraged by Jefferson—resumed writing for various newspapers, including the Richmond *Examiner.* His Antifederalist *The Prospect before Us* led to his prosecution and martyrdom under the sedition law in June 1800. His Republican supporters used his trial to gain maximum political sympathy, but Callender was sentenced by Justice Samuel Chase to six months in jail and a fine of $200. He continued his propaganda from his cell.

Having served his sentence, Callender expected some reward for his efforts toward Jefferson's presidential triumph. He was soon disillusioned. Loathed by the Federalists and scorned by the moderate Republicans, he was left isolated and bitter by Jefferson's policy of political consensus, which required the jettisoning of immoderate Republican militants. In February 1802 he entered a partnership with the Federalist newspaper editor Henry Pace and soon earned the enmity of the Virginia Republican planter elite by exposing their peccadilloes. He also unremittingly attacked the *Examiner,* the Republicans' major mouthpiece in Virginia. In the Richmond *Recorder,* however, Callender did not abandon his ideals. He continued to promote his extreme democratic politics, attacking both parties but directing his most scathing criticism at the Republicans, who now controlled both the state and federal governments. When in September he obtained evidence that his erstwhile Republican colleagues had spread malicious gossip about his marriage (that his wife had died of venereal disease while he cavorted drunkenly in the next room), Callender gained revenge by publishing the rumors about Jefferson's liaisons with a slave that he had learned from anonymous correspondents. The Sally Hemings story, greatly embellished since Callender's rather prosaic comments, remains the subject of controversy.

Callender's reputation as a brilliant but unscrupulous editor peaked with these revelations. In December 1802 he was soundly beaten by George Hay, one of his lawyers in 1800 whom Callender had threatened to publish stories about, and spent several days in jail as a martyr for the concept of a free press. Thereafter his fortunes declined. Callender never invented stories for his own purposes, and once the gossip died down he began to lose his readership. Drinking heavily, he quarrelled with Pace and broke the partnership. Callender was found drowned in the James River, probably a suicide. He left a note, which was later published in the *Examiner,* in which he expressed remorse for some of his excesses. But he did not apologize for maligning Jefferson; nor did he retreat from the extreme democratic republicanism to which he had adhered since his first years as a radical, but misanthropic, agitator.

• A few letters from Callender can be found in the correspondence of Andrew Stuart, National Library of Scotland, and in the Thomas Jefferson Papers, Library of Congress. His most important pamphlets are *Deformities of Dr. Samuel Johnson* (1782), *The Political Progress of Britain,* Part 1 (1792), *The History of the United States for 1796* (1797), and *The Prospect before Us,* (2 vols., 1800). He contributed prolifically to the following newspapers: the Philadelphia *Aurora* (1794–1798), the Richmond *Examiner* (1799–1801), and the Richmond *Recorder* (1801–1803). The only full-length biography is Michael Durey, *"With the Hammer of Truth": James Thomson Callender and America's Early National Heroes* (1990), but see also Charles A. Jellison, "That Scoundrel Callender," *Virginia Magazine of History and Biography* 64 (1959): 295–306.

MICHAEL J. DUREY

CALLENDER, John (1706–26 Jan. 1748), Baptist clergyman and historian, was born in Boston, Massachusetts, the son of John Callender, a shopkeeper, and Priscilla Man. His grandfather, Ellis Callender, was lay preacher at the First Baptist Church from 1708 to 1726. At the age of thirteen, Callender entered Harvard College. As a scholarship student, he was supported with the income from the benefactions of Thomas Hollis and later with funds supplied by Thomas Brattle. At graduation in 1726, he was awarded the honor of presenting an address on the proposition, "Scriptura credendi et agendi est norma perfecta et sola." ("The perfect and only rule for believing and acting is Scripture.") After leaving Harvard, Callender was baptized by his uncle, Elisha Callender, minister of the first Baptist church. He then taught school briefly in the Swansea, Massachusetts, area and preached for a while in Newport, Rhode Island. In August 1728 he was invited to preach for the church in Swansea, the oldest Baptist church in Massachusetts. There he remained until 1730, when, to the surprise of his congregation, he declined the call to settle. After leaving Swansea, he married Elizabeth Hardin of that town and commenced the practice of a physician. The couple had nine children.

Soon thereafter, in October 1731, Callender reentered the ministry and was ordained by his uncle Elisha as pastor of the Baptist church in Newport, Rhode Island, which was the second-oldest church of that denomination in the United States. He served there until his death, preaching a gentle and tolerant form of "Old Light" theology, fully sympathetic to and in substantial agreement with New England Congregational leaders in spite of the controversies inspired by the Great Awakening. The characteristic enthusiasm of the Great Awakening, with its emphasis on evangelism and perfectionism, and its attendant emotionalism, spontaneous expression, and disdain for rationalism, was alien to the decorum and respect for tradition, learning, and reason so evident in the person of Callender. As an Old Light, he identified with inherited institutions and saw preaching as a way to preserve the social order. Callender drew attention for his belief in free communion, published in his sermon on the occasion of Jeremiah Condy's ordination in 1739 to the Baptist church in Boston, that godly non-Baptists should be permitted to take communion in Baptist churches. He was widely esteemed in his community, and he got along well with his ministerial colleagues and fellow Harvard graduates, especially with his classmate, Samuel Mather, son of Cotton Mather. He was a member of the Society for Promoting Virtue and Knowledge by a Free Conversation, in Newport, which later became the Redwood Library. It is likely that this urbane clergyman could have prospered only in his Newport church, which, unlike other New England Baptist churches, had several wealthy members, who undoubtedly appreciated Callender's learning and gentility.

Callender was a friend of the Boston clergyman and antiquarian Thomas Prince and shared the latter's interest in the history of New England. Indeed, the favorable reaction to Callender's sermon delivered in 1738 on the centennial of Rhode Island's founding persuaded him to write his full-scale history of the colony. Callender's *Historical Discourse on the Civil and Religious Affairs of the Colony of Rhode Island and Providence* (1739) was an important contribution to Rhode Island history; he also collected much historical material relating to the colonial history of Baptist churches. Mindful of the difficult earlier relations between Puritans and Baptists, and equally mindful of the sensibility of his friend Samuel Mather, grandson of Increase Mather, who had persecuted the earliest Baptists in Massachusetts, Callender employed a restrained, reasonable tone and made a strong plea for freedom of conscience.

Callender's text was a model of impartiality. It proved a valuable source for Isaac Backus when he wrote his history of the Baptists in New England many years later. The importance of Callender's writing lay in its marking a change from conflict between Baptists and Congregationalists to one among groups within both churches. Delineated primarily by education and socioeconomic standing, differing attitudes toward social and theological issues became the fault lines within those respective churches as they were overtaken by the Great Awakening.

Callender was appointed by the Rhode Island General Assembly in 1743 to serve on a committee to revise and print the colony's laws. He was also elected schoolmaster in 1746 by the citizens of Newport. He died in Newport after a long illness and was buried there. He was eulogized in the *Boston Gazette* (9 Feb. 1748) as a "gentleman of . . . natural Accomplishments, and extensive Learning; of the greatest Integrity and Modesty" and, in the *Boston Evening-Post* (15 Feb. 1748), as one of "superior good Sence, and very Extensive Knowledge" who was also "an entire Stranger to Cunning and Artifice." The epitaph on his tomb noted that he was "distinguished as a shining and very burning light by a true and faithful ministry."

Callender was symbol of rapprochement between Baptists and Congregationalists in the first half of the eighteenth century, as his gentle, tolerant theology, along with his *Historical discourse* . . . and its emphasis on freedom of religious expression, tended to produce an alliance among educated New Englanders who saw in the existing churches a force for social order as well as salvation.

• Some of the historical materials collected by Callender and used by Isaac Backus for his historical research are now in the Yale University Library. The characteristically balanced and informative sketch by Clifford K. Shipton in *Sibley's Harvard Graduates Biographies*, vol. 7 (1945), is the best source of information on Callender, though the "Memoir" by Romeo Elton in Rhode Island Historical Society, *Collections*, vol. 4 (1888), pp. 9–25, also contains some useful information.

WILLIAM L. JOYCE

CALLIMACHOS, Panos Demetrios (4 Dec. 1879–13 Oct. 1963), Greek Orthodox priest and journalist, was born in Madytos, Dardanelles, Turkey, the son of Panagiotis Paximadas and Grammatiki (maiden name unknown). Following studies in Constantinople and Smyrna, Callimachos received his doctorate in theology from the University of Athens in 1902, only four years after Greece was defeated in its war with Turkey.

Greatly influenced by the Greek desire to regain the region of Asia Minor from Turkey, Callimachos was an ardent champion of the Greek cause. He became the editor of the newspaper sponsored by Hellenismos, a society dedicated to the propagation of Greek territorial aspirations. As a lecturer for the political movement known as Regeneration, he traveled throughout Greece as well as Asia Minor, the Middle East, and Egypt. He served as the secretary of Patriarch Photios of Alexandria from 1906 to 1914. During this period, he married Olga Andres in 1908 in Cairo and had two sons. Subsequently ordained a priest, Callimachos served as a chaplain during the Balkan Wars of 1912–1913.

Callimachos came to New York in December 1914 at the invitation of the Panhellenic Union, a society devoted to preserving Greek identity among the immigrants from Greece and Asia Minor. While his initial intention may have been only to stay briefly to bolster the work of the union, Callimachos came to believe that he and his family should remain in America to aid the Greek immigrants who were deeply divided over politics in their native country. In 1915 he became editor of the New York Greek daily *National Herald*, a new publication created to espouse the position of the Greek Republican cause led by Prime Minister Elevtherios Venezelos and to oppose the *Atlantis*, a pro-Royalist publication. The two Greek dailies served the Greek immigrant population, although they frequently engaged in bitter attacks on each other. Callimachos championed a more democratic government in Greece and advocated that Greece join the Allies in World War I as a means of gaining greater territory.

As a result of a dispute with the *National Herald*'s management, Callimachos left his editorial position in 1918 and became pastor of St. Constantine Church in Brooklyn. He also edited a Greek language monthly, *National Renaissance*, and taught briefly at St. Athanasius Seminary in Astoria. Returning to the *National Herald* as editor in 1922, Callimachos became the chief spokesman for the movement opposing assimilation of Greek immigrants and the greater Americanization of the Greek Orthodox church. He became one of the leaders of the church during the period when Archbishop Athenagoras Spyrou sought to heal divisions resulting from the old Vennazelist-Royalist debate that had divided parishes.

Resigning from the *National Herald* again in 1944, Callimachos became the editor of the Greek-language weekly *Eleutheros Typos*. He strongly opposed the Greek Communists during the Greek civil war. In 1947 he became editor emeritus of the *National Herald*. He died in New York City.

Callimachos championed democratic values and supported the notion of larger territory for the Greek nation. With regards to Greek immigrants in the United States, he called for the preservation of the Greek language and culture in the face of the overwhelming movement toward greater assimilation. His support for the legitimate leadership of the Greek Orthodox church in America during the 1930s and 1940s contributed greatly to the overcoming of fraternal divisions rooted in Old World politics.

• Assessments of Callimachos's activities can be found in George Papaioannou, *The Odyssey of Hellenism in America* (1985), and Theodore Saloutos, *The Greeks in the United States* (1964). For information on the Greek Orthodox church in America, see Miltiades Efthimiou and George Christopoulos, *History of the Greek Orthodox Church in America* (1984).

THOMAS FITZGERALD

CALLOWAY, Cab (25 Dec. 1907–18 Nov. 1994), jazz and popular singer and bandleader, was born Cabell Calloway III in Rochester, New York, the son of Cabell Calloway, a lawyer who also worked in real estate, and Martha Eulalia Reed, a public school teacher and church organist. Around 1914 the family moved to Baltimore, Maryland. His father died around 1920, and his mother married John Nelson Fortune, who held a succession of respectable jobs. Calloway sang solos at Bethlehem Methodist Episcopal Church, and he took voice lessons at age fourteen. He was nevertheless an incorrigible teenager, and in 1921 his stepfather sent him to Downingtown Industrial and Agricultural School, a reform school run by his granduncle, a pastor in Downington, Pennsylvania. In the spring of 1922 Calloway returned home on his own initiative, by his own account not reformed, but now a man rather than a boy. He thereafter moved comfortably between the proprieties of mainstream American life and the depravities of American entertainment.

After studies at Laureville School in Wilson Park, a suburb of Baltimore, Calloway moved with his family back into the city in the summer of 1924 and enrolled at Frederick Douglass High School. He took further voice lessons, began to play drums, and sang, eventually working professionally in local vaudeville venues with a small band. Concurrently he starred in basketball at Frederick Douglass and as a guard with the Baltimore Athenians of the Negro professional basketball league. At the start of his last semester, a child was born illegitimately to Calloway and his high school sweetheart, Zelma Steptoe.

Shortly after Calloway's graduation in June 1927, his sister Blanche Calloway came through Baltimore with the Plantation Days revue, which he joined, replacing a singer in a quartet. Calloway toured to Chicago in August, studying acting under Blanche's tutelage and appearing with her in the Plantation Days show on the understanding that in September, when the show ended, he would enroll at Crane College, ostensibly in preparation for the law. During his short stay at Crane he played on the college basketball team and performed nightly in Chicago clubs. Early in 1928 he sang at the Dreamland Café. At the Sunset Café he became house singer with trumpeter Louis Armstrong's band. He served temporarily as the café's relief drummer and then became its master of ceremonies. During this period he began taking saxophone lessons. In 1928 he married Wenonah "Betty" Conacher. After a fun-loving start, Calloway regretted the marriage. They were in many ways ill suited to each other, and Calloway was a chronic womanizer.

When Armstrong went with Carroll Dickerson's band to Connie's Inn in New York in the spring of 1929, the Alabamians came into the Sunset, and Calloway soon took over their leadership. From May 1929 he toured with the Alabamians to New York, where in October 1929 they had a disastrous engagement at the Savoy Ballroom, owing to the band's unfamiliarity with dance music then current in Harlem. The group disbanded after a battle of the bands with the Missourians.

Renewing his association with Armstrong, Calloway secured a part in the revue *Connie's Hot Chocolates* in which he sang "Ain't Misbehavin'." His performances were a great success on Broadway and on tour to Philadelphia and Boston. He was invited to return to New York to lead the Missourians at the Savoy Ballroom in March 1930. While working at lesser-known venues, Calloway became affiliated with promoter Irving Mills and made his first recordings, with the Missourians, now billed as Cab Calloway and his orchestra. Titles such as "St. Louis Blues," from July, and "Some of These Days" and "St. James Infirmary," from December, feature trumpeters Roger Quincy Dickerson, Lammar Wright, Sr., and Wendell Culley; trombonist De Priest Wheeler; and reed players William Thornton Blue and Walter "Foots" Thomas.

In February 1931 Mills brought the band into the Cotton Club, where over the course of a year it appeared, or left for touring, in alternation with Duke Ellington's orchestra, also managed by Mills. Ellington left the Cotton Club permanently in 1932, but Calloway continued there regularly to 1936, when the Harlem location of the club closed, and again from the fall of 1936 to 1940, during the lifespan of the Cotton Club as a midtown venue.

Shows at the Cotton Club were built around Calloway's singing, his jive talk and zany behavior, and his dancing. He became a national celebrity as a consequence of network radio broadcasts from the club, together with recordings and, soon thereafter, films. The aforementioned "St. James Infirmary" became his first hit, featuring his piercing and eccentric interpretation of the lyric. This title was immediately overshadowed by "Minnie the Moocher," which presented the first of what would become a series of musical portraits of imaginary Minnie's lowlife experiences and which featured an unforgettable imitative exchange between Calloway and his bandsmen, who scat-sang "hi-de-hi-de-hi-de-ho" and other nonsense lyrics. Developed in performance during his first month at the Cotton Club, "Minnie the Moocher" was recorded early in March 1931. Other recordings from this year include "Black Rhythm" and "Six or Seven Times."

Calloway became the "King of Hi-de-ho" and thereby inspired the character of Sportin' Life in George Gershwin's *Porgy and Bess* (1935). In 1932 he continued Minnie's story in "Minnie the Moocher's Wedding Day." That same year he repeated the original "Minnie the Moocher" in a cartoon of the same name starring Betty Boop and including an appearance by Calloway and his orchestra, and in 1933 he performed the song in the full-length movie *The Big Broadcast* and in an excellent new recorded version. His colorful fantasies about the drug trade in Harlem included "Reefer Man," recorded on 9 June 1932 and slotted into the film *International House* in 1933, and "Kicking the Gong Around" (that is, smoking opium), recorded in December 1933. Calloway noted that despite the experience that these and other such titles apparently revealed, he himself never took drugs, having seen the effect on others, and instead indulged in women, gambling, cars, and clothes. The recording session of 9 June 1932 also yielded "Old Man of the Mountain," made into a delightful Betty Boop cartoon the following year. In Calloway's finest perversion of the American norm, "St. James Infirmary" reappeared in 1933 in Betty Boop's cartoon version of "Snow White." Calloway himself was also parodied and caricatured in a number of cartoons from the mid-1930s.

In seasons off from the Cotton Club, Calloway took his band on tour throughout the nation, into Canada, and, in March and April 1934, to Europe. He made the film short *Cab Calloway's Jitterbug Party* in 1935. New faces in the band during the early 1930s included trumpeter Doc Cheatham, reed player Eddie Barefield, pianist Benny Payne, and bassist Al Morgan. Trombonists Claude Jones and Keg Johnson, reed players Garvin Bushell and Ben Webster, guitarist Danny Barker, and bassist Milt Hinton were among the new band members in the mid-1930s. Calloway's most significant hiring was tenor saxophonist Chu Berry, who joined in 1937 on the condition that Calloway never again play alto saxophone with the band, and whose high standard of musicianship methodically improved the orchestra's stature as jazz instrumentalists in accompaniment to the leader and occasionally in performances without him. Among many actions, Berry made a private agreement with drummer and bandleader Chick Webb, trading items from Webb's personal band library for instrumental parts that Berry secretly had copied from Calloway's books.

In 1937 Calloway made the film shorts *Hi De Ho* and *Manhattan Merry-Go-Round*, the latter presenting "Mimmie the Minnie." In this same year Calloway and his wife adopted a daughter in an unsuccessful attempt to rescue their marriage. In 1938 he published the first edition of *Cab Calloway's Hepsters Dictionary*. He explained that he mainly assembled it from language heard on the street, but in some instances he claimed to have coined words, including "jitterbug." In 1939 he published *Professor Cab Calloway's Swingformation Bureau*, teaching how to apply the vocabulary in the dictionary. It went through six editions to 1944, the last as *The New Cab Calloway's Hepsters Dictionary: Language of Jive*, by which point it had been adopted as the official jive language reference book of the New York Public Library. Millions of copies were distributed. At some unknown date New York University gave Calloway the honorary title of "Dean of American Jive."

From the perspective of instrumental jazz, rather than American popular song and entertainment, the orchestra's greatest years stretched from mid-1939, when trumpeter Dizzy Gillespie joined, to the fall of 1941, when Berry died in an automobile accident and Gillespie left after literally getting into a fight with Calloway and knifing him. This band had an exceptional rhythm section comprising Payne, Barker, Hinton, and drummer Cozy Cole. Recordings from this period include Benny Carter's bouncy arrangement of Leonard Feather's composition "Calling All Bars"; the energetic "Bye Bye Blues," with sparkling solos from Berry, Gillespie, and vibraphonist Tyree Glenn; the ballads "A Ghost of a Chance" and "Lonesome Nights," both featuring Berry (1940); and "Jonah Joins the Cab," written for trumpeter Jonah Jones (1941).

In 1941 Calloway's group performed in the movie *Roadshow*. In 1942 he had an NBC network radio show, "The Cab Calloway Quizzicale," satirizing bandleader Kay Kayser's "College of Musical Knowledge" radio quiz show. In 1943 he costarred with Lena Horne in *Stormy Weather*, his most important film role. From that year into 1944 he held engagements in Manhattan and Cedar Grove, New Jersey. In 1942 Calloway had met Nuffie (maiden name unknown), a secretary in the Department of Housing in Washington, D.C. By 1943 they were living together. He was legally separated from Betty in 1944, but Betty fought the divorce, and his first two children with Nuffie were born out of wedlock. When the divorce was finalized in 1949, they married immediately and had a third daughter (Calloway's fifth).

Calloway continued leading his orchestra until April 1948, when the big band business crashed. After a solo visit to England in the summer, he formed a six- or seven-piece group while reconstituting the big band for special occasions, including an engagement in Miami early in 1949. With only four players—Jones, pianist Dave Rivera, Hinton, and drummer Panama Francis—he made the film short *St. James Infirmary* in 1950 and toured Cuba. He re-formed the big band for a festival performance in Montevideo, Uruguay, in 1951. In 1952 the quartet played at Birdland in New York and then disbanded.

Through the 1950s Calloway often played Sportin' Life in revivals of *Porgy and Bess*, both on Broadway and on tour. He returned to England as a soloist in 1955. Later in the decade he played occasional big band jobs in New York and Las Vegas. He continued acting in the 1960s with a small part in the movie *The Cincinnati Kid* (1965) and a leading role in an African-American production of *Hello Dolly!* He also toured with the Harlem Globetrotters show. Calloway led a big band at the Newport Jazz Festival in 1973. In 1975 he toured Catskill and Pocono mountain resorts and Florida theaters and clubs on his own, while also participating in a national tour with drummer Ray McKinley's big band.

New generations discovered "Minnie the Moocher" when Calloway starred as mentor to comedians John Belushi and Dan Aykroyd in the movie *The Blues Brothers* (1980). He subsequently appeared on the children's television show "Sesame Street," and he hosted a television retrospective on Harlem nightclubs, "Of Minnie the Moocher and Many, Many More" (1981). He delivered yet another rendition of "Minnie the Moocher" in Francis Ford Coppola's *The Cotton Club* (1984) while denouncing the film's inauthenticity. In 1987 he toured for six weeks with one of his daughters, singer and actress Chris Calloway, in a revue, *His Royal Highness of Hi-de-ho*: *The Legendary Cab Calloway*. He hosted the public television series "The Soundies," made in Los Angeles, as well as the episode "The Cotton Club Remembered" in the PBS "Great Performances" series. In 1989 he appeared as singer Janet Jackson's partner in the music video "Alright." On 12 June 1994 Calloway suffered a severe stroke at home in White Plains, New York. He died at a nursing home in Hockessin, Delaware.

Despite the occasional well-publicized fight, Calloway was one of America's most beloved bandleaders, showing an unusual capability to combine discipline with sensitivity. He insisted on tidy and clean uniforms, personal responsibility, and timeliness, and yet he showed himself able to accommodate his musicians' needs. Among African-American bands, Calloway's payroll was probably the highest and certainly the most reliable, and he gave his musicians yearly paid vacations, even as the big band business was failing in the mid-1940s.

Jazz critics have often echoed the complaint Eddie Barefield expressed to writer Albert J. McCarthy: "The men were not given the chances to play that they should have had. . . . He took all the limelight with his singing" ("Eddie Barefield Story," p. 12). This view was especially felt during 1939–1941, when Calloway's jazzmen might have been much more of a match for the Duke Ellington and Count Basie orchestras than the recorded legacy indicates. Writer Gunther Schuller, however, praises Calloway highly for his singing skills, his arrangers, and his instrumental soloists. Though he offered an ear-opening corrective to earlier assessments, Schuller perhaps went too far in asserting that "Calloway, amazingly, even in his most extravagant vocal antics, never left the bounds of good taste"

(p. 330). One might argue rather that Calloway made grotesque tastelessness into an extraordinary personal style.

In any event, as Hinton told writer Stanley Dance, "Music was secondary to Cab's act" (p. 367). He had a voice that could cut through any situation, without need of a microphone. He was not merely handsome but style setting, his trademark being a flashy white or canary yellow zoot suit, and this sense of style was tied directly to the cutting-edge hepness (later, hipness) that his dictionary documents. On stage he was shrewdly spontaneous, hilarious, and completely uninhibited, as McCarthy indicates in retelling a story of how Calloway turned a battle of the bands in his favor: "He made a spectacular entry, leaping over chairs, turning somersaults, and so on, all the while singing in his most bizarre manner" (p. 8). Calloway was unquestionably one of the greatest showmen of the twentieth century.

• Calloway's papers are held at Boston University. Cab Calloway and Bryant Rollins, *Of Minnie the Moocher and Me* (1976), reproduces as an appendix to the autobiography both *Professor Cab Calloway's Swingformation Bureau* (1939) and *The New Cab Calloway's Hepsters Dictionary* (1944 ed.). Additional information is in Steve Voce, "The Marquis of Harlem," *Jazz Journal*, June 1958, pp. 9–11; Albert J. McCarthy, "The Big Band Era: 1. Cab Calloway," *Jazz Monthly*, Feb. 1960, pp. 7–9, 31, repr. in McCarthy, *Big Band Jazz* (1974), pp. 210–14; George T. Simon, *The Big Bands*, 4th. ed. (1981), pp. 110–12; and Ben Fong-Torres, "Cab Calloway Is No 'Moocher' Off Life," *San Francisco Chronicle Datebook*, 24 Nov. 1985, pp. 39–40. Calloway's sidemen give detailed accounts of the band in McCarthy, "The Eddie Barefield Story," *Jazz Monthly*, May 1959, pp. 11–12; Stanley Dance, *The World of Swing* (1974), pp. 366–75; Dizzy Gillespie, with Al Fraser, *To Be, or Not . . . to Bop: Memoirs* (1979); Danny Barker, *A Life in Jazz*, ed. Alyn Shipton (1986); Garvin Bushell and Mark Tucker, *Jazz from the Beginning* (1988); and Milt Hinton and David G. Berger, *Bass Lines: The Stories and Photographs of Milt Hinton* (1988). For details of the 1934 European tour, including a bibliography of articles bylined by Calloway, see Howard Rye, "Visiting Firemen: 3 (a) Cab Calloway and His Orchestra," *Storyville*, Oct.–Nov. 1980, pp. 30–31. For musical analysis, see Gunther Schuller, *The Swing Era: The Development of Jazz, 1930–1945* (1989), pp. 326–50. Jay Popa catalogs recordings in *Cab Calloway and His Orchestra* (1976; rev. 2d. ed., 1987). Obituaries are in the *New York Times*, the *Washington Post*, and the *San Francisco Examiner*, 20 Nov. 1994.

BARRY KERNFELD

CALVERT, Cecilius (8 Aug. 1605–30 Nov. 1675), second Lord Baltimore and founder and first proprietor of Maryland, was born probably in Kent County, England, the son of Sir George Calvert, first Lord Baltimore, and Anne Mynne. Little is known of Cecilius's childhood. Named Cecil for Sir Robert Cecil, the most powerful man in the government of James I, he was baptized in the Church of England on 2 March 1606. As his father steadily advanced in government service to membership on the Privy Council and a position as one of the principal secretaries of state, the family conformed to the Church of England. Calvert attended Trinity College (Oxford) but did not take a degree. When he made the decision to live openly as a Roman Catholic remains problematic. He may have decided in advance of his father, who resolved his religious commitment in November 1624. Earlier that year Calvert traveled to the Continent, and while his pass contained the usual prohibition against visiting Rome, there is reason to suspect that he did. Certainly by 1625 young Calvert openly worshiped as a Catholic. In so doing, he identified with an outlawed, but never socially ostracized, minority within the English community. He took the name Cecilius when confirmed into the Catholic faith.

The Calverts made their mark as Catholic colonizers in seventeenth-century America. Cecilius Calvert, who remained in England to manage the family enterprises, did not participate in the family's efforts to colonize in Avalon in Newfoundland between 1627 and 1629. In 1628 he married Anne Arundell, the daughter of Lord Arundell of Wardour, solidifying the Calverts with the small but socially prominent Catholic community. They had at least five children, two of whom lived to adulthood. In 1629 the elder Calvert removed his family from Avalon to the Chesapeake region in search of a more favorable climate for a new colony. Returning to England, he initiated the process to secure a charter for land along the Chesapeake Bay. He died in 1632, shortly before the government of Charles I granted a generous charter to colonize in Maryland. Cecilius Calvert inherited not only his father's title and what little was left of the family fortune but the dream to establish a prosperous colony in the New World. Unlike his father, Calvert lacked experience in government service and colonizing. To him fell the responsibility of launching the Maryland enterprise.

A lack of financial resources, a hostile coalition that supported the claims of the defunct Virginia Company, and an inability to attract potential colonists—Protestant or Catholic—hampered implementation of the undertaking. Lord Baltimore intended to sail with the first ships, which left in November 1633, but his adversaries forced him to remain in England to protect his charter. During the early years of his proprietary rule, the impoverished Baltimore lived at Hook House on his father-in-law's estate. He attempted to govern his colony through his younger brother, Leonard Calvert, who served in his place.

Circumstances, as much as philosophical considerations, dictated Lord Baltimore's contribution to developing a concept of the separation of religious and political loyalties. From the beginning Catholics were a minority of the Maryland population, and Baltimore intended to keep the peace by removing religious animosities from the political realm. Although priests from the Society of Jesus accompanied the first settlers for the primary purpose of converting the natives, the government supported no religious denomination, and religion remained a private matter. The charter invested Lord Baltimore with feudal powers through which he attempted to recreate the English manorial system he knew so well. His charter enabled him to create a number of manors, self-contained administrative units based on the distribution of land to parties loyal to him. In this way he hoped not only to attract substantial settlers to the enterprise but also to ensure a degree of economic, social, and political stability that was frequently absent in fledgling colonies. Lord Baltimore may have seen the judicial powers invested in the manorial lords as a means of keeping potentially disruptive religious quarrels from becoming public events. He instructed the governor to avoid any controversies involving religion, and undoubtedly he expected the lords of the manors to comply with those instructions. Such confrontations during the first decade, however, could not be avoided. In two notorious cases his government ruled in favor of the Protestants, an indication that Baltimore's policies could work.

During the English civil wars and the Interregnum, Baltimore faced his severest challenges as proprietor of the nascent colony. He envisioned that under his charter he alone held title to the land in Maryland. The Jesuits, as a result of their missionary efforts to the Maryland Indians, were acquiring land from the natives independent of the proprietor. In addition, he considered the Jesuits' demands for religious privileges to be excessive. Their bitter quarrel came to a head in 1642 when Baltimore came close to expelling the defiant priests. Later, in 1645 an interloper named Richard Ingle, claiming authority from the Protestant Parliament, invaded the colony. Forcing the governor to flee, he plundered the colony and kidnapped a number of priests and prominent Catholics, whom he transported to England. As a political entity, Maryland had been destroyed. The governor restored order in 1646, but within a year of Calvert's death in 1647, Baltimore revolutionized his government by appointing a Protestant governor and council in an effort to stem further challenges to his government based on spurious religious claims. To ensure that the Catholics who ventured to Maryland would continue to enjoy their property and civil rights Baltimore required his officers to take an oath not to interfere with any Christian's free exercise of religion and sent the Act Concerning Religion to the Maryland Assembly. After concerted debate the 1649 act passed. The enactment signaled the end of Baltimore's effort to ensure religious freedom through private means. Still, the act was a major breakthrough in contemporary thinking about the relationship between religious and political institutions. For the first time in the English world, a legislative enactment guaranteed all Christians their right to worship without molestation from secular authorities.

The triumph was short lived. Radical Protestants from Virginia, denied freedom in their own colony, in 1649 accepted Baltimore's offer to immigrate to Maryland. In 1652 they turned against his government, instigating a rebellion that temporarily brought an end to Baltimore's liberal rule. Catholics and Anglicans no longer enjoyed full political benefits under the restrictive 1654 Act Concerning Religion. In England in 1658 Baltimore used his influence with the government of Oliver Cromwell to regain control of his colony. With the restoration of Charles II in 1660 and a more relaxed attitude toward Catholics in England, Baltimore's little colony began to flourish. Under his leadership an effort was made to develop St. Mary's City into a baroque city with the building of a brick Roman Catholic chapel and a brick statehouse. By the time of Baltimore's death near London, England, Maryland was not the land of large manors dominated by a new world nobility he had envisioned; rather it was a prospering colony of small tobacco farms.

Although he never ventured to America, Baltimore pioneered in developing the concept of religious freedom by creating a society in Maryland based on religious toleration. This bold experiment of colonizing with a religiously pluralistic population, first attempted by his father in Newfoundland in the 1620s, lasted until a Protestant association overturned the proprietorship of his son Charles Calvert in 1688. Thereafter, the newly formed government, under a Protestant royal governor, forced Catholics to worship in a clandestine fashion.

• A small number of official papers are held in the Hugh Hampton Young Collection in the Enoch Pratt Free Library, Baltimore. The Public Record Office houses important documents relating to Baltimore and his colony. The Wentworth papers, housed in the Sheffield City Library, Sheffield, England, contain a small number of Baltimore's letters. The Maryland Historical Society maintains the largest collection of family papers, but it has limited material on the second Lord Baltimore. For a description of these papers, see Richard J. Cox, *A Guide to the Microfilm Edition of the Calvert Papers* (1973). A major portion of the family papers disappeared in the nineteenth century. See Cox, "A History of the Calvert Papers MS. 174," *Maryland Historical Magazine* 68 (Fall 1973): 309–22. The Maryland Historical Society published some documents relevant to the second Lord Baltimore in *The Calvert Papers* (3 vols., 1889–1899). His official correspondence is in William Hand Browne et al., eds., *The Archives of Maryland* (76 vols., 1883–). Clayton Coleman Hall reprinted many important documents in *Narratives of Early Maryland, 1633–1684* (1910). The best biographical study remains Browne's dated *George Calvert and Cecilius Calvert: Barons Baltimore of Baltimore* (1890). For two more recent assessments of Baltimore, see John D. Krugler, "Lord Baltimore, Roman Catholics, and Toleration: Religious Policy during the Early Catholic Years, 1632–1649," *Catholic Historical Review* 65 (Jan. 1979): 49–75, and Russell R. Menard and Lois Green Carr, "The Lords Baltimore and the Colonization of Maryland" in *Early Maryland and the Wider World*, ed. David B. Quinn (1982), pp. 167–85.

JOHN D. KRUGLER

CALVERT, Charles (27 Aug. 1637–20 Feb. 1715), third Lord Baltimore and second proprietor of Maryland, was born in England, the son of Cecil Calvert, second Lord Baltimore, and Anne Arundel, the daughter of Sir Thomas Arundel of Wardour, England. Calvert spent his youth in England with the advantages of affluence and social status, but he experienced the disadvantages of being Catholic in a country that severely limited the rights of those professing his religion. Calvert was well educated and explicitly groomed by his father to become the head of the family's proprietary colony of Maryland.

Following marriage around 1656 to Mary Darnall of Herefordshire, Calvert moved with his wife and a retinue of friends to Maryland in 1661. The couple had no children. Although only twenty-four years old, Calvert began his public career by serving as governor, the highest local officer in the province. It was a daunting assignment for the young Calvert, even with the counsel of Philip Calvert, his father's half-brother, who had arrived in Maryland just a few years earlier. Cecil Calvert had been without effective and dependable leadership in the colony for over a decade and was hopeful that these two family members could fill the vacuum.

Calvert's first decade as governor was primarily an apprenticeship, during which he managed slowly to reestablish proprietary authority following years of civil disruption in Maryland, rule by parliamentary commissioners, and a rebellion put down just a year before his own arrival. Calvert restored considerable religious toleration, particularly halting the persecution of Quakers, protecting the rights of Catholics, and welcoming to the colony other dissenters, who helped to increase the population and secure territorial claims in the northern regions of Maryland. Often during the 1670s, however, Calvert lamented the scarcity of men of education and social standing in the colony. The absence of what he considered a suitable core of leaders limited what he felt he could accomplish in providing stable government and resisting demands of the general public for policies more responsive to their perceived needs.

Calvert's imperial style and obvious close ties to Lord Baltimore, as well as an adeptness for detecting, isolating, and skillfully combating opposition, served him well in his early years as governor. Nonetheless, this frontier colony was steadily maturing, and the growing population, overwhelmingly Protestant, increasingly challenged proprietary procedures and policies. Dissidents especially cited the charter's provision for freemen to have a voice in the governance of Maryland and demanded a greater role for the elected representatives. A particularly assertive and divisive assembly in 1669 prompted Calvert to sail to England to consult more closely with his father on how to deal with the mounting opposition.

Calvert's return to Maryland by November 1670 marked a new stage in his administration. He took aggressive steps to build a cadre of officeholders closely bound to him and his father by blood, marriage, or patronage. His first wife having died (year unknown), Calvert arranged marriages between aspiring colonists and the five stepchildren he had acquired through his marriage in 1666 to Jane Lowe, widow of his good friend Henry Sewall. The Calverts had four children together. Several of Calvert's cousins immigrated to the colony in these years, and the governor immediately appointed them to powerful positions. Calvert was also generally astute throughout the 1670s in recruiting some Protestants into this emerging oligarchy, which was nonetheless predominantly Catholic, but by the late 1680s he unwisely allowed the number of Protestants in high offices to dwindle. He also extended the tenures of loyal sheriffs and other local officeholders rather than continuing his earlier policy of rotation in office. Individuals who questioned proprietary policies failed to obtain appointments or found their commissions promptly revoked.

Besides fashioning a new governing elite after 1670, Calvert attempted to forestall the mounting pressure from the colony's freemen by limiting their political power. Copying an English precedent, he issued an ordinance requiring ownership of a fifty-acre freehold or equivalent wealth in order to vote. He also reduced the number of representatives per county and instituted other measures that enabled him more easily to control elections, the assembly's membership, and the election of the Speaker of the lower house. Calvert then convened the legislature less frequently than had been the earlier custom. These measures antagonized many colonists, while limiting their means of legal opposition.

Calvert and the elected representatives to the assembly became particularly embattled in 1675. The spread of plantations and creation of new counties had inevitably provoked tensions with neighboring Indians, themselves pressed by tribes migrating from the north where they had been displaced. The need for frontier defense prompted Calvert to summon an assembly. He pressed for new taxes despite serious problems with an economy that was increasingly dependent on tobacco, which was falling in price. The delegates grudgingly granted the revenues but demanded more power in exchange. Cecil Calvert died in late 1675, and a few months later Charles Calvert returned to England for formal investiture as the third Lord Baltimore. During the two years of his absence, Bacon's Rebellion in neighboring Virginia threatened to spill over into Maryland. The hard economic times intensified the colonists' other longstanding frustrations, and only the capable intervention of Protestant Thomas Notley, who had acceded to the post of deputy governor, forestalled rebellion.

Following Calvert's return to Maryland in late 1678, he presided as resident proprietor for another six years, continuing the policies he had pursued since 1670. As long as he remained in the colony, opponents had little success in challenging his rule. Their fortunes improved, however, when Calvert again returned to England in the late spring of 1684 to confront serious problems from outside the colony. Imperial authorities were dissatisfied with Maryland's lax enforcement of the navigation acts, and the proprietary charter itself was threatened by colonial bureaucrats in Whitehall who wished to assert a stronger royal presence and central authority throughout the English colonies. In addition, William Penn, the proprietor of Pennsylvania, was questioning the boundary between the two provinces and disputing Calvert's land claims.

Before Calvert's departure for England, he established a deputy government with powers shared among several councillors. The lack of a single authoritative executive proved disastrous over the next few years, as the deputies mishandled a number of situations. One councillor, related to Calvert, murdered a customs collector and was then allowed to escape capture. This controversial incident provided additional ammunition for Calvert's opponents in Maryland and in London and further delayed his return to the colony.

In 1688 Calvert dispatched a new governor to Maryland, William Joseph, but he proved to be a poor choice. A strident advocate of divine right theories of government, he clashed immediately with local elected officeholders. Later that year, when Joseph and the council failed to acknowledge the new Protestant monarchs William and Mary, longstanding suspicions about the loyalty of the colony's Catholic leadership finally caused a group of proprietary opponents to seize power in a bloodless revolution. They organized as the Protestant Associators and removed all Catholics from office, proclaimed the authority of William and Mary, and appealed to the Crown to make Maryland a royal colony. Despite active lobbying by Calvert, the Crown did ultimately decide to assume control of Maryland as "a case of necessity." By a commission issued in June 1691, Calvert lost all political control of the province, although he retained rights to the land and to some revenues.

Calvert never returned to Maryland. After the death of Jane Calvert in 1700, he married twice more, in 1701 to Mary Thorpe, who died in 1710, and thereafter (year unknown) to Margaret Charleton, who survived Calvert. There were no additional children from these marriages. Periodically, Calvert petitioned the Crown in efforts to regain his original charter rights or to protect his land revenues from covetous imperial placemen or colonists. He became increasingly estranged from his son Benedict Leonard, who converted to Protestantism during the reign of Queen Anne and successfully appealed to her for financial assistance. As a result, after Charles Calvert's death in England, his son, then the fourth Lord Baltimore, achieved what had eluded his father for twenty-five years, restoration of proprietary authority in Maryland.

• Much of Calvert's surviving correspondence and other personal documents are printed in *The Calvert Papers*, vol. 1 (1889), and in the volumes of the *Archives of Maryland* covering the years 1660 to 1715. Secondary treatments include Clayton Colman Hall, *The Lords Baltimore and Their Maryland Palatinate* (1902); Charles M. Andrews, *The Colonial Period of American History*, vol. 2 (1937); and David W. Jordan, *Foundations of Representative Government in Maryland, 1632–1715* (1987).

DAVID W. JORDAN

CALVERT, Charles (29 Sept. 1699–24 Apr. 1751), fifth baron of Baltimore and proprietor of Maryland, was probably born at "Woodcote Park," the family estate in Epsom, Surrey County, England, the son of Benedict Leonard Calvert, fourth baron of Baltimore and a Tory member of Parliament, and Lady Charlotte Lee, a granddaughter of King Charles II. Charles was reared in an aristocratic but troubled Roman Catholic family. Charles's father divorced his wife in 1705, fathered children with a housekeeper, and in 1713 professed himself an Anglican, abandoning the family's Roman Catholic faith. He used his conversion to secure the return of full governing rights over the family's colony of Maryland, which his father had lost in the wake of the Glorious Revolution of 1688. But Calvert's father died in 1715, leaving the daunting task of reestablishing control over the colony to Calvert, who at age fifteen became the fifth baron of Baltimore and the proprietor of Maryland.

Until Calvert reached age twenty-one, his guardian Francis North, second baron of Guilford, made most of the decisions affecting the administration of Maryland. Not long after he came of age, however, Calvert made it clear that he intended to exert his influence in the colony. This would be no mean feat. Throughout the quarter-century of royal rule following the Glorious Revolution and during the years of Calvert's minority, strong leadership had been lacking in Maryland. Popularly elected members of the lower house of the General Assembly had exploited the political vacuum, vastly increasing their power and influence. Now Calvert announced his intent to correct the imbalance between the colonists' rights and his prerogatives. He planned to do this by reasserting the nearly kingly powers granted the proprietor by the Maryland charter, which the king had given to Calvert's great-grandfather in 1632.

To strengthen his ties to the colony, Calvert first sent a cousin in 1720 and then his younger brother Benedict Leonard in 1727 to the colony as governor. Benedict Leonard was a careful observer, and in detailed reports to his brother he described the major issues facing the colony, urging his brother to do something about the lack of a circulating medium of exchange in the colony, which many people considered an important impediment to economic growth. He observed that the need to secure assembly approval for the schedule of fees paid to proprietary officials and for the salary of the governor imperiled the proprietor's authority in the colony. And he warned his brother that an important source of proprietary revenue—the export duty on tobacco that since 1671 had been collected in lieu of the annual quitrent on land—was also dependent on assembly action every few years. As Calvert studied his brother's reports, he became convinced that resolution of these critical issues required him to visit the colony personally. In 1730 Calvert married Mary Janssen, daughter of Theodore Janssen; they had two sons and three daughters. Before his marriage Calvert had fathered a son, who was known as Benedict Swingate in childhood but who later assumed his father's surname. Historians have cited evidence that Calvert was a homosexual, who traveled to Russia in 1739 with a homosexual companion.

Calvert arrived in Annapolis in December 1732. His visit caused great excitement since he was the first proprietor to visit the colony since his great-grandfather had left in 1684. Calvert only stayed in Maryland for about seven months, but in that brief period he dramatically altered Maryland politics.

Well prepared by the detailed intelligence and thoughtful recommendations of his brother, Calvert moved quickly to address the major problems facing the colony. Soon after the general assembly convened in March 1733, it passed a paper-money bill providing £90,000 in small-denomination notes. To the delight of legislators and the public alike, Calvert promptly assented to this popular measure.

This was to be the last good news the colonists received from the proprietor. Calvert refused the assembly's offer to pass another equivalency bill for the quitrents. Instead he ordered an immediate return to the pre-1671 form of direct payments of the quitrents and promptly established a bureaucracy to collect it. To ensure that the annual revenue would make it worth his trouble, he announced a 250 percent increase in the quitrent.

Addressing the issue of the governor's salary and officers' fees, Calvert again exercised the kingly powers vested in him by the Maryland charter. He designated the source and means of collecting the revenue needed to fund each of them, independent of the General Assembly. Thus by fiat Calvert solved, at least to his own satisfaction, two of the thorniest issues facing the colony.

Then Calvert tackled the problem of the lower house itself. He believed that when he returned to England, the lower house would quickly resume its efforts to increase its power and influence at the expense of his prerogatives. Calvert approached the leader of the lower house, Daniel Dulany the Elder, and offered him three important posts in the proprietary establishment. The positions were so lucrative that Dulany could not refuse. By accepting, Calvert's most powerful enemy in the assembly became his staunchest ally. Gratified by his success with Dulany, Calvert launched a calculated program of using patronage to influence Maryland politics, a strategy that he employed successfully for the rest of his life.

When Calvert sailed for home in July 1733, he left a colony much changed by his visit. There was no longer any doubt about who was in charge of Maryland's government. He had resolved all of the major issues facing the colony without divisive public debate. He had reassured his officials and placemen that they were important to the proprietary establishment and that their incomes would be protected. And he left the leadership of the lower house shaken and compromised.

Calvert must have been pleased with his accomplishments on his brief visit to Maryland. However, by asserting so forcefully the absolute prerogatives of the proprietor, he had also polarized Maryland politics as never before. Virtually since the beginning of settlement in Maryland, popular interests had been pitted against the proprietary prerogative. But each side had always claimed a willingness to work together for the greater good of the colony. Now Calvert had shown that he intended to rule Maryland in the way that would most benefit him, without fear of retaliation from the lower house of the assembly or concern for the sensibilities of its members.

Initially weakened and dispirited, the lower house soon drew strength from Calvert's visit. His naked use of arbitrary power provided a rallying point for popular leaders, and Maryland politics quickly degenerated into stalemate. One commentator characterized the relationship between the lower house and the proprietor in the years after Calvert's visit as "the politics of irreconcilabilities." Whatever the proprietor wanted, the lower house opposed, and vice versa.

Virtually no important legislation passed the Maryland assembly for the rest of Calvert's proprietorship. The single exception was the Tobacco Inspection Act of 1747, a bill that established a system of tobacco inspection stations in the colony. Virginia had passed an inspection act in 1730, making a Maryland inspection act an economic imperative. Nevertheless, passage of the Maryland bill took years of negotiations before the lower house and proprietor finally agreed on terms.

In 1746 Calvert was appointed cofferer to Frederick Prince of Wales, a lord of the Admiralty. He was also elected a fellow of the Royal Society. He died in England.

• The largest collection of papers from Calvert's years as proprietor of Maryland are in the Calvert papers, MS. 174, at the Maryland Historical Society in Baltimore. The collection has been microfilmed and is cataloged in Donna M. Ellis and Karen A. Stuart, *The Calvert Papers: Calendar and Guide to the Microfilm Edition* (1989). Relations between the proprietor and the upper and lower houses of the Maryland General Assembly are detailed in William Hand Browne et al., eds., *Archives of Maryland*, vols. 25, 28, 33–40, 44, and 46 (1883–1972). A brief biographical sketch of Calvert is in Edward C. Papenfuse et al., eds., *A Biographical Dictionary of the Maryland Legislature, 1635–1789*, vol. 1 (1979; rev. ed., 1985). The best treatments of Maryland during Calvert's proprietorship are Charles Albro Barker, *The Background of the Revolution in Maryland* (1940), and Aubrey C. Land, *Colonial Maryland: A History* (1981). Calvert's use of political patronage to neutralize political opponents in the lower house of assembly is detailed in Aubrey C. Land, *The Dulanys of Maryland* (1955). An interesting study that combines extensive historical research on the Calvert family with the results of archaeological work at the Governor Charles Calvert House in Annapolis is Anne Elizabeth Yentsch, *A Chesapeake Family and Their Slaves: A Study in Historical Archaeology* (1994). Information on Calvert's homosexuality is in the Reverend Paul K. Thomas's letter to the editor, *Maryland Historical Magazine*, Summer 1996, pp. 244–45.

GREGORY A. STIVERSON

CALVERT, Charles Benedict (23 Aug. 1808–12 May 1864), politician and agricultural reformer, was born at the family plantation, "Riversdale," in Prince George's County, Maryland, the son of the Belgian-born heiress Rosalie Eugenia Stier and George Calvert, a lineal descendant of Maryland proprietors.

Calvert's grandfather Benedict was an illegitimate, although acknowledged, son of Charles Calvert, the fifth Lord Baltimore. But Riversdale, the thousand-acre tobacco plantation graced by an elegant Georgian mansion, had been developed by the wealthy Stiers who fled Europe when the army of revolutionary France threatened their native Antwerp in 1794; they later turned the plantation over to their daughter and son-in-law. In 1838, when his father died, Charles Benedict bought the estate after he and his older brother George Henry agreed to a division of their parents' assets.

Tutored at home by his mother and a succession of outsiders, Charles displayed an early appreciation for both farming and horses. He attended school in Philadelphia and at the nearby Bladensburg Academy, and in 1827 graduated from the University of Virginia where he studied agriculture. Returned to Riversdale, for the next ten years Charles helped his widowed father manage the plantation and its forty-six slaves. In 1839 he married Charlotte Augusta Norris, a Baltimore heiress who died in 1876. The couple raised their five children at Riversdale, which remained in the family until 1887 when it was sold to land developers.

In 1838 Charles Benedict Calvert was elected to the Maryland House of Delegates as a Whig and, after his defeat for reelection in 1840, he won election to both the 1843 and 1845 legislatures. Soon identified as an agricultural reformer who encouraged crop diversification for Maryland's exhausted tobacco lands, Calvert was a member of the legislature's committee on agriculture. In the 1850s when the Whigs disappeared, Calvert was attracted to the Know Nothings whose flame burned brightly but briefly in Maryland. As he wrote in his local newspaper, "Americans must support a movement bringing back the government to its original purity." Accordingly he voted for the Know Nothing presidential candidate Millard Fillmore in 1856.

As civil war threatened, like many other Marylanders who feared their state would serve as a bloody battleground (Riversdale was only nine miles north of the Capitol), Calvert became a Unionist who opposed secession and the creation of the Confederacy. In 1861 as a member of the newly created Union party, he was elected to the Thirty-seventh Congress. He took his seat in the special session convened by President Lincoln on 4 July.

A vigorous advocate of a federal department of agriculture, Calvert argued on the floor of the House that only when a "cabinet minister was appointed would the farmer be appreciated by the government and proper steps be taken to advance his noble calling." But soon this farmers' friend became absorbed in the issue of emancipation, which personally affected his plantation. Calvert opposed Lincoln's recommendation for gradual emancipation, and in the famous meeting in March 1862 that Lincoln called with border state representatives to advance the concept of federal compensation for slaveowners, Calvert spoke against the freeing of slaves on the grounds that such action was beyond the government's authority and would disrupt Maryland's society and economy. In December 1862 he voted against a resolution supporting Lincoln's preliminary emancipation proclamation, believing it unconstitutional even as a war measure. Later, as slaves freed themselves and public opinion even in the border state of Maryland shifted to oppose slavery, Calvert supported a plan to compensate slaveowners.

In 1863, the year before his death at Riversdale, Calvert ran again as a conservative Unionist for reelection to Congress from Maryland's Fifth District on the platform of "the Union as it was and the Constitution as it is." Calvert was defeated by an Unconditional Unionist, but his support of the Lincoln administration, though a plantation owner, displayed the depth of Unionist sentiment in Maryland.

Throughout his life Calvert worked to transform Riversdale into a model of progressive agriculture. He served as the first president of the Maryland Agricultural Society and helped found the United States Agricultural Society, where he promoted the importance of planting legumes that rested the soil. Before the war he sold one of his several farms to the state of Maryland for an agricultural college, which became the forerunner of the University of Maryland.

Important in the early 1860s as a border-state slave-owning representative in Congress, Calvert made what were in the long run equally crucial contributions to the University of Maryland and to agricultural reform.

• Few letters and manuscripts relating to Charles Benedict Calvert remain, although there are some relevant materials in the massive Calvert papers at the Maryland Historical Society and the Riversdale Historical Society in Prince George's County. An account of Riversdale is available in a Historic Structures Report of the National Capital Park and Planning Commission. See also Margaret Law Callcott, ed., *Mistress of Riversdale: The Plantation Letters of Rosalie Stier Calvert, 1795–1821* (1991), and Jean H. Baker, *The Politics of Continuity: Maryland Political Parties, 1858–1870* (1973).

JEAN HARVEY BAKER

CALVERT, Frederick (6 Feb. 1732–4 Sept. 1771), sixth and last Lord Baltimore and the proprietor of Maryland, was born in Epsom, Surrey, England, the son of Charles Calvert and Mary Janssen. Calvert was tutored privately at home as well as during travels throughout Europe. His poetry and other writings (as bad as they were) reveal a solid education in the classics, history, and languages. His inheritance on his father's death in 1751 included the proprietorship of Maryland, vast wealth, and important connections at court.

Frederick Calvert led a life of leisure at the expense of his responsibilities as proprietor of Maryland. Although his guardians included reputable men such as Arthur Onslow (Speaker of the House of Commons) and lawyer John Sharpe (whose brother George Sharpe was chaplain to George III), Calvert grew up to be "a dissolute but generous man . . . a traveler who never visited his province, a writer and a rake" and "frivolous, conceited, and dissipated, but sometimes generous and sympathetic." He professed the Anglican faith to which his grandfather had converted from Catholicism to help regain his proprietary colony, which the Crown had taken over following the Protestant Associators rebellion in 1689. Calvert traveled extensively throughout Europe, particularly in Italy where he stayed for extended periods, living in high style. He also lived in Constantinople for a time. He sustained his lifestyle with his inherited wealth, including huge tracts of land in Maryland, an annual income of about £10,000 sterling from quitrents and other taxes, his Woodcote Park estate in Surrey, and considerable Bank of England stock.

Calvert's contacts went well beyond the court in London or the tourist circuits of Europe. Several Maryland governors were among his kin. His aunt married Thomas Bladen, his sister married Robert Eden, and his guardian was the brother of Horatio Sharpe. These connections account for the appointment of Sharpe as governor and his replacement by Eden in 1768. Secretary Hugh Hammersley wrote Sharpe after his dismissal that Lord Baltimore had no complaints against him, but that "a similitude of pursuits and partiality for his sister" accounted for Calvert's appointment of Eden. Although Calvert chose Sharpe and Eden for personal reasons, the appointees proved politically sound. Both Sharpe and Eden often found themselves mediating between the proprietor and the colonists of Maryland.

While Calvert never set foot in Maryland, his attitudes, actions, and policies shaped Maryland's reaction to the imperial crisis that led to the Revolution. He abused the trust his colony had in its proprietor. However capable or popular his appointed governors in Maryland might have been, they were constantly frustrated by Calvert's actions, which alienated his colonial subjects. Claiming that he was a sufficient representative, Calvert refused to allow Maryland to have a colonial agent in London as so many of the other colonies did, including Penn's proprietorship. Claiming taxation of his property to be a violation of his prerogative, Calvert denied that his private lands or income could be taxed to support the war against France. He even refused to have the income from ordinary licensing redirected from his private income to defray military costs. The colonials resented these policies as unfair, while the Crown saw Calvert as an obstruction to the war effort.

Calvert's large-scale land sales indicated that he saw the province only as a source of money and that he had no long-term interest in the colony. His appointments caused resentment among the colonists and even the governors. Bennet Allen (an Anglican clergyman and friend of Calvert) engaged in pluralism, serving as rector of two lucrative parishes simultaneously, despite Maryland law and custom. Allen's personal effrontery led to one confrontation after another with members of the Maryland aristocracy. Allen frequently threatened his opponents with the displeasure of the proprietor if they did not cooperate, using his personal connections to Calvert, the extent of which are in question although they appeared then to be substantial. Each clash reduced the colonists' respect for Lord Baltimore and strengthened the antiproprietary party in the province. The same opposition party also led the resistance to imperial taxation. Even relations between Calvert and his governors were strained. His own provincial secretary had difficulty locating him to conduct business.

Calvert's personal habits made him hard to reach. He traveled abroad, often moving about to avoid his growing disrepute. He failed in his attempts at poetry, which brought him only derision among the critics and London society. His marriage in 1753 was a disaster. He usually lived apart from his wife, Lady Diana Egerton (daughter of the duke of Bridgewater), citing "a helpless disagreement of temper." After her death in 1758, Calvert lived with Hester Whalen of Ireland, with whom he had an illegitimate son and daughter. By 1770 he had twins by a different woman and a daughter by yet another. Calvert left Constantinople after a scandal broke involving an illegitimate child and accusations of having a private seraglio, a charge brought against him in London as well. He did at least support his illegitimate children, even making payments to the stepfather of his heir Henry (by Whalen). In 1768 Calvert was the center of another great public scandal, this time at home. Sarah Woodcock, a London milliner, charged him with abduction and repeated rape. The trial was conducted as much in the press as in the courtroom. Although the jury acquitted him, reportedly believing that Woodcock had not made adequate attempts to escape or to report the crime (and perhaps because of his station), Calvert retreated to the Continent to avoid further disgrace.

Calvert caused problems for his colony even after his death in Naples. While living, he had named his illegitimate son Henry Harford as his heir. He took elaborate steps to ensure Henry's inheritance, barring the entail on the province of Maryland and instructing Governor Eden to declare for Harford on Calvert's death. Although Maryland recognized Harford, his cousins the Brownings did not. The Brownings contested Calvert's will but were bought off. Eden, one of the executors, left Maryland in 1774 during a crucial phase in the coming of the Revolution. Eden chose to pursue his own interests by pressing for his wife's claims on her brother Frederick's estate in court, but in doing so, he abandoned his colony to the revolutionaries. In his absence, the Loyalist cause lost the pacifying and stabilizing force Eden had so far exerted on Maryland during the early stages of the Revolution. Calvert was thus responsible at least in part for the unrest in Maryland that contributed to the anti-imperial attitudes leading to American independence. However, once satisfied with successfully displacing the proprietor's authority, Marylanders were hesitant to join the rest of the colonies against the king of England.

• The Calvert papers, MS 174 at the Maryland Historical Society, contain several items regarding Frederick Calvert. The papers are also available on microfilm. See also the biographical files in the Special Collections at the Maryland State Archives. The best sources concerning Calvert's administration of Maryland are Charles A. Barker, *Background of the Revolution in Maryland* (1940), and James Haw, "Politics in Revolutionary Maryland" (Ph.D. diss., Univ. of Virginia, 1972). For an examination of Calvert's character and personal life, see Wallace Shugg, "The Baron and the Milliner . . . ," *Maryland Historical Magazine* (Winter 1988): 310–30. Vera Foster Rollo gathered considerable information on Calvert's inheritance in *The Proprietorship of Maryland* (1989), and has transcribed several pertinent original documents including Calvert's will. For information on all the proprietors, as well as the governors and other legislative officeholders in colonial and revolutionary Maryland, see Edward Papenfuse et al., eds., *A Biographical Dictionary of the Maryland Legislature, 1635–1789* (1979).

R. J. ROCKEFELLER

CALVERT, George (1580?–15 Apr. 1632), first Lord Baltimore and colonial entrepreneur, was born in Kiplin, Yorkshire, the son of Leonard Calvert, a gentleman of modest means, and a woman named Crossland, perhaps Alicia or Alice, or Grace. Calvert received a broad education through formal study and extensive travel. He earned a bachelor's degree from Trinity College, Oxford, in 1597 and in 1605 an honorary master's degree from that university. He gained fluency in Spanish, French, and Italian in his sojourns on the European continent. By his mid-twenties this preparation and his obvious talents in administration and diplomacy brought appointment as private secretary to Sir Robert Cecil, a privy councilor and secretary of state, through whom Calvert acquired still other patronage and the attention of the king. Marriage by 1605 to Anne Mynne of Hertfordshire probably also assisted Calvert's career; she was related to several prominent families active in government circles and in early trading and colonizing ventures.

In 1609 Calvert won the first of what would be three elections to the House of Commons. He represented the constituency of Bossiney in Cornwall. After 1621 he served for Yorkshire, a seat he obtained largely through the efforts of another patron, Sir Thomas Wentworth, later earl of Strafford. Following defeat in a reelection bid there in 1624, Calvert promptly secured election as a member for the University of Oxford. During the reign of James I, Calvert undertook a number of important assignments for the Crown in France, Spain, and Ireland. Appointed clerk of the Privy Council in 1613, he traveled the next year to Ireland on a special committee to study religious grievances of the Irish Parliament and its workings. Such services brought a knighthood in 1617 and appointment as a secretary of state in 1619. He assisted in negotiating international religious issues, political questions, and the possible marriage of Prince Charles of England to the daughter of the king of Spain, an alliance opposed by many in England who wanted neither closer ties with Spain nor marriage to a Catholic. Calvert's distinguished career in government ended in 1625 with the failure of the negotiations for the Spanish alliance and public announcement of his own conversion to Catholicism. The king accepted Calvert's resignation as secretary but retained him as a member of the Privy Council and made him baron of Baltimore, an Irish peerage, as a reward for his "fidelity and obedience." King James died shortly thereafter, and while his son, Charles I, offered to dispense with the oath of supremacy to retain Calvert on the Privy Council, Calvert refused and retired from the government.

For some years, Calvert had been interested in England's colonial ventures in Ireland and the Western Hemisphere, and he had become involved in several colonizing efforts, including investment in the Virginia Company and service on the council of the New England Company. In the mid-1620s Calvert briefly considered settling permanently in Ireland, but he soon turned his attention to North America. Calvert's most significant contribution to imperial policy came from his desire for a colonial charter that would provide greater flexibility and sovereignty for principal investors than was afforded by the joint stock companies then prevalent in colonizing and trading ventures. First in the charter for Avalon that Calvert received in April 1623 and then in the charter for Maryland that he helped to draft before his death, Calvert established the model for the proprietary charter that would prevail for many colonial entrepreneurs to follow.

Both as a shrewd investor and a Catholic, Calvert wanted independence, flexibility, and certain protections in his colonizing ventures. From his own political experiences and convictions, he wished to extend to any settlers in his colony basic English rights, particularly a voice in their own governance, but not ones that would significantly circumscribe proprietary powers. Moreover, Calvert believed that frontier settlements in America would not be ready for many decades for the fully developed political institutions of contemporary England, which required a more mature society. As Calvert focused his interest on the peninsula of Avalon in Newfoundland, where he had first invested in 1620, he formulated his theories of colonial government. He located a promising precedent for his New World vision in the palatinate of Durham, where the bishop of Durham's authority reached its zenith in the 1300s, yet where an assembly also met annually with limited legislative powers. The Avalon charter, which King James gave Calvert in 1623, incorporated at Calvert's request proprietary powers equivalent to any the bishop of Durham ever held; these royal powers were to become commonplace in later charters for other New World colonies and enabled the proprietor to declare war, institute martial law, regulate trade, issue ordinances, establish courts, and appoint judicial and military officers.

The Avalon experiment itself was less successful, in large part because of the inhospitable climate. Calvert visited the province in 1627 and returned to Avalon the following year with his second wife, Joan (last name unknown), whom he had married after the death of Anne in 1622, and with all of his children except his oldest son, Cecil Calvert. Other settlers in the young colony were predominantly Catholic and Irish. A single winter in Avalon was enough to convince Calvert that the colony would never be suited for anything but a seasonal fishery.

Sailing south with his family late in the summer of 1629, Calvert's entourage arrived in Jamestown on 1 October. As Catholics, the Calverts were not welcomed in Anglican Virginia. Calvert returned to England determined to acquire land in a more temperate climate than Newfoundland afforded. By now, his financial and imperial interests had been joined by a desire to assist other Catholics in avoiding persecution and in enjoying political and religious liberties. Calvert eventually decided to ask for a grant of land just north of Virginia and enlisted the support of friends in his negotiations with King Charles and others. The king ultimately agreed to give Calvert a colony extending from the Potomac River north to the fortieth parallel. At the king's particular request, Calvert named the colony "Mariland" in honor of the queen, Henrietta Maria.

Cecil, the second Lord Baltimore, would actually be the first proprietor of Maryland, because George Calvert died in England before the charter passed the royal seal on 30 June 1632. George Calvert had, however, played the major role in shaping the contents of that charter. It successfully retained the features he had found most advantageous in the Avalon charter while altering other provisions, such as the terms of land tenure from knight service to free and common socage, and adding new language that allowed him to make land grants and to erect manors. The results of these changes were to afford the proprietor greater rights and fewer obligations while at the same time extending to Roman Catholics greater protections for their civil and religious rights.

Calvert was survived by his wife, four sons (three sons from his first marriage predeceased him), and five daughters. All four sons participated in the settlement of Maryland—Cecil as proprietor; his second son, Leonard Calvert, as governor; his third son, George, as a gentleman adventurer; and a fourth son from his second marriage, Philip, who was later governor.

• No substantial body of Calvert's personal papers has survived. Charles M. Andrews, *The Colonial Period of American History*, vol. 2 (1936), remains the standard source on Calvert's extensive involvement in colonial enterprises. John D. Krugler, in a series of recent articles, has undertaken a broader study of this man: "Sir George Calvert's Resignation as Secretary of State and the Founding of Maryland," *Maryland Historical Magazine* 68 (1973): 239–54; "'Our Trusty and Well-Beloved Counsellor': The Parliamentary Career of Sir George Calvert, 1609–24," *Maryland Historical Magazine* 72 (1977): 470–91; "'The Face of a Protestant and the Heart of a Papist': A Reexamination of Sir George Calvert's Conversion to Roman Catholicism," *Journal of Church and State* 20 (1978): 507–31; and "The Calvert Family, Catholicism and Court Politics in Early Seventeenth-Century England," *Historian* 43 (1981): 378–92.

DAVID W. JORDAN

CALVERT, George Henry (2 June 1803–24 May 1889), author, was born on his family's estate near Bladensburg, Maryland, the son of George Calvert, a planter and politician, and Rosalie Eugenia Stier. As a child, Calvert was raised to be mindful of his aristocratic heritage—his paternal great-grandfather was the fifth Lord Baltimore, the founder of Maryland, and on his maternal side he was a descendant of Peter Paul Rubens—and his childhood years were spent in a style befitting a young man of wealth and gentility. In 1819 Calvert entered Harvard College, where he remained until 1823, at which time he was dismissed along with thirty other students for participating in the "Great Rebellion," a protest aimed at limiting the restrictions over student activities, but which ultimately led to the students protesting the quality of the education that they were receiving at Harvard. After leaving Harvard, Calvert journeyed to Europe and stayed with an uncle in Antwerp before spending fifteen months studying history and philosophy at the University of Göttingen. Concurrent and subsequent to his time at Göttingen, Calvert traveled to Weimar, where he met Goethe, and he then visited Edinburgh, Paris, and Antwerp again before returning to America in 1827. Calvert settled in Baltimore, where he served as editor of the *Baltimore Times*, and where he married Elizabeth Steuart in 1829.

While living in Baltimore Calvert published the first of his more than thirty books, *Illustrations of Phrenology* (1832), a collection of essays from the *Edinburgh Phrenological Journal*. His next work, however, was more ambitious, and although published anonymously, *A Volume from the Life of Herbert Barclay* (1833) was the first of a number of original works of literature; yet it was the only novel that he would write, the balance of his fiction being poetry and drama. After the publication of *Herbert Barclay*, Calvert limited himself to periodical publications until 1840, at which time he produced in quick succession two volumes of poetry and a drama, *Count Julian*.

In 1840 Calvert not only reentered the publishing world with a flourish, but he took his second European tour as well. In England Calvert spent several days with William Wordsworth, and he later traveled extensively in Germany and Italy. Returning to the United States in 1843 and settling in Newport, Rhode Island, he entered the most prolific phase of his literary career, and one of the earliest works to emerge after his second European tour was *Scenes and Thoughts in Europe. By an American* (1846). This work was immensely popular. Not only was it revised and republished several times, but it prompted a third European tour in 1851–1852, which spawned *Scenes and Thoughts in Europe. By an American. Second Series* in 1852.

After his third European tour, Calvert returned to Newport, where he took up permanent residence in 1853. In Newport he served as the chairman of the school board for a number of years, and he was also elected as the city's mayor in 1853 and 1854. While he continued to publish both poetry and drama during the next decade, it was his allegorical exposition *The Gentleman*, published in 1863 during the most crucial days of the Civil War, that was to make him a household name. In its discussion of the lifestyle and behavior of gentlemen throughout history, *The Gentleman* was of interest to readers at the time in its treatment of honor as a standard of a gentleman's behavior, especially in that for many Americans honor, and not slavery, had long been the central issue in the Civil War. Reprinted four times, *The Gentleman* was by far Calvert's most popular work.

While Calvert continued to write various works of poetry and prose, it was the publication of *Goethe: His Life and Works* (1872) that heralded a new phase of his literary career; henceforth he would write a substantial number of critical biographical studies of famous historical figures. Like his study on Goethe, his early biographies were on individuals of whom he had some personal knowledge or relationship, hence *The Life of Rubens* (1876) and *Wordsworth: A Biographic Aesthetic Study* (1878). Subsequently Calvert published biographical studies on Shakespeare (1879) as well as Samuel Taylor Coleridge, Percy Shelley, and Goethe again (1880). His last published work, the drama *Brangonar, a Tragedy* (1883), was about Napoleon, and thus in the latter stages of his career even his fictional works had taken on a biographical aspect. Calvert published no major works of literature after 1883, in part because critics and readers felt that he was out of touch with current literary trends—an opinion that Calvert himself only reinforced by published statements such as his opinion that "Walt Whitman is an enormous joke." Openly bitter and disappointed that his own work was no longer valued or wanted, he spent the last years of his life in retirement with his wife at his home in Newport, where he died.

While the great diversity of Calvert's work indicates that he was a man of impressive intellect and many talents, it was perhaps his ability to write on so many subjects that has left modern critics with an opinion that he was perhaps too much the literary dilettante. In his own time he was often subject to mixed reviews concerning his literary abilities, hence Edgar Allan Poe's comments that some of Calvert's poetry "did him no credit," and that he was "essentially a feeble and commonplace writer of poetry, although his prose compositions have a certain degree of merit." Yet despite the fact that he is little-known today, Calvert was unquestionably regarded as one of the most promising of America's literati during the nineteenth century, and as evidence that he was regarded as such one only need remember that he numbered among his friends and acquaintances not only Goethe and Wordsworth, but also Ralph Waldo Emerson, Thomas Carlyle, and Margaret Fuller. Thus, though Calvert is now regarded as a literary figure of only marginal importance, as a novelist, playwright, poet, biographer, and critic, he was unquestionably a foundational figure in the development of nineteenth-century American literature.

• The majority of Calvert's surviving letters are at Brown University, although there are also holdings at Columbia University, Harvard, Johns Hopkins, Yale, and Duke. Ida G. Everson, *George Henry Calvert* (1944), is not only a valuable biography but includes excellent bibliographic matter as well. In addition, Calvert is mentioned in Orie W. Long, *Literary Pioneers: Early American Explorers of European Culture* (1935), and Bayard Quincy Morgan, *A Critical Bibliography of German Literature in English Translation, 1481–1927* (1938). On his relationship with Goethe, see H. W. Pfund, "George Henry Calvert, Admirer of Goethe," in *Studies in Honor of John Albrecht Walz* (1941), and for further information on Poe's opinion of him, see Poe, *A Chapter on Autography* (1841).

JAMES R. SIMMONS, JR.

CALVERT, Leonard (c. 1606–9 June 1647), first governor of the colony of Maryland, was born in England, the son of George Calvert (1580–1632), the first Lord Baltimore and a colonial entrepreneur, and Anne Mynne. His exact place of birth and details of his early education are unknown. The young Calvert had a privileged upbringing; his father held important political appointments under King James, including secretary of state, and served three terms in the Parliament. Leonard himself received preferment as prothonotary and keeper of writs in Connacht and Thurmond, Ireland, in 1621. Prospects for the Calverts changed considerably in 1625, when George Calvert announced his conversion to Catholicism, which effectively terminated his officeholding career in England. Leonard Calvert and his siblings all became professed Catholics as well.

The senior Calvert, now Baron Baltimore, increasingly directed his attentions to investment ventures in North America. Leonard in 1628 accompanied his father and other family members to Newfoundland, where Lord Baltimore had received a proprietary charter for the colony of Avalon. The brutal climate discouraged the Calverts, who sailed southward in 1629 to Virginia, where religious prejudice prompted them to return to England. Later that year, Leonard Calvert captained a ship carrying provisions to Ferryland and was taken and briefly held by the French. Meanwhile, Lord Baltimore was lobbying for a land grant and charter to establish a new colony on the Chesapeake, north of Virginia. King Charles issued the charter for Maryland in 1632, shortly after Calvert's death. His son—Leonard's older brother Cecil Calvert—became the first proprietor. The second Lord Baltimore never visited Maryland and was to rely heavily on Leonard as the chief proprietary representative and family member in the colony during its critical early years.

On 22 November 1633 Leonard Calvert departed England with the first band of colonists. Their two ships, the *Ark* and the *Dove*, sailed up the Chesapeake

Bay the first week of March 1634. After exploring the region in search of the most suitable location and conferring with local Indians, Calvert officially took possession on 27 March in the name of King Charles and settled the immigrants at what became St. Marys City on the Potomac River. Calvert devoted most of the next three years to those tasks essential for the colony's secure future. He supervised the laying out of the settlement and construction of a fort and other necessary facilities, the planting of crops, the negotiating of treaties with Indians, and the establishing of trade relations with New England, New Netherlands, and Virginia.

The first settlers, approximately 150 in number, included seventeen gentleman adventurers, probably all Catholics and among them Calvert's younger brother George Calvert (1613–1634), and two or three Jesuit priests. The remaining immigrants consisted of an uncertain number of less affluent free men and women and indentured servants, most of whom were Protestants. Even with continuing immigration, the population never exceeded 500 during Leonard Calvert's lifetime and dropped as low as 100 in the mid-1640s. It was a fragile and fractious colony with very divergent interests that he was assigned to lead.

The governor's responsibilities were delineated most fully in a subsequent commission issued in April 1637 by Lord Baltimore. Leonard Calvert was the commander in chief of armed forces, the chief magistrate with substantial powers of appointment, the chancellor and chief justice of the judicial system with personal authority to try all criminal and civil cases not involving life or member, and the head of the land office designated to grant patents and to appoint places for ports of entry and other purposes. Calvert also received authority to issue edicts and ordinances and to summon an assembly, with provisional power to approve or reject laws passed by that body. In this young colony, administration was very personal, and most of the responsibility devolved on Calvert himself, although Lord Baltimore also formally created a council in 1637 to advise his brother. Before that, Calvert had the assistance of two commissioners, Jerome Hawley and Thomas Cornwaleys. Nonetheless, it was primarily Calvert who implemented the procedures and led the institutions of early Maryland.

Calvert's initial directions from the proprietor were quite limited and granted little leeway. The governor was to cultivate friendly relations with the neighboring colony of Virginia, to establish the young province on a sound economic and political footing, to give no offense to Protestants, and to restrict Catholics from any public displays of worship or open discussion about religious matters. From the outset, however, Calvert exercised greater flexibility than his brother intended, because of both his own differences with the proprietor and local circumstances and personalities that quickly made impossible any efforts to adhere literally to his instructions. For example, many Virginians disputed Maryland's land claims, especially on Kent Island in the Chesapeake Bay, where William Claiborne (c. 1587–c. 1677) had established a trading post in 1631. Differences led ultimately to Calvert's heading a military force in February 1638 that subdued Kent Island. This brought under Maryland authority still more free Protestants and created an angry enemy in Claiborne, who lobbied effectively in England against Maryland interests. Prominent settlers protested trade policies that discriminated clearly in favor of the proprietor, especially when the initiatives failed for a prosperous fur trade and tobacco became the more profitable commodity. Many Catholics, freed from the constraints against them in England, practiced their religion quite openly, perhaps emboldened by the governor's allowing a public mass to celebrate the safe arrival in Maryland, and the Jesuit priests proselytized aggressively among Protestants and Indians, angering many colonists. These and other tensions prompted Calvert to summon an assembly of freemen, 26 February 1635, before he had official authority from Lord Baltimore to do so. The governor sided with critics of proprietary policies on several disputed matters. Lord Baltimore vetoed the legislation that ensued and sent John Lewger to Maryland as secretary of the province with drafts of preferred laws and instructions to see that Lord Baltimore's wishes and interests were pursued more faithfully. Thereafter, disputes over the proper role of freemen in the assembly and in the colony joined with differences on religion, economy, and defense to divide still further the colonists. Leonard Calvert found himself the moderate attempting to balance the more extreme positions of others in the province. These efforts at compromise did not always please his brother but forestalled major disruptions in the young colony. Still, seven assemblies before 1643 failed to develop a code of laws acceptable to local parties and to the absentee proprietor.

In the spring of 1643 Calvert recrossed the Atlantic Ocean to confer directly with Lord Baltimore. He came to appreciate better the implications of the changing political scene in England, where the outbreak of civil war had successfully challenged the authority of Charles I. Militant Protestants in the ascendancy in the Long Parliament were exerting greater pressure on Lord Baltimore and threatening an end to the Calverts' proprietorship, particularly in response to the aggressive policies of the Jesuits in Maryland and the growing anger and opposition of neighboring Virginians. By the time Calvert returned to Maryland in the fall of 1644, the local situation had further deteriorated. Catholic Giles Brent, whom he had left in command, had vigorously upheld the cause of King Charles and had arrested Richard Ingle, a Protestant mariner. This controversial action had split the council and the populace at large. Calvert dismissed Brent and tried to restore order, but despite his conciliatory efforts, the colony entered an unsettling period known then as "the time of troubles" and "the plundering times" and by many since as Ingle's Rebellion. The province was effectively without a government for more than two years, during which time Calvert was exiled in Virginia, where he had the support of Governor William Berkeley. In the early spring of 1646, forces under Captain Edward Hill of Virginia finally reestablished authority, which passed back to Calvert the following December. The governor died six months later in St. Marys. Calvert's value as a balancing figure became even more obvious in the following years. No other person proved capable of providing the necessary leadership until the 1660s, when Charles Calvert (1637–1715), the son of the proprietor, migrated to the colony as governor and imposed a stable government.

During his years in Maryland, Calvert acquired 9,000 acres, including three manors. On his deathbed he appointed as executrix of his estate Margaret Brent. At that time, no mention was made of a spouse or children, but later a son, William, and a daughter, Anne, appeared. They were apparently offspring by a woman named Ann, perhaps a relation of Margaret Brent and her brother Giles Brent, and may have been illegitimate. The two children immigrated to Maryland in the early 1660s and made strategic political marriages to prominent colonists.

• Primary materials on Calvert are printed in *The Calvert Papers, Number One* (1889); Clayton Colman Hall, ed., *Narratives of Early Maryland, 1633–1684* (1910); and William Hand Brown et al., eds., *Archives of Maryland*, vols. 1 (1883), 3 (1885), and 4 (1887). The most thorough accounts of Calvert's governorship are Russell R. Menard and Lois Green Carr, "The Lords Baltimore and the Colonization of Maryland," *Early Maryland in a Wider World*, ed. David B. Quinn (1982); David W. Jordan, *Foundations of Representative Government in Maryland, 1632–1715* (1987); and Thomas J. Hughes, *History of the Society of Jesus in North America* (4 vols., 1907–1917).

DAVID W. JORDAN

CALVERTON, Victor Francis (25 June 1900–20 Nov. 1940), socialist writer and editor, was born George Goetz in Baltimore, Maryland, the son of Charles Goetz, a German-American tailor, and Ida Geiger, the granddaughter of a left-wing refugee from the German 1848 revolution. Radicalized by his father's denunciations of the Spanish-American War, Calverton read voraciously throughout high school in the Baltimore public schools, transferring his allegiance from Lutheranism to socialism. Although he was tempted to become a professional baseball player, he decided to earn money for college by working as a timekeeper with the Bethlehem Steel Company. In 1921 he graduated from Johns Hopkins University with a degree in English and then spent a year studying psychology at Hopkins. After a brief membership in the Socialist Labor party, he began teaching in the public schools. In 1923 he published the first issue of the *Modern Quarterly* (originally to have been called the "Radical Quarterly"), for which he adopted his pseudonym to protect his teaching job, although his friends continued to call him "George."

Although he wrote several volumes of literary criticism, fiction, history, sociology, and anthropology, he is remembered mostly for his journal, the *Modern Quarterly*, which in the 1920s and 1930s was "a kind of intellectual brokerage house for the revolution" (Aaron, p. 322). Calverton had a wide range of interests, including psychology, literature, medicine, African American culture, Marxism, and sex, which were well represented in his journal. These preoccupations were also the subjects of eighteen books he wrote or edited, among them *The Newer Spirit* (1925), *Sex Expression in Literature* (1926), and *The Liberation of American Literature* (1931). At times Calverton interpreted Marxism in a coarse or common way, and he was lax about properly crediting his sources. He also wrote highly personal fiction, such as the stories collected in *Three Strange Lovers* (1930) and the novel *The Man Inside* (1936). His last book, published posthumously, was a history of Utopian colonies in the United States called *Where Angels Dared to Tread* (1940).

In 1921 Calverton married Helen Letzer, but he prided himself on his sexual independence and experimentation. The couple divorced in 1930; they had no children, but Calverton had one child, out of wedlock, with Una Corbett. The last years of his life were spent with Nina Melville, and he gave 1931 as the year they entered a common-law marriage.

From 1926 to 1932 Calverton was closely allied with the Communist party. Spending four days a week in New York, he wrote reviews, lectured, worked for publishers, and was a steady contributor to the Saturday *Daily Worker*. Regular gatherings at his apartment brought Communists and non-Communists together for intellectual and political exchanges. In July 1927 he visited the Soviet Union. Calverton refused to join the Communist party, and despite his avowed support of Joseph Stalin, the Communists grew suspicious of him. He encouraged "Americanizing" party tactics, and both the party and the Communist International believed his work somehow supported the Trotskyists and other malcontents, who were seen as threats. In a series of articles published in 1932–1933 the party and the International attacked him as a fascist. Calverton responded by printing in his *Modern Quarterly* (which was known as the *Modern Monthly* from 1933 to 1938) articles by opposition Communists, such as followers of Leon Trotsky and Nikolai Bukharin. He also joined an independent revolutionary organization, the American Workers party, led by A. J. Muste.

Lionel Trilling, James Rorty, Elliot Cohen, Anita Brenner, and Lewis Corey were among the Communist dissidents who contributed to Calverton's journal. Editorial board members included Edmund Wilson, Max Eastman, and Sidney Hook. Eastman and Hook conducted a famous philosophical debate over dialectical materialism. Calverton longed to be recognized as a major intellectual force, a status he never achieved. He died suddenly of pernicious anemia in New York City.

In his influential *Writers on the Left*, Daniel Aaron dubbed Calverton "The Radical Impresario," and more recent studies have sought to enlarge his reputation to that of intellectual fugleman for the Great Depression generation, and also as a prophet for concerns that would preoccupy the post–World War II generations of radicalized intelligentsia. Calverton is also remembered for his healthy respect for debate and disagreement, and his pragmatic radicalism. His preoccupation with "Americanizing" socialism and his bohemian way of life are themes that are represented in the lives and work of many others of his generation.

• The central depository of Calverton's manuscripts and letters is the New York Public Library. In addition to Daniel Aaron's chapters on Calverton in *Writers on the Left: Episodes in American Literary Communism* (1961), the two major studies are Leonard Wilcox, *V. F. Calverton: Radical in the American Grain* (1992), and Philip Abbott, *Leftward Ho! V. F. Calverton and American Radicalism* (1993). The "V. F. Calverton Memorial Issue" of *Modern Quarterly* 11, no. 7 (Autumn 1940), contains over forty assessments by his contemporaries. An obituary is in the *New York Times*, 21 Nov. 1940.

ALAN M. WALD

CAMBRELENG, Churchill Caldom (24 Oct. 1786–30 Apr. 1862), member of Congress, was born in Washington, Beaufort County, North Carolina. Details regarding his parents and his early education are unavailable. Cambreleng attended school in New Bern, North Carolina, before moving to New York City in 1802. From 1806 to 1809 he worked as a clerk in Providence, Rhode Island. While in Providence, he joined a literary society that included both students and faculty from Brown University and discussed books, engaged in writing compositions, and held formal debates. Earning about $600 a year, he undertook to educate his younger brothers at Union College in Schenectady, New York, and funded one brother's attendance at the law school at Litchfield, Connecticut.

Returning to New York, Cambreleng established the commercial houses of Cambreleng & Chrystie and Cambreleng & Pearson, and he became a director of Farmers Fire Insurance and Loan Company. He engaged in cotton speculation briefly before working for John Jacob Astor. He married (date unknown) a woman with the surname Glover, but they had no children.

Working with Astor, Cambreleng traveled extensively in both the United States and overseas. Astor planned to open a trading house in Canton, China, at the mouth of the Colombia River. Astor sent Cambreleng to Europe to observe the negotiations, mediated by the Russians, between the United States and Britain over the Oregon Territory. He arrived in Sweden and traveled to Germany, where he observed the retreat of Napoléon's forces toward Paris. This trip took him to Prussia, Silesia, Bohemia, France, Holland, and England. In 1815 and 1816, in connection with trips for Astor, he visited France, Italy, and Asia Minor. In 1825 he made a tour of Great Britain, visiting Scotland and Wales.

In the winter of 1820–1821 Cambreleng worked on a publication regarding a set of proposed higher tariffs, arguing forcefully for a low-tariff position. The publication, *An Examination of the New Tariff Proposed by the Hon. Henry Baldwin* (1821), was nearly 300 pages in print and received wide circulation.

Cambreleng was elected to Congress in 1821 as a Republican supporter of Andrew Jackson. He was subsequently reelected as a Democrat, serving in the Twentieth through the Twenty-fifth Congresses (1821–1839). As a member of Congress, he held a number of important committee chairmanships, including the Committees on Commerce and Navigation, on Ways and Means, and on Foreign Affairs. Through the 1830s he was the House leader for both Jackson and Martin Van Buren, and he continued to fight for low tariffs.

Like Jackson, Cambreleng opposed the renewal of the charter of the Bank of the United States, and he also opposed the high tariffs of 1824 and 1828. He supported U.S. claims to the Oregon Territory, probably reflecting his association with Astor. During his term of office, he became identified with the hard money advocates, who blamed both the Bank of the United States and the state banks for the overissue of bank notes and the inflation of currency. Cambreleng and other businessmen-politicians of the era illustrate that the hard currency and antibanking policies of Jackson and Van Buren received support not only from frontier interests and the rising Workingmen's movement but also from some conservative eastern businessmen. Interpretation of the position of such men became a key issue in debates among historians over the political base of the Jacksonian movement.

In the late 1820s Cambreleng argued against higher tariffs on wool and wines, and he developed the argument against protective tariffs more fully by 1830. Several of his published speeches and essays received wide circulation, including *Report of the Committee on Commerce and Navigation of the United States* (1930), which was reprinted in London in 1830. Extensive extracts from a speech he delivered in favor of hard currency and an independent Treasury in 1837 were reprinted in 1839 in the periodical *United States Democratic Review*. Basing his argument on both statistics and personal observation, he roundly criticized the British system of banknotes and credit and argued for the elimination of paper money in favor of specie.

In 1838 Cambreleng was defeated for reelection to Congress. He traveled to Europe, and while he was there, President Van Buren appointed him minister to Russia. He served in this post from 20 May 1840 to 13 July 1841. In 1846 he was a member of the New York State constitutional convention as a representative of Suffolk County.

At the 1847 Democratic party national convention, a political split between "Hunkers" and "Barnburners" led to the walkout by the Barnburners, who held a separate convention, over which Cambreleng presided. Among other stands, this faction strictly opposed allowing banks to issue notes without adequate specie reserves, a continuation of the hard money policies that Cambreleng had advocated for decades. In 1848 he again supported Van Buren for the presidency at a Barnburner convention in Utica, a forerunner to the formation of the Free Soil party. Like others in the Barnburner–Free Soil faction, Cambreleng opposed the expansion of slaveholding territory that would come with war with Mexico. Cambreleng was an associate and political ally of William Cullen Bryant, editor of the New York *Evening Post*, a fellow "radical" northern Democrat, and an opponent of high tariffs. An underlying theme of the rhetoric of Cambreleng and his fellow Barnburners was opposition to "aristocracy," whether represented by bankers or by the growing power of slaveholders. In his speeches Cambreleng sometimes referred to the aristocratic and monarchical systems he had observed in Europe.

Cambreleng's career spanned the period of the 1820s, when his low tariff and hard money doctrines attracted him to the Jacksonian Democratic party, through the 1840s, when the northern Democrats began to coalesce into a component of the eventual antislavery Republican party, which emerged in the 1850s. Cambreleng died at his home in Suffolk County, New York, near Huntington.

• Cambreleng's published writings include *Speech on the Proposition to Amend the Constitution of the United States Respecting the Election of President and Vice President* (1826), *Duties on Woolens* (1828), *Speech on the Subject of the Removal of the Public Deposits from the Bank of the United States* (1834), *Speech on the Bill Regulating the Deposits of the Public Money in Certain Local Banks, and on the Abuses and Corruptions of Government* (1835), and *Speech on His Motion to Provide for the Armament of Our Fortifications* (1836). Other sources include "Churchill Caldom Cambreleng, Political Portraits No. XIV," *United States Democratic Review* 6, no. 20 (Aug. 1839): 144–59.

RODNEY P. CARLISLE

CAMBRIDGE, Godfrey (26 Feb. 1933–29 Nov. 1976), actor and comedian, was born in New York City, the son of Alexander Cambridge, a bookkeeper, and Sarah (maiden name unknown), a stenographer. His parents emigrated from British Guiana in the West Indies to Sydney, Nova Scotia, Canada, later settling in Harlem. Although his parents were trained professionals, neither could secure work in their fields. Consequently his father became a day laborer, digging ditches, unloading coal cars, and unpacking trucks; his mother worked in the garment district.

Critical of New York's Harlem schools, Cambridge's parents sent him to Sydney for grammar school, where he lived with his grandparents until age thirteen, when he returned to New York to enroll at Flushing High School in Queens. He excelled academically and engaged in a variety of extracurricular activities. He was dubbed the "Unforgettable Godfrey Wonder Boy Cambridge" in his high school yearbook, which foresaw his penchant for comedy by adding that he always had "a laugh, a chat, a gay retort, perhaps sometimes a pun" for everyone.

Cambridge began Hofstra College on a scholarship in 1949, but to his parents' utter dismay dropped out in his junior year and turned later to a career in acting. In 1956 he won acclaim for his role as a bartender in the off-Broadway revival of *Take a Giant Step*. Thereafter came parts in many highly rated television dramas but, as always, roles for black actors were scarce. In desperation Cambridge accepted any available performance work, including one time entering a "laughing contest" in which he was voted one of the country's four "laugh champions." He translated his experiences in menial day jobs into nighttime stand-up routines at small clubs and coffeehouses.

After appearing on Broadway in prominent dramas but in small roles, Cambridge's big break came in 1961 in the off-Broadway production of Jean Genet's *The Blacks*. He played the character Diouf, an elderly black man who assumes the role of a white woman, wearing a blonde wig and grotesque white face makeup, who is raped and murdered. His performance earned him the *Village Voice*'s coveted Obie Award. The following year he was nominated for a Tony Award for his portrayal of Gitlow, the archetypal Uncle Tom in Ossie Davis's satire of plantation life, *Purlie Victorious*. Later he would perform the role in the film version, *Gone Are the Days!* (1963).

For the next several years, Cambridge appeared in *The Living Premise*, an improvisational satirical revue; was booked at the Blue Angel and Village Vanguard clubs, and performed on the college-campus circuit as a stand-up comic. His stature soared in 1964 as a result of three stints as a guest on the highly popular "Jack Paar Show" on late-night television. The response led to many bookings in nightclubs and films, and a long-term recording contract with Epic records. His first album, *Ready or Not, Here's Godfrey Cambridge*, was among the top five bestselling albums of 1964.

After *Gone Are the Days!* Cambridge announced in the mid-1960s that he would seek roles that delineated him "as a man, rather than as a Negro." His national popularity broadened his options. He was cast as an Irishman in *The Troublemaker* (1964), a CIA agent in *The President's Analyst* (1967), a gangster in *The Busy Body* (1967), a concert violinist in *The Biggest Bundle of Them All* (1968), and as a Jewish taxicab driver in *Bye, Bye Braverman* (1968). He received high praise for his performance as the lawman Gravedigger Jones in *Cotton Comes to Harlem* (1970) and in *The Watermelon Man* (1970), in which he plays a white bigot who awakens to find himself turned into a black man overnight. On stage Cambridge was applauded by critics for his playing of the slave Pseudolus in a road production of *A Funny Thing Happened on the Way to the Forum* (1967) and in the play *How to Be a Jewish Mother* (1967), in which he costarred with Molly Picon.

Cambridge married Barbara Ann Teer, an actress, in 1962, but the marriage ended in divorce two-and-a-half years later; the couple had no children. He died in Hollywood of a heart attack while making a film.

Physically, Cambridge was heavyset, sometimes overweight—his girth adding dimension to his satirical approach. His own comedy was filled with irony and he was particularly fond of lampooning the stereotypes of both whites and blacks: "Nothing worries [a white] more than the sight of a Negro walking down his street carrying the real estate section of the *New York Times*." Nevertheless, Cambridge insisted that his comedy transcended racial issues and reflected rather the travails of the little man, indistinguishable by race. "I attack whatever is attackable. I take up the cudgels for the common man, black or white, and deal with his problems," Cambridge said. Mel Watkins noted, "Cambridge did not avoid racial issues. . . . he was a brilliant satirist, and although he did not concentrate on them, the contradictions and absurdities of bigotry often entered into his expansive social satire" (p. 509).

• Besides *Ready or Not*, Cambridge's comedy is captured on three other Epic albums: *Them Cotton Pickin' Days Is Over*, *Godfrey Cambridge Toys with the World*, and *The Godfrey Cambridge Show*. A talented writer who generated his own materials, he also contributed to a short-lived satirical magazine, *Monocle*. His book *Put-Downs and Put-Ons* was published in paperback in 1967. An excellent contemporary biography appears in Charles Moritz, ed., *Current Biography* (1969).

Vignettes of Cambridge's life and career appear in articles published in various magazines. Especially see *Ebony*, Oct. 1967, pp. 160–70; *Esquire*, Nov. 1964, p. 94; and the *New York Times* magazine, 20 Nov. 1966, pp. 13, 92. Evaluations of Cambridge's place in African-American humor can be found in Nancy Levi Arnez and Clara B. Anthony, "Contemporary Negro Humor as Social Satire," *Phylon* 29 (Winter 1968): 339–46; and in Mel Watkins, *On the Real Side* (1994).

JOSEPH BOSKIN

CAMDEN, Johnson Newlon (6 Mar. 1828–25 Apr. 1908), oil company executive, pioneer industrialist, and U.S. senator, was born in Collins Settlement, Lewis County, Virginia (now Jacksonville, W.Va.), the son of John Scrivener Camden, a justice of the peace, and Nancy Newlon. Camden's father bought a house and tavern in Sutton, Braxton County, and moved the family there in 1837.

During the years of his youth in Sutton, Camden attended subscription schools in and around the village. In 1842, at the age of fourteen, he became an assistant in the office of the clerk of Lewis County, serving as an errand boy and learning the business of keeping county records. From 1843 to 1845 he attended the Northwestern Academy in Clarksburg. He returned to Sutton in 1845 and served two years as deputy clerk of the county court in Braxton County. In 1847 Camden enrolled at the U.S. Military Academy at West Point, New York, but finding mathematics an insuperable obstacle, he returned to Sutton in 1849 to read law. In 1851 he was prosecuting attorney in Braxton County. In 1852 he enjoyed his first success at politics, when he was elected as the Democratic candidate for prosecuting attorney of Nicholas County. In 1853 he resigned that position to move to Weston, Lewis County, where he served as a bank clerk, practiced law (specializing as a collector for Baltimore wholesale houses), and speculated in land during the depression of 1857, when he bought land at depressed prices. In 1858 he married Anne Gaither Thompson; they had three children.

In 1858 Camden joined the speculative enthusiasm for cannel coal, a carbon-rich mineral that could be refined into oil and other lucrative by-products. Although he did not find cannel coal in sufficient quantity for commercial production, his interest led him into the petroleum business, and in 1860 he joined in a partnership that became one of the pioneer oil producers at Burning Springs on the Little Kanawha River in Wirt County.

Caught up in the feverish excitement of the oil rush, Camden gave little attention to the growing sectional crisis. When the Civil War came, he went against sentiment and family tradition and took his stand on the side of the Union, no doubt judging that his burgeoning business interests would best be served by that course. His choice was a painful one, however. Four of his brothers fought for Virginia, and an uncle was elected by the secessionist convention to the Confederate congress.

Camden's firm made regular oil shipments to eastern cities until a Confederate raid on 9 May 1863 demolished the Burning Springs works. He led the way in rebuilding the damaged wells and in opening new wells in Wood and Ritchie counties, and he helped found a new bank in Parkersburg, which financed much of the work. In 1866, convinced that the peak of oil production had passed on the Little Kanawha, Camden turned to oil refining, establishing J. N. Camden and Company at Parkersburg, which built up an extensive trade in petroleum products. In 1875 his refinery became a part of John D. Rockefeller's Standard Oil Company, and Camden became Rockefeller's chief lieutenant in West Virginia, lobbying both the state legislature and Congress on Standard Oil's behalf.

Camden also pioneered in the development of central and northern West Virginia's railroads and coal fields. He played a leading role in such enterprises as the Ohio River Railroad, which started in Wheeling in 1882 and reached a terminus at Huntington in 1888; the West Virginia and Pittsburgh Railroad, which sought to link the Baltimore and Ohio and the Chesapeake railroads; and the Monongahela Railroad and the Monongah Coal and Coke Company, which developed coal mines in the Upper Monongahela Valley in the 1880s.

In addition to his wide-ranging business activities, Camden helped shape West Virginia politics during the late nineteenth century. During Reconstruction he became a leader of the Democratic party in the new state of West Virginia, opposing laws proscribing former Confederates and running unsuccessfully for governor in 1868 and 1872. Though Democrats controlled the state from 1870 to 1897, the party was torn by bitter factional conflict, and Camden's chief political opposition sometimes came from other Democrats, who branded him a "monopolist." An indifferent speaker, Camden fared best in behind-the-scenes maneuvering rather than on the campaign hustings. With his ally Henry Gassaway Davis, he strengthened the state Democratic party by investing in newspapers, cultivating editors, funding candidates, and dispensing patronage, and he saw to it that West Virginia remained friendly to business and industrial interests.

In 1875 Camden sought election to the U.S. Senate. He had to step aside when a deal to return the state capital from Charleston to Wheeling provided for southern West Virginia to be compensated with a Senate seat. After a referendum determined that the capital would be permanently located at Charleston, the way was open for Camden to attain his goal, and the legislature elected him in 1881.

In the Senate Camden belonged to the group called incidental protectionists. These conservative Democrats straddled the tariff issue by rejecting Republican protectionism while advocating a tariff for revenue only, which would provide incidental protection to, as Camden put it, "the various productive interests of the country." He remained a spokesman for Standard Oil, defending its practices in an article in the *North American Review* in February 1883. Despite an attempt to pose as a reformer by sponsoring a ban on discrimination between long and short hauls in the Interstate Commerce Act of 1887, he was denied reelection in that year by a determined Democratic coalition of disappointed office seekers, antimonopolists, and agricultural interests.

Stung by the defeat, Camden nevertheless continued to work for the success of the Democratic party in West Virginia. In 1893 the legislature rewarded his service to the party with election to a two-year unexpired Senate term to replace John E. Kenna, who had died in office. Camden hoped to win a full term in 1895, but a Republican sweep of the 1894 legislative elections led to his defeat by Stephen Benton Elkins. Elkins's victory marked the beginning of a long period of Republican rule in West Virginia and effectively ended Camden's political career.

As one of West Virginia's richest and most powerful men in its formative years, Camden wielded substantial influence in shaping the state's political system and in determining the nature of its economic development. He died in Baltimore, Maryland.

• Camden's papers are in the West Virginia and Regional History Collection, West Virginia University Library, Morgantown. Festus Paul Summers, *Johnson Newlon Camden, A Study in Individualism* (1937), is a thoroughly researched and readable biography. A recent critical account is John Alexander Williams, *West Virginia and the Captains of Industry* (1976).

JERRY BRUCE THOMAS

CAMERON, Andrew Carr (28 Sept. 1836–28 May 1892), labor leader and editor, was born in Berwick-on-Tweed, England, the son of a Scots printer (his father's occupation and nationality are all that are known about his parents). After only a brief time in school, Cameron went to work in his father's shop. In 1851 he emigrated with his parents to the United States, settling just outside of Chicago.

Cameron first worked on the *Young American*, which later became the Chicago *Times*. In 1864, during a printers' strike, he was hired as the editor of the newly established *Workingman's Advocate*, a labor newspaper "Devoted to the Interests of the Producing Classes of the Northwest." Two years later Cameron became the *Advocate*'s publisher. During the 1860s the *Workingman's Advocate* functioned as the official organ of both the Trades' Assembly of Chicago and the National Labor Union (NLU), which Cameron had helped to launch. Led by a broad-based national movement of trade unionists and reform sympathizers, the annual congresses of the NLU represented through the 1860s and 1870s the principal labor-reform aspirations of the day. Cameron belonged to Typographical Union No. 16 in Chicago, headed the Illinois Grand Eight Hour League and the State Labor Association, and, for four years, presided over the Trades' Assembly of Chicago. In 1869 he represented the NLU at the Fourth Congress of the International Workingmen's Association in Basle, Switzerland.

Committed to building a strong labor movement, Cameron, as chair of the NLU's committee on trades' unions and strikes in 1866, recommended "the formation of unions in all localities where the same do not now exist, and the formation of an international organization in every branch of industry as a first and most important duty of the hour." He also advocated organizing unskilled, female, and black workers. Even so, Cameron considered unions and strikes to be inherently "defensive in character" and not a "panacea" for all the evils faced by workers. Closely associated with the efforts to organize a National Labor party, Cameron insisted that American workers could not "battle victoriously against capital" unless they "began shaping laws in the interests of labor."

At the top of Cameron's political agenda for labor reform was constituting eight hours "as the standard of a legal day's work." According to the "Address to Workingmen," prepared by Cameron and issued by the NLU in July 1867, workers would continue to "occupy their present menial position" until they were able to "devote more time to their own advancement, and less to the enrichment of the drones of society." In this address Cameron also voiced concern over the prevailing "false, vicious financial system." However, monetary reform was an issue that was taken up more fully in August 1867 in the NLU's "Declaration of Principles," which was drafted by the committee on political organization chaired by Cameron. To protect America's "democratic republican institutions" against erosion by the money monopoly, "the parent of all monopolies," the NLU adopted ideas on political economy introduced in the late 1840s by Edward Kellogg as modified by Alexander Campbell in *The True American System of Finance* (1864). The NLU endorsed such "soft-money" principles as the substitution of legal-tender treasury notes, or greenbacks, as the "exclusive currency of the nation" and the payment of the nation's debts in interconvertible bonds issued at low interest rates.

Cameron remained sympathetic to the cause of labor to the end of his life, although after the demise of the *Workingman's Advocate* in 1877 he became editor of the *Inland Printer*, a technical trade journal. He was publishing the *Artist Printer* when he died in Chicago of a brain hemorrhage after a severe attack of grippe.

Cameron, cited by the labor economist John R. Commons as the "greatest labour editor of his time," molded the *Workingman's Advocate* into a national platform for labor reformers during the 1860s and 1870s. Through his close association with Chicago's trade unions and the NLU, Cameron helped set the agenda for the postbellum labor movement.

• The *Workingman's Advocate* and the proceedings of the National Labor Union, reprinted in John R. Commons et al., *A Documentary History of American Industrial Society*, vol. 9 (1958), are essential primary sources for Cameron's public life and ideas. An entry on Cameron is included in Gary M. Fink, ed., *Biographical Dictionary of American Labor Leaders* (1974). The best discussion of Cameron and the events of his life are John R. Commons et al., *History of Labour in the United States*, vol. 2 (1918); David Montgomery, *Beyond Equality: Labor and the Radical Republicans, 1862–1872* (1967); and Irwin Unger, *The Greenback Era: A Social and Political History of American Finance, 1865–1879* (1964).

BRIAN GREENBERG

CAMERON, Don (14 May 1833–30 Aug. 1918), U.S. senator and political boss, was born James Donald Cameron in Middletown, Pennsylvania, the son of Simon Cameron, a politician and businessman, and Margaret Brua. After graduating from Princeton in 1852, Cameron worked as a clerk in the Bank of Middletown, established by his father, soon rising to the post of cashier and then president. As a result of his father's mounting political ambitions, Don Cameron also took charge of the Northern Central Railroad, the so-called Cameron Road, serving as president of the company from 1863 until its absorption by the Pennsylvania Railroad in 1874.

Cameron also became a junior partner in his father's political enterprises. During this period Simon Cameron was in the process of forging the Republican machine that was to dominate Pennsylvania politics for the next half-century. To the attainment of this goal Don Cameron made a significant contribution. His skillful management of the Cameron forces in the state legislature made possible his father's election to the Senate in 1867 and again in 1873. In 1876 he led the Pennsylvania delegation to the Republican National Convention at Cincinnati, where he held his forces together long enough to frustrate the presidential ambitions of James G. Blaine, to the ultimate advantage of Rutherford B. Hayes. As a reward for his father's political influence rather than his own achievements, Cameron was appointed in May 1876 as secretary of war in the cabinet of President Ulysses S. Grant. During the election dispute of 1876–1877, he unashamedly used his position to support his party's claim to the electoral votes of Florida, Louisiana, and South Carolina, promptly ordering extra federal troops to protect Republican officials in the contested states. Not only did Cameron insist on his party's right to the electoral votes, but he staunchly maintained until the day of his departure from the War Department that it was the federal government's duty to sustain, by force if necessary, the Republican regimes in Louisiana and South Carolina in the face of Democratic majorities secured by intimidation and fraud. Neither Grant nor Hayes, on his accession to the presidency, was willing to go so far. Despite intense pressure from Pennsylvania Republicans, the new president, who at this point was quite out of sympathy with Cameron's stalwart defense of southern Republicanism, declined to reappoint him, whereupon Simon Cameron seized the opportunity to bequeath his Senate seat to his son. Having rapidly secured pledges of support from Republican members of the legislature, Simon Cameron suddenly resigned. The following day Don Cameron was nominated to succeed him by a nearly unanimous vote of the Republican caucus. Although the so-called Cameron Transfer, in the words of the *Nation*, "must have seemed quite natural and logical to those who know anything of Pennsylvania politics," it stood nevertheless as a striking demonstration of the power of the machine (24 Mar. 1877).

With his accession to the Senate, Don Cameron also took his father's place at the head of the organization. "Indeed, there is not a political leader in any State whose mandates are so implicitly obeyed as are Cameron's in Pennsylvania to-day," remarked the Philadelphia *Times* (29 Jan. 1878). Within a few years, however, the fragility of his grasp became apparent. In 1880 he committed the organization to Grant's quest for a third term in the White House. At the state convention the machine forced through a resolution ordering delegates to the national convention to vote as a unit for Grant, despite the widespread support for Blaine among Pennsylvania Republicans. Grant supporters, like Senators Roscoe Conkling of New York and John A. Logan of Illinois, hoped to exploit Cameron's newly won position as chairman of the national committee to impose the "unit rule" on the convention, thereby compelling dissident members of their own delegations to vote for the "Hero of Appomattox." Suspecting such a scheme, the supporters of other candidates, who constituted a majority of the national committee, challenged Cameron to state his intentions and forced the nomination of a neutral presiding officer who would not apply the unit rule to the organization of the convention. Once more, however, Cameron and his Stalwart allies, though unable to nominate Grant, were powerful enough to block the nomination of Blaine. Cameron's arbitrary leadership provoked a reaction that left the Pennsylvania Republican party for some years dangerously divided between Stalwart and Half-Breed factions, resulting in the defeat of organization candidates for the Senate in 1881 and the governorship in 1882. Though able, enterprising, and courageous, the younger Cameron lacked the flexibility and sensitivity to the public mood shown by either his father, who preceded him, or Matthew S. Quay, who succeeded him. Reticent by nature and a poor speaker, he shunned contact with crowds, but he also disdained the regime of letter writing and small-group meetings that was essential to the smooth running of the machine. Few party activists knew Don Cameron by sight. During the course of the 1880s he gradually withdrew from active political management, leaving both the distribution of patronage and management of the legislature to Quay.

During his long senatorial career (20 Mar. 1877–3 Mar. 1897), Cameron spoke rarely, introduced few bills of national importance, served on no great committee, and was absent as often as not when the roll was called. Only occasionally did he depart from this record of anonymity. In 1890 he voted against the Federal Elections Bill, ostensibly because he did not wish to see sectional antagonisms reopened but more likely because he desired to clear a path for a protective tariff bill, which was precious to his Pennsylvania constituents, and for the Silver Purchase Bill, which was precious to Cameron himself, who had invested heavily in silver. Three years later he was the only eastern Republican to vote against repeal of the Silver Purchase Act. His growing political heterodoxy and his increasing remoteness from the political life of the state effectively removed him from consideration for a further senatorial term, and in March 1897 he retired to private life.

In truth Cameron had largely devoted himself to his private affairs for some years. His first wife, Mary McCormick, having died four years earlier (the date of this marriage and the number of their children, if any, are unknown), in 1878 he married Elizabeth Sherman (the niece of Senator John Sherman of Ohio and William Tecumseh Sherman), an accomplished young woman of inexhaustible vitality and charm, whose Washington salon attracted luminaries such as Henry B. Adams and John Hay. They had one daughter. Cameron's later years were divided between periods of European travel and residence on his houseboat on the South Carolina coast and his farm near Middletown, where he died.

• Few of Cameron's private papers survive, so the events of his life must be pieced together from various printed sources. There are brief references to Cameron in the memoirs of some of his contemporaries, such as James G. Blaine, *Twenty Years of Congress* (1886); George F. Hoar, *Autobiography of Seventy Years* (1903); and Alexander McClure, *Old Time Notes of Pennsylvania* (1905), which offers a remarkably balanced assessment for so persistent a political opponent. For information about Cameron's early life see Erwin S. Bradley, *Simon Cameron, Lincoln's Secretary of War* (1966), which also traces his involvement in state politics. Also on state politics see Frank B. Evans, *Pennsylvania Politics, 1872–1877* (1966); James A. Kehl, *Boss Rule in the Gilded Age: Matt Quay of Pennsylvania* (1981); and Robert Harrison, "Blaine and the Camerons: A Study in the Limits of Machine Power," *Pennsylvania History* 49 (1982): 157–75. The fullest account of his service as secretary of war is in Allan Nevins, *Hamilton Fish: The Inner History of the Grant Administration* (1936); his brief career as an aspiring president-maker is described in Robert D. Marcus, *Grand Old Party: Political Structure in the Gilded Age* (1971). Useful information about Cameron's later life appears incidentally in Ernest Samuels, *Henry Adams* (1948–1964).

ROBERT HARRISON

CAMERON, Donaldina Mackenzie (26 July 1869–4 Jan. 1968), missionary and social reformer, was born on the South Island of New Zealand, the daughter of Allan Cameron and Isabella Mackenzie, sheep ranchers. The family relocated to the San Joaquin Valley in California in 1871 and began raising sheep. After his wife's death in 1874, Allan Cameron and his children moved to the San Jose area, where he worked for other ranchers and his older daughters kept house. Donaldina attended a local girls' school, and after the Camerons moved to Oakland she went to high school. Her father became manager of a sheep ranch near Los Angeles, and the family relocated once again when Donaldina was age fifteen. She then began studying to become a teacher at Los Angeles Normal School, but in 1887 she discontinued her studies after the death of her father.

In 1895 Mary Ann Frank Browne, the mother of an Oakland schoolmate, introduced the idea of mission work to Cameron, a devout Christian. Browne served as president of the Woman's Occidental Board of Foreign Missions, an organization established in 1873 in San Francisco to provide a refuge for Chinese women. Cameron accepted a position as assistant to the mission's directors and, in 1900, became superintendent. Having twice before declined marriage proposals because of her devotion to religious work, in 1911 she agreed to marry a wealthy supporter of missionary efforts. His sudden death, however, strengthened Cameron's commitment to the mission.

The location of the mission on the edge of Chinatown gave Cameron a base for working toward the discontinuation of the importing of Chinese slaves to the United States. With the help of Chinese and American friends she became a famous crusader, following up on appeals for help by breaking into gambling clubs and brothels. She brought the rescued women and girls to the mission, sued for legal custody in court, and helped to prosecute slave importers. She also supported in many ways the girls assigned to her as foster daughters. In 1925 she also established a refuge for young children in Oakland.

As a result of Cameron's work, the United States and China were no longer able to ignore the slave trade, which led to its discontinuation. The burning of old Chinatown in the San Francisco fire of 1906 and the institution of reforms prohibiting slavery that followed the Chinese Revolution of 1911 weakened the trade. By the 1920s the mission had become increasingly involved in community activities, and in the 1930s it served as the base for social service operations of the Presbyterian church.

Cameron left the mission in 1934, at the mission board's mandatory retirement age of sixty-five. She assisted her successor until moving to Oakland in 1939 to care for her three older sisters. After the death of one sister, she and her two other sisters relocated in 1942 to Palo Alto. That same year Cameron agreed to the renaming of the mission as the Donaldina Cameron House. She died in Palo Alto.

In a memorial address before the California legislature, Representative March Fong lauded Cameron as a "distinguished Californian," noting her importance "in the history of San Francisco and the Chinese community." Cameron's efforts, although intruding upon the accepted practices of Chinese culture, reflected her Christian belief in working toward the welfare of a common humanity. At once a strict taskmaster and an affectionate "Lo Mo" (Mama); a firm superintendent and a humble Presbyterian; a British citizen and an American heroine; a distinguished public figure and a reserved private citizen; the youngest sister of a close family and an independent woman seeking her way, she lived a life that resolved the potential sources of conflict in her complex personality.

• Cameron's papers are held by her niece Caroline Bailey in Palo Alto. The Cameron House holds the files of the Woman's Occidental Board of Foreign Missions, and its *Annual Reports* (1874–1921) are in the San Francisco Theological Seminary Archives, San Anselmo, Calif. Other correspondence by Cameron can be found in the Presbyterian Church Archives in Philadelphia. For studies of Cameron's life, see Carol Green Wilson, *Chinatown Quest* (1931; repr. 1974); Lorna E. Logan, *Ventures in Mission* (1976); and Mildred Crowl Martin, *Chinatown's Angry Angel* (1977). An obituary is in the *Oakland Tribune,* 6 Jan. 1968.

GUNTHER BARTH

CAMERON, Simon (8 Mar. 1799–26 June 1889), secretary of war, U.S. senator, and ambassador to Russia, was born in Lancaster County, Pennsylvania, the son of Charles Cameron, a tailor and tavern keeper, and Martha Pfoutz. Growing up in an often impoverished family, Cameron received little formal schooling. At age eleven he was placed as a ward in the family of a local doctor. Subsequently he apprenticed himself to several printers in the Lancaster-Harrisburg area, and he became the editor of a newspaper. In Harrisburg he caught the attention of important state politicians who helped his journalistic career. At age twenty-three he moved to Washington, D.C., where he worked for the printing firm of Gales and Seaton, which printed the *Annals of Congress* (later the *Congressional Globe*). The opportunity for a part-ownership in the *Pennsylvania Intelligencer* (later the *Pennsylvania Reporter*) took Cameron back to Harrisburg in 1822. That year he met and married Margaretta Brua, the daughter of a director of the Harrisburg Bank. They had ten children, one of whom, J. Donald Cameron, followed his father into politics.

Astute and ambitious, Cameron began his long public career in 1824, when he served as a delegate from Dauphin County to the state Democratic convention. In 1829 he was appointed adjutant general of the commonwealth of Pennsylvania. Amassing enough capital to invest in banking and business ventures, he founded the Bank of Middletown in 1832 and was one of several organizers of the Northern Central Railroad in 1854. Through his business and political activities, he won a contract with the state in 1826 to build canals in Pennsylvania. By this time Cameron had adopted an enduring principle of his politics—support of protective tariffs as a means of simultaneously helping American business and protecting the jobs of Pennsylvania workers from international competition.

Increasingly active in state politics and at Democratic conventions, Cameron lost his canal-building contract because of his partisanship, but in its place he received in 1830 a patronage position as the superintendent of the Mississippi River–Lake Pontchartrain canal in Louisiana. In 1838 he served as a federal commissioner to the Winnebago Indians to adjudicate the tribe's claims. From this episode arose the first of many charges that Cameron engaged in corrupt practices. In this case he was accused of purchasing at discount rates drafts issued to Indians and then paying off the notes at inflated rates from his own bank. Although no criminal proceedings were brought against him, Cameron's reputation was forever tainted by these claims of corruption.

In 1845 Cameron was selected by a coalition of Democrats, Whigs, and Know Nothings to oppose the regular Democratic candidate for the U.S. Senate seat of James Buchanan, who became secretary of state in James Polk's administration. Cameron was successfully elected by the Pennsylvania legislature, but he lost favor with Buchanan and the regular Democrats. In the Twenty-ninth and Thirtieth Congresses Cameron was known in Pennsylvania for his support of the Mexican-American War and protective tariffs. He received national attention when, after being interrupted by Senator Henry Foote, he knocked the Mississippian to the Senate floor.

In 1849 Cameron was not reelected. He formally retired from public life for eight years and began to organize a following based on personal loyalty to him. This machine, built on both his control over official patronage and his wealth, made him an important factor in state politics for over forty years. During the party realignment of the 1850s, his economic resources permitted him to give generous contributions to other candidates as he maneuvered to return to public office.

In 1855 Cameron left the Democratic party and sought office in the U.S. Senate as a member of the Know Nothing party, a change possible only in the fluid partisan conditions of the 1850s, when Pennsylvania parties numbered as many as five. Yet his move to nativism struck some Pennsylvanians as motivated not by any commitment to the anti-immigrant and anti-Catholic policies of the Know Nothings but by political opportunism. Although he endorsed the Democratic presidential candidate Franklin Pierce in 1852, two years later he supported the nativist policy of extending the residency requirement for naturalized voters from seven to twenty-one years. He opposed the

Kansas-Nebraska Act of 1854, supported efforts to keep slavery out of the territories, and advocated revision of the prosouthern Fugitive Slave Act.

In 1856 Cameron joined the Republican party, which absorbed many Know Nothings, and that year John Frémont, the first presidential candidate of the new party, briefly favored him for vice president. In 1857 Cameron returned to the U.S. Senate after a campaign that Thaddeus Stevens likened to "wholesale private bribery." Charges of bribing voters were too vague for official action, although a brief investigation was conducted. Despite his unsavory reputation, through hard work and the use of his personal contacts Cameron emerged as an important national leader of the Republicans and one of the party's national strategists. In the Senate he opposed the English Bill, which would have admitted Kansas immediately if the territory accepted the proslavery Lecompton constitution and a reduced land grant. He was best known for his active lobbying for tariffs protecting his state's coal and iron interests.

By 1860 Cameron had presidential aspirations, though at the Republican convention he received only the votes of his Pennsylvania delegation. When he threw his support to Abraham Lincoln instead of William Seward, Lincoln's managers promised him the cabinet post of secretary of the treasury. In early January 1861 the president-elect rescinded the invitation, claiming he had not agreed to the bargain. A confusing sequence followed, in which Cameron fought for a place in the cabinet and Lincoln balanced the importance of having a Pennsylvanian in the cabinet against Cameron's reputation for corruption. Ultimately the president asked Cameron to join his cabinet as secretary of war.

With the outbreak of war in April 1861, Cameron was overwhelmed with the necessity of modernizing an unprepared War Department of eight bureaus, only ninety employees, and an archaic bookkeeping system. While the secretary's former business experience suggested that he might be an efficient administrator, Cameron instead proved a poor manager. He kept records in his head, was overwhelmed by the hordes of officeseekers, and used personal friendship as the rationale for many appointments. The process of rapidly expanding the department led to abuses in the authorization of contracts for horses and buying supplies at inflated prices. Cameron also used special agents who were not government officials to purchase supplies, and in the chaotic early days of the war he approved military units raised by private individuals. Under growing criticism and hoping to gain congressional support, he further embarrassed the president by arguing in his December 1861 report for enrolling slaves in the Union army.

By this time Cameron had become a liability for Lincoln, who, to be rid of him, appointed Cameron as minister to Russia in January 1862. "I have done my best," Cameron wrote Lincoln concerning his service in the War Department. "It is impossible, in the direction of operations so extensive, but that some mistakes happen and some complications and complaints arise." In the spring of 1862 the Republican-controlled House of Representatives passed a resolution of censure against Cameron for the letting of unsupervised contracts to inappropriate persons, though he was not charged with profiting personally. He remained ambassador until February 1863, even as his Republican friends in Pennsylvania worked unsuccessfully during that year for his return to the Senate. Upon leaving Russia, he returned to Harrisburg.

After the war Cameron remained active in politics, and his efforts were rewarded when he was reelected to the Senate in 1867 and again in 1873. In the Fortieth Congress he opposed efforts to modify the Radical Republicans' policies of military Reconstruction, arguing that the South did not deserve clemency. In 1871, despite charges that he was not appropriate for the post, he became chairman of the Senate Foreign Relations Committee, and four years later he successfully accomplished his goal of getting the House to rescind his earlier censure. An authoritative figure in the Ulysses S. Grant administration because of his friendship with the president, he successfully placed his son J. Donald Cameron as secretary of war. When Rutherford Hayes wanted to remove his son, Cameron engineered a final deal, resigning from the Senate in 1877 so the Pennsylvania legislature could appoint his son to his seat.

Only after 1877 did the millionaire Cameron abandon his consuming interest in party politics, replacing it with travels abroad and the enjoyment of "Lochiel," his estate outside of Harrisburg, and his mansion in town. The tall, thin, sharp-faced "Eagle of the Susquehanna" died at his estate. Controversial, hard-working, consumed by politics, Cameron represented the new kind of nineteenth-century politicians who pursued public life as a career.

• The bulk of the Simon Cameron Papers are in the Library of Congress and in the Dauphin County Historical Society in Harrisburg, Pa. Material relating to Cameron is also in the Salmon Chase, John Forney, Andrew Johnson, and Robert Todd Lincoln papers in the Library of Congress. The most substantial biographies are Lee Crippen, *Simon Cameron: The Ante-Bellum Years* (1942), and Erwin Bradley, *Simon Cameron Lincoln's Secretary of War: A Political Biography* (1966). Obituaries are in the *New York Times*, 27 June 1889, and the *Harrisburg Daily Patriot*, 27 June 1889.

JEAN BAKER

CAMINETTI, Anthony (30 July 1854–17 Nov. 1923), California legislator and U.S. commissioner general of immigration, was born in Jackson Gate, near Jackson, California, the son of Italian immigrants Roche "Rocco" Caminetti, a farmer and miner, and Batistina Guisto. Caminetti was raised in the heart of the Mother Lode region in the turbulent frontier atmosphere of the gold rush, which had lured his parents from Boston to California in 1849 via the Cape Horn route. Young Anthony attended primary schools in Jackson until the age of ten. His parents then sent him to San Francisco, where he completed his grammar school education in 1867. Returning to Jackson, Caminetti spent the next three years working in a store owned by his uncle Biagio Caminetti. In 1870 Caminetti journeyed once again to San Francisco to begin the study of law as a clerk in the offices of Leander Quint and James H. Hardy. He remained with them until March 1871, when he enrolled at the University of California. Withdrawing in October 1873 because of poor health and finances, Caminetti resumed working in his uncle's store and studying law under the tutelage of James T. Farley, a prominent Jackson attorney and Amador County politician.

The former Know Nothing Speaker of the California state assembly, Farley was elected to the state senate as a Democrat in 1875. He took Caminetti with him to Sacramento, ensconcing his young aide as assistant journal clerk of the senate during the 1875–1876 legislative session. Caminetti continued to read law with Farley until 1877, when his mentor won a seat in the U.S. Senate. In May of that same year Caminetti launched his own career by gaining admission to the state bar and running successfully for district attorney. Reelected in 1879, he served as Amador County's chief prosecutor for five years. In 1881 he married Eliza Ellington Martin, a schoolteacher. The couple had two sons and a daughter; the daughter died in childhood.

Rather than seek a third term as district attorney, Caminetti ran for the state assembly in 1882 and won. Quickly establishing himself as a prominent member of the lower house, he secured passage of a bill in 1883 that laid the foundation of California's modern system of public secondary education. Because the state constitution provided only for the funding of primary and grammar schools, fewer than twenty public high schools existed in California. Caminetti's bill allowed local districts to circumvent the constitutional limitation by adding three years to their grammar curricula, creating, in effect, the equivalent of a high school. By the time his "grammar school course law" was repealed in 1891, fifty-five "Caminetti schools" flourished across the state.

Declining a second term in the assembly, Caminetti opened a private legal practice in Jackson. Two years later, in 1886, he returned to public life and was elected to the state senate. There he introduced successful legislation to boost funding for his Caminetti schools and to build the Preston School of Industry at Ione. He also secured an agricultural experiment station for Jackson to promote the fruit and wine industries in his constituent counties of Amador and Calaveras. In a similar vein, Caminetti helped organize the Amador County Board of Trade and served as secretary of the state board of trade from March to September 1890, when he resigned to run for Congress.

Elected to two consecutive terms from the sprawling fifteen-county Second District, Caminetti became the first native-born Californian of non-Hispanic descent to serve in the House of Representatives. He was also the second Italian American elected to Congress, following fellow Democrat Francis Spinola of New York (1887–1891).

Serving a huge rural district where mining and agriculture competed for preeminence, Caminetti took a deep interest in resolving the long-running feud between farmers and miners over hydraulic goldmining. Developed in the early 1850s as an efficient means of exposing the rich tertiary deposits buried along the Sierra Nevada's western slope, hydraulic mining techniques created a booming but destructive industry. By washing tons of mud, sand, and gravel into the tributaries of the Sacramento and San Joaquin rivers, hydraulic mining interfered with commercial navigation, destroyed fisheries, ravaged downstream cities and towns, and flooded productive farmlands, leaving them inundated with infertile mining debris or "slickens." Opponents fought for years to tame the industry before finally emerging victorious in 1884, when federal judge Lorenzo Sawyer issued a permanent injunction against uncontrolled hydraulic mining. Sawyer's decision met with bitter resistance, however, and defiant miners continued to operate illegally.

Hoping to rescue hydraulic mining without antagonizing its many critics, Caminetti introduced a landmark piece of legislation that anticipated the dramatic rise of federal regulatory authority during the Progressive Era. Signed into law by President Benjamin Harrison in March 1893, the Caminetti Act established the California Debris Commission, a federal agency composed of three U.S. Army engineers empowered to inspect, license, and reopen the state's languishing hydraulic mines. Mining companies that agreed to build special containment dams to impound their slickens could resume operation.

Hailed as a brilliant compromise, the Caminetti Act did much more to promote flood control and navigation than to restore hydraulic mining. Most companies could not afford to build expensive containment dams, and the commission was quick to revoke the licenses of those whose dams failed to meet its strict standards. By 1905 the hydraulic revival was over. Nevertheless, the Caminetti Act firmly established the federal government as the chief protector and manager of California's inland waterways.

Meanwhile, despite his achievement, Caminetti was swept from office by the Republican landslide of 1894. He bounced back two years later, however, by recapturing his old seat in the state assembly. Reelected in 1898, Caminetti declined to seek a third term in 1900. Then, over his strenuous objections, the Democrats drafted him in 1904 for another ill-fated congressional race, which he lost to future California governor James Gillette. Once again, however, defeat proved temporary. In 1906 Caminetti returned to the state senate, where he served for the next six years, laboring successfully to protect the Calaveras Big Trees and to build state highways between Sacramento and Jackson and from Jackson to Carson Pass in the Sierra. Most important was his 1907 bill that enabled high schools to extend their course offerings to include the equivalent of the freshman and sophomore years at the University of California. This legislation spawned California's remarkable community college system, which became the largest in the nation.

In the state elections of 1910, the triumph of progressive Republican forces led by gubernatorial candidate Hiram Johnson touched off a veritable revolution in California politics. Though a member of the opposition party, Caminetti lent vital support to the flood of reform legislation enacted by Johnson and his followers in the legislative sessions of 1911 and 1913. A staunch progressive in his own right, Caminetti boasted solid credentials as a reformer who had battled the California progressives' bête noire, the Southern Pacific Railroad, for nearly thirty years in Sacramento and Washington. More than most progressives, Caminetti also enjoyed a reputation as an ardent champion of organized labor. Indeed, one of his few rifts with Johnson involved Caminetti's controversial anti-injunction bill of 1911, which failed because it lacked a firm commitment from the governor's office.

As a reward for his early support of Woodrow Wilson's presidential candidacy, Caminetti was appointed commissioner general of immigration following Wilson's election in 1912. Resigning from the state senate in May 1913, Caminetti departed once more for Washington. Unfortunately, his first year as commissioner general was marred by the arrest and conviction of his son, Farley Drew Caminetti, for violating the federal White Slave Traffic Act of 1910, better known as the Mann Act. The resulting scandal proved embarrassing not only to Caminetti but to the entire Wilson administration.

A longtime and hostile opponent of Asiatic immigration, Caminetti worked diligently and successfully to convince Congress to bar Indians and other East Asians from entering the United States. Winning his objective in 1917, Caminetti then turned his attention to the deportation of alien anarchists and Communists during the post–World War One red scare. Working closely with Attorney General A. Mitchell Palmer and his assistant investigator J. Edgar Hoover, Caminetti played a key part in the notorious Palmer raids of 7 November 1919 and 2 January 1920. These nationwide dragnets resulted in the sudden arrests of over 10,000 people, 800 of whom were subsequently deported. The most sensational of these expulsions occurred on 21 December 1919, when anarchists Emma Goldman, Alexander Berkman, and 247 others left Ellis Island aboard the army transport *Buford* with Caminetti and Hoover there to personally see them off.

The departure of the "Soviet Ark" for Russia crowned Caminetti's tenure as commissioner general, which ended with the close of the Wilson administration in March 1921. In poor and deteriorating health, Caminetti retired to his home in Jackson, where he died.

• The Amador County Archives in Jackson, Calif., has a small collection of Caminetti's papers. The best available sources are Joseph P. Giovinco, "The California Career of Anthony Caminetti, Italian-American Politician" (Ph.D. diss., Univ. of California, Berkeley, 1973), and Miriam E. Young, "Anthony Caminetti and His Role in the Development of a Complete System of Free Public Education in California" (Ed.D diss., Univ. of Denver, 1966). Useful published sources on Caminetti's life include brief sketches in J. D. Mason, *History of Amador County, California* (1881); *A Memorial and Biographical History of Northern California* (1891); and *A Volume of Memoirs and Genealogy of Representative Citizens of Northern California* (1901). Brief but revealing accounts of Caminetti's service as immigration commissioner are in Joan Jensen, *Passage from India: Asian Indian Immigrants in North America* (1988), and William Preston, Jr., *Aliens and Dissenters: Federal Suppression of Radicals, 1903–1933* (1963). Other valuable sources on Caminetti include those dealing with his son's arrest and conviction, especially Robert L. Anderson, *The Diggs-Caminetti Case, 1913–1917: For Any Other Immoral Purpose* (1990); Norbert Macdonald, "The Diggs-Caminetti Case of 1913 and Subsequent Interpretation of the White Slave Trade Act," *Pacific Historian* 29 (Spring 1985): 30–39; and Joseph P. Giovinco, "The Diggs-Caminetti Case," *Manuscripts* 48 (Summer 1996): 207–12. An obituary is in the *Sacramento Bee*, 17 Nov. 1923.

MICHAEL MAGLIARI

CAMM, John (21 June 1718–22 May 1779), Anglican clergyman, professor, and college president, was born in Hornsea, Yorkshire, England, the son of Thomas Camm, and Ann (or Anna) Atkinson. He received a B.A. at Trinity College, Cambridge, and may also have held an M.A. and a D.D. He arrived in the colony of Virginia in 1745 to fill the post of rector of Newport Parish, Isle of Wight County. Within four years, he was appointed to one of two professorships of divinity at the College of William and Mary, first appearing in the faculty minutes on 18 September, 1749. He also became rector of Yorkhampton Parish, whose church stood in Yorktown, some twelve miles distant from Williamsburg, the seat of the college and of the government of the colony.

By the early 1750s, the college entered a period of intense controversy that did not altogether abate until American independence. The struggle was between a heavily British and clerical faculty and a governing body, the Board of Visitors, which was largely dominated by Virginia laymen, many of whom were the political and social leaders of the colony. The contest predictably involved such issues as student discipline, curriculum and academic requirements, election of presidents, and the qualifications and personal character of the faculty, and, ultimately, who would govern the institution. From the beginning Camm emerged as an articulate and contentious advocate for faculty, church, and empire. Although attacked and satirized in newspaper and pamphlet debates, Camm was, unlike some of his colleagues, never criticized on matters of morality or professional competence. One of the royal governors who tangled with Camm, Francis Fauquier, aptly described him as "a Man of Abilities but a Turbulent Man who delights to live in a Flame" (*The Official Papers of Francis Fauquier*, ed. George Reese, vol. 1 (1983), p. 145).

The conflicts at the college first reached a crisis in the summer and fall of 1757 when the visitors removed the entire faculty, ostensibly over the expulsion of two students, although broader issues of control of the college were clearly at stake. Camm successfully appealed his dismissal to the Privy Council in Britain, but review of the case took until 1763 before he was reinstated.

In the interim Camm remained as rector of Yorkhampton Parish, continuing his challenge to the Virginia leadership in the Parsons' Cause. This dispute stemmed from two years of very short tobacco crops in 1755 and 1758 with resultant high prices. Since public obligations in Virginia, including the salaries of Anglican clergymen, were paid in pounds of tobacco rather than currency, the colonial legislature sought to control what it would have to spend by commuting public obligations to cash value at a lesser and more normal rate of two pence per pound of tobacco. Bridling at the loss of a potential windfall, several clerics, led by Camm, appealed to Britain for an overturn of the laws. Camm took the appeal to London, while he and several others also brought suits in Virginia courts against their vestries for recovery of the lost income. In the ensuing controversy, Camm also engaged in a vigorous pamphlet war with two veteran legislators and defenders of the acts, Landon Carter and Richard Bland. Their views of the extent to which the British government could override the acts of a colonial legislature foreshadowed the political debates of the American Revolution. Camm, in response, advanced a vigorous and uncompromising defense of imperial authority.

Once reinstated on the faculty, Camm for the most part avoided involvement in the deepening imperial controversy to concentrate on the contest between faculty and visitors that took on renewed intensity between 1763 and 1770. The quarrel focused on the visitors' intention of stripping the faculty of its powers of governance and weakening academic requirements in classical languages and the pure sciences. Except for a brief exchange of letters with Arthur Lee in the *Virginia Gazette* during the spring of 1768, Camm contented himself with private appeals to British authorities and to writing various faculty statements that challenged the visitors. By 1771 Camm had also become an active partisan in a brief, ill-fated effort by a few Virginia clerics to secure the appointment of an Anglican bishop for the colony.

Thereafter Camm ceased his engagement in such controversies. Two years earlier in 1769, at age fifty-one, the seemingly confirmed bachelor surprised everyone by taking a fifteen-year-old wife, Elizabeth "Betsy" Hansford, of Yorktown. In 1771 Camm became acting president, and on 30 July 1772 he received a permanent appointment as president. For a few years the college seemed to prosper, its enrollment increased, its faculty was at full strength, and its budget balanced. With his election as president Camm also received appointments as commissary, the representative of the bishop of London in ecclesiastical affairs in the colony, and as a member of the Council, the small elite group who sat as the upper house of the legislature, the high court of Virginia, and advisers to the governor.

With the outbreak of the revolutionary war in the spring of 1775, the college was seriously disrupted, losing students who joined the American cause or simply returned home. Williamsburg became an armed camp, and before the end of 1775 two key faculty members who were Loyalists fled to Britain. Camm's sympathies were no less Loyalist, but he was now an old man with five young children, had lived in Virginia for more than a quarter century, and was in no position to return to Britain. He remained at the college until the spring of 1777, when the visitors removed him on grounds of "neglect and misconduct." He continued to hold his parish living until his death in York County, Virginia.

John Camm played a substantial role in bringing the College of William and Mary to perhaps its greatest strength during the colonial period, but it proved a fleeting achievement. What seems in the end most significant about his Virginia years is that his various writings, published and unpublished, likely constitute the best extant body of Loyalist thought in the colony. While he said almost nothing about the immediate revolutionary crisis itself, his strong defense of the Anglican church, including the proposed American bishopric, of a more traditional and hierarchical British culture and the educational means of supporting it, and of British imperial authority, provides a significant insight into one brand of loyalism during the American Revolution.

• A number of Camm's letters are in the Virginia portions of the Fulham Palace Papers in the Lambeth Palace Library, London (microfilm copies in Virginia Colonial Records Project). The Journals of the Meetings of the President and the Masters of William and Mary College, 1729–1784, College Archives, Earl Gregg Swem Library in Williamsburg, Va., contain extensive material on Camm's activities at the college. Camm's two pamphlets in the Parsons' Cause debate are *A Single and Distinct View of the Act Vulgarly Called the Two-Penny Act* (1763) and *Review of the Rector Detected; or The Colonel Reconnoitred* (1764). Lester J. Cappon and Stella F. Duff, eds., *Virginia Gazette Index* (2 vols., 1950), lists references to Camm or pieces by him in the Williamsburg newspapers. Information regarding Camm's family is in *William and Mary Quarterly* 4 (July 1895): 61–62, and 4 (Apr. 1896): 275–78. Robert Polk Thomson, "The Reform of the College of William & Mary, 1763–1780," *Proceedings of the American Philosophical Society* 115 (1971): 187–213, is the best account of the college in Camm's era. Although unsympathetic to Camm, Richard L. Morton, *Colonial Virginia*, vol. 2 (1960), pp. 784–819, affords a full account of the Parsons' Cause and of Camm's role in it.

THAD W. TATE

CAMP, Walter Chauncey (7 Apr. 1859–14 Mar. 1925), football coach and administrator, was born in New Britain, Connecticut, the son of Leverett L. Camp, a schoolmaster and publisher, and Ellen Cornwell. Camp attended Hopkins Grammar School in New Haven, Connecticut, before enrolling at Yale University in 1876. On graduation with a B.A. in 1880 and the honor of being named class poet, he studied medicine for two years at Yale. He gave up his medical studies and joined the Manhattan Watch Company, a New York City firm, in 1882. The following year he began a lifetime career with the New Haven Clock Company, becoming president in 1903. Camp married Alice Graham Sumner, sister of the famed Yale economist and sociologist William Graham Sumner, in 1888. They had two children.

Although a successful entrepreneur, Camp gained fame from his association with Yale athletics and American football. He performed in baseball, track, class crew, and tennis at Yale, but he attracted national recognition only in football. Camp was a starter on the Yale team for six years, his final two as a medical student. As a freshman in 1876 he played halfback in the first Harvard-Yale game played under Rugby Union rules established by the newly formed Intercollegiate Football Association. As team captain for three years and as representative to the national football rules-making body from 1877 until 1925, Camp led the movement that transformed rugby football into American football. More than any other person, Camp created the American version of football that became the dominant college sport; he thus helped shape the course of all intercollegiate sports in the United States. He was the leader of football's transformation from a relatively insignificant fall pastime in colleges to a gigantic commercial attraction that was the most visible sign of college life.

As the leading football innovator, Camp in 1880 proposed changing the number of players from fifteen to eleven. More important, he made football more structured with his proposal the same year creating the line of scrimmage, in which one team had undisputed possession of the ball to begin each play. The scrimmage, in which the quarterback was the dominant figure, replaced the chance possession found in the rugby scrummage. When possession made it possible for one team to keep the ball an entire half, Camp proposed the system of downs in 1882. A team was given three attempts, or downs, to make five yards or surrender possession. The lines placed on the field to determine yardage created a gridiron effect.

The resulting game of a limited number of downs and a specific number of yards to be gained led inventive collegians to create efficient, machinelike tactics and strategy. Much as Harvard dropout Frederick W. Taylor was scientifically managing the workplace at the Midvale Steel Company in Philadelphia, Camp was producing "work" efficiency on the "play" field. Yale had a smooth-running football machine, which emphasized team cooperation rather than individual effort. Signals for calling plays, when a team had undisputed possession, followed naturally. Camp first devised four plays that were indicated by nonsense sentences such as "Look out quick, Deac," directing a specified back through a position in the line. He also was instrumental in developing the concept of interference, or blocking, which he called the "keynote of the American game." In rugby football, players were not allowed to be ahead of the ball carrier and interfere with those attempting to tackle the runner. Most American athletes, though, lacked the English upper-class "spirit of the rules" and were more likely to follow only the "letter of the rules." Camp was no exception, and he advocated guarding the ball carrier by running alongside him and interfering with tacklers. "The Rugby code," Camp once noted, "was all right for Englishmen who had been brought up upon traditions. . . ." As much a "gamesman" as a "sportsman," Camp nevertheless played the role of gentleman's sportsman to the public. He often quoted the following, as found in *Walter Camp's Book of Football* (1910):

> Who misses or who wins the prize,
> Go lose or conquer as you can;
> But if you fail or if you rise
> Be each, pray God, a gentleman!

Camp helped create the present point system for touchdowns, field goals, points after touchdowns, and safeties (a rule he revised to penalize a team for retreating behind its goal line). In 1887 he also proposed permitting tackling below the waist, a decision that led to surer tackles in the open field. This led to mass momentum and brutal plays attacking the middle of line that flourished from the 1880s until the early 1900s. In 1905 Camp was the principal figure in a White House conference with President Theodore Roosevelt (1858–1919). The president attempted to get athletic leaders from Harvard, Yale, and Princeton to lead the nation toward more ethical and less violent practices in football. Following that season, Camp became a reluctant reformer, "the leader of the conservative forces," when brutality and unethical play threatened the game's existence. He unsuccessfully opposed introduction of the forward pass, which was put into effect in 1906 and eventually led to a more open and interesting game for spectators. He was, rather, the prime advocate for extending the yardage needed for a first down to ten yards (which also took place in 1906), believing it would accomplish similar purposes. He also opposed creation in 1906 of the National Collegiate Athletic Association, which would take power away from the football rules-making body he had dominated for nearly three decades.

At Yale, Camp was associated in some capacity, officially or unofficially, with its football team from 1876 through 1909. He was at times an official coach with a salary, but generally he was an unpaid adviser who coached the coaches. During this 34-year period Yale won more than 95 percent of its games, losing only fourteen times. When Camp advised the football team, the captain, coaches, and quarterback generally spent Sunday afternoons at his home to discuss the previous game and to plan strategy for future opponents. From across the country people wrote for Camp's advice. One, a Notre Dame football coach, wrote Camp in 1892 asking: "Will you kindly furnish me with some points on the best way to develop a good football team?" Camp served as treasurer of the Yale Field Corporation and the Yale Financial Union, positions formed among alumni and students to help run Yale athletics. All athletic funds were channeled through Camp as head of the Financial Union, and until 1905 he kept a huge secret athletic fund accumulated from surplus income. Thus, Yale athletics, although nominally under student management, were governed by Camp as director of athletics. Princeton's Parke Davis, the first historian of American football, described Camp as the "father of the game, the Nestor of its counsellors, the dean of its sages. . . ." But in many ways he was the benevolent dictator of Yale athletics. He had a powerful position in the higher councils of the Yale Corporation acting "analogist to that of an independent dean," as Yale President Arthur Hadley once noted.

Camp strongly influenced the long-term commercialization of intercollegiate sports. He published more than 250 magazine articles and numerous newspaper pieces that constantly extolled the virtues young men acquired by playing football and other sports. One of the highest-paid nonfiction writers of his day, he wrote close to two dozen books during a thirty-year span and edited *Spalding's Official Intercollegiate Football Guide*. He also published seven works of fiction, the most popular among them *The Substitute* (1908) and *Jack Hall at Yale* (1909). In all of his writing he emphasized the qualities of character, determination, and fair play. In 1894 he published a study of the degree of brutality in football. His *Football Facts and Figures*, a biased compilation on the subject, helped allay fears that football was injurious to athletes' health. With Harvard football innovator Lorin F. Deland he wrote *Football* (1896), which offered a detailed description of football-playing techniques. Of major importance were the annual All-America football teams that he personally selected; these mythical teams inspired great interest in the sport and its stars throughout the country.

Camp pulled back from most of his activities in Yale's athletic programs after 1910. When the United States entered World War I, he was named director of the U.S. Navy Training Camps Physical Development Program. His pamphlet, "Daily Dozen," based on his well-known exercise and calisthenic regimen, sold nearly a half-million copies after the war; through that program he probably had a greater impact than any other individual of his time on daily physical activity in the United States.

Camp remained active on the Intercollegiate Football Rules Committee until his death, which occurred at a committee meeting. In 1928 the Walter Camp Memorial Gateway was dedicated at Yale Bowl, recognizing the man who dominated the development of college football.

• Camp's extensive papers are housed in the Yale University Archives. They have been microfilmed by Yale and include a *Guide to the Walter Camp Papers* by Robert O. Anthony (1982) that contains a lengthy biography. The only book-length published biography is Harford Powell, Jr., *Walter Camp: The Father of American Football* (1926). Richard Borkowski's unpublished dissertation is titled "Life and Contributions of Walter Camp to American Football" (Ed.D., Temple Univ., 1979). For the system of Yale athletics and Camp's role in it, see Lewis S. Welch and Walter Camp, *YALE: Her Campus, Class-rooms, and Athletics* (1899). For football, see John S. Martin, "Walter Camp and His Gridiron Game," *American Heritage* 12 (Oct. 1961): 50–55, 77–81; Parke H. Davis, *Football: The American Intercollegiate Game* (1911); Thomas G. Bergin, *The Game: The Harvard-Yale Rivalry, 1875–1983* (1984); Tim Cohane, *The Yale Football Story* (1951); and Ronald A. Smith, *Sports and Freedom: The Rise of Big-Time College Athletics* (1988). Obituaries are in the *New York Times*, 15 Mar. 1925, and the *Yale Alumni Weekly*, 20 Mar. 1925, p. 768.

RONALD A. SMITH

CAMPANELLA, Roy (19 Nov. 1921–26 June 1993), Negro League and major league baseball player, was born in Philadelphia, Pennsylvania, the son of John Campanella, an Italian-American fruit stand owner, and his African-American wife, Ida Mercer. Campanella grew up in the Germantown and Nicetown neighborhoods of Philadelphia. There he caught briefly for the Simon Gratz High School team before joining a black semiprofessional team, the Bachrach Giants, at the age of fifteen. A year later he quit high school and joined the Baltimore Elite Giants in the Negro National League (NNL). There Biz Mackey, one of the greatest catchers in the Negro Leagues and player-manager for the Elite Giants, schooled Campanella in the art of catching.

Soon the Elite Giants' starting catcher, Campanella played eight years in the NNL (1937–1942 and 1944–1945), where he was an adept defensive receiver and a powerful hitter. He appeared in the Negro League all-star game, known as the East-West Classic, in 1941, 1944, and 1945. During the winter months Campanella usually played either in Mexico, Venezuela, Puerto Rico (Caguas in 1940–1941 and 1941–1942, Santurce in 1944–1945, and San Juan in 1946–1947), or Cuba (Marianao in 1943–1944). He also played for Monterrey in the Mexican League for parts of the 1942 summer season and again in 1943. He learned Spanish and sometimes managed his winter ball clubs. In 1941 Campanella married Ruthe Willis; the couple had three sons and two daughters.

Campanella was in Venezuela in early 1946 when Brooklyn Dodgers general manager Branch Rickey asked him to return to the United States, where the Dodgers offered him a contract to play for their Class B farm club in Nashua, New Hampshire. Rickey had signed Jackie Robinson to play for the Dodgers' Class A club in Montreal, Quebec, Canada, only months before. Campanella played in 1946 for Nashua and the next year in Montreal, where his manager, Paul Richards, said that "Campanella is the best catcher in the business—major or minor leagues." The 5′9½″, 195-pound Campanella joined the Dodgers in 1948. He was sent to St. Paul, Minnesota, after three games in order to integrate the American Association, but in July Brooklyn manager Leo Durocher insisted that Campanella return to his club. He had nine hits, including two home runs and a triple, in his first three games after being promoted. Campanella anchored the fabled Brooklyn "boys of summer," who won the National League pennant five times between 1949 and 1956. He was catching for the Dodgers when they won the 1955 World Series over the New York Yankees.

The second black player in the majors, Campanella was one of the major leagues' first black superstars. During his ten seasons, he won three Most Valuable Player awards (1951, 1953, and 1955) and in 1953 established single-season records for a catcher by hitting 41 home runs, collecting 142 runs batted in, and recording 807 putouts. Campanella was selected to eight consecutive All-Star teams (1949–1956). His career batting average was .276, with 1,161 hits, 242 home runs, and 856 runs batted in. Campanella also established a record for durability by becoming the first man to catch at least 100 games for nine consecutive seasons, despite a series of injuries.

Campanella opened a liquor store in Harlem during his Brooklyn career. While driving home from the store on 28 January 1958, his car skidded into a telephone pole and overturned. Two of Campanella's vertebrae were crushed, leaving him paralyzed from the waist down. But his courageous struggle to live and regain an active life made him an inspiration and symbol for those with disabilities. Campanella told his story in *It's Good to Be Alive*, published in 1959 and made into a television movie in 1974.

An 8 May 1959 exhibition game between the Dodgers and the Yankees to raise funds to help pay Campanella's considerable medical expenses drew a crowd of 93,103 paying fans, setting a record for the largest game attendance in baseball history. In 1969 Campanella became the second black player ever voted into the National Baseball Hall of Fame. Campanella moved to Los Angeles in 1978 to work in the Dodgers' community services department. He was also an instructor for the club during spring training, despite being confined to a wheelchair.

Campanella's first wife died in 1963. At the time of his death in Woodland Hills, California, he was survived by his second wife Roxie Doles, whom he had married in 1964, and his five children. Known for the infectious joy he had for the game as much as for his skills, Campanella said "To play in the big leagues, you got to be a man, but you got to have a lot of little boy in you, too."

Campanella might have been the greatest catcher in major league baseball history despite playing only 10 seasons in the majors. Though baseball's color line blocked Campanella's entry at the beginning of his career and a tragic car accident prematurely brought it to an end when he was thirty-six, fellow Hall of Famer Ty Cobb captured the opinion of many in the baseball world when he said that "Campanella will be remembered longer than any catcher in baseball history."

• A clipping file on Campanella is at the National Baseball Library in Cooperstown, N.Y. A second edition of Campanella's *It's Good to Be Alive* was published in 1995, with an introduction by Jules Tygiel. Campanella's career statistics are in John Thorn and Pete Palmer, eds., *Total Baseball*, 4th ed. (1993); and *The Baseball Encyclopedia*, 10th ed. (1996). A biography is Milt Shapiro, *The Roy Campanella Story* (1958). For information on Campanella, see Tygiel, *Baseball's Great Experiment: Jackie Robinson and His Legacy* (1983); Donn Rogosin, *Invisible Men: Life in Baseball's Negro Leagues* (1983); and Jim Riley, *Biographical Dictionary of the Negro Baseball Leagues* (1994).

ROB RUCK

CAMPANIUS, Johan (15 Aug. 1601–17 Sept. 1683), thought to have been the first European to translate a religious document into a Native-American language, was born in Stockholm, Sweden, the son of Reverend Jonas Peter Campanius, rector of St. Klara's Church. (His mother's name is unknown.) He was ordained in 1633 after graduating from the University of Uppsala. The name Holm was often added to his name to indicate that he was from Stockholm.

Campanius went to Russia in 1634 as chaplain to the Swedish diplomatic mission and then became a teacher at Norrtälje, just north of Stockholm. He was chaplain and teacher at the Stockholm Orphan's Home in 1642, when he was chosen by the New Sweden Company to accompany the newly appointed governor, Johan Printz, to the New Sweden colony on the South River, as the Delaware was then called. Campanius had married by that time (his wife's name and the number of children the couple had are unknown). Several sources state that his family accompanied him on the *Fama*, which left Sweden in November 1642 and reached Fort Christina (now Wilmington, Del.) on 15 February 1643.

He was given land near present-day Chester, Pennsylvania, where he farmed and raised cattle to provide for his "numerous little children," as Amandus Johnson translated his letter in *Swedish Settlements on the Delaware, 1638–1664* (1911). These settlements were from fourteen to thirty miles apart. He supervised the building of a wooden church at Tinicum, about twenty miles north of Fort Christina, and consecrated it and the burial ground on 4 September 1646. Seven weeks later he presided over the first burial there.

Campanius kept detailed records of his life in New Sweden, his travels to and from the colony, the lives of the Native Americans, the climate, the flora and fauna, and his twice daily astronomical observations. Much of his writing has been preserved because his grandson, Thomas Campanius, who never came to America, used Johan Campanius's journals and notes to write *A Short Description of the Province of New Sweden* (1702). Included were Johan Campanius's descriptions of snakes that could bite off a person's leg, and of "sea spiders," probably horseshoe crabs, with tails like double-edged swords that could fell trees.

When Campanius held services, the nearby Lenape Indians came to observe and were greatly impressed that his listeners would allow him to speak for so long without asking for or permitting their advice. His apparently enormous importance made the Native Americans both uneasy and curious about him. Campanius reciprocated this curiosity. Drawing upon lessons from the Lenape and his own interest in the similarities between some Lenape and Hebrew words, Campanius soon learned their customs and language. Though he desired, according to his grandson, to acquaint an American Indian man and woman with Sweden, the native peoples required him first to swear to return the visitors intact or they would kill all the Swedes in the colony, and he could not risk having everyone killed.

He translated Martin Luther's *Shorter Catechism* into the Lenape language and appended ten lists of vocabulary and phrases: God, heaven, and the seasons; man and the parts of the human body; men and women (which included the verbs *to quarrel, make war, sit, weep*, and *laugh*); clothing; houses and furniture; water; animals, fishes and birds; trees and fruits; and numerals. He also included dialogues of sentences and questions, about eighty words, and the numbering system of the neighboring Mingua Indians. The catechism was not published until 1696, when the Swedish government decided to send 500 copies to America.

Despite his successes in learning the American Indians' languages and customs, Campanius was unable to convert many to Christianity. He reasoned that they had strong beliefs of their own; for their part, the Lenape observed that Europeans often lied and cheated. Campanius knew that other missionaries had failed to learn the intricacies of the American Indian languages and that some had stayed only as long as there were skins to trade. After five years of hard work, Campanius wrote to his bishop asking to be recalled. By then he was the only minister in the New Sweden colony and was in poor health. His request was granted, and he left for Sweden in May 1648 with a good recommendation from Governor Printz.

Campanius reached Sweden in July and was made First Preacher to the Admiralty one month later. In 1649 he became rector of the churches at Frösthult and Hernevi, where he served for thirty-four years. He died in Frösthult.

No parishioner in the colony is known to have written of Campanius's work, but settlers who arrived after his departure heard of his diligence and concern for others and considered him the most important of the early New Sweden missionaries. His observations helped to illuminate for European leaders new land, and his translation of the catechism is a monument to his belief in the value of the souls and the lives of Native Americans.

• Johan Campanius's journals, notes, and letters are kept in the Royal Archives in Stockholm, Sweden. The church records of Campanius's ministry at Frösthult and Hernevi are kept at Landsarkivet in Uppsala. The University of Pennsylvania Museum has a 1696 copy of his translation of the catechism with vocabulary. Amandus Johnson included a photocopy of the frontispiece to the catechism in *Swedish Settlements on the Delaware*. This book also contains a short biography of Campanius and an extensive bibliography. According to Israel Acrelius, *A History of New Sweden* (1874), probably the first English translation of the catechism was published by Charles Magnus von Wrangel in Benjamin Franklin's printing office in Philadelphia between 1759 and 1768. An English translation of Thomas Campanius's *A Short Description of the Province of New Sweden* is included in the *Memoirs of the Historical Society of Pennsylvania*, vol. 3 (1834), and is available at the Historical Society of Delaware in Wilmington.

DOROTHY ROWLETT COLBURN

CAMPBELL, Alexander (12 Sept. 1788–4 Mar. 1866), religious reformer and principal founder of the Disciples of Christ, was born in County Antrim, Ireland, the son of Thomas Campbell, a clergyman in the Antiburgher sect of the Seceder Presbyterian church, and Jane Corneigle. The foundations of Campbell's lifelong commitment to liberty, religious reformation, and education were laid in his native Ulster. In his formative years, the Irish Rebellion of 1898 was violently suppressed. He came to maturity in one of Ireland's most violent areas (northeastern County Armagh) at a time when sectarian and political violence was at its peak.

Campbell's active mind and exceptional memory were disciplined by scrupulous religious and moral education in his home and the independent academies of Markethill in County Armagh and Newry in County Down. In 1805 his father and he opened Richhill Classical and Mercantile Academy, promising in a broadside advertisement to "prepare their charges for the university or compting house in half the normal time." The academy combined classical and practical education.

His introduction in adolescence to the works of John Locke and to the philosophy of the Scottish Common Sense Realists was made indelible by a year of study at Glasgow University. Building on Locke's theory of the mind, the Scottish Common Sense Realists asserted that human perceptions of the natural and moral worlds had validity and that inductive reasoning about particular observations would lead to truth. Thus, one studied behavioral or moral questions in the same way one studied botany, for example, by looking at the evidence, classifying and analyzing that evidence logically, and inducing generalizations only from evidence.

Campbell believed that God disclosed himself through the Bible and had made the human mind an unfailing mechanism to determine truth. Impacted by the self-authenticating text of the Bible, the mind apprehends the truth of God's self-revelation through Scripture. Faith, then, is neither an emotion nor a precondition for understanding Scripture. Faith is the result of induction; it "is the intelligent belief in divine testimony," the result of a rational process of the mind's apprehension of the truth revealed in Scripture.

Campbell's father immigrated to the United States in 1807. Attempting to follow in 1808, the family was shipwrecked on the Isle of Islay and was forced to winter in Glasgow. During the shipwreck off the coast of Scotland, Campbell made his commitment to the

Christian ministry. He broke with the Antiburgher Seceder Presbyterian church in 1809 over the issue of the right of the individual to determine his own worthiness to commune, but the break doubtlessly involved other issues, since he also associated it with his conversion to Independency in church government.

When the family was reunited in the United States in 1809, Campbell embraced enthusiastically the Christian Association of Washington, Pennsylvania, and evangelical society newly initiated by his father. The principles stated in *The Declaration and Address of the Christian Association of Washington, Pennsylvania* (1809), were a millennial mission to preach the Christian gospel, Christian union, the restoration of primitive New Testament faith and practice, and liberty. These four principles became watchwords of Campbell's life and thought. They were also the central distinguishing concepts of the early Second Evangelical Revival, a Protestant renewal and reform movement that became widespread in Western Europe and in the United States in 1790–1830, partially in response to the American and French Revolutions, and that culminated in the birth of the foreign missionary and the antislavery movements, among other religious and social reforms.

On 4 May 1811 the Christian Association reorganized itself into the Brush Run Church, the first church of the Disciples of Christ. Campbell had preached his first sermon a year earlier and was ordained to the ministry on 1 January 1812. By 1814 he had replaced his father as the primary leader of the Disciples. Campbell married Margaret Brown of Brooke County, Virginia (later part of West Virginia), in 1811 and made her family homestead his residence until his death; the couple had eight children. Following her death in 1827, he married Selina Bakewell; they had six children. Only four of Campbell's fourteen children survived him.

Campbell's postmillennial philosophy of history provided the integrating framework for his varied career as religious reformer, educator, debater, postmaster, sheep farmer, convention delegate, and editor. Postmillennialism, a common worldview in the early nineteenth century, was a progressive view of history which believed that science, education, technology, and the development of republican institutions, augmented and, to some degree, driven by the progress of the Christian religion, would lead to a final golden age.

Campbell observed progress in God's successive self-revelations in the Bible, a process that he believed pointed to a millennial utopia before the Second Coming of Jesus. Each successive age, according to Campbell, was instituted by a decisive new divine revelation and had its own constitution or covenantal law. He insisted that the Bible had to be read in the light of this progressive philosophy of history. Thus, Campbell's controversial *Sermon on the Law* (1816) undercut much of the biblical foundation for Calvinism by denying the authority of the Mosaic Law for Christians.

Campbell's postmillenialism was not a midlife development but a constant from his earliest preaching to his final essay published shortly before his death. He believed the American Revolution was a significant preparatory step leading to a future millennium but resisted all efforts to predict an inaugural date for the new age. In the 1829 *Prospectus* of the *Millennial Harbinger*, Campbell indicated that the publication would have "for its object the development, and introduction of that political and religious order of society called THE MILLENNIUM, which will be the consummation of that ultimate amelioration of society proposed in the Christian Scriptures." In this *Prospectus*, he asserted that the four evangelical principles mentioned above, plus freeing the Christian scriptures from dogmatic systems of interpretation, educational reform, political justice, and emancipation of African slaves would be the millennial concerns of the new publication. These eight millennial principles or causes were also the dominant and integrating concerns of his highly productive adult career.

His extended speaking tours, public debates, and editorial activity spread Campbell's fame throughout the English-speaking world. Convinced that Christian preaching was the most essential preparation for the millennial age, Campbell preached more than 100 times in his first year, 1810–1811, and made extended preaching tours, almost annually, throughout the United States (and the United Kingdom in 1847). To maintain a commitment not to accept remuneration for preaching, he became a successful sheep farmer and ran an extensive printing operation.

Campbell's public debates gave him an international reputation. His early decision to embrace believer's immersion as biblical baptism provoked great controversy. Believing debates to be antithetical to Christian union, he refused all challenges at first, but in 1820 he agreed to meet the Reverend John Walker at Mt. Pleasant, Ohio, stipulating only that the debate be published. His debates on Christian baptism with the Reverend William L. McCalla (1823) and with L. N. Rice (1843) were also published. Henry Clay presided at the Campbell-Rice debate. The published transcripts of each debate were widely distributed in several printings. "One debate is worth a year of preaching," Campbell observed.

Campbell's 1829 debate with the British social reformer Robert Owen of New Lanark, Scotland, and his 1837 debate with Archbishop Jean Baptiste Purcell of Cincinnati attracted the most attention. The former dealt with the ideal social order and the evidences for the Christian religion; the latter was a disputation on Roman Catholicism. Campbell shared the common anti-Catholic prejudices of his era. Both debates were held in Cincinnati, Ohio, and the ensuing transcripts were distributed widely in the United States and the United Kingdom.

Recognizing the utility of the press to his evangelical mission, Campbell initiated a monthly journal, the *Christian Baptist*, on 4 July 1823. Iconoclastic and satirical, it held up to ridicule the foibles of the religious leaders with whom he disagreed. As his reformation grew, he replaced the *Christian Baptist* with the *Millennial Harbinger* in 1830, a monthly with a more constructive tone. Most of Campbell's journalistic essays were reprinted in the *British Millenial* Harbinger.

Although he greeted favorably the formation of the Evangelical Alliance for the United States of America in 1847, Campbell was convinced that councilar efforts could not restore the broken unity of the church because such associations were based on creedal or doctrinal unity. Unity, he believed, was of the essence of the church and would not be realized until the various denominations surrendered their human creeds and "inventions" and returned to New Testament faith and practice.

His systematic explication of the restoration of the New Testament church was, to Campbell's associates, his unique contribution. Beginning in the second volume of *The Christian Baptist*, Campbell wrote thirty essays on "A Restoration of the Ancient Order of Things" and ten essays on the "Ancient Gospel." In the first essay of the former series, he asserted that a restoration of New Testament faith and practice would lead to "the long and blissful Millennium." In 1835 he published *Christianity Restored*, better known as *The Christian System* (1839), the title of later revised editions. This book is a summary of Campbell's basic theology.

After Campbell adopted believer's baptism, a relationship with the Baptists was natural. In 1815 Brush Run Church was admitted to Redstone Baptist Association, albeit with an extensive list of exceptions to traditional Baptist faith and practice. Among the Baptists, Campbell and his associates were known as Reformers.

The relationship between Campbell and the Baptist clergy was stormy from the beginning. Early it appeared that the Reformers might prevail; they made great headway in Baptist associations in Ohio and Kentucky. Ultimately, however, Redstone Association expelled Brush Run and other Reformer churches in 1826–1827 in a series of acrimonious sessions. The separation of Baptists and Disciples of Christ in Virginia, Pennsylvania, Ohio, and Kentucky was complete by 1830.

As union with the Baptists faltered, Kentucky Disciples were developing relationships with Barton W. Stone's Christian Connection churches. The two groups differed primarily in emphasis. The union, initiated 1 January 1832, brought together almost 10,000 Disciples and 8,000 Christians in Kentucky.

Although committed to Independency in principle and often critical of Sunday schools and denominational societies, Campbell always recognized the importance of voluntary connectional relationships between Christian congregations. With his encouragement, the Disciples began to establish state and regional conventions during the late 1830s and 1840s. Meeting in Cincinnati in 1849, they organized a General Convention and the American Christian Missionary Society and elected Campbell president of both organizations.

"He gave the Bible to the people" summarized Campbell's own view of his most important work. Implied were three things: (1) he insisted that each individual had the right and the ability to interpret the Bible; (2) he devoted much energy to teaching the hermeneutical principles necessary for reliable scriptural interpretation; and (3) he expended much effort in preparing and publishing a New Testament translation in American English. Dean Luther Weigle, general editor of the Revised Standard Version (RSV), regarded Campbell's translation, *The Living Oracles*, first published in 1826 and revised in many later editions, to be one of the better American translations prior to the RSV (1956). Campbell's last major work was a translation of *The Acts of the Apostles* (1858), published by the American Bible Union.

Campbell criticized the educational institutions of his era for their failure to adapt methods to fit what was known about learners and to prepare graduates adequately to make responsible, moral contributions to a democratic society. Using the Richhill Classical and Mercantile Academy as a model, he established Buffalo Seminary (1818) and Bethany College (1840), a private liberal arts college. Campbell spent his final twenty-five years primarily involved with Bethany College—managing, teaching, soliciting adequate endowment, and obtaining state-of-the-art science apparatus.

Campbell was committed to the education of all persons. At the 1829 Constitutional Convention of Virginia, he led an unsuccessful effort to mandate constitutionally a statewide, publicly supported educational system. For more than a decade, Campbell served as vice president of the Western Literary Institute and College of Professional Teachers, a pioneer voluntary society organized to foster and guide nascent public schools in the West.

Campbell was embroiled in the slavery issue more than he wished. Believing slavery antidemocratic, he manumitted his slaves early. As a delegate to the Virginia Constitutional Convention, he had hoped to secure a constitutional provision eliminating slavery. In the 1830s he supported the American Colonization Society. In Charleston, South Carolina, in 1835, he warned that civil war was inevitable if the slavery issue was not settled. Written with the knowledge that his Disciples of Christ were numerous there, his *A Tract for the People of Kentucky* (1849) urged a constitutional end to slavery in that state.

Campbell's last decade was deeply marked by the slavery crisis. His opposition to slavery coupled with his refusal to become an abolitionist or to disown his slave-owning colleagues led to his vilification by both sides. When the Civil War came, his own family was divided and Bethany College almost closed. And the conflict sowed seeds of the first permanent division within the Disciples of Christ, a division completed in 1906.

The religious reformation led by Campbell grew rapidly in his lifetime. When he died in Bethany, West Virginia, the Disciples of Christ in the United States had 210,000 members in some 2,400 churches with 1,800 ministers. There were also congregations and members in the United Kingdom, Canada, Australia, and New Zealand.

Although a strong and effective controversialist, Campbell was by nature genial, hospitable, and an exceptional conversationalist. Henry K. Rowe observed, "He was well adapted by courage, energy, conviction, fine public presence, and eloquence" to be the leader of a great reformation. Today, three major Christian denominations with almost 5 million members and congregations in more than 100 countries trace their origins to his work. He is widely recognized as a pioneer of the modern ecumenical movement, as well as the most effective example of those radical reformers who sought to democratize American religion in the early days of the Republic.

• The most complete collection of Campbell's writing, including his unpublished letters, ledgers, and notebooks, is in the Alexander Campbell Collection of Thomas W. Phillips Memorial Library at Bethany College in Bethany, W.Va. In addition to the works and journals cited above, Campbell also wrote or edited *Psalms, Hymns and Spiritual Songs* (1828), *Delusions: An Analysis of the Book of Mormon* (1832), *The Christian Preacher's Companion* (1836), *The Christian Hymnbook* (1843), *Christian Baptism—Its Antecedents and Consequents* (1851), *Memoirs of Elder Thomas Campbell* (1861), *Popular Lectures and Addresses* (1863), and *Familiar Lectures on the Pentateuch* (1867). Robert Richardson, *Memoirs of Alexander Campbell* (1870), although dated, is still the standard biography; all later biographies are dependent on it. See also T. Dwight Bozeman, "Alexander Campbell: Child of the Puritans?" in *Lecturers in Honor of the Alexander Campbell Bicentennial, 1788–1988* (1988), on Campbell's break with Calvinism; Nathan O. Hatch, *The Democratization of American Christianity* (1989), and Hatch, "The Christian Movement and the Demand for a Theology of the People," *Journal of American History* (1980): 545–67, for Campbell's role in the radical reform of American religion after the Revolution; William J. Richardson, "Alexander Campbell as Advocate of Christian Union," in *Lecturers in Honor of the Alexander Campbell Bicentennial, 1788–1988* (1988), pp. 101–26, for his views on Christian unity; Cecil K. Thomas, *Alexander Campbell and His New Version* (1958), on his preparation and publication of an American translation of the New Testament; Robert Frederick West, *Alexander Campbell and Natural Religion* (1948), on the style of the *Christian Baptist* and the Campbell-Owen Debate; Richard T. Hughes, "From Primitive Church to Civil Religion: The Millennial Odyssey of Alexander Campbell," *Journal of the American Academy of Religion* (1976), pp. 87–103; Richard T. Hughes and C. Leonard Allen, *Illusions of Innocence: Protestant Primitivism in America, 1630–1875* (1988), on his postmillennialism and restorationism in the context of these movements in American culture; Hughes, *Reviving the Ancient Faith: The Story of the Churches of Christ in America* (1996), for an assessment of Campbell and his enduring influence in the Churches of Christ; and David E. Harrell, Jr., *Quest for a Christian America: The Disciples of Christ and American Society to 1866* (1966).

HIRAM J. LESTER

CAMPBELL, Angus (10 Aug. 1910–15 Dec. 1980), psychologist and educator, was born Albert Angus Campbell in Leiters, Indiana, the son of Albert Alexis Campbell, a public school superintendent, and Orpha Brumbaugh. He grew up in Portland, Oregon, and received a B.A. in 1931 and an M.A. in 1932 in psychology at the University of Oregon. In 1936 he completed his doctoral training as an experimental psychologist at Stanford University, where he trained under psychologists Ernest R. Hilgard and Kurt Lewin, among others.

He began to teach at Northwestern University in 1936 and soon became interested in a broader range of the social sciences, including the burgeoning new field of social psychology and such neighboring disciplines as anthropology and sociology. In 1939–1940 he studied social anthropology at Cambridge University, England, and did fieldwork on the interplay of culture and personality among blacks on St. Thomas in the Virgin Islands. He married Jean Lorraine Winter in 1940; they had three children.

The advent of World War II interrupted Campbell's academic career and set him on the intellectual path that would occupy him for the rest of his life. In 1942 he left Northwestern for Washington, D.C., joining a galaxy of young social scientists converging on the capital from all over the country to participate in the war effort. Campbell had applied for a position with the Division of Program Surveys in the Department of Agriculture, by this time under the direction of Rensis Likert, also a "refugee" from academic psychology and one of the central figures in attitude measurement and public opinion. Agriculture Secretary Henry Wallace had originated the division a few years earlier to exploit the new techniques of sample surveys for keeping track of the feelings and life situations of American farmers. Now the unit was taking on a wider wartime role, monitoring the reactions of the full national population to features of the war mobilization. Likert hired Campbell as his assistant.

In this period statisticians at the Department of Agriculture and the Census Bureau were devising practical ways of applying rigorous probability theory to the selection of respondents over the extensive national territory. The Division of Program Surveys, as one of the first agencies to put these ideas about area probability sampling into practice, thereby replaced the crude quota-sampling procedures of the first pollsters. Campbell and his colleagues were also central in the design of new questionnaire procedures, emphasizing more searching interviews with "open-ended" items that invited respondents to answer questions in their own words rather than select among a few fixed alternative responses offered by the investigator. Himself active both as an interviewer in the field and as a top administrator in a growing survey research organization, Campbell learned firsthand every practical aspect of the trade.

Shortly after the war, congressional budget cuts closed the Division of Program Surveys, along with a number of other wartime offices. Likert and his top staff decided to return to academic life as a group, establishing the Survey Research Center at the University of Michigan in 1946. This fledgling group was soon joined by the Research Center for Group Dynamics, dedicated to small-group experimentation under the original inspiration of Lewin. The two centers were united under a new umbrella organization, the Institute for Social Research, in 1948. This grouping was awarded by the University of Michigan the rare privilege of retaining its own indirect cost recovery on grants and contracts.

Likert assumed directorship of the new institute, and Campbell became director of the Survey Research Center, a post he held for the next twenty-two years. During Campbell's tenure, the center grew from a small and struggling collection of researchers to an institution of high national and international repute and the largest university-based center for the conduct of survey research in the world. Among its hallmarks under Campbell was an emphasis on "programmatic research," featuring an evolving series of cumulative studies in the same domain, such as consumer psychology and behavior, rather than assorted studies on disconnected subjects.

Though a consummate administrator, Campbell was primarily dedicated to a life of research and writing based on the new kinds of information about the U.S. population—its preferences, attitudes toward public issues, and aspirations—that scientific survey research had suddenly made possible. The influence of his broad-ranging scholarly interests reached well beyond social psychology. Shortly after the Survey Research Center was organized in the 1940s, Campbell and his local colleagues launched a program of studies in political behavior involving national surveys of the American electorate taken just before and just after each presidential and biennial congressional election. In contrast to earlier election studies that focused on vote variation by social attributes, Campbell envisioned the voting decision within the terms of Lewinian field theory, as a proximal resultant of an array of attitudinal forces largely represented by the triad of party, candidate, and issue orientations. This posture delighted such political scientists as V. O. Key, because it brought back into the picture straightforward political objects that could account for short-term variability in voting, unlike the social groupings that differed little in size between adjacent elections.

These election studies produced a sequence of collaborative monographs culminating in *The American Voter* (1960), which made landmark conceptual contributions to the study of grass-roots democratic process in the United States that became known as the "Michigan Model." In addition to designing the general architecture of the studies, Campbell in particular developed the concept of party identification, devised what remains the standard mode of its measurement, and studied its short-term primacy in vote choice and its long-term intergenerational transmission. He also illuminated the microbehavior that produced various repetitive features of aggregate voting outcomes in the United States, such as the occasional intrusion of realigning elections or the empirical rule that the party in the White House would almost invariably lose seats in the next congressional election. The general program of election studies has more or less been directly emulated in all of the world's democracies in subsequent decades. And as carried on by Campbell's collaborators after he turned his own attention elsewhere, the core series of U.S. surveys was in 1976 named a "national resource" by the U.S. National Science Foundation, the first such designation for any program of social science research.

Campbell spent the last decade of his life directing an imaginative series of surveys to assess the sense of fulfillment and frustration experienced by the adult American population in connection with jobs, health, economic situations, housing, marriages, friendships, and other domains of their daily lives. He believed that ultimately, as he was fond of putting it, "the quality of life is in the eye of the beholder." The major purpose of the 1972 study was to establish benchmarks for domain satisfaction levels in the early 1970s that could be compared in a spirit of social monitoring with replications in later eras. The structure of the measurements, in which the various domain satisfactions were combined as components of a more generalized sense of well-being, was presented by Campbell and his collaborators in *The Quality of American Life* (1976). A follow-up study conducted in 1978 formed the basis of *The Sense of Well-Being in America* (1981), which Campbell prepared shortly before his death in Ann Arbor.

One of the pioneers in pushing the new capabilities of survey research beyond the short-term, topical focus of most early public-opinion polls, shaping the method into a serious instrument for the scientific investigation of the human condition in social, psychological, and political terms. His emphasis on programmatic research strengthened the cumulativity of the social sciences, while providing the first rigorous view of the mental life of the national population.

• Campbell's papers and professional correspondence are in the Bentley Historical Library at the University of Michigan. Other major monographs authored by Campbell with various collaborators include *The Voter Decides* (1954) and *Elections and the Political Order* (1966), from the studies of national elections; *White Attitudes toward Black People* (1971), from the Koerner Commission work; and an edited volume on social indicators from survey research, *The Human Meaning of Social Change* (1972).

PHILIP E. CONVERSE

CAMPBELL, Arthur (3 Nov. 1743–8 Aug. 1811), frontiersman, soldier, and politician, was born in Augusta County, Virginia, the son of David Campbell and Mary Hamilton, immigrant Scotch-Irish Presbyterian farmers. He was not quite fifteen when, during the French and Indian War, he joined a company of Virginia rangers stationed in western Augusta County. At Fort Young on the Jackson River in September 1758,

Campbell was captured by Wyandot Indians and spent two years in captivity in the vicinity of Detroit before escaping.

After the war Campbell attended Augusta Academy and was trained as a surveyor and lawyer. About the year 1770 he and his family moved to a site on the middle fork of the Holston River, then called Royal Oak, located one mile east of what is now Marion, in Smyth County, Virginia. The Campbells were among the first pioneers to settle in the region. In 1773 he married his cousin Margaret Campbell; the couple had twelve children.

During Lord Dunmore's War, Campbell, a major in the militia, was responsible for protecting southern Fincastle County, Virginia, against Indian raids, mainly Cherokee. When the First Continental Congress urged the colonies to organize committees in opposition to British policy, Campbell was elected by the freeholders of Fincastle to serve on the county Committee of Safety. The committee took vigorous action against those who opposed the Patriot cause.

The voters of Fincastle elected Campbell and William Russell to represent the county at the Fifth Virginia Convention. This convention instructed Virginia's delegates in the Second Continental Congress to call for independence. The convention also adopted Virginia's first constitution and bill of rights, and organized the revolutionary state government. Campbell, now a lieutenant colonel in the militia, served on a variety of committees and was recognized as the best-informed man at the convention on issues concerning Indians.

Fincastle County voters elected Campbell to the fall 1776 term of the Virginia House of Delegates, the first of six terms he was elected to that body. During the fall session he fought in vain against a bill creating Kentucky County out of Fincastle County. Campbell speculated in land and supported Richard Henderson's Transylvania scheme in Kentucky. It is probable that he obtained land in Transylvania from Henderson. Also, Campbell's interests in Kentucky came in conflict with those of other Fincastle County leaders, among them county lieutenant William Preston. Apparently Campbell believed it would be to his personal advantage if the Kentucky bill failed and Transylvania survived. Consequently, he did what he could to defeat the measure. His obstinance made him long-lasting enemies, among them George Rogers Clark, who campaigned for the creation of Kentucky County.

Some of the details surrounding the passage of the Kentucky bill are complex and cloudy, but ironically, Campbell's status increased significantly as a result of its passage. Perhaps to pacify Campbell, Washington County, Virginia, was also created out of Fincastle County. Campbell was commissioned county lieutenant and a justice of the peace for Washington County, and he became the presiding justice of the county court. Perhaps to pacify Preston, a third county, Montgomery, was also formed out of Fincastle.

As county lieutenant, Campbell was the commanding officer of the Seventieth Regiment of the Virginia militia and responsible for the defense of Washington County, a large region from which other counties would later be carved. Throughout the American Revolution the Seventieth Regiment protected the frontier from both Indians and Loyalists. Campbell's policy toward Loyalists, expressed in orders to his men, was to "disarm, distress and terrify" those most active in joining the British (*Virginia Magazine of History and Biography* 27 [Apr. 1919]: 161). So zealous was he in suppressing Loyalists in Washington County that he sometimes helped to route them in neighboring Montgomery. Although he did not go on the campaign himself, Campbell cooperated with Isaac Shelby and John Sevier of western North Carolina in organizing an expedition commanded by William Campbell (1745–1781) that resulted in a major defeat of Loyalists at King's Mountain, South Carolina, on 7 October 1780.

In December 1780, with a force of Virginia and North Carolina militia, Arthur Campbell and Sevier invaded the Cherokee country, burning towns and destroying food supplies as far south as Hiwassee, in present-day Tennessee. Campbell introduced a new method of fighting the Indians by attacking them with mounted riflemen. The devastation resulting from the campaign led to a peace agreement in the Treaty of Long Island on the Holston on 20 July 1781.

Campbell was the leader of a secession movement in Southwest Virginia during the Confederation era, and he greatly influenced the movement in what was then North Carolina, now Tennessee, that culminated in the temporary state of Franklin. To a lesser extent he was involved in a separate state movement in Kentucky. In his campaign for a new state Campbell frequently argued that the inhabitants of Southwest Virginia received no benefit from the unfair and burdensome taxes placed on them by the distant, eastern-dominated, Virginia government. He stressed the view that the people in the East were indifferent toward the difficulties and dangers the western inhabitants faced and the many sacrifices they made to keep the East safe from Indian attacks. He also expressed opposition to the Virginia government's authority over the disposition of western land. Therefore, he urged the Southwest Virginia counties to secede and join the state of Franklin. It was only after Virginia governor Patrick Henry threatened to charge him with treason that the separate-state movement in Southwest Virginia ended. Henry removed Campbell from the offices of county lieutenant and judge, but he was fully reinstated within three years. In 1786 and again in 1787, at the height of the controversy over his separate-state activities, Campbell was elected to the House of Delegates, a clear indication of his popularity in Washington County.

Campbell was a nationalist and supporter of the Federalist party. During George Washington's presidency, he was commissioned an Indian agent and awarded a contract to establish a mail route from Staunton to Abingdon. He had been instrumental in Abingdon's incorporation in 1778. About the time Thomas Jefferson was elected president in 1800,

Campbell retired, and by 1809 had moved to Yellow Creek near Cumberland Gap, the future site of Middlesboro, Kentucky. Here he lived the remainder of his life.

Arthur Campbell was extremely controversial. David Campbell, a former governor of Virginia and a nephew, in 1840 described him as "hasty and excitable . . . , disposed to be overbearing, and . . . often engaged in violent personal quarrels." Nevertheless, for a quarter of a century Campbell was the spokesman for many of the people of Southwest Virginia. He represented them at the Fifth Convention and in the Virginia Assembly at the most crucial times during the Revolution and several times thereafter. He protected area settlers during years of bloody Indian warfare and by vigorously suppressing Loyalists helped to ensure that the entire region remained firmly in the Patriot camp. Also significant was his influence on the growth of democracy on the frontier. Campbell took literally the philosophy of the Declaration of Independence, insisting that the people in the West had the natural right to govern themselves. While the secessionist movement failed in Southwest Virginia, his separate-state activities contributed to the formation of the states of Kentucky and Tennessee admitted into the Union in 1792 and 1796, respectively.

• The Arthur Campbell Papers are located at the Filson Club, Louisville, Ky. Other valuable sources are the Campbell family papers, among them the David Campbell Papers, Duke University, Durham, N.C.; Lyman C. Draper Manuscript Collection, Wisconsin State Historical Society, Madison, of which the King's Mountain Papers, DD, and the Preston papers, QQ, are the most useful; and W. P. Palmer et al., eds., *Calendar of Virginia State Papers . . .* (11 vols., 1875–1893; repr. 1968). For a biography see H. L. Quinn, *Arthur Campbell: Pioneer and Patriot of the Old Southwest* (1990). See also R. L. Kincaid, "Colonel Arthur Campbell: Frontier Leader and Patriot," *Historical Society of Washington County Virginia Publications*, 2d ser., 2 (Fall 1965). Books concerning Campbell's role in the Revolution are E. G. Evans, "Trouble in the Backcountry: Disaffection in Southwestern Virginia during the American Revolution," in *An Uncivil War: The Southern Backcountry during the American Revolution*, R. Hoffman et al., eds. (1985); A. H. Tillson, Jr., *Gentry and Common Folk: Political Culture on a Virginia Frontier, 1740–1789* (1991); E. L. Sayers, *Pathfinders and Patriots* (1983); and H. M. Wilson, *Great Valley Patriots: Western Virginia in the Struggle for Liberty* (1976). His secessionist activities are examined in S. C. Williams, *History of the Lost State of Franklin* (1924), and Frederick Jackson Turner, "Western State-Making in the Revolutionary Era," *American Historical Review* 2 (Oct.–Jan. 1896): 70–87, 251–69. L. P. Summers, *History of Southwest Virginia, 1746–1786, Washington County, 1777–1870* (1903), is invaluable for many aspects of Campbell's career.

HARTWELL L. QUINN

CAMPBELL, Bartley, Jr. (12 Aug. 1843–30 July 1888), playwright and producer, was born in Allegheny City, Pennsylvania, the son of Bartley Campbell, the owner of a brickyard, and Mary Eckles. The family had emigrated from Ireland in 1840. Campbell received little formal education, spending much of his childhood working with his two older brothers in their father's brickyard.

At the age of fifteen Campbell took a job as an office boy at the *Pittsburgh Post*, for which he was soon put to work as a staff writer. He developed a keen interest in politics and wrote numerous articles attacking political corruption. While still a teenager Campbell was called to testify before investigative committees in Harrisburg, Pennsylvania. He developed a close attachment to the Democratic party and gained a reputation for his rabble-rousing campaign speeches.

In 1865 Campbell left the *Post* to become cofounder of a rival daily, the *Pittsburgh Leader*, for which he served as drama critic. So severe were his criticisms of actors that the paper was sued by several who charged unjust damage to their careers. Campbell's coeditors were said to be relieved when he left the *Leader* in 1868 to start his own paper, the *Mail*. At age twenty-five, he was the youngest newspaper owner in the United States. Also in 1868 he married Elizabeth Woodhouse. They had two children.

The *Mail* was the first of several publications that Campbell founded and saw fail within a year. Immediately after the *Mail* folded in 1868, Campbell and his wife moved to Philadelphia, where he began writing for the *Philadelphia Press*. Within weeks of beginning his work there, he was sued for slander by an actor whom he had criticized severely. Campbell argued so forcefully in his own defense in the courtroom that he was sentenced to a thirty-day jail term for contempt. Penniless and unemployed following his release from jail, he moved with Elizabeth to New Orleans, Louisiana. Campbell secured a position at the *New Orleans Picayune* but soon left to start a literary magazine that he called simply the *Southern Monthly Magazine*. It folded after its second issue. He then took a job as recorder for the Louisiana state legislature. When the Campbells had saved enough money they returned in 1870 to Pittsburgh, where he started yet another daily newspaper, the *Paper*, which quickly went bankrupt. With the birth of his second son in 1871, Campbell redoubled his writing efforts. He edited cookbooks, wrote advertising jingles, and ghostwrote speeches for political candidates.

Also in 1871 Campbell wrote his first play, a "Grand Historical Allegory" called *America*. He followed this the same year with *Peril; or Love at Long Branch* and the "sensation play" *Through Fire*, both of which ran briefly at the Pittsburgh Opera House. A short run of *Peril* in Chicago attracted the attention of the Irish-born minstrel performer R. M. Hooley, who brought Campbell to Chicago in 1872 to assist in converting Hooley's Chicago theater to "legit" drama. Between 1872 and 1876 Campbell wrote and directed six plays for Hooley's company: *Fate*, *Risks*, *On the Rhine*, *The Virginian*, *Hearts*, and *Bulls and Bears*. During the same period Campbell also wrote plays for other managers. These included *Little Sunshine*, *Gran Uale*, *The Orphans*, *The New World*, and *The Rising Moon*. Thus he completed eleven full-length plays in four years.

In 1875 the Hooley company went to San Francisco, where Campbell came to know writers Bret Harte and Samuel Clemens (Mark Twain). That same year Campbell became involved in his first copyright lawsuit when producer-playwright Augustin Daly sued him over the right to be the sole American adapter of the German play *Ultimo*. A San Francisco judge declined to block production of the Campbell version, which opened in June 1875 and ran for three weeks.

In 1876 Campbell returned east with the Hooley company. He left Hooley's employ and in May 1876 sailed to London, where he supervised a production of *The Virginian* and wrote two new plays, *How Women Love* and *A Heroine in Rags*. In the fall of 1877 Campbell returned to the United States and presented a season of his own plays at the Arch Street Theatre in Philadelphia. He organized tours for the next two seasons and wrote two new plays, a farce called *My Foolish Wife* and *Clio*, a spectacle play. But the tours proved unprofitable, and by 1879 Campbell was nearly destitute. His failure to secure a New York opening greatly hampered his drawing power.

Campbell's next play radically changed his life. *My Partner* opened at the Union Square Theatre in New York on 16 September 1879. Its enormous popularity rocketed Campbell to fame and provoked demand for more work by him. *The Galley Slave* opened to great acclaim only two weeks after *My Partner*; *Fairfax* opened in December and drew praise from Campbell's hero, poet Henry Wadsworth Longfellow. Over the next six years Campbell published a succession of melodramas, farces, and spectacles. At one time in 1882 Campbell had six companies touring the nation with his plays. His writing then continued at a slower pace: *Matrimony* (a revised version of the earlier *Peril*) opened in 1880, *My Geraldine* and *Government Bonds* in 1881, *The White Slave* and *Siberia* in 1882, *Separation* in 1884. *Paquita; or, The Dude Husband* opened Campbell's first New York theater, the Fourteenth Street Theatre, in August 1885. At the time of the play's opening Campbell's net worth was estimated at $500,000, and he was by many measures the most popular American dramatist.

The failure of the bizarre spectacle-melodrama *Paquita* and the financial collapse of Campbell's Fourteenth Street Theatre coincided with a growing strangeness in his personality. He had become deeply involved in spiritualism, telling friends that he conversed with spirits on a daily basis. Campbell began claiming that his plays had been written under the "spiritual influence" of French playwright Jean Racine and that the Greek writers Sappho and Aristophanes often gave him writing advice. On 13 May 1886 a warrant was sworn, declaring Campbell to be "irresponsible and likely to harm himself and others." He was confined by the court to Bellevue Hospital for treatment. By September of that year his condition had worsened, and a doctor testified that Campbell was incurably insane. He was moved to Middletown (New York) State Hospital for the Insane. He died there two years later. The cause of death was listed as "General Paresis."

Campbell was a talented and energetic popular dramatist. His plays, like those of other melodramatists, are exaggerated in their emotionality and wildly sentimental in their conclusions. Campbell was no innovator in the mold of such sophisticated contemporaries as James A. Herne and William Dean Howells. Instead, his talent lay in reading the popular mind and providing drama that was emotionally gripping and morally satisfying to that audience. The plays are especially valuable as barometers of public tastes of the later nineteenth century.

• Five of Campbell's plays are published in Napier Wilt, ed., *The White Slave and Other Plays*, vol. 19 of the *America's Lost Plays* series (1941). Also included in the collection are *The Virginian*, *My Partner*, *The Galley Slave*, and *Fairfax*, and the volume contains invaluable production and biographical data, such as dates of openings and cast lists. A guide to finding other plays in manuscript is provided in Don Hixon and Don Hennessee, *Nineteenth-Century American Drama: A Finding Guide* (1977). The best sources of information on Campbell and his work are Wayne H. Claeren, "Bartley Campbell: Playwright of the Gilded Age" (Ph.D. diss., Univ. of Pittsburgh, 1975), and Homer Bower, "Bartley Campbell: Successful American Playwright" (M.A. thesis, Stanford Univ., 1952). Wilt and Bower both worked with the assistance of Campbell's son Robert in gathering biographical information. A thorough guide to reviews of the plays is in Patricia Marks, *American Literary and Drama Reviews: An Index to Late Nineteenth Century Periodicals* (1984). An obituary is in the *New York Dramatic Mirror*, 4 Aug. 1888.

MARK FEARNOW

CAMPBELL, Charles Macfie (8 Sept. 1876–7 Aug. 1943), psychiatrist, was born in Edinburgh, Scotland, the son of Daniel Campbell, a banker, and Eliza McLaren. After preparation at George Watson's Boys College in Scotland, Campbell entered the University of Edinburgh in 1893. He received an M.A. in philosophy in 1897. He then stayed on at the university, earning a B.S. in 1900 with distinction in anatomy, physiology, and anthropology. After his training in the life sciences, Campbell continued at Edinburgh to pursue a medical education, graduating summa cum laude in 1902 with an M.B. and a Ch.B.

Campbell had already spent some of his summers as a university student on the Continent learning French and German. After completing Edinburgh's version of an elementary medical education (which was really quite advanced), Campbell crossed the Channel once again to spend a year in the laboratories and clinics of leading European neurologists such as Pierre Marie in France and Wilhelm Erb in Germany, from whom he gained further knowledge in his chosen specialty, neurology. Following his continental sojourn, Campbell returned to Scotland, where he spent a year as a resident at the Royal Edinburgh Infirmary. In 1904 Campbell moved to the United States to accept an employment offer from Adolph Meyer, a prominent American psychiatrist who directed the Pathologic Institute (later called the Psychiatric Institute) of the

New York State Hospital for the Insane on Ward's Island in New York City. In 1907 Campbell returned to Scotland to serve in the prestigious post of assistant physician at the Royal Edinburgh Asylum. In 1908 he was elected as a member of the Royal College of Physicians of Edinburgh. That year he married an Edinburgh physician, Jessie Deans Rankin; they had four children.

Campbell's return to Scotland was, however, only temporary; soon after Campbell's wedding, Meyer lured the Scotsman back to Ward's Island with an offer to join the Psychiatric Institute as an associate. In 1909 Campbell also took a part-time position as an instructor in psychiatry at Cornell University Medical School in New York City, which he held until 1913. In 1911 Campbell traded his clinical appointment at the Psychiatric Institute for a position as a psychiatrist at the Bloomingdale Hospital in White Plains, New York. During the same year Campbell finished his thesis, "Focal Symptoms in General Paralysis," which he successfully presented at the University of Edinburgh for an M.D. (considered an advanced medical degree in Britain).

In 1913 Campbell resigned from his positions in New York to join Meyer, who had already departed for Johns Hopkins in Baltimore. Meyer had recruited Campbell to serve under him as an associate director of the newly established Phipps Psychiatric Clinic at the Johns Hopkins Hospital. Campbell simultaneously accepted an appointment as an associate professor of psychiatry in the Johns Hopkins Medical School. While at Johns Hopkins, Campbell's intellectual orientation shifted from neuropathology to a greater emphasis on social and emotional maladjustment as causes of mental disorder. He urged his colleagues and students to pay attention to the influence of personality and life experiences in their therapeutic interactions with patients suffering from psychiatric problems. Campbell was also a pioneer in stressing the significance of psychosomatic illness, emphasizing on many occasions the need for all physicians to accept the possibility that problems in general medicine might be manifestations of mental disturbance. Campbell did not strictly follow any of the schools of psychiatric thought that were popular in the early twentieth century, although he was well versed in the work of major figures such as Sigmund Freud and Carl Jung. Instead, Campbell used and taught an eclectic approach, drawing widely on what he perceived as the most useful insights of prominent contemporary psychiatric theorists.

During World War I Campbell initially contributed to the war effort by serving as a "civil surgeon," working with military medical officers who came to the Phipps Clinic at Johns Hopkins for training in neuropsychiatry. As the war progressed, Campbell decided that he should join more directly in the military operations of his adopted country. In November 1918 he entered the U.S. Army as a private and became a citizen of the United States. The peace treaty signed in the same month brought both the Great War and Campbell's plans to seek a commission as a medical officer to an end.

In 1920 Campbell moved to Boston to accept a joint appointment as the chair of psychiatry at Harvard Medical School and the medical director at the Boston Psychopathic Hospital. During his years in Boston, Campbell focused most of his investigative energies on schizophrenia. He published a number of papers on this vexing disease, but his sudden death prevented him from publishing a large synthetic work on the topic—a source of considerable regret among his colleagues. Campbell had planned to write his magnum opus on schizophrenia during his retirement, which was scheduled to begin in September 1943. However, a fatal heart attack brought an end to these plans twenty-four days before Campbell was due to become a professor emeritus.

Campbell served as president of the Boston Society of Psychiatry and Neurology (1924), the Massachusetts Psychiatric Association (1935), and the American Psychiatric Association (1937). He also left a legacy of the many physicians he had trained during his more than thirty years as a popular and widely respected teacher. And even though he never had the opportunity to write his planned synthetic work on schizophrenia, he left a lasting intellectual mark through over seventy publications, including five books.

• Campbell's publications include *Human Personality and the Environment* (1934) and *Destiny and Disease in Mental Disorders* (1935). Informative obituaries of Campbell include Gaylord P. Coon, *Journal of Nervous and Mental Diseases* 98 (1943): 561–64; Harry C. Solomon and Stanley Cobb, *Archives of Neurology and Psychiatry* 50 (1943): 711–14; and Solomon, *American Journal of Psychiatry* 100 (1943): 438–41.

JON M. HARKNESS

CAMPBELL, Douglas Houghton (16 Dec. 1859–24 Feb. 1953), botanist, was born in Detroit, Michigan, the son of Cornelia Hotchkiss and James Valentine Campbell, a judge of the supreme court of Michigan. The fifth of six children, he was named after geologist Douglas Houghton, a close friend of Judge Campbell's. Campbell developed an early interest in natural history, which he pursued during the summer months on Grosse Isle, Michigan. Having read extensively in his family library, Campbell's interest in natural history and exploration of the tropics was fueled by reading Alfred Russel Wallace's *Malay Archipelago.* After graduating in 1878 from Detroit High School, Campbell attended the University of Michigan, where he studied botany, a field especially well developed at the University of Michigan. His lifelong interest in cryptogamic botany came as a result of reading a translation of Hofmeister's celebrated text on the morphology of archegoniate plants while he learned microscopic techniques (then a new introduction to botanical studies) as a result of enrolling in Volney Spalding's introductory survey of botany. Other teachers included Joseph B. Steere in zoology and Calvin Thomas in classics. After he received his master's degree in 1882, Campbell supported himself as a teacher of botany at Detroit

High School while he continued graduate research on the morphology of fern gametophytes, completing his Ph.D. in 1886. Having saved enough money (he lived frugally and under parental care), he took a two-year trip to Germany to learn the latest botanical techniques with noted German botanists like Eduard Strasburger in Bonn and Wilhelm Pfeffer in Tübingen, as well as visiting Carl Ignaz Leopold Kny in Berlin. During these two years he learned not only the latest microscopical techniques, but he adapted a technique from zoologists and developed a method of embedding material in paraffin in preparation for serial sections (a sequence of cross sections through plant material that permits more continuous imaging). He also helped to develop vital stains used in preparing material for microscopical analysis.

Returning from Germany, Campbell was first appointed as professor of botany at Indiana University (1888–1891) and then became head of the botany department at the new Stanford University in Palo Alto, California, where he stayed until his death. In 1890 he completed a laboratory manual and textbook, *Elements of Structural and Systematic Botany*, which earned him some attention as a teacher of botany. At Stanford, Campbell quickly distinguished himself at the new university. He reorganized and chaired the botany department at the same time that he threw himself into teaching and research. He remained head of the department until 1925, receiving some administrative assistance from George J. Pierce. His work was heavily supported by the president of Stanford, David Starr Jordan.

Beginning with his first publication in 1881 to his last in 1947, Campbell's botanical career was long and productive. He took advantage of his West Coast location to fulfill his childhood interest in the tropics by making frequent trips to collect interesting botanical specimens. During his first year at Stanford he visited Hawaii and subsequently took numerous trips to the tropics. His early interest in ferns widened to mosses and liverworts, which he found in abundant quantities after the first wet season in California. The culmination of a year-long trip to the British Museum of Natural History, where he studied the literature on mosses, liverworts, and ferns, was *The Structure and Development of Mosses and Ferns*, which was published in 1895 with the support of British botanist F. O. Bower. The book became the authoritative source on mosses and ferns and a very popular textbook that went through several editions. As a result of this book, Campbell became an internationally known botanist.

While most of Campbell's work was concerned with cryptogams, he eventually turned to the study of gametophyte development in flowering plants, which he used to determine phylogenetic relationships. Campbell's interest in phylogenetic construction led to the publication of a second very popular book, *Lectures on the Evolution of Plants* (1899), which became widely adopted as a textbook for introductory students. Campbell included important discussions of ecological factors, frequently linking environmental, morphological, and cellular matters.

Over the course of his long life, Campbell traveled extensively and collected numerous specimens. Though he traveled to Australia, New Zealand, the West Indies, and the Mediterranean and took trips around the world at least twice to collect specimens along the way, his favorite collecting region was the famous mountain laboratory run by the Botanical Garden and Buitenzorg, Java. He published his observations on the geographic distributions of the flora he visited and compiled all these in a book published in 1926, *Outline of Plant Geography*. Because it did not cover theories about plant geography popular at the time—Campbell had intended his book to be about his own observations—the book was deemed rather superficial and was not generally well received.

In addition to his widely read textbooks, Campbell distinguished himself by his high-quality smaller studies into cryptogamic botany. He was renowned for his technical microscopic abilities: he could cut extra thin hand sections for examination under the microscope. Campbell is largely known for his phylogenetic work linking various fern groups with the primitive hepatics, the Anthocerotales. From his detailed study of the reproductive structures of *Anthoceros* and ferns, Campbell was the first to suggest the close relationship of the Anthocerotales with eusporangiate ferns. Campbell suggested that the eusporangiate ferns were a more primitive group than the leptosporangiates because their embedded archegonia and antheridia more closely resembled the primitive Anthocerotales.

In 1913 Campbell became president of the Botanical Society of America. Other honors included election to the National Academy of Sciences, membership in the Linnaean Society of London, the Royal Society of Edinburgh, the Deutsche Botanische Gesellschaft, the International Association of Botanists, and the American Philosophical Society.

Campbell appears to have had a small circle of close friends with whom he socialized, frequently attending concerts and other musical events. In his leisure, he read nonbotanical literature and exercised strenuously; one of his favorite sports was riding his horse. Campbell never married, but he shared a home with a colleague, Professor Robert E. Allardice, until Allardice's death in 1928. The two built their home on Stanford property; Campbell remained there until his death.

• Campbell's personal correspondence and administrative records of the department are housed at the University Archives of Cecil Green Library at Stanford University. For a detailed biographical sketch and list of publications, see Gilbert M. Smith, "Douglas Houghton Campbell," National Academy of Sciences, *Biographical Memoirs* 29 (1956): 45–63; see also the entry in Harry Baker Humphrey, *Makers of North American Botany* (1961). For a discussion of Campbell's scientific work, see Smith, *Cryptogamic Botany*, vol. 2 (1938). Obituary notices are William C. Steere, *Bryologist* 56 (1953): 127–33; Steere, "Douglas Houghton Campbell and Especially His Work on Bryophytes," *Asa Gray Bulletin* 2 (1953):

137–40; Ira L. Wiggins, "Twenty-eight Years with Douglas Houghton Campbell," *Asa Gray Bulletin* 2 (1953): 121–28; and Wiggins, "Douglas Houghton Campbell, in the Classroom and on the Campus," *American Fern Journal* 43 (1953): 97–103.

VASSILIKI BETTY SMOCOVITIS

CAMPBELL, George Washington (8 Feb. 1769–17 Feb. 1848), lawyer and statesman, was born in Tongue Parish, Sutherlandshire, Scotland, the son of Archibald Campbell, a physician, and Elizabeth Mackay. He immigrated with his family to America in 1772 and settled with them near the present city of Charlotte, North Carolina, where his father farmed and practiced medicine. After several years of teaching in a small school near his home, he was admitted at the age of twenty-three to the junior class of the College of New Jersey (now Princeton) and graduated in 1794 with high honors. He taught in New Jersey for a year or two but soon returned to North Carolina, where he studied law. By 1798 he had moved to Knoxville, Tennessee, a bustling commercial center of about fifty homes, where he achieved immediate success at the bar. Knoxville was the capital of the state for more than another decade, and this fact, in addition to the city's significant growth during that time, was a factor in his success.

From 1800 to 1820 Campbell's interests centered largely on politics and public service. He was defeated in 1801 in his quest for Tennessee's only congressional seat, but in 1803, when the state was allotted two additional places, he was elected to represent the Hamilton District, which consisted of the state's twelve eastern counties. He soon became a respected "spokesman for the West" and was a strong supporter of Thomas Jefferson nationally and Andrew Jackson locally. Early in his career he supported westward expansion, and by 1810 he embraced the "War Hawks"—principally southern and western congressmen who aggressively sought expansion into Florida and Canada and were willing to fight England and Spain to accomplish this. He also, as a leader in the House, soon became chair of the Ways and Means Committee, where he made enemies among lawmakers of the Northeast. By February 1808 his defense of the embargo and his strong War Hawk position generally became the immediate cause for a duel with Barent Gardenier, an Upstate New Yorker who represented an area enjoying a brisk and profitable trade with England. Suffering a mild chest wound, Gardenier was hospitalized for a few days in the nearby home of Benjamin Stoddert, who had been President John Adams's secretary of state. While visiting the wounded duelist, as was becoming a gentleman, Campbell met and fell in love with Stoddert's daughter Harriet Stoddert, and they were married in 1812. They had six children.

Campbell declined reelection to the House in 1809 and moved to Nashville—a developing western town that soon became the capital of the state. He had no sooner established a law practice there than he was appointed to the Supreme Court of Errors and Appeals for the state, where he served for a few months and then was elected to the U.S. Senate. Once back in Washington, he continued his War Hawk proclivities and helped plunge the country into war with Great Britain. By November 1812 he was chair of the Senate Committee on Military Affairs, where he devoted considerable attention to a much-needed reorganization of the army. Soon thereafter, he also became chair of the Committee on Foreign Relations.

In February 1814 Campbell replaced Albert Gallatin as secretary of the treasury but was not effective in raising funds necessary to prosecute the war, mainly because northern and eastern bankers failed to cooperate. He remained at the treasury for two years but was back in the Senate by December 1815. There he remained until 1818, when he was appointed minister to Russia.

Campbell was successful in gaining respect for his country during his two years in Russia. Czar Alexander I had been concerned about the movement in South America for independence from Spain and also about the desire of the United States for Spanish Florida. Campbell effectively represented his country's position, however, and was partly responsible for changing Alexander's mind to positions friendly toward the United States on both matters. Although one child was born to the Campbells while they were in Russia, three children died there of typhus fever. These deaths no doubt were a strong reason for Campbell's asking for a recall from his diplomatic post after only two years of service.

Once back home, Campbell entered vigorously into the practice of law and achieved immediate success. His business and land ventures also were successful, and within a few years he owned thousands of acres in a dozen counties in and around Nashville and in the newly acquired Jackson Purchase, located between the Tennessee and Mississippi rivers.

Although Campbell lived for two decades after his return from Russia, he did not enter public service again except briefly in 1832, when he was appointed by President Jackson to work out provisions of the Rives Treaty with France. Campbell died in Nashville.

Although an able and respected public servant of his day, Campbell has not received the acclaim other westerners, such as Henry Clay, Jackson, John Sevier, and Felix Grundy, have. This may be due in part to the fact that he was not a military hero like Jackson or Sevier or an orator like Clay or Grundy. A man of culture and refinement, he was perhaps best known for his strong defense of the West—a major factor in his failure to win the confidence of easterners such as John Quincy Adams. But his public service for the most part was superior or at least comparable to that of many of the other public figures of his time.

• Weymouth T. Jordan is the recognized scholar on Campbell. His *George Washington Campbell of Tennessee: Western Statesman* (1955) is authoritative, as are several of Jordan's articles, including "The Public Career of George Washington

Campbell," *East Tennessee Historical Society Publications* 10 (1938): 3–15, and "The Private Interests and Activities of George Washington Campbell," *East Tennessee Historical Society Publications* 13 (1941): 47–65. See also Joshua W. Caldwell, *Sketches of the Bench and Bar in Tennessee* (1898), and "Proclamation of the Nashville Bar, in Relation to the Death of Hon. G. W. Campbell," in 27 *Tenn. Reports* (1848): xxi.

ROBERT E. CORLEW

CAMPBELL, Helen Stuart (4 July 1839–22 July 1918), author and home economist, was born in Lockport, New York, to Jane E. Campbell and Homer H. Stuart, a banker and lawyer. She attended New York public schools and two private schools, the Gammell School in Warren, Rhode Island, and Mrs. Cook's Seminary in Bloomfield, New Jersey.

Campbell's writing career began shortly after her marriage in 1859 or 1860 to Grenville Mellen Weeks, an army surgeon; they had no children. In 1862 she began publishing stories in children's magazines under her married name, Helen C. Weeks. Over the next two decades she wrote many children's stories and several children's books, including in 1868 and 1869 the *Ainslee Series*, a four-volume collection that sold particularly well. During this time she also published several light adult novels and short stories as Campbell Wheaton and Helen Stuart Campbell, the name she used throughout the remainder of her life. She separated from her husband around 1871 and they eventually divorced.

Campbell's career took another direction in the late 1870s when she became active in the new home economics movement, which addressed ways of making homemaking more "scientific," rewarding, and socially beneficial. Campbell studied home economics under Juliet Corson, and her growing expertise rapidly led to new professional opportunities. In 1880 she helped found a Washington, D.C., mission cooking school and diet kitchen; she published a home economics textbook, *The Easiest Way in House-keeping and Cooking* (1881) that sold well; from 1882 to 1884 she was the literary and household editor of *Our Continent* magazine. In 1893 she helped found the National Household Economics Association, and later, in 1896, she published *Household Economics*, essays based on a series of college lectures.

Campbell's strongest interest was in what she called "survival economics"—ways in which home economics knowledge could be used to improve the lives of poor working women in urban ghettos—and she believed that advancements related to sanitation, diet and nutrition, and health care and budget management had particular application. She argued, "The knowledge that is broad enough to ensure good food is broad enough to mean better living in all ways; and not till such knowledge is the property of all women can we look for the 'emancipation' from some of the deepest evils that curse the life of woman in the slums and out" (*The Problem of the Poor*, p. 229).

In 1879 and 1880 Campbell wrote a series of twelve dramatic articles titled "Studies in the Slums" for *Sunday Afternoon* and *Lippincott's* magazines; in 1882 an expanded version of the articles was published as *The Problem of the Poor*. The book used dialogue and vivid details to describe Campbell's personal exploration of the slums and the difficult lives of the poor women she met. Three final chapters suggested specific social and economic reforms, as well as applications of home economics to slum women's problems. She continued to write investigative articles and books about slum conditions for the rest of the decade. Her novel, *Mrs. Herndon's Income* (1886), addressed many of the same subjects covered in *The Problem of the Poor*. That same year she began "Prisoners of Poverty," a 21-part series for the *New York Tribune* that dealt compellingly with women's tenement life. She focused on garment industry sweatshop workers and salesgirls, combining poignant individual stories with detailed economic and demographic data. Campbell's proposed solutions to poverty began to be more radical, drawing on socialist ideas and strongly arguing that middle-class women must cease exploiting the cheap labor of poor women. These articles were published in book form under the same title in 1889.

Two years later Campbell wrote one of the three studies of New York slum life that formed a book titled *Darkness and Daylight* (1891). The editor's introduction captured something of Campbell's personal knowledge of and emotional involvement with her subjects: "Her interest in missions and her labors among the lower classes have brought her face to face with squalor and misery among the hopelessly poor, as well as with degraded men and women in their own homes; while her ready sympathy gained for her access to their hearts, and thus gave her a practical insight into their daily life possessed by few." Campbell published two related works on poor women: *Prisoners of Poverty Abroad* (1889) reported on the working women she had encountered during an eighteen-month-long trip to England, France, Italy, and Germany; *Women Wage-Earners* (1893), a survey of the state of women workers in America and Europe, won an award from the American Economic Association. It carried an introduction by a prominent economist, Richard T. Ely, with whom Campbell had studied. Ely arranged for Campbell to teach home economics at the University of Wisconsin in the spring of 1895 and also aided in her appointment as professor of home economics at Kansas State Agricultural College in 1897.

Before moving to Wisconsin Campbell had settled in 1894 in San Francisco, where she began to work with one of the country's premier women's rights advocates, Charlotte Perkins Gilman. In 1894 the two women, who were living together, became coeditors of the *Impress*, the official journal of the Women's Press Association. Under their editorship the publication became increasingly activist, advocating Populist and socialist reforms. Campbell's responsibilities included writing a weekly column in which she further developed her ideas on home economics. She also was a prolific magazine writer in the 1890s. She continued to address the issues of slum life and slum labor, particularly as they affected women, in magazines such as *Worthington's Illustrated, Kate Field's Washington*, and *Land of Sunshine*. Her most frequent and significant articles appeared in the *Arena*, the key reform periodical of the period. By this time Campbell was well known as a lecturer, and she continued the extensive speaking schedule that had begun two decades earlier.

Having resigned from her University of Kansas position in March 1898 in part because of ill health, Campbell was much less productive for the rest of her life. She continued to lecture and produce magazine articles but in far smaller numbers. She did, however, begin writing for a new magazine, the *Nationalist*, the official publication of the Nationalist movement. Campbell had earlier joined the First Nationalist Club of Boston, founded by followers of Edward Bellamy's utopian socialism.

Campbell lived on and off with Charlotte Perkins Gilman in New York City from around 1900 until she moved to the Boston area in 1912. She died in Dedham, Massachusetts.

Heavily involved in the home economics movement almost from its beginnings, Campbell made substantial contributions to it. From the early 1880s on, that movement can be traced through much of her speaking and writing, especially her journalism, which addressed the social and economic ills of the poor at a critical moment. When the articles that were to become *The Problem of the Poor* were first published, urban tenement life had seldom been seriously examined in American magazines and newspapers. The subject did not begin to receive sustained attention until the late 1880s and 1890s and, even then, few writers focused on women's problems to the extent that Campbell did. She was able to utilize her novelist's skills to depict poor women's lives in ways that helped readers see them vividly and sympathetically. Campbell was not a gifted or subtle writer, and she was much better at showing the human cost of social problems than at carefully analyzing the reasons for such problems. Still, historians note that her work played a role in the formation of consumers' leagues, in the passage of legislation protecting children and other factory laborers, and in housing reform. And there is no doubt that her publications and speeches succeeded in touching the consciences of many middle-class Americans.

• Campbell's life is described briefly in Frances E. Willard and Mary A. Livermore, eds., *A Woman of the Century*, vol. 1 (1893), and in *The National Cyclopaedia of American Biography* (vol. 9, 1907). Her journalism is studied in Susan Henry, "Reporting Deeply and at First Hand: Helen Campbell in the 19th-Century Slums," *Journalism History* 11 (1984): 18–25. See also Frank Luther Mott, *A History of American Magazines* (vols. 3 and 4, 1938–1957), and a book by Campbell's editor at the *Arena*, B. O. Flower, *Progressive Men, Women, and Movements of the Past Twenty-Five Years* (1914), which also describes Campbell as a person. Her writings and lectures are mentioned in a reform context in Elizabeth Faulkner Baker, *Protective Labor Legislation, With Special Reference to Women in the State of New York* (1925); Robert H. Bremner, *From the Depths: The Discovery of Poverty in the United States* (1964); Susan Estabrook Kennedy, *If All We Did Was Weep at Home: A History of White Working-Class Women in America* (1979); Arthur Mann, *Yankee Reformers in the Urban Age* (1954); Annie Nathan Meyer, ed., *Women's Work in America* (1891); and Walter Fuller Taylor, *The Economic Novel in America* (1942).

Her long association with Charlotte Perkins Gilman is in Mary A. Hill, *Charlotte Perkins Gilman: The Making of a Feminist, 1860–1896* (1980), and Charlotte Perkins Gilman, *The Living of Charlotte Perkins Gilman: An Autobiography* (1935). For her home economics activities, see Mary J. Lincoln, "The Pioneers of Scientific Cookery," *Good Housekeeping*, Oct. 1910; Julie A. Mathaei, *An Economic History of Women in America* (1982); Mary I. Wood, *The History of the General Federation of Women's Clubs* (1912); and Laura Shapiro, *Perfection Salad* (1986). An obituary appears in the *Boston Evening Transcript*, 23 July 1918.

SUSAN HENRY

CAMPBELL, James (1 Sept. 1812–27 Jan. 1893), jurist and U.S. postmaster general, was born in the Southwark section of Philadelphia, Pennsylvania, the son of Anthony Campbell, an affluent shopkeeper, and Catherine McGarvey. James, an Irish-Catholic by birth and upbringing, was educated privately, studied law in the Philadelphia law offices of Edward D. Ingraham, and was admitted to the Pennsylvania bar on 14 September 1833. He then opened a legal practice that grew rapidly and brought him increasing prominence. As a result, he was appointed to various local political positions and gradually emerged as the spokesman for Philadelphia's Catholics.

Ethnic and religious factors were often decisive in Philadelphia's politics in that era, and Campbell skillfully welded Catholic voters into a solid bloc, becoming one of Philadelphia's most influential politicians. Given the Whig flirtation with nativism in the period, Campbell regularly delivered the Catholic vote to the Democratic party. Consequently, when a vacancy arose on the Philadelphia Court of Common Pleas, Democratic governor David R. Porter, in 1842, appointed Campbell. Campbell continued his political activities throughout the decade and was an important element in Democratic triumphs in both city and statewide contests. In 1845 he married Emilie S. Chapron; they had two children.

In 1850 Pennsylvania amended its constitution to provide for the popular election of judges, and the Democratic party nominated Campbell as one of five candidates for the state supreme court. All of the Democrats won handily except Campbell, who was defeated by Whig Richard Coulter. His defeat was generally attributed to his religion, and Campbell and other Catholics were outraged. Campbell drew some solace, however, from the victory in the gubernatorial contest of Democrat William Bigler, whom he had supported vigorously over incumbent governor William F. Johnston, who had enjoyed nativist support. In gratitude, and in an effort to placate angry Catholic voters, Bigler named Campbell his attorney general.

Party politics in both the state and nation in these years was intensely factional, and within the Democratic party Campbell was a James Buchanan loyalist. By 1850 Buchanan was an acknowledged leader of his party, and his name had been placed before two Democratic presidential nominating conventions. In 1852 he made his most determined bid for the nomination, an effort to which Campbell gave unstinted support. When Buchanan's cause became hopeless, however, Campbell backed Franklin Pierce, who obtained the nomination on the forty-ninth ballot. He subsequently stumped Pennsylvania for Pierce, defending him against Whig-inspired charges that he was anti-Catholic. Pierce won the election, carrying both Philadelphia and the state, and named Campbell postmaster general on Buchanan's recommendation.

The post office department, when Campbell assumed its leadership, was a sprawling and inefficient enterprise with nearly 25,000 employees and with offices in virtually every hamlet in the United States. It routinely operated at a loss, relying on annual congressional subsidies of approximately $2 million, and had long since been politicized.

To his new responsibilities, Campbell brought a strong sense of purpose, determination, a methodical efficiency, a capacity for hard work, and a reputation for integrity. All are reflected vividly in his annual reports to Congress. He was, however, neither a charismatic leader nor a particularly social person. Dignified and somewhat retiring, he shunned Washington's social whirl for the support and companionship of his family.

Campbell was determined that his department would be both efficient and self-supporting. To those ends, he terminated ineffectual postmasters, discontinued excessively expensive mail routes, fined delinquent contractors, and overhauled the department's accounting system. To Congress, Campbell proposed rate increases, the discontinuance of congressionally mandated discounts, and even the abolition of the franking privilege. He appeared indifferent to the fact that these initiatives offended powerful interests.

Among Campbell's innovations were the introduction of prestamped envelopes, perforated sheets of stamps to replace printed sheets, and the registry system for the shipment of valuables through the mails. The registry system, which held the individual postmaster responsible for any valuables handled, was a significant innovation that, in its essentials, has survived to the present.

Under Campbell's direction, postal service improved and expanded, but the department did not become self-supporting. Those affected by his cost-cutting measures resisted them, and Congress declined to enact the measures proposed. To his keen disappointment, annual subsidies continued throughout his tenure.

A matter of immense importance to Campbell and to Pierce was the distribution of patronage through the appointment of postmasters and other personnel. Campbell made 24,288 appointments, the most sweeping realignment in the department's history. While he rewarded his Catholic followers and rigorously excluded nativists, his constant goal was to build a national organization committed to the reelection of Pierce. Despite his efforts, however, the Democrats in 1856 rejected Pierce for Buchanan, who was subsequently elected.

In Buchanan's administration, understandably, there was no place for ex-Pierce men, and for Campbell the political wars were over. He returned to Philadelphia and resumed his law practice. Except for a failed bid for a U.S. Senate seat in 1863, he never sought public office again. A respected elder statesman but increasingly a political anachronism, Campbell died in Philadelphia. Although not a politician of the first rank, he helped shape events in a tumultuous era and served creditably in national office.

• There is no known collection of Campbell's papers. Letters from Campbell can be found in the James Buchanan Papers and the William Bigler Papers, both in the Historical Society of Pennsylvania, in the Franklin Pierce Papers and the Jeremiah S. Black Papers, both in the Library of Congress, in the Franklin Pierce Papers in the New Hampshire Historical Society, and, less frequently, in the papers of his most prominent contemporaries. His four annual reports (1853–1856) as postmaster general are in *U.S. Senate Executive Documents*, for the pertinent sessions of Congress. Campbell's son's evaluation of his father is John M. Campbell, "Biographical sketch of Hon. James Campbell," *Records of the American Catholic Historical Society of Philadelphia* 5 (1894): 265–303. A more scholarly assessment is John F. Coleman, "The Public Career of James Campbell," *Pennsylvania History* 29 (1962): 24–39.

JOHN F. COLEMAN

CAMPBELL, James Edwin (28 Sept. 1867–26 Jan. 1896), African-American poet and educator, was born in Pomeroy, Ohio, the son of James Campbell, a laborer, and Lethia Stark. He graduated from the Pomeroy Academy, having completed the course in Latin and German, in 1884. Entering teaching, Campbell spent the next two years in schools near Gallipolis, Ohio, and also in Rutland, Ohio, where he was offered a position as principal of the white schools, an offer he declined.

In 1886 Campbell briefly left teaching to edit the *Pioneer*, a newspaper published in Charleston, West Virginia, and, subsequently, the *West Virginia Enterprise*, also published in Kanawha County. Neither was to last, however, and within a short time Campbell returned to Pomeroy, where he involved himself heavily in politics. A notable public speaker who had made his debut shortly after his graduation from high school, Campbell took to the stump in 1887 on behalf of the Ohio Republican party, and, during the 1888 election, he spoke in both Ohio and West Virginia. In 1890 he served as a delegate and secretary to the Meigs County, Ohio, Republican convention and as a delegate to the party's convention for the Twelfth Ohio Congressional District.

Campbell's early years were also notable for the beginning of his poetic career. He had begun to write poetry while in school. Subsequently his work appeared in newspapers and periodicals as well as in his first volume, *Driftings and Gleanings,* published in Charleston in 1887. Campbell's verses from this time were modeled on typical Victorian popular poetry and dealt with common themes of love and nature as well as classical topics. Unlike most of his African-American contemporaries, Campbell at first wrote little on racial themes, although he was among the first African-American poets to focus on the inflammatory issue of interracial love, notably in "The Pariah's Love," a lengthy poem appearing in the April 1889 *A.M.E. Church Review*.

In 1890 Campbell returned to his work as an educator, becoming principal of the Langston School in Point Pleasant, West Virginia, on the Ohio River. A short time later, in August 1891, he married Mary E. Champ, herself a teacher at Wilberforce College. Then, in 1892, he became principal of the newly founded West Virginia Colored Institute, later to become West Virginia State University, in Charleston. Adding to his fame as a speaker, Campbell used his position to spread ideas of discipline and uplift throughout the state's black communities while attempting to attract students to the school. He also became active in the West Virginia Teachers' Association and was elected its president in 1893.

In 1894 Campbell's career at the institute and as an educator came to an end as, after some administrative controversy, he was forced to resign as principal. Moving to Chicago the following year, he returned to journalism, joining the literary staff of the *Chicago Times-Herald* and writing for other newspapers and periodicals.

It was during this time that Campbell made his most important contribution as a poet, through his innovative work in African-American dialect. Dialect poetry, when Campbell came to it, was problematic, having close ties to the "plantation tradition" writing of the late nineteenth century—a tradition developed by white writers that glorified the Old South and entrenched dominant racial stereotypes. Nevertheless, dialect poetry began to attract African-American practitioners and became by the end of the century a major form among black poets. When Campbell began to write dialect poetry in the late 1880s, he was one of the first African-American poets to do so. He published his major collection of such works in a book entitled *Echoes from the Cabin and Elsewhere* (1895).

The significance of Campbell's poetry grew out of its faithfulness to folk rather than to literary sources. While most African-American dialect writers avoided the excesses of the plantation tradition, they remained fairly close to that tradition's generally idyllic focus on antebellum life and, especially, to its language, using a version of dialect that suggested more than it represented black folk speech. In his language, in particular, Campbell moved further than most from the conventions of the form, his version of dialect more closely representing, grammatically and phonetically, actual speech. To be sure, like most other African-American dialect poets, Campbell evoked quaint themes and took comfort in a belief that African Americans were quickly casting off the speech and customs his poetry portrayed. Nevertheless, although his own fame was quickly eclipsed by the phenomenal success of the most noted black writer in the form, Paul Laurence Dunbar—a man he knew and liked—Campbell was one of the first American poets to try to capture and to give poetic shape to a vision of African-American folk life and society.

Campbell's career showed great promise during the last year of his life, but on a brief visit to his parents' home in Pomeroy during the 1895 Christmas season, he fell ill, initially manifesting symptoms of pneumonia, followed by typhoid symptoms and peritonitis. He died a few weeks later. Nevertheless, though his potential was to be unfulfilled, Campbell remains an important figure in the creation of an African-American literary tradition.

• The main sources for Campbell's life and work consist of brief sketches, including his obituary in the Pomeroy *Tribune-Telegraph,* 29 Jan. 1896; an account in the *Cleveland Gazette,* 24 Jan. 1891; and, the standard source, Carter G. Woodson, "James Edwin Campbell: A Forgotten Man of Letters," *Negro History Bulletin* 2, no. 2 (Nov. 1938): 11. The best recent discussions are in Joan Sherman, *Invisible Poets* (1989); Jean Wagner, *Black Poets of the United States* (1973); Eugene Redmond, *Drumvoices* (1976); and, especially useful, Lorenzo Thomas, "James Edwin Campbell," *Dictionary of Literary Biography*, vol. 50 (1986), pp. 32–36.

DICKSON D. BRUCE, JR.

CAMPBELL, James Hepburn (8 Feb. 1820–12 Apr. 1895), congressman, was born in Williamsport, Pennsylvania, the son of Francis C. Campbell, a lawyer, and Jane Hepburn. After graduating from the law department of Dickinson College, he established a legal practice at Pottsville, Pennsylvania, in the heart of Schuylkill County's coal-mining region. In 1843 he married Juliet Lewis, the daughter of Ellis Lewis, chief justice of the Pennsylvania Supreme Court, and herself a poet, whose published works were praised for their "purity of sentiment and diction" (Thomas B. Reed, *Female Poets of America* [1894], p. 217). They had five children, two of whom survived into adulthood.

A Whig by political preference, Campbell was a delegate to his party's 1844 convention and supported the nomination of his political idol, Henry Clay. In 1854 he was elected to Congress from the normally Democratic Eleventh District, consisting of Schuylkill and Northumberland counties. In return for his efforts on behalf of Nathaniel P. Banks in the bitter Speakership contest, he was appointed to the influential Ways and Means Committee, where he supported the industrial interests of his state by vigorous advocacy of the protective tariff.

Defeated for reelection in 1856, Campbell was returned to Congress as a Republican in 1858 and in 1860. He strongly opposed slavery expansion and President James Buchanan's Kansas policies, and he continued to promote higher tariffs. "Let our motto," he urged the House on 24 April 1860, "be *protection to everything American, against everything foreign*." The following year he was active in support of the Morrill tariff.

During the turbulent months following the election of Abraham Lincoln and the first stirrings of secession, Campbell stood firm for the Union and against proposed concessions to the slave interest, such as the Crittenden Compromise. The inauguration of Lincoln, he insisted, must proceed "without terms, without negotiations, without compromise, and without apology" (Speech to House of Representatives, 14 Feb. 1861). Appointed as Pennsylvania's representative to the House Special Committee of Thirty-three, he continued to resist all but the most modest measures of sectional conciliation, defiantly declaring that his state would uphold the Union "to the last of her sons and her treasure."

True to his word, Campbell dashed to the defense of Washington as soon as he learned of the commencement of hostilities at Fort Sumter. With prosecessionist mobs out of control in Maryland, the beleaguered capital was virtually cut off from the rest of the nation. Campbell's train was the last to pass safely through Baltimore, and from its windows he could see scenes of devastation that left his "blood on fire" with patriotic indignation. He immediately enlisted in Cassius Marcellus Clay's band of superannuated volunteers and for five sleepless nights patrolled the otherwise defenseless public buildings until relieved by Federal soldiers. On 1 May 1861 Campbell was elected major of the Twenty-fifth Pennsylvania Volunteer Infantry, a three-month regiment drawn mainly from his Schuylkill County constituents. Assigned primarily to garrison duty at the Washington Arsenal and at Fort Washington on the Potomac, it also participated in a bloodless sortie into Maryland.

Upon the expiration of his regiment's term of enlistment, Campbell returned to his congressional seat on a full-time basis. Disgruntled at what he considered to be inferior committee assignments from House Speaker Galusha Grow, a Pennsylvania rival, Campbell at first rejected all committee service, but later in the session he was persuaded to take charge of the Select Committee on the Pacific Railroad. The bill he introduced—providing federal aid for the building of a line through Nebraska, Wyoming, Utah, Nevada, and California—became, with some modifications, the basis on which the first transcontinental railroad link was constructed.

A vigorous supporter of all measures to support the war effort, including conscription, Campbell incurred the hostility of elements in his district, where opposition to the draft had erupted into riots. Defeated for reelection in 1862, he was offered a diplomatic mission by the administration as a reward for his loyal support. He declined Lincoln's initial offer of judge on the Court for the Suppression of the Slave Trade, which sat in Cape Town, South Africa, but he accepted an appointment as minister to Sweden and Norway.

Before he could assume his diplomatic duties, Campbell served a final brief stint as a soldier. To help meet Confederate general Robert E. Lee's invasion of the North, Pennsylvania governor Andrew Curtin called for an emergency muster of volunteers. Campbell helped recruit the Thirty-ninth Pennsylvania Volunteer Militia Regiment and was commissioned lieutenant colonel on 4 July 1863. The regiment did little other than to participate in the futile chase of Lee's retreating troops after the battle of Gettysburg and was mustered out of service on 2 August 1863.

Campbell's diplomatic mission to Scandinavia passed without incident and was terminated in November 1867. Declining President Andrew Johnson's offer of an assignment to Colombia because of political differences with the administration, Campbell retired from public life to devote himself to his Philadelphia legal practice and his country estate, "Aeola," near Wayne, Pennsylvania, where he died after a lengthy, useful career that touched upon, though did not shape, the main currents of his time.

• Campbell's Civil War letters to his wife, comprising a detailed, day-by-day description of his activities, are at the Clements Library of the University of Michigan. Selected excerpts from this correspondence are printed in Allan Peskin, ed., "Two White House Visits," *Lincoln Herald* 94 (Winter 1992): 157–58, and "Lee Has Escaped!" *Pennsylvania History* 61 (Jan. 1994): 102–11. A smaller collection of papers is at the Pennsylvania Historical Society. For a contemporary sketch of his career, see Charles Robson, ed., *The Biographical Encyclopedia of Pennsylvania in the Nineteenth Century* (1874). A lengthy obituary is in the *Philadelphia Inquirer*, 13 Apr. 1895.

ALLAN PESKIN

CAMPBELL, John (1653–4 Mar. 1728), journalist, evidently born in Scotland, was probably the son of Duncan Campbell, the postmaster of Boston. His mother's identity is unknown. In 1702 John Campbell succeeded the deceased Duncan Campbell and became, with the approval of Governor Joseph Dudley, postmaster of Boston. As postmaster, Campbell was commissioned by the Massachusetts General Court not only to deliver the handwritten "public letters" but also to circulate maritime and mercantile information and political news (mostly from Europe) to other postmasters and to regional leaders. Following the model of the English newspaper press, especially the *London Gazette*, Campbell began, on 24 April 1704, to print the *Boston News-Letter*. Printed every Monday, the *News-Letter* was timed to take advantage of the arrival of the weekly post and was mailed with Campbell's franking privileges.

Campbell produced the *Boston News-Letter* as an effort, in the phrase of Arthur Schlesinger, to "improve and commercialize" the flow of public, if mostly maritime, information. The news published in the *News-Letter* was aimed principally at the economic, political, and social elite of Massachusetts. As the economy was so dependent on the sea, the news, primarily in the form of accounts simply lifted from the London papers and reprinted, featured European wars and alliances, piracy, poor weather, the movement of ships more generally, events in the Caribbean, domestic events, and market conditions in London. Comparatively little news came from the American colonies.

The *News-Letter* was a printed half-sheet (about 12″ by 8″ with two columns on each page) that followed closely the physical appearance (including the organization of the content) of the *London Gazette*. Though not the first attempt to produce a newspaper (Benjamin Harris's *Publick Occurrences* appeared briefly in Boston as a broadsheet before being suppressed in 1690), Campbell's enterprise was to become the first successful newspaper in North America. Campbell noted that his newspaper was "published by authority," and he was careful not to give offense to his governmental patrons. Nevertheless, through the *News-Letter*, he transformed what was essentially private correspondence into a public activity of gathering and disseminating the news to whoever wanted to pay for it. In so doing, he created the institution of the newspaper in North America. The *News-Letter*, surviving until 1776, focused initially, to be sure, on events in London and the other European capitals, but it was firmly fixed as well on providing useful information to those who had no other ready source of such information.

While not an "official" publication, Campbell's *News-Letter* appears to have been published with the approbation of the royal governor and seems to have served official needs on occasion by publishing proclamations and official notices, even publishing stories that reflected an official point of view, such as publicizing punishment of a drover who did not keep the Sabbath. The General Court often did not reimburse Campbell fully for publishing official notices, and on at least one occasion in 1722 (when he was no longer postmaster but still publishing the *News-Letter*) it refused to reimburse him at all. The *News-Letter* was first printed (until 1707) by Bartholomew Green, who used pica types; the publisher for the first few issues was Nicholas Boone, until Campbell later included his own name in the notice at the end of each issue.

The *News-Letter* was not well written. It was published weekly, and accounts of political developments in Europe were reprinted generally in chronological order, in order to provide a "thread of occurrences." Some maritime news from the colonial American ports and a few brief local items were also included. There was little advertising (often no more than one or two advertisements per issue in the early years), though the use of blank pages (or at least blocks of blank space) allowed readers space for writing their own letters. Initially the *News-Letter* was two printed pages but soon (by 1705) expanded to four before reverting by 1707 back to two.

The *News-Letter* remained two pages until 1719, when Campbell sought to make his "thread of occurrences" more current by producing both supplements and four-page numbers. As Campbell himself observed in a notice in the issue of 10 August 1719, "It was impossible with half a Sheet a Week to carry on all the Public Occurrences of Europe, with those of this, our Neighboring Provinces, and the West Indies." The expanded editions continued well into 1720; soon after, his newspaper resumed its two-page appearance. It was a constant struggle for Campbell to find sufficient subscribers (he complained in 1719 that he could not find 300 subscribers, compared to the "thousands" who read English newspapers).

Green was succeeded as printer of the *News-Letter* by John Allen, who published it for four years, from 10 November 1707 through 1 October 1711; Campbell's post office and Allen's printing shop were then consumed in the great fire of 2 October 1711. With the following issue, Bartholomew Green resumed printing the newspaper, adding his name as printer to the imprint in 1715.

In 1718 Campbell was replaced as postmaster (thereby losing considerable advantage of using the mails to circulate his newspaper free of postage), and his successor as postmaster, William Brooker, started a rival newspaper, the *Boston Gazette*, which was printed by James Franklin. Brooker's tenure as postmaster was brief, and when he was replaced by Philip Musgrave, the printing of the *Boston Gazette* went to Samuel Kneeland, nephew of Bartholomew Green. Soon thereafter, in 1720, Campbell printed the *News-Letter* on half a sheet, advising his customers to use the other half for their own correspondence, thereby saving money by combining the newspaper and the letter for only one postage charge. In this way, Campbell sought to minimize the competitive edge that he had lost when he was removed as postmaster. The appearance of the *Gazette* precipitated the first journalistic controversy in British North America when Brooker attacked Campbell and his newspaper for being unresponsive to the needs of its readers. If readers were pardonably bored with its details, the controversy nonetheless heralded a new age of journalism in the colonies.

In 1721 a third newspaper, the *New England Courant*, was started in Boston by James Franklin, who promptly criticized Campbell's newspaper for its dullness. Campbell was quick to respond and waged battle with Franklin for the duration of his tenure as publisher of the *News-Letter*. Indeed, Campbell supported Cotton Mather against Franklin in the smallpox inoculation controversy of 1721, briefly publishing a full sheet weekly before reducing it back to a half sheet, like the *Gazette* and the *Courant*. By the end of 1722, Campbell had turned the *News-Letter* over to Bartholomew Green, who had remained as its printer since resuming that activity in 1711.

Campbell held a number of civic positions, including justice of the peace. He was married twice, perhaps three times, and his surviving spouse was Mary Clarke Pemberton. He appears to have died in Boston.

Campbell deserves historical attention as publisher of the first successful newspaper in the British North American colonies, however marginal its financial standing. Campbell's initiative was quickly imitated, and within a generation New England was home to a number of newspapers.

• The recent work of Charles E. Clark has broadened understanding of the advent of newspapers in British North America and provides the broad context for Campbell's career and achievement. Clark, "The Newspapers of Provincial America," in the American Antiquarian Society, *Proceedings*, vol. 100 (1991), pp. 367–89, is an excellent and compact summary that blends the broadest developments with recent historiography, while his more recent *The Public Prints: The Newspaper in Anglo-American Culture, 1665–1740* (1994) provides a wider political and cultural context in which to set Campbell's pathbreaking activity. Information about Campbell may be gleaned from a variety of sources, including Clarence S. Brigham, *History and Bibliography of American Newspapers, 1690–1820* (2 vols., 1947); Isaiah Thomas, *The History of Printing in America*, repr. ed. (1970); Joseph T. Buckingham, *Specimens of Newspaper Literature* (1850); and John T. Winterich, *Early American Books and Printing*, repr. ed. (1974). A source of conveniently compiled information is Benjamin Franklin V, ed., *Boston Printers, Publishers, and Booksellers, 1640–1800* (1980).

WILLIAM L. JOYCE

CAMPBELL, John Allen (8 Oct. 1835–14 July 1880), Wyoming's first territorial governor, was born in Salem, Columbiana County, Ohio. Little is known about Campbell's parents. After attending public schools, he entered the newspaper profession, and by the beginning of the Civil War he was an editorial writer for the *Cleveland Leader*. In April 1861 he enlisted in the Union army as a private. He quickly earned a promotion to first lieutenant and then major. In November 1862 he became adjutant general on the staff of Major General John Schofield, with whom he remained until the end of the war. Campbell participated in engagements at Rich Mountain, Shiloh, Perryville, and Stones River as well as most of the actions during the Atlanta campaign in 1864. That same year he was breveted brigadier general.

After the war Campbell remained on the staff of Schofield, who was in command of the Fifth Military District, which comprised the state of Virginia. From May 1868 to March 1869 Campbell served as assistant secretary of war. Through this service he came to the attention of President Ulysses Grant, who, on 3 April 1869, appointed Campbell, a loyal Republican, as the first governor of the territory of Wyoming. The Senate confirmed Campbell four days later. He took the oath of office on 15 April and left for the territory, which had been in existence for less than one year. Arriving in Cheyenne a month later, Campbell organized the territorial government, designating Cheyenne as the temporary capital. The governor also authorized the taking of a census. On 3 August 1869 Campbell issued a proclamation that called for an election to be held on 2 September of members of the first territorial legislature.

The first legislature met from October to December 1869. This session passed laws regulating mining and protecting miners, selected Laramie as the site for the penitentiary, legalized gambling, and adopted a general property tax law, but its most noted piece of legislation granted women the right to vote and hold office, the first such law in the nation. The representative from South Pass City, William Bright, president of the territorial council, introduced the suffrage bill late in the first session. The all-Democratic legislature passed the bill and sent it to the governor's office on 6 December. Campbell, although not a supporter of woman suffrage, reluctantly signed the bill on 10 December 1869. His diary entry for that day simply stated, "Signed Woman Suffrage Bill." Two years later he explained, "I approved the bill giving suffrage to woman without looking favorably upon it, owing to my early prejudices."

The legislature passed the suffrage bill for a number of reasons. Some expected the new law to advertise the territory and attract more settlers, especially women, to the new and sparsely populated territory. Still others claimed it was an attempt to embarrass the Republican governor by forcing him to face such a sensitive issue early during his administration. Others said the bill was regarded as a joke by many of the legislators, who clearly expected the governor to veto it. Finally, some legislators did exhibit a genuine concern for the rights of women. The same legislature passed laws, signed by Campbell, that protected the property of married women and stipulated that all teachers were to be paid equally, regardless of gender.

Wyoming felt the effects of the new suffrage law almost immediately. Early in 1870 Esther Morris took the office of justice of the peace at South Pass City and became the first woman in the nation to hold such a position. That same year women served on juries in Laramie and the following year in Cheyenne. This experiment ended, however, in 1871. Also in 1871 the Democrats in the legislature, no longer maintaining a monopoly and believing that most women voted for Republicans, passed a bill repealing suffrage. Campbell vetoed the bill. By then much more of a suffrage supporter, Campbell stated in his veto message, "For the first time in the history of our country we have a government to which the noble words of our Magna Charter of freedom may be applied, not as a mere figure of speech, but as expressing a simple truth, for it is a government which derives all just powers from the consent of the governed." The house overwhelmingly overrode his veto, but the council failed by one vote in its attempt to override.

During most of Campbell's years as governor, the Wyoming Republican party was split into two factions, one led by Campbell and the other by Herman Glafcke, the secretary of the territory. Campbell's inept efforts to remove his opponents from offices and his failure to ensure that Republicans were elected to the legislature and Congress contributed to this infighting. Campbell was able to get legislation passed that formed a territorial militia and created a commissioner of immigration, whose job it was to publicize the attractions of Wyoming, but the Republican squabbling prevented some federal assistance from benefiting the new territory.

During his third year in office, Campbell married in 1872 Isabella Crane Wunderly. President Grant appointed Campbell to a second term as Wyoming's governor in 1873. Campbell took the oath of office on 7 April 1873, only one week before the birth of his only child. He resigned as governor in February 1875, after almost six years in office, and accepted Grant's appointment as third assistant secretary of state under Secretary Hamilton Fish. The U.S. Senate confirmed him on 24 February. In December 1877, because of failing health, Campbell accepted an appointment as American consul at Basel, Switzerland, hoping the change of climate would restore his health. The climate proved too severe, however, and early in 1880 he returned to Washington, D.C., where he died several months later.

On 13 February 1911 Wyoming's state legislature honored Governor Campbell by creating Campbell County in northern Wyoming. Campbell's real importance, however, is his role in the passage of the nation's first woman suffrage law. In 1889 Wyoming's constitutional convention included a suffrage provision in the aspiring state's constitution. When it joined the Union on 10 July 1890, Wyoming became the first state to grant women the right to vote and hold office. Wyoming became known as "the Equality State," a legacy to which Campbell contributed.

• Campbell's gubernatorial papers and his personal diary for the years 1869 to 1875 are in the Wyoming State Archives, Cheyenne. Portions of his diary were printed in Nina Moran, ed., "Diary: John A. Campbell, 1869–1875," *Annals of Wyoming* 10 (1938): 5–11, 59–78, 120–43, 155–85. See also Harry B. Henderson, Sr., "Wyoming Territorial Governors," *Annals of Wyoming* 11 (1939): 237–53; Lewis L. Gould, *Wyoming: A Political History, 1868–1896* (1968); Marie H. Erwin, *Wyoming Historical Blue Book* (1946); and T. A. Larson, *History of Wyoming*, 2d ed. (1978). For examinations of the passage of Wyoming's suffrage law in 1869 see Michael A. Massie, "Reform Is Where You Find It: The Roots of Woman Suffrage in Wyoming," *Annals of Wyoming* 62 (1990): 2–22; and Sidney Howell Fleming, "Solving the Jigsaw Puzzle: One Suffrage Story at a Time," *Annals of Wyoming* 62 (1990): 23–72. See also Larson, "Petticoats at the Polls: Woman Suffrage in Territorial Wyoming," *Pacific Northwest Quarterly* 44 (1953): 74–78; Miriam Gantz Chapman, "The Story of Woman Suffrage in Wyoming, 1869–1890" (master's thesis, Univ. of Wyoming, 1952); and Beverly Benton, "Woman Suffrage in the American West: 1869–1896" (Ph.D. diss., Univ. of Utah, 1976). An obituary is in the *Cheyenne Daily Sun*, 15 July 1880.

RICK EWIG

CAMPBELL, John Archibald (24 June 1811–12 Mar. 1889), associate justice of the U.S. Supreme Court, was born in Washington, Georgia, the son of Duncan Green Campbell, a lawyer and state legislator, and Mary Williamson. Young John, a product of his parents' money and influence, enrolled at the University of Georgia, then Franklin College, at the age of eleven. He graduated with honors in 1825 and was appointed to a cadetship in the U.S. Military Academy at West Point. Duncan Green Campbell died the day before he was widely expected to be elected governor of Georgia in 1828, and John resigned from West Point to teach in Florida for a year to help pay off his father's financial responsibilities. He returned to Georgia, studied law, and was admitted to the bar in 1829.

Campbell moved to Montgomery in 1830, was admitted to the Alabama state bar, and began to practice law. That same year he married Anna Esther Goldthwaite. They had five children. In 1836 he was elected as a Democrat to the state legislature and moved to Mobile the following year. While in Mobile Campbell argued high profile cases before the state supreme court, federal courts, and the U.S. Supreme Court, where in a much celebrated inheritance case involving a two-decade long court battle between a daughter and her father's estate, *Gaines v. Relf* (1852), he was opposed by Daniel Webster. Twice he turned down nominations by the governor to sit on the Alabama Supreme Court. In 1850 he was a delegate to the Convention of the Southern States held at Nashville, Tennessee, where he introduced the resolutions articulating the position of the people of the southern states with regard to slavery.

In 1852 Justice John McKinley of the U.S. Supreme Court died. President Millard Fillmore was unable to gain Senate confirmation for his nominee, North Carolina senator George E. Badger, and the seat remained unfilled as the new president, Franklin Pierce, took office the following year. In what was then a highly unusual move, Justices James Catron and Benjamin Robbins Curtis wrote letters of recommendation urging the new president to nominate Campbell for the vacant seat. Pierce agreed and the Senate confirmed Campbell's nomination on 25 March 1853. He joined a Court led by the 73-year-old chief justice Roger B. Taney. Campbell undertook a strict constructionist philosophy of judicial review during his years on the Court and became known as a dissenter. In *Dodge v. Woolsey* (1856) his dissent argued that state legislatures, not the federal government, should have jurisdiction over state-chartered corporations. In *Dred Scott v. Sandford* (1857) he voted in conference against hearing the case but was outvoted. Once the case was argued, he sided with the majority led by Chief Justice Taney in overturning the Missouri Compromise, declaring that blacks could not be citizens of the United States and that slaves were property protected by the Constitution. Campbell had owned household slaves but emancipated them upon his appointment to the Supreme Court. (Since Alabama did not allow private manumission within the state, Campbell was made guardian of his freed slaves.) While riding circuit, he upheld statutes prohibiting the slave trade. He believed that slavery should not cause the dissolution of the union, that it was a transitory institution that would be changed in time, and that it had been receding to the South and Southwest since the adoption of the Constitution. He did believe, though, that slavery, as well as secession, was an issue for the states to decide. In 1860 he was mentioned as a possible compromise candidate for president of the United States, as palatable to Democrats of both the North and South. On 11 January 1861 Alabama seceded. Campbell was a steadfast believer in states' rights, and though personally opposed to secession and the war, he felt it his duty to resign from the Court and join his home state of Alabama in the Confederate cause. He resigned on 26 April 1861.

In October 1862 Campbell agreed to become assistant secretary of war for the Confederate States of America, a post he took because he believed he might have some influence in promoting peace. The post was basically a legal, administrative position, and Campbell had nothing to do with military operations or the conduct of the war. He attempted to resign a year later but was persuaded to stay. Campbell was part of a commission that met with President Abraham Lincoln to try and avert war. He finally resigned upon the Confederate evacuation of Richmond in April 1865. He knew the war was nearly over and again met with Lincoln, in February 1865, to discuss peace. Days later, General Robert E. Lee surrendered and the president was assassinated. Campbell was arrested and imprisoned in May 1865 as many in Washington believed that he had suggested, in the recent peace talks with Lincoln, that the Virginia legislature reconvene. He had in fact discussed reconvening the legislature with Lincoln, but only in so far as it would cooperate in ending the war and submit to national authority. Campbell did not desire an independent "rebel" legislature as his detractors claimed. In August, Justices Benjamin Robbins Curtis and Samuel Nelson wrote President Andrew Johnson lobbying for Campbell's release. Soon thereafter, the president acceded. Campbell, whose Mobile, Alabama, property was destroyed, went to New Orleans to practice law, never to return to public office again.

Campbell's private practice flourished, and he soon found himself arguing cases before his former brethren at the U.S. Supreme Court. In December 1872 in the *Slaughterhouse Cases* Campbell represented before the Court a New Orleans butchers' association of more than 1,000 workers who were prohibited from practicing their trade by a state law granting a monopoly to a small company. He argued that the newly ratified Fourteenth Amendment guaranteed persons economic liberty that states could not restrict. Campbell lost the 5–4 decision. His reasoning prevailed two decades later when the Court overturned similar state regulations on due process grounds. He continued to practice in New Orleans until his wife's death in 1884. At age seventy-three he retired from general practice and moved to Baltimore, Maryland. He still accepted retainers and continued to argue cases before the U.S. Supreme Court. He died at his residence in Baltimore.

Loyal to his home state and the South, Campbell was not unlike many men during the period surrounding the Civil War. His struggle for peace, however, set him apart. Campbell's view that personal liberties were, for the most part, best protected by the states, placed him on the losing end of many arguments throughout his career, hence his classification as a dissenter. Though he served on the U.S. Supreme Court, it is widely agreed that his best and most important work occurred while he was a practicing attorney during the postwar years and in those cases he argued before the Court.

• The initial biography is Henry G. Connor, *John Archibald Campbell* (1920; repr. 1971). A more recent account is Justine S. Mann, "The Political and Constitutional Thought of John Archibald Campbell" (master's thesis, Univ. of Alabama, 1966), which includes an extensive list of the various locations of Campbell's papers. For references to various letters, articles, and briefs written by Campbell, see Mann, "The Political Thought of John Archibald Campbell: The Formative Years, 1847–1851," *Alabama Law Review* 22 (Spring 1970): 275–302. On his departure from the Court, see Thad Holt, Jr., "The Resignation of Mr. Justice Campbell," *Alabama Law Review* 12 (1959): 105–18. The following cases can be found in *United States Reports: Gains v. Relf*, 12 How. 474 (1852); *Dred Scott v. Sandford*, 19 How. 60 U.S. 393 (1857); *Dodge v. Woolsey*, 18 How. 59 U.S. 331 (1856); *Slaughterhouse Cases*, 16 Wall. 83 U.S. 36 (1873). An obituary is in the *Baltimore Sun*, 13 Mar. 1889.

ARTEMUS E. WARD

CAMPBELL, John Wilson (23 Feb. 1782–24 Sept. 1833), Ohio congressman and judge, was born in Augusta County, Virginia, the son of William Campbell and Elizabeth Wilson, pioneer farmers. His parents, immigrants from northern Ireland, moved to Kentucky in about 1791. Disliking farm work, young Campbell left home and became an apprentice carpenter in Cincinnati, but this so distressed his mother that he returned home and later moved to southern Ohio with the family. He paid for his schooling by clearing land and teaching school, becoming an excellent Latin scholar, although he had no college education. After studying law in Morgantown, Virginia, with his uncle, Thomas Wilson, he was admitted to the Ohio bar in 1808 and took up practice in West Union. Appointed prosecuting attorney for Adams and Highland counties, he built a profitable practice dealing mainly with disputed land titles in Ohio's Virginia Military District, where he also acted as land agent for nonresident proprietors. In 1811 he married Eleanor W. Doak. They adopted one child.

In 1810 Campbell was elected to the Ohio Assembly, where he identified himself with the conservative Republican faction, which insisted on the legitimacy of judicial review and opposed the attempt of the Tammany Society to impose a dictatorial party discipline. After brief war service he ran unsuccessfully for Congress in 1812, winning a large majority in the two counties where he was known but failing in other parts of the still-scattered district. In 1813 and 1815 he was elected once more to the Ohio lower house; in December 1814 he ran a respectable third in a legislative election for the U.S. Senate. In 1816 he was at last elected a congressman and was reelected "by an almost unanimous vote" on four consecutive occasions (Campbell, pp. 4–5).

In Congress Campbell deprecated the "astonishing . . . jealousy" with which "Western interests are viewed by many" and supported demands for federal appropriations for internal improvements (*Old North-*

west Genealogical Quarterly 10: 261). At the same time he advocated cuts in official salaries, proposing in 1821 a 20 percent reduction in those of congressmen. Serving on several committees, he spoke frequently, concisely, and sensibly. In the 1824 presidential campaign he supported Henry Clay, but when the election was thrown into the House of Representatives he followed the preference of his district in voting for Andrew Jackson. In December the Jacksonians in the House ran him as their candidate for Speaker, but he attracted only forty-two of the ninety-seven votes needed for election. Later in the session he joined in the first attack on the John Quincy Adams administration in a speech opposing the new president's proposal to send U.S. delegates to the pan-American congress that was to be held in Panama.

Refusing to run again for Congress in 1826, Campbell retired to a farm in Brown County, but he continued to be regarded as a leading Jacksonian. In 1828 he hesitatingly accepted nomination as the party's gubernatorial candidate, only to be defeated because its vote was not fully mobilized in northern Ohio. In December 1828 the Jacksonian caucus unanimously nominated Campbell for the U.S. Senate, but he lost, 56–50, on a strict party vote. Finally, in 1829 President Jackson named him U.S. district judge for Ohio, and the Senate confirmed the appointment unanimously. As judge he suffered initially from his lack of recent practice, but he soon won praise for the "unbending integrity and good sense" of his decisions. In 1831 he was awarded an honorary D.C.L. by Augusta College and in the same year moved to Columbus, where he opposed the drift of the Jackson party toward "whole-hog" partyism and an excessively centralized discipline (Campbell, pp. 124–27).

Always studious in his habits—regularly rising at four in the morning to study—Campbell began preparing a biographical work on Ohio's early pioneers. Some of these *Biographical Sketches* were published by his widow in 1838, together with other essays, poems, and speeches, as a memorial to his literary sensitivity and reflective judgment. Campbell was a regular Presbyterian but no sectarian enthusiast, a leading supporter of the American Colonization Society's scheme to resettle freed slaves in Liberia, and an active philanthropist. During the cholera epidemic of 1833 (which carried off his adopted daughter and his brother), he insisted on visiting "the abodes of distress" in Columbus. Shortly after, on a restorative trip to Delaware Springs in Ohio, he caught a severe chill and died from a "high fever" (Campbell, pp. 9–11). Equable and fair-minded, Campbell was praised even by political opponents for his "public-spirited, obliging and benevolent" character and conscientious public service (Columbus *Ohio State Journal*, 28 Sept. 1833).

• Some of Campbell's letters may be found in the papers of his contemporaries, and a few are reprinted in *Old Northwest Genealogical Quarterly* 9 (1906): 230, and 10 (1907): 45, 261. The volume of *Biographical Sketches; with Other Literary Remains of the Late John W. Campbell, Compiled by His Widow* (1838), includes the fullest sketch of his life. Margaret Campbell Pilcher, *Historical Sketches of the Campbell, Pilcher and Kindred Families* (1911), adds little beyond genealogical background. His literary and educational interests are explored in Gerald S. Greenburg, "Literary Bequests in Early Ohio Wills," *Ohio History* 102 (1993): 22–25.

DONALD J. RATCLIFFE

CAMPBELL, Joseph (26 Mar. 1904–30 Oct. 1987), teacher and author, was born in New York City, the son of Charles William Campbell, a businessman, and Josephine Lynch. Raised a Roman Catholic, Campbell as a boy was attracted to Native American art and culture and read Indian historical and ethnographic literature while still in grade school. After a year at Dartmouth, he went to Columbia (B.A., 1925), where he studied literature and became a track star. He remained at Columbia for two more years, earning an M.A. in 1927 with a thesis on medieval Arthurian literature. Planning to pursue his Ph.D., he accepted a two-year fellowship to study Old French and Provençal at the University of Paris (1927–1928) and Sanskrit and Oriental philosophy at the University of Munich (1928–1929).

In Europe, Campbell discovered modern art, literature, and thought, reading James Joyce, Thomas Mann, Freud, and Jung, among others. He lost interest in pursuing a specialized program of study on the Middle Ages. He also became disillusioned with doctrinaire Christianity because of its incompatibility with modern science and its intolerance of other spiritual paths. He returned to the United States in 1929.

For a time Campbell tried to be a writer, with little success. A cross-country drive in 1931 took him to Monterey, California, where he met novelist John Steinbeck and marine biologist Ed Ricketts. He continued his wide reading in all his areas of interest: mythology, literature, psychology, history, modern art, and, increasingly, Eastern religion.

In 1934 Campbell began teaching at Sarah Lawrence College, a women's college in Bronxville, New York, first instructing in literature classes but later teaching courses on mythology and religion. At Sarah Lawrence he also met dancer and choreographer Jean Erdman, whom he married in 1938. They had no children.

In 1940 Campbell began working with German Indologist Heinrich Zimmer, whom he later called his "master." Zimmer encouraged Campbell's interest in mythology and psychology and by example showed how he could bring his various interests together in a synthetic approach to world mythology. After Zimmer's sudden death in 1943, Campbell edited his mentor's notes into a series of volumes on Asian Indian art and philosophy. Also during the early 1940s Campbell and novelist Henry Morton Robinson wrote *A Skeleton Key to Finnegan's Wake* (published 1944), a useful and thorough commentary on Joyce's enigmatic novel.

Campbell's own fully mature and characteristic original work began in 1949, when he published *The Hero with a Thousand Faces*. In this influential and extraordinarily popular work, Campbell traced the theme of the hero's journey (which he called the "monomyth") through the world's mythologies. Bringing to bear the insights of Freud and Jung, he also compared the patterns of myth to those of dreams. The book thus combined a serious appreciation of the spiritual values available in all religions with a sophisticated approach derived from modern psychology and science. Like most of Campbell's later work, it is written in a style that moves from the easy discursivity of a storyteller to ecstatic identification with the content of myth.

Campbell's next major work was *The Masks of God*, a study of world mythology in four volumes: *Primitive Mythology* (1959), *Oriental Mythology* (1961), *Occidental Mythology* (1964), and *Creative Mythology* (1968). Here he extended his earlier perspective on myth while vastly increasing the range of his references and dividing his material along broad regional and historical lines. In the final two volumes, Campbell wrestled with the relatively intolerant monotheistic religions of the West and with the modern rationalism that would dismiss all mythology as false. Increasingly, Campbell developed the theme that dominated his later work: mythology could redeem modern men and women by giving them authentic experience, but only if myths were read spiritually. Western religions, including Judaism, Christianity, and Islam, insisted on the literal truth of their myths and so lost their power.

In 1972, with his retirement from Sarah Lawrence, Campbell embarked on a second career as a full-time writer and lecturer. His later books included *The Mythic Image* (1974), written with M. J. Abadie, and the unfinished *Historical Atlas of World Mythology* (volumes published in 1983 and 1988). He lectured widely at conferences, schools, and sites such as the Esalen Institute, dedicated to "New Age" psychology and medicine. In 1983 he moved to Honolulu, Hawaii, although he maintained a full schedule of traveling, lecturing, and writing well past his eightieth birthday. He died in Honolulu. Six television interviews broadcast after his death reached a huge audience, and the accompanying book, *The Power of Myth* (1988), written with Bill Moyers, was a bestseller.

A writer on world mythology who did no original work on any single culture, Campbell was criticized or ignored by most professional anthropologists and students of comparative religion. On the other hand, his approach to the study of myth influenced a number of writers, artists, and filmmakers, who acknowledged their debt to his works. Robert Bly, poet and author of *Iron John: A Book about Men* (1990), novelist Richard Adams, author of *Watership Down* (1972), and filmmaker George Lucas, writer and producer of the *Star Wars* films, all credited Campbell with having inspired them. His politics were conservative, and some critics after his death charged Campbell with personal attitudes of racism, sexism, and anti-Semitism; these charges were vehemently denied by his friends. Whatever the truth, there is no question that as a compelling teacher and lecturer, he had a profound personal influence on the lives of many of his hearers.

• Many letters to and from Campbell along with his personal journals are housed in the Joseph Campbell Archive and Library in Carpinteria, Calif., and the Joseph Campbell Foundation in Honolulu, Hawaii. Besides those mentioned above, Campbell edited and wrote many other works, the most important of which are two collections of essays, *The Flight of the Wild Gander* (1969) and *Myths to Live By* (1972), and his late meditation on modern mythologies, *The Inner Reaches of Outer Space* (1986). A full biography, authorized by his widow, is Stephen Larsen and Robin Larsen, *A Fire in the Mind: The Life of Joseph Campbell* (1991). Campbell recalls his life and discusses his work in Phil Cousineau, ed., *The Hero's Journey* (1990), a volume that supplements the Larsens' biography. A full bibliography of works by and about Campbell, along with a discussion of his major books, can be found in Robert A. Segal, *Joseph Campbell: An Introduction* (1987). Obituaries are in the *Los Angeles Times*, 3 Nov. 1987, and the *Chicago Tribune*, 4 Nov. 1987. A controversial memoir of Campbell by Brendan Gill appeared in the *New York Review of Books*, 28 Sept. 1989.

HENRY S. LIMOUZE

CAMPBELL, Josiah Adams Patterson (2 Mar. 1830–10 Jan. 1917), jurist and a founding father of the Confederacy, was born in South Carolina (sources vary as to location), the son of Robert B. Campbell, a Princeton-educated Presbyterian minister, and Mary Patterson. A precocious child, he spent some time as a student at Davidson College in North Carolina before joining his parents at their new home in Madison County, Mississippi, in 1845. After reading law in the office of a local attorney for two years, he was admitted to the bar at the age of seventeen and began practicing in Kosciusko in Attala County. In 1850 he married Eugenia E. Nash; they had seven children.

At twenty-one, the earliest age permitted by the state's constitution, Campbell was elected to represent Attala County in the Mississippi House of Representatives. In 1859, still not yet thirty, he was chosen to be the speaker. In that capacity, on 30 November 1860, along with the president of the senate and the governor, he signed the resolution that called for Mississippi's secession from the Union. In January 1861 he traveled to Montgomery, Alabama, as a member of Mississippi's seven-man delegation to the constitutional convention that created the Confederacy. One of the forty-nine signers of the Confederate constitution, he served first in Montgomery and then in Richmond, Virginia, in the Confederate provisional congress, chairing the committees on territories and accounts, until November 1861.

Unsuccessful in a bid for election to the first regular congress, Campbell enrolled in the Confederate army in March 1862 and was appointed a lieutenant colonel of the Fortieth Mississippi Infantry Regiment. Later that year, he fought in the battle of Iuka and at Corinth, where he was wounded. Early in 1863 he was summoned back east to serve, with the rank and pay of a colonel of cavalry, on the legal staff of General Leonidas Polk's corps.

A few months after the war ended, Campbell was elected to fill an unexpired term as circuit judge for the Fifth Judicial District, which included Attala and four other mid-Mississippi counties. Reelected for a full term in 1866, he was forced out of office in 1869 because he could not take an oath, which was required of all state officeholders under Mississippi's Reconstruction constitution, that he had always been loyal to the Union. Settling down to practice law in his parents' hometown of Canton in Madison County, he declined an invitation in 1870 to fill the chair of law at the University of Mississippi. He did, however, agree to serve as one of the commissioners that drew up a new code of laws for the state in 1871.

Politically, Campbell was at this time one of Mississippi's moderate Democrats, who, though they disliked Reconstruction, were prepared to accept it as the inevitable result of military defeat. He recalled some years later how white Mississippians at the time, "were sick and tired of war, weary and worn out . . . the feeling of an overwhelming majority of our people was one of readiness to be faithful to the government" (Garner, p. 155). To him and to other like-minded whites it seemed that the wisest policy would be "to make the most of the situation and form an alliance with the negroes politically by a full recognition of their rights to vote and hold office, acquire ascendancy over them, and become their teachers and controllers instead of allowing the Republicans to do so" (Garner, p. 179). In the spring and summer of 1872, he campaigned in several mid-Mississippi counties on behalf of the national Democratic ticket.

By the mid-1870s, however, a Republican near-monopoly of the black vote, an economic depression, and extremely high taxes, convinced Campbell and many Mississippi whites that moderate policies had failed. In 1875 he was serving on the executive committee of the state Democratic party when, in what he later recalled as "the glorious campaign," by a combination of threatened and sometimes actual physical intimidation, plus, where necessary, ballot box stuffing, the Democrats won control of the state legislature in elections that were held in November of that year.

Campbell was rewarded the following spring with an appointment to a seat on the state's supreme court. From 1878 to 1880 he presided over a commission that drafted yet another new version of the Mississippi code, whose important changes included giving married women absolute control over their own property and clarifying conveyancing procedures. In 1882 he became chief justice of the supreme court under a rule that gave the position to the justice whose term was closest to expiring. He was reappointed to the court in 1885. Because he was a supreme court justice, Campbell could not become openly involved in the deliberations of the convention that drafted Mississippi's 1890 constitution, which was primarily designed to ensure white political supremacy. But because his onetime Canton law partner, Solomon Saladin Calhoon, presided over the convention, and his second son, Robert Bond Campbell, was one of the delegates, he may well have had some unofficial input into its framing.

When Campbell retired from the court in 1894, a loss of hearing prevented him from resuming his law practice. Instead, he consulted frequently, pleaded an occasional case before the supreme court, and delivered many public speeches. He died in Canton, Mississippi. The *Jackson Clarion Ledger* carried a front-page obituary that described him as a man of "imposing figure whose appearance attracted attention in any crowd," and noted that he had been "the author of more legal reforms than any other lawyer" in the state in his day. Certainly he was one of the outstanding leaders of his generation in Mississippi through a very stormy period in the state's history.

• Campbell's papers, including a five-page handwritten autobiography, are in the Southern Historical Collection in Wilson Library at the University of North Carolina at Chapel Hill. The fullest account of Campbell's life is in *Biographical and Historical Memoirs of Mississippi*, vol. 1 (1891), pp. 496–98. Shorter accounts of his life can be found in the *Biographical Register of the Confederate Congress* (1975) and *A History of the Mississippi Supreme Court* (1973). His opinions on Reconstruction politics are quoted in J. W. Garner, *Reconstruction in Mississippi* (1901; repr. 1964). An obituary is in the *Jackson Clarion Ledger*, 11 Jan. 1917.

MICHAEL DE L. LANDON

CAMPBELL, Lewis Davis (9 Aug. 1811–26 Nov. 1882), congressman and diplomat, was born in Warren County, Ohio, the son of Samuel Campbell and Mary Small, farmers. Educated in Ohio's common school system, Campbell left the family farm in 1828 to become an apprentice printer with the *Cincinnati Gazette*. Three years later he became the publisher of the *Hamilton Intelligencer*, a staunchly Whig newspaper. While serving as publisher, Campbell read law and was admitted to the bar in 1835. A forceful orator with a keen interest in politics, Campbell built a flourishing law practice and acquired a reputation as a skilled stump speaker. His marriage in 1836 to Jane H. Reily, the daughter of John Reily, an influential Ohio politician, enhanced a growing social prestige. The couple had three daughters.

Strongly committed to the Whig philosophy of government, Campbell unsuccessfully ran for Congress in 1840, 1842, and 1844. Finally, in 1848 he succeeded and was subsequently reelected in 1850, 1852, and 1854, representing agricultural Butler County. During his fourth term, he unsuccessfully campaigned for Speaker, served as chairman of the Ways and Means Committee, and was a member of the select committee assigned to investigate Representative Preston S. Brooks's assault on Senator Charles Sumner.

In the campaign of 1856 Campbell defeated Democratic challenger Clement L. Vallandigham by a scant nineteen votes. Returning to Washington, Campbell held his seat from 7 Dec. 1857 until 25 May 1858, when he was succeeded by Vallandigham, who had successfully contested the 1856 results. Two years later, he unsuccessfully campaigned to regain the seat.

In Congress, Campbell supported the 1846 Wilmot Proviso, arguing that "all powers of the Constitution" ought to be exercised to prevent the extension of slavery into the territories. He contended, however, that the institution must be protected where it already existed and that the slave states should be accorded "in good faith, all that is guaranteed to them by the American bond of Union," including northern cooperation with enforcement of the Fugitive Slave Law of 1850. Even though slavery was odious, Campbell believed that no individual could nullify legally enacted legislation. The only legitimate avenues of opposition were repeal or judicial review. "The spirit" that attempted to abrogate laws "through forcible resistance" would produce "civil war" and "anarchy." Outraged by the repeal of the Missouri Compromise and the specter of opening additional territory to slavery, Campbell vigorously opposed the Kansas-Nebraska Act, vowing to resist it "to the last extremity, and the bitter end."

The nativist movement of the 1850s also focused national attention on Campbell. With the demise of the Whig party, he ran for reelection in 1854 as an American party candidate on an Anti-Nebraska or fusion ticket. Charging that the Roman Catholic church, "governed by a head in a foreign land, holding no sympathy" with democratic institutions, endangered "civil" and "religious" liberty, Campbell quickly became a national leader of the nativist movement, apparently hoping to be its standard bearer for the presidency. He allied with the Republican party in 1856 and served as party floor leader, but his continuing emphasis on nativism, endless personal quarrels, and differences with party leaders over specific legislation undercut his influence in the Republican party and eventually led to his estrangement from the party. He supported John Bell and the Constitutional Union party in the 1860 elections.

During the Civil War, Campbell served as a colonel in the Sixty-ninth Ohio Volunteer Infantry in 1861 and 1862. After the war, he supported the policies of President Andrew Johnson and served as a delegate to the National Union Convention in 1866. Although not the president's first choice, Campbell served as minister to Mexico from 4 May 1866 until 18 June 1867. Sent to make contact with the republican government-in-exile of Benito Juárez, Campbell's mission was a comedy of errors that ended in total failure. He never met with Juárez and spent the last few months of his ambassadorship at the St. Charles Hotel in New Orleans, Louisiana. His repeated refusal to take up his post prompted demands that he resign, which he finally did.

Two years later Campbell resumed active participation in politics. In 1869 he was elected to the state senate, won a congressional seat as a Democrat in 1870, supported Horace Greeley in the 1872 presidential election, and was chosen as a delegate to the Ohio constitutional convention in 1873, serving as its vice president. After the convention, he retired from politics and returned to farming. He died in Hamilton, Ohio. Praised as a man "who was honest in all opinions and vigorous in supporting his views," Campbell saw his political career cut short because of his extreme sensitivity, overdeveloped vanity, excessive combativeness, and persistent focus on personal animosities.

• Letters from Campbell are in the Lewis D. Campbell Papers in the Ohio Historical Society. The major source of information for his political career is William E. Van Horne, "Lewis D. Campbell and the Know-Nothing Party in Ohio," *Ohio History* 76 (Autumn 1967): 203–21 and 270–73. For his role in the abortive mission to Mexico, see Ellis Paxson Oberholtzer, *A History of the United States since the Civil War*, vol. 1 (1926), and Martin Hardwick Hall, "The Campbell-Sherman Diplomatic Mission to Mexico," *The Historical and Philosophical Society of Ohio* bulletin 13 (October 1955): 254–70. Copies of Campbell's official correspondence as minister to Mexico are reprinted in *House Executive Document No. 1*, 39 Cong., 2d sess. (Serial 1283); *House Executive Document No. 76*, 39 Cong., 2d sess. (Serial 1294); and *House Executive Document No. 30*, 40 Cong., 1st sess. (Serial 1311). Campbell's speeches in the House of Representatives are reprinted in the *Congressional Globe* for the 31st, 32d, 33d, 34th, 35th, and 42d Congresses. In addition to the *Congressional Globe*, a number of Campbell's speeches were issued in pamphlet form. Obituaries and related stories are in the *Cincinnati Enquirer*, 27 Nov. 1882; the *Cincinnati Commercial*, 27 and 30 Nov. 1882; and the *New York Times*, 28 Nov. 1882.

THOMAS W. KREMM

CAMPBELL, Loraine Leeson (12 May 1905–10 Feb. 1982), birth control movement leader, was born in Newton Center, Massachusetts, the daughter of Robert Ainsworth Leeson, a corporate executive, and Mildred Dix. She enjoyed a privileged childhood as a member of a socially prominent Boston family, excelled in academics and sports at the Winsor School, where she was student body president, and spent a year "coming out" as a debutante before entering Vassar College in 1924. She majored in psychology, shocked her parents by joining pickets at strikes, and was elected Phi Beta Kappa and student body president. She turned down job offers to conduct child development research after her mother died in the spring of her senior year, and her father urged her to return to Boston to help rear three younger siblings.

She sought to fulfill her ambition to do research on language development in brain-damaged children by renting space in the Harvard Medical School laboratory of Stanley Cobb. Although her tutorial in neurological research ended with administrative objections to her self-financed presence in Cobb's department, she developed strong friendships among members of the Harvard medical community who were active in the effort to provide contraceptive services to the indigent through birth control clinics. In 1934 she married Walter E. Campbell, an architect; they had three sons.

Marriage made it socially acceptable for Loraine Campbell to assume leadership roles in the Massachusetts birth control movement as vice president of the state league and as chair of the executive committee of the state's first birth control clinic. Birth control advocates in Massachusetts had mobilized in 1928 to defend Antoinette Konikow, a physician with a large middle-class clientele, who was arrested following a lecture on family planning. The newly formed Birth Control League of Massachusetts lobbied in 1931 for a change in the 1879 state Comstock law to guarantee the right of physicians to provide contraceptive information to married clients. After they failed to get their bill out of committee, in 1932 the birth controllers tested public tolerance by opening a birth control clinic in Brookline for those unable to afford the services of a private physician. Three thousand women were served in seven urban clinics throughout the state, but rising concern among Roman Catholic clergy led to a series of police raids in 1937 that closed the clinics. An appeal to the state supreme judicial court failed in 1938, so birth controllers returned by necessity to the search for legislative relief through initiative and referendum. As president of the state birth control league (1940–1943, 1945–1949), Campbell led sophisticated campaigns that demonstrated widespread support for change and mobilized a majority of the members of the Massachusetts Medical Society in support, but reform referenda failed in 1942 and 1948 by seven-to-five margins that reflected the firm Roman Catholic opposition to public recognition of contraception as a legitimate social practice. Campbell remained actively involved in efforts to legalize family planning in Massachusetts through 1966, when a reform bill recognized the legality of medical prescription of contraception, and then in the effort to provide services through clinics. Much of her energy after 1948, however, went to national work with the Planned Parenthood Federation of America, which she served as a director (1941–1969) and as president (1956–1959).

Campbell's career as a social activist illustrates some of the difficulties in bringing women into the historical canon. She always worked as a volunteer during a period when there was a self-conscious effort to replace unpaid workers with professionals, often men, who presumably would bring greater prestige and effectiveness to the movement. Campbell contributed executive services of a high order at both the state and national levels, but she usually wrote or spoke as a representative of a committee or organization and as such presented consensus positions that often differed from her personal views. Although she was drawn into the birth control movement as a self-conscious and sexually active young woman who wanted to defend the reproductive autonomy of all women, Campbell presented herself as a concerned citizen rather than as an ardent feminist. She always sought to build heterosexual coalitions, was respectful of medical expertise, and was willing to make concessions to Roman Catholics and male authority figures in order to move public policy toward acceptance of planned parenthood.

Within the birth control movement, Campbell was important as a mediator who negotiated disruptive conflict among competing personalities and interests. During the 1930s she bridged the gap between an older cohort of feminists and younger enthusiasts for eugenics. Although she personally escorted Margaret Sanger on a 1940 barnstorming tour in support of the proposed state birth control referendum—and thus aroused militant Roman Catholic opposition—Campbell worked tirelessly to maintain communication with liberal Catholic clergy. As president of national Planned Parenthood, she mediated between the New York office and Connecticut activists who were initiating the test cases that led to *Griswold v. Connecticut* (1965), a landmark in the development of the constitutional right to privacy, and she quietly had Morris Ernst replaced as the national organization's principal legal counsel when his sexist and anticommunist attitudes threatened the working relationship with progressive litigators. In the 1970s, when Cold War enthusiasts such as Joseph Sunnen, the manufacturer of a spermicidal foam, sought to enlist Planned Parenthood in their cause, Campbell reminded them that the movement's basis was humanitarian concern for the rights of women, but she also found room for their concern over rapid population growth in her public presentations.

Admired among her women friends as an intrepid campaigner who kicked off her proper shoes at every opportunity, Campbell's commitment to gradual social change reflected her situation as a social insider who valued her strong marriage but needed the opportunity for social service provided by the fight for birth control. She died in Cambridge, Massachusetts.

• Campbell's oral history and some personal papers are in the Schlesinger Library, Cambridge, Mass. Her reform career is documented in the Planned Parenthood League of Massachusetts Papers and in the Planned Parenthood Federation of America Papers in the Sophia Smith Collection, Northhampton, Mass. An obituary is in the *Boston Globe*, 12 Feb. 1982.

JAMES W. REED

CAMPBELL, Lucie E. (1885–3 Jan. 1963), gospel composer and teacher, was born in Duck Hill, Mississippi, the daughter of Burrell Campbell, a railroad worker, and Isabella Wilkerson. Her mother was widowed several months after Lucie's birth, and the family soon moved from Carroll County to Memphis, the nearest major city. Lucie and her many siblings struggled to survive on their mother's meager wages, which she earned by washing and ironing clothing. Given the family's insubstantial income, it could afford a musical education for only one child: Lucie's older sister Lora. Lucie eventually learned to play piano, however, through her own persistence, a gifted ear for music, and a little help from Lora.

Lucie Campbell was a bright student who easily mastered elementary school and middle school, winning awards in both penmanship and Latin. Even before graduating from Kortrecht Senior High School (later Booker T. Washington) as the class valedictorian, she began teaching classes at Carnes Grammar School. Although Campbell taught full time to support herself, she still maintained a keen interest in music and the Baptist church, of which she remained a lifelong member. In 1904 Campbell founded the Music Club in Memphis, which was intended to promote local musical activity in the black community. By this time she was singing at First Baptist Church as well as playing the organ for Central Baptist Church. In later years she also helped to organize the Bethesda Baptist Church. Campbell continued to teach history and English for the Memphis public school system, moving to Booker T. Washington High School in 1911. She remained there for many years and was considered a well-respected, devoted, and strict instructor.

In 1916 Memphis was the site for the Baptist church's newly formed Sunday School Congress. This body had emerged the previous year as the result of a huge internal schism within the denomination, in which the National Baptist Convention was rent in two during a bitter dispute over the ownership of its publishing board. The organization consequently became two entities: the National Baptist Convention, U.S.A., Incorporated, and the National Baptist Convention of America, Unincorporated. Campbell remained affiliated with the former branch and was asked to join eight others in organizing the crucial meeting of the congress. Because she was both an active church musician and a well-recognized singer, Campbell was quickly elected as the first music director of the Sunday School and National Baptist Training Union, the Baptist organization devoted to the dissemination of church doctrine and music. Publishing gospel songbooks and hymnals became an integral part of this organization's mission, and eventually important works such as *Gospel Pearls* (1921), *Spirituals Triumphant Old and New* (1927), and *Inspirational Melodies #2* (n.d.) were published by a variety of allied houses (especially the Sunday School Publishing Board of Nashville, Tenn.) and then publicized through the congress. In addition to her duties as music director, Campbell also served on the committee in charge of choosing the music for *Gospel Pearls*.

Within three years Campbell herself began writing and publishing gospel songs, one of the first African-American women to do so. "The Lord Is My Shepherd," written and copyrighted in 1919 but not published until 1921, was her initial offering, appearing first in *Gospel Pearls*. Campbell continued to compose and publish gospel songs during the 1920s, and two of her best-known numbers, "Just to Behold His Face" and "Heavenly Sunshine," premiered in 1923. During this period not only did Campbell remain active in her church and at Booker T. Washington High, but she became a student as well, enrolling at Rust College, a predominantly black school some fifty miles southeast of Memphis. In 1927 Campbell graduated with a liberal arts degree. Much later, in 1951, she earned an M.S. from Tennessee State.

Campbell's style added significantly to the development of African-American gospel music during the seminal decades of the 1920s and 1930s. She loved the older lined hymns and slower paced songs, which reflected not only her affection for the older performance practices but her respect for her own musical heritage. Campbell also composed more moderately paced hymns, such as "When I Get Home" (1947), that are generally marked by her use of light syncopation and responsorial structure. Like Thomas A. Dorsey, she was a deft lyricist who stressed self-sufficiency and introspection as important parts of the Christian life. Her compositions, with lyrics so strongly relevant to contemporary black life, helped to bridge the gap between the older hymns and the modern gospel song form. Campbell's penchant for waltz times and other triple meters proved to be another of her major contributions to the tradition.

During a remarkable 32-year stretch from 1930 to 1962, Campbell managed to present one new composition at each of the annual meetings of the National Baptist Convention. "He Understands; He'll Say, 'Well Done,'" certainly her most widely performed composition, debuted at the 1933 convention. Her contributions to the annual conventions were not limited to presenting newly composed songs, however. Campbell also directed choruses, chorales, and other large congregational singing groups. At the June 1932 convention held in Memphis, Campbell wrote, produced, and directed *Ethiopia*, a grand musical pageant with scores of participants. This production, along with *Memphis Bound*, were among several musical extravaganzas that Campbell orchestrated during her career.

Gospel compositions continued to flow from Campbell's pen at a steady rate until her death. In 1947 she published no fewer than nine compositions, including "In the Upper Room," which was often performed during the late 1940s and well into the 1950s. In 1954, just as the popularity of this song was fading, Campbell retired from the Memphis school system after more than four decades. She was widely hailed as a positive role model for thousands of her students, in whom she strove to instill a strong sense of pride by engendering self-esteem. Campbell was often called on to speak at nonschool functions, especially on one particular topic that was close to her heart, the importance and virtues of Christian womanhood.

Following her retirement Campbell continued to write songs and serve as the music director of the Sunday School and National Baptist Training Union. In 1960 she married the Reverend Countee Robert Williams, a lifelong friend, and, after living nearly all of her life in Memphis, moved to Nashville, where she died. Her passing was most widely noted in Memphis, where she was highly praised during the large funeral service held in her honor. Twenty years later a group of friends placed a commemorative stone on her grave as part of a heartfelt memorial honoring her life and accomplishments.

Campbell's importance as a pioneer in twentieth-century black gospel music is difficult to understate. She was one of a handful of women accorded first class status in the largely male-dominated world of the National Baptist Congress. This status was especially uncommon in the 1920s when her early compositions and the national leadership she provided helped to shape the direction taken by the organization. Furthermore, Campbell stands out as a highly respected gospel composer whose work built a bridge between older hymns and modern gospel songs. She is remembered as an outstanding teacher, a talented singer and composer, and a female leader in the Baptist congress, on both the local and national level, for more than forty years.

• There is material on Campbell, including interviews and photographs, at the Archive Center of the National Museum of American History, Smithsonian Institution. For a collection of Campbell's songs, see Niani Kilkenny and Rebecca E. Curzon, eds., *The Songs of Lucie E. Campbell: Gospel Music Composer* (1984). In the same volume, Campbell's place in gospel music is discussed in an essay by Luvenia George, "Lucie E. Campbell and the Enduring Tradition of Gospel Hymnody." Campbell is also the subject of three essays in Bernice Johnson Reagon, ed., *We'll Understand It Better By and By* (1992): Horace Boyer, "Lucie E. Campbell: Composer for the National Baptist Convention"; George, "Lucie E. Campbell: Her Nurturing and Expansion of Gospel Music in the National Baptist Convention, U.S.A., Inc."; and Charles Walker, "Lucie E. Campbell Williams: A Cultural Biography." See also George, "Lucie E. Campbell: Baptist Composer and Educator," *Black Perspective in Music* 15, no. 1 (Spring 1987): 24–49, and Kip Lornell, *"Happy in the Service of the Lord": African-American Sacred Vocal Harmony Quartets in Memphis*, 2d ed. (1995).

KIP LORNELL

CAMPBELL, Mrs. Patrick (9 Feb. 1865–9 Apr. 1940), actress, was born Beatrice Stella Tanner in Kensington, London, the daughter of John Tanner, a rarely present ordnance manufacturer and speculator, and Luigia Romanini. She was educated in Brighton, Hampstead, and Paris, and she won a music scholarship from the Guildhall School of Music to study in Leipzig for three years. She forsook the scholarship to marry Patrick Campbell in 1884; they had two children. Patrick Campbell went to South Africa in 1888 to relieve his tuberculosis, and Mrs. Campbell turned to the theater to support herself. After achieving some success in amateur dramatics, she secured an engagement with Ben Greet's company in 1887 and made her professional debut in Liverpool on 22 October 1888 as Sophia Moody in *Bachelors*.

Campbell's first notable success was her performance in the title role of Arthur Wing Pinero's *The Second Mrs. Tanqueray* in 1893. Other actresses had avoided the role, that of a heroine with a lurid past, but Campbell's portrayal of the character marked a milestone in the English theater and a turning point in the depiction of women on stage. She acted with Beerbohm Tree in *John O'Dreams* and with John Hare in Pinero's *The Notorious Mrs. Ebbsmith*. She costarred with Sir Johnston Forbes-Robertson in 1896 in *Romeo and Juliet* and later appeared with him as Ophelia in *Hamlet* and as Lady Teazle in Richard Brinsley Sheridan's *The School for Scandal*.

Campbell first visited the United States in 1901 to appear for six months with a repertory company that performed such works as *The Notorious Mrs. Ebbsmith* and *The Second Mrs. Tanqueray*. The company opened in Chicago, then visited the major eastern cities. Campbell caused a sensation by violating the taboo against women smoking in public and generated a comparable stir by winning $20,000 in a bridge game. A year later, while appearing in New York in the title role of *Magda*, Campbell demanded that a layer of tanbark be applied to Forty-second Street because the street noises disturbed her performance.

In 1904 Sarah Bernhardt asked Campbell to appear with her in *Pelléas et Mélisande*; Campbell agreed, performing in French with Bernhardt in London. In 1907 she appeared with her daughter, Stella, in *The Ambassador's Wife*, written by her son Alan. Patrick Campbell died in the Boer War, and in 1914 Campbell married George Cornwallas-West, the divorced husband of Lady Randolph Churchill. The marriage took place within two hours of his divorce from his first wife. The union between Campbell and Cornwallas-West was not a happy one; they became estranged several years before separating.

George Bernard Shaw had written *Caesar and Cleopatra* in 1907 with Campbell and Forbes-Robertson in mind, but she never played Cleopatra. Instead, in 1914 she performed Eliza Doolittle in the premiere of Shaw's *Pygmalion*, the high point of her London career. When in 1922 Campbell published her memoirs, *My Life and Some Letters*, her inclusion of several supposed "love letters" from Shaw caused another sensation. Campbell appeared in revivals of *Mrs. Tanqueray* and in 1927 appeared in New York in *The Adventurous Age*, by Frederic Witney. Receiving poor reviews, she left for England, vowing never to return to the United States. A few years later, however, she did return, making her Hollywood film debut in 1930 in *The Dancers*. She alienated most of the Hollywood stars who could have helped to further her career by refusing to kowtow to them. Alexander Woollcott compared Campbell to "a sinking ship firing on its rescuers." She made several motion pictures and toured the United States, lecturing on diction, while still finding time to appear occasionally on Broadway and in London. Campbell's last stage appearance was in *The 13th Chair* in Milford, Connecticut, in the late 1930s, after which she retired, except to deliver occasional lectures. She died in Pau, France.

Critics described Campbell as a dark, passionate beauty, who reputedly inspired Sir Edward Coley Burne-Jones to paint and Rudyard Kipling to write *The Vampire*. Others considered her a "merry madcap whose elfin exploits taunted and beleaguered the leading personalities of her day." An often-told anecdote depicts her storming out of a rehearsal and lashing out at the vegetarian Shaw by exclaiming, "One day you'll eat a pork chop, Joey, and then God help all women!" Campbell later incurred Shaw's wrath by tampering with the last line of *Pygmalion*.

When Campbell first appeared in the United States, New York critic J. Rankin Towse, in his column for the *Critic*, spoke of her "rare faculties and power of expression," calling her voice "a charming instrument, rich, soft, and musical, with sufficient volume." He also praised "her eyes, large and dark and deep, often partly veiled . . . by the drooping lids." Towse added, "Her great height, her graceful, sinuous figure, and her long arms make her poses singularly picturesque and her gestures uncommonly eloquent and striking."

William Winter in *The Wallet of Time* gave detailed descriptions of Campbell in *Magda*, referring to her as "tall, lithe, slender, alert in movement, nervous, restless, impetuous, possessed of an expressive countenance and of a peculiar voice, . . . clever in posing and proficient in sudden swirls of vehement motion and fervent loquacity." Winter described Campbell in the role of Electra as pervading the stage, "pouring forth a torrent of lachrymose loquacity, and seeming to be a kind of human exotic." Summing up Campbell's career, Winter, whose sense of Victorian propriety colored his judgments, claimed to have seen nothing but a "long procession of hussies and fools, some of them dissolute in conduct and unsavory in repute, and all of them morbid in fibre and unhealthy in influence."

• The University of Chicago holds a collection of Campbell's papers, mostly correspondence, clippings, programs, and photographs, totalling 160 items. The most substantial biography of Campbell is Margot Peters, *Mrs. Pat: The Life of Mrs. Patrick Campbell* (1984), which contains a valuable bibliography of unpublished source materials. See also Alan Dent, *Mrs. Patrick Campbell* (1961; repr. 1973). William Winter, *The Wallet of Time* (1913), contains detailed descriptions of Campbell in several plays, among them *Magda*, *Beyond Human Power*, *Mariana*, *Pélleas and Mélisande*, *Aunt Jeannie*, *The Joy of Living*, *The Sorceress*, and *Electra*. Jerome Kilty, *Dear Liar* (1960), dramatized the correspondence between Campbell and Shaw, which Dent had previously edited for *Bernard Shaw and Mrs. Patrick Campbell: Their Correspondence* (1952). Leigh Woods, " 'The Golden Calf': Noted English Actresses in American Vaudeville, 1904–1916," *Journal of American Culture* (Fall 1992): 61–71, describes Campbell in that branch of show business; and Alan Brock, "This Very Old Lady: The Last Years of Mrs. Patrick Campbell," *New Theatre Quarterly* (Feb. 1990): 57–63, describes how Brock became her agent. Substantial obituaries are in the *New York Times*, 11 Apr. 1940, and *Variety*, 17 Apr. 1940.

STEPHEN M. ARCHER

CAMPBELL, Oliver Samuel (25 Feb. 1871–11 July 1953), tennis player, was born in Brooklyn, New York, the son of Frederick Hudson Campbell, a dry goods merchant who died in 1872, and Emily Barber. "Ollie" was raised amidst affluence in Brooklyn. He began playing lawn tennis at age twelve and entered his first public tournaments shortly before his fifteenth birthday. Despite his youth, he performed well in adult competition. When he lost to the experienced Harry Slocum, after winning one set, in the first round of the U.S. championship at the Newport (R.I.) Casino, Campbell became the youngest to play in national mens singles until Vinnie Richards competed in 1918. At Newport, Campbell so admired the volleying skill of champion Dick Sears that he resolved to develop a style based on persistent net rushing and hard-paced volleys. The strategy paid off in the fall of 1886 when Campbell, representing the Brooklyn Heights Tennis Club, won his first tournament, the New York Tennis Club open.

Campbell won four singles and three doubles events in 1887. At the Orange (N.J.) Tennis Club open, he defeated Clarence Hobart and Ed MacMullen to win in singles and teamed with Vallie Hall to capture the doubles. That fall he entered the School of Mines at Columbia University. In 1888 Campbell won three singles and five doubles tournaments, including the U.S. and the Intercollegiate doubles titles with Hall, and reached the U.S. singles semifinals before Slocum defeated him. An unofficial national ranking that year placed Campbell eighth. In 1889 he won only one singles tournament, but the unofficial national ranking made him third. This ranking was obviously influenced by Campbell's strong performances at the U.S. championship, in which he defeated Howard Taylor, Joe Clark, and visiting Englishman Ernest G. Meers before losing the all-comers final to Quin Shaw. Campbell gained five doubles titles that year, including the Intercollegiate championship for Columbia while partnered with Empie Wright.

In 1890 Campbell defeated seven opponents, including defending champion Slocum, to win the U.S. singles crown, the youngest to secure the title (at nineteen years, six months, and nine days) until Pete Sampras won it one hundred years later. Campbell's match record for the entire season was 34 wins and four losses, bowing only to Bob Huntington twice, Hobart, and Fred Hovey. With Huntington he captured four doubles events, including the New England and Long Island (N.Y.) championships. During the spring of 1891 Campbell graduated from Columbia with a bachelor of arts degree. That year Campbell and Huntington won the U.S., Eastern, and Long Island doubles titles. As the defending U.S. titleholder that year, Campbell played few singles matches before the championship challenge round. He then beat Hobart after the latter tired badly in the fourth and fifth sets; Hobart later claimed that this was due to his strenuous play in winning the all-comers tournament.

In March 1892 Campbell played in a handicap tournament at Beau Site, Cannes, on the French Riviera, after which he enjoyed a leisurely sightseeing tour of western Europe. In May a sprained ankle kept him out of the Irish championship in Dublin. During June and July, he competed in six English tournaments, failing to reach any singles finals and winning but two doubles events, the Northumberland championship with Harold Mahony and the Exmouth open with Ernest Renshaw. During this period his singles record against ranking players was 4–8. He beat George Hillyard, ranked 12th by *Pastime*, England's premier sports periodical, and Arthur Gore, ranked 16th, but subsequently Gore bested him in straight sets in the All-England Championship at Wimbledon. He also lost to players *Pastime* ranked second, fourth (twice), fifth, seventh, 10th, and 20th. *Pastime* ranked Campbell 17th, in contrast to his unofficial American ranking of first for 1890, 1891, and 1892.

Campbell arrived home in time to practice at Newport before successfully defending his U.S. championship against Hovey, another persistent net rusher,

7–5, 3–6, 6–3, 7–5, in what was called "one of the finest matches on record in this country." Also in 1892 he won the doubles championship with Vallie Hall. Turning to business interests, Campbell competed seldom thereafter. In 1893 he won the New Jersey doubles title with Bill Larned, and in 1894 he captured the Tropical singles and doubles championships in St. Augustine, Florida.

A slender, 5′11½″ right-hander, Campbell consistently followed his serves to the net, where he volleyed decisively with power; however, his eagerness to hurry there cost him many double faults. His groundstrokes were comparatively weak except with regard to handling high bounces. Although Campbell's success prompted many Americans to emulate his net rushing style, English players—who were sounder, steadier, and more experienced baseliners—exposed his basic weakness of rushing in behind nonforcing groundstrokes and passed him repeatedly. Americans in England were handicapped somewhat by climatic and court surface differences, but Campbell readily conceded that the English and Irish regular tournament competitors were simply much better players than the Americans. Campbell wrote one tennis text, *The Game of Lawn Tennis and How to Play It*, published in 1893. His incentive may have been *Campbell's Lawn Tennis and the Way to Play It*, published in 1891 with no author stated. Evidently marketed to trade on Campbell's popularity, its text was a verbatim reprint of H. W. W. Wilberforce's *Lawn Tennis* (1889).

Campbell maintained offices in New York City in the late 1890s as a lawyer and, after 1900, as a broker. He and his brother, Frederick Barber Campbell, both lifetime bachelors, resided in the same Manhattan apartment for several decades. For 34 years Campbell vacationed during the summer months at the prestigious Restigouche Salmon Club near Matapedia, Quebec, Canada. While on a fishing trip from the club, he died in Campbellton, New Brunswick, Canada. He was posthumously elected to the National Lawn (later International) Tennis Hall of Fame in 1955.

• Campbell discussed his early tennis competition in "The All-Net Attack Succeeds," in U.S. Lawn Tennis Association, *Fifty Years of Lawn Tennis in the United States* (1931), pp. 49–52, and provided an assessment of American and English tennis in "America vs. English Lawn Tennis," *Harper's Weekly*, 27 Aug. 1892. A comprehensive resume of Campbell's tennis career and importance appears in Bud Collins and Zander Hollander, eds., *Bud Collins Modern Encyclopedia of Tennis*, 2d ed. (1994), pp. 410–11. A discussion of Campbell's style of play and scores of his U.S. championship singles matches is in Bill Talbert with Pete Axthelm, *Tennis Observed* (1967), pp. 15, 64–67. J. Parmly Paret, *Lawn Tennis* (1904), pp. 19–21, contains an evaluation of Campbell's influence on early American tennis. *The American Cricketer*, vols. 9–16 (1886–1892), provides the best-detailed coverage of Campbell's tournament career.

FRANK V. PHELPS

CAMPBELL, Persia Crawford (15 Mar. 1898–2 Mar. 1974), economist and consumer leader, was born in Nerrigundah, Australia, the daughter of Rodolph Campbell and Beatrice Harriet Hunt, schoolteachers. She was the first of two children. Her parents were strong Presbyterians and instilled in her at an early age a love of learning. Before she entered high school her father died, leaving her mother as the sole breadwinner. Persia tried to help by making and selling dolls' clothes. With her excellent grades she was able to enter a state scholarship high school for girls from families of modest incomes.

Campbell entered the University of Sydney in 1914. She earned an A.B. with first-class honors in history and English in 1919 and an A.M. in history and economics in 1920. She then won a two-year traveling fellowship in economics to the London School of Economics, from which she earned an M.Sc. in economics in 1923. That year Campbell published her thesis, *Chinese Coolie Emigration to the Countries within the British Empire*. In this heavily factual and remarkably objective book, she revealed few opinions of her own—except in the preface, in which she expressed a hope for better understanding among the peoples and nations of the Pacific.

In 1924 Campbell held a one-year fellowship at Bryn Mawr College in Pennsylvania to study American immigration. In 1925 she returned to Australia and became the assistant editor of the *Australian Encyclopedia*. Between 1926 and 1928 she was a research economist for Justice A. B. Piddington, the head of the Industrial Commission of New South Wales (N.S.W.), a wage-fixing tribunal. Between 1928 and 1929 Campbell was a research economist at the N.S.W. Bureau of Statistics. In 1927 she became a cofounder and secretary of the N.S.W. branch of the Institute of Pacific Relations, an organization for improving understanding among the peoples and countries of the Pacific region.

Through her activities and contacts at the institute, Campbell traveled to Washington, D.C., where she decided to study American agricultural policy under the auspices of the Brookings Institution. In 1930 she went to Harvard on a two-year Rockefeller International Scholarship to study American agricultural policy and its impact on rural living standards. Her resulting book was the authoritative *American Agricultural Policy* (1933).

In 1931 Campbell met and married Edward Rice, Jr., an American engineer, inventor, and member of the Institute of Pacific Relations. She gladly became the mother of his three children and had two children of her own. They soon established their home in Manhattan, and she became an American citizen in 1936.

As her husband's inventions brought in little income, and as she was eager to prepare herself for a career, Campbell began taking courses in public law at Columbia. She soon began research for a Ph.D. dissertation on the Consumers Advisory Board (CAB) of the National Recovery Administration (NRA).

While working on her dissertation, Campbell became the unpaid executive secretary of the Consumers National Federation, organized in the spring of 1937. The federation's executive committee was made up of progressives such as Helen Hall, who served as its chairman and was also the president of the National Federation of Settlements, and the head of the Henry Street Settlement; Robert Lynd, its vice chairman, a professor at Columbia, and Campbell's thesis adviser; and representatives of such organizations as the Consumers Union and the American Association of University Women (AAUW). Hall saw Campbell as the driving force of the organization. The federation hoped to be the nucleus for the first national consumers' organization. Although it made some progress toward that end, a lack of funds, the turn of public attention to war, and Campbell's resignation after her husband's death in 1939 brought about the federation's demise in 1940.

After her husband died, Campbell had to finish her dissertation quickly and get a paying job to support her family. Her dissertation, published in 1940 as *Consumer Representation in the New Deal*, analyzed why consumer representation, especially in the CAB, was so ineffective in its goal to keep industrial production higher and wages and prices lower so as to further the interests of workers, when viewed as consumers. To overcome this ineffectiveness of consumer representation in government, Campbell advocated the same objectives the federation had pursued: the development of a comprehensive body of knowledge of the economy from a consumer viewpoint, so that consumers and their leaders would know what consumer interests are; the creation of a major agency in the federal government to promote consumer needs; and the organization of a nationwide consumer movement. Through these she hoped to initiate the formation of what she often referred to as the "consumer interest" to counter the well-organized manufacturing, agricultural, commercial, and labor interests and to ensure that the economy fulfills its primary purpose of producing goods that consumers desire, thereby becoming more democratized.

In 1940 Campbell received her Ph.D. from Columbia and was hired to teach economics at Queens College. During the war she was also the director of Consumer Services of the Greater New York Civilian Defense Volunteer Office, a member of the National Consumer Advisory Board of the Office of Price Administration (OPA), and the vice chairman of the OPA's New York Consumers Committee. In 1947 she helped found the National Association of Consumers along with Hall, other consumer advocates, and leaders of national women's organizations. This association promoted the same goals as its predecessor, the Consumers National Federation. In 1948 she became the association's vice chairman. Lacking sufficient members, it came to an end in the 1950s.

In her most ambitious book, *The Consumer Interest: A Study in Consumer Economics* (1949), Campbell tried to create an example of consumer economics for consumer activists. She demonstrated in impressive detail, breadth, and clarity how many sectors of the economy met or failed to meet consumers' needs, especially those of lower-income families.

In 1954 the Democratic governor-elect of New York, Averell Harriman, upon the recommendation of Hall, appointed Campbell as his consumer counsel with cabinet rank. This was the first time a consumer leader attained such a high official position in state government. Harriman's action was due to his having been impressed with the objectives his sister Mary Harriman Rumsey had brought to her chairmanship of the CAB of the NRA.

Although Campbell's staff was small and short of funds, the governor gave her solid political support. Her office accomplished much. It carried out research on consumer problems, educated consumers through a variety of programs, coordinated consumer programs scattered throughout the state government, and initiated and coordinated efforts to pass consumer protection laws—most notably, eight laws passed in 1956, 1957, and 1958 to regulate installment credit, which rapidly expanded in ways unfair to consumers after World War II. Campbell's office became a model for most consumer affairs offices subsequently created in other states and the federal government, starting with California and Massachusetts, whose governors relied on her advice.

In 1959 Campbell returned to the Queens College faculty, where she became the chairman of the economics department in 1962. In 1964 she retired from teaching. In the 1960s and the early 1970s she was a consultant on various high-level New York City consumer boards, where she especially promoted the interests of lower-income groups.

In 1962 President John F. Kennedy appointed Campbell to his new Consumers Advisory Council, which was attached to the Council of Economic Advisers. After consulting with her, he set up a Consumer Counsel's Office in in the executive office and appointed Esther Peterson as its head. President Lyndon B. Johnson created a new Consumers Advisory Council separate from the Council of Economic Advisers and appointed Campbell to it. He appointed Peterson as his special assistant for consumer affairs, and she chaired the council. Peterson, who was new to consumer affairs, consulted closely with Campbell. The council and Peterson's office lacked power and adequate funding. In order to strengthen the position of the council and Peterson's office, consumer activists on and off the council, including Campbell, organized in 1967 the Consumers Federation of America, thus fulfilling one of Campbell's cherished objectives of an effective and long-lasting national consumers' organization.

After the late 1950s, Campbell had begun concentrating most of her consumer activities on international concerns. Her early interest in promoting international understanding had been intensified by the way she had seen World War II and the Cold War diverting resources from improving living standards. Most of her United Nations (UN) work was centered upon improving the living standards of lower-income people in underdeveloped nations. As early as 1948 she was a consumer adviser to the U.S. delegation at the

Food and Agricultural Organization (FAO), the goal of which was to increase agricultural productivity in the Third World. In 1951 she was the cochairman of the National Conference of Non-Governmental Relations working with the FAO.

As a board member since 1959 of the Consumers Union, the producer of *Consumer Reports*, Campbell was very active in the International Organization of Consumers Unions and was elected in 1966 as the chairman of its committee to the UN. Having worked with the AAUW on consumer issues for many years, she was made in 1968 the UN representative for the International Federation of University Women. She was also a widely traveled chairman of the Pan Pacific and Southeast Asia Women's Association. Campbell died in Queens, New York.

Guided by her reliance upon a rational, scholarly approach as the basis for discovering and promoting consumer interests, Campbell sometimes seemed impersonal even to her best friends. She was also a private person who did not easily discuss her inner feelings or personal life. Her reserved style also made it difficult for her to further her consumer reforms through emotional pleas. But those who worked with her found her to be a warm, gracious, intelligent person with inexhaustible energy and a buoyant optimism regarding her causes. She was a dedicated leader whose belief in the consumer cause inspired her coworkers.

Peterson rightly saw Campbell "as the one who really brought about the birth of the modern consumer movement in its modern dress" (Wolfe, p. 88). This "modern dress" was a national consumer organization, consumer offices possessing real power and influence at all levels of government, and, above all, the creation of a body of factual, rigorously presented economic data that would enable consumers to understand their interests and to act upon this understanding.

• Campbell's papers are in the Consumers Union Archives in Yonkers, New York. They include materials such as her letters, published and unpublished articles and speeches, legislative testimony, personal library, and some rather scattered and brief material on her private life. The University of Sydney has her official student records. Materials on her work as state consumer counsel of New York are in the Averell Harriman Papers at Syracuse University. Also see her book *Mary Williamson Harriman* (1960). Allis R. Wolfe, *Persia Campbell: Portrait of a Consumer Activist* (1981) is brief but very useful and sound. It contains a bibliography of most of her published articles and is partly based on interviews that are deposited in the Consumers Union Archives. See also Helen Hall, *Unfinished Business* (1971). Obituaries are in the *New York Times*, 3 Mar. 1974, and the *Washington Post*, 4 Mar. 1974.

PAUL C. TAYLOR

CAMPBELL, Prince Lucien (6 Oct. 1861–14 Aug. 1925), college president, was born in Newmarket, Missouri, the son of the Reverend Thomas Franklin Campbell and Jane Eliza Campbell, a first cousin of Alexander Campbell, cofounder of the Disciples of Christ. In 1879 Campbell graduated from Christian College in Monmouth, Oregon, where he remained as instructor in the classics for the next three years. (His father was president of the college from 1869 to 1882.) In 1882 he entered Harvard as a sophomore. After a year-long job reporting for the Kansas City *Star* between his junior and senior years, he received the A.B. degree in 1886. He then returned to Oregon to teach ancient and modern languages at the Oregon State Normal School at Monmouth, the successor to Christian College. In 1887 he married Eugenia J. Zieber of Forest Grove, Oregon. The couple had two children, a son who died in infancy and a daughter. In 1891 Campbell's wife died a few weeks after giving birth, and in 1908 he married a widowed cousin, Mrs. Susan Campbell Church of San Francisco.

Campbell became president of the Normal School in 1889 and served in that capacity for twelve years before becoming the fourth president of the University of Oregon in Eugene in 1902. During his twenty-three year tenure as president, Campbell was known as an indefatigable campaigner for the cause of public higher education in a state with a long tradition of denominational colleges and a citizenry habituated to private provision of education. Recognizing that the progress of state-supported universities depended on sufficient numbers of qualified student applicants and adequate funding, he actively promoted free public high schools throughout the state and helped to convince the legislature and the public to increase university appropriations.

In large degree, the administrative structure and educational ideology necessary for expansion were already in place when Campbell arrived at Oregon. His task was to win support for a broader vision of the university. Many Oregonians felt that the traditional functions of universities were antithetical to the broad economic and social values of society, and Campbell chose to expand the institution in practical directions that would prove its usefulness to the state. Between 1902 and 1921 Campbell added the schools of music, education, journalism, architecture and allied arts, business administration, sociology, and health and physical education to the already existing College of Liberal Arts and School of Engineering (in Eugene) and the schools of law and medicine (in Portland). In addition, he established the Extension Division, the Department of Correspondence (for correspondence courses), summer sessions in both Eugene and Portland, and brought the Law School to Eugene.

Campbell's solid achievements in service-oriented institution-building marked him as an avid educational statesman rather than scholar. He derived such pleasure from his work that he once commented he had "a 'sneaking' feeling about accepting a salary for doing it." In addition to his presidential duties, he served on the Emergency Council on Education during World War I and maintained lifelong avocational interests in philosophy, art, poetry, and mountain climbing. Campbell died in Eugene, Oregon.

• The papers of Prince Lucien Campbell are housed in the University of Oregon archives. A pamphlet detailing his philosophy of public education, *Education and the State* (1927), was published posthumously. The only biography is Joseph Schafer, *Prince Lucien Campbell* (1926), a celebratory work by a close friend and colleague. See also Henry D. Sheldon, *History of University of Oregon* (1940), for a laudatory account of Campbell's presidency, and Helen Butler Jones, "The Contributions of Certain Leaders to the Development of the Oregon Normal School, 1850–1930" (master's thesis, Univ. of Oregon, 1947), for a description of his tenure at the Oregon Normal School. Obituaries are in the 15 Aug. 1925 issues of the *New York Times*, the Portland *Morning Oregonian*, and the Eugene *Morning Register*.

C. H. Edson

CAMPBELL, Thomas (1 Feb. 1763–4 Jan. 1854), one of the early leaders of the Restoration movement in American Protestantism, was born in County Down, Ireland, the son of Archibald Campbell, a soldier, and Alice McNally. Little is known about Campbell's early life, but from a young age he was pious and studious. His father had converted from Roman Catholicism to Anglicanism, but Thomas joined the Seceder branch of the Presbyterian church as a young man. After teaching Latin and Greek near his home town, Thomas was allowed to attend the University of Glasgow, where he studied for the Presbyterian ministry. Following the normal three-year theological program, he received special training provided by the Antiburgher faction of the Seceder Presbyterian church. When his formal education was completed, he returned to Ireland, where he taught at Ballymena in County Antrim. There he married Jane Corneigle, probably in 1787. They had ten children, two of whom died in infancy. In 1798 he accepted the pastorate of Ahorey Church and also began an academy at Rich Hill.

Campbell had a good reputation as a teacher of classical languages and literature and was acquainted with the philosophy of Thomas Reid of the Common Sense school of thought. During his pastorate at Ahorey, he studied John Locke's *Letters on Toleration* (1689, 1690, 1692) and became increasingly dissatisfied with the factionalism of his Presbyterian church. He failed in an attempt to unite the Burgher and Antiburgher factions of the Seceder church at the synod of 1805. This failure made him even more convinced of "the awful consequences of distracting, disturbing, and dividing the flock of the Lord's heritage by sectarianism." He gave up on his native church, and in 1807 he immigrated to America, leaving his Rich Hill Academy in the hands of his nineteen-year-old son, Alexander Campbell.

The Associate Synod of North America of the Seceder Presbyterian Church assigned Campbell to the presbytery of Chartiers in southwest Pennsylvania. He immediately became the center of controversy and was censured by the presbytery in 1808 on the charge that he rejected a number of Presbyterian practices and beliefs, such as creeds, confessions, and fast days, asserting that they were based only on human authority, not on Scripture. Campbell defended himself by the Reformation claim of *sola scriptura*, but he was forced to resign from the Presbyterian ministry on 13 September 1808. He continued to preach as an independent itinerant, and on 17 August 1809 he formed the Christian Association of Washington (Pa.), which was intended to promote his new plan for church union on the basis of the Bible alone. Campbell officially renounced creeds and confessions as impediments to church union. The motto of the association was simply: "Where the Scriptures speak, we will speak; where the Scriptures are silent, we are silent."

Campbell's principles were published by the Christian Association in *A Declaration and an Address* (1809), providing the clearest statements of Campbell's theology and vision of creedless Christianity. The *Declaration* was written by a man "tired and sick of the bitter jarrings and janglings of a party spirit" who wanted to "restore unity, peace, and purity, to the whole church of God" (Garrison and De Groot, p. 146). Campbell's argument in the address shows the influence of both his Calvinist background and reading of Common Sense philosophy. For Campbell, true Christianity must be "very far remote from logical subtleties and metaphysical speculations" and instead be established "on the plainest and most obvious principles of common sense." In summary, the address argues that the Bible is a clear document that can be understood by any rational person; the New Testament governs the practice of the Christian church, just as the Old Testament had governed the practice of Judaism; the Bible expresses the divine will, and all practices and doctrines that arose after the New Testament are human inventions; and, therefore, the New Testament alone forms the basis for the union of all Christians. Campbell earnestly believed that his Restorationist program would inaugurate a reformation among the Protestants in America that would produce a church "free from all mixture of human opinions and inventions of men."

However, Campbell's Christian Association did not become the planned leaven within the churches. Instead it became a separate church after Campbell was denied admission to the Pittsburgh Presbytery in 1810. On 4 May 1811 the Christian Association became the Brush Run Church. During this time, Campbell sent for his family from Ireland. Alexander Campbell soon became a leader in his father's growing movement. They both itinerated and established small academies in Guernsey County, Ohio; Pittsburgh, Pennsylvania; and Brooke County, Virginia. Alexander took his father's principle of allowing only practices that were clearly attested in the New Testament one step further than his father and renounced infant baptism. Eventually he convinced Thomas that a believer's baptism was the only norm in the New Testament, and on 2 June 1812 all of the Campbells were immersed by a local Baptist minister. This led to a brief merger with the Redstone Baptist Association that soon failed because of tension between the rationalism of the Campbells and the emotionalism of the Baptists. Eventually Barton Stone and his followers joined with the Campbellites, and the Disciples of Christ denomination was born. Thomas and Alexander Campbell worked closely together until the former's death in Bethany, Virginia (later W.Va.). Thomas assisted his son in running the Buffaloe Seminary, which closed in 1822. He also served as a teacher and trustee for Alexander's Bethany Seminary, founded in 1840. Moreover, he was a frequent contributor and occasional editor of the *Christian Baptist* magazine and its successor, the *Millennial Harbinger*, which helped spread the idea of primitive Christianity throughout the frontier.

Campbell played a major role in the formation of American Christianity by developing and spreading Restorationist ideas on the frontier. Campbell hoped that his concept of a creedless, principled church would unite Christians; however, he found himself involved in controversies with other evangelicals. For instance, during his sojourn in Kentucky and Ohio in 1816–1817, he was very critical of Baptist emotionalism. Both Campbells stressed the rational aspect of Christianity. The Disciples of Christ church, which grew out of the Campbellite movement, continued to promote Campbell's dream of a unified Christian church; however, Campbell's view of Scripture also became one of the foundations of the Fundamentalist movement.

• The archives of Bethany College in W.Va. contain many original sources related to Campbell and the early Restorationist movement. One of the major sources on Campbell is Alexander Campbell, *The Memoirs of Elder Thomas Campbell* (1861), which includes extracts from his diary, letters, addresses, and *A Declaration and an Address*. The work is marred by the son's desire to glorify his father. Information is also contained in R. Richardson, *Memoirs of Alexander Campbell* (1868). A number of small, popular biographies of Campbell have been produced by the Disciples of Christ, but the most complete biography available is William Hebert Hanna, *Thomas Campbell, Seceder and Christian Union Advocate* (1935; repr. 1977). The chapters on the Campbells in Winfred Ernest Garrison and Alfred T. De Groot, *The Disciples of Christ: A History*, rev. ed. (1958), are very helpful, as is the bibliography.

CRAIG D. ATWOOD

CAMPBELL, Tunis Gulic (1 Apr. 1812–4 Dec. 1891), abolitionist and Georgia politician, was born free in Middlebrook, New Jersey, the son of John Campbell, a blacksmith, and an unknown mother. From 1817 to 1830 he attended an otherwise all-white Episcopal school in Babylon, New York, where he trained to be a missionary to Liberia under the auspices of the American Colonization Society. Rebelling against his training and calling himself "a moral reformer and temperance lecturer," Campbell moved to New Brunswick, New Jersey, converted to Methodism, joined an abolition society, and began to preach against slavery, colonization, alcohol, and prostitution. He joined with Frederick Douglass on speaking tours and participated in the Colored Convention Movement that aimed to uplift African Americans to equality with whites.

From 1832 to 1845 Campbell lived and worked in New York City as a steward at the Howard Hotel. Later, for an undetermined period, he worked at the Adams House in Boston, where he wrote *Hotel Keepers, Head Waiters, and Housekeepers' Guide* (1848), the first American-written book on how to run a first-class hotel. Appended to the text was a recommendation from his New York employer calling Campbell "an unusually intelligent, dignified, attentive, and obliging man . . . of unblemished moral character, with a disposition to elevate the condition and character of persons of his color." While living Boston, Campbell married Harriet (maiden name unknown), with whom he had two children and adopted another. In 1861 Campbell relocated his family to New York City, where he managed a bakery.

Early in the Civil War, Campbell volunteered to join the army, but the nation accepted no black soldiers at that time. After Lincoln's Emancipation Proclamation, a white friend of Campbell's persuaded Secretary of War Edwin Stanton to commission Campbell to report to General Rufus Saxton and help resettle black refugees around Port Royal, South Carolina. Campbell worked with Saxton for nearly eighteen months before Congress established the Bureau of Refugees, Freedmen, and Abandoned Lands in March 1865. Saxton appointed him as a bureau agent and assigned him to supervise resettlement on five Georgia islands.

Campbell transported settlers to Ossabaw, Delaware, Colonel's, Sapelo, and St. Catherine's islands, where he approved land divisions in forty-acre plots, distributed food from the bureau and northern philanthropic groups, organized the men into militia companies, established schools, oversaw planting, and instructed the former slaves on representative government. His wife and sons joined him as teachers in the schools on St. Catherine's. By December 1865 nearly 1,000 newly freed people were learning to be free in families and on land of their own.

In Washington, President Andrew Johnson reversed the gains of blacks by pardoning white planters and ordering their property returned to them. The bureau revoked the land deeds held by freedmen and encouraged blacks to sign labor contracts with their former masters. Campbell used his militia units to resist, but when U.S. troops confronted him, he was forced to capitulate. Removed from his position for defying Presidential Reconstruction, Campbell moved to mainland Georgia and signed a rent-to-own agreement for "BelleVille" plantation in McIntosh County. He began his own resettlement program, offering settlers the chance to grow crops on plots of their own, using the proceeds of the harvest to buy the land. Once the mortgage was paid, the land would be theirs. Incessant rains spoiled these plans.

When Congress took charge of Reconstruction in March 1867, Campbell registered freedmen to vote in McIntosh, Liberty, and Tatnall counties in southeastern Georgia. In this capacity he strengthened his position as the most prominent black man in an area with a two-to-one black majority. On the state level Campbell was elected vice president of Georgia's Republican party. In ensuing elections, voters elected him to the state constitutional convention, the Georgia Senate, and to the position of justice of the peace.

From 1868 to 1873 Senator Campbell worked diligently for the elevation of blacks. He spoke personally with Senator Charles Sumner and President Ulysses S. Grant about the necessity for establishing and enforcing the Fifteenth Amendment. He testified before the congressional committee investigating the Ku Klux Klan. Within the state Campbell promoted laws to establish equal educational opportunities, abolish imprisonment for debt, revise the judicial selection process to include intelligent jurors of both races, stop discrimination on public conveyances, and provide protection at polling places to ensure fair voting.

From his office as a local justice of the peace and his pulpit in the African Methodist Episcopal church, from his new house in Darien and in his capacity as the local political boss of the black community, Campbell tried to protect freed people from physical abuse. He fined or jailed whites who assaulted them. He held frequent meetings to advise the people on labor contracts, religion, politics, and militancy. He ran a cohesive black power structure that counseled blacks to advance "without compromise" but "in harmony" with whites as far as possible.

In 1872 conservative white Georgians surged back into power and began a concerted effort to remove prominent black politicians. In a series of extraordinary moves that culminated in 1876, Campbell was stripped of his senate seat; then after his election to the state house, a fraudulent recount took that seat too. He was indicted and jailed for malfeasance in his position as justice of the peace, which stemmed from a year-old case in which Campbell had jailed a white man for contempt of court.

After a failed intervention by armed black supporters and an unsuccessful effort by the U.S. attorney general to make the government of Georgia correct the injustice, Campbell spent nine months in a Savannah jail and a year as a convict hired out by the Georgia penitentiary to a rich farmer in middle Georgia. Afraid to return to Darien after his release in January 1877, Campbell left the state for Washington, D.C. He wrote a short autobiography and returned to preaching.

In 1882 Campbell traveled to McIntosh County to campaign against an old rival. Local authorities quickly put him in jail for a few days, as a warning, before releasing him. The local newspaper printed an assessment: "Do not fear . . . he is not boss now." But one month later, the same paper acknowledged: "The colored people of this county have the greatest confidence in Tunis G. Campbell, and are willing to let him . . . do just as his sweet will dictates." Campbell picked the opposition candidate for the state legislative contest, and voters overwhelmingly voted for his choice, Hercules Wilson, a black man. Campbell left the state for good on 30 December 1882. The events of his life thereafter are unknown. He died in Boston.

Campbell was a significant actor in his roles as abolitionist lecturer, Freedmen's Bureau agent, state senator, black adviser, and community organizer. During the Reconstruction period, few African Americans gained more power or accomplished as much in helping their constituents gain equal treatment. Even after he was removed, his political machine controlled local elections until 1907, when the state of Georgia disfranchised blacks. At that time, the only African American in the legislature was Amos Rodgers of McIntosh County. The historical image of Campbell has shifted from that of a black carpetbagger who exploited blacks for personal gain to that of an honest reformer committed to equality.

• No cache of Campbell papers exists. For an account of his ordeals see his brief autobiography, *Sufferings of the Rev. T. G. Campbell and His Family in Georgia* (1877). Russell Duncan, *Freedom's Shore: Tunis Campbell and the Georgia Freedmen* (1986), is a full-length biography. A more negative evaluation of him can be found in E. Merton Coulter, *Negro Legislators in Georgia during the Reconstruction Period* (1968). See also Edmund L. Drago, *Black Politicians and Reconstruction in Georgia: A Splendid Failure* (1982), for the most comprehensive view of black politics in Georgia, and Eric Foner, *Reconstruction: America's Unfinished Revolution, 1863–1877* (1988), for Campbell's place in a national context.

RUSSELL DUNCAN

CAMPBELL, Walter Gilbert (8 Nov. 1877–19 Mar. 1963), federal food and drug regulatory official, was born in Knox County, Kentucky, the son of Charles Christopher Campbell and Sallie Hoskins. (Nothing is known about what his parents did for a living.) Graduated from the University of Kentucky (1902), Campbell secured a law degree from the University of Louisville (1905) and began practice in that city. He was retained by the Kentucky Experiment Station to help enforce the state food and drug law. In 1907 Campbell took the first Civil Service examination for inspectors to enforce the federal Food and Drugs Act of 1906. When they first met, Campbell so impressed Harvey W. Wiley, chief of the Bureau of Chemistry of the Department of Agriculture, that Wiley appointed Campbell chief inspector. During the early days of enforcement in 1907, Wiley became upset at seeing barrels of rectified whiskey, which he deemed adulterated, on a sidewalk in downtown Washington, and he demanded something be done about it. When the district attorney did not know how to proceed, Campbell prepared the first libel for seizure under the law. He also drafted the first inspectors' manual. When Wiley became embroiled in high-level controversies, he left the placement of inspectors and the establishment of inspectional routines to Campbell.

After Wiley's resignation, Campbell became head of the Eastern District, one of three regions set up in 1914 for field enforcement operations. "When we first started," he recalled, "it was a sort of gum shoe method, because we could bring down game no matter where we aimed." Campbell developed a project plan for his region, setting priorities and time allotments based on the urgency of food and drug problems. This system he extended nationwide when he became assistant chief of the Bureau of Chemistry in 1916 then acting chief in 1921. In 1916 he married May Ashby Lambert; there were no children in the marriage.

During the first decade and a half under the law, some sixty food products warranted special investigations, the most troublesome being milk, eggs, vinegar, oysters, tomato products, stock feed, olive oil, and other canned vegetables. Crises involved spoiled canned salmon and ripe olives contaminated with a toxin-causing botulism. On the drug side, many outrageous patent medicines were removed from the marketplace, and inspections targeted adulterated crude botanicals gathered in American forests and fields. In the 1920s pesticide residues, especially on apples, became a major problem.

Campbell refused appointment as chief of the bureau, believing a chemist should hold this post and arguing that law enforcement and chemical research did not belong in the same bureaucratic body. In 1927 Congress accepted Secretary of Agriculture William M. Jardine's recommendation to split the bureau, the regulatory half becoming the Food, Drug, and Insecticide Administration (FDIA) with Campbell as chief. He continued also as director of regulatory work for the Department of Agriculture, a responsibility he held from 1923 to 1933. The FDIA became the Food and Drug Administration (FDA) in 1930 and in 1940 was transferred from Agriculture to the Federal Security Agency, Campbell becoming commissioner of food and drugs.

Campbell was a consummate administrator. A close associate gave him this accolade: "His experience in solving administrative problems, his skill in directing the work of the staff, his diplomacy in dealing with other Federal officials, his fairness with the trade, his adherence to the best interests of the consumer, his integrity, and his quickness of perception commanded the respect of all who knew him" (Linton, *FDC Law Journal* 5:328). While Campbell's manner struck subordinates as sometimes brusque, he traveled through the field and came to know members of his agency by name, even sharing their poker games.

Campbell fought fiercely against fraud, such as pepper adulterated with ground shells by McCormick & Company and the common weed horsetail promoted under the name Banbar to cure diabetes. However, if science was uncertain, or if illegal actions were accidental or the work of a minority of producers, Campbell cooperated with industry and strove to educate it to curb questionable practices and improve consumer protection. With contact committees from the two major pharmaceutical manufacturers associations, he worked out state-of-the-art standards governing injectable drugs, and with processors of canned salmon and their trade association he negotiated a Better Salmon Control Plan to maintain quality in the industry. Campbell was a skillful negotiator. He could say no to unjustifiable requests so subtly that his negative was accepted without resentment—his staff termed this "administering the ether." Campbell did not always succeed in his goals. After a long FDA campaign had reduced levels of arsenic and lead residues from pesticides on fruits and vegetables to acceptable tolerance levels, Congress in the late 1930s, lobbied by apple growers, canceled FDA's research into pesticide hazards, and the agency was forced to double tolerances.

Campbell recognized inadequacies in the 1906 law from the beginning of his career, and during the 1920s he fought successfully bills intended to weaken it further, for example, proposed legislation that would have barred the bureau from making multiple seizures to clear the market quickly of an objectionable product. He worked closely with members of Congress and proved to be an effective witness before committees. With the arrival of the New Deal, Campbell directed the strategy in the five-year campaign for a more adequate statute that led to the Food, Drug, and Cosmetic Act of 1938. He did not achieve all his legislative aims. For example, he unsuccessfully sought the authority for FDA to police food and drug advertising. The law greatly strengthened consumer protection, however, and medical devices and cosmetics came under FDA control. The law also increased penalties and gave FDA a new weapon, the injunction. Foods injurious to health could be more stringently regulated, and FDA was given authority to establish standards of identity and quality for most foods. The government no longer needed to prove fraudulent intent concerning false therapeutic claims in the labeling of proprietary drugs, and labeling was now required to include adequate warnings. New drugs could not be marketed until their manufacturers had persuaded FDA that they were safe. Campbell devised enforcement plans under the new law and trained the three commissioners who followed him. Thus, even though he retired in 1944, it can be said that Campbell's concepts governed federal regulation under food and drug statutes from 1907 to 1966.

In retirement the Campbells lived in Orlando, Florida, where Walter Campbell died.

• Food and Drug Administration records (Record Group 88) in the National Archives and the Washington National Records Center contain many of Campbell's letters and speeches. FDA's annual reports are collected in *Federal Food, Drug and Cosmetic Law: Administrative Reports, 1907–1949* (1951). See also Ruth deForest Lamb, *American Chamber of Horrors* (1936); Fred B. Linton's series on "Federal Food and Drug Laws—Leaders," in *Food Drug Cosmetic Law Quarterly* 4 (1949): 451–70, and *Food Drug Cosmetic Law Journal* 5 (1950): 103–15, 326–39, 479–93, 771–87; Paul B. Dunbar, "Memories of Early Days," *Food Drug Cosmetic Law Journal* 14 (1959): 87–138; Charles O. Jackson, *Food and Drug Legislation in the New Deal* (1970); and James Harvey Young, "From Oysters to After-Dinner Mints: The Role of the Early Food and Drug Inspector," *Journal of the History of Medicine and Allied Sciences* 42 (1987): 30–53, and "Food and Drug Enforcers in the 1920s: Restraining and Educating Business," *Business and Economic History* 2d ser., 21 (1992): 119–

28. The FDA periodical *Food and Drug Review* chronicled key events in Campbell's career; for his retirement, 4 (1944): 107–8, 112–14; for an obituary, 47 (1963): 93, 120.

JAMES HARVEY YOUNG

CAMPBELL, Walter Stanley (15 Aug. 1887–25 Dec. 1957), historian and author, was born Walter Stanley Vestal near Severy, Kansas, the son of Walter Mallory Vestal, a lawyer, and Isabella Louise Wood, a teacher. His father died shortly after his birth. In 1895 his mother met James Robert Campbell, whom she married in August 1896, and Walter assumed his stepfather's name. James Campbell's research work for H. H. Bancroft fostered Walter Campbell's love for the Old West and developed his sympathetic views toward Native Americans.

In August 1898 the Campbell family moved to Guthrie, Oklahoma Territory. Here Campbell developed the lifelong habit of collecting firsthand stories from Old West frontiersmen and Native Americans. During the summer of 1899 and the following three summers, Campbell visited and lived among a Cheyenne tribe near his uncle's home. By age fifteen, he was well versed in Cheyenne life and customs.

In 1903 the Campbell family moved to Weatherford, Oklahoma, after James Campbell was appointed president of the new Southwestern State Normal School. Here Walter Campbell befriended John Washee, an Indian scout for General Custer, and George Bent, regarded by western Americana historians as the best Native American historian of the southern Plains tribes. At the 1904 World's Fair in St. Louis, Campbell talked with the Apache Geronimo and learned the customs, dress, and crafts of various other tribes at the fair.

In 1908 Campbell won a Rhodes Scholarship. In 1911 he received a bachelor of arts from Oxford and returned to the United States. He taught at Mechanical High School and later at Male High School in Louisville, Kentucky, until 1914. Unhappy with teaching, Campbell returned home to Arapaho, Oklahoma, to live with his parents and conduct research among the Native Americans living there. He published two articles for the *American Anthropologist* in 1915, but debts forced him to accept a teaching position at University of Oklahoma that same year. He achieved modest success with articles he published in newspapers and the *Oklahoma Monthly*. At this time he began publishing under his birth name, Stanley Vestal. In 1916 Campbell was awarded an honorary master of arts degree from Oxford. In 1917 he volunteered for the first Reserve Officer Training Corps calvary unit during World War I. That same year he married Isabel Jones; they had two children, both daughters.

After the war Campbell returned to Weatherford to teach at Southwestern State College. In 1922 he began his first book-length project based on research material he had started to collect on the Cheyennes when he was twelve. He also began a biography of Kit Carson and a book of Old West ballads, while teaching full time, editing John Homer Seger's *Early Days among the Cheyenne and Arapaho Indians*, and conducting research for future projects.

In 1925 Campbell's publishing success began. H. L. Mencken, editor of *American Mercury*, and Harriet Monroe, editor of *Poetry: A Magazine of Verse*, bought several ballads for their periodicals. He also published articles and stories in other publications. In 1927 his first book, *Fandango: Ballads of the Old West*, was published by Houghton Mifflin Company. In 1928 *Kit Carson* and *Happy Hunting Grounds* were published, and in 1929 *'Dobe Walls* appeared. All were critically well received.

In 1930 the Guggenheim Foundation awarded Campbell a grant to study the Plains Indians and work on a biography of Sitting Bull. *Sitting Bull: Champion of the Sioux* (1932) established him as a leading historian of the Plains tribes. In 1934 *Warpath*, a biography of White Bull, and *New Sources of Indian History, 1850–1891* were published. After the publication of *Mountain Men* in 1937, Campbell was selected for membership in the Oklahoma chapter of Phi Beta Kappa for his achievements as a writer, teacher, and scholar.

Campbell established a creative-writing school in 1938 at University of Oklahoma based on his book *Professional Writing*. Macmillan brought out two editions of his book in 1938, one for schools and one for the trade. That same year Houghton Mifflin published Vestal's final historical novel, *Revolt on the Border*. *The Old Santa Fe Trail* (1939) resulted in his selection to *World Biographical Encyclopedia* and charter membership in the Society of American Historians. Campbell and his wife divorced at this time.

Campbell's stature and fame grew with the success of both his publications and his writing program at University of Oklahoma. He went on to write *Short Grass Country* (1941), *Bigfoot Wallace* (1942), and *The Missouri* (1945). For his contribution to literature, Campbell was inducted into the International Mark Twain Society in 1945. In 1947 he received a Rockefeller Foundation award for work on the advancement of literature in the South, and in 1956 he received the National Achievement Award from The Westerners for helping preserve the cultural heritage of the American West through his work. He was a member of the League of American Writers, the British *Who's Who*, the Author's Club (London), the Author's League of America, and the Association of University Professors; he was inducted into the Oklahoma Hall of Fame and the Western Writers of America. He was also included in *Who's Who in the Western Hemisphere*. Campbell continued writing until his death in Oklahoma City.

Campbell's biographies and histories continue to be the standard work in their areas because his sources were firsthand witnesses to the people and events he outlines. His research was so exhaustive that he left little to be uncovered after one of his books was published. His compassion and respect toward Native Americans, and the frontiersmen who lived their way of life, led him to write a history of the American West from a Native American perspective.

• Campbell's unpublished letters, diaries, and miscellaneous papers are located in the Campbell collection, Division of Manuscripts, University of Oklahoma Library, Norman, Okla. Other books by Campbell include *Warpath* (1934), *The Wine Room Murder* (1935), *Sallow Moon* (1937), *King of the Fur Traders: Pierre Esprit Radisson* (1940), *Jim Bridger* (1946), *Wagons Southwest* (1946), *Warpath and Council Fire* (1948), *Joe Meek* (1952), and *Queen of the Cow Towns: Dodge City* (1957). Ray Tassin, *Stanley Vestal: Champion of the Old West* (1973), is a valuable biography that traces Campbell's career and works; it also contains an extensive bibliography of primary and secondary sources.

ELIZABETH A. ARCHULETA
SUSAN E. GUNTER

CAMPBELL, William (1730?–?5 Sept. 1778), last royal governor of South Carolina, was the son of John Campbell, the fourth duke of Argyll, and Mary Bellenden. As the younger son of a duke, Campbell was not a peer, and "lord" was thus given to him as a courtesy title. With no expectation of an inheritance, he sought to make his fortune in the military. Between 1752 and 1760 he served in India as an officer of the East India Company. He participated in two naval actions against the fleet of comte d'Aché and took part in the battle of Plassey.

In December 1760 Campbell was commissioned a lieutenant in the Royal Navy. His rise in rank was meteoric. By August 1762 he held a captain's commission. Early in 1763, as commander of the HMS *Nightingale*, he visited the province of South Carolina, where he met Sarah Izard, daughter of the wealthy and prominent planter Ralph Izard. After a brief courtship, the two were married that April. The union produced three children.

In 1764 Campbell was elected to the House of Commons as a representative of the Shire of Argyll. Two years later he resigned from Parliament when he was appointed governor of Nova Scotia. He assumed his new position in November 1766 and served until 1773. In part because the cold climate at Halifax aggravated an eye injury suffered "whilst a boy at school," Campbell was often away from his post. He made multiple trips to Boston, London, and the southern colonies and was away from Nova Scotia for almost two years. During Campbell's frequent absences, Lieutenant Governor Michael Francklin dominated provincial affairs. Though generally popular with his constituents, Campbell proved at best an adequate governor. He did encourage road construction to create closer ties among the inhabitants of Nova Scotia. Without concrete success, he attempted to address the province's imposing debt and to curb smuggling and illicit trade. The latter policy did not endear him to local merchants or sea captains. As one strong faction launched an effort to secure Campbell's removal, the governor himself lobbied for transfer to a more prestigious position. In June 1773 his wish was fulfilled, and he was appointed governor of South Carolina.

On 17 June 1775 Campbell arrived in Charleston to a chilly reception. He found the province in the midst of revolutionary activity. The Provincial Congress, which now constituted the government, had appointed a Council of Safety to supervise defense efforts. Campbell called the Commons House of Assembly into session but was unable to persuade the hostile representatives to uphold royal government. South Carolinians, the governor discovered, feared that the British would utilize both the black slave majority and American Indians to reassert control. This paranoia resulted in the trial and execution of Thomas Jeremiah, a free black harbor pilot accused of plotting a slave revolt. To no avail, Campbell, who believed Jeremiah was innocent, pleaded that the pilot be treated with clemency.

Soon after his arrival, Campbell opened communications with loyal settlers in the South Carolina backcountry. He encouraged Loyalists to maintain their allegiance to the Crown but cautioned them to avoid armed encounters with the rebels. Militant Loyalists, such as Thomas Brown and Moses Kirkland, proposed that the British military act in coordination with backcountry Loyalists to restore royal authority. Campbell supported these suggestions and submitted reports to the British ministry that proved influential in its strategic decision to utilize southern Loyalists and Indians to extinguish the rebellion.

After the Council of Safety received confirmation of Campbell's secret communications with both Loyalists and Indians, there were numerous calls for his arrest. Fearful for his own safety, Campbell dissolved the assembly and fled to the sloop *Tamar* on 15 September. The Council of Safety invited him to return on the condition that he not act against the revolutionary movement. "I never will return to Charles-Town till I can support the King's authority and proteck [*sic*] his faithful and Loyal Subjects," replied Campbell. He remained in Charleston Harbor until January 1776, when the revolutionaries, having discovered that the British concealed escaped slaves, refused to provide further provisions to the fleet of six ships.

One month later Campbell joined Major General Henry Clinton's expedition against the southern provinces. Clinton initially hoped to coordinate a campaign with Loyalists in North Carolina, but the rebel victory at Moores Creek Bridge in late February eliminated any chance for a British rendezvous with their allies in that province. At that point Clinton preferred operations in Virginia, but Campbell urged an attack on Charleston. Campbell's arguments, coupled with the endorsement of commodore Sir Peter Parker, the naval commander of the expedition, convinced Clinton to move against Charleston. At the British defeat in the battle of Sullivan's Island on 28 June, Campbell volunteered to command the lower deck guns on HMS *Bristol*. The American gunners in Fort Sullivan directed much of their fire at the *Bristol*, and Campbell was among 111 casualties. In a dispatch to the British admiralty, Parker commended Campbell, who "received a contusion on His Left Side, but I have the Happiness to inform Their Lordships, That it has not proved of much Consequence."

Parker was wrong, for Campbell never fully recovered. With his family he returned to England, where he continued to press for renewed British efforts against South Carolina. In August 1777 Campbell and James Wright, the royal governor of Georgia, submitted to Lord George Germain a memorial that proposed an immediate attack against the southernmost rebellious provinces. The governors argued that both Georgia and South Carolina contained large numbers of Loyalists who would help restore British rule. Campbell died at Southampton, apparently from complications caused by his wound.

A man of unquestioned bravery, as a governor Campbell was well intentioned but largely ineffectual. In that sense he was typical of the British officials who encountered the tide of revolution in America. His persistence in championing the Loyalists as an untapped military resource was among the factors that led British war planners to launch their southern strategy in 1778, when they redirected their major military efforts toward the southern states.

• Campbell letters concerning revolutionary South Carolina are housed in the British Public Records Office, Colonial Office Papers (CO5/396 is readily available on microfilm). Campbell correspondence is also in the Clinton papers, William L. Clements Library, University of Michigan, Ann Arbor. Campbell's early career and tenure in Nova Scotia can be followed in John Bartlet Brebner, *The Neutral Yankees of Nova Scotia: A Marginal Colony during the Revolutionary Years* (1937). On Campbell in South Carolina, consult *The Papers of Henry Laurens*, ed. David R. Chesnutt, vol. 10 (1985). His role in the formulation of British military strategy is discussed in Paul H. Smith, *Loyalists and Redcoats: A Study in British Revolutionary Policy* (1964). The battle of Sullivan's Island is covered in William J. Morgan, ed., *Naval Documents of the American Revolution*, vol. 5 (1970).

GREGORY D. MASSEY

CAMPBELL, William (Aug. 1745–22 Aug. 1781), revolutionary war officer, was born in Augusta County, Virginia, the son of Charles Campbell, a farmer and landowner, and Margaret Buchanan. Campbell's grandfather came to America from northern Ireland in 1726 and settled in Lancaster County, Pennsylvania. In 1733 Campbell's father settled in Augusta County, Virginia (then part of Orange County). Campbell was baptized on 1 September 1745; the exact date of his birth is unknown. From the tutorship of David Thompson and attendance at Augusta Academy (the nucleus of the later Washington and Lee University), Campbell gained a mastery of the English language and became known as an excellent writer. Possessing a tall, rugged physique, sandy red hair, and blue eyes, Campbell had a great source of confidence that made him ideally suited as a leader of Virginia's frontiersmen.

In 1769, two years after his father died, Campbell moved with his mother and four sisters to rich farm land near the Middle Fork of the Holston River. Here Campbell established a plantation, which he called "Aspenvale," twenty-one miles east of Abdington, Virginia. On 6 July 1773 Campbell was appointed a justice of the peace for the newly created Virginia county of Fincastle, which included most of southwestern Virginia and all of Kentucky.

As a militia captain in 1774, Campbell served in the campaign against Indians known as Dunmore's War. He raised a company in a regiment, commanded by Colonel William Christian, that would join Colonel Andrew Lewis's army on the Ohio River as it prepared to invade the Shawnee Indian country. Christian's force arrived at Lewis's camp at midnight just after the battle of Point Pleasant, 10 October 1774. Campbell stayed with the army until after Lord Dunmore, Virginia's royal governor, concluded the Treaty of Camp Charlotte nine days later.

After the Revolution began in April 1775, Campbell raised another company of militia from Bedford, Botetourt, Fincastle, and Pittsylvania counties. With this company he joined Colonel William Woodford's militia near Norfolk in mid-December 1775, just after the battle of Great Bridge, to fight against Lord Dunmore's troops. Campbell was appointed 28 February 1776, at his same rank of captain, to serve in the First Virginia Regiment of the Continental army. In April 1776 Campbell married Elizabeth Henry, the sister of Patrick Henry; they had two children. Campbell stayed with the Virginia troops until Lord Dunmore and his forces fled Virginia in July 1776.

In order to help defend his frontier home from possible attack by Cherokee Indians, Campbell resigned his army commission on 9 October 1776. Had he remained in military service he would have joined Virginia forces already with George Washington's army in New York. A Cherokee war did not materialize, however, and Campbell served as one of the commissioners that determined a boundary line between Virginia and Cherokee territory. In 1777 Campbell was a lieutenant colonel of militia. From 28 January 1777 to 19 April 1780 he was a justice of the peace for the new Washington County, as well as its county lieutenant. In 1780 he achieved the rank of full colonel of the militia.

During 1779 and 1780 Campbell led his neighbors on mounted raids against Tories in southwestern Virginia. The vigilante militia apprehended spies in the service of the British as well as Tory robbers; meted out punishment; and plundered and confiscated Tory property, which was later auctioned off. Called the "bloody tyrant of Washington County," Campbell executed about a dozen Tories. Once, while he, his family, and some neighbors were returning home from church, he encountered a known British spy and chased him. After fierce hand-to-hand combat, Campbell subdued the fugitive, who was immediately hanged by the roadside. Campbell also led about 500 militia from several counties to break up a Tory effort to seize the state's lead mines in Montgomery County. Instead of censuring the brand of military justice administered by Campbell and several other frontier leaders, the Virginia assembly voted its approval.

Campbell was elected to the Virginia House of Delegates in 1780 and 1781, but he had little time to attend legislative sessions. In the summer of 1780, under orders from Governor Thomas Jefferson, Campbell led militia into the Cherokee country, which resulted in negotiations for peace. During much of the last year of his life Campbell commanded militia in conjunction with regular army troops as they resisted the British invasion of the Carolinas and Virginia.

Campbell achieved lasting fame at the battle of Kings Mountain on 7 October 1780 in North Carolina. His Washington County militia had linked up with similar volunteers from western Virginia, eastern Tennessee, and North Carolina. On 2 October Campbell was voted to be in command of an expedition against a Tory military force under Major Patrick Ferguson. Many years later an American soldier commented that, under Campbell's leadership, "the whole army appeared to be renovated; discipline was more strict; and our troops appeared more like a well organized army . . . our marches were more rapid, and the whole force seemed to gain new animation" (quoted in Malgee, p. 134). Campbell led his men up the right side of the small plateau ridge occupied by Ferguson's men, with Campbell entreating his militiamen to "shout like hell and fight like devils!" During the last twenty minutes of the battle Campbell stayed at the head of his troops and fought the enemy at the close range of 20 to 30 yards. Although he was party to some of the slaughter of enemy troops who had attempted to surrender, Campbell is credited with preventing to some extent further butchery.

Not long after the battle of Kings Mountain, Campbell answered a summons from General Nathanael Greene for assistance to the Continental army in the South. Greene said that Campbell could "add new splendor to your own glory and give the world another proof of the bravery of the Mountain Militia" (*Greene Papers*, vol. 7, p. 218). Campbell joined his force with other militia, all under the command of General Otho Williams. In North Carolina at Wetzell's Mill on 6 March 1781, Campbell helped to hold off attacking British cavalry while the rest of the American force sought better ground. At the battle of Guilford Courthouse on 15 March 1781, near Greensboro, North Carolina, Campbell's militia and Henry Lee's legion held firm in engaging the left flank of General Charles Cornwallis's army. Lee, however, suddenly abandoned Campbell, leaving Campbell's men to sustain heavy casualties. Campbell was most embittered by Lee's decision. After the battle Greene praised Campbell's heroism, and his cousin Arthur Campbell declared that had other troops fought as did those under Campbell, "the British army must have met with a total defeat" (quoted in Malgee, p. 221).

Appointed brigadier general by the Virginia General Assembly on 14 June 1781, Campbell joined the army of the marquis de Lafayette, which was confronting Cornwallis's invasion of Virginia. Commented Lafayette, "I have put all the Riflemen under Campbell." Campbell himself was not involved at the battle of Green Spring (6 July 1781), near Williamsburg, in which troops under General Anthony Wayne were ambushed by Cornwallis's army; however, several of his riflemen were among the casualties. Campbell did not accompany Lafayette's army as it followed the British down the peninsula, resulting in the siege of Yorktown. Complaining of a pain in his chest he went to the home of his wife's half-brother, Colonel John Syme, at Rocky Mills in Hanover County, where he died of an apparent heart attack.

Campbell played a major role in the Revolution, both in securing southwestern Virginia for the patriot cause and in his role as a militia commander. Although slightly hot-tempered and given to full vengeance against Tories, Campbell was an inspiring military leader who earned the plaudits of Congress. Campbell County, Virginia, created in 1782, was named for him.

• Manuscripts and various materials relating to Campbell are in the Lyman C. Draper Collection at the State Historical Society of Wisconsin. Campbell's army career is documented in Reuben G. Thwaites and Louise P. Kellogg, eds., *Documentary History of Dunmore's War* (1905); Robert L. Scribner and Brent Tartar, eds., *Revolutionary Virginia, the Road to Independence*, vols. 5–7 (1979–1983); Richard K. Showman, ed., *The Papers of General Nathanael Greene*, vol. 7 (1994); and Stanley J. Idzerda, ed., *Lafayette in the Age of the American Revolution: Selected Letters and Papers, 1776–1790*, vol. 4 (1981). For the battle of Kings Mountain, see Lyman C. Draper, *King's Mountain and Its Heroes* (1881), pp. 378–402, which contains a sketch of Campbell; and Samuel C. Williams, *Tennessee during the Revolutionary War* (1944). Campbell's effort to subdue Tories in southwestern Virginia is covered in Emory G. Evans, "Trouble in the Backcountry: Disaffection in Southern Virginia during the American Revolution," in Ronald Hoffman et al., eds., *An Uncivil War: The Southern Backcountry during the American Revolution* (1985), pp. 179–212. Two excellent, thoroughly researched biographies are David G. Malgee, "A Frontier Biography: William Campbell of King's Mountain" (M.A. thesis, Univ. of Richmond, 1983); and Agnes G. S. Riley, *Brigadier General William Campbell, 1745–1781*, Historical Society of Washington County Publication, ser. 2, no. 22 (May 1985). Of less value is Fran Russell, "A Commentary on the Life of General William Campbell," *Northern Neck of Virginia Historical Magazine* 4, no. 1 (Dec. 1954): 338–50. Hartwell L. Quinn, *Arthur Campbell: Pioneer and Patriot of the "Old Southwest"* (1990), has information on Campbell's early life and on the alleged rivalry between William Campbell and his cousin. John S. Pancake, *This Destructive War: The British Campaign in the Carolinas, 1780–1782* (1985), provides context for Campbell's participation in the southern military campaigns, and Lewis P. Summers, *History of Southwest Virginia, 1746–1786, Washington County, 1777–1890* (1903), does the same for Campbell and his home locale.

HARRY M. WARD

CAMPBELL, William (24 June 1876–16 Dec. 1936), metallurgist, was born in Gateshead-on-Tyne, England, the son of Thomas Campbell and his American-born wife, Franciska Albrecht, occupations unknown. Campbell's extensive formal schooling began at the

Civil Service Department of King's College in London in 1892, followed by two years at St. Kenelm's College, Oxford. He then entered Durham University College of Science, where he completed an associate of science degree in 1896 and his bachelor's degree in 1898. From 1899 to 1901 he was the 1851 Royal Exhibition research scholar at the Royal School of Mines in London. There he worked with Sir William Chandler Roberts-Austen who, along with other pioneer metallurgists, was still developing the field's basic scientific tools and proving their value to manufacturers in the form of improved products and processes. It was an exciting time to enter the field.

Campbell's connection to Roberts-Austen led him to begin work in 1902 with Henry Marion Howe, a leading American metallurgical pioneer, at Columbia University. Within a year Campbell was lecturing in European geology and had become an instructor in metallurgy. Howe himself recognized Campbell's ability in the preface to his *Iron, Steel and Other Alloys* (1903), "Let me thank . . . Dr. William Campbell, a non-resident lecturer on Metallurgy, for much valuable information, for many of the micrographs, and indeed, for the original suggestion to write the book." Campbell also received the endorsement of the British Society of the Chemical Industry, which awarded him its Saville Shaw Medal in 1903. That same year he received his doctorate, followed by an A.M. in 1905, both from Columbia. Also in 1905 he received an Sc.D. from the University of Durham and a Carnegie Scholarship from the British Iron and Steel Institute.

Clearly comfortable at Columbia, Campbell remained on that university's faculty for the remainder of his professional career, rising to adjunct professor in 1907, associate professor in 1912, and full professor in 1914. He also edited the *Columbia School of Mines Quarterly* during 1910–1911 and remained on its editorial board until 1915. Fittingly, Campbell became the first Henry Marion Howe Professor of Metallurgy in 1924. With interests in all aspects of ferrous and nonferrous physical metallurgy, he was considered a fine teacher, especially of advanced graduate students. His special interest, which continued the work of Roberts-Austen and Howe, was metallography, the branch of the field that sought to understand the crystal structures of metals using microscopic analysis. Of Campbell's more than fifty papers, perhaps his most noted was "A List of Alloys" (*American Society for Testing Materials* [1922; rev. ed., 1930]).

Like most leading academic metallurgists, Campbell was not strictly a university teacher. He especially liked trouble-shooting investigations of real world problems, including failures. Along with Howe and John Howe Hall, he also developed a low-manganese alloy steel and invented a microscope for the examination of ores. In further efforts to connect academia and the real world, Campbell served as a consulting metallographer to federal agencies: the U.S. Geological Survey from 1907 to 1911, the Bureau of Mines from 1912 to 1918, the National Research Council committee on alloy steels, and the advisory committee to the U.S. Bureau of Standards. He also was an advisory metallurgist to Ingersoll Rand from 1916 to 1928. In 1913 he lectured at the U.S. Naval Academy's postgraduate school and in 1917 became a metallurgist in the Brooklyn Navy Yard, a post that led to a commission as lieutenant commander in the navy reserve a year later. Promoted to commander in 1919, Campbell retained his commission until 1929.

Campbell was active in the professional societies that served the field of metallurgy, especially the American Society for Testing Materials, which was formed in 1899 and eventually became a leading setter of materials standards. His long connection to ASTM centered on its Committee on Nonferrous Metals and Alloys, which Campbell chaired from its inception in 1909 until 1934, when he was elected honorary chair. He also served on ASTM committees on heat treatment of iron and steel (after 1905), corrosion of iron and steel (after 1906), metallography (beginning in 1916), and on ASTM's executive committee from 1924 to 1926.

Campbell participated in many other organizations, including the American Institute of Mining and Metallurgical Engineers, the American Society of Metals, the American Society of Steel Treating, the British Institute of Metals, and the British Iron and Steel Institute. He was elected vice president of the New York Academy of Sciences and was a member of the Sigma Xi and Tau Beta Pi honorary fraternities. He also served for a time as an editor of the *International Journal of Metallography* and of the *Journal of Industrial and Engineering Chemistry*. Appropriately indicative of his stature was the invitation to deliver the third Howe Memorial Lecture to the AIMME in 1926.

In 1918 Campbell had married Estelle M. Campbell, but the couple divorced in 1930. They had no children. Campbell studied ancient metallurgy as a hobby and became an expert on metal weapons and armor as well as a collector of ancient and modern coins. He was also a stamp collector, a watercolor painter, and an excellent photographer, and he played golf, tennis, and handball.

Campbell was one of the generation of metallurgists who, after the turn of the twentieth century, built an academic discipline on a foundation provided by the field's pioneers. His main contribution came in the classroom, but he typified the close connections between academic metallurgists and corporations, professional organizations, and government agencies. His home was Columbia University, which bestowed on him an honorary doctorate in 1929, and to which he bequeathed his entire estate. He died in New York City. The pallbearers at his funeral included leading figures from Columbia and American engineering education such as Columbia president Nicholas Murray Butler; electrical engineer Dugald Jackson of MIT; and secretary of the American Institute of Mining and Metallurgical Engineers, A. B. Parsons.

• A collection of about 1,000 items, including letters, notebooks, financial records, and memorabilia spanning the years from 1900 to 1925, are in the William Campbell Papers, Rare Book and Manuscript Room, Butler Library, Columbia University. Campbell's 1926 Howe lecture, published as "Twenty-five Years of Metallography," *Transactions of the American Institute of Mining and Metallurgical Engineers* 73 (1926): 1135–78, contains some biographical information. Indicative of Campbell's other interests was his *Greek and Roman Plated Coins*, American Numismatic Society Notes and Monographs No. 57 (1933). A contemporary account of Campbell's career is in "Professor Campbell Honored by Committee," *ASTM Bulletin* 70 (Oct. 1934): 3. Additional information can be found in the entry on Campbell in *Who's Who in Engineering*, 3d ed. (1931). Obituaries and related articles are in *Mining and Metallurgy* 13 (Apr. 1937): 226–27 and the *New York Times*, 17 and 18 Dec. 1936.

BRUCE E. SEELY

CAMPBELL, William Bowen (1 Feb. 1807–19 Aug. 1867), congressman and governor, was born in Sumner County, Tennessee, the son of David Campbell and Catherine Bowen, farmers. The family was related by marriage to David Campbell (1779–1859) of Abingdon, Virginia, governor of Virginia from 1837 to 1840, who took responsibility for the education of his wife's nephew. After studying law with the famed Henry St. George Tucker (1780–1848) in Winchester, Virginia in 1827–1828, in 1829 Campbell returned to Carthage, Smith County, Tennessee, to practice. In 1835 he married Frances Isabella Owen; they had seven children.

Campbell became involved in politics during the early 1830s and was elected to the state legislature from Smith County in 1835. He favored the 1836 presidential candidacy of Tennessee senator Hugh Lawson White, thereby siding with the nascent Whig party. Campbell was elected in 1837 to the first of three consecutive terms in the U.S. House of Representatives, representing the Sixth District of middle Tennessee, which included Sumner, Smith, and Jackson counties. His voting record placed him among the more conservative southern Whigs. He did support a new national bank, but he opposed a high tariff, internal improvements, and depression relief.

Campbell, who in 1836 had led a company of volunteers in the Seminole War, was elected colonel of the volunteer First Tennessee Regiment soon after the start of the Mexican War. In the battle of Monterey on 21 September 1846, the "Bloody First" suffered over a hundred casualties, including more than thirty deaths. According to tradition, Campbell successfully rallied his men with the cry, "Boys, follow me!" The regiment subsequently participated in the siege of Vera Cruz and the battle of Cerro Gordo.

Campbell's military stature made him a leading prospect to run for governor of Tennessee in 1847, but he was discouraged from doing so by the powerful John Bell. Campbell instead deferred to Neill S. Brown, who won the post in 1847 but lost it two years later. In 1851 Tennessee Whigs turned to Campbell to challenge the incumbent Democratic governor, William Trousdale. Campbell took advantage of popular support for the Compromise of 1850 and for state aid to railroads, issues which divided the Democrats and on which Trousdale had equivocated. Although prevented by illness from completing a grueling public campaign, Campbell won narrowly and became the last Whig governor of the state. He held the post only for a single two-year term and did not seek reelection. After working as a cotton factor for about two years in New Orleans, by 1855 he returned to live in Lebanon, Wilson County, Tennessee, and became president of the Bank of Middle Tennessee.

In 1860 Campbell supported the presidential candidacy of his longtime political ally Bell on the Constitutional Union party ticket. Following Abraham Lincoln's victory, Campbell became a staunch antisecessionist who opposed even allowing a state convention to meet. After Lincoln's call for troops in April 1861, a patriotic clamor swept middle Tennessee, as most former Unionists spurned Lincoln's "coercive" policy and promptly sided with the Confederacy. Judging that he could not change the course of events, Campbell rebuffed pleas for assistance from the dwindling minority of unconditional Unionists. At the same time, however, he refused to acquiesce in the new order, rejecting the offer of a Confederate generalship.

The Union offensive of February and March 1862 restored middle Tennessee to federal control. Lincoln promptly appointed Tennessee senator Andrew Johnson as military governor of the state. Notwithstanding their earlier partisan disagreements, Johnson had Campbell appointed to a brigadier generalship in the Union army in June 1862. Because Campbell had misgivings about exercising active military command in the field, Johnson dispatched him to visit Tennessee prisoners of war in the North to obtain the release of those willing to pledge loyalty to the Union.

Campbell reacted indignantly when Lincoln issued his preliminary Emancipation Proclamation in September 1862. Fearing that it created "great danger of revolt in the Army," Campbell and like-minded Tennessee Unionists lobbied successfully to exempt their entire state from Lincoln's January 1863 edict (*Johnson Papers*, vol. 6, pp. 46–47, 85–86). Campbell resigned from the army in January 1863 and was soon prominent among Tennessee's antiemancipation Unionists. In 1864 he opposed Lincoln's reelection and supported George B. McClellan (1826–1885).

Campbell was elected to Congress from the Nashville district in August 1865. He opposed black testimony in court, complained about emancipation without compensation, and attacked the legitimacy of the state government under William G. Brownlow, which maintained power by disfranchising many former Confederates. Campbell was not seated in Congress until December 1866, after Tennessee ratified the Fourteenth Amendment. As one of Johnson's outnumbered allies, Campbell was appointed the minority member of the House committee that investigated the New Orleans riot of 30 July 1866. His term ended in March 1867.

Campbell, who had suffered intermittent ill health for many years, died at his home near Lebanon. He never recaptured the popularity and influence he enjoyed during his term as governor. His wartime Unionism was tentative and qualified, especially after Union war aims expanded to include emancipation. After the war the one-time Unionist allied openly with ex-Confederates.

• A quantity of manuscript material to and from Campbell may be found in the Campbell Family Papers, William R. Perkins Library, Duke University. Some items now in this collection were published in St. George Sioussat, ed., "Mexican War Letters of Col. William Bowen Campbell, of Tennessee, Written to Governor David Campbell, of Virginia, 1846–1847," *Tennessee Historical Magazine* 1 (1915): 129–67; and Sioussat, ed., "Letters of John Bell to William B. Campbell, 1839–1857," *Tennessee Historical Magazine* 3 (1917): 201–27. Some biographical information about Campbell may be found in *Sketch of the Life and Public Services of Gen. Wm. B. Campbell, of Tennessee* (1851) and in Margaret Campbell Pilcher, *Historical Sketches of the Campbell, Pilcher and Kindred Families* (1911). In the absence of a full biography, information about Campbell's career must be gleaned from the following: Joseph Howard Parks, *John Bell of Tennessee* (1950); Charles Grier Sellers, Jr., *James K. Polk: Jacksonian, 1795–1843* (1957) and *James K. Polk: Continentalist, 1843–1846* (1966); Thomas B. Alexander, *Thomas A. R. Nelson of East Tennessee* (1956) and *Political Reconstruction in Tennessee* (1950); Joel H. Silbey, *The Shrine of Party: Congressional Voting Behavior, 1841–1852* (1967); Arthur Charles Cole, *The Whig Party in the South* (1912); Mary Emily Robertson Campbell, *The Attitude of Tennesseans toward the Union, 1847–1861* (1961); Paul H. Bergeron, *Antebellum Politics in Tennessee* (1982); and Daniel W. Crofts, *Reluctant Confederates: Upper South Unionists in the Secession Crisis* (1989).

DANIEL W. CROFTS

CAMPBELL, William Henry (14 Sept. 1808–7 Dec. 1890), college president and clergyman, was born in Baltimore, Maryland, the son of William Campbell, a merchant, and Ann Ditchfield. His mother died when Campbell was less than a month old, and he was subsequently raised by his sisters. After attending a private academy conducted by the Reverend John Gibson, he continued his education at Dickinson College in Carlisle, Pennsylvania, graduating in 1828. Anticipating a career in the ministry, Campbell studied at Princeton Theological Seminary but left abruptly in 1829 when his father declared bankruptcy. Denied the opportunity for formal instruction, he continued his studies under his brother-in-law, the Reverend Thomas M. Strong, who later obtained for Campbell the post of assistant teacher at Erasmus Hall in the Flatbush section of Brooklyn, New York. In 1831 Campbell secured his license to preach from the Second Presbytery of New York, and also that year he married Katherine Elsie Schoonmaker. They had four children.

In 1831 Campbell secured a co-pastorship (with the Reverend Andrew Yates) at Chittenango in upstate New York, where he served until 1833, when chronic bronchitis forced a career detour. He returned to Erasmus and served as principal of the school until 1839, when he assumed pastoral duties in East New York (in Brooklyn). Remaining there until 1841, he also served as schoolmaster, since his church was unable to pay him an adequate salary for ministerial duties alone.

Returning to upstate New York in 1841, Campbell assumed pastoral duties at the Third Reformed Church in Albany, remaining there until 1848. He reentered education as principal of Albany Academy from 1848 to 1851. In 1851 he became professor of oriental literature at the New Brunswick (N.J.) Theological Seminary, replacing his Dickinson College mentor Alexander McClelland, and served concurrently as professor of belles-lettres at Rutgers College. He remained in both posts until 1863. As a teacher Campbell was noted for his spirited and orderly instruction. He actively promoted separating the seminary from Rutgers, a change that was accomplished to the satisfaction of both institutions by 1864.

Well known and widely respected, Campbell was elected president of Rutgers in July 1862. He accepted with reluctance after the college trustees agreed to allow him to continue his seminary teaching duties for an additional academic year. Immediately setting out in 1863 on what he perceived as the college's greatest need, fundraising, Campbell successfully raised nearly $430,000 in gifts and bequests, largely from congregations of the Dutch Reformed church, with which Rutgers held close ties. The success of the "New Endowment" campaign was even more remarkable given the fact that the trustees of Rutgers were seeking to sever the formal ties between the Dutch Reformed church and the college. An agreement was reached in June 1864, wherein the General Synod reconveyed to the college the main building, Queen's, which had been acquired by the synod in 1823, during a period of distress for Rutgers, and in exchange, three-quarters of the college trustees would hold membership in the church.

With full control over the physical plant and a newly enlarged endowment in hand, Campbell then focused on his next challenge, creating the Rutgers Scientific School. The Morrill Act of 1862 had made federal funds available to each state for the purpose of establishing within a college a curriculum of agriculture and mechanic arts. Rutgers was named as the New Jersey land-grant college by the state legislature in April 1864, and the first class entered what is now Cook College in 1865. While engineering (or mechanic arts) proved immediately successful, the demand for agricultural instruction lagged for years.

Campbell's administration also accomplished the construction of several new buildings on campus, most notably the Geological Hall and the college chapel, and the founding of a Phi Beta Kappa chapter. Many Rutgers traditions date from his administration, including the founding of the student newspaper *Targum* (1867); the selection of scarlet as the school color (1869); and the first intercollegiate football game (1869), in which Rutgers beat Princeton 6–4. "On the Banks of the Old Raritan," perhaps the most famous Rutgers song, was written in 1873.

Upon assuming the presidency, Campbell hired many new faculty members, including Jacob Cooper, Theodore S. Doolittle, and George W. Atherton, who served the college well for years. While the overall number of students fluctuated during the Campbell years (reaching a high of 188 in 1875), the newly enlarged faculty did instruct the first Japanese exchange students. Beginning in 1866 some forty students from Japan experienced Western education and culture firsthand.

With declining vision, Campbell resigned as president in June 1881, remaining in office until his successor, Merrill Edward Gates, was installed in June 1882. In retirement Campbell, although nearly blind, organized the Suydam Street Reformed Church in New Brunswick. He served as its pastor until 1888, when his son Alan Campbell succeeded him. Campbell died at his home in New Brunswick. While not as well known as his nearby contemporary, James McCosh of Princeton, Campbell provided Rutgers with solid and substantial advances.

• A small collection of Campbell papers is at the Rutgers University Archives in New Brunswick, N.J. His career at Rutgers is documented at length in William H. S. Demarest, *History of Rutgers College, 1766–1924* (1924), and Richard P. McCormick, *Rutgers: A Bicentennial History* (1966). An obituary is in the *New Brunswick Daily Home News*, 8 Dec. 1890.

EDWARD L. LACH, JR.

CAMPBELL, William Wallace (28 Dec. 1862–14 June 1938), astronomer, was born on a farm near Fostoria in northwestern Ohio, the son of Robert William Campbell and Harriet Welch, farmers. The family was poor, and Wallace (as he was known all his life) was the sixth of seven children. Robert Campbell died when Wallace was four, and his sister Isabel (fifteen years older than he), took care of him and the other younger children while their mother managed the farm. Campbell liked arithmetic and was considered a near prodigy in the small country schools he attended and at Fostoria High School. He entered Ohio State University in 1881 but lasted only one term. In 1882 he started over at the University of Michigan, where he completed his bachelor's degree in civil engineering in four years. Campbell was still deeply interested in mathematics and spent much of his spare time studying it. But between his junior and senior years he read Simon Newcomb's *Popular Astronomy* (in forty-eight consecutive hours, according to his later memory) and decided then and there to devote his life to astronomy.

In his last year at Michigan, Campbell was able to fit a course in astronomy (taught by John M. Schaeberle) into his schedule, and on graduating in 1886 he got a job as professor of mathematics at the University of Colorado. In 1888 he returned to the University of Michigan as an instructor in astronomy, although it meant a large reduction in salary; he was determined to do research. Campbell went to Lick Observatory, which then had the largest refracting telescope in the world, on Mount Hamilton, California, as a volunteer assistant in the summer of 1890. There he learned to be an astronomical spectroscopist, working under astronomer James E. Keeler. Campbell was able, intelligent, quick to learn, and dedicated, and when Keeler left Lick to become director of the Allegheny Observatory in Pittsburgh, the University of California hired Campbell to do astronomical spectroscopy in 1891, giving him the title of assistant astronomer. A year later Campbell married Elizabeth Ballard Thompson, a Michigan native who had been a student in one of the mathematics courses he had taught at Colorado. They had three children.

At Lick, Campbell converted the visual spectroscope into a photographic spectrograph and began getting important new results on stars, nebulae, planets, and comets with the 36-inch refractor. His lack of training in physics was little handicap; the subject was new, and discoveries were waiting to be made by the hard-working observer with the big telescope at the clear Mount Hamilton site. Campbell designed and had built a new spectrograph, optimized for measuring the radial velocities ("velocities in the line of sight") of stars from the minute Doppler shifts of the lines in their spectra. Here his engineering training and mechanical skills served him well. He systematized every step of the data taking and reduction procedures, and soon Lick was famous in the astronomical world for measuring more stars' radial velocities more accurately and more quickly than anywhere else.

Keeler returned to Lick Observatory as its director in 1898 but died unexpectedly in 1900; Campbell was immediately put in charge and succeeded to the directorship in 1901. He remained director for twenty-nine years and converted Lick Observatory into a radial-velocity factory. Campbell, his assistants, and his students measured thousands of stars' velocities and discovered hundreds of previously unknown spectroscopic binaries (apparently single stars, revealed by the periodic velocity shifts and doublings of their spectral lines to be two stars in orbits about one another). Campbell raised the money to build and operate a Lick Observatory southern station in Chile, to measure the radial velocities of stars in the southern skies that cannot be observed from California. These measurements, of stars all over the sky, are necessary for a full statistical discussion of stellar motions. Campbell designed the telescope and spectrograph for the Chile observatory and intended to take them to Santiago and erect them there himself, but he was badly injured in testing the telescope in southern California in 1903. The heavy glass mirror fell and nearly crushed him; his back was permanently injured and he continued to suffer pain for many years afterward. But his assistants took the telescope south and sent back the radial velocity results; Campbell discussed them and found many of the now well known correlations between stars' spectral types and motions.

Campbell's style as director was perhaps best described by Paul W. Merrill, one of his Lick Ph.D.s who became an outstanding, long-term Mount Wilson Observatory stellar spectroscopist. He wrote of Campbell, "Scotch granite was a basic constituent of his moral character. . . . This gave him the reputation, more or less deserved, of being austere. He never, even in the slightest degree, camouflaged the facts or his own beliefs." All of the Lick Observatory astronomers respected Campbell; few of them liked him. His wife, far more outgoing and sympathetic than he, did her best to humanize him.

In addition to the radial velocity program that he planned, organized, and directed, Campbell carried out another program throughout his long life that took him all over the world. It was observing solar eclipses, which required being exactly on the path of the eclipse, with the specialized equipment in place and ready to begin operating at precisely the right moment. All the Lick expeditions were planned to obtain direct images of the solar corona, ordinarily hidden in the glare from the bright sun itself, and spectrograms of the chromosphere (the outermost layers of the sun, just inside the corona) and the corona. Campbell headed seven Lick eclipse expeditions, beginning with one to Jeur, India, in 1898 and ending with Wallal, Australia, in 1922. His wife often accompanied him, acting as observing assistant and major domo of living arrangements. At each eclipse (except for Brovary, Russia, in 1914), Campbell had clear weather. His instruments and local volunteer assistants, whom he drilled thoroughly in countless rehearsals before the big event, worked to perfection, and he brought back better and better data from each eclipse. He himself published little in the way of results beyond the accurately measured wavelengths of the chromospheric and coronal spectral lines and direct photographs of the corona, but these spectrograms and images formed the basis for Donald H. Menzel's pioneering Lick Observatory analysis of the physical nature and structure of the outer layers of the sun.

After 1912 Campbell's main effort at these total solar eclipses went into testing Albert Einstein's general theory of relativity, which predicted a gravitational deflection of light from the stars at the edge of the sun. The photographs necessary to measure the effect could be obtained only at an eclipse, with the sun's bright glare removed from the sky, leaving the stars observable. In his first attempt to detect the deflection in 1914, Campbell was clouded out. His second attempt, at Goldendale, Washington, in 1918, was a failure, largely because the best Lick eclipse-camera lenses were unavailable; Campbell had barely gotten out of Russia in 1914 when World War I broke out, and he had left the lenses there for safekeeping until the war ended. In 1919 two British expeditions, one headed by Arthur S. Eddington, apparently confirmed the general theory, but only a few star images had been measurable, the observational errors were large, and many astronomers, particularly outside the United Kingdom, were skeptical of the announced result. At the Wallal eclipse in 1922, Campbell and Robert J. Trumpler were spectacularly successful; they had new, improved cameras and lenses especially designed for the project, the star field around the sun was rich so that many stars were measurable, and they confirmed the predictions of the general theory with very high precision. Their result was convincing to all but the most reactionary Einstein-haters.

Campbell also made many contributions to the spectroscopic study of the planets, especially the search for traces of water vapor in the atmosphere of Mars. This culminated in his expedition to the summit of Mount Whitney in 1909 to obtain spectrograms of the red planet at an unusually favorable close approach to the earth from a high, dry site with almost no terrestrial water vapor above it. He was able to set an extremely small upper limit to the amount of Martian vapor, far less than the optimistic estimates of the seekers for life on Mars of those days.

In 1923 Campbell was named president of the University of California. He had not sought the post; the regents chose him because they knew him for his integrity, character, competence, drive, organizational ability, and high scientific reputation. Campbell was not eager to begin a new career at the age of sixty, but he felt it his duty to accept. However, he retained the Lick directorship as well. He moved to the president's office in Berkeley, and Robert G. Aitken became associate director in charge of operations on Mount Hamilton. Campbell retained overall control and played a large role in new appointments to the Lick faculty, particularly that of Menzel to analyze the eclipse data. As president, Campbell began the buildup of the University of California into a great research institution and supervised the transformation of what was referred to simply as the southern branch into UCLA, the second campus of the university.

When he retired from the presidency in 1930 at the age of sixty-seven, Campbell intended to return to Mount Hamilton and do research, but he found that he was too old and too tired to do so. In 1931 he was elected president of the National Academy of Sciences, and he and his wife moved to Washington, D.C., for part of each year, returning each summer to their apartment in San Francisco. Campbell, a conservative Republican, battled with Democratic president Franklin D. Roosevelt, who he thought was trying to bypass the National Academy of Sciences and rule American science through an appointed committee. Campbell's term as academy president was not a happy one.

When he returned to San Francisco in 1935, he was very tired. He had become blind in one eye and was losing the sight in the other. He suffered frequently from aphasia. Fearing that he would become a burden on his wife, he left a note for her and then committed suicide in San Francisco.

Campbell was one of the most generally powerful figures in American astronomy, but his greatest contribution was the pioneering spectroscopic results he obtained on the motions of the stars and on the physical properties of the sun, the planets, the stars, and the universe.

• The largest collection of Campbell's letters is in the Mary Lea Shane Archives of the Lick Observatory at the University of California, Santa Cruz Library. His correspondence as president of the University of California is in its archives, at the Bancroft Library, Berkeley. Among the most important of Campbell's works are "Spectra of the Great Nebula in Orion and Other Well-Known Nebulae," *Astronomy and Astro-Physics* 13 (1894): 384–98, 494–501; "The Spectrum of Mars as Observed by the Crocker Expedition to Mount Whitney," *Lick Observatory Bulletins* 5 (1909): 149–64; *Stellar Motions, with Special Reference to Motions Determined by Means of the Spectrograph* (1913); and, with J. H. Moore, "Radial Velocities of Stars Brighter Than Visual Magnitude 5.51 as Determined at Mount Hamilton and Santiago," *Publications of the Lick Observatory* 15 (1928): 1–399. The most nearly complete published memorial biographies are Robert G. Aitken, "William Wallace Campbell, 1862–1938," *Publications of the Astronomical Society of the Pacific* 50 (1938): 204–9; Paul W. Merrill, "William Wallace Campbell," *Monthly Notices of the Royal Astronomical Society* 99 (1939): 317–21; Joseph H. Moore, "William Wallace Campbell, 1862–1938," *Astrophysical Journal* 89 (1939): 143–51; and William H. Wright, "William Wallace Campbell, 1862–1938," *National Academy of Sciences Biographical Memoirs* 25 (1949), pp. 35–74. The latter contains a complete bibliography of Campbell's published scientific papers and books. See also J. H. Moore, "Fifty Years of Research at the Lick Observatory," *Publications of the Astronomical Society of the Pacific* 50 (1938): 189–203, and Donald E. Osterbrock et al., *Eye on the Sky: Lick Observatory's First Century* (1988).

DONALD E. OSTERBROCK

CAMRYN, Walter (22 July 1903–29 Feb. 1984), dancer, choreographer, and teacher, was born Walter Cameron in Helena, Montana, the son of Angus Cameron, a cattle rancher, and Rose Ann Hodge. Camryn's early years in Montana among pioneer homesteaders influenced the style and themes of his dancing and choreography. From the age of six he witnessed and participated in the rural dances of the community. The early twentieth century was the heyday of vaudeville, and young Camryn saw much popular dance of that genre, also an influence on his distinctive choreography.

After attending public elementary and high schools, Camryn worked in a florist shop and took part in amateur theatricals. His theater activities, combined with his early experiences with dance, led Camryn to seek a career in theater dance. In 1927 he moved to Chicago, changed his last name, and with the money he had saved from working at the florist shop he enrolled in the summer course at the Adolph Bolm school. Bolm found Camryn to be talented and gave him a scholarship to continue his studies at the school. Camryn admired Bolm, whose supremacy as a character dancer made him the logical mentor for Camryn. Camryn also received training in classical ballet from Bolm's assistant, Alexandra Maximova. For a few years Camryn continued his studies and worked as an usher in a vaudeville theater, where he gained insight into the movement quality intrinsic to American performers.

Male dancers were in demand, and probably in 1930 Camryn became a member of the corps de ballet of the Chicago Civic Opera. During the opera seasons of the 1930s and 1940s Camryn danced under a succession of ballet directors, including Laurent Novikoff, Vecheslav Swoboda, Muriel Stuart, and Ruth Page. He appeared in the standard dance episodes in the operas as well as in the all-ballet programs presented by Novikoff and Page. Between opera seasons Camryn found dance opportunities in Chicago's cabarets and the stage shows in the cinema palaces.

The 1930s was an era of experimentation in dance, and Camryn appeared in solo concerts with fellow avant-garde dancers. His first choreography, touching on memories of his early years, was *Hot Afternoons Have Been in Montana*, in which he depicted a farm worker with a pitchfork. Camryn evoked another phase of American history in the solo *Boston John the Shaker*, which depicted the characteristic movements of the Shaker religious sect. Dancer Bentley Stone created for Camryn two essays in Americana, *Turkey in the Straw* and *Casey at the Bat*.

Stone had been teaching in a dance school in the Chicago suburb of Oak Park for a number of years. When an additional teacher was needed Stone recommended Camryn, who spent the next seven years teaching at what he described as a "factory," an institution with hundreds of pupils, large classes, and half-hour lessons. Before he began teaching full time, Camryn's teaching duties had been sandwiched between opera ballet rehearsals, concerts, and various dance activities.

Unhappy in the dance factory, Stone and Camryn left the Oak Park school and in 1941 opened the Stone-Camryn School of Dance in Chicago, which in the four decades of its existence became a leading American dance school. Camryn developed his unique method and materials for teaching character dance, an art for which he became famous. He emphasized the importance of posture and gait, rather than steps, as the essence of national styles, and he encouraged the lilting expansiveness of American dancing, which differed from the stamping footwork of the commonly taught eastern European character dancing.

Camryn established himself as a teacher of dance teachers through summer courses at the Stone-Camryn school and through classes at the national conventions of teacher organizations. He wrote a pamphlet, *Analytical Study of Character Movement and Dances*, explaining his principles and describing several of his dances. The school was an important part of his life, but Camryn also pursued his performing career, dancing until well over seventy years of age in many kinds of programs. In 1934 at the Chicago World's Fair he appeared as a soloist in *A Century of Dance*, choreographed by Edward Caton.

After appearing as a guest artist in 1938–1939, in 1939 Camryn was appointed director of the Federal Theater Project's dance program in Chicago. For the program's large dance group he choreographed *Thunder in the Hills*, a ballet portraying an American revival meeting, set to music by Stephen Foster. Before the piece could be presented, however, the Federal Theater was terminated by Congress. Nevertheless, a sympathetic public official, Alderman (later Senator) Paul Douglas, came to the rescue, paying for the Camryn-designed costumes and arranging for a successful series of performances at a University of Chicago venue in the fall of 1939. From 1941 to 1951 Camryn directed the Children's Civic Theatre in Chicago, for which he choreographed dances and directed plays. A number of talented dancers, including Joan Ehemann, Audre Deckmann, Sheila Reilly, Billy Reilly, and Darrell Notara, emerged from this program and went on to achieve success dancing in ballet companies and Broadway musicals.

During World War II Camryn volunteered for service in the U.S. Medical Corps. After some months he found this unsatisfactory, resigned, and took up defense work. He worked nights, leaving his afternoons free to teach at his school.

During the following decades Camryn created a repertory of some twenty Americana solos and group dances. He choreographed dances for the Stone-Camryn Ballet, a company consisting of professional-level students and guest artists: Camryn himself appeared in his own repertory and in dances choreographed by Stone. The ensemble performed both classical dances and lively works with American themes. The large-cast works Camryn created for the company include *Alice in Wonderland* (1950s) and the autobiographical *In My Landscape* (1960).

In 1958 the Stone-Camryn school began publishing a quarterly, the *Upstairs Club Bulletin*, most of it written by Camryn. He was a compulsive reader and writer, and in the bulletin he presented news items and bits of wisdom gleaned from his readings of well-known and obscure writers. Camryn also included chapters of the Chicago dance history he had been a part of. Publication of the bulletin stopped when the school closed in 1981. Camryn died in Chicago. He had never married.

Camryn was a pioneer in the presentation of American themes in theater dance and in the use of intrinsically American movements. Although he taught classical ballet, Camryn was not particularly distinguished as a ballet performer. Rather, his lasting impact on dance lies in his unique way of teaching character dance.

• Camryn's diaries, scrapbooks, films, and other effects are in the Dance Archives of the Newberry Library in Chicago. A complete run of the *Upstairs Club Bulletin*, edited by Camryn, is in the collection of dance periodicals at the Newberry. A collection of Camryn photographs and programs are in the Dance Collection of the New York Public Library for the Performing Arts, Lincoln Center.

ANN BARZEL

CANADAY, Ward Murphey (12 Dec. 1885–28 Feb. 1976), industrialist, was born in New Castle, Indiana, the son of Miles Murphey Canaday, a banker, and Sarah Helena Smith. Canaday graduated from New Castle High School in 1903 and studied at the University of Colorado at Boulder for two years, after which he transferred to Harvard University, where he received an A.B. cum laude in 1907.

Canaday landed his first job in Philadelphia, selling classified advertisements for *Munsey's* magazine. In 1908 he moved to New York City to become eastern sales agent for the Hoosier Kitchen Cabinet Company. This job provided him with experience in dealing with financial crises, such as the 1907 collapse of the Knickerbocker Trust Company in New York, which helped to trigger a nationwide panic. In response to this crisis, Canaday helped to structure a pioneering time-payment plan called the "Hoosier Club Plan." In 1910 Canaday left the Hoosier Company and worked briefly as advertising manager for Reed and Barton, silversmiths, in Taunton, Massachusetts. He rejoined the Hoosier Company later the same year, this time working as an assistant sales manager and advertising manager in his home town of New Castle, Indiana, where he stayed for the next six years. In 1912 he married Miriam Louise Coffin; they had one daughter.

In 1916 Canaday accepted an offer from John North Willys, chairman of the board of Willys-Overland Motors, to become advertising manager for that corporation. He moved to Toledo, Ohio, where he was to spend the rest of his life. Willys wanted to sell his automobiles on a time-payment plan, and he charged Canaday with the responsibility of creating the country's first automobile time-payment corporation. In 1921 Canaday also started his own advertising agency, the United States Advertising Corporation, after his advertising staff at Willys-Overland had been drastically slashed. The company later became Canaday-Ewell-Thurber, Incorporated, with offices in New York, Chicago, and Baltimore. In 1921 Canaday formed the Dealers' Finance Company, his own time-payment company, and merged it with the Commercial Credit Company (CCC) of Baltimore. Canaday served as a director of CCC until 1960. From 1933 to 1935 he was also an administrator and director of public relations for the Federal Housing Administration.

Willys-Overland Motors fell on hard times during World War I. It had entered the war as the number-two automaker in the country, after the Ford Motor Company, but emerged from the war in twenty-eighth place because of difficulties it encountered in converting to postwar civilian production. In 1932, struggling during the Great Depression, the company was put into receivership. Canaday reorganized the corporation and raised $3 million in new funds; in 1936, after the death of John Willys the previous year, Canaday became chairman of the board of the newly organized Willys-Overland Motors, Incorporated. He ordered a full restyling of the company's line for 1937, the result of which was the Model 37, an odd-looking car with a bulging front and a rounded body. In 1941 the company began to manufacture a successful line of four-cylinder automobiles called the "Willys-Americar," a fuel-efficient model that sold for only $395. When the United States entered World War II, Canaday led Willys-Overland to become the first automobile plant in the country to convert completely to war production. During the war Willys-Overland produced over $760 million of war material, including its most important single contribution to the war effort, the Jeep. This four-wheel-drive, "general purpose" military vehicle was designed to replace the cavalry horse by offering four-wheel drive and maneuverability over a wide range of field conditions. The Jeep, which Canaday credited with resuscitating Willys-Overland, was used again extensively during the Korean War and was also successfully parlayed into a civilian vehicle, the first version of which was a Jeep station wagon.

After the war, as a result of a policy disagreement with Willys-Overland president Charles Sorensen, Canaday vacated the position of chairman of the board to assume a newly created post, chairman of the finance committee. In 1949 James Mooney became president of Willys-Overland and Canaday returned as chairman of the board, while retaining his position as chairman of the finance committee. Canaday's activity was curtailed for half a year in 1952 when he suffered a heart attack. That year Willys-Overland made a more determined effort to return to the passenger car market by introducing the Aero-Willys, a small, fuel-efficient car that Canaday selected after reviewing numerous design proposals. In 1953 the Kaiser-Frazer Corporation, an ailing automobile manufacturer, bought Willys-Overland for $62.3 million and formed the Kaiser-Willys Sales Corporation, which concentrated all of its manufacturing operations in Willys-Overland's Toledo plant. Just two years later, Kaiser-Willys abandoned the U.S. automobile market and made automobiles exclusively for export.

Canaday left Willys-Overland at this time but used its name in starting an investment company, the Overland Corporation, serving as its president and chairman of the board. In 1965 he directed the merger of the Overland Corporation with the State Street Investment Corporation of Boston. After the merger he served as chairman of the board of a new company, the Overland Investment Corporation, while his daughter, Doreen C. Spitzer, was its president.

Canaday owned a lavish 42,000-acre estate, "Annaly Hill," on St. Croix Island in the Virgin Islands. He developed a new breed of cattle there and grew crops such as sugar cane and tomatoes. In 1948, when the domestic tomato crop was poor, Canaday was able to make a profit by flying tomatoes from his plantation to New York for sale in the United States. President Harry S. Truman visited Annaly Hill in 1948 and, impressed with Canaday's familiarity with the Virgin Islands, appointed him chairman of the U.S. section of the Caribbean Commission, a group designed to strengthen American-Caribbean relations and to solve economic and social problems in the region. In 1949 Truman appointed Canaday as one of three directors of the Virgin Islands Corporation, an economic development agency; President Dwight D. Eisenhower reappointed him in 1953.

Canaday had a deep interest in the arts and in archaeology. He was chairman emeritus of the board of the American School of Classical Studies in Athens, Greece, and in that capacity supported the excavation and reconstruction of the ancient Stoa of Attalos, a large, colonnaded building near Athens that was built in 143 B.C. and that had served as the marketplace and civic center of ancient Athens. Excavations had discovered the Stoa in 1861, and in 1956 it was dedicated as a museum. At the dedication ceremonies, Canaday and his wife were guests of the king and queen of Greece and were also personal representatives of President Eisenhower. Canaday also contributed to the Toledo Symphony Orchestra and was a former chairman of the board of the Toledo Museum of Art, where he was an honorary trustee.

Canaday was also a patron of American education and gave generously to Harvard University, his alma mater; Bryn Mawr College, his wife's alma mater; the University of Toledo; Wooster College; and several other colleges and universities. His donations to Harvard helped to finance a $3 million freshman dormitory complex there, Canaday Hall, which was dedicated in 1974. Canaday died in Ottawa Hills, Ohio.

• Canaday's daughter, Doreen C. Spitzer, wrote a book about her parents, *By One and One* (1984). The main branch of the Toledo-Lucas County Public Library maintains a file on Canaday in its local history department. The file contains newspaper clippings on Canaday, mostly from the *Toledo Blade*. Obituaries are in the *Toledo Blade*, 28 Feb. 1976, and in the *New York Times*, 29 Feb. 1976.

YANEK MIECZKOWSKI

CANBY, Edward Richard Sprigg (9 Nov. 1817–11 Apr. 1873), Civil War general, was born in Piatt's Landing, Kentucky, the son of Israel T. Canby, a land speculator and politician, and Elizabeth Piatt. Canby received an appointment to West Point and graduated thirtieth out of thirty-one in the class of 1839. Shortly after graduation he married Louisa Hawkins; they had one child, who died young. He began his military career as a second lieutenant with the Second Regiment of the U.S. Infantry. Canby gained his first military leadership experience during the confrontation with the Seminole Nation in northern Florida, 1840–1842, and his first administrative experience in the Adjutant General's Office during garrison duty at Fort Niagara, 1842–1846. At the end of this duty, in June 1846, he received promotion to first lieutenant and, in 1847, to captain as assistant adjutant general. During the Mexican War Canby fought beside Winfield Scott in the invasion army. He saw action at the siege of Veracruz and in the battles of Cerro Gordo, Contreras and Churubusco, and Belen Gate. On 3 March 1847 Canby was brevetted to captain in the adjutant general's department. He was assigned to Colonel Bennett Riley's Second Brigade on 12 March as its assistant adjutant general and ex officio chief of staff. During the battle of Cerro Gordo on 17–18 April, Canby led a charge against the Mexican army that resulted in the capture of three field guns and helped cause the Mexican army's general retreat from the battlefield. At the battle of Contreras and Churubusco, Canby played an integral role in keeping the brigade organized and bringing reserves up to the front. He was a part of the Second Brigade's garrison of Mexico City after General Winfield Scott captured the capital in September 1847. He received two citations for gallant and meritorious conduct. Between 1849 and 1851, at the height of the gold rush, he was stationed in California.

In June 1851 Canby turned down a promotion to captain in the infantry to keep his captain's rank in the Adjutant General's Office. In turning to the administrative side of the military, he focused on his organizational talents and understanding of government bureaucracy. On 21 June 1851 he was brevetted lieutenant colonel and soon after undertook a series of inspection tours in the South and Southeast. In the years before the American Civil War, he fought to suppress the 1857–1858 Mormon rebellion in Utah and participated in the campaign against the Navajo.

On the outbreak of the Civil War, Canby remained with the Union. In June 1861 he was charged with the affairs of the Department of New Mexico and promoted to colonel of the Nineteenth Regiment. He experienced problems with supplies, munitions, and money in his department. In one major engagement during Canby's command, the battle of Valverde on 21 February 1862, Confederate general Henry Hopkins Sibley defeated Canby's army while attempting to reach the gold supplies in California.

The 26 March 1862 battle for Glorieta Pass, known as the Gettysburg of the Southwest, was another significant battle during Canby's tenure in the Department of New Mexico. Canby had ordered Colonel John P. Slough of the First Colorado Volunteers to stay at Fort Union until he could meet with the colonel to review strategy. Slough misinterpreted Canby's orders and searched for the invading Confederate forces. At Glorieta Pass, the Colorado volunteers stumbled on the Confederate supply train and destroyed it. This forced the invading Texans to stop their advance into the New Mexico territory. After the engagement, Canby ordered Slough not to pursue the Confederate force and to wait for reinforcements. Slough obeyed but resigned in protest. At Peralta, New Mexico, Canby and Colonel Gabriel R. Paul combined forces and had the opportunity to eliminate the Texan threat. Canby, however, wanted a victory without the loss of men and declined to permit a general assault against the town. Instead, Canby allowed Sibley to withdraw across the border.

Canby did not win the majority of engagements he faced with the Texans, but his ability to keep his army intact and disrupt the Confederate plans enabled him to eliminate their threat to New Mexico. He received a promotion to brigadier general of volunteers on 31 March 1862 and relinquished command on 18 September 1862 to begin service as assistant to Secretary of War Edwin M. Stanton. Canby presided over a series of inspection tours and gained prominence helping to maintain peace in New York City after riots caused by the National Conscription Act on 3 March 1863.

On 11 May 1864 Canby assumed command, as brevet major general of volunteers, in the Military Division of West Mississippi, which included the Gulf states and the Southwest. His purpose was to strengthen the scattered forces, to support General William Tecumseh Sherman's campaign, and to maintain order in the division. His duties were interrupted on 6 November 1864, when a Confederate guerrilla wounded him while aboard the gunboat *Cricket* on the White River in Arkansas. Canby administered his responsibilities fully with the limited forces and materials available, but he still earned General U. S. Grant's displeasure. During the campaign that resulted in the capture of Mobile, Alabama, on 12 April 1865, Grant complained that Canby acted too slowly, lost too many men, and caused an excess of property destruction. Despite Grant's displeasure, Canby earned a brevet to major general on 13 March 1865 for his feat. He accepted the surrender of Edmund Kirby Smith, Confederate commander of the Department of the Trans-Mississippi, on 26 May 1865 in New Orleans, ending hostilities in his military district. Canby relinquished command on 28 May 1866 and was assigned to the Department of Washington, where he headed a special commission directed to examine war claims. He received promotion to brigadier general in the regular army on 28 July 1866.

After the defeat of the Confederacy, Canby played a significant role in the Reconstruction period. He commanded the Second Military District, comprising North Carolina and South Carolina, from 27 August 1867 to 8 May 1868; the Fifth Military District, which covered Texas, from 12 November 1868 to 8 April 1869; and the First Military District in Virginia from 20 July 1869 to 27 January 1870. He was the only person to command more than one military district. Under the congressional acts of 2 and 23 March 1867 and 19 July 1867, Canby guided the former Confederate states into the Union. He oversaw state elections and the writing of new constitutions. His contemporaries applauded his evenhanded approach that employed noninterference.

On 8 August 1870 Canby took command of the Department of Columbia, which included Oregon and the territories of Washington, Idaho, and Alaska. One of his tasks was to quell Keintpoos, commonly referred to as "Captain Jack," of the Modoc tribe, who resisted the efforts of the U.S. government to resettle his people. After a series of skirmishes between the Modoc and settlers, the government ordered Canby to mediate directly with Keintpoos. Their chance meeting on 23 March 1873 in the lava beds in Siskiyou County, northern California, afforded Canby his opportunity. The two sides talked for nearly three weeks without result. On 11 April 1873 Canby and three other men met with Keintpoos and eight of his men. The meeting was to be a friendly one, and Canby went without a sidearm. After the initial formalities, Keintpoos produced a revolver and shot Canby. Only one of Canby's entourage escaped death. Canby became the first general to die at the hands of the American Indians. His assassination caused much public fervor for revenge, which was satisfied many weeks later when Keintpoos was captured and executed for his act.

Canby spent his life in the service of his country. His rise in the military was a slow one until the Civil War. His contribution to the United States was not exceptional, but, as his biographer Max L. Heyman noted, Canby performed his responsibilities in the clearest, most professional manner possible. Ovander J. Hollister, one of Canby's contemporaries, noted that he was a man of "foresight and judgment—patient, prudent, and cautious—of great courage, both moral and physical, and as true to the Government as any man."

• The standard biography of Canby is Max L. Heyman, *Prudent Soldier: A Biography of Major General E. R. S. Canby, 1817–1873* (1959). Articles on Canby's service in the Department of New Mexico during the Civil War include David Perrine, "The Battle of Valverde, New Mexico Territory, February 21, 1862," *Journal of the West* 19, no. 4 (1980): 26–38; and Charles Bennett, "The Civil War in New Mexico," *Palacio* 96, no. 2 (1991): 8–15. *The War of the Rebellion: A Compilation of the Official Records of the Union and Confederate Armies* (128 vols., 1880–1901) also provides an excellent source for Canby's wartime activities. For information on the Modoc War see Maurice Fitzgerald, "The Modoc War," *Journal of the Shaw Historical Library* 4, no. 2 (1990): 8–23. An obituary is in the *New York Times*, 24 May 1873.

RONALD BRUCE FRANKUM, JR.

CANBY, Henry Seidel (6 Sept. 1878–5 Apr. 1961), educator, author, and editor, was born in Wilmington, Delaware, the son of Edward Tatnell Canby, a founder and president of the Delaware Trust Company, and Ella Augusta Seidel. Though reared in an Episcopalian family, Canby attended Quaker schools and then entered Yale, where he edited two undergraduate literary papers and earned his Ph.B. in 1899. While studying for his Ph.D. in English literature (1905) and afterward, he taught at Yale (1900–1916). He was the first professor at Yale to offer courses in American literature. Early in his career, he championed the work of Willa Cather, Robert Frost, and Edwin Arlington Robinson, among other American authors he regarded as neglected by academics.

Canby married Marion Ponsonby Gause in 1907; the couple had two children. His wife published books of poetry. When Wilbur L. Cross founded the *Yale Review* in 1911, he hired Canby as his assistant editor (1911–1920). Aiming between the academic and technical on the one hand, and the journalistic on the other, Canby sought in the *Review* to make popular scholarship available to a public he regarded as too commercially oriented. In the last years of World War I Canby served in Ireland and France under the auspices of the British Commission of War Information, after which he again taught at Yale on an irregular basis (1918–1920 and later).

When the *New York Evening Post* began to publish the *Literary Review* as a weekly supplement in 1920, Canby served as its respected editor, assisted by William Rose Benét, Amy Loveman, and Christopher Morley. Following the demise of the *Literary Review* in 1924, Canby and Morley founded, that same year, the *Saturday Review of Literature*, with Canby as its editor until 1936. This influential review maintained a balance between high aesthetic standards and open-minded criticism of current literary and cultural developments, thus appealing to ordinary intelligent readers. Among contributors were Harold Ickes, James Harvey Robinson, H. G. Wells, and George Santayana, while works by authors as diverse as James Branch Cabell, John Dos Passos, Robinson Jeffers, and William Faulkner were reviewed evenhandedly.

Canby became chair of the board of the Book-of-the-Month Club, founded in 1926. The board included Loveman and Morley; judges for selections, in addition to Canby, were Heywood Broun, Dorothy Canfield Fisher, Morley, and William Allen White. The club concept was so appealing that net sales grew from $503,000 the first year to $1.5 million the second; membership grew to 100,000 by 1928 and to 900,000 by 1946. Until the outbreak of World War II in 1939, a foreign advisory board, which included Arnold Bennett, Thomas Mann, and André Maurois, made special recommendations. Even so, the club was criticized for being neither highbrow nor lowbrow, for being middlebrow and dictatorial, for not knowing whether to appeal to the masses or to cults, and for promoting standardization and mediocrity. Such criticism was unfair, since books by Pearl Buck, Ellen Glasgow, T. E. Lawrence, Sinclair Lewis, Erich Maria Remarque, and George Santayana were among the hundred million sold by 1949. Canby retired from the board in 1955.

Canby, who suffered a minor breakdown in 1930, grew increasingly dismayed by cultural, economic, and political developments in the 1930s, both in the United States and abroad, and turned his critical attention mainly to nineteenth-century authors. However, he remained a discriminating champion of certain liberal causes. In 1935 he was one of 300 persons who signed a petition to the U.S. Supreme Court to declare the Internal Security Act unconstitutional and a threat to American liberty. During World War II he served as a liaison officer of the U.S. Office of War Information in Australia and New Zealand, where he also lectured on American culture and on the importance of national literatures. He was a representative of the National Institute of Arts and Letters on the National Commission of the United Nations Educational, Scientific and Cultural Organization (UNESCO) until 1948. That same year he joined a protest against the New York Board of Education for banning the *Nation* from public school libraries. During his final years Canby remained active in promoting international understanding and intellectual cooperation and fought unceasingly against all forms of censorship but did support anti–avant-garde scholarship in the wide realm of American culture. Obviously the most personally revealing of his thirty-two books is *American Memoir* (1947), a healthy, nostalgia-filled narrative of his varied life. Also nicely sentimental are sections of Canby's *The Brandywine* (1941, part of the Rivers of America Series), revealing his obvious love for the history-laden river flowing into the Delaware River near his birthplace. Canby died in Ossining, New York.

Canby influenced a generation of students with critical books on the short story and textbooks on grammar and composition—published from 1902 to 1918. He joined fellow editors Thomas H. Johnson, Robert E. Spiller, and Willard Thorp in assembling essays by many scholars for the *Literary History of the United States* (2 vols., plus bibliographical vol., 1948; 2 vols. rev. as 1 vol., 1953; bibliography supp., 1959). This publication was a standard-setting handbook for graduate students for many years. Even more important were Canby's three separate critical studies: *Thoreau: A Biography* (1939; Spanish trans., 1944), *Walt Whitman, an American: A Study in Biography* (1943), and *Turn West, Turn East: Mark Twain and Henry James* (1951). *Thoreau*, the most complete factual account of its subject's life to its date, is notorious for suggesting that Thoreau was in love with Ralph Waldo Emerson's wife Lidian. The thesis of *Walt Whitman* is that the great poet's everyday activities were less important than aspects of his inner life and the creative processes resulting in his holding a mirror to a rambunctious America. *Turn West, Turn East* is an amiable Plutarchian study, which, though sometimes slighting James, shows well his resemblance to and divergence from Twain. Modern criticism has gone beyond Canby's insights, as well as his often easy generalizations, but his desire to encourage more readers to appreciate the best of America's past and his undeviatingly lucid style remain examples of committed scholarship.

• Most of Canby's papers are in the Sterling Library and the Beinecke Library, Yale University; the Butler Library, Columbia University; the Van Pelt Library, University of Pennsylvania; and the American Academy of Arts and Letters, N.Y. An unsigned article titled "Has America a Literary Dictatorship?" *Bookman* 65 (Apr. 1927): 191–99, ridicules Book-of-the-Month Club editors in general, and Canby in particular, as "clever publicists and literary boosters," but Charles Lee, *The Hidden Public: The Story of the Book-of-the-Month Club* (1958), extols the club and praises Canby for his part in its success. Norman Foerster, "The Literary Historians," *Bookman* 71 (July 1930): 365–74, divides literary critics into slapdash impressionists and thoughtful scholars, places Canby among the latter, and calls him one of the best academic *and* journalistic "literary historians," particularly for his work on the *Literary Review* and the *Saturday Review of Literature*. Norman Cousins, *Present Tense: An American Editor's Odyssey* (1967), describes Canby's perceptive, balanced editorial work on the *Saturday Review of Literature*. An obituary is in the *New York Times*, 6 Apr. 1961.

ROBERT L. GALE

CANDEE, Leverett (1 June 1795–27 Nov. 1863), rubber manufacturer, was born in Oxford, Connecticut, the son of Job Candee, a politician, and Sarah Benham. His father, locally prominent, was a revolutionary war veteran who later served as a captain in the militia and as a member of the state legislature. After receiving a meager education in the local district schools, in 1810 Candee relocated to New Haven, Connecticut, where he found employment with Captain Gad Peck, a leading merchant in the import-export trade. He then entered the dry goods trade—a profession that he would follow for the next twenty-five years—with the firm of Root & Atwater. Candee afterwards entered into a series of short-lived partnerships—in the fashion of the day—the first of which was the firm of Candee, Dean & Cutler, which he formed with clerical co-workers William Cutler and James E. P. Dean.

Departing New Haven for the first time in his professional career, Candee left his firm in 1833 and removed to New York City, where he entered into another dry goods partnership. He remained in New York for two years and then returned to his adopted hometown, where he entered into yet another dry goods partnership, this time with Timothy Lester and Abraham Murdock. Following the dissolution of this partnership, Candee entered into the new (for him) field of book-paper manufacturing. Centered in the town of Westville, Connecticut, his firm, trading under the name Candee, Page & Lester (by 1840 known as Candee & Lester), was initially successful. The deterioration of business conditions following the panic of 1837, however, caused the firm to struggle, and by 1842 it failed completely. The collapse of his business nearly ruined Candee; at the then-advanced age of forty-seven, almost all of his fortune (accumulated over the previous twenty-five years) was lost.

Despite the setback, Candee remained undaunted. In the same year (1842) he began the manufacturing of men's elastic suspenders and at some point met fellow New Havenite Charles Goodyear. Goodyear's accidental discovery of the process of vulcanization in 1839 offered great promise to potential manufacturers of rubber products, and years of experimentation had left Goodyear nearly destitute and eager to license his discovery for cash returns. However, potential problems still had to be addressed by anyone seeking to capitalize on the new process. The biggest difficulty was the lingering consumer perception of rubber-based products as being inferior. Formerly, rubber products—mostly shoes imported from South America—had proven themselves brittle in winter cold and foul smelling in summer heat. Additionally, British advances in rubber manufacturing, as well as nebulous American patent laws, promised controversy and litigation to any manufacturer bold enough to enter the field.

With the blessings of Goodyear and the financial backing of Henry and Lucius Hotchkiss, Candee established a manufacturing facility in Hamden, Connecticut. The plant, which was shortly relocated to East Street in New Haven, initially produced only footwear. Operating under the name of L.Candee Rubber Company, the firm, one of the earliest to produce products under the Goodyear patent, overcame consumer resistance by covering New England with an army of peddlers who often left free samples of the shoes (the first variety produced was in the "buskin" style) with retailers, who in turn provided the goods to their most influential customers. By word of mouth, the Candee line (benefiting from a careful attention to quality) soon grew in popularity and made the practice of discounting unnecessary. Candee also developed a type of elastic varnish that, when applied to his products, added greatly to their durability and appearance.

With the growth and development of the rubber industry, patent infringers soon appeared on the scene. In an effort to combat this practice, on 1 July 1848 Candee banded together with the Hayward Rubber Company, the Newark India-Rubber Manufacturing Company, and Ford and Company to form a Shoe Association. Goodyear granted the association the exclusive rights to manufacture shoes for $10,000 and a royalty of ½ cent per pair of shoes produced. The association also pooled its financial resources to combat the problem of patent infringement; but the matter was not fully resolved until 1852, when Daniel Webster won a court decision on behalf of Goodyear.

In that same year, Candee & Company was formally organized. Capitalized at $200,000, the firm had four partners: Candee, who served as managing partner and (with the exception of one year) as president of the firm; the Hotchkiss brothers; and Timothy Lester. Candee remained with the firm until his retirement shortly before his death; in the last year of his career he had also joined James Brewster in the purchase of the G. and D. Cook & Co. carriage manufacturing firm. Later known as Henry Hooker & Co., the company prospered for years thereafter, selling to both foreign and domestic markets. Candee & Company remained active and profitable in the production of footwear until after World War I, when changes in technology caused a rapid decline in sales; the firm was sold to United States Rubber in 1928. Candee had married Jane Caroline Tomlinson (date of marriage unknown). They had at least one son.

After suffering a serious financial setback in midlife, Leverett Candee joined forces with another struggling entrepreneur—Charles Goodyear—and created a useful consumer line of products that remained popular for more than half a century. His contributions to the early development of the American rubber industry stand as his greatest legacy.

• The papers of Leverett Candee are held at the New Haven Colony Historical Society, New Haven, Conn. Secondary sources on Candee's life and career include Roy Nuhn, "Historic New Haven: The L. Candee Rubber Co.," *Business Digest of Greater New Haven* (Mar. 1988): 28–30; Glenn D. Babcock, *History of the United States Rubber Company* (1966); and Ralph F. Wolf, *India Rubber Man: The Story of Charles Goodyear* (1939).

EDWARD L. LACH, JR.

CANDLER, Allen Daniel (4 Nov. 1834–26 Oct. 1910), politician and compiler of records, was born in Auraria, Georgia, the son of Daniel Gill Candler and Nancy Caroline Matthews, farmers. Candler worked on the family farm, taught school, and attended Mercer University, where he earned an A.B. in 1859 and an M.A. in 1866. During the Civil War he served in the Confederate Army of Tennessee. A wound in 1864 resulted in the loss of one eye. That same year he married Eugenia Thomas Williams; they would have eleven children. At the war's end he said, "I counted myself quite wealthy [with] . . . one wife, and baby, one eye, and one silver dollar."

In 1870 Candler moved to Gainesville, Georgia, where he developed interests in street railways, railroads, and construction. Two years later he was elected mayor, and later in the decade he served four terms in the state legislature.

In 1882 Candler won a seat in Congress, running as a regular Democrat against Emory Speer, the independent incumbent. Unlike independent Democrats, who were primarily small farmers, regular, or Bourbon, Democrats advocated "New South" industrialism. During the campaign Speer dubbed Candler the "one-eyed plowboy of Pigeon Roost," and Candler pledged "an eye single to duty." Candler served four terms before retiring in 1891. During his congressional career he played an important role in the unification of the Democratic party in his district.

After serving as Georgia's secretary of state from 1894 to 1898, Candler was elected governor in 1898 and again in 1900. As a conservative regular Democrat, he advocated law enforcement, government retrenchment because of low state income, industrial development, and white supremacy. However, the legislature ignored most of his recommendations, and he demonstrated little executive leadership. After he left office he claimed credit for Georgia's white primary, instituted by the Democratic party in 1900 as a means of nominating Democratic candidates in primary elections open only to whites.

As governor, Candler was instrumental in creating the office of compiler of records, and his successor, Joseph M. Terrell, appointed him to that position in 1902. Despite advancing years and failing sight in his single eye, Candler laboriously began the work. Since many of Georgia's records had been lost over the years through neglect, he secured copies of Colonial period documents from the British Public Record Office in London. He published these as *The Colonial Records of the State of Georgia* (20 vols., 1904–1910). He also published three volumes of *The Revolutionary Records of the State of Georgia* (1908) and five volumes of *The Confederate Records of the State of Georgia* (1901–1911). With Clement A. Evans, he coedited *Georgia: Comprising Sketches of Counties, Towns, Events, Institutions, and Persons* (3 vols., 1906).

Like many self-made men of his generation, Candler was an advocate of business, but he also advocated a child labor law and claimed to be a friend of education. The publication of the state's records is what he is best remembered for today and may well be his most important contribution. He died in Atlanta.

• Candler's official papers and correspondence are in the Georgia Department of Archives and History. For biographical information, see Elizabeth Hulsey Marshall, "Allen D. Candler, Governor and Collector of Records" (M.A. thesis, Univ. of Georgia, 1959), and E. H. Marshall, "Governor and

Compiler of Records Allen D. Candler, an Image of an Age," *Atlanta Historical Journal* 25 (Summer 1981): 73–94. Additional information can be found in William J. Northen, ed., *Men of Mark in Georgia*, vol. 4 (1908; repr. 1974); Kenneth Coleman and Charles Stephen Gurr, eds., Dictionary of Georgia Biography (1983); and Theodore H. Jack, "The Preservation of Georgia History," *North Carolina Review* 4 (July 1927): 239–51. Obituaries are in the *Atlanta Constitution*, 27 Oct. 1910, and the *Atlanta Journal*, 26 Oct. 1910.

KENNETH COLEMAN

CANDLER, Asa Griggs (30 Dec. 1851–12 Mar. 1929), businessman and civic leader, was born near Villa Rica, Carroll County, Georgia, the son of Samuel Charles Candler, a farmer and merchant, and Martha Beall. Three of Asa Candler's brothers also rose to prominence: one became a Methodist Episcopal bishop; one a justice on the Georgia Supreme Court; and the third a U.S. congressman. Candler married Lucy Elizabeth Howard in 1878, and they had five children. Lucy Candler died in Atlanta in 1919. Candler married Mary Little Reagan in 1923.

Growing up in the poverty and hardship of rural Georgia during the Civil War and Reconstruction, Candler had no formal education beyond the elementary grades. Unable to fulfill his dream of becoming a physician, Candler apprenticed himself to two physicians in Cartersville, Georgia, in 1870 to learn pharmacy. In July 1873 Candler left Cartersville for Atlanta, where he found work as a clerk in the drugstore of George J. Howard, his future father-in-law. The death of Candler's father in November 1873 forced him to return to the family farm to help his mother, but in January 1875 he resumed his position with Howard. In March 1877 Candler and Marcellus B. Hallman formed a wholesale and retail drug company, Hallman & Candler. In 1881 Candler bought out Hallman, who retired. In 1882 he sold one-half interest in the business to his father-in-law, and the firm became Howard & Candler. When Howard retired in 1886, Candler bought out his interest and became sole proprietor of Asa G. Candler & Company. As a growing New South commercial center, Atlanta prospered, and so did Candler's business. Candler expanded his business by investing in the enterprise all income not required for living expenses, and by 1889 Candler had become the sole owner of one of the largest drug businesses in Atlanta. Candler sold several proprietary products, including a new elixir, Coca-Cola, created in 1886 by Atlanta druggist John Styth Pemberton, in which Candler acquired one-third interest in April 1888. In 1890 Candler closed his drug business to focus his efforts on the marketing of Coca-Cola, and in April 1891 he became the sole owner of Coca-Cola, controlling its formula, trademark, and all other rights in the product. In January 1892 the Coca-Cola Company was chartered. Candler's careful attention to quality control and aggressive marketing turned a little-known beverage dispensed from drugstore soda fountains in Atlanta into a popular drink consumed by Americans across the nation. Candler was an innovator in advertising, using billboards, point-of-sale posters, calendars, and novelty items to keep the Coca-Cola trademark before the public. In 1909 the Associated Advertising Clubs of America declared Coca-Cola to be "the best advertised article in America."

In July 1909 the U.S. government launched a landmark case under the new Pure Food and Drug Act, charging that Coca-Cola was a threat to public health because its caffeine content made the drink addictive. After a trial in 1911 and numerous appeals culminating in a hearing before the U.S. Supreme Court, the case was settled in November 1918, and Coca-Cola agreed to reduce the amount of caffeine in its formula. This case and federal regulations stipulating that public-held corporations like Coca-Cola must distribute financial surpluses to stockholders as dividends convinced Candler that the conditions that had made possible Coca-Cola's success were being swept away by increasing government regulation of business. In 1916 Candler resigned as an officer of the Coca-Cola Company, and in September 1919 the company was sold for $25 million to Atlanta investors led by banker Ernest Woodruff.

With the success of Coca-Cola, Candler organized other businesses and became Atlanta's leading businessman. Candler was a principal investor in suburban real estate in Atlanta as a partner in the development of Inman Park in 1886 and Druid Hills in 1909. Candler established the Central Bank & Trust Corporation of Atlanta in 1905, which merged with the Citizens & Southern Bank in 1922.

As a philanthropist and lay leader of the Methodist church in Georgia, Candler demonstrated his belief that "the wealth we win in commerce is not to be used as a toy, it is stored power for the benefit of mankind" ("The City Is the Nerve Center of Civilization," n.d., Asa Griggs Candler Papers). In 1903 Candler was named treasurer of the Board of Missions of the North Georgia Conference of the Methodist Church. Since 1889 Candler had served on the Board of Trustees of Emory College, then a small Methodist-owned liberal arts college in Oxford, Georgia, and devoted much of his energy and wealth to the development of the institution. When the Methodist Episcopal Church, South decided to establish a university east of the Mississippi River, Candler in 1915 contributed a tract in Druid Hills and $1 million to the endowment of the university, making it possible for Emory College to move to Atlanta to become Emory University. From 1919 to 1929 Candler was a vice president of the American Bible Society.

In his public career Candler was an influential civic leader and booster of Atlanta. Candler was a founder of the Atlanta Chamber of Commerce, and in 1908 and 1909 he served as its president. On two occasions Candler committed his financial resources to relieve the suffering of the people of Atlanta and Georgia. To prevent a crash in real estate values in Atlanta during the economic crisis of 1907, Candler bought the homes of families threatened with foreclosure. Spending at least $1 million of his own funds, Candler purchased about 250 homes, which he later sold to homeowners on easy terms. In 1914, when the advent of World War I closed the European market to southern cotton, and the price of cotton plummeted, Candler pledged $30 million, his entire wealth, for the relief of cotton farmers. Through the Central Bank & Trust Company Candler lent farmers six cents per pound for every bale of cotton they stored in his warehouses. Candler's Atlanta Warehouse Company built a forty-acre warehouse for the storage of cotton. In 1916, when the city of Atlanta faced bankruptcy and municipal services were neglected, local business leaders turned to Candler because of his managerial qualities and selfless devotion to Atlanta to end the political bickering in city government and put the city's affairs in order. In answering the call to run for mayor, Candler did not propose specific programs but promised "to apply the same energy, the same thought, the same business judgement and the same care to it that I have always applied to every other corporation over which I have been called to preside" (Candler, p. 324). As mayor from 1917 to 1918, Candler introduced a program of economy in municipal government to address the operating deficit and debt of the city. Candler died in Atlanta.

Candler's devotion to using his wealth for the betterment of the community prompted the Atlanta *Journal* to comment at his death, "Service . . . was the master motive of his well-nigh four score years, born of his heart, nurtured by his faith, exemplified in his daily life" (Candler, p. 460). Shaped by the southern rural evangelicalism of his family upbringing, Candler in his public career linked the moral life of the community with its material prosperity. According to Candler, commerce, the key to community advancement, was corrupted when conscience did not guide individual behavior in the marketplace. Advocating "conscientious conservatism," Candler promoted civic responsibility that offered conservative measures that benefited all members of the community while respecting the rights of property and labor. As a successful businessman and active civic leader, Candler provided a model of private success and civic involvement for Atlanta's business leaders whom he admonished to lead their fellow citizens toward material and moral improvement.

• Candler's letters and speeches are collected in the Asa Griggs Candler Papers in the Robert W. Woodruff Library of Emory University. The only biography of Candler is written by his son, Charles Howard Candler, *Asa Griggs Candler* (1950). The entry on Candler in William J. Northen, ed., *Men of Mark in Georgia* vol. 4 (1908), is also helpful. Candler's prominent role in the affairs of Atlanta is described in Franklin M. Garrett, *Atlanta and Environs: A Chronicle of Its People and Events* (2 vols., 1954). Pat Watters, *Coca-Cola: An Illustrated History* (1978), provides an account of Candler and the Coca-Cola Company. A succinct analysis of Candler and the 1909 Food and Drug Administration case is in James Harvey Young, "Three Southern Food and Drug Cases," *Journal of Southern History* 49 (Feb. 1983): 3–36. An obituary is in the *New York Times*, 13 Mar. 1929.

MICHAEL SHIRLEY

CANDLER, Warren Akin (23 Aug. 1857–25 Sept. 1941), educator and clergyman, was born in Villa Rica, Georgia, the son of Samuel Charles Candler, a farmer, real estate speculator, merchant, and politician, and Martha Bernetta Beall. Samuel Candler was a slaveholder and Union Democrat who supported the South during the Civil War. While the war and Reconstruction brought temporary hardship, Warren enrolled in Emory College in 1873 with advanced standing and graduated three years later. Although intending to study for the bar, he felt a "calling" in his senior year and entered the ministry. Candler married Sarah Antoinette Curtright in 1877, a year after he graduated and began his career in the church. They had five children.

Entering the North Georgia Conference of the Methodist Episcopal Church, South, on trial in December 1875, Candler received appointments to Covington (1876) and then Watkinsville circuit (1877). Ordained as deacon in December 1877, he moved from Atlanta (1877–1880) to the Dahlonega District (1881), where he served as presiding elder overseeing the work of other ministers. Candler next moved on to Sparta (1882) and finally to Augusta (1883–1886). Influential Bishop George Foster Pierce became his mentor and encouraged him to emphasize the evangelical message of salvation, the authority of bishops, and proper personal conduct.

While in Augusta, in 1884 Candler and Pierce helped found Paine College, an institution with a liberal arts curriculum geared toward training African-American teachers, lawyers, and ministers. Created jointly with the Colored Methodist Episcopal church, Pain had a biracial board of trustees and faculty. Candler supported this policy of limited integration, serving as a member and as president of the board. A conservative proponent of an organic society in which all persons had their proper roles, Candler believed that black people should be encouraged to reach their (to him, limited) potential. Thus paradoxically (since this was the era of Jim Crow), the paternalistic Candler supported the integration of administration and teaching at Paine College. This position was more similar to that later espoused by W. E. B. Du Bois (albeit with a decidedly different rationale) than to that of Booker T. Washington during an era of segregation. Candler later denounced lynching on the grounds that it destroyed law and order and was unjust, yet he also opposed the union of southern and northern Methodist churches, partly because he decried the supervision of white ministers by black bishops.

During the 1880s Candler fostered missions in the cities, created a tract society, and flirted with the Holiness movement, a force within Methodism that emphasized the need for an experience of "entire sanctification." He ultimately broke with the Holiness party over theological differences, but he continued to denounce personal "vices" and "temptations," including intemperance, dancing, the theater, circuses, and gambling. Candler thus linked righteousness and holiness and eased his way into the position of assistant editor of the denomination's Nashville *Christian Advocate* (1886–1888). In his editorials and in sermons in a Nashville pulpit, he objected to the Social Gospel (because it did not stress sanctification and faith), biblical criticism (because it questioned the divinity of the Scriptures), labor union violence, and state institutions of higher education. He also advocated greater support for church colleges. While Candler was never one to shun controversy, his views reflected rural fears of change in the late nineteenth century South.

In 1888 Candler won election to the presidency of Emory College, which was located in Oxford, Georgia, east of Atlanta. Over the next decade he reorganized Emory's financial system; enlarged the endowment; brought renewed emphasis to the liberal arts and sciences, theology, and law; created a student loan fund; doubled the number of library holdings; and increased enrollment and faculty by almost one-third. During his tenure, Candler supported new degree options and more stringent requirements. He also encouraged extracurricular activities but banned intercollegiate sports because gambling had earlier disrupted a baseball game and because he believed that coaches were overpaid and that competitive sports detracted from the college's primary educational mission. Under Candler's leadership, Emory subsequently emerged as a pioneer in the intramural movement of "athletics-for-all." As the advocate of a "Christian education" to train gentlemen-leaders, Candler was a transitional president who set Emory on a sound footing and prepared it for future change.

Typically, Candler's Oxford years were marked by conflict, especially with Rebecca Latimer Felton, wife of an Independent politician and first woman to serve in the U.S. Senate. Candler and Felton battled for decades over state support for higher education, women's rights, lynching, and other issues. At the turn of the century, for example, he supported his son-in-law, Andrew Sledd, a young Emory College teacher, against Felton. Felton had called Sledd to task for writing an article denouncing lynching and supporting black rights.

Candler was voted into the Southern Methodist Episcopal bishopric in 1898. During the next thirty-six years he served as secretary to the College of Bishops and oversaw churches throughout the Southeast. His supervision of missions in Cuba, Mexico, and the Orient included creation of Candler College in Havana and the introduction of native ministers in many lands. During this period, he also wrote weekly columns for Atlanta newspapers and fifteen books, several of which were biographies of bishops he had known.

Candler's episcopal duties included ex officio membership on the Vanderbilt University Board of Trustees. In 1904, he served as chairman of the board's committee on faculty nominations. In this capacity, Candler became embroiled in the controversy over the ownership and control of Vanderbilt University. While considering and then accepting two nominations submitted by Chancellor James Kirkland, Candler urged that attention be paid in future faculty nominations to church membership in addition to scholarly credentials. His committee's report indicated that Southern Methodists were underrepresented on the Vanderbilt faculty. Kirkland viewed the recommendation as a challenge to his authority and the direction that he wanted the school to follow. Candler lost his position on the board in 1905. During the ensuing decade friction continued, with Kirkland enjoying the support of the majority of the board and certain elements within the church itself. Candler and his supporters wanted the school to maintain its identity as a denominational institution with the church electing trustees and controlling policies, while Kirkland strove to make Vanderbilt a secular university with nominal religious affiliation. Candler believed that the school was still a Methodist institution and had been since its founding by Bishop Holland N. McTyeire in 1872. Unlike Kirkland, Candler did not believe continued Methodist identity and ownership precluded academic excellence. While the issue of school ownership was before the Tennessee Supreme Court (which eventually decided against church authority), the Carnegie Foundation offered one million dollars to Vanderbilt's medical school if it broke denominational ties. This outside interference simplified the Vanderbilt controversy in Candler's perception. He now viewed the confrontation between church and school as part of the larger battleground between the forces of secular materialism and religion. He no longer considered any compromise that might have allowed any continued association between the university and the Southern Methodist church. Under his leadership the College of Bishops vetoed Carnegie's offer (a position Kirkland and the board ignored) and later renounced further claims to the university in 1914.

To counteract these events the Methodist Episcopal Church, South, established an educational commission, with Candler as chairman, to further its mission on behalf of higher learning. Southern Methodist University in Dallas, Texas, was expanded as the major denominational school west of the Mississippi River, and Emory College was moved to Atlanta (1914–1919) to be transformed into a university to serve church needs in the East.

With the support of his brother, Asa G. Candler, the builder of Coca-Cola, Warren Candler first became chancellor of Emory University in 1914. Candler oversaw the addition of theology, law, and medical schools to the original college. Wesley Memorial Enterprise, an institutional church and hospital established by the brothers, provided part of the school's foundation. Between 1914 and 1918 the endowment more than doubled, the assets of the school multiplied by two and one-half times, and enrollment jumped from 631 to 1323. During his Emory leadership, Candler hired faculty who were graduates of the best universities, and he defended their academic freedom.

Candler became senior bishop of the Methodist Episcopal Church, South, in 1922, an honor he held for the next twelve years before his mandatory retirement. During the 1920s he supported fundamental values against the inroads of theological modernism and materialism and in opposition to the unity of the southern and northern Methodist churches. Confronted with changing cultural perspectives on religion, the government, and the family, he conducted a rearguard action in an attempt to maintain traditional nineteenth-century values and institutions.

Warren Candler's life spanned eight decades during which the country experienced dramatic changes. The study of his life throws light on the trials and tribulations of transition. He ultimately rejected the new ways, and thus most of his positions became anachronistic. Nonetheless many of his conservative ideas concerning family values and religion were reinvigorated during the 1980s and 1990s. Until the last two decades of his life, when he felt largely powerless and met repeated defeats, Candler's actions illustrated the positive contributions that the conservative as idealist could make. He opposed lynching, supported academic freedom, and helped build several enduring institutions. He died in Atlanta.

• The largest collection of Candler papers is housed at Emory University, with smaller but still helpful collections at Duke University, the University of Virginia, and the University of North Carolina at Chapel Hill. Collections of Candler's sermons, articles, lectures, and commencement addresses appeared in 1901, 1921, 1922, 1926, 1927, and 1930. In these writings and in *Great Revivals and the Great Republic* (1904), *Christus Auctor: A Manual of Christian Evidences* (1909), and *Practical Studies in the Fourth Gospel*, 2 vols. (1913), Candler explicated his world view and the qualities necessary for a valuable life. There are two biographies, Mark K. Bauman, *Warren Akin Candler: Conservative as Idealist* (1981), and the authorized Alfred M. Pierce, *Giant against the Sky* (1948). Articles by Bauman include "A Famous Atlantan Speaks Out against Lynching: Bishop Warren A. Candler and Social Justice," *Atlanta Historical Bulletin* 20 (Spring 1976): 24–32; " 'The Inherent Disposition of Racial Consciousness': Bishop Candler's Changing Attitude toward Lynching," *Atlanta Historical Bulletin* 21 (Fall 1977): 24–31; "John T. Scopes, Leopold and Loeb, and Bishop Warren A. Candler," *Methodist History* 16 (Jan. 1978): 92–100; "Prohibition and Politics: Warren Candler and Al Smith's 1928 Campaign," *Mississippi Quarterly* 31 (Winter 1977–1978): 109–17; "Vanderbilt, Emory and Southern Methodist University through the Eyes of Methodist Episcopal Church, South, Bishop Warren A. Candler," *Milestones* 1 (Dec. 1988): 71–75; and "Race and Mastery: The Debate of 1903," in *From the Old South to the New*, ed. Walter J. Fraser, Jr., and Winfred B. Moore, Jr. (1981). Charles H. Candler, *Asa Griggs Candler* (1950), offers family background, and Henry M. Bullock, *A History of Emory University* (1936), Thomas H. English, *Emory University, 1915–1965* (1966), and Boone M. Bowen, *The Candler School of Theology* (1974), provide insights into Emory and Candler's experiences there. Obituaries are in the Atlanta *Journal* and the Atlanta *Constitution*, 26 Sept. 1941.

MARK K. BAUMAN

CANE, Melville Henry (15 Apr. 1879–10 Mar. 1980), lawyer and poet, was born in Plattsburgh, New York, the son of Henry William Cane, a merchant, and Sophia Goodman. Cane's family moved to New York City when he was six years of age. He received a bachelor of arts degree from Columbia University in 1900 and a bachelor of laws from the same institution in 1903. Cane demonstrated an early interest in writing. As an undergraduate at Columbia, he served as editor in chief of the *Literary Monthly* and composed lyrics for John Erskine's variety shows. During that time he also contributed light verse to *Puck* and *Judge*.

In 1905 Cane began practicing law with the firm of Ernst, Cane, Berner & Gitlin. In 1909 he married Florence Naumbury, and they had two daughters. Despite a demanding career and a new marriage, the literary connections Cane had previously forged at college remained strong. His classmates at Columbia had included Alfred Harcourt and Donald Brace. As their lawyer, Cane drew up incorporation papers for their publishing house in 1919. Other clients included Sinclair Lewis, Thomas Wolfe, William Saroyan, and Upton Sinclair, whom Cane advised on copyright and invasion of privacy concerns.

As he practiced law, Cane also wrote poetry. His first collection, *January Garden*, was published by Harcourt Brace in 1926. Cane used free verse in most of the volume, and the poems reflect his transition from the lighthearted style he had previously adopted in college to a more serious, introspective one.

This collection was followed by *Behind Dark Spaces* (1930) and *Poems: New and Selected* (1938). The poems in both of these collections are examples of Cane's ability to paint succinct pictures. Cane wrote in his autobiography that he learned the discipline of conciseness from drawing contracts and legal briefs. In both, he said, there has to be a precise inspection of the object. The poems in these volumes convey a somber tone, and much like the mood Cane's poetry addresses serious themes; including the uncertainty man perceives in nature, winter, and the night. In his autobiography, Cane noted that snow is his most recurrent symbol; he looked on it as a "benign miracle." Despite the dark tone of most of the poems, *Poems: New and Selected* and successive volumes like *A Wider Arc* (1947) reflect Cane's transition to a poetic style that combined somberness with the light touch he had developed earlier. Many are relieved by an insistent spirit of hopefulness. Although much of his poetry is written in couplets, many times he suspended form for his message.

He became a member of the board of directors of Harcourt Brace Jovanovich, which incorporated in 1940, and continued to write. Not restricting his writing to poetry, his prose includes *Making a Poem* (1953). Along with Harry E. Maule and Philip Allan Friedman, Cane also edited *The Man from Main Street: A Sinclair Lewis Reader*, an anthology of selected essays and writings by Lewis. Cane had been Lewis's literary executor and referred to him as "a great man for research."

A review of Cane's *And Pastures New* (1956), which was printed in the *New York Times Book Review*, garnered him the appellation "lyric philosopher" from Robert Hillyer, referring to Cane's tendency to gently examine serious subjects. Hillyer also linked Cane's poetry to the imagists because of his use of colorful, sharp language. However, Hillyer felt that Cane subordinated his use of language to the moods and emotions his poems embodied. Cane himself acknowledged the technical influence of the imagists in his poetry, including their "heightened accuracy" and "sharper sensuous awareness." Still, Cane felt that beyond these contributions his own verse differed from the imagists' work, which he often found "static" and "lacking in overtones that cause a poem to linger on and become memorable."

The 1960s and 1970s were prolific years for Cane during which he produced seven major texts, *Bullet-Hunting* (1960), co-edited with John Farrar and Louise Townsend Nicholl; *The Golden Year: The Poetry Society of America Anthology* (1960); *To Build a Fire* (1964); *So That It Flower: A Gathering of Poems* (1966); *Eloquent April: New Poems and Prose* (1971); *The First Firefly: New Poems and Prose* (1974); and *Snow toward Evening* (1974). During this period Cane also contributed poems, articles, and stories to various publications, including *Sporting News*, *Saturday Review*, *American Scholar*, *Virginia Quarterly Review*, and *Southwest Review*.

Cane belonged to the Association of the New York Bar, the Poetry Society of America, the Columbia University Club, and Phi Beta Kappa, an eclectic list that demonstrates his attraction to both law and letters. The honors awarded him also reflect his double love. Among them are the Columbia University medal for conspicuous alumni service (1933) and the medal for excellence in law and literature (1948). Harcourt Brace Jovanovich established the Poetry Society of America's Melville Henry Cane Award in 1960, designated to be given annually to honor new books of verse or critical studies of poetry. In 1971 the Poetry Society of America also awarded Cane its gold medal "for longtime contributions to poetry" shortly after his ninety-second birthday and the publication of *Eloquent April.* Charles A. Wagner, the Poetry Society's executive secretary and a poet himself, called the recognition of Cane "the culmination of decades dedicated to poeticizing." Cane died in New York City.

Cane saw a strong relationship between writing poetry and practicing law. According to Ian T. Macauley in his obituary of Cane for the *New York Times*, Cane once wrote, "You have to be accurate in law, and you have to be accurate in a poem."

While Cane was a prolific poet, his work is not widely known. Still, the balancing trait he created between the serious and the lyric in his poetry makes its examination relevant to succeeding generations. Although noted for his "technical control," Cane's craftsmanship also showed a playful side. Gorham Munson noted in the *Saturday Review* (16 June 1956) that Cane "is truly a serious poet, but he is saved from gravity by his playfulness, the playfulness that makes his light verse delightful and his serious verse springy in spirit."

• Several recordings of Cane reading or discussing his poetry have been made. A copy of the City College of New York recording of 28 Feb. 1941 was made for the Archive of Recorded Poetry and Literature at the Library of Congress in 1953. In 1969, as part of the motivational series titled Authors and Their Books, Cane discussed *All and Sundry* with columnist Robert Cromie. Likewise, the Columbia University oral history collection, *Reminiscences* (1972), includes a transcript of an interview conducted with Cane in 1956 by personnel from the Oral History Research Office. Columbia University also marked the ninety-first birthday of its alumnus by establishing the Cane Collection, which documents his career and contains his memorabilia. For biographical information concerning Cane's life, see his autobiography, *All and Sundry: An Oblique Autobiography* (1968), a collection of vignettes from his life along with some of his poetry. Henry Morton Robinson, *Poetry and Personality* (1951), also provides useful commentary on Cane's work. See also Cane's *How "Humbly, Wildly" Was Born* (1951). Obituaries are in *Newsweek*, 24 Mar. 1980; the *New York Times*, 11 Mar. 1980; and *Publishers Weekly*, 21 Mar. 1980.

LINDA K. WRIGHT

CANFIELD, Cass (26 Apr. 1897–27 Mar. 1986), publisher and writer, was born in New York City, the son of Augustus Cass Canfield, an engineer and sportsman, and Josephine Houghteling. When Cass Canfield was eight years old, his father died; several years later his mother married Frank Jay Griswold, a sportsman credited with inventing the tuxedo, and Griswold took an active role in raising his stepson.

Canfield was educated privately in Manhattan and prepared for college at Groton; he entered Harvard University in 1915. His attendance at Harvard was interrupted in 1918, when he left to serve as a second lieutenant during World War I, but he returned to graduate with his class the following year. After a year's study at Oxford University, Canfield spent several months in Paris, then traveled around the world. During his journeys in the Far East, he retraced on foot the route of Marco Polo, walking more than 1,200 miles through Burma and China.

Following his return to New York City in 1921, Canfield began work as a securities analyst at the investment firm Harris, Forbes and Company. A year later he joined the staff of the *New York Evening Post*, working first as a reporter and then transferring to the business department, where he sold advertising. In 1924 one of the *Post*'s clients, Harper & Brothers, a distinguished American book and magazine publishing company founded in 1817, was in the process of reorganizing; Canfield, who was independently wealthy—a consequence of the Cass family's extensive landholdings—became a major investor in the company. Shortly afterward he left the *Post* and became manager of Harper's London office. During his three years there, Canfield added a number of British authors to Harper's list, among them novelist J. B. Priestley, biologist Julian Huxley, and political scientist Harold Laski.

Canfield returned to New York in 1927 to become an assistant book editor at Harper's Manhattan office. This position, however, was only temporary, preparing him for increasing responsibilities within the company. He rose swiftly; two years later he was promoted to executive vice president, which involved him in the business management of *Harper's Magazine*, and in 1931 he became president of the company. In 1932–1934 Canfield also served as president of the National Association of Book Publishers.

Canfield held the Harper's presidency until 1945, interrupting his tenure several times during World War II. In May 1942 he took a fifteen-month leave of absence to serve on the Board of Economic Warfare, an assignment that took him to Stockholm and London. During the war he was also a special consultant to the Foreign Economic Administration in Washington, D.C., and for several months at the beginning of 1945 he was on leave to serve as director of informational activities in France for the Office of War Information.

After the war Canfield served for a decade as chairman of the board at Harper's; during this time *Harper's Magazine* was sold to Cowles Publishing. He became chairman of Harper's executive committee in 1955. In 1961, midway through Canfield's tenure in this role, the company merged with a textbook publisher, Row, Peterson and Company, and became known as Harper & Row. In 1967, at the age of seventy-one, Canfield relinquished his executive role to become senior book editor, a position he held until his death. He went to his office daily until September 1985, when he suffered a stroke.

Although his responsibilities at Harper's were largely administrative for much of his tenure there, Canfield was always active in the editorial department. He is credited with recruiting a number of authors for publication, among them James Thurber, Thornton Wilder, E. B. White, and John Gunther, who wrote *Inside Europe* at Canfield's request. Canfield's keen interest in politics—he was one of the founders of the journal *Foreign Affairs* in the early 1920s—also led him to solicit and publish works by such well-known public figures as Eleanor Roosevelt, Adlai Stevenson, John F. Kennedy, Sumner Welles, Henry Stimson, and Allen Dulles. Canfield enjoyed the craft of editing, and many of the books that he published were personally edited by him.

In 1969 Canfield's memoir *The Publishing Experience* was published; a companion volume, *Up and Down and Around*, appeared two years later. Canfield subsequently wrote five more nonfiction works: *The Incredible Pierpont Morgan* (1974); *Samuel Adams' Revolution* (1976); *The Iron Will of Jefferson Davis* (1978); *Outrageous Fortunes* (1981); and *The Six* (1983).

Throughout much of his adult life, Canfield was a supporter of the Democratic party; he played an active role in the 1956 presidential campaign of Adlai Stevenson. Another of his major interests outside publishing was birth control. He was chairman for many years of the executive committee of the Planned Parenthood Foundation, and he traveled widely for that organization, making speeches and raising money. He was also a member of the board of New York University.

Canfield was married three times. He and his first wife, Katharine Emmet, whom he married in 1922, had two sons, one of whom became an editor at Harper's; they were divorced in 1937. He married Jane White Fuller in 1938; she died in 1984, and later that year he married Joan H. King, who survived him. He died in New York City.

Cass Canfield is considered one of the giants of twentieth-century American publishing, along with Alfred Knopf and Bennett Cerf, and he was widely respected for his integrity as well as his abilities and accomplishments. In 1948, at the height of his career, he offered the following statement as his professional credo: "To present to the public the work of new authors of talent; to publish books of cultural and historical value; to keep in print worthwhile books; to present in book form every point of view that has validity and is worthy of expression."

• Biographical information on Cass Canfield appears in *Current Biography* (1954) and in the *Saturday Review of Literature*, 17 Apr. 1948. An obituary is in the *New York Times*, 28 Mar. 1986.

ANN T. KEENE

CANFIELD, Dorothy. *See* Fisher, Dorothy F. Canfield.

CANHAM, Erwin Dain (13 Feb. 1904–3 Jan. 1982), editor, was born in Auburn, Maine, the son of Vincent Walter Canham and Elizabeth May Gowell, journalists. In addition to adopting his parents' career choices, the young Canham followed their choice of religious practice, converting from Methodism to Christian Science along with his parents.

In an account in *Editor & Publisher*, Canham described how as a youth he helped his father take information or interview residents for news stories using a rural telephone. When he was eight his father became editor and publisher of the *Sanford Star-News*, a weekly intended to disseminate the liberal views of the Maine citizens who published it, and from that time on Canham never considered another career.

At age fourteen Canham was, as he described, "grossly over-promoted" to the position of reporter on the *Lewiston Sun-Journal* because the "real reporters" were serving on the battlefields of World War I. After he received his A.B. from Bates College in 1925, he won a Rhodes scholarship and received advanced degrees at Oxford University in 1936 while working on and off for the Boston-based *Christian Science Monitor*. As a cub reporter, he rented an apartment with columnist Roscoe Drummond, who gave Canham the nickname "Spike." He married Thelma Whitman Hart in 1930, and they had two daughters. After her death in 1967 he married Patience Daltry in 1968. They had no children.

During his years at Oxford, Canham covered the 1930 London Naval Disarmament Conference for the *Christian Science Monitor*. In 1932 Canham became the chief of the *Monitor*'s bureau in Washington, D.C., where he covered the 1932 presidential election and the first seven years of the New Deal. He became the managing editor in 1941, the editor in 1945, and the editor in chief in 1964.

One of Canham's first jobs as editor was to attend the 1945 organizational meeting of the United Nations held in San Francisco; he referred to himself in his reports as "our man." On his return from San Francisco he stopped in Los Angeles to receive an award for the *Monitor*'s noteworthy achievements in the realm of sports. In his remarks he stressed that his intention for the *Monitor*'s sports pages was to show that keen competition can take place without ill feelings or bad sportsmanship.

In his leadership positions, Canham strengthened coverage of foreign news and trained staff specialists in many areas. As a Christian Scientist he followed the philosophy of founder Mary Baker Eddy "to injure no man, but to bless all mankind." This meant that Canham encouraged greater attention to topics that would remain significant in the long term and discouraged focus on crime, violence, and disasters.

Because of Canham's activity in a number of professional organizations, including the American Society of Newspaper Editors (ASNE), which he served as its eighteenth president in 1948–1949, he was esteemed by his colleagues as a competent and unbiased journalist. Along with Roy A. Roberts of the *Kansas City Star*, N. R. Howard of the *Cleveland News*, Wilbur Forrest of the *New York Herald Tribune*, and John Knight of the Knight Newspaper group, Canham helped make the years between 1944 and 1950 the golden years of globalism for the ASNE. He later conceded that despite the long years of involvement, the promotion of press freedom in foreign countries by ASNE and American journalists had generally been unsuccessful.

During his years with ASNE, Canham was a leader of a majority group that opposed enforcement of ethics codes in the press, believing that such codes should remain voluntary. Diverging from the stronger ASNE position of Willis Abbot, another *Christian Science Monitor* editor and ASNE leader, Canham concluded "with the utmost earnestness that self-control is working among American newspapers through organized self-analysis, self-improvement and a voluntary sense of accepted responsibility which means long-run survival."

As a practicing Christian Scientist and editor of its newspaper, Canham faced problems unlike those of most editors. Among his biggest challenges was to make the newspaper lively for the great mass of readers outside of Boston who received the paper late, while staying competitive with local news publications. According to one account, "Canham had to see that the contents of the *Monitor* passed theological as well as journalistic tests [which were] not always, in the eyes of those outside the faith, . . . reconcilable." He understood, though, that his task was not to proselytize, and so the paper's religious message appeared as a single piece, clearly labeled as the *Monitor*'s "Daily Religious Article" and composed by church members outside the staff.

Canham served as editor in chief until 1974 and then as editor emeritus. During his editorial tenure he helped make the *Christian Science Monitor* a nationally and internationally respected newspaper. Canham saw no conflict of interest between his newspaper position and his involvement in numerous government and business organizations, including service as the U.S. delegate to the United Nations, the president of the U.S. Chamber of Commerce, a director of the John Hancock Mutual Life Insurance Company and the Federal Reserve Bank of Boston, and the president of the Christian Science church (1966). The *New York Times* once called Canham's career an unusual combination of two deep interests: "religious concern and a nose for the news." From 1975 to 1978 he served as resident commissioner of the Northern Marianas Islands. He died in Agana, Guam.

• Two of Canham's books reveal his personal and professional philosophy: *Commitment to Freedom: The Story of the Christian Science Monitor* (1958) and *The Christian Science Way of Life with a Christian Scientist's Life* (1962), coauthored with DeWitt John. For an overview of his life see Kenneth Stewart and John Tebbel, *Makers of Modern Journalism* (1952). For an understanding of Canham's leadership role see Paul Alfred Pratte, *Gods within the Machine: A History of the American Society of Newspaper Editors, 1923–1993* (1995). An obituary is in the *New York Times*, 4 Jan. 1982.

ALF PRATTE

CANIFF, Milton Arthur Paul (28 Feb. 1907–3 Apr. 1988), cartoonist, was born in Hillsboro, Ohio, the only son of John William Caniff, a printer, and Elizabeth Burton. Caniff apprenticed in the art department of the *Dayton Journal* while in high school, where he excelled in both art and drama courses, and he worked as an artist at the *Columbus Dispatch* while at Ohio State University (1925–1930). Graduating with a degree in fine art, he married his high school sweetheart, Esther Frances "Bunny" Parsons, in 1930; they had no children. In April 1932 Caniff became a staff artist for the Associated Press in New York. There, he did miscellaneous illustrations and panel cartoons (including *Mister Gilfeather, Puffy the Pig*, and *The Gay Thirties*) until 31 July 1933, when the AP launched his first nationally syndicated strip, *Dickie Dare*, which dramatized a boy's dreams of adventures with such heroes as Robin Hood, Robinson Crusoe, and Aladdin.

Then in October 1934 Joseph Patterson of the *New York Daily News* asked Caniff to create a strip about "real" adventuring. Beginning on 22 October, *Terry and the Pirates* embodied a formula suggested by Patterson: a kid hero (Terry) with a rugged and handsome adult mentor (Pat Ryan), wandering through China ("Anything can still happen out there," Patterson said) and encountering dangers and femmes fatales at every pagoda. But Caniff went beyond Patterson's prescription and virtually redefined the adventure continuity strip—so thoroughly did he improve on the genre's basic ingredients. Inspired by the work of his studiomate, Noel Sickles, Caniff developed an impressionistic style of drawing that suggested reality economically with shadow rather than with painstakingly rendered particulars. To the realism of this graphic technique, he added realism of detail, striving for absolute authenticity in depicting every aspect of the setting of *Terry*, whether Oriental or, later, military, and amassing a research library of several thousand volumes on these matters. He polished the prose of his dialogue, and as speech balloons grew larger, he resorted to cinematic techniques to rejuvenate visual excitement in the strip—shifting his "camera" rapidly from panel to panel to portray scenes from dramatically different distances and angles.

But Caniff's signal accomplishment was as storyteller: he enriched the simple adventure story by making character development integral to action-packed plots. To weave into the tapestry of Terry's history such an intriguing character as an alluring but ruthless pirate queen called the Dragon Lady was to add a powerful enhancement to the strip's exotic locale: her characterization complemented the mysteriousness of the Orient with the inscrutability of her personality. Still, the Dragon Lady's personality seemed so true-to-life that it lent the authority of its authenticity to the strip's stories, making the most improbable adventures seem real.

Disqualified from military service on medical grounds, Caniff reached the pinnacle of his fame during World War II. In the strip, Terry joined the U.S. Air Force, and Caniff's realistic and sympathetic treatment of military life championed the achievements of ordinary men and women in uniform. *Terry*'s trenchant, pragmatic patriotism warmed hearts and steeled nerves on the home front as well as at the battlefront. The Sunday page for 17 October 1943 so incisively captured the wartime spirit of the day that it was read into the *Congressional Record*. One of Caniff's most celebrated creations came about through one of his numerous contributions to the war effort: Miss Lace, a curvaceous bundle of civilian camaraderie, was the central figure of *Male Call*, a mildly risqué weekly strip he drew without remuneration for distribution as a morale booster to camp and unit newspapers (Mar. 1943–Mar. 1946). The strip was published regularly in more than 3,000 papers, the greatest circulation in number of publications attained by any comic strip.

After the war, Caniff abandoned *Terry*, which was owned by the Chicago Tribune-New York Daily News Syndicate, to create for Field Enterprises a new strip that, in a departure from the proprietary custom of the industry, he would own himself. Caniff's work was held in such high esteem that his new creation was bought sight-unseen by nearly 200 newspapers. Starting 13 January 1947, *Steve Canyon* debuted with a storytelling tour de force: Caniff built suspense by postponing his hero's appearance for the first week. Deliberately contrived to appeal to a postwar audience of former GIs, Canyon was an ex-Army Transport Command pilot, and, like thousands of other veterans, he had set himself up in business—operating his own cargo airline. His vocation gave him a plausible excuse for being a globe-trotting soldier of fortune.

When the Korean War broke out, however, Caniff put Steve back into uniform in the air force, and, from then on, *Steve Canyon* was a military strip; henceforth, Canyon's adventures took place in military settings and with such an authentic representation of the military point of view that he became an unofficial spokesman for the air force. Caniff's propagandizing was entirely unforced. Military life was amicable to the themes of courage, resourcefulness, and (above all) loyalty that had predominated in Caniff's work all his life; in the military context, dramatic expression of these values was achieved naturally in patriotic as well as personal terms.

Maintaining the high standards of craftsmanship he had set in *Terry*, Caniff also continued to explore the medium's potential. He introduced the repertory theater concept, rotating stories among several leading players (including Poteet Canyon, Steve's "kissin' cousin" and ward). In later years he also sometimes let his characters dream themselves into adventures in other times and places. By such devices, Caniff shifted the focus of the strip to hold reader interest with highly topical stories, keeping pace with changing public tastes—until the Vietnam war, when antimilitary sentiment undermined the appeal of his air force hero, and papers canceled by the score. He nonetheless continued to produce the strip until his death in New York City. By then, Caniff had been in print every weekday for fifty-five years. His support of the U.S. Air Force earned him many accolades, including the USAF Exceptional Service Award (the highest for a civilian). He was twice (1946 and 1971) named "outstanding cartoonist of the year" by the National Cartoonists Society, an organization he helped found, serving as its second president (1948–1949) and as honorary chairman for seventeen years. Caniff is one of the few authentic giants in the history of cartooning. His achievements in the newspaper comic strip form shaped the adventure strip genre and set standards by which all storytelling strips were subsequently judged.

• Much of Caniff's oeuvre has been collected in book form: *Dickie Dare* in a single volume (1986), *Terry and the Pirates* in twelve volumes (1984–1987), *Male Call* (1987), and *Steve Canyon* in magazine format (Jan. 1983–Dec. 1988), the remainder in paperback (1989–). The only published biography is the brief *Milton Caniff: Rembrandt of the Comic Strip* (1946; repr. 1989), by "John Paul Adams" (Charles Kinnaird); written to promote *Steve Canyon*, it covers only Caniff's early career. Similar material is treated in more detail by Caniff's friend Paul Ackerman, writing in *Sigma Chi Magazine*, Jan.–Feb. 1935, July 1937; the magazine's Feb.–Mar. 1945 issue collects and reprints numerous articles about him. "Escape Artist," *Time*, 13 Jan. 1947, discusses the introduction of *Steve Canyon* and reviews Caniff's career. In "Secrets of a Comic-Strip Artist," *Coronet*, Apr. 1947, Caniff writes about how he invented his hero. And in Lesson 20 of *The Famous Artists Cartoon Course*, Caniff writes about his life and about drawing an adventure comic strip. Two lengthy interviews with him by other cartoonists appear in Will Eisner, *Spirit Magazine #34–35*, Apr. and June 1982, and Arn Saba, *Comics Journal #108*, May 1986 (a 1978 interview). All of the works listed here, as well as Caniff's papers and much of his original art, are in the Cartoon, Graphic and Photographic Arts Research Library at Ohio State University. In the same collection is the typescript of an unpublished authorized biography, two-thirds of which had been written in time to be approved by Caniff before he died—*Meanwhile: The Life and Art of Milton Caniff*, by Robert C. Harvey; it is the only single source of biographical information on the last forty years of his life. An obituary is in the *New York Times*, 5 Apr. 1988. The most complete review of Caniff's career and evaluation of his contribution to the art is by Robert C. Harvey and appears in the *Comics Buyer's Guide*, 29 Apr. 1988. The best collection of reminiscences is in the *Dayton Daily News*, 4 Apr. 1988.

ROBERT C. HARVEY

CANNAN, Robert Keith (18 Apr. 1894–24 May 1971), biochemist, was born in Fowler, California, the son of David Cannan, a physician, and Mary Cunningham. Cannan's parents were British subjects, and in 1896 they moved the family to Asheville, North Carolina, before returning to London, England, in 1897. In 1911 he matriculated at the University of London's East London College and received his B.Sc. in chemistry in 1914. He then joined the British Expeditionary Force as a second lieutenant of infantry and distinguished himself in combat in France. In 1916 he was promoted to captain and completed World War I as a divisional trench mortar officer.

In 1919 Cannan became affiliated with University College in London as a graduate student and as an assistant in biochemistry. In 1920 he married Catherine Ann Smith; they had one child. He received his M.Sc. in biochemistry in 1923 and was promoted to senior assistant of physiology and biochemistry. He returned briefly to the United States in 1924 as a Rockefeller Foundation traveling fellow and conducted research at the U.S. Public Health Service in Washington, D.C., and at Woods Hole Marine Biological Laboratories in Falmouth, Massachusetts. He returned to his teaching duties at University College in 1925 as a senior lecturer of medical students and completed his graduate studies by receiving his D.Sc. from the college in 1930.

While at University College Cannan experimented with oxidation-reduction reactions, which involve the transfer of either oxygen atoms, hydrogen atoms, or electrons between two substances; the results of this research earned him a reputation as the leading biochemist in Great Britain. However in 1930 he made a decision that steered him away from a promising career as a biochemist and into a career as a teacher and administrator. Upon completion of his studies, he accepted a position as professor and chairman of the Department of Biochemistry at the New York University and Bellevue Hospital Medical College, later renamed the New York University Medical Center. The position had been vacant for two years, so Cannan's major task involved reorganizing the department. One of the most promising students to pass through the department while Cannan was chairman was Jonas Salk. Under Cannan's supervision Salk conducted experiments regarding the inactivation of viruses by formaldehyde that led directly to the development of the polio vaccine.

Although primarily a teacher and administrator, Cannan continued to conduct research of his own. He began investigating the physical chemistry of proteins and was particularly interested in the relationship between acid-base reactions, which involve the exchange of hydrogen ions, and the amino acid composition and structure of proteins. He took a leave of absence from the medical center from 1943 to 1945 to direct the study of chemical warfare agents at the University of Chicago's Toxicity Laboratory for the U.S. Office of Scientific Research and Development. From 1948 to 1950 he served as the medical center's vice chairman of research and from 1950 to 1952 as its assistant director.

While performing his duties at the medical center, Cannan became involved with the work of the National Academy of Sciences's National Research Council. From 1945 to 1952 he served in various capacities on its Division of Medical Sciences's Committee of Growth as it implemented a cancer research program. In 1952 he left New York University and moved to Washington, D.C., to become the division's vice chairman. In 1953 he was appointed chairman; he was also divorced from his first wife and married a former research collaborator at the medical center, Hildegard Newcomb Wilson; they had no children. As division chairman he appointed and oversaw the work of forty committees whose primary research concerns ranged from anesthesia to tissue transplants.

Cannan also served as chief administrator of two important projects. From 1956 to 1957 he was the executive director of the Atomic Bomb Casualty Commission, a research group that had been studying for ten years the health of the survivors of the bombings of Hiroshima and Nagasaki. The commission's researchers were working without well-defined goals as to how their work should be conducted or what sort of results their work might be expected to yield. During Cannan's brief tenure, the commission's mission was redefined, and its work was revitalized when he affiliated it with the medical schools of Yale University and the University of California at Los Angeles.

From 1962 to 1967 Cannan oversaw the work of the Drug Efficacy Study. When Congress amended the Food, Drug and Cosmetic Act of 1938 to require the Food and Drug Administration (FDA) to approve the effectiveness as well as the safety of all new drugs before they could be sold to the public, the FDA asked the National Academy of Sciences to help it comply with this directive. Consequently, Cannan recruited 180 experts to serve on thirty panels covering the range of human illness and disease; he also played a major role in authoring the guidelines by which they proceeded. During the next five years these experts worked closely with members of the medical and pharmaceutical communities to evaluate the efficacy of approximately 3,600 drugs. In 1967 Cannan resigned from the division to serve as a special assistant to the president of the National Academy of Sciences, and in this capacity he helped to organize the academy's Institute of Medicine. He retired in 1971 and died in Washington, D.C.

Cannan received several awards and honors for his contributions to medical research. He was given medals by the University of Hiroshima in 1961, the Armed Forces Institute of Pathology in 1962, and the Atomic Bomb Casualty Commission and the Japanese National Institute of Health in 1969. He became a member of the National Academy of Sciences in 1969 and of the American Association for the Advancement of Science.

Cannan contributed to the development of American science through exercising his skills as an administrator. His ability to organize large research projects and keep them running smoothly over a period of years advanced important research efforts concerning the treatment of cancer, the effects of nuclear radiation, and the development of pharmaceutical drugs.

• Some of Cannan's correspondence is in the W. M. Clark Papers in the Library of the American Philosophical Society in Philadelphia, Pa. A good biography that includes a complete bibliography of his work is John T. Edsall, National Academy of Sciences, *Biographical Memoirs* 55 (1985): 107–33. An obituary is in the *New York Times*, 25 May 1971.

CHARLES W. CAREY, JR.

CANNON, Annie Jump (11 Dec. 1863–13 Apr. 1941), astronomer, was born in Dover, Delaware, the daughter of Wilson Lee Cannon, a prosperous merchant and shipbuilder, and Mary Elizabeth Jump. As a young child Annie showed interest and talent in science. Aided by her mother, she began observing the skies and recognizing the constellations. Encouraged by her father, she enrolled in 1880 in Wellesley College, which had recently been founded to provide sound academic education for women. As an undergraduate she studied physics and astronomy with Sarah F. Whiting. After her graduation in 1884, Cannon returned to her family home and remained there for ten years; by the end of that time she had become seriously deaf. After the death of her mother, She returned to Wellesley as assistant to Whiting. The following year she began graduate work in astronomy at Radcliffe College in Cambridge, Massachusetts, which had been established to provide young women with an education equivalent to that available to young men at nearby Harvard College. In 1896 Edward C. Pickering, director of the Harvard College Observatory, offered Cannon a position examining photographic plates of stellar spectra. She remained associated with the observatory until her retirement in 1940.

Cannon was an early member of a group of women hired by Pickering to study the photographic plates obtained when starlight passed through both a telescope and a spectroscope. The combining of photography and spectroscopy with astronomy in the late nineteenth century opened a fertile new area of study for astronomers. The group of women Cannon joined was headed by Williamina Fleming; when Fleming died in 1911, Cannon succeeded her as curator of astronomical photographs at the observatory. Under Cannon's supervision the collection grew from 200,000 to 500,000 plates.

The work done by Cannon and the other "computers," as they were called, involved examining and classifying each star's spectral image. Cannon modified and improved the classification system used at the observatory so that it became recognized and used worldwide. Cannon was such a meticulous and careful worker that she discovered five novae and more than 300 variable stars in the course of her examination of the photographic plates.

The spectral classification of stars that engaged Cannon and her co-workers was made possible by a generous grant, the Henry Draper Memorial, established by Mary Anna Palmer Draper to ensure the continuation of her late husband's interest. Henry Draper, a physician practicing in New York City, was an amateur astronomer who had made the first photograph of the spectrum of a star in 1872. Publication of *The Henry Draper Catalogue* began under Cannon's supervision in 1918 and continued until 1924. This provided the spectral classes for about 350,000 stars. Cannon began an *Extension* of this catalog in 1925, which was continued until 1949 by others after her death. Because of the reliability and consistency of the data collected by the single group of analyzers under Cannon's direct supervision, the information provided in these catalogs was especially valuable to the rising number of astrophysicists in the early twentieth century who sought to understand the evolution of stars and the history of the universe. The Hertzsprung-Russell diagram organized Cannon's classifications in an especially useful way.

Cannon, well known and respected in the worldwide community of astronomers, was the recipient of many honors. Among these were two honorary degrees, doctor of astronomy from the University of Groningen (1921) and doctor of science from Oxford University (1925). Valuable as her work was to the Harvard College Observatory, she was not given a regular university appointment by the Harvard Corporation until 1938, when she was officially designated William Cranch Bond Astronomer. She was one of the first women to achieve recognition in Harvard's male bastion. Although elected to membership in the American Philosophical Society, the American Academy of Arts and Sciences, and the Royal Astronomical Society of Great Britain (honorary), she was never elected to the National Academy of Sciences, even though she received its Draper Medal in 1931. When Cannon received the Ellen Richards Prize from the Society to Aid Scientific Research by Women, she gave the monetary award to the American Astronomical Society to establish the Annie J. Cannon Prize, to be awarded triennially to a woman astronomer who had made significant contributions.

Despite the handicap of her deafness, Cannon traveled widely, lecturing and attending professional meetings. She also did work at Arequipa, Peru, where Harvard had an observatory that photographed the stars of the Southern Hemisphere. She died in Cambridge, Massachusetts, where she had made her home close to the observatory.

Cannon entered the world of astronomy in an era when women were accepted as workers but were not given genuine professional status. Encouraged by the example of her work, however, women who came after her, such as Dorrit Hoffleit, Cecilia Payne-Gaposchkin, and Vera Rubin, sought and in some cases achieved full acceptance. In the later decades of the twentieth century Cannon received considerable attention from feminist scholars seeking to document the experiences of talented women scientists of earlier generations.

• The Harvard University Archives has a large collection of Cannon's papers, including diaries, autobiographical writings, personal and professional correspondence, manuscripts, and photographs. The article on Cannon by astronomer Dorrit Hoffleit in *Notable American Women, 1607–1950*, ed. Edward T. James et al., vol. 1 (1971), gives an excellent summary of her life and work. Bessie Z. Jones and Lyle Gifford Boyd, *The Harvard College Observatory: The First Four Directorships 1839–1919* (1970), contains a biographical sketch of Cannon with a photograph and describes Edward C. Pickering's employment of women as astronomical assistants and the Henry Draper Memorial. Marilyn B. Ogilvie, *Women in Science through the Nineteenth Century: A Biographical Dictionary with Annotated Bibliography* (1986), has a list of sources, including obituary notices, and a summary of Cannon's career. See also Pamela E. Mack, "Strategies and Compromises: Women in Astronomy at Harvard University, 1870–1920," *Journal of the History of Astronomy* 21 (1990): 65–76; Peggy Aldrich Kidwell, "Three Women of American Astronomy," *American Scientist* 78 (1990): 244–51; and Margaret Rossiter, *Women Scientists in America: Struggles and Strategies to 1940* (1982). An obituary is in the *New York Times*, 14 Apr. 1941, as is an editorial tribute in the issue of 15 Apr. 1941.

KATHERINE R. SOPKA

CANNON, Charles James (4 Nov. 1800–9 Nov. 1860), author, was born in New York City, the son of an Irish Catholic couple whose names are unknown. A sickly child who received scanty education, Cannon soon began a lengthy career as a customhouse clerk. In his spare time, he wrote tales, novels, poetry, and plays. Having "never known the advantages of education" and having composed his works "in the intervals of labour or disease," as he noted in the preface to his *Facts, Feelings, and Fancies* (1835), the young author feared criticism and therefore routinely prefaced his writings with meek apologies for any "faults and anachronisms" that might be evident to an educated reader.

Cannon's first attempt at literature consisted of poetry, which appeared in the minor periodicals of his time. Although he subsequently collected his early verse into a volume entitled *Poems by a Proser* (1831), the work apparently attracted little notice, as *Facts, Feelings, and Fancies* is commonly identified as his first published work. Cannon himself characteristically declared his early writings to have been presented in "an imperfect form before the public" and hoped that his new volume, generously revised, would "correct" the faults. Comprising both poems and tales, his work possesses a moody, melodramatic quality. He abandoned one poem, "Evert Van Schaik," in midstream, worried that it would be "condemned" as a poor imitation of Fitz-Greene Halleck's "Fanny."

In 1841 Cannon's next offering, *The Poet's Quest and Other Poems*, was published. The volume includes forty short, melancholic poems, mainly inspired by the death of several of Cannon's friends or acquaintances. Critics decried the author's "Byronic moodiness." Two years later, Cannon published *The Crowning Hour and Other Poems*, a collection noticeably lighter in tone. Advertising matter following one of Cannon's later publications describes *The Crowning Hour* as being "characterized by that chaste and quiet beauty which so favorably distinguishes his poetical productions." The long title poem deals with Christopher Columbus's first sight of the new land, while the other lengthy poem, "Love," presents a successful poet's quest. The remaining poems are chiefly religious, a theme to which Cannon frequently returned, being a deeply pious man.

Mora Carmody; or, Woman's Influence followed in 1844. A staunch Catholic, Cannon hoped by his work "to show that the professors of the Ancient Faith might be, at least, as good as their neighbours." Apparently not content to let his preface suffice, the writer added a brief, third-person postscript, in which he declared that, through the "simple arguments" of his heroine, he wished to "induce [the] sincere inquirer after truth, to examine upon what grounds the Catholic rests his faith."

Of *Mora Carmody*, a critic in *Brownson's Quarterly Review* observed, "This is a very pleasant little book, written with a serious intention, and with an ability and genius from which we have much to hope." The *Truth Teller* elaborated: "a very pleasing, well-written, and interesting tale, introducing many of the controverted points between Catholics and Protestants. We recommend it to our female readers." Cannon followed his well-received work with another religious tale, *Father Felix* (1845), a stilted story that he was convinced would lead any earnest reader to convert to Catholicism.

In 1851 Cannon brought out *Poems: Dramatic and Miscellaneous* but claimed that he would soon be leaving the "unprofitable trade of ballad-making." Indeed, on 18 March 1850 his tragedy *The Oath of Office* was "successfully produced" at the Bowery Theatre and was subsequently published in 1854. The powerful tragedy, set in fifteenth-century Ireland, has long been considered Cannon's best work. Yet Cannon, sensitive and insecure, bitterly abandoned theatricals, resigning himself to publishing his tragedies in a collection simply named *Dramas* (1857). Thus, his other plays were not staged. Unlike his *Oath of Office*, Cannon's other tragedies lacked memorable characters and realistic details. They were more like tales of horror than like real dramas. His one attempt at humor, "Better Late Than Never" (*Dramas*), failed as well.

On a different note, and under the pseudonym "Grandfather Greenway," Cannon published a collection of tales known as *Ravellings from the Web of Life* (1855). An entertaining work, *Ravellings* comprises six tales composed and told by a group of family members to pass the time. The tales were well received; a critic in *Brownson's Quarterly* declared that they possessed "nice observation, deep feeling, happy descriptive powers and now and then something of the witchery of romance."

The quality of Cannon's fiction varies. His narrative style is simple and often engaging, as in *Mora Carmody*. Yet Cannon also occasionally uses long-winded sentences devoid of charm and dialogue that sounds awkward. *Father Felix*, admittedly a didactic text, serves up the unlikely sounding admonition from one lover to another: "It grieves me deeply, Julia, to see a mind like yours bend itself to the influences of a gloomy fanaticism." It extends the strain with Julia's reply: "But he has, through the mercy of God . . . kindled, by the fervour of his eloquence, a flame in my cold and worldly heart that will increase in strength and brightness through the endless round of eternity!"

The same qualities are found in Cannon's poetry. At times it achieves a certain grace, a felicity of expression, while at other times it sounds trite. Nevertheless, Cannon produced a considerable body of literature, no worse, and occasionally better, than much of the passing literature of his day. In addition, he is historically interesting for his defense of Catholicism. Virtually nothing is known of Cannon's personal life. According to Trow's *Directory*, he was still working as a clerk in 1850. With the exception of a short residence in Brooklyn toward the end of his life, Cannon lived in or near Greenwich Village until his death.

• Cannon's other works include the sketch *Harry Layden* (1842); the story *Scenes and Characters from the Comedy of Life* (1847); the novels *Tighe Lyfford* (1859) and *Bickerton; or, The Immigrant's Daughter* (1855); and, for the "Catholic Educational Series," *The Practical Spelling Book, a Manual of Instruction in the Rudiments of the English Tongue* (1852) and *Lessons for Young Learners* (1853), the first of a series of readers. Cannon's prefaces, forewords, and postscripts to his various works provide some information on his life and work. For reviews of his publications, consult *Brownson's Quarterly Review*, Jan. 1845, Jan. 1846, and Oct. 1857; and *Spirit of the Times*, 23 Mar. 1850.

KAREN N. SCHRAMM

CANNON, Clarence Andrew (11 Apr. 1879–12 May 1964), congressman, was born in Elsberry, Missouri, the son of John Randolph Cannon, a farmer and merchant, and Ida Glovina Whiteside. Reflecting his family's influence and his rural, border-state background, Cannon maintained a lifelong devotion to the Southern Baptist faith and the Democratic party. He also possessed a firm belief in the superiority of the agrarian lifestyle and small-town values.

Intelligent, ambitious, and articulate, Cannon earned high marks at two Missouri junior colleges before obtaining a B.A. (1903) and an M.A. (1904) from William Jewell College in Liberty, Missouri. After working as a high school teacher and principal, he served as an instructor of history at Stephens College in Columbia, Missouri (1904–1908). Though he retained a lifelong interest in the American past and wrote several books on family and local history, Cannon deemed the academic life too sedentary. Accordingly, he studied law at the University of Missouri while teaching at Stephens College. He earned an LL.B. and joined the bar in 1908. He established a law practice in Troy, Missouri, but soon transferred it to his home town of Elsberry.

In 1906 Cannon married Ida Dawson Wigginton; they had two daughters. The couple formed a close working relationship. Ida Cannon became her husband's most trusted political adviser. Starting in the 1920s she traveled extensively over the back-country roads of northeastern Missouri campaigning for her spouse, while he remained at his congressional desk in Washington, D.C.

Cannon eagerly sought elective office, but his first two campaigns, for county school superintendent and state representative, ended in defeat. His political fortunes changed after his congressman, Champ Clark, hired him as a confidential secretary in 1911. When Democrats elected Clark Speaker of the House that year, Cannon found himself near the center of power in Washington.

Enjoying Clark's patronage, Cannon advanced to the positions of House journal clerk (1914–1917) and House parliamentarian (1917–1920). A quick study, he rapidly established himself as a leading authority on parliamentary procedure. His skills proved so impressive that the Republicans retained him after winning the House in 1918. In 1920 he became parliamentarian of the Democratic National Convention, a position he held through 1960. Cannon exercised lasting influence over the workings of Congress through publications such as *Procedure in the House of Representatives* (1920) and *Cannon's Precedents of the House of Representatives* (1936).

After resigning as House parliamentarian, Cannon returned to his law practice in Elsberry. In 1922 voters in Clark's old congressional district elected Cannon to his mentor's seat in the House of Representatives. Popular with his constituents, he repeatedly won reelection, often without opposition, until his death.

Heeding the concerns of his rural district, Cannon emerged as a leading advocate of agricultural interests. He supported parity payments to maintain farmers' incomes, low-interest federal farm loans, and soil conservation and flood control projects. The latter two were of special concern in Cannon's district, and one of the congressman's most enduring legacies involved securing federal funding for what eventually became the Clarence Cannon Dam and Reservoir in northeastern Missouri. Cannon also played a major role in the establishment of the rural electrification program and in obtaining government funds for agricultural research. "No farm legislation was approved by Congress during the Cannon years," a contemporary observer noted, "that did not bear the impress of Cannon's knowledge of parliamentary procedure and his influence in Congress."

With the notable exception of farm supports, the Missourian primarily gained a reputation as a budget-slashing fiscal conservative, especially after he became chair of the House Appropriations Committee in 1941. Cannon retained this powerful position, except for four years of Republican control, until his death. He urged a quick reduction in military expenditures immediately after World War II, denounced foreign aid as waste, and ridiculed the space program as "moondoggle." Cannon's desire to hold tight the nation's purse strings grew with the years. In 1962 he bitterly denounced the first "$100-billion Congress" in a much-publicized speech on the House floor, angering House Speaker John W. McCormack and other fellow Democrats.

Always outspoken, sometimes irascible, Cannon earned a reputation for pugnacity. He once lampooned a fellow House member, "Of all the 'piddlin' politicians that ever piddled 'piddlin' politics on this floor, my esteemed friend, the gentleman from Wisconsin, is the greatest piddler that ever piddled." During an argument in 1945 Cannon punched in the face Representative John Taber of New York, the ranking Republican member of the House Appropriations Committee. Cannon noted gleefully that Taber ran out of the room with a bleeding lip. In 1962 Cannon engaged in an unseemly and well-publicized dispute with Senator Carl Hayden of Arizona, another octogenarian Democrat, over obscure matters of parliamentary precedent.

Cannon's irascibility extended beyond the halls of Congress. In January 1964 Jacqueline Kennedy wrote to him expressing her appreciation for his help in establishing the John F. Kennedy Center for the Performing Arts, adding, "I know the fight was not easy." Cannon barked back to the recently widowed first lady: "You say the fight was not easy, but on the contrary, we had cooperation from everyone. It was done practically by acclamation."

Cannon died in Washington, D.C., remaining an active congressman to the very end of his life, as he had wished. He had already announced his intention to seek reelection later in the year. His lengthy service in Congress made him an influential if somewhat contradictory representative. During his 41-year congressional career, he served well his rural Missouri constituents, securing passage of farm supports and funding for local projects that some critics denounced as "pork barrel" politics. At the same time, he advocated stricter fiscal responsibility in other branches of the federal government. Beyond the scope of legislation, Cannon's publications on congressional procedure have achieved the status of holy writ for successive generations of lawmakers. His contributions to agricultural and appropriation policies and parliamentary procedure, enhanced by his colorful personality, have ensured him a place as one of the major congressional figures of the twentieth century.

• Cannon's papers are deposited at the Western Historical Manuscripts Collection, University of Missouri, Columbia. In addition to his volumes on parliamentary procedure, Cannon wrote at least a half-dozen works of genealogy and local history, the most significant of which is *History of Elsberry, 1673–1955* (1955), a study of his hometown. C. Herschel Schooley, *Missouri's Cannon in the House* (1977), contains a welter of poorly organized facts and anecdotes. More scholarly is Stephen Ray Lilley, "The Early Career of Clarence Cannon, 1879–1924" (M.A. thesis, Northeast Missouri State Univ., Kirksville, 1976). Useful for various aspects of Cannon's career are William M. Fulkerson, "A Rhetorical Study of the Appropriations Speaking of Clarence Andrew Cannon in the House of Representatives, 1923–1964" (Ph.D. diss., Michigan State Univ., 1969); Charles A. Jarvis, "Clarence Cannon, the Corn Cob Pipe, and the Hawley-Smoot Tariff," *Missouri Historical Review* 84 (1990): 151–65; Lilley, "A Minuteman for Years: Clarence Cannon and the Spirit of Volunteerism," *Missouri Historical Review* 75 (1980): 33–50; and Michael D. Shulse, "The History and Development of the Clarence Cannon Dam and Reservoir, 1957–1968" (M.A. thesis, Northeast Missouri State Univ., Kirksville, 1975). Obituaries are in the *St. Louis Post-Dispatch*, 12 May 1964; the *New York Times*, 13 May 1964; *Time*, 22 May 1964; and *Newsweek*, 25 May 1964.

RICKY EARL NEWPORT

CANNON, Cornelia James (17 Nov. 1876–1 Dec. 1969), novelist and birth control activist, was born in St. Paul, Minnesota, the daughter of Henry Clay James and Frances Haynes. While her father practiced law and speculated in land, her mother helped out the family fortunes by painting; some of her watercolors are now at the Minnesota Historical Society. Cannon grew up in St. Paul and Newport. At Radcliffe College Cannon studied philosophy with William James and zoology with Charles Davenport and took courses in a wide variety of fields as well. Following nineteenth-century notions of education for women, she strove for breadth rather than depth. Her social life at college was very active; she joined almost every club and held almost every office her class had to offer. In 1899 she received her B.A. In 1965 she received one of Radcliffe's first Founder Awards.

For two years she taught Latin at the St. Paul Mechanic Arts High School. In 1901 she married Walter Bradford Cannon, a physiologist at the Harvard Medical School. On their wedding trip they climbed 10,000-foot Goat Mountain, which was later renamed "Cannon Mountain," in Glacier National Park. They settled in Cambridge, later spending their summers at a farm they bought in Franklin, New Hampshire. Between 1907 and 1915 they had five children, and Cannon spent her time taking care of her family and supporting her husband's career.

When her children entered school, however, Cannon, an ardent believer in public education, became involved in school committee work, serving as secretary of the Cambridge Public School Association and writing hundreds of letters for the *Cambridge Chronicle* on public school education and on the work of the association. She also started her campaigns against corruption in city government, becoming, according to her daughter, Marian Cannon Schlesinger, "the scourge of City Hall." Her ideas found their way into print in provocative articles that were published by *Atlantic Monthly, North American Review*, and *Harper's* in the 1920s, among them "Philanthropic Doubts," "Can Our Civilization Maintain Itself?," and "The Crabbing of Youth by Age." In the early 1920s she also launched her career as a monologuist, performing her unconventional poetry in women's clubs and libraries all over New England.

During her husband's absence to serve in World War I, Cannon took full responsibility for her family; she also organized host and educational programs for American soldiers who were stationed in Cambridge before their departure to Europe. Her wartime experiences were expressed in her first (unpublished) novel, *The Clan Betrays*, which she wrote after her husband's return. Although the novel attempts to describe too many things at once—men's and women's differing war experiences, problems of a Protestant–Irish Catholic marriage, and corruption in local politics—it nevertheless documents both Cannon's willingness to take on the most controversial political and social issues of her day and her keen awareness of gendered experience.

In 1925, after a trip with her sister to New Mexico, Cannon started work on children's books about the Spanish conquest of the Southwest, the four *Pueblo* novels: *The Pueblo Boy* (1926), *The Pueblo Girl* (1929), *Lazaro in the Pueblos* (1931), and *The Fight for the Pueblo* (1934). Her greatest commercial success, however, was *Red Rust*, a bestseller published in 1928. The novel's protagonist, a Swedish farmer in Minnesota, struggles successfully to develop a strain of wheat resistant to the rust disease. He is supported by his wife; through her experiences Cannon portrayed both the hardships of pioneer women and (an autobiographical element) the challenges faced by the wife of a devoted investigator. *Heirs* (1930), a novel conceived as a contribution to the nativism debate, depicted the confrontation between old and sophisticated but exhausted New Englanders and a vigorous pioneer race of Poles in a New Hampshire town. This book, Cannon's most mature, unfortunately suffered from the decline in book sales during the early years of the depression.

Cannon's last novel, *Denial*, never published, reflected her most controversial political concern, birth control. After attending Margaret Sanger's Birth Control Conference in New York in 1921, Cannon became a convert, but she refrained from active participation in the movement out of consideration for her husband's career. Motivated both by feminist anger at a state that denied women the right to control their fertility and by her eugenic conviction that the high birth rates of the nation's poor and ethnic minorities ought to be reduced, she did, however, do pioneer work in the movement of the 1930s. She served as president of the Massachusetts Mothers' Health Council from 1933 to 1935, later worked on the board of directors of the Planned Parenthood League of Massachusetts, and traveled the world as a "missionary" of birth control. *Denial* was a polemic written in the mid-1930s to support the Massachusetts campaign for the Doctor's Bill, which intended to give Massachusetts physicians the right to distribute birth control information to married women. The novel delineates in graphic detail the fate of a working-class Massachusetts woman who falls victim to the state's rigorous birth control laws: though suffering from a heart disease, she is refused birth control information; after several abortions she finally commits suicide and murder, gassing herself and her children. In addition to novels, Cannon wrote poetry, plays, travelogues, and thousands of letters, most of which were preserved by her family. Her oeuvre is a fascinating record of nineteenth- and twentieth-century American womanhood.

Cannon was an enthusiastic traveler. With the proceeds from *Red Rust* she took her family on a European tour in 1929–1930, during which she treated her daughters to three months of travel in Italy. Among her European travels with her husband, a trip to Spain led to their support of the Medical Bureau to Aid Spanish Democracy. The couple also visited Central and South America in the 1930s and 1940s, and in 1935 a lecture tour took them to Japan, China, and the USSR. After her husband's death, Cannon traveled around the world several times—the last time at age eighty-five—usually alone, and still acting as a champion of birth control by distributing condoms and birth control information wherever she went. At eighty-two she returned to the USSR. She left unpublished accounts of all her tours, among them "Art Awheel in Italy," "A Grandmother Visits the Philippines," and "Feast with the Bear."

Intellectually curious and adventurous, Cannon published only a small part of her extensive writings. In many ways she was the quintessential faculty wife of the early twentieth century, pursuing her social goals primarily through her family life and through wide-ranging volunteer activities. Her published work remains of interest, and several of her books merit rereading—*Heirs* and *Red Rust* for their literary strengths, and *Denial* and *The Clan Betrays* for their sociohistorical significance. Cornelia James Cannon died in a Franklin, New Hampshire, rest home.

• Most of Cornelia James Cannon's manuscripts and correspondence are held by her daughter Marian Cannon Schlesinger, Cambridge, Mass.; additional material is in the Walter B. Cannon Papers in Countway Library, Harvard Medical School, and in the Cornelia James Cannon Papers in the Radcliffe College Archives. Additional biographical information was acquired in interviews with Cornelia James Cannon's daughters Wilma Cannon Fairbank, Linda Cannon Burgess, Marian Cannon Schlesinger, and Helen Cannon Bond and in an interview with John King Fairbank. For a personal impression, see Marian Cannon Schlesinger, *Snatched from Oblivion: A Cambridge Memoir* (1979). For further biographical information see Saul Benison et al., *Walter B. Cannon: The Life and Times of a Young Scientist* (1987). An obituary is in the *Boston Herald*, 8 Dec. 1969.

MARIA DIEDRICH

CANNON, Harriett Starr (7 May 1823–5 Apr. 1896), Episcopal sister, was born in Charleston, South Carolina, the daughter of William Cannon and Sally Hinman. Very little is known about her parents since both of them died on or about 24 November 1824, when she was little more than a year old. Captain James Allen, the brother-in-law of Sally Cannon, took Harriett and her sister Catherine Ann to Bridgeport, Connecticut, where they were raised by their aunt, Mrs. Hyde, a sister of their mother. In 1855 Catherine Ann died, and this major crisis for Harriett left her convinced, as she later recalled, that "God had a purpose for me" (Dix, p. 15). This purpose was to establish the first permanent Episcopal sisterhood in the United States.

On 6 February 1856, Ash Wednesday, Cannon was received as a candidate for the Sisterhood of the Holy Communion, in the oratory of the sisters' house, by William Augustus Muhlenberg. The order had been organized eleven years earlier by Muhlenberg and Anne Ayres but had operated in secret until 1852 because of opposition in the Episcopal church to monasticism and religious orders. Some Episcopalians believed that monasticism was a Roman Catholic invention and tended, instead, toward salvation by the righteousness of works. On the Feast of the Purification, 2 February 1857, Cannon was admitted into full membership in the sisterhood.

Several of the sisters, led by Sister Harriett, wanted to give a more devotional character and traditionally monastic quality to the sisterhood, and they prepared to organize the sisterhood similar to a Roman Catholic order. In April 1863 Sister Anne resigned from her position as first sister, and Muhlenberg declared that her resignation dissolved the organization. Sister Harriett and her followers withdrew from the Church of the Holy Communion, and on 9 April 1863 Sister Harriett, Sister Mary B. Heartt, Sister Jane C. Haight, and Sister Sarah C. Bridge left the Sisterhood of the Holy Communion and St. Luke's Hospital, where they worked. On 1 September 1863 these four sisters took charge of the House of Mercy, a shelter "for the reception of and reformation of destitute women who may wish to abandon a vicious course of life" (Hilary, *Ten Decades of Praise*, p. 17). In 1864 they took over the Sheltering Arms of Jesus, a home for children.

During these years of work, 1863–1864, the sisters began the process of setting up a new sisterhood. The Sisterhood of the Holy Communion had been an extension of parish ministry, not needing the sanction of the episcopate. It had remained Protestant, and its purposes were Christian mercy and charity work. Sister Harriett and her companions wanted a more balanced life, incorporating both active ministry and personal and communal devotions. They wanted a more Catholic spirituality with more structured worship. On 2 February 1865 Sisters Harriett, Mary, Jane, and Sarah, along with Amelia W. Asten, were received into the Sisterhood of St. Mary (now called the Community of St. Mary) at a profession service held at St. Michael's Church in New York City. This was the first official establishment of a religious community in the Episcopal church and the first instance of the profession of sisters by a bishop since the time of the Reformation in the Anglican tradition.

In May 1865 the sisterhood was incorporated, and in September 1865 Sister Harriett was elected mother superior, a position to which she was frequently reelected and which she held when she died. On 11 June 1865 the sisters took charge of St. Barnabas' House, a home for women and children. On 2 February 1867 Sister Harriett took her formal life vows.

In 1866 the Reverend Morgan Dix, rector of Trinity Church in New York City, became chaplain to the sisters, and on 4 April 1866 he presented the sisterhood with its first Rule, which he had written. They also had the *Book of Hours*, which Dix had composed and which enabled them to recite the hours of the breviary. The printing of the *Book of Hours* and the use of a Rule caused considerable opposition to the community, and they were accused of being "popish" and "ritualistic." They were forced out of St. Barnabas' House and the Sheltering Arms, but public suspicion began to decline because of their work at St. Mary's Free Hospital for Poor Children.

The great work of the sisterhood, under Sister Harriett's leadership, in the education of girls was begun in May 1868, when St. Mary's School opened on West Forty-sixth Street. St. Gabriel's School, Peekskill, New York, opened in 1872; St. Mary's School, Memphis, Tennessee, opened in 1873; and Kemper Hall, Kenosha, Wisconsin, opened in 1878. Sister Harriett died at the Peekskill convent, the headquarters of the community.

Sister Harriett was one of the leading Episcopal women of the nineteenth century. She established the first religious community in the Episcopal church, persisted against opposition to monasticism, and helped to found numerous schools for girls. At the time of her death there were more than one hundred sisters working in thirteen houses in New York, Tennessee, and Wisconsin.

• Cannon's papers are in the archives of St. Mary's Convent, Peekskill, N.Y. The major study of her life is Morgan Dix, *Harriett Starr Cannon, First Mother Superior of the Sisterhood of St. Mary* (1896), but see also an undated manuscript by Sister Mary Hilary, "The Life of Harriett Starr Cannon," in St. Mary's archives. A helpful article by a contemporary is George F. Seymour, "Mother Harriett of the Sisterhood of St. Mary," *Church Eclectic* 24 (June 1896): 235–45. Two articles treat the founding of the order: Mary Theodora, "The Foundation of the Sisterhood of St. Mary," *Historical Magazine of the Protestant Episcopal Church* 14 (Mar. 1945): 38–52, and Lawson Carter Rich, "The Community of St. Mary," *Churchman* 95 (1907): 171–79. The major study of the order is Hilary, *Ten Decades of Praise: The Story of the Community of Saint Mary during Its First Century, 1865 to 1965* (1965). Henry C. Potter also discusses the community in *Sisterhoods and Deaconesses at Home and Abroad* (1873).

DON S. ARMENTROUT

CANNON, Ida Maud (29 June 1877–9 July 1960), social worker, was born in Milwaukee, Wisconsin, the daughter of Colbert Hanchett Cannon, a traffic controller, and Sarah Wilma Denio. When she was four her mother died, and her father remarried. Her father was employed by the Great Northern Railroad, and the family's circumstances were comfortable. Ida Cannon completed high school in St. Paul, Minnesota, in 1896, the same year that her brother Walter graduated from Harvard College (he had a distinguished career as a physiologist and Harvard professor). Ida graduated from the St. Paul County Hospital Training School for Nurses in 1898 and took a position at the State School for the Feeble-minded in Faribault, Minnesota, where she established a hospital unit. From 1900 to 1901 she took courses in psychology and sociology at the University of Minnesota. It was as a visiting nurse for the Saint Paul Associated Charities from 1903 to 1906 that she became aware of the desperate lives of the poor and saw the limitations of both traditional social work and medicine.

Leaving for Boston in 1906 to take a course at the Boston School of Social Work (later Simmons College), Ida Cannon met Dr. Richard Cabot, whose pioneering department of social service at the Massachusetts General Hospital (MGH) seemed to offer exactly the kind of "social medicine" she believed in. Cannon became a volunteer; then, after graduation in 1907, she became head worker in 1908. In 1915 she became chief of social service, a position she held until her retirement in 1945.

Ida Cannon established medical social work as an accepted subspecialty of social work at the MGH and eventually in the nation. Her career was closely associated with the development of medical social work that combined the skills of the nurse, the social worker, the social investigator, and the psychologist. By 1912 she had developed a specialized medical social-work curriculum at the Boston School of Social Work; she herself taught at the school from 1937 to 1945. Meanwhile she continued to train nurses and social workers at the MGH. Cannon was a tireless publicist for the new field, frequently traveling to speak at conventions of physicians and social workers. By 1918, when she helped found the American Association of Hospital Social Workers, there were 286 social service departments in North America and several abroad.

Cannon advocated broadening the function of the hospital to include preventive and public health work: clinical work with individual patients could not solve, for example, the problems of tuberculosis and syphilis, which were community-based. Overcoming entrenched opposition, she showed the value of her methods in the social service department of the Massachusetts General. In 1919 the hospital finally accepted financial and administrative responsibility for her department. Although Cannon always gave Cabot credit for this success, she continued to develop the medical social work program further after his departure for a Harvard teaching position in 1921. By the time she retired in October 1945, the Massachusetts General social service department employed thirty-one social workers and served 8,000 patients a year.

In combining social casework with health work and investigation, Cannon was following the precedent set by early women doctors like Elizabeth Blackwell. In fact, her career can best be understood in the context firstly of the increasing hostility toward women physicians in the early twentieth century and secondly in that of the professionalization of social work. The development of hospital social work partly compensated women for the fact that their opportunities in medicine were narrowing during these years. Social workers were usually nurses, but they enjoyed higher status than either nurses or charity workers. Both of Cannon's published books make a self-conscious effort to define and justify the new field as a profession for women. In *Social Work in Hospitals: A Contribution to Progressive Medicine* (1913), she boldly claimed that the diagnostic casework of the social worker was as important for treatment of the patient as was the clinical diagnosis of the doctor. "As hospital problems are social as well as medical, two expert professions, not one alone are needed," she wrote.

Not surprisingly, relations between the new specialty and physicians were problematic. Not only were social workers intruders in an established, hierarchical institution in which most doctors either opposed their presence or were indifferent to them, but also the purpose of the hospital, to treat as many patients as efficiently as possible, clashed with the social workers' goal of painstaking casework with individuals. Cannon soon learned to be more guarded about her claims for social work in the hospital. In her 1952 reminiscence she wrote that she and her colleagues had "learned our lesson": that they had to work closely with, and under the authority of, the doctor. Cannon credited Cabot with creating hospital social work, a claim that has been repeated by historians. But her deference to her mentor and friend also indicates the extent to which medical social workers were, like nurses, increasingly subordinated to doctors in the hospital's hierarchy. The status of women professionals in both social work and medicine remained problematical.

Ida Cannon's strong advocacy of professionalization for medical social work was based not on the sympathy or class position of social workers, but on their expertise in medicine, psychology, and sociology. Her success has been attributed to her persistence and her tact, qualities that enabled her to deal with physicians, nurses, social workers, volunteer workers, and hospital administrators. A colleague, Harriett M. Bartlett, described her as "wise and warmly sympathetic." Personal charm made her an effective advocate and publicist. Ida Cannon never married but lived for many years (together with her sister Bernice) with her brother and his wife, Cornelia James Cannon (a novelist) in Cambridge, Massachusetts. She died in Watertown, Massachusetts.

• The Ida Cannon papers at the Massachusetts General Hospital are the best source of information on Cannon's life and career. There are personal papers including correspondence and some diary entries. The archives of the hospital's social service department also contain the department's annual reports, from 1906, and many reprints. The Richard Clarke Cabot Papers at Harvard University contain some correspondence between Cannon and Cabot. In addition to the work cited in the text, Cannon's other major published work is *On the Social Frontier of Medicine: Pioneering in Medical Social Service* (1952).

Roy Lubove, "Ida Maud Cannon," in *Notable American Women: The Modern Period*, ed. Barbara Sicherman and Carol Green Hurd (1980), pp. 133–35, gives details of Cannon's life and career and includes material from interviews with her nieces, Marian Cannon Schlesinger and Linda Burgess. Harriet M. Bartlett, a member of the social service department of MGH from 1921 to 1943, wrote the sympathetic but thorough "Ida M. Cannon: Pioneer in Medical Social Work," *Social Service Review* 49 (June 1975): 208–29. The origins of medical social work are also sketched in Lubove, *The Professional Altruist: The Emergence of Social Work as a Career, 1880–1930* (1965). See also, Richard C. Cabot, *Social Work: Essays on the Meeting-Ground of Doctor and Social Worker* (1919). Mary Roth Walsh, "*Doctors Wanted: No Women Need Apply": Sexual Barriers in the Medical Profession, 1835–1975* (1977), which focuses on Boston, gives useful background about women and professionalization.

RUTH HUTCHINSON CROCKER

CANNON, James, Jr. (13 Nov. 1864–6 Sept. 1944), southern Methodist bishop and temperance crusader, was born in Salisbury, Maryland, the son of James Cannon and Lydia Robertson Primrose, merchants. The family was prosperous and prominent in Delaware, where James's uncle, William Cannon, was governor from 1863 to 1865. Possessed of strong southern sympathies, the Cannons moved to Salisbury, Maryland, at the time of the Civil War, where the family business continued to thrive. Longtime Methodists, the family abandoned the Methodist Episcopal church and helped to found the local congregation of the Methodist Episcopal Church, South. They were active in this congregation, in the Democratic party, and in the emerging local temperance movement.

In 1881 Cannon entered Randolph Macon College, a Southern Methodist institution in Virginia, to study law, but he had a religious conversion and began instead to prepare for the ministry. He also assisted the college president, W. W. Bennett, in the publication of the *Southern Crusader*, a temperance newspaper. After graduating in 1884 (A.B.), he attended Princeton Theological Seminary (B.D., 1888) and the College of New Jersey, later renamed Princeton University (M.A., 1890).

Cannon formed a deep attachment to Virginia during his college years and joined the Virginia Conference of the Methodist Episcopal Church, South, in 1888. During the same summer he married Lura Virginia Bennett, the daughter of his college president. The couple had nine children, seven of whom survived to adulthood. Cannon was appointed to a series of significant pastoral charges until, in 1894, he became principal and president of the Blackstone Female Institute in Virginia, a position he held from 1894 to 1911 and again from 1914 to 1918. During the intervening three years he founded and served as the first superintendent of the Southern Assembly at Lake Junaluska, a Methodist summer recreation and retreat center in North Carolina. He was indefatigable in the service of both of these causes, working long days and devoting his considerable energies to strengthening them financially and morally. He is credited with the success of both institutions, although his single-minded efforts often led him into conflict with established church leaders.

Cannon's unflinching advocacy of moral causes, especially temperance, won him a following in the Virginia Conference, which elected him a delegate to the 1902 General Conference. In 1904 he became editor of the Conference newspaper, the *Baltimore and Richmond Christian Advocate*, writing about a variety of moral and social issues in the church. The General Conference of 1918 elected him bishop. In this role he advanced an agenda that included reunification of the northern and southern Methodist churches, concern for foreign missions, and temperance.

Cannon's greatest fame came from his work in the Prohibition movement. His interest in the cause can be traced back to his twelfth year, when he watched his mother being berated by a drunken saloon keeper. He vowed at the time to fight for the temperance cause, a promise he kept from his college days until his death. As a minister he regularly preached against the evils of alcohol. In 1910 he founded the *Richmond Virginian*, an anti-saloon daily newspaper. He became a leading southern spokesman for the new Anti-Saloon League, ultimately serving as the executive director of the Virginia branch and chairperson of the national legislative committee. He lobbied the Virginia legislature and governor for a variety of measures, including local option for the sale of alcohol, and succeeded in promoting a statewide referendum on the sale of alcohol in 1914. The "dry" forces won an overwhelming victory, catapulting Cannon into national prominence. Many credited him with leading five southern states in defecting from "wet" presidential candidate Alfred E. Smith in the election of 1928, ensuring the election of Herbert Hoover. His political activism earned him powerful enemies among both antiprohibitionists and southern Democrats.

The following year Cannon was attacked by such potent enemies as the William Randolph Hearst newspaper organization, Senator Carter Glass of Virginia, and many members of the Methodist Council of Bishops. Opponents charged him with risking church funds in stock market speculation, regarded as a form of gambling by the church, and misuse of campaign and church funds. He endured a series of investigations and hearings by church bodies and by the Senate Lobby Committee. He mounted a vigorous defense, becoming the first witness ever to walk out on a Senate hearing. His wife died in 1928, and Cannon supplied more ammunition for his detractors two years later when he married his private secretary, Helen Hawley McCallum, a much younger woman. Accused of adultery, he endured another series of church and civil proceedings, which exonerated him of all charges, but his career was ruined. Although his opponents twice failed to force him to retire from his episcopacy, they succeeded in dissolving the church Board of Temperance and Social Service, which had served as a platform for Cannon's efforts. This, along with the failure of the Prohibition experiment, led to his disappearance from public life. He continued to write and speak, but found few interested in the message. He died while attending an Anti-Saloon League meeting in Chicago and was buried in Richmond, Virginia.

• Cannon's papers are housed in the Duke University Library, while other relevant collections include Carter Glass Papers, Virginius Dabney Papers, and Collins Denny Papers in the library of the University of Virginia. Cannon's publications include many brief articles in Methodist organs and in the newspapers he edited. His unfinished autobiography, *Bishop Cannon's Own Story: Life as I Have Seen It*, ed. Richard L. Watson (1955), was released by his family in response to the uncomplimentary biography by Virginius Dabney, *Dry Messiah: The Life of Bishop James Cannon, Jr.* (1949). Other useful treatments of Cannon's life include the article by Daniel Swinson in *Twentieth-Century Shapers of American Popular Religion*, ed. Charles H. Lippy (1989); Norman H. Clark, *Deliver Us from Evil: An Interpretation of American Prohibition* (1976); and K. Austin Kerr, *Organized for Prohibition: A New History of the Anti-Saloon League* (1985).

MICHAEL R. MCCOY

CANNON, James William (25 Apr. 1852–19 Dec. 1921), textile manufacturer, was born near Sugar Creek Church in Mecklenburg County, North Carolina, the son of Eliza Long and Joseph A. Cannon, farmers. As a child he worked on his father's farm and attended private school. At the age of fourteen Cannon took a job as a clerk and errand boy at a grocery store in Charlotte. In 1868 he went to Concord, North Carolina, and worked at Cannon, Fetzer, and Wadsworth, the general store in which his brother David Franklin Cannon was part owner. Before the age of nineteen, after working at the store fewer than three years, he had purchased an interest in his brother's mercantile business. Cannon was a successful merchant and became an involved and respected leader within the city of Concord, and his store became one of the leading businesses in Cabarrus County. He married Mary Ella Bost in 1875; they had ten children.

Like other merchants in the South, Cannon grew concerned over the role of the cotton trade in the southern economy. Northern textile mills bought cotton at cheap prices and sold finished cotton goods to the South at large profits. Cannon became intrigued with the idea of saving transportation costs in the production of cotton by establishing cotton mills in the South, thus improving the southern economy.

Cannon built his first mill (which later became Plant No. 2 in the huge Cannon Mills Company) in 1888 and operated it through the Cannon Manufacturing Company, which he founded in 1887 with the aid of $75,000 from northern banks and the assistance of the Philadelphia firm of McGill and Wood Manufacturing Company. The spinning mill was located on Franklin Avenue in Concord and operated around 4,000 spindles. Cannon involved himself in all aspects of the operation of the mill. He took responsibility for sales and management and even slipped into overalls to learn about and later repair spinning frames and other equipment. Cannon decided to manufacture the finished textile product and not complete only one step of the manufacturing process. To meet this end, he added looms and other necessary machinery to the mill. Instead of merely manufacturing cloth and selling it, he decided that Cannon Manufacturing Company would market branded products. The Cannon name appeared on all cloth manufactured so that women who were pleased with the product could ask specifically for it. "Cannon cloth" soon became a favorite with southern women because of its versatility. The fabric was used for everything from bedding to clothing.

Expansion came rapidly to the Cannon Manufacturing Company. It completed the Cabarrus Cotton Mill around 1892, followed by two other mills in Concord, Gibson Manufacturing Company and Franklin Cotton Mill. It also built mills in other Carolina cities, such as Patterson Manufacturing Company in China Grove, Wiscassett Mills Company in Albemarle, Kesler Manufacturing Company in Salisbury, and Tuscarora Cotton Mill in Mount Pleasant.

In 1898, with the demand for Cannon cloth still strong, Cannon decided to begin manufacturing the first towels ever produced in the South. This decision was made based upon his belief that there was a demand for affordable cotton towels. He realized that the period of home-sewn clothing was coming to an end and that the market demand for Cannon cloth had peaked. For a time he produced both cloth and towels, but the demand for cloth declined while the demand for towels increased. In 1904 Cannon opened a sales office in New York City with the goal of expanding and reading markets for Cannon products outside the South.

After deciding to concentrate on towel production, Cannon purchased six hundred acres of land near the Cabarrus and Rowan county lines and established the textile town of Kannapolis (Greek for "City of Looms") in 1906. E. S. Draper and Company planned the town, and the mills operated solely from electric power provided by the Southern Power Company (later known as Duke Power). Cannon built seventy-five mill houses and the Young Men's Christian Association (YMCA) as the mills were completed. The Kannapolis YMCA became one of the world's largest. By 1910 Cannon was involved in the creation of a police department, a railway station, a postal service, and a road to Concord. Cannon gave the land and funds to the Cabarrus School Board to found the first school in Kannapolis in 1907. He offered encouragement and assistance in the establishment of churches, volunteer organizations, and parks. Such practices were characteristic of southern industrialists at the time, and Cannon repeated them as his company expanded into Georgia, Alabama, and South Carolina and became the world's largest manufacturer of towels, with Kannapolis as its headquarters. Cannon was a member of the First Presbyterian Church in Concord, politically independent, and a Mason. He died in Concord.

• The Cannon Collection at the Duke University Library Archives has some personal papers. *A Century of Progress: Fieldcrest Cannon, Inc. Salutes Cannon Mills Company and Its Employees, Past and Present* (1987), pp. 5–11, contains information on James William Cannon, as does James Moore and Thomas Wingate, *Cabarrus Reborn* (1940), pp. 50–88.

STEVEN W. USSELMAN

CANNON, Joseph Gurney (7 May 1836–12 Nov. 1926), Speaker of the House, was born in New Garden, Guilford County, North Carolina, the son of Horace Franklin Cannon and Gulielma Hollingsworth. His father, a country school teacher and self-taught doctor, hated slavery. Cannon moved with his Quaker parents to Bloomingdale, Indiana, in 1840, studied law at the Cincinnati Law School, and was admitted to the bar in 1858. He then moved to Tuscola, Illinois, in 1859 and served as state's attorney for the Twenty-seventh Judicial District of Illinois from March 1861 to December 1868. In 1862 he married Mary Pamela Reed; they had three children. In 1869 he settled in Danville, Illinois. Elected as a Republican in 1872 to the Forty-third Congress, Cannon served, with the exception of two terms (Fifty-second Congress, 1891–1892, and Sixty-third Congress, 1913–1915) when he was defeated for reelection, until 1923, when he retired from public life. In all, Cannon served a total of forty-six years in Congress, the longest tenure of any member prior to World War II.

No significant piece of legislation bears Cannon's name. As a conservative Republican gaining seniority, Cannon moved to positions of enhanced prestige and power from chairman of the Committee on Expenditures in the Post Office Department (Forty-seventh Congress) to that of the Committee on Appropriations (Fifty-fourth through Fifty-seventh Congress). Seniority brought him to the Speaker's chair and to the chair of the Rules Committee in 1903. As Speaker he was both the presiding officer and Republican party leader, and as chairman of the Rules Committee he controlled access to the floor for all major bills. Cannon vigorously exploited the authority of his position, taking full advantage of his power over committee assignments and his right to determine which members could speak on the floor. His resolution of voice votes was arbitrary. He once ruled, "The Ayes make the most noise, but the Nays have it." The term "Cannonism" came into widespread use during his tenure to describe his ironfisted rule. As Speaker, Cannon was not sympathetic to the progressive wing of his party and considered himself, as a seasoned poker player, a standpatter hostile to insurgent efforts, for example, to lower tariff rates or to modify the rules. As a party leader with some friction he went along with Theodore Roosevelt's (1858–1919) legislative program and strongly endorsed that of Roosevelt's successor, William Howard Taft. Since Taft was not as active an executive as his predecessor, Cannon found himself in a stronger position to oppose insurgent efforts at reform.

By fully utilizing the dictatorial powers of his office, Cannon raised the authority of the Speaker to its highest peak, though he introduced few parliamentary changes. However, Cannonism came to an end in March 1910, when insurgent Republicans joined by the Democrats revolted against the Speaker's authority, removing him from membership on the Rules Committee and ending his power to select committee members and to direct floor action. George William Norris, a Republican insurgent from Nebraska, through a parliamentary maneuver, bested the usually astute Speaker when he asked permission to introduce a measure privileged by the Constitution. Cannon laughingly agreed. Norris's resolution called for removing the Speaker from the Rules Committee.

After twenty-nine hours of debate, Cannon, recognizing that the motion could not be defeated, offered to resign. His offer was not accepted, and Cannon retained his post until the end of the Sixty-first Congress. He lost his bid for reelection in 1912 but was successful in 1914 and in succeeding elections until his voluntary retirement at age eighty-seven at the conclusion of the Sixty-seventh Congress on 3 March 1923. He retired to Danville, where he joined the Methodist church and was visible in the Second National Bank, which he helped found with his brother, William Cannon, or on his daily walk or motor outing. He died in Danville.

As Speaker, Cannon, known as "Uncle Joe," exhibited a jauntiness in his dress and deportment. A fiscal conservative, a strict constructionist of the law and the Constitution, opposed to special privileges for any group or class, Cannon was an obstinate, ruthless, and resourceful member of Congress. At times he was coarse in remarks and aroused the enmity of those in and out of Congress whom he thought sought special favors. But he bore no grudges and was respected and even well liked by both Republicans and Democrats.

• The Joseph G. Cannon Papers are on deposit in the State Historical Library in Springfield, Ill. See too, *Uncle Joe Cannon: The Story of a Pioneer American* as told to L. White Busbey (1927); Blair Bolles, *Tyrant from Illinois: Uncle Joe Cannon's Experiment with Personal Power* (1951); William Rea Gwinn, *Uncle Joe Cannon, Archfoe of Insurgency: A History of the Rise and Fall of Cannonism* (1957); and Richard Lowitt, *George W. Norris, The Making of a Progressive, 1861–1912* (1963). Extensive obituaries are in the *Washington Post* and the *New York Times*, both 13 Nov. 1926.

RICHARD LOWITT

CANNON, Newton (22 May 1781–16 Sept. 1841), congressman and governor of Tennessee, was born in Guilford County, North Carolina, the son of Minos Cannon, a farmer and revolutionary war veteran, and Letitia Thompson. In 1784 the Cannon family moved to what is now Tennessee but soon returned to North Carolina. About 1790 the family again journeyed westward, staying at Fort Nashboro (present-day Nashville) until about 1798, when they moved near Nelsonville in Williamson County. Cannon had limited formal education. After working as a saddler, clerk, and merchant, he became a land surveyor and, using his knowledge to advantage, acquired large holdings and established a plantation on the Big Harpeth River in Williamson County.

During this time Tennessee politics were more a matter of personalities than issues. By the time Cannon was elected a state senator in 1811, Andrew Jackson was a leading member of the dominant faction, and Tennessee politicians increasingly identified themselves as either Jackson allies or enemies. The reasons for the antagonism between Cannon and Jackson are not certain. One story relates Cannon's loss of a $5,000 bet to Jackson on an 1811 horse race. Another story concerns Cannon's vote as a member of a jury to acquit the murderer of Jackson's friend Peyton Anderson, reportedly prompting Jackson to single Cannon out with the warning, "I'll mark you, young man." In 1813 Jackson supported Felix Grundy over Cannon for Congress; Cannon lost. Whatever animus existed between the two before 1813 was made manifest that year during the Creek War. Jackson, major general of the Tennessee militia, commanded Cannon, a colonel of Mounted Rifles. A dispute arose over the length of service owed by Cannon's regiment. Short of supplies, Cannon requested permission to send his troops home, but Jackson, wanting to maintain an effective force, initially refused. Thereafter each man disdained the other.

The following year Cannon won a special election to Congress, replacing Grundy, who had resigned. Cannon served in Washington from 1815 to 1817 and again from 1819 to 1823. Throughout his congressional career, Cannon's positions conflicted with Jackson's views. Cannon repeatedly sought to reduce the size of the military, a move undoubtedly aimed at Jackson, who, since 1815, had been one of two major generals in the regular army. In 1816 Cannon supported a Cherokee Indian treaty that accepted claims of depredations committed by Jackson's Tennessee troops. On the national level Cannon aligned himself with Jackson's antagonist William H. Crawford, who, as secretary of war, had negotiated the 1816 Cherokee treaty. By 1819, when President James Monroe appointed him a commissioner to treat with the Chickasaw Indians, Cannon was a leader of the anti-Jackson faction in Tennessee.

Cannon retired from Congress in 1823 and devoted the next few years to his growing family. In 1813 he had married Leah Pryor Perkins, who died three years later, leaving him two children. In 1818 he married Rachel Starnes Wellborn, a niece of North Carolina senator Montford Stokes; they had eight children. By 1827 Cannon was back in the political fray, losing to Sam Houston in a three-man race to replace retiring governor William Carroll. Cannon returned to the Tennessee State Senate in 1829, did not seek reelection in 1831, but failed to recapture the seat in 1833. Meanwhile, President Jackson was at the height of his power and influence in Tennessee, and Cannon's political career seemed finished.

A convergence of circumstances during the next two years facilitated Cannon's return. In 1834 he represented Williamson County at a convention called to revise the 1796 constitution, serving as chair of the Committee of the Whole. Cannon played a key role in retaining the generally conservative features of the former charter while adapting the new constitution to the more democratic times. Perhaps the most significant reform (backed by Cannon) was the adoption of one tax rate for all types of property, eliminating the lower rate heretofore granted landowners.

The constitutional revision created an opening for William Carroll who, in 1835, was completing a second set of three consecutive two-year terms, the constitutional maximum under both charters. Carroll maintained that the new constitution wiped the slate clean, and he ran for another term. In 1835 Cannon challenged the popular governor and would have had little chance of success had not the Jacksonians been divided among themselves over Jackson's designation of Vice President Martin Van Buren as his successor. Carroll endorsed Van Buren, but disaffected Jacksonians in Tennessee and the always present anti-Jackson element formed the nascent Whig party and put forward Tennessee's popular U.S. senator Hugh Lawson White as a presidential candidate. In Tennessee, Whigs supported Cannon, and he won the governor's chair, 41,970 to 31,205.

Cannon sought to improve the state's road, banking, and educational systems, but a downturn in the economy and the resulting panic of 1837 prevented full implementation of his program. Nevertheless, the legislature incorporated new railroads, reformed the state's supreme court, settled the boundary between Tennessee and Mississippi, and laid the foundation for a statewide system of public education. Cannon called out the militia to fight in the so-called Second Seminole War and lobbied (unsuccessfully) for the elimination of Tennessee's remaining death penalties. In 1837, taking advantage of the public's disillusionment with the Van Buren administration, Cannon defeated Robert Armstrong, commander of the Tennessee militia in Florida, and the Whigs took control of the state's general assembly. Two years later, however, a unified Democratic party selected congressman James K. Polk, who, after a series of joint appearances with Cannon, defeated the governor and overconfident Whigs by some 2,600 votes.

Cannon returned home and contemplated a rematch with Polk in 1841, but the state's Whig leaders declined to support him. Cannon died in Nashville. At his death he owned more than 5,500 acres of land in Tennessee and Mississippi and 127 slaves. Cannon's mark on Tennessee history is remarkably slight given the length and prominence of his career. A competent congressman and governor, Cannon is chiefly remembered not for his accomplishments but for his steadfast opposition to Jackson and the Democratic party.

• No significant collection of Cannon's papers has been located. For his official messages as governor with a commentary and overview of his administration, see Robert H. White, ed., *Messages of the Governors of Tennessee*, vol. 3 (1954). Other insights into Cannon's career can be gained from the *Correspondence of Andrew Jackson*, ed. John S. Bassett (7 vols., 1926–1935); and *The Papers of Andrew Jackson*, ed. Sam B. Smith et al., vols. 3 and 4 (4 vols., 1980–). See also *The Correspondence of James K. Polk*, ed. Herbert Weaver et al., vols. 4 and 5 (8 vols., 1969–). The most complete overview is John E. Harkins, "Newton Cannon, Jackson Nemesis," *Tennessee Historical Quarterly* 43 (1984): 355–75. For genealogical information see Virginia M. Bowman, "Governor Newton Cannon," in *Historic Williamson County: Old Homes and Sites* (1971); and Robert M. McBride and Dan M. Robison, eds., *Biographical Directory of the Tennessee General Assembly*, vol. 1 (1975). For assessments of Cannon's political career see Robert Cassell, "Newton Cannon and the Constitutional Convention of 1834," *Tennessee Historical Quarterly* 15 (1956): 224–42; Cassell, "Newton Cannon and State Politics, 1835–1839," *Tennessee Historical Quarterly* 15 (1956): 306–21; and E. Bruce Thompson, "Reforms in the Penal System of Tennessee, 1820–1850," *Tennessee Historical Quarterly* 1 (1942): 307–8.

GEORGE H. HOEMANN

CANNON, Walter Bradford (19 Oct. 1871–1 Oct. 1945), physiologist, was born in Prairie du Chien, Wisconsin, the son of Colbert Hanchett Cannon, a railroad official, and Sarah Wilma Denio, a schoolteacher who died when Walter was ten years old. Cannon attended public schools in Milwaukee and St. Paul, where his high school English teacher, May Newson, encouraged him to seek a scholarship at Harvard College and helped him to secure financial aid. At Harvard Cannon studied biology and zoology under professors George H. Parker and Charles B. Davenport, who directed Cannon's first research project, a study of phototropism (the movement of organisms toward or away from light) for which Cannon received a master's degree in 1897.

Cannon entered Harvard Medical School in 1896 and immediately approached physiologist Henry Pickering Bowditch about possibilities for research. At Bowditch's suggestion, Cannon, together with fellow student Albert Moser, proposed to test a new theory about the nature of swallowing by using the newly discovered X rays. By introducing the use of gelatin capsules containing bismuth subnitrate and, later, barium sulphate—substances opaque to X rays—Cannon and his coworkers were able to visualize for the first time the movements of the digestive organs. Cannon offered an informal demonstration of viewing the swallowing process in a goose by means of X rays at the 1896 meeting of the American Physiological Society in Boston.

The X ray also played a role in Cannon's personal life. According to his daughter Marian Cannon Schlesinger his marriage proposal to Cornelia James was accompanied by an X-ray picture of his hand over his heart. The two were married in June 1901, two years after James's graduation from Radcliffe College. Despite initial difficulties in starting a family, perhaps related to Cannon's X-ray exposure, they had five children.

During his years as a medical student, Cannon was also responsible for innovation in medical education. Envious of the active educational experiences of students at Harvard Law School, Cannon imported the case study method to medical education, using actual case histories and data from various hospitals to replace the "dreary and benumbing process" of listening passively to lectures. His 1900 paper "Case Method of Teaching Systematic Medicine," published in the *Boston Medical and Surgical Journal*, was incorporated into a number of medical texts, and several departments at the Harvard Medical School implemented such instruction.

Upon graduating from medical school in 1900, Cannon, who was already teaching zoology and comparative vertebrate anatomy to Harvard students, was appointed instructor in physiology at Harvard Medical School. In 1902 he became assistant professor, and four years later, when Cornell Medical School attempted to lure him to New York, Cannon succeeded Bowditch as George Higginson Professor of Physiology and chair of the Department of Physiology at Harvard Medical School. He remained in this position until his retirement in 1942.

As a young investigator, Cannon continued his research on the digestive system. Working extensively with radiographic methods, he investigated gastrointestinal motility, the nature of gastric peristalsis, the mechanism of swallowing, and control of the pylorus. Cannon published his observations and explanations in an influential 1911 text, *The Mechanical Factors of Digestion*, often identified as a classic work on gastrointestinal physiology and radiology. His final research on digestion was a study of hunger contractions in human beings. With the aid of medical student Arthur L. Washburn, who trained himself to swallow a rubber tube with an attached balloon connected to a pressure gauge, Cannon measured the contractions of the stomach and esophagus in an effort to explain hunger and thirst. Many of his experimental observations were later substantiated and extended by University of Chicago physiologist Anton J. Carlson.

Throughout his research on digestion, Cannon had observed how emotional states influenced the digestive process. He noted that when animals became frightened or aroused, the movements of the stomach and intestines ceased. In the 1910s he actively investigated this topic, beginning with a series of studies on the release of adrenaline into the blood during stress. Cannon's investigations of the bodily function of adrenal secretion led to his elaboration of the emergency function of the sympathetic nervous system, the body's response of "fight or flight." Public notice was drawn by his proposal that international athletic events could provide "a physiological equivalent for war" by channeling emotions and aggression into more socially acceptable forms and by his 1915 book *Bodily Changes in Pain, Hunger, Fear, and Rage*.

World War I interrupted Cannon's researches. Approached by the National Research Council to organize a committee of physiologists to develop a research program to enhance the health and welfare of the armed forces, Cannon selected the problem of wound shock, one of the most pressing surgical problems of the day, as his research topic. In 1917 he traveled to France as a member of the Harvard Hospital Unit and became director of a surgical research laboratory in Dijon. Cannon and his associates studied the respiratory and cardiac changes in traumatic shock and advanced the adoption of intravenous administration of gum acacia, an early blood volume expander, for emergency treatment of wounded soldiers.

After the war Cannon returned to his earlier research on the sympathetic nervous system, which had been harshly criticized by physiologists George N. Stewart and Julius Rogoff. Beginning in 1917 Stewart and Rogoff, both at Western Reserve University, questioned the methods of the Harvard group and challenged Cannon's claims about increased adrenal secretion in conditions of asphyxia, pain, and emotional excitement. Cannon later credited the controversy, ultimately resolved in his favor, with useful results. The attack on his methodology encouraged Cannon to develop a new experimental preparation, the denervated cat heart, in order to obtain confirmatory evidence about increased adrenal secretion. Evidence from the denervated heart preparation in turn stimulated the development of the operation of complete sympathectomy (surgical removal of an animal's sympathetic nerves) and to further work on hormonal secretion of the sympathetic nervous system. Work on the denervated heart brought Cannon to the brink of a major discovery. In 1921 he and his coworker Joseph Uridil reported that stimulation of the nerves to the liver produced acceleration of the denervated heart, suggesting that some factor or chemical substance mediated the transmission of nerve impulses. British physiologist Henry Dale, who shared the 1936 Nobel Prize with Otto Loewi, later acknowledged how close Cannon had come to the discovery of chemical neurotransmission, for which Loewi received the prize.

In the 1920s Cannon increasingly focused on other features of the autonomic nervous system and on efforts to explain the ability of the body to maintain itself in a state of equilibrium. Extending French physiologist Claude Bernard's concept of the *milieu interieur*, Cannon introduced the term "homeostasis" (first used in print in 1926) to describe the stability of the internal environment and the processes through which such constancy is maintained. He provided an extensive discussion of homeostasis in a 1929 paper in *Physiological Reviews*. At the persistent urging of publisher W. W. Norton, Cannon authored a popular book, *The Wisdom of the Body* (1932), in which he expressed his ideas about "social homeostasis," the need for the body politic, like the physiologic body, to develop automatic, regulatory means to maintain social stability.

In the 1930s Cannon resumed his efforts to identify and isolate the sympathetic transmitter. In work undertaken with Mexican physiologist Arturo Rosenblueth, his major collaborator in the last fifteen years of his life, he developed an alternative theory to explain the mediation of sympathetic nerve impulses. Challenging the growing consensus that adrenaline was the substance responsible for nerve transmission, Cannon and Rosenblueth concluded that two other substances (two different sympathins, one excitatory and one inhibitory) were necessary for the mediation of nerve impulses. Work done by Swedish investigator Ulf von Euler in the late 1940s (for which he received the 1970 Nobel Prize), demonstrated that the neurotransmitters sought by Cannon and Rosenblueth were epinephrine and norepinephrine.

In addition to his research and educational activities at Harvard, Cannon devoted considerable energy to defending animal experimentation. In 1908, following a vigorous attack on the recently opened Rockefeller Institute for Medical Research, the American Medical Association established a Council on the Defense of Medical Research, composed of representatives of various scientific disciplines and chaired by Cannon. Cannon worked strenuously to defend animal experimentation and to undermine the efforts of American antivivisectionists to restrict access to and use of laboratory animals. His efforts included circulating regulations for the use of experimental animals to American medical schools and monitoring research publications to alert authors and editors to language that could be misunderstood by people unfamiliar with laboratory practices. He organized a series of papers by medical experts outlining the importance of animal experimentation to advances in surgery and the treatment of both human and animal diseases, and he advised researchers around the country about effective responses to antivivisectionist challenges. After his resignation as chair of the AMA committee in 1926, Cannon continued in an advisory capacity to influence organized medicine's defense of animal experimentation.

In the 1930s and 1940s Cannon, who throughout his career had worked collaboratively with physiologists from around the world, grew increasingly troubled by the growing threat to the scientific community from fascist governments. After a 1930 visit during which he met Juan Negrin, professor of physiology at the University of Madrid and later premier of the Spanish republic, Cannon closely followed political developments in Spain. When Francisco Franco launched a counterrevolution against the Spanish Republican government, Cannon joined a number of prominent physicians in organizing a medical division affiliated with the American Friends of Spanish Democracy. A new Spanish relief organization, the North American Committee in Aid of Spanish Democracy, was formed, and in 1937 Cannon became chair of its reorganized Medical Bureau and threw himself into efforts to petition the U.S. government to allow the shipment of medical supplies to the Spanish government and to raise funds to purchase such supplies for the Spanish people. In addition, Cannon participated in other political activities considered suspect by some Americans: he lent his support to efforts to aid displaced Jewish scientists and to foster closer scientific ties with the Soviet Union.

In 1942 Cannon retired from Harvard, but he continued his research collaboration with Rosenblueth. During World War II he served as chair of the National Research Council's Committee on Shock and Transfusion and as an adviser to the program for blood procurement for U.S. troops.

By 1909 Cannon had ceased his use of X rays as a research method, but he suffered from radiation damage for much of his life. In addition to burns on his hands and knees from primitive X-ray tubes, Cannon developed mycosis fungoides, a chronic, progressive lymphoma, diagnosed by his physicians in 1932. He subsequently developed three other cancerous conditions, including leukemia and basal cell carcinoma, traced to his X-ray exposure. During the last fourteen years of his life he received radium and low voltage X-ray treatments for his disease and underwent several experimental therapies. He died in Franklin, New Hampshire.

Cannon identified regulation of the organism as the central problem in physiology. In the first half of the twentieth century he was a central figure in the international medical research community. A pioneer in the field of gastric research, he was also a major contributor to the understanding of nerve transmission and hormonal regulation of the body. Cannon delivered the Kober Lecture in 1934, and he was mentioned several times as a contender for the Nobel Prize in Medicine (in 1920, 1934, 1935, and 1936), although he was never awarded the prize.

• The Walter B. Cannon Archive at the Francis A. Countway Library at Harvard University holds the most extensive collection of Cannon's papers, including correspondence, diaries, and manuscripts. Collections at the Rockefeller Archive Center, North Tarrytown, N.Y., and at the American Philosophical Society, Philadelphia, are also useful.

In addition to the works mentioned above, Cannon's major scientific publications include *Digestion and Health* (1936), *Autonomic Neuro-Effector Systems* (1937), written with Arturo Rosenblueth, and *Supersensitivity of Denervated Structures* (1949), also written with Rosenblueth. An autobiography, *The Way of an Investigator: A Scientist's Experiences in Medical Research*, appeared in 1945. Personal recollections are in accounts by his daughter Marian Cannon Schlesinger, *Snatched from Oblivion: A Cambridge Memoir* (1979), and his son, Bradford Cannon, "Walter Bradford Cannon, M.D.: Reflections on the Physician, the Man, and His Contributions," *Gastrointestinal Radiology* 7 (1982): 1–6.

A bibliography of Cannon's publications, together with a list of obituaries and biographical notices, appears in Chandler McC. Brooks et al., eds., *The Life and Contributions of Walter Bradford Cannon, 1871–1945: His Influence on the Development of Physiology in the Twentieth Century* (1975). A comprehensive discussion of Cannon's early career is Saul Benison et al., *Walter B. Cannon: The Life and Times of a Young Scientist* (1987); for his later career, see Benison, "Walter B. Cannon and the Politics of Medical Science, 1920–1940," *Bulletin of the History of Medicine* 65 (1991): 234–51; and Benison et al., "Walter B. Cannon and the Mystery of Shock: A Study of Anglo-American Co-Operation in World War I," *Medical History* 35 (1991): 217–49.

For Cannon's political activities, see Susan E. Lederer, *Subjected to Science: Human Experimentation in America before the Second World War* (1995); and Peter J. Kuznick, *Beyond the Laboratory: Scientists as Political Activists in 1930s America* (1987). Cannon's work on homeostasis is discussed in Stephen J. Cross and William R. Albury, "Walter B. Cannon, L. J. Henderson, and the Organic Analogy," *Osiris* 3 (1987): 165–92; and Donald Fleming, "Walter B. Cannon and Homeostasis," *Social Research* 51 (1984): 609–40. For speculation about Cannon's failure to receive the Nobel Prize, see Horace W. Davenport, "Signs of Anxiety, Rage, or Distress," *Physiologist* 24 (1981): 1–5.

SUSAN E. LEDERER

CANONCHET (?–1676), Narragansett sachem and leader of the Indian forces during King Philip's War (1675–1676), also known as Quananchit, Nauntenoo, or Nanuntenoo, was the son of Miantonomo, who was executed by Mohegans on the orders of English colonists in 1643. Little is known of Canonchet before King Philip's War except that he was involved in some land transactions in the 1660s.

By 1675, as grand sachem of the Narragansetts, Canonchet was leader of the most powerful tribe in New England. Rich in corn, the Narragansetts may have numbered as many as 3,000 warriors. Nevertheless, they tried to remain neutral at the beginning of the war between the colonists and King Philip's Wampanoags, even agreeing to turn over to the colonists enemy Indians who sought refuge in their country. Canonchet possibly confirmed this agreement in Boston in October 1675, albeit perhaps under coercion, and the English gave him a lace coat. But when the Wampanoags sent their women and children into Narragansett country, the Narragansetts gave them refuge, refusing to hand them over to slavery. The English interpreted this as a breach of faith and an act of hostility, although it is likely that they were more concerned that the Narragansetts' corn supplies might be used to feed Philip's Indians during the winter.

Arguing that Canonchet was on the brink of entering the war, troops from the United Colonies of Plymouth, Massachusetts Bay, and Connecticut launched a preemptive strike against the main Narragansett village, near present-day South Kingston, Rhode Island. In the "Great Swamp Fight" in December 1675, the Puritans burned the village and killed as many as 700 men, women, and children. With Canonchet and his warriors fast approaching from their stronghold at Pettaquamscutt, the English retreated. The attack did the very thing it was supposed to prevent: in January 1676 Canonchet and the Narragansetts joined King Philip.

As leader of the strongest warrior contingent, Canonchet probably surpassed Philip to become commander of the Indian forces. Increase Mather, in his *Brief History of the Warr with the Indians in New-England* (1676), said that Canonchet "was a principal Ring-leader in the *Narragansett* War, and had as great an interest and influence, as can be said of any among the Indians." Canonchet and his warriors ambushed

Captain Michael Pierce's force in March 1676, attacked the towns of Warwick and Rehoboth, and even burned Providence, despite the entreaties of Roger Williams to spare the town. Captains James Avery and George Denison of Connecticut led a retaliatory expedition, amply supported by Indian allies, against Canonchet's camp in the Pawtucket Valley. Canonchet was captured by an Indian scout and turned over to the English, "so that there was a gracious smile of providence in this thing," wrote Mather in his *Brief History*.

Canonchet refused to surrender the Narragansetts in exchange for his life and held himself aloof from his captors, saying that "he was born a Prince, and if Princes came to speak with him he would answer" ("N. S.," *A New and Further Narrative of the State of New England* [1676]). The English sent him to Stonington, Connecticut, to be executed. Canonchet apparently resolved to die "before I speak anything unworthy of myself." Accounts of the execution differ, although there is no doubt that Indians did the killing. Some say that Canonchet requested as his executioner the son of the Mohegan who had killed his father and that the Mohegan dispatched him with an axe. Mather said the English employed a firing squad of their Mohegan, Pequot, and Niantic allies to further divide the Indians and bind the killers to them in common fear of retribution. Others agreed: "That all might come under the Glory of destroying so great a Prince, and come under the Obligation of Fidelity each to other, the Pequods shot him, the Mohegins cut off his Head and quartered his Body, and the Ninnicrofts Men [Niantics] made the Fire and burned his Quarters; and as a Token of their Love and Fidelity to the English, presented his Head to the Council at Hartford" (*New and Further Narrative*).

Canonchet's death was a major blow to the Indian war effort. In the months that followed the Indians were defeated piecemeal, and Philip was killed. Canonchet's enemies described him as "that famous but very bloudy and cruel Sachem" (*New and Further Narrative*), but the Narragansett won grudging respect from the English even during the war and lived on in New England lore. In 1829 the "heroic and enterprising" Canonchet figured as a prominent character in James Fenimore Cooper's *The Wept of Wish-ton-Wish*.

• The details of Canonchet's participation in the war are scattered in the standard histories of the conflict, from William Hubbard, *The History of the Indian Wars in New England from the First Settlement to the Termination of the War with King Philip* (1677), and Charles A. Lincoln, ed., *Narratives of the Indian Wars, 1675–1699* (1913), to, more recently, Douglas Edward Leach, *Flintlock and Tomahawk: New England in King Philip's War* (1958), and Russell Bourne, *The Red King's Rebellion* (1990). George Mason Bodge, *Soldiers in King Philip's War* (1906), includes a chapter on "Philip, Canonchet, and Other Hostile Indians." Increase Mather, *Brief History of the Warr with the Indians in New-England* (1676), is reprinted in Richard Slotkin and James K. Folsom, eds., *So Dreadful a Judgment: Puritan Responses to King Philip's War, 1676–1677* (1978); "N. S.," *A New and Further Narrative of the State of New England* (1676), is reprinted in Lincoln, *Narratives of the Indian Wars*.

COLIN G. CALLOWAY

CANONICUS (c. 1562–4 June 1647), senior chief of the Narragansett tribe inhabiting the western shore of Narragansett Bay, presided over some 30,000 members in partnership with his nephew Miantonomo. This may have been according to the arrangement common among Indians for an elder sachem to let a younger, more vigorous man be his spokesman.

In 1621 Canonicus sought friendship with the colonists of newly founded New Plymouth. They elected, however, to ally with Chief Massasoit (Ousamequin) of the nearby Wampanoags. Lacking a royal charter to validate their colony, Plymouth's settlers interpreted the Wampanoag treaty as ceding territory to them. As the Wampanoags had formerly been tributaries to the Narragansetts, Plymouth's action signified enmity to the latter. Nevertheless, Canonicus swallowed the affront.

In 1622 Plymouth governor William Bradford sent to Canonicus a rattlesnake skin wrapped around powder and shot, a symbol of defiance and a challenge to fight. According to the colony's devious propagandist Edward Winslow, this act had been preceded by Canonicus's sending arrows wrapped in the skin as a sign of Narragansett bellicosity, but this evidence is doubtful, especially because neither Canonicus nor any other Narragansett would accept Bradford's challenge. Had they done so, the outcome of the ensuing war could hardly have been in doubt at odds of 30,000 against a couple of hundred. Rather, historian Neal Salisbury has called the Narragansetts "committed pacifists," attributing their hegemonic status to "persuasion rather than violence" (p. 148). Soon, however, their situation involved them in conflicts with various neighbors.

Wampanoags contended over islands in Narragansett Bay and territory on its eastern shore. To the west, Pequots disputed hunting lands with the Narragansetts. Europeans colonized all about them; New Plymouth was soon followed by Massachusetts Bay in the east, New Netherland on the west, and Connecticut in the interior, high on the Connecticut River. Each of these armed camps dealt in various ways with Indians between them and the Narragansetts. Canonicus tried to gain English friends by alliance with Massachusetts and by welcoming settlers in his own territory. In 1634 Boston's magistrates aimed at a foothold in the Indian trade by accepting the Pequots as clients and "mediated" peace between Pequots and Narragansetts. The Narragansetts accepted Boston's mediation as a treaty of friendship, but it was quickly strained when the town of Dorchester hived off to begin the colony of Connecticut, which defied Massachusetts's presumption of control. Canonicus was never able to gain a decent working relationship with Connecticut because its founders coveted his tribe's lands.

In 1633 Captain John Oldham journeyed from Boston to the upper Connecticut River, after which a catastrophic epidemic wiped out most of the Indians resident there. About 700 Narragansetts died in the same epidemic, seemingly a variant of smallpox, and Canonicus came to believe that the disease had been "sent" by Englishmen. His belief has been sneered away as a savage superstition, and certainly it is unprovable today, but Canonicus may have had unrecorded information. His belief seems to have been shared by his councillors who got hold of John Oldham and executed him on Block Island, thus precipitating threats of angry retribution from Boston. Whatever the truth may be, the heavy casualties of the disease seriously weakened the Narragansetts and their relations with Massachusetts. Maintaining independence became more difficult.

Heresy hunts in Massachusetts caused some persons to flee to what is now the state of Rhode Island, among them Roger Williams, who in 1636 settled at the head of Narragansett Bay on the Providence River. He courted favor of Canonicus and Miantonomo, who gave permission to settle though no deed was then made, nor was any payment given. A. B. Patton calls it "a conveyance after the manner of a tribal grant" (p. 157). It was followed by the first formal deed in Rhode Island's history, also conveyed by Canonicus and Miantonomo, 24 March 1638. In 1637 another refugee, William Coddington, bought Aquidneck (the island of Rhode Island) from the two chiefs. The deed, dated 24 March 1637, specified payment of forty fathoms of white wampum beads and stipulated that Miantonomo would order Indian inhabitants to remove, compensating them with twenty hoes and ten coats. Like Roger Williams, Coddington dealt with the Wampanoag competing claim by gifts to Massasoit also. The hospitality of the chiefs for English dissidents in these and later cases led gradually to a transition from tribal to colonial jurisdiction. Sydney V. James remarks, "It is quite realistic to think of the colony of Rhode Island as in part a product of Narragansett Indian policy" (p. 8).

These proceedings annoyed the Puritan magistrates in both Boston and Hartford, as they projected incorporating the Narragansett country into their own jurisdictions. Roger Williams tried to mollify Massachusetts governor John Winthrop, Sr., by purchasing Chibachuwese (Prudence Island) from the chiefs, 10 November 1637, which he presented to Winthrop personally. Winthrop's plans were set aside temporarily because of difficulties between the Pequots and Connecticut. The Pequots solicited alliance with their former enemies the Narragansetts against the English colonists. Roger Williams heard about it and interceded. He claimed to have prevented the alliance; Neal Salisbury attributes that result to the policies of Canonicus and Miantonomo. Instead, when in 1637 English troops marched against the Pequot stockade on Mystic River, Canonicus allowed a hundred or more Narragansett warriors to march with them. They were shocked by the massacre perpetrated there and protested, "It slays too many men."

In 1643 Canonicus resented the involvement of the English colonists in the killing of Miantonomo by hostile Mohegans. When summoned peremptorily to Boston, Canonicus refused to go. Aided by the Rhode Island colonists called "Gortonoges," he wrote to Massachusetts, "Our late brother [Miantonomo] was willing to stir much abroad, and we see a sad event at the last thereupon." He declared his people under the direct protection of the king of England and rejected further orders from Boston. The surprised magistrates sent messengers to inquire into this show of independence, and Canonicus made them stand in the rain for two hours before he would admit them to his lodge. The royal protection to which the Narragansetts had appealed failed to materialize because England was in the throes of the Puritan revolution there. Massachusetts declared war and by a show of strength imposed a bloodless capitulation requiring a large payment of wampum and subsequent annual tribute.

Among the scant documentation for Canonicus personally is the account of his grief when a son died in 1642. The mourning father buried his son and burned his "palace" with all the goods in it.

At the end of his life in 1647 Canonicus was no longer in charge of policies, while his people became more and more dependent on political protection by heterodox Englishmen among them who feared Puritan domination almost as much as did the Indians.

• *The Winthrop Papers*, ed. Allyn B. Forbes (5 vols., 1929–1947), and *The History of New England from 1630 to 1649* (1690), ed. James Savage, 2d ed. (2 vols., 1853), both by John Winthrop, Sr., must be consulted but with care. He was a lawyer who crafted his side's case with everything he wrote, and he believed in compiling history "according to truth with due weight." For balance, see the writings of the Puritan challengers in Rhode Island. *The Correspondence of Roger Williams, 1629–1682* (1988) is now conveniently compiled and edited by Glenn W. La Fantasie. Other data are scattered in *Publications of the Narragansett Club*, *Collections of the Rhode Island Historical Society* (especially vol. 3), and *Rhode Island Colonial Records*. The best nineteenth-century account is Samuel G. Drake, *The Biography and History of the Indians of North America*, 11th ed. (1856). Good but contrasting accounts are Neal Salisbury, *Manitou and Providence* (1982), and Francis Jennings, *The Invasion of America* (1975). See also Sydney V. James, *Colonial Rhode Island: A History* (1975), and A. B. Patton, "The Early Land Titles of Providence," *Narragansett Historical Register*, ed. James N. Arnold, vol. 8 (1890), pp. 157–75.

FRANCIS JENNINGS

CANOVA, Judy (20 Nov. 1916–5 Aug. 1983), hillbilly singer, was born Juliette Canova in Starke, Florida, the daughter of Joseph Canova, a cotton broker and contractor, and Henrietta Perry, a concert singer. The family was quite musical, and Canova and her brother Zeke and sister Annie studied piano, voice, violin, and horn. Judy, an extrovert—or, as her mother put it, "a natural ham"—from age three, performed at family and church socials. At age twelve she and her best friend entered a series of Jacksonville amateur nights, often taking first place. When the friend dropped out,

Zeke and Annie took her spot and the Canova Cracker Trio was born. They sang and did hillbilly comedy and were signed to do local radio. She claimed to have picked up her cornpone lingo from sharecroppers who patronized her father's cotton gin.

Canova said, "Growing up, I was funny but not at the top of anyone's date list. I was awkward and plain but I got smart and not only accepted my lack of glamour, but made the most of it." After graduation in 1930, her mother took her to New York where Judy learned tap and planned to enter Juilliard to study opera, a plan that was cut short when her mother died.

Two years later, Judy returned to New York with her brother and sister, who attempted to exclude her from the act, arguing she wasn't "high-tone enough." However, it was her hillbilly antics and songs collected while vacationing in the North Carolina mountains that got the trio booked into Greenwich Village's Village Barn. "We wondered how New York would take to us," said Canova, "but fortune smiled on us. It was like ants to a picnic! But the club was so small that when you sat down, you found a customer in your lap."

Canova, billed as the Duse of the Sticks, sang in a nasal twang, did her hair in braids, sported a straw hat, and wore a plain skirt, bobby sox, and ankle boots. She carried a well-worn suitcase and usually had a piece of straw in her mouth. Thanks to her comedy, the trio's engagement was extended for almost two years.

"After our landlady almost evicted us for rehearsing," Canova said, "we took our yodels, grunts, caws, and hog calls to Central Park. East Side and West Side, people stared out of their windows wondering what jungle animals had invaded."

Rudy Vallee signed Canova and siblings to a one-year contract on his radio show, and they played the vaudeville circuit. Brother Pete joined the act in 1934 when they made their Broadway debut in a revue, *Calling All Stars*. Canova stole the show with a novelty song, "Last of the Hill Billies." Warner Bros. studio, which financed the show, signed the act for the movies.

In their second film, 1935's *In Caliente* starring Dolores Del Rio and Pat O'Brien, one of Canova's soundstage antics was caught on film and proved so funny it was left in. In a number choreographed by Busby Berkeley, she popped from behind a pillar dressed as a Mexican hillbilly and parodied the singer. The scene sent audiences into convulsions of laughter.

Warner's didn't renew the Canovas' contract, but Paramount signed them for *Artists and Models* (1937), the first of a two-picture deal. They earned $6,000 a week, but Judy wasn't disappointed when their option wasn't renewed. "I would have done better getting eighteen bucks a week and a good part," she said.

The family played London's Palladium, then Judy returned to Broadway solo, costarring with Bob Hope, Fannie Brice, Josephine Baker, and Eve Arden in the Ziegfeld *Follies* of 1936. In 1938 the Canovas joined Edgar Bergen, to whom Judy was briefly engaged, on radio for thirty weeks, earning over $4,000 a week. More and more, Judy emerged as the act's main attraction.

Republic Pictures signed her in 1939 to a five-year contract. She starred in eight low-budget comedies with music that capitalized on her hillbilly image. Canova revived a vanishing type of American humor, playing the country rube who chases but never quite catches her man. She washed floors by attaching brushes to rollerskates, used a lawnmower to clean a kitchen floor with grass growing between the cracks, ate soap-filled creampuffs, and endeared herself to audiences with her zany singing and slapstick.

Republic was among the handful of small, independent studios that produced inexpensive "hillbilly musicals," as they were called, to fill out double bills in small-town movie theaters, which typically booked them with other B movies, such as singing-cowboy westerns. Although critics dismissed such material, Canova became the studio's fourth-highest grossing star, behind Gene Autry, Roy Rogers, and John Wayne. When *Joan of Ozark*, with Canova hunting down a Nazi ring, was released in 1942, she ranked ahead of such stars as Rita Hayworth and James Stewart in popularity polls. However, Canova wanted to grow as an actress but found herself persistently typecast. "It was like a life term at Alcatraz," she said. "You only cease being that particular character when you cease to be. A lot of my act was tongue-in-cheek, but I guess I did it so well that people took me seriously."

CBS Radio signed her in 1943 for a weekly variety show, which was canceled after a season. She also toured army camps and promoted U.S. bands during the remainder of the war. Canova also had a recording contract with RCA Victor, and in 1945 NBC Radio put her in a situation comedy as a man-hungry, love-starved gal from Unadella, Georgia. It ranked in the ratings' top ten even into the early years of television. She returned to Republic in 1951, making six more formula comedies before the studio closed. She guest starred on TV in November 1952 on NBC's "Colgate Comedy Hour," battling wits and insults with Zsa Zsa Gabor. The network planned a series, which never materialized. In 1953, when the comedienne left her radio show to have a baby, she was earning $8,500 a week. Canova continued to work sporadically in films, including *The WAC from Walla Walla* (1952), *Carolina Cannonball* (1955), and *The Adventures of Huckleberry Finn* (1960).

In addition to twenty-two movies, Canova guest-starred in rodeos and on the Grand Ole Opry. In 1947 she toured Latin America, earning $10,000 a week. Her Las Vegas debut was at the Sahara in 1954. She did TV commercials, game shows, and appeared on series as diverse as "Alfred Hitchcock Presents," "Love, American Style," "Police Woman," and "Love Boat." In 1968 Canova was hospitalized for a respiratory ailment. In 1970 she shot a pilot for a proposed TV series that never came to be. Then in 1973 she appeared in the national tour of *No, No, Nanette* in the part originated in the 1970 Broadway revival by Patsy Kelly. She died, after a lengthy bout with cancer, in Hollywood.

Canova was married and divorced four times. In 1936 she married William Burns and divorced him three years later. In 1941 she married James H. Ripley, whom she denied marrying, but a month later began annulment proceedings. She had no children with Burns or Ripley. In 1943 she married Chet (Chester) England, with whom she had one daughter before their divorce in 1949. She had one other daughter, television actress Diana Canova (Rivero), with her fourth husband, Filiberto (Philip) Rivero, whom she married in 1950. Rivero was a Cuban bandleader who became a notable anti-Castro leader in the United States. Conova blamed her career for her numerous failed marriages. She told an interviewer, "It's almost impossible to maintain a marriage when you're in the limelight and separated because of a career from your husband."

Canova was a country bumpkin with an ear-shattering yodel, a heart of gold, and the tact of a grizzly bear. Her ability to make people laugh and her homespun comic persona allowed her to reach the zenith of popularity in the great era of radio comedy. And, though she didn't make the transition to television, Canova's style and material clearly established her as the forerunner to such popular television programs as "The Beverly Hillbillies," "Petticoat Junction," and "Green Acres."

• Extensive biographical information about Canova and some of her comedy routines are in James Robert Parish, *The Slapstick Queens* (1973), and Linda Martin and Kerry Segrave, *Women in Comedy* (1986). Her musical career, with and without her siblings, is treated in Robert Oermann and Mary A. Bufwack, *Finding Her Voice: The Saga of Women in Country Music* (1993). See also Mary Unterbrink, *Funny Women: American Comediennes, 1860–1985* (1987). An obituary is in the *New York Times*, 7 Aug. 1983.

ELLIS NASSOUR

CANSINO, Angel (1898?–19 Mar. 1956), dancer and dance teacher, was born in Madrid, Spain, the son of Antonio "Padre" Cansino and Carmen (maiden name unknown), Spanish dancers. Antonio was the patriarch of three generations of Spanish dancers (both classical and exhibition ballroom) and teachers, many of whom lived and worked in the United States around the middle years of the twentieth century. Angel began to dance professionally with the Cansino family in Madrid at age eight. He emigrated to America around 1915 as part of a troupe known as the "Dancing Cansinos," made up of his older brother Eduardo and older sister Elisa. The Dancing Cansinos performed primarily on the vaudeville circuit, but Angel soon left the troupe to settle permanently in New York City as a teacher. He married an American ballet dancer, Susita, in New York. (Her last name and the date of their marriage are unknown.) They had one child, Carmina Susanne, who had the distinction of actually being born in Carnegie Hall, where the Cansinos had an apartment and studio. Susita taught with Angel in New York, and Carmina later had a career as a performer and teacher as well.

Broadly speaking, the second generation of the Cansino family was responsible for making Spanish dancing popular in the United States during the twentieth century. Indeed, according to Barbara Cohen-Stratyner the second-generation Cansinos toured so extensively from the twenties through the fifties that they were all in the same place only twice between 1925 and 1945, when family reunions were held in Seville, Spain, and Los Angeles. The range of Spanish dance styles that the Cansino family members performed was, as the critic Ann Barzel puts it, a "revelation" to Americans. Angel Cansino, the preeminent and most influential teacher of the family, taught "peasant" dancing, classical Spanish dancing, and flamenco as well as the art of playing castanets and finger cymbals (he was his niece Rita Hayworth's first dance teacher). In the United States, he used the traditional Spanish method of teaching dancing, in which a dance in its entirety is presented to the student and then, as Barzel describes it, "gone over so many times that finally the pupil knows it." The technique and style required for performing the dance correctly is essentially "picked up along the way." As it happened, Cansino's traditional Spanish teaching method was adopted by many other expatriate dance teachers in the United States so that they could teach the complete "routines" demanded by American students, whose training and patience for long study were limited.

In addition to teaching at his own studio on West 54th Street in New York, Cansino taught at the famous, as well as famously eclectic, Chalif dancing school in the twenties and thirties. The Chalif school's influence extended not only from Louis Chalif's large New York studio but also from his many and widely distributed textbooks on dance and his teaching at dancing masters' conventions. Cansino also helped to popularize Spanish dancing by teaching at these conventions held throughout the United States. At dancing masters' conventions, the students were themselves teachers who then returned to their own schools all over the country to teach what they had learned. The influence of the dancing masters' conventions on the popularization of Spanish dancing on Broadway and in the movies should not be underestimated. From the twenties through the forties, many of the Spanish dances performed by numerous American dancers could be traced to one or another member of the Cansino family, often Angel. Indeed, by the fifties, Angel Cansino's reputation as a teacher extended from the United States back to Europe, where he also occasionally taught.

Cansino continued to perform into the 1950s, although usually in the context of teaching. He performed and taught several times, for example, on the Jacob's Pillow summer dance festival program in Massachusetts. He was at Jacob's Pillow the year before his death. Angel Cansino died in New York City of pneumonia following a heart attack.

• For information on the Cansino family see Ann Barzel, "European Dance Teachers in the United States," *Dance Index*, Apr.–June 1944, pp. 56–100; Donald Duncan, "The Name Dropper," *Dance Magazine*, Sept. 1958, p. 18; and Barbara Naomi Cohen-Stratyner, *Biographical Dictionary of Dance* (1982), pp. 141–48. An obituary is in *Dance News*, Apr. 1956.

ADRIENNE L. MCLEAN

CANTOR, Eddie (Sept. 1892?–10 Oct. 1964), entertainer, was born Israel Iskowitz in New York City, the son of Mechel Iskowitz, a violinist, and Meta Kantrowitz. Orphaned at the age of three, he was raised by Esther Kantrowitz, his maternal grandmother. He was educated in the public schools of New York's Lower East Side. His grandmother registered him as "Israel Kantrowitz," but the name was subsequently anglicized to "Isidore Kanter" by a school official. Kanter, who altered the spelling of his name to "Cantor" upon embarking on a show business career in 1911, grew up on the streets. His grandmother, an Orthodox Jew, earned a living selling candles and other household items and by securing employment for young immigrants as maids in East Side homes.

Cantor made his New York stage debut at the Clinton Music Hall in partnership with his friend Daniel Lipsky in 1907 and appeared in the burlesque show *Indiana Maidens* in 1908–1909. He was a singing waiter at Carey Walsh's café on Coney Island in the summer of 1909 and worked for J. C. Weir and Co. and the National Cloak and Suit Company in 1910. Returning to show business in early 1911, he secured small-time vaudeville bookings as a comedian and singer and then joined the big-time comedy juggling act of (Jean) Bedini and (Roy) Arthur.

Cantor played the butler in Gus Edwards's *Kid Kabaret*, a show that featured the juvenile talents of Eddie Buzzel and George Jessel, among others. In 1914 Cantor married Ida Tobias, with whom he had five daughters. Cantor and Sammy Kessler sailed for England and opened at London's Oxford Music Hall. When their act proved unsuccessful, Cantor's American agent, Max Hart, got him a spot in Andre Charlot's revue *Not Likely*, where he scored a success with the song "To the Ladies." Hart teamed Cantor with straight man Al Lee on his return to the United States.

Cantor and Lee were partnered for two seasons, playing the Orpheum Theatre in Los Angeles in the spring of 1916. Earl Carroll saw their act there and offered Cantor a major role in *Canary Cottage*, a musical comedy starring Trixie Friganza. Cantor stole the show when the production opened in Los Angeles. Following the show's run in San Francisco, he left for New York for what would prove to be a 27-week engagement in Florenz Ziegfeld's *Midnight Frolic*.

Cantor appeared in the Ziegfeld *Follies* of 1917, scoring great successes with the songs "The Modern Maiden's Prayer" and "That's the Kind of a Baby for Me." He also appeared in the *Follies* of 1918 and 1919. Subsequently Cantor helped lead the strike that established the Actor's Equity Association on Broadway. He played an important role in actors' unions for more than twenty years, becoming president of the Screen Actors' Guild, the American Federation of Radio Artists, and the American Guild of Variety Artists.

Cantor's relations with Ziegfeld, ruffled by the actors' strike, were severed in the fall of 1920, and he appeared in Rufus LeMaire's *Broadway Brevities* for several weeks until the Messrs. Shubert gave him his first starring tour in the *Midnight Rounders* (1920–1922). The Shuberts then starred Cantor on Broadway in the revue *Make It Snappy* (1922) before he returned to the Ziegfeld banner in 1923.

Cantor reached Broadway superstardom in *Kid Boots*, a show about a bootlegging caddy at a country club that became one of the decade's longest-running hit musicals. He starred in a silent motion picture version of the show for Paramount in 1926 and in a second silent film, *Special Delivery*, early the following year.

Cantor returned to the Broadway stage in the Ziegfeld *Follies* of 1927, becoming the first and only performer to receive featured billing in that annual revue. The show was built entirely around Cantor; when he came down with pleurisy Ziegfeld canceled the road tour. Cantor spent several months recuperating, returning to the Broadway stage on 4 December 1928 in *Whoopee*, a musical comedy based on Owen Davis's play *The Nervous Wreck*.

The stock market crash of October 1929 wiped out Cantor's fortune, leaving him more than a quarter million dollars in debt. In 1930, following a brief road tour in *Whoopee*, he returned to Hollywood to star in a sound version of that show.

Cantor became the first major Broadway star to have his own weekly radio show when he went on the "Chase and Sanborn Hour" in the fall of 1931. His success in the early to mid-1930s in both film and radio was truly phenomenal, and for a time he reigned as the number one box-office star in both media—making him probably the most important star in the world. Cantor was on the "Chase and Sanborn Hour" through the end of 1934, continuing on radio for Pebeco (1935–1936), Texaco (1936–1938), and Camels (1938–1939). His contract with the last-named sponsor was allowed to expire after he made a speech calling Father Charles E. Coughlin, the popular and controversial radio priest, "un-American" at the New York World's Fair in June 1939. Off the air the following season, he returned with a new sponsor, Bristol Myers, in November 1940.

His success led to five more Samuel Goldwyn film vehicles: *Palmy Days* (1931), *The Kid from Spain* (1932), *Roman Scandals* (1933), *Kid Millions* (1934), and *Strike Me Pink* (1936). After leaving Goldwyn, he starred in *Ali Baba Goes to Town*, a political satire utilizing themes from *Roman Scandals* and *Kid Millions*, for Twentieth Century-Fox in 1937. In 1940 MGM released *Forty Little Mothers*, in which Cantor played an unmarried professor who, with the help of his students, attempts to look after an abandoned baby. This was a major departure for Cantor, who had made his mark performing in sketch comedy and singing uptempo songs. He played an essentially straight role in *Forty Little Mothers* and had only one song, a ballad called "Little Curly Hair in a Highchair." This film was not successful and marked the last time he would play a solo starring movie role.

Cantor returned to the Broadway stage as the star of *Banjo Eyes* during the season of 1941–1942, but the show closed owing to Cantor's physical collapse. He continued on radio and performed for wounded GIs in hospitals across the country, creating the "Purple Heart Circuit" in the process. Cantor appeared in several motion pictures during the 1940s, including *Thank Your Lucky Stars* (1943), *Show Business* (1944), *Hollywood Canteen* (1945), and *If You Knew Susie* (1948). Pabst Beer replaced Bristol Myers as his radio sponsor in 1946. Cantor starred in "The Eddie Cantor Pabst Blue Ribbon Show" until 1949, when he hosted "Take It or Leave It," a popular radio game show, and then made the transition to television.

Cantor became one of four rotating star acts on the "Colgate Comedy Hour" in the fall of 1950, concurrent with touring in *My Forty Years in Show Business*, a one-man show he had performed at Carnegie Hall the previous season. Cantor continued his rapid pace until October 1952, when a severe heart attack forced him to cut down on his schedule and adopt a more sedate style of performance. He recorded the soundtrack for *The Eddie Cantor Story*, which Warner Bros. released to a lukewarm response in 1953, and continued on the Colgate show until the spring of 1954. Cantor then starred in "The Eddie Cantor Comedy Theatre," a series of filmed half-hour comedy programs, hosting all the shows and starring in a third of them.

Cantor starred in "George Has a Birthday" and "Sizeman and Son," two television dramatic shows, in 1956 but was forced into retirement by a second heart attack after an appearance on "The Jackie Gleason Show" in January 1957. He wrote several books in his remaining years, but the deaths of his eldest daughter in 1959 and of his wife in 1962, in addition to his own declining health, made those last years sad and painful. He died in Los Angeles, having been awarded the Medal of Freedom by President Lyndon B. Johnson earlier that year.

Cantor was the first performer to establish a continuous record of success in several performance media—stage, film, radio, and to a lesser extent, recordings and television. He was also the first star to take definite and often controversial stands on major social issues and to adopt causes, such as sending needy children to Surprise Lake Camp, raising money for the transportation of Jewish children out of Nazi-occupied territories prior to World War II, and many other charitable projects. He was the founder of the March of Dimes, launched to fight polio.

As a performer, Cantor carried on the tradition of harlequin musical comedy, balancing the shrewdness and self-reliance of that character with the homey pedestrianism of the common man and the "lamb being led to the slaughter" aspect that helped make him such a popular favorite. The spontaneous energy he put into his songs has seldom been equaled, and his skill as a comedy pantomimist has been matched by only a few.

Cantor's films seem dated on television, though they play better on large screens in front of large audiences. Although he was successful in a variety of media, his style was best suited to the theater. A transitional performer, he was instrumental in bridging the gap between the "old" show business of the stage and vaudeville and the modern world of mass media entertainment.

• Cantor's private scrapbooks (dating from the 1930s) and other items, including numerous awards, are in the collection of the University of Southern California. The Magic Castle in Los Angeles has many of his radio scripts, and both the Theatre Collection of the New York Public Library for the Performing Arts and the Academy of Motion Picture Arts and Sciences have collections of newspaper clippings. The Shubert Archive (Lyceum Theatre Building, New York) contains correspondence, contracts, and other items relating to Cantor's employment by the Shuberts. Cantor's writings include two autobiographies, *My Life Is in Your Hands* (1928) and *Take My Life* (1957). The first book was ghost-written by David Freedman; the second, written with Jane Kesner Ardmore, is more reliable and retains much of the author's personal style. Cantor's other books include *The Way I See It* (1959), a volume of personal philosophy, and *As I Remember Them* (1963), anecdotes and reminiscences of past contemporaries in the world of entertainment. Both books include additional autobiographical material. (Cantor also wrote *Ziegfeld: The Great Glorifier* [1934], a biography of the famed producer, and numerous shorter "gag" books, including, most notably, *Caught Short: A Saga of Wailing Wall Street* [1929].) Cantor's professional activity was well covered in contemporary trade newspapers, and the daily press reported his charitable and political activities with admirable regularity.

HERBERT G. GOLDMAN

CANTRIL, Hadley (16 June 1906–28 May 1969), psychologist and public opinion researcher, was born Albert Hadley Cantril in Hyrum, Utah, the son of Albert Hadley Cantril, a physician, and Edna Mary Meyer. He grew up in Douglas, Wyoming, and graduated from Dartmouth College in 1928. He then spent two years studying in Berlin and Munich. After receiving his Ph.D. in psychology from Harvard in 1931, he served for one year as instructor of sociology at Dartmouth. In 1932 he married Mavis Katherine Lyman; they had two children. In the fall after his marriage he returned to Harvard as instructor in psychology. He then moved to Teachers College, Columbia University, in 1935, the year that he coauthored his first book, *The Psychology of Radio,* with Gordon W. Allport. The book reported on a number of experiments studying listeners' responses to this "psychological novelty," which were supplemented by a general analysis and interpretation of psychological and cultural factors shaping radio programs as well as audience behavior.

In 1936 Cantril accepted a position as assistant professor at Princeton University. At Princeton he became involved in public opinion research through his contact with George Gallup, who had just begun his career as opinion pollster during the 1936 presidential election campaign. In 1937 Cantril became one of the founders of the *Public Opinion Quarterly,* which was later chosen to be the journal of the American Association for Public Opinion Research. When Orson Welles's radio play "War of the Worlds" created widespread panic on the East Coast, Cantril combined interview data from listeners and content analysis of the program in an attempt to account for the surprising turn of events in his book *Invasion from Mars* (1940). In the same year he set up, with support from the Rockefeller Foundation, the Office of Public Opinion Research at Princeton University. Developing small sample techniques and the collection of trend data for opinion research, he provided information and advice for President Franklin D. Roosevelt on the shifting opinions of the public in this country during World War II. In later years he would perform similar consulting work for presidents Dwight D. Eisenhower and John F. Kennedy. He also helped to initiate opinion surveys for policy research in Latin America, studying the effects of Nazi propaganda on the public there. An analysis of shortwave news and propaganda broadcasts in Europe led eventually to the establishment of the Foreign Broadcasting Monitoring Service, which analyzed Axis propaganda during the war and in part aimed at predicting future Axis military moves. He was even involved in some clandestine opinion surveys in Axis territory. Cantril's work of this early phase was reported in two books, *The Psychology of Social Movements* (1941) and *Gauging Public Opinion* (1944), the latter a classic on the methods and results of early public opinion studies. His wartime exploits, which were highly confidential at the time, were described much later in *The Human Dimension: Experiences in Policy Research* (1967).

In 1944 Cantril was promoted to full professor and became Stuart Professor and chair of the psychology department at Princeton in 1953. In this period, he collaborated with social psychologist Muzafer Sherif on *The Psychology of Ego-Involvements* (1947). He became enthralled with Adelbert Ames's demonstrations of the "assumptive" nature of visual perception, such as the rotating, "trapezoid window," which invariably is misperceived as an oscillating rectangular shape, based on our expectations of right-angled carpentry. He would show these demonstrations to his near-neighbor in Princeton, Albert Einstein, and to President Eisenhower, among others. Cantril also attempted, together with psychologists Ames, Albert H. Hastorf, and William H. Ittelson, to work out a new approach to the basic issues in the scientific understanding of human beings. Rejecting both a behaviorist and a psychoanalytic determinism in favor of a third, "humanistic" psychology, he developed a "transactional" approach (a term borrowed from John Dewey), implying organic interchanges among organisms-in-environments rather than mechanical actions and reactions between solid objects in empty physical space, described in his book *The "Why" of Man's Experience* (1950). Under the auspices of UNESCO, he began a public opinion research project in Europe. The results were published in *How Nations See Each Other* (1953); Cantril also edited a companion volume, *Tensions That Cause Wars* (1950).

In 1955 Cantril received an offer of ample funding for research from Nelson Rockefeller. Appreciating the independence it provided, Cantril left academia to become chairman of the Institute for International Social Research, which he founded with pollster Lloyd Free. The institute carried out extensive cross-national studies on several continents during the next fifteen years. One of the earlier surveys produced *The Politics of Despair* (1958), an analysis of the appeals of the Communist parties to the voters of Italy and France, which was remarkably free of Cold War rhetoric. Similarly, after a visit to the Soviet Union in connection with his book *Soviet Leaders and Mastery over Man* (1960), Cantril recommended to President Eisenhower an approach to the Soviets that would be firm but free of ideological combativeness and would reinforce any positive moves on their part. Later *The Political Beliefs of Americans: A Study of Public Opinion* (with Lloyd Free, 1967) reported a major study of the U.S. voting public's attitudes, ideological leanings, and party affiliations during the 1964 campaign.

Cantril was one of the academic pioneers of public opinion research and the initiator of its use for advice to policy makers. A prolific writer, he authored or coauthored some twenty books—many of them translated or reissued in paperback—and numerous journal articles. He contributed conceptual refinement, critical analyses, and a variety of methodological innovations to the emerging specialty of opinion polling and survey research. Though not always appreciated by his academic colleagues, he also contributed important ideas to psychological theorizing. His main goals were to find a middle way between rigorous narrowness and broad-gauge speculation, to combine public opinion data with results from experimental perception studies and new developments in neurophysiology, and to create an adequate framework for the understanding of human experience. While working on a manuscript that addressed these issues, he died in Princeton. His obituary in the *Public Opinion Quarterly* was written by George Gallup.

• Cantril's correspondence with President Roosevelt is at Dartmouth College. The rest of his papers are in the custody of Albert H. Cantril of Washington, D.C. A complete list of Cantril's publications is given in Albert H. Cantril, ed., *Psychology, Humanism, and Scientific Inquiry: The Selected Essays of Hadley Cantril* (1988), which also contains a biographical statement of his transactional views in the epilogue. An obituary is in the *Journal of Individual Psychology* 25 (1969): 219–25.

FRANZ SAMELSON

CANTWELL, Robert Emmett (31 Jan. 1908–8 Dec. 1978), writer and historian, was born in Little Falls (now Vader), Washington, the son of Charles James Cantwell, a teacher and engineer, and Nina Adelia

Hanson, a former teacher. His paternal grandfather founded Little Falls in the 1840s. In 1912 the family moved to Onalaska, a lumber-company town, where Charles Cantwell became a builder, then the superintendent of the lumber mill and the town. Later he was the superintendent of Carlisle, another company town nearby. Robert Cantwell attended schools in Onalaska, Chehalis, and Aberdeen, all in Washington, and beginning at age sixteen studied for one year at the University of Washington in Seattle, where his older brother James was also a student. Their father's illness forced them to leave school, however, and Cantwell spent the next four years primarily as a veneer clipper operator in a plywood factory in Hoquiam, Washington. His father died in 1927.

Having read widely because of his mother's influence and his studies at the university, Cantwell began writing fiction. An Aberdeen friend placed one of his stories, "Hang by My Thumbs," in the *New American Caravan* (Spring 1929). F. Scott Fitzgerald praised the story to Maxwell Perkins, his editor at Scribner's. Cantwell was encouraged by a book contract to go to New York City in late 1929. He married Mary Elizabeth Chambers of Baton Rouge, Louisiana, in 1931 (the couple eventually had three children) and was pleased when his first novel, *Laugh and Lie Down*, was published later that year. An autobiographical story, it concerns two brothers whose father's efforts to spare the family impoverishment come to naught when he dies. Compelled to abandon their education at a university, the brothers spiral into disillusionment. In the end, one of the brothers causes chaos and multiple tragedy, having been required by fate to grow up too fast; the other brother and his wife suffer similarly. Reviews of *Laugh and Lie Down* were favorable, but sales were not. At this point a vociferous anti-fascist, Cantwell joined Malcolm Cowley to report for the *New Republic* on the National Hunger March of 1932 and happily—if prematurely—predicted that on 4 March 1933 the United States would go bankrupt. During the time he was literary editor for the *New Outlook* (1931–1935), he published *The Land of Plenty* (1934), an ironically titled proletarian novel sympathetic to lumber-mill strikers in the Northwest. A power failure in a Northwest plywood factory at the start brilliantly symbolizes the failure of the capitalist system itself. Although the night-shift workers are dangerously trapped in the plant amid stilled machines, they can cope better than their inept foreman and superintendent. When fifteen of the workers are fired, the others call a strike and seize the factory. Outgunned, the laborers are soon crushed by the police. Because of Cantwell's thorough understanding of the workers' psychology and his sympathy with their sense of hopelessness, *The Land of Plenty* remains one of the most authentic and accurate proletarian novels ever written.

Cantwell soon began to demonstrate ideological inconsistency. He went to Boston in 1935 to help his friend Lincoln Steffens with research on a procapitalist, abortive biography of E. A. Filene, the merchant-reformer. Despite Cantwell's apparent defection from the communist cause, *The Land of Plenty* sold well and was influential, and its author was touted as a strident voice favoring the cause of organized labor. While continuing to contribute articles to various periodicals, Cantwell established a long-standing, profitable relationship with the Time & Life organization. He was literary editor of *Time* (1935–1936), an editor of *Fortune* (1937), and an associate editor of *Time* (1938–1945). He took an extended leave, moved to Sherman, Connecticut, and freelanced again (1945–1950). He moved back to Manhattan and became literary editor of *Newsweek* (1949–1954) and briefly an editor of the Limited Editions Club (1956). He returned to Time & Life to work for its new magazine, *Sports Illustrated*, as an editorial consultant (1957–1961), as senior editor (1961–1972), and as a prolific special contributor during those years and until 1978.

Very shortly after his wife died, Cantwell in 1974 was briefly married to but soon divorced from Allison Semmes Joy (1977). He married Eva Stolz late in 1978 but died five weeks later in New York City.

Cantwell must be regarded as a writer of immense but unfocused talents, whose nervous breakdown in 1943–1944 might have permanently diminished his creative energy. He never followed his two promising novels with another, although there is evidence that he planned more. He left unfinished a study of contemporary literature, to be called "Poets and Killers," and had unrealized plans for a biography of Mark Catesby, the English naturalist and student of American flora and fauna. What Cantwell did accomplish, however, is significant. Five books are especially noteworthy. *Nathaniel Hawthorne: The American Years* (1948), the first of a projected two-volume biography, is an exhaustive study of Hawthorne's ancestors and his life to the year 1850, when he published *The Scarlet Letter*. Cantwell nicely reveals Hawthorne's less reclusive side, but his theory that Hawthorne was a government spy was so ridiculed that he never wrote his second volume. In his *Famous American Men of Letters* (1956), Cantwell explains to young readers the worth of thirteen American literary masters, from Washington Irving and James Fenimore Cooper to O. Henry and Jack London. Cantwell's *Alexander Wilson: Naturalist and Pioneer* (1961) is a thorough, appreciative biography of the wild, idealistic Scotsman who came to the United States in 1794 to paint birds, after which he published his landmark *American Ornithology*. (Cantwell was an avid birdwatcher as well as an adept chess player.) An outgrowth of some of his *Sports Illustrated* articles was *The Real McCoy: The Life and Times of Norman Selby* (1971), about the American boxer who defeated Tommy Ryan in 1896 for the world welterweight title. Finally came *The Hidden Northwest* (1972), Cantwell's proud and melancholy western masterpiece, also partly an outgrowth of *Sports Illustrated* articles. It concerns treatment by early explorers and writers of the land comprising Oregon, Washington, and British Columbia, erroneous myths about the region, proconservationist optimism, and pertinent travel literature. Well-researched and beautifully written, *The Hidden Northwest* will undoubtedly be Cantwell's most enduring book.

• Many of Cantwell's manuscripts and much of his correspondence are in the library of the University of Oregon. Walter B. Rideout, *The Radical Novel in the United States, 1900–1954* (1956), which contains the best general account of proletarian novels in the 1930s, includes an excellent discussion of Cantwell's *Laugh and Lie Down* and *The Land of Plenty*. David Madden, ed., *Proletarian Writers of the Thirties* (1968), contains two essays featuring Cantwell: Jack Conroy, "Robert Cantwell's *Land of Plenty*," pp. 74–84, and Frederick J. Hoffman, "Aesthetics of the Proletarian Novel," pp. 184–93. Harvey Swados, "Cantwell Redivivus," *Novel: A Forum on Fiction* 6 (Fall 1972): 92–94, is a fine, measured review of *The Land of Plenty*. Richard H. Pells, *Radical Visions and American Dreams: Culture and Social Thought in the Depression Years* (1973), contains superb commentary on Cantwell's early intellectual development and his novel *The Land of Plenty*. Malcolm Cowley, *The Dream of the Golden Mountains: Remembering the 1930s* (1980), pp. 126–33, describes Cantwell's activities during the National Hunger March. Merrill Lewis, *Robert Cantwell* (1985), concentrates on Cantwell's western writings. The *New York Times* published a brief obituary, 10 Dec. 1978, but Kelso F. Sutton's "Letter from the Publisher" in *Sports Illustrated*, 18 Dec. 1978, is a fuller, loving obituary of Cantwell by a colleague and friend.

ROBERT L. GALE

CANZONERI, Tony (6 Nov. 1908–8 Dec. 1959), boxer, was born in Slidell, Louisiana, the son of Sicilian immigrants George Canzoneri and Josephine (maiden name unknown), occupations unknown. He grew up on the streets of New Orleans, working as a bootblack, and began boxing at age eleven. He took part in impromptu matches held in the yards of tenement houses, where he was seen by bantamweight champion Pete Herman, a fellow Italian American, who perceived his potential. Herman gave Canzoneri his first boxing lessons and started him in amateur boxing.

In 1923 the Canzoneri family moved to Brooklyn, New York, and Tony, only fourteen years old, carried with him a letter of introduction from Herman to Sammy Goldman, who became the manager of his amateur and professional career. Canzoneri won the amateur bantamweight championship of New York in 1924. In 1925 he got a professional license by exaggerating his age by four years, and he immediately became a consistent winner.

After winning thirty-six of his first forty fights (including victories over Bushy Graham, André Routis, and Archie Bell), Canzoneri boxed Bud Taylor in Chicago on 26 March 1927 for the vacant bantamweight title. The fight was a draw, and Taylor won the rematch, also in Chicago, on 24 June 1927. Finding himself unable to maintain the bantamweight limit, Canzoneri began to box as a featherweight and quickly won several important victories, including a one-round knockout of the Filipino sensation Pete Sarmiento. On 24 October 1927 he fought Johnny Dundee for the vacant featherweight title in New York and won. After one successful defense against Benny Bass, he lost the title to Routis in 1928. Once more he moved up a weight division to lightweight and gained a series of impressive victories, including wins over Joey Sangor, Routis, and Ignacio Fernandez. On 2 August 1929 at Chicago, he challenged Sammy Mandell for the lightweight title but lost the decision.

Always resilient, Canzoneri rebounded from the Mandell loss quickly. In the next year he won fourteen fights, including triumphs over Stanislaus Loayza, Bass, and Joe Glick, losing close fights only to Jack "Kid" Berg and Billy Petrolle, to earn another lightweight title fight. This time he won the championship by knocking out Al Singer in one round on 14 November 1930 in New York. On 24 April 1931 he fought Berg, then the junior welterweight champion; with his own lightweight title and Berg's title at stake, Canzoneri scored a sensational three-round knockout.

Later in 1931 he defended both titles successfully against Berg (twice), Cecil Payne, and Kid Chocolate. On 18 January 1932 he lost the junior welterweight title to Johnny Jadick in Philadelphia but regained it on 21 May 1933 by defeating Battling Shaw at New Orleans. He finally lost it for good to Barney Ross in Chicago on 23 June 1933. Still the holder of the lightweight title, Canzoneri made a successful defense in New York against Billy Petrolle on 4 November 1932. In his June 1933 fight with Ross, the lightweight title also was at stake and was lost simultaneously with the light welterweight title. Canzoneri failed to regain the titles from Ross in a rematch on 12 September 1933.

Once more refusing to leave the championship scene, Canzoneri won fourteen of his next sixteen fights, including a spectacular knockout of Kid Chocolate. On 10 May 1935 he regained the lightweight title by defeating Lou Ambers, defended it successfully against Al Roth, then lost it again to Ambers in 1936. He failed in an attempt to regain the lightweight title from Ambers in 1937. In all, Canzoneri engaged in twenty-two professional championship fights. He is generally rated among the three or four best lightweights in boxing history.

Canzoneri was perhaps the most popular fighter of the late 1920s and early 1930s. He was friendly, unassuming, and spoke with a southern drawl. His trademarks were a big smile on his ruggedly handsome face, persistent good humor, and a cigar in his hand. His fights were invariably action-packed, and, in an era when criminal influence in big-city boxing was pervasive, there was never a question about the honesty of Canzoneri's matches.

Canzoneri was versatile. He could nullify clever tactics by fighting aggressively, and he coped with aggressive, hard-hitting opponents by using superior boxing technique. However, his pride sometimes caused him to try to beat his opponents at their own games by, for instance, trying to outslug Petrolle or outbox Chocolate, and his foolish tactics occasionally led to defeat. He was fearless, indomitable, and remarkably consistent. Above all, Canzoneri always gave his best and sent the fans home happy.

Canzoneri boxed exciting series with nearly every important lightweight and some of the notable welterweights of the decade from 1928 to 1937. One of his greatest triumphs and gamest performances came on 8 May 1936 when he decisively outboxed the great welterweight Jimmy McLarnin under difficult circumstances; Canzoneri's head collided with the suspended ring microphone just before the fight started, leaving him stunned and with a deep gash on his forehead. He won 143 of 175 fights, with ten draws, and was knocked out only once, in his last fight on 1 November 1939, by Al Davis.

Although Canzoneri's career peaked during the depression, when purses were slim, he took home more than $500,000 in ring earnings and was in good financial shape when he retired from boxing. But he later lost his money through bad investments. A clothing business and a restaurant he opened both failed. He appeared in one Broadway comedy and later served as the straight man and stooge for a comedian. At times he even directed a dance band. In 1936 he had married dancer Rita Ray, with whom he had one child before they divorced in the early 1950s.

Canzoneri, a familiar face on Broadway during the thirties and forties, sank gradually into poverty and loneliness. He lived his final years in a cheap Broadway hotel, where his body was found on 10 December 1959. He had been dead of natural causes for about two days. Canzoneri was an inaugural inductee to the International Boxing Hall of Fame in 1990.

• An accurate and complete version of Canzoneri's record is in Herbert G. Goldman, ed., *1986–87 Ring Record Book and Boxing Encyclopedia*. Contemporary descriptions of most of Canzoneri's important fights are in the *New York Times*, the *Chicago Tribune*, and other leading newspapers. The best sources of information are articles published in the *Ring* magazine, including Francis Albertanti, "Tony Canzoneri Seeks to Emulate Teacher, Pete Herman, Former Champion," July 1927, pp. 16–17, 19; Tony Lawrence, "Tony Canzoneri—The Lad Who Smiles at Reverses," Jan. 1930, pp. 6–7; Eddie Borden, "Tony Canzoneri—A Gent of the Old School," Apr. 1936, pp. 6–7; Nat Fleischer, "Tony Canzoneri Passes," Feb. 1960, pp. 30–31, 49; Ted Carroll, "Tony Canzoneri," Mar. 1961, pp. 14–15, 47; Sam Andre, "Pictures Never Before Seen of Tony Canzoneri," Apr. 1962, pp. 14–19; and Goldman, "Tony Canzoneri: The Best Roman Warrior of All," July 1982, pp. 66–79. An obituary is in the *New York Times*, 11 Dec. 1959.

LUCKETT V. DAVIS

CAPA, Robert (22 Oct. 1913–25 May 1954), photographer, was born Endre Ernö Friedmann, in Budapest, Hungary, the son of Dezsö Friedmann and Julianna Henrietta Berkovits, proprietors of a fashionable dressmaking salon. Bandi, as Capa was called in his youth, attended the Imre Madàch Gymnasium. At fifteen he was introduced to documentary photography by his neighbor, Eva Besnyö, whom he accompanied while she photographed workers and the destitute. In 1929 he met the socialist artist and writer Lajos Kassàk, whose art journal *Munka* often included "Szociofoto" (social photography) such as images of poor laborers. In his last two years at the Gymnasium Capa became part of a group of followers who marched in pro–trade union, anti-fascist demonstrations organized by the journal's contributors. In the spring of 1931, as a result of his involvement in activist politics, he was arrested and beaten by the police.

In July 1931, after passing his university-qualifying exams, Capa fled the climate of political oppression in Budapest for Berlin, where he planned to study journalism at the Deutsche Hochschule für Politik, an independent college of political science. After a few months his parents found they could no longer support him, and he became a photographer, "the nearest thing to journalism for anyone who found himself without a language," as he later said. A fellow Hungarian émigré, the painter and photographer György Kepes, lent him a Voightländer camera, and Capa's career was launched. His first job in Berlin was with Simon Guttmann's photo agency Dephot (later Degephot), where he began as a darkroom assistant in 1931. Soon he was promoted to photographer, and in November 1932 the agency sent him to Copenhagen to cover a rare appearance by the exiled Leon Trotsky for the Berlin weekly magazine *Der Weltspiegel*.

When Hitler assumed power in February 1933, Capa left Berlin, going first to Budapest to visit his family and then to Paris. There, now calling himself André Friedmann, he was befriended by the photographers Henri Cartier-Bresson and André Kertész and struggled to support himself as a freelancer. In November 1934 he traveled with the photographer Gorta to the Saar, then under the supervision of the League of Nations, to record the tense atmosphere surrounding the elections to decide the question of reunification with Germany. Their photographs were printed in the French magazine *Vu*.

In 1934 Capa met and fell in love with Gerda Taro, a German who had also come to Paris to escape Nazism. Taro first acted as Capa's agent, but later, under his tutelage, she became a photographer herself. In 1936 Capa assumed the name by which he is now known, choosing it for its lack of any national or ethnic identity. He encouraged confusion of his surname with that of the Hollywood director Frank Capra and was able to extract a higher price from French publishers by representing himself as a successful American photographer; he then told American publishers he was French.

In August 1936 Capa and Taro went to Barcelona to document the outbreak of the Spanish Civil War for *Vu*. The pictures Capa took on this trip included one of a Loyalist militiaman in the act of falling to the ground after being struck by an enemy bullet near Córdoba. In subsequent years, however, the authenticity of this famous shot, hailed at the time of its publication as the greatest photograph of battle action ever taken, has sometimes been questioned. In 1937 Capa became a staff photographer for the Paris daily newspaper *Ce Soir* but continued to publish his pictures of the Spanish struggle in several French, British, and German magazines as well as the American magazine *Life*. In July Taro was killed near Brunete, Spain, when her car collided with a tank. Her death devastated Capa, who memorialized their war experiences in the book *Death in the Making* (1938), a collection of the photographs they had taken at the front. As a result of Capa's dramatic coverage of the war and his sensitive studies of civilian suffering, he was lauded by critics. *Time* called him "one of the world's great photographers" in February 1938, and the December 1938 issue of the British magazine *Picture Post* ran a photo of him with the caption "The Greatest War-Photographer in the World."

In 1938 Capa traveled to China to record the Chinese defeat of the invading Japanese forces at Tai'erzhuang. He returned to Spain in October to photograph the fall of Barcelona, where he met and became friends with Ernest Hemingway; he then followed the Loyalist soldiers and refugees to France to record their experiences in the internment camps. With the signing of the Russo-German nonaggression pact in August 1939, European war seemed imminent, and Capa joined his mother and his brother Cornell in New York, where he worked for *Life*. In March 1940, when his visa expired, he arranged a marriage of convenience with the fashion model Toni Sorel; they never lived together and were divorced in 1945.

In April 1941 Capa went to London with the writer Diana Forbes-Robertson to chronicle the experiences of an average family during the Blitz; their work was published later that year as *The Battle of Waterloo Road*. In 1942 *Collier's* hired Capa to photograph the war effort in England. When he became an accredited photographer to the U.S. Army in 1943, the magazine sent him to cover the North African campaign and the Allied invasion of Sicily; he also photographed the fighting on the Italian mainland. His understated portraits of soldiers on the convoys and in battle gave a human face to the war.

On D-Day, 6 June 1944, Capa landed with the first wave of American troops on Omaha Beach. Only eleven of his seventy-two photographs survived a darkroom accident, but those few blurred images, filled with soldiers' faces, shrapnel smoke, and sinking ships, powerfully evoked the chaos of the landing and the soldiers' bravery and were considered the best shots of the invasion. Capa accompanied the French troops on their march to liberate Paris, and in December he covered the Battle of the Bulge. In April 1945 he parachuted into Germany with the 17th Airborne Division. There he photographed what he believed to be the last soldier to die in the European struggle, an American corporal on duty on an apartment balcony shot by a sniper moments before.

Capa became a naturalized American citizen in 1946 and legally changed his name to Robert Capa. In 1947, with the photographers Cartier-Bresson, David Seymour, George Rodger, and Bill Vandivert, he founded Magnum, a cooperative agency, with offices in New York and Paris. That year Capa and the novelist John Steinbeck traveled in the Soviet Union and collaborated on a book about their experiences, *A Russian Journal*. Capa's work from this time also includes intimate portraits of celebrities, such as Pablo Picasso on the beach in Nice with his mistress Françoise Gilot and their son, and Henri Matisse sketching in bed at his house in Cimiez, France.

The Israeli war for independence drew Capa back to the front from 1948 to 1950. His photographs of the fighting in Palestine and the arriving refugees appeared in the British magazine *Illustrated* and in Irwin Shaw's 1950 book *Report on Israel*. From 1950 to 1953 he served as the director of the Magnum office in Paris. Capa went to Vietnam in 1954 to cover the French Indochina War for *Life*; in the course of photographing French maneuvers on the Red River delta, he stepped on a land mine and was killed.

In 1955 *Life* and the Overseas Press Club established the Robert Capa annual prize for "superlative photography requiring exceptional courage and enterprise abroad." In 1977, in his brother's memory, Cornell Capa (who had adopted Capa's name when he too became a photojournalist) created the International Center for Photography in New York to support documentary photographers. Capa was a controversial figure who often exaggerated and embellished the stories behind his photographs, yet the power of the images themselves, along with the courage and compassion they evince, is undisputed.

• Capa's photographs are in collections worldwide; his negatives and papers are archived at the International Center for Photography. In addition to his works already mentioned, he published an autobiography, *Slightly Out of Focus* (1947). Richard Whelan, *Robert Capa* (1985), is the most detailed biography and includes a comprehensive bibliography. *Robert Capa/Photographs* (1996) contains many previously unpublished photographs. Two published exhibition catalogs, Cornell Capa and Bhupenda Karia, eds., *Robert Capa* (1974), and Anna Farova, ed., *Robert Capa* (1969), are also useful. An obituary appears in the *New York Times*, 26 May 1954.

BARBARA LEE WILLIAMS
SARAH WALL

CAPEHART, Homer Earl (6 June 1897–3 Sept. 1979), U.S. senator, was born in Highbanks, Pike County, Indiana, the son of Alvin Thomas Capehart and Susanna A. Kelso, small farmers. The elder Capehart moved the family to Daviess County, where he became a tenant on the Graham farm, near Washington, Indiana. Homer's parents could not afford to send him to college, so after graduation from high school he took a job selling baking powder door to door. When the United States entered World War I he enlisted in the army and served as supply sergeant at Camp Lewis, Washington.

After the war Capehart worked for various companies, demonstrating his remarkable skills as a salesman and promoter. By 1927 he was general sales manager for Holcomb and Hoke Manufacturing Corporation of Indianapolis, which produced electric popcorn and peanut toasters. Meanwhile, Capehart's rugged appearance—heavy frame, ruddy face, a cigar jammed into the corner of his mouth—became his trademark. In 1922 he married Irma Mueller, the daughter of a prominent citizen of Wrightstown, Wisconsin; they had three children.

Capehart's business success began during the Jazz Age of the 1920s when during a trip to Cleveland he discovered a man who had invented a device that could automatically turn over and play the reverse sides of a pile of records. Capehart purchased the invention for $500 plus royalties and subsequently formed the Capehart Automatic Phonograph Corporation of Huntington, Indiana. In 1930 he moved the company to more spacious quarters in Fort Wayne, Indiana, and introduced several new lines for the home and dance hall. The Capehart phonograph gained international fame for high-quality sound. The onset of the Great Depression and an accompanying drop in sales, however, caused the board of directors to remove him as president in 1932. Almost immediately he organized another company, the Packard Manufacturing Company, and soon accepted a proposal made by the Rudolph Wurlitzer Corporation to become its vice president and head of its jukebox division. By 1939 the public's love of recorded music had made Wurlitzer the nation's largest producer of jukeboxes and Capehart a millionaire. His financial success allowed him to purchase a large farm in southern Indiana near where he had lived as a child and begin a political career. He continued to own and operate his Packard corporation, moving it to Indianapolis. The company produced equipment for the jukebox industry, and during World War II, after conversion to defense manufacturing, it produced items such as slip rings for tank turrets and cartridge slides for the M-1 carbine rifle.

Capehart had turned his attention to politics in 1936 to combat the federal government, which he considered paternalistic. Later, working with the state Republican chairman, he staged a rally on his farm, the "Capehart Cornfield Conference," the kickoff for the 1938 Republican congressional campaign. The event, which brought together precinct committeemen from throughout the state and national Republican leaders, signaled the beginning of a national shift toward conservative, anti–New Deal politics. It also gave Capehart a political identity.

In the next six years he spoke at Republican rallies; organized a large celebration at Elwood, Indiana, at which fellow businessman Wendell Willkie accepted the 1940 Republican presidential nomination; and was elected to the Republican state committee. In 1944, campaigning against what he considered to be a left-leaning, three-term president with dictatorial aspirations and for the creation of "real" jobs in private industry, Capehart defeated one of Indiana's most popular politicians, Governor Henry F. Schricker, for the U.S. Senate. Capehart would be reelected twice, becoming the first individual elected by the people of Indiana to serve three terms.

Moving to Washington, D.C., Capehart opposed President Harry S. Truman's various liberal reform policies, such as the Employment Act of 1946 and federal intervention in disputes between management and organized labor, calling them no different from the New Deal, which he considered "socialistic." Private enterprise and not the government, he believed, was the source of jobs and production. He opposed Truman's program of aid to Europe, including the Marshall Plan and the concept of collective security. Then during the early 1950s, the Hoosier senator joined with right-wing GOP colleagues William E. Jenner of Indiana and Joseph R. McCarthy of Wisconsin in condemning Truman for allegedly allowing Communists to infiltrate the U.S. government.

Fortunately, this strident, partisan side of Capehart did not last. With the Republicans' successes in the 1952 elections leading to GOP control of the Eighty-third Congress of 1953–1954, he softened his tone and repudiated the red-baiting of McCarthy and Jenner. As chairman of the Banking and Currency Committee in those years, he initiated fruitful studies of trade relations with Latin America and of fraud in the Federal Housing Administration. He supported the domestic and foreign policies of the recently elected Republican president, Dwight D. Eisenhower, and in 1955 he was instrumental in the passage of a military housing bill. He also became a member of the Foreign Relations Committee, and by the time he left office he was the senior GOP member.

His third term in the Senate (which began in 1957) coincided with a lessening of public confidence in the Eisenhower administration, highlighted by accusations by Senator John F. Kennedy that President Eisenhower had allowed the Soviet Union to forge ahead in nuclear missiles. Capehart tried to defend the president but also criticized him for inviting the Soviet leader, Nikita Khrushchev, to the United States in 1959. He reserved his sharpest criticisms for Kennedy following his election to the presidency, first condemning the failed Central Intelligence Agency–sponsored Bay of Pigs operation of 1961 and then accusing the president in 1962 of allowing the Soviets to install missiles in Cuba. Capehart advocated a Cuban blockade to obtain the removal of the Soviet weapons. Kennedy, as he undertook this very course during the Cuban missile crisis of October 1962, worried that events had made Capehart look like a prophet.

Capehart suffered defeat in his 1962 bid for reelection at a time when hope was sweeping urban Indiana and a new generation was entering politics. His successful opponent, Birch E. Bayh, was young, handsome, and an aggressive debater. Bayh projected the same dynamism as Kennedy, while Capehart appeared as the paunchy, balding, elder politician. Nonetheless, Bayh won by only 10,944 votes. Retiring from politics, Capehart lived in Indianapolis, developed real estate, farmed (commuting to Daviess County on weekends), served as a court-appointed trustee of pension funds, and was a guest speaker in college classes at Indiana University. He died in Indianapolis.

As a senator and businessman, the self-made Capehart made mistakes but balanced them with his enthusiasm and an ability to learn. He contributed to the atmosphere in which McCarthy stifled civil liberties.

And he failed until 1953 to see that the United States could not retreat from world affairs. But he was attractive to businessmen, midwestern farmers, veterans, and middle-class Americans to whom he had demonstrated by his personal experience as an entrepreneur that Americans could overcome economic depression and foreign aggression. (He attributed the allied victory in World War II to the combination of military prowess and American industrial strength.) In the absence of evidence from the Soviet archives one can only speculate, but had policymakers heeded his advice regarding the threat of Communist expansion and excessive American spending, the Cold War might have been made less dangerous and costly. He wanted the United States to remain strong militarily, but, seeing the Soviet competition as primarily political and economic, he felt the Truman and later the Kennedy administrations misunderstood the threat and relied too heavily on building military force.

• The primary material on Capehart's life and career is located in Indianapolis; his personal papers are in the possession of his son Homer Earl Capehart, Jr., and his senate papers are in the manuscripts department of the Indiana Division of Indiana State Library. The Lilly Library at Indiana University in Bloomington contains the tapes and transcripts of an oral history of Capehart produced by the Indiana University oral history project. For additional information see William B. Pickett, *Homer E. Capehart: A Senator's Life, 1897–1979* (1990). Capehart's childhood appears in "A Little Sound Ignorance" (unpublished ms., 1943), a study done for a campaign biography. His business creed appears in *Creative Selling* (1929), a manual he wrote for his salesmen. "The Capehart," *Fortune*, Feb. 1941, pp. 122–25, and John Krivine, *Jukebox Saturday Night* (1977), describe his activities in the jukebox industry. For Indiana politics at the time of Capehart's entry into it, see James H. Madison, *Tradition and Change: A History of the Hoosier State and Its People 1920–1945* (1982). Capehart's activities as a supporter of McCarthy appear in David M. Oshinsky, *A Conspiracy So Immense: The World of Joe McCarthy* (1975), and Robert Griffith, *The Politics of Fear: Joseph R. McCarthy and the Senate* (1970). For a discussion of Capehart's conflicts with Kennedy, see Herbert Parmet, *JFK: The Presidency of John F. Kennedy* (1983), and Arthur M. Schlesinger, Jr., *Robert F. Kennedy and His Times* (1978). Capehart's role in the Cuban missile crisis is in Thomas G. Patterson and William J. Brophy, "October Missiles and November Elections: The Cuban Missile Crisis and American Politics, 1962," *Journal of American History* (June 1986): 87–119. A summary of his life and contributions appeared in the *Indianapolis Star*, 5 Sept. 1979.

WILLIAM B. PICKETT

CAPEN, Samuel Paul (21 Mar. 1878–22 June 1956), first director of the American Council on Education and college chancellor, was born in Somerville, Massachusetts, the son of Elmer Hewitt Capen, then president of Tufts College, and Mary Leavitt Edwards. Capen grew up in an academic family. The only son of a college president known for his broad interests and progressive ideas, Capen witnessed at close hand his father's educational policies and practices at Tufts. Capen himself attended Tufts, where he received both an A.B. and A.M. in 1898, with honorable mention in German and French. He was president of his senior class and one of four students chosen to deliver a commencement address. In 1900 Capen received another A.M. from Harvard, and, following a year at Leipzig, received his Ph.D. in modern languages at the University of Pennsylvania.

Capen began his career in 1902 as an instructor in modern languages at the newly formed Clark College, an experimental undergraduate school formed within Clark University. Since its founding in 1889 in Worcester, Massachusetts, the university had existed without any undergraduate department. Clark College was organized in an effort to link the university with a conventional liberal arts college. Capen's experiences and observations while at Clark would later provide fertile ground for the development of many of his ideas about colleges and universities. After twelve years at Clark, Capen had risen to the rank of professor of German and broadened his teaching to include educational administration. In 1908 he married the president's daughter Grace Duncan Wright. They had one child.

In 1914 Capen left Clark for Washington, D.C., where he took the post of specialist in higher education in the Bureau of Education (precursor to the U.S. Office of Education). He was in charge of the division dealing with colleges and universities. Because his work entailed preparing annual reports on educational movements and conditions throughout the country, preparing statistics, and conducting special investigations of university and college problems, Capen quickly gained a reputation as a systematic observer and adviser. Requests for information from the various state educational authorities began to increase, and, as they did, Capen's influence broadened. From 1915 to 1919 he directed surveys in Washington, Oregon, Nevada, Arizona, South Dakota, Iowa, North Carolina, and Alabama. All dealt wholly or in part with state institutions. He made subsequent recommendations not only for changes in organization but also for fundamental reforms in teaching methods and the modernization of standards and curricula. With these studies Capen was tilling new ground, for there were no precedents to follow.

With World War I came establishment of the Committee on Education under the direction of the Council of National Defense. The committee was charged with coordinating the university interests of the country, avoiding duplication, and using the resources of America's colleges and universities to further various war enterprises. Capen, appointed the first executive secretary, inherited a difficult assignment. Apart from the Bureau of Education there was as yet no central cooperative organization to provide the forum necessary to carry out the charge of the committee. During the last few months of the war, representatives of the Association of American Colleges, the Association of American Universities, the Catholic Education Association, and the National Association of State Universities formed the American Council on Education (ACE). In 1918 Capen was appointed temporary chairman of the new organization and, from 1919 to

1922 served as director until leaving to assume chancellorship of the University of Buffalo. At the next annual meeting in 1923 he was elected chairman, a post that carried with it membership on the executive committee. Even after his tenure as chairman had expired, he continued to be reelected to this committee until 1940. In 1920 Capen founded the ACE journal *Educational Record* and served as editor until 1922. Though his tenure at ACE was brief, throughout his career Capen was regarded as its chief designing architect and the one who outlined the philosophical underpinnings of the organization.

When Capen arrived at the University of Buffalo he found a collection of professional schools that were dependent on tuition fees. Buildings and equipment were so antiquated that some faculty feared a loss of accreditation. Students numbered about 900, full-time faculty not more than twenty. Here was Capen's opportunity to assume leadership of a major institution and to put into practice the educational ideas he had developed through his experiences at Clark, the Bureau of Education, and ACE.

Capen had already turned down several college presidencies but was intrigued by the University of Buffalo offer because the struggling institution was at a crossroads. The prospect of reform moved him to go there. In his inaugural address on 28 October 1922 he said, "A few American colleges are now experimenting with honors courses. . . . But none of these experiments . . . yet goes far enough. . . . professional schools also stand in need of reconstruction." And later, in reference to Buffalo's standing among America's colleges and universities, he commented, "Has the University of Buffalo the courage to be different? . . . a university may be developed here that will challenge nation-wide attention."

Though the University of Buffalo did not achieve great national fame, Capen's initiatives characterized measures that brought coherence and academic excellence to the modern American university in its distinctive combination of undergraduate collegiate education integrated with graduate and professional studies. His accomplishments there hinged on more selective admissions and curricular innovations in all units. Within the undergraduate college he implemented a tutorial system—unique at the time—whereby students could pursue independent study under the direction of individual faculty members. By 1931 all upperclassmen were taking a combination of course work and independent study. Capen also strengthened the professional schools, particularly those in medicine and dentistry, by hiring a full-time faculty. And, as part of his vision of the contemporary urban university, he created strong relationships between the campus and the community. He retired from the university in 1950 and died in Buffalo six years later.

As a young instructor at Clark College, Capen had been honored in 1911 by the senior class as their favorite professor, the brightest, the most pleasant, the best lecturer, the best teacher. He was a strong academic administrator with a sense of purpose, one who defined the role of a college president as that of "a champion of freedom for teachers and students." In criticizing his politics, a colleague once said that Capen "ought to have lived in the nineteenth century," to which Capen replied, "Oh, longer ago than that, in the eighteenth" (Park, p. 52). Capen's career reflects an era in American higher education that has long since passed: an era of growth predicated on the freedom to experiment and to go in new directions. He provided leadership during an era when higher education was fueled by optimism.

Capen served as chancellor of Buffalo for twenty-eight years. By the time of his retirement he had become a nationally known authority in college and university planning whose commitment to academic freedom was matched only by his dislike of the growing "standardization" in higher education, particularly as reflected in mechanistic procedures adopted by some accrediting agencies. Throughout his career—from instructor at Clark College through bureaucratic service with the federal government through his tenure at the American Council on Education to his lengthy tenure at Buffalo—Capen sought out opportunities to put into practice his pioneering ideas in educational administration.

• In 1953, on Capen's seventy-fifth birthday, the University of Buffalo published a volume of his essays and addresses, *The Management of Universities*, a distillation of his philosophy of college administration. The archives of SUNY–Buffalo contain Capen's "Undated Biography to 1922" as well as Douglas Crone's 1967 D.Ed. dissertation, "An Historical Study of the Development of the Educational and Administrative Ideas of Samuel Paul Capen." Also the reader is directed to Julian Park, "Samuel P. Capen, 1878–1956," *University of Buffalo Studies* (Oct. 1957): 5–58. For substantive discussion of Capen and the ACE, see Hugh Hawkins, *Banding Together: The Rise of National Associations in American Higher Education, 1887–1950* (1992). An obituary is in the *New York Times*, 23 June 1956. Tributes were also run in *Educational Record*, July 1956 and Jan. 1957.

JOHN R. THELIN
SHARON THELIN-BLACKBURN

CAPERS, Ellison (14 Oct. 1837–22 Apr. 1908), Confederate soldier and Episcopal clergyman, was born in Charleston, South Carolina, the son of William Capers, a Methodist bishop, and Susan McGill. After attending the private schools of his native city, he was graduated in 1857 from the South Carolina Military Academy. He taught mathematics at his alma mater and for a year was on the staff of a college in Winnsboro, South Carolina. Early in 1859 he married Charlotte Palmer; they had nine children.

Following South Carolina's secession in December 1860, Capers joined a volunteer regiment, of which he was soon elected major. The following April the unit participated in the bombardment of Fort Sumter; for his commendable service, Capers became lieutenant colonel of the outfit into which his original unit evolved, the Twenty-fourth South Carolina Infantry. For two years thereafter, he served with the regiment in defending his native state. In early June 1862 Capers distinguished himself during a skirmish on the southern end of James Island, leading the Twenty-fourth South Carolina and some attached troops in a charge that captured parts of three Union regiments. Two weeks later, during the battle of Secessionville, Capers's regiment held the Confederate left flank and helped repulse a series of Union attacks.

In May 1863, following the repulse of a major enemy effort to take Charleston by sea, Brigadier General S. R. Gist's brigade, which included the Twenty-fourth South Carolina, was transferred to Mississippi to augment the army of Joseph E. Johnston at a critical phase of the Vicksburg campaign. Due to feeble transportation facilities, the South Carolinians failed to reach Johnston in time for the battle of Raymond (12 May), but two days later they engaged Ulysses S. Grant's Federals near the state capital of Jackson. Although the fight ended in Union victory, General Gist lauded Capers's regiment, particularly those companies under his personal leadership that created confusion among several Union regiments and drove them from the field. In the fight Capers sustained a wound that failed to keep him out of action for long.

After Vicksburg's fall, Gist's command was sent to Braxton Bragg's Army of Tennessee for the Chickamauga-Chattanooga campaign. On the second day at Chickamauga (20 Sept.), the brigade advanced to the support of embattled comrades and held its ground throughout the engagement despite devastating fire. The Twenty-fourth South Carolina was at the forefront, and Capers was again wounded, recovering to lead his regiment two months later at Missionary Ridge. In January 1864, following Bragg's retreat to northern Georgia, Capers's combat record gained him the colonelcy of his outfit, succeeding the recently promoted Brigadier General Clement H. Stevens. At the start of the spring 1864 campaign, Capers noted, "Gist's brigade was in fine condition for the work before it, and no part of it in better trim than the Twenty-fourth."

At his new rank, Capers commanded his South Carolinians throughout the Atlanta campaign. The regiment fought effectively on 16 May in the aftermath of Resaca, when it charged and forced the retreat of a Union battery. The high point of Capers's participation in the Atlanta campaign occurred on 1 September at Jonesboro, where his outfit, holding the extreme right of Lieutenant General William J. Hardee's corps, stood firm against an afternoon-long series of attacks. At Hardee's order the regiment finally withdrew in good order, even amid the confusion of Confederate defeat.

At the start of John Bell Hood's autumn campaign, Capers for a time commanded Gist's brigade before reverting to regimental command early in October. On the march that eventually took the Army of Tennessee to Nashville, the brigade performed ably in many engagements, especially on 16 October at Ship's Gap and on 30 November at Franklin. In the latter engagement, Gist was mortally wounded, and Capers took another wound leading his regiment up to the enemy's works under a blizzard of rifle and artillery fire. The colonel noted proudly, "No command of the army fought with more spirit and heroic determination at Franklin than the Twenty-fourth South Carolina Volunteers."

On 1 March 1865, having recovered from his latest wound, Capers was promoted to brigadier general and assigned permanent command of Gist's brigade, which he led through the remainder of the war in the West. Returning in May to his home in Anderson, South Carolina, he contemplated a legal and political career; seven months later he was elected South Carolina's secretary of state. In 1867 he sought a higher constituency by entering the Episcopalian ministry, the religion of past generations of his family. For twenty years (broken only by a one-year ministry in Selma, Ala.) he served as rector of Christ Church, Greenville, South Carolina. From 1887 to 1893 he was the rector at Trinity Church, in Columbia, during which time he received a doctor of divinity degree from the state university. In 1893 he was consecrated assistant bishop of South Carolina, and in 1904 he was elected chancellor of the University of the South, Sewanee, Tennessee. Until his death Capers also served as chaplain general of the Society of Confederate Veterans. A member of the Southern Historical Society, he wrote many articles for regional journals and in 1899 compiled the South Carolina volume in the series *Confederate Military History* (ed. Clement A. Davis).

In many of his sermons, especially those he delivered in the last decade of the nineteenth century, Capers protested social evils such as alcoholism and homicide. Perhaps his best-known attack on crime occurred in December 1897 when he addressed to the clergy of his diocese a ringing denunciation of "the crime of murder, now so prevalent in our State," an act that "degraded the sacredness of life and dishonored the courage and character of our people." Critics termed Capers's appeal "unusual and striking . . . one with few precedents, if any, in the history of the Protestant Church."

By all accounts, Capers was one of the most able and inspiring regimental and brigade leaders in the western armies of the Confederacy. His commands distinguished themselves on virtually every field, and on numerous occasions they and their leader reaped the praise of senior officers. Throughout the war, in the midst of great privation and suffering, Capers also maintained a devotion to the Christian faith; his piety inspired many of his troops as well as superiors, including Generals Gist and Hardee. Capers's ability to balance the duties of military officer and the responsibilities of a Christian layman earned him the respect of all who knew him. He died at his home in Columbia, South Carolina.

• Capers is represented by numerous collections of personal correspondence. The largest of these is a trove of almost 200 missives, including his wartime letters to his wife, at Duke University. Another large collection is in the South Caroliniana Library, University of South Carolina; the Citadel Archives-Museum contains not only much correspondence but also Capers's wartime journal. Capers's reports as regimental and brigade commander are included in *The War of the Rebellion: A Compilation of the Official Records of the Union and Confederate Armies* (128 vols., 1880–1901); his report of the battle of Jonesboro was reprinted in the *Southern Historical Society Papers* 11 (1883): 481–84. The only full-length biography is Walter B. Capers, *The Soldier-Bishop, Ellison Capers* (1912), seven chapters of which cover his war service. More modern studies of campaigns in which Capers distinguished himself include E. Milby Burton, *The Siege of Charleston, 1861–1865* (1970); Albert Castel, *Decision in the West: The Atlanta Campaign of 1864* (1992); and Wiley Sword, *Embrace an Angry Wind: The Confederacy's Last Hurrah—Spring Hill, Franklin, and Nashville* (1991). A recent biography of Capers's brigade commander, Walter Brian Cisco, *States Rights Gist: A South Carolina General of the Civil War* (1991), contains much information about Capers.

EDWARD G. LONGACRE

CAPERS, William (26 Jan. 1790–29 Jan. 1855), Methodist bishop, editor, and missionary, was born at Bull-Head Swamp plantation in St. Thomas Parish, South Carolina, the son of William Capers, a planter and former revolutionary war officer, and Mary Singeltary. William was only two years old when his mother died, and he was reared primarily by his stepmother, Mary Wragg. After being tutored at home, he attended schools in Georgetown, South Carolina, and in the High Hills, Santee. At age sixteen he entered South Carolina College, but he found his preparation in classical studies inadequate. After dropping out to study law with John S. Richardson of Stateburg, South Carolina, Capers soon abandoned that career for the ministry in the Methodist Episcopal (ME) church.

Awakened to the spiritual life at a camp meeting at Rembert's settlement in 1806, Capers joined the denomination two years later and moved immediately into exhorter's and local preacher's roles before being admitted on trial into the South Carolina Annual Conference in December 1808. Successful as a preacher to both white and black converts, he held appointments on the Wateree Circuit, in Fayetteville and Wilmington, North Carolina, and in Charleston. In 1810 the conference ordained him as a deacon in full connection, and two years later he became an elder in the ME church. In 1813 he married Anna White; they had one child.

In 1814 Capers left the traveling ministry to tend to his father's farm and to relieve his wife from the burden of being the spouse of a Methodist itinerant. Capers's wife died in childbirth on 20 December 1815. For the next two years he combined farming, teaching, and local ministerial work before rejoining the South Carolina Methodist Conference in January 1818. He married Susan McGill in October 1816; they had eight children.

Following pastorates in Columbia and Savannah, Capers served as the superintendent of missions to the Creek Indians in Georgia and Alabama from 1821 to 1825. He spent the next four years in Charleston as a preacher, a presiding elder, and the editor of the *Wesleyan Journal* (Oct. 1825–Mar. 1827). The *Journal* was a weekly Methodist newspaper that ceased being published when it merged with the *Christian Advocate and Journal* of New York. In 1829 Capers allied himself with Charles Cotesworth Pinckney and other planters to begin Methodist plantation missions in South Carolina. The evangelization of the slaves spread to other states, becoming for white Christians in the South the religious alternative to emancipation. In 1832 Capers published the first of several catechisms for the program.

While Capers was pastor for a third time in Charleston in 1833–1834, a controversy arose over seating arrangements for slave, free black, and white communicants. It provoked a secession by some white members, who tried but failed to seize control of the church property held in trust for the South Carolina Methodist Conference. The conflict resulted in Capers becoming involved in a local pamphlet war with the seceders, with whom he had struggled to find a solution. After moving to Savannah to escape the crisis, Capers became a professor of moral and intellectual philosophy at South Carolina College. Expecting that the presidency of the school was to accompany the appointment, Capers declined the offer after being reassigned to the school chaplaincy and a teaching post in evidences of Christianity and sacred literature. From 1836 to 1840 he was the first editor of the *Southern Christian Advocate*, a Methodist weekly in which Capers opposed abolitionist influences in the denomination, supported the right of slaveholders to be church members and clergymen, and championed plantation missions. From 1840 to 1844 he was the superintendent of missions across the South.

By 1844, when the ME church split sectionally over the question of slavery, Capers had become a major spokesman for white southern Methodists. He had been a delegate to all quadrennial General Conferences since 1820, and he was the fraternal representative from the American church to the British Wesleyan Conference in 1828. If he had not been a slaveholder, he might have been elected as a bishop or as the editor of the national *Christian Advocate and Journal*. When the General Conference of 1844 requested that his friend, Bishop James O. Andrew, resign because he owned slaves, Capers urged otherwise, saying "his resignation would inflict an incurable wound on the whole South and inevitably lead to division in the Church" (George G. Smith, *Life of James Osgood Andrew* [1882], p. 343). When the national church divided as he predicted, Capers assumed new leadership, chairing the organizing convention of the Methodist Episcopal Church, South (MECS) in 1845 and advancing into its episcopacy at its General Conference the next year.

For eight years as bishop, Capers traveled the region to hold conferences, kept his catechisms in print, celebrated the success of slave missions, and enjoyed the achievements of his children. Espousing the spiritual identity of the church as a protection against overt involvement in politics, Capers advocated the removal of all Methodist rules about slavery for the southern church. He did correspond with Secretary of State John C. Calhoun over the consequences of the sectional division of Methodism in 1844. And in February 1851 he publicly cautioned South Carolina secessionists not to undermine national unity. An alleged letter from him in 1854 forecasting the doom of slavery and the probability of civil war was published in the *Methodist* in New York in 1875. (Despite his family's approval to publish it, most southern Methodists and the only modern biographer of Capers did not consider the letter authentic.)

When Capers died of a heart attack in Anderson, South Carolina, he had earned the reputation of being a founder of Methodist missions to the slaves across the South and of the MECS—a denomination that existed as a separate body until 1939.

• Capers's manuscripts are in several collections, but most are held at the South Carolina Methodist Historical Society at Wofford College in Spartanburg. William D. Wightman, *Life of William Capers* (1859), contains his autobiography to 1821. A complete bibliography of his writings, except for specific contributions to the Methodist newspapers that he edited, is in the only modern study of Capers: Duncan Alexander Reily, "William Capers: An Evaluation of His Life and Thought" (Ph.D. diss. Emory Univ. 1972). A study of his ideas is Harmon L. Smith, "William Capers and William A. Smith: Neglected Advocates of the Pro-Slavery Argument," *Methodist History* 3 (1964): 23–32.

WILL GRAVELY

CAPERTON, William Banks (30 June 1855–21 Dec. 1941), admiral, U.S. Navy, was born in Spring Hill, Tennessee, the son of Samuel B. Caperton and Mary Jane Childress. Following Caperton's early education at Spring Hill Academy, in 1871 Congressman Washington C. Whitthorne gave him an appointment as midshipman at the U.S. Naval Academy. Caperton graduated from the academy in 1875 and served for two years as a passed midshipman on board the USS *Hartford* under the command of Captain Stephen B. Luce. Commissioned an ensign in 1877, Caperton was at sea for the next five years, serving successively on board the screw steamer USS *Powatan*, the frigate USS *Constellation*, and the USS *Tennessee*, the flagship of the North Atlantic Squadron. In January 1880 he received orders to serve with the Coast Survey. Over the next three years he served on the survey steamers *Gedney* and *Bache*, making hydrographic surveys on the coasts of Texas, Florida, South Carolina, North Carolina, and in Long Island Sound.

In November 1883 Caperton reported on board the screw sloop USS *Ossipee* for duty on the China Station. In January 1884, in Chemulpo, Korea, he joined the USS *Trenton*, on which he served until the spring of 1887. Returning to the United States, he took up naval duties as inspector of steel at the Homestead Steel Works and the Linden Steel Works in Pittsburgh, Pennsylvania, where he remained until 1888. In November of that year he went to Washington, D.C., and took up new duties as secretary of the Steel Inspection Board. He remained in Washington until 1891. There he served as a member of the Bunce Board on Navy Yard Reorganization before briefly serving as recorder of the Naval Examining Board in Norfolk, Virginia, during the summer of 1891.

In October 1891 Caperton began three years of sea duty in the North Atlantic, the West Indies, and in European waters, serving on the monitor USS *Miantonomah*, the dynamite cruiser USS *Vesuvius*, and the sail training ship USS *Essex*, respectively. In January 1895 he reported to the Office of Naval Intelligence. While assigned to that office Caperton attended the Naval War College at Newport, Rhode Island, in 1896. In November of that year he was sent to the cruiser USS *Brooklyn*, then being fitted out for its first assignment as flagship for Rear Admiral Joseph N. Miller, representing the U.S. Navy at Queen Victoria's Diamond Jubilee in 1897.

In September 1897 Caperton was assigned as executive officer of the newly built schooner-rigged gunboat USS *Marietta* on the Pacific Station, cruising in Alaska and in Central and South American waters. At the outbreak of the Spanish-American War the *Marietta* joined the battleship USS *Oregon* in April 1898 and sailed with it through the Straits of Magellan for duty off the coast of Cuba. During the war the *Marietta* participated in the blockade of Havana, cleared mines in Cuban waters, and visited Latin American ports.

Caperton returned to shore duty in October 1899 as inspector of ordnance at the Naval Gun Factory in the Washington Navy Yard. Leaving that assignment in July 1901, he joined the steam training ship USS *Prairie* as executive officer, serving in that capacity until May 1904, when he again attended the course at the Naval War College. Leaving Newport, Rhode Island, in October 1904, Caperton traveled to St. Louis, Missouri, where he became inspector of the Fifteenth Light House District for the Mississippi, Illinois, and Missouri rivers; he remained in that post until 1907. A few years later, *Waterways Journal* recalled that in this position, Caperton "was one of the most popular navy officials we ever had the pleasure of meeting" (25 [June 1912]: 1).

Caperton took up his first command in April 1907 with the cruiser USS *Denver* (C-14), sailing through the Suez Canal to the Mediterranean for assignment on the Asiatic Station. Promoted to captain in July 1908, he immediately took command of the battleship USS *Maine* (BB-10) at Cavite, Philippines, while the ship was on the world cruise of the "Great White Fleet." Owing to the *Maine*'s high coal consumption, the Navy Department ordered Caperton to return with the ship to the United States in October 1908, well in advance of the rest of the fleet, to serve as flagship of the Third Squadron, Atlantic Fleet. Upon the decommissioning of the *Maine*, Caperton became secretary of the Light House Board in October 1909, with an office at the Department of Commerce and Labor in Washington, D.C. In June 1910 he attended the summer course at the Naval War College for the third time and then returned to Washington for duty as a member of the Naval Examining and Naval Retiring Board.

From May 1912 to October 1913 Caperton served as commandant of the Second Naval District and commandant of the naval station in Newport and Narragansett Bay, Rhode Island. While in that position he was promoted to rear admiral. He took command in November 1913 of the Atlantic Reserve Fleet, flying his flag in the battleship USS *Alabama* (BB-8) while training the naval militia of several states. A year later Caperton took command of the Atlantic Fleet Cruiser Squadron with the armored cruiser USS *Washington* as his flagship.

In January 1915 Caperton, on the *Washington*, commanded the forces that President Woodrow Wilson had ordered to Haiti in response to unrest in that republic. Authorized to act on his own discretion and believing that the United States should keep forces in Haiti indefinitely to maintain stability, Caperton and his chief of staff, Captain Edward L. Beach, intervened in local politics to ensure the election of Haitian Senate president Philippe Sudre Dartiguenave as president of the republic. Subsequently they negotiated a treaty for U.S. officials to administer government services.

Upon news of the outbreak of civil war in the Dominican Republic in May 1916, Caperton sailed to Santo Domingo in the dispatch boat USS *Dolphin* (PG-24). He directed the landing and occupation of the country after the collapse of political stability there.

In July 1916 President Wilson promoted Caperton to full admiral as commander in chief of the Pacific Fleet, flying his flag in the armored cruiser USS *Pittsburgh*. When the United States entered World War I, the Navy Department ordered Caperton, with the Pacific Fleet, to the South Atlantic. There he supervised patrols of the east coast of South America to guard against German raiders. In addition, he used the fleet in diplomatic duties to help foster better relations with Latin American countries. President Wilson named Caperton ambassador extraordinary and plenipotentiary, as the representative of the United States for the inauguration in 1919 of President Francisco Rodrigues Alves of Brazil, and as special naval delegate at the inauguration of President Baltasar Brum of Uruguay. In 1919 Acting Secretary of the Navy Franklin D. Roosevelt awarded him the Distinguished Service Medal for his service as fleet commander "in establishing friendly diplomatic relations with the countries of South America."

Caperton officially retired from the navy on 30 June 1919 but continued on temporary active duty to serve as naval aide to President-elect Epitácio Pessôa of Brazil during his official visit to the United States following the death of President Alves. Caperton then remained on temporary active duty in the office of the chief of naval operations, serving as a witness before the Senate Committee on the Occupation of Haiti. Relieved of all active duty in November 1921, Caperton retired to Newport, Rhode Island, where he eventually made his home in an apartment at the Hotel Viking.

Caperton's personality was most aptly captured by Jesse S. Cottrell, a journalist for the *Nashville Banner* (9 Oct. 1915): "there is nothing unusual about Admiral Caperton when devotion to duty is regarded the usual complement of a naval officer. But all who know him, admire and like him and his kindly ways and quiet unassuming manner." His hobby has been "a clean ship and fit men," and he "despises the highbrow crowd in the Navy."

Caperton was married to Georgie Washington Langhorne Blacklock. They had one child.

Caperton was a founder and honorary member of the Military Order Foreign Wars of the United States and served as commanding general from 1914 to 1917. He died in Newport, Rhode Island, and was buried in Arlington National Cemetery.

• Caperton's papers are in three locations. The largest and most important collection is in the Naval Historical Foundation Collection at the Library of Congress. The remainder are divided between the Tennessee State Museum in Nashville and the Naval Historical Collection at the Naval War College. David Healy, *Gunboat Diplomacy in the Wilson Era: The U.S. Navy in Haiti, 1915–1916* (1976), gives a detailed account of Caperton and the occupation along with a detailed bibliography. This is placed in broad perspective in Donald A. Yerxa, *Admirals and Empire; The United States Navy in the Caribbean, 1898–1945* (1991), pp. 39–49, 80–81. Robert E. Johnson, *Thence Round Cape Horn: The Story of United States Naval Forces on Pacific Station, 1818–1923* (1963), discusses Caperton's command during World War I. A long obituary is in the *Newport Mercury*, 26 Dec. 1941.

JOHN B. HATTENDORF

CAPONE, Al (17 Jan. 1899–25 Jan. 1947), Chicago bootlegger and symbolic crime figure, was born Alphonse Capone in Brooklyn, New York, the son of Gabriel Capone, a barber, and Teresa Raiola, both immigrants from the Naples region of Italy. At age fourteen, Capone dropped out of school, joined the gang life of the streets, and soon worked as a bartender and bouncer on Coney Island. In 1917, in a brawl with a customer, he received the knife wound that earned him the media nickname "Scarface" (although his friends called him "Snorky"). In December 1918 he married Mary "Mae" Coughlin, the daughter of a laborer.

There is disagreement concerning when Capone arrived in Chicago to work in the rackets run by John Torrio, another transplanted New Yorker. Torrio was a partner of James "Big Jim" Colosimo, a famous Chicago restaurateur and entrepreneur in Chicago's notorious South Side redlight district. In May 1920, shortly after the beginning of Prohibition, Colosimo was assassinated, and Torrio thereafter oversaw the redlight activities while expanding rapidly into bootlegging. By most accounts, Capone was in Chicago in time to assist Torrio in planning Colosimo's assassination, and he certainly worked with Torrio afterward in managing redlight activities in Chicago and the suburbs and in developing the illegal liquor business. As the bootlegging expanded, Capone brought his brothers, Ralph and Salvatore (Frank), to Chicago to assist in the operations. Emphasizing wholesaling, the Torrio operation supplied liquor to speakeasies in the downtown Loop and in several suburbs west and south of the city while also selling liquor to bootleggers in other parts of the city. By 1923 Torrio had patched together a loose territorial agreement with other bootleggers.

In April 1924 Capone began to capture the headlines that would make him America's most famous criminal. He organized gunmen to control an election in Cicero, a town west of Chicago. Although his brother Frank was killed in a shootout with the police, his candidates won, and Capone and his associates expanded their participation in Cicero gambling houses.

Soon afterward the truce among Chicago bootleggers collapsed. In January 1925 Torrio pleaded guilty to an earlier bootlegging charge and a week later was shot and seriously wounded in front of his home. On release from the hospital in February, he began a nine-month sentence and made plans to return to New York. In late 1925 Capone became the most famous member of the coalition that took over Torrio's Chicago operations.

To coordinate their varied enterprises, Capone and his associates worked out a set of partnerships within an essentially decentralized system. There were four senior partners—Al Capone, his older brother Ralph, their cousin Frank Nitti, and Jack Guzik—who split their profits more or less evenly. These four supported an entourage that hung out at their headquarters in Chicago's Metropole Hotel beginning in 1925 and the Lexington Hotel in 1928. To operate their enterprises, the senior partners gave a share of the profits to those who provided day-to-day oversight of a gambling house, bootlegging operation, parlor house, or other activity. Among the senior partners, Capone often exercised leadership because of his dominating personality, his occasionally volcanic temper, and his willingness to take decisive action. Because he was frequently absent from the city, however, the other partners assumed much of the oversight.

Capone achieved notoriety in part because Chicago's bootlegging wars were more violent and persistent than those in other cities. Among the high points of the beer wars were the 10 November 1924 shooting of North Side bootlegger Dion O'Banion in his flower shop; the April 1926 assassination of Assistant State Attorney William H. McSwiggin; the widely reported October 1926 peace treaty of two months' duration, negotiated by leading Chicago bootleggers in a hotel room; the April 1928 "Pineapple Primary" bombings to aid the candidates backed by Capone ally Mayor William Hale "Big Bill" Thompson; and finally the notorious St. Valentine's Day massacre of 1929, which eliminated the North Side gang as a serious rival. Through it all, Capone was available to the press, acknowledged the cheers of the crowds at sporting events, drove down Michigan Avenue in his armored car, threw large tips to waiters and newsboys, and gloried in the attention he received.

Through it all, too, Capone and his growing network of associates expanded their business activities and political influence. As their wholesale activities grew, they developed contacts to obtain imported liquor from Detroit, New York, and Miami; diverted industrial alcohol from Philadelphia; and purchased beer from towns in Wisconsin and downstate Illinois. After the St. Valentine's Day massacre, Capone's associates expanded the wholesaling of liquor to the growing nightclub district on the Near North Side, and some became owners of nightclubs. In 1927, in addition, the senior partners joined Edward J. O'Hare to establish the Hawthorn Kennel Club in Cicero for dog racing. Extending their influence, members of Capone's group provided protection for labor racketeers or became labor racketeers themselves.

Capone's notoriety, however, placed him under pressure and removed him from daily oversight of operations. In autumn 1927 Mayor Thompson, pursuing unrealistic presidential ambitions, ordered his police chief to harass Capone out of Chicago. That winter Capone moved to Florida and in March 1928 purchased a mansion on Palm Island in Miami Beach. Although he periodically returned to Chicago, he mostly lived in informal exile, and his influence waned. In May 1929, after attending a conference of leading bootleggers in Atlantic City, Capone was arrested while changing trains in Philadelphia and received a year's sentence for carrying a concealed weapon.

When Capone left the Philadelphia jail on 17 March 1930, his partners were in trouble for tax evasion, and federal authorities were under instructions from President Herbert Hoover to put Capone in prison. The Internal Revenue Service probed his Chicago and Florida finances while the Prohibition bureau investigated his bootlegging. In March and June 1931 Capone was indicted for income tax fraud. At first he agreed to plead guilty in return for a short sentence, but when the judge refused to be bound by the agreement, Capone withdrew his plea. In October a federal jury found him guilty on five of twenty-three counts. The judge sentenced him to eleven years in prison plus fines and court costs.

When the U.S. Supreme Court refused to hear his appeal on 2 May 1932, Capone was transferred from the Cook County jail to the federal penitentiary in Atlanta, Georgia. In August 1934, when a maximum-security prison was opened at Alcatraz in San Francisco Bay, Capone was among its first occupants. In early February 1938, doctors confirmed a diagnosis of syphilis of the brain. Released on 16 November 1939 (with reduced time for good behavior), he sought treatment in a Baltimore hospital and then retired to his Palm Island estate with his wife and only son. Before dying from a stroke in Miami, he alternated between periods of recovery and periods of increasing mental and physical deterioration.

Capone was a major underworld leader from late 1925 until late 1927, when his absence from Chicago reduced his involvement. At age thirty-two, Capone's influence ended completely with his last tax-fraud conviction, but his myth, exaggerating his brief career, had barely begun. Through media coverage, numerous exciting biographies, several movies, and a popular television series ("The Untouchables"), he came to represent the violence of Chicago in the 1920s and the place of crime in American society during and after Prohibition.

• There are two important manuscript sources for studying Capone. One is the extensive files of the Chicago Crime Commission, which assembled newspaper clippings and investigative files on Capone and his associates through the 1920s and after. The other is the raw investigative file (no. SI 7085-F) assembled by the Intelligence Bureau of the IRS during its income tax investigation. This file—containing grand jury testimony, informants' reports, records seized from gambling houses, and other materials—has been closed since 1973.

The most thoroughly documented biographies of Capone are Robert J. Schoenberg, *Mr. Capone* (1992), and Laurence Bergreen, *Capone: The Man and the Era* (1994), both of which also include lists of primary sources. A careful earlier study is John Kobler, *Capone: The Life and World of Al Capone* (1971). All three books deal chiefly with the beer wars and assassinations rather than with Capone's business activities. Capone's life has also been the subject of numerous popular and journalistic studies that helped create his notoriety. Among these are Fred D. Pasley, *Al Capone: The Biography of a Self-Made Man* (1930); James O'Donnell Bennett, *Chicago Gang Land: The True Story of Chicago Crime* (1929); Walter Noble Burns, *The One-Way Ride: The Red Trail of Chicago Gangland from Prohibition to Jake Lingle* (1931); and Edward D. Sullivan, *Rattling the Cup on Chicago Crime* (1929). While these books contain inside information based on the reporters' knowledge, none is footnoted.

There have also been works looking at Capone from the point of view of law enforcement. Best known is Eliot Ness, with Oscar Fraley, *The Untouchables: The Real Story* (1957). One of the IRS agents described the income tax investigation in Elmer L. Irey, as told to William J. Slocum, *The Tax Dodgers: The Inside Story of the T-Men's War with America's Political and Underworld Hoodlums* (1948), chap. 2. For an analysis by a reporter who had access to the IRS files, see Hank Messick, *Secret File* (1969), chap. 2. Robert Ross, *The Trial of Al Capone* (1933), provides excerpts and summaries of Capone's trial and appeal. For an analysis of the official investigations, see Dennis E. Hoffman, *Scarface Al and the Crime Crusaders: Chicago's Private War against Capone* (1993), and James Calder, *The Origins and Development of Federal Crime Control Policy* (1993).

Some scholarly studies place Capone in a historical context. Most important is David E. Ruth, "Inventing the Public Enemy: the Gangster in American Culture, 1918–1934" (Ph.D. diss., Northwestern Univ., 1992), which uses Capone as the chief example in an incisive exploration of the mythology that surrounded the criminals of the 1920s. Humbert S. Nelli, *Italians in Chicago, 1880–1930: A Study in Ethnic Mobility* (1970), places Capone's activities in the context of the Chicago Italian community. Mark H. Haller, "Illegal Enterprise: A Theoretical and Historical Interpretation," *Criminology* 28 (May 1990): 215–23, briefly analyzes the structure of Capone's business operations.

MARK H. HALLER

CAPOTE, Truman (30 Sept. 1924–25 Aug. 1984), writer, was born Truman Streckfus Persons in New Orleans, the son of Arch Persons, a salesman and drifter, and sixteen-year-old Lillie Mae "Nina" Faulk. His parents' turbulent marriage dissolved when Truman was six. After his mother entered business colleges in Selma, Alabama, and Bowling Green, Kentucky, in 1929, Truman—who had been neglected and psychologically abused—was relegated a year later to her distant cousins in Monroeville, Alabama, population 1,355. "This was a very strange household," he commented once. "It consisted of three elderly ladies and an elderly uncle. They were the people who had adopted my mother—her own parents had died when she was very young. I lived there until I was ten, and it was a very lonely life, and it was then that I became interested in writing" (Roy Newquist, *Counterpoint* [1964], p. 76). In Monroeville his chief companions were his childlike guardian Sook Faulk and the young and tomboyish Harper Lee, who in later life wrote the novel *To Kill a Mockingbird* and who in the 1960s assisted Truman by gathering facts for his documentary *In Cold Blood* (1965).

When Truman's mother won a three-month scholarship to the Elizabeth Arden cosmetology school in New York in 1931, she resumed a friendship with a Cuban-American textile broker named Joseph Capote, who may have been one of her numerous lovers during Truman's infancy. They were married in 1932. In 1934, when he was not yet ten, Truman allegedly wrote his first book, a roman à clef he titled *Old Mr. Busybody*, the first installment of which appeared in the *Mobile Press Register*. The piece was strangely prophetic of his incomplete, posthumously published *Answered Prayers: The Unfinished Novel* (1987), in part an exposé of wealthy and famous people who had offended him in some way. So too in *Old Mr. Busybody*, Capote commented, when "somebody realized that I was serving up a local scandal," the story was killed.

In the meantime, a protracted custody battle ended after Arch Persons pled guilty to forging post office money orders. In 1935 Truman Streckfus Persons became Truman Garcia Capote when he was legally adopted in New York. His literary interests continued unabated, however, and by the age of eleven he claimed to have formed a devotion to Willa Cather, Gustave Flaubert, and Marcel Proust. In Monroeville, where he continued to spend his summers until 1939, he was rightly regarded as effeminate. "I didn't feel as if I were imprisoned in the wrong body. I wasn't transsexual. I just felt things would be easier for me if I were a girl," he once remarked (Clarke, p. 43). In New York, Capote attended the private boys' Episcopal Trinity School for three years, and then St. John's Military Academy in Ossining for three unpleasant months in 1936, during which he was sexually exploited by other boys.

He nevertheless returned to St. John's in 1937 and apparently alluded to this school and others when he referred in "A Christmas Memory" (1956) to having attended "a miserable succession of bugle-blowing prisons." But in English classes at St. John's he continued to evidence some emergent literary talent. When the Capotes moved to Greenwich, Connecticut, he was fortunate to come under the abiding and compassionate influence of a Greenwich High School English teacher named Catherine Wood, who encouraged his writing talent and to whom "A Christmas Memory" is fondly dedicated. Other Capote tendencies later in life are traceable to his youth and childhood as well. His addiction to alcohol, he told interviewer Gloria Steinem, began when as a ten-year-old he wrote through the night (something he continued to do as a mature writer) and found himself unable to relax until he "discovered whiskey." His mother also discovered whiskey and carried on her own lifelong battle with alcoholism.

As a teenager living in Greenwich, Capote made no secret of his homosexuality—something his mother once proposed to eradicate by ordering injections of male hormones. When the family returned to New York in 1942, Capote attended the Franklin School, where he befriended Oona O'Neill (daughter of playwright Eugene O'Neill) and Gloria Vanderbilt. These friendships were an early indication of his penchant for cultivating the company of celebrities. About the age of eighteen he became a copyboy at the *New Yorker*, although his role at the magazine is clouded by contradictions that Capote himself invented. He received only rejections of his early fiction there. Editor Harold Ross dismissed him after he raised the hackles of poet Robert Frost, who mistakenly presumed Capote to be a writer on assignment from the *New Yorker* to interview him at the Bread Loaf Writers' Conference.

Returning to Monroeville, he abandoned a half-written novel and turned instead to the composition of *Other Voices, Other Rooms* (1948), a psychological and autobiographical project that absorbed three years during which he lived on the charity of relatives. He labored on the book in rented quarters on Royal Street in New Orleans's French Quarter, then continued to write in the company of scholar Newton Arvin on Nantucket Island and at the Yaddo writers' colony near Saratoga Springs, New York. *Other Voices*, he explained later, "was an attempt to exorcise demons," meaning that his protagonist Joel Knox was a modified self-portrait of the artist as a young man. During the early stages of the novel, while he was working in Alabama, he also began to publish some of his earlier fiction, such as "Miriam" (published in 1945 and recipient of an O. Henry Memorial Award), "A Tree of Night" (1945), and "Shut a Final Door" (1947). These selections alone were sufficient to launch his literary career. "The Walls Are Cold" appeared in the 1943 fourth-quarter edition of *Decade of Short Stories*. The wryly comical "My Side of the Matter" turned up in *Story* in 1945, the year that the *Prairie Schooner* carried "Preacher's Legend." "Shut a Final Door" was published in the 1946 O. Henry Memorial Award volume, the same year Capote received a $1,500 advance on *Other Voices*. At the age of twenty-three he made a first foray into criticism through an assessment of the 1946 New York theatrical season with an essay called "This Winter's Mask" in the December issue of *Harper's Bazaar*.

Random House published *Other Voices*, replete with the now famous homoerotically suggestive Harold Halma photograph of its author posed supine on a Victorian divan. "There were so many cruel things written about me at the time," he said later, "and a great deal of comment about the photograph on the back of the book (which was perfectly innocent)" (Newquist, p. 77). Initial reviews of the novel were barbed. Carlos Baker wrote in the *New York Times* that "the story of Joel Knox did not need to be told except to get it out of the author's system." An anonymous *Time* reviewer remarked that "the distasteful trappings of its homosexual theme overhang it like Spanish moss." Seemingly indifferent to critical reception, however, Capote saw to the publication of *A Tree of Night and Other Stories* (1949), a collection of seven tales; and *Local Color* (1950), an early gathering of experiments in reportage.

In a first attempt at playmaking, Capote's *The Grass Harp*, a short-running drama based upon his novel of the same title set in the rural South, was published in 1952, the same year Capote was on location with Humphrey Bogart and director John Huston in Ravello, Italy, struggling over the script for an adventure-spoof film called *Beat the Devil*. It was released in 1954, the year after his mother died from a barbiturate overdose. Also in 1954, Capote assembled another short-running Broadway musical called *House of Flowers*, a spinoff from his 1950 short story.

Prose writing was what Capote did best, and in 1955 he went on assignment for the *New Yorker* to follow the colorful exploits of the American *Porgy and Bess* company's Russian tour. The result was *The Muses Are Heard* (1956), a continuing experiment with depth-reporting, written with a mind to blending the arts of fiction and investigative journalism. His autobiographic "A Christmas Memory" was in a similar vein. When in the company of Cecil Beaton Capote journeyed to Japan to write an account of the filming of *Sayonara*, he did not focus on the movie itself but upon an interview with Marlon Brando called "The Duke in His Domain" (1957).

Truman Capote claimed once that his second career began with *Breakfast at Tiffany's* (1958), the novel that in his view delivered him at last from an arduous literary apprenticeship, from which he sought to escape. "I am not a keen rereader of my own books: what's done is done," he later wrote. "Moreover, I am always afraid of finding that my harsher detractors are correct" (*The Dogs Bark*, p. 10). *Breakfast at Tiffany's* introduced the irrepressible Holly Golightly and took place in New York City, a setting quite different from the gothic surroundings of *Other Voices* and most of his early short fiction.

For the next seven years Capote's energy focused mainly on Holcomb, Kansas, and the 1959 Clutter family murders, including the motives for, and appreciation of, murderers Perry Smith and Richard Hickock. One of the more distinguished achievements in reportage by any writer, *In Cold Blood* first appeared serially in the *New Yorker*, where it examined with extraordinary depth, precision, and drama the victims and their killers. So immense was the stress of the editorial undertaking, however, that Capote became addicted to tranquilizers and developed an emotional attachment to the criminals, whose deaths by hanging he witnessed at the Kansas state penitentiary. From more than four thousand pages of typewritten notes gathered with Harper Lee, Capote's celebrated "non-fiction novel" won the Mystery Writers of America Edgar Allan Poe Award and exacted enough of a psychological toll upon its author to preclude much sustained work in the future. While working on *In Cold Blood* he had taken on a number of other projects, including a group of biographic sketches for Richard Avedon's *Observations* (1959), and collaborated with William Archebald on a screenplay adaptation of the gothic novella *The Turn of the Screw*, by Henry James (1843–1916). Retitled *The Innocents*, the film appeared in 1961 and starred Deborah Kerr and Michael Redgrave. Simultaneously, Paramount issued *Breakfast at Tiffany's*, with Audrey Hepburn and George Peppard.

Capote's means of alleviating some of the *In Cold Blood* stress was to orchestrate the fabled "Party of the Decade" at New York's Plaza Hotel in 1966, when he entertained five hundred of his most celebrated "real friends." Gentlemen were instructed to arrive in black tie and black mask; ladies were asked to don black or white dresses and white masks and to carry a fan. His penchant for celebrity gathering was never more evident, and the extent to which his psyche had been depleted by the stress of *In Cold Blood* was never more clear. Regardless, *The Dogs Bark: Public People and Private Places* (1973), his next major publication, consisted of prose essays of uniformly high quality.

"The Tiny Terror," as he became known in some circles, played a character role in Neil Simon's film *Murder by Death* in 1976 and within a year sought treatment for alcoholism. On his projected novel *Answered Prayers*, for which he drew a $25,000 advance from Random House and another $350,000 up front from Twentieth Century–Fox, he offered a manuscript only partially completed yet one that contained enough scandalous assertions aimed at his high-living former friends as to render him socially ostracized for the rest of his days. While *Answered Prayers* continued to hang fire, *Music for Chameleons*, consisting of some of his most effective prose, was published in 1980. Capote died, apparently of a drug overdose, at the Los Angeles home of Joanne Carson, former wife of television personality Johnny Carson. Dwarfish and fey, he had for a lifetime perceived the carnival sideshow freakishness that defined him. Years before, he mused that he might be reincarnated as a buzzard, a creature that "doesn't have to bother about his appearance or ability to beguile and please; he doesn't have to put on airs. Nobody's going to like him anyway; he is ugly, unwanted, unwelcome everywhere" (*Music for Chameleons*, p. 257).

• Truman Capote manuscripts are deposited with the Library of Congress, the New York Public Library, the Columbia University Library, and the Smith College Library. Because Capote offered different versions of his own history, reconstructing the facts of his life is a biographic minefield. Gerald Clarke, *Capote: A Biography* (1988), is a remarkable effort to sort out fact and myth. William L. Nance, *The Worlds of Truman Capote* (1970), offers a blend of biography and criticism based in part on firsthand interviews. Helen Garson, *Truman Capote* (1980), and Kenneth T. Reed, *Truman Capote* (1981), advance varying biographical and critical perspectives. Marianne M. Moates, *A Bridge of Childhood: Truman Capote's Southern Years* (1989), is a recollection of Capote's Monroeville, Alabama, childhood. Interviews with Capote abound, but the accuracy of his testimony is sometimes questionable. An obituary written by Reed appears in the *Dictionary of Literary Biography Yearbook* (1985).

KENNETH T. REED

CAPP, Al (28 Sept. 1909–5 Nov. 1979), cartoonist, was born Alfred Gerald Caplin in New Haven, Connecticut, the son of Otto Caplin, an unsuccessful salesman, and Matilda Davidson. Moving to Bridgeport and then Boston, the family lived near poverty much of the time. Young Alfred began drawing at an early age, a recreation he turned to increasingly (also reading voraciously) after the age of nine, when he lost his left leg under the wheels of a streetcar. After high school, he attended a series of art schools, including the Pennsylvania Academy of Fine Arts, the Boston Museum School of Fine Arts, and the Designers Art School, where he met Catherine Wingate Cameron, whom he married in 1932; they had three children. Tiring of the succession of art courses, Capp (the pen name he adopted as his legal name in 1949) went to New York City to seek his fortune.

Capp eked out a living for months by selling advertising cartoons until he was hired by the Associated Press early in 1932 to produce a panel cartoon called *Colonel Gilfeather*. Discouraged by his inexperience and the incompatible material, Capp quit after about six months and returned to Boston for more art classes and marriage. Back in New York in the spring of 1933, he was hired by Ham Fisher to assist in producing his comic strip, *Joe Palooka*. Shortly after working on a sequence involving backwoods mountain people (which may have been inspired by Capp's recollections of a trip he had made as a teenager through the Cumberland Mountains or by a vaudeville show he and his wife attended—or both), Capp began developing a comic strip of his own. *Li'l Abner*, featuring the outlandishly harrowing adventures of a family of hillbillies, started on 13 August 1934; within six months, Capp had achieved both fame and wealth.

Li'l Abner Yokum, a red-blooded nineteen-year-old with the mature physique of a bodybuilder and the mind of an infant, lives contentedly with his diminutive Mammy, the pipe-smoking matriarch of the family, and his simpleton Pappy in poverty-stricken Dogpatch, a backwoods community perched precariously on the side of Onnecessary Mountain. The only cloud in the youth's idyllic everyday blue sky is Daisy Mae

Scragg, a skimpily clad blonde mountain houri who is forever pursuing him with ("gulp") matrimony in mind; Li'l Abner, too stupid to realize even that he loves her, shuns the nuptial bond as well as her embrace, imagining them as somehow unmanly. Daisy Mae drags him before Marryin' Sam at least once a year, but the ceremony is invariably nullified by some clanking plot contrivance; Capp finally married them for good on 29 March 1952.

Capp's Candide, Li'l Abner is fated to wander often into a threatening outside world, where he encounters civilization—politicians and plutocrats, scientists and swindlers, mountebanks, bunglers, and love-starved maidens. By this device, Capp contrasts Li'l Abner's country simplicity against society's sophistication—or, more precisely, his innocence against its decadence, his purity against its corruption. Throughout, the comedy is circumstantial, arising from the preposterousness of Abner's predicaments and his simplicity in dealing with them, rather than carefully structured jokes. Capp's effort was not so much to end his daily strips with punchlines as it was to finish with extravagant cliffhangers.

As a satirist, Capp ridiculed the pretensions and foibles of humanity—greed, bigotry, egotism, selfishness, vaulting ambition. All of humankind's baser instincts, which the cartoonist saw manifest in many otherwise socially acceptable guises, were his targets. And he undertook to strip away the pretensions that masked those follies, revealing society (all civilization perhaps) as mostly artificial, often shallow and self-serving, usually avaricious, and ultimately, inhumane. Li'l Abner is the perfect foil in this enterprise: naive and unpretentious (and, not to gloss the matter, just plain stupid), Li'l Abner believes in all the idealistic preachments of his fellowman—and is therefore the ideal victim for their practices (which invariably fall far short of their noble utterances). He is both champion and fall guy.

Capp's vehicle was burlesque, a mode of satirical comment that allows no fine gray shadings. Painted in stark blacks and whites, the world he revealed was divided simply into the Good (the Yokums) and the Bad (almost everybody else). Because he attacked the conventions of modern civilized society and because the most conspicuous upholders of those values were the wealthy and powerful members of the establishment, and because America's establishment was mostly political conservatives, most of the icons Capp smashed so exultantly were those of the political Right. Consequently, Capp was extremely popular among liberals.

A protean talent, Capp invented a host of memorable Dickensian characters and introduced a number of cultural epiphenomena. Perhaps the most famous of his secondary characters was the one that threatened at times to take over the strip—Fearless Fosdick, a razor-jawed parody of another comic strip character, Dick Tracy. Among Capp's contributions to popular culture is Sadie Hawkins Day, an annual November foot-race in which the unmarried women of Dogpatch pursue unmarried men across the countryside like so many hounds after the hare, marrying those whom they catch. Capp also invented Shmoos, cuddly, pliant, pear-shaped creatures who cheerfully die to supply everyone's needs. And he created Lower Slobbovia, a perpetually snowbound country of abject poverty and starvation. All provided grist for his satiric mill.

Not content with the outlet *Li'l Abner* afforded him, Capp launched in 1937 another comic strip, a somewhat more serious narrative about a crusty old spinster and her manly nephew called *Abbie and Slats*, which he wrote and Raeburn Van Buren drew; after nine years, Capp's brother Elliot took over the scripting, continuing until the strip ceased in 1971. In 1954, Capp started writing yet another strip, *Long Sam*, starring a female version of Li'l Abner; drawn by Bob Lubbers, it ran until 1962. Capp also wrote a syndicated newspaper column and was a frequent guest on radio and television talk shows, regaling his audiences with his analyses of contemporary events, outrageous commentaries that he punctuated with jubilant hoots of self-appreciative laughter.

In the 1960s Capp was roundly criticized by his traditional constituency of liberals for the unyielding rigor of his attacks on the New Left, particularly college youth (which, in *Li'l Abner*, were all members of S.W.I.N.E., "Students Wildly Indignant about Nearly Everything"). It was assumed that Capp had defected and gone over to the Right. But Capp's objective as a satirist remained constant: the fanaticism of the New Left was no less a human folly in his eyes than was the rigidity of the Right in seeking to preserve the conventions of its social order. Capp took folly where he found it and unceremoniously ripped the veils of self-righteousness away, roaring with rabelaisian laughter all the while. In ill health, Capp discontinued *Li'l Abner* on 13 November 1977. Two years later, Capp died in Cambridge, Massachusetts, after a long illness complicated by emphysema.

• Several books reprinting various sequences of *Li'l Abner* have been published: *The Life and Times of the Shmoo* (1948), *The World of Li'l Abner*, with prefatory matter by John Steinbeck and Charles Chaplin (1952), *From Dogpatch to Slobbovia: The (Gasp!) World of Li'l Abner* (1964), and *The Best of Li'l Abner* (1978). A collection of Capp's newspaper writing, illustrated by Capp, was published as *The Hardhat's Bedtime Story Book* (1971). And a posthumous anthology of autobiographical essays, including Capp's notorious attack on Ham Fisher, appeared as *My Well Balanced Life on a Wooden Leg: Memoirs* in 1991. The chief events of Al Capp's life and career are rehearsed in the standard histories and reference works about the medium, *The Comics* (1947) by Coulton Waugh, *Comic Art in America* (1959) by Stephen Becker, and *The Encyclopedia of American Comics* (1990) by Ron Goulart. Additional details can be found in "Die Monstersinger," the cover story for *Time*, 6 Nov. 1950; "Recap on Al Capp" by William Furlong in the *Saturday Evening Post*, Winter 1971; "The Truth about Al Capp" by Richard Marschall in *Cartoonist PROfiles* 37 (Mar. 1978); "We Called Him Alfred" by Elliot Caplin in *Cartoonist PROfiles* 48 (Dec. 1980); and "The Storyteller" by Dave Schreiner, the introduction to the first of a multivolume reprinting of *Li'l Abner* (1988). An obituary is in the *New York Times*, 6 Nov. 1979.

ROBERT C. HARVEY

CAPPA, Carlo Alberto (9 Dec. 1834–6 Jan. 1893), bandleader and trombonist, was born in Alessandria, Italy. Little is known of his parentage. He began studies in the rudiments of music at the age of eight. Two years later he began studying the trombone, and that same year he entered the Royal Academy in Asti, a school to which admission was limited to the sons of soldiers. His father's position as a major in the Sardinian army gave him the right to matriculate at the prestigious institution. At age fifteen he left the academy and enlisted in the Italian army as a trombonist with the band of the Sixth Lancers, whose duties consisted of performing at both public and private functions of Victor Emmanuel, the king of Sardinia and Italy. Cappa remained in the military for six years. He resigned from service when he received an invitation to join the band of the U.S. Navy frigate *Congress*, which was visiting Genoa at the time. The ship cruised for two years before returning to the United States on 22 February 1858, at which time Cappa decided to make the United States his home.

Immediately following his arrival in the United States, Cappa joined the band of the famous Boston keyed bugle player Ned Kendall, with whom he toured principal American cities for two years before settling in New York City and becoming a member of Shelton's Celebrated New York Band, led by the esteemed Claudio Grafulla. In December 1859 Grafulla was hired to organize the New York Seventh Regiment Band of the National Guard, and he invited Cappa to play with the ensemble. Their first concert was in February 1860. Cappa served with the band throughout its tour of active duty during the Civil War. Upon his return to New York City, Cappa continued to pursue musical engagements. He was the first trombonist for the Theodore Thomas Orchestra and the euphonium soloist with the Mapleson Opera Company, performed with both the New York and Brooklyn philharmonic societies, and was a frequent soloist with the Dodworth Band.

In November 1881 Cappa assumed leadership of the Seventh Regiment Band and for the next decade proceeded to enhance its reputation nationwide. The concert series he produced each summer in Central Park was well received, as were his yearly summer concert residencies at Brighton Beach on Coney Island and his winter promenade concerts at the Seventh Avenue Armory. In August 1883 Cappa took his band to Louisville, Kentucky, for the opening of the Southern Exposition, where they performed for seven weeks. He returned to Louisville each of the next five seasons for similar extended visits. In 1887 Cappa undertook a transcontinental tour to San Francisco, performing in major cities en route. He traveled to the West Coast again in 1892 for an exposition engagement in Tacoma, Washington. Cappa's band, like other professional bands in the nineteenth century, often provided the general public with its first hearing of much of the classical orchestral literature, albeit in transcription for wind instruments. Cappa's programs included works by Mendelssohn, Beethoven, Wagner, Berlioz, Liszt, Rossini, Ponchielli, Bizet, and other internationally recognized composers.

Cappa composed several short pieces, including *Veteran's Seventh Regiment Guard Mounting March* (1884), *Seventh Regiment Knapsack Quickstep* (1887), *Pro Patria et Gloria Quickstep* (1888), and *Col. Appleton's March* (1890). He died in New York City of a heart attack brought on by fatigue and a severe cold after having been in charge of the music for the New York City Columbian quadricentennial festivities. He was buried in Evergreen Cemetery, Brooklyn. Cappa was knighted by the king of Italy and the government of Venezuela, and his gentlemanly bearing, obliging manner, and superb musicianship endeared him to all who knew him. He was known for his ability to present concerts of outstanding musical merit and interest to the general public, earning him the title of "educator of the people" (Rossi, p. 10).

• There is no known repository of papers or collection of music for Cappa. An assessment of his life and work can only be made through the various articles that appeared during his lifetime or immediately following his death. These include "Carlo Cappa," *American Art Journal* 44, no. 14 (1886): 1; "Bandmaster Cappa," *American Music Journal*, 6 Feb. 1886; "Opera, Concert and Band Items," *Metronome* 3, no. 9 (1887): 3; Emmons Clark, *History of the Seventh Regiment of New York, 1806–1889* (1890); T. Rossi, "An Educator of the People," *Musical Courier* 25 (1892): 10; "Death of Carlo A. Cappa," *American Art Journal* 60, no. 14 (1893): 307; obituary, *Musical Courier* 26 (1893): 21; and the obituary and funeral coverage in the *New York Times*, 7, 8, and 10 Jan. 1893.

FRANK J. CIPOLLA

CAPPER, Arthur (14 July 1865–19 Dec. 1951), governor and U.S. senator, was the first native-born Kansan to serve his state in these offices. He was born in Garnett, Anderson County, the son of Herbert Capper, an English-born tinner and hardware merchant, and Isabella McGrew. Arthur Capper learned the printing trade and graduated from Garnett High School in 1884. He found work with the Topeka *Daily Capital*, soon becoming a cub reporter, then city editor. He fully developed his talents and reported local news from a prohibitionist, Republican slant. For about a year he worked for the *New York Tribune* and as a correspondent in Washington, D.C. In 1892 Capper married Florence Crawford, the only daughter of former Kansas governor Samuel J. Crawford.

In 1893 Capper used his own resources to purchase the weekly North Topeka *Mail*. His capacity for endless hours of hard work began to pay off. The Populist party controlled much of Kansas, while Capper's Republican paper prospered, and he acquired other journals, the most important being the Topeka *Daily Capital*. Capper either absorbed each journal's subscription list into an established paper or operated it independently with improved reading matter and an enlarged circulation, thus increasing advertising revenue. Until World War I, costs remained low, and income grew rapidly. He owned the second automobile in Topeka, built a new publishing plant, which cost $355,000, and a $75,000 Topeka Avenue mansion, all paid for with his current income. With increases in expenses in later years, Capper's personal wealth did not grow like his business.

Capper's early reputation was based on his editorial opposition to railroad domination of Kansas politics. He supported Progressive reform, but he did not run for public office until 1912 when he became the Republican candidate for governor. He lost to the Democrat, George Hodges, by twenty-nine votes, his only loss in sixteen statewide primary and general elections. He was elected governor in 1914 and reelected in 1916, although he made no notable reforms. In 1918 he was elected to the first of five consecutive terms in the U.S. Senate, enjoying phenomenal support from the Kansas electorate.

As publisher, Capper owned as many as twelve newspapers at one time. His list in 1923 included the Topeka *Daily Capital*, Kansas City *Kansan*, *Capper's Weekly*, *Household*, *Capper's Farmer*, *Kansas Farmer*, *Oklahoma Farmer*, *Missouri Ruralist*, *Nebraska Farm Journal*, *Ohio Farmer*, *Michigan Farmer*, and *Pennsylvania Farmer*. His journals supported rural youth clubs until 4-H clubs replaced them. Later, in 1928, Capper Publications sold some journals and expanded into radio. Capper maintained that the North Topeka paper was the only journal purchase he initiated.

In 1912 Capper employed 600 persons in his publishing empire and maintained an "open door" policy for everyone. He interpreted his role as publisher broadly and provided substantial leeway for his writers. He always encouraged correspondence, and his mail was voluminous. Answers were prompt, and Capper queried correspondents on specific questions. His speaking ability was marginal, but campaigning was something he did all the time.

One of his first Senate votes was for the League of Nations, with reservations, but it lost. He was a leader in the Farm Bloc, but his primary bent was committee work, not speaking on the Senate floor. His name is associated with the Capper-Volstead Acts of 1922 and 1926, considered the "magna charta" for agricultural cooperatives, and the Capper-Ketchum Act of 1928, supporting 4-H clubs. Capper always responded quickly to voter correspondence, just as he had as a publisher. During the New Deal years he backed new government initiatives, but he was a persistent isolationist, a stand that changed when World War II began. As a long-time member of the District of Columbia Committee he developed civil rights legislation. Republicans had been a majority when Capper was a junior member of the Senate; his party regained control in 1947, when he served as chairman of the Agricultural Committee. He retired from the Senate in 1949.

Capper's wife died in 1926, and they had no children, so he willed the bulk of his estate to the Capper Foundation for Crippled Children and to some employees. By the time of his death in Topeka, circulation of his journals was almost five million, and his employees numbered 1,200. When the Capper heirs sold out in 1956, the Capper Foundation built a fine building for services to crippled children, the principal memorial to Arthur Capper. A school in Topeka and Arthur Capper Dwellings in Washington, D.C., also bear his name. He is remembered in Congress for his advocacy of the farming family, his support for civil rights, and his general opposition to war.

• Arthur Capper was listed as the author of *The Agricultural Bloc* (1922). His publishing empire put out about 450 volumes of different newspapers and magazines between 1893 and 1951. His principal biography is Homer E. Socolofsky, *Arthur Capper: Publisher, Politician, Philanthropist* (1962). The Capper papers, including many pictures, are in the manuscript department of the Kansas State Historical Society in Topeka.

HOMER E. SOCOLOFSKY

CAPPS, Edward (21 Dec. 1866–21 Aug. 1950), classical scholar and administrator, was born in Jacksonville, Illinois, the son of Stephen Reid Capps and Rhoda Smith Tomlin. His father was a successful manufacturer and philanthropist. He received his B.A. in 1887 from Illinois College, Jacksonville, where Edward B. Clapp won him over to the study of classics. He earned his Ph.D. from Yale in 1891 with an outstanding dissertation on the stage in the ancient Greek theater. At Yale he met William Rainey Harper, who appointed him to the University of Chicago upon its inception in 1892. There he became a colleague of the great Hellenist Paul Shorey, one of the founders of scientific philology in the United States, and rose to full professor. In 1892 he married Grace Alexander. Four children resulted from this union. He did postdoctoral study at the American School of Classical Studies in Athens (1893–1894) and later at Halle, Berlin, and Munich (1903–1904). In 1901 he published *From Homer to Theocritus: A Manual of Greek Literature*. This was the first history of Greek literature written by an American and one of the very few in any language written by so young a scholar. In 1906 he became the first managing editor of the journal *Classical Philology*. In 1907, after a widely publicized trial in which he successfully sued the University of Chicago over a question of summer salary, Capps left Chicago for Princeton, where he was professor of Greek until his retirement in 1936.

At Princeton he made the astute decision to side with Woodrow Wilson in his dispute with Capps's classical colleague Dean Andrew Fleming West and to abandon his family's allegiance to the Republican party. He won a second influential supporter when, through John Williams White, he met the wealthy philanthropist and Hellenophile James Loeb. Loeb appointed him to the advisory board of the newly founded Loeb Classical Library in 1912 and in 1914 made him American editor of the series, a well-paid post that gave him control over extensive patronage. In the same year he was elected president of the American Philological Society. In 1920 he became the first president of the American Association of University Professors, which he had helped to found in 1915.

In 1918, with Wilson's support, he became American Red Cross Commissioner in Greece (1918–1919). In 1920–1921 he served as Wilson's envoy extraordinary and ambassador plenipotentiary in Greece and Montenegro. During this time he made the acquaintance of powerful and influential men, like the prime minister of Greece, Eleutherios Venizelos, and helped found Athens College, an American-Greek elite boys school, whose alumni served in every Greek cabinet until 1967. Capps's Hellenic connections made his appointment in 1919 as chairman of the managing committee of the American School inevitable. He has been called "the second founder" of the school. He increased the endowment more than tenfold. In 1922 he secured for the school the library of the wealthy bibliophile Dr. J. Gennadius and raised the funds to house what would be called the Gennadeion. In 1928 he secured the Agora Excavation, which has been the center of the school's scholarly activity ever since. As a result, generations of Americans have excavated the marketplace and civic center of ancient Athens, one of the most important archaeological sites in the Greco-Roman world, equaled only by the Roman Forum. He insisted on prompt, expert publication of finds and founded the journal *Hesperia* as an organ for such publication.

Capps played a decisive and influential role in American classics. Until 1914 he was a brilliant, productive scholar, a pioneer in the discipline of scenic antiquities, that is, the ancient staging of tragedy and comedy. Here he anticipated the work of English scholars like A. W. Pickard-Cambridge and T. B. L. Webster. In his *Four Plays of Menander: The Hero, Epitreportes, Periceiromene and Samia* (1910), according to the greatest Hellenist of modern times, Ulrich von Wilamowitz-Moellendorff, Capps interpreted the newly discovered *Epitrepontes* "in a way worthy of the highest praise, with expertise and taste." He provides a rare example of a successful scholar, not a failed one, who deserted scholarship for administration. The American School and the Loeb Classical Library flourished under his aegis. Because of his friendship with Woodrow Wilson, he achieved international prominence and became one of the few American classicists who played a part in the larger history of his time. In this he is comparable to Edward Everett and among the English to Benjamin Jowett and Gilbert Murray. Wilson said of him: "I would trust his judgment most of the time and his intentions always." He died in Princeton, New Jersey.

• Capps's dissertation was published as "The Greek Stage according to the Extant Dramas," *Transactions and Proceedings of the American Philological Association* 22 (1891): 5–80. For his life and scholarship, see G. H. Chase, *American Journal of Archaeology* 55 (1951): 101; Louis E. Lord, "The Chairmanship of Edward Capps," in *A History of the American School of Classical Studies at Athens 1882–1942: An Intercollegiate Project* (1947), pp. 130–270; B. D. Meritt, *Transactions and Proceedings of the American Philological Association* 81 (1950): xiv–xv; the *New York Times*, 22 Aug. 1950; Ulrich von Wilamowitz-Moellendorff, *Menander: Das Schiedsgericht (Epitrepontes)* (1925; repr. 1958), p. 8.

WILLIAM M. CALDER III

CAPRA, Frank (18 May 1897–3 Sept. 1991), filmmaker, was born in Bisacquino, Sicily, the son of Salvatore Capra and Rosaria Nicolosi, farmers. The family immigrated to the United States, settling on a farm outside Los Angeles, when Capra was six years old. Capra was the only of his parents' fourteen children to attend college; he obtained a scholarship and graduated from Throop College of Technology (later California Institute of Technology) in 1918 with a degree in chemical engineering.

Capra obtained an army commission and served as an artillery school instructor until the end of World War I. He was unable to find employment as an engineer after being discharged, so he worked as a door-to-door salesman and at other menial jobs until he persuaded a San Francisco filmmaker to allow him to direct short films. His first film was a dramatization of a Rudyard Kipling poem, *Fultah Fisher's Boarding House* (1922). He directed several other forgettable silent shorts and then worked in a film laboratory for room and board while he learned photographic technique.

Capra moved to Hollywood in 1923 to work as a gag writer on the "Our Gang" comedies at the Hal Roach studios. Six months later he joined the Mack Sennett Studio to write gags and screenplays for Harry Langdon. Capra wrote screenplays for more than two dozen Langdon films and directed the hits *Tramp, Tramp, Tramp* (1926), *The Strong Man* (1926), and *Long Pants* (1927). After Langdon and Capra quarreled over who was responsible for the success of these films, Capra left for New York to make an independent production, *For the Love of Mike* (1927). It was unsuccessful, and he returned to the Mack Sennett studio as a writer.

Capra married actress Helen Edith Howell in 1925; they had no children and were divorced in 1928. Capra married Lucille Warner Reyburn, a widow, in 1932. The couple had four children, one of whom, Frank Capra, Jr., later became a motion picture and television producer.

In 1928 Columbia Pictures mogul Harry Cohn hired Capra to direct films for his "Poverty Row" studio. The contract paid Capra the relatively small fee of $1,000 per film (a sum that vastly increased after subsequent hits) but granted him total artistic control over his work. Capra's first films for Columbia were minor but profitable comedies that gave him experience with the new sound technology. Capra also directed *Flight* (1929), *Dirigible* (1931), and several other action films, but he hit his stride with social comedies involving wise-cracking and sexually forthright actresses like Barbara Stanwyck in *Ladies of Leisure* (1930) and Jean Harlow in *Platinum Blonde* (1931).

Many of Capra's films used screenplays by Robert Riskin, a Broadway playwright who joined Capra on *Platinum Blonde* and worked with him for the next fifteen years. Capra had a similarly productive long-term collaboration with cinematographer Joseph Walker, who implemented Capra's visual style.

Capra tried his hand at melodrama in *The Bitter Tea of General Yen* (1933), an erotic drama dealing with anarchy, murder, racism, and miscegenation in warlord China. Although critically acclaimed, particularly for its opulent set design and cinematography, it was not as profitable as the earlier comedies. Capra returned to romantic comedy with *It Happened One Night* (1934), a blockbuster hit that was the first ever to win five Oscars, including best film, director, screenplay, actor, and actress. The film helped to make Columbia Pictures a major studio, and it engendered a new genre of films, the screwball comedy. Capra became Hollywood's most sought-after director, and the film's two leads, Claudette Colbert and Clark Gable, were transformed into major sex symbols.

The following year saw a hiatus in Capra's work when he developed appendicitis and peritonitis. He later claimed that while recovering he was visited by an unknown man who told him to use his "God-given talents for His purpose." Thereafter, Capra eliminated sensuality and sexual innuendoes from his work. Most of his subsequent films were whimsical, almost fablelike comedies that preached a belief in the basic goodness of humankind. *Mr. Deeds Goes to Town* (1936) set out the formula for most of his subsequent films: an honest and idealistic—although somewhat naive—hero encounters problems from corrupt men and institutions but ultimately prevails with the help of a more cynical, but nonsexual, girlfriend. The film starred Gary Cooper and Jean Arthur and won an Oscar for best director.

Capra's next film was the fantasy *Lost Horizon* (1937), based on Ronald Hilton's popular novel and one of the most expensive films produced by Columbia. Like *General Yen*, it dealt with the confrontation of West and East in an exotic locale but carried a more inspirational message of hope and harmony. Although nominated for best picture, the film was not a popular success. Capra returned to the genre of social comedy during the remainder of the decade. *You Can't Take It with You* (1938) won Oscars for best picture and best director, and *Mr. Smith Goes to Washington* (1939) garnered nominations for best picture and best director.

Capra served as the president of the American Academy of Motion Picture Arts and Sciences from 1935 to 1939, and he was head of the Directors Guild from 1938 to 1940. In the latter capacity he was preoccupied during 1939 in a bitter dispute with the producers and studios that resulted in directors gaining more credit and artistic control over their work. The dispute took so much of his time that he did not direct another film until *Meet John Doe* (1941), which he produced as an independent filmmaker. In 1941 he directed the movie version of the popular stage drama *Arsenic and Old Lace*, but it was not released until it closed on Broadway in 1944.

Immediately after the Japanese attack on Pearl Harbor, the 44-year-old Capra volunteered for service in the U.S. Army. He was initially assigned to the army's Signal Photographic Detachment but soon rose to become head of the Army Pictorial Service. Capra directed and produced Why We Fight, a series of propaganda documentaries that were initially planned for exclusive viewing by U.S. troops. His work, however, was more artful and skillful than most propaganda films and transcended the genre. When Why We Fight was eventually screened for general audiences it won critical acclaim. *Prelude to War* won him an Oscar for best documentary of 1942, and the entire Why We Fight series won a special award from the New York Film Critics. Capra was discharged in 1945 with the rank of colonel and was awarded the Distinguished Service Medal, Order of the British Empire, and the French Legion of Merit.

Upon returning to Hollywood, Capra set up another independent production company, Liberty Films, Inc., with directors William Wyler, George Stevens, and Sam Briskin. Capra was president of the new venture, and he co-scripted, produced, and directed its first production, *It's a Wonderful Life* (1947). The film was Capra's personal favorite, and although it was initially unpopular with both critics and the public, it was eventually revived and shown on television every Christmas.

Financial losses from *It's a Wonderful Life* and *State of the Union* (1948) eventually forced the sale of Liberty Films to Paramount Studios. Capra made three other films for Metro-Goldwyn-Mayer and Paramount, but these failed to hold audience interest. For most of the 1950s his motion picture career was on hold. Critics panned his films as old-fashioned and out of touch with the more abrasive mood of the postwar movie audiences; journalists coined the word "Capracorn" to deride his optimistic outlook. Capra was unable to obtain financing for any more films, and his only work during the mid-1950s was a series of television documentaries for the Bell System: "Our Mr. Sun" (1956), "Hemo the Magnificent" (1957), "The Strange Case of the Cosmic Rays" (1957), and "The Unchained Goddess" (1958).

In 1959 Capra set up a partnership with Frank Sinatra to produce *A Hole in the Head*, directed by Capra and starring Sinatra. Critics panned the comedy, but it was a popular hit, and its song "High Hopes" received an Oscar nomination for best song. The film's financial success allowed Capra to find financing for another independent production, *Pocketful of Miracles* (1961). This remake of his earlier hit *Lady for a Day* (1933) was rejected by the public and critics and ended his career in Hollywood. His only other production was the documentary *Rendezvous in Space*, produced for the 1964 New York World's Fair.

Capra left Hollywood in 1966 to retire in La Quinta, California, a suburb of Palm Springs. He published an autobiography, *The Name above the Title* (1971), and wrote the introduction to *The Man Who Invented Hollywood: The Autobiography of D. W. Griffith* (1972) and several other books about movies. In 1982 the American Film Institute awarded him a Lifetime Achievement Award, and NBC broadcast a television special, "The American Film Institute Salute to Frank Capra." His revived popularity prompted Capra to begin a lecture tour on college campuses, but after his wife died in 1984 Capra became a recluse. He died seven years later in La Quinta.

• The Frank Capra Archives are at Wesleyan University, Middletown, Conn. He is interviewed on videotape in Center for Cassette Studies, *Focus on Frank Capra: The Famous Film Director Discusses the Art* (1971). Transcripts of other interviews are located at the Oral History Research Center, Columbia University, and at the Brigham Young University Archives, Provo, Utah. The best biography is Joseph McBride, *Frank Capra: The Catastrophe of Success* (1992). Other useful works include Raymond Carney, *American Vision: The Films of Frank Capra* (1986); Lee Lourdeaux, *Italian and Irish Filmmakers in America* (1990); Leland Poague, *The Cinema of Frank Capra: An Approach to Film Comedy* (1975); Robert Glatzer and John Raeburn, eds., *Frank Capra: The Man and His Films* (1975); Dennis Bohnenkamp and Sam Grogg, eds., *Frank Capra Study Guide* (1979); "How Frank Capra Makes a Hit Picture," *Life*, 19 Sept. 1938; and George A. Phelps, "The 'Populist' Films of Frank Capra," *Journal of American Studies* 12 (1979). Jeanine Basinger's *The "It's a Wonderful Life" Book* (1986) is a detailed analysis of the production of his most famous film. Obituaries are in the *New York Times*, 4 Sept. 1991, and *Variety*, 9 Sept. 1991.

STEPHEN G. MARSHALL

CAPTAIN JACK (1837?–3 Oct. 1873), Modoc war chief who led the Indians in the Modoc war of 1872–1873, was born Kintpuash. His place of birth and the names of his parents are unknown. He was called Captain Jack because he resembled a white man named Jack and liked military decorations.

In 1864 the Modoc, led by Chief Schonchin, were forced to accept a reservation in southern Oregon with their cousins, the Klamath. This treaty proved bitter for the Modoc. They were harassed by the more numerous Klamath, and the Indian agent refused to intervene. In April 1870 Jack and 150 Modoc, about sixty of them warriors, fled to the old Modoc homeland in the vicinity of Tule Lake in northern California.

For two years all peaceful efforts to get Jack and his followers back to the reservation failed, and on 28 November 1872, thirty-six soldiers under Captain James Jackson were sent to compel their return. After a skirmish the next day, in which both sides suffered fatalities, Jack fled with his warriors in two groups into nearby lava beds (now the Lava Beds National Monument) south of Tule Lake, one band killing eighteen civilians on the way. Eventually Jack had some eighty warriors in the lava beds, a natural fortress filled with caves and fissures that served as tunnels and trenches.

Soldiers under Brevet Major General E. R. S. Canby surrounded the lava beds, and on 17 January 1873 began a daylong battle in which forty-nine regulars and volunteers were killed or wounded, but there was no Indian casualty. President Ulysses S. Grant then ordered a peace commission to resolve the problem, and it met with Jack on 11 April. Against Jack's wishes, the war party among his followers insisted on attacking the commissioners. General Canby and the Reverend Eleazer Thomas were killed, and another commissioner was wounded. Only Indian Agent L. S. Dyar escaped.

The attack on these commissioners caused a public clamor for a war of extermination against the Modoc. Colonel Jefferson C. Davis took command and with more than 1,000 soldiers and volunteers pressed the attack. The Modoc abandoned the lava beds and, beset by soldiers, quarreled among themselves. In May they began surrendering in small bands, some joining the hunt for the remaining hostiles. Jack surrendered on 1 June.

He and five other Modoc warriors were court-martialed on 1 July for murdering the peace commissioners. During this trial, in which the accused had no attorney and could not understand most of the charges because the proceedings were in English, some of the warriors who had forced the war on Jack testified for the prosecution. On 9 July all six Modoc defendants were sentenced to death by hanging. President Grant commuted to life imprisonment the sentences of two of the condemned, but they were not told of this until they stood at the foot of the gallows on 3 October. The other four—Jack, John Schonchin, Black Jim, and Boston Charley—were hanged. Jack's head was severed and sent to the army medical museum for study.

At his last conference with a chaplain, Jack said, "When I look in my heart I see no crime." Today his defenders say he was pushed into a war he did not want to fight by whites who coveted Modoc land.

• See Richard Dillon, *Burnt-Out Fires: California's Modoc Indian War* (1973); Keith A. Murray, *The Modocs and Their War* (1959); and Odie B. Faulk and Laura E. Faulk, *The Modoc People* (1988). A. B. Meacham, one of the peace commissioners, wrote a sympathetic account of the Modoc plight in *Wigwam and War-Path* (1875); T. B. Odeneal, one of the agents at the Klamath reservation, wrote a self-justification that contains the white viewpoint in *The Modoc War: Statement of Its Origin and Causes* (1873). A good ethnological study is Verne F. Ray, *Primitive Pragmatists: The Modoc Indians of Northern California* (1963).

ODIE B. FAULK

CAPTAIN JOHNNY. *See* Kekewepelethy.

CAPTAIN PIPE (c. 1725–1794), Delaware chief of the Wolf phratry, was prominent during the American Revolution. He was also known as Hopocan or Kageshquanohel. Pipe earned his reputation fighting against the British during the French and Indian War and in Pontiac's War of 1763–1764. As tensions between Indians and whites increased in the Ohio Valley, he and White Eyes, of the Turtle phratry, worked as mediators between Virginia and the Shawnees, trying in vain to prevent Lord Dunmore's War in 1774. On the eve of the American Revolution, Pipe succeeded his uncle, Custaloga, as head of the Wolf phratry.

Like other Indian peoples in the Ohio Valley, the Delawares occupied a precarious position, caught in a diplomatic tug-of-war between the Americans operating out of Fort Pitt and the British and their Indian allies around Detroit. White Eyes leaned toward the Americans and cultivated good relations with George Morgan, the Continental Congress's Indian agent at Fort Pitt. Pipe assumed the position of war captain in the Revolution, and he has often been portrayed as throwing in his lot with the British early in the war. In fact, Pipe endeavored to keep his people neutral in the early years of the conflict. In the fall of 1777, Americans killed some of his relatives in General Edward Hand's notorious "squaw campaign," during which militia attacked camps of Delaware women and children, but Pipe still refused to go to war. He attended conferences with the Americans at Fort Pitt and signed a controversial treaty there with the United States in September 1778. The Americans interpreted the treaty as a formal commitment by the Delawares to a defensive and offensive alliance with the United States; the Delaware signatories seem to have believed they were conferring to the Americans only the right to cross their lands in return for trade and a fort to protect their women and children. Americans murdered White Eyes in 1778, but as late as 1779 Pipe was regarded as "a Virginian" (that is, pro-American) by Indians in the British camp. By that time, however, he was moving increasingly toward allegiance with the British. He began to argue the merits of a British alliance in the Delaware national council and took up residence near Pluggy's Town, a stronghold of pro-British warriors in the Sandusky country. The Americans' failure to provide the trade and protection they had promised allowed him to increase his influence, at the expense of John Killbuck, the pro-American head of the Turtle phratry. Delaware warriors filtered away from the villages clustered around the capital at Coshocton and joined Pipe's village on the Sandusky River, where they received supplies and support from the British at Detroit.

In 1781 Pipe joined the Wyandot Half King in removing Moravian mission communities from the Muskingum Valley to the Sandusky. The British regarded the pro-American Moravians as a strategic threat. At Detroit Pipe interrogated the missionaries as to their activities. The missionaries saw him as a tool of the British. Nevertheless, Moravian missionary John Heckewelder recorded a speech made by Pipe to Arent Schuyler De Peyster, the British commander at Detroit, in which he denounced the redcoats for unleashing the Indians on the Americans while contemplating peace themselves. In 1782 he played a prominent role in the defeat of Colonel William Crawford's expedition into the Sandusky region. Pipe's Delawares ritually tortured and executed Crawford in retaliation for the slaughter by American militia of almost 100 Moravian Delawares at Gnadenhutten earlier in the year.

Pipe appears to have been losing influence among the Delawares by the end of the Revolution, and some accused him of bringing disaster on the nation by espousing the British cause. He began to resume the role of a civil chief rather than a war captain. In 1785 Pipe signed the Treaty of Fort McIntosh with the United States. The American commissioners, acting on the assumption that the Indians had forfeited their lands by siding with Britain in the Revolution, dictated punitive terms to the Delawares, Wyandots, Chippewas, and Ottawas. Some of his people accused Pipe of selling out to the Americans. Pipe also signed the Treaty of Fort Harmar in 1789. Heckewelder said Pipe died a few days before Anthony Wayne defeated the confederated Indians at the battle of Fallen Timbers on 20 August 1794.

Like many other Indian leaders who have been depicted as unswervingly hostile to the Americans in the Revolution, Pipe endeavored to remain neutral until such a position became untenable, at which point he made common cause with the British as the best chance for the Delawares' survival. British abandonment of their Indian allies in 1783 left leaders like Pipe with little alternative but to try to chart a new course of accommodation with the victorious Americans. In the tumultuous times of the revolutionary era, Indian peoples in the Ohio Valley were constantly adjusting to new realities.

• C. A. Weslager, *The Delaware Indians: A History* (1972), provides the standard context for Pipe's life, although he shares the Moravian missionary perspective of Pipe as scheming a British alliance. Richard White, *The Middle Ground: Indians, Empires, and Republics in the Great Lakes Region, 1650–1815* (1991), contains a discussion of Pipe's shifting roles as civil chief and war captain. Colin G. Calloway, *The American Revolution in Indian Country: Crisis and Diversity in Native American Communities* (1995), provides a broad context for the Delawares' experience in these years. Calloway, ed., *Revolution and Confederation, 1775–1789*, vol. 18 of *Early American Indian Documents: Treaties and Laws, 1607–1789*, ed. Alden T. Vaughan (1979–), contains treaties and other documents relating to Delaware diplomacy in the Revolution. Other relevant documents are scattered through the *Collections of the State Historical Society of Wisconsin*, ed. Reuben G. Thwaites and Louise P. Kellogg: *Revolution on the Upper Ohio* (1908), *Frontier Defense on the Upper Ohio* (1912), *Frontier Advance on the Upper Ohio* (1916), and *Frontier Retreat on the Upper Ohio* (1916). The account of Pipe's speech at Detroit is in John Heckewelder, *History, Manners, and Customs of the Indian Nations Who Once Inhabited Pennsylvania and the Neighboring States* (1876).

COLIN G. CALLOWAY

CARAWAY, Hattie Ophelia Wyatt (1 Feb. 1878–21 Dec. 1950), U.S. senator, was born on a farm near Bakerville, Tennessee, the daughter of William Carroll Wyatt, a farmer and shopkeeper, and Lucy Mildred Burch. At the age of four she moved with her family to Hustburg, Tennessee. After briefly attending Ebenezer College in Hustburg, she transferred to Dickson (Tenn.) Normal College, where she received her B.A.

degree in 1896. She taught school for a time before marrying in 1902 Thaddeus Horatius Caraway, whom she had met in college; they had three children.

The Caraways settled in Jonesboro, Arkansas, where he established a legal practice while she cared for the children, tended the household and kitchen garden, and helped to oversee the family's cotton farm. Upon Thaddeus Caraway's election to the U.S. House of Representatives in 1912, the family established a second home in Riverdale, Maryland. Although she took an interest in her husband's political career, Hattie Caraway avoided the capital's social and political life as well as the campaign for woman suffrage. She recalled that "after equal suffrage I just added voting to cooking and sewing and other household duties."

In 1921 Thaddeus Caraway was elected to the U.S. Senate and served there until his death on 6 November 1931. Following the precedent of appointing widows to temporarily take their husbands' places, Arkansas governor Harvey Parnell appointed Hattie Caraway to the vacant seat, and she was sworn into office on 9 December. With the Arkansas Democratic party's backing, she easily won a special election in January 1932 for the remaining months of the term, becoming the first woman elected to the Senate.

In May 1932 Caraway surprised Arkansas politicians by announcing that she would run for a full term in the upcoming election, joining a field already crowded with prominent candidates who had assumed she would step aside. She told reporters, "The time has passed when a woman should be placed in a position and kept there only while someone else is being groomed for the job." Lacking any significant political backing, Caraway accepted the offer of help from Louisiana senator Huey P. Long, whose efforts to limit incomes and increase aid to the poor she had supported. Long was also motivated by sympathy for the widow as well as by his ambition to extend his influence into the home state of his rival, Senator Joseph Robinson. Bringing his colorful and flamboyant campaign style to Arkansas, Long stumped the state with Caraway for a week just before the Democratic primary, helping her amass nearly twice as many votes as her closest opponent. She went on to win the general election in November.

Caraway's Senate committee assignments included Agriculture and Forestry, Commerce, and Enrolled Bills and Library, which she chaired. She sustained a special interest in relief for farmers, flood control, and veterans' benefits, all of direct concern to her constituents, and cast her votes for nearly every New Deal measure. Her loyalty to President Franklin D. Roosevelt, however, did not extend to racial issues, and in 1938 she joined fellow southerners in a filibuster against the administration's antilynching bill. Although she carefully prepared herself for Senate work, Caraway spoke infrequently and was sometimes portrayed by patronizing reporters as "Silent Hattie" or "the quiet grandmother who never . . . said anything or did anything." She explained her reticence as unwillingness "to take a minute away from the men. The poor dears love it so."

In 1938 Caraway entered a tough fight for reelection, challenged by Representative John L. McClellan, who argued that a man could more effectively promote the state's interests. With backing from government employees, women's groups, and unions, Caraway won a narrow victory in the primary and took the general election by a large margin. She supported Roosevelt's foreign policy, arguing for his lend-lease bill from her perspective as a mother with two sons in the army. While encouraging women to contribute to the war effort, Caraway insisted that caring for the home and family was a woman's primary task. Yet her consciousness of women's disadvantages was evident as early as 1931, when, upon being assigned the same Senate desk that had been briefly occupied by the first widow ever appointed to take her husband's place, she commented privately, "I guess they wanted as few of them contaminated as possible." Moreover, in 1943, Caraway became the first woman legislator to cosponsor the Equal Rights Amendment.

In her bid for reelection in 1944, Caraway placed a poor fourth in the Democratic primary, losing her Senate seat to freshman congressman J. William Fulbright, the young, dynamic former president of the University of Arkansas who had already gained a national reputation. Roosevelt then appointed her to the Employees' Compensation Commission, and in 1946 President Harry Truman gave her a post on the Employees' Compensation Appeals Board, where she served until suffering a stroke in January 1950. She died in Falls Church, Virginia, and was buried in West Lawn Cemetery in Jonesboro, Arkansas.

Caraway's defiance of the Arkansas establishment in insisting that she was more than a temporary stand-in for her husband enabled her to set a valuable precedent for women in politics. Although she remained at the margins of power, Caraway's diligent and capable attention to Senate responsibilities won the respect of her colleagues, encouraged advocates of wider public roles for women, and demonstrated that political skills were not the exclusive property of men.

• A small collection of Caraway's papers, including scrapbooks, a few letters, and a partial autobiography, are at the University of Arkansas at Fayetteville. Diane D. Kincaid, ed., *Silent Hattie Speaks: The Personal Journal of Senator Hattie Caraway* (1979), covers her first year in office. Two Little Rock newspapers, the *Arkansas Democrat* and the *Arkansas Gazette*, report on many aspects of Caraway's career. The most thorough secondary source is Betty Marie Sneed, "Hattie Wyatt Caraway: United States Senator, 1931–1945" (master's thesis, Univ. of Arkansas, 1975). The 1932 campaign is covered in David Malone, *Hattie and Huey: An Arkansas Tour* (1989). General treatments include George Creel, "The Woman Who Holds Her Tongue," *Colliers'*, 18 Sept. 1937, pp. 22, 55; Annabel Paxton, *Women in Congress* (1945); Hope Chamberlin, *A Minority of Members: Women in the U.S. Congress, 1917–1972* (1973); and "The Last of the First," *Time*, 7 Aug. 1944, p. 19. An obituary is in the *New York Times*, 22 Dec. 1950.

SUSAN M. HARTMANN

CARBO, Frankie (10 Aug. 1904–10 Nov. 1976), Italian-American gangster and "underworld czar of boxing," was born Paul John Carbo and reared on New York's Lower East Side. His parents' names and occupations are unknown. Carbo was first arrested at age eleven and spent much of the next four years at the Juvenile Catholic Protectory. Arrested again in his late teens for felonious assault and grand larceny, he then became an enforcer for a Bronx taxicab protection racket. In 1924 he murdered a cab driver who resisted a shakedown, and he served twenty months in Sing Sing for the crime. Thereafter, he was involved in beer-running and bookmaking and was indicted four more times for murder, but he was never convicted.

In 1939 Carbo, Bugsy Siegel, and Champ Segal were indicted for the gangland execution of Harry "Big Greenie" Greenberg, allegedly at the behest of Louis Lepke Buchalter, head of Murder, Inc. The first trial, despite eyewitness testimony by getaway driver Allie Tannenbaum and corroboration by Abe Reles, a close associate of Buchalter, ended in a hung jury. A second trial resulted in no decision, largely because Reles, despite 24-hour police protection, fell from a sixth-story window of a Coney Island hotel before he could testify.

Carbo's principal source of income by the mid-1930s was from boxing. He had a highly regarded ability to identify talent and took advantage of underworld connections, a power vacuum among managers and matchmakers in the middle and lower weight classifications, and the absence of an effective independent regulatory commission to become a major figure in prizefighting from the mid-1930s through 1960. Because as an ex-felon he could not get a managerial license, he had to secretly gain control of several champions and most of the leading contenders. In so doing he dominated the middleweight division. He subsequently expanded his influence into all weight classes, and by the late 1940s he wielded unrivaled power. While considered soft-spoken and retiring, he had no qualms about using violence or threats to get his way.

Carbo was known in boxing circles as "Mr. Gray," a name often mentioned in government wiretaps of organized crime figures. His front men included underworld characters and "respectable" businessmen. His right-hand man was Gabe Genovese, first cousin of Vito Genovese, head of the most powerful New York crime family; Gabe Genovese acted as an unlicensed manager who operated through front men. Carbo's other principal aide was Philadelphia gambling kingpin Frank "Blinky" Palermo, whose champions included Ike Williams, Johnny Saxton, and Sonny Liston. Williams was an outstanding lightweight who was blacklisted by Carbo in 1946 until he agreed to work for Palermo. Palermo helped him become champion by arranging key fights, but he cheated Williams financially. Other managers who fronted for Carbo included such ostensibly legitimate businessmen as Herman "Mink" Wallman, a New York furrier, and *Ring* magazine's 1957 Manager of the Year Bernard Glickman, a Chicago awnings dealer.

Carbo's clout got his fighters good bouts—particularly prestigious television matches—to advance their careers; he also arranged for the assignment of cooperative referees and judges. However, recalcitrant fighters were dealt with sternly. In 1951 welterweight contender Billy Graham rejected Carbo's offer of the championship for 20 percent of his earnings. In response, the mob ordered a judge in the Graham–Kid Gavilan title fight to vote for Gavilan, who won a split decision. Carbo was Gavilan's secret manager, and in 1954, after Gavilan opted for a dancing tour instead of training, Carbo punished him by arranging to have his title taken away in his next defense against Johnny Saxton, a surprising winner in a controversial decision.

Carbo prearranged other bouts, including the Jake LaMotta–Billy Fox match in 1947, aimed at setting up Fox for a light heavyweight championship fight. For years LaMotta was the number one middleweight contender, but he never got a title bout because of his independence. However, this time he accepted Carbo's offer of $100,000 and a title match if he would take a dive. The referee stopped the fight in the fourth round after LaMotta made no effort to defend himself. The outcome was so suspicious that LaMotta had to wait two years before the New York State Boxing Commission would approve a championship fight.

Carbo's control over top fighters and his influence in the hiring of prominent matchmakers like Billy Brown of Madison Square Garden gave him enormous influence with the men who planned bouts, and they consulted with him on a regular basis. His power was primarily in New York and Chicago, the major centers of prizefighting, but it extended to the West Coast through Babe McCoy, the leading Los Angeles matchmaker, who in 1941 had managed a Carbo fighter.

Carbo developed close ties to all the top promoters because of his influence with the leading managers, fighters, and matchmakers. Virtually every notable bout required his approval and financial involvement. Carbo even had clout with Mike Jacobs, the principal boxing promoter in the United States from the mid-1930s until 1946. In 1949 James Norris, Jr., and Arthur Wirtz established the International Boxing Club (IBC) to replace Jacobs, who had suffered an incapacitating stroke. The IBC dominated world championship fights between 1949 and 1953, promoting four-fifths of those staged in the United States and nearly monopolizing the booming television market. Norris worked closely with Carbo, who had an office at IBC headquarters in Madison Square Garden. The IBC paid Carbo's future wife, Viola Masters, $45,000 from 1954 to 1957 for no apparent duties. Carbo's role in the IBC escalated after 1954, and one year later he took it over. In 1956 he married Masters; they had no children.

Carbo's downfall began in July 1958 when he was indicted in New York as an unlicensed boxing manager. He went underground to avoid prosecution, and in August the Internal Revenue Service sued him for tax evasion. Carbo was arrested in Haddon Township,

New Jersey, in May 1959. Shortly thereafter, Gabe Genovese became the first person convicted as an unlicensed manager, and Carbo subsequently pleaded guilty and received a two-year prison sentence.

In mid-1960 Carbo was at the center of a major U.S. Senate investigation of boxing, during which he took the Fifth Amendment twenty-five times. While in prison, he and four coconspirators were charged in a federal indictment with extortion for using intimidation to seek control of welterweight champion Don Jordan. In 1962, based on wiretap evidence, Carbo received a 25-year sentence to the McNeil Island, Washington, federal prison. He was also convicted of tax evasion for the years 1944–1946 and 1949–1952. The mob's control of boxing ended with Carbo's conviction, although other nefarious characters later took over his place. Shortly after Carbo was pardoned from prison for ill health, he died in Miami Beach, Florida.

• On Carbo's career, see U.S. Senate, Judiciary Committee, *Professional Boxing, Hearings before the Subcommittee on Antitrust and Monopoly*, 86th Cong., 2d sess., 1960 (1960–1961). For Carbo's place in boxing history, see Steven A. Riess, "Only the Ring Was Square: Frankie Carbo and the Underworld Control of American Boxing," *International Journal of the History of Sport* 5 (May 1988): 29–52; Jeffrey T. Sammons, *Beyond the Ring: The Role of Boxing in American Society* (1988); and Barney Nagler, *James Norris and the Decline of Boxing* (1964). On Carbo and the International Boxing Club, see Robert Coughlin, "How the IBC Runs Boxing," *Sports Illustrated*, 17 Jan. 1955, pp. 47–48. Carbo's relations with LaMotta are described in Jake LaMotta, with Pete Savage, *Raging Bull* (1970). On Carbo's legal problems, see the *New York Times*, 25 July 1958, 31 Oct. 1959, 15 Mar. and 31 May 1961, and 31 Mar. 1962. For his obituary, see the *New York Times*, 11 Nov. 1976.

STEVEN A. RIESS

CARDER, Frederick (18 Sept. 1863–10 Dec. 1963), glassmaker and founder and managing director of Steuben Glass Works in Corning, New York, was born in Brockmoor, Kingswinford, Staffordshire, England, the son of Caleb Carder and Ann Wadelin. Caleb Carder's father owned Leys Pottery in Brierley Hill, Staffordshire, and bequeathed it to his two brothers. Frederick Carder was attracted to art, particularly drawing and sculpting, at an early age. He quit school at the age of fourteen to work in the pottery, where he was assigned menial tasks. Quickly realizing his mistake, he determined to leave the pottery and began taking night school classes at the Stourbridge School of Art and at the Dudley Mechanics Institute. A visit in 1878 to the studio of the glass carver and decorator John Northwood, where he saw Northwood's glass copy of the Roman cameo glass "Portland Vase," attracted him to work in glass.

In 1880 Carder joined the Stevens & Williams glass factory in Brierley Hill as a designer and draftsman. Rising gradually to the position of chief designer, Carder initiated the production of colored glass at Stevens & Williams, perfecting many of the formulas and developing numerous designs for decorative glassware during his 23-year association with the factory. He continued his night art classes, receiving a gold medal and an art master's certificate in 1897. He established the Wordsley School of Art in the same year, serving as headmaster until 1903. In 1887 Carder married Annie Walker; they had three children.

In 1902 Carder was sent by the South Staffordshire County Council to survey the state of glassmaking in Austria and Germany and in 1903 to glassmaking centers in the United States. In Corning, New York, he met Thomas G. Hawkes, who convinced him to leave England and establish a new glasshouse in Corning to supply the Hawkes's glass-cutting firm with blanks. Carder quit Stevens & Williams, emigrated with his wife, daughter, and son in July 1903 (one child having died in 1899), and started the Steuben Glass Works the same year. He was a minority stockholder and served as manager. Although the factory was founded primarily to produce colorless blanks for Hawkes, Carder also quickly began making a line of colorful wares in the art nouveau and classical styles. Principal among them were several types of iridescent colored glass, including "Aurene," "Tyrian," and "Verre de Soie." Carder, determined to make better glass than anyone else, developed all of the company's formulas and most of the decorating techniques; he also designed all of the glass shapes and decorations. By 1932 more than 140 colored glass formulas and decorating techniques had been perfected, and nearly 8,000 forms and more than 500 engraving, cutting, and acid-etching designs had been produced.

Because of the impossibility of buying lead and other materials during World War I, the factory was sold to Corning Glass Works in 1918. It became the Steuben Division of Corning. During the war years, plant production shifted from decorative tableware to essential commodities such as sheet glass, light bulbs, and tubing (which did not require scarce lead in the formula). From 1918 to 1932, Carder remained manager. When Steuben again faced serious financial difficulties in 1932, Carder was promoted to art director of Corning Glass Works. He resented the "promotion," saying that he was "kicked upstairs."

Corning Glass Works considered liquidating Steuben but instead reorganized it as a separate company, Steuben Glass, Inc., and named Arthur A. Houghton, Jr., as president in 1933. Houghton, a great-grandson of the Corning Glass Works' founder, argued that Steuben was failing principally because it lacked a definable style and because it was marketed haphazardly. He hired architect John Monteith Gates and sculptor Sidney Waugh as its first designers. Using a lead crystal perfected at Corning in 1932, Houghton set out to "balance material, workmanship and design" in Steuben's products. A massive, fluid style that showed off the perfection of the material was developed; that design aesthetic is still apparent in Steuben glass. It achieved international recognition as *the* American glass and a rival of famous European factories such as Baccarat, Lalique, Orrefors, and Venini. It retains that distinction.

After 1932, Carder began to experiment with new glass-forming techniques, such as casting by the lost-wax method, in his own office-laboratory, using equipment and materials that he developed himself. He likewise participated in the development of glass for architectural installations for Corning. Among the important commissions was the glass panel above the main entrance of the RCA Building in Rockefeller Center (designed by Lee Lawrie), which was completed in 1933.

Carder was a Fellow of the Royal Society of Arts from 1900 on, a member of the Chemical Society in England, the Art Masters Association of Great Britain, the Ceramic Society, the Society of Glass Technology, a Thirty-third Degree Mason, founder of the City Club in Corning (serving as its president for ten years), founding member and first president of the Corning Rotary Club, and member of the Corning Board of Education (serving as president from 1934 to 1951). He received the Friedsam Gold Medal of the Architectural League of New York and the Binns Medal of the American Ceramic Society, and he was a delegate in the Hoover Commission to the 1925 world's fair in Paris.

Carder, mentally alert and using peppery language to the end, continued working in his factory office-studio until 1959, when, at the age of ninety-six, he finally "retired" to painting and gardening. He died in Corning, New York.

Carder is often referred to as a "glassmaker's glassmaker," reflecting his simultaneous roles as chemist, technician, designer, and manager of Steuben. The designs of his products were rooted in a classical aesthetic and rarely embraced the lush art nouveau style fully. They are typically cool, intellectual exercises emphasizing classical forms and proportions, precise workmanship, and elegant surface finish and color. Louis Comfort Tiffany, Carder's chief competitor in the production of iridescent glass, is generally given the nod for artistic creativity. Carder is acknowledged more for his technical expertise and for the myriad forming and decorating techniques he developed that have continued to be studied and adapted by artists working with glass.

• An unpublished manuscript autobiography is in the Corning Museum of Glass. The most comprehensive work dealing with Carder's life and work is Paul V. Gardner, *The Glass of Frederick Carder* (1971). Additional surveys include W. E. S. Turner, "The Art of Frederick Carder," *Journal of the Society of Glass Technology* 23 (1939): 41–43; Thomas Scharman Buechner, *Frederick Carder, His Life and Work* (1952; repr. 1985); Paul N. Perrot et al., *Steuben: Seventy Years of American Glassmaking* (1974); and Gardner, *Frederick Carder: Portrait of a Glassmaker* (1985). The most complete obituary is in the *Corning Leader*, 11 Dec. 1963.

DWIGHT P. LANMON

CARDOZO, Benjamin Nathan (24 May 1870–9 July 1938), lawyer and jurist, was born in New York City, the son of Albert Cardozo, a lawyer, and Rebecca Washington Nathan. Cardozo's mother died when he was nine, his father when he was fifteen. His sister, Ellen, ten years his senior, assumed much of the responsibility for raising him. Cardozo never married but resided with Ellen; she died in 1929 and thereafter he lived alone. The Cardozos were Sephardic Jews, congregants of Shearith Israel (Remnant of Israel), often called the Spanish-Portuguese Synagogue. Rabbi Henry Pereira Mendes prepared Cardozo for his bar mitzvah, celebrated when he reached the age of thirteen. He remained a member of Shearith Israel all his life but was not a deeply religious man or one who observed Jewish rituals.

Most writers have claimed that Cardozo's choice of a legal career and his behavior as a judge were crucially influenced by his reaction to a scandal involving his father. In 1872 Albert Cardozo, a justice of the New York State Supreme Court, resigned to avoid probable impeachment for malfeasance in office. The most serious allegation was that he assigned lucrative receiverships to a relative in return for kickbacks amounting to nearly $30,000. Albert Cardozo, however, always regarded himself as innocent, the victim of a political vendetta, as did other members of his family. Consequently, the suggestion that Benjamin Cardozo consciously set out to vindicate his father and restore honor to the family name is not persuasive.

As a youth Cardozo did not attend school but was educated at home. Horatio Alger, Jr., whose rags-to-riches formula made him the most widely read author of books for young readers in the late nineteenth century and who privately tutored the children of several prominent Jewish families, prepared Cardozo for admission to Columbia College. Matriculating in 1885, Cardozo was graduated in 1889 with honors in four subjects and then received a master's degree in 1890 from the School of Political Science. He studied at Columbia's School of Law from 1889 to 1891 but did not receive a law degree. A member of only the second class that was required to take a three- rather than a two-year course of study, Cardozo elected to withdraw after two years. After passing the bar examination, he entered private practice.

Over the next two decades Cardozo established himself as one of the most knowledgeable attorneys in New York City's legal community. Since his personal style—restrained, detached, scholarly—was ill-suited to the adversarial atmosphere of the courtroom, Cardozo specialized in preparing briefs for lawyers who were appealing cases to higher courts. In all, he submitted briefs in 197 such cases, 128 of them at the intermediate-court level and 69 to the state's highest court, the Court of Appeals. Nearly all of his suits dealt with real property and aspects of civil law rather than with criminal law. In 1903 Cardozo published *The Jurisdiction of the Court of Appeals of the State of New York*, in which he explained that the function of the court was "not of declaring justice between man and man, but of settling the law. . . . The wrongs of aggrieved suitors are only the algebraic symbols from which the court is to work out the formula of justice."

In 1913 Cardozo, a Democrat, was nominated by the newly formed anti–Tammany Hall Fusion party as a candidate for the New York State Supreme Court, the same court from which his father had resigned. He was elected by a plurality of fewer than 3,000 out of more than 300,000 votes cast. In February 1914, only a month after Cardozo took his seat, Governor Martin Glynn appointed him to a vacancy on the Court of Appeals. Designated to serve a three-year term, he was elected in his own right in 1917 and was appointed chief judge in 1926, moving to Albany, New York.

During the eighteen years he served on the Court of Appeals Cardozo wrote more than 500 opinions. Many of his rulings in the areas of torts, contracts, and liability influenced courts throughout the United States. He was universally regarded as a judge who remained faithful to settled traditions yet he was capable of adapting the law to modern social and economic needs. Indeed, his two most influential and frequently cited decisions, *MacPherson v. Buick Motor Company* (1916) and *Palsgraf v. Long Island Railroad Co.* (1928), brought about profound changes in the law. *MacPherson* made automobile manufacturers responsible for the safety of their cars not only to the dealers to whom they actually sold the cars but also to the customers who ultimately bought them. In *Palsgraf* Cardozo redefined the law of negligence. He reasoned that a railroad company could not be expected to take precautions against unforeseeable hazards, and therefore a passenger who was injured while waiting on a platform did not have a right to recover damages. "The risk reasonably to be perceived defines the duty to be obeyed," Cardozo wrote, "and risk imparts relation."

During Cardozo's years on the Court of Appeals his many speeches, writings, and extrajudicial activities helped him to achieve a national reputation. He was the author of *The Nature of the Judicial Process* (1921) and *The Growth of the Law* (1924), both deriving from lectures delivered at the Yale Law School; *The Paradoxes of Legal Science* (1928), based on lectures at Columbia University; and a collection of essays and addresses, *Law and Literature* (1931). He was a founder and vice president of the American Law Institute, an organization dedicated to codifying legal principles. "What is it that I do when I decide a case?" Cardozo asked in *The Nature of the Judicial Process*. His answer made it clear that he accepted the view, controversial at the time, that judges did not "find" a preexisting law, but rather "made" the law. At the same time, Cardozo argued, judges were not free to make law as they pleased or "travel beyond the walls of the interstices, the bounds set to judicial innovation by precedent and custom." Judges must draw their inspiration from "consecrated principles," he asserted, and not yield to a "vague and unregulated benevolence."

On 15 February 1932 President Herbert Hoover nominated Cardozo to fill the vacancy on the U.S. Supreme Court created by the resignation of Oliver Wendell Holmes, Jr. Hailed as the most suitable successor to the venerable Holmes, Cardozo won quick and unanimous Senate confirmation. Although cautious in outlook and moderate in manner, Cardozo eventually came to be regarded as among the most liberal of justices, chiefly because his belief in judicial restraint usually led him to approve New Deal measures. Along with Associate Justices Louis D. Brandeis and Harlan Fiske Stone, Cardozo was the member of the Court most likely to uphold state and congressional statutes regulating the economy.

Cardozo outlined his position in *Stewart Dry Goods Co. v. Lewis*, a 1935 case in which a majority of the justices declared that a state could not impose a tax based on a business's gross sales rather than its profits. Cardozo dissented, reasoning that such a tax was constitutional so long as the legislature had not acted "in a perverse or vengeful spirit" but had rather sought to pursue "legitimate ends by methods honestly conceived and rationally chosen." This outlook led Cardozo to side with the Franklin D. Roosevelt administration in related matters as well. In 1936 Cardozo wrote dissenting opinions for himself, Brandeis, and Stone when a conservative majority struck down a measure establishing minimum wages and maximum hours in the bituminous coal industry (*Carter v. Carter Coal Co.*) and when it nullified a statute designed to provide bankruptcy relief to state and local governments (*Ashton v. Cameron County Water Improvement District I*).

In 1937 the Supreme Court began to approve important New Deal measures. Cardozo wrote the majority opinion in *Helvering v. Davis* that upheld the government's authority to impose taxes on employees and employers to fund old-age pensions under the Social Security Act. Congress had a right to use the spending power to aid the "general welfare," Cardozo said, and this necessarily involved both a measure of discretion and a willingness to take account of changing circumstances: "The hope behind this statute is to save men and women from the rigors of the poor house as well as from the haunting fear that such a lot awaits them when journey's end is near."

Cardozo's philosophy of judicial restraint, which led him to side with liberals on issues involving economic regulation, produced a different outcome when questions of individual rights came before the Court. *Palko v. Connecticut*, decided in December 1937, was Cardozo's most influential Supreme Court opinion and the last one he ever wrote. A man was accused of murdering a policeman. Connecticut asked for a first-degree murder conviction, but the jury returned a verdict of second-degree murder after the trial judge had ruled that a confession was inadmissible. A higher court ruled that the judge had erred, a new trial was held, the confession was admitted, a verdict of first-degree murder was returned, and the death sentence was pronounced. Cardozo's decision held that this did not constitute double jeopardy, but in any event that prohibition in the Bill of Rights did not apply to the states (through the Fourteenth Amendment's due process clause) because protection against double jeopardy was not "of the very essence of a scheme of ordered liberty." Rights that were "implicit in the concept of ordered liberty"—Cardozo listed freedom of speech and press, peaceable assembly, free exercise of religion, and benefit of counsel—were, however, protected against encroachment by the states.

Shortly after delivering this opinion Cardozo suffered a heart attack, followed by a stroke in January 1938. He was never able to resume his duties on the Supreme Court. He died in Port Chester, New York, at the home of his friend Irving Lehman, an associate judge of the New York State Court of Appeals. Never one who felt comfortable revealing his innermost feelings—he was, in Lehman's words, "a man of fastidious reticence"—Cardozo had lived a lonely life, especially after he moved from Albany to Washington, D.C. "He never quite wanted anybody to penetrate into his inner life," Lehman noted, and to make sure nobody ever did, Lehman arranged to have the bulk of Cardozo's private papers destroyed. Consequently, the scholarly attention paid to Cardozo has focused on his professional career rather than his personal life. The career surely merits the attention, for all writers—those who admire Cardozo and those who are more critical—agree that he had a profound influence on the development of American law.

• There are small collections of Benjamin Cardozo's papers at Columbia University and the American Jewish Archives. Since most of his own papers were destroyed, his letters can only be found in other collections, including the papers of Harlan Fiske Stone (Library of Congress), Annie Nathan Meyer (Barnard College), Stephen S. Wise (American Jewish Historical Society), Charles C. Burlingham and Learned Hand (Harvard Law School), Jerome Frank (Yale University), Karl Llewellyn (University of Chicago Law School), George S. Hellman (New York Public Library), and Oscar Cox (Franklin D. Roosevelt Library). An informative although uncritical biography is George S. Hellman, *Benjamin N. Cardozo: American Judge* (1940). For a more recent assessment, see Richard A. Posner, *Cardozo: A Study in Reputation* (1990). Stanley Charles Brubaker's "Benjamin Nathan Cardozo: An Intellectual Biography" (Ph.D. diss., Univ. of Virginia, 1979) is a first-rate study. An obituary is in the *New York Times*, 10 July 1938.

RICHARD POLENBERG

CARDOZO, Francis Louis (1 Feb. 1837–22 July 1903), minister, educator, and politician, was born in Charleston, South Carolina, the son of a free black woman (name unknown) and a Jewish father. It is uncertain whether Cardozo's father was Jacob N. Cardozo, the prominent economist and editor of an "ardently anti-nullification newspaper in Charleston during the 1830s" (Williamson, p. 210), or his lesser-known brother, Isaac Cardozo, a weigher in the city's customhouse. Born free at a time when slavery dominated southern life, Cardozo enjoyed a childhood of relative privilege among Charleston's antebellum free black community. Between the ages of five and twelve he attended a school for free blacks, then he spent five years as a carpenter's apprentice and four more as a journeyman. In 1858 Cardozo used his savings to travel to Scotland, where he studied at the University of Glasgow, graduating with distinction in 1861. As the Civil War erupted at home, he remained in Europe to study at the London School of Theology and at a Presbyterian seminary in Edinburgh.

In 1864 Cardozo returned to the United States to become pastor of the Temple Street Congregational Church in New Haven, Connecticut. That year he married Catherine Rowena Howell; they had six children, one of whom died in infancy. During his brief stay in the North, Cardozo became active in politics. In October 1864 he was among 145 black leaders who attended a national black convention in Syracuse, New York, that reflected the contagion of rising expectations inspired by the Civil War and emancipation.

In June 1865 Cardozo became an agent of the American Missionary Association (AMA) and almost immediately returned to his native South Carolina. His brother Thomas Cardozo, the AMA's education director, was accused of having an affair with a student in New York, and Francis Cardozo replaced him while also assuming the directorship of the Saxton School in Charleston. Within months the school was flourishing under his leadership, with more than one thousand black students and twenty-one teachers. In 1866 Cardozo helped to found the Avery Normal Institute and became its first superintendent.

Unlike many South Carolina mulattoes, Cardozo made no distinction between educating blacks who were born free and former slaves, nor did he draw conclusions, then common, about intellectual capacity based on skin color gradations. Instead, he was committed to universal education regardless of "race, color or previous condition," a devotion he considered "the object for which I left all the superior advantages and privileges of the North and came South, it is the object for which I have labored during the past year, and for which I am willing to *remain* here and make this place my home."

Despite the fact that he claimed to possess "no desire for the turbulent political scene," Cardozo soon found himself in the middle of Reconstruction politics. In 1865 he attended the state black convention in Charleston, where he helped draft a petition to the state legislature demanding stronger civil rights provisions. In 1868, following the passage of the Reconstruction Acts by Congress, he was elected as a delegate to the South Carolina constitutional convention. From the onset he was frank about his intentions, "As colored men we have been cheated out of our rights for two centuries and now that we have the opportunity I want to fix them in the Constitution in such a way that no lawyer, however cunning, can possibly misinterpret the meaning."

Cardozo wielded considerable influence at the convention. As chair of the Education Committee, he was instrumental in drafting a plan, which was later ratified, to establish a tax-supported system of compulsory, integrated public education, the first of its kind in the South. Despite his support for integration, however, he also understood the logic articulated by black teachers of maintaining support for separate schools for blacks who wanted to avoid the hostility and violence that often accompanied integration. Consistently egalitarian, he opposed poll taxes, literacy tests, and other forms of what he called "class legislation." Moreover, he fought proposals to suspend the collection of wartime debts, which he thought would only halt the destruction of "the infernal plantation system," a process he deemed central to Reconstruction's success. In fact, Cardozo argued: "We will never have true freedom until we abolish the system of agriculture which existed in the Southern States. It is useless to have any schools while we maintain the stronghold of slavery as the agricultural system of the country." Thus, he called for a tripartite approach to enfranchisement: universal access to political participation and power, comprehensive public education, and reform initiatives that guaranteed equal opportunity for land ownership and economic independence.

After the convention, Cardozo's career accelerated. A "handsome man, almost white in color . . . with . . . tall, portly, well-groomed figure and elaborately urbane manners" (Simkins and Woody), Cardozo played a central role in the real efforts to reconstruct American society along more democratic lines. In 1868 he declined the Republican nomination for lieutenant governor in the wake of white claims of Reconstruction "black supremacy." Later that year he was elected secretary of state, making him the first black state official in South Carolina history, and he retained that position until 1872. In 1869 Cardozo was a delegate to the South Carolina labor convention and then briefly served as secretary of the advisory board of the state land commission, an agency created to redistribute confiscated land to freedmen and poor whites. In this capacity, he helped to reorganize its operations after a period of severe mismanagement and corruption. As secretary of state, he was given full responsibility for overseeing the land commission. In 1872 he successfully advocated for the immediate redistribution of land to settlers and produced the first comprehensive report on the agency's financial activities. By the fall of 1872, owing in large part to Cardozo's efforts, over 5,000 families—3,000 more than in 1871—had settled on tracts of land provided by the commission, one of the more radical achievements of the Reconstruction Era.

In 1870, the same year that the federal census estimated his net worth at an impressive $8,000, Cardozo was elected president of the Grand Council of Union Leagues, an organization that worked to ensure Republican victories throughout the state. His civic activities included serving as president of the Greenville and Columbia Railroad, a charter member of the Columbia Street Railway Company, and a member of the Board of Trustees of the University of South Carolina. Some sources report that he enrolled in the university's law school in October 1874, however, no evidence exists that he ever received a degree.

From 1871 to 1872 Cardozo was professor of Latin in Washington, D.C., at Howard University, where he was considered for the presidency in 1877. In 1872 and 1874 he was elected state treasurer, vowing to restore South Carolina's credit. During his first term as treasurer he oversaw the allocation of more money than had been spent "for the education of the common people by the government of South Carolina from the Declaration of Independence to 1868, a period of ninety-two years" (Cardozo, *The Finances of the State of South Carolina* [1873], pp. 11–12). In the words of one conservative newspaper editor, Cardozo was the "most respectable and honest of all the state officials." Despite his longstanding reputation for scrupulous financial management, he was accused in 1875 of "misconduct and irregularity in office" for allegedly mishandling state bonds. Though he claimed reelection as treasurer in 1876, he officially resigned from the office on 11 April 1877. Subsequently tried and convicted for fraud by the Court of General Sessions for Richland County in November 1877, Cardozo was eventually pardoned by Democratic governor Wade Hampton before his sentence, two years in prison and a fine of $4,000, was commuted.

Following the ascendancy of the new Democratic government and the final abandonment of Radical Reconstruction in 1877, Cardozo moved in 1878 to Washington, D.C., and secured a clerkship in the Treasury Department, which he held from 1878 to 1884. Returning to education in the last decades of his life, he served as principal of the Colored Preparatory High School from 1884 to 1891 and from 1891 to 1896 as principal of the M Street High School, where he instituted a comprehensive business curriculum. A prominent member of Washington's elite black community until his death there, Cardozo was so revered by his peers, black and white, that a business high school opened in 1928 was named in his honor.

• The Francis L. Cardozo Family Papers are held at the Library of Congress. *Proceedings of the 1868 Constitutional Convention of South Carolina* (Charleston, 1868) help to locate Cardozo's ideas within the context of Reconstruction debates. The *Twentieth Annual Report on the Educational Condition in Charleston, American Missionary Association* (1866) contains Cardozo's assessment of black education in the aftermath of the Civil War. For good biographical sketches of Cardozo's activities, see William C. Hine, "Black Politicians in Reconstruction Charleston, South Carolina," *Journal of Southern History* 49 (1983); Joe M. Richardson, "Francis L. Cardozo: Black Educator during Reconstruction," *Journal of Negro Education* 48 (1979): 73–83; and Edward F. Sweat, "Francis L. Cardoza—Profile of Integrity in Reconstruction Politics," *Journal of Negro History* 44 (1961): 217–32. Useful secondary works include Francis Simkins and Robert H. Woody, *South Carolina during Reconstruction* (1932); W. E. B. Du Bois, *Black Reconstruction in America, 1860–1880* (1935); Joel Williamson, *After Slavery: The Negro in South Carolina during Reconstruction, 1861–1877* (1965); Carol K. Rothrock Bleser, *The Promised Land: The History of the South Carolina Land Commission, 1869–1890* (1969); Peggy Lamson, *The Glorious Failure: Black Congressman Robert Brown Elliott and the Reconstruction in South Carolina* (1973); Thomas Holt, *Black Over White: Negro Political Leadership in South Carolina during Reconstruction* (1979); and Eric Foner, *Reconstruction: America's Unfinished Revolution, 1863–1877* (1988).

TIMOTHY P. MCCARTHY

CARDOZO, Jacob Newton (17 June 1786–30 Aug. 1873), economist and journalist, was born in Savannah, Georgia, the son of David N. Cardozo, a member of the Sephardic Jewish mercantile community who had served in the South Carolina militia during the American Revolution (the identity of his mother is unknown). Cardozo had a modest formal education; he left school at the age of twelve and subsequently became a lumber clerk. From an early age he displayed a remarkable intellectual curiosity and a talent for writing. His career in journalism began in 1816 when he joined the staff of the *Southern Patriot*, published in Charleston, South Carolina. He became the owner of this newspaper in 1823 and served as its editor and publisher until 1845. From 1845 to 1861 he was affiliated with the *Charleston Evening News*; initially as founder-owner and subsequently as commercial editor. Cardozo was also a contributor to antebellum journals of opinion such as the *Southern Review* and the *Southern Quarterly Review*.

Cardozo first attracted widespread attention in 1826 with the publication of *Notes on Political Economy*, one of the pioneering treatises on this subject to be written by an American. Cardozo was well read in the theories propounded by the British classical school of economists. He insisted, however, that the "statesmen of the new world" should "not be implicitly guided by the results of investigations pursued by European writers into the sources of wealth." He saw his own contribution as a direct challenge to David Ricardo's line of analysis, holding that "if the principles of this theory (which are founded on circumstances completely contrasted to those that are peculiar to our own country) should be adopted as texts for lectures in our Colleges and Universities, it will greatly retard the progress of this important science among us" (*Notes on Political Economy* [1826], pp. iii–iv). Cardozo took particular exception to Ricardian teaching on the theory of rent, which maintained that agricultural output per acre would fall as the area under cultivation was extended. This conclusion did not apply in the United States where land abundance—not land scarcity—was a fundamental reality. Even on the inferior soils yields could be expected to rise through time as improved technologies were applied to them. Cardozo's analysis offered an optimistic vision for sustained economic progress in the New World.

While Cardozo disputed properties of the Ricardian theoretical system, he still endorsed most of the policy conclusions of the orthodox classical tradition. In particular, he was an articulate spokesman for free trade, serving on the committee that drafted the first southern petition to Congress to protest against the "Tariff of Abominations" in 1827–1828. But he parted company with the more militant South Carolinians over the question of nullification. In his view at that time, "we should consider it a lesser evil to have this system of protection, with all its attendant losses and prospective risks, to a separation of the States" (*The Tariff: Its True Character and Effects Practically Illustrated* [1830], p. 50). Though he was a southern loyalist in his defense of slavery, he opposed reopening the transatlantic slave trade. He was outspoken, however, in his editorial denunciation of abolitionists, whose agitation he regarded as a "conspiracy against property." In the decade before the Civil War he reluctantly concluded that secession was inevitable.

By the 1840s and 1850s Cardozo was persuaded that the survival of slavery was dependent on the South's success in increasing its economic power. While he recognized the crucial contribution of plantation-grown cotton to southern economic life, he argued in support of diversifying the region's production pattern. Industrial development should be promoted actively. In his view, southern manufacturing could be competitive because of the cost advantages of slave labor. Thus strengthened economically, the South would be better positioned to defend its social institutions. Cardozo's thinking on this matter stood in sharp contrast to that of northern contemporaries (such as Henry C. Carey) who insisted that growth in the demand for labor spurred by an expanding manufacturing base would convert slaves into emancipated wage employees.

During the Civil War Cardozo enthusiastically embraced the Confederate cause. His editorial commentary, appearing in *Southern Confederacy* (published in Atlanta, Ga.), included advice on the management of the South's war economy. He then denounced efforts to contain inflationary-pressures through price-fixing and faulted the Confederate government for its excessive issue of currency. Arguing that the southern economy could not bear the strain of financing the war through current taxation, he urged the Confederate government to borrow abroad—a prospect he held to be feasible. His essays on this subject were collected in pamphlet form in 1863 under the title *A Plan for Financial Relief, Addressed to the Legislature of Georgia, and Confederate States Congress*. His last book-length work, *Reminiscences of Charleston* (1866), was a nostalgic lament for the passing of the old order.

Details about Cardozo's personal life are sparse. He is known to have fathered a son by a woman of mixed African-American and Native-American blood. The son, Francis L. Cardozo, served as a South Carolina secretary of the state and state treasurer during the Reconstruction period. Jacob Newton Cardozo's uncle was the great-grandfather of Benjamin N. Cardozo, an associate justice of the U.S. Supreme Court (1932–1938). Jacob Newton Cardozo died in Savannah, Georgia.

Twentieth-century students of the history of economic thought have recognized Cardozo as a fresh and original voice, whose sophistication in formal economic theorizing was superior to that of most American contemporaries. While he was the ablest economic thinker in the antebellum South, in his attitudes toward the overriding practical issues of his day, he was the captive of his cultural environment. In southern intellectual circles, however, he enjoyed a reputation as a one-man "Brain Trust."

• No personal papers or correspondence are known to exist. A review of Cardozo's major contributions to economic debate is in Joseph Dorfman, *The Economic Mind in American Civilization*, vol. 2 (1946). Dorfman has added biographical details in his preface to the reissue of Cardozo's *Notes on Political Economy* (1960). Melvin M. Leiman, *Jacob N. Cardozo: Economic Thought in the Antebellum South* (1966), offers a more extended survey of his life and work. The paternity of Francis L. Cardozo is discussed in Rayford W. Logan and Michael R. Winston, eds., *Dictionary of American Negro Biography* (1982).

WILLIAM J. BARBER

CAREY, Henry Charles (15 Dec. 1793–13 Oct. 1879), economist, publisher, and social scientist, was born in Philadelphia, Pennsylvania, the son of Mathew Carey, an economist and publisher, and Bridget Flavahan. His father, an Irish patriot and political exile, also worked periodically in social science. Carey never received any formal education and instead was taught by his father. In addition, he read many of the books that made their way through his father's publishing house, Carey & Lea (later known as Carey, Lea & Carey). In 1802 he went to work for his father, eventually becoming a partner and head of the firm, which was at the time the largest publishing and bookselling house in the country. Carey became the American publisher for Thomas Carlyle, Sir Walter Scott, and Washington Irving. He continued running the family firm until he retired in 1835.

After leaving the publishing business, in which he had amassed a considerable fortune, Carey devoted the rest of his life to the study of political economy. His first published effort was his *Essay on the Rate of Wages* (1835), which advocated a laissez-faire approach to economic affairs and also adopted the wage-fund theory. Carey rejected the Ricardian rent theory, which held that farmers would choose the most fertile land to farm on first, progressively going down with corresponding returns on the land, by announcing his belief that capital and invention would make up for the infertility of poorer land. Carey's earliest work left little doubt that he was an ardent supporter of the concept of free trade. Each of his publications stressed his conviction that governmental interference in economics would cause great damage and that only unfettered commerce between countries would maintain peace and property rights.

Carey expanded his *Essay on the Rate of Wages* into the *Principles of Political Economy*, which came out in three separate volumes from 1837 to 1840. Among the ideas propounded in this set was Carey's unusual distribution theory, which called for progressive dispersal of wealth among the poorest families in a society. This work was especially popular in Europe, where it was translated into Swedish and Italian and appeared in numerous political/economic journals. Throughout his life, Carey's works experienced global circulation and were translated, additionally, into German, Japanese, Portuguese, and Russian. Carey believed that *Principles of Political Economy* influenced the 1850 publication of *Harmonies Economiques* by French economist M. Bastiat. Bastiat denied the charge, stating that Carey's *Principles* merely confirmed his own, already established opinions.

In 1842, still holding firm to his laissez-faire views, Carey forecast that dire circumstances would result from that year's protective tariff. Some historians believe that, after the tariff was enacted, Carey noticed that it was beneficial and thus was forced to rethink his ideas of political economy. In contrast, William Elder, in his biography, *Memoir of Henry C. Carey* (1880), wrote that Carey's conversion from the free-trade system to protectionism came practically out of nowhere in 1844. Regardless, Carey renounced his belief in laissez-faire for good in his book *Past, Present and Future* (1848) despite the fact that during this era the idea of free trade was gathering considerable momentum worldwide.

Carey continued to trumpet the cause of protectionism. He began working as an editorial writer for Horace Greeley's *New York Tribune* in 1849, during Greeley's protectionist phase. Greeley would later support the tariff of 1857, which represented a change of heart for him because that tariff reduced rates. Carey also helped finance a protectionist journal, *The Plough, the Loom, and the Anvil.* In *Harmony of Interests: Agricultural, Manufacturing, and Commercial* (1851), he further honed his principles of protectionism, putting forth his belief that the closer the proximity of manufactures and agriculture to each other, the more effective economic development would be. He felt that American security was threatened by the economic power of England, thus any economic ties to Great Britain must be severed to achieve the goal of economic independence for the United States.

Carey also became involved in politics. In 1856 he served as a delegate to the Republican National Convention, where he received three votes for vice president. In 1860 he was considered a potential candidate for president or for governor of Pennsylvania. Those candidacies never materialized, and the only public office Carey held was as a delegate to the Pennsylvania constitutional convention in 1872.

Although it is unclear what, if any, enduring effect Carey had on the theory of international trade, his writings contributed to the debate in the United States of protectionism versus free trade, which was in many ways a political question rather than strictly a question of economic theory. More than most other economists, Carey grasped the link between politics and economics. In his *Principles of Social Science*, which appeared in three volumes in 1858 and 1859, he wrote: "The system of this country being based upon the idea of entire political equality, we might, perhaps, be warranted in looking to our teachers for something different, even if not better; but if we should, in general, be disappointed. With few and slight exceptions, our professors teach the same social science that is taught abroad by men who live by inculcating the divine right of kings." This insightful work showed how the economic shift from autocratic to democratic rule coupled with the effect of democratic political theory on economic conditions led the United States to move from political economy to what he termed social science. Carey believed that political economy was only a practical art, while social science was something akin to natural science. This elevation from political economy to social science meant that social science itself was merely a part of universal knowledge and moral philosophy. "All science will prove to be but one," he wrote in *Principles of Social Science*, "its parts differing as do the colors of the spectrum, but producing, as does the sun's ray, undecomposed, one white and brilliant light."

Thereafter Carey's creativity diminished, and the remainder of his works basically restated the same ideas. His final book was the *Unity of Law* (1872), but he continued churning out his economic writings in pamphlet form until his death.

It is difficult to clearly state Carey's proper place in the annals of political economy given the lack of consensus among historians. Rodney J. Morrison wrote: "In advocating protection and in developing a complete economic system, Carey's theoretical arguments cannot withstand the scrutiny of absolute criteria. He was undoubtedly the best example of a nationalist economist in nineteenth century America, but in no way was he on the side of angels. . . . [His] career is shrouded by the possibility of vested interests." A more mixed review comes from J. R. Turner in *The Ricardian Rent Theory in Early American Economics* (1921). Turner wrote: "Desire to find the truth seems to be his one motive. Let an unfavorable doctrine come his way, however, and he remonstrated with a spartan-like vigor. That he was positive in his convictions, dogmatic, wanting in judicial temperament, over-confident, and too much one-sided on many questions cannot be denied . . . [but h]e was honest, profoundly in earnest, he labored with zeal for the betterment of man." A kind appraisal comes from O. F. Boucke in *The Development of Economics, 1750–1900* (1921): "H. C. Carey was the first to unite with a general knowledge of natural science a deep interest in philosophy as well as originality in the treatment of economic problems. No American of the nineteenth century can claim more justly our high regard for labors well done than this zealous champion of monism. . . . What [August] Comte was to France and [John Stuart] Mill to England, Carey, in a way, meant to America."

The reason for the divergent views on Carey's contributions is likely the inability of anyone to articulate precisely what he stood for. Perhaps Arnold Wilfred Green put it best:

> In the case of Carey . . . there would appear to be unusual difficulties in seeking summary formula. He was a determined, headstrong, impulsive partisan, whose writings and activities are so elusive in logical, moral, or ideational consistency that . . . various previous attempts to assess the man have selected valid aspects of his character to form general statements which stand poles apart. Exactly what Carey's historical mission was . . . appears difficult to determine. [He] devoted his life to his fellow man, to a vision of the better society which would emerge if the future were to actualize the principle he enunciated. He was also the most effective mouthpiece a growing capitalist class could claim for its own, making a special plea for their, and not too incidentally his own, interests. And there the matter must remain.

The full name of Carey's wife, a sister of the artist C. R. Leslie, and the date of their marriage are unknown. They had no children. Carey died in Philadelphia.

• Carey's library was bequeathed to the University of Pennsylvania. Numerous biographical sources chronicle his economic theories in addition to the facts of his life, including Rodney J. Morrison, *Henry C. Carey and American Economic Development* (1986), which contains a complete list of Carey's works; Arnold Wilfred Green, *Henry Charles Carey, Nineteenth-Century Sociologist* (1951); Ernest Teilhac, *Pioneers of American Economic Thought in the Nineteenth Century*, trans. E. A. J. Johnson (1936); A. D. H. Kaplan, *Henry Charles Carey: A Study in American Economic Thought* (1931); and William Elder, *A Memorial of Henry C. Carey* (1880).

FRANCESCO L. NEPA

CAREY, Joseph Maull (19 Jan. 1845–5 Feb. 1924), U.S. senator and governor of Wyoming, was born in Milton, Delaware, the son of Robert Hood Carey, a merchant and farmer, and Susan Davis. He attended public schools in his hometown. At the age of seventeen, Joseph left Delaware to study at the Fort Edward Collegiate Institute in New York before entering Union College, where he studied for two years. In 1867 he graduated from the University of Pennsylvania with a degree in law and was admitted to the bar that same year. After practicing law for two years in Philadelphia with Benjamin F. Temple and others, he was appointed by President Ulysses S. Grant as U.S. attorney for the new Wyoming Territory. In 1872, at the age of twenty-seven, he was appointed associate justice of the territorial supreme court and served on the bench until 1876, when he resigned to devote his energies to his expanding cattle empire. In 1877 he married Louisa David, and they had two sons. The elder, Robert D. Carey, served as governor of Wyoming from 1919 to 1923 and as U.S. senator from 1931 to 1937.

After his arrival in Wyoming, Carey observed that any man with a little capital and "with but ordinary luck" would find cattle ranching on the open range "a sure road to fortune" (Gould, *Wyoming*, p. 76). He entered the cattle business in 1871, driving herds north from Texas into the Wyoming Territory. His famous CY brand was among the very earliest registered in the Wyoming Territory. Quickly becoming one of the West's greatest cattle barons, he formed a partnership with his brother, R. Davis Carey (another brother, Dr. John F. Carey, joined the partnership in the late 1880s). In 1876 Joseph Carey drove 15,000 head of cattle from central Wyoming into open rangelands north of the Platte River and Chugwater Creek, from which American Indians had recently been forcibly removed to reservations. Two years earlier he had been one of the principal organizers of the Wyoming Stock Growers Association (WSGA), and during the 1870s Carey played a central role in the formation of what became known as the American National Livestock Association. Both organizations successfully fostered state and national legislation aimed at protecting the interests of the cattle ranchers. In 1878 an associate observed Carey to be "still wholly absorbed in the cattle business to such an extent that he can do and does little to help his friends in the political or any other field" (Gould, *Wyoming*, p. 77). During the 1880s, while he represented the Wyoming Territory as its congressional delegate in Washington, Carey served, simultaneously, as chairman of the Committee on State and National Legislation for the national cattlemen's group. He was president of the WSGA from 1883 to 1888 and a member of its secretive committee that employed livestock detectives or regulators to suppress those suspected of rustling cattle. In 1885 Carey founded the Wyoming Development Company to irrigate lands for the production of grain along the Laramie River and Chugwater Creek in eastern Wyoming. He eventually bought out his brothers' interests and became sole proprietor of a vast ranching enterprise that included the first purebred Hereford cattle in Wyoming. Throughout the boom era of the cattle kingdoms, Carey frequently joined fellow aristocrats of the open range at the notorious Cheyenne Club, where Canadian waiters served the world's finest wines and champagnes accompanied by caviar and pickled eel and where visitors arriving at Cheyenne via the Union Pacific Railroad were amazed at the splendor the cattlemen had arranged for themselves on the rugged Wyoming frontier.

While never wavering in his support of measures to assist the western cattle industry, Carey's political career displayed an interest in progressive social legislation and government reform measures. He was mayor of Cheyenne from 1881 to 1884 and served from 1885 to 1890 as Wyoming's delegate to Congress, where he authored the acts that admitted Wyoming and Idaho to statehood in 1890. His efforts to secure Wyoming's admission to the Union won him acclaim as the "Father of Wyoming Statehood." Chosen the first U.S. senator from the new state of Wyoming in 1890, Carey secured passage in 1894 of the Carey Arid Lands Act. Popularly known as the Carey Act, it authorized the secretary of the interior to patent lands to states with desert areas, provided that the land would be reclaimed and irrigated. Large areas in Wyoming were patented to various land companies almost immediately as a result of this legislation.

When the WSGA saw its power threatened by homesteaders and those suspected of rustling, Carey used his influence on behalf of the big ranchers in the brief but violent dispute known as the Johnson County War. In 1892 the WSGA employed a band of ruffians from Texas and Oklahoma, known as the "Invaders," to hunt down suspected rustlers and intimidate homesteaders on the open range in the area around Buffalo, Wyoming. The extent to which Carey was involved in the planning of this sordid adventure is unknown, but one of his ranch managers, Edward David, played a central role in recruiting gunmen and cutting the telegraph lines to Buffalo. According to David, the "Invaders" were instructed to shoot or lynch at least thirty men whose names appeared on a WSGA list and to eliminate Sheriff W. G. "Red" Angus and three Johnson County Commissioners, replacing them with "a proper set of officials" who would be more sympathetic to the WSGA. After murdering two luckless settlers in a cabin near Kaycee, the "Invaders" found themselves surrounded on the TA Ranch by a huge, well-armed posse comprised of local citizens and led by Sheriff Angus. In panic, the WSGA turned to Washington to avoid disaster. Acting Governor Amos W. Barber, who undoubtedly knew in advance of the WSGA plans to invade Johnson County, sent an urgent telegram to President Benjamin Harrison on 12 April 1892 declaring "an insurrection exists in Johnson county . . . against the government," and he pleaded that federal troops from Ft. McKinney be sent "to assist in suppressing the insurrection" (quoted in Smith, p. 224). Arriving at the White House in the middle of the night, Carey and fellow Wyoming senator Francis E. Warren, also a wealthy and powerful rancher, successfully persuaded President Benjamin Harrison (1833–1901) to order federal troops to rescue immediately the WSGA's besieged band of hired gunmen.

For a brief time, the "Invaders" were held in custody, but no charges were ever brought against them and all were eventually released. However, public outrage over the actions of the WSGA assisted in sweeping Republicans from control of both houses in the Wyoming legislature. Meanwhile, Asa S. Mercer, an eccentric publicist for the WSGA, became so disillusioned by the entire Johnson County affair that he turned against his employers. In 1894, he attacked their brutal and high-handed methods in a vitriolic diatribe entitled *Bandetti of the Plains; or, The Cattlemen's Invasion of Wyoming in 1892 (The Crowning Infamy of the Ages)*. The WSGA attempted to destroy all copies of Mercer's privately published booklet and the author received various threats and a severe beating for his literary effort.

The Johnson County War did not end the WSGA's efforts to intimidate settlers, rustlers, or anyone else who threatened their interests; and the continuing conflict between the cattle barons, settlers, and rustlers became a central theme of American western folklore. The large ranches, many controlled by absentee owners and foreign syndicates, continued to hire gunmen to work as "regulators" or "stock detectives," and they employed cowboys who were skilled with firearms. For example, Carey's extensive cattle operations continued to draw the attention of real rustlers, such as the notorious "Wild Bunch" whose hide-out in cliffs along a dissolute tributary of the Powder River was known as "The Hole in the Wall." In the summer of 1897, the foreman of Carey's CY ranch led a team of tough, well-armed cowhands into the "Hole in the

Wall," successfully retrieving CY cattle and killing at least one rustler in an episode of vigilante justice.

Carey was not returned to the Senate in 1895, because he had supported Democratic president Grover Cleveland in opposing the unlimited coinage of silver. In addition, the state's Republicans, wanting only one senator from Cheyenne, favored Warren over Carey. Carey also lost the seat on the Republican National Committee he had held since 1876. This rebuke by his party initiated a lasting feud between Carey and Warren, who had already built a powerful Republican "machine" in the new state. Carey was not capable of building an enthusiastic political following, since even his friends found him tough, stern, and aloof, although they viewed him as fair-minded and reasonable. His more popular rival in politics and ranching, Warren, claimed to have "known Carey from the time he stepped off the train in 1869, a green boy," and considered him "the most seductive and successful hypocrite and the most infernal liar" he had ever known (Gould, *Wyoming*, p. 78).

Carey returned to the political arena in 1910 and was elected governor of Wyoming on the Democratic ticket, after failing to secure the Republican party's nomination for that office. A progressive on many issues, Carey supported woman suffrage, the direct primary, a secret ballot, a commission form of government for cities, a corrupt practices act, and the direct election of U.S. senators. However, he remained a conservative on economic matters and opposed efforts at government regulation of business. In 1912 he was one of seven governors calling for the nomination of Theodore Roosevelt (1858–1919) for president, and he supported the Progressive ticket. At a Roosevelt rally in Sheridan, Wyoming, Carey stated, "It is the duty of every man to turn his back on what is bad in his own party." He continued with an attack on Warren's domination of the Republicans, saying, "A one-man power has overhung Wyoming and driven men elsewhere" (Carey manuscripts, Univ. of Wyoming). Carey did not seek reelection in 1914 and instead supported the successful candidacy of Democrat John B. Kendrick. He returned to his many lucrative business ventures, including banking and a partnership with Sir Horace Plunckett in a land development company, which opened huge tracts of land near Wheatland, Wyoming, to cultivation by means of elaborate irrigation projects. Carey died at his home in Cheyenne.

• Two manuscript boxes related to Carey's public career are held at the American Heritage Center (formerly the Western History Research Center) at the University of Wyoming, which also holds the extensive collection of F. E. Warren, including correspondence with Carey. The Wyoming State Archives holds Carey's official correspondence as governor (available on microfilm). Also see Betsy Ross Peters, "Joseph M. Carey and the Progressive Movement in Wyoming" (Ph.D. diss., Univ. of Wyoming, 1971); A. W. Spring, "Carey Story Is a Wyoming Saga," *Hereford Journal* (5 July 1938), pp. 10–11, 30–31; Lewis L. Gould, *Wyoming: From Territory to Statehood* (1989); Gould, "Joseph M. Carey and Wyoming Statehood," *Annals of Wyoming* 37 (Oct. 1965): 157–69; George W. Paulson, "The Congressional Career of Joseph Maull Carey," *Annals of Wyoming* 35 (Apr. 1963): 21–81; and T. A. Larson, *History of Wyoming*, rev. 2d ed., (1978). The most thorough account of the Johnson County War is Helena Huntington Smith, *The War on the Power River* (1966). An obituary is in the *Wyoming State Tribune and Cheyenne Leader*, 7 and 8 Feb. 1924; testimonials and reminiscences appear in the same paper on 17 Feb. 1924.

MICHAEL J. DEVINE

CAREY, Matthew (28 Jan. 1760–16 Sept. 1839), publisher and economist, was born in Dublin, Ireland, the son of Christopher Carey, a prosperous baker, and Mary Sherridan, both Catholics. He was an avid reader but not a good student. He was taunted at school because of his lameness (the result of having been dropped by a nurse) and his small stature; for the rest of his life he was quick to take offense at any imagined slight to his dignity. In 1775 he was apprenticed to a bookseller who was also copublisher of the *Hiberian Journal*, which in 1777 printed his first work, an essay against dueling. In 1781 he wrote an anonymous pamphlet, *The Urgent Necessity of an Immediate Repeal of the Whole Penal Code*, denouncing the anti-Catholic legal code. (In his autobiography he remembered the date as 1779, but internal evidence contradicts him.) It was suppressed, a reward was offered for the discovery of its author, and Carey was spirited off to Paris for a year. There he was introduced to Benjamin Franklin, who put him to work briefly on his press at Passy, and to the marquis de Lafayette. In 1783, back in Dublin, Carey worked for the *Freeman's Journal* and then established his own *Volunteer's Journal*. Passionately nationalistic and anti-English, it had the second largest newspaper circulation in Ireland. In 1784 he printed a cartoon depicting the prospective chancellor of the Exchequer hung as a traitor for his opposition to a protective tariff bill. Carey was imprisoned for sedition and only released after lengthy proceedings in Parliament. Further prosecution for libel was pending, so (supposedly dressed as a woman) he crept aboard a ship bound for Philadelphia in September 1784.

Carey landed in Philadelphia with only a dozen guineas in his pocket. Lafayette heard of his predicament, sought him out, and loaned him $400 with which to start a newspaper. (When the marquis returned impoverished to America in 1824, Carey publicly repaid the loan.) Carey published the *Pennsylvania Evening Herald* from 1785 to 1787. Its success was assured when it began printing full transcripts of the debates in the general assembly, taken in shorthand by Carey. Its politics were democratic and anti-English. Colonel Eleazer Oswald, editor of a rival and more aristocratic paper, mocked Carey's politics, nationality, and appearance in his columns. Carey replied with a bitter verse satire on Oswald, *The Plagi-Scurriliad* (1786). The colonel challenged Carey to a duel and wounded him severely in his game leg.

In 1786 Carey, in partnership with others, launched the monthly *Columbian Magazine*. After a few issues he quarreled with his partners and in 1787 started a competing magazine on his own, the *American Museum*. The *Museum* was a strong proponent of the Federalists, who endorsed it and solicited subscribers in every state.

In 1790 Carey published the first American edition of the Catholic Douay Bible; he also founded the Hibernian Society for the relief of Irish immigrants and helped found the first Sunday school society in America. In 1791 he married Bridget Flahavan; they had nine children, two of whom died in infancy. He greeted the French Revolution with joy; the pro-English reaction of George Washington and Alexander Hamilton moved Carey and the *Museum* toward the Thomas Jefferson camp. After the presidential election of 1792, possibly as a retaliation, the Philadelphia postmaster ruled that magazines could no longer be entered at the cheap newspaper rate. Despite its prestige, the *Museum* had never made a profit, and this blow ended it.

During the yellow fever epidemic of 1793, Carey was one of the committee of citizens that governed the city. The crisis was barely past when he issued his *Short Account of the Malignant Fever*, including a list of those who had died. In it he stated that the assistance given by the black community in nursing the sick and burying the dead demanded public gratitude, and though a few black nurses had been guilty of extortion and theft, it was unjust to censure the whole community, as many had done. He intended his remarks to be evenhanded, but they prompted a spirited rejoinder from black clergyman Richard Allen and Absalom Jones. They pointed out that whites had been equally guilty of these crimes (as Carey acknowledged in his next edition) and argued that in general his account undervalued the black contribution and unwittingly fostered racial prejudice.

Meanwhile Carey had begun to import books from Britain on long credit, which he used to finance the publication of two large and expensive books, a geography with an atlas and an illustrated natural history. They were reprints of English books, part of an economic nationalist effort to replace imported books with native manufactures. In 1794 he realized he could not be both printer and publisher, so he sold his printing office and henceforth hired others to print for him. His publishing venture was risky, his capital was small, and local sales did not meet expectations. In 1796 he engaged the colorful and compelling itinerant bookseller Mason Locke Weems to push his books out into Philadelphia's Chesapeake hinterland.

Carey had finally broken with the Federalists in 1795 over Jay's Treaty and cast his lot with Jefferson's party. In 1798 William Cobbett accused Carey of being one of the radical United Irishmen, and a prosecution under the Alien and Sedition Acts loomed. Carey again struck back with satire in *A Plumb Pudding for . . . Peter Porcupine* and *The Porcupiniad* (1799). After Jefferson's election in 1801, Carey was rewarded for his support with a seat on the board of the Bank of Pennsylvania. This afforded him extensive credit, which allowed him to place his business on a firm foundation at last.

In 1801 Carey summoned the booksellers of America to a literary fair designed to foster the exchange of books among publishers in distant parts of the country and to encourage the circulation of American editions in place of imports. Though the semiannual fairs lasted only a few years, they formed the first national book distribution network. In 1801 Carey also published the first edition of his quarto family Bible, followed by a smaller-format school Bible. Over the next twenty years he published several editions of the Bible each year from standing type, capturing the lion's share of the American Bible market. His other publications included a variety of atlases, schoolbooks, and almanacs; reprints of English fiction, drama, biography, and travel; and the two great American bestsellers of the age, Weems's *Life of Washington* and Susannah Rowson's *Charlotte Temple*. When the New England states threatened to secede in 1814, Carey wrote *The Olive Branch; or, Faults on Both Sides, Federal and Democratic*. Its impartiality established him as an independent beholden to neither party. It was the most widely read American political tract since *Common Sense* and is said to have done much to save the Union. In 1817 he took his son Henry Charles Carey as a partner and began to withdraw from business. In his leisure he wrote a scholarly tome, *Vindiciae Hibernicae* (1819), which argued that the massacres said to have been committed by the Irish in the insurrection of 1641—justification for much later repression—had never taken place. In 1822 he officially retired. Henry Charles, in partnership with his brother-in-law Isaac Lea, took over the firm's stock, out of which they paid Carey a handsome annuity. He quickly overspent his income printing the many pamphlets he was now writing on economics.

Carey's efforts to influence national economic policy had begun in earnest in reaction to the panic of 1819. That year he helped found the Philadelphia Society for the Promotion of National Industry and wrote for it an influential series of thirteen addresses on protective tariffs. Throughout the 1820s he wrote scores of pamphlets on tariffs, replete with statistics and case studies, under pseudonyms such as Hamilton and Colbert.

In 1824 Carey founded the Pennsylvania Society for the Promotion of Internal Improvements, through which he swayed public opinion in favor of a canal rather than a railroad link between Philadelphia and Pittsburgh. As the opposition of southerners to tariffs grew after 1828, he tirelessly refuted their arguments. He believed that a combination of colonization and the employment of free blacks in factories would gradually end both slavery and the South's dependence on foreign cotton markets. In 1832 he deplored nullification but favored compromise on tariffs to save the Union. Most of his positions were later incorporated into the platform of the Whig party, but he gradually withdrew from public life after 1832.

From 1833 to 1835 he published serially an autobiography that Edgar Allan Poe likened to Franklin's. In 1838 he wrote a guide to domestic happiness, *The Philosophy of Common Sense*, which shows the beneficent and tolerant side of a personality that was often petulant and vituperative. He died in Philadelphia as a result of injuries sustained in a carriage accident. His many public and private acts of philanthropy were remembered in a funeral procession that was, after Stephen Girard's, the largest the city had ever seen.

Though he is often viewed as the founder of the more famous firm of Carey and Lea, Matthew Carey was the leading book publisher in America in the formative years of that industry. Though Carey never sought high office, Henry Clay and James Madison, among many others, acknowledged his political influence. He left no systematic work of economic theory, but Henry Charles Carey's later economic works show a deep debt to his father, so that Matthew Carey must be reckoned as one of the founders of the nationalist school of American economic thought.

• Carey's business archive (1785–1822) is one of the largest surviving private archives of the early national period; it is divided between the Historical Society of Pennsylvania (correspondence) and the American Antiquarian Society (bills and receipts). Weems's letters to Carey were edited by Emily E. F. Skeel, *Mason Locke Weems, His Works and Ways* (1929). A diary of political activities from 1822 to 1826 is at the University of Pennsylvania. Other personal papers are at the Library Company of Philadelphia and the Clements Library. The Library Company has the largest collection of books and pamphlets written or published by Carey. See William Clarkin, *Matthew Carey: A Bibliography of His Publications* (1984; 1,527 entries). Carey's autobiography appeared in the *New England Magazine*, July 1833–Dec. 1834 (repr. 1942). See also Earl L. Bradsher, *Matthew Carey, Editor, Author, and Publisher* (1912); Kenneth W. Rowe, *Matthew Carey: A Study in American Economic Development* (1933), which lists some 450 of his pamphlets on economics; Julius Rubin, "Canal or Railroad?" *Transactions of the American Philosophical Society*, n.s., 51 (1961): 7; Edward C. Carter, "The Political Activities of Matthew Carey, Nationalist, 1760–1814" (Ph.D. diss., Bryn Mawr College, 1962); James N. Green, *Matthew Carey, Publisher and Patriot* (1985); and Richard C. Cole, *Irish Booksellers and English Writers* (1987).

JAMES N. GREEN

CAREY, Max George (11 Jan. 1890–30 May 1976), Hall of Fame baseball player, known as Scoops, was born Maximillian Carnarius in Terre Haute, Indiana, the son of contractor Frank August Ernst Carnarius and Catherine Augusta Astroth. That Carey pursued a career in baseball was unexpected, given that he began a six-year program in 1903 to prepare for the Lutheran ministry. But the 5′11½″, 170-pound student also played for Concordia College and sought a tryout with the South Bend team of the Central League in the summer of 1909.

Using the name Max Carey to preserve his amateur status, which he would have lost by playing professional ball, Carey started at shortstop for the rest of the season, hitting only .148 and committing 24 errors. After graduation from college in 1910, Carey returned to South Bend, where as an outfielder he hit .293 and stole 36 bases in 96 games. Purchased by the Pittsburgh Pirates at the end of the season, he appeared in two games that October and opted for baseball instead of the ministry. He would remain in Pittsburgh's lineup as leadoff hitter and center fielder until 1926, establishing himself as the Tris Speaker of the National League for his defensive brilliance and as the most consistently successful base stealer of his era.

A switch-hitter with little power but a good eye and the ability to hit to all fields, Carey maintained a career .285 batting average and drew 1,040 walks in 2,469 games. He hit far more triples, 159, than home runs, 69, and batted above .300 in five full seasons. Among the all-time Pirates' leaders in virtually every offensive category but home runs and RBIs, he remains the team's leader in career steals.

"Stealing bases," he said, "is the art of picking up little things—things like a spitball pitcher who never threw to first if he was going to throw a spitter to the plate." On the advice of Pirate veteran Honus Wagner, Carey ran regularly during the winter to maintain his speed. He first led the National League in stolen bases in 1913, then repeated four times in a row (1915–1918). Injuries kept him on the bench for more than half of the 1919 season, but he regained the base stealing crown in 1920 and again each season from 1922 through 1925.

In 1922, Carey hit .329 with 140 runs scored and 207 hits, and he stole 51 bases in 53 attempts, one of the best consistency marks in major league history. His 738 career stolen bases were the record total in the National League until Lou Brock overtook him in 1974. Overall, he stole home 33 times.

Carey also made major contributions in the field. He led National League outfielders in putouts for nine seasons in a row and in assists four times. Carey's 6,363 career putouts led that category until Willie Mays surpassed him, while his 339 career assists remained the record into the 1990s. His nickname of Scoops came from his ability to rush in and scoop short fly balls into his glove before they hit the grass as well as the similarity of his name to that of an earlier player, George "Scoops" Carey. Carey signed his contracts as Max George Carey.

The pinnacle of his career came in 1925 when Carey hit a career-high .343, scored 109 runs, led the league in stolen bases, and helped lead the Pirates to the World Series against the Washington Senators. Carey hit .458 with 11 hits and three stolen bases during the seven games, despite playing the last two with broken ribs. In the final game, Carey scored three times, drove in two runs, and stole a base as the Pirates won 9–7.

But Carey's career with Pittsburgh ended the following season. Team vice president Fred Clarke joined manager Bill McKechnie in the dugout that year as, more or less, a comanager. Some of the players resented Clarke's presence, including Carey, who as team captain called a players' meeting to vote for either Clarke or McKechnie. For that, he was suspended without pay and waived by the club. He finished his playing career with the Brooklyn Dodgers in 1929 and returned to the Pirates as a coach in 1930. In 1932, he managed the Dodgers, who finished third in 1932 and sixth in 1933. He was replaced by Casey Stengel for the 1934 season.

Carey then retired to Florida with his wife, Aurelia Behrens, whom he had married 22 June 1913, and their two sons. The couple had lived in Miami Beach during the off-season since 1920. Although he had invested in Florida real estate and made more than $100,000, he lost most of it during the 1929 stock market crash.

Carey returned to baseball in 1940, managing the Miami team in the Florida East Coast League. He served as the commissioner of the All-American Girls Professional Baseball League during World War II and managed Cordele in the Georgia-Florida League in 1955 and Louisville of the American Association in 1956. He worked as a dog racing commission steward for three years at the Miami Beach Kennel Club and was general manager of dog tracks in Key West and Colorado.

Fluent in German and able to translate Greek and Latin, he wrote several books about baseball, including *Fifty Baseball Secrets*. On hearing of his election to the Hall of Fame in 1961, he thanked J. G. Taylor Spink, publisher of the *Sporting News*, who had campaigned for the election of deserving old-time players before "they go into the obscurity that comes with the passage of time." Carey died in Miami Beach.

• There is no book-length biography of Max Carey, but his life and career are described in Frederick G. Lieb, *The Pittsburgh Pirates* (1948); Lowell Reidenbaugh, *Cooperstown: Where Baseball's Legends Live Forever* (1983); and in the *Sporting News*, 25 Jan. and 8 Feb. 1961. Information on Carey also is available in the National Baseball Library at the Hall of Fame in Cooperstown, New York.

ROB RUCK

CAREY, Mutt (1891–3 Sept. 1948), jazz trumpeter, was born Thomas Carey in Hahnville, Louisiana, a small town west of New Orleans. Nothing is known of Carey's parents, but, of seventeen siblings, five of his brothers, including legendary trombonist and bandleader Jack Carey, were also musicians. Carey's first instruments were drums, guitar, and alto horn, but around 1912 he started playing cornet, working in his brother Jack's ragtime marching band and other similar groups. In 1914, along with clarinetist Johnny Dodds and bassist Pops Foster, he played in trombonist Kid Ory's band and in 1917 toured with Billy and Baby Mack's Merrymakers revue in a group that included Dodds and pianist Steve Lewis. After leaving the Merrymakers, on the suggestion of cornetist Joe "King" Oliver, Carey took a job with clarinetist Lawrence Duhé's Original Creole Band at the Pekin Café in Chicago, but, not liking the northern climate, he returned to New Orleans in 1918. Subsequent local work included jobs with trumpeter Chris Kelly's band at the Bulls' Club and with clarinetist Wade Whaley at the Bucktown Tavern in Jefferson Parish, a tough lakeside resort area on the West End.

In November 1919 Carey went to Los Angeles to join Kid Ory's group at the Cadillac Café on Central Avenue. In 1920 or 1921 the band played at the Creole Café in Oakland and while on a later engagement at the Wayside Park Café, also in Oakland, participated in the very first recording session by a black jazz band. Recorded in June 1922 in Los Angeles and first issued on the Nordskog label under the name of Spikes' Seven Pods of Pepper, the two instrumental sides, "Ory's Creole Trombone" and "Society Blues," were quickly re-released with a new pasted-over label reading Ory's Sunshine Orchestra. Also recorded at the same session were four sides on which the band accompanied blues singers Roberta Dudley and Ruth Lee. Although far less important musically than the pacesetting 1923 recordings by King Oliver's Creole Jazz Band, the Ory coupling does present Carey in a favorable light. His tone is broad, his phrasing relaxed and rhythmic, and though he does no improvising his lead is both confident and assertive. In addition to being the first black band to record jazz, in 1923 Ory's group was also the first jazz band of any kind to play for radio broadcast.

In late 1925, when Ory left for Chicago to record with Louis Armstrong's Hot Five and to work in King Oliver's Dixie Syncopators, he turned his band over to Carey. In his new capacity, Carey changed the name of the group to "Pop" Mutt and his Jeffersonians, enlarged the personnel, and worked fairly steadily at various venues in Los Angeles through the late 1930s. In 1927, while working at the Liberty Dance Hall under the name of Papa Mutt's Liberty Syncopators, Carey's band, after the departure of former Ory bassist Ed "Montudi" Garland, consisted of trombonist Leon White, reedmen Joe Darensbourg and Leonard Davidson, pianist Elzie Cooper, guitarist and banjoist Frank Pasley, and drummer Minor "Ram" Hall. In addition to playing in cabarets and at taxi dance halls, during the silent film era the band was frequently hired to play on Hollywood film sets, providing atmospheric music for such stars as Greta Garbo, although there is no indication that they ever appeared on screen. Unfortunately, since Carey did no recording at all during this lengthy period, the sound of his band must be left to speculation.

With the advent of World War II, Carey left music full-time and took a job as a Pullman porter with the Southern Pacific railroad line, but he also continued to play musical engagements whenever possible. Carey became active again as a full-time musician in early 1944, when Ory re-formed his Creole Jazz Band for a contracted thirteen-week run of appearances on Orson Welles's "Mercury Theater" on CBS. Regulars in the band were Carey, pianist Buster Wilson, guitarist Bud Scott, bassist Garland, and drummer Zutty Singleton. Seminal New Orleans virtuoso Jimmie Noone played clarinet with the band until his death in April, being succeeded by Wade Whatley, Ellington star Barney Bigard, and finally Joe Darensbourg.

In addition to the Welles broadcasts, the Ory band worked regularly at such Los Angeles venues as the Tip Toe Inn, the Jade Palace, and the Beverly Cavern, while recording extensively for Crescent, Exner, Decca, Good Time Jazz, Columbia, and V-Disc. Between May 1944 and January 1946 the band also participated in a series of specially recorded performances for Standard Oil Company of California. With supporting educational lectures on the music's history, these shows were specifically designed for direct broadcast to elementary and secondary schools in an attempt to bolster appreciation of American folk music. Surviving discs from this series were released in 1991 on the American Music label. The only recordings the trumpeter made during this period that were not with Ory were those on Riverside accompanying pianist-singer Hociel Thomas in August 1946. From the spring of 1946 through February 1947 the Ory band worked at the Green Room in San Francisco, and unauthorized recordings of the band's closing night performances were released in 1992, also on the American Music label. Although technically flawed, these recordings are the only examples of how the band actually sounded on the job.

After leaving Ory in the summer of 1947, Carey went to New York and by November had recorded his first and only leader dates under the name of Mutt Carey and his New Yorkers. For these sessions Carey used the house band of the "This Is Jazz" radio series: trombonist Jimmy Archey, clarinetist Albert Nicholas, pianist Hank Duncan, guitarist Danny Barker, bassist Pops Foster, and drummer Baby Dodds. On the second of the two recording dates, Nicholas and Duncan were replaced by Edmond Hall and Cliff Jackson, respectively. Following this session and a few concert appearances, Carey returned to Los Angeles, where he worked intermittently with his own bands. While in the process of forming a new band, he died in Elsinore, California, a vacation resort near Los Angeles.

From the Welles broadcasts of early 1944 through his last sessions in November 1947, Carey displayed a characteristically penetrating sound, with and without the use of his plunger mute, but his notes often cracked and his range was limited. For the most part, though, his spare, rhythmically relaxed expositions of the melody, albeit phrased in a raggy rather than swinging manner and with a wide, shuddering vibrato, set a reliable lead for the ensemble. Carey appears at his best on Ory's 1944–1945 Good Time Jazz recordings, with Omer Simeon and Darnell Howard as guest clarinetists, on the 1946 Columbia album with Bigard, and finally on his own final sessions for Century, later reissued on Savoy. Here, on "Shim-Me-Sha-Wabble," "Slow Drivin'," "Ostrich Walk," and "Cake Walking Babies," he is the epitome of the tonally distinctive New Orleans lead trumpet player, while the band's relatively straight readings of "Joplin's Sensation," "Chrysanthemum," and "The Entertainer" are among the first and finest revivals of orchestral ragtime on record.

• For information about Carey's career see Barney Bigard, *With Louis and the Duke* 1985; repr. (1986); Joe Darensbourg, *Jazz Odyssey: The Autobiography of Joe Darensbourg* (1987); Baby Dodds, *The Baby Dodds Story*, as told to Larry Gara (1959); and Pops Foster, *Pops Foster: The Autobiography of a New Orleans Jazzman*, as told to Tom Stoddard 1971; repr. (1973). The best source of information on New Orleans jazz in California in the 1910s and 1920s is Stoddard, *Jazz on the Barbary Coast* (1982). Complete discographical listings for Carey are in Brian Rust, *Jazz Records, 1897–1942*, 5th ed. (1982), and Walter Bruyninckx, *Traditional Jazz Discography, 1897–1988* (1989). An obituary is in *Jazz Journal* 1, no. 11 (1948): 10.

JACK SOHMER

CARLES, Arthur B. (9 Mar. 1882–18 June 1952), modernist painter and teacher, was born Arthur Beecher Carles, Jr., in Philadelphia, Pennsylvania, the son of Arthur Beecher Carles, a designer of watch covers and an amateur painter, and Janet Buchanan. His parents supported his artistic aspirations and those of his younger sister Sara, who also became a painter.

Arthur Carles studied at the Pennsylvania Academy of Fine Arts, where he enrolled on scholarship in late 1900. His teachers included William Merritt Chase, Cecilia Beaux, Thomas Anshutz, Hugh Henry Breckinridge, and Henry McCarter, all of whom shared their awareness of the principles of abstract design and modern European art in addition to the academic basics. Carles began to exhibit his work as a student and won traveling scholarships to England, France, and Spain in the summer of 1905 and for two years beginning in 1907. He extended his stay through 1910 by receiving a commission to copy Raphael's *Transfiguration* for a Philadelphia church. His academic competence enabled him to produce a faithful copy, but his personal interest lay in capturing the French landscape with strokes of vivid color in such paintings as *L'Eglise* (1908, Metropolitan Museum of Art). In Paris he exhibited at the Salon d'Automne, met Henri Matisse, and was friendly with other American modernists, such as Edward Steichen and John Marin.

Carles was one of the American artists living in France who carried European modernism back to the United States before the First World War. Interested primarily in the interactions of color, he was most influenced initially by fauvism, especially the work of Paul Cézanne and Henri Matisse. Upon his return, his paintings were exhibited in New York, first by Alfred Stieglitz at his "291" gallery in 1910, then at a solo exhibition in 1912, and later at the historic Armory Show in 1913. After another stay in France in 1912, Carles settled in Philadelphia, where he focused his energy on entering academic exhibitions, earning recognition across the country for his bold nudes and portraits, such as *An Actress as Cleopatra* (1914, Museum of American Art at the Pennsylvania Academy of Fine Arts). Success led to a teaching position at the Pennsylvania Academy, which he held from 1917 to 1925. His costumed sketch class was one of the most popular in the school, and his individualized teaching about color and the dynamics of composition made a lifelong impression on many students. His largest and most dramatic painting, *The Marseillaise* (1918–1919, Philadelphia Museum of Art), was painted at the end of World War I. A trip to France in 1921 renewed his enthusiasm for painting freely with color and greater boldness of form, as is evident in *Flower Composition* (1922, Philadelphia Museum of Art). He brought the flower still life to renewed prominence and participated along with Leopold Stokowski, conductor of the Philadelphia Orchestra, in the flourishing of culture in Philadelphia in the 1920s. Carles attracted attention with his artistic temperament and appearance, characterized by a progressively less-kempt beard. He was intense, witty, outspoken, impulsive, and often impractical. Although he refused to work with a dealer, his work was acquired by many loyal supporters in Philadelphia, the most important of whom were the wealthy painter Carroll Tyson and lawyers Maurice Speiser and Alexander Lieberman.

Carles brought modern American and European art to the students at the Pennsylvania Academy by helping to organize three major exhibitions, culminating in the controversial showing of recent acquisitions of work by Amedeo Modigliani, Chaim Soutine, Matisse, and Picasso by Albert C. Barnes in 1923. After losing his teaching position at the academy, Carles continued to teach privately to small groups and individuals. Although his painting was disrupted by periods of increasingly severe alcoholism, he participated in numerous national exhibitions and had major solo exhibitions in New York in 1922, 1936, and 1944. His first one-man shows in Philadelphia in 1935 were followed by four others in the 1940s, culminating with a memorial exhibition in 1953.

Carles produced his most pioneering and powerful work from the late 1920s when he began to break up forms with cubist planes of color, as exemplified by *Arrangement* (1925–1927, Art Institute of Chicago). His final stay in Paris lasted from 1929 to 1931. Many of his late paintings, such as *Composition No. 5* (1935, Philadelphia Museum of Art), were built up of many layers of changes, and much of his late work, including *Abstraction (Last Painting)* (1936–1941, Hirshhorn Museum and Sculpture Garden), was prophetic of abstract expressionism, anticipating the rough brushwork of Willem de Kooning and the drips of Jackson Pollock, both of which had an enormous impact only a few years later. Carles was admired by other painters, such as Hans Hofmann. His career was abruptly halted by a fall and paralytic stroke in 1941 that left him an invalid. Romantically involved with numerous women, Carles was married twice, first to artist Mercedes de Cordoba, from 1909 to 1926, and then to Caroline Robinson, from 1927, and had a daughter by each. His elder daughter, Mercedes Carles Matter, born in 1913, also became a painter and teacher; she was a founder of the New York Studio School. He died in a nursing home on the outskirts of Philadelphia.

Carles painted intuitively. Although he sometimes developed ideas in a series, he rarely repeated himself. Because his work even within a single period could vary in style and approach, and because he rarely signed and almost never dated his work, questions regarding attribution and chronology often arise. His best signature is his characteristic vibrant palette of greens and blues contrasted with warm violets. In his dynamic compositions the backgrounds are as full of color and motion as the foreground objects, and curving lines lead the viewer's eye through space.

• Correspondence on microfilm from two lenders and from his widow's estate, as well as research notes and slides, are in the Archives of American Art, Smithsonian Institution; the Archives of the Pennsylvania Academy of the Fine Arts contains information about his student years and exhibitions. The majority of Carles's work is in private collections, but he is represented in most major museums. The Pennsylvania Academy of the Fine Arts, the Philadelphia Museum of Art, and the Hirshhorn Museum and Sculpture Garden hold the largest collections of his paintings. Significant articles include "'True Art Emotional,' Carles Says: Nature and Life as a Post-Impressionist Sees Them," *Philadelphia Press*, 21 July 1913, and Jo Mielziner, "Arthur Carles: The Man Who Paints with Color," *Creative Art* 2 (Feb. 1928): 30–35. Early exhibition catalogs are Pennsylvania Academy of the Fine Arts and Philadelphia Museum of Art, *Memorial Exhibition: Arthur B. Carles* (1953), and Graham Gallery, New York, *Arthur B. Carles, 1882–1952: Retrospective Exhibition* (1959). Research on Carles began with Elizabeth C. W. O'Connor, "Arthur B. Carles, 1882–1952: Colorist and Experimenter" (M.A. thesis, Columbia Univ., 1965), followed by Henry G. Gardiner, "Arthur B. Carles: A Critical Biography," *Bulletin of the Philadelphia Museum of Art* 64 (Jan.–Mar. 1970); it continued with Joshua C. Taylor and Richard R. Boyle, *Pennsylvania Academy Moderns* (1975), and Abraham A. Davidson, *Early American Modernist Painting: 1910–1935* (1981). The major publication on Carles is Barbara A. Wolanin, *Arthur B. Carles, 1882–1952: Painting with Color* (1983), based on her Ph.D. dissertation with preliminary catalogue raisonné (Univ. of Wisconsin–Madison, 1981). The major obituary is Henry Clifford, "Prophet with Honor," *Art News* 52 (Apr. 1953): 48.

BARBARA ANN BOESE WOLANIN

CARLETON, Henry Guy (21 June 1856–10 Dec. 1910), playwright, was born in Fort Union, New Mexico, the son of James Henry Carleton, a general in the U.S. Army, and Sophia Garland Wolfe. He was educated at Santa Clara College in California, where he majored in engineering, and graduated in 1871. In 1873 he entered the military as a second lieutenant with the Eighth U.S. Cavalry and fought in Indian campaigns in the Southwest, particularly against the Apache, Comanche, and Kiowa tribes.

Carleton resigned from the army in August 1876 and embarked on a new career as a newspaperman. From 1876 through 1879 he wrote for the *New Orleans Times*. Then in 1880 he went to the *Chicago Tribune*, remaining until 1882, at which point he moved to the *New York Times* as an editorial writer. From 1883 through 1885 he was a literary editor for *Life*. While at *Life* he became known for his humorous sketches titled "The Thompson Street Poker Club." These were printed in book form in 1884 as the *Thompson Street Poker Club Papers*. In 1886 he joined the *New York World*, staying through 1889.

Playwriting had long held a fascination for Carleton. When he was fifteen, he made a youthful attempt at the form with a work titled *The Age of Gold*. In 1881 he embarked on a career as a dramatist with his first play, *Memnon*, a blank verse tragedy about a prophet of ancient Thebes. The actor-manager John McCullough paid Carleton $5,000 for the play, but it was never produced. *Victor Durand*, his next play, opened in New York in December 1884 at Wallack's Theatre with a cast that included noteworthy performers such as John Gilbert, Rose Coghlan, and Osmond Tearle. Set in Paris, this drama about false imprisonment for murder ran for two seasons and established Carleton as an important new voice in the American theater. The *New York Times* reviewer particularly praised it as a first-produced work, calling it "a remarkably ingenious and interesting play" (19 Dec. 1884). Over the next two decades—the span of his playwriting career—came a remarkable flow of works in various dramatic genres, totaling about sixteen original plays and three adaptations. (Scanty records make an exact count difficult.)

In 1889 *The Pembertons* appeared. This was followed by almost one play a year, some with major stars of the American stage. According to first production dates, next came *The Lion's Mouth* and then *Ye Earlie Trouble* (both 1891); *The Princess of Erie* (1892); *A Gilded Fool* (1892), with Nat Goodwin; *A Bit of Scandal* (1893); *The Butterflies* (1893), with John Drew and Maude Adams; *Lem Kettle* (1894); *Ambition* (1895), with Nat Goodwin; *That Imprudent Young Couple* (1895), with Maude Adams, Ethel Barrymore, and Arthur Byron; *Two Men of Business* (1896); *Colinette* (1898), with Julia Marlowe; *The Cuckoo* (1898); *Jack's Honeymoon* (1903); and his last play, *The Trap and the Bait* (?). Also credited to him are four works that cannot be dated: *The Adventurers* and the adaptations *Never Again*, *Ladies First*, and *The Girl from Maxim's*.

Carleton regarded the craftsmanship of his plays as paramount in his writing. He stated that a play should be "a versimilitude of human life, with diverse human interests and human emotions tangled in one skein; words subservient to action, and individual values made tributory to the general effect" (*Dramatic Mirror*, 1 Feb. 1890). And his craftsmanship won praise from critics, such as the one who commented in 5 May 1905: "Those of his plays which were successful showed skillful portraiture and nice adjustment of parts, coupled with marked clearness of purpose, graceful handling, and logical development."

Carleton frequently returned to a favorite theme, that of exposing financial malefaction, as in *A Gilded Fool* and *That Imprudent Young Couple*. Yet he did not believe in the drama as a form for expounding strong intellectual or moral stances. "A play," he asserted in an interview, "is written for the purpose of affording amusement to the public. I will repeat this: A play is written for the purpose of affording amusement to the public" (*Illustrated American*, 24 Mar. 1894).

In addition to his careers as soldier, journalist, and playwright, Carleton was also an inventor. He was admitted to the California Academy of Sciences in 1872 and over the years invented a number of devices, such as a double-fluid barometer and an early type of electric chair for executing criminals.

Carleton was married and divorced three times. His first wife was Helen S. Hubbard (dates of marriage and divorce unknown). Then in 1890 he married Effie Shannon, an actress; they divorced in 1892. Lastly, in 1894 he married Olive May, an actress; they divorced in 1898. He had one child (by which wife is not known). In his later years he developed severe rheumatism. This culminated in paralysis, and he died from this condition in Hot Springs, Arkansas.

Carleton was one of the most prolific American dramatists of the late nineteenth century. As his obituary in the *New York World* (10 Dec. 1910) states: "For years he held a prominent place in the little group of American writers for the stage, having the art to be smart without vulgarity, light without levity and witty without coarseness." Yet with all the contemporary newspaper references to him as a brilliant American dramatist well versed in a variety of forms, from blank verse tragedy to comedy to serious drama, most of his plays were failures when produced. He left no theatrical legacy.

• The Billy Rose Theatre Collection of the New York Public Library at Lincoln Center contains clipping files dealing with Carleton. See also Henry Guy Carleton, "The Dramatic Millennium," *New York Dramatic Mirror*, 1 Feb. 1890; an interview in the *Illustrated American*, "Dramatists at Home," 24 Mar. 1894, pp. 317–18; and N. C. Goodwin, *Nat Goodwin's Book* (1914). Contemporary information about productions of *Victor Durand*, *Ye Earlie Trouble*, *A Gilded Fool*, and *The Butterflies* may be found in George C. D. Odell, *Annals of the New York Stage*, vols. 12 and 15 (1940, 1949). In addition to the one cited in the text above, an obituary appears in the *New York Dramatic Mirror*, 14 Dec. 1910.

WILLIAM GREEN

CARLILE, John Snyder (16 Dec. 1817–24 Oct. 1878), lawyer and politician, was born in Winchester, Virginia; his parents' names are unknown. He was educated at home by his mother. His father died when Carlile was young, and at the age of fourteen Carlile worked in a country store as a clerk to help support his mother. When he was seventeen he started his own business as a merchant, but that failed, leaving Carlile in debt. He paid his debts in full, even after all legal obligations had ceased.

Fortunately, Carlile had also begun to read law, and in 1840 he was admitted to the Virginia bar. In the early 1840s, to further his legal prospects, he moved to Beverly, Virginia, then to Philippi, and finally to Clarksburg, where he began his political career. He was a forceful and persuasive speaker and was quickly successful. A member of the American party, he began as a state senator (1847–1851), was elected as a delegate to the 1850 Virginia constitutional convention, and was elected to the U.S. House of Representatives in 1855. In 1857 he was defeated for reelection, however, on the eve of secession he was again elected to the House.

Carlile's most prominent role was as a vociferous opponent of secession and an early advocate of West Virginia statehood. When asked to comment on the possibility of Virginia secession in early 1861, he responded, "Oh! for [Andrew] Jackson to say and make good the saying, 'The Federal Union; it must and shall be preserved'" (McGregor, p. 86). As a delegate to the Richmond convention that considered an ordinance of secession in the spring of 1861, Carlile maintained a firm Unionist position, which placed him in physical danger from the state's rabid secession element. Returning to Clarksburg, he penned the "Clarksburg Resolutions," which rejected the ordinance of secession and called for a Unionist convention to meet in Wheeling, Virginia, in May 1861.

Although Carlile was an advocate of a plan to immediately separate West Virginia from Virginia, a more cautious spirit prevailed at this First Wheeling Convention. A Second Wheeling Convention convened in June 1861, after the ordinance of secession had been adopted by the state of Virginia. Led by Francis H. Pierpont, Waitman T. Willey, and others, this group argued that the loyal government of Virginia ought to first be restored. After that was accomplished, a convention could be called to draft a constitution for West Virginia and to apply to Congress for admission. Although he was the most popular Unionist leader in Virginia, Carlile was unwilling to divide Unionist support for a separate state, and he acquiesced to Pierpont and the others. At the Second Wheeling Convention, Carlile was appointed to the Committee of Thirteen that drafted "A Declaration of the People of Virginia," providing the legal justification for reorganizing the government of Virginia.

In return for his support for the more cautious approach, Carlile was elected senator from the newly reconstituted state of Virginia, replacing the secessionist senator Robert M. T. Hunter, and he resigned his House seat. Meanwhile, a constitutional convention met in Wheeling in November 1861 and began drafting a constitution for the state of West Virginia, which was completed in the spring of 1862.

In the U.S. Senate, Carlile was a member of the Committee on Territories, chaired by Ohio Republican Benjamin F. Wade. Carlile played a major role in drafting the bill for West Virginia statehood in the summer of 1862. Some of his actions in crafting the bill have puzzled historians. For instance, his bill added thirteen counties to the forty-eight counties approved by the West Virginia constitutional convention, even though many of the additional counties probably contained a majority of southern sympathizers.

Even more puzzling, however, was Carlile's eventual decision to vote against the very bill he had drafted. His opposition was the result of the incorporation of an amendment introduced by Virginia's other replacement senator, Willey. This amendment would have eliminated the thirteen additional counties proposed by Carlile, and more importantly, it would have made congressional acceptance of West Virginia statehood contingent upon the approval of the state constitution's gradual emancipation provision by a majority of West Virginia voters. Carlile rejected the whole statehood bill on the grounds of congressional interference. Congress, he argued, had no right to impose any conditions on a state applying for admission to the Union, especially since slavery existed in the other Border States of the country. "I would never consent to have the organic law of a State framed for its people by the Congress of the United States," he declared during the Senate debate. When the Senate voted on the West Virginia statehood bill with the Willey amendment, Carlile voted against his pet project. Ironically, when West Virginia was officially accepted into the Union in June 1863, Carlile, the earliest supporter of independent statehood, no longer advocated the project.

Although Carlile spurned party labels during the Civil War and called himself a Unionist, he espoused a strict constructionist view of the Constitution and regarded the war solely as an attempt to restore the Union, not as a crusade to abolish slavery. This position earned him the contemptuous "Copperhead" label among Radical Republicans. It also explains why he opposed the final form of the West Virginia statehood bill. Carlile's view of the Constitution allowed each state sufficient latitude to frame its own constitution without conditions dictated by the U.S. Congress. He saw Congress forcing West Virginia to accept gradual emancipation prior to statehood as a dangerous usurpation of power by the central government. Although this position was more indicative of Democratic opponents of the Abraham Lincoln administration, it also resonated among some conservative Republicans and Border State Unionists.

Following the expiration of his Senate term in March 1865, Carlile never again held political office. Although he became a Republican after the war, his opposition to the Willey amendment had earned him the contempt of Radical Republicans. That fact combined with the increasing domination of West Virginia by the Democratic party in the late 1860s to keep him from an active political role. In 1868 he stumped the state on behalf of Republican presidential nominee Ulysses S. Grant, and in return Grant nominated Carlile as minister to Sweden. However, the opposition of Radical Republicans, particularly Charles Sumner, denied him confirmation. Little is known of Carlile's retirement except that he spent it in relative obscurity on his Clarksburg farm. He was married and had at least one son. He died in Clarksburg.

Carlile's career was marked by controversy and seeming inconsistency. In his native Virginia, he was seen as a "radical" for his opposition to secession and support of separate statehood for West Virginia. In the Republican dominated Congress in Washington, however, he was denounced as a southern sympathizer and supporter of slavery. Carlile could be seen in both of these roles, because he simultaneously endorsed the sanctity of the Union and advocated a strict constructionist view of the Constitution that did not allow the central government to trample on states' rights. His political banishment after the Civil War was the price he paid for his convictions.

• Small collections of Carlile's papers are at the Library of Congress, Manuscripts Division, Washington, D.C.; the Rush Rhees Library, University of Rochester, Rochester, N.Y.; the Pierpont Morgan Library, New York City; the Alderman Library, University of Virginia, Charlottesville, Va.; the Virginia Historical Society, Richmond, Va.; and the West Virginia University Library, Morgantown, W.Va. The *Congressional Globe* contains a number of Carlile's Senate speeches and contributions to debates; see particularly 37th Cong., 2d sess., pt. 4, 1862, pp. 2959, 3309–18. A short biography of Carlile's life written by his son is in William P. Willey, *An Inside View of the Formation of the State of West Virginia* (1901). Several books provide a wealth of information about Carlile's role in W.Va. politics, including James C. McGregor, *The Disruption of Virginia* (1922); Charles H. Ambler, *Francis Pierpont* (1929); Richard O. Curry, *A House Divided: A Study of Statehood Politics and the Copperhead Movement in West Virginia* (1964); and Otis K. Rice, *West Virginia: A History* (1985). Obituaries are in the *New York Herald* and the *New York Times*, 25 Oct. 1878.

BRUCE TAP

CARLISLE, Cliff (6 May 1904–5 Apr. 1983), pioneer country musician and songwriter, was born Clifford Raymond Carlisle in Mt. Eden, Kentucky. Many members of his family were musicians, and his younger brother Bill would later join Cliff in the ranks of early professional musicians. Cliff attended several rural grade schools near Wakefield, Kentucky, eventually transferring to larger schools in Louisville, Kentucky, between 1921 and 1924. Unlike many early musicians, he did not serve an apprenticeship in another field before taking up music; from his earliest days he aspired to be a professional musician, and he emerged as one of the first such professionals in the field of country music.

As a child growing up in eastern Kentucky, Carlisle was exposed to a national fad for Hawaiian music and to a widespread popularity of the Hawaiian guitar—an acoustic guitar customarily noted with a steel bar instead of picks. Early Hawaiian-style record artists like Sol Hoopi and Frank Ferera became favorites of young Carlisle, who would play their records "until they scratched so badly you couldn't hear them." By the time he was sixteen, in 1920, he had formed a partnership with Wilbur Ball, another guitarist and singer from Louisville. During this period, around 1924, Cliff married Alice Henrietta Smith; the couple had three children. From 1920 to 1930, Carlisle and Ferera worked together, singing and playing on various tent shows and vaudeville tours, including the Continental Red Path Chautauqua and the B. F. Kieth shows. Their tours carried them nationwide, and they were able to play hillbilly or country music in the South and do Hawaiian shows when in the North. By 1930 they were appearing on Louisville's WHAS radio under the name "The Lullaby Larkers."

By this time the Hawaiian fad had spent itself, and the new trend in country music was the country blues and "blue yodels" of singers like Jimmie Rodgers. Carlisle had been exposed to several African-American bluesmen as a youth and found that he could adapt their singing styles to the kind of song Rodgers was doing. This talent won Carlisle his first record contract, with the independent Gennett Company, who encouraged him to record several "cover" versions of Rodgers hit songs. He was so good at this that the following year, in 1931, he was chosen to actually back Rodgers himself on one of his sessions.

This break launched Carlisle on a recording career that would make him one of the most prolific record makers in the 1930s and would create a discography of more than 300 sides. As early as 1932 he began establishing an independent reputation and emerging from the shadow of Rodgers and his songs; he was now being billed in record advertisements as "The Yodelin' Hobo," and his company, known then as the American Record Company, was announcing his releases as a "new song series." These new songs included many Carlisle originals, songs that were somewhat cruder than those of Rodgers but delighted blue-collar audiences. Gone were the sentimental themes and rural images of the country music of the 1920s, and in their place were lyrics that dealt with such modern problems as drinking, divorce, domestic abuse, barroom brawls, gangsters, faithless lovers, and hard times. "Seven Years with the Wrong Woman" (1932) was one of the first country songs about a familiar theme in modern country, divorce. "Pay Day Fight" (1937) described a violent fight between wife and husband over who got the pay envelope and "Wildcat Woman and a Tomcat Man" (1936) was another blow-by-blow account of a domestic brawl. One of his most popular records was "The Girl in the Blue Velvet Band" (1934), Carlisle's reworking of an old English ballad, which told a Dashiel Hammett-like tale of a boy in San Francisco who is framed for robbery by a *femme fatale*.

Although the huge number of Carlisle's records included everything from hobo songs to gospel tunes, he became most notorious for his series of off-color or double-entendre songs. At first, such songs were couched in terms of animal references, a classic technique in risque American humor from the vaudeville or burlesque stage. "Shanghai Rooster Yodel" (1931) and "Tom Cat Blues" (1932), the latter with its famous line "If you got your heat turned up,/You better turn your damper down," were his first two hits in this mode. Chickens became favorite images, with titles like "It Takes an Old Hen to Deliver the Goods" (1937), and amphibians were also targets in a song like "When I Feel Froggy I'm Gonna Hop" (1936). Other songs were more direct; two 1933 records, "Mouse's Ear Blues" and "Sal Got a Meatskin," were about deflowering virgins. The prim Victorian maidens sung about by Rodgers were replaced with robust redneck girls: "String Bean Mama," "Copper Head Mama," "Onion Eating Mama" (all 1934). For the raunchier titles, the American Record Company released sides under the pseudonym "Bob Clifford." On some of these Carlisle was also accompanied by the rhythm guitar and singing of his brother Bill.

One of Carlisle's children, Tommy, became a child prodigy and joined him in his act, although the addition later caused Carlisle to run afoul of child labor laws in several states. As his records sold thousands of copies—many through the mail order giants of Sears and Montgomery Ward—Carlisle bounced around from radio station to radio station during the 1930s. His homes ranged from Louisville to Chicago, from Cincinnati to Knoxville, and from Charlotte to Asheville. By the end of the decade, the Carlisle brothers were presenting themselves on radio as a family group, and their records began to include more and more gospel songs, such as "the Blind Child's Prayer," "Valley of Peace," and "The Unclouded Day."

During the 1940s the brothers began to focus their activities more on stations in Knoxville (where they joined "The Mid-Day-Merry-Go-Round") and in Memphis. They had a last big hit in 1946 on King, "Rainbow at Midnight," and Cliff spent more time writing his own songs. Often he worked with pioneer publishers Fred Rose and Wally Fowler, but he eventually retired from music in the early 1950s. His retirement years were devoted to interior decorating and painting in Lexington, Kentucky, where he died.

Carlisle's place in country music history rests on several achievements. He was one of the genre's first true professionals; he was a pioneer in the steel guitar; he was an influential white bluesman; he was an innovative songwriter who helped to move country song themes into the modern era; and he was a versatile and accomplished singer.

• Carlisle's personal scrapbook—a huge compendium of letters, flyers, and clippings—is held at the Country Music Foundation in Nashville. A good account of his career is in Charles K. Wolfe, *Kentucky Country: Folk and Country Music of Kentucky* (1982). See also Charles Wolfe, "Cliff Carlisle," *Bluegrass Unlimited*, Dec. 1984, pp. 56ff.

CHARLES K. WOLFE

CARLISLE, John Griffin (5 Sept. 1834–31 July 1910), U.S. congressman, senator, and secretary of the treasury, was born in Campbell (now Kenton) County, Kentucky, the son of Lilbon Hardin Carlisle and Mary A. Reynolds, farmers. He attended common schools and taught school before studying law under the distinguished lawyer (later governor and U.S. senator) John White Stevenson, with whom he became a close friend. After Carlisle was admitted to the bar in 1858, he entered the law firm of the prominent judge William B. Kinkead in Covington, Kentucky. In 1857 he married Mary Jane Goodson, with whom he had two sons who lived to adulthood.

Although Carlisle lacked formal education, his keen intellect and native ability soon won him prominence among Kentucky lawyers. Joining the Democratic party, he made speeches against the Know-Nothings before his twentieth birthday. In 1859 he won election to the state legislature and was reelected the following year.

During the secession winter of 1861, Carlisle endorsed sectional compromise and joined other Kentucky legislators in opposing federal coercion of departing states. After Fort Sumter he backed the assembly's declaration of neutrality. Although the Unionist-leaning voters of Carlisle's Ohio River district denied him reelection in 1861, he stood by his neutrality and joined neither the Union nor the Confederate army.

Like many other Kentuckians, Carlisle bristled at the perceived offenses of military occupation and cast his lot with the Peace Democrats. He refused, however, appointment as an elector for the 1864 Democratic presidential nominee, George B. McClellan (1826–1885). He was elected to the state senate in 1866 and reelected in 1869. In that body he achieved enough visibility to win election as lieutenant governor in 1871. For four years he presided over the state senate, thereby acquiring insights into parliamentary procedures he later applied in his congressional career.

In 1876 Carlisle was elected to the U.S. House of Representatives where he served until 1890. Entering Congress at a time when the money issue dominated public concern, he advocated the repeal of the Specie Resumption Act of 1875. Echoing western sentiments, he argued that government payment of gold for depreciated greenback currency, scheduled to begin 1 January 1879, would work severe hardships on debt-ridden farmers and laborers. He also opposed the federal government's lavishing bonds and land grants on railroad builders. He took a moderate position on the silver issue in the 1870s, favoring the use of silver along with gold coins but opposing the free coinage of silver.

In the off-year elections during the term of President Rutherford B. Hayes, the Democrats won control of both houses of Congress. They immediately sought to undo civil rights legislation passed during Reconstruction. Carlisle vigorously championed the movement to attach repeal measures to appropriations bills, and even though Hayes steadfastly vetoed bills with such "riders," Carlisle's speeches on that issue increased his stature with House Democrats.

At the beginning of his second term in Congress, Carlisle took a seat on the Ways and Means Committee. There he ardently advocated tariff reduction. Following the logic of generations of southern Democrats, he argued that a protective tariff unjustly favored special interests at the expense of farmers and working-class consumers. When Republican president Chester A. Arthur appointed a commission to study the question and suggest rates, Carlisle suspected a plot in favor of protected interests. In fact, the commission advocated lower import duties. Rancorous debate ensued, culminating in the passage of the so-called Mongrel Tariff of 1883. In the course of this struggle, Carlisle emerged as a leading spokesman for the low-tariff wing of the Democrats.

When the 48th Congress opened in December 1883, the Democrats elected Carlisle Speaker over protectionist Samuel J. Randall of Pennsylvania, thereby signaling the party's further embrace of tariff reduction. Carlisle was reelected Speaker twice. In that post he earned a reputation for fairness, but he also employed his power to recognize members on the floor selectively in order to further the Democrats' agenda. At the Democratic National Convention in 1884, Kentucky offered his name for the presidency, but he received only twenty-seven votes. The party then turned to Grover Cleveland, who went on to win the White House.

Cleveland sided with Carlisle on the tariff, but Randall's protectionist supporters, numbering roughly forty in the House, continued to unite with Republicans to hinder reduction measures. Although government revenues mounted, Carlisle, as Speaker, blocked efforts to reduce internal taxes or to pass appropriation measures he considered extravagant. Thus, the treasury surplus continued to grow and threaten the economy.

In December 1887 Cleveland devoted his entire annual message to an impassioned plea for tariff reduction. In the ensuing congressional session, Carlisle again threw himself into the fight for lower duties. He and his allies at last secured House passage of the Mills Bill in 1888, but the measure had no chance in the Republican Senate. In the election that year, Cleveland lost to Benjamin Harrison (1833–1901), and the Republicans took both houses of Congress, although Carlisle retained his seat.

In the new House, Minority Leader Carlisle strenuously opposed Republican Speaker Thomas B. Reed's imposition of new rules permitting the Speaker to defeat obstructionist tactics by the minority. Afterward, Carlisle fought vainly to block passage of the McKinley Tariff Bill with its record-high peacetime rates. Carlisle had a unique opportunity to vote against the McKinley Tariff in both houses, for in May 1890 the Kentucky legislature elected him to fill the Senate vacancy created by the death of James B. Beck. In the Senate he opposed other Republican activist measures, including the Lodge Federal Elections Bill and appropriations for veterans' pensions.

The voters' overwhelming rejection of the Republican program in the 1890 congressional elections augured a Democratic victory in the 1892 presidential race, and many party members considered Carlisle a strong contender. The party chose Cleveland again, however, and he won an easy victory over Harrison. With the tariff and currency questions certain to loom large in his second term, Cleveland asked Carlisle to become secretary of the treasury.

In the last months of the Harrison administration, the overheated economy slowed down. When the new administration took office in March 1893, the nation's finances teetered on the brink of disaster. The confidence that had led many businesspeople to overextend their enterprises and their debts turned to despair. Frightened, people sought safety in the possession of gold, and the Treasury Department witnessed a severe drain on its reserves. Less than two months after taking office, Carlisle saw treasury holdings dip below $100 million—the level considered essential to maintain the gold standard and the nation's economic health. By early May panic gripped the country's financial markets, triggering a deep depression that lasted half a decade.

In pre–Federal Reserve days the government had little power to combat a deflationary spiral. Carlisle did issue a small quantity of National Bank notes to banks holding U.S. bonds, but he and Cleveland settled on what they considered a more fundamental solution: repeal of the Sherman Silver Purchase Act of 1890. This would halt the exchange of silver certificates for gold at the treasury, supposedly strengthen faith in the government's solvency, and generally contribute to a restoration of business confidence. Carlisle had pushed for repeal in his final months in the Senate and was a leader in the administration's fight for repeal at a special session of Congress in 1893. The effort succeeded but only after a bruising battle that split the Democratic party into gold and silver wings.

The Sherman Act repeal did not restore economic confidence, and neither did the badly bungled administration effort to undo the excesses of the McKinley Tariff. Having dissipated their leverage in the repeal fight, Cleveland and Carlisle could not prevent passage or secure improvement of the protectionist Wilson-Gorman Tariff, which became law without Cleveland's signature. As the gold reserve continued to fall, Carlisle and Cleveland concluded that their only recourse was the sale of government bonds to replenish the stock. Two sales in February and November 1894 did little to help because most of the buyers purchased bonds with gold obtained from the treasury in exchange for greenbacks or other government paper. A third sale of bonds directly to a banking syndicate headed by J. P. Morgan (1837–1913), with great profit to the bankers, evoked a storm of criticism and raised the gold reserve only temporarily. In early 1896 Carlisle floated a fourth bond issue to the public, and the gold reserve began to hold steady.

As the Cleveland administration drew to a close, the split in the Democratic party was complete. Carlisle, who earlier in his career had seen a place for silver in the nation's currency, became irrevocably identified with the supporters of gold. In 1896 many Democrats supported him for president, but he withdrew from the nomination race. When the party chose silverite William Jennings Bryan, Carlisle backed an opposing Gold Democratic ticket.

Carlisle's currency policies alienated his constituents in Kentucky. At the end of his term as treasury secretary, he moved to New York City to practice law. He largely withdrew from politics except for participation in the movement against expansionism after the Spanish-American War, when he served as vice president of the Anti-Imperialist League. He died in New York City.

Carlisle's successful career symbolized the resurgent South in the nation's politics. His principal concerns in the House of Representatives and the Treasury Department mirrored the primacy of financial issues in the postwar decades. Yet his embrace of conservative money policy, and the opposition it evoked, reflected tensions within the Democratic party that undermined its strength and helped the Republicans achieve a national majority they maintained for a generation.

• Letters from Carlisle are in the Grover Cleveland Papers and the W. C. P. Breckinridge Papers in the Library of Congress. Papers relating to his service in Congress and the Treasury Department may also be found in the National Archives. The only full-length biography is James A. Barnes, *John G. Carlisle: Financial Statesman* (1931).

CHARLES W. CALHOUN

CARLISLE, Una Mae (26 Dec. 1915–7 Nov. 1956), jazz pianist, singer, and composer of popular songs, was born in Zanesville, Ohio, the daughter of Edward E. Carlisle and Mellie (maiden name unknown), a schoolteacher. (The assertion that she was born in Xenia, Ohio, published in many references, does not conform to family records.) With piano training from her mother, she sang and played in public at age three in Chillicothe, Ohio. After participating in musical activities at church and school in Jamestown and Xenia, Ohio, she began performing regularly on radio station WHIO in Dayton while still a youngster. In 1932 she came to the notice of Thomas "Fats" Waller in Cincinnati and quickly became his protégée and the beneficiary of his counsel. Until the end of 1933 she worked alongside the well-known entertainer, both on tour and on his *Rhythm Club* broadcasts for Cincinnati station WLW, which boasted the highest wattage of any radio station in the country. She soon came to emulate his keyboard style as well as his witty delivery of novelty songs. In a biography of his father, Waller's son contends that Carlisle came to his father's attention as a backup singer on the Waller recording of "Mean Old Bedbug Blues" made in New York in July 1932, during Carlisle's summer vacation from high school. This special relationship with Waller, while notably tempestuous, continued on a personal level until his death in 1943; in her professional life his influence extended much longer as she made recordings with ensembles patterned after her mentor's and with instrumentalists associated with him.

After graduation from high school in 1933, Carlisle moved to Chicago and then New York City. She was employed for a brief period in 1934 as a showgirl at the Cotton Club. Disenchanted, she then worked for a short time as a copyist-arranger for music publisher Irving Mills before joining a touring company of Lew Leslie's *Blackbirds* revue for a London run in 1936. (Leslie's famous *Blackbirds* series, like many others at this time, featured songs, dances, and "plantation" skits by an all-black cast for the benefit of white audiences.) Remaining in Europe between 1937 and 1939, Carlisle accepted club engagements as a soloist in as many as eighteen countries and was known to sing in seven languages; her repertoire reflected the crowd-pleasing Waller approach and included such humorous numbers as "Two Old Maids in a Folding Bed." In Paris, where she enjoyed a lengthy residency at the Boeuf sur le Toit, she reportedly studied harmony at the Sorbonne and operated her own nightclub in Montmartre. In May 1938 her recording career as a leading artist was launched in London by Leonard Feather with a set of recordings influenced by the combo style championed by Waller. Carlisle also appeared in several films in England and France in minor musical roles; in *Crossroads*, she introduced the song "Darling, je vous aime beaucoup" (1935), by Anna Sosenko, to European audiences. During her stay on the Continent she formed friendships with many celebrities in show business and high life, such as Josephine Baker, Maurice Chevalier, and the duke of Kent. In 1937 she was the guest of the Egyptian royal family in Cairo for three weeks during festivities surrounding the lavish nuptials of King Farouk and performed at the royal wedding reception.

Deteriorating conditions in Europe in 1939 hastened Carlisle's return to the United States, where she established a reputation in New York City clubs, such as the Village Vanguard, Kelly's Stables, the Plantation Club, and Hotel Dixie, and made recordings. She sang on Waller's evergreen hit "I Can't Give You Anything but Love" (1939) and, more importantly, led her own all-star combo on the Bluebird label during 1940 and 1941. Among her illustrious collaborators in this endeavor were saxophonists Lester Young and Benny Carter and bass player John Kirby. The most successful of her fifteen recordings, "Walkin' by the River" (1940) and "I See a Million People" (1941), were renditions of her own compositions, tuneful ballads with lyrics by Robert Sour, and earned BMI awards; arrangements of both were heard nationally on "Your Hit Parade," the radio program that identified the ten most popular songs in America each week. Carlisle was the first African-American woman to achieve such a distinction as a composer of popular songs. Subsequent recordings of these songs, in particular by such notable musicians as Benny Goodman, Ella Fitzgerald, and Cab Calloway, contributed to her growing reputation. Carlisle composed as many as 500 songs before 1952. She appeared in three full-length musical films devoted to performances by prominent African-American artists: *Stars on Parade* (1944), *This Joint Is Jumpin'* (1947), and *Boarding House Blues* (1948). Her celebrity and stature are also suggested by her inclusion in the short documentary *The Negro in Entertainment* (1950), for which she shared billing with W. C. Handy, Ethel Waters, Louis Armstrong, Duke Ellington, and Fats Waller.

In 1950 Carlisle's popularity earned her a radio series in her own name originating in New York City and syndicated coast-to-coast by the American Broadcasting Corporation; she hosted a similar radio program from 1951 until 1953. Her work in radio was of historic significance as she was the first African-American musician to be featured on her own nationally syndicated radio program. In 1950 she began to record on the Columbia label with saxophonists Don Redman and Bob Chester. Forced by chronic illness to retire in 1954, she returned to her family in Ohio but died in Harlem. At the time of her death, she was married to John Bradford, a one-time dancer.

Carlisle, known for her striking appearance and feisty personality, possessed a clear, vibrant, rich voice and was equally adept in performing love ballads and up-tempo dance songs. In spite of her collaboration with seasoned jazz musicians of the first order, her recorded performances do not identify her as a dynamic improviser in the jazz tradition. Gunther Schuller assesses her work as a jazz artist as "second-rate." In his autobiography, however, jazz critic Leonard Feather, who produced her earliest recordings, remembered Carlisle as an "uncommonly capable" pianist and singer. Periodically there are suggestions of the poignancy of Billie Holiday and of those inflections that characterize the African-American tradition, but in general the interpretative style and the emotional content of her singing are more influenced by the commercialized mainstream of popular music of the day. Her keyboard playing is grounded in the "bouncy" stride style; her instrumental solos demonstrate an easy command of conventional material without calling much attention to her ingenuity. Long after Carlisle's death, Feather lamented her failure to realize the full extent of her promise as a musician: "Perhaps because of a lifestyle as self-indulgent as Fats' own, Una Mae never reached the plateau of fame to which her talent and beauty might have been expected to bring her" (p. 128). Nevertheless, in a career that stopped rather suddenly in her prime, Carlisle distinguished herself as a nightclub entertainer, a recording artist, a song composer, and a radio personality.

• A folder of newspaper clippings and memorabilia compiled under the supervision of Carlisle's sister and nephew is in the Greene County Room of the Greene County Public Library in Xenia, Ohio. Her relationship with Fats Waller is described in Maurice Waller and Anthony Calabrese, *Fats Waller* (1977), and Joel Vance, *Fats Waller: His Life and Times* (1977). Information about her recording career is found in H. Smith, "Una Mae Carlisle Takes Final Bow," *Record Research* 11, no. 5 (1957): 24; Leonard Feather, *The Jazz Years: Earwitness to an Era* (1987); Bruce Bastin, *Never Sell a Copyright: Joe Davis and His Role in the New York Music Scene, 1916–1978* (1990); and Bruce Bastin, liner notes to *Una Mae Carlisle, Maxine Sullivan & Savannah Churchill, 1942–1944* (Harlequin CD 19 [1992]). The greatest detail about her recording sessions appears in the writings of Bastin. A useful discography is in Roger D. Kinkle, *The Complete Encyclopedia of Popular Music and Jazz, 1900–1950* (1974). Carlisle is treated in a broader context in "Women in Music: 71 of the Key Creators," *BMI: The Many Worlds of Music* (1977), pp. 9–10; Henry T. Sampson, *Blacks in Blackface: A Source Book on Early Black Musical Shows* (1980); D. Antoinette Handy, *Black Women in American Bands and Orchestras* (1981); Sally Placksin, *American Women in Jazz, 1900 to the Present: Their Words, Lives, and Music* (1982); Linda Dahl, *Stormy Weather: The Music and Lives of a Century of Jazzwomen* (1984); Gunther Schuller, *The Swing Era: The Development of Jazz, 1930–1945* (1989); and Virginia L. Grattan, *American Women Songwriters* (1993).

MICHAEL J. BUDDS

CARLSON, Anton Julius (29 Jan. 1875–2 Sept. 1956), physiologist, was born in Bohuslan, Sweden, the son of Carl Jacobson and Hedvig Andersdotter, farmers. Carl Jacobson died when his six children were still very young, after which the modest family farm was lost and his children went to work for neighbors to support the family. From as young as age seven, Carlson spent the summer months herding sheep on neighboring farms but also took time to learn from his mother, a devout Swedish Lutheran, how to read and write, and to appreciate the value of work. At age sixteen, leaving his mother, whom he would never see again, and speaking no English, Carlson immigrated to the United States to join his older brother Albin as a carpenter's helper in Chicago.

Encouraged by a young Lutheran minister in Chicago, Carlson used his meager savings to attend Augustana Academy and College, a Swedish Lutheran preparatory school and college in Rock Island, Illinois, from which Carlson received a B.A. in 1898 and an M.A. in philosophy in 1899. While at Augustana, Carlson met Esther Sjogren; the two married in 1905 and had two sons and a daughter. During his studies at Augustana, Carlson's growing skepticism of Lutheran dogma led his teachers and peers to rescind his election as class valedictorian. Despite his spiritual confusion, Carlson went to Anaconda, Montana, to serve as a minister in the city's Swedish Lutheran church but left the position a year later, in 1900, to begin graduate studies in physiology at Stanford University.

An intensely serious student, Carlson lived in the physiological laboratory of his mentor, O. P. Jenkins, where his research involved measuring the nerve conduction rate of invertebrate pseudopods. For a dissertation concluding that the conductive substance in the nerve fiber must be a liquid rather than a solid, Carlson received a Ph.D. in 1902. Joining the Carnegie Institution as a research associate after graduation, Carlson spent 1903 and 1904 studying the coordination and the conduction of the cardiac impulse in the Limulus, or horseshoe crab. Carlson became internationally known for his research demonstrating that the cardiac nerves are responsible for the coordination and conduction of the heartbeat, helping to settle the debate over the neurogenic and myogenic theories of cardiac conduction.

Carlson's research led to his appointment in 1904 as associate in the Department of Physiology at the University of Chicago. The remainder of Carlson's professional career was spent at the University of Chicago, where he was promoted to associate professor in 1909, professor in 1914, and physiology department chair in 1916, and from which he retired in 1940 as the John P. Hixon Distinguished Service Professor of Physiology Emeritus.

After 1908, Carlson's research began to shift to questions in mammalian physiology, particularly seminal studies on lymph formation and on the thyroid and pancreas. At this time, accidental removal of the parathyroid glands during surgery on the thyroid often led to fatal tetany. Carlson and his students Arno B. Luckhardt and Lester R. Dragstedt studied the onset of tetany, and Luckhardt and Dragstedt developed techniques to prevent the condition. Other research on the internal secretion of the pancreas came close to isolating insulin. Although Carlson had no formal training in medicine, his colleagues and students considered him astute about clinical medicine, a quality that was evident in his teaching of physiology to medical students and in the frequent requests from clinical societies to appear at their paper discussions.

When World War I broke out, Carlson sought to join the military but was advised that his abilities were of most use in the army's medical department. Enlisting as a captain in the newly organized Sanitary Corps, Carlson went to England and France as an inspector of the food supplied to army camps. In 1919 he was promoted to lieutenant colonel in the Medical Corps. After the war, Carlson spent a year working for the Hoover Commission charged with distributing food in defeated European nations. While visiting countries in central and eastern Europe, children and women—the innocent and defenseless victims of war—and the Christian prejudice against Muslims moved Carlson to speak out against the hypocritical actions of military and civilian leaders in the Allied war effort. Returning to Chicago and his laboratory in 1919, Carlson began studies on the origins of the sensation of hunger, Pursuing clinical reports that insulin overdose produced hunger pangs, Carlson and his students demonstrated that insulin hypoglycemia resulted in contractions in the empty stomach much like those during starvation and that insulin hypoglycemia stimulated the secretion of gastric acids if the vagus nerves were intact.

Although Carlson continued to direct the research efforts of numerous graduate students over the next two decades, his own research subsided after his work on hunger. Turning his attention to public health efforts in Chicago and across the nation, Carlson was instrumental in promoting a free lunch program for poor children in Chicago's public schools and a variety of other children's programs, including the activities of the National Foundation for Infantile Paralysis. He also worked on efforts to curb the use of lead arsenate as an insecticide by fruit growers and to mediate conflicts between butter producers and margarine manufacturers. An outspoken and vigorous supporter of humanitarian causes, Carlson opposed Mussolini's invitation for the International Physiological Congress to meet in Rome and supported the activities of the Association of University Professors (as president) and the American Civil Liberties Union. When antivivisectionists threatened medical and biological research efforts, Carlson and his student Andrew C. Ivy founded the National Society for Medical Research to promote the need for research on animals.

Carlson was widely recognized for his humanitarian and scientific achievements. In addition to being awarded the Distinguished Service Award by the American Medical Association in 1946, Carlson was also elected to the National Academy of Sciences (1920) and the American Philosophical Society. As president of the American Association for the Advancement of Science, the American Physiological Society, the Federation of American Societies for Experimental Biology, the Institute of Medicine of Chicago, and other organizations, Carlson championed the need for increased scientific research and the social responsibilities of scientists. In the period after World War II, when the lay public grew to distrust the potential benefits of science, Carlson served as a moral compass in the scientific community, advocating that socially responsible scientific research was possible and could lead to a better understanding of the human condition. He died in Chicago.

• Among Carlson's most important papers are, in the *American Journal of Physiology*, "The Rhythm Produced in the Resting Heart of Molluscs by the Stimulation of the Cardio-accelerator Nerves," 12 (1904): 55–66; "The Nervous Origin of the Heartbeat in Limulus and the Nervous Nature of Coordination or Conduction in the Heart," 12 (1904): 67–74; "Contributions to the Physiology of the Stomach. I. The Character of the Movements of the Empty Stomach in Man," 31 (1912): 151–68; "Contributions to the Physiology of the Stomach. II. The Relation between the Contractions of the Empty Stomach and the Sensation of Hunger," 31 (1912): 175–92; and "The Secretion of Gastric Juice in Man," 37 (1915): 50–73. His book *On the Nervous Control of the Hunger Mechanism* (1917) was followed by "A Few Observations of Certain Conditions in Europe after the War," *Journal of the Missouri Medical Association* 17 (1920): 229; "Child Health and Protection: The Physician's Responsibility," *Journal of the Iowa Medical Society* 22 (1932): 450–52; "Experimentation and Medicine: Man's Debt to the Animal World," *Hygeia* 13 (1935): 126–28; and "Role of Fundamental Sciences in Medical Progress," *Scientific Monthly* 50 (1940): 59–64. The most comprehensive biography is Lester R. Dragstedt, "Anton Julius Carlson," National Academy of Sciences, *Biographical Memoirs* 35 (1961): 1–32, which includes a complete list of Carlson's publications; see also Carlson's autobiographical article, "Anton Julius Carlson (1875–)—Missionary to the Heathen," *Postgraduate Medicine* 1 (1947): 159–63.

D. George Joseph

CARLSON, Chester Floyd (8 Feb. 1906–19 Sept. 1968), inventor and patent lawyer, was born in Seattle, Washington, the son of Olof Adolph Carlson, a barber, and Ellen Josephine (maiden name unknown). His father had emigrated from Sweden and suffered from severe arthritis, and both parents developed tuberculosis. The family moved briefly to Mexico for the warmer weather but returned to the United States in 1912 to settle on a rented farm near San Bernardino, California. For a time Carlson was the only student in a country school, and he rode into town on a bicycle to work at odd jobs. His mother died when he was seventeen, and he supported his father.

One of Carlson's jobs during high school was as the janitor in a printing shop, where he developed an interest in graphic arts and printing. Using an old printing press that had been given to him, he published a newsletter on chemistry for his fellow students. He also worked in the testing laboratory of a nearby cement plant. In 1925 he attended Riverside Junior College, where he concentrated on chemistry and physics. A special program allowed him to alternate course work and employment every six weeks in the testing laboratory at the Riverside Cement Company. In 1928

Carlson transferred to the California Institute of Technology, where he worked on outside jobs to support the costs. He received a B.S. in physics in 1930.

Carlson moved to New York City after his father died and began work at Bell Telephone Laboratories in 1930. After researching the chemistry of carbon in telephone microphones for a few months, he became assistant to an attorney in the patent department. He held this position until 1933, when the company reduced its work force during the depression. Carlson found a similar job at a company named Austin & Bix; he then moved in 1934 to the patent department of P. R. Mallory and Co., a builder of rectifiers, electrolytic condensers, and batteries.

Noting the higher salaries paid to patent attorneys, Carlson decided to get a law degree. He took evening courses at New York Law School, reducing expenses by reading textbooks at the public library. After receiving a law degree in 1939, he was admitted to the state bar in 1940 and became head of Mallory's patent department.

The necessity of creating many copies of drawings and specifications in patent applications and the tediousness of manual copying from law textbooks created a yearning in Carlson for a rapid copying process. He read a paper by Hungarian inventor Paul Selenyi, who had created an electrostatic image on a coated rotating drum. Carlson decided to try to devise a machine that could produce an image on a photoconductive plate that had been exposed to light and transfer the image to a sheet of paper. In 1934 he set up a laboratory in the kitchen of his rented apartment and began experimenting. The odor of spilled chemicals brought Linda (maiden name unknown), the daughter of his landlady, to his door, and they soon developed a friendship. Later that year he married her; they had no children.

Some experimental accidents led his wife to urge him to set up a laboratory elsewhere. He moved his experiments in 1935 to a "dreary little building" in Astoria, Long Island, which was owned by his wife's mother. There he worked for long hours alone. At first he coated a zinc plate with a thin layer of sulfur after rubbing it with a cloth to give it an electrostatic charge. He then exposed the plate for a few seconds to a bright floodlight. In 1937 Carlson applied for a patent on this "electro-photography" (the patent was issued in 1942). In 1938 he hired Otto Kornei, a German physicist and engineer who had left Germany to avoid the Nazi regime. They successfully produced their first image on 22 October 1938, using a sulfur-coated metal plate dusted with a vegetable-based powder, called lycopodium, from a glass slide inscribed "10–22–38 Astoria." They promptly reproduced this on wax-coated paper. The process proved effective, although the image was quite blurry.

Kornei found that anthracene was a more satisfactory conductor than sulfur. He could not afford to continue at the low salary Carlson could pay him and soon took a position with IBM. Carlson continued experimenting with improvements in chemical coatings and in lighting, and he obtained several more patents. He tried to interest various companies in his copying technique but they did not see a need for such equipment, and during his demonstrations there were often technical problems.

Russell W. Dayton of Battelle Memorial Institute in Columbus, Ohio, learned of Carlson's invention when he visited P. R. Mallory and Company in 1944. The institute was seeking inventions to develop with private industry or government funds. Following a demonstration, Roland M. Schaffert, the head of Battelle's graphic arts division, wrote that the invention had possibilities, that business applications existed, and that, in fact, "this process looks like a good research gamble." In August 1944, Battelle agreed to spend $3,000 for its own further research and development of electrophotography, to try to find an industrial sponsor, to pay $1,000 a year to Carlson, and to guarantee him 25 percent of all profits or royalties. Battelle increased the research funds in later years and, with Carlson's participation, tried to find a commercial sponsor. The company's engineers improved the original process by using selenium for the photoconductive plate, by using a dim light, and by setting up a more effective transfer of the powder from the plate to the paper.

In 1945 Carlson left P. R. Mallory and Company and was divorced. In April of that year John H. Dessauer, head of the research and engineering division of Haloid Company in Rochester, New York, read a brief description about Carlson's process in *Kodak's Monthly Abstract Bulletin*. The small company manufactured photographic paper and related products. Dessauer brought the item to the attention of Haloid's president, Joseph C. Wilson. In 1946, following discussions with engineers at Battelle and various negotiations, Haloid agreed to pay Battelle $25,000 a year for its research work on electrophotography, for which Haloid would receive limited copying rights and would pay Battelle a royalty of 8 percent on future revenues from the technique. Carlson became a consultant to Haloid and assigned some additional patents to it. As Dessauer noted, Battelle engineers continued to improve the system, and Carlson "would watch these experiments, hovering over work benches, making suggestions over people's shoulders" (Dessauer, p. 47). The suggestions were often significant. Carlson married Dorris Hudgins in the latter 1940s; they had no children.

Officials of Battelle and Haloid, with the advice of a Greek scholar at Ohio State University, coined the word "xerography" ("xeros" for dry, "graphos" for writing or picture) for the new technique in 1947. According to Dessauer, someone at Haloid suggested the trade name "Xerox" (for a few years it was "XeroX").

Haloid introduced the copying machine at a meeting of the Optical Society of America on 22 October 1948, the tenth anniversary of Carlson's initial success. The first commercial machines that the company marketed in the late 1940s proved to be most suitable for offset duplicating, at a cost well below that of previous machines for this purpose. In 1950 Battelle and Haloid agreed that Haloid would be the sole licensing agency for all patents in the xerographic field, while Battelle would receive 8 percent royalty on Haloid's licensing. Carlson, by borrowing from relatives, picked up a previously negotiated option to receive 40 percent of everything that Battelle earned on his invention.

In 1956 Haloid acquired from Battelle the full rights of the Carlson patents for 50,000 shares of Haloid common stock. In 1958 the company changed its name to Haloid-Xerox. It continued to sell an increasing number of the other products with which it had started and which it had been continually improving. In 1959 the company placed on the market the Xerox 914 Office Copier, a piece of equipment primarily intended to be leased (914 referred to the page size of 9 inches by 14 inches that it could handle). Sales and leases soared. In 1961 income from xerographic products reached more than 75 percent of its business, and the company changed its name to Xerox Corporation. That year its stock was first traded on the New York Stock Exchange.

Through the years Carlson did not participate in the creation of the company's policies, although he frequently advised on new patents from ideas that began in its research facilities. As he put it, "I'm really a patent attorney. Inventing was something I did in my kitchen after hours" (Dessauer, p. 152).

After a childhood of poverty and decades of financial struggle, Carlson became wealthy through Xerox Corporation. From the latter 1950s he was a philanthropist, although he was shy and his gifts were usually anonymous. He gave money to the California Institute of Technology for a new building, he donated to agencies of the United Nations in health programs and to various causes for peace, and he contributed heavily to the Center for the Study of Democratic Institutions. He also gave money for studies in psychical research, extrasensory perception, and Zen Buddhism.

Carlson obtained forty-two U.S. patents, most related to xerography. He received the Edward Longstreth Medal of Franklin Institute in 1953. He lived for some years in a suburb of Rochester, New York, and he died in New York City while working for a philanthropic cause.

• A summary of Carlson's life is in John H. Dessauer, *My Years with Xerox* (1971). James E. Brittain's account of Carlson's achievements in the *Dictionary of American Biography* is helpful. An obituary is in the *New York Times*, 20 Sept. 1968.

ELIZABETH NOBLE SHOR

CARLSON, Evans Fordyce (26 Feb. 1896–27 May 1947), army and Marine Corps officer and writer, was born in Sidney, New York, the son of Thomas Alpine Carlson, a Congregationalist minister, and Joetta Viola Evans. He grew up in New England and left home at fourteen to work on a farm near Vergennes, Vermont, where he attended but did not graduate from the local high school. After working as an assistant freight master in New Haven, Connecticut, and as a chainman in New Jersey, he joined the army in 1912, at age sixteen, with the reluctant permission of his parents. Stationed in the Philippines and in Hawaii, he was discharged with the rank of master sergeant in 1915.

After working with an artesian well–digging outfit and a surveying crew, Carlson was recalled to duty in 1916 during the U.S. border conflict with Mexico. He served as an instructor to the National Guard Artillery at Fort Bliss in El Paso, Texas. When the United States entered World War I in April 1917, he was commissioned a second lieutenant and was assigned to the Thirteenth Field Artillery. Following duty at several camps in the United States, he was sent to France, where he served briefly on the staff of General John J. Pershing as assistant adjutant general. Discharged at the age of twenty-three with the rank of captain, Carlson was awarded French and Italian decorations and a citation from General Pershing.

Carlson worked for two years as a salesman and then, in 1922, enlisted in the Marine Corps as a private. It was as a marine that Carlson earned public distinction. Commissioned as a second lieutenant in 1923, he held several domestic assignments over the next four years.

From 24 February 1927 to 24 September 1929 Carlson served as operations and intelligence officer in Shanghai, China, as part of the Fourth Marine Regiment. He was promoted to first lieutenant on 20 September 1927—ten years to the day of his promotion to that grade in the army. Carlson began an intensive study of Chinese history and language and wrote articles on China's political situation. He also spent several months preparing a detailed map of the International Settlement.

From 1930 to 1933 Carlson served in Nicaragua. He was an adviser and patrol leader in the Guardia Nacional, the Nicaraguan National Guard, trained by the U.S. Marine Corps. Carlson received the Navy Cross for "extraordinary heroism" during the Pasmata patrol, in which, using novel night-fighting tactics, he led a dozen men against a force of nearly 100 Nicaraguan rebels and succeeded in recovering stolen property and in dispersing the rebel band across the Honduran border without sustaining any losses. Carlson also served informally as a judge in the district of Jalapa, hearing cases ranging from murder to family disputes. In December 1930 Carlson became commander of the guardia's Department of Managua. When the earthquake of 31 March 1931 devastated Managua, he swiftly helped build a relief organization and brought law and order to the devastated city. Carlson was awarded Nicaragua's Presidential Medal of Merit. From December 1931 until his departure, he served as Managua's chief of police and tried to rid the city of graft and corruption.

In March 1933 Carlson returned to Shanghai as an intelligence officer with the Fourth Regiment. Restless to see more of China, he received a transfer to Peking (Beijing) and duty with the Legation Guard. He began a legation language school and succeeded in reducing the number of altercations between marines and townspeople as their attitudes changed.

Brought back to the United States in 1935, Carlson was promoted to captain and designated second in command to the Marine detachment at the Warm Springs, Georgia, retreat of President Franklin D. Roosevelt, with whom he enjoyed a cordial personal relationship. He also studied at the Marine Corps Schools and took graduate classes in international law at George Washington University, despite his lack of a high school diploma.

Carlson left for his third tour of China in summer 1937 as a naval intelligence observer of Chinese and Japanese military tactics. With the navy's permission, Carlson became the first foreign military observer of the Chinese Communist Eighth Route Army operations. He made two extended tours throughout the Northwest in December 1937 and early 1938, often accompanying Communist guerrillas behind Japanese lines. In a secret correspondence, initiated at President Roosevelt's request, Carlson kept the president informed of his activities. His public praise of the Communist troops' resourcefulness and flexible tactics brought censure from his superiors and resulted in his resignation in April 1939 so that he could freely write and speak about China. For the next two years he lectured and wrote two books on China. As a civilian he returned in 1940 and 1941 to China, primarily to inspect 600 industrial cooperatives in eight provinces. There he learned the term *gonghe*, the pinyin spelling for "work together," which he popularized in the United States as "gung ho."

Convinced that war with Japan was likely, Carlson reenlisted in the Marine Corps and was commissioned a major in the reserves in April 1941. Early in 1942 he was promoted to lieutenant colonel in command of the newly formed 2d Marine Raider Battalion, with the president's son James Roosevelt as his executive officer. Carlson called his volunteer, handpicked force the "gung ho" battalion, modeled after the Eighth Route Army. Discipline was firm but informal. At weekly "gung ho" meetings, raiders were encouraged to discuss battle plans and, after completing missions, to engage in self-criticism.

The Carlson Raiders first saw action on 17–18 August 1942 in a hit-and-run raid against the Japanese on Butaritari in the Makin Atoll of the Gilberts. In the only landing raid made by Marines in rubber boats launched from submarines, Carlson led 222 raiders against 86 Japanese. Thirty hours later the raiders returned home heroes, having killed nearly all the Japanese and having destroyed a radio station, aviation fuel, and a seaplane base. However, nine raiders who remained were later captured by the Japanese and beheaded. Marine losses totaled thirty, which was unacceptable to the hierarchy and raised doubt about the value of raiders.

On 4–30 November 1942 the raiders again operated behind Japanese lines in Guadalcanal, killing nearly 500 enemy troops while suffering only sixteen deaths in one of the greatest combat patrols in history. Despite a navy citation for their skill and aggressiveness, the raiders were consolidated with three other battalions into a Marine Raider Regiment. Carlson never received another command. After hospitalization for malaria, he became an official adviser to Universal Studios during the filming of a movie on the Makin raid, *Gung Ho*. In 1943–1944 he was an observer during the assaults at Tarawa, Kwajalein, and Saipan. At Tarawa he carried vital information through enemy fire, and he was seriously wounded at Saipan while rescuing a wounded enlisted man. Physical disability caused Carlson's retirement on 1 July 1946. He was advanced to brigadier general rank on the retired list.

Carlson became increasingly active in supporting American troop withdrawal from China and opposing U.S. aid to Nationalist forces as chair of the Committee for a Democratic Far Eastern Policy and other organizations. At the time of his death he planned to seek a U.S. Senate seat from California.

Carlson's marriage to Dorothy Seccombe in 1916 lasted four years, ending in divorce. His only child, Evans Charles Carlson, served with him as a raider at Guadalcanal. A second marriage, in 1924, to Etelle Sawyer ended in divorce in 1943. In 1944 Carlson married Peggy Tatum Whyte, and they settled in Brightwood, Oregon. Carlson died of heart failure in Portland, Oregon. He was buried with full military honors at Arlington National Cemetery.

Carlson remains a controversial figure. Critics, notably Senator Joseph McCarthy, who branded him the "Red General," portrayed him as a dupe of the Chinese Communists. Nonetheless, most contemporary observers discounted these unfounded charges and praised him as an unparalleled motivator of men, developer of innovative tactics in guerrilla warfare, and expert on China.

• Carlson's voluminous correspondence with Roosevelt is at the Roosevelt Library at Hyde Park, N.Y. Carlson's works include two books, *The Chinese Army: Its Organization and Military Efficiency* (1940) and *Twin Stars of China: A Behind-the-Scenes Story of China's Valiant Struggle for Existence by a U.S. Marine Who Lived and Moved with the People* (1940), and over a dozen articles, including "Marines as Aid to Diplomacy in China," *Marine Corps Gazette* 20 (Feb. 1936): 27–30, 47–53; and "America Faces Crisis in the Orient," *Amerasia*, Feb. 1940, pp. 555–60. The only biography, Michael Blankfort, *The Big Yankee: The Life of Evans Carlson of the Raiders* (1947), is a valuable though romanticized source. Zheng de Hou, *Harmonica and Dagger: A Biography of E. Carlson* (1991), in Chinese, only covers Carlson's years in China. See also Kenneth E. Shewmaker, *Americans and Chinese Communists, 1927–1945* (1971); Helen Foster Snow, "Carlson of (the 'Gung Ho') Carlson's Raiders: His Own Sketch" (1940), an unpublished manuscript at the Marine Corps Historical Center, Washington, D.C.; and Phyllis A. Zimmerman, "Braiding the Cord: The Role of Evans F. Carlson's Second Marine Raider Battalion in Amphibious Warfare," *Marine Corps Gazette* 78 (Nov. 1994): 90–95. The most substantive obituary is in the *Washington Post*, 1 June 1947.

PHYLLIS A. ZIMMERMAN

CARLSON, Frank (23 Jan. 1893–30 May 1987), governor of Kansas and U.S. senator, was born near Concordia, Kansas, the son of Swedish immigrants

Charles Eric Carlson and Anna Johnson, farmers. He studied agriculture at Concordia Normal and Business College and Kansas State College at Manhattan before serving as a private in the U.S. Army in World War I; he was discharged in 1919, having seen no overseas action. That same year, he married Alice Frederickson; they had one daughter and one foster son.

Returning to Concordia after his military service, Carlson purchased a large wheat and livestock farm, which he owned until his death. Throughout the 1920s he was both a successful farmer and a local Republican party leader, serving first as a precinct committeeman and then as Cloud County chairman, before being elected in 1928 to the first of two terms in the Kansas state legislature. As a legislator, he specialized in issues of taxation and agriculture, areas on which he focused most of his efforts and attention throughout his forty-year political career. Briefly leaving elective office, Carlson served from 1932 to 1934 as chairman of the Kansas State Republican Central Committee, in which capacity he managed Alf Landon's successful campaign for governor. When Landon offered him a cabinet position, Carlson declined, saying, "I don't want a political job. I've got a five-hundred-acre farm which will take all my time."

In 1934, however, Carlson changed his mind, running successfully for the U.S. House of Representatives from the Sixth District. Subsequently, he was reelected five times. In the House, he continued to build his reputation as a master of tax and farm legislation and as a champion of national flood control and water conservation measures. Like nearly all congressional Republicans, he opposed most New Deal measures as well as amendment of the Neutrality Acts to permit the president greater latitude prior to World War II. During the war, he was one of the legislative architects of the federal income tax withholding system.

Carlson gave up his House seat to run for governor in 1946, a year when controversy raged in Kansas over whether the statewide prohibition law should be repealed. Though a teetotaler, Carlson urged in his campaign that a state referendum be held and soundly defeated his opponent, former governor Harry Woodring, who advocated outright repeal. After the referendum in November 1948 ended prohibition in the state, Carlson (who was easily reelected to a second term as governor in the 1948 election) won approval of an effective liquor control bill that provided for licensing, regulation, and taxation of the liquor trade. An activist postwar governor, he won passage of such wide-ranging measures as expansion of the rural school program, initiation of a twenty-year state highway construction program, reorganization of the state's mental health and social welfare services, and strengthening of state law enforcement.

In 1950 Carlson was elected to the U.S. Senate with 54.3 percent of the vote. He took his seat immediately after the election through the cooperation of interim senator Harry Darby, whom he had appointed one year earlier to complete an unexpired term. A moderate among Senate Republicans on both foreign and domestic policy questions, Carlson was a prominent early supporter of Dwight Eisenhower for the 1952 presidential nomination and, after Eisenhower's election, was among his most loyal congressional supporters. In the Senate, Carlson was the prototypical farm-state Republican, relatively conservative on fiscal and welfare matters but vigorously supportive of federal aid for farmers. As the ranking Republican on the Post Office and Civil Service Committee, he also came to be regarded as an advocate for federal employees, for whom he regularly championed pay increases and other benefits.

Reelected by increasing margins in 1956 (with 58 percent) and 1962 (with 62 percent), Carlson never emerged as a major force in the Senate and rarely sought the limelight. Even as one of the three Republicans on the select committee to investigate censure of Senator Joseph R. McCarthy in 1954, he maintained a low profile, though in the end voting for censure. For most of his tenure in the Senate, he held seats on the prestigious Finance and Foreign Relations committees and for a time was a member of the Joint Congressional Committee on Internal Revenue Taxation. In the sixties, he voted against most of the major New Frontier–Great Society legislation, including the Economic Opportunity Act, Medicare, Appalachian Redevelopment, and creation of the Department of Housing and Urban Development, but he was a supporter of both the 1964 Civil Rights Act and the Voting Rights Act. He remained to the end the quintessential middle-of-the-road Republican; in virtually every session of Congress in which he was a member, *Congressional Quarterly* boxscores placed him almost exactly in the middle of Republicans in terms of support for the conservative coalition.

Carlson decided not to seek reelection to a fourth Senate term in 1968, retiring with an unbroken string of thirteen electoral victories. He returned to Concordia, where he actively worked his farm for the first ten of the remaining nineteen years of his life. He died in Concordia.

• Carlson's senatorial papers are available for research at the Kansas State Historical Society, and a second collection of miscellaneous papers and memorabilia is housed in the Frank Carlson Library in Concordia. There is no biography of him, nor did he publish memoirs. An informative obituary is in the *Washington Post*, 31 May 1987.

GARY W. REICHARD

CARLSON, Henry Clifford (4 July 1894–1 Nov. 1964), college basketball coach and physician, was born in Pitsburg, Ohio, a mere crossroad in the west-central part of the state, the son of Harold Carlson and Martha (maiden name unknown). When he was two his family moved to Murray City, Ohio, where his father went to work in the coal mines. Tragedy and near poverty plagued the family. When Henry was five his father died in a mining accident. His mother remarried, and the family moved to Fayette City, Pennsylvania, where his stepfather also lost his life in the mines. Unlike many of his friends, Carlson completed high school, graduating in 1912. Unable to afford college, he enrolled in the Bellefonte Academy in Fayette, Pennsylvania. At Bellefonte the young redhead pursued a college preparatory curriculum for two years and excelled in three sports before entering the University of Pittsburgh on an athletic scholarship in 1914.

As a collegian Carlson earned nine varsity letters in football, basketball, and baseball while pursuing a premedical curriculum. While Carlson excelled in all sports, his size at 6′2″, and keen savvy for the game made him an outstanding football player under the legendary coach Glenn "Pop" Warner. During his gridiron career, the Pitt Panthers lost only one game. As captain of the 1917 undefeated squad, Carlson earned All-America honors at the end position.

Following his college graduation in 1918, "Doc," as he was affectionately called, enrolled at the University of Pittsburgh Medical School. To finance medical school, Carlson coached Pitt's freshman football team in 1918, played professional football for the Cleveland Indians during the 1919 season, and coached high school and industrial league basketball in and around Pittsburgh. Carlson received his medical degree in 1920 and married Mary Hyatt. They had two children. He began private practice in Braddock, Pennsylvania, and served eleven years as corporate physician to the Carnegie Steel and U.S. Steel corporations from 1921 to 1932.

Despite Carlson's devotion to medicine, his love of sport was equally strong. In 1922, while continuing his medical practice, he became freshman football coach at Pitt and succeeded Andy Kerr as the school's head basketball coach. Over a 31-year coaching career, Carlson's basketball teams compiled 369 wins and 247 losses. He was an innovative coach and made numerous contributions to the game of basketball, most notably the first pattern offense, the "figure-8" system. While the style was quickly adopted by other schools, Carlson's teams ran this offense to perfection, and it provided for much of his success. In his sixth season, 1928, the Panthers compiled a perfect 21 and 0 campaign and were declared national champions. This distinction was repeated in 1930.

Carlson also applied his medical knowledge to basketball. He was a strong advocate of physical conditioning and nutrition. Following rigorous workouts he fed his players quantities of ice cream to replenish energy levels, and he administered oxygen on the bench during games. Carlson developed a fatigue curve test to determine the fatigue rate of his players related to their work during practice. The test later was incorporated into President Dwight Eisenhower's physical fitness program.

Carlson was a strong advocate for national basketball competition. In 1931–1932, following his retirement from medical practice, Carlson became the first eastern coach to take a team west of the Mississippi River. Pittsburgh's victories over highly respected western teams such as Stanford and the Universities of Kansas, Colorado, and Southern California helped restore prestige to eastern college basketball.

Adding to Carlson's coaching success was his showmanship on and off the court. His colorful actions, especially at away games, not only sold tickets and sparked interest but also provoked opposing fans. A master of the "deep freeze," Carlson frequently instructed his players to control the ball for several minutes without taking a shot. Opposing fans were enraged. But Carlson ignored their protests and embellished the tactic by having his players sit down on the court or bring out a card table and play cards. Following a Pitt victory over Washington and Jefferson, a fan assaulted Carlson with her umbrella. A personality unto himself, Carlson's quarrels with officials were historic. He once ventured the opinion that "the referee is the boil on basketball's nose," and he was especially suspect of road game officials. At West Virginia University during the 1937 season, in response to what Carlson perceived as partisan officiating, he repeatedly shouted to the referee, "This burns me up." To douse Carlson's flames a spectator showered him with a bucket of water.

While each year brought fame and success on the court, tragedy again entered Carlson's life during the 1946 season with the death of his wife. He coached the Panthers through seven more basketball campaigns, retiring following the 1953 season. He had married Alice Martsolf in 1950. They had no children. After leaving coaching, Carlson applied his medical training as director of student health services and athletic medical chief at the University of Pittsburgh. He retired permanently from the university in September 1964. He died at home in Ligonier, Pennsylvania.

Carlson's life and professional career revolved around the university and city of Pittsburgh, and he gave extensive service to each. While his coaching success won him the limelight, Carlson frequently donated his medical expertise to the less fortunate and bought groceries for the hungry, especially during the depression years. He was a Presbyterian church leader and served on numerous local and national medical association boards.

Off the court Carlson contributed to numerous basketball organizations, serving as president of the National Association of Basketball Coaches in 1937. For his athletic and coaching achievements, Carlson was awarded dozens of accolades. He was named to the University of Pittsburgh's Dapper Dan Hall of Fame in 1957 and the Basketball Coaches Hall of Fame in 1955, and in 1960 he was inducted into the Naismith Memorial Basketball Hall of Fame.

Carlson's contribution to basketball extended beyond his coaching innovations and techniques. Unique among coaches in his medical skills and extensive humanitarian interests, Carlson drew on each of these passions and effectively incorporated them to form a foundation for their continued advancement in sport.

• The Henry C. Carlson File, Naismith Memorial Basketball Hall of Fame, Springfield, Mass., contains articles and newspaper accounts pertaining to his life and specific games and records. Carlson's *Basketball: The American Game* (1938) provides some insight into his coaching philosophy and techniques. Neil D. Isaacs, *All The Moves: A History of College Basketball* (1984), provides statistics, his record, and comparison with other coaches. Obituaries are in the *Pittsburgh Post Gazette and Sun Telegraph* and the *Pittsburgh Press*, 2 Nov. 1964.

JERRY JAYE WRIGHT

CARMAN, William Bliss (18 Apr. 1861–8 June 1929), poet, was born in Fredericton, New Brunswick, Canada, the son of William Carman, registrar of the New Brunswick Supreme Court, and Sophia Mary Bliss. He spent his earliest years with a private tutor, and then was educated in a local private school and the University of New Brunswick, from which he received his B.A. in 1881, his M.A. in 1884, and his LL.D. in 1906. He also studied briefly at Oxford and Edinburgh, in 1882 and 1883, and for a longer period at Harvard, where he studied English literature under Francis Child from 1886 to 1888.

Carman had a love for the waters and landscape of the eastern Canadian shoreline and a lasting attachment to Greek and Roman mythology. The lessons of his youth, combined with those received at Harvard, where he read the works of poets writing in English, exercised tremendous influence on his poetry. From his early wanderings through the landscapes of eastern Canada, Carman created poems with widely varying yet identifiable settings, populated by common people, ancient deities, and not so ancient poets.

Over thirty books of Carman's poetry and prose were published beginning in 1893 and continuing after his death. It is a poetry of uneven merit, strictly metrical but not always logical, and highly varied in form, meter, and genre. Carman wrote elegies, haunting ballads, sonnets (unrhymed), masques, and occasional pieces. The prose, at least as it is found in his two principal books of essays, *The Kinship of Nature* (1903) and *The Friendship of Art* (1904), is packed into short pieces of approximately ten pages each. It consists of pleasant, didactic ramblings about life, often religious in the heterodox, homiletic Christianity called "Personal Harmonizing."

Carman published his first, and best known, poem, "Low Tide on Grand Pré," in 1887, the year before he left Harvard. For the next decade he traveled and worked on the editorial staff of a number of different New York magazines. During this time he also saw the publication of six volumes of poetry, beginning with *Low Tide on Grand Pré: A Book of Lyrics* (1893) and including *Songs from Vagabondia* (1894), *More Songs from Vagabondia* (1896), and *Last Songs from Vagabondia* (1900). The Vagabondia books, of which there were finally four, shared covers with poems by Richard Hovey, whom Carman had met at Harvard and who proved to be his closest male friend.

In 1896, on his voyage back from a walking tour in Europe, Carman met Dr. and Mrs. Morris King, newly married. Drawn by Mrs. King, the former Mary Perry, he would remain in their vicinity and company for practically the rest of his life, either at or near their winter home in New Canaan, Connecticut, or their summer home in Haines Falls, New York. At Haines Falls, in the exclusive summer community known as Twilight Park, he lived from June to October every year in the small house the Kings built for him a few yards from their residence. Mrs. King was an aspiring actress and author and a religious philosopher, and the productions she and Carman wrote and produced in her spacious parlor were the delight of Twilight residents each summer. A quotation from Carman still graces the area above the fireplace in the Park recreation room.

The qualities of his poetry may be seen first in "Low Tide on Grand Pré," particularly its last stanza:

The night has fallen, and the tide . . .
  Now and again comes drifting home,
Across these aching barrens wide,
  A sigh like driven wind or foam:
  In grief the flood is bursting home.

And the qualities of his contributions to the four Vagabondia books are best represented in the first stanza of "The Wanderers," which also appeared in the "Grand Pré" volume:

We are the vagabonds of time,
  And rove the yellow, autumn days,
When all the roads are gray with rime
  And all the valleys blue with haze.

His elegies are shown to best advantage in the title poem of *By the Aurelian Wall, and Other Elegies*, published in 1898. Its epigraph reads "In Memory of John Keats," and it uses a meter that is almost prose, with a felicity that is rare in Carman's poems. In fact, his elegies, to Percy Bysshe Shelley, William Blake, Robert Louis Stevenson, and others, are among his finest poetry.

Carman's ballads, best represented in the volume *Ballads of Lost Haven* (1897), are mostly sea pieces and go well with "Low Tide on Grand Pré" to show why Carman has been so beloved in Canada. A few of the titles alone are almost all one needs to grasp the sweep and tragic depth of his ballads: "The Gravedigger," "The Yule Guest," "A Sailor's Wedding," "The King of Ys," "The Ships of St. John," "The Kelpie Riders," "The Nancy's Pride," "The Shadow Boatswain."

Carman died in New Canaan, attended, even at the last, by Mary Perry King, who wished to have him buried in New Canaan, but bowed to his family's wishes to have him interred in Fredericton. He never married.

Perhaps his poetic merit can best be assessed by late-twentieth-century standards if he is looked at as a regional poet, a poet of place, with at least three favorite locales: the Atlantic coast of Canada, the Catskills, and Fairfield County, Connecticut. His poems will continue to be read by residents of and visitors to those areas, and in those regions his reputation as person and poet will continue to be strong. He was a great walker and traveler, and in his regional poems he pays careful attention to the lay of the land, making it possible for his readers to recognize landmarks and to participate in the poet's appreciation of them. This poetic gift is displayed well in his poems about foreign places like Rome or Simla, India, as well as places closer to home.

• There are seven letters to Carman in the Pierpont Morgan Library in New York, a fine collection of signed essays and books in the possession of the Haines Falls Public Library, Haines Falls, N.Y., and a small collection of materials in the New Canaan Public Library, New Canaan, Conn. The New York Public Library also has some manuscripts of occasional pieces.

Though much study of Carman begins and ends with *Low Tide on Grand Pré*, some of his best poetry is to be found in *Behind the Arras: A Book of the Unseen* (1895) and *A Seamark: A Threnody for Robert Louis Stevenson* (1895). The unconventional Carman may be found in *Sappho: One Hundred Lyrics* (1905) and *The Pipes of Pan (Definitive Edition)* (1906). Late collections of Carman's poetry include *Later Poems* (1921), *Sanctuary* (1929), *Bliss Carman's Poems* (1931), and *The Selected Poems of Bliss Carman* (1954). The philosophy he and Mary King shared may be seen in *The Making of the Personality* (1908), a book of essays he published with Mary Perry King.

The principal biography of Bliss Carman is Donald Stephens, *Bliss Carman* (1966). While Stephens admits that he does not value Carman's poetry highly, he concentrates on Carman's "poetic contribution to Canadian letters." The bibliography, albeit a "selected bibliography," is excellent, particularly on Canadian repositories. Alfred H. Marks, "Poet of the Catskills," in *Kaaterskill: From the Catskill Mountain House to the Hudson River School*, published for the Mountain Top Historical Society (1993), analyzes some of Carman's poetry and prose for descriptions of the local scene. An obituary is in the *New York Times*, 9 June 1929.

ALFRED H. MARKS

CARMER, Carl Lamson (16 Oct. 1893–11 Sept. 1976), poet and historian, was born in Cortland, New York, the son of Willis Griswold Carmer, the superintendent of schools in Albion, New York, and Mary Lamson. He graduated from Hamilton College in 1914 with a Ph.B. and returned for a Ph.M. in 1917, after receiving an M.A. from Harvard two years earlier. In 1914 he married Doris Geer; they had no children.

Carmer taught English at Syracuse University, the University of Rochester, Hamilton College, and the University of Alabama at Tuscaloosa, interrupting his teaching career only shortly to serve as an officer in field artillery in World War I. In 1927, however, he left the teaching profession and turned to writing and editing full time. When his first marriage ended in divorce, Carmer married Elizabeth Black, an artist who later illustrated several of his books, in 1928. They had no children.

In his new career, Carmer worked first as a columnist for the *New Orleans Morning Tribune*, moving to *Vanity Fair* as an assistant editor in 1928. Carmer then moved to *Theater Arts Monthly* in 1929, again as assistant editor, working there until 1933. Some of the tribulations of changing careers are hinted at in Carmer's book *The Screaming Ghost and Other Stories* (1956). During this early period Carmer's first book, *French Town*, a collection of poems, was published in New Orleans in 1930. In *Stars Fell on Alabama* (1934), however, he established his mature approach, which was based on what Carmer later described in *The Boy Drummer of Vincennes* (1972) as his "deep commitment to literary creativity in the writing of history." *Stars Fell on Alabama* is filled with his gleanings of local folkways from six years of wanderings in the Alabama countryside. It is best described as a miscellany filled with songs, rambling conversations, and poetry about Alabama people, both black and white. The text also illustrates what Carmer would continue to do in thirty or so volumes of poetry and prose for both children and adults throughout the rest of his life.

With the publication of *Listen for a Lonesome Drum* (1936), subtitled *A York State Chronicle*, Carmer returned to the New York state he knew, meaning the Finger Lakes and the Genesee Valley, and all the way to the Buffalo area. This book also had the "miscellany" structure, which Carmer would return to much later in *Dark Trees to the Wind* (1949) and *My Kind of Country* (1966). The first essay of *Dark Trees to the Wind*, "York State Is a Country," may be the piece that best describes Carmer's message and program. *My Kind of Country*, although its first essay is titled "Upstate Is a Country," is much more downstate than other works by Carmer and contains a tribute to New York City mayor Fiorello La Guardia and the essay "The Mad Poet of Broadway." The latter text's essays "How Boscobel Was Saved" and "Three Decades and a River" show something of Carmer's involvement in preserving history and the land in the lower Hudson Valley during his mature years.

In the meantime Carmer became editor of Farrar and Rinehart's Rivers of America series, succeeding its founder, Constance Lindsay Skinner, in 1939. *The Hudson* (1939) was written in a more straightforward style than Carmer's earlier works and was his first individual contribution to that series. Still, the text was governed by Carmer's approach to history as historical fact combined with anecdote and folklore and a dash of the occult. He later published two other books, *The Susquehanna* and the anthology *Songs of the Rivers of America*, in the series, which would eventually include approximately forty volumes. Carmer also edited the Regions of America series.

World War II caused Carmer to move his attention to writing and research more directly involved with the hostilities. In 1943 he edited a collection of essays, *The War against God*, directed primarily at Adolf Hitler, and in 1945 Carmer wrote the poetic text for the CBS broadcast "Taps Is Not Enough." In 1946 he and Carl Van Doren edited a collection of basic statements on American democracy, *The American Scriptures*; in 1947 Carmer also produced *For the Rights of Men*. Another notable digression from Carmer's main work was his book *The Farm Boy and the Angel*, a history of

Mormonism from Joseph Smith through Brigham Young.

In 1963 Carmer became president of Boscobel Restoration, Inc., across the swamp from West Point and the Hudson. That same year he was appointed to the board of overseers of the College of the Virgin Islands. He spent the last three decades of his life in a spectacular octagonal house in Irvington, New York. The house was reconstructed after Carmer's death in a hospital in Bronxville, New York, and is now one of the showpieces of the Hudson Valley.

• The Carmer papers and personal library are in the library of the New York State Historical Association, Cooperstown. The papers, divided into folders, each marked for the appropriate volume, show the meticulous detail with which the author approached a writing task. Carmer's novel *Genesee Fever* (1941), is built around historical events that took place in the area of *Listen for a Lonesome Drum*. *The Tavern Lights Are Burning: Literary Journeys through Six Regions and Four Centuries of New York State* (1964) is a comprehensive presentation of New York history and scenic description. *Rebellion at Quaker Hill: A Story of the First Rent War* (1954) is concerned with the Catskill region. Carmer also wrote more than ten books for children, one of which, *The Boy Drummer of Vincennes* (1972), seems to have been published by Carmer himself. An obituary is in the *New York Times*, 12 Sept. 1976.

ALFRED H. MARKS

CARMICHAEL, Hoagy (22 Nov. 1899–28 Dec. 1981), composer, was born Hoagland Howard Carmichael in Bloomington, Indiana, the son of Howard Clyde Carmichael, a horse-and-buggy driver, and Lida Mary Robison. His mother played silent-film accompaniments, and Carmichael began learning to play the piano at age six. Following an undistinguished high school career in Bloomington and Indianapolis and tutoring by Reggie Duval, a ragtime pianist, he worked odd jobs. The slender Carmichael gained enough weight to be accepted into the wartime army—one day before the armistice. After returning to Bloomington in 1919 he played for high school dances.

Like many midwestern youths, Carmichael traveled to Chicago speakeasies to hear jazz, which had "come up the river from New Orleans." He particularly admired African-American cornetists King Oliver and Louis Armstrong. But the "hot" jazz of midwestern college bands developed in a stream parallel to the New Orleans variety: midwestern jazz was mainly played, improvised, and written by whites.

Involvement in "twenties jazz" carried fringe benefits: Carmichael financed his 1922 entry to Indiana University's law school (he never did earn his A.B.) by smuggling champagne. Forming a five-piece band, he became a fixture at Bloomington's bookstore and jazz spot, the Book Nook. In 1923 at Northwestern University he met a teenaged cornet player from Iowa named Bix Beiderbecke. Already renowned for his powerful attack and his round, bell-like tone, Beiderbecke, in Carmichael's words, "showed me that jazz could be musical and beautiful as well as hot."

In 1924 Carmichael began booking Beiderbecke for college dances. According to Carmichael, it was Beiderbecke who suggested that he write music; by 1926 Carmichael's "Riverboat Shuffle" (originally titled "Free Wheelin'") was becoming a classic for Bix and his Wolverines. Beiderbecke's melodic jazz echoes in Carmichael's subsequent popular songs. Composer and musicologist Alec Wilder said that "of all the better song writers, I can think of very few who have any emotional kinship with the jazz musician and his bittersweet, witty, lonely, intense world. . . . Hoagy Carmichael certainly did."

In 1926, armed with his new law degree, Carmichael opened a practice in Palm Beach, Florida. En route to Florida he stopped in New York, leaving the music for "Washboard Blues" with bandleader Red Nichols. Nichols made it a hit, and Carmichael abandoned law and returned to Bloomington.

In 1927 Carmichael recorded with a number of midwestern orchestras. With Jean Goldkette's he played a ragtime-paced piano solo called "Barnyard Shuffle," which according to legend originated on the Indiana campus after Carmichael had parted from a longtime girlfriend. The Isham Jones Orchestra recorded it as a ballad. In 1929 "Barnyard Shuffle" was renamed "Star Dust," and romantic lyrics were added by Mitchell Parish. A classmate from Bloomington, Stuart Gorrell, provided the title, telling Carmichael, "That one's all the girls, the university, the family, the old golden oak, all the good things gone, all wrapped up in a melody." Newspaper columnist Walter Winchell commended "Star Dust," and the song's popularity soared.

"Star Dust" became the most recorded song of the century, identifiable with no particular artist, although a sweet 1940 instrumental version by clarinetist Artie Shaw's orchestra sold 2 million copies, and later Frank Sinatra underlined the song's exceptional richness by recording only its verse. It is the improvisational quality of the Beiderbecke-like verse, cascading and leaping through a remarkable range—in Wilder's words "not in any way vocal"—that takes "Star Dust" into another realm.

Carmichael moved to New York in 1929, and a procession of hit songs—jazz based but increasingly varied—followed: the low-down "Rockin' Chair" (1929), Carmichael's first lyric and inspired by the aged proprietor of an illegal Bloomington beer hall; the nostalgic "Georgia on My Mind" (1930); the Jerome Kern–like "One Morning in May" and the rolling "Lazy River" (1931); and the laconic "Lazy Bones" (1933), a development of Carmichael's piano solo on "Washboard Blues." Carmichael wrote that "there was a year or two when my music amounted to about 1.5 percent of all music played on the air."

In 1936, the year he contributed "Little Old Lady" to the Broadway revue *The Show Is On*, Carmichael married Ruth Meinardi in his New York apartment to musical accompaniment by George Gershwin and Carmichael's mother, who played "The Maple Leaf Rag"; they had two sons and were divorced in 1959. Also in 1936 Carmichael signed with Paramount Pictures and moved to Hollywood; from then on his songs usually appeared in dramatic films, the jazz element modulating from "hot" to "sweet swing." Among these songs were the romantic "The Nearness of You" (1937); the playful "Two Sleepy People," "Small Fry," and the atypically jingly "Heart and Soul" (1938); the rangy "Blue Orchids" and "I Get Along without You Very Well" (1939). In 1940 Carmichael collaborated with lyricist Johnny Mercer on the score for a Broadway musical, *Walk with Music*. In 1942 came Carmichael and Mercer's classic "Skylark," featuring a buoyant, Beiderbecke-like release. Written in the same year, the insinuating "Baltimore Oriole" was in 1944 included, along with the 1939 "Hong Kong Blues" and "How Little We Know," in the film *To Have and Have Not*. Carmichael made his performing debut on film as Cricket in the same film.

Between 1944 and 1955 Carmichael appeared, usually as a dissolute-looking piano player with an attractively worn singing style, in ten films, including *The Best Years of Our Lives* (1946). He gave a notable performance as Smoke in the 1950 dramatization of a novel about Beiderbecke's life, *Young Man with a Horn*. His public persona, personally described as "one part dead-end kid, one part lawyer, one part musician," had solidified.

After 1945 Carmichael was mainly known for this public persona, although one of his songs, the springy jazz waltz "My Resistance Is Low" (1951), was as original as anything he had ever done; another song, the novelty (with Mercer) "In the Cool, Cool, Cool of the Evening" (1951), won an Academy Award. Carmichael became a regular performer on radio and television, and his 1948 radio and 1953 television series were moderately successful. His impressionistic autobiography, *The Stardust Road*, was published in 1946; its British publication was particularly well received.

Billboard magazine named Carmichael the best male singer of 1948. That same year he made his first London variety appearance. Between 1959 and 1962 he played a character role for television's "Laramie." In 1965 he collaborated with jazz author Stephen Longstreet on an update of *The Stardust Road* titled *Sometimes I Wonder*. In 1977 Carmichael married Wanda McKay; they had no children. A play about Carmichael by British poet Adrian Mitchell, *Hoagy, Bix and Wolfgang Beethoven Bunkhaus* (1980), further solidified his British popularity and was performed in Los Angeles. Carmichael died in Rancho Mirage, California.

Carmichael was the jazz poet of American popular song. His compositions were endlessly improvised upon by instrumental groups large and small, and his songs—particularly "Star Dust," "Skylark," and "The Nearness of You"—were the property of singers capable of the astounding leaps and discoveries belonging to instrumental jazz.

• Some of Carmichael's manuscripts and sheet music, as well as discussions of Indiana's role in jazz history, can be found in the archives of Indiana University in Bloomington. Carmichael's art is usefully discussed in Alec Wilder, *American Popular Song: The Great Innovators, 1900–1950* (1972). The insider's version of midwestern jazz is incomparably found in Mezz Mezzrow and Bernard Wolfe, *Really the Blues* (1946). An obituary is in the *New York Times*, 29 Dec. 1981.

JAMES ROSS MOORE

CARMICHAEL, Leonard (9 Nov. 1898–16 Sept. 1973), experimental psychologist and institutional administrator, was born in Germantown, Pennsylvania, the son of Thomas Harrison Carmichael, a physician, and Emily Leonard, a teacher and administrator. He entered Tufts College in 1917, volunteered as a private in the U.S. Army in 1918, and received his B.S. in biology summa cum laude in 1921. His Ph.D. in psychology was awarded by Harvard University in 1924, and he joined the Princeton University psychology department that same year. While still in graduate school, he was identified as an especially promising scholar, and he rose rapidly through the academic ranks. In 1927 he moved to Brown University as director of the Psychological Laboratory and was promoted to professor the following year.

Carmichael's research focused on the relative contributions of heredity and environment in the development of patterns of behavior. His demonstration that swimming movements in salamanders and frog tadpoles emerged in the absence of practice were (and continue to be) widely quoted. He later devised techniques for observing reactions of fetal guinea pigs and other mammals, thus providing for the first time a description of the maturation of species-typical sensory and response capabilities of mammals during early development and before environmental stimulation provided opportunities for specific experience. From these investigations came the conclusion that genetic coding provides for the maturation of structures to be ahead of the maturation of the adaptive behavior that utilizes those structures (sometimes referred to as Carmichael's law of anticipatory function). Although he also did pioneering research in such areas as electroencephalography, and in reading and visual fatigue, evaluations of the relative influences of nature and nurture on the development of behavior and perception characterized most of the research conducted by Carmichael and his students for almost fifty years. That these publications have continued to be cited by researchers and textbook authors attests to the significance and robustness of the work.

Carmichael carried on a lifelong pattern of daily research, writing, and editing in spite of heavy teaching loads when he was a junior faculty member and despite heavy administrative responsibilities in his later years. He published several books, scores of scientific and technical articles, and countless administrative reports. He was married in 1932 to Pearl Kidston, who assisted him in his research and writing. They had one child.

In 1936 Carmichael was appointed dean of the Faculty of Arts and Sciences and chairman of the psychology department at the University of Rochester. In 1938 he became president of Tufts University and director of the Tufts Laboratory of Sensory Psychology and Physiology. In addition to his university duties, he was asked to organize and, from 1939 to 1945, to serve as director of the National Roster of Scientific and Specialized Personnel. This agency was responsible for the mobilization of thousands of scientists and engineers for the nation's war effort and grew to have an office staff of more than 400 persons. During this same period, Carmichael also directed military research projects that evaluated synthetic training devices (for example, full-sized models of shipboard control stations), and he headed a group that developed procedures for measuring aptitudes for specific types of military training. Carmichael made one or two round-trips a week between Boston and Washington, D.C., by railway sleeping car to fulfill his multiple administrative responsibilities. "The human brain can stand a good deal of shaking" was Carmichael's wry comment (1967, p. 48) on the travel demands of his wartime commitments.

In 1952 he resigned the presidency of Tufts to accept appointment as secretary of the Smithsonian Institution (the chief administrative officer of the institution). Under Carmichael's leadership, the Smithsonian's museums and the National Zoological Park were modernized, making their treasures more available to the public. The annual number of visitors rose from 3.5 million to more than 10 million during his tenure. At the same time, he further strengthened the Smithsonian's research functions, through key appointments, expanded research fellowships and grants, and (perhaps most important) by example, for he continued his own investigations and scientific publications while serving as secretary. He was an effective lobbyist with Congress and with private foundations, increasing the operating budgets for each of the Smithsonian's various bureaus by several hundred percent over his eleven-year tenure and obtaining the funding and the land for the construction of modern facilities to complement the restored, historically significant buildings of the Smithsonian.

In 1964, on his retirement from the Smithsonian, he was appointed vice president for research and exploration by the National Geographic Society. In this capacity he organized and administered programs of research in anthropology, archaeology, human prehistory, and animal behavior as well as in the society's traditional fields of geology and geography. He was instrumental in obtaining support for the study of nonhuman primates (including chimpanzee and gorilla populations) in their natural habitats and in raising worldwide concern for the preservation of wilderness regions on all continents.

At six feet three inches, Carmichael was taller than most of his generation, and he was endowed with a resonant, powerful voice. It was impossible for him to be inconspicuous, nor did he have any desire to be so. In his earlier years, although he was unusually formal in his interpersonal relationships, undergraduates at Brown and at Tufts several times voted him "favorite professor." One former student and associate recalled that "during and after the Tufts years, he became much less formal (but not *very* informal)" (Mead, p. 522). He was comfortable in positions of responsibility and authority, and he enjoyed the formalities of ceremonial occasions and the meetings with foreign dignitaries and with leaders in the Washington power structure that were a necessary part of his Smithsonian responsibilities.

Among his honors were election to the National Academy of Sciences (1943) and the presidency of the American Psychological Association (1940) and of the American Philosophical Society (1970–1973). He received two Presidential Citations of Merit; was decorated by Spain, Germany, Denmark, and Italy; and was awarded honorary doctorates by twenty-three universities. He died in Washington, D.C., and his ashes were interred in the Washington National Cathedral, for which he served as a trustee.

• Carmichael's personal papers are archived with the American Philosophical Society, Philadelphia. He listed a representative sample of his publications in his autobiographical chapter in E. G. Boring and G. Lindzey, eds., *A History of Psychology in Autobiography*, vol. 5 (1967). Observations by two of his colleagues are given in Leonard Mead, "Leonard Carmichael: 1898–1973," *American Journal of Psychology* 87 (1974): 517–25, and in Melvin M. Payne, "Leonard Carmichael: An Appreciation," *National Geographic Magazine* 144 (Dec. 1973): 870–74. An obituary is in the *Washington Post*, 17 Sept. 1973.

J. W. KLING

CARMICHAEL, Oliver Cromwell (3 Oct. 1891–25 Sept. 1966), educator, was born near Goodwater, in Clay County, Alabama, the son of Daniel Monroe Carmichael and Amanda Delight Lessley, farmers. After attending a country school, Carmichael (later nicknamed "Mike") worked his way through college. He studied at Alabama Presbyterian College in Anniston for two years before transferring to the University of Alabama in Tuscaloosa, where he earned his B.A. in 1911 and his M.A. in 1914. As a senior and graduate student, he held a teaching fellowship in Romance languages; in 1912 and 1913 he was acting modern languages professor at the Normal School in Florence, Alabama. From 1913 to 1917 Carmichael was a Rhodes scholar at Wadham College, Oxford University, where he earned a B.S. and a diploma in anthropology. During the first year of World War I he served with the Commission for Relief in Belgium and became a friend of Herbert Hoover. Carmichael joined the Young Men's Christian Association and in 1915 went to Bombay, where he assisted the British army, and then to East Africa in 1916, learning Urdu and Swahili. He then received a fellowship in languages at Princeton University, but he resigned it to enter officers' training at Fort Oglethorpe, Georgia. While at Camp Jackson in Columbia, South Carolina, Carmichael met Mae Crabtree of Atlanta, whom he married in July 1918. He then went to France, where he served with the Intelligence Section of Division Staff. The Carmichaels had two sons.

Because being married made him ineligible for the Princeton fellowship, Carmichael never earned a doctorate. From 1919 to 1922 he was successively head of the foreign language department at Birmingham Central High School, principal of the Henley Grammar School, and principal of Woodlawn High School. He also ran unsuccessfully for Congress.

In 1922 Carmichael began a thirteen-year career at Alabama State College for Women (later the University of Montevallo), first as dean and assistant to the president and then, from 1926 to 1935, as president. Popular with the students, he successfully led the college's "Million Dollar Drive." In 1935 he became dean of Vanderbilt University's graduate school and senior college in Nashville, Tennessee; in 1936 he was named vice chancellor as well. During his chancellorship from 1937 to 1946, Vanderbilt expanded its curriculum and research program and collaborated with Scarritt College for Christian Workers and George Peabody College for Teachers to establish a central university library in Nashville. Heavily involved in fundraising for Vanderbilt's liberal arts college and law school, Carmichael became a friend of John D. Rockefeller, Jr.

Carmichael's growing national reputation brought him the presidency of the Carnegie Foundation for the Advancement of Teaching (1946–1953). His goals were to develop American graduate education according to the European model, which emphasized research; to promote American studies programs, and to expand scholarship in international relations. Governor Thomas E. Dewey appointed Carmichael vice chairman of the Temporary Commission on the Need for a State University, and Carmichael chaired the board of trustees of the New York State University System (1948–1953). He was also a member of President Harry Truman's Commission on Higher Education (1946–1947). He delivered a number of important lectures, including "Background and Opportunity of the State University of New York," at its organizational meeting (1949). *The Changing Role of Higher Education* (1949) compiles four lectures given for a Kappa Delta Pi lecture series. He envisioned higher education, which had vastly expanded its responsibilities since 1900, as the catalyst for democratization and social progress. In 1952 he was Spaulding Lecturer at Yale University.

In 1953 Carmichael accepted the presidency of the University of Alabama as an opportunity to serve his native state. By the time Carmichael arrived on campus, the board of trustees had retained an influential law firm (and would later hire detectives) in an effort to prevent the court-ordered admission of a black student, Autherine Lucy, and her friend Pollie Anne Myers, whose lawsuit was supported by the National Association for the Advancement of Colored People. Powerful trustees were determined that Carmichael should follow their lead, even though he recognized that the university might soon have to desegregate in the aftermath of the U.S. Supreme Court's decision in *Brown v. Board of Education* (1954). However, neither he nor the trustees were prepared to deal with the riot on 6 February 1956—the first at a major southern state university—that drove Lucy from the campus and ultimately resulted in her expulsion for charging Carmichael and the trustees with conspiracy. Characterizing Carmichael as temperamentally conciliatory, personally indecisive, and publicly ambiguous on integration, historian E. Culpepper Clark blamed the riot partly on the president's segregationist sentiments, his unwillingness to lead the board of trustees, and his failure to take advantage of earlier opportunities to adopt alternative courses of action. By 1956, given the massive white resistance generated by the concurrent Montgomery bus boycott, the university could not ensure peaceful integration without substantial assistance from the state or federal government. Despite his attempt to deal with the integration issue more openly than other contemporary Deep South university presidents, Carmichael was buffered on the one hand by criticism from northern liberals and moderates for not doing more to keep Lucy at the university, and on the other by denunciations from segregationists for allowing her to enter. Feeling that he had been made to look ineffectual, Carmichael resigned on 31 December 1956.

Becoming a consultant to the Fund for the Advancement of Education, Carmichael wrote *Universities, Commonwealth and American: A Comparative Study* (1959), based on his visits to fifty-six universities in eight British Commonwealth nations. He urged that a Commonwealth-American Commission on University Education be established to exchange information. He also published *Racial Tensions: A Study in Human Relations* (1959). In *Graduate Education: A Critique and a Program* (1961), which received both the American Council Book Award gold medal and the 1961–1962 higher education prize of the American Council on Education, he proposed reorganizing and strengthening graduate education. Appointed in 1960 to the Southern Regional Educational Board's commission on higher education in the South, Carmichael contributed his views to its report, *Within Our Reach* (1961). He believed that through expanded opportunities, education for effective citizenship, and better teaching and scholarship, the South could improve economically and deal with its social and racial problems. Carmichael died in Asheville, North Carolina.

• Carmichael's papers are at the University of Alabama Library, the Jean and Alexander Heard Library at Vanderbilt University, and the Carnegie Corporation and Ford Foundation in New York. Among Carmichael's important publications not cited above are "Some Educational Frontiers; Address before the Graduate Convocation, Brown University, June 19, 1948," published in *School and Society* 68, no. 1761 (25 Sept. 1948): 193–96; and *Education and International Understanding* (1950), an address delivered on the forty-third anniversity of the University of Hawaii's founding, 7 March 1950. He also wrote "What Constitutes an Educated Man," *American Mercury* 66, no. 291 (Mar. 1948): 347–52; "The State University: Its Problems and Prospects," *National Association of State Universities Transactions and Proceedings* 52

(1954): 28–34; and "College for Americans: A Hundred Years of the Land-grant Movement," *Saturday Review*, 21 April 1962, pp. 58–59, 71–72. See also *Proceedings of the Symposium on Legal Education at Vanderbilt University, Held at the School of Law in Connection with the Inauguration of Oliver C. Carmichael as Chancellor* (1938). The best treatment of Carmichael's role in the 1956 desegregation crisis is E. Culpepper Clark, *The Schoolhouse Door: Segregation's Last Stand at the University of Alabama* (1993). For information on his family, see John Leslie Carmichael, *The Saga of an American Family* (1982). An obituary is in the *New York Times*, 27 Sept. 1966.

MARCIA G. SYNNOTT

CARMICHAEL, William (?–9 Feb. 1795), diplomat and adventurer, was born at "Round Top" in Queen Anne's County, Maryland, the son of William Carmichael, a Scottish immigrant, and Brooke (maiden name unknown), a niece of the second wife of Richard Bennett, a wealthy landowner. Owing to the land and property that came to Carmichael from his mother's side of the family, he was able to obtain a top-notch American education and to be admitted to the bar in Maryland. Carmichael also traveled to Ireland in 1768 and studied in Edinburgh, Scotland. He traveled throughout the British Isles for a time and when the American Revolution began, he was enjoying a pleasant life in London (where he was known for frequenting alehouses and soliciting the services of prostitutes).

Carmichael hardly appeared to be a likely candidate for a diplomatic career, but he must have possessed some charm of manner for he was given the important task of bringing dispatches for Arthur Lee from London to Paris. Once in Paris, Carmichael became a regular member of the American entourage there, and after 1777 he became an intimate of Benjamin Franklin. He rendered an important service to the American cause in late 1776 and early 1777 when he actively and successfully encouraged the young marquis de Lafayette to go to America.

There seems to be little doubt, however, that Carmichael was playing a double game. He was well known to the British Secret Service, and he engaged Captain Joseph Hynson, also of Maryland, to serve in the American cause; Hynson soon proved to be a complete traitor. For this reason, Carmichael was later charged by a historian with "going to the verge, if not over the edge, of treason" (Bemis, p. 480). Little was suspected of Carmichael at the time, however, and early in 1778 he sailed from France to the new United States, where his services were regarded as at least satisfactory.

After his return to America, Carmichael was a member of the Continental Congress from Maryland (19 Nov. 1778–27 Sept. 1779), in which he served on the important Committee on the Treasury. In September 1779 he was chosen by the Congress to go to Spain with John Jay and to serve as the secretary of the American legation to be founded there. Carmichael sailed with John and Sarah Jay aboard the *Confederacy* in late October 1779. During a crossing filled with stormy weather and anxiety over the possibility of meeting with British warships, Carmichael and Jay came to mutually distrust one another, a condition that persisted after they landed at Cádiz on 22 January 1780.

Upon their arrival in Spain, Jay and Carmichael negotiated with the Spanish foreign minister, Count Floridablanca. The count was personally gracious to both of the Americans but he and his monarch, King Charles III, declined to formally receive the legation. It became clear that Bourbon Spain was anxious about the status of its possessions in North America, New Orleans and the mouth of the Mississippi River in particular. Jay was able to obtain nearly $200,000 in Spanish loans for the United States, but in May 1782 he departed for Paris and, on the advice of Franklin, left Carmichael in the position of chargé d'affaires in Madrid.

Although he lacked the formal title of minister, Carmichael initially had somewhat more success than had Jay. In February 1783 the marquis de Lafayette arrived in Madrid. Mindful of the assistance Carmichael had rendered him six years earlier, Lafayette lobbied the Court of Spain on the American's behalf. Lafayette's assistance gained Carmichael an invitation to a diplomatic dinner—the first for an American in Madrid. Even after Lafayette's departure, Carmichael's standing continued to improve; on 23 August 1783 he was formally presented to King Charles III and the Spanish royal family.

Unfortunately, that was the high point of Carmichael's long service in Spain (1780–1794). Although he maintained the good will of Floridablanca, Carmichael failed to win concessions from the Spanish Court. In addition, his lack of standing at home (he was never granted the title of minister and his pay was usually in arrears) rankled Carmichael. During his later years in Madrid, Carmichael fell behind in his diplomatic correspondence. Relieved of his duties on 5 June 1794, he planned to return to America but fell ill in early 1795. Carmichael died in Madrid, where he was buried in a lot adjoining the Catholic Cemetery.

Carmichael married twice; the first time to a Miss Stirling of Maryland and the second time, as a widower, to Antonia Reynon in Spain, with whom he had one daughter. Carmichael's widow and daughter went to America soon after his death and lived in Maryland.

Some mystery and speculation still surround Carmichael's career. It seems clear that he acted in a duplicitous fashion while he was in Paris (1775–1778), and it is certain that he was unable to get along with his superior John Jay in Spain. In response to Carmichael's death, Jay wrote, "William Carmichael—a man who mistook cunning for wisdom; and who in pursuing his Purposes, preferred the Guidance of artifice and Simulation to that of Truth and Rectitude." Such a biased judgment can be balanced only by looking at Carmichael's record in the years that he was in Spain on his own. In fairness, it must be conceded that few diplomats could have gained much in negotiations with the Spanish Court during the 1780s and early 1790s. It is ironic, to say the least, that the Pinckney Treaty (1795) granted the United States much for which both Jay and Carmichael had labored. While an unequivocal evaluation of the amateur diplomat from Maryland is difficult, it may be concluded that Carmichael did both good and harm to the American cause during his years in Paris and Madrid.

• Carmichael's papers are in the Library of Congress, Manuscript Division. The single most important source is Samuel G. Coe, *The Mission of William Carmichael to Spain* (1928). It is important to check the work of Samuel Flagg Bemis, "British Secret Service and the French-American Alliance," *American Historical Review* 29 (Apr. 1924), and that of Cecil B. Currey, *Code Number 72/Ben Franklin: Patriot or Spy?* (1972), both of which consider Carmichael to have been traitorous in his actions. Other important studies are Elmer Bendiner, *The Virgin Diplomats* (1976), Richard B. Morris, *The Peacemakers: The Great Powers and American Independence* (1965), Morris, *John Jay: The Winning of the Peace: Unpublished Papers 1780–1784* (1980), and Franco Venturi, *The End of the Old Regime in Europe, 1776–1789*, vol. 1: *The Great States of the West* (1991).

SAMUEL WILLARD CROMPTON

CARNAP, Rudolf (18 May 1891–14 Sept. 1970), philosopher, was born in Ronsdorf, near Barmen, Germany, the son of Johannes S. Carnap, a prosperous merchant, and Anna Dörpfeld, formerly a teacher. His home environment was deeply religious, but religion was much more a matter of attitude than belief in a particular creed. The atmosphere was one of tolerance. In his youth he relinquished religion, but the tolerance remained and manifested itself in his later technical work. In secondary school he was attracted to mathematics, he said, "by the exactness of its concepts and the possibility of proving results by mere thinking" and to Latin on account of its "rational structure." These preferences foreshadowed the philosophical work to which he devoted his life; it was characterized throughout by ratiocination of exquisite precision.

From 1910 to 1914 Carnap attended the Universities of Jena and Freiburg in Breisgau, where he studied mathematics, philosophy, and physics. He was deeply impressed by the lectures and writings of Gottlob Frege—at the time an obscure mathematician over sixty years of age whose work was virtually unknown—who was subsequently recognized as a superlatively creative pioneer in mathematical logic, a subject to which Carnap later made significant contributions. In 1913 Carnap began a project in experimental physics, but it was terminated by the outbreak of World War I in August 1914 and never completed. During the war he did military service; after the war he resumed his studies but did not return to experimental physics because his inclinations were more theoretical. He continued to be interested in theoretical physics, as well as mathematics and philosophy. He received his Ph.D. from the University of Jena in 1921, and his doctoral dissertation, *Der Raum* (1922), was on the concept of space in physics, mathematics, and philosophy. At that time he was strongly influenced by Immanuel Kant, but soon thereafter he became a strict empiricist.

Carnap's philosophical career spanned the years from 1921 to 1970; he was a productive scholar until the end of his life. His chief claim to fame is as one of the two leaders of the group of scientific philosophers that originated in Germany in the early 1920s (Hans Reichenbach was the other) later known as logical positivists or logical empiricists. Carnap dated the beginning of this movement to March 1923, on the occasion of a conference at Erlangen at which he first met Reichenbach. Members of this group believed that philosophy should aspire to the same standards of precision as mathematics and natural science, and they rejected as cognitively meaningless the kind of speculative metaphysics and theology that was dominant in Europe at that time. However, Carnap never condemned religion (in contrast to theological doctrine) as a source of psychological support or spiritual inspiration. At the invitation of Moritz Schlick he moved to Vienna in 1926, joined the famous Vienna Circle of logical positivists, and became its leading spokesperson (especially after the tragic assassination of Schlick by a deranged student in 1936). He and Reichenbach (who had stayed in Germany until 1933 but fled Adolf Hitler's regime at that time, eventually moving to California) remained in close contact; in 1930 they jointly founded and subsequently coedited the journal *Erkenntnis*, the chief organ of scientific philosophy prior to World War II.

During the early 1920s, stimulated mainly by Bertrand Russell, Carnap composed a magnum opus, *Der logische Aufbau der Welt* (The logical structure of the world, 1928), attempting to show how the entire universe, including physical, psychological, and social phenomena, could be defined in terms of a sequence of momentary experiences of one person. He was attempting to carry out in precise detail a program that others, especially Russell, had only sketched. It was a heroic effort, but it was unsuccessful; Carnap later abandoned the project as futile. This "failure" was in fact a major achievement; it showed convincingly that a program widely thought to be "possible in principle" actually was not possible. It should be added, however, as an instance of his "principle of tolerance," that he tried to show how such a construction could be carried out, not only in terms of Russell's phenomenological language, but also in terms of other languages, including the physicalistic language that Carnap himself later preferred.

In 1931 Carnap moved to the German University in Prague, Czechoslovakia. Two years later he married Elizabeth Ina von Stöger; they had four children. Late in 1935, because of the increasing influence of Nazism in the German-speaking world outside of Germany, he left for the United States, taking a position at the University of Chicago. The rise of Nazism drove scientific philosophy from most of Europe; a number of the most influential figures in the movement came to America. Carnap became a U.S. citizen in 1941.

Language was one of Carnap's major concerns throughout his career, especially the precise formal languages that can be used in mathematics, natural science, and philosophy. After the publication of the *Aufbau*, during the time he was in Prague, and for his first few years at Chicago, he concentrated on formal syntax and semantics. He steadfastly adhered to his "principle of tolerance," according to which the choice of language is a matter of practical efficiency that has no metaphysical implications concerning the existence of various sorts of entities, such as propositions, numbers, or atoms.

Beginning in the early 1940s Carnap undertook a project concerning probability and confirmation that largely occupied his philosophical efforts for the rest of his life. In 1950 he published another magnum opus, *Logical Foundations of Probability*. His aim was to construct a system of inductive logic as precise as systems of deductive logic available at the time; indeed, his construction was a combined system of inductive and deductive logic. The work of Frege, Russell, and others in deductive logic had provided a precise systematic foundation for mathematics; Carnap aspired to provide the same sort of foundation for the empirical sciences in his theory of confirmation. The 1950 book turned out to be a preliminary study; for the remaining twenty years of his life Carnap sought to enrich and perfect it.

Following Reichenbach's death in 1953, Carnap was invited to fill his chair at the University of California at Los Angeles, which he assumed in 1954 and held until his retirement in 1961. He resided in the Los Angeles area until his death in Santa Monica. He will be remembered as a leading contributor to a philosophical movement that has profoundly affected philosophy—especially Anglo-American philosophy—throughout most of the twentieth century.

• Carnap's papers, along with those of Reichenbach and other scientific philosophers, are housed in the Archive for Scientific Philosophy in the Twentieth Century, Hillman Library, University of Pittsburgh. Carnap received the highest honor available to philosophers, namely, a volume in Paul Arthur Schilpp's series *The Library of Living Philosophers—The Philosophy of Rudolf Carnap* (1963), which includes Carnap's "Intellectual Autobiography," the richest available source of biographical information, and a comprehensive bibliography of his publications from 1921 to 1961. The most accessible exposition of Carnap's philosophy is in his *Philosophical Foundations of Physics*, ed. Martin Gardner (1966), reissued in paperback under the title *Introduction to the Philosophy of Science* (1974). The paperback version was altered slightly to remove errors in the hardback original issue. The book is based on tape recordings of one of Carnap's graduate seminars at UCLA, which were substantially rewritten by Gardner for a popular audience. Carnap then examined and revised Gardner's text. As Carnap remarked in a letter, this book was read by more people than any other of his works. Rolf George's English translation of *Der logische Aufbau der Welt* was published as *The Logical Structure of the World* (1967), along with a translation of a less technical work from about the same period of Carnap's career, *Pseudoproblems in Philosophy*. Carnap's most important work in logic is *Der logische Syntax der Sprache* (1934), translated into English by A. Smeaton and published in 1937 as *The Logical Syntax of Language*. Norman Martin's article on Carnap in *The Encyclopedia of Philosophy* (1967) gives an excellent summary of Carnap's technical work.

WESLEY C. SALMON

CARNEGIE, Andrew (25 Nov. 1835–11 Aug. 1919), industrialist and philanthropist, was born in Dunfermline, Scotland, the son of William Carnegie, a handloom weaver, and Margaret Morrison. William Carnegie was sufficiently prosperous to have four looms in his shop and to employ three apprentices. Although shunning political activism, he was an enthusiastic supporter of the political views of his wife's father, Thomas Morrison, Sr., an early leader of the Chartist movement and a friend of William Cobbett to whose journal, *Cobbett's Register*, Morrison was a frequent contributor. Margaret Carnegie's brother, Tom, Jr., preferred the soapbox to the pen by which to disseminate the same radical views of abolishing the monarchy and the House of Lords, disestablishing the state church, and nationalizing all lands in Britain. One of Andrew's earliest memories was being awakened by a neighbor shouting that Tom had just been hauled off to jail for disturbing the peace with his incendiary harangues in the public square. Andrew later confided to a friend that he then determined to "get to be a man and kill a king."

Another of Andrew's uncles, George Lauder, a fairly prosperous shopkeeper, exerted a different influence on the boy by reciting to him heroic sagas of Scotland's past and by requiring him to memorize Robert Burns's poems. Under Lauder's tutelage, Andrew became incurably romantic in his love of all things Scottish.

Promised by his indulgent parents that he need not attend school until he was ready to do so, Andrew was nearly eight before he indicated he wanted to go, prompted perhaps by the birth of his brother Tom. Andrew was sent to a Lancastrian one-room school in the neighborhood and quickly made up for lost time. Teacher Martin acquired his brightest pupil, and Andrew's classmates gained a conspicuous "teacher's pet" to taunt.

The year 1844 marked a turning point in the family's fortunes. Industrialism was only then revolutionizing the linen textile trade. The recent arrival of a steam-power loom factory was rapidly making the Dunfermline handloom weaver obsolete. One by one William's looms were sold and his apprentices dismissed. There was barely enough demand to keep one loom operating. Andrew's mother supplemented the family's income by selling ha'penny candy and mending shoes, a skill she had learned from her father. Still hoping for a Chartist Utopia, William Carnegie at first refused to listen to his wife's urging that they join her two sisters who had earlier emigrated to America. In the harsh winter of 1847–1848, however, poverty finally crushed his resistance, and the Carnegies made plans for the "flitting," as many other Scots had already done. From that moment, Margaret became the true head of the family. It was she who sold off their few possessions and borrowed the additional funds necessary to take them across the Atlantic. "I'll make a spoon or spoil the horn," was her terse epigrammatic response to those who scoffed at her plans.

On 17 May 1848 the Carnegies departed from Glasgow on the small sailing vessel *Wiscasset*. After an arduous ten-week journey, they reached Pittsburgh. They were provided with two rooms rent-free in a house that sister Annie owned on a back alley in Allegheny, across the river from Pittsburgh. One glance at their new home must have convinced even the determined Margaret that she had indeed "spoiled the horn," for here was slum poverty that exceeded anything she had ever seen in Scotland. But there could be no retreat. Her husband must swallow his pride and take a job in a cotton textile factory, and twelve-year-old Andrew must join him as a bobbin-boy in the same factory, earning $1.20 a week. The four years at Teacher Martin's school would be all the formal education Andrew Carnegie would ever have.

The boy was not disheartened. He was proud to be earning his own keep, and he never questioned his ability for self-advancement. This optimism was bolstered by his discovery that Allegheny's richest citizen, Colonel James Anderson, had opened his personal library free of charge to any working boy, and Andrew became the colonel's most frequent customer. Arriving in the United States in the midst of the 1848 presidential election, Andrew was an avid observer of American democracy in operation. In one of his frequent letters to his cousin George "Dod" Lauder, Jr., he pictured his new country as the realization of their family's political dream. "We have perfect political equality . . . We have the Charter which you have been fighting for for years as the Panacea for all Britian's [*sic*] woes, the bulwark of the people" (18 Aug. 1853, Carnegie papers, Library of Congress, vol. 1).

No record of the Carnegie family's ever having taken out naturalization papers exists, but Andrew simply assumed American citizenship, and in record time he became as thoroughly Americanized as any child whose family had been in residence for two centuries. Carnegie's flag-waving patriotism would earn for him the sobriquet "the Star-Spangled Scotsman."

William Carnegie could not adapt to factory routine and returned to the hand loom, weaving linen tablecloths that he himself peddled from door to door in the forlorn hope of finding customers. Andrew left the mill to take a job as a steam engine tender for two dollars a week. Release came from this hated job when he became a messenger boy at a local telegraph office, where he quickly earned the reputation of being the company's fastest delivery boy, having memorized the location of every business office in Pittsburgh. He was next promoted to telegraph operator, excelling again and becoming one of the first operators in the country who could take messages directly by ear from the sound of the clicking key rather than waiting to translate the message from the printed tape the receiver produced. This remarkable talent caught the attention of Thomas A. Scott, superintendent of the Western Division of the Pennsylvania Railroad. Scott promptly hired him to be his personal telegrapher and private secretary at $35 a month.

Carnegie was fortunate to become the protégé of one of the country's most able and daring railroad executives. Scott gave him valuable lessons in business management and stock investment. When Carnegie received his first dividend from the ten shares of Adams Express stock that Scott had loaned him the money to buy, he shouted, "Eureka! Here's the goose that lays the golden eggs." It was the first money that anyone in his family had ever received that had not been earned, as he said, "by the sweat of the brow."

So rapidly did "Scott's Andy" learn all of the intricate details of managing a railroad line that when Scott in 1859 returned to Philadelphia to become general superintendent of the Pennsylvania Railroad, Carnegie was appointed his successor as superintendent of the Western Division. At twenty-two, Carnegie now had a salary that enabled him to make other investments: an oil well in western Pennsylvania and a one-eighth ownership of Theodore Woodruff's sleeping car company.

At the outbreak of the Civil War, Scott was appointed assistant secretary of war in charge of military transportation. He brought Carnegie to Washington to head up telegraphic communications with the army. But Carnegie suffered a sunstroke early in the war and returned to his railroad duties in Pittsburgh.

Although Carnegie would later make famous the aphorism "put all your eggs in one basket and then watch that basket," in these mid-century years he became wealthy by placing his eggs in so many baskets that he soon had neither time nor interest in remaining a salaried employee. In March 1865 he resigned as superintendent of the Western Division to devote full time to his various business ventures. With George Pullman he fashioned the Pullman Palace Car Company in 1867. At the same time he was investing heavily in the Pacific & Atlantic Telegraph Company, which he later sold to Western Union at great profit. He also made several trips to Europe to sell railroad bonds for Junius Morgan, and in 1862 he organized a bridge company to build the United States's first iron railroad bridges, most notably the Eads Bridge in St. Louis.

William Carnegie died in 1855, but Margaret Carnegie reveled in her son's prosperity. Carnegie had promised his mother that someday she would ride pridefully in her own carriage and that never would he leave her as long as they both lived. When Carnegie moved from Pittsburgh to New York in 1867 to tend to the increasing complexities of his financial affairs, his mother went along to share his palatial suite in the St. Nicholas hotel.

Carnegie's parents had instilled in him two quite different sets of values. His father had given him his political views—a commitment to social equality and grass roots democracy. His mother gave him her hard realistic appraisal of life as a brutal struggle for existence. Only those tough and determined enough to take advantage of every opportunity, shrewd enough to cut corners at every turn, and brutal enough to elbow themselves to the head of the line would survive and prosper. These contradictory philosophies of humanitarian idealism and self-centered realism continued to coexist, and they created a persistent tension in his life.

Late in December 1868 Carnegie totaled up his assets. It was an impressive account—$400,000 in stocks and bonds, giving him an annual income of $56,110. He had come a long way in the twelve years since he had received his first $10 dividend check. This realization brought him pleasure, but it also raised nagging doubts as to what he was doing with his life. Having assessed his net worth, he promptly wrote himself a memorandum:

> Thirty-three and an income of 50,000$ per annum . . . Beyond this never earn—make no effort to increase fortune, but spend the surplus each year for benovelent [*sic*] purposes . . . Man must have an idol—The amassing of wealth is one of the worst species of idolitary [*sic*]. No idol more debasing than the worship of money. Whatever I engage in I must push inordinately therefor should I be careful to choose that life which will be the most elevating in its character. To continue much longer overwhelmed with business cares and with most of my thoughts wholly upon the way to make more money in the shortest time, must degrade me beyond hope of permanent recovery. I will resign business at Thirty five . . . (copy of the original in the Carnegie papers, New York Public Library).

Carnegie wrote this memorandum only for self-admonition. He did not intend for it to be seen by anyone else, most certainly not his mother. Over the next thirty years none of his business associates would suspect that he had ever entertained such thoughts, for Carnegie continued to "push inordinately" until he had amassed one of the world's greatest fortunes. But that memorandum, lying undisturbed in his desk drawer, was not forgotten. It continued to disturb his self-esteem.

Only by chance did Carnegie find the one big basket in which to collect his fortune. Early in the war two of his boyhood friends, Tom Miller and Henry Phipps, had entered into partnership with a German immigrant, Andrew Kloman, who owned a small forge shop producing railcar axles. Carnegie's younger brother Tom had subsequently been invited into the firm only to discover that there were serious personal disagreements among the three partners, especially between Miller and Phipps. Tom asked his brother to step in as arbiter. Reluctantly, Andrew did so, but without success. His involvement, however, had brought Carnegie directly into the iron business where before he had only been a customer for rails and structural beams. It then occurred to Carnegie that here might be the opportunity for his Keystone Bridge Company, which had now become his major interest, to produce its own iron beams. He proposed to Miller that since there appeared to be no hope for harmony within the Kloman company the two of them should pool their resources and form a rival iron company. Miller jumped at this opportunity to destroy his former partners. In October 1864 the Cyclops Iron Company was created, and an iron mill was rapidly constructed a half mile from the Kloman plant. Cyclops was a larger and more efficient mill and could have proved a deadly competitor to Kloman. Carnegie, however, did not want to destroy; he wanted to expand, for now he was committed to the iron trade. Always eager to acquire good men, Carnegie wanted the mechanical skills of Kloman and the business acumen of Phipps. Against the protests of Miller, Carnegie offered them not competition but consolidation. Seeing no alternative, Kloman and Phipps agreed, and in March 1865 the two companies merged to form the Union Mills. Carnegie's efforts to keep Miller in the partnership were to no avail. Miller sold his shares to Carnegie, who now found himself with a controlling interest in an iron company he had initially entered into only as an arbiter. It was a control he would not relinquish for the next thirty-five years.

In later years Carnegie was to coin another famous adage for business management, "Pioneering don't pay," but this was hardly applicable to his rise as an iron and steel entrepreneur. No one proved to be a more adventurous pioneer than Carnegie as he pushed ahead in this new field. He was at first determined to keep iron in its long-held preeminence as the basic material for rails. He tried to sell the railroad companies the Dodd, and later the Webb, process of facing iron rails with a thin coating of steel, but neither process proved satisfactory. Railroad managers were looking to England for the Bessemer all-steel rails, because though steel rails cost more, they lasted far longer than Carnegie's processed substitutes. To meet British competition, Carnegie began plans for the construction of the largest Bessemer steel plant in the United States. A site was selected a dozen miles south of Pittsburgh. Carnegie named his mill after the president of the Pennsylvania Railroad, J. Edgar Thomson, in the expectation that the railroad would be Carnegie's best customer.

Construction had barely begun when the depression of 1873 brought most business expansion to an abrupt halt. Carnegie, however, regarded the depression as an opportunity. With prices tumbling, he was able to build his blast furnaces and rolling mills at only three-fourths the amount they would have cost two years earlier. In this period of low wages and unemployment Carnegie could also attract the skilled workmen he needed, and at a time when no one else was building, he could employ the world's greatest Bessemer engineer, Alexander Holley, to design the most modern and efficient steel mill. Holley brought with him a young Welshman, Captain William Jones. Over the next two decades Captain Bill became the best and most inventive steelmaker in the history of the industry. With Holley to design his plant and Jones to get production rolling, Carnegie was ready to dominate the steel trade when prosperity returned.

In later years Carnegie credited his success to what he called the "young geniuses" whom he employed.

"Take from me all the ore mines, railroads, manufacturing plants," he said, "but leave me my organization, and in a few years I promise to duplicate the Carnegie company." Holley and Jones certainly were geniuses, and in later years, Henry Clay Frick and Charles M. Schwab also were worthy of that title. It was, however, typical Carnegie hyperbole to dub most of his partners young geniuses. Most were quite ordinary men who could be, and frequently were, easily replaced. Carnegie's success must be attributed to other factors, not the least of which was Carnegie himself. It was the intensity of his drive, his greed for ever more production, his brilliant competitive tactics, and his spectacular good luck in being in the right place at the right time that made him, as one associate called him, the Napoleon in the battle for industrial supremacy.

At a time when big business was adopting the modern corporate structure, managed by highly paid executives but owned by absentee stockholders, Carnegie maintained a simple partnership and made it pay. His partners had to be active managers of the company; instead of big salaries, they received a small percentage of the ownership. This bound them as firmly to the future growth of the company as a medieval serf was bound to the land. Partners who proved successful could not be lured away by high salaries because they would then forfeit their interest in the company. Partners who failed on the job were summarily ousted, receiving only the minuscule book value instead of the true worth of their interest.

With no outside stockholders to pressure him for dividends, Carnegie could put profits back into the plant. Profits for Carnegie were never the end but only the tool for development. What mattered were costs. To reduce costs, he would quickly scrap any machine, process, or even an entire mill in favor of more efficient operations. He would also reward a partner with a larger percentage of ownership if that young genius could reduce the cost of a particular operation by even a fraction of a cent per ton.

Initially interested only in the manufacture of steel ingots and converting those ingots into steel rails and structural beams, Carnegie was obsessed with the cost of production. He was thereby led to extend the principle of "verticality" by gaining control of the ingredients used in the manufacture of steel and the transportation facilities to get those raw materials to the mills. Never holding less than 52 percent of the total capitalization of his company, Carnegie did not fear that his partners would gainsay his policies.

It was Carnegie's drive for verticality that brought Henry Clay Frick into the company in 1881. Frick had begun buying up coal lands near Connellsville in 1870 and in less than a decade had emerged as Coke King of Pennsylvania. Carnegie needed Frick's coke for the manufacture of steel, and Frick in turn needed Carnegie's capital to further expand his own operations. From this union, Frick in a very short time held a 6 percent interest in the Carnegie partnership, the second largest holding of any of Carnegie's partners, while Carnegie's interest in the Frick Coke Company was increased to 50 percent. Carnegie wrote to Frick soon after the latter became chairman of Carnegie Brothers Steel, "I have found THE MAN," as indeed he had, but unlike Carnegie's previous managers, a man who would remain his own man.

Under Frick's supervision, Carnegie's steel empire in the 1880s made spectacular advances. Homestead, a potentially dangerous rival, was purchased in 1883; Hartman Steel, a finishing mill for wire and nails, was acquired in the same year; and in 1889 the Duquesne steelworks was added. Giving no heed to his own stricture against pioneering, Carnegie continued to welcome advances in the technology of steel manufacture, including the Gilchrist Thomas process for removing phosphorus from iron ore and the Siemens open hearth furnace to produce steel to precise specifications. Carnegie also was the first to employ an academically trained chemist as a permanent member of his staff. These innovations paid handsomely, and by 1890 the company's annual profits had reached $4.5 million.

Carnegie had "pushed inordinately" to reach this pinnacle of success, but that old memorandum of 1868 still haunted him with the fear that his empire-building had indeed degraded him "beyond hope of permanent recovery." Only by directing his increasing surplus toward benevolent purposes could he hope for moral recovery. As a first step he sought to fulfill the dream of his father and grandfather by giving to Britain the charter of democracy they had striven for in vain fifty years earlier. In the early 1880s he formed a newspaper syndicate of seven daily and ten weekly journals covering a territory that extended from Portsmouth on the southern coast of England to Newcastle in the northeast. All of these papers promoted the same Carnegie-Morrison radical liberalism aimed at the disestablishment of the state church and the creation of the Republic of Great Britain. It was one of Carnegie's few ventures in which he lost money. After only three years as a newspaper proprietor, he beat a hasty retreat. Having failed in his appeal to British politicians to adopt the charter, Carnegie then attempted to persuade the people that democracy was in their best economic interest. In 1886 he published *Triumphant Democracy*, which he would always consider his magnum opus. His argument, bolstered by statistical tables, was that political forms determine material success. By establishing a democracy the United States was achieving economic supremacy over outdated European monarchies. The book became a bestseller both in the United States and in Britain.

Carnegie also published two articles in 1886 on labor policies in *Forum* proclaiming the right of labor to organize and decrying the use of strikebreakers. "There is an unwritten law among the best workers: 'Thou shalt not take thy neighbor's job,'" Carnegie pontificated. These articles created a sensation on both sides of the Atlantic. Labor hailed Carnegie's pronouncements as a new Magna Carta for the workingman, while the managerial class and the conservative press heaped scorn on him as a traitor to free enterprise. Only six years later, however, Carnegie betrayed his own noble sentiments regarding the rights of labor. Before leaving for his annual summer vacation in Scotland in April 1892, he told Frick that he wanted the union at Homestead broken when its contract came up for renewal in June, an order that Frick was happy to carry out. As the 30 June deadline approached, negotiations with the Amalgamated Association of Iron and Steel Workers were abruptly terminated, and the plant was closed. Frick then attempted to bring in Pinkerton guards to protect scab workers entering the plant to take their neighbors' jobs. The result was a bloody battle on the banks of the Monongahela River on 6 July 1892. The Homestead strike became for labor everywhere the symbol of the perfidy and cruelty of the capitalist boss. Carnegie blamed Frick for having hired Pinkertons and strikebreakers, and this was the beginning of the rift between the two men. But Carnegie's efforts to shift the responsibility for the fiasco onto others did not convince the public. He was called the "arch-hypocrite of the age," and no amount of self-exculpation could efface the scar that Homestead left on his reputation.

It was not until he published his "Wealth" articles in the *North American Review* for June and December 1889 that Carnegie at last was satisfied that he had found a way to reconcile plutocracy with democracy and thus earn final absolution from self-reproach. His two-part essay was promptly reprinted in England under the title "Gospel of Wealth." Carnegie argued that the accumulation of great wealth was justified in the modern industrial society providing the holders regarded themselves only as trustees of that wealth and returned it to society from whence it came. "Don't shoot the millionaire for he is the bee that gathers the honey," was his counsel to the populists. The honey, however, must be returned to the hive only in the ways that Carnegie specified. Ideally, the accumulator himself should dispense his largesse and not leave the task to others. The most reprehensible practice, but unfortunately the most common, was to will it to one's own family. Nor should the millionaire waste his fortune on gifts of individual charity to those whom Carnegie called "the submerged tenth." Better to throw one's dollars into the sea than drop them into the tin cup of beggary. According to Carnegie society benefits only when wealth is used to provide opportunities for that "swimming tenth" determined to advance itself by its own ambitious drive.

Carnegie obligingly provided a list of "the best fields of philanthropy." In descending order of importance they were universities and other institutions "to encourage investigations, research and discovery"; free public libraries; medical education and health service facilities; parks and arboretums; concert halls; public swimming baths; and churches. The specificity of his list aroused a storm of criticism, particularly from the clergy, who resented being provided for last, just after swimming baths. But Carnegie was sure that through this gospel he had found salvation. As he so succinctly stated, here was "refuge from self-questioning."

Carnegie had made his first gifts of a library and a swimming bath to his native town of Dunfermline in 1881, followed by gifts of a library to Braddock, Pennsylvania, and a pipe organ to the small Swedenborgian church his father had attended in Allegheny. After his retirement from business in 1901 Carnegie would begin in earnest to practice what he had preached in 1889.

Although Carnegie's business activities and writing projects might explain why he was not a conspicuous figure on the New York social scene, the truth was he never had any interest in high society nor, unlike most wealthy men, was he a collector of art, rare books, or antique furniture. He did, however, always find time for the kind of recreation he enjoyed—travels around the world, coaching trips in Britain, and long summers of relaxation at his cottage in Cresson, high up in the mountains of western Pennsylvania. Carnegie was no recluse, but the company he sought was not that as defined by Ward McAllister's New York 400. He sought friendship with those who could provide intellectual stimulation, and he found most businessmen exceedingly dull. The one thing he had gained of value from his newspaper venture was an introduction into an elite circle of the British intelligentsia. His money gained him admission but his quick wit, insatiable curiosity, and political views let him move with ease in the company of a diverse group of notables such as William Gladstone; Matthew Arnold; Rudyard Kipling; his mentor, the social evolutionist Herbert Spencer; the eccentric editor of the *Pall Mall Gazette*, W. T. Stead; and his closest friend of all, the historian and statesman John Morley. In the United States he collected an equally distinguished and eclectic list of companions, including Mark Twain; Senator James G. Blaine; Theodore Roosevelt; Cornell University president Andrew White; and the African-American educator Booker T. Washington. This immigrant with only four years of schooling now dared to tread where other American businessmen not only feared but had no desire to go.

In Carnegie's busy schedule of making money and cultivating men of distinction there seemed to be little time for female companionship other than that of his mother, who continued to live with him both in New York and at their Cresson summer home as well as accompanying him on his numerous trips to Britain. In 1880, however, Carnegie met Louise Whitfield, the daughter of a New York merchant. They discovered a mutual interest in horseback riding, and on their frequent early morning rides through Central Park, to his own surprise, at forty-five Carnegie found himself in love. It was a troubled and protracted courtship, for although Whitfield, twenty-two years his junior, was happy to accept his proposal of marriage, she soon realized that their union could never be so long as Margaret Carnegie held the tie that truly bound her son.

In the late summer of 1886, while at the Cresson cottage, Margaret died of pneumonia. At the time Carnegie was seriously ill of typhoid fever and lay for weeks in a semiconscious state, unaware that his mother had died. When he had recovered enough by November to learn of his mother's death, he at once scrawled a note to Louise, "I am now wholly yours—all gone but you . . . Till death, Louise, yours alone" (24 Nov. 1886, letter in possession of the Carnegie-Miller family).

On 22 April 1887, Andrew, at the advanced age of fifty-one, and Louise were married. At the even more advanced age of sixty-one, Carnegie became the father of his only child, a daughter.

Carnegie never returned to Cresson following the death of his mother, but his sensitivity to heat forced him to seek out another summer retreat. For the first ten years of their marriage, the Carnegies leased Cluny Castle in the Scottish Highlands for six months every year. Following the birth of their daughter, Louise insisted that they have their own castle, and Carnegie purchased the ancient estate of "Skibo" on Dornoch Firth in northeastern Scotland. The old castle was rebuilt and greatly enlarged, and every summer Skibo became the kind of social center that Carnegie most enjoyed. Through its impressive portals passed educators, poets, artists, politicians, pacificists, and—of least interest to Carnegie—business associates of both continents. There Carnegie also did much of his writing—articles on history, economics, foreign policy for leading journals, his biography of James Watt, his collected essays on *Problems of Today*, and in the last years of his life, his autobiography. From 1881, when his first book, a travel journal of his trip around the world appeared, until 1916, Carnegie produced sixty-three articles and eight books—a bibliography that his academic friends might well have envied.

The winters in New York were largely devoted to his business affairs. Expansion remained the key word, and with Frick as chairman and Charles Schwab as president of Carnegie Steel, Carnegie had found the right team to carry out his orders. In the 1890s the rich iron ores of the Mesabi range in Minnesota were acquired by the company, and Carnegie constructed his own railroad from Pittsburgh to the dock facilities on Lake Erie, allowing him to escape the monopolistic stranglehold in which the Pennsylvania Railroad had long held his mills.

Although Carnegie's respect for Frick's managerial skills remained high, their personal relationship cooled after the Homestead strike and became even chillier in 1899 when Frick attempted to buy Carnegie Steel at Carnegie's asking price of $320 million by forming a syndicate with three of the most notorious stock manipulators on Wall Street, John "Bet a Million" Gates and the two Moore brothers, William and James. The syndicate was given three months to raise the money, which it was unable to do. Carnegie, to Frick's disgust, kept the deposit of one million dollars, which he had insisted on as a pledge of good faith. The final break between Carnegie and Frick came soon thereafter when the Frick Coke Company attempted to raise the price of coke sold to Carnegie Steel from $1.35 a ton to $1.75 a ton. Even though this was still considerably below the price other steel companies were paying, Carnegie insisted he had a gentleman's agreement with Frick that Carnegie Steel would never have to pay above $1.35 a ton. There was, however, no formal contract to that effect, and Frick refused to budge. With his majority interest in both companies, Carnegie in retaliation forced Frick out of the chairmanship of Carnegie Steel and pushed through a contract with the coke company establishing the fixed price he demanded. Not content with that, using the "Iron Clad Agreement" that all of his partners had had to sign, Carnegie attempted to buy out Frick's 11 percent in Carnegie Steel at the book value of $5 million, only a fraction of its real worth. Frick took the matter to court in a suit that became a national sensation. Pressure from the entire business community as well as the Republican party facing an election in 1900 brought about an out-of-court settlement. In the terms of the settlement, the Frick Coke Company and Carnegie Steel were merged into the Carnegie Company, capitalized at $320 million. Frick kept his 11 percent interest in the new company, now worth $30 million instead of the $5 million previously offered, but could never hold any position within the new company. Schwab, the big winner, became chief executive officer with an enlarged interest.

At sixty-five Carnegie appeared to have emerged from this imbroglio with Frick eager for a new start and with no thought of retirement. To meet the threat of a powerful new combine of steel plants, Federal Steel, which J. P. Morgan had recently effected, Carnegie proposed to push verticality still farther by producing finished steel products on a massive scale. Schwab was put in charge of building such a plant at Conneaut, Ohio, even though Carnegie's associates had little enthusiasm for this new venture. The older partners—Phipps and Lauder in particular—were eager to get out with their long-promised but not yet realized fortune, and Schwab was more than ready to take over. It was he who served as the negotiator between Morgan, greatly disturbed by Carnegie's proposed Conneaut venture, and Carnegie to bring about an amalgamation of their interests. In early January 1901, with the enthusiastic support of Louise Carnegie, Schwab informed Carnegie that Morgan had asked for him to name his price. Carnegie scrawled on the back of an envelope the figure $480,000,000, which Schwab rushed back to Morgan. Without a moment's hesitation, Morgan said, "I accept the price." Just that simply the largest merger in American industrial history to that time was accomplished. Carnegie's own share amounted to more than $225 million in 5 percent gold bonds, secured by a first mortgage on all the properties of the forthcoming giant steel trust. On 2 March 1901, the United States Steel Corporation was born, America's first billion-dollar corporation, with Schwab as president.

Carnegie could at last turn to the task of putting into practice his gospel of wealth. With this fortune he could cover most of the seven items on his list of "the best fields of philanthropy." His personal priority was free public libraries. He provided 2,811 libraries to the English-speaking world, including 1,946 in the United States, 660 in Great Britain, and 156 in Canada, at a total cost of over $50 million. Carnegie donated only the buildings, and gave solely to those communities willing to tax their citizens for the purchase of books and the cost of operation. Libraries proved to be the best known and most popular of all of Carnegie's philanthropies. He liked to boast that the sun never set on his chain of libraries reaching from northern Scotland to the Fiji islands. In addition to libraries, his first gifts following his retirement went to a pension fund for his former steelworkers and to pensions for college teachers distributed by the Carnegie Foundation for the Advancement of Teaching. The Carnegie Institution of Washington was created in 1902 to advance scientific research and discovery. Even churches, last on his list of best fields, were remembered with gifts of 7,689 pipe organs.

Although Carnegie had insisted there was no place for sentiment in his concept of "scientific" philanthropy, nevertheless, Scotland and especially his native Dunfermline received very special consideration. The Carnegie-Dunfermline Trust, established in 1903, was to give the town, in addition to the library and swimming bath already donated, the Pittencrieff estate, containing the historic ruins of Scotland's first capital, a technical college, a medical clinic that provided free care for the children of the town, a Women's Institute, and a concert hall. For all of Scotland he endowed a trust to provide free tuition to the four Scottish universities. For all of Great Britain, he established the United Kingdom Trust, a counterpart to the Carnegie Institution of Washington. Pittsburgh also got special recognition—the Carnegie Institute, which provided for an art gallery and concert hall as well as a library and the Carnegie Institute of Technology.

Carnegie's initial giving was as highly diverse as had been his earliest ventures in capitalism. But just as he had found the single basket of steel on which to concentrate his interest, so he was now to find in philanthropy a single specialty—world peace. In his pursuit of international justice and the abolition of war, Carnegie created four foundations: the Carnegie Endowment for International Peace, the Carnegie Hero Fund to reward civilian heroes who saved lives, the Church Peace Union, and the Simplified Spelling Board in the belief that if the spelling of English could be made more phonetic it would become the universal tongue for the promotion of international understanding. He also built what he called his three "Temples of Peace": the Pan American Union building in Washington for the promotion of peace in the Western Hemisphere, the Central American Court of Justice in Costa Rica to arbitrate differences among those five frequently quarreling little republics, and, most important, The Hague Peace Palace in the Netherlands to house the World Court.

Carnegie had entered into this last great enterprise of his life with high enthusiasm. He loved the fanfare that accompanied his gifts, and he was to set an all-time record of receiving more Freedom of the City awards in Britain (fifty-seven in all) than any other person, including Winston Churchill. It came as a shock to Carnegie to discover, however, that his generous giving aroused more public criticism than had his aggressive getting. How Carnegie got his wealth, most believed, was his own business; how he gave it away was everybody's business. There was also the sobering fact that as fast as he dispensed his fortune his remaining bonds were earning more. "The final dispensation of one's wealth preparing for the final exit," he wrote his Scottish solicitor, John Ross, "is I found a heavy task—all sad . . . You have no idea the strain I have been under" (11 Feb. 1913, Carnegie papers, Library of Congress, vol. 213). He gratefully accepted his friend the statesman Elihu Root's suggestion that he create one great philanthropic foundation in which to place the remainder of his fortune. The Carnegie Corporation of New York was established in 1911 with an endowment of $125 million. Carnegie had once written, "The man who dies thus rich, dies disgraced." Carnegie had finally found grace by dispensing nine-tenths of his fortune.

Carnegie had begun his quest for peace in the naive belief that with his wealth he could buy international justice and harmony for the world. Prospects for that achievement never seemed brighter to him than in what proved to be his last summer at Skibo. Carnegie subscribed to the Carlylean view of history that every age finds its great hero, and in that summer of 1914, he believed he had found two heroes of peace. Given his commitment to republicanism, his choices were curious—the Democratic president of the United States, Woodrow Wilson, and the emperor of Germany, Wilhelm II. Carnegie was just finishing the last chapter of his autobiography in which he sang the praises of Kaiser Wilhelm when he received the news that world war had begun. He hastily added a postscript to the manuscript: "The world convulsed by war as never before! Men slaying each other like wild beasts. I dare not relinquish all hope." As Louise Carnegie was to write in a preface to the autobiography, published posthumously in 1920, "the world disaster was too much. His heart was broken." Carnegie died five years later at his new summer home in Lenox, Massachusetts, and was buried in Sleepy Hollow cemetery, Tarrytown, New York.

Carnegie made significant contributions in his three major areas of interest. As an industrialist, he emphasized the importance of cost of production over the value of profits, he pushed for verticality within his company structure, and he welcomed technological innovation. As a philanthropist, he attempted a scientific analysis of the art of giving, pioneered in the development of the modern philanthropic foundation, and placed education and free inquiry as primary fields of importance in creating a better society. Finally, as a pacifist, Andrew Carnegie pushed for a summit meeting of the great powers, Great Britain, the United States, and Germany, long before such meetings would become a common occurrence in the late twentieth century, and he correctly saw the arbitration of international disputes as the only rational option to the irrational recourse to war.

• The major collection of Andrew Carnegie's papers (239 volumes) is in the Manuscript Division of the Library of Congress. Another important collection, consisting of letterbooks of his business correspondence prior to 1881, is the USX Corporation collection in the Annandale Archives, Boyers, Pa. Smaller collections are in the Manuscript Division of the New York Public Library and in the Carnegie Museum, Dunfermline, Scotland. Personal letters from Carnegie to his mother and brother (1865–1866) and letters between Carnegie and Louise Whitfield prior to their marriage (1880–1886) are in the possession of the Carnegie-Miller family.

Carnegie's own writings were edited and published by Burton J. Hendrick in ten volumes in 1933. Included in this series are Carnegie's books, with first publication dates in parentheses: *Round the World* (1881), *An American Four-in-Hand in Britain* (1883), *Triumphant Democracy* (1886), *James Watt* (1903), *Problems of Today* (1908), and *Autobiography of Andrew Carnegie* (1920). Carnegie's articles also are republished in this series under the titles *The Gospel of Wealth*, *The Empire of Business*, and *Miscellaneous Writings of Andrew Carnegie* (2 vols.). A collection of Carnegie's writings published in a single volume is *The Andrew Carnegie Reader*, ed. Joseph F. Wall (1992).

Secondary sources on Carnegie's career are legion. Two biographies covering all aspects of his life are Joseph Frazier Wall, *Andrew Carnegie* (1970; repr. 1989), and Burton J. Hendrick, *The Life of Andrew Carnegie* (1932). Books that emphasize his business career but are strongly biased against Carnegie are John K. Winkler, *Incredible Carnegie* (1931), and James H. Bridge, *The Inside History of the Carnegie Steel Company* (1903; repr. 1991). A more balanced account of Carnegie as an industrialist is Harold C. Livesay, *Andrew Carnegie and the Rise of Big Business* (1975). Books dealing with Carnegie's business associates are William B. Dickson, *History of the Carnegie Veterans Association* (1938); Robert Hessen, *Steel Titan: Charles M. Schwab* (1975); and Jeanne McHugh, *Alexander Holley and the Makers of Steel* (1980). Much has been written on the Homestead strike; especially important are David Brody, *Steel Workers in America: The Non-Union Era* (1960); Paul Krause, *The Battle for Homestead 1880–1892* (1992); and David P. Demarest, Jr., ed., *"The River Ran Red": Homestead 1892* (1992). Carnegie's philanthropies are detailed in *A Manual of the Public Benefactions of Andrew Carnegie*, comp. Carnegie Endowment for International Peace (1919); Robert M. Lester, *Forty Years of Carnegie Giving* (1941); and Simon Goodenough, *The Greatest Good Fortune* (1985). Books dealing with Carnegie's personal life are John B. Mackie, *Andrew Carnegie: His Dunfermline Ties* (1916); Burton J. Hendrick and Daniel Henderson, *Louise Whitfield Carnegie* (1950); and Joseph F. Wall, *Skibo* (1985). An obituary is in the *New York Times*, 12 Aug. 1919.

JOSEPH FRAZIER WALL

CARNEGIE, Dale (22 Nov. 1888–1 Nov. 1955), author and teacher of public speaking, was born Dale Breckenridge Carnegey in Maryville, Missouri, the son of James William Carnegey and Amanda Elizabeth Harbison. In 1919 he changed his name to Carnegie in honor of his hero, Andrew Carnegie. Carnegie grew up on a farm that offered poverty as a character-builder. His mother was a devout Methodist who met each disaster with a "stout-hearted hymn" and took her troubles to God. She wanted Dale to be a minister, and early in his life he practiced public speaking by reciting in Sunday school pieces such as "The Saloon: Offspring of Hell." Dale was not a strong student, nor was he athletic, and his farm chores took up much of his time. He early took to public speaking and debate in high school, having been influenced by the Chautauqua speakers in his rural area. In 1908 Carnegie graduated from the State Teacher's College in Warrensburg, Missouri (now Central Missouri College). One prophet in the college yearbook wrote that Carnegie was "sure to win fame, makes all the students think he can declaim."

Carnegie's early life was checkered; he tried his hand at many things, eagerly searching for the one career that would bring him the fame and fortune he felt he deserved. For a short time he worked as a salesman in western Nebraska and Wyoming—not a fertile area—for the International Correspondence School. He earned $500 peddling bacon and lard for Armour & Company in the Dakota Badlands, another area of poor prospects. He then decided that his future lay in the East and went to New York City to study drama. He spent a year on the road in a theater vehicle called "Polly of the Circus." Back in New York he briefly sold Packard trucks, a job that he hated and did poorly. He attended the American Academy of Dramatic Arts and took courses at Columbia University and New York University.

In 1912 his career took a turn at the 125th Street YMCA, where he was able to sell the director on a program in public speaking after he recited elocution pieces with piano accompaniment. Carnegie also began his writing career, publishing essays in periodicals. While giving courses in public speaking at the YMCA, he discovered the key to his success—"have the students speak." Carnegie was an organizing genius. In a short time he organized classes in public speaking and wrote several pamphlets on the subject that served as texts. The public speaking program caught on and spread to YMCAs in other cities. By 1914 Carnegie was averaging $400 per week, and he began offering special courses about public speaking and influencing people for clubs, chambers of commerce, and business organizations in New York City, Philadelphia, and Washington, D.C. He began to train sales forces and executives including the New York Telephone Company, Westinghouse Electric & Manufacturing, Brooklyn Union Gas Company, the Cornell Club, New York's Junior League, and the Sun Oil Company. He served briefly in the U.S. Army during World War I, although, surprisingly, he never said much about this military experience. He wrote a great deal during this time but was not very successful with his writing. His novel *Blizzard* was given an icy reception by most editors. He did special research into Abraham Lincoln, and wrote *Lincoln the Unknown* (1932). Historian Allan Nevins, however, called the book "a sentimental portrait."

Among Carnegie's early writings that did fairly well was *Public Speaking and Influencing Men in Business* (1926). Carnegie lectured in the United States, Canada, and Great Britain, where he presented Sir Ross Smith at the Philharmonic Hall in London and served as Lowell Thomas's manager. He traveled extensively in Europe, Asia, and the Arctic regions, later claiming that he had almost reached the North Pole. Back in the United States, Carnegie continued his public speaking and writing. One of his early popular books was *Little Known Facts About Well-Known People* (1943), which led to a radio program of the same name. In 1921 Carnegie had married a German divorcée, Lolita Baucaire, but the marriage was not a happy one and ended in divorce in 1931. In 1944 he married Dorothy Prince Vanderpool, who was a graduate of his course. The couple had one daughter, and Mrs. Carnegie had a daughter by a previous marriage. Carnegie's second wife was a strong supporter of his career.

In 1936 Carnegie hit the jackpot with his book *How to Win Friends and Influence People*. It was an immediate bestseller, and brought a great demand for lectures, periodical articles, and even a syndicated newspaper column. In a short period this book of "common-sense advice" was translated into thirty languages, and by 1986 it had sold more than 15 million copies. It was even adopted by the Army Air Corps Forces Officer's Candidate School in Miami, Florida.

The book's theme is quite simple: smile, support the ethic of cooperation, see others' points of view, avoid criticism, and emphasize the golden rule. The emphasis was on positive thinking, and the book was a lineal descendant of nineteenth-century success books like the Horatio Alger series. The structure of the book was also simple, using biographical sketches of great figures from history. Carnegie sold enthusiasm, and his exuberant style offered inspirational stories as a secret formula for success. There were a few minor critics. Author James Thurber accused Carnegie of producing "disingenuities," and writer Sinclair Lewis protested that Carnegie "feigned altruism."

One reviewer of Carnegie's work summarized Carnegie's philosophy as "Push button-Smile, be Friendly." His glittering eyeglasses resembled those of Harry S. Truman, a fellow Missourian. Carnegie spoke with a midwestern drawl and wore dapper double-breasted suits.

By 1940 this "barefoot boy from Missouri" had become wealthy, yet he lived in a modest stucco house in Forest Hills, Queens, in New York City.

The Carnegie Course in Effective Speaking contributed to Carnegie's wealth. Remaining active long after his death, the course had by 1988 produced more than 165,000 graduates in the United States alone and, during the 1990s, was being conducted in more than sixty other countries around the world. The course was Carnegie's laboratory with people, where he concentrated his life experiences, his philosophy, and the techniques of the rural minister. Carnegie could not resist giving advice. His last book was *How to Stop Worrying and Start Living* (1948), published when he was sixty. He died in Forest Hills.

Although Carnegie's work was ignored by the academic world, he was the most important and influential success writer in the decades following 1940. He appealed to the American longing for success, and taught many Americans how to substitute "smiles" for Hobbes's political authority. Carnegie had critics such as Thomas Luck, who considered Carnegie's work a "collection of platitudes," but Gilcs Kcmp called him "one of the greatest teachers of all time." Carnegie was a pioneer in the field of public speaking and the psychology of the successful personality. A child of the rural oratorical tradition of the nineteenth century, he left his mark on the twentieth century.

• Most information about Carnegie's early life and experiences at Central Missouri State College was lost in a 1915 fire that destroyed all student records. Most of Carnegie's papers are retained by the Dale Carnegie Institute for Effective Speaking and Human Relations, Garden City, N.Y. Carnegie's other books include *The Art of Public Speaking*, with Joseph Berg Esenwein (1915); *Public Speaking: A Practical Course for Business Men* (2 vols., 1926), his key work, which was later renamed *Public Speaking and Influencing Men in Business* (1932); *Lincoln the Unknown* (1932); *Little Known Facts About Well-Known People* (1934), which led to his radio program; *Five Minute Biographies* (1937), consisting of sketches that he used in his course; and *Biographical Round-Up* (1945), a collection of sketches. Two of Carnegie's best pieces are "Enthusiasm and Appreciation," *Vital Speeches* 19 (15 Jan. 1953): 216–21, from a speech he gave before the Chicago Executive Club; and "Fool Things I Have Done," *Reader's Digest*, Apr. 1947.

Two good sources on Carnegie are Donald Meyer, *The Positive Thinkers: A Study of the American Quest for Health, Wealth, and Personal Power from Mary Baker Eddy to Norman Vincent Peale* (1965); and Richard M. Huber, "How to Win Friends and Influence People," chap. 16 in *The American Idea of Success* (1971). Also useful are John G. Cawelti, *The Apostles of the Self-Made Man* (1965); and Giles Kemp and Edward Claflin, *Dale Carnegie: The Man Who Influenced Millions* (1989). Unique contemporary books are Bruce Barton, *The Man Nobody Knows* (1925); and Ralph W. Trine, *The Power That Wins* (1928). A useful analysis of Carnegie is in Laurie Di Mauro, ed., *Twentieth Century Literary Criticism* (1994).

From 1925 to 1955 a flood of periodical literature about Carnegie was published. Important articles from this period include A. E. Mayer, "How Dale Carnegie Made Friends," *American Mercury*, July 1943, pp. 40–48; M. E. Harrison, "He Sells Hope," *Nation*, 19 Mar. 1938, pp. 325ff; James Thurber, "The Voice with a Smile," *Saturday Review of Literature*, 30 Jan. 1937; and Richard Coniff, "The So-so Salesman Who Told Millions How to Make It Big." *Smithsonian*, Oct. 1987, pp. 82–93.

An obituary is in the *New York Times*, 1 Nov. 1955.

NICHOLAS C. POLOS

CARNEGIE, Hattie (15 Mar. 1886–22 Feb. 1956), fashion designer and merchandiser, was born Henrietta Könengeiser in Vienna, Austria, the daughter of Isaac Könengeiser and Hannah Kraenzer. The family emigrated to the United States, settling on New York's Lower East Side in 1892. Hattie's first job was as a messenger at R. H. Macy's, where she encountered the heady new world of modern retailing and the lifestyle of affluent New York. That experience may have inspired her to assume the name Carnegie; Andrew Carnegie was one of the richest men in the country.

In 1909 Carnegie and Rose Roth, a seamstress, opened a custom dress and millinery shop. Carnegie was not the designer; she worked as a salesperson. By 1913 the business had moved to the opulent Upper West Side of Manhattan. Five years later Carnegie bought out Roth and began to focus on her own designs and adaptations of Paris fashion. She made her first trip to Paris in 1919, and after that her design sensibility was deeply influenced by French fashion and carried the cachet of French taste, modulated to the American spirit. In 1923 Carnegie moved the business to its longtime site, a townhouse at Forty-ninth Street off Park Avenue.

By this time Carnegie's company had become widely known among chic clients and was attracting socialites and movie stars. Her taste-making reputation led I. Magnin, a California department store, to ask her to create products under the Magnin private label and the Hattie Carnegie brand; Carnegie went wholesale in 1925. In 1927, after two failed marriages, Carnegie married Major John Zanft. In 1928 she initiated her label "Hattie Carnegie Originals," maintaining her custom clothing business but profiting from the market's move to ready-to-wear clothes. Thousands of "little Carnegie suits," party dresses, and fashionable accessories were sold nationwide.

In the 1930s Carnegie's New York salon was a beacon for the most stylish clients. Carnegie hired designers Norman Norell, Bruno, Travis Banton, Jean Louis, and Claire McCardell, among others. Bruno made Carnegie's stylish, practical sportswear under the "Spectator Sports" label. Carnegie brought back suits, dresses, and coats from Paris; the designers modified and generally simplified their designs.

In 1941 Carnegie shrewdly expanded her business with a "jeune fille" department, ostensibly for young women but also appealing to the budget-minded. The same year she produced a mail-order Christmas catalog offering her accessories, cosmetics, and even men's gifts. In 1945 she added a fragrance line. She established a Blue Room in her custom shop to sell ready-to-wear clothing. In 1947 *Life* called Carnegie the "undisputed leader" of American fashion, with more than 100 stores selling her products.

In the 1950s Carnegie designed the habit for an order of Carmelite nuns and the WAC uniform, a modification of the classic Carnegie suit. In 1955 she created Hattie Carnegie Costume Jewelry, extending her authority from hat to hem: the "Carnegie look" was one-stop shopping. By the time of her death in New York, Carnegie presided over a multimillion-dollar fashion company with more than 1,000 employees in wholesale, made-to-order, accessories, and perfume divisions.

Although she began as an imitator enthralled by Paris fashion, Carnegie became—through a workshop staffed by the best young designers—a distinctly American fashion maker, reflecting the democratic trends of mass marketing, a broad desire for stylishness, and the importance of ready-to-wear fashion. She counted as clients socialites—the duchess of Windsor, Mrs. Paul Mellon, and Clare Booth Luce—as well as Hollywood stars like Joan Crawford, Tallulah Bankhead, and Norma Shearer. She also, however, established an ideal that attracted almost every American woman. A parvenue and public personality, Carnegie captured the new spirit of democratic fashion by making high style available at a reasonable price. Carnegie meant good taste and decorum realized by luxurious materials and expert craft, but she also had a flair for the dramatic. Her image—a charismatic, media-savvy tastemaker presiding over a fashion empire—became American fashion's model.

• Carnegie is the subject of a biographical account by Madelyn Shaw, "Hattie Carnegie," in *Contemporary Fashion*, ed. Richard Martin (1995). An exhibition, Hattie Carnegie: American Style Defined, was held at the Fashion Institute of Technology in New York City, 16 Feb.–27 Apr. 1996. An obituary is in the *New York Times*, 23 Feb. 1956.

RICHARD MARTIN

CARNEGIE, Louise Whitfield (7 Mar. 1857–24 June 1946), philanthropist, was born in New York City, the daughter of John William Whitfield, a wholesale merchant, and Fannie Davis. Louise enjoyed a nurturing, upper-class home life, where her parents stressed industry and public spirit. Her playmates in Gramercy Park included Theodore Roosevelt and his sister Corinne. Louise was enrolled at age six in Miss Henrietta Haines School. In addition to lessons in manners, deportment, and French conversation and literature, she took lessons in science from the geologist Arnold Henry Guyot. She excelled at her studies and at age sixteen was taken on a European tour by her parents.

In 1875, just as Louise completed her school work, her mother became ill and the care of her two siblings fell to her. Despite these responsibilities, she maintained an active social life until 1878 when her father died. The family entered a prolonged period of mourning, and Louise withdrew from society. Bright spots in Louise's life were visits with Andrew Carnegie. She had first met the steel magnate in the early 1870s when he called on her family with Alexander and Agnes King. He continued to call on the family each year on New Year's Day. By the early 1880s Louise and Andrew formed a friendship based on their mutual love of books, music, and horses.

Andrew Carnegie began inviting Louise Whitfield to ride with him in Central Park. Though she was twenty-two years younger and three inches taller, the romance blossomed, and in 1883 they became secretly engaged. The Scottish-born industrialist grew increasingly attentive, but his devotion to his elderly mother, with whom he lived at the Hotel Windsor in Manhattan, precluded marriage. Tensions mounted and the engagement was broken in the spring of 1884, then renewed the following fall.

The death of Andrew's mother in December 1886 liberated him. He and Louise were married in a private ceremony at the Whitfield home in April 1887. Many years after Andrew's death Louise confessed that his mother was the most unpleasant person she had ever met. As a wedding present, Andrew gave his wife stocks and bonds with an annual income of $20,000 and a house at 5 West Fifty-first Street. Though Louise regretted that she had not been there to help her husband at the start of his career, she found that her new life had ample challenges.

Louise Carnegie was used to running one household, but now she had to learn to run several households, entertain a succession of guests, and bolster her husband's spirits in times of crisis. During the violent strike at the Carnegie Company's Homestead plant in July 1892, Andrew relied on his wife for comfort. In addition, he sought Louise's advice in planning his philanthropic bequests, from libraries to New York City's Carnegie Hall, where she laid the cornerstone in 1891. Following the death of her mother in 1890, Louise's siblings moved in with the Carnegies. Seven years later the couple had their only child, Margaret. Louise was overjoyed and Andrew resolved to create glorious abodes for his family.

Beginning in 1887 the Carnegies had spent nearly every summer in Scotland, renting Cluny Castle. After Margaret's birth, Carnegie purchased "Skibo" in Sutherland, Scotland. Both the 22,000-acre estate and the imposing castle required an extensive overhaul. Louise Carnegie oversaw every detail from the landscaping, which included a nine-hole golf course, to the creation of the library and the installation of the organ. She also insisted on the renovation of a nearby cottage, which served as the family's private retreat.

The Carnegies took up residence at Skibo in the summer of 1899 and began entertaining lavishly. The guest list at Skibo in a single summer before the start of World War I included trustees of all the Carnegie trusts, presidents of the four major Scottish universities, ambassadors, physicians, and musicians. Rudyard Kipling wrote *Kim* while staying at Skibo. The castle's renowned comfort and elegance prompted King Edward VII of England to visit in 1903, seeking inspiration for the impending renovation of Buckingham Palace.

While Skibo was being renovated, construction began in New York City on the Carnegie mansion at Ninety-first Street and Fifth Avenue, with Louise Carnegie again overseeing every detail. She began to hope that her husband would leave their Fifty-first Street residence and his business simultaneously. She urged him to fulfill his pledge in his *The Gospel of Wealth* (1889) and give up industry for philanthropy. She orchestrated one of the meetings that resulted in Andrew's decision to sell his share of the Carnegie Company. The deal, which led to the creation of U.S. Steel in 1901, netted him approximately $270 million.

Once settled in their new homes, the Carnegies embarked on a mission to promote education and peace. Bequests included $10 million to the Carnegie Institute of Washington for Fundamental Scientific Research in 1903; $10 million to the Carnegie Endowment for International Peace in 1910; $125 million for the endowment of the Carnegie Corporation of New York in 1911; and at Louise's particular urging, $2 million for a Church Peace Union in 1915.

The onset of World War I shattered the Carnegies' dream of world peace and interrupted the family's summer trips to Scotland. When Andrew's health failed, Louise devoted herself to his comfort. Their daughter's marriage to Roswell Miller in April 1919 brightened the Carnegies' final days together. Andrew Carnegie died the following August.

The births of four grandchildren between June 1920 and July 1926 revived Louise Carnegie. She was inspired to return to Skibo in the hope that the Millers would make the castle their summer home. The family returned almost every summer up to the start of World War II. In order to have the Millers nearby in the winter, Louise bought for them a house on Ninetieth Street in New York City that adjoined the mansion.

As the steward of Andrew Carnegie's wealth, Louise Carnegie continuously considered causes to support. In 1928 she created a birthplace memorial to her husband in Dunfermline, Scotland. As a devout Presbyterian she donated the parish house to the Brick Church in New York City. She also supported the New York Ophthalmic Hospital, the American Red Cross, the Young Woman's Christian Association, the Community Service Society, and the Union Theological Seminary. She bequeathed her Ninety-first Street residence to the New York School of Social Work. In helping to distribute more than $311 million, Louise Carnegie played a subtle but significant role in shaping American philanthropy. She died at home in New York City.

• Though two writers, Burton J. Hendrick and Daniel Henderson, have used Louise Carnegie's diaries and letters, there appears to be little primary source material in the public domain about her. The best secondary sources are a sympathetic biography by Hendrick and Henderson, *Louise Whitfield Carnegie* (1950), and two more objective books by Joseph Frazier Wall, *Andrew Carnegie* (1970) and *Skibo* (1984). An obituary is in the *New York Times*, 25 June 1946.

SARAH HENRY LEDERMAN

CARNELL, Edward John (28 June 1919–25 Apr. 1967), theologian and educator, was born in Antigo, Langlade County, Wisconsin, the son of Herbert C. Carnell and Fannie Carstens, a fundamentalist minister and his wife who struggled to support their family by serving several Baptist churches in the Upper Midwest. Carnell attended Wheaton College from 1937 to 1941 and received an A.B. in philosophy. Although he sometimes worked thirty-five to forty hours a week in the dining hall as an undergraduate, Carnell was able to excel in philosophy under the tutelage of Professor Gordon Haddon Clark, whose philosophical defense of Christianity made a lasting impact on a generation of evangelical leaders who attended the midwestern fundamentalist liberal arts college during these years. From Wheaton, Carnell went to Westminster Seminary in Philadelphia, an institution that had been founded in opposition to Princeton Seminary in 1929 during the fundamentalist controversy. At Westminster he studied theology with the Dutch Calvinist Cornelius Van Til, whose system of theology stressed the intellectual differences between believers and nonbelievers, and he earned both a Th.B. and a Th.M (1944). Because the U.S. government deferred the draft of seminarians, Carnell did not serve in World War II. In 1944 he married Shirley Rowe, a schoolteacher; they had two children. Carnell went on to complete two doctorates. He first earned a Th.D. at Harvard University (1948), where he wrote a dissertation on the theology of Reinhold Niebuhr. Then he received a Ph.D. at Boston University (1949) for a study of Søren Kierkegaard.

While studying in eastern Massachusetts, Carnell was appointed professor of religion and philosophy at Gordon College in 1945. Three years later he joined the faculty of the newly founded Fuller Seminary in Pasadena, California, an institution with which he would be affiliated for the rest of his life, first as professor of theology and later as president from 1954 to 1959. During his tenure at Fuller, Carnell emerged as a leader of the resurgence of intellectual evangelicalism after World War II. The seminary became synonymous with a new kind of fundamentalism, often called the new evangelicalism, which was less sectarian in its dealings with mainline Protestants, more open to the intellectual currents of the academy, and more interested in shaping public life. In the view of evangelicals like Carnell, revivalist fundamentalism was too narrow and negative to have a lasting impact on American society. If conservative Protestants were to have any influence on the culture, they needed to join rather than remain separate from established institutions, especially within higher education.

Carnell's academic pursuits typified the desire of new evangelicals to abandon the anti-intellectualism of fundamentalism, engage the most recent theological and philosophical developments, and show that the old certainties of conservative Protestantism provided answers to the questions of modern science and philosophy. In his first book, *An Introduction to Christian Apologetics* (1948), Carnell, still in his twenties, elaborated a philosophically informed defense of fundamentalist beliefs, which earned the much-heralded Eerdman's Evangelical Book Award of $5,000 and established him as one of the bright lights of the new evangelical movement. In his next major book, *A Philosophy of the Christian Religion* (1952), Carnell turned from logical and metaphysical grounds for Christianity to an argument that linked orthodox theology to the human heart's desire for meaning and values.

These efforts to refurbish the image of conservative Protestantism, however, did not please older fundamentalists, and during the 1950s a major controversy erupted among conservative Protestants over cooperation with mainline denominations. The actions of the young and popular evangelist Billy Graham proved to be especially divisive when, during his 1957 crusade in New York City, he enlisted the support and resources of mainstream Protestant congregations.

What Graham was doing through his evangelistic campaigns, Carnell was attempting to do as president of Fuller Seminary. During his tenure as chief administrator, he moved the new seminary into the mainstream of Protestant theological education by convincing the American Association of Theological Schools that the new institution was sufficiently committed to academic freedom and scholarly endeavor to merit accreditation. Carnell's efforts drew immediate criticism from many fundamentalists. Some believed he had departed significantly from orthodoxy. Others feared that the seminary was not theologically safe. *The Case for Orthodox Theology* (1959), written toward the end of his term as president, reflected the theological strains within fundamentalism. In it Carnell responded to his more conservative critics by calling old style fundamentalism "orthodoxy gone cultic." His aim in *The Case for Orthodox Theology* was similar to previous books: to demonstrate that historic Christianity was intellectually respectable, but he took this argument one step farther by trying to distance orthodox theology from "the intellectual dishonesty and ethical hypocrisy of fundamentalism."

Carnell represented a mediating influence within second-generation fundamentalism. Whereas more sectarian fundamentalists continued to ridicule the modern university and mainline denominations, Carnell strove to defend Protestant conservatism while also making it more palatable to mainstream Protestants and intellectuals.

Controversies eventually took their toll. Conflicts with his detractors accentuated psychological problems that had plagued Carnell for much of his adult life. On the verge of a physical and emotional collapse, he resigned from Fuller in 1959. Although eventually he would resume his teaching responsibilities, he never regained his intellectual vigor. Shock treatments for deep depression as well as dependence on sleeping pills cut short what had been a promising career. Carnell died alone during an ecumenical conference in Berkeley, California, from an overdose of barbiturates. Some believe he committed suicide; others think Carnell's death was accidental.

• Carnell's personal papers were destroyed. In addition to his works cited above, see *Television: Servant or Master?* (1950), *The Theology of Reinhold Niebuhr* (1950), *Christian Commitment* (1957), *The Burden of Søren Kierkegaard* (1965), and *The Case for Biblical Christianity* (1969). For a critical assessment of Carnell, see Rudolph Nelson, *The Making and Unmaking of an Evangelical Mind: The Case of Edward Carnell* (1987), which contrasts with John A. Sims, *Edward John Carnell: Defender of the Faith* (1979), a more hagiographical treatment. On Carnell's influence at Fuller Seminary and within the new evangelicalism, see George M. Marsden, *Reforming Fundamentalism: Fuller Seminary and the New Evangelicalism* (1987).

D. G. HART

CARNEY, Harry Howell (1 Apr. 1910–8 Oct. 1974), jazz baritone saxophonist, was born in Boston, Massachusetts. His mother's given name was Jenny; other details of his parents are unknown. Carney studied piano at age six, switched to clarinet, and then took up alto saxophone in the seventh grade, when he met saxophonist Johnny Hodges. Soon he was working professionally in Boston.

In late June 1926 Duke Ellington heard Carney, hired him for a local job, and obtained permission from Carney's parents to take him on the road. While with Ellington, Carney took up baritone saxophone, which gradually became his principal instrument. He resumed his schooling in the fall but returned to Ellington when his schedule allowed, including a trip to New York City during Christmas vacation in 1926, when he first recorded with the band.

On 8 March 1927 saxophonist Charlie Holmes and Carney left Boston for New York. Carney worked at the Savoy Ballroom and then with Henry Saparo's band at the Bamboo Inn while making further recordings with Ellington and occasionally joining him at the Kentucky Club. Impressed that Carney already had a car and his own instruments, Ellington hired him permanently, commencing with a summer 1927 tour of New England. Then followed the band's famous stand at the Cotton Club (1927–1931) and over four decades of national and international touring, during which Carney's career paralleled Ellington's closely.

Among Carney's few independent or semi-independent activities were two recording sessions with singer Billie Holiday and pianist Teddy Wilson (1936 and 1937), participation in a jam session at Benny Goodman's Carnegie Hall concert in January 1938, and a number of recordings with bands led by musicians closely associated with Ellington, including clarinetist Barney Bigard, cornetist Rex Stewart, trumpeter Cootie Williams, and Hodges. None of this work approached the significance of his performances for Ellington, including recorded solos on "East St. Louis Toodle-oo" (1927); "Doin' the Voom Voom" (1929); "Harlem Speaks" and "Jive Stomp" (both 1933); "Saddest Tale" (1934), playing bass clarinet; "In a Sentimental Mood" (1935); "Solitude" (1938); "Perdido" (1942); "Prelude to a Kiss" (1945); and "Sophisticated Lady" (1969), on the album *Duke Ellington's 70th Birthday Concert*. He may be seen and heard with the band in the film shorts *Black and Tan* (1929), *Salute to Duke Ellington* (1950), *Solitude* and *Sophisticated Lady* (both 1952), and *Duke Ellington and His Orchestra* (1965) and the films *Monterey Jazz* (1973) and *Memories of Duke* (1980).

Carney was widely admired as a nice, responsible gentleman. One such testimony among many came from Stewart, who wrote that Carney "is cultured, knowledgeable, and also blessed with such an abundance of good nature that he enriches most scenes by his presence" (p. 134). He loved to drive, and from around 1949 he doubled as Ellington's chauffeur. Later in life he became fond of golf, which he played whenever the band held residencies in Las Vegas. Not long after Ellington's death, Carney died in New York City. He was survived by his wife Dorothy; details of the marriage are unknown.

Carney was the first great jazz baritone saxophonist. Under Ellington's leadership, he took an instrument that had elsewhere been used mainly in a splatty bass role and instead made it into the gruff, full-voiced foundation of a big-band saxophone section. So authoritative was his playing that he could sometimes be heard leading the section from below. (The lead instrument in a big-band section usually plays the highest-pitched melody, as Hodges or Bigard normally did with Ellington's reeds.) Carney also established the baritone saxophone as a convincing solo instrument, particularly in his gorgeous interpretations of ballad melodies.

• Surveys and interviews are by Bill Coss, "An Evening with Harry Carney," *Down Beat*, 25 May 1961, pp. 14, 45; Don DeMichael, "Double Play: Carney to Hodges to Ellington," *Down Beat*, 7 June 1962, pp. 20–21; Jimmy Staples, "Harry Carney," *Crescendo* 2 (July 1964): 28; Valerie Wilmer, "Harry Carney," *Jazz Monthly* 10 (Apr. 1964): 8, 10; Stanley Dance, *The World of Duke Ellington* (1970; repr. 1981); Barry McRae, "Harry Carney," *Jazz Journal* 24 (June 1971): 30, 44; Rex Stewart, *Jazz Masters of the Thirties* (1972; repr. 1982); Duke Ellington, *Music Is My Mistress* (1973); Niels Nielson, "Before Baritone Madness, *Jazz Journal International* 35 (July 1982): 16–17; and Johnny Simmen, "Harry Carney," *Cadence* 13 (July 1987): 14–17. Details of his first affiliations with Ellington appear in Mark Tucker, *Ellington: The Early Years* (1991). See also Tucker, ed., *The Duke Ellington Reader* (1993). Dick M. Bakker, *Duke Ellington on Microgroove*, vol. 1: *1923–1936* (1977), identifies Carney's early recorded solos. For musical analysis, see Gunther Schuller, *Early Jazz: Its Roots and Musical Development* (1968), and Schuller, *The Swing Era: The Development of Jazz, 1930–1945* (1989). An obituary is in the *New York Times*, 10 Oct. 1974.

BARRY KERNFELD

CARNEY, Thomas (20 Aug. 1824–28 July 1888), second governor of Kansas, was born near Tipton, in Delaware County, Ohio, the son of James Carney and Sarah (maiden name unknown), farmers. His boyhood was one of meager education, grueling labor, and poverty. At nineteen he became a clerk in a dry-goods store in Columbus and by the age of thirty was a partner in a dry-goods firm in Cincinnati, Ohio. In 1851 he married Rebecca Ann Canaday, with whom he had five children, one of whom died in infancy. In 1858 he transferred his business operations to Leavenworth, Kansas, where in partnership with Thomas C. Stevens he established a wholesale firm that made him reputedly the richest man in Kansas.

Transferring his ambition to politics, in the fall of 1861 Carney became a member of the Kansas legislature. On 4 November 1862 he was elected governor as the candidate of the regular Republican party. After assuming office on 12 January 1863 he applied his business acumen to liquidating the state's debt through bond transactions, from which he profited personally. He presided over the raising of several new regiments for the Union army and spent $10,000 of his own money (subsequently reimbursed) for a border patrol to guard against guerrilla raids from Missouri. In mid-August 1863 he disbanded the patrol, having been advised by the military authorities that it no longer was needed; a few days later, on 21 August, William C. Quantrill's guerrillas massacred 150 men at Lawrence, Kansas.

In 1864 Carney sought to obtain the U.S. Senate seat held by James H. Lane, the Republican political boss of Kansas. On 9 February he induced the legislature to elect him senator even though Lane's seat was not to become vacant until March 1865. Public reaction to this maneuver, however, was so adverse that he soon had to renounce his claim to the seat. He then endeavored to use patronage, in the form of officers' commissions to the new regiments, to gain control of the state's Republican party. This too failed when President Abraham Lincoln backed Lane because he believed, with cause, that Carney was in league with antiadministration Republicans. Finally, during the fall election campaign, which took place while a large Confederate army was advancing through Missouri, Carney concluded that Kansas was in no actual danger of invasion. He became convinced instead that the calling out of the militia, which he had done at the request of Major General Samuel R. Curtis, the Union army commander in the state, was merely a trick of Lane's to prevent militia members from voting. Hence on 20 October Carney asked Curtis to revoke martial law, with a view to sending the militia home. His timing could not have been worse: that very same day word arrived that the Confederates were indeed moving toward Kansas, and within a week several battles, the only regular ones of the war, took place in the state. This fiasco ensured the defeat of the anti-Lane Republicans and with it Carney's last hope of supplanting Lane, who was reelected by the legislature in March 1865. To quote a contemporary observer, "If [the people of Kansas] cannot have an honest man in the Senate they prefer that the *rascal* who represents them, should be a man of brains."

On 9 January 1865 Carney completed his term as governor. After serving as mayor of Leavenworth in 1865–1866 and making an unsuccessful bid (interestingly enough with Lane's backing) for the Republican congressional nomination in 1866, he retired from politics and devoted himself to business. He was much better suited to this course, as his prewar career demonstrated. When he died in Leavenworth he possessed what a journalist who interviewed him in 1886 described as an "ample fortune."

• Carney's official correspondence as governor is in the Kansas State Archives, Kansas State Historical Society. The papers of James L. McDowell, Carney's chief political lieutenant, also at the Kansas State Historical Society, contain revealing letters by and about Carney. A detailed account of Carney's career as governor is in Albert Castel, *A Frontier State at War: Kansas, 1861–1865* (1958). The best contemporary account of his career, and the main source of all subsequent biographical sketches, appears in an interview with him by a journalist in the *Chicago Times*, 10 July 1886.

ALBERT CASTEL

CARNEY, William Harvey (1840–after 1901), Union army sergeant and first African American awarded the Congressional Medal of Honor, was born in Norfolk, Virginia, the son of William Carney and Ann, a former slave. Little is known of his early years. As a young boy he expressed an interest in the ministry, and at the age of fourteen, in 1854, he attended a covertly run school under the tutelage of a local minister. Later he moved to New Bedford, Massachusetts, where he took odd jobs in the hope of saving sufficient funds to acquire his religious training.

In 1862, despite strong opposition, Abraham Lincoln signed a bill authorizing the recruitment of African-American troops. Parties attempting to suppress the bill argued that African Americans were incapable of being trained, that in battle they would cower from the enemy, and that arming them was tantamount to giving them the means for insurrection. In January 1863 Governor John Andrew of Massachusetts was authorized to raise a regiment of African Americans. Since the African-American community was relatively small in that state, recruiters also turned to enlisting men from other states. It took some time to convince enough African Americans to enlist, given the availability of employment in the North for African Americans, the threat of being put to death by the Confederate army if they were captured as Union soldiers, and the fact that they would have to serve under white commissioned officers. With such prominent individuals as Frederick Douglass, William Lloyd Garrison, and Wendell Phillips acting as recruiting agents, by the end of April the ranks of the Fifty-fourth Massachusetts Regiment were filled, and Governor Andrew began securing men to fill the Fifty-fifth Massachusetts Regiment. In February 1863 Lieutenant James W. Grace, a businessman turned recruiting agent, opened a recruiting office in New Bedford, a town considered ideal for enlisting suitable men because of the large community of educated African Americans residing there. That year, at the age of twenty-three, Carney joined the Morgan Guards, which eventually became Company C of the Fifty-fourth Massachusetts Regiment rather than a separate regiment. Evidently Carney was viewed as having strong potential, for when the New Bedford enlistees left for camp he was listed on the roster with the rank of sergeant.

Within two months of active duty, Carney participated in one of the bloodiest battles witnessed by African-American soldiers during the Civil War, the assault of 18 July 1863 on Fort Wagner on Morris Island near Charleston, South Carolina. Two days prior to the assault, the men of the Fifty-fourth were first put to the test, seeing action on James Island, South Carolina. Under heavy fire they came to the aid of the Tenth Connecticut Regiment, possibly saving three companies from total annihilation by the Confederate forces. The unwavering front of African Americans coupled with the shower of mortar from the Union navy forced the enemy to retreat. The performance of the African-American regiment impressed General Alfred H. Terry, commander of the 4,000-man division, and as the Union troops withdrew, the Fifty-fourth received its orders to proceed to Morris Island, which controlled the harbor entrance to Charleston.

From its inception, the Fifty-fourth Massachusetts Colored Infantry, under the command of Colonel Robert Gould Shaw, the scion of a wealthy Boston merchant family, had to prove itself worthy of entering the battlefield in Union blues. Thus, even though they had been deprived of sleep, food, and water for several days, Shaw volunteered his men to lead the charge on the bastion, a mission that exacted a terrible toll because of the lack of normal assault preparation. Although open at the rear, Fort Wagner, or Battery Wagner, was only approachable from the south and presented a formidable structure. Equipped with sixteen to twenty guns mounted on the ramparts, its bombproof interior could house an entire regiment of men. Moreover it had artillery support from other Confederate strongholds nearby, including Fort Sumter, James Island, Sullivan's Island, and Fort Gregg. To compound the difficulties of an assault, any frontal invasion would encounter unfavorable terrain, with marshland on the left, sea and then sand stretching in front, and a ditch that forced men advancing from the right flank to wade through knee-high water.

The Union orders were to take the fort by storm with the Fifty-fourth leading the way, followed closely by other units and aided by artillery support from the navy. Thus the men of the Fifty-fourth entered the battlefield, muskets loaded but not capped, bayonets fixed, only to find later that the 9th Maine, 10th Connecticut, 63d Ohio, and 48th and 100th New York were not in position to lead the second wave of the assault. At 7:45 P.M. on 18 July the assault unfolded as the Fifty-fourth Massachusetts Regiment, following the lead of Colonel Shaw, marched toward the fort. When the advancing line was within approximately two or three hundred yards of the perimeter, the Confederate troops opened up a barrage of fire, quickly bringing down the formation. Despite heavy casualties from shell and musket fire, the men of the Fifty-fourth pressed forward.

Prior to the assault Brigadier General George C. Strong, the field commander for whom the battery was later renamed, had addressed the Fifty-fourth, telling the recruits to do honor to the nation. When he asked who would carry the national flag in case the color bearer fell in action, Shaw replied that he would. Shaw was one of the first to reach the summit, but as he raised his sword to rally his men on, shouting "Forward, Fifty-fourth," he was fatally struck in the chest. At the same time the color sergeant, John Wall, who was carrying the flag, also began to fall. Carney was close enough to see both men start to topple, and he heroically commandeered the colors and prevented the flag from falling to the ground. Despite wounds in both legs, his chest, and his right arm, he determinedly forged ahead, clutching the flag, which he planted on the crest next to the regimental colors. He managed to keep it aloft even as he lay on the outer slope surrounded by a hail of bullets. The lines of the Fifty-fourth Massachusetts were decimated by the time a second charge of reinforcements reached them. Only then was Carney able to creep back to friendly lines, albeit on one knee, still determined to protect the colors. When he eventually staggered into a hospital tent, he collapsed, uttering the words, "Boys, the old flag never touched the ground."

For his act of courage, Sergeant Carney was one of four soldiers from the Fifty-fourth Massachusetts who received the Gilmore Medal, and he was the first African American awarded the Congressional Medal of Honor. The citation of the latter read, "For conspicuous gallantry and intrepidity at the risk of life, above and beyond the call of duty, in action involving actual conflict with an opposing armed force."

When Carney was discharged from the army in 1864, he returned to New Bedford, Massachusetts. After spending some time at home he moved, for no known reason, to California. He returned to New Bedford in 1870. For the remainder of his years he resided in Massachusetts, where he worked as one of four African-American letter carriers, retiring in 1901 after thirty-one years of service. Following his retirement from the postal service he worked as a state employee in Boston. He died probably in Boston.

Carney's home in Norfolk, Virginia, is a historic site, officially known as the "Sergeant Carney Memorial House." The American flag saved by Carney resides in Memorial Hall, Boston, Massachusetts, and his features are enshrined on Boston Common in the monument sculpted by Augustus Saint-Gaudens that pays tribute to Colonel Shaw and his warriors.

• Two informative biographical sketches of Sergeant Carney are in Robert Ewell Greene, *Black Defenders of America 1775–1973: A Reference and Pictorial History* (1974), and Wilhelmena S. Robinson, *Historical Negro Biographies* (1970). Descriptions of the assault on Fort Wagner are in Luis F. Emilio, *A Brave Black Regiment: History of the Fifty-fourth Regiment of Massachusetts Volunteer Infantry, 1863–1865* (1894); Corporal James Henry Gooding, *On the Altar of Freedom: A Black Soldier's Civil War Letters from the Front* (1991); Hondon B. Hargrove, *Black Union Soldiers in the Civil War* (1988); and Charles H. Wesley and Patricia W. Romero, *Negro Americans in the Civil War: From Slavery to Citizenship* (1967). The best depiction of the history and struggles of the Fifty-fourth Regiment is in the feature film *Glory* (1989), based partially on Peter Burchard, *One Gallant Rush: Robert Gould Shaw and His Brave Black Regiment* (1965).

DALYCE NEWBY

CARNOCHAN, John Murray (4 July 1817–28 Oct. 1887), surgeon, was born in Savannah, Georgia, the son of John Carnochan, a planter and merchant, and Harriet Frances Putnam. His weak constitution led his parents to take him to his father's ancestral home in Galloway, Scotland, where he lived with two maiden aunts until he turned eleven. After completing his secondary education in Edinburgh, Scotland, he matriculated at the University of Edinburgh, where he studied philosophy, chemistry, and anatomy and graduated in 1834. He was then granted admission to the Royal College of Surgeons of Edinburgh but for unknown reasons was compelled to return to Savannah that same year. Shortly thereafter he enrolled in the College of Surgeons and Physicians in New York City, where he studied with Valentine Mott, a master at reconnecting and tying off blood vessels. Carnochan was so deft an operator that while still a student he dissected a human foot in such minute detail that the individual nerve fibers could be seen. He received the M.D. in 1836 and spent the next six years studying surgery at the École de Medicine in Paris, France. In 1842 he went to London, England, where he studied surgery for another five years.

In 1847 Carnochan turned down the opportunity to become the partner of the eminent British surgeon Robert Liston, a pioneer in the use of ether as an anesthetic, and returned to New York City to open his own medical and surgical practice. His interest in birth defects involving that part of the thighbone that fits into the hip socket led him to perform several innovative operations to redress this problem, the results of which he described at length in *Etiology, Pathology, and Treatment of Congenital Dislocation of the Head of the Femur* (1850).

In 1850 Carnochan took on the additional duties of surgeon in chief at the recently opened State Emigrant Hospital on Ward's Island, at the time the largest hospital in the United States. In 1851, the same year he became professor of surgery at the year-old New York Medical College, he performed two particularly unusual operations. When a patient's thigh swelled to dangerously abnormal size following a parasitic infestation in the veins, he devised a way to save the limb from amputation by successfully tying off the femoral artery. When another patient's lower jaw began to decay as a result of a bacterial infection arising from typhoid fever, he removed it in its entirety; though a similar operation had been performed thirty years earlier by Mott, the procedure remained a difficult one.

In 1856 Carnochan married Estelle Morris, with whom he had no children. That same year he became the first surgeon to relieve a patient from severe and chronic facial pain by removing the Meckel's ganglion and a lengthy branch of the maxillary nerve. He also pioneered the relief of abnormal swelling of the head, face, neck, and tongue by tying off the various carotid arteries; removed two bones from a forearm without costing the patient the loss of that limb's use; experimented with ways to eliminate stones by removing them surgically and by crushing them in the bladder; and developed several techniques for removing diseased ovaries and ovarian tumors. He detailed many of these groundbreaking procedures in *Contributions to Operative Surgery and Surgical Pathology* (9 vols., 1858–1878); the accompanying illustrations were drawn by his wife.

Carnochan's Scottish upbringing and many years of residence in Europe and New York offset whatever sympathy his southern birth and his association with the college's predominantly southern student body may have engendered for the Confederate cause. He served during the Civil War as a surgeon with the Union Army of the Potomac and proved to be a brilliant operator under battlefield conditions. He distinguished himself particularly in 1864 during ten days of intermittent but ferocious fighting near Spotsylvania Court House, Virginia, that included action at the "Bloody Angle."

After the war Carnochan returned to his medical practice and the emigrant hospital; he did not resume his teaching career because the medical college had closed its doors in 1863 for lack of students. In 1870–1871 he also served as health officer for the Port of New York. Although he continued to practice privately until his death, in 1875 he gave up his position at the hospital in order to devote more time to completing the remaining volumes of *Contributions*. Late in his career he became interested in the possibility that a physical defect in a specific portion of the brain causes mental illness, a topic he addressed in *Cerebral Localization in Relation to Insanity* (1884). He died in New York City.

Carnochan was one of the foremost surgeons of his day. He contributed to the development of American medicine by performing several innovative operations and disseminating the details as a teacher and author.

• Carnochan's papers have not been located. His contributions are discussed in Francis R. Packard, *History of Medicine in the United States* (1931; repr. 1963). An obituary is in the *Medico-Legal Journal* 5 (1887–1188): 346.

CHARLES W. CAREY, JR.

CARONDELET, Báron de (bap. 29 July 1747–10 Aug. 1807), governor of Louisiana and West Florida, was born Francisco Luis Héctor Carondelet into a distinguished Burgundian family in Noyelles, Flanders, the son of Jean Louis Nicolas de Carondelet, baron de Carondelet et de Noyelles, and Marie-Angélique Bernard de Rasoir. His family was a branch of the Carondelets who had maintained their loyalty to Spain. At sixteen, Carondelet entered the Spanish Walloon Guards and soon was assigned to Madrid. In 1767 he became an *alférez* (sublieutenant) and the next year entered the Knights of Malta. In 1775 he participated in General Alejandro O'Reilly's ill-fated attack on Algiers, for which he won praise from O'Reilly. From his 1777 marriage to María de Castaños y Aragorri, he acquired important ties to the Spanish military and court.

During Spain's participation in the American Revolution, Carondelet served in the 1781 battle of Pensacola under Bernardo de Gálvez against Britain and again distinguished himself. Several years later he petitioned the king for a post and received the intendancy of San Salvador in Central America. During his two years as intendant, he supervised the world's leading producer of indigo, resettled Indians in new towns and promoted their assimilation, improved food and water supplies, created a local mail system, established a disciplined militia, and tried to administer the province for both the Crown and local interests. In 1791 he was named governor and intendant of Louisiana and West Florida, replacing Esteban Miró.

His work in San Salvador gave him experience as an administrator, and he did much in Louisiana. It did not, however, prepare him for the complex problems he would face. His inability to speak English also hurt him as governor. Soon after he assumed office on 30 December 1791, Miró and Manuel Gayoso de Lemos, governor of the Natchez district in West Florida, briefed him on conditions in the colony: a boundary controversy with the United States; possible invasion by Britain, France, or the United States; Indian and slave unrest; and the presence of radical Frenchmen inspired by the French Revolution. Within Louisiana he needed to maintain the strength of the Fixed Louisiana Regiment, rebuild fortifications, attract immigrants to increase Louisiana's small population, and promote economic well-being. For several years he had the support of his immediate superior, his brother-in-law Luis de las Casas, captain general of Cuba, who helped Carondelet by sending troops to Louisiana, permitting him to build defenses, and by providing money.

From the start of his governorship, Carondelet spent large sums to ensure the security of Louisiana. He strengthened fortifications, called for new recruits and troops from Havana, reorganized the militia, and tried to attract loyal European, as opposed to dubious American, immigrants. He attempted to use the Southern Indians and the powerful but often hostile Osage Indians as sepoys in the protection of Spanish lands. He rebuilt New Orleans's defenses, lighted the city streets, and established syndics to assist post commandants throughout lower Louisiana. When French Jacobinism surfaced, he deported suspected revolutionaries, often dispensing with legal formalities, and brought militiamen from the lower Louisiana posts to quell revolutionary ardor in the capital city. The growth of New Orleans, a surge in commerce, particularly with the United States, the establishment of a theater and newspaper, construction of a canal that linked the city to Lake Pontchartrain, and new regulations in a variety of areas showed his dedication as an administrator.

Carondelet built Fort San Fernando de las Barrancas (at modern Memphis), finished the forts at Nogales (modern Vicksburg) and at the mouth of the Mississippi River, and kept a squadron of gunboats on the river, all for protection against foreign invasion. He initially refused to evacuate the Mississippi's left bank down to the thirty-first parallel as called for in the 1795 Treaty of San Lorenzo (Pinckney's Treaty) because it meant surrendering the important forts of San Fernando, Nogales, and Natchez, in addition to Confederación and San Esteban in West Florida. Evacuation finally occurred after he left Louisiana.

The governor, however, made errors in judgment, overreacting to rumors of invasion or conspiracy and refusing to follow sound advice. He mistakenly revived James Wilkinson's languishing conspiracy to separate Kentucky from the United States, and his attempts to use the Indians as a buffer against U.S. encroachment failed. His efforts to enforce Spain's humanitarian slave laws alienated the planter class, which later refused to support him against revolutionaries. Carondelet's relatively lenient attitude toward slaves and the French Revolution helped to trigger the abortive slave insurrection at Pointe Coupee, which was punished harshly. As a result, Carondelet issued a new, stern slave code that placed slaves under the authority of any whites, not just slave masters. His permissiveness, which let Louisiana trade more freely than Spanish laws allowed, led to his removal as intendant but not as governor in October 1793. Despite his failures, the Crown promoted him to brigadier general in 1793, and the New Orleans Cabildo set up a plaque honoring him in 1796, the only governor it singled out for praise in this way.

A controversial governor, Carondelet has been called quick tempered, gullible, and impulsive. But he was also vigorous and provided leadership where a more cautious governor would have waited for royal approval before acting. The situation in Louisiana in the 1790s was often fluid, demanding answers to complex and sometimes intractable problems. Frequently cut off from Spain and even Cuba by enemy naval blockades and short of manpower, money, and instructions, Carondelet had to act on his own. Perhaps his greatest legacy was that Louisiana and West Florida were still Spanish when his term ended, and when they were lost, it was not because of his governorship.

On 5 August 1797 Carondelet surrendered his office to Gayoso and soon departed for Quito, Ecuador, where he had been named commandant general of Quito and president of the Audiencia of Quito. He died there.

• Archival information on Carondelet is in the Archivo General de Indias, Seville; the Archivo Historico Nacional, Madrid; and the Archivo General de Simancas, near Valladolid. Aside from Thomas M. Fiehrer, "The Baron de Carondelet as Agent of Bourbon Reform: A Study of Spanish Colonial Administration in the Years of the French Revolution" (Ph.D. diss., Tulane Univ., 1977), Carondelet has not received the attention that is due him. Useful information on him, however, can be gleaned from Charles E. Gayarré, *History of Louisiana*, 5th ed. (1965); James Thomas McGowan, "Creation of a Slave Society: Louisiana Plantations in the Eighteenth Century" (Ph.D. diss., Univ. of Rochester, 1976); Ernest R. Liljegren, "Jacobinism in Spanish Louisiana," *Louisiana Historical Quarterly* 22, no. 1 (1939): 3–53; Gilbert C. Din and A. P. Nasatir, *The Imperial Osages: Spanish-Indian Diplomacy in the Mississippi Valley* (1983); Din, "Spain's Immigration Policy in Louisiana and the American Penetration, 1792–1803," *Southwestern Historical Quarterly* 76, no. 3 (1972–1973): 255–76; and Carl A. Brasseaux,

"François-Louis Hector, Baron de Carondelet et Noyelles," in *The Louisiana Governors: From Iberville to Edwards*, ed. Joseph G. Dawson III (1990).

GILBERT C. DIN

CAROTHERS, Wallace Hume (27 Apr. 1896–29 Apr. 1937), chemist, was born in Burlington, Iowa, to Ira Hume Carothers, an educator, and Mary Evalina McMullin. The family moved to Des Moines, Iowa, when he was five so that his father could accept a teaching position at Capital City Commercial College. In 1914 Wallace enrolled at Capital City to study accounting, and in 1915 he matriculated at Tarkio (Missouri) College, where he studied chemistry and physics and taught accounting. After receiving his B.S. degree from Tarkio in 1920, he enrolled in the University of Illinois, receiving his M.S. in 1921 and his Ph.D. in organic chemistry in 1924.

Carothers began teaching college chemistry while he was still an undergraduate. Having taken every chemistry course Tarkio had to offer as a freshman and sophomore, he spent his junior and senior years teaching them when the department's sole professor resigned and the college was unable to hire a suitable replacement. After receiving his M.S., he taught analytical and physical chemistry at the University of South Dakota for a year in order to earn enough money to complete graduate school. He taught organic chemistry at the University of Illinois from 1924 to 1926 and at Harvard University from 1926 to 1928.

Although Carothers was an effective classroom teacher, he much preferred to spend his time in the research laboratory. As a student he dreamed of opening a laboratory of his own where he could "test some ideas of vast commercial importance" (Hounshell and Smith, p. 230). His interest in both chemistry and physics led him to investigate the theory, first propagated by Gilbert N. Lewis in 1916, that chemical bonds could be formed by the sharing of electrons as well as by their transfer. This line of inquiry led to the publication in 1924 of Carothers's findings concerning the nature of the double covalent bond, by which the atoms of certain organic molecules share two pairs of electrons instead of only one.

The article apparently brought Carothers to the attention of Charles M. A. Stine, chemical department director of the E. I. du Pont de Nemours Company. In 1927 the company committed itself to promoting fundamental research in colloid chemistry, catalysis, organic synthesis, and polymerization; however, the chemists with established reputations in these fields were college professors who either disdained the commercial applications of their work or preferred the independence of an academic situation. Consequently, Stine began recruiting young chemists who he believed had the potential to do great things; he offered Carothers escape from the drudgery of teaching undergraduates and an opportunity to conduct pure research as Du Pont's director of research in organic chemistry. At first Carothers did not want to leave the security of academia, but he changed his mind in 1928 when he became convinced of the complete intellectual freedom and financial support that Stine and Du Pont intended to give him.

Before leaving Harvard, Carothers began preparing for his new job by investigating the construction of polymers—complex molecules consisting of long chains of simple molecules arranged in repetitive configurations. Inspired by the work of Leo Baekeland, who in 1907 polymerized the first known commercial plastic, and Hermann Staudinger, whose experiments with polymers eventually won him the Nobel Prize for chemistry in 1953, Carothers hoped to synthesize many useful organic compounds through molecular bonding. After joining Du Pont, he made long chains of polyesters by combining alcohols and acids in such a way that the molecule on one end of the chain was always capable of further reaction. By 1929 he and his eight-man research team had shed much light on the nature of polymers; specifically, they demonstrated conclusively that polymeric molecules were held together by simple covalent bonds, instead of by some unknown force peculiar to polymers (as had been suspected), and that there was no theoretical limit to the length of a polymeric chain.

In April 1930 Carothers's research group made an accidental discovery that led to the development of the first high-grade synthetic rubber. Earlier that year, Carothers had been asked to investigate the chemical structure of divinylacetylene (DVA), a short-chain polymer that had attracted the attention of earlier Du Pont researchers seeking a way to synthesize rubber. While producing high-grade DVA, Arnold M. Collins, a member of the group, recovered a liquid byproduct that emulsified into a white, rubbery mass a few days later. Named "chloroprene" by Carothers, the liquid was soon found to possess a molecular structure analogous to that of isoprene, the chemical constituent of rubber. Further experimentation showed that chloroprene resulted from the reaction between monovinylacetylene, a derivative of DVA, and cuprous chloride. Chloroprene was turned over to Du Pont's Jackson Laboratory later that summer and was developed commercially into neoprene, an oil-resistant synthetic rubber compound used to make shoe soles, industrial hoses, and adhesives.

Also in April 1930, Carothers and his associates made another important discovery, which eventually led to the invention of the first commercially acceptable synthetic fiber. While trying to make the longest polymeric chain ever produced in a laboratory, Carothers discovered that the water formed during the production of polyesters impeded the reaction between alcohols and acids in such a way as to impose an upper limit on the length of a chain. Accordingly, he and Julian W. Hill, another group member, developed a "molecular still" to condense the water from the polymerization mixture. In the process, they created a molten polyester that could be drawn into pliable filaments that, when cooled, could be stretched to form very strong fibers. Despite their strength, these fibers were unsuited for commercial use because their melting temperature was too low. Other fibers produced from polyamides—ammonia-acid compounds that can be molded while hot but assume a permanent shape when cooled—possessed melting temperatures so high that they could not be spun into yarn. In 1934 Carothers and Donald D. Coffman, another member of the group, finally polymerized a carefully purified amino acid ester that produced the tough, elastic, heat-resistant synthetic fiber known today as nylon. Other Du Pont chemists developed nylon into a vast array of products, the most popular one being women's hosiery. Over the next twenty years, the commercial development of nylon, which led to that of other synthetic fibers such as Orlon and Dacron, allowed Du Pont to increase net sales 600 percent and to triple its net income.

Unfortunately, Carothers did not live to see the full impact of his discoveries. He had suffered bouts of depression long before joining Du Pont, but they intensified after mid-1930, when Stine was replaced as the director of the fundamental research program by Elmer K. Bolton, whose style and philosophy differed significantly from Stine's. Bolton believed that research should pay for itself by solving specific, well-defined problems that had commercial applications, and that researchers should therefore be managed rather than allowed to pursue whatever line of inquiry struck their fancy. This was what Carothers had feared when he rejected Stine's first overture. Although Bolton was largely responsible for directing Carothers's research toward the development of nylon, Carothers felt his reputation as a scientist was cheapened by the change in operation, particularly when Bolton was reluctant to let him publish his findings. Nonetheless, when offered the opportunity to become chairman of the University of Chicago's chemistry department in 1934, Carothers elected to remain at Du Pont. Shortly after the development of the first nylon fibers, he became depressed enough to seek psychiatric help. The bouts of depression grew worse and more frequent and culminated in a nervous breakdown in 1936, just a few months after his marriage to Helen Everett Sweetman. His wife's pregnancy with their one child and his sister's death the following year compounded his melancholia, and two weeks after filing the basic nylon patent application, he committed suicide in Philadelphia, Pennsylvania.

Carothers published his findings concerning polymers in more than thirty scholarly articles, and the work of his research group resulted in the filing of more than seventy patents. He served as associate editor of the *Journal of the American Chemical Society* from 1929 to 1937 and as an editor of *Organic Syntheses* from 1930 to 1937. He was a member of the American Academy for the Advancement of Science and was elected to the National Academy of Sciences in 1936. In 1946 Du Pont named its synthetic fiber research laboratory in his honor.

Carothers was a pioneer in the field of polymer science and was considered by many to be the best organic chemist of his day. His pivotal role in the development of commercial polymers, especially nylon and neoprene, led to the creation of the synthetic fiber and synthetic rubber industries.

• Carothers's papers are in the Wallace H. Carothers Correspondence Collection and the Du Pont R&D History Project Collection in the Hagley Museum and Library, Wilmington, Del. His laboratory notebooks and related materials are in the E. I. du Pont de Nemours and Company Records. Many of his technical papers are in *Collected Papers of Wallace Hume Carothers on High Polymeric Substances*, ed. H. Mark Whitby and G. S. Whitby (1940). His biography and a complete bibliography of his work appear in Roger Adams, "Wallace Hume Carothers," National Academy of Sciences, *Biographical Memoirs* 20 (1939): 293–309. His scientific contributions are discussed in David A. Hounshell and John Kenly Smith, Jr., *Science and Corporate Strategy: Du Pont R&D, 1902–1980* (1988), and Graham D. Taylor and Patricia E. Sudnik, *Du Pont and the International Chemical Industry* (1984). An obituary is in the *New York Times*, 30 Apr. 1937.

CHARLES W. CAREY, JR.

CARPENTER, Cyrus Clay (24 Nov. 1829–29 May 1898), politician and farmer, was born in Harford, Susquehanna County, Pennsylvania, the son of Asahel Carpenter, a farmer, and Amanda Thayer. Orphaned during his early teens and raised by relatives, Carpenter attended public school in Harford. Between 1848 and 1851 he alternated teaching jobs with attendance at Harford Academy. During these early years he developed the temperance and antislavery views that he held during his adult years.

Chronic money shortages motivated Carpenter to migrate to Fort Dodge, Iowa, in 1854 via Johnstown, Ohio, where he spent the years 1851–1854 teaching school. His first employment at Fort Dodge was as a farm laborer, surveyor, and schoolteacher. In partnership with his brother, Robert Emmett, he opened an office in 1855 as land agent and surveyor but achieved only limited financial success. Active in the newly organized Republican party, Carpenter was elected Webster County surveyor in 1855 and also served as a delegate to a district convention that selected a representative to the state's constitutional convention.

The year 1857 was an eventful one for Carpenter. In March he enhanced his local reputation by participating in a difficult rescue mission to aid survivors of a massacre at Spirit Lake in Dickinson County perpetrated by Ink-pa-do-tah and a group of Sioux seeking revenge for an earlier murder of a Sioux and his family. In August he attended the state Republican convention as a member of the Webster County delegation. In October he won election to the state legislature. At Des Moines he supported the Republican party agenda but did not especially distinguish himself. Persistent money concerns prompted him to decline a second term in the legislature, and he did not attend the state Republican convention in 1859. In 1860–1861 he spent twenty months in the Colorado gold fields but failed to acquire his desired fortune.

During the Civil War Carpenter entered the Union army as a captain of commissary and served under a number of notable commanders, including Grenville M. Dodge, who later became a major leader of the Iowa Republican party. During a furlough in 1864, Carpenter married Susan Catherine "Kate" Burkholder following a six-year engagement period; they had no children. At this point he accepted his wife's Methodist denomination; he had been a Congregationalist. After his release from military service, Carpenter ran for election to the state legislature in 1865 but lost by sixteen votes. Until his election in 1866 to the first of two terms as register of the State Land Office, Carpenter lived off his military savings, farming, and livestock operations. Politically, he aligned himself with the Radical wing of the Republican party, supporting African-American suffrage and opposing Andrew Johnson's presidency.

Geographical as well as political considerations combined to encourage Carpenter to seek his party's gubernatorial nomination in 1871: he was a resident of northwestern Iowa, whose leaders sought to place a local resident in the governor's office; he had a reputation for honesty; he had the endorsement of Republican state party leaders; and he was acceptable to the rank-and-file party membership across the state. Carpenter's margin of victory at the October election was strong.

As governor Carpenter supported the establishment of a "normal institute" to train teachers, efforts to attract industry to Iowa, equitable taxation of railroad property, and the elimination of the death penalty. He took a neutral stance on the major goal of the state Grange: he did not oppose the regulation of railroad freight rates but believed the U.S. Congress should deal with the matter. Such regulation was deadlocked in the Iowa legislature during Carpenter's first term.

A Liberal Republican minority clashed with the Radical Republicans, mainly on national issues. The Liberals opposed a second term for President Ulysses S. Grant and sought civil service reform, amnesty for the South, and free trade legislation. For president they nominated Horace Greeley, whom the Democrats also endorsed. Carpenter maintained his Radical credentials partly by endorsing his party's state and national candidates and partly by opposing the demands of the Liberals.

Carpenter's reputation for honesty and integrity was sorely tested by the alleged embezzlement of state funds by Treasurer Samuel E. Rankin and Deputy Treasurer Isaac Brandt. Uncovered in December 1872, the scandal dragged on for three years and almost engulfed the state Republican party along with Carpenter's administration. Eventually a jury exonerated Rankin, while the Iowa Supreme Court voided Brandt's conviction. In such an atmosphere Carpenter managed to win reelection as governor in 1873, but his margin of victory was smaller than in 1871. Again, as in the previous campaign, national issues dominated the election. On the state level, both parties called for regulation of railroad freight rates in their platforms.

Following his gubernatorial service, Carpenter was appointed second comptroller of the U.S. Treasury, a reward for loyal support of his party. He had campaigned for Republican state and national candidates in Iowa during various elections since 1866. After serving in Washington, D.C., for twenty months, Carpenter resigned to return to Iowa to campaign for the congressional seat from his northwestern district. Prior to his election to Congress in the fall of 1878, Carpenter served as president of the Board of Railroad Commissioners.

Carpenter entered the Forty-sixth Congress as a member of the Republican minority. As a freshman congressman he took part in no debates, and he voted on bills and amendments as his party caucus dictated. His only committee assignment was membership on the Committee of War Claims. Except to eulogize a late member of the Iowa congressional delegation, Carpenter delivered no memorable speeches during his first term in the House. He easily won election to a second term as Republicans swept all congressional seats in Iowa in 1880.

During his second term in Congress, Carpenter was placed on more prestigious committees, such as the Agriculture and Education and Labor committees, and was more vocal on the floor. He spoke in support of an appropriation to improve the Missouri River and the creation of a Department of Agriculture with cabinet status, but he opposed the Chinese exclusion bill. He introduced legislation to divide Iowa into two judicial districts, a goal of Iowans since 1870. Following the expiration of this term, Carpenter faced a losing battle for another nomination to Congress, because his old Ninth Congressional District had been merged into a newly created Tenth District.

Upon leaving Congress in early 1883, Carpenter returned to Fort Dodge to become a partner in the Fort Dodge Loan and Trust Company. In the fall of 1883 he was elected to the Iowa legislature, where his service was far more significant and effective than it had been during his initial experience in Iowa's lower house. He was floor leader of the Iowa House, chairman of the Ways and Means Committee, and chairman of the Republican legislative caucus. He retired from active politics following the expiration of his legislative term but continued to campaign for his party when requested, especially in behalf of his protégé, Jonathan Dolliver, a future congressman and senator.

Needing a steady source of income as his business venture and farm were uncertain bases for financial security, Carpenter agreed to serve as postmaster of Fort Dodge, a position he held from 1889 to 1894. During his final years he attended to his correspondence, stumped the state for Republican candidates, and wrote articles for the *Annals of Iowa*. He died at his home in Fort Dodge.

Carpenter spent most of his adult life in a variety of elective or appointive offices on the state or national levels. Yet it cannot be said that his career was markedly distinguished. His importance, perhaps, was more subtle. Viewed by party leaders and voters as reliable, honest, and trustworthy, Carpenter contributed an important element to the maintenance of Republican political power in Iowa and on the national level during the years after the Civil War.

• Carpenter's papers, including his diary, are in the State Historical Society of Iowa in Iowa City. Benjamin F. Shambaugh compiled his official papers as governor in *The Messages and Proclamations of the Governors of Iowa*, vol. 4 (1903). Mildred Throne's fine biography, *Cyrus Clay Carpenter and Iowa Politics, 1854–1898* (1974), was published after her death by the State Historical Society of Iowa. Leland Sage, *William Boyd Allison* (1956), provides additional information on Carpenter and the Iowa Republican leadership. An obituary is in the *Fort Dodge Messenger*, 3 June 1898.

MORTON M. ROSENBERG

CARPENTER, Frank George (8 May 1855–18 June 1924), journalist and author of travel books, was born in Mansfield, Ohio, the son of George F. Carpenter, an attorney, and Jeannette Reid. Frank attended public school in Mansfield and then went on to the University of Wooster, earning a Phi Beta Kappa key and graduating in 1877. He did further study at Ohio State University. In 1878 or 1879 he was hired as the Columbus (Ohio) correspondent for the *Cleveland Leader*. With an insatiable curiosity coupled with wanderlust, Carpenter began roaming the world in search of stories in 1881, traveling first to Asia. In 1882 he returned to the United States, and from then until 1888 he was the *Leader*'s Washington correspondent. In 1883 he married Joanna Condict. They had two children.

Carpenter's lively dispatches were widely reprinted. His style was chatty, and he preferred the human interest story to political analysis. Of President Grover Cleveland's 1886 marriage he wrote, "The President's matrimonial affairs are the chief topic of this week's gossip over the tea tables of Washington. Veteran know-alls . . . report that Miss [Frances] Folsom is laying in a Paris trousseau of extravagant dimensions. Others hint that Cleveland is footing all the expenses of this European trip" (*Carp's Washington*, p. 46). A friend wrote that Carpenter "cast a wide net" and everything "is fish that comes in his direction, to be written of now or stored away for use later on." Twentieth-century social critic Cleveland Amory said of him, "In his search for news and human interest, Carp meets everybody, goes everywhere, sees everything."

Hired by the American Press Association in 1885 and the *New York World* in 1887, Carpenter was able to secure enough assignments to pay for an around-the-world trip in 1888–1889. His task was to send one "letter" each week to twelve periodicals, describing life as he saw it. He covered the aftermath of hurricanes, famines, and political revolutions.

Following the Spanish-American War in 1898, Americans became interested in learning about the world, including its various cultures and inhabitants. Although most could not learn about their global neighbors firsthand, many turned readily to Frank Carpenter's enthusiastic and sympathetic descriptions of foreign peoples and places.

Carpenter's first book, *South America: Social, Industrial, and Political*, was published in 1900. Apparently unedited, it was criticized in *The Nation* as being "destitute of literary finish and also lacking in systematic arrangement." His later books, published by Doubleday, were polished and well organized. They were written for the armchair traveler in the style of a nineteenth-century essayist, always aware of his audience. His book, *Java and the East Indies* (1923), opened, "In beginning our travels in these far-away lands, I shall ask you to imagine ourselves connected by a radio so strong that it will carry a whisper halfway round the globe. You are comfortably seated in your own home, and I am . . . south of the Equator. . . . You can almost hear the rustling of the coconut palms over my head as their long leaves sway to and fro under the winds of the tropical sea."

In 1919 he reported on the devastation in Europe following World War I. During his travels he interviewed such luminaries as the king of Korea, the king of Greece, the khedive of Egypt, and Prince Otto von Bismarck of Prussia. More often he described day-to-day life from the point of view of a good-hearted American who believed implicitly in progress through industry and who enjoyed the adventure of new experiences. His wife accompanied him and was described by a contemporary as a good companion, "putting up with hardship and helping her husband gather valuable information."

Carpenter also compiled a series of geographical readers for youngsters, introducing them to exotic cultures. All were published by American Book Company and were popular enough to go through many reprintings. The titles include *Africa* (1905), *Around the World with Children: An Introduction to Geography* (1917), *Asia* (1897), *Australia* (1904), *Europe* (1902), *North America* (1898), *South America* (1915), *How the World Is Clothed* (1908), *How the World Is Housed* (1911), and *How the World Is Fed* (1907). His general trade books, all published by Doubleday, include *Alaska, Our Northern Wonderland* (1923), *Along the Paraná and the Amazon* (1925), *The Alps, the Danube and the Near East* (1924), *Australia, New Zealand and Some Islands of the South Seas* (1924), *The British Isles and the Baltic States* (1927), *Cairo to Kisuma: Egypt–the Sudan–Kenya* (1923), *Canada and Newfoundland* (1926), *China* (1925), *France to Scandinavia* (1923), *From Bangkok to Bombay* (1924), *From Tangier to Tripoli* (1923), *The Holy Land and Syria* (1922), *Java and the East Indies* (1923), *Lands of the Andes and the Desert* (1924), *Lands of the Caribbean* (1927), *Mexico* (1924), *The Tail of the Hemispheres: Chile and Argentina* (1923), *Through the Philippines and Hawaii* (1925), and *Uganda to the Cape* (1924).

Frank Carpenter was a fellow of the Royal Geographical Society of Washington and a member of Beta Theta Pi. In 1940 he was inducted into the Ohio State University Journalism Hall of Fame. He died while in Nanking, China.

Carpenter is remembered as a populizer of cultural anthropology and geography, although he probably would have described himself as just a reporter having a good time. It is difficult to estimate how many lives he reached with his books or what impact they had on the generation of school children who read them. He was a small part of the general movement from parochialism to internationalism in the first half of the twentieth century.

• *Carp's Washington* (1960), reprints of his dispatches on social affairs, gossip, and human interest stories, was compiled and edited by his daughter Frances Carpenter. His papers relating to that book are in the Library of Congress. A biographical reference can be found in William Coyle, *Ohio Authors and Their Books* (1962). An obituary is in the *Mansfield (Ohio) News*, 18 June 1924.

BETTY BURNETT

CARPENTER, John Alden (28 Feb. 1876–26 Apr. 1951), composer, was born in Park Ridge, Illinois, the son of George B. Carpenter, the president of a large chandlery, and Elizabeth Curtis Greene, an amateur singer and organist. He was named after a distant forebear, the legendary pilgrim John Alden.

Carpenter began piano lessons with his mother at age five and subsequently studied piano with Amy Fay and piano, theory, and composition with William C. E. Seeboeck. While at Harvard (1893–1897), he studied music with John Knowles Paine and published a few songs and piano pieces. In 1897 he entered his father's business, becoming a partner in 1901 and vice president in 1909. He retired in 1936, after almost forty years of juggling careers in music and business. In 1900 he married Rue Winterbotham, an artist, interior designer, arts collector, and admired hostess. The Carpenters collaborated on two sets of children's songs—*When Little Boys Sing* (1904) and *Improving Songs for Anxious Children* (1907)—whose whimsical humor and sweet nostalgia became earmarks of the composer's music.

Carpenter pursued his musical studies with Edward Elgar in Rome (1904–1907) and then with theorist Bernard Ziehn in Chicago (1908–1912). Under Ziehn's tutelage, Carpenter's music became both more expert and daring, resulting in such works as the 1911 Violin Sonata and many sensitive songs and culminating in the 1913 song cycle, *Gitanjali*, based on poems by Rabindranath Tagore, which brought Carpenter to the front ranks of America's most advanced and sophisticated composers.

In 1914 Carpenter composed his first large orchestral work—the six-movement tone poem, *Adventures in a Perambulator*—for the Chicago Symphony Orchestra and its conductor, Frederick Stock. The music, which depicts a day in the life of a baby from the baby's point of view, derived from Strauss and Debussy but also quoted Irving Berlin's "Alexander's Ragtime Band." In part inspired by the composer's only child, Ginny, *Perambulator* became a huge success, delighting young and old around the world. In 1915 Carpenter had another success with his sparkling Concertino for Piano and Orchestra, whose use of various popular idioms made it a landmark in the development of American music. During World War I, Carpenter helped supervise music for the armed services, and in 1917 he composed the popular patriotic anthem, "The Home Road."

By this time Carpenter had begun to feel the influence of Stravinsky, and in 1917–1918 he collaborated with the Russian choreographer Adolph Bolm and the set designer Robert Edmond Jones on the ballet, *The Birthday of the Infanta*, after a fairy tale by Oscar Wilde. Although it was one of the first important ballets created in the United States, its score failed to enter the repertory despite repeated revisions and arrangements by the composer. In 1921 Carpenter collaborated with Bolm and the American cartoonist George Herriman on another landmark, the ballet *Krazy Kat*, after Herriman's newspaper comic strip of the same name. Subtitled "A Jazz Pantomime," *Krazy Kat* became one of the first concert works to openly make use of jazz (by which Carpenter primarily meant popular songs and society dance music).

In 1923–1924 Carpenter collaborated once again with Robert Edmond Jones on his third and last ballet, *Skyscrapers: A Ballet of Modern American Life.* Originally commissioned by Sergei Diaghilev for the Ballets Russes (the only such commission ever granted an American composer), the Metropolitan Opera successfully launched the work in 1926 after Diaghilev refused a timely mounting. The ballet begins with a depiction of menial labor set against mechanical sounds, changes scene to an amusement park, where the sounds and images of industrial work are transformed into play, and concludes with a return to work. As a ballet, the work was only occasionally revived, as in Munich in 1928, but in concert form *Skyscrapers* enjoyed numerous performances in the United States and elsewhere.

Carpenter further experimented with "jazz" in *A Little Bit of Jazz* (1925), composed for Paul Whiteman and his Palais Royal Orchestra, and in his poignant 1926–1927 settings of four Langston Hughes poems, *Four Negro Songs.* However, by 1926, Carpenter had begun to regard the use of jazz as somewhat faddish, comparable to the use of the whole-tone scale in the 1910s. The stylish 1927 String Quartet marked a transition to the composer's more romantic and intimate work of the 1930s. In 1931 Carpenter composed a choral tribute to George Washington, *Song of Faith*, commissioned by the U.S. Congress in honor of Washington's two-hundredth birthday, and in 1932, he completed *Patterns* for orchestra, a belated offering to Koussevitzky and the Boston Symphony Orchestra in celebration of the orchestra's fiftieth anniversary.

In 1931 Rue Carpenter died suddenly of a cerebral hemorrhage, and in 1933 Carpenter married Ellen Waller Borden, the mother-in-law of Adlai Stevenson by a previous marriage and one of Chicago's wealthiest women. It was sometimes asserted that Carpenter's abilities declined without Rue by his side, but in fact, since 1913, Carpenter had carried on an impassioned love affair with Ellen, who inspired many of his most successful works. Honeymooning on the French Riviera in 1933, Carpenter composed one of his masterpieces, the elegiac tone-poem *Sea Drift*, based on Walt Whitman's poem of the same name. In the 1930s Carpenter, long a world traveler, became more and more interested in non-Western musics. This new enthusiasm was reflected in the use of an Algerian tune in the 1934 Piano Quintet and Chinese-inspired materials in both the 1935 *Danza* for piano and the 1936 Violin Concerto composed for Zlatko Balokovic.

From 1937 to his death, Carpenter occupied himself largely with revising and arranging earlier scores. As a result, at least two versions exist for nearly all of the composer's larger chamber and orchestral works. For the most part, Carpenter limited his revisions to cutting material, adding pickups, lightening textures, and fine-tuning details of tempo and dynamics. G. Schirmer, Inc., the composer's principal publisher, declined to put out new editions of these revisions, relying instead on holographs through their rental department. The more substantial of these revisions and arrangements include the Symphony No. 1 (1940) from an unsuccessful Symphony No. 1 (*Sermon in Stones*) of (1917), the Symphony No. 2 (1942), based on material from the Piano Quintet (1934), and the 1948 *Carmel Concerto* from the Violin Concerto and a little piece for piano, the 1916 *Little Indian*. Carpenter continued to compose some totally new compositions, most notably *The Seven Ages* for orchestra (1945), inspired by the famous soliloquy in Shakespeare. A distillation and summary of the composer's work, *The Seven Ages*, like most of Carpenter's later output, was successful with critics and public but failed to enter the standard repertory.

For many years, Carpenter served as a director of the Illinois Children's Home and Aid Society, but his principal philanthropic activity was in championing the arts in his native Chicago. Between the two world wars, he guided the musical activities of the Chicago Arts Club, making it the city's premiere forum for new music: Stravinsky, Honegger, Prokofiev, Schoenberg, Hindemith, and Bartók, among others, arrived under club auspices to discuss and play their music. Carpenter also founded and directed the Chicago Allied Arts, which, in the three years of its existence (1924–1927), staged dances by Bolm and Ruth Page to the music of Falla, Satie, Schoenberg, and others.

From 1919 to 1933 Carpenter also served as president of the Society for the Publication of American Music, which published new music intended for amateurs as well as professionals. During World War II, Carpenter became president of the Choral and Instrumental Association of Chicago, which sponsored concerts in the Chicago parks. "I recommend prayer and a return to religion and art as solution to today's problems," Carpenter wrote in the last year of his life. "They speak to the best that is in us. These troubled times are not a healthy period for the creator. Artists cannot be afraid of today and afraid for tomorrow and express themselves freely."

In his lifetime, Carpenter won a success almost unparalleled for an American composer of concert music. The period's leading conductors—Walter Damrosch, Frederick Stock, Leopold Stokowski, Serge Koussevitzky, Fritz Reiner, Artur Rodzinski, Pierre Monteux, Otto Klemperer, and Bruno Walter—performed his music repeatedly. Such acclaimed singers as Kirsten Flagstad, Conchita Supervia, and Rose Bampton sang and recorded his songs. Percy Grainger performed the Concertino for Piano and Orchestra for decades. Carpenter's honors were many, including the Chevalier of the French Legion of Honor (1921) and the Gold Medal of the National Institute of Arts and Letters (1947).

Although some of Carpenter's music, including *Gitanjali*, *Skyscrapers*, and *Sea Drift*, is revived from time to time, the majority of his scores have fallen into obscurity. He remains nonetheless an important figure in the history of American music over and above the success of individual pieces: for his early appreciation of Debussy, Stravinsky, and other European moderns; for assimilating aspects of American popular music and culture; and for creating musical works recognized as distinctly American both at home and abroad.

• Most of Carpenter's papers, including manuscripts and correspondence, are in the Carpenter Collection at the Music Division of the Library of Congress and, to a lesser extent, in the Carpenter Collection at the Newberry Library, Chicago, which also holds extensive archival material on the Chicago Arts Club. A comprehensive study of the composer is Howard Pollack's *Skyscraper Lullaby: The Life and Music of John Alden Carpenter* (1995). See also Felix Borowski, "John Alden Carpenter," *Musical Quarterly* 16 (Oct. 1930): 449–68, and Thoms C. Pierson, "The Life and Music of John Alden Carpenter" (Ph.D. diss., Univ. of Rochester, 1952). Joan O'Connor, *John Alden Carpenter: A Bio- Bibliography* (1994), provides a comprehensive guide to the composer's works and sources. An obituary is in the *New York Times*, 27 Apr. 1951.

HOWARD POLLACK

CARPENTER, Karen (2 Mar. 1950–4 Feb. 1983), singer, was born Karen Anne Carpenter in New Haven, Connecticut, the daughter of Harold Bertram Carpenter, a printing pressman, and Agnes Reuwer Tatum. In June 1963 the family moved to Downey, in southern California. Karen joined her high school band, opting, with characteristic individuality, to learn to play the drums, which soon became a passion. In 1965 her brother Richard, a pianist, formed a pop jazz instrumental group, the Richard Carpenter Trio, with Karen and fellow musician Wes Jacobs. Karen was on occasion required to sing while she drummed. Although her voice was strong and she was taking voice lessons, she was a reluctant singer, regarding herself primarily as a drummer. For a time the trio hired a female vocalist to relieve Karen of singing. Despite this, her voice came to the attention of a local record label company, Magic Lamp, and in 1966 Karen was signed to them as a solo singer. A single, *Looking for Love/I'll Be Yours*, was issued, but Magic Lamp folded soon after. In June 1966 the trio earned brief acclaim at the Hollywood Battle of the Bands, where they took three awards, including the sweepstakes. This resulted in a record contract with RCA, but it was then terminated, as RCA questioned the commercial viability of a jazz instrumental group.

In 1967 Karen and Richard formed a new group, Spectrum, with four other musicians, concentrating less on jazz, or the Big Band sound, and more on pop. Karen enrolled at California State University in Long Beach, majoring in music, although her distraction with Spectrum caused a temporary suspension in the spring of 1968. That same year Richard and Karen re-formed as the Carpenters, the group that would make them famous. In a friend's garage they produced multitrack, overdubbed vocal recordings to create harmony effects, reminiscent of the Beach Boys. Richard, by now aware of the potential of Karen's voice, arranged orchestral settings, using piano, woodwind, and strings as a counterpoint to the somber resonance of her voice. They won three appearances on television's "Your All American College Show" between 1968 and 1969 but were met with skepticism from record producers, who felt their sound was too soft, too "easy listening," in contrast to the hard rock of the time. The Carpenters' professed influences were the "Three Bs"—the Beatles, the Beach Boys, and Burt Bacharach. But when Herb Alpert heard a demo tape in 1969, Karen's contralto depth reminded him of Patti Page. Despite misgivings concerning the Carpenters' commercial potential, a contract was offered with Alpert's record label, A&M. Legally underage at nineteen, Karen's parents countersigned for her on 22 April 1969. At this point Karen abandoned her degree course.

Success on a national and global scale followed, first with a Bacharach song, "Close to You," which reached number one in July 1970 and went gold worldwide and platinum. The album of the same name also reached number one. Their second number-one song, "We've Only Just Begun," followed soon after, also went gold, and became their signature song. Critics tended to describe the Carpenters' sound as bland and sentimental. Yet the romantic, sometimes nostalgic tenor of their music found a large audience. Throughout the 1970s all their albums went into the charts, and their singles were placed in either the top ten or twenty. They earned forty-nine gold records worldwide. They won three Grammy Awards: for best new artist and best contemporary vocal group in 1970, and one for their *Carpenters (The Singles, 1969–1973)* album in 1971, which had "instant gold" status. Much of their popularity rested in their wholesome image. President Richard Nixon invited them to perform at the White House in May 1973 and described them as "young America at its very best."

In 1971, after their third gold success, "For All We Know," Richard persuaded Karen to sing at the front of the stage, rather than behind the drums. Despite her reticence, Karen agreed, having confidence in Richard's technical expertise and his belief in her voice. Karen was a perfectionist, absolutely committed to success in her craft. She was intelligent and humorous but also subject to many personal insecurities, and those qualities that helped bring success—her determination, resilience, and obstinacy on occasion—also fueled an anorexic condition that eventually killed her. This began to take hold of Karen in the mid-1970s. By 1975 Karen was physically drained, and her thinness startled her audiences, although her condition never affected the strength of her voice or her perfect pitch. But the Carpenters' commercial success, too, was in decline by this time. "Only Yesterday" in 1975 was their last top-ten single.

Karen left her parents' home relatively late, moving to Century City, Los Angeles, in 1976. In September 1980 she married Thomas J. Burris, a real estate developer. The marriage lasted a little over a year, and they had no children. She lived in New York City during 1982 for the sole purpose of attending psychotherapeutic sessions with a specialist for her anorexia nervosa. She ended this in November, having gained thirty pounds. But the following February she died of heart failure, and her previous anorexic condition was a clear factor. She collapsed at her parents' home in Downey the day she was to sign divorce papers.

While many of the Carpenters' songs were composed by Richard and his associate John Bettis, Karen had planned to write songs, although this never materialized. She worked through 1979 on a solo album but relinquished the effort in order to concentrate on another album with Richard, *Made in America* (1981). Her "magical God-given voice," as Alpert described it, was essential to the Carpenters' sound, and her success made her a millionaire.

After her death, her family established the Karen A. Carpenter Memorial Foundation for research into eating disorders.

• Other Carpenters' singles not already mentioned include "Rainy Days and Mondays" (1971), "Superstar" (1971), "Goodbye to Love" (1972), "Sing" (1973), "Yesterday Once More" (1973), "Top of the World" (1973), "Please Mr. Postman" (1974), "There's a Kind of Hush" (1976), "Calling Occupants of Interplanetary Craft" (1977), and "Touch Me When We're Dancing" (1981). Other albums include *Now and Then* (1973), *Horizon* (1975), and *Voice of the Heart* (1983). Much biographical material is in Ray Coleman, *The Carpenters* (1994), which includes a complete listing of the Carpenters' singles A-sides and album tracks. Extensive obituaries and assessments are in the *Los Angeles Times*, 5–13 Feb. 1983, and the *Washington Post* and the *New York Times*, 5 Feb. 1983.

JOANNA HAWKE

CARPENTER, Matthew Hale (22 Dec. 1824–24 Feb. 1881), lawyer and politician, was born in Moretown, Vermont, the son of Ira Carpenter, a farmer and local politician, and Esther Anne Luce. Christened Decatur Merritt Hammond Carpenter, he changed his name in 1850 for reasons that are not clear. Known for his skill at public speaking, Carpenter at fourteen studied law under Paul Dillingham of Waterbury, a distinguished lawyer who served a term as governor. He entered the

U.S. Military Academy at West Point in 1843, but he grew dissatisfied with the curriculum's emphasis on mathematics and natural sciences and withdrew after two years to resume his legal studies. Admitted to the Vermont bar in 1847, Carpenter spent six months studying under Rufus Choate in Boston before he traveled west to the new state of Wisconsin, settling in Beloit. Temporary blindness compelled him to return east for treatment in New York and recuperation in Vermont; in 1850 he came back to Beloit and commenced building his legal practice. Five years later, on 27 November 1855, he married Caroline Dillingham, the daughter of his legal mentor; the couple had four children.

Carpenter gained a reputation as a shrewd, articulate, and informed advocate. He also became involved in politics as a Democrat, vigorous in his support of states' rights. In 1850 he won election as district attorney of Rock County, a position he held intermittently. In 1854 he missed being nominated for Congress by a single vote at the district convention. The next year he drew attention when he commenced litigation based on the assertion that all contracts that conveyed preempted lands prior to a patent being issued were invalid because one could not trade away what one did not yet legally possess. The implications of the case for land titles throughout the West were tremendous; Carpenter claimed that his objective was to ruin land speculators. Among the lawyers who opposed Carpenter were Abraham Lincoln and James R. Doolittle; eventually Carpenter's client (none other than Paul Dillingham) withdrew his case after the U.S. Supreme Court held against Carpenter's view in a similar case in Louisiana. Even more important was his role in defending Democratic Wisconsin governor William A. Barstow from *quo warranto* proceedings instituted by his Republican rival, Coles Bashford, who claimed that Barstow's appointees had manipulated the voting returns from the 1855 contest. Although the court rejected Carpenter's argument that it did not possess jurisdiction and ejected Barstow, Carpenter's prominence gained him more work, including several lucrative railroad cases. In 1858 he moved to Milwaukee and joined forces with Edward G. Ryan, a leading Democrat.

Despite his Democratic affiliation, Carpenter grew increasingly uneasy with the rising influence of southern Democrats and their advocacy of slavery; moreover, the emerging Republican majority in Wisconsin doomed him to a minority position in politics. In the aftermath of Fort Sumter he came out foursquare for the Lincoln administration; as early as August 1861 he advocated emancipation as essential to securing Confederate defeat. Throughout the conflict he spoke on behalf of the war effort, a position that led to a break with his law partner Ryan. Unable to establish an independent Union party, in 1863 Carpenter led Wisconsin Democrats who favored the war into coalition with Republicans under the Union label. Although he was unwilling to do so during the war, by 1866 he had ventured into Republican ranks. Nevertheless, in appearances before the Supreme Court on issues related to Reconstruction, he revealed that his conversion was not complete. In *Ex parte Garland* (1866), he joined Reverdy Johnson to argue successfully Augustus H. Garland's petition to try cases before the Supreme Court, thus challenging the ironclad oath. In *Ex parte McCardle* (1869), however, Carpenter served with Lyman Trumbull and James Hughes as counsel for the federal government in defending the basis of Reconstruction legislation; the Court never issued a decision, because Republicans in Congress hurriedly repealed the law under which the case had made its way to the Court. Nevertheless, Carpenter's argument endeared him to Wisconsin Republicans, who rewarded him in 1869 with election to the U.S. Senate over the conservative Doolittle.

In the Senate, Carpenter soon allied himself with supporters of the Grant administration, often battling Charles Sumner. Although his personal loyalty to Grant was constant, he did not always support the administration. He opposed efforts to place conditions on Congressional readmission of the former Confederate states, arguing that it would be better to keep them under direct federal supervision until Congress deemed them ready to be readmitted without conditions. He also resisted Grant's efforts to commence civil service reform. Carpenter advocated woman suffrage and opposed efforts to deny Chinese immigrants citizenship. In May 1871 he gained a measure of infamy among reporters when he held two *New York Tribune* correspondents in contempt of Congress for their refusal to name the source who had leaked to them the provisions of the Treaty of Washington.

Although Carpenter supported the passage of the Ku Klux Klan Act in 1871, his position on Reconstruction wavered. In 1873 he argued on behalf of the state of Louisiana in the Slaughterhouse Cases, successfully advocating a narrow construction of the citizenship clause of the Fourteenth Amendment. Although his position was consistent with his prewar states'-rights beliefs, it had significant implications for Reconstruction, because it established the basis for striking down legislation essential to federal protection for freedmen. Two days later, the Court ruled against his client Myra Bradwell, who was seeking to practice law in Illinois. In his willingness to take on challenges on a case-by-case basis, he often contradicted himself and did not always consider the long-term impact of his actions.

During Grant's second term Carpenter denounced Louisiana Republicans and questioned their claim to office, calling for new elections in the wake of the disputed 1872 contest. He also assailed antiblack violence in that state. His inept defense of the so-called Salary Grab of 1873 and ill-advised remarks concerning Crédit Mobilier, along with a series of press attacks impugning his personal morals and friction in Wisconsin Republican ranks, led to his defeat for reelection to the Senate in 1875. He remained prominent in political circles, however, defeating congressional efforts to convict former war secretary William W. Belknap of charges of corruption by successfully asserting that Belknap's resignation precluded impeachment. Early the following year, he argued on behalf of Samuel J. Tilden's claim for the electoral votes of Louisiana before the electoral commission constructed in the wake of the disputed presidential election of 1876. Although suffering from diabetes and Bright's disease, Carpenter was returned to the Senate in 1879. The following session saw flashes of the old warrior on the Senate floor, but his health steadily declined in 1880. He died early the following year in Washington.

• A good deal of Carpenter's correspondence is scattered through the papers of Elisha W. Keyes, George B. Smith, and Charles D. Robinson at the State Historical Society of Wisconsin. Two biographies worth consulting are Frank A. Flower, *Life of Matthew Hale Carpenter* (1883); and E. Bruce Thompson, *Matthew Hale Carpenter: Webster of the West* (1954). For broader context, see Alexander MacDonald Thomson, *A Political History of Wisconsin* (2d ed., 1902).

BROOKS D. SIMPSON

CARPENTER, Rhys (5 Aug. 1889–2 Jan. 1980), professor of classical archaeology, was born in Cotuit, Massachusetts, the son of William Henry Carpenter, a provost of Columbia University, and Anna Morgan Douglass. Graduating from Columbia at the age of nineteen, Carpenter went as a Rhodes Scholar to Balliol College, Oxford University, where he took a second bachelor's degree in Greats (1911) and subsequently an M.A. (1914). During those years at Balliol he published his first poem in the *North American Review* (1910). Other poems and three volumes of verse followed during the pre- and postwar years. *The Tragedy of Etarre* (1912), *The Sun Thief and Other Poems* (1914), and *The Plainsman and Other Poems* (1920).

A year at the American School of Classical Studies at Athens (1912–1913) focused Carpenter's classical interests on archaeology, and in 1913 he accepted the invitation of Bryn Mawr College president M. Carey Thomas to establish a department of classical archaeology. In 1916 he received his Ph.D. from Columbia with a dissertation published as *The Ethics of Euripides*. He rose rapidly at Bryn Mawr, becoming full professor in 1918. In that same year he married Eleanor Houston Hill, an alumna of the college; they had no children. Until her death in 1976, Eleanor was to accompany Carpenter on his travels, her strong interest in the arts and dog breeding providing him with opportunities for the creative activity in which he delighted.

Carpenter was away from Bryn Mawr from 1917 to 1919 on war leave, and from 1918 to 1919, as an expert on Greek-Albanian territorial problems, he served in Paris on the American Commission to Negotiate Peace. During this time he also took the thousand-mile muleback tour of archaeological sites in Guatemala that he recorded in *The Land beyond Mexico* (1920).

With his first archaeological publication, *The Esthetic Basis of Greek Art of the Fifth and Fourth Centuries B.C.* (1921), an induction of general aesthetic principles from an examination of Greek sculpture and architecture, Carpenter demonstrated the originality that would characterize his subsequent contributions in a number of fields. His archaeological exploration in Spain resulted in *The Greeks in Spain* (1925), and during these years he also translated Pindaric odes and investigated certain works of sculpture and architecture. These led to his appointment first as annual professor at the American Academy in Rome (1926–1927) and then as director of the American School of Classical Studies at Athens (1927–1932). His term there resulted in various publications and was notable for numerous innovations: the building of a student dormitory, the establishment of the school's journal, *Hesperia*, and the beginning of the American excavations in the Athenian Agora. Louis E. Lord, the school's first historian, recalled that it "had never known a quinquennium so exciting."

Upon his return to Bryn Mawr in 1932, Carpenter continued his original investigations in many areas, from alphabetic origins to Parthenon pedimental sculptures. His articles on the Greek alphabet overturned conventional scholarly opinion, arguing for a now generally accepted eighth-century B.C. date rather than an earlier dating. In the Martin Classical Lectures at Oberlin College, published as *The Humanistic Value of Archaeology* (1933), Carpenter helped to define and justify the still youthful discipline of classical archaeology. In 1939–1940 he served as professor in charge of the Classical School of the American Academy in Rome; the result was *Observations on Familiar Statuary in Rome* (1941). His continued work on the Greek alphabet later led to an original and provocative study of Homer as a prealphabetic poet who combined various strands of oral tradition and invention. Carpenter's Sather Classical Lectures at the University of California at Berkeley, which expanded further on the poet and his work, resulted in *Folk Tale, Fiction and Saga in the Homeric Epics* (1946).

Carpenter's *Art, a Bryn Mawr Symposium* (1940), *The Bases of Artistic Creation* (1942), and *The Age of Diocletian* (1953) sprang from his participation in symposia and discussions concerned with aesthetics in theory and practice. In addition to his tenure at Bryn Mawr and American schools abroad, Carpenter held an Andrew W. Mellon professorship at the University of Pittsburgh (1961–1962) and professorships at the University of Pennsylvania (1960) and the University of Washington (1963–1964). He was a member of many societies and in 1969 became gold medalist of the Archaeological Institute of America.

Carpenter was most productive in the fifteen years after his retirement from Bryn Mawr in 1955. The six books and dozens of seminal articles that he published during that time show the great range of his interests and expertise. The combination of learning and originality that characterize his other work is also exemplified in his last book, *The Architects of the Parthenon* (1970), which hypothesizes a Cimonian Parthenon (built under the jurisdiction or during the floruit of Cimon, a fifth-century Athenian general and statesman).

It is fitting that his final book should take up what Carpenter called "this symbol of Greek genius."

Quietly and almost diffidently, Carpenter showed his students and colleagues new ways of understanding the ancient Mediterranean world by the very breadth and interaction of his interests: aesthetics and art in general or sculpture in particular; cultural geography and alphabetic origins; and the making, translating, and interpreting of literature. Acknowledging no disciplinary boundaries and immensely creative in his approach to both texts and stones, he inspired others to challenge his provocative ideas while emulating his rigorous scholarly standards. Carpenter died in Devon, Pennsylvania.

• A collection of some of Carpenter's unpublished papers is in the Bryn Mawr College archives. In addition to those mentioned in the text, Carpenter's major publications include *Korinthos: A Guide to the Excavations and Museum* (1928); *The Sculpture of the Nike Temple Parapet* (1929); with A. Bon and A. W. Parsons, *The Defenses of Acrocorinth and the Lower Town*, vol. 3., pt. 2 of the Corinth series (1936); *Greek Sculpture: A Critical Review* (1960); *Greek Art: A Study of the Formal Evolution of Style* (1962); with J. S. Ackerman, *Art and Archaeology* (1963); and *Beyond the Pillars of Heracles: The Classical World Seen through the Eyes of Its Discoverers* (1966). A complete bibliography appears in *Hesperia* 38, no. 2 (1969): 123–32. See also the bibliographical memoir in the *American Philosophical Society Yearbook* (1980), pp. 555–60. An obituary is in the *New York Times*, 4 Jan. 1980.

MABEL L. LANG

CARPENTER, Stephen Cullen (?–1820?), editor and publisher, was born in Ireland of English parents whose names are unknown. Before moving to Charleston, South Carolina, by 1802 Carpenter had established his reputation by brilliant reporting of the parliamentary speeches at the Warren Hastings trial. In the United States in 1803, he edited the *Courier*, a strongly Federalist newspaper based in Charleston. However, Carpenter was not primarily a political journalist, and his second venture, the *Monthly Register and Review of the United States*, which began in Charleston in January 1805, concentrated on history and literature, especially French literature. He moved this journal to New York in July 1806, retitled it the *Monthly Register, Magazine and Review of the United States*, and published six issues. At the same time he edited the *People's Friend* from 1 September 1806 to 3 August 1807.

In the *Monthly Register*, Carpenter included a history of the American Revolution, but he was primarily interested in reaffirming the genteel tastes of his aristocratic readers. He would not discuss the "new" romantics, like William Wordsworth, Samuel Taylor Coleridge, and Robert Southey, whom he believed were corrupters of society and debauchers of taste. His duty was to heighten readers' sensitivity to moral literature and to express appropriate sentimentality.

Carpenter returned to magazine editing in January 1810 with the Philadelphia *Mirror of Taste and Dramatic Censor*, where he continued to judge the theater by the same standards. Historian Frank Luther Mott observed that the *Mirror of Taste*, which ran for twenty-four issues, was "the most important magazine devoted chiefly to the drama of this period, and the only one which outlasted a single theatrical season" (it lasted one full season and parts of two others). Carpenter opened each of the first eighteen issues with successive installments in a survey of drama from the Greeks to eighteenth-century France. He reviewed plays performed locally, profiled actors playing locally, reported general news about the theatrical world, and published a new play in each issue.

This potpourri was, in the *Mirror of Taste* as in the earlier *Monthly Register* and the later *Bureau: Or Repository of Literature, Politics, and Intelligence* (28 Mar. 1812–30 Dec. 1812), handled expansively in an ornate and wordy style. In his historical writings and political reporting, Carpenter consistently eschewed open partisanship, although by opting to present the world through a moralistic and sentimental prism, he reinforced aristocratic and Federalist attitudes just on the eve of Jacksonian democracy.

Nothing is known of Carpenter's personal life save that he held government positions in Washington, D.C., until his death there.

• Carpenter left no papers. Copies of every issue of the two newspapers and three magazines that he edited are extant. Carpenter edited *Memoirs of the Honorable Thomas Jefferson* (2 vols., 1809) and *Select American Speeches Forensic and Parliamentary with Prefatory Remarks; A Sequel to Dr. Chapman's Select Speeches* (1815). The best essay about Carpenter is David E. Matchen's in the *Dictionary of Literary Biography*, ed. Sam G. Riley, vol. 73, *American Magazine Journalists, 1741–1850* (1988). Frank Luther Mott, *A History of American Magazines*, vol. 1 (1938), and Sam G. Riley, *Magazines of the American South* (1986), place Carpenter in perspective.

WILLIAM F. STEIRER, JR.

CARR, Benjamin (12 Sept. 1768–24 May 1831), composer, organist, and music publisher, was born in Holborn, England, the son of Joseph Carr, the owner of a music store in London, and Mary Jordan. Born into a musical family, Carr studied music with Samuel Arnold, a well-known opera composer, and Charles Wesley, an organist and composer of Methodist hymns. In addition to singing in concerts, Carr was involved with the London musical stage and wrote an opera, *Philander and Silvia; or, Love Crown'd at Last*, which was performed at Sadler's Wells Theatre in London on 16 October 1792.

Carr immigrated to Philadelphia by the summer of 1793, followed by his parents and brother Thomas, who settled in Baltimore to continue the family's music-publishing business. Benjamin opened the Musical Repository, Philadelphia's earliest musical store, under the name of B. Carr & Co. in 1793. Carr was active in Philadelphia's New Theatre, composing accompaniments for plays such as *Macbeth*. In 1794 he was allied with the Old American Company, singing the role of Young Meadows in Thomas Arne's ballad-opera *Love in a Village* both in Philadelphia and New York.

He received a good review in *New York Magazine* (Dec. 1794). By 1795 he established himself as a music and musical instrument seller in New York, printing music and selling pianofortes imported from London.

With William Dunlap as librettist, Carr composed the music for *The Archers; or, The Mountaineers of Switzerland*, an operatic treatment of the William Tell legend. It was highly acclaimed at its first performance by the Old American Company in New York's John Street Theatre on 18 April 1796. The work was staged several times in New York and twice in Boston. Little of the music remains except for the romantic song "Why, Huntress, Why?" which was printed in Carr's *Musical Journal for the Piano Forte* (1800–1801). Another of his operas, *Bourville Castle; or, The Gallic Orphan*, was produced in New York in 1797.

A dynamic force in early American music, Carr introduced amateur musicians to noted European composers by printing selections from the works of Haydn, Mozart, Hummel and others, as well as popular English songs and arrangements of ballad-operatic songs. In April 1794 he began publishing his *Gentleman's Amusement*, a monthly selection of solos, duets, and overtures. After selling his New York store to James Hewitt in 1797, Carr continued publishing in Philadelphia until 1800.

Carr was a productive and inventive composer whose works were, in Oscar Sonneck's view, "distinguished by a pleasing softness" (*Miscellaneous Studies in the History of Music* [1921], p. 65). His numerous compositions encompassed secular pieces such as the "Dead March and Monody" for the funeral of George Washington in 1799 and his setting of Walter Scott's poem "Allen a Dale" to music (c. 1813). "Poor Richard," which he originally composed in London, was his most popular song.

Carr responded to the intense political fervor of the 1790s by producing the *Federal Overture*, a highly skilled blending of patriotic songs such as "The Marseilles Hymn" and "Ca Ira," popular with pro-French Jeffersonian Republicans, with Federalist favorites such as "The President's March" and "Yankee Doodle," in its first known American printing. His medley was enthusiastically cheered by a Philadelphia theater audience at its initial performance on 20 September 1794. In 1806 he caught the spirit of the Tripolitanian naval war with his *Siege of Tripoli, an Historical Naval Sonata*.

Carr energetically supported the growth of American musical culture, directing his efforts after 1800 to "those who are desirous to forward the advancement of music in this country" ("To the Patrons of Music," *Baltimore Federal Gazette*, 2 Nov. 1800). To encourage amateur musicianship, he joined his father in founding the *Musical Journal*, which appeared in two editions, one for the pianoforte and one for flute or violin. From 1800 to 1804 he edited the publication, selecting and arranging the music.

Until 1800 he often appeared as a singer in local concerts, not always winning accolades. He then turned his vibrant energies to composing church music, which he published in *Masses, Vespers, Litanies, Hymns . . . for . . . the Catholic Churches . . .* (1805) and *The Chorister* (1820), designed for Episcopal churches. Constantly striving to improve the quality of choruses while serving as organist in leading Philadelphia churches, he directed choirs in Saint Augustine's Roman Catholic Church (1801–1831), Saint Mary's Catholic Church (1807–1811), and Saint Peter's Episcopal Church (c. 1820–1831).

Conscious that church choirs were strongly influenced by "that dull monotony of style introduced by the gloomy Calvin" (letter to John R. Parker, 31 May 1821), Carr promoted high standards in sacred music through trained musicians. In June 1810 he conducted excerpts from Handel's *Messiah*. With a sizable orchestra for the time, including twenty-one violins, six violas, five cellos, and a choir of thirty-four, it was a celebrated performance.

In addition, in 1816 Carr founded the Musical Fund Society of Philadelphia with the aim of helping impoverished musicians and elevating the quality of choral performance. Following Carr's death in Philadelphia, the society erected a monument to "a distinguished professor of music" who was held in "high esteem" by his associates. There is no record of his having married.

• Copies of Carr's published music are at Columbia University, the New York Public Library, the University of Michigan, and the Library of Congress. For information on Carr's musical career, see Carroll J. Lehman, "Benjamin Carr: His Contribution to Early American Solo Vocal Literature" (D.M.A. diss., Univ. of Iowa, 1975), which explores his vocal compositions and includes the texts of some five letters of Carr's housed at the University of Pennsylvania. Carr's activities as an organist and choral director are treated in Ronnie L. Smith, "The Church Music of Benjamin Carr" (D.M.A. diss., Southwestern Baptist Theological Seminary, 1970). Virginia Larkin Redway, "The Carrs, American Music Publishers," *Music Quarterly* 18 (Jan. 1932): 150–64, presents the known data about the multiple publishing activities of the Carr family. Stephen Siek, "Benjamin Carr's Theatrical Career," *American Music* 11 (1993): 158–84, presents new material on Carr's multifaceted professional life to 1800. Irving Lowens, *Music and Musicians in Early America* (1964), contains information on Carr's composition of the *Federal Overture*. Louis C. Madeira, *Annals of Music in Philadelphia and History of the Musical Fund Society* (1896), details Carr's role as founder of the society and contains a portrait of Carr from a mezzotint by John Sartain, taken from a painting by J. C. Dailey (1831), reproduced as the frontispiece.

WINFRED E. A. BERNHARD

CARR, Charlotte Elizabeth (3 May 1890–12 July 1956), social worker and reformer, was born in Dayton, Ohio, the daughter of Joseph Henry Carr, a successful businessman, and Frances Carver. Carr developed an early sensitivity to problems of poverty and injustice, and when her parents insisted on her becoming a debutante instead of going to college she ran away and got a job in Pittsburgh. Her parents relented and enrolled her at Vassar College. Carr later said she learned little at Vassar; her higher education began in 1915 when she graduated and started "bumming around." After serving as a matron in an Ohio orphan asylum Carr moved to New York, where she worked for the State Charities Aid Association and then for the New York Probation and Protective Association. Next came a stint as a policewoman, doing night patrols in the Brooklyn Bridge area. She then did personnel work at the American Lithographic Company and Knox Hat Company in New York (1921–1923) and at Stark Mills in New Hampshire (1923).

In 1923 Carr became assistant director of the Bureau of Women in Industry, New York State Department of Labor, serving under Frances Perkins. Among other tasks, she helped Perkins document the deleterious effects of factory work on children. In 1925 she was recruited by Governor Gifford Pinchot to create a Women's Bureau for the Pennsylvania State Labor Department, but she was ousted four years later by Pinchot's successor when she refused to make the required political contributions. When Pinchot returned to office in 1931 he made her deputy secretary of labor and industry. It was new territory for a woman—particularly a "fat Irishwoman," as Carr called herself—and many found her unfeminine, with her outspoken humor and forceful manner. More serious opposition arose over her vigorous advocacy for improved working conditions; one critic nicknamed her "Scarlet" Carr. In 1933 she attacked the labor practices of a firm owned by Joseph Grundy, president of the Pennsylvania Manufacturers Association and one of the Republican party's major fundraisers. In retaliation the legislature stopped her salary, but Pinchot rewarded her by firing the department secretary and promoting her to that position.

As Pinchot's term drew to a close in 1934, Carr moved to New York to advise Governor Herbert Lehman on relief programs. The following year Mayor Fiorello LaGuardia appointed her assistant director of New York City's Emergency Relief Bureau. Within a few months the director retired, and Carr inherited the job, which involved managing an annual budget of more than $100 million, supervising 18,000 employees, and providing assistance to nearly one million people. With the help of newly-created federal work programs she was able to cut the number of home-relief cases nearly in half, while helping (and sometimes pressing) many unemployed New Yorkers to find jobs for the first time in several years. She also decreased the bureau's overhead costs while raising its welfare allowances. Some conservatives criticized Carr for being too sympathetic to Communists and for spending too much money. At the same time she drew opposition from liberals for policies such as her insistence that children's wages be deducted from a family's relief allotments. By the end of her tenure, however, a dozen top civic and labor organizations spoke out in her support, and LaGuardia praised her for "administering relief intelligently and kindly without humiliation to the recipients."

In 1937 Carr accepted one of the most notable jobs in private social welfare: head of Chicago's Hull-House, succeeding its renowned founder, Jane Addams. Carr did not think that private institutions could meet the majority of society's needs, but she felt they could play an important role in demonstrating new approaches that could be adopted by public agencies. Then, she explained, "the settlement writes the past off the books and moves on to new frontiers." Hull-House had been fearlessly controversial in its early days, but in later years it had become more cautious. Carr set out to rekindle the fire, instituting courses in labor law and collective bargaining, organizing community groups to fight for physical improvements in the neighborhood, and forcing the institution to address the fact that few blacks used the settlement. She persuaded a Chicago journalist and his social worker wife to become Hull-House's first black residents, aggressively encouraged black participation in settlement activities, and set up satellite centers in parts of the neighborhood where blacks predominated. The effort had only modest success, in part because of opposition from both white participants and staff. Carr's administrative changes antagonized many longtime supporters of Hull-House, just as the personal style that had led one observer to describe her as "a feminine counterpart" of labor leader John L. Lewis proved abrasive in the genteel world of the settlement. Her highly visible campaigning for Democratic candidates in 1940 troubled the board, as did the fact that her program costs required the use of endowment funds to cover operating expenses. Her departure in 1942 was described by the board as a resignation, but she herself said, "Hell, I was fired!"

In 1943 Carr became assistant to the vice chair of the War Manpower Commission, and during the 1944 presidential campaign she headed the Congress of Industrial Organization's Political Action Committee for the New York region. In 1945 she became the first director of the Citizens Committee on Children of New York City, helping win approval for health and child-care services in public housing projects, a foster-home program in the Welfare Department, and new juvenile services within the Police Department. During this period she also served on the Mayor's Committee on Management Survey (1950–1953), the National Child Labor Committee (1943–1956), and the board of the Northside Center for Child Development (1946–1956). In 1954 she became a consultant to the city welfare commissioner, a job she held until her death. Never marrying, Carr died in New York City just one day after representing the department at a community meeting.

Carr lived her life at a high pitch, struggling courageously for the causes she believed in, accepting the enmity that her politics and her style evoked, bouncing back after each defeat to take up the fight again in a new arena. Having chosen to battle against poverty, injustice, and inequality, she won few unequivocal victories, but she touched millions of lives and left many of them better for her efforts.

• No personal papers on Carr are available, but material on her years at Hull-House can be found in the Jane Addams Memorial Collection, University of Illinois, Chicago. Discussion of her career appears in Milton Mayer, "Charlotte Carr—Settlement Lady," *Atlantic Monthly*, Dec. 1938, pp. 741–48; George Britt, "Charlotte Carr at Hull-House," *Survey Graphic* 27 (Feb. 1938): 80–82; Mary Bryan et al., eds., *100 Years at Hull-House* (1990); and M. Nelson McGeary, *Gifford Pinchot: Forester, Politician* (1960). A *New York Times* obituary appears 13 July 1956.

SANDRA OPDYCKE

CARR, Dabney (27 Apr. 1773–8 Jan. 1837), jurist, was born in Spring Forest, Goochland County, Virginia, the son of Dabney Carr, a lawyer and revolutionary patriot, and Martha Jefferson, a younger sister of Thomas Jefferson. Carr's father died only three weeks after his birth, and he was raised by his mother at Spring Forest and at "Monticello." Jefferson, his uncle, acted as legal guardian and foster father to him, closely supervising his education. In 1784, when Jefferson went to France, he entrusted Carr to James Madison, and the next year Madison sent Carr to the academy at Hampden-Sydney. (Madison was a trustee of Hampden-Sydney College.) Carr then attended Hampden-Sydney College from 1787 to 1789 but did not remain to receive a degree. Madison kept Jefferson informed of Carr's academic progress throughout Jefferson's residency abroad. In 1790 Carr was sent to the well-known boarding school of the Reverend Matthew Maury in Albemarle County to study Greek and French; he was already an accomplished Latinist.

Carr returned home three years later and began a course of reading law using books borrowed from his uncle. He was admitted to the bar in 1796 and began the practice of law in Charlottesville and Albemarle County. His practice was successful and soon spread to the neighboring counties of Fluvanna, Buckingham, and Amherst and to the chancery court in Staunton. He married his first cousin, Elizabeth Carr, in 1800, and they had two children. From 1801 to 1811 he served as the commonwealth's attorney for Albemarle County. It was during this early period that he met William Wirt, Francis Walker Gilmer, and James Barbour, who were also lawyers in the area. They remained intimate friends for the remainder of their lives, sharing interests in literary matters as well as the law.

On 26 March 1811 Carr was appointed by Virginia's governor to sit on an interim basis as a judge on the general court, but when the general assembly convened in April, he was not confirmed. Carr's talents were recognized, however, and the legislators created a new chancery court in Winchester and Clarksburg and on 29 January 1812 appointed him to that bench. Carr moved to Winchester in March and distinguished himself there professionally and socially.

Carr was not drawn to politics but instead devoted his leisure time to literature, particularly the Latin classics. He contributed an essay to Wirt's *The Old Bachelor* (1814) under the signature of Obadiah Squaretoes.

In February 1824 Carr was elected to the court of appeals, the highest court in Virginia. At that time judges served for life during good behavior. He accordingly moved to Richmond, where he remained until his death. He bought a house on the outskirts of the city to have the benefit of the exercise of walking to and from court; Carr was told that this daily exercise would alleviate kidney stones. (The court of appeals occupied a room in the capitol building, which had been designed years before by his famous uncle.) In 1825 Carr was asked to be the first law professor at the new University of Virginia, but he declined, which turned out to be a wise choice considering the low salary and later student disturbances.

Carr was known for his personal modesty and urbanity. His dealing with counsel during argument was always courteous, fair, and self-effacing. His judicial opinions, which are reported in volumes twenty-three through thirty-four of the *Virginia Reports*, are learned, thoughtful, and thorough. In an article in the *Southern Literary Messenger* a year after his death it is written that

> his deportment on the bench was characterized by that modesty, and forbearance, and deference for the opinions of others, which marked his conduct through life. He rarely interrupted the counsel, and when he ventured to suggest a difficulty, he always did it in such a manner as neither to embarrass or to damp their ardor. . . . He was indeed not hasty in making up his opinions, or in yielding to the first suggestions of his mind upon the arguments of a case, though when his judgment was once formed, it was inflexible. . . . The mind of Judge Carr was clear, vigorous, and accurate; his style was pure, classical, and strong; his learning was extensive, well digested, and profound; his acquirements in every field of literature considerable.

He was active on the bench until a few weeks before his death. He died at his residence and was buried in Richmond.

• Correspondence to, from, and about Carr is located in the Carr–Cary collection and the Jefferson papers at the University of Virginia Library; correspondence to Carr from Wirt and Gilmer is in the Virginia State Library and Archives. The primary source for Carr's life is a lengthy anonymous article, "Dabney Carr," in the *Southern Literary Messenger* 4 (Feb. 1838): 65–70. His friendships with William Wirt and Francis Walker Gilmer are described in John Pendleton Kennedy, *Memoirs of the Life of William Wirt* (1849), and Richard Beale Davis, *Francis Walker Gilmer* (1939). See also Davis, *Intellectual Life in Jefferson's Virginia, 1790–1830* (1964). Genealogical data is in *Virginia Magazine* 2 (1894): 221–24, and *William and Mary Quarterly*, 1st ser., no. 15 (1906): 119. For Carr's education, see *The Letters of Thomas Jefferson*, ed. Julian P. Boyd, vols. 7–16 (1953–1961), and Dumas Malone, *Jefferson the Virginian* (1948), pp. 161, 393, 396, 431. For how Carr was active in the practice of law, see W. Hamilton Bryson, ed., *Miscellaneous Virginia Law Reports* (1992), pp. 74, 126, 128.

W. HAMILTON BRYSON

CARR, Elias (25 Feb. 1839–22 July 1900), North Carolina governor, Farmers' Alliance leader, and planter, was born at "Bracebridge," the family plantation near Old Sparta, Edgecombe County, North Carolina, the son of Jonas Johnston Carr and Elizabeth Jane Hilliard, planters. Within four years both parents died, and with his sister Mary and brother William, Carr moved to Warren County to live with his mother's sister, Temperance, and her husband, John Buxton Williams. Carr's first education was at a school established by Williams. Later Carr attended the Bingham School in Orange County, spent two years at the University of North Carolina, and took courses at the University of Virginia, but he did not get a college degree. In 1857 he returned to Bracebridge, and in 1859 he married Eleanor Kearny; they had six children. In September 1861, after the Civil War had started, Carr enlisted as a private in Company G, Forty-first Regiment, North Carolina Troops, known as the Scotland Neck Mounted Riflemen. In June 1862 he left the army to supply the Confederacy with farm products.

Though the South's defeat deprived Carr of his slaves and Confederate bonds, neither his house nor his farm were damaged, and this fortune as well as his scientific farming practices enabled him to operate profitably. Carr produced cotton principally, but he also grew pale peas, peanuts, and in the 1890s, tobacco. He operated a commercial dairy, and Bracebridge plantation produced most of the food consumed by Carr's family and employees.

An overseer supervised Carr's workers, whether share tenants or wage earners. His laborers received top wages, but he exacted cash penalties from those workers who abused any of his properties, crops, animals, or land. A commissary he ran sold goods at near cost levels, earning for him a reputation for fairness and honesty with his employees and the public.

Carr purchased quality seed and modern farm equipment and practiced diversification, rotation, and fertilization of crops. In his continuous search for efficiency, he consulted authorities such as the North Carolina Agricultural Experiment Station, established in 1877 under the newly authorized Department of Agriculture. He kept detailed records of his operations and wrote articles and made speeches on farm subjects. His most popular article, entitled "Plan for a Silo," was first published in the Raleigh *Progressive Farmer* (12 Feb. 1889).

Not only interested in farming, Carr invested in the Rocky Mount Mills, a textile manufacturing company, serving at one time as chairman of its board of directors. In 1888 he became part owner of the Farmers' Co-Operative Manufacturing Company, a cottonseed oil mill, and he invested in the Tar River Navigation Company, which operated a boat on the Tar River. From 1877 to 1892 Carr served on the Board of Commissioners of Edgecombe County. In 1887 the North Carolina Farmers' Association, of which he was president (1887–1889), secured passage of a bill establishing the Agricultural and Mechanical College in Raleigh. Carr became a charter member of its board of trustees.

Carr's leadership of the Farmers' Alliance in North Carolina brought him state and national attention. He became active at all levels of the hierarchical organization, known as the Southern Alliance, whose purpose was improving social and economic conditions for farmers. In 1887 he joined the North Carolina Farmers' State Alliance (NCFSA) and served as chairman of the executive board (Oct. 1887–Aug. 1889). He is credited with founding the Alliance Business Agency, through which members bought and sold merchandise. Carr was the first president of the Sparta Sub-Alliance (Dec. 1887–Jan. 1890) and the Edgecombe County Alliance (Mar. 1888–Mar. 1890). In August 1889 he was elected president of the NCFSA and served two, one-year terms. As president he guided the organization through its most active period, answering inquiries about its operation, especially membership requirements, devised to keep the alliance closely knit and effective. He directed its educational work, primarily the activities of lecturers, who instructed members in modern farming methods and about alliance legislative demands.

After his term as president ended, Carr continued to manifest interest in the flourishing national farm movement. He opposed the St. Louis platform adopted by the alliance and other reform groups in 1892 because it advocated government ownership and operation of railroads, ignored the tariff issue, and propelled the organization toward a third party. His moderate position on issues won him support from both alliance and straight-out Democrats, who in 1892 nominated him for governor. Carr won election with a plurality of the votes.

Ironically Carr, who detested political controversy and possessed little political experience, served as North Carolina governor during the most turbulent period after Reconstruction. Still he achieved a number of reforms. His proposal for financing roads received modest support, but he did persuade the general assembly to increase the school tax from fifteen to eighteen cents on property valued at $100. The State Board of Health was redefined in an 1893 law and given increased funding and expanded functions. Carr advocated modern facilities and practices in the care and treatment of inmates in charitable and penal institutions. At the end of 1896 the penitentiary had become self-supporting, a long-sought goal, and North Carolina was a model in treatment of the mentally ill.

Carr sought to make North Carolina more attractive to both settlers and investors. He attended a convention of southern governors in Richmond, Virginia, in April 1893 for the purpose of encouraging immigration. Afterward he published a pamphlet, *Resources and Advantages of NORTH CAROLINA* (1893), and attracted the Waldensians, who planted a colony at Valdese in Burke County that year. During Carr's term the North Carolina Geological and Economic Survey assessed the state's mineral, timber, and water resources, and its many publications encouraged both conservation of resources and capital investment in the state.

The Fusionists, a coalition of Populists and Republicans, won control of the general assembly in 1895, and Carr looked with disfavor on their attempts to expand their patronage. Distrust of the Fusionists and memories of railroad scandals during Reconstruction probably motivated him to support a 99-year lease of the North Carolina Railroad to the Southern Railway System in 1895, before the existing lease expired. This action proved the most controversial of his governorship, since it enabled enemies to portray him as a friend of railroad corporations even though in 1893 Carr had made the railroads surrender their tax-exempt status. Modest and reserved, with no flair for oratory, he proved a strong administrator. Retiring from office in January 1897, Carr returned to Bracebridge, where he died.

• Carr's papers, numbering more than 7,000 items, are located in the East Carolina Manuscript Collection, Joyner Library, East Carolina University, Greenville, N.C. The Governor's Papers and Letterbooks (1893–1897), located in the Department of Cultural Resources, Division of Archives and History, Raleigh, are quite extensive. Three other collections in the archives illuminate Carr's childhood and family life, the papers of John Buxton Williams, the Polk family, and Thomas Merritt Pittman. Some correspondence is in the Zebulon B. Vance Papers in the archives and in the Southern Historical Collection, University of North Carolina at Chapel Hill. Printed material on the alliance includes the North Carolina Farmers' State Alliance *Proceedings* (1888–1893) and NCFSA *Constitutions* (1888–1893). Study of government documents is requisite for Carr's governorship. Informative newspapers include the *Tarboro Southerner* (1866–1900), the Raleigh *Progressive Farmer* (1887–1897), and the Raleigh *News and Observer* (1887–1900).

Secondary sources on Carr include articles written by Lala Carr Steelman, "The Life-Style of an Eastern North Carolina Planter: Elias Carr of Bracebridge Hall," *North Carolina Historical Review* 57 (1980): 17–42; "The Role of Elias Carr in the North Carolina Farmers' Alliance," *North Carolina Historical Review* 57 (1980): 133–58; and "Elias Carr: A Profile," *Journal of the Association of Historians in North Carolina* 1 (1993): 29–60, which is a synopsis and assessment of the subject. Two works by the same author, although not focused on Carr, include information on his alliance activities. *The North Carolina Farmers' Alliance: A Political History, 1887–1893* (1985) treats Carr's political philosophy and his activities in the 1892 campaign. "Leonidas Lafayette Polk, North Carolina Alliancemen, and Some Conflicts of Agrarian Leadership, 1887–1892," in *Of Tar Heel Towns, Shipbuilders, Reconstructionists and Alliancemen*, ed. Joseph F. Steelman (1981), discusses controversy and conflict within the NCFSA with Polk as the central figure. An obituary is in the Raleigh *News and Observer*, 24 July 1900.

LALA CARR STEELMAN

CARR, Emma Perry (23 July 1880–7 Jan. 1972), chemist, was born in Holmesville, Ohio, the daughter of Edmund Cone, a general practitioner from a family of physicians, and Anna Mary Jack. Her family moved fifty miles south to the somewhat larger town of Coshocton about a year after Carr was born. She graduated from public schools and then went to Ohio State University in 1898, where she studied chemistry with William McPherson. At the end of her freshman year she transferred to Mount Holyoke College, becoming part of a tradition that supported women's education in science and that, as a faculty member, she would sustain and expand.

Carr completed two more years of study in chemistry at Mount Holyoke and then stayed on as an assistant in chemistry from 1901 to 1904. Encouraged by the faculty, she went to the University of Chicago for her senior year, receiving a B.S. in 1905. She returned to Mount Holyoke as an instructor in chemistry for three years before retracing her path to Chicago for graduate study. Working in physical chemistry, she completed her course work and a thesis in 1910 under the direction of Julius Stieglitz, a distinguished chemist and educator. Mount Holyoke welcomed her back as an associate professor, and Carr committed herself fully to a combined program of teaching and research in physical chemistry that made Mount Holyoke a notable center for both. In 1913 she was promoted to full professor and became chair of the department, a position she held until her retirement thirty-three years later. Although her graduate work had not included spectroscopy, her lifelong research was on the relationship between the structure of organic compounds and their ultraviolet spectra. She thus joined an emerging group of physical chemists seeking to measure the absorption of certain wavelengths of light by atomic groups within specific molecules as a way of understanding their electronic structure.

Carr was pioneering in her decision to involve undergraduate students in research and deliberately chose to work on the absorption spectra of simple hydrocarbons because her students could be taught the techniques and be assigned particular projects. The program she designed after 1913 initiated advanced honors students and master's degree candidates cooperatively in ultraviolet spectroscopy using analytical techniques introduced in Europe but only beginning to be used in the United States. Granted money from a fund donated to the college by a pioneering woman scientist at Mount Holyoke, Lydia Shattuck, Carr was able to buy a small spectrograph for research and very quickly Mount Holyoke faculty and students were accomplished in the skilled technical work and tedious data gathering required of that early equipment. In 1919, determined to learn more spectral theory and techniques, Carr contacted A. W. Stewart in Glasgow. Because he was about to move to Queens University in Belfast, he urged her to join him there, where she spent half a year learning the most advanced ultraviolet techniques available.

In 1924 Carr was asked to become a cooperating expert on the International Critical Tables (ICT) project dealing with absorption spectra, collaborating with Victor Henri of the University of Zurich and his colleague Jean A. E. M. Becquerel in Paris. Once again, Carr decided to go abroad, this time to Switzerland, so that she could work in a well-equipped laboratory and concentrate on the ICT assignment. She coordinated the work of the team and made a lifelong friendship with Henri and his family during her half year in Zurich in 1925, and in 1929 returned to work in his laboratory, sponsored by a fellowship from the American Association of University Women. Carr shifted her research interests slightly in the late 1920s, turning to a series of more simple unsaturated hydrocarbons in the hope of contributing to theoretical discussions. With funds from the National Research Council (NRC) she was able to buy a vacuum spectrograph. Over the course of the next decade, the research group at Mount Holyoke disproved Morris S. Kharasch's electromer theory and provided important data in the very high frequency region of the ultraviolet. With her students and some fellow faculty members, Carr published a steady stream of papers and received an NRC grant in 1934 for technical assistance as well as funds from the Rockefeller Foundation for equipment and laboratory support. She spent her sabbatical leave in 1937–1938 working at Harvard, in Liège where Henri was acting as director of the Institute of Physical Chemistry, and in Australia visiting chemical laboratories. During World War II, the Mount Holyoke group spent much of its time working, unsuccessfully as it turned out, to find an antimalarial compound that might substitute for quinine. In 1944, sponsored by the Rockefeller Foundation, Carr visited the new Institute of Chemistry in Mexico City and made professional friendships there that continued for several years.

Under Carr's leadership, Mount Holyoke hired a number of women on the faculty, some exceptional classroom teachers and others productive research chemists. Carr had no doubts about women's capacities for science and, as chair of a committee of the American Association for University Women, helped produce *Women in Chemistry: A Study of Professional Opportunities* (1922). Mount Holyoke's chemistry department was exceptional in producing women chemists during Carr's leadership; forty-three undergraduates went on for Ph.D.s in chemistry, nearly half of the total number of women who took Ph.D.s during the period from 1913 to 1946, when Carr retired.

Among the women hired by Carr was Mary Lura Sherrill. Within a few years after being hired in 1929, she and Carr had become close friends and frequently collaborated in the laboratory. They also established a home that was a social center for students and alumnae in South Hadley. Summers were often spent doing research and relaxing in Coshocton. Sherrill succeeded Carr as department head, but Carr continued her research efforts well into her seventies. She was remembered as a campus leader, outspoken on occasion, as when, for example, a man was hired to replace Mary E. Woolley in 1937, breaking the tradition of women presidents at Mount Holyoke.

Carr was the first to receive the Garvan Medal (1937), honoring "an American woman for distinguished service in chemistry." She was a member of the American Chemical Society and the American Association for the Advancement of Science, and she was honored at the dedication of the Carr Laboratories at Mount Holyoke. Intense, sociable, and demanding, Carr was much loved and respected by her students who saw in her a woman for whom work was truly "an exciting adventure" even as she traveled extensively, played tennis, followed baseball, and was active in campus and civic affairs. After retirement Carr was elected representative from her district to the South Hadley Town Meeting. She moved in 1964 to Evansville, Illinois, to be near her brother's family; she died there of heart failure.

• Mount Holyoke College archives contain records, reports, and unpublished materials relating to Carr and her career there. Biographical sketches include those by students in the *Mount Holyoke Alumnae Quarterly* 30 (Aug. 1946): 53–55; and 46 (Spring 1972): 23–25. Carr wrote several essays about science education at Mount Holyoke, including "Chemical Education in American Institutions: Mount Holyoke College," *Journal of Chemical Education* 25 (1948): 11–18; her major scientific publications are cited in *Chemical Abstracts*. Other references include Bojan Hamlin Jennings, "The Professional Life of Emma Perry Carr," *Journal of Chemical Education* 63 (Nov. 1986): 923–27, and Carole B. Shmurak and Bonnie S. Handler, "'Castle of Science': Mount Holyoke College and the Preparation of Women in Chemistry, 1837–1941," *History of Education Quarterly* 32 (Fall 1992): 315–42. Multiple references and background information are provided in Margaret Rossiter, *Women in Science: Struggles and Strategies to 1940* (1983). An obituary is in the *New York Times*, 8 Jan. 1972.

SALLY GREGORY KOHLSTEDT

CARR, Eugene Asa (20 Mar. 1830–2 Dec. 1910), army officer, was born in Concord, Erie County, New York, the son of Clark Murwin Carr and Delia Ann Torrey (occupations unknown). He entered the U.S. Military Academy in 1846, graduating four years later, nineteenth in his class of forty-four. Assigned to the Regiment of Mounted Rifles as a brevet second lieutenant, Carr received his regular commission on 30 June 1851. Joining his regiment at Jefferson Barracks, Missouri, he served in two military expeditions to the Rocky Mountains during 1852–1853. The following year, Carr was wounded while serving as second in command during Captain John A. Walker's pursuit of Apaches west of newly created Fort Davis, Texas. Though his wound was initially presumed to be fatal, Carr recovered and was promoted to first lieutenant, First Cavalry Regiment.

Carr served in the Sioux expedition of 1855 before moving to Kansas, where he worked briefly as aide-de-camp to Governor Robert J. Walker. In 1858 Carr was promoted to captain and served in the Utah expedition. Transferred with his unit to Fort Washita, Indian Territory, he participated in several campaigns against the Comanches and Kiowas in 1859 and 1860.

With the outbreak of the Civil War, Carr joined General Nathaniel Lyon's command in southwestern Missouri. Brevetted a lieutenant colonel for his actions at the battle of Wilson's Creek, in August 1861 he was appointed colonel of the Third Illinois Volunteer Cavalry and was soon commanding a full brigade and eventually a division in General Samuel R. Curtis's Army of the Southwest. At the battle of Pea Ridge, Carr suffered three wounds but refused to leave the field; for having held his position despite heavy losses, he was promoted to brigadier general of volunteers and would subsequently (1894) be awarded the Medal of Honor for gallantry. Carr commanded a division in the Vicksburg campaign, where he distinguished himself in fighting at Edwards' Station, Port Gibson, Big Black River Bridge, and Champion Hill. Promoted to brevet colonel (regular army), Carr fought in several engagements in the Department of Arkansas until 1865, when he led a division during General Edward R. S. Canby's campaign against Mobile, Alabama. In the process, Carr was ultimately promoted to brevet major general of volunteers on 13 March 1865.

Carr reverted to his regular rank of major as part of the massive army reductions following the Civil War. Commanding a detachment at Raleigh, North Carolina, from March 1866 to April 1867, Carr then took several staff assignments in Washington, D.C. He returned to Kansas and rejoined his Fifth Cavalry, taking an active role in the southern Plains campaigns of 1868–1869. In one of the regular army's most decisive victories against the American Indians, on 11 July 1869 Carr's command routed a group of Cheyenne Dog Soldiers at Summit Springs, Colorado.

Stationed in Nebraska and later Arizona, in early 1873 Carr was promoted to lieutenant colonel. After taking a leave of absence to visit Europe, he returned to his regiment, stationed at Fort Hays, Kansas, in June 1875. During the Great Sioux War (1876), Carr briefly commanded the District of the Black Hills and fought at the battle of Slim Buttes. He later served a brief stint with troops in Chicago during the 1877 railway strike.

In 1879 Carr received full colonelcy of the Sixth Cavalry Regiment and proceeded to Arizona. There he participated in numerous campaigns against the Apaches, the most famous of which occurred on 30 August 1881 at Cibicu Creek. During that controversial engagement, the American Indian auxiliaries serving with Carr mutinied, killing or mortally wounding one officer and seven enlisted men and nearly annihilating his entire command. An official investigation largely exonerated Carr of any substantial charges, tempering its criticism of his judgment with praise for his bravery and quick thinking once the affair actually began. Transferred with his regiment in 1883 to New Mexico, Carr and the Sixth were rushed north to participate in the Wounded Knee campaign of 1890–1891.

Appointed brigadier general on 19 July 1892, Carr retired from active duty on 15 February 1893. He died in Washington, D.C., survived by his wife, Mary P. Maguire, whom he had married in 1865, and two children. During the 1870s, one newspaper correspondent had described him as "short, fairly stout, full-bearded, and lavish while in conversation of graceful and energetic gestures" (Altshuler, p. 60). Carr, like so many of his fellow officers, had found the transition from the promotions and fame of the Civil War to the more frustrating monotony of the frontiers difficult. Angry that others had gained more public recognition and quicker promotion for fighting American Indians than he, Carr was troubled by bouts with alcoholism during the postbellum years (J. C. Kelton to John M. Schofield, 5 Feb. 1873, John M. Schofield Papers, Library of Congress). In his prime, however, Carr, called "War Eagle" by the American Indians, had ranked among the army's most effective American-Indian fighters. Phil Sheridan once described him as "always active, competent and brave" (Hutton, p. 314).

• The Eugene A. Carr Papers are located at the U.S. Army Military History Research Collection, Carlisle Barracks, Pa. The standard biography of Carr is James T. King, *War Eagle: A Life of General Eugene A. Carr* (1963). Shorter biographical accounts may be found in Constance Wynn Altshuler, *Cavalry Yellow and Infantry Blue: Army Officers in Arizona between 1851 and 1886* (1991) and *Records of Living Officers of the United States Army* (1884). A good survey of the army during Carr's career is Paul Andrew Hutton, *Phil Sheridan and His Army* (1985).

ROBERT WOOSTER

CARR, John Dickson (30 Nov. 1906–27 Feb. 1977), writer of mystery and detective novels, was born in Uniontown, Pennsylvania, the son of Wooda Nicholas Carr, a lawyer, Democratic congressman (1913–1915), and then U.S. postmaster for Uniontown, and Amanda Julia Cook. A precocious child, he gained a name among his father's colleagues in the lower house of Congress by reciting poetry from table tops at age eight. His impulsive activities continued through college, where he devoted less energy to law, his supposed course of study, than to developing his talent for investigative journalism, an interest perhaps spurred by the combined influence of his father's law office and his grandfather's part ownership of a newspaper. He is particularly remembered for staging fake murders, complete with "dead bodies," to lure the police. Nonetheless, he graduated from Haverford College in 1928 and moved to Paris, where he attended the Sorbonne.

Carr did not fit in with the radical fringe of foreign writers who frequented the Paris cafés, so he took rooms on the Right Bank, where he wrote prodigiously, though taking time off to proselytize, in a good-natured manner, to the Left Bank bohemians. Dissatisfied at the time with the quality of his work, Carr burned all his manuscripts before or shortly after completing them, an action he later regretted, and returned after two years to the United States. He completed his first mystery novel, *It Walks by Night* (1930), in a New York hotel room. At a time when average sales for such novels ranged from 3,000 to 5,000 copies, the 24-year-old Carr became a bestselling author as his first book quickly sold more than 15,000. He went on to write, at times, up to six books a year.

Carr traveled continuously between France, the United States, and England, spending money prodigiously and frequently running out of funds. In 1931 he married Clarice Cleaves, an Englishwoman from Bristol, with whom he had three daughters. The couple lived in Bristol until an excellent review by Dorothy Sayers in the *Sunday Times* (London) soon launched Carr onto the British literary scene. The family moved to London, where they lived until 1948, during which time Carr wrote most of his books, using not only his own name, but also the pseudonyms "Carr Dickson" and "Carter Dickson." During World War II he also wrote propaganda broadcasts for the BBC; a weekly radio mystery show, "Appointment with Fear"; and initiated the "Suspense" series on American radio. Despite being bombed out of his house three times during the 1940–1941 blitz, Carr, described by a *National Review* critic in 1971 as "an unapologetic Tory—an old-fashioned champion of gentility, taste, standards and romance," remained in London until his objections to the policies of postwar Labor governments led him to return to the United States in 1948.

Carr objected to the disparaging way in which writers of detective fiction were frequently discussed in literary circles. He himself successfully attempted other genres: he wrote in 1949 a bestselling authorized biography of Sir Arthur Conan Doyle and in the 1950s a number of historical mysteries set in the Restoration and Regency periods. He is best known for what has been called his infinite and varied exploitation of the "locked room" puzzle in mystery and detective fiction and for his sleuth heroes, Sir Henry Merrivale (whom Carr claimed embodied "a lot of Winston Churchill . . . and even a little of me") and Dr. Gideon Fell (whom he clearly modeled on his personal hero, the British writer G. K. Chesterton).

At a time when much American detective fiction was predictable and riddled with clichés and British mystery writing centered mainly on the upper classes, Carr's novels broke the mold, combining a particular sense of the macabre—dealing with such topics as devil worship, witchcraft, and the supernatural—with a new depiction of women as sexually suggestive, even frank. It was perhaps this originality that led to the decisions to award him two Mystery Writers of America "Edgars" (Edgar Allan Poe awards) and two Ellery Queen awards for short fiction, among many other awards and honors.

Some critics have objected that Carr's obsession with the intense logic of the plot leaves little room for characterization, and that while Carr's earlier novels emulate many of the finer aspects of Poe and Chesterton (two of his particular influences), such imaginative depth is frequently overwhelmed in his later works by what almost seems to be a passion for intellectualism. He had a tendency to allow plots to turn on minutely specific—although technically accurate—details, mined from his own extensive library of reference works on crime, punishment, eighteenth-century trial proceedings, the medical effects of poison, and other such vital areas of inquiry. Modern scholars may investigate Carr's work for the expressions of class, gender, and race that, for example, allow Sir Henry Merrivale to tell Joan Bailey she has "a figure that would make Aphrodite look like a laundry bag in a thunderstorm," or that led Carr himself to say that he had "never met a really good-looking adventuress with slant eyes."

Carr died in Greenville, South Carolina, leaving behind a reputation as one of the finest mystery writers of the twentieth century. A number of his books, radio scripts, and short stories have been made into films (*The Emperor's Snuffbox* was filmed as *City after Midnight* in 1959). Whether it is a feature of their ingenuity, their constant ability to surprise the reader at every turn, their pioneering combination of horror and suspense with detective fiction, or the fact that Carr invariably and somewhat nostalgically invokes a sense of morality and justice eventually triumphing, his books continue to be reprinted and to find a wide audience.

• For an extensive bibliography of Carr's writings, see James Lesniak, ed., *Contemporary Authors*, new rev. ser., vol. 33 (1991). Carr is best known for his Dr. Fell series and Sir Henry Merrivale books. *The Devil in Velvet* (1951), a historical mystery, remains one of his most popular works and was Carr's personal favorite. Carr is the subject of a two-part profile in the *New Yorker*, 8 and 15 Sept. 1951, and a *Life* magazine profile, 29 Dec. 1953. More recent treatments include Douglas G. Greene, *John Dickson Carr: The Man Who Explained Miracles* (1995), and S. T. Joshi, *John Dickson Carr: A Critical Study* (1990). See also Howard Haycraft, *Murder for Pleasure: The Life and Times of the Detective Story* (1941); C. A. Hoyt, ed., *Minor American Novelists* (1970); Julian Symons, *Mortal Consequences: A History—from the Detective Story to the Crime Novel* (1972); James Kingman, "John Dickson Carr and the Aura of Genius," *Armchair Detective*, Spring 1981; Kingsley Amis, "The Art of the Impossible," *Times Literary Supplement*, 5 June 1981; and Edmund Miller, "Stanislaw Lem and John Dickson Carr: Critics of the Scientific World-View," *Armchair Detective*, Fall 1981. An obituary is in the *New York Times*, 1 Mar. 1977.

PETER E. MORGAN

CARR, Joseph F. (22 Oct. 1880–20 May 1939), sports executive, promoter, and sportswriter, was born in Columbus, Ohio. Little is known about Carr's parentage or early life except that after attending high school in Columbus he went to work as a machinist for the Panhandle Division of the Pennsylvania Railroad. From 1900 to 1906 he also was employed as a sportswriter for the *Ohio State Journal*, rising to the rank of assistant sports editor. In 1901 he organized the Panhandle White Sox baseball team, a Columbus semiprofessional organization that played in the Ohio State League (OSL). The team featured six brothers named Nesser who worked for the Panhandle Division. Carr also served as secretary of the league in 1906 and president in 1908. In 1910 Carr married Josephine Marie Sullivan; they had two children. After a six-year absence the OSL returned in 1922 with Carr again president. He was also president of the Columbus franchise through the 1931 season. In 1933 Carr became director of the National Baseball Association's promotional department and served in this position until his death. The number of minor leagues had shrunk to only 12 when Carr took the job, but under his leadership 41 leagues were in business by the end of the decade. During the 1930s Carr was also a member of the executive committee of the American Baseball Federation.

An avid sports enthusiast, Carr became a basketball promoter in the 1920s when he organized the American Basketball League (ABL) in 1925 with teams in nine cities. The Chicago team was owned and coached by George Halas, who was Carr's colleague in building the National Football League (NFL). "Joe talked me into it," Halas recalled. "I didn't know much about basketball but Joe said it had the potential to be a big league sport. If Joe said so, that was good enough for me." Carr served as president of the ABL from 1925 to 1928 before his commitment to professional football forced him to resign. During that time, he introduced pro basketball to New York's Madison Square Garden by arranging for ABL games to be played there.

Carr's most significant venture in sports promotion came with his involvement in the NFL. In 1904 he organized the Columbus Panhandle football team built around the six Nesser brothers. For a number of years the Panhandles were one of the top teams in pro football. In 1920 Columbus became a charter member of the American Professional Football Association (APFA), which became the NFL in 1922. Although a popular choice to become first president of the new league, Carr instead favored Jim Thorpe for the position, believing that Thorpe's name would enhance the APFA's popularity. After a disappointing initial season, in 1921 Carr became president of the league, a position he held until his death. At that time pro football had been largely confined to small midwestern towns and cities and plagued by contract jumping among players, unstable franchises, the practice of raiding college rosters, and gambling. As NFL president, Carr nurtured the game into a respectable big-time sport.

Under Carr's leadership all NFL franchises had moved to large metropolitan areas by 1934 with the exception of the Green Bay Packers. In 1925 Carr was personally involved in establishing a franchise in New York City, to be known as the Giants, which improved the league's credibility. To provide stability to the league, in 1921 he instituted the standard player contract, which helped end the practice of players jumping from team to team. Later he introduced a fixed schedule of games determined by the league as well as game officials hired by the NFL. One of the most persistent criticisms of pro football was that teams frequently hired college players who used assumed names to compete in the games, which were mainly played on Sundays. Carr cracked down on this practice by disqualifying the original Green Bay franchise in 1922 for using college men and the Milwaukee franchise in 1925 for employing high school players. When Red Grange signed to play for the Chicago Bears immediately after his last college game in 1925, college officials again cried foul. Carr immediately instituted a rule that prohibited NFL teams from signing college players until their class had graduated. This rule did much to mitigate the charge that pro football undermined the college amateur ethic.

During the mid-1920s Carr fought off a challenge by the American Football League (AFL), organized by Red Grange and his agent, Charles C. Pyle. When Grange and Pyle proposed to establish an NFL franchise in New York in 1926 that would compete with the Giants, Carr denied the request, which led to the establishment of the AFL. By helping to force the collapse of the AFL after only one season, Carr strengthened the NFL by reinforcing the principle that teams would not be challenged by other league franchises in their territorial areas. During the 1930s Carr oversaw the beginning of divisional play within the NFL and an annual championship playoff. League rules were also refined to place greater emphasis on the offensive aspect of the game; two of the most important changes were the implementation of the hash mark procedure and the relocation of the goal posts to the goal lines.

Carr died of cardiac arrest in Columbus. In 1963 he was posthumously named a charter member of the Professional Football Hall of Fame.

• A newspaper file on Carr is in the Professional Football Hall of Fame in Canton, Ohio. The best published sources on Carr are David S. Neft and Richard Cohen et al., *Pro Football, the Early Years: An Encyclopedic History, 1895–1959* (1987); Arthur Daley, *Pro Football's Hall of Fame* (1963); George Sullivan, *Pro Football's All-Time Greats: The Immortals in Pro Football's Hall of Fame* (1968); and Roger Treat, ed., *The Official National Football League Football Encyclopedia* (1979). See also Marc Maltby, "The Origin and Early Development of Professional Football, 1900–1920" (Ph.D. diss., Ohio Univ., 1987); and Robert Peterson, *Cages to Jump Shots: Pro Basketball's Early Years* (1990). An obituary is in the *New York Times*, 21 May 1939.

JOHN M. CARROLL

CARR, Wilbur John (31 Oct. 1870–26 June 1942), State Department official, was born near Taylorsville, Ohio, the son of Edward Livingston Carr and Catherine Fender, farmers. An elder son from whom much was expected, Carr grew up not far from Zanesville in southeastern Ohio. Aiming toward a business career, he graduated from the Commercial College of the University of Kentucky in 1889 and polished his shorthand and typewriting skills at Chafee's Phonographic Institute in Oswego, New York. The following year, Carr accepted a position as secretary of the Peekskill Military Academy. Having passed the federal civil service examination, in 1892 Carr departed the bucolic environment of a preparatory school and Dutchess County, New York, for Washington, D.C. He had secured a clerkship in the State Department, an organization that was beginning to emerge from decades of lethargy.

On 1 June 1892 Carr reported for duty, was assigned to address envelopes, and found himself immediately rebuked for using elaborate Spencerian penmanship rather than the plain calligraphy customary in the department. He acknowledged in a personal diary that the daily routine was "dwarfing to the mind."

Although Carr's goal was to use this opportunity to pursue the study of law—he earned an LL.B. from Georgetown University in 1894 and the LL.M. from Columbian (later George Washington) University in 1899—he became reconciled to government service and, indeed, demonstrated himself early to be an able and innovative administrator. Carr married Mary Eugenia Crane of Washington in 1897.

Added responsibility and advancement came quickly. He had participated as early as 1894 in embryonic attempts to reform the consular and diplomatic services, then crippled by lack of professional standards, excessive politicization, and even widespread corruption. After 1902, when Carr was appointed head of the Consular Bureau and assigned oversight of some 300 U.S. consular posts abroad, he took a leading role in the movement for reform. His efforts were instrumental in passage of the Lodge Act of April 1906, which classified all consular posts by size and functions, placed consuls on salaries, and prohibited supplementary financial endeavors for those earning more than $1,000 annually. He also played a role in drafting President Theodore Roosevelt's executive order of November 1905 that sought to eradicate political influence by requiring competitive examinations for appointments and promotions.

Carr was appointed chief clerk of the State Department in 1907, a position he held until his retirement in 1937; he received formal designation as director of the Consular Service in 1909. During most of the department's existence, responsibility for its daily affairs and, thus, enormous power resided with the chief clerk. Indeed, three departmental officials (William Hunter, Alvey A. Adee, and the last and most influential, Carr) together accumulated 152 years of service. Carr presided over momentous changes in administration of the State Department's consular and diplomatic services. After his wife's death in 1911, he married Edith Adele Koon in 1917. No children were born to either marriage, and Carr's interests aside from the department were limited to the poetry of Dante and photography.

Carr's vision of a professional consular service and a modern, efficient system of departmental administration was only slowly realized. It suffered a serious setback during the stewardship of William Jennings Bryan (1913–1915), who was eager to award consular and diplomatic posts to "needy Democrats." Although Carr himself did not go abroad until 1916, any campaign for professionalization had to contend with mossbacks—conservative timeservers in the department and their supporters in Congress—who possessed little knowledge of or interest in world affairs. Persevering, Carr won a signal victory with passage in 1924 of the Rogers Act, which greatly restricted opportunities for political patronage by merging the consular and diplomatic services into one Foreign Service. Armed with the authority conferred by his appointment in July 1924 as assistant secretary of state and head of the new Foreign Service, Carr beat back repeated attempts to impose a dual salary system and to block the assignment of former consular personnel to diplomatic posts. So widely regarded for fairness and unswerving commitment was Carr by the late 1920s that congressional committees tended to accept without challenge his recommendations on budgetary and administrative issues. To Francis M. Huntington-Wilson, a State Department contemporary, Carr was the quintessential bureaucrat: "He toed in slightly, as if from so many years of walking the straight line of Civil Service duty."

Near-universal admiration for Carr led President Franklin D. Roosevelt to grant a special dispensation so that he could continue in office after the mandatory retirement age of sixty-five. Two years later, in July 1937 Carr released administration of the Department of State and accepted an appointment as U.S. minister to Czechoslovakia. Carr enjoyed this singular opportunity to represent his country as a diplomat and, according to George F. Kennan who served with him in Prague, he performed his duties with "imperturbable patience . . . and transparent integrity." Carr returned to Washington after the Nazi occupation of Czechoslovakia in March 1939. While undergoing treatment for complications from chronic asthma, he died in Baltimore, Maryland. Although Congress did not approve the Foreign Service Act, which fully integrated the consular and diplomatic services and thus completed the program of reform to which Carr had devoted much of his career until 1946, four years after his death, Wilbur John Carr is correctly acknowledged as one of its chief architects.

• Carr's papers, including a handwritten diary that is helpful for personal matters and personalities in the Department of State, are in the Library of Congress. Katharine Crane, *Mr. Carr of State* (1960), though blatantly admiring and chatty in tone, remains essential for Carr's life and career. Insightful comments about Carr are in Francis M. Huntington-Wilson, *Memoirs of an Ex-Diplomat* (1945); Waldo H. Heinrichs, *American Ambassador: Joseph C. Grew and the Development of an American Diplomatic Tradition* (1966); and George F. Kennan, *Memoirs, 1925–1950* (1967). *Professional Diplomacy in the United States, 1779–1939: A Study in Administrative History* (1961), Warren F. Ilchman's treatment of the efforts to modernize the Department of State and of Carr's role, is extremely helpful. See also Graham H. Stuart, *American Diplomatic and Consular Practice* (1952); Rachel West, *The Department of State on the Eve of the First World War* (1978); Robert D. Schulzinger, *The Making of the Diplomatic Mind: The Training, Outlook, and Style of United States Foreign Service Officers, 1908–1931* (1975); and Richard H. Werking, *The Master Architects: Building the United States Foreign Service, 1890–1913* (1977).

THEODORE A. WILSON

CARREL, Alexis (28 June 1873–5 Nov. 1944), scientist, was born Marie Joseph Auguste Carrel in Sainte-foy-Lès Lyon, France, the son of Alexis Carrel-Billiard, a manufacturer of textiles, and Anne-Marie Ricard. In 1890 Carrel entered the Faculty of Medicine at the University of Lyon, completing his training in 1900. While still a medical student, he began research on the problems of joining severed blood vessels. His interest in this area was supposedly aroused because surgeons had failed to save the life of Marie-François-Sadi Carnot, the French president who was fatally wounded by an assassin while visiting Lyon in 1894. Carrel's triangulation method (1902) required inserting single threads at three points on the circumference of each vessel, pulling gently on each thread so that the circular vessels became triangular, and finally sewing the straight edges together.

Carrel twice failed the difficult qualifying examinations for surgery and became increasingly frustrated with what he perceived as the narrowness and conservatism of the society in which he lived and worked. In 1904 he emigrated to Montreal and later the same year moved to Chicago, where he continued his research on joining severed blood vessels. He worked with Charles Guthrie at the University of Chicago, where they performed organ transplants in dogs, especially of kidneys. Carrel became a member of the Rockefeller Institute of New York in 1906 and remained there for the next thirty-three years. He won the Nobel Prize in physiology or medicine in 1912 for his research in transplantation and the repair of blood vessels. In 1913 he married a widow, Anne-Marie Laure Gourlez de la Meyrie (her maiden name was de la Motte). The couple had no children.

Carrel's surgical skills were put to use during World War I, when he was called back to France to serve in the French army. He established a hospital at Compiègne, where he carried out research on the best means to treat war wounds. Carrel devised a means by which wounds could be continuously perfused with a saline solution ("Dakin solution") that was intended to clear the wounds of bacterial infection. After the war Carrel returned to the Rockefeller Institute to continue his surgical research. A highlight of this later research was his collaboration with Charles A. Lindbergh in the development of a perfusion apparatus for the organs—the so-called Glass Heart (1935). The newsmaking combination of Lindbergh, Carrel, and the glass heart was irresistible to the press, and Carrel's name was featured prominently in the headlines.

The second of Carrel's major contributions to biomedical research was his enthusiastic espousal of tissue culture and the technical advance he made to the field. Tissue culture was developed by Ross G. Harrison and used by him to investigate the growth and nerve fibers. Carrel took up tissue culture to investigate wound healing, and he showed that cells from a wide variety of tissues and organisms, including human tissues, could be grown in vitro (1910). He introduced a water extract of chick embryos as a medium in which to grow cells (1913); a technique using glass flasks to hold the cultures (1923); and a method for subdividing a growing culture so that it could be maintained for a long time (1912). Carrel made headlines with his claim that he could grow chicken heart cells indefinitely (1913), a feat that has never been repeated and what success he believed he had was probably due to living cells present in the chick embryo extract used to grow the cells. Carrel's emphasis on the need for a rigorous aseptic technique may have deterred others from taking up cell culture.

Carrel used his position as one of the United States' most prominent biomedical researchers to make known his views on a wide variety of social issues. His controversial book, *Man, the Unknown* (1935), included praise for Benito Mussolini, advocacy of eugenics, the claim that mental disorders were to be feared because "they profoundly weaken the dominant white races," and the suggestion that criminals, including those who "misled the public in important matters . . . should be humanely and economically disposed of in small euthanasic institutions supplied with the proper gases." Carrel's views found a sympathetic audience, for, as he wrote, "After all, scientists are only men. They are saturated with the prejudices of their environment and of their epoch." The book became a best-seller, and his public lectures on sociopolitical topics became so popular that large forces of police had to be called out to control the crowds. His second book, *Reflections on Life*, was published posthumously (English ed., 1952). Carrel also wrote articles on medical and health matters for popular journals such as *Reader's Digest*.

In 1903 Carrel acted as physician to a party traveling to France to the religious shrine at Lourdes and witnessed the apparently miraculous recovery of a young girl suffering from what appeared to be terminal tuberculous peritonitis. He saw other remarkable cures on subsequent visits and maintained a lifelong interest in the spiritual aspects of healing and psychic phenomena. In 1935 Carrel began planning for an institute that would combine rigorous scientific research with investigations of mystical and paranormal phenomena, but no reputable scientists were prepared to be associated with this enterprise. Carrel reached retirement age in 1938 and left the Rockefeller Institute, where his colleagues found his political views distasteful and did not urge him to stay. Returning to France, he created the Fondation Francaise pour l'Etude des Problems Humains in 1939. Studies at his foundation included telepathy, extrasensory perception, and water divination. More conventional subjects were studied there as well, including nutrition, demography, and occupational medicine. Throughout World War II Carrel remained as director of the foundation, which received support from the Vichy government. After France was liberated he was accused of being a collaborator. Whether these suspicions were justified was never determined, for Carrel died at his home in Paris before he could be brought to trial.

Carrel's important contributions to experimental surgery and tissue culture have withstood the test of time. His willingness to attempt difficult procedures, his manual dexterity, and his insistence on maintaining scrupulously aseptic conditions in the preantibiotic era contributed to his success. However, his reputation as a philosopher, mystic, and sociopolitical commentator suffered a decline that is unlikely to be reversed.

• The principal collection of Carrel's papers is in the Special Collections Division of the University Library of Georgetown University. In addition, the Archives Office of Rockefeller University has a small collection of his papers, including Carrel's scientific reports made annually to the scientific directors of the Rockefeller Institute. Accounts of Carrel's career tend to be hagiographic and should be read with a healthy degree of skepticism. The principal biographies are W. Sterling Edwards and Peter D. Edwards, *Alexis Carrel: Visionary Surgeon* (1974), and Theodore I. Malinin, *Surgery and Life: The Extraordinary Career of Alexis Carrel* (1979). In addition, good accounts of Carrel's work at the Rockefeller Institute are in George W. Corner, *A History of the Rockefeller Institute, 1901–1953* (1964). Corner includes interesting comments on Carrel's personality and interactions with his colleagues. A brief but comprehensive review of Carrel's surgical research is Julius H. Comroe, "Who Was Alexis Who?" *American Review of Respiratory Diseases* 118 (1978): 391–402. An assessment of Carrel's contributions to tissue culture is Jan A. Witkowski, "Alexis Carrel and the Mysticism of Tissue Culture," *Medical History* 23 (1979): 279–96. The myth of the immortality of Carrel's chick heart cells persists despite evidence suggesting that self-deception, if not fraud, was a factor in the supposed success of these cultures; see Witkowski, "Dr. Carrel's Immortal Cells," *Medical History* 24 (1980): 129–42. The "glass heart" for perfusing organs was devised by Carrel and Charles A. Lindbergh between 1931 and 1935; the most complete account is their book, *The Culture of Organs* (1938). Carrel's methods for treating war wounds were described in his collaboration with G. Dehelly, *The Treatment of Infected Wounds* (1917). Carrel's controversial *Man, the Unknown* was also his most popular; it went through at least forty editions.

JAN A. WITKOWSKI

CARREÑO, Teresa (22 Dec. 1853–12 June 1917), pianist, was born in Caracas, Venezuela, the daughter of Manuel Antonio Carreño, a Venezuelan minister of finance, and Corinda García de Sena y Toro. Although the young Carreño exhibited musical talent as a toddler, she did not begin studying the piano with her father, a talented amateur, until she was six. Manuel Antonio devised clever technical and musical exercises for his precocious daughter, which included improvisation, harmony, and variation techniques. His educational methods created a foundation of meticulous work habits from which Carreño would never stray.

In July 1862 the political situation in Venezuela became untenable for Manuel Antonio and he moved his family to New York. It was there, on 25 November 1862, that Teresa, not quite nine years old, made her piano debut at Irving Hall. The resounding success of the recital brought invitations for four repeat performances and drew the attention of Louis Moreau Gottschalk, America's foremost pianist. Gottschalk not only offered lessons to Carreño but became her most influential publicist. While introducing his protégé he once wrote: "On hearing her one sees, one feels at once that Teresa plays the piano as the bird sings, as the flower opens its petals. She is born to music, she has the instinct of the beauty—she devines it!" After performing in Cuba, completing a series of twelve recitals in Boston and a short tour of New England, Carreño was invited to the White House in 1863 to play privately for President Abraham Lincoln and his family. The program, including works of Bach and Gottschalk, ended with a series of brilliant improvisations on the president's favorite song, "Listen to the Mockingbird."

In March 1866, with her reputation firmly established in the United States, Carreño and her family moved to Paris. By May of the same year, she had become the darling of the French artistic community. Embraced by such patrons as Giocomo Rossini, Madame Érard, Franz Liszt, and her first European teachers, Georges Mattias and Emmanuel Bazin, Carreño ascended to the elite cadre of European performers swiftly and effortlessly. For the next four years the Carreño family maintained a residence in Paris, although Teresa's performances took her throughout the Continent and frequently to England. In 1868 she was introduced to Anton Rubinstein who, as a master teacher and devoted friend, guided her career. With the outbreak of the Franco-Prussian War in July 1870, Carreño established residency in London, her home for the next four years.

By this time Carreño had developed into a pianist of incredible strength and virtuosity, features which earned her the title "the Valkyrie of the piano." She played with such power and passion that she drew criticism from some musicians. Paderewski commented that "Carreño was one of the women pianists who had a very big tone, but it was not a beautiful tone, because a beautiful tone must include tenderness, and there was none of that, just brilliance." She was a pianist with a large hand who played in the tradition of Franz Liszt and Anton Rubinstein and never felt restrained by the composer's manuscript. Changes in tempo, dynamics, or rhythm were often dictated by her emotions, and she improved upon some passages by improvisation or rescoring. Edward Greig once wrote of her playing that "the devil is in these virtuosos who always want to improve on everything." But there was never a doubt that she was a formidable musician, not merely a pianist. Carreño also composed virtuosic "salon pieces" that she used as encores. While not profound, they are well-crafted, pleasant vignettes.

In 1872, while on tour with the operatic impressario James Henry Mapleson, Carreño substituted for an ailing mezzo-soprano and, without benefit of rehearsal, sang the role of the Queen in Meyeberr's *Les Hugenots*. On 25 February 1876 her formal career as an operatic artist was launched when she performed Zerlina in Mozart's *Don Giovanni*. For the next decade she often neglected the piano to sing, conduct, and eventually codirect an ill-fated operatic troupe with her second husband, the baritone Giobani Tagliapietra.

Carreño first marriage, to the violinist Émile Sauret, was stormy and brief. After touring the United States and Canada together for several months in 1872, they married in 1873 and had two children (only the first survived). By 1875 Carreño had moved into a common-law marriage with Tagliapietra. Her second marriage lasted until 1889 and produced three children, the second of which, Teresita, became a noted pianist.

After separating from Tagliapietra, Carreño resumed her career as a concert pianist with her German debut in Berlin on 18 November 1889. Her performance of the Grieg concerto with the Berlin Philharmonic orchestra drew the attention of Hans von Bülow, who acclaimed her as "the most interesting pianist of the present age, a phenomenon. She sweeps the floor clean of all piano paraders who, after her arrival, must take themselves elsewhere." Eventually settling in Berlin, she soon embarked upon a number of concert tours which established her as the leading female pianist of the period.

It was in Berlin in 1892 that Carreño met and married her third husband, the brilliant pianist and composer, Eugen d'Albert. Of this couple a Berlin music critic once wrote: "Frau Carreño yesterday played for the first time the second concerto of her third husband at the fourth Philharmonic concert." Although the marriage was to last only three years (and produce two more daughters), Carreño benefited greatly by her musical association with d'Albert. Her sense of style was refined as she began to explore the more subtle realms of pianism; her tone softened, her tempo became more relaxed and consistent, and she learned to restrain and control her excesses.

Carreño married a fourth and final time in 1902, to Arturo Tagliapietra, the younger brother of her second husband. The event was somewhat scandalous but proved to be the only marriage in which Carreño was truly happy. Tagliapietra served as a business manager and companion not only to Teresa but to her daughter, Teresita, as well. For the next fifteen years Carreño toured arduously, often playing more than seventy recitals and concerts a year. Her repertoire was immense as was the energy she expended to survive the constant travel, performance schedules and rigorous practice routines. By 1910 she had also established a large studio of students: she was considered an outstanding teacher. Her treatise, "Possibilities of Tone Color by Artistic Use of Pedals" (1909), is considered one of the finest pedagogical works available to teachers. Music of her most famous student, Edward MacDowell, was often included in her programs, beginning with the First Modern Suite in 1883 and including performances of his first concerto in 1888 and the second concerto, dedicated to Carreño, in 1890.

Carreño also traveled to Australia, New Zealand and the United States for concerts in 1907–1908, again in 1909–1911, and extensively toured the United States in 1913–1914. With the outbreak of the First World War, Carreño's concert schedule was curtailed dramatically and in 1916 she moved to New York in search of a larger audience. She played her last American concert with the New York Philharmonic Society in 1916 and her final recital in Havana, Cuba, on 12 March 1917. Her death in New York City followed a brief illness. Her ashes were first interred in Union Hill, New Jersey, later moved to Berlin, and finally, according to her wishes, moved to the Cementerio del Sur in Caracas, Venezuela, in 1938.

Carreño's legacy is that of the consummate musical artist whose entire life was dedicated to the expression of her art. Her concerts were spectacles that inspired audiences to shout boisterously, throw bouquets of flowers, and demand repeated encores. Her pianistic showmanship was rivaled only by the bravura styles of Franz Liszt, Ignace Paderewski, Anton Rubinstein, and Ferruccio Bustoni, and it was frequently remarked that "she played like a man." During her lifetime more than thirty of her compositions, mostly for solo piano, were published by the publishing houses of Heugel in Pris and Ditson in Boston. Carreño's artistic contributions were vast and, along with Clara Schumann, Wanda Landowska, and Myra Hess, she will always be considered as one of the "grandes dames" of the keyboard.

• The Teresa Carreño Collection at Vassar College contains manuscripts, papers, photographs, music, costumes, clippings, and other memorabilia of the pianist, which the college purchased from the Carreno estate in 1941; a detailed list of holdings may be found in Brian Mann's article in *Music Library Association Notes* 47 (1990–1991). The most complete biography is Marta Milinowski, *Teresa Carreño: By the Grace of God* (1940), but a number of shorter biographies, in Spanish, should be consulted: Lucilia Palacios, *Teresa Carreño* (1975); two works by Milanca Guzmán, *Teresa Carreño* (1987) and *Quién fué Teresa Carreño?* (1990); Juan Bautista Plaza, *Teresa Carreño* (1938); Israel Pena, *Teresa Carreño* (1953); Rosario Marciano, *Teresa Carreño* (1966); Carmen Clemente Travieso, *Teresa Carreño* (1953); and A. Marques Rodriquez, *Esbozo Biográfico de Teresa Carreño* (1953). Valuable descriptions of Carreño's life are contained in David Ewen, *Musicians Since 1900*, and Harold Schonberg, *The Great Pianists* (1963). Periodical sources include R. Stevenson, "Carreño's 1875 California Appearances," *Int. American Music Revue* 5 (1983); M. S. Fainshtein, "Teresa Carreño's Russian Visits," *Int. American Music Revue* 3 (1981); and N. Bergenfeld, "Piano Mastery—Profiles of Twentieth-Century Artist-Teachers," *Piano Quarterly* 19 (1971). Earlier articles, many of which were published shortly after Carreño's death, include two by William Armstrong, "The Best Musical Investment," *Musician*, Mar. 1917, and "Teresa Carreño's Reminiscences," *Musical Courier*, 28 June 1917 and 6 July 1917; and Yetta Dorothea Giffen's "Wisdom and Wit from the Lips of Teresa Carreño," *Musical Courier*, 8 Mar. 1917, "Teresa Carreño's Death Ends Notable Career," *Musical America*, 23 June 1917, and "Idealism in Music: An Interview with Teresa Carreño," *Etude*, June 1917. Obituaries are in the *New York Times*, 13, 15, and 17 June 1917.

ROBERT WYATT

CARRÈRE, John Merven (9 Nov. 1858–1 Mar. 1911), architect, was born in Rio de Janeiro, Brazil, the son of a prosperous American coffee trader of French descent. After pursuing an exclusive European education, Carrère chose to begin a career in architecture, gaining admission to the preeminent design academy of the era, the École des Beaux-Arts in Paris, in 1878. In 1881 Carrère sought out American "compatriot" Thomas Hastings as a partner in a student design project. Hastings later noted that his fellow student "both looked and spoke like a Frenchman," in spite of his

U.S. citizenship ("John Merven Carrère," p. 65). After attaining the rank of student of the first class, Carrère left the École des Beaux-Arts in 1882.

Little is known of the circumstances that led Carrère to New York, but by the time Hastings arrived at the office of McKim, Mead and White in late 1883, Carrère had already established himself as a draftsman for the firm. While at the École Carrère had absorbed the academy's classically based principles, which were reinforced by further training under McKim, another École alumnus steeped in the French method of design. Teamed on several projects, Carrère and Hastings soon discovered that their talents were complementary, with the former handling administration, management, and finance and the latter concentrating on design and rendering. The two broke away from McKim, Mead and White in 1885 and soon established themselves as their mentors' chief rivals in the influential and profitable New York architecture scene of the turn of the century. In 1886 Carrère married Marion Dell; they had two daughters.

The period from 1890 to World War I in American architecture was dominated by the "Beaux-Arts movement," of which Carrère and Hastings were leading practitioners. Their firm did not ascribe to a single style but used Beaux-Arts planning methods that focused on creating monumental buildings based on a rigidly ordered plan. These structures were often cross-axial, with a clearly defined hierarchy of interior spaces and a heavy reliance on Italian Renaissance and eighteenth-century French models for exterior articulation and ornament. Cosmopolitan and École-trained architects like Carrère, Hastings, and McKim believed that demonstrating venerable standards of design in monumental commissions could help bring U.S. architecture into concert with the best of the European architectural tradition. In the hundreds of public buildings, grand residences, and commercial works it produced, the firm of Carrère and Hastings played a leading role in the establishment of Beaux-Arts planning and design as the standard for American monumental architecture of the period.

Carrère's role in the firm was almost exclusively managerial; the only design attributed to his own hand being that of his own residence, "Red Oak" (White Plains, N.Y., 1906–1908). In spite of a temperamental personality, unanimously described by contemporaries as "difficult" and "forceful," Carrère successfully maintained working relationships with powerful clients such as oil tycoon Henry Flagler (most notably the Ponce de Leon Hotel in St. Augustine, Fla., 1887; and "White Hall," Flagler's Palm Beach residence, 1901), rubber magnate Frank Goodyear (residence, Buffalo, N.Y., 1903), railroad heir William K. Vanderbilt, Jr. (residence, Great Neck, Long Island, 1903), and Secretary of State Elihu Root (residence, N.Y., 1903). Carrère's administrative skills and fierce dedication to the highest standards of construction and design contributed greatly to the success of such monumental projects as the Russell Senate Office Building (Washington, D.C., 1894–1906) and the firm's best-known work, the New York Public Library (1897–1911).

Carrère labored tirelessly for the advancement of his profession. An active member of the American Institute of Architects, a trustee of the American Academy in Rome, a founding member of the Beaux-Arts Society of Architects and of the Municipal Art Commission of the City of New York, Carrère privately gave financial support and encouragement to aspiring architects and artists. Carrère's stature in his profession was such that, on his death in a taxicab accident in New York City, the trustees of the New York Public Library permitted his body to lie in state in the building so closely associated with his name. Although Carrère's contribution to American architecture does not rest with his work as a designer, his efforts in management, professional advancement, and the promotion of Beaux-Arts standards of design made him one of the most influential figures in American architecture of the early twentieth century.

• Little scholarly attention has been given to John Carrère, the exception being Curtis Channing Blake's "The Architecture of Carrère and Hastings" (Ph.D. diss., Columbia Univ., 1976). For his contemporaries' tributes, see "John Merven Carrère," *New York Architect* 5 (May 1911): 65–72. "The Works of Carrère and Hastings," *Architectural Record* 27 (Jan. 1910): 1–120, illustrates many of the firm's important commissions and provides a general discussion of its perceived importance to the profession at that time. An obituary is in the *New York Times*, 2 Mar. 1911.

J. LAURIE OSSMAN

CARRICK, Samuel Czar (17 July 1760–17 Aug. 1809), Presbyterian minister and educator, was born in York (now Adams) County, Pennsylvania. Nothing is known of his parents. Shortly after his birth his family moved to Virginia's Shenandoah Valley, where he studied under the tutelage of the Reverend William Graham at Liberty Hall (now Washington and Lee College). He was a member of the school's first graduating class. In 1779 he married Elizabeth Moore, and they had three children. In 1782 Carrick was licensed to preach by the New Providence Presbyterian Church, and the following year he was ordained and installed as minister of the Rocky Spring and Wahab Presbyterian Church in Augustana County, Virginia.

Carrick ministered to Scotch-Irish Presbyterians on his itinerant horseback tours throughout Virginia and the Tennessee Territory. His ministry was part of a larger attempt by the Presbyterian church to plant congregations among the Scotch-Irish population then settling in the growing southwestern frontier. He was a popular itinerant, drawing large crowds wherever he preached. In 1787 the Reverend Samuel Doak, a Presbyterian minister in Tennessee and founder of Washington College, convinced Carrick to settle in this developing region and start a Presbyterian church. After a brief self-imposed hiatus from the ministry, owing to what he believed to be his slackened spiritual condition, Carrick in 1791 accepted Doak's challenge and settled, with his family, along the junction of the Holston and French Broad rivers in Tennessee. In the same year he established the Lebanon-in-the-Fork Church at Gilliam Station, a settlement located a few miles from the growing town of Knoxville. The church grew rapidly under Carrick's leadership, and soon the young Presbyterian had gained a reputation as an inspiring preacher and defender of Calvinist orthodoxy. The young community faced a series of attacks by Native Americans, and in 1793 Carrick's wife was killed during a raid by Creek and Cherokee Indians.

In 1793 Carrick began in his home a school designed to educate young men in the rudiments of Latin, Greek, geography, logic, astronomy, rhetoric, and natural and moral philosophy. His school operated on a semester schedule, with five months allotted for each term. He charged seven dollars per semester for education, room, and board. His most famous student was Hugh Lawson White, who would marry Carrick's daughter and become a U.S. senator and presidential candidate.

In 1794 Carrick married Anne McLellan. They had no children. That same year he was appointed by the Tennessee Territorial legislature as the first president of Blount College, an institution of higher education named for Tennessee governor William Blount. The school met in Carrick's house until proper facilities could be obtained. Blount College welcomed both male and female students, making it one of the first coeducational institutions of higher learning in the country, but the college struggled continually with financial problems and low enrollments, graduating only one student in its nine-year existence. As a result, in 1803 the school was closed, and in 1807 the institution was renamed and incorporated into what became East Tennessee College, the institutional forerunner of the University of Tennessee at Knoxville. The legislature asked Carrick to remain in his presidential role at the new institution, a position he would retain until his death.

Shortly after forming the Lebanon-in-the-Fork Church, Carrick organized the First Presbyterian Church of Knoxville. He served as pastor of both churches until 1803, when he left the Lebanon Church to focus his attention solely on the Knoxville congregation. He also played an important role in denominational affairs within the Presbyterian church. He was active in the Abington Presbytery and was influential in the formation of the Union Presbytery in 1797. Carrick fulfilled several responsibilities in the Presbyterian General Assembly. He authored pastoral letters on its behalf to the country's Presbyterian ministers, helped write the church's disciplinary regulations and codes of conduct, and served in 1806 as a commissioner. He prayed before several important political meetings of the Tennessee Territorial legislature related to the fate of Tennessee statehood.

In 1798 Carrick left his farm on the Holston River and moved to Knoxville to be closer to his work. He was known for doctrinal sermons grounded in biblical texts, a commitment to the growth of the Presbyterian church, and a cultured lifestyle even on the frontier. He also had some knowledge of medicine. Commonly referred to by his contemporaries as a "healer," he provided medical treatment and advice to friends and parishioners. Carrick died of a stroke in Knoxville. His ministry brought some institutional stability to the southwestern frontier by organizing churches and by encouraging a staid and sober version of Presbyterian faith in a region known for either its enthusiastic evangelicalism or for its lack of religion.

• Little is available concerning Carrick's life and career outside of his sporadic mention in records of the Presbyterian church. Some information is available in the Hanover, Abington, and Union Presbytery Minutes at the Office of History, Presbyterian Church in America, Montreat, N.C., and in Guy S. Klett, ed., *Minutes of the Presbyterian Church in America, 1706–1788* (1976). A chapter-length study of his ministry is in Earle W. Crawford, *An Endless Line of Splendor: Profiles of Six Pioneer Presbyterian Preacher-Educators* (1983). Other works that briefly address his career include William Henry Foote, *Sketches of North Carolina: Historical and Biographical* (1846); Foote, *Sketches of Virginia: Historical and Biographical* (1856); William Sprague, *Annals of the American Pulpit* (1859); and Ernest Trice Thompson, *Presbyterians in the South* (1963).

JOHN FEA

CARRIER, Willis Haviland (26 Nov. 1876–7 Oct. 1950), inventor, was born in Angola, New York, the son of Duane Williams Carrier, a dairy and fruit farmer, and Elizabeth Haviland, a schoolteacher. From an early age, Carrier showed an interest and ability in mechanics. Graduating in 1893 from Buffalo's Central High School, he was eager to pursue an engineering course at Cornell University, but the onset of a nationwide depression forced him to spend almost four years teaching at a local school.

Carrier later liked to tell interviewers he headed to Cornell in 1897 with five dollars in his pocket, although he had in fact won scholarships that paid his tuition and afforded a small stipend. He financed the rest with odd jobs. As a senior, Carrier and another student set up a cooperative laundry service that netted them almost $1,000 each.

In June 1901 Carrier received the degree of mechanical engineer in electrical engineering. He had hoped to work for General Electric but accepted an interview with Buffalo Forge, a major manufacturer of fans, blowers, and industrial heating equipment. That interview became the stuff of Carrier's personal and corporate legend. On a streetcar headed toward the plant, the new graduate asked directions of another young man who proved to be a Buffalo Forge engineer. With his assistance, Carrier secured an engineering position at ten dollars a week. J. Irvine Lyle, the chance acquaintance, became a lifelong friend and business partner.

Carrier was put to work on 1 July designing heating plants and drying equipment for industrial use. He soon realized that sketchy and inaccurate data based on old "rule of thumb" methods of measuring such variables as air pressure, humidity, and heat were crippling the operational efficiency of his firm's products. The young engineer worked extra hours to devise a fan design that required less horsepower. He presented his findings at a 1901 winter sales meeting attended by Buffalo Forge's top executives. By January 1902 the company had doubled Carrier's salary and let him start an industrial research laboratory.

Meanwhile, Lyle, now Buffalo Forge's New York City sales manager, had a humidity problem. Sackett-Wilhelms Lithographing and Publishing Co. of Brooklyn, printers of the popular humor magazine *Judge*, had suffered serious quality lapses during the unusually hot and muggy summers of 1900 and 1901. Ink would often fail to adhere to the paper, slowing the printing process and ruining quantities of stock. Lyle asked Carrier to propose a remedy.

Using Weather Bureau data, Carrier in July 1902 presented a plan for what was probably the first scientific air conditioning system. The printing process, he determined, needed an indoor temperature in summer of 80°F at 55 percent relative humidity, requiring the removal of 400 pounds of water from the air every hour. To achieve these conditions, Carrier installed two sections of chilled coil in the print shop. One circulated cold artesian well water; the other was connected to an ammonia refrigerating compressor.

The system worked and soon Buffalo Forge was approached by other industries needing moisture regulation for optimal production. Textile mills and the Detroit pharmaceutical maker Parke, Davis & Co. were early clients; the Celluloid Company, makers of film stock, and tobacco processors came later. To succeed, Carrier insisted, Buffalo Forge must guarantee its customer not just its equipment but the conditions of temperature and humidity the equipment would produce. It was the beginning of what Carrier would later advertise as "manufactured weather." Also in 1902, Carrier married Cornell classmate Edith Claire Seymour of Gloversville, New York. They had no children.

In 1906 Carrier was awarded the first of his more than 80 patents. Patent #808897, Apparatus for Treating Air, produced a fine spray of chilled water that cooled the air around it. Because air's ability to hold moisture declines as it gets colder—air at 70°F holds only half as much water vapor as 90°F air—wetting the air actually lowered its humidity. "He Dries Air with Water," marveled John Janney in a worshipful profile that appeared in the *American Magazine* (Feb. 1933, p. 37). Carrier's often counterintuitive approach to everyday physical phenomena was a key to his success as both inventor and publicist.

Carrier's most enduring theoretical breakthrough was the Psychrometric Chart, formally presented at the American Society of Mechanical Engineers' convention on 3 December 1911. The chart became the bible of the heating and air conditioning industry and, in modified form, is still in use. It graphically represents the relationships of five key variables associated with air temperature and humidity, enabling the engineer to accurately plot optimum combinations of heat and moisture for any industrial process or human activity.

In 1907 Buffalo Forge named Carrier vice president of a wholly owned subsidiary, the Carrier Air Conditioning Company of America. Sales had doubled by 1914, but the outbreak of war persuaded Buffalo Forge to return to its fundamental business of manufacturing rather than designing and installing systems. The separation was friendly. Carrier took with him six key employees including Lyle and a promise that Buffalo Forge would sell his undertaking most of the apparatus it required. With a capital stake of $32,600, Carrier and his six associates launched the Carrier Engineering Corporation on 1 July 1915. By the end of 1915 it had forty signed contracts.

Carrier's first wife had died in 1912, and in 1913 he married Jennie Tifft Martin of Angola, a relation of his stepmother, and they adopted sons Vernon and Earl.

Human comfort had been only an accidental byproduct of industrial air conditioning. In the 1920s, Carrier helped improve summer comfort when his expanding firm began installing cooling systems in urban movie palaces. New York City's plush Rivoli Theater was Carrier's biggest challenge. As the air conditioning went into operation at the Rivoli's Memorial Day opening in 1925, 2,000 patrons, including movie mogul Adolph Zukor, put aside the fans they had brought to keep cool.

Two Carrier inventions helped make comfort cooling possible. The centrifugal compressor, unveiled in May 1922, was more compact, efficient, and durable than previous machinery. Carrier's biographer, Margaret Ingels, called it the "first major advance in mechanical refrigeration since David Boyle designed the original ammonia compressor in 1872" (p. 61). An early model is in the permanent collection of the Smithsonian's National Museum of American History. At the same time, Carrier associate L. Logan Lewis engineered a new method of distributing refrigerated air without cold drafts. In 1928 Carrier used these innovations to air-condition the U.S. Capitol.

Movie air conditioning was most Americans' first real exposure to summer cooling. Carrier would insist all his life that proper air conditioning included winter heating and humidification but from the 1920s on "air conditioning" and "Carrier" became synonymous with cooling in the public mind.

In December 1930 Carrier Engineering merged with two competitors, Brunswick-Kroeschell and York Heating & Ventilating, to form the Carrier Corporation. The merger was conceived during a golf outing at a 1928 refrigeration convention. Carrier was a stalwart in an array of trade and engineering societies. In 1932 he was the first recipient of the American Society of Heating & Ventilating Engineers' highest honor. Carrier enjoyed being called "the Chief" at the office and actively encouraged his public image as "father of air conditioning."

Described by Cloud Wampler in the foreword to Ingels's biography as a handsome man, almost six feet in height with "powerful shoulders, a majestic head topped with tousled hair," Carrier smoked cigars and spent as much time as he could outdoors, fishing, hunting, and golfing. Notwithstanding his business acumen, he was famously absentminded, forgetting meals, appointments, train schedules, and items of clothing. His admirers attributed this to his intense concentration on scientific problems that could seize him at any time of day or night.

Carrier and his company suffered during the depression; he cut salaries and released staff during the disastrous year of 1932. But he never lost faith in the ultimate success of his products and the new way of life they promised. His ability to explain the new technology in terms most people could understand was as crucial to the success of the industry as his patents and engineering savvy.

In an August 1936 radio interview with John Black on WABC in New York City, Carrier described "the air-conditioned life of the future." At any time of year, he predicted,

> the average business man will rise, pleasantly refreshed, having slept in an air-conditioned room, he will travel in an air-conditioned train and toil in an air-conditioned office, store, or factory—and dine in an air-conditioned restaurant. In fact, the only time he will know anything about heat waves or Arctic blasts, will be when he exposes himself to the natural discomforts of out-of-doors.

Despite his lifelong aspiration to the acclaim achieved by his personal hero, Thomas Edison, Carrier could be refreshingly modest. "I've never bothered about planning my career far in advance," he told interviewer Milton Lomask ("An Industrial Pioneer," *Future: The Magazine for Young Men*, Sept. 1939). "For one thing I'm too lazy. For another, if you worry too much about the future you bungle the present."

Carrier's second wife died in 1939 and in 1941 he married Elizabeth Marsh Wise. They had no children.

During World War II, Carrier aided the war effort with what he called his greatest engineering achievement. He installed a system capable of cooling 10 million cubic feet of air per minute to $-67°F$ in a Cleveland wind tunnel used to test fighter planes. In February 1948, already ailing from the heart condition that would cause his death, Carrier was named chairman emeritus of the international corporation that bore his name. He died in New York City and was buried in a family plot in Buffalo's Forest Lawn Cemetery.

Willis Carrier neither invented air conditioning nor named it. The 1906 coinage is attributed to cotton mill engineer Stuart Cramer. He was, however, quick to grasp the importance of controlled climate in modern industry and to understand the potential of the human comfort market. A gifted and prolific engineer, he taught others how to use the physics of temperature and moisture to achieve controlled conditions. A third edition of his authoritative *Modern Air Conditioning, Heating and Ventilating*, written with Walter A. Grant and Realto E. Cherne in 1940, appeared nine years after his death. Most of the 109 articles he published between 1903 and 1953 were on technical subjects, but a large number were aimed at general audiences in such publications as *Good Housekeeping*, *Popular Mechanics*, and *Scientific American*.

Carrier's gift for prophecy and his enthusiastic promotion of air conditioning's utopian possibilities left an enduring mark on American life. Although air conditioning is sometimes blamed for energy waste and has been linked to indoor air pollution, there are few in the United States who willingly do without it.

• The Carrier Corporation Records, 1875–1964, are housed at Cornell University. Although not strictly the papers of Willis H. Carrier, this archive contains 121 folders of personal data, including a voice recording, speeches, articles and technical papers, family information, profiles, and interviews. Carrier's publications include "Air Conditioning," *Encyclopaedia Britannica*, 14th ed.; "Air Conditioning: New Prospects for an Established Industry," *Heating, Piping, and Air Conditioning*, May 1929, pp. 29–30; and, with Margaret Ingels, "Making Weather to Order in the Home," *Good Housekeeping*, Mar. 1931, 92+. A published biography is Carrier engineer Margaret Ingels's hagiographic but invaluable *Willis Haviland Carrier, Father of Air Conditioning* (1952). It includes a nine-page list of books and articles written by Carrier and a 48-page chronology from the year 1500 of developments that "led to modern air conditioning." Robert Friedman, "The Air-Conditioned Century," *American Heritage*, Aug.-Sept. 1984, pp. 20–33, is a good survey of air-conditioning's development and social impact and Willis Carrier's role in making both happen. Kathy Bodovitz and Ed Hardy's short profile, "Doing Something about the Weather" appeared in *Cornell Alumni News*, June 1992. An obituary is in the *New York Times*, 8 Oct. 1950.

MARSHA E. ACKERMANN

CARRINGTON, Elaine Sterne (14 June 1891–4 May 1958), author and radio scriptwriter, was born in New York City, the daughter of Theodore Sterne, a merchant, and Mary Louise Henriquez. Even as a young child, Elaine displayed a natural talent for storytelling. Before writing her first words she created fanciful tales to tell her grandmother and romantic stories for her father's dinner guests. In her teens Elaine began writing instead of telling. A deluge of manuscripts arrived at publishing houses from Elaine Sterne, G. A., the initials standing for "Great Author." A novel, a musical comedy, and many other stories were all rejected until she sold "King of the Christmas Feast" to *St. Nicholas* magazine in 1910.

Educated at local New York schools, Elaine attended Columbia University from 1910 to 1911. In 1911 she won a $1,000 first prize when she submitted an outline for a play called "Sins of the Mothers" in a scenario-writing contest sponsored by the *New York Evening Sun*. As the year progressed she won two additional prizes, one for a scenario and one for a short story. Her stories and scripts centered on topics such as romance and courtship, marriage and families. Plots involved the elements of secrecy as couples eloped, the doom of relationships between different classes, and conflicts between parent and child.

Over the next few years Elaine's writing career blossomed. She wrote scripts for Hollywood movies and sold her short stories to a number of magazines, including *Good Housekeeping*, *Redbook*, and the *Saturday Evening Post*. She also wrote a play, *Nightstick*, under the name John Ray, which was adapted into the 1929 movie *Alibi*. In 1920 she married George Dart Carrington, an attorney whom she had known since childhood. The couple had two children.

A prolific writer, Elaine Carrington wrote *The Gypsy Star* in 1928 and a play, *Five Minutes from the Station: A Comedy of Life That Comes Close to Being a Tragedy*, in 1930 in addition to the many short stories she wrote for magazines. Her radio career began in 1932 when she was caught in a rainstorm and ducked into the National Broadcasting Company's (NBC) offices. She happened to have a number of one-act plays that she had written with her and left the manuscripts with NBC. After reviewing them NBC asked Carrington to write a serial for radio.

Patterning the script after her own experiences as a middle-class wife and mother, Carrington wrote "Red Adams," which went on the air in October 1932 and ran three nights weekly. When Beechnut became the program's sponsor the show was renamed "Red Davis." A new sponsor, Proctor & Gamble, changed the name to "Forever Young," and in 1936 the name underwent a final change, to "Pepper Young's Family." The show began as a comedy but soon became a popular soap opera that dramatized a family's problems associated with understanding children, raising an adolescent, and surviving daily money matters.

Carrington's serials were said to be of a higher literary quality than other radio serials. Still, she geared the material to the listeners and the situations they encountered. She told one interviewer that "the story must be one that tugs at the heart . . . [bringing] the listener back day after day." By 1938 "Pepper Young's Family" had won over its audiences, was picked up by NBC in 1933 (it ran simultaneously on the Columbia Broadcasting System [CBS] from 1942 to 1944), and played at three different times each day. Injecting humor and creating stories heavy on plot, Carrington added new dimensions to her shows by often inventing new youthful characters. The program aired until 1959.

Carrington's popularity led to additional scripts, and in 1939 she wrote "When a Girl Marries," which became the number-one soap opera for five consecutive years and ran until 1956. From 1944 to 1955 Carrington's serial "Rosemary" was aired on NBC. The program began with a dedication to "all the women of today." She used the show as a forum for her patriotism, encouraging her audience to buy war bonds. Her success tabulated into gross earnings of $2,500 weekly in 1944. Her daytime programs eventually reached 2 million listeners, and she became known as the Queen of the Soapers. In 1950 Carrington received an award for radio achievement from the National Conference of Christians and Jews.

Although always busy, Carrington managed to take on public service assignments such as writing scripts for the U.S. Treasury Department during World War II. She relayed subtle messages through her characters that could be either informative, for instance, detailing emergency medical treatment, or a way to relate her own personal social views, such as her advocacy of racial integration. Accepting all people regardless of their racial origins or religious preferences, she brought to life a young African-American character (on "When a Girl Marries") who did not meet sponsor approval and appeared only twice. Carrington felt a responsibility to audiences, knowing that many accepted what the characters said at face value.

The estimated 38,000 words she produced each week were done largely by Carrington lying on her "seven-foot bed" and speaking into a dictaphone while rendering a dramatic enactment in which she played all the parts herself. Once dictated, she never replayed the script, rarely listened to one of her own broadcasts, and never heard any of the other soap-opera serials. However, she did attend some rehearsals where she defended her dialogue and refused to allow changes or cuts. Her workload became so great that she eventually hired a writer to help her with the programs.

In 1939 Carrington wrote *All Things Considered*, an anthology of ten short stories. In the mid-1940s she established "The Carrington Playhouse," which allowed young writers to present their material in a weekly contest that aired the winner's play on radio. When television gained in popularity Carrington moved into that medium. Her program "Follow Your Heart" went on the air in late 1953 on NBC but was canceled after three months. By the time of her death in New York City, Carrington was earning over $200,000 a year and owned a Manhattan penthouse, a Long Island estate, and a home in Florida.

Known as the originator of the radio soap opera, Carrington had great business sense and self-marketing abilities. She was a woman of wit and radiant personality. Her soap operas offered subtle moral messages at the same time they provided millions of Americans a momentary escape from the harsh realities of the depression and war.

• Carrington left no papers. In addition to her other writings, she also published a detective novel, *The Crimson Goddess* (1936). For information on her life and career see Frances Willard Kerr, *Women in Radio: A View of Important Jobs in Radio Held by Women* (1947); James Thurber, *The Beast in Me and Other Animals* (1948); Mary Jane Higby, *Tune in Tomorrow* (1968); Frank Buxton and Bill Owen, *The Big Broadcast: 1920–1950* (1972; 2d ed., 1997); Madeline Edmondson, *The Soaps* (1973); Edmondson and David Rounds, *From Mary Noble to Mary Hartman: The Complete Soap Opera Book* (1976); Raymond William Stedman, *The Serials: Suspense and Drama by Installment* (1977); Robert LaGuardia, *Soap World* (1983); and Jeff Kisseloff, *The Box: An Oral History of Television, 1920–1961* (1995). An obituary is in the *New York Times*, 5 May 1958.

MARILYN ELIZABETH PERRY

CARRINGTON, Henry Beebee (2 Mar. 1824–26 Oct. 1912), army officer and author, was born in Wallingford, Connecticut, the son of Miles M. Carrington and Mary Beebee. Young Carrington was converted into a determined abolitionist upon hearing a speech by John Brown. Carrington had a strong interest in the military, but weak health prevented him from entering West Point. Accordingly, he entered Yale College in 1840. Hampered by frequent illness, he finally graduated in 1845. For the rest of that year and most of the next, he taught at Irving Institute, Tarrytown, New York, where Washington Irving encouraged him to study military history. The association with Irving inspired Carrington to be a writer, but his studies deepened his ambition to be an army officer. For the time being, however, after leaving Irving Institute, Carrington taught at the New Haven Collegiate Institute while studying at Yale Law School.

Carrington moved to Columbus, Ohio, in 1848 and took up the practice of law. He enjoyed success in his legal career and also played an important role in founding the Republican party in Ohio, attending an 1854 convention called to protest the Kansas-Nebraska Act. Sometime during this period he married Margaret Irvin Sullivant; they had seven children. He also began writing books. In 1849 he published *American Classics* and in 1851 *Russia among the Nations*. Friendship with prominent Republicans, notably Governors Salmon P. Chase and William Dennison, the latter a former law partner of Carrington's, brought him a position with the state militia. In 1857 he was appointed adjutant general.

At the outbreak of the Civil War, Carrington quickly organized nine regiments of Ohio militia and sent them across the Ohio River to aid General George B. McClellan in securing western Virginia against the secessionists. This service earned him the thanks of Secretary of War Simon Cameron and Generals Winfield Scott and John E. Wool. Not long after, he was commissioned as colonel of the newly created Eighteenth U.S. Infantry. Thus, unlike most civilians who rose rapidly to positions of rank in the army, Carrington held his commission as a regular rather than as a volunteer. Despite this promotion, he continued to function as adjutant general of Ohio, organizing that state's troops for service. In 1862 he published *Hints to Soldiers Taking the Field*. Later that year Governor Oliver P. Morton of Indiana requested his services, and Carrington proved even more useful in that state. On 29 November 1862 he was promoted to brigadier general of volunteers and, continuing in his role as recruiter and organizer of troops, prepared over 100,000 Indiana troops for service before the war was over.

By far his most controversial duty was suppressing antiwar and Copperhead agitation in Ohio and Indiana, particularly an organization known as the "Sons of Liberty." This "Northwest Conspiracy" may or may not have posed a genuine threat to the government, but since its members certainly intended for it to, Carrington took them at their word. He energetically had suspected conspirators apprehended and tried by military tribunals. Eventually the decisions of these tribunals were overturned by the U.S. Supreme Court in *Ex Parte Milligan* (1866) on the grounds that neither Ohio nor Indiana had then been technically "in rebellion" and the local courts there were still open. By the time of the decision, however, the war was over and the danger past. Throughout the war, Carrington's duties were legal and organizational and kept him exclusively in rear areas.

When the Civil War ended, Carrington was ordered west, once again as colonel of the Eighteenth Infantry. He had apparently used his influence to secure such orders in pursuit of his dream of a combat command. He assignment was to build forts Reno, C. F. Smith, and Phil Kearny in central Wyoming as part of the army's effort to protect traffic on the Bozeman Trail. The trail, which led to the gold fields of Montana, also led through the heart of Sioux country, and its presence, as well as that of the forts, enraged the American Indians. Building and defending these forts in the midst of the resulting conflict, called Red Cloud's War, was no job for a bookish man who had never seen combat before. The Sioux all but besieged the outposts, including Carrington's headquarters at Fort Phil Kearny.

Disaster struck in December 1866, when an 81-man detachment under Captain William Fetterman was ambushed and annihilated outside Fort Phil Kearny by hostile Sioux and Cheyenne. Controversy surrounds the incident. Carrington claimed Fetterman, in pursuing the Indians, exceeded orders that called only for relieving a woodcutting party the Indians had attacked. Certain scholars have suggested, however, that Carrington may have ordered Fetterman's aggressive movement and then, after the latter's death, shifted blame to him, charging disobedience to orders.

Though Carrington personally led the detachment that recovered the eighty-one grotesquely mutilated bodies the day after the massacre, his superiors were not impressed with his overall performance. General Philip St. George Cooke assessed Carrington as "an energetic, industrious man in garrison; but it is too evident that he has not maintained discipline, and that his officers have no confidence in him." General William T. Sherman was even blunter, "I know enough of Carrington to believe that he is better qualified for a safe place than one of danger." Commanding general Ulysses S. Grant thought Carrington should be court-martialed, and though an Interior Department inquiry absolved him of blame, Carrington continued to be regarded poorly by his fellow army officers.

The following year Carrington helped negotiate a treaty with many of the Sioux. Not long after, he was granted a year's leave of absence because of an injury to his hip. Carrington was known as a humane officer who forbade his noncommissioned officers to use "profane swearing, verbal abuse, kicks and blows" in dealing with the privates. In 1869 he was detailed as a professor of military science at Wabash College in Indiana, which amounted to a separation from the army. He remained in this post for twenty years. In 1870 his first wife died, and in 1871 he married Frances Courtney "Fannie" Grummond, who was, interestingly, the widow of Lieutenant G. W. Grummond, who had been killed in the Fetterman massacre. They had three children. During his years at Wabash College and thereafter, Carrington continued to write articles and books, including *Battles of the American Revolution* (1876), *Battle Maps and Charts of the American Revolution* (1881), *The Six Nations* (1892), and *Washington, the Soldier* (1898). He died in Hyde Park, Massachusetts.

• Both of Carrington's wives wrote memoirs of their lives with him on the Great Plains, Frances C. Carrington, *Army Life on the Plains* (1910), and Margaret I. Carrington, *Absaraka, Home of the Crows*, ed. Milo M. Quaife (1950). Don Rickey, Jr., mentions Carrington's decency toward common soldiers in *Forty Miles a Day on Beans and Hay: The Enlisted Soldier Fighting the Indian Wars* (1963). Carrington's role in suppressing Copperhead activity during the Civil War is detailed in *The War of the Rebellion: A Compilation of the Official Records of the Union and Confederate Armies* (128 vols., 1880–1901). The critics of Carrington's tenure as commander on the plains are legion. Robert M. Utley, *Frontier Regulars: The United States Army and the Indian, 1866–1890* (1973), criticizes the treaty Carrington helped make with the Sioux. Dee Brown, *Fort Phil Kearny: An American Saga* (1962), and Jesse Wendell Vaughn, *Indian Fights: New Facts on Seven Encounters* (1966), arraign him for everything from doddering incompetence to outright duplicity in his handling of the affairs at Fort Phil Kearny and in the events surrounding the Fetterman massacre.

STEVEN E. WOODWORTH

CARROLL, Anna Ella (29 Aug. 1815–19 Feb. 1894), writer and political lobbyist, was born in Somerset County, Maryland, the daughter of Thomas King Carroll, a plantation owner and, later, governor of Maryland, and Julianna Stevenson, daughter of a prominent Baltimore physician. The eldest of nine children, Carroll received an unusually thorough education from her father, including the subjects of history, geography, philosophy, and law. Although little evidence remains of her life prior to midcentury, Carroll was clearly fascinated by politics at a precocious age, writing at fourteen to her governor father, "It is my principle, as well as that of Lycurgus, to avoid 'mediums'—that is to say people who are not decidedly one thing or the other. In politics they are the inveterate enemies of the state" (Blackwell, *Life of a Military Genius*, p. 18). As financial problems plagued her family, Carroll used her skill as a writer to hire herself out as a lobbyist for railroad promoters and other private interest groups. By the early 1850s, she had become an unpaid political pamphleteer for the nativist Know Nothing, or American, party. Her most important work for them was *The Great American Battle; or, The Contest Between Christianity and Political Romanism* (1856), a book delineating the anti-Catholic, anti-immigrant platform of the American Party. She held salons in New York City and Washington, hosting such political notables as American party presidential candidate Millard Fillmore, William Henry Seward, Jefferson Davis, Thurlow Weed, and minor politicians connected with the Know Nothings as well as the rising Republicans.

After Fillmore lost the election in 1856, Carroll turned to what she hoped would be more lucrative writing, publishing *The Star of the West* (1857), a collection of essays on various political topics such as filibustering and the transcontinental railroad. She also began to promote the candidacy of John Minor Botts of Virginia, a former Whig and Unionist who had apparently hired her as his publicist. As Botts's star faded, Carroll latched onto the Republicans as best she could, writing fulsome letters of praise to all and sundry in an attempt to establish political connections. Her primary goal during these years was to find a patronage position for her father, who had long since run through the family fortunes.

Carroll worried that Abraham Lincoln might be an abolitionist, since, like many border states politicians, she was a Unionist but did not support emancipation because of its social and economic ramifications. After the Civil War began, however, she turned her considerable political skill to crafting longer pamphlets in support of the president's policies. The most important, *Reply to Breckinridge*, was published in August 1861. In it, Carroll argued that the president could use all the powers he held as commander in chief to fulfill his duties as executor of the laws. Thus the naval blockade, the call for volunteers, and the suspension of the writ of habeas corpus, criticized as acts of war committed by the president when the power to declare war belonged to Congress, were in reality legitimate actions under the Constitution's mandate that the president enforce the laws. This pamphlet, detailing the same argument used by Lincoln and his attorney general, Edward Bates, was so well regarded by the administration that Secretary of State Seward ordered copies of it to be laid on every desk in Congress. (A year later, noted lawyer Horace Binney published a better-known pamphlet on the same subject.)

The recognition of the value of Carroll's work led to a peculiar verbal contract with Assistant Secretary of War Thomas A. Scott that she would be paid for any labor on behalf of the administration. Carroll relied on the contract to promote herself as an agent of the government. She continued to publish pamphlets, including one indirectly attacking Lincoln for his support of the Confiscation Acts, which freed slaves captured by Union troops. At the same time, she was in the private employ of Aaron Columbus Burr, a leading New York merchant, one of many who sought a government contract for establishing a colony for freed slaves. Burr used Carroll to lobby the president to choose the land Burr held in British Honduras for the colony, but her campaign failed.

Carroll's fame stems not from her theorizing and pamphleteering but from her claim that, under her contract with the War Department, she devised a military strategy to invade Tennessee by traveling up the Tennessee and Cumberland rivers, rather than down the Mississippi. Carroll traveled to St. Louis in the fall of 1861, interviewed riverboat captain Charles M. Scott, and together with him and her companion, former congressman Lemuel D. Evans, a Texas Unionist, devised a plan for the Union invasion. Carroll argued not only that her scheme would move Union forces deeper into the South, since the Tennessee went clear to northern Alabama, but that any damaged Union gunboats would float north, downstream, instead of falling into the hands of the Confederates. While Carroll's plan was good, commonsense military strategy, it reiterated not only a plan published in the *New York Times* two weeks earlier, on 17 November 1861, by someone signing himself "A Tennessean," but also the overall strategy being practiced by the Union army in the region. While Carroll always claimed it was her plan that had guided the Union forces in their invasion, which began the following February and did in fact follow much the same line of attack she had suggested, General Ulysses Grant, who had been in charge of the campaign, had been progressing toward the invasion during the fall, first capturing the towns at the mouths of the rivers, then waiting for shallow-draft gunboats so he could travel on the inland waters.

Nevertheless, Carroll pursued her claim against the federal government, arguing that they owed her considerable money for her work on behalf of the Union. While her early dunning of the administration was for her expenses in publishing her pamphlets, after the war was over and the appropriate parties largely dead and gone, she began to portray herself as the woman who had saved the Union by devising the Tennessee invasion. Suffragists soon joined the cause, and Carroll became the symbol of women's oppression by men who could not accept that a woman and a civilian had pointed out the military strategy that had presented the Union with its first major victories. Carroll's claims against the government grew until she asked for $250,000, a major generalship, and an appropriate pension. She never succeeded in obtaining any money, and the numerous bills, in both the House and the Senate, that were introduced for her relief all died before reaching a vote. A last-ditch federal lawsuit was decided against her in 1885.

Carroll remained a cause for the suffragists who published articles and books on her behalf and took up collections of money to support her in her old age. Even after her death in Washington, the controversy continued, as literally dozens of books, articles, plays, radio dramas, and novels have all sought to portray Carroll as a victim of man's injustice to woman.

Carroll's true importance, however, lies in her early political writings. Not only did she articulate the positions of the Know Nothing party in the 1850s, but she also articulated to Lincoln the concerns of the border states and their fears regarding the effect of abolition. (Carroll freed her family's slaves in 1855.) Her strong personality, her gift for promoting herself as well as others, and her ability to keep herself in the public eye until her death contributed to the legend surrounding her work. She was buried in Old Trinity Churchyard, Church Creek, Maryland, where on her gravestone the year of her death is misdated 1893.

• Carroll's papers are in two separate collections at the Maryland Historical Society: the Anna Ella Carroll Papers and the Carroll, Cradock, Jenson Collection. Her other important published works include *The War Powers of the General Government* (1861) and *The Relation of the National Government to the Revolted Citizens Defined* ([1862]). Her political writings have been edited by James B. Whisker in *Anna Ella Carroll: American Political Writer of Maryland* (1992). The only scholarly full-length biography of Carroll is Janet L. Coryell, *Neither Heroine nor Fool: Anna Ella Carroll of Maryland* (1990). Other important biographical information can be gained from Sarah Ellen Blackwell, *Life and Writings of Anna Ella Carroll* (1895) and *Life of a Military Genius: Anna Ella Carroll of Maryland* (1891). Sidney Greenbie and Marjorie Barstow Greenbie, *Anna Ella Carroll and Abraham Lincoln: A Biography* (1952), while widely cited, is wildly speculative and simply unreliable. Scholarly assessments of Carroll's military strategy can be found in Kenneth Williams, "The Tennessee River Campaign and Anna Ella Carroll," *Indiana Magazine of History* 46 (Sept. 1950): 221–48, and E. B. Long, "Anna Ella Carroll: Exaggerated Heroine?," *Civil War Times Illustrated* 14 (July 1975): 28–35, while her role as woman oppressed can be seen in Lucinda B. Chandler, "Anna Ella Carroll: The Great Unrecognized Genius of the War of the Rebellion," *Godey's Magazine* 133 (Sept. 1896): 250–67, and Ida Tarbell, "The American Woman: How She Met the Experience of War," *American Magazine* 69 (Apr. 1910): 801–14.

JANET L. CORYELL

CARROLL, Charles (22 Mar. 1723–23 Mar. 1783), politician and landowner, was born in Annapolis, Maryland, the son of Charles Carroll, a physician, and Dorothy Blake. The Carrolls and the Blakes were among the most prominent Roman Catholic families in Maryland. In 1734 Dr. Carroll sent his son to Europe for a Catholic education at the English College at Bairro Alto, Lisbon, Portugal. In 1738, after a violent falling out with other Carrolls in Annapolis, Dr. Carroll became a member of the Anglican church and transferred his son to Eton. After Eton the young Charles Carroll went to Clare College, Cambridge, returning to Annapolis in 1746. From 1751 until 1753 he studied law at the Middle Temple, London.

At his father's death in 1755, Carroll, as his father's sole surviving son, inherited property in Annapolis; a one-fifth interest in the Baltimore Company, a highly profitable ironworks; and over 15,000 acres, including three working plantations and land for speculation in western Maryland, making him one of the wealthiest men in the province. Four prominent men named Charles Carroll lived in or near Annapolis in the mid-eighteenth century. They were all related, partners in various business enterprises, and political allies during the Revolution. Each added a "Particular Distinction" to his name, and Carroll has always been referred to as "Charles Carroll, Barrister." Although his legal papers have not survived, he is known to have had an active legal career. He practiced before the Provincial Court of Maryland, the Court of Chancery, and the Anne Arundel County Court. His later activities during the

American Revolution attest to the high regard in which his legal experience and ability were held.

In 1756 Carroll was elected to the lower house of the Maryland Assembly to fill his late father's term and was reelected in 1757 and 1758. He did not stand for election after 1761 because of his opposition to the policies of Lord Baltimore, the lord proprietor of Maryland, although he always maintained a personal friendship with the governor of the province.

In addition to the profits from his plantations and the ironworks, Carroll's income came from a variety of sources. His investment property in Annapolis included a bakery, a warehouse, and a dock. He operated two gristmills and a shipyard on the outskirts of Baltimore. He added several thousand acres to those inherited from his father until he held 15,400 acres in Frederick County, Maryland. At that time, this rich Piedmont land was on the western frontier. It was sold in approximately 200-acre lots as settlers arrived from Europe or moved west from worn-out Tidewater lands. In the prerevolutionary years when there were no banks in the colonies, Carroll, along with other well-to-do men, loaned money. In 1769 he listed his outstanding loans totaling 654 pounds sterling and 5,621 pounds in Maryland currency.

In 1763 Carroll married his cousin, Margaret Tilghman, daughter of Matthew Tilghman. The couple had two children, who died in infancy. The Tilghmans were wealthy, politically prominent plantation owners, and Margaret Tilghman possessed a fortune in her own right. The Carrolls maintained a town house in Annapolis and a summer residence at "Mount Clare," their plantation near Baltimore. Mount Clare was one of the outstanding mid-eighteenth-century houses in Maryland, stretching over 250 feet above terraced gardens. George Washington later partly based the plan and details of his orangery at "Mount Vernon" on the Carrolls' at Mount Clare.

Carroll was one of the Annapolis patrons who paid to send the budding artist Charles Willson Peale to England for training. Carroll later sent Peale additional funds along with letters of introduction and advice on his future painting career in America. Peale painted several portraits of Mr. and Mrs. Carroll.

Along with other major eighteenth-century landowners, Carroll was actively interested in improving the materials and methods of agriculture. He ordered seeds for grains, grasses, and vegetables as well as fruit trees from his London agent, describing himself as one of the "Experiment making Farmers." He was also interested in breeding and racing horses. He ordered a stopwatch in 1764 and four years later imported an Arabian stallion through his London agent, the "cost not Exceeding one hundred Guineas."

In June 1774 Carroll represented Anne Arundel County in a convention called to determine Maryland's response to the Boston Port Bill. This convention was effectively the beginning of a provisional government. Eight further conventions were called through August 1776, and the "Barrister" served in all of them. Shortly after the ninth convention met in August 1776, Carroll resigned, because he considered the views of his democratic-minded constituents incompatible with good government and the public peace and happiness." He served on the first four Councils of Safety, August 1775–July 1776.

In January 1776 Carroll hosted a dinner party to which the colonial governor, Robert Eden, was invited. Also present were members of the Council of Safety; Thomas Johnson, who would become the first governor of the state of Maryland; and Samuel Chase and Thomas Stone, both of whom would sign the Declaration of Independence six months later. The purpose of the dinner was to quietly discuss ways by which they could "disperse the cloud that has almost overshadowed and is ready to bust upon us."

Carroll is credited with framing Maryland's declaration of independence, which was adopted on 3 July 1776 and was the major influence in the committee that wrote Maryland's first constitution later the same year. He was a delegate to the Continental Congress in 1776–1777 and served in the state senate from 1776 until his death. The Barrister played an important role in keeping moderates in control in Maryland during the Revolution. John Ridout, an Annapolis neighbor and a Loyalist, accurately summed up Carroll's activities during the Revolution as "very moderate and honorable."

All his adult life, Carroll suffered from "fevers and agues" thought to be a form of malaria contracted while a student in Portugal. In 1777 he declined his appointment as a judge of the General Court of Maryland because of his ill health. He died at Mount Clare from a fever brought on by a cold caught several days earlier. He was buried in the Carroll vault in St. Ann's churchyard in Annapolis. In his will the Barrister left Mount Clare to his widow for life as well as half the income from his estate. The estate was left to two of his sister's sons on the condition that the Maryland legislature pass a bill changing their names to Carroll and granting them the Carroll coat of arms. This was done in 1783 and was the first example of a state legislature granting a coat of arms.

• Carroll's letters are in the Letterbooks of Dr. Charles Carroll of Annapolis, MS 208, Maryland Historical Society. Also helpful are the Carroll-Maccubbin papers, MS 219, Maryland Historical Society, and the Ridout papers, D371, Gift Collection, Maryland State Archives, Annapolis. Biographical information is in W. Stull Holt, "Charles Carroll, Barrister: The Man," *Maryland Historical Magazine* 31 (1936): 112–26, and Edward C. Papenfuse et al., *A Biographical Dictionary of the Maryland Legislature, 1635–1789*, vol. 1 (1979). See also Edward S. Delaplaine, "The Life of Thomas Johnson," *Maryland Historical Magazine* 15 (1920): 262–63, and George Washington, *The Writings of George Washington from the Original Manuscript Sources, 1745–1799*, ed. John C. Fitzpatrick (39 vols., 1931–1944).

MICHAEL F. TROSTEL

CARROLL, Daniel (22 July 1730–7 May 1796), planter and merchant, was born in Upper Marlboro, Maryland, the son of Daniel Carroll I, a large plantation owner and merchant, and Eleanor Darnall. Carroll lived at a time when Maryland law denied Catholics the right to vote, hold office, worship, erect churches, or provide a formal education for their children. Aristocratic families sent their sons to the Jesuit-owned Bohenia Manor Academy in Cecil County, Maryland, for elementary schooling and then to St. Omer's College in French Flanders for a solid scholastic education. Daniel Carroll, his brother John Carroll, his second cousin Charles Carroll of Carrollton, and the sons of many other prominent Catholic families in Maryland endured many years of separation from family and home to receive this education.

After six years of study abroad, Daniel Carroll returned to the colonies in 1748. In 1752 he married his first cousin, Eleanor, daughter of Daniel Carroll of Duddington, who bore them a son and daughter. Carroll inherited his father's prosperous merchant business, which was located on the Patuxent River in Upper Marlboro. Besides the property he had inherited from his father, Carroll purchased large landholdings in Maryland. Some of this land he sold after the Revolution to provide funds to invest in the acquisition of confiscated British property; Carroll was one of the larger investors in this property in the urban area and one of the largest investors in a single lot. It also enabled him to become a land speculator in the Mississippi and Potomac Land companies. At the time of his death Carroll owned approximately 7,804 acres in Prince George's, Montgomery, and Frederick counties and thirty-two slaves.

Carroll held no public office until the American Revolution, when the state constitution of Maryland (1776) gave Catholics the right to vote and to serve their state in political office. From 1777 until the end of his life Carroll was an active public servant. The governor and the Executive Council to which Carroll was elected in 1777 controlled the executive department of Maryland. During the war the council had charge of the state's military forces and directed the raising of supplies, foodstuffs, and monies—tasks that proved to be as important to the war effort as the military action on the battlefront.

In 1781 Carroll was elected to his first five-year term as a state senator. The same year, he was also elected a state delegate to the Continental Congress. As president of the senate in 1783 and again in 1786, Carroll represented a conservative, aristocratic element that sought to strengthen the centralized government at the expense of local and foreign interests. In 1785 he became a member of the commission for the Potomac Canal Company, which sought to open and extend navigation on the Potomac River. Carroll later became a member of the Bank Stock Company, which attempted to recover stock belonging to Maryland that was still held in England. Finally, Carroll advocated that financial aid be given to Catholic and Protestant churches and members alike to ensure freedom for all religions.

In February 1781, Carroll arrived in Philadelphia to take his seat in the Continental Congress. His wealth was a necessary factor in his appointment as delegate, since the Constitution required representatives in Congress to own property valued at over £1,000, and the House and Senate forbade members to engage in foreign trade. Carroll played a role in the decisions for financial, military, economic, and foreign affairs. Carroll also played a key role in the issue of sovereignty over western lands. He insisted that the right of absolute sovereignty over the territory be vested in the United States, and refused to sign the Articles of Confederation until "the states holding back lands, ceded them to the United States as common property." After strong resistance, particularly from Virginia, all of the states with western land claims acceded to Maryland's demand. Carroll again emphasized his belief in a stronger central government when he supported the proposed amendment to the Articles of Confederation that would give Congress the power to levy a small tariff (an impost duty) in order to obtain a natural revenue and free the government from dependency on the states. Carroll signed the Articles on 1 March 1781, with John Hanson, the other delegate from Maryland.

The weakness of the Articles of Confederation was soon evident, necessitating another convention, which met in Philadelphia in May 1787. Carroll was again chosen to represent Maryland. In his notes characterizing the various delegates, William Pierce, a delegate from Georgia, wrote that Carroll "is a Man of large fortune and influence in his State. He possess plain good sense, and is in the full confidence of his Countrymen." Carroll was appointed a member of a committee on representation chaired by James Madison. To prevent any dissatisfaction with the eastern and middle states Carroll voted against the proposal to count slaves as three-fifths of all other free citizens. Although his part in the convention was not significant, Carroll did speak for two critical provisions. He consistently stressed a need for a centralized government safeguarded by a strong Constitution, and, like delegates James Madison of Virginia and James Wilson of Philadelphia, he adhered firmly to the belief that the sovereignty of the people was essential for good government and had to be preserved and guaranteed.

Carroll signed the final draft of the Constitution on 17 September 1787, but much work lay ahead to ensure the ratification of the proposed Constitution by the citizens of Maryland. Carroll requested that the unanimous consent of all thirteen states be required to ratify the Constitution since it had been established unanimously by all states. His proposal was defeated ten to one, but he continued to work earnestly for the ratification of the federal Constitution. Using the pseudonym, "A Friend of the Constitution," Daniel Carroll spearheaded a successful campaign of letter writing in the *Maryland Journal* of 1787. Carroll was absent, however, when the majority of delegates to Maryland's ratification convention approved the proposed Constitution on 26 April 1788, making Maryland the seventh state to ratify.

On 13 January 1789 Carroll was elected to the first session of the U.S. House of Representatives. The first meeting was held on 4 March 1789 in New York, where the House convened until its move to Philadelphia for the third session. At James Madison's insistence, the First Congress drafted a Bill of Rights. Carroll contributed much to clarifying the wording of the First and Tenth Amendments. In the First Amendment, Carroll succeeded in strengthening protections for civil rights and for equal rights in matters of conscience. Likewise, convinced that power must rest with the people, Carroll requested that the Tenth Amendment state emphatically that the powers not delegated to the Constitution be reserved for the states and the people. This was accepted.

On 22 January 1791, President George Washington appointed Carroll to serve as one of three commissioners to survey the District territory as the permanent seat of government. Carroll agreed to serve, despite the fact that several of his relatives figured conspicuously among the wealthy landowners in the District. Major Pierre Charles L'Enfant had been chosen to lay out the city; his "Grand Plan" stated that all public edifices were to be seen from twenty miles away, that all streets be 160 feet in width, and that the federal city was to be made the most beautiful one in the world. As one of the commissioners responsible for the purchase and sale of District land, Carroll feared that L'Enfant's plan would require the destruction of the homes of many wealthy District families without compensating them. Carroll constantly confronted L'Enfant about the injustice of his "Grand Plan," and he repeatedly wrote to Washington and Madison to express his distress over this matter and the "infamous slander" L'Enfant was circulating about him. Washington agreed that the design was too grandiose. L'Enfant's refusal to submit to the authority of the commissioners and the president and constant bickering among the board members caused President Thomas Jefferson to terminate L'Enfant's services. Carroll served for four years and was the last of the original commissioners to resign. He became ill in early 1795 and on 21 May resigned his position.

Carroll outlived his wife, who had died thirty-three years before his death, and his children, Daniel and Mary. His estate passed to Notley Young and Robert Brent, relatives by marriage, and to his three grandchildren.

Carroll's important efforts in helping to establish the government of his state and nation went unrecorded by the *Federal Gazette* and the *Baltimore Daily Advertiser*; upon his death they simply reported that "he was a gentleman of unbounded philanthropy and possessed of the esteem of all who had the pleasure of his acquaintance."

• The political letters of Daniel Carroll are in the Library of Congress, in the Red Books in the Maryland State Papers at the state archives in Annapolis, in the Emmet Bound Collection at the New York Public Library, and in the Gratz collection, the Etings papers, the Dreer collection, and the Canarroe papers at the Historical Society of Pennsylvania in Philadelphia. Two biographies of Carroll are by Virginia Geiger, *Daniel Carroll, a Framer of the Constitution* (1943) and *Daniel Carroll, One Man and His Descendants* (1979). Carroll's family, public office holding, and wealth are outlined in his biography in Edward C. Papenfuse et al., *A Biographical Dictionary of the Maryland Legislature*, (1979), 1:199–200. See also Richard Purcell, "Daniel Carroll, Framer of the Constitution," *Records of the American Catholic Historical Society* 52 (1941): 65–87; 137–60.

VIRGINIA GEIGER

CARROLL, Earl (16 Sept. 1893–17 June 1948), theatrical producer and songwriter, was born in Pittsburgh, Pennsylvania, the son of James Carroll and Elizabeth Wills, hotelkeepers. At thirteen, Carroll became a program boy at a Pittsburgh theater. At seventeen, having graduated from Allegheny High School, he was assistant treasurer and box-office manager at another theater. He worked his passage around the world doing odd jobs, wrote for an English-language newspaper in the Orient, and, after visiting New York, became treasurer at Pittsburgh's Nixon Theater.

In 1912 Carroll returned to New York, hoping that his musical play *Lady of the Lamp* would be produced. (He eventually produced it himself in 1919.) He stayed, working for music publisher Leo Feist; the first of his more than four hundred songs was interpolated into *The Passing Show of 1912*. In 1913's *Ziegfeld Follies* Jose Collins made a minor hit of the florid "Isle d'Amour" by Carroll and Leo Edwards. Carroll became a charter member of the American Society of Composers, Authors, and Publishers (ASCAP). His "Dreams of Long Ago" was popularized by Enrico Caruso. *The Pretty Mrs. Smith*, with book and lyrics by Carroll, was taken up by California producer Oliver Morosco as a star vehicle for Fritzi Scheff. Carroll's first major Broadway hit score, for Morosco's *So Long, Letty* (1916), helped launch Charlotte Greenwood's starring career. *Canary Cottage* (1917), also for Morosco, starred Eddie Cantor. Musical theater historian Gerald Bordman wrote that Carroll's book, *The Love Mill* (1918), was cynical about marriage while the lyrics overflowed with "reverence, truth and sweetness." Carroll married French actress Marcelle Hontabat in October 1916; the couple had no children. She left him in 1927 and returned to France.

After serving in the U.S. Army Air Corps during World War I, Carroll became a producer in 1919. In 1923 he built his first Earl Carroll Theater at Seventh Avenue and Fiftieth Street and moved into a penthouse off Times Square. Though Carroll also presented plays that were daring for their time—such as *White Cargo*, whose heroine, Tondelayo, wore the briefest of sarongs and engaged in simulated sex onstage—his definitive style developed in his own revues. The first of eleven *Earl Carroll Vanities* opened in 1923, starring comic Joe Cook, the juggling, shaggy-dog proponent of "one-man vaudeville," featuring socialite Peggy Hopkins Joyce in a chinchilla coat, and presenting forgettable songs such as "Girls Were Made for Dancing." Carroll's *Vanities* usually enjoyed lengthy runs and became sure draws on the road. He featured flashy settings, oddments such as bird ballets, and a heterogeneous collection of stars: Cook, Fanny Brice, William Demarest, Joe Frisco, W. C. Fields, Lillian Roth, Jimmy Savo, Sophie Tucker, Smith and Dale, Jack Benny, Patsy Kelley, Ken Murray, and George Moran and Charlie Mack, the "Two Black Crows."

Carroll employed various ruses to disguise the nudity of the "most beautiful girls." A girl might swing to and fro on a pendulum behind a lace curtain, or chorines might parade strategically wrapped in cellophane. Theater critic John Mason Brown wrote, "It is undeniably true that every mother's daughter of them is beautiful. But just as surely as each and every one of Mr. Carroll's sylphs, Olympias and figurines is beautiful, so almost the whole of his new *Vanities* is dumb." The tired visiting businessman loved it. The 1926 *Vanities*, running until midnight, commanded a $100 ticket top.

In the same year, Carroll spent four months in the federal penitentiary at Atlanta because of a predawn onstage party during which chorus girl Joyce Hawley was alleged to have taken a champagne bath. (The only political stand ever taken in a Carroll revue came in the 1930 *Vanities*: against Prohibition.) Carroll's lawyer remarked that the producer had lied "like a gentleman" to protect Hawley. During the commotion, Carroll's 1927 *Vanities: International Edition*, an uncomfortable mixture of girlies and the sophistication of André Charlot's London troupe, failed, stranding the Charlot company and ending Charlot's American success.

Carroll's fortunes quickly rebounded. His 1929 *Earl Carroll Sketch Book*, benefiting from Jay Gorney and E. Y. Harburg's score, was the season's biggest hit. In 1931 he opened the second Earl Carroll Theater built on the same site as the first (the first theater he demolished to build the second). It claimed to be the world's biggest legitimate (as opposed to cinema) theater, with air conditioning and chrome fixtures; its 3,000 seats boasted individual reading lights; its black velvet walls contained 5,000 acoustical disks; its orchestra pit could be raised or lowered; its ticket sellers wore tuxedos and its militarily uniformed ushers were all over six feet tall; its checkroom was free and so were the soft drinks. Five months later, because he failed to pay its opening bills, he lost the theater to Florenz Ziegfeld, who erased all trace of Carroll; Ziegfeld staged one show there—his last. The *Earl Carroll Sketch Book* (1935) presented a "chorus girl's version of history" ("Now bear us out and you will see / Our little book of history"). The last, unsuccessful *Vanities* (1940) balefully introduced microphones to the Broadway stage. For many years Carroll judged the Miss America beauty pageant.

Carroll's interest gradually shifted westward. His 1933 Broadway revue-within-a-mystery, *Murder at the Vanities*, was filmed in 1934, its unlikely star, Bela Lugosi, replaced by Carl Brisson. Carroll was associate producer of the 1935 Shirley Temple film *Stowaway*, and in 1941 he appeared in *A Night at Earl Carroll's*. In 1938 he opened the Earl Carroll Theater-Restaurant on Sunset Boulevard in Hollywood. Designed by the architect of the Santa Anita racetrack, the streamlined theater boasted broad stairways and inside terraces. In 1940 he sought to fix celebrity autographs in the sidewalks around his theater. Denied by government, he hung the 2½ × 4-foot concrete slabs on the building's front, creating an instant landmark. In 1948 he announced plans for a "Radio City West," seating 7,000, but the huge building was never built.

Carroll died in an airplane crash in Pennsylvania en route to New York to cast another *Vanities* road show. Forty-two others, including his longtime companion Beryl Wallace, the star of most of his Hollywood revues, also died. The fading Carroll tradition was carried on for a time in Hollywood by his former star and biographer Ken Murray, who staged many editions of *Blackouts*.

Carroll's funeral featured life-sized "Candlelight Girls" of 6,000 sweetpea and carnation blossoms and a floral blanket of 3,000 red roses. A succession of unsuccessful lawsuits contested Carroll's will and alleged airline negligence. In 1951 Carroll's and Wallace's ashes, together with those of Carroll's brother James, were placed in a marble tomb topped by a bronze likeness of Wallace. His theater-restaurant endured many metamorphoses, among them a boxing arena.

A prolific and formulaic composer, Carroll won his greatest fame purveying "innocent vulgarity" in a series of revues staged in his own flamboyant theaters "through [whose] portals pass[ed] the most beautiful girls in the world." A restless self-publicist credited with more than six hundred theatrical productions, Carroll, alongside rivals such as George White, further trivialized a theatrical genre that was lightweight to begin with. Florenz Ziegfeld had "glorified" the American girl, dressing her stylishly and surrounding her with gorgeous sets. Carroll removed most of her clothing and played for easy laughs. If he did not invent the "dumb chorine," he perfected the stereotype.

• The clippings file of the *Los Angeles Times* has material on Carroll, as does the Harvard University Theatre Collection. The only biography of Earl Carroll is Ken Murray's rare *The Body Merchant: Earl Carroll* (1976). Stanley Green's books—especially *Broadway Musicals of the 30s* (1971; rpt. 1982) and *Broadway Musicals Show by Show* (1985)—are excellent evocations of the style and substance of the Carroll revues. Gerald Bordman's *American Musical Theatre: A Chronicle* (1990; 2d ed. 1992) is a useful compilation of most of Carroll's contributions.

JAMES ROSS MOORE

CARROLL, James (5 June 1854–16 Sept. 1907), bacteriologist and military physician, was born in Woolwich, England, the son of James Carroll, a royal artillery gunner, and Harriet Chiverton. Having attended the Albion House Academy until the age of fifteen, Carroll left Britain for Canada, where he is said to have been a blacksmith, railroad laborer, and backwoodsman. He migrated to the United States in 1874 and volunteered for the U.S. Army, serving with the First Infantry in Montana. He reenlisted in 1879 and eventually was appointed hospital steward at Fort Douglas in Utah.

Carroll enlisted in the army for a third time, and during this stint, with the encouragement of Assistant Surgeon James Calahan at Fort Snelling, he started to pursue an interest in medicine. He studied first at the Medical College of St. Paul, Minnesota, and in the fall of 1886 he embarked on a course in microscopy at the University of New York and one on physical diagnosis at Bellevue Hospital. In 1888 he married Jennie M. G. Lucas; they had seven children.

In 1889, after fifteen years of military service, Carroll reenlisted once again. He was sent to Washington barracks and eventually Fort Henry in Maryland. From 1890 to 1891 he undertook a course at the University of Maryland Medical School, receiving his clinical instruction at Bay-View, Lying-in, and University hospitals. He graduated in 1891 and the following spring he took, along with Walter Reed, the course on bacteriology and pathology taught by William Welch at Johns Hopkins Medical School. In 1893 he took the course again.

Also in 1893 Reed was appointed to teach a course on clinical and military microscopy at the U.S. Army Medical School, and Carroll acted as his assistant. Two years later Reed was appointed to the position of professor of pathology and bacteriology at Columbia University; Carroll also accepted a position there as an assistant professor.

In 1897 Giuseppe Sanarelli, an Italian bacteriologist working in Uruguay, announced that he had discovered the etiologic agent of yellow fever, a bacillus he termed *Bacillus icteroides*. George Sternberg, surgeon general from 1893 to 1902, had a long-standing interest in yellow fever and asked Reed and Carroll to investigate Sanarelli's claim. Injecting animal subjects with Sanarelli's bacillus, they found the lesions and symptoms of hog cholera and concluded that *Bacillus icteroides* was in fact *Bacillus Cholerae Suis*.

In 1900 the surgeon general of the U.S. Marine Hospital Service, Walter Wyman, ordered a commission, headed by Eugene Wasdin and Henry D. Geddings, to test the validity of Sanarelli's findings. They confirmed Sanarelli's claim. Sternberg responded by asking the War Department to select a U.S. Army board to conduct research in infectious diseases in Cuba. Reed was asked to be chairman and Carroll a member of the board along with Assistant Surgeon Jesse Lazear and Astrides Agramonte, who was in charge of Military Hospital Number One in Havana. Reed and Carroll left for Cuba in the early summer of 1900 and met the other board members there. Although the board was to investigate infectious diseases in general, they spent much of their time on yellow fever. At the end of three weeks, the board reached the previous conclusion: Sanarelli's *Bacillus icteroides* was not the etiologic agent of yellow fever, but it was the germ responsible for cholera in hogs.

Soon after the members arrived the board met two scientists from the Liverpool School of Tropical Medicine, H. E. Durham and Walter Myers, who were on their way to Brazil to conduct research on mosquitoes. These two scientists strongly supported the theory of Carlos Finlay, who suggested that yellow fever was transmitted by mosquitoes. The board visited Finlay in Havana and decided to test his claim. Reed left for the United States, leaving Carroll, Lazear, and Agramonte to conduct the mosquito experiments. Lazear allowed mosquitoes to feed on the blood of yellow fever patients and then to bite a volunteer. At the end of August Carroll volunteered, and within a few days he was acutely ill with yellow fever. Lazear used the same mosquito that had bitten Carroll on another volunteer, Private William H. Dean, and he, too, developed yellow fever. Lazear then concluded that mosquitoes were responsible for the transmission of yellow fever. Soon after Carroll recovered from the disease, Lazear contracted a fatal case. Reed returned to Cuba, and, using Lazear's papers and notebooks, he wrote a paper on the etiology of yellow fever that appeared in the *Philadelphia Medical Journal*. Wasdin, among others, claimed that Reed had proved nothing. After publishing the paper, Reed, Carroll, and Agramonte conducted controlled experiments using mosquitoes and volunteers.

After the experiments Reed and Carroll returned to Washington, D.C., and resumed teaching. In 1901 Carroll returned to Havana to study the morphology of the agent for yellow fever. He found that the serum of a yellow fever patient passed through a Berkefeld filter. This meant that, according to one of Carroll's contemporaries, the organism belonged to a "mysterious class of organisms, known as ultra-microscopic" (Kelly et al., p. 4).

In 1902, after twenty-eight years in the army, Carroll applied to be a commissioned officer in the U.S. Army Medical Corps, and with the age limitations waived, he became a lieutenant of the corps. He was named professor of bacteriology and curator of the Army Medical Museum, and, after Reed's death in 1902, he was appointed professor of pathology and bacteriology of the George Washington University Medical School.

Reed and Carroll, long-time collaborators, did not have an easy relationship. During his life Reed took much of the credit for finding the agent responsible for causing yellow fever, overshadowing other scientists who conducted research on the disease. In an obituary on Carroll, William Welch called him "the real hero" of the yellow fever commission (J. C. Hemmeter, "Major James Carroll of the United States Army, Yellow Fever Commission, and the Discovery of the Transmission of Yellow Fever by the Bite of the Mosquito 'Stegomyia Fasciata'," *Janus* 13 [1908]: 68).

Author and coauthor of many papers on yellow fever, Carroll published on few other topics. He was a member of a number of professional organizations, including the American Medical Association, the American Public Health Association, and the American Association for the Advancement of Science. Just before he died, he was promoted, by an act of Congress, to major. Carroll never fully recovered from his attack of yellow fever. He died in Washington, D.C., of an organic heart lesion, brought on by his attack of the disease.

In the last decade of the nineteenth century the question of how yellow fever was transmitted concerned scientists all over the world, and many deserve credit for describing the etiology of the disease: Finlay, Reed, Agramonte, Durham, Myers, Lazear, and others. No one individual was entirely responsible for determining the etiology and transmission of yellow fever. Carroll played an important part in delineating the role of the mosquito in transmitting the disease, and he defined the size limit of the agent responsible for yellow fever.

• Some of Carroll's papers are in the University of Maryland historical library. The rest remain in the possession of Jan Snelling of Albany, Georgia. These include about 300 pages of typescript, ten photographs, sixty-three letters, and twelve documents. A list of these papers, including the origins and dates of the letters, are at the University of Virginia in the Hench Yellow Fever Collection and in the University of Maryland Medical School library.

Much of what Carroll wrote on yellow fever was coauthored with Walter Reed and others. For example, Reed et al., "The Etiology of Yellow Fever: A Preliminary Note," *Philadelphia Medical Journal* 6 (1900): 790–96, and Reed et al., "The Etiology of Yellow Fever: An Additional Note," *Journal of the American Medical Association* 36 (1901): 431–40. Carroll's other important works include "The Transmission of Yellow Fever: A Reply to Dr. Agramonte," *Journal of the American Medical Association* 41 (1903): 1429–33, and "Yellow Fever," in *Systems of Medicine*, ed. William Osler (1907), pp. 730–56.

The most recent source on Carroll's life is J. A. del Regato, "James Carroll," *Bulletin of the Cuban Medical Convention* 1 (1992): 72–85. Other sources include Howard A. Kelly, *Proceedings of the Washington Academy of Sciences* 10 (1908): 204–7, and John C. Hemmeter, *Master Minds in Medicine* (1927). An obituary is in the *Bulletin of the Johns Hopkins Hospital* 19 (1908).

M. P. SUTPHEN

CARROLL, John (8 Jan. 1736–3 Dec. 1815), first bishop and archbishop of Baltimore, was born in Upper Marlboro, Maryland, the son of Daniel Carroll, a wealthy merchant, and Eleanor Darnall, a member of one of Maryland's oldest and most distinguished families. At age eleven John was enrolled in the short-lived Jesuit school at Bohemia Manor in Cecil County, Maryland, but in 1748 he was sent to the Jesuit college of St. Omer in French Flanders. On 7 September 1753 he entered the novitiate of the Society of Jesus at nearby Watten and made his first vows two years later. At the house of studies for Jesuits, the English College at Liège, he followed the ordinary three years of philosophy and four of theology. On 14 February 1761, during the usual third year of theology, he was ordained priest by the auxiliary bishop of Liège in the chapel of the episcopal palace.

Carroll taught philosophy and theology at the English College until about 1767, when he was listed as "preceptor" for sons of the English gentry at the Jesuit college in Bruges. After a year's preparation in Ghent, he pronounced his solemn vows on 2 February 1771, renouncing in the process any claim to family property. For the next two years he was chaperon for the continental tour of the son of an English nobleman, for Carroll a broadening experience. A good part of this time he resided at the Jesuits' College of Nobles in Bologna, but he spent the early months of 1773 incognito in Rome in order to be close to the negotiations for the suppression of the Society of Jesus. "What a revolution of ideas," he wrote a friend, "do all these proceedings produce in a mind accustomed to regard this city as the seat of religion." Back in Bruges news of the act of suppression (21 July 1773) caused him to write his mother: "The greatest blessing which in my estimation I could receive from God, would be immediate death." Thereafter he referred to the pope of the suppression, Clement XIV, by no other name than Ganganelli.

With the expulsion of the former Jesuits from the college at Bruges, Carroll, his "own man," went to England and enjoyed for a time the hospitality of Lord Arundell at Wardour Castle before returning to Maryland in the spring of 1774. For some thirteen years he lived with his mother at Rock Creek; for most of that time he served the surrounding Catholics from a church built on the Carroll property by his brother Daniel Carroll. In 1776 the Continental Congress requested him to accompany a mission to Canada composed of Benjamin Franklin (1706–1790), Samuel Chase, and his cousin Charles Carroll (1736–1832) of Carrollton, the purpose of which was to win the Canadians to the American cause. Though he believed that ministers of religion should not involve themselves in politics and entertained small hope for the success of the enterprise, he considered it his patriotic duty to go. The mission failed to accomplish its purpose, but Carroll's solicitude for the ailing Franklin on their return journey earned the latter's friendship, later an important factor in the selection of Carroll as the first Catholic bishop in the United States.

When it was obvious in 1783 that ecclesiastical ties with Britain would soon be broken, Carroll, deploring the apathy and irresolution of the former American Jesuits, who lived in Maryland and Pennsylvania, and concerned for the security of their extensive properties, called a meeting of several priests at White Marsh, Maryland. From a plan he had outlined, they drew up a constitution that provided for a chapter of the clergy elected from three districts that would have charge of all temporal affairs. Only then did the ex-Jesuits, at Carroll's prompting, petition the Holy See to grant the necessary faculties, or ritual powers, to their former superior, Father John Lewis.

Rome meanwhile, through time-honored diplomatic channels, approached the American representatives in Paris. At Franklin's suggestion the pope in June 1784 named Carroll, instead of Lewis, superior of the American mission. As superior Carroll succeeded in averting the appointment of a vicar apostolic, a missionary bishop under the Propaganda Fide, the Roman congregation charged with mission lands, which had appropriated former Jesuit properties.

At the same time, Carroll composed a lengthy rebuttal to a work published by a cousin and former Jesuit, Charles Henry Wharton, who had justified his conversion to the Episcopal church by claiming that the Catholic church was inimical to the freedom espoused by Americans. In his *Address to the Roman Catholics of the United States of America* (1784), Carroll argued that "America may come to exhibit a proof to the world, that general and equal toleration, by giving a free circulation to fair argument, is the most effectual method to bring all denominations to an unity of faith." At this point in his career Carroll also favored a liturgy in the language of the people and a recognition of the powers of the pope as purely spiritual. He fought a tax for the support of clergymen in Maryland and wrote articles for American journals demanding equal rights for Roman Catholics.

Difficulties in New York, where two factions fought for control of a new parish, and in Philadelphia, where the Germans demanded a church of their own, plus the growing number of clerical adventurers drawn to the new nation convinced Carroll of the need for a bishop. In 1788 he petitioned the pope for the creation of an ordinary bishop directly under the Holy Father who would be elected by the American clergy. The election was allowed, and the nearly unanimous choice fell upon Carroll. On 6 November 1789 he was named bishop of the new diocese of Baltimore, an ordinary bishop as requested but under the Congregation of the Propaganda. Carroll chose to be ordained a bishop in the private chapel of the Weld family in Lulworth Castle, Dorset, England. On 15 August 1790 he was raised to the episcopacy by Bishop Charles Walmesley.

In November 1791 Carroll held his first and only synod. Though it dealt mostly with the uniform administration of the sacraments, Carroll's principal concern was education. About a month before the synod the Sulpicians, at Carroll's invitation, had opened St. Mary's Seminary in Baltimore, the first Catholic seminary in the United States, and about a month after some former Jesuits began classes at Georgetown College founded earlier by Carroll in the District of Columbia. In 1805 Carroll, without informing the Propaganda, effected a partial restoration of the Society of Jesus in the United States by securing an affiliation with the Jesuits who had avoided suppression in Russia. To the society he entrusted not only Georgetown College but the properties controlled by the chapter of the clergy created in 1783, chartered in 1792 as the Corporation of the Roman Catholic Clergy of Maryland.

Carroll invited other religous orders to labor in the United States. In 1805 he persuaded English Dominicans to open a priory and college in Kentucky to serve the hundreds of Marylanders migrating there annually. For English Carmelite nuns who had come to Maryland from Flanders in 1790 Carroll acquired papal permission to teach, but they chose to remain strictly cloistered. Carroll encouraged the founding of the Sisters of the Visitation to take charge of a school in Georgetown and the Sisters of Charity, who under Elizabeth Ann Seton established a motherhouse and academy in Emmitsburg, Maryland.

Over and above the care of a diocese that was coterminous with the United States, the Holy See in 1804 charged Carroll with the administration of the Virgin Islands and in 1805 with the Louisiana Territory. The coadjutor bishop, Leonard Neale, granted to Carroll in 1795 but not raised to episcopal rank until 1800, proved of little help to Carroll. Finally, on 8 April 1808, the diocese of Baltimore was made an archdiocese and from it was carved four suffragan sees: Boston, New York, Philadelphia, and Bardstown, Kentucky. Carroll himself chose and ordained all but the bishop of New York. Difficulties in New York and Philadelphia continued to involve Carroll in the affairs of the new dioceses. Though he came to appreciate the support of the Congregation of the Propaganda, Carroll and his suffragans still sought to deal directly with the pope.

Many of the problems of Carroll's administration arose from the trustee arrangement that he himself had encouraged as the best manner of securing church property and involving the laity in the governance of the church. Trustees proved unruly, even defiant, in New York, Philadelphia, Charleston, and Baltimore. Despite assertions to the contrary, Carroll never repudiated the system. The conflicts of these port cities were the exceptions. In most places the system worked well. Carroll, in fact, was grateful for the assistance of the trustees of the cathedral parish in securing the talents of Benjamin Henry Latrobe (1764–1820), architect of the Capitol, and in overseeing the construction of the magnificent cathedral Carroll envisioned. Begun in 1806, it was not completed until six years after his death.

Problem priests and not trustees provided the greatest worries of Carroll's administration, causing him on more than one occasion to modify his goals and principles. The arrogant John Ashton, for example, for many years the fiscal agent for the Corporation of the Roman Catholic Clergy, caused Carroll to play more than simply the spiritual role he had originally designed for himself in the affairs of incorporated bodies. It was undoubtedly the prevalence of such troublemakers that also induced Carroll not to press for a continuation of the election of bishops by the clergy.

Carroll also had to deal with the contention that developed between the Sulpicians, whom Carroll came to admire and to depend upon, and the Jesuits, largely the result of national feelings and academic rivalry. With difficulty Carroll persuaded the Sulpicians to remain in the United States despite their inability for several years to attract candidates to the seminary, for which they blamed in part the Jesuits' decision to offer philosophy at Georgetown to prospective seminarians. A strain developed between Carroll and the Jesuits because of his refusal to grant them the independence they sought before a full restoration of the Society of

Jesus on the part of Rome. When the restoration came in 1814, Carroll still hesitated to grant them the powers, properties, and parishes to which their superior claimed they were entitled. Carroll's last year was also troubled by the intrusion of European ecclesiastics into the selection of bishops for New York and Philadelphia, which he declared "a very dangerous precedent."

Despite a greater conservatism as bishop than he had shown as priest, Carroll was the architect of the "Maryland tradition" in American Catholicism. He accepted without qualification such American principles as freedom of conscience and separation of church and state and sought in his relationship with the Holy See a measure of autonomy for the American church. Totally committed to interfaith harmony, he contributed more than anyone to the public's acceptance of Roman Catholicism. His sense of civic duty placed him on the board of such institutions as St. John's College, Annapolis, and Baltimore College, where he was president of the board, and led him to promote such enterprises as the Baltimore Library Company, the Female Humane Association, and the Baltimore General Dispensary.

"His manners were mild, impressive and urbane," an obituary in the *Baltimore Telegraph* read. "The various stores of knowledge came from his lips with uncommon classical grace and richness. . . . His charities were only bounded by his means" (1815; repr. in Baltimore *Catholic Mirror*, 25 Dec. 1858). He died in Baltimore.

• The Carroll papers are located in the archives of the archdiocese of Baltimore, but many of Carroll's letters and other writings can be found in the archives of the Congregation of the Propaganda Fide (now Evangelization of Peoples) in Rome and the archives of the University of Notre Dame. With some omissions the Carroll papers are published in *The John Carroll Papers*, ed. Thomas O'Brien Hanley (3 vols., 1976). The best biographies of Carroll are Peter Guilday, *The Life and Times of John Carroll, Archbishop of Baltimore (1735–1815)* (1922), and Annabelle M. Melville, *John Carroll of Baltimore: Founder of the American Catholic Hierarchy* (1955). See also Thomas W. Spalding, *The Premier See: A History of the Archdiocese of Baltimore, 1789–1989* (1989); Thomas Hughes, *History of the Society of Jesus in North America: Colonial and Federal* (3 vols., 1907–1917); Christopher J. Kauffman, *Tradition and Transformation in Catholic Culture: The Priests of Saint Sulpice in the United States from 1791 to the Present* (1988); Spalding, "John Carroll: Corrigenda and Addenda," *Catholic Historical Review* 71 (1985): 505–18; and Spalding, "'A Revolution More Extraordinary': Bishop John Carroll and the Birth of American Catholicism," *Maryland Historical Magazine* 84 (1989): 195–222.

THOMAS W. SPALDING

CARROLL, Leo G. (18 Oct. 1892–16 Oct. 1972), actor, was born Leo Grattan Carroll in Weedon, England, the son of William Carroll, a British army officer, and Catherine (maiden name unknown). Although Carroll's education ended at age fifteen, he was introduced to the theater through school productions of Gilbert and Sullivan, all of which he referred to as "intelligently done." However, later, as an apprentice wine merchant, he had no intention of choosing the stage as a profession until in London he ran into an actor friend who said: "*The Prisoner of Zenda* is going on tour. Would you like to come along?" Carroll accepted as an understudy of many parts in 1911 when he was nineteen. Thus began his six-decade acting career.

Carroll's proper London stage debut in March 1912 occurred in *The Blindness of Virtue*. That same year he traveled to the United States for the first time as stage manager and actor in *Rutherford and Son*. His first American review on 4 January 1913 said that he played his bit part "sincerely and effectively." But for the next fifteen years his training, mostly in repertory, and performance was back on the London stage. His career was interrupted only once when he served in the infantry in World War I. He fought in France, Greece, and the Holy Land, where in 1916 as a lieutenant he was wounded and invalided home. After two years of hospitalization, he was able to resume his acting career.

In 1924 Carroll made his home in the United States, but he always retained his British citizenship. His early American stage work consists of *The Vortex* (1925), starring and written by Noël Coward, and *The Constant Nymph* (1926). His performance as a butler in *The Green Bay Tree* (1933) resulted in a contract with Metro-Goldwyn-Mayer and a rush trip to Hollywood to play Joan Crawford's butler in *Sadie McKee* (1934)—Carroll's first movie. Even when plays like *Storm Over Patsy* (1937) were run-of-the-mill, Carroll got stellar reviews. He was an adroit performer who could adapt to any part, all of which kept him employed and in demand. His best-known Broadway roles were as Detective Inspector Rough in *Angel Street* (1941), as a Boston Brahmin in *The Late George Apley* (1944), and as Professor White in *The Druid Circle* (1947).

Following his first Hollywood film in 1934, Carroll went on to make dozens more, most notably *The Barretts of Wimpole Street* (1934), *Clive of India* (1935), *Wuthering Heights* (1939), *The House on 92nd Street* (1945), *Father of the Bride* (1950), *The Desert Fox* (1951), *The Bad and the Beautiful* (1952), *We're No Angels* (1954), and *The Parent Trap* (1961). In all, he appeared in six of director Alfred Hitchcock's American films—*Rebecca* (1940), *Suspicion* (1941), *Spellbound* (1945), *The Paradine Case* (1947), *Strangers on a Train* (1951), and *North by Northwest* (1959)—more screen credits for Hitchcock than any other actor.

Carroll married former actress Nancy de Silva in 1948. They had one child.

In the mid-fifties, in the series title role of "Topper" (1953–1955) Carroll scored a hit on network television. Later, as Mr. Waverly, the absent-minded spy director, he was featured in "The Man from U.N.C.L.E." (1964–1968), for which he received an Emmy nomination. When he appeared in that show's spin-off, "The Girl from U.N.C.L.E." (1966–1967), he became one of the few actors to costar simultaneously in two TV series.

Back in 1935 Carroll discussed acting in terms of the intricacies of the voice and the possibilities yet to be brought forth through improving motion picture technology. He also said that an actor should never mingle social life and acting but should always be an observer. With shaggy eyebrows, a lugubrious countenance, a bulldog jaw, a tweedy mellowness, and a mischievous manner, he was urbane and droll, a master of understated performance. He possessed class and charm, qualities that surfaced in his acting and his life. By the end of his career he had appeared in literally hundreds of stage plays, films, and television shows.

Once, reflecting on his family and career, he said: "I owe the theatre a great deal. It owes me nothing."

Carroll died in Hollywood.

• Carroll's career is fully documented in the clipping files at the Library for the Performing Arts, Lincoln Center, New York Public Library. Useful biographical references include David Inman, *The TV Encyclopedia* (1991); Tim Cawkwell and John M. Smith, eds., *The World Encyclopedia of Film* (1972); and Gerald Boardman, ed., *The Oxford Companion to American Theatre* (1984). Obituaries appear in the *New York Times* and *Times* (London), 19 Oct. 1972; *Newsweek* and *Time*, 30 Oct. 1972; *Variety*, 25 Oct. 1972; and, by theater critic Richard Watts, *New York Post*, 18 Nov. 1972.

PATRICIA FOX-SHEINWOLD

CARROLL, Mother Austin (23 Feb. 1836?–29 Nov. 1909), educator and author, was born Margaret Anne Carroll in Clonmel, County Tipperary, Ireland, the daughter of William Carroll, a shop owner and mill manager, and Margaret Mary Strahan. Clonmel, Ireland's largest inland town during Margaret's childhood, was a bustling grain-shipping center where William Carroll's business ventures, like his nine children, thrived. In this comfortable merchant-class family noted for staunch devotion to both faith and learning, Margaret shared in family charity by carrying food supplies to the needy long before the famine years. Attending private schools in Clonmel, she acquired facility in four languages then earned Ireland's Teacher Certification in the National Model School.

In 1853 Carroll decided to dedicate her life to assisting others as a member of Catherine McAuley's Mercy Institute. She entered the Convent of Mercy in Cork, received the name Mary Austin, and in 1856 professed her religious vows for life. Within a few months she was one of several Cork sisters assigned to the American missions to aid the pioneer Sisters of Mercy there. Mary Austin, occasionally adding Teresa to avoid the confusion of duplicate names in one convent, assisted the Irish sisters as they spread schools and social services in Providence, Rhode Island, Hartford, Connecticut, and Manchester, New Hampshire, in New England, in Rochester and Buffalo in New York, and later from Florida to Texas.

From 1869 to 1902 Carroll served as one of the compassionate and dynamic Mercy leaders in New Orleans and Mobile. She opened shelters for immigrant girls in 1869, for needy women, orphans, and toddlers in day care in successive years, and for newsboys and street waifs in 1879. She and her sisters regularly visited the poor sick in their homes with bread, soup, and assistance and risked their lives nursing in every yellow fever epidemic. By using the power of the press through the courtesy of local newspapers, Carroll effected reforms such as a separate facility for women and the hiring of matrons instead of male guards in the women's sections of local prisons during the late 1870s and 1880s.

Carroll challenged high school girls with a more solid curriculum in mathematics and science then encouraged them to continue with higher education. In 1887 she planned a Catholic women's college in New Orleans but was unable to bring her dream to reality. In the 1870s and the following decade, she offered free evening classes for newsboys, job training and placement aid for girls and women, night school for working youths, and in Belize, Central America, from 1882 on both academic and vocational training schools for girls.

Most numerous of Carroll's educational outreach programs, however, were the schools that she opened for African Americans in the small towns of Alabama, Florida, Louisiana, and Mississippi, where blacks had no other option. Although these black schools caused turmoil during the Reconstruction era, when racists often torched black schools at night, Carroll courageously placed each of her black schools adjacent to the local Mercy Convent. Her combination of compassionate concern plus daring determination in the face of opposition preserved her schools into the twentieth century while she struggled to finance them as a writer.

In Ireland Carroll had begun translating for her sisters the French spiritual works of Charles Daniel, S.J., and Jean-Baptiste St. Jure, S.J. While in New England, again for her sisters, she had researched and written the *Life of Catherine McAuley*, the Mercy founder. A few years after its publication in 1866, Carroll realized that its appeal to the general public had provided considerable funds for the sisters' charitable works. Her sisters encouraged her to publish her translations specifically to aid the fever orphans temporarily sheltered in the convent. Between 1869 and 1875 Carroll sent three of her translations plus several small prayer collections to the New York publishers. The books sold surprisingly well, possibly because the people of New Orleans wished to thank Carroll and her sisters for their assistance during the yellow fever epidemics.

Just before 1870 Carroll wrote four collections of stories in response to childrens' entreaties for nice lively characters who misbehaved now and again as real children tend to do. In writing to please her young readers, she helped to bridge the gap between earlier tales of sugar-sweet darlings and Mark Twain's happy Tom and Becky (1876) and Huck Finn himself. Carroll's *Happy Hours* (1867), *Angel Dreams* (1868), and *By the Seaside* (1869) were republished in London and

New York in the 1890s. The fourth and largest collection, *Glimpses of Pleasant Homes* (1869), which had Ireland as its setting, seems to have characterized the Carroll children's pleasant home. These books were some of the staple titles in the fifteen circulating parish libraries and thirty-six school collections Carroll established through the years.

Although Carroll wrote four school plays and several lives of saints in the 1880s, her lasting work was a historical series called *Leaves from the Annals of the Sisters of Mercy*. Describing the work of the Mercies in different parts of the world, she presented Ireland in vol. 1 (1881); England plus Crimean War nursing and Australia in vol. 2 (1883); and North, Central, and South America in vol. 3 (1889) and vol. 4 (1895). By 1900 Carroll had published a total of twenty books. Reprints in the United States included *Cottage Controversy*, a book by Mercy founder Catherine McAuley, extant only because Carroll had unearthed a copy even though the original edition had been lost.

Even with numerous historical articles in the Dublin *Irish Monthly*, the *American Catholic Quarterly Review*, and other journals, Carroll was long known only by the initials M. A. C. Her books carried, instead of her name, a phrase typical of the time, "by a Member of the Order of Mercy." Such anonymity brought her recognition only after her works appeared in literary displays in World's Fairs in New Orleans in 1885 and later in Atlanta. Invited to prepare papers for both the 1892 Columbian Exposition in Chicago and the Apostolate of the Press Meet in New York the same year, she chose the latter. During her last decade, she wrote three more books and a half-dozen articles before a final stroke stilled her hand in the Convent of Mercy in Mobile, Alabama.

Obituaries in the North praised Carroll as author, educator, and founder of institutions, schools, and libraries. Across the South editors had seen her provide epidemic nursing, combat racism, encourage higher education for women, and fight for prison reform, justice for her Mercies, and schools for blacks. Her successes were many, her failures few. Her sisters appreciate her as their historian who gathered their scattered threads, wound them into a cord, a rope, then a cable uniting in one spirit Mercies all over the world.

• A collection of photocopied letters to and from Carroll is in the archives of Sisters of Mercy, New Orleans. See also Mary Hermenia Muldrey, RSM, *Abounding in Mercy: Mother Austin Carroll* (1988); and Matthew Russell, "Mother Austin Carroll," *Irish Monthly* 14 (Mar. 1886): 159–60. Obituaries are "Mother Austin Carroll, Famous in Charity, Education, and Literature," *New Orleans Daily Picayune*, 30 Nov. 1909; "Eulogies for Mother Austin Carroll, Beloved Superior," *Mobile Daily Register*, 2 Dec. 1909; and "Distinguished Nun and Successful Author," *Boston Pilot*, 8 Dec. 1909.

MARY HERMENIA MULDREY

CARROLL, Samuel Sprigg (21 Sept. 1832–28 Jan. 1893), soldier, was born in Washington, D.C., the son of William Thomas Carroll, a clerk of the U.S. Supreme Court. He was a descendant of Charles Carroll of Carrollton. He received an appointment to West Point in 1852 and graduated near the bottom of his class in 1856. Following graduation, he was brevetted second lieutenant in the Ninth U.S. Infantry. In October he received promotion to second lieutenant in the Tenth U.S. Infantry, with which he served at Fort Ridgely, Minnesota, in 1857, and on the Utah expedition from late 1857 through 1859. He was subsequently assigned to duty at West Point as quartermaster in January 1860. While serving at this post, he was promoted to first lieutenant on 25 April 1861 and to captain in the Tenth Infantry on 1 November 1861.

With the enlargement of the army after the outbreak of the Civil War, Carroll saw greater opportunity in the volunteer service than the regular army. He secured an appointment as colonel of the Eighth Ohio Volunteer Infantry, effective 7 December 1861. The historian of the regiment recalled of Carroll, "He was a dashing officer, anxious to distinguish himself, and above all to qualify his regiment for its duties." Carroll molded the regiment into a fine body of soldiers that gave an excellent account of itself on many battlefields of the war, including the Union victory over Thomas J. "Stonewall" Jackson in the action at Kernstown, Virginia, on 22–23 March 1862. Two months later, on 24 May, Carroll was assigned to command of a brigade in General James Shields's division, and he was nominated for the rank of brigadier general of volunteers. Carroll proved to be one of the few officers to distinguish themselves in the dismal Shenandoah Valley campaign against Confederate general Jackson. He led his brigade through the Union defeats at Port Republic, Virginia, on 9 June 1862 and Cedar Mountain, Virginia, on 9 August 1862. He was wounded five days later while inspecting picket posts along the Rapidan River, and he spent nearly one month recovering.

Upon his return Carroll was assigned to command the Second Brigade of Amiel Weeks Whipple's division in the Third Army Corps. He led the brigade through the fall campaign and the battle of Fredericksburg (13 Dec. 1862). In January 1863 he went on sick leave, possibly because of his wound. During his absence his brigade was broken up, and the regiments were transferred to other commands. Carroll requested assignment to the Second Army Corps and was placed in command of the First Brigade in William Henry French's division. The First Brigade, which contained Carroll's old regiment, the Eighth Ohio, participated in the Union defeat at Chancellorsville (2–4 May 1863). Throughout this period Carroll remained a colonel; his nomination as a brigadier general of volunteers was not confirmed.

At the battle of Gettysburg, on 2 July 1863, Carroll's brigade was ordered to reinforce Cemetery Hill, which had been attacked and nearly captured by Confederate troops. His timely and skillfully handled counterattack helped drive the Confederates off the hill and secure possession of that important position. Although he had earned a reputation as a fearless and aggressive officer and had won brevets to major and lieutenant colonel for gallant and meritorious service at Chancellorsville and Gettysburg, he still did not win a general's star. The men of his command revered him. The historian of the Fourth Ohio Infantry wrote, "Every man in the brigade loved him and gloried in him, and would have followed him wherever he might go against the enemy, and he would go wherever he was ordered or die in the attempt." This same historian wrote that, despite his aggressive demeanor as a soldier, Carroll was "as tender in feeling as a woman, whole-souled and true." His flaming red hair earned him the nickname "Bricktop" with his men. He led them through the fall campaign at Bristoe Station and Mine Run, Virginia. Carroll's brigade was heavily engaged on 5–6 May 1864 at the battle of the Wilderness. He was wounded in the arm on 5 May but refused to leave the field. He remained with his command through the savage fighting at Spotsylvania Court House until 13 May. Early on the morning of that day, while his brigade was skirmishing, Carroll's arm was shattered above the elbow by a Minié ball. The day before Carroll was wounded, the Army of the Potomac commander, General George G. Meade, had submitted Carroll's name for promotion to brigadier general. Carroll's promotion was approved, but his wound prevented him from returning to the field. Following his recovery from his wounds, Carroll served on court-martial duty, temporarily commanded the Department of West Virginia (Feb.–Mar. 1865), and briefly commanded a division in the Army of the Shenandoah at the end of the war.

Following the war, Carroll was assigned to the District of Central Virginia until 22 January 1866, when he was mustered out of the volunteer service and was appointed lieutenant colonel of the Twenty-first U.S. Infantry. He was acting inspector general of the Division of the Atlantic in 1868. By 1869 his wounds compelled him to retire.

Carroll spent his retirement at his family estate, "Belle View," in Takoma Park, Maryland. He remained a bachelor. He died in Takoma Park and was buried at Arlington National Cemetery. Union general Oliver O. Howard aptly summarized Carroll's ability as a soldier in March 1864: "For fearlessness and energetic action, Col. Carroll has not a superior."

• Carroll's Civil War reports and some correspondence are in U.S. War Department, *The War of the Rebellion: A Compilation of the Official Records of the Union and Confederate Armies* (128 vols., 1880–1901). Biographical information is in George W. Cullum, *Biographical Register of the Officers and Graduates of the Military Academy, from 1802 to 1867* (1879), and the supplement to this volume, also published in 1879. Two sketches of Carroll's military career and character are Augustus Buell, "Gen. S. S. Carroll," *National Tribune*, 16 Feb. 1893; and *Tribune* editor, "Gen. S. S. Carroll," *National Tribune*, 23 Mar. 1893. A lengthier sketch of his military career is in William H. Powell and Edward Shippen, eds., *Officers of the Army and Navy Who Served in the Civil War* (1892). Franklin Sawyer, *A Military History of the 8th Ohio Regiment Ohio Vol. Inf'y* (1881), offers some observations on Carroll's character and the role he played in molding this regiment into soldiers. See also William Kepler, *History of the Fourth Regiment Ohio Volunteer Infantry* (1886), for more commentary and a detailed description of the action in which Carroll was wounded at Spotsylvania. An in-depth examination of the part played by Carroll's command at Gettysburg is Gary Lash, *The Gibraltar Brigade on East Cemetery Hill* (1995). An obituary of Carroll is in the *National Tribune*, 2 Feb. 1893.

D. Scott Hartwig

CARROLL, William (3 Mar. 1788–22 Mar. 1844), soldier, businessman and governor of Tennessee, was born near Pittsburgh, Pennsylvania, the son of Thomas Carroll, a farmer and businessman, and Mary Montgomery. Although his formal education was meager, his letters, papers, and public documents exhibit an unusual clarity of thought and facility of expression. His father formed a partnership with Albert Gallatin in the operation of a general hardware store, and William, as a teenager, was a part of the firm. In 1810 he moved to Nashville and opened a branch of the Pittsburgh store. In 1813 he married Cecelia Bradford; they had four children.

Soon after his arrival in Nashville, Carroll became a close friend of Andrew Jackson, and when in 1812 he fought a duel with Jesse Benton (in which neither was seriously hurt), Jackson served as his second. Carroll joined the state militia, probably at Jackson's suggestion, and by the time war against Great Britain had been declared (18 June 1812) he had become captain of the Nashville Volunteers. In the fall of the following year, Jackson, as commander of one of Tennessee's two major divisions, marched to defend the southern frontier, and he appointed Carroll as inspector general. Carroll fought during the ensuing war against the Creek Indians with conspicuous bravery. In 1814 Jackson became a major general of the U.S. Army, and Carroll took command of the Tennessee militia with the rank of major general. When British troops assaulted New Orleans early in 1815, Carroll had been placed in command of the center where most of the fighting eventually took place, and he emerged with a reputation in Tennessee second only to that of Jackson.

By midsummer of 1815, Carroll had reopened his business in Nashville, and not long thereafter he bought a steamboat—which he named the *General Jackson*—to participate in the river traffic on the Cumberland. The panic of 1819 reduced him to the verge of bankruptcy, however. Two years later he was a candidate for governor. His comprehensive platform showed compassion for the common person and debtor classes, pledging a revision of the banking laws, the construction of a "penitentiary house," a revision of the penal code, state care for the insane, reorganization of the courts, internal improvements, and the establishment of a public school system. The common people received him gladly as he talked his way across the state, and he defeated wealthy lieutenant governor Edward Ward by a margin of 4 to 1. For twelve years he presided as governor, setting a record for the longest tenure of such an elected official in Tennessee. He encountered no opposition in 1823, 1825, and 1829 and had little difficulty in gaining reelection in 1831 and 1833.

A fiscal conservative, Governor Carroll turned his attention first to ending the effects of the panic of 1819. He criticized banks as operating in "too loose" a fashion, and he announced that all would be "carefully watched" and those found to be unsound would be prohibited from reopening and continuing operation. A resumption of specie was required by 1824. Economic liberals must have quaked as he told legislators in his first message to the general assembly that the cultivation of "industrious habits and the practice of rigid economy are the only means by which individuals can be relieved from pecuniary embarrassments."

Carroll was able to accomplish most of the reforms he advocated. The penal code was revised to eliminate the branding iron, whipping post, pillory, and stocks. By 1831 a state penitentiary was in operation in Nashville where authorities believed that "solitary confinement, coarse food, and hard work" would rehabilitate a felon so that he or she would live a normal life upon release. As significant as any accomplishment was the revision of the constitution in 1834 that reflected the growing democratic spirit of the times. Property qualifications for office holding were removed, the franchise was extended to all free white men, and taxation was made more equitable. The outcome represented a culmination of the efforts of many people toward constitutional democracy.

Carroll, as a Jacksonian Democrat, may have worked with John Overton and others of the "Nashville Junto" to promote the political fortunes of Jackson soon after his return from New Orleans. There is ample evidence that Carroll visited in surrounding states while governor to promote the Old Chief's candidacy for president. His gubernatorial victories in 1821 and 1823 helped prepare voters for the Jackson candidacy in 1824 and 1828.

Carroll was defeated in 1835 when he sought a fourth consecutive term. The constitution clearly stated that no one could serve as governor for more than three consecutive terms, but Carroll argued that the "new" constitution of 1834 gave him the right to serve again. Perhaps more important in his defeat than the technicality of the constitutional issue was the beginning of the Whig revolt against Jacksonian Democrats as represented by the new Whig party.

Carroll campaigned vigorously in 1836 for Jackson's choice of Martin Van Buren as president and, sometime thereafter, vainly sought an appointment as minister to Mexico. In 1840 he was chosen as chairman of the national Democratic party. He supported Van Buren's bid for reelection, but the president's defeat put Whigs in control both in the White House and in Tennessee's state house. Although friends urged him to run again for governor, Carroll refused. He died in Nashville.

• A fairly complete collection of Carroll's papers as governor are found in Robert H. White, *Messages of the Governors of Tennessee, 1821–35*, vol. 2 (1952). A few of his letters may be found in John Spencer Bassett, ed., *Correspondence of Andrew Jackson* (7 vols., 1926–1935). Two articles, although prepared seventy or more years ago, are helpful: Gabriel H. Golden, "William Carroll and His Administration: Tennessee's Business Governor," *Tennessee Historical Magazine* 9 (1925): 9–30, and Emma Carroll Tucker, "Governor William Carroll," *American Historical Magazine* 7 (1902): 388–96. Graduate studies concerning Carroll include Wallace R. Rogers, "A History of the Administration of William Carroll, Governor of Tennessee" (master's thesis, Univ. of Tennessee, 1925); Margaret L. Walker, "The Life of William Carroll" (master's thesis, Univ. of Tennessee, 1929); and Isabelle G. Kegley, "The Work of William Carroll as Governor of Tennessee" (master's thesis, Vanderbilt Univ., 1933).

ROBERT E. CORLEW

CARROLL OF CARROLLTON, Charles (19 Sept. 1737–14 Nov. 1832), planter, businessman, investor, and the only Roman Catholic signer of the Declaration of Independence, as well as the last of the signers to die, was born in Annapolis, Maryland, the son of Charles Carroll of Annapolis, a planter, and his common-law wife, Elizabeth Brooke. An only child, Carroll was sent at the age of ten to the Jesuit college of St. Omers, in French Flanders, where Maryland's Catholic gentry sent their sons because the colony's laws, which denied "papists" the right to vote, hold office, practice law, and worship publicly, also forbade them to maintain religious schools. Young Carroll studied abroad for sixteen years, ending with a thesis in philosophy at the college of Louis le Grand in Paris in 1757. After reading civil law in Bourges and Paris, he moved to London in September 1759 to pursue the common law at the Inns of Court. However, his antipathy for the discipline, which he regarded as "founded upon and still subsisting by villainy," became so intense that he ultimately defied his father's intention that he formally enter the Inner Temple, one of the four Inns of Court. Finding the paternal insistence on his acquiring the social graces more to his liking, he became adept at dancing, drawing, and fencing and mastered Italian, bookkeeping, and surveying, practical skills the elder Carroll deemed essential for success as a landowner and man of business.

Charles Carroll of Annapolis married Elizabeth Brooke in 1757. Her death in 1761 shattered the fond hopes of her son for a reunion with his parents once he had completed his education. Profoundly shaken by the news of his mother's demise and afraid of losing his father as well, Carroll pled earnestly to come home, but "Papa" insisted that he finish his legal studies in England. It was not until February 1765 that he finally returned to Annapolis.

To differentiate himself from other similarly named relatives, Carroll appended to his name "of Carrollton," the family's 10,000-acre tenanted manor in Frederick County. He turned his attention to family affairs and, under his father's meticulous tutelage, began to learn the intricacies of administering their wide-ranging interests: the growing and marketing of tobacco; the management and cultivation of their 12,500-acre dwelling plantation "Doohoregan (later Doughoregan)

Manor" with its nearly 300 slaves; the leasing of land and supervision of tenants on Carrollton; the lending of money; and the direction of the Baltimore Company ironworks. In 1768 he married Mary Darnall, a first cousin once removed. They had seven children, only three of whom survived to adulthood.

A provincial controversy catapulted Carroll into public view. Early in 1773 Maryland's provincial secretary, Daniel Dulany defended in the *Maryland Gazette* Governor Robert Eden's unilateral decision to raise the fees charged by public officials for their services. Carroll, using the pseudonym "First Citizen," published a series of responses that attacked the higher rates and criticized Dulany's self-interest in supporting them. The contest between "First Citizen" and "Antilon," the name Dulany adopted, continued through the spring and led to the formation of a new political coalition centered around Carroll. Composed of ambitious young men, among them Samuel Chase, Thomas Johnson, Jr., William Paca, and Matthew Tilghman, this "popular party" managed to triumph over Dulany's supporters in the May elections to the general assembly's lower house.

Although Maryland law still barred Roman Catholics from voting and holding office, the events of 1773 brought Carroll actively into politics. As the mounting imperial crisis superseded provincial disputes, he became an advocate of separation from Great Britain. Beginning in November 1774 he served in all but the first and seventh of the provincial conventions that formed Maryland's provisional government. In March 1776 the Second Continental Congress sent Carroll, his cousin Father John Carroll, Chase, and Benjamin Franklin to Montreal in a vain attempt to persuade the Canadians to join the American cause. The trip brought Carroll further attention, and after his return to Maryland in June, he used his growing prestige to help Chase and other popular leaders convince the eighth convention to vote for independence. Appointed to Congress early in July, he signed the Declaration of Independence on 2 August. Later in 1776 Carroll played a major role in drafting the state's declaration of rights and its highly conservative constitution.

Carroll endured months of intense anxiety and racking doubt as the civil disorder unleashed by the Revolution threatened to plunge Maryland into anarchy. Certain at first that chaos could be avoided only through reunion with Great Britain, he shortly acknowledged the impossibility of that solution and began to work with considerable skill and sensitivity to save both the political and economic power of the elite and the patriot cause. After securing the adoption of a state constitution that guaranteed political hegemony to men of property, Carroll and his allies worked to popularize the Revolution by enacting fiscal policies that shifted the burden of taxation from polls to land and slaves and made paper currency legal tender for the payment of prewar sterling debts. The second measure brought Carroll into sharp conflict with his father, who opposed any law that threatened to deprive him of approximately a third of his fortune, which he had lent at interest.

Carroll's father and his wife died within two weeks of each other in 1782, leaving him with four children. He never remarried.

A delegate to Congress in 1776 and 1777–1778, Carroll remained in public life until 1800, serving continuously in the Maryland Senate and as a U.S. senator from 1789 to 1792. He was elected to the Philadelphia convention in 1787 but declined the post. However, he fervently supported the Constitution, which he considered the supreme guarantor of the rights of men of property. Confident that he would be chosen a delegate to the state's ratifying convention, he prepared a lengthy speech advocating adoption of the Constitution as the best means of restraining the "excesses of an uncontrolled Democracy," thereby assuring "respectability abroad and stability at home." Although a vigorous anti-Federalist campaign prevented his election and denied him the chance to deliver his oration, Carroll's draft of his intended remarks reflects his determination that the powerful egalitarian forces unleashed by the American Revolution would never again threaten his class.

The causes Carroll supported during his three years in the U.S. Senate, such as a strong chief executive, a standing army, and Alexander Hamilton's plan for funding the war debt, as well as the views he expressed in private correspondence after his retirement from politics all reveal his unwavering allegiance to a central government powerful enough to protect the interests of propertied men and his undiminished distaste for popular rule. Writing to Thomas Jefferson in 1791, Carroll noted that he regarded the proceedings of France's national assembly with "anxious care" and predicted that country's "new system" had less to fear from "the opposition of the dignified Clergy and noblesse" than from "the fear of disunion, the side views and factions, combinations and cabals amongst the popular party." Displeased by Jefferson's continuing attachment to the French and amazed by his "strange sentiment" favoring periodic revolutions as a means of preserving the "liberties of a people," Carroll hoped the Virginian would not be elected president in 1801. He characterized Jefferson as a "poor creature" who "will be afraid of using his constitutional powers in defence of the people, lest he may offend these ignorant and suspicious sovereigns." Writing to his son in 1806, he commented that it was "impossible for a man tainted with democratic principles to possess an elevated soul and dignified character." His priorities for the new nation are perhaps best revealed in his correspondence with his son-in-law Robert Goodloe Harper, to whom he complained in 1820 that, instead of wasting time on the "Missouri question," Congress should attend to "matters of more importance to the Union," namely, passage of a bankruptcy law, preventing abuses in the banking system, and ensuring that purchasers of western lands would "pay ready money for them." Although he acknowledged that slavery was "a great evil," he wondered impatiently why the question should be kept alive. "Let an effectual mode of getting rid of it be pointed out," he told Harper, "or let the question sleep forever." In 1830, at the age of ninety-three, Carroll accepted the presidency of the American Society for Colonizing the Free People of Color of the United States. Yet of the 334 slaves he owned at his death, his will freed only one, his "servant Bill."

The disfavor with which Carroll regarded the democratic tendencies of the Republic he had helped create did not prevent him from taking advantage of the opportunities its economy provided for making money. In addition to continuing his agricultural operations, he invested in banks, insurance, railroads, and turnpike and canal companies and also bought foreign stocks, one of the more interesting of these acquisitions being the 5 percent British navy stock, worth more than $25,000, that was part of his portfolio during the War of 1812. Vigilantly guarding his capital against the material appetites of his family, he kept meticulous accounts of the gifts he made to his son and daughters, lectured them incessantly about the virtues of frugality, and did not hesitate to assume control of their assets in exchange for settling their debts, even as his substantial contributions continued to make possible the gracious style of life to which all of them felt entitled. Deeply disappointed in his only son, Charles Carroll of Homewood, whose lack of self-discipline and fondness for strong drink periodically threatened to make him a public embarrassment as well as a private tragedy, Carroll greatly enjoyed the international success garnered by three of his granddaughters. Dazzling British society on their arrival in London in 1816, these women eventually contracted marriages with members of the aristocracy, thereby wedding their grandfather's New World money to Old World titles.

With the deaths of John Adams and Jefferson on 4 July 1826, Carroll became the sole living signer of the Declaration of Independence, a distinction that inspired Daniel Webster to venerate him as "an aged oak, standing alone on the plain" and his countrymen to name their sons, towns, and counties after him. Following Carroll's demise in Baltimore, President Andrew Jackson ordered the federal government closed to mark his passing, an honor previously accorded only to George Washington. Carroll's estate included some 30,000 acres of land in Maryland, another 45,000 acres in Pennsylvania and New York, and personal property worth nearly $1.5 million.

• The bulk of Carroll's papers is deposited at the Maryland Historical Society, Baltimore. The most significant prerevolutionary collection contains his correspondence with his father, 1749–1782, while postrevolutionary materials include some 200 letters written to his son between 1797 and 1825 and considerable correspondence with his son-in-law Harper for the years 1801–1825. In addition, the Library of Congress and the University of San Francisco own valuable, though less extensive, collections of papers pertaining to Carroll and his family. Two microfilm editions of Carroll manuscripts are available. The most recent and comprehensive, Ronald Hoffman and Eleanor S. Darcy, eds., *The Charles Carroll of Carrollton Family Papers: A Microfilm Edition of Documents Located at the Maryland Historical Society* (1985), includes correspondence, business and land papers, manuscripts concerning the Baltimore Company, ledgers and account books, and Carroll's estate papers. Thomas O'Brien Hanley's microfilm edition, *The Charles Carroll Papers* (1971), is limited to correspondence but does contain some Carroll letters from repositories other than the Maryland Historical Society. Ronald Hoffman et al., eds., *Dear Papa, Dear Charley* (1997), is a documentary edition of Carroll's correspondence for the years 1749–1782. An earlier volume of Carroll correspondence, Thomas Meagher Field, comp., *Unpublished Letters of Charles Carroll of Carrollton, and of His Father, Charles Carroll of Doughoregan* (1902), contains many errors and should be used with extreme caution. See the essays by Sally D. Mason, Hoffman, and Edward C. Papenfuse in *"Anywhere So Long As There Be Freedom": Charles Carroll of Carrollton, His Family, & His Maryland*, cat. Ann C. Van Devanter (1975), as well as Hoffman's *Princes of Eile, Planters of Maryland: The Carroll Saga, 1500–1782* (1997), which takes the family from its origins in the Irish midlands through the American Revolution. Hoffman, *A Spirit of Dissension: Economics, Politics, and the Revolution in Maryland* (1973), contains a perceptive analysis of Carroll's revolutionary political career.

RONALD HOFFMAN

CARRUTH, Hayden (31 Oct. 1862–3 Jan. 1932), writer, was born Fred Hayden Carruth near Lake City, Minnesota, the son of Oliver Powers Carruth and Mary Veeder, farmers. After receiving elementary and secondary education locally, young Fred, as he was then called, taught for several years in area schools. Although he had little interest in pursuing a college degree, he had shown skill as a writer from an early age, and he attended the University of Minnesota for one year, in 1881–1882, in preparation for a career in journalism.

Upon leaving the university, Carruth joined the staff of a Minneapolis newspaper, where he worked for a year. Then, in 1883, he moved to the prairie town of Estelline, Minnesota, where he established his own weekly newspaper, the *Estelline Bell.* The paper attracted nationwide attention for its humorous features written by Carruth, and other newspapers reprinted some of his pieces. However, it was not a financial success, and Carruth sold it in 1886. That same year he moved to Sioux Falls, where he founded a humorous weekly, the *Dakota Bell.* Once again lack of adequate financial support forced Carruth to give up the publication. He moved to New York City, where he joined the staff of the *New York Tribune* and dropped his first name.

From 1888 to 1892 Hayden Carruth wrote a humorous editorial daily for the *Tribune*, then left to become a freelance writer. For the next thirteen years he contributed short stories, essays, serials, and verse to periodicals such as *Harper's Weekly*, *Century*, *Cosmopolitan*, the *Saturday Evening Post*, and *Youth's Companion*. In 1900–1902 Carruth also edited a feature called "The Drawer" for *Harper's Magazine*.

Carruth's first book, a collection of his stories, was *The Adventures of Jones*, published in 1895. This was followed four years later by *Mr. Milo Bush and Other*

Worthies, Their Recollections. Both books were works of humor, collections of tall tales featuring stock frontier characters. Unlike similar works by his contemporaries Bret Harte and Mark Twain, however, Carruth's stories were written solely to entertain rather than to moralize or offer social criticism.

During this period Carruth also wrote two books for boys. The first, *The Voyage of the Rattletrap*, published in 1897, is a humorous account of a trip by prairie schooner through Nebraska and the Dakotas. The second, *Track's End*, was serialized that same year in *Youth's Companion* and made Carruth famous. *Track's End* is an adventure story about an eighteen-year-old boy left behind to guard the bank and the hotel in his hometown, called Track's End, in Dakota Territory, when the rest of its inhabitants go east for the winter. Comparing it favorably with *Kidnapped* and *Robinson Crusoe*, critics hailed Carruth's story when it was published in book form in 1911; the *New York Times* reviewer called it "the best book of the season."

In 1905 Carruth became the literary editor of *Woman's Home Companion* and ten years later began writing "The Postscript," a column of commentary about the passing scene that appeared regularly on the last page of the magazine. In 1917 he resigned as literary editor in order to devote himself full time to the column, which he wrote until his death. As the most popular feature of a nationally circulated women's magazine, "The Postscript" made Carruth widely liked and respected. Although often light in tone, Carruth incorporated into the column his concerns for domestic social issues, in particular his strong support of child-labor legislation. The source of his appeal lay in his ability to communicate with the average reader and to empathize with her concerns. Following his death, an editorial in *Woman's Home Companion* singled out for praise his "sympathetic interest in everything and everybody."

Carruth married Ettie Leah Gorton of Lake City in 1884; she died in 1929. The couple had four children, and Carruth's concern for his family was often reflected in his magazine column. A grandson and namesake, Hayden Carruth, became a well-known poet.

Carruth contributed the article on South Dakota to *These United States*, a two-volume work edited by Ernest Gruening and published in 1923–1924. He died at his home in Briarcliff Manor, New York.

• Biographical information on Hayden Carruth can be found in *Who Was Who in America*, vol. 1 (4th printing, 1960); "Hayden Carruth, Author of Good Cheer," *National Magazine*, July–Aug. 1932, pp. 167, 176; and *Woman's Home Companion*, Mar. 1932, p. 59. An obituary is in the *New York Times*, 4 Jan. 1932.

ANN T. KEENE

CARSE, Matilda Bradley (19 Nov. 1835–3 June 1917), temperance worker, editor, and entrepreneur, was born near Belfast, Ireland, the daughter of John Bradley and Catherine Cleland, Scottish merchants whose ancestors had migrated to Ireland in the seventeenth century. Educated in Ireland, Carse emigrated in 1858 to Chicago. In 1861 she married Thomas Carse, a railroad manager with whom she had three sons. After her husband's death in 1870, her youngest son was killed by a drunken drayman, propelling Carse into the temperance cause just as the Woman's Christian Temperance Union (WCTU) was organizing. She devoted much of the rest of her life to business and volunteer activities related to that organization.

Carse was president of the Chicago Central Union, one of the strongest WCTU locals, from 1878 to 1913 and superintended its myriad charitable and reform activities, including a nursery school for working mothers, two kindergartens, a shelter for "wayward" girls, a dispensary, and reading rooms. In 1880 she founded and became president of the Woman's Temperance Publishing Association (WTPA), a stock company owned solely by women and staffed largely by women. It published the *Signal* (*Union Signal* after 1882), the weekly organ of the national organization, the WCTU's other serial publications, and many books and pamphlets related to temperance and reform. The organization flourished, reaching over 100 employees in 1890.

In 1887 Carse launched another ambitious project, a thirteen-story Loop office building designed by the eminent architect John W. Root and called the Woman's Temple. The building served as the national and local headquarters of the WCTU and the WTPA. Chicago businessmen and WCTU women subscribed the original $900,000 in capital, and the building was expected to pay for itself and generate additional funds through rental of its choice office space. It was a magnificent achievement, a symbolic structure that affirmed the power of American womanhood by its sheer grandeur. However, completed just at the onset of the panic of 1893, it proved a financial disaster that vastly overextended the resources of the WCTU. The Temple's financial difficulties almost split the WCTU in the 1890s, a split Frances Willard was able to avoid. But after Willard's death in 1898, Carse no longer commanded the support of the national union. In 1898, because of its severe financial difficulties, the Temple enterprise was taken over by Marshall Field, a Chicago businessman and a major stockholder in the venture; thereafter the Temple's connections to the WCTU and Carse were severed. Carse's presidency of the WTPA was terminated at the same time, and the publishing corporation was dissolved in 1903, the WCTU directly assuming many of its publishing functions.

Carse continued to head the Chicago Union and was also active in Chicago reformist circles. She was president of the Chicago Foundling Home Association, the first woman to serve on the Chicago Board of Education, and one of the Lady Managers of the Columbian Exposition of 1893. In 1913 she retired from active life and left Chicago to make her home in New York with her son. She died at Park Hill-on-Hudson. Despite her ultimate business failures, Carse was a spectacular entrepreneur. Both in her publishing ventures and as the leader of the Chicago WCTU, she made a significant contribution to the women's movement, including woman suffrage, as well as to social reform movements generally.

• All papers relating to Carse's life are in the Willard Memorial Library, WCTU Headquarters, Evanston, Ill. The *Union Signal* (the chief publication of the WTPA) and the correspondence, *Minutes*, and scrapbooks of the WCTU, which contain much information on Carse, the Temple, and her publishing activities, are also available on microfilm as part of the *Temperance and Prohibition Papers* (1977). Carse and the Woman's Temple are discussed in Ruth Bordin, *Woman and Temperance: The Quest For Power and Liberty, 1873–1900* (1981; repr. 1990) and *Frances Willard: A Biography* (1986); and in Mary Earhart Dillon, *Frances Willard: From Prayers to Politics* (1944). The most complete biographical sketches of Carse are in *Notable American Women* (1971), and Frances Willard and Mary Livermore, eds., *A Woman of the Century* (1893). An obituary is in the *Chicago Tribune*, 4 June 1917.

RUTH BORDIN

CARSON, John (23 Mar. 1868–11 Dec. 1949), early country fiddler, vocalist, and entertainer, known professionally as "Fiddlin'" John, was born in Fannin County, Georgia, the son of J. P. Carson and Mary Ann Beaty, subsistence farmers. Carson was raised on the family farm, where he learned the rudiments of music-making. His early education was spotty, and the extent of his training unknown. Although he worked as a professional entertainer, he also held odd jobs such as painter and carpenter and probably worked as a subsistence farmer. In 1894 he married Jenny Nora Scroggins (or Scoggins). They had at least nine children.

Carson's first recording was released in 1923, when he was fifty-five years old, after about forty years of semiprofessional fiddling, singing, and entertaining in rural Georgia. Polk Brockman, the Atlanta-based local dealer for OKeh records, sent a telegram to New York requesting that the company record Carson because he knew the music would sell well in Georgia. Carson recorded the sentimental song "Little Old Log Cabin in the Lane" along with a novelty fiddle number, "The Old Hen Cackled (and the Rooster's Gonna Crow)," featuring birdlike sound effects. Legendary producer Ralph Peer oversaw the session but believed that the music was so bad that he had the records pressed without labels or a master number and shipped copies only to Brockman as a favor. When the records quickly sold out, Peer realized his mistake and quickly signed Carson to the label.

For his first two years of recording, Carson primarily worked as a soloist, using traditional tunings and uneven rhythms in his accompaniments to his own rough-hewn vocals. He also performed in a duo with his daughter Rosa Lee Carson (dubbed "Moonshine Kate" by OKeh executives), a fine singer in a deadpan country style who also played the banjo and guitar.

As stringbands were becoming increasingly popular in the mid-1920s, Carson formed his own band, the Virginia Reelers, a floating ensemble of musicians who were mostly younger and played in a style more modern than their leader's. Chief among the members of this group were fiddlers Earl Johnson and "Bully" Brewer, banjoists Land Norris and Bill White, and guitarists "Peanut" Brown and Rosa Lee Carson. Many of the band's members doubled or even tripled on other instruments (Brewer played fiddle, banjo, and guitar), so that they could fill in for one another. On his band recordings, Carson continues to play using the older tunings and his own unique sense of rhythm, while the band often struggles to follow his lead. The result is a sometimes chaotic meeting of two traditions, the older unaccompanied songster matched with a jazzy, driving stringband sound.

Carson's repertoire reached back into the mid-nineteenth century and was an amalgam of traditional dance tunes, ballads, and songs and recently composed sentimental, comic, and vaudeville numbers. He performed and recorded traditional dance tunes such as "Cotton-Eyed Joe," "Fire in the Mountain," "Sugar in the Gourd," and "Arkansas Traveler" and topical and protest songs such as "The Honest Farmer," "There's a Hard Time Coming," "The Death of Floyd Collins," "Taxes on the Farmer Feeds Them All," and "My Ford Sedan." His selections also included nineteenth-century sentimental songs and early twentieth-century popular and novelty items like his first recording, "Little Old Log Cabin in the Lane" (although Carson typically transforms it into an almost ancient-sounding celebration of life in the backwoods). He performed "The Baggage Coach Ahead," "When You and I Were Young, Maggie," "Bully of the Town," and "I'm Glad My Wife's in Europe" and traditional songs such as "Bachelor's Hall," "900 Miles Away from Home," "Old Joe Clark," and "Goin' Where the Weather Suits My Clothes" (Carson's title for "Worried Man Blues").

By the 1930s Carson's style of performing was considered outdated. Thanks to a long relationship with local politicians (many of whom used Carson's performances to attract voters to rallies), he was given a job as an elevator operator in the Georgia state capitol in Atlanta. By the 1940s he had retired; he died in Atlanta.

Carson set the stage for later country stars in many crucial ways. He was a unique personality with a humorous, although deadpan delivery style, who transformed the material that he performed through his own unique sound. His sense of rhythm and tonality, influenced by his boyhood in rural Georgia and his years of professional performing in tent shows and fiddlers' contests, gives even the most recently composed of his songs a country sound. Finally, Carson's music is often both topical and humorous, commenting on the everyday experiences of his listeners. As a performer, Carson came from the people and, although he achieved great celebrity, he never "took on airs" or acted like a star. His popularity convinced countless others that they, too, could become country performers.

• Eugene Earle, *Fiddlin' Georgia Crazy* (1986), gives the life story of this pioneering musician. Unattributed liner notes (perhaps by Mark Wilson) to the Rounder Records release, *The Old Hen Cackled* (Rounder 1003), and Norm Cohen, "Fiddlin' John Carson: An Appreciation and Discography," *JEMF Quarterly* 10 (1974), are also useful. An obituary is in the *Atlanta Journal*, 15 Dec. 1949.

RICHARD CARLIN

CARSON, Joseph (19 Apr. 1808–30 Dec. 1876), physician and botanist, was born in Philadelphia, Pennsylvania, the son of Joseph Carson, a merchant, and Elizabeth Lawrence. After obtaining his A.B. from the University of Pennsylvania in 1826, he went to work in the drugstore of Edward Lowber in Philadelphia where he developed an interest in botany. He studied medicine with Thomas T. Hewson and obtained his M.D. from the University of Pennsylvania in 1830. After a period as physician to the hospital of the Philadelphia almshouse, he served as ship's surgeon on the *Georgiana* on a voyage that took him to India (and on which, in his own words, he "played both the part of Merchant and Doctor" and which provided opportunities for drawing the flora and fauna he encountered). He returned to Philadelphia in 1832 and entered the practice of medicine.

Carson gained prominence as an obstetrician. In 1849 he was elected to the obstetrical staff of the Pennsylvania Hospital and served in that post until the Lying-In Department was closed in 1854 due to an outbreak of puerperal fever. He gave up obstetrics in favor of the materia medica, a branch of medicine closely related to his interests in botany and which he deemed "indispensable in the scheme for the acquisition of medical knowledge, secondary to none." He held the posts of professor of materia medica and pharmacy from 1836 to 1846 and of professor of materia medica from 1846 to 1850 at the Philadelphia College of Pharmacy. He also was lecturer on the materia medica at the Philadelphia Medical Institute from 1844 to 1848. In 1850 he became professor of materia medica and therapeutics at the University of Pennsylvania and remained there until ill health forced his retirement in 1876.

In 1833 Carson was elected to the Academy of Natural Sciences of Philadelphia and remained active in the academy throughout his life. At various times he served the academy as librarian, secretary, member of the publications committee, and, from 1869 to 1875, as one of the vice presidents. He was a frequent contributor to the academy's library and museum. In 1838 he was elected fellow of the College of Physicians of Philadelphia. He served at times on its committees on the materia medica and on the pharmacopoeia, as a censor, as a delegate of the college to the National Medical Convention held at Philadelphia in 1847 that became the American Medical Association, and often as delegate to the American Medical Association. He became a member of the American Philosophical Society in 1844 and served as its curator from 1859 until the year of his death. He served as president of the Philadelphia County Medical Society in 1861.

Carson gained a considerable reputation in botany and especially in medical botany. This derived not only from his prestigious professorships but also from his publications. His two-volume, large-format *Illustrations of Medical Botany: Consisting of Coloured Figures of the Plants Affording the Important Articles of the Materia Medica*, containing 100 leaves of hand-colored lithographs, appeared in 1847. He edited, introduced U.S. Pharmacopoeia nomenclature and formulas, added histories of American indigenous medical botanicals, and otherwise augmented three American editions of Jonathan Pereira's (whom Carson called "the modern Dioscorides") *The Elements of the Materia Medica* in 1843, 1846, and 1852–1854. He also edited one of John Forbes Royle's *Materia Medica and Therapeutics* in 1847. The *Lecture Introductory* and *Synopsis* of his courses were published many times between 1839 and 1867. The Smithsonian Institution asked his advice on medical-botanical matters on several occasions, and his botanical correspondence included savants in France and Germany. He served as editor of the *American Journal of Pharmacy* from 1836 to 1850 and regularly contributed original papers to it. Several of his papers gained the distinction of inclusion in the *Catalogue of Scientific Papers* of the Royal Society of London.

Carson was appointed a delegate of the College of Physicians to national convention for revising the pharmacopoeia in 1840 and 1850. In 1860 he served on the revision committee of the convention, and in 1870 he was president of the convention and chairman of its revision committee.

In 1869 Carson published *A History of the Medical Department of the University of Pennsylvania from Its Foundation in 1765*, a work highly esteemed by his contemporaries. He also copied into a large notebook documents pertaining to the medical affairs of the American Revolution, apparently with the intention of writing a medical history of the Revolution. In addition, he assembled a large collection of portraits and holograph letters (a small proportion to himself) of notables, mainly physicians and scientists, reflecting an awareness and appreciation of what was going on in the world of science.

In 1841 Carson married Mary Goddard, who died the next year; their son died in infancy. In 1848 he married Mary Hollingsworth, with whom he had a son and two daughters who survived him. Carson died in Philadelphia.

• Both the College of Physicians of Philadelphia and the American Philosophical Society have Carson papers that include memoranda, lists of specimens, manuscript lecture notes, lecture notes kept by students, and incoming correspondence. A few Carson letters are in the collections of their recipients. The College of Physicians has the original of Carson's collection of portraits and autographs; the American Philosophical Society has a microfilm of it. The chief biographical sources are W. S. W. Ruschenberger, "Obituary Notice," *American Journal of the Medical Sciences*, n.s., 73 (1877): 568–70; James Darrach, "Memoir of Joseph Carson, M.D.," *Transactions of the College of Physicians of Philadel-*

phia, 3d ser., 4 (1879): xlv–lxvii, which includes a bibliography of Carson's publications; and J. W. Harshberger, *The Botanists of Philadelphia and Their Work* (1899), pp. 199–208.

DAVID L. COWEN

CARSON, Kit (24 Dec. 1809–23 May 1868), mountain man, army officer, and Indian agent, was born Christopher Houston Carson in Madison County, Kentucky, the son of Lindsey Carson, a farmer and revolutionary war veteran, and Rebecca Robinson. In 1811 Lindsey Carson moved his family to Howard County, Missouri, to find "elbow room." He died in 1818, hit by a falling limb while clearing timber from his land. Christopher enjoyed no schooling and never learned to read or write, other than signing his name to documents. In 1825 his mother and stepfather apprenticed him to David Workman, a Franklin, Missouri, saddler whom Kit described as a kind and good man. Nevertheless, he ran away because he found saddlemaking tedious and distasteful work and yearned to travel. Following in the footsteps of a brother and a half-brother who were in the Santa Fe trade, Carson joined a caravan as a "cavvy boy" (an assistant to the wrangler in charge of the horse and mule herd). Though not unsympathetic, Workman was obliged by law to advertise for his runaway. But he misleadingly suggested to readers of the *Missouri Intelligencer* (6 Oct. 1826) that Kit had headed north, then offered only a one-cent reward for his apprehension.

In New Mexico, Carson worked as a teamster and cook, then served a new and welcome apprenticeship with Ewing Young as a fur trapper on his 1829 expedition across the southwestern desert to California's Sacramento and San Joaquin rivers. In 1831 he entered the Rocky Mountain fur trade as a free trapper with Tom Fitzpatrick. He later worked with John Gantt and Jim Bridger. Carson was never the leader of a fur company but won respect for his great skill and courage, both as a hunter and Indian fighter. He was seriously wounded only once, in a fight in 1833 with the Blackfeet near the Snake River in what is now Idaho. In 1836 he married an Arapaho woman, known as Alice, or Waa-nibe (Singing Grass), with whom he had two children, only one of whom survived. When his wife died in 1842, Carson married a Cheyenne, but the marriage was brief and unhappy. So he took his daughter Adaline to live in St. Louis with his sister and receive the education that he had missed. All told, Carson trapped for about eight years, "commuting" between the northern Rockies and his adopted hometown, Taos, New Mexico, where he was baptized a Catholic and married Josefa Jaramillo in 1843. They had eight children, one of whom died young.

The turning point in carson's life came on a St. Louis steamboat in 1842. Explorer John C. Frémont hired him as a guide and hunter for his 1842 expedition to the Wind River Mountains in Wyoming. With Fitzpatrick, Carson was also Frémont's guide on his second expedition (1843–1844), to California and Oregon; he again scouted and guided for him on his controversial 1845–1846 California expedition, which ended in filibustering and a court-martial for the so-called Pathfinder. Meanwhile, Kit was becoming famous because Frémont lauded him in his government reports, which became the equivalent of bestsellers, so hungry was the public for information on the West. Unfortunately, they were also the stimulus for a raft of fictional tales, potboiler novels, and dime magazines, which created a rival, mythical Kit Carson to the real article.

While serving with Frémont in the 1846 Bear Flag Revolt, the "first act" of the Mexican War in California, Carson's reputation was indelibly blackened when, out of his unquestioning loyalty to Frémont, he obeyed his distracted commander's (implied) order to take no prisoners and had three noncombatant *Californios* shot at San Rafael. Sent to Washington with dispatches, he was intercepted in New Mexico by General Stephen W. Kearny, who ordered him to guide his Army of the West to California. Carson did so and, with two others, slipped through enemy lines for reinforcements when Kearny's dragoons were besieged and badly mauled by Don Andrés Pico's lancers at the battle of San Pascual in December 1846. After helping in the conquest of southern California, Carson twice carried dispatches to Washington. There, he found himself hailed as a hero, and President James K. Polk appointed him a lieutenant in the mounted rifles regiment. However, the Senate rejected the appointment, not because of the incongruity of a semi-illiterate becoming "an officer and gentleman," but because political rivals wished to embarrass Frémont and his father-in-law, Senator Thomas Hart Benton.

By 1849 Carson had settled down near Taos to farm, but he also scouted for army units fighting hostile Indians. He made one last trapping expedition in 1852 and, in 1853, drove 6,500 sheep from New Mexico to California. Appointed Indian agent for the Southern Ute, Jicarilla Apache, and Pueblo, he began his duties in 1853 or 1854 while continuing to scout for the army. In 1856 he dictated his memoirs, which were made into a much embellished book, *The Life and Adventures of Kit Carson, the Nestor of the Rocky Mountains* (1858), by Dr. De Witt C. Peters, who wildly exaggerated Carson's actual exploits.

At the outbreak of the Civil War in 1861, Carson resigned as Indian agent and in June was appointed a lieutenant colonel (promoted to colonel three months later), commanding the First New Mexico Volunteer Infantry Regiment. He fought at the battle of Valverde against Confederates invading New Mexico (1862), then, under the direction of General James H. Carleton, directed successful campaigns against the Mescalero Apache and Navajo (1862–1864), forcing them to migrate to Carleton's (ultimately unsuccessful) "colony" (reservation) on the Pecos River, Bosque Redondo. In November 1864 Carson fought his last fight, the battle of Adobe Walls in the Texas panhandle. Technically a defeat, it was actually a brilliant strategic withdrawal. After fighting thousands of Kiowas, Comanches, and Apaches to a draw with his small force, he withdrew with few casualties from what might have ended as another Little Big Horn had a reckless officer like George Armstrong Custer been in command.

For his valor at Valverde and elsewhere, Carson was promoted to brevet brigadier general of volunteers. He took command of Fort Garland, Colorado, in 1866 but had to resign from the army in 1867 because of ill health. The following year, he was appointed superintendent of Indian affairs for Colorado Territory but died that summer at Fort Lyon from a hemorrhage caused by an aneurysm of the aorta. He was buried in nearby Boggsville, but in 1869 his body was reinterred in Taos, where it remains, the site of pilgrimages by aficionados of the history of the West.

The freckle-faced Carson was short, weighing only 145 pounds in his prime, and was both bow-legged and pigeon-toed, the very opposite of his image in dime novels. Although he was not pious like Jed Smith, he was unlike most mountain men in that he was temperate in the use of alcohol and profanity, although he was addicted to tobacco. He was soft-voiced, reticent, and genuinely modest in contrast to such braggarts as Jim Bridger. Handicapped as he was by small stature and illiteracy, Carson was universally respected by Americans, Canadians, Mexicans, and Indians and loved by many of them because of his strong character. He was not a leader in the ordinary sense but an exemplar. His honesty, loyalty, courage, decency, and sense of duty—in short, his personal integrity—so elevated him in public esteem, even during his lifetime, that he became and has remained the equal of Daniel Boone as an American frontiersman, almost *sans reproche*. The one black mark on his record remains his execution of three civilians, on Frémont's orders, in California in 1846.

• Since Carson was illiterate, he left no holograph documents; there is no archive of Carson manuscripts. His dictated autobiography, ruined by Peters in 1858, was rescued by Blanche C. Grant, ed., *Kit Carson's Own Story of His Life* (1926). But it has been superseded by Harvey L. Carter, *Dear Old Kit* (1968), an expansion of the original memoir, and by Carter Guild and Thelma S. Guild's biography, *Kit Carson, a Pattern for Heroes* (1984). See also Edwin Legrand Sabin, *Kit Carson Days (1809–1868)* (1914), for its documentary sources.

RICHARD H. DILLON

CARSON, Rachel Louise (27 May 1907–14 Apr. 1964), writer and scientist, was born in Springdale, Pennsylvania, the daughter of Robert Warden Carson, a salesman, and Maria Frazier McLean, a teacher. Her father was never successfully employed. He sold real estate and insurance and worked for the local public utility company. Her mother, who had had the benefit of a fine education at the Washington Female Seminary, was an avid naturalist and passed on her deep respect for the natural world and her love of literature to her daughter. Mother and daughter, who never married, lived together almost continuously until Maria Carson died in 1958.

As a child, Carson read and wrote stories about farm animals and woodland creatures that she and her mother encountered on their frequent outdoor excursions. She won the first of several literary prizes at age ten for a story published in *St. Nicholas Magazine*. By the time she graduated from high school she was a skilled naturalist and a student with recognized literary talent.

In 1925 Carson entered Pennsylvania College for Women (now Chatham College) in Pittsburgh as a scholarship student. She was a reserved but self-confident English major whose social life was limited by her impecuniousness, but she excelled academically. A required course in biology given by Mary Scott Skinker, a brilliant young zoology professor, inspired Carson to change her major to biology in her junior year. Skinker had a profound impact on Carson, who modeled her life and career after her teacher. Carson graduated magna cum laude in 1929 and won a place that summer as "beginning investigator" at the Woods Hole Marine Biological Laboratory in Woods Hole, Massachusetts, where she saw the ocean for the first time and embarked upon a lifelong study of marine life. She won a small stipend for graduate work at Johns Hopkins University, where she began a master's degree program in zoology in the fall of 1929.

Carson was single-minded about preparing for a career in science at a time when very few women could find professional positions. She consulted with established scientists at Woods Hole and sought advice from Skinker, who sent her to biologist Elmer Higgins, her future supervisor, at the Bureau of Fisheries. Carson completed an M.A. in zoology in 1932 while teaching part-time at Johns Hopkins and at the University of Maryland. Although she intended to continue graduate work, her family's financial situation and the depression precluded it. When her father and older sister died suddenly in 1935 and 1937, respectively, Carson became the sole support of an extended family that included her mother and her sister's two young daughters.

Carson found a part-time job as an aide at the Commerce Department's Bureau of Fisheries field office in Baltimore, Maryland, in 1935. She wrote radio scripts for a series on marine life called "Romance under the Waters" and, to supplement her government income, natural history features for the *Baltimore Sunday Sun Magazine*. The following year she entered the federal service as a junior aquatic biologist after placing first on the women's register. At that time she was one of two female professionals at the bureau, which in 1939 was combined with the U.S. Biological Survey to create the U.S. Fish and Wildlife Service.

Carson worked her way up the bureaucratic ladder as a science writer and editor rather than a field biologist. Higgins encouraged her to submit an essay she had written for government publication to the *Atlantic Monthly*, which published it in 1937. The essay, "Undersea," received critical notice and the interest of Quincy Howe, an editor at Simon and Schuster who suggested that she expand it into a book. *Under the Sea-Wind* appeared just before the outbreak of World War II in 1941. It was hailed by scientists such as oceanographer William Beebe, but because of the war, it sold poorly.

In 1946 Carson was promoted from the Office of Fishery Coordination to the Division of Information where by 1949 she was the editor of all Fish and Wildlife Service publications. She developed a series of pamphlets on the nation's refuge system called "Conservation in Action." The four pamphlets Carson wrote herself are distinguished by their scientific accuracy and sensitivity to ecological relationships. Carson's editorial work demanded both wide-ranging knowledge and scientific breadth. It required that she be familiar with the scientific background of every subject that came across her desk. It also exposed her to a variety of field environments that she later used in her writing. Carson was temperamentally suited to the routine of the federal bureaucracy and enjoyed the collegial atmosphere. Her writing was encouraged in this supportive environment, and her emotional and intellectual connection with nature was given both an outlet and a framework.

Her increasing editorial responsibilities, however, dramatically slowed the pace of her own writing. It took her a decade to produce her next and most popular sea book, *The Sea Around Us*, published in 1951. One chapter, "The Birth of an Island," had appeared earlier in the *Yale Review* and won Carson the George Westinghouse Science Writing Award of the American Association for the Advancement of Science. *The Sea Around Us* was serialized in the *New Yorker*, where it captivated scientists and the public alike. It remained on the *New York Times* bestseller list for a record eighty-six weeks. Its success resulted in the reissue of *Under the Sea-Wind*, which also became a bestseller, the same year. There was almost no precedent for a book of such scientific scholarship that was at once a lyrical description of the wonders of nature and fine literature. Through Carson's synthesis of the extant knowledge of marine life, readers became sensitive to the fragile interdependence of life. Carson was awarded the John Burroughs Medal and the National Book Award and was chosen "woman of the year in literature" by the Associated Press. *The Sea Around Us* established Carson as the preeminent natural science writer of the day and won her international acclaim.

Royalties from *The Sea Around Us* enabled Carson to retire from government service in 1952 and to build a cottage on the Sheepscot River in Maine, where she retreated to work each summer. The last volume in the sea's biography, *The Edge of the Sea*, was completed in 1955 and like its predecessor was a bestseller. It contains her finest poetic evocation of life along the shore as well as the delicate ecological balance between sea and shore. Although it did not garner the record sales of *The Sea Around Us*, it was the book she most enjoyed writing because she was able to work on it in Maine, surrounded by close friends.

Carson was fascinated by the ocean and its mysteries as well as by the shoreline of life between the sea and the land. Her nature writing enthralled millions of readers, introducing them to the myriad of intricate interrelationships that were basic to the science of ecology. Embedded within her writing was the view that human beings were but one part of nature, distinguished primarily by their power to alter it, in some cases irreversibly. Believing that science and literature were equal in their ability to illuminate and inspire, Carson sought to educate the public about the natural world in terms that, while scientifically accurate, also embodied the poetic truths she found in nature.

Uncertain which of several projects to pursue next, Carson completed an important article in 1956 on preserving a child's sense of wonder in nature, which was posthumously published as *The Sense of Wonder* (1965). She produced a television script for the "Omnibus" series on clouds and a juvenile edition of *The Sea Around Us* and advocated the preservation of certain areas of seashore as wilderness in an essay for *Holiday* magazine. Before her death, she leant her support to legislation for the humane treatment of animals, particularly those used in scientific experiments. A series of unforeseen events determined that Carson's next project would not continue her mystical exploration of the natural world but warn of the potential for ecological disaster as a result of the careless misuse of chemical pesticides.

Synthetic hydrocarbon pesticides, products of wartime technology, revolutionized domestic agriculture in the 1950s because of their persistence and effectiveness. As a Fish and Wildlife editor, Carson had been on the periphery of scientific debates over the use of such chemicals as DDT, but her interest in pollutants and poisons began as early as 1938. Her immediate attention to pesticide abuse was directed by a friend in Duxbury, Massachusetts, who complained of the disastrous effects that DDT had had on birds during a state mosquito control program and who had asked Carson to help gather information about the pesticide and its effects. Carson's research was assisted by material collected as a result of a suit brought against the federal government's insect eradication program on Long Island, New York, by concerned amateur scientists Marjorie Spock, sister of Dr. Benjamin Spock, and Mary Richards and joined by ornithologist Robert Cushman Murphy. About the same time pesticides made political news when the Department of Agriculture was publicly criticized for its ill-conceived extermination campaign against the imported fire ant in the southeastern United States, which resulted in much harm to wildlife and the water supply. Carson took part in local conservation protests against the government program.

Reluctantly concluding that no magazine would publish an article on such a distasteful subject as pesticide pollution, she embarked on a book, originally proposed to her Houghton Mifflin editor Paul Brooks as "The Control of Nature" in 1958. As her research progressed, however, Carson came to believe that everything that meant the most to her was being threatened by the careless use of these new chemicals. Likening the effects of pesticides to those of atomic radiation, she became an unabashed crusader for change in the government's policy of pesticide approval and use. The result, *Silent Spring* (1962), was a powerful critique of the Cold War culture that condoned such crude and short-sighted tampering with the natural world. The book indicted the chemical industry, the government, and agribusiness for indiscriminately using pesticides without knowing more about their long-term effects. Once again serialized by the *New Yorker* in advance of publication, the book caused a sensation. In clear, often beautiful prose Carson demonstrated that chemical pesticides were potential biocides that threatened humankind and nature with extinction. She used the impact of pesticides to illustrate that man, like other species, was a vulnerable part of the earth's ecosystem.

Silent Spring and its author were immediately attacked by the scientific establishment and the powerful agrichemical industry. Mounting a quarter-million-dollar publicity campaign, the industry attacked her as an hysterical woman as well as a poor scientist and accused her of needlessly alarming the public. Nonetheless, *Silent Spring* caught the attention of President John F. Kennedy, who called for an investigation of the issues it raised. The 1963 report of a special panel of the President's Science Advisory Committee supported Carson's conclusions. Regulatory hearings by a U.S. Senate subcommittee chaired by Connecticut senator Abraham Ribicoff at which Carson testified followed. The public responded by calling for state and federal regulation of pesticide control programs and the elimination of the use of some compounds. Carson was acclaimed by the public and received numerous scientific and literary awards, including election to the American Academy of Arts and Letters.

Writing *Silent Spring* was an act of extraordinary moral and physical courage for Carson, who endured what she called a "catalogue of illnesses." Belatedly diagnosed breast cancer, crippling arthritis, and iritis plagued her throughout the four years of research and writing. She died in Silver Spring, Maryland, just eighteen months after its publication.

Carson's meticulous scientific research and her spiritual connection with nature inspired a group of younger activists to demand that the government act to protect human health and regulate activities that affect the environment. Her work also helped expand the definition of environmental protection, and it encouraged conservation organizations to embrace a broader ecological orientation that included wilderness, habitat, and species preservation. Generally credited as being the fountainhead of the environmental movement, Carson helped democratize science by challenging scientists, government officials, and industry executives to understand the impact of new technologies and by forcing the citizenry to become part of the growing debate over technological advances of all kinds. She demonstrated that government had failed to protect the public adequately and that new policies were necessary. Although some of the research Carson used has been refined, her fears about chemical pollution were stated conservatively. Some chemicals have been banned from the United States, yet more powerful ones have taken their place, and some that were banned have returned to these shores via an agricultural import "cycle of poison." Americans still struggle to heed her warnings, but her witness for the whole of nature has continued to inspire later generations. Carson was awarded the Presidential Medal of Freedom posthumously by President Jimmy Carter in 1980.

• Carson's letters, papers, and manuscripts are part of the Yale Collection of American Literature, Beinecke Rare Book and Manuscript Library, Yale University. Family and professional photographs, college correspondence, miscellaneous reviews, newspaper clippings, and a manuscript account of the *Silent Spring* controversy are part of the Rachel Carson History Project, Rachel Carson Council Inc., Chevy Chase, Md. Frank Graham, Jr., *Since Silent Spring* (1970), is the best published account of the pesticide controversy. H. Patricia Hynes provides a feminist interpretation of Carson and the controversy in *The Recurring Silent Spring* (1989), and the government and industry reaction is reevaluated in G. Marco et al., eds., *Silent Spring Revisited* (1987). The critical relationship between atomic pollution and pesticides is addressed by Ralph Lutts, "Chemical Fallout: Rachel Carson's *Silent Spring*, Radioactive Fallout and the Environmental Movement," *Environmental Review* 9 (Fall 1985): 211–25. Linda J. Lear gives an appraisal of the federal bureaucratic reaction to *Silent Spring* in "Bombshell in Beltsville: The USDA and the Challenge of *Silent Spring*," *Agricultural History* 66 (Spring 1992): 151–70. Lear's article "Rachel Carson's *Silent Spring*," *Environmental History Review* 17 (Summer 1993): 23–48, puts Carson and the pesticide controversy in the context of the times. The most complete biography is by Carson's friend and publisher, Paul Brooks, *The House of Life: Rachel Carson at Work* (1972). It includes a complete bibliography of Carson's publications, including magazines and foreign editions; his chapter on Carson in *Speaking for Nature* (1983) is a fine evaluation of her naturalist legacy. Mary McCay, *Rachel Carson* (1993), is a brief literary biography focusing on Carson's nature writing, and Vera Norwood, *Made from this Earth* (1993), devotes a chapter to Carson's interpretation of nature from the perspective of gender, and her assessment of Carson in *The American Radical*, ed. Mary Jo Buhle et al. (1994), discusses the revolutionary aspects of Carson's critique. Martha Freeman has edited the correspondence between Carson and her grandmother in *Always, Rachel: The Letters of Rachel Carson and Dorothy Freeman* (1995), which provides an intimate account of Carson's activities from 1953 to her death. Cheryll Glotfelty's splendid literary analysis of Carson's life and work in *Scribner's Encyclopedia of Nature Writing* (1995) is an important addition to Carol Gartner's earlier literary study, *Rachel Carson* (1983). Two television documentaries also are noteworthy. CBS Reports, "The Silent Spring of Rachel Carson" (1963), is an invaluable tool for understanding the participants, and the PBS "American Experience" documentary "Rachel Carson's Silent Spring" (1993), contains important interviews with Carson's colleagues and critics. An obituary is in the *New York Times*, 15 Apr. 1964.

LINDA J. LEAR

CARTER, Amon G. (11 Dec. 1879–23 June 1955), newspaper publisher, was born in Crafton, Texas, the son of William Henry Carter, a farmer and part-time blacksmith, and Josephine Ream. His parents named him Giles Amon Carter, but he despised his first name and banished it to its status as a middle initial. He shuttled between a grandmother's house and his father's home after his mother's death in 1892. He attended country schools until age eleven or twelve, then tried his hand at blacksmithing and working at a hotel in Nocona, Texas. As a teenager he started his first business—selling lunches to the railroad passengers who passed through the north Texas town of Bowie.

Carter was a smooth-talking entrepreneur who graduated from peddling chicken sandwiches to photographic portraits and picture frames door to door. His confidence and stubbornness were his biggest assets. "To me, 'No' is just a word in the dictionary," Carter said. "I don't often consult the dictionary." He married Zetta Thomas, the daughter of a prominent north Texas family, in 1902. They had one child and were divorced in 1917. In 1918 Carter married Nenetta Burton. They had two children and were divorced in 1941. He married Minnie Meacham Smith in 1947.

Carter moved to Fort Worth, Texas, in 1905, from San Francisco, where he had been having trouble selling advertisements. Arriving in the booming livestock town, he opened a one-man advertising office that doubled as his bedroom. While attending a demonstration of the fuel potential of combustible cow manure—which Fort Worth's stockyards had in abundance—he met two reporters who were covering the event. The experimental fuel was a failure, proving too pungent to be practical, but Carter and the reporters struck up a friendship and agreed to start a new afternoon paper in Fort Worth. They called it the *Star*. Carter borrowed $250 from a bank, pledging a small diamond ring as security, to get the paper started. He sold all of the advertisements for the first edition, which appeared on 1 February 1906.

The *Star* merged with the successful *Telegram* in 1909. Carter was the business and advertising manager. He acquired controlling interest of the *Star-Telegram* in 1923 and became president and publisher. He believed that promoting his city would benefit his newspaper. Vice President Jack Garner once said, "That man wants the whole government of the United States to run for the exclusive benefit of Fort Worth and, if possible, to the detriment of Dallas."

Carter's boosterism took many forms. When a group of oil executives met in Forth Worth, Carter published a photograph of them eight columns wide. During World War II *Star-Telegram* war correspondents were instructed to find and write about Texans. On the first day of the Korean War the paper devoted the top half of the front page to an upbeat report on the growth of Fort Worth.

The slogan atop the front page of the *Star-Telegram* was "Where the West Begins." Carter promoted that phrase nationwide with the help of his friend, humorist Will Rogers. According to Jerry Flemmons, Carter's biographer, the publisher "created the modern fictional Texan portrayed in movies and books and on stage." When trying to make an impression, Carter dressed like a dime-store cowboy complete with silver spurs, bandanna, leather chaps, and pearl-handled pistols. He wore a huge cowboy hat and gave away copies of it to visiting dignitaries. At the 1928 Democratic convention in Houston, his showmanship went too far when he fired a pistol through the doors of an elevator that did not stop at his floor in a crowded hotel. No one was hurt, but "the elevator incident" became part of Amon Carter lore.

Carter's persistence brought to Fort Worth the corporate headquarters of South West Air Craft Corporation, which later became American Airlines and of which he became a director and one of its largest stockholders. He secured an aircraft factory for the city's west side that in later years became General Dynamics. His newspaper was instrumental in establishing Texas Tech University in Lubbock and in making Big Bend a national park.

Carter took the most pleasure out of getting the best of Dallas, the larger and more prosperous twin city of Fort Worth. His coup occurred in 1936. A Texas Centennial Commission chose Dallas as host city for the state's hundredth birthday party. Outraged, Carter set up a rival celebration in Fort Worth. He hired Broadway producer Billy Rose, for $1,000 a day, to produce a fun show that would dwarf the one in Dallas. Rose hired American Indians, cowgirls, dancers, and Sally Rand's Nude Ranch. With Carter's blessing, 11,000 billboards trumpeting Fort Worth's Frontier Centennial blanketed nine states. They pictured nearly nude cowgirls and said, "Go elsewhere for education, Come to Fort Worth for fun." Nearly 2 million visitors did, between July and November 1936, when the Frontier Centennial closed. Rose told Carter, "As a producer, you will pardon me if I envy you. I build shows. Christ! You built a city."

Carter built the *Star-Telegram* into the largest-circulation paper in Texas and made it required reading at Franklin Roosevelt's White House. Between 1923 and 1952 the circulation rose from 5,000 to 250,000. At its peak, the paper served 375,000 square miles, from the Colorado border to the Rio Grande and from north central Texas to El Paso. Carter never bought another paper, although he tried to purchase the *Washington Post* in 1933. After his death in Fort Worth, his son, Amon, Jr., became publisher of the *Star-Telegram*. The paper was purchased by Capital Communications Incorporated in the 1970s for $70 million—a record price for a newspaper at that time.

Carter made a fortune on an oil strike but gave much of the money to the community through philanthropy and the Amon G. Carter Foundation. Fort Worth is home to the Amon G. Carter Museum, which houses his magnificent collection of western art including paintings by Frederic Remington and Charles Russell.

Carter was "at any and all times ebullient, gracious, intractable, . . . phenomenal, mesmerizing, dictatorial and genius," Flemmons writes. His chamber-of-commerce brand of journalism would have been ridiculed in New York or Washington, but Carter's paper had a different mission and served a different public. His obituary in the *New York Times* described him as "the best town booster in the country."

• Most of Amon Carter's papers are at Texas Christian University, Fort Worth. They are not available to the public, but they are available for scholarly research. Papers dealing with his role in the creation of Big Bend National Park are at Sul Ross State University in Alpine, Tex., and his Texas Tech papers are at that university, in Lubbock. See also Jerry Flemmons, *Amon: The Life of Amon Carter Sr. of Texas* (1978), a book-length biography. The book is rare and out of print. Short profiles appear in the *Saturday Evening Post*, 26 Nov. 1938, and in *Time*, 25 Feb. 1952. Obituaries are in *Time* and *Newsweek*, both 4 July 1955, and the *New York Times*, 24 June 1955.

MIKE SWEENEY

CARTER, A. P. (15 Dec. 1891–7 Nov. 1960), and **Sara Carter** (21 July 1898–8 Jan. 1979), musicians and songwriters, were the founding members of the early country music singing group the Carter Family. A. P. Carter was born Alvin Pleasant Delaney Carter near the Appalachian hamlet of Maces Spring, Scott County, Virginia, the son of Robert C. Carter and Mollie Arvelle Bays, both local farmers whose families had been in the region since the late eighteenth century. As a youth, A. P. was exposed to music by both sides of his family. His father had been a well-known local banjo player who later turned to sacred music; his mother's family included an uncle, Flanders Bays, who taught rural singing schools for area churches; and his mother was a repository of old ballads, both those brought over from Great Britain and newer ones derived from Native American Sources. By 1913 A. P. was singing bass in a local church choir and had learned to play both the guitar and fiddle—the latter in a light-bowed, skirling style associated with older Scotch styles. A restless and curious young man, A. P. traveled to Indiana in around 1910–1911, worked on a railroad crew near Richmond, Virginia, for a time, and eventually returned home, suffering from typhoid fever. His schooling consisted of sporadic attendance at local country schools in the Poor Valley. By 1915 he was trying to make a living selling fruit trees to area residents.

Sara Carter was born Sara Dougherty in Flat Woods, near the modern town of Coeburn, in Wise County, Virginia, the daughter of Sevier Dougherty, a sawmill operator, and Elizabeth Kilgore. When her mother died prematurely, young Sara was reared by her aunt and uncle, Milburn and Melinda Nickles, in the Copper Creek area of nearby Scott County. There she became interested in music and learned to play the autoharp—a stringed instrument then new to the folk music of the mountains—from her neighbor Eb Easterland. Family history tells that one day, probably in 1914, while Sara was at a relative's house playing her autoharp and singing the train-wreck ballad "Engine 143," A. P. appeared with his fruit trees for sale. The pair hit it off and, after an exchange of letters and visits, were married in 1915 at Milburn and Melinda Nickles's house in Copper Creek.

For the next several years the young husband and wife entertained informally in the area; they would sing many of the old songs and ballads, but, unlike many of the older singers who sang unaccompanied, Sara and A. P. sang in harmony and backed their singing with guitars or autoharp. Much of this early work was at churches and most of it yielded little money; neither of them yet thought about trying to make a living from their music. By 1925 they were being joined by a third musician, Sara's first cousin Maybelle Addington. She was a skilled guitar player and singer as well, and after she married A. P.'s brother Ezra, she joined the group and the Carter Family was born.

By this time phonograph records were making their way into the mountains, and the Carters began to hear on records some of the old tunes that they had been singing. The commercial record companies, looking for authentic mountain music to put on their new discs, were sending talent scouts into the Appalachians, and in early 1927 A. P. and Sara auditioned for the Brunswick company in nearby Norton. The company wanted to develop A. P. as a fiddle player, but he felt his talents were as a singer and song arranger and spurned the offer. A. P. was by now interested in making records, though, and began to correspond with Ralph Peer, the artists and repertory (A&R) man from the Victor Talking Machine Company. When Peer decided to come to nearby Bristol, on the Tennessee-Virginia line, to set up a field studio and record local talent in July 1927, he invited the Carter Family to come in for an audition. This they did, and one of music history's most important events ensued: a session that yielded the first recordings by the Carters as well as by Jimmie Rodgers, the two acts that would in effect define modern country music.

Most of the Carter Family vocal arrangements were built around Sara's lead singing, and it was her voice that impressed Peer. On many of the early recordings, vocal duties were shared by her and A. P.; on later arrangements, Sara and Maybelle carried the burden of the singing, with A. P. occasionally (to use his own words) "bassin' in." Their very first professional recording was an old folk lyric, "Bury Me under the Weeping Willow" (Victor 21074), and it was typical of their repertoire: an old song known in the mountains for years but rearranged by A. P. Within a few years they would record numerous songs for Victor that would become country music, folk, and bluegrass standards: "The Storms Are on the Ocean" (Victor 20937, 1927); "Keep on the Sunny Side," their theme song (Victor 21434, 1928); "Wildwood Flower" (Victor 40000, 1928); "John Hardy Was a Desparate Little Man" (Victor 40190, 1928); "I'm Thinking Tonight of My Blue Eyes" (Victor 40089, 1929); "Wabash Cannonball" (Victor 23731, 1929); and "Worried Man Blues" (Victor 40317, 1930).

From 1927 until 1941 the Carter Family recorded more than 300 songs for RCA Victor (and its Bluebird subsidiary), Decca, and the American Recording

Company. Their songs and their sparse but elegant arrangements made them the most famous singing group in country music history. While A. P., and occasionally Sara, would create original songs, most were older tunes that had been arranged or even rewritten by A. P. At one time it was assumed that most of the songs were old folk songs, but recent research has revealed that many were old popular songs from the late nineteenth century, written and at one time published in songsters and sheet music. Many of the gospel songs came from the paperbacked shape-note songbooks published by companies like James D. Vaughan of Tennessee.

During the height of their popularity, the Carters were often separated and beset with personal problems. As early as 1931 Maybelle and her husband were living as far away as Washington, D.C., where her husband's work took him; the group sometimes came together only for recording sessions. Then, in early 1933, Sara and A. P. separated, with Sara returning to Copper Creek and working with A. P. only on professional occasions. They would later divorce, and in 1939 Sara married one of A. P.'s cousins. Both Sara and Maybelle were busy raising their families during this time as well.

The Carter Family career also encompassed radio shows throughout the 1930s, many of them on the various "border radio" stations in Texas, such as XERA in Del Rio. Such stations skirted federal broadcasting regulations by having their transmitters across the Rio Grande in Mexico, allowing them to broadcast at hundreds of thousands of watts. These stations carried the Carter Family music to every hamlet and home in the southern United States. During these years—the late 1930s—the Carters involved their children in the group. Sara's daughter Janette performed, as did Maybelle's children Helen, June, and Anita.

The Carters broke up permanently in 1943. A. P. returned to Maces Spring to open a country store; Sara moved to California with her new husband. Maybelle started her own career featuring herself and her daughters. Though A. P. and Sara were effectively retired from music, they did reunite in 1952 for a series of recordings on the independent Acme label, but these recordings were not commercially successful. Through the offices of Johnny Cash, who had married Maybelle's daughter June, Sara and Maybelle did a reunion album in 1967.

• The Carter Family's songs were collected in Alvin Pleasant Carter's *The Carter Family Album of Smokey Mountain Ballads* (1934–1937) and *The Carter Family Album of Smokey Mountain Ballads, No. 3* (1944). For additional information on A. P. and Sara's career, see John Atkins, "The Carter Family," in *Stars of Country Music*, ed. Judith McCulloch and Bill C. Malone (1975); Atkins, ed., *The Carter Family* (1973); and Charles K. Wolfe's liner notes for *The Carter Family: The Complete Victor Recordings* (Rounder Records; 9 vols., 1995–1996).

CHARLES K. WOLFE

CARTER, Bo (21 Mar. 1893–21 Sept. 1964), blues singer, was born Armenter Chatmon in rural Hinds County, Mississippi, about fifteen miles west of Jackson, the son of Henderson Chatmon and Eliza Jackson, farmers. His father was a musician whose reputation as a fiddler dated back to country dances in the days of slavery. His mother played guitar. All nine brothers and one sister in the family played various instruments. Armenter, nicknamed "Bo," played violin, guitar, bass, banjo, and clarinet, learning mainly from an older brother, Lonnie. Another brother, Sam, whose later recollections constituted the main body of information about the family, said Lonnie was born early in the 1890s and was the first to learn music, so he taught each of the younger siblings.

It was Bo who first organized the musical siblings as a business enterprise around 1917. Working in various groupings as they came of age, brothers Bo, Lonnie, Willie, Edgar, Lamar, Sam (whose given name was Vivian), Larry, Harry, and Charlie (a stepbrother) played parties, picnics, and resorts, relying heavily on white audiences and the square-dance repertoire they had learned from their father. As their popularity grew, the brothers added blues, fox trots, and pop hits, learned mostly from Lonnie, the only sibling who could read music. To handle multiple bookings, the brothers began to divide up into two or more groups. They also began to include a musical cousin and neighbor, Walter Vincson, a guitar prodigy who worked around Jackson in the early 1920s with such accomplished blues artists as Tommy Johnson, Ishmon Bracey, and Charlie McCoy.

According to Vincson, disagreements over how earnings should be divided caused the brothers to disband at some point in the mid-1920s. Bo moved north to the Delta region of the state and got a job on a plantation near Hollandale. Lonnie, Sam, and Vincson followed, and by 1928 the four were playing in the Hollandale area.

In December 1928 Bo went to New Orleans and launched the family's recording career, cutting three issued sides as the vocalist and leader in a string-band format—violin, guitar, and mandolin—for the Brunswick label. It is most likely that Bo was the violinist, accompanied by Vincson on guitar and Charlie McCoy on mandolin. Vincson, by this time, was considered an adopted Chatmon, and McCoy would continue to work with the family, off and on, until the mid-1930s.

Within a year or so after the initial Brunswick session, a talent scout for OKeh Records heard a Chatmon group playing at a white square dance in Itta Bena, Mississippi, and arranged a recording session in Shreveport, Louisiana. The session, held on 17 February 1930, was supervised by record distributor Polk Brockman, who suggested that the musical family adopt a catchy name. They settled on the Mississippi Sheiks, "sheik" being then-current slang for a ladies' man. That session, featuring Lonnie on violin with Walter Vincson on guitar, and possibly Bo on second violin, was a huge success. It yielded eight issued sides, among them the hits "Stop and Listen" and "Sitting on Top of the World," the latter of which would become an American standard, reprised by bluegrass, swing, rock, pop, and blues groups.

Lonnie and Walter Vincson continued to form the core of the Sheiks over the next five years, although Sam and Harry Chatmon and Charlie McCoy often joined them at recording sessions. Bo, who by then had changed his musical persona to Bo Carter, also participated in many of the sessions and toured extensively with the Sheiks. Still, Bo maintained an identity separate from the group, recording as a featured artist or as the Mississippi Sheiks with Bo Carter. As a solo artist, Bo produced more than one hundred recorded titles between 1928 and 1940, displaying an intricate and richly textured picking style on guitar and a seemingly inexhaustible talent for risqué lyrics—"Banana in Your Fruit Basket" was a typical title.

Bo also played on a number of recordings that were issued under fanciful pseudonyms. In late 1930, for example, when he and the Sheiks recorded for OKeh in Jackson, the session included McCoy on a half-dozen instrumentals attributed to the "Mississippi Mud Steppers." McCoy also backed Bo and Sam at a January 1931 session for Brunswick in Chicago, with sides attributed to the "Mississippi Blacksnakes" and the "Tennessee Shakers."

In 1931 alone Bo produced twenty-four issued sides for OKeh and played with the Sheiks on twelve additional sides. As the Great Depression deepened, however, recording dates dropped off. The Chatmons traveled to Grafton, Wisconsin, in 1932 to record for Paramount, a once-thriving blues label that had fallen on hard times. The session produced a dozen issued sides but failed to save Paramount, which folded that same year. In 1933 the brothers went to New York City for what turned out to be their final session for OKeh. The next year, in San Antonio, Texas, Bo and the Sheiks recorded for Bluebird, a low-budget label started by RCA Victor. It was around this time that Bo acquired a steel-bodied National guitar, an instrument well suited to his increasing output of blues-oriented material.

Although the Chatmons recorded for the last time as the Mississippi Sheiks in January 1935, they were far from finished as recording artists. Bo recorded a dozen sides for Bluebird in February 1936 and a dozen more in October. The October session, at the St. Charles Hotel in New Orleans, also resulted in ten sides by Lonnie and Sam, recording as the Chatmon Brothers. Walter Vincson was at the October session, too, recording as a featured artist with piano accompaniment. When not recording, Bo and the Sheiks were on the move throughout the 1930s, touring Mississippi, Louisiana, and Texas and as far north as Illinois and New York. Even after the Sheiks no longer issued records, they continued to perform with traveling minstrel and medicine shows.

Bo recorded for Bluebird until 1940, but his eyesight was failing and his popularity was in decline. In 1936 he settled in Glen Allan, Mississippi, about twenty-five miles south of Greenville. In the early 1940s he moved to Walls, Mississippi, just south of Memphis, and later moved into Memphis, where he faded into obscurity and poverty. When British blues researcher Paul Oliver located him in 1960, he was blind and barely able to play guitar. He died four years later of a cerebral hemorrhage at a Memphis hospital and was buried in Sharkey County, Mississippi, in the Nitta Yuma Cemetery, between Anguilla and Hollandale.

As for Lonnie Chatmon, he moved to Anguilla in 1937. He operated a juke joint there and later opened a second place near his family's original homestead in Hinds County. In failing health with heart trouble, he died around 1951.

Walter Vincson, the adopted Chatmon, moved to Chicago in 1941. He recorded for Bluebird in August of that year, then dropped out of the music business for nearly two decades. He resurfaced during the 1960s-era blues revival, recording an album for Riverside in 1961 and playing on a Sheiks reunion album issued by Rounder in 1972. He died in a nursing home in 1975 and was buried in Holy Sepulchre Cemetery in Worth, Illinois.

Part-time Sheik Charlie McCoy also landed in Chicago. He worked as an accompanist to such major blues artists as Memphis Minnie and John Lee "Sonny Boy" Williamson, formed a jazz, blues group known as the Harlem Hamfats, and remained active in music through the 1940s. He later entered a psychiatric hospital, where he died of a paralytic brain disease in 1950. He was buried in Restvale Cemetery, also in Worth.

The last of the original Sheiks, Sam Chatmon, remained in Mississippi for a number of years, working as a plantation supervisor in Arcola before moving back to Hollandale. He, too, resurfaced during the blues revival, playing in California, touring on the festival circuit, and recording for Arhoolie, Blue Goose, Rounder, and Advent. He appeared on network television in 1976 as a spokesman for Mississippi, was featured in the documentary film *Good Morning Blues*, and became the principal interpreter of his family's history for music researchers. He died in Hollandale in 1983. He was survived by a son, Singing Sam Chatmon Junior, who recorded in Chicago in the 1960s.

Bo Carter and the Mississippi Sheiks were among the most prolific recording artists of their day and were enormously popular with African Americans. The Sheiks put out almost one hundred sides—not counting the many sides issued under pseudonyms. Bo's record output put him in a league with Memphis Minnie and other top blues artists of his era. Bo was also a superb guitarist, adorning his vocals with sophisticated runs and chords. Along with Charlie McCoy, he ranks among the best instrumentalists ever to come from the Jackson–Hinds County area of Mississippi. Walter Vincson, who on his own records was often identified as Walter Vinson or Walter Jacobs, was a fine guitarist, too, but he always relinquished the lead to Lonnie Chatmon's fiddle when recording as a Sheik.

Early critics and record collectors, impressed by the more hard-edged blues of musicians such as Tommy Johnson and Charley Patton, tended to downgrade Carter and the Sheiks because of their blending of black and white styles, their heavy doses of double entendre, and their repertoire of good-time dance blues. Even their huge record output was held against them, as if commercial appeal precluded historical importance. Later researchers, more attuned to the African-American string-band tradition and the deep cultural roots of so-called "party blues," accorded the Chatmons and their colleagues a more prominent niche in musical history.

The Chatmon family's music spanned more than 120 years. It originated in a string-band tradition that was served up for white consumption; it then evolved into a good-natured blues style that catered almost exclusively to the African-American "race market" during the depression; and later, with Singing Sam Chatmon Junior, it melded into the big-city electric blues sound that presaged rock 'n' roll.

• For more biographical information, see Sheldon Harris, *Blues Who's Who: A Biographical Dictionary of Blues Singers* (1979; fifth printing, 1989); Margaret McKee and Fred Chisenhall, *Beale Black and Blue: Life and Music on Black America's Main Street* (1981); Galen Gart, "Sam Chatmon," *Blues Unlimited*, July 1971, pp. 9–10; and Robert Javors, "Sam Chatmon: The Mississippi Sheik Is Alive and Well," *Sing Out* 26 (May–June 1977): 10–11. For discographical information, see Robert M. W. Dixon and John Godrich, *Blues and Gospel Records: 1902–1943* (1982); Mike Leadbitter and Neil Slaven, *Blues Records 1943–1970: A Selective Discography*, vol. 1 (1987); and Mike Leadbitter et al., *Blues Records 1943–1970: "The Bible of the Blues,"* vol. 2 (1994). For an interview with Bo Carter, see Paul Oliver, *Conversations with the Blues* (1964). For samples of the music, try *Bo Carter—Greatest Hits 1930–1940*, Yazoo 1014, and *Mississippi Sheiks: Stop and Listen*, Yazoo 2006. An obituary on Sam Chatmon, by Lou Curtiss, is in *Living Blues*, Autumn 1983, p. 24.

BARRY LEE PEARSON
BILL MCCULLOCH

CARTER, Caroline Louise Dudley (10 June 1862–13 Nov. 1937), actress, professionally known as "Mrs. Leslie Carter," was born in Lexington, Kentucky, the daughter of Orson (or Orison) Dudley, a wealthy businessman, and Catherine Roth. When she was seven she moved with her parents to Dayton, Ohio, where her mother's well-to-do family were leading citizens. Her father died in 1870. She attended the Episcopal Convent of St. Mary in New York City for four years and the Cooper Female Seminary in Dayton for another four. A vivacious "belle," she made her debut in Dayton society during the winter of 1876–1877.

While vacationing in Wisconsin in summer 1879, seventeen-year-old Caroline Dudley met Leslie Carter, a wealthy Chicago socialite in his early thirties and heir to an industrial fortune. They were married the following year. A son was born in 1881. The couple proved extremely incompatible, and the marriage ended in 1889 in a highly publicized divorce trial so salacious that the judge barred women and children from the courtroom. The divorce cost Caroline Dudley, now known as Mrs. Leslie Carter, a fortune in legal fees. She also lost custody of her son and her position in Chicago society. To earn a living, she decided to go on the stage and gained an interview with David Belasco, an up-and-coming playwright and stage manager. Although impressed by the society woman's natural emotive ability, mellifluous voice, and luxurious red hair, Belasco only agreed to become her acting coach and manager after a wealthy Chicago benefactor came forward to underwrite her training. To spite her former husband and to capitalize on the notoriety gained in her divorce trial, she continued to use her married name as her stage name.

Mrs. Leslie Carter's acting debut was in *The Ugly Duckling*, which opened at the Broadway Theatre in November 1890. The short-lived play, concocted by David Belasco and others, was poorly received, but critics were surprised by Mrs. Carter's competent, if not brilliant, performance. A year later she opened at the Star Theatre in *Miss Helyett*, a musical farce adapted by Belasco from the French. Though her husky voice could not carry a tune (she never appeared in another musical), the show was a minor success. Belasco withdrew Carter from the stage at the close of the national tour of *Miss Helyett* in early 1893. For two and a half years Belasco tutored her in dozens of roles, including those in Shakespeare and other classics. A company of actors was hired to rehearse with the indefatigable actress, whose willingness to work long hours reinforced Belasco's belief that she could be a major star if she were presented in the proper vehicle.

To showcase Carter's talent, Belasco wrote *The Heart of Maryland*, a Civil War drama about a southern woman who falls in love with a Union officer. Belasco felt so strongly about her potential that he turned down an offer from the powerful theatrical manager Charles Frohman, who had produced many of Belasco's previous works, to produce the play with a different actress in the lead. This rift with Frohman laid the groundwork for Belasco's career as an independent manager. Belasco eventually obtained the financial backing of a theatrically inexperienced businessman, and *The Heart of Maryland*, which costarred matinee idol Maurice Barrymore, opened at the Herald Square Theatre in October 1895. Critical reaction was mixed, but audiences responded to the play's heavy theatricality. Its climax featured Carter, as Maryland Calvert, saving the life of her beloved by grabbing hold of the clapper of the bell that was set to toll his death knell (that she was actually suspended thirty-eight feet above the stage heightened the dramatic effect). As Belasco predicted, *The Heart of Maryland* made Carter a star. She toured with the play for two seasons. Equal success followed with *Zaza* (1899–1901), *DuBarry* (1901–1903), and *Adrea* (1905–1906), all fanciful melodramas devised by Belasco to suit his protégé's innate sensuality and effusive acting.

Though her peak years of fame extended into the early twentieth century, Carter was the last of the great emotional actresses of the nineteenth century. While her more "modern" contemporaries, such as the acerbic, cerebral Minnie Maddern Fiske and the diffident, ethereal Maude Adams, were forging new styles of acting, Carter carried on the fading tradition of Clara Morris and Fanny Davenport, to whom she was sometimes compared. Carter "had the ability to lose herself in the emotions of her role and to involve an audience in the hysteria of her own feelings" (Wilson, p. 137). Although her thick red hair became a trademark, Carter depended more on earthy sex appeal than classic beauty.

The Carter-Belasco partnership came to an abrupt end in summer 1906, when Carter, while on vacation in New Hampshire, impulsively married William Louis Payne, an unknown actor about a dozen years her junior. Belasco, now one of the theater's most powerful managers, never spoke to the actress again. A devastated Carter hounded Belasco, whom she affectionately called "Mr. Dave," with a steady stream of letters begging forgiveness and reconciliation but to no avail. The letters continued for a quarter century, only stopping at Belasco's death in 1931. Without the support and guidance of her mentor, Carter's career faltered. Now in her middle forties and having been more than a decade at the top, her career might have slowed down anyway. She declared bankruptcy in 1907, and in April 1908 many of her personal possessions, including a polar bear fur coat, were auctioned off. Associations with other managers, including Charles Dillingham and John Cort, did not work out. She made screen versions of *DuBarry* (1914) and *The Heart of Maryland* (1915) and toured the vaudeville circuit in one-act abridgments of her past stage triumphs to which Belasco had given her the rights. In early 1916 Carter announced her retirement. She spent the next five years living in France and England with her husband and their adopted daughter.

A chance meeting with producer Arch Selwyn at a Paris café led to Carter's return to Broadway in W. Somerset Maugham's sophisticated comedy *The Circle* in September 1921. Though not experienced at lighter fare, Carter acquitted herself well in the supporting role of Lady Katherine, a worldly-wise older woman. She toured with *The Circle*, in which she played opposite John Drew, the aging master of high comedy, until May 1923. After spending a year in one-act plays, Carter was given the lead in John Colton's drama *The Shanghai Gesture*. Disagreements with director Guthrie McClintic caused her to be replaced by Florence Reed during out-of-town tryouts. She owned a share of the rights to the play and gained financially by its long run on Broadway. Carter's final New York appearance came as Mrs. Hardcastle in a brief revival of *She Stoops to Conquer* in May 1928. She then starred in a national tour of *The Shanghai Gesture* through November 1929.

Carter spent the last years of her life in California. In 1935 the resourceful and resilient former leading lady, now in her early seventies, played a supporting character role in the Paramount Pictures western *Rocky Mountain Mystery* with Randolph Scott and Ann Sheridan. In the same year she made her final stage appearance, taking the role of Good Deeds in a benefit production of *Everyman* at the Hollywood Bowl. Two years later Mrs. Leslie Carter died of pneumonia.

• The most complete source of information on Carter is Charles H. Harper, "Mrs. Leslie Carter: Her Life and Acting Career" (Ph.D. diss., Univ. of Nebraska, 1978). Craig Timberlake, *The Bishop of Broadway: The Life and Work of David Belasco* (1954), includes chapters on Carter and an appendix of many of her numerous letters to Belasco. *Notable Women in the American Theatre* (1989) offers an informative biographical essay on Carter. Also of value are Garff B. Wilson, *A History of American Acting* (1966), and Lewis C. Strang, *Famous Actresses of the Day in America*, 1st ser. (1899) and 2d ser. (1902). A series of lively but somewhat unreliable autobiographical articles by Carter entitled "Portrait of a Lady with Red Hair" appeared in *Liberty*, 15 Jan. 1927 through 19 Mar. 1927. A motion picture based on these articles, *The Lady with Red Hair* (1940), starred Miriam Hopkins as Mrs. Carter and Claude Rains as David Belasco. An obituary is in the *New York Times*, 14 Nov. 1937.

MARY C. KALFATOVIC

CARTER, Dad (25 Sept. 1889–28 Apr. 1963), southern gospel singer, was born David Parker Carter in a small mill town near Columbia, Kentucky, and moved westward to Texas as a small child. His mother died when he was sixteen, but other details of his early life are lacking. He came of age in Clay County, Texas, and met his wife, Carrie Brooks, at a singing school there. They married in 1909.

The young couple took up farming in Tioga, Texas, and then moved to Noel, Missouri, where Carter took a job as a brakeman on the Rock Island Line railway. After he was seriously injured in a railroad accident in 1927, he and his growing family returned to the land and took up cotton farming. Nine children were eventually born to the couple: Ernest (1910), Clellon (1913), Rosa Lola (1915), Effie (1917), Eddie (1919), Anna (1922), Ruth Ellen (1924), Roy (1926), and Bettye (1930). Of these, Ernest (or Jim, as he was called), Rosa Lola (Rose), Effie (called Anna), Ruth Ellen, and Roy would all play important roles later in the family singing group.

As the children grew up, different combinations of them began to sing informally for churches in the area, and when they returned to cotton farming, they would often gather in the front room of the farmhouse and sing to the accompaniment of guitar, mandolin, and even banjo. Older children taught the younger ones, and Carter usually led the ensemble with his tenor voice. In 1935, when one of the children fell ill and the family had no money for medicine, Carter approached the manager of radio station KFYO in Lubbock, Texas, and talked him into letting the Carters play for $12.50 a week. Rose and Anna sang soprano and alto, Carter sang tenor, and Jim sang bass. Their early repertoire included sentimental secular songs like "Mother of the Valley" as well as gospel songs. Originally, they were called simply the Carter Quartet, but in 1936 they moved to the larger station WBAP at Ft. Worth. There they were sponsored by a local company called Flour Mills, which sold Bewley's Best Flour, and changed their name to the Chuck Wagon Gang.

As a "mixed quartet" (both male and female vocalists), the Chuck Wagon Gang soon set themselves apart from many of the other gospel quartets on southern radio at that time. Their use of guitar and mandolin, instead of piano, made them especially appealing to country-music fans; their frequent use of new songs from Dallas's Stamps-Baxter publishing company gave them a renewable repertoire of singable, buoyant songs. On 25 November 1936 they made their first recordings for the American Recording Company, which released them on several labels, including Columbia, Vocalion, and Okeh. Later sessions soon followed, and by the outbreak of World War II, the Chucks, as they were now being called by their fans, had forged a distinctive style and won a large share of the gospel and country audience.

The group disbanded temporarily during the war and did not record commercially again until 1948. Though Rose and Anna had both by now married, the basic personnel remained the same. Among the several classics recorded at the 1948 Columbia session were "If We Ever Meet Again," "I'll Fly Away," and "Looking for a City." Throughout the 1950s, the group recorded for Columbia on a regular basis, though they seldom toured to support their records. They were content to remain radio entertainers and record artists, getting onto the concert stage only when they began working for Wally Fowler's All-Night Sings around 1950. Carter himself formally retired from the group in 1955, with son Eddie replacing him for a time. During this time, the Chucks were often featured on the popular radio show conducted by the Reverend J. Bazzell Mull, out of Knoxville, Tennessee; Mull also sold truckloads of Chuck Wagon Gang 45s and LPs through his show.

For a time, family members and in-laws provided personnel for later editions of the Chuck Wagon; by the time the original group finished their recording career, they had amassed some 408 recordings. In the 1980s and 1990s the family authorized the re-formation of a new Chuck Wagon Gang, which recorded several award-winning albums. Carter, in the meantime, passed away at a singing program in Oklahoma City. Many historians credit the Chuck Wagon Gang as the first singing group in the late 1930s to fully professionalize their music and to perform without the sponsorship of churches or song-book publishers.

• The only substantial source is Bob Terrell's book, *The Chuck Wagon Gang: A Legend Lives On* (1990). The author also relied on unpublished personal interviews with Bill Timmons, Roy Carter, Bill C. Malone, the Reverend J. Bazzell Mull, Don Cusic, and Bob Pinson. Discographical details are in copies of the notebooks of Columbia producer Arthur E. Satherley, in the author's files.

CHARLES K. WOLFE

CARTER, Eunice Hunton (16 July 1899–25 Jan. 1970), attorney, was born in Atlanta, Georgia, the daughter of Canadian-born William Alphaeus Hunton, an executive with the Young Men's Christian Association (YMCA), and Addie Waites, a field-worker with the Young Women's Christian Association (YWCA) in Europe. Carter's parents, who were African American, had three other children, but only Carter and her younger brother lived to adulthood. After the race riots of 1906, Carter's family left Atlanta for Brooklyn, New York. In Brooklyn Carter attended public schools. When her mother went to Strasbourg, Germany, to study at Kaiser Wilhelm University from 1909 to 1910, Carter accompanied her.

Carter attended Smith College in 1917, graduating cum laude with a B.A. and an M.A. in 1921. Her master's thesis was titled "Reform of State Government with Special Attention to the State of Massachusetts." Following in her parents' footsteps, Carter went into public service. For eleven years she was employed as a social worker with family service agencies in New York and New Jersey. She married Lisle Carter, a Barbados native, in 1924. A dentist, Lisle Carter practiced in New Jersey. The couple had one child.

Carter took occasional classes at Columbia University, finally committing herself to night classes at the Fordham University law school, where she completed her LL.B. in 1932. She was admitted to the New York bar in 1934. That same year Carter made an unsuccessful bid for a seat in the New York state assembly. Between 1935 and 1945 she belonged to the National Association of Women Lawyers, the National Lawyers Guild, the New York Women's Bar Association, and the Harlem Lawyers Association. She served as secretary of the Committee on Conditions in Harlem after the riots there in the spring of 1935.

An Episcopalian and a Republican, Carter began a private practice after law school and also started her active career in social organizations. In August 1940 an *Ebony* article listed Carter as one of seventy known Negro women who had become lawyers since 1869 ("Lady Lawyers," p. 18). Carter remained in private practice only briefly before William C. Dodge hired her to be a prosecutor for New York City magistrate's or criminal courts. As a prosecutor, Carter tried many cases against prostitutes, most of which she did not win. Because the same bail bondsman and lawyer represented these women, Carter suspected that a bigger organization was controlling prostitution. She told her boss, who dismissed her suspicions. However, Thomas Dewey, a special prosecutor investigating organized crime, took her suspicions seriously and eventually hired Carter as an assistant district attorney. She became part of a team that Dewey organized to investigate rackets and organized crime, particularly as it involved "Dutch" Schultz (Arthur Flegenheimer). She is also acknowledged for developing valuable evidence in the case against "Lucky" Luciano. Because of Carter's skills, in 1941 Dewey named her head of a Special Sessions Bureau overseeing juvenile justice. Eventually supervising more than 14,000 criminal cases per year, Carter served as a trial prosecutor until 1945.

Carter then returned to private practice and greater involvement in civic and social organizations and the movement for equal rights for women. She was a charter member, chairperson, and trustee of the National Council of Negro Women (NCNW), founded in 1935, and a member of the NCNW's Executive Board, the Roosevelt House League of Hunter College, the National Board of the YWCA (1949), the YWCA's administrative committee for its Foreign Divisions, the Panel on Women in Occupied Areas under Communism, and the Association of University Women. In 1945, as the chair of the NCNW's committee of laws, Carter, with her close associate Mary McLeod Bethune, attended a San Francisco conference that organized the United Nations. She was also very active in the local YWCAs of Harlem and Manhattan. Carter served as the secretary of the American Section of the Liaison Committee of International Organizations and the Conference on the Group of U.S. National Organizations; as a consultant to the Economic and Social Council for the International Council of Women (1947); as the chairperson of the Friends of the NAACP (National Association for the Advancement of Colored People); as the vice president of the Eastern Division of the Pan-Pacific Women's Association and the National Council of Women of the U.S. (1964); and as the cochair of the YWCA's Committee on Development of Leadership in Other Countries. In 1954 Carter visited Germany to serve as an adviser to the German government on women in public life. In 1955 she was elected to chair the International Conference of Non-Governmental Organizations of the United Nations. She was also a trustee of the Museum of the City of New York and a member of the Urban League. Carter retired from law in 1952. She died in New York City.

• Consult these collections for information on Carter: a vertical file on Carter in the Woodruff Library of the Atlanta University Center; the National Council of Negro Women papers at the National Archives for Black Women's History in Washington, D.C.; and the Eunice Carter portrait collection in the New York Public Library Research Library. For details about Carter's work against organized crime, see the *New York Herald Tribune*, 6 Aug. 1935, and Karen Berger Morello, *The Invisible Bar: The Woman Lawyer in America, 1638 to the Present* (1986). Obituaries are in the *New York Times*, 26 Jan. 1970; *Jet*, 12 Feb. 1970, and the *New York Amsterdam News*, 31 Jan. 1970.

FAYE A. CHADWELL

CARTER, Henry Alpheus Peirce (7 Aug. 1837–1 Nov. 1891), merchant and diplomat, was born in Honolulu, Kingdom of Hawaii, the son of Captain Joseph Oliver Carter, a Pacific trader and master mariner, and Hannah Trufant Lord. At age three, Henry and his older brother were sent to Boston, Massachusetts, to be educated, but owing to their father's subsequent financial losses, they had to return to Hawaii in 1849.

At age twelve, Carter, realizing that he had a responsibility to help support the family, sought every opportunity to improve his knowledge and his situation. In 1851, while working as a postal clerk in Honolulu, he devoted his leisure time to learning to set type at the government printing office next door. The following year he sailed to California, where for a short while he worked as a clerk in a grocer's shop in Stockton. At that time his employer wrote his mother in Honolulu, "You have every reason to be proud of such a son. He has the mind of a man with deep-fixed moral principles which will always make him beloved by everyone, and carry him safely through the troublesome world. . . . He will make a noble man" (Sullivan, p. 120). This prophesy proved correct.

By 1854 Carter had returned to Honolulu, where he was offered a clerkship in the well-established mercantile firm of C. Brewer & Co., one of the "Big Five," the most important business firms in the Hawaiian Islands (the others were Castle & Cooke, Alexander & Baldwin, Theo H. Davies, and H. Hackfield). Eight years later, he was taken into the firm as a partner and in 1867 became the senior partner.

In the 1860s the whaling industry, which had been the mainstay of the Hawaiian economy for forty years, was declining due to the discovery of an alternative source of oil in petroleum and the decimation of the whaling fleet during the American Civil War and in the Arctic ice. The mercantile firms in Hawaii had served as factors for the whaling industry, providing ships with produce, fuel, and chandlery, as well as transshipping whale products to U.S. markets. Carter envisioned sugar production as an alternative to whaling and guided C. Brewer & Co. into a major role in the development of the sugar plantations, turning their factoring skills and organization to servicing the sugar industry. From initially handling sugar on a commission basis, Brewer pioneered the sugar factor system under which the Hawaiian firms bought equipment and supplies for the plantations, found markets for their produce, and acted as financing agents.

While deeply engrossed in business, Carter also concerned himself with civic affairs, speaking at political rallies and serving as a corporal in a volunteer militia company and as secretary of the Honolulu Men's Debating Society. In 1862 he married Sybil Augusta Judd, a descendant of one of the foremost missionary families in the islands. They had five children, one of whom, George R. Carter, was appointed the second governor of the territory of Hawaii.

Carter's interest in promoting the sugar industry led to his involvement in Hawaiian government affairs. By 1872 the sugar industry was in the doldrums. Labor was hard to obtain, transportation costs were high, and so were tariffs. In 1874 King Kalakaua appointed him to his privy council, a position he retained until his death. That same year he was designated Hawaii's special commissioner to the government of the United States to assist Chief Justice Elisha H. Allen in negotiating a reciprocity treaty between Hawaii and the United States that was designed to allow Hawaiian sugar to enter the United States duty free. When the treaty was activated in 1876, the U.S. tariff on Hawaiian sugar was removed, which gave the sugar industry an enormous advantage and solved its marketing problems for the next decade.

In 1871 Carter had recruited into the firm of C. Brewer & Co. an able businessman, Peter Cushman Jones, in whose judgment he had such faith that thereafter he felt free to leave Hawaii on government assignments. Although he retained his predominant interest in the firm, from 1874 on he was largely preoccupied with government affairs. He was considered by his contemporaries to be "a moderate, profoundly imbued with the enthusiasm and devotion necessary to a successful advocate" (Sullivan, p. 135). His social gifts, a quick intelligence and sound judgment, and his ability to reason and persuade were of great assistance to him, not only in business but also in his work for the kingdom, particularly in diplomatic endeavors.

Following the negotiation of the reciprocity treaty with the United States, the governments of Great Britain, France, and Germany expressed concern over trade advantages accorded to the United States. Carter was dispatched by the Hawaiian government to Europe to placate those governments and to negotiate new treaties with them. Upon returning to Hawaii in December 1876, Carter was appointed minister of foreign affairs and later served as minister of the interior (1880–1881).

As a result of the Reciprocity Treaty of 1876, which assured the U.S. market to Hawaiian sugar, the plantations needed more laborers than were available in the islands. King Kalakaua again turned to Carter for advice. He was first appointed to the Bureau of Immigration (1876) and then to the Commission to Aid the Development of the Resources of the Kingdom (1877). In 1879 the first Portuguese immigrants were recruited as additions to the labor market, and some of these immigrants complained to their home government that recruiting promises were not being fulfilled. In 1881 Carter had to call on all his diplomatic skills when he was sent to Portugal as Hawaii's envoy, with the task of reassuring that government that the Portuguese immigrants were being accorded fair treatment. Carter traveled to Lisbon, mollified the Portuguese officials, and negotiated a treaty regulating Portuguese immigration into the islands.

The following year Kalakaua appointed him Hawaii's envoy to France, and from then until his death Carter spent most of his time in Europe or in Washington, D.C., with only occasional visits to his home in Hawaii. He succeeded Allen as the Hawaiian minister at Washington, D.C., in January 1883; from 1885 to 1887 he was accredited to the government of Germany. He then returned to Washington, again as minister resident, where he negotiated the renewal of the reciprocity treaty in 1887 and was Hawaii's delegate to a number of commissions and congresses, including the Pan-American Congress in 1890.

Late in September 1891 Carter returned from Europe suffering from heart trouble. He moved into the Everett House in New York City, where he died. His wife and children brought his body home to Hawaii, where his funeral was attended by Queen Liliuokalani and a multitude of dignitaries and friends.

• Carter's official papers are in the Archives of Hawaii in a number of files pertaining to the kingdom of Hawaii. The most important are those of the Hawaiian Ministry of Foreign Affairs, the Ministry of the Interior, and the attorney general. In addition, Carter's official life is recorded in the minutes of the Privy Council and the reports of the various commissions on which he served, including the Bureau of Immigration, the Commission on Crown Lands, the Commission to Aid Development of Resources of the Kingdom, and the Board of Health. Carter's private papers are also held in the Archives of Hawaii, Private Collections M-23. An account of Carter's business life is contained in Josephine Sullivan, *A History of C. Brewer & Company Limited: One Hundred Years in the Hawaiian Islands, 1826–1926* (1926), and an account of his family is in George R. Carter, *Joseph Oliver Carter: The Founder of the Carter Family in Hawaii* (1915).

RHODA E. A. HACKLER

CARTER, Henry Rose (25 Aug. 1852–14 Sept. 1925), sanitarian and epidemiologist, was born in Caroline County, Virginia, the son of Henry Rose Carter and Emma Coleman, planters. Carter graduated from the University of Virginia in 1873 with a degree in mathematics and engineering. A leg injury at that time led him to abandon plans for the active life that engineering entailed. After teaching for three years he earned a medical degree from the University of Maryland in 1879. He then entered government employment in the Marine Hospital Service, later the U.S. Public Health Service. Carter's engineering education had equipped him for this competitive post, which offered a steady salary, travel, and the challenge of public health work. His career spanned the time during which the Marine Hospital Service evolved from an agency that ran hospitals for the merchant marine (and hired doctors to work in them) to the national public health service, maintaining quarantine stations and fighting epidemics along the American coast. Carter was a central figure in that expansion, acquiring and systematizing the knowledge needed to combat the principal foes: yellow fever and later malaria with a uniform public health code backed by federal authority. Although he often suffered from ill health, which included a disability from his leg injury, Meniere's disease, syphilis acquired during a surgical procedure, and, at the end, angina, Carter traveled widely and lived a vigorous professional life.

Carter's early postings in the service included Cairo, Illinois, where he first learned of yellow fever. He married Laura Hook in 1880; they had three children. In 1888 he was sent to Ship Island Quarantine Station off the coast of Mississippi, the key defense in the protection of New Orleans and the Mississippi Valley from yellow fever. At Ship Island he first explored the question of yellow fever's incubation period, which was central in deciding how long to detain ships in quarantine. He also worked to establish uniform quarantine practices and disinfection methods along the southern coast. His activities were hampered by his acceptance of the prevailing theory that yellow fever was caused by a bacterium whose mode of spread was unknown. It took another twelve years to find the mosquito vector and even longer to recognize the viral nature of the disease.

Carter organized the defense against yellow fever along the southern coast during the 1890s, and his prompt action helped limit damage from the disease during small epidemics that occurred from 1897 to 1899. These epidemics gave him the opportunity to study yellow fever in limited outbreaks in which the order of events could be recognized with precision. From his documentation of the period of time between the first exposure to a yellow fever source and the appearance of secondary cases in several small Mississippi towns, the extrinsic incubation time of yellow fever was established. Walter Reed, the U.S. Army physician whose research team established that yellow fever was spread by mosquitoes, cited Carter's discovery as a central inspiration to his own theory since it suggested an intermediate host.

Carter spent the rest of his career applying mosquito control measures to eradicate yellow fever. He held important administrative positions in the Cuba (1899–1900) and Panama (1904–1909) campaigns for which William Crawford Gorgas became famous. Gorgas, Carter, and co-workers organized efforts that, by killing mosquitoes with pyrethrum compounds, screening sickrooms, and destroying breeding grounds, broke the vector chain and ended the threat of yellow fever in Cuba and the Canal Zone. From 1913 to 1919 he turned his hand to controlling malaria in the South, especially around military bases and key defense industries. While yellow fever's mosquitoes prefer the clean water of cisterns and barrels, malaria's vector breeds in swamps and marshes. Carter drew what he could from his yellow fever experience in fighting malaria, but new technologies had to be developed to battle the primarily wetland-based problem of malaria. The success of these campaigns established that malaria was not an inevitable feature of the southern landscape. In 1915 he achieved his highest rank, assistant surgeon general.

In 1919 Carter retired from the Public Health Service to devote himself to the international fight against yellow fever. He also began a seminal work on the history of the disease, published posthumously as *Yellow Fever: An Epidemiological and Historical Study of Its Place of Origin* (1931). By the time of his death in Washington, D.C., he had published over thirty works on tropical medicine and sanitation. Carter's epidemiological research remains a model of careful field investigation, while his success in eradicating yellow fever and malaria through federally funded public health projects based on the latest in scientific developments contributed significantly to the reputation and power of the fledgling U.S. Public Health Service.

• Carter's letters and reports are well represented in the papers of the Marine Hospital Service (National Archives) and its publications. Carter's classical epidemiological paper establishing the extrinsic incubation time of yellow fever is titled, "A Note on the Interval between Infecting and Secondary Cases of Yellow Fever from the Records at Orwood and Taylor, Miss., in 1898," *New Orleans Medical and Surgical Journal* 52 (1899–1900): 617–36. Walter Reed's comments citing Carter's discovery as having benefited his own research appeared in "The Etiology of Yellow Fever: A Preliminary Note," *Philadelphia Medical Journal* 6 (1900): 790–96. Obituaries are in the *American Journal of Tropical Medicine* 5 (1925): 385–88, and the *Virginia Medical Monthly* 53 (1926): 398–402.

MARGARET HUMPHREYS

CARTER, James Coolidge (14 Oct. 1827–14 Feb. 1905), lawyer, was born in Lancaster, Massachusetts, the son of Solomon Carter and Elizabeth White. Little is known about his parents. Although his father died when James was only two years old, James still attended Derby Academy in Hingham, Massachusetts, and in 1846 he enrolled at Harvard College. Graduating fourth in his class in 1850, Carter then lived a year in New York, tutoring and studying in the office of Kent and Davis. In 1851 he returned to Harvard for law school, where, despite his apparent success at his studies, he preferred the tangible aspects of law over abstract legal theory. In the spring of 1853, during Carter's last term, Judge Henry E. Davies summoned him to New York to become the managing clerk in his office, Davies and Scudder. Carter accepted the invitation, was admitted to the state bar that same year, and became a member of the firm in 1854, after Davies's retirement. In one capacity or another Carter remained in the same office for the next fifty-two years, watching the firm change names, partners, and personnel as he made a place for himself among the top lawyers of New York.

Early in his legal career Carter attracted the attention of Charles O'Conor, then the leader of the New York bar, who requested Carter's help as an associate in various cases. The most famous of these was the Madame Elizabeth Jumel will case, which stretched over twenty years and earned Carter celebrity status. Jumel's impressive estate in the upper part of Manhattan was continuously under siege by various claimants after her death. One elderly claimant said he was Jumel's illegitimate child. Carter unearthed inconspicuous documents and facts dating back to the eighteenth century to defend his client. Taking the case eventually to the Supreme Court in 1878, he won a victory for both his client and himself.

After the Jumel case, Carter was special counsel in cases, both for and against New York City, resulting from the downfall of William Marcy Tweed's Tammany Hall. The conspirators, who had looted the city's treasury, faced criminal charges, and private parties sued the city for payment for various services. Because of conflicts of interest, the New York corporation counsel could not handle the cases, and Carter served as special counsel through the terms of six corporation counsels.

Carter's most important case was the *People v. Tweed* (1876), which sought to recover the money stolen from the city's treasury. David Dudley Field, the man whom Carter would later battle over the codification of common law, was in charge of the defense. The trial, which continued for many weeks, eventually culminated in a verdict for the city of over $6.5 million.

While Carter was embroiled in a myriad of civil and criminal cases for the city, Governor Samuel Tilden appointed him in 1875 to a commission in charge of reforming the government of New York State's cities. The commission report was harshly criticized for recommending that boards of finance, elected by a limited class of property-owing voters, be given control of the cities' funds. Nevertheless, over the next twenty-five years, Carter pushed for municipal reform, claiming that national and state politics should not intrude into a city's affairs.

In 1870 Carter helped form the Association of the Bar of the City of New York. He then undertook the battle for which he is best remembered, his fight to prevent the codification of the common law of New York State. The new civil code, drafted by Field, had been twice approved by the New York legislature only to be promptly vetoed. Carter called the fight for the enactment of the civil code "the endeavor of a few men, it might almost be said, of one man, to abrogate our system of unwritten law, to discard the principles and methods from which it has sprung, and to substitute in its place a scheme of codification borrowed from the systems of despotic nations" (Miller, p. 18). In 1883 the city's bar association passed a unanimous resolution opposing the civil code and its passage, calling it "the greatest misfortune which has ever threatened the State of New York" (Horwitz, p. 118). Consequently, Carter wrote a pamphlet entitled *The Proposed Codification of Our Common Law* (1884) and distributed it extensively in an attempt to prove that common law reasoning differed from political reasoning and therefore the common law should not be codified. Although Carter appealed to the "democratic spirit" of the common law, arguing that "in free, popular States, the law springs from, and is made by, the people," at the root of his conservative argument was the fear that codification would somehow bring about the redistribution of wealth, thus, according to Carter, diminishing the stability provided to property and business by the common law. Carter did not address the specifics of the proposed code in detail, opting instead to discuss the nature and function of law in terms of evolutionary determinism. He argued that law, as well as the procedures governing it, was an inductive science that should be allowed to develop, unfold, and adapt itself according to the circumstances of society. Largely because of Carter's efforts, the civil code did not make it through both houses of the legislature again, and eventually it died in committee.

Throughout his career, Carter remained singularly focused on the law and never married. In addition to his success at the bench, he was elected by his colleagues as president of the American Bar Association in 1894–1895 and was president of the Association of the Bar of New York City for five years (1884–1886, 1897–1900). The pinnacle of his professional career, however, was his representation of the United States before the Bering Sea Fur-Seal Tribunal of Arbitration in Paris during February 1893. According to the English press and members of the commission, Carter's opening argument for the United States was the best of any delivered. During the last part of his career Carter argued several cases before the Supreme Court. The most famous was the Income Tax Case of 1895, in which he identified what he deemed hypocritical about the current methods of national taxation. Although he ultimately lost the case, his argument in favor of the income tax, as well as its constitutionality, was evidenced by the dissents of several justices.

After his retirement in 1904, Carter spent numerous hours preparing a series of lectures on jurisprudence for presentation at Harvard in the spring of 1905. He died in New York City before delivering the lectures, which were printed posthumously in 1907 under the title *Law: Its Origin, Growth, and Function.*

A thorough researcher and a perfectionist when it came to the details of a particular case, Carter was also an eloquent speaker who used both irony and earnestness in an unlikely but effective combination. He once said, in words indicative of his own sincerity at the bench: "It is difficult to prescribe methods by which the art of commanding attention may be acquired. I think that the first requirement is that the man should be *in earnest*—that is, that he should really believe what he says" (Miller, p. 37).

• For Carter's philosophical and legal views on the codification of common law see his "The Provinces of the Written and the Unwritten Law," *Report of Virginia State Bar Association* (1889); and "The Ideal and the Actual in the Law," *Report to the American Bar Association* (1890). For a warm tribute by his former partner and friend see George Alfred Miller, "James Coolidge Carter," in *Great American Lawyers*, ed. William Draper Lewis (1909). A brief but thorough discussion of the battle over codification of common law in the United States is in Morton J. Horwitz, *The Transformation of American Law 1870–1960: The Crisis of Legal Orthodoxy* (1992). George Martin, *Causes and Conflicts: The Centennial History of the Association of the Bar of the City of New York, 1870–1970* (1970), discusses Carter's career and activities in the New York City bar association. An obituary is in the *New York Times*, 15 Feb. 1905.

DONNA GREAR PARKER

CARTER, James Gordon (7 Sept. 1795–21 July 1849), educational reformer, was born in Leominster, Massachusetts, the son of James Carter and Betsy Hale, farmers. Carter's boyhood summers were spent helping his parents eke out a meager income from the land. He received his basic elementary education in the town's winter school. Carter's days on the farm came to an end in 1812 when he enrolled in Groton Academy. He supported himself there and later at Harvard College by teaching at various district and singing schools and by lecturing on the history of Masonry. Upon graduating from college with honors in 1820, Carter opened a school in Lancaster, Massachusetts, devoted to helping Harvard students overcome academic difficulties. He continued to teach there for ten years. Carter had experience with students with special needs, for during his final year at Harvard he taught a class of disruptive older students, most of them sailors, in Cohasset. At the end of the term his pupils joined with the school committee in presenting him with a letter of thanks for his effectiveness as a disciplinarian and teacher.

Carter's teaching experiences undoubtedly played a role in shaping the career that earned him his place in educational history, that of propagandist and activist for school reform. He entered this phase of activity in 1821 with a series of letters in the Boston *Transcript* that decried the growth of private academies in the state and the lack of support for and the declining quality of the commonwealth's common (public elementary) schools. He identified the most serious deficiencies of the common schools as poor textbooks and incompetent teachers. The solutions he urged were very much along the lines promoted by the Swiss reformer Johann Heinrich Pestalozzi; these included more emphasis on pupils actively discovering knowledge inductively rather than by endless, rote memory drills and more attention to the selection and training of teachers. The *Transcript* letters were published in pamphlet form as *Letters to the Hon. William Prescott, LL.D., on the Free Schools of New England, with Remarks on the Principles of Instruction* (1824). In another literary venture that year, Carter and Theophilus Parsons (1797–1882) established *The United States Literary Gazette*, whose pages became a vehicle for writings on education, with particular emphasis on the relationship between free public schooling and the maintenance of an intelligent electorate. In 1824 Carter also initiated a series of articles in the Boston *Patriot* under the name Franklin, which were later published as a sixty-page pamphlet entitled *Essays upon Popular Education; Containing a Particular Examination of the Schools of Massachusetts, and an Outline for an Institution for the Education of Teachers* (1826). Carter's critique of education was well received in reform circles. His proposal for normal schools to train future pedagogues in the "science" of education and the art of teaching was greeted with particular enthusiasm.

Following the publication of the *Essays* Carter became increasingly and more directly active in the cause of public school reform. In 1827 he submitted a memorial to the state legislature urging the implementation of his teacher-training proposals. A bill for funding a normal school and associated model elementary school failed by a single vote in the senate. The private normal school Carter established in Lancaster shortly after the legislative defeat was short-lived, though he continued to offer private lessons in pedagogy for many years. In 1827 he married Anne M. Packard; they had one child. In 1830 Carter authored a series of illustrated geography textbooks on Pestalozzian principles. That same year he played a leading role in founding the American Institute of Instruction.

In 1835 Carter was elected to the Massachusetts House of Representatives, where he served for three years before moving to the state senate (1838–1839). Carter was clearly the legislature's leading advocate for the public schools, and as chairman of the house committee on education he was able to report out a number of important bills, including an annual appropriation to support the activities of the American Institute of Instruction and "an act to provide for the better instruction of youth, employed in manufacturing establishments." By far his most significant achievement was steering through the bill establishing the state Board of Education in 1837. Carter expected to be named secretary to the board, and most friends of public schooling considered him the logical choice. However, Governor Edward Everett appointed Horace Mann, who had no previous association with school matters, to the position. Carter was given a one-year appointment to the eight-member board. Disappointed at the outcome, he soon after shifted his attention away from the cause of educational reform.

During his last years Carter was active in a number of reform causes, most notably the temperance movement. He also devoted considerable time and effort to mostly unsuccessful financial ventures. He died while on a visit to Chicago.

Horace Mann deserves credit for leading a largely successful crusade to improve public education in Massachusetts and for being the era's leading spokesperson for school reform. However, it was a crusade launched in large measure by Carter. The goals he set and the arguments he employed were extremely influential in his own state and beyond long after he left the scene. Henry Barnard credited Carter with alerting New Englanders to the declining quality of the region's public schools, to the threat to social unity posed by the growing number of private academies, and to the need for teacher-training seminaries.

• The most complete treatment of James Gordon Carter's life and career is Henry Barnard, ed., *Memoirs of Teachers, Educators, and Promoters and Benefactors of Education, Literature and Science* (1859). Also useful are David Wilder, *History of Leominster* (1853), and Abijah P. Marvin, *History of the Town of Lancaster, Massachusetts, 1643–1879* (1879). For a thorough analysis of Carter's ideas about teaching, see J. J. Chambliss, "James G. Carter on Baconian Induction," *History of Education Quarterly* 3 (1963): 198–209. Other aspects of Carter's career in education are considered in Thomas F. Flaherty and John J. Flaherty, "James Carter: Champion of the Normal School," *Resources in Education* (June 1974): 1–13, and in Jonathan C. Messerli, "James G. Carter's Liabilities as a Common School Reformer," *History of Education Quarterly* 5 (1965): 14–25.

FREDERICK M. BINDER

CARTER, Jesse Benedict (16 June 1872–20 July 1917), educator and classical scholar, was born in New York City, the son of Peter Carter, a publisher, and Mary Louise Benedict. He entered New York University in 1889 but after a year transferred to Princeton, where his studies gravitated toward literature and the arts but especially classical studies. He graduated at the top of his class in 1893. He then went to Germany, where the best training for a career as a classicist was to be found, and studied for a year at Leipzig (1893–1894) and a year at Berlin and Göttingen (1894–1895). He then returned to Princeton, where he was an instructor in Latin for two years (1895–1897), and then returned to Germany for a year to take his Ph.D. at Halle in 1898. At Halle he was a pupil of the great German student of Roman religion, Georg Wissowa, whose influence permeated his work for the rest of his life. His dissertation *De Deorum Cognominibus* (1898) was written on the surnames given to Roman divinities. He also studied archaeology under Carl Robert.

Carter returned to Princeton as assistant professor of Latin (1898–1902) and then as professor of Latin (1902–1907). In 1900 he was lecturer on Roman religion at the summer school of the University of Wisconsin, and the same year he published an annotated edition of *Selections from the Roman Elegiac Poets*, which he described as the fruit of several years of undergraduate teaching. In 1902 he married Kate Benedict Freeman of New York City; they had no children. The following year he published a school text, *Virgil's Aeneid* (1903). While still professor of Latin at Princeton, he went to Rome in 1904 as annual professor of Latin at the American School of Classical Studies, remaining in that position until 1907, when he left his professorship at Princeton to become director of the American School (1907–1912). While annual professor he produced *The Religion of Numa* (1906), a study of early Roman religious institutions and perhaps his most important book, and an English translation of Christian Huelsen's *The Roman Forum* (1906). When the American School of Classical Studies merged with the American Academy in Rome in 1911, Carter continued as director of the Classical School until 1912, and on 1 January 1913 he became director of the American Academy. The same year he was awarded an L.H.D. by Princeton. At that time the academy was housed in Villa Mirafiori on Via Nomentana, but following the merger work was begun on the construction of the new academy building at Porta San Pancrazio on the Janiculan hill. The Carters moved into Villa Bellacci there, although he was accustomed to giving his address as Villa Aurelia, which had been Giuseppe Garibaldi's headquarters in the defense of Rome in 1849.

Of medium height, stout, and round faced, Carter took great pride in his dress and had a flamboyant manner that made him a popular lecturer. A woman Fellow of the academy at the time later remarked, "The ladies swooned over him; he was a spell-binder." He was also known to be fond of the good life and convivial. His books were essentially published lectures. But he was a serious and highly respected scholar, and although inclined to extravagances that sometimes irritated the academy's trustees, he was an energetic and highly effective administrator and ably served the American Academy in Rome in a period of change and upheaval. Under his directorship the academy became an important intellectual and artistic center. In 1911 he produced his most popular book, *The Religious Life of Ancient Rome*, based on lectures given at the Lowell Institute in Boston in January of that year; this was a survey of Roman religion from its beginnings to the death of Gregory the Great in A.D. 595. In 1916, at the invitation of the French minister of public instruction, he gave a series of lectures at the Sorbonne and other universities in France on the growth of humanism in the United States.

In 1916, like some of the Fellows of the American Academy in Rome, Carter became actively involved in war relief work in northern Italy, and in recognition of this he was named Commendatore della Corona d'Italia by Victor Emmanuel III in 1917 at a ceremony at Villa Mirafiori. Shortly thereafter he departed for the north on a commission of the American Red Cross connected with the organization of its activities on the Italian front, but on the journey he died suddenly in Cervignano near Aquileia of heart trouble brought on reportedly by sunstroke. His last work, "The Reorganization of the Roman Priesthoods at the Beginning of the Republic," appeared in the first volume of the *Memoirs of the American Academy in Rome* (1917).

In addition to his other work Carter was a contributor to volumes 4 and 5 of W. H. Roscher's *Ausführliches Lexikon der griechischen und römischen Mythologie* (1909–1915 and 1916–1924) and wrote the supplement volume *Epitheta Deorum quae apud Poetas Romanos Leguntur* (1902). He was also a contributor to James Hastings's *Encyclopaedia of Religion and Ethics* (1908–1926). He was a member of the American Philological Association, the American Archaeological Society, the Imperial German Archaeological Institute, the British and American Archaeological Society of Rome, and Psi Upsilon. His excellent library was donated by his widow to the library of the American Academy together with a bronze bust of Carter.

• There is little written about Carter except what he himself includes in the prefaces to his books. Somewhat fuller accounts of his years at the American Academy in Rome appear in the *Memoirs of the American Academy in Rome 1916–17*, pp. 31–33, 41–42, and Lucia and Alan Valentine, *The American Academy in Rome, 1894–1969* (1973), pp. 62–75. There are obituaries in the *New York Times*, 23 July 1917, and the *American Journal of Archaeology* 21 (1917): 337, 340.

L. RICHARDSON, JR

CARTER, John (21 July 1745–19 Aug. 1814), printer and editor, was born in Philadelphia, Pennsylvania, the son of John Carter, a naval officer killed in battle two months before his son's birth, and Elizabeth Spriggs. During the late 1750s, he was apprenticed in the shop of Benjamin Franklin and David Hall. In 1767 Carter moved to Providence, Rhode Island, where printer Sarah Goddard took him as a partner. Starting on 19 September 1767, Carter began helping her publish the *Providence Gazette*. Fourteen months later, she sold Carter her printing equipment and withdrew from their partnership. Carter continued publishing the *Gazette* on his own "at the Sign of Shakespear's Head." In his first solo issue (12 Nov.

1768), Carter included a prospectus explaining his grand design: "To plead and defend the glorious Cause of *Liberty*, and the inestimable Blessings derived from thence." Throughout the next four decades Carter never lost sight of his vision. During the revolutionary war, the *Gazette* animatedly urged readers to support the cause of patriotism; after the war, the paper continued to defend liberty throughout Carter's tenure as printer and publisher. In May 1769 Carter married Amey Crawford; they had twelve children.

Other early products of Carter's press confirm his ideological stance. In 1774 he reprinted Henry Care's *English Liberties; or, The Free-Born Subject's Inheritance*, which had not been printed in the United States since Franklin's 1721 edition. He also printed Thomas Paine's *Common Sense* (1776) in two editions. Carter supported early American science by printing Benjamin West's account of the 1769 transit of Venus, a copy of which was presented to the Royal Society (Raymond Phineas Stearns, *Science in the British Colonies of America* [1970], p. 667). The *New-England Almanack* was a staple of his printing business for forty-five years. Carter also printed occasional sermons, religious pamphlets, textbooks, and Latin catalogs of graduates for Rhode Island College (later Brown University). In 1775 he began printing laws and statutes for the Rhode Island colony. From 1764 to 1783 Carter was among the most productive American printers. During that period, he printed more than 40 percent of all Rhode Island imprints. Carter supplemented his printing trade by becoming postmaster in July 1772, a position he held until June 1792.

Carter was a levelheaded businessman, and his four-and-a-half decades as a printer were remarkably trouble free. One significant personal challenge came in 1779, when Solomon Southwick, formerly a printer in Rhode Island and Massachusetts, came to Providence. He set up a press with Bennet Wheeler in late February or early March of 1779 and did some printing for the Rhode Island General Assembly, thus taking business away from Carter. Resenting the competition, Carter vigorously attacked Southwick in the *Gazette* from 6 March through 20 March 1779. Overall, Carter's confrontation with Southwick was a relatively minor skirmish. He preferred controversies that directly concerned individual liberty. After the revolutionary war, Carter turned his energies to the battle against slavery. He printed the "Constitution of the Providence Society for Abolishing the Slave-Trade" both separately and in the *Gazette* (21 Feb. 1789). He also printed several antislavery tracts, including Jonathan Edwards's *Injustice and Impolicy of the Slave-Trade* (1792), Samuel Hopkins's *Discourse upon the Slave-Trade* (1793), and William Patten's *On the Inhumanity of the Slave-Trade* (1793). Much of Carter's other printing business during the early 1790s was designed to help serve the public. He apparently had little desire to print popular books, such as practical manuals or belletristic works.

Carter's printing activity greatly increased in 1793, and in October or November of that year he formed a partnership with William Wilkinson. Carter's partner had a good sense of late eighteenth-century American taste in books, and he helped to enlarge the business, printing such colonial bestsellers as Robert Dodsley's *Oeconomy of Human Life* (1795) and Alexander Pope's *Essay on Man* (1796); practical works, including the *Seaman's Journal-Book* (1795) and Josiah Twamley's *Dairying Exemplified* (1796); and Wilkinson's own *Federal Calculator, and American Ready Reckoner* (1795). After the partnership was dissolved in May 1799, Carter continued to publish the *Gazette* on his own. He also continued publishing separate works, including several sermons by Philip Doddridge, small jobs for local philanthropic organizations, laws for the state of Rhode Island and the city of Providence, library catalogs, various jobs for Brown University, and several Fourth of July orations. Carter's book output, however, decreased significantly after Wilkinson's departure. He preferred to devote his waning energies to his newspaper.

Writing near the end of Carter's life, printer Isaiah Thomas remarked that the *Gazette* "zealously defended the rights of the colonies before the revolution, ably supported the cause of the country during the war, and has weekly diffused federal republican principles since the establishment of independence." Carter continued publishing the paper after the death of his wife in 1806 and into early 1814, when he announced his retirement. For the 14 February 1814 issue, Carter wrote a retrospective of the *Gazette* in which he described the paper as "open for the reception of temperate discussions of public affairs; respectful remonstrances to government . . . and appeals to the people when their independence has been endangered. It has . . . abounded with original essays on political, literary, moral and religious subjects; and . . . has unceasingly disseminated the orthodox political principles of the Washington school." After Carter's death, an obituary in the *Gazette* (20 Aug. 1814) praised his "sterling integrity, genuine patriotism, and the pure philanthropy of his nature."

• For Carter's eighteenth-century imprints, see John Eliot Alden, *Rhode Island Imprints 1727–1800* (1949), and Roger P. Bristol, *Supplement to Charles Evans' American Bibliography* (1970). For Carter's nineteenth-century imprints, see Ralph R. Shaw and Richard H. Shoemaker, *American Bibliography: A Preliminary Checklist for 1801 [–1819]* (22 vols., 1958–1966). Biographical sources include Isaiah Thomas, *The History of Printing in America*, ed. Marcus A. McCorison (1970); John Carter Brown Woods, "John Carter," *Rhode Island Historical Society Collections* 11 (1918): 101–7, which reprints Carter's valedictory from the *Providence Gazette* and his obituary; and G. Thomas Tanselle, "Some Statistics on American Printing, 1764–1783," in *The Press and the American Revolution*, ed. Bernard Bailyn and John B. Hench (1980). The *Providence Gazette* is discussed in Clarence S. Brigham, *History and Bibliography of American Newspapers 1690–1820* (1947).

KEVIN J. HAYES

CARTER, Landon (18 Aug. 1710–22 Dec. 1778), patriot and diarist, was born in Lancaster County, Virginia, the son of Robert "King" Carter, a planter-merchant member of the King's Council, and Elizabeth Landon. The young Landon was sent to England for schooling when aged nine. Showing special promise as a scholar, he continued there for seven years before returning to Virginia in 1726, where he enrolled at the College of William and Mary in 1727 before settling to learn the tobacco planter and consignment business as assistant and companion to his aged father. In 1732 Carter's father died, and Carter received a large inheritance. That year he married Elizabeth Wormeley. After Elizabeth's death in 1740, he married Maria Byrd in 1742, and they had one child. Following Maria's death in 1744, he married Elizabeth Beale in 1746; they had three children before she died around 1755. In all he had eight children. Carter was a widower for a long period at the end of his life, the years of his diary keeping. The three marriages brought substantial increases in property holding.

In 1733 Carter settled in Richmond County, where he was immediately made a justice and one of the quorum on the county court. Before long he was a vestryman of his church parish and also colonel in command of the militia, appointments he received in recognition of his status as a leading gentleman of wealth, high family, and notable educational attainments. Drawing on the resources of his growing estate, Carter sometime in the 1740s built a fine Georgian family seat called "Sabine Hall" in Richmond County. In 1752 he won election as a legislator and represented his county in the House of Burgesses continuously for sixteen years. In 1768, during the turbulent times following the Stamp Act crisis, he was defeated at the polls. Despite being an early mover in colonial opposition to British encroachment on the liberties of Americans, he was too aloof from the people. During his time as a leading legislator and for a decade longer, Carter engaged in a series of political campaigns. He was active in supporting resistance to the lieutenant governor's attempt to exact a pistole fee on land grants, zealous in mobilizing Virginia's efforts in the French and Indian War, a supporter of colonial legislative autonomy in the Two-Penny Act controversies, and a staunch patriot in the series of struggles from the Stamp Act crisis onward. As a strong believer in the British constitution of King, Lords, and Commons and in the rights of the colonists as "British" freemen, Carter disliked the writings of Thomas Paine and zealous activism for independence. Although wary of the movement for a new, more radical republican constitution that was mounting in early 1776, he continued to support the American cause unwaveringly to the end of his life.

During his years as a legislator Carter published some four political pamphlets, the first two anonymously and the later two over his own name, and nearly fifty newspaper essays. In his political writings he clung to the conventional Whig view that society is a simple community, and its wisest and most virtuoso members could discern its single true interest. These natural leaders were the gentry owners of land; merchants he distrusted as systematically dishonest. The collective virtue of the legislators and the fact of their own subjection to the laws they made should enable the legislature to act as a necessary check on the otherwise inevitable abuses into which the greed and ambition of human nature would lead men in government. Outsiders, including the British Parliament and ministry, could neither know the distant community's interest nor act as a check on power. Therefore, the king, whose right to be the government Carter did not question, must both tax and legislate only as determined by the elected representatives in his colonial legislatures. For his scientific writings Carter was elected to the American Philosophical Society in 1769 and, upon its founding in 1773, to the Virginia Society for the Promotion of Useful Knowledge.

Although only a minor notable in American history for his part in the affairs and the published patriot polemics of his day, Carter has an undoubted preeminence in one respect. This planter gentleman kept a journal whose evolving forms over twenty-five years make the accumulating text deeply revealing of the intellectual and emotional currents of his times. Its strong writing exhibits in an everyday setting the moral and affective attachments of the patriarchalism that guided the American Revolution. The truisms of these white gentlemen—though already contending with turbulent popular democracy, New Light evangelicalism, and publicly articulated women's points of view—were powerful in shaping the new Republic. Since the twentieth-century discovery and publication of this series of journals, Carter has stood forth among the greatest American diarists.

The first surviving diary Carter acquired when he went to Williamsburg as a county representative in the Virginia Assembly. He evidently intended it as a journal of procedures to help him master the protocols of the House of Burgesses. Soon it became also a rich personal record of debates and his participation in them. After four years, perhaps because he felt he now had more procedural expertise than even the Speaker, he in the fall of 1756 converted this volume to a plantation procedures book headed "Farming Observations etc. continued." So began the copious plantation diary that assures Carter a place in American history. True to its heading, this journal is a record of attempted scientific management of agriculture. He added to it until October 1758, when its pages were filled. The descriptions of weather, crop experiments, medical treatments, and labor management and a series of inventive engineering designs are deeply personal in their intensity and unmatched by any other known day-to-day agricultural record from anywhere in the English-speaking world. The fullness and vigor of the writing reveals the Enlightenment on the farm—the lived experience of engaging in the "agricultural improvement" for which this age is famous. As an example of the American "moderate Enlightenment," with its strenuous insistence on joining the new science to the old biblical religion, the diary shows Carter, even as he recorded his striving for rational control, imbued with a deep sense of God's omnipotence and of his own need to learn "to kiss the rod" that chastised him with bereavement, drought, wind, flood, and frost.

No journal survives for the five years between October 1758 and November 1763, and another gap exists for the years 1765, 1768, and 1769. Beginning in January 1770 Carter made his own notebooks or "little monthly diaries," in which, in addition to the continuing Enlightenment observations toward methodizing of the plantation, he began to tell stories, artfully presented in full. The subjects were various: plantation conflicts with slaves and overseers, domestic quarrels with his son and daughter-in-law and their children, neighborhood feuds over straying cattle, merchants' fraudulent contrivances, and the contests and jealousies among magistrates and patriot leaders in the county.

The great series of diary stories in some sense culminates with the old colonel finding himself up against revolution and a world being remade in ways very disturbing to him. The great stock of stories in the later diaries on the one hand presents a Virginia version of a rich and ancient manor-house folklore, a gentry counterpart to trickster tales in which squires pondered whether their servants were most knaves or fools, and on the other hand suddenly shows an emergent new order in which rights proclaimed in revolution would be claimed by those for whom the proclaimers had certainly not intended them.

This diarist, keeping up his outpourings until shortly before his death at Sabine Hall, was truly remarkable in his generation for the way he continually followed out his thoughts on paper. Carter was a copious writer of pamphlets and newspaper essays in defense of "the Cause of American Liberties," an elder statesman to the generation that launched the Revolution, and the keeper for more than twenty-five years of one of the most remarkable diaries in American history.

• The bulk of Carter's surviving papers are in the Sabine Hall Collection, Alderman Library, University of Virginia, Charlottesville. A smaller but still important collection of his papers is included in the Carter Family Papers, College of William and Mary Library, Williamsburg, Va. These two manuscript collections, including most of the surviving portions of the diary, and the papers at the Virginia Historical Society in Richmond have been published in microform as "The Carter Family Papers, 1659–1797, in the Sabine Hall Collection," Microfilm Publication no. 3, University of Virginia. Carter's diary was published in book form under the auspices of the Virginia Historical Society, Jack P. Greene, ed., *The Diary of Colonel Landon Carter of Sabine Hall, 1752–1778* (1965; repr. 1987). The "Introduction," a fine appraisal of the political and moral themes traceable in the diary and other writings of Carter, was reissued as Greene, *Landon Carter: An Inquiry into the Personal Values and Social Imperatives of the Eighteenth-Century Virginia Gentry* (1967), which identifies and lists in text and notes all the surviving writings. Carter's published pamphlets are *A Letter from a Gentleman in Virginia, to the Merchants of Great Britain . . .* (1754), *A Letter to a Gentleman in London, from Virginia* (1759), *A Letter to the . . . Lord B[isho]p of L——n* (1760), and the satiric *Rector Detected* (1764). Studies that include Carter are Gerald W. Mullin, *Flight and Rebellion in Eighteenth-Century Virginia* (1972); Rhys Isaac, *The Transformation of Virginia, 1740–1790* (1982); and Isaac, "Imagination and Material Culture: The Enlightenment on a Mid-18th-Century Virginia Plantation," in *The Art and Mystery of Historical Archaeology*, ed. Anne Elizabeth Yentsch and Mary C. Beaudry (1992).

RHYS ISAAC

CARTER, Maybelle (10 May 1909–23 Oct. 1978), country-music singer and instrumentalist and matriarch of a music performing dynasty, known as Mother Maybelle, was born Maybelle Addington around Nicklesville, Scott County, Virginia, a few miles north of the Tennessee-Virginia state line. Both of her parents, Hugh Jack Addington and Margaret Elizabeth Kilgore, had deep roots in rural Scott County. Maybelle was one of ten children, many of whom grew up playing various stringed instruments. Maybelle's mother was a banjo player, and when Maybelle was still a child she joined in as the family band played for local square dances. She played the autoharp as well, but her real fascination came when she was about twelve and one of her older brothers gave her a guitar. "I started trying different ways to pick it," she later recalled, "and came up with my own style, because there weren't many guitar pickers around." The guitar was just becoming popular in the mountains, and the style Maybelle came up with—what would become known as the "Carter lick" or "thumb-brush" technique—allowed the thumb to pick the melody on the bass strings while the fingers keep rhythm downstroking the higher strings. This permitted the guitarist to pick a melody and keep rhythm at the same time, and eventually it became the most copied guitar style in country music.

Maybelle sang with her cousin Sara Dougherty, who lived about a quarter of a mile from her home. Maybelle was only six years old when Sara married A. P. Carter in 1915, and she continued to see Sara as she grew up. In 1926 seventeen-year-old Maybelle married A. P. Carter's brother Ezra, and after her marriage she began singing with Sara and A. P. on a more regular basis. Most of the time in such gatherings Maybelle—by now a small, quiet, dark-eyed girl—was content to provide the guitar leads for the group while Sara played either the autoharp or kept up a rhythm on the second guitar. Later, Maybelle began to sing more, often performing duets with Sara.

In July 1927 A. P. Carter drove the group to nearby Bristol, on the Tennessee-Virginia line, where they made their first six phonograph records for the Victor Talking Machine Company, on 1 August. Sara and A. P. did all the singing on this first session, with Maybelle joining in only on "Bury Me under the Weeping Willow" and "The Storms Are on the Ocean." These records were the first in a long series and launched the Carter Family on its way to fame. The next few years saw dozens of popular and influential recordings, though Maybelle did not regularly begin singing duets with Sara until late 1929. On 10 May 1928, recording in Camden, New Jersey, Maybelle crafted what was perhaps her best-known guitar passage, on the old song "Wildwood Flower" (Victor V-40000). Her style on this cut exemplified the Carter lick and made the song a testing piece for generations of young guitar players. A second such piece came on 24 May 1930, when Maybelle crafted an influential part to "The Cannonball" (Victor V-40317), a tune that would become known as "Cannonball Rag." By this time Maybelle was learning various blues and picking techniques from African-American guitarist and songster Leslie Riddles, who lived in nearby Kingsport, Tennessee, and often visited the Carters.

Maybelle's marriage with Ezra continued to be fruitful and rewarding during her time with the Carter Family. A mail clerk for the railway, Ezra was often transferred, spending time in Washington, D.C., and then in Bluefield, West Virginia; at such times, Maybelle would have to travel back and forth to join the Family at recording sessions or at important concerts and radio shows. During these years, three daughters, Helen, June, and Anita, also resulted from the union. All three inherited their mother's musical talent, and all three continued the Carter tradition by forging their own careers that would extend into the 1990s.

After the original Family disbanded in 1943 and both A. P. and Sara retired from music, Maybelle determined to forge her own career, along with her three daughters. Though all three were still in their teens, they had gained radio experience while working with the Family in the late 1930s on the border radio stations (stations with transmitters in Mexico, allowing them to evade U.S. broadcasting regulations). Billing themselves as Mother Maybelle and the Carter Sisters, they soon found work on regional radio barn dance programs: from 1943 to 1946 they worked in Richmond, Virginia, eventually on "The Old Dominion Barn Dance"; in 1947 they moved to Knoxville, Tennessee, where they appeared on WNOX; the following year saw them at KWTO in Springfield, Missouri, where they appeared on "The Ozark Jubilee" and joined forces with a young guitarist named Chet Atkins. In 1950 they arrived in Nashville, where they settled in at the Grand Ole Opry and resumed their recording career. Helen, Anita, and June also began to work with other country singers as soloists and duet partners.

In 1961 Maybelle Carter and her daughters began to tour and work with Johnny Cash, then at the height of his popularity; this, as well as a folk revival, led to another round of LP albums, both by Carter alone and with her family. Though she had never played autoharp on the original Carter Family recordings, she now began to feature the instrument and found herself much in demand at prestigious venues like the Newport Folk Festival. Her guitar work received new acclaim as she often joined forces with bluegrass greats Earl Scruggs and Lester Flatt; Scruggs, best known for his banjo playing, was a devotee of Carter's guitar style and used it on many of his group's gospel recordings. In 1973 Carter participated in the popular album set *Will the Circle Be Unbroken* with the country-rock group the Nitty Gritty Dirt Band.

By the 1970s, suffering from arthritis and Parkinson's disease, Carter began to drop out of music. She died in Nashville.

• Mary A. Bufwack and Robert K. Oermann, *Finding Her Voice: The Saga of Women in Country Music* (1993), is a useful source on Carter.

CHARLES K. WOLFE

CARTER, Robert (1663–4 Aug. 1732), merchant-planter and public official, was born in Lancaster County, Virginia, the son of John Carter, a wealthy merchant-planter and attorney, and Sarah Ludlow. John Carter died in 1669 leaving Robert 1,000 acres and one-third of his personal estate. He also provided that an indentured servant be "bought for him . . . to teach him his books either in English or Latine according to his capacity." Later, probably around 1672, he was sent to London by his elder brother John where he spent six years receiving a grammar school education. In London Robert lived with Arthur Bailey, a prosperous merchant, from whom he must have learned about the intricacies of the tobacco trade. Little else is known about his early years, but in 1688 he married Judith Armistead, with whom he had five children. In 1701 he married Elizabeth Landon Willis; this union produced an additional ten children. Five sons and five daughters lived to maturity, and all the sons received an English education. The death of his brother John in 1690, followed shortly by the death of his daughter and half brother, resulted in Carter inheriting the bulk of a large estate that included more than 9,000 acres of land and 115 slaves. Carter, already a man of substance, quickly added to his wealth through planting and mercantile activity, including a significant involvement in the slave trade. He also began to acquire large amounts of land, a process that was aided by the two terms he served as agent (1702–1712, 1719–1732) for the Fairfax family, the proprietors of the Northern Neck. The Northern Neck was that vast area of land between the Rappahannock and the Potomac rivers, stretching to the headwaters of the latter. At Carter's death it was reported that he left 300,000 acres of land, 1,000 slaves, and £10,000 in cash, and it appears that this estimate was not far off the mark.

In acquiring this vast wealth Carter was aided by the fact that from early on he held a variety of key public offices. He became a justice of the peace in Westmoreland County in 1688 and soon thereafter in Lancaster County. In 1691 Lancaster County elected him to the House of Burgesses, where he continued for most of the decade, serving as its Speaker in 1696–1697 and 1699. In 1699 he was appointed to the council of state, the highest office a Virginian could hope to attain, and remained on the council for the rest of his life. After the death of Lieutenant Governor Hugh Drysdale in 1726, as senior member on the council Carter served as acting governor for over a year. Other offices he held included treasurer of the colony, naval officer for the Rappahannock River, and colonel and lieutenant of the militia in Lancaster and Northumberland counties. These posts, and his wealth, made Carter the most powerful Virginian in public life in the first third of the eighteenth century. If his detractors are to be believed he did not hesitate to use his power and position. They referred to his "extraordinary Pride & Ambition" as well as his "haughtiness" and asserted that he was sometimes called "King Carter . . . even to his face."

Carter was certainly a driven and ambitious man for himself and for his family. In 1722 he played a key role in the appointment of his eldest son John as solicitor of Virginia affairs and then secretary of the colony. The latter office was the most remunerative one in Virginia, and it cost Robert Carter £1,500. Soon thereafter he pushed for his son to be appointed to fill a vacancy on the council of state. Since "he is Secretary there seems to be a sort of Justice in it" he wrote an English correspondent, and if he were not appointed "I shall consider it an Injustice to my son." John Carter joined his father on the council in 1724. While acting governor Carter arranged for the appointment of his son Robert as naval officer for the Rappahannock River, over the vocal objection of one of the council. When Robert resigned that post in 1729 he was replaced by his brother Charles. Such arrangements and the large fortune he left his children and grandchildren assured the family's important political, economic, and social role until the end of the century.

But Carter worked not only for himself and his progeny but for the wider public as well. A staunch Whig, he gloried in the "English Nation" while at the same time vigorously defending Virginia's rights within the British empire. As his tombstone epitaph succinctly states, "He defended with equal justice the royal authority and the common freedom." A responsible, affectionate, and generous father he also valued education, read widely, and possessed a library of well over 500 volumes. Deeply religious, at his death he had almost completed the building, at his expense, of the handsome brick Christ Church, which still stands near the site of his home in Lancaster County.

When he died at his home in Lancaster County, Virginia, at a ripe old age for the time, Carter had served himself and Virginia well.

• Major collections of Carter papers, largely for the 1720s, can be found at the Alderman Library, University of Virginia, Charlottesville, and the Virginia Historical Society. See also Paul P. Hoffman, ed., *Guide to the Microfilm Edition of the Carter Family Papers, 1659–1797, in the Sabine Hall Collection* (1967). Copies of other letters are in the Wormeley Estate Papers, 1701–1710, 1716, Christ Church Parish, Lancaster County, at the Virginia State Library, and in Louis B. Wright, ed., *Letters of Robert Carter: The Commercial Interests of a Virginia Gentleman* (1940). His extensive will and the inventory of his estate are in the *Virginia Magazine of History and Biography* 5, 6, and 7. His education is discussed in Alan Simpson, "Robert Carter's Schooldays," *Virginia Magazine of History and Biography* 94 (Apr. 1986): 161–88. Good and complimentary descriptions of his life are in Louis B. Wright, *The First Gentleman of Virginia: Intellectual Qualities of the Early Colonial Ruling Class* (1940); Clifford Dowdey, *The Virginia Dynasties: The Emergence of "King" Carter and the Golden Age* (1969); and Research Staff, Historic Christ Church, *Robert "King" Carter—Builder of Historic Christ Church* (1986). Family background and genealogy can be pursued in Christine A. Jones, comp., *John Carter II of "Corotoman" Lancaster County, Virginia* (1978); Noel Currer-Briggs, *The Carters of Virginia* (1979); and Robert R. Carter and Marion Oliver, *The Carter Family Tree* (1897).

EMORY G. EVANS

CARTER, Robert (5 Feb. 1819–15 Feb. 1879), author and editor, was born in Albany, New York, the son of Irish immigrants (names unknown). Although most of the details of Carter's early life remain sketchy, he was apparently raised in conditions of wretched poverty. His education came from his sporadic sojourns at public schools, until he eventually attended the Jesuit College of Chambly in Canada. He quit school at fifteen, and he was appointed assistant librarian in the state library in Albany, where he remained until 1838. By age twenty he had decided to embark on a career in journalism, having already published some poetry and essays in the Albany newspapers. In 1841 he moved to Boston, and there he met James Russell Lowell, a similarly idealistic young man with whom he had his first brush with literary fame.

In January 1843 Carter and Lowell published the first issue of their ill-fated literary journal, *The Pioneer*. Although the journal had a run of only three issues and ceased to exist after March 1843, the quality of the literature that *The Pioneer* contained was enough to make those three issues legendary. In addition to original compositions by Lowell, among the journal's highlights were first printings of Edgar Allan Poe's "The Tell-Tale Heart" and "Lenore," Nathaniel Hawthorne's "The Birthmark," and original verse by John Greenleaf Whittier, W. W. Story, and Elizabeth Barrett (later Barrett Browning), as well as Carter's own story "The Armenian's Daughter," of which three numbers had appeared when the periodical ceased publication. While the magazine's failure left Lowell some $1,800 in debt—a substantial sum in 1843—Carter emerged from the experience relatively unscathed. Carter held a variety of jobs over the next several years, among them chief clerk in the Cambridge post office, freelance literary adviser, and private secretary to the famous historian William H. Prescott.

After marrying the writer Ann Augusta Gray in 1846, Carter served as secretary to Prescott in 1847. After leaving this position, he became more active politically. By 1848 he was not only allied with the Free Soil party, but he was, with John G. Palfrey, made editor of the *Boston Commonwealth*, a paper known for espousing the Free Soilers' platforms. During this period he also published *The Hungarian Controversy* (1852), a collection of essays that had originally appeared in the *Boston Atlas* in 1850. These essays, which were a rebuttal to *North American Review* editor Francis Bowen's articles attacking the Hungarian revolutionaries, were a significant milestone in the careers of both men. Carter's essays not only increased his own reputation, but they were also a severe setback to Bowen, whose election to the McLean Chair of History at Harvard was vetoed after the overseers of the college determined that Carter had made Bowen appear as a man of only marginal intelligence.

His rising reputation made Carter a natural choice for the position of Free Soil party secretary, and true to form, Carter made a significant impact after his appointment in 1854. Using the influence that this position afforded him, Carter sent thousands of circulars to men of all political parties who were opposed to slavery, and he subsequently organized a meeting of these men in Worcester on 20 July. Carter drafted the antislavery platform used by the Free Soilers, Whigs, and Democrats who met that day, and he also suggested that they change their name to the "Republican" party. Until his death, Carter remained a staunch supporter and an active member of that group.

Ever restless and looking for new challenges, Carter next served as editor of the *Boston Telegraph* (1855) and the *Boston Atlas* (1856), then as the Washington correspondent for Horace Greeley's *New York Tribune* from 1857 through 1859. In 1859 Carter joined George Ripley and Charles A. Dana as editors for the first edition of *The American Cyclopedia*, where he stayed until 1863, the same year that his wife died. After briefly working for Secretary of the Treasury Salmon P. Chase in 1864, he became editor of the *Rochester (N.Y.) Democrat*, and while there in 1864 he married his second wife, Susan Nichols, herself an author and the daughter of printer and publisher George Nichols. (As in the case of Carter's first marriage, this second marriage was childless.) While editor of the *Democrat* he published his book *A Summer Cruise on the Coast of New England* (1864), which was immensely popular and went into subsequent editions in 1865, 1888, and 1889. While his tenure as editor of the *Democrat* was relatively long by Carter's standards—he stayed there until 1870—he left that position to become editor of *Appleton's Journal*. In 1873 he left *Appleton's* to work once again on *The American Cyclopedia*, which was his final professional position. By 1874 his failing health forced him to retire, and thereafter he traveled for much of the remainder of his life. He died in Cambridge.

Carter had an impact on many aspects of American life in his time, and his presence was felt both passively (as an editor of works by literary figures such as Poe and Hawthorne) and from an active position as well (his instrumental role in Massachusetts politics). As an editor, author, and politician, Carter was unquestionably an important figure in nineteenth-century America.

• The majority of Robert Carter's papers are in the Houghton Library at Harvard, although some can be found in the Schlesinger Library at Radcliffe College. Much of the information extant on Carter is in reference to his days as the editor of *The Pioneer*, and the best work for biographical information is Sculley Bradley, *The Pioneer: A Literary Magazine* (1947). Frank Luther Mott, *A History of American Magazines* (1957), also discusses Carter's involvement with *The Pioneer*, as well as his disagreement with Francis Bowen's articles in the *North American Review*. Horace Scudder's *James Russell Lowell* (1901), a biography, includes numerous references to Carter, not only in regard to *The Pioneer* but also to his and Lowell's relationship after the failure of the periodical. In addition, see Rossiter Johnson's introduction to the 1888 edition of Carter's *A Summer Cruise*, and Carter's obituary in the *Boston Transcript*, 17 Feb. 1879.

JAMES R. SIMMONS, JR.

CARTER, Samuel Powhatan (6 Aug. 1819–26 May 1891), naval and army officer, was born in Elizabethton, Carter County, Tennessee, the son of Alfred Moore Carter, an iron manufacturer, and Evalina Belmont Perry or Parry. Carter's middle name is given as Powhatan on his gravestone, but Carter family descendants insist he bore his mother's maiden name, Powhatan being a nickname acquired during the Civil War. As a middle initial only appears in his signature and on all extant documents, the question cannot be resolved, but the nickname story is plausible.

Carter's family was locally prominent. Carter County was named for his grandfather, Landon Carter, a local revolutionary war leader, while the county seat, Elizabethton, was named for his grandmother. Alfred Carter was one of the wealthiest men of East Tennessee, giving Samuel and his brothers, William Blount Carter and James Patton Taylor Carter, educational advantages. Samuel Carter attended Washington College, a nearby Presbyterian school, and enrolled in Princeton in 1837. For reasons not known, he gave up the social prominence and wealth connected with his family's circumstances to become a midshipman in the then diminutive U.S. Navy.

Carter's appointment dated from 14 February 1840. Starting a naval career at the late age of twenty-one without patrons in the service placed him at a severe disadvantage, but he rose steadily. His early service included cruises in the Pacific, the Great Lakes, and the Atlantic. From 1845 to 1846 he attended the new U.S. Naval Academy at Annapolis, graduating with its first class. As a passed midshipman he participated in the naval operations against Veracruz during the Mexican War. From 1847 to 1861, Carter performed a variety of duties, ashore and afloat. He was detached to the Washington Naval Observatory for a year and was briefly an assistant professor of mathematics at the naval academy. Commissioned a lieutenant in 1855, he led men from the *San Jacinto* in a storming party against the Barrier Forts in the Canton River, China, the following year. He was stationed with the Brazil Squadron in 1861, when orders brought his ship back to the United States at the outbreak of the Civil War.

During the secession crisis, Carter's brothers had been active in rallying local support for the national government, but by the time of Carter's return in July 1861, Tennessee had left the Union. Apparently as the result of arrangements made by his brothers, Carter was detached from the navy to the War Department and commissioned a brigadier general of volunteers without relinquishing his naval rank. Carter attempted to reach East Tennessee to raise recruits for Federal service, but Confederate troops already occupied the region. He, therefore, set up a recruiting camp in the Kentucky mountains, which attracted hundreds of East Tennessee refugees. According to legend, Carter adopted the nom de guerre Powhatan in secret correspondence with those who remained in his home region as resistance fighters.

For the next three years, the Carter brothers lobbied the Lincoln administration and the military authorities in Kentucky on behalf of the oppressed loyalists in East Tennessee. Although Abraham Lincoln fully endorsed their pleas for an immediate, permanent occupation of the region, larger strategic circumstances and the forbidding mountain terrain gave Union commanders in Kentucky good reason to assign a low priority to such schemes. Carter received command of the brigade of East Tennesseans he raised, and with support and funding from Lincoln, William Carter secretly arranged an uprising of East Tennesseans in November 1861. Although a number of railroad bridges were burned and armed Unionists gathered, the planned simultaneous invasion by forces including Samuel Carter's brigade was canceled at the last minute, and the Unionists suffered severe reprisals. Carter's brigade was part of the force under Brigadier General George W. Morgan that captured Cumberland Gap in June 1862, but the Confederate invasion of Kentucky that fall negated plans for advancing into East Tennessee.

In November 1862 Carter proposed the operation that became known as "Carter's Raid." In addition to testing a possible invasion route, the raid was designed to encourage continued loyalist resistance in the South. Carter's goal was to destroy a full one hundred miles of railroad between Knoxville, Tennessee, and the Virginia border, thereby crippling the major east-west Confederate logistical and communications line between the eastern and western theaters of the war simultaneous with the advance of Union forces in Middle Tennessee for what became the Stones River campaign.

In the last weeks of December and the first weeks of January 1863, Carter led a force of almost 1,000 cavalrymen over a torturous mountain route in brutal winter weather to destroy bridges on the East Tennessee and Virginia Railway at Blountville, Union (now Bluff City), and Carter's Depot (now Watauga), Tennessee. Although an occupation force was poised to follow, Carter regretfully reported the route impracticable for infantry. As the first successful large-scale, long-distance Union raid of the Civil War, Carter's operations marked a shift in the employment of mounted troops away from minor tactical activities toward larger strategic objectives. A last-minute reduction of Carter's force from 3,000 to 1,000 men, due to a scarcity of cavalry, limited the damage he was able to inflict, but subsequent Union cavalry raids built upon his bold and courageous example.

As a reward for his accomplishment, Carter was promoted to lieutenant commander in the navy. When Union forces finally occupied most of East Tennessee later in 1863, Carter reluctantly accepted an appointment as provost marshal in Knoxville. He took the field again in 1865, commanding one wing of the Union forces that won the battle of Kinston, North Carolina, in March 1865. At the war's end he was a brevet major general commanding the XXIII Corps and the military district of Beaufort, North Carolina.

Worried that his service on land had jeopardized his naval career, Carter immediately sought and obtained sea duty. His fears were groundless. With the special thanks of the secretary of the navy, he was promoted to commander. A captain in 1870, he was for three years commandant of the U.S. Naval Academy. He reached commodore in 1878 and, after commanding a number of vessels, retired in 1881 at the age of sixty-two. Carter settled in Washington, D.C., where in 1882 he was promoted to rear admiral on the retired list by special legislation, to reward him for remaining loyal to the government during the war.

A devoted Christian, Carter was active throughout his life in the Presbyterian church, the denomination in which his brother William was ordained. In the 1850s Carter married Caroline C. Potts; they had one son. Following Caroline's death in 1875, Carter married Martha Custis Williams. Carter died in Washington, D.C. No other American had previously held both the rank of major general in the army and rear admiral in the navy. Carter upheld the highest traditions of each service.

• No public collection of Carter's papers exists, although Carter family descendants preserve a few items. Carter wrote a brief account of his Civil War experiences, "A Sketch of the Military Services of Samuel P. Carter, Brig. Genl. & Brevt. Maj. Genl. of U.S. Vols. during the Rebellion of the Southern States, 1861–5." This is part of the Naval Historical Foundation Collection in the Library of Congress. A biography of Carter has yet to be published.

Carter's military correspondence and reports are preserved in the War Department's *The War of the Rebellion; A Compilation of the Official Records of the Union and Confederate Armies* (128 vols., 1880–1901). The report of his raid, together with observations by an officer who accompanied it, is also in "Doc. 92: General Carter's Expedition," in *The Rebellion Record*, vol. 6, ed. Frank Moore (1862–1871). Two regimental histories chronicle the raid from the perspective of units that participated in it: Marshall P. Thatcher, *A Hundred Battles in the West, St. Louis to Atlanta, 1861–65, the Second Michigan Cavalry* (1884), and John W. Rowell, *Yankee Cavalrymen: Through the Civil War with the Ninth Pennsylvania Cavalry* (1971). The raid also receives considerable attention in Robert L. Kincaid, *The Wilderness Road* (1951). The most complete accounts, however, are Campbell H. Brown, "Carter's East Tennessee Raid: The Sailor on Horseback Who Raided His Own Back Yard," *Tennessee Historical Quarterly* 22 (Mar. 1963): 66–82; and William Garrett Piston, *Carter's Raid: An Episode of the Civil War in East Tennessee* (1989).

WILLIAM GARRETT PISTON

CARTER, Sara. *See* Carter, A. P., and Sara Carter.

CARTER, Thomas Henry (30 Oct. 1854–17 Sept. 1911), U.S. senator, was born near Portsmouth, in Scioto County, Ohio, the son of Edward C. Carter and Margaret Byrnes, farmers. He moved with his parents in 1865 to Pana, Illinois, where he later engaged in farming, teaching, and railroading. Carter left home in 1878 to study law at Burlington, Iowa. In 1882 he relocated to Helena, Montana, where four years later he married Ellen L. Galen. They had two children. Also in 1882 he formed a law partnership with John B. Clayberg and Fletcher Maddox. Becoming interested in politics, he entered that arena at the formative stage of Montana's statehood and during a turbulent period in the state's political history. Carter, who balanced his public career with a domestic life that included his family and the Catholic faith, earned a reputation as a tenacious politician and party loyalist.

Carter's political career began in 1888 when he secured the Republican nomination as territorial delegate to Congress. He won a surprising victory over William A. Clark, a wealthy mining baron, who blamed his defeat on fellow Democrat Marcus Daly, who had urged his supporters to vote for Carter on the theory that a Republican would be more influential during a Republican administration. When Montana gained statehood in 1889, Carter sought the lone congressional seat. Once again he triumphed at the polls. As a member of the House of Representatives, he advocated liberal legislation for homesteaders and endorsed the free and unlimited coinage of silver. A loyal ally of House Speaker Thomas B. Reed, Carter was chairman of the Committee on Mines and Mining in the Fifty-first Congress. Defeated in 1890 in his bid for reelection, Carter returned to his Helena law practice. Shortly thereafter, President Benjamin Harrison selected Carter to serve as commissioner of the General Land Office, in which capacity he worked to satisfy the complaints of western farmers, miners, and timbermen.

In 1892 President Harrison asked Carter to coordinate his renomination efforts with Louis T. Michener, a former attorney general of Indiana who served as Harrison's political manager. Following Harrison's renomination at the Republican National Convention in Minneapolis, Carter became chairman of the Republican National Committee. "The President seems to have absolute confidence in my capacity to do the work and my associates on the Committee are my friends," he assured his wife. In this position, Carter spearheaded efforts to placate discordant elements within the party while trying unsuccessfully to garner support from southern Populists in order to disrupt the Democrats. His most troublesome episode occurred when Michener charged him with incompetence, particularly with regard to the political situation in Indiana, Harrison's home state. There John K. Gowdy, chairman of the Indiana Republican State Committee, complained bitterly over a lack of money and an inadequately staffed headquarters. The simmering tensions among Gowdy, Michener, and Carter finally exploded when Carter wrote a caustic letter to Elijah W. Halford, private secretary to the president, on 1 November, defending his record and castigating both Gowdy and Michener.

Harrison lost the election in 1892. He owed his defeat in part to the defection of labor and farming elements upset with strikes and high tariffs and to the failure of the Republican party to capitalize on these woes. Unable to stir the party faithful, the beleaguered incumbent had infuriated too many party leaders and in the process provided an easy target for the Democrats. A disappointed Carter remained as national chairman for the next few years, but he returned to Montana in 1893 to consolidate his hold there on Republican politics and to practice law.

Elected to the U.S. Senate, Carter sat in the upper chamber from 1895 to 1901 and again from 1905 to 1911. He drafted the National Forest Act of 1897 and was instrumental in establishing Glacier National Park. Although he opposed high protective tariffs, Carter supported the Dingley Tariff of 1897 and the Payne-Aldrich Tariff of 1909, but only after adequate amendments had been added to protect western raw materials. Although Carter declined to join the Silver Republicans in 1896, he fought for international bimetalism and allied himself with copper and large capitalistic and business interests in his state. The senator also favored civil service reform, helping to extend the regulations and opposing those who attacked its purpose. Carter endorsed the Australian secret ballot but voiced disapproval of the direct election of senators and primary elections, which put him at odds with progressive Republicans. He resisted attempts at extensive conservation and thought that President Theodore Roosevelt's conservation policies primarily benefited large lumber companies. In addition, Carter piloted through the Senate the Postal Savings Bank Act of 1910, which he considered the most important legislation of his career. The senator served on various committees, such as appropriations, public lands, military affairs, census, post offices, irrigation, and relations with Canada. Throughout his years of senatorial service, Carter attempted to convince the government to aid in reclaiming arid western lands. Near the close of his term, Carter engaged in a noted filibuster, speaking for fourteen hours against a river and harbor bill, thereby preventing its passage.

Unwilling to recognize the progressive tides sweeping across the country, Carter by 1910 was out of step with the times. He had not adapted his political ideas to reflect the changing circumstances in the nation. As a result, Carter, an apostle of old guardism, shared more in common with the status quo conservative Democratic governor of Montana at the time than with his progressive Republican colleague, Senator Joseph M. Dixon, a leading figure of the Montana progressive movement, who clashed with Carter over fundamental reform issues and patronage, including direct election of senators and preferential primaries. In fact, the political differences between Carter and Dixon by 1910 on the state level mirrored to some extent the surging conservative-progressive divisions within the national party.

In 1900 and again in 1910 Carter was the caucus nominee for reelection by his party, which held a minority position in the state legislature. In 1910 he lost his seat to Democrat Henry L. Myers. President William Howard Taft appointed him chairman of the U.S. section of the International Joint Commission created to prevent disputes regarding the use of boundary waters between the United States and Canada. Shortly afterward Carter died of an infarction of the lungs in Washington, D.C. Although not among the great men his age produced, Carter received recognition beyond his rural state. Along with Dixon, Thomas James Walsh, Burton K. Wheeler, and Mike Mansfield, Carter was one of Montana's adopted sons who rose to national prominence in one hundred years of statehood.

• Carter's papers are in the Library of Congress and in the manuscript collections of various contemporaries, such as Benjamin Harrison. A small collection of his letters is available at the Montana Historical Society Archives in Helena. His speeches are in the *Congressional Record*. See his "The Republican Outlook," *North American Review* 158 (1894): 423–32. The best study of Carter is Leonard Schlup, "Gilded Age Republican: Thomas H. Carter of Montana and the Presidential Campaign of 1892," *Midwest Review* 15 (1993): 51–70. Also see Richard B. Roeder, "Thomas H. Carter, Spokesman for Western Development," *Montana: The Magazine of Western History* 39 (1989): 23–29. Information about Carter may also be found in Jules A. Karlin, *Joseph M. Dixon of Montana* (1974), and Harry J. Sievers, *Benjamin Harrison, Hoosier President* (1968). An obituary is in the *Helena Daily Independent*, 18 Sept. 1911.

LEONARD SCHLUP

CARTER, William Beverly, Jr. (1 Feb. 1921–9 May 1982), newspaper publisher and ambassador, was born in Coatesville, Pennsylvania, the son of William Beverly Carter and Maria Green. Carter grew up in Philadelphia and graduated in 1944 from historically African-American Lincoln University. As a student, he was a member of Alpha Boule, Sigma Pi Phi, and Kappa Alpha Psi, and he served as executive secretary of the alumni association from 1952 to 1955. He attended Temple University Law School from 1946 to 1947 and the New School for Social Research from 1950 to 1951.

Early in his professional career Carter worked as a reporter for the *Philadelphia Tribune*, from 1943 to 1945. He was city editor of the Philadelphia *Afro-American* from 1945 to 1948 and publisher of the Pittsburgh *Courier* newspaper group from 1955 to 1964. In 1958 he served as president of the National Newspaper Publishers Association. He made an unsuccessful run for Congress in 1954.

Carter devoted the remainder of his professional life to diplomatic service, especially in Africa, which had long held his interest. His first trip there was in 1952; eventually he visited forty countries. After joining the United States Information Agency (USIA), his first overseas post was as press attaché at the U.S. embassy in Nairobi, Kenya, from 1965 to 1966. From 1966 to 1969 he was assigned to the embassy in Lagos, Nigeria, and from 1969 to 1972 he was a department assistant to the secretary of state for African affairs in Washington, D.C. In 1972 President Richard M. Nixon appointed him ambassador to Tanzania, a post he held until 1975, when he was recalled because of his involvement in a hostage crisis controversy.

In May 1975 the Central Committee of the People's Revolutionary Party, a Marxist group that had been waging a guerrilla war for about six years against the repressive government of General Joseph Mobutu Sese Seko of Zaire, seized three Stanford University students and a French woman from an African research center. In defiance of a State Department standing order against negotiating with terrorists, Carter became involved with hostage negotiations and permitted an embassy aide to take part in the ransom payment.

Secretary of State Henry Kissinger, affronted by this individual decision making, intended to dismiss Carter but was dissuaded from doing so by aides. Instead, he slated Carter for demotion to a lower-paying post with the USIA. Carter's supporters rallied behind him, and a dinner in his honor was attended by 250 persons. The Congressional Black Caucus, contending that the U.S. position on Africa was unclear, met with Kissinger and received assurances that nothing would be done to impede Carter's State Department career. In 1976, after Senate Foreign Relations Committee hearings, at which Representative Charles Rangel (D.-N.Y.) testified for the caucus, Carter was appointed ambassador to Liberia, where he remained until 1979.

This reappointment to Liberia was still considered a demotion; Carter had been slated to be named ambassador to Denmark until Kissinger withdrew his nomination in the wake of the hostage controversy. At that time African-American senior members of the State Department represented only 4 percent of the department's total staff and were concentrated in African assignments. Nevertheless, in this new post he was honored with Liberia's highest civilian decoration, the Order of African Redemption.

Committed to civil rights both at home and abroad, Carter served from 1972 until his death as a member of the United Nations Subcommittee on Prevention of Discrimination and Protection of Minorities. In this capacity Carter was again embroiled in controversy with the U.S. government when he voted in September 1979 with the subcommittee's majority on two resolutions critical of Israeli policy. These resolutions urged Israel to negotiate with the Palestine Liberation Organization, to restore the rights of self-determination to the Palestinians, and to stop the bombardment of southern Lebanon. The U.S. State Department disassociated itself from his votes, contending that Carter was just one member of an international panel of experts who were under no instructions from their governments.

From 1979 to 1981 he served as ambassador at large, the first African American to hold that office, and as head of the State Department's Office for Liaison with State and Local Governments. When he retired from the State Department in 1981, he was given the agency's highest civilian citation, the Distinguished Honor Award. In April 1982 he received the Reverend James Robinson Award for Operation Crossroads, Africa, in recognition of his role in improving relations between the United States and the nations of Africa. At home his civil rights activities included involvement in the National Association for the Advancement of Colored People and the National Urban League; the Urban League of Philadelphia cited him for his work on human rights.

When Carter died in Bethesda, Maryland, he left a wife, the former Carlyn Brown Pogue, whom he had married in 1971, a son (by a previous marriage to Rosalie A. Terry), and two stepchildren. At the time of his death he was director of development and international affairs for the Inter-Maritime Group based in Geneva, Switzerland. In both the African hostage situation and the UN subcommittee hearings, Carter had established himself as an independent thinker unwilling to follow State Department mandates with which he did not agree. More broadly, Carter worked toward the advancement of human rights at home and abroad.

• Carter's oral history interview was presented to the New York Public Library's Schomburg Center for Research in Black Culture on 19 Apr. 1984. Obituaries are in the *New York Times*, *Washington Post*, and *Philadelphia Tribune*, all 11 May 1982; the national edition of the *Afro-American*, 15 May 1982; and *Jet*, 24 May 1982.

ARLENE LAZAROWITZ

CARTER, William Hodding, II (3 Feb. 1907–4 Apr. 1972), newspaper editor and author, was the son of William Hodding Carter, a farmer and one-term legislator, and Irma Dutartre. Born in Hammond, Tangipahoa Parish, Louisiana, he grew up in a violent frontier town where his parents taught him that Christianity and education were the superior virtues. After graduating as valedictorian of his Hammond High School class, he attended Bowdoin College in Brunswick, Maine, from 1923 to 1927. A southerner in New England, he became extremely self-conscious about his Louisiana background. He studied journalism and literature at Columbia University from 1927 through 1928, taught freshman English at Tulane University in New Orleans in 1929–1930, became a reporter for the *New Orleans Item* in 1929, and took a job with United Press International in New Orleans as night bureau manager in 1930. He served as manager of the Associated Press Bureau in Jackson, Mississippi, 1931–1932. More liberal than his contemporaries, he earned the reputation for being a "Louisiana Yankee."

In 1931 Carter married Betty Brunhilde Werlein of New Orleans. Daughter of the owners of the Werlein Music Company and graduate of Sophie Newcomb College, Betty was a talented researcher and writer and a remarkable assistant to her husband. Together they had three sons.

On 18 April 1932, in the first issue of his and Betty's newly founded *Hammond Daily Courier*, Hodding Carter promised "to make men think, to make men ashamed, and to keep men free." A man with a quick temper and a strong sense of fairness, he called Senator Huey P. Long for political tyranny. A "crawfish" who employed a corrupt machine to control the state's politics and establish himself as a virtual dictator. Long was assassinated in September 1935, and the next year his surviving political machine withdrew from the Carters' small daily newspaper, taking with it a state printing contract that was vital for the paper's survival. A shrewd businessman, Carter sold the newspaper in which he and Betty had invested less than $400 to pro-Long investors for $16,000.

Answering an invitation from writers David Cohn and William Alexander Percy, Hodding and Betty Carter moved to Greenville, Mississippi, in 1936. In the heart of the Mississippi Delta they found themselves surrounded by a small group of creative people, a few Episcopalians like themselves, and a majority of impoverished African Americans. Within the prevailing conservative social attitudes they saw the opportunity to establish an outrageously successful controversial newspaper. They founded the *Delta Star*, bought their rival *Democrat Times*, and in 1938 merged them into the *Delta Democrat-Times*. Carter traveled the country giving speeches about the South, widely publicizing his paper. For the next thirty-five years, the "*DDT*" became nationally famous as a rare liberal voice of the South.

At the beginning of World War II, Carter's strong sense of patriotism drove him to join the National Guard. When his unit was called to active duty in 1940, he went with it to Cairo, Egypt, for the war years. During that time he coauthored, with Richard Ernest Dupuy, *Civilian Defense of the United States* (1942), wrote a popular history of the Mississippi River south of Cairo, Illinois, entitled *Lower Mississippi* (1942), and penned an autobiographical novel, *The Winds of Fear* (1944).

At the end of the war in 1945, Carter returned to Greenville, where both he and his newspaper rose to national prominence. In 1946 he won the Pulitzer Prize in journalism for "Go for Broke," an editorial he had published on 27 August 1945, in which he argued that Japanese Americans should not be mistreated. He traveled around the country making speeches, which he said explained the North to the South and the South to the North. He openly debated Mississippi's reform-minded, but racist, Senator Theodore G. Bilbo, and in 1947 published *Flood Crest*, a novel in which the villain was patterned after Bilbo. Although Carter believed that African Americans should be treated fairly and equally with white citizens, he did not favor the complete integration of the races. He thought that blacks should have fair treatment in the courts and schools, and that they should have incomes equal to those of whites, but in a segregated society.

In the 1950s Carter leaped to the forefront of the national debate over civil rights. Still arguing for separate but equal facilities for both whites and blacks, he condemned Mississippi's efforts to close public schools after the U.S. Supreme Court, in *Brown v. Board of Education of Topeka* (1954), ordered them integrated. Likewise, he excoriated the popular White Citizens' Council as "a wave of terror" that threatened the South (*Look*, 22 Mar. 1955). An enraged Mississippi State House of Representatives resolved by a vote of 89 to 19 that Hodding Carter was a liar. He was "the most hated white man in Mississippi." Both amused and angry, Carter responded, with a front-page editorial in his newspaper (3 Apr. 1955), that eighty-nine of the legislators were "jackasses," and that he had voted 1 to 0 that there were eighty-nine liars in the Mississippi House. Likewise, Carter condemned black nationalists of the 1960s whose tactics reminded him of the Ku Klux Klan. Radical for his time and place in the Mississippi Delta, he was by national standards a conservative who opposed forced integration.

Carter capitalized on his fame by building his newspaper into a lucrative enterprise, making speeches for pay, and writing popular books. He wrote three books for children: *Robert E. Lee and the Road of Honor* (1955), *The Marquis de Lafayette: Bright Sword for Freedom* (1958), and *The Commandos of World War II* (1966). His popular histories include *Gulf Coast Country* (with Anthony Ragusin, 1951), *John Law Wasn't So Wrong: The Story of Louisiana's Horn of Plenty* (1951), *So Great a Good: A History of the Episcopal Church in Louisiana and of Christ Church Cathedral, 1805–1955* (with Betty Werlein Carter, 1955), *The Angry Scar: The Story of Reconstruction* (1959), *Doomed Road of Empire: The Spanish Trail of Conquest* (with Betty Werlein Carter, 1963), *Their Words Were Bullets: The Southern Press in War, Reconstruction and Peace* (1969), and *Man and the River: The Mississippi* (1970). He wrote an informal autobiography, *Where Main Street Meets the River* (1953); published a volume of poetry, *The Ballad of Catfoot Grimes, and Other Verses* (1964); and edited *The Past as Prelude: New Orleans, 1718–1968* (1968). He commented on his efforts to bring change to the South, and native resistance to it, in *Southern Legacy* (1950), *First Person Rural* (1963), and *So the Heffners Left McComb* (1965).

In the 1960s when other advocates of civil rights for African Americans demanded complete racial equality, Carter surrendered most of the editorial writing for the *Delta Democrat-Times* to his oldest son, Hodding Carter III. "Big" Hodding, as the father was nicknamed, supported Presidents John F. Kennedy and Lyndon B. Johnson and the presidential candidacy of Robert F. Kennedy in 1968. He gleaned prizes and honorary degrees. Before his death in Greenville, however, he lived to see the beginning fulfillment of his dream, his demand, that his region and nation give complete freedom to all of its citizens.

• The William Hodding Carter II Papers are located in Special Collections, Mitchell Memorial Library, Mississippi State University, near Starkville. James E. Robinson, "Hodding Carter: Southern Liberal, 1907–1972" (Ph.D. diss., Mississippi State Univ., 1974), gives a comprehensive account of his public career. Other useful sources include Carter's autobiographical writings; his obituary in the *Delta Democrat-Times*, 5 Apr. 1972; and Gene Lyons, "The Other Carters," *New York Times Magazine*, 18 Sept. 1977.

E. STANLY GODBOLD

CARTERET, Philip (1639–Dec. 1682), first deputy governor of New Jersey, was born on the island of Jersey in the Channel Islands, the son of Helier de Carteret, attorney general of Jersey, and Rachel La Cloche. He was a cousin of Sir George Carteret who, with John, Lord Berkeley, was awarded the proprietary colony of New Jersey by the duke of York in 1664. Philip Carteret was commissioned by them as deputy governor of New Jersey at the age of twenty-five. He arrived in the colony in August 1665 with thirty colonists from Jersey.

During his first period as deputy governor (1664–1672), Carteret helped to charter towns in New Jersey, encouraged immigration to the colony from Long Island and New England, sanctioned a court of judicature at Bergen, issued orders restraining the sale of liquor to American Indians, and granted large land patents to half a dozen wealthy men. The colony's government was based on the "Concessions and Agreements" of February 1665, which allowed for an elected legislative assembly, a council appointed by the governor, religious liberty, and a land system under which quitrents were paid to the proprietors.

The first assembly met in Elizabethtown in May 1668 but soon dispersed when Carteret refused council permission to sit with the representatives. Further legislative sessions were held in 1669, 1670, and 1671. The Dutch at Bergen accepted Carteret's authority, but the deputy governor faced much hostility to the collection of quitrents from New England settlers in New Jersey. These immigrants, used to free ideas of settlement and land tenure, alleged that they held land not from the proprietors but from the Indians and from grants issued by Governor Richard Nicholls, who had governed New Jersey as part of New York until 1665. In 1670 many colonists, especially those in Middletown, Shrewsbury, and Newark, refused to pay quitrents because they thought Carteret wanted to repudiate their system of town government.

In 1671 a rebellion occurred against the proprietary interest in which Captain James Carteret, the second son of the proprietor, was chosen by deputies as "president of the country." Several "Declarations" rejected the rebels' claim to exercise authority. The assembly was stripped of its power over appointments, land distribution, and charter incorporation. Governor Carteret appointed John Berry as acting deputy governor and returned to England, where he successfully defended his right to office by consulting George Carteret, who disowned his son's conduct.

James Carteret left New Jersey in 1673, and the rebellion was crushed. Political difficulties nevertheless continued. New Jersey was overtaken by the Dutch as part of their reconquest of New York in August 1673.

For some months New Jersey and New York were governed by a council of war and by a Dutch governor, Anthony Colne. After New Jersey was restored to English rule, Philip Carteret returned to assert his authority in November 1674. He reassembled his council and established it at Elizabethtown.

The original province had now split into two, with Sir George Carteret retaining the proprietorship of East Jersey, the northern portion, and Quaker assigns of Berkeley taking charge of West Jersey, the southern portion. The two divisions remained separate until they were combined in 1702 to form the royal province of New Jersey. When the partition came into effect in 1676, Philip Carteret became deputy governor of East Jersey, a position he retained until 1680 and again held in 1681–1682.

Carteret administered East Jersey with some success, but his authority was challenged by Sir Edmund Andros, lieutenant governor of New York. From August 1678 Andros, acting on behalf of the duke of York, considered he had jurisdiction over all of the Jerseys and wanted to impose his authority on both divisions. He insisted that all vessels bound for East Jersey should put in at New York to pay customs, a claim Carteret rejected on the grounds that "it was by His Majesty's command that this government was established."

Andros and Carteret soon became locked in a battle over who had the right to govern New Jersey. Andros provoked Carteret greatly by claiming that the latter was governing illegally under the duke's patent. Refusing to surrender East Jersey, Carteret was seized and taken into custody, on Andros's orders, in 1680 and tried in New York by a special court of assize. The jury found Carteret not guilty but ruled, under Andros's pressure, that Carteret could return to East Jersey but not assume any jurisdiction there. Andros informed the East Jersey assembly that they would be subject to the duke's laws; he met little opposition.

Unfortunately for Carteret, the proprietor Sir George Carteret died in January 1680, just when he needed to enlist his help. Then came a stroke of luck. Andros was recalled to England in August 1680 on the duke's order after William Penn and his associates had virtually forced the duke of York to relinquish his claims to New Jersey. Philip Carteret resumed his position in East Jersey in March 1681. Also in 1681 Carteret married Elizabeth Smith Lawrence; they had no children.

In October 1681 Carteret quarreled with the assembly because he refused to restore some of the powers taken away from it in 1672. He and his council lost the confidence of the people and their representatives. He dissolved the assembly in November 1681 after it insisted that its full powers be restored. Carteret also antagonized the New York government by asserting a claim to Staten Island. Whereas in his first years in New Jersey he could claim to be at the mercy of conflicting proprietorial claims beyond his control, in these final years as deputy governor he courted controversy by acting high-handedly. His political career in New Jersey began and ended in turmoil. In November 1682 he relinquished his position to Thomas Rudyard, deputy governor for the twenty-four proprietors who now owned the province. Carteret died in Elizabeth, New Jersey.

• The main source of printed information on Carteret's activities is ed. William A. Whitehead et al., *Archives of the State of New Jersey*, 1st ser., vol. 1, *Documents Relating to the Colonial, Revolutionary and Post-Revolutionary History of the State of New Jersey* (1880). A slim pamphlet containing some of his correspondence is *New Jersey: Autograph Letters from Philip Carteret, First Governor of New Jersey, 1672–1682* (1934), a limited edition of fifty copies. His family background is outlined in Catharina Romana Baetjer, *Carteret and Bryant Genealogy* (1887), and Willis Fletcher Johnson, "The Story of the Carterets," *New Jersey Historical Society Proceedings*, n.s., 9 (1924): 328–33. John E. Pomfret wrote several good appraisals of Carteret's career, *The Province of East New Jersey 1609–1702: The Rebellious Proprietary* (1962; repr. 1981); *The New Jersey Proprietors and Their Lands* (1964), and "Philip Carteret," in *The Governors of New Jersey 1664–1974*, ed. Paul A. Stellhorn and Michael J. Birkner (1982). Essential context is in John A. Latschar, "East New Jersey 1665–1682: Perils of a Proprietary Government" (Ph.D. diss., Rutgers Univ., 1978); Edwin P. Tanner, *The Province of New Jersey, 1664–1738* (1908); and Aaron Leaming and Jacob Spicer, eds., *The Grants, Concessions, and Original Constitutions of the Province of New Jersey* (1758).

KENNETH MORGAN

CARTER FAMILY. *See* Carter, A. P., and Sara Carter; and Carter, Maybelle.

CARTWRIGHT, Alexander Joy, Jr. (17 Apr. 1820–12 July 1892), baseball pioneer and businessman, was born in New York City, the son of merchant ship captain Alexander Joy Cartwright and Ester Rebecca Burlock. At age sixteen, when his family suffered financial reverses, Cartwright left school to clerk for a Wall Street brokerage firm. In 1842, now a teller at New York's Union Bank, he married Eliza Ann Gerrits Van Wie; they had five children. Three years later, in partnership with his younger brother Alfred, he opened a bookstore on Wall Street. For recreation he played "base ball," a relatively unsophisticated ball and bat game descended from the British children's game of rounders.

In the spring of 1845 Cartwright proposed to his ballplaying friends that they organize formally. During the summer he helped recruit additional members for the club, and on 23 September the Knickerbocker Base Ball Club was established. The club's innovative playing rules were very possibly devised by Cartwright, although this chief claim to his fame cannot be verified, and transformed baseball from casual recreation for children and youth into sport for adults. The Knickerbocker rules form the foundation of the modern game. They established a more "manly" distance between bases (29.7 paces, about the same as today's ninety feet), a distance 50 percent greater than that typical of earlier versions of the game. The rules also divided the field into fair and foul territory, narrowing the playing area. The division encouraged a more disciplined style of play and created a place for the spectators that the game soon attracted. And the Knickerbocker rules eliminated the practice of putting out baserunners by hitting them with a thrown ball, a change that not only promoted greater dignity on the field, but also led to the use of a harder ball, and concomitantly swifter play.

Cartwright did not witness the explosion of baseball clubs throughout New York and Brooklyn that the Knickerbocker game inspired in the 1850s, or the rapid expansion of baseball into the Midwest and South in the 1860s. In March 1849, lured by the discovery of gold in California, he set off overland for the West Coast, introducing baseball to settlers and travelers along the way. Upon his arrival at San Francisco in August, however, he contracted dysentery and left almost immediately for the Sandwich (Hawaiian) Islands to recuperate. Hired as bookkeeper to a ship chandler in Honolulu, Cartwright was induced to accompany a cargo of sweet potatoes bound for California. He had planned to remain in the United States, but the lure of Hawaii overcame him. After one more voyage to California, he returned to Honolulu permanently and sent for his wife and children.

Within a year of his arrival in Hawaii Cartwright founded Honolulu's fire department, which he directed as fire chief for several years. In 1852 he laid out a baseball field in the city's Makiki Park and—using the ball and the Knickerbocker rules he had brought with him from New York—introduced baseball to the receptive Hawaiians before the game was known in most of the United States.

Cartwright prospered in Hawaii. Until the whaling industry abandoned the islands, he served as an agent for New York whaling ships. He helped found numerous businesses, including Bishop and Company, which grew into a prominent Honolulu bank. Through his principal firm, Cartwright and Company, he engaged in banking, insurance, and estate management. He developed a close friendship with Hawaii's King Kamehameha IV and served as financial advisor and diplomat for successive generations of Hawaii's royal family.

Among Cartwright's many civic activities were founding and administrative roles in Honolulu's American Seaman's Institute, the Honolulu Library and Reading Room, the Queen's Hospital, and the Masonic Hawaiian Lodge No. 21. He retained his interest in baseball beyond his playing days and attended the games of clubs he had organized. Although he was long one of Honolulu's most prominent and respected residents, Cartwright rejected Hawaiian citizenship, remaining "an enthusiastic American" until his death a few months before the Hawaiian monarchy was overthrown and the islands became American territory.

Cartwright's contribution to the creation of modern baseball was all but forgotten until the latter 1930s. A grandson wrote to the newly organized National Baseball Hall of Fame in Cooperstown, New York, challenging the claim that General Abner Doubleday had invented baseball and setting forth his grandfather's qualifications for the honor. The evidence proved sufficiently persuasive to gain Cartwright election to the Hall of Fame in 1938. He was enshrined the following year in the Hall's first induction ceremonies, which formed, ironically, a focus for baseball's centennial celebration of General Doubleday's alleged invention of the game. In Honolulu, Makiki Park was renamed Cartwright Park.

• The Alexander Cartwright file at the National Baseball Library, Cooperstown, N.Y., contains copies of articles, documents, and letters by and about Cartwright. Robert W. Henderson, *Ball, Bat and Bishop: The Origin of Ball Games* (1947), first explored in a scholarly way the origins of baseball and Cartwright's role in founding the Knickerbocker Club. Harold Peterson's biography, *The Man Who Invented Baseball* (1973), slights Cartwright's Hawaiian years but employs Cartwright's journal to trace in detail his 1849 trek across America. The *Hawaiian Gazette* (19 July 1892) contains Cartwright's obituary and reprints a biographical sketch from Hawaii's *Commercial Record*.

FREDERICK IVOR-CAMPBELL

CARTWRIGHT, Peter (1 Sept. 1785–25 Sept. 1872), Methodist clergyman, was born in Amherst County, Virginia, the son of Peter Cartwright and Christiana Garvin Wilcox, poor farmers of English descent. In 1791 the family moved to Lincoln County and then to Logan County, Kentucky, where Cartwright attended camp meetings. In 1801 he experienced a conversion and joined his mother's Methodist society. Within a year he received a license as a Methodist exhorter to assist preachers in worship. When his parents moved again, he organized a Methodist circuit in Livingston County. The next year he felt called to preach and in 1804 joined the Western Annual Conference, being appointed by Bishop Francis Asbury to the Salt River and Shelby circuit. Along with his pastoral duties he read theology and studied grammar with his presiding elder, William McKendree. In 1806 Asbury ordained him deacon, and in October 1808, McKendree, now a bishop, ordained him elder. Although early Methodists discouraged clerical marriage, Cartwright had in August married Frances Gaines, with whom he would have nine children. Settling with his wife on a farm in Christian County, Kentucky, he continued to ride Methodist circuits.

In 1812 Cartwright became presiding elder of a district that extended into Indiana Territory. There he supervised about twenty circuit preachers, while continuing to preach and hold quarterly conferences. The next two decades saw him advance in the denomination, as his colleagues elected him a delegate to the 1816 General Conference, the first of thirteen that he attended as a delegate. He defended Methodist theology and practice both in oral and pamphlet debates, notably in an 1822 conflict over predestination with Presbyterians in Kentucky. Sporting a broad-brimmed, Quaker-style hat, he would publicly excoriate Baptists and Calvinists, declaiming as well against whiskey, slavery, and "superfluous ornament, or extravagant dress of any kind."

While serving as a presiding elder in the Tennessee Conference (1812–1816) and in the Kentucky Conference (1821–1824), Cartwright censured fellow Methodists who accepted slavery. His dislike for the institution led him to transfer in 1824 to the Illinois Conference. He and his family moved to Sangamon County, settling fifteen miles northwest of Springfield in a community that he called "Pleasant Plains," his home until his death. After two years as preacher in charge of the Sangamon circuit, Cartwright in 1826 became presiding elder of Illinois District, and he held the same office continuously in other districts in the Illinois Conference until 1869.

Unlike Kentucky, Illinois allowed clergy to hold public office. Cartwright joined the antislavery forces and aligned himself, alongside other Methodists, with factions that drifted toward the Whig party, where they became known as the "Methodist Militia." Cartwright ran four times for election to the lower house of the state legislature, winning twice (1828, 1832) and losing twice (1826, 1830). In the 1832 campaign, he placed fourth in an at-large contest to elect four; eighth, and thus defeated, was Abraham Lincoln.

As a legislator, Cartwright promoted canals, roads, and bridges; he also introduced a bill to found a state university at Springfield. He sponsored legislation against "vice and immorality," designed to prevent drunks and rowdies from disturbing church meetings. He joined the majority that applauded President Andrew Jackson for moving against nullification in South Carolina, and by the mid-1830s he was a Jacksonian Democrat. An unsuccessful candidate in 1835 for the state senate, Cartwright later reflected that "I left politics years ago, or rather politics left me." But he avowed that "if the people . . . would select honest and capable men, I can not see the impropriety of canvassing for office on Christian principles" (*Autobiography*, p. 261).

In church politics, Cartwright joined the successful drive between 1820 and 1824 to retain for bishops their power of appointing presiding elders—a victory that led the opponents of episcopal power to form a separate Methodist Protestant church. He supported efforts to prevent abolitionists from discussing slavery at the General Conferences of 1836 and 1840, but he also supported the 1844 conference decision to ask slave-holding bishop James O. Andrew to refrain from episcopal duties while he held slaves. After southerners in 1846 formed the Methodist Episcopal Church, South, Cartwright joined the forces that refused to accept the legality of their action, denouncing "these slavery-loving preachers" as "ungodly seceders."

In 1846 Cartwright returned briefly to secular politics, running as a Democrat for the U.S. House of Representatives against Abraham Lincoln, alleging that his opponent's religious views made him unacceptable. Cartwright received only 42 percent of the vote. The next year he failed to gain election as a delegate to the state constitutional convention. He had continuing victories, however, within his denomination. Having launched the *Central Christian Advocate* in 1852 at St. Louis as virtually his own periodical, with his son-in-law as editor, Cartwright succeeded in persuading the 1856 General Conference to adopt the paper officially.

Cartwright gained an almost mythic status within Methodism after the publication in 1856 of *Autobiography of Peter Cartwright, the Backwoods Preacher*, a book that rehearsed his experiences, beginning with the rough life of the early West. He launched a series of lecture tours that eventually extended from the Midwest to the East Coast and then back to Nebraska. From the platform, the pulpit, and in at least one autograph-book sentiment, he delighted in presenting himself as "a good old Methodist preacher" who was "fully opposed to all innovations." In 1859 Cartwright was called to testify in the trial of a grandson accused of murder. The youth was acquitted; his attorney was Abraham Lincoln.

During the secession winter of 1860–1861, Cartwright rallied to the cause of the nation as a self-described "War Union Douglas Democrat." He ran unsuccessfully as a delegate to the 1862 constitutional convention in Illinois, but his clerical colleagues, after failing to send him to the 1864 General Conference, elected him again as a delegate in 1868. The Illinois Conference in 1869 acclaimed his fifty-year ministry in the office of presiding elder with a jubilee celebration. He responded to the denomination's adulation by compiling *Fifty Years as a Presiding Elder* (1871) and by continuing to preach and lecture as conference missionary.

Cartwright died at Pleasant Plains, two days after his conference renewed his missionary appointment. A half century later the United Methodist church designated as a "national heritage landmark" the Peter Cartwright Church in Pleasant Plains. His autobiography gave him the status of the archetypal frontier Methodist circuit preacher, colorful in his actions and colloquial in his language. The *St. Louis Republican* summed up his repute: "A great number of anecdotes are told concerning this singular man, many of which are true" (Agnew [1953], p. 443).

Cartwright declared in his last will and testament that he was "by profession a farmer," but he was also an example of upward mobility who cherished his honorary doctorate from McKendree College even while ridiculing the pretensions of refined clergy. He typified a chapter in the history of American eccentric personality into being a major actor in the folklore of America.

• The largest collection of Cartwright's papers is in the Archives of the Illinois Great Rivers Annual Conference (United Methodist church) and the Illinois State Historical Library, Springfield. The manuscript of his autobiography is in the Ohio Historical Society Archives Library. The most detailed biography is Theodore L. Agnew, "Peter Cartwright and His Times, the First Fifty Years, 1785–1835" (Ph.D. diss., Harvard Univ., 1953), which has bibliographical data. See also Philip M. Watters, *Peter Cartwright* (1910), Helen Hardie Grant, *Peter Cartwright, Pioneer* (1931); Agnew, "Methodism on the Frontier," in *The History of American*

Methodism, ed. Emory S. Bucke, vol. 1 (1964); M. H. Chamberlin, "Rev. Peter Cartwright, D.D.," *Illinois State Historical Society Transactions* (1902): 27–56; Harry E. Pratt, "Peter Cartwright and the Cause of Education," *Illinois State Historical Society Journal* 28 (1935–1936): 271–78; Marie S. White, "The Methodist Antislavery Struggle in the Land of Lincoln," *Methodist History* 10, no. 4 (1972): 33–65; Robert Bray, "Beating the Devil: Life and Art in Peter Cartwright's *Autobiography*," *Illinois Historical Journal* 78 (1985): 179–94; Katharine L. Dvorak, "Peter Cartwright and Charisma," *Methodist History* 26 (1987–1988): 113–26; and Richard Chrisman, "Peter Cartwright as a Presiding Elder," *Methodist History* 27 (1988–1989): 151–62. A summary of genealogical data appears in Harry G. Newman, Jr., "The History and Heritage of the Reverend Peter Cartwright," *Historical Messenger* 26 (1994): 1–4.

THEODORE L. AGNEW

CARTWRIGHT, Samuel Adolphus (3 Nov. 1793–2 May 1863), physician and slavery advocate, was born in Fairfax County, Virginia, the son of John S. Cartwright, a minister; his mother's name is unknown. His early medical studies with a local physician, John Brewer, were interrupted by the War of 1812. While serving with Tanson's artillery, Cartwright was wounded in the battle of North Point (12 Sept. 1814) and discharged.

Enrolling at the University of Pennsylvania, Cartwright was introduced to the theories of Benjamin Rush. He then pursued further study in Baltimore and at Transylvania University in Lexington, Kentucky. He practiced briefly in Huntsville, Alabama, and Hamilton, Mississippi, before settling in Natchez, Mississippi, in 1822. A year later he won a prize for an essay recounting a yellow fever epidemic in Monroe County. Cartwright's diagnosis of yellow fever later proved incorrect, but the article launched his career as a medical author. In the 1820s he wrote on treatments for yellow fever, syphilis, cholera, emphysema, and epilepsy; "Whether the Veins Perform the Function of Absorption"; the uses of iodine; and diseases endemic to the South. His reputation grew as he garnered more prizes, and he turned down offers of professorships at several northern universities. Work during an 1832–1833 cholera epidemic increased his prominence.

In 1825 Cartwright married Mary Wren, the daughter of a Natchez physician, with whom he had two children who survived to adulthood. An ardent Democrat, he helped found the first Jacksonian newspaper in the state, the *Mississippi Statesman and Natchez Gazette*, and served as coeditor during its existence (1826–1830). Well-versed in Latin, Greek, and Hebrew, he was also a classical and biblical scholar of some repute.

An eighteen-month tour of Europe in 1836 and 1837 allowed Cartwright to study and lecture at leading hospitals. His treatise on yellow fever was officially endorsed by the French government. In Paris, while undergoing treatment for increasing deafness that had plagued him since the war, he received word that the New Orleans bank that held his considerable fortune had collapsed. Financial problems thus necessitated a recommitment to his Natchez practice, but Cartwright continued his writing and research, increasingly focusing on what he believed to be predominantly southern diseases. He served as president of the Mississippi Medical Society in 1846 and treated several well-known patients, including Governor John A. Quitman, Jefferson Davis, and their families. Although he labeled self-medication and quackery the "main cause of the great mortality of this valley" (*Western Journal of Medicine and Surgery*, 3d ser., 1[1848]), Cartwright employed many of the drastic and dubious treatments common to his day. When called to aid one of Quitman's daughters, her sister recorded that "he told us that her head was affected and that leeches must be applied"; he also suggested that she take castor oil, spirits of wormwood, and "powders" (James, p. 270). Cartwright followed the monistic approach of Benjamin Rush, proposing that black tongue, erysipelas, spotted fever, putrid sore throat, cold plague, typhoid pneumonia, and malignant scarlet fever were all actually the same disease—diphtheria.

During an 1848 visit to New Orleans to conduct cholera studies at the Charity Hospital, Cartwright decided to relocate his practice. His 1849 pamphlet, *Pathology and Treatment of Cholera*, attracted national attention, and a year later he started publishing his series "Report on the Diseases and Physical Peculiarities of the Negro Race" (*New Orleans Medical and Surgical Journal* 7–10 [1850–1853]), beginning the most notable and controversial period of his career. Cartwright, who had already been dubbed by physician John Bell the "champion of states' rights medicine" in 1846, mixed philosophy, religion, patriotism, elitism, and white supremacy with medicine into his racial theories. He declared that blacks were immune to many diseases because God had ordained them for "drudgery work under a Southern sun." The "differences in the organic or physical characters" were "imprinted by the hand of Nature on the two races." This "immutable law" had "made the white race rulers, and enjoined on them a life of temperance and self-control, to qualify them for the high and responsible trust, of preserving in all their purity those wise institutions founded on virtue, economy and the fitness of things, bequeathed them by Washington and the sword of their fathers" (*New Orleans Medical and Surgical Journal* 10 [1853]: 312–13). Whites who did not respect this natural order and engaged in labor that Cartwright felt was intended for blacks were susceptible to the plagues of the lower classes. He attributed various forms of typhus to despotism, ignorance, vice, extravagance, high taxes, poverty, filth, and disregard of natural law.

However, black immunity did not extend to ailments peculiar to the race, such as drapetomania, "the disease causing negroes to run away," and dysaesthesia, lethargy or rascality. "Like children," wrote Cartwright, blacks "require government in every thing; food, clothing, exercise, sleep—all require to be prescribed by rule, or they will run into excesses." He also pointed out that "the blackest negroes were always the healthiest, and the thicker the lips and the flatter the nose the sounder the constitution." He believed the Negro race to be "more like the monkey tribes and the lower order of animals than any other species of the genus man" (Elliott, p. 707).

The sectional strife of the 1850s created an audience willing to believe Cartwright's theories. In 1851 he was appointed professor of "diseases of the Negro" at the University of Louisiana (now Tulane), adding scholarly weight to his conclusions. The *New Orleans Medical and Surgical Journal* served as the primary vehicle for his medically related ideas, while he championed slavery in *De Bow's Review*. Cartwright also became a proponent of what he called the "sugar-house cure," whereby patients with consumption could be healed by spending time in Louisiana sugar houses during refining season (*Boston Medical and Surgical Journal* 47 [1853]).

Early in the Civil War Cartwright proclaimed that troops needed sugar and molasses to prevent disease (New Orleans *Daily Delta*, 22 Sept. 1861), and the following year he advised his friend Jefferson Davis that slaves should be used as soldiers in place of "our tenderly bred gentlemen" (*Davis Papers*, vol 8; p. 143). In January 1863 Davis secured an appointment for Cartwright as a Confederate medical inspector in Mississippi. Nearly deaf and weakened by an extended illness the previous summer, he threw himself too vigorously into the work, became incapacitated while visiting a Vicksburg encampment, and died at a private residence near Jackson, Mississippi. Although a respected physician during his time, Cartwright is remembered primarily for his racial theories.

• Cartwright's papers are at Louisiana State University. Cartwright's "Slavery in the Light of Ethnology," in *Cotton is King, and Pro-Slavery Arguments*, ed. E. N. Elliott (1860), summarizes his medical-racial theories. He also authored *Some Account of the Asiatic Cholera* (1832) and *Essays, Being Inductions Drawn from the Baconian Philosophy Proving the Truth of the Bible* (1843), in addition to numerous articles. Though not entirely accurate, Mary Louise Marshall, "Samuel A. Cartwright and States' Rights Medicine," *Louisiana State Medical Society Journal* 93 (1940): 74–78, remains the most complete account of his career. His European travels are the subject of Robert L. Savant, ed., "A Southerner's Sojourn in Europe: The Journal of Samuel Adolphus Cartwright, 1836–1837" (M.A. thesis, Northwestern State Univ., 1974). Much of his correspondence with Davis appears in vols. 4–9 of *The Papers of Jefferson Davis* (1983–1997). D. Clayton James, *Antebellum Natchez* (1968), includes several references to Cartwright's service in that community. An obituary is in the New Orleans *Daily Picayune*, 13 May 1863.

KENNETH H. WILLIAMS

CARTY, John Joseph (14 Apr. 1861–27 Dec. 1932), electrical engineer and research administrator, was born in Cambridge, Massachusetts, the son of Henry Carty, a machinist and metal founder, and Elizabeth O'Malley. Carty grew up in Cambridge, graduating from the Cambridge Latin School before a temporary vision impediment sidetracked plans for a college education. After working for a Boston philosophical apparatus (scientific instrument) maker, he began his career in the infant telephone industry in 1879 as an operator for the Boston Telephone Despatch Company. This company was a licensee of the New England Telephone Company, which was formed by the original Bell Telephone Company.

Carty quickly applied himself to many of the technical problems that plagued early telephone transmission, proving himself a creative and resourceful engineer, though he had no formal education as such. His first significant contribution was developing (though not discovering) the "metallic" or two-wire circuit. Previously, telephone transmission had used a single wire with an earth ground—just as telegraph systems did. The metallic circuit reduced interference and allowed for longer transmission distances, though it required twice as much wiring as before. In 1881 he demonstrated this technique with a line between Boston and Providence, Rhode Island. The metallic circuit became the standard for long-distance telephone lines, and slowly local exchanges converted their single-wire systems to metallic. In 1884 Carty became superintendent of the Boston exchange. He continued developing and implementing new techniques, such as using a centralized "common battery" for multiple phones (rather than requiring separate batteries in each phone). This development, like the metallic circuit, would shape telephone system design well into the next century.

In 1887 Carty transferred to the cable department of the Western Electric Company, the equipment manufacturing arm of the American Bell Telephone Company, in New York City. Two years later he became electrician for the Metropolitan Telephone and Telegraph Company, which was the local Bell company for New York, and in 1893 he became chief engineer at Metropolitan. Here he designed a "bridging ringer"—a high-impedance bell wired in parallel across the telephone circuit. With this device, a relatively high voltage signal would ring the bell, while low-voltage voice transmission would largely bypass the high-impedance device. This achievement made possible the party line (multiple telephones on a single circuit). He received the Edward Longstreth Medal of Merit from the Franklin Institute in 1903 for this work. He also found a practical way to implement a phantom circuit, a method of using two sets of circuits (four wires) to carry a third (phantom) circuit, without interfering with the original two circuits. Finally, in 1891 he developed a theory for the removal of "cross-talk" or electrostatic interference from lines that are strung in close proximity. He achieved this through the simple method of crossing the lines at set intervals (dependent on the total distance of the lines). In total, Carty was awarded twenty-four patents, all between the years 1883 and 1896. In 1891 he married Marion Mount Russell; they had one child.

Carty slowly migrated from engineering to management positions within the Bell system. Though much of the technology was rapidly outpacing his on-the-job education, he took with him a great respect for the potential that scientific and engineering research held for telephony. At a time when business leaders were only beginning to understand the relationship between science and industry, Carty was a strong proponent of commercial research and development. As early as the 1890s Carty saw the growing importance of the engineer within the corporate structure. In the next decade Carty advocated science and fundamental research as part of the corporate mission.

When Theodore M. Vail became president of American Telephone and Telegraph (AT&T) in 1907, he replaced the company's chief engineer, Hammond Hayes, with Carty. Vail and Carty had known each other from their days working in Boston, where Vail was general manager of Bell Telephone. While Carty's appointment reflected a corporate shift toward increased industrial research, Carty himself saw an opportunity to expand AT&T's technological control of telephony through an aggressive research program. At the same time he ambitiously centralized control of research within the company. Carty held the position of chief engineer until 1919, forging the path for what would become Bell Laboratories in 1925. His first major task was to centralize the disparate engineering functions of the company, closing the Chicago and Boston offices and moving most of their functions to the New York laboratory.

Carty was pivotal in the institution of the Research Branch within the Engineering Department of the Western Electric Company in 1911. The impetus behind the Research Branch was Carty's belief that AT&T's long-term growth depended on new technologies. The company could acquire innovations through the purchase of patents or by producing their own in-house. AT&T ultimately did both, though Carty was important in eliciting support from upper management for "fundamental" research, all the while keeping AT&T's business imperative in mind. Though the swiftly changing field of electrical engineering meant that Carty was no longer performing a significant engineering function within the company, he instead used his management position as a bridge between upper management and the scientists and engineers. Working underneath Carty and keeping him abreast of scientific and technological developments were notable figures such as Frank Jewett, Edwin Colpitts, and Harold Arnold.

Behind the establishment of the Research Branch lay AT&T's goal of transcontinental telephone transmission. As of 1911 AT&T's trunk lines could handle a call from New York to Denver (making use of loading coils) but nothing longer. Carty sought an improved repeater, a device to receive the original signal and retransmit it with renewed electrical strength, and received the support of the board of directors to pursue this line of research. This was the first task of the Research Branch. The branch ultimately bought the rights in 1913 for Lee de Forest's "audion" (an early vacuum tube) and improved and adapted it for telephone use. In 1915 the first commercial transcontinental line was opened using the audion. Carty's role was not that of researcher, but as a manager and proponent of research. He tightly coordinated managerial support for directed research aimed at technologies that would aid AT&T or produce valuable patents. He also went to great lengths to publicize such technical achievements, a move that garnered further corporate support and respect for AT&T's research capacity (not to mention Carty himself).

At the same time that the Research Branch was developing the audion, Carty pushed the company to explore radio transmission. Though AT&T was not in the radio business, he believed that the technology, if sufficiently improved by others, could interfere with AT&T's telephone market. The laboratory researched radio from 1913 to 1915, in the process successfully transmitting voice messages across the Atlantic Ocean. The knowledge gained by AT&T was used not to commercially exploit radio, but to protect its telephone business by holding key radio transmission patents.

After the United States became embroiled in World War I, Carty assisted the U.S. military in technical matters. He entered the Army Signal Corps in 1917 as a major in the Officers' Reserve Corps and coordinated efforts by Bell's research staff to meet the wartime needs of the army and navy. He helped select and organize the twelve battalions of AT&T personnel who would serve the Signal Corps and advised the army and navy on technical matters relating to communication. In August 1917 he was promoted to colonel. In addition to his duties for the Signal Corps, Carty served on the newly created National Research Council as chair of its executive committee. Carty received his discharge in 1919, though he remained in the Officers' Reserve Corps. In 1921 he was promoted to brigadier general. He received the Distinguished Service Medal from General John Joseph Pershing and the Cross of the Legion of Honor from France for his contributions to the war.

Carty's numerous other awards, honors, and positions included honorary fellow, American Electro-Therapeutic Association, 1893; president, New York Electrical Society, 1903–1904; honorary member of the Franklin Institute and recipient of its Franklin Medal, 1916; president, American Institute of Electrical Engineers (AIEE), 1915–1916; fellow, American Academy of the Arts and Sciences; Edison Medal (AIEE), 1917; John Fritz Medal (AIEE), 1928; member, board of trustees, Carnegie Corporation; trustee, Carnegie Institution of Washington; member, National Academy of Sciences; and recipient of the Japanese Imperial Order of the Rising Sun, 1909, the Japanese Imperial Order of the Sacred Treasure of the Meiji, 1912; and the Carty Medal (named for him) from the National Academy of Sciences in 1932.

Carty retired from his position as chief engineer in 1919 and became vice president in charge of AT&T's Department of Development and Research. In 1925, when Bell Telephone Laboratories was officially formed, Carty became its first board chair. He retired from both positions in 1930. Carty died at Johns Hopkins in Baltimore, Maryland, and was buried at Arlington National Cemetery.

Carty was instrumental to the development of telephony and helped shape the emerging field of industrial research. In the late nineteenth century Carty produced a number of technical advances for what would later become the American Telephone and Telegraph Company. As he progressed from engineering positions to management positions, his abilities and leadership became increasingly important to the formation of a dedicated research capacity within AT&T. In the early twentieth century his outspoken belief in the value of science and engineering to industry made him a prominent public figure in the rise of American industrial research.

• The AT&T Bell Laboratories Archives in Murray Hill, N.J., hold a great deal of primary source material, including Carty's executive files. Another fruitful source is the Federal Communications Commission, *Investigation Pursuant to Public Resolution #8*, 74th Cong. (77 vols., 1937–1938), FCC Library, Washington, D.C. A bibliography of Carty's writings and speeches is in Frank B. Jewett, "Biographical Memoir of John Joseph Carty, 1861–1932," National Academy of Sciences, *Biographical Memoirs* 18 (1938): 69–91. The standard, though uncritical, source of biographical information is Frederick Leland Rhodes, *John J. Carty: An Appreciation* (1932). For technical achievements, see M. D. Fagen, ed., *A History of Engineering and Science in the Bell System: The Early Years (1875–1925)* (1975). For Carty's role in the growth of industrial research, see Leonard S. Reich, "Industrial Research and the Pursuit of Corporate Security: The Early Years at Bell Labs," *Business History Review* 54, no. 4 (Winter 1980): 504–29.

ROBERT G. FERGUSON

CARUS, Paul (18 July 1852–11 February 1919), editor, author, and philosopher, was born in Ilsenburg, Germany, the son of Dr. Gustav Carus, the first superintendent-general of the Church of Eastern and Western Prussia, and Laura Krueger. As the son of a well-known theologian and state church official, Carus was afforded an appropriate Gymnasium education, which focused on mathematics and the classics. He studied at the Universities of Greifswald, Strasbourg, and Tübingen, eventually earning his Ph.D. degree from Tübingen in 1876. His first professional position was as an educator at the military academy in Dresden, an appointment he soon resigned because of conflicts over his liberal religious views. He then lived briefly in England (1881–1884) before traveling to the United States and settling in LaSalle, Illinois, where he lived for the remainder of his life.

At the outset of his literary career in America, Carus published several articles in a new journal called *Open Court*, founded in 1887 by Chicago manufacturer Edward C. Hegeler and devoted to current issues in religion and ethics. Shortly thereafter Carus became editor of *Open Court*, a position he maintained from 1887 until his death. His personal relationship with the manufacturer was enhanced by his marriage to Hegeler's daughter Mary in 1888. He also edited the *Monist*, a somewhat more technical quarterly, from 1890 to 1919. In addition, he was instrumental in founding the Open Court Publishing Company in LaSalle, a rather eclectic press that published inexpensive reprints of philosophical classics and new philosophical works influenced by scientific discovery.

Not merely an editor, Carus was an author of significant if unconventional reputation. Although a virtually lifelong monist (i.e., a proponent of the philosophical viewpoint that there is only one ultimate reality), he not only rejected the transcendent but also suggested that philosophy could be treated as objectively as any science. As such, he sought a scientific conception of God and, in so doing, failed to leave a profound mark on academic philosophy. One might postulate that his failure to influence academe was based on the notion that he was essentially an "outsider," or intellectual intruder, and that his rationalism was contrary to the then predominant pragmatism.

Carus was especially interested in the Buddhist religion. More particularly, he sought to defend its integrity from a variety of well-known but somewhat misguided critics and detractors, including such figures as Sir Monier Monier-Williams (compiler of the still standard *A Sanskrit-English Dictionary*) and the Reverend Spence Hardy. Carus thought that Monier-Williams, for example, sought to deride the Buddha by continually emphasizing the supremacy of Christ. Additionally, however, his criticism did not stop with these figures, as he attacked even more traditional and established scholars of Buddhism, such as the great Pāli scholar Hermann Oldenberg, arguing that Oldenberg, despite his knowledge of Buddhist philology, understood little of Buddha and as a result incorrectly understood Buddhism's genuine meaning. Nonetheless, Carus was *not* a Buddhist but emphasized the unity of all major religious traditions.

It must be noted that Carus was instrumental in bringing a variety of Asian Buddhists to the United States, including such individuals as Anagarika Dharmapala, Soyen Shaku, and D. T. Suzuki. He was fortunate to meet most of these individuals at the World Parliament of Religions, held in Chicago in 1893 as part of the Columbian Exposition. Many of these Buddhists stayed with Carus at his home in LaSalle, working on various projects for Open Court. It was there, for example, that Suzuki began work on his famous *Outlines of Mahayana Buddhism*, his first English-language book.

Along with his tasks as editor, Carus was a prolific author with more than fifty titles to his credit, a number of which continue to be widely read today. Included among his publications are *Fundamental Problems* (1889), *The Soul of Man* (1891), *The Gospel of Buddha* (1894), *Buddhism and Its Christian Critics* (1897), *Chinese Thought* (1907), *God: An Enquiry . . . and a Solution* (1908), and *Truth on Trial* (1911). In summarizing his effect on scholarship, Winston King notes: "At a time when there was little interest in Buddhism outside academic circles, and in the face of a prevalent denominational Christian prejudice against anything which sounded like religious syncretism, he pioneered in his studies and writing about Buddhism in a sympathetic vein." (*A Thousand Lives Away* [1964], pp. 44–45). The combination of all aspects of Carus's work seems to reflect an overarching attempt to bring Buddhism to the West in a fashion that was meaningful, understandable, and in keeping with Buddha's original intent, which Carus felt had diminished in Asia. Thus, as a publisher, editor, and writer, Carus had a particularly influential role in popularizing Buddhism and other Eastern religions in the West.

• In addition to those mentioned in the text, Carus's books included *Kant and Spencer: A Study of the Fallacies of Agnosticism* (1899), *The History of the Devil and the Idea of Evil* (1900), *The Foundations of Mathematics* (1908), *Philosophy as Science* (1909), and *Goethe, with Special Consideration of His Philosophy* (1915). An anthology of some of his writings was edited by Catherine Cook and published as *The Point of View* (1927). An interesting sketch of Carus is presented in William Peiris's *The Western Contribution to Buddhism* (1973). His impact on American Buddhism is considered in Rick Fields's *How the Swans Came to the Lake: A Narrative History of Buddhism in America* (1981).

CHARLES S. PREBISH

CARUSO, Enrico (25 Feb. 1873–2 Aug. 1921), opera singer, was born (and christened) Errico Caruso in Naples, Italy, the son of Marcellino Caruso, a mechanic, and Anna Baldini. When Caruso was ten his mother sent him to school for rudimentary lessons and voice training; he also studied voice privately. He became an apprentice at a mechanical plant, where his drawing ability attracted attention. He appeared in an amateur opera when he was fourteen and later sang at church services. Within months of his mother's death in 1888 Caruso's father remarried (Caruso was devoted to his stepmother). Working as a mechanic and then a factory accountant, Caruso also sang in churches and cafes for substantial pay. In 1891 he took lessons from Maestro Guglielmo Vergine, who forced him to sign a contract that amounted to extortion. At age twenty Caruso was drafted into the Italian army but was released a few weeks later when his voice was praised by a friend of his major. Caruso debuted in Naples in 1895, performing in a poor opera written by a wealthy local composer. Substantial operatic roles at Caserta and Naples followed.

Before the spring of 1896 Caruso had appeared in at least eleven different operas in Naples, Caserta, and Trapani, Italy, and also in Egypt. Although his acting ability did not equal the quality of his voice, it improved, and the speed with which he mastered roles was proof of his talent and stamina. His "golden voice" increasingly pleased the critics and the public. He extended his range from mezza voce and subsequently attained the status of a true tenor. He sang in Naples and its environs and then in Sicily. Caruso went on to win favor in several northern Italian cities and was accorded international recognition for his performance in the world premiere of Umberto Giordano's *Fedora* in Milan (1898). That same year Caruso and soprano Anna Giachetti-Botti, having starred together in Giacomo Puccini's *La Bohème*, had a child, although she was already married. (They never married but had one more child, Enrico, Jr.) In 1899 Guglielmo Vergine faced Caruso with his contract from his early days. Caruso settled out of court with Vergine by paying him 20,000 lire, thereby negating the contract.

For the next several years Caruso dazzled audiences not only in Italy but in foreign cities as well: St. Petersburg (1899, 1899–1900), Buenos Aires (1899, 1900, 1901, 1903), Moscow (1900), Warsaw (1901), Monte Carlo (1902, 1903), London (1902), Lisbon (1903), Montevideo (1903), and Rio de Janeiro (1903). Caruso made his American debut in 1903. His initial successes were substantial both at the Metropolitan Opera, where he debuted as the Duke of Mantua in Giuseppe Verdi's *Rigoletto* (23 Nov. 1903), and at Philadelphia's Academy of Music. Most notable were his performances in Verdi's *Rigoletto*, *La Traviata*, and *Aida*; Puccini's *Tosca* and *La Bohème*; Ruggero Leoncavallo's *I Pagliacci*; and Gaetano Donizetti's *Lucia di Lammermoor* and *L'Elisir d'amore*. Though contrasting sharply with New York's then-favorite star, the elegant Polish tenor Jean de Reszke, Caruso soon reigned supreme by virtue of his passionate voice, despite his round face, portly build, and ungainly acting. He eventually learned to sing roles in English, French, Latin, Neapolitan, and Spanish. In 1904 Caruso performed in Monte Carlo, Paris, Barcelona, Prague, Dresden, London, and Berlin. In 1904–1905 he returned to the United States, appearing in ten cities coast to coast. A whirlwind pattern of touring established itself during the next decade, and from late spring through early autumn he performed in Europe, followed by engagements in New York and other American cities.

World War I limited Caruso's European appearances and prompted him to return more often to South America. His generosity with fans, relatives, friends, and charities was legendary. He was sincerely amiable to well-wishers and autograph-seekers in hotel lobbies. Caruso and a good friend, baritone Antonio Scotti, were known to burst into song on the street, to the delight of their followers. Caruso also pleased his public by publishing his own clever cartoons on a weekly basis. He bought more than forty adjacent farms near Florence, Italy, where he supported more than a dozen family members and many acquaintances. He loaded his villa with furniture, art objects, stamps, coins, old costumes, and memorabilia. Caruso regularly bought Metropolitan tickets and gave them away to friends. He eventually commanded up to $2,500 per appearance at the Metropolitan and as much as $15,000 per performance in Cuba, Mexico, and South America. In addition, it is estimated that he earned $2 million by making successful recordings between 1904 and 1920; many have been reissued on modern recordings. During World War I he donated $5 million to the Italian Red Cross, and he raised money for the Allied cause by making many gratis concert appearances.

Caruso faced many personal difficulties. In 1906 he was arrested for allegedly molesting a woman in Central Park in New York. Even though the woman failed to appear in court, he was found guilty and was fined $10. His father's death in 1908 caused him great anguish, and that same year Anna deserted him for another man. In 1909 Caruso proposed marriage to a teenage shopgirl in Milan. He then had second thoughts and in 1911 was sued for breach of promise; though acquitted, he was publicly shamed. In 1910 he defied the New York Mafia's extortion demand for $15,000 on pain of death. Later that year he suffered knee and head injuries on a Munich stage (unrelated to the Mafia threat). In 1911 Anna sued him unsuccessfully for attempting to kidnap their sons. Caruso filed a countersuit for libel but soon dropped it.

In 1918 Caruso married Dorothy Park Benjamin, twenty years his junior and the daughter of Park Benjamin, a rich New York author who disinherited her a year later. The couple had one child. Caruso's performance at the Metropolitan in Fromental Halévy's *La Juive* in 1919 was acclaimed as his greatest artistic triumph. By this time Caruso had become ill, but despite the effects he continued to fulfill engagements in the United States and abroad. In 1920 he performed in *L'Elisir d'amore* at Brooklyn's Academy of Music with a broken blood vessel in his throat, and although he sang a few times more, he was never well again. While evidently recovering from pleurisy, pneumonia, and peritonitis, he returned to Naples, where he died of a ruptured internal abscess. Caruso is widely regarded as the greatest tenor in the long history of grand opera.

• The Centro Studi Carusiani in Milan, Italy, and the Enrico Caruso Museum in Brooklyn, N.Y., have a wealth of material concerning Caruso, including memorabilia, photographs, paintings, and correspondence to and from him. Literature on him is vast. Dorothy Caruso, *Enrico Caruso: His Life and Death* (1945), touchingly combines objectivity and deep affection. (She describes his singing as "a shower of stars.") Howard Greenfeld, *Caruso* (1983), is a full-scale, authoritative biography, based on meticulous research. Enrico Caruso, Jr., and Andrew Farkas, *Enrico Caruso: My Father and My Family* (1990), is richly informative, with a balanced treatment of Caruso and also of the life of Enrico Caruso, Jr., after his father's death; it includes a definitive discography, by William R. Moran, of Caruso's original recordings and also a discography, by Richard Koprowski, of post-1950 reissues. Francis Robinson, *Caruso: His Life in Pictures* (1957), and Greenfeld, *Caruso: An Illustrated Life* (1991), contain a variety of personal and professional photographs and other illustrative material, with informative captions. An obituary is in the *New York Times*, 3 Aug. 1921.

ROBERT L. GALE

CARUTHERS, Robert Lee (5 Jan. 1864–5 Aug. 1911), baseball player, was born in Memphis, Tennessee, the son of James P. Caruthers, a lawyer and judge. His mother, whose maiden name was McNeil (or McNeill), came from Kentucky. Caruthers's childhood provided few clues of his future prowess. He was a sickly child from a solid middle-class family. Concerned with propriety, his mother objected when a Memphis doctor prescribed rigorous exercise for her frail son. She especially took umbrage to Robert's pursuit of baseball, a sport that at the time was generally associated with immigrants, gambling, drinking, and rowdiness. Sports agreed with Robert, however, and though he was physically slight at 5′7″ and 138 pounds, he developed a compact, wiry body.

Caruthers's baseball career began in earnest after his family moved to Chicago. In 1882 he played amateur ball with the North End Club. The following year he moved to the Lake Views, before signing a professional contract with Grand Rapids in the Northwestern League in 1894. That year he played right field and batted .288. The next year in Minneapolis, Caruthers began to pitch as well as play the outfield. Before the season ended, his contract was purchased by the St. Louis Browns of the American Association. He appeared in 23 games, 13 as a pitcher, and had a 7–2 record while batting .256.

In 1885 Caruthers had one of the greatest years in baseball history, compiling a phenomenal 40–13 pitching record and leading the Browns to the league pennant. On a team that also included Arlie Latham and Charles Comiskey, Caruthers shared right field duties with fellow hurler Dave Foutz, and the two became the league's premier pitching duo. After the season he traveled to France with catcher Doc Bushong; from there he conducted contract negotiations with the Browns' parsimonious owner Christian Von der Ahe. His $3,200 long-distance contract earned him the nickname "Parisian Bob."

Caruthers's 30–14 pitching record in 1886 more than justified his contract. Moreover, his .334 batting average was the league's fourth highest, and his .527 slugging percentage was just one percentage point below league leader Dave Orr. On 16 August he became the first major league pitcher to collect four extra-base hits in a single game when he clouted a double, a triple, and two home runs. Only two other pitchers have duplicated that feat. Through these efforts Caruthers spearheaded the Browns to their second straight league pennant.

Caruthers led the Browns to a third consecutive pennant in 1887 when he compiled a 29–9 record as a pitcher and batted .357. (His published average was actually .459, but during this time walks were calculated as hits.) Although Caruthers was enormously popular in St. Louis, he and Foutz were sold to the Brooklyn Bridegrooms during the off-season. Ostensibly, Browns' owner Von der Ahe was angered by his team's poor performance in a 15-game World Series against the Detroit Wolverines in which St. Louis won only five games. Caruthers, whose record in that series was 4–4, further angered Von der Ahe when he and several teammates refused to play the all-black Cuban Giants in a series of exhibition games. But given that Von der Ahe sold Caruthers and Foutz for $13,500, a significant amount at that time, profit may have been his real motive.

Caruthers helped the once lowly Bridegrooms finish second in 1888 with a 29–15 record, though his batting fell off. He was strictly a pitcher during the 1889 season, and his sensational 40–11 record propelled Brooklyn to the American Association crown. The

Bridegrooms transferred to the National League for the 1890 season (they would later be renamed the Superbas, then the Dodgers), and Caruthers helped Brooklyn win the pennant with a 23–11 pitching record. It was his last stellar year in the major leagues. In 1891 he fell to 18–14, and in 1892 he returned to the Browns, who had joined the National League. That season he compiled a losing pitching record for the first time. He appeared briefly for Chicago and Cincinnati in 1893, but he finished his career in 1898 after playing for four years in the minor leagues, mostly as first baseman.

Caruthers's departure from the majors coincided with changes he was unlikely to survive. In 1893 the pitcher's mound was moved from 50 feet to 60 feet, 6 inches, from home plate, thus ushering in changes in delivery and speed characteristic of the so-called "modern game." Caruthers depended on craft, location, and what he called "headwork" to get hitters out. In more than 2,800 innings, Caruthers struck out 900 batters, logged 25 shutouts, and won 218 games while losing only 97. His lifetime .692 winning percentage is one of the highest recorded among all major league pitchers and second only to Albert Spalding's .787 among nineteenth-century pitchers.

Little is known of Caruthers's personal life other than the fact that he married and fathered at least one child. Upon retiring as a player, Caruthers worked as an umpire in several minor leagues and, in 1902 and 1903, in the newly-formed American League. While umpiring a game in the Three-I League in Peoria, Illinois, he suffered what newspapers called a "nervous collapse" and died.

• The National Baseball Library in Cooperstown, N.Y., maintains files on Caruthers. His career statistics are in *The Baseball Encyclopedia* (1985). More information is also available in Hy Turkin and Sherley Clark Thompson, *The Official Encyclopedia of Baseball* (1951); Microsoft Corporation's computer software *Complete Baseball* (1994); and David Quentin Voigt, *American Baseball*, vol. 1: *From Gentlemen's Sport to the Commissioner System* (1966). Obituaries are in the *Peoria Evening Journal*, 5 Aug. 1911, and *Sporting Life*, 12 Aug. 1911.

ROBERT E. WEIR

CARUTHERS, William Alexander (23 Dec. 1802–29 Aug. 1846), novelist, was born in Lexington, Virginia, the son of William Caruthers, a merchant and farmer, and Phebe Alexander. Caruthers was the fourth of eleven children born into the prosperous and influential family. From 1817 to 1820, he attended Washington College (later named Washington and Lee University) but did not graduate. In 1823 he received a medical degree from the University of Pennsylvania. In the summer of that year, the young physician married Louisa Catharine Gibson, daughter of a wealthy planter from Whitemarsh Island, Georgia. The couple settled in Lexington and eventually had five children.

Caruthers eagerly involved himself in numerous town functions, participating in the literary and debating societies of the college and in the village Franklin Library Company and engaging in politics as a member of the Whig party. A town trustee, Caruthers was a responsible public citizen, but his private affairs were not so secure. By the closing months of 1829, despite his wife's resources, the doctor's finances compelled him to move his family to New York City to improve his prospects.

In the plague year of 1832, Caruthers was kept busy treating cholera patients. New York City also proved important to his nonmedical career, for he befriended the prominent author James Kirke Paulding. According to Caruthers's own testimony, the two "published books together" through the press of Harper and Brothers, though some mystery surrounds the results of that collaboration. Desirous of establishing a literary name for himself, Caruthers produced his two-volume romance *The Kentuckian in New-York; or, The Adventures of Three Southerns* (1834). This humorous novel in epistolary form is significant on several counts: it contains an enlightened discussion on the wickedness of slavery; it spoofs the character of the "backwoodsman" (Davy Crockett was an acquaintance of Caruthers's aunt and uncle); and it emphasizes the African origin of the slaves, a topic that deeply engaged the author's interest. Yet Caruthers minimized the work, explaining in the epilogue that the Kentuckian was but a humorous character introduced to ensure the book's popularity.

Of greater importance are Caruthers's two historical romances, *The Cavaliers of Virginia* (1834–1835) and *The Knights of the Golden Horseshoe, a Traditionary Tale of the Cocked Hat Gentry in the Old Dominion* (1845). The first of these works focused on Bacon's Rebellion of 1676; the well-received and widely read romance was the first book-length treatment of the rebellion, the incident that Caruthers believed to be "the first germ of the American Revolution." Although the two-volume work possesses a good-natured style, it suffers from verbosity, as in the following: "'Mine host' made sundry equivocal contortions of the countenance, and practiced by anticipation several downward motions of the muscles of deglutition." As the brief excerpt suggests, Caruthers's wordiness could be annoying. Yet his writing is appreciated for its extraordinarily genial and conciliatory treatment of such issues as slavery and harmony between the North and the South. That the southern gentleman's novels attracted some notice in the North is a testimonial to his pleasant manner, especially since he once noted that "there is evidently a current in American literature, the fountainhead of which lies north of the Potomac, and in which a southerner is compelled to navigate upstream if he jumps in too far south."

The author's second, and superior, historical romance centered on the 1716 "tramontane" expedition of Lieutenant Governor Sir Alexander Spotswood and originally bore the title *The Tramontane Order*. As with *The Cavaliers*, the account proved to be of literary-historical import, for it was the first extended treatment of Spotswood's career. Caruthers stressed that remembrance and celebration of the exploits of the Virginia colony's past were incumbent on Virginians. Accordingly, he went to work researching the circumstances of the lieutenant governor's Blue Ridge expedition. By 1837, he had finished gathering his materials and was working them into a manageable format. Unfortunately, a fire destroyed his manuscript, necessitating a thorough rewrite. The story eventually ran serially in the Savannah monthly, the *Magnolia*, in 1841, receiving favorable reviews. Owing to sectional pride, however, Caruthers then allowed a Virginia-born editor in Alabama to publish the work in book form; there, for lack of distribution, it received less than its fair share of discussion.

The Knights of the Golden Horseshoe is an important work. It contains Caruthers's usual literary flaws, including young ladies' prolix commentaries filled with unlikely diction, numerous "eye-beams" and incidents of gratuitous tear-dashing (hallmarks of the sentimental school), and rather mechanical scene-shifting. In addition, the true subject of the novel resists development until the second volume, to accommodate all the love stories. Nevertheless, with its theme of heroic adventure, Caruthers's historical novel captures the imagination. The sense of excitement and divine mission to cross the wild mountains into the Valley of Virginia resonates deeply with the notion of Manifest Destiny emerging in mid-nineteenth-century America. In the inspiring words of the protagonist:

> Rouse ye up, Virginians, and sleep no longer at the portals of the world. It is not merely to explore a few insignificant water-courses, and thread an unknown mountain pass, that I would urge you, but it is to enter upon that grand inheritance which Providence opens to our acceptance. Beyond the mountains, spreads out the most wonderful country ever dreamed of by the most daring imagination.

The Knights is notable also because of its treatment of the Indians who attack Spotswood and his crew. Caruthers characteristically presents a dialogue between hero Frank Lee and the backwoodsman scout, Joe Jarvis, in which each is given a chance to voice his opinions of the "red devils." The fair Lee is inclined to grant the Indians respect and dignity; not so the scout. While the humorous Jarvis is so animated by his dislike of "Ingins" that, in dealing with a captive warrior, he begs the governor to let him "hang him a little—just a little," he appears more for local color than to express the others' attitude toward the natives. Certain diversions from historical truth do exist: Spotswood and his men encountered no great Indian threat and were not even the first white group to arrive at the Shenandoah Valley. Still, the work is an admirable, if not wholly accurate, account. Most intriguing of all, *The Knights* inaugurated an ongoing search for the tiny garnet-studded horseshoes of gold that Spotswood bestowed upon his men of the Tramontane order.

Some years prior to the publication of *The Knights*, Caruthers and his family had moved to Savannah, for in the spring of 1837 he was a charter member of the Georgia Historical Society and a member of the Georgia Medical Society, the city's board of health, and the board of aldermen. Caruthers lived a full but brief life. Contracting that great scourge of the nineteenth century, tuberculosis, he died while seeking relief at a health resort in the Georgia mountains. For his literary attention to the events of Virginia's history, Caruthers deserves some renown, having helped to shape its legendry.

• Caruthers wrote several short works, most notably, "Climbing the Natural Bridge. By the Only Surviving Witness of That Extraordinary Feat," *Knickerbocker Magazine* 12 (July 1838): 32–35. This essay, celebrating the 1818 ascent of the Virginia landmark by Washington College classmate James Hayes Piper, achieved as much celebrity as had the original climb. Caruthers also penned "Daniel Boone," in *The National Portrait Gallery of Distinguished Americans*, ed. James Herring and James B. Longacre (4 vols., 1834–1839), vol. 2, unpaged; as well as a handful of articles in *Magnolia; or, Southern Monthly*, including "The Ruins of Jamestown," *Magnolia* 3 (Jan. 1841): 14–15, and "Mesmerism," *Magnolia* 4 (Mar. 1842): 178–82.

Curtis Carroll Davis is the best source of information on Caruthers; his *Chronicler of the Cavaliers: A Life of the Virginia Novelist, Dr. William A. Caruthers* (1953) includes bibliographies. Other sources to consult include E. A. Alderman and J. C. Harris, *Library of Southern Literature*, vol. 2 (1908); Russell Blankenship, *American Literature as an Expression of the National Mind* (1931); Alexander Cowie, *The Rise of the American Novel* (1948); Richard Beale Davis, *Intellectual Life in Jefferson's Virginia, 1790–1830* (1964); Jay B. Hubbell, *South and Southwest* (1965) and *The South in American Literature, 1607–1900* (1954); J. G. Johnson, *Southern Fiction Prior to 1860* (1909); and William R. Taylor, *Cavalier and Yankee: The Old South and the American National Character* (1961).

KAREN N. SCHRAMM

CARVEL, Thomas Andreas (14 July 1906–21 Oct. 1990), corporation chairman, was born Thomas Andreas Carvelas in Athanossos, Greece, the son of a wine chemist. When he was four years old, his family moved to New York City. During the 1920s Carvel played drums and toured with a Dixieland band in the Catskill Mountains. He also worked as a mechanic in his older brother's automobile garage and served as a test driver for Studebaker automobiles. In the early 1930s Carvel contracted tuberculosis and convalesced at a sanitarium in Saranac Lake, New York. Following medical advice that he work outdoors in the countryside, he began selling ice cream from a truck as well as from a hand cart he pushed around neighborhoods in Hartsdale, New York. On Memorial Day in 1934 his truck developed a flat tire, and he stopped in a vacant parking lot, where he plugged his freezer unit into a nearby pottery shop and continued to sell ice cream. At this point he developed the idea of opening his own ice cream store. He soon earned enough money to buy the pottery store, and his first Carvel ice cream store opened at that site. Carvel credited his father's background in chemistry with encouraging him to experiment with different flavors and toppings in order to offer a wide variety of choices to consumers. While

Carvel conducted experiments and did mechanical work, Agnes Stewart, whom he married in 1937, often ran the store.

Carvel's mechanical inclinations enabled him to invent the world's first soft-serve machine, which did not pump the ice cream full of air as other machines did. Carvel sold his ice cream machine to stores, although owners found it difficult to operate, and many went into debt. Carvel soon began to sell his knowledge as well as his products, for a flat fee plus a percentage of profits. In 1941 Carvel initiated a franchise system, teaching franchise owners how to operate the machine while selling his ice cream under the Carvel name. Thus, he was among the first to employ the franchise system, which soon spread to other corporations in the food service industry. Carvel's franchise system grew steadily, so that by 1951 he had 100 stores on the East Coast.

Carvel developed a reputation as a domineering franchise owner who forced his merchants to buy virtually all of their supplies from him at prices they considered exorbitant. Carvel defended his practices, saying, "You can't run a business unless you're a tyrant" (Burstein, p. 88), and arguing, "The product has my name on it, so I get to control what goes into it" ("Old King Cone," p. 64). The tension between Carvel and his franchisees bubbled to the surface in 1957, when a group of Carvel merchants in California sued him for illegally restricting their operations with his stringent franchise contracts and purchasing requirements. The legal struggle proved long and costly, dragging on for eight years and draining Carvel's financial resources. The Supreme Court finally decided the case in Carvel's favor.

Carvel operated his franchise system out of headquarters in Yonkers, New York. Most Carvel stores were located on the East Coast, although the company operated outlets throughout America and overseas as well.

Carvel's innovations, which were legion, helped to explain his success and steady endurance in the ice cream industry. Besides serving as a model for the franchise industry, the company became famous, not only for the standard ice cream fare, such as cones and sundaes, but especially for its novelty ice cream products. Among these were the first round ice cream cookie (the Carvel "flying saucer"), the "Fudgie the Whale" ice cream cake, and specialty cakes for occasions such as Easter, Mother's Day, and Halloween (which featured creations such as "Dumpy the Pumpkin" and "Nutty the Ghost"). Carvel also pioneered successful "Buy One, Get One Free" promotions, which he introduced in 1937, and gift certificates, which he began in 1954. Carvel pioneered the use of plastic packaging in the ice cream industry, and in 1947 the corporation opened a store with an all-glass facade and a pitched roof, a design that other restaurant chains subsequently imitated. Later, in 1972, Carvel unveiled two low-fat products, "Lo-Yo" frozen yogurt and the "Thinny-Thin" frozen dietary dessert.

In 1949 the Carvel Corporation became the first franchise chain to advertise on television, with a spot on New York's WPIX. When in 1955 Carvel heard an advertisement for the opening of one of his new stores, he became irritated that the radio announcer had failed to specify that the store was located in the borough of Manhattan. As a result, he began narrating his own television and radio commercials for his corporation. These advertisements were distinguished by Carvel's gravelly voice and mangled syntax. He performed without a script, without rehearsing, and without editing his work for mistakes. Critics chided his diction and delivery, but Carvel just scoffed at the barbs, saying, "All words are just noise flying through the air" (Burstein, p. 88). Moreover, he noted, "the ice cream is good, so who cares that I sound lousy?" ("Old King Cone," p. 101). The advertisements made Carvel's voice and his products familiar to millions of Americans and became a trademark for the corporation. In addition, Carvel's advertising work pioneered the practice of corporate chiefs acting as their own spokesmen in commercials, a technique that Lee Iacocca of the Chrysler Corporation and Dave Thomas of Wendy's Hamburgers successfully followed.

In 1949 Carvel also began to operate a school for new and prospective storeowners, at first called the "Sundae School" and later dubbed "Carvel College," located in Yonkers. There potential licensees learned production and management techniques, machinery repair and maintenance, cake decoration, refrigeration, and other skills. Carvel delivered the commencement address at the school's graduation exercises, imparting his standard admonition that a storeowner should be frugal until a store becomes lucrative.

In 1956 Carvel's friend Ray Kroc asked him to join Kroc in establishing a chain of McDonalds hamburger restaurants. At the time, Carvel's ice cream business was flourishing, with over 250 franchises in the United States, so he declined Kroc's offer, opting to concentrate on the ice cream business. But Carvel did recommend to Kroc that he adopt the same building design that Carvel used (the all-glass facade with a pitched roof), as well as the franchise system for expanding his operation, advice that Kroc gainfully followed.

Carvel began public stock offerings in his corporation in 1969. However, dissatisfied with the corporation's subsequent performance on the stock market, Carvel and his wife bought back most of the stock, and the company went private in 1977, with the couple holding 93 percent of the shares.

In later years the relationship between Carvel and his franchisees remained strained, as they criticized him for being stubbornly averse to change and slow to meet the demands of competitors such as Dairy Queen, Haagen-Dazs, and TCBY (The Country's Best Yogurt). Many franchisees felt the company was stagnating and needed revitalization. In November 1989 Carvel sold his corporation, which comprised 700 franchises and was the third largest ice cream chain in the country, for over $80 million to Investcorp, an investment bank in the Middle Eastern country of Bahrain. Two years later Investcorp relocated the Carvel Corporation's headquarters to Farmington, Connecticut.

Carvel owned three homes: a 710-acre estate in Pine Plains, New York, a converted slate-roofed stable in Ardsley, New York, and a home in West Palm Beach, Florida. He died in Pine Plains.

• Several articles profile Carvel: Chris Anderson, "Meet the Presidents: Tom Carvel," *Good Housekeeping*, Nov. 1986; Patricia Burstein, "Teacher," *People*, 31 July 1978, pp. 87–88; "Old King Cone," *Forbes*, 26 June 1978; and Walter Taylor, "The Marvel of Carvel," *Westchester Illustrated*, Mar. 1981. Ronnie Telzer's "Carvel's Commercial Charisma," *Marketing Communications*, Nov. 1981, describes Carvel's advertising. Obituaries are in the *(Yonkers, N.Y.) Herald Statesman* and the *New York Times*, both 22 Oct. 1990.

YANEK MIECZKOWSKI

CARVER, George Washington (c. 1864–5 Jan. 1943), African-American scientist and educator, was born in Diamond (formerly Diamond Grove), Missouri, the son of Mary Carver, who was the slave of Moses and Susan Carver. His father was said to have been a slave on a neighboring farm who was accidently killed before Carver's birth. His mother was apparently kidnapped by slave raiders while he was very young, and he and his older brother were raised by the Carvers on their small farm.

Barred from the local school because of his color, Carver was sent to nearby Neosho in the mid-1870s to enter school. Having been privately tutored earlier, he soon learned that his teacher knew little more than he did, so he caught a ride with a family moving to Fort Scott, Kansas. Until 1890 Carver roamed around Kansas, Missouri, and Iowa seeking an education while supporting himself doing laundry, cooking, and homesteading.

In 1890 Carver entered Simpson College in Indianola, Iowa, as a preparatory student and art major. Convinced by his teacher that there was little future in art for a black man, he transferred the next year to Iowa State, where he was again the only African-American student. By the time he received his masters degree in agriculture in 1896, Carver had won the respect and love of both faculty and students. He participated in many campus activities while compiling an impressive academic record. He was employed as a botany assistant and put in charge of the greenhouse. He also taught freshmen.

The faculty regarded Carver as outstanding in mycology (the study of fungi) and in cross-fertilization. Had he not felt obligated to share his knowledge with other African Americans, he probably would have remained at Iowa State and made significant contributions in one or both of those fields. Aware of deteriorating race relations in the year of *Plessy v. Ferguson*, he instead accepted Booker T. Washington's offer in 1896 to head the agricultural department at Tuskegee Normal and Industrial Institute in Macon County, Alabama. Carver brought both his knowledge and professional contacts to Tuskegee. Two of his former teachers, James Wilson (1836–1920) and Henry C. Wallace, became U.S. secretaries of agriculture, as did Wallace's son, Henry A. Wallace. All three granted Department of Agriculture aid to Tuskegee and provided access to such presidents as Theodore Roosevelt and Franklin D. Roosevelt.

Carver's strong will led to conflicts with the equally strong-willed Washington over Carver's incompetence at administration. His contacts and flair for teaching and research protected Carver from dismissal. In both his teaching and his research his primary goal was to alleviate the crushing cycle of debt and poverty suffered by many black farmers who were trapped in sharecropping and cotton dependency. As director of the only all-black agricultural experiment station, he practiced what was later called "appropriate technology," seeking to exploit available and renewable resources. In the classroom, in such outreach programs as farmers' institutes and a wagon equipped as a mobile school, and in agricultural bulletins Carver taught how to improve soil fertility without commercial fertilizer, how to make paints from native clays, and how to grow crops that would replace purchased commodities. He especially advocated peanuts as an inexpensive source of protein and published several bulletins containing peanut recipes.

In 1905 Carver considered marrying, but he never did. Tuskegee students became his "adopted family." He was mentor to many, providing financial aid and personal guidance. Devoutly religious in a nonsectarian way, he also taught a voluntary Bible class on campus.

At the time of Booker T. Washington's death in 1915, Carver was respected by agricultural researchers but largely unknown to the general public. Long in the shadow of Washington, Carver became the heir to the principal's fame after being praised by Theodore Roosevelt at the funeral. In 1916 he was inducted into the Royal Society for the Arts in London. Then the peanut industry recognized his usefulness. In 1921 a growers' association paid his way to Washington so that he could testify at congressional tariff hearings, where his showmanship in displaying peanut products garnered national publicity. In 1923 Atlanta businessmen founded the Carver Products Company, and Carver won the Spingarn Medal of the National Association for the Advancement of Colored People. The company failed but obtained one patent and much publicity. In 1933 an Associated Press release overstated Carver's success in helping polio patients with peanut oil massages. Carver became one of the best-known African Americans of his era.

His rise from slavery and some personal eccentricities—such as wearing an old coat with a flower in the lapel and wandering the woods at dawn to commune with his "Creator"—appealed to a wide public. Advocates of racial equality, the "New South," a religious approach to science, the "American Dream," and even segregation appropriated Carver as a symbol of their varied causes. Carver made some quiet, personal stands against segregation, but he never made public statements on any racial or political issues. Thus his name could be used for contradictory goals. He relished the publicity and did little to correct the exaggerations of his work, aside from humble protestations regarding his "unworthiness" of the honors that came in increasing numbers.

Though some of this mythology was unfortunate, Carver served as a role model to African Americans and as a potent force promoting racial tolerance among young whites. The Commission on Interracial Cooperation and the Young Men's Christian Association sent him on lecture tours of white campuses in the 1920s and 1930s. On these occasions Carver adopted some white "children" into his "family" and converted dozens to the cause of racial justice. To them Carver was no "token black" but a personal friend and confidant. Indeed, many people who met Carver, Henry Ford among them, were made to feel they were "special friends."

Carver never earned more than $1,200 a year and refused compensation from peanut producers. Nevertheless he was able to accumulate almost $60,000 because he lived in a student dormitory and spent very little money. In 1940 he used his savings to establish the George Washington Carver Foundation to support scientific research—a legacy that continues at Tuskegee University. He died three years later in Tuskegee. Although his scientific contributions were meager relative to his fame, Carver's work did help hundreds of landless farmers improve the quality of their lives. And his magnetic personality and capacity for friendship inspired and enriched countless individuals.

• Carver was a prolific correspondent and saved most of the letters he received and carbons of many of his replies. These letters are in the Tuskegee University Archives along with copies of his lectures, articles, agricultural bulletins, and miscellaneous other materials, including typescripts of interviews conducted by Tuskegee personnel in the 1950s. In the 1970s the National Historical Publication Center provided funds to obtain copies of Carver materials from other archives and to microfilm the entire collection. Included in the *Microfilm Edition of the George Washington Carver Papers* are copies from the National Archives; the Library of Congress; the George Washington Carver National Monument in Diamond, Missouri; Simpson College; Iowa State University; and various individuals. Significant materials not in the microfilm edition can be found at the Michigan Historical Collections at Ann Arbor, Michigan; the Lucy Cherry Crisp Papers at East Carolina University in Greenville, North Carolina; the George Washington Carver National Monument (tapes of interviews and new acquisitions); and in two document boxes collected by Jessie P. Guzman in the Tuskegee University Archives that were not filmed. See also Rackham Holt, *George Washington Carver: An American Biography* (1943; rev. ed., 1963); Linda O. McMurry, *George Washington Carver: Scientist and Symbol* (1981); and Gary R. Kremer, *George Washington Carver in His Own Words* (1987). Obituaries appeared in most national newspapers.

LINDA O. MCMURRY

CARVER, John (c. 1576–12 Apr. 1621), *Mayflower* Pilgrim and first governor of Plymouth, was born in Doncaster, Yorkshire, England, less than ten miles up the Great North Road from Scrooby. His parents' names are unknown. He was not a member of the Scrooby (Separatist Puritan) congregation. In 1600 he married Catherine White Leggatt, and they went to London to seek their fortune in business.

As merchants, Carver and his wife made their way to Holland, and they must have been living in Leyden for some time when the Scrooby congregation arrived in 1609. Carver may have influenced the group's decision to come to Leyden through John Robinson, the pastor, whose wife Bridget was Catherine Carver's younger sister. The Carvers probably became members of the congregation in 1610 or 1611. Like many respectable Puritans of the time, Carver probably strongly adhered to purely reformist principles for some time before finally deciding to take on the radical Separatist ideas. He was first mentioned in Leyden documents in 1616 as a man of "singular Piety and Rare for humillitie." As a deacon he was immediately ranked third among the officers of the church, following Robinson and William Brewster. A successful businessman, Carver was the richest man among the Pilgrims, and his fortune helped maintain the congregation financially. He purchased the house used as the pastor's residence and the place of worship.

In September 1617, when the congregation was entertaining the possibility of immigrating to America, Carver went to England with another deacon, Robert Cushman, to obtain permission from the Virginia Company of London to settle in their country and to secure funds from a group of merchants to finance the venture. Carver, Cushman, and Christopher Martin, who was appointed as the third agent, frequently quarreled, and their original plans failed. But eventually these three men contributed in their own ways to secure a grant.

On 15 July 1620 Carver sailed on the *Mayflower* from London with the group, including Miles Standish and John Alden, to meet the Leyden contingent of thirty-five Pilgrims at Southampton. John Robinson stayed in Leyden with more than half of the congregation. Carver's wife sailed with him. On 16 September 1620 the *Mayflower* set sail from Plymouth with a combined London-Leyden group of 102 Pilgrims.

After a stormy two-month voyage, the Pilgrims came in sight of Cape Cod, having gone farther north than the Hudson River, the designated region. In order to avoid "dangerous shoals and roaring breakers" to go down to their destination, they made a temporary landing at Provincetown. The patent obtained from the Virginia Company of London now became useless, and some men threatened disobedience. The Pilgrims on 11 November drew up and signed the Mayflower Compact, pledging to form a government and to place themselves under it. Carver signed first, and altogether forty-one men, including all the free adult males and some servants, signed the document. Thereafter Carver was unanimously chosen to serve as the first governor. The choice was an easy one because Carver, an older man, a successful merchant, and a leading member of the church in Leyden, was the most substantial and respectable among them.

Although vigorous young men like William Bradford thought it vital to get the *Mayflower* to Plymouth harbor immediately, Governor Carver, older and less decisive, was anxious to give everyone a voice in the final decision. On 15 December, after full debate and deliberation, they finally voted to settle in Plymouth as their new home.

The winter of 1620–1621 was milder than average, but a viral disease similar to influenza swept through the colony in epidemic proportions. Carver, Bradford, and other leaders were among the sick, and they were nearly killed on 14 January, when a spark caught the thatched roof of the common house, where they were lying. Before the end of December six people died, in January another eight died, February claimed an additional seventeen, and in March thirteen more perished, reducing the population to almost half of the original number.

One of Carver's major accomplishments was the treaty he negotiated with the Wampanoag Indian chief, Massassoit, in March 1621. This treaty of peace and friendship, which provided mutual assistance and also secured for the colonists extraterritoriality within the settlement, served as the basis for their future security. It lasted for the remaining forty years of Massassoit's life and was renewed until 1675 by his sons.

On 25 March, the first day of the year according to the old Julian calendar, Carver was reelected as governor for a full year. Eleven days later he made the first major decision of his new term, allowing the *Mayflower* to sail for home, because he was convinced that the colony would survive without the help of the ship.

A week after the *Mayflower* sailed, while at work planting corn with many other people on an unusually hot day, Governor Carver laid down his hoe and came in from the fields complaining of a severe headache. He soon sank into a coma and died. He was buried with a simple ceremony, according to Bradford, "in ye best manner they could, with some vollies of shott by all that bore armes." His wife, a frail woman who was totally dependent on him, survived him by only five or six weeks and died of a broken heart. Carver was succeeded by Bradford, aged thirty-two, who was unanimously elected as the new governor.

Although the Carvers were childless, they brought with them to the New World six servants, all "bound out" to him. Roger Wilder and a little boy, Jasper More, died of the common infection before Carver and his wife died. Desire Minter returned to England in 1625 but died soon after. Another servant boy, William Latham, stayed in Plymouth for more than twenty years, returned to England, then went to the Bahamas, where he and some others starved to death. Catherine Carver's maid servant married in Plymouth but died a year or two later. The Carvers left their entire estate to John Howland, the thirteenth signer of the Mayflower Compact, who promptly bought his freedom. In 1624 he married Elizabeth Tilley, the daughter of John Tilley, and they had nine children. He lived a long life as one of Plymouth's leaders until 1672.

• Primary materials with valuable information on Carver are William Bradford, *Of Plymouth Plantation, 1620–1647*, ed. Samuel E. Morison (1952), and Alexander Young, *Chronicles of the Pilgrim Fathers of the Colony of Plymouth, from 1602 to 1625* (1841). Major secondary works that deal with Carver are John Demos, *A Little Commonwealth: Family Life in Plymouth Colony* (1970); Francis Dillon, *The Pilgrims* (1975); Crispin Gill, *"Mayflower" Remembered: A History of the Plymouth Pilgrims* (1970); Thomas J. Fleming, *One Small Candle: The Pilgrims' First Year in America* (1976); George D. Langdon, Jr., *Pilgrim Colony: A History of New Plymouth, 1620–1691* (1966); and George F. Willison, *Saints and Strangers* (1945).

YASUHIDE KAWASHIMA

CARVER, Jonathan (13 Apr. 1710–31 Jan. 1780), explorer, was born in Weymouth, Massachusetts, the son of David Carver, a town government official, and Hannah Dyer, a member of a prominent Connecticut family. Little is known of Carver's youth. The family moved to Canterbury, Connecticut, and it was there that Jonathan grew up. He apparently had some formal schooling, for he wrote quite well, and his writing indicates a broad range of interests from religion to natural history. Carver's father died when Carver was eighteen years old, and Colonel John Dyer, his uncle, became his guardian. From that point in his life until his marriage to Abigail Robbins in Canterbury on 20 October 1746, nothing is known of him. About 1749 they moved to Montague in northwestern Massachusetts, and they probably lived for a time in nearby Deerfield. Seven children were born to them between 1747 and 1762. He appears to have earned his living as a shoemaker.

With intensification of hostilities on the frontier in the 1750s, Carver served several enlistments in the military, participating in engagements at Crown Point, Lake George, Fort William Henry (where he was taken prisoner), and Fort Edward. He had risen to the rank of captain by the end of the war in 1763. It is possible that he met Major Robert Rogers during his military career.

Carver received no pension for his military service, and he perceived future opportunity on the frontier as a surveyor, so he studied drafting and mathematics in the hope of employment in the western lands newly ceded to Great Britain by France. The dominant element in the western economy was the fur trade, and British policy hoped to manage this business as a closely regulated trade. A key point in its management was Fort Michilimackinac near the juncture of lakes Michigan, Huron, and Superior. Major Rogers secured command of this fort from the Board of Trade in London in recognition of his military service. His intention was to make it a gathering point for furs from the western Great Lakes area and a base for further westward exploration in the hope of finding a west-flowing river leading to the Pacific Ocean. To these ends he planned an expedition to be commanded by Captain James Tute, a former military commander, and Carver was signed on as the expedition's draftsman.

Carver left Boston on 20 May 1766 for Michilimackinac, arriving there on 28 August. He departed on 3 September with orders to proceed up the Fox and down the Wisconsin rivers to the Mississippi, then to go northward to the Falls of St. Anthony and to winter in that vicinity. Tute and the remainder of the company were to winter farther south along the Mississippi. Joining forces in the spring, they were to go northward to the head of Lake Superior and await further supplies from Rogers as support for a westward expedition in search of the river leading to the Pacific.

Carver spent the winter of 1766–1767 near the Minnesota River in what is now west-central Minnesota, among Dakota people, seeking to persuade them of the advantages of taking their furs to Michilimackinac in the spring. In May he joined Captain Tute at Prairie du Chien, Tute having wintered near there. Together they went on the Chippewa, Namekagon, and Brule rivers to Lake Superior to await supplies from Rogers. The supplies did not come, for Rogers had come under suspicion of treasonous dealings with France and would shortly be arrested. With no hope of further supplies, the expedition returned to Michilimackinac along the northern shore of Lake Superior, arriving there on 31 August 1767. Carver spent the winter of 1767–1768 at Michilimackinac. His appeals to colonial officials for payment for his services were denied on the grounds that Rogers had not been authorized to send out such an expedition. Returning to Boston, he sought subscribers for an edition of the journal of his travels that he proposed to publish, but the subscriptions were insufficient to pay for it.

In February 1769 Carver sailed for London, hoping to be paid for his services, and after more than a year of bureaucratic delay he appears to have received £1,376 6s. 8d. He also found some employment as a cartographer, but continuing financial distress led him to fabricate a land grant in the present state of Wisconsin from Indians west of the Mississippi. In 1774, probably for financial reasons, he was married a second time, to a Mrs. Mary Harris, by whom he had two children, despite having a wife in Massachusetts.

Carver hoped to increase his income through the publication of his journals. With the help of Sir Joseph Banks they were published in 1778 as *Travels through the Interior Parts of North America in the Years 1766, 1767 and 1768*, an account of his journey and return from Boston to the Minnesota River, including his wintering among the Dakota. Much of this area at that time was known only from French sources. Attempting to make the book more impressive both in size and in style, the publishers engaged Alexander Bicknell, an undistinguished author, as editor. Bicknell added large sections of material from the works of Louis Hennepin and Louis Armand de Lom d'Arce, baron de Lahontan, without indicating his additions. As a result the book was soon under criticism as a flagrant plagiarism, despite its considerable popularity at the outset and its translation into German, Dutch, and French. Sixteen editions had appeared by 1798. German educator Joachim Heinrich Campe adapted it as a children's text, and it enjoyed wide popularity in several languages in this form. The criticism continued nonetheless, and Carver's reputation was damaged further by land claims made by his heirs and others after his death in London, apparently in great poverty.

Carver's reputations as an explorer and as an author were restored in 1909 with documentation by John Thomas Lee proving that Carver had made the journey he claimed to have made, that he had the literary skills to write about it, and most importantly, that his journals had been acquired by the British Museum and remained there in four states of preparation for publication, none of them including material from other sources. Bicknell in his book *Doncaster Races* subsequently identified himself as the editor of Carver's *Travels*. Subsequent studies have confirmed which portions of the *Travels* come from the journals and which are editorial additions. A noteworthy feature of both the journals and the *Travels* is a detailed map of the western Great Lakes–upper Mississippi Valley area. A facsimile edition of the 1781 edition of the *Travels* was published in 1956.

• The only known manuscript sources relating to Carver's travels and his book are the manuscript journals in the British Library and a collection of papers relating to Robert Rogers in the William L. Clements Library, University of Michigan. Carver's only other book is *A Treatise on the Culture of the Tobacco Plant* (1779). John Thomas Lee's published documentation of Carver's *Travels* is "A Bibliography of Carver's Travels," State Historical Society of Wisconsin, *Proceedings 1909* (1910): 143–83, and "Captain Jonathan Carver: Additional Data," State Historical Society of Wisconsin, *Proceedings 1912* (1913): 87–123. The literature concerning the controversy over *Travels*, with a bibliography of its many editions, is in John Parker, ed., *The Journals of Jonathan Carver and Related Documents, 1766–1770* (1976). Additional material on Carver's time in London is in Parker, "New Light on Jonathan Carver," *American Magazine and Historical Chronicle*, Spring-Summer 1986, pp. 4–17.

JOHN PARKER

CARVER, Raymond (25 May 1938–2 Aug. 1988), writer, was born Raymond Clevie Carver in Clatskanie, Oregon, the son of Clevie Raymond Carver, a sawmill worker, and Ella Beatrice Casey, a retail clerk and waitress. Like his "companion soul" Anton Chekhov, Carver was a child of the working poor. During the Great Depression his parents had migrated from the Arkansas dust bowl to the Pacific Northwest. Raymond, the first of their two sons, was born in a mill town of 700 on the Columbia River. In 1941 his family moved to Yakima, a hub town in the fruit lands of central Washington.

Carver married Maryann E. Burk at nineteen, and they had two children before he turned twenty-one. In pursuit of higher education he moved his family to northern California in 1958. At Chico State College he took creative writing with John Gardner. Through part-time study he received his A.B. degree from Humboldt State College in 1963. A year of graduate school at the Iowa Writers' Workshop followed. During these years of "unrelieved responsibility and permanent distraction" Carver struggled to write while laboring as a delivery man, mill hand, and hospital janitor. Later, after working as a textbook editor at Science Research Associates in Palo Alto, he held temporary lectureships in creative writing at the Santa Cruz and Berkeley campuses of the University of California and at the Iowa Writers' Workshop.

In this "first life," as he later called it, Carver faced many of the hardships depicted in his early writings: spirit-breaking disillusionment, domestic "dis-ease" leading to divorce, and near-fatal alcoholism. What he termed his "second life" began on 2 June 1977. On that day, estranged from his wife and grown children, he stopped drinking. His companion of the next decade was Tess Gallagher, a poet who like him had grown up poor in Washington. During these productive years Carver gained recognition as the foremost short-story writer of his generation, the successor to John Cheever. He held visiting appointments at Goddard College and the University of Texas at El Paso before accepting a full professorship at Syracuse University in 1980. In 1983 the American Academy acknowledged his achievement by granting him one of its first Strauss "Livings," a fellowship bringing five years' support and relief from his teaching duties at Syracuse University. Carver and Gallagher were married in 1988, shortly before his death in Port Angeles, Washington, from lung cancer.

Carver's development as a writer parallels the course of his two lives. The bulk of his early fiction is contained in his first short-story collection, *Will You Please Be Quiet, Please?* (1976). There, in twenty-two stories written over fifteen years, Carver fuses Chekhov's lucid realism with the cryptic expressionism of Franz Kafka. This deceptively simple mode of storytelling invests ordinary experience with strange undertones, typically with a note of menace. For the most part, Carver's early characters are laconic service workers whose sensibilities exceed their powers of expression. In the course of everyday activities they find their lives transformed by seemingly trivial events. Sometimes, as in "Fat," the change is positive, a step toward liberation. More often, as in "Neighbors," what follows is a loss of identity. For this oddly arresting book Carver received a National Book Award nomination.

A transitional middle period in Carver's fiction begins with the cessation of his drinking. Over the course of several overlapping books, stories such as "So Much Water So Close to Home" pass through the refining fires of textual expansion, compression, and reexpansion in new forms. The process begins in *Furious Seasons* (1977), a collection of eight stories, seven of which Carver rewrote for inclusion in later books. Next, following the "theory of omission" proposed by Ernest Hemingway, Carver cut his stories "to the marrow, not just to the bone" for *What We Talk About When We Talk About Love* (1981). In the words of Donald Newlove the result was "seventeen tales of Hopelessville, its marriages and alcoholic wreckage, told in a prose as sparingly clear as a fifth of iced Smirnoff." By slashing his stories, Carver exposed a chasm separating talk and love in the lives of men and women whose intimate relations have been sullied by infidelity, alcohol, and the death of youthful dreams. The striking unity of voice and vision won him recognition as a "full-grown master" by distinguished critics such as Frank Kermode. At the same time, the pared-down stories prompted some to call him a "minimalist," a label he rejected as false to the spirit of his work. Worse yet, the radically understated writing left his characters with nothing more to say. To exit this dead end Carver executed a stylistic turnabout. Between 1981 and 1983 he restored and expanded many of the stories he had cut. In addition, he wrote a group of new "more generous" stories in a richer, fuller, and more hopeful style. The first signs of this "opening up" appeared in a volume aptly titled *Fires* (1983). Conclusive evidence followed in *Cathedral* (1983), a book that received nominations for the Pulitzer Prize and National Book Critics Circle Award. There, in twelve new and expanded stories, characters feel their lives enhanced as loneliness and silence give way to community, compassion, and spiritual communion.

Carver won acclaim for his fiction, but his first love remained poetry. Writing in the vernacular lyric-narrative mode of William Carlos Williams, he published three books of poetry before his first short-story collection appeared: *Near Klamath* (1968), *Winter Insomnia* (1970), and *At Night the Salmon Move* (1976). Moreover, even as he concentrated on fiction, Carver remained a poet. In 1984, after years away from his birthplace, he returned to the Pacific Northwest and to poetry. Carver settled in Gallagher's home town of Port Angeles on the north shore of Washington's Olympic Peninsula. There he completed two new poetry collections, *Where Water Comes Together with Other Water* (1985) and *Ultramarine* (1986). These richly reflective books chart the shifting currents of his life and art, including his deepening preoccupation with the mysteries of love and death.

Carver took up fiction again in 1986–1987, publishing seven new stories collected in *Where I'm Calling From* (1988). This burst of creativity opened new territory and heralded further work to come. In retrospect, however, Carver's untimely death marks this resurgence as his final phase. His late stories are typically longer, looser, and more reflective than his previous work. Their texture is novelistic and their tone autumnal, with first-person narrators exploring the interplay of character and incident. The capstone of the group is "Errand," Carver's last work of fiction. There, taking for his subject the death of Chekhov, Carver blurs the boundary separating life and art. In the process, he shows how imagination can transcend a wrenching loss. Even as his own health declined, he continued writing, completing a final book of poems, *A New Path to the Waterfall* (1989), only weeks before his death.

Despite his foreshortened career, Carver's contributions to American literature are substantial. Carver reinvented realism for postmoderns, prompted a revival of the short story form, and bore witness to the losses and longings of working people on the dark side of the American dream. By precept and example, he inspired a younger generation of writers whose fiction is, like his, both lyrical and realistic. Working in the tradition of Chekhov, Hemingway, and Cheever, Carver set himself a modest but enduring goal. "Good fiction," he said, "is partly a bringing of the news from one world to another."

• Carver's papers are in the Charvat Collection at Ohio State University. His further works include *Dostoevsky: A Screenplay* (1985), with Tess Gallagher; *No Heroics, Please: Uncollected Writings* (1991); *Carnations: A Play in One Act* (1992); and *All of Us: The Collected Poems* (1996). Several books shed light on Carver's life: *Carver Country: The World of Raymond Carver* (1990), with photographs by Bob Adelman and an introduction by Gallagher; Marshall Bruce Gentry and William L. Stull, eds., *Conversations with Raymond Carver* (1990); Stull and Maureen P. Carroll, eds., *Remembering Ray: A Composite Biography of Raymond Carver* (1993); and Sam Halpert, ed., *Raymond Carver: An Oral Biography* (1995). Critical studies include Arthur M. Saltzman, *Understanding Raymond Carver* (1988); Randolph Paul Runyon, *Reading Raymond Carver* (1992); Ewing Campbell, *Raymond Carver: A Study of the Short Fiction* (1992); Kirk Nesset, *The Stories of Raymond Carver* (1995), and Adam Meyer, *Raymond Carver* (1995). The motion picture *Short Cuts* (1993), directed by Robert Altman, is adapted from a selection of Carver's writings. Two documentaries, *Raymond Carver: Dreams Are What You Wake up From* (BBC 1, 1989; expanded 1996) and *To Write and Keep Kind* (PBS/KCTS Seattle, 1992), examine his life and work. An obituary is in the *New York Times*, 3 Aug. 1988.

WILLIAM L. STULL

CARY, Alice (26 Apr. 1820–12 Feb. 1871), writer, was born in Hamilton County, Ohio, the daughter of Robert Cary and Elizabeth Jessup, farmers. The family farm was located near a village called Mount Healthy, which was the basis for the town of Clovernook, the setting of her popular short fiction. Cary's education was haphazard; although both mother and father were literate, formal education for their daughters was not a priority. As Cary wrote in an early letter to Rufus Griswold, her education "was limited to the meagre and infrequent advantages of an obscure district school" from which she was "removed altogether at a very early age" (Griswold, p. 239). The family subscribed to the *Trumpet*, a Boston-based Universalist periodical, and according to Cary's sister and fellow poet, Phoebe Cary, the *Trumpet* was "for many years the only paper seen by Alice, and its poet's corner the food of her fancy and the source of her inspiration."

The Cary sisters developed an interest in reading and writing poetry at an early age. After publishing poetry in local papers, they drew the attention of Griswold, who published their verse in *Female Poets of America* in 1848. Cary also found an encouraging friend in John Greenleaf Whittier, who urged her to print their first volume of poems, *Poems of Alice and Phoebe Cary* (1849), and subsequently championed the book. In Edgar Allan Poe's review of this volume, he cited Cary's poem "Pictures of Memory" as "decidedly the noblest in the collection." The literary acclaim the book received was a major factor in Cary's decision to leave Ohio for New York City in 1851. She moved to a modest home on Twentieth Street in 1855 and was joined by sisters Phoebe and Elmina, her lifelong companions.

In 1852 Cary published a series of short sketches based on her childhood reminiscences, the first series of *Clovernook Papers*. This volume was successful enough to merit a second series of the *Clovernook Papers* (1853) and a volume for younger readers titled *Clovernook Children* (1854). Cary thought of herself as a poet first and foremost, however, and she continually produced poetry as well: *Lyra and Other Poems* (1853) was well received, and Poe again singled out a number of verses—"Lyra," "In Illness," "Hymn to Night," and "Winter"—as inferior to none written in America. Her *Collected Poems* appeared in 1855, followed by *Ballads, Lyrics and Hymns* (1866) and *The Lover's Diary* (1868). She wrote sentimental verse with rhyming stanzas often of four lines with regular meter. Cary also wrote several novels: *Hagar: A Story of To-day* (1852), *Hollywood* (1855), *Married, Not Mated* (1856), and *The Bishop's Son* (1867). She also published *Pictures of Country Life* (1859), a collection of her contributions to leading periodicals, and *Snowberries* (1867).

Of all this work, the Clovernook sketches are widely recognized as Cary's most lasting achievement. They bear, said Whittier, "the true stamp of genius—simple, natural, truthful—and evince a keen sense of the humor and pathos, of the comedy and tragedy, of life in the country." The sketches place Cary among the first prominent women regionalist writers; her work is characterized by an emphasis on depiction of character and landscape over plot and the use of a distinct, first-person narrative consciousness. She is also notable in her articulation of the need for a new literature that is distinctly American in subject and style. In the preface to *Clovernook*, she allied herself with other writers who saw unique literary potential in the American landscape and character: "There is surely as much in the simple manners, and the little histories every day revealed, to interest us in humanity, as there can be in those old empires where the press of tyrannous laws and the deadening influence of hereditary acquiescence necessarily destroy the best life of society." What Cary promised was a literature that mixed "shadow and sunbeams," a view of rural Ohio that was realistic in focus. Faulting those who had earlier written of rural life for knowing "scarcely anything of it from participation" and for producing brilliant but untrue pictures, she noted that hers would have a "natural and probable" air. Although the work is primarily realistic, one must note that Cary's definition of "probable" reflects a belief in dreams and visions, which were often integral elements of her sketches.

Cary's fiction is also notable for the distinctive narrative consciousness that unifies the sketches, typically that of an observer not directly involved in the action and events she records. Cary's narrators focused on the grimmer aspects of country life and everyday battles for survival. The act of storytelling tends to ease the pain of these grim realities and to build understanding and community among a series of disconnected individuals. In "Ghost Story, Number II," for example, the narrator tells of a number of scattered residents who gather briefly to share tales and bits of experience and leave with "kindly feeling stirred up, and hearts strengthened and steadied for the work and the warfare of life."

During Cary's later years, the Cary home became a gathering place for literary figures of New York. The well-known Sunday evening receptions were attended by figures such as Horace Greeley, William Lloyd Garrison, Sara Helen Whitman, Gail Hamilton, James T. Fields, and Whittier. Cary died in her New York City home after being bedridden for eighteen months with tuberculosis. She is buried in Brooklyn's Greenwood Cemetery beside her sisters Phoebe and Elmina.

• The correspondence between Cary and Griswold can be found in William McGrillis Griswold, ed., *Passages from the Correspondence of Rufus W. Griswold and Other Papers* (1898). Cary's final volume of published poetry, *The Last Poems of Alice and Phoebe Cary* (1874), was compiled by a personal friend and member of the Cary literary circle, Mary Clemmer Ames. Ames also wrote what is still the standard biography of the Cary sisters, *A Memorial of Alice and Phoebe Cary, with Some of Their Later Poems* (1874). See also Phoebe Cary's tribute to her sister, "Alice Cary," *Woman's Journal*, 5 Aug. 1871. For additional biography and a discussion of Cary's short fiction, see *Clovernook Sketches and Other Stories* (1987), edited and with an introduction by Judith Fetterley. Cary's short fiction is largely recognized as being her most enduring work, but in Robert Bain, ed., *Whitman's and Dickinson's Contemporaries: An Anthology of Their Verse* (1996), Wilson Somerville places a selection of Cary's poetic output in a historical context. Poe's review of Cary's work is in the *Southern Literary Messenger* 15 (1849), and Whittier is quoted in Fred Lewis Pattee's consideration of Cary in *A History of American Literature* (1896).

DEBORAH EVANS

CARY, Annie Louise (22 Oct. 1841–3 Apr. 1921), contralto, was born in Wayne, Kennebec County, Maine, the daughter of Nelson Howard Cary, a physician, and Maria Stockbridge. After being graduated from Gorham Seminary in Gorham, Maine, in 1860, Cary determined to pursue a singing career and moved to Boston to begin voice lessons, procuring a position as a church soloist to help support herself. She also joined the chorus of the Handel and Haydn Society. Appearing as a soloist with this organization in a performance of Handel's *Messiah* in January 1863, she caught the attention of John Sullivan Dwight, who wrote that the heretofore unknown singer had "a large and rich contralto, with considerable execution" (*Dwight's Journal of Music* 22, no. 14 [Jan. 1863]: 319).

Wishing to continue her studies in Europe, Cary organized a concert in 1866 and raised enough funds for a year of tuition under Giovanni Corsi in Milan. She then accepted an engagement in Copenhagen, where she debuted as Ulrica in Verdi's *Un Ballo in Maschera* in January 1868. This led to additional operatic debuts in Stockholm, Hamburg, and Brussels from the spring of 1868 to the fall of 1869, punctuated by summer study with Pauline Viardot-Garcia (Baden-Baden, 1868) and Giovanni Bottesini (Paris, 1869). On 12 April 1870 she made her Covent Garden debut under the name Mlle. Cari, appearing as Orsini in Donizetti's *Lucrezia Borgia*. Following her London engagement Cary joined a concert company managed by impresarios Max Strakosch and Maurice Strakosch and sailed for the United States in the summer of 1870. Cary made her professional American concert debut with this organization on 19 September 1870 at Steinway Hall in New York City. In addition to world-famous soprano Christine Nilsson, the troupe contained several other notable musicians: the violinist Henri Vieuxtemps, tenor Pasquale Brignoli, and conductor Luigi Arditi.

Though the reviews focused on Nilsson, Cary nevertheless attracted favorable comments from New York critics, the *New York Times* noting that "Miss Cary . . . won great favor before the evening was ended. Her voice is even, extended, and of a most sympathetic quality, and she uses it in a manner indicating a culture very complete" (20 Sept. 1870). After giving several more concerts in New York, Max Strakosch took the company on an extended tour of the East and Midwest. By way of this and subsequent tours, Cary gained a nationwide reputation and became one of the public's most beloved performers.

For the 1871–1872 season, Max Strakosch hired Cary as a member of an opera company that included Nilsson and tenors Brignoli and Victor Capoul. As a member of this troupe, Cary made her American operatic debut as Frederick in Friedrich von Flotow's *Martha* on 27 October 1871 at the Academy of Music in New York. Her other roles during this season included Siebel in Gounod's *Faust*, Nancy in Daniel Auber's *Fra Diavolo*, and one of her most famous, Azucena in Verdi's *Il Trovatore*. In addition, she sang the role of the Queen in the U.S. premiere of Ambroise Thomas's *Hamlet*, given at the Academy of Music on 22 March 1872.

In the 1872–1873 season, Cary returned to the concert stage, touring under the management of Max Strakosch with such luminaries as soprano Carlotta Patti, tenor Giovanni Mario, and pianist Teresa Carreño. She also made the first of many appearances at the Cincinnati Festival, singing in the inaugural concerts of May 1873. Returning to the operatic stage the following season, Cary joined a star-studded company that included Nilsson and Capoul, as well as tenor Italo Campanini and baritone Giuseppe Del Puente. The highlight of this season was the U.S. premiere of Verdi's *Aida*, given at the New York Academy of Music on 26 November 1873, in which Cary performed what was perhaps her most famous role, the Egyptian princess Amneris. Within four months she became the first American woman to perform a Wagnerian role in the United States, singing Ortrud in the Italian-language premiere of *Lohengrin* on 23 March 1874 in New York City.

During 1874–1875 Cary was on the road again with the Strakosch Italian Opera Company, touring with singers like Emma Albani and Del Puente. The winters of 1875–1876 and 1876–1877 found her and Adelina Patti singing operatic roles in Russia. Nevertheless she managed to chalk up three American concert premieres during this period: Verdi's *Requiem* on 17 November 1874 in New York City, Bach's *Magnificat* in D on 13 May 1875 in Cincinnati, and Bach's *Christmas Oratorio* on 17 May 1877 in Boston.

Cary returned to the United States for the 1877–1878 and 1878–1879 seasons, touring with soprano Clara Louise Kellogg in opera and concert. She sang an average of three to four nights per week and often earned $2,000 to $3,000 per month.

During her last two operatic seasons, 1879–1880 and 1880–1881, Cary sang under the management of British impresario James Henry Mapleson. Her appearances under his direction included the roles of Marta and Pantalis in the first Italian-language performance of Arrigo Boito's *Mefistofele*, given at the New York Academy of Music on 24 November 1880. Cary's final operatic appearance took place in Philadelphia on 22 April 1881, when she sang Ulrica in *Un Ballo in Maschera*. Thereafter a recurrent throat ailment of an unspecified nature caused her to cancel a number of engagements during the 1881–1882 season. She made her last public appearance at a New York Music Festival matinee concert on 6 May 1882. A few weeks later she married New York banker Charles Monson Raymond and retired from the stage. She and her husband had no children.

Well liked by the public and her fellow artists, Cary enjoyed a reputation for honesty and amiability. Her outlook toward her profession was revealed in an interview in St. Louis in 1878. Approached by the *Globe-Democrat* concerning rumors of jealousy between Clara Louise Kellogg and herself, Cary replied: "What's the use? . . . Life is too short to be embittered by such troubles. . . . I try to be affectionate with everybody I have to be with and I'm sure I don't feel at all envious of anybody else's success" (24 Feb. 1878).

American-born singers first began to make their mark in the musical world during and shortly after the Civil War. Performing with a distinguished generation of American sopranos, Annie Louise Cary stood out as the earliest native-born contralto to achieve international prominence. Perhaps the best summary of her achievement appeared in the *New York Herald*: "She was the foremost contralto who trod the lyric stage within the memory of living operagoers. No other has quite equalled her in the splendor of her tone, the excellence of her vocal technic, her command of the grand style and her heroic delivery of tragic music" (10 Apr. 1921).

• The Scarborough Public Library, Scarborough, Maine, has a scrapbook with clippings, correspondence dated 1916–1917, and an autographed 1876 concert program from Unity Church, Chicago. A number of clippings, programs, and photographs are held in the Theatre Collection, Widener Library, Harvard University. No biography of Annie Louise Cary exists; however, G. T. Edwards, *Music and Musicians of Maine* (1928), is a rich source of biographical material. Though sprinkled with incorrect dates, Oscar Thompson, *The American Singer* (1937), contains a good deal of biographical information. For accurate reporting of her engagements and the names of her associates, an excellent source is George C. D. Odell, *Annals of the New York Stage*, vols. 9–11 (1937–1939). Reviews of her performances can be found in many newspapers, including the *New York Times* and the London *Times*. Two obituaries are in sections 3 and 6 of the *New York Times*, 10 Apr. 1921.

HARLAN F. JENNINGS, JR.

CARY, Lott (c. 1780–10 Nov. 1828), Baptist preacher and missionary to Africa, was born on a plantation in Charles City County, Virginia, thirty miles from Richmond, the son of slave parents, names unknown. His grandmother Mihala had a strong influence on Lott's early religious development. He married around 1800 and with his first wife (name unknown) had two children. Lott's master sent him to Richmond in 1804 as a hired slave laborer. He worked in the Shockoe Tobacco Warehouse first as a laborer, then as a shipping clerk.

Cary attended the predominantly white First Baptist Church, as did other blacks in Richmond. He experienced conversion in 1807 after hearing a sermon on Jesus and Nicodemus. Allowed to earn money by selling waste tobacco, Cary purchased his freedom and that of his two children in 1813. His wife had died by this time. Anxious to study the Bible, Cary enrolled in a night school taught by William Crane. There he learned to read, write, and do elementary arithmetic. His studies allowed him to assume greater responsibilities at the tobacco warehouse and achieve more economic independence; he eventually rose to the position of foreman with a salary of $800 per year. He remarried about 1815; his second wife's name also is unknown; they had one child.

Cary felt called to the Christian ministry and began to hold meetings for Richmond's African-American residents. The First Baptist Church licensed him around 1814 after a trial period. Contemporaries credited him with extraordinary abilities as an extemporary speaker. Cary's strong interest in foreign mission work began when he heard Crane report on the plans of the American Colonization Society (ACS) for establishing colonies of African Americans in West Africa and conducting Christian missions. Cary sought to arouse interest in Africa among fellow blacks in Richmond and along with Crane was instrumental in organizing the Richmond African Baptist Missionary Society in 1815. Because of white opposition to unregulated black organizations in the wake of the insurrection of Gabriel in 1800, Crane, one of the white members of First Baptist, served as president of the missionary society. Cary was recording secretary.

Cary developed an even stronger interest in going to Africa as a Christian missionary after the visit of Luther Rice to Richmond in 1817. He sought support from the white Baptist General Missionary Convention. When asked why he should want to leave America for the uncertainties of Africa, Cary said: "I am an African, and in this country, however meritorious my conduct, and respectable my character, I cannot receive the credit due to either. I wish to go to a country where I shall be estimated by my merits, not by complexion; and I feel bound to labor for my suffering race" (Gurley, p. 148). The Baptist Board of Foreign Missions and the ACS endorsed Cary in 1819. The ACS had been organized in December 1816 by whites who were interested primarily in removing blacks (especially free blacks) to West Africa; most ACS members did not oppose slavery as an institution. Cary's reservations concerning the policies of the ACS apparently were overshadowed by his desire to see Africa and conduct mission work there. He served the ACS without pay.

Cary and a group of twenty-eight colonists, plus a number of children, departed Norfolk, Virginia, on board the brig *Nautilus* bound for Sierra Leone in January 1821. Before leaving America, Cary and six other colonists, including his close friend Colin Teague, organized a missionary Baptist church. As he boarded ship Cary told those who had assembled to see the *Nautilus* off, "It may be that I shall behold you no more on this side of the grave, but I feel bound to labor for my brothers, perishing as they are in the far distant land of Africa. For their sake and for Christ's sake I am happy in leaving all and venturing all" (Gurley, p. 149). The Richmond African Baptist Missionary Society gave $700 to support Cary. This was the first effort by black Baptists in America to do mission work in Africa.

After a voyage of forty-four days, Cary and the other colonists arrived at Freetown, Sierra Leone, which the British government had taken over in 1808 for the settlement of "Liberated Africans" whom the British navy freed from captured slave ships. Agents of the American Colonization Society had urged the U.S. government to establish a freed-slave colony on Sherbro Island down the coast from Freetown, but when Cary arrived in 1821 no provisions had been made for them. The new arrivals were required to cultivate farms and do other labor in Sierra Leone. Soon after their arrival, Cary's second wife died of tropical fever, leaving him to care for three children. While in Sierra Leone, Cary did missionary work among the Vai tribe at Cape Grand Mountain.

By December 1821 arrangements had been made for the purchase of land from King Peter, the principal chief around the cape, for another settlement. This later became part of the Republic of Liberia. In early 1822 Cary and his family moved to Mesurado (now Cape Monrovia). Jehudi Ashmun, a representative of the ACS, served as colonial agent of the colony of about 130 members, and Cary acted as health officer and inspector. In addition to assisting Ashmun in defense of the colony against the forces of King Peter, who was resentful of the colony's expansion, in 1822 Cary established a Baptist church in Monrovia that grew to about seventy members by 1825. Known as Providence Baptist, the church had its nucleus in the missionary congregation Cary and fellow Baptists had organized before leaving the United States. Cary also established a day school in Monrovia, which was moved to Cape Grand Mountain in 1827, but eventually closed because of insufficient funding.

In 1823 conflict developed between the earliest colonists and Ashmun, who attempted to redistribute town lots because of the arrival of additional settlers. The controversy escalated to the point where some colonists were charged with sedition and stealing rations. Though Cary initially opposed Ashmun, he mediated the dispute between the disgruntled colonists and the governing authorities. Liberia was established with a permanent government in 1825 as a colony of the United States; Ashmun became governor. Cary was elected vice agent of the colony in September 1826. When Ashmun became ill and left for the United States in March 1828, the entire administrative responsibility of the colony fell into Cary's hands. After Ashmun's death in August 1828, Cary was appointed governor of the more than 1,200 settlers of Liberia.

In late 1828 a native group known as the Bassa, with whom the colonists had been having periodic conflict, robbed a factory at Digby, a settlement north of Monrovia. Cary called for a show of force by the settler militia. On 8 November 1828 he was making cartridges in the old agency house when a candle was accidentally upset. The ammunition exploded. Seriously injured, Cary died two days later; he was buried in Liberia. A monument was later erected that bore the inscription "Lott Cary's self-denying, self-sacrificing labors, as a self-taught Physician, as a Missionary and Pastor of a Church, and finally as Governor of the Colony, have inscribed his name indelibly on the page of history, not only as one of Nature's Noblemen, but as an eminent Philanthropist and Missionary of Jesus Christ." In 1897 black Baptists in America organized the Lott Cary Foreign Missionary Convention in honor of Cary's pioneering labors in Liberia.

• The most important primary sources of information on Cary are James B. Taylor, *The Biography of Elder Lott Cary* (1837), and Ralph Randolph Gurley, *Life of Jehudi Ashmun, Late Colonial Agent in Liberia, with an Appendix Containing Extracts from His Journal and Other Writings, with a Brief Sketch of the Life of the Rev. Lott Cary* (1835). Gurley was secretary of the American Colonization Society. Additional primary sources can be found in "Letters, Addresses, and the Like Throwing Light on the Career of Lott Cary," *Journal of Negro History* 7 (Oct. 1922): 427–48. Miles Mark Fisher collected much of the available information on Cary in his seminal essay, "Lott Cary, the Colonizing Missionary," *Journal of Negro History* 7 (Oct. 1922): 380–418. See also William A. Poe, "Lott Cary: Man of Purchased Freedom," *Church History* 39 (Mar. 1970): 49–61. The most comprehensive recent study is Leroy Fitts, *Lott Carey: First Black Missionary to Africa* (1978). The spelling of Cary's name as "Carey" is probably due to confusion in some primary sources with the well-known English Baptist, the Reverend William Carey. Lott Cary, however, signed his name as "Cary."

MILTON C. SERNETT

CARY, Mary Ann Camberton Shadd (9 Oct. 1823–5 June 1893), African-American educator, journalist/editor, and lawyer, was born in Wilmington, Delaware, the daughter of Abraham Doras Shadd and Harriet Parnell. Although the eldest of thirteen children, Mary Ann Shadd grew up in comfortable economic circumstances. Little is known about her mother except that she was born in North Carolina in 1806 and was of mixed black and white heritage; whether she was born free or a slave is unknown. Shadd's father was also of mixed-race heritage. His paternal grandfather, Jeremiah Schad, was a German soldier who had fought in the American Revolution and later married Elizabeth Jackson, a free black woman from Pennsylvania. Abraham Shadd had amassed his wealth as a shoemaker, and his property by the 1830s was valued at $5,000. He was a respected member of the free black community in Wilmington and in West Chester, Pennsylvania, where the family had moved sometime in the 1830s, and he served as a delegate to the American Anti-Slavery Society in 1835 and 1836.

Mary Ann Shadd continued her family's activist tradition by devoting her life to the advancement of black education and the immediate abolition of slavery. As a youth she attended a private Quaker school for blacks taught by whites, in which several of her teachers were abolitionists. During the 1840s she taught in schools for blacks in Wilmington, West Chester, New York City, and Norristown, Pennsylvania. When passage of the Fugitive Slave Act of 1850 endangered the freedom of free blacks as well as fugitive slaves, Shadd joined the faction of black abolitionists who promoted the controversial cause of voluntary black emigration to Canada. This movement illustrated the depth of disillusionment with the United States that had developed among many blacks since the 1840s. Angered and disappointed in the continued tolerance of slavery and the upsurge of violence against free blacks, a faction of black activists broke from the American abolitionist organization and from those black abolitionists who preferred to stay and fight oppression in the United States.

Between 1850 and 1860 approximately 40,000 blacks fled to southern Ontario. Shadd found employment in 1851 as a teacher of blacks in Windsor, Ontario, and was later joined by several members of her family. Shadd taught school and became a fervent spokeswoman for the emigration movement. Like most teachers in the black settlements, she had to struggle to keep her schools open, facing such obstacles as inadequate supplies, ramshackle school buildings, inclement weather, and the frequent outbreak of cholera and measles.

In addition to teaching, Shadd was a talented writer. One of the most important enterprises was her participation with Rev. Samuel Ringgold Ward in the founding in 1853 of the *Provincial Freeman*, a newspaper dedicated to promoting the interests of Canadian blacks, in Toronto, Ontario. The *Provincial Freeman* functioned as Shadd's vehicle for promoting Canada as a haven for the oppressed and for condemning the United States. In addition, she wrote extensively on the topics of temperance, antislavery, anticolonization, black education, and women's rights.

Shadd also used the podium effectively for promoting her ideas, despite the resistance she often encountered against women who engaged in the traditionally male activity of public speaking. After much debate, for example, she was given the opportunity to address the all-male delegation at the Eleventh Colored National Convention in Philadelphia in 1855. One man in the audience noted that her eyes were "small and penetrating and fairly flash when she is speaking." He described her as a "superior woman . . . however much we may differ with her on the subject of emigration." At another engagement, an observer praised her as "a woman of superior intellect, and the persevering energy of character." On her lecture trips, however, she often found the platform closed to women. While in Rockford, Illinois, she wrote to her brother Isaac that the citizens were "so conservative . . . as not to tolerate lectures from women." In both her writings and her speeches, Shadd spoke her mind, often roundly criticizing leading black males in the United States and Canada for providing inadequate support for Canadian black communities.

Her outspoken and candid manner often brought her into conflict with other black Canadian activists during the 1850s over such issues as the appropriate means for funding black schools and for raising money to help newly arrived blacks. Her most publicized feud was with Henry Bibb and Mary Bibb, American-born free black activists who had helped in the establishment of the black settlement in Windsor the year before Shadd arrived. What began as a disagreement over policies escalated into a bitter personal feud between Shadd and the Bibbs that was well publicized in their rival newspapers and in Shadd's lengthy correspondence with George Whipple, secretary of the American Missionary Association. In his *Voice of the Fugitive*, Bibb chastised her for criticizing him, calling her unladylike, while Shadd described him as "a dishonest man."

The Bibbs favored all-black schools sponsored by the Canadian government, but Shadd sought to break down all racial barriers, favoring privately funded nongovernment schools that made no distinctions about color. Although she encouraged black parents to make concerted efforts to sustain the schools, finding the necessary funds was a formidable barrier. Shadd finally was forced to appeal to the American Missionary Association for assistance.

Shadd also criticized the activities of the Refugee Home Society, an organization that Henry Bibb had started in 1850 to distribute land, clothing, and money to black refugees. Shadd accused Bibb of corruption and of perpetuating a "begging scheme." According to Shadd, who charged that corrupt agents pocketed the money, few such resources actually went to the refugees. She argued further that too much assistance would prevent black settlers from becoming self-reliant.

Her marriage in 1856 to widower Thomas F. Cary, a barber and bathhouse proprietor from Toronto, did not prevent her from continuing to write, lecture, and teach. When at home in Chatham she worked on the newspaper and cared for his three children. They had two children of their own, one in 1857 and another in 1860. Shadd Cary continued to lecture and write for the *Provincial Freeman*. She also operated her school until 1864. During the Civil War she traveled to the United States to help recruit soldiers for the Union army. In 1869, Mary Ann Shadd Cary, by now a widow, moved to Washington, D.C., with her two children. Later, she lived with her older daughter, Sarah E. Cary Evans, a schoolteacher. Between 1869 and 1871 she began her studies in law at Howard University but stopped for unknown reasons. She resumed her studies in 1881 and received her degree in 1883, the only black woman in a class of five, although there is no evidence that she actually practiced law. She also continued her support for women's rights. In 1878 she delivered a lecture at the annual National Woman Suffrage Association Conference. She died at home in Washington.

Mary Ann Shadd Cary stands as one of the most significant, yet least recognized, abolitionists who worked on behalf of black emigration and the sustenance of black settlements in Canada. At the same time, her lifelong challenge of racism and sexism made Cary an important figure in the struggle for racial and sexual equality during the nineteenth century.

• Manuscript collections on the life of Mary Shadd Cary are located at the Moorland-Spingarn Library at Howard University in Washington, D.C., and the Ontario Black History Society in Toronto. The *Provincial Freeman* and Cary's correspondence with George Whipple are available in Peter C. Ripley and George Carter, eds., *Black Abolitionist Papers* (5 vols., 1885–1992). Letters by and about her are also available in Dorothy Sterling, ed., *We Are Your Sisters: Black Women in the Nineteenth Century* (1984). See also Jim Bearden and Linda Jean Butler, *Shadd: The Life and Times of Mary Ann Shadd Cary* (1977). An obituary is in the Washington, D.C., *Evening Star* and is housed with city directories, and her death certificate in the Mary Ann Shadd Cary Papers in the Ontario Black History Society.

SHIRLEY J. YEE

CARY, Phoebe (4 Sept. 1824–31 July 1871), writer, was born in Hamilton County, Ohio, the daughter of Robert Cary and Elizabeth Jessup, farmers. The farm was located near the village of Mount Healthy, eight miles outside Cincinnati. At an early age Cary lost her mother and two sisters to tuberculosis. After her father remarried and moved to another house on their farm in 1839, the five remaining Cary children maintained an independent household, with their elder sister, Alice, nineteen, as its head.

Phoebe Cary's poetic career is almost inextricably linked with that of her sister, fellow writer Alice Cary. Although neither of the sisters had any formal training beyond that offered by a limited country school education, they developed an early interest in poetry. They published in local papers but gained a far broader readership when Rufus Griswold included their verse in his anthology *The Female Poets of America* (1849). When the sisters published their first joint volume, *The Poems of Alice and Phoebe Cary* (1850), the response was so favorable that one critic reported, "No 'first volume' by any American writers experienced a more satisfactory reception" (Orville J. Victor, *Poets and Poetry of the West* [1864], p. 343).

In 1851 the women made an important personal change, leaving their native Ohio and moving to a more active life in New York City, where they resided for the remainder of their lives. Neither woman ever married, and they developed an interdependent, almost symbiotic relationship. Alice, known as the more industrious of the sisters, was responsible for providing an income for the household; various contemporaries describe Phoebe as the more "feminine" and animated of the sisters. Both were known in their later years as hostesses of popular Sunday evening literary gatherings, frequented by figures such as Horace Greeley, John Greenleaf Whittier, James T. Fields, Sarah Helen Whitman, and William Lloyd Garrison, among others.

Although in their day Alice gained a greater share of public acclaim, some critics have singled out Phoebe's verse for particular notice. Griswold's early assessment of Phoebe's poetry rings true. He notes that she "writes with vigor, and a hopeful and genial spirit. . . . She refers more than Alice to the common experience, and has perhaps a deeper sympathy with that philosophy and those movements of the day, which look for a nearer approach to equality, in culture, fortune, and social relations" (*Female Poets of America*, p. 372). These concerns reflect her private advocacy of temperance, women's issues, and human rights. Although she rarely became a public figure in these popular movements, she did participate actively, serving as assistant editor for *Revolution*, Susan B. Anthony's suffrage paper, for a few months. Cary addresses the role of woman in her poetry as well. For instance, in "A Woman's Conclusions" a single woman looks back on a life without "the highest and purest bliss" of marriage and without children, and concludes,

> And who knows how a life at the last may show?
> Why, look at the moon from where we stand!
> Opaque, uneven, you say; yet it shines,
> A luminous sphere, complete and grand!
>
> So let my past stand, just as it stands,
> And let me now, as I may, grow old;
> I am what I am, and my life for me
> Is the best—or it had not been, I hold.

She does not apologize for an unmarried life but instead asserts her faith that the life of a single woman is not half-lived, but complete in its own right.

During her lifetime Cary was best known, however, not as an activist but as the author of popular hymns such as "Nearer Home," beginning, "One sweetly solemn thought." Charles Noble cites this as "one of the treasured possessions of religious spirits in all the English-speaking world" (*Studies in American Literature* [1898], pp. 285–86). Her religious poetry reflected a conventional sentimental piety; it was recognized for its simple, unadorned style that critics regarded as a reflection of its author's humble beginnings.

She was also adept at ballads, hymns, and lyrics. Her love of fun and wit can be seen in her parodies of contemporary classics such as Edgar Allan Poe's "Annabel Lee," Henry Wadsworth Longfellow's "The Day Is Done," and William Wordsworth's "She Dwelt among the Untrodden Ways." Although Cary was not the consistent writer that her sister was, and in fact left writing for eight years, she did publish two volumes of poetry independently of her sister: *Poems and Parodies* (1854) and *Poems of Faith, Hope, and Love* (1868).

Cary died in Newport, Rhode Island, just months after Alice's death.

• After the sisters' death, Mary Clemmer Ames, a member of the Cary literary circle, compiled *The Last Poems of Alice and Phoebe Cary* (1873). Ames also wrote what is still the most complete biography of the Carys to date, *A Memorial of Alice and Phoebe Cary, with Some of Their Later Poems* (1873). For more on the Cary sisters, see Janice G. Pulsifer, "Alice and Phoebe Cary, Whittier's Sweet Singers of the West," *Essex Institute Historical Collections* 109 (Jan. 1973), and Judith Fetterley's excellent introduction to her selection of Alice Cary's short fiction, *Clovernook and Other Sketches* (1987). Phoebe Cary is considered independently of her sister and placed in historical context in Robert Bain, ed., *Whitman's and Dickinson's Contemporaries: An Anthology of Their Verse* (1996).

DEBORAH EVANS

CARY, Thomas (?–1718), deputy governor of northern Carolina, was born probably in Chipping Wycombe, Buckinghamshire, England, the son of Walter Cary and Ann Dobson. After the death of his father (date unknown) his mother in 1673 married John Archdale, proprietor and governor of Carolina. Although his stepfather was a noted Quaker, Cary was apparently an Anglican. Cary settled in southern Carolina in Charles Town sometime before 1695 when Archdale, who had assumed the governorship, appointed him to be secretary of the council. Other posts that he held in Carolina were provincial treasurer (1697–1698) and register of the admiralty court (1698). Cary became a successful merchant and shipowner, acquiring considerable wealth by 1702, when he was able to post a £2,000 bond for the new governor of Carolina, Sir Nathaniel Johnson, and also for the governor of the Bahamas.

Because of the great distances in Carolina, the proprietary executive of the province resided in the south at Charles Town and appointed a deputy to govern the northern Albemarle County settlement. Governor Johnson named Cary deputy governor of Albemarle in March 1705, and Cary set out for a colony torn by religious and political dissension. Encouraged by the religious tolerance granted by the proprietary charter, the Quakers had been the first organized church in Albemarle, and many other dissenters, chiefly Baptists and Presbyterians, had been attracted to the colony. Through the influence of proprietor Archdale, Quakers had dominated the assembly and council of Albemarle. The Anglicans finally succeeded in passing a vestry act in 1703, establishing the Anglican church. To secure their political ascendency, the Anglicans wrote into the act, in accordance with prevailing English law, requirements that assemblymen must be Anglican and must take an oath of allegiance to the Crown, provisions totally unacceptable to the dissenters. In addition to the religious factionalism, the rapidly growing Bath County south of Albemarle Sound had emerged to challenge the political hegemony of Albemarle County.

Cary's relationship to the highly respected Archdale engendered the false impression that he would be more lenient in enforcing the test oath, but shortly after his arrival in the colony in March, he backed the Anglicans, excluding the dissenters from the government. A Quaker leader, John Porter, was dispatched to England to persuade the proprietors to remove Cary. In 1707 Cary was in Charles Town, where he was elected to the assembly and served as Speaker of the house. While Cary was away, Porter returned in October with confirmation of Cary's ouster by the proprietors, and William Glover was elected president of the council (acting governor). Within the year Glover's identification with the Anglican-Albemarle faction enabled Cary to gather a base of power from Bath County, where he was then residing. Cary became the colonel of the county militia. He established himself in the Indian trade and also had built several ships that were engaged in the colonial coastal trade.

With the armed support of the Bath County faction, Cary regained power in October 1708, forcing Glover to flee the colony to Virginia. He effectively governed northern Carolina as president of the council until the arrival in January 1711 of Edward Hyde (1650–1712), a cousin of the queen and the intended new deputy governor. Hyde had not received his commission prior to the unexpected death of the governor of Carolina, but he was accepted by the colony and elected president of the council. Cary's retirement to Bath County might have ended the conflict had not his former enemies in Albemarle convinced Hyde to arrest him and his key supporters, touching off the Cary Rebellion. In May Hyde led an armed force into Bath County but withdrew after a half-hearted attempt against Cary's fortified plantation. In June Cary sailed north in an armed fleet to attack Hyde and overthrow his government but was repulsed in a skirmish on the Chowan River. Hyde secured marine reinforcements from Virginia in July and in a second expedition into Bath defeated Cary. Cary fled into Virginia, where Governor Alexander Spotswood found him and his fellow fugitives living with Indians on the James River. Although Cary was sent to England to be tried by the Carolina proprietors, following desultory hearings over the span of a year, charges were finally dropped for lack of evidence.

In July 1712 during the Tuscarora War, a devastating Indian war, Governor Hyde pardoned all of the rebels except Cary and four of his chief lieutenants. By the time Cary returned in early 1713 the colony was at peace and his nemesis Hyde had died. Cary continued to live in Bath County until his death. Although it is not known whom he married, he was survived by a son.

Cary governed northern Carolina during a time of political turmoil and instability. He seems to have been motivated more by political ambition than by principle, but he never exhibited the vindictiveness that his opponents dealt him. In his second term of office his willingness to compromise with his political opponents established effective government in the colony. Cary also made a significant contribution to the economic development of Bath County and the future of Carolina by his residence and interest in the region south of Albemarle Sound.

• The public papers of Thomas Cary are published in William L. Saunders, ed., *The Colonial Records of North Carolina*, vols. 1–2 (1887); Robert J. Cain, ed., *Records of the Executive Council, 1664–1734*, The Colonial Records of North Carolina, 2d ser., vol. 7 (1984); and William S. Price, Jr., ed., *North Carolina Higher-Court Records*, The Colonial Records of North Carolina, 2d ser., vols. 4–5 (1974). Personal information on Cary is in Fairfax Harrison, *The Virginia Carys: An Essay in Genealogy* (1919); Stephen B. Weeks, *Southern Quakers and Slavery: A Study in Institutional History* (1896; repr. 1968); and Beaufort County, North Carolina Deeds, North Carolina State Archives, Raleigh, vol. 1.

LINDLEY S. BUTLER

CARY, William de la Montagne (30 June 1840–7 Jan. 1922), documentary artist, was born in Tappan, New York, the son of William Cary, an architect, and Susan de la Montagne. The family moved to New York City when Cary was a small child. His formal education is unknown; he may have been coached in painting by his father. At fourteen he was apprenticed to an engraver and later assisted in carving the stone birds used on staircases on the mall in Central Park.

Urged by his parents to study abroad, Cary chose instead to go West in April 1861 with two friends—William Henry Schieffelin, scion of a wholesale drug company, and Emlen N. Lawrence—on an adventurous expedition that set the pattern for Cary's career. The youths traveled 3,575 miles up the untamed Missouri River to hunt game and observe Native American tribal customs before the expansion of the railroads settled the wilderness. They survived the explosion and sinking of the steamboat *Chippewa* and several skirmishes with hostile Indians before reaching Fort Benton. They traveled alone to Hell Gate (near present-day Missoula, Montana) where they were able to join a military supply train bound for Fort Walla Walla, Washington. They arrived in San Francisco by steamer in November with twenty-five cents among them.

On their return to the East, Schieffelin entered active service in the Civil War as a major with the Seventh New York Regiment; he later took over the family business. No records explain Cary's failure to take part in the war. Until his marriage to Jessie S. Henderson in 1870, Cary lived in Hoboken, New Jersey. The couple lived on Long Island and in upper Manhattan. He maintained a Manhattan studio throughout his career.

Painting from field sketches based on his earlier adventures, Cary was recognized as outstanding among New York illustrators. He furnished illustrations for many books and periodicals, including *Harper's Weekly, Scribner's*, and Frank Leslie's publications.

In 1874 Cary returned to Bismarck, Dakota Territory, to join the Northern Boundary Survey with a commission from *Harper's Weekly* to do twenty-two illustrations on Montana scenes. Eighteen days on the Missouri in a fleet of mackinaw boats bearing prominent ethnologists and scientists provided Cary with sketches for his most famous paintings such as *Fire Canoe at Fort Berthold, Return of the Northern Boundary Survey, The Winter Supply Train for Boundary Survey*, and *Northern Boundary Survey under Major Twining*. The last painting includes likenesses of Twining, astronomer Francis Vinton Greene, and Dr. Elliott Coues, naturalist and assistant surgeon for the U.S. Army.

Sketches made on his westward trip to join the survey party and on the party's return downriver furnished material for the documentary oils that Cary painted during the remainder of his career. For years he maintained a studio in the Holbein Building, which housed the studios of Albert Bierstadt, Elihu Vedder, and George Brown Inness, Jr.

In 1885 Cary's oil *The Contested Game*, showing a grizzly bear challenging Indian hunters for a buffalo, was exhibited in the Royal Academy in London and in Berlin. Two of his bronzes were exhibited in the Fine Arts Building at the Chicago World's Fair in 1893. George Bird Grinnell may have been instrumental in arranging for a Cary exhibition of oil paintings at the Museum of Natural History of New York in 1917.

The Carys, who had five children, were separated several years before her death in 1914, presumably on account of the artist's inability to make an adequate living with his brush and because of his worsening drinking problem. Most of his oils were family-owned until they became the nucleus of Thomas Gilcrease's collection.

In his declining years, Cary corresponded with frontiersmen prominent in Montana's history to authenticate details in his work. He died at a daughter's home in Brookline, Massachusetts.

Cary's 1861 expedition, prompted by boyhood dreams, yielded sketches of Indians and wildlife on the plains before a way of life was changed forever by the massive westward movement following the Civil War. His vision of the West, evidenced in his illustrations for popular periodicals, contributed to that of the nation as a whole. His sympathy for Native Americans, particularly for the lot of Indian women, became more obvious late in the century in paintings such as *Enroute to the Trading Post* and *Enroute to Winter Camp*.

• All of Cary's papers and his 1874 journal are in files of the Gilcrease Institute of American History and Art, Tulsa, Okla. The Gilcrease also is the repository for the bulk of Cary's work, consisting of more than 200 paintings and drawings and two sculptures. A biography, *William de la Montagne Cary: Artist on the Missouri River*, by Mildred D. Ladner, was published in 1984. See also George Bird Grinnell, "Recollections of the Old West," *American Museum Journal* 17, no. 5 (1917): 332–40, and "American Genre of the Victorian Period," *Antiques*, June 1935, pp. 228–29; Lee Silliman, "William de la Montagne Cary," *American West* 17, no. 5 (1980): 34–47; and Mildred D. Ladner, "Missouri River Lured Artists of Two Continents," *Gilcrease Magazine of American History and Art* 2, no. 4 (1980): 20–28, "Artists on the Missouri," *Southwest Art* 12, no. 5 (1982): 116–23, and "William Cary," *American History Illustrated* 20, no. 1 (1985): 22–29.

MILDRED D. LADNER

CARY, William Lucius (27 Nov. 1910–7 Feb. 1983), chairman of the U.S. Securities and Exchange Commission and law professor, was born in Columbus, Ohio, the son of William Lincoln Cary, a utilities lawyer and executive, and Ellen Taugher. At the age of sixteen Cary enrolled at Yale College, where he received his A.B. in 1931. In 1934 he received his J.D. from Yale Law School, where he took one of the last corporate finance courses taught by William O. Douglas.

Upon graduating Cary went into private practice at the Cleveland law firm of Squire, Sanders & Dempsey. In 1936 he left practice to enter Harvard Business School, where he earned his M.B.A. in 1938. Immediately afterward Cary embarked on a series of assignments for the federal government, beginning as a staff counsel for the Securities and Exchange Commission (SEC) in Washington, D.C., under Douglas, who had become the chairman. In 1940 Cary was appointed as a special assistant to the head of the Tax Division of the Justice Department. Two years later he became the counsel to the Office of the Coordinator of Inter-American Affairs in Rio de Janeiro, Brazil. In 1943 he joined the U.S. Marine Corps, serving until 1946 and rising to the rank of major. While in the military he was assigned to the Office of Strategic Services and conducted espionage operations in Rumania and Yugoslavia.

At the end of World War II Cary launched his academic career, accepting an appointment as a lecturer at Harvard Business School in 1946. The following year he joined the faculty at Northwestern University School of Law, where he taught until 1955. From 1951 through 1952 Cary took leave from Northwestern to serve as a deputy department counselor for procurement at the Department of the Army in Washington, D.C. He married Katherine Lemoine Fenimore Cooper, a great-great-granddaughter of James Fenimore Cooper, in 1954; they had two children.

While at Northwestern Cary earned the respect of academics and the bar for his incisive knowledge of taxation and corporate law. Along with J. Keith Butters and John Lintner, he authored *Effects of Taxation: Corporate Mergers* in 1951. A prolific scholar, he also published numerous articles on topics ranging from bankruptcy to the Public Utility Holding Company Act and government financing of defense contractors. His most ambitious works during that period, dealing with sales-leasebacks and corporate mergers, displayed a sophisticated command of intricate business transactions and the laws that governed them. Those works presaged the law and economics movement of the 1980s and 1990s by analyzing how tax and corporate laws shaped companies' incentives when structuring major corporate transactions. Cary's 1955 article on pressure groups and the revenue code, which attacked preferential tax amendments, displayed a moral conscience that epitomized his later years at the SEC and his subsequent scholarly work.

Based on his contributions to tax and corporate law, Columbia Law School persuaded Cary to accept a professorship there in 1955. Cary spent the rest of his career at Columbia, apart from his years at the SEC. While in New York City, Cary also practiced law one day a week at Patterson, Belknap, Webb and Tyler, where he was counsel to the firm from 1959 to 1961 and again beginning in 1964. The textbook, *Cases and Materials on Corporations*, which he first coauthored with Ralph J. Baker in 1959, became the leading casebook on corporate governance and sealed Cary's reputation as a leading corporate law scholar.

In 1952 and 1956 Cary campaigned for Adlai E. Stevenson for president, and the two eventually became close friends. Later Cary worked with Robert M. Morgenthau in John F. Kennedy's bid for the presidency in 1960. After the election, on 3 February 1961 President Kennedy appointed Cary as the chairman of the SEC.

The SEC of the 1930s had been famed for its vigor and activism, but by the 1950s the agency had lapsed into lethargy, decimated by budget cuts and the appointment of political cronies. Cary arrived determined to reinvigorate the agency; in the words of John Brooks, he brought to the SEC "a vigor and drive that it had lacked for years" (p. 83). In three short years Cary persuaded Congress to increase the SEC's appropriations and staff by nearly one-half. His additions to the staff included a cadre of bright new law graduates, personally recruited by Cary, who imbued the agency with a spirit of scholarly reform.

Cary's tenure at the SEC ushered in an aggressive new era of enforcement. In 1961 Cary personally authored the SEC's decision in *In re Cady, Roberts & Co.*, in which the commission first held that insider trading by a stockbroker constituted securities fraud in violation of Section 10(b) of the Securities Exchange Act of 1934 and SEC Rule 10b-5. *Cady, Roberts* was unprecedented, among other reasons, for prohibiting trading based on confidential information before such information was disclosed to the general public. If disclosure was "improper or unrealistic," according to Cary (because, for example, the sale was conducted on an exchange rather than face-to-face), then "the alternative [was] to forgo the transaction."

Concerned that the SEC had lost sight of its mission, Cary also commissioned outside experts to conduct the landmark Special Study of the Securities Markets in 1961. Upon the release of the Special Study in 1963, Cary used its findings to lobby successfully for the Securities Acts Amendments of 1964, which extended SEC jurisdiction to the over-the-counter market and gave the commission authority to regulate stockbrokers and their firms.

On 20 August 1964, the day the amendments were signed, Cary resigned from the SEC and returned to Columbia Law School, where he was named as the Dwight Professor of Law. A decade later Cary wrote the article for which he was most renowned, titled "Federalism and Corporate Law: Reflections Upon Delaware." In the article, which appeared in the *Yale Law Journal* (83 [1974]: 663–705), Cary argued that the states had diluted the duties of loyalty and care for corporate directors, and he called for uniform federal standards of corporate responsibility to replace state law. Cary's proposal was never implemented, but his description of a "race for the bottom" among the states spurred copious debate among the succeeding generation of corporate law scholars. Cary formally retired from Columbia in 1979 but continued to teach there until his death in New York City.

Cary was one of the preeminent corporate law scholars of his time. Respected for combining scholasticism and pragmatism, he often quoted legal theorist Karl Llewellyn to the effect that "technique without ideals is a menace; ideals without technique are a mess." By virtue of his practicality and ideals, Cary became "a pivotal figure" at the SEC, who, according to Professor Joel Seligman, "picked up the [SEC] at a point where it had become a dreary, unaggressive overseer of Wall Street, and transformed it into an institution that worried about the really serious problems in the securities field" (*New York Times*, 9 Feb. 1983). As such, he continued the legacy of the SEC's first chairman Douglas and was the father of the modern Securities and Exchange Commission.

• In addition to the works mentioned above, Cary's major works include *Politics and the Regulatory Agencies* (1967); "Corporate Financing through the Sale and Lease-back of Property: Business, Tax, and Policy Considerations," *Harvard Law Review* 62 (1948): 1–41; "Motives Affecting Form of Sales and Purchases of Businesses," with Butters, *Harvard Law Review* 64 (1951): 697–726; and "Pressure Groups and the Revenue Code: A Requiem in Honor of the Departing Uniformity of the Tax Laws," *Harvard Law Review* 68 (1955): 745–80. A bibliography of Cary's writings appears in the *Columbia Law Review* 79 (1979): 614. Secondary accounts include John Brooks, *The Go-Go Years* (1973); Securities and Exchange Commission, " . . . *Good People, Important Problems and Workable Laws: 50 Years of the U.S. Securities and Exchange Commission* (1984); and Joel Seligman, *The Transformation of Wall Street* (1995). Obituaries are in the *Columbia Law Review* 83 (1983): 765–71, and the *New York Times*, 9 Feb. 1983.

PATRICIA A. MCCOY

CARYLL, Ivan (12 May 1861–29 Nov. 1921), theatrical composer, was born Felix Tilkin in Liege, Belgium. His parents' names are unknown. After attending conservatories in Liege and Paris, where he studied with Camille Saint-Saëns and won a gold medal, Tilkin moved to London in 1882. There he changed his name and struggled for a time, giving piano lessons to suburban housewives. Soon, however, after contributing songs to West End shows, he became a conductor at the Comedy and Lyric theaters.

In 1886 Caryll's operetta *The Lily of Leoville*, with a "light and pretty" score, achieved a six-week run. In the same year he became music director of the musical play *Dorothy*, which ran for 931 performances at the Gaiety Theatre. Between 1887 and 1892 Caryll wrote seven one-act curtain-raising operettas for *Dorothy*, for its successor *Doris*, and for *The Red Hussar*.

Caryll's interpolations overwhelmed the original score of the French *La Cigale* (1890), a show that co-starred the "vivacious and arch" American Geraldine Ulmar, known in her homeland for playing Gilbert and Sullivan heroines. Caryll and Ulmar soon married. They had no children. Caryll's second wife was Gaiety star Maud Hill; they had five children. After the death of composer Alfred Cellier, Caryll collaborated with W. S. Gilbert to complete *The Mountebanks* (1892).

By this time the Gaiety's impresario George "Guv" Edwardes had developed the musical comedy format, a lightly plotted form employing broader comedy and less demanding music than operetta. For the next twenty years the adaptable, tune-filled Caryll was a Gaiety mainstay.

Caryll's first full musical comedy score, for *Little Christopher Columbus* (1893), was called more evocative of the "vulgar" music hall than the operatic stage. When *Little Christopher Columbus* traveled to New York it became the 1895 season's most popular show. Jerome Kern's biographer believes it may have been the twelve-year-old Kern's introduction to the musical theater.

As a Gaiety composer Caryll became part of a factory that rarely gave one librettist, lyricist, or composer entire responsibility for a show. In *The Shop Girl* (1894) Caryll's sentimental waltzes were first supplemented by Lionel Monckton's graceful songs. Caryll's well-crafted but not particularly memorable melodies eventually underpinned more than forty shows on both sides of the Atlantic.

As the Gaiety's musical director, according to British musical historian Alan Hyman, Caryll would "drive up to the theatre every night . . . in a pair-horse Victoria with two men on the box, and used to walk on to the stage looking like a fashion plate in his dress clothes, with his black beard parted on both sides of his chin" (*The Gaiety Years*, p. 68). A ferocious presence, he would stare intently at the performers throughout the show.

Caryll's versatility was further displayed in the opera bouffe *Dandy Dick Whittington* (1895) and the farcical adaptation of *The Gay Parisienne* (1896), for which he produced jaunty new music for the American Moore and Burgess minstrel song "Mary Jane's Top Note." In the Gaiety comedies *The Circus Girl* (1896) and *A Runaway Girl* (1898) Caryll produced solid, singable numbers, and Monckton wrote all the hits.

By 1899 Sir Edward Elgar was writing original compositions for Ivan Caryll's Light Orchestra. *The Lucky Star* (1899) found Caryll adapting Emmanuel Chabrier's score of the operetta *L'Etoile* so thoroughly that only one Chabrier number remained. In 1901 *The Ladies' Paradise*, with a score by Caryll, became the first musical comedy performed at the Metropolitan Opera House in New York. In *The Girl from Kay's* (1902) Caryll's "Semi-Detached" and "Mrs. Hoggenheimer" proved his ability to write comic songs. In 1903 Caryll's last operetta, written in 1897, *The Duchess of Dantzig*, starring Billie Burke, was called by the *Stage* "sometimes Offenbachian." Richard Traubner called the patter songs "Sullivanesque." Caryll's 1903 scores for *The Orchid* and *The Earl and the Girl* were supplemented with interpolations of American hits. Caryll's "By the Shores of the Mediterranean" from *The Earl* is a swooping comic waltz ("They clang their guitars and light your cigars"). When *The Earl* traveled to Broadway, Kern interpolated his first hit, "How'd You Like to Spoon with Me?" *The Cherry Girl* (1903) included "Goodbye Little Yellow Bird," a song so evoking its era that it was used in the 1945 American film of Oscar Wilde's *The Picture of Dorian Gray*.

Caryll's lively, tuneful scores found increasing favor in the United States, with Kern's songs frequently added. For London's *Nelly Neil* (1907) American producer Charles Frohman teamed Caryll with Charles McLellan who, as "Hugh Morton," had written the hugely successful *The Belle of New York* (1899). The last great Gaiety show, *Our Miss Gibbs* (1909), starred Gertie Millar, Monckton's wife. In 1910 Caryll left for the United States.

At a time when all major Broadway scores except George M. Cohan's were being written by transplanted Europeans such as Gustave Kerker, Victor Herbert, and Ludwig Englander, Caryll's move seemed to liberate his hit-making qualities. With McLellan he wrote *Marriage à la Carte* (1911) and *The Pink Lady* (1911), which produced Caryll's most famous song, the surging waltz "Beautiful Lady" ("Glide, glide, beautiful lady") and made pink a fashionable color, thanks to the costumes of its star, Hazel Dawn. Also written with McLellan was the highly successful *Oh! Oh!! Delphine!!!* (1913), one of several adaptations of French farces that displayed a dazzling variety of waltzes and an authentic can-can. Against *Delphine, The Red Petticoat*, with the young Jerome Kern's first full score, quickly closed.

Caryll became a box-office asset, collaborating with lyricist Anne Caldwell in the lavish *Chin-Chin* (1914). The Aladdin story featured knockabout comics Dave Montgomery and Fred Stone and introduced the catch-line "very good Eddie." For *Chin-Chin* Caryll wrote "Ragtime Temple Bells" and the hit "Good-bye Girls, I'm Through." After *Papa's Darling* (1914), with the prolific librettist Harry B. Smith, Caryll teamed with Caldwell again for Charles Dillingham's *Jack o' Lantern* (1917), which produced "Wait till the Cows Come Home," which was for several decades the theme of radio's "Carnation Contented Hour."

Caryll enjoyed spending money to entertain himself and his friends, and it was not long before he owned main residences on Long Island and in Paris, as well as a villa in Deauville. According to Hyman, when he was hatching a new score, Caryll would take a suite at the Knickerbocker Hotel and invite managers there to make him an offer. According to P. G. Wodehouse, who dubbed him "Fabulous Felix," his huge beard hypnotized all the bidders.

Caryll was so successful that he was passed over by producers Elizabeth Marbury and Ray Comstock for their series of intimate musical comedies at the Princess Theatre because they could not afford him. After Kern got the job, the most important era of American musicals to date started without Caryll.

Caryll's first outing with Guy Bolton and Wodehouse, *The Girl behind the Gun* (1918), was a relative failure, and in general his American shows were not popular in London, except *Kissing Time* (1919), the revised version of *The Girl behind the Gun*, which opened the Winter Garden Theatre. Its score included mild syncopation, gallops, Sullivanesque sounds, a genteel rag, a promenading song, and thundering waltzes. "Women Haven't Any Mercy on a Man" is a mock operatic recitative prefiguring by thirty-five years Frederick Loewe's "A Hymn to Him" in *My Fair Lady*.

Caryll was rehearsing *Little Miss Raffles* (subsequently *The Hotel Mouse*, 1922) in New York when he collapsed in the orchestra pit; he died of cancer ten days later. The score for the show incorporated jazzier American dance rhythms than he had previously attempted, demonstrating that this transitional era in the musical theater had no more versatile craftsman.

• Caryll is profiled in Alan Hyman's *The Gaiety Years* (1975) and *Sullivan and His Satellites* (1978). Lists and evaluations of Caryll's musical accomplishments are in Kurt Gänzl, *British Musical Theatre* (1986); Gerald Bordman, *American Musical Comedy* (1982) and *Jerome Kern* (1980); Richard Traubner, *Operetta* (1984); and Ethan Mordden, *Broadway Babies* (1985). Periodicals such as the *Playgoer and Society Illustrated* and *Play Pictorial* review many of Caryll's shows and offer biographical insights. Because American recording practice lagged far behind Britain until the 1940s, recordings of Caryll's works are located in Robert Seeley and Rex Bunnett's *London Musical Shows on Record 1889–1989* (1989) and at the British National Sound Archive, a division of the British Library.

JAMES ROSS MOORE

CASALS, Pablo (29 Dec. 1876–22 Oct. 1973), cellist and conductor, was born Pau Carlos Salvador Defilló de Casals in El Vendrell (Catalonia), Spain, the son of Carlos Casals i Riba, a musician, and Pilar Ursula Defilló i Amiguet. Casals demonstrated his musical gift early, joining his father's church choir at age five and later studying violin, piano, and organ with his father. He discovered the cello in 1888 and entered the Municipal School of Music in Barcelona. Casals studied cello with José García, his only teacher on the instrument, but even then he was rethinking accepted techniques of cello playing. He was joined in Barcelona by his mother and brother, helping support the family by playing in a café. He graduated in 1893 with highest honors in cello, piano, and composition.

Upon graduating, Casals went to Madrid with a recommendation from Isaac Albéniz to meet the Count of Morphy, a noted arts patron. Morphy secured Casals a pension from Queen María Cristina, whom Casals often visited. Morphy tutored Casals for two years, helping to finish his general education. Casals also studied chamber music with Jesús de Monasterio at the Royal Conservatory in Madrid. He pursued further musical study at Brussels Conservatory at Morphy's urging but the additional training proved unnecessary. Casals and his family then moved to Paris, but he found launching a career there impossible with his family in tow. He returned to Barcelona in early 1896 and became a cello teacher at the Municipal School of Music and first cellist in the Gran Teatro del Liceu. By 1897 he was touring in Spain with a chamber ensemble and as a soloist.

In May 1899 Casals moved to Paris alone, playing with the noted Lamoureux Orchestra and making his London debut. His extensive touring began in 1900. One of his first partners was pianist Harold Bauer, with whom he played often. For ten months in 1901–1902, Casals toured North America with other musicians. A serious injury to his left hand in San Francisco ended the tour for Casals, but by age thirty he had performed throughout Europe, Russia, and the Americas, often playing 150 to 200 concerts per year. He played at the White House for President Theodore Roosevelt in 1904. In 1906 he began playing in a trio with violinist Jacques Thibaud and pianist Alfred Cortot, forming a celebrated piano trio that performed together off and on until 1933. Casals often resided in Paris between 1906 and 1910, maintaining a relationship with Portuguese cellist Guilhermina Suggia (the couple lived together but never married).

Casals's relationship with Suggia ended in 1913, and in 1914 he married American soprano Susan Scott Metcalfe; they had no children. They were separated in 1928 and divorced in 1957. Like many European artists, Casals lived and toured in the United States during World War I. In 1919 he assisted Cortot in founding the École Normale de Musique in Paris and gave summer master classes there for a number of years.

After World War I Casals did not wish to continue such extensive touring and settled in Barcelona. In 1919 he founded the Orquestra Pau Casals, the first orchestra he conducted on a regular basis. The orchestra played seasons in the fall and spring until the Spanish Civil War (1936–1939) and reached out to the lower classes through the Workingmen's Concert Association, which grew to 300,000 members. During these years Casals continued touring in the United States, England, and elsewhere, using his earnings to support the orchestra. Late in the 1930s Casals made most of his important recordings as a cellist, especially those of J. S. Bach's Suites for Unaccompanied Cello (1936–1939) and Antonín Dvořák's Cello Concerto in B Minor (1939), recorded with the Czech Philharmonic conducted by George Szell.

Casals continued to live in Catalonia throughout the 1930s and during the Spanish Civil War but still toured. He shared his father's Republican political beliefs and was forced into exile at the end of the war. He became active in refugee relief efforts and spent World War II in Prades, a village in French Catalonia. His life became difficult after the German occupation of the town in late 1942. After France was freed, Casals performed numerous concerts in England and France, but by the end of 1946 he was disillusioned by the world's acceptance of the Franco government in Spain and withdrew from public performance. He was openly hostile toward musicians who had appeared to collaborate with fascist governments, most notably Cortot. Casals retired to Prades, where he began to compose again and teach cello. His companion in Prades was Franchisca Capdevila, a close friend and confidante for many years, who lived with Casals from 1928 until her death in 1955.

Casals's return to the concert stage was largely the work of violinist Alexander Schneider. Unable to lure Casals to the United States for concerts, he took the advice of Casals's lifelong friend, pianist Mieczyslaw Horszowski, and planned a Bach Festival in 1950 that brought many musicians to Prades. The festival included a chamber orchestra that Casals directed, many chamber music performances, and solo concerts by Casals. The early Prades Festivals were subsidized heavily by Columbia Records, which released many discs of the performances. The Prades Festivals helped reestablish Casals's position in the musical world. Although his greatest years as a cellist were behind him, his best work as a conductor was just beginning. Many performances that he directed were recorded, and sometimes they were filmed.

The last period in Casals's life began when an eighteen-year-old Puerto Rican cellist, Marta Montañez, arrived in Prades to study in late 1954. She rapidly moved from favorite student to secretary. After traveling together in Europe in the summer of 1955, in December Casals and Montañez sailed for Puerto Rico. Casals visited the family of his mother, a native Puerto Rican, and found the island a worthy substitute for his native Catalonia. Before he left Puerto Rico in March 1956, the first Festival Casals had been planned there for April 1957, again with the help of Schneider. Casals moved to Puerto Rico in 1957 and lived there the rest of his life. He suffered a heart attack on the eve of the first festival but fully recovered. Casals married Marta Montañez in 1957; they had no children. There is little doubt that the domestic happiness this brought Casals kept him a productive musician into extreme old age.

Casals spent the last sixteen years of his life working on the festivals he helped create and teaching a regular schedule of master classes. The Festival Casals in San Juan took place each spring and the Prades Festival each summer. Beginning in the early 1950s he taught in August at the Zermatt Summer Academy in Switzerland, and after 1960 he taught at the Marlboro Music Festival in Vermont in July. Eventually Marlboro replaced Prades on Casals's schedule; a number of his later recordings were made as a chamber musician and conductor at Marlboro.

Casals's reputation as a humanitarian stems from his refugee relief efforts in the years around World War II and his work for peace in the last two decades of his life. In 1958 he signed a letter with Albert Schweitzer that called for an end to atomic weapons testing, and later that year he participated in a United Nations Day concert broadcast throughout the world. In 1958 he was nominated for the Nobel Peace Prize, and in November 1961 he performed in a highly publicized, televised concert at the Kennedy White House. Beginning in 1960 he conducted his oratorio, *El Pessebre* (The manger), in a crusade for peace, leading the work thirty-three times in a number of countries before his death. He spent more time in Puerto Rico after 1966 but took part in dozens of performances after his ninetieth birthday, including his third concert at the United Nations in 1971 and his last visit to Israel in September 1973. Casals died in San Juan.

Casals's influence as a musician and teacher was monumental. He redefined cello technique, freeing players from unnecessarily confining practices in the right and left hands. He was among the first successful touring solo cellists, helping codify the cello's solo repertory and especially championing Bach's Suites for Unaccompanied Cello. He taught many important cellists and influenced most players of the instrument. He had an important career as a conductor in Spain before World War II and throughout the world late in his life. Although Casals was a fine pianist and fertile composer, few of his compositions were published during his lifetime. His musical taste as a performer and composer was profoundly conservative, but because of the integrity that he brought to his music making he transcended the conflict between traditional musical sounds and the avant-garde. A man of deep principles, Casals had many devoted friends both in and out of music, but his relationships were sometimes strained by his inability to compromise significantly. Few musicians have had the same impact as a humanitarian and spokesman for peace.

• Collections of Casals's papers are at the Fundació Pau Casals in San Salvador, Spain, and in the personal possession of his widow, Marta Casals Istomin. Some of Casals's published interviews include J. Ma. Corredor, *Conversations avec Casals* (1955), later published in English as *Conversations with Casals* (1956); and Albert E. Kahn, *Joys and Sorrows: His Own Story* (1970), also published as *Joys and Sorrows: Reflections* (1974). Both of these works provide useful pictures of the musician, but Casals controlled the selection of material to be included. A major biography is H. L. Kirk, *Pablo Casals* (1974), written in the last years of Casals's life with his cooperation. Although mostly laudatory, the book nevertheless touches on most aspects of Casals's life, including those he hesitated to discuss in interviews. Other useful biographies include the brief but extensively illustrated Bernard Taper, *Cellist in Exile: A Portrait of Pablo Casals* (1962), and Robert Baldock, *Pablo Casals* (1992), a detailed and evenhanded study that provides a list of Casals's recordings available on compact disc. Enric Casals, *Pau Casals: dades biogràfiques inèdites, cartes íntimes I records viscuts* (1979), provides an intimate portrait written by his brother, who used unedited sources, letters, and descriptions of his relationships with many important musicians. An interesting photographic essay concerning Casals's music making and domestic life in the mid-1960s is Vytas Valaitis, *Casals* (1966), which includes text by Theodore Strongin. Casals's musical thoughts and personality are the subject of David Blum, *Casals and the Art of Interpretation* (1977), a study intended for the musically literate. Obituaries are in the *New York Times*, 24 Oct. 1973, and *Time*, 5 Nov. 1973.

PAUL R. LAIRD

CASE, Adelaide Teague (10 Jan. 1887–19 June 1948), religious educator, was born in St. Louis, Missouri, the daughter of Charles Lyman Case, the American manager of the London Assurance Company, and Lois Adelaide Teague. When Adelaide was an infant the Cases moved with their six children to New York City, where she was raised as an Anglican. Case attended the Brearley School in New York City and graduated from Bryn Mawr College (A.B., 1908). She then taught for a year at St. Faith's Episcopal Boarding School for Girls in Poughkeepsie, New York. In 1910 she enrolled in the graduate program of Columbia University to study history and sociology, but due to tuberculosis, which she had contracted in childhood, she withdrew from the program after one year. She underwent treatment for nearly a year and partially convalesced during a trip to Europe with her parents. From 1914 to 1916 Case worked as a librarian for the Christ Missions House in New York, but she continued to suffer health problems and underwent a serious knee operation in 1916.

In the fall of 1917 Case enrolled in graduate school again—this time at Columbia University's Teachers College, specializing in religious education. During this time (1917–1919) she also began teaching religious education at the New York Training School for Deaconesses, owned and run by the Order of Deaconesses of the Episcopal church. After taking the Ph.D. from Teachers College in November 1924, she accepted a teaching appointment there in the religious education department. Among the courses she taught were Principles of Religious Education, Use of the Bible in Religious Education, Major Course for Directors of Religious Education, and Professional Problems in Religious Education. Case advanced through the academic ranks to full professor and became departmental chair by 1935. In 1941 she joined the faculty of the Episcopal Theological School in Cambridge, Massachusetts, becoming the first woman to be appointed to full professorial rank in any Episcopal or Anglican seminary in the United States.

Case was very much involved in religious and civic organizations. She served on the directing boards of the International Council of Religious Education, the Student Christian Movement, the American Jewish Congress and Beth Hayaled of New York City, the Religious Education Association, the Federal Council of Churches, the Riverside Colored Orphanage, and the Church League for Industrial Democracy (later known as the Episcopal League for Social Action). She was also on the board of Windham House, an unofficial training center for women interested in the teaching profession.

Case's numerous writings indicate that she advocated the then fairly recently developed "progressive" philosophy of education that emphasized, among other things, the importance of child-centered, as opposed to teacher-focused, curricula and agenda. In her 1924 dissertation, "Liberal Christianity and Religious Education," she creatively related the progressive philosophy to religious education in her challenge to persuade educators and religious leaders that "the aims of religious education must concern themselves with issues alive in the present social environment of children."

Case also took scholarly interest in social ethics, during her time a popular subfield in theological studies. According to her dissertation adviser, educationist and theologian George A. Coe, she concerned herself with liberalism that was both "intellectual and social." In her mature writings Case also applied her progressive religious-education philosophy to issues having to do with moral and ethical formation and the role she thought the critical study of the Bible should have in it: "As an element in religious teaching critical study of the Bible has an important function, but it must be subordinate to human values" ("When Is Education Religious?" [1929]). This article reflected not only her religious intellectualism and modernism but also her deep humanity, a synthesis few in her time pursued.

An illuminating example of the professional and personal tightrope Case was forced to walk can be seen in the fact that although she personally favored ordination for women in the Episcopal church, she never pressed it as an issue in her writings. She was a member of a generation of highly trained, committed, and determined religious women who, having the door to ordination and church leadership closed to them, nevertheless pursued a religious vocation and challenged the patriarchy and traditionalism of all types through other creative paths. Case's path was teaching and scholarship. She worked zealously in her commitment to make religious education comprehensive. Her commitment is reflected in the following passage from "When Is Education Religious?": [T]he time has come for the churches to set up a seven-day plan for religious education which will utilize the public school, the home, the playground, and the church school, integrating the religious aspects of all these experiences and directing them toward the realization of Christian purposes."

Case's legacy lies primarily in writings of this sort—deeply felt, prophetic, but also reasoned and engaging about a wide range of contemporary social and political issues. They exemplify the activist life of the female religious liberal intellectual during a time when figures such as Reinhold Niebuhr, Henry Pit Van Deusen, and Paul Tillich loomed large as American religious public intellectuals. Here beyond the pulpit she found her niche and—as the many female religious academics who modeled their careers after hers suggest—made a lasting contribution.

Case never married. She died in Boston.

• Some of Case's correspondence is in the files of William Russell, Teachers College Library, Columbia University, and the papers of George Coe, Yale Divinity School Library. In addition to the works mentioned above, Case's books include *As Modern Writers See Jesus: A Descriptive Bibliography of Books about Jesus* (1927), *Seven Psalms* (1935), *Servant of the Lord* (1940), and *Teaching That Touches Life* (n.d.). She also published chapters in *Religion, the Dynamic of Education*, ed. Walter M. Howlett (1929); *Our Children*, ed. Dorothy Canfield Fisher and Sidonie M. Gruenberg (1932); *Liberal Catholicism and the Modern World*, ed. Frank Gavin (1934); and *The Church through Half a Century*, ed. Samuel McC. Cavert and Henry P. Van Deusen (1936). For biographical data see Sydney Temple, ed., *Peace Is Possible: Essays Dedicated to the Memory of Adelaide T. Case* (1949); J. C. Schwarz, ed. *Religious Leaders of America*, vol. 2 (1941–1942); James A. Muller, *The Episcopal Theological School, 1867–1943* (1944); W. A. Nichols, "Theological Seminary Called Woman Professor, *New York World-Telegram*, 14 June 1941; and Charles L. Taylor, Jr., "Adelaide T. Case: An Appreciation," *Living Church*, 8 Aug. 1948, p. 11. An obituary is in the *New York Times*, 20 June 1948.

VINCENT L. WIMBUSH

CASE, Clifford Philip (16 Apr. 1904–5 Mar. 1982), U.S. senator, was born in Franklin Park, New Jersey, the son of Clifford P. Case, Dutch Reformed minister, and Jeannette McAlpin Benedict. Case spent much of his childhood in Poughkeepsie, New York, where his father had a pastorate. Graduating from Rutgers University in 1925, he received his law degree from Columbia University in 1928. He joined the prestigious New York firm of Simpson, Thacher & Bartlett and later became a partner.

In 1928 he married Ruth Miriam Smith. They had three children and resided in Rahway, New Jersey.

Case first ran for public office in 1937, winning a seat on the Rahway Common Council. In 1942 he was elected as a Republican to the New Jersey Assembly, and in 1944 he won the 6th Congressional District race for the U.S. House of Representatives. Over the next ten years he compiled a fairly liberal voting record, particularly in the areas of civil rights and immigration reform, and supported a bipartisan foreign policy. He was an early leader of the movement to draft Dwight Eisenhower for the Republican presidential nomination in 1952. In the November election Case, backed (despite his support of the Taft-Hartley Act) by the AFL, CIO, and Americans for Democratic Action, ran ahead of Eisenhower in his district.

In early 1953 Case announced his candidacy for the New Jersey governorship, but he soon dropped out when state Republican leaders failed to support him. He resigned his House seat in August 1953 to accept the presidency of the Fund for the Republic, a Ford Foundation offshoot dedicated to eliminating restrictions on freedom of thought and expression.

With the Republicans having lost the 1953 contest for governor, as well as the special election in Case's old congressional district, he became the choice of party leaders for the U.S. Senate in 1954. But he then created a furor by announcing that, if elected, he would vote to deny Senator Joseph R. McCarthy membership on any committee with investigative functions. Conservatives in the state GOP denounced him as a "pro-Communist Republicrat," but President Eisenhower and Vice President Richard Nixon spoke up vigorously on his behalf, and Case won by 3,507 votes, out of 1.8 million cast. For the next two decades Case, as a self-styled champion of "middle-of-the-road progressivism," was well-positioned to appeal to a New Jersey electorate fairly evenly split between the two major parties. The Republican label he inherited from his father, his own liberal stance on most issues, and his ability to communicate his conscience-driven approach to policy left his Democratic opponents with only a narrow base in the electorate. He gained reelection in 1960, 1966, and 1972 by comfortable margins.

In the Senate, Case championed civil rights and social legislation. He was the only Republican to endorse President John F. Kennedy's proposal to provide medical insurance for the elderly. A supporter of President Lyndon Johnson's Great Society programs, he later often found himself at odds with President Nixon. He opposed the supersonic transport (SST) and three of Nixon's six appointments to the U.S. Supreme Court; he also voted to override Nixon's veto of a day-care funding bill. In the early 1970s Case was the only Republican senator given a zero rating by the conservative Americans for Constitutional Action.

Serving on the Foreign Relations Committee, of which he became the ranking Republican member, he took an increasingly dim view of American involvement in Vietnam and the powers that presidents Johnson and Nixon exercised to escalate the fighting there. Reflecting this disenchantment, Case in 1972 initiated legislation requiring the president to report any executive agreement reached with a foreign country to Congress within sixty days. In 1973 Congress approved legislation drafted by Case and Frank Church (D-Idaho) cutting off appropriations for American military operations anywhere in the former Indo-China. Case also was a strong advocate of the War Powers Act adopted later that year. He later gave his backing to the Panama Canal treaties negotiated by President Jimmy Carter, although his long-standing support for Israel led him to oppose the Carter administration's plan to sell military aircraft to Egypt and Saudi Arabia.

Known for both his quiet manner and political independence, Case was an early sponsor of efforts to make Congress and the public more aware of the possible conflicts-of-interest facing legislators as they carried out their responsibilities. Years before it was mandated by law, Case made public his personal finances.

Up for reelection in 1978, he knew that he faced a difficult battle against his likely Democratic opponent, former basketball star Bill Bradley, but he took the Republican primary contest—as he had in the past—lightly. This proved to be a mistake. After twenty-four years in the Senate and almost thirty-four years in Washington, Case was becoming a remote figure in his home state. And New Jersey, the nation's most suburbanized state, was ripe for the taxpayers' revolt beginning to sweep the country. Jeffrey Bell, Case's 34-year-old GOP rival, who had served on Ronald Reagan's 1976 presidential campaign staff, found a receptive audience for his advocacy of the Kemp-Roth tax reduction plan. Presaging the conservative direction of the GOP nationally, Bell narrowly defeated Case, although Bradley won the general election.

Case remained in Washington, resuming the practice of law. He served as the head of Freedom House, an organization devoted to encouraging democracy around the world. He also led the unsuccessful fight against the Reagan administration's decision to sell AWACs to Saudi Arabia.

Case was representative of the moderate-to-liberal northeastern Republicans who, from the 1940s through the 1970s, dominated the party in the region—and to some extent nationally—and offered voters an attractive alternative to old-fashioned Democratic machine candidates. They helped to blur partisan lines in this era and were critical to the enactment of reform legislation. With the decline of liberalism generally by the early 1980s, Republicans like Case had been consigned to the margins of their party.

• The Case papers, mainly office records of his years in Congress (1945–1979), but including some personal material, are at the Rutgers University Library. There are no scholarly articles or books detailing Case's career; his activities are best followed in the annual volumes of the *Congressional Quarterly*. His brief tenure at the Fund for the Republic is described in Thomas C. Reeves, *Freedom and the Foundation: The Fund for the Republic in the Era of McCarthyism* (1969). A sketch of him appeared in *Current Biography 1955*, and the *New York Times* and the *Washington Post* ran obituaries on 7 Mar. 1982.

MARK I. GELFAND

CASE, Everett Norris (21 June 1900–30 Apr. 1966), basketball coach, was born in Anderson, Indiana, the son of Samuel H. Case and Emma Norris. Case played tennis at Anderson High School, but, surprisingly, he did not play basketball, either in high school or in college.

For more than two decades he coached high school basketball in his native state, where he became a controversial legend. He began that career in 1919–1920 as an assistant in Connersville, Indiana. The following season he became head coach at Columbus High School, and he went on to coach at Smithfield High School (1921–1922), Frankfort High School (1922–

1931, 1934–1942), and Anderson High School (1931–1933). He had his greatest success at Frankfort, where his teams captured state titles in 1925, 1929, 1936, and 1939. The innovative Case was accused frequently of illegal recruiting, and his 1929 Frankfort team was placed on probation for that reason; his Anderson team was put on probation for the 1932–1933 season for using an ineligible player. The best evidence indicates that Case's high school record as a head coach was 467 wins, 124 losses, and 1 tie (a .789 winning percentage).

While coaching, Case attended a number of colleges and received a bachelor's degree in physical education in 1923 from the University of Wisconsin. He was an assistant coach at the University of Southern California in 1933–1934 while he was obtaining his M.A. degree; his thesis was on free throw shooting.

Commissioned a lieutenant in the U.S. Navy in 1942, he headed the navy's physical fitness program at DePauw University in 1943–1944 and coached the V-5 basketball team to a 29–3 record. The following season he was athletic director at the Naval Air Station at Ottumwa, Iowa, where he coached the base basketball team to a 27–2 mark.

Case was discharged in 1946 with the rank of commander. That summer he became head basketball coach at North Carolina State College (later University) in Raleigh. He had an immediate catalytic affect on college basketball at that school and in the state by introducing a rarely seen, up-tempo brand of basketball along with a sophisticated recruiting network and a promotional flair. Early in his State career, fire marshals canceled several games because of overcrowding.

Case's first North Carolina State team won twenty-six games, only two fewer than the number for the previous four seasons combined. Relying in large part on players brought in from the high school basketball hotbeds of Indiana, North Carolina State captured the Southern Conference (SC) tournament championship from 1947 through 1952—an unprecedented six consecutive seasons. The school joined the newly formed Atlantic Coast Conference (ACC) in the autumn of 1953 and won the first three ACC tournament titles in 1954, 1955, and 1956.

Case's first decade at North Carolina State was one of almost total dominance of its opponents. His overall won-lost record from 1946–1947 through 1955–1956 was 267–60, and his teams had third-place finishes in the 1947 National Invitation (NIT) and the 1950 National Collegiate Athletic Association (NCAA) tournaments. His teams also competed in the 1948 and 1951 NIT and the 1951, 1952, 1954, and 1956 NCAA tournaments.

Case's impact was felt widely. Rival schools upgraded their programs to keep pace. After losing fifteen consecutive games to their arch-rivals from Raleigh, the University of North Carolina (UNC) hired successful St. John's University coach Frank McGuire to oversee its program. Case established and hosted the Dixie Classic, a popular three-day holiday tournament. His team won the event's inaugural in 1949 and repeated as winners in 1950, 1951, 1952, 1954, and 1955.

North Carolina State's program began to exhibit problems during the mid-1950s. The NCAA placed the Wolfpack on probation for the 1954–1955 season because of recruiting violations. More serious recruiting troubles in 1956 resulted in a four-year NCAA probation, which kept State out of the 1959 NCAA tournament. Competition from other ACC teams stiffened. UNC captured the NCAA title in 1957, a championship that always eluded Case. In 1959 Duke University hired one of his former players and assistant coaches, Vic Bubas, who quickly moved Duke's program past that of State. The most telling blow, however, fell in 1961 when four of Case's players admitted to taking money from gamblers for shaving points during the 1960–1961 season. Ironically, Case had long taken the lead in combating gambler influence on college basketball. As a result of this scandal, which also involved UNC, the Dixie Classic was canceled permanently, and recruiting restrictions were placed on both schools.

Case called the scandal "the darkest day in my basketball coaching career." His program never recovered its earlier luster. He completed the 1963–1964 season, but ill health forced him to retire after two games in December 1964. His record for eighteen seasons at North Carolina State was 377–134. He died in Raleigh. A bachelor, he left a significant portion of his estate to all of his former college players who had graduated. He was inducted into the Naismith Memorial Basketball Hall of Fame, the North Carolina Sports Hall of Fame, and the Indiana Basketball Hall of Fame.

Case approached basketball with the fervor of an evangelist. His promotional abilities enabled him to transplant the basketball hysteria so characteristic of Indiana into his adopted state. Only five years after he arrived in North Carolina, the Raleigh *News and Observer* wrote: "Since the little man came here from Indiana . . . basketball has almost replaced politics as a favorite topic of discussion." Case was innovative, energetic, meticulous, and so crafty that rivals dubbed him the "old gray fox." Most of all, he was fiercely competitive—a characteristic that led him to cross ethical lines on more than one occasion. He left an indelible mark on college basketball.

• Extensive newspaper and magazine clipping files on Case can be found at North Carolina State University in the Sports Information Department and the University Archives. There is no biography of Case. The most complete discussions of his career can be found in Smith Barrier, *On Tobacco Road: Basketball in North Carolina* (1983); William H. Beezley, *The Wolfpack: Intercollegiate Athletics at North Carolina State University* (1976); and Ron Morris, *ACC Basketball: An Illustrated History* (1988). Beezley discusses the point-shaving scandal in "The 1961 Scandal at North Carolina State and the End of the Dixie Classic," in *Sport and Higher Education*, ed. Donald Chu et al. (1985). Also see Jim L. Sumner, "Everett Case

Conquers Dixie: Hoosier Basketball in North Carolina," *Traces of Indiana and Midwestern History* 5 (Fall 1993): 4–17. An obituary is in the *New York Times*, 1 May 1966.

JIM SUMNER

CASE, Francis Higbee (9 Dec. 1896–22 June 1962), journalist and politician, was born in Everly, Iowa, the son of Rev. Herbert L. Case, a Methodist minister, and Mary Ellen Grannis. In 1909 his family moved to Sturgis, in South Dakota's Black Hills. Entering Dakota Wesleyan University in 1914, he displayed skills as an orator and writer. Upon graduation in 1918, Case enlisted in the Marine Corps and served eight months but saw no service in World War I. Following the war he resumed his studies and in 1920 earned an M.A. degree in history from Northwestern University. While at Northwestern, Case served as assistant editor of the *Epworth Herald*, a Chicago-based Methodist periodical, and published several works related to church advertising. Returning to South Dakota, he purchased an interest in the *Rapid City Daily Journal* in 1922 and, over the next twenty years, served as editor and publisher of several other South Dakota newspapers.

Case entered politics in 1924, when he was elected Republican chairman of the state's Third Congressional District as a compromise choice between his party's feuding progressive and conservative factions. In 1926 he gained statewide prominence by succeeding in convincing President Calvin Coolidge to vacation in the Black Hills. That year he married Myrle Lucille Graves, with whom he had two children.

His emerging political career initially faltered with an unsuccessful bid for the U.S. House of Representatives in the 1928 Republican primary and then a defeat as the Republican nominee for a House seat in 1934. In the 1936 Democratic landslide, however, he rode a wave of home-state Republican resurgence and defeated the Democratic incumbent, attracting 51.7 percent of the vote. Winning the next six elections with margins ranging from 61 to 73 percent, he served in a district including his state's western counties from 1937 to 1951.

Early in his House career, Case secured a valued place on the Appropriations Committee and championed a program to renegotiate war contracts that achieved savings of $9 billion for the treasury. His "Case Resolution" of 1939–1940 led to passage of the 1944 Missouri River Flood Control Act. In foreign affairs, Case followed his region's isolationist proclivities until several weeks before the United States entered World War II. After the war he advocated a strong nuclear deterrent of Soviet-inspired communism. On the home front, he gained national prominence with his Case Labor Bill, introduced in 1945 to curb spreading labor unrest he feared would imperil the nation's postwar economy. Congress subsequently incorporated major provisions of his bill into the Taft-Hartley Act of 1947, which provided a sixty-day cooling-off period while a federal mediation board reviewed labor-management disputes.

Desiring to move to the U.S. Senate, Case defeated his party's incumbent, Senator Chan Gurney, in the 1950 primary and won the general election easily. Serving in the Senate from 1951 until his death, Case served on the Armed Services and Public Works committees and earned a reputation as the "amendingest senator" and "Senator comma" for his close attention to legislative details. A member of a special committee created in 1954 to consider censure of Senator Joseph R. McCarthy, he continued his support of McCarthy's underlying anticommunism and subsequently voted against one of the two condemning resolutions that the Senate adopted in December 1954.

From 1953 to 1955, the only period of his service during which the Republicans controlled the Senate, Case chaired two committees: the District of Columbia Committee, where he became a strong advocate of home rule for that city; and the Public Works Subcommittee on Roads and Highways, where he shaped the Federal-Aid Highway Act of 1956 that established the interstate highway system. Case also promoted water-conservation projects, carrying on his career-long interest in irrigation and reclamation legislation.

Case again achieved national prominence in February 1956, as a result of a controversy precipitated by his sponsorship of a bill to remove controls on prices producers charged for natural gas. An early supporter of this legislation, Case admitted during floor debate on the legislation to having received a $2,500 contribution to his reelection campaign fund from an oil company lobbyist. Considering the offer improper, he changed his announced position and voted against the bill. Case's refusal to identify the lobbyist led the Senate to establish a bipartisan committee to investigate possible bribery. The committee, however, made no substantive recommendations, preferring to allow Case's constituents to decide in the upcoming 1956 elections whether he had acted improperly. But Case's resulting 2 percent majority (far less than his usual comfortable victory margins) was more a consequence of voter dissatisfaction with the Eisenhower administration's farm policies at a time of a farm depression.

A low-profile, colorless, behind-the-scenes legislator, Case was best known as a watchdog of the federal treasury and an advocate of precisely worded legislation. His principal success came in obtaining for his state significant federal funding for construction of flood control, irrigation, and highway projects. He died in Bethesda, Maryland.

• The principal collection of Case's papers is at Dakota Wesleyan University, with a smaller holding at the South Dakota State Historical Society. See also Richard R. Chenoweth's biography of Case in *South Dakota Historical Collections*, vol. 39 (1979). An obituary is in the *New York Times*, 23 June 1962.

RICHARD ALLAN BAKER

CASE, Jerome Increase (11 Dec. 1818–22 Dec. 1891), manufacturer, was born in Williamstown, New York, the son of Caleb Case and Deborah Jackson, pioneer farmers. When he was barely sixteen years old, Jerome became manager of a threshing company, utilizing a horse-treadmill threshing machine purchased by his father. Although he had always displayed an uncommon interest in and aptitude for the mechanics of farm implements, Case's only formal training consisted of an eight-month-long "engineering" course at Rensselaer Academy in Mexico, New York in 1841. The following year, having read of the burgeoning wheat yield of the newly opened Wisconsin territory, he purchased six horse-powered threshers, popularly known as "ground hogs," and headed to the western shores of Lake Michigan via Chicago. Along the road to Wisconsin, Case sold five of the machines to area farmers and kept the sixth, with the goal of supporting himself by threshing while he sought to improve the equipment.

Locating in the village of Rochester in western Racine County, Case and manufacturer Richard Emerson Ela soon designed, built, and operated a combined thresher-separator machine that beat out the wheat kernels, separated them from the straw, and blew the straw and chaff into a stock. When the village fathers, desirous of monopolizing the water power of the Fox River for their sawmill and gristmill, refused to grant Case permission to build a threshing machine "manufactory" on its banks in 1844, he moved his operation to the larger village of Racine, situated where the Root River flowed into Lake Michigan. Beginning in a rented shop, Case experienced three difficult years during which he sold a few units and gave hundreds of threshing demonstrations before acquiring enough capital to build his own manufacturing plant. Ten years later, it had become the largest thresher factory west of Buffalo, producing 1,600 machines a year. In 1849 Case married Lydia A. Bull of nearby Yorkville, with whom he had four children.

In 1863 Case formed a partnership with three employees, his brother-in-law Stephen Bull, Massena B. Erskine, and Robert Baker, calling it the J. I. Case Company. Two years later, the company adopted the American bald eagle astride the globe as its company trademark, patterning the bird after "Old Abe," the mascot of Company C of the Eighth Wisconsin Division during the Civil War. As the company grew into a nationwide supplier of threshing machines, Case added his own foundry and machine shop, warranted his product with the claim that it was "the best in use," and advertised in agricultural publications.

So devoted was Case to the reputation of his machines that, at age sixty-five, he reportedly traveled to Faribault, Minnesota, to fix a thresher that had broken down. Unable to repair the machine, Case poured kerosene on it and burned it to the ground, awarding the startled farmer a brand new thresher. A former competitor later described Case as "an austere man, very set in his ways, abrupt in manner, hard to work for or with," but also "as honest as the day, both in personal and business matters."

In 1869 Case pioneered the steam-powered thresher, some fifteen years before its general adoption; the original Number One stands in the Smithsonian Institution. Shortly after his death, the Case Company developed its first gasoline-powered engine, eventually switching all of its implements to that mode of power and branching out into automobile manufacturing. The centennial year of 1876 was a banner one for Case, as he formed a second company, the J. I. Case Plow Works, and his new traction engine earned a gold medal for excellence at the Philadelphia Exposition. In 1880 he dissolved his partnership with Bull, Erskine, and Baker and incorporated the firm as the J. I. Case Threshing Machine Company. By the time of his death, both enterprises were shipping products all over the world and, together, constituted Wisconsin's largest manufacturing complex.

Branching into the banking business in 1871, Case established the Manufacturers' National Bank of Racine and the First National Bank of Burlington, Wisconsin, and later became associated with national banks in Minnesota, South Dakota, and California. His reputation as a financier led to membership on the board of trustees of the Northwestern Mutual Life Insurance Company of Milwaukee, and he served as a Wisconsin state commissioner to the Centennial Exposition. A staunch Republican, Case was elected to three terms as mayor of Racine—in 1856, 1858, and 1860—and served as state senator from 1865 to 1867. Although virtually without formal education, he was one of the founders of the Wisconsin Academy of Science, Arts, and Letters. Fascinated by horse racing, Case established a 200-acre farm called Hickory Grove in the mid-1870s and purchased the Glenview Stock Farm in Louisville, Kentucky, in order to breed trotters and pacers. His most famous champion, named Jay Eye See, set the mile record for both trotting and pacing, a feat never since duplicated.

Case died in Racine at his home. When the state of Wisconsin founded its Hall of Fame in 1937, he was one of the first four inductees, along with political leader Robert M. La Follette (1855–1925), novelist Hamlin Garland, and historian Frederick Jackson Turner.

• Case's papers are housed in the J. I. Case Company archives in Racine. Although no full-scale biography exists, Stewart H. Holbrook (updated by Richard G. Charlton), *Machine of Plenty: Chronicle of an Innovator In Construction and Agricultural Equipment* (1955), while largely uncritical, contains much valuable information. Brief profiles appear in *Western Monthly* 4, no. 21 (1869–1870), and in *National Magazine: A Monthly Journal of American History* 15 (May 1898). The obituary in the Milwaukee *Sentinel,* 23 Dec. 1891, is helpful.

JOHN D. BUENKER

CASE, Leonard (27 June 1820–6 Jan. 1880), philanthropist, was born in Cleveland, Ohio, the son of Leonard Case, Sr., a prominent businessman, and Elizabeth Gaylord. He received his early education in local schools, including the academies of the Reverend Colley Foster and Franklin T. Backus. A Yale graduate, Backus encouraged Case to attend his alma mater, which he entered in 1838. After beginning his studies in New Haven as a member of the sophomore class, in the following year Case was forced to withdraw from school due to poor health, a problem that plagued him his entire life. He returned to Yale, however, in time to graduate with the class of 1842. He then entered the Cincinnati Law School, remaining there until 1844. After passing the Ohio bar examination that year, he opened a law office in Cleveland in 1845.

Although a potentially promising career in law beckoned, due in no small part to the business activity generated by his wealthy father's real estate, banking, and railroad interests, the younger Case had little interest in either the business world or legal practice. Freed from the need to struggle for wealth, he returned his attention to his own independent course of study. Interests in literature (he wrote essays and poetry and could read French, German, Greek, Italian, and Latin) and travel meshed nicely with his interests in mathematics and the natural sciences. With his older brother William and a group of friends, Case founded the "Ark," an informal association, turning his office into a meeting place and natural history museum, replete with mounted specimens of birds and animals, where he and the other "Arkites" discussed a wide variety of natural history topics.

With the passage of time, Case became interested in philanthropy. He worked with his brother in 1859 to open Case Hall, a civic and cultural center for the city of Cleveland, and provided space for the Cleveland Academy of Natural Sciences, for the Cleveland Library Association, which had previously received an endowment from Case of $20,000, and for the Ark. Other local charities benefiting from Case's largesse included the local Young Men's Christian Association, the Cleveland Orphan Asylum, the Old Stone Church, the Cleveland Female Seminary, and the Industrial Aid Society.

Upon the death of his father in 1864, Case inherited $15 million. Determined to expand his charitable work, Case was one of the early benefactors of the Western Reserve Historical Society upon its founding in 1867. Although his attentions were increasingly drawn away from the world of commerce as the years went by, Case was instrumental in creating the Case Block in 1875. This large commercial building, located on Superior and Wood streets, provided both retail and office space and was also used, until 1916, as Cleveland's city hall.

The Case Block played an important role in Case's greatest philanthropy, the founding of the Case School of Applied Science. Despite his own classical training Case, through his years of activities with the Ark, fully realized the value of a technical education in a world that was becoming increasingly industrialized. Although the trust deed creating the school's endowment was signed in February 1877, the gift, because of Case's intense dislike of publicity, did not become public knowledge until after his death. Rental income from the Case Block provided an annual income to the new school, which opened in 1881 at the former Case residence on Rockwell Avenue. The institution remained at that location until 1885, when it moved to University Circle. Founded with the intent of providing technical education for impoverished boys, it enjoyed solid growth before merging with Western Reserve University to form the modern-day Case Western Reserve University. The somewhat eccentric Case, who never married, successfully maintained his father's wealth, his only indulgence being a stable of expensive race horses, which, due to his frail health, he never rode. He died in Cleveland of lung disease.

The life and career of Leonard Case reflected the outlook of many men of similar means and background in the latter portion of the nineteenth century. Driven by intellectual interests, a premonition that science would figure large in the future, and a warm generosity, Case used both his own and his family's fortune to make a series of fiduciary contributions that had a long-reaching effect on his community's life.

• The papers of Leonard Case are divided between the Western Reserve Historical Society and the Case Western Reserve University archives, both in Cleveland, Ohio. Information on the life and career of Case is scarce; however, information regarding his activities can be gleaned from Clarence H. Cramer, *Case Institute of Technology: A Centennial History, 1880–1980* (1980), and Claude T. Martin, *From School to Institute: An Informal Story of Case* (1967).

EDWARD L. LACH, JR.

CASEY, James E. (29 Mar. 1888–6 June 1983), corporation executive, was born in Candelaria, Nevada, a small mining town where his father worked as a part-time prospector and part-time innkeeper. While Casey was still an infant, his father moved the family to Seattle, Washington. With his father in poor health, Casey had to leave school at age eleven to support the family. After working in Seattle as a delivery boy for a department store and as a messenger for the American District Telegraph Company, Casey went to Nevada and prospected for gold. He returned to Seattle where, in August 1907, he and fellow teenager Claude Ryan began a messenger service, which they called the American Messenger Company. Ryan's uncle allowed the boys to establish an office in a space 6 feet by 17 feet beneath a tavern that he operated at Main Street and Second Avenue in Seattle.

Casey and Ryan put posters promising "Best Services at Lowest Rates" near public phones and advertised 24-hour service seven days a week, including holidays. The two entrepreneurs slept in their cramped office quarters, using a lunch counter as a bed. Their six employees, who walked or used bicycles or streetcars to deliver messages and packages, were trained to be courteous and wore visored caps bearing the company name. In 1911 George Casey, James's younger brother, joined the business.

The American Messenger Company quickly built a reputation for fast and reliable service, and by 1912 it had opened a second office in Seattle, which George Casey managed. James Casey and Ryan remained in charge of the original office. The following year, the company merged with one of its main competitors,

Evert McCabe's Motorcycle Delivery Service. They closed the two American Messenger Company offices, consolidating operations at the Motorcycle Delivery Service's office, and changed the name to Merchants' Parcel Delivery (MPD). Casey became the company's first president. The company soon acquired its first delivery truck, a 1913 Model T Ford automobile, and replaced the chassis with a delivery truck body that could hold fifty packages. MPD's delivery truck was an unusual sight and something of a novelty item. Casey recalled, "The new vehicle created a lot of interest among Seattle residents and was good advertising for us" (Buckley, p. 13). As operations expanded the company added to its fleet of delivery vehicles. By 1915 MPD had four cars, five motorcycles, and twenty foot messengers and was Seattle's largest delivery service. While Casey originally wanted MPD's fleet of vehicles to be painted yellow, Charlie Soderstrom, another employee and stockholder in the company, convinced him to adopt a more conservative color. In order to make the vehicles look as clean as possible during use, Soderstrom suggested and MPD adopted a brown hue that eventually became synonymous with United Parcel Service.

In 1917 Ryan resigned as a director of MPD to enter the insurance business. Casey remained with the company and two years later presided over its first expansion outside of Seattle when MPD purchased the Motor Parcel Delivery Company in Oakland, California. Because a San Francisco company already had the name of Merchants' Parcel Delivery, the new branch was called United Parcel Service. That name was used for other branches that subsequently opened in cities on the West Coast, including San Diego, California, and Portland, Oregon. In 1925 the Seattle headquarters followed its branches by officially changing its name to United Parcel Service (UPS). In 1929 UPS opened United Air Express, offering deliveries to many West Coast cities and as far inland as Texas. After the stock market crash that year, however, UPS suspended air service until 1953. In 1930 Casey moved UPS headquarters to New York City. Already a major presence on the West Coast, UPS thus expanded its clientele in the East. The headquarters later moved to California and then to Atlanta. As UPS expanded its operations, stores throughout the country abandoned their own delivery services and opted to rely on UPS efficiency and reliability. In the 1950s customers began to carry their own packages home with them, so UPS branched out, delivering packages for commercial and private customers between all addresses. Reinstituting air deliveries, UPS offered that service in all states by the late 1970s and extended into international deliveries in the 1980s. Next Day Air service was available in forty-eight states by 1985.

Casey's management of UPS involved innovations that later spread to other companies. His desire to treat his employees as more than just hired hands led him to start one of the first profit-sharing programs in an American company. Moreover, during discussions or meetings, Casey solicited opinions from executives and managers from various levels of the corporation. "Ideas of our company cannot be carried out from the top alone," he once explained. "They must become a part of the makeup of our entire organization. They must be instilled in the minds of all men down the ranks" (*New York Times*). Casey's policies and dedication to service were the foundation of the company's success. He remained active in UPS operations until his death in Seattle.

A bachelor his entire life, Casey carefully guarded his privacy and shunned publicity. With his brother and sister he established the Annie E. Casey Foundation and the Casey Family Program, through which he gave generously to causes related to child welfare. He also supported civic improvements in downtown Seattle. The site of the original office he shared with Ryan became Waterfall Park, which was built through philanthropic contributions from Casey and his family.

• An article on Casey and the history of United Parcel Service is Dan Buckley, "The Messenger Company That Became United Parcel Service," *Portage: The Magazine of the Historical Society of Seattle and King County*, Summer 1982, pp. 10–15. Another article on Casey and the founding of UPS is in the *Puget Sound Business Journal*, 2 Apr. 1993. An obituary is in the *New York Times*, 7 June 1983.

YANEK MIECZKOWSKI

CASEY, Joseph (17 Dec. 1814–10 Feb. 1879), lawyer and jurist, was born in Ringgold's Manor, Washington County, Maryland, the son of Joseph Casey, an educator and native of Ireland, and Rebecca McLaughlin of Pennsylvania. Casey's family separated after experiencing what were probably financial difficulties when he was a young child. In 1819 Casey was sent to live with a blacksmith's family in Newville, Pennsylvania, where his family had moved. He remained there until he was fourteen years old, when he returned to his father's house in Shippensburg, Pennsylvania. Casey's formal education was sparse, but he showed intelligence and became an enthusiastic reader, memorizing much of the Psalms and New Testament. He was a lifelong Presbyterian, but "free from all sectarian bigotry or bias" (*Bio. Encyc.*, p. 472).

Between 1828 and 1831 Casey attended a common school for about one year, but without the funds to continue his education, he became apprentice to a hat manufacturer in Shippensburg in 1831. He made hats until 1835 in Shippensburg, in Williamsport, Maryland, and in Newville, where he also taught school. In 1835 he became assistant manager of a factory in Chambersburg, Pennsylvania, and in 1836 began his professional education by reading law in the office of Charles B. Penrose in Carlisle, Pennsylvania. Continuing to teach school during his legal studies, Casey was called to the Pennsylvania bar in November 1838. He married Mary A. Krettle in 1841; they had three children.

Casey practiced law in Bloomfield, Pennsylvania, until 1845, when he moved to the more promising town of New Berlin in Union County, Pennsylvania, where he became a leader of the bar. In 1848 Casey was elected to represent his home district in the Thirty-first Congress as a Whig, winning by a large margin after a difficult campaign among a largely Democratic electorate. During his single term in Congress, Casey was a moderate who generally supported the Taylor and Fillmore administrations, endorsed the Compromise of 1850, but opposed slavery and the Fugitive Slave Law. Declining renomination to Congress, Casey returned to Pennsylvania and lost the 1851 election for district judge of Mifflin and Union counties.

Casey resumed his law practice at New Berlin but in 1855 moved to the Pennsylvania capital of Harrisburg. In 1855 the governor appointed him commissioner to settle the "Erie Railroad War," a significant dispute between Pennsylvania and railroad companies. Casey successfully accomplished the task. He served as "state reporter" of the *Pennsylvania State Reports* from 1856 to 1861, editing volumes 25–36 of the commonwealth's supreme court decisions. These volumes, known as "Casey's Reports," were favorably received by the bar at a time of uneven quality among privately prepared law reports. He continued in his demanding law practice while undertaking his official duties in Harrisburg. In his preface to the first volume of the *Reports*, he noted that his reporting task had "devolved upon me, in the midst of numerous business and professional engagements previously assumed. In consequence of which I have not been able to bestow as much time and labour upon the preparation of this volume as I otherwise would have done."

Sometime after 1851 Casey abandoned his Whig affiliation to become a Republican. President Abraham Lincoln appointed him in May 1861 to the U.S. Court of Claims in Washington, D.C. The court of claims was reorganized and its jurisdiction extended in 1863, when Casey became its first chief justice. The court adjudicated claims made against the federal government by private individuals and businesses, which was a novel, sensitive, and difficult task, especially during the Civil War. During his tenure on the court, Casey's fairness both to the government and to private litigants earned him praise as a jurist.

Casey resigned from the court of claims in December 1870 as a result of ill health and pressing business interests "of the most extensive and lucrative nature" (*Bio. Encyc.*, p. 472). He remained in Washington, D.C., where he resumed his law practice, taught at the National University, and eventually died.

Casey's life exhibits a remarkable tenacity as he rose from very modest beginnings to great honor and success through self-education and perseverance. His most lasting public achievement was launching the new court of claims as an effective and fair tribunal that has survived to the late twentieth century and occupies an important, if limited, niche in American jurisprudence. As lawyer, judge, and court historian, Casey led a distinguished life in the law that was characteristic of the best of American attorneys.

• *The Biographical Encyclopedia of Pennsylvania of the 19th Century* (1874) has a long entry about Casey. See also B. P. Poore, comp., *Political Register and Congressional Directory, 1776–1878* (1878). An obituary is in the *National Republican*, 11–12 Feb. 1879.

FRANCIS HELMINSKI

CASEY, Silas (12 July 1807–22 Jan. 1882), soldier, was born in East Greenwich, Rhode Island, the son of Wanton Casey, an international merchant. His mother's name and occupation are unknown. At age fifteen he was appointed to the U.S. Military Academy, supposedly through the influence of its superintendent, a longtime friend of his father. Casey was graduated in 1826, ranking thirty-ninth in a class of forty-one. Despite his low standing, Casey served in the army for forty-six years, forging a career as a "gallant soldier," a scholar in higher mathematics, and an authority on tactical theory.

Casey's military career began slowly: for ten years after leaving West Point he remained a second lieutenant, and when the Mexican War broke out in 1846, he had advanced only as far as captain. More rapid advancement came as a result of his distinguished service under Winfield Scott at Contreras, Churubusco, Molino del Rey, and in the fighting outside Mexico City. In the assault on the castle of Chapultepec, 13 September 1847, Casey was severely wounded while leading one of two 250-man storming parties, which, sent forward as a "forlorn hope," were critical to Scott's victory.

In the years leading up to the Civil War, Brevet Lieutenant Colonel Casey did garrison duty on the western frontier and along the Pacific Coast. In the mid-1850s he became involved in revising the army's system of infantry tactics. His work, first published in 1862, was based heavily on earlier manuals by General Scott and Major William J. Hardee. The basic value of *Casey's Tactics* was that it made his predecessors' systems widely available at a time when thousands of volunteer officers were pouring into the Union armies. Casey did attempt to adapt and expand upon existing tactical theory. He sought to make modifications responsive to the realities of combat, such as by expediting the process of moving a military unit from marching column into line of battle. He also tried to adapt Scott's and Hardee's tactics to larger units than they had considered. Even so, Casey's manual was characterized neither by originality nor by innovation. Its largest deficiency was its failure to address adequately the impact that the long-range rifle was exerting on traditional skirmishes and assault tactics.

In 1855 an army reorganization resulted in the creation of the Ninth U.S. Infantry, with Casey as its lieutenant colonel. By the outbreak of the Civil War, he had risen to colonel of the regiment, then serving in the Pacific Northwest. When his outfit was called east in the spring of 1861, Casey, widely regarded as an "able drill master," was put to work organizing and training the volunteer regiments flocking to Washington, D.C. On 31 August he was named a brigadier general of volunteers, and on 6 December he was assigned to command a division that became part of the

Fourth Corps in March 1862 in Major General George B. McClellan's Army of the Potomac.

In March 1862 Casey accompanied McClellan's mammoth command to Fort Monroe on the tip of the Virginia Peninsula and from there trudged northwest toward the enemy capital at Richmond. His troops saw sporadic action along the road to Yorktown, and on 5 May they were ordered up as McClellan clashed with the Confederates of Joseph E. Johnston outside Williamsburg. Conflicting orders marred the 54-year-old Casey's first combat as a field commander. McClellan directed him to reinforce the Union right flank; McClellan's senior corps commander, Major General Edwin V. Sumner, instructed Casey to bolster the left; and Casey's immediate superior, Major General Erasmus D. Keyes, assigned his division a position in the rear. Unable to determine a course of action, Casey did not make a contribution to the battle until late in the day, a circumstance that brought him unmerited criticism.

Casey received immeasurably greater censure as a result of the battle at Seven Pines (or Fair Oaks), a crossroads location seven miles from Richmond, on the last day of May. Having advanced so near to his objective, McClellan should have anticipated an enemy foray. Yet he maneuvered his army so incautiously that on 31 May three of his five corps lay along the north bank of the Chickahominy River; the other two corps, including Keyes's, held a vulnerable position south of the rain-swollen stream. Casey's division—two-thirds of which was composed of raw troops whose reliability had been compromised by unusually fatiguing service and a long sick list—occupied the most advanced post, at the intersection of the Williamsburg Stage Road and Nine Mile Road.

Casey's unfinished line of breastworks and entrenchments at Seven Pines drew the attention of Johnston, who exploited the tactical opportunity his opponent had granted him. At 1:00 P.M. on the thirty-first, the inexperienced Federals were taken by surprise when four brigades led by Major General D. H. Hill, supported by two brigades under Major General Richard H. Anderson, struck them in front and on their heavily wooded left flank. One of Casey's soldiers later recalled that "bullets flew in myriads around us, humming deadly songs, hitting our men, and splintering the trees around us." After resisting for over two hours, most of Casey's men fled to the rear in panic; only the timely arrival of reinforcements, the majority from the north side of the river, stemmed the rout and the following day salvaged a stalemate for McClellan.

Although Casey's personal conduct at Seven Pines was not a factor in the defeat, his standing in the army plummeted. An inquiry by the assistant inspector general of the army into the causes of the rout—which had cost his command more than 1,800 casualties, mostly in missing or captured—revealed "both gallant and bad conduct in this division," blame for which adhered to its commander. On 23 June Casey was relieved and sent to dispose of government stores at White House Landing, McClellan's soon-to-be-abandoned base of supply on the Pamunkey River. Then, on 4 July, McClellan "reluctantly" ordered Casey back to Washington, informing Adjutant General Lorenzo Thomas that, although he had "great respect" for Casey's experience and acumen, "I have no command which can be given him with a beneficial result to the public service." Ironically, Casey attained a major generalship to rank from the day of his defeat.

The deposed commander served in and near the capital for the balance of the war. At first he resumed the work of "receiving and encamping" newly arrived volunteers. He then served on the court that tried Major General Fitz-John Porter for disobedience and misbehavior during the Second Bull Run campaign (Second Manassas), commanded a provisional division in the Washington defenses, and presided over a board to examine candidates for commissions in the U.S. Colored Troops. He later adapted his tactical manual to what he regarded as the peculiar requirements of black outfits. Like many of his military associates, Casey considered black troops and their officers to possess below-average intelligence; he therefore oversimplified his manual almost to the point of uselessness.

In August 1865 Casey was mustered out of the volunteer ranks, reverting to the post of colonel, Fourth Infantry, which he had attained late in 1861. Casey served with his regiment in New York Harbor, along the Great Lakes, and in the Department of the Platte, except for occasional stints of special duty, until his retirement in 1868. He died in Brooklyn, New York. His first wife was Abby Perry; they had five children. His second spouse was Florida Gordon; they had one child. The dates of his marriages are unknown. Casey was remembered as a modest and unassuming man, a conscientious soldier, and a theorist who failed to appreciate the power of the rifled musket until thousands of them, in enemy hands, blew his career to pieces.

• A collection of Casey family papers is maintained by the Society for the Preservation of New England Antiquities in Boston, while other letters from the general can be found in the Winfield Scott Papers, U.S. Military Academy (USMA) Library. The USMA Archives at West Point contain documents that help flesh out the scanty published sources on his pre–Civil War years. *The War of the Rebellion: A Compilation of the Official Records of the Union and Confederate Armies*, ser. 1, vol. 12, pt. 1 (128 vols., 1880–1901), contains Casey's after-action reports of Williamsburg and Fair Oaks as well as the findings of the inspector general, Army of the Potomac, as to the debacle of 31 May 1862. The latter event is also examined in several works, including Gustavus W. Smith, *The Battle of Seven Pines* (1891); George D. Harmon, "General Silas Casey and the Battle of Fair Oaks," *Historian: Phi Alpha Theta* 4 (1941): 84–102; and Stephen W. Sears, *To the Gates of Richmond: The Peninsula Campaign* (1992). One of the best assessments of Casey's infantry tactics is Grady McWhiney and Perry D. Jamieson, *Attack and Die: Civil War Military Tactics and the Southern Heritage* (1982). The standard career reference is George W. Cullum, comp., *Biographical Register of the Officers and Graduates of the U.S. Military Academy* (1891). An obituary is in the *New York Times*, 23 Jan. 1882.

EDWARD G. LONGACRE

CASEY, Thomas Lincoln (10 May 1831–25 Mar. 1896), military engineer, was born at the Madison Barracks, Sackett's Harbor, New York, the son of General Silas Casey and Abby Sophia (maiden name unknown). The Caseys' three sons all became army or navy officers, and their two daughters married army officers.

In 1852 Casey graduated first in his class from the U.S. Military Academy at West Point, New York, and was immediately brevetted a second lieutenant in the U.S. Army's Corps of Engineers. His first assignment was as assistant engineer for the construction of Fort Delaware and for improvements to the harbor of the Delaware River and bay. He was promoted to second lieutenant on 22 June 1854 and spent the next five years as an assistant professor of engineering at West Point. In 1856 he married Emma Weir, daughter of the artist Robert W. Weir, who taught at West Point. The couple had three sons. Casey's promotion to first lieutenant took place on 1 December 1856. From 1859 to 1861 he commanded the troops who constructed a wagon road from Vancouver, Washington, to Cowlitz River, Oregon, the first land route connecting the Columbia River and Puget Sound.

Casey was commissioned a captain on 6 August 1861, and appointed staff engineer at Fortress Monroe, Virginia. Subsequently he was assigned to oversee the construction of permanent defenses and forts along the Maine coast, Forts Scammel, Gorges, and Preble in Portland Harbor; Fort Popham at the mouth of the Kennebec River; and Fort Knox on the Penobscot River. In 1863 Casey was called to Washington to serve with the North Atlantic Squadron, which harried sea coast fortifications in Confederate hands. He participated in the first expedition to capture Fort Fisher, North Carolina, which was successful. Casey received his majority on 2 October 1863 and was brevetted lieutenant colonel and colonel on 13 March 1865, in recognition of his wartime service. He took a seven-month leave from the army at the close of the war to work for the Portland Company, an iron and machine works that manufactured locomotive and marine engines, but then returned to his post at Portland Harbor to complete work on the Maine forts.

Casey was posted to the Chief of Engineers Office in Washington, D.C., on 18 November 1867, and placed in charge of the Division on Fortifications. That same year the duties of the defunct Commissioner of Public Buildings were transferred to the Chief of Engineers. He remained in Washington for the remainder of his life, with only short assignments elsewhere, including an official trip to Europe in 1873 to examine torpedo defense systems.

The most significant part of Casey's career began on 27 February 1877, when he was placed in charge of the Office of Public Buildings and Grounds for the District of Columbia. For the next two decades he completed construction of some of the city's most important landmarks. On 3 March 1877 Casey was charged with overseeing the final stages of the Washington Aqueduct, designed by fellow military engineer Montgomery C. Meigs. The same day he was appointed to complete construction of the State, War, and Navy Building, now the Old Executive Office Building located on the west side of the White House grounds. The State, War, and Navy Building was begun in 1871 following designs by Alfred B. Mullett, supervising architect of the Treasury, who resigned in 1874. When Casey took over, the south wing had been completed and occupied, and foundations for the east wing had been laid. Superintending many of the same draftsmen and engineers as had worked for Mullett, Casey completed the three remaining wings efficiently and economically by May 1888. Architectural variations in the wings, both externally and internally, are minor because the chief draftsman, Richard von Ezdorf, was both the ornamental designer and a structural engineer during most of the building's construction.

While construction of the State, War, and Navy Building was under way, Casey was assigned two additional projects. On 25 June 1878 he was charged by a commission appointed by Congress with completing the Washington Monument. Originally designed by Robert Mills in 1848, the monument had had its construction halted at 173 feet in 1855. Casey's first task was to strengthen the original foundations by inserting concrete piers under them and buttressing them with splayed concrete slabs. He changed the original plan slightly, removing Mills's Egyptian Revival door frames, designing a fifty-foot-tall pyramid for the obelisk's apex, and setting its height at 555 feet, ten times the width of each side at ground level. The monument's 3,300-pound capstone was put in place on 6 December 1884, under Casey's direction. Casey's third project in Washington during the 1880s was to build, on the mall, the Army Medical Museum, which was replaced by the Hirschhorn Museum in 1966. The Victorian brick museum was designed by Adolf Cluss and Paul Schulze; Casey was in charge of construction from April 1885 until October 1886.

Casey's renown as a competent engineer and reliable cost estimator led to several smaller commissions. Between 1882 and 1886 he erected an obelisk replacing the original one over Thomas Jefferson's grave at Monticello. He was in charge of building the monument at Washington's Headquarters in Newburg, New York (1883–1884), and the one that marked Washington's birthplace in Westmoreland County, Virginia (1883–1886). In 1887 Casey oversaw setting up the base and statue of the Chester A. Garfield Monument in Washington. In none of these projects was Casey the designer; rather his expert knowledge of contemporary building practices often led to minor modifications.

From 1886 to 1888 Casey served as president of the Board of Engineers for Fortifications and Public Works in New York City, where he resided for eighteen months. Shortly after he was appointed brigadier general and named chief of engineers on 6 July 1888, Casey was placed in charge of constructing the Library of Congress Building. John Smithmeyer and Paul Pelz had won the 1873 competition and continued to provide several designs for alternate sites for fifteen years.

In 1888 Casey fired Smithmeyer and continued Pelz as the architect until 1892, when he replaced him with his son, Edward Pearce Casey. Although Casey was retired from active duty on 10 May 1895, by an act of Congress he continued to work in a private capacity on the library's construction until his death. Hundreds of drawings at the Library of Congress demonstrate that the basic spaces, decorative schemes, and engineering solutions were established by Smithmeyer and Pelz. Casey's forte was his organizational ability linked with his knowledge of modern construction methods and materials.

Casey served as president of the American Society of Civil Engineers and was the member of several learned societies, including the National Academy of Sciences, the Philosophical Society of Washington, the New England Historic Genealogical Society, and the Century Association of New York. He was a member of the Legion of Honor of France and the Massachusetts Chapter of the Society of the Cincinnati. Locally in Washington, Casey served on the Light House Board and as president of the Rock Creek Park Commission. He died in Washington, D.C.

• The Thomas Lincoln Casey Papers at the Society for the Preservation of New England Antiquities in Boston, Mass., is the major private collection of Casey's reports, correspondence, and drawings. The pre–revolutionary war Casey Farm in Saunderstown, R.I., is administered by the SPNEA. His official papers are scattered among several record groups in the National Archives, principally RG 77 and RG 42. The Library of Congress contains some Casey materials. The Office of History, U.S. Army Corps of Engineers, Alexandria, Va., has substantial research files on Casey. The best synopsis of Casey's career, "In Memoriam of General Thomas L. Casey," written by his longtime assistant Bernard R. Green, was delivered before the Association of the Graduates of the U.S. Military Academy, 11 June 1896; copies are held at both the SPNEA's headquarters and the Office of History, U.S. Army Corps of Engineers. Much of his Washington career is outlined in George W. Cullum, *Biographical Register of the Officers and Graduates of the U.S. Military Academy*, vol. 4, ed. Edward S. Holden (1901); Albert E. Cowdrey, *A City for the Nation: The Army Engineers and the Building of Washington, D.C., 1790–1967* (1978); Mary-Jane M. Dowd, comp., *Records of the Office of Public Buildings and Public Parks of the National Capital* (1992); Sacket Duryee, ed., *A Historical Summary of the Work of the Corps of Engineers in Washington, D.C., and Vicinity, 1852–1952* (1952); Frederick L. Harvey, *History of the Washington National Monument and the Washington National Monument Society* (1903); and, Louis Torres, *"To the Immortal Name and Memory of George Washington": The United States Army Corps of Engineers and the Construction of the Washington Monument* (1984). Obituaries are in the *Washington Evening Star*, 26 Mar. 1896; *Engineering and Mining Journal* 61 (1896): 307; the *Engineering Record* 33 (1895–1896): 291, 309–10; the *Railroad Gazette* 28 (1896): 241; *Scientific American* 74 (1896): 211; and the *New York Times*, 26 Mar. 1896.

PAMELA SCOTT
MARTIN K. GORDON

CASEY, William Joseph (13 Mar. 1913–6 May 1987), lawyer and government official, was born in New York City, the son of William Joseph Casey, Sr., a city official and Democratic party functionary, and Blanche La Vigne, a department store stock buyer. The eldest of three surviving children, William Casey, familiarly known as "Bill," eschewed the suffix "junior."

Except for his last two years of high school, Casey received a Roman Catholic education. He returned to a Catholic venue at New York's Fordham University, from which he graduated with honors in philosophy in 1934. He went on to graduate school in social work at Catholic University in Washington, D.C., but found actual casework for the New York City Department of Welfare more engaging and dropped out. Shifting to the law, he enrolled in courses at St. John's University, receiving his LL.B. in 1937; he was admitted to the New York bar that September. He then found work as a writer for and later chief of the board of researchers of the Research Institute of America, a specialty publisher of data on business trends and related matters. Illustrating what became a frequent pattern, Casey did not inform his employer when he began doing free-lance legal work outside of business hours. Casey's bosses appreciated his ability to extract simple explanations or descriptions from complex masses of detail and lavished promotions and raises on the young analyst. In 1941 he married Sophia Kurz, with whom he had one child.

During World War II, the U.S. Office of Strategic Services (OSS), forerunner of the Central Intelligence Agency (CIA), needed an administrative specialist to routinize the work of its forward base in London. Casey, who had an aptitude for organizing paperwork, heard about the job, lobbied for it, and was sent to London with a commission as a navy junior officer. That placed him on the scene in late 1944 when personnel transfers opened up the position of chief of OSS secret intelligence operations for Europe. Taking over as the northwestern Europe campaign was reaching its height at the Battle of the Bulge, Casey organized training and made preparations for agent teams to be infiltrated into Germany. Before the end of the European war in May 1945, Casey's OSS unit had mounted a total of 102 missions; its report rated sixty-two of these as successful, eleven as results unknown, and twenty-nine as failures. Bill Casey received the French Croix de Guerre for his wartime service, which also brought him renown as a spy chieftain.

Resigning on the day Japan surrendered in August 1945, Casey returned to the Research Institute of America, where he continued to work until 1950, save for a leave of absence during 1948 when he served as associate general counsel for the European Cooperation Administration, which, headquartered at Paris, administered Marshall Plan foreign aid disbursements. Beginning in 1948 through the next decade and into the early 1960s, Casey periodically lectured on tax law at New York University and published books on business practice and tax shelters that earned him a fortune. In 1966 he ran for the Republican nomination for Nassau County's Third Congressional District but lost in the primary against Steven B. Derounian, a

Goldwater ally more conservative than Casey himself. From 1954 through 1971 he was president of the Institute for Business Planning, and from 1957 to 1971 he was a partner in the law firm of Hall, Casey, Dickler & Howley. From 1976 until 1981 he was a partner in the law firm of Rogers & Wells.

Throughout this period Casey gradually broadened his political involvement. He contributed to Richard Nixon's presidential campaign in 1960 and 1968, conducting research for the latter campaign and subsequent GOP election efforts. Casey's active involvement in foreign policy matters appears to have begun in 1962, when he was a founder and board member of the National Strategy Information Center, a conservative, New York–based defense policy think tank. Seven years later Casey founded an advocacy group called the Citizens Committee for Peace and Security, which pressed the United States to deploy a ballistic missile defense system, the military effectiveness of which was being hotly debated.

Casey's government service began in 1971 when President Nixon appointed him chairman of the Securities Exchange Commission. For about a year starting in 1973 he moved to the State Department as undersecretary for economic affairs, and in 1974 President Gerald Ford appointed him chairman of the Export-Import Bank. Casey also worked on the Murphy Commission, a blue ribbon foreign policy review chaired by diplomat Robert Murphy (1974–1975), and in 1976 he was appointed to the President's Foreign Intelligence Advisory Board (PFIAB), a group of private consultants to the president on intelligence matters. After President Jimmy Carter abolished PFIAB in 1977, Casey's primary links to intelligence were through OSS veterans' associations.

All that changed after the 1980 election, in which Casey managed the GOP campaign for Ronald Reagan following the early demise of political operative John Sears. Reagan won the election and made Casey a senior official of his transition team. Casey was disappointed at not being offered the position he preferred, secretary of state, or even secretary of defense. Instead, he was offered the job of director of central intelligence (DCI), chief of the U.S. intelligence community, including the CIA. With some hesitation Casey took the job and became the longest-serving DCI since Allen Dulles in the 1950s.

Dispute dogged Bill Casey throughout his tenure, partly because of his own secretiveness and partly because of the Reagan administration's controversial policies, particularly in Central America. During his Senate confirmation process it was learned that the secretive, free-wheeling Casey had not disclosed the names of all his legal clients, as required by law, or registered as an agent for the many foreign governments he had represented. Later there were controversies over the way Casey dealt with congressional oversight committees; over certain subordinates he appointed; over his refusal to put his financial assets into a blind trust; over his trading in stocks of companies that had CIA contracts; over his role during the 1980 campaign, when documents were stolen from the Carter campaign organization and some believed that the GOP had made private deals with foreign powers to help Reagan get elected; and over Casey's access to President Reagan and his actions in Reagan's name with foreign officials such as then-President Ferdinand Marcos of the Philippines.

Casey's biggest controversy came in the affair called Iran-Contra, in which members of the White House staff made private deals with Iranian arms traders and funneled the profits to the Nicaraguan contras, or rebels. In the hearings that resulted, witnesses claimed that Casey had been involved in the affair and alleged that his intent had been to create a "private, off the shelf" covert operations entity not subject to U.S. constitutional checks and balances. Called to testify, Casey gave false testimony to Congress under oath. As U.S. Senate investigators prepared to call him to explain himself, on 15 December 1986, in his office at CIA headquarters, Casey suffered a stroke that was found to have been caused by a brain tumor. Hospitalized, Casey never returned to work; he resigned in January 1987, suffered a relapse that April, died the following month in a Washington hospital without clearly answering the allegations against him.

William J. Casey's legacy is a decidedly mixed one. On the one hand, he built the CIA into a larger organization than it had ever been and restored agency morale after the shocks of the Iran hostage crisis and the CIA investigations of the 1970s. However, Casey's political attitudes led him to interfere directly in CIA analytical efforts, demoralizing a different segment of the agency, while his preoccupation with covert operations meant that he left the intelligence community's roles and missions essentially the way he found them in 1981. Of Casey's covert operations themselves, only Afghanistan was a clear military success, and there political consequences followed largely the path Casey's critics had predicted. Iran-Contra was a huge disaster, robbing the CIA of much of the credit Casey had restored to it. Finally, the funding and personnel increases Casey had secured proved unsustainable in the post–Cold War era.

• At this writing Bill Casey's papers remain in family hands. Herbert E. Meyer, an admiring former special assistant to Casey, has collected his public speeches in *Scouting the Future* (1989). Casey's own writings include a manuscript published after his death, *The Secret War against Hitler* (1988), and an earlier travelogue, *Where and How the War Was Fought: An Armchair Tour of the American Revolution* (1976). Casey's business writings include many volumes of financial advice, among them, *Tax Sheltered Investments* (1952), *The Accounting Desk Book* (1956), and *The Tax Shelter in Real Estate* (1957). A full-length biography is Joseph E. Persico, *Casey: From the OSS to the CIA* (1990). Journalist Bob Woodward authored a study of the Casey era at the CIA titled *Veil: The Secret Wars of the CIA 1981–1987* (1987), which contains disputed revelations concerning deathbed statements attributed to Casey. An obituary is in the *New York Times*, 7 May 1987.

JOHN PRADOS

CASH, W. J. (2 May 1900–1 July 1941), journalist and writer, was born in Gaffney, South Carolina, the son of John William Cash, a store manager, and Nannie Lutitia Hamrick. Named Joseph Wilbur, Cash reversed the order of his given names and usually used his initials. His staunchly Baptist parents raised him in the textile mill region of the Carolina Piedmont until they moved to Boiling Springs, North Carolina, in 1912. Cash attended Gaffney's public schools and was graduated from a Baptist academy in Boiling Springs in 1917. Nicknamed "Sleepy," Cash was bookish, unathletic, eccentric, and imaginative.

After briefly attending Wofford College (1918–1919) and Valparaiso University for one term in 1919, Cash went to North Carolina's Wake Forest College, earning a bachelor of arts degree in 1922. At first hesitant about entering a "preacher's school," Cash discovered at the small Baptist college a lively intellectual atmosphere presided over by President William Louis Poteat, a biologist who accepted Darwinian evolution, and dedicated professors who encouraged critical thinking. Cash read Joseph Conrad, James Branch Cabell, and other modern writers, including H. L. Mencken, whose iconoclastic style permanently influenced him. As an editor of the student newspaper and campus bohemian, he hurled Menckenian brickbats at Baptist pieties.

Following graduation Cash drifted through the 1920s, first attending law school for a year, then teaching, working intermittently as a journalist, battling chronic depression, failing at love, traveling abroad, and reading voraciously—Sigmund Freud, Fyodor Dostoyevski, Theodore Dreiser—all the while pursuing the elusive dream of writing fiction. During the heated presidential election campaign of 1928, Cash edited the *Cleveland Press*, a short-lived county newspaper in Shelby, North Carolina. His editorials decried the campaign's anti-Catholic bigotry and violence. Afterward, he poured out his heart in articles for Mencken's *American Mercury*, including "The Mind of the South" (1929), a topic on which he had written as an undergraduate. "A thinker in the South is regarded quite logically as an enemy of the people," wrote Cash, as he announced what would become central themes of his later thought. Mencken brought Cash's writings to the publisher Alfred A. Knopf, who immediately proposed that Cash do a book. While working on his book, Cash wrote caustic essays of social criticism for the *American Mercury*, struggled with neurasthenia, hyperthyroidism, loneliness, and the awareness that he was a burden on his parents, who were hard hit by the depression. He lived at home until taking a position as associate editor and book reviewer for the Charlotte *News* in 1935.

At the *News* Cash reviewed an array of books; roamed discursively and perceptively over Conrad, William Faulkner, Thomas Wolfe, Erskine Caldwell, and other contemporary writers; and wrote stinging editorials that denounced Hitler and fascism. He enjoyed the camaraderie of the newsroom, where he was something of a celebrity, though his drinking and sudden, enraged outbursts damning Hitler raised eyebrows. He socialized with Charlotte's small, cosmopolitan set of writers, which included Mary Ross Northrop, a vivacious, recent divorcee, who fell in love with Cash at first sight. They agreed to be married as soon as he finished his book.

After much agonizing, and much prodding from an exasperated Knopf, Cash, a perfectionist, finished *The Mind of the South* in July 1940. Although slashingly critical of the region's "savage ideal" of intolerance, its "proto-Dorian" bonding of prejudiced whites, its racism, violence, religious fundamentalism, and hostility to the "modern mind," the book was praised everywhere, even in the South. His brilliant style, bold overarching thesis about the unity and continuity of the "mind" of the South, his psychological insights, tragic tone, and subtle probing of paradox and irony made his book a classic in historical interpretation.

Cash and Northrop were married on Christmas day 1940. He was awarded a Guggenheim Fellowship the following spring. In May the couple left for Mexico City, where Cash planned to write a novel. He had toyed with writing a Civil War epic but settled on charting the rise of a cotton mill family in the Piedmont.

In Mexico City Cash immediately fell victim to a combination of exhaustion, severe digestive disorders, anxiety, and dizziness from the altitude. He was unable to write. In addition, he developed a sudden intolerance for alcohol, and it appears that he was suffering from acute alcohol withdrawal (delirium tremens). He began hallucinating about hearing threatening voices and the presence of Nazis who wanted to kill him. He disappeared on 1 July 1941 and was later found hanging in a nearby hotel room.

Some scholars have challenged Cash's major arguments, faulting his imprecise definition of "mind" and contending that he confused mind with "temperament" or "culture." Yet other historians continue to read him, finding considerable value in his insights into southern "honor" and into the centrality of race in the South.

• Cash's papers are in the Southern Historical Collection at the University of North Carolina at Chapel Hill. The most thorough critical biography is Bruce Clayton, *W. J. Cash: A Life* (1991). Joseph L. Morrison, *W. J. Cash, Southern Prophet: A Biography and Reader* (1967), briefer and less analytical, reprints a representative sampling of Cash's journalism. For insight into the continuing appeal and controversy of *The Mind of the South* see C. Vann Woodward, "The Elusive Mind of the South," in *American Counterpoint: Slavery and Racism in the North-South Dialogue*, ed. C. Vann Woodward (1971); Paul Escott, ed., *W. J. Cash and the Minds of the South* (1992); and Charles W. Eagles, ed., *The Mind of the South: Fifty Years Later* (1992).

BRUCE CLAYTON

CASPARY, Vera (Nov. 1899–6 June 1987), author, screenwriter, and playwright, was born in Chicago, the daughter of Paul Caspary, a department store buyer, and Julia Cohen. Although most references list her as being born in 1904, Caspary writes in her autobiography that she was "born by accident in the nineteenth century" and that "no one expected her on that November day."

Caspary was educated in Chicago public schools and after business school (1917) obtained work as a stenographer. She held numerous jobs, quitting some and being fired from others because of her outspoken, independent nature. In 1921 she became a copywriter for a mail-order operation and part-time editor of *Trianon Topics*, a magazine that advertised "The World's Most Beautiful Ballroom." In 1924 she became Chicago editorial representative for Bernarr MacFadden Publications, and she later edited *Dance Magazine* (c. 1926) in New York City and wrote freelance articles. Over her lifetime she lived in a variety of places—Hollywood, New York, and London among them—and she traveled extensively.

Among her novels were *The White Girl* (1929), *Ladies and Gents* (1929), *Music in the Street* (1930), *Thicker than Water* (1932), *Laura* (1942), *Bedelia* (1945), *Stranger than Truth* (1946), *The Weeping and the Laughter* (1950), *Thelma* (1952), *The Husband* (1957), *Evvie* (1960), *A Chosen Sparrow* (1964), *The Man Who Loved His Wife* (1966), *The Rosecrest Cell* (1967), and *Final Portrait* (1971). Her first novel, *The White Girl*, was unusual in its time in having a black heroine, a woman who had left the South for Chicago, passing as white. In *Thicker than Water* she delved into the problems of a Portuguese-Jewish family in Chicago. In all, she wrote eighteen novels.

Caspary also wrote for the stage. Her four plays were *Blind Mice* (1931), on which she collaborated with Winifred Lenihen; *Geraniums in My Window* (1934), with Samuel Ornitz; an adaptation of her novel *Laura* (1946), with George Sklar; and *Wedding in Paris* (1956).

In one of her earlier jobs she had written a series of correspondence school courses on photoplay writing, and eventually she completed a photoplay of her own. During her lifetime she worked on many movies, including several adapted from her novels. From 1932 until 1961 she received eighteen screen credits, more than half of them for story or co-story preparation, four for co-writing original film scripts, and three for adaptations. Nearly all of her work was done for Hollywood studios, but in 1945 she spent seven months in England adapting her novel *Bedelia* for a 1946 release. The better-known movies in which she had a hand were *Easy Living* (1937), *Laura* (1944), *A Letter to Three Wives* (1949), *The Blue Gardenia* (1953), and *Les Girls* (1957).

In her later writing years Caspary became known as a mystery writer, although she was quick to note that she used elements from outside that genre. After her first mystery novel, *Laura*, she wrote mystery serial stories for *Colliers* (1946) and for other publications; because of her psychological insights, they never were considered run-of-the-mill detective yarns. *Bedelia*, for one, was a curious, skillfully told tale in which she managed to present a pathological case history without using psychiatric terminology.

She believed *Evvie* to be one of her best novels, although it was declared obscene by one Chicago reviewer. In her autobiography, *The Secrets of Grown-Ups* (1979), Caspary noted that this judgment was odd, since *Evvie* included no graphic sexual descriptions. The novel, she said, was drawn from her own experiences in the 1920s when morality was more rigid and inhibition more binding than later when women declared greater independence.

During the 1930s Caspary became a member of the Communist party, as did many of her fellow writers. In part, she was influenced by the anti-Semitic pogroms in Russia and by the humiliating circumstances of apple-sellers on New York streets during the depression. She noted in her autobiography that no official body openly accused her of being a Communist, nor was she called before a court or legislative investigating committee. However, accusations were published. She herself scoffed at the charges. "How could I," she said, "who could not learn to play poker, understand dialectical materialism?"

She admitted, though, that she hated party secrecy. She said that her reasons for joining the party—the search for honesty, the questioning of values—were denied by the discipline of silence. As a party member, her name was Lucy Sheridan. After a trip to the Soviet Union in 1939 and subsequent disagreements, she asked to be "out." To be released from the party, however, she was forced to threaten her "cultural commissar" with writing a scathing piece about all she had seen and heard as a member unless he stopped trying to keep her within the ranks. Her bravado succeeded.

In 1949, after living together for seven years, Caspary and I. G. "Igee" Goldsmith, a movie producer, were married. She died in New York City.

• Biographical information on Caspary can be found in the *Wilson Library Bulletin* (1947), *Current Biography* (1947), *Current Biography Yearbook* (1987), *Contemporary Authors* (1975), and *American Authors and Books* (1972). Critical works on her writings are Jane S. Bakerman, "Vera Caspary's Chicago: Symbol and Setting," *Midamerica XI* (1984) pp. 81–89, and Ann L. Warren, "Word Play: The Lives and Works of Four Writers in Hollywood's Golden Age" (Ph.D. diss., Univ. of Southern California, 1988). Obituary feature articles are in the *Chicago Tribune* and the *Detroit News*, 18 June 1987.

MARY A. GARDNER

CASS, George Washington (12 Mar. 1810–21 Mar. 1888), engineer and business leader, was born near Dresden, Muskingum County, Ohio, the son of George W. Cass and Sophia Lord, farmers.

Cass received a good education. His parents sent him to Detroit at the age of fourteen, and from 1824 to 1827 he attended the highly regarded Detroit Academy while living with his uncle, Lewis Cass, the governor of Michigan Territory. Following his graduation, he secured an appointment to the U.S. Military Academy in West Point, from which he graduated in 1832 with special honors in mathematics.

Following a brief stint in 1832 with the Department of Topographical Engineers, Cass secured a choice position with the Army Corps of Engineers. He assisted Captain Richard Delafield in overseeing improvements on the federally funded Cumberland Road, also known as the National Road. Cass also helped to design an 80-foot bridge in Brownsville, Pennsylvania, over Dunlap Creek, a tributary of the Monongahela River. The first cast-iron bridge in the United States, this structure remained standing at the end of the twentieth century and was designated a National Civil Engineering Landmark in 1979.

Cass resigned from the military in 1836, having attained the rank of first lieutenant. Taking advantage of what he had learned about western Pennsylvania during his stint with the Army Corps, he settled in Brownsville, a growing commercial center on the route of the National Road. He established himself as a merchant and also continued to work as an independent engineer. Among the projects he supervised was a series of locks to improve the navigability of the Monongahela River, which Cass undertook first for the state of Pennsylvania and later for a private firm.

During this time Cass shifted his attention from improving the means of transportation to providing transportation services for the public. Having helped to facilitate the navigation of the Monongahela, he then organized the first steamboat line on the river. In 1849 he established the first fast stagecoach line west of the Allegheny Mountains and extended the parcel delivery service of the New England-based Adams & Co. from Baltimore to Pittsburgh. Cass's efforts led to his appointment as president of the successor Adams Express in 1855. During his presidency Cass helped to consolidate the firm's various lines, which by this time stretched from Boston west to St. Louis and south to Richmond, Virginia.

Cass moved to Pittsburgh in 1856 and soon applied his engineering and administrative talents to the burgeoning railroad industry. The following year he resigned the presidency of Adams Express and secured the presidency of the Pittsburgh, Fort Wayne & Chicago Railroad, a new firm that had been formed from the consolidation of a number of smaller lines. Cass remained its president, with the exception of one brief interval, from 1856 until 1881. he was very successful; this may have prompted party leaders to nominate him, unsuccessfully, in 1863 and 1868 as the Democratic gubernatorial candidate for Pennsylvania.

During the Civil War Cass worked to preserve labor peace on the Pittsburgh, Fort Wayne & Chicago. When railroad engineers considered organizing a strike, Cass responded by threatening to have them drafted into the Union army. Cass's action helped forestall interruption in service on this crucial route.

Following the Civil War Cass again expanded the scope of his activities. In 1867 he was appointed director of the struggling Northern Pacific Railroad, which had just begun to build its main line between Minnesota and the West Coast. In 1872 he was appointed president, a position he held until 1875. As president, Cass helped choose Tacoma, Washington, as the western terminus of the line. Like many of his contemporaries, Cass assumed that the line would not be completed within his lifetime, but it reached the Pacific in 1883, five years before his death.

Cass's forthright administrative style is illustrated by some of the positions he articulated during his presidency. He denounced the railroad's policy of granting free passes to influential politicians and newspaper editors, as well as its cozy relationship with contractors, land companies, and Washington lobbyists. In justification of his opposition to one particularly questionable business arrangement, Cass declared, "Monopolies are always odious under a Republican form of government" (Cochran, p. 205). Cass even questioned the desirability of the Northern Pacific's various government subsidies, preferring to rely entirely on private funds.

Cass's efforts failed to prevent the Northern Pacific from defaulting on its bonds in 1873 as the result of a combination of weak management, high construction costs, and the dislocations caused by the Franco-Prussian War. Following the firm's subsequent reorganization, Cass was named its receiver. In this capacity he took advantage of a land-for-bonds deal engineered by director Frederick Billings. This scheme enabled Cass and his fellow director Benjamin P. Cheney to secure an enormous tract of land in the Red River Valley of Dakota Territory; there they successfully grew wheat.

Cass's personal life was equally busy and productive. Though conservative by temperament, he was active in local affairs and a generous benefactor of various charities. He married twice, first to Louisa Dawson in 1843, and later to Louisa's sister Ellen, both from Brownsville. He had thirteen children from the two marriages. Like many business leaders of the period, he lived in stately style; in 1863 he built a large mansion, "Casella," with an impressive garden in Sewickley, Pennsylvania, a site favored by railroad leaders. It was his summer residence until 1873. A devoted Episcopalian, Cass helped establish St. Stephen's Church, the first Episcopal church in the area. During the last years of his life his principal residence was New York City, where he died, having served for several years as a senior warden of Christ Church.

Cass's principal legacy lay in the various transportation improvements he helped to oversee. Roads, rivers, steamboats, stagecoaches, express services, and railroads commanded his attention. Like many entrepreneurs of his day, he grew up with the country and illustrated the enduring influence of military education on nineteenth-century American business.

• Much business correspondence is in the Northern Pacific Collection at the Minnesota Historical Society. For a brief discussion of the National Road project, see Charles Hendricks, "Corps Builds Road," *Engineer Update* (Nov. 1987): 4–5. The cast-iron bridge is the subject of Martin P. Burke, Jr., "Dunlap's Creek Bridge: Enduring Symbol of American

Endeavor," *TR News*, no. 141 (Mar. Apr. 1989): 3–8. See also Frances C. Robb, "Cast Aside: The First Cast-Iron Bridge in the United States," *IA: The Journal of the Society of Industrial Archaeology* 19, no. 2 (1993): 48–62. Information on Cass's Pennsylvania years, as well as on his wives' families, is in Franklin Ellis, ed., *History of Fayette County, Pennsylvania* (1882) and *History of Allegheny County, Pennsylvania*, vol. 2 (1889), pp. 292–93. The threatened military draft is touched on in Theodore R. Parker, "A Glimpse of Railroading in the Civil War," *Western Pennsylvania Historical Magazine* 20 (Sept. 1937): 220. The most complete assessment of Cass's years with the Northern Pacific, including correspondence, is in Thomas C. Cochran, *Railroad Leaders, 1845–1890* (1953). See also Eugene V. Smalley, *History of the Northern Pacific Railroad* (1883), pp. 190–97. On Cass's summer home, see Franklin Taylor Nevin, *The Village of Sewickley* (1929), and Agnes L. Ellis, *Lights and Shadows of Sewickley Life* (1893). An obituary is in the *New York Times*, 22 Mar. 1888.

MAUREEN A. BRIDGES

CASS, Lewis (9 Oct. 1782–17 June 1866), political leader and presidential candidate, was born in Exeter, New Hampshire, the oldest child of Jonathan Cass, a skilled craftsman, revolutionary war veteran, soldier, and landowner, and Mary Gilman, daughter of a wealthy merchant. Both parents' families had emigrated to New England in the seventeenth century. Cass was educated at Phillips Exeter Academy between 1792 and 1799, briefly taught school in Delaware, and then moved to Marietta in the Ohio territory, where his family had gone while his father served in the army on the frontier. Cass studied law in a local law office and established a practice in Zanesville, Ohio, where he married Elizabeth Spencer, a doctor's daughter, in 1806. The family grew to include four daughters and one son.

In the same year as his marriage, Cass was elected to the Ohio legislature as its youngest member. He served one term, distinguishing himself as a loyal supporter of Jeffersonian republicanism and as a vocal opponent of Aaron Burr and the latter's separatist schemes. For most of his career, Cass held a series of federal administrative appointments, beginning in 1806 when President Thomas Jefferson named him federal marshal for Ohio. He became colonel of the Third Ohio Regiment at the outset of the War of 1812, fighting in the major battles along the Great Lakes border with Canada and against the Indian tribes allied with the British. He achieved the rank of major general of volunteers. For his war service, he was appointed governor of Michigan territory in 1813, establishing himself in Detroit. He served in that post until 1831.

As governor, Cass vigorously pursued the normal duties of the post, supervising Indian and defense matters and promoting the settlement and development of the territory. He showed shrewd concern for the Indians in his area and was determined to wean them from their British allies, to "reclaim them as far as practicable, from the savage situation in which they are placed," and, finally, as the pressures of white settlement intensified, to move them from the territory. During his regime Cass entered into a series of treaties with the tribes in which the latter ceded much of their remaining land claims. He also invested heavily in land, becoming very wealthy over the years.

In 1831, President Andrew Jackson, impressed by Cass's record as a loyal partisan and competent administrator, appointed him secretary of war. The post placed Cass in charge of Indian affairs at the national level, federal internal improvements, and army matters. Deeply committed to the Jacksonian ideology and program, Cass supervised the Indian removal policy and the building of roads and forts to protect the frontier. At the same time, he was drawn into the controversies over the national bank and South Carolina nullification. He disagreed with Jackson over the bank but never played a critical role in the contentious defining issues of the early and mid-1830s. In 1836 Jackson appointed him minister to France. Cass spoke French fluently and became friendly with King Louis-Phillipe during a period of relative calm in French-American relations. Cass repeatedly demonstrated his deep and persistent anglophobia, honed by his long years on the Canadian frontier. He stayed on as minister after the Whig William Henry Harrison succeeded Martin Van Buren as president in 1841 but resigned the next year in a dispute with Secretary of State Daniel Webster over Cass's opposition to the Webster-Ashburton treaty with England and his very public anti-British activities in the French capital.

When Cass returned to Detroit, he again became involved in Democratic party politics. His truculance toward England and his territorial expansionist sentiments won him wide support in party circles and made him a candidate for the party's presidential nomination in 1844. His powerful letter to Senator Edward Hannegan of Indiana, supporting the annexation of Texas, solidified his claim to speak for western Democrats. At the party's bitterly divided national convention, he led on several early ballots over the antiexpansionist Van Buren but lost the nomination when the delegates surged to the compromise choice, the dark horse James K. Polk. The Van Burenites blamed Cass for their loss and ever after hated him with a party-debilitating bitterness.

In 1845 the Michigan legislature elected Cass to the U.S. Senate, his first elective post since his service in the Ohio legislature almost forty years before. In the Senate, as in the cabinet, Cass pursued a policy of unswerving party regularity, echoed traditional Jacksonian and western orientation, espoused a strong nationalism, and remained always suspicious of England. He was committed to limiting the use of federal power in domestic matters, although, like other westerners, he sometimes favored federal appropriations for river and harbor improvements. In the Senate he usually acted as a spokesman for the Polk administration, particularly on territorial expansion issues, although he pressed to acquire all of Oregon against Polk's more moderate course. During the Mexican war he, along with other western Democrats, favored annexing even more of Mexican territory than the United States won in the peace treaty.

As the issue of slavery extension intensified as a result of the Mexican war, Cass followed the conservative Democratic line. He resisted the Wilmot Proviso and sought to resolve sectional differences through popular sovereignty. He championed the determination of slavery's place in an area by the local population as the best means of handling the issue in newly acquired territories. In late 1847, his letter to Tennessee politician A. O. P. Nicholson, proposing the application of popular sovereignty in the Mexican Cession, strengthened his place as a potential presidential candidate by bringing him southern Democratic support.

Cass was nominated for the presidency on the fourth ballot by the Democratic National Convention in Baltimore in 1848 on the traditional party platform of limited government, resistance to centralization, and acceptance of slavery where it existed while tolerant of its possible expansion. The split in the party over slavery expansion and the Free Soil candidacy of Martin Van Buren doomed Cass's chances, however. He lost to Zachary Taylor in a close race. Returning to the Senate, he sought to end the sectional crisis of 1850, strongly supporting the various compromise measures, which embodied his original notions of popular sovereignty.

Cass was reelected to the Senate in 1851. He was again considered for the presidency at the 1852 Democratic National Convention but lost the nomination to Franklin Pierce. In the acrimonious debates over Kansas in 1854, Cass generally supported Stephen A. Douglas's policies as part of the bloc of northern Democrats who continued to resist federally imposed restrictions on slavery's extension. He remained in the Senate until 1857 as a leader of the Democrats. He was defeated for reelection in 1857 as a result of a powerful backlash against the Democrats and the emergence of the antislavery Republican party in his state and throughout the North.

In 1857 President James Buchanan appointed Cass secretary of state. During his tenure, however, he was overshadowed by the president's own initiatives in foreign policy and by his own increasing feebleness. He remained a loyal party man, however, and in 1860 went with the administration in supporting John C. Breckinridge as the Democratic candidate over Stephen A. Douglas. Subsequently, however, Cass argued with Buchanan over the defense of American military posts in the face of southern secession. Taking his traditional strong nationalist position, he pushed hard to reinforce the beleaguered forts at Charleston and Pensacola and resigned in disgust over Buchanan's hesitations about doing so—a resignation the latter accepted with alacrity. He returned to Michigan to spend the rest of his life, dying at his home in Detroit.

• The Cass papers are split between the University of Michigan and the Detroit Public Library. The only two biographies are very out of date: Andrew McLaughlin, *Lewis Cass* (1891), and Frank Woodford, *Lewis Cass: The Last Jeffersonian* (1950). There is, however, much about Cass in more recent biographies of his contemporaries. One aspect of Cass's public career is covered in Francis P. Prucha, *Lewis Cass and American Indian Policy* (1967).

JOEL H. SILBEY

CASS, Melnea Agnes Jones (16 June 1896–16 Dec. 1978), civic leader and civil rights activist, was born in Richmond, Virginia, the daughter of Albert Jones, a janitor, and Mary Drew, a domestic worker. Seeking broader employment and educational opportunities, the Jones family moved to Boston, Massachusetts, when Melnea was five years old. Her mother died when she was eight, and she and her two sisters were entrusted to the care of an aunt, Ella Drew. After one year at Girls' High School in Boston, she was sent to St. Francis de Sales Convent School, a Roman Catholic school for black and Indian girls in Rock Castle, Virginia. There household management was taught in addition to the academic curriculum; she graduated as valedictorian of her class in 1914.

When she returned to Boston, she was unable to find work as a salesgirl because of her race. Instead, she was employed as a domestic worker until her marriage to Marshall Cass in December 1917; she resumed domestic work during the depression, when her husband lost his job as a dental laboratory technician. The marriage lasted until his death in 1958. The couple had three children.

While her husband was serving in World War I, Cass moved in with her mother-in-law, Rosa Cass Brown, who introduced her to community and church activities and persuaded her of the importance of the vote for women. At Brown's urging, Cass became a leader in the local suffrage movement and also joined the National Association for the Advancement of Colored People (NAACP).

In the 1920s Cass joined the Kindergarten Mothers, later renamed the Friendship Club, of the Robert Gould Shaw House, in the heart of the black community in Boston's South End. With other neighborhood mothers, she raised money for Shaw House. Cass served twice as president and also as secretary of the Friendship Club. The group established the first nursery school in the black community, which became a model for later day care centers. The motto she selected for the Friendship Club, "If we cannot do great things, we can do small things in a great way," exemplified Cass's personal philosophy.

Her work at Shaw House started Cass on a lifetime of community service. She served as secretary, vice president, president, and chairman of the board for the Northeastern Region of the National Association of Colored Women's Clubs and in the 1960s was vice president of the national organization. During World War II, she was one of the organizers of Women in Community Services; in the 1960s she was community resources chairman and was active in recruiting girls for the Job Corps. In 1949 she was a founder and charter member of Freedom House, a private social service and advocacy agency, initiated by Muriel S. Snowden and Otto Snowden to aid and develop the black community. In the 1950s she joined the Women's Service Club and was its sixth president, serving for seventeen years, during which time she oversaw the development of the Migrant Service Program and the initiation, in 1968, of a federally funded homemaker training program. It was said of Cass that "it would be difficult to find a single successful black individual in Boston who hadn't been given a boost by her"; indeed, she was available to lend a helping hand to every individual in need, whatever his or her station in life.

The city of Boston began to call upon Cass's talents in the 1950s when she was appointed the only female charter member of Action for Boston Community Development, an agency that was established to help people displaced by urban renewal and that later administered the city's poverty program; she served as its vice president for eight years, retiring in 1970. For ten years she was a member of the Board of Overseers of Public Welfare for the city of Boston, an advisory group to the mayor and the Welfare Department.

Throughout her adult life, Cass was a leader in the struggle against racial discrimination. She participated in A. Philip Randolph's drive to organize the sleeping car porters. In 1933, nearly twenty years after she was denied employment as a salesgirl, she joined demonstrations led by William Monroe Trotter to get Boston department stores to hire blacks. The next year she demonstrated in favor of the hiring of black doctors and nurses at Boston City Hospital. For many years she was on the board of the Boston YWCA but left the organization in 1951 because of its discriminatory practices; she rejoined years later only after many policy changes had been made. A life member of the NAACP, she served in many capacities in the Boston branch and held the presidency from 1962 to 1964, when the NAACP organized demonstrations against the Boston School Committee and held sit-ins to support desegregation and protest inequality in the curriculum for black children. She continued the tradition started by William Monroe Trotter of annually laying a wreath in honor of Crispus Attucks, and she successfully lobbied for Boston to observe the birthday of Frederick Douglass.

In her seventies, Cass became a spokesperson for the elderly, serving as president of the Roxbury Council of Elders, chairperson of the Mayor's Advisory Committee for Affairs of the Elderly (1975), and chairperson of the Massachusetts Advisory Committee for the Elderly (1975–1976). National recognition came in 1973 when Elliott Richardson appointed her to represent consumers' Medicare interests on the National Health Insurance Benefits Advisory Council.

Patriotic and church organizations also benefited from her participation. Among other affiliations and offices, as state president of the United War Mothers of America, she was the first black woman to hold that office in a national patriotic organization. She was also the first woman, black or white, elected state president of the Gold Star and War Parents of America. At St. Mark Congregational Church in Roxbury she was a charter member of the Mothers' Club and chaired the Social Action Committee. In 1967 she was the first woman to deliver a sermon for Woman's Day from the pulpit of the Ebenezer Baptist Church in Boston.

On many occasions, the community expressed its appreciation for her contributions. As early as 1949 the Friendship Club of Shaw House gave a banquet in tribute to her "efficient leadership, wise counsel, dependability, and fair judgment." In 1966 Mayor John Collins proclaimed 22 May "Melnea Cass Day," and more than 1,000 people attended a salute to the "First Lady of Roxbury." In 1974, at the recommendation of the Massachusetts State Federation of Women's Clubs, she was named Massachusetts Mother of the Year, and in 1977 she was designated one of seven "Grand Bostonians." Several facilities were named in her honor: the Melnea A. Cass Metropolitan District Commission Swimming Pool and Skating Rink (1968), the Melnea A. Cass Clarendon Street Branch of the YWCA (1976), and Cass House, a mixed-income apartment development (1989). Malnea A. Cass Boulevard opened in Boston in 1981.

At age seventy-nine Cass expressed the philosophy that had guided her life of service: "I am convinced that my life belongs to the whole community, and as long as I live, it is my privilege to do for it whatever I can, for the harder I work the more I live" (funeral program, St. Mark Congregational Church). She died in Boston. "By doing many small things in a great way" she had improved life for Boston's black community and won the respect and admiration of Bostonians of all races.

• The major source of information on Cass is her oral history recorded with Tahi L. Mottl in 1977 and published in *The Black Women Oral History Project*, ed. Ruth Edmonds Hill, vol. 2 (1991). The original tapes and two folders of newspaper clippings and memorabilia are in the files of the Black Women Oral History Project, Schlesinger Library, Radcliffe College. The only published biography of Cass is the entry by Hill in *Notable Black American Women*, ed. Jessie Carney Smith (1992). See also the *Sunday Herald Advertiser* (Boston), 20 June 1976. Obituaries are in the *Bay State Banner*, 21 Dec. 1978, and the *Boston Globe*, 20 Dec. 1978.

PATRICIA MILLER KING

CASSADY, Neal (8 Feb. 1926–4 Feb. 1968), laborer and source of inspiration to two American subcultures, was born in Salt Lake City, Utah, the son of Neal Cassady, Sr., a barber, and Maude Scheuer Daly. At the time of his birth, Cassady's father was moving the family from Des Moines, Iowa, to Hollywood. The family later completed its move to California and opened a barbershop. His alcoholic father struggled in the new environment, however, and the sale of the shop and a relocation to Denver, Colorado, in 1928 did not improve the family fortunes. During the depression, the business failed completely.

Cassady's childhood was chaotic. The dual burdens of alcohol and deprivation weighed heavily on the family, and his mother, who had seven children from her first marriage, was unable to hold the family together.

Cassady's older half siblings tormented him, and he eventually ended up living with his father in a rundown Denver flophouse. He later traveled throughout the country with his father, hitchhiking, riding freight trains, and sleeping with hoboes. Cassady sought escape from his surroundings in the fantasy world within his own imagination, taking particular pleasure in the western movies shown at the local theater.

Given his background, it is not surprising that Cassady ran afoul of the law. He endured three stints in reform schools (his formal education largely over after the eighth grade), and he had, by his own admission, stolen 500 cars during his adolescence. While in reform school, he had a nightmare that changed his life. In the dream, he viewed himself as an old man who had become his father's sad duplicate. Utilizing the manic energy that he was to display for the rest of his life, Cassady embarked on an intensive period of self-education. He studied Marcel Proust, William Shakespeare, and Arthur Schopenhauer and could soon more than hold his own in conversations with college-educated individuals.

In August 1945 Cassady married LuAnne Henderson in Denver, Colorado. They had no children. The couple immediately hitchhiked to the Midwest, where they both found jobs as laborers. After a short stay in Sidney, Nebraska, the Cassadys left for New York City in late 1946, hoping to visit some friends and possibly establish themselves. During this period Cassady first encountered the group of bohemian writers and hangers-on who were later to be labeled the "Beat Generation."

Cassady, who harbored vague ambitions as a writer, was immediately integrated into the group. His most profound influence was on Allen Ginsberg and Jack Kerouac. Kerouac found in Cassady "the energy of a new kind of American saint" and thought him to be "more like Dostoevsky than anyone I know." While the Beats came from a wide variety of backgrounds and experiences, all shared a sense of restlessness and found American society in the late 1940s rigidly confining, if not stifling. Seeking outlets for their creative energies, the Beats flaunted societal mores by experimenting with drugs and free love. They also found release in an endless search for "kicks," which included spur-of-the-moment crosscountry automobile trips, all-night discussions, and an infatuation with jazz. In Cassady, the Beats (who also included William S. Burroughs, Lawrence Ferlinghetti, and John Clellon Holmes, among others) found their role model.

In 1947 Cassady returned to Denver, having been deserted by his wife, and met Carolyn Robinson, whom he married in San Francisco in April 1948 before his previous marriage had been annulled. They had three children and were divorced in 1963.

During the late 1940s Cassady and Kerouac made several long-distance automobile trips that were later immortalized in Kerouac's most famous book, *On the Road*, which was published in September 1957 and caused an immediate sensation. Readers had never encountered a persona like Dean Moriarty (the name of Cassady's character), and Americans were thus formally introduced to a group of individuals who refused to be bound by conventional social limits. Cassady also served as the inspiration for Kerouac's *Visions of Cody* (1959) and for Ginsberg's famous 1956 poem "Howl," which was dedicated to "N. C., the secret hero."

Ironically, as the Beat genre took shape during the 1950s, Cassady was engaged in a constant struggle between a life of quiet domesticity in Los Gatos, California (where he worked as a brakeman for the Southern Pacific Railroad, then as a tire recapper), and periodic escapes to the open road. He left his family and, while in New York, married Diana Hansen in July 1950, again committing bigamy and fathering another child. Having failed in an attempt to settle all three wives past and present in close proximity in California, Cassady moved back in with Carolyn, and Diana departed for New York.

A nominal Roman Catholic, Cassady later became fascinated by the psychic teachings of Edgar Cayce, an interest he shared with Carolyn as they struggled to keep their marriage intact. Cassady's outside interests, which included growing marijuana in his backyard, finally caught up with him. He was arrested on 8 April 1958 in San Francisco on a drug smuggling charge and ended up with a two-year prison term. Released on 4 July 1960, he began frequenting the Palo Alto, California, area and met author Ken Kesey in the summer of 1962, shortly after Kesey's novel *One Flew over the Cuckoo's Nest* had been published. Cassady soon fell in with Kesey and his group that was later dubbed the "Merry Pranksters." Traveling around the country in a psychedelically painted bus named "Further," Cassady (newly nicknamed "Speed Limit") joined the other prototypical counterculturists in conducting "acid tests," which involved large crowds consuming LSD and other drugs at sound and light shows.

Kesey was arrested in April 1965 on drug charges and, while the case was being appealed, drifted into Mexico with Cassady and the rest of the Pranksters. Years of drug abuse, which in later years included heavy usage of amphetamines, had taken their toll, however, and Cassady was found unconscious near a set of railroad tracks in San Miguel de Allende. He died in a nearby hospital the same day.

Neal Cassady as a literary figure hardly rates a footnote. His sole published work, *The First Third*, was an autobiography published posthumously in 1971. His significance remains the catalytic effect of his personality on the Beat Generation and later on the newly emerging hippie movement. These two movements stand as evidence that life in the United States was not limited to the dull conformity characteristic of the 1950s and much of the 1960s.

• Cassady's correspondence is scattered. Allen Ginsberg collected a sample of the correspondence between them and published it in *The Visions of the Great Rememberer* (1974). A solid biography that does a good job of analyzing Cassady's complex personality is William Plummer, *"The Holy Goof":*

A Biography of Neal Cassady (1981). All scholarly treatments of Jack Kerouac include extensive discussions of Cassady; the definitive biography of Kerouac is Ann Charters, *Kerouac* (1973). A personal view of Cassady, the Beat Generation, and their interpersonal relationships is provided by Carolyn Cassady, *Off the Road: My Years with Cassady, Kerouac, and Ginsberg* (1990).

EDWARD L. LACH, JR.

CASSATT, Alexander Johnston (8 Dec. 1839–28 Dec. 1906), railroad president, was born in Pittsburgh, Pennsylvania, the son of Robert Cassatt, a banker, and Katherine Johnston. With his parents and five brothers and sisters, Alexander moved to Philadelphia in 1848 then to Paris, France, in 1851. He graduated from a private academy in Darmstadt, Germany, in 1856. Returning to the United States that year, he enrolled at Yale University, but, unhappy with the technical curriculum, he transferred to Rensselaer Polytechnic Institute and graduated with a degree in civil engineering in 1859.

Cassatt became a surveyor's assistant for the Georgia Railroad, then under construction, but he moved north in 1861, on the eve of the Civil War, and took a similar job with the Pennsylvania Railroad (PRR). In 1863 he served as assistant civil engineer in charge of building a connection between the PRR and the United Railroads of New Jersey, near Trenton, by which the Pennsylvania gained an all-rail route to the Hudson River. In 1864 Cassatt was made chief civil engineer of the middle division of the Philadelphia & Erie Railroad (P&E), a PRR subsidiary. Two years later he served briefly as chief civil engineer of a P&E affiliate, the Warren & Franklin Railroad, before becoming the P&E's superintendent of motive power. This was his first mechanical engineering position, but it also included significant managerial responsibilities. He performed ably and won commendation from PRR president J. Edgar Thomson, who in 1867 named Cassatt superintendent of motive power for Lines East (of Pittsburgh and Erie), with headquarters in Altoona, site of the railroad's main shops. There Cassatt oversaw the design, construction, and maintenance of hundreds of steam locomotives. In 1868 he married Maria Lois Buchanan, a niece of President James Buchanan. They had four children.

Cassatt was an early advocate of replacing locomotives built for specific applications with more general-use, standard designs, that is, a few basic classes of locomotives that would employ interchangeable parts and could be used in many types of service systemwide. The PRR later adopted this cost-saving approach on a massive scale and set a precedent for locomotive standardization that would inspire not only other railroads but also builders of diesel-electric engines in the mid-twentieth century. Cassatt also put the PRR in the forefront of the adoption of the air brake, first by sponsoring trials of the new device (invented by George Westinghouse) and then, in 1870, by ordering all the railroad's passenger trains to be equipped with air brakes.

Late in 1870 Cassatt was promoted to general superintendent of Lines East. Although he was still based in Altoona, he was assigned by Thomson to negotiate the purchase of a controlling interest in the Camden & Amboy Railroad, which would assure the PRR's control of the rail line across New Jersey. The Erie and the New York Central railroads tried to block the purchase, but Cassatt prevailed. In 1871 Thomson brought him to company headquarters in Philadelphia as general manager of Lines East.

As general manager (1871–1874) and third vice president (1874–1880), Cassatt became acquainted with virtually all aspects of the railroad business. In the realm of labor, for example, he went to Pittsburgh in 1877 to represent the PRR during the trainmen's strike, which saw the burning of the city's passenger station and repair shops. Although he preferred a shirt-sleeves management style—even to the point of serving as locomotive engineer or fireman on many of his vice presidential inspection trips—his vigorous defense of private property during the strike earned him the enmity of railroad labor. This was not without irony, for Cassatt himself showed a distaste for many so-called "captains of industry." His quiet demeanor, modest lifestyle, and loathing of publicity contrasted markedly with the conspicuous consumption so amply displayed by the Vanderbilts, Goulds, and others. He was particularly irked by John D. Rockefeller, whom he dealt with in a vain effort to curb the oil magnate's demand for rebates, or givebacks, by the PRR on petroleum hauled not only for Rockefeller's Standard Oil Company but for other oil producers as well. Cassatt came to regard rebating—a widespread practice among rail shippers—as a critical problem for the railroad industry. He estimated the PRR alone had lost $10 million in revenue to Standard Oil over eighteen months.

Many observers expected Cassatt to succeed Thomas A. Scott as PRR president when the latter stepped down in 1880. Instead, the board of directors selected First Vice President George B. Roberts and named Cassatt the new first vice president. The two men were longtime rivals and personally distant. Cassatt considered Roberts to be unimaginative and unnecessarily cautious. Roberts regarded Cassatt as impetuous and too eager to expand the railroad. In 1881 Roberts reacted with indifference to Cassatt's plea to buy the Philadelphia, Wilmington & Baltimore Railroad (PW&B), over which the Pennsylvania ran its trains between Philadelphia and Washington, D.C. Cassatt had long advocated acquiring this line to protect it from control by the Baltimore & Ohio or another unfriendly road. In fact, the B&O did make an energetic attempt to capture the line but was foiled when Cassatt, backed by his board of directors, at the last minute shrewdly maneuvered some PW&B stockholders into the Pennsylvania's camp.

In 1882 Cassatt resigned and retired to his Haverford estate to spend time with his family. He also devoted much time to breeding and racing horses and to traveling in Europe with his sister, the painter Mary

Cassatt. He remained as a director of the PRR and served four years (1885–1889) as president of the New York, Philadelphia & Norfolk Railroad, a lightly trafficked line (later a PRR subsidiary) that ran down the Delmarva Peninsula to Cape Charles and a ferry connection with the Norfolk & Western. When Roberts died in 1897, Cassatt's name again came to the fore as a possible successor, but he did not seek the presidency, which went to Frank Thomson, J. Edgar Thomson's nephew. Thomson died two years later, however, and the first vice president, John P. Green, lacked the engineering expertise the directors preferred in their company's chief executive. Cassatt at last was named president on 9 June 1899.

One of Cassatt's first priorities was to eliminate rebates. In a rare accord with archrival New York Central, the two large eastern roads bought controlling shares in most smaller lines. The PRR thus acquired substantial ownership of the B&O, Norfolk & Western, and Chesapeake & Ohio railroads. This "community of interest," as Cassatt termed it, enabled the railroads to present a united front against Standard Oil, the Carnegie steel combine, and other large shippers. It served as a major stabilizing force in the railroad industry in the East and predated by several years the better-known integration of western railroads under E. H. Harriman. When the shippers were no longer able to play one line against a rival in a search for givebacks, rebating all but ceased. Although President Theodore Roosevelt (1858–1919) shared Cassatt's hatred of rebating, he saw the community of interest as dangerously monopolistic and called for federal regulation. Cassatt assumed any railroad-conceived antirebating scheme to be temporary and imperfect. He broke with many of his fellow railroad chiefs and supported Roosevelt's program, which was implemented through the Elkins Act (1903) and the Hepburn Act (1906). Evidence shows that Cassatt helped to draft the Elkins Act, which prohibited rebates. The Hepburn Act gave the Interstate Commerce Commission the power to set maximum rates. Cassatt viewed it as the only realistic and long-term solution to the rate wars that for years had been sapping the railroads' financial strength.

Meanwhile Cassatt, drawing on his civil engineering experience, presided over one of the most extensive capital improvement projects yet undertaken in the railroad industry. The single most expensive ($150 million) venture involved boring tunnels beneath the Hudson and East rivers and building the magnificent Pennsylvania Station in Manhattan. The PRR pioneered electric traction in the United States by introducing direct-current locomotives to pull the trains through these tunnels. The project finally gave the company an all-rail route into Manhattan, eliminating cumbersome passenger ferries and enabling it to compete more effectively with the New York Central. Monumental passenger stations also were erected in New York, Washington, Baltimore, and Pittsburgh. One of the world's largest freight classification yards was built at Enola, near Harrisburg, Pennsylvania. From there, the railroad broadened its heavily traveled main line to Pittsburgh from two to three and four tracks, reduced curvatures, and eased grades. Freight bypass lines were constructed to the north and west of Philadelphia. Steel freight and passenger cars replaced wooden rolling stock, and, in the same way that the air brake had overtaken hand brakes thirty years earlier, virtually all other railroads followed the PRR's lead.

Cassatt set these improvements in motion but did not live to see most of them bear fruit. He died in Philadelphia and was succeeded in the presidency by James McCrea. Cassatt's legacy is mixed. Under his leadership, the PRR in effect rebuilt itself physically and became the nation's best-engineered railroad. His insistence on keeping pace with railroading's changing technology—from locomotives to air brakes to electrification—paid for itself many times over and helped to make the Pennsylvania one of the world's most profitable and efficient transportation systems. During his seven-year presidency, annual gross income climbed from $71 million to $146 million. Cassatt also was in the vanguard of railroad executives who favored government regulation as a solution to the railroad industry's constant, debilitating rate wars. Although he could not have foreseen the outcome, the legislation he championed ultimately crippled the industry's ability to compete with other forms of transportation and within fifty years brought the railroads perilously close to ultimate ruin as economic enterprises.

• Board of directors minutes, letterbooks, miscellaneous managerial papers, and engineering records are in the Pennsylvania Railroad Collections of the Pennsylvania Historical and Museum Commission in Harrisburg and the Hagley Museum and Library in Wilmington, Del. See also Annual Reports of the Pennsylvania Railroad for the years under discussion. The only biography is Patricia T. Davis, *End of the Line: A. J. Cassatt and the Pennsylvania Railroad* (1978), but it is highly simplified and contains numerous factual errors. The best corporate history is George H. Burgess and Miles C. Kennedy, *Centennial History of the Pennsylvania Railroad Company* (1949). Obituaries are in *Railway Age*, 4 Jan. 1907; the *New York Times*, 29 Dec. 1906; and the *Philadelphia Inquirer*, 29 Dec. 1906.

MICHAEL BEZILLA

CASSATT, Mary (22 May 1844–13 June 1926), artist, was born Mary Stevenson Cassatt in Allegheny City (now part of Pittsburgh), Pennsylvania, the daughter of Robert Simpson Cassatt and Katherine Kelso Johnston. At the time of her birth, her father was a forwarding merchant, buying raw materials from the frontier states and selling them to eastern manufacturers, but in later years he opened an investment firm in Philadelphia. Her mother was the daughter of Alexander Johnston, the first director of the Bank of Pittsburgh.

When Cassatt was four years old, the family moved to Lancaster, Pennsylvania, and two years after that to Philadelphia. In 1851 they embarked on a lengthy sojourn in Europe where Cassatt received her basic education. Returning to Philadelphia in 1855, she was allowed to leave school at the age of sixteen so that she might study at the Pennsylvania Academy of the Fine Arts (1860–1864). At the conclusion of the Civil War, she traveled to Europe to finish her training in France and Italy. Except for a few short trips back to the United States in 1870–1871, 1875, 1898, and 1908, she practiced as an artist in Europe, primarily in Paris, for the rest of her life.

Although Cassatt was an expatriate, she was not divorced from American culture. Both as a student and as a professional, she was part of a larger contingent of American artists, intellectuals, and patrons who frequented the prestigious art schools and galleries abroad. Throughout her life she sent her work back home to American exhibitions and sold to American collectors. After 1900 her fame was such in her own country that she was regularly visited by American art students seeking advice. She never gave up her American citizenship and continued to be keenly interested in American politics, including the American woman suffrage movement.

However, it was her participation in the French impressionist group from 1879 to 1886 that set her apart from the other American artists abroad and has provided the basis for her lasting reputation. During the first years of her professional career (1868–1876), she competed successfully for recognition within the art establishment of Paris. She had paintings accepted regularly into the annual state-sponsored exhibition, the Paris Salon, and was considered by her teachers, Charles Chaplin, Jean-Léon Gérôme, and Thomas Couture, as well as by some critics, to be among the best young artists of her generation. But the rigidity of the current styles as well as the politics of the established system offended the independent young woman, and by 1874 she was already known as an outspoken critic of the official art world. In turn, the salon juries began rejecting her increasingly experimental paintings. In 1877, after hearing that she would not be represented at the salon for the first time in seven years, she accepted an invitation by Edgar Degas to join the impressionists.

Cassatt had discovered Degas's work in 1875 but does not seem to have met him until two years later. Meanwhile, she began acquainting herself with the art of Claude Monet, Auguste Renoir, Camille Pissarro, Berthe Morisot, and their friends who had turned their backs on the salon to form their own renegade exhibiting group. They were unified in their belief that art should capture a more immediate image of modern life around them, and they had developed a lighter palette and choppier brushstrokes to convey a sense of spontaneity. Dubbed the "impressionists" after the title of one of Monet's paintings in their first group exhibition in 1874, they quickly attracted the attention of the Paris art world, which was undergoing a period of disarray and reorganization during the Third Republic.

Cassatt became the only American to join the group; the other famous American expatriates, John Singer Sargent and James McNeill Whistler, both friends of Cassatt, were invited but declined in order to follow more conservative paths. For Cassatt, it was the opportunity of a lifetime. As she told her biographer Achille Segard, "I accepted with joy. . . . I began to live." She learned the style quickly, adopting the impressionist subjects of the theater, the drawing room, and the flower-filled garden. When she debuted with the group in their next exhibition in 1879, she was hailed by critics as a welcome addition. "Mlle. Mary Cassatt is fond of pure colors and possesses the secret of blending them in a composition that is bold, mysterious, and fresh," wrote the impressionist sympathizer Arsène Houssaye in *L'Artiste* (May 1879).

That same year, after the close of the impressionist exhibition, Cassatt joined Degas, Pissarro, and other artists and writers in a project to publish a "journal" of modern life, called *Le Jour et la Nuit*. The artists were to contribute original etchings that would be bound into the publication and would appeal to print collectors. Cassatt, who had never previously investigated printmaking as an art, launched wholeheartedly into the mastery of etching, aquatint, drypoint, and lithograph. Although the journal was never published, Cassatt's interest in prints continued for the next twenty-five years, and she became one of the finest printmakers of her generation.

Cassatt's participation in the impressionist group brought her further into French artistic circles than Americans tended to go. Although accepted as students, professional American artists were kept at arm's length by the French. They were expected to stay within the American colony in Paris for their social and professional contacts as well as for patronage. But Cassatt's deep knowledge of and enthusiasm for French culture, particularly modern French literature, allowed her to participate in the highly intellectual discussions that bound the members of the impressionist group together socially as well as artistically. She formed lifelong friendships with Degas, Morisot, Pissarro, and Renoir. Her acceptance by the group was aided by her equally engaging parents and older sister who had come in 1878 to make their home with her in Paris. The Cassatts' apartment in the artists' quarter near the Place Pigalle was the site of many an afternoon or evening party of the kind that drew the impressionist artists together several times a month.

Mary Cassatt exhibited in impressionist exhibitions in 1879, 1880, 1881, and in the last group exhibition in 1886. By the mid-1880s, the shift toward symbolism in art and literature led all the impressionist artists to move on to new themes and styles. Cassatt had already begun investigating more stable compositional devices for her portraits and figure studies when, in 1888, she began a series of mother-and-child paintings and prints. This new subject gave her figure studies a monumentality and symbolic dimension that had previously been absent from her impressionist representations of modern life. In claiming this theme as her own, she joined a large number of both European and American artists who were also interested in bringing the revered Old Master theme back into modern art. But Cassatt's ability to capture the nuances of both adult and child body language in an affectionate but stately embrace has made her works outlive those of her many rivals.

Cassatt's success with the mother-and-child theme caused the spread of her reputation throughout Europe and the United States in the 1890s. She was taken on by the influential dealer of the impressionists, Paul Durand-Ruel, who arranged her first solo exhibition in 1891 in Paris. This small but impressive installation consisted of four mother-and-child paintings and pastels and a series of ten color prints. The avant-garde critic Félix Fénéon praised Cassatt's acute observations of the women she depicted in the ten prints that, like the Japanese ukiyo-e woodcuts they resembled, showed scenes of daily life. "It is without self-consciousness that the letter-writer is caught going over what she has just written in the letter and how she hesitates to finally seal it; or how this 'young Woman Trying on a Dress' betrays a fugitive restlessness that comes from her curiosity to turn and see the whole" (*Le Chat Noir*, Apr. 1891). Unlike Japanese woodblock prints, Cassatt's series was done in drypoint and aquatint, but the principle of printing in color was the same. Each composition required several plates upon which the colored inks were hand painted and then printed one after another to complete the color scheme. Cassatt labored for almost a year to design and print an edition of twenty-five of each of the ten images. Today they are among the most prized of nineteenth-century prints.

In 1892 Cassatt was invited to paint one of the two large murals that would decorate the hall of honor of the Woman's Building, a pavilion in the World's Columbian Exposition held in Chicago in 1893. Cassatt's theme, "modern woman," would face a mural depicting "primitive woman" to show the great strides women had made in education and the professions. Although her adaptation of "picking fruit from the tree of knowledge" in modern dress and bright colors was not understood by all visitors, it was noticed and admired by avant-garde artists and critics and served to reintroduce her to American audiences at home.

A large exhibition in Paris in 1893 organized by Durand-Ruel and another held two years later in New York were also signs of Cassatt's prominence in the art world of both countries. Her sales to both French and American collectors were sufficient by 1894 to fund her purchase of a country home, "Mesnil-Beaufresne," about fifty miles northwest of Paris. She was to lose the last remaining member of her Paris family—her mother—in 1895, but she remained close to her two brothers in Philadelphia and made them, their wives, and their children her models during their almost annual visits to Paris. She continued an active social life with her old impressionist colleagues, particularly Degas, and the wider circle that included the poet Stéphane Mallarmé and the statesman Georges Clemenceau. But more Americans infused her social schedule during the 1890s as her many American relatives, as well as her growing acquaintance among American "impressionists," such as J. Alden Weir and William Merritt Chase, sought her out.

Cassatt's best friend during the 1890s and for the last decades of her life was the American collector and suffragist Louisine Elder Havemeyer. Although Havemeyer lived in New York, she made frequent trips abroad with her husband to study and purchase art. Cassatt introduced her to French realist and impressionist paintings and helped her to purchase some of the finest works by Gustave Courbet, Edouard Manet, and Degas that would come to the United States. Cassatt did not have the personal fortune nor, indeed, the zeal necessary to become a collector herself, but she enjoyed shaping her friend's collection and took great personal pride in it. She felt competitive toward the other great American art amateurs of this era, such as Henry Walters of Baltimore and Isabella Stewart Gardner of Boston, who she felt had not achieved the proper balance of Old Master and modern art.

Cassatt's reputation continued to grow in the early twentieth century, particularly in the United States. As if to acknowledge her new stature, her paintings also grew larger and weightier. Her study of the Old Masters during collecting trips with the Havemeyers shows in the rich fabrics and elaborate costumes of her new mother-and-child compositions. This trend toward traditional art also signals her loss of interest in the newer styles developing in Paris, particularly fauvism as it was defined by Henri Matisse, whose works she singled out for censure. Her conservatism, however, won her the praise of American critics and the appellation in the magazine *Current Literature* (Feb. 1909) as "the most eminent of living American women painters."

Just as Cassatt received such international acclaim, her health became significantly impaired by the combination of a taxing voyage through Egypt in 1911 and the onset of cataracts. She recovered her health long enough to produce one more year of work in 1913–1914, but her eyesight continued to fail despite repeated operations, leaving her functionally blind for the last ten years of her life. Deprived of her art in her seventies when she was otherwise still very active, she was found to be bitter and temperamental by younger Americans who knew her only at this period of her life.

However, Cassatt maintained an active interest in many spheres of life. In response to World War I, which made a battle zone out of the area around her country house, she organized humanitarian aid for local families and, in addition, invented and acquired a patent for a hammock for the convalescence of wounded soldiers. She also followed the suffrage campaign in the United States and participated in a benefit exhibition of her work, hung alongside Degas's and Old Master paintings, which was organized by Havemeyer in New York in 1915.

After the war, Cassatt spent most of her time in her country house entertaining visitors ranging from the family to important art world figures. When she died in Mesnil-Théribus, France, memorial exhibitions were organized in Paris, New York, Philadelphia, and Chicago. The obituaries and tributes show that her reputation as an impressionist, a mother-and-child painter, and an independent woman had not waned even a dozen years after she stopped painting. Successive generations have interpreted her work and her life according to their own values, but she continues to be ranked as an important figure in the art of her period.

• Cassatt's own papers were not preserved after her death, but large groups of letters concerning Cassatt may be found in the Cassatt Family Papers at the Philadelphia Museum of Art and in the Havemeyer papers at the Metropolitan Museum of Art. Most of the known letters by and about her in various collections have been recorded on microfilm by the Archives of American Art. The earliest monograph published during her lifetime was Achille Segard, *Mary Cassatt: Un peintre des enfants et des mères* (1913), which is partially based on interviews with her. See also Adelyn Breeskin, *Mary Cassatt: A Catalogue Raisonné of the Graphic Work* (1948; rev. ed., 1979) and *Mary Cassatt: A Catalogue Raisonné of the Oils, Pastels, Watercolors, and Drawings* (1970). The color prints have been published in an updated catalogue raisonné, *Mary Cassatt: The Color Prints* (1989), by Nancy Mowll Mathews and Barbara Shapiro. An authoritative biography is Mathews, *Mary Cassatt: A Life* (1994). See also Mathews, ed., *Cassatt: A Retrospective* (1996), an anthology of writings about Cassatt during her lifetime.

NANCY MOWLL MATHEWS

CASSAVETES, John (9 Dec. 1929–3 Feb. 1989), actor, screenwriter, director, and filmmaker, was born in New York City, the son of Nicholas John Cassavetes, the owner of a travel business, and Katherine Demitri. Although his father, a Greek immigrant, had a "knack" for making and losing millions, Cassavetes grew up in the affluent Long Island towns of Sands Point and Port Washington, where he went to public schools. He attended Mohawk College and Colgate University, majoring in English. He left college for a brief stint as a sports announcer, but after reading the plays of Robert E. Sherwood he decided to become an actor and enrolled at the New York Academy of Dramatic Arts, where he met his future wife Gena Rowlands. They married in 1954 and had three children. Cassavetes graduated in 1950. Unable to find work in New York City, he joined a stock company in Providence, Rhode Island.

Cassavetes broke into film in 1951 as an extra; his first speaking part was in *Taxi* (1953), directed by Gregory Ratoff. Ratoff also hired him as assistant stage manager for the Broadway play *The Fifth Season* (1953). Later that same year he was chosen to play the lead, a "brooding young bullfighter," in "Pasa Doble," a segment of *Omnibus* on CBS television. His success in this role led to others. In two years Cassavetes appeared in more than eighty teleplays, usually as a troubled youth. His unsmiling face and intense demeanor typecast him as a perfect "psychopathic young hoodlum." Some of these teleplays were remade into films; his role in "Crime in the Streets" for *The Elgin Hour* in 1955 brought him to Hollywood, where he played the same part in the film version of 1957. Other teleplays that brought him film parts were *The Night Holds Terror* (1955) and *Edge of the City* (1956). In 1959–1960 Cassavetes starred in his own weekly television series *Staccato*, later titled *Johnny Staccato*, about a Greenwich Village jazz musician turned amateur detective.

Yet Cassavetes needed something more than acting. He had always wanted to "express things that I think may be of value" and was concerned with "problems confronting real people." In 1956 Cassavetes began conducting classes in method acting at Burt Lane's Drama Workshop in New York City. The classes were going so well that the students suggested making a film. With the money he made from *Johnny Staccato* and loans from friends, Cassavetes began the project.

The resulting film, *Shadows* (1960), was an undertaking that took three years. Cassavetes, working as both producer and director, used the actors from his workshop to build the film from a series of dramatic improvisations. There is nothing "Hollywood" about this film, which cost a mere $40,000 and was shot with a handheld sixteen-millimeter camera. When the picture was blown up to thirty-five millimeter, it achieved a grainy, "rough-hewn" quality. Cassavetes was not able to get an American distributor and sent the film to Europe, where it was hailed as a triumph of cinema verité. *Shadows* won the Critics' Award at the 1960 Venice Film Festival and made a respectable profit. It was released in the United States in 1961.

Impressed by Cassavetes's success, Paramount hired him to make a series of "high-quality, low-budget films." *Too Late Blues* (1961) was not received well, either by the critics or the public, and Paramount canceled its contract with Cassavetes. His next directing job in Hollywood was *A Child Is Waiting* (1963). Cassavetes was given only two weeks to edit the film. When he objected, he was fired, and the film was "edited" by the producer, Stanley Kramer. Cassavetes renounced the film and resolved to never again direct a film whose ultimate form was in the hands of others. Hollywood, in turn, blackballed the "difficult" Cassavetes.

Although Cassavetes would no longer direct in Hollywood, he continued to act, using his income to finance his own films. During this time he appeared in *The Killers* (1964) with Ronald Reagan, who played a villain in his final role as an actor; and *Devil's Angels* (1967). His portrayal of yet another psychopathic killer in *The Dirty Dozen* (1967) brought him an Oscar nomination for best supporting actor. That same year he played the husband who sells his wife to the devil in *Rosemary's Baby*. Cassavetes was also doing episodes on a variety of television series, including *Rawhide*, *Dr. Kildare*, *Burke's Law*, *Alfred Hitchcock Theater*, and *The Virginian*.

During this time Cassavetes was writing, shooting, and editing his next film, *Faces* (1968), starring John Marley; Lynn Carlin; his wife Rowlands, who would be his lifelong star and collaborator; and Cassavetes himself. It is a hard and unrelenting look at the disintegration of a marriage. The final product took three years of editing time and 300,000 feet of film to produce what one critic described as "the most brilliant home movie ever made." *Faces* was shown at film festivals in New York City, San Francisco, and Venice, where it received five awards. Cassavetes was nominated for an Academy Award for the screenplay.

After *Faces*, Cassavetes, in the six years between 1969 and 1975, made four major independent feature-length films. *Husbands* (1970) is the only one of his films in which he gave himself a major role. He recruited his friends Peter Falk and Ben Gazzara to play with him as a trio of affluent Long Island suburbanites who, following a wake, impulsively visit London for gambling and sex. Some critics see *Husbands* as his best film. In *Minnie and Moskowitz* (1971) Cassavetes proves he can do comedy. The film is a family affair, with Rowlands, Cassavetes, Cassavetes's mother, Rowland's mother, and various other family members playing parts. *A Woman under the Influence* (1974) was originally written at Rowland's request as a vehicle for her to return to the stage. But as the work developed, it was apparent that the central role was so taxing that it would be impossible for an actress to play the part night after night. Cassavetes rewrote the play as a film, mortgaging his house and borrowing from his friends to finance it. The film is a tour de force for Rowlands and also stars Peter Falk. It became Cassavetes's biggest commercial success and won the National Board of Review best picture award. It also brought Cassavetes another Oscar nomination, this time for his directing, making him one of the few filmmakers to earn nominations in acting, writing, and directing. *The Killing of a Chinese Bookie* (1976), starring Gazzara, described as Cassavetes's venture into film noir, was not as well received.

Other films include *Opening Night* (1978), starring Rowlands in yet another "bravura performance." The film impressed English reviewers, but some American critics called it a disaster. *Gloria* (1980), which Cassavetes wrote, produced, and directed, was co-winner at the Venice Film Festival. Critic David Ansen called it "Cassavetes's loopy version of an action movie." It is loaded with straight-faced humor and a larger than life heroine, played by Rowlands, as a hilarious version of a Gloria Swanson "wanna be." *Love Streams* (1984), written with Ted Allen, won the top prize at the Berlin Film Festival.

In 1986 Cassavetes, as a personal favor to the producer Michael Lobell, stepped in to direct *Big Trouble* (1986) after scriptwriter and director Andrew Bergman left the project. During the filming Cassavetes was already ill. In 1988 he was writing a sequel to *Gloria* as well as reworking a romantic comedy he wrote in 1980, "She's De Lovely." Neither project was completed. He died in Los Angeles of cirrhosis of the liver, exacerbated by years of alcohol abuse.

Although Cassavetes was a highly regarded actor, it was as a filmmaker that he achieved renown. He was the first since Orson Welles to challenge the established way of making movies. Director Peter Bogdanovich reflected that Cassavetes "believed in letting a picture find itself" and called him an "American Renoir." Cassavetes was a perennial outsider. As an actor, he played misfits; as a filmmaker he challenged Hollywood, stating that Hollywood made films the way Detroit manufactured cars: mass produced to maximize profits. He made films his way, and they are still playing, although to a limited audience. When asked about his life, Cassavetes once said: "My life? It's not very exciting. The excitement is the work. I live through my films. They are my life."

• The largest single collection of Cassavetes's own statements about his life and work (including material previously unpublished) is in *John Cassavetes: Autoportraits*, ed. Ray Carney (1992). Carney is also the author of two books that include material about Cassavetes's life but more about the films he made: *American Dreaming: The Films of John Cassavetes and the American Experience* (1985) and *The Films of John Cassavetes: Pragmatism, Modernism, and the Movies* (1994). Both contain bibliographies and filmographies. Biographical articles are in David Thomson, *A Biographical Dictionary of Film* (1994), and John Wakeman, ed., *World Film Directors*, vol. 2 (1988). Tributes to Cassavetes as a director that also include biographical information are Janet Maslin, "Cassavetes, a Model of Defiance," *New York Times*, 19 Feb. 1989; Lisa Katzman, "Moment by Moment," *Film Comment*, May 1989, pp. 34–39; Carney, "Complex Characters," *Film Comment*, May 1989, pp. 29–33; and Jacob Levich, "John Cassavetes: An American Maverick," *Cineaste* 20 (1993): 51–53. Obituaries are in the *New York Times*, 4 Feb. 1989; *Variety*, 8 Feb. 1989; *People Weekly*, 20 Feb. 1989; *American Film*, May 1989; and *Sight and Sound* 58 (Spring 1989): 102–3.

MARCIA B. DINNEEN

CASSIDY, Butch (13 Apr. 1866–1908? or 1937?), outlaw and rancher, was born Robert LeRoy Parker in Beaver, Utah, the oldest of thirteen children of Maximillian Parker and Ann Gillies, small ranchers. His British-born parents were Mormons who pulled handcarts across the Great Plains to Utah in 1856. As a teenager growing up near Circleville, Utah, Parker was influenced by cowhand Mike Cassidy, who taught him to ride, shoot, rope, brand, and rustle cattle and horses. Under suspicion by local authorities, Parker and Cassidy left Utah in 1884. Parker went to Telluride, Colorado, where he found employment with a mining company. There he met Tom McCarty, a bank robber, and soon joined the McCarty Gang. On 24 June 1889, he participated in a bank robbery at Telluride, after which he drifted into Wyoming. Because he was now wanted by the law, Parker took the surname of his boyhood idol, calling himself George Cassidy. While working in a butcher's shop in Rock Springs, Wyoming, he became Butch Cassidy.

During this period he met several of the men who later joined him to form a band of horseback outlaws widely known as the Wild Bunch. At the time of the 1892 war between cattlemen and homesteaders in Johnson County, Wyoming, Butch Cassidy and the Wild Bunch found themselves in the midst of the conflict, their sympathies with those who rustled cattle from the big ranchers. The outlaws and the fugitive homesteaders both took refuge in a hideout behind a high ridge that could be entered only through an easily defended defile known as the Hole-in-the-Wall. For years afterward, the Wild Bunch was also known as the Hole-in-the-Wall Gang.

In 1892 Cassidy was arrested for stealing a horse valued at five dollars. His defense was that he had unknowingly bought the animal from a rustler. He was convicted, but because of legal delays he was not sentenced to the Wyoming Penitentiary until 1894. According to some of his friends, this confinement, which he considered unfair, helped to deepen his contempt for the law.

After Cassidy's release in 1896, bank and train robberies charged to the Wild Bunch increased in number. Scores of Pinkerton detectives joined sheriffs' posses in futile pursuit of the gang throughout the West, from Montana to New Mexico. After a daring robbery of a Winnemucca, Nevada, bank in September 1990, several members of the band rendezvoused at Fort Worth, Texas. Cassidy and four companions posed there for a studio photograph and then sent a print of it to the Pinkerton Detective Agency. Weary of being continually harassed, however, Cassidy and another member of the gang, Harry Longabaugh (the Sundance Kid), decided to go to South America.

At this point in Cassidy's career, the Pinkerton Agency's profile described him as being flaxen-haired, blue-eyed and of light complexion, 5′7″ tall, weighing 165 pounds, with a "sandy beard, if any." By all accounts he was a handsome and affable man. Evidence exists that he courted women, but apparently he never married.

Cassidy, Longabaugh, and the latter's mistress, Etta Place, sailed to South America from New York City in 1901. In a letter from Cholila, Argentina, to a friend in Utah, dated 10 August 1902, Cassidy described a well-stocked ranch they had purchased in the Patagonian grasslands.

Evidently the ranch proved unprofitable. At any rate, Cassidy and Longabaugh turned to robbing banks again. In December 1907, they sold the ranch and vanished from the Cholila area. A year later they were reported to be working for a tin mine in Bolivia. From there, the trail of Butch Cassidy becomes lost in undocumented and controversial legends. Possibly he and the Sundance Kid robbed again and were tracked down at San Vicente by Bolivian cavalry and killed. But even accounts that agree in citing this as their fate, vary in dating their deaths anywhere from 1908 to 1911.

In the years that followed, "sightings" of Cassidy were occasionally reported by persons who had known him. William T. Phillips, an engineer in Spokane, Washington, claimed to be Cassidy and wrote an account of his life. He died on 20 July 1937. Cassidy's sister, Lula Parker Betenson, who published an account of her brother's life, told an interviewer in 1970 that Cassidy had visited her in 1925. She said he had lived under an assumed name in the Northwest and that he had died in 1937, but that William Phillips was not her brother.

Like other romantic outlaws, including Jesse James, whose ends appear to be controlled by an inexorable destiny, Butch Cassidy has achieved a place in American mythology.

• See Larry Pointer, *In Search of Butch Cassidy* (1977); Lula Parker Betenson, as told to Dora Flack, *Butch Cassidy, My Brother* (1975); C. Bruce Chatwin, *In Patagonia* (1977).

DEE BROWN

CASSIN, John (6 Sept. 1813–10 Jan. 1869), ornithologist and printing company executive, was born near the present site of Media, Pennsylvania, the son of Thomas Cassin, a Quaker farmer, and Rachel Sharpless. Cassin attended a Quaker School in Westtown, Pennsylvania, and studied under private tutors. His interest in natural history developed as the result of the emphasis placed on the subject by Quaker schools at that time; this proved decisive in Cassin's choice of avocation. He began observing and identifying birds on the family property in his mid-teens, and as an adult he regretted that he had not gotten out into the field more often to go birdwatching. At age twenty-one he went to Philadelphia, where he worked first in merchandising and then at the U.S. Customs House. When J. T. Bowen, an engraver and lithographer, died, Cassin assumed the management of Bowen's firm and continued to supply illustrations for various scientific books and periodicals and for federal government publications.

In 1842 Cassin was named curator at the Academy of Natural Sciences of Philadelphia, a position that he retained until his death. He also served the academy as corresponding secretary (1848–1852) and as vice president (1864–1869). During the late 1840s Dr. Thomas B. Wilson, a well-to-do benefactor who later served as the academy's president, began collecting a substantial number of bird specimens, ultimately numbering 26,000, together with as complete a library of ornithological books and periodicals as could then be purchased. Cassin, who was considered, in the terminology of the time, a "closet naturalist," organized and mastered this material. He published a succession of technical papers, focusing on the classification of birds, most of which were North American. Cassin also dealt with birds collected by the American explorer Paul du Chaillu, who had gone to Africa under the sponsorship of the Academy of Natural Sciences. During Cassin's lifetime it was generally understood that the academy collections were his private domain, inasmuch as few others, especially those with whom he was professionally at odds, were given access to either the specimens or the books without his expressed approval. Until the late 1850s, when specimens from around the nation, and especially the West, began accumulating at the Smithsonian, the Academy of Natural Sciences had what was probably the outstanding institutional collection in the nation. Cassin not only developed a reputation as one of the nation's leading ornithologists, but he was also considered politically adept in scientific circles.

When the U.S. Exploring Expedition, led by Captain Charles Wilkes, returned to the United States in 1842, a thirty-year effort to publish its scientific results got under way. Titian Peale, a naturalist who had accompanied the expedition, published a volume in 1848 concerning the mammals and birds collected by Peale and others in the Pacific Ocean region. Unhappy with both Peale and his book, Wilkes suppressed it, and Cassin, one of several authorities who had been consulted about the matter, agreed, following several years of negotiations, to prepare a replacement volume. This Cassin accomplished, after requesting and receiving a salary of $2,000 per year over a period of five years, and his book *Mammalogy and Ornithology*, dealing with the findings of the expedition, was issued in 1858. In it, Cassin acknowledged his debt to Peale's notes, observations, and drawings, many of which appeared in the text and in the atlas of engravings prepared to accompany the book.

Cassin's other publications included *Illustrations of the Birds of California, Texas, Oregon, British, and Russian America* (1856), in which he described birds newly identified since the publication of John James Audubon's *Birds of America* two decades before. This was also the first American book in which trinomials were employed to describe what later became known as subspecific forms. In 1857 Cassin was invited to join Spencer F. Baird of the Smithsonian and George N. Lawrence of New York in coauthoring what became a classic volume summarizing what was then known concerning North American birds. Cassin contributed a number of descriptions to the volume, first published as "Reports of Explorations and Surveys to Determine a Route for a Railroad from the Mississippi River to the Pacific Ocean," vol. 9, part 2 (1858). It was issued in expanded form two years later as *The Birds of North America*. He also contributed descriptions of birds collected to the second volume of "Narrative of the Expedition of an American Squadron to the China Seas and Japan" (1856), and to the second volume of "United States Naval Astronomical Expedition to the Southern Hemisphere" (1855).

Despite his age and domestic status—he was forty-seven years of age and had married Hannah (maiden name unknown), with whom he had several children—Cassin enlisted in the Union army soon after the Civil War broke out in 1861. He was captured and held in the infamous Libby Prison in Richmond, Virginia, until the end of the war, an experience that permanently affected his health. He died in Philadelphia. Two decades after his death, the journal *Cassinia* was established by the Delaware Valley Ornithological Club.

• Biographical summaries of Cassin include an obituary by Thomas M. Brewer in *Proceedings of the Boston Society of Natural History* (1869); and Witmer Stone, "John Cassin," *Cassinia* 5 (1901). See also Barbara Mearns and Richard Mearns, *Audubon to Xantus* (1992), and the introduction by Robert McCracken Peck in his new edition of Cassin's *Illustrations of the Birds of California, Texas, Oregon, British, and Russian America* (1991).

KEIR B. STERLING

CASTAÑEDA, Carlos Eduardo (11 Nov. 1896–3 Apr. 1958), historian, was born in Ciudad Camargo, Tamaulipas, Mexico, the son of Timoteo Castañeda, a Mexican teacher of Yucatecan birth who had been educated in San Antonio, Texas, and Elise Leroux. In 1908 the Mexican Revolution drove the Castañeda family north to Brownsville, Texas, where Castañeda received his primary and secondary education in the public schools. Though his parents died when he was in the eighth grade, Castañeda persevered. Raised by family members, he was the valedictorian—and the only Mexican American—of the 1916 graduating class of Brownsville High School.

Castañeda entered the University of Texas in 1917 on an academic scholarship, initially planning to study engineering. The next year he volunteered for service in the U.S. Army, though he remained stateside during World War I. He returned to the University of Texas after the war, but a lack of funds forced him to drop out of school. He spent a year working in the oil fields, finally earning his bachelor of arts degree in history from the University of Texas in 1921 and a Phi Beta Kappa key. That same year Castañeda married Elsa Rios and began working as an engineer in the tropical marshlands near Tampico, Mexico. The couple had three children. Disliking the life of an engineer, Castañeda quit and returned to Texas. He taught Spanish in high schools in Beaumont and San Antonio while pursuing graduate studies and received his M.A. from the University of Texas in 1923. Castañeda's first college appointment was as associate professor of Spanish at the College of William and Mary in Virginia, where he remained for four years. It was there that Castañeda wrote his first article, a history of the Franciscans in Texas. He followed it with a biography of Antonio Margil de Jesus, one of the founders of the Texas missions. Castañeda continued his research in Latin American history at the University of Havana and in Mexico.

In 1927 Castañeda and his family returned to the University of Texas as a librarian in the newly established Latin American Collection. He was assigned to the Genaro García Collection, which comprised rare books, manuscripts, and newspapers dealing with Mexican history. The following year Castañeda's first book was published, *The Mexican Side of the Texas Revolution*, a collection of Mexican leaders' accounts of the 1836 revolution. In addition to building the university's collections, he wrote articles and book reviews and published in 1929 an edition *Historia de Todos los Colegios de la Ciudad de Mexico* (History of All Colleges of Mexico City) by Felix Osores and in 1930 an edition of *Guerra de Reforma Segun el Archivo del General Doblado* (The War of Reform according to the General Doblado Archive). At the invitation of the National Library of Mexico, Castañeda represented the University of Texas at a meeting in 1930 in Mexico City where scholars were assembled to sort documents from a huge Franciscan library at the Convento Grande. It was there that Castañeda discovered the unpublished history of Texas by Fray Juan Agustin Morfi, who had visited Texas in 1780.

In 1932 Castañeda completed his Ph.D., based on editing and translating Morfi's *History of Texas*. The Morfi book was published by the Quivira Society of New Mexico in a two-volume edition. Castañeda gained critical acclaim for this translation, and the following year the Knights of Columbus Historical Commission chose him to write a multivolume history of the Catholic church in Texas for the state's centennial. From that information Castañeda produced his monumental six-volume work, *Our Catholic Heritage in Texas*, which was completed between 1936 and 1950. This series remains the classic work of Catholicism's development and influence in Texas. While working on this project, Castañeda continued teaching at the University of Texas, having been named a member of the history department in 1939. Castañeda was elected president of the American Catholic Historical Association that same year. He also was assigned to editorships on the *Hispanic American Historical Review*, the *Americas*, and the *Handbook of Latin American Studies*.

From 1943 to 1946 Castañeda served on President Roosevelt's Fair Employment Practices Committee (FEPC). The FEPC appointed him to oversee its field investigations of job discrimination in the United States against Spanish-speaking workers in the Southwest. He testified that in Arizona, Mexicans comprised 60 percent of the state's mine workers but the majority worked in less-skilled and lower-paying jobs. Castañeda recommended that the FEPC employ Spanish-speaking field investigators knowledgeable in the history and culture of the Southwest to facilitate interviews with Mexican-American copper workers. Castañeda disapproved of the case-by-case approach of the FEPC and instead argued for public hearings to be held in Phoenix. Notwithstanding the shortcomings of the FEPC, an understaffed and underfunded government agency whose investigations of discrimination in the Southwest could have jeopardized the Good Neighbor Policy, Castañeda helped improve opportunities and working conditions for Mexican Americans in the Southwest.

During World War II Castañeda also participated in community organizations such as the League of United Latin American Citizens, which had been founded to seek equal rights and political and economic advancement for Mexican Americans. He, along with Mexican-American scholars George Sánchez, Arturo Campa, and Ernesto Galarza, wrote various essays on the conditions of Mexican Americans in the Southwest, challenging the discrimination against Mexican Americans in education, employment, and political representation. Castañeda called for cooperation and understanding between Anglo Americans and Mexican Americans, appealing to the Anglos to be tolerant of cultural differences. Castañeda extended this philosophy of peaceful relations between Anglos and Mexicans in calling for the recognition of the economic and cultural ties between Latin America and the United States. He was one of several Mexican-American educators and elected officials to participate in national conferences funded by the Spanish-Speaking Peoples' Division of the Office of the Coordinator of Inter-American Affairs, headed by Nelson D. Rockefeller. Their efforts were to influence legislative action guaranteeing civil and human rights for Mexican Americans. In 1946 Castañeda retired from his position as librarian of the Latin American Collection at the University of Texas to have more time for his work and that same year was promoted to professor of Latin American history at the university, a position he would hold until his death.

Castañeda devoted his life to historical scholarship, publishing twelve books and more than eighty-five articles on the American Southwest and Mexican history and culture. His lasting contributions are his advocacy of civil rights for Mexican Americans and his revision of Texas and borderlands history to incorporate the Spanish colonial experience. Castañeda died in Austin, Texas, while starting work on volume seven of *Our Catholic Heritage in Texas*. In 1977 the University of Texas named its main library building in his honor.

• Carlos Castañeda's personal papers are available at the Benson Latin American Studies Library at the University of Texas, Austin. For more information see Félix D. Almaráz, Jr., "Carlos Eduardo Castañeda, Mexican-American Historian: The Formative Years, 1896–1927," *Pacific Historical Review* (Aug. 1973): 319–34, and "The Making of a Boltonian: Carlos Castañeda of Texas—The Early Years," *Red River Valley Historical Review* (Winter 1974): 329–50; and Mario T. García, "Carlos E. Castañeda and the Search for History," in his *Mexican Americans: Leadership, Ideology, and Identity, 1930–1960* (1989), pp. 231–51.

ZARAGOSA VARGAS

CASTIGLIONI, Luigi (3 Oct. 1757–22 Apr. 1832), naturalist, author, and politician, was born in Milan, Italy, the son of Count Ottavio Castiglioni and Teresa Verri, both of distinguished families. In childhood, after the death of his father, Castiglioni and his older brother, Alfonso, were adopted by their mother's brother, Pietro Verri, whose political ideas and writings placed him and his brother, Alessandro, among the central figures of the Italian Enlightenment. Although Verri provided his nephews with material comfort and intellectual guidance, their relationship was sometimes contentious.

Castiglioni first studied at the Collegio dè Nobili, under the Barnabite priests, and possibly later with Giovanni Scopoli, a professor of chemistry and botany, at the University of Pavia. Along with his brother, Castiglioni developed an early interest in Linnaean botany. In 1784, in pursuit of scholarly knowledge, he traveled first to France and England and in April of the following year to the United States, where he remained until 1787. During these years, he made the acquaintance of leading scientists and public figures, who noted Castiglioni with praise in their own correspondence. Among the Americans Castiglioni met and described were Thomas Jefferson, Benjamin Franklin, George Washington, John and Samuel Adams, John Hancock, John Jay, and Robert Morris. While in the United States, Castiglioni was elected a member of the American Academy of Arts and Sciences in Boston and the American Philosophical Society in Philadelphia, with Benjamin Rush and John Vaughan among his supporters.

As a result of this voyage, Castiglioni wrote his best-known work, *Viaggio negli Stati Uniti dell' America settentrionale fatto negli anni 1785, 1786, e 1787*. Published in Milan in 1790, this lengthy travel journal describes the physical and natural environment of the new nation, the histories of its separate states, the social institutions and customs of the people, and the species of plant life that might be introduced to Italy.

In Italy Castiglioni resumed other scholarly interests. He translated ancient Latin writings on antiquities, agriculture, and numismatics and pursued an interest in agronomy by experiments in his gardens. Castiglioni also led an active public life in the early years of the Risorgimento. After being arrested and deported to Nice by the French, Castiglioni was nominated to an appointment, which he refused, as a member of the Junior Council of the Cisalpine Republic. With the establishment of an Italian Republic in the northern regions in 1802, Castiglioni began a period of intense involvement in public affairs. Although he published an endorsement of republican values, Castiglioni espoused only a moderate form of these sentiments. When Napoleon assumed the imperial crown, Castiglioni continued to serve the new Italian kingdom. In subsequent years, he held other posts in the government in Milan, among them the director of the Royal Printing House. Castiglioni's public life reached its pinnacle when he was nominated to the senate of the kingdom in 1809 and Napoleon conferred on him the title of count the next year. With the defeat of Napoleon, Castiglioni was appointed a delegate to plead for the preservation of Italian independence at the meeting of the Allies in Paris in 1814. When the Treaty of Paris granted Austria possession of Milan, Castiglioni's political career ended. But even the new Austrian government bestowed honors upon Castiglioni, by knighthood in 1819 and an appointment as an imperial chamberlain in 1820. He still served in other civic positions almost to the end of his life, most notably as the president of the Academy of Fine Arts, the famed Brera Gallery of Milan, from 1807 to 1831. Castiglioni also appears to have been elected to membership in scientific academies and scholarly societies in Bologna, Leghorn, Copenhagen, Geneva, and Vienna.

From his marriage in 1800 to a distant relative, Teresa Castiglioni, Castiglioni had two children, one of whom died as an infant. On his death in Milan, Castiglioni left a major collection of rare and precious coins to that city. But to his native city, social historians, and botanists, Castiglioni also left the legacy of his scholarly reflections.

In the *Viaggio*, in the final entry before he sailed from London to Boston, Castiglioni aptly expressed his principal intention, as well as his physiocratic aspirations: "Happy me, . . . if I can observe things that deserve to pass down to the memory of posterity, and if I shall not have thrown away in vain my labor and my time."

Unlike other European contemporaries who traveled to North America, Castiglioni confidently anticipated a strong future for the United States. He concluded the *Viaggio* with the argument that the advantages of its natural environment and the influence of its government would soon enable the young nation to emerge as one of the most powerful and civilized in the world. Castiglioni believed that the American Revolution was not only one of the most important events of the century, but that it would eventually also have great consequences for all of Europe.

Castiglioni's observations failed, however, to make him an earlier, Italian version of Alexis de Tocqueville. While he often began an important point, Castiglioni tended to remain at a relatively shallow level of description without reaching a more incisive examination of American society and its institutions. He provided illuminating vignettes and brief fragments on aspects of culture and social structure, including languages of Native Americans, agricultural practices, commerce and exports, architecture, and social ecology, but no extended, systematic analysis. Perhaps, as one critic has observed, Castiglioni's temperament and training, as his distinguished uncles had feared, left him intellectually timid.

While Castiglioni's social and political observations were noted by Italian writers in the final years of the eighteenth and the early decades of the nineteenth centuries, the information on plants and trees, along with the seeds, with which he had returned had potentially greater importance, particularly for the depleted forests of northern Italy. But Castiglioni twice lost much of his specimen collection while attempting river crossings. Several other factors, such as language, place of publication, and his intellectual conservatism may have also contributed to lessening his influence on subsequent botanical research. By the mid-nineteenth century, Castiglioni appeared to have lost his scientific relevance to modern botany.

After a period of some neglect, Americans, beginning with the influential Henry T. Tuckerman in 1864, rediscovered and paid gradually increasing attention to Castiglioni and his writings. In the twentieth century, writers in Italy and the United States noted Castiglioni's significance for social and botanical issues, such as ethnographic observation, criminal and penal philosophy, botanical history, and plant transference from one country to another. In recent years an English language version of his *Viaggio* has been published. When compared to what travel literature often provides to its readers, the rediscovery and reassessment of Castiglioni may even reflect a judgment that was rendered in his native city, when his work first appeared: "This is really contributing to one's native country by travels, from which others often bring back only vices and fashions."

• Castiglioni's major work is now available in an English language edition as *Luigi Castiglioni's Viaggio—Travels in the United States of North America, 1785–87* (1983). The volume contains an invaluable critical introduction by Antonio Pace, the translator and most authoritative scholar of Castiglioni's work, as well as an extensive bibliography. Also worth consulting is the article by Pace, "The Fortunes of Luigi Castiglioni, Traveler in Colonial America, with an Extract from a Recently Discovered Manuscript of His *Viaggio nell' America Settentrionale (1785–1787)*," *Italian Americana* 1 (1975): 247–64. For an attempt to place Castiglioni and other Italian scholars and intellectuals in a broader context provided by the times and their events, and in particular the relationship between Italy and the United States, see Pace's *Benjamin Franklin and Italy* (1958). For a brief, but important, assessment of Castiglioni's life and a useful bibliography of Italian sources, the entry by C. Capra in the *Dizionario Biografico degli Italiani*, vol. 22 (1979), should also be examined.

RICHARD N. JULIANI

CASTLE, Irene (7 Apr. 1893–25 Jan. 1969), and **Vernon Castle** (2 May 1887–15 Feb. 1918), ballroom dancers, were born, respectively, Irene Foote in New Rochelle, New York, and Vernon Blythe in Norwich, England. Irene was the daughter of Hubert Townsend Foote, a physician, and Annie Elroy Thomas. Vernon was the son of William Blythe, a tavern owner, and Jane (maiden name unknown). Vernon immigrated with his father and sister to the United States in 1906; the next year he took the name Castle. Although he had trained as an engineer at the University of Birmingham, Castle established himself as a promising musical comedy soloist soon after his arrival in the United States. His specialty was comedic dance; however, he was a highly versatile and talented performer, adept in several styles of popular dance. In productions such as Lew Fields's *About Town* (1906), *Old Dutch* (1909), and *The Midnight Sons* (1909) he displayed a penchant for highly physical comedy such as the "gentlemanly drunk" who tries to maintain his composure while bumping into furniture and sliding down staircases. Castle's unique acrobatic-eccentric dance style prompted a reviewer in *Variety* to describe him as "an attenuated youth with voluble legs" (Sime, undated clipping). The skills associated with eccentric dance—timing, balance, and precision—would serve him well on the ballroom floor.

Irene Castle also aspired to a professional theater career. She had studied theatrical dance technique with Rosetta O'Neill, of the famous Dodworth family of dance teachers, and had performed in several amateur theatricals. Irene Foote and Vernon Castle were introduced through a mutual theatrical acquaintance; it was Vernon, in fact, who had helped her get her first professional role in the Fields production *The Summer Widowers* (1910). When an actress in a minor role suddenly dropped out, Fields cast Irene in the part. After they were married, in May 1911, the Castles performed together in several theatrical productions, including Fields's *The Hen-Pecks* (in which Vernon had a principal comic role). Their first performances of exhibition ballroom specialties were in the 1911 Parisian production *Enfin . . . une Revue*, a melange of variety acts featuring Vernon's well-known barbershop scene from *The Hen-Pecks*, in which as a magician he dodges the slapdash habits of a barber. It was here also that they introduced several ragtime couple dances, such as the Grizzly Bear and the Turkey Trot, at that time the rage in America.

The show closed unexpectedly, but the couple secured an engagement at the fashionable Parisian nightclub Café de Paris, performing impromptu routines of popular American social dances. These improvised ballroom renditions delighted the Parisians, and the Castles soon found themselves performing nightly at the club. For Vernon this was professionally a lucky opportunity; he was able to prove his versatility as a performer and expand his range beyond the comic-dance roles with which he had become associated. By chance it propelled both of them into prominent roles as exhibition ballroom stars as that form of dance was becoming popular.

When the *New York Times* (10 July 1910) reported on their earlier success in France and their minor involvements with European nobility, the public was primed for the Castles' return to the United States. At Louis Martin's, a popular Broadway area restaurant-cabaret, the Castles performed their latest dances and, along with a host of other popular teams, helped to popularize social dancing with the public. A unique pattern developed in the cabarets: on the heels of the ballroom teams' performances, couples crowded the dance floor to imitate them. Sometimes the audience's mood demanded an on-the-spot creation. The Castles supposedly "invented" their renowned Castle Walk during an engagement in 1912 at Louis Martin's. While doing the basic one-step, a series of smooth walking steps taken to each beat of the music, they simply hopped up on each beat. A novel dance yet easy to perform, the Castle Walk caught on instantly with the public.

The Castles were considered to be the quintessential exhibition ballroom team in their graceful demeanor, poise, and synchronicity of movement. They popularized and theatricalized the basic social dances of the day, including one-steps, hesitation waltzes, tangos, and fox trots. The Castles typically opened their act with the Castle Walk—their signature dance—and followed it with an exhibition one-step, an Argentine tango, and a Brazilian maxixe (a dance combining steps of the tango and two-step). Their act featured the celebrated ragtime bandleader James Reese Europe, who had composed music for several of their dances, including the Castle Walk and the Castle House Rag.

In addition to the cabaret, the Castles became equally well known in the popular theater of their day. During the 1913–1914 season they became headliners on the Keith vaudeville circuit, one of the national chains that owned theaters and controlled bookings. Their vaudeville acts reflected their consciousness of their identity as one of America's best-loved ballroom teams: Vernon typically prefaced their performances with advice on how their dances could be performed should audience members attempt the dances themselves. Their musical theater productions included *The Sunshine Girl* (1913) and *Watch Your Step* (1914), which boasted not only the Castles but also a score composed by Irving Berlin. Said the *New York Herald*, "If there were ever doubt that the tango and the fox-trot would resist becoming a musical comedy theme it was dispelled by Mr. Dillingham's stroke of genius in making the Castles his two stars" (undated clipping). The Castles were also one of the first exhibition ballroom teams to produce motion-picture shorts of their dancing. These fifteen-minute films of their best-known exhibition dances generally appeared as a featured act on a typical vaudeville bill.

By the mid-teens the Castles' popularity as an exhibition ballroom team and as cultural role models was enormous. They had published one of the first texts on contemporary ballroom dance, *Modern Dancing* (1914); operated their own dancing school, Castle House; owned their own cabaret; and even starred in a film biography, *The Whirl of Life* (Pathé, 1915). The mastermind behind the Castles' successful marketing campaign was Elizabeth Marbury, a literary agent and New York socialite. By promoting the team as a model of elegance and social grace, Marbury made them appealing to high society (earning them the title of "society dancers"). At the same time, the franchising of the Castle name won them a large following among the middle classes; they copyrighted merchandise ranging from Castle Corsets to Castle Dance Records. Irene was a trendsetter in women's fashion and hairstyles (she is credited with having introduced "bobbed" hair), and photo layouts of her clothing designs and dance dresses frequently graced the pages of the *Ladies Home Journal* and other women's and fashion magazines.

Although the Castles experienced great success, it was short-lived. During the run of *Watch Your Step* in 1915, with World War I under way, Vernon enlisted in the British Royal Flying Corps. At this time Irene embarked on a solo career. She performed on Broadway in *Miss 1917* and made her film debut in *Patria* (Pathé, 1917–1918), a fifteen-part movie serial, in which she played a glamorous spy. In 1917 Vernon returned to the United States as a flight instructor at Fort Worth, Texas, but he was killed tragically the following year during a routine flight lesson. Through the late teens and early twenties, Irene Castle continued her film work and appeared in several film serials and features for Pathé and Warner Brothers.

From 1922 to 1924 Irene formed a dance partnership with William Reardon, performing in a vaudeville act choreographed by Fred Astaire and Adele Astaire called *Let's Dance*. She still performed the specialty fox trots and waltzes that had previously won her fame, but she was never able to reignite with Reardon the excitement produced by her partnership with Vernon. Irene had a short-lived marriage to Robert E. Treman, of Ithaca, New York, from 1919 until their divorce in 1923. She was immediately remarried the same year to Frederic McLaughlin, a Chicago coffee magnate. They had three children, one of whom died in infancy; these were her only children. McLaughlin died in 1944, and in 1946 she married George Enzinger, an advertising executive.

Although she had officially retired by the mid-1920s, Irene maintained her ties to the theater world. She made a brief appearance at the 1939 Chicago World's Fair, where she was partnered with Alex Fisher. In 1939–1940 she appeared in several plays, including a summer theater production of Noël Coward's *Shadow Play*, and in the early 1950s she choreographed the ballroom dances for the play *Josephine*, starring Norma Shearer. During her later years Irene Castle became particularly active in the antivivisectionist movement. She devoted considerable fundraising efforts to her organization Orphans of the Storm, dedicated to preventing cruelty to animals. Although Irene Castle claimed that her animal-rights work was her most important accomplishment, she is best remembered for her renowned dance partnership with Vernon Castle. She died in Eureka Springs, Arkansas.

Irene and Vernon Castle epitomized the grace and glamour of contemporary ballroom dance of the 1910s, helping to promote ballroom dance as a popular social as well as theatrical dance form. Their style represented the essence of the American ballroom "dance craze" sweeping the country, characterized by a new freedom of movement and expression on the dance floor.

• For the most complete account of the career of Irene and Vernon Castle, see the Irene and Vernon Castle scrapbook series at the Billy Rose Theatre Collection at the New York Public Library for the Performing Arts, Lincoln Center. Memorabilia as well as newspaper and magazine clippings are also housed in the Theatre Collection of the Museum of the City of New York. The Museum of Modern Art Film Collection contains the Castles' 1915 biographical film *The Whirl of Life*. In addition, see Irene Castle, *Castles in the Air* (1958), and *My Husband* (1919; repr. 1979); Irene and Vernon Castle, *Modern Dancing* (1915); and Irene Castle, "What Is a Thé Dansant?" *The Delineator*, May 1914, p. 10. Articles and books about them by others include Elroy Foote, "The Story of the Castles," *Theatre Magazine*, Mar. 1915, pp. 112–15; Frederic Lewis Allen, "When America Learned to Dance," *Scribner's Magazine*, Sept. 1937, pp. 11–17, 92; Lewis A. Erenberg, "Everybody's Doin' It: The Pre–World War I Dance Craze, the Castles, and the Modern American Girl," *Feminist Studies* 3 (Fall 1975): 155–70; and Julie Malnig, *Dancing Till Dawn: A Century of Exhibition Ballroom Dance* (1992). An obituary for Irene Castle is in the *New York Times*, 26 Jan. 1969.

JULIE MALNIG

CASTLE, William Ernest (25 Oct. 1867–3 June 1962), biologist, was born near Alexandria, Ohio, the son of William Augustus Castle and Sarah Fassett, farmers. Learning about livestock at the farm probably sparked young Castle's interest in breeding and led him to appreciate its relevance to studies of evolution and heredity. After graduating with an A.B. in 1889 from Denison University in Granville, Ohio, he taught Latin at Ottawa University in Ottawa, Kansas, for three years before entering Harvard for graduate work. He earned a second A.B. in 1893, an A.M. in 1894, and a Ph.D. in zoology in 1895. His dissertation on the embryology of the ascidian *Ciona intestinalis*, which was directed by E. L. Mark, showed that the sperm and eggs produced by a single individual were not able to unite in fertilization, a phenomenon comparable to self-sterility in plants that had not yet been observed in animals. Castle married Clara Sears Bosworth in 1896; they had three children.

Castle taught zoology for one year at the University of Wisconsin and for another year at Knox College before returning to Harvard in 1897, where he became assistant professor in 1903 and professor in 1908. He remained at Harvard until his retirement in 1936, when he became research associate at the University of California at Berkeley.

At Harvard, Castle was influenced by the zoologist Charles Davenport, who defined experimental evolution as the study of the dynamics of the germ plasm; Castle called himself an experimental evolutionist. When Davenport left Harvard in 1901, Castle aimed to fill his place. He worked as a research associate for the Station for Experimental Evolution, which was directed by Davenport and founded by the Carnegie Institution of Washington, D.C. The institution supported Castle's work from 1904 to 1943.

With a strong commitment to Darwinian evolution, Castle studied evolutionary problems through the analysis of heredity, testing, and extending Gregor Mendel's principles of inheritance. In 1901 Castle was the first researcher to use *Drosophila*, or fruit flies, in the laboratory to study the influence of inbreeding and cross-breeding on fertility and variability. While studying the sex ratio in mammals, he discovered that sex was inherited in Mendelian fashion. In a 1903 paper he discussed the laws of heredity as set forth by Sir Francis Galton and Mendel. Here he argued that in the absence of selection and under random mating, a population remains in equilibrium, basically the thesis that later became known as the Hardy-Weinberg law. In 1908 Castle helped to organize Harvard's Bussey Institution of Applied Biology, where he worked until his retirement in 1936.

In 1909 Castle and his associate John C. Phillips transplanted the ovaries from a pure black guinea pig into a pure white guinea pig whose ovaries had been removed. The offspring produced by the latter were all black, thus providing support for August Weismann's thesis on the separation between the individual's germ plasm and somatoplasm, which therefore provided evidence against the inheritance of acquired characteristics.

Castle also worked on the effects of selection on the hereditary factors, or genes, from 1907 until 1919. He experimented with 50,000 piebald, or hooded, rats, which are white with a black hood and thin back stripe. Castle was struck by the great variation in this pattern and wondered whether selection could change it. He selected rats in opposite directions: a plus series for an increase of the hood and back-stripe pigmentation and a minus series for a decrease of these characteristics. Soon Castle had one set of rats almost completely pigmented and another set almost all white. Rejecting the idea of gametic purity, he argued that selection caused permanent genetic change by modifying the genes responsible for the hooded pattern. The close proximity of the genes in the gametes, he suggested, allowed them to mix and contaminate one another. Convinced that selection plays a strong role in evolution, he thought that it was the instability of genes that allows selection to act in a "creative" and not only in a "destructive" way.

Castle knew that what he called "blending inheritance" could also be explained by the multiple-factor hypothesis, the idea that a phenotypic characteristic can be influenced by several genetic factors, but he rejected this view. In 1919, though, some of Castle's experiments showed that the genes had not been changed by selection, and he tentatively accepted the multiple-factor hypothesis. In later years, however, he became skeptical again. Although he strongly influenced the development of Mendelian studies in the United States, on several occasions Castle questioned the view that all inheritance could be explained in Mendelian terms. His experiments with hooded rats, however interpreted, were important for clarifying the relation between the genotype and the phenotype and the way in which selection acted on them.

In the 1920s Castle worked on the inheritance of size in mammals, arguing against the thesis that differences in total size were due to the sum of independent effects of genes on different parts of the body. He also worked on genetic linkage and on the construction of genetic maps of the rabbit and the rat. His work on the albino and pink-eye loci in the mouse first showed linkage in mammals. His pioneer work on guinea pigs, rabbits, rats, cows, and horses made him the founder of mammalian genetics in the United States. Castle's research in California focused on linkage systems in the rat and on the genetics of color in the coat of the palomino horse. He died in Berkeley, still active in research.

Castle shared with his contemporaries an interest in the practical applications of biological knowledge to human affairs. However, he was skeptical of the feasibility and desirability of eugenics to improve the human race through the control of reproduction. His friendship with Davenport probably kept him from being more openly critical of eugenics than he was. Although he was a member of the American Eugenics Society until 1928, he argued that issues like racial crossing were primarily sociological, not biological, problems and that the way to achieve progress was to improve the social environment. He also attacked the racist and classist assumptions held by many eugenicists.

Castle's most important contribution to biology was his early understanding that experimental breeding and the analysis of heredity were essential to understanding the evolutionary process. He studied central problems in evolution: the effects of inbreeding, the power and nature of selection, the inheritance of quantitative characteristics, among others. More important than his particular conclusions was his approach to these problems. He developed experimental evolution so that evolutionary and genetic problems illuminated each other. This approach clearly influenced his students, many of whom became leaders in the study of evolution and genetics, including John H. Detlefsen, E. Carleton MacDowell, Clarence Little, Sewall Wright, L. C. Dunn, W. H. Gates, Gregory Pincus, Paul Sawin, George D. Snell, and Sheldon C. Reed. Soft-spoken, kind, devoted to his family and his work, direct, unassuming, and very tolerant of other viewpoints, Castle enjoyed the respect and admiration of his colleagues and students. He published 242 papers, three books, and a laboratory manual. His book *Genetics and Eugenics* (1916) was widely used and went through four editions.

Castle was a member of the National Academy of Sciences, the American Academy of Arts and Sciences, the American Philosophical Society, the American Society of Naturalists (president in 1919), the Genetics Society of America, and the American Genetics Association (vice president in 1924). In 1955 he received the Kimber Award from the National Academy of Sciences. He was a founder of the American Breeders' Association and of the journal *Genetics* and a member of the editorial board of the *Journal of Experimental Zoology* from its initial issue in 1904 until his death.

• Castle apparently destroyed his papers when he moved to California. Some of his letters can be found in the correspondence of students and colleagues. The single most important collection is the Castle papers at the American Philosophical Society (APS) in Philadelphia. The APS also contains the Davenport papers, which include extensive correspondence with Castle. Among Castle's writings, see "The Laws of Heredity of Galton and Mendel, and Some Laws Governing Race Improvement by Selection," *Proceedings of the American Academy of Arts and Sciences* 39 (1903): 223–42, "The Mutation Theory of Organic Evolution from the Standpoint of Animal Breeding," *Science* 21 (1905): 521–25, "A Successful Ovarian Transplantation in the Guinea-Pig and Its Bearing on Problems of Genetics" (with J. C. Phillips), *Science* 30 (1909): 312–13, "Can Selection Cause Genetic Change?" *American Naturalist* 50 (1916): 248–56, *Genetics and Eugenics: A Text-Book for Students of Biology and a Reference Book for Animal and Plant Breeders* (1916; repr. 1920, 1924, 1930), "Piebald Rats and Selection, a Correction," *American Naturalist* 53 (1919): 370–75, and *Mammalian Genetics* (1940). The most extensive biography on Castle was written by his student L. C. Dunn, "William Ernest Castle, October 25, 1867–June 3, 1962," in National Academy of Sciences, *Biographical Memoirs* 38 (1965): 31–80. See also Garland Allen's entry on Castle in *Dictionary of Scientific Biography* 32 (1971): 120–24, and Sewall Wright, "William Ernest Castle 1867–1962," *Genetics* 48 (1963): 1–5. No comprehensive presentation of Castle's work exists except for Terry H. Taylor, "William Ernest Castle, American Geneticist: A Case-Study in the Impact of the Mendelian Research Program" (M.A. thesis, Oregon State Univ., 1983). An assessment of his ideas and influence is in Elof A. Carlson, *The Gene: A Critical History* (1966), and William Provine, *Sewall Wright and Evolutionary Biology* (1986).

MARGA VICEDO

CASTLE, William Richards, Jr. (19 June 1878–13 Oct. 1963), diplomat, was born in Honolulu, Hawaii, the son of William Richards Castle, a business executive, and Ida Beatrice Lowrey. His father was prominent in the revolution against Queen Liliuokalani in 1892 and took a treaty of annexation to Washington, only to see it refused by President Grover Cleveland. In 1902 Castle, Jr., married Margaret Farlow; they had one child.

Graduating in 1900 from Harvard, Castle became assistant dean of Harvard College, serving from 1906 until 1913. He was the author of two novels, *The Green Vase* (1912) and *The Pillar of Sand* (1914). His *Hawaii, Past and Present* (1913) enjoyed a wide readership, and he edited *Essays in Memory of Barrett Wendell* (1926). In 1915–1917 he was editor of the *Harvard Graduates' Magazine*.

After U.S. entry into World War I, Castle served overseas with the Red Cross. The experience brought him in touch with officials in the War and State Departments, turning his attention to government service. He entered the Department of State in 1919. There his responsibilities increased rapidly: chief of the Division of Western European Affairs, assistant secretary of state for Western Europe beginning in 1927, and under secretary in 1931–1933. He was temporary ambassador to Japan in 1930 at the time of the London Naval Conference, because the post was unfilled and Japan was one of the leading nations represented at the conference.

Castle's principal contribution to American diplomacy was his effort to create a corps of dedicated officials both in the department and abroad. Until his time in the department, ministers and ambassadors were usually political appointees, rewarded for campaign contributions. Sometimes they were sent abroad because they possessed sufficient wealth to afford the expenses of their posts. For the important diplomacy prior to, during, and after World War I, these qualifications no longer sufficed. Moreover, the increasing foreign commerce of the United States demanded skilled representation.

Castle's era in the department coincided with the passage of the Rogers Act of 1924, which combined the old diplomatic and consular services into a foreign service. Castle helped with that task. He corresponded assiduously with American representatives in Western Europe and, as under secretary, around the world, helping give them a sense of professionalism and a feeling of the department's concern for their problems. He was a member of the foreign service board that passed on appointments and promotions. Castle sought to give attention to merit but favored Ivy League graduates. He was against women as diplomats. Like other members of the board, he discriminated against consuls in favor of diplomatic personnel. Critics believed that consular appointments went to graduates of inland institutions.

In dealing with foreign policy, Castle opposed American membership in the League of Nations, believing the league dominated by the victorious powers of the war and that it could not accomplish anything serious in preserving European or world peace. He considered the league a minor addition to the traditional procedures of diplomacy.

Castle saw the principal American contribution to peace as limitation of naval arms; because of the small size of the U.S. Army, he saw no advantage to participating in league efforts to limit land forces. He favored collection of the war debts and opposed any linking, as the European nations desired, of debts to reparations owed by Germany to the former Allies. In 1931, however, when America's debtors threatened to default on the debts because the Germans were unable to pay reparations, he became the principal negotiator of the Hoover moratorium, a standstill on debts and reparations.

The single large effort of the United States to offer European and other nations a multilateral treaty to prevent war, the Kellogg-Briand Pact of 1928, Castle regarded only as a device to rid the United States of a proposal by the French foreign minister, Aristide Briand, of a bilateral treaty to renounce war between France and the United States. This Castle saw as a negative military alliance, a promise of the United States not to go to war against France in some future European crisis. Unlike his chief in 1925–1929, Secretary of State Frank B. Kellogg, he considered the multilateral treaty, apart from its special usefulness, as no more than an international kiss.

During the Manchurian crisis of 1931–1933, Castle sided with President Herbert Hoover against the efforts of Secretary of State Henry L. Stimson to bring Japan to the bar of world opinion. At instruction from the president and during Stimson's absence in Europe, Castle announced the Hoover Doctrine, which declared that the country would take no part in economic sanctions. His year as ambassador in Japan convinced him that the Japanese people and their leaders desired respect above all else as well as friendship with the United States. He was close to President Hoover, who gave Castle more attention than he gave Stimson, whom the president considered an apostle of the late Theodore Roosevelt.

Upon the coming in of the Franklin D. Roosevelt administration, Castle resigned and soon joined the Republican isolationists. He advocated a pro-Japanese policy and noninvolvement with Europe, even after the fall of France. He opposed aid to Great Britain.

In the years after the war, as in those beginning in 1933, Castle held no posts in government. He maintained a large correspondence with his former isolationist friends, notably former president Hoover. He died in Washington, D.C.

• Castle's papers are at the Herbert Hoover Library in West Branch, Iowa, and his voluminous diary is at the Houghton Library, Harvard University. See L. Ethan Ellis, *Republican Foreign Policy: 1921–33* (1968); Robert H. Ferrell, *American Diplomacy in the Great Depression* (1957); and Justus D. Doenecke, *When the Wicked Rise* (1984). An obituary is in the *New York Times*, 14 Oct. 1963.

ROBERT H. FERRELL

CASWELL, Alexis (29 Jan. 1799–8 Jan. 1877), science professor and administrator, was born in Taunton, Massachusetts, the son of Samuel Caswell and Polly Seaver, farmers. The boy attended an academy in Taunton, then entered Brown University. There he "bore the highest honors of his class," said his biographer William Gammell. He gave the valedictory address at his graduation in 1822. During his college years he joined the First Baptist Church in Providence, Rhode Island, with which he was associated for the rest of his life.

In 1822 Caswell was appointed tutor at Columbian College (now George Washington University) in Washington, D.C., which had opened the previous year. From 1825 to 1826 he was professor of ancient languages there, and during his time at the college he studied theology with its president, William Staughton, a Baptist clergyman from England. In Washington Caswell enjoyed attending some sessions of Congress and visiting nearby areas, meeting former presidents James Madison and Thomas Jefferson.

When the college had financial problems in 1827, Caswell left it and returned to Massachusetts. He was invited to become minister of a newly established Baptist church in Halifax, Nova Scotia, Canada; he was ordained and served there from October 1827 to the following August. He then returned to Providence to assist the ailing pastor of its Baptist church. He filled the post temporarily, but before he agreed to take it permanently, Brown University offered him the post of professor of mathematics and natural philosophy, which he accepted in 1828. Caswell married Esther Lois Thompson in 1830; of their six children, three survived infancy.

Brown University was then enlarging its curriculum, especially in the sciences, but had not obtained professors for all new courses, so in addition to his own classes Caswell at different times taught chemistry, natural history, ethics, and constitutional law. He established a museum of natural history at the university. He was noted for taking great interest in students and their welfare and was much admired and respected by them. He was also helpful to the administration in fundraising efforts, especially for the library. During an absence of Brown's president, Francis Wayland, in 1840, Caswell was acting president.

Caswell's strongest scientific interest was astronomy. He made observations without the advantage of an observatory, and he maintained correspondence with others in that field. His title was changed to professor of mathematics and astronomy in 1850 and to professor of natural philosophy and astronomy in

1855. In 1858 he presented a course of four lectures on astronomy at the Smithsonian Institution ("Lectures on Astronomy," *Annual Report of Smithsonian Institution for 1858* [1859]: 85–137). Through the years Caswell maintained daily observations of temperature, barometric pressure, rainfall, wind speed, storms, and the aurora, which were published as "Meteorological Observations Made at Providence, Rhode Island, Extending over a Period of Twenty-eight Years and a Half, from December 1831 to May 1860" (*Smithsonian Contributions to Knowledge* 12, art. 4 [1860]: 1–179). He published only a few scientific papers and resisted the urging of publishers and colleagues to write textbooks on the scientific subjects he taught. Devoutly religious, Caswell's "religious faith and his scientific conclusions were never seriously at variance with each other," according to Gammell (p. 11). Unlike some scientists of his time, he believed that the teachings of the Bible were consistent with scientific discoveries. In the introduction to his lectures at the Smithsonian Institution, he wrote: "The mechanism of the heavens, in proportion as we comprehend more and more of its vastness and seeming complexity, bears witness to the enduring order and harmony of the universe, and points with unerring certainty to the superintending agency of an intelligent and infinite Creator."

In 1850 Caswell joined the American Association for the Advancement of Science, established two years before; he was its vice president in 1855, and in 1858 he gave the presidential address in the absence of the senior officers. In 1863 he was chosen as one of the fifty incorporators of the National Academy of Sciences, for which he served as temporary secretary in its first year and then as chairman of the committee of organization. For the academy he also served on a committee to determine methods of preparing and publishing charts of ocean winds and currents for the Navy Department. In 1866 he presented a memorial tribute to Benjamin Silliman (National Academy of Sciences, *Biographical Memoirs* 1 [1877]: 99–112).

Caswell's first wife died in 1850, and in 1855 he married Elizabeth Brown Edmands; they had no children. In 1860 Caswell and his wife spent a year in Europe, where he visited scientists and astronomical observatories and enjoyed attending scientific meetings. He resigned from Brown University as professor in 1863. That year he became president of both the National Exchange Bank and the American Screw Company in Providence. When the president of Brown University resigned in 1867, Caswell was chosen to succeed him in January 1868. During his tenure until 1872, student enrollment, the number of professors, and funding increased, and the museum of natural history was enlarged. Caswell served the university as a trustee from 1873 to 1875 and as a fellow in its corporation from 1875 until his death. In addition to supporting missionary programs for his church, for many years he was active in civic and educational projects, serving as trustee and president of the city hospital and inspector of the state prison. He died in Providence.

• Some biographical material on Caswell is at Brown University. Biographies include William Gammell, "Memoir of Alexis Caswell, D.D., LL.D., Ex-President of Brown University," *New England Historical and Genealogical Register* (July 1877): 1–12, and Joseph Lovering, "Biographical Memoir of Alexis Caswell," *Proceedings of the American Academy of Arts and Sciences* 12 (1877): 307–13, which is reprinted in National Academy of Sciences, *Biographical Memoirs* 6 (1909): 365–72.

ELIZABETH NOBLE SHOR

CASWELL, Hollis Leland (22 Oct. 1901–22 Nov. 1988), professor and college president, was born in Woodruff, Kansas, the son of Hollis Caswell, a postmaster, and Lotta Hood. Caswell was raised in McDonald, a small town in northwest Kansas, where his father worked as a rural mail carrier and later as postmaster. After completing high school in 1918, Caswell spent the next two years at the Kansas State College in Fort Hayes. He then transferred to the University of Nebraska at Lincoln, where he graduated in 1922 with a bachelor's degree in English. During the next four years, Caswell held administrative positions in two rural Nebraska school systems, first as principal of the high school in Auburn and then as superintendent of schools in Syracuse.

By 1926 Caswell had settled on a career in education and had decided to pursue graduate study. He enrolled in what was then one of the nation's most distinguished centers for graduate study in education, Columbia University's Teachers College. He earned his master's degree in school administration in 1927 and his doctorate, also in administration, two years later. Caswell married a fellow graduate student at Teachers College, Ruth Allen, in 1928. They had two children.

In 1929 Caswell joined the faculty of George Peabody College for Teachers in Nashville, Tennessee, where he taught for the next eight years. It was during this period that he first assumed national prominence as a leader in the emerging field of curriculum development. A promoter of educational progressivism, he questioned whether the existing school curriculum, which was organized around the traditional academic disciplines, met the needs or appealed to the interests of twentieth-century youth. He favored instead a curriculum that integrated the disciplines around such key problems of life as economic production, conservation, recreation, and social integration. Between 1929 and 1937, Caswell promoted this view of the curriculum as a consultant for statewide curriculum revisions in Alabama, Florida, Virginia, Mississippi, and Arkansas.

In 1935 Caswell and his colleague, Doak Campbell, coauthored a textbook in curriculum planning titled *Curriculum Development*. Two years later, they coedited *Readings in Curriculum Development*, a collection of essays to accompany the text. *Curriculum Development*, as it turned out, was the fullest statement of Caswell's educational thinking. The American public school, Caswell and Campbell argued, had become in the twentieth century the vehicle for adjusting children to the realities of an urban, industrial society. The task of the curriculum, they asserted, was to instill within students a cooperative impulse, to offset the kind of selfish individualism that had brought about the economic disruptions of the day.

In 1937 Caswell left Peabody to become chair of the newly formed Department of Curriculum and Teaching at Teachers College, Columbia University. After serving nine years as chair, he became associate dean and in 1949 was appointed dean of Teachers College. In 1954 Caswell assumed the presidency of Teachers College. During his quarter-century career at Columbia, Caswell continued to work as a curriculum consultant as well as to write. Among his books were *Education in the Elementary School* (1942), *The American High School* (1946), and *Curriculum Improvement in Public School Systems* (1950). In these books and elsewhere, Caswell addressed, as he had in the 1930s, the school's role in building a more cooperative society. Writing against the backdrop of World War II and then the Cold War, Caswell noted that the nation's schools required a curriculum that would promote understanding and harmony among the world's people. In 1962 Caswell resigned the presidency and returned to the Teachers College faculty as the Marshall Field, Jr., Professor of Education. Retiring from Teachers College in 1967, Caswell spent his remaining years in Santa Barbara, California, where he died.

Caswell was one of a few professional educators of the early twentieth century who helped establish curriculum as a field of study in the university and as an occupational role in the schools. A champion of the progressive education movement, he promoted efforts to create an integrated curriculum organized around the important social issues of the day. Such a program, he believed, would appeal to the interests of youth as well as instill in them the cooperative impulses needed to address the problems of urban, industrial society. Toward this end, Caswell popularized the twin concepts of scope and sequence to depict the relationship between curricular content and grade level. Scope was his term for depicting the diverse array of social functions that composed the content or topics of the curriculum. The scope of the curriculum that he proposed in Virginia included such topics as the consumption of goods and services, the communication and transportation of goods and services, and recreation. Caswell used the term sequence to refer to the time dimension during which this content was to be taught. In his Virginia elementary curriculum proposal, sequence included a number of what he called "centers of interest" existing at different grade levels. Among these centers were home and school life (grade 1), community life (grade 2), and the adaptation of life to the environmental forces of nature (grade 3). Caswell used these two concepts to depict the curriculum as a matrix that displayed the scope vertically and the sequence horizontally. The intersection between any one component of the scope with any one component of the sequence yielded the specific subject matter that was to be taught at a particular grade level. These two concepts freed Caswell from the constraints that traditional disciplinary boundaries placed on curriculum planning. The curriculum did not have to be composed on the traditional academic disciplines. Instead, it could be made up, as was the case in Virginia, of an array of social problems arranged in accordance with the age and interest of children.

Caswell continued to lecture and write for another decade after his retirement. Yet his influence and popularity began to wane with the demise, in the late 1950s and early 1960s, of the brand of educational progressivism that he so favored. Caswell is best remembered for using the curriculum as an instrument of social reform and for his readiness to take childhood interest into account in selecting curricular content.

• Caswell's papers are housed in the American Heritage Center at the University of Wyoming Library. For the most complete exploration and assessment of Caswell's life, career, and intellectual contributions, see Barry M. Franklin, *Building the American Community: The School Curriculum and the Search for Social Control* (1986), and Mary Louise Seguel, *The Curriculum Field: Its Formative Years* (1966). Other, less extensive treatments are to be found in Arthur W. Foshay, "Hollis Leland Caswell: An Appreciation," *Teaching Education* 1 (Feb. 1987): 76–79, and Herbert M. Kliebard, *The Struggle for the American Curriculum, 1893–1958* (1986). An obituary is in the *New York Times*, 24 Nov. 1988.

BARRY M. FRANKLIN

CASWELL, Richard (3 Aug. 1729–10 Nov. 1789), revolutionary militia general and state governor, was born in Baltimore County, Maryland, the son of Richard Caswell, a merchant, and Christian Dallam. Educated in the Anglican parish school, Caswell at an early age was involved in his family's mercantile business. In 1745 he moved with his family to North Carolina, and within two years he secured a position as deputy surveyor general. Caswell married Mary Mackilwean, the daughter of his mentor James Mackilwean, the surveyor general, on 21 April 1752. From this marriage he had one surviving son, William. Since he had lived with the Mackilwean family on the Neuse River adjacent to the present city of Kinston, Caswell located his plantation seat nearby and began accumulating property, eventually owning more than 3,000 acres. Following Mary's death in 1757, Caswell married on 20 June 1758 Sarah Heritage, the daughter of William Heritage, under whose tutelage Caswell read law and passed the bar. Eight children were born to this marriage.

Caswell began four decades of public service on the local level as deputy clerk of the Johnston County court (1749–1753), and he served briefly as county sheriff. From his county office Caswell soon moved to the state arena and in 1754 began a distinguished career in the North Carolina General Assembly, serving in every subsequent session of the colonial assembly and as speaker of the house (1770–1771). A consummate politician, he was simultaneously a confidant of the royal governor and a member of the inner circle of the developing revolutionary leadership. He sided with Governor William Tryon against the Regulator rebellion, a backcountry uprising that protested eastern political domination, unfair taxes, and unjust government. Caswell, then colonel of the Dobbs County militia, commanded a wing of the provincial army in the battle of Alamance (16 May 1771), in which the insurgents were defeated. After the insurrection Caswell was appointed a judge of the special court of oyer and terminer by the new royal governor Josiah Martin.

As the revolutionary unrest mounted in the 1770s, Caswell emerged as a key figure, serving on the provincial committee of correspondence, in all five of the provincial congresses, in both Continental Congresses, and as state public treasurer. Governor Martin described him in this period as "the most active tool of sedition." As colonel of the New Bern militia district, he commanded the force that defeated a loyalist army at the battle of Moore's Creek Bridge on 27 February 1776. Following this significant victory, the provincial congress appointed him brigadier general. Caswell also served as colonel of the North Carolina Partisan Rangers throughout the war. He was chosen to preside over the Fifth Provincial Congress in November 1776, which framed the state constitution, and in December he was elected the first state governor. An effective wartime executive, Caswell devoted extraordinary effort to raising and equipping troops for the field. He eventually served seven annual terms from 1777 to 1780 and from 1785 to 1787, longer than any other governor until the late twentieth century. Beginning in 1780 he was in eight sessions of the state senate, presiding over five of these.

When the British invaded South Carolina in 1780, Caswell was appointed major general of the state militia, becoming the only person to hold that rank in North Carolina during the war. He took charge of the state's defense and raised troops to support the southern command of General Horatio Gates. Although ill, Caswell led the state militia in the battle of Camden (16 Aug. 1780), where the American army was crushed primarily because of the faulty troop dispositions of General Gates. The panicked flight of the North Carolina militia at Camden, for which Caswell shouldered the blame, led to his temporary relief from duty. Although Caswell eventually returned to militia command, his chief participation in the later war effort was as chairman of the Council Extraordinary, an emergency war board.

In the postwar period the state continued to call on Caswell. In addition to serving as a state senator and governor, he also acted as comptroller general from 1782 to 1785. He declined to represent the state in the federal constitutional convention and did not support the ratification of the new federal Constitution in 1788. A Mason since 1754, he was elected second grand master of the state in 1788. He sympathized with the effort of the transmountain counties (the future Tennessee) to establish an independent state, and if his health had not begun to decline, he might have moved to that region. While presiding over the state senate he had a stroke and died a few days later. He was buried in an unmarked grave on his plantation in Lenoir County near the present city of Kinston. A contemporary, the distinguished congressman Nathaniel Macon, wrote of him that he "was one of the most powerful men that ever lived in this or any other country." Caswell dominated the revolutionary era in North Carolina and fully deserves the sobriquet "father of his state."

• For Caswell's correspondence and official documents see William L. Saunders, ed., *The Colonial Records of North Carolina*, vols. 8–10 (1890), and Walter J. Clark, ed., *The State Records of North Carolina*, vols. 11–22 (1896–1907). Biographical sketches are by Eugene C. Brooks in *The Biographical History of North Carolina*, ed. Samuel A. Ashe, vol. 3 (1906), pp. 65–79; Robert D. W. Connor, *Revolutionary Leaders of North Carolina* (1916); and the following three articles by Clayton B. Alexander: "The Training of Richard Caswell," *North Carolina Historical Review* 23 (1946): 13–31; "Richard Caswell: Versatile Leader of the Revolution," *North Carolina Historical Review* 23 (1946): 119–41; and "Richard Caswell's Military and Later Public Services," *North Carolina Historical Review* 23 (1946): 287–312.

LINDLEY S. BUTLER

CATALDO, Joseph Maria (17 Mar. 1837–9 Apr. 1928), Jesuit missionary and founder of Gonzaga University, was born in Terrasini, Sicily, the son of Antonio Cataldo and Sebastiana Borruso. Little is known about his parents. At the age of fifteen, on 22 December 1852, he entered the Society of Jesus in Palermo, Sicily, where he both studied and taught rhetoric, philosophy, and other arts for eight years. He took his first vows while at Palermo, on 6 January 1855. In 1860 revolutionists under Garibaldi banished the Jesuits from Italy; Cataldo was sent to Louvain, Belgium, to continue his studies. He was permitted ordination at an early age, twenty-five, because of ill health; Right Reverend Monsignor d'Argentcau, bishop of Liege and former officer in the army of Napoleon I, ordained Cataldo on 8 September 1862. The following day, Cataldo said his first mass in Maestricht, Holland.

Cataldo is best known for his missionary and educational efforts among Indian tribes in the United States. His early dream was to do missionary work among the Indians of the Rocky Mountains. In 1862 he went to Boston to continue his studies in theology and the English language in preparation for this work. In January 1863 he contracted a bad cold; he was sent to the warmer climate of California and labeled an incurable consumptive. He finished his studies at Santa Clara College, where he also taught philosophy.

Though still ill, Cataldo pleaded with Rome to go work among the Rocky Mountain Indians. His wish was granted; in 1865 he traveled north by boat and arrived at the Old Coeur d'Alene Mission (later renamed Sacred Heart), near present-day Cataldo, Idaho, where he immediately began studying the Kalispell language, native tongue of several Rocky Mountain Indian tribes. From 1865 to 1877 he worked mainly among the Coeur d'Alene, the Spokane, and the Nez Perce in Idaho, teaching Catholicism and converting numerous Indians. He founded the Spokane Mission on Peone Prairie in November 1866 for the Spokane Indians. A letter from Rome intended for another Jesuit but erroneously delivered to Cataldo, led him for most of 1867 to Montana, where he worked among the Flathead at the St. Ignatius Mission. Following his mission in Montana, he traveled the Mullan Road back to Idaho, where he founded St. Joseph's Mission at Slickpoo, Idaho, for the Nez Perce in 1868. Many of the Nez Perce were not on friendly terms with white settlers. Friction escalated, and in 1877 the Nez Perce War began when a few Indians killed two whites on the Salmon River. Just before the outbreak of war, Cataldo had traveled numerous miles by horseback among the tribes of the Spokane, Coeur d'Alene, and Colville Indians to keep them from joining the war; he received presidential commendations for his peacekeeping efforts. Also in 1877, on 16 June, Cataldo was appointed general superior of all the Northwest Jesuit missions.

In addition to his extraordinary missionary work, Cataldo was also a major influence in education; in 1881 he bought land from the Northern Pacific Railroad for the site of Gonzaga College and St. Michael's Mission School for Indians (Spokane Mission was moved to this new site and renamed St. Michael's). Construction of Gonzaga College began in 1883; it opened in 1887. Cataldo is frequently credited as the chief factor in the building of Spokane, Washington, because of his efforts in establishing Gonzaga there.

From 1884 to 1904 Cataldo expanded his missionary work in the Northwest by initiating a building program for Indian missions in Washington, Oregon, Wyoming, and Alaska. In addition, he spent time among the Crow Indians at St. Xavier's Mission in Montana. From December 1884 to August 1885 he traveled to Europe to recruit Jesuits to join missionary efforts in the Northwest; fifty Jesuits heeded his call. In 1886 Cataldo founded the Indian Missions of Alaska and appointed the first two Jesuit missionaries to Alaska.

Cataldo inaugurated two other institutions of higher learning: a novitiate in DeSmet, Idaho, in 1891 and the Immaculate Conception College in Seattle, Washington, in 1892. The DeSmet training house for missionaries was the crowning point of his administration as superior, according to G. F. Weibel. After his superiorship ended in 1893, at his request he set his sights again on Alaska; he made a second trip there in 1896, spending fourteen months as general inspector of the missions in the Yukon region. He made yet a third trip to Alaska in 1901, serving as superior in Nome, where he celebrated his fiftieth year in the Jesuit order. He was superior in Nulato in 1902.

Cataldo's aspirations to spread Catholicism in the Northwest took him on a recruiting trip for young religious women in 1904 to Philadelphia; he returned with twelve postulates and founded the Sisters of St. Joseph. By 1907 he had founded a school where the sisters taught Nez Perce children.

In 1907 Cataldo obeyed a desperate summons to serve as pastor of the Italian-speaking parish of the Holy Family in San Jose, California. His stay in California was short-lived, however. In 1908 he was called to assist an ill priest at St. Mary's in Pendleton, Oregon, and while there he oversaw the construction of a new church. From 1915 to 1916 he worked among the Umatilla Indians at St. Andrew's near Pendleton. In 1915 he achieved a notable first with the publication of his *Jesus-Christ-Nim*, a translation of *The Life of Jesus Christ, from the Four Gospels* from English into Nez Perce. From 1915 until his final year of life, Cataldo worked mainly among the Nez Perce at Slickpoo.

On 28 March 1928, though in failing health, Cataldo answered a request for another mission to the Umatilla Indians at St. Andrew's near Pendleton. He suffered a fainting spell Easter morning but insisted on saying mass; another priest held him up during the service. That evening he was taken to the hospital in Pendleton, and he died the following day. Four days later he was interred at St. Michael's, the site of his sixteen-year superiorship and the first mission he founded.

Through relentless determination, Cataldo overcame chronic health problems and fulfilled his missionary dream. During his seventy-five years as a Jesuit missionary, he studied twenty languages, including European and Indian languages. He traveled extensively to teach Catholicism, enduring numerous hardships. Three times he had serious falls that resulted in broken bones; the Nez Perce nicknamed him "Kuailks-Metatcopun" (Black Robe Three-Times-Broken).

• Cataldo's papers, including his manuscript sermons and diaries, are in the Gonzaga University Library Rare Book Room. Additional papers and manuscript collections are available in the special collections of Idaho State University and the Spokane Public Library. Important sources include G. F. Weibel, *Rev. Joseph M. Cataldo, S.J.: A Short Sketch of a Wonderful Career* (1928); Laurence E. Crosby, *Kuailks Metatcopun (Black Robe Three-Times-Broken)* (1925); and Michael O'Malley, *Missionary Life of Father Cataldo in the Inland Empire (1865–1928)* (n.d.). See also Lucia Ahern's master's thesis, "The Long Harvest: The Life of Joseph M. Cataldo, S.J." (Nebraska State Teachers College, 1958).

MARY ANNE HANSEN

CATESBY, Mark (31 Dec. 1682–23 Dec. 1749), naturalist, botanist, and ornithologist, was born in Castle Hedingham, Essex, England, the son of John Catesby, a former town clerk, justice of the peace, and mayor of Sudbury, England, and Elizabeth Jekyll. He may have attended the local grammar school in Sudbury, but little is known of his educational record. It is thought that he had no university-level or formal legal training, although his eldest brother was a student at Cambridge University and the Inns of Court in London. Catesby was reasonably proficient in Latin, and it is possible that he either had some training in botany or some early experience in that field. It is also probable that he met and learned from the celebrated English naturalist John Ray sometime prior to the latter's death in 1705.

Until his late thirties Catesby was primarily a collector of plant specimens and seeds for his own use and for other naturalists and collectors. In 1712 he went to Virginia to learn something of its natural history. He lived for a time with his older sister Elizabeth and her husband William Cocke, a physician who was secretary to the colony and later a member of the governor's council. Here he met a number of prominent Virginians, including William Byrd II, who shared with Catesby his knowledge of the colony's fauna and flora. Catesby spent much time collecting plant specimens and seeds, most of which were sent to collectors in England, principally Sir Hans Sloane, then head of the Royal Society.

In 1714 Catesby made his first trip to the Appalachians, the Bahamas, and Jamaica, where he continued to study native plants and animals. From 1716 to 1718 he appears to have been heavily involved in the management of his brother-in-law's personal affairs while the latter was in London on business for the colony. Catesby himself returned to England in 1719.

In 1720 a group of prominent plant collectors in England, notably Sloane, William Sherard, Samuel Dale, Charles Dubois, and several others, decided to underwrite a second trip by Catesby to the Carolinas and the West Indies. His objective was to collect specimens and information about the natural history of the southeastern American colonies and the Bahamas. Discussions about this project had been ongoing for at least ten years, and Catesby was not the group's first choice for this assignment, but he accepted and departed for the colonies in January 1722. Much of his time was spent as a middleman between plant and seed collectors in England and America, packing specimens for shipment to his patrons in England. He also began drawing and painting watercolors of many birds, insects, animals, and plants. In addition, Catesby was interested in domesticating certain American plants, trees, and shrubs in England, and he also selected some plants for shipment to England that had commercial or medicinal value. By 1724 Catesby was extending his collecting and research into the neighboring Spanish colonies. During parts of 1725 and 1726 he was in the Bahamas, making additional collections and illustrations.

Catesby returned to England from his second stay in the colonies in 1726, and he remained there for the remainder of his life. He had hoped that his backers would underwrite an illustrated account of his findings, but having supported his travels for more than four years, they concluded that this was as much as they were prepared to do. Catesby therefore undertook to do the job himself, and this was exacting and time-consuming work for one who had no experience in engraving and publishing. He received excellent guidance in etching and engraving from the French-born Joseph Goupy, and the Quaker merchant Peter Collinson loaned the impecunious artist funds that enabled him to continue with his project. William Sherard briefly aided Catesby with questions of Latin nomenclature prior to Sherard's death in 1728. Catesby did much of his own coloring to save scarce funds.

Catesby was invited to exhibit the initial twenty plates of his projected book before the Royal Society in 1729. The book was published in parts and sold by subscription at a price of two guineas per part. During much of this period, Catesby supported himself by working in a nursery owned by Thomas Fairchild near London. He also grew many plants on his own, the proceeds from the sale of which also helped him eke out a living.

The first volume of *The Natural History of Carolina, Florida, and the Bahama Islands* was finally published at the end of 1732. This led to his election as a fellow of the Royal Society in April 1733. Catesby defrayed some of the expenses of membership by providing illustrations for the society's *Register Book* and by reviewing foreign publications to be distributed to the membership. In 1735 he was asked to assess the first edition of Linnaeus's *Systema Naturae*, a task he declined, in part because he felt his lack of a scientific background. It is possible, however, that the two men met when Linnaeus visited England in the summer of 1736.

Catesby continued work on the second volume of his *Natural History* for eleven years, completing it in December 1743. Three years later an illustrated *Appendix*, essentially a compilation of work done by John Bartram and other botanists, was published. Catesby then spent his remaining years working on his *Hortus Britanno-Americanus, or, a Curious Collection of Trees and Shrubs, the Produce of the British Colonies in North America; Adapted to the Soil and Climate of England*, a catalog of eighty-five domesticated American trees and shrubs in England. A few parts of this book had been printed when Catesby died; the completed project, with his illustrations, appeared posthumously in 1763. This work gave Catesby an opportunity to publish some of his more mature and accurate ideas about American flora, but it was not as successful, principally because he did not live to see the entire work through to final publication. Various foreign editions of the *Natural History*, some of them pirated, together with some plagiarisms, were published during Catesby's life and later; but neither he nor his family derived any pecuniary benefit from them. His friend George Edwards published revised editions of the *Natural History* in 1754 and 1771. Some of Catesby's errors were corrected, but the quality of the illustrations was inferior.

Catesby was not a well-trained naturalist, and his artistry was not distinguished. Nevertheless, his *Natural History*, containing as it did illustrations of plants and animals in their natural settings, was a major achievement, adumbrating John James Audubon's great work a century later. Catesby's reputation rests primarily on this book. Though less successful, some of his ornithological theorizing was superior to that of many of his contemporaries. His birds were not painted with an accuracy that would meet modern scientific standards, but he depended almost entirely on his own observations and had little comparative data with which to work. His bird illustrations, however, were equal or superior to those done by his contemporaries. His botanical work did not fare as well. His plant illustrations lacked sufficient detail to meet the requirements of the Linnaean system of classification. In addition, the caliber of contemporary botanical work done in the colonies was far more advanced than its zoology.

Catesby's *Natural History* was for many years a major source of information for those interested in American plants and animals. Other late eighteenth- and early nineteenth-century naturalists, including Linnaeus, Brisson, Buffon, and Kalm, cited and depended upon his work. Long considered the father of American ornithology, he is also regarded as a pioneering American ecologist.

Catesby married Elizabeth Rowland, a widow whom he had known for some years, in 1747. The couple had two children, the eldest of whom, a son, was eight years of age when Catesby died in London.

• Few if any of Catesby's papers are extant. Some of his manuscripts, and letters of those associated with him, particularly the five-volume *Dr. [William] Sherard's Philosophical Letters*, are in the Library of the Royal Society, London, and the Sloane collections at the British Museum. See also the *Richardson Correspondence, MS Radcliffe Trust*, at the Bodleian Library, Oxford University, and *The Sherardian Pinax*, at the Library of the Oxford Botanical Garden. Research notes on Catesby assembled for her study of early ornithologists, are in the Elsa G. Allen Papers, Cornell University. The principal biography is George F. Frick and Raymond P. Stearns, *Mark Catesby: The Colonial Audubon* (1961). See also Elsa G. Allen, "History of American Ornithology before Audubon," *Transactions of the American Philosophical Society* (1951); Robert Elman, *First in the Field* (1977); William H. Goetzmann, *New Lands, New Men: America and the Second Great Age of Discovery* (1986); Joseph Kastner, *A Species of Eternity* (1977); Raymond P. Stearns, *Science in the British Colonies of America* (1970); Louis B. Wright and Marion Tinling, eds., *The Secret Diary of William Byrd of Westover, 1709–1712* (1941); and Henrietta McBurney, *Mark Catesby's Natural History of America: The Watercolours from the Royal Library, Windsor Castle* (1997).

KEIR B. STERLING

CATHER, Willa (7 Dec. 1873–24 April 1947), novelist and short-story writer, was born in Back Creek Valley (now Gore), Virginia, the daughter of Charles Cather, farmer, and Mary Virginia Boak. Cather's family moved to Nebraska in 1883. She later told an interviewer that after the mountains of Virginia the prairie made her feel that she had "come to the end of everything—it was a kind of erasure of personality. . . . I thought I would go under." But she did not, and for the first eighteen months of her life in Nebraska she lived on her grandfather's farm, surrounded by immigrant farm families whom she came to know and love and whom she eventually turned into memorable fictional characters. When her father moved the family to the prairie village of Red Cloud and opened an insurance and real estate office, Cather began the next phase of her life. The town appears in six of her novels and a good many stories.

After high school Cather moved to Lincoln to spend a year prepping for college and entered the University of Nebraska in 1891. When her professor, unbeknownst to her, published one of her essays in the newspaper, she dropped plans for a scientific career and thenceforth considered herself a writer. "What youthful vanity can be unaffected by the sight of itself in print!" she later wrote.

Early in her junior year, she began writing drama criticism and a column for the *Nebraska State Journal*. She was largely self-supporting from then on. After graduating from the university in 1895 she continued her journalistic career in Lincoln and in 1896 was hired to edit a magazine in Pittsburgh. The next year she moved to the Pittsburgh *Leader*, where she worked as telegraph editor, drama and music critic, and book reviewer. About this time Cather met Isabelle McClung, the socially prominent daughter of a Pittsburgh judge. Isabelle became Cather's most ardent admirer, her lifelong best friend, and the person for whom, Cather said, she had written all her books. In 1900 Cather started teaching high school English in Pittsburgh. This job gave her summers to write and travel and resulted in her first book, *April Twilights* (1903), a collection of forgettable verse, and her first trip to Europe in 1902. Traveling with Isabelle McClung, she spent most of the summer in France. The visit, the first of five between 1902 and 1935, reinforced her lifelong love affair with France and French culture that had begun in college. Cather's first book of fiction, *The Troll Garden* (1905), was a collection of stories about art, music, and artists, two of which, "The Sculptor's Funeral" and "Paul's Case," have often been reprinted.

Cather completed her odyssey from farm to metropolis when S. S. McClure hired her to help edit his magazine in New York. Her permanent home then became New York City. She loved it for its cultural advantages but hated it for its noise and dirt; she left the city often to travel. From 1906 through 1911 she was a *McClure's* executive. McClure made her managing editor soon after she joined the staff. While she was on assignment for the magazine in Boston in 1908, she met Sarah Orne Jewett, who became a major influence. But editing a muckraking magazine was not what Cather wanted to do with her life. In 1912 she left *McClure's* and took a long trip to the Southwest, the first of many visits to this area. This journey had a major effect on her subsequent fiction. After this trip Cather and Edith Lewis, her friend and companion for thirty-nine years, moved into a Greenwich Village apartment on Bank Street where they lived until 1927. Lewis, who worked for magazines and in advertising, was a self-effacing assistant who made reservations, bought tickets, and packed trunks.

Cather's career as a novelist properly begins after this visit, but she had written a short novel, *Alexander's Bridge*, before leaving *McClure's*. Although she later disparaged this story of a man torn between love for his Boston wife and a London actress, it is a competent work and contains a number of themes and situations that she later developed more powerfully.

After living in Pittsburgh and New York for seventeen years, Cather turned to Nebraska as a subject and her memories of her youth in the prairie state came flooding back. The result was *O Pioneers!* (1913). Cather always maintained that a writer's most important material was acquired before the age of fifteen. *O Pioneers!* is the story of Swedish immigrants who tame the wild land. The protagonist, Alexandra Bergson, is a strong, capable woman of mythic proportions. The novel evokes memorably the spirit of the pioneers, contrasting it with the materialism of the next generation—a theme that figures prominently in Cather's later fiction.

The Song of the Lark (1915), about the career of a famous singer, combined Cather's use of Nebraska in pioneer times, her recent discovery of the Southwest, and her consuming interest in music. The singer as child and adolescent is Cather herself growing up in Red Cloud; the adult singer is based on Olive Fremstad, then the leading Wagnerian soprano at the Metropolitan Opera.

Cather's *My Ántonia* (1918), which has become a modern classic, captures poignantly the life of Czech immigrants in Nebraska, most notably the title character, who in real life was Cather's close friend Anna Pavelka. It is a superb drama of memory. Antonia, a madonna of the wheat fields, is described as the mother of races.

My Ántonia was followed by a collection of stories, *Youth and the Bright Medusa* (1920), which contains four tales reprinted from *The Troll Garden* and several new ones dealing with the lives of singers. *One of Ours* (1922), which takes place during World War I, was inspired by the death of a cousin in France in 1918. In it, an idealistic Nebraska farm boy enlists in the army after an unhappy life on the farm and a failed marriage. He engages in the struggle against Germany and dies thinking he is helping save the world for democracy. The Nebraska scenes are vintage Cather, but the battle scenes had to be based on secondary sources, a method alien to Cather's best work. Writing it cost her four years of effort, and it received mixed reviews. Yet the novel won the Pulitzer Prize.

Cather described 1922, without explaining, as the year her world broke in two. Critics have seen this as a midlife crisis, caused perhaps by unfavorable criticism of *One of Ours*, her sudden financial success after years of struggle, dissatisfaction with the materialism and what she saw as the vulgarity of the 1920s, and simply approaching the age of fifty. Cather found refuge in the Episcopal church, and went on to write one of her best novels, *A Lost Lady* (1923), which critics acclaimed as a minor masterpiece. The lost lady of the novel, Marian Forrester, is based on Leila Garber, wife of Silas Garber, governor of Nebraska, and a woman Cather had greatly admired. This short novel illustrates a narrative principle Cather described in her essay "The Novel Démeublé," where she argues for the elimination of excess furniture, a principle based on the elder Alexandre Dumas's remark that "to make a drama, a man needed one passion and four walls."

After *A Lost Lady*, Cather wrote what she called a middle-aged novel, *The Professor's House* (1925). Her protagonist is a historian who has just won an important prize for a book on the Spanish in North America. Yet he is strangely dissatisfied with his life, the victim, like his creator, of a midlife crisis. After nearly being asphyxiated at the end of the novel, the professor comes to terms with life as a diminished thing.

The Professor's House was followed by *My Mortal Enemy* (1926), a short, bitter novel that drained the last bit of gall that had accompanied Cather's midlife crisis. It is the story of Myra Driscoll, who elopes with the Protestant Oswald Henshawe and is consequently disinherited by her rich, bigoted Irish Catholic great uncle. Myra lives to regret marrying for love, and the story ends in defeat and death.

Cather's passion for the Southwest was most fully expressed in *Death Comes for the Archbishop* (1927). She considered this book her best, as do many critics. It is an experimental modernist work, loosely episodic, with no conventional plot and laced with inset stories. Cather said she was trying to write a novel that was like a series of frescoes by Puvis de Chavannes depicting the life of Ste. Geneviève, which she had seen in Paris in 1902. She also drew on the way the lives of the saints were written in *The Golden Legend*, in which their martyrdoms are no more emphasized than the trivial events of their lives. The immediate inspiration for the book, however, was the biography of a priest who had been vicar to the first bishop (later archbishop) of New Mexico. The novel fictionalizes the lives of Jean Baptiste Lamy and Joseph Machebeuf, missionary priests from France, as they organize and minister to the new diocese of New Mexico after its annexation by the United States following the war with Mexico. Beautifully told in Cather's simple but eloquent style, it is one of the classics of modern American literature.

Soon after Cather finished this novel, her father died, her mother had a stroke, and she had to move from the Greenwich Village apartment she had lived in for fifteen years. Life seemed to be falling apart. Her salvation was the writing of *Shadows on the Rock* (1931), a novel laid in seventeenth-century Quebec. It is remarkable for its descriptions of Quebec at various times of the year and a fine example of writing in the style of impressionistic painting.

After her mother died in 1931, Cather returned to Red Cloud for a family reunion at Christmas but thereafter never returned to Nebraska. She lived in New York but summered on Grand Manan Island in the Bay of Fundy, where she built a cottage, and spent part of each autumn at the Shattuck Inn in Jaffrey, New Hampshire. A collection of three stories, *Obscure Destinies* (1932), was her final major work using the prairie setting for which she is famous. "Neighbour Rosicky" describes a Czech farmer and his family. It is a kind of sequel to *My Ántonia*. "Old Mrs. Harris," the best of all her short stories, re-creates Cather's grandmother, Cather's mother, and Vicki (Cather herself), a teenager getting ready to go to college. "Two Friends" is a lesser tale, inspired by Cather's memory of listening to two Red Cloud businessmen talk in the evenings outside a store. After *Obscure Destinies* appeared, Cather and Lewis ended five years of camping out in the old Grosvenor Hotel and moved into a Park Avenue apartment, where Cather spent her final years.

Two more novels, *Lucy Gayheart* (1935) and *Sapphira and the Slave Girl* (1940), complete the Cather canon. The former, one of Cather's lesser works, is the story of a musician who goes to Chicago to study. *Sapphira and the Slave Girl*, however, is one of Cather's best and the only one in which she used her native Virginia as a setting. It is laid in the village of her birth in the decade before the Civil War. The story involves the conflict between Sapphira's efforts to sell her servant Nancy and her husband's refusal to consent to the transaction. Sapphira and Henry Colbert are drawn from Cather's maternal great-grandparents, and the character of Mrs. Blake is a fictional portrait of Grandmother Boak. In the climax, Mrs. Blake helps Nancy escape to Canada. Plot, setting, and character are handled with exceptional skill in this novel, even though Cather was at the end of her career and her health was failing.

In all her works Cather carries out the principle she learned from Sarah Orne Jewett: "If [a writer] achieves anything enduring, it must be by giving himself absolutely to his material. And this gift of sympathy is his great gift."

In her old age Willa Cather wrote a friend that she had pretty well gotten out of life what she wanted. She had achieved recognition by the writers she most admired and had lived the kind of life she preferred. She had escaped the things she most violently did not want, such as too much money, noisy publicity, and the bother of meeting lots of people. She knew at the end that she was leaving behind a significant body of work, including twelve novels and fifty-eight stories. Politically active critics in the sociological 1930s charged her with writing escapist fiction, but in the years after World War II her stature grew steadily. She is generally regarded as one of the major American writers of the twentieth century.

After publishing *Sapphira*, Cather wrote only a few more stories and left unfinished a novel that was destroyed after her death by her longtime companion Edith Lewis. She died in New York and was buried in Jaffrey, New Hampshire.

Few writers have been so dedicated to their art as Cather. From the time she was in college, she maintained that an artist had to sacrifice everything for art. This in her case included matrimony and children, for though she had proposals during her Pittsburgh years, she remained single throughout her life. In recent years some critics have concluded that she was lesbian, and though it is true that her strongest emotional attachments (outside of her father and brothers) were to women, all the evidence points to a celibate writer, married only to her art. Fanny Butcher wrote in her memoirs of Cather: "I never knew anyone who seemed to be more wrapped around by her work. . . . Once she said to me that nothing mattered to her but writing books, and living the kind of life that makes it possible to write them."

• Although Cather's will forbids the publication of her letters, there are significant collections of them at the Willa Cather Pioneer Memorial, Red Cloud; the Nebraska State Historical Society, Lincoln; the Newberry Library, Chicago; and the University of Virginia Library. A few manuscripts are available at the New York Public Library. Published works by Cather not mentioned above are Georgine Milmine's *The Life of Mary Baker G. Eddy* (1909), written for *McClure's* from an unpublishable manuscript; the ghostwritten autobiography of S. S. McClure (1914); *April Twilights and Other Poems* (1923), a later collection of verse; *Not under Forty* (1936), a collection of essays; and *The Old Beauty and Others* (1948), three posthumously published stories.

The original authorized biography by E. K. Brown, *Willa Cather: A Critical Biography* (1953) has been superseded by James Woodress, *Willa Cather: A Literary Life* (1987). Important memoirs by friends are Edith Lewis, *Willa Cather Living* (1953), and Elizabeth Sergeant, *Willa Cather: A Memoir* (1953). Three good critical studies are David Stouck, *Willa Cather's Imagination* (1975); Susan Rosowski, *The Voyage Perilous: Willa Cather's Romanticism* (1986); and Hermione Lee, *Willa Cather: A Life Saved Up* (1989). Criticism is collected in John Murphy, ed., *Critical Essays on Willa Cather* (1983); and two useful reference works are Marilyn Arnold, *Willa Cather: A Reference Guide* (1986), and Joan Crane, *Willa Cather: A Bibliography* (1982). Sharon O'Brien, *Willa Cather: The Emerging Voice* (1987), which deals with the lesbian issue, is an important psychological biography of Cather's first forty years. The University of Nebraska Press makes available all the stories Cather did not collect herself and much of her journalism, interviews, and speeches: *Collected Short Fiction, 1892–1912*, ed. Virginia Faulkner (1970); *Uncle Valentine and Other Stories: Willa Cather's Uncollected Short Fiction, 1915–1929*, ed. Bernice Slote (1973); *The Kingdom of Art: Willa Cather's First Principles and Critical Statements, 1893–1896*, ed. Bernice Slote (1967); *The World and the Parish: Willa Cather's Articles and Reviews, 1893–1902*, ed. William Curtin (1970); and *Willa Cather in Person: Interviews, Speeches, and Letters*, ed. Brent Bohlke (1986).

JAMES WOODRESS

CATHERWOOD, Mary Hartwell (16 Dec. 1847–26 Dec. 1902), fiction writer, was born in Luray, Ohio, the daughter of Marcus Hartwell, a physician, and Phoebe Thompson. In the mid-1850s the Hartwells moved to Illinois, where in 1857 both parents died within a few months of each other. Mary and her siblings were returned to Ohio and raised by maternal relatives in Hebron, an apparently difficult time for Mary and one on which she later drew in her realistic stories.

At fourteen Mary began teaching and publishing verses in the Newark, Ohio, newspaper. With the help of Milton L. Wilson, editor of the *Newark North American*, she gained admission to the Granville Female Seminary in 1865 and completed a four-year program in only three years while supporting herself with her teaching. Catherwood earned the distinction of being the first woman writer born west of the Alleghenies and the first woman writer of prominence to graduate from college. After graduation she returned to teaching at Danville, Illinois. In 1871 she won a prize from *Wood's Household Magazine* for her short stories and three years later moved to Newburgh, New York (headquarters of *Wood's*), to begin a career as a freelance writer. Finding ready acceptance for her fiction, she published her previously serialized novel *A Woman in Armor* (1875). In spite of the novel's melodramatic plot, it established Catherwood's satiric method of describing small-town life, this time in Little Boston, the scene of the novel's action.

Moving to Cincinnati, Mary found success as a writer until the national economic depression of the mid-1870s forced her return to Danville and to reliance on relatives. There in 1877 she married James Steele Catherwood, a merchant in the village of Oakwood, Indiana. The Catherwoods later moved to Indianapolis, where Mary Catherwood became a drama critic for *Saturday Review* and mingled with Indiana writers, among them James Whitcomb Riley, with whom she remained an intimate literary friend throughout her lifetime. In 1882 the Catherwoods moved to Hoopeston, Illinois, where their daughter and son were born; the son did not live beyond infancy.

Early in her career Catherwood produced children's books that disavowed the expected sentimental and religious strains of juvenile fiction and instead offered realistic portrayals of her region and its people (*The Dogberry Bunch* [1879], *Rocky Fork* [1882], *Old Caravan Days* [1884], and *The Secrets at Roseladies* [1888]), but her major focus was local-color stories about the farms and villages of the Corn Belt. These stories, published in *Atlantic*, *Harper's*, and *Lippincott's*, among other periodicals, remain mostly uncollected but illustrate her early bent toward realism and exemplify some of her best work. Fred Patee suggests that had she continued to write in this mode, Catherwood might have ranked with Sarah Orne Jewett or Mary Freeman as a leading regionalist.

Her 1881 novel, *Craque-'o-Doom*, was a critical portrait of the provinciality and aesthetic aridity of the Hebron, Ohio, of her childhood. As Robert Price points out, this Ohio village was "probably the first of all Winesburgs," establishing Catherwood as a precursor to the "revolt from the village" writers. Serialized stories such as "A Little God" (1878–1879) satirized the boomtown mentality of Whoopertown (a thinly veiled Hoopeston), and eighteen years later this story became the basis for her novella *The Spirit of an Illinois Town*, a piece that a *Critic* reviewer found unsurpassed in showing "convincingly the squalor, the rush, the intensity, the intoxication of life in a growing western town" (10 Apr. 1897). Catherwood's feminist concerns surface in this same period in stories such as "The Monument of the First Mrs. Smith" (1878), a bitter sketch of a farm wife's life on the prairies. Catherwood's early realistic works would later be overshadowed by her romantic historical fiction, but they serve as "chronological firsts," predating Joseph Kirkland's *Zury* (1887) and Edgar Howe's *The Story of a Country Town* (1883), both critical studies of the stifled intellectualism and culture in small towns of the farm belt.

In 1886 Catherwood joined other midwestern writers in establishing the Western Association of Writers, a group that later supported her commitment to romance as the proper vehicle for exploring the individual's ability to confront universal and timeless human problems. In 1889 Catherwood's work took a decided turn toward historical romance with the publication of *The Romance of Dollard*, a novel influenced by the works of Francis Parkman, who also wrote the novel's introduction. Meticulously attentive to historical record and fascinated by the ancien régime of French Canada, Catherwood devoted the remainder of her career and nine subsequent novels to romantic subjects and particularly to tales of the French in early America. Her summer sojourns to Mackinac Island, a place rich in French and Indian tradition, inspired much of her work of this period. In the preface to her 1891 novel, *The Lady of Fort St. John*, Catherwood claimed reality "stranger than fiction," but her romances, although documented by historical record, are riddled with fictionalized details of her characters' lives. While such characterization appears in her story collections *The Chase of Saint-Castin and Other Stories of the French in the New World* (1894) and *Mackinac and Lake Stories* (1899), the latter is arguably her best work in the genre.

Coming under attack from Hamlin Garland and the realists at the 1893 Columbia Exposition in Chicago, Catherwood defended the "aristocratic in literature," privileging the fanciful over the realistic. Garland had asserted that her work made a piteously direct appeal to readers, did not have truth on its side, and dripped of ambrosia and nectar. Catherwood replied, "Is looking at the beautiful side of life insincere?" She argued for an "uplifting" presentation of life in fiction rather than for the common and unclean that would trample down or deny Yesterday. To Garland's claim that only realism sells and that the West—"the home of Milwaukee beer and Chicago pork"—had no place for romantic idealism, Catherwood defended her heroes from the past as practical men, such as Robert Chevalier LaSalle, who confronted real-life hardships: "If Mr. Garland would look at these great men of the past he would see the same human soul struggling with human problems that he sees to-day" (Dennis, pp. 130–32). As she wrote in *The Romance of Dollard*, "All localities have their romance, their unseen or possible life, which is hinted to the maker of stories alone," a view that prompted Eugene Field to proclaim Catherwood "the queen of Western romanticism."

With a Thomas Hardy–like ability to make picturesque settings into characters, Catherwood recounted the stories of LaSalle (*The Story of Tonty* [1890]), the young Abraham Lincoln (*Spanish Peggy: A Story of Young Illinois* [1899]), and even Joan of Arc (*The Days of Jeanne D'Arc* [1897]). Catherwood's most popular novel, *Lazarre* (1901), is a skillful blending of historical panorama and fictionalized drama of the lost

French dauphin's repudiation of the throne for the love of a woman and the freedom of the American West. Although Catherwood's historical romances met with popular success, they suffered from frequent lapses into melodrama and sentimentalism.

In her later years Catherwood separated from her husband, traveled abroad and in Canada, and established residence in Chicago, where she edited the magazine the *Graphic*. She died in Chicago of cancer.

Catherwood's place in American fiction is secure as one of the earliest women writers from the western regions to support herself by writing. Publishing more than thirty books in twenty years, she was a versatile writer who pioneered the romantic historical novel that became the bestselling genre of the 1890s. Catherwood's ability to present authentic details of time and place while celebrating the ennobling traits of sentimentalized characters calls for reconsideration of the conventional terms "romance" and "realism." Of greater importance than her historical novels, though, is her early short fiction, which establishes her as a regionalist whose understanding of and disaffection for small-town and rural life predict the "revolt from the village" movement. Her place in American literary history hinges on new appraisals of her early ventures into realism and her appropriation of feminist themes.

• Selected personal papers of Catherwood are in the Newberry Library, Chicago, and the Ohioana Library, Columbus. Robert Price, "A Critical Biography of Mary Hartwell Catherwood" (Ph.D. diss., Ohio State Univ., 1943), provides the most reliable biographical information, while a short memoir by Catherwood's friend Milton L. Wilson, *Biography of Mary Hartwell Catherwood* (1904), offers more personal insights. Of literary historians, Fred Lewis Patee gives the most complete overview of her work in *A History of American Literature since 1870* (1915). In regional literary studies, Arthur W. Shumaker provides the most comprehensive study in *A History of Indiana Literature* (1962), while Kenny Williams concentrates on Catherwood's Chicago connections and interests in *Prairie Voices: A Literary History of Chicago from the Frontier to 1893* (1980), and Dorothy Dondore's *The Prairie and the Making of Middle America* (1926), places Catherwood within the regional school. See also Beverly Seaton, "'In Canaan's Land': Images of Granville, Ohio," *Old Northwest* 5 (1979): 3–17, and Robert Price, "Mary Hartwell Catherwood and Cincinnati," *Cincinnati Historical Society Bulletin* 22 (1964): 162–68. Brief analyses and annotated bibliographies of four of Catherwood's principal works appear in Bernice E. Gallagher, *Illinois Women Novelists in the Nineteenth Century* (1994). The most significant scholarship on Catherwood's early stories comes from Robert Price, "Mrs. Catherwood's Early Experiments with Critical Realism," *American Literature* 17 (1945): 140–51. Accounts of Catherwood's 1893 debate with Garland on the issue of realism versus romanticism are recorded in Garland, *Roadside Meetings* (1930), and, more objectively, in Charles H. Dennis, *Eugene Field's Creative Years* (1924). Peggy B. Treece has broached the subject of both Catherwood's regionalism and feminist concerns in two articles in *Midwestern Miscellany*: "A Hidden Woman of Local Color: Mrs. Mary Hartwell Catherwood," 3 (1975): 24–31, and "Mary Hartwell Catherwood's Disguised Handbooks of Feminism," 7 (1979): 7–14.

MARY R. RYDER

CATLEDGE, Turner (17 Mar. 1901–27 Apr. 1983), newspaper editor, was born in New Prospect, Mississippi, the son of Lee Johnston Catledge and Willie Anna Turner, farmers. Catledge grew up in Philadelphia, Mississippi, and worked at a variety of jobs for his uncles, who owned a market, a drugstore, a hardware store, and an automobile dealership. Following graduation from Philadelphia High School, Catledge decided to attend Mississippi A & M (now known as Mississippi State University). He worked as an assistant to the school's agricultural editor producing bulletins while majoring in business administration. Shortly after graduation in 1922 he was offered a job in his hometown as a reporter for the *Neshoba Democrat*. He spent the next eighteen months as a reporter, advertising solicitor, mechanical supervisor, and managing editor, in quick succession, for the *Neshoba Democrat*, the *Tunica* (Miss.) *Times*, and the *Tupelo* (Miss.) *Journal*.

Catledge obtained a reporting job with the *Memphis Press* in February 1924. One month later he secured a reporting position with the competing *Memphis Commercial Appeal*. His early assignments included covering city and county government. An opportunity came his way during the 1927 flood of the Mississippi River. He filed several stories on the flood's devastation of the area. Because of his knowledge of the Mississippi Valley, Catledge accompanied Secretary of Commerce Herbert Hoover on an airplane survey of the region.

A change in the *Commercial Appeal*'s ownership caused Catledge to look for other opportunities, and in the summer of 1927 he joined the *Baltimore Sun* as a features writer and reporter. After a few months in Baltimore, he was reassigned to Washington, D.C., as a correspondent to cover the 1928 presidential campaign. A year and a half after he arrived in the District of Columbia as a Washington correspondent for the *Sun*, Catledge received an offer to work for the *New York Times*. The *Times* was not the dominant New York paper at that time. In fact, it ranked fourth in circulation for New York papers, but New York was the newspaper capital of the world. Catledge accepted the offer, and in August 1929 he began his long career with the *Times*. Four months later he was back in Washington again as a correspondent. His reassignment to Washington allowed him to resume a courtship, and in 1931 he married Mildred Turpin. They had two children.

In January 1932 Catledge was promoted to chief Capitol correspondent. He followed Herbert Hoover's campaign during the 1932 presidential election and the campaign trail of Alfred Landon in 1936.

During President Franklin D. Roosevelt's administration, Catledge was responsible for sorting out the barrage of bills and new legislation coming through Congress as a result of the New Deal. One piece of legislation, known as the "court-packing" bill, was a challenge from the Roosevelt administration to the Supreme Court, which was consistently finding Roosevelt's New Deal programs unconstitutional. Catledge followed the bill for more than five and a half months, filing stories on its progress seven days a week from the inception of the bill until it was defeated in August 1937. Catledge and his fellow correspondent Joseph Allsop collected their writings and expanded them into a book titled *The 168 Days*.

In 1940 Catledge returned to presidential election coverage and followed Wendell Willkie's campaign. In October 1941 Catledge accepted an offer as Washington chief correspondent for Marshall Field's new paper, the *Chicago Sun*. A few months later he was named editor of the *Sun*. He never felt comfortable being editor of a city paper in a city he did not know, and in May 1943 he returned to the *New York Times* Washington bureau, this time as national correspondent. He covered the presidential campaign of Thomas E. Dewey in 1944. After the election he accompanied the *Times*'s publisher, Arthur Hays Sulzberger, on a five-week tour of the Pacific theater of the war. At the conclusion of the trip, Sulzberger informed Catledge that he would not be returning to Washington; instead, he was to be the new assistant managing editor of the *Times*. After thirteen years with the *New York Times*, Catledge had spent only four months in the New York offices.

Catledge immediately began implementing changes at the *Times*, while he expanded the role of the assistant managing editor. He instituted meetings between shift editors to coordinate decisions; changed reporters' assignments to cover news topically rather than along geographical bounds; and limited the news dependency from Washington, D.C., while expanding national reporting.

In May 1951 Catledge was promoted to executive managing editor, and in December 1951 he became managing editor. Catledge recognized that under the leadership of previous managing editors the *Times* had grown in recognition and prestige, but he saw that administratively there were numerous problems. He organized meetings and communication channels to resolve such difficulties. He maintained a strong working relationship with Sulzberger throughout the reorganization. Catledge worked to fill positions with strong managers and talented editors. Among those promoted by Catledge were Harrison Salisbury, James "Scotty" Reston, and Abe Rosenthal. In early 1958 Catledge was divorced, and he married Abby Ray Izard on 19 February 1958. They had no children.

On 1 September 1964 Catledge was promoted to executive editor. During his tenure he continued to build the *Times* as a prestigious paper, and on 1 June 1968 he became vice president of the New York Times Company. He resigned a year and a half later and worked on publishing a semiautobiographical book, *My Life and the Times*, which was published in 1971. He remained on the board of directors of the New York Times Company until 1973. Catledge died in New Orleans, Louisiana.

• Sources on Catledge include Meyer Burger, *The Story of the New York Times, 1851–1951* (1951); Gay Talese, *The Kingdom and the Power* (1969); and Harrison Salisbury, *Without Fear or Favor: The New York Times and its Times* (1980). An obituary is in the *New York Times*, 28 Apr. 1983.

EDWARD E. ADAMS

CATLETT, Big Sid (17 Jan. 1910–25 Mar. 1951), drummer, was born Sidney Catlett in Evansville, Indiana, the son of John B. Catlett, a chauffeur. His mother (name unknown) was a cook. He briefly studied piano before playing drums in school, an activity he continued at Tilden Technical High School after the family moved to Chicago. There he studied under theater orchestra drummer Joe Russek. He worked with lesser-known bands and on occasion substituted for Zutty Singleton in Carroll Dickerson's band, which included Louis Armstrong, at the Savoy in 1928. Late that year he joined Sammy Stewart's orchestra at the Michigan Theater. In 1930 the band toured from Chicago to New York, picking up tenor saxophonist Leon "Chu" Berry along the way. Catlett left Stewart in New York and began working with banjoist Elmer Snowden at Smalls' Paradise. He joined Benny Carter's big band, recording in June 1932 and then playing in New York. Carter, moving from the leader's position into the saxophone section, allowed Fletcher Henderson to lead the band from December 1932 to January 1933. Catlett remained associated with Carter in 1933, including recordings under Spike Hughes's leadership, in an eight-piece group known as the Chocolate Dandies, and under Carter's name ("Symphony in Riffs").

Catlett played in Rex Stewart's big band at the Empire Ballroom from summer 1933 to autumn 1934, during which time he recorded four titles with Eddie Condon, including "The Eel." He joined Sam Wooding's dance orchestra briefly and then McKinney's Cotton Pickers (1934–1935). In Chicago he again played with lesser-known groups and led his own sextet at the Stables in 1935. He joined the big bands of Jeter-Pillars in St. Louis (1935?–1936), Henderson at the Grand Terrace Ballroom in Chicago (Mar.–mid-July 1936), Don Redman (fall 1936–late 1938), and Armstrong (late 1938–spring 1941). In November 1938 he recorded with Roy Eldridge in Berry's quartet, contributing a solo on "Forty-six West Fifty-two." Around 1939 he also played on Sundays with Jelly Roll Morton's band at Nick's in New York. He made recordings intermittently with Sidney Bechet (1939–1941), including "Old Man Blues," on which, paying homage to Duke Ellington, he played a passage on tom-tom drums (1940). He participated in Carter's reincarnation of the Chocolate Dandies—this time as a sextet with Eldridge and Coleman Hawkins—for their finest session of 25 May 1940, including "I Can't Believe That You're in Love with Me" (the master take). According to Stewart, at some point, perhaps during this period in New York, Catlett became the favorite drummer for chorus girls at the Apollo Theatre, owing to his sensitivity in accompanying dancing.

After a short stay with Eldridge's big band, he joined Benny Goodman (mid-1941–Oct. 1941); among his recordings with Goodman is "The Count."

He returned to Armstrong's big band (Nov. 1941–summer 1942) and then played in New York with Teddy Wilson's small group (c. Aug. 1942–early 1944). Except for a brief attempt to establish a big band late in 1946, he led small swing groups from 1944 into 1947 at jazz clubs on Fifty-second Street in New York, at the Streets of Paris in Hollywood, and in Chicago, Detroit, and other cities. Ben Webster often worked as his sideman, and from this association came an acclaimed recording session in March 1944, with Catlett soloing on "Sleep." According to Mary Lou Williams, while leading at the Three Deuces in New York, probably in the mid-1940s, Catlett got into an argument with the band and temporarily fired them all, then successfully played the night as a soloist, an unusual feat for a drummer of that era and a testimony to his musicality.

As a freelance musician he recorded "Afternoon of a Basie-ite" with Lester Young at the end of 1943. He was featured in the film *Jammin' the Blues* (1944). He participated in one of the first studio sessions in the new bebop style, recording "Salt Peanuts" and "Shaw Nuff" with Charlie Parker under Dizzy Gillespie's leadership (May 1945); his usual deft cymbal work and penetrating, irregular snare and bass drum accents fit in perfectly. Another reincarnation of Carter's Chocolate Dandies in August 1946, in a group including Webster and Buck Clayton, found Catlett drumming forcefully on "Cadillac Slim" and revealing a hidden talent by singing a ballad, "Out of My Way," in a clear-toned, full, handsome baritone.

Catlett starred in a concert with Armstrong in February 1947 at Carnegie Hall in which he was particularly showcased on "Tiger Rag." The success of the concert was one factor leading to the formation of Armstrong's All Stars, with Catlett as one of its founding members, in August of that year. The group performed at the jazz festival in Nice, France, in 1948, and unusually for Catlett, who was widely regarded as one of the most tasteful accompanists in jazz, he was publicly criticized by Armstrong for drumming overexuberantly.

Catlett had to retire from the group because of heart and kidney ailments in April 1949, returning to his father's home in Chicago. One month later he was working with Eddie Condon in New York on NBC television and in the recording studio. Back in Chicago he became the house drummer at Jazz, Ltd., playing traditional jazz and dixieland with Bechet, Miff Mole, Georg Brunis, and Muggsy Spanier. During this period he and his wife, Gladys (maiden name and marriage date unknown), had their son, Sid Catlett, Jr. (later a basketball star at the University of Notre Dame). Early in 1951 Catlett contracted pneumonia. He was apparently recovering when he suffered a fatal heart attack while attending a jazz concert at Chicago's Opera House.

Catlett was a superb showman who twirled, threw, and caught the drumsticks and who walked around playing from odd angles or keeping the beat on objects other than the drum set (including fellow musicians), without disrupting the rhythm. More significantly, he was one of the most precise and musical drummers of his era, comfortable playing in any of the prevailing styles or with any size of ensemble. Clarinetist Barney Bigard, who played with Catlett in Armstrong's All Stars, reports, "He was just lovable. . . . He knew all the musicians and was real popular with them all. . . . When he took a solo it was like you could hear that melody line right through it all. . . . He was good for a soloist because he'd push you. He would never get in your way. . . . Sid . . . was one of the best time keepers. Just fantastic" (Bigard, pp. 106–7).

• Whitney Balliett gives a colorful description of Catlett's drumming style in "Big Sid," in *The Sound of Surprise* (1959), pp. 143–48. Summaries of his career are George Hoefer, "Big Sid," *Down Beat*, 24 Mar. 1966, pp. 26–29, which draws from an interview with Catlett in Aug. 1941 for *Music & Rhythm*; and Bill Esposito, "Big Sid Catlett," *Jazz Journal* 22 (May 1969): 10–11. Personal remembrances appear in Nat Shapiro and Nat Hentoff, eds., *Hear Me Talkin' to Ya: The Story of Jazz as Told by the Men Who Made It* (1955), pp. 363–64; Arnold Shaw, *The Street That Never Slept* (1971; repr. as *52nd Street: The Street of Jazz* [1977]), including Mary Lou Williams's reminiscence; Rex Stewart, "My Man, Big Sid (Sidney Catlett)," in *Jazz Masters of the Thirties* (1972), pp. 160–67; Balliett, "Big Sid," in *Improvising: Sixteen Jazz Musicians and Their Art* (1977), pp. 139–50, which has further colorful descriptions of his drumming (repr. in *American Musicians: Fifty-six Portraits in Jazz* [1986], pp. 179–87); Stanley Dance, *The World of Earl Hines* (1977); Barney Bigard, *With Louis and the Duke: The Autobiography of a Jazz Clarinetist*, ed. Barry Martyn (1985); and D. Russell Connor, *Benny Goodman: Listen to His Legacy* (1988), pp. 122–28. Many of these reminiscences are collected, with greater detail added, in Burt Korall, *Drummin' Men: The Heartbeat of Jazz: The Swing Years* (1990), pp. 163–203. Further details of his various affiliations are scattered through Walter C. Allen, *Hendersonia: The Music of Fletcher Henderson and His Musicians: A Bio-Discography* (1973); Dance, *The World of Swing* (1974); Albert McCarthy, *Big Band Jazz* (1974); Morroe Berger et al., *Benny Carter: A Life in American Music* (1982); and Gunther Schuller, *The Swing Era: The Development of Jazz, 1930–1945* (1989). An obituary is in the *New York Times*, 27 Mar. 1951.

BARRY KERNFELD

CATLETT, Walter L. (4 Feb. 1889–14 Nov. 1960), actor, was born in San Francisco, California, the son of George C. Catlett, a banker, and Mary Noonan. He studied history at St. Ignatius College in San Francisco (later the University of San Francisco), but he did not graduate. He made his theatrical debut in San Francisco in *Brownies in Fairyland* (1906). After further roles in San Francisco and Los Angeles, in 1907 Catlett joined a touring stock company run by Denis O'Sullivan. In 1908 he toured with McKee Rankin and Nance O'Neil's troupe. He claimed to have played 104 different roles during these two years.

Following a season with the Columbia Minstrels, Catlett made his Broadway debut in 1911 in *The Prince of Pilsen*, an English operetta. For the next two years he toured in similar shows, *Madame Sherry* and *The Red Rose*. By the time he appeared at the Shubert Theater in *So Long, Letty* (1916), the American musical comedy that made Charlotte Greenwood a star, the wiry Catlett had established himself as a brisk, smooth supporting comic.

Catlett played sketches in the Ziegfeld Follies of 1917. After three more American musical comedies, in 1919 he joined the post–World War I American invasion of Britain in Nat Ayer and Clifford Grey's *Baby Bunting*. As William Pye, the jaunty bookkeeper in Bunny Bunting's Soeesi Furnishing Company, Catlett was entrusted with cynical, slangy lyrics such as these to newborns in general: "If you're a boy, you'll have to try and earn your living / If you're a girl, you needn't save a blessed sou; / If you're a boy, you'll have to work to keep a fam'ly / If you're a girl, you'll kid some boob to work for you."

After a tour of *Keyhole Kameos*, Catlett returned to New York City for composer Jerome Kern's *Sally* (1920), as the first of many slick theatrical agents, Otis Hooper, passing off a dishwasher as a leading lady and singing the charming P. G. Wodehouse lyric to "The Little Church around the Corner." *Sally* ran for 570 performances. After the short-lived Kern musical comedy *Dear Sir* (1924), in which he was praised for his brash comedy, Catlett became J. Watterson (Watty) Watkins, a garrulous lawyer spouting the snappy patter of librettists Guy Bolton and Fred Thompson in the Gershwins' first Broadway hit, *Lady, Be Good!* (1924). A man perfectly willing to represent both sides in a lawsuit, Watty introduced the peppy title song.

During the run of *Lady, Be Good!* Catlett began his film career, supporting Alfred Lunt and Lynne Fontanne in *Second Youth* (1924). After an engagement in San Francisco, Catlett played a flirting husband in the film *Summer Bachelors* (1926). Back on Broadway in 1927, he appeared in the failed musical comedy *Lucky* and the hit *Rio Rita*. Catlett created the first of his medicine show barkers in the 1927 film *The Music Master*.

After two more 1928 musicals, *Here's Howe* and the Gershwins' puzzling flop *Treasure Girl*, Catlett joined the Broadway exodus to all-talking, all-singing, all-dancing Hollywood. After three 1929 films, including *Happy Days*, as the interlocutor of a Mississippi riverboat show, Catlett considered directing a series of comedy shorts for RKO, but Fox Studios' character parts proved more to his liking.

Catlett's adroit singing and dancing were rarely utilized in film. Instead, he became known for his comic portrayals of insecure, fast-talking types—promoters, producers, managers, agents, newspapermen. He was a Hollywood director in *Let's Go Places* (1930). In 1931 he was twice a newspaper hack. Among eight 1932 films were Howard Hughes's *The Cock of the Air*, as Col. Benjamin Wallace, a comic airman distracted by femme fatale Billie Dove, and *The Sport Parade*, as a shifty wrestling manager double-crossed by his conscience-stricken client. As Ned Flynn in *Arizona to Broadway* (1933), he impersonated real-life reigning comic Ed Wynn.

By 1934 Catlett was a freelancer much in demand. In *The Affair of Susan* (1935), he played a drunk who inadvertently advanced the course of true love. Departing from type, he was the villainous informer Barsad in the Metro-Goldwyn-Mayer production of *A Tale of Two Cities* (1935). Although he played a substantial role as Warfield Scott, the philandering photographer, in *Banjo on My Knee* (1936), Catlett increasingly specialized in cameo roles—dominating a single comic scene that twists the plot. In director Frank Capra's *Mr. Deeds Goes to Town* (1936), he was a sneering poet who got the naive hero, Gary Cooper, into trouble by conning him into a drunken binge.

Though Catlett played in film musicals, he was always in secondary roles. In *On the Avenue* (1937), he played Dibble, a blustery revue producer, and for Warner Brothers' *Varsity Show* (1937), Professor Sylvester Biddle, the pompous director of a college variety show who temporarily blocks the students from taking it to Broadway.

Perhaps Catlett's most memorable role was the fidgety Constable Slocum in director Howard Hawks's *Bringing Up Baby* (1938). A master of rapid-fire crosstalk and doubletake, in the climactic jailhouse scene Catlett helped whip this screwball comedy to its pitch of lunacy. In the same year's *Going Places* he played a sporting goods salesman involved with a horse named Jeepers Creepers that could not win unless the Johnny Mercer song of that name was being played.

Supporting such disparate stars as Mae West, Bert Lahr, and Deanna Durbin in 1939–1940, Catlett claimed a further film immortality in Walt Disney's comedy *Pinocchio* (1940), as the voice of the fox J. Worthington Foulfellow who, singing "Hi, Diddle-Dee-Dee, an Actor's Life for Me," lured the puppet-made-boy into a life of debauchery.

Though there were exceptions—the George M. Cohan biography, *Yankee Doodle Dandy* (1942), and comedian Danny Kaye's first film, *Up in Arms* (1944)—the overall quality, though not the quantity, of Catlett's films declined throughout the 1940s and early 1950s. Working at smaller studios such as Monogram, he supported the Andrews Sisters, ice skaters Belita and Vera Hruba Ralston, hillbilly comic Judy Canova, and anarchistic comics Olsen and Johnson. His one starring role came as a medicine man in a B-movie, *My Gal Loves Music* (1943).

Catlett made a sort of comeback in *Beau James* (1957), the biography of former New York City mayor Jimmy Walker. Supporting Bob Hope, Catlett was sharp and funny as New York governor and presidential candidate Al Smith. He was married three times—to Zanetta Watrous, Ruth Verney, and Kathlene Martin (or Martyn)—and he had one child. Catlett was a lifelong gambler who, according to *Variety*, never had much money in his bank account and once bet his false teeth (valued at $350) in a poker game (he won). Catlett died in the Motion Picture Country Home and Hospital in Woodland Hills, California.

• Aside from his films themselves and their useful description in the catalogs of the American Film Institute, Catlett's quality is best glimpsed in such biographies as Gerald Bordman, *Jerome Kern* (1980), and Edward Jablonski, *Gershwin* (1987), and discussions of individual shows such as Stanley Green, *Broadway Musicals, Show by Show* (1985). Information regarding Catlett's brief British career is available in the files of the Theatre Museum, London. An affectionate obituary is in *Variety*, 16 Nov. 1960.

JAMES ROSS MOORE

CATLIN, George (26 July 1796–23 Dec. 1872), artist, was born in Wilkes-Barre, Pennsylvania, the son of Putnam Catlin, a lawyer, farmer, and minor office-holder, and Polly Sutton. Catlin grew up in northwestern Pennsylvania and Broome County, New York. He entered law school in Litchfield, Connecticut, in July 1817, and the next year he was admitted to the bar in Connecticut and Pennsylvania.

Catlin abandoned his law practice within a few years, sold his law books, and in 1821 moved to Philadelphia, determined to make his mark as an artist. He had dabbled as a painter in the past, but now art became his profession. He brought to it an unquenchable romanticism and at most, a rudimentary talent. Catlin specialized in miniatures (those of some of his family members show him to advantage), exhibited regularly, and became a member of the Pennsylvania Academy of the Fine Arts in 1824. But portraiture was dull, and miniatures were inadequate to the scope of his ambition. Catlin was already nurturing the idea of becoming a historical painter when he moved to New York in 1827, the year after he was elected a member of the newly founded National Academy of Design.

In 1828 Catlin married Clara Gregory, the daughter of a prominent Albany family. Recognition had already come his way with a commission from the New York Common Council to paint a full-length portrait of Governor DeWitt Clinton (City Hall, N.Y.). Modest success was in the offing, but Catlin was still restless, still in search of an animating purpose for his life and art. He found it, he recalled, when he spotted a delegation of western American Indians on a visit to Philadelphia: their appearance captivated him, and he resolved to paint Indians, "thus snatching from a hasty oblivion what could be saved for the benefit of posterity, and perpetuating it, as a fair and just monument, to the memory of a truly lofty and noble race" (*Letters and Notes*, vol. 1, p. 3). Realism was never Catlin's strong suit. He was a dreamer, wildly impractical, and a driven man beset by contrary impulses, at once exploitive and tenderhearted, negligent and loving, self-centered and altruistic. His stated goal was to win fame and fortune by creating an Indian Gallery. Confident his endeavor would command public support, in the spring of 1830 he moved to Saint Louis, Missouri, to launch his career as a painter of Indians.

Catlin polished his artistic skills on visiting members of various tribes (he was good at painting faces but weak at anatomy), and then he boarded a steamboat on 26 March 1832 for the 1,800-mile trip up the Missouri River to Fort Union, in the heart of Indian country. He painted Blackfeet, Crow, and all the river tribes, concentrating on the Mandan, whose devastation by smallpox five years later confirmed the importance of his visionary enterprise. Subsequently he toured the southern plains (1834), the Mississippi River and the Great Lakes region (1835), and the sacred red pipestone quarry on the Coteau des Prairies (1836). He described his travels in letters to the newspapers, which were collected in his 1841 classic *Letters and Notes on the Manners, Customs, and Conditions of the North American Indians*, and between trips he exhibited his growing collection of Indian paintings to help cover expenses.

Catlin's Indian Gallery was a novelty. Artists before him had painted Indian dignitaries visiting in Washington, D.C., or had portrayed them in council with American officials in the field. Catlin's claim to originality turned on the nature and extent of his coverage. Besides more than 300 portraits of men and women from some fifty tribes, he displayed 200 paintings of Indians on their own turf, going about their everyday activities. His catalogs and advertising emphasized these "beautiful Landscapes of the Prairies of the 'Far West'—Views of Indian villages—Dances, Sports and Amusements" (*New York Morning Herald*, 27 Nov. 1837). He rightfully insisted that he was the first artist to offer the world a representative picture of Indian life based on personal observation. Though he described his paintings in his 1837 catalog as "rather as *fac similes* of what he has seen, than as finished works of art" (p. 36), his best portraits (*Black Hawk*, *Buffalo Bull*, *Red Bear*, *Mint*, *Mountain of Rocks*, *Sky-se-ro-ka*, *Osceola*, and *Little Wolf*, for example) show people, not romantic stereotypes, and the ethnographic value of his work has only appreciated with the passage of time.

Catlin formed his Indian Gallery without government patronage, but he turned to Congress in May 1838 confident it would reward his enterprise by purchasing his collection. Frustrated in this hope, he nevertheless became a regular supplicant, petitioning Congress with an urgency that mounted with his debts. Certain he would find a more receptive audience in Europe, he moved to England in November 1839. After touring his gallery throughout Great Britain, he took his collection in April 1845 to Paris, where he was entertained by King Louis-Philippe. But fame never translated into fortune for Catlin, and in 1848, fleeing ahead of a revolution that swept Louis-Philippe off the throne, he returned to London with his three daughters; his wife and only son had died during his stay in France. His gallery was no longer a novelty in England, and though a book recounting his experiences abroad (*Notes of Eight Years' Travels and Residence in Europe, with His North American Indian Collection* [1848]), lectures, and American emigration schemes kept his name before the British public, Catlin continued to slide toward financial ruin. His 1852 appeal to the U.S. Congress—his fifth in seven years—was thus a desperate one. "My Collection is in the hands of and at the mercy of, my creditors," he wrote Daniel Webster, "I have not the power to save it—but the Congress of My Country has, provided their action is quick" (15 Apr. 1852, Webster papers). Congress rejected Catlin's latest plea for purchase, and his life's work was lost to his creditors.

Bereft of his Indian Gallery, Catlin entered a period of obscurity and frequent despair, punctuated by three trips to South America in the 1850s that are still shrouded in mystery (his primary motive may have been a search for precious minerals). He lived by his wits, selling compilations ("albums unique") of pencil outlines previously copied from his Indian portraits and publishing two successful children's books recounting his travels, *Life amongst the Indians* (1861) and *Last Rambles amongst the Indians of the Rocky Mountains and the Andes* (1867). He wrote a quirky self-help manual that was an unlikely popular success, *The Breath of Life; or, Mal-Respiration* (1861); a book defending his Mandan studies against charges of inaccuracy, *O-Kee-Pa: A Religious Ceremony; and Other Customs of the Mandans* (1867); and another advancing a theory of geological catastrophe in the creation of the Western Hemisphere, *The Lifted and Subsided Rocks of America* (1870). He also painted a second Indian gallery, a group of 600 "cartoons," half recapitulating his original collection, the rest showing Indians of the Northwest Coast and South America, which he exhibited in Brussels in 1870. The next year, after an absence of more than three decades, he returned to America and showed his Cartoon Collection in New York and in February 1872, at the invitation of the Smithsonian Institution, in Washington, D.C. That May he petitioned Congress to purchase his original gallery, thereby allowing him to redeem it from storage in Philadelphia, where his principal creditor resided. Congress had taken no action before Catlin died in Jersey City, his daughters by his side.

Amazingly, Catlin's two Indian collections have survived in Washington largely intact, the Indian Gallery owned by the National Museum of American Art and the Cartoon Collection owned by the National Gallery of Art. They attest to Catlin's peculiar genius. He had set out to show "a vast country of green fields, where the *men* are all *red*" (*Letters and Notes*, vol. 1, p. 59). In paintings sometimes naive and awkward, sometimes poignant and profound, he fashioned the prism through which Americans still view a vanished world.

• The Catlin papers are scattered. The Smithsonian Institution holds an important collection that is readily accessible in the Archives of American Art microfilm series, rolls 2136–37. The principal family collection is in the Bancroft Library, University of California, Berkeley, and has been published in Marjorie Catlin Roehm, *The Letters of George Catlin and His Family: A Chronicle of the American West* (1966). Some of his letters are in the Daniel Webster Papers at Morristown National Historical Park, Morristown, N.J. Besides his own books, the most useful works on Catlin are Thomas Donaldson's huge compilation *The George Catlin Indian Gallery in the U.S. National Museum (Smithsonian Institution) with Memoir and Statistics, Annual Report, Smithsonian Institution, 1885*, pt. 2 (1886); John C. Ewers, "George Catlin: Painter of Indians of the West," *Annual Report, Smithsonian Institution, 1955* (1955); Harold McCracken, *George Catlin and the Old Frontier* (1959); and William H. Truettner's masterly *The Natural Man Observed: A Study of Catlin's Indian Gallery* (1979). Brian W. Dippie, *Catlin and His Contemporaries: The Politics of Patronage* (1990), examines Catlin's unsuccessful quest for patronage and places the artist in a broad historical context. Helpful for understanding Catlin's artistic goals is Joan Carpenter Troccoli, *First Artist of the West: George Catlin Paintings and Watercolors* (1993). For a compilation of Catlin's paintings and writings from the 1850s, see Marvin C. Ross, *George Catlin: Episodes from Life among the Indians and Last Rambles* (1959). For an entire "album unique" in facsimile, see Peter Hassrick's edition of George Catlin, *Drawings of the North American Indian* (1984), and for a case study in Catlin's South American rambles, see Edgardo Carlos Krebs, "George Catlin and South America: A Look at His 'Lost' Years and His Paintings of Northeastern Argentina," *American Art Journal* 22, no. 4 (1990): 4–39.

BRIAN W. DIPPIE

CATRON, John (1781?–30 May 1865), lawyer and Supreme Court justice, was born according to some accounts in Pennsylvania, and according to others in Virginia. The year of his birth is variously given between 1778 and 1787, although his niece reported that before he died Catron told his family he was born in 1781. Nothing is known of his parents. His early life was spent in Virginia. He later moved to Kentucky and then to Tennessee, where in 1807 he married Matilda Childress of Nashville. They had no children.

Catron studied law in 1812 with attorney George W. Gibbs. He served under Andrew Jackson in the conflict against the Creek Indians and, according to some sources, in the War of 1812 at the Battle of New Orleans. He was admitted to the bar in 1815. He worked as a local prosecutor and later moved to Nashville, where he built a large private practice.

Catron was elected by the state legislature to the Tennessee Supreme Court of Errors and Appeals in 1824 and was selected as the court's first chief justice, serving from 1831 to 1834. He was an expert on disputed land titles and favored rules that would give stability to existing titles. In an early case disbarring a lawyer for killing another lawyer in a duel, he wrote a strong opinion condemning dueling as murder. In another early case, he denounced any form of gambling.

Catron's opinion in *Cornet v. Winton* (1826) contained positive statements concerning Cherokee civilization and self-government, but he later supported and justified President Jackson's policy against Native Americans. He authored an opinion in *State v. Foreman* (1835) vindicating Jackson's policy and attempting to bring before the U.S. Supreme Court a case that would provide an opportunity for overruling *Worcester v. Georgia* (1832). In *Foreman*, Catron held that the state government, not the national government, was the "controlling authority" in Indian matters. He agreed with Jackson that a national bank was unconstitutional and supported Jackson in his stand against the South Carolina Nullification Ordinance of 1832. Perhaps recalling the bitterness of Tennessee politics at a time when Catron was an ardent supporter of Jackson, an article in 1893 referred to Catron as "a most intense partisan" and "one of the best-hated men of his day."

From 1827 to 1833 Catron was one of three partners in the profitable Buffalo Iron Works, based near Nashville. He returned to private practice in Nashville in 1834, when the Court of Errors and Appeals was abolished. He supported Martin Van Buren's 1836 presidential campaign in Tennessee.

President Jackson appointed Catron to the U.S. Supreme Court in 1837. He is generally considered to have been an unexceptional justice. He was assigned to the Eighth Circuit, which consisted of Kentucky, Tennessee, and Missouri (1837–1861), and later to the Sixth Circuit, which consisted of Kentucky, Tennessee, Louisiana, Arkansas, and Texas (1862–1865). Only one of his circuit opinions was officially published. As a justice, he authored 157 majority opinions, twelve concurring opinions, and twenty-six dissents.

The best-known case in which Catron played a prominent role was *Dred Scott v. John F. A. Sanford* (1857). Catron, himself a slaveholder, had written early opinions narrowly construing the rights of slaveholders when he was a Supreme Court justice in Tennessee. He later construed state statutes authorizing the freeing of slaves narrowly and referred to free African Americans in Tennessee as living "without motive and without hope" in *Fisher's Negros v. Dabbs*. Nonetheless, he was not as extreme as some: in 1860 he publicly denounced a proposal introduced in the Tennessee legislature to enslave all free blacks.

Catron had joined in the Supreme Court's opinions enforcing the fugitive slave acts of 1793 and 1850. In his separate opinion in *Dred Scott*, he did not join Chief Justice Taney's opinion asserting that African Americans could never be citizens; rather, he held that this matter was not properly before the court. Privately, Catron had once expressed the opinion that slavery could be prohibited in U.S. territories. In his separate opinion in *Dred Scott*, however, he found that the Treaty of 1803, under which the United States acquired the Louisiana Purchase, guaranteed the right of slavery and therefore prohibited the Missouri Compromise of 1820. He also suggested that the Missouri Compromise (which admitted Missouri as a slave state but barred slavery from new territories north of a stated latitude) was prohibited by the principles of equality of rights among the states and equality of citizens under the "privileges and immunities" clause of Article Four of the U.S. Constitution.

During the pendency of the *Dred Scott* decision, Catron wrote to ask President James Buchanan to lobby fellow Pennsylvanian and Democrat Justice Robert Grier to vote with the Taney majority. Later he disclosed the nature of the decision to the President before it was announced. Catron even drafted a statement that President Buchanan could use in his inaugural address, asking the public to abide by whatever decision the Supreme Court rendered in *Dred Scott*. Buchanan therefore knew the outcome of the case when he asked the public to follow the Supreme Court's decision, no matter what the outcome.

Many historians mitigate Catron's actions in disclosing the decision in *Dred Scott* by documenting similar incidents of disclosure of confidential information by other justices and by noting Catron's close relationships with most of the vice presidents and presidents of his time. In 1835, when sitting on the Tennessee Supreme Court, he sent a copy of one of his opinions to Martin Van Buren. He was a frequent correspondent of Jackson, Polk, and Buchanan. He gave President Benjamin Pierce early warning of the outcome in the Wheeling Bridge Case in 1852. But even if the sharing of the results of the decision was justified, this would not excuse the solicitation of Buchanan's help to influence Grier's vote.

During the Civil War Catron remained loyal to the Union. On his return to Nashville in 1860, there were threats against his life, and he was advised to leave the area for safety. His property, valued at approximately one hundred thousand dollars, was later confiscated by Confederate authorities. Unlike Chief Justice Taney, he did not use the writ of habeas corpus to interfere with the war effort. As a circuit judge he upheld the constitutionality of the Federal Confiscation Act, which provided for the confiscation of property, including slaves, of those engaged in the rebellion. In the *Prize Cases* (1863), however, Catron joined Justice Nelson's dissenting opinion, indicating that the president could not close or blockade Southern ports without the authorization of Congress.

Catron was able to return to Tennessee again to hold court in Nashville. He died there soon afterward.

• Some of Catron's letters are in the John McLean, Andrew Jackson, and James Polk manuscript collections of the Library of Congress. The Tennessee State Library and Archives contains twelve items in its collection of John Catron Papers. His Tennessee decisions are reported in *Yerger's Reports*. His one reported circuit court opinion is *In re Klein*, 14 Federal Cases 716, no. 7, 865 (C.C.D.Mo. 1843). His Supreme Court opinions are in the *United States Reports*. Biographical sketches appear in Bicentennial Committee of the Judicial Conference of the United States, *History of the Sixth Circuit* (1976), pp. 52–53; Leon Friedman and Fred L. Israel, eds., *The Justices of the United States Supreme Court*, vol. 1 (1969), p. 737; Elder Witt, *Congressional Quarterly's Guide to the U.S. Supreme Court* (2d ed., 1989); Albert, D. Marks, "The Supreme Court of Tennessee," *Green Bag* 5 (1893): 127; Walter Chandles, *The Centenary of Associate Justice John Catron of the United States Supreme Court* (1937); and Henry H. Ingersoll, "John Catron," in *Great American Lawyers*, ed. William D. Lewis, vol. 4 (1908), p. 264. Statistical information is found in Albert P. Blaustein and Roy M. Mersky, *The First One Hundred Justices* (1978). An account of the Supreme Court in Catron's time is Carl B. Swisher, *History of the Supreme Court of the United States*, vol. 5 (1974). For the *Dred Scott* case, see Don Fehrenbacher, *Dred Scott* (1978), and Kenneth M. Stampp, *America in 1857* (1990). An obituary is in the *New York Times*, 10 Dec. 1865.

RICHARD L. AYNES

CATRON, Thomas Benton (6 Oct. 1840–15 May 1921), U.S. senator and New Mexico territorial politician, was born near Lexington, Missouri, the son of John Catron and Mary Fletcher, farmers. Thomas Catron graduated from the University of Missouri in July 1860 and had just begun to read law when the Civil War broke out. Two months after Fort Sumter, he joined a Confederate infantry brigade that experienced frequent action throughout the war, including participation in the battle of Vicksburg.

Paroled out of the army in 1865, Catron quickly realized that loyalty to the Democratic party would only hamper any future political career. The first Reconstruction legislature in Missouri sealed his fate by prohibiting ex-rebels from practicing law. As a result, young Catron lit out for New Mexico Territory, lured by a college friend, Stephen B. Elkins, who wrote often that talented lawyers there were few and far between. Catron studied Spanish along the way, since New Mexico had only been ceded to the United States by Mexico in 1846, and legal documents were predominantly written in that language. He arrived in Santa Fe in July 1866. On 1 June 1867 Catron was named district attorney for the Third Judicial District but was not admitted to the bar until 15 June. In similar fashion, Catron became territorial attorney general on 12 January 1869 and one day later was admitted to practice law before the New Mexico Supreme Court.

Catron arrived with two wagonloads of flour, which he sold for $10,000. He used this nest egg, his Santa Fe law practice with Elkins, and his official offices to accumulate a land empire that eventually equaled in size the states of Delaware and Rhode Island combined. Catron and Elkins invested in and soon controlled the First National Bank of Santa Fe. They also procured interests in numerous New Mexico coal, copper, and gold mining operations.

Like many lawyers in New Mexico, Catron profited from the complex Spanish land grant situation and the lucrative government contracts awarded to ranchers to supply American Indian reservations and army posts. Before Mexican independence in 1821, Spain endowed some inhabitants with huge tracts of unsurveyed land. In 1848 the Treaty of Guadalupe Hidalgo granted citizenship to former Mexican citizens living within the borders of New Mexico and allowed them to retain their land. American lawyers often complicated the process of obtaining title under U.S. law, however, then took land and cattle in lieu of cash payments for services rendered. Catron was no exception. His involvement in ranching and government contracts also embroiled him in the notorious 1878 Lincoln County War, where two factions struggled to monopolize beef sales to Fort Stanton and the Mescalero Apache reservation. Catron held the mortgage on and acted as silent partner to the established group, and he used his position as attorney general to arrest challengers and entangle them in lengthy litigation.

Catron's growing wealth translated into political influence. New Mexico politics before 1866 was dominated by individuals, not parties, but since Republicans dominated Washington, D.C., after the war, they also controlled New Mexico's future. Allied with ranchers, bankers, and mine owners, Catron helped form a strong Republican party ruled by this loose coalition of wealth, dubbed "the Santa Fe Ring." Thus, Catron dominated New Mexico politics for the next fifty years and was generally acknowledged as "ring" boss. In 1877 Catron married Julia A. Walz; they had four children who survived infancy.

Catron served in the territorial legislature during the twenty-sixth, twenty-ninth, thirty-third, and thirty-sixth sessions and helped draft much of New Mexico's legal structure. He was elected to Congress for the 1895–1897 term as a nonvoting delegate. Increasingly verbal regarding statehood, he participated in an 1869–1870 bid to admit New Mexico as the state of Lincoln. Statehood, he believed, would only enhance economic development, and besides, Catron wanted to be New Mexico's first U.S. senator. Nevertheless, he opposed a 1904 bill proposing joint statehood with Arizona. When President William Howard Taft visited Albuquerque in 1909, Catron made a prostatehood speech at a dinner in his honor. Catron then journeyed to Washington to encourage passage of an enabling bill, which Taft signed on 20 June 1910, allowing New Mexico to call a constitutional convention. Although the convention was a typical rough and tumble political battle, the delegates wrote the only bilingual state constitution in the United States, and New Mexico was admitted to the Union in January 1912.

Catron was elected U.S. senator by the state legislature on 27 March 1912 and served until March 1917, when party infighting destroyed his bid for reelection. A conservative standpat Republican, Catron backed Taft over Theodore Roosevelt (1858–1919) in the 1912 election, supported a high protective tariff, favored military intervention into Mexico after 1913, and wholeheartedly criticized President Woodrow Wilson's World War I policies.

Catron's fortune and health declined after 1917, but when he died in Santa Fe, New Mexico, he had just asked the State Department for appointment as American minister to Chile. For over half a century, Catron was associated with the dirty politics and shady business practices of the Santa Fe Ring. His reputation, therefore, remains somewhat tarnished. A talented lawyer, he used his practice and judicial offices to amass wealth and solidify his political strength. Faced with a wide-open, anything goes frontier in 1866, Catron took full advantage.

Nevertheless, Catron's legacy is mixed. He helped develop the laws and legal structure of New Mexico, a composition that benefited Spanish-speaking and Anglo citizens alike. He worked diligently for statehood and became New Mexico's first U.S. senator, although perhaps overshadowed by fellow senator Albert Bacon Fall, who was later convicted in the Teapot Dome scandal. Catron accumulated the largest library in the Southwest, containing hundreds of rare manuscripts, which eventually went to the New Mexico Historical Society, and his law library was considered the best in New Mexico. He possessed a brilliant legal mind with an aggressive, resourceful personality to match and was undoubtedly the most powerful man in New Mexico during the second half of the nineteenth century.

• The University of New Mexico's Center for Southwest Research houses 325 boxes of Catron's personal papers, which include land title records, territorial and senatorship papers, New Mexico Supreme Court records, and correspondence. The only biography is Victor Westphall, *Thomas Benton Catron and His Era* (1973), which unfortunately dismisses negative aspects of Catron's life. Also see Vioalle C. Hefferan, "Thomas Benton Catron" (master's thesis, Univ. of New Mexico, 1940). Short sketches are in William A. Keleher, *The Fabulous Frontier: Twelve New Mexico Items* (1945); and Frederick Nolan, *The Lincoln County War, A Documentary History* (1992). Because the Lincoln County War has been so thoroughly explored, many sources offer extensive accounts of Catron's role. Most recent are the aforementioned Nolan, *Documentary History*; Joel Jacobsen, *Such Men as Billy the Kid: The Lincoln County War Reconsidered* (1994); and Robert M. Utley, *High Noon in Lincoln: Violence on the Western Frontier* (1987). Land grant involvement is detailed in Keleher, *The Maxwell Land Grant: A New Mexico Item* (1984); Charles L. Briggs and John R. Van Ness, *Land, Water and Culture: New Perspectives on Hispanic Land Grants* (1987); and Malcolm Ebright, *The Tierra Amarilla Grant: A History of Chicanery* (1993). For Catron's pursuit of statehood see Robert W. Larson, *New Mexico's Quest for Statehood, 1846–1912* (1968). For political scandals see Simeon H. Newman III, "The Santa Fe Ring: A Letter to the *New York Sun*," *Arizona and the West* 12, no. 3 (1970): 269–88. A good obituary is in the *Santa Fe New Mexican*, 16 May 1921.

KATHLEEN EGAN CHAMBERLAIN

CATT, Carrie Chapman (9 Feb. 1859–9 Mar. 1947), suffragist leader and peace activist, was born Carrie Clinton Lane in Ripon, Wisconsin, the daughter of Lucius Lane and Maria Clinton, farmers. In 1866 the family moved to a farm outside Charles City, Iowa, and Carrie thereafter identified herself as an Iowan. She was graduated from Iowa State Agricultural College (now Iowa State University) in 1880 with a B.S. She was a feminist long before she knew the word; at thirteen she was indignant when she realized that her mother could not vote in the presidential election. At college she organized a debate on woman suffrage and broke tradition by joining a public-speaking society. After graduation she read law for a year, then taught high school in Mason City, Iowa. She soon became the school's principal as well as the superintendent of schools. In these posts she developed her organizational and administrative talents. They were the keystones to her success as a leader of women for the next sixty years.

In 1885 she married Leo Chapman, editor of the weekly *Mason City Republican* and became coeditor of the paper. She instituted a feature called "Woman's World" in which she discussed woman's rights issues. During the November elections Leo Chapman alleged in an editorial that the County Auditor Henry Shepard, who was running for reelection, had been involved in some fraudulent county money manipulations. Shepard sued Chapman for criminal libel. His demurrer to the indictment was overruled, and his trial was set for March. The Chapmans sold the paper and left Mason City. Carrie stayed with her parents in Charles City while Leo sought work in San Francisco. Before he was settled he caught typhoid fever. Carrie was en route by train to be with him when she received word that he had died.

She stayed in San Francisco for a year, working as a freelance reporter, and started a career as a lecturer. Then she returned to Charles City where she continued to lecture and to write for (and occasionally edit) local newspapers. At this time she also joined the Woman's Christian Temperance Union, the only local organization interested in woman suffrage. The experience was valuable when she decided to devote her life to getting the franchise.

In October 1889 she attended the Iowa Woman Suffrage Association convention. She was elected state lecturer and organizer at a modest salary and within a few months had created ten new Political Equality Clubs. Her first national convention was the landmark 1890 meeting, which united the two leading organizations for votes for women. The movement had been divided by two strategies; Lucy Stone and Henry B. Blackwell favored winning the franchise state by state, whereas Susan B. Anthony and Elizabeth Cady Stanton were convinced that a constitutional amendment was the way. The new National American Woman Suffrage Association (NAWSA) recognized the necessity of using both approaches.

In Seattle in June 1890 Carrie Chapman married George Catt, an engineer whom she had known in college and met again in San Francisco. A brilliant and financially successful engineer, Catt supported his wife's work strongly and spoke occasionally at suffrage conventions himself. "We made a team to work for the cause," she often said.

Her first election campaign under NAWSA was in 1891 in South Dakota where she went with several other suffragists to gain support for a referendum to enfranchise women. The campaign was disastrous. It was poorly organized, full of petty rivalries, and rife with politicians who reneged on their promises of support. She talked and talked but only to the convinced and the voteless. It was hard and dispiriting work. She saw local politicians marking the ballots for recent immigrants to successfully defeat woman suffrage. It was a searing experience and intensified her conviction that floods of male immigrants from paternalistic cultures were imposing their prejudices on issues that could be determined only by an informed electorate of women and men.

In 1892 the Catts moved to New York. Carrie Catt increased her work for the NAWSA and strengthened it by her genius for organization and administration. She improved the local suffrage branches, started new ones, promoted new methods of work, and encouraged women to be active in the movement. She was a charismatic speaker with great stage presence and a well-modulated voice that could be heard in a hall or an outdoors meeting. Although many of her lectures and much of her writing in these early years reflected a xenophobic oversimplification that made scapegoats of immigrants, she developed diplomatically and politically as her experience grew.

The 1892 NAWSA convention was the real beginning of a transition in which new members with fresh ideas began to replace the old guard. Susan B. Anthony, the new president, was the most conspicuous survivor of the women who had begun and led the suffrage movement. Her first major change was to replace the old executive committee with a business committee headed by Catt, who was responsible for recruiting and educating suffragists through a network of organizer-lecturers. Catt hired the speakers, planned their trips, made local arrangements, and raised money. She wrote detailed instructions for starting suffrage clubs and maintaining enthusiasm in them and made suggestions for the conduct of the meetings and broad plans for future work. Catt was strong on detail but never entrapped by it; she always kept her broad vision of equal rights. She continued to revitalize local clubs and inspire fresh interest in suffrage while she was president of the NAWSA from 1900 until 1904. She resigned her office then because of George Catt's ill health. He died in 1905.

In 1893 a Congress of Representative Women of All Lands had opened the World's Columbian Exposition in Chicago. It was a turning point in Catt's life. There she saw women from twenty-seven countries representing more than a hundred organizations. She began thinking about an international organization of women that would strengthen them all by sharing their experiences and expertise. In 1902 she founded the International Woman Suffrage Alliance (IWSA) at a meeting in Washington, D.C. This was perhaps her greatest contribution to the woman's movement; it was singularly her own, accomplished in spite of opposition from her friend and mentor Susan B. Anthony. By 1904, when the IWSA met in Berlin, it had become an important and influential support for women throughout the Western world.

After her husband's death Catt continued her active national and international work for women, but her own health began to deteriorate. In 1911 she began a trip around the world. Ostensibly it was to rest, but in actuality it was to see for herself what women were doing in countries beyond the United States and Europe. In South Africa she and a friend and traveling companion, Aletta Jacobs, a Dutch physician, held meetings and organized suffrage conferences. She talked to women in Jerusalem, Egypt, India, Java, the Philippines, China, Japan, and Korea. She met intelligent women everywhere who were in sympathy with the woman's liberation movement although many of them had never heard of it as an organized process and had never heard it discussed. She saw children and women exploited by slave-like working conditions; at the other extreme she saw women members of the Assembly of Canton Province in session. Any lingering traces of jingoism were demolished on that trip, and she acknowledged that she no longer thought America had a monopoly on all that stood for progress. "This battle for equal justice is not for ourselves alone," she said, "but for the women of the entire world. Our cause is one."

Catt finished her trip in San Francisco in November 1912, when California women voted for the first time in a national election. Equal suffrage states by then numbered ten (each victory a struggle but up from four in 1896). Back in New York she resumed her work with new vigor and determination. In 1915 she again became head of the NAWSA and remained its president through the successful enactment of the Nineteenth Amendment in 1920.

During the last years of the fight for woman suffrage, the national movement again split into two factions. The women of the NAWSA sought the vote by constitutional means, winning it state by state while at the same time pressing Congress to enfranchise women nationally. Catt emphasized this two-pronged approach because she knew that ultimately the ratification of a constitutional amendment would depend on the approval of individual states. The more states with woman suffrage that could put pressure on their national representatives to ratify the federal bill, the greater were the chances of success. On the other hand, because it would be impossible to get every state to enfranchise women, the goal of national suffrage was necessary. This ambition required the cooperation of both major political parties, neither of which had an unsullied record of support for woman suffrage, but neither of which was completely opposed to it. Individuals in each party were helpful to the suffragists.

Seeking change by other means were women, led by Alice Paul, who thought the cause needed more visibility and media exposure. In 1913 Paul, who had chaired the congressional committee of the NAWSA, formed the Congressional Union (later the Woman's party). This group adopted the British policy of holding the party in power responsible and in 1917 began picketing the White House. They did not destroy property as their British counterparts did, but even mild demonstrations and peaceful picketing by women earned them the title "militant." Whether their actions helped or hindered the movement was a matter of opinion, but there was no question that the Woman's party made news and brought the cause publicity.

When the United States declared war on Germany in 1917, most of the women of the NAWSA agreed with their executive council to stand by the government and do what war work they could but at the same time continue suffrage work. Catt had been opposed to war all her life and in 1915 had been a cofounder with Jane Addams of the Woman's Peace party, but she was concerned that suffragists not be deflected from their primary cause. Catt was widely criticized for her decision. Pacifists accused her of selling out to the war machine, and antisuffragists accused her of not doing her share of war work. She followed her own conscience.

Suffrage work continued with a critical campaign in New York State, which Catt led through the New York Woman Suffrage party she had founded on her return from her worldwide trip. The state was crucial because there was no hope of any action on the federal amendment that war year. The last great suffrage parade was held in October in New York City; in November woman suffrage won. There were victories in six other states in 1917, and the number of presidential electors for whom women were entitled to vote had increased from 91 to 232. The way seemed open for the submission and passage of the federal amendment. A Woman Suffrage Committee was established in the House, and a new amendment resolution, which was introduced and sent to committee, reported favorably. The House approved it in January 1918, but the Senate dallied and finally turned it down in October and again in February 1919. Victory finally came in the next Congress, the House ratifying it in May and the Senate in June 1919. Detailed ratification plans had been in place for months, and on 26 August 1920 the Nineteenth Amendment became part of the Constitution.

The Fourteenth Amendment expressly specified that voters should be male. To get that word out had taken fifty-two years and, according to Catt's summation,

> fifty-six campaigns of referenda to male voters; 480 campaigns to urge Legislatures to submit suffrage amendments to voters; 47 campaigns to induce State constitutional conventions to write woman suffrage into State constitutions; 277 campaigns to persuade State party conventions to include woman suffrage planks; 30 campaigns to urge presidential party conventions to adopt woman suffrage planks in party platforms, and 19 campaigns with 19 successive Congresses.

It took three generations of women to conduct those 909 campaigns. Catt was a leader of the last two generations. The work of the NAWSA was finished, and the suffrage association became the League of Women Voters, dedicated to Catt's dream of an informed and active electorate. She thought the new organization should be run by younger women, and although she wrote and spoke for the league, she devoted her major efforts to working for peace.

In 1925 Catt organized the first annual Conference on the Cause and Cure of War, which she chaired. Now that women could vote, she claimed, they could be a political power; a large group of knowledgeable women who were determined to live in a peaceful world could have some influence. She especially wanted to reach women of good will who were as yet uncommitted to the peace movement. The initial conference had 450 delegates who represented five million women members of the nine sponsoring organizations. Many prominent men and women spoke, and the delegates were received by President Calvin Coolidge. Throughout the 1920s and 1930s, the Committee on the Cause and Cure of War lobbied for the World Court, the League of Nations, the Kellogg-Briand Pact, and other international solutions to conflict.

In the early 1930s Catt thought that the Committee on the Cause and Cure of War should disband because the conferences had been designed to educate many people for a few years, not to be perennial. However, although she resigned as chair in 1932 she continued her support until its dissolution in 1941. Many honors came to Catt in the last decades of her life. She died at her home in New Rochelle, New York.

Catt led women throughout the world as well as the United States in organizing to get universal suffrage, which she saw as an essential tool in achieving equal rights for women. When that goal was achieved in 1920 at home, she devoted her life to working for peace as the basis for human rights. Her unique contribution to the women's movement was her global view and her certainty that the world's people had to live equitably and peacefully together if the species were to survive. Her feminism was a worldwide revolt against all artificial barriers that laws and customs interpose between women and human freedom. The impact of her ideas and organization of women has continued to influence the lives of millions.

• Most of Catt's papers are in the Library of Congress, as are the records of the National American Woman Suffrage Association. The Sophia Smith Collection, Smith College; the Schlesinger Library, Radcliffe College; the State Historical Society, Des Moines, Iowa; and the Manuscript Division, New York Public Library, also have a significant amount of material. Other manuscripts are in dozens of libraries throughout the United States. Albert Krichmar, *The Women's Rights Movement in the United States 1848–1970*, is an excellent guide to sources. Catt was a prolific writer of articles and reports, many of which were published in *Woman's Journal*, *Jus Suffragii*, and other feminist publications as well as general readership magazines and papers. She wrote introductions to books and a chapter in *Why Wars Must Cease* (1935). With Nettie Rogers Shuler, she wrote *Woman Suffrage and Politics: The Inner Story of the Suffrage Movement* (1923). Biographies include Mary Gray Peck, *Carrie Chapman Catt* (1944); Robert B. Fowler, *Carrie Catt, Feminist Politician* (1986); and Jacqueline Van Voris, *Carrie Chapman Catt: A Public Life* (1987). Among the many obituaries are ones in the *New York Times* and the *New York Herald Tribune*, 10 Mar. 1947.

JACQUELINE VAN VORIS

CATTELL, James McKeen (25 May 1860–20 Jan. 1944), psychologist and editor, was born in Easton, Pennsylvania, the son of William C. Cattell, a Presbyterian minister and president of Lafayette College in Easton, and Elizabeth McKeen, the daughter of James McKeen, the college's most generous benefactor. Cattell grew up as the scion of Easton's leading family, and even as a student at Lafayette (A.B., 1880) he came to expect the deference of others. His family's closeness led him to study the ethics of Comtean positivism, which idealized the mother's sacrifice in childbirth as the model of all altruistic behavior. At Lafayette, the teaching of philologist Francis Andrew March—especially March's emphasis on the philosophy of Francis Bacon—impressed him. Cattell developed an approach to science that combined a Comtean emphasis on quantification with a Baconian appreciation for the hypothesis-free collection of empirical "facts" and the usefulness of science. Throughout his career he adopted methods that produced quantitative data about psychological phenomena, even if he often could not explain them.

Cattell studied for one semester each at the universities of Göttingen and Leipzig before his father won for him a fellowship at Johns Hopkins University in 1882. There Cattell timed simple mental processes, but he lost his fellowship the following year in part because he complained that Johns Hopkins president Daniel Coit Gilman had "not taken as much interest in me as he might have." He returned to Leipzig, where in 1886 he became the first American to earn a German Ph.D. with Wilhelm Wundt in the new experimental psychology. Cattell's first experiments extended his earlier work. He timed individuals' reading of letters and words and claimed that people naturally read whole words, rather than syllables. (This study led many later reading teachers to abandon phonics for the "whole-word" approach.) For his dissertation, he measured reaction times under varying conditions more precisely than had any previous investigator and, despite Wundt's preference, made no use of *innere Wahrnehmung* (often translated as "introspection"). These experiments thus emphasized their subjects' behavior and set a precedent that many later psychologists followed.

Unable to find a suitable American position, Cattell became a fellow-commoner at St. Johns College, Cambridge, England, in 1886. While there, he assimilated into his approach to science English polymath Francis Galton's concern for differences among individuals. Galton developed this concern into a program of positive eugenics that called for intelligent men and women to marry each other and have many children, and this idea resonated with Cattell's early experience. In 1888 he married Josephine Owen, an Englishwoman who had studied voice at the Mendelssohn Conservatory in Leipzig; they had seven children.

After assuming a professorship at the University of Pennsylvania in 1889, Cattell began two elaborate series of experiments. With biologist Charles S. Dolley, he extended his reaction-time studies in an attempt to measure the velocity of the nervous impulse. With philosopher George S. Fullerton, he reassessed standard psychophysical methods, whose proponents claimed that they measured the relation between physical stimulus and mental sensation. By arguing that these techniques really measured errors of observation, Cattell again emphasized his subjects' behavior over their mental activity.

Cattell moved to Columbia University in 1891, where he used standard laboratory procedures in the first self-identified program of "mental tests." These gathered quantitative data about individuals' reaction times, short-term memory, and the sensitivity of the senses and soon attracted much professional attention. But because Cattell and his collaborators never considered how these traits helped people live their lives, their tests produced no useful results, and psychologists soon abandoned them for more "functional" procedures. Despite this failure, Cattell continually urged his colleagues to apply their science to practical problems, and those who developed later tests and an explicitly applied psychology often emphasized Cattell's inspiration. In 1901 he became the first psychologist elected to the National Academy of Sciences.

From 1894 (when he founded the *Psychological Review* with Princeton colleague James Mark Baldwin), Cattell owned, edited, and eventually published many major scientific journals. These publications often had professional goals—the *Psychological Review* challenged Clark University president G. Stanley Hall's leadership of the American psychological community—but Cattell was usually more interested in their profitability. In late 1894 he took control of the failing weekly *Science*, which in 1900 became the official journal of the American Association for the Advancement of Science. This arrangement greatly increased AAAS membership, *Science*'s circulation, and Cattell's advertising income. Before 1920, he used *Science* to set the terms of and draw participants into debates over major policy issues. After 1915, *Science* emphasized serious discussions about support for scientific research. Attracted by a growing readership and a weekly publication schedule, many American scientists began to publish their best work in *Science*.

Taking over another failing journal, *Popular Science Monthly*, in 1900, Cattell used his editorship of *Science* to attract prominent contributors. (In 1915 he sold the journal's name but continued it as the *Scientific Monthly*.) In 1901 he established the Science Press to publish the newly acquired journal; it soon published all of his journals, and the demands of these activities gradually led Cattell to withdraw from laboratory work. In 1903 he began collecting data for what emerged in 1906 as the first edition of *American Men of Science*, a directory of the country's scientific workers. He also used these data in his studies of the psychology of scientific eminence, through which he identified the 1,000 most eminent American scientists. He repeated these procedures (with modifications) for the later *American Men of Science* editions that he oversaw. In 1904 he sold his share of the *Psychological Review* and in 1907 took over *American Naturalist*, which he initially hoped would encourage positive eugenics. Under the editorial guidance of Columbia colleague Thomas H. Morgan, however, the journal instead promoted Mendelian genetics. In 1915 Cattell founded *School and Society* to serve educators as *Science* served scientists. These publications, which he edited through the 1930s (and *Science* through the early 1940s), defined his position in the American scientific community.

Although American scientists respected Cattell's scientific and editorial achievements, they resented his often arrogant approach to others, and in 1909 Columbia president Nicholas Murray Butler wrote that "Cattell is chronically opposed nowadays to anything that anybody does." At times this opposition emerged as a defense of academic freedom, and in 1913 Cattell collected a series of *Science* articles in a volume entitled *University Control*. When his ad hominem attacks led Butler to try to force Cattell's retirement in 1913, friends admitted Cattell's personal shortcomings but rushed to his defense. But his public statements gradually alienated even longtime supporters at Columbia such as anthropologist Franz Boas and philosopher John Dewey. In 1917, when the university finally fired Cattell, ostensibly for opposing U.S. conscription policy during World War I, he found few allies. He sued Columbia for libel and in a 1922 out-of-court settlement won an annuity in lieu of a regular pension. He used Columbia's lump-sum payment of installments due from 1917 to finance the Psychological Corporation, which he founded in 1921 to implement his interest in applied psychology. Cattell, however, emphasized the firm's organization and never could explain how psychologists actually applied their science. The corporation floundered until 1926, when psychologists with significant experience with "real world" problems assumed its control.

In his last years, Cattell continued to edit and publish his journals, and in 1923 he founded the Science Press Printing Company to produce them. He chaired the AAAS Executive Committee from 1920 through 1941 and acted as psychology's grand old man, but he continued to alienate colleagues. For example, the AAAS under his leadership hired and fired four permanent secretaries, and his public attack (as president of the 1929 International Congress of Psychology) on the scientific integrity of Duke University researcher William McDougall scandalized American psychologists. Cattell died in Lancaster, Pennsylvania, where he had moved to oversee his business interests. But even as Cattell's Baconian approach to science and his self-centered approach to others always limited his influence, his psychological experiments and programmatic statements helped set his science's course through the first half of the twentieth century, and the American scientific community relied heavily on his editorial labor throughout this period.

• The Library of Congress holds an exceptionally large and valuable collection of Cattell papers. Other collections are in Columbia University's manuscripts library, central files, and Columbiana Collection. Much of Cattell's correspondence can be found in the collections described in *A Guide to Manuscript Collections in the History of Psychology and Related Areas* (1982). Many of Cattell's most important scientific papers are collected in A. T. Poffenberger, ed., *James McKeen Cattell: Man of Science* (2 vols., 1947), which also reprints significant obituaries by two of Cattell's most eminent students, Frederic L. Wells and Robert S. Woodworth. See also "*Science* and James McKeen Cattell, 1894–1945," *Science* 209 (1980): 43–52; "The Unpublished Autobiography of James McKeen Cattell," *American Psychologist* 26 (1971): 626–35; *An Education in Psychology: James McKeen Cattell's Journal and Letters from Germany and England, 1880–1888* (1981); "The Origins of the Psychological Corporation," *Journal of the History of the Behavioral Sciences* 17 (1981): 54–67; "James McKeen Cattell and the Failure of Anthropometric Mental Testing, 1890–1901," in *The Problematic Science: Psychology in Nineteenth-Century Thought*, ed. William R. Woodward and Mitchell G. Ash (1982); and "Star-Gazing: James McKeen Cattell and *American Men of Science*, 1906–44," in *Psychology, Science, and Human Affairs: Essays in Honor of William Bevan*, ed. Frank Kessel (1993).

MICHAEL M. SOKAL

CATTELL, William Cassady (30 Aug. 1827–11 Feb. 1898), clergyman and college president, was born in Salem, New Jersey, the son of Thomas Ware Cattell, a merchant and banker, and Keziah Gilmore. Cattell received his early education at local schools and also studied under a brother in Virginia for two years. He returned home to enter the College of New Jersey (now Princeton University), from which he graduated with an A.B. in 1848. After spending a year teaching in Goochland County, Virginia, he again returned to New Jersey, entering the Princeton Theological Seminary, where he completed his studies in 1852. Cattell remained in Princeton for the following academic year and undertook special Oriental studies with Professor J. Addison Alexander.

Cattell began his career as an academic administrator in 1853, when he became associate principal at Edgehill Preparatory School in Princeton. He remained there until 1855, when he became professor of Latin and Greek at Lafayette College in Easton, Pennsylvania. The following year he was ordained by the Presbytery of Newton, New Jersey, and finally entered into the ministry on a full-time basis in 1860. Cattell spent the next three years at the Pine Street Presbyterian Church in Harrisburg, Pennsylvania, where he was held in high esteem by the congregation. He retained ties with Lafayette, however; none was more significant than his marriage in 1859 to Elizabeth McKeen, the daughter of James McKeen, a member of the Lafayette College Board of Trustees and the head of a prominent Easton family. They had two children. Cattell became a trustee himself in 1861 and remained one until his death.

A state of crisis prevailed in October 1863, when Cattell returned to Lafayette as its newly elected president. As was the case with many small, church-related colleges in the period, Lafayette College's finances were uncertain. The advent of the Civil War with the corresponding loss of both students and tuition fees exacerbated an already severe burden of debt. Cattell immediately set out on a fundraising expedition—a difficult task during wartime—and managed to raise enough money to keep the college afloat in his first year. A critical donation of $20,000 from businessman Ario Pardee proved to be the turning point. The gift generated badly needed momentum for Cattell's fundraising efforts, and his continued fieldwork combined with forbearance on the part of the faculty concerning overdue salaries saved the college.

The Cattell administration was marked by clear direction and permanent influence. Thanks in part to the Pardee gift, the Pardee Scientific Department was established in 1866, making Lafayette College one of the early leaders in the field of applied sciences and engineering. Cattell also supervised the beginning of a full, formal four-year course in biblical studies. The faculty, which had placed its sustenance at such risk, obtained modest salary increases, and an ambitious building and landscaping program began under Cattell's direction. After conducting research, Cattell standardized the spelling of the college name as "Lafayette," and with the advent of intercollegiate athletics, he also selected the school colors of maroon and white.

The stressful nature of the position took its toll, however, and Cattell was forced to resign the presidency owing to poor health in June 1883, remaining with the college as both professor emeritus and trustee. A year spent in Europe proved helpful in his recuperation, and Cattell returned to the United States to find that he had been elected corresponding secretary of the Presbyterian Board of Ministerial Relief in absentia. Assuming his new position in December 1884, he moved to Philadelphia, Pennsylvania, and worked tirelessly for the benefit of retired ministers and their dependents until 1896, when health problems compelled his resignation from these duties as well.

Cattell continued to contribute to religious and academic activities long after his retirement. He served as moderator of the Presbyterian Synod in 1871. On several occasions he served as a delegate of the Presbyterian General Assembly to churches in Bohemia, Moravia, and Scotland. He served as president of the Presbyterian Historical Society from 1890 until 1898 and was a member of the Board of Directors of the Princeton Theological Seminary from 1864 until his death. Cattell assisted in the founding of the alumni association of the seminary and served as its president in 1881.

While Cattell served in many capacities during his lifetime, his work as president of Lafayette College is his most enduring legacy. An effective and well-liked teacher, minister, and administrator, he was widely mourned following his death in Philadelphia. A street near the college bears his name.

• A small collection of Cattell's papers are at the Lafayette College Archives in Easton, Pa. His *Memoir of William C. Cattell* was published in 1899. The best source of information concerning his career at Lafayette College is David Bishop Skillman, *The Biography of A College: Being the History of the First Century of the Life of Lafayette College* (2 vols., 1932). Obituaries are in the *Philadelphia Public Ledger*, 11 Feb. 1898, and the *Presbyterian*, 16 Feb. 1898.

EDWARD L. LACH, JR.

CATTON, Bruce (9 Oct. 1899–28 Aug. 1978), historian and editor, was born Charles Bruce Catton in Petoskey, Michigan, the son of George Robert Catton, a Congregational minister and educator, and Adella Maude Patten. As a youth, Catton lived in Benzonia, a small community in Michigan's Lower Peninsula. In a later interview, he remembered it as "about as small a small town as there ever was, and I think about as pleasant a place, in the last of the preautomobile age, for a child to grow up" (*Wilson Library Bulletin*, June 1954, p. 834). In Benzonia he regularly encountered old soldiers of the Civil War. In a later letter to a colleague, Oliver Jensen, Catton recalled: "I grew up amidst a regular flowerbed of Civil War veterans. . . . I used to hear the old gentlemen tell war stories until I felt as if the whole affair had taken place in the next county just a few years ago." As a result of these childhood experiences, he developed what would be a lifelong fascination with the war.

In 1916 Catton graduated from Benzonia Academy, a small preparatory school directed by his father, and entered Oberlin College in Ohio. However, he left Oberlin the following year to enlist in the U.S. Navy, serving as a gunner's mate in World War I. After two years of military service, he returned to Oberlin but left at the end of his junior year in order to begin a career as a professional journalist.

From 1920 to 1926 Catton was a reporter for the *Cleveland News*, the *Boston American*, and the *Cleveland Plain Dealer*. In August 1925 he married Hazel H. Cherry; they had one child. From 1926 to 1941 he worked for the Newspaper Enterprise Association as a Washington, D.C., correspondent, book reviewer, and editorial writer. By 1939 he was writing a syndicated newspaper column.

Following the United States's entry into World War II, Catton became the director of information for the War Production Board; after the war he held similar positions in the Departments of Commerce and the Interior. By 1948 he was a special assistant to the secretary of commerce. His firsthand observations of the federal bureaucracy were the basis for his first book, *The War Lords of Washington* (1948), which focused on the conflict between civilian and military authorities during the war. Although the book received mixed reviews, its favorable reception by some critics led him to leave government service and turn his longtime passion into a new occupation.

Catton decided that he wanted to write books about the Civil War. He had collected and studied a wide range of Civil War material, including diaries, letters, and regimental histories, while also reading *War of the Rebellion: A Compilation of the Official Records of the Union and Confederate Armies* (1880–1902) and the existing literature on the war. He first attempted to write a novel about the war but soon became dissatisfied with the result and gave up. He subsequently turned his attention to the Army of the Potomac, but his first Civil War book, an account of the army's early years, was initially rejected by several publishers. It was eventually published by Doubleday as *Mr. Lincoln's Army* (1951), the first volume of what would be a trilogy. This was followed by *Glory Road* (1952), which traced the story of the Army of the Potomac from autumn 1862 to the Gettysburg campaign. While both books received generally favorable reviews, neither sold well. However, his concluding volume, *A Stillness at Appomattox* (1953), won both the National Book Award and the Pulitzer Prize for history in 1954. The book was acclaimed by both literary critics and professional historians and became a national bestseller as well.

In 1954, at the urging of friends, Catton joined with others to organize a new hardcover magazine of popular history, *American Heritage*. He was its first editor, and in 1959 he became senior editor, serving in this capacity until his death. He was also a frequent contributor, writing numerous articles, book reviews, and columns for *American Heritage* during his twenty-four years with the magazine. Meanwhile, he and his wife left the Washington, D.C., area and moved to New York City, which would be his home for the remainder of his life.

Despite his editorial duties, requests for lectures, and other growing demands on his time, Catton continued to write Civil War books. These included *U. S. Grant and the American Military Tradition* (1954), which was part of the Library of American Biography series. It was followed by *This Hallowed Ground* (1956), an account of the Union side of the war, and *America Goes to War* (1958), a collection of essays on the war based on lectures Catton delivered as a visiting professor of history at Wesleyan University in Middletown, Connecticut, during the spring of 1958. In 1959 former president Harry S. Truman presented him with an award for "meritorious service in the field of Civil War History."

At the recommendation of the widow of historian Lloyd Lewis, Little, Brown and Company selected Catton to complete a trilogy on Ulysses S. Grant, which Lewis had begun with his book *Captain Sam Grant* (1950). Catton used Lewis's extensive notes and conducted further research on his own. The result was *Grant Moves South* (1960), a narrative of Grant's early war years up to the Vicksburg campaign. He later completed the trilogy with *Grant Takes Command* (1969), an account of Grant's subsequent Civil War campaigns.

Catton's emergence as a popular chronicler of the Civil War was soon followed by the nation's observance of the war's centennial. In 1960 Governor Nelson Rockefeller named Catton chairman of the New York State Civil War Commission. He also wrote the narrative for *The American Heritage Picture History of the Civil War* (1960). In 1961 this work won a special Pulitzer citation for both Catton and Stephen W. Sears, the book's picture editor. Catton also wrote a three-volume *Centennial History of the Civil War*, which included *The Coming Fury* (1961), *Terrible Swift Sword* (1963), and *Never Call Retreat* (1965). The first volume of this trilogy won for Catton a 1962 nonfiction award from the Ohioana Library Association. He collaborated with his son William Bruce Catton, a professor of history at Middlebury College in Vermont, on *Two Roads to Sumter* (1963), an account of events leading to the war as seen from the perspectives of Abraham Lincoln and Jefferson Davis.

In his later years, Catton continued to write on the Civil War while examining other aspects of the American past. His wife Hazel died in 1969, and contemplation of his own mortality led him to write a memoir, *Waiting for the Morning Train: An American Boyhood* (1972). In it he stated that "early youth is exactly like old age; it is a time of waiting before a big trip to an unknown destination. The chief difference is that youth waits for the morning limited and age waits for the night train." In this work he offered reminiscences of both his boyhood in Benzonia and the technological changes that ended the world in which he grew up, discussing what he saw as technology's potentially dire consequences for humankind. His final books included *Gettysburg: The Final Fury* (1974), an account of the climactic Civil War battle; *Michigan: A Bicentennial History* (1976), a volume in the State and Nation series; and, in collaboration with his son, *The Bold and Magnificent Dream: America's Founding Years, 1492–1815* (1978). In 1977 President Gerald R. Ford presented Catton with the Presidential Medal of Freedom. He died in Frankfort, Michigan, during a vacation at his summer home.

Catton helped Americans rediscover the nature and meaning of the Civil War. He was a highly disciplined and prolific writer who produced powerful narratives based upon extensive research. His books include vivid portraits of a wide range of personalities, from statesmen and generals to ordinary enlisted men. Moreover, he did not repeat himself in his numerous Civil War books; instead, he consistently offered new insights into the war not found in his previous works. In a memorial article, his colleague Jensen remembered him as "a thoroughly professional editor [whose] knowledge of history . . . was prodigious and by no means confined to the war whose Homer he had been proclaimed," as well as a kind and approachable man "with the faintly courtly good manners of the old Midwest" ("Working with Bruce Catton," *American Heritage*, Feb. 1979, pp. 44–51).

• Catton's papers are located at the Citadel in Charleston, S.C. His other books include *Banners at Shenandoah* (1955) and *Prefaces to History* (1970). Insights into Catton's personality and work may be found in Fred J. Eckert, "What I Learned from Bruce Catton," *Writer's Digest*, Nov. 1964, pp. 39, 76–7; and Eckert, "Unforgettable Bruce Catton," *Reader's Digest*, Sept. 1991, pp. 115–20. An obituary is in the *New York Times*, 6 Nov. 1978.

THOMAS I. CRIMANDO

CAULKINS, Frances Manwaring (26 Apr. 1795–3 Feb. 1869), author, was born in New London, Connecticut, the daughter of Joshua Caulkins, a seagoing trader who died in Haiti before her birth, and Fanny Manwaring. Her mother married Philemon Haven in 1807. Caulkins attended schools in Norwichtown and Norwich, Connecticut. She was a voracious reader and began early in life to collect information about history and genealogies. She lived with a maternal uncle in New London, where she began to publish essays in local newspapers about people and events of regional interest.

When her stepfather died in 1819, Caulkins began to teach school and perform school administrative work to provide needed funds for her family. She worked at girls' schools in Norwichtown (1820–1829 and 1832–1834) and New London (1829–1832). Experiencing profound religious impulses beginning in 1831, Caulkins joined a Congregational church in New London. From 1836 to 1842, she lived in New York City, staying with a cousin and writing popular booklets for the American Tract Society. In 1842 she returned to New London to live with Henry Philemon Haven, her half brother. He was a whaling merchant and a Sunday school superintendent. Circa 1848 Caulkins published *The Tract Primer* in the Tract Society's *American Messenger*; she later published it with the title *The Pictorial Tract Primer*. The work was popular and was translated into French in 1852. An example of one of its exhortations to children is the "GOLD'-EN RULE":

> To do to all men as I would
> That they should do to me,
> Will make me kind and just and good,
> And so I'll try to be.

Caulkins's other religious writings include *The Child's Hymn Book* (1835), *Children of the Bible: As Examples, and as Warnings* (1842), *The Bible Primer* (1854); and *Eve and Her Daughters of Holy Writ; or, Women of the Bible* (1861). Her *Bible Primer* (sometimes titled *Youth's Bible Studies*) consists of six small "volumes": "Primer of the Pentateuch," "Primer of the Historic Books," "Primer of the Prophets," "Primer of the Poetical Books," "Primer of the Gospels," and "Primer of the Acts, Epistles, Etc." Her method of helping children was to tell stories, often in verse; to ask and answer questions, the latter sometimes directly from the Scriptures; to lecture gently; and to make it a point to avoid tedious wordiness. She sought to challenge her young readers to better themselves.

Caulkins also wrote many poetic works for older readers. One, *Bride Brook, a Legend of New London, Connecticut* (1852), describes a marriage ceremony beside a snowy stream in the winter of 1646–1647. In this short poem Caulkins writes, "Forth steps the conscious, blushing bride" toward "her fearless lover, bold and free." In the 1850s she also published "Colporteur Songs" in the *American Messenger*. In one of the four little poems, the "porteur," carrying Psalms, children's songs, and copies of the Bible into the wilderness, muses, "O how sweet to dwellings lonely/ Leaves of heavenly truth to bear!" and hopes "the Gospel's clear sun-light [will] illumine the world!" Caulkins's verses, though utterly sincere, are often too shallow and sweetly devout to appeal to the taste of later readers.

For twenty years, while Caulkins was a secretary for the Ladies' Seamen's Friend Society of New London, she found time to accomplish painstaking research on regional history. She published two compendious books on the subject. The first was *The History of Norwich, Connecticut, from Its Settlement in 1660, to January 1845* (1845); she expanded this work as *The History of Norwich, Connecticut: From Its Possession by the Indians to the Year 1866* (1866). (In an 1874 reprint, an appendix containing notes and sketches was added, continuing the history to 1873.) Her second book was *The History of New London, Connecticut, from the First Survey of the Coast in 1612, to 1852* (1852); an 1860 edition continued the history to that date.

Caulkins's 1845 and 1852 histories total nearly 1,400 pages. The works, well written and solidly based on original documents, remain authoritative. In them she discusses Indian tribes, their varying relationships with English colonists, and their own intertribal disputes over leadership. Far from seeing encroachments by the settlers as a misfortune for the Indians, Caulkins views interracial dealings that resulted in advantages to the whites as proof of God's providence and His desire to see the Indians Christianized. She regards white leaders as superior to the Indians, who willingly followed them. Caulkins also discusses religion in Connecticut, including the loss of religious enthusiasm in the waning years of the seventeenth century, the Great Awakening in the eighteenth century, church leadership, revivalism, separatist activities, the persecution of extremists, and the influence of economic forces on religion.

In 1849 Caulkins was nominated for corresponding membership in the Massachusetts Historical Society by James Savage, its president and a future genealogist of New England. She was easily elected, becoming the first woman to be thus honored and the only one up to the time of her death. In her later years she was in poor health but never complained, remaining cheerful and continuing to read and write. Having never married, she died in the home of her half brother in New London.

• Some of Caulkins's workbooks and manuscripts are in the New London County Historical Society collections. One of Caulkins's minor works is *Memoir of the Rev. William Adams, of Dedham, Mass., and of the Rev. Eliphalet Adams, of New London, Conn., and Their Descendants, with the Journal of William Adams, 1660–1682* (1949). Posthumous publications are "Poems on Local Scenes and Incidents," *New London County Historical Society Records and Papers* 1 (1890–1894): 37–70; and Emily S. Gilman, ed., *Stone Records of Groton* (1903). She may also have been the author of *Ye Antient Buriall Place of New London, Conn.* (1899). A reprint of her *History of New London* (1895) contains a short biography. A partial bibliography of her works is in *New London County Historical Society, Records and Papers* 1 (1890–1894): 33–36. Many of her seventeenth-century Caulkins and Manwaring forebears are listed in James Savage, *A Genealogical Dictionary of the First Settlers of New England, Showing Three Generations of Those Who Came before May, 1692, on the Basis of Farmer's Register* (4 vols., 1860–1862). An obituary is in the *Massachusetts Historical Society Proceedings* 10 (1869): 473–74.

ROBERT L. GALE

CAVANAUGH, John Joseph (23 Jan. 1899–28 Dec. 1979), priest and educator, was born in Bennington Township, Shiawasee County, Michigan, the son of Michael Francis Cavanaugh and Mary Ann Keegan, farmers. His father died when John was five years old, and his mother was forced to sell their small farm and move with four young children to nearby Owosso, taking in boarders for a time to meet expenses. After completing parish grammar school, young John enrolled in an accelerated commercial course of typing, shorthand, and bookkeeping and, at thirteen, entered the work force, eventually serving as a business secretary.

In 1917 he contacted Rev. John W. Cavanaugh, C.S.C. (no relation), president of the University of Notre Dame, where his younger brother was studying for the priesthood, and the elder Cavanaugh agreed to take him on as his secretary. He passed the university's entrance examination in 1919, continued his secretarial work part-time, and graduated as president of the student government in 1923. He joined the sales staff of the Studebaker Corporation of South Bend and, in less than three years, rose to the position of assistant advertising manager. In January 1925 he entered the seminary, received a master's degree in English from Notre Dame in 1927, and was ordained a priest for the Congregation of Holy Cross (C.S.C.) in 1931.

After two additional years of graduate study in philosophy at the Gregorian University in Rome, Cavanaugh returned to Notre Dame, first as assistant prefect of religion and then as prefect of religion from 1934 to 1938. He published a one-page *Religious Bulletin* of spiritual advice and encouragement each day, took surveys of student religious practices, arranged inquiry classes for interested non-Catholic students, and remained available much of the day to hear confessions and distribute Holy Communion.

After serving as assistant provincial superior in the Congregation of Holy Cross for two years and as Notre Dame vice president for six, Cavanaugh was named president of Notre Dame in 1946. His most notable achievement as president, said one commentator, "was simply that he led Notre Dame into the twentieth century" (Stritch, p. 29). Undergraduate enrollment increased from 3,200 to more than 5,000, and the university's administrative structure was reorganized under five new vice presidencies. In 1947 he established a central fundraising office, the Notre Dame Foundation, and undertook a $9 million construction program, renovating several buildings and erecting a new science hall, a liberal and fine arts building, an additional residence hall, and a public inn for the university's use.

Cavanaugh was equally concerned with academic growth. He organized advisory councils for the individual colleges to advise the president on curriculum strengths and weaknesses, and he inaugurated a Great Books program to bring tighter unity to the liberal arts curriculum. He established specialized centers of learning and research—the Medieval Institute, the Natural Law Forum, a Committee on International Relations, and the germ-free Laboratories of Bacteriology (LOBUND)—and he increased postgraduate enrollment fourfold. With newly acquired resources, he undertook a Distinguished Professors program to attract major scholars from other universities to Notre Dame.

From his early experience in advertising, Cavanaugh understood the importance of public relations, and he was a frequent speaker before alumni groups and religious, business, and civic gatherings. He opposed universal military training but championed Cold War preparedness and defended the use of atomic weapons against armed aggression. Amid allegations of Communist infiltration of American universities, he insisted that no one espousing the overthrow of the U.S. government had a right to teach others. He consistently stressed the value of religious schools and favored tax relief for those supporting them, since he believed only religious schools could educate youths fully as children of God destined for eternity. A truly educated person, he believed, was "one who knows what God wants him to do and has the discipline to do it."

Limited by church law to six years as religious superior, Cavanaugh relinquished the presidency in 1952 to his hand-picked successor, Rev. Theodore Hesburgh, C.S.C. Cavanaugh remained at the university as director of the Notre Dame Foundation from 1953 to 1960 and as student counselor at Notre Dame and nearby Saint Mary's College from 1960 to 1973. A speech he delivered in Washington in 1957 was given national publicity when he strongly criticized the deficiencies in Catholic education and asked rhetorically: "Where are the Catholic Salks, Oppenheimers, Einsteins?"

Cavanaugh retained a close friendship begun in the early 1940's with the Kennedy family: he offered Mass with the Kennedy family in the East Room of the White House the day after President Kennedy's assassination, flew to Hyannis Port to be with the president's father during the funeral itself, assisted at the funeral of Senator Robert Kennedy in St. Patrick's Cathedral in New York five years later, and offered Mass in the family home in Hyannis Port on the death of family patriarch and former ambassador Joseph Kennedy in 1969.

Cavanaugh was a member of the Board of Visitors of the U.S. Naval Academy, the Board of Directors of the Ford Foundation's Fund for Adult Education, the Citizens Advisory Commission on Manpower Utilization in the Armed Services, and the National Commission on Public Controls in Higher Education, and he was a trustee of the Great Books Foundation.

Traditional and even conservative in theology, he was liberal on questions of civil rights, ecumenism, and the place of women in society. More administrator than scholar, he readily sought the academic advice of others. His favorite pastimes were reading, bridge, and occasionally golf, and he thoroughly enjoyed the company and conversation of others. Even in the midst of controversy, he remained calm and soft-spoken. "The charm president," one writer called him, a person who made his point but rarely made an enemy. He died in a retirement home for priests and brothers on the campus of Notre Dame near South Bend, Indiana.

• The major collection of Cavanaugh papers, including an extensive 1973 oral history interview, is preserved in the archives of the University of Notre Dame. A shorter oral history interview detailing Cavanaugh's friendship with the Kennedy family is preserved in the John F. Kennedy Library in Boston. Cavanaugh himself published very little. His M.A. thesis was entitled "The Thomistic Philosophy in the Divine Comedy" (Univ. of Notre Dame, 1927), and he summarized his educational views in a popular pamphlet, *The Blasphemous Thing* (1949). A good source for Cavanaugh's early years is Arthur J. Hope, *Notre Dame: One Hundred Years*, rev. ed. (1948). His work as prefect of religion is discussed in Thomas P. Jones, *The Development of the Office of Prefect of Religion at the University of Notre Dame from 1842 to 1952* (1960). For Cavanaugh's years as Notre Dame president, see John J. Powers, "The Charm President," *Notre Dame Magazine* 21 (Spring 1992): 14–16; Thomas J. Schlereth, *The University of Notre Dame: A Portrait of Its History and Campus* (1976); and Thomas Stritch, *My Notre Dame: Memories and Reflections of Sixty Years* (1991). James E. Armstrong, *Onward to Victory: A Chronicle of the Alumni of the University of Notre Dame du Lac, 1842–1973* (1974), discusses Cavanaugh both as president and as director of the Notre Dame Foundation. Popular articles on Cavanaugh can be found in *Time*, 28 Apr. 1952, pp. 78–80, and 30 Dec. 1957, pp. 49–50. The *New York Times*, 16 Dec. 1957, summarized Cavanaugh's Washington speech critical of Catholic education.

THOMAS E. BLANTZ

CAVERLY, Charles Solomon (30 Sept. 1856–16 Oct. 1918), physician and public health officer, was born in Troy, New Hampshire, the son of Abiel Caverly, a physician, and Sarah Goddard. Caverly attended public school in Concord, New Hampshire, and in Brandon, Vermont, and then prepared for college at Kimball Union Academy in Meriden, New Hampshire. He graduated from Dartmouth College in 1878 and studied medicine in his father's office until his father's death in 1879. He continued his studies with Dr. Middleton Goldsmith of Rutland, Vermont, and then attended the University of Vermont, from which he received an M.D. in 1881. He married Mabel Tuttle in 1885; they had one son. After some postgraduate study at the College of Physicians and Surgeons in New York, Caverly in 1883 went into practice with his old friend Goldsmith in Rutland. He remained a busy and respected physician there until his death in Rutland during the influenza epidemic of 1918.

Known for his interest in preventive medicine and communicable disease, Caverly was Rutland's first health officer, a member and then president of the Vermont State Board of Health from 1891, president of the Vermont State Medical Society in 1892, and a director of the American Public Health Association. He was special professor of hygiene from 1903 to 1910, and from 1911 to 1918 he was professor of hygiene and preventive medicine, both positions at the University of Vermont. He played a major role in the establishment in 1907 of the tuberculosis sanatorium in Pittsfield, Vermont, and the Preventorium, a home for children whose parents were ill with tuberculosis, was named for him in 1918.

Caverly is most remembered for his pioneering work in the epidemiology of poliomyelitis, then more commonly known as infantile paralysis, and the care and treatment of children affected by it. In 1894 he became aware that doctors in the Otter Creek Valley, particularly in Rutland and Wallingford, were seeing an acute nervous disease associated with fever and then paralysis of one or more extremities. The first case appeared in about mid-June, and by the middle of July other towns in the same general region were reporting similar illnesses. As a practicing physician himself in that area, respected for his knowledge of communicable disease, and as president of the Vermont State Board of Health, Caverly was able to induce physicians to report their cases to him, and he decided to devote a major effort to recording each case in as much detail as possible and to making whatever epidemiological observations he could, becoming the first American physician to make a systematic study of a large epidemic.

By the end of the summer Caverly was able to report 132 cases, the largest number reported anywhere in the world up to that time. The disease was not entirely unknown; smaller outbreaks had been noted in Scandinavia and during the previous summer in Boston. The name "poliomyelitis" had already been attached to the paralytic form. But Caverly's report received worldwide attention both because of the large number of cases covered and because they had been so well studied. The majority of these patients eventually recovered, but thirty of the 132 remained permanently paralyzed to some degree. By careful clinical study Caverly was able to identify six or seven children who were never paralyzed at all but whom he considered to have had the same disease because of the signs and symptoms in the acute phase. The nonparalytic cases had not been recognized before, but later researchers confirmed that they should be included in descriptions of the disease.

The incidence of polio in Vermont slackened in the fall as it had in other places. During the following years a few cases were seen each summer, but another epidemic struck in 1910, and by 1914 Caverly was able to report more than 300 cases from Vermont. By this time the disease had become a major national problem, and more research attention began to be paid to it during the next few years than to any other disease, with the possible exception of tuberculosis.

Caverly's efforts during the decade after the first epidemic were chiefly that of recording as many of the cases as possible, being aware of the world literature on the disease, and as president of the board of health sending out bulletins to local physicians on the management of quarantine and the disinfection of the homes of affected patients. He and others were helpless as far as treatment was concerned. But Caverly became associated with another big advance after the large epidemic of 1910. Realizing that further research was urgently needed, he was able to convince Emily Dutton Proctor of the Vermont marble industry family to fund a research effort devoted not only to the disease itself but to management of the sick children. Proctor, who remained anonymous for many years, started in

1914 an annual grant to the board of health that allowed Caverly to consult with Simon Flexner of the Rockefeller Institute in New York for research into the epidemiology and virology of the disease and to ask Robert Lovett, Harvard professor of orthopedics, to help with the study of how the paralytic cases might be treated. Vermont's board of health notified all physicians who had cases of paralytic disease that there would be a series of clinics attended by Lovett as well as local physicians and nurses. The board set up treatment plans, and because of the rural nature of Vermont, the clinics met in several cities around the state, providing patients and their families easier access to services. The resulting program, which came to be known as the Vermont plan of management, attracted the attention of public health agencies from around the country.

While gaining recognition as an important contributor to the understanding of polio, Caverly remained a caring physician who took seriously his responsibility to the community for help with hygiene and preventive medicine. In his biography, his friend Lovett wrote of him as a "quiet and cultivated man."

• Caverly's publications include an article in *Preventive Medicine with a Study of the Infectious Diseases Prevalent in Vermont in Transactions of the Vermont State Medical Society* (1881); and "History of Medicine and Surgery," in the *Vermonter* 8 (May 1903): 311–35. *Infantile Paralysis in Vermont* (1924), published by the state department of public health as a memorial to Caverly, contains reprints of most of his papers, as well as those of his co-workers and a short biography by Robert Lovett. John R. Paul, *A History of Poliomyelitis* (1971), pp. 79–87, discusses Caverly's contributions. An obituary is in the *Rutland Herald*, 17 Oct. 1918.

LESTER J. WALLMAN

CAVERT, Samuel McCrea (9 Sept. 1888–21 Dec. 1976), Presbyterian minister and ecumenical leader, was born in Charlton, New York, the son of Walter I. Cavert, a successful farmer-businessman who was conspicuous in local affairs, and Elizabeth Brann. Small of stature and somewhat delicate in health as a boy, Cavert contributed to the family farm primarily by helping his father with its business aspects. Educated at Union College in Schenectady, New York (B.A., 1910), Cavert excelled in debating, was president of his class and of the student YMCA, and was elected to Phi Beta Kappa. After two more years on campus working as director of the student Y and teaching Greek, he entered New York City's Union Theological Seminary (B.D., 1915), while also taking courses at Columbia University (M.A., 1914). He was ordained to the ministry by the presbytery of Albany in 1915. As winner of the seminary's traveling fellowship for 1915–1917, he remained at the seminary for a year as assistant to systematic theologian William Adams Brown, then spent a year of study and travel abroad, becoming acquainted with various forms of religious and cultural life and visiting Christian missions in India, China, and Japan.

In the fall of 1917 he joined the staff of the General War-Time Commission of the Churches, an agency that helped coordinate the work of religious bodies during World War I. His abilities as organizer and leader were immediately appreciated, but he resigned to become an army chaplain in October 1918. His active service at an army hospital in Colorado was brief, for his former teacher, William Adams Brown, persuaded him to resign in January to become secretary of the Committee on the War and the Religious Outlook, organized by the Federal Council of the Churches of Christ in America (FCC), to help its members face the problems of postwar reconstruction. In November 1918 he had married Ruth Miller, but early in 1920, soon after the birth of a healthy daughter, his wife died of fever; the baby was cared for by her maternal grandparents.

Early in 1921 Cavert was named a general secretary of the FCC. He proved to be an effective partner to Charles S. Macfarland, FCC senior general secretary. The two complemented each other well, for the forceful, outspoken Macfarland emphasized the council's leadership in social thought and action, while the evangelical liberal Cavert, though never neglecting the FCC's Social Gospel role, paid close attention to the educational, evangelistic, and mission aspects of church cooperation and soon took over and continued for more than fifteen years to edit the monthly *Federal Council Bulletin*. As the FCC became increasingly aware of racial tensions, Cavert worked closely with its Commission on Negro Churches and Interracial Relations (formed in 1921). He traveled frequently at home and abroad, attending many meetings of the various member churches and interchurch movements. He became deeply interested in Eastern Orthodoxy; in 1923 the FCC appointed a Committee on Relations with Eastern Churches, which helped prepare the way for the first Orthodox body to join the council in 1938. In June 1927 he and Ruth Twila Lytton, then dean of students and professor of English at Lawrence College in Appleton, Wisconsin, were married and settled into an apartment in New York City.

When Macfarland resigned from the FCC in 1930, Cavert carried on, and in January 1933 he was confirmed as senior general secretary, the council's top administrator. He assumed primary executive responsibilities for the interpretation of the FCC's role in American church life, for public relations, for major organizational and personnel decisions, and for budget making and fundraising. The latter responsibility was especially difficult in the lean years of the Great Depression, and his thoughtful persistence was important to the continuation of major FCC programs. Throughout his career Cavert maintained a remarkable balance of diplomacy and decisiveness in administration. A good public speaker and a clear writer, he never lost the art of listening to others. He was often called on to defend the council against criticisms and attacks by some who believed it was not the business of the churches to focus their attention on social and reform matters that had liberal racial and political overtones. His effective leadership throughout the difficult depression years led to a higher level of institutional morale in the later thirties and contributed significantly to the continuation in FCC membership of almost all of its member denominations as well as the addition of a few new ones.

In the 1930s Cavert emerged as a major architect of the World Council of Churches (WCC) and in 1937 was the first to suggest the name that later was officially adopted. He was actively involved in many ecumenical conferences and planning committees in preparing for the WCC, frequently traveling to Europe. He was an official participant in the Oxford Conference on Church, Community and State (1937), a major world conference of the Life and Work movement, which was concerned especially with practical matters of interdenominational church action in service to humanity, matters of great importance to Cavert. He was somewhat less interested in the parallel gathering that followed soon after in Edinburgh: a world conference of the Faith and Order movement, which sought Christian unity by openly facing theological and dogmatic issues. He did participate in it, however, and both conferences voted to have the two movements integrated into what would become the WCC.

The next year Cavert was deeply involved in the follow-up advisory conference held at Utrecht in the Netherlands, during which he was named to the provisional committee formed to bring the WCC into existence, presumably in 1941. The outbreak of World War II in Europe in 1939 interrupted that plan and increased Cavert's duties as the FCC supported the work of the WCC "in process of formation" by strengthening its ministry to prisoners of war and providing aid to refugees. After the United States entered the war, Cavert facilitated FCC cooperation in the work of military chaplains, services to men and women in uniform, ministries to unpopular minorities, and the relocation of interned Japanese. He continued to serve as an important link between European and American churches, taking a risky trip through some Nazi-held territory to Switzerland early in the fall of 1942 to coordinate and strengthen American church efforts for interchurch aid and relief programs for displaced peoples. After the war he was "loaned" to the Geneva staff of the developing WCC for the latter half of 1945 to assist in the reconciliation of former enemies and simultaneously to serve as the first official Protestant governmental liaison between the German Protestant churches and the U.S. Office of Military Government in Germany. He was deeply involved in preparing for the WCC's formal first assembly in Amsterdam in 1948 and competently chaired its committee on arrangements.

Two years after that milestone in world Christian unity Cavert was deeply involved at home with the merger of the FCC with seven other major North American Protestant cooperative agencies to form the National Council of the Churches of Christ in the United States of America (NCC), becoming its first general secretary. His mediatorial style and administrative expertise were important to the early success of the enlarged council. The inclusion of three Lutheran and four Eastern Orthodox churches in the NCC membership illustrated the inclusiveness that Cavert had long sought. After his organizing skill had successfully brought the merging agencies into a viable working relationship, he retired from that post in 1954. He then served for four years as executive secretary of the WCC in the United States, giving significant attention to the North American Study Conference, which dealt with faith and order concerns in 1957.

After "retirement" from executive posts, Cavert remained active for years, attending the third assembly of the WCC at New Delhi in 1961 and, as an observer, the third session of the Second Vatican Council in 1964, which he found thrilling and which led him to anticipate "a new era in Protestant-Catholic relations." He died in Bronxville, New York, where the Caverts had long made their home.

Cavert was one of the major religious leaders of his time. In his early career he was strongly influenced by liberal theology and the Social Gospel. Without losing his commitment to personal freedom and to freedom of religious thought or his belief that religious faith should address social and economic injustices, he also benefited from other points of view, such as neoorthodox theological movements, which focused on keeping the personal and social aspects of Christian faith in creative tension. His untiring commitment to and action toward continuing cooperation among churches through participation in federative structures on national and world levels made Cavert one of the leading figures of the ecumenical movement as embodied in the work of national, regional, and world councils of churches. Always concerned about a fuller unity among Protestants, increasingly he broadened his perspective to include Eastern Orthodox and Roman Catholic churches.

• Extensive materials on Cavert are in the files of the FCC and the NCC at the Department of History, Presbyterian Church (U.S.A.), Philadelphia. William J. Schmidt has written the informative biography, *Architect of Unity: A Biography of Samuel McCrea Cavert* (1978). Among Cavert's early books are *Securing Christian Leaders for Tomorrow: A Study in Present Problems in Recruiting for Christian Life-Service* (1926) and *The Adventure of the Church: A Study of the Missionary Genius of Christianity* (1927). Major works completed during his retirement are *On the Road to Christian Unity: An Appraisal of the Ecumenical Movement* (1961), *The American Churches in the Ecumenical Movement, 1900–1968* (1968), and *Church Cooperation and Unity in America: A Historical Review: 1900–1970* (1970). An obituary is in the *New York Times*, 23 Dec. 1976.

ROBERT T. HANDY

CAWEIN, Madison Julius (23 Mar. 1865–8 Dec. 1914), poet, was born in Louisville, Kentucky, the son of William Cawein, a German-born herbalist and compounder of herbal-based medicines, and Christiana Stelsly, also of German parentage. Early acquaintance with rural life and his father's interest in herbs contributed to Cawein's lifelong love of the outdoors and his dedication to nature. The supernatural fantasies in much of Cawein's poetry may have had their origin in the spiritualist beliefs and practices of his mother, who saw herself as a medium. In 1872 the Caweins moved to Oldham County, Kentucky, then a year later to New Albany, Indiana, and finally back to Louisville in 1879. Cawein began to write poetry when only a boy. As a teenager, he discovered the Romantic poets, who greatly influenced his own poetry. Fond of books, Cawein read widely in English and German literature while attending the Louisville Male High School, from which he graduated as class poet in 1886. After graduation, he worked for a time as a cashier in the local Newmarket Pool Hall, a site of off-track betting, which was legal at the time.

While working in the poolroom, Cawein wrote and published his first volume of verse, *Blooms of the Berry* (1887), which William Dean Howells lauded in the pages of *Harper's Monthly* (May 1888). This encouragement led Cawein to dedicate his second volume of poetry, *The Triumph of Music, and Other Lyrics* (1888), to Howells. Though Howells commended this work as well as *Accolon of Gaul, with Other Poems* (1889), more years of apprenticeship passed before Cawein was accorded much notice by other critics. During this short, busy period, Cawein published at least a volume of poetry annually: *Lyrics and Idyls* (1890), *Days and Dreams* (1891), *Moods and Memories* (1892), *Poems of Nature and Love* (1893), and *Intimations of the Beautiful* (1894).

Never earning more than a small income from his writings, Cawein had to make a living in the workaday world. To escape from the poolroom, he took up real estate and the stock market. He devoted the morning to his business activities; the afternoons he reserved for writing, often walking in the woods as he composed his verses. The criticism of his poetry, favorable and otherwise, that did appear during the half-dozen years after he published *Blooms of the Berry* did not go unnoticed by Cawein. *Moods and Memories* and *Poems of Love and Nature*, both compilations from earlier volumes in which many poems are revised, reveal Cawein striving to make improvements in style, diction, meter, and harmony. By the end of his years of apprenticeship, he had begun to attract the notice of critics, fellow poets, and publishers of magazines. He had established friendships with literary figures such as Howells, James Whitcomb Riley, Edwin Arlington Robinson, and Harry van Dyke.

In 1895 Cawein published a volume of translations from German poetry under the title *The White Snake, and Other Poems*. Volumes of his own verse followed in rapid succession: *The Garden of Dreams* (1896), *Undertones* (1896), *Idyllic Monologues* (1898), *Shapes and Shadows* (1898), *Myth and Romance* (1899), and *One Day & Another* (1901). Edmund Gosse collected what he considered Cawein's best poems and published them in London under the title *Kentucky Poems* in 1902. In his critical introduction to the volume, Gosse held Cawein to be "a poet who stands alone in his generation." In 1903 Cawein married Gertrude Foster McKelvey; they had one child.

Despite growing critical commendation for his work, Cawein did not find great popular favor, leading him to blame the materialism of the times. Though discouraged, he continued to publish prolifically, hoping to attract a wider public. *Weeds by the Wall* (1901) was followed by *A Voice on the Wind, and Other Poems* (1902) and *The Vail of Tempe* (1905), which Cawein considered his best single work. His *Nature-Notes and Impressions*, in prose and verse, appeared in 1906. The same year, Cawein suffered serious financial losses as a result of the San Francisco earthquake. Undaunted, he brought out a five-volume edition of *The Poems of Madison Cawein* in 1907. Election to the National Institute of Arts and Letters came soon thereafter.

Individual volumes of Cawein's verse followed the publication of his collected poems in rapid succession: *The Giant and the Star, Little Annals in Rhyme* (1909), *New Poems* (1909), *Poems* (1911), *So Many Ways* (1911), and *The Poet, the Fool and the Fairies* (1912). In failing health, Cawein lost heavily in a stock market crash in 1912. The threat of poverty led him to move with his wife and son from their attractive home into an apartment. Continuing financial strain caused him to sell part of his library. In 1914 the Authors Club of New York City placed him on their relief list and awarded him a monthly check. Yet ill health and deep financial troubles did not keep him from writing and publishing his verse. Three volumes of poetry appeared in 1913 alone: *The Message of the Lilies, Minions of the Moon*, and *The Republic; a Little Book of Homespun Verse*. The poems in *The Cup of Comus*, published posthumously in 1915, found Cawein experimenting with more current verse forms. Cawein died in Louisville after a fall in his bathroom. It is not known whether his death was caused by a stroke or by hitting his head on the tub.

Many of Cawein's poems of nature evoke the distinct atmosphere of a poet who writes about a land he knows. This impression is due in part to his craftsmanship, to a lesser degree to a large body of sustained work over a long period. Yet there is something incongruous about Cawein's filling the forests of Kentucky with sprites, elves, nymphs, and other airy spirits. This use of folklore and mythological beings no doubt foreshortened his reputation. Cawein wrote too easily, repeated himself, and lacked the faculty of self-criticism. He penned some 2,700 lyrics, about 1,500 of which were originals, the rest revisions. Publishing thirty-six volumes in twenty-eight years proved to be far too much. Occasional sensitive lyrics and a real richness of imagery are buried under a welter of mediocre verse. Nevertheless, Cawein was the first Kentucky poet to garner a national and international reputation. He was regarded by fellow poets such as Joyce Kilmer and critics alike as the foremost contemplative nature poet of his time.

• Cawein's papers are in the libraries of the University of Kentucky and the University of Virginia. Biographical material on Cawein is found in Otto A. Rothert, *The Story of a Poet, Madison Cawein* (1921); H. Houston Peckham, "Madison Cawein," *South Atlantic Quarterly* 14 (1915): 279–84; and Madeline Covi, "Madison Cawein: A Landscape Poet," *Kentucky Review*, no. 3 (1982): 3–19. Also of interest are William N. Guthrie, "A Southern Poet," *Sewanee Review* 1 (May 1893): 290–308, and William Dean Howells, "The Poetry of Madison Cawein," *North American Review* 187 (January 1908): 124–28. An obituary is in the *Boston Transcript*, 19 Dec. 1914.

L. MOODY SIMMS, JR.

CAYCE, Edgar (18 Mar. 1877–3 Jan. 1945), psychic "reader" and influential figure in "alternative" medicine and spirituality, was born near Hopkinsville, Kentucky, the son of Leslie B. Cayce, a tobacco farmer and small-town businessman, and Carrie Elizabeth Major. Cayce was raised in the Christian church (Disciples of Christ), taught Sunday school, and always saw himself as a Christian and active churchgoer. He left school while a teenager to become apprenticed to a photographer and pursued photography as a career for the first part of his life. He married Gertrude Evans in 1903; the union produced three sons. The couple initially made their home in Bowling Green, Kentucky, where Cayce set up a photography business. In 1909 he moved the business to Selma, Alabama.

According to his own later reports, Cayce experienced trances and visions in childhood. He was to claim that at age sixteen he prescribed for himself in a semiconscious state a poultice that healed an injury he had suffered in a ball game. He also was to say that in 1900 he cured himself of chronic laryngitis through diagnosis and hypnotic remedies given him in a self-induced trance. Thereafter he performed similar trance-diagnoses and prescriptions for others, and his reputation grew. In 1909 he treated in like manner a homeopathic physician, Wesley Ketchum, who publicized Cayce's cures widely and was quoted on the subject in a sensational article in the *New York Times* in October 1910.

Thereafter Cayce, now commonly called the "Sleeping Prophet," had to devote the greater portion of his time to the thousands who came to his door expecting that he would go into a sleeplike trance, say "We can see the body," and then describe his client's ailment and its cause minutely. Cayce would often offer some cure, usually a home remedy in the form of a syrup, poultice, or ointment; or he would provide psychic treatment; or he would recommend that the patient see a particular doctor. Increasingly, Cayce's treatments would "travel" in response to letters from faraway suppliants. In sessions conducted on behalf of those clients, Cayce would be accompanied by his wife, who controlled the questioning, and a secretary who would take careful minutes of the readings. The voluminous notes of some 14,000 psychic readings form the real basis of Cayce's posthumous fame; they are available for study at the Edgar Cayce Foundation in Virginia Beach, Virginia.

In 1923, in Dayton, Ohio, Cayce met and talked at some length with Arthur Lammers, a wealthy student of Theosophy and Eastern religions. Thereafter Cayce commenced giving "Life Readings," which dealt with the reincarnations, past lives, and karma of clients and included references to Atlantis and "Earth Changes," or predicted dramatic transformations in the configurations of the continents. These have proved to be highly significant to later students of Cayce's corpus. Presumably in order to be near his new sponsor, Cayce moved to Dayton for a couple of years.

In 1925, however, Lammers suffered financial reverses, which caused him to withdraw his support of Cayce, and at the same time a New York stockbroker named Morton Blumenthal offered to finance a hospital and study center for Cayce in a resort area on the East Coast. The choice of Virginia Beach as the place where Cayce and his family would settle seems to have been obtained by psychic means. Although the Cayce Hospital and Atlantic University were established with Blumenthal's backing, both failed and had to be closed in 1931, casualties of the Great Depression. But Cayce's fortunes gradually recovered. In 1931 his family and friends established the Association for Research and Enlightenment with the aim of underwriting his work as a psychic and the study by others of his readings and teachings.

After Cayce's death in Virginia Beach, his sons—especially Hugh Lynn Cayce—aggressively promoted his name and legacy, which prospered in the atmosphere of post–World War II affluence. The Edgar Cayce Foundation, with its archives and its revived school, health facilities, and conference center, became a magnet for those interested in "alternative" medicine and spirituality. By the 1960s Cayce was spoken of as "America's best-known psychic." Such books as *Edgar Cayce on Prophecy* (1967) and *Edgar Cayce on Atlantis* (1968) provided guidance about spiritual themes that had won renewed popular attention at the time they were published. Edited by his son Hugh and others, the numerous volumes appearing under Cayce's name draw on his carefully recorded pronouncements, especially the later "Life Readings." A figure with roots deep in American folk medicine and popular culture, Cayce represents a key link connecting the psychic healing of an earlier day with the "counterculture" of the 1960s and the "New Age" spirituality of the last decades of the twentieth century.

• Cayce's papers are preserved by the Edgar Cayce Foundation in Virginia Beach, Va. His autobiography, *The Lost Memoirs of Edgar Cayce*, was published in 1997. The Association for Research and Enlightenment has sponsored the publication of many volumes; besides those mentioned in the text, representative titles include *Edgar Cayce on Dreams* (1968), *Edgar Cayce on ESP* (1969), and *Edgar Cayce on Reincarnation* (1967). Biographies of Cayce include Thomas Sugrue, *There Is a River: The Story of Edgar Cayce* (1942); Hugh Lynn Cayce, *Venture Inward: Edgar Cayce's Story and the Mysteries of the Unconscious Mind* (1964); Jess Stearn, *Edgar*

Cayce: The Sleeping Prophet (1969); and Harmon Hartzell Bro, *A Seer Out of Season: The Life of Edgar Cayce* (1989). See also "Illiterate Man Becomes a Doctor When Hypnotized—Strange Power Shown by Edgar Cayce Puzzles Physicians," *New York Times*, 9 Oct. 1910.

JAMES R. LEWIS

CAYTON, Horace Roscoe (12 Apr. 1903–22 Jan. 1970), sociologist and writer, was born in Seattle, Washington, the son of Horace Roscoe Cayton, a newspaper reporter, and Susie Sumner Revels, an instructor at Rust College. Horace's maternal grandfather, Hiram R. Revels, was elected senator from Mississippi at the height of Reconstruction; through the years, the family remained in the upper classes of African-American society. At the time of Horace's birth, the Cayton family was prosperous, middle-class, and living in the heart of white Seattle.

Soon after Horace's birth, however, the family experienced financial distress accentuated by the racism of Seattle. Growing up, Horace had various scrapes with the law, culminating in his arrest for driving a getaway car in a gas station robbery. As a teenager, Cayton attended, and soon dropped out of, reform school. He traveled widely, supporting himself as a manual laborer. Eventually Cayton returned to Seattle, where he finished high school at a Young Men's Christian Association preparatory school, and entered the University of Washington in 1925. Supporting himself financially as a sheriff's deputy, he received a B.A. in sociology from Washington in 1931. That year Cayton won a fellowship to study sociology at the University of Chicago.

Cayton never completed his doctoral degree. He worked for two years in the sociology program at the University of Chicago and then as an editor for a Tuskegee Institute newsletter. In 1934 he worked as a special assistant to Secretary of the Interior Harold Ickes, attempting to discover how the New Deal affected African-American labor. After a brief stay in Europe, Cayton taught economics at Fisk University, until returning to Chicago in 1936.

From 1936 to 1939 Cayton led a Works Projects Administration project that studied the social structure of the African-American family. He was joined in this project by St. Clair Drake, an African-American anthropologist from the University of Chicago. In 1941 a grant from the Julius Rosenwald Fund allowed Cayton and Drake to organize the materials from the WPA project and to supplement it with information from the 1940s. Their efforts resulted in a volume coauthored by Drake and Cayton: *Black Metropolis* (1945).

Black Metropolis blended the two dominant social scientific methodologies used during the interwar years for the study of race relations: the Chicago school of sociology, which saw race relations as a dynamic process of assimilation; and the relatively static model of anthropological studies of caste-and-class. The book examined the effects of the rapid migration of African Americans into Chicago. Drake and Cayton argued that racism prevented African Americans from assimilating into the dominant culture, which made them unique among ethnic groups in the United States. Drake and Cayton included a series of participant-observer interviews with African Americans in Chicago which revealed that Chicago's race relations closely resembled the caste system of the American South. Drake and Cayton closed their volume with a call for the government to do more to help African Americans achieve equality in American culture.

This call in *Black Metropolis* reflected Cayton's ongoing concern for racial equality and civil rights. Since 1934 he had been a regular columnist for the *Pittsburgh Courier*, often arguing forcefully for civil rights for African Americans. In 1940 he became the director of Chicago's Parkway House, which soon became a focus of African-American cultural life, frequently visited by such luminaries as Langston Hughes, Arna Bontemps, Paul Robeson, and Richard Wright. Wright and Cayton became particularly close friends during the 1940s.

Although his time in Chicago was successful professionally, Cayton was a profoundly disconsolate individual. His personal unhappiness was evident in a series of failed marriages: he first married Bonnie Branch, a white social worker in 1931; they were divorced in 1936. In the two decades following World War II, Cayton and Irma Jackson were twice married and twice divorced. He last married and divorced Ruby Wright. He had no children.

Cayton was in psychoanalysis from 1943 to 1949, grappling with his profound feelings of loneliness and hostility toward white America. In 1945, just as *Black Metropolis* was about to bring some measure of national recognition to his professional life, Cayton's personal life began to disintegrate. He began seeing his work at the Parkway House as nothing more than a sop thrown to the African-American community by the white power structure. In 1949 he left Chicago and moved to New York City.

During the 1950s Cayton was in and out of various New York treatment centers for alcoholism and drug addiction, conditions he had been battling throughout his adult life. Although he kept up with his regular column for the *Pittsburgh Courier*, he was unable to keep steady employment in New York. He worked a series of jobs: researcher for the American Jewish Committee (1950–1951), correspondent to the United Nations for the *Pittsburgh Courier* (1952–1954), researcher for the National Council of Churches (1954–1958), and instructor for the City College of New York (1957–1958).

In 1960 Cayton moved to California, for a time depending on his brother Revels for financial support. Again he was in and out of treatment centers for alcoholism. In 1961 he ended his regular column with the *Pittsburgh Courier* and began working, in various capacities, for the University of California at Berkeley. During this time, Cayton began working on his autobiography, *Long Old Road* (1965), which he saw as a form of therapy, a way to grapple with the demons of racism and loneliness that had plagued him for most of his adult life. In it, frankly and openly, he discussed his alcoholism, failed marriages, stormy relationship with the rest of the Cayton family, and his stark feelings on American racism.

In 1968 Cayton received a grant from the National Foundation for the Arts and Humanities for a biography of Richard Wright, his estranged friend. He traveled to Paris, France, in connection with the Wright biography, and there he died of natural causes.

Through both his academic and personal writings, Cayton powerfully and relentlessly attacked American racism. However, his personal demons, alcoholism and difficulties in maintaining personal relationships, often overcame him, and likely overcame the keen and penetrating insights he might have shared with the world.

• Many of Cayton's papers are lost. The largest single collection of his papers is deposited at the Vivian G. Harsh Research Collection of Afro-American History and Literature in Chicago. The Harsh collection includes a complete file of Cayton's columns for the *Pittsburgh Courier* as well as many records for the Parkway House. Cayton's correspondence with Wright can be found in the collection of Wright's papers deposited at the Beinecke Library at Yale University. Finally, there is a small collection of Cayton's letters at the Bancroft Library of the University of California at Berkeley. Cayton's autobiography, *Long Old Road* (1965), contains many details of Cayton's life; however, it is not always historically accurate, particularly for the post–World War II years. The most extensive biographical work on Cayton is Richard Stanley Hobbs, "The Cayton Legacy: Two Generations of a Black Family, 1859–1976" (Ph.D. diss., Univ. of Washington, 1989). An obituary is in the *New York Times*, 25 Jan. 1970.

JOHN P. JACKSON

CAZENOVE, Théophile (13 Oct. 1740–6 Mar. 1811), speculator, was born in Amsterdam, the Netherlands, the son of Théophile Cazenove and Marie de Raspin-Thoyras. His marriage in 1763 to Margaretha Helena van Jever, a member of a noted mercantile family, helped Cazenove secure a comfortable spot within Amsterdam's commercial circles. He worked as a broker and trader through the following decades, evidently spending some time in the 1780s in Paris, where he became acquainted with the cleric and future statesman Charles Maurice de Talleyrand-Périgord.

In the late 1780s Cazenove's trafficking in the U.S. revolutionary era debt to France bankrupted him. However, he quickly rebounded with the aid of a consortium of Dutch bankers equally eager to profit from the young nation's public debt and economic potential but weary of working through third parties. Appointed purchasing agent for the combined interests of four Dutch financial houses, Pieter Stadnitski & Son, Nicolaas and Jacob Van Staphorst, P. & C. Van Eeghen, and Ten Cate & Vollenhoven, Cazenove landed in America in 1790. Basing himself in Philadelphia, he initially bought up depreciated federal and state securities, investments that seemed destined to afford a nice profit given Secretary of the Treasury Alexander Hamilton's intention to fund the federal debt at par and have the national government assume the obligations of the states. Less happily, Cazenove proceeded to pour Dutch money into canal companies and the Society for Establishing Useful Manufactures, all of which ultimately proved to be losing propositions. As Hamilton's financial program brought stability to the treasury, the potential rewards of speculation in the public debt diminished, and Cazenove's attention turned to the booming market in western land. The Dutch combine, which eventually included the firms of W. & J. Willink and Rutger Jan Schimmelpenninck, became equally convinced that the westward movement of the American population promised large returns on the purchase and resale of frontier real estate, and by 1792 Cazenove began his remarkable career as a land speculator. The six Dutch houses formed a joint stock company that in 1796 was incorporated as the Holland Land Company (*Hollandsche Land Compagnie*).

Cazenove purchased huge swaths of undeveloped land, in the course of which he involved his backers' fortunes with those of some of the more prominent personages of the early national period. Primarily through James Wilson, signer of the Declaration of Independence, delegate to the Constitutional Convention, and associate justice of the U.S. Supreme Court, he bought up 1.5 million acres in northern and western Pennsylvania. In addition to 200,000 acres in central New York, in the midst of which the eponymous town of Cazenovia was founded, Cazenove arranged for the purchase of some 1.5 million acres further to the west from Robert Morris, erstwhile "financier of the Revolution" and by that time an increasingly harried U.S. senator. Together with the real estate the Dutch bankers bought directly from Morris's son, the Holland Land Company established a claim to almost all of New York west of the Genesee River, the huge tract becoming known as the Holland Purchase. This sale was considerably complicated by Morris's disordered finances, the fact that the Iroquois had not yet yielded their own claim to the land, and the laws of New York, which forbade alien landownership. In the course of an ultimately successful attempt to have the law changed, Cazenove employed the legal and lobbying talents first of Alexander Hamilton and then of Aaron Burr. He also pursued numerous other business ventures, a few in the company of the émigré Talleyrand, who later recalled Cazenove as "a man of a rather enlightened, though slow, mind, and of a timid and most careless nature," who, all the same, was "very useful to me" (Talleyrand, vol. 1, p. 175). Others in Philadelphia apparently found Cazenove more charming than Talleyrand did, or at least equally useful, for he cut quite a swath in Federalist high society.

As Talleyrand's remark might suggest, Cazenove's acquisitive energy was not matched by scrupulous attention to how much he spent, whose money he used, or precisely what he was buying. The company's vast tract in Pennsylvania proved to be mountainous, isolated, not uniformly arable, and, consequently, entirely unprofitable. This was not the case with the tracts Cazenove secured in western New York, but the complications of settling with Morris and with the Indians meant that years passed before much of the land could even be surveyed and parceled out, much less begin to generate a substantial return. In the meantime, the men whose money Cazenove was spreading about became increasingly distressed with the sloppiness of his accounting. After the directors called a halt to further ventures and ordered strict retrenchment late in 1798, Cazenove returned to Europe. The considerably more cautious Paul Busti thereafter headed the company's operations in the United States.

The balance of Cazenove's life would be all anticlimax. He continued for several years to work for the Dutch financiers, though on a much shorter leash. He afterward resided chiefly in Paris, where he conjured up a livelihood out of his continuing association with Talleyrand, by then a most influential figure. Cazenove died in Paris.

Cazenove's activities in the United States are notable for the light they shed on the less statesmanlike aspects of certain statesmen's careers. They also stand as a symbol of the significance of foreign capital in the United States' westward development whether invested in land speculations or, later, in railroad construction. In more practical terms, the territory acquired during Cazenove's tenure as agent general allowed the Holland Land Company to play an influential role in the development of western New York, though that role was not always celebrated by the many settlers beholden to the firm.

• Cazenove's correspondence and the records of the Holland Land Company are in Amsterdam's municipal archive, *Gemeentearchief*. One of his journals has been published by Rayner Kelsey, ed., *Cazenove Journal 1794* (1922). The standard discussion of Cazenove's activities in the United States is Paul Evans, *The Holland Land Company* (1924), but see also William Chazanof, *Joseph Ellicott and the Holland Land Company* (1970). Talleyrand's estimation of Cazenove is in *Memoirs of the Prince de Talleyrand* (1891).

PATRICK G. WILLIAMS

CAZNEAU, Jane Maria Eliza McManus Storms (6 Apr. 1807–12 Dec. 1878), journalist, was born near Troy, New York, the daughter of William McManus, an attorney and later a member of the U.S. House of Representatives, and Catharina Coons. Little is known of her early years, although an aunt in Connecticut appears to have been partly responsible for raising her. Jane McManus married Allen B. (or William F.) Storms in 1825. They had one son before divorcing in 1831.

In 1832 Jane Storms (who sometimes went by her maiden name following the divorce) became involved with her father, her brother, and an aged Aaron Burr in a plan to develop a colony of immigrants in Texas. She went to Texas with her brother, but their plans were thwarted by the reluctance of the German settlers to move inland from the coastal town of Matagorda. In 1834 Storms was named in a suit for divorce brought against Aaron Burr by his second wife. While there is no clear evidence of a romantic interest between Burr and Storms, the two were very close after her divorce, and the former vice president thought highly of her. Burr was only the first of a number of male politicians whom Storms sought to recruit to her causes.

Following the failure of the Texas colony, Storms returned to New York City. She turned to journalism after 1840, receiving her initial entrée through her close friendship with the publisher of the *New York Sun*, Moses Y. Beach. She wrote articles under the name "Cora Montgomery" for the *Sun*, the *U.S. Magazine and Democratic Review*, and other journals and was an editorial writer at the *Sun* from 1844 to 1849. Her principal subject was U.S. expansion in the South and West, a cause she championed in strident and nationalistic fashion. In a remarkable letter to George Bancroft, secretary of the navy, Storms wrote in 1846 that "to a certain point I can and do control over half of the entire daily circulation and from my position thus hold the balance of opinion on any man and measure." This bombastic celebration of her own powers was no doubt an exaggeration, but it indicates the scope of her ambition.

During the Mexican War, Storms, a lifelong Democrat, established close ties to a number of officials in Washington, D.C., and in late 1846 she helped arrange the appointment of Moses Beach as an agent to Mexico. Storms spoke Spanish and accompanied Beach on a secret peace mission to Mexico City. The mission proved fruitless, and she then traveled alone to Vera Cruz, where she may have met General Winfield Scott. Storms later claimed that she provided Scott with an invasion route to Mexico City, but there is no way of documenting this contention. She did, however, write thirty-one letters to the *Sun*, making her the only correspondent behind enemy lines during the entire war. The Treaty of Guadalupe Hidalgo greatly disappointed Storms, who believed that the United States should have annexed the northern half of current-day Mexico as well as California and New Mexico.

Storms next turned her attention to Cuba, then under the control of Spain. In concert with other U.S. citizens and some Cubans, Beach had made plans for a Cuban exile newspaper to be published in New York. Storms was named editor of the journal, *La Verdad*, in early 1848. She used that platform and the columns of the *New York Sun* to propagandize on behalf of U.S. annexation of Cuba and made the same case in *The Queen of the Islands and the King of the Rivers* (1850). In late 1849 Storms married William Leslie Cazneau, a merchant and politician from Texas, and returned to live with him in Eagle Pass. They had no children. She wrote of her experiences in Texas in *Eagle Pass; or, Life on the Border* (1852).

In 1853 William Cazneau was named special commissioner to the Dominican Republic. Jane Cazneau took an active role in diplomacy behind the scenes, promoting an unsuccessful effort to secure a U.S. naval base and keeping up her own correspondence with officials in Washington. Although William Cazneau's appointment ended in late 1854, the couple remained there for the next two decades, living on a plantation outside Santo Domingo. Jane Cazneau was, as ever, a proponent of American expansion. She and her husband advocated U.S. annexation of the Dominican Republic. In the meantime, they pursued schemes to exploit Dominican resources and bring in U.S. settlers. Jane Cazneau painted a rosy picture of the island in *Life in the Tropics; by a Settler in Santo Domingo* (1863). In 1866 Secretary of State William Seward (whom Jane knew from her years in New York) visited the couple's home and indicated his support for annexation. An annexation treaty was presented to the U.S. Senate, where it faced bitter opposition and was killed in 1871. The Cazneaus moved to Jamaica, where William died in 1876. Jane died in a shipwreck off Cape Hatteras.

Jane Cazneau saw little success in the projects she pursued, from the Texas colony in the 1830s to the annexation of the Dominican Republic several decades later. Nonetheless, in promoting those causes she achieved a level of influence that was remarkable for a woman of her era; she distinguished herself in journalism and maintained a network of connections to powerful politicians. Like many of her male counterparts, she used the language of American nationalism and manifest destiny to promote the acquisition of new territories and at the same time pursued schemes of self-enrichment in those places.

• Some of Jane Cazneau's papers are at the New-York Historical Society, but her most important letters are found among the papers of the policymakers with whom she corresponded: George Bancroft (papers at the Massachusetts Historical Society), James Buchanan (papers at the Historical Society of Pennsylvania), and various officials of the State Department, in General Records of the Department of State, Record Group 59, National Archives. In addition to the books mentioned in the text, her published works include *The Prince of Kashna: A West Indian Story* (1866) and *Our Winter Eden: Pen Pictures of the Tropics* (1878). Cazneau was almost totally overlooked by historians until the 1950s, but since then the literature on her role has grown. Some of the best works are Edward S. Wallace, *Destiny and Glory* (1957); Frederick Merk, *Manifest Destiny and Mission in American History: A Reinterpretation* (1963); and Edward P. Crapol, ed., *Women and American Foreign Policy* (1987). There are a number of valuable articles, including Anna Kasten Nelson, "Mission to Mexico: Moses Y. Beach, Secret Agent," *New-York Historical Society Quarterly* 59 (1975): 227–45, and "Jane Storms Cazneau: Disciple of Manifest Destiny," *Prologue* 18 (1986): 25–40; Tom Reilly, "Jane McManus Storms: Letter from the Mexican War, 1846–1848," *Southwestern Historical Quarterly* 85 (1981): 21–44; and Robert E. May, "Lobbyists for Commercial Empire: Jane Cazneau, William Cazneau and U.S. Caribbean Policy, 1846–1878," *Pacific Historical Review* 48 (1979): 383–412.

SAMUEL WILLARD CROMPTON

CECIL, Russell LaFayette (13 Oct. 1881–1 June 1965), physician, was born in Nicholasville, Kentucky, the son of Russell Cecil, a Presbyterian minister, and Alma Miller. He received an A.B. cum laude from Princeton University in 1902 and an M.D. in 1906 from the University College of Medicine in Richmond (later Medical College of Virginia). In 1923 he married Eileen Cumming; they had one child. After serving a residency in pathology at Presbyterian Hospital of New York from 1907 to 1910, he became an instructor in clinical medicine at the Columbia University College of Physicians and Surgeons in 1912. In 1916 he joined the faculty of Cornell University College of Medicine as an instructor in clinical medicine; he became a professor in 1933 and remained until his retirement in 1950.

Cecil's career had four overlapping phases: research in infectious diseases; research in the diagnosis and treatment of rheumatoid arthritis; medical education; and organizational activities pertaining to the rheumatic diseases. Despite his training in pathology, all of his faculty positions were in internal medicine. His early work, while he was an assistant visiting physician at Presbyterian Hospital from 1911 to 1916, pertained to the pathology of the pancreas and various parasitic and bacterial infections. Upon joining the Cornell faculty in 1916 he became an assistant visiting physician at Bellevue Hospital. When Cecil began his career as a clinical and laboratory investigator of respiratory tract infections in 1915, antibiotics had not yet been discovered, and Cecil's projects, at the forefront of infectious disease research, sought to develop vaccines to combat pneumonia. He enlisted in the Army Medical Corps in 1917, and during his two years of active duty he headed the surgeon general's commission for the study of pneumonia. This work included the testing of pneumococcus vaccines both for preventive immunization and treatment of pneumonia at two army camps, which was reported in Cecil and J. H. Austin, "Results of Prophylactic Innoculation against Pneumococcus in 12519 men," *Journal of Experimental Medicine*, 28 (1918): 19–41. Cecil and Francis G. Blake, a future professor of medicine at Yale University, published ten further reports on this work, which were reprinted as *Studies on Experimental Pneumonia* (1920). Cecil returned to Cornell that year as an assistant professor, but also received appointment as chairman of the U.S. Public Health Service Hygiene Laboratory's commission to study pneumonia, a position which he held until 1928. During most of this period he continued research to improve the efficacy of antipneumococcal vaccines.

In 1917, while already deeply involved in the pneumonia research, Cecil published his first paper on the treatment of rheumatoid arthritis. In 1922 he established both an arthritis clinic at the Cornell University Clinic, then an innovative undertaking, and a bacteriologic research laboratory at Bellevue Hospital. The cause of rheumatoid arthritis was (and remains) unknown. Inconsistent evidence that had been accumulating since the 1890s suggested that the disease resulted from a bacterial infection, so it was referred to as "chronic infectious arthritis." In 1927 Cecil redirected his laboratory from pneumococcus research to investigation of the cause of rheumatoid arthritis, which by then was commonly believed to be due to a streptococcus. His first report, in 1929, described the recovery of streptococci from the blood and/or joint fluid of nearly two-thirds of cases of rheumatoid arthritis, but none from control cases. Most of the streptococci were considered to be of the same variety and were designated the "typical strain." The causal significance of these bacteria was supported by the development of arthritis in rabbits into which the typical strains had been injected. In 1931 Cecil, E. E. Nicholls, and W. J. Stainsby reported that "to our surprise we found that the serum of practically every patient with well-developed rheumatoid arthritis gave a strongly positive agglutination [test reaction] with the typical strains of streptococci" (*American Journal of Medical Sciences* 181 [1931]: 12–25). While this was confirmed in some laboratories and seemed to be conclusive evidence that rheumatoid arthritis was a streptococcal disease, Martin H. Dawson's research group at Columbia University concluded from their replication of Cecil's bacteriologic studies that no bacterial growth except for accidental contaminants could be demonstrated. They also showed that the agglutination reaction with serum from cases of rheumatoid arthritis also occurred with other than the "typical strains" of streptococci (*Journal of Immunology* 23 [1932]: 205–28). In 1940, without proposing an explanation for the difference in bacteriologic results between rheumatoid and control subjects, Cecil agreed that these years of research had been based on errors in laboratory techniques. Ultimately his work on the agglutination reaction led to the discovery of the "rheumatoid factor," which is of diagnostic and prognostic, though not of etiologic, importance.

An important paper by Cecil, "The Necessity of Establishing Specific Criteria by which to Evaluate Treatments for Arthritis" (*Annals of Internal Medicine* 10 (1936): 637–42), advocated the necessity of establishing specific criteria by which to evaluate treatments for arthritis. This concern evolved from his experiences with various supposedly antirheumatic agents, especially gold compounds. French physician Jacques Forestier, who in 1928 had introduced this group of drugs for treating rheumatoid arthritis, visited Cecil in 1931 and encouraged him to try this therapy. Although Cecil was not impressed initially, he eventually became a leading popularizer of this treatment, which continued to be a mainstay into the 1980s.

In 1927 Cecil edited *A Textbook of Medicine by American Authors*. In a departure from preceding American textbooks of medicine, this was a multi-author work in a single volume. Its content did not differ substantially, but it was immediately successful. A new edition was published every three to four years, with eleven editions appearing during Cecil's lifetime and under his editorship. In 1929 he also published the monograph *The Diagnosis and Treatment of Arthritis*. Except for receiving a wider appreciation by physicians with a special interest in rheumatic diseases, Cecil's name became virtually synonymous with the *Textbook*, which for medical students had hardly any competition into the 1950s. He also was coeditor with Howard F. Conn of a companion text, *The Specialties in General Practice*, first published in 1951.

In 1929 Cecil chaired the Section of Medical Practice of the American Medical Association. In 1934 he became a charter member of the American Association for the Study and Control of Rheumatic Diseases and served as this organization's third president from 1936 to 1937, when it was renamed the American Rheumatism Association. He was elected the first president of the New York Rheumatism Association in 1943. Soon thereafter Cecil began to foster the concept of a national foundation to fund and coordinate research and education in the rheumatic diseases. The Arthritis and Rheumatism Foundation was chartered with these goals in 1948. Cecil was its medical director from 1949 to 1951 and from 1955 to 1958, and remained as consulting medical director until 1965.

Recognition of Cecil's services to American medicine included the Gold Medal of the American Medical Writers Association in 1954 and the Distinguished Service Award of the American Medical Association in 1962. The latter award cited that "not only has he made original scientific contributions in this most important area [rheumatology], but he has served unselfishly and most effectively as a counselor and advisor in the whole field and particularly in the guidance of the rapid expansion of research in arthritis." Cecil died in New York City.

• Among Cecil's works that have not already been mentioned are, with Nicholls and Stainsby, "The Bacteriology of the Blood and Joints in Chronic Infectious Arthritis," *Archives of Internal Medicine* 43 (1929): 571–605, and, with W. H. Kammerer and F. J. DePrume, "Gold Salts in the Treatment of Rheumatoid Arthritis: A Study of 245 Cases," *Annals of Internal Medicine* 16 (1942): 811–27. Cecil's brief retraction of the results of his bacteriological studies of rheumatoid arthritis appeared in the *Proceedings of the American Medical Association* (10 June 1940); reprinted in *Journal of the American Medical Association* 115 (1940): 2113. For his contributions to rheumatology, see C. J. Smyth, R. F. Freyburg, and C. McEwen, *History of Rheumatology* (1985). Obituaries are in the *Journal of the American Medical Association* 192 (14 June 1965): 43, and *Arthritis and Rheumatism* 8 (1965): 577–80.

THOMAS G. BENEDEK

CELESTE, Mme. (6 Aug. 1810–18 Feb. 1882), performer and theater manager, also known as Mlle. Celeste and Celine Celeste, was born Anastasie Céleste des Rousselles in Marcilly sur Compagne, France, the daughter of Jeanne Marie de Rousselles, a couturière, and Jean Christophe Keppler, a stocking maker. Celeste studied at the Académie de Musique in Paris and also performed in children's roles at the Paris Opéra, eventually assuming minor corps and pantomime roles.

The earliest of an influx of European ballerinas to appear before American audiences, Celeste's first performance in the United States was a solo dance (*pas seul*) from *Les Pages du duc de Vendôme* at the Bowery Theater in New York in June 1827. In other pieces, Celeste appeared alongside dancers Francisque Hutin and Joseph Barbiere at the Bowery and three months later in Boston. Barbiere choreographed a *pas seul* for her appearance at the Chestnut Street Theatre in Philadelphia in March 1828.

Celeste married Henry Elliott of Baltimore in 1828 and had a daughter, but during a tour in 1830 she left for England amid rumors concerning the restrictive circumstances of her personal life. She retained her married name in private life but performed in the United States and Europe as Mlle. or Mme. Celeste. In 1830 she began an extended career in England, first appearing in Liverpool as Fenella the mute girl in Auber's opera *Masaniello* and then making her London debut in the ballet *La Bayadere* at the Queen's Theatre. In 1831 she danced in Paris, Manchester, Liverpool, Dublin, and London. That same year Celeste also assumed multiple roles in *The French Spy*, transformations that would become her trademark in many plays that were written especially for her. She also performed men's roles *en travesti* ("breeches roles"). Among the writers who provided her with star vehicles were James Robinson Planché, Tom Taylor, John Baldwin Buckstone, and Charles Selby.

From 1834 to 1837 Celeste again toured America, dancing roles in *La Sylphide* and Auber's *Le Dieu et la Bayadère*. In New York, Celeste performed her version of *La Bayadère* at the National Theatre, while her rival Mlle. Augusta danced the same role at the Park. Estimates of her financial success for this tour placed her profits at $200,000, a fortune at that time. Her contract fees, usually half of the theater's receipts, indicated her popularity and marketability. In 1836 she had an audience with President Andrew Jackson in Washington, D.C., which was later satirized in an extant lithograph titled "The Celeste-al Cabinet."

Returning to London in 1837, Celeste was featured in an assortment of pantomimes, mute roles, and divertissements at the Haymarket Theatre, also making some appearances in Paris. The death of her husband in 1842, however, prompted Celeste to return to Baltimore to settle his estate and to bring back her daughter. While in the United States, she performed at the Bowery Theatre in New York and at the Walnut Street Theatre in Philadelphia before returning to the Haymarket.

In 1843 Celeste assisted Benjamin Webster in managing the Theatre Royal in Liverpool, a collaboration that continued in London, where Webster set her up as manager of the Adelphi in 1844. The association was romantic as well as professional: their liaison was not clandestine, although Webster was already married. Profits from the popular Adelphi seasons helped to support Webster's ventures at the Haymarket. In addition to melodramas and divertissements, Celeste commissioned dance plays that burlesqued the latest ballets or dancers featured at rival London theaters. She was also the first recorded woman to dance the part of Harlequin in 1855 in an annual Christmas pantomime entitled *Harlequin à la Watteau*. Although manager in name, Celeste also frequently took leave to tour.

In 1853 Webster relinquished the management of the Haymarket to Buckstone, who had long been associated with the theater as actor and dramatist. The Webster-Celeste personal and professional partnership at the Adelphi dissolved in 1857 with his decision to take back the reins and renovate the theater.

Taking some members of the Adelphi company with her, Celeste engaged the Lyceum, renovated it, and began performing there in 1859. When in 1861 the theater returned to Edmund Falconer's management, Celeste arranged engagements at other theaters in London, including the Sadler's Wells in 1863 and the Victoria in 1865. She then spent most of 1865 to 1868 performing in the United States and the Antipodes. Considering retirement, Celeste gave twelve farewell performances of Stirling Coyne's *Woman in Red* at the St. James in 1868, but she continued to perform in 1869 at the Princess. In 1870 she performed her signature role of Miami in a revival of Buckstone's *The Green Bushes* and yearly performed in farewell benefits in the same role at the Adelphi from 1872 to 1874. Celeste retired permanently from the stage in 1874 and moved to Paris, where she died.

Of her acting, critics attributed "that high finish that elevates even melodramatic acting to the dignity of histrionic art" to Celeste's portrayals. The "remarkable power of her pantomimic expression" gave her the versatility to impersonate characters with contrasting emotions: love, despair, joy, indignation, fidelity, duplicity. Her classical ballet technique seems to have been wanting, but she found success as an "intelligent interpreter of the mysteries of the ballet."

Celeste's popularity and financial success arose from her combination of performance ability and marketing acuity. Her repertoire responded to current trends in popular taste for stage and social dance. Celeste performed versions of most of the solo character dances that captured the public's admiration: the cachucha and the tarantella, for example. She also capitalized on the popularity of social dances by performing stage versions of the polka (in *The Trumpeter's Daughter* at the Haymarket) and the mazurka (in *Taming a Tartar* at the Adelphi). She circumvented her difficulties with English by commissioning mute or foreign-accent roles in melodramas and burlettas, thereby also ensuring a performance career when her dance technique deteriorated in her later years. Her use of London as home base also gave Celeste access to the latest fashionable dances and performance pieces, materials that she then successfully took on tour to the United States, where foreign artists were preferred to domestic products.

• The papers of the Benjamin Webster family, on which Margaret Webster based her account *The Same Only Different* (1969), are located in the Library of Congress; the New York Public Library Dance Collection also holds photographs and engravings of Celeste. Charles E. Pascoe, *The Dramatic List: A Record of the Principal Performances of Living Actors and Actresses of the British Stage* (1880; repr. 1969 and 1971), includes Celeste's biographical information, as well as excerpts from major performance reviews, although some of the dates are questionable. George C. D. Odell, *Annals of the New York Stage* (1927–1949); Arthur Herman Wilson, *A History of the Philadelphia Theatre, 1835 to 1855* (1935); and Noah M. Ludlow, *Dramatic Life as I Found It* (1880), provide records of Celeste's appearances in the United States. The *Illustrated London News* and the *Theatrical Examiner* (London) provide transatlantic anecdotes of Celeste's tours and reviews of the minor London theaters at which she predominantly performed. The most reliable secondary source on Celeste's American career is Mary Grace Swift, *Belles and Beaux on Their Toes* (1979). An obituary is in the *Era* (London), 25 Feb. 1882.

LIBBY SMIGEL

CELESTIN, Papa (1 Jan. 1884–15 Dec. 1954), bandleader and trumpeter, was born Oscar Philip Celestin in Lafourche Parish, Louisiana, the son of Joseph Celestin, a sugar-cane cutter, and Lucy (maiden name unknown). About 1900 Celestin got his first cornet and for a few years worked as a cook for a railroad. In 1902 he moved to St. Charles Parish, where he got his first job as a musician with J. C. Trist's band. In 1906 he moved to New Orleans and worked first as a longshoreman and, in 1909, as a musician at Josie Arlington's saloon in the local red-light district. The first New Orleans band of which he was a regular member was the Indiana Brass Band. Then he joined Jack Carey's band, where he began to play jazz. He also worked with other New Orleans bands, including Henry Allen's Brass Band, the Silver Leaf Band, and Armand Piron's band. Originally called "Sonny," Celestin gradually affected a paternal bearing and became known among musicians as "Papa."

In 1910 Celestin joined the Tuxedo Band at the Tuxedo Dance Hall in the Storyville district. A year later he was joined by future musicians such as Johnny Lindsay and Pops Foster to form the Original Tuxedo Brass Band. Appearing with them were Louis Armstrong, Roy Palmer, Lee Collins, and King Oliver; Armstrong called it the best brass band in town. The band donned black tuxedos, derbies, and white shirts, and their attire and good manners helped develop their reputation. It became the prototypical New Orleans jazz band.

During and after World War I, the band played at debutante parties, carnival balls, country clubs, fraternity and sorority dances, yacht clubs, fine hotels, and, on every Sunday of the baseball season, Heinemann Park. In July 1924 two members of the band squeezed into an airplane with the Gates Flying Circus and gave a concert of sorts—the first musicians, ostensibly, to play from an airplane. In 1922 Celestin had married Ophelia Jackson; they did not have children.

Celestin served as musical director and William "Baba" Ridgley as booking agent and business manager, a division of duties and talents that precipitated a split following an angry recording session in January 1925. Some of the musicians went with Ridgley, forming Ridgley's Original Tuxedo Jazz Orchestra, and others joined Celestin's Original Tuxedo Jazz Orchestra. Both bands were successful, but Ridgley abandoned his project after six years.

In his own band, Celestin's sweet, melodic style was contrasted by a second cornetist, who played a hotter, more modern style. Some members read music, and others did not; they generally played from memory, but they also counted measures and beats.

During the 1930s Celestin worked at college dances, carnival parties, and similar society jobs. Although he toured neighboring states, he refused many offers to leave town permanently. The depression and the proliferation of bands with white musicians forced Celestin to work under the Works Progress Administration as a laborer.

Though Celestin played occasionally during World War II, he also had to work as a longshoreman, drive a truck, and become a chauffeur. In 1944 he was hit by a car when leaving his job at a defense plant and was kept in bed for two years while both of his broken legs mended. His wife nursed him back to health and encouraged his return to the horn.

During the 1946–1947 tourist season Celestin began work at the Paddock Lounge on Bourbon Street. Soon the New Orleans jazz revival was under way, and crowds flocked into the nightclub. Although the band used Celestin's name, he was not the actual leader; he did lead another band that played private engagements, especially the departure of luxury ships. In 1951 he left the Paddock to concentrate on these other engagements but worked an occasional Bourbon Street nightclub job. He also appeared on radio and television, and his band was in the 1953 film *Cinerama Holiday*. In May 1953 Celestin played for the White House Correspondents' Association, receiving a certificate of appreciation signed by President Dwight D. Eisenhower. When Celestin died in New Orleans, trombonist Eddie Pierson became the band's new manager; but Celestin's widow was considered its leader and received a share of its pay.

Celestin was a showstopper. When his band rendered "Tiger Rag," Celestin would claw, then roar and shake. He excelled at entertaining as well as bandleading, and his showmanship was a major reason for his popularity and success. Armstrong and "Sweet Emma" Barrett praised his fairness and courtesy, and he was known for developing young musicians. While critics sometimes complained that his work was too melodic and predictable, Celestin knew what the audience wanted. Sid Davilla, a clarinetist and Bourbon Street nightclub owner, told David Brinkley that when Celestin put a tight mute in his trumpet and played "Just Telephone Me," the cash register fell silent and no one ordered a drink. Celestin's popularity with New Orleaneans was so great that his records and his legend have been passed down to younger generations, both in the United States and around the world.

• The William Ransom Hogan Jazz Archive in Tulane's Howard-Tilton Memorial Library has a collection of Celestin material in various forms, including recordings, oral histories, correspondence, photographs, and printed sources. John G. Curren, "Oscar 'Papa' Celestin," *Second Line*, Jan.–Feb. 1955, pp. 1, 3–6, 20, tells much of his life story, but some details are contradicted in other sources. Peter R. Haby, "Oscar 'Papa' Celestin 1884–1954," *Footnote*, June–July 1981, pp. 4–15, gives many details of Celestin's life; the recordings suggested for listening are useful, and Haby's acknowledgments might help in bibliographical work. John Chilton's brief biography of Celestin in the *New Grove Dictionary of Jazz*, ed. Barry Kernfeld, vol. 1 (1988), contains a list of selected recordings as well as a brief bibliography. Alan Ward, with Richard B. Allen, "Hot Tuxedoes," *Footnote*, June–July 1987, pp. 4–9, is another biography with much detail up to 1923. Louis Armstrong, *Satchmo: My Life in New Orleans* (c. 1954), relates Armstrong's experience in the Original Tuxedo Brass Band and describes Celestin's help with reading music. Oren Blackstone, "Papa Celestin Comes Back," *Jazzfinder*, Apr. 1948, pp. 11–13, has a brief Celestin biography, followed by a discography. Also see later discographies and Chris Botsford, with William Russell, "Sweet Emma's 1968 Interview," *Jazz Beat*, Fall–Winter 1990–1991, pp. 5–6. Obituaries are in the *New York Times*, and the *New Orleans Times-Picayune*, both 16 Dec. 1954.

RICHARD B. ALLEN

CELLER, Emanuel (6 May 1888–15 Jan. 1981), lawyer and politician, was born in Brooklyn, New York, the son of Henry H. Celler, a liquor and wine merchant, and Josephine Müller. Celler grew up in a prosperous Jewish family. After attending public schools in Brooklyn, he entered Columbia University. While Celler was enrolled at Columbia College, he had to take on the role of head of household after both parents died. Attending classes in the mornings, he sold wine in the afternoons. In 1910 he received his bachelor's degree, and two years later he earned his law degree from Columbia. He passed the bar in 1912 and opened a law practice in New York City. In 1914 he married Stella B. Baar; they had two children.

For the next eight years Celler concentrated on building his law practice. In 1922 he was asked by James J. Sexton, tax collector of New York City, to consider running for the U.S. House of Representatives as a Democrat from the Tenth Congressional District of Brooklyn. Although the district was primarily Republican, its constituents included many immigrant families, and Celler agreed to run. After conducting a vigorous campaign, he won an upset victory by over 3,000 votes, and he began his first term in Congress on 4 March 1923. In subsequent elections he won by wide margins, sometimes as great as 3 to 1 after the district's boundaries were changed. In later years the district increasingly became a Jewish middle-class area. Celler would serve for fifty years in the House of Representatives, working under nine presidents.

When Celler entered Congress the mood of the nation was conservative. Frustrated during his early years in Congress, in one of his first speeches he attacked the Johnson Reed Immigration Act that further limited the national origins quotas that had been instituted in 1921 by the Emergency Quota Act. As finally put into effect in 1929, national origins quotas gave European countries immigrant quotas based on their percentage of the white American population in 1920. The provision, which provided a total of only 150,000 visas, favored European nations like Great Britain, Ireland, and Germany and left southern and eastern European nations with small allotments. He also opposed monopolies and abuses by big business, but his proposals on these issues had little chance for success in this era. During his time in Congress he also continued his law practice, worked for a bank, and served briefly as a trustee, counselor, and vice president of the Reliance Investment Company.

With the coming of the New Deal era, Celler found fellow legislators and a president in sympathy with his liberal views. He backed Franklin D. Roosevelt's New Deal measures with enthusiasm. He favored laws to regulate business and became a strong supporter of federal relief for the unemployed, the Tennessee Valley Authority, the Works Progress Administration, the Social Security Act, the National Labor Relations Act, and other measures helpful to labor unions. Celler did not approve of Supreme Court decisions declaring New Deal legislation unconstitutional, but on ethical grounds he opposed Roosevelt's Supreme Court packing scheme.

Celler sided with the administration on foreign policy issues, supporting Roosevelt's lend-lease strategy and measures to build up the national defense. He later backed Roosevelt's leadership during the war. Celler was converted to Zionism during his twenties, and in the 1940s he was a strong supporter of the establishment of the state of Israel.

Celler's standing in the House grew over time. Under the seniority system he became the ranking Democrat on the House Judiciary Committee in 1940 and then chairman of that important committee during the years that the Democrats were in the majority. By 1965 he was the senior member in the House of Representatives.

As the Cold War developed, Celler supported President Harry S. Truman's proposals for the Marshall Plan, the National Atlantic Treaty Organization, and foreign aid. However, he opposed a loan to Great Britain because of British policy toward Palestine during the 1940s. In other Cold War issues, Celler found himself in a minority, especially on matters dealing with communism and alleged Communist influence in the United States. He attacked Senator Joseph R. McCarthy and voted against the Internal Security Act of 1950 and the Mundt-Nixon Communist registration bill. He also spoke out against the House Un-American Activities Committee and its investigations and opposed its establishment as a permanent standing committee.

He became coauthor of the Celler-Kefauver Anti-Merger Act of 1950, which barred mergers achieved by acquisition of assets and led to less competition. Later in the decade, as civil rights issues loomed large, Celler played a key role in the drafting and passing of the Civil Rights Acts of 1957 and 1960, which created the Civil Rights Commission and provided some protection for African-American civil rights. He was a major figure in guiding through Congress the Civil Rights Act of 1964, with its far-reaching provisions against racial segregation and job discrimination. The act banned segregation in most public places, prohibited discrimination by employers and labor unions, gave the government the power to withhold federal funds from public programs that practiced discrimination, and created the Equal Employment Opportunity Commission. He also supported measures in President Lyndon Johnson's War on Poverty. Celler is best known as one of the key figures in the enactment of the Immigration and Nationality Act of 1965, known as the Hart-Celler Act. He had long favored the immigration liberalization that the act instituted. The Hart-Celler Act abolished the national origins quotas, giving each nation the same quota of 20,000 visas, not counting immediate family members of American citizens, and based immigration on family unification, economic considerations, and refugee status.

Celler had angered some constituents by supporting the Vietnam War and opposing the Equal Rights Amendment. Moreover, in his later terms he lost touch with many constituents, failing to use the mail effectively to keep the voters informed and not attending meetings of various organizations in his district. Nonetheless, in 1972 Celler and his supporters predicted another easy victory. He was challenged in the Democratic primary by Elizabeth Holtzman, a young attorney who ran a tough campaign. The result was a surprising upset by Holtzman; he lost the primary in a close vote, thus ending twenty-five terms in the House of Representatives. Celler then returned to New York City, where he continued to practice law until shortly before his death at his home in Brooklyn.

• No collection of Celler's papers exists. For personal accounts, see a 1957 oral history conducted by the Herbert Lehman Project, "Reminiscences of Emanuel Celler," at Columbia University, and his autobiography, *You Never Leave Brooklyn* (1953). See also *Current Biography* (1966). An obituary is in the *New York Times*, 16 Jan. 1981.

DAVID REIMERS

CELLI, Vincenzo (4 May 1900–28 Feb. 1988), dancer and dance teacher, was born Vincenzo Yacullo in Salerno, Italy. The family (his parents' names are unknown) emigrated to Chicago when he was a young child. As a teenager Celli performed in Shakespearean and other theatrical performances at Hull-House, the famous settlement house directed by Jane Addams. Aspiring to be an actor, Celli moved to New York in 1916 and joined the Washington Square Players. There the ballet director Adolph Bolm coached the young man in movement, then hired him to appear in a production of *Le Coq d'Or* at the Metropolitan Opera and encouraged him to continue his studies at his Chicago school. A small group of patrons gathered funds to sponsor the young man's formal dance study in Europe. His journey began in Paris, where he met the opera singer Marion Ivell, who became his wife in 1925. They had no children. Celli studied in Milan with Raffaele Grassi and made his debut as a dancer in 1920 at the Dal Verme Theater. The production was Manzotti's popular ballet-spectacle *Excelsior*. In 1922 Celli was engaged as a dancer at La Scala, where he first partnered the ballerina Cia Fornaroli. Celli joined a small group of dancers from the opera who toured for six months in Spain and Italy. He then took an engagement at the Vienna Volksoper, where he danced under the direction of Irene Sironi, again partnering Fornaroli.

During this period Celli met the great teacher Enrico Cecchetti, the favored teacher of Diaghilev's Ballets Russes. Cecchetti epitomized the Italian style of dancing, but for nearly two decades he had also been the ballet master of the Imperial Ballet in St. Petersburg. He agreed to take Celli as a student for six months of intensive training. Celli recalled that the daily class sometimes extended to four hours. After the first six months the lessons continued in Milan, Turin, Monte Carlo, and Venice, whenever and wherever their engagements would allow, and Celli remained a devoted pupil until Cecchetti's death in 1928.

A misunderstanding about his 1924–1925 season contract at La Scala left Celli out of work, and he went to Paris, where he performed with the great Russian ballerina Olga Spessivtseva. There, he also met the legendary ballerina Anna Pavlova and was engaged to join her company for the 1925 London season, followed by a tour of England, Scotland, and Ireland. Celli then returned to La Scala, where he continued to perform for the next eight years as a leading dancer. He was particularly known for his interpretations of the title roles in *Petrouchka*, conducted by Igor Stravinsky in a spectacular production in 1927, and *The Legend of Joseph*, directed by Richard Strauss in 1929. Celli was appointed choreographer as well as principal male dancer at La Scala in 1931, but pressures to join the Fascist party made him increasingly uneasy.

Celli's attempts to return to the United States were complicated because he had retained his nationality of birth and had never become an American citizen. In 1933 he joined a small concert group with Fornaroli, who with her in-laws, the Toscanini family, was also in exile from Milan. He finally managed to enter the United States in the autumn of 1934 and returned to Chicago to care for his parents in the final years of their lives. Celli remained active as a dancer over the next few years with small concerts in the Chicago area. In 1937 he rented a New York studio at Fifty-ninth Street and Madison Avenue and started to offer classes. Students came, and with his growing following he moved to Studio 61 at Carnegie Hall. Léonide Massine, director of the Ballet Russe de Monte Carlo, learned that Celli was teaching and offered him a position with the company. For two years Celli toured all over the United States, teaching the daily company technique class and dancing a few roles.

In the early 1940s, Celli established a studio on Fifty-ninth Street in New York, where he attracted a cosmopolitan mixture of students from stars to neophytes and perpetuated the Cecchetti style. Among the dancers who attended his classes regularly were Alicia Markova, Anton Dolin, Rosella Hightower, Royes Fernandez, Lupe Serrano, Mia Slavenska, Marge

Champion, and Moscelyne Larkin. In a tribute to Cecchetti published in *Dance Index*, Celli defined the teaching method that had been bequeathed to him: "The Cecchetti method adheres to a strict program—definite rules and sequences of exercises to be learned by every pupil, excluding the preference or habit of any given master. . . . By varying the types of steps, no one set of muscles is ever overtrained or forced. The development is gradual but positive."

In the late 1980s, after the death of his wife, Celli's health began to decline, and during his last years he lived with a friend in Greenwich, Connecticut, where he died.

• Celli recorded a book-length oral history with Dale Harris for the Dance Collection of the New York Public Library for the Performing Arts, where his scrapbooks, photographs, and personal papers also are kept. A film by Léonide Massine records a class taught by Celli in 1940, and correspondence and various papers are in the Walter Toscanini Collection of Research Materials in the Dance Collection. Celli published tributes to two of his partners in *Dance Magazine*, Cia Fornaroli in Jan. 1955 and Olga Spessivtseva in Nov. 1941, as well as an extensive portrait of Enrico Cecchetti in *Dance Index*, July 1946. An obituary is in the *New York Times*, 1 Mar. 1988.

MONICA MOSELEY

CÉLORON DE BLAINVILLE, Pierre Joseph (29 Dec. 1693–12 Apr. 1759), explorer, was born in Montreal, Canada, the son of Captain Jean Baptiste Céloron de Blainville of the French colonial regulars and Hélène Picoté de Belestre. Pursuing the usual career path of a Canadian noble, Céloron de Blainville followed his father into the Compagnies franches de la Marine, the colonial garrison troops of the French Ministry of the Navy and Colonies. Granted the rank of cadet in 1707 at the age of thirteen, he was promoted to first ensign in 1715, commissioned a lieutenant in 1731, and promoted to captain, the highest official rank in his corps, in 1738, a few months after his appointment as commander of Fort Michilimackinac (Mackinaw City, Mich.). In 1724 he married Marie-Madeleine Blondeau in Montreal; they had six children.

In 1739–1740 Governor Jean Baptiste Le Moyne de Bienville of Louisiana organized a campaign against the Chickasaws, who were undermining France's position in the Mississippi Valley. On orders from Canada, Céloron de Blainville descended the Mississippi with a contingent of 200 Canadians and 300 Great Lakes Indians to rendezvous with the Louisianians at Fort Assomption (Memphis, Tenn.). Delays in advancing on the Chickasaw stronghold (Tupelo, Miss.) nearly resulted in the campaign ending in a humiliating failure. Fortunately for Bienville, Céloron's success in a battle on 22 February 1740 helped to persuade the Chickasaws to negotiate for peace. The following year Louis XV awarded the Canadian nobleman the coveted cross of the military order of Saint-Louis. Céloron's first wife had died in 1733, and in 1743 he married Catherine Eury de La Pérelle in Montreal; they had seven children.

In 1742 Governor General the Marquis de Beauharnois placed Céloron in command of Fort Pontchartrain or Detroit and in 1744 transferred him to Fort Niagara (Youngstown, N.Y.), where he remained until late in 1745. Although Céloron gained the esteem of the Ottawa chiefs at Michilimackinac, at Detroit and Niagara he angered the Canadian fur traders, who claimed that he interfered with their business. In 1747, during the War of the Austrian Succession, Beauharnois appointed Céloron to command Fort Saint-Frédéric (Crown Point, N.Y.) on Lake Champlain. In the spring of 1748, however, Governor General the Marquis de La Galissonière gave Céloron command of troops sent to quell France's native allies in the Great Lakes region, who were furious about the rising cost and increasing shortage of trade goods and La Galissonière's tactless assertions of authority.

La Galissonière then ordered Céloron to mount a show of force on the Ohio, where the Indian nations, many former allies, openly traded with the Pennsylvanians and Virginians. The captain was to intimidate the local peoples into allying themselves with France, expel British traders, map the area more accurately, and bury a series of engraved lead plates proclaiming French sovereignty. On 15 June 1749 Céloron left Montreal for the Ohio in command of about 200 Canadian militia and colonial regulars and thirty Mission Iroquois and Abenaki. After a stop at Fort Niagara, the small force landed on the south shore of Lake Erie (Westfield, N.Y.), portaged to Lake Chautauqua, and paddled down the Allegheny and Ohio rivers. It quickly became apparent that the French were too weak to make much of an impression on the Indians or even the traders, whose goods Céloron did not dare to confiscate in the face of native opposition. He gave one group of traders a letter to the governor of Pennsylvania informing him that Pennsylvanians were trespassing on French soil, but the pro-British stance of the Mingo, Shawnee, and Miami peoples made French claims illusory. At the end of August Céloron turned north, meeting the hostile Miami chief Memeskia or La Demoiselle at Pickawillany (Piqua, Ohio). The French force stopped for a short while at Fort des Miamis (Fort Wayne, Ind.) before returning to Montreal, arriving there on 9 November 1749. The Jesuit professor Joseph Pierre de Bonnécamps, who accompanied the expedition as chaplain, cartographer, and secretary, called Céloron "a man born to command," a statement borne out by the officer's success in traveling more than 3,000 miles (5,000 km) through unmapped and unfriendly territory with the loss of only one man drowned. Nevertheless, Céloron was only too conscious that instead of overawing the Ohio Indians, they had humiliated him. Although he feared that a further show of force might drive the Ohio nations further into the arms of the British, he recommended in his report that an expensive chain of military posts be built linking Lake Erie and the upper Ohio, a project that La Galissonière strongly supported.

La Galissonière's successor, the Marquis de La Jonquière, appointed Céloron town major of the Canadian settlement of Detroit, and in 1751 La Jonquière ordered him to attack and destroy the pro-British Miamis. Céloron, however, failed to muster any native support for the expedition and declined to follow orders, claiming that 1,800 colonial regulars and militia were necessary for success and that failure would destroy French prestige in the entire West. In 1753 the next governor general, the Marquis Duquesne, recalled the now elderly Céloron and gave him the less rigorous post of town major of Montreal. Duquesne and others characterized Céloron as a courageous and intelligent military leader but also haughty, injudicious, and poorly suited to routine administrative duties.

Céloron did not take an active part in the Seven Years' War and died in Montreal near the end of the conflict, leaving his family little money. His eldest son from his first marriage, a captain also named Pierre Joseph, moved to France after the British conquest, but Céloron's widow remained in Canada, joining the Congregation of the Sisters of Charity, or Gray Nuns.

Céloron de Blainville played a significant role in maintaining French power in the Great Lakes region during the mid-eighteenth century. His expedition and report of 1749 paved the way for the French occupation of the upper Ohio in 1753, which precipitated the Seven Years' War.

• Correspondence relating to Céloron de Blainville can be found at the Archives Nationales in Paris, Fonds des Colonies C11A, D2C, D2D, and F3; much of this material is also on microfilm at the National Archives in Ottawa, Canada. A biography of Céloron de Blainville has yet to be published. The most detailed sources concerning his career are Céloron's and Bonnécamps' journals of 1749, Céloron de Blainville, "Journal de la campagne," in *Découvertes et établissements des Français dans l'ouest et dans le sud de l'Amérique septentrionale*, ed. Pierre Margry (1879–1888), vol. 6, pp. 666–726, and Joseph Pierre de Bonnécamps, "Relation du voyage de la Belle Rivière faite en 1749, sous les ordres de M. de Céloron," in *The Jesuit Relations and Allied Documents*, ed. Reuben G. Thwaites (1898), vol. 69, pp. 150–98. Also important are O. H. Marshall, "De Céloron's Expedition to the Ohio in 1749," *Magazine of American History* 2 (1878): 129–50; an account of Céloron's family in Pierre G. Roy, *La famille Céloron de Blainville* (1909); and a detailed reference biography, William J. Eccles, "Céloron de Blainville, Pierre-Joseph," *Dictionary of Canadian Biography*, vol. 3, pp. 99–101.

A number of secondary works place Céloron's activities in their historical context. Michael J. Foret, "The Failure of Administration: The Chickasaw Campaign of 1739–1740," *Revue de Louisiane/Louisiana Review* 11 (1982): 49–60; Joseph L. Peyser, "The Chickasaw Wars of 1736 and 1740: French Military Drawings and Plans Document the Struggle for the Lower Mississippi," *Journal of Mississippi History* 44 (1982): 1–25; and Daniel H. Usner, *Indians, Settlers, and Slaves in a Frontier Exchange Economy: The Lower Mississippi Valley before 1783* (1992), deal with the Chickasaw campaigns. Richard White, *The Middle Ground: Indians, Empires, and Republics in the Great Lakes Region, 1650–1815* (1991), and George F. G. Stanley, *New France: The Last Phase, 1744–1760* (1968), provide an overview of Céloron's activities in the Great Lakes and Ohio Valley, and D. Dale Standen, *Charles, Marquis de Beauharnois de la Boische, Governor General of New France, 1726–1747* (1975), examines Céloron's relationship with Beauharnois.

MARTIN NICOLAI

CERF, Bennett Alfred (25 May 1898–27 Aug. 1971), publisher and author, was born in New York City, the son of Gustave Cerf, a lithographer, and Frederika Wise, an heiress. Although Frederika had money that accrued from a parental trust fund, Gustave insisted that the family live modestly on his lithographer's salary. When Cerf was in his teens, his mother died, shortly after giving birth to his sister, who also died. Consequently, sixteen-year-old Cerf became the sole beneficiary of his mother's sizable trust fund of $125,000.

With familial connections, a cadre of influential personal friends, and financial freedom, Cerf's interests took two diverse paths—finance and business on one hand and literature and the theater on the other. His paramount interest, however, was monetary, and he dropped out of high school to work for an accountant while taking classes at the Packard Commercial School for Business. Although the experience was enriching, he found the work dull and, at the insistence of his uncle Herbert Wise, pursued classes for high school credit until he was accepted into Columbia University. In 1919 he earned two degrees simultaneously, a bachelor of arts from Columbia and a bachelor of literature from the School of Journalism. Although he was elected Phi Beta Kappa in his junior year, it was his journalistic activity, as columnist for the campus newspaper, the *Daily Spectator*, and editor of the humor magazine *The Jester*, that eventually shaped the path his life would take.

Still a man with multiple interests, Cerf took a position in a Wall Street brokerage and wrote a financial column for the *New York Tribune*. After only a few months he was dismissed by the *Tribune* for giving inaccurate financial advice and for not following directives about what to write. His life was altered permanently, however, when Richard L. Simon, a friend from school, introduced him to Horace Liveright, owner of Boni and Liveright Publishers. Fascinated by the world of books and authors, Cerf acquiesced to Liveright's invitation to alleviate the firm's financial woes by investing in the business and accepted the position of vice president that went with the offer. His initial investment was $25,000, followed by an additional $25,000 in partnership. A mere two years later, Liveright was once again in financial duress, and once again Cerf came to his rescue by offering to purchase the Modern Library subsidiary for $215,000. Having no other recourse, Liveright agreed, and Cerf with another college colleague, Donald Klopfer, became the owner of a publishing house in 1925.

The Modern Library series was the predecessor of paperbacks because the editions were physically smaller and often less expensive than the original works. It was such a financial success that Cerf and Klopfer recouped their investment after only two years and decided to expand, initially as a distributor for others. Inevitably, feeling the need for a challenge, Cerf suggested they publish a few new books—at random—and thus Random House was born in 1926.

The first years were invested in publishing limited editions of classic works such as Melville's *Benito Cereno* and Dante's *Divine Comedy* that were marketed at a high price, but that commercial avenue was promptly closed by the stock market crash of 1929. Although the firm was not drastically affected by the disastrous financial climate, the collectors of expensive editions were, and Cerf, always the entrepreneur, sought new venues. Perhaps his most outstanding contribution to the world of letters came in 1933, when he and Random House engaged in court action to lift the censorship ban on James Joyce's *Ulysses* and to secure the right to publish the first American edition in 1934.

After a one-year bicoastal marriage to actress Sylvia Sidney—she lived in Hollywood; he, in New York—ended in divorce, in 1940 Cerf married Phyllis Fraser (née Helen Nichols), a cousin of the actress Ginger Rogers. She became an editor at Random House, and the couple had two sons.

The history of Random House and the personal history of Cerf are inseparable. He gave encouragement, succor, and advice freely to the authors who published under his imprint, among them William Faulkner, Gertrude Stein, Robert Penn Warren, and James Michener. With seemingly boundless energy, a passion for humor, and a penchant for self-promotion, Cerf wined and dined the most famous people in the world and called them friends.

Never being one to enjoy the stagnation produced by success, Cerf launched a new career in 1948 as author and editor of a series of humor anthologies and collections of plays and short stories, beginning with the *Pocketbook of War Humor*, which he edited. The first collection of his own work, compiled in 1943 from anecdotal columns he created for *Saturday Review of Literature*, was *Try and Stop Me*, which topped the bestseller list. To alleviate a comparison between his personal promotional efforts and those of his authors, Cerf did not publish his own books, placing them instead with Richard Simon, his old friend and an owner of Simon and Schuster. His later books were published mainly by Doubleday; one was published by Harper.

As his personal fame increased, Cerf became the focus of other offers. He hosted a radio show, "Books Are Bullets," on which he interviewed authors of war books; he became indispensable on the lecture circuit; and, in 1951, he became a permanent panelist on the television quiz show "What's My Line?," which ran to summer 1967 and earned him national public recognition. There were periods during this time when he claimed the need to remind the public of his primary position as a publisher, and there were those who considered him less than dignified when he accepted questionable positions, such as product spokesperson for advertising campaigns and a faculty position for the mail-order Famous Writer's School.

Despite public criticism of his role as raconteur and dilettante, Cerf was lauded in a *New York Times* front-page obituary as a "powerful shaper of the country's literary and cultural life." His equal flair for commerce and promotion led to the purchase by Random House of Grosset and Dunlap and eventually of Alfred Knopf, culminating in the sale of the firm to RCA for $40 million in 1966.

His other accomplishments notwithstanding, it is his bon vivant flair, remarkable optimism and honesty, and raucous sense of humor for which Bennett Cerf will be remembered. In his autobiographical *At Random* (1977), he wrote his own epitaph: "He left people a little happier than they were when he came into the room" (292). Bennett Cerf died at his estate in Mt. Kisco, New York, of unknown causes.

• Bennett Cerf's personal papers are in the library at Columbia University in New York City. The best source of information is Cerf's own reminiscence, *At Random* (1977). Other biographical works merely reiterate much of the same information. Among articles of interest are Thomas Morgan, "The Long Happy Life of Bennett Cerf," *Esquire*, Mar. 1964, pp. 112–18, and Robert Corrigan, "What's My Line: Bennett Cerf, Ezra Pound and the American Poet," *American Quarterly* (Mar. 1972): 101–13, which discusses Cerf's exclusion of Pound from a poetry anthology. Lengthy obituaries are on page 1 of the *New York Times*, 29 Aug. 1971, and in *Publishers Weekly*, 6 Sept. 1971, pp. 30–31.

JOYCE DUNCAN

CERMAK, Anton Joseph (9 May 1873–6 Mar. 1933), mayor of Chicago, Illinois, was born in Kladno, Czechoslovakia (then a province in the Austro-Hungarian Empire), the son of Anton Cermak, a miner, and Catherine Frank. Cermak's family arrived in the United States in 1874 and settled in Braidwood, Illinois, where young Cermak had a few years of schooling before he moved to Chicago in 1889. He engaged in a number of businesses including wood hauling, real estate, and insurance. In 1894 he married Mary Horejs, with whom he had three children. He began his political career in 1894 as an assistant precinct captain and gradually worked his way up until 1902 when he won election as state representative. From then until his death he always held one or more elective appointments in Chicago, Cook County, or the state of Illinois, as well as Democratic party offices. Beginning in 1902 he won four successive elections to the Illinois state legislature. In 1909 he was elected alderman in Chicago, representing a predominantly Czech ward. The Czech ethnic group was to be the base for his political success at the city, county, and state levels.

Cermak's first citywide elective office came in 1912 as bailiff of the municipal court. In 1922 he won a seat on, and became the president of, the Cook County Board of Commissioners. In 1928 Cermak wanted the Democratic nomination for governor but could not get it. Instead he reluctantly accepted nomination for U.S. senator but lost the election. When the leader of the Cook County Democratic party, James Brennan, died in the midst of the campaign, Cermak seized the opportunity, and within a year and a half he had become the leader of the Cook County Democratic machine.

Cermak was now in position to achieve his ultimate goal, the mayoralty of Chicago, which he won in 1931 by defeating the Republican incumbent, William Hale Thompson. As mayor from April 1931 until his death, Cermak had to cope with the critical financial situation caused by the depression. He spent most of his term trying to borrow money and collect back taxes in order to keep the city from going bankrupt. His mayoralty was also marked by a sharp drop in municipal employment and the combining of various city bureaus in order to reduce the payroll. In February 1933 Cermak visited Miami to confer with President-elect Franklin D. Roosevelt about federal aid for Chicago and Democratic politics, when he was shot by Giuseppe Zangara in an attempt on the president-elect's life. Cermak died in the hospital in Miami several weeks later.

Cermak was the ultimate ethnic and urban political leader in Illinois, if not the nation, during the 1920s and early 1930s. He built his political power on a coalition of ethnic groups led by fellow Czechs and with strong support from Jews, Germans, and Poles, as well as the newer immigrants of the 1890–1920 period. While he had no overall political ideology or program, he used the strong opposition of many European immigrant groups to Prohibition as an ideological position. Besides his superior abilities as an organizational politician, Cermak was considered an energetic, hardworking, and careful administrator who strongly supported urban public works and education. Cermak's control and administration of the Democratic party in Chicago set the model for the city's long-standing Democratic political domination that began in 1931.

• There are no remaining Cermak letters or manuscripts. Alex Gottfried, *Boss Cermak of Chicago: A Study of Political Leadership* (1962), is a full-scale biography. Additional material about Cermak's role as mayor and Chicago political leader is in John M. Allswang, *Bosses, Machines, and Urban Voters* (1977; rev. ed., 1986), and Allswang, *The Political Behavior of Chicago's Ethnic Groups, 1918–1932* (1967; rpt. 1980). A lengthy obituary is in the *Chicago Tribune*, 6 Mar. 1933.

ALBERT ERLEBACHER

CESAR (c. 1682–?), South Carolina slave and medical practitioner who developed primitive pharmaceuticals, was born possibly in Africa or the Caribbean and transported to the southern colonies as a slave, or perhaps he was born into slavery in South Carolina. (His name is often spelled Caesar.) His parents are unknown; he may have been the descendant of skilled medicine men, who transferred medical knowledge from their native cultures to the colonies, sharing drug recipes and folk remedies that used herbs and roots, or of slave midwives, who had performed Caesarian sections in Africa and taught other slaves that procedure.

Cesar might also have had Native American ancestors because many Carolina slaves had intermarried with native tribes. Southern Native Americans were known for their potent herbal remedies. Slave physicians were either self-taught or acquired some training from fellow slaves or masters, and they became celebrities within their communities for their healing powers. Their reputation boosted their social rank, and whites became aware of their "curative knowledge."

Cesar was well known in his community for his use of roots and herbs as an antidote to poison. His pharmaceutical prowess attracted the attention of colonial leaders, and his successes were preserved in colonial records. The 24 November 1749 journal of the South Carolina Commons House of Assembly in Charleston noted that a "Member acquainted the House that there is a Negro Man named Caesar belonging to Mr. John Norman of Beach Hill, who had cured several of the Inhabitants of this Province who had been poisoned by Slaves." The legislator stated that Cesar "was willing to make a Discovery of the Remedy which he makes Use of in such Cases for a reasonable Reward." The following day the assembly appointed a committee to investigate the claim and "report what Reward the said Negro Man Caesar shall merit for his Services." By Wednesday, 29 November, the assembly "Ordered that Doctor Glen and Doctor Brisband be added to the Committee who were appointed to . . . examine into the Services lately done by a Negro Man called Caesar . . . who have it in charge to desire the Aid and Observations of any skilful Physicians they shall think fit."

Committee member Mr. Austin delivered a report to the clerk, which was read to the legislators. William Miles had informed the committee that his sister and brother had been poisoned, and Cesar saved their lives. Miles's son had recently been poisoned and "wants Caesar to his Relief." Other testimonials included "Henry Middleton, Esq., [who] believed he was poisoned and after two doses was cured. His overseer had also been cured." A Mr. Sacheverell "informed the Committee that Caesar had undertaken to cure a Man who was violently afflicted with Fits, and, in Appearance, will effect it."

Cesar's master, John Norman, told the committee that "to his Knowledge, Caesar had done many Services in a physical Way, and in particular had frequently cured the Bite of Rattle Snakes, and never knew him to fail in any one Attempt." Norman elaborated that "Caesar had been frequently called upon as a Doctor in many Cases by the Neighbours," mentioning an "Instance to the Committee of a Negro Man that had been cured of the Yaws by Caesar when he had been twice salivated, and was covered with an intire [*sic*] Scab from Top to Toe." The committee noted that "another Point Caesar is very famous in is the Cure of Pleurisies many of which he had undertaken to the Knowledge of Mr. Norman which had had very deadly symptoms."

Cesar was then asked "on what Conditions he would discover his Antidotes, and such other useful Simples as he was acquainted with," and he replied "that he expected his Freedom, and a moderate Competence for Life, which he hoped the Committee would be of Opinion deserved one hundred Pounds Currency per

Annum." Cesar told the assembly that "he proposed to give the Committee any satisfactory Experiment of his ability they please, as soon as he should be able to provide himself with the necessary ingredients."

The committee supported Cesar's request, suggesting that "he shall have his Freedom, and an annual Allowance of one hundred pounds for Life with such a further Allowance for any other useful Discovery he may make to the Public as this House shall think fit." The house approved the committee's recommendation and "Resolved that this House will make Provision for Payment to the said John Norman of the appraised Value of the said Negro Caesar." Cesar was appraised by four people, two nominated by the house and two by Norman.

On 7 December 1749 the house issued a statement "that upon due Consideration of all the Advantages the said Negro Slave Caesar (aged near sixty-seven Years) might be of to the Owner by his knowledge and Skill may be worth the Sum of five hundred Pounds Current Money of South Carolina," which the public treasurer was ordered to pay "immediately" and also "advance the Sum of fifty Pounds to be paid to the Negro Man named Caesar."

The house also requested that the *South Carolina Gazette* print Cesar's prescription for public use, which appeared in the 14 May 1750 issue. Most historians consider this the first publication of a medical cure developed by an African American; the person who actually wrote the instructions is unknown but probably was Cesar's master, an assemblyman, a local doctor, or the printer. One year later, issue number 877 of the *South Carolina Gazette*, dated 25 February to 4 March 1751, stated, "There having been so great a Demand for our Gazette of the 14th of May 1750, (wherein was published, by Order of the Commons House of Assembly, the Negro Caesar's Cure for Poison) that none were left in a short time, 'tis hoped the Re-publication of that Cure, may not be unacceptable at this Time."

Cesar described the symptoms of poisoning and revealed how he prepared his cure for poison, which called for boiling the "roots of Plantane and wild Hoarhound, fresh or dried" and straining it. "Of this decoction let the patient take one third part three mornings fasting successively, from which if he finds any relief, it must be continued, 'till he is perfectly recovered," Caesar prescribed. "During the cure, the patient must live on spare diet, and abstain from eating mutton, pork, butter, or any other fat or oily food." He advised that they boil Goldenrod roots with sassafras and "to this decoction, after it is strain'd, add a glass of rum or brandy, and sweeten it with sugar, for ordinary drink." For fevers that accompany poisoning, he suggested a wood ash mash.

For rattlesnake bites, Cesar told physicians to "take of the roots of Plantane or Hoarhound, (in summer roots and branches together) a sufficient quantity, bruise them in a mortar, and squeeze out the juice, of which give as soon as possible, one large spoonful: if he is swell'd you must force it down his throat." He noted that "this generally will cure; but if the patient finds no relief in an hour after, you may give another spoonful which never fails." He also recommended that "to the wound may be applied, a leaf of good tobacco, moisten'd with rum."

Cesar's cures became well known and were also published, probably near the time of his death, in 1789 at Philadelphia and in the 1792 *Massachusetts Magazine*. They were also mentioned in William Buchan's *Domestic Medicine* (1797), which noted that Cesar's detailed description "was in the grand tradition of Sydenham, the great English clinician of the seventeenth century." Cesar's work provided a foundation for future black physicians, including James Derham, considered the first African-American doctor, who practiced in New Orleans after the American Revolution, and an unknown man described in the 22 June 1797 Charleston, South Carolina, *City Gazette and Daily Advertiser* as "He passes for a Doctor among people of his color and it is supposed practices in that capacity about town." Cesar's career preceded by a century and a half the acceptance of African Americans into U.S. medical schools.

• Primary source material on Cesar can be found in *The Colonial Records of South Carolina: The Journal of the Commons House of Assembly March 28, 1749–March 19, 1750*, ed. J. H. Easterby, vol. 9 (1962). Secondary sources include M. O. Bousefield, "An Account of Physicians of Color in the United States," *Bulletin of the History of Medicine* 17 (1945): 61–84; James L. Curtis, *Blacks, Medical Schools, and Society* (1971); Leonard Johnson, Jr., "History of the Education of Negro Physicians," *Journal of Medical Education* 42 (1967): 439–46; Kelly Miller, "The Historic Background of the Negro Physician," *Journal of Negro History* 1 (Apr. 1916): 99–109; Herbert M. Morais, *The History of the Afro-American in Medicine* (1976); Ronald L. Numbers and Todd L. Savitt, *Science and Medicine in the Old South* (1989); and Savitt, *Medicine and Slavery: The Diseases and Health Care of Blacks in Antebellum Virginia* (1978).

ELIZABETH D. SCHAFER

CHACE, Elizabeth Buffum (9 Dec. 1806–12 Dec. 1899), antislavery activist and reformer, was born in Providence, Rhode Island, the daughter of Arnold Buffum, the first president of the New England Anti-Slavery Society, and Rebecca Gould. Elizabeth Buffum's Quaker ancestry stretched back for many generations. Married in 1828 to a Quaker textile manufacturer, Samuel Buffington Chace of Fall River, Massachusetts, she gave birth to ten children during the years 1830 to 1852. The oldest five children died of scarlet fever and other diseases before the younger five were born.

Chace first became publicly active in 1835 when she and two sisters helped to organize the Fall River Female Anti-Slavery Society, which was allied with the radical wing of the antislavery movement led by William Lloyd Garrison. After moving to Valley Falls, Rhode Island, in 1840 Chace became active in the abolitionist movement there, organizing meetings and bringing illustrious antislavery agitators to the state. Among the friends and colleagues who stayed at her home were Garrison, Sojourner Truth, Lucy Stone, Abby Kelley Foster, and Wendell Phillips. In 1843 Chace resigned from the Society of Friends because of Providence Quakers' antipathy to her antislavery activism. Her home was a station on the Underground Railroad, and she raised her five surviving children to be ardent antislavery sympathizers.

After the Civil War Chace, like other abolitionists, became involved in a plethora of reform activities. She and reformer Paulina Wright Davis founded the Rhode Island Woman Suffrage Association (RIWSA) in 1868; Chace served as president of the organization from 1870 until her death. Throughout her presidency, Chace and her colleagues in RIWSA worked tirelessly to gain the vote for women through an amendment to the state constitution. Chace did not limit her reform agenda to woman suffrage, however; she used her post as president of RIWSA to address the needs of disadvantaged women and children in the state. She was appointed in 1870 by the governor of Rhode Island to serve on the first Board of Lady Visitors to state institutions where women were confined, but she resigned in 1876 when it became clear that the board was strictly advisory and had no real power. She also worked to have women appointed directly to the boards of state institutions where underprivileged women resided. In the 1870s Chace lobbied for the establishment of a model institution where dependent wards of the state could be instructed and cared for. Her vision was realized in 1885 when the legislature voted funds to establish a state Home and School for Dependent Children. In the 1890s RIWSA women joined with others in the Rhode Island Council of Women to press for legislation to protect women factory workers.

Along with Lucretia Mott and others, Chace was an organizer of the Free Religious Association, a nonsectarian group founded in Boston in 1867 that stressed intellectual inquiry on religious subjects. An ardent temperance advocate, Chace never affiliated formally with the Women's Christian Temperance Union, but preferred to wield influence through personal letters and individual efforts. Chace was a deeply principled woman. In 1877 she resigned her membership in the Providence Woman's Club, a social and philanthropic institution, when members refused to admit an African-American schoolteacher to the club. She also worked for the admission of women to Brown University. She wrote numerous letters and articles for Providence newspapers on a variety of subjects, often advocating for disadvantaged individuals and groups. In an address prepared for the Woman's Congress in Buffalo in 1881, Chace urged her sister reformers to take note of conditions in factories and mills—like those owned by her own family—especially as they related to women and children. Although she was not present at the congress, Chace's address was read, and it concluded by admonishing the reformers that "wherever we live, it is our duty to interest ourselves in the welfare of the people among whom our lives are cast, especially if in the race of progress, they are behind us." In 1876 Chace founded the first kindergarten in Rhode Island, for the children of factory workers in Valley Falls.

Active mainly in Rhode Island and New England, Chace served one term as president of the American Woman Suffrage Association (1882–1883) and was a vice president of the Association for the Advancement of Women. In her only trip abroad she was a delegate to an international conference on prison reform held in London in 1872. From 1880 until 1894 she spent summers in Wianno, Massachusetts, at her "Sabbatia Cottage," where she visited with other reformers and their children. After being housebound for several years, she died at her home in Valley Falls. Despite the class privilege that accompanied her marriage, Elizabeth Buffum Chace labored continuously for those on the margins of society. Her Rhode Island suffrage colleague and labor organizer Frederic A. Hinckly wrote of her, "Wherever a question of justice, or of morality was concerned she rose at once to the largeness of the issue, and showed herself superior to the prejudices of class" (RIWSA Papers, R.I. State Archives). She was notable for her willingness to take unpopular stands on controversial issues, and she worked unceasingly for the causes she believed in. Chace was typical of a group of middle-class women who first became publicly active in the antislavery movement in the pre–Civil War era and who then went on to spearhead a multiplicity of reform initiatives at the state and national levels in the decades following the Civil War. Her life as a social activist spanned some sixty years.

• A few of Chace's letters, one diary, and a scrapbook with clippings on her suffrage activities are in the John Hay Library at Brown University. A smattering of letters are at other repositories, including the Rhode Island Historical Society and the Antislavery Collection at the Boston Public Library; others are in private hands. Before the Civil War, a few of Chace's writings appeared in the *Liberator*; after the war, her numerous articles and letters were published in the *Providence Journal* and other Providence newspapers. She also wrote letters and articles for the *Woman's Journal*, a reform paper published by her colleagues Lucy Stone and Henry B. Blackwell. The most widely used source on her life has been *Elizabeth Buffum Chace, 1806–1899: Her Life and Its Environment* (2 vols., 1914) written by Chace's daughter, Lillie Buffum Chace Wyman, and grandson, Arthur Crawford Wyman. Chace herself wrote one book, *Antislavery Reminiscences* (1891), that covers the period of her prewar abolitionist work. The text of *Antislavery Reminiscences* is reproduced in Malcolm Lovell, ed., *Two Quaker Sisters* (1937). The only modern study on Chace is Elizabeth C. Stevens, "'From Generation to Generation': The Mother and Daughter Activism of Elizabeth Buffum Chace and Lillie Chace Wyman" (Ph.D. diss., Brown Univ., 1993). An obituary is in the *Woman's Journal*, 23 Dec. 1899.

ELIZABETH C. STEVENS

CHACE, Marian (31 Oct. 1896–19 July 1970), dancer and dance therapist, was born in Providence, Rhode Island, the daughter of Daniel Chace, a journalist, and Harriet Edgaretta Northrop, a teacher and writer. Chace was encouraged by her parents to attend Pembroke College and did so for one year starting in the fall of 1914. Dissatisfied, she moved with her family to the Washington, D.C., area and went to the Corcoran School of Art in 1915. She hurt her back in a diving accident, making it painful for her to paint or draw. Her physician suggested she take dance classes to strengthen her back and from that time she focused all her attention on dance. This became her "natural means of communication." Now in her late twenties, she made the decision to attend the Denishawn School of Dance in New York City. She began her studies in the summer of 1923, greatly broadening her learning and developing a philosophy of movement. Chace came to believe that there are infinite ways of moving related to cultural, religious, and philosophical motivation. Her studies of the body and how it functions led to correct body use parallel to sensing that all movement emerges from the center so that, used correctly, the dance emerged with clear structure and integration of the dancer.

The following year, on 29 July 1924, Chace married Lester Shafer, another Denishawn dancer. Soon after, they left the school for an opportunity to dance in vaudeville, where dancers were welcomed as performers at that time. A year later, on 13 June 1925, their only child was born to the couple, and they returned to teach and perform in the Washington, D.C., area so that Chace's family could care for their daughter. They rejoined the Denishawn School in New York in late 1927 or early 1928 and stayed until 1930. They were among the avant-garde artists of the period.

In 1930 Chace and her husband returned to Washington and opened a branch of the Denishawn School. It was a period of artistic growth for them. There were many classes to teach, and they performed regularly with their own company, including several pageants. They were known for lavish costuming. Their choreography began to be influenced by other leaders of the time such as Martha Graham, Mary Wigman, and Harald Kreutzberg.

Lester Shafer remained involved in the New York Denishawn performance group but eventually, for personal and financial reasons, left Chace to go off on his own. The marriage dissolved in 1938. Chace remained committed to continuing her dance company, but bouts of depression and a lack of funds made it difficult. She began teaching in institutions for children and adolescents and her work began to develop in new directions.

She wondered why people came to study dance but had no intention of being performers. As she observed these individuals more closely, she began to shift her classes to enable the movement to better meet their needs. The focus became the person dancing rather than dance technique. Her reputation as a special teacher spread so that soon pediatricians and psychiatrists were sending her patients for classes. In 1942 she was invited to work under the auspices of the American Red Cross at St. Elizabeths Hospital in Washington, D.C., a federal psychiatric hospital that housed many of the psychological casualties of World War II. It was before the advent of psychotropic drugs, and there was an openness to new methods of treatment, particularly through group processes. It was there that "Dance for Communication" was first offered. This was the start of what became a new mental health profession—dance/movement therapy. Chace was made the first full-time dance therapist in 1944, working for the Red Cross at St. Elizabeths. In 1947 she was to join the official staff at St. Elizabeths in the Psychotherapy Section.

During this period, Chace studied psychodrama and enrolled at the Washington School of Psychiatry, where she met Dr. Frieda Fromm-Reichmann, a leader in the work with schizophrenic patients at Chestnut Lodge, a private psychiatric hospital in Rockville, Maryland. In 1946 Chace was invited to lecture at Chestnut Lodge and was immediately offered the opportunity to work there.

She continued to work in her studio teaching, choreographing, and leading a dance company until she made the decision, early in the 1950s, to devote all her time to her new work. Chace began to write articles, offer workshops, and teach in two- or three-week sessions at such places as the Turtle Bay Music School in New York City. She accepted interns and trained many people at St. Elizabeths Hospital. In addition to the dance therapy groups on the wards and in her dance therapy studio, she gave annual theatrical productions with the patients. One of these was about Dorothea Dix, a pioneer in mental health treatment; it was filmed and shown on television.

In recognition of her dedication to creating a new form of treatment for the benefit of many individuals, Chace was awarded the St. Elizabeths Hospital Award for Outstanding Service in 1954 and the St. Elizabeths Oveta Culp Hobby Award in 1955. The U.S. Department of Health, Education and Welfare recognized her achievements in 1956 with an award for outstanding service.

Chace's work was her life. Although she feared that her use of dance as therapy would be trivialized and applied superficially rather than with a depth of understanding of movement, she eventually supported the development of the American Dance Therapy Association and served as its first president from 1966 to 1968. The Marian Chace Memorial Fund, which serves to enable scholarship and research in dance/movement therapy, was established as a tribute to her essential contributions.

Chace continued to work at St. Elizabeths Hospital, using dance as a means of therapy and communication, until she was required by law to retire on 31 October 1966. She went on with her full-time work at Chestnut Lodge until the day of her death at her Washington, D.C., home.

Marian Chace was a seminal figure in the development of the profession of dance/movement therapy. An original thinker, she evolved a theory of clinical practice that used basic dance to engage those who are severely disturbed. She thought of herself first as a dancer and maintained that one needed to have the art form well integrated within oneself in order to then make use of it as a therapeutic modality. From her own experiences, she extrapolated those concepts and principles that are basic to facilitating therapeutic change. She understood the essence of the art form of dance and how it relates to the needs of human beings for communication and understanding. Her ability to observe these communications in movement led to responses that unlocked or structured many feelings such as anger, confusion, and isolation. Chace offered dignity and compassion in surroundings bereft of such. Her intuitive trust of the body and its expression in movement led to a way of thinking that evolved into structures that could be taught to others. She was a woman of conviction and courage, and she unflinchingly shared her truths despite personal insecurities.

An important idea that Chace contributed was that tensions and distortions in the body are reflections of traumatic experience. She understood that movement was symbolic of the unconscious and that by reflecting and building on the movement offered, the patient could begin to claim the expression as his own and explore new possibilities. She understood how to integrate the verbal and nonverbal in a way that allowed one to flow into the other without awkward shifts. Her use of kinesthetic empathy was basic to the process.

These principles and structures have since been elaborated by others and modified to meet different problems. However, her vision of dance as therapy and the concepts she evolved are core precepts that can be applied to any behavioral theory.

• Articles by Chace were published in journals and magazines primarily in the 1950s. All her published and unpublished papers were collected in a book edited by Harris Chaiklin entitled *Marian Chace: Her Papers* (1975). A revised and expanded version of the book, *Foundations of Dance/Movement Therapy: The Life and Work of Marian Chace*, ed. Susan Sandel et al. (1993), includes added biographical material and recent articles written by other dance/movement therapy practitioners that build on her clinical concepts; all her papers and articles about her from the previous volume were preserved. Martha M. Schwieters, "Art and Empathy: The Early Career of Marian Chace" (M.A. thesis, American Univ., 1984), discusses Chace's dance experiences and life up to the time she became totally involved in dance therapy. Her work is discussed in relation to the dance/therapy profession in Fran J. Levy, *Dance Movement Therapy: A Healing Art* (1988).

SHARON CHAIKLIN

CHADWICK, French Ensor (29 Feb. 1844–27 Jan. 1919), naval officer, was born in Morgantown, West Virginia, the son of Daniel Clark Chadwick, a grocer, and Margaret Elizabeth Evans. At age seventeen he entered the U.S. Naval Academy, which because of the Civil War had moved from Annapolis, Maryland, to Newport, Rhode Island. He graduated fourth in his class in November 1864. He was a veteran of the war only in the sense that he served on the small steamer *Marblehead* while it hunted for Confederate warships in the Atlantic—unavailingly.

After the Civil War, Chadwick served in the South Atlantic and Caribbean until 1872, taught mathematics at the academy for three years, then had a three-year tour as the executive officer of a steamer. When he met Cornelia Jones Miller, twelve years his junior, remains unknown, but they were married in 1878. They had no children. She being the daughter of a consular official helped his career.

In 1879 Chadwick visited Europe and reported on how the British, French, and Germans trained sailors for their navies and merchant marines. The report resulted in the creation of a training squadron at Newport. While serving as the assistant inspector for the Third Lighthouse District, he wrote a history of the Lighthouse Service that revealed his ability to do research, write, and sketch. While studying the lifesaving and lighthouse systems of the nations of northern Europe, on 15 July 1882 he became the first U.S. naval attaché. His tenure from 1882 to 1889 has never been equaled. From London he reported on what he learned in England, France, and Germany. He obtained British plans useful for building the first four warships of the new American navy and additional plans for the cruiser *Charleston*, the first American warship to be built without sails. Lastly, he suggested improving naval administration by subordinating the bureaus, which often competed while conducting the navy's daily affairs, to a chief of staff—a suggestion that went unanswered until 1915.

In February 1889 Chadwick obtained command of the new gunboat *Yorktown*. The ship served in the Squadron of Evolution, 1889–1891, which tested strategic and tactical principles determined at the Naval War College and decided which would be followed by the ships of the modern steel navy. Chadwick then headed the Office of Naval Intelligence, 1892–1893, and for four years the Bureau of Equipment.

Promoted to captain in November 1897, Chadwick obtained command of the heavy armored cruiser *New York*, flagship of the Atlantic Squadron. After the battleship *Maine* was destroyed in Havana harbor on 15 February 1898, he took his ship there. As a member of a board of investigation into the tragedy, he agreed that the *Maine* had been destroyed by an external explosion—which fueled the flames of war against Spain. When Rear Admiral William T. Sampson assumed command of the fleet, he rode the *New York*, and Chadwick served as his chief of staff as well as the ship's captain.

After war was declared against Spain on 25 April 1898, Sampson established a blockade around Havana. On learning that Admiral Pasquale Cervera had left the Cape Verdes Islands on 29 April, Sampson sought him at San Juan, Puerto Rico, but missed him there. He then learned that Cervera had reached Curaçao, West Indies, and estimated that he would try to reach Cienfuegos, Cuba. After Commodore Winfield S. Schley, commanding a flying squadron at Norfolk, failed to find the Spaniard, as Sampson had ordered, Chadwick supported Sampson's decision to go to Santiago de Cuba, where Cervera sought refuge. Seeking to escape on 3 July, Cervera lost his four cruisers and two torpedo boats to Schley. Because the *New York* had been taking Sampson to meet with the American army commander, it missed the opening actions. Schley's and others' claim that he rather than Sampson had won the victory sufficed for the secretary of the navy to call for a court of inquiry in which Chadwick heartily supported Sampson. Chadwick's permitting a reporter to see some confidential data and criticizing Schley to a reporter who violated "off the record" procedure sat very badly with the officer corps and damaged his career. Chadwick was usually affable, but his brusque criticism of official inefficiency also made him persona non grata to many.

From 1900 to 1903 Chadwick was president of the Naval War College, commandant of the Second Naval District, and member of the new general board of the navy. While Chadwick was at the college, war games and the study of amphibious operations were added to its curriculum; in Washington he helped draft war plans.

Chadwick's last sea duty, 1904–1905, was to command the South Atlantic Squadron and show the flag during a trip via the Mediterranean and Suez to Capetown, South Africa. While he was in the Canaries, President Theodore Roosevelt ordered him to Tangier, Morocco, where Raisuli, lord of the Rif, had captured a rich Greek of American nationality. There Chadwick helped obtain release of the captive.

Chadwick made rear admiral on 6 October 1905. Billets for men of his rank were few, and when junior men were selected to command the three main squadrons, he requested detachment. He was detached on 23 November and on 28 February 1906 was placed on the retired list.

Chadwick then began a second career as a historian. *The Causes of the Civil War*, his three-volume "monument to Sampson," was issued in 1907. *The Relations of the United States and Spain: Diplomacy* (1911) and *The Relations of the United States and Spain: The Spanish-American War* (1911) are still acclaimed as definitive. Other writings show him to have been a racist (Spanish peoples were decadent and underdeveloped), an anti-Semite (Jews ruled America like patriarchs), and a male chauvinist (women teachers were dangerous).

Unlike most American naval officers, during the Great War Chadwick demanded justice for Germany as well as for the Allies. In July 1917 he suffered a mild stroke. With the victory of the Allies he cheered President Woodrow Wilson's objective of having a "navy second to none" to allow a renewed merchant marine to enjoy the freedom of the seas.

Chadwick had well served his navy for forty-six years. Between 1914 and 1918 he published four articles and a history of the American navy, contributed several chapters to a history of the Great War, and edited the papers of Admiral Sir Thomas Graves. He died in New York City.

• A collection of Chadwick's papers has been beautifully edited by Doris Maguire, *French Ensor Chadwick: Selected Letters and Papers* (1981). A full biography is Paolo E. Coletta, *French Ensor Chadwick: Scholarly Warrior* (1980). A perceptive essay is Malcolm Muir, Jr., "French Ensor Chadwick: Reformer, Historian, and Outcast," in *Admirals of the New Steel Navy: Makers of the American Naval Tradition, 1880–1930*, ed. James C. Bradford (1990). His career may also be followed in William B. Cogar, *Dictionary of Admirals of the U.S. Navy*, vol. 2, *1901–1919* (1991). Chadwick is mentioned particularly in works dealing with the Office of Naval Intelligence and with the Spanish-American War. An obituary is in the *New York Times*, 28 Jan. 1919.

PAOLO E. COLETTA

CHADWICK, George Whitefield (13 Nov. 1854–4 Apr. 1931), composer and music educator, was born in Lowell, Massachusetts, the son of Alonzo Calvin Chadwick, an insurance agent, and Hannah Godfrey Fitts. Both his parents were musically inclined. His father had been the president of the Martin Luther Music Association of Boscawen, New Hampshire, and was a sponsor of a singing school, where he had met his wife. Chadwick's mother died eleven days after he was born. His father remarried and sent Chadwick, still an infant, to live with his grandparents for the next three years. When Chadwick was reunited with his father and stepmother, the family moved downriver to Lawrence, Massachusetts, where Alonzo became an insurance agent and participated in the local choral society, which performed at Patrick Gilmore's celebrated Peace Jubilee in Boston in 1869.

Chadwick's interest in music was encouraged by his father's activities and by his elder brother, who was also a musician. He quit high school after his sophomore year, joined his father in the insurance business, and began taking organ and harmony lessons while on trips to Boston. His acceptance of an opportunity to substitute-teach at Olivet College in Michigan from 1876 to 1877 began a rift between him and his father that became final when Chadwick, determined to pursue a musical career despite its uncertainties, went to study in Germany, funded only by savings from his one-year's salary. Studying at the conservatory in Leipzig from 1877 to 1879 under Carl Reinecke and, especially, Salamon Jadassohn, Chadwick miraculously transformed himself from an amateur dabbler into a prizewinning professional with his overture "Rip Van Winkle" (1879), which evoked American scenes and moods. He also studied at the Royal Academy in Munich under Josef Rheinberger in 1879–1880. Perhaps just as significant as his work with Rheinberger was a chance encounter at the academy with a group of young American painters, the "Duveneck Boys," which resulted in lasting friendships and aesthetic inclinations.

Returning to Boston in 1880, Chadwick began his new musical life as a composer, organist, conductor, and teacher. His return was coincident with a golden musical era in Boston, exemplified by the founding of the Boston Symphony Orchestra and the New England Conservatory of Music, and the beginning of erudite music criticism. In 1882 Chadwick was made instructor in harmony and composition at the conservatory.

In 1886 Chadwick's Symphony no. 2 in B-flat Major, which he himself had conducted at the Boston Symphony concerts, was published by Arthur P. Schmidt of Boston. This work, along with his tragic overture *Melpomene* (1887), established Chadwick as the logical successor to John Knowles Paine as the American symphonist. In 1897, when a political upheaval at the New England Conservatory resulted in the resignation of Carl Faelten, Chadwick was chosen to replace him as director, a post he held until 1930. During his 33-year tenure, Chadwick altered the course of collegiate music education through the amalgamation of American practical pedagogy with the highest continental standards of aesthetics. He created the first student symphony orchestra on professional lines and used it as a medium for presenting contemporary works as well as classical repertory. He organized the first opera studio workshop and inaugurated novel courses in orchestration and composition. Under Chadwick's leadership a new neoclassical building was erected near Symphony Hall. The changes effected by Chadwick symbolized the transformation of the conservatory from a women's boarding school into America's premier institution for music.

Notwithstanding the demands of teaching and administrative duties, Chadwick proved himself a prolific and versatile composer in all genres. He was the first American successfully to reconcile cosmopolitan expectation for craft with clearly audible American musical traits, as evinced in his *Symphonic Sketches* (1894–1904) and his Fourth String Quartet (1896). More surprising from a "Boston" composer are Chadwick's works for the stage. The first, *The Peer and the Pauper* (1884), was an obvious imitation of Gilbert and Sullivan operettas and was set to a libretto by the novelist Robert Grant. Chadwick then established his reputation as an academic who could also write saucy tunes, in *Tabasco* (1894) and the Broadway extravaganza *Everywoman* (1912). His lyric drama *Judith* (1901) and his tragic masterpiece *The Padrone* (1913), a work dealing with pre–World War I Italian immigrants that was rejected by the Metropolitan Opera, reveal Chadwick as a man of feeling with a fine sense of the theater and of the natural prosody of English speech.

Except for leading the New England Conservatory orchestra, Chadwick's career as a conductor was largely limited to the Springfield and, later, the Worcester music festivals. He had arrived on the scene too early for consideration as director of any of the premier symphony orchestras. Besides his music, Chadwick left the legacy of legions of students, many of whom have, in their own time, contributed greatly to American cultural history. These students include Horatio Parker (teacher of Charles Ives); Frederick S. Converse; the three Arthurs: Bird, Shepherd, and Whiting; Sidney Homer (uncle and mentor of Samuel Barber); Henry Hadley; Margaret Ruthven Lang; Wallace Goodrich; Daniel Gregory Mason; William Grant Still; Mabel Daniels; Edward Burlingame Hill; and Leroy Robertson.

Chadwick married Ida May Crocker in 1885; they had two children. During the concert season Chadwick was busy with academic duties, but he found time to write and revise a textbook, *Harmony* (1897), that went through seventy-four editions and is notable for its clarity, keyboard format, and examples taken from actual pieces of music. During the summers Chadwick and his family lived in a modest house in West Chop, Martha's Vineyard, where Chadwick had the time and isolation to write. He received an M.A. from Yale University in 1897 and the Gold Medal of the American Academy of Arts and Letters in 1928. After Edward MacDowell's withdrawal from creative activity at about the turn of the century, Chadwick succeeded him as the Dean of American composers. But even before Chadwick's death, the changing winds of fashion seemed to have swept him and his colleagues aside. Not until the late twentieth century did Chadwick's reputation begin to be rehabilitated and his works again performed and made available on recordings. Chadwick died in Boston.

• The bulk of Chadwick's musical manuscripts are in the Library of Congress. The Spaulding Library of the New England Conservatory also has some materials. Steven Ledbetter's list of Chadwick's musical works in the *New Grove Dictionary of American Music* (1986) contains a valuable index to the composer's vocal pieces. Two noteworthy dissertations are Douglas G. Campbell, "George Whitefield Chadwick: His Life and Works" (Ph.D. diss., Univ. of Rochester, 1957), and Victor F. Yellin, "The Life and Operatic Works of George Whitefield Chadwick" (Ph.D. diss., Harvard Univ., 1957). Articles containing information derived directly from Chadwick are in F. O. Jones, *A Handbook of American Music and Musicians* (1886) and *Musical Quarterly* 10 (July 1924): 438–57. See also Louis C. Elson (a colleague of Chadwick's at the New England Conservatory), *The History of American Music* (1904), pp. 170–76, and John Tasker Howard, *Our American Music* (1930). A valuable eyewitness account is by a New England Conservatory student and later a member of the Boston Symphony Orchestra: Allan Lincoln Langley, "Chadwick and the New England Conservatory of Music," *Musical Quarterly* 21 (Jan. 1935): 39–52. Later published works based on archival and analytical research are Yellin, *Chadwick: Yankee Composer* (1991); and a stylistic reassessment: Yellin, "Chadwick, American Musical Realist," *Musical Quarterly* 61 (Jan. 1975): 77–97.

VICTOR FELL YELLIN

CHADWICK, Henry (5 Oct. 1824–20 Apr. 1908), baseball sportswriter, was born in Jessamine Cottage, St. Thomas, Exeter, England, the son of Sir James Chadwick, a newspaper editor (mother's name unknown). Chadwick and his parents came to the United States in September 1837 and settled in Brooklyn. Although trained to be a music teacher, Chadwick soon gravitated toward journalism. In 1844 he started contributing to the *Long Island Star*, a Brooklyn newspaper. Over the course of his career he wrote for more than twenty magazines and newspapers, including the *New York Times*, and he had long associations with the daily *Brooklyn Eagle* and the *New York Clipper*, a weekly devoted to sport and the theater. On 19 August 1848 he married Jane Botts of Richmond, Virginia. They had two children.

Chadwick brought with him from England a youthful enthusiasm for the games of cricket and rounders and for outdoor recreation in general, a predilection that was part of an urban attitude toward physical fitness and exercise born in the mid-nineteenth century. Discarding the notion that sport was useless and improper, those who held to this view endorsed recreation as an antidote to the harmful effects of life in industrial cities.

Chadwick was at first devoted to cricket, whose participants he lauded for their British standards of sportsmanship, but he came to criticize the English game for its slow play and the reluctance of immigrant English cricketers to popularize their sport. Early on, he had been exposed to baseball, but it was not until 1856 that he saw the possibilities inherent in the new sport. "I chanced to go through the Elysian Fields during the progress of a contest between the noted Eagle and Gotham Clubs," he recalled in *The Game of Baseball* (1868), "and I watched it with deeper interest than any previous ball match between clubs that I had seen. I was struck with the idea that base ball was just the game for a national sport for Americans."

By 1860 he had stopped covering cricket entirely to concentrate on baseball. He became, in effect, a one-man publicity firm boosting the developing sport. He attended many games in New York and Brooklyn and sold accounts of them to whatever newspapers would print them. Gradually, the daily press began to devote regular space to baseball, and some papers hired their own reporters.

Chadwick's zeal and his dry, precise writing style got him appointed to the rules committee of the National Association of Base Ball Players, an organization founded to bring order to the relations among the growing number of amateur clubs. In this capacity he wrote the first baseball rules book (1859), and, nearly simultaneously, he assembled *Beadle's Dime Base Ball Player* (1860), the sport's first annual reference guide.

After a short interlude in Richmond as a Civil War correspondent for the *New York Tribune*, Chadwick returned to Brooklyn and to baseball with prolific intensity. He published his own weekly, the *American Chronicle of Sports and Pastimes*, but it lasted only thirteen months. He compiled *Haney's Base Ball Book of Reference* (1866–1870) and *DeWitt's Base Ball Guide* (1869–1880), and from 1881 to 1908 he edited *Spalding's Official Base Ball Guide*, the foremost statistical compendium the sport had yet seen. All of these publications were supplemented with a variety of instructional booklets, plus a guide to the game's emerging slang prepared for British writers covering the odyssey of two teams led by Albert G. Spalding to England in 1874.

Chadwick was profoundly instrumental in developing methods to describe baseball performance with statistics, thereby helping to imbue the game with a seriousness that appealed to adults. At first, he relied on his cricket background and tallied only runs and outs, arranging these totals in a primitive version of the box score. After a few years, he added additional columns and augmented this simple counting with baseball's first average, runs per game. This statistic, rooted in cricket where a hit and a run are synonymous, gained wide acceptance. Beginning in 1867 the official batting champion as declared by Chadwick was the player with the highest average of runs per game. A few years later, Chadwick changed the standard, first to average number of hits per game, and then to hits per at bat, the present-day batting average.

Chadwick's tall, imposing figure lent a certain authority to his opinions. He assumed the guardian's role for baseball's image and weighed in heavily against behavior that he considered disruptive or immoral. One of the initial crises that he and the baseball hierarchy had to face was the game's evolution from amateur to professional status. The first organized baseball teams had been called clubs because they were composed mainly of workers and clerks who played baseball with their peers for recreation. Before long, these clubs began to hire outsiders and to pay them for playing. Chadwick did not oppose the rise of professionalism or the concomitant move by clubs to fence in their playing grounds and charge admission to games. He saw "no reason whatever why a professional ball player should be ashamed of his position" so long as the player kept "in the honest path of the English cricket professional."

Chadwick was willing to recognize professional baseball as a business, but its success, he reasoned, depended on a game free from corruption. He viewed professionalism as one way to promote players' loyalty to their clubs and dissuade them from gambling or taking bribes. He railed against contract jumping or "revolving," as it was then called, and he condemned "hippodroming," fixing the outcome of games in advance and then playing them as legitimate competitions. His campaign to rid baseball of gambling was so vociferously insistent that when club owners formed the National League in 1876, they took an extremely hard line against all kinds of betting.

Chadwick's passion for baseball was based in part on his belief that it was particularly suited to the American national character. But he did not agree with other observers that baseball was indigenous to the United States. Rather, he argued that baseball was derived from the English schoolyard game of rounders. The rounders theory was opposed most notably by Spalding, who declared baseball to be purely American in origin.

The debate raged rather steadily for years until it was settled, albeit temporarily, in 1907 by the Mills Commission, a special body formed to investigate the question. Chaired by Abraham G. Mills, former president of the National League, the commission determined that baseball was invented on a summer day in 1839 by Abner Doubleday in Cooperstown, New York. This conclusion has been thoroughly discredited by historians, and Chadwick's evolutionary view is now fully accepted.

Well before the turn of the century, "Father" Chadwick was a revered figure within the baseball establishment. In 1894 the National League made him an honorary member, and two years later the league granted him an annual $600 pension. In 1904 the St. Louis World's Fair awarded him the only medal given to a journalist.

Chadwick remained active to the end of his life. In 1887 he was elected the first vice president of the Base Ball Reporters Association of America, an organization pledged to a standard method of scoring games and advancing the interests of baseball through the press. In 1889 he lauded the game's contemporary players, praising their skills over those of players from decades past. One year later, however, he criticized many of these same players for their involvement in the Brotherhood of Professional Base Ball Players, the first players' union.

Throughout his life, Chadwick kept an office at the *Brooklyn Eagle*. In 1908 he attended opening day in inclement weather, caught a cold that turned into pneumonia, and died within a few days. He was elected to the National Baseball Hall of Fame in 1938, the only sportswriter so honored until the establishment of the J. G. Taylor Spink Award, given annually since 1962.

• Chadwick's papers, including scrapbooks, diaries, and related materials, were given by his widow to Albert G. Spalding. They are now part of the Albert G. Spalding Baseball Collection, Manuscript Division, New York Public Library, and are available in microform. There is no bibliography of Chadwick's writings and no critical biography. Chadwick's name and contributions are cited frequently in several histories of early baseball, including Harold Seymour, *Baseball: The Early Years* (1960); David Quentin Voigt, *American Baseball: From Gentleman's Sport to the Commissioner System* (1966); and George B. Kirsch, *The Creation of American Team Sports: Baseball and Cricket, 1838–72* (1989). Shorter assessments include John B. Foster, "Henry Chadwick: 'The Father of Base Ball,'" *Spalding's Official Base Ball Guide* (1909), pp. 6–20; Thomas S. Rice, "Henry Chadwick, the 'Father of Baseball,' Also Grand Dad of Diamond Chroniclers," *Sporting News*, 21 May 1936; and John Thorn and Pete Palmer, eds., *Total Baseball*, 4th ed. (1995): 642–56. Obituaries are in the *Brooklyn Eagle*, 20 Apr. 1908; the *New York Times*, 21 Apr. 1908; *Sporting News*, 23 Apr. 1908; and *Sporting Life*, 25 Apr. 1908.

STEVEN P. GIETSCHIER

CHADWICK, James Read (2 Nov. 1844–23 Sept. 1905), gynecologist and medical librarian, was born in Boston, Massachusetts, the son of Christopher Champlin Chadwick and Louisa Read, the daughter of a well-to-do Boston merchant. James was named after his grandfather, with whom in 1844 his father entered into partnership as domestic goods commission merchants, the firm of Read and Chadwick then commencing a period of great prosperity. James Read Chadwick was educated in the Boston schools and at Harvard College, graduating with an A.B. in 1865. After an extended trip abroad, he entered the Harvard Medical School in 1867 and received an M.D. in 1871, submitting a thesis on tracheotomy, as illustrated by cases in the records of the Massachusetts General Hospital. That same year he married Katherine M. Lyman, daughter of Dr. George H. Lyman, one of the pioneers in Boston in treating the diseases of women, a field in which Chadwick then began to train. The couple had four children.

In the summer of 1871 Chadwick took his wife for a period of two years to Europe, where he undertook postgraduate study in Germany, Austria, France, and the British Isles. His studies brought him into contact with some of the leaders of the newly established field of gynecology: Franz K. L. W. Winckel in Munich, Wilhelm A. Freund in Breslau, John Braxton Hicks in London, and Spencer Wells in Edinburgh. While in Britain, Chadwick witnessed or assisted in ovariotomies and other gynecological procedures that were just being made practical through the introduction of antiseptic surgery.

Returning to Boston in the summer of 1873, the Chadwicks built a house on Clarendon Street, which remained their lifelong home. From 1875 to 1882 Chadwick was physician to outpatients in the Gynecological Department of the Boston City Hospital. For many years he conducted a dispensary for the treatment of the diseases of women at which he gave instruction to students at the Harvard Medical School, holding the appointment of instructor in gynecology at Harvard from 1873 to 1880 and from 1883 to 1887. Imparting to students the advantages of his training abroad, he taught them to observe and exercise independent judgment. He conceived the idea in 1876 of forming the American Gynecological Society and served as its secretary from its founding that year until 1882 and as its president in 1897.

An ardent book lover and omnivorous reader, Chadwick believed that the library was the heart of any system of education. In medicine, he felt, the library allowed the deductions drawn in the lecture room, the laboratory, and the clinic to be permanently recorded; here were collected and stored the treasures of the past and year-by-year records of science in the process of evolution. This interest led Chadwick in 1875 to help reestablish the Boston Medical Library, an institution originally founded in 1805 but which in 1829 had deposited its books and periodicals in the Boston Athenaeum. By 1874, however, the introduction of bacteriology, antiseptic surgery, and other innovations in medicine had resulted in an explosion of scientific literature, and the physicians of Boston once more felt the need of a library of their own. At the urging of Henry I. Bowditch and other senior physicians and under the titular direction of Oliver Wendell Holmes, its first president, the library opened its doors in 1875, with Chadwick serving as librarian, a position he held until his death thirty years later.

Under Chadwick's brilliant and enthusiastic leadership, the Boston Medical Library grew by leaps and bounds. The seeds he sowed and the traditions he established resulted, in the sixty years following his death, in the growth of the Boston Medical Library into one of the largest and most complete medical libraries in the United States and throughout the world. It became especially known for the size and completeness of its periodical collection and for its rare and historical collections, which Chadwick had done much to foster. His work in increasing the collections brought him into contact with William Osler, John Shaw Billings (then building the library of the surgeon general's office), Silas Weir Mitchell, and other leading physicians of that time.

Chadwick spent many hours a day, including Sundays and holidays, collecting and making contacts for the acquisition of books and seeing to their cataloging. On trips throughout the country and abroad, he carried his "want book," recording the contents of periodical sets, so that he could acquire volumes that were missing. His quest to acquire as complete a record of the literature of medicine as possible resulted in continual space problems that were finally solved in 1903 through the erection of a new building at No. 8 The Fenway. This served the needs of the Boston Medical Library until 1965, when its collections were merged with those of the Harvard Medical Library in the newly constructed Francis A. Countway Library of Medicine.

Cremation was another of Chadwick's interests. In 1892 he was responsible for reorganizing the New England Cremation Society, and he also served as clerk of the Massachusetts Cremation Society, which erected a crematory and chapel at Forest Hills Cemetery in 1893; later serving as its president, he did much to popularize cremation, which he saw as an orderly, practical, and sanitary means of disposing of the dead. Broad-minded for his time, he wrote many articles and letters championing the admission of women to medical schools and into medical societies. Preserved among his manuscript papers are scrapbooks containing correspondence and printed literature documenting his activity in this area. Chadwick was also founder of the Harvard Medical Alumni Association, serving as its president from 1890 to 1893.

Chadwick wrote approximately seventy-five articles, mainly on topics of gynecology, libraries, medical history, and cremation. On his return from study abroad, he translated Winckel's treatise on puerperal fever, which was published in 1876 under the title *The Pathology and Treatment of Childbed: A Treatise for Physicians and Surgeons*.

Possessing something of the temperament of the poet and artist, Bohemian in taste, and unconventional in dress, Chadwick presented a notable yet commanding presence wherever he went. Described as having progressive ideas and fresh purposes, he was known for his clever conversation, sense of humor, lightheartedness, and good fellowship. When he was found dead outside his summer residence at Chorocua, New Hampshire, his death was attributed to abdominal hemorrhage caused by an accidental fall from the balcony outside his second-story bedroom, where he was thought to have gone for air after becoming sick. He left behind, as his greatest and most enduring monument, the Boston Medical Library.

• The bulk of Chadwick's preserved papers is in the Boston Medical Library. The most extensive biographical treatment of him is Walter L. Burrage, "James Read Chadwick, M.D. (1844–1905)," published, along with a bibliography, in the *Transactions of the American Gynecological Society* 31 (1906): 437–45. Detailed discussion of Chadwick's important role as a medical librarian appears in histories of the Boston Medical Library: John W. Farlow, *The History of the Boston Medical Library* (1905), and Joseph E. Garlan, *The Centennial History of the Boston Medical Library* (1975). Memorial remarks by Clarence J. Blake are contained in Boston Medical Library, *Thirtieth Annual Report* (1905), pp. 14–18. Obituaries are in the *Boston Medical and Surgical Journal* 153, no. 14 (5 Oct. 1905), the *Journal of the American Medical Association* 45 (7 Oct. 1905), and *Lancet* (14 Oct. 1905).

RICHARD J. WOLFE

CHAFEE, Zechariah, Jr. (7 Dec. 1885–8 Feb. 1957), professor of law and civil libertarian, was born in Providence, Rhode Island, the son of Zechariah Chafee, an industrialist, and Mary Dexter Sharpe. For generations his father's family owned and ran the Builders Iron Foundry, and his mother's family owned the Brown and Sharpe Manufacturing Company. Chafee attended Brown University, graduating Phi Beta Kappa in 1907. For three years he worked at the family foundry but discovered that he was temperamentally unsuited to the life of an industrialist. He entered Harvard Law School in 1910 and again showed intellectual prowess by graduating at the top of his class in 1913. In 1912 he married Bess Frank Searle; they had four children. Chafee practiced at a law firm in Providence until 1916 when he joined the Harvard Law School faculty, where he would remain until his retirement in 1956. He was made a full professor in 1919, eventually occupied the prestigious Langdell Chair, and became a University Professor in 1950.

Chafee is most famous for his advocacy of free speech, and his work is a primary doctrinal source for modern First Amendment protection of speech and the press. Chafee's interest in the subject was galvanized soon after he went to Harvard by the repressions of dissent during World War I. He saw that freedom of speech and press was a significant, and largely unexplored, area of constitutional legal development. In a 1919 article in the *Harvard Law Review*, and in *Freedom of Speech*, first published in 1920 (revised edition published in 1941 under the title *Free Speech in the United States*), Chafee recast the debate over the First Amendment. He argued that the framers of the Bill of Rights intended to abolish the English law of seditious libel, which prohibited restraints on speech prior to publication but allowed punishment of seditious speech after the fact. The real message of the First Amendment, Chafee maintained, was that freedom of speech allows for the vigorous pursuit of truth. "One of the most important purposes of society and government is the discovery and spread of truth on subjects of general concern," he wrote in *Freedom of Speech*. "This is possible only through absolutely unlimited discussion, for . . . once force is thrown into the argument, it becomes a matter of chance whether it is thrown on the false side or the true, and truth loses all its natural advantage in the contest." Chafee is credited with liberalizing Justice Oliver Wendell Holmes's (1841–1935) views on free speech as documented by an extensive correspondence that they and Judge Learned Hand conducted from 1918 through 1921.

Chafee did not advocate absolute protection for all speech. He was one of the first to use balancing tests in constitutional analysis. When free speech was inconsistent with other valid governmental interests, such as "order, the training of the young, [and] protection against external aggression," Chafee asserted, it was proper to balance the conflicting state interest against the interest in free expression, "but freedom of speech ought to weigh very heavily in the scale."

Broadly speaking, Chafee's vision has become the law of the land. In case after case over the last seven decades, the U.S. Supreme Court has endorsed Chafee's ideas, from Justice Holmes's statement that "the best test of truth is the power of the thought to get itself accepted in the competition of the market" (*Abrams v. United States, 1919*), to Justice William Brennan's holding that the unconstitutionality of the law of seditious libel is "the central meaning of the First Amendment" (*New York Times v. Sullivan, 1964*).

Chafee's free speech theory has not been entirely immune from attack. His 1919 law review article prompted charges of radicalism by law alumni in 1920. Harvard president Abbott Lawrence Lowell defended the young professor, and the board of overseers dismissed the charges after a dramatic "trial" at the Harvard Club. Since Chafee's death, some scholars have questioned the accuracy of his analysis of the First Amendment. Especially among legal historians, Chafee's emphasis on the World War I years as the beginning of thoughtful judicial consideration of attempts to suppress speech has been criticized as overlooking important state court decisions in the latter half of the nineteenth century. Further, it remains a matter of debate whether or not the framers actually intended to outlaw prosecutions for seditious libel. Nonetheless, the greater part of his scholarship still stands as a pillar of twentieth-century thought on the jurisprudence of free speech.

Chafee's work went well beyond the First Amendment, or even civil liberties. The two areas of law on which he spent the bulk of his time, as a classroom teacher and as a practitioner, were equity and the complex system of rules that regulate litigation among multiple parties in the federal courts. Chafee was the author of the Federal Interpleader Act of 1936. He also wrote about and taught subjects as diverse as evidence, commercial paper, copyright, and trademark. Indeed, Chafee was eager to avoid a label, including that of champion of civil liberties. For example, he refused to become a member of the National Advisory Committee of the American Civil Liberties Union, although he made financial and scholarly contributions to the organization.

Chafee was also very much a man of his time, place, and class. A product of the New England industrial elite, he was ever conscious of his wealth and privilege, and he was deeply committed to the concept of private property. He remained active in his family business throughout his life. His advocacy of free expression was based in part on a patrician sense of obligation to help the less fortunate. "When I am loafing around on my boat, or taking an inordinately large number of strokes on the golf course, I occasionally think of these poor devils [jailed for seditious libel] who won't be out for five or ten years and want to do a bit to make the society less heavy on them," he wrote to a friend in 1923. Further, he believed that limiting free speech was more likely to foster resentment of authority than to dissipate it: "Nothing adds more to men's hatred for government than its refusal to let them talk, especially if they are the type of person anarchists are, to whom talking a little wildly is the greatest joy of life" (*Free Speech in the United States*). Ever the gentleman, Chafee never talked "wildly"; he was unfailingly polite and controlled in public settings. On a substantive level, Chafee's faith in the existence of some easily discoverable truth through discussion sounds almost naive to modern ears.

It would be a mistake to assume that Chafee was little more than an especially perspicacious moderate. His highly successful marriage to Bess Frank Searle, the impecunious daughter of an avowedly socialist woman, his profound grief at the suicide of his son, his own emotional troubles in the 1930s, and his lifelong inability to turn away when confronted with injustice all suggest that Chafee was a complex man. Among many other activities, he served on the Wickersham Commission, which studied law enforcement during Prohibition, he was a delegate in 1948 to the United Nations Conference on Freedom of Information and of the Press, and he fought diligently against the excesses of McCarthyism in the years after World War II.

Chafee died in Cambridge, Massachusetts.

• Chafee's papers are in the manuscript collections at Brown and Harvard Universities. Important works by Chafee not mentioned in the text include "Freedom of Speech in War Time," *Harvard Law Review* 32 (1919): 932–73, and "A Contemporary State Trial: The United States versus Jacob Abrams et al.," *Harvard Law Review* 33 (1920): 747–74. For a collection of his writings, see Edward D. Re, ed., *Freedom's Prophet: Selected Writings of Zechariah Chafee, Jr., University Professor, Harvard Law School* (1981). For information on his life and career, see Donald L. Smith, *Zechariah Chafee, Jr.: Defender of Liberty and Law* (1986); Leonard W. Levy, *Legacy of Suppression: Freedom of Speech and Press in Early American History* (1960); David M. Rabban, "The First Amendment in Its Forgotten Years," *Yale Law Journal* 90 (1981): 1205–36; and Jerold S. Auerbach, "The Patrician as Libertarian: Zechariah Chafee, Jr., and Freedom of Speech," *New England Quarterly* 42 (1969): 511–31.

NORMAN DORSEN

CHAFER, Lewis Sperry (27 Feb. 1871–22 Aug. 1952), Presbyterian minister and founder of Dallas Theological Seminary, was born in Rock Creek, Ohio, the son of Thomas Franklin Chafer, a Congregational clergyman, and Lomira Sperry. Raised in a secure, loving, musical home, he experienced a religious conversion as a child. The serenity of his early years was shattered when his father succumbed to tuberculosis in 1882. The resulting financial and emotional distress shaped his adolescence by limiting the extent of his education and unsettling the family. Also, the impression that was made on him by an obscure evangelist by the name of Scott, who was near death with tuberculosis, encouraged his sense of a calling into religious work.

Determined to maintain and educate her family, Lomira Chafer taught in the local Rock Creek school and, later, operated boardinghouses in New Lyme, Ohio, where her children attended New Lyme Institute, the equivalent of a secondary school, and in Oberlin, Ohio, where Lewis studied at Oberlin College. After a semester in the preparatory school (1889), he attended the college's conservatory of music for one semester each in 1890 and 1891.

Leaving college before completing a degree, he went into religious work, mainly with Arthur T. Reed, a YMCA state evangelist in Ohio working as advance man, choir director, and soloist. When in 1896 he married Ella Lorraine Case of Ellington, New York, whom he had met in college, he settled briefly as minister of music in the Painesville, Ohio, Congregational Church. Soon, however, the couple formed their own evangelistic team and traveled intermittently for several years, Chafer slowly moving from music ministry to preaching. After a brief interim in the Lewiston, New York, Presbyterian church in 1898, he became an associate minister in the First Congregational Church, Buffalo, New York, where he was officially ordained in 1900.

In 1901 Chafer moved to East Northfield, Massachusetts, where he became active in the annual Northfield Conferences, part of Dwight L. Moody's evangelistic empire. Of special significance was his encounter there with Cyrus I. Scofield, pastor of the Trinitarian Congregational Church and director of the Northfield Training School. Enamored of Scofield's teaching skills ("I had never heard a real Bible teacher . . . It was a crisis for me. I was captured for life"), he quickly identified himself with his mentor. While he continued to lead the music at the summer conferences, where his wife was the organist, and to teach music in Moody's two Northfield schools, he yearned to associate with Scofield, particularly after 1909 when both shared the platform at the Southfield Conference in Crescent City, Florida. In 1911 Chafer joined his teacher, who was basking in the success of the Scofield Reference Bible (1909), to serve as an extension teacher conducting conferences through the South; in 1914 he assisted his mentor in founding the Philadelphia School of the Bible (now Philadelphia College of Bible). In 1907 Chafer had transferred his ministerial credentials to the Presbyterian Church U.S.A. (the northern church). In 1912 he again transferred his ministerial credentials, to the southern church, the Presbyterian Church, U.S., as had his mentor; the primary reason for this shift was Chafer's increased ministry among Presbyterians in the southeast.

With his increasing activities in the Bible conference movement, holding seminars called "Bible institutes," Chafer also ventured into the field of publication. His first influential book was *True Evangelism* (1911), a critique of the methods of contemporary evangelists (that is, the prevalence of manipulation instead of persuasion and the distortion of the gospel message). That was followed by *The Kingdom in History and Prophecy* (1915), a discourse on his eschatological views, which were premillennial (that Christ would return *before* the 1,000 years mentioned in Rev. 20); dispensational (a teaching that the Bible reveals seven periods, or dispensations, of history and shows that we are living in the final period before Christ's return); and pretribulational (that Christians will be "raptured," or caught up, to be with Christ before the tribulation as indicated in 1 Thess. 4). He also published *Salvation* (1919), a delineation of the content of his evangelistic message; *He That Is Spiritual* (1918), a defense of Keswick Theology, a teaching concerning the possibility of success or victory over sin in the Christian's experience through a second, subsequent spiritual awakening by a crisis dedication and submission (that is, lordship); and *Grace* (1922), published the year after Scofield's death and dedicated to him, in which Chafer offered a defense of Scofield's dispensationalism (against the reaction to his teaching primarily from Presbyterian covenantalists), which was identical with his own.

In 1922 Chafer moved to Dallas, Texas, where he assumed the leadership of Scofield's former church (First Congregational, renamed the same year the Scofield Memorial Church) and directed a foreign missionary society his mentor had established in 1890, the Central American Mission. His major focus, however, was a dream spawned through his Bible conferences and conversations with pastors about their education: to establish a "distinctly new departure" in ministerial preparation, a curriculum that would combine the elements of seminary education with the distinctive doctrines and methods of the Bible institutes and Bible conferences (a "graduate school" of the emerging nondenominational evangelical movement). Chafer founded in 1924 the Evangelical Theological College (renamed in 1936 the Dallas Theological Seminary), a school that until late in the twentieth century was singularly prominent in the fundamentalist segment of the evangelical movement, and served as its president and professor of systematic theology until his death.

In addition to *Major Bible Themes* (1926), a doctrinal survey, and the editorship of *Bibliotheca Sacra*, the seminary's journal, Chafer's major literary contribution was his magnum opus, the multivolume *Systematic Theology* (1947), the first major attempt to set forth a definitive dispensational theology. (Dispensationalism is an attempt to establish the coherency of Scriptures, or to demonstrate an overarching grid, for interpretive insight. Seeing the working of God in distinct economies or eras, the system emphasizes a cleavage between the Old and New Testament, two peoples of God with two distinct destinies: Israel as the earthly people, the Church as heavenly). In Chafer's case, and true of most dispensationalists, he embraced pretribulationalism and premillennialism. Chafer's theology may be seen as an attempt to delineate systematically Scofield's version of Protestant orthodoxy.

Although diminutive in size, Chafer possessed enormous energy and oratorical skills. While he did not have children of his own, his students formed deep and enduring affectionate bonds with him (as he had with his mentor). His lasting contributions to American evangelicalism were the establishing of a school that would train hundreds of pastors, teachers, and missionaries and the systematizing of the dispensationalist strand of American evangelicalism that had emerged from the Bible Conference movement and was enshrined in Scofield's reference Bible. Chafer continued to teach and lecture until his death in Seattle, Washington, while on a speaking tour.

• There is no standard biography available on the life of Chafer, only a variety of short articles. Among them, the following are the best: Chafer's "When I Learned from Dr. Scofield," *Sunday School Times*, 4 Mar. 1922, p. 120; C. Fred Lincoln, "Biographical Sketch of the Author," in Chafer's *Systematic Theology*, vol. 8 (1947), pp. 3–6; John D. Hannah, "The Early Years of Lewis Sperry Chafer," *Bibliotheca Sacra* 144 (1987): 3–23; John F. Walvoord, "Lewis Sperry Chafer," *Sunday School Times* (11 Oct. 1952), pp. 855, 868–70; and John A. Witmer, "'What God Hath Wrought' Part I: God's Man and His Dream," *Bibliotheca Sacra* 131 (Jan.–Mar. 1974): 3–13. Jeffrey J. Richards, *The Promise of Dawn: The Eschatology of Lewis Sperry Chafer* (1991), is an excellent treatment of Chafer's views on his most unique theological contribution. Several histories of Dallas Theological Seminary also are pertinent: Chafer, "Twenty Years of Experience," *Dallas Theological Seminary Bulletin* 19 (July–Sept. 1943): 3–4; Rudolf A. Renfer, "A History of Dallas Theological Seminary" (Ph.D. diss., Univ. of Texas, 1959); and John D. Hannah, "The Social and Intellectual History of the Origins of the Evangelical Theological College" (Ph.D. diss., Univ. of Texas at Dallas, 1988).

JOHN D. HANNAH

CHAFFEE, Adna Romanza (14 Apr. 1842–1 Nov. 1914), army officer, was born in Orwell, Ashtabula County, Ohio, the son of Truman Bibbins Chaffee and Grace Hyde, farmers. He was raised on his father's farm, receiving only a rudimentary education. Upon the outbreak of the Civil War, Chaffee left home intending to join an Ohio regiment, but he met the Sixth U.S. Cavalry and enlisted as a private on 22 July 1861. He rode with the Sixth for the next twenty-seven years. By dint of good soldiering, Chaffee became sergeant within weeks and, following service in the Peninsula and Antietam campaigns, rose to first sergeant. On 12 May 1863 he was commissioned second lieutenant at the behest of Secretary of War Edwin M. Stanton. Chaffee subsequently fought at Brandy Station and Gettysburg, being wounded at both battles and captured near Fairfield, Pennsylvania. Refusing to accept parole, he escaped, rejoined his outfit, and received brevet promotion to first lieutenant on 3 July 1863. In this capacity Chaffee accompanied General Philip H. Sheridan throughout the 1864 Shenandoah Valley campaign, rising to first lieutenant on 22 February 1865. The following month he obtained brevet promotion to captain for distinguished service at the battle of Dinwiddie Court House, Virginia. By the war's end, Chaffee had participated in no less than fifty-four major battles and skirmishes.

Chaffee remained in the army as regimental adjutant and quartermaster until March 1867, when he resigned his commission to pursue a business career. Soon afterward his commanding officer prevailed upon him to rejoin the service. Chaffee rose to captain on 12 October 1867 and spent the next two and a half decades on the southwestern frontier, gaining a reputation as a peerless Indian fighter. On 7 March 1868 he distinguished himself in combat with the Comanches at Paint Creek, Texas, and was brevetted major. Chaffee then rode with General Nelson A. Miles against the Cheyenne from August 1874 to February 1875 and subsequently commanded the San Carlos Indian Reservation from July 1879 to May 1880. Chaffee won official commendation for helping subdue the White Mountain Indians in November 1881, fought at the July 1882 battle of Big Dry Wash, Arizona, and accompanied General George Crook (1829–1890) during his expedition into the Sierra Madre, Mexico, in 1883. Chaffee was promoted to major on 7 July 1888, transferred to the Ninth Cavalry, and received brevet promotion to lieutenant colonel for meritorious services on February 27 1890. That year he joined the Department of Arizona as inspector general and in 1896 transferred to the service school at Fort Leavenworth, Kansas. Chaffee advanced to lieutenant colonel, Third Cavalry, on 1 June 1897 and thereafter served as commandant of the cavalry school at Fort Riley, Kansas.

Following commencement of the Spanish-American War in 1898, Chaffee was commissioned brigadier general of volunteers and assigned to the Third Brigade of General Henry W. Lawton's Second Division. Arriving in Cuba, Chaffee fought in the battle of Santiago and was delegated the capture of El Caney, a strongly fortified post on the American right. On 1 July the Americans succeeded after a tenacious ten-hour struggle with entrenched Spanish troops, and the following week Chaffee was promoted to major general of volunteers. He returned briefly to the United States before being recalled back to Cuba at the behest of General John R. Brooke, the military governor. There Chaffee functioned as chief of staff to General Leonard Wood until May 1900. Postwar reductions cost Chaffee his general's rank, but on 8 May 1899 he advanced to colonel, Eighth Cavalry.

In July 1900 Secretary of War Elihu Root dispatched Chaffee to command American forces in China, then wracked by the so-called Boxer Rebellion. He arrived at Tientsin and, in concert with English,

French, Italian, German, and Japanese troops, marched on the imperial capital of Beijing (Peking) to rescue foreign legations from the rebels. On 14 August Chaffee's contingent stormed the city's gates and secured the beleaguered diplomats. His skill in battle and his tactful treatment of inhabitants were openly praised by Chinese and foreign observers alike. Chaffee became a major general on 4 February 1901 and, departing China, served briefly as military governor of the Philippines.

Chaffee returned to the United States in October 1902 and assumed command of the Department of the East. He concurrently served as chief of the army general staff with the rank of lieutenant general as of 9 January 1904. The following year he ventured to France as acting secretary of war to observe the French army on maneuvers. Chaffee retired from the military on 1 February 1906, settled in Los Angeles, and served several years as head of the city's board of public works. He died in Los Angeles and was buried at Arlington National Cemetery.

Chaffee was a consummate professional soldier and was regarded as a model career officer for the army. In forty-two years of dedicated service, he remains the only American soldier to have risen to lieutenant general from the rank of private. Stern, uncompromising, yet popular with the troops, Chaffee was distinguished as much for his humanity toward captives and civilians as for his aplomb in battle. He was married twice, to Kate Haynie Reynolds in 1867 and, after her death in 1869, to Anna Frances Rockwell in 1875. This second union produced four children, of whom Adna Romanza Chaffee, Jr. (1889–1941), became a distinguished army officer and the father of American armored forces.

• Chaffee's official correspondence is in the Old Army and Navy Branch, National Archives. A collection of personal letters is at the Arizona Pioneers Historical Society, Tucson, with scattered materials in the James E. Babb Collection, Yale University Library, and the Henry C. Corbin Papers, Manuscript Division, Library of Congress. His account of the Boxer Rebellion is in *Extracts from the Report of Major General Adna R. Chaffee* (1900). A biography is William H. Carter, *The Life of Lieutenant General Chaffee* (1917). Details on his military activities appear in William H. Carter, *From Yorktown to Santiago with the Sixth U.S. Cavalry* (1900); John B. B. Trussell, "At the Gates of the Manchus," *Field Artillery Journal* 40 (1950): 72–75; Sarah P. Conger, *Letters from China* (1909); and Aaron S. Daggett, *America in the China Relief Expedition* (1903).

JOHN C. FREDRIKSEN

CHAFFEE, Adna Romanza, Jr. (23 Sept. 1884–22 Aug. 1941), army officer, was born in Junction City, Kansas, the son of Adna Romanza Chaffee (1842–1914), an officer who became army chief of staff, and Annie Frances Rockwell. Young Adna spent his childhood at a variety of army posts, becoming an expert equestrian under his father's tutelage. He attended West Point from 1902 to 1906, graduating thirty-first in a class of seventy-eight. Chaffee married Ethel Warren Huff on 15 December 1908. The couple had one son, also named Adna Romanza.

Chaffee was assigned to the cavalry upon graduation from West Point. His early military service included tours of duty in Cuba (1906–1907) and the Philippines (1914–1916). Recognized as one of the army's finest horsemen, he represented the cavalry in equestrian competitions and was selected to attend the French cavalry school at Saumur from 1911 to 1912. He subsequently taught at the U.S. Army Mounted Service School (1912–1913) and at West Point (1916–1917). Chaffee returned to France in 1918 as part of the American Expeditionary Force. He proved himself a skilled administrator, serving as the operations officer on division and corps staffs. In the decade following the war, he continued to excel in a variety of staff, command, and instructor positions. He graduated from the Army War College in 1925.

Although he remained an enthusiastic horseman, Chaffee recognized that the cavalry of the future would ride vehicles, not horses. From 1931 to 1934 he served as executive officer and then commander of the experimental First Cavalry Regiment (Mechanized). Promoted to brigadier general in 1938, he organized and trained a larger test unit, the Seventh Cavalry Brigade (Mechanized). This force included tanks, motorized (truck-transported) infantry, and motorized artillery. In 1939 and 1940, Chaffee led this brigade in a series of maneuvers against traditional cavalry and infantry units, establishing himself as the army's leading expert in armored warfare. He came to believe that a properly constituted armored force was capable of delivering decisive blows in battle. Although more conservative officers disputed Chaffee's claims, he was vindicated when German armored divisions spearheaded the blitzkrieg that conquered Poland and France in the early campaigns of World War II.

On 10 July 1940, the War Department established a full-fledged armored force of its own and named Chaffee to command it. Promotion to the rank of major general followed in October. In the process of organizing and training this force, Chaffee developed concepts of armored warfare that served the army well in World War II and have remained a part of armored doctrine ever since. He massed tanks into divisions that included elements of the other combat arms, and he employed these divisions in powerful, highly mobile operations against the enemy's flanks and rear. The wartime armored force eventually attained a strength of sixteen divisions and played a major role in American operations, but Chaffee did not live to see the culmination of his efforts. Stricken with cancer in 1940, his death was undoubtedly hastened by his attempts to continue working, against the advice of physicians. He died in Boston, Massachusetts. Although he never led his troops into battle, Chaffee is justifiably remembered as the father of the U.S. Army's armored branch.

• For a more detailed biographical sketch of Chaffee, see the entry by Timothy K. Nenninger in Roger J. Spiller et al., eds., *Dictionary of American Military Biography* (1984). Mildred Hanson Gillie, *Forging the Thunderbolt* (1947), is a partly biographical treatment of Chaffee in the creation of the armored force. An obituary is in the *New York Times*, 23 Aug. 1941.

CHRISTOPHER R. GABEL

CHAILLÉ, Stanford Emerson (9 July 1830–27 May 1911), physician, medical educator, and sanitarian, was born in Natchez, Mississippi, the son of William Hamilton Chaillé, a planter, and Mary Eunice Stanford. Chaillé's father died when he was six, and after his mother's death in 1844 he went to live with relatives in Boston. He graduated from Phillips Academy, Andover, Massachusetts, and attended Harvard University, where he received his B.A. in 1851 and his M.A. in 1854.

Chaillé was known as an ardent defender of the southern cause during his Harvard years, so it is perhaps not surprising that he chose to return to the South for his medical training. He lived with an uncle in New Orleans while completing the two-year course at the University of Louisiana medical school (M.D. 1853). When arguing for medical education reform in later years Chaillé pointed to the poor quality of training he received in these two years. He supplemented his education with internships at Circus Street Hospital and Marine Hospital. In 1860 and again in 1866 he traveled to Europe to study with famed physiologist Claude Bernard as well.

Chaillé married Laura E. Mountfort in 1857; she died in 1858 after giving birth to his only child. He would marry Mary Louise Napier in 1863. His first professional position was attendance at the Circus Street Hospital, a dispensary in New Orleans. Chaillé joined with two other local physicians in 1857 to found the *New Orleans Medical and Surgical Journal*, which he edited for the next ten years (with a hiatus during the war). He became a demonstrator in anatomy at the University of Louisiana medical school in 1858, beginning an association with the school that would end only with his retirement in 1908.

Chaillé was in Europe when the Civil War broke out, and he hurried home to join a Louisiana troop as a private. His superior officers quickly recognized that he was of greater value as a physician and appointed him surgeon general of the Louisiana troops. He then moved to the staff of General Braxton Bragg and later to administer hospitals in Atlanta and Macon, where he was captured in 1865.

Chaillé returned to New Orleans and helped his colleagues resurrect the medical school. He held the chair of obstetrics and gynecology for one year and continued as demonstrator in anatomy. In 1868 he became professor of physiology and pathological anatomy; with the later addition of hygiene to his assignment he held this chair until 1908. In 1886 he became dean of the medical school, which was renamed Tulane University, after a generous benefactor of the early 1880s.

Chaillé's greatest contribution to medicine was as an educator and reformer. Under his guidance Tulane gained a place in the forefront of American medical schools. His writings reveal both zeal for improvement and pragmatism about what was possible. At the time he had completed his medical studies, students were required to attend two years of lectures and faced no prerequisites to medical study. Students could enter the course of lectures late in the year and still be granted credit. The examinations were lax, and laboratory work, dissection, and clinical experience were not required. In all this the University of Louisiana was typical of its time, but by the 1870s the better medical schools were toughening their requirements. Chicago, Harvard, Pennsylvania, and others began to require a high school degree and increased the course of study to three years. Chaillé wanted Tulane to follow suit, but he recognized that if Tulane's requirements were too onerous, students would go elsewhere, thereby further threatening the perilous financial situation of the school.

Chaillé came at reform indirectly by introducing optional courses: a year of premedical work in the sciences (including microbiology), optional instruction in anatomy and microscopy, and additional clinical teaching. By the 1890s the school required a high school degree and had increased the term to three years; more than half the students were taking the optional courses, so making them required courses represented a small change. In 1899 the course was extended to four years. The introduction of state licensing in the 1890s added to the pressure on students, because an adequate preparation was necessary to pass the examination. Chaillé worked to keep the school abreast of new knowledge in microbiology and surgical technique, and he was successful in wooing benefactors to upgrade the physical plant in response to the greater spatial needs of laboratory medicine. When he retired he left a school that offered the best medical education in the South.

Chaillé's other major professional agenda was the promotion of "state medicine." By this he meant the government's responsibility for sanitation, vital statistics, inspection of food products, regulation of medical practice, forensics, and public education regarding hygiene. His was an active voice in urging the American Medical Association to advocate public health measures on the state and national levels. He continually pushed his state medical society into political activism, especially in support of laws governing the collection of vital statistics and the licensing of physicians. Chaillé wrote several papers extolling the value of vital statistics as a means of judging the efficacy of public health interventions, claiming that in no other way could public hygiene be grounded in scientific data. He was a firm believer in the sanitary gospel—that the way to a healthy populace was through the provision of pure water, cleansing of the streets, and government inspection to ensure food purity. He was quick to assimilate new scientific information, such as the microbiological discoveries of the 1880s, and to apply them to public health practice. By 1902 he was a major supporter of Walter Reed's 1900 work on the mosquito as the vector in yellow fever, while most of the Louisiana public health establishment was clinging to the older fomite theory.

Chaillé achieved fame as a national figure in public health after the 1878 yellow fever epidemic devastated the South. He was appointed to federal commissions to study the disease first in the South and then in Havana, Cuba. When Congress created the National Board of Health in 1879 in response to the yellow fever threat, Chaillé was made inspector for the port of New Orleans. This led him into direct conflict with the head of the Louisiana State Board of Health, Joseph Jones, who used states' rights arguments to claim that the national board had no right to tell him how to run his quarantine station. Chaillé's reasoned approach is evident in his summary of this affair, and it won him the respect of his New Orleans colleagues. When the National Board of Health lost its appropriation in 1882, Chaillé's national role ended, but he kept up the pressure for reform on the local level until his retirement in 1908. He died in New Orleans.

Chaillé was an important voice for raising the standards of excellence in medical education and public health practice in New Orleans for more than fifty years. If in 1874 he could call medical education in the United States a "very sick patient," then by his retirement in 1908 he must have been heartened by that patient's convalescence, in which he had played such a large role.

• The Rudolph Matas Medical Library at Tulane has a collection of reprints of many of Chaillé's works. It also has his manuscript papers. There are many letters to and from Chaillé in the forty-nine microfilm reels of the National Board of Health Papers, National Archives, R. G. 90. Chaillé published numerous articles in the *New Orleans Medical and Surgical Journal* on public health, vital statistics, medical jurisprudence, and medical education. In addition there are papers in the publications of the American Medical Association, the American Public Health Association, and the National Board of Health. The "very sick patient" comment is from "The Medical Colleges, the Medical Profession, and the Public," *New Orleans Medical and Surgical Journal*, n.s. 1 (1873–1874): 818–41. An account of his early career is Kenneth R. Whitehead, "A Biography of Stanford Emerson Chaillé, 1830–1876" (master's thesis, Louisiana State Univ., 1961). Chaillé's role at Tulane is described in depth in John Duffy, *The Tulane University Medical Center: One Hundred Fifty Years of Medical Education* (1984). Chaillé's National Board of Health role and the conflict with Joseph Jones is discussed in Margaret Humphreys, *Yellow Fever and the South* (1992). The most useful obituaries are by F. W. Parham and George Denegre in the *New Orleans Medical and Surgical Journal* 65 (1912–1913): 42–57.

MARGARET HUMPHREYS

CHALFANT, Jefferson David (6 Nov. 1856–3 Feb. 1931), painter, was born in Sadsbury Township, Chester County, Pennsylvania, the son of Franklin Chalfant, a cabinetmaker, and Lydia Nelson. He attended public schools in Lancaster, Pennsylvania. For a time he made a living by cabinetmaking, and he returned to cabinetmaking to support himself at various times throughout his life. By 1879 Chalfant had moved to Wilmington, Delaware, possibly at the urging of his sister, Aribell Bullock, who had married a Wilmington blacksmith.

Chalfant was introduced to painting through his job as a decorative painter for a car and sash works. With no formal training, he opened a studio in Wilmington in 1883. It was at this time that he experimented with media and subjects. From 1883 to 1886 Chalfant's work reflected his attempts to learn how to paint. These attempts were most often landscapes or still lifes. It was also during this period that he became close friends with two other Wilmington artists, Robert Shaw and Henry Lea Tatnall, both of whom were landscape artists.

In 1886 Chalfant painted the first of his trompe l'oeil works. They were extremely accomplished and represent a tremendous change from his earlier landscapes. Like many artists of the period, he was influenced by William Harnett's realist images. Chalfant produced only about a dozen trompe l'oeil paintings, and of these the best known are the four violin paintings created between 1887 and 1889. His compositions are simply arranged with only a few objects painted in a linear and incredibly realistic style.

Because his work was so true to life, Chalfant was arrested in 1886 for alleged counterfeiting of U.S. currency. Nonetheless, Chalfant continued to paint images of money after his arrest: *Perfect Counterfeit* (1888), for instance, depicts in trompe l'oeil style a treasury note pinned on an old wooden panel. In the late 1880s he began his long association with Haines Woodruff Sullivan, a Brooklyn, New York, businessman who acted as Chalfant's agent. Chalfant remained in Wilmington while Sullivan encouraged him, and he soon became financially successful. After Sullivan's death in 1903 Chalfant married Katherine Braunstein of Wilmington.

In 1890, with the financial assistance of New York art patron Alfred Corning Clark, Chalfant went to Europe to study art. He remained in France for nearly two years studying with Jules Lefebvre and William Bouguereau, concentrating on drawing and depicting the human figure. His work remained highly traditional, and he did not develop any interest in the avant-garde styles then prevalent in France.

Upon his return to the United States, Chalfant began creating genre paintings, making use of both his practical knowledge of the realist still life tradition and his new understanding of the human figure. Chalfant executed only two to four paintings a year, but he earned a good living. His genre paintings were smaller in size in the beginning, with rougher, more painterly surfaces than his earlier smoothly polished trompe l'oeil works. During the 1890s Chalfant also established himself as an inventor and experimenter, developing a series of innovations, including a type-justifying machine and improvements on a bicycle saddle and pedal crank attachment.

Chalfant based many of his images on photographs, and he kept many props in his Wilmington studio. His genre themes were mostly American in nature, often featuring images of tradesmen, black children, cavaliers, musicians, and chess players. Chalfant constructed sets, often placing figures in them, and then had the entire scene photographed. One writer from the period described his studio as a large room with floors covered in rugs of skin or wool, and with easels, chairs, tables, and draperies all about. In the midst of this lay china, swords, pistols, coats, hats, and other props.

By 1900 Chalfant moved to the more lucrative field of portrait painting. He received numerous portrait commissions and even worked from photographs of deceased individuals. With Sullivan no longer available to promote his work, Chalfant began to depend on prominent Wilmington families for his portrait commissions rather than trying to market his work outside of Wilmington. Although paintings from this last period produced the most income, they were not his most significant works. While Chalfant's work can be divided into distinct periods based on subject and style, he is best known for his trompe l'oeil images created between 1886 and 1890. The fact that he initially had no art school training and that he came from a craftsman tradition no doubt influenced him in his vision of art as a means to make a living. As a result, Chalfant was an astute follower of the public's taste and shifted subjects and style accordingly.

Chalfant retired to his suburban home "Ashley," near Wilmington, in 1927, and he died there in 1931. Knowledge of his career was lost until the late 1950s, and only in the 1970s did historians and scholars begin to recognize Chalfant's contributions. Many consider Chalfant one of the best of the considerable number of Harnett followers.

• Good sources of information are the Jefferson David Chalfant Files, at the Helen Farr Sloan Library, Delaware Art Museum, Wilmington, Del. See also Joan H. Gorman, *Jefferson David Chalfant*, 1856–1931 (1979).

J. SUSAN ISAACS

CHALIF, Louis Harvey (25 Dec. 1876–24 Nov. 1948), ballet dancer and teacher, was born in Odessa, Ukraine. His parents' names are unknown. A graduate of the Russian Imperial Ballet School, Chalif was a child dancer in the ballet *Excelsior* with ballerina Virginia Zucchi at the Odessa Municipal Theater in 1887. He studied at the ballet school connected with the theater under Alfred Bekefi, Ivan Savitsky, and Thomas Nijinsky, father of Vaslav Nijinsky and Bronislava Nijinska. He graduated in 1893 and became ballet master of the troupe four years later. He was still dancing with the company when a year later Tchaikovsky was in the audience. The composer, impressed by Chalif's vigor and expressiveness, asked Chalif to dance in his ballets.

Chalif served in the Russian army from 1899 to 1902. That year he returned to civilian life and married Sara Katzhof; they had six children. He was named a premier danseur the following year, but in 1904 he elected to emigrate to the United States, the first Russian-born teacher of ballet and dance to do so. Communication was not a problem because in addition to his own language he spoke English, French, and Italian. He was deeply familiar with the stories and choreography of virtually all the major ballets up to that time as well as operas and their libretti, folk and national dances, and their costumes.

Once in the United States, Chalif was instrumental in promoting a number of career advancements in quick succession. He volunteered his services to Lillian Wald, founder of the Henry Street Settlement House in New York. Impressed by his talent and industry, Wald introduced Chalif to Luigi Albertieri, director of the Metropolitan Opera House Ballet. Albertieri named Chalif first dancer of the company and assistant ballet master at a princely salary of $50 a week. Chalif danced in the 1904–1905 season and at the same time began to give private lessons to children and young adults destined to become teachers.

Chalif also began to teach folk dancing in the physical education department of New York University and wrote a syllabus on the subject. The staff felt that the course of instruction was too difficult and preferred the so-called "baby dances" that Chalif taught at the settlement house. These simple dances were, according to Chalif's catalog, brief "garlands of fancies" for young children, set to music arranged for the piano. The NYU teachers believed boys could be brought into such an activity. During this period Chalif continued to perform, and he taught at Columbia University Teachers College.

He founded his first school, the Chalif Normal School of Dancing, in 1905 at an address on 42nd Street just west of Fifth Avenue, New York City. An early catalog described it as "Professional Courses in Esthetic Greek, National, Interpretive, Character, Folk, Contra and Fine Ballroom Dancing." The school later moved to studios at 163 West 57th Street, then to Rockefeller Center with a faculty of ten and four accompanists, as well as the secretarial staff.

Soon after Chalif had arrived in the United States he sent for his wife and family, which by this time included two children.

Although Chalif did not stress classical ballet as practiced in the Imperial Russian Ballet, neither did he slight it. He choreographed in the genre but devoted the major portion of his system and intellect to the major aims set forth in his writings: "To teach dancing, to give technique, strength and grace, to impart an understanding of the laws of the art, and the ability to obey them, and to develop that central soul of dancing, self expression. To provide a repertory, surprisingly large in proportion to the time expended, of truly excellent dances, and to teach how to teach. It is constantly borne in mind that the teacher-pupil must be enabled to pass on the instruction given." None of these aims is antithetical to the purpose of the classroom today, but he expressed these ideals in 1905, when organized dance was still in its infancy in the United States; self-expression was recognized mainly in the field of physical education or in such free-form movement as that identified with the dancer Isadora Duncan. All of Chalif's children were given dance instruction and training as a matter of course. Later, three of them, Edward, Frances, and Amos, taught in the school. By the 1930s, the 500 hours required for graduation included successful completion of "modern ballet, character and national dance, children's material, tap and musical comedy, classical ballet and toe technique, ballroom, modern, Spanish and body conditioning."

Chalif sought to form an amalgam of his own training with ideals toward which dancers in this country were groping. To this end he gave lessons at various academies and schools in addition to his own. During his lifetime he made 1,200 dances ranging from the simplest to the most advanced and choreographed 35 ballets and 120 folk dances, and he also arranged six collections of piano reductions from the classical repertoire as accompaniments. He also wrote six textbooks, one of them on Russian folklore and costumes, and sent 20,000 mail-order catalogs (containing descriptions of the faculty members, Chalif's philosophy and methodology, the various styles of dancing taught, classes, fees, and textbooks) to public and dance schools throughout the world, using in part the mailing lists of dance societies of which he was a member. The sum of this massive output is in the Library of Congress.

His son Amos said it was nothing for Chalif to work sixteen hours a day juggling his various enterprises. By 1915 Chalif had amassed sufficient funds to design and see to the construction of his own five-story building on 57th Street across from Carnegie Hall; it was completed in 1918. Chalif taught mainly in New York City but occasionally ventured to nearby locales such as the Barn Studio, founded in rural Bernardsville, New Jersey, in 1931. The structure had originally been a horse barn but was remodeled by Mrs. Howard G. Hull, a patroness. Edward took charge and carried out the Chalif method until his retirement in 1968. Amos and his wife, who had maintained a dance studio in nearby Chatham, New Jersey, took over and were carrying on the tradition as late as 1994. Louis Chalif gave classes in both places.

Chalif enjoyed an immense reputation early on and during the World War I years worked with Sol Hurok, Anna Pavlova, and the Mordkin Ballet, among other Russian troupes. The Soviet Union approached him officially in 1936 with a proposal to become the commissar of all dance in the USSR. By then an American citizen, prosperous and in love with his adopted country, Chalif declined. He died in New York City.

Although Chalif's school flourished during the same period as those of Isadora Duncan and Ruth St. Denis, the latter were more involved with developing disciples. Chalif's aim was to spread the joy of dance as epitomized on the title page of his first textbook: "Dance—To Live. Let dancing ever be pure beauty—so shall it best interpret the aspirations of our soul. And let it be studied with all the ardor and the science worthy of so great an art."

• Chalif's textbooks and other tracts dealing with folk dances, choreographies, scores, and works for students of all ages are in the Library of Congress and the Dance Collection of the New York Public Library for the Performing Arts. The latter also contains catalogs and announcements from Chalif's schools (1911–1938); numerous newspaper clippings about Chalif and his career; a comprehensive article by Ann Barzel, "Louis H. Chalif," in the July 1945 issue of *Dance Magazine*; and Albertina Vitak, "In Memoriam: Louis H. Chalif," *Dance Magazine*, Jan. 1949. Photographs of Chalif may be found in the Dance Collection and in the Museum of Modern Art, New York.

JOSEPH GALE

CHALLENGER SHUTTLE CREW, comprising seven astronauts, died in the explosion of their spacecraft during the launch of STS-51-L from the Kennedy Space Center, Florida, at about 11:40 A.M., EST, on 28 January 1986. The explosion occurred seventy-three seconds into the flight as a result of a leak in one of two solid rocket boosters that caused the main liquid fuel tank to ignite. The crew members of the *Challenger* represented a cross section of the American population in terms of race, gender, geography, background, and religion. The explosion became one of the most significant events of the 1980s, as billions around the world saw the accident on television and empathized with the crew members killed.

Francis Richard "Dick" Scobee, spacecraft commander, was born on 19 May 1939 in Cle Elum, Washington, the son of Francis W. Scobee, a trainmaster and railroad engineer. After graduating from the public high school in Auburn, Washington, in 1957, he enlisted in the U.S. Air Force, training as a reciprocating engine mechanic but longing to fly. He took night courses and in 1965 received a B.S. degree in aerospace engineering from the University of Arizona. This made it possible for Scobee to receive an officer's commission and enter the air force pilot training program. He received his pilot's wings in 1966 and began a series of flying assignments with the air force, including a combat tour in Vietnam. Scobee married Virginia June Kent of San Antonio, Texas; they had two children. He attended the USAF Aerospace Research Pilot School at Edwards Air Force Base, California, in 1972 and thereafter was involved in several test programs. As an air force test pilot Scobee flew more than forty-five types of aircraft, logging more than 6,500 hours of flight time.

In 1978 Scobee entered NASA's astronaut corps and was the pilot of STS-41-C, the fifth orbital flight of the *Challenger* spacecraft, launched from the Kennedy Space Center on 6 April 1984. During this seven-day mission the crew successfully retrieved and repaired the ailing Solar Maximum Satellite and returned it to orbit. This was an enormously important mission because it confirmed, as NASA had long claimed, that the space shuttle could be used to repair satellites in orbit.

Michael J. Smith, shuttle pilot, was born on 30 April 1945 in Beaufort, North Carolina, the son of Robert and Lucille Smith. A commander in the U.S. Navy at the time of the *Challenger* accident, Smith had been educated at the U.S. Naval Academy, class of 1967, and received an M.S. in aeronautical engineering from the Naval Postgraduate School in 1968. He was married in 1967, and he and his wife, Jane Jarrell, had three children. Smith underwent aviator training at Kingsville, Texas, and received his wings in May 1969. After a tour as an instructor at the navy's Advanced Jet Training Command between 1969 and 1971, he flew A-6 "Intruders" from the USS *Kitty Hawk* in Southeast Asia. Later he worked as a test pilot for the navy, flying twenty-eight different types of aircraft and logging more than 4,300 hours of flying time. Smith was selected as a NASA astronaut in May 1980, and a year later, after completing further training, he qualified as a space shuttle pilot. The *Challenger* flight was his first shuttle mission.

Judith A. Resnik, one of three *Challenger* mission specialists, was born on 5 April 1949 in Akron, Ohio, the daughter of Marvin Resnik, an optometrist, and Sarah Resnik. Educated in public schools, Resnik attended Carnegie-Mellon University, where she received a B.S. in electrical engineering in 1970, and the University of Maryland, where she earned a Ph.D., also in electrical engineering, in 1977. Resnik, who never married, worked in a variety of professional positions with the RCA corporation in the early 1970s and as a staff fellow with the Laboratory of Neurophysiology at the National Institutes of Health in Bethesda, Maryland, between 1974 and 1977.

Selected as a NASA astronaut in January 1978, the first cadre containing women, Resnik underwent the training program for shuttle mission specialists during the next year. Thereafter she filled a number of positions within NASA at the Johnson Space Center in Texas, working on aspects of the shuttle program. Resnik became the second American woman in orbit on the maiden flight of *Discovery*, STS-41-D, between 30 August and 5 September 1984. During this mission she helped deploy three satellites into orbit and also was involved in biomedical research. Afterward, she began intensive training for the STS-51-L mission, on which she was killed.

Ronald E. McNair, the second *Challenger* mission specialist, was born on 21 October 1950 in Lake City, South Carolina, the son of Carl C. McNair, Sr., and Pearl M. McNair. In the segregated public schools that he had to attend, he achieved early success as both a student and an athlete. Valedictorian of his high school class, he attended North Carolina A&T State University, where in 1971 he received a B.S. in physics. He went on to study physics at MIT, where he specialized in quantum electronics and laser technology, completing his Ph.D. in 1976. As a student he conducted some of the earliest work on chemical HF/DF and high-pressure CO lasers, publishing pathbreaking scientific papers on the subject. He married Cheryl B. Moore of New York, with whom he had two children.

After completing his Ph.D., McNair was employed as a physicist at the Optical Physics Department of Hughes Research Laboratories in Malibu, California, where he conducted research on electro-optic laser modulation for satellite-to-satellite space communications. This research led him into contact with the space program, and when the opportunity presented itself, he applied for astronaut training. In January 1978 NASA selected him to enter the astronaut cadre, one of the first three black Americans chosen. McNair became the second black American in space when he flew on the *Challenger* shuttle mission STS-41-B between 3 and 11 February 1984. During this mission McNair operated the maneuverable arm used to move payloads in space. The 1986 *Challenger* mission was his second shuttle flight.

Ellison S. Onizuka, the third *Challenger* mission specialist, was born on 24 June 1946 in Kealakekua, Kona, Hawaii. He attended the University of Colorado, receiving B.S. and M.S. degrees in engineering in June and December 1969, respectively. While at the university he married Lorna Leiko Yoshida of Hawaii; the couple had two children. He also participated in the U.S. Air Force ROTC program, leading to a commission in January 1970. While on active duty with the air force during the early 1970s, he was an aerospace flight test engineer at the Sacramento Air Logistics Center. After July 1975 he was assigned to the Air Force Flight Test Center at Edwards Air Force Base, California, as squadron flight test officer and later as chief of the engineering support section.

In January 1978 Onizuka was selected as a NASA astronaut and entered a one-year training program, after which he became eligible for assignment as a mission specialist on future space shuttle flights. He worked on orbiter test and checkout teams and launch support crews at the Kennedy Space Center for the first two shuttle missions. Because he was an air force officer on detached duty with NASA, Onizuka was a logical choice to serve on the first dedicated Department of Defense classified mission. He was a mission specialist on STS-51-C, which was flown on the *Discovery* orbiter from 24 to 27 January 1985. The *Challenger* flight was his second shuttle mission.

The last two members of the *Challenger* crew were not federal government employees. Gregory B. Jarvis, payload specialist, was born on 24 August 1944 in Detroit, Michigan, the son of Bruce and Lucille Jarvis. Educated at the State University of New York at Buffalo, he received a B.S. in electrical engineering in 1967; at Northeastern University in Boston he received an M.S. in the same field in 1969; and at West Coast University in Los Angeles he completed course work for an M.S. in management science in 1973. He was married in 1975; he and his wife, Marcia G. Jarboe, had no children. Jarvis became an employee of Hughes Aircraft Corporation in 1973 and served in a variety of technical positions until 1984, when he was accepted into the astronaut program under Hughes's sponsorship after competing against 600 other Hughes employees for the opportunity. Jarvis's duties on the *Challenger* flight involved gathering new information on the design of liquid-fueled rockets.

Christa McAuliffe, a schoolteacher, was born Sharon Christa Corrigan on 2 September 1948 in Boston, Massachusetts, the daughter of Edward Corrigan, an accountant, and Grace Corrigan. As a youth growing up in the Boston suburb of Framingham, she registered excitement over the Apollo moon landing program and years later wrote on the astronaut application form, "I watched the Space Age being born and I would like to participate."

In 1970, a few weeks after graduating from Framingham State College, Christa Corrigan married her longtime boyfriend, Steven McAuliffe, with whom she had two children. They then moved to the Washington, D.C., metropolitan area, where he attended the Georgetown University Law Center while she taught in secondary schools, specializing in American history and social studies. The McAuliffes stayed in the Washington area for the next eight years, during which time Christa continued to teach and earned an M.A. in education from Bowie State University in Maryland in 1978. That same year the couple moved to Concord, New Hampshire, where Steven accepted a job as an assistant to the state attorney general. In 1982 Christa McAuliffe took a teaching post at Concord High School and two years later learned about NASA's search for an educator to fly on the shuttle, the intent being to find a gifted teacher who could communicate with students from space. She was one of 11,000 educators who applied for entrance into the astronaut ranks.

NASA selected McAuliffe for the position in the summer of 1985, and in the fall she took a yearlong leave of absence from teaching in order to train for an early 1986 shuttle mission. As a result of her immediate rapport with the media, the teacher-in-space program received tremendous popular attention. It is in part because of the excitement over McAuliffe's presence on the *Challenger* that the accident had such a significant impact on the nation.

• A useful collection of biographical materials about the 1986 *Challenger* crew, including news clippings and obituaries, can be found in the NASA History Division Reference Collection and at the Archives of the National Air and Space Museum, Smithsonian Institution, both in Washington, D.C. Books dealing with the subject include Joseph D. Atkinson, Jr., and Jay M. Shafritz, *The Real Stuff: A History of the NASA Astronaut Recruitment Program* (1985); Robert T. Hohler, *"I Touch the Future . . . ": The Story of Christa McAuliffe* (1986); William P. Rogers et al., *Report of the Presidential Commission on the Space Shuttle Challenger Accident* (5 vols., 1986); staff of the *Washington Post*, *Challengers: The Inspiring Life Stories of the Seven Brave Astronauts of Shuttle Mission 51-L* (1986); Daniel Cohen and Susan Cohen, *Heroes of the Challenger* (1986); David Shayler, *Shuttle Challenger* (1987); and Joseph J. Trento, with reporting by Susan B. Trento, *Prescription for Disaster: From the Glory of Apollo to the Betrayal of the Shuttle* (1987).

ROGER D. LAUNIUS

CHALMERS, James Ronald (11 Jan. 1831–9 Apr. 1898), Confederate general and U.S. congressman, was born in Halifax County, Virginia, the son of Joseph W. Chalmers, a lawyer, and Fannie Henderson. In 1839 the family moved to Holly Springs, Mississippi; his father became a prominent attorney there and served in the U.S. Senate. James Chalmers attended South Carolina College, graduating in 1851. Returning to Holly Springs, he studied law and was admitted to the bar in 1853. Between 1853 and 1858 he practiced law in Holly Springs. In 1858 he was elected district attorney and served in this office until 1861. He married Rebecca Arthur around 1865; they had one daughter. A Democrat in politics, he supported secession after Lincoln's election and served as chairman of the committee on military affairs in the state convention of 1861 that took Mississippi out of the Union.

When the Civil War began, Chalmers raised a company, was elected captain, and soon was appointed colonel of a Mississippi regiment in western Florida. In 1862, having been promoted to brigadier general, he commanded a brigade of infantry at the battle of Shiloh. After the Confederate retreat from Corinth, Mississippi, he was placed in command of a cavalry brigade and played an important role in General Braxton Bragg's Kentucky campaign. In the bloody battle of Murfreesboro in late 1862, he distinguished himself, leading to his selection as commander of the Military District of Mississippi and East Louisiana.

In 1864 Chalmers commanded a division under General Nathan Bedford Forrest. Chalmers participated in the military action that led to the massacre of surrendering black and Tennessee Union soldiers at Fort Pillow, Tennessee. His role in this infamous affair is still unclear.

After the war Chalmers settled in Friar's Point, Mississippi, and practiced law. At first he did not engage in Reconstruction politics, but in the 1875 campaign that "redeemed" Mississippi from Radical rule, he played a prominent role and was elected to the state senate. In 1876 he won election to Congress as a Democrat from the Delta. He was twice reelected, but the last time, in 1880, his election was successfully challenged by black leader John R. Lynch, a Republican, on the grounds of election fraud. Chalmers believed that Senator Lucius Q. C. Lamar, a state Democratic leader, had failed to support him in his contest to be seated in Congress.

When the Democratic legislature gerrymandered Chalmers's district to punish him for criticizing Lamar, he abandoned the party and in 1882 ran for Congress on the Independent ticket of disaffected agrarians. Supported by white Republicans, Chalmers defeated the Democratic candidate in an election in which both sides charged intimidation and fraud. Despite the use of his Fort Pillow record against him, the Republican leadership in Congress, as part of a southern strategy to divide the "Solid South," embraced Chalmers, and he was seated. But the alliance was so anomalous that, in 1884, when he sought reelection, he was decisively defeated by a combination of black and white votes. In 1885 he moved to Memphis, where he practiced law until his death.

• Brief biographical sketches of Chalmers can be found in Dunbar Rowland, ed., *Mississippi: Comprising Sketches of Counties, Towns, Events, Institutions, and Persons, Arranged in Cyclopedic Form* (3 vols., 1907), and Ezra J. Warner, *Generals in Gray: Lives of the Confederate Commanders* (1959). Chalmers's political career in historical context is described in Albert D. Kirwan, *Revolt of the Rednecks: Mississippi Politics, 1876–1925* (1951); C. Vann Woodward, *Origins of the New South, 1877–1913* (1951); and William C. Harris's introduction to John R. Lynch, *The Facts of Reconstruction* (1970).

WILLIAM C. HARRIS

CHALMERS, William James (10 July 1852–10 Dec. 1938), businessman and philanthropist, was born in Chicago, Illinois, the son of Thomas Chalmers, a machinist and mining manufacturer, and Janet Telfer. Educated in the Chicago public schools until the age of fourteen, he then worked as an apprentice machinist in the Eagle Works Manufacturing Company (Chicago), where his father was superintendent. Upon completing his apprenticeship, he spent a year traveling in Europe. He returned to Chicago in 1871, where he took charge of the finances for his father's newly formed company, Fraser, Chalmers & Co., which designed machines for milling, smelting, and refining ores.

One of Chalmers's tasks in his position was to oversee the activities of the Chicago Relief and Aid Society to support the 1,200 employees at Fraser and Chalmers in the days after the Chicago fire, which occurred in October 1871. His service after the fire earned him a reputation for being especially "liberal" in issues concerning children and their care. He also came into contact with many of Chicago's leading businessmen and philanthropists. His membership in Chicago's elite society was ensured in 1878, when he married Joan Pinkerton, the socially prominent daughter of Allan Pinkerton, head of the Pinkerton Detective Agency. They had two children.

As the business activities of Fraser, Chalmers & Co. grew, so did Chalmers's responsibilities in the company. In 1882 he was made a partner, and in 1891 he became its president. By then the company had constructed a second manufacturing plant in England especially for the South African mining market and had branch offices in New York City, London, Denver, Helena, Salt Lake City, Mexico City, and Tokyo. The company's products equipped the largest gold and silver mines in the western United States and South Africa. Under Chalmers's innovative and entrepreneurial leadership, the company's product line expanded to include pumping engines, boilers, crushing equipment, and a variety of equipment for roasting, smelting, and refining minerals and metals. The company was also willing to custom fit their equipment for virtually any situation, a fact that made it a dominant force in the mining industry.

In 1900 Chalmers and Edwin Reynolds of the Allis Engine Works of Milwaukee, Wisconsin, began discussing the possible merger of the two companies. The merger of the largest steam engine building company in the United States with Fraser, Chalmers & Co. seemed to be a practical way to deal with what appeared to be the saturation of the mining equipment market that Chalmers foresaw. As the merger took shape, two other companies that produced related equipment were invited to join the new company: the Gates Iron Works Company of Chicago and the Dickson Works of Scranton, Pennsylvania. The new company, incorporated in May 1901 and known as Allis Chalmers, immediately became a world leader in the manufacture of mining and milling equipment, steam engines, and—with the subsequent acquisition of Bullock Electric and Manufacturing Company—electrical equipment and steam turbines. Chalmers served in various executive offices of the new company until his retirement in 1905, when the firm offices moved to Milwaukee.

Before his retirement Chalmers had been actively involved in a variety of Chicago's civic and charitable organizations. He was a member of the Chicago Board of Education and a director of the 1893 World's Columbian Exposition, serving both on the Ways and Means Committee and the Committee on Mines and Mining. After his retirement he became even more involved, both in Chicago and abroad. In 1911 he founded a country home for convalescent children near the Chicago suburb of Wheaton. He served as a life trustee of the Field Museum of Natural History and was actively involved in the Presbyterian church. Following World War I, Herbert Hoover asked Chalmers to coordinate the raising of relief funds for Belgium children, which he did with great success; he was eventually decorated by the King of Belgium for his efforts. These decorations were part of his 1933 gift to the Chicago Historical Society of World War I medals for a new department commemorating the valor of American and foreign soldiers. Chalmers died in Chicago.

• Some limited biographical materials are available in the Chalmers Family Collection, Archives and Manuscripts, Chicago Historical Society; limited business materials are available in the Allis Chalmers Corporation Records, Milwaukee County Library. Sketches of Chalmers's life appear in volumes and newspaper articles devoted to prominent Chicagoans and American businessmen. Chalmers's role in the creation of Allis Chalmers is detailed in C. H. Wendel, *The Allis Chalmers Story* (1993). Obituaries are in the *Chicago Tribune* and the *New York Times*, both 11 Dec. 1938.

JANICE REIFF

CHALOFF, Serge (24 Nov. 1923–16 July 1957), jazz baritone saxophonist, was born in Newton, Massachusetts, the son of Julius Chaloff, a musician with the Boston Symphony Orchestra, and Margaret Stedman, a professor at the Boston University School of Music. He took lessons in piano and clarinet (or alto saxophone) formally but taught himself to play the baritone saxophone. Initially influenced by Harry Carney and Jack Washington, he played in lesser-known big bands from 1939 to 1944 and then joined Boyd Raeburn's orchestra in 1945. While with the big bands of Georgie Auld (1945–1946) and Jimmy Dorsey (1946), he was deeply influenced by alto saxophonist Charlie Parker, whose agile bop style Chaloff adapted to the more cumbersome baritone saxophone.

In September 1946 Chaloff recorded "Dial-ogue" and "Blue Serge" with members of Woody Herman's band, under the direction of arranger Ralph Burns. In Chicago he joined Auld's sextet, which included trumpeter Red Rodney and tenor saxophonist Allen Eager, and he recorded "Elevation" and "Fine and Dandy" under Rodney's name in New York in January 1947. That March he led a recording session that produced two takes each of "Pumpernickel," "Gabardine and Serge," "Serge's Urge," and "A Bar a Second," showcasing his bop improvisations.

Chaloff is best known for his membership from September 1947 to December 1949 in Woody Herman's big band, the Second Herd, in which Chaloff and tenor saxophonists Stan Getz, Zoot Sims, and Herbie Steward formed a saxophone section known as the Four Brothers. (Al Cohn replaced Steward in January 1948.) Chaloff can be heard in numerous brief solos recorded with Herman, including "Keen and Peachy," "The Goof and I," "Four Brothers," "That's Right," "Lemon Drop," and "Keeper of the Flame." His skills as an improviser are better documented in his earlier small group recordings as well as in a March 1949 session under his own name that produced "Chickasaw," "Bop Scotch," and "The Most."

By this time Chaloff was addicted to heroin. In his case the addiction created, or at least reinforced, an ugly personality. Herman and his sidemen recalled both humorous and vicious incidents involving Chaloff. Of greatest relevance to his career, his peers remembered that Chaloff threw his music, which he had memorized, into the Charles River in Boston after Herman attempted to fire him, thereby assuring that he could not be replaced and could continue to support his habit until Herman disbanded the Second Herd late in 1949. Swedish trumpeter Rolf Ericson remembered the impact of drug and drink on Chaloff and several other members of Herman's band: "When the band started a night's work they sounded wonderful, but after the intermission, during which they used the needle or lushed, the good music for the night was over. It was horrible to see them sitting on the stage like living dead, peering into paper envelopes when they weren't playing" (Morgan, p. 25).

Chaloff returned to Boston. After a brief tour with Count Basie's octet from May to June 1950, he settled in Boston, where he married Linda Black, a local model; they had a daughter. He suffered from his debilitating drug habit until late in 1954, when he overcame his addiction during a four-month-long hospital stay. Nevertheless he worked regularly in the Boston area and on tours ranging as far as the Midwest and the West Coast. Four appearances as a leader in the recording studio found him inventing brilliant bop lines with a more expansive timbral and emotional palette than evidenced in his improvisations of the late 1940s. These recordings include "Love Is Just Around the Corner" and "Easy Street" (late Mar. 1954), the title track and "Let's Jump" on the album *The Fable of Mabel* (Sept. 1954), "Body and Soul" on *Boston Blow-up* (Apr. 1955), and especially *Blue Serge*, with versions of "The Goof and I" and "Stairway to the Stars" (Mar. 1956).

By 1955 Chaloff was divorced from Linda Black. Near the end of his life he married Susan Black (no relation to his first wife). In May 1956 he suffered spinal paralysis as a result of pressure from a cancerous tumor. He was confined to crutches and eventually to a wheelchair but continued to perform and record. He died of cancer in Boston.

Together with baritone saxophonist Cecil Payne, in parallel with slide trombonist J. J. Johnson and following what Dizzy Gillespie had already done for the trumpet, Chaloff was a leading figure in the mid-1940s transformation of the rather unwieldy baritone sax into a vehicle for sleek and heady bop improvisation.

• The essential biographical and musical surveys and catalogs of recordings are Alun Morgan, "Serge Chaloff," *Jazz Monthly* 3 (Oct. 1957): 24–28, 31, and Vladimir Simosko, pamphlet notes to *The Complete Serge Chaloff Sessions* (1993). Additional surveys are Max Harrison, "Serge Chaloff," *Jazz Monthly* 9 (May 1963): 10–12, repr. in Harrison, *A Jazz Retrospect* (1976; rev. 2d ed., 1977); Jim Burns, "Serge Chaloff," *Jazz Journal* 21 (Mar. 1968): 14; and Alan Groves, "Blue Serge Blues: The Recorded Evidence of the Great Serge Chaloff," *Jazz Journal International* 32 (June 1979): 8–9. Morgan's catalog is updated in Pete Moon, "Serge Chaloff Discography," *Discographical Forum*, no. 38 (1977): 3; no. 39 (1977): 7; no. 40 (1978): 1–2, 7; and no. 41 (1978): 7, 20; and in G. von Jena, *Discografie of Serge Chaloff* (1986). Further glimpses into his career may be gleaned from James A. Treichel, *Keeper of the Flame: Woody Herman and the Second Herd, 1947–1949* (1978). See also Chris Sheridan, *Count Basie: A Bio-discography* (1986); Steve Voce, *Woody Herman* (1986); and Woody Herman and Stuart Troup, *The Woodchopper's Ball: The Autobiography of Woody Herman* (1990). An obituary is in the *Boston Daily Globe*, 19 July 1957.

BARRY KERNFELD

CHAMBERLAIN, Alexander Francis (12 Jan. 1865–8 Apr. 1914), anthropologist, was born in Kenninghall, Norfolk, England, the son of George Chamberlain, a businessman, and Maria Anderton. The family emigrated to the United States around 1870 and lived for one year in Bushnell's Basin, New York, near Rochester, where Chamberlain first attended school. The family soon moved to Canada and settled in Peterborough, Ontario. Chamberlain won his high school's graduation scholarship and enrolled in the University of Toronto.

Sir Daniel Wilson, the new president of the university, who had founded the first North American department of ethnology, became Chamberlain's mentor. Chamberlain thrived in this milieu and developed the characteristics that were to be the foundations of his career: a facility with foreign languages, an appetite for compiling and organizing diverse information, and concern for the survival of the world's smaller cultures and for the humans who lived in those cultures. He won many academic prizes and completed a B.A. with honors in 1886. The following year he was appointed a fellow in modern languages and began studies of the Missisauga Indians of Ontario, resulting in an M.A. in 1889.

In 1890 Chamberlain was appointed a fellow in anthropology at newly founded Clark University in Worcester, Massachusetts. In 1891 he presented a course of lectures, "The Relation of Linguistics to Psychology." Also that year he began studies of the Kootenay Indians of British Columbia. He wrote his doctoral dissertation under the supervision of Franz Boas, receiving in 1892 a Ph.D. in anthropology, the first ever in North America. Boas moved to Columbia University that year, and Chamberlain took his position at Clark, beginning as lecturer in anthropology and becoming full professor in 1911. However, the anthropology curriculum at Clark was small, and Chamberlain was handicapped by lack of student majors and graduate students. The university had a very strong reputation in child psychology, and that may explain his shift in that direction. From 1891 to 1900 he was the most prolific contributor to the child psychology journal *Pedagogical Seminary*. Two of his books were *Child and Childhood in Folk Thought* (1896) and *The Child: A Study in the Evolution of Man* (1900).

In 1898 Chamberlain married Isabel Cushman; they had two daughters. He idealized family and community life. From his student days in Toronto, he had been active in various reform movements, including those favoring prohibition, woman suffrage, labor unions, Henry George's single tax, anti-imperialism, and international peace. He participated in the local politics of Worcester as alderman-at-large and was a leader of the left wing of the city's Democratic party, serving as party chairman. He was also an active member of the Unitarian church. He often quoted inspirational verse and published a volume of his own poetry in 1904.

Chamberlain was renowned among his colleagues and students for his encyclopedic reading of ethnographic literature, based on his command of French, German, Dutch, Scandinavian languages, Italian, Spanish, Portuguese, and Russian. He annually compiled bibliographies for *American Anthropologist*, *Current Anthropological Literature*, and *Journal of American Folk-Lore*, which he edited. He was also coeditor of the *Journal of Religious Psychology*. Cross-cultural comparisons and encyclopedic summaries were necessary, Chamberlain argued, because the goals of anthropology and psychology were to understand the "generically human" condition, to differentiate it from the surface manifestations seen in the diversity of world cultures. The socialization of children and the development of civilization obscured the generically human condition. The similarity of children worldwide demonstrated the physical unity of our species as well as our psychic unity.

But Chamberlain was also a defender of cultural diversity. According to survival-of-the-fittest arguments often used to justify imperialism and racism, if a people could be conquered and oppressed, then that was proof that they should be conquered and oppressed. Chamberlain stood this evolutionary argument on its head and argued that continuing human progress requires the preservation of cultural diversity. The so-called lower races were the gene pool for future cultural and political-economic development. Hence, he emphasized the study of intercultural transfer, particularly the influences of minority and aboriginal peoples on the cultures of the dominant society. For example, he identified the Uncle Remus stories as Cherokee legends that were adapted to African-American story telling, eventually becoming popular literature for the dominant Anglo-Saxon society.

If Chamberlain had lived longer and if he had had graduate students to continue the development of his ideas, his impact on psychology and anthropology might have been greater.

Certainly, many of his ideas and observations were subsequently rediscovered, although no credit was given to him. He had argued that the psychological theories of aboriginal peoples should be treated as science, for example, the explanation that handedness is determined by the orientation of the head at birth. This would now fit the subfield of ethnopsychology. He had also observed and experimentally studied changes in the perception of environmental sounds when bilingual subjects switched languages. Gestalt theorists were later to describe this as perceptual set, the readiness to perceive in a specific way. Perhaps his most enduring contribution to anthropology was to develop the argument that race is distinct from culture, that cultures should be classified by the languages the people speak, not by the physical characteristics of their bodies.

Chamberlain's career was terminated abruptly by diabetes. A few weeks after it was first diagnosed, he died in Worcester of diabetic gangrene.

• There is a collection of Chamberlain papers at Clark University. In his brief career, Chamberlain published more than 700 articles and books. See his article "North American Indians" in the eleventh edition of the *Encyclopaedia Britannica*, vol. 14 (1910), pp. 452–82. He was working on a similar classification of South American native peoples at the time of his death. See also his "Linguistic Status of South American Indians, with Distribution Map," *American Anthropologist* 16 (1913): 236–47. For an example of his advocacy on behalf of minority peoples, see his article "Contact of 'Higher' and 'Lower' Races," *Pedagogical Seminary* 9 (1902): 507–20, in which he castigates U.S. occupation policies in the Philippines. For a bibliography and brief account of his life, see Albert N. Gilbertson, "In Memoriam," *American Psychologist* 16 (1914): 336–48. Clark University published a bibliography and collection of essays on Chamberlain, *In Memory of Alexander Francis Chamberlain*, ed. Louis N. Wilson (1914).

FLOYD W. RUDMIN

CHAMBERLAIN, Charles Joseph (23 Feb. 1863–5 Jan. 1943), botanist, was born near Sullivan, Ohio, the son of Edsell Whitmore Chamberlain and Mary Ella Spencer, farmers. His father had an aptitude for mechanics and mathematics and invented or improved several farm machines. Chamberlain's parents moved to Oberlin for their two sons' education, and his father became secretary-treasurer of a farm mutual insurance company.

Chamberlain initially intended to attend the Oberlin Conservatory of Music; a cornet soloist, he had written and arranged music. After a year in Oberlin College's Preparatory Department, he matriculated in the Classical Course in 1884. One of his professors, Albert A. Wright, who taught biological sciences and geology, interested him in botany. Meanwhile, Chamberlain participated in musical activities, as he would throughout life, playing the cornet in bands and the French horn with the conservatory orchestra. Upon receiving his A.B. in 1888, Chamberlain married Mary Ella Life; they had one daughter.

After teaching at the Pittsfield, Ohio, Central School for a year, Chamberlain became principal of the Crookston, Minnesota, State High School (1889–1893), also teaching Latin, Greek, mathematics, and other subjects. In the summers he worked in Wright's laboratory at Oberlin, gaining familiarity with microscopy and histological techniques; he decided to pursue graduate study in botany and earned a master's degree from Oberlin in 1894.

When Chamberlain entered the University of Chicago in 1893 for further graduate work, botany was not yet taught there, but he attended zoology lectures by Charles Otis Whitman and Jacques Loeb, vertebrate embryology with William Morton Wheeler, cytology, and histology as background for his future investigations in plant morphology. Lectures in botany were first given on a weekly visiting basis by John Merle Coulter, who had been taught by Asa Gray and who in 1895 became head of the newly-established department of botany. Chamberlain studied with Coulter, and they collaborated in teaching, dividing the responsibility, with Chamberlain in charge of the laboratory and Coulter lecturing. Communicating his enthusiasm for firsthand observation of plants in the wild, Chamberlain led frequent collecting trips to gather material for the herbarium and for morphological studies. He published numerous articles from 1895 on. In 1897 Chamberlain received the first Ph.D. given by the department of botany at Chicago; he then joined the faculty, rising from assistant and then associate in botany to professor of plant morphology and cytology in 1915. Coulter and Chamberlain together published morphologies of the spermatophytes (1901) and the angiosperms (1903), and a volume on the morphology of the gymnosperms (1910).

In 1901 the Chamberlains left for Germany so he could obtain specialized training in cytology. He spent a year working in the laboratory of Eduard Strasburger, and their friendship and correspondence continued. From 1902 Chamberlain was American editor for plant cytology of the *Botanisches Zentralblatt*, and for years he was associate editor of the *Botanical Gazette*.

Chamberlain's outstanding investigations over four decades were largely devoted to the cycads, a family of the gymnosperms that have been called "living fossils," practically unchanged descendants of palmlike Paleozoic plants. Widely dispersed in Mesozoic times, nine genera now survive in tropical and semitropical regions of the Eastern and Western hemispheres. Chamberlain's interest in cycads stemmed from his early work with Coulter on the gymnosperms, when he could find little information on these plants. He discussed it with a colleague in Strasburger's laboratory, who described to him a cycad locale he had seen years before near Jalapa, Mexico. "I was attracted to an investigation of the group partly by its great antiquity and partly because so little was known about it," Chamberlain wrote in *The Living Cycads* (1919, p. 3). He embarked on botanical explorations throughout the world to study and collect material on cycads in the field, for in his words, "The 'norm' of a plant can be determined only by studying it thoroughly in its natural surroundings."

In 1904 Chamberlain made his first trip to Mexico to investigate cycads. He collected botanical material, photographed, and gathered other information; afterward he had cycad cones and seeds sent periodically to Chicago. He journeyed to Mexico in 1906, 1908, and 1910 to learn more about the ecology, comparative morphology, and life histories of the cycads. In 1911 and 1912 he saw all the oriental cycad genera and most of the species during an extended trip to the Hawaiian Islands, Fiji Islands, New Zealand, and Australia, then to South Africa and Tenerife; he also became widely acquainted with foreign botanists and collections. He learned that cycad populations were increasingly restricted and threatened. In 1914 and 1922 he visited Cuba to study *Microcycas* there. In the laboratory, he employed evidence from cytology, embryogeny, and paleobotany to study cycads and their origins. The cycads in the greenhouses at the University of Chicago, meanwhile, formed a comprehensive collection that contained all the genera and more than half of the known species.

Chamberlain received an honorary Sc.D. from Oberlin College in 1923, and was chairman of the botanical section and vice president of the American Association for the Advancement of Science that year. He became emeritus professor in 1929, taught and lectured at several universities, and worked for two summers at the Puget Sound Biological Station. From 1931 to 1932 Chamberlain served as president of the Botanical Society of America. He held membership in the botanical societies of a number of countries and received many honors. In 1931 Chamberlain's first wife died; he married Martha Stanley Lathrop in 1938.

In forty-five years in the department of botany at the University of Chicago, Chamberlain trained many students who became members of botany faculties in other universities. He published his comprehensive work, *Gymnosperms: Structure and Evolution*, in 1935. At the time of his death in Chicago, he had nearly completed a book on taxonomy and his long-planned large work on the cycads.

• Autobiographical manuscripts and biographical material are in the Charles J. Chamberlain Papers in the Department of Special Collections of the University of Chicago Library. There is biographical information in the Student Files (Charles Joseph Chamberlain), Alumni and Development Records, Oberlin College Archives. Some of his notebooks, including research material on cycads, are in the department of botany of the Field Museum of Natural History, Chicago. Coulter and Chamberlain coauthored *Morphology of Spermatophytes, Part I: Gymnosperms* (1901), *Morphology of Angiosperms, Part II* (1903), and *Morphology of Gymnosperms* (1910, 1917). Chamberlain published several editions of *Methods in Plant Histology* (1901, 1905, 1915, 1924, 1932), a standard text outlining microscopical techniques for the laboratory and educational principles, as well as *Elements of Plant Science* (1930), and *Gymnosperms: Structure and Evolution* (1935, repr. 1957). For biographical sketches, see J. T. Bucholz, "Charles Joseph Chamberlain," *Botanical Gazette* 104 (1943): 369–70; Arthur W. Haupt, "Charles Joseph Chamberlain," *Chronica Botanica* 7, no. 8 (1943): 438–40; and an obituary in the *New York Times*, 6 Jan. 1943.

GLORIA ROBINSON

CHAMBERLAIN, Daniel Henry (23 June 1835–13 Apr. 1907), governor of South Carolina, was born in West Brookfield, Massachusetts, the son of Eli Chamberlain and Achsah Forbes, farmers. He worked on the farm and attended several schools intermittently. At age twenty-one he entered Worcester High School, one of the country's few public secondary schools, where he was a superior student. With the help of a part-time teaching job and loans from teachers and others, he entered Yale College in 1858; he was an outstanding debater and studied classics and English composition. After graduation in 1862, he studied at Harvard Law School for a year but felt compelled to enlist in the Union army. He was commissioned as a lieutenant and served as adjutant under Colonel Charles Francis Adams in the Fifth Massachusetts, a regiment of black troops. He saw little action and left the army as a captain.

After the war, Chamberlain visited the Sea Islands of South Carolina to find and return the body and effects of a Yale classmate who had accidentally drowned there. Hoping to pay off his debts, he decided to stay and raise cotton on Wadmalaw Island. In December 1867 he went north to marry Alice Ingersoll of Bangor, Maine, with whom he later had four children. On his return, he served as a delegate to the state constitutional convention required under Reconstruction. Representing Berkeley, an overwhelmingly black district, Chamberlain, who was a white northerner, supported elimination of qualifications for holding office, election of judges, and provision of land for freedmen, although only the first of these radical proposals was actually adopted.

In 1868 the newly formed Republican party nominated Chamberlain for attorney general. He won the election and served two terms until 1872. As attorney general, he was a member of two important and controversial bodies: the financial board, which issued state bonds, mainly to build railroads, and the land commission, which bought and distributed land to the landless. Although both boards were accused of corruption and incompetence, he emerged with his reputation intact. In 1871 he publicly reprimanded the Republicans for their conduct of government and joined leading Democrats in organizing a taxpayers' convention to demand retrenchment and reform.

After losing the Republican gubernatorial nomination to Franklin J. Moses in 1872, Chamberlain opened a law practice in Charleston. Two years later he was elected governor with the support of Republican reformers, including the African-American congressman Robert Brown Elliot, and with the discreet support of many Democrats, particularly Francis W. Dawson, editor of the *Charleston News and Courier*. His aim was to build a coalition to reform and reorganize the Republican party by attracting to it some of the more conciliatory Democrats. As governor, he vetoed patronage and spending bills. Moderate Democrats supported him, but many Republicans and partisan Democrats resisted. After a courageous campaign against the Democrats, who now openly employed terror and violence and advocated white supremacy, he polled a narrow plurality in his 1876 reelection campaign. But the Democrats challenged the results and his efforts to form a government, and eventually President Rutherford B. Hayes abandoned him as a part of the contested 1876 presidential election and the subsequent bargain with southern Democrats known as the Compromise of 1877.

After that defeat, Chamberlain moved to New York City, where he became a successful lawyer; he also taught a course in constitutional law on an annual basis at Cornell University. Over the next twenty years, he published articles on law and public issues, particularly Reconstruction, which he came to view as misguided. He died of cancer in Charlottesville, Virginia, one of a number of places in America as well as abroad where he lived briefly during the last years of his life.

• Chamberlain's official papers as governor are in the South Carolina Department of Archives in Columbia. The Perkins Library at Duke University houses a small collection of his papers as well as much of his correspondence with Francis W. Dawson, which is in the Dawson papers. Walter Allen, *Governor Chamberlain's Administration in South Carolina* (1888), contains speeches and documents from his two terms. Chamberlain's recollections and changing views on Reconstruction are in "Reconstruction and the Negro," *North American Review*, Feb. 1879, pp. 161–73; "Reconstruction in South Carolina," *Atlantic Monthly*, Apr. 1901, pp. 473–84; and "Some Conclusions of a Free Thinker," *North American Review*, Oct. 1907, pp. 176–92. Monographs include Thomas Holt, *Black over White: Negro Political Leadership in South Carolina during Reconstruction* (1977), and Richard N. Current, *Those Terrible Carpetbaggers: A Reinterpretation* (1988).

MICHAEL PERMAN

CHAMBERLAIN, George Earle (1 Jan. 1854–9 July 1928), lawyer and politician, was born near Natchez, Mississippi, the son of Charles Thomson Chamberlain, a physician, and Pamelia H. Archer. He received both the bachelor of arts and bachelor of law degrees from Washington and Lee University in 1876. He sought broader opportunities outside his native region and shortly after graduation moved to Albany, Oregon, where he took a job as a teacher. In 1878–1879 he served as the Linn County (Ore.) deputy clerk. Although he returned to Mississippi briefly in 1879 to marry Sallie Newman Welch (they would have six children), he never really went home again.

In Oregon Chamberlain rose steadily in Democratic politics. He served in the Oregon House of Representatives from 1880 to 1884 and was elected state attorney general in 1892. In order to secure office in traditionally Republican Oregon, Chamberlain had to draw support across party lines. Accordingly, in 1902 he ran for governor as something of an antiestablishment progressive Democrat. He supported electoral reform, attacked the infamous timber barons, and warning of the "yellow peril," called for an end to Asian immigration. Such a populist strategy appealed to the antimonopolists and the conservationists and was not uncommon on the West Coast; it served him well in Oregon politics for almost two decades. He was reelected governor in 1906 and in 1909 was appointed by the Republican-dominated Oregon legislature to the U.S. Senate. In 1915, primarily because of a fissure in Oregon between conservatives and progressives in the Republican party, he won a second term by direct election.

Colleagues often labeled the sturdily built Oregonian with pince-nez glasses a Bull Moose Democrat. After Woodrow Wilson was elected president in 1912, Chamberlain became chairman of the Senate Committee on Military Affairs. A nativist, he feared the effects of the recent massive influx of immigrants. He championed universal peacetime military service, an unprecedented and revolutionary change in American military manpower policy, to indoctrinate those "strangers in the land" with current conceptions of patriotism and to help assimilate them into American society. Chamberlain, a friend of the new General Staff system, was politically closer to Chief of Staff Leonard Wood than he was to Secretary of War Lindley M. Garrison. His later poor relations with Garrison's successor, Newton D. Baker, nearly culminated in political disaster for the Wilson administration.

Chamberlain wanted root and branch reform of the army, and the outbreak of the Great War in 1914 gave him an opportunity to act. In 1915 he introduced a bill in the Senate for universal military service. While it had no chance of passage, the bill positioned him well for the debates over preparedness. He demanded a full War Department investigation of the state of the army and incorporated many of the recommendations of the resulting study, "A Proper Military Policy for the United States," into his next legislative proposals. Although he failed to secure universal training, some of his recommendations, such as formal training of reserve officers in the nation's colleges (ROTC) and an organization to coordinate industrial mobilization, the Council of National Defense (CND), were included in the National Defense Act of 1916. Chamberlain continued to press for universal military training and led the successful fight in the Senate to introduce selective service when the United States entered the war in April 1917.

Chamberlain's subsequent career has long puzzled students of the Wilson Era. After initially supporting the administration, Chamberlain, by the end of December 1917, was leading the congressional attack on Wilson and Secretary of War Baker. His speeches enumerating the failures of the first year of war mobilization surpassed in vitriol even those of Republican senator Henry Cabot Lodge (1850–1924). Perhaps, as Chamberlain later asserted, he was merely a patriot protecting the interests of the young, drafted soldiers of the army. He was also well aware of the views of critical elements such as the Bull Moose faction in Oregon politics, and an antiadministration position could improve his standing in that traditional bulwark of independent Republicanism. Though Chamberlain's calls for reorganization of the war effort, appointment of a minister of munitions, and resignation of Secretary Baker failed, they invoked a response from the administration and the War Department that culminated in the passage of the Overman Act in May 1918. This legislation gave President Wilson the power to reorganize the government in any way necessary to assure the successful prosecution of the war. Thus, regardless of his reasons, the senator from Oregon had a positive effect on the war effort. Meanwhile Chamberlain had become anathema to the Democratic party. His later opposition to certain parts of the Versailles treaty further alienated President Wilson, who cast him into the political darkness, sending a letter just before the upcoming election asking voters to defeat Chamberlain. Oregon Republicans also proved ungrateful. Chamberlain lost his Senate seat in the general Democratic debacle of 1920 and never held elective office again.

In 1926 Chamberlain married Carolyn E. Shelton, a former clerk of the Military Affairs Committee (his first wife died in 1924). A member of the U.S. Shipping Board from 1921 to 1923, he practiced law in Washington, D.C., until his death there.

• Chamberlain's papers are located at the Oregon State Historical Society. For his work on preparedness and his wartime Senate career see John Garry Clifford, *The Citizen Soldiers: The Plattsburg Training Camp Movement, 1913–1920* (1972); John P. Finnegan, *Against the Specter of a Dragon: The Campaign for American Military Preparedness 1914–1917* (1974); and Daniel R. Beaver, *Newton D. Baker and the American War Effort 1917–1919* (1966). An obituary is in the *New York Times*, 10 July 1928.

DANIEL R. BEAVER

CHAMBERLAIN, Joseph Perkins (1 Oct. 1873–21 May 1951), professor of public law, was born to affluence in Cleveland, Ohio, the son of Robert Linton Chamberlain and Ellen Steele Perkins. After graduation from the Belmont School, a year of study at Harvard, and another year at the University of California at Berkeley, he earned a degree in law at Hastings Law School in San Francisco and was admitted to the California bar in 1898. Chamberlain spent two further years in the study of international law in Paris, Berlin, and Leipzig. While in Germany he met Elisabeth Stillman, a music student, whom he married in 1905. She died in 1928. They had no children.

Chamberlain practiced law in San Francisco from 1902 to 1905, and in 1907–1908 he served as a lecturer in the School of Jurisprudence at the University of California. In 1911, with Professors John Bassett Moore and Harlan Fiske Stone, Chamberlain established the Legislative Drafting Research Fund at the Columbia Law School. To assure the fund's early viability, Chamberlain financed its first five years from his own resources and later gave additional money to support ongoing operations. This fund has since prepared generations of students, serving as a laboratory for developing in future lawyers a capacity for practical participation in the legislative process, a goal that drew renewed emphasis in American legal education in the final decades of the twentieth century.

As a "meticulous legislative technician," Chamberlain was engaged at every level of government, international, national, state, and local. The scope of his professional work and interests was extraordinarily broad, but his deepest interest was in international law. *The Regime of International Rivers: Danube and Rhine* (1923), a monograph he prepared in 1917 for use by the State Department at the Versailles Peace Conference, established him as an authority on the law of international waterways. He later also became an expert in international law on the control of narcotics. With James Shotwell, also of Columbia, he helped prepare a draft treaty that became the Kellogg-Briand Pact, denouncing war as an instrument of national policy.

Initial fund research focused on workers' compensation legislation at the national and state levels. An early publication coauthored by Chamberlain for the New York State Constitutional Convention Commission was an *Index-Digest of State Constitutions* (1915). State constitutions became a subject in which the Research Fund retained a consistent interest over decades. After the fund assisted several committees of Congress in drafting legislation between 1916 and 1918, Middleton Beaman and Thomas I. Parkinson of its staff became, respectively, the first legislative counsel to the House of Representatives and the first head of the U.S. Senate legislative drafting service, significantly professionalizing legislative drafting at the national level. Parkinson's departure from the Columbia Law faculty was temporary, but it left Chamberlain as the fund's sole director in 1918. He retained the post until his death.

As counsel to the New York City Charter Commission in 1935–1936, Chamberlain took a principal role in drafting a reform city charter that, when accepted at the polls, accomplished the first major revision of that municipality's government in a third of a century. In 1936 he published *Legislative Processes: National and State*, a book praised for its "lucidity" and reliance on the author's "practical experience." It was reprinted as a classic in the field in 1969.

Chamberlain studied problems of slavery and forced labor as a member of an International Labor Office Committee in the 1920s. In 1933 President Franklin D. Roosevelt appointed him as the American member of the International High Commission for Refugees. Throughout the 1930s and 1940s Chamberlain was active as an advocate on behalf of Jewish refugees from Western Europe, founding and heading voluntary organizations, raising funds, and interceding with the government to a degree unusual for a person of his class and background. For example, he was a founder in 1934 of German-Jewish Children's Aid, an organization that sought visas and raised money to bring to the United States 250 children "not only in want, but also in danger." In 1943 he became chairman of the American Council of Voluntary Agencies for Foreign Service, an organization instrumental in settling thousands of displaced persons in the United States.

Chamberlain earned his doctorate when he was fifty-two years old. Columbia simultaneously awarded this degree and appointed Chamberlain professor of law in the Department of Public Law and Government in 1923. He had earlier taken and passed oral examinations to legitimize his role at the Research Fund he founded, because he did not wish to be dismissed as a rich dilettante. After steps were taken to declassify his 1917 monograph for the State Department, it was published and accepted by the university as the equivalent of a doctoral dissertation. Colleagues later remembered that the dissertation "defense" never mentioned the research but was a celebration of the man and his work. This "shy," "gentle," but "strong willed" and "dedicated" scholar, teacher, humanitarian, and public servant died at home in New York City.

Two parallel threads are evident in Chamberlain's professional career: a desire to bring a practical focus to the teaching and study of law, and an effort to develop and institutionalize the role of the expert legislative draftsperson in the American public policy process. A third focus of his life and work, perhaps the most important, was Chamberlain's early and consistent leadership as a humanitarian activist in the cause of European refugees, especially children, before and during World War II.

• Unpublished material is in the files of the YIVO Institute for Jewish Research in New York City, especially RG 278, "Register of the Papers of Joseph P. Chamberlain." Some unpublished materials are still retained by the Legislative Drafting Research Fund at the Columbia Law School. Additional works by Chamberlain are Chamberlain et al., *The Judicial Function in Federal Administrative Agencies* (1942), and a memorial volume, Chamberlain and P. C. Jessup, eds., *International Regulation of Economic and Social Questions* (1955). For biographical material see Philip C. Jessup, "Professor Joseph P. Chamberlain," *Arbitration Journal* 2 (Spring 1947): 77–78; and John M. Kernochan, "A University Service to Legislation: Columbia's Legislative Drafting Research Fund," *Louisiana Law Review* 16 (1956): 623–38. See also Ruth Gruber, *Haven: The Unknown Story of 1000 World War II Refugees* (1983); Lindsay Rogers, "In Memorium," *American Political*

Science Review 45 (Sept. 1951): 833–35; and an editorial in the *New York Times*, 23 May 1951. Obituaries are in the *New York Times*, 22 May 1951, with a portrait; *Survey*, June 1951, p. 252, with a portrait; and *Political Science Quarterly* 62 (Dec. 1951): 640–42.

GERALD BENJAMIN

CHAMBERLAIN, Joshua Lawrence (8 Sept. 1828–24 Feb. 1914), soldier, politician, and educator, was born in Brewer, Maine, the son of Joshua Chamberlain, a farmer and shipbuilder, and Sarah Dupee Brastow. After attending a military academy in Ellsworth, Chamberlain entered Bowdoin College in 1848, graduating in 1852. Three years later, after graduating from the Bangor Theological Seminary, he joined Bowdoin's faculty and taught a broad range of subjects, including logic, natural theology, rhetoric, oratory, and modern languages. In 1855 he married Frances Caroline Adams; of the couple's five children, three survived to adulthood.

Chamberlain's initial efforts to enlist in the Union army at the outbreak of the American Civil War met resistance from Bowdoin faculty and administrators. Finally, he secured a leave from Bowdoin, ostensibly to study abroad, but instead he volunteered for military service. He was commissioned lieutenant colonel of the Twentieth Maine Infantry on 8 August 1862. Joining the Army of the Potomac on the eve of Antietam, Chamberlain participated in the battles of Shepherdstown Ford and Fredericksburg, where he was wounded, and won promotion to colonel and regimental command on 20 May 1863. At Gettysburg, on 2 July 1863, Chamberlain and the Twentieth Maine were directed to hold the extreme left flank of the Army of the Potomac, resting on Little Round Top. The colonel's able defense of this position played a significant role in turning back the Confederate assault, and in 1893 he was awarded the Medal of Honor for his personal heroism. Wounded during the battle, Chamberlain remained with his command until repeated attacks of malaria forced him to take medical leave from November 1863 to May 1864. Rejoining his regiment during the battle of Spotsylvania, Chamberlain was soon elevated to the command of a brigade, and he fought in the battles of the North Anna and Cold Harbor. On 18 June 1864 he was seriously wounded while leading an assault on the Petersburg fortifications, winning a battlefield promotion to brigadier general from Ulysses S. Grant. After recovering from his wounds, Chamberlain played a prominent role as a brigade commander in the Appomattox campaign, suffering yet another wound, and he commanded the Union forces designated to accept the formal surrender of the Army of Northern Virginia on 12 April 1865. His service during this final campaign earned him the brevet rank of major general of volunteers, a fitting coda to his distinguished military record.

Refusing a commission in the regular army, Chamberlain retired in 1866 with the brevet rank of major general. Returning to Maine, he joined the Republican party and that fall won the first of four consecutive terms as governor (1867–1870). During his tenure in the governor's mansion he resisted measures to enforce state liquor laws, claiming that they infringed upon individuals' constitutional rights, and aroused controversy when he enforced capital punishment. In 1871 he returned to Bowdoin as its president, a position he held until 1883. During his dozen years in office he pressed for curriculum reform, especially in the areas of natural science and modern languages, with some success. His efforts to introduce mandatory military drill to the student body met with more resistance and less success. Appointed as a professor of philosophy, he taught several subjects, even after retiring as president. During his tenure as president he served as a U.S. commissioner to the Paris Exposition of 1878. As major general of the state militia, he was instrumental in keeping the peace during the disputed state election of 1879, when an alliance between Democrats and Greenbackers challenged election returns and threatened the Republican control of the governorship and legislature, resulting in an armed confrontation between the factions in January 1880. His refusal to recognize the claims of either party promoted a peaceful resolution of the crisis but effectively curtailed his future in Maine's Republican party. In 1885 he resigned his professorate as lecturer in political science and public law at Bowdoin, bringing to an end an academic career during which he had taught every subject except mathematics and physical science.

After his retirement from Bowdoin, Chamberlain became involved in a number of business enterprises interested in construction, transportation, and development, most notably as president of a Florida land development company (1885–1892). At the same time he pursued various cultural and literary interests, serving as president of the Institute for Artists and Artisans, writing and compiling essays on topics ranging from the Civil War to education, and delivering public addresses. Active in veterans' organizations, he served as president of the Society of the Army of the Potomac (1889), wrote extensively on his military experiences, and took special pains to commemorate the actions of the Twentieth Maine at Little Round Top. In 1900 he was appointed surveyor of the port of Portland, Maine. He died in Portland.

• Chamberlain's papers are at the Library of Congress, the Rutherford B. Hayes Presidential Center in Fremont, Ohio, and the Maine Historical Society in Portland, Maine. Several of his orations and addresses were published in pamphlet form, but his account of the Appomattox campaign, *The Passing of the Armies* (1915), remains his most lasting contribution to literature. More recently, a collection of his essays appeared under the title of *"Bayonet! Forward": My Civil War Reminiscences* (1994). Willard M. Wallace, *Soul of the Lion: A Biography of General Joshua L. Chamberlain* (1960), is the standard biography, but Alice Rains Trulock, *In the Hands of Providence: Joshua L. Chamberlain and the American Civil War* (1992), offers a closer look at his military service. Also worth consulting are John J. Pullen, *The Twentieth Maine: A Volunteer Regiment in the Civil War* (1957), a model unit history; and Harry W. Pfanz, *Gettysburg: The Second Day* (1987), which includes an account of the fighting at Little Round Top.

BROOKS D. SIMPSON

CHAMBERLAIN, William Isaac (11 Feb. 1837–30 June 1920), agriculturalist and editor, was born in Sharon, Connecticut, the son of Jacob Chamberlain and Anna Nutting, farmers. When Chamberlain was only fifteen months old, his parents moved from Connecticut to Hudson, Ohio, where they purchased and maintained a 147-acre farm. He received an A.B. from Western Reserve College (located in Hudson) in 1859 and an A.M. from the same school two years later. For three years he taught Greek and Latin at Shaw Academy in East Cleveland, Ohio, then became a member of the Western Reserve College faculty teaching the same languages. In 1863 he became superintendent of the Cuyahoga Falls, Ohio, schools, a position he held for two years, but with a decline in his health and his elderly parents needing more care Chamberlain resigned that position to teach languages at Western Reserve College and to maintain the family farm, which he had purchased in 1863. Also in 1863 he married Lucy Jones Marshall, daughter of publisher David Marshall, in Pittsburgh, Pennsylvania. They had five children.

Chamberlain reorganized the family farm into a profitable enterprise that was also a private experimental station devoted to the improvement of farm productivity. Despite his classical education, he became a student of agriculture and an advocate of scientific methods and business practices as applied to farming. He frequently tested and experimented with new procedures and applications, especially those concerning dairy cattle, wheat production, fertilizers, and apple production, because he believed the poor soil of the farm and the climate were suited for these enterprises. He also installed an extensive network of drainage tiles to increase the land available for agriculture. He began writing for regional agricultural journals in 1865, using the activities on his farm as the basis of his numerous articles. His clear prose and his emphasis on efficiency and practicality made him one of the most recognized agriculturalists in Ohio.

In 1880 the Ohio Board of Agriculture elected Chamberlain as its secretary and asked him to extend its work. During his six years as secretary he developed a system of monthly crop reports, secured passage of a state law controlling commercial fertilizers, helped to establish the Ohio Agricultural Experimental Station, purchased land for a state fairgrounds in Columbus, and increased dramatically the revenue of the state fair. Chamberlain's most important contribution was the creation of Farmers' Institutes (1880), in which agriculture professors and successful local farmers conducted lectures and discussions on farm practices in all eighty-eight Ohio counties. Ohio was the first state to hold numerous Farmers' Institutes on the local level.

In 1886 the Iowa State College of Agriculture and Mechanical Arts (later Iowa State University) named Chamberlain as its president. During his four-year tenure he oversaw the construction of Morrill Hall, an increase in enrollment, and the establishment of a federally funded agricultural experimental station, but growing campus dissent and problems with fraternities led to his resignation in 1890. Chamberlain returned to Hudson and resumed his career as an advocate of improved agricultural practices, using his farm as a model. In six weeks he wrote *Tile Drainage* (1891), a practical guide to the subject. He became an associate editor of the *Ohio Farmer* in October 1891, commuting to Cleveland twice a week to work at the paper, while also maintaining his farm. He produced a regular column, "Notes from Our Experimental Farm," that championed scientific agriculture and the application of business practices to farming. His favorite topics included the use of fertilizers, the development of an apple orchard, maple sugar production, the cultivation of wheat and potatoes, and the profitable marketing of farm products. While offering reports on experiments (always undertaken with financial constraints in mind), Chamberlain's popular column also emphasized education, suggested practical advice in a question-and-answer format, and advocated agricultural diversity and the maintenance of careful records. He remained with the *Ohio Farmer* until 1908, when he accepted an associate editorship with the *National Stockman and Farmer* of Pittsburgh, Pennsylvania, a position he held until 1919. In September 1919 he returned to the *Ohio Farmer* as a corresponding editor and remained there until his death. In addition to his editorial duties, Chamberlain contributed articles to the *Rural New Yorker*, the *Country Gentleman*, *Outlook*, and the *American Agriculturalist*. He was also an active and popular participant in many Farmers' Institutes held in the winter months throughout Ohio and occasionally in Pennsylvania, Michigan, and New York, and he maintained a demanding lecture schedule until late in life. Some of his lectures were published in agricultural journals. Chamberlain also held monthly meetings at his home to discuss agricultural practices with area farmers.

Chamberlain was a trustee of Western Reserve University, Ohio State University, the Ohio Agricultural Station (also serving on its board of control), and Western Reserve Academy. Rutgers College (1885) and Ohio State University (1887) conferred the honorary LL.D. on him, after which he was publicly called Dr. Chamberlain. He was a member and trustee of the Congregational church. Politically, he was a Republican. He maintained his love of the classics, reading works in Greek and Latin nearly every day. Chamberlain devoted his life to the improvement of agricultural practices through education and the sharing of practical experiences. He was known for his generosity, high ideals, and staunch loyalty to the interests of farm progress. He died at his daughter's home in Cleveland, Ohio, a few weeks after his wife's death.

• The Iowa State University Archives has a limited number of Chamberlain papers, mostly to do with his presidency of Iowa State College of Agriculture and Mechanical Arts. For Chamberlain's reports as secretary of the Ohio Board of Agriculture, see *Report of the Ohio State Board of Agriculture* (1880–1886). Chamberlain's presidency of the Iowa State College of Agriculture and Mechanical Arts is discussed in Clarence Ray Aurner, *History of Education in Iowa*, vol. 4 (1916). His efforts as an agricultural reformer are discussed in Lester S. Ivans and Albert E. Winship, *Fifty Famous Farmers* (1924). See also William A. Doyle, *Centennial History of Summit County, Ohio and Representative Citizens* (1908). Obituaries are in the *Cleveland Plain Dealer*, 1 July 1920, and the *Ohio Farmer*, 10 July 1920.

RAYMOND M. HYSER

CHAMBERLIN, Clarence Duncan (11 Nov. 1893–31 Oct. 1976), aviation pioneer and aircraft industry executive, was born in Denison, Iowa, the son of Elzie Clarence Chamberlin and Jessie Duncan, watchmakers and mechanics. He worked for his parents in their shop and proved adept at engineering and mechanics. Able to carry on his education after most other men in his age group at Denison had entered the workforce, Chamberlin attended Normal and Business College in Denison, graduating in 1911, and Iowa State College, graduating with a B.S. in engineering in 1914. Not long after automobiles made an appearance in Denison, in 1912 he took time off from school to open his own automotive sales and repair business. He ran this business and continued his studies until he graduated from Iowa State College.

An early enthusiast of aviation, Chamberlin learned to fly while serving in the Aviation Section of the U.S. Army Signal Corps during World War I. He began with balloon training at Fort Omaha, Nebraska, and later was trained as a pilot in Texas. After serving a stint as an instructor pilot at Kelly Field, Texas, Chamberlin was mustered out of service in 1919. He then began working as a transport pilot and barnstormer. At the same time, in 1921–1922 he was a partner, mechanic, and test pilot for an aircraft repair shop in Hasbrouk Heights, New Jersey, but he sold out and founded the Chamberlin-Rowe Corp., involved in aviation services, in New York City in 1923.

Chamberlin began to make a name for himself as an aviator in 1925 when he did well in the Mitchel Field Air Races near New York. The next year he participated in the Philadelphia Air Races, and in 1927 he undertook three record-setting flights. On 14 May he set an endurance record for circling over Roosevelt Field, New York, with co-pilot Bert Acosta for 51 hours, 11 minutes, and 20 seconds. Chamberlin also made the first transatlantic airmail flight on 8 August.

In addition to these two record-setting activities, Chamberlin made his most significant flight that year. He had been in a race with several other flyers to make the first solo nonstop transatlantic flight but lost to Charles A. Lindbergh, who made the flight on 20 May. Two weeks later Chamberlin and passenger Charles A. Levine, a wealthy New York junk dealer who financed the flight, flew from New York to Eisleben, Germany, where they landed in a farmer's field after running out of fuel. Flying the Wright Aeronautical Corp. *Columbia* monoplane designed by Giuseppe Bellanca, they flew a record 3,905 miles in 42 hours and 45 minutes. While it was a significant achievement—Chamberlin had made the first nonstop transatlantic flight to Germany and carried the first nonstop transatlantic passenger—Lindbergh's earlier achievement garnered most of the celebrity, while Chamberlin's flight was quickly forgotten by all but a few aviation enthusiasts. In 1928 he published an account of his experiences, *Record Flights*, but was unsuccessful in rescuing his own exploits from obscurity.

Chamberlin continued in the aeronautics business from his base in New York in the latter 1920s and in the 1930s. He formed the Chamberlin Aircraft Corp., not a manufacturing company as the name implies but an umbrella organization under which he carried out most of his business activities, such as continued exhibition, stunt, and record flying. For instance, in 1932 he set a world altitude record of 19,363 feet, but that record was soon broken by other pilots flying more advanced aircraft. He also used whatever name recognition he possessed from his transatlantic flight to hawk aviation products, serving as a consultant and public spokesman for a succession of aviation firms during the depression. In addition he served as chairman of the New York City Mayor's Aviation Committee in 1933, as director of the Floyd Bennett Airport in Brooklyn during the middle part of the 1930s, and as a member of the Baker Board that in 1934 investigated the quality of the Army Air Corps. In all these endeavors he was a capable, if somewhat mundane performer. Chamberlin also was an avid proponent of the importance of aviation to the economic and cultural development of the United States, and he lectured widely to school and civic groups. He also worked as a consultant for some eastern cities on airport planning and problem solving.

During World War II Chamberlin entered into an agreement with the Army Air Forces to open several training centers for pilots, and he personally directed the center at Bendix Airport, New Jersey; the contract netted him his first steady income in nearly twenty years. After the war, Chamberlin, while still active in publicizing aviation, entered the real estate business. He died at his home in Derby, Connecticut.

Clarence Chamberlin was one of the many second-echelon stunt pilots who operated before the Second World War. He had attained some stature with record-making flights but was never able to break into the ranks of such famous flyers as Charles A. Lindbergh and Amelia Earhart or even Roscoe Turner. Accordingly, he eked out a living on the margins of the expanding aviation industry. He was not able to make the transition to the airline or aircraft industry, as did so many other flyers of his stature, and after his 1927 transatlantic flight he was unable to duplicate the fame he had briefly enjoyed. He stayed with the aeronautical business because of his love of flying, and only in

World War II, when the military was desperate to train pilots, did he find a ready market for his skills.

• There is no formal collection of Chamberlin's papers. Material by and about him can be found in scattered collections at the Library of Congress and the National Air and Space Museum, Smithsonian Institution. Short sketches of his career can be found in the various editions of *Who's Who in American Aviation* through 1945. Obituaries are in the *New York Times* and the *Washington Post*, both 1 Nov. 1976.

ROGER D. LAUNIUS

CHAMBERLIN, Guy (16 Jan. 1894–4 Apr. 1967), professional football player and coach, was born Berlin Chamberlin in Blue Springs, Nebraska, the son of Elmer E. Chamberlin and Ana I. Tobyne. He grew up in a large farm family. Tall and fast, Chamberlin had the makings of a fine athlete, but the local high school was too small to field a football team. Relegated to sandlot play against nearby teams and lacking confidence, he entered a small college, Nebraska Wesleyan, in 1912. There he blossomed as a football star, winning all-state honors in his first season and attracting the attention of Jumbo Stiehm, football coach at the University of Nebraska, who recruited Chamberlin to the larger state institution.

During Chamberlin's tenure at Nebraska he was known for playing the entire sixty-minute game, as a defensive end and halfback or end when on offense. The 1914 and 1915 Nebraska football teams enjoyed undefeated seasons. Nebraska's rise to national prominence was affirmed by its defeat of Notre Dame, 20–19, in 1915 on the strength of two touchdowns by Chamberlin. Chamberlin, the most valuable player in the Missouri Valley Conference and winner of All-America honors in both 1914 and 1915, amassed 25 touchdowns over that period.

Following graduation Chamberlin entered the U.S. Army during World War I. He was discharged in 1919. Around this time he married Bernyce W. Watkins, with whom he had a daughter.

In 1919 Chamberlin joined the Canton Bulldogs, a professional football team. Chamberlin was allegedly recruited by his idol, Jim Thorpe, who also played for the Canton club. The 6′2″, 210-pound Chamberlin proved a fast ballcarrier and good pass catcher. His long runs on end around plays and his tenacious defensive play excited fans and won the admiration of his teammates. The Bulldogs had a 7–4–2 overall record.

In 1920 the fourteen professional football teams formed a loose affiliation, the American Professional Football Association, mostly centered in the Midwest. The organization evolved into the National Football League, but its early years were marked by instability. George Halas, one of the association's founders, lured Chamberlin and other players, including future Hall of Famers Paddy Driscoll and George Trafton, to his team, the Decatur Staleys, by providing work at the team's sponsor, the Staley Starch Company. During the two years that Chamberlin spent with the Staleys they enjoyed a 21–2–2 record and won the undisputed championship in 1921 on a 70-yard touchdown by the speedy Chamberlin. Calculated, daring, and aggressive play on defense typified Chamberlin's career.

Chamberlin returned to Canton as player-coach for the next two seasons. Under his guidance Canton posted undefeated seasons of 10–0–2 in 1922 and 11–0 in 1923, winning the league championship in both years. Other stars on the Canton team included future Hall of Fame members Wilbur "Pete" Henry, a massive lineman and kicker, and Roy "Link" Lyman, a tackle.

Before the 1924 season the Canton team was sold to a Cleveland promoter and assumed the name of the Cleveland Bulldogs. As player-coach, Chamberlin brought a greater sense of professionalism to the enterprise by requiring daily practices. His disciplined, conscientious approach resulted in a third consecutive championship but produced no financial gain. The team returned to Canton in 1925, but Chamberlin moved on to become player-coach of the Frankford Yellow Jackets, a Philadelphia entrant in a 20-team league. Frankford, overscheduled by its management, played 25 games for the season and plunged to sixth place. The Yellow Jackets rebounded as champions in 1926 with a 14–1–1 record and triumphed 7–6 in an end-of-season game against the Bears when Chamberlin twice blocked the opponents' game-winning kicks. The win put the team in first place, and the following week they clinched the title. In five years Chamberlin won four titles with three different teams.

Chamberlin joined the Chicago Cardinals as a player in 1927 and coached the team briefly in 1928. Team and financial problems (owner Chris O'Brien had trouble meeting the payroll and sold the franchise in 1929) caused him to quit the position after a few games and return to his Nebraska farm. In later years he held government positions as a state livestock inspector and reformatory foreman. He died at his Lincoln, Nebraska, home.

Chamberlin had already been honored for his accomplishments as a player and coach. He was chosen as a member of the 1920s all-decade team. In 1962 the National Football Foundation inducted him into its College Football Hall of Fame; the Pro Football Hall of Fame followed suit in 1965. At the time of his induction his winning percentage as a coach (60–16–6) ranked him above all others. After his death the state of Nebraska created the Guy Chamberlin Athletic Scholarship, to be awarded annually to its best high school football player.

• The Pro Football Hall of Fame in Canton, Ohio, has archival materials, including newspaper clippings and biographical information, in its file on Chamberlin. Accounts of his exploits as a player and coach are in Tom Perrin, *Football: A College History* (1987), John D. McCallum, *Big Eight Football* (1979), Richard Whittingham, *The Chicago Bears* (1986), William S. Jarrett, *Timetables of Sports History: Football* (1989), and Beau Riffenburgh, *The Official NFL Encyclopedia* (1986).

GERALD GEMS

CHAMBERLIN, Rollin Thomas (20 Oct. 1881–6 Mar. 1948), teacher, editor, and structural and glacial geologist, was born in Beloit, Wisconsin, the son of Alma Isabel Wilson and Thomas Chrowder Chamberlin, a geologist and educator. He was married in 1922 to Dorothy Ingalls Smith; they had three children.

Despite the potential handicap of a son having to follow a famous father, Rollin Chamberlin was able to carve his own niche in the earth sciences. He began his early college training in Geneva and Zurich in 1899 and 1900 but returned to the University of Chicago for his B.S. and all advanced education. His first paper, on glacial deposits in Wisconsin, was published in 1905 while he was still in graduate school.

Chamberlin's doctoral dissertation in 1907, on the nature and amount of volatile components trapped within rocks, was published the following year by the Carnegie Institution of Washington. This publication, "The Gases in Rocks," was significant in the major theoretical problem of the origin of the atmosphere. Possible changes through time in the atmosphere could cause climatic change and thereby help to explain such phenomena as worldwide cooling and glaciation. This theoretically based study promptly led to a U.S. Geological Survey *Bulletin* in 1909 concerned with mine explosions, for it provided a better understanding of the release of methane gas from coal during mining. It included the practical recommendation of sprinkling limestone dust in coal mines to react with the methane. As a direct result the number of disastrous coal mine explosions decreased dramatically. His last published paper (posthumous) was on geologic evidence bearing on evolution of the atmosphere.

Chamberlin was an academic whose entire career was associated with the Department of Geology at the University of Chicago, headed since its inception by his father. He was appointed instructor in 1912, assistant professor in 1914, associate professor in 1918, professor in 1923, and professor emeritus in 1947. Chamberlin enjoyed teaching students at all levels and was not confined to his specialty. In 1926 he wrote part of the material for an undergraduate survey course on the nature of the world and man. With an associate, in 1927 he revised part one of the T. C. Chamberlin and Salisbury—another famous Chicago geologist—textbook *College Geology* and in 1930 revised part two; he made further revisions of part one in 1933 and 1937. According to one memorialist, he inspired more doctoral dissertations than any other member of the departmental staff.

At the University of Chicago, Chamberlin was also closely associated with the *Journal of Geology*, a scientific periodical that was founded by his father at the same time the geology department was formed. He became a member of the editorial board in 1912, managing editor in 1923, and he served as editor from 1929 until mid-1947, exceeding his father's length of service. In addition to his major published works, Chamberlin wrote innumerable reviews of books and treatises for the *Journal*, many of which were in the form of essays that included his own ideas on the subject.

Throughout his career, Chamberlin traveled extensively and conducted fieldwork on every continent except Antarctica. He wrote on aspects of geology in China, Samoa, western Canada, Brazil, and the Andean chain in South America. He was involved in the investigations at Vero, Florida, concerned with dating the occurrence of early man in America.

Chamberlin's scientific interests were focused particularly on problems of formation of mountains and the structural features, such as folds and faults of the rocks within mountain ranges; his first paper on the subject was in 1910 and considered the folded rocks of the Appalachian Mountains in central Pennsylvania. Chamberlin noted that some mountain ranges showed little igneous activity, showed lateral movement of the rocks, and appeared "thin-skinned." In contrast, "thick-skinned" ranges were characterized by vertical movement of the rocks and more igneous activity; he also noted that a range could change from "thin-" to "thick-skinned" along its length.

At the University of Chicago, Chamberlin conducted laboratory experiments using petroleum jelly and paraffin to model rock strata that were then mechanically deformed. Combined with his field investigations, this led to a 1925 paper in which he envisioned mountain chains as downward narrowing and downward wedge-shaped masses that then moved laterally along gently inclined breaks; such a break is called a low-angle overthrust in the geological literature. Chamberlin also influenced the study of glaciers and their movement, treating glacial ice as a rock, a concept now generally accepted.

In many mountain ranges, large igneous masses, or batholiths, are present. They had been interpreted as bodies steadily increasing in size downward. Chamberlin studied them in the field and in 1927 concluded that molten rock came from below through a relatively narrow channel but then spread out relatively close to the earth's surface, melting its way through the crust and affecting vertical and lateral movements in "thick-skinned" mountains.

Chamberlin was also interested in the concept of isostasy, the gravitation equilibrium of the earth's crust, particularly in regard to the issue of erosion and subsequent uplift of mountains by the loss of weight. His various structural studies led him to conclude that continents were stable in position and had not moved through geologic time; Wegener's view of continental drift, modified to the concept of plate tectonics, is the prevailing view today.

In his later years, Chamberlin was a member of the Yellowstone-Bighorn Research Association for a decade. This group investigated the structure of the area while teaching field geology to students. His studies led to another significant paper in 1940 on the structure of the Bighorn Basin in Wyoming that had implications for interpreting the structural geology of other basinal deformations.

At one time Chamberlin was handball champion of the university, but his forte and hobby was mountain climbing. He had sixty-three notable ascents to his credit, including several first ascents in the Canadian Rockies. During one season in Switzerland, to fill in the time between measurements of the movement of ice on a glacier, he participated in twenty-two climbs.

Numerous climbs and work at high altitude contributed to development of thrombosis before Chamberlin was sixty. Though he could no longer engage in fieldwork, Chamberlin used a telescope and in 1945 published a note on the absence of folded mountains on the moon.

• Bibliographical sources include N. L. Bowen, "Memorial to Rollin Thomas Chamberlin," *Proceedings of the Geological Society of America for 1948* (1949), pp. 135–43, which contains a portrait and bibliography of major publications; and F. J. Pettijohn, "Rollin Thomas Chamberlin 20 October, 1881–6 March, 1948," National Academy of Sciences, *Biographical Memoirs* 41 (1970): 89–110.

ELLIS YOCHELSON

CHAMBERLIN, Thomas Chrowder (25 Sept. 1843–15 Nov. 1928), geologist, was born in Mattoon, Illinois, the son of John Chamberlin, a farmer and Methodist circuit rider, and Cecilia Gill. When he was three years old, Chamberlin's family moved to Beloit, Wisconsin, where his interest in natural history developed as he grew older. He pursued the traditional classical curriculum at Beloit College but augmented these studies with science classes and developed a keen interest in geology. Upon graduation in 1866, Chamberlin became principal of a nearby high school and significantly changed the curriculum to include elementary science courses. The following year, he married Alma Isabel Wilson of Beloit; the couple had one child who also became a geologist.

Recognizing the inadequacy of his science education, Chamberlin spent the 1868–1869 academic year at the University of Michigan, taking a wide variety of science classes and studying with the noted geologist Alexander Winchell. He then became professor of natural science at the state normal school at Whitewater, Wisconsin, where he had responsibility for the entire science curriculum. In 1873 Chamberlin joined the newly established Wisconsin Geological Survey as assistant geologist. Assigned the southeastern portion of the state (the region of least interest to the survey because of its lack of economically important resources), Chamberlin discovered an intriguing research topic in the evidence of glaciation in the area. Three years later, he became chief geologist of the survey, coordinating field work and publications. Chamberlin presented a report on his glaciation research at the 1878 International Geological Congress in Paris, after which he pursued field research in the Alps. While serving on the geological survey, he also taught part-time at Beloit College.

Chamberlin's research on Wisconsin glaciation attracted significant professional attention and led to the establishment of a separate glacial division of the U.S. Geological Survey. Director John Wesley Powell appointed Chamberlin as chief geologist of this new division, effective following the end of the Wisconsin Geological Survey in 1882. Chamberlin continued in this post until 1904, despite holding various other positions, and soon established himself as the nation's leading glaciologist. Actively involved in field work from the Atlantic coast west to Montana, Chamberlin also coordinated the activities of a large staff and directed the publication of a series of reports that remain classics in the geological literature.

Chamberlin's most active service in the U.S. Geological Survey ended in 1887, when he became president of the University of Wisconsin. The university was a small, relatively nondescript college at this time, a situation Chamberlin began to change through an ambitious program of reorganization and redirection. He established and encouraged graduate education, initiated extension programs, and attracted the faculty necessary for active research and teaching in several fields. Although Chamberlin encouraged the natural sciences, he also initiated the growth of the social sciences on campus. He formed the School of Economics, Political Science, and History, successfully recruiting noted economist Richard T. Ely of Johns Hopkins University to head the new division. Chamberlin also convinced young history instructor Frederick Jackson Turner to pursue doctoral work at Johns Hopkins, laying the foundation for Turner's later emergence as one of the major figures in the historical profession.

Although Chamberlin was effective and successful as president, the details of his administrative responsibilities became increasingly burdensome. When William R. Harper, who was organizing the newly established University of Chicago in 1891, offered Chamberlin the chairmanship of the geology department, the geologist eagerly accepted the invitation. Moving to the new school in the fall of 1892, Chamberlin hoped to return to his research pursuits, but administrative duties followed him to Chicago. He held positions as dean and museum director, while playing an active role in establishing a strong science component in the curriculum. In 1893 he founded the *Journal of Geology* and for the next three decades served as its editor in chief. This position proved especially time-consuming in the early years, as Chamberlin was responsible for organizing the editorial board and soliciting manuscripts for the journal.

Despite administrative responsibilities, the years at the University of Chicago were very profitable in Chamberlin's career as a scientist. He accompanied the Peary Relief Expedition to Greenland in 1894 and made significant observations concerning the glaciers of the area. He was active in the efforts to detail the multiple glacial episodes in North America, adding significantly to this aspect of geological knowledge. Beginning in the mid-1890s as well, Chamberlin examined the implications of his work in glaciology. He was especially interested in glacial climates and how they related to climatic changes in the geologic past.

Geologists had recently discovered evidence of glaciation in the earliest time periods, indicating cold climates. Chamberlin developed an explanation for these climates based on the fluctuations of atmospheric carbon dioxide concentrations, providing a workable mechanism for this important geologic and climatologic phenomenon.

The consideration of cold climates in the distant past led Chamberlin to develop a theory that arguably represents his most important contribution to science. The existence of such climates clashed with the accepted concept of the early earth as a molten globe. This concept was an outgrowth of Pierre-Simonde Laplace's nebular hypothesis, which attributed the origin of the earth and the other planets to the condensation of a gas cloud surrounding the sun. The nebular hypothesis implied that the earth was very warm in the distant past, an implication seriously challenged by evidence of early glaciation. Working with University of Chicago mathematician and astronomer Forest R. Moulton, Chamberlin examined the nebular hypothesis carefully. By 1900 he and Moulton had abandoned Laplace's ideas and soon developed the alternative explanation known as the "planetesimal hypothesis." The close approach of a star had drawn off material from the sun into the space surrounding that body. The small particles ("planetesimals") in orbit around the sun then coalesced to form the planets, creating a much cooler early terrestrial climate that would explain the evidence of glaciation in the distant geologic past.

Published discussions of the planetesimal hypothesis began to appear in 1904. Growing professional interest in the new explanation convinced Chamberlin to prepare a book-length treatment of the topic, which appeared in 1916 as *The Origin of the Earth.* Although less technical than the discussions in the professional periodical literature, this volume provided a complete account of the origin and early evolution of the earth based on the planetesimal hypothesis. By the mid-1920s the nebular hypothesis had largely been replaced among astronomers by the Chamberlin-Moulton theory. The new theory supplied the basis for future investigations and more complete theories of terrestrial and solar system evolution.

The planetesimal hypothesis guided much of Chamberlin's later work. The last two volumes of his three-volume treatise, *Geology* (written with Rollin D. Salisbury), appeared in 1906. The discussion of the history of the earth in these volumes was guided by the implications of the planetesimal hypothesis. Chamberlin and his son examined the terrestrial conditions that might have aided organic synthesis, contributing several additional studies based on the new cosmological perspective. A series of fifteen articles that appeared in the *Journal of Geology* between 1913 and 1921 discussed the geologic history of the earth from the perspective of the planetesimal hypothesis, examining climatic changes and the impact of geological evolution on the origin of life. Chamberlin's last publication was *The Two Solar Families* (1928), the first volume of a proposed two-volume expansion of *The Origin of the Earth.* The completed volume focused on the origin of the solar system, based on the continued development of Chamberlin's thought concerning the planetesimal hypothesis.

In addition to his research and administrative duties, Chamberlin remained active in other areas related to science. He served as president of the Geological Society of America (1895), the Chicago Academy of Science (1897–1915), and the Illinois Academy of Science (1907). He was elected a vice president (1885–1886) and president (1908–1909) of the American Association for the Advancement of Science. In 1909 he served as a member of the commission to visit China on behalf of the Rockefeller Foundation, which was attempting to determine how best to appropriate funds for work in that nation. Despite his age, Chamberlin traveled throughout China for five months and contributed significantly to the report that led to foundation support for medical science in China.

In 1918 Chamberlin retired from the University of Chicago. Although he remained as senior editor of the *Journal of Geology*, he spent most of the remainder of his life pursuing various research projects and publishing widely. His health slowly deteriorated over the next decade, with stomach ulcers and cataracts becoming increasingly troublesome. A month after the publication of *The Two Solar Families*, he became sufficiently ill to require hospitalization and died in Chicago two weeks later.

During his long career, Chamberlin received many honors for his scientic contributions. He was elected to the National Academy of Sciences, the American Philosophical Society, and the American Academy of Arts and Sciences. Chamberlin also received numerous medals for his geological publications and professional achievements.

• The primary collection of Chamberlin's papers is in the University of Chicago Library. Earlier papers, including his notebooks from the Wisconsin Geological Survey, are in the State Historical Society of Wisconsin. His most important publications include "Preliminary Paper on the Terminal Moraine of the Second Glacial Epoch," *Third Annual Report: United States Geological Survey* (1882): 291–402; "An Attempt to Frame a Working Hypothesis of the Cause of Glacial Periods on an Atmospheric Basis," *Journal of Geology* 7 (1899): 545–84, 667–85, 751–87; "Fundamental Problems of Geology," *Yearbook of the Carnegie Institution of Washington* (1905): 195–258; and "The Age of the Earth from the Geological Viewpoint," *Proceedings of the American Philosophical Society* 61 (1922): 247–71. The most complete biographical study of Chamberlin, written by his son and including an extensive bibliography, is Rollin Thomas Chamberlin, "Biographical Memoir of Thomas Chrowder Chamberlin, 1843–1928," National Academy of Sciences, *Biographical Memoirs* 15 (1934): 307–407. Also of interest is Bailey Willis, "Memorial of Thomas Chrowder Chamberlin," *Bulletin of the Geological Society of America* 40 (1929): 23–45. An obituary is in the *New York Times*, 16 Nov. 1928.

GEORGE E. WEBB

CHAMBERS, George (24 Feb. 1786–25 Mar. 1866), lawyer, was born in Chambersburg, Pennsylvania, the son of Benjamin Chambers, an investor and plantation owner, and Sarah Brown. His grandfather, also named Benjamin, a native of Antrim, Ireland, had purchased land from the Penn family and founded Chambersburg in 1734. George Chambers was raised in an atmosphere rich in education and material goods, and many opportunities were available for him to excel. Ambitious and studious, Chambers learned to read and write at an early age. His outstanding academic record at the Chambersburg Academy enabled him to enter Princeton's junior class at age sixteen. Graduating in 1804 with high honors, Chambers studied law under William M. Brown in Chambersburg and a Judge Duncan in Carlisle. George Chambers was perceived as a promising young attorney, and after admission to the bar on 9 November 1807, he began specializing in Pennsylvania's intricate land laws. Also taking an interest in civil and orphans' court litigation, he led all members of his bar in these types of cases. Chambers was characterized in his section of the state as a hard-working and thorough attorney.

Chambers married Alice Armstrong Lyon in 1810; they would have six children. After Chambers was wed he became very interested in his town's future. In 1814 the town elected him manager of the Chambersburg Turnpike Road Company, and he later became the president of the business. Chambers also organized and established the Franklin County Bible Society in 1814. He became an officer shortly afterward. In 1815 he became a trustee at his alma mater, the Chambersburg Academy, and soon after he became the school's president, an office he would hold for forty-five years. Also in 1815 Chambers served as a trustee of the Presbyterian Church of Chambersburg, later becoming actively involved as president until 1864. In 1821 he was a member of the town council, and he was a burgess of Chambersburg from 1829 to 1833.

In 1832 he was elected to the U.S. House of Representatives, where he served until refusing a third nomination in 1836. During his years in Congress, Chambers came to respect, admire, and befriend many influential individuals, including Henry Clay. Believing Clay should attain the Whig nomination for president, Chambers rallied for a Clay Convention in Pennsylvania. Because of his efforts the Whigs held their convention in Chambersburg and had Chambers preside. Although Clay was eventually defeated, contemporary chronicler John M. Cooper noted that Chambers's ability, dignity, and courtesy would have been rewarded with a post in Clay's cabinet.

After leaving Congress in 1836 Chambers returned to Pennsylvania, where he continued to engross himself in public matters. He became the director and then president of the Bank of Chambersburg. Later in 1836 Chambers's constituency asked him to represent Franklin County as a member of the convention to amend Pennsylvania's constitution. When work began in 1837 Chambers was appointed a member of the subcommittee to revise the constitution's judicial article. Believing that the judiciary should remain appointed, therefore impartial and independent, he argued eloquently for that cause.

In 1842 Chambers made a public profession of his faith. Although he had always supported religion, his faith became the guiding principle of his life. At the same time Chambers became a staunch supporter of the temperance movement. In 1851 Governor William Freame Johnston appointed Chambers a justice on the Supreme Court of Pennsylvania. Filling a vacancy created by a death on the bench, Chambers only served from April to December 1851. He attempted to remain on the court by running on the Whig ticket. Vying for election, a process he had fought against during the constitutional convention, Chambers was unsuccessful. After his service on the bench, he retired from his law practice and state-level public service.

Chambers's prominence as a lawyer and a civic leader was unmatched in his section of the state. Toward the end of his life he became an ardent friend of the Historical Society of Pennsylvania, eventually becoming a vice president of this organization in 1858. Interested in his cultural history and heritage, he endeavored to discredit Irish and Scotch stereotypes by publishing a book titled *A Tribute to the Principles, Virtues, Habits, and Public Usefulness of the Irish and Scotch Early Settlers of Pennsylvania; by a Descendant* (1865). In honor of his lifelong service, George Chambers was awarded an LL.D. in 1861 from Washington College in Washington, Pennsylvania. As the son of patriots, Chambers was a devout Unionist at the outbreak of war with the South. Because he was known as an outspoken opponent of rebellion, Confederate forces purposefully burned many of his properties and landholdings during their attack on Chambersburg on 30 July 1864. (Chambersburg was the only northern town to be decimated by the Confederates.) He died less than two years later, presumably in Chambersburg.

As the perennial public servant of Franklin County, and more specifically Chambersburg, George Chambers was also a leading member of his bar, a business entrepreneur, a congressman, and a judge. Chambers not only accomplished his forefathers' dream by nurturing their settlement of Chambersburg, but he also served his nation on a federal level.

• The most significant work written about George Chambers the man is James McDowell Sharpe, *A Memoir of George Chambers of Chambersburg, Late Vice-President of the Society* (1873). General family studies are William D. Chambers, *Chambers History: Trails of the Centuries* (1925), and G. O. Seilhamer, "Some Studies of Early Surveys," in his short-lived *Kittochitinny Magazine: A Tentative Record of Local History and Genealogy West of the Susquehanna*, Apr. and July 1905, pp. 136–57 and 279–95, respectively. (The magazine was discontinued after two issues.) See also John M. Cooper, *Recollections of Chambersburg, PA: Chiefly between the Years 1830–1850* (1900).

RONALD W. FISCHER, JR.

CHAMBERS, John (6 Oct. 1780–21 Sept. 1852), U.S. congressman and territorial governor, was born at Bromley Bridge in Somerset County, New Jersey, the son of Rowland Chambers, a farmer and storekeeper, and Phoebe Mullican. After the Revolution, Chambers's family suffered economic reverses and moved to Kentucky. Aged fourteen and barely literate, he found a job as a clerk. Supported by his brother William, John spent four months at Transylvania University in Lexington, leaving in the summer of 1795 to resume his position in the store. Two years later he apprenticed himself to the clerk of the county court. He read law in his spare time and gained admittance to the Kentucky bar in 1800. In his rise from store clerk to attorney, he followed the pattern of many ambitious young men on the frontier.

In 1803 Chambers married Margaret Taylor of Maryland; they had two stillborn children. She died in March 1807, and in October 1807 he married Hannah Taylor of Hagerstown, Maryland, the half sister of his first wife. They had twelve children.

Chambers built an estate near Washington, Kentucky, where he practiced law with increasing success. During the War of 1812 he served as aide on the staff of General William Henry Harrison at the battle of the Thames. Although he made his reputation by organizing Harrison's records, Chambers effectively used the title "Major" in his future political career.

In the decade after the war, Chambers's legal practice thrived. He also found himself increasingly involved in political issues as spokesman for the Anti-Relief party, which represented sound conservative financial and judicial principles. The Kentucky laws that favored debtors by stays of judgment and by establishing forty independent banks empowered to issue notes without state control were particular targets of Chambers and his party. At the end of the 1820s Chambers turned to politics. Capitalizing on his military reputation and strong Whig principles, mixed with his skills as a stump speaker, he was elected to the state legislature (1812–1818, 1830–1834) and the U.S. House of Representatives (1828–1829, 1835–1839). In Congress he espoused Whig programs and criticized the Martin Van Buren administration for its expedients in coping with the panic of 1837, especially the Sub-Treasury Bill and the distribution of national funds to select banks. Chambers also opposed congressional meddling in the slavery issue. Growing weary of service so far from home and increasingly depressed by the death of his wife in 1832, he refused to stand for reelection in 1839.

With the nomination of Harrison for president in 1840, Chambers came out of retirement to campaign energetically for a fellow Whig and his old commanding officer. After the decisive victory, Chambers accepted an office to please his president. He received his commissions as governor of the Iowa Territory and superintendent of Indian affairs there shortly before Harrison's death.

On 12 May 1841 Chambers entered on his duties at Burlington, Iowa Territory. During his four years in office, he presided over the growth and expansion of the infant territory, brought a degree of civility to an acrimonious political climate, and settled an inflammatory boundary dispute with Missouri. As superintendent of Indian affairs, he sought a measure of justice in the chaotic process of distributing annuity payments to Indians, recognized the disastrous influence of traders on Native American life, and presided over the treaty of 1842, in which the Sac and Fox Confederated Tribes relinquished what remained of their lands in Iowa Territory. Chambers emerged from his experiences with much sympathy for the American Indians but did little to protect them from the outrages of traders and trespassing settlers. Reappointed to office in 1844 by President John Tyler, he was removed the following year after the election of Democrat James Polk.

Declining health led Chambers to return to Kentucky. Enfeebled by age but with a tireless sense of public duty, he accepted the office of commissioner to negotiate with the Sioux in Minnesota and went there in 1849. In his final years as elder statesman, he remained a fiscal conservative and a strong defender of slavery, although he favored compromises to preserve the Union. He died at his daughter's house in Paris, Kentucky.

• Original Chambers letters and copies of letters are in the collections of the State Historical Society of Iowa, Iowa City. The two major sources for Chambers are John Porter Bloom, ed., *Territorial Papers of the United States* (2 vols., 1836–1848), available in a 1971 microfilm version; and Territorial Papers of Iowa, National Archives (1975), microfilm. Among the published materials are Chambers's "Autobiography," *Iowa Journal of History and Politics*, no. 2 (Apr. 1908): 247–86, and John Carl Parish, *John Chambers* (1909).

MALCOLM J. ROHRBOUGH

CHAMBERS, Paul (22 Apr. 1935–4 Jan. 1969), bassist, known as "Mr. P. C.," was born Paul Laurence Dunbar Chambers, Jr., in Pittsburgh, Pennsylvania. Little is known of his parents and early life. After his mother died, Chambers moved to Detroit, Michigan, with his family when he was thirteen. In high school he played the baritone saxophone and then the tuba, but sometime in 1949 he began to play the string bass. He was soon working professionally with guitarist Kenny Burrell, trumpeter Thad Jones, pianist Hank Jones, and other musicians in the Detroit area. In 1952 he began taking lessons with a bassist in the Detroit Symphony and played with a classical group called the Detroit String Band. Between 1952 and 1955 he also studied, off and on, at Cass Tech and played in the school's symphony orchestra and other student groups.

By this time Chambers had fully absorbed the bop lessons of Charlie Parker and Bud Powell, his first influences, as well as the innovations in bass playing pioneered by Jimmy Blanton with the Ellington Band of a decade earlier. In 1955 he toured with tenor saxophonist Paul Quinichette and also traveled through the South with trombonist Bennie Green. He moved to New York City the same year and immediately attracted attention, playing with noted musicians like Sonny Stitt, J. J. Johnson, and George Wallington. In October Chambers joined the Miles Davis Quintet, a legendary association that would last for eight years. He appeared on all of Davis's well-known albums of the period, including *Cookin'*, *Relaxin'*, *Workin'*, and *Steamin'* (all 1956); *Porgy and Bess* and *Milestones* (both 1958); and *Kind of Blue* (1959). On *Milestones*, his seven-chorus, beautifully melodic bowed solo on "Dr. Jekyll" is particularly notable. But he is best remembered for his six-note solo at the beginning of "So What" on *Kind of Blue*. Few phrases in music immediately evoke the feeling of an entire tune as this one does.

In addition to his work with Davis, Chambers appeared as a sideman on numerous other recordings and led several sessions of his own. His first session as a leader was for Blue Note in 1955 and included an appearance by John Coltrane. After a 1956 recording for Jazz West titled *A Delegation from the East*, he returned to Blue Note for a series of outstanding sessions: *Whims of Chambers* (1956); *The East-West Controversy* (1957); *The Paul Chambers Quintet*, *Chambers Music*, and *Bass on Top* (all 1957). The personnel on all of these sessions featured the best modern jazz musicians of the day, including at various times Coltrane, guitarist Kenny Burrell, pianist Hank Jones, drummers Art Taylor, Philly Joe Jones, and Elvin Jones, pianist Horace Silver, and trumpeter Donald Byrd. Chambers signed with Vee Jay records in 1959 and recorded three albums that year—*Ease It*, *Just Friends*, and *Go*, all with superior performers, including his partners in the Davis rhythm section, pianist Wynton Kelly and drummer Philly Joe Jones. In 1960 he waxed one final session for Vee Jay, *1st Bassman*.

As a sideman, Chambers was the most recorded bassist of his era. His sessions included the following albums: Sonny Rollins, *Tenor Madness* (1956) and *Volume Two* (1957); John Coltrane, *Blue Train* (1957) and *Giant Steps* (1959); Sonny Clark, *Sonny's Crib* (1957) and *Cool Struttin'* (1958); Wynton Kelly, *Kelly Blue* (1959); Hank Mobley, *Roll Call* and *Soul Station* (1960–1961); Art Pepper, *Art Pepper Meets the Rhythm Section* (1960), notable for Chambers's walking bass solo on "Softly, as in a Morning Sunrise"; and albums by Bud Powell, Jackie McClean, Dexter Gordon, Ike Quebec, Benny Golson, Kenny Dorham, Lee Morgan, and Johnny Griffin, all for Blue Note. The leaders of all these sessions, appreciative of his talents, afforded Chambers far more solo space than was the norm for bassists.

In 1963 Chambers left Davis and formed a trio with Wynton Kelly and drummer Jimmy Cobb, known as the Wynton Kelly Trio. The group recorded several outstanding albums, particularly the classic *Someday My Prince Will Come* (1965). They also recorded as a back-up rhythm section for guitarists Kenny Burrell and Wes Montgomery. Suffering from tuberculosis and plagued by the ravages of heroin and alcohol problems, Chambers curtailed his activity during the second half of the 1960s. He died in New York City.

Paul Chambers was one of the most important postbop bassists. He contributed a solid harmonic/melodic foundation to any group he played with and also helped popularize the use of the bow among jazz bassists. Though not as innovative as his contemporary Scott LaFaro, nor as fiery as such bassists as Charles Mingus and Ray Brown, he helped bring horn-like, bop phrasing to the bass, often beginning his phrases between the first and second beats, or on the second and fourth beats instead of the first and third. Such versatility made him a crucial figure in the Miles Davis groups, and his presence energized the Davis recordings and many other influential sessions of the late 1950s and early 1960s.

• Relatively little has been written about Chambers; much of what there is appears in the contexts of discussions about Davis's various groups. See the discussion in Thomas Owens, *Bebop: The Music and Its Players* (1995), and Leonard Feather's liner notes for *Whims of Chambers* (1956). Also see Nat Hentoff, "Detroit Producing Stars: Paul Chambers Big One," *Down Beat* 23, no. 1 (1956): 12; B. Gardner, "Paul Chambers: Youngest Old Man in Jazz," *Down Beat* 27, no. 15 (1960): 31; and Val Wilmer, "Paul Chambers," *Jazz Journal* 14, no. 3 (1961): 15. An obituary is in *Jazz Journal* 22, no. 4 (1969): 5.

RONALD P. DUFOUR

CHAMBERS, Robert William (26 May 1865–16 Dec. 1933), artist and writer, was born in Brooklyn, New York, the son of William Chambers, a lawyer, and Caroline Boughton. His younger brother was noted architect Walter Boughton Chambers. He was educated at the Brooklyn Polytechnic Institute and was one of the first students to enroll at the Art Students League in New York City; one of his classmates was Charles Dana Gibson (creator of the Gibson Girl), and the two became lifelong friends. In 1886 Chambers went to Paris, spending the next seven years studying at the École des Beaux-Arts and at the Académie Julian. Success came early; he exhibited at the Paris Salon when he was twenty-four. He returned to New York in 1893. A story published in the *New York Times* (28 Dec. 1913) states that Chambers and Gibson simultaneously submitted sketches to *Life*, but Gibson's was turned down while Chambers's was accepted. Chambers provided illustrations for *Life*, *Truth*, *Vogue*, the *New York Times*, and other newspapers and magazines. He married Elsa Vaughn Moller in 1898; they had one son.

It is not known why Chambers chose to abandon painting to write, but a contemporary states that Chambers found storytelling easy. Under the literary influence of Henri Murger's *La Vie de Boheme*, Chambers wrote *In the Quarter* (1894), whose events were based on his life as an art student in Paris. It was followed in 1895 by Chambers's most famous work, *The King in Yellow*, a collection that included several prose poems and five fantastic stories, four of which are linked by a consistent mythological pattern involving the Lake of Hali, Hastur, the shadowed city of Carcosa, the mystery of the Hyades, and the dreadful

King in Yellow, simultaneously a drama so terrible that it shatters the mind of all those who encounter it and a supernatural being of the utmost malignancy. Although many of the names were derived from the works of Ambrose Bierce and the content and style were partially inspired by the work of Theophile Gautier and the ornate prose of the French decadents, Chambers's results are completely original and defy ready categorization. *The King in Yellow* is one of the most significant volumes of supernatural fiction in American literature, integral in the transition between the standard Victorian fantasy and the more modern concentration on the nightmare. It has been read by virtually every American writer of supernatural fiction, influencing noted fantasists H. P. Lovecraft, Robert E. Howard, A. A. Merritt, and Marion Zimmer Bradley.

Fantastic elements are present in some of Chambers's later work, notably *The Maker of Moons* (1896), *The Mystery of Choice* (1897), *In Search of the Unknown* (1904), *The Green Mouse* (1910), *The Gay Rebellion* (1913), and *Police!!!* (1915), but the majority of his output is grounded in reality. He wrote some seventy-two books, and although he was never a bestseller he achieved popularity for his historical novels. Chambers wrote with equal facility about acts of derring-do and spies during the colonial period and the revolutionary, Civil, and First World wars. *Cardigan* (1901) was acclaimed for its description of Sir William Johnson and the Six Nations. In *The Man They Hanged* (1926) Chambers wrote in defense of Captain Kidd, arguing that Kidd was made a scapegoat by the British government. His numerous romance novels featuring New York socialities were devoured by the shopgirl market but were less popular with critics, who attacked them for their vulgarization of marriage, divorce, alcoholism, and the morality of posing nude for artists. Calculatedly trivial though these works may be, they nonetheless provide insight into the attitudes of pre-Titanic America.

Chambers did not limit himself to novels. He wrote short stories, articles, verse, and two librettos for operas. He maintained an interest in the theatre, and for Ada Rehan he adapted "The Witch of Ellangowan" from Sir Walter Scott's *Guy Mannering*; it was directed in 1897 by John Augustin Daly, and, had Daly not died in 1899, it is probable that he would have staged Chambers's dramas. Chambers's comedy *Iole* was produced in 1913, and he assisted on the sets and wrote the story and titles for D. W. Griffith's epic motion picture *America* (1924), also writing the novelization of the screenplay. His most durable literary creation is probably the private detective, Bayard Keene. Introduced in *The Tracer of Lost Persons* (1906), Keene's cases were dramatized for radio during the 1930s and later adapted for television.

Virtually all of Chambers's later works are light romances; at their strongest, they are mildly melodramatic. Despite frequent painterly touches in his descriptions, Chambers was not particularly gifted at narrative. His plots and stories were repetitive, and his characters were simple and shallowly drawn. In comparison with *The King in Yellow*, the rest of his works are pallid, insipid, and unmemorable. Nevertheless, the backgrounds to Chambers's stories are largely unimpeachable. Chambers was a serious researcher and was personally knowledgeable about Chinese and Japanese antiques, rare paintings, fishing, hunting, and North American butterflies. Furthermore, almost all of the money he acquired from writing was spent in restoring "Broadalbin," the 800-acre estate in Fulton County, New York, that was established by his grandfather William Chambers in the nineteenth century. It is said that Robert Chambers planted between 20,000 and 30,000 trees at the estate before his death in New York City.

Despite some interest in the fantastic elements in his later works, criticism of Chambers has tended to focus on *The King in Yellow*. The majority of Chambers's books are simply ignored, and Chambers himself is dismissed as a hack. In his *Supernatural Horror in Literature*, H. P. Lovecraft provided what has become the standard critical appraisal, stating that "one cannot help regretting that he did not further develop a vein in which he could so easily have become a recognised master" (p. 72). Chambers himself maintained that some of the greatest literature was written for money, and he would have genuinely objected to Lovecraft's attitude, for he made no claims of greatness. A possibly apocryphal interview quotes him as stating, "I am a story-teller. I have no other gift. Those who imagine that they have seen in my earlier work some quality of literary distinction or some unrealized possibility as an artist missing from my later work, are wrong. . . . A story-teller I began, and a story-teller I remain" (Overton, pp. 366–67).

Like his contemporary John Kendrick Bangs, Chambers was an intelligent and literate man who deliberately chose to write fluff, only occasionally permitting hints of a more serious, more socially conscious man to filter through his prose. His 1896 "A Pleasant Evening" reveals that he was well aware of New York City's contemporary social problems, but he chose not to grapple with such serious issues in his fiction. Despite the care that Chambers is said to have spent on his writing, there is no evidence that he made any attempts at recapturing the energy that permeated his earlier material, and, had he not written *The King in Yellow*, he would today be completely forgotten. This early work, however, reveals an artist of the highest ability and guarantees that he will be remembered.

• Despite some claims to the contrary, Chambers was not reclusive, but interviews with him do not achieve any depth. One of the most significant of these, conducted by Joyce Kilmer, appears in the *New York Times*, 9 May 1915, and was later reprinted in Kilmer's *Literature in the Making* (1917). Contemporary reactions to Chambers are in Duffield Osborne, "A Writer of Romance," *Overland Monthly* 31, no. 181 (Jan. 1898): 86–87; Frederic Tabor Cooper, *Some American Story Tellers* (1911); Charles C. Baldwin, *The Men Who Make Our Novels* (1919; rev. ed., 1925); Blanche Colton Williams, *Our Short Story Writers* (1922); and Grant Overton,

Authors of the Day (1924). A partial bibliography is given in Kenneth Clark, "Robert W. Chambers Re-Classified," *Journal of the Long Island Book Collectors* 3 (1975): 18–20. Significant modern criticism of Chambers's supernatural fiction begins with E. F. Bleiler's introduction to *The King in Yellow and Other Horror Stories* (1970), and Marion Zimmer Bradley's pamphlet, *The Necessity for Beauty: Robert W. Chambers and the Romantic Tradition* (1974). Chambers's fantastic fiction has been discussed in David Punter, *The Literature of Terror: A History of Gothic Fictions from 1765 to the Present Day* (1980); Brian Stableford discusses *The King in Yellow* in *Survey of Modern Fantasy Literature*, ed. Frank N. Magill (1983); and Bleiler describes Chambers's supernatural oeuvre in *The Guide to Supernatural Fiction* (1983). Also see Lee Weinstein in *Supernatural Fiction Writers: Fantasy and Horror*, ed. Bleiler (1985). A lengthy obituary is in the *New York Times*, 17 Dec. 1933.

RICHARD BLEILER

CHAMBERS, Thomas (fl. 1834–1866), folk artist, was born in London, England. He was forty-seven years old in June 1855, according to the New York state census, and thus would have been born either in 1807 or 1808. Nothing is known of his parents or family background or of his artistic training, if any. He came to the United States in 1832. At an unknown date before his departure from England he married Harriet Shellard of London, who followed him to America in 1834. Presumably Chambers wished to establish himself in this country before bringing his wife. No children are recorded in the 1855 census. Harriet Chambers died in New York City in 1864.

Chambers is first listed in the New York City directory for 1834, where he is identified as a landscape painter. He was so listed until the 1838 directory, where his occupation is given as marine painter. He is not listed in the New York City directory after 1840. From 1843 to 1851 he is listed in the Boston directories, where his occupation is given merely as "artist." In 1851 he moved to Albany, New York, where he lived and worked until 1857. By 1858 he was back in New York City and worked there until 1866 or 1867. He is last listed in *Trow's New York City Directory* for the year ending 31 May 1867, and nothing further is known of him after that date.

Although he worked in the United States for more than thirty years, Chambers never exhibited his work at any of the organizations that sponsored exhibitions of art, such as the National Academy of Design or the Boston Athenaeum. He appears to have been self-taught, although he may have had some training as a decorative painter, and his work would today be categorized as folk art. Only a few of his paintings are signed or dated, but he painted in such an individual style that over 100 paintings can safely be attributed to him. All of his works are landscapes or seascapes. His paintings are characterized by bold colors and a strong sense of design. Although most of his work is derived from engravings, Chambers was no slavish copyist and often altered elements of his source to create a more effective composition. *The Birthplace of George Washington* (c. 1845, versions owned by the Abby Aldrich Rockefeller Folk Art Center, Williamsburg, Va., and the Fruitlands Museum, Harvard), for example, is based on an engraving after an 1834 painting by John Gadsby Chapman. Whereas the engraving is a matter-of-fact depiction, in black and white, of the site of Washington's birth as it looked in the 1830s, Chambers endowed the scene with a moodiness not apparent in his source. He set the time at sunset, with twilight fast approaching; the sky and clouds are pink, while the silver reflection of Pope's Creek suggests moonlight. The overall mood is calm and serene, but the rust-colored vines in the foreground suggest decay and death. Chambers is not known to have traveled to Washington's birthplace, and his depiction is certainly based on an engraving, but through his use of color he has captured the feeling of melancholy and neglect often commented on by visitors to the site during the early nineteenth century.

The Connecticut Valley (c. 1850, National Gallery of Art, Washington, D.C.) depicts the Connecticut River near Northampton, Massachusetts, a location also painted by well-known landscape artists Thomas Cole and William Henry Bartlett. Chambers did not copy either Cole or Bartlett; he may have based his painting on his own observation of the area. His view makes for an interesting contrast to Cole's. Cole painted a panoramic landscape whose main features are the oxbow of the Connecticut River and a thunderstorm passing away to the left. Chambers's depiction is quieter and more intimate. The oxbow occupies a minor place in the background at right; the main feature is a mountain in the center foreground with green foliage slowly turning to an autumnal red-brown.

Threatening Sky, Bay of New York (c. 1840, National Gallery of Art) makes particularly effective use of color. New York Harbor, with Castle Williams at left and Staten Island in the background, is shown primarily in tones of red. The threatening sky of the title, the waters of the harbor that largely reflect that sky, and Castle Williams—the circular fortification at far left—are all painted in the same basic russet tones, which Chambers used to depict the distinctive atmosphere often seen before a thunderstorm. The placid waters contrast with the turbulent storm clouds.

Most of Chambers's seascapes depict harbor scenes or merchant ships at sea, but he did paint two naval engagements of the War of 1812: *The Constitution and the Guerriere* (Metropolitan Museum of Art, New York) and *The United States and the Macedonian* (National Museum of American Art, Washington, D.C.). These are thought to have been painted around 1845, and both derive from engravings after paintings by Thomas Birch. Chambers did not copy the engravings exactly but, as was his custom, made several changes that improved upon them. He simplified details and telescoped Birch's composition in order to focus more closely on the action. The paintings were executed with Chambers's characteristically bold coloring. A brilliant blue sky contrasts with the dark green water, and he altered the shape of the clouds to a diagonal pattern that contrasts as well with the diagonal pattern of the waves. He also increased the number of cannonball holes in the sails of the ships, emphasizing the violence of the battles.

Chambers appears to have earned a good livelihood. The 1855 census noted that his house was worth $2,500, a fairly substantial sum in those days. As none of his paintings can be traced to its original owner, it is not known who his clients were. It is presumed they were middle-class professionals and businessmen desiring relatively inexpensive but attractive works of art for the walls of their homes, and perhaps their offices as well. There are no known contemporary references to Chambers's work, and his career as an artist was forgotten until 1942, when a group of his paintings were exhibited in New York City. He is now recognized as one of the most original and distinctive American folk artists of the nineteenth century.

• Chambers's paintings can be found in many public collections, including the National Gallery of Art; the National Museum of American Art; the Abby Aldrich Rockefeller Folk Art Center; the Metropolitan Museum of Art; the New York State Historical Association, Cooperstown; the Fruitlands Museum; the Smith College Museum of Art, Northampton, Mass.; and the Albany Institute of History and Art, Albany, N.Y. The definitive study of Chambers's life and career is Howard S. Merritt, "Thomas Chambers, Artist," *New York History* 37 (Apr. 1956): 212–22. Nina Fletcher Little wrote three pioneering articles on Chambers, all of which were published in *Antiques*: "T. Chambers: Man or Myth?" 53 (Mar. 1948): 194–97; "Earliest Signed Picture by T. Chambers," 53 (Apr. 1948): 285; and "More about T. Chambers," 60 (Nov. 1951): 469. Good biographical sketches are in *American Folk Paintings from the Abby Aldrich Rockefeller Folk Art Center* (1988), pp. 19–21; *American Naive Paintings*, National Gallery of Art, Washington, D.C. (1992), pp. 43–58; and *American Paintings in the Metropolitan Museum of Art*, vol. 1 (1994), pp. 522–24.

DAVID MESCHUTT

CHAMBERS, Whittaker (1 Apr. 1901–9 July 1961), magazine editor and anti-Communist, was born Jay Vivian Chambers in Philadelphia, Pennsylvania, the son of Jay Chambers, a staff artist on the *New York World*, and Laha Whittaker, an actress. Shortly after his birth, his family moved to Brooklyn, New York, then settled in Lynbrook on Long Island's south shore. The family home was spartan and contentious, and his parents separated around 1908. It was at this time that he took the name David Whittaker. After graduating from high school, Chambers, now calling himself Charles Adams, and a friend obtained work for four months as day laborers in Washington, D.C. They then unsuccessfully sought employment in New Orleans. Late in 1919 Chambers returned to Lynbrook, agreeing to work at his father's advertising firm in New York City. Now known as Whittaker Chambers, he also enrolled at Columbia University. Discarding the conservative Republicanism of his parents and influenced by a cadre of young intellectuals, he was attracted to Marxism. As editor in chief of the *Morningside*, the student literary publication, Chambers was denounced for a purportedly blasphemous issue that portrayed Jesus as a weary soul, and he withdrew from the university in January 1923. That summer he wandered through Europe with a pair of friends from Columbia. In the fall he returned to the United States, taking a job at the New York Public Library. He briefly returned to Columbia in the fall of 1924 and experienced a pair of difficult love affairs, fathering a child he never lived with.

Experiencing a series of emotional crises, Chambers joined the Communist party in 1925. The suicide of his brother Richard in September 1926 led him to turn to communism more fully than before. In April 1927 he informed a friend, "I have gone quite over [to] the revolutionary movement." During that same period, he was fired from the New York Public Library for stealing books. He began working as a journalist and translator, translating Felix Salten's *Bambi* (1923), served as news editor of the *Daily Worker* by 1929, and taught journalism classes on behalf of the party. After a two-year hiatus from the Communist party, which proved traumatic for him, he rejoined it in 1931, becoming involved with the John Reed Club for radical writers and artists. In 1931 he married Esther Shemitz, a painter who worked for the pacifist publication the *World Tomorrow*. They had two children. In 1931 Chambers became an editor of the *New Masses*, a Communist-dominated publication, and in early 1932 he and his wife moved to a farmhouse at Glen Gardner, New Jersey.

In 1932 Chambers joined the Communist underground headed by Joseph Peters, beginning a six-year odyssey that purportedly brought him in contact with sympathetic figures in high governmental circles in Washington, D.C. Employing a string of aliases, such as Karl Phillips and Harold Phillips, he foresaw the possibility of a Soviet America during a period when capitalism appeared to be failing miserably. He now appeared to live multiple lives, ranging from his espionage work to his family life to numerous short-lived homosexual encounters. On several occasions he informed friends about his assignment, even sending postcards from Moscow, where he and Esther had gone in April 1933 so he could either be trained at the International Lenin School or briefed by Soviet military intelligence. Chambers later testified that he dealt with secret Communists who worked for New Deal agencies during the 1930s, including a group headed by Harold Ware at the Agricultural Adjustment Administration and supposedly numbering Alger Hiss among its ranks. Through Peters, Chambers claimed, important information was passed on to Soviet intelligence.

In mid-1937 Chambers, increasingly disillusioned and fearful that he might become another victim of Joseph Stalin's purges, evaded a party order to return to Moscow and began his break from communism. By November he had acquired a temporary job with the National Research Project and began withholding some government documents from Russian agents. He also turned to anti-Stalinist friends, like Robert Cantwell and Meyer Schapiro, who helped him get work as a translator for Oxford University Press. Chambers employed his own name once more but lived furtively, in fear of Communist machinations. His defection evidently caused consternation in Soviet intelligence circles.

By late 1938 Chambers began working on a series of articles concerning the Communist underground in the United States and in September 1939 sought unsuccessfully to expose its enterprises to Assistant Secretary of State Adolf A. Berle, Jr., naming Alger Hiss and Donald Hiss as secret Communists. In April 1939 Chambers had been hired as a writer for *Time* Magazine, earning $100 a week, and in 1942 he became senior editor of the magazine in charge of the books section. He also attended a Quaker meeting, and in 1942 he suffered his first heart attack. His editorial slant was stridently anti-Communist, as he summarily lumped together New Deal liberals, anti-Stalinist radicals, and Communists. In May 1942 two Federal Bureau of Investigation (FBI) agents visited Chambers, and he again indicated that the Hiss brothers and other federal employees were connected to the Communist underground. In 1945 Chambers, whose annual salary approached $15,000, achieved his long-sought ambition when publisher Henry Luce named him editor of foreign news for *Time*, where his ideological perspective was still more influential. A battle with the magazine's distinguished senior correspondents, including John Osborne, John Hersey, and Theodore H. White, ensued, and Chambers's control of foreign policy coverage lessened. He also had a second heart attack and another, more extended encounter with FBI agents regarding the Communist underground. After a convalescence, he was named an editor at large on special projects, saw his salary reach $21,000 by 1948, and produced some well-regarded treatises on historical and theological issues and a series of biographical sketches.

In August 1948 the accusations Chambers had earlier made to the FBI and State Department security officers regarding Alger Hiss and the Communist underground received public exposure in testimony before the House Committee on Un-American Activities (HUAC). Hiss, who by 1945 had become a high-ranking State Department official before resigning to become president of the Carnegie Endowment for International Peace, indignantly denied the charges. Chambers revealed intimate details about Alger and Phyllis Hiss to a subcommittee headed by freshman Republican congressman Richard Milhous Nixon. When recalled before the committee, Hiss now suggested that perhaps Chambers was an individual with bad teeth known as George Crosley whom the Hisses had known during the 1930s. Following a dramatic encounter on 17 August, Hiss declared that Chambers was Crosley while still denying any Communist affiliation on his part.

Challenged by Hiss to repeat his charges outside the halls of Congress, Chambers complied on the television program "Meet the Press," declaring Hiss had been a Communist "and may still be one now." Hiss initiated a slander suit against Chambers, and early developments led Chambers to attempt suicide. During pretrial hearings, Chambers produced typewritten copies and handwritten summaries of State Department documents that he claimed to have received from Hiss. Then in December 1948 Chambers reappeared before HUAC and dramatically introduced the so-called pumpkin papers, microfilm that had been stored at his farmhouse in Maryland that contained confidential governmental information. Hiss was indicted for perjury by a federal grand jury on 15 December 1948. During the subsequent trial, an old Woodstock typewriter owned by the Hiss family turned up and appeared to match the typescript of the microfilmed materials. After the initial court proceedings ended in a mistrial, Hiss was convicted of perjury at a second trial in January 1950 and sentenced to five years in a federal penitentiary. The Hiss case boosted Nixon's career, provided conservatives with ammunition to attack the Harry Truman and Franklin D. Roosevelt administrations, and fed domestic fears of Communist subversion.

In December 1948 Chambers had resigned from *Time*, and Luce subsequently refused to allow him to return to the magazine, considering him too controversial a figure. In his 1952 bestselling autobiographical work *Witness*, Chambers, increasingly despairing about the fate of Western civilization, proclaimed that only one who had experienced hell could warn about its evils. He wrote, "Those who do not inform are still conniving at that evil." In 1957 he joined the staff of William F. Buckley's *National Review*, serving as a senior editor. In the fall of 1959 Chambers stopped contributing to the journal and determined to complete his undergraduate degree at Western Maryland College. Continuing to be appalled at Hiss's unwillingness to acknowledge guilt, Chambers believed his "defiance perpetuates and keeps from healing a fracture in the community as a whole." Chambers died on the family farm near Westminster, Maryland, deeply despondent about world events. In 1984 President Ronald Reagan posthumously awarded Chambers the Medal of Freedom and, along with Buckley, praised him as a great American hero. In the 1987 Public Broadcasting System (PBS) documentary "The Conservatives," Buckley declared that Chambers "reified the hard spiritual case against Communism more successfully than anyone in that generation." Others continued to view Chambers in a less charitable fashion as a pathological liar who was driven by class resentment to destroy Hiss.

• A massive Federal Bureau of Investigation file housed at the FBI's reading room in Washington, D.C., relating to the case of *Whittaker Chambers v. Alger Hiss* contains tens of thousands of pages of documents. Other governmental papers of significance include those released by the Central Intelligence Agency (CIA), the Department of Justice, and the Department of State. Chambers's own writings provide insight into his makeup, especially articles he penned for the *New Masses*, *Time*, and *Look* from the 1920s onward. More revealing still are his *Cold Friday* (1964) and *Odyssey of a*

Friend (1970), which contains correspondence with Buckley. A full treatment of Chambers's life is Sam Tanenhaus, *Whittaker Chambers: A Biography* (1997). Allen Weinstein's controversial *Perjury: The Hiss-Chambers Case* (1978) provides illuminating biographical information and psychological analyses of the two combatants. An important chapter, "The Strange Case of Whittaker Chambers," is in Sidney Hook, *Out of Step: An Unquiet Life in the 20th Century* (1987). Brief but noteworthy descriptions of Chambers as an underground agent are in Harvey Klehr et al., *The Secret World of American Communism* (1995). Significant passages discussing Hiss and Chambers are in Tom Wicker, *One of Us: Richard Nixon and the American Dream* (1991), and Herbert S. Parmet, *Richard Nixon and His America* (1990). A good summary of the Hiss-Chamber clash is in Richard M. Fried, *Nightmare in Red: The McCarthy Era in Perspective* (1990). An earlier analysis, Leslie Fielder, "Hiss, Chambers, and the Age of Innocence," *Commentary*, Dec. 1950, indicted the left and radicalism in general. Works highly critical of Chambers's role in the affair include William A. Reuben, *The Honorable Mr. Nixon and the Alger Hiss Case* (1956); Fred J. Cook, *The Unfinished Story of Alger Hiss* (1958); Walter Goodman, *The Committee* (1968); and John Cabot Smith, *Alger Hiss: The True Story* (1976). A brief but significant discussion of the conflicting interpretations of the Hiss-Chambers case is in Neil Jumonville, *Critical Crossings: The New York Intellectuals in Postwar America* (1991). Examinations of Chambers's historical impact are in *Time*, 21 July 1961, and the *New York Times*, 12 July 1961.

ROBERT C. COTTRELL

CHAMPION, Albert (2 Apr. 1878–27 Oct. 1927), inventor and businessman, was born in Paris, France, the son of Alexander Champion. Available sources reveal no other information about his family or his early life. No doubt he received an early education in Paris. When he was about twelve years old, he obtained employment as an errand boy for a bicycle manufacturer.

In 1894, at age sixteen, Champion began entering bicycle races, inspired by his employer's financial support and encouragement. With victories in French racing he became the middle-distance champion, which took him to the United States in 1899 to compete with bicycle riders there. He achieved both a U.S. and a world championship. Champion took not only his bicycles but also motorcycles and motor magnetos. He also participated in automobile and motorcycle races. He returned to France with a new focus for his ambitions, having seen the potential in automobile manufacturing and particularly in the sale of automotive accessories in the United States.

Champion briefly returned to the United States in 1900 when his interest in speed led him to race both motorcycles and automobiles, including the famous Packard "Gray Wolf." At Brighton Beach, he drove it through a fence and was seriously injured. He returned to France, where he resumed his study of automobile mechanics and drove in eighteen races, all of which he won.

Champion's reputation as an expert on automobiles preceded him when he returned to the United States. By the last months of 1904 he was initiating his plans to manufacture equipment that would improve automotive performance and speed. In 1905, with financial backers, he started a small plant in Boston, Massachusetts, for the manufacture of "sparking plugs"; he also instituted a system for importing magnetos. Apparently no one in the United States had attempted to make spark plug insulators. The demand for his products brought such success to the Boston plant that a second plant was opened in Toledo, Ohio.

In 1908 William C. Durant, founder of General Motors, convinced Champion to sever his connection with the Champion company and open an independent manufacturing firm in Flint, Michigan, where he would produce ignition devices, spark plugs, and other electrical equipment for Buick cars. The Champion Ignition Company began production with only fifteen employees in the manufacturing operations. The process involved assembling fired clay insulators between the steel shells and gland nuts, which the employees machined and threaded in the plant.

Champion's clay insulators were especially valued for their high quality. This was achieved by a special method of clay firing that produced the proper strength and size. The clay was imported from France and was fired by Champion Ignition's specially trained kiln operator, who closely guarded the secret of the process. Champion himself was excluded from the kiln room when the operator was at work, to guard against any possible leak of his trade secrets.

To meet the demands of a rapidly expanding automobile industry, Champion Ignition embarked on a physical plant expansion initiative. Significantly its first structure was completed in 1909, the year after Durant founded General Motors (GM). The complete lineup of GM cars—Buick, Oldsmobile, Cadillac, and Oakland—all needed multiple spark plugs. In 1910 Buick purchased control of Champion Ignition, and it began to operate as a GM subsidiary—AC Division—with Champion remaining as general manager.

In the beginning, the company had a contract for supplying a few hundred plugs a day to only one manufacturer. This situation changed by the mid-1920s when the company not only supplied General Motors' needs but also provided spark plugs for more than 200 independent automobile manufacturers. During the same period company records also indicate that it was the world's largest manufacturer of speedometers, which constituted part of the original equipment of GM, Chrysler, Gray, Maxwell, and other motor cars.

In May 1927 Charles A. Lindbergh made a statement after crossing the Atlantic on his historic nonstop flight that secured AC's reputation as a manufacturer of a reliable and dependable product. According to Lindbergh, "AC Spark Plugs functioned perfectly during the entire flight."

During Champion's tenure as president, AC purchased control of two of the oldest established spark plug factories operating in Europe: Sphinx Sparking Plug Company in England and Oleo Company in France.

On 1 October 1927 Albert Champion and his wife, Edna, set sail on his annual trip to Europe, during which they toured the London and Paris automobile shows. Champion also visited his new Paris factory, which had opened during the summer of 1927. By all reports he appeared to be healthy when he set sail. Upon entering the Hotel Maurice's dining room, where the Champions were to have dinner with friends, Champion collapsed into the arms of a business friend. In a moment he was dead. According to the diagnosis, he died of an embolism, the sudden clotting of blood in an artery. At the time of his death and after, a cloud of rumor, speculation, and gossip about a romantic triangle involving Charles L. Brazelle surrounded the tragedy. Paris police never suggested or stated that the death was by violence or by other than natural causes.

The truth about the sudden death of Albert Champion may never surface. Nevertheless, his place in history is secure. He will be remembered as a leader of industry and an innovator. His initials are preserved in one industry that he founded, and another company continues to bear his name.

• The key repository for primary materials related to Champion's life is the GMI Alumni Foundation Collection of Industrial History in Flint. The chapter in W. C. Durant's unpublished memoir is especially informative. Published works include Arthur Pound, *The Turning Wheel* (1934); Frank Rodolf, *An Industrial History of Flint* (c. 1944); Lawrence R. Gustin, *Billy Durant: Creator of General Motors* (1973); Clarence Young and William Quinn, *Foundation for Living* (1963); Bernard A. Weisberger, *The Dream Maker: William C. Durant, Founder of General Motors* (1979); and Richard P. Scharchburg, *W. C. Durant: The Boss* (1973).

RICHARD P. SCHARCHBURG

CHAMPION, Gower (22 June 1921–25 Aug. 1980), dancer, director, and choreographer, was born in Geneva, Illinois, the son of John W. Champion, an advertising executive, and Beatrice Carlisle. Following his parents' divorce, Champion was raised in Los Angeles by his mother. At the age of twelve he began studying dance with Ernest Belcher, a well-known dance director in films of the 1930s. Some of Belcher's other students included Betty Grable, Shirley Temple, and Cyd Charisse. Champion's training encompassed ballet, acrobatic, tap, and Spanish dance. At age fifteen Champion and Jeanne Tyler, who were both students at Hollywood High School, made their professional dancing debut as a couples act. When Tyler quit in 1941 to get married, Belcher's daughter, Marge, also a student at Hollywood High, took her place in the act. They borrowed $30 from a friend for airfare, flew to Montreal for their first scheduled performance, and went on to become one of the most popular dancing couples in the 1940s and 1950s.

In the beginning of their careers, Champion and Belcher played three- and four-star hotels around the country, receiving good notices. They married in 1947 and had two children. The same year that they were married the Champions were hired for their first Broadway show, *Lend an Ear*, choreographed by Gower. It won Champion his first Tony Award and helped establish the Champions on Broadway as a formidable song-and-dance act.

Between two more Broadway shows, *Small Wonder* (1948) and *Make a Wish* (1951), the Champions segued to television, beginning with *Admiral Broadway Revue* (1949), starring comedians Sid Caesar and Imogene Coca. The Champions' dances on the show—romantic and comedic pas de deux in which their characters would meet and fall in love—foretold the kind of narrative choreography that would distinguish Champion's later work on Broadway.

By the early fifties, the Champions were actively working in theater and television, but it was their film work that brought them to a larger public and made them stars. Under contract with Paramount, they danced together in *Mr. Music* (1950); they then signed with MGM for *Showboat* (1951), *Lovely to Look At* (1952), and *Everything I Have Is Yours* (1952), in which they received star billing. In 1952 the Champions were on the cover of *Newsweek* and appeared on many television variety shows, including those hosted by Ed Sullivan, Perry Como, Steve Allen, and Dinah Shore. They also appeared in *Jupiter's Darling* (1954) and *3 for Tonight* (1955). In 1960 *Variety* reported that they were one of the highest-paid dance teams in the world.

What was it about the Champions and their dancing that drew audiences to the box office? Unquestionably, their chemistry stayed true to the romantic partnering conventions of decades past while offering glimpses of a provocative, playful physicality. As for Gower's choreography (early in her career Marge preferred dancing to choreography, leaving Gower to stage the dances), the Champions were professed cat lovers and claimed that observing cats informed their dance routines. In a 1954 *People & Places* magazine cover story, Gower Champion called cats "the most graceful of animals." He admitted that he scrutinized every movement of his seven felines and sometimes filmed them. "Some people make home movies of their children," Marge said. "We make movies of our cats."

Still, the Champions' dances were not simply catlike; their appeal stemmed from Gower's ability to make the most conventional dance routines seem inspired. *New York Times* theater critic Brooks Atkinson wrote of the Champions' performances in *3 for Tonight*, in which Gower danced, directed, and choreographed: "As everyone knows, Mr. and Mrs. Champion are effortless dancers. But they are also people of intelligence who hate the hackneyed and despise the pretentious."

The Champions dissolved their couples act in the sixties to pursue different projects. They eventually separated and were divorced in 1973. Gower Champion later married Carla Russell.

Gower's status as a sought-after director-choreographer was cemented with *Bye Bye Birdie* (1960), an affectionate Broadway spoof of rock 'n' roll, which garnered him Tony Awards for directing and choreography. A year later he directed and choreographed

Carnival!, based on the film musical *Lili*. After a failed attempt to direct a drama—*My Mother, My Father and Me* (1963)—Champion rebounded with his greatest success ever, *Hello, Dolly!* In that 1964 musical, which starred Carol Channing, Champion kept alive old-fashioned music-hall traditions. *Hello, Dolly!* was a Busby Berkeley–type show business extravaganza that boasted dazzling staging without losing sight of the show's storyline. Channing's charisma as the irrepressible matchmaker Dolly Levi, the lavish sets, and Jerry Herman's eminently hummable score dovetailed with Champion's staging, and *Hello, Dolly!* went on to become one of Broadway's longest-running musicals. Again, Champion won Tony Awards for outstanding direction and choreography.

Champion had other successes on Broadway, including *I Do! I Do!* (1966), *The Happy Time* (1968), and *Irene* (1972)—and three significant flops, *Sugar* (1972), *Mack and Mabel* (1974), and *Rockabye Hamlet* (1976)—but he waited sixteen years for his next runaway hit musical, *42nd Street*. This 1980 David Merrick production, based on Busby Berkeley's 1933 movie starring Ruby Keeler, would be Champion's last project. As he had shown in *Hello, Dolly!*, he was fond of old-fashioned, no-expense-spared musical comedy numbers, exuberantly realized in *42nd Street*'s "We're in the Money" and the title song. Sadly, the show's public and critical praise was offset by an announcement on opening night that Champion had died earlier that day in New York City of a rare cancer of the lymphoid cells. Of Champion's accomplishments as a Broadway director-choreographer, *New York Times* theater critic Frank Rich wrote in 1980 that while Champion was not an innovator like Jerome Robbins or Michael Bennett, nor did he develop his own style of dancing like Bob Fosse, "he almost single-handedly kept alive the fabled traditions of Broadway's most glittery and innocent past."

• Information about Champion's career can be gleaned from the Dance and Theater Collections at the Library of the Performing Arts at Lincoln Center. Little information about his life is available in published form. See the article on Champion in *Current Biography* (1953), and the obituaries in the *New York Times*, 27 Aug. 1980, and *Variety*, 27 Aug. 1980.

KEVIN B. GRUBB

CHAMPION, Henry (19 Jan. 1723–23 July 1797), political and military leader who played an important role in provisioning the Continental army, was born in East Haddam, Connecticut, the son of Lieutenant Henry Champion and Mehitable Rowley. Little is known about his early life and education.

Champion was elected ensign in his local militia company at the age of eighteen and, after moving to Colchester, served with distinction as a captain in the expeditionary force raised in 1758 to attack the French at Ticonderoga. On his return to Connecticut he was made a captain in the militia and in May 1772 was promoted to major. In the intervening years he appears to have taken a leading role as a merchant intermediary in introducing commercial livestock raising to his section of eastern Connecticut. On the eve of hostilities with Britain in 1775 he was made lieutenant colonel of the twelfth militia regiment and in May 1776 colonel of the newly constituted twenty-fifth regiment. He also served in the Connecticut General Assembly as a deputy for Colchester in 1761 and from 1765 to 1780, again in 1781 and 1783, and as justice of the peace for Hartford County from 1767 to 1787.

The General Assembly appointed him one of nine commissioners charged with supplying Connecticut's troops during the siege of Boston in 1775. Their success in providing for Connecticut's forces led George Washington to recommend that Joseph Trumbull, the governor's eldest son and the commissary general for Connecticut's forces, be appointed commissary general of the Continental army. Acting under Trumbull and his deputy commissary general, Jeremiah Wadsworth, Champion specialized in the procurement of meat and eventually in live beef. He quickly developed a network of agents that eventually extended throughout New England. These agents successfully stimulated beef production by placing contracts with cattle fatteners at competitive prices. The fatteners in turn encouraged local producers to increase their herds, which allowed the commissariat in the early years of the war to keep up with the expanding demand of the army. Champion's central supervision of this network allowed him to dispatch droves when and where they were needed with an efficiency unmatched by the rest of the supply services.

In 1777 the Continental Congress, rebelling against the rising cost of the war, reorganized the commissary department, forcing Trumbull's resignation. Wadsworth and Champion refused to accept commissions under the new arrangement, but did help to supply forces in the northern department that played a role in forcing John Burgoyne's surrender at Saratoga in October 1777. Early in 1778 Champion resumed procuring beef in the old manner under the General Assembly's authority and in the spring of 1778 he was able to relieve the severe meat shortage experienced by the Continental army at Valley Forge. When Congress appointed Jeremiah Wadsworth commissary general in early 1778, Wadsworth again vested Champion with responsibility for procuring beef throughout all of the northern department.

Champion's procurement system continued to work effectively in the face of dramatic currency depreciation. Cattle raisers were under pressure to move one generation of animals off the land to make room for the next and found the continental currency useful in freeing themselves from debt and in meeting tax obligations, as well as in local exchanges, provided higher prices were given to compensate for the depreciation. Attempts at price fixing to control the escalating costs of the war repeatedly threatened Champion's system. And the system eventually broke down in the wake of Congress's decision in September 1779 not to issue any further currency. Champion now found himself unable to honor the contracts his agents had made and unable to make the advances to fatteners necessary to maintain the old system of procurement. As a result many producers started to cut back on their herds and Champion quickly lost the capacity to provide the troops with meat.

Though designated as purchaser for the eastern department by the new commissary general, Ephraim Blaine, and by the Connecticut General Assembly in 1780, Champion was forced to rely principally on taxation in kind for what little meat he was able to procure for the army during the remainder of the war. Champion's sons, Henry, Jr., and Epaphroditus, had more success acting as Wadsworth's agents in supplying the French expeditionary force under Jean Baptiste Donatien Rochambeau's command. Since the French had money with which to pay for their supplies, the Champions simply reactivated their father's old purchasing system for the French. They also participated as subcontractors in the contracts let by Robert Morris (1734–1806) for provisioning the army in 1782. But in the later phases of the war Champion's agents proved less effective because of Congress's inability to make effective provision for the enormous debts they had previously contracted.

After the war Champion retired to private life in Colchester. Few clues remain in the surviving documentation about his personality, suggesting a secretive streak, perhaps motivated by a desire to protect the centralized character of his procurement system from political jealousies. But he was obviously well known and well regarded by the Trumbull family in neighboring Lebanon as well as by Jeremiah Wadsworth. In 1746 he had married Deborah Brainard, with whom he had nine children, six of whom grew to maturity. Though Champion remained prominent locally as deacon of the Westchester Society church and occasionally represented the town in the General Assembly, his energies after the war took a more private turn, focusing on the building of a family house that still stands. After Deborah's death in 1789 Champion married Sarah Brainard Lewis in 1791. She outlived him by more than twenty years. When he died, his estate was appraised at $48,933.61. The sum suggests that Champion was a merchant of above average prosperity, but it was hardly the princely estate of which his enemies and critics throughout the war had repeatedly accused him of accumulating through self-interested extravagance in procurement.

• The Connecticut Historical Society holds a small collection of Henry Champion Papers, but they pertain mostly to a prominent son's rather than to the colonel's life. Important fragments of Colonel Champion's correspondence can be found in the Joseph Trumbull Papers and Jeremiah Wadsworth Papers in the Connecticut Historical Society, Hartford; in the Jonathan Trumbull Papers and Connecticut Archives Revolutionary War Series in the Connecticut State Library, Hartford; and in the papers of the Continental Congress and the George Washington Papers in the Library of Congress. In addition, the Connecticut State Library has a manuscript journal and some accounts pertaining to his service as a company officer during the Seven Years' War. His public career is best traced in the relevant volumes of J. H. Trumbull and C. J. Hoadly, eds., *Public Records of the Colony of Connecticut, 1636–1776* (15 vols., 1850–1890); and C. J. Hoadly et al., eds., *Public Records of the State of Connecticut* (1894-). A short life of Colonel Champion has been published in *Encyclopedia of Connecticut Biography; Genealogical-Memorial* (10 vols., 1917), but the best secondary treatment of his career is Chester M. Destler, "Colonel Henry Champion, Revolutionary Commissary," *The Connecticut Historical Society Bulletin* 36 (1971): 52–64. Destler's *Connecticut: The Provisions State* (1973) also refers frequently to Champion.

RICHARD BUEL, JR.

CHAMPLAIN, Samuel de (c. 1567–1570–25 Dec. 1635), explorer and colonizer, probably was born at Brouage, Saintonge (Charente-Maritime), France, the son of Anthoine de Champlain, allegedly a naval captain, and Dame Marguerritte Le Roy. Champlain may have been baptized a Huguenot, but if so he was early converted to the Church of Rome. Little is known of his early years except that he acquired the skills of a draftsman and cartographer. In 1632 he declared that he had served in Brittany for several years (until 1598) with the army of Henri IV against the Catholic League in the French Wars of Religion. Yet, when the Spanish army occupying Britanny returned to Spain at the end of those wars, Champlain went with them, for in 1601 he was in Cadiz. In 1603 he accompanied François Gravé Du Pont on a fur-trading venture up the St. Lawrence River to Tadoussac at the mouth of the Saguenay. It had become the customary summer rendezvous for European traders and the Montagnais Indians, who provided furs in exchange for metal goods, cloth, and trinkets.

During the few weeks that he was there Champlain made brief trips up the Saguenay and Richelieu rivers and the St. Lawrence as far as the island of Montreal. By somehow questioning the Indians he encountered, with the aid of French interpreters whose command of the Montagnais language could hardly have been comprehensive, Champlain managed to gain a remarkably accurate concept of the geography of the northeastern third of the continent; of a large bay to the north, soon to be named Hudson Bay; and of the Great Lakes. He then leapt to the conclusion that these lakes would prove to be the ardently desired water route across the continent to the Pacific Ocean and thence to the riches of Cathay. He subsequently declared to Louis XIII that were the French to control this route they could charge customs tolls for its use. Every maritime nation in Europe would have to pay rather than make the long, dangerous voyage around Africa or South America. This was a chimera that would endure among the French down to the mid-eighteenth century.

Champlain subsequently published journals of his voyages and experience in New France. They were written for a gullible French audience unable to check their accuracy and were manifestly intended to enhance his reputation and advance his career by impressing influential personages at the royal court. Not everything that he wrote can be accepted at face value, yet they are one of the few sources that we have for the period.

On their return to France, Du Pont and Champlain paused at Gaspé, where they learned from the Indians of a land to the south, with a more agreeable climate than that at Tadoussac. They were shown tantalizing pieces of copper and silver, imagined mines to equal those of Mexico and Peru, and were told of great bays and rivers that surely had to lead to the Pacific. Thus when Pierre du Gua de Monts received a commission as lieutenant general of New France and a monopoly of its trade on condition that he establish a permanent settlement there, Champlain apparently persuaded him to base it on the Atlantic coast, in what came to be called Acadia.

In 1604 de Monts, accompanied by Champlain, established a base on an island at the mouth of the Saint-Croix River. It was a poor choice because it lacked fresh water and firewood; thirty-five of the seventy-nine men who wintered there died of scurvy. When the Bay of Fundy was free of ice in the spring, the survivors moved to an inlet on the south side of the bay, where they established a base that they named Port-Royal. Champlain remained there for three years. While there he established North America's first gastronomic society, the Order of Good Cheer. He also systematically mapped the coast south as far as Cape Cod. He ventured up a large river flowing from the north that he named the Saint-Jean and somehow gathered from the Indians that it was a route to the St. Lawrence. That filled in another gap in the map of the continent that he was forming in his mind.

De Monts's trade monopoly was revoked in 1607, and he gave up on Port-Royal. The following year he made another attempt to establish a secure base for the fur trade, this time farther up the St. Lawrence, where interloping fur traders could be forestalled. In 1608 Champlain chose a site where the St. Lawrence narrows to a cannon shot in width. It came to be called Quebec. Here, too, scurvy took its toll. Of the twenty-five men who wintered there, sixteen died, but the base was maintained. Everything that followed in New France was built on it.

Champlain's main aims in life were to explore and map that part of the world, find a viable water route across it, and convert the Indians to Christianity. These objectives depended on a commercial alliance with the northern Indian nations, which could supply the furs that would finance the entire enterprise. These nations, Montagnais, Algonquin, Huron, Nipissing, and Ojibway, demanded military support in their interminable war with the Iroquois Confederacy. It was for this reason that in June 1609 Champlain with two of his men set out with a war party of some sixty Indians on a sortie into the country of the Mohawks. They ascended the Richelieu River to a lake that Champlain named after himself. The Indians explained, likely by means of crude maps drawn on birch bark with a charred stick, that they could go from that lake to yet another and thence to a river that flowed down to the ocean.

Late at night, according to Champlain's account, he and his Indian allies encountered a large Iroquois war party at what came to be known as Crown Point (Pointe à la Chevelure). Champlain's account of what then ensued stretches credulity beyond all reasonable limits. He states that the two parties agreed to give battle the next day. Champlain also claims that he and his two companions, with their clumsy matchlock muskets, enabled his grossly outnumbered allies to rout the Mohawks. If so, it was a costly victory for the French. Later, first the Dutch and then the English established themselves in the area and became allies of the Iroquois.

Champlain then returned to France to regain financial backing for the Canadian enterprise. The following year he was back at Quebec, where he took part in an attack on a marauding Iroquois war party. According to his account, the Iroquois were defeated with heavy losses. His account of this and other events leave the reader with the impression that there was no language barrier.

In August he sailed again for France, where on 30 December 1610, in his forties, he married Hélène Boullé, aged twelve, with the understanding that the marriage would not be consummated until two years hence. The 6,000 livres dowry was what mattered. During these years he spent a few summer months in Canada, more months in France, and three or more going back and forth. In France he assembled merchants willing to finance the commercial base at Quebec. At Quebec he had to whip lazy workers into doing the work that they had neglected in his absence, such as repairing old buildings and restoring damaged relations with the Indian allies.

In 1613 Champlain embarked on a voyage up the river of the Ottawas to Huronia but got no farther than Lac aux Allumettes. He mapped the Ottawa River, which was the main route to the west for two centuries.

Back in France later that year he persuaded the Recollet branch of the Franciscan order to send four missionaries to Canada. He accompanied them to Quebec in 1615 and then set off with two of his men on his epic voyage to the country of the Hurons south of Georgian Bay. Once there, fulfilling his promise to support them in their war with the Iroquois, he accompanied a war party in an attack on a village south of Lake Ontario. It failed dismally. This Champlain attributed to the Hurons' failure to heed his orders. During the affray he received two arrow wounds in the leg and had to be carried by a Huron warrior for some days during the retreat to Huronia.

Champlain spent that winter with the Hurons, acquiring much knowledge of their country, customs, way of life, and religious beliefs. He never made an attempt to comprehend their sophisticated cosmology. Since they had no edifice set aside for worship, he assumed that they had no religion. Nor did he make an attempt to master any Indian language; always he relied on interpreters who were of dubious competence. He wanted to discover what lay west of Huronia, but the Hurons were at war with the nations there and would not allow the French to have any dealings with them. Thus the map that he eventually produced was largely a product of his imagination.

Back in France Champlain found that the prince de Condé, viceroy of New France, was incarcerated in the Bastille; his company, the Compagnie des Marchands de Rouen et de Saint-Malo, in disarray. Champlain had been stripped of his lieutenancy. He may have visited Quebec briefly in 1717, but he was back in Paris that July. The following February he presented his famous reports to the king and the chamber of commerce. In them he espoused a grand colonizing policy, the establishment of a town at Quebec with 300 families, a garrison of 300 soldiers, and 15 Recollet missionaries. Thus France would control access to a vast country, the pagans would be converted to Christianity, and wealth would pour into the kingdom from the country's fish, timber, silver, iron, copper, precious stones, and furs. Most important, the wealth to be garnered once the short water route to China was found would surpass all the rest combined. The chamber was persuaded, and the king gave the proposal his support.

Champlain spent a few weeks at Quebec that summer but had to spend the following two years in France combating the chicanery of his associates in the trading company. When the duc de Montmorency, admiral of France, succeeded Condé as viceroy of New France, he confirmed Champlain's commission as his lieutenant and appointed him commandant of the colony. From this time on he devoted himself to that task.

In July 1620 Champlain, accompanied by his wife, was at Quebec, where he tried to resolve disputes between rival trading factions, curb the depredations of interlopers, and mend French relations with the Indians. Somehow he managed to keep this flicker of French imperialism alive in North America. Four years later he and his wife were back in France. Hélène, who had had her fill of the American wilderness, never returned to Canada, but in 1626 Champlain was back at Quebec coping with a multitude of mundane problems.

At long last, in 1627 someone competent took charge of the French colonial enterprise. It was Cardinal Richelieu, the king's first minister. He established the Compagnie de la Nouvelle-France (commonly known as the Compagnie des Cent-Associés) with 100 associate members, each of whom invested 3,000 livres in the venture. Champlain was one of them and, while Richelieu retained the title of governor, Champlain was duly appointed acting governor of New France. The settlers in Canada and Acadia were estimated to number 107; to the south the Dutch and English numbered at least 2,600. Thus it was that in 1629 Champlain was forced to surrender Quebec to a force of Anglo-Scottish freebooters led by the Kirke brothers. Champlain was taken prisoner to England, where he discovered that peace had been declared between England and France before he had surrendered Quebec. In France, at his urging, Richelieu and the king obliged England to restore Canada and Acadia to France as a term of the Treaty of Saint-Germain-en-Laye in 1632. The following year Champlain returned to Quebec as Richelieu's acting governor once more. There he had first to repair the depredations of the Kirkes' men; they had not been good tenants, and all had to be rebuilt.

In 1635 Champlain's health failed. Paralyzed, his mind obviously gone, he dictated a new will bequeathing all his possessions to the Virgin Mary. He died in Quebec. His will was annulled two years later.

Champlain, an intrepid navigator and explorer and a skilled geographer and cartographer, was the first person to map the Atlantic coast from Newfoundland to Cape Cod and the eastern Great Lakes. He established an enduring alliance with the northern Indian nations and laid the foundations on which others built a vast, if short-lived, empire.

• The best edition of Champlain's works is *The Works of Samuel de Champlain*, ed. H. P. Biggar (6 vols., 1922–1936). That series provides the best available French text with an English translation. There is no good biography of Champlain. That by Narcisse-Eutrope Dionne, *Samuel de Champlain, fondateur de Québec et père de la Nouvelle-France. Histoire de sa vie et de ses voyages* (2 vols., 1891–1906), as the title indicates, is hagiographic and also outdated. Morris B. Bishop, *Champlain, the Life of Fortitude* (1948), is hagiography, a mixture of facts and fiction, but very readable. Samuel Eliot Morison, *Samuel de Champlain: Father of New France* (1972), is another hagiographic work, riddled with misconceptions. The best work in English on Champlain and his times is contained in Marcel Trudel, *The Beginnings of New France 1524–1663*, trans. Patricia Claxton (1973), a condensation of the first four volumes of Trudel's magisterial *Histoire de la Nouvelle-France* (1963–1983). An excellent study of Champlain's mysterious *Brief Discours* is Luca Codignola, "Samuel de Champlain et les mystères de son voyage aux Indes occidentales, 1599–1601. L'état de la recherche et quelques routes à suivre," in *La découverte de nouveaux mondes: aventures et voyages imaginaires au XVIIe siècle. Actes du XXIIe Colloque du Centre Méridional de Rencontres sur le XVIIe Siècle*, ed. Cecilia Rizza (1992).

Robert le Blant and René Baudry, *Nouveaux documents sur Champlain et son époque*, vol. 1, *1560–1622* (1967), is an important collection. Other sources are Reuben Gold Thwaites, ed., *The Jesuit Relations and Allied Documents* (73 vols., 1896–1901). Marc Lescarbot was a contemporary of Champlain's in Acadia. His *Histoire de la Nouvelle-France* was published in 1609. It appeared with an English translation, notes, and appendices by W. L. Grant as *The History of New France* (3 vols., 1907–1914). An intriguing contemporary account of a sojourn with the Hurons in Champlain's day is Gabriel Sagard, *Le Grand Voyage du pays des Hurons*. The best edition is that edited and annotated by Réal Ouellet and Jack Warwick (1990).

WILLIAM ECCLES

CHAMPLIN, Stephen (17 Nov. 1789–20 Feb. 1870), naval officer, was born in South Kingston, Rhode Island, the son of Stephen Champlin and Elizabeth Perry. His parents' occupations are unknown. He was cousin to the celebrated commodores Oliver Hazard Perry and Matthew Calbraith Perry. Champlin resided on a farm in Lebanon, Connecticut, until he ran away to join the merchant marine at the age of sixteen. By 1806 he had completed several cruises to Demerara, Newfoundland, and Buenos Aires and acquired the rank of second mate. Champlin was afforded a chance to demonstrate his sailing prowess in 1811 when, during a voyage to the West Indies, his captain died of yellow fever. He assumed command of the brig *Dove*, returned it safely to port, and was appointed captain at the age of twenty-two. The following year impending hostilities with Great Britain induced Champlin to seek a naval commission, and on 22 May 1812 he became a sailing master. His first assignment was with Captain Oliver Hazard Perry's gunboat squadron at Newport, Rhode Island.

After the War of 1812 commenced, Champlin was occupied with carrying important dispatches to New London and Boston. He fulfilled his assignments with alacrity and in February 1813 accompanied his cousin to Sackets Harbor, New York, as part of Commodore Isaac Chauncey's Lake Ontario squadron. He conducted a party of forty-two sailors overland in record time and became second in command of the schooner *Asp*. In this capacity Champlin fought at the 27 April 1813 capture of York (now Toronto) and the 27 May battle of Fort George, Upper Canada. On 18 July 1813 Chauncey ordered Champlin to transfer seventy-four men to Erie, Pennsylvania, as part of Perry's embryonic Lake Erie fleet. When Champlin completed this arduous task in only five days, he was rewarded with his first independent command, the schooner *Scorpion*.

On 10 September 1813 Champlin fought conspicuously in the decisive battle of Lake Erie. *Scorpion* took post as a flanking vessel to Perry's flagship *Lawrence*, and Champlin fired the first American shots of the battle. He remained hotly engaged until the British surrender at 3:00 P.M. and, assisted by Lieutenant Daniel Turner, pursued and secured two fleeing enemy vessels, *Chippewa* and *Little Belt*. The shots he fired during this capture were also the last of the engagement. For his role in Perry's victory, Champlin received a sword from Congress and a considerable share of the prize money.

After the battle, Champlin provided naval transport to the army of General William Henry Harrison. He ran the *Scorpion* forty miles up the Thames River in support and subsequently transported the severely wounded Richard Mentor Johnson back to Detroit. Champlin then skillfully navigated the captured British vessels *Queen Charlotte* and *Detroit* back to Erie amidst boisterous weather. In the summer of 1814 he assumed command of the schooner *Tigress* and accompanied Commodore Arthur Sinclair on his ill-fated Mackinac expedition. Champlin and Lieutenant Turner of the *Scorpion* established a naval blockade and spent several weeks cruising the upper lakes. Either by negligence or surprise, both vessels were captured on 3 September 1814 while anchored near St. Joseph Island. Champlin sustained a serious grapeshot injury to his thigh and was conveyed to Mackinac a prisoner. Following forty-seven days of close confinement, he was paroled and returned to Connecticut in March 1815.

Champlin had been promoted to lieutenant on 9 December 1814, and he received orders to join Perry on board the frigate *Java* for Mediterranean service. Unfortunately, his wound required several operations, and he returned to Connecticut to recuperate. By 1816 Champlin had recovered sufficiently to allow a return to active duty, and he commanded the schooner *Porcupine* while surveying the national boundaries of the Great Lakes. Champlin then sailed to Buffalo, New York, where he met and in 1817 married Minerva L. Pomeroy, with whom he had six children. His wound again forced him to convalesce in Connecticut until 1828, when he briefly served aboard the steam battery *Fulton* in New York City. Champlin subsequently requested a transfer back to Buffalo in 1834 and was allowed to remain there for the rest of his active career.

Despite intermittent health problems, Champlin continued to receive important naval assignments. He rose to commander on 22 June 1838 and four years later assumed control of the Buffalo recruiting depot. When the Canadian "Patriot War" erupted in 1838, Champlin cruised the lakes in the steamers *Fulton* and *New England*, enforcing a strict neutrality. In 1845 he was entrusted with the new ironclad vessel *Michigan* and on 4 August 1850 acquired his captaincy. Plagued by illness, Champlin retired on 13 September 1855 with leave of absence pay. Six years later the old sailor tendered his services to the Union at the outbreak of the Civil War. These were politely declined, but Champlin nonetheless received the rank of commodore on 4 April 1867. He died at Buffalo, the last surviving officer of Commodore Perry's squadron.

Like many contemporaries, Champlin was a skilled and resourceful sailor. He rendered valuable service while covering Perry's flank on Lake Erie and defended his vessel the following year until resistance was no longer possible. Champlin never overcame his wartime injuries, but his devotion to duty, adroitness in action, and unflagging patriotism exemplify U.S. Navy professionalism at its best.

• Champlin's official correspondence is in Record Group 45, Captains' Letters, National Archives. Other materials are in the Oliver Hazard Perry Papers, Clements Library, University of Michigan; and the Buffalo and Erie County Historical Society. An informative panegyric is George W. Clinton, "The Life of Stephen Champlin," *Buffalo Historical Society Publications* 8 (1905): 381–99. For details on War of 1812 operations consult William J. Walsh and David C. Skaggs, eds., *War on the Great Lakes* (1991). For an excellent overview of the navy in which Champlin served see Christopher McKee, *A Gentlemanly and Honorable Profession* (1991).

JOHN C. FREDRIKSEN

CHANCE, Frank Leroy (9 Sept. 1877–15 Sept. 1924), baseball player and manager, was born in Fresno, California, the son of a bank president. His parents' names and details of his early life are unknown. He played on the Fresno High School baseball team in 1893 and subsequently played for Washington College in Irvington, California, where he studied dentistry.

Chance, who stood six feet tall and weighed approximately 200 pounds, dropped out of college to play semiprofessional baseball in his native state. Major league right fielder Bill Lange saw him play and in 1898 Chance began a professional career by joining Lange's team, the Chicago Orphans (later called the Cubs), as a catcher. He came to be regarded as an extremely capable handler of pitchers, an astute student of hitters, and a rough-and-tumble performer at the game's most rugged position. Nicknamed "Husk" (as in husky), Chance was aggressive at bat as well, crowding home plate and sustaining thirty-six career beanings in the sport's pre-batting helmet era. Coupled with his off-season career as a boxer, the beanings affected Chance's hearing, speech, and disposition. Moreover, they led to lingering headaches and blood clotting, culminating in surgery near the end of his playing career.

Cubs manager Frank Selee converted Chance from a catcher to a first baseman in 1903. Chance balked at the change, but a raise in salary eased his compliance. At first base, Chance was particularly adept at scooping balls out of the dirt. His participation in the double play combination that included second baseman Johnny Evers and shortstop Joe Tinker inspired one of baseball's most famous poems, New York writer (and New York Giants fan) Franklin P. Adams's lament entitled "Baseball's Sad Lexicon" (1910): These are the saddest of possible words, / Tinker-to-Evers-to-Chance. / Trio of Bear Cubs fleeter than birds, / Tinker-to-Evers-to-Chance. / Ruthlessly pricking our gonfalon bubble, / Making a Giant hit into a double, / Words that are weighty with nothing but trouble. / Tinker-to-Evers-to-Chance.

The Chicago infielders' defensive renown seemingly owes more to timing—to their ability to execute the double play at critical points of games—than to prolificacy (only 54 double plays from 1906 through 1909, according to the research of Chicago sportswriter Warren Brown).

Despite his bowleggedness, Chance was an excellent baserunner, leading the National League with a team record 67 stolen bases in 1903 and with 57 in 1906. He also tied for first base fielding honors with a .990 percentage in 1904, led National League players with 103 runs scored in 1906, and paced the league's first basemen with a .992 fielding percentage the following season. Conversely, in 1903 Chance led the league in errors at his position with 36.

Offensively, Chance, who batted fourth in the order, hit over .300 in five different seasons, peaking with .327 in 1903. In 1906 he achieved a career high for hits in a season with 151 in 474 times at bat. Chance's career statistics included nine seasons of ten or more doubles and four seasons of ten or more triples. Playing in the dead ball period, he hit a personal high six home runs—the third best figure in the league—in 1904. A career .297 hitter, Chance averaged .310 through four World Series, including a .421 average in 1908 when the Cubs defeated the Detroit Tigers. In the Cubs-Giants game that determined the National League pennant that year, Chance managed three hits against Christy Mathewson.

Previously chosen by his peers as team captain, Chance replaced the tubercular Selee as Cubs manager during the 1905 season, at the relatively boyish age of twenty-seven. He fashioned the Chicago club into a dynasty that won four National League pennants and two World Series during a five-year span (1906–1910). In 1906 the Cubs set a major league record for most wins in a season with 116 but lost to the "hitless wonders" of the Chicago White Sox in the World Series. The exacting "Husk" earned another nickname, "The Peerless Leader," for his managing. Given to challenging umpires, Chance earned respect, and their best efforts, by displaying loyalty to his players and treating them as adults. Quick to rid his teams of recalcitrants, Chance physically fought at least one dissenting Cubs player, the infamous Heinie Zimmerman, promising to quit as manager if Zimmerman were to triumph. Chance, whose off-season boxing regimen was praised by heavyweight champion James J. Corbett, easily won the fight.

While as a manager, Chance might occasionally brood or even tear up a locker room after a loss, he would also treat his players to drinks at Chicago's old West Side Park after games. A poker player who once fined himself for continuing a card game beyond the curfew he had established, Chance liked ballplayers who also played poker or bet on the horses, considering such activities valuable as mental exercises.

Chance's .593 winning percentage as a major league manager with the Cubs (1905–1912), New York Yankees (1913–1914) and Boston Red Sox (1923) is among the highest such averages in baseball history. Besides managing in the big leagues, Chance—after trying his hand at operating orange groves on a California ranch—was manager and part-owner of the Los Angeles team of the minor Pacific Coast League in 1916 and 1917, after which he returned to the ranch. He was scheduled to return to Chicago in 1924 as manager of the White Sox, but he contracted tuberculosis. Chance died in Los Angeles before the season concluded. He was married to a woman named Edith (maiden name unknown). After falling seven votes shy of enshrinement in 1945, he was elected to the National Baseball Hall of Fame the following year, along with his double play partners Evers and Tinker.

• A clipping file on Chance is at the National Baseball Library, Cooperstown, N.Y. Chance wrote one book, *The Bride and the Pennant: The Greatest Story in the History of America's National Game* (c. 1910). Peter Golenbock, *Wrigleyville* (1996), is a valuable source on Chance's fifteen-year professional affiliation with the Chicago Cubs. Harvey Frommer, *Baseball's Greatest Managers* (1985), sheds light on personal aspects of Chance's life. For other useful overviews, see Donald Dewey and Nicholas Acocella, *The Biographical History of Baseball* (1995); and Lowell Reidenbaugh, *Cooperstown* (1983).

THOMAS D. JOZWIK

CHANDLER, Albert Benjamin (14 July 1898–15 June 1991), governor, senator, and commissioner of major league baseball, was born near Corydon, Kentucky, the son of Joseph Sephus Chandler and Callie Sanders, farmers. When Chandler was four years old his mother abandoned the family. He and his younger brother at first stayed with relatives; later they lived with their father. Beginning at age seven, Chandler worked at odd jobs to earn additional income for the family.

In the fall of 1917 Chandler entered Transylvania University in Lexington, Kentucky. As he delighted in recalling throughout his career, he arrived on campus with nothing more than "a red sweater, a five-dollar bill, and a smile." His grades there, though not stellar, nonetheless won him entry into Harvard Law School, where he enrolled in August 1921. Chandler remained at Harvard only one year. Desperately short of funds, he transferred to the law school of the University of Kentucky in Lexington, from which he graduated in 1924.

Chandler began the practice of law in the small town of Versailles, twelve miles from Lexington. During his first year there he met Mildred Watkins, a native Virginian who was teaching in an elite girls' school. The couple married in 1925, and they would have four children. His gracious and astute wife—known to most everyone as "Mama Chandler"—became an invaluable asset to his career.

Like his father, Chandler took an interest in Democratic politics. He first sought elected office in 1929, when he won a seat in the Kentucky Senate. Two years later his party's convention nominated him to run for lieutenant governor on a ticket headed by Ruby Laffoon. Sworn into office in December 1931, Chandler soon broke with Laffoon over the state sales tax, which Chandler opposed. A bitter feud ensued, in which the governor's forces stripped Chandler of most powers. In 1935 Chandler seized the opportunity of Laffoon's absence from the state to convene a special session of the legislature to enact a primary election law. He subsequently defeated Tom Rhea to capture the Democratic nomination for governor. In the general election that November he scored a landslide victory over his Republican challenger, King Swope, winning 55 percent of the vote.

Chandler was inaugurated on 10 December 1935, at age thirty-seven. Hailed as "the boy governor," he compiled a substantial record of progressive reform. He reorganized state government, reducing the number of departments from twenty-six to eleven. He funded the construction of badly needed schools, hospitals, roads, and charitable institutions and established the state teachers' retirement system. Honoring his campaign pledge, he repealed the state's 3 percent sales tax. To finance his initiatives he supported luxury, inheritance, and income taxes. With the repeal of statewide Prohibition, additional revenues resulted from excise taxes levied on whiskey. Chandler's record, combined with a colorful, winning personality perfectly expressed in his nickname of "Happy," made him the most popular political figure in Kentucky.

Limited by the state constitution to a single term as governor, Chandler set his sights on the U.S. Senate. In 1938 he decided to challenge the two-term incumbent, Alben W. Barkley, a fellow Democrat. Barkley, his party's majority leader in the Senate, received the endorsement of his close friend and ally, Franklin D. Roosevelt. Indeed, the president journeyed to Kentucky to campaign on his behalf. The popularity of Barkley, FDR, and the New Deal proved insurmountable, and Chandler experienced his first electoral defeat.

When the state's other senator, Marvel Mills Logan, died unexpectedly in October 1939, Chandler was handed the opportunity he had been seeking. He resigned the governorship and, by prior arrangement, was then appointed to an interim seat. In 1940 he won a special election to complete the remaining two years of Logan's term. Following a hard-fought contest in 1942, Chandler defeated former congressman John Y. Brown, Sr., to secure a full six-year term.

In the Senate Chandler usually voted in support of the Roosevelt program, though he never forgave the president for supporting Barkley in 1938. A member of the military affairs committee, Chandler in 1943 joined four of his colleagues on a globe-circling inspection tour of U.S. troops and bases. He returned an ardent admirer of General Douglas MacArthur and convinced that a greater proportion of Allied men and matériel should be devoted to the Pacific theater.

Shortly after the war, in November 1945, Chandler surprised most observers—and himself, too, he said—by resigning to become commissioner of major league baseball. He left the Senate, he insisted, out of financial necessity. With four children he found the offer of $50,000 a year—five times the salary of a U.S. senator—impossible to turn down. The lure of the game doubtless attracted him as well. Throughout high school and college Chandler had been a star athlete, good enough, in fact, to play several summers of minor league baseball.

Chandler's years as commissioner were turbulent. His establishment of a pension fund and a minimum salary made him a favorite of players. But his one-year suspension of Brooklyn Dodgers manager Leo Durocher in April 1947, for what Chandler termed "conduct detrimental to the game," angered fans and owners alike. An outspoken proponent of "breaking the color line" in baseball, he authorized the transfer of Jackie Robinson, an African American, from Montreal to Brooklyn. When Chandler's contract came up for renewal in 1951, he received the support of a majority of the owners but fell short of the three-fourths required. He soon resigned and returned to practice law in Versailles.

But politics remained first in Chandler's heart. In the 1955 Democratic primary he defeated Bert T. Combs, a state court of appeals judge, to win the nomination for governor. In the general election that November he secured a landslide victory over an ineffectual Republican candidate, Edwin R. Denney. But Chandler's second term lacked the stirring successes of his first. He supported the Supreme Court's *Brown V. Board of Education* decision, on several occasions sending in the National Guard and state police to enforce desegregation efforts. His crowning achievement was the establishment of a medical school and hospital at the University of Kentucky, later named in his honor.

The outspoken Chandler inspired passionate devotion as well as distrust. His colorful personality captured the attention of a national audience. Nominated for president at the 1956 Democratic National Convention, he received votes from eight state delegations. In 1968 George C. Wallace encouraged him to accept the vice presidential nomination on his American party ticket. Chandler eventually declined, realizing the two were incompatible on the race issue.

Constitutionally prohibited from seeking reelection, Chandler left the governorship in December 1959 and never again held elected office. On three occasions—in 1963, 1967, and 1971—he failed to secure his party's nomination for governor. He remained active in civic affairs well into his eighties. The highlight of his later years was his 1982 induction into the National Baseball Hall of Fame in Cooperstown, New York. He died at his home in Versailles.

• An extensive collection of Chandler's papers and audiotape interviews, especially rich on Kentucky politics and major league baseball, is at the University of Kentucky Library. The National Baseball Library, Cooperstown, N.Y., has a file on Chandler. Chandler collaborated with Vance Trimble on an autobiography, *Heroes, Plain Folks, and Skunks: The Life and Times of Happy Chandler* (1989). Significant aspects of his career are discussed in three articles published in the *Register of the Kentucky Historical Society*: Walter L. Hixson, "The 1938 Kentucky Senate Election: Alben W. Barkley, 'Happy' Chandler, and the New Deal," 80 (1982): 309–29; William J. Marshall, "A. B. Chandler as Baseball Commissioner, 1945–51: An Overview," 82 (1984): 358–88; and Charles P. Roland, "Happy Chandler," 85 (1987): 138–61. An essential source regarding Chandler's role in the integration of major league baseball is Jules Tygiel, *Baseball's Great Experiment* (1983). Obituaries are in the *Louisville Courier-Journal* and the *New York Times*, both 16 June 1991.

THOMAS H. APPLETON, JR.

CHANDLER, Charles Frederick (6 Dec. 1836–25 Aug. 1925), chemist, was born in Lancaster, Massachusetts, the son of Charles Chandler, the owner of a dry goods store, and Sarah Whitney. Chandler was raised in New Bedford, Massachusetts, where he attended public schools. A high-school teacher encouraged him in chemistry, and especially after hearing lectures by Louis Agassiz in New Bedford, Chandler took a keen interest in science. He helped in his father's store before school in the morning, and he tended the family vegetable garden. From his earnings he bought equipment for a chemical laboratory in the attic. During summers at his grandfather's home in Lancaster, he began collecting local minerals, and he acquired more from ballast in whaling ships.

After completing high school Chandler was tutored for a year in Latin and Greek, and in 1853 he entered the new Lawrence Scientific School at Harvard to learn chemistry. The program, essentially an unsupervised laboratory course, did not satisfy him, so he accepted the advice of Charles A. Joy of Union College, who, when visiting Harvard, urged the chemistry students to study in Europe. In 1854 Chandler went to the University of Göttingen, where he became assistant to chemist Friedrich Wöhler and attended lectures on several scientific subjects. The next year, at the University of Berlin, he was assistant to chemist Heinrich Rose. Chandler received an A.M. and a Ph.D. from the University of Göttingen in 1856. His dissertation was on analyses of nine unusual minerals from the United States and Europe.

In 1857 Chandler became assistant to Joy at Union College in Schenectady, New York. His job title was janitor, so he also cleaned the laboratory. Joy started a new chemistry course that year with six students and almost immediately accepted a professorship at Columbia University. Chandler replaced him at Union College as adjunct professor in 1857 and soon became a professor. Through seven years he offered courses in organic and inorganic chemistry, analytical and agricultural chemistry, blowpipe analysis, geology, and mineralogy. Besides publishing several papers on minerals and chemistry, he wrote the useful text *A Manual of Qualitative Analysis* (1860; repr. 1873) with D. K. Tuttle of the University of Virginia. In 1862 Chandler married Anna Maria Craig; they had one child.

A visit to the excellent collection of minerals at Union College by mining engineer Thomas Egleston in 1864 led to an offer for Chandler to found a School of Mines at Columbia University, which he accepted. While such schools were common in Europe then, none existed in the United States. The new school opened in 1864 with equipment paid for by donors, a good collection of donated minerals, and three professors. Chandler taught geology, analytical and applied chemistry, and assaying. Financial support was through fees from registered students. At the school's opening the professors hoped for twelve students and were inundated by twenty-four, which increased to forty-seven at the year's end. In 1866 John Strong Newberry became professor of geology, while Chandler continued teaching chemistry courses. At some time he became dean of the school, retaining that position until 1897. He was its "all-pervading genius and chief driving force," according to his biographer Marston Taylor Bogert (Bogert, p. 139). Columbia University soon made the school a regular teaching unit and provided a new building, designed by Chandler. Students admired and respected him, and one noted that he "led them through a course of Chemistry, Ethics and Humor, so cleverly combined that it has made men of them" (Bogert, p. 141). In 1866 Chandler developed a standard system of weights for assaying metal in ores, a significant contribution to chemistry.

In 1866 Peter W. Bedford, a professor at the New York College of Pharmacy, approached Chandler for advice. As a result, Chandler lectured on chemistry at the College of Pharmacy three nights a week, at first without pay. He became vice president and later president of the college while continuing at Columbia. The number of students increased, and the college was able to build a larger facility, with support from the city's druggists. In 1905 Columbia University invited the school to join it as the College of Pharmacy, and Chandler continued to teach at the college until 1910. After his wife's death he married Augusta P. Berard in 1905. They had no children.

In 1872 Chandler also became an adjunct professor of chemistry and medical jurisprudence at the New York College of Physicians and Surgeons. Four years later he advanced to professor, conducting his teaching in late afternoons. He led the college to the adoption of a four-year course for medical students, and he provided students with information on sanitation and hygiene. In 1891 Columbia University took over this facility as its College of Physicians and Surgeons, and Chandler retired from that college in 1897.

In addition to his several teaching appointments, Chandler did consulting work for sugar companies, Standard Oil Company, and the New York Gas Company among others. He advised the New York Central Railroad on incrustations in boilers in the engines, and he analyzed the waters of many mineral springs in New York State, especially those at Saratoga. He was also a chemical expert in many patent suits.

The Metropolitan Board of Health of New York City sought Chandler's advice in 1866 on sanitation problems, and thereafter he had an impact on health and sanitation. In 1867 he was paid as the first chemist on the board of health. He became its president in 1873 and was reappointed from 1877 to 1883. He first examined kerosene, which came into use about 1860 as a replacement for whale oil in lamps and which frequently exploded. Chandler found that grocers often diluted kerosene, which was safe to burn, with cheaper petroleum distillates such as naphtha and benzine, which were explosive. His report "Dangerous Kerosene" (*American Gas Light Journal*, 2 Feb. 1869) was widely distributed in the United States and Europe and brought about a dramatic decrease in lamp explosions.

When an epidemic of smallpox struck New York City in 1874, Chandler set up improved nursing care for victims and, after vaccinating himself, arranged for door-to-door vaccinations. He then helped persuade the board of education to require vaccinations before children could attend school. He set up a corps of fifty physicians to visit tenement houses in summers to treat illnesses and advise on health conditions. He determined that much of the milk in the city was diluted with water and ended the practice by rigorous enforcement of standards. He required gas and petroleum companies and rendering plants to clean up their foul odors. He invented the flush toilet but chose not to patent it. He had filthy public markets destroyed, tenement buildings inspected and improved, plumbing systems reconstructed, and street cleaning increased. He encouraged the construction of a few large slaughter houses instead of many small ones throughout the city, prohibited driving cattle on city streets, and persuaded the slaughter houses to dry and market blood as fertilizer. When the New York subway opened, he analyzed its air, which some claimed was unhealthy, and he declared it as pure as air at the surface.

For the state of New York Chandler pushed for a state board of health and served as chairman of its sanitary committee. In that position he urged legislation to prohibit adulteration of foods and other products and to provide enforcement. For the federal government he studied wood preservation for the navy, waterproofing of paper currency for the Treasury Department, and the sanitation of hog products at the request of President Chester A. Arthur. Chandler successfully urged the creation of a commission on cholera to check immigrants at U.S. ports of entry. When stories circulated that stamps were poisonous to lick, he tested them at the request of the postmaster general and declared them safe. In 1880 and again in 1903 he examined the original Declaration of Independence for the Secretary of the Interior, who requested Chandler's advice on preventing it from fading. However, Chandler could only recommend reinking the signatures, which was not done.

Chandler and his brother William H. Chandler of Lehigh University began publishing *American Chemist* in 1870. In 1874 the chemical section of the New York Lyceum of Natural History honored the centennial of the discovery of oxygen by Joseph Priestley at his grave site in Northumberland, Pennsylvania. Chandler was president of the ceremony, which was well attended by chemists, and he led a movement to found a nationwide society. The American Chemical Society was established at a meeting in New York in 1876, and he was elected a vice president. He served as president in 1881 and 1889. The brothers discontinued *American Chemist* in 1877 in favor of the new *Journal of the American Chemical Society.*

Chandler was chairman of the chemistry department at Columbia for some years, probably beginning in 1897, and retired in 1911. He was elected to the National Academy of Sciences in 1874, and in 1899 he was president of the British-based Society of Chemical Industry, which awarded him its Perkin Medal in 1920. Columbia alumni established a medal in his name for recognition in chemistry. After a distinguished career in teaching and in public health service, Chandler died in Hartford, Connecticut.

• Files of administrative correspondence of Chandler from 1890 to 1917 are in the archives of Columbia University. The primary biography is Marston Taylor Bogert, "Charles Frederick Chandler," National Academy of Sciences, *Biographical Memoirs* 14 (1931): 125–81.

ELIZABETH NOBLE SHOR

CHANDLER, Elizabeth Margaret (24 Dec. 1807 2 Nov. 1834), poet and essayist, was born in Centre, Delaware, near Wilmington, the daughter of Thomas Chandler, a physician and farmer, and Margaret Evans. Her father was a man of means; he descended from Quaker settlers on the Delaware River. Her mother died while Chandler was a baby.

In 1816 Chandler's father moved to Philadelphia and placed his children in the care of their maternal grandmother. As a girl, Chandler was serious and contemplative; she attended a school run by the Society of Friends. Her father died when she was nine years of age (the same age as when the precocious poet wrote "Reflections on a Thunder-gust"), and her mother's three sisters helped rear her.

Although she left school at age thirteen, Chandler continued to read and write for entertainment and expression. Friends respected her shyness and published her essays without attribution. By the age of sixteen Chandler was still avoiding society except for Quaker meetings, but she was writing more for publication.

When Chandler was eighteen years old, "The Slave Ship," perhaps her best known work, was published in *Casket*. The monthly journal awarded her poem third prize. "I still consider it equal to those which were exalted above it," she wrote later. Chandler, who became the first female poet to concentrate on the theme of slavery, cited "The Slave Ship" as her first on the subject; its impetus, she recalled, had been a minister's sermon.

Benjamin Lundy, who edited a Philadelphia newspaper, *Genius of Universal Emancipation*, reprinted the poem and, on its strength, hired Chandler as a contributor in 1827. Her poems on slavery appeared often in the *Genius*, including "The Recaptured Slave," "The Slave's Appeal," and "The Wife's Lament." Modern critics compare her work to that of Lydia Maria Child, who also began to write poetry in her adolescence.

In 1829 Chandler was hired to edit "The Female Repository," the "woman's page" of the *Genius*, making her one of the first female editors in the United States. At the *Genius*, she worked with—and agreed with—William Lloyd Garrison on the subject of abolition. She opposed slavery absolutely as, in her words, "the only means of avoiding a participation in guilt." She fought against efforts to colonize freed slaves in Africa and Canada.

Although she wrote most of the Repository section herself, Chandler rarely gave herself credit as editor. For the Repository, she penned her "Appeal to the Ladies of the United States": "We wish to impress you with a firm, steady conviction of the manifest injustice and pernicious effects attendant on slavery, and with a deep sense of your own responsibility in either directly or indirectly lending it your encouragement." Reportedly, the article caused a few female readers to free their slaves. Critics have thus compared her influence to that of Harriet Beecher Stowe. Chandler gained international attention when "An Appeal" was reprinted in Europe. At the same time she was editing for the *Genius*, she published *The Poetic Works*, a collection of her poems that include such paeans to Delaware as "The Brandywine."

In 1830, her health weakening, Chandler moved with a brother Thomas and her Aunt Ruth to the Territory of Michigan, settling on a farm she named "Hazelbank," in Lenawee County, about sixty miles southwest of Detroit. Chandler continued to correspond, especially to her intimate friend, Hannah Townsend Longstreth, and she edited the newspaper by mail.

Encouraged by a visit by Lundy in 1832 to her retreat, Chandler formed the Logan Anti-Slavery Society, which advocated full participation by African Americans in society. The only thing that stopped her work was the so-called "remittent fever," which she caught in the fall of 1834. She died in Lewanee County.

Chandler was one of the earliest American women to address women, Native Americans, and African Americans. Fully half her output concerns slavery. Her poems were set to music and sung at abolitionists' meetings, owing to both their sentiment and their measured pace (for example, the anapestic tetrameter of "The Battlefield" never wavers).

Her essays, too, addressed her chosen theme at every opportunity. For example, for 4 July 1827, she contrasted the lives of slaves and Indians with the promises of the Declaration of Independence. Chandler also encouraged a boycott of products made by slaves to eliminate the economics of the system. Chandler reasoned that, because women usually controlled household purchases of clothing and food, they could refuse to buy anything produced by slave labor. In a series of essays written as "Letters to Isabel," an invented "friend," Chandler chastised her for not refusing to eat dessert made from slave-produced sugar. She appealed to women to put their intelligence to work in the fight for freedom. Another series of essays published in the *Genius* exhorted women to take up humanitarian causes. Chandler's tracts, written more for politics than rhetoric, were often reprinted in the humanitarian press, which was especially influential among women.

Lundy pronounced Chandler to be "an able author, and editor; in fact, one of the most accomplished and powerful female writers of her time." He declared her "language . . . appropriate, her reasoning clear, her detections logical, and her conclusions impressive and convincing." In 1836 Lundy published *Essays, Philanthropic and Moral* and *The Poetical Works of Elizabeth Margaret Chandler*, which he introduced with a *Memoir of Her Life and Character*.

• Chandler's unpublished correspondence (125 pieces) is in the Michigan History Collections of the University of Michigan. Although she is often included in lists of nineteenth-century writers, Chandler's poems are rarely anthologized, even among modern collections specializing in women or in the Civil War era. However, Chandler is described in Mary Sam Ward, ed., *Delaware Women Remembered* (1977); Rufus W. Griswold, *The Female Poets in America* (1859); Sarah Josepha

Hale, *Woman's Record* (1853); and Merton L. Dillon, "Elizabeth Chandler and the Spread of Anti-slavery Sentiment to Michigan," *Michigan History* (Dec. 1955). George W. Clark, *The Liberty Minstrel* (1844), includes her poems set to music.

MARTHA K. BAKER

CHANDLER, Happy. *See* Chandler, Albert Benjamin.

CHANDLER, John (1 Feb. 1762–25 Sept. 1841), soldier, U.S. congressman, and senator, was born in Epping, New Hampshire, the son of Joseph Chandler and Lydia Eastman. His father, a subsistence farmer and soldier, died in 1776, leaving a destitute widow and ten children. To help support the family, John, upon turning fifteen, enlisted in the Continental army, engaging in the 1777 Saratoga campaign that resulted in the defeat and capture of General John Burgoyne's army. In January 1779 he sailed on the *Arnold*, a privateer out of Newburyport, Massachusetts, which took several prizes before being captured in May by a British warship. Chandler spent the next four months on an overcrowded prison ship anchored in the Savannah River. In September, after many prisoners had died from disease and starvation, he and a few desperate inmates overpowered the guards and escaped. After a cross-country trek lasting more than four months, Chandler arrived back at Epping in February 1780. He subsequently enlisted for a final six-month term in the army. On 28 August 1783 Chandler married Mary Whittier, with whom he would have seven children. Anxious to improve their economic prospects, the newlyweds left the unpromising Epping farm in early 1784 and moved to the frontier District of Maine, settling on a farm in Kennebec County in what became the town of Monmouth.

Apprenticed very young to a blacksmith, Chandler had only a rudimentary education. What he lacked in education, however, he made up in industry, frugality, and ambition. Frontier Maine afforded plenty of opportunities for him to improve his fortune. He engaged in a variety of employments—farming, blacksmithing, sawmilling, and operating a tavern and store. At the same time, he studied under the local schoolmaster to improve his education. His hard work, resourcefulness, and shrewd business acumen soon paid off. Within a decade he had become a prosperous and respected community leader. His self-education created opportunities for career advancement: when the town of Monmouth was incorporated in 1792, he was made town clerk, assessor, and selectman, and when a post office was established in the town two years later, he was appointed postmaster. These positions were stepping-stones to more important political offices.

A Jeffersonian Republican in politics, Chandler was elected to the Massachusetts Senate in 1803. Chafing under the Federalist party's domination of the statehouse, he won election in 1805 to Congress, where he served in the House of Representatives from 4 March 1805 through 3 March 1809. He did not stand for reelection in 1808 because the governor of Massachusetts persuaded him to accept an appointment as sheriff of Kennebec County. A combination of circumstances—disputes among inhabitants over land titles, corruption in the sheriff's office, and a breakdown in governmental authority—had reduced Kennebec County to a state of lawlessness that exceeded what was normal for a frontier community. Chandler moved energetically to restore law and order, at one point employing armed force to prevent a riot. He resigned as sheriff in 1812 as war approached.

When war was declared in June 1812, Chandler was a major general in the Massachusetts militia. He resigned to accept a commission as brigadier general in the U.S. Army, a political appointment that reflected the dearth of experienced military officers in 1812. The troops he commanded fought principally on the Niagara frontier. In May 1813 his brigade helped to capture Fort George, which forced the British to evacuate the other nearby garrisons, Fort Chippewa, Fort Erie, and Queenstown. American forces suffered a major setback on 6 June 1813 at Stoney Creek, where the British army surprised the troops under Chandler and General William Winder. Chandler showed courage under fire, but his forces were outnumbered. He had his horse shot from under him and was injured. Chandler, Winder, and General James Winchester were all captured and imprisoned at Quebec, where they remained until exchanged in April 1814.

The injuries he received at Stoney Creek, from which he never fully recovered, prevented Chandler from returning to active duty until August 1814. Placed then in command of regular army troops in Maine, he helped to devise a plan for defending the exposed port of Portland. In September he was assigned responsibility for defending Portsmouth, New Hampshire. His command at both places was complicated by militia politics, especially in Maine, where the strongly Republican militia insisted on serving under their own elected officers rather than under federal command. Chandler handled these difficulties with skill and diplomacy.

At war's end Chandler returned to Monmouth to resume his political and business pursuits. Like most Maine Republicans, he favored separation of his district from Massachusetts. Reelected to the Massachusetts General Court in 1819, he actively supported statehood for Maine. He attended two separate conventions called to consider the question of separation and was a leader of the convention that met in October 1819 to draw up Maine's constitution. Elected first president of the Maine Senate, he was chosen along with his friend John Holmes to represent Maine in the U.S. Senate after Maine became a state in 1820. Reelected in 1823, he served from 4 June 1820 until 3 March 1829, when he retired, having declined to stand for reelection in 1828.

In the Senate Chandler took a strong interest in the militia and served from the Eighteenth through the Twentieth Congresses as chairman of the Committee on Militia. He worked in that capacity to strengthen the militia and promoted select internal improvements, such as the construction of a military road from the Penobscot River in upper Maine to Houlton on the Canadian border. Otherwise, he opposed internal improvements, especially the ambitious federal internal-improvements program advocated by President John Quincy Adams. A strong supporter of Andrew Jackson, he opposed recharter of the national bank, although he served as a member of the board of directors of its Portland branch in the late 1820s. President Jackson rewarded him with appointment as collector of customs for the ports of Falmouth and Portland, a lucrative post he held from 1829 until 1837, when he declined reappointment. A strong advocate of education, he served for many years as a trustee of Bowdoin College. He died in Augusta.

• The John Chandler Papers at the Boston Public Library have three items of marginal value; the largest collection of Chandler papers, at the Maine Historical Society, Portland, contains some political correspondence and business papers, mostly to do with Chandler's career as sheriff of Kennebec County, and only a few personal and political letters. The William King Papers at the Maine Historical Society contain a few valuable letters between King and Chandler. The only account of Chandler's life is his manuscript autobiography at the Maine Historical Society, published (with corrections and revisions) in *Maine Historical Society Collections* 9:167–206.

CHARLES D. LOWERY

CHANDLER, Julian Alvin Carroll (29 Oct. 1872–31 May 1934), historian and president of the College of William and Mary (1919–1934), was born near Guinea in Caroline County, Virginia, the son of physician Joseph Alsop Chandler and Emuella Josephine White. Raised on a farm, Chandler entered the College of William and Mary intent upon a medical career, but by the time he graduated, in 1891, had decided to teach. He taught English and history at William and Mary while working on his M.A. (1892). He earned his doctorate in history at Johns Hopkins University in 1896.

Chandler served Virginia education in a variety of positions. He was dean of the faculty (1896–1899) and acting president (1899–1900) at the Women's College in Richmond; professor of history and literature (1897–1900) and professor of English (1900–1904) at Richmond College; and dean of the Richmond Academy (1902–1904). He left teaching to become an editor at Silver, Burdett & Co. in New York City (1904–1907) and then returned to Virginia to head the Department of History and Education for the Jamestown Exposition. He next edited the *Virginia Journal of Education* (1907–1909) and taught history at Richmond College (1908–1909). He wrote a number of books during this time, including *Representation in Virginia* (1896) and *The History of Suffrage in Virginia* (1901), and was the coauthor of several additional volumes. The bulk of his historical writing concentrated on school textbooks, but his earliest scholarly writing on the history of electoral representation and voting in Virginia was infused with the spirit of the new scientific, progressive history, which examined the past with an eye toward contemporary social and political reform. In *Representation in Virginia*, for example, he argued that Virginia's constitution provided no basis for representation in the legislature, leaving the matter in the hands of the legislature and thus affording opportunities for fraud in the form of periodic gerrymandering for the aggrandizement of the party in power. He favored reforms to bring about more equitable representation.

Chandler became superintendent of the public schools of Richmond in July 1909. A proponent of progressive educational reform, he initiated an extensive building program, established junior high schools, and pushed for expanded vocational training, business training, and physical education and for higher standards for teachers.

In July 1919 Chandler became president of the College of William and Mary. During the next fifteen years he modernized and greatly expanded the small college. Described by his friend Douglas S. Freeman as "the modern college administrator incarnate," Chandler was a tireless builder and promoter of the school. He worked to raise an endowment, lobbied state officials for increased appropriations, solicited the support of the college's friends, alumni, and such philanthropies as the General Education Board to fund his plans, and persuaded John D. Rockefeller, Jr., to include college buildings in the plans to restore Colonial Williamsburg. He also added extension classes in Richmond, Petersburg, Norfolk, and Newport News.

Chandler's expansive plans for both the Richmond schools and the College of William and Mary sparked opposition from teachers, politicians, and others who were concerned about the costs of his changes, their effect on academic standards, and the heavy-handed nature of his administration. A politically astute administrator, however, he was urged by some but did not run for governor in 1928 as the successor to Harry F. Byrd, who supported Chandler's plans for William and Mary. Shortly before Chandler died, a state audit was highly critical of his handling of the school's finances, finding that the school was in debt because recent expansion had far exceeded available resources. Subsequent presidents resolved the financial difficulties through financial retrenchment and a reduction in extension work.

Chandler was married in July 1897 to Lenore Burten Duke of Churchland, Virginia. They had four children, one of whom, Alvin D. Chandler, also served as president of the College of William and Mary (1951–1960). Chandler died in Protestant Hospital in Norfolk after a long illness.

• The University Archives at the College of William and Mary in Williamsburg, Virginia, contain the Julian Alvin Carroll Chandler Papers, his President's Office Papers (1919–1934), and the Columbia University Oral History Tapes (1930), which contain an interview with Chandler.

Both the General Education Board records and the Rockefeller Family Archives at the Rockefeller Archive Center in North Tarrytown, New York, contain material on Chandler's promotional and fundraising efforts on behalf of the College of William and Mary. Besides those mentioned above, Chandler published several books on Virginia and U.S. history. Biographical sketches of Chandler appear in *Virginia Biography* (1924), pp. 629–30, and Marshall Wingfield, *A History of Caroline County, Virginia* (1924; repr. 1975); pp. 148–50. The *William and Mary Quarterly Historical Magazine*, 2d ser., 14, no. 4 (Oct. 1934), includes the tribute by Douglas S. Freeman, "This Dreamer Cometh," and a biographical sketch. More substantive accounts of his life are by Solomon R. Butler and Charles D. Walters, *The Life of Dr. Julian Alvin Carroll Chandler and His Influence on Education in Virginia* (1973), which is based in part upon Butler's unpublished 209-page manuscript, "The Life of Dr. Julian Alvin Carroll Chandler and His Influence on Education in Virginia" (1961), located in the University Archives at the College of William and Mary; and John M. Craig and Timothy H. Silver, "'Tolerance of the Intolerant': J.A.C. Chandler and the Ku Klux Klan at William and Mary," *South Atlantic Quarterly* 84, no. 2 (Spring 1985): 213–22. Obituaries appeared on 1 June 1934 in the major Virginia newspapers as well as the *Washington Post*.

KENNETH W. ROSE

CHANDLER, Lucinda (1 Apr. 1828–9 Mar. 1911), social reformer and feminist, was born Lucinda Banister in Potsdam, New York, the daughter of Silas Banister and Eliza Smith. She attended St. Lawrence Academy until age thirteen, when she was forced to withdraw because of a spinal injury she had received as an infant. This injury was to cause Chandler recurring invalidism but never impeded her feminist efforts. She married John Chandler of Potsdam in 1858 and had one child.

Chandler participated in the post–Civil War reconstruction of American society that feminists attempted through communal efforts, control of sexual behavior, and the reform of marriage laws. A devout evangelical Christian, she did not believe that a parent could leave a child's salvation to the church. For her divergence, she earned the label "feminist spiritualist reformer." Chandler believed that women must achieve the right to govern themselves and their children through their spiritual role as mothers in order to thwart the social evils that resulted from a society based on male dominance and female subservience. She considered marriage a spiritual union that was hampered by the male sex drive. She wanted women to have control of their bodies, but unlike proponents of birth control, such as Mary Gove Nichols, who endorsed the use of contraception, Chandler believed that women were obliged to control their sexuality by resisting male sexual desire.

Later, Chandler supported dress reform by discouraging women from wearing clothes that emphasized their gender and enticed men. Since a woman's sexual abstinence would lead to the purification of both parents, she argued, children could then be raised with an understanding of marriage as a spiritual union, a microcosm of a planned world based on respectful cooperation, rather than as an institution that served the interests of men and capitalism. Chandler's booklet *Motherhood: Its Power over Human Destiny* (1870) received the approbation of society women in Vineland, New Jersey, the home of a number of active female reformers. Its influence spread. The booklet was serialized in 1871 in *Woodhull and Claflin's Weekly*, a radical feminist journal devoted to women's rights, organized labor, spiritualism, and free love, and established Chandler's as a decisive voice of moral education.

Chandler gained notoriety lecturing on parenthood and the elevation of moral standards to intellectual women of Boston. She delivered her lectures in parlor meetings in the style of Margaret Fuller. In 1871 Chandler was a founding member of the Boston Moral Education Society, which emphasized the prevention of moral decay through education and child rearing. It also supplied women with a space in which they could discuss marriage, sex, and birth control without the censorious gaze of men. In 1872 the Boston Moral Science Committee commissioned Chandler to lecture in Philadelphia and Chicago on the need for women to enlighten themselves on matters of marriage, maternity, and sexual relations. Chandler declared the need for sex education in high schools for girls so that they had full knowledge of their maternal role. She went on to help establish moral education societies in New York, Philadelphia, and in Washington, D.C., the branch that started *Alpha*, which became the official journal of the societies. Chandler wrote on moral education for almost every major feminist periodical including *Revolution*, in which she published both "Marital Equality" (1871) and "Motherhood and Its Duties" (1871).

Having contributed to feminism in the specific area of moral education, in 1873 Chandler was ready to join forces with other prominent feminists in the national feminist movement. She attended the meetings of the Association for the Advancement of Women, then became a member of the National Woman Suffrage Association in order to formulate a new contract for sexual relations between husband and wife. Like the suffragists, Chandler believed in equality of the sexes but an equality based on a specific distribution of roles. Meaningful social reform required that women's roles as mothers had to be recognized as equivalent to roles dominated by men. Like Elizabeth Cady Stanton, Chandler advocated a woman's right to her own property and equal access to education, and she believed that the government should legislate and enforce equity between men and women. At the first Woman's Congress of 1873 Chandler delivered her essay "Enlightened Motherhood—How Attainable," in which she insisted that a woman needed access to all the opportunities for education granted to men in order to raise children to the best of her ability. In her "Woman's Sphere of Motherhood" in *Woman's Journal* (1873), Chandler argued for women's right to legal ownership of property. She lobbied in Washington for the repeal of the law of coverture (which placed a married woman under the cover, protection, and authority of her husband) so that women would have the right to protect themselves and their children from abuses. In 1877 Chandler was appointed vice president of the National Woman Suffrage Association.

Chandler's early work focused on the relations between men and women, and she conceived of personal and marital reform as a means of changing society. By 1880 she went still further. That year she analyzed the U.S. Constitution and turned her attention to economic, land, and industrial reform. She wanted a cooperative system to replace capitalist individualism. Since she believed that it was within women's power as mothers to affect social change, she proposed that women be educated in government and economic reform. Children, she argued, should learn to appreciate natural resources more than private property. As a founding member of Chicago's first Margaret Fuller Society, Chandler lectured on the nationalization of railroads, highways, and communications. In 1882 she became the first president of the Chicago Moral Education Society and was vice president of the Woman's Christian Temperance Alliance of Illinois. Chandler advocated total abstinence and, as a Christian socialist, believed that religious tenets should be the guiding force in decisions made in the private and public spheres. In 1888 Chandler was considered as a candidate for editorship of *Lucifer*, a journal of sexual radicalism. She died in Chicago, Illinois.

Chandler was known among social reformers as inexhaustible in her fight for a woman's right to equal access to the educational and business opportunities in the world. In addition to her active participation in organizations for the moral education of America, through her writings she contributed an invaluable archive on the debates about birth control and the rationalization of sexual desire.

• For Chandler's role in the first Margaret Fuller Society of Chicago, see its *Proceedings*, 1880–1881, at the Schlesinger Library, Radcliffe College, which also holds the papers and letters of the first Woman's Congress of 1873. See also Lucinda Chandler, "The Margaret Fuller Society," *Inter-Ocean*, 18 Oct. 1880. Chandler is quoted in Linda Gordon, *Woman's Body, Woman's Right* (1976). A portrait of Chandler is included in Frances E. Willard and Mary A. Livermore, eds., *A Woman of the Century* (1893; repr., 1967). William Leach offers a thorough description of Chandler's accomplishments in *True Love and Perfect Union: The Feminist Reform of Sex and Society* (1980). In *Purity Crusade* (1973) David J. Pivar mentions Chandler's contribution to moral education in the 1870s. An obituary is in the *Chicago Tribune*, 16 Mar. 1911.

BARBARA L. CICCARELLI

CHANDLER, Raymond Thornton (23 July 1888–26 Mar. 1959), detective novelist, was born in Chicago, Illinois, the son of Maurice Benjamin Chandler, a railroad engineer, and Florence Dart Thornton. Chandler lived in Nebraska until age seven, when his father disappeared. His mother took him to live with her Irish relations outside London. After an exceptional public school education at Dulwich College, Chandler took civil service exams. Among 600 candidates, he placed first in classics and third overall. His reward, a clerkship in the British Admiralty, did not agree with him, and he took up poetry writing and book reviewing for small journals. A die-hard romantic, he disparaged realism and was apparently unaware of avant-garde writing.

In 1912 Chandler returned to the United States. Befriended by a Los Angeles family, Chandler discovered Theosophy, writers, musicians, and the strikingly bohemian Cissy Pascal, ex-wife of West Indian pianist Julian Pascal. In 1917 Chandler enlisted in the Canadian army and saw dramatic action in World War I. A German artillery barrage killed everyone in his unit except Chandler, who received only a concussion. He was decorated and promoted.

Discharged in 1919, Chandler attempted to start a literary career in Los Angeles but ended up working for Dabney Oil Syndicate. His interest in Cissy Pascal was rekindled; she divorced in 1920, but Chandler did not marry her until after his mother died in 1924. Cissy was seventeen years his senior, but this union became the central fact of his life. Rising quickly at Dabney Oil, he became accountant, office manager, and general factotum, earning $1,000 a month and commanding two cars despite the depression. Initially he ran a superb operation, but later he became depressed, womanizing and drinking excessively, until he was fired in 1932.

"Wandering up and down the Pacific Coast in an automobile," he wrote about the period following his dismissal from Dabney, "I began to read pulp magazines, because they were cheap enough to throw away. . . . This was in the great days of the *Black Mask* . . . and it struck me that some of the writing was pretty forceful and honest" (*Selected Letters*, p. 236). Always an exceptional student, Chandler enrolled in a correspondence course, then spent five months perfecting "Blackmailers Don't Shoot," his first story, which he sold to *Black Mask* in 1933.

Over the next four years, Chandler published fifteen stories in *Black Mask* and *Dime Detective*. His first detective was named Mallory, and although he experimented with other names before arriving at Philip Marlowe, the chivalric template remained. Blackmail and kidnapping were his preferred crimes, usually set against a romantic triangle in which one woman manipulates two men. Though he combined the plots of his stories for novels, in dialogue and characterization Chandler was always highly original. The crackling repartee of Philip Marlowe and his opponents was a major influence on film dialogue and popular speech in the 1930s and 1940s.

In 1938 Chandler began *The Big Sleep*, a novel using the oil industry as background. Knopf published the book in 1939 in its prestigious Borzoi line. Despite this success, Chandler was hesitant to begin another novel. He started *Farewell, My Lovely* but stopped to write *The Lady in the Lake*, interrupting this work to rewrite *Farewell* twice. Published in August 1940, *Farewell, My Lovely* had excellent reviews but disappointing sales. "I think *Farewell, My Lovely* is the top," he later wrote, "I shall never again achieve quite the same combination of ingredients" (*Selected Letters*, p. 192). Besides presenting grotesque characters like Moose Malloy and Second Planting, the novel epitomized Chandler's metaphoric brilliance. In one scene, Malloy looks "about as inconspicuous as a tarantula on a slice of angel food."

The High Window appeared in 1942 and was sold to Hollywood, as was *Farewell*, inaugurating Chandler's film career. He worked as a screenwriter with Billy Wilder on *Double Indemnity*, with Frank Partos on *And Now Tomorrow*, with Hagar Wilde on *The Unseen*, and with John Houseman on *The Blue Dahlia*. Of his own work, Chandler scripted only part of *The Lady in the Lake* (1943), though he consulted with Howard Hawks on *The Big Sleep*. Problems with alcohol and women reemerged during this period, but Chandler also wrote a celebrated essay "The Simple Art of Murder" (1944).

By 1946 Chandler had earned enough to leave scriptwriting and Los Angeles, buying his first and only home, outside San Diego overlooking the ocean. There he dedicated himself to writing, to a daily round of chores, and to caring for Cissy, now an invalid. Despite medical problems of his own, including shingles and an eczema so severe that he had to wear gloves to type, Chandler produced a novel about Hollywood, *The Little Sister* (1949); wrote articles for the *Atlantic Monthly*; and collaborated with Alfred Hitchcock on *Strangers on a Train*.

In 1950 and 1951 Chandler worked on a new book, but Philip Marlowe bored him. When his own agents rejected the manuscript, Chandler revised it but refused to produce the old Marlowe. "There is no doubt that Chandler intended to put all of himself into [the book]," his biographer remarked. "He knew it was his last chance to do so" (MacShane, p. 197). *The Long Goodbye* (1953) was a landmark, introducing a conscience-driven detective and making social criticism part of the genre.

After a long illness, Cissy died in 1954, and Chandler grew depressed and resumed drinking. Thinking to begin a new life, he went to England in 1955. The trip reacquainted him with his origins, but Chandler was unable to acclimate. He traveled back and forth between England and California in 1955–1956, finally staying in Palm Springs to finish a lesser work, *Playback* (1958). Though he wanted to return to England, tax problems prevented him from doing so.

Chandler spent his last days in San Diego. He died at the Scrippts Clinic of pneumonia brought on by alcoholism and a cold. "I do not see who can succeed Raymond Chandler," wrote Somerset Maugham. He saved the detective genre after Dashiell Hammett from descending again into the popular slough, and he made social criticism a major function of the form. Through his language, Chandler summoned up a host of allusions that gave his work a thematic resonance out of proportion to its structural integrity. This language provided what he thought most important in writing, "a quality of redemption."

• The largest collections of Chandler's manuscripts, screenplays, and letters are those of Helga Greene, his heir and executrix, and the Department of Special Collections, Research Library, University of California, Los Angeles. Much of this material is reprinted in *The Notebooks of Raymond Chandler and English Summer: A Gothic Romance* (1976), *Raymond Chandler Speaking* (1977), and *Selected Letters of Raymond Chandler* (1981). For his English apprentice work, see *Chandler before Marlowe: Raymond Chandler's Early Prose and Poetry* (1973). The principal collections of Chandler's short stories are *Five Murderers* (1944), *Five Sinister Characters* (1945), *Finger Man and Other Stories* (1946), *The Simple Art of Murder* (1950), *Pickup on Noon Street* (1952), and *Killer in the Rain* (1964). The only screenplay published is *The Blue Dahlia* (1974). The major biography of Chandler is Frank MacShane's *The Life of Raymond Chandler* (1976), although Philip Durham's earlier *Down These Mean Streets a Man Must Go: Raymond Chandler's Knight* (1963) and Gavin Lambert's *The Dangerous Edge* (1976) contain biographic sections. Matthew J. Bruccoli, *Raymond Chandler: A Descriptive Bibliography* (1979), is the major reference work, but Robert E. Skinner, *The Hard-Boiled Explicator* (1985), also is valuable. Book-length studies of Chandler's oeuvre include Jerry Speir, *Raymond Chandler* (1981), William Marling, *Raymond Chandler* (1986), and Peter Wolfe, *Something More Than Night: The Case of Raymond Chandler*, ed. Miriam Gross (1977), while David Madden, *Tough Guy Writers of the Thirties* (1968), contains several key essays. Among specialized studies Keith Newlin's *Hardboiled Burlesque: Raymond Chandler's Comic Style* (1984), Stephen Pendo's *Raymond Chandler on Screen* (1976), and Dennis Porter's *The Pursuit of Crime: Art and Ideology in Detective Fiction* (1981) are notable.

WILLIAM MARLING

CHANDLER, Seth Carlo, Jr. (16 Sept. 1846–31 Dec. 1913), astronomer, geodesist, and actuary, was born in Boston, Massachusetts, the son of Seth Carlo Chandler, Sr., a businessman, and Mary Cheever. Chandler attended the English High School at Boston, graduating in 1861. During his last year in high school he became associated with Benjamin Pierce of the Harvard College Observatory, for whom he performed mathematical computations. Upon graduating, he became a private assistant to Benjamin Apthorp Gould, one of the best-known American astronomers of that time. Gould was assisting the U.S. Coast Survey develop improved procedures for the determination of astronomic longitude, and in 1864 Chandler joined the survey as an aide.

In 1866 Chandler was assigned to an astronomic survey party, which he served as an observer and performed computations. He participated in a historic determination of the astronomic longitude at Calais, Maine, in which the new transatlantic cable was used to relate the local clock to the master clock at the Royal Greenwich Observatory in England. His party also traveled by ship to New Orleans to make longitude determinations, again using telegraph signals to synchronize the local clock with the Coast Survey's master clock. It was an exciting period in geodetic astronomy, and young Chandler had the opportunity to learn the latest computational techniques, develop his observational skills, and acquaint himself with state-of-the-art instrumentation.

When Chandler fell in love with Carrie Margaret Herman, he decided to leave the Coast Survey and accept a position in New York City as an actuary with the Continental Life Insurance Company. He married Carrie Herman in October 1870; they would eventually have seven daughters. Chandler corresponded regularly with his old mentor B. A. Gould, who had moved to Argentina to establish the Cordoba Observatory. With Gould's encouragement, Chandler published his first technical paper, on the development of an analytical expression for computing a person's life expectancy from his current age, an alternate method to using actuarial tables.

Even though he was employed as an actuary, Chandler continued his interest in geodetic astronomy, designing an instrument that he called an Almucantar for determining astronomic latitude. The Almucantar had a telescope very much like the zenith telescope that Chandler had used during his work at the Coast Survey, but it was mounted with a mercury flotation bearing, making it self-leveling. Chandler's goal was to eliminate the costly and troublesome level vials that had to be read before and after every observation on a star.

In 1876 Chandler moved his family to Boston, where he continued his actuarial work as a consultant to the Union Mutual Life Insurance Company of Boston. He contracted for the construction of a 25 mm aperture Almucantar and performed a series of test observations from which he concluded that the mercury bearing worked well. Well enough, in fact, that he ordered the construction of a 75 mm aperture instrument.

In 1880 Chandler renewed his association with the Harvard College Observatory and in 1881 moved into a newly built house in Cambridge, within a short walking distance of the observatory. When his new Almucantar was completed, he mounted it on a pier near the main telescope dome and in 1885 made a series of latitude determinations. He reduced the observations and published a very detailed account of the work in a special report, "The Almucantar," published by Harvard Observatory in 1887. Chandler pointed out an apparent variation in the observed latitude for which he could find no explanation but stopped short of claiming to have detected "variation of latitude," that is, the complex wobble of the earth on its axis of rotation now known as polar motion. Five years later when the German astronomer Friedrich Kustler published a paper in which he claimed to have detected a change in the latitude of the Berlin observatory during 1885, Chandler reexamined his observations and those of several other observatories and announced the discovery of a fourteen-month oscillation of the pole. This paper was followed by two dozen more in which Chandler correctly identified an annual variation that beats with the fourteen-month component to cause the path of the pole to spiral outward and then inward approximately every six years, semiannual polar motion, secular polar motion, and nearly every other facet of polar motion known today.

Chandler's interests were much broader than polar motion, and he made substantial contributions to diverse areas of astronomy such as cataloging and monitoring variable stars, the independent discovery of the nova T Coronae, improving the estimate of the constant of aberration, and computing the orbital parameters of nearly every minor planet and comet detected. Chandler argued strongly that skilled observers were critical to the collection of astronomical observations, and ultimately his criticism of flaws in a Harvard star catalog led in 1894 to a public dispute with Edward Charles Pickering, then director of the Harvard Observatory. By 1904 Chandler's association with the observatory ended, but he continued his observations with a telescope mounted in a cupola atop the roof of his own home. It was also from his home that he carried on the duties of associate editor of the *Astronomical Journal* while Gould was editor, and later as editor after Gould's death. He used his own funds to help continue to publish the journal during difficult financial periods. In 1909 he turned the editorship over to Lewis Boss but continued to serve as an associate editor.

In 1904 the Chandlers moved to a new home in the small town of Wellesley Hills, today a residential suburb of Boston, where he died. Chandler was best known for his discovery of the variation of latitude. His achievements were well recognized by his contemporaries, as documented by the many prestigious awards that he received: honorary doctor of law degree, DePauw University; recipient of the Gold Medal and Foreign Associate of the Royal Astronomical Society of London; life member of the Astronomische Gesellschaft; recipient of the Watson Medal and Fellow, American Association for the Advancement of Science; and Fellow, American Academy of Arts and Sciences.

• An extensive collection of Chandler's private and professional correspondence has been assembled and is available on microfilm from the American Institute of Physics, Center for History of Physics, New York City. Chandler was an active member of the amateur astronomy community, and his earliest articles, which often included detailed instructions for making various types of observations, were published in *Science Observer* during the period 1877 to 1882. During the period 1882 to 1885 he published a series of papers dealing with comets, variable stars, and fundamental star catalogs in the German journal *Astronomische Nachrichten*. Beginning in 1886 Chandler published predominantly in the *Astronomical Journal*, where, as associate editor and then editor, he did not hesitate to include very pointed responses to his detractors in the next installment of his latest scientific findings. By the time he retired in 1904, he had published some 150 articles in the *Astronomical Journal*. For more complete biographies of Chandler, see W. E. Carter, "Seth Carlo Chandler, Jr.: Discoveries in Polar Motion," *Transactions of the American Geophysical Union* 68 (23 June 1987): 603–5, and W. E. Carter and M. S. Carter, "Seth Carlo Chandler, Jr.," National Academy of Sciences, *Biographical Memoirs* 66 (1995), which includes an extensive bibliography of Chandler's works. Obituaries are in Astronomical Society of the Pacific, *Publications* 26 (1914): 39–41, and *Astronomical Journal* 28 (July 1913–Jan. 1915): 101–2.

W. E. CARTER

CHANDLER, William Eaton (28 Dec. 1835–30 Nov. 1917), lawyer, politician, and secretary of the navy, was born at Concord, New Hampshire, the son of Nathan Chandler, a prosperous innkeeper and owner of a stagecoach line, and Mary Ann Tucker. A product of local academies and common schools, he studied law privately until admitted to Harvard Law School, from which he graduated in 1854. Admitted to the bar the next year, he returned to Concord and went into private practice. Helping establish the Republican party in the state, he became a member of its controlling clique. Henceforth, politics became Chandler's greatest delight in life, as he became Republican State Committee secretary from 1858 to 1859 and then was elected to the state assembly, over which he presided as Speaker from 1863 to 1864. He ensured legislative support for the national programs of the administration of President Abraham Lincoln (including emancipation, prosecution of the war, and suppression of dissent), and his loyalty to Lincoln's reelection campaign led to his appointment as solicitor and judge advocate general of the Navy Department on 9 March 1865. Andrew Johnson continued Chandler's federal appointments as assistant secretary of the Treasury, a position he occupied until 1867. Certainly two marriages contributed to his political career, the first in 1859 to Ann Caroline Gilmore, daughter of the New Hampshire governor Joseph Albree Gilmore, and three years after Ann's death in 1871 to Lucy Lambert Hale, daughter of U.S. senator John P. Hale.

As secretary of the Republican National Committee, Chandler was in practical command of the party forces that placed Ulysses S. Grant in the White House. Witness to the ineptitude of that president, Chandler devoted his principal attention to private business as Washington lobbyist for various western railroads, shipping interests, the Atlantic Cable Company, and the Plate Iron Manufacturers Association, for example. As part of inner Washington political circles, he was too busy to practice law. He remained attentive to New Hampshire as well as national politics and participated in that state's constitutional convention in 1876. He acquired control of the Republican Press Association (the party's communications device) and, in terms of issues, stood squarely against corrupt government and for black political equality in the reconstructed South. He became campaign manager for candidate James G. Blaine, declined further service as national party secretary that year, but remained a loyal stalwart Republican.

In the 1876 presidential contest, Chandler proved an adroit manager of the pivotal Florida electors in the disputed victory of Rutherford B. Hayes. He was instrumental in swinging the Florida electoral vote into the Hayes column. Notwithstanding his subsequent disenchantment with the new president's southern policy (which abandoned black suffrage and citizenship enforced by federal law), Chandler always regarded his contribution to the defeat of Democrat Samuel Tilden as his greatest service to the nation. Preferring manipulation behind the scenes to high public office, Chandler's party loyalty won him nomination as solicitor general by President James A. Garfield on 23 March 1881. He failed to receive Senate confirmation because of opposition from southern senators, the independent press, and even some conservative members of his own party over Chandler's role and image in partisan politics. He was more successful a year later, when President Chester Arthur chose him to succeed William H. Hunt as secretary of the navy. Taking office on 17 April 1882, Chandler was still termed a "hack politician" by enemies in both parties.

Chandler's stewardship of the navy proved equally controversial. Appearing at a pivotal moment in the naval renaissance of the period, he presided over initial steps in transforming a wooden, sail-powered collection of obsolete vessels into a new fleet of steel and steam warships. One of a series of influential late nineteenth-century secretaries in that regard, Chandler's tenure was marked by stormy government-contractor relations, continuing political control of the shore establishment, and imprecise technical and policy directions. More fundamental reforms still lay in the future, but Chandler's aggressive pursuit of his duties indicated a determination to apply civil control over the navy and executive rather than congressional direction to naval reconstruction programs.

Nothing so appropriately captured the spirit of the Chandler period than the first controversial steel warships, popularly called the "ABCD" cruisers. Small, under-gunned, and unarmored in comparison with some European vessels, the *Chicago, Boston, Atlanta,* and *Dolphin* formed a nucleus for a new navy. Chandler proclaimed them experimental, yet they reflected a tentative marriage between the navy and domestic steel and shipbuilding industries. They evolved from nothing more complex than a congressional mandate to limit repair outlays for old wooden hulks by moving to new construction technologies. Chandler's approach was to bypass barnacled old navy bureaucrats, create a technical advisory board, and negotiate the ABCDs with industrialists ill prepared for new directions and skeptical of government contracts. A bidding war between private Delaware River contractors led to the questionable award of all four vessels to Chandler's political crony John Roach of Chester, Pennsylvania. A "contract scandal" ensued, and the propriety, ethics, and award procedures of the Roach contract might still seem questionable. The contract supposedly saved the government money, though only the *Dolphin* reached the water during Chandler's term. It then suffered engine breakdowns, a cracked propellor shaft, and other maladies indicative of maritime technology of the age. The plans for the other ships drew like criticism for inadequate motive power (half sail, half steam), their classification as unarmored or protected cruisers, and eventual cost overruns.

Still, Chandler's cruisers provided a first step in modernization. They stimulated development of high-velocity, breech-loading, rifled naval ordnance and the naval-industrial linkage so necessary for modern warfare. Inspirational to younger naval officers and an enthusiastic public alike, these warships literally symbolized the dawn of a new period in U.S. naval power. While his politician's instincts caused him to duck navy yard reform, Chandler's internal administration of the department showed a progressive intent to streamline organization to support the new fleet. Foremost among his accomplishments was the establishment in 1884 of the Naval War College at Newport, Rhode Island, which, under the able leadership of Rear Admiral Stephen B. Luce and Captain Alfred Thayer Mahan, received the mission of training high-ranking officers in strategic planning, national security policy making, and other intellectual underpinnings necessary for naval service in the future. Chandler also established a second advisory board (patterned after that of his predecessor) for advice on fleet construction and development and displayed a willingness to revolutionize the process whereby the U.S. Navy could begin to rise from its "dark ages" after the Civil War.

Chandler's naval service terminated with the inauguration of Democrat Grover Cleveland in 1885. He returned to his Concord law practice until elected to the U.S. Senate, serving there from 1887 to 1901. Among the causes he espoused in that body were freedom of the ballot in the South, the immigration station at Ellis Island, and continued fleet modernization (although sometimes at odds with his own party's advocacy of battleships rather than lighter and less costly cruisers). He also advocated bimetallism, the war of 1898 with Spain to free Cuba, and development of government-owned armaments plants to offset price gouging by the private steel industry. Defeated by railroad interests in New Hampshire, he retired from the Senate but not from public life. President William McKinley appointed him almost immediately to the Spanish Treaty Claims Commission, on which he remained until 1907. This body deliberated over $65 million in claims by U.S. citizens resulting from Spanish responsibility in the Cuban insurrection and the Spanish-American War. Problems of law and equity and access to Spanish records prolonged the activity, yet Chandler regarded his tenure as among the most leisurely and intellectually stimulating of his life. Thereafter Chandler retired to his law practice and some offstage political advising and manipulating but no longer with the power and energy of his early years. He especially fell from grace with party politicians such as Theodore Roosevelt (1858–1919), since the New Hampshire ex-senator hardly reflected the political reformist tendencies now gripping the Republican party. He died in Concord, New Hampshire.

Earning the sobriquet of the "Stormy Petrel of New Hampshire Politics," over the years Chandler's energy and untiring industry on behalf of the Republican party was coupled with a highly assertive nature that denied any association with a particular cause or movement unless he rose to a position of leadership therein. Slight in height and build and often in frail health, he preferred the role of manipulative politician, and while representative of stalwart political loyalty, he also stood with the harbingers of change. Though not a genuine navalist or internationalist, he enthusiastically pursued progressive administrative reform of the U.S. Navy. One of a succession of capable lawyer-politicians who managed the Gilded Age fleet, Chandler combined intelligence with political sagacity, courage to overcome the narrow interests of both civilian political colleagues and entrenched senior naval officers, and a determination to improve efficiency and ability in the professional organization of the sea service. While creating the first U.S. steel warships, a naval war college, and the gradual modernization of naval thinking, he also oversaw the fitful beginnings of a modern military-industrial complex.

• Chandler's papers are in the Library of Congress, his diaries are in the New Hampshire Historical Society, and official naval documents for his tenure are in the National Archives. Pertinent published works include Leon B. Richardson, *William E. Chandler: Republican* (1940); George F. Howe, *Chester A. Arthur: A Quarter-Century of Machine Politics* (1935); Leonard A. Swann, Jr., *John Roach, Maritime Entrepreneur: The Years as Naval Constructor, 1882–1886* (1965); Walter R. Herrick, *The American Naval Revolution* (1966); Herrick's sketch of Chandler in *American Secretaries of the Navy*, ed. Paolo E. Coletta (1980); and Benjamin Franklin Cooling, *Gray Steel and Blue Water Navy: The Formative Years of America's Military-Industrial Complex 1881–1917* (1979).

B. FRANKLIN COOLING

CHANDLER, Winthrop (6 Apr. 1747–29 July 1790), folk artist, was born at Chandler Hill, the family farm located on the town line between Woodstock and Thompson, Connecticut, the son of William Chandler, a farmer and surveyor, and Jemima Bradbury, a descendant of Governor John Winthrop of Massachusetts, for whom he was named.

Nothing is known of Chandler's training as an artist, although a nineteenth-century source indicates that he learned to paint portraits in Boston. This may well be true, for Chandler's name is absent from the Woodstock town records between 1762 and 1770 and he received an important commission to paint portraits of the Reverend Ebenezer Devotion and his wife (both Brookline Historical Society, Brookline, Mass.) shortly after he reappears in the Woodstock records. Since he worked as a carver, gilder, and professional draftsman in addition to being a painter, Chandler presumably received some sort of instruction in all of these areas. The portraits of the Devotions are his earliest-known paintings and are strong characterizations with well-modeled faces. The minister and his wife each hold a book. Behind Devotion is his library. Chandler carefully delineated each book and lettered them so clearly that some of them can be matched to books that still survive. He subsequently painted portraits of the couple's son Ebenezer Devotion, Jr.; his wife Eunice

Huntington, with their daughter; and individual portraits of their sons Ebenezer III, John, and Jonathan.

In 1772 Chandler married Mary Gleason of Dudley, Massachusetts; they had five sons and two daughters. Chandler's main source of income derived from painting houses, but he continued to paint portraits, primarily of relatives and an occasional neighbor. He did not travel seeking commissions but lived most of his life in Woodstock. Early on he suffered financial difficulties that continued throughout his life, and he may have painted some portraits in partial payment of debts. A unique work from the pre–Revolutionary War period is a pine carving of the British coat of arms, which he executed in 1773 for a Loyalist cousin, Gardiner Chandler. Winthrop himself appears not to have taken part in the Revolution, although he evidently favored the American side.

Around 1780 Chandler painted what are generally considered to be his finest portraits: likenesses of his brother Samuel and Samuel's wife Anna Paine (both National Gallery of Art, Washington, D.C.). Like most of his work, they are seated and shown at full length. Anna is seated beside a table in her finest dress, which the artist has meticulously painted. The background is largely dark, but shelves filled with books can clearly be seen, and one book has been faced outward so that its pages, rather than its spine, are shown. The darkness of the background is relieved not only by this book but also by a voluminous blue drapery that frames the composition. The companion portrait of his brother Samuel is an arresting portrayal of a Revolutionary War veteran. He is depicted in uniform, his sword in his right hand and his hat on a table to his left. Through the window in the background at right is a battle scene, presumably an engagement in which the captain took part. The battle is rendered with a grim realism unusual in the eighteenth century and may be construed as a commentary on the brutality of war.

Chandler painted a small number of landscapes. The earliest-known of these is *The Homestead of General Timothy Ruggles* (c. 1770–1775, Worcester Art Museum, Worcester, Mass.). This almost qualifies as a genre painting: the artist has included men and women in bright clothing engaged in conversation and horseback riding; two dogs are shown tracking the scent of a large hare seen disappearing into nearby bushes. This painting is unique among Chandler's landscapes because it was painted on canvas. More common are his over-mantel landscapes, painted on a wood panel for placement above a fireplace. Most of these are fanciful views, but in one instance he painted a reasonably accurate depiction of the battle of Bunker Hill (Museum of Fine Arts, Boston).

In 1785 Chandler moved with his family to Worcester, Massachusetts. It was probably after this move that he painted portraits of himself and his wife (both American Antiquarian Society, Worcester, Mass.). These display the strong modeling and ability to capture character evident in his earlier work, but they are bust-length rather than full-length portraits. The unusually strong, almost harsh lighting indicates that he painted them by candlelight, possibly to demonstrate to potential customers his skill at taking a likeness. No other paintings can be assigned to his years in Worcester, but in 1788 he gilded the courthouse weathervane for a fee of sixteen shillings.

Chandler's wife died in 1789, and he returned to Chandler Hill, where he died the following year. Destitute, he executed a quit-claim deed eight weeks before his death in which he bequeathed all of his property to the selectmen of Thompson in exchange for his medical and funeral expenses. At his death, he was described in this way: "The world was not his enemy, but as is too common, his genius was not matured on the bosom of encouragement. Embarrassment, like strong weeds in a garden of delicate flowers, checked his enthusiasm and disheartened the man" (Little, p. 88).

Despite the obscurity in which he lived and worked, Chandler is considered to be one of the most important artists of New England in the latter part of the eighteenth century. His paintings, although not greatly appreciated during his lifetime, are much appreciated today. The tight but sophisticated modeling seen in his work and the strong, invariably somber characterizations of his portraits continue to be admired.

• Nina Fletcher Little, "Winthrop Chandler, Limner of Windham County, Connecticut," *Art in America* 35 (Apr. 1947): 75–168, is a detailed account of the artist's life and career. The sketch by Little in Jean Lipman and Tom Armstrong, *American Folk Painters of Three Centuries* (1980), is based on her earlier article.

DAVID MESCHUTT

CHANDLER, Zachariah (10 Dec. 1813–1 Nov. 1879), U.S. senator, was born in Bedford, New Hampshire, the son of Samuel Chandler and Margaret Orr, farmers. He was educated in local schools. He farmed briefly, taught school, worked as a clerk, and then in 1833 followed the Erie Canal to Michigan. He settled in Detroit and opened a successful dry goods business. He worked so hard that he sometimes slept on the shop counter at night. He also built profitable toll roads in the area.

In 1844 Chandler married Letitia Grace Douglass of New York; they had one child. Though gruff and quick-tempered, Chandler had an affectionate nature, passionate ideals, and a generous commitment to public causes. In 1851, as a Whig, he won his first bid for public office, becoming mayor of Detroit; in 1852 he lost a race for governor. An early opponent of slavery, Chandler participated in the Underground Railroad, raised money for abolitionists convicted of harboring fugitive slaves, and opposed the extension of slavery into the territories. When the Kansas-Nebraska Act passed in 1854, he helped unite anti-Nebraska Whigs, Democrats, and Free Soilers into a new Republican party. In 1856 he attended the party's first national convention and the following year was elected to the U.S. Senate.

Once in the Senate, Chandler vigorously opposed secession and welcomed a war to save the Union. "Without a little blood-letting this Union will not, in my estimation, be worth a rush," he said in February 1861. Impatient, he spent much of the war prodding Abraham Lincoln and the generals to act. Trusting more in Congress, Chandler in December 1861 proposed creation of the Joint Committee on the Conduct of the War and became a leading member of it. In mid-1862 he attacked George B. McClellan's (1826–1885) competency and nerve in a widely publicized Senate speech. As Radical Republican, he questioned Lincoln's plans for Reconstruction. Chandler wanted to confiscate Confederate property, punish Confederate officeholders, and grant suffrage to the freedmen. Lincoln's assassination shocked him, but he thought Andrew Johnson might be "a better man to finish the work." Johnson's actions soon changed his mind, and he voted for Johnson's impeachment.

From 1861 to 1875 Chandler chaired the influential Committee on Commerce, where he pressed for a system of national banks, hard money, higher tariffs, and federal aid to economic growth. Business interests in Michigan prospered in his committee. A fervent expansionist, Chandler hoped to annex Canada, Santo Domingo, and other lands; he also urged retaliation against Great Britain for actions during the Civil War. The 1874 Democratic landslide removed him from the Senate, but Ulysses S. Grant promptly named him secretary of the interior. Though opponents called him a "spoilsman," he was an honest and effective secretary. He improved efficiency, rooted out abuses in the distribution of government lands and pensions, and worked to reform the Bureau of Indian Affairs.

In 1876 Chandler chaired the Republican National Committee and managed Rutherford B. Hayes's campaign against Samuel J. Tilden. In the electoral crisis that followed, he oversaw the successful effort to swing the disputed states to Hayes, then broke publicly with Hayes over his attempts as president to conciliate the South. In February 1879 Chandler won reelection to the Senate, but he served for only a few months. In one of his last speeches on the Senate floor, he assailed a proposal to grant a government pension to Jefferson F. Davis. He died in Chicago while campaigning for the Republican party. Chandler was one of the wealthiest men in Michigan, and he left an estate worth nearly $2 million, which included bank stocks, timberlands, and large real estate holdings.

A man of bulldog tenacity, Chandler combined successful careers in business and politics. Like others of his generation, he became deeply involved in the fight against slavery and secession, an experience that molded him for life. Chandler possessed courage; out to cheer a Union victory at the first battle of Manassas (First Bull Run), he stood in the road to halt the Union rout. Lacking subtlety, he attacked problems head-on. A founder of the Republican party, Chandler held to its early principles of federal authority, moral force, economic nationalism, and concern for civil rights. He achieved his greatest influence as a Radical Republican who demanded vigorous prosecution of the war, stern punishment for treason, and ongoing protection for the freedmen. That influence waned in the closing years of Reconstruction, as northerners and southerners joined in a reconciliation that came, he believed, at the expense of his ideals.

• Chandler's surviving correspondence is in the Zachariah Chandler Papers in the Library of Congress. There are three biographies: *Zachariah Chandler: An Outline Sketch of His Life and Public Services*, prepared by the *Detroit Post and Tribune* (1880); Wilmer C. Harris, *The Public Life of Zachariah Chandler, 1851–1875* (1917); and the most recent and best, Sister Mary Karl George, *Zachariah Chandler: A Political Biography* (1969). Chandler figures largely in histories of the Civil War and Reconstruction. Older studies, such as T. Harry Williams, *Lincoln and the Radicals* (1941), tended to be critical; later ones, such as Hans Trefousse, *The Radical Republicans: Lincoln's Vanguard for Racial Justice* (1969), have viewed Chandler and the Radicals in a more positive light. An obituary is in the *New York Times*, 2 Nov. 1879.

R. HAL WILLIAMS

CHANDRASEKHAR, Subrahmanyan (19 Oct. 1910–21 Aug. 1995), astrophysicist, was born in Lahore, India, the son of Chandrasekhara Subrahmanya, Ayyar, a civil servant, and Sitalakshmi Balakrishna. Following Hindu tradition as the firstborn son, he took the name of his paternal grandfather; however, he is best known as simply Chandra. The family was highly educated; his father rose to a high position in the Indian railways and was a noted musicologist specializing in the Karnatic music of southern India. His uncle Chandrasekhara Venkata Raman, a physicist, discovered the Raman effect in light scattering and received the 1930 Nobel Prize in physics. Chandra showed a marked aptitude for mathematics and at the age of fifteen entered Presidency College of the University of Madras. There, at the insistence of his father, he pursued an honors degree program in physics and graduated at the top of his class with a B.A. (subsequently awarded an M.A.) in 1930. His outstanding record earned him a Government of Madras Research Scholarship to enable him to study at Trinity College in Cambridge, England. He received his doctorate in 1933 following his studies in Cambridge, which included a year spent at Niels Bohr's Institute for Theoretical Physics in Copenhagen (1932–1933). His dissertation on stellar structure, "Polytropic Distributions," was supervised by Ralph H. Fowler. In 1936 Chandra married Lalitha Doraiswarmy in Tiruchanur, India. They had met while they were both students at Presidency College, and she was a physicist employed in the Bangalore Laboratory of his uncle Sir Chandrasekhara Raman. They had no children.

Upon completing his doctoral work Chandra was a fellow of Trinity College (1933–1937), which included a period spent at Harvard Observatory as a lecturer (1935–1936). He then moved to the University of Chicago, where he served successively as research associate (1937–1938); assistant professor (1938–1941); associate professor (1941–1943); and professor of astronomy (1943–1946). He became a distinguished service professor of theoretical astrophysics (1946–1952) and finally the Morton D. Hull Distinguished Service Professor of Astrophysics (1952–1985). He spent the first twenty-seven years of this time at Yerkes Observatory conducting research in astronomy, while he spent the last thirty-one years on the Chicago campus performing various excursions into theoretical physics. During World War II he worked on the theory of shock waves at the Ballistic Research Laboratories of the U.S. Army at Aberdeen Proving Ground (1943–1945); and he consulted with his Chicago colleagues (notably Enrico Fermi) who were engaged in the Manhattan Project. His wartime service was complicated by security considerations since he did not become a naturalized U.S. citizen until 1953. From 1952 to 1971 he was managing editor of the *Astrophysical Journal*, which he succeeded in raising from a parochial publication of the astronomy department to the national journal of the American Astronomical Society.

Chandra's research began before his departure from India, and one of his greatest discoveries was made on his voyage to England in 1930. He found that a class of stars, technically known as white dwarfs, could by relativistic degeneracy exist only up to a certain limiting mass—the so-called Chandrasekhar mass limit—of about 1.44 solar masses. This proved controversial; his mentor at Cambridge, Sir Arthur Eddington, publicly ridiculed this result after Chandra had presented it at a January 1935 meeting of the Royal Astronomical Society. Although Eddington's conclusion was wrong, his prestige was such that it took astrophysicists almost three decades to accept the validity of Chandra's analysis.

Chandra soon turned to other areas of astronomy and astrophysics, a full account of which would require a lengthy recitation of the history of astrophysics in the twentieth century. As he noted in his biographical account for the Nobel Foundation, his work naturally fell into seven periods, in which he directed his attention to a particular topic. Each of these periods lasted for eight to ten years, during which he wrote a number of research papers; when he had accumulated a sufficient body of knowledge and attained a certain perspective, he summarized his views in a definitive research book. He then regarded the subject as closed and looked for a new area of possible study. The resulting volumes were *An Introduction to the Study of Stellar Structure* (1939); *Principles of Stellar Dynamics* (1942); *Radiative Transfer* (1950); *Plasma Physics* (1960); *Hydrodynamic and Hydromagnetic Stability* (1961); *Ellipsoidal Figures of Equilibrium* (1969); and *The Mathematical Theory of Black Holes* (1983).

Chandra's intense style of working followed a fixed routine. Dressed in a dark suit, a white shirt, and a dark tie, he would be at his desk by 6:00 each morning. He usually worked ten to twelve hours each day, frequently seven days a week, during which virtually everything was sacrificed in his effort to achieve a coherent account of the order, form, and structure of the theory. His approach was one of phenomenal persistence, in which he battered his way through problems no one else could solve. The final product was a highly condensed and logical account of the material that exhibited remarkable ingenuity and insight. However, the account was also lean, sparse, and almost devoid of prose. For example, in the treatise on black holes, his prologue and epilogue together fill less than one page, in which one is simply told that black holes constitute the most perfect macroscopic objects in the universe and that their subsequent description was inexorably mathematical and demanding. Thus Chandra's technical books were difficult reading requiring careful study.

Chandra was much honored in his lifetime. He was elected a fellow of the Royal Society (1944) and a member of the National Academy of Sciences (1955). He also won numerous medals and prizes for his research, including the 1983 Nobel Prize in physics, which he shared with William F. Fowler.

In 1982 Chandra delivered the Centenary Lectures at Trinity College, and these subsequently appeared in his book *Eddington: The Most Distinguished Astrophysicist of His Time* (1983). For his own time the same appellation is applicable to Chandrasekhar himself. He contributed significantly through his publications (ten books and almost 400 papers) and his tutelage (fifty-one doctoral students). However, he was also one of the first people to attack the issues making use of the full apparatus of modern physics. In doing so he transformed a seemingly esoteric field of astronomy into a vigorous and vital area of theoretical physics, and literally he can be regarded as the father of modern astrophysics. In person, Chandra was a slender man of patrician bearing having rather sorrowful dark eyes. He had a perfect upper-class English accent, and, notwithstanding his appearance, he could easily have been mistaken for a very energetic Cambridge don. His relations with colleagues were formal and reserved, although he had a few close friends who perceived his inner warmth. However, he had a great fondness for children; as he admitted, he often had warmer relations with his colleagues' children than with their parents. He possessed a soft-spoken, gentle charm accompanied by an innate orderliness and precision and an unending passion for the search for beauty in nature.

In his later years Chandra's health began to fail; he had a heart attack in December 1974 and heart bypass surgery in the fall of 1976. Following his retirement, he remained active, although his interests tended to shift toward historical and philosophical writings. These include a collection of essays, *Truth and Beauty: Aesthetics and Motivations in Science* (1987), and his last book, *Newton's 'Principia' for the Common Reader* (1995). The latter is a modern reconstruction of Newton's treatise that brings into sharp focus the beauty, clarity, and economy of Newton's methodology. It also reveals much about Chandra's taste in science and his profound admiration for a scientist whom he believed was unsurpassable. In a very real sense this characterization of Newton is equally applicable to

Chandra himself in his chosen field, and the book is a fitting monument to him. Chandra died in the University of Chicago Hospital.

• Chandra's papers are at the University of Chicago Library. An authorized biography is Kameshwar Wali, *Chandra* (1991). Chandra also participated in the preparation of the six-volume *Selected Papers of S. Chandrasekhar* (1989–1990). The volumes, arranged in a topical manner, include expert commentaries and assessments of his work. The titles give a succinct overview of the breadth of his scientific activities: vol. 1, *Stellar Structure and Stellar Atmospheres*; vol. 2, *Radiative Transfer and Negative Ion of Hydrogen*; vol. 3, *Stochastic, Statistical, and Hydromagnetic Problems in Physics and Astronomy*; vol. 4, *Plasma Physics, Hydrodynamic and Hydromagnetic Stability, and Applications of the Tensor-Virial Theorem*; vol. 5, *Relativistic Astrophysics*; and vol. 6, *The Mathematical Theory of Black Holes and of Colliding Plane Waves*. Obituaries are in the *New York Times*, 22 Aug. 1995; *Nature* 377 (12 Oct. 1995): 484; and *Physics Today* 48 (Nov. 1995): 106–8.

JOSEPH D. ZUND

CHANEY, Lon (1 Apr. 1883–26 Aug. 1930), actor, was born Leonidas Chaney in Colorado Springs, Colorado, the son of Frank H. Chaney, a barber, and Emma Alice Kennedy. Chaney dropped out of school before the fifth grade in order to help support his bedridden mother, taking a job as a tour guide at Pike's Peak. In 1895 he began working as a prop boy and scene painter at a local theater in Colorado Springs. In 1901 he joined the stock company owned and managed by his older brother John; he made his acting debut in *The Little Tycoon*. In 1905 Chaney married actress Cleva Creighton, and the couple had a son, Creighton Tull Chaney, who later became an actor under the name Lon Chaney, Jr.

John Chaney sold his share of the theater during the 1905–1906 season, but Lon Chaney remained with the company for another season before moving to Chicago with the hope of becoming a song and dance man in variety musicals. Chaney joined a vaudeville troupe that took him to California, where, sometime in 1909, he joined the company of German comedians Kolb and Dill in San Francisco. Chaney also appeared briefly with the Ferris Hartmann Opera Company. In 1913 Chaney began his film career appearing in one- and two-reel slapstick films, including *Poor Jake's Demise* and *The Sea Urchin* (both 1913). The following year Chaney began a professional relationship with directors Joseph DeGrasse and Ida May Park. Beginning with *The Pipes of Pan* (1914), they made at least sixty films together over the next four years. During these years, influenced by DeGrasse and Park, Chaney began experimenting with the makeup techniques that soon became his trademark. In 1914 Chaney and Creighton divorced, and the next year he married actress Hazel Bennett Hastings, whom he had met while with the Ferris Hartmann Company. The couple had no children.

Chaney's work in film was diverse. In 1915 he became a regular member of Universal's stock company. He appeared in numerous films every year and directed a series of seven western pictures starring J. Warren Kerrigan. Even after Chaney starred in the highly successful *Riddle Gawne* (1918), Universal refused Chaney's request for a raise in salary. Chaney then moved to Adolf Zukor's Paramount–Artcraft studio and in 1919 achieved success as the crippled Frog in *The Miracle Man*. In *Photoplay* (Feb. 1928) Chaney related that the director of the film, George Loane Tucker, had not wanted Chaney for the role but had hoped rather to cast a contortionist. Chaney, however, willing to endure great pain for a role, practiced contortions in a mirror until he convinced Tucker. The scene in the film in which the Frog is cured became a classic.

Appearing in more than 149 films during his career, Chaney is best known for character roles such as the legless criminal Blizzard in *The Penalty* (1920), Quasimodo in *The Hunchback of Notre Dame* (1923), the Phantom in *The Phantom of the Opera* (1925), Echo in *The Unholy Three* (1925), and the title role in *Mr. Wu* (1927). Chaney's use of makeup for these roles was innovative but often painful for the actor. In *Photoplay* (Feb. 1928) Ruth Waterbury wrote that "in this visible suffering Lon was plainly an artist in the exquisite travail of creation. To endure pain for his work brought him strange joy." For the role of Quasimodo, Chaney spent four and a half hours daily putting on his makeup and costume—a twenty-pound hump attached to a leather harness and buckled to breast and leg plates, which held him in a stoop, reducing him from a height of 5′9″ to a mere four feet. Over this he wore medieval clothing. He used layers of cotton and collodion to distort his cheekbones, cigarholder ends in his nostrils, and gutta-percha to achieve his jagged teeth and protruding jaw. In *Phantom of the Opera*, Chaney used wire forced into his nose and eye sockets to create the illusion of a badly scarred face. The egg skin Chaney often used in his eyes to white out his pupils and the putty used in *Hunchback* and for his numerous Oriental roles eventually caused such eye damage that he had to wear glasses. His makeup abilities earned Chaney the title "The Man of a Thousand Faces," and indeed he often played multiple roles in his films. In 1930 he was approached to appear in the talking remake of his 1925 hit *The Unholy Three*. Chaney, who had built his career on creating characters that obscured the man behind them, was reluctant, saying, "When you hear a person talk you begin to know him better. My whole career has been devoted to keeping people from knowing me. It has taken me years to build up a sort of mystery surrounding myself, which is my stock in trade. And I wouldn't sacrifice it by talking" (*New York Times*, 6 July 1930). In addition, Chaney was concerned that the extensive makeup he used inside his mouth would somehow distort his voice. The movie was made with Chaney playing the ventriloquist and his dummy, an old woman, a girl, and a parrot—with none of the voices heard on screen his own natural voice.

Other important roles in Chaney's film career include Blind Pew in *Treasure Island* (1920); Black Mike Silva and Joe Wang in *Outside the Law* (1921); Singapore Joe in *Road to Mandalay* (1926); Sergeant O'Hara in *Tell It to the Marines* (1926), Chaney's favorite starring role and, ironically, one that required no special makeup; Burke in *London after Midnight* (1927); and Tito in *Laugh, Clown, Laugh* (1928). Chaney's popularity was exploited by Paramount during its early years, and his *London after Midnight* boosted the newly formed Metro-Goldwyn-Mayer studio.

Chaney's reluctance for the public to hear his voice revealed a man who preferred an unpublic life and was uncomfortable with his stardom. He gave interviews only when relating to a new role and rarely made personal appearances. Colleagues said he seemed more comfortable with the stagehands than with the other actors, and he proudly remained a member of the backstage unions he had joined as a youngster. He died suddenly of bronchial cancer in Los Angeles soon after finishing *The Unholy Three*.

During the 1920s Chaney was one of the biggest draws at the box office. His talent as an actor and his skill as a makeup artist—enabled him to bring personal and sympathetic realism to the most bizarre and physically distorted characters. The pathos he gave his characters lifted them above the ghoulish monsters in ordinary horror films, causing audiences to respond with sympathy rather than fear. Chaney's characters, no matter how deformed or wretched, broke away from Hollywood stereotypes. His films remain classics of the horror genre. His pantomimic abilities were often attributed to the fact that his parents were deaf-mutes, and he thus learned facial and physical expressiveness at a young age.

Chaney's innovations in the art of theatrical makeup made him a legend. He turned makeup into an art form—a difficult feat in an age in which special film cosmetics had yet to be developed. Chaney demonstrated the possibilities of theatrical makeup, leading the way for other makeup artists and for manufacturers to advance and perfect both the materials and the techniques of makeup for film.

• Robert G. Anderson, *Faces, Forms, Films: The Artistry of Lon Chaney* (1971), and Michael F. Blake, *Lon Chaney: The Man behind the Thousand Faces* (1993), which includes a complete bibliography, are the most informative sources on his life and career. Chaney also appears in DeWitt Bodeen, *From Hollywood: The Careers of Fifteen Great American Stars* (1976), and Carlos Clemens, *An Illustrated History of Horror Film* (1967). Informative articles include Herbert Howe, "A Miracle Man of Make-Up," *Picture Play*, Mar. 1920, pp. 37–39; 96–97; Kathleen Ussher, "Chaney the Chameleon," *Pictures and Picture Goer*, Dec. 1927, pp. 18–21; and DeWitt Bodeen, "Lon Chaney: Man of A Thousand Faces," *Focus on Film*, May/Aug. 1970, pp. 21–39. A rare interview with Chaney appears in *Motion Picture Magazine*, Dec. 1922, pp. 32–33, 110–14, and his contribution to film makeup is discussed in John Baxter, *Stunt* (1973). A complete listing of films in which Chaney appeared or directed can be found in *The International Dictionary of Films and Filmmakers*: vol. 3, *Actors and Actresses* (1985). Obituaries are in the *New York Times*, the *New York Herald Tribune*, and the *Los Angeles Times*, 27 Aug. 1930.

MELISSA VICKERY-BAREFORD

CHANEY, Lon, Jr. (10 Feb. 1906–12 July 1973), actor, was born Creighton Tull Chaney near Oklahoma City, Oklahoma, the son of Lon Chaney and Cleva Creighton, actors. As a child Chaney toured with his parents and at age three joined his father in a circus trapeze act. His parents separated when he was a small child, and he remained with his father, who began working in films in 1912 in Hollywood. Chaney grew up in the film capital and attended Hollywood High School. During his teen years he worked at a variety of jobs, including butcher's boy, fruit picker, and poultry dresser. Since his father did not want him to become an actor, Chaney attended Commercial Experts Training Institute in Los Angeles, where he studied plumbing. At age nineteen he became secretary-treasurer of Los Angeles's General Water Heat Corporation. In 1926 he married Dorothy Hinckley, with whom he had two sons, his only children.

Following the death of Lon Chaney in 1930, Creighton Chaney continued in the business world, but by 1932 he accepted a contract with RKO Radio Pictures, where he made *Bird of Paradise* (1932), *Lucky Devils* (1933), *Scarlet River* (1933), *Son of the Border* (1933), and *Captain Hurricane* (1935), as well as starring in RKO's only serial, *The Last Frontier* (1932). Chaney proved to be an athletic leading man type, and to hone his abilities he attended acting classes. In 1935 he was signed by the producer Ray Kirkwood to star in two dozen feature films over the next three years. He also changed his name to Lon Chaney, Jr. He later said, "I am most proud of the name Lon Chaney, because it was my father's and he was something to be proud of. I am *not* proud of Lon Chaney Jr. because they had to starve me to make me take this name" (quoted in *Films in Review* [Nov. 1973]: 531).

Standing slightly over six feet tall and weighing around 200 pounds, Lon Chaney, Jr., had a physically imposing appearance that often lead to his being cast as villains, and later in the monster roles that brought him stardom. After starring in *The Shadow of Silk Lennox* and *Scream in the Night* in 1935 for Kirkwood, the series terminated. Chaney then began working not only as an actor but also as a stuntman and extra and later claimed he was in more than 400 films in these capacities.

In 1936 Chaney's marriage ended. The next year he wed a former model, Patsy Beck, and signed a player's contract with Twentieth Century-Fox, where in the next two years he had small parts in thirty films. His contract was not renewed in 1939, but that year he landed the plum role of Lennie in the West Coast production of John Steinbeck's *Of Mice and Men*, the part having been played two years earlier on Broadway by Broderick Crawford. Chaney proved to be superb as Lennie, and when the producer Hal Roach purchased the screen rights Chaney re-created the role on celluloid. The actor drew critical acclaim for his work; regarding Chaney's performance, the *New York Herald Tribune* said, "He gives so knowing a characterization of the giant Lennie . . . that you will not forget it for a long time." As a result of the film's success Chaney had hoped to play his father's part of Quasimodo in RKO's remake of *The Hunchback of Notre Dame*, but the role went to Charles Laughton. Nor did plans for Roach to star him in a screen version of John Steinbeck's book *Cup of Gold* materialize. However, he did appear to advantage as a caveman in Roach's *One Million B.C.* (1940).

Universal signed Chaney to a long-term contract in 1941, and he starred in *Man Made Monster*. Next the studio assigned him the title role in *The Wolfman* (1941), a part that required hours of makeup application to turn Chaney into a werewolf. The film, however, proved to be the studio's biggest success of the year and launched Lon Chaney, Jr., as the "King of Horror Films," a title that had been held by his father during the 1920s. For the next five years he played a variety of monsters in box-office successes such as *Ghost of Frankenstein* (1942), *The Mummy's Tomb* (1942), *Frankenstein Meets the Wolf Man* (1943), *Son of Dracula* (1943), *The Mummy's Ghost* (1944), *House of Frankenstein* (1945), *The Mummy's Curse* (1945), and *House of Dracula* (1945), as well as features based on radio's "Inner Sanctum" series: *Calling Dr. Death* (1943), *Weird Woman* (1944), *Dead Man's Eyes* (1944), *The Frozen Ghost* (1945), *The Strange Confession* (1945), and *Pillow of Death* (1945). Chaney almost singlehandedly kept alive the popularity of horror films during the World War II era. In addition, Universal kept him busy in programs like *Too Many Blondes* (1941), *Badlands of Dakota* (1941), *North to the Klondike* (1942), *Eyes of the Underworld* (1943), *Frontier Badmen* (1943), *Cobra Woman* (1944), *Here Come the Coeds* (1945), and *The Daltons Ride Again* (1945), as well as the serials *Riders of Death Valley* (1941) and *Overland Mail* (1942). During his tenure at Universal, Lon Chaney, as he was billed, was one of the studio's movies' top attractions, and his salary reached $2,000 per week.

When Chaney's contract with Universal expired in 1946, he freelanced and returned to the stage, touring in *Born Yesterday*. He also continued in films, becoming a much-sought-after character actor in features like *My Favorite Brunette* (1947), *Only the Valiant* (1951), *High Noon* (1952), *A Lion Is in the Streets* (1953), *Passion* (1954), *Not As a Stranger* (1955), *The Defiant Ones* (1958), and *Welcome to Hard Times* (1967). He continued as a horror headliner in *Abbott and Costello Meet Frankenstein* (1948), *Bride of the Gorilla* (1951), *Manfish* (1956), *The Indestructible Man* (1956), *La Casa Del Terror* (1959), *The Alligator People* (1959), *The Haunted Palace* (1963), *Witchcraft* (1964), *Spider Baby* (1968), and *Dracula vs. Frankenstein* (1971). From 1951 to 1971 Chaney was a frequent guest star on a variety of television programs and was in three series: "Hawkeye and the Last of the Mohicans" (1956–1957), the Swedish-made "13 Demon Street" (1961), and "Pistols 'n' Petticoats" (1967–1968). In addition to acting, Chaney wrote the story on which a biopic of his father called *The Man of a Thousand Faces* (1957) was based, and in later years he worked on an uncompleted pictorial family history, *A Century of Chaneys*, as well as his autobiography and a biography of his father. Chaney's final years were plagued by ill health before he died at his home in San Clemente, California.

Chaney's accomplishments have typically been overlooked by film historians and critics. He created one of the screen's most memorable portrayals, that of Lennie in *Of Mice and Men*, and he became one of filmdom's busiest character actors. But he is best remembered for his horror films and for his ability to make believable and sympathetic the many monsters he portrayed.

• Chaney's personal papers are not available. His brief essay, "My Father—Lon Chaney," is in Forrest J. Ackerman, *Lon of 1000 Faces!* (1983). Chapters on Chaney appear in Calvin Thomas Beck, *Heroes of the Horrors* (1975); Paul Welsh, *The Spine Chillers: Chaney Jr., Cushing, Lee and Price* (1975); John Brosnan, *The Horror People* (1976); Michael R. Pitts, *Horror Film Stars* (1981; rev. ed., 1991); and Gregory William Mank, *The Hollywood Hissables* (1989). An essay on Chaney by Reginald LeBorg, "Lon Chaney, Jr.: A Man Living in a Shadow," is in Danny Peary, *Close-Ups: Intimate Profiles of Movie Stars by Their Co-stars, Directors, Screenwriters, and Friends* (1978). Among articles about Chaney are Nancy Pryor, "Is Lon Chaney's Son Fated to Suffer for Films, Too?," *Movie Classic*, Jan. 1933, pp. 54–55; Ding Scully, "Lon Chaney Jr. Finally Clicks," *Motion Picture*, Jan. 1940, pp. 54, 72, 76; Charles Darnton, "Chaney the Second," *Screenland*, May 1941, pp. 51–52, 79; William Lynch Vallee, "Sentimental Monster," *Silver Screen* 13, no. 9 (July 1943): 42–44, 74–77; Richard Bojarski and John Cocchi, "Son of Chaney," *Castle of Frankenstein* 3 (1963): 20–23, 4 (May 1964): 8–9, 42–45, 6 (1965): 14–27, and 7 (1965): 38–45; Don Sheppard, "Chaney, Champion of Chills," *Mad Monsters* 8 (Summer 1964): 27–33; Ron Haydock, "The Life and Times of Lon Chaney Jr.," *Monster Times* 24 (July 1973): 10–13, 31; James Robert Parish and Michael R. Pitts, "Lon Chaney, Jr., 1906–1973," *Films in Review* 24, no. 9 (Nov. 1973): 529–48; Ron Haydock, "Lon Chaney: Beyond the Wolfman," *Monsters of the Movies* 4 (Dec. 1974): 24–30; Michael R. Pitts, "Lon Chaney Jr.: A Filmography," *Classic Images* 81 (Mar. 1982): 30–33, 82 (Apr. 1982): 22–24, 83 (May 1982): 38–41, and 84 (June 1982): 32–33; and Jack Gourley and Gary Dorst, "Lon Chaney Jr.," *Filmfax* 20 (May 1990): 50–58, 94–95, and 21 (July 1990): 68–77.

MICHAEL R. PITTS

CHANFRAU, Frank (22 Feb. 1824–2 Oct. 1884), actor, was born Francis S. Chanfrau in New York City, the son of a French naval officer who settled in New York as an eating house proprietor, and Mehitable Trenchard. It is not insignificant that Chanfrau grew up in a tenement known as "The Old Tree House" at the corner of the Bowery and Pell Street, for it was Bowery life that inspired one of his greatest stage successes and the Bowery Theatre that launched his professional career.

After a basic education in city schools, Chanfrau headed west in his teens, when his father's business failed, to try to make a living on his own. First a driver on the Ohio Canal, he then learned the ship carpenter's trade in boatyards around the Great Lakes. Before leaving New York, and perhaps for a time upon his return, Chanfrau played minor roles in the amateur theatricals of The Dramatic Institute, a group that rented the Franklin Theatre "where they murdered Shakespeare to poor houses" (Wemyss, p. 172).

The theatrical contacts that Chanfrau made as an amateur thespian together with the carpentry skills he acquired while away from New York combined to secure for him his first professional stage employment, as both a properties assistant and supernumerary at the Bowery Theatre in 1840. He gained attention there for his uncanny ability to imitate in voice, gesture, and facial expression the leading actors of the day, notably Edwin Forrest, Tom Hamblin, and such British touring stars as William Charles Macready and Charles Kean. Hamblin, then manager of the Bowery, recognized Chanfrau's gift and promoted him to "utility man," playing minor parts, but parts in which Chanfrau could freely interpolate his imitations, to the great delight of the Bowery audiences. Accepting engagements at theaters in Buffalo, Detroit, New Orleans, and Boston, Chanfrau worked his way up to larger, but still secondary roles, this phase of his career culminating in his playing Laertes to the Hamlet of James W. Wallack, Jr. at New York's Chatham Theatre on 17 June 1844.

But classical repertory did not make Frank Chanfrau a star. From the time he had worked at the Bowery Theatre, the young actor-cum-stagehand had been a member of the Volunteer Fire Department, attached to Engine No. 15 in the Bowery. At Mitchell's Olympic Theatre he played numerous parts, including Jeremiah Clip in *The Widow's Victim*—a role that gave Chanfrau license to mimic every notable actor in New York. During rehearsal breaks or relaxing in the greenroom at Mitchell's, he would often amuse the company with tales of the "fire b'hoys," replicating the peculiar dialect, slang, mannerisms, and appearance (including hair slicked down into two "soap-locks") of this distinct and distinctive subculture of New York society. These anecdotes and impersonations inspired Benjamin A. Baker, the Olympic's prompter, to write a dramatic sketch especially for Chanfrau, to be presented at a benefit performance for Baker himself. On 15 February 1848, with the premiere of *A Glance at New York*, Mose the Bowery Boy was born, making Chanfrau an immediate star.

So great was Chanfrau's popularity as Mose that a month into the run Baker expanded the sketch into a full-length entertainment and began work on a second "Mose" play. Meanwhile, with two partners Chanfrau had leased the Chatham, renaming it Chanfrau's National Theatre. For a considerable time he appeared nightly as Mose in both theaters, first in Baker's new piece *New York As It Is* at the National, then at a later hour in *A Glance at New York* at Mitchell's.

Mose became a theatrical folk hero, with Chanfrau inextricably linked to the role. He took his Bowery Boy on tour to all the major theatrical cities in the East, both in his original incarnation and in plays written subsequently by Baker and others as a vehicle for Chanfrau as Mose: *The Mysteries and Miseries of New York*, *Three Years and After*, *Mose Married*, and *Mose in California*. Chanfrau's familiarity with the real Bowery fire boys, his keen powers of observation and imitation, and his natural attributes of a handsome, rugged appearance and an excellent voice combined to make Mose an enduring stage success. Chanfrau played Mose steadily in New York and on the road for at least three and a half years after the character's 1848 debut, and Mose remained a staple of Chanfrau's repertory for nearly two decades.

In June 1858 Chanfrau married Henrietta Baker (born Jeannette Davis), already an established actress, when they were both playing at the National Theatre in Cincinnati. Generally Chanfrau and his wife preferred to star in separate plays, though they did appear together in an acclaimed production of *London Assurance*. The Chanfraus had two sons, the elder of whom, Henry, was an actor who recreated some of his father's most popular roles after Chanfrau's death.

As the vogue for the Bowery Boy character was waning, Chanfrau accepted another role in 1865 that kept him at the pinnacle of popularity, the title character in Thomas B. DeWalden's *Sam*, a comic type described in Chanfrau's *New York Times* obituary as "scarcely a specimen of mental activity." Chanfrau could tour Sam even more widely than Mose, since the character had more broad-based appeal, requiring no familiarity with the vagaries of life on the Lower East Side. Both in New York and on tour Chanfrau played Sam 783 times.

But Chanfrau's most widely popular starring turn was yet to come in another role written specifically for him—Kit Redding in *Kit the Arkansas Traveller*, by Edward Spencer and C. W. Tayleure, Chanfrau's own business manager. From its New York premiere at Niblo's Garden on 9 May 1871, until two nights before his death in Jersey City, New Jersey, Chanfrau continuously played this role in every major theatrical center in the country. According to his *Times* obituary, "he never had to seek another play after obtaining 'Kit.'"

The esteem in which the theatrical community held Chanfrau was clear from the luminaries who assembled at his funeral, including not only New Yorkers but also theatrical managers from Philadelphia, Baltimore, Boston, and even Chicago's great entrepreneur, J. H. McVicker. Chanfrau was one of the first true stars of the American popular theater, a star whose fame extended far beyond New York and whose acting powers and versatility were unflagging until his death.

• Two contemporary accounts of Chanfrau, excellent as descriptions and assessments of his work as an actor, but unreliable in their presentation of factual material, are those in Francis Courtney Wemyss, *Theatrical Biography of Eminent Actors and Authors* (n.d.), and Charles Gayler, "Early Struggles of Prominent Actors," *New York Dramatic Mirror* (no date given by editor), both reprinted in William C. Young's *Famous Actors and Actresses of the American Stage: Documents of American Theater History*, vol. 1 (1975), pp. 172–173, and 173–176. Other contemporary accounts with a strong factual content are Joseph Norton Ireland, *Records of the New York Stage* (1866), and T. Allston Brown, *History of the American*

Stage (1870). George C. D. Odell, *Annals of the New York Stage*, vol. 5 (1931), pp. 372–75, describes in detail the circumstances surrounding the production of the first two "Mose" plays, and there are scattered references to Chanfrau and the roles he played in all volumes covering the years of his theatrical career. Chanfrau's obituary in the *New York Times*, 3 Oct. 1884, contains an extensive account of his life, and an article on 6 Oct. 1884 gives a full account of his funeral, including a comprehensive list of the theatrical personalities who attended.

JOHN BUSH JONES

CHANFRAU, Henrietta Baker (1837–21 Sept. 1909), actress, was born Jeannette Davis in Philadelphia, Pennsylvania. Her parents' name are not known, and details about her early years are sketchy. In 1854, under the name Henrietta Baker, she made her debut as a vocalist at the Assembly Buildings in Philadelphia under the management of a Professor Mueller. A few months later, on 19 September, she made her debut as an actress in the role of Miss Apsley in *The Willow Copse* at the City Museum. She then joined the company at the Arch Street Theatre, remaining for the following two seasons. For the 1857–1858 season she performed with the company at the newly formed National Theatre in Cincinnati under the management of Lewis Baker. There she enjoyed great popular success, especially in domestic dramas. While with Baker's company she met Francis S. Chanfrau, an actor acclaimed as "Mose the fire fighter." They were married in 1858, and after her marriage she acted under the name Mrs. Chanfrau.

Performing primarily in Boston, New York, and Philadelphia, Chanfrau played both as a headliner and in supporting roles. Later in 1858 she played Jane Chatterly in *The Widow's Victim* at Wallack's Theatre in New York City. During the 1863–1864 season she played successfully at the Boston Theatre under the management of Wyzeman Marshall. In New York Chanfrau joined brothers Junius, Edwin, and John Wilkes Booth on 25 November 1864 as Portia in the famous production of *Julius Caesar* at the Winter Garden. The next evening she played Ophelia to Edwin Booth's Hamlet. The show ran for one hundred nights—the longest run of the play until that time—and it was dubbed the "hundred nights *Hamlet*." Starting on 16 May 1866 Chanfrau performed with Charles Dillon at Niblo's Garden, and on 5 August 1867 she premiered as Esther Eccles in T. W. Robertson's *Caste* at the Broadway Theatre. According to theater historian George C. Odell, Chanfrau made "an ideal Esther," and the role became one of her standards. Following her triumph at the Broadway Theatre Chanfrau played a successful season at John H. Selwyn's Theatre in Boston. During the 1869 season she appeared in New York with Augustin Daly's company at his newly opened Fifth Avenue Theatre. Chanfrau reprised the role of Esther and played Lady Alice in *Old Heads and Young Hearts*, Countess d'Autreval in *Checkmate*, Mrs. Dorillon in *Wives As They Were*, and Blanche in *The Duke's Motto*. The season closed with *Don Caesar de Bazan*, but Chanfrau was forced to leave after opening night owing to illness. Chanfrau's popularity and success at Daly's, Wallack's, and the Boston theaters made the 1860s the pinnacle of her career. Other popular roles of this period were the title roles in *Dora* and *Christie Johnstone* and Isabel in *East Lynne*.

During the 1870s Chanfrau spent less time as a member of a permanent company, instead playing two- or three-week engagements at various theaters. Her career often took a back seat to that of her more famous husband—historian Gerald Bordman calls her a "fine actress long content to play in her husband's shadow"—and she frequently performed in matinee performances while her husband starred in the evenings. Throughout the 1870s she played at the Court Square Theatre, the Novelty Theatre, the Park Theatre, Booth's Theatre, the Eagle Theatre, and other New York City theaters. Her most popular roles continued to be Esther, Dora, and Christie Johnstone, but she added May Edwards in *The Ticket to Leave Man* and played both Grace Shirley and Josephine in *Parted*.

As her husband became more and more popular, first as Mose and later in roles such as Kit Redding in *Kit*, Chanfrau's star gradually faded. By the late 1870s reviews often referred only to her early success and her inability to maintain it—Odell describes her as "the great favorite of the Sixties." When her husband died in 1884 Chanfrau retired briefly from the stage, but she returned two years later to tour Europe. After returning to the United States she appeared at the Union Square Theatre in New York in *The Scapegoat*. Bordman states that Chanfrau was "not yet fifty and still attractive . . . she had every reason to hope for success." Critics praised Chanfrau's performance, but the play lasted only two weeks, and she "was seen no more on New York Stages." After her retirement Chanfrau purchased the *Long Branch News* and became active as a Christian Science healer in Philadelphia. She died in Burlington, New Jersey.

Called "one of the most natural actresses on the American stage," Chanfrau supported actresses such as Charlotte Cushman and Mrs. John Drew and acted opposite Edwin Forrest, Edwin Booth, William Warren, E. L. Davenport, and Charles Fechter. Chanfrau successfully played the classical roles of Portia and Ophelia, but she was better known for her portrayal of the heroine in domestic dramas. After entering the theater world at a young age, Chanfrau rose to stardom in the 1860s. Even though she did not enjoy such success in her later career, she was always well liked and popular with both audiences and critics.

• The best sources of information on Chanfrau's life and career are T. Allston Browne, *History of the American Stage* (1870); Gerald Bordman, *American Theatre* (1994); Arthur Hornblow, *A History of the Theatre in America* (1965); Eugene Tompkins, *History of the Boston Theatre 1854–1901* (1908); P. Phelps, *Players of a Century* (1880); and George C. Odell, *An-*

nals of the New York Stage, vols. 8–11 (1937–1942). Obituaries are in the *New York Clipper*, 9 Oct. 1909; the *New York Tribune*, 23 Sept. 1909; and *Theatre Magazine*, Nov. 1909.

MELISSA VICKERY-BAREFORD

CHANG (11 May 1811–17 Jan. 1874) and **Eng** (11 May 1811–17 Jan. 1874), Siamese twins, were born in Meklong, Siam (now Thailand), the sons of Ti-eye, a Chinese-born fisherman, and Nok, who was half-Chinese and half-Malay. Chang and Eng were born connected at the chest by an armlike ligament of flesh that, later in their childhood, was pliable enough to allow the brothers to stand side by side. Since no one in the village had seen joined twins before, the brothers were looked upon with horror and suspicion. Some conjectured their birth was a portent of evil or a sign that the apocalypse would soon follow. Although people came from all around Siam to see the brothers, Nok treated the babies like all her other children and, fearing that separation would mean certain death for the twins, dismissed doctors who wanted to experiment with knives or hot wire. Overcoming normal childhood obstacles was doubly hard for Eng and Chang. Perhaps most difficult was learning to get along, as they were of different temperaments, with Chang lordly and volatile and Eng docile and mellow. In 1819 cholera killed their father and five of the twins' seven siblings, and soon after the brothers were forced to work as fishermen and then as merchants to help support the surviving family. Becoming locally famous, Chang and Eng were summoned to appear before King Rama III in 1825, and two years later, at the request of the king, the twins accompanied a diplomatic mission to Cochin China (now Vietnam).

Not long after Eng and Chang's return, Scottish merchant Robert Hunter, who had first met the brothers in 1824 and sensed moneymaking opportunities inherent in exhibiting the twins abroad, enticed Eng and Chang with plans to tour them in the United States and Great Britain. Having secured ship captain Abel Coffin as a business partner, Hunter obtained permission for the trip from both the king and Nok, who was persuaded in part by an assurance that her sons would return within three years. Eng and Chang set sail for the United States on Coffin's ship *Sachem* on 1 April 1829. They never returned.

Chang and Eng arrived in Boston after a 138-day journey during which the twins learned a smattering of English from the crew. Their first appointment in Boston, and in nearly every other city in which they appeared, was with the area's best physician, who poked, prodded, and examined the mysterious band that connected the brothers. Indeed, Coffin teased prospective customers with doctors' reports about the viability of separating them. Medical tests over the years found that Eng and Chang's vital signs were similar; that they were about 5′3½″, with Chang standing about an inch shorter (he wore shoes with lifts); that they moved in unison, no doubt a tendency carved out of necessity; and that, in the opinion of most doctors, separation of the twins would prove fatal to one or both of them, though this did not seem to overly concern Eng and Chang, who, at least in their younger days, insisted they had no desire to be cut apart. After overcoming a dubious public who suspected that they somehow faked their predicament, the Siamese twins were a success in the United States, drawing many who gladly paid fifty cents to see the "most wonderful and extraordinary human curiosities."

In October 1829 Coffin took the twins to Great Britain, where again they appeared before packed houses and to much journalistic fanfare. Most reviews were positive, but one observant reporter pronounced the twins "doomed to pass their lives in a species of slavery." After captivating England, the twins journeyed to Scotland and Ireland but were barred from France because the government feared pregnant women who viewed them would have children that were similarly affected. In March 1831 they returned to New York City.

In May 1832, having become disgusted with Coffin and his wife Susan, who the twins believed were swindling them, Eng and Chang discontinued their contact with the captain (Hunter had sold out to Coffin the year before). They continued to tour on their own for the next few years, becoming more irritable and less popular, probably on account of a shrinking audience who had not seen them already. Eng and Chang apparently sought release from the tensions of constant travel with prostitutes and fine cigars, and Chang earned a reputation as a heavy drinker. Also to ease the drudgery of answering the same questions asked by the audience day after day, Eng and Chang had earlier added games of checkers and some acrobatics to their act. In 1835 the twins exhibited in Cuba; later that year they finally were allowed to go to Paris, which was followed by Belgium and the Netherlands.

During many of their tours of the United States Eng and Chang held long-running engagements at Peale's Museum in New York City, a former art and natural history museum that now featured circus-type acts and other curiosities. There the brothers met James Calloway from Wilkesboro, North Carolina, who convinced them to visit the rural, farming area. They fell in love with its serenity, southern hospitality, and bountiful hunting. In 1839 they built a two-story home complete with slave quarters on a large parcel of land on nearby Trap Hill and, after an unsuccessful attempt to open a retail operation, established themselves as gentlemen farmers. That same year the brothers had obtained U.S. citizenship and a year later took "Bunker" as their surname, probably in honor of some friends named Bunker.

Not long afterward Chang and Eng shocked their rural community when they announced their engagements to Adelaide Yates and her sister Sarah, respectively. Though the twins had always flirted with women, they believed that no "modest girl" would be willing to enter a marriage in which "the pleasures of her bridal bed would be exposed, as ours would have to be" (Wallace, p. 168). Wilkesboro farmers David and Nancy Yates, the sisters' parents, and the neighbors were appalled, no doubt envisioning the "sexual perversion" that would occur in their shared marital bed, but according to Chang and Eng the prejudice was due more to their ethnicity. David Yates finally relented, however, and the two couples were married in April 1843. Since no documentation exists as to their sexual habits, except that an especially wide bed was built for the foursome, one can only speculate on how they conducted their intimate relations. One fact not in doubt is the twins' virility: both women were pregnant within a month, and the two families had twenty-one children between them.

For the next several years the Bunkers prospered as well-to-do farmers, reportedly becoming the first in the region to produce bright-leaf tobacco. In 1845 they bought a larger house near Mount Airy in Surry County to house their growing family and increasing number of slaves. Fervent states' rights supporters, Eng and Chang owned at least twenty-eight blacks between them by the beginning of the Civil War, gaining reputations as hard-driving and sometimes cruel masters. Though active in the White Plains Baptist Church, they were not devout, practicing their own blend of Christianity and Buddhism. As they grew older Eng and Chang fought more often and more violently, and Chang's drinking worsened. As if animosity between the twins was not enough, their wives also began to quarrel, necessitating the 1857 construction of a second house for Chang one mile away. For the rest of their lives the Siamese twins, when in North Carolina, stuck to a strict schedule of three days at one twin's house, three days at the other. Perhaps owing to the growing anger between the two Bunker families, on later trips abroad Chang and Eng seriously sought medical opinions on the feasibility of being separated. No doctor would agree to perform the surgery.

In 1849, finding their finances strained by supporting such a large family, Eng and Chang, with two of their daughters, began an unsuccessful six-week engagement in New York City, and four years later a daughter and a son accompanied them on a yearlong tour of New England. In October 1860, before embarking on a trip to the Far West, including California, the brothers began what was overall an insignificant relationship with P. T. Barnum by appearing for a month at the latter's American Museum on Broadway in New York City. Their only other association with Barnum was when the showman promoted them on an 1868 tour of Great Britain that included Scotland, Ireland, and England.

Fearing for their property after the onset of the Civil War, Eng and Chang abandoned hopes of journeying from California to Siam and returned to North Carolina in 1861. Their anxieties were realized when, after the war, they lost their slaves, who constituted a good part of their estate. Forced again to tour, Eng and Chang left in 1865 for a long eastern and midwestern jaunt. Only five months after their 1868 tour for Barnum they embarked on a successful trip to Germany, then journeyed to Russia.

In 1870, on board the ship returning them to the United States, Chang suffered a stroke that paralyzed his right side. Since Chang's paralysis for all practical purposes incapacitated the healthy Eng, they had a cart built for Chang in order to increase the pair's mobility. On the early morning of 17 January 1874, after an especially restless night at the Chang household during which Chang had trouble breathing, the paralyzed twin died. Upon seeing his dead brother, Eng said, "Then I am going," and died a couple of hours later. An autopsy revealed that Chang died of a cerebral hemorrhage; doctors believed Eng died of fright. The Siamese twins, who were initially buried at Chang's farm, were reinterred in 1917 at the White Plains Baptist Church cemetery, where Chang's wife also rests.

Eng and Chang were neither the first nor the last twins born conjoined, but they are certainly the most famous. Possibly the most celebrated nineteenth-century Asian Americans, the twins, unlike other "human curiosities" who exhibited for profit, worked for the better part of their careers independently, exploited by no one. Their story endures not only because of its peculiarity but because of the terminology they left us. The congenital defect in which twins are conjoined was named for their country of birth.

• Information on Eng and Chang can be found in the North Carolina Collection at Wilson Library, University of North Carolina, Chapel Hill. The papers of James W. Hale and Susan A. Coffin at the Clements Library at the University of Michigan contain a few letters written by Hale, who served as business manager for Eng and Chang, to Coffin and her husband. A complete biography is Irving Wallace and Amy Wallace, *The Two* (1978). An earlier account is Kay Hunter, *Duet for a Lifetime* (1964). A book for young people is David R. Collins, *Eng and Chang: The Original Siamese Twins* (1994). James W. Hale wrote the pamphlet *An Historical and Descriptive Account of the Siamese Twin Brothers from Actual Observations* (1831). Philip B. Kunhardt, Jr., et al., *P. T. Barnum, America's Greatest Showman: An Illustrated Biography* (1995), has a small section on the twins but has general information on the climate in which they worked. Maudy Benz, "Chang and Eng: A Love Story," *Oxford American*, Oct.–Nov. 1996, pp. 40–46, tells of one woman's visit to a reunion of Eng and Chang's descendants.

STACEY HAMILTON

CHANNING, Edward (15 June 1856–7 Jan. 1931), historian, was born in Dorchester, Massachusetts, the son of William Ellery Channing, a poet, and Ellen Kilshaw Fuller, a sister of the famous reformer Margaret Fuller. Channing married Alice Thatcher in 1886; they had two daughters. Much of Channing's life was centered around Harvard University, from which he had graduated in 1878 with honors in history. As an undergraduate Channing had been especially drawn to the teaching style and critical stance of Henry Adams and equally repulsed by the orthodoxy of Henry Cabot Lodge. By the time he received his Ph.D. in 1880, with a dissertation on the Louisiana Purchase, Channing knew that he wanted to teach U.S. history at Harvard. It took him just three years to secure such a position, during which time he traveled to Europe, wrote articles on geography for *Science*, and nurtured his connections with the Harvard faculty. He remained at Harvard until his retirement in 1929.

Channing's historical writing began in the same year as his teaching career. In 1883 he won the Robert N. Toppan Prize for an essay titled "Town and County Government in the English Colonies." Published the following year as a volume in the Johns Hopkins University Studies in Historical and Political Science, this short work also helped Channing gain election to the elite Massachusetts Historical Society. Channing presented the work in briefer form in 1884 as the first paper at the first meeting of the American Historical Association. In 1897 he coauthored *Guide to the Study of American History* with Albert Bushnell Hart and that same year published a small textbook on America from 1765 to 1865 in the Cambridge Historical Series. Over the next two decades Channing published an English history text with Thomas Wentworth Higginson and numerous textbooks, short histories, articles, and document collections on the United States. Channing's most popular textbook, *A Student's History of the United States* (1898), went through five editions by 1924. *The Jeffersonian System, 1801–1811* (1906), was Channing's contribution to Hart's famous American Nation Series.

Once Channing began his "Great Work," as he and his students habitually referred to his mammoth *History of the United States*, he took little time for anything else. The first of a projected eight volumes, *The Planting of a Nation in the New World, 1000–1660*, was issued in 1905. The volumes then appeared at approximately four-year intervals until the Pulitzer Prize–winning volume six, on the Civil War era, was published in 1925. Thereafter, Channing's age slowed him down considerably. He was laboring at his desk on volume seven on the day before his death of a cerebral hemorrhage in Cambridge, Massachusetts.

Channing's preface to volume one of *History* foretold a great deal about the finished product. He intended to treat the growth of the nation as one continuous development, he announced, "from the political, military, institutional, industrial and social points of view." Channing's belief in progress, doubtless influenced by the evolutionary climate of opinion in his day, was made clear in what he called the "guiding idea" of his *History*: "to view the subject as the record of an evolution, . . . [as] the story of living forces, always struggling onward and upward toward that which is better and higher in human conception." Closely related to this guiding idea was what Channing saw as "the most important single fact in our development," which he described as "the victory of the forces of union over those of particularism." Finally, Channing knew that "the time and place of one's birth and breeding affect the judgment [of the historian], and the opportunity for error is frequent." In light of this he always tried, and urged others to try, to judge historical figures by the standards of their own time: "To estimate them by the conditions and ideas of the present day is to give a false picture."

In both volume three, *The American Revolution, 1761–1789* (1912), and volume six, *The War for Southern Independence* (1925), Channing's narrative has a strong central theme, weighted toward the political history that he understood best. While he devotes more than half of volume five to the topics of society and culture, his efforts in these areas seem strangely disconnected from the overall emphasis of his *History*. Examining in volume three the economic causes of the revolutionary break in America's evolution within the British Empire, he writes, "Commercialism, the desire for advantage and profit in trade and industry, was at the bottom of the struggle between England and America." In the work's preface he had already placed himself within the "Imperial School" of colonial historians, writing that he "considered the colonies as parts of the English empire, as having sprung from that political fabric, and as having simply pursued a course of institutional evolution unlike that of the branch of the English race which remained behind in the old homeland across the Atlantic."

Although volume six stresses his theme of union over particularism, Channing is unable to offer as coherent an explanation of the Civil War as he had offered of the Revolution in volume three. His theory, though complex, may offer a more realistic picture of how the war came about than those of historians who seek succinct explanations. According to Channing, the war resulted from a natural, environmentally produced sectionalism in which the two leading factors were slavery (in the economic and social arenas) and divergent views over the nature of the union (in the political arena). Soon after it began, however, the war became purely emotional: "The psychology of men's actions is often beyond the ken of the historian; but in this case sentiment overruled every other consideration in the North—and in the South."

The day after Channing's death, the *Boston Herald* declared, "The most eminent of contemporary American writers of history is gone." While historians have challenged Channing's faith in progress, questioned many of his judgments, and added significant new historical actors and dilemmas to his narrative, Channing was, in his own time, a distinguished teacher, a pioneering textbook author, and a tireless chronicler of the evolution of America.

• No single collection of Channing's papers exists, but substantial materials are in the Harvard University Archives and the Macmillan Authors Collection in the Manuscript Division of the New York Public Library. Davis D. Joyce, *Edward Channing and the Great Work* (1974), is a thorough study of Channing's life and writings. In 1993 Joyce also edited and abridged into a single volume Channing's *A History of the United States*. Of several brief assessments of Channing, the best is John A. De Novo, "Edward Channing's 'Great Work' Twenty Years After," *Mississippi Valley Historical Review* 39 (Sept. 1952): 257–74. George W. Robinson provides a comprehensive list of Channing's major and minor works in

Bibliography of Edward Channing (1932). Obituaries are in the *Boston Transcript* and the *Boston Herald*, 8 Jan. 1932, and by S. E. Morison in *Proceedings of the Massachusetts Historical Society* 64 (1932).

DAVIS D. JOYCE

CHANNING, William Ellery (7 Apr. 1780–2 Oct. 1842), Unitarian clergyman and author, was born in Newport, Rhode Island, the son of William Channing, a lawyer, and Lucy Ellery. His father, a prominent Federalist, had been attorney general of Rhode Island and U.S. district attorney; George Washington and John Jay (1745–1829) were among the guests entertained in the household. Channing's father died when he was thirteen, and his maternal grandfather, William Ellery, a signer of the Declaration of Independence, became the boy's principal father figure. Ironically for one who would become known for his denunciation of slavery, the Newport where Channing grew up was a center of the slave trade. His parents had owned several slaves but manumitted them after the Revolution.

Channing attended Harvard College, belonged to the Porcellian and Hasty Pudding clubs there, and graduated in 1798 at the head of his class. He worked as a tutor in Richmond, Virginia, where he spent an unhappy year and a half, lonely and ill. He later recalled that this miserable period was the only time in his life when he felt any inclination toward a Calvinist view of existence. He returned north a convinced critic of slavery. For the next three years he studied divinity in preparation for a ministerial career and became attracted to the theology of the liberal wing of the standing order in Massachusetts (the Congregational church), to which he had been exposed at Harvard. During this time he also heard the preaching of Samuel Hopkins (1721–1803), whose Calvinist theology Channing rejected but whose character and antislavery principles he admired. The assertion, made by some historians, that Channing underwent a religious conversion experience is contradicted by his own account (*Memoir*, 1:129).

In 1803 two liberal parishes in Boston, the Brattle Street Church and the Federal Street Church, encouraged Channing to settle; he accepted the latter, although at the time it was the less distinguished. Under his leadership the Federal Street Church (relocated after his death and renamed the Arlington Street Church) became a center of the Unitarian movement. Channing's writing and preaching during the decades to come were critical in defining the doctrines and characteristics of this emergent denomination.

Channing has rightly been judged "the single most important figure in the history of American Unitarianism" (David Robinson, *The Unitarians and the Universalists* [1985], p. 229). This role began when, in 1815, he replied to Calvinist critics of the religious liberals in a public *Letter to Samuel C. Thacher*; he followed this with other writings directed against the theological opinions and ecclesiastical policies of New England Calvinist leaders, among them Jedidiah Morse, Jeremiah Evarts, and Samuel Worcester. Noteworthy among Channing's statements were "The System of Exclusion and Denunciation in Religion Considered" (1815) and "The Moral Argument against Calvinism" (1820). In 1819 Channing delivered a sermon at the ordination of Jared Sparks in Baltimore, Maryland; published as a pamphlet under the title *Unitarian Christianity*, it enjoyed a wide circulation and became the virtual manifesto of the liberal movement in theology, now explicitly Unitarian. The following year he organized the Berry Street Conference, a precursor of the American Unitarian Association, founded in 1825. In the course of these controversies, what had been merely an informal liberal (or Arminian) group within the Congregational church took on a heightened level of self-consciousness and reorganized itself into a new Unitarian denomination, with Channing as its most respected leader. The new Harvard Divinity School, which Channing (as a Fellow of the Harvard Corporation) helped establish in 1816, trained its ministers.

In 1814 Channing married his first cousin, Ruth Gibbs, daughter of a wealthy merchant and distiller. Her income gave the couple financial independence; they had four children. Beginning in 1824, Channing arranged for his pastoral duties to be gradually taken over by his associate, Ezra Stiles Gannett, leaving himself freer to concentrate on his writings.

Channing had an image of the clergyman as an intellectual, cultural, and moral leader of the community, and he exercised this leadership through his writing and preaching. His "Remarks on a National Literature" (1830) constituted an early summons to the creation of an authentic American literature that would celebrate the dignity and self-awareness of humanity. Essays on Milton (1826), Napoleon (1827–1828), and Fénelon (1829) had already gained him an audience. On his travels abroad, Channing won the admiration of leading European intellectuals; Coleridge declared of Channing, "He has the love of wisdom and the wisdom of love." In France, where his writings were repeatedly translated, he enjoyed a substantial following in both Roman Catholic and Protestant circles.

Channing articulated a clear-cut theological position. Reacting against New England's Calvinist inheritance, he affirmed the freedom of the will and rejected the doctrine of original sin; he also denied the necessity for an identifiable conversion experience. Although a Unitarian, he emphatically considered himself a Christian, with an Arian Christology. Like the other New England Unitarians of his day, he accepted the Old and New Testaments as divine revelation. His views on the authority of Scripture, strongly influenced by the Anglican William Paley (1743–1805), were well stated in the Dudleian Lecture Channing delivered at Harvard in 1821, "The Evidences of Revealed Religion." He was a Christian humanist, both in the sense of respecting classical education and in the sense of believing in the dignity of the individual. His strong sense of human potential is apparent in his ordination sermon for Frederick A. Farley, "Likeness to God" (1828).

Channing's social views derived from his religious ones and centered on his dedication to the full development of the potential of every human being. Accordingly, he was a strong supporter of education for all classes of the population. His remarks on "Self-Culture," delivered as a Franklin Lecture in 1838, summarized his belief that education is a lifelong process and includes the full range of human faculties: moral, spiritual, social, and artistic, as well as intellectual and physical. (When Channing arranged his collected works for publication, he placed this lecture at the head.) Various philanthropic and reform activities engaged Channing's sympathies, including prison reform, temperance, working-class education, and ministry to the urban poor. He was acquainted with virtually all the leading American artists, intellectuals, and reformers of his day. Although not active in the nascent feminist movement, he admired Mary Wollstonecraft and was respected in turn by such prominent women reformers as Julia Ward Howe and Elizabeth Palmer Peabody. In politics Channing was first a Federalist, later an independent Whig of the John Quincy Adams (1767–1848) sort. He opposed United States acquisition of Texas in his *Letter to the Hon. Henry Clay on the Annexation of Texas* (1837). This was one of the earliest statements of an opposition to annexation that eventually became widespread among Whigs.

Given Channing's moral commitments, it was inevitable that he should speak out against slavery. After a visit to the West Indies confirmed his detestation of the institution, he published a short volume entitled *Slavery* (1835), demonstrating its ethical indefensibility. Temperate in tone though this statement was, it came early enough to offend not only southern whites but even conservative northerners, including some of Channing's parishioners. Despite such opposition, he persevered in other antislavery pronouncements, including "Remarks on the Slavery Question" (1839), "Emancipation in the British West Indies" (1840), and "The Duty of the Free States" (1842).

Channing never worked through abolitionist organizations, and he found William Lloyd Garrison tasteless. Even so, by the last years of his life Channing's antislavery views had estranged him from his congregation. In 1840, following the church's refusal to hold a memorial service for the German scholar and antislavery spokesman Carl Follen, a close friend of Channing's, he resigned the stipend he had been receiving in his semiretirement, retaining only a nominal connection with the church until his death on a visit to Bennington, Vermont, two years later.

Channing was slightly built and a semi-invalid much of his life. But his eyes and voice commanded attention, and he captured the imagination of the rising generation of young New England intellectuals. Those who became Transcendentalists, such as Ralph Waldo Emerson, Theodore Parker, and Margaret Fuller, came to feel that they had moved beyond his patrician reformism and pre-Romantic sensibility, but they always remembered the impression he had early made on them and the liberating value of his humane opinions. Channing himself never became a Transcendentalist, though many other Unitarian clergy did. In addition to the Transcendentalists, Channing also influenced such important contemporaries as Charles Sumner, Horace Mann, James Russell Lowell, Henry Wadsworth Longfellow, Lydia Maria Child, and Dorothea Dix. As this list indicates, the characteristic New England mixture of individual self-culture and social reform owed much to Channing's precept and example.

Channing synthesized Protestant moralism with the Enlightenment's commitment to human dignity. His formal philosophical views were shaped by Scottish moral philosophy and Arminian theology, but he was widely read and receptive to humane ideas from whatever source (as illustrated by his admiration for the French Catholic bishop Fénelon). Channing marshaled the resources of the Protestant intellectual tradition to encourage two major developments while both were in their infancy: the emergence of American literature and the emergence of Victorian social reform. As a result his cultural significance far transcends the small religious body whose spokesperson he became. American Unitarianism, with which Channing will always be identified, has retained a cultural and moral influence out of all proportion to its size.

• The six-volume edition of Channing's *Works* (1843 and many subsequent editions) omits much of his early writing (the omissions are listed in William Sprague, *Annals of the American Pulpit*, vol. 8 [1865], p. 366); it also needs supplementing with the sermons collected by his nephew William Henry Channing under the title *The Perfect Life* (1873). Channing's papers were accidentally destroyed by fire after his death, but not before some of them had been printed: see William Henry Channing, ed., *A Memoir of William Ellery Channing* (3 vols., 1848); *Correspondence of William Ellery Channing and Lucy Aiken* (1874); Elizabeth Palmer Peabody, *Reminiscences of Rev. William Ellery Channing* (1880); and Grace Ellery Channing, ed., *Dr. Channing's Notebook* (1887). A convenient brief selection is William Ellery Channing, *Unitarian Christianity and Other Essays*, ed. Irving Bartlett (1957).

The secondary literature on Channing is uneven in quality. The following are recommended: John White Chadwick, *William Ellery Channing* (1903); Madeleine Hooke Rice, *Federal Street Pastor* (1961); Conrad Wright, *Three Prophets of Religious Liberalism: Channing, Emerson, Parker* (1961); and Jack Mendelsohn, *Channing: The Reluctant Radical* (1971). For Channing in his context, see Conrad Wright, *The Liberal Christians* (1970); David Robinson, "The Legacy of Channing," *Harvard Theological Review* 74 (1981): 221–39; and Daniel Walker Howe, *The Unitarian Conscience*, rev. ed. (1988).

DANIEL WALKER HOWE

CHANNING, William Ellery, II (29 Nov. 1817–23 Dec. 1901), poet, was born in Boston, Massachusetts, the son of Dr. Walter Channing, professor of obstetrics at Harvard Medical School, and Barbara Perkins. Like his reverend uncle and namesake, William Ellery Channing (1780–1842), he was given the name of his maternal grandfather, William Ellery of Rhode Island, a signer of the Declaration of Independence. When he was five years old, his secure world was shattered by his mother's death. Ellery and his three sisters were distributed among relatives. He attended several good schools, including Round Hill of Northampton, which encouraged walking expeditions and nature study.

In September 1834 Channing entered Harvard College; but the solicitude his family and teachers had shown him from childhood had persuaded him he was a special case, and he rebelled against attendance regulations that he believed violated his freedom. He left that December without giving notice. His father discovered him among family friends at Curzon's Mill in Newburyport.

Back in his father's house, he read and wrote extensively. From April to December 1835, he published nineteen pieces of prose and verse in the Boston *Mercantile Journal* under the pen name Hal Menge. With the publication of "The Spider" in the *New England Magazine* that October, Channing felt himself a dedicated poet. Dr. Channing, doubting that his son had found his true vocation, attempted to steer him in new directions. One was homesteading in Illinois. There the young Channing weathered the winter of 1839–1840, but left at planting time for Massachusetts.

In 1841, when Channing was in Cincinnati seeking guidance from his uncle James Handasyd Perkins (1810–1849), he met Ellen Fuller, the frail but attractive sister of Sarah Margaret Fuller, the Transcendentalist. Both unemployed, they found consolation in each other, marrying in September 1841 against the advice of both families. Once an accomplished fact, the marriage was accepted graciously by Dr. Channing and by Margaret, speaking for the Fullers.

The previous year the *Dial*, a Transcendentalist journal, had been established with Margaret Fuller as editor. To the first issue, Ralph Waldo Emerson had contributed an article entitled "New Poetry," including, coincidentally, five poems by Channing. He welcomed the fresh voice, noting—but downplaying—deficiencies in meter and syntax. Sam Ward (1814–1884), whom Channing had known at Round Hill, had brought Emerson's attention to the young poet. Ward would soon offer to pay publication costs for a volume of poems.

Following their marriage, Channing and his wife continued to live in Cincinnati, where Channing had a subeditorship on the *Gazette*. That winter another of Channing's poems appeared in the *Dial*. The Channings became eager to return to Massachusetts, preferably to live in Concord, near Emerson. In July 1842 Channing left for the East to explore professional and residential possibilities. That same July the *Dial* carried seven more of his poems.

When Channing knocked on Emerson's door in midsummer, the two poets were barely acquainted personally. But Emerson was curious about Channing, the man. He welcomed him cordially, offering him a bedroom as headquarters while Channing foraged for more permanent shelter. This would give Emerson a chance to sample him as a walking companion and to introduce him to Henry David Thoreau, A. Bronson Alcott, and Nathaniel Hawthorne. They all found Channing's comments perceptive and original. Emerson was outspoken in support of Channing: his untamed wit, his independence of convention. Even Hawthorne, who preferred Channing's originality in small doses, missed him when he was absent.

Channing's wife joined him in September 1842 and agreed that they should pass the winter in Cambridge, near Margaret Fuller, and settle in Concord the next spring. In April 1843 they moved into the Red Lodge, a cottage adjoining Emerson's garden. It would be an eventful year, including the publication of *Poems*, Channing's first book. Unfortunately that book is remembered chiefly as having inspired Poe's most contemptuous review. He said of the contents: "They are full of all kinds of mistakes of which the most important is that of their having been written at all. They are not precisely English—nor will we insult a great nation by calling them Kickapoo; perhaps they are Channingese." The same year, "The Youth of the Poet and Painter," Channing's pleasantly amusing semiautobiography, appeared serially in the *Dial*.

Ellen bore five children between 1844 and 1856, receiving no help from her husband in raising them, though there is little doubt that Ellery Channing's father provided the family with a modest allowance. Channing was an artist at escape. He felt the woods were his true home; but another refuge was the *New-York Tribune*, where he served from November 1844 to March 1845. Deciding then that he needed poetic stimulation, he raised $300 from friends to take him to Rome and back, though the excursion gave him only sixteen days in the Eternal City.

Before that trip produced any literary results, Emerson made possible a second volume of Channing's verse by attaching a rider to a contract for the publication of his own poems. This time Channing's volume (*Poems, Second Series*, 1847) was reviewed by several critics along with Emerson's, resulting in mixed reviews for both.

Conversations in Rome between an Artist, a Catholic, and a Critic also appeared in 1847. In a talk-fest on the arts, with poetry interspersed, the three characters express divergent opinions, all voiced by Channing, who could defend tradition when the occasion demanded. Reviewers found the book quite readable. They were friendly though often patronizing.

In 1853, exhausted and consumptive, Ellen escaped with her four children to the protective home of her sister-in-law Mary and Mary's husband, Thomas Wentworth Higginson. In 1855 a repentant Channing persuaded her to revive their marriage at a new address, in Dorchester. He accepted a position on the New Bedford *Mercury*, within commuting distance by rail. But Ellen died three months after the birth of her fifth child. The relatives praised Channing's efforts to be helpful during that final year. After Ellen's death, they took over all responsibility for the children—no doubt to his relief.

Channing returned to Concord. From the spring of 1845, when he helped Thoreau build the cabin at Walden, he had been Thoreau's most consistent walking companion, including trips to the Berkshires, the Catskills, Cape Cod, and Canada. In 1860 they camped together for five nights on Mt. Monadnock. By the close of 1861, when Thoreau was confined to his daybed, Channing visited him daily. When death came in May 1862, Channing wrote four stanzas for the funeral.

Henceforth his life would be dedicated to the memory of his friend. Immediately Sophia Thoreau sought his help in editing her brother's journals, from which they produced *The Maine Woods* (1864) and *Cape Cod* (1865). In 1871 Channing published *The Wanderer*, the best of his longer poems, with Thoreau the featured character. It was financed by Emerson and edited by Channing's friend and neighbor Franklin B. Sanborn. More coherent and pictorial than any of his other poems, it was almost completely sold out within a month, the remaining copies destroyed in the great Boston fire of 1872. Most important was his biography, *Thoreau, the Poet-Naturalist*, in 1873, a series of biographical essays with numerous supplements—an invaluable source for all later biographers.

From 1865 to 1891 Channing lived in frugal solitude in a house provided by his father, who, dying in 1876, left him the income from a modest trust fund. For years the poet regularly had Sunday supper with the Emersons, and on weekdays he commuted by rail to Boston, avidly reading and note-taking at the Public Library and the Athenaeum. He rejected all overtures from his children. In 1891, ill and unable to care for himself, Channing was received into the home of his friend Sanborn, where he died.

Channing remains an integral part of the Transcendental movement, even though his life and his work often seem to caricature its high aims. He wrote a few good poems; and his poetry, as he said of himself, made tracks in the snow for others to walk in—by helping create a climate of freedom that made experimentation respectable. Finally, his tributes to Thoreau are given a special authority by their twenty years of intimate companionship.

• Manuscripts abound (letters, notebooks, miscellaneous poetry and prose), especially in collections at the Houghton Library of Harvard University, the Concord, Mass., Free Public Library, and the Massachusetts Historical Society. Books by Channing not mentioned above are *The Woodman, and Other Poems* (1849), *Near Home, a Poem* (1858), *Eliot, a Poem* (1885), and *John Brown and the Heroes of Harpers Ferry, a Poem* (1886). F. B. Sanborn reprinted *Thoreau, the Poet-Naturalist* in an enlarged edition in 1902 and in the same year issued *Poems of Sixty-Five Years*, a collection of Channing's verse combined with a biographical sketch. Also see *The Collected Poems of William Ellery Channing the Younger*, ed. Walter Harding (1967), and *Selected Letters of Ellery Channing the Younger*, ed. Francis C. Dedmond, which appeared serially in *Studies in the American Renaissance* from 1987 to 1992. Two books on Channing complement each other in emphasis: Frederick T. McGill, Jr., *Channing of Concord* (1967), which is mainly biography, and Robert N. Hudspeth, *Ellery Channing* (1973), which is mainly literary criticism.

FREDERICK T. MCGILL, JR.

CHANNING, William Henry (25 May 1810–23 Dec. 1884), Unitarian minister and reformer, was born in Boston, Massachusetts, the son of Francis Dana Channing, an attorney, and Susan Higginson. Although his father died in 1810, Channing was well-connected with influential New England families through both parents and was raised in an atmosphere of privilege. He grew up in the household of his maternal grandfather Stephen Higginson, a merchant, and his education was directed to a significant extent by his uncle William Ellery Channing, minister of Boston's Federal Street Church and the period's leading Unitarian thinker. His schooling conformed to a standard pattern for young Unitarian men of intellectual inclinations. He attended Boston Latin School, graduated from Harvard College in 1829, and completed Harvard Divinity School in 1833.

During the remainder of the 1830s Channing struggled to find a place in a changing society. Like many young Unitarian ministers, he was inspired by a vision of concurrent spiritual and social reform. In 1834 he participated briefly in the Cambridge Antislavery Society, a group led by Unitarian ministers who opposed both slavery and the radical methods of the Garrisonian abolitionists. In 1837 he opened a free church for the poor in New York City, but failed to gather a congregation. He was more successful in his efforts to help establish Unitarianism in the West. He served as minister of the First Congregational Church of Cincinnati, Ohio, from 1838 to 1841 and worked as an editor of the *Western Messenger*. These activities were punctuated, however, by periods of indecision. During the winters of 1834–1835 and 1841–1842 Channing withdrew to his mother's home in Cambridge, Massachusetts, to try to resolve his religious doubts through study. He married Julia Allen of Rondout, New York, in 1836; they had three children. However, family life did not bring stability to Channing. His wife's loyalty to the Episcopalianism of her childhood led to reservations about her husband's ministry. The Channings often lived apart in future years, and their children were raised in the Episcopal church.

Channing made his most vigorous contribution to American religion and reform during the 1840s. The decade began with a spiritual crisis, centered in Channing's skepticism about traditional Unitarian proofs of the authority of Jesus and Christianity, that led to his resignation from the Cincinnati church. As he read contemporary European philosophy, however, he formulated a Christian organicism infused with a sense of the presence of the supernatural in history. His "confession of faith," published in the opening number of his periodical, *The Present*, acknowledged his debt to such intellectuals as Pierre Leroux, Emanuel Swedenborg, and Charles Fourier and affirmed his belief in "the unity of the human race—the threefold life of man—Jesus Christ as the divine type of glorified humanity—the kingdom of Heaven on earth—the duty of this nation to establish united interests" (Sept. 1843, p. 10). Jesus was the mediator who brought grace to humanity and made progress possible by harmonizing social relations.

Channing's emphasis on religious sentiment, historical progress, and social amelioration strengthened his connection with a group of Transcendentalists that included Margaret Fuller and the residents of the Brook Farm community. At the same time, his insistence on the infusion of spirit in nature distanced him from Theodore Parker's humanism, a philosophical view Channing characterized as "mere Naturalism" in his 1860 eulogy "Lessons from the Life of Theodore Parker." Most important, Channing's new philosophical synthesis became the groundwork of a variety of activities. He served as minister of a congregation devoted to "Christian Union" in New York City from 1843 to 1845 and led the Religious Union of Associationists in Boston from 1847 to 1850. Both groups gave a Christian theological and liturgical dimension to Fourierist social reform. "The Christian Church and Social Reform," a sermon Channing delivered to the Religious Union of Associationists in 1848, was typical of this outlook. The church, which he defined broadly as spiritual Christendom, was the channel through which grace would work to perfect society. He edited two periodicals, *The Present* (1843–1844) and *The Spirit of the Age* (1849–1850), and contributed frequently to the principal Fourier journals published in the East, *The Phalanx* (1843–1845) and *The Harbinger* (1845–1849). He lived briefly at Brook Farm in 1846 and at the North American Phalanx, a Fourier community in New Jersey, in 1850. Channing left his mark on the reforms of the 1840s less as a social activist, however, than as an intellectual and religious leader.

When Channing's hopes through social transformation were disappointed, he searched once again for new ways to act on his principles. He ministered to the Unitarian society of Rochester, New York, from 1852 to 1854. In that role he advocated antislavery, women's rights, and temperance. In 1854 he accepted the first of four appointments as a minister to English Unitarian churches: Renshaw Street (1854–1857) and Hope Street Chapels (1857–1861), Liverpool; New Oakfield Road Church, Clifton (1865–1866?); and Free Christian Church, Kensington and later Notting Hill (1867–1869?). One advantage of residence in England was that his wife enjoyed English society, and they lived together. Their son Francis became a member of Parliament, and their surviving daughter Fanny married Sir Edwin Arnold. Channing, however, felt uneasy about resuming his affiliation with the Unitarians and uncomfortable with the formality of the British Unitarian liturgy. The Civil War soon stirred his patriotism, as he revealed in a sermon preached to his Liverpool congregation, "The Civil War in America" (1861). He moved to Washington, D.C., where he served as minister to the Unitarian society and later chaplain to the House of Representatives. When he failed to find an American congregation willing to offer him a position at the end of the war, he returned to England.

Channing had a reputation among his contemporaries as a mystic and social visionary. Although observers often voiced this assessment as criticism, the description contained some truth. Channing remained faithful to his belief, crystalized in the 1840s, that if sectarianism, materialism, and other human impediments to divine power were removed, regeneration of the race would follow. His interest in non-Western religions after the war, exemplified by an address, "Religions of China" (1870), delivered to the Free Religious Association in Boston, reflected his continuing conviction that a richly cultivated spirituality must be the center of personal and social experience. Despite this religious sensibility, Channing's book-length works were historical in nature, specifically memoirs of his kin and friends. He compiled a meticulous memoir of his uncle, *The Life of William Ellery Channing* (1848); published a life of his cousin, *The Memoir and Writings of James Handasyd Perkins* (1851); and coedited *Memoirs of Margaret Fuller Ossoli* (1852) with Ralph Waldo Emerson and James Freeman Clarke. The prominence of these memorials among his writings attests to the continuing influence of his privileged family background as well as the importance of private relationships in energizing his public reform activities.

Channing visited America occasionally after the Civil War and lectured at the Lowell Institute (1869–1870), the Free Religious Association (1870, 1880), and the Concord School of Philosophy (1880). He died in London and was buried in Boston. Although the distance between Channing's ideals and his modest social and literary accomplishments might suggest that he was out of step with his time, his efforts were in fact part of some of the decisive movements of the nineteenth century. Intellectually, Channing reformulated his commitment to Christianity in light of European and Asian philosophy; socially, he viewed Christianity as a blueprint for an ethical society. This combination of his cosmopolitanism and reforming zeal may have deterred sustained practical commitments. Nonetheless, Channing was influential in opening up American culture to new ideas and persuading many of his contemporaries that religion should guide social change.

• Some Channing manuscripts are located in the Channing Family Papers, Houghton Library, Harvard University. Additional writing by Channing of particular importance include "Ernest the Seeker," *Dial* 1 (1840): 48–58, 233–42; *The Gospel of To-day* (1847); and "Edwards and the Revivalists: A Chapter of New England Ecclesiastical History," *Christian Examiner* 43 (1847): 374–94. For a biography of Channing see Octavius Brooks Frothingham, *Memoir of William Henry Channing* (1886). Frothingham's book is especially useful because it includes long quotations from Channing's manuscripts, that have since been lost. Information on Channing's role in establishing Unitarianism in the West may be found in

Charles Lyttle, *Freedom Moves West: A History of the Western Unitarian Conference, 1852–1952* (1952), and Robert D. Habich, *Transcendentalism and the "Western Messenger": A History of the Magazine and Its Contributors, 1835–1841* (1985). The Transcendentalist and Fourierist reform contexts of the 1830s and 1840s have been explored by Anne C. Rose, *Transcendentalism as a Social Movement, 1830–1850* (1981), and Carl J. Guarneri, *The Utopian Alternative: Fourierism in Nineteenth-Century America* (1991). Perry Miller published a few selections of Channing's writings in *The Transcendentalists: An Anthology* (1950).

ANNE C. ROSE

CHANUTE, Octave (18 Feb. 1832–23 Nov. 1910), engineer and aeronautical experimenter, was born in Paris, France, the son of Joseph Chanut, an educator and historian, and Elise Sohpie de Bonnaire. His parents separated in 1838, when six-year-old Octave moved to New Orleans with his father, who was appointed vice president of Jefferson College. In 1844 father and son resettled in New York, where Octave was educated in a private school. He added a final "e" to his patronym during this period as a mark of Americanization and a means of suggesting the proper pronunciation of his name.

Determined to become a civil engineer, in 1849 Chanute traveled to Ossining, New York, where he convinced Henry Gardiner, chief engineer of the Hudson River Railroad, to employ him as a member of a surveying crew. Energetic and eager to learn, Chanute quickly rose through the ranks. By 1853 he was serving the railroad as a division engineer in charge of facilities and maintenance-of-way at Albany. In September 1853 he moved west, accepting a position as division engineer with the Chicago and Mississippi Railroad. Over the next decade he would fill a series of increasingly responsible engineering positions with a variety of western railroads, notably the Chicago and Alton. He married Annie James, of Peoria, Illinois, in 1857; they had four children.

In 1867 Chanute was hired as chief engineer of the Kansas City Bridge, the first railroad bridge across the Missouri River. Working with a talented team of assistants, Chanute successfully completed the task in 1869. He then became chief engineer and representative for the enterprises of John F. Joy, one of the most important promoters extending rail lines west into Kansas. In that capacity Chanute was responsible not only for matters specifically related to engineering, but also for land acquisition, property management, negotiations with local town and county governments, and a variety of other business matters. His contributions to the economic infrastructure of western America ranged from the planning and construction of the Kansas City stockyards to the provision of water, sewer, and gas systems for cities and small towns across the region.

In 1873 Chanute was appointed chief engineer of the reorganized Erie Railroad. As he prepared to take up his new duties, newspapers across the West praised his contributions to the growth of the region. The *Parsons* (Kans.) *Star* protested "against New York taking from us one of the ablest and best brain-men in the state," while other local journals pronounced him one of "the ablest as well as one of the most popular men in the West," "a universal favorite," and "the best civil engineer in the West."

Chanute would spend ten difficult years with the Erie. While he was plagued by political and business problems during this period, he also enjoyed some successes—double tracking the entire line, planning the construction of several notable bridges, and undertaking a number of special engineering projects, including involvement in planning an elevated train system for New York City. He served as president of the American Society of Civil Engineers (1891) and was involved in the work of other professional organizations, notably the Civil Engineering Section of the American Association for the Advancement of Science (AAAS).

After a decade of service to the Erie Railroad, Chanute returned to Kansas City and, eventually, to Chicago, where he worked as a consulting engineer on several major bridge projects and established a company specializing in wood preservation. He also began to spend an increasing amount of time on his hobby, the investigation of aeronautics.

Chanute's interest in flight can be dated to the early 1870s, when, during the course of a European vacation with his family, he became aware of the aeronautical experiments undertaken by French and English engineers. Chanute immersed himself in the literature of the field and began to correspond with virtually every major flying machine experimenter in the world. By 1885 he had begun to lecture on the subject at leading American engineering schools including Cornell University, and had organized the first major session on aeronautics at the meeting of the Engineering Section of the AAAS at Buffalo, New York. His activities during this period drew other leading American scientists and engineers into the field, most notably Robert Thurston of Cornell and Samuel Pierpont Langley of the Western University of Pennsylvania and the Smithsonian Institution.

In 1886 Matthias Forney, editor of the *American Railroad and Engineering Journal*, invited Chanute to publish a series of articles on aeronautics. Twenty-seven installments of the series "Progress in Flying Machines" were published in the journal beginning in October 1891. Forney republished the entire series, revised and expanded by the author, as a book of the same title in 1894. The volume, combined with Chanute's involvement in planning a major conference on the subject at Chicago in August 1893, established him as one of the world's leading authorities on flight.

Chanute not only wrote, spoke, and organized conferences on flight, but he also began to plan his own course of aeronautical experiments. He provided small sums of money to Louis Mouillard, Augustus M. Herring, and other promising experimenters in Europe and the United States. On 22 June 1896 Chanute, accompanied by a group of young enthusiasts, established a glider testing camp in the sand dunes on the southern shore of Lake Michigan, near Miller, Indiana. His associates, all temporary employees of Chanute, included Herring, William Avery, William Paul Butusov, and James Rickets, a Chicago physician with, as Chanute explained, "a slack practice and a taste for aviation."

The men tested a series of man-carrying gliders, constructed or refurbished at Chanute's expense. The tests attracted the attention of Chicago reporters, who filled the city's newspapers with accounts of the flights being conducted in the dunes. Anxious to escape the attention of the press and to construct other gliders based on the lessons learned during the first weeks in the dunes, Chanute and his associates returned to Chicago on 4 July.

They established a second camp deeper in the dunes on 20 August. During the intervening weeks in Chicago, Avery had constructed a new glider, jointly designed by Herring and Chanute. Precise credit for the design of the craft would be a point of contention between Chanute and Herring for the rest of their lives. Originally flown as a triplane with a special stabilizing tail, the glider was first tested on 29 August. The lower wing was removed in an effort to improve performance, transforming the craft into a biplane. It quickly proved to be the most successful man-carrying glider constructed to date, capable of flying distances of up to 359 feet and remaining in the air up to fourteen seconds at a time. The basic design of the craft, biplane wings linked into a single beam by means of a bridge truss system, established the structural form that would be adapted for the world's first powered airplanes.

The most important association of Chanute's life began in May 1900, when he received a letter from Wilbur Wright, who, with his brother Orville, was the owner of a small bicycle shop and manufacturing facility in Dayton, Ohio. The letter, in which Wilbur introduced himself to Chanute and outlined his plans for a series of flying-machine experiments, marked the beginning of the most influential friendship in the history of aeronautics.

Between Wilbur Wright's first letter of 13 May 1900 and Chanute's last letter to the brothers on 14 March 1910, a total of 435 letters, notes, and telegrams passed between them. The sheer bulk of the correspondence was overwhelming, averaging a letter every eight or nine days over a decade. Chanute served as an important sounding board for the Wrights. He also introduced them to the larger international circle of aeronautical experimenters. He arranged for Wilbur to offer one of the most important lectures in the early history of flight to the members of the Western Society of Engineers in Chicago in 1901. He visited them at home in Dayton and in their camp at Kitty Hawk, North Carolina.

In spite of the important role that the friendship had played in their lives, Chanute became alienated from the Wright brothers after 1903. In part the conflict began when the Wrights recognized that Chanute was considerably overstating his contributions to their success. In an important speech before the members of the Aero Club de France in Paris on 2 April 1903, for example, he had described the brothers as his "devoted collaborators" and as his "young, intelligent and daring pupils." Moreover, the Wrights doubted that Chanute had ever fully understood the intricacies of their invention.

Chanute seems to have regarded the Wright brothers as ungrateful. He also came to believe that they were too secretive, hiding their invention from public view in an effort to improve their financial position rather than sharing information with other flying-machine experimenters. Wilbur attempted to heal the breach with his old friend in 1910. The process was still under way when Chanute died at his home in Chicago. Wilbur attended the funeral.

Through his efforts to draw professional engineers into aeronautics, to publicize the experiments of others, and to directly encourage a new generation of talented young technicians to enter the field, Chanute helped to set the stage for the invention of the airplane. "By the death of Mr. O. Chanute the world has lost one whose labors had to an unusual degree influenced the course of human progress," Wilbur Wright remarked in January 1911. "No one was too humble to receive a share of his time. In patience and goodness of heart he has rarely been surpassed. Few men were more universally respected and loved."

• The papers of Octave Chanute, a major collection containing the bulk of his correspondence, notebooks, scrapbooks, and photographs, are maintained by the Manuscript Division of the Library of Congress. The Manuscript Division of the Denver Public Library contains additional materials, as well as valuable information gathered by Pearl I. Young for a biography that was never written. The archive of the Illinois Institute of Technology, Chicago, contains some additional Chanute papers of interest.

Copies of Young's manuscript bibliography of materials written by Chanute are in the archive of the National Air and Space Museum (NASM), the Library of Congress, and the Denver Public Library. The NASM library also contains a multivolume, typed transcript of Chanute's aeronautical correspondence.

Although Chanute has not yet inspired the publication of a full-scale biography, Tom D. Crouch, *A Dream of Wings: Americans and the Airplane, 1875–1905* (1979), provides an overview of his career set against the backdrop of early American aeronautical efforts. Additional information is in Marvin W. McFarland, ed., *The Papers of Wilbur and Orville Wright* (2 vols., 1953); *Chicago Inter-Ocean*, 24 Nov. 1910; *Men and Women of America* (1910); "The Life and Work of Octave Chanute," *Aeronautics* (Jan. 1911): 3; James Means, "Octave Chanute's Work in Aviation," *Aeronautics* (Jan. 1911): 3; and *Octave Chanute: Aviation Pioneer* (1940). An obituary by Wilbur Wright is in *Aeronautics*, Jan. 1911.

TOM D. CROUCH

CHAPELLE, Dickey (14 Mar. 1918–4 Nov. 1965), foreign correspondent and photojournalist, was born Georgette Louise Marie Meyer in Milwaukee, Wisconsin, the daughter of Paul Gerhard Meyer, a building materials salesman, and Edna F. Engelhardt. "Dickey" became her nickname as a young girl. In

1935 she graduated valedictorian at the age of seventeen from Shorewood (Wis.) High School and won a full scholarship to study aeronautical engineering at the Massachusetts Institute of Technology. Writing news stories for the *Boston Traveler* was more important to Chapelle than studying, however, and she became academically ineligible to return to MIT in her sophomore year. After going home, she worked for the *Milwaukee Journal* for a year and then began writing articles and books about aviation. She obtained a pilot's license at age twenty-one.

Chapelle moved to Florida to live with her grandparents but in 1938 landed a job in New York City with the publicity bureau of Transcontinental and Western Airlines. In 1939 she took a photography course with Anthony Chapelle, TWA's publicity photographer. They were married in October 1940; they had no children together.

When her husband reenlisted in the navy following Pearl Harbor and was stationed in Panama, Chapelle got press credentials to cover maneuvers there for *Look* magazine. From 1943 to 1945 Chapelle wrote and contributed to books on aviation. She spent time in 1945 in Iwo Jima, Okinawa, and Guam photographing for Fawcett Publications, making her one of the youngest American war correspondents.

In 1946 and 1947 Chapelle served as associate editor for *Seventeen* magazine. Then she worked for two years for the American Friends Service Committee in fourteen European countries, freelancing stories with her husband for humanitarian agencies such as UNESCO and the American Friends Service Committee. In 1951 Chapelle was a photographer/writer for the Red Cross Blood Program. She and her husband then spent two years as writers/photographers in Iraq, Iran, and India at the U.S. Technical Co-operation Administration in the Department of State, generating public information and publicity materials. *Reader's Digest* published many of her articles during the 1950s, and in 1953 the Chapelles were published in the *National Geographic* magazine.

By the mid-1950s the Chapelles experienced serious marital trouble. They separated in 1955, and in July 1956 their fifteen-year marriage was annulled by the New York State Supreme Court.

That same year Chapelle covered life in India for the *National Geographic* and then became director of public information for the Research Institute of America in New York City. While holding this position, she went to Hungary to cover the Revolution of 1956 for *Life* magazine and as the publicist for the International Rescue Committee. While carrying penicillin with "freedom fighters," Chapelle was captured on 5 December 1956 and was charged with illegally crossing the Hungarian border. She was imprisoned in a Hungarian jail for fifty-two days, thirty-eight of which were spent in solitary confinement. She was released on 27 January 1957. This ordeal is described in great detail in Chapelle's 1962 autobiography, *What's a Woman Doing Here? A Reporter's Report on Herself*.

Later in 1957 Chapelle went to Algeria to photograph the Scorpion Battalion of the Algerian Federation of National Liberation. In 1958 she photographed Fidel Castro's revolution in Cuba. The following year Chapelle parachuted into Korea with an army airborne division.

Chapelle went on to have contract jobs with at least six magazines and one news syndicate, writing stories, taking pictures, and assembling story/photo packages on trouble spots throughout the world, including Algeria, Cuba, Lebanon, Okinawa, Kashmir, the Dominican Republic, Korea, Greece, Laos, and Vietnam. Her work appeared in such wide-ranging publications as the *Reader's Digest*, *Life*, *Mademoiselle*, the *National Observer*, and *Leatherneck*, among others. Chapelle became the first female journalist accredited to the Sixth Fleet and, at the time of her death, was the only woman authorized to jump with U.S. airborne forces.

Although she championed the military, Chapelle was not simply a mouthpiece of the U.S. government. Official briefings were of little interest to her; she felt she could only get the true story out in the field. The short, gravel-voiced, chain-smoking Chapelle was well known to many marines, and she frequently traveled without the normally required military escort. Chapelle's photographs and articles had a "you are there" quality, as did her first-person accounts. As a freelancer she usually had to hunt for stories on her own, skirting legalities and taking great personal risks.

When not on assignment covering U.S. soldiers overseas in the late 1950s and early 1960s, Chapelle spent several months a year on the lecture circuit, mostly in the East and Midwest, describing her experiences abroad and relating her grim view of Communism.

Government control of information became a major concern during the last few years of Chapelle's life. While working for the *Reader's Digest* in Laos and Vietnam for seven months in 1961, Chapelle shot hundreds of rolls of film and produced no fewer than six articles. She submitted her work to the Departments of Defense and State for review. The government's evaluation of one of her articles on Laos took about ten weeks, and she was told 800 of her photographs were "missing in censorship." "It was not surprising that the articles Dickey wrote from Laos and Vietnam, all of which were confrontational about American policy, were suppressed by the *Reader's Digest* and waylaid by the Pentagon, nor that her photographs were 'lost' by the Defense Department," wrote Roberta Ostroff (p. 329). Chapelle's November 1962 *National Geographic* article and photographs, "Helicopter War in South Viet Nam," were the first time Americans had seen in print other Americans fighting in Southeast Asia. The State Department tried to no avail to get the magazine editors to omit some of her pictures.

The $500 George Polk Memorial Award, the highest honor of the Overseas Press Club, was given to Chapelle in 1962. The following year "Helicopter War" won first place in the Magazine News Picture

Story category of the National Press Photographers Association competition.

Chapelle persuaded the *National Geographic* to send her back to Vietnam in 1964. From late 1964 through early 1965 she was paid a monthly guarantee for time spent in Southeast Asia, but she fought for months trying to get another article published. Angered at being put off repeatedly by *National Geographic* editors, Chapelle went to work for the *National Observer*, which assigned her to Vietnam for her fifth and final time in the fall of 1965. She was killed while on patrol with the marines near Chu Lai, South Vietnam. The *National Geographic* finally published "Water War in Vietnam" in the February 1966 issue.

Chapelle's hatred of Communism and love of the Marines compelled her to cover wars and rebellions over a twenty-year period. Unlike most foreign correspondents, she both photographed and wrote stories. As editor Bill Giles said after her death, "She had the rare gift of articulating what we call the 'feel' of a story. With her, I suspect, it came easy because she had a natural feel for people and events." Chapelle was the first woman and the fourth journalist to be killed while covering Vietnam.

• Chapelle's manuscripts and photographs are in the State Historical Society of Wisconsin, Madison. The National Geographic Magazine Archive, Washington, D.C., has a Chapelle file.

The work she published as a freelancer includes two articles with Tony Chapelle in the *National Geographic*: "Report from the Locust Wars," Apr. 1953, pp. 545–62, and "New Life for India's Villagers," Apr. 1956, pp. 572–88.

Roberta Ostroff, *Fire in the Wind: The Life of Dickey Chapelle* (1992), the only biography, tends to emphasize the personal more than the professional. There are chapters on Chapelle in Julia Edwards, *Women of the World: The Great Foreign Correspondents* (1988), and Virginia Elwood-Akers, *Women War Correspondents in the Vietnam War, 1961–1975* (1988). See also Frederick Ellis, "Dickey Chapelle: A Reporter and Her Work" (master's thesis, Univ. of Wisconsin, 1968); Stanley P. Friedman, "Dickey Chapelle: Two Wars and Four Revolutions," *Ms.*, Apr. 1976, pp. 24–27; and William D. Bevis, "Dickey Chapelle: Memories of an Extraordinary Woman," *Retired Officer*, Apr. 1986, pp. 26–29.

Obituaries are in the *New York Times*, 4 Nov. 1965; *Time*, 12 Nov. 1965; and *Newsweek*, 15 Nov. 1965. Eulogies appeared in the *National Observer*, 8 Nov. 1965; the *National Review*, 30 Nov. 1965; and the *National Geographic*, Feb. 1966.

C. Zoe Smith

CHAPELLE, Placide-Louis (28 Aug. 1842–9 Aug. 1905), Roman Catholic archbishop of New Orleans, was born at Runes, Lozère, France, the son of Jean Baptiste Chapelle and Marie Antoinette de Viala (occupations unknown). After receiving a classical education at Mende, France, he was sent by his uncle, the future bishop of Port-au-Prince, Haiti, to complete his studies at the college of Enghien in Belgium. This same uncle later encouraged him to move to the United States. Chapelle arrived in Baltimore in 1859 and entered St. Mary's Seminary, from which he received a doctorate in 1869. He was ordained to the priesthood in 1865 by Archbishop Martin J. Spalding. In 1866 he served as theologian to Spalding at the Second Plenary Council of Baltimore. From 1865 until 1881, he served at parishes in Rockville, Maryland, and Baltimore. In 1882 he was appointed pastor of St. Matthew's Parish in Washington, D.C., where he rose to prominence as one of the most important Catholic clergymen in the capital city. While serving as secretary to Cardinal James Gibbons, Chapelle was also secretary of the Bureau of Catholic Indian Missions and a promoter of the Catholic University of America in Washington, D.C.

Plans to send Chapelle to assist Archbishop Francis X. Leray of New Orleans in 1886 were curtailed due to the opposition of Bishop John Keane of Richmond, who preferred another candidate. James Gibbons, archbishop of Baltimore, acceded to Keane's request after initially supporting Chapelle's candidacy, but assuaged Chapelle's loss by having him appointed coadjutor, with right of succession, to the failing Archbishop John Baptist Salpointe of Santa Fe in 1891. Upon Salpointe's resignation in 1894, he briefly assumed this position. Three years later Rome appointed him to head the Archdiocese of New Orleans, which had once again become vacant. A few weeks after he formally took possession of his office, the United States went to war with Spain. Pope Leo XIII commissioned Chapelle to represent the Catholic church in the peace negotiations between Spain and the United States. At the same time, the pontiff appointed him the apostolic delegate to Cuba and Puerto Rico and the envoy extraordinary in the Philippines. In early 1899, his diplomatic rank in the Philippines was upgraded to the rank of apostolic delegate. At the Paris peace conference, he managed to have a clause inserted in the treaty that confirmed to the Catholic church the possession of all properties to which she had a right under the Spanish government.

In 1899 Chapelle made a tour of the Carribbean, and in 1900 he visited the Philippines. The Philippine archipelago was beset by armed revolution, which the American military and civilian officials were eagerly trying to subdue. One of the major demands of the Filipino revolutionaries was the confiscation of lands held by Spanish friars, religious communities of men, who had acquired vast landholdings in the colonial period. American officials, eager to pacify the country without antagonizing Catholic interests, impaneled two insular commissions to study this and other issues involved in administering the newly acquired islands. In these complex negotiations, Chapelle clearly favored the cause of the friars. He found his position undercut, however, by Archbishop John Ireland of St. Paul, Minnesota, who had close contacts with the McKinley administration, and American diplomat Bellamy Storer and his wife. The Storers were converts of Ireland's and were well connected with high ecclesiastics in Rome as well as with government officials. The American commissioner in the Philippines, William Howard Taft, also disliked Chapelle and exerted what influence he could to have the prelate recalled. Chapelle's identification with the friars' cause led to his dismissal from the Philippine post by Cardinal Mariano Rampolla del Tindaro, secretary of state of Pope Leo XIII. Rampolla recognized that Chapelle had lost credibility with the American negotiators. As an accommodation to Washington, Chapelle was replaced by the more pliant Archbishop Donato Sbaretti. Once the rebellion was quelled, the issue of the lands faded. Eventually, Taft dealt directly with Vatican officials, and the U.S. government confiscated the lands while reimbursing the friars for their losses.

Returning to New Orleans, Chapelle dedicated his remaining years to working with the people of his diocese, who felt neglected by his absence on far-flung diplomatic duties. He wiped out a huge diocesan debt and visited every parish in the diocese. Chapelle met his death in New Orleans during a yellow fever outbreak.

• Much about Chapelle can be gleaned from John Tracy Ellis, *Life of James Cardinal Gibbons* (2 vols., 1951), which is especially helpful in discussing Chapelle's association with Gibbons and his diplomatic work. Additional information about Ireland, the Storers, and Chapelle may be found in Marvin R. O'Connell, *John Ireland and the American Catholic Church* (1988). A significant amount of information about Chapelle's work in the Philippines is found in a two-part article by John T. Farrell, "Background of the Taft Mission to Rome I," *Catholic Historical Review* 36 (Apr. 1950): 1–32, and "Background of the Taft Mission to Rome II," *Catholic Historical Review* 37 (Apr. 1951): 1–22. See also Frank T. Reuter, "American Catholics and the Establishment of the Philippines Public School System," *Catholic Historical Review* 49 (Oct. 1963): 365–81.

STEVEN M. AVELLA

CHAPIN, Charles Value (17 Jan. 1856–31 Jan. 1941), public health officer and epidemiologist, was born in Providence, Rhode Island, the son of Joshua Bicknell Chapin, who was successively a physician, pharmacist, photographer, and Rhode Island Commissioner of Public Schools, and Jane Catherine Louise Value, a portrait painter. After graduating with a B.A. from Brown University in 1876, Chapin remained in Providence for another year reading medicine under preceptors. He then continued his medical training with a year at the College of Physicians and Surgeons of New York, followed by a year at the Bellevue Hospital Medical College, where he studied pathology under William H. Welch and received his M.D. in 1879. During the following year he interned at Bellevue Hospital under such physicians as Abraham Jacobi, Edward G. Janeway, and the elder Austin Flint.

Between 1880 and 1884 Chapin practiced medicine in Providence. During that period he joined the regular city and state medical societies, in both of which he went on to play creative and lengthy roles as reformer, scientific contributor, and president. In his first few years in medicine he also served as part-time pathologist at the Rhode Island Hospital and did medical charity work for the Providence Dispensary. Between 1882 and 1895 he was also part-time professor of physiology at Brown University, for which institution he helped organize a pioneering program of premedical studies. In 1886 Chapin married Anna Augusta Balch of Providence; they had one son.

Admittedly lacking a comforting bedside manner with patients, and impatient with the routine of private practice, Chapin in 1884 welcomed appointment as superintendent of health of Providence, and in 1888 he became city registrar as well. An energetic, conscientious, and highly innovative public servant, he remained in these positions through successive political changes for forty-eight and forty-four years, respectively. And during that extraordinarily lengthy public career he gained international stature as a role model for the modern municipal health officer.

Chapin's early reputation rested largely on his vigorous efforts to eradicate the unsanitary conditions in his city as well as on his success in updating sanitary technologies and systematizing the standard urban sanitary measures of the day. One prominent activity was his campaign to eliminate Providence's malodorous and unhygienic privies and to expedite the introduction of indoor plumbing. He also experimented with chemical and mechanical methods of garbage disposal, and he became a pioneer in the testing of filtration and other modes of protecting public water supplies in the United States. In 1902 he summarized his own and other city health officers' experiences with contemporary sanitary activities in a large volume entitled *Municipal Sanitation in the United States*, a work that became a standard text in the field.

During this same period, however, Chapin moved steadily away from traditional environmental sanitation to carve out a more significant career as one of the earliest American health officers to apply the findings and techniques of bacteriology to sanitation and public health work generally. With Gardner T. Swarts he established, in 1888, the first municipal bacteriological laboratory in the United States. There, among more routine work, they performed pioneer tests of mechanical water filters and examinations of disinfectants. And then, as laboratory diagnostic methods developed elsewhere in the 1890s, initially for typhoid fever and tuberculosis, Chapin made bacteriological analysis a key element in the campaign to control the common infectious diseases.

By the early years of the twentieth century, Chapin had become widely known as a public health iconoclast. This was due to the vigor of his attack on some of the era's most tenacious epidemiological and sanitary theories: among them, the idea that filth per se caused urban communicable disease; that such diseases were indiscriminately transmitted through the air, often accompanied by bad smells; and that disinfection was a cure-all for many sanitary evils. To evaluate such theories, Chapin conducted extensive field studies and statistical analyses of the incidence and behavior of diseases in Providence and then integrated his findings with the pertinent laboratory research results of the day. He concluded that the ordinary infectious diseases of temperate climates were spread principally through quite direct contact between persons. And, in the continued absence of sera or vaccines for most such diseases, he believed that the most effective means of preventing their spreading were the isolation of individuals having specific diseases; the monitoring of well carriers when discovered; and especially, the strict observance of personal cleanliness. As a corollary, he concluded that most of the standard sanitary measures of the day against generalized filthy conditions had little if anything to do with preventing specific diseases. He urged that these measures should no longer be regarded as responsibilities of health departments but should be transferred to other municipal departments, at least in cities where the basic sanitary facilities or infrastructures were already in place.

Chapin synthesized these and related ideas in a landmark book, *The Sources and Modes of Infection* (1910). At about the same time he incorporated many of them in his planning for the Providence City Hospital, an up-to-date isolation facility for patients with infectious diseases. When it opened in 1910, the hospital became a showcase for the systematic application of aseptic nursing principles and as such became a model for other similar institutions around the United States.

Chapin's concepts formed much of the theoretical underpinning for and substance of what came to be known, particularly among the better-trained health officers, as the "new public health." This collection of concepts, strategies, and measures, in turn, informed many broad community health projects focussing on specific problems, enterprises that combined the efforts of health officials and professionals with those of lay reformers at national, state, and local levels. Chapin played a direct, long-term role in the development of several of these—notably, the antituberculosis campaign, the infant hygiene movement, and the school health movement.

Chapin was equally known to his contemporaries as an authority in the field of vital statistics. In part this was a result of his efforts in the American Public Health Association to improve disease nomenclature and classification and to standardize birth and death certificates. But to a much greater extent it resulted from his routine work as city registrar of Providence. In that position he was able to make the city's reporting of birth and mortality statistics among the most accurate and complete of any American community. And, through his analyses of the unbroken series of mortality reports begun in 1856 by his predecessor, Edwin M. Snow, and continued by himself, Chapin provided the early twentieth-century public health community with more accurate information on urban disease trends than was available from almost any other American source.

After 1900 Chapin also attracted professional attention with his development of precise modes for evaluating given public health measures, particularly in terms of such criteria as cost and their effectiveness in reducing disease. His principal application of these methods came in the nationwide survey of health in the various states that he conducted between 1913 and 1915 for the American Medical Association. Results of the survey were published in his *Report on State Public Health Work* (1916). Chapin's numerical ratings of the states in that work made for no little controversy, but the report as a whole went on to exert considerable influence in stimulating broader state public health legislation and in strengthening health departments around the country. During the 1920s Chapin went on to refine and extend his appraisal techniques for the American Public Health Association.

Chapin served as president of the American Public Health Association (1926–1927) and as president of the American Epidemiological Society (1927). In 1932 he retired from his positions as Providence's superintendent of health and city registrar. He died in Providence.

Chapin's administrative and evaluative innovations were practical contributions both to good city government and to public health professionalism in Progressive-era America and ones that remained as durable standards in subsequent generations. His analyses of urban diseases, while carried out with simple arithmetical methods rather than sophisticated mathematical statistics, were nevertheless of much importance as models for a revived science of epidemiology during the early twentieth century. At the same time, the new laboratory-based approach to health work that Chapin did so much to shape became after 1900 the acknowledged basis for the activities of most of America's organized public health professionals. However, as the twentieth century went on, the almost exclusive preoccupation of these professionals with specific diseases attracted increasing criticism, particularly because of the conspicuous tendency of those in the field to neglect the general causes of ill health, including the social and environmental factors in health.

• There are collections of Chapin's papers in the Rhode Island Medical Society Library, the Brown University Library, and the Rhode Island Historical Society. Chapin also wrote *How to Avoid Infection* (1917) and, with his wife, *A History of Rhode Island Ferries* (1925). *The Papers of Charles V. Chapin, M.D.*, ed. Clarence L. Scamman (1934), contains a short biographical account and a good bibliography. A full-length study is James H. Cassedy, *Charles V. Chapin and the Public Health Movement* (1962). Among professional appreciations are those by Wade H. Frost, "The Familial Aggregation of Infectious Diseases," *American Journal of Public Health* 28 (Jan. 1939): 7–13; an address by George E. Vincent in the *Rhode Island Medical Journal* 10 (Mar. 1927): 35–45; and Charles-Edward A. Winslow, *The Conquest of Epidemic Disease* (1943), chapter 18. See also Barbara G. Rosenkrantz, "Cart before Horse: Theory, Practice and Professional Image in American Public Health, 1870–1920," *Journal of the History of Medicine and Allied Sciences* 29 (Jan. 1974): 55–73.

JAMES H. CASSEDY

CHAPIN, Francis Stuart (3 Feb. 1888–7 July 1974), sociologist, was born in Brooklyn, New York, the son of Charles B. Chapin and Florence Johnson. Chapin was tempered by a Protestant work ethic passed down from his clergyman father and a love of poetry and painting from his mother. Chapin's early interests included mathematics and chemistry. At twenty-one he received a B.S. in science at Columbia (1909). He continued at Columbia and earned his M.A. (1910) and then Ph.D. (1911) in sociology. *Education and the Mores*, based on his dissertation, was published in 1911. That same year he married Nellie Estelle Peck; they would have three children.

At the time during which Chapin developed intellectually, the United States was in transition, with monumental changes taking place. Urbanization, immigration, and large-scale industrialization combined to create rapid growth, poverty and other social problems, and institutional disorganization. The times required a new breed of social thought. Studying under both sociologist Franklin Giddings and anthropologist Franz Boas, Chapin made his mark at Columbia as a twentieth-century empirical thinker.

Best known for his contributions as author, administrator, researcher, teacher, and public servant, Chapin taught economics at Wellesley College in 1911, served as professor at the Smith College of Social Work beginning in 1912 and then as director from 1918 until 1921, when he fell ill and took a leave of absence. In 1922 he became chairperson of the Department of Sociology at the University of Minnesota (1922–1951), teaching from 1922 to 1953. In this capacity Chapin became known as "Mr. Sociology," the man who gave both Minnesota sociology and American sociology its scientific character. In conjunction with his position in the Department of Sociology, Chapin also served as director of the University of Minnesota School of Social Work from 1922 to 1949. His first wife died in 1925, and in 1927 he married Eula Elizabeth Pickard; the couple had no children together.

Chapin's research interests were broad and rich. He studied individual attainment in university faculties, the impact of war on community leadership, individual participation in the community, housing, small-group experiments, organizational structures, latent and manifest social patterns, and more. During the course of his career he wrote ten books and 170 articles. His greatest contributions have to do with the subjects of structure, change, culture, and methodology.

Chapin considered education to be an institution that promoted social stability. As a social organ, it institutionalized custom and exerted control. In the past, Chapin argued in *Education and the Mores*, education had preserved the mores of the clan, tribe, or dominant class, but due to the impact of evolutionary science, mores had become less powerful and education as an institution had become disorganized. By the time he published *An Introduction to the Study of Social Evolution* (1913), however, Chapin's notion of education had begun to change. Early on he had become convinced that education was the cradle of stability. Interested in group survival, Chapin also adopted Giddings's concept of behavioral pluralism. The group or nation with the strongest bonds (customs and morals) would be the most likely to survive.

Chapin's early works were dominated by an emphasis on biology and evolutionism. Organic evolution ensured the inheritance of characteristics from generation to generation with variation, while the struggle for survival perpetuated the fittest of the species. "Biologically, survival means the individual reaches maturity and has offspring to which he transmits the favorable characteristics that aided him in the struggle" (*Social Evolution*, p. 26). Chapin stressed the impact of both the physical and the cultural environment. He argued that human beings are shaped primarily by social heredity in that through socialization the individual receives standards and customs, and thus culture, from the collective experience.

Chapin's strict evolutionary view of human nature was modified somewhat in *An Historical Introduction to Social Economy* (1917). Here he maintained that, in modern society, conditions of both natural and social selection are at work, but social selection is more prominent and also more dependent on social control. The Industrial Revolution changed material culture and, as a consequence, all aspects of everyday life, including society's attitudes toward social problems. These changes, he believed, had caused charity to give way to social legislation. Massive poverty was declining, he argued, thanks to industrial and social organization. Poverty was ending, "in large measure at least, not so much of its own accord as because of intelligent efforts to abolish the causes" (p. 280).

Three years later, Chapin published *Field Work and Social Research* (1920), his landmark work in promoting the use of statistics in social science research. This work helped to earn him the label "incorrigible quantifier." For Chapin, there were three major methods of research: historical, fieldwork, and statistical analysis. Chapin and other pluralistic behaviorists emphasized the use of statistical analysis and promoted the use of graphs, scales, ratios, averages, coefficients, and so on. For Chapin, science had three tasks: to discover laws, to determine causes, and to predict effect. Like other scientists, the social researcher would develop a working hypothesis, collect data, classify data for comparative uses, and make generalizations from the data to produce some law or formula.

In 1928 Chapin returned to the topic of culture in *Cultural Change*, one of his major theoretical contributions. He studied the subject within a scientific framework, identifying cycles during which material and nonmaterial culture undergo changes and social forms, institutions, and customs both rise and fall. Cultural change, both material and nonmaterial, could be thought of as cyclical, with each cultural form abiding by its own laws of change. Societies must react to the cultural changes either by attempting to enforce mores, by trying out different expedients, or by integrating trial and error into a stable plan. Likewise, the changing patterns required different leadership. For Chapin, the laws of each cultural cycle could be expressed quantitatively.

Contemporary American Institutions (1935) is considered by many to be Chapin's second major theoretical contribution. Here, he attempted to integrate the theoretical problem of structure. Starting with small, concrete units of social behavior, Chapin used an inductive scientific approach to examine institutional behavior, change, cycles of the social process, and group reaction. This particular contribution has been described as Chapin's beginning of an approach to both collective psychology and leadership styles. Chapin found three cycles of the social process (i.e., stability inertia, experimentation, and integration). As each phase becomes increasingly complex, attitudes and behaviors of the masses change, requiring different leadership styles that reflect the needs of their particular cycle.

Although Chapin continued to write for and to edit prominent journals and to conduct lectures, his last book, *Experimental Designs in Sociological Research*, was published in 1947 and revised in 1955. In it he returned to methodology and introduced cross-sectional, projected, and ex post facto designs, again focusing on hypotheses, empirical measures, laws, and predictions. Althouse considered this work to be Chapin's "methodological high point" (p. 217).

Chapin retired to Asheville, North Carolina, in 1953 and remained active in the community until his death there. He served as a consultant to and board member of various organizations and commissions, lectured and published on occasion, and enjoyed fishing and spending time with his family.

His no-nonsense approach to sociology resulted in a transformation for Chapin over the years. Initially focusing on abstract singular units such as evolution, by the 1930s Chapin had begun to abandon such concepts for smaller concrete units that he believed could be defended methodologically. Believing that sociology should be as scientific, as quantifiable, and as objective as possible, Chapin disdained qualitative "subjective" approaches, which he found to be unscientific. Chapin was regarded as one of the most important contributors to the transition of sociology from prescience to science.

• Chapin's papers are located at the University of Minnesota Archives Collection. The standard work on Chapin, from which much of the material for this essay derives, is Ronald Althouse, "The Intellectual Career of F. Stuart Chapin: An Examination of the Development and Contribution of a Pluralistic Behaviorist" (Ph.D. diss., Univ. of Minnesota, 1964). For additional sources see Gary Alan Fine and Janet Severance, "Great Men and Hard Times: Sociology at the University of Minnesota," *Sociological Quarterly* 26, no. 1 (1985): 117–34, and Don Martindale, *The Romance of a Profession: A Case History in the Sociology of Sociology* (1976) and *Nature and Types of Sociological Theory* (1981).

LORI HOLYFIELD
GARY ALAN FINE

CHAPIN, Harry Forster (7 Dec. 1942–16 July 1981), popular singer and writer of topical songs, was born in New York City, the son of James Forbes Chapin, a big-band percussionist, and Elspeth Burke. As a high school student, Chapin sang in the Brooklyn Heights Boys Choir and, later, played guitar, banjo, and trumpet in a band that included his father and brothers Stephen Chapin and Tom Chapin. He attended the U.S. Air Force Academy briefly and studied at Cornell University from 1960 to 1964. Chapin was best known for his popular ballads, films, and cultural and humanitarian work for the cause of eradicating world hunger. He married Sandra Campbell Gaston in 1968; they had five children.

During the late 1960s, Harry and his brothers performed in clubs in New York's Greenwich Village. Around this time, he developed a strong interest in documentary film. In 1969, *Legendary Champions*, a film he made with Jim Jacobs, won first prizes at the New York and Atlanta film festivals and was nominated for an Academy Award as the best feature documentary of the year.

Chapin's first album with his own band, *Heads and Tails*, was released in 1972, featuring the introspective ballad "Taxi," which became a top-twenty hit. This song, with its exploration of the themes of personal loss and assessment of past and present, typified Chapin's style, which appealed to young audiences. The musical style was a variant on the form of the 32-bar popular song, with an interlude in a contrasting key that revealed the narrator's struggle for understanding himself and his path in life. Chapin was nominated in 1972 for a Grammy Award as the year's best new artist. He received another Grammy nomination in 1975 as best male vocalist for his recording of the single "Cat's in the Cradle" from the *Verities and Balderdash* album, which was his first to sell more than a million copies. Other albums include *Sniper and Other Love Songs* (1972), *Short Stories* (1973), *Portrait Gallery* (1975), *On the Road to Kingdom Come* and *Harry Chapin's Greatest Stories Live* (1976), *Dance Band on the Titanic* (produced by his brother Steve in 1977), *Living Room Suite* (1978), *Legends of the Lost and Found* (1979), and *Sequel* (1980). In addition to recording and performing, Chapin wrote the music for the television series "Make a Wish," of which his brother Tom was the host. From the show, the song "Circles" (1971), later titled "Circle," became popular. He also wrote music for the plays *Zinger* and *The Night That Made America Famous*.

Chapin was the recipient of the Rock Music Award for public service in 1976 and 1977 and a Humanitarian Award from B'nai B'rith in 1977. A longtime Long Island resident, he was selected as the Long Island Advertisers Man of the Year in 1977, received the Lone Eagle Award of the Long Island Public Relations Society in 1978, and was named one of the Ten Outstanding Young Men by the U.N. Jaycees in 1977.

During the last years of his career, Chapin performed more than 200 concerts a year, many of them for cultural and humanitarian organizations such as the National Multiple Sclerosis Society. He maintained this demanding schedule of fundraising and humanitarian activities even as he continued to compose new songs and record new albums. Chapin was honorary chair of the Suffolk County (Long Island) Hunger

Hearings, a trustee of the Performing Arts Foundation of Long Island, a founding trustee of the World Hunger Year, and a member of the President's Commission on International, Domestic, and World Hunger. From 1979 to 1981 he served on the boards of the Eglevsky Ballet and the Long Island Business Association.

Harry Chapin suffered a heart attack while driving on the Long Island Expressway on the way to a benefit concert. His car was subsequently hit by a truck. Chapin is remembered both for the poignancy of his storytelling ballads and for his commitment to using his talents to support local and national cultural and humanitarian causes.

• After Harry Chapin's death, his brothers, Tom and Steve, edited *Harry Chapin: A Legacy in Song* (1987). Peter Coan wrote a popular biography, *Taxi: The Harry Chapin Story* (1987). See Harry Chapin's obituaries in the *New York Times*, 17 July 1981; *Time*, 27 July 1981; and *Newsweek*, 27 July 1981.

BARBARA L. TISCHLER

CHAPIN, Henry Dwight (4 Feb. 1857–27 June 1942), physician, was born in Steubenville, Ohio, the son of the Reverend Henry Barton Chapin, a Presbyterian minister, and Harriet Ann Smith. He graduated from the College of New Jersey (later Princeton University) in 1877 and studied medicine with a preceptor (possibly Dr. Stephen Smith) for two years. Chapin subsequently attended the College of Physicians and Surgeons (later Columbia University Medical School) and received his M.D. in 1881.

After serving several internships Chapin began private practice in 1884. Over the course of his career he served as attending physician or consulting physician at numerous New York area institutions. From 1885 until 1890 he was professor of the diseases of children at the Women's Medical College of the New York Infirmary. His primary affiliation, however, was with the New York Post-Graduate Medical School and Hospital. The association began in 1885 when he taught a course on diseases of children; the following year he became professor of pediatrics, a position he held until 1920, when he became professor emeritus. Chapin also served as director of pediatrics in the hospital's Babies' Ward from 1885 until 1917. In addition, he was a member of the hospital's board of directors and chair of its social service committee. As an educator, Chapin was known for his Monday pediatric "demonstrations," in which he lectured to as many as one hundred general practitioners. At a time when pediatrics was not medicine practiced by specialists but specialized medical knowledge applied by general practitioners, Chapin's educational endeavors helped transport knowledge obtained at the hospital bedside and in the clinical laboratory to the homes of young patients.

Chapin helped to define the emerging specialty of pediatrics with its age-based focus and its attention to social welfare as well as science. He has been called "the first socially conscious American pediatrician," which captures his own commitment to improving the lives of children through the application of medical science and alludes to the fact that he worked within a larger Progressive Era movement that sought to impose professional leadership on a variety of humanitarian reforms. Chapin's progressivism manifested itself in efforts to improve the care provided to poor, sick, and dependent infants and children in order to lower the infant mortality rate and increase the chances that youngsters would grow up to become productive citizens. Throughout his career, he played a prominent role in the leadership of medical and social welfare organizations. One of the founders of the American Pediatric Society in 1888, he served as its president in 1910. In 1912 he served as chair of the pediatric section of the American Medical Association and in 1913 was named chair of the pediatric section of the New York Academy of Medicine. From 1909 to 1920 he was president of the Working Woman's Protective Union, and he served on the advisory council of the Public Education Association of New York and the boards of the New York Juvenile Asylum, the Havens Relief Fund Society, the Life Saving Benevolent Association, the Hospital Service Association of New York, and the Children's Welfare Federation, which he served as president in 1924.

Chapin's writings display his interest in advancing pediatric science and promoting child welfare. He wrote two pediatrics textbooks, *The Theory and Practice of Infant Feeding* (1902) and *Diseases of Infants and Children* (1909) with the first four editions coauthored with Godfrey R. Pisek and the fifth and sixth with Lawrence T. Royster. He also wrote three popular works, *Vital Questions* (1905), *Health First: The Fine Art of Living* (1917), and *Heredity and Child Culture* (1922). In addition, Chapin published over 120 articles on a variety of subjects, including diseases of children, infant nutrition, public schools, care of foundlings, and hospital social services.

The enduring legacy of Chapin resides not in his organizational efforts or his publications but in his efforts to unite medicine and social welfare both inside and outside the hospital. At the Post-Graduate Hospital he inaugurated such reforms as visiting hours for the parents of hospitalized children and the first hospital social work effort in the country. The latter began in 1890 with female visitors who investigated the circumstances of discharged patients. They were soon replaced by a trained nurse, and by 1905 the hospital had a formal social service program. Another of Chapin's innovations was the privately run Speedwell Society, created in 1902 to board convalescent infants with rural foster families. While boarding-out systems were not new, the Speedwell Plan was unique in its careful medical regulation. Female managers inspected the homes of foster families, and local physicians and nurses provided additional oversight. By 1940 over twenty thousand children had entered Speedwell homes and the work of the society was widely known thanks to Chapin's efforts to publicize the program.

In 1907 Chapin married Alice Delafield. They had no children but a full nursery. In 1910 the Chapins took in an abandoned baby girl, caring for her until she was in good health and overseeing her adoption. Shortly thereafter they established a large nursery. The Alice Chapin Adoption Nursery oversaw 1,700 adoptions and placed 2,000 other children. After Henry Dwight Chapin's death, it merged with the Spence Alumni Association to become the Spence-Chapin Adoption Service. According to Chapin, placing infants was his "true life work." Through the Alice Chapin Adoption Nursery and Speedwell Society he played a critical role in shifting the care of dependent infants and children from institutions to foster or adoptive homes. He also contributed substantially to the development of pediatrics through his leadership, scholarship, and teaching. Chapin died at his home in Bronxville, New York.

• There are no manuscript holdings for Chapin. The records of the New York Post-Graduate Hospital and Babies' Ward are located at the New York University Medical Center Archives, which also contains some photographs of Chapin and a letter. See also "Dr. and Mrs. Chapin," *Review of Reviews* 78 (Aug. 1928): 182–83; Marshall Carleton Pease, "An Early Undertaking in Hospital Social Service," *American Journal of Diseases of Children* 44 (July 1932): 176–80; "Henry Dwight Chapin (1857–1942): Pediatric Social Service Pioneer," *Medical Press*, Feb. 1957, p. 119; and Peter Romanofsky, "Infant Mortality, Dr. Henry Dwight Chapin, and the Speedwell Society, 1890–1920," *Journal of the Medical Society of New Jersey* 73 (Jan. 1976): 33–38.

Obituaries appear in the *American Journal of Diseases of Children* 64 (Sept. 1942): 535–38; and in the *New York Times*, 28 June 1942; an obituary of Alice Delafield Chapin is in the *New York Times*, 21 Feb. 1964.

JANET GOLDEN

CHAPIN, James Paul (9 July 1889–5 Apr. 1964), ornithologist, was born in New York City, the son of Gilbert Granger Chapin, a fresh produce dealer, and Nano Eagle. Although the family home was situated fewer than twenty blocks from the American Museum of Natural History, with which Chapin would be associated for nearly sixty years, much of his childhood and young manhood was spent on Staten Island. There he developed a strong interest in natural history, delivering his first paper before the local natural history society at the age of sixteen. That same year (1905) Chapin completed high school.

Deciding to take a year off before entering Columbia University, Chapin secured a temporary appointment in the American Museum's exhibit preparation department. He began his undergraduate career at Columbia in the fall of 1907, but his studies were interrupted in the spring of 1909 when an unusual opportunity arose. Arrangements had been made for an American Museum expedition to carry out a biological survey of the Belgian Congo. Herbert Lang, the expedition's leader and Chapin's former supervisor at the museum, suggested that the nineteen-year-old Chapin accompany him on what was projected as a one- to three-year trip. Chapin accepted this invitation, which would prove decisive in his choice of career. The expedition in fact lasted until nearly the end of 1914 and gave him a thorough grounding in the ornithology of the Congo region, which ultimately became the area of his professional specialization.

Often Lang and Chapin worked together, but there were periods of time during their five and a half years in Africa during which the two men worked in different parts of the Congo. The two men made an effective team, and the results they achieved were impressive. They traveled a total of 15,000 miles, employed 38,000 native porters, and collected more than 126,000 specimens. Four-fifths of these were invertebrates, though there were also 6,400 birds and 5,800 mammals, together with nearly 11,000 other vertebrates and 3,800 items of anthropological material, nearly 10,000 photographs, and detailed field notes. Complex logistical challenges were encountered in getting this mass of material back to New York in the midst of World War I, but this task was successfully accomplished early in 1915.

Chapin resumed his studies at Columbia, completing his A.B. in 1916 and his M.A. in 1917, but his efforts to resume work on the Congo materials were further delayed by U.S. entry into World War I. Chapin, who spoke fluent French, served in the Allied Expeditionary Force as a first lieutenant. A billeting officer in France, he returned to New York in 1919.

Appointed an assistant in ornithology at the American Museum on his return from Africa in 1915, Chapin was promoted to assistant curator of ornithology in 1919 and to associate curator in 1923. He retained this post for twenty-five years until being forced to retire in 1948. His doctoral dissertation, completed at Columbia in 1932, dealt with the bird specimens he had brought back to New York from the Congo in 1915 and constituted a zoological account of the colony's bird fauna. Chapin's was the first doctorate ever awarded by Columbia for work in field ornithology. Additional research led to the publication of Chapin's *Birds of the Belgian Congo*, a four-part, 3,055-page effort with more than 400 illustrations. The first two volumes were issued in 1932 and 1938, the last two in 1953 and 1954. The substance of Chapin's doctoral dissertation formed the basis for the first half of the first volume of this work. This project is regarded as one of the outstanding works of zoological research ever completed on any African region, and the best done by an American.

Chapin returned to Africa and the Congo for additional research on five occasions, in 1926–1927, 1930, 1937, 1942, and finally from 1953 to 1958. The 1942 trip was undertaken on behalf of the Office of Strategic Services in order to complete a war-related project. Chapin's travels also took him to western Canada (1915), Panama (1923), and the Galapagos Islands (1930). During an expedition to Polynesia in 1934–1935 he collected a number of specimens that were mounted in the American Museum's Hall of Oceanic Birds.

Chapin was noted for the care, precision, and tenacity exhibited in his work. In 1913, for example, he was given a solitary flight feather of a bird unknown to him by a native in the Congo. For twenty-three years he was unsuccessful in identifying it until he came across two old dust-covered mounted peacock-like birds stored in the Congo Museum in Belgium. He determined that the feather in his possession matched ones found on these birds, which proved to be of a new species. For many years Chapin exemplified the study of African ornithology to the many younger colleagues who consulted him. His field notes and some of his letters often included clearly drawn illustrations. He enjoyed the respect and affection of many of his professional colleagues.

Chapin was president of the American Ornithologists' Union from 1939 to 1942 and of the Explorer's Club of New York from 1949 to 1950. He was an honorary member of the British, French, and German ornithological societies and of the Cercle Zoologique Congolaise, and was active in other scientific organizations. His accomplishments brought him several medals and honors from the Belgian government, the National Academy of Sciences, and the Explorer's Club of New York.

Chapin met Suzanne Drouël in France during World War I and married her in 1921. They had four children, one of whom died in childhood, and were divorced in 1939. Chapin's second wife, whom he married in 1940, was Ruth Trimble, who had been an assistant curator of birds at the Carnegie Museum in Pittsburgh, Pennsylvania. The couple had no children.

In poor health during the last several years of his life, Chapin nevertheless continued with his ornithological researches until the day before his death, which occurred in New York City.

• The American Museum of Natural History holds Chapin's notes on his fieldwork and a good deal of his correspondence. Biographical sketches are in *Natural History*, Jan. 1942; *Audubon*, July 1946; and *Auk*, Apr. 1966; the latter incorporates a bibliography of Chapin's scientific publications, save for book reviews. His obituary is in the *New York Times*, 7 Apr. 1964.

KEIR B. STERLING

CHAPIN, Roy Dikeman (23 Feb. 1880–10 Feb. 1936), auto industry pioneer and secretary of commerce, was born in Lansing, Michigan, the son of Edward Cornelius Chapin, a successful local attorney, and Ella King. In 1899 Chapin enrolled in the University of Michigan, but he left in the spring of 1901 to take a position with the Olds Motor Works in Detroit. Chapin worked as a photographer, helped out in the factory in May during a machinists' strike, and served as a test driver. It was in the latter capacity that Chapin drove an Oldsmobile runabout from Detroit to New York in seven and a half days in 1901, arriving in time to display it at the National Automobile Show. This trip, the one event for which Chapin is best remembered, promoted sales of the frail, 600-pound car while providing a boost to Chapin's career.

In 1902 Chapin was given a top sales position with the Olds company, despite the objections of R. E. Olds, who thought he was too young and inexperienced for the job. Olds was overruled by Frederic Smith, the secretary-treasurer, an early sign of the rift between Olds and Smith, whose family controlled a majority of the company stock. This rift led to Olds's departure in 1904 and Smith's assumption of the position of general manager. Smith then named Chapin sales manager. His skill as a salesman had helped make the Oldsmobile the world's bestselling car, with sales doubling from 2,500 in 1902 to 5,000 in 1904.

However, in 1906 Chapin persuaded the Buffalo automaker Edwin R. Thomas to back a new company that Chapin and three other Olds employees wanted to form to produce a new runabout designed by one of the four men, Howard E. Coffin, chief engineer for Olds. Chapin was general manager of the resulting E. R. Thomas–Detroit Company, but distribution of the company's cars was handled by Thomas's Buffalo company. To free the Detroit firm from this arrangement, Chapin in 1908 persuaded Hugh Chalmers to buy half of Thomas's interest, with the company reorganized as Chalmers-Detroit. It distributed its own cars, and Chapin continued as general manager.

In February 1909, Chapin, Chalmers, Coffin, and other investors formed the Hudson Motor Car Company, which was named after Joseph L. Hudson, a wealthy Detroit merchant and principal investor in the new business. Later that year Chapin became president of Hudson, which quickly emerged as one of the industry's stronger companies. Production rose from 1,000 cars in 1909 to nearly 13,000 in 1915, at which time Hudson was reportedly the world's largest producer of six-cylinder cars, which it had introduced in 1912.

With his newfound wealth, Chapin took more time to enjoy himself. He and Howard Coffin, a close friend as well as business colleague, took trips to Europe. On a trip to Georgia, Coffin introduced Chapin to Inez Tiedeman, whom Chapin married in 1914.

From the outset of his career, Chapin took an active interest in automobile trade association work and would become the industry's recognized spokesman on many issues. He also became a champion of the good-roads cause. In 1913, together with Henry B. Joy of the Packard company, he took the leadership in forming the Lincoln Highway Association, whose goal was a coast-to-coast all-weather road.

Too much attention to outside interests probably explains Chapin's failure to note the rising costs that brought a sharp drop in Hudson profits in 1915. His first reaction was to involve Hudson in a merger that William C. Durant was trying to put together in 1916. When that deal fell through, Chapin moved to regain full control of Hudson, but his plans for restoring the growth of the earlier years were delayed by American entry into World War I in April 1917. During the war, Chapin was chairman of the Highway Transport Committee of the Council on National Defense. To ease the critical shortage of freight cars, he persuaded manufacturers of trucks bound for the war to have them driven to East Coast ports rather than shipping them by rail. The result was a dramatic demonstration of the possibilities of trucks as long-distance freight haulers.

After the war Chapin turned his attention to company matters. In 1917 he and his colleagues had formed a separate company, Essex Motor Car Company, to provide Hudson dealers with a lower-priced, four-cylinder car. Essex's production soon surpassed Hudson's. The popularity of Essex and Hudson cars after the war was due to the introduction in 1922 of closed-body models, a development that constitutes Chapin's most important contribution to the industry. Up to this time, closed cars were limited to luxury makes, but Chapin priced closed Essex and Hudson makes at only $100 more than the open models. Producers of other lower-priced cars had to follow suit, and by 1925 over half the cars produced in the United States were closed, not open models.

Hudson's success led Chapin and his partners to go public in 1922 with Chapin handling the negotiations. The stock offering provided the remaining original partners with $7 million in cash and $16 million in Hudson stock. In 1923 Chapin, while still firmly in control of the company, stepped down as president and took the less demanding role of chairman.

Chapin devoted more time to his family (which by 1930 included six children) and his mansion in the Detroit suburb of Grosse Pointe Farms. Chapin also helped organize the Pan-American Conference for Highway Education in 1924, chaired the World Transport Committee in Paris in 1927, and presided over the Sixth International Road Congress in Washington in 1930. The last caused the French government in 1931 to name him an officer in the Legion of Honor.

In July 1932 President Herbert Hoover appointed Chapin as secretary of commerce. Chapin is best remembered in this position for his unsuccessful effort to persuade Henry Ford to agree to participate in a federal plan to save one of Detroit's two major banking groups, Guardian Detroit Union. Ford's rejection of Chapin's appeal precipitated a crisis that led to the Michigan bank holiday, precedent for the national bank holiday proclaimed by Franklin D. Roosevelt in March 1933.

Upon Chapin's return to Detroit in 1933 at the end of the Hoover administration, he resumed active command of Hudson. The company's production had plummeted from 300,000 cars in 1929 to only 40,000 in 1933 during the depths of the Great Depression. While many of the remaining smaller auto companies were driven out of business by the economic collapse, Chapin was able to raise production to 100,000 by 1935 and to once again turn a profit. At the same time he was actively involved with industry affairs as a member of the committee that drew up the auto industry code required under the provisions of the National Industrial Recovery Act.

Chapin died in Detroit of pneumonia a few days short of his fifty-sixth birthday. One of the leaders of the auto industry during its formative years, he could claim as his most important achievement the Hudson company, which he created and which he headed for a quarter century, staving off the economic forces that destroyed most of the auto companies in existence when Hudson was organized. His eldest son, Roy D. Chapin, Jr., later became an executive with Hudson and served as chief executive officer of American Motors Corporation, its successor, from 1967 to 1977.

• The papers of Roy D. Chapin are in the Michigan Historical Collections of the Bentley Historical Library, University of Michigan, Ann Arbor. It is one of the most complete and revealing collections available for any of the leading auto executives. The only book-length biography, John C. Long, *Roy D. Chapin* (1945), was commissioned and privately published by Chapin's widow. Factually it is reasonably adequate, but a new study, providing a more objective interpretation of Chapin's work, is much needed. For a comparison of Chapin's importance with other industry pioneers, see John B. Rae, *American Automobile Manufacturers: The First Forty Years* (1959). See also George S. May, "The Detroit–New York Odyssey of Roy D. Chapin," *Detroit in Perspective* 2 (Aug. 1973): 5–25; and, for insights into the formation of E. R. Thomas-Detroit, Eugene W. Lewis, *Motor Memories* (1947).

GEORGE S. MAY

CHAPIN, Sarah Flournoy Moore (14 Mar. 1830?–19 Apr. 1896), reformer and temperance worker, known by the nickname Sallie, was born in Charleston, South Carolina, the daughter of George Washington Moore, a wealthy Methodist minister, and Elizabeth Martha (Vigneron) Simons, who was of Rhode Island Huguenot ancestry. Sallie spent her childhood in Cokesbury, South Carolina, where she was educated at the Cokesbury Academy. In 1847 she married Leonard Chapin, a prominent Charleston businessman and philanthropist who was instrumental in founding the Charleston Young Men's Christian Association (YMCA). They had one adopted child.

Sallie Chapin was active in the Sunday school movement and worked in hospitals for the Soldiers' Relief Society during the Civil War. Though she would later write many pamphlets on temperance, in 1872 she published her only book, the popular *Fitz-Hugh St. Clair: The South Carolina Rebel Boy; or, It Is No Crime to Be Born a Gentleman.* She dedicated her partly autobiographical but also didactic novel to the children of the Confederacy and attempted to explain what she saw as the causes of the Civil War. She also continued her public work as an active supporter of the Ladies' Christian Association, the auxiliary of the YMCA. Chapin attended a national temperance convention and camp meeting at Ocean Grove, New Jersey, in 1879. Here she met Frances Willard, president of the Woman's Christian Temperance Union (WCTU), and was introduced to the scope of women's temperance work in the North. The next year Chapin organized the Charleston WCTU, and when Willard embarked on her first southern tour in 1881 Chapin accompanied her much of the time, giving Willard the cachet that only a woman from the Charleston establishment could provide.

Chapin lectured, wrote, and organized for temperance all over the South. She was constantly on the road in the 1880s. At the 1885 WCTU convention she reported traveling 16,775 miles on union business the previous year. She developed a truly charismatic personality on the public platform, becoming the most important single force in the WCTU's growing success in the South. Her well-modulated voice and southern love of imagery made her speech "almost a poem." She lobbied southern legislators for temperance education, local option laws, and state prohibition. Working with black as well as white WCTU groups, she went from church to church organizing black unions. She became president of the South Carolina WCTU in 1883 and was chairman of the National WCTU's Department of Southern Work until 1889, when it was abolished because the South was no longer considered a "missionary" field that needed special help from the national organization. Chapin was a major figure in bringing southern women into a large national movement, where they worked on a common cause with their northern sisters for the first time since the Civil War. At the same time, her many successful speaking engagements in northern cities interpreted the South to northern audiences.

The fact that Chapin spoke often and with great eloquence to northern WCTU's did much to convince northern women that rapprochement with southern women was desirable and that their former positions on the question of slavery did not make it impossible for them to work together in a good cause. Chapin's impeccable social background and the fame she had acquired through her popular novel opened doors for her everywhere. Southern women, like northern women, had been introduced to public activity through the Civil War, and with Chapin as a chief catalyst, they were ready to find fulfillment in a new cause. Chapin also served as president of the Women's Press Association of the South, member of the first executive committee of the Prohibition Home Protection Party, and campaigner for woman suffrage and women's higher education. She died in Charleston, following a successful legislative campaign (which she led while she was already very ill with cancer) to raise the age of legal consent from ten years to sixteen.

• Chapin's personal papers are still in the hands of her family. The South Carolina WCTU Records, which contain material on Chapin, are in the University of South Carolina Caroliniana Library. Early biographical sketches can be found in Frances Willard, *Woman and Temperance* (1883); Frances Willard and Mary Livermore, eds., *A Woman of the Century* (1893); and Ernest Cherrington, ed., *The Standard Encyclopedia of the Alcohol Problem* (1925–1930). The most complete biography is in *Notable American Women* (1971). Chapin's work is discussed in Ruth Bordin, *Woman and Temperance: The Quest for Power and Liberty, 1873–1900* (1981; repr. 1990). An obituary is in the *Union Signal*, 7 May 1896.

RUTH BORDIN

CHAPLIN, Charlie (16 Apr. 1889–25 Dec. 1977), motion picture actor and director, was born Charles Spencer Chaplin in London, England, the son of Charles Chaplin, Sr., and Hannah Harriet Pedlingham Hill. His parents were singers in the English music halls. His father, after separating from the family in 1890, provided little child support and died an alcoholic in 1901. After her singing career ended, Chaplin's mother worked as a seamstress. From 1895 on, however, she was frequently hospitalized for physical and emotional difficulties. During this period Chaplin was placed in several different institutions, including the Hanwell School for Orphans and Destitute Children, and intermittently obtained over four years his only formal education.

Chaplin first performed before an audience in 1894, substituting for his mother when her voice failed. Late in 1898 he obtained his first paying job with a child clog-dancing group called the Eight Lancashire Lads. Between 1900 and 1908 he acted in a variety of plays, most notably in several productions of *Sherlock Holmes*. In 1908 he joined Fred Karno's group of renowned comic pantomime troupes, twice traveling to North America. While working with Karno in English music halls, Chaplin—a handsome, small, wiry, and physically graceful man—polished his pantomime. In 1913, on his second North American tour, producer Mack Sennett, head of Keystone Studios, home of the popular Keystone Kop films, signed Chaplin to work in comic movies for $150 per week, about twice his salary with Karno.

But that was just the beginning, for Chaplin arrived at Keystone just as the movie-producing companies were beginning to develop a star system aimed at helping attract a larger audience. Under this new mode of marketing movies, Chaplin became within a half decade one of the cinema's most popular and wealthiest stars, as the terms of his next three contracts demonstrate. After a year at Keystone, Chaplin signed a one-year contract with Essanay that paid him a salary of $1,250 per week, plus a $10,000 bonus. During this year U.S. filmgoers experienced a case of what one observer called "Chaplinitis"—manifested in fan-magazine articles, Chaplin hit songs and look-alike contests, and Charlie imitators. By early 1916 the Mutual Film Corporation paid him a bonus of $150,000 and $10,000 a week to make twelve two-reel films. Finally, in 1917 the First National Exhibitors' Circuit, a buying agent for twenty-four of the largest owners of first-run theaters, signed Chaplin to make eight short films with complete creative autonomy for more than a million dollars. This meant that the legal ownership of the First National films would remain in Chaplin's hands, as did the ownership of all the films he made for the rest of his career. Shortly thereafter, Chaplin constructed his own studio at La Brea Avenue and Sunset

Boulevard, gaining in the process a degree of financial and creative control nearly unparalleled in Hollywood history.

Chaplin's films became so popular (and such valuable commodities) during this period because of the screen persona he developed and the stories built around that persona. Shortly after he arrived at Keystone, Chaplin assembled a costume that became his trademark. It consisted of a coat a size too small, loose trousers, oversized shoes, a derby, a cane, and a thin moustache, which made him look like a man of good breeding down on his luck. The resulting comic screen persona—known variously as Charlie, the Tramp, the Little Fellow, or, in France, Charlot—served as the anchor for Chaplin's silents and the nondialogue films, *City Lights* (1931) and *Modern Times* (1936).

In 1914 Chaplin made thirty-five movies for Keystone and directed all his films after April 1914. These Keystone films, mostly one- and two-reelers, contained broad slapstick and what some genteel viewers of the time considered vulgar humor. At Essanay he made fourteen short films in 1915 and the first months of 1916. As early as *The Tramp* (1915), he started to blend comedy with the pathos of unrequited love, which would become another Chaplin trademark. At Mutual, in what he later described as the happiest period of his life, Chaplin made twelve two-reel films, including such outstanding comedies as *The Vagabond*, *One A.M.*, *The Pawnshop*, and *The Immigrant*. Film historians and critics who prefer Chaplin's short comedies to his later features often find the Mutual films to be among his greatest work.

In 1918 First National began to release Chaplin's new motion pictures, including *A Dog's Life*, a three-reeler, and *Shoulder Arms*, in which the Charlie persona plays a soldier who imagines capturing the German kaiser. After Chaplin had been criticized in some quarters for not enlisting, *Shoulder Arms*, helped show his support for the American and British involvement in World War I, as did a short Liberty Loan fundraising film called *The Bond* and an April tour of the eastern and southern United States selling Liberty Bonds.

In January 1919 Chaplin, fellow film stars Mary Pickford and Douglas Fairbanks, and the director D. W. Griffith set up United Artists to enable them to remain independent financially and creatively at a time when the movie industry was becoming consolidated. United Artists was the distributor of every Chaplin film from *A Woman of Paris* (1923) to *Limelight* (1952).

Before beginning work with United Artists, however, Chaplin ran into personal and professional problems as he struggled to fulfill his First National contract. His first marriage, to Mildred Harris in 1918, began to disintegrate following the death of their only child three days after it was born in 1919. They were divorced in 1920. Some critics and filmgoers were dissatisfied with his two 1919 releases, *Sunnyside* and *A Day's Pleasure*, but Chaplin rebounded with a six-reeler, *The Kid* (1921), described in the opening title as "a comedy with a smile—and perhaps a tear." In this critically acclaimed film containing veiled autobiographical resonances from his own difficult childhood, Chaplin played the Tramp raising an orphan son. He completed his First National contract with *The Idle Class* (1921), *Pay Day* (1922), and *The Pilgrim* (1923).

Chaplin did not star in his first United Artists film. Instead, *A Woman of Paris* (1923) was designed as a vehicle for Edna Purviance, who had starred opposite Chaplin in many of his comic shorts. Although this serious and deft melodrama in a French setting failed to satisfy filmgoers the way his comedies usually did, it was critically well received and enlarged the circle of Chaplin's artistic and intellectual admirers. With *The Gold Rush* (1925), Chaplin returned to his trademark blend of comedy and pathos; he came to consider it his most memorable comic feature. Here the Charlie persona struggles during the Klondike gold rush of 1898 to survive cold, deprivation, and human brutality and to find romantic love. The film includes famous scenes of Charlie eating a boot for Thanksgiving dinner and performing the Oceana Roll (a pantomime dance using forks as legs and bread rolls as feet) for his dinner guests.

Chaplin and Lita Grey had married in late 1924 and had two children. But in January 1927 she filed for divorce because of his obsession with his work and other strains. Much publicity attended the suit, which resulted in a divorce that August. In the interim Chaplin postponed production of *The Circus*, a film in which Charlie works in a traveling circus. His last film produced during the silent era, *The Circus* was released in January 1928.

In response to the advent of talking motion pictures, Chaplin made a sound film, *City Lights*, with sound effects and a musical score but without dialogue. Released early in 1931, this comedy contrasts two different moral universes by having Charlie function in both the world of a millionaire who befriends him only when drunk and that of a blind flower girl who falls in love with him. Famous comic scenes include the opening sequence of Charlie atop statuary during a dedication ceremony and his boxing to raise money for the blind girl. Its ending constitutes one of the most exquisite scenes of pathos in Chaplin's work. Despite the gamble he took in making a nondialogue film well after Hollywood had shifted to sound pictures, *City Lights* was successful at the box office and with most reviewers.

Following the film's release Chaplin immediately began a world tour, which lasted until June 1932. Now one of the world's most famous people, he met with celebrities in politics and the arts, drawing huge crowds everywhere. Chaplin observed some of the effects of the worldwide depression on the trip, and when he returned to the United States, many observers were calling for art that grappled with the serious social problems of the day. These pressures influenced Chaplin's next three films, beginning with *Modern Times* (1936), his last predominantly nondialogue film. The depression is constantly present in this satire: factories close; people are homeless, starving, and unemployed; and police shoot at rioting strikers. Except for a song of comic gibberish sung by Charlie, the only dialogue consists of orders spoken through such machinery as a phonograph, a radio, and a public address system, which helps further the film's implicit critique of technology's effects on human beings. During this period Chaplin secretly married actress Paulette Goddard, who starred in *Modern Times* and Chaplin's next feature film, *The Great Dictator* (1940).

Work on *The Great Dictator*, his first genuine dialogue film, actually began in 1938. In his scathing parody of Adolf Hitler, Chaplin played the parts of both the dictator, Adenoid Hynkel (the Phooey of Tomania), and the sort of person Hitler was bent on destroying, a peaceable barber who happens to be Jewish. As Hynkel, Chaplin displayed verbal virtuosity, mimicking Hitler's bombastic oratorical style using a sort of pidgin German. Chaplin's most overtly topical film—Chaplin even briefly considered scrapping the project when World War II broke out in 1939—*The Great Dictator* concludes with a four-minute speech by the barber, disguised as Hynkel, calling for human kindness and rational resistance to totalitarianism. No other film of Chaplin's equaled its success at the box office. During the 1940s Chaplin's public standing was severely damaged by the suit actress Joan Barry brought against him. Chaplin's marriage to Goddard ended in an amicable divorce in 1942, about a year after he met Barry. After a federal grand jury charged him with violation of the Mann Act (crossing state lines with a woman to engage in immoral acts) and infringing on Barry's civil rights, Chaplin was nominally exonerated by blood tests of being the father of Barry's child. Despite extensive FBI investigations of these federal charges, they were dropped. But California state courts did not recognize the validity of the blood tests, and the paternity suit went forward. After the first trial ended in a 7–5 hung jury in January 1945, a retrial was ordered, and the second jury decided in Barry's favor. The charges and trials received extensive press coverage, much of it negatively portraying Chaplin as an immoral womanizer. His image was further tarnished because in 1943, while the litigation was in full swing, Chaplin and Eugene O'Neill's eighteen-year-old daughter Oona were married. They remained married until Chaplin's death and had eight children.

Publicity surrounding Chaplin's political activity during World War II also contributed to the deterioration of his public reputation among a significant segment of Americans. In public speeches he offered passing references to the courage and fighting spirit of America's Soviet allies and advocated that an eastern front in Europe be opened in order to stretch German troops as far as possible. When the Cold War set in immediately following the end of armed conflict, Chaplin's positive comments about the Russians, as well as the fact that he was still a British citizen after living in the United States for more than thirty years, made him vulnerable to attack from conservative groups and veteran organizations like the American Legion.

In this changed climate, Chaplin's fortunes in the United States reached their lowest ebb. There were protests and movie theater boycotts against Chaplin's next two films, the "comedy of murders" *Monsieur Verdoux* (1947), in which he plays a bluebeard who murders rich widows to support his family, and the autobiographical *Limelight* (1952), dramatizing the fate of a comedian in Edwardian England who is well past his prime. Both films failed badly in the United States but did quite well in Europe. In fact, *Limelight* won the Foreign Film Critics' Best Film Award for 1952. In that same year Chaplin was effectively banished from the United States. Officially classified as a resident alien, he had applied for and received a reentry permit from the Immigration and Naturalization Service in order to travel abroad for the London and Paris premieres of *Limelight*. Two days after Chaplin and his family set sail for England, however, U.S. Attorney General James P. McGranery revoked Chaplin's reentry permit and announced that Chaplin would not be permitted to return to the United States until he faced an INS board about political and moral questions. Finding himself welcome in England and France, Chaplin, after securing his U.S. assets, surrendered his reentry permit in April 1953 to the U.S. embassy in Switzerland.

Chaplin's permanent residence for the rest of his life was in Vevey, Switzerland. Although he sold his studio in 1953 and his remaining interest in United Artists in 1955, he directed two more films while living abroad. He played a deposed monarch visiting New York City in *A King in New York* (1957), which contained a pointed satirical attack on badgering congressional investigative tactics during the McCarthy era. He made only a cameo appearance in his last film, *The Countess from Hong Kong* (1967), which featured Sophia Loren and Marlon Brando and did poorly both with critics and at the box office.

During the 1960s interest in Chaplin and his films began to grow again, owing in large part to a limited New York retrospective of his films in 1963–1964 and to *My Autobiography*, which was published in the United States in 1964. A shifting political climate more sympathetic to his views also contributed to the reappraisal. Chaplin visited the United States in April 1972 after an absence of two decades; just the year before, the American re-release of his early work in films had begun. He was celebrated in New York at the Lincoln Center, and in Los Angeles he was granted a special Oscar for his central role in making movies the most important art form of the twentieth century. In 1974 he completed a book consisting largely of film stills and other visual materials, *My Life in Pictures*. Knighted by Queen Elizabeth in 1975, he died two years later in Vevey.

Chaplin remains an important figure in American film and cultural history. As a director, Chaplin disliked flamboyant camera work, preferring a functional and unobtrusive style that emphasized narrative and character, particularly as embodied by the Tramp. He should be remembered as one of the first in the Hollywood star system to achieve genuine international acclaim. In addition, his mythic alter ego, the Tramp, has appealed to both a mass moviegoing audience and the intelligentsia, principally because of Chaplin's remarkable performance skills, which combined graceful physical movement and nuanced facial expressions, and because of his ability as writer and director to create in his films a broad emotional range of comedy and pathos as well as a thematic richness. Although he and Buster Keaton have often been regarded as the two most gifted figures in American silent film comedies, Chaplin had a longer career, a greater creative range, and a more varied repertoire in his filmmaking. His achievements as director and actor are due in part to his independence from major studio control. Because all of Chaplin's films from the First National period on remain available and in good condition, his work will continue to figure prominently in the history of American film.

• Although Chaplin's personal papers are not available to scholars, extensive clipping files may be studied in the Robinson Locke Collection at the New York Public Library for the Performing Arts, Lincoln Center, while relevant studio records are located in the United Artists Collection at the Wisconsin State Historical Library. Four books appear under Chaplin's name: *My Trip Abroad* (1921), *A Comedian Sees the World* (1933), *My Autobiography* (1964), and *My Life in Pictures* (1974). Theodore Huff, *Charlie Chaplin* (1951), is a valuable early biography. The standard biography is *Chaplin: His Life and Art* (1985) by David Robinson, who had access to Chaplin's personal papers and records. See also Georges Sadoul, *Vie de Charlot: Charles Spencer Chaplin, ses films et son temps* (1952, 1978); Roger Manvell, *Charlie Chaplin* (1974); Raoul Sobel and David Francis, *Chaplin: Genesis of a Clown* (1978); Charles J. Maland, *Chaplin and American Culture* (1989); and Kenneth S. Lynn, *Charlie Chaplin and His Times* (1997). Two useful bibliographical works survey the many writings on Chaplin: Timothy Lyons, *Charles Chaplin: A Guide to References and Resources* (1979), and Wes Gehring, *Chaplin: A Bio-Bibliography* (1983). An obituary is in the *New York Times*, 26 and 27 Dec. 1977.

CHARLES J. MALAND

CHAPLIN, Ralph Hosea (30 Aug. 1887–23 May 1961), radical labor editor and artist, was born in Cloud County, Kansas, the son of Edgar Chaplin and Clara Bradford, farmers. Hard times forced his family to leave Kansas when Chaplin was an infant, and he was raised in Chicago, where his family moved frequently and struggled against poverty.

Chaplin's involvement in labor and radical activities began at age seven when he threw brickbats at strikebreakers and Pinkertons during the Pullman Strike, which had cost his father his railroad job. As a youth he attended Socialist party meetings and distributed socialist pamphlets on the streets of Chicago. His formal schooling ended at the age of thirteen when he found work in a local portrait studio and began training for his lifelong career as an artist. While still in his teens, he interrupted this work to roam through the West finding menial work where he could, an experience that fed his sympathy for the workers whose lot he shared and fostered his attraction to labor organization as a way to improve their lives. Upon his return to Chicago, he married Edith Medin in 1905. Interested in the revolutionary stirrings in Mexico, he left for that country to work as an artist in a portrait studio in Mexico City.

Back in Chicago in 1910 he developed ties with left-wing writers at the *International Socialist Review* and became a close friend of Bill Haywood, a founder of the Industrial Workers of the World (IWW). Encouraged by his association with the city's labor activists, Chaplin worked to establish a union of commercial portrait artists in Chicago. When this effort ended in a failed strike, he found himself blacklisted by local studios and left Illinois to work as an artist in West Virginia. There he actively supported the coal miners' strike in Kanawha, wrote an article for the *International Socialist Review* on the struggle, and began writing the lyrics of "Solidarity Forever," which he would complete in 1915. From Kanawha, Chaplin moved his wife and young son (the couple's only child) to Cleveland, where he joined the IWW and wrote his first article for that union's official paper, *Solidarity*. Increasingly he became convinced that the IWW program of revolutionary industrial unionism and direct-action tactics offered the best hope for the country's workers.

In the winter of 1913–1914 Chaplin found work as an artist in Montreal and was there when war broke out in Europe. He returned to Cleveland as a staff writer for *Solidarity* in 1914 but left after a few months when he became caught in a dispute between editor Ben Williams and General Secretary Haywood concerning where the paper's office should be located. When Williams resigned in 1917 Chaplin accepted Haywood's offer to replace him at IWW headquarters in Chicago.

Within weeks after Chaplin became editor of *Solidarity*, the United States entered the war, and he became a leader in the IWW's antiwar activities. In Cleveland Chaplin had designed a propaganda device, the "stickerettes," as part of the IWW drive to organize agricultural workers. With the country at war, he designed a new series of stickers, drawn in the union's red and black colors, as part of the IWW's antiwar protest. Such IWW opposition, on stickers and in publications and speeches, led to nationwide raids by the Justice Department on union offices in September 1917. When indictments were returned against 166 IWW members for violations of the Espionage Act of 1917, Chaplin and Haywood were among those arrested and held for trial on the charge of interfering with the war effort. The Chicago mass trial of IWW activists began on 1 April 1918 and continued for five months. All the defendants were found guilty, and, on his thirty-first birthday, Chaplin was given the maximum sentence of twenty years in federal prison. Released on bail pending appeal, Chaplin rejected the opportunity to join Haywood in flight to the Soviet Union. Instead he traveled extensively to raise support for the IWW defense. When the convictions were upheld, Chaplin and the others were imprisoned at Leavenworth in Kansas. By the time his sentence was commuted in 1923, he had spent more than four years behind bars.

During the period of Chaplin's appeal and incarceration, IWW ranks split on the union's position vis-à-vis the international communist movement. Chaplin was among those who were dubious about the Communists' urge for power over the union. Although he joined the party for a brief time, he ended his affiliation in the late 1920s. Concerned with communism's "dictatorial bureaucracy" and "Russian dictatorship," he would for the rest of his life be a vocal opponent of communism and the Soviet Union. Chaplin remained in the IWW, becoming editor of its *Industrial Worker* in 1932, but in 1936 he severed all connections with the union and its radical agenda, convinced that a less revolutionary union movement offered more promise for the American worker.

In 1937 Chaplin was recruited by young, non-Communist workers in California to be editor of the *Voice of the Federation*, the organ of the Maritime Federation of the Pacific Coast. In that capacity he came into conflict with Harry Bridges, head of the International Longshoremen's Association, who was seeking control of the West Coast maritime unions. When Bridges prevailed over his opponents in the federation, Chaplin was forced out of the *Voice*, and he returned to Illinois. In June 1941, working once again at a Chicago portrait studio, he accepted the editorship of the Tacoma, Washington, *Labor Advocate*, the official journal of the city's American Federation of Labor (AFL) Central Labor Council. As editor he became a vocal supporter of the war effort and a staunch advocate of national unity.

Chaplin's editorship of the *Labor Advocate* ended in 1947. In his last years he became active in the Indian rights movement, published his autobiography, and served as curator of manuscripts for the Washington State Historical Society. He died in Tacoma.

Ralph Chaplin's sympathy for the plight of the American worker led him to prominence in the early twentieth century labor movement, particularly within the IWW. As editor of major union publications, author of hundreds of poems, illustrator for numerous radical journals and causes, and author of "Solidarity Forever" and "Joe Hill," he was a major figure in labor's early battles. His drift toward conservatism and his vocal opposition to communism alienated some of his early IWW associates, but this warm and dedicated man remained true to his lifelong commitment to the labor movement.

• Ralph Chaplin's publications include his autobiography, *Wobbly: The Rough and Tumble Story of an American Radical* (1948); *The Centralia Conspiracy* (1920); *American Labor's Case against Communism* (1947); and "Why I Wrote 'Solidarity Forever'," *American West* 5, no. 1 (1968): 19–25. His poems are in *When the Leaves Come Out, and Other Rebel Verses* (1917); *Bars and Shadows: The Prison Poems of Ralph Chaplin* (1922); *Somewhat Barbaric, A Selection of Poems, Lyrics and Sonnets* (1944); and *Only the Drums Remembered: A Memento for Leschi* (1960). Material regarding Chaplin's IWW period can be found in the Joseph Labadie Collection at the University of Michigan and at the Labor-Management Documentation Center, Cornell University. His papers are at the Washington State Historical Society, which has published the *Inventory of the Ralph Chaplin Collection* (1967). Articles on Chaplin include John R. Salter, Jr., "Reflections on Ralph Chaplin, the Wobblies, and Organizing in the Save the World Business—Then and Now," *Pacific Historian* 30, no. 2 (1986): 4–19, and Tony Bubka, "Time to Organize: The IWW Stickerettes," *American West* 5, no. 1 (1968): 21–22, 25–26. Information on his IWW role can be found in such standard works on the union as Melvin Dubofsky, *We Shall Be All* (1969), and Joseph R. Conlin, *Bread and Roses Too* (1969). An obituary is in the *New York Times*, 28 Mar. 1961.

ANNE HUBER TRIPP

CHAPMAN, Alvan Wentworth (28 Sept. 1809–6 Apr. 1899), botanist, was born in Southampton, Massachusetts, the son of Paul Chapman and Ruth Pomeroy. Chapman received a bachelor's degree from Amherst in 1830. For the next two years he served as a private tutor in Georgia and then became principal of an academy for several years before undertaking the study of medicine. In 1835 he relocated to Florida and began practicing medicine. In 1839 Chapman married Mary Ann Simmons Hancock, with whom he had one daughter who died in childhood.

Like many physicians of the day, Chapman took an interest in botany and by the late 1830s was corresponding with Asa Gray and John Torrey. He supplied both with specimens from the relatively unknown flora of western Florida. He suffered greatly during the Civil War because he was a Unionist who chose to stay in the South. His wife, a secessionist, left him for the duration of the war. The townspeople's dependence on his medical skills meant that they kept him safe during raids. He helped those escapees from the Confederate prison at Andersonville, Georgia, who made it downriver as far as Apalachicola, Florida, where he was then living, by rowing them or having them rowed out to northern ships blockading the coast.

Because he was cut off from direct contact with the national scientific community by living in the rural South and more dramatically by the war, Chapman's career and his ability to publish were both significantly hampered. As he was to other southern botanists, Gray proved Chapman's benefactor, saving the plates of the first edition of Chapman's *Flora of the Southern States*, which was near publication when the war broke out. The *Flora*, first published in 1860 and then in revised editions in 1883 and 1897, served as Gray's grand scheme for a national flora. In the wake of the war he gradually ceased to practice medicine, perhaps because of growing deafness. His interest in botany grew to fill his time and attention. In time he became the South's leading botanist.

Chapman was a passionate collector and both Gray and Torrey, as well as leading southern botanists like Moses Ashley Curtis, visited to collect with him. Specimens that he collected are well represented in the Gray Herbarium at Harvard and even more so at Columbia University and the New York Botanical Garden. A woman who had been his neighbor and protégé as a child reminisced after his death about the rigor of collecting with him even in his old age. She had served as assistant, since he was severely colorblind and needed help both with descriptions and with identification. Chapman died in Apalachicola from a heart attack, which was reputed to have been triggered by too vigorous a collecting trip.

Chapman had no students and his sole publication of note was the *Flora*. His chief contribution—in addition to the *Flora*, which was well regarded—were the specimens he sent to Gray and Torrey and those that eventually found their way into herbaria, all of which greatly expanded the knowledge of the flora of western Florida.

• No collection of Chapman's manuscripts or papers exists, but correspondence can be found in the Asa Gray Collection at Harvard University, the George Engelman Letters at the Missouri Botanical Garden, and the John Torrey Letters at the New York Botanical Garden. Winifred Kimball, a friend and protégé of Chapman, published a reminiscence of him in the *Journal of the New York Botanical Garden* 22 (1921): 1–12. The *Dictionary of Scientific Biography*, vol. 2, includes a short but valuable sketch by Joseph Ewan. Retrospectives on Chapman's life and career are F. H. Knowlton in *Plant World* 2 (1899): 140–43 and by Charles Mohr in the *Botanical Gazette* 27 (1899): 473–78.

LIZ KEENEY

CHAPMAN, Caroline (1818?–8 May 1876), actress and entertainer, was born in London, England, the purported daughter of William Chapman, a long-term performer and manager of the Theatre Royal, Covent Garden, and Penelope Britt. (A family biographer contends that she was in reality the illegitimate child of William B. Chapman, Jr., the eldest son of William Chapman.) From infancy, Caroline Chapman was raised as a performer. In 1827 Chapman accompanied her purported father, along with William B. Chapman, Jr., and three other siblings, to the United States. All family members initially pursued acting careers in New York and Philadelphia, and Chapman made her New York debut in 1829 at the American Opera House, where for a short time she performed juvenile roles under the name "Miss Greenwood."

In 1831 William Chapman decided to take the entire family west, to inaugurate a new phase of their collective career as the manager and repertory company of a flatboat theater designed to operate on the Ohio and Mississippi rivers. Launched in Pittsburgh, the novel venture proved successful, in part as a result of the high quality of entertainment provided by the talented and experienced performers. It was on a series of crude flatboats and then on a more sophisticated river steamer known as "Chapman's Floating Palace" that the teenage Chapman served her apprenticeship under the tutelage of older family members. Chapman acted primarily in soubrette roles initially, in which she excelled as a comedienne, dancer, and singer. Later she began playing dramatic leads as well and ultimately won great acclaim in a starring engagement at the St. Charles Theater in New Orleans. In 1846 Chapman returned east for her adult debut in New York on 5 June at the Greenwich Theater, and from 1848 to 1852 she served in the company of Burton's Theater, where she gained enormous popularity as a soubrette.

Chapman then moved west in the company of "Uncle Billy" Chapman—her purported brother—to pursue a joint career in California. She made her California debut on 24 March 1852 at Maguire's Jenny Lind Theater in San Francisco, where she was an immediate sensation. Over the next five years she performed in San Francisco (where she earned the affectionate sobriquet "Our Caroline"), Sacramento, and the mining towns and camps of the Gold Coast. In her work *Troupers of the Gold Coast* (1928), Constance Rourke contends that the Chapman team went on to "dominate the California stage through a bright heyday."

Over time Chapman's repertoire came to include Shakespearean tragic heroines and Restoration comedy roles, as well as romantic leads in popular melodramas of the day. According to the San Francisco *Herald* (15 June 1853), "the versatility of this admirable actress is astonishing. In tragedy, in comedy, in melodrama and burlesque she appears equally at home and in all *natural*, piquant and attractive." Her expressive range appears to have been broad. In the course of her California career, Chapman performed with all the major touring stars of the day, including a very young Lotta Crabtree, Laura Keene, Junius Brutus Booth, and J. B. Booth, Jr. She played Ophelia in Edwin Booth's first performance as Hamlet in 1853. When Lola Montez, a notorious "exotic dancer" and self-styled actress, arrived in California in 1853, Chapman and "Uncle Billy" produced stinging burlesques of Montez's best-known performances, including her notorious "Spider Dance," in a successful effort to compete for audiences. The Chapman-Montez feud, thus inaugurated, persisted for several years.

As the definitive itinerant trouper, Chapman was initially known and loved for her lively, vivacious, even boisterous stage manner and for her radiant smile, both of which compensated for her lack of real physical beauty. She was also acclaimed for her "modesty"—rare indeed among Gold Coast troupers. Following the death in 1857 of her longtime partner, "Uncle Billy," however, Chapman began to lose popularity. Over time, her performance style came to be deemed overly physical, unsophisticated, old-fashioned, and dated. At the same time, she was confronted with the onslaught of the ubiquitous touring minstrel shows. (To compete with the minstrels Chapman actually played a blackface Topsy in a production of *Uncle Tom's Cabin*, with J. B. Booth, Jr., as Uncle Tom.) An ill-timed effort at an eastern tour produced only a few New York performances, none to any acclaim. Chapman ultimately returned to San Francisco, where she performed infrequently until 1870, when she retired altogether. She never married and left no offspring. By the time of her death in San Francisco, according to a memorialist Chapman was "alone and forgotten."

• Biographical material on Chapman is varied and often distorted and questionable. Among the more reliable accounts of her early career, *San Francisco Theatre Research Monographs*, vol. 3 (1938), is the most complete. George D. Ford, *These Were Actors* (1955), contains material on the Chapman family, including the matter of Chapman's parentage. The showboat years are best treated in Philip Graham, *Showboats* (1951), and in Noah M. Ludlow's classic *Dramatic Life as I Found It* (1880). Chapman's New York career may be traced in Joseph N. Ireland, *Records of the New York Stage*, vol. 2 (1867), and in George C. D. Odell, *Annals of the New York Stage*, vols. 3 (1928) and 6 (1931). Several works on the California stage include material on Chapman, including George R. MacMinn, *The Theater of the Golden Age in California* (1941), and Edmund M. Gagey, *The San Francisco Stage* (1950).

JAMES H. DORMON

CHAPMAN, Conrad Wise (14 Feb. 1842–10 Dec. 1910), artist, was born in Washington, D.C., the son of John Gadsby Chapman, an artist, and Mary Elizabeth Luckett. Chapman's older brother, John Linton Chapman, also became an artist. Conrad spent most of his childhood in Rome, where his family settled in 1850. He greatly admired his father and received his earliest instruction in art from him. Residence in Rome also gave him ample opportunity to study the works of the Italian Old Masters.

Chapman's parents were natives of Virginia and he always considered himself a Virginian, "which would have been the case [even if] I had been born in Italy" (Holzer and Neely, p. 36). At the beginning of the Civil War he returned to America to offer his services to the Confederate cause. Unable to travel to Virginia after landing in New York City, he went instead to Kentucky where, on 30 September 1861, he enlisted as a private in Company D of the Third Regiment, Kentucky Infantry. (A border state, Kentucky sent regiments to both the Union and Confederate armies.) Chapman continued to paint for practice and improvement and received much encouragement from his fellow soldiers, who nicknamed him "Old Rome." He fought in the battle of Shiloh, where he accidentally wounded himself, although not seriously, while reloading his gun.

Chapman's father, meanwhile, had written to Brigadier General Henry A. Wise—from whom Chapman had received his middle name—asking him to look after his son. Wise arranged for Chapman's transfer to Company A, Forty-sixth Regiment, Virginia Volunteers, which was part of Wise's command. During the winter of 1862–1863 he was on active duty in the area of Virginia below Richmond. He continued to draw, his subjects being scenes of life in camp, and it was at this time that he sketched a sentry on duty. He subsequently worked this up into an oil painting in which he depicted himself as the sentry. The result, *Picket Post: Self-Portrait* (Valentine Museum, Richmond, Va.) became perhaps his best-known work. Chapman appears sitting on an earthwork and holding his rifle, his right trouser leg torn at the knee, a dejected expression on his face. The painting captures the boredom of a soldier's routine and seems to foretell the ultimate futility of the Confederate cause.

In September 1863 Wise's brigade was transferred to Charleston, South Carolina, where Chapman sketched during the next six months. In March 1864 he received a furlough to visit his family in Rome. There he worked up his Charleston sketches into a series of twenty-five oil paintings (Museum of the Confederacy, Richmond, Va.), his most important artistic achievement. (An additional six paintings in the series were painted by Chapman's father from his sketches.) The paintings depict military activity at Charleston's harbor fortifications. The titles include *Flag of Fort Sumter, October 20, 1863*, which shows a tattered Confederate flag flying defiantly over the ruined fort; *Quaker Battery*, so named because the "guns" are actually large logs painted to resemble cannon; and *Submarine Torpedo Boat H. L. Hunley, December 6, 1863*, a depiction of the Confederate submarine subsequently lost after it sank a U.S. naval vessel in Charleston Harbor. These paintings are valuable because Chapman was both a skilled painter and an eyewitness to the scenes he rendered, making his work a rare and presumably accurate portrayal of Confederate military life.

Chapman had intended to rejoin his unit when his furlough was over, but he had gotten no further than Texas when he learned of Robert E. Lee's surrender in April 1865. With neither the desire to remain in a vanquished South nor the funds to return to Rome, he traveled to Monterey, Mexico, where he painted two views of that city. W. R. Jolly, an English engineer working in Mexico, commissioned Chapman to paint his factory in the Valley of Mexico. Chapman produced a large (seven by fourteen feet) painting of the valley. With the money he received for this, he was able to return to Rome in 1866.

Desirous of improving his skill, Chapman moved to Paris in 1869 in order to study with the noted artist and teacher Jean-Léon Gérôme. He lived there for several years, but on a visit to England around 1872 he temporarily lost his sanity and was placed in an asylum in London. He eventually recovered and was released after three years. After a short visit to his family in Rome, he returned to Paris, where he met and married Anne Marie Martin. The couple had no children. In 1883 Chapman and his wife moved to Mexico City, where he continued to work as an artist but never earned more than a modest income. Like his father during the latter part of his career in Italy, Chapman painted small landscapes mainly as souvenirs for American tourists.

Chapman's wife died in 1889 and the artist spent the next several years living alternately in Mexico and Paris. In March 1892 he married Laura Seager, an Englishwoman residing in Mexico City whom he had known since 1866. They had no children. Until 1898 they lived in Mexico City, where Chapman spent most of his time coloring photographs by hand for resale. The Chapmans then moved to Richmond, Virginia, where Chapman had not been for more than thirty years. In 1901 they settled in New York City. Unable to earn a decent livelihood in either place, they returned to Mexico in 1904; but in 1909, wishing to spend his last days in Virginia, Chapman and his wife settled in Hampton. His return inspired thoughts of the Civil War and he planned a large painting of Confederate generals Stonewall Jackson and Barnard Bee at the first battle of Manassas, but a lack of money and failing health prevented him from executing it. He died in Hampton.

Chapman, owing to hardship, poor health, and poor luck, was never able to live up to his early promise, and his post-1866 work is of no great interest. However, his service in the Confederate army afforded him access to locations and events available to very few other artists of comparable skill. Although a number of artists subsequently painted the Southern point of view in the decades following the Civil War, Chapman painted scenes of Confederate military life during the war itself, thus creating a pictorial record that has proven to be invaluable to historians.

• Some of Chapman's letters from the latter part of his career and a journal that he kept during the last year of his life are owned by the Valentine Museum, Richmond, Va. A few other papers, including two letters from Chapman to John S. Wise, belong to the Museum of the Confederacy, Richmond. Most of Chapman's surviving work is in Richmond in the collections of the Valentine Museum, the Museum of the Confederacy, and the Library of Virginia (formerly called the Virginia State Library). The most detailed accounts of Chapman's life are a memoir by his second wife, Laura Seager Chapman, written in 1920, the manuscript of which is in the Valentine Museum; and *Conrad Wise Chapman: An Exhibition of His Works in the Valentine Museum* (1962). Chapman's Civil War paintings are also discussed in Harold Holzer and Mark E. Neely, Jr., *Mine Eyes Have Seen the Glory* (1993).

DAVID MESCHUTT

CHAPMAN, Frank Michler (12 June 1864–15 Nov. 1945), ornithologist and museum curator, was born in Englewood Township, New Jersey, the son of Lebbeus Chapman, Jr., a partner in a New York City law firm, and Mary Augusta Parkhurst. His father died when his son was eleven. In addition to possessing a strong ornithological interest from the age of eight, Chapman inherited a musical ear from his mother, and his daughter-in-law, Gladys Swarthout, for many years a soloist with the Metropolitan Opera, later stated that Chapman was "an almost infallible critic and commentator."

Chapman's home until 1905 was a forty-acre fruit farm, to which his father had added a great many trees. Chapman then moved into the town of Englewood and later lived in New York City. He attended Englewood Academy for ten years, save for one term following his father's death in 1876, when the family lived in Baltimore. He had little interest in his studies but was encouraged in his growing fascination with nature by his mother. On graduating from Englewood Academy in 1880, he elected not to go to college and was employed by a New York bank for which his father had been counsel.

As his ornithological avocation grew stronger, Chapman began a collection of bird skins. When in 1884 Dr. Clinton Hart Merriam, chairman of the Committee on Migration of the newly formed American Ornithologists' Union (AOU), asked for volunteers to make observations on the migration of birds, Chapman eagerly signed up. The report he submitted on these observations impressed the AOU committee. He was elected an associate member of the AOU in 1885; he also became a member of the Linnaean Society of New York.

By 1886 Chapman had decided to devote himself to ornithology. He resigned from the bank, supported himself with a modest inheritance from his father, and spent part of the next several years collecting birds in Florida. He also volunteered his services identifying and cataloging birds for Joel Asaph Allen, the newly appointed curator of birds and mammals at the American Museum of Natural History. In 1888 Chapman was made an assistant to Allen at a salary of $50 a month, beginning an association with the American Museum that would last more than half a century. In 1901 he became associate curator of birds and mammals, and in 1908, when the museum work in ornithology and mammalogy was formally divided, he became curator of birds. The Department of Birds was created at the American Museum in 1920; Chapman was named its first chairman, and he remained in this position until 1942. The fundamentally shy Chapman, who possessed a number of personality quirks, enjoyed the affectionate respect of his museum colleagues, to whom he was known as "the Chief." During his long tenure, the number of bird skins held by the American Museum grew through assiduous effort by staff members and by purchase from some 10,000 specimens to more than 750,000, making it the leading collection in the world.

Once he had a thorough grounding in ornithological systematics and distribution, Chapman reorganized the museum's bird displays to differentiate between the 350 species found in the New York City region and those found elsewhere. There was also a seasonal exhibit that focused on "birds of the month," divided between permanent resident and migratory species. In 1900, or soon thereafter, a wealthy museum patron suggested placing bird mountings in more lifelike settings. Chapman developed the concept of habitat groups, first conceptualized by artist Charles Willson Peale in the early nineteenth century. Mounted specimens were displayed in lifelike imitations of their habitat, with well-executed painted backgrounds, so that they could be understood in relation to their environment. A well-written museum handbook explaining his system went through many editions. This approach to museum display gradually became standard throughout the United States and other parts of the world.

For the growing audience of bird watchers in the field, Chapman published a series of popular volumes beginning in the mid-1890s. His *Handbook of Birds of Eastern North America* (1895) was the most detailed and went through several editions and reprintings. More introductory works included *Bird Life: A Guide to the Study of Our Common Birds* (1897), *Color Key to North American Birds* (1903), and *What Bird Is That? A Pocket Museum of the Land Birds of Eastern United States Arranged According to Season* (1920). All of these were several times revised or reprinted and reached a very wide audience until the early 1940s. Several of these volumes were illustrated by leading illustrators of the day, notably Louis Agassiz Fuertes, Ernest Thompson Seton, and Chester A. Reed. *Bird Studies with a Camera* (1900) dealt with bird photography, while *Camps and Cruises of an Ornithologist* (1908) was an early account of his experiences as a bird observer. *The Warblers of North America* (1907) reflected a research interest of long standing. In all Chapman published seventeen books and 225 articles. In 1899 he founded *Bird Lore*, a popular journal that he used to advocate his views on conservation and to educate the public about birds; he served as the journal's publisher until 1935. This journal was sold to the National Audubon Society and became *Audubon Magazine* and later *Audubon*. His other writings for a general audience appeared in popular periodicals such as *National Geographic* and *Popular Science Monthly*. As a result of his many writings for general audiences, Chapman was recognized as one of the most effective exponents of nature study in the nation.

Chapman had begun his research on birdlife outside the United States with trips to Cuba, Mexico, and Trinidad in the early and mid-1890s, and again after 1910. He first visited South America in 1911. Chapman's biogeographical studies, particularly on the discontinuous geographical ranges of birds, dealt in part with earlier geographical barriers to their distribution. His fieldwork in the Andean region of South America also demonstrated the importance of various plant and animal associations, climate, and altitude in certain "life zones." These findings were reflected both in displays at the American Museum and in a series of published studies, notably *The Distribution of Bird Life in Colombia* (1917), *The Distribution of Bird Life in the Urubamba Valley of Peru* (1921), "The Distribution of Bird Life in Ecuador" (1926), and "The Upper Zonal Bird Life of Mts. Roraima and Duida" (1931). Chapman was president of the AOU in 1912 and was awarded the AOU's William Brewster Medal in 1933. Other honors included the first Medal of the Linnaean Society of New York, of which he had been president (1912), and the Daniel Giraud Elliott Medal of the National Academy of Sciences (1917). He was elected to the National Academy of Sciences, in 1921, and he received an honorary membership in the British Ornithologists' Union. He also received the Roosevelt Medal (1928) and the John Burroughs Medal for his writing about nature (1929). In 1913 he received an honorary doctorate of science from Brown University. As an American Red Cross volunteer during World War I, Chapman was first director of its Department of Publications in Washington and later a special representative of the Red Cross in Latin America.

In 1898 Chapman married Fannie Bates Embury, a widow with four children; the couple had one son. Chapman died in New York.

• Field notes, manuscripts of Chapman's books, and correspondence are in the Department of Ornithology, American Museum of Natural History, N.Y. Chapman covered many of the events of his life in three autobiographical volumes: *My Tropical Air Castle: Nature Studies in Panama* (1929), *Autobiography of a Bird Lover* (1933), and *Life in an Air Castle* (1938), his last book, which perhaps most ably sets forth his philosophy of nature study. Several colleagues wrote useful biographical sketches, including William K. Gregory's lengthy memoir in National Academy of Sciences, *Biographical Memoirs* 25 (1948), to which is appended a complete bibliography; J. T. Zimmer's in *American Naturalist* (1946); and several by Robert Cushman Murphy in the *Yearbook* of the American Philosophical Society (1946) and the *Auk*, July 1950. See also Paul R. Cutright, *The Great Naturalists Explore South America* (1940); Victor W. von Hagen, *The Green World of the Naturalists* (1948); Geoffrey T. Hellman, *Bankers, Bones & Beetles: The First Century of the American Museum of Natural History* (1968); and J. M. Kennedy, "Philanthropy and Science in New York City: The American Museum of Natural History, 1868–1968" (Ph.D. diss., Yale Univ., 1968). Elizabeth S. Austin edited some of Chapman's letters and journals from his early years in Florida in *Frank M. Chapman in Florida* (1967). Obituaries are in the *New York Times* and *New York Herald Tribune*, both 17 Nov. 1945.

KEIR B. STERLING

CHAPMAN, John (26 Sept. 1774–10 Mar. 1845), pioneer nurseryman and folk hero known as "Johnny Appleseed," was born in Leominster, Massachusetts, the son of Nathaniel Chapman, a farmer and carpenter, and Elizabeth Simons (or Simonds). No authenticated account of Chapman's childhood has come to light. It is likely, however, that he began to develop his remarkable woodsman's skills during his childhood and youth along the Connecticut River near Longmeadow, Massachusetts, to which the family had moved following his father's remarriage. As a young man, Chapman established an appletree nursery along the Allegheny Valley (1797–1798) in northwestern Pennsylvania. From there he gradually extended his operations into central and northwestern Ohio and then into eastern Indiana.

Chapman's scouting and plantings in Ohio were the fruition of methods he had been developing on the Allegheny—shrewdly judging along what routes pioneers would be likely to settle and planting apple seedlings just ahead of settlements from which homesteaders could start their orchards. These Ohio settlements, aided by the building of Zane's Trace and the sale of U.S. military lands, were growing rapidly. In the rough environment of the first decade of the 1800s, Chapman's resourcefulness, wilderness skills, and endurance of pain and hardship won him admiration; but his nondescript clothing (sackcloth shirt with holes for head and arms, tow-linen smock, and—when he wore them at all—worn-out shoes) and his kindness to creatures of the wild, even to rattlesnakes, struck his contemporaries as eccentric.

The tributaries of the Muskingum River gave Chapman ready access to the north central part of Ohio, in particular to the environs of Mansfield. During this period legends about him proliferated. He had become familiar to settlers as an intrepid frontiersman, ready to help them with apple seedlings (free to those unable to pay the five cents' charge) and medicinal plants or with a practiced axe when needed. But during the War of 1812 a major element of the legend developed as a result of his daring as a scout: he traveled through the wilderness from Mansfield to Mount Vernon at the risk of his life to warn backwoods settlers of impending Indian massacres and to seek reinforcements.

Tales of Chapman's preaching extemporaneous sermons when staying with a family overnight were given a heightened dimension through his devotion to the writings of the Swedish theologian Emmanuel Swedenborg. Chapman's renown reached the Manchester, England, Swedenborg Society, which published a vivid account of the missionary zeal of this primitive preacher in 1817. Chapman would pull apart Swedenborgian tracts (sent by William Schlatter of Philadelphia, a wealthy merchant) so as to leave a section at each cabin he visited and when he returned take that section to the next cabin.

These tracts may have been particularly appealing to him since their doctrines seemed to sanction and confirm his own qualities. His kindness to animals found confirmation in Swedenborg's view that "God has made all things for good," and his concern for his frontier neighbors was articulated in the doctrine that "the life of religion is to do good" and that "there is a heavenly happiness in doing good without a view to recompense."

Popular impressions of Chapman's eccentricities of dress and manner, of his apparent impecuniousness (though his various holdings added up to 1,200 acres), and of his heroic exploits and missionary zeal had been expanding into legend before he began to move in the early 1830s along the St. Marys, Auglaize, and Maumee rivers into northwestern Ohio and northeastern Indiana. These impressions were later enhanced by literary accounts—as in Henry Howe's *Historical Collections of Ohio* (1847, 1889–1891, 1896); W. D. Haley's article in *Harper's New Monthly Magazine* (Nov. 1871), which made Chapman a national figure; several novels, including James F. M'Gaw's *Philip Seymour* (1858, 1877) and Eleanor Atkinson's very popular *Johnny Appleseed: The Romance of a Sower* (1915); and the poetry of Vachel Lindsay (*In Praise of Johnny Appleseed* [1921]) and Rosemary and Stephen Benét (*Johnny Appleseed* [1933]). Chapman's life was idealized: he was portrayed as the tragic victim of unrequited love; his plantings were seen as furthering his mission of disseminating the gospel; and his benevolences—the expression of an apparently innate decency and gentility—took on spiritual dimensions.

Typical of the growth of the Johnny Appleseed legend was his metamorphosis from pioneer planter of apple seeds to patron saint of horticulture, a transformation into a cultural hero who made the wilderness habitable by providing settlers with the means of subsistence. Behind the legend lay the facts that apples and cider were an indispensable part of the frontier diet and that an apple orchard could stand as a legal prerequisite to a claim. Chapman's transformation into cultural hero owed much also to the feeling that he embodied the more humane impulses of his society as well as its tough frontier skills.

Despite being idealized and romanticized, Chapman emerges from popular reminiscences and literary treatments as an authentic folk figure, one who not only paved the way for cultivation of the wilderness but who symbolized as well the civilizing traits of the new West. Literary fantasy has Johnny Appleseed planting his saplings across the continent to the Pacific. Though there is some evidence that he may have gone as far west as Illinois and Iowa, his final years were spent in the neighborhood of Fort Wayne, where he died at the cabin of a friend, William Worth. He is believed to have been buried not far north of Fort Wayne.

• The most thorough and balanced treatment of John Chapman is Robert Price, *Johnny Appleseed, Man and Myth* (1954). A lively account, based almost exclusively on Price, is Edward Hoagland, "Johnny Appleseed," *American Heritage* 31 (1979): 61–73. Curt J. Gronner, "Illinois Commentary: Johnny Appleseed's Visit to Whiteside County," *Journal of the Illinois State Historical Society* 71 (1978) uses local records to authenticate the claim that Johnny Appleseed came through Illinois in 1843. D. W. Garber explores Jedediah Smith's association with Mike Fink and Johnny Appleseed in "Jedediah Strong Smith, Johnny Appleseed and Tylertown," *Pacific Historian* 16 (1972): 47–58.

FRANK R. KRAMER

CHAPMAN, John Gadsby (11 Aug. 1808–28 Nov. 1889), artist, was born in Alexandria, Virginia, the son of Charles T. Chapman, a businessman, and Sarah Margaret Gadsby. He was named for his maternal grandfather John Gadsby, a well-known tavern keeper. Chapman grew up in Alexandria and attended the academy there. Early on he displayed an interest in art, which was encouraged by the artists Charles Bird King and George Cooke, both of whom resided in nearby Washington, D.C. In 1827, while still only in his teens, Chapman moved to Winchester, Virginia, where he began working professionally as an artist. There he met Henry A. Wise, later the governor of Virginia but at the time a law student, and David Holmes Conrad, a Winchester lawyer; they became his closest friends.

A portrait that Chapman painted at this time, *George H. Smoot*, shows that his level of skill was similar to that of a folk artist. He was aware that he needed to improve, and on advice from Thomas Sully, he spent six months studying with Peter Ancora, a well-regarded drawing master in Philadelphia. Chapman aspired to be a history painter, however, and he realized he needed to study in Europe. He raised sufficient funds from his friends and departed for Italy in the latter part of 1828. There he studied and copied the works of the Old Masters. He met James Fenimore Cooper, who commissioned a copy of Guido Reni's well-known *Aurora*, and Samuel F. B. Morse, whom Chapman accompanied on two sketching trips, one through the mountains east of Rome and the other to Naples. He also studied life drawing in one of the academies in Rome, and in 1830 he painted his first major picture, *Hagar and Ishmael Fainting in the Wilderness*. He met and painted the sculptor Horatio Greenough; Chapman presented the portrait in 1832 to the Boston Athenaeum.

Chapman returned to the United States in 1831. The following year he married Mary Elizabeth Luckett, with whom he had three children. Both of their sons, John Linton and Conrad Wise (who was named for his father's two closest friends), also became artists.

In 1832 and 1833 Chapman traveled around Virginia, painting portraits and landscapes. He visited James Madison's home, "Montpelier," and painted a portrait of the former president; he also did a drawing of Madison's summer house. Among Chapman's works of this period are nine paintings depicting the sites of George Washington's birthplace in Westmoreland County and boyhood home outside Fredericksburg; Washington's mother's home in Fredericksburg; views of Yorktown; and Washington's home and tomb at Mount Vernon. These are among Chapman's best works, successful both as landscapes and as historical documents. He also during this time copied Charles Willson Peale's 1772 portrait of George Washington and painted *The Family of Mrs. John Augustine Washington of Mount Vernon*. He also worked in Washington, D.C., where he painted two portraits of David Crockett, then a congressman from Tennessee: a bust-length and a small full-length work showing him holding his rifle in his left hand and waving his hat with his right.

Chapman was not content to be a portrait painter, but he was unable to obtain commissions to paint the great history paintings he dreamed of creating. He therefore moved to New York to do illustrations for books—if he could not get the opportunity to do history paintings in the grand manner, he would do them in the small. He contributed illustrations to James Kirke Paulding's *Life of Washington* (1835) and *A Christmas Gift from Fairy Land* (1838); to *The Poets of America*, edited by John Keese (1840); and to various periodicals. He also undertook 1,400 wood engravings for Harper's *Illuminated Bible* (1843–1846). His etchings for *A Christmas Gift* and *The Poets of America* are his finest work in this field; in the words of his biographer William P. Campbell, they display "an inventiveness and delicacy of execution seldom to be found elsewhere in his graphic work" (p. 11).

Chapman was elected to the National Academy of Design in 1836. The following year he received the commission he had long sought, a history painting for the rotunda of the U.S. Capitol. He chose as his subject *The Baptism of Pocahontas* and worked on it for three years; it was completed in 1840. Measuring 12 by 18 feet, it became his best-known work. The painting was generally well executed, especially considering that Chapman had never worked on such a large scale before. However, a certain awkwardness in the handling confirms that his talents lay in working on a smaller scale. He returned to depicting early Virginia history in 1841 with *The Hope of Jamestown* (also known as *The Landing at Jamestown*), a small painting measuring 8⅝ by 12¼ inches, which was engraved and published in the *New-York Mirror* (8 May 1841).

In 1843 Chapman began a labor of love, *The American Drawing-Book*, which became a very successful instructive drawing manual. Chapman's idea was to present a simple method of teaching the basics of drawing. According to the critic Henry Theodore Tuckerman, drawing manuals before that time were not very helpful, but Chapman's book "brings out the whole subject, from its simplest to its most complex relations, illustrating the process at every stage with great felicity" (p. 219). It was published in 1847 and reissued several times over the next thirty years. Among Chapman's other accomplishments during this period were a portrait of his fellow artist Alexander Anderson, the first professional wood engraver in the United States, which he painted in 1844; and a wax relief of President James K. Polk (1846), which served as the model for the presidential likeness on the Indian Peace Medal issued during Polk's administration.

Though he never lacked for work, Chapman had difficulty making ends meet and often took on more assignments than he could handle. The increasing pressures from publishers wanting more illustrations undermined his health and left him no time for serious painting. He decided to move to Europe in the hopes of restoring his health and lessening the demands on his time. The Chapman family sailed in the spring of 1848 for London, where they resided for a few months before moving on to Paris, where they spent a year. In 1850 they settled in Rome, where the "few years" of living abroad turned into thirty-four.

In Italy Chapman concentrated on small paintings and etchings of the Italian countryside and of Italian peasant life. He sold most of these pictures to American and British tourists. He also painted larger landscapes, such as *Pines of the Villa Barberini* (1856), *The Roman Campagna* (1864), and *Harvesters on the Roman Campagna* (1867). These larger paintings are well executed; but in general Chapman's Italian pictures seem less inspired than his earlier work in the United States, and the subject matter is not as interesting as that of his American landscapes and history paintings. He was taking life much easier, content to earn a reasonably good living catering to tourists in order to remain in the sunny Italian climate. The outbreak of the Civil War, however, drastically reduced the number of American travelers to Italy. Chapman had depended on them for his livelihood, and his finances never recovered from the loss, even after the war ended in 1865.

Chapman's health remained uncertain, which probably explains his reluctance to return to the United States. In 1874 his wife died. Chapman visited the United States briefly in 1877 but returned to Rome the following year and continued to reside there until 1884, when he returned to the United States for good. He spent his last years living in Brooklyn with his son John Linton Chapman; though he was listed in the city directory as "John G. Chapman, artist," the only pictures known from this period are a few pen-and-ink drawings of foliage and one of a church in Mexico, where he visited in 1888. Chapman died in New Brighton, Staten Island, New York, and was buried in Green-Wood Cemetery in Brooklyn.

Though never in the front rank of American artists, Chapman was a talented painter and engraver whose best works are the scenes of his native Virginia. He was a leading figure in the New York art world, highly regarded by his peers, and he was the first artist of great skill and reputation to work in the field of American illustration.

• The Valentine Museum, Richmond, Va., owns a collection of Chapman's papers and a number of his paintings and etchings. A self-portrait probably painted at the time of his election to the National Academy of Design in 1836 belongs to that institution, while the Valentine Museum owns a self-portrait etching that shows the artist in his Rome studio in May 1881. The best modern account of Chapman's life and career is William P. Campbell, *John Gadsby Chapman: Painter and Illustrator*, the catalog of an exhibition at the National Gallery of Art (1962). A sympathetic appraisal of Chapman's career is in Henry Theodore Tuckerman, *Book of the Artists* (1867), pp. 216–22. Georgia Stamm Chamberlain, *Studies on John Gadsby Chapman: American Artist, 1808–1889* (1963), is a collection of her articles on Chapman published in various magazines between 1957 and 1961.

DAVID MESCHUTT

CHAPMAN, John Jay (2 Mar. 1862–4 Nov. 1933), essayist and poet, was born in New York City, the son of Henry Grafton Chapman, a well-to-do stockbroker and later president of the New York Stock Exchange, and Eleanor Jay, the great-granddaughter of John Jay, the first chief justice of the United States. From 1874 to 1877 Chapman studied at St. Paul's School in Concord, New Hampshire, where he suffered a nervous breakdown. After then being tutored privately for college, he entered Harvard in 1880 and profited intellectually by touring Europe as an undergraduate. He received his bachelor's degree in 1885 and studied at Harvard Law School for the next two years. In January 1887 he mistook the harmless attentions of Percival Lowell, the future Orientalist and astronomer, toward Minna Timmins, his own close friend, and he beat Lowell with a heavy cane. Learning of his error in judgment, Chapman punished himself by burning his left hand in a coal fire so severely that it had to be amputated. After vacationing in Europe that summer, he was admitted to the New York bar the following year. He married Timmins in 1889 and lived with her in New York. The couple had three children. He practiced law in New York until 1898 but preferred to read and involve himself in political reform.

Partly because his wife was half Italian, he studied Italian literature and published "The Fourth Canto of the *Inferno*" (*Atlantic Monthly*, Nov. 1890) and "Michael Angelo's Sonnets" (*Bachelor of Arts*, June 1895). In the 1890s he also published *The Two Philosophers* (1892), a comedy based on an incident involving the Harvard faculty, and essays on William Shakespeare (1896), Robert Browning (1896), and Walt Whitman (1897). A major work was his "Emerson Sixty Years After" (*Atlantic*, Jan.–Feb. 1897). In March 1897 he also began to edit and privately publish a monthly periodical titled the *Political Nursery*, rebuking Tammany Hall chicanery in New York City and promoting suggestions by the local Good Government Club. He discontinued the magazine in January 1901. Chapman's wife died in 1897. A year later he married Elizabeth Chanler. The couple had one child. He published *Emerson and Other Essays* in 1898. Ralph Waldo Emerson had become the most important single influence on Chapman's self-reliant moral, social, and intellectual stance. His *Causes and Consequences* (1898) and *Practical Agitation* (1900) reflect his disgust at the unholy alliance of party politics, commercialism, and conservative writers. No longer a Republican but now an independent, he was outraged when he and others persuaded his friend Theodore Roosevelt in 1898 to run for governor of New York as an independent only to see him switch back to the Republican party. Meanwhile, Chapman was viewing with dismay America's steady drift toward imperialism after the Spanish-American War.

Chapman was stricken in 1901 with a mysterious physical and nervous breakdown, was bedridden for a year, and walked only with crutches for a year after that. He was devastated when his nine-year-old son drowned in Austria while the family was vacationing there in 1903. During this period he received psychological help from his friend William James.

Chapman's work on the stage began in 1907 with seven plays he wrote for children. Mostly comic, romantic, and unoriginal, they feature lost children, witches, hermits, knights, and the like, have passages of blank verse, and praise idealists and reformers. The plays, which were performed by vacationing groups and in schools, were published in 1908 and 1911. Chapman also wrote three adult dramas, one of which, *The Treason and Death of Benedict Arnold: A Play for a Greek Theatre* (1910), retains its value. It depicts a heroic figure gone tragically astray, and its use of varied rhythms, episodes, chorus, and intermezzo provides variety and excitement. Writing plays was undoubtedly of therapeutic value to Chapman.

In 1910 he suddenly felt well again. He published *Learning and Other Essays* that year and took a trip to Italy and North Africa the next. In 1912 he made a penitential pilgrimage, in an effort to cleanse the American soul, to Coatesville, Pennsylvania. He rented a room in a vacant store, advertised a meeting, and on 18 August read a moving address to memorialize the unusually brutal lynching one year earlier of Zacharia (or Ezekiel) Walker, an African American who killed a white man during a robbery. Chapman's speech urged love in response to hate and reverence for human nature and in the process exposed a black corner of the American soul. He spoke to an audience of two people. Getting a better response was his spirited, well-documented *William Lloyd Garrison* (1913), in praise of unpopular, but occasionally necessary, violent action against evil, in this instance abolitionist Garrison's war against slavery.

In June 1914 Chapman and his wife visited his son Victor, an architecture student in Paris. In July the couple were in Germany. When that country invaded France, the Chapmans returned home via London, but Victor joined the Lafayette Escadrille and was killed in action in June 1916—the first American aviator to die in World War I. Earlier, Chapman had published *Deutschland über Alles; or, Germany Speaks . . .* (Nov. 1914), in which he mostly lets Germany condemn itself by quoting bellicose German statesmen, writers, and militarists. He also more sanely, if vainly, asked American leaders—including President Woodrow Wilson in person—to seek, first, disarmament, and then, after America entered the war, unvengeful treatment of Germany, the predestined loser.

After Victor's death, Chapman never regained his previous creative energy. He edited and published Victor's letters from France (1917). He revealed surprising prejudices, wanting names of German students kept off the Harvard War Memorial (1917), objecting when a Roman Catholic was seated on Harvard's Board of Overseers (1924), and opposing the nomination of Alfred E. Smith as Democratic candidate for president because of his Catholicism (1927). More endearingly, he published a book on Shakespeare (1922), *Letters and Religion* (1924), a study of Dante (1927), and three books concerned with Greek literature (1928, 1929, 1931). He visited Europe three more times (1919, 1925, 1930). He died in Poughkeepsie, New York.

Chapman was a brilliant, honest man of letters and advocate of reform. His interests were varied, and none of his twenty-five books is representative. His main, self-imposed challenge was to understand and reform the American mind. Everything he wrote is graceful, vigorous, and implicitly autobiographical.

• Most of Chapman's voluminous papers are at the Huntington Library in San Marino, Calif., and in libraries at Columbia University, Johns Hopkins University, the University of Pennsylvania, and Yale University. *The Selected Writings of John Jay Chapman*, ed. Jacques Barzun (1957), reprints representative works by Chapman with an analytical introduction. Owen Wister, *Two Appreciations of John Jay Chapman* (1934), is a tribute by a lifelong friend. M. A. DeWolfe Howe, another close friend, in *John Jay Chapman and His Letters* (1937), quotes extensively from "Retrospections," Chapman's unpublished autobiography. Richard B. Hovey, *John Jay Chapman: An American Mind* (1959), is the standard biography and contains a select bibliography. Edmund Wilson, *The Triple Thinkers: Ten Essays on Literature* (1938; rev. ed., 1948), contains the best short essay on Chapman. Daniel Aaron, "'Strongly-Flavored Imitation Cynicism': Henry Adams's *Education* Reviewed by John Jay Chapman," *New England Quarterly* 93 (June 1990): 288–93, prints for the first time and comments on Chapman's adverse opinion of *The Education of Henry Adams*. An obituary is in the *New York Times*, 5 Nov. 1933.

ROBERT L. GALE

CHAPMAN, John Wilbur (17 June 1859–25 Dec. 1918), evangelist, was born in Richmond, Indiana, the son of Alexander Hamilton Chapman, an insurance adjuster, and Lorinda McWhinney. As a youth, Chapman worked at odd jobs—delivering milk, selling newspapers, keeping books, and producing and marketing household items. He graduated from Lake Forest University in 1879. While a student at Lane Seminary in Cincinnati he did supply preaching and was licensed for the ministry by the presbytery of Whitewater, Ohio, in April 1881. After receiving his B.D. from Lane in 1882 he became the pastor of two small Presbyterian congregations, one in College Corner, Ohio, and the other in Liberty, Indiana. In 1882 Chapman married Irene Steddom, who died in 1886, a month after the birth of their first child.

Calls to other churches soon followed. From 1883 to 1885 he was pastor of the Reformed Church of Schuylerville, New York, and from 1885 to 1890 of the First Reformed Church of Albany, New York. During Chapman's pastorate at Albany, more than 500 people joined the congregation. In 1890 Chapman became the pastor of Bethany Presbyterian Church in Philadelphia, popularly known as "John Wanamaker's church," after the merchant and philanthropist who for years served as an elder and superintendent of its Sunday school. Under Chapman's leadership the church grew from 1,700 to 2,800 members by 1893. He organized a men's brotherhood, taught 800 men in a Sunday school class, and expanded the institutional facilities of the church to include a hospital, an employment bureau, a savings bank, and Bethany College. Chapman married Agnes Pruyn Strain in 1888; they had four children.

As a result of his successes in Philadelphia, Chapman received many requests to hold revival meetings. With college classmate and close friend B. Fay Mills, Chapman conducted successful revivals in the Cincinnati-Covington area and Minneapolis and worked with Dwight L. Moody's evangelistic campaign at the Chicago World Fair. In 1893 Chapman resigned from Bethany and during the next three years held revivals on his own at Montreal; Saginaw, Michigan; Burlington, Vermont; Fort Wayne, Indiana; and other cities.

In 1896 Chapman helped found the Winona Lake Bible Conference and became vice president of the Moody Bible Institute in Chicago. That same year he returned to Bethany Presbyterian Church, where he remained until 1899, when he accepted a call from the fashionable Fourth Presbyterian Church of New York

City, whose membership had dwindled to a mere handful. By the time Chapman resigned in 1903 the congregation had added about 700 members and had achieved financial stability. In 1901 the Presbyterian General Assembly appointed him corresponding secretary of the newly created Committee on Evangelism.

Chapman's effective supervision of more than fifty Presbyterian evangelists led other denominations to request his assistance, and in 1903 he entered evangelistic work full time, conducting hundreds of revival campaigns in the United States and around the world. His experiences with Moody and Mills helped him improve the organizational techniques of urban evangelism, especially through his development of the "simultaneous campaign." Using this method, a city was divided into as many as thirty districts, each of which held simultaneous revival meetings. Teaming with musician Charles Alexander from 1908 on, Chapman preached at a large, centrally located auditorium while other pairs held meetings in the surrounding districts. Chapman's crusades employed advertising campaigns and featured prayer meetings; songfests; and noon meetings for special groups such as businessmen, college students, office workers, prostitutes, and drunkards in addition to the regular nightly services. His greatest results were achieved in Philadelphia (a six-week crusade in 1908 supported by more than 40 congregations with approximately 1.47 million attenders and 8,000 converts), Boston, and Chicago. By 1911 the simultaneous campaign technique began losing popularity, primarily because most of Chapman's associates did not have his preaching ability. By 1912 Billy Sunday, who in the mid-1890s had worked as Chapman's advance man, surpassed him in popularity and influence. From 1909 to 1914 Chapman and Alexander held revivals in Australia, Korea, the Philippines, China, New Zealand, Tasmania, Ceylon, England, and Scotland. Chapman's wife Agnes died in 1907, and he married Mabel Cornelia Moulton in 1910.

In addition to his work as an evangelist, Chapman wrote or edited more than thirty books and many articles and pamphlets, most of which were collections of sermons, manuals on evangelism, or discussions of devotional and theological topics. His most significant books include *Received Ye the Holy Ghost?* (1894); *The Power of a Surrendered Life* (1897); *From Life to Life* (1900); *The Life and Work of Dwight L. Moody* (1900); *Revivals and Missions* (1900); *Present-Day Evangelism* (1903); *And Judas Iscariot* (1906); *S. H. Hadley of Water Street* (1906), a description of the great rescue mission; *The Problem of the Work* (1911), a discussion of Bethany's success; *Revival Sermons* (1911); *The Personal Touch* (1911); and *When Home Is Heaven* (1917). Chapman also wrote numerous hymns and gospel songs and compiled several hymnbooks.

Chapman's success was attributable to his methods, his message, his personality, and his style of preaching. Both his churches and his crusades benefited from his excellent planning and wise delegation of responsibility. Irenic in temperament and appreciative of various theological traditions, Chapman attracted people from different denominations to work together. Known as the "pastors' evangelist," he was especially effective in enlisting the cooperation of clergy in his crusades.

Chapman was a theological conservative who stressed the divinity, Atonement, and Second Coming of Christ; sin; repentance; the efficacy of prayer; and the importance of righteous conduct. Like Moody and Sunday, he skillfully explained the Scriptures, used many biblical illustrations and pictorial images, and knew how to tell a good story. Unlike most professional evangelists of his day, his "tone was usually pleading and friendly," as William McLoughlin, Jr., put it, rather than aggressive and fiery (*Modern Revivalism*, p. 385). His breadth of knowledge, travel experience, and education exceeded that of other revivalists of his era. While his sermons were filled with sentimental stories, they were clearly outlined and based upon careful study and solid textual exposition. His colleague and biographer Ford Ottman described Chapman as naturally reserved but "gracious and genial," as having "great energy, zeal, and conviction" but few close friends. His greatest contribution was undoubtedly helping to "make mass evangelism an accepted part" of the institutional structure of Protestantism (McLoughlin, *Billy Sunday Was His Real Name* [1955], p. 40). Billy Graham appropriated several of Chapman's methods, including the thorough training of personal workers and the use of decision cards. After experiencing numerous health problems and being continually warned by physicians to slow the pace of his relentless schedule, Chapman died following emergency surgery in a New York City hospital.

• Many of Chapman's personal papers, including sermon typescripts, outlines, notebooks, and correspondence, are at the Presbyterian Historical Society in Philadelphia. Chapman's major published works, in addition to those mentioned above, include *"And Peter" and Other Sermons* (1895); *The Lost Crown* (1898); *The Life of Blessing* (1899); *The Bible Readers' Aids, Prepared for the New Century Bible* (1900); *Day by Day* (1901); *Fishing for Men* (1904); *Another Mile, and Other Addresses* (1908); *The Minister's Handicap* (1918); and *Day after Day* (1919). He compiled *Present Day Parables* (1900).

The most complete accounts of Chapman's life, work, and significance are Ford Ottman, *J. Wilbur Chapman: A Biography* (1920), and John C. Ramsay, *John Wilbur Chapman: The Man, His Methods and His Message* (1962), which contains a useful bibliography. To understand Chapman's place in and contribution to revivalism, see William McLoughlin, Jr., *Modern Revivalism: Charles Grandison Finney to Billy Graham* (1959). A. Z. Conrad, *Boston's Awakening* (1909), and Dale Soden, "Anatomy of a Presbyterian Urban Revival: J. W. Chapman in the Pacific Northwest," *American Presbyterians* 64 (1986): 49–57, provide in-depth analyses of specific crusades. Also of interest is *Awakening Sermons of J. Wilbur Chapman*, ed. Edgar Work (1922). An obituary is in the *New York Times*, 26 Dec. 1918.

GARY SCOTT SMITH

CHAPMAN, Maria Weston (26 July 1806–12 July 1885), abolitionist and reformer, was born in Weymouth, Massachusetts, the daughter of Warren

Weston and Anne Bates. Maria Weston was educated in England, where she lived with the family of her uncle Joshua Bates. She returned to the United States in 1828 to become the principal of the newly founded Ebenezer Bailey's Young Ladies' High School. Two years later she married Henry Chapman, a progressive Boston businessman; they had four children.

The Chapmans became active in the various reform movements of the late 1830s, especially the antislavery crusade. The impassioned speeches of visiting British abolitionist George Thompson and the mob violence directed at him and other opponents of slavery in 1835 apparently shaped and intensified Maria's antislavery commitment. As corresponding secretary of the Boston Female Anti-Slavery Society in October 1835, when a meeting of the society was threatened by a mob, Chapman rallied the women to walk calmly through the mob, black and white together. The meeting relocated to the Chapman house, which escaped attack because the violent anti-abolitionists were diverted by discovering William Lloyd Garrison in his office. "The Question now," Chapman wrote, "is the right of whites as well as the right of blacks—therefore we must *strongly assert our right to plead for the blacks*." And strongly assert she did.

In 1835 Chapman took over the management of the annual Antislavery Fairs, which had been launched the year before as a way of raising revenue for the American Anti-Slavery Society through the sale of everything from fruit and free-labor sugar to gift books and artwork. The fairs also included lectures and exhibitions that, along with the sales, helped raise $4,000 per year for the society. That the fairs were the antislavery movement's major source of income was largely due to the energy and vision of Chapman, who ran them virtually single-handedly until 1858 when, without consulting her colleagues, she instituted what she thought would be a more lucrative money-raising venture, the Subscription Anniversary. This became the new annual antislavery entertainment—a soiree with music, refreshments, and morally uplifting speeches—and it raised significantly more money than the fairs had.

In addition, between 1835 and 1865, Chapman served for varying lengths of time on the business and executive committees of the Massachusetts Anti-Slavery Society, the New England Anti-Slavery Society, and the American Anti-Slavery Society. She was active in the petition campaigns of the late 1830s, calling for the abolition of slavery in Washington, D.C., the end of racial discrimination on railroads, and the repeal of antimiscegenation laws in Massachusetts. Beginning in 1836, Chapman wrote the annual reports of the Boston Female Anti-Slavery Society, and from 1839 to 1858 she edited the *Liberty Bell*, a giftbook annual containing stories, essays, and poems written by well-known abolitionists that popularized the antislavery cause. She also served as the acting editor of the *Liberator* when Garrison was ill or traveling, and between 1844 and 1848 she was on the editorial committee of the *National Anti-Slavery Standard*, the official newspaper of the American Anti-Slavery Society.

Chapman was a central figure in the "Boston Circle," a small band of young, gifted, experienced, and, for the most part, financially independent Garrisonian abolitionists that included reformer Wendell Phillips, lawyer Ellis Gray Loring, merchant Francis Jackson, minister Samuel May, Jr., and poet James Russell Lowell as well as Anne and Deborah Weston, Maria's sisters. These men and women were committed to the immediate and uncompensated abolition of slavery and full civil liberty for blacks. They also advocated universal reform, including women's rights, as distinct from the more narrowly focused one-issue wing of the antislavery movement.

The Boston Circle sought to achieve its goals through moral suasion, which, in Chapman's words, meant "the propagation of principle, the spreading of information, the presenting of argument, appeal, entreaty, denunciation, as the case may require, through agents, newspapers, books, tracts, and lectures." Moral suasion also meant nonresistance, a rejection of political or institutionally coercive means to free the slave. Chapman, especially after 1840 and the formation of the abolitionist Liberty party, rejected the belief that abolitionists could use established national institutions, including churches, political parties, and the federal government with its "proslavery" Constitution, to further the cause of the slave. Moral suasion did not preclude moral coercion, however, and Chapman also supported a "come-outer" and later a disunionist position, both of which rejected association with slaveholders. In her nonresistance principles and in her "come-outerism," she was rigidly dogmatic and self-righteous, believing that "when one is perfectly right one neither asks nor needs sympathy."

Although she was at times overbearing, Chapman displayed great skill and strength. Even she, however, could not always handle the burdens and stresses of antislavery work. In 1838, after months of rigorous antislavery labors and increasing distress over the worsening tubercular condition of her husband as well as over the death of his sister, who had been a fervent and loyal supporter of their efforts, Chapman gave her first and only public address at Pennsylvania Hall in Philadelphia while a mob threatened. The next day the building was ransacked and burned. Chapman was soon hospitalized, apparently suffering from a serious nervous disorder. She recovered quickly, however, and threw herself back into the movement with undiminished vigor and single-mindedness.

In 1840 divisiveness within the Boston Female Anti-Slavery Society, mainly between nonresistance Garrisonians and their opponents, led to the society's dissolution. Chapman, however, facetiously dubbed the "great goddess" by her enemies and "Lady Macbeth" even by her friends, marshaled the Garrisonian forces, outmaneuvered the opposition and presided over a rump session capturing control of a resurrected organization with the old name.

In 1841 and 1842 the Chapmans spent considerable time in Haiti for Henry's health, but Maria's antislavery work continued even there. After Henry's death in 1842, Maria was undaunted, pursuing reform activities for the next two decades. Between 1848 and 1855, when Chapman was abroad giving her daughters the same kind of education and social exposure she had enjoyed, she systematically solicited aid for the American abolitionist cause from members of British and French society. Through her efforts, Lady Byron, Harriet Martineau, Alexis de Tocqueville, and Alphonse de Lamartine all contributed to the antislavery movement.

Soon after Chapman's return to the United States in 1855, slavery became a national issue with the crisis in Kansas and the rise of the Republican party. By 1857 Chapman was endorsing direct political action to create support for the Republican party and Republican support for antislavery. She continued to call herself a Garrisonian, however, insisting that the American Anti-Slavery Society, unlike the political abolitionists, embraced "the truth, the whole truth, and nothing but the truth, and is not afraid or ashamed to proclaim it." Perhaps she hoped that a Republican victory would lead simply to southern secession and thus to the disassociation with slavery and slaveholders that she had championed since the 1830s. After the war came, however, Chapman went so far as to counsel wholehearted support for using force, abandoning nonresistance and even the defense of civil liberties, which she called a hindrance to the military effort. She also accepted Abraham Lincoln's proposal for gradual, compensated emancipation in 1862. The state, after all, was the social agency best suited to fulfill the promise of the antislavery movement. Unlike Garrison and many of his followers who appeared to be torn between the principle of noncoercion and the temptation during the Civil War to kill slavery once and for all, Chapman was apparently as rigid in her new conviction as she had been in her old, admitting neither ambivalence nor error.

Chapman had fulfilled her goal of helping instill an antislavery consciousness in the American public that led to the end of slavery. But despite her newfound faith in the power of the state, she felt it had little or no obligation to assist the former slaves in realizing their freedom. In 1863, at the age of fifty-seven, except for a continuing interest in the Massachusetts Anti-Slavery Society, she dropped out of the antislavery movement. For the last twenty years of her life Chapman savored the perceived success of her cause and, equally, her own role in the victory. She died in Weymouth.

• Chapman correspondence and other important materials are in the Weston Family Papers, the Chapman Family Papers, the William Lloyd Garrison Family Papers, the Estlin Papers, and the Samuel May, Jr., Papers, all in the Anti-Slavery Collection of the Boston Public Library. Writings by Chapman include *Right and Wrong in Massachusetts* (1839) and *How Can I Help to Abolish Slavery?* (1855). See also Harriet Martineau, *Autobiography, with Memorials by Maria Weston Chapman* (2 vols., 1877). The best biographical essay is Jane H. Pease and William H. Pease, "The Boston Bluestocking: Maria Weston Chapman," in *Bound with Them in Chains: A Biographical History of the Antislavery Movement* (1972). Important information is available in W. P. Garrison and F. J. Garrison, *William Lloyd Garrison* (4 vols., 1885–1889). An obituary is in *Woman's Journal*, 18 July, 1885.

GERALD SORIN

CHAPMAN, Nathaniel (28 May 1780–1 July 1853), physician and medical educator, was born in Fairfax County, Virginia, the son of George Chapman and Amelia Macrae. As a youth Chapman attended the Classical Academy in Alexandria, founded by George Washington. In 1795 he began his medical studies under the tutelage of John Weems and then of Elisha Cullen Dick. Two years later he traveled to Philadelphia and studied medicine under Dick's mentor, Benjamin Rush. He received his medical degree from the University of Pennsylvania on 8 June 1801. His thesis, "An Essay on the Canine State of Fever," was on rabies and represented a defense of Rush's neo-Brunian medical system. According to Rush, diseases were commonly the result of overstimulation of the body and should be treated by purging and bloodletting. The same year Chapman also published two articles in the pro-Federalist magazine *Port Folio*, in which he criticized an earlier pro-Bonaparte contribution to the periodical. He next traveled to England, where he studied under John Abernethy in London for almost a year; after that, he traveled to Edinburgh and continued his medical studies for two more years.

Chapman returned to Philadelphia in 1804 and practiced medicine and surgery for two years with the First Troop Philadelphia City Cavalry. He taught midwifery to supplement the material received by medical students from William Shippen at the University of Pennsylvania. Shortly after his return, Chapman began to attack Rush's medical system publicly, and the once felicitous relationship between mentor and pupil turned acerbic. Rush opposed the traditional classification of diseases (nosology) by promoting the unity of diseases, and he considered all drugs to act in a similar fashion, differing only in the degree of their activity; Chapman ultimately classified diseases according to the various anatomical and physiological systems of the body, and he held drugs to exhibit activities specific for each of the bodily tissues.

Chapman began another literary project during this time, editing British political speeches. His multivolume *Select Speeches, Forensick and Parliamentary with Prefatory Remarks* appeared in 1808. The work was a success, and Chapman promised a sequel featuring American speeches; it appeared in 1815, edited not by Chapman but by Stephen Cullen Carpenter. On 1 September 1808 Chapman married Rebecca Cornell Biddle; the couple had six children, but only three of them reached adulthood. That year Chapman also assisted Thomas C. James in the teaching of midwifery.

Chapman's academic ambition was to occupy the chair of theory and practice of medicine at Pennsylvania's medical school, then held by Rush. In April 1813

Rush died, and the chair was then open. In anticipation of receiving the appointment, Chapman hastily edited Anthelme Richerand's *Elements of Physiology*, which he dedicated to Thomas Tickell Hewson, an influential member of the Philadelphia medical community. However, the appointment went to Benjamin Smith Barton, while Chapman received the chair of materia medica. Several years later the rotation of the faculty deanship fell to Chapman. Barton died in 1816, and this time Chapman won his coveted appointment on 7 March 1816. He occupied the chair of the theory and practice of medicine for more than thirty years. As a teacher Chapman was popular with the students, who presented their instructor with a bust of himself.

In 1817 and 1819 Chapman published his two-volume *Discourses on the Elements of Therapeutics and Materia Medica*, which he dedicated to his students. He distinguished his work on materia medica from others: "There is no one which I have seen, precisely on the plan of mine, uniting to some of the more useful pharmaceutical details, copious practical instructions, adapted to the management of diseases, modified, as they confessedly are, by the peculiarity of the state of society, and climate, of our own country" (p. vi). The textbook went through six editions, with the last appearing in 1831. Chapman founded his theory of medicine on the "doctrine of vitality," in which a "primordial principle of life" maintained the integrity of the body. He also published his lectures on the theory and practice of medicine as *Lectures on the More Important Diseases of the Thoracic and Abdominal Viscera* (1844) and *Lectures on the More Important Eruptive Fevers, Haemorrhages and Dropsies, and on Gout and Rheumatism* (1844). In 1846 Chapman's student Nathan Dow Benedict published the balance of the lectures as *A Compendium of Lectures on the Theory and Practice of Medicine*.

In 1817 Chapman was instrumental in founding the Medical Institute of Philadelphia, where lectures in medicine were given to continue courses taught at Pennsylvania's medical school. Chapman taught theory and practice, while William Horner taught anatomy. The institute was successful and still in operation at the time of Chapman's death. In 1820 Chapman founded the *Philadelphia Journal of the Medical and Physical Sciences*, acting as its editor for seven years; the name of the periodical was changed in 1827 to the *American Journal of the Medical Sciences*, as it is known today. The journal was an important avenue for the communication of American contributions to medicine.

Chapman was active during two epidemics in Philadelphia—yellow fever in 1820 and Asiatic cholera in 1832. He was codirector of a hospital on Bush Hill for patients infected with yellow fever, and again in charge of a hospital during the cholera epidemic. For his efforts during the latter he received a silver pitcher from the city. In 1848 Chapman became the first president of the newly founded American Medical Association. He resigned the post a year later, expressing the wish that no president would preside longer than a year. Owing to failing health, he resigned from the University of Pennsylvania in 1850 and died a few years later in Philadelphia. Samuel D. Gross, in his *Autobiography* (1887), assessed him: "Nathaniel Chapman will ever be remembered as an eloquent and popular teacher, as a facile writer, as a great practitioner, and as a man of versatile mind, full of wit, humor, and *bonhomie*" (vol. 2, pp. 281–82).

• For an exhaustive biographical account of Chapman that includes archival material as well as primary and secondary sources, see Irwin Richman, *The Brightest Ornament: A Biography of Nathaniel Chapman, M.D.* (1967). For an assessment of Chapman by a contemporary, see Samuel Jackson, *A Discourse Commemorative of Nathaniel Chapman* (1854).

JAMES A. MARCUM

CHAPMAN, Oscar Littleton (22 Oct. 1896–6 Feb. 1978), humanitarian, politician, and secretary of the interior, was born in Halifax County, Virginia, the son of James Jackson Chapman and Rosa Blount, farmers. Portending his future liberalism, young Chapman rebelled against his southern heritage, choosing a picture of Abraham Lincoln as a gift for his school, an act that led to his temporary suspension. Even so, he went on to prep school and Randolph-Macon Academy, from which he graduated in 1918.

Chapman immediately joined the wartime navy, serving as a pharmacist's mate, but he contracted tuberculosis after eighteen months. Sent to Denver to recuperate, he remained in that city and joined the staff of juvenile court judge Ben Lindsey. Chapman assisted the judge for four years without pay, and Lindsey, as a reward, named him assistant chief probation officer in 1924 and chief probation officer in 1926. During this period of his life, in December 1920, Chapman married Olga Pauline Edholm; they had no children. In 1929 he earned a law degree at Westminster Law School and was admitted to the Colorado bar.

That same year Chapman was taken into partnership by the liberal Democrat Edward P. Costigan, who was intrigued by Chapman's political skills. It was a neat fit, because Chapman favored progressive politics more than lawyering. He founded a Spanish-American League to combat exploitation of Mexican workers, organized world war veterans who had been his fellow patients, and captured one of Denver's Democratic precinct organizations. So it was that Costigan chose Chapman to manage his successful campaign for the U.S. Senate in 1930.

Less than three years later, Chapman's partnership with Costigan and, doubtless, his successful management of Alva Adams's Senate campaign in 1932 paid off. President Franklin Roosevelt appointed him assistant secretary of the interior. For thirteen years he carried out Secretary Harold L. Ickes's policies loyally and effectively, but Ickes did not appoint him first assistant secretary or undersecretary when those openings occurred.

Icke's's refusal to promote Chapman reflected their temperamental differences, Ickes's displeasure with his subordinate's access to the president, and what Ickes believed was Chapman's excessive involvement in outside activities at the expense of his Interior Department duties. These activities ranged from seeking other jobs in Washington and considering a race for the Senate to promoting the interests and rights of ethnic minorities. In the late thirties that meant aiding fugitives from Nazi Germany by forming a branch of the Emergency Committee to Save the Jewish People and working with others to combat racism by arranging for the famed black singer Marian Anderson to perform on the Mall between the Lincoln Memorial and the Washington Monument. These were unofficial battles for social justice, but they were closely matched by Chapman's support in that era, as supervisor of the Bureau of Indian Affairs within the Interior Department, of John Collier's "Indian New Deal." In 1940, eight years after his first wife died, Chapman married Ann Kendrick; they had one child.

When Ickes resigned in February 1946, President Harry Truman reputedly offered Chapman the secretaryship, only to be turned down. Chapman lacked Ickes's tough skin and thus may have decided that, as a liberal endorsed by liberals, he would inherit Ickes's enemies and their attacks. At the same time, he would be charged by Ickes's friends with having connived to get him out. Chapman agreed, however, to serve as acting secretary until Truman found a permanent replacement. In March 1946 Chapman reverted to undersecretary when Truman named Julius Krug to the top post. Though Krug had a superb reputation as an administrator, he soon lost interest in his new job, and by early 1947 Chapman was, effectively, making policy.

As de facto secretary, Chapman made little effort to prevent the undoing of many programs for which he and Ickes had once fought. Assimilation replaced cultural pluralism in the department's policy toward dependent peoples; the department began to abandon Collier's Indian New Deal; and the preservation of natural resources as the dominant theme of conservation policy evolved toward a utilitarian approach more favorable to business.

If Chapman bent before the cultural conservatism and emphasis on economic growth that enveloped Cold War America, he was hardly alone. Liberalism itself was shifting ground, shedding its New Deal priorities. Nonetheless, as a postwar liberal, he took policy positions that were controversial if not dangerous. In 1948 he endorsed statehood for Hawaii, inviting attacks from some racially fearful Republicans and southern Democrats; he called for compensation for the many Japanese Americans who suffered losses because of their relocation during World War II; and, finally, he fought segregation in the District of Columbia and discrimination wherever it existed.

Chapman's career might have peaked but for his contributions to Truman's election in 1948. In June 1948 Chapman received a phone call from the president of the University of California at Berkeley that led to Truman's "nonpolitical" trip to California, which forecast the value of what became Truman's autumn "whistlestop" tour. Further, in September, when the president's campaign committee could not pay a national radio network to carry his critical Labor Day speech, Chapman took charge. Learning of the problem only two days before the event, he phoned an old friend, Oklahoma governor Roy Turner, who quickly raised the $50,000 that saved the day. So ended the first of Chapman's "arrangements." Over the next two months he served as the president's advance man, traveling 26,000 miles on his behalf.

When Krug resigned in November 1949, Truman understandably asked Chapman to take Krug's job, and Chapman accepted. Now secretary, he served through the remainder of Truman's tenure, pursuing the policies for which he had become noted while undersecretary.

After March 1953 Chapman became a partner in a Washington law firm. He remained active until slowed by heart problems in the mid-1970s. He died in Washington, D.C.

• Chapman's papers are in the 125-box Chapman collection at the Harry S. Truman Library, Independence, Mo.; the National Archives in Washington, D.C.; and the Franklin D. Roosevelt Library, Hyde Park, N.Y. A study of Chapman's career is Clayton Koppes, "Oscar L. Chapman: A Liberal at the Interior Department, 1933–1953" (Ph.D. diss., Univ. of Kansas, 1974), which bears the imprint of numerous interviews and reflects the biases of contemporary radical historians. Also see *Current Biography, 1949* and Cabell Phillips, *The Truman Presidency* (1966). An obituary appears in the *New York Times*, 9 Feb. 1978.

STUART L. WEISS

CHAPMAN, Reuben (15 July 1799–17 May 1882), lawyer and politician, was born in Caroline County, Virginia, the son of Colonel Reuben Chapman, a revolutionary war veteran, and Ann Reynolds. Educated at Bowling Green, Virginia, he, like many other young men, migrated to Alabama, arriving on horseback in 1824. He read law with his brother Samuel Chapman in Huntsville, was admitted to the bar in 1825, and began to practice law at Somerville, Morgan County. Tall, red-headed, and conspicuous, he was keenly interested in politics and in 1824 was selected to carry Alabama's electoral vote to Washington, D.C.

Like most residents of the Tennessee Valley, Morgan County voters were strong supporters of Andrew Jackson, and Chapman was in tune with popular feeling. In 1832 he was rewarded with election to the state senate, a post he held until he went to Congress in 1835. A working senator, he opposed efforts to drag Alabama into the nullification controversy, reported proposals to reduce the minimum price of public lands, and displayed a willingness to regulate the emancipation and possible colonization of slaves. He was consistently a member of the Judiciary Committee (a tribute to his legal knowledge) and was chosen for two special committees appointed to examine the affairs of the Bank of Alabama.

As a congressman, Chapman proved to be a Jacksonian with southern rights leanings. On a practical level he served his constituents, maintained an interest in public lands, and worked (somewhat Whiggishly) to secure internal improvements for the Tennessee Valley. Yet in the eyes of his colleagues and the public, he was increasingly an ally of John C. Calhoun, Dixon Hall Lewis, and William Lowndes Yancey. Indeed, he was one of Yancey's seconds in the latter's 1845 duel with North Carolina congressman T. L. Clingman. States' rights extremists were not always popular in North Alabama, but Chapman's rapport with the voters made him unbeatable. In his first bid for reelection he defeated former governor Gabriel Moore by 6,300 votes; thereafter he was usually unopposed. In the meantime he was enjoying stability in his personal life. In 1838 he married Felicia Pickett of Limestone County; they raised four daughters and two sons.

Chapman served in Congress for twelve years, returning to state-level politics just when his combination of skills and stances was particularly welcome. For years the shaky condition of the state bank had been an issue transcending political parties. In the 1840s revelations of fraud and favoritism by bank officers had stirred up a furor that resulted in significant reforms, notably the formation of a well-regarded commission to supervise liquidation of the bank. During these years the state Democratic party split into probank and antibank factions, and such was the confusion that antibank Democrat Joshua Lanier Martin won the gubernatorial election of 1845 by running as an Independent. Chapman, Lewis, Yancey, and other states' rights men approved of Martin's attitude toward the bank; but divisions in the party were so deep that Martin was denied a second term. Chapman was nominated instead as an experienced and available candidate popular in both sections of the state. He was elected over the North Alabama Whig Nicholas Davis.

As governor, Chapman worked to pay off state debts and to cooperate with Francis Strother Lyon, who was made sole banking commissioner. Otherwise Chapman's administration was marked by heated discussion of the problems relating to the westward extension of slavery. In February 1848 Chapman's friend Yancey succeeded in pushing through a state Democratic convention his "Alabama Platform," which declared that slavery should be allowed to exist in the territories conquered from Mexico. For a time it seemed that public opinion might be moving toward Yancey's radical sectionalism.

The southern rights men overreached themselves, at least temporarily, and Chapman shared in their defeat. His appointment of South Alabama states' rights politician Benjamin Fitzpatrick to the U.S. Senate (to replace the deceased Lewis) had been very unpopular in North Alabama. Unable to secure the necessary two-thirds majority at the Democratic State Convention of 1849, Chapman withdrew his name from consideration for renomination. In his parting message, he urged the legislature to call a special convention if Congress took action limiting the expansion of slavery into the new territories. Following Calhoun and Yancey's lead, he opposed the Compromise of 1850, and he was one of a handful of Alabamians who attended the second session of the Nashville Convention in November 1850.

Chapman's role thereafter was largely that of elder statesman, though he won election to the legislature in 1855, defeating the Know Nothing candidate, former U.S. senator Jeremiah Clemens. The deepening of the national crisis apparently failed to cool his southern rights ardor. However, as a delegate to the Democrats' Baltimore convention in 1860, he opposed the breakup of the party. Once secession was an accomplished fact, he was a loyal Confederate. When Union troops invaded the Tennessee Valley, his property was burned, and he was sent back to Confederate-held territory. After the war was over, he settled in Huntsville and resumed his support of the Democratic party. He died in Huntsville.

Chapman shared the preoccupations of many Alabama politicians, whose chief concerns were the state bank, states' rights, and service to faction or party. He was energetic, reasonably consistent, and (by his lights) public-spirited. He simply failed to understand, until it was too late, where the southern rights doctrine was leading Alabama. On the other hand, he lived long enough to see both the Reconstruction of his state and its "Redemption" from Republican rule. Politically, he died a happy man.

• Chapman's gubernatorial papers are at the Alabama Department of Archives and History in Montgomery. Information on his legislative work is in the printed records of the Alabama Senate and the U.S. House of Representatives. A number of his speeches survive in pamphlet form, including *Speech of Mr. Chapman, of Alabama, on the Bill to Grant Preemption Rights to the Settlers on the Public Lands* (1838), *Speech of Hon. R. Chapman, of Alabama, in Defence of the Alabama Volunteers in Mexico* (1847), and *The Inaugural Address of Governor Chapman* (1847). Biographical sketches of Chapman include articles and information in Willis Brewer, *Alabama: Her History, Resources, War Record, and Public Men* (1872); William Garrett, *Reminiscences of Public Men in Alabama for Thirty Years* (1872); *Northern Alabama: Historical and Biographical* (1888); and Thomas M. Owen, *History of Alabama and Dictionary of Alabama Biography* (4 vols., 1921). John Witherspoon DuBose, *The Life and Times of William Lowndes Yancey* (1892), also contains significant information.

PAUL M. PRUITT, JR.

CHAPMAN, Sydney (29 Jan. 1888–16 June 1970), geophysicist and applied mathematician, was born in Eccles, Lancashire, near Manchester, England, the son of Joseph Chapman, chief cashier of a textile firm, and Sarah Louisa Gray. Chapman's early education emphasized mathematics and science. He entered the Royal Technical Institute in Lancashire in 1902. He was awarded a competitive scholarship to study at Manchester University, where he earned a B.Sc. with first class honors in engineering in 1907 and another in mathematics in 1908. At Manchester he studied under the well-known scientists Osborne Reynolds, Horace Lamb, and J. E. Littlewood.

In 1908 Chapman moved to Trinity College, Cambridge, on advice from Littlewood that a degree from Cambridge University was necessary if he wished to become a mathematician. As he later reflected, at Cambridge he began to live. He began on a partial scholarship and in 1909 was promoted to a full scholarship. He completed his studies and examinations in two years, but a third year was required for his degree, a B.A. in mathematics (1911). He studied with Joseph Larmor and G. H. Hardy, and associated with A. N. Whitehead, Bertrand Russell, and Lancelot Hogben. He also obtained a D.Sc. at Manchester (1912) and an M.A. at Cambridge (1914).

Chapman's ability to see uses for mathematics in physical science characterized his research. His early work with G. H. Hardy at Cambridge concerned nonconvergent series. His future path was indicated more directly by his simultaneous investigation of gas theory related to the flow of rarefied gases in narrow tubes. In 1916 and 1917 he published a complete theory of nonuniform gases and a study of gas mixtures, predicting thermal diffusion. These results, independently and simultaneously developed by the Swede David Enskog, were later used to separate isotopes. Chapman explored the implications of these results for diffusion in the Earth's upper atmosphere, the damping of sound waves, the electrical conductivity of the ionosphere, and the solar corona.

In 1910, before Chapman had completed his degree requirements, the Royal Astronomer, Frank Dyson, selected him as one of his two chief assistants (the other was Arthur Eddington). Dyson assigned Chapman to establish a new geomagnetic observatory at Greenwich. This first contact with geomagnetic instruments and measurements determined the direction of the rest of Chapman's career. This position connected him with the foremost geomagnetic theorist of the day, Arthur Schuster, who sat on the Board of Visitors of Greenwich. Chapman held this position until 1914, and again from 1916 to 1918.

Chapman's primary research thereafter lay in geomagnetic theory. He changed institutions many times during his career, going to Manchester in 1919 as professor of mathematics; to Imperial College of Science and Technology in London in 1924, also as professor of mathematics; to Queen's College, Oxford, in 1946 as Sedleian Professor of Natural Philosophy; to the California Institute of Technology in 1950 as a research associate; to the Geophysical Institute at the University of Alaska, Fairbanks, in 1951; to the High Altitude Observatory in Boulder, Colorado, in 1955; and to the University of Michigan's Institute of Science and Technology as senior research scientist from 1959 to 1965. The last three positions were held simultaneously, and Chapman traveled extensively as a visiting scientist throughout his career. The common thread was his investigation of geomagnetism (a word he himself coined) and related phenomena.

Chapman concentrated on theoretical questions to counterbalance others' emphasis on observation. With few exceptions, geomagnetic research since the 1830s had focused on measurement of geomagnetic variables and their mapping on the globe. In a time when most geomagnetic investigators were minimally trained in physics, Chapman was one of an emerging number of theoretical physicists interested in explaining Earth's magnetic phenomena. He focused early on periodic changes in the geomagnetic field, such as the daily variations due to the Sun and the Moon. He simultaneously investigated atmospheric tides, another phenomenon to which mathematical series could be applied. His exploration of the role of electrical currents induced in the atmosphere was based on earlier ideas of Balfour Stewart and Arthur Schuster.

By 1918 Chapman had become interested in magnetic storms, sudden disturbances of the magnetic field. Dyson had pointed out to him that these storms recur every twenty-seven days, the period of the Sun's rotation. In the 1920s this interest broadened to solar-terrestrial relations generally. His first theory followed Kristian Birkeland's idea that magnetic storms are caused by the Sun's ejecting a stream of particles of a uniform electrical charge. Chapman later developed a theory based on an ejected ionized gas, with both positive and negative ions.

In the late 1920s the Adams Prize question at Cambridge University was set: to develop a theory of geomagnetic phenomena. This was probably proposed with Chapman in mind. He submitted an essay and won the prize. From 1929 he cooperated on the theory of magnetic storms with his student Vincenzo C. A. Ferraro. Throughout the 1930s he also worked with Julius Bartels, ultimately publishing the classic two-volume text *Geomagnetism* with him in 1940.

Chapman received an extraordinary number of honors beyond those already listed. The old geophysics building at the University of Alaska was named in his honor. He was a fellow of Trinity College, Cambridge. The Royal Society of London elected him a fellow in 1919 and awarded him its Royal Medal (1934) and its Copley Medal (1964). The American Geophysical Union chose Chapman for its Bowie Medal (1962), the Royal Meteorological Society for its Symons Memorial Gold Medal (1965), and the Smithsonian Institution for its Hodgkins Medal in the same year. He served as president of the International Association of Meteorology and Atmospheric Physics (1936–1948), the International Association for Terrestrial Magnetism and Electricity, the International Union for Geodesy and Geophysics, the Commission for the International Geophysical Year, and ten other learned societies.

Chapman's simple tastes and austere manner were common knowledge among scientists, as were his persistence, his joy in work, and his love of exercise. He swam and walked every day and rode a bicycle from Montreal to Washington, D.C., in 1939 for the meeting of the IUGG. Chapman was a religious nonconformist and pacifist early in life, then an evangelical Anglican, and finally, progressively less religious. He forswore pacifism to support the battle against fascism during World War II. He married Katharine Nora

Steinthal in 1922; they had three sons and one daughter. Chapman died in Boulder, Colorado.

• The main collection of Chapman's letters and papers is at the University of Alaska, Fairbanks. In addition to *Geomagnetism*, Chapman published six more books and more than 400 scientific articles. His scientific career, especially the details of his geomagnetic research, are discussed in T. G. Cowling, "Sydney Chapman, 1888–1970," *Biographical Memoirs of Fellows of the Royal Society* 17 (Nov. 1971): 52–89, which includes a nearly complete bibliography of Chapman's publications. Scores of his colleagues offered reminiscences and analyses of Chapman's work in a very useful book, Syun-Ichi Akasofu et al., eds., *Sydney Chapman, Eighty: From his Friends* (1968). Obituaries are in the *Times* (London), 18 June 1970, and the *New York Times*, 20 June 1970.

GREGORY A. GOOD

CHAPPEL, Alonzo (1 Mar. 1828–4 Dec. 1887), artist, was born in New York City, the son of William Pelton Chappel, a tinsmith and amateur painter, and Maria Louise Howes. The family was of Huguenot descent, and the name is pronounced CHAP-pel, with the accent on the first syllable. He demonstrated artistic ability early; he is said to have contributed a painting titled *The Father of His Country* to the American Institute Fair when he was only nine years old. By the time he was twelve Chappel was working on the sidewalks of New York, where for five to ten dollars he would paint the portrait of anyone willing to sit. He left school in 1842 in order to learn the trades of japanning and window shade painting. He was first listed as an artist in the 1844 New York City Directory; at this time he was painting mainly portraits and charging $25 for a likeness. In 1845 he enrolled in the antique class of the National Academy of Design, where he learned the basics of anatomy by drawing from casts of antique sculpture. This was apparently the only formal artistic training he received. By 1848 he had settled in Brooklyn, New York (then an independent city), where he continued to paint portraits and took on additional work painting stage scenery. During this period he married Almira Stewart; they had four children.

Through the early 1850s Chappel exhibited genre paintings at the American Art-Union, the National Academy of Design, and the prestigious firm of Goupil and Company. Among the paintings he created at this time were *The Strolling Minstrels* (1849, unlocated); *Little Jack Horner* (1995, Philadelphia Art Market), and *A Militia Cavalryman Preparing His Mount for a Fourth of July Parade* (1854, West Point Museum, U.S. Military Academy, West Point, N.Y.). They are typical of the genre painting popular in the United States at that time.

In 1856 Chappel met the Reverend Elias Magoon, a noted collector of American art, who apparently introduced the artist to the New York publisher Henry Johnson. Johnson commissioned Chappel to illustrate John Frederick Schroeder's *Life and Times of Washington*, published by Johnson, Fry and Company in 1857. Chappel's talents were ideally suited to historical illustration, and he spent the rest of his career creating illustrations to be engraved for books on American history published by the Johnson firm. Among these were Henry B. Dawson's *Battles of the United States* (1858); Jesse Ames Spencer's *History of the United States* (1858); and several books by Evert A. Duyckinck, including *National Portrait Gallery of Eminent Americans* (1862), *National History of the War for the Union* (1861–1865), *History of the World, Ancient and Modern* (1871), and *Portrait Gallery of Eminent Men and Women of Europe and America* (1872–1873). Chappel painted both portraits and historical events, and his pictures reveal the results of painstaking research. He did not rely solely on the books he was illustrating to provide information on the subject at hand; he consulted other sources as well in order to ensure that his depictions were as accurate as possible.

None of the portraits Chappell did as illustrations was from life (not even those of his contemporaries), but they were based on the best available life portraits, engravings, and photographs. A rare instance of a life portrait from his hand is that of his friend and fellow artist William Marshall Swayne, painted in 1864–1866 (Chester County Historical Society, Pa.). The skill with which it was painted indicates that Chappel could have earned a steady income as a portraitist had he not been so busy as an illustrator.

Chappel usually worked in oils (occasionally in chalk or crayon), and, while a number of his oils are in color, the bulk of his surviving illustrations were created in *grisaille* (grey or grayish monotone), in order to assist the engravers in translating them into black-and-white engravings. He exhibited several of his illustrations at the National Academy of Design and the Brooklyn Art Association in the 1860s. Chappel also painted an occasional history painting. His most ambitious work in this genre is *The Last Hours of Lincoln*, painted in 1865–1868 (versions owned by Brown University and the Chicago Historical Society). It depicts the mortally wounded president lying on his deathbed, surrounded by top government officials, congressmen, and his wife and sons.

Chappel's wife died in 1863. Some years later he married Abby J. Briggam, a widow who had one son; whether any children resulted from this second marriage is not known. From 1863 to 1864 he served in the New York National Guard. He was active in the Brooklyn art world and belonged to the Brooklyn Art Association, but a disagreement with its policies led Chappel and others to set up the Brooklyn Academy of Design in 1866. He was elected second vice president of that organization and donated a number of antique casts to the new school. Chappel eventually left Brooklyn, however, driven out by a steep rise in his rent. In 1869 he purchased land in Middle Island, Long Island, along the shore of Glover's Pond, a body of water subsequently renamed "Artist's Lake" in his Honor. He built a house there and moved in with his family the following year. He continued to work for the next decade and a half, but he appears to have retired in 1885, the year he sold his 343-volume reference library at an auction. Two years later he died in Middle Island and was buried in the local Presbyterian cemetery.

Chappel's reputation virtually evaporated within a few years of his death, primarily because of the low esteem in which illustration was held. The artist Albert Sterner noted that "there is serious danger in the tendency to consider illustration as something apart from serious art work, something mechanical, something partaking of business rather than art, and I fight against it as hard as I can" (*Bookbuyer* 11 [June 1894]: 246). Another factor was the lack of public access to his originals; they were retained by his publisher and not exhibited, and most have now dropped from sight. Yet his work remained popular even as awareness of the artist faded. Engravings of his illustrations have continued to be reproduced in both scholarly and popular books and even on postage stamps, and in recent decades his surviving originals have also been reproduced in books and on television programs. Such paintings as *Capture of Fort Ticonderoga* (private collection), *Battle of Long Island* (Brooklyn Historical Society, Brooklyn, N.Y.), *Battle of Bennington* (Bennington Museum, Vt.), and *Death of Captain Lawrence: Don't Give Up the Ship* (Franklin D. Roosevelt National Historic Site, Hyde Park, N.Y.) have become the best known, even definitive, depictions of these events. Chappel may be said to rank, in skill and reputation, second only to Felix Octavius Carr Darley among American illustrators of the mid-nineteenth century.

• The only located likenesses of Chappel are two *carte-de-visite* photographs that belonged to his friend William Marshall Swayne and are now owned by the Chester County Historical Society, West Chester, Pa. Swayne executed a bas-relief of Chappel that is presently unlocated. Two letters from Chappel to John B. Bachelder are in the possession of David Meschutt, and a letter from Chappel to Elias Magoon is in the library of Vassar College, Poughkeepsie, N.Y. The largest collection of Chappel's original paintings belongs to the Chicago Historical Society. Other originals by him are in various private collections and a number of other institutions, including the Virginia Historical Society, Richmond; the National Portrait Gallery, Washington, D.C.; the National Museum of American Art, Washington; the U.S. Naval Academy Museum, Annapolis, Md.; the Brandywine River Museum, Chadds Ford, Pa.; the New-York Historical Society, New York City; the Museum of Fine Arts, Boston; the Museum of Our National Heritage, Lexington, Mass.; and the Museum of Art, Rhode Island School of Design, Providence. In 1992 the Brandywine River Museum mounted the first retrospective exhibition of Chappel's work; it subsequently traveled to the Maryland Historical Society in Baltimore and the Virginia Historical Society in Richmond. The accompanying catalog, by Barbara J. Mitnick and David Meschutt, is the most complete account of Chappel's life and career and contains a full bibliography. The author is indebted to Chappel's great-grandniece, Mrs. Hester Halstead Pier of New Haven, Conn., for information on Chappel's siblings that corrects the account given in the exhibition catalog cited above.

DAVID MESCHUTT

CHARLES, Ezzard (7 July 1921–27 May 1975), heavyweight boxer, was born Ezzard Mack Charles in Lawrenceville, Georgia, the son of William Charles, a truck driver and later a janitor, and Alberta Foster. His parents were divorced when he was five years old, and at the age of nine he went to live with his grandmother and great-grandmother in Cincinnati, Ohio. There he received his education, which included three years of attendance at Woodward High School.

Not a street fighter, young Charles trained himself at home and learned boxing as an amateur. In 1937, guided by Bert Williams, he began winning amateur titles; in 1939 he became the National Amateur Athletic Union middleweight champion. In March 1940, having won all 42 of his amateur bouts, he began his professional boxing career. His first manager was Max Elkus, owner of a men's clothing store, for whom he also worked at various jobs.

A middleweight from 1940 to 1943, Charles was fighting in main events by the end of 1940. In 1941 he defeated former world middleweight champion Teddy Yarosz but lost to another former champion, Ken Overlin. In 1942 he knocked out a former light heavyweight title claimant, Anton Christoforidis; drew with Overlin in a return fight; knocked out middleweight contender Jose Basora; twice beat welterweight contender Charley Burley; and twice outpointed future world light heavyweight champion Joey Maxim. His only loss that year was to Kid Tunero of Cuba. However, in early 1943 his progress was interrupted by losses to two highly rated light heavyweights, Jimmy Bivins and Lloyd Marshall. After the Marshall loss, Charles was inducted into the U.S. Army and served until 1945.

Charles returned to the ring in 1946 under the management of Jake Mintz, a Cincinnati businessman. Now a light heavyweight, he won 10 consecutive fights, during which he knocked out Marshall, defeated Bivins, and outpointed future champion Archie Moore. In 1947 Charles scored a spectacular one-punch knockout of Bivins and beat Moore again. Although the leading contender for the light heavyweight title, he had never fought in New York City. In his debut there on 25 July, his winning streak ended when he was the victim of a poor decision in a fight with heavyweight contender Elmer Ray. Charles won all of his remaining fights in 1947 and started 1948 with a one-punch knockout of Moore in Cleveland.

On 20 February 1948 Charles knocked out Sam Baroudi in 10 rounds, and Baroudi died of injuries sustained in the fight. Although Charles, who always fought cleanly, was not blamed for Baroudi's death, he was greatly upset by it. He returned to the ring in May, knocked out Ray in a return fight, and donated his entire purse to the Baroudi family. Following three more winning bouts, Charles won his second New York appearance by stopping heavyweight contender Joe Baksi on 10 December.

Although weighing only about 180 pounds, barely more than the light heavyweight limit, Charles had now established himself as a leading heavyweight contender when long-reigning champion Joe Louis retired on 1 March 1949. Charles then, in a fight recognized in some quarters as being for the heavyweight title, decisively won a cautiously fought, dull 15-round decision over Jersey Joe Walcott at Chicago on 22 June 1949. Charles defended his heavyweight title claim successively against Gus Lesnevich in New York City on 10 August 1949, Pat Valentino in San Francisco on 14 October 1949, and Freddie Beshore in Buffalo, New York, on 15 August 1950, stopping all three of these opponents. But his performances, although skillful, failed to bring him popularity or the plaudits of sportswriters.

On 27 September 1950 in New York City, Charles faced Joe Louis, who had decided to return to the ring, in a fight that would produce a universally accepted heavyweight champion. Charles outpunched and outboxed Louis from the first round to the last, winning by a large margin. However, even this victory failed to bring him acclaim, with more publicity being given to Louis's failing abilities.

Charles was a calculating ring tactician whose style somewhat resembled that of another unpopular heavyweight champion, Gene Tunney. Although a good puncher, as shown by his career record of 58 knockouts in 122 fights, he was content to outpoint opponents unless a solid chance to score a knockout appeared. Consequently he came to be regarded as an unexciting plodder. Furthermore, Charles had an unassuming, quiet, gentlemanly personality, and he chose to avoid the public eye whenever possible. He continued to live with his grandmother and great-grandmother, even after he married Gladys Gartrell in 1949. Charles kept the marriage a secret until his pregnant wife insisted that it be made public; they eventually had three children. He read, played the bass violin, listened to music, and attended church regularly.

An active heavyweight champion, Charles made successful defenses against Nick Barone, Lee Oma, Jersey Joe Walcott, and Joey Maxim, all between December 1950 and May 1951. He gave Walcott a second chance to win the title at Pittsburgh, 18 July 1951, and was surprisingly knocked out in the seventh round. The two men met for the fourth time on 5 June 1952 at Philadelphia, with Walcott's title at stake, and, after a close fight, Walcott won the unanimous vote of the officials even though most of the sportswriters favored Charles.

After losing the heavyweight title, Charles continued to fight and won 11 of his next 14 fights. Then on 17 June 1954 he lost a 15-round decision to Rocky Marciano in New York City, but only after one of the most thrilling heavyweight title fights in history, in which Charles built up a big early advantage that Marciano overcame in the later rounds. In a rematch on 17 September 1954, also in New York City, Marciano suffered a very severe nose injury but scored an eighth-round knockout. Charles continued his career until 1959, but by 1956 he was no longer a heavyweight contender.

Charles earned more than $2 million in purses during his boxing career, but by 1961 he was penniless. For a while he was a professional wrestler, then a greeter in a nightclub, then was appointed the coordinator of the boxing clubs in Chicago's Commission on Youths. Soon he began to suffer from the effects of amyotrophic lateral sclerosis (Lou Gehrig's disease), and by the mid-1960s he was unable to walk and had impaired speech. No longer able to work or to meet the expenses related to his illness, he was supported by the city of Chicago until his death there.

Charles is remembered for his unassuming personality, his work ethic, and his honesty. He described himself as "a simple, square sort of fellow, who believed in playing the game by the rules." Efficient and talented in the ring, he lacked the "killer instinct" and probably was at his best from 1946 to 1948, before becoming a heavyweight. He was an inaugural inductee to the International Boxing Hall of Fame in 1989.

• Charles's complete professional boxing record is in Herbert G. Goldman, ed., *The Ring Record Book and Boxing Encyclopedia* (1987). Two informative magazine articles are W. C. Heinz, "The Strange Case of Ezzard Charles," *Saturday Evening Post*, 7 June 1952, and Daniel M. Daniel, "Ezz's Personality Story Stresses His Humility, " *The Ring* magazine, Jan. 1951. Charles's championship fights and many of the incidents of his career are detailed in *The Ring*. His obituary is in the *New York Times*, 29 May 1975.

LUCKETT V. DAVIS

CHARLESTON, Oscar McKinley (12 Oct. 1896–6 Oct. 1954), African-American baseball player and manager, was born in Indianapolis, Indiana, to Tom Charleston, a construction worker, and Mary Thomas. The seventh of 11 children, Charleston served as a batboy for a local professional team before enlisting in the army at age 15. While stationed in the Philippines with the black 24th Infantry, Charleston honed his athletic skills in track and baseball, becoming the only African-American player in the Manila baseball league in 1914. Following his army discharge a year later, he joined the Indianapolis ABCs at a salary of $50 per month. The American Brewing Company sponsored the ABCs, but C. I. Taylor, Negro League pioneer, directed day-to-day operations.

Charleston, nicknamed Charlie, was a 5′11″ 185-pound center fielder who batted and threw left-handed. Described as barrel-chested, he would have difficulty maintaining his weight as his career progressed. He played a very shallow center field in his fielding heyday and counted on his speed to reach balls hit over his head. During his first year with the ABCs, he married Helen Grubbs from Indianapolis, but the marriage ended in an early divorce. Although described by his peers as basically a quiet man off the field, he displayed a fiery competitive temper as a player. He fought umpires, opponents, and fans, contesting calls, sliding hard into bases, and battling spectators for balls hit into the stands. Likened to contemporary Ty Cobb for his baseball skills and competitiveness, Charleston, for some sportswriters, was not the "black Ty Cobb," but rather Cobb was the "white Oscar Charleston."

After three years with the ABCs, Charleston in 1919 joined the Chicago American Giants run by Negro National League entrepreneur Rube Foster. It was common "blackball" practice for players, lured by better money offers, to change teams. Contracts were either poorly written or ignored, and barnstorming teams often made the most money. In 1921 Charleston moved to the St. Louis Giants and apparently gained superstar status, reportedly batting .434 in the 60-game season, including 14 doubles and league-leading 11 triples, 15 home runs, and 34 stolen bases. Although box score statistics for the Negro leagues are fragmentary, available numbers give Charleston a career hitting average of .350 in the Negro leagues from 1919 through 1937, .365 in Cuban League winter ball, which he played annually from 1919 through 1928, and .318 versus white major leaguers in 53 exhibition games from 1915 through 1936.

Charleston began the 1922 season in St. Louis but returned mid-year to Indianapolis, earning $325 per month, $125 above any teammate and one of the highest salaries in black baseball. In 1924 he jumped to the Harrisburg Giants of the Eastern Colored League for four years as player-manager, batting .391 in 1924, .418 in 1925 with a league-leading 15 doubles and 16 home runs, and .335 in 1927 with 18 doubles and 12 home runs. In Harrisburg he married Jane Blaylock, daughter of a Methodist bishop. The couple had no children and divorced after about 20 years. In 1928 and 1929 Charleston was on the roster of the Philadelphia Hilldales and hit .360 and .339, respectively.

As the depression made the financial life of teams in the Negro leagues especially precarious, independent, barnstorming clubs raided their ranks. The Homestead Grays of Pittsburgh, owned by Cum Posey, signed Charleston and other top players from failing franchises for the 1930 season. Because added weight had reduced his outstanding skills as a center fielder, Charleston moved to first base. Yet during the 1930 and 1931 seasons he hit a combined .371. In time, Posey and his successor, Gus Greenlee, who bought out Posey in 1932 to stock up his Pittsburgh Crawfords, accumulated the best black team in history, including future Hall of Famers Satchel Paige, Josh Gibson, James "Cool Papa" Bell, Judy Johnson, and Charleston, who was player-manager for the "Craws" from 1932 through 1937. As his skills began to diminish, Charleston batted .376 in 1933, .333 in 1934, and .288 in 1935. When the Dominican Republic Summer League in 1937 enticed many of the Crawford stars to move south, the team collapsed. Charleston moved to the Toledo Crawfords in 1938, but that franchise folded in mid-season 1939; the manager-first baseman joined the Philadelphia Stars, remaining for five seasons.

During World War II Charleston worked at the Philadelphia quartermaster depot. In 1945 he managed the Brooklyn Brown Dodgers, Branch Rickey's cover team set up to scout Jackie Robinson and other African-American players. As the Negro leagues faded away, Charleston's career ended with managing stints with the Philadelphia Stars (1946) and the Indianapolis Clowns (1947–1948). In 1949 he retired and worked in the baggage department of Philadelphia's Pennsylvania Railway Station. He died in Philadelphia following a heart attack and stroke. Charleston's election in 1976 to the Baseball Hall of Fame in Cooperstown New York, as the second Negro league player after Josh Gibson, finally brought recognition to his career and supported sportswriter Grantland Rice's earlier observation, "It's impossible for anyone to be a better ball player than Oscar Charleston."

• Short personal profiles of Oscar Charleston appear in Martin Appel and Burt Goldblatt, *Baseball's Best: The Hall of Fame Gallery* (1977); John Holway, *Blackball Stars: Negro League Pioneers* (1988); James Bankes, *The Pittsburgh Crawfords* (1991); *Dictionary of American Negro Biography* (1982); and *Black Sports* (July 1977). An obituary is in the *Pittsburgh Courier*, 16 Oct. 1954.

DAVID BERNSTEIN

CHARLEVOIX, Pierre-François-Xavier de (24 Oct. 1682–1 Feb. 1761), Jesuit priest and historian, was born at Saint-Quentin, France, the son of François de Charlevoix, a member of the old nobility and deputy king's attorney, and Antoinette Forestier. He studied at the Collège des Bons-Enfants in Saint-Quentin and moved to Paris when he began (15 Sept. 1698) his two-year novitiate with the Society of Jesus. He then moved to the Collège Louis-le-Grand, where he studied rhetoric and philosophy.

Ordained deacon, Charlevoix, then almost twenty-three, was sent to New France to teach grammar at the Jesuit college. He arrived at Quebec on 7 September 1705. A general peace treaty with the Iroquois had been signed on 4 August 1701, but during Charlevoix's stay in the colony the War of the Spanish Succession, or Queen Anne's War as it was called in North America (1702–1713), was being fought. Charlevoix seems to have traveled in the colony, although we know only that he was in Montreal in September 1708. During his stay he met the then retired first bishop of Quebec, François de Laval, and a number of veteran Jesuit missionaries. Although the power and the influence of the church were waning, its members, and especially the Jesuits, were still prominent members of the colonial society.

Returning to France in 1709, Charlevoix completed his studies, was ordained priest in 1713, taught classics and philosophy at Collège Louis-le-Grand, and began his scholarly career with the publication of *Histoire de l'établissement, des progrès et de la décadence du christianisme dans l'empire du Japon* (3 vols., 1715; repr. 1828, 1836, 1842, 1853). In 1719 the Crown entrusted him with the task of recommending boundaries for Acadia, which France had partially ceded to England at the Treaty of Utrecht (1713). The original report, now lost but known through a summary, was sent by Charlevoix to Paris from Quebec on 19 October 1720. It maintained that France had ceded only peninsular Nova Scotia and that France should continue to support and trade with the Abenakis. In 1720 Philippe, duke of Orléans and regent of France, asked Charlevoix to investigate the rumors relating to the existence of a western sea between the Great Lakes and the Pacific Ocean.

Charlevoix sailed from Rochefort on 1 July 1720, reached Quebec on 23 September, and returned to Le Havre two and a half years later, on 26 December 1722. His trip is described in *Journal d'un voyage fait par ordre du Roi dans l'Amérique septentrionnale*, volume 3 of *Histoire et description générale de la Nouvelle-France*, published more than twenty years later (1744). In its final form, following a literary device of its times, the *Journal* consisted of thirty-six letters addressed to Gabrielle-Victor de Rochechouart de Mortemart, duchesse de Lesdiguières.

After spending the winter of 1720–1721 in Quebec, Charlevoix left for the West in early March 1721. On his way to Michilimackinac (Mackinaw City, Mich., reached by 28 July 1721), he visited Fort Chambly, Sault-Saint-Louis (Kehnawake, Que.), Fort Frontenac (Kingston, Ont.), the Niagara region, and Lake St. Clair. Along the eastern shore of Lake Michigan, he began his descent toward the mouth of the Missouri River (reached 10 Oct. 1721), passing through Baie des Noquets (Big Bay De Noc, Mich.), Fort Saint-Joseph (Niles, Mich.), along the Theakiki (Kankakee) and Illinois rivers. He then proceeded to Cahokia (East St. Louis, Ill.) and Kaskaskia, spent Christmas at Natchez, reached New Orleans (10 Jan. 1722), and from there Biloxi (Ocean Springs, Miss.) in early February. It took Charlevoix the remainder of 1722 to reach France. The *Adour*, which was to take him back to Quebec, was shipwrecked off the Florida Keys (14 Apr.), and it took him fifty days to return to Biloxi. Charlevoix left again on the *Bellone* (22 June); but when he reached Saint-Domingue at the end of September, it was too late in the season. He decided to go to France instead. Charlevoix set sail from the Cap (Cap-Haitien) on 25 September in the *Louis de Bourbon*, reached Plymouth on 2 December, did not manage to leave England for three weeks, and eventually made it to Le Havre on 26 December.

Although he had not found the western sea, Charlevoix maintained its existence somewhere between 40° and 50° north latitude (roughly between Winnipeg and Kansas City) and that it could be found either through the Missouri River or by posting a mission among the Sioux. Meanwhile, he had gained a firsthand knowledge of an immense territory and of the Indian nations that lived there.

For the rest of his life Charlevoix lived in France, except for three years he spent in Rome (1725–1728). He was a teacher, from 1734 the editor of the Jesuit monthly publication, *Mémoires pour servir à l'histoire des sciences et des beaux-arts* (better known as *Mémoires de Trévoux* or *Journal de Trévoux*), and from 1742 to 1749 the procurator in Paris for the Jesuit missions and Ursuline convents in Canada and Louisiana. He spent his retirement and died at the Jesuit college of La Flèche.

Charlevoix is mostly remembered for his historical works. In 1724 he published *La vie de la mère Marie de l'Incarnation, institutrice & première superieure des Ursulines de la Nouvelle France* (repr. 1735, 1862); in 1730–1731, *Histoire de l'isle Espagnole ou de S. Domingue. Ecrite particulierement sur des Memoires du P. Jean-Baptiste Le Pers* (2 vols., repr. 1733, 1744); in 1736, *Histoire et description générale du Japon* (2 vols., repr. 1754, 1839, 1841, 1844, 1852); in 1744, *Histoire et Description Générale de la Nouvelle-France* (3 or 6 vols., repr. 1976; trans. 1962); and in 1756, *Histoire du Paraguay* (3 vols., repr. 1757).

Charlevoix was a careful, thorough, and honest historian. He consulted archival documents, listed his bibliographical sources, used footnotes, interviewed eyewitnesses, and relied, whenever possible, on personal observations. Given his firsthand knowledge of the country, his major achievement is *Histoire et description générale de la Nouvelle-France*, used by subsequent historians to this date as a primary source for the history of New France and for the ethnography of the North American Indians. The work is subdivided into 3 volumes. Volumes 1 and 2 include twenty-two books (the chronological history of the colony to 1731) and a valuable description of the North American flora. Volume 3 includes an essay on the origin of the Indians, the journal of his 1720 voyage, the chronology of the history of the New World (1248–1739), and a bibliographical essay.

• Selections of Charlevoix's works were edited by Léon Pouliot, *Charlevoix (1682–1761)* (1959), and Charles Edwards O'Neill, *Charlevoix's Louisiana* (1977). A book-length biography has yet to be published. The best original study of Charlevoix's life and works, including a full bibliography and the list of known archival sources, is David M. Hayne's very good entry in Francess G. Halpenny, ed., *Dictionary of Canadian Biography*, vol. 3, *1741–1770* (1974), pp. 103–10. Jean Delanglez, *The French Jesuits in Lower Louisiana (1700–1763)* (1935), pp. 88–90, also uses archival sources for a short sketch of Charlevoix's "transit" in Louisiana. Marie-Aimée Cliche's entry in Maurice Lemire, ed., *Dictionnaire des oeuvres littéraires du Québec*, vol. 1, *Dès origines à 1900* (1980), pp. 366–73, deals with Charlevoix's *Histoire et description générale de la Nouvelle-France* and demonstrates its influence on later historians. This point is also stressed in Bruce Graham Trigger, *Natives and Newcomers: Canada's "Heroic Age" Reconsidered* (1985), pp. 23–25.

LUCA CODIGNOLA

CHARLOT (1830?–10 Jan. 1910), head chief of the Bitterroot Salish (who are also known by the misnomer "Flatheads"), was known in the Salish language as "Claw of the Small Grizzly Bear," the son of Victor, or "Plenty Horses," head chief of the Salish from 1854 to 1870, and Agate (?). He was also known as Victor Charlot, and his name is sometimes rendered as Charlo. Little is known of Charlot before he succeeded his father in 1870. Charlot's early life, like that of all Salish by the nineteenth century, was based in the Bitterroot Valley of southwestern Montana, although the tribe utilized an immense territory and often made two trips annually to hunt bison on the plains east of the Continental Divide. The Salish suffered heavily during this period from successive epidemics of smallpox and other European diseases, and from raids by the Blackfeet, a larger tribe with better access to firearms. Due in part to these losses, the Salish made several arduous journeys to St. Louis seeking the "powers" of the "Blackrobes," and in 1841, Jesuits established a mission in the Bitterroot Valley.

In 1855 Isaac Stevens, the first governor of newly formed Washington Territory, moved through the inland Northwest negotiating treaties with many of the region's tribes. Stevens was intent on placing the Salish, Pend d'Oreille, and one band of the Kootenai onto a single reservation whose center would be the St. Ignatius mission and the nearby Hudson's Bay trading post of Fort Connah. Chief Victor, however, surprised Stevens with his unbending determination that the Salish remain in the Bitterroot Valley. Victor, like Charlot after him, maintained a resolute policy of peace with the whites but also refused to cede control of the tribe's beloved valley, coveted by whites as the most promising agricultural land in the region. Stevens, Victor, and other tribal leaders finally agreed on a treaty that contained a complicated scenario for the Bitterroot, establishing a "conditional reservation" unless a presidentially authorized survey should decide that the "Jocko" or Flathead Reservation was better suited to the needs of the tribe. When the government did nothing over the next fifteen years, the Salish concluded the valley would remain their permanent home.

In 1870 Victor died during one of the annual bison hunts east of the mountains. As Charlot assumed leadership of the tribe, the Salish were still the predominant single force in the area, but the balance of power was shifting dramatically with the construction of military roads, the onset of the Montana gold rush, and the beginning of the cattle industry. At the urgings of white settlers and the territorial delegates, President Ulysses S. Grant issued an executive order on 14 November 1871 that falsely stated that the required survey had been carried out, that the Bitterroot had been determined "not to be better adapted to the wants of the Flathead Tribe," and that the Salish were therefore to be removed to the reservation. However, when future president James Garfield was sent to Montana in 1872 to negotiate the removal, Charlot refused to sign the agreement, in spite of threats and pressure. Two subchiefs did sign: Arlee, a Nez Percé by birth, and Adolphe. Although the original copy of the agreement showed no mark beside Charlot's name, the copies published for the Senate, which were used for the vote on ratification, had Charlot's mark forged onto them. The false appearance of an agreement spurred many white settlers to crowd onto Salish lands in the Bitterroot Valley. To Charlot's further outrage, the government treated Arlee as the head chief and extended to him a house, land, and a stipend. Over the following two years, about twenty Salish families joined Arlee on the Jocko reservation.

Until Senator George G. Vest confirmed the forgery of Charlot's mark in 1883, the chief was vilified in Montana's press as a liar and a treaty violator. Missoula County, which claimed jurisdiction over the area, used this as a pretext for various efforts to force the Salish out, including an attempt in 1876 to tax Salish property. Charlot, according to an account in the *Daily Missoulian* (26 Apr. 1876), responded bitterly, saying "the white man wants us to pay him . . . for the things we have from our god and our forefathers; for things he never owned and never gave us . . . he spoils what the spirit who gave us this country made beautiful and clean . . . To take and to lie should be burned on his forehead."

Despite his deep and growing resentment, Charlot stuck to his policy of nonviolent resistance. This was sorely tested in July 1877, when Chief Joseph and the nontreaty Nez Percé, pursued by the army, moved east over Lolo Pass and approached the Bitterroot Valley. White settlers in Montana, the memory of Custer's defeat fresh in their minds, frantically raised alarms about a supposed Salish alliance with the Nez Percé to exterminate all whites in the region, who had minimal defenses. Charlot, however, refused to ally with his ancient allies and close relations and in fact warned them not to harm any whites, or the Salish would fight against them.

Whites, however, continued to view the Salish only as a problem, and pressures on the tribe only intensified with the elimination of the Plains bison and the completion of the Northern Pacific Railroad and spur lines into the Bitterroot Valley. Charlot nevertheless continued to reject repeated government efforts to evict the Salish. He told Senator Vest in 1883, "You want to place your foot upon our neck, and grind our face in the dust, but I will not go" (Fahey, p. 233). In 1884 Agent Peter Ronan took Charlot and a number of his headmen to Washington, D.C., for meetings with the Secretary of the Interior and President Chester Arthur. Charlot was not swayed during the meetings, but he reaffirmed that he would not try to stop other Salish people from moving to the reservation. By 1889 the social cohesion of the tribe was beginning to disintegrate as elders died and younger people moved away, and in November, Charlot finally agreed to move.

Expecting removal, the Salish planted no crops in 1890. Inaction by Congress, however, delayed removal for another two years, and according to some observers, the tribe's desperation reached a level of outright starvation. On 15 October 1891 General Henry B. Carrington and troops from Fort Missoula finally forced Charlot and the forty remaining Salish families to leave their ancestral lands. They reached the reservation two days later, where Charlot directed the Salish to present themselves in their finest ceremonial dress. In a great flourish, they rode into the Jocko Valley, where Charlot then solemnly shook hands with each of the Pend d'Oreille, Salish, and Kootenai people who had waited to greet his band. He then led everyone to a mass conducted by the Jesuit fathers. Charlot had long before devoted himself to the exceedingly strict version of Catholicism brought to the Salish by the Jesuits.

The government again failed to honor its promises to the Salish of housing, livestock, and agricultural equipment and assistance, or even to replace the equipment and household items that the people had been told to leave behind in the Bitterroot Valley. Nevertheless, the Salish gradually rebuilt a life for themselves on the Flathead Reservation, establishing a number of farms and ranches, most producing for subsistence needs.

From 1895 to 1901 Charlot and other tribal leaders had to rebuff the efforts of a congressional commission seeking further cessions of reservation lands. "You all know that I won't sell a foot of land," Charlot told the commission. "You had better hunt some people who want money more than we do." In 1904, Representative Joseph Dixon pushed the Flathead Allotment Act through Congress. The bill called for the allotment of individual tracts of lands to Indians on the Flathead Reservation, and then the opening of any "surplus" lands to white homesteaders. From 1904 to 1907 Charlot fought the allotment and opening of the reservation through letters and visits to Washington, where President Theodore Roosevelt rebuffed him. After 1907 Charlot appears to have become dispirited, and other Salish men, including Sam Resurrection, picked up the mantle of resistance, but to no avail.

Charlot's death at his home near Evaro spared him the agony of seeing even the Flathead Reservation opened to white settlement. Numerous prominent white Montanans lauded Charlot at his death, even as many of them pushed or supported policies that would dismantle the reservation. Three months later, homesteaders poured into the Jocko and Mission valleys, where they quickly outnumbered tribal people and assumed a dominating social and economic position.

The U.S. Indian agent soon moved to evict Charlot's widow, Isabel, from the chief's residence, which the government asserted was only granted to Charlot for use during his lifetime. Isabel was Charlot's second wife, having married him in Stevensville in 1888. She had no children with Charlot. Charlot had three children from his first marriage to Margaret, who died before 1888. Among them was Martin (1856–1941), who was chosen to succeed his father as head Chief.

Both politically and personally, Chief Charlot was a complex mix of accommodation and resistance, reflecting the difficult choices the Salish faced in their struggle for political and cultural survival. Regarded as courageous and principled by his admirers, inflexible and stubborn by his enemies, Charlot threaded a course for the Salish through a perilous time, seeking to avoid annihilation and yet preserve the Salish land base and traditional way of life.

• Information on Charlot is scattered. The most important federal records, through 1881, were organized by Indian Agency and Superintendency, and have been microfilmed by the National Archives; the Flathead Agency fell under numerous Superintendencies during this period. The largest single body of primary information after 1881 remains at the National Archives in the records of the Office of Indian Affairs (later the Bureau of Indian Affairs). Especially important are the extremely inaccessible "Letters Received [from Indian Agencies], 1881–1907," though much information can also be gained from the *Annual Reports of the Commissioner of Indian Affairs* for this period; the 1872 volume contains minutes of the 1872 negotiations. Extensive references to Charlot are in *Report of a Select Subcommittee of the Senate Concerning the Condition of the Indian Tribes in the Territories of Montana and Dakota* (48th Cong., 1st sess., SR 283). Sen G. G. Vest described his encounters in "Charlot: Chief of the Flathead Indians: A True Story," *Washington Post*, 26 July 1903. Yale University's Manuscripts and Archives contains the papers of General Carrington, who arranged the Salish removal and met repeatedly with Charlot.

One of the few sources for Salish commentaries on Charlot is J. Verne Dusenberry's "Sample of Pend d'Oreille Oral Literature and Salish Narratives," in *Lifeways of Intermontane and Plains Montana Indians*, ed. Leslie B. Davis (1979). Duncan McDonald (Salish-Nez Perce-Scottish) commented on the role of Charlot and the Salish in the 1877 War in "The Nez Perce, the History of Their Troubles and the Campaign of 1877," *New North-West*, 26 Apr. 1878–28 Mar. 1879; it was reprinted in *Idaho Yesterday* 21, no. 1 (1977): 2–15, 26–30; and no. 4 (1978): 2–10, 18–28. A native perspective on Charlot and the forced exodus from the Bitterroot Valley is in the tribe's newspaper, *Char-Koosta News*, Apr. 1975.

The standard secondary work, John Fahey, *The Flathead Indians* (1971), provides a useful history of the tribe through 1910, including much information on Charlot. Similar information is in Ellsworth H. Brown, "The History of the Flathead Indians in the Nineteenth Century" (Ph.D. diss., Michigan State Univ., 1975). Secondary articles on Charlot include Helen Addison Howard, "Indians and the Indian Agent: Chief Charlot and the Forged Document," *Journal of the West* 5, no. 3 (July 1966): 379–97; and Michael Harrison, "Chief Charlot's Battle with Bureaucracy," *Montana: The Magazine of Western History* 10, no. 4 (Autumn 1960): 27–33. A tribal secondary work is Flathead Culture Committee, *A Brief History of the Flathead Tribes* (1978; 1983). An obituary is in *Daily Missoulian*, 11 Jan. 1910.

THOMPSON R. SMITH

CHARLOT, André (26 July 1882–20 May 1956), theatrical impresario, was born Eugene André Maurice Charlot in Paris, France, the son of Maurice Charlot, a journalist and theatrical manager, and Sargine Battu. After failing his exams at Paris's Lycée Condorcet, Charlot gave up his dream of being a composer like his prizewinning grandfather and undertook an apprenticeship in Paris in theater management and public relations. In 1912 he assumed the managership of London's Alhambra Theatre, anglicizing French spectacular topical revue. In 1908 he married Florence Gladman, one-half of an English sister act; they had two children.

By 1915 Charlot was producing inexpensive revues in smaller theaters; these allusively lit shows, literate, topical, and playful, caught the escapist spirit of wartime London. Charlot's small choruses, funny and versatile, became the training ground for a generation of theatrical headliners, including Jessie Matthews and Anna Neagle. Critics likened the informal atmosphere of his productions, depending on shared values and experience, to gatherings of old friends, hence the title "intimate revue." Charlot sketches—playlets that broke new ground in being published—were ironic and snappy.

Perhaps even more than economy and taste, Charlot was known for his ability to develop talent. Among his discoveries were Beatrice Lillie (for forty years "the funniest woman on earth") and the chorus graduate Gertrude Lawrence, her era's most popular stage star. Lawrence, Lillie, and the singer-dancer Jack Buchanan came to New York for *Charlot's London Revue*; Noël Coward, who had written his first revue for Charlot, contributed many of its songs and sketches.

When *Charlot's London Revue*, subtitled *The Revue Intime*, opened at the Selwyn Theatre in January 1924, the vast revues staged by Florenz Ziegfeld and Charles Dillingham were still the Broadway standard. Lawrence wrote, "We were . . . rather frightened by the obvious lavishness of the productions in comparison with our intimate revue. . . . We wondered if we could compete with our tiny show and our British humor."

Of the revue's impact, theatrical historian Gerald Bordman wrote, "Charlot made the evening seem to move at a lightning-like pace by flying in the face of Broadway practice and steadfastly refusing to allow encores." The *New York Evening Telegraph*'s critic noted that after the company's opening number, "there was an immediate response between actors and audience. That cordial relationship continued throughout the evening and when the curtain fell, the fact was established that in Charlot's Revue, Broadway has something new."

Before long, a New York women's clothier advertised the Charlot suit: "Today's Fashion News. The suit that confers youth because it is youth." There followed a Charlot necklace and Charlot gown; Charlot wrote, "When two New Yorkers met on the avenue, it was a compliment for one to say to the other, 'Say, you're looking real Buchanan.'" Soon there were Buchanan ties, shirts, and socks. Several Algonquin Round Table wits opened a revue "on the lines of Mr. Charlot's entertainment." Charlot's revue ran nine sold-out months. There was a 1926 nationwide tour, culminating in Hollywood, where the show opened the new El Capitan Theatre.

Charlot's stars achieved American success. Lillie made silent films and Broadway musical comedies. Buchanan starred in films such as *Monte Carlo* (1929). After the Gershwin musical comedy *Oh, Kay!* in 1927, Lawrence made her home and career principally in the United States. Coward's revue *This Year of Grace* (1928) continued the tradition and affirmed Coward as a Broadway near-regular.

Stanley Green called *The Little Show* (1929; songs by transatlantic veterans Arthur Schwartz and Howard Dietz, sketches by George S. Kaufman) "something of an American counterpart to the Charlot revues and *This Year of Grace*." By the end of the 1930s, such quick-paced, topical productions had entirely replaced the larger, more vulgar works of Earl Carroll and George White; such revues, frequently starring Charlot veterans like Lillie and Reginald Gardner, remained Broadway's most popular musical productions until 1943, when *Oklahoma!* began the trend to serious book shows, wherein plot, song, and dance were integrated.

Charlot's American success faltered with an ill-considered partnership with Earl Carroll in the latter's 1927 *Vanities, International Edition*. In 1928 Charlot pioneered radio revue, winning the largest audience response recorded to that date by the British Broadcasting Corporation. In the same year he gave Lawrence her first dramatic role, in Owen Davis's *Icebound*. Charlot continued to discover talent, made several comebacks, and suffered several setbacks. His last British shows (1937) were "non-stop revue," a debased form created in response to all-day cinema programs and featuring sexual humor and near-nudity.

In 1937 Charlot came to Hollywood where he worked briefly as a technical adviser for Paramount Pictures. He became an American citizen in 1944 and remained in Hollywood until his death, attempting to revive his sort of show on screen, radio, stage, and eventually television. With the exception of *Charlot's British War Relief Revue* (at the El Capitan) in 1940, an all-star affair mixing his material and alumni with performers such as Fanny Brice, Henry Fonda, Bob Hope, Buster Keaton, and Rita Hayworth, he did not succeed. Between 1942 and 1953 he appeared, often as a European clergyman, diplomat, businessman, or inventor, in more than three dozen American films, including *The Constant Nymph*, *The Song of Bernadette*, and several Falcon detective films.

Charlot's London Revue remains a landmark of American theater. Intimate revue as pioneered by Charlot remains the British standard, though in the 1960s the impact of television and a rise in the fortunes of the British book musical carved it into several subdivisions.

• Reviews and programs of Charlot's productions and miscellaneous records are kept in such archives as the Theatre Museum, London, and the Special Collections Department of the University of California, Los Angeles, Research Library. His unpublished works are held by family members. He is mentioned in theatrical histories and in the autobiographies of Gertrude Lawrence, *A Star Danced* (1945), and Beatrice Lillie, *Every Other Inch a Lady* (1973), as well as biographies such as Michael Marshall, *Top Hat and Tails: The Story of Jack Buchanan* (1978). Charlot's life to the mid-1930s was chronicled in British newspapers, including the Manchester *Evening News* (July–Aug. 1928) and the London *Sunday Express* (20 and 27 Dec. 1931, 3 Jan. 1932). The British Broadcasting Corporation has produced two radio programs dealing with Charlot, the most recent being James Ross Moore's "Buzz Buzz: The Lives of André Charlot" in Oct. 1993.

JAMES ROSS MOORE

CHARNEY, Jule Gregory (1 Jan. 1917–16 June 1981), atmospheric scientist, was born in San Francisco, California, the son of Ely Charney and Stella Littman. Both parents were Yiddish-speaking Russian Jews who worked in the garment industry. The family moved to the Los Angeles area in 1922. All of Charney's earned degrees were from the University of California at Los Angeles: an A.B. in mathematics in 1938, an M.A. in mathematics in 1940, and a Ph.D. in meteorology in 1946. From 1942 to 1946 Charney was an instructor in physics and meteorology at UCLA. His dissertation, "Dynamics of Long Waves in a Baroclinic Westerly Current," comprised the entire October 1947 issue of the *Journal of Meteorology*. This paper was influential, first because it emphasized the influence of "long waves" in the upper atmosphere on the behavior of the entire atmosphere rather than the more traditional emphasis on the polar front and, second, because it provided a simplified way of analyzing perturbations along these waves, which proved both physically insightful and mathematically rigorous.

After graduation Charney served for a year as a research associate at the University of Chicago. In 1946 he married Elinor Kesting Frye, who already had one son; together the couple had two other children. During the academic year 1947–1948 he held a National Research Council postgraduate fellowship at the University of Oslo in Norway. During this year he developed a technique known as the "quasi-geostrophic approximation" for calculating the large-scale motions of planetary-scale waves. He returned from Norway to the Institute for Advanced Study in Princeton, where he was a member and then director of its theoretical meteorology project from 1948 to 1956. His supervisor, the noted mathematician John von Neumann, was in charge of a project to develop an electronic computer. Charney's group constructed a successful mathematical model of the atmosphere and demonstrated that numerical weather prediction was both feasible (using the ENIAC computer, which took twenty-four hours to generate a forecast) and practicable (using von Neumann's stored-program computer to generate a forecast in five minutes). In 1954 Charney helped establish a numerical weather prediction unit within the U.S. Weather Bureau.

Charney was professor of meteorology at the Massachusetts Institute of Technology from 1956 to 1981 and was Alfred P. Sloan Professor there from 1966. His research focused on the dynamics of atmospheres and oceans. From 1963 to 1966 he was chair of the National Research Council's Panel on International Meteorological Cooperation, and from 1968 to 1971 he was chair of the U.S. Committee for the Global Atmospheric Research Programme. GARP was a series of international experiments conducted by the World Meteorological Organization to measure the circulation of the atmosphere, model its behavior, and improve predictions of its future state. Charney was instrumental in articulating the global goals and vision of GARP, and he consistently argued that scientists needed to view the atmosphere as a single, global system.

Charney was elected to Phi Beta Kappa in 1937. He was a fellow of the American Academy of Arts and Sciences, American Geophysical Union, and American Meteorological Society. He was a member of the U.S. National Academy of Sciences and a foreign member of the Norwegian and Royal Swedish Academies of Science. Among his many awards were the Meisinger Award and the Rossby Medal of the American Meteorological Society (1949 and 1964), the Losey Award of the Institute of Aeronautical Sciences (1957), the Symons Medal of the Royal Meteorological Society (1964), the Hodgkins Medal of the Smithsonian Institution (1969), and the International Meteorological Organization Prize (1971). He was much in demand as a visiting professor and guest lecturer. Charney died in Boston.

• Charney's personal papers are located in the archives of the Massachusetts Institute of Technology. They include a tape recorded interview with Charney, transcribed as "Conversations with Jule Charney," ed. George W. Platzman, National Center for Atmospheric Research, *Technical Note* 298 (1987). On Charney's scientific contributions see Norman A. Phillips, "Jule Charney's Influence on Meteorology," *Bulletin of the American Meteorological Society* 63 (1982): 492–98. A memorial volume is Richard S. Lindzen, Edward N. Lorenz, and George W. Platzman, eds., *The Atmosphere, a Challenge: The Science of Jule Gregory Charney* (1990). This volume contains Charney's vita, reprints of some of his most important papers, and articles by scientists who knew him.

JAMES RODGER FLEMING

CHARTERS, W. W. (24 Oct. 1875–8 Mar. 1952), educator, was born Werrett Wallace Charters in Hartford, Ontario, Canada, the son of Alexander Maxwell Charters, a well digger and grain farmer, and Mary Ann Mealley. His parents were of Scottish and Irish descent and were Baptist, a religious affiliation that Charters actively maintained in his adulthood. Charters was reared in a rural community in the southern part of the province of Ontario. He completed his formal schooling at the Hartford Village School and Hagersville High School (1894) and was a teacher (1894–1895) in Rockford, Ontario, before embarking on his university studies. He earned his bachelor of arts from McMaster University (then located in Toronto, Ontario) in 1898; his teacher training certificate from the Ontario Normal College in Hamilton, Ontario, in 1899; and his bachelor of pedagogy from the University of Toronto in 1901. After earning his teacher certification with distinction, Charters served as principal of the Hamilton Normal School (1899–1901), during which time he was responsible for training many Ontario teachers.

Charters, later to be known more formally as W. W. Charters and Wallace W. Charters, began his graduate education at the University of Chicago in 1901 and earned his Ph.M. (1903) and Ph.D. (1904). His doctoral adviser was renowned philosopher and educational theorist John Dewey, whose ideology differed considerably from Charters's own bent for scientific curriculum making and educational engineering.

Between 1904 and 1942, Charters was employed at seven institutions. He served at the State Normal School in Winona, Minnesota, from 1904 to 1907 as principal of the Laboratory Elementary School and supervisor of practice teaching. He then moved to the

University of Missouri, Columbia, where he became professor of the theory of teaching (1907–1917) and dean of the School of Education (1910–1917). He served briefly at the University of Illinois at Urbana-Champaign as professor of education (1917–1919) and dean of the School of Education (1918–1919) before moving to the Carnegie Institute of Technology in Pittsburgh (later Carnegie-Mellon University) as professor of education and director of the Research Bureau for Retail Training (1919–1923). In 1923 he went to the University of Pittsburgh, where he became dean of the Graduate School in 1924. In 1925 he became professor of education at the University of Chicago, and in 1928 he moved to the Ohio State University in Columbus, where he served as professor of education and director of the Bureau of Educational Research until he retired in August 1942. Charters also served as the director of research at Stephens College in Columbia, Missouri (1920–1945); Rochester Mechanical Institute in Rochester, New York (1928–1945); and Muskingum College in New Concord, Ohio (1942).

Charters married Jesse Blount Allen in December 1907, and they had four children. They had met at the University of Chicago as graduate students, and his wife, known formally as Dr. Jesse A. Charters, was an academic in her own right, most specifically as a professor of adult education at the Ohio State University. Education was apparently important in the family, and all their children received postsecondary education. Also important to Charters were a number of enduring hobbies, which included reading, stock market analysis, membership in the Paul Bunyan Society, stamp collecting, and crossword puzzles. He also maintained his Canadian associations, even though he had become a naturalized American.

Charters was an internationally renowned leader, entrepreneur, and man of action during the first half of the twentieth century. He conducted his career through the emerging American machine age, depression, and wars, and he adapted and contributed to the changing scientific and technological needs for advancements, job analysis, efficiency, and utility. By the time of his death in Livingston, Alabama, Charters had made a number of noteworthy contributions to education and curriculum. He served as a mentor to many future leaders in education who were his students and associates, and he had considerable influence on recognized contributors to the field of media and educational communication, such as William H. Cowley, Edgar Dale, Sidney L. Pressey, I. Keith Tyler, and Douglas Waples. Likewise, the fields of curriculum and teacher education have felt the influence of the contributions of such individuals as Wilford M. Aikin, Ross L. Mooney, Louis E. Raths, Hilda Taba, and Ralph W. Tyler, all of whom were closely associated with Charters.

Charters made a number of significant contributions to education that served as a foundation for contemporary thought and action. He organized an "invisible college" of American educators who were interested in curriculum, and this group of curricularists contributed to the study of and future advancements in curriculum as a field of inquiry and practice. In 1929–1930 he was the founding director of the Institute for Education by Radio; radio became a demonstrated means of educational technology and later served as a model for the use of more advanced educational media. He was instrumental in promoting the move of his alma mater, McMaster University, from Toronto to Hamilton in 1930 and was the founding editor of the *Journal of Higher Education* and the editor of the *Educational Research Bulletin*, both of which published current research and scholarship during his time. Charters also engineered from behind the scenes the design and evaluation of the significant Eight-Year, 30-School Study (1932–1940), and he was responsible for hiring the majority of the principal researchers for the longitudinal study. In addition to these accomplishments, Charters directed the Bureau of Educational Research at Ohio State so successfully that it became a model for university teaching services that assist university faculty and staff with teaching and efficient use of facilities, and he personally instructed the first course on college teaching. Upon his retirement from Ohio State, Charters served as the chair of the Bureau of Educational Training for the War Manpower Commission and was responsible for mainstreaming war veterans into American life through educational training programs.

Charters's research and writing spanned five decades, and he wrote more than 570 published books, studies, articles, reviews, and editorials, as well as numerous unpublished papers, speeches, and an unfinished manuscript on educational engineering. While individuals who knew him noted his writing as being less substantial than his other contributions, his early work contributed to contemporary curriculum organization and implementation, teacher education, behavioral objectives, competency-based education, systems concept, job analysis, the research project method, and evaluation.

Finally, Charters serves as an exemplar of the professional about whom he wrote: the educational engineer. He would be a worthy case study in education, psychology, and business administration, for he was a model leader, entrepreneur, grantsman, consultant, resource developer, delegator, and man of action. Furthermore, his writing, research, and projects within various educational, business, health, and military institutions were precursors to the "action research" conducted by his students, associates, and ensuing generations.

• The Charters papers are in the Special Collections at William Oxley Thompson Memorial Library, Ohio State University, Columbus. Sheldon A. Rosenstock, "The Educational Contributions of W(errett) W(allace) Charters" (Ph.D. diss., Ohio State Univ., 1983), includes a complete listing of Charters's writings and writings about him. Other sources include Raymond E. Callahan, *Education and the Cult of Efficiency* (1962); Lawrence A. Cremin, *The Transformation of the School: Progressivism in American Education, 1876–1957* (1964); Barry M. Franklin, *Building the American Communi-*

ty: The School Curriculum and the Search for Social Control (1986); Herbert M. Kliebard, *Forging the American Curriculum* (1992) and *The Struggle for the American Curriculum: 1893–1958* (1986); William L. Patty, *A Study of Mechanism in Education* (1938); William H. Schubert, *Curriculum: Perspective, Paradigm, and Possibility* (1986) and *Curriculum Books: The First Eighty Years* (1984); Mary Louise Seguel, *The Curriculum Field: Its Formative Years* (1966); Daniel Tanner and Laurel Tanner, *The History of the School Curriculum* (1990) and *Curriculum Development: Theory into Practice* (1980); Alan R. Tom, *Teaching as a Moral Craft* (1984); and Norman Woelfel, *Molders of the American Mind* (1933).

SHELDON ROSENSTOCK

CHASE, Agnes (20 Apr. 1869–24 Sept. 1963), botanist and suffragist, was born Mary Agnes Meara (Mera) in Iroquois County, Illinois, the daughter of Martin J. Meara, a railroad worker and farmer, and Mary Cassidy Brannick. After her father's death in 1871, the family (which included six children) moved to Chicago and changed their name to Merrill. Agnes, as she was called, finished eight years of public school and held odd jobs to help her mother support the family.

After a short time proofreading for the *School Herald*, a periodical for rural teachers, she married its editor, William Ingraham Chase, in 1888. After only one year of marriage William Chase died, and his young widow, although not accountable for her husband's debts, felt duty-bound to repay them all. She proofread, often by night, for the *Inter-Ocean* newspaper of Chicago, while living frugally on a spartan diet. She then worked briefly in her brother-in-law's general store in Wady Petra, Illinois, where her nephew, Virginius Chase, sparked her interest in identifying the plants of Stark County.

In 1890 she returned to her job with the *Inter-Ocean*. At the Columbian Exposition of 1893, she and Virginius learned how to collect plant specimens and prepare a herbarium. By 1897 Chase began to keep field notes and the following year, while collecting specimens near the Des Plaines River, she met Ellsworth Jerome Hill, an Episcopal priest and bryologist. During the next five years Hill taught her botany and Latin, while employing her to illustrate many of the new species that he described. He introduced her to Charles Frederick Millspaugh, then curator of botany at the Field Museum of Natural History, who recognized Chase's native talent with pen and microscope and hired her as collaborator on his *Plantae Utowanae* (1900) and *Plantae Yucatanae* (1904). Both works treated large numbers of grasses and species of the aster family. It was here that her childhood fascination with grasses metamorphosed into scientific study. In November 1903, after a short stint as a meat inspector at the Chicago stockyards office of the U.S. Department of Agriculture (USDA), she transferred to the Forage Crops Division of the USDA Bureau of Plant Industry in Washington, D.C. In 1905 she began working with Albert Spear Hitchcock, rising from illustrator to scientific assistant in systematic agrostology to assistant and then to associate botanist, finally succeeding Hitchcock in 1936 as principal scientist in charge of systematic agrostology.

Chase's scientific career spanned nearly sixty years. Her contributions to the knowledge of grasses, especially those of the Americas, can be summarized in four words—collections, illustrations, identifications, and publications. By her last collecting trip in 1940 (to Venezuela at age seventy-one), Chase had gathered over 12,200 sets of plants, mostly grasses. From 1905 to 1912 she concentrated on the eastern and southern coasts of the United States, then the southwestern states, northern Mexico, and parts of California. Her work joined Hitchcock's to produce a *Manual of the Grasses of the United States* (1935) and to generate monographs on the North American species of *Panicum* (1910, 1915) and *Paspalum* (1929).

Chase was an intrepid explorer who financed most of her expeditions to Puerto Rico (1913) and to Brazil (1924–1925, 1929–1930), where she collected over 4,500 species for the grass herbarium of the USDA, many of which were not known before. These collections and her careful work on them helped to make the Washington grass herbarium the finest for studying grasses of the Western hemisphere. Like Hitchcock, Chase donated her own library in agrostology to the U.S. National Herbarium at the Smithsonian, where the grass herbarium was transferred, and with it her office, in 1912.

Agnes Chase worked on specific taxonomic problems in European herbaria in 1922 and again in 1925. She supplied them with needed monographs and in return received valuable duplicates of type specimens which are now at the Smithsonian. Besides her nearly seventy publications in agrostology, Chase made important contributions to botany in general. She wrote a popular *First Book of Grasses* (1922) and, with Cornelia D. Niles, a three-volume *Index to Grass Species* (1962), a bibliographic register of types. She also revised the 1935 *Manual of the Grasses of the United States* (1950). Many foreign students interested in grasses came to study with Agnes Chase and often stayed at her house in Washington.

Chase championed civil rights for blacks and women and supported prohibition and pacifism. Friends said that her version of Christianity was socialism, and she consistently supported Norman Thomas for the presidency. She marched with Alice Paul (1885–1977) and her contingent of suffragists and was jailed and forcibly fed. She vowed to burn any publication by Woodrow Wilson in which the words liberty and freedom appeared until he supported woman suffrage. Although raised a Roman Catholic, she lived her Christian principles by active support of the NAACP, the Fellowship of Reconciliation, the National Woman's party, and the Women's International League for Peace and Freedom. Although officially retired in 1939, Chase continued working into the last years of her life. She cared for her handicapped sister Rose from 1936 until Rose's death in 1954. After 1953 she shared her Washington home with Florence Van Eseltine, a longtime friend and the editor-typist for the *In-*

dex to Grass Species. Agnes Chase died in Bethesda, Maryland.

With neither diplomas nor degrees, she learned from nature, people, and literature. The Botanical Society of America awarded her, one of its charter member in 1906, a certificate of merit in 1956 "for distinguished achievement in the contributions to the advancement of botanical science." In 1958 the University of Illinois conferred on her the honorary D.Sc.; that same year the government of Brazil awarded her a distinguished service medal, and the Smithsonian Institution made Chase its eighth honorary fellow. Lastly, in 1961 the Linnean Society of London unanimously elected her a fellow.

• Chase's manuscripts can be found in the Albert S. Hitchcock and Mary Agnes Chase Papers at the Smithsonian Institution Archives. Microfilm copies of these papers as well as some additional documents are held by the Hunt Institute for Botanical Documentation, Carnegie Mellon University, Pittsburgh. Chase's bound field notebooks (7 vols., 1897–1959) are in the botany branch of the Smithsonian Institution Libraries. Reprints of articles and various unpublished talks and papers are in the Hitchcock-Chase-McClure Library, Division of Grasses, Smithsonian Institution. Letters between Chase and C. F. Millspaugh can be found in the botany department, Field Museum of Natural History, Chicago. They collaborated on papers that appeared in the *Field Columbian Museum Botanical Series*, no. 50, Aug. 1900, pp. 113–24; no. 69, Feb. 1903, pp. 15–84; no. 92, Apr. 1904, pp. 85–151. Transcripts of interviews (1977, 1979) with friends of Chase are in the Oral History Collection of the Hunt Institute.

Chase's *First Book of Grasses* (rev. 1937, 1968) was reissued in 1977. Her article, "Eastern Brazil through an Agrostologist's Spectacles," appeared in the *Annual Report Smithsonian Institution, 1926* (1927), pp. 383–403. Chase's "Rev. E. J. Hill," *Rhodora*, Apr. 1917, pp. 61–69, offers some information on her early association with Ellsworth Hill. See also her illustrations in E. J. Hill, "A New Biennial-Fruited Oak," *Botanical Gazette*, Mar. 1899, pp. 204–8, and her memorial to Hitchcock, *Science*, 6 Mar. 1936, pp. 1–6. F. R. Fosberg and J. R. Swallen compiled a bibliography and brief biography in "Agnes Chase," *Taxon*, 8 (June 1959): 145–51. See also M. T. Stieber, "Manuscripts Written and/or Annotated by Agnes Chase Pertinent to the Grass Collections of the Smithsonian Institution," *Huntia* 3 (1979): 117–25. Leonard Carmichael's foreword to the *First Book of Grasses*, 3d. ed., includes a biographical sketch. See also Marcia Bonta, *Women in the Field: America's Pioneering Naturalists* (1991); Liz Hillebrand, "87-Year-Old Grass Expert Still Happy with Subject," *Washington Post and Times Herald*, 30 Apr. 1956; Bess Furman, "Grass Is Her Life-Root," *New York Times*, 11 June 1958; Gladys Baker, "Women in the U.S. Department of Agriculture," *Agricultural History* 50 (Jan. 1976): 190–201. An obituary is in the *New York Times*, 26 Sept. 1963.

MICHAEL T. STIEBER

CHASE, Edna Woolman (14 Mar. 1877–20 Mar. 1957), magazine editor, was born in Asbury Park, New Jersey, the daughter of Franklyn Alloway and Laura Woolman. Her parents divorced during her infancy, and her mother remarried and moved to New York City, leaving Edna to be brought up by her maternal grandparents in New Jersey. Her mother's family were members of the Society of Friends—Laura Woolman was a descendant of John Woolman, a prominent eighteenth-century Quaker—and young Edna was raised in an environment that emphasized plain living and frowned on personal adornment. Years later, she recalled that her interest in fashion was inspired by the chic clothing that her mother wore during visits to her daughter.

Edna was tutored at home by her grandparents and attended area private schools. At the age of eighteen she moved to New York City to live with her mother, and at that time took Woolman as her surname. Through a friend she found a clerical job at *Vogue*, a weekly fashion magazine founded three years earlier, and moved into a boardinghouse. The temporary position turned into full-time employment, and Edna Woolman found herself at home among the society people who made up the magazine staff. Soon she was working closely with the publisher, Arthur Turnure, who relied on her advice about deadlines and layout, and she was gradually given more editorial authority after Turnure's sister-in-law Marie L. Harrison became editor in 1901.

Edna Woolman married Francis Dane Chase, the son of a Boston banker, in 1904; they had one daughter, Ilka, born in 1905, who later became a well-known actress and author. Motherhood, however, did not hinder Edna Woolman Chase's advancement at *Vogue*. When publishing magnate Condé Nast bought the magazine in 1909, Chase was retained as an employee and in two years' time had assumed the duties of managing editor. Up to this time *Vogue* had been a magazine that reported fashion news and illustrated outfits worn by society women. Over the next few years Chase enlivened its pages by commissioning artists to invent and portray new designs of fancy costumes. Impressed by her abilities, Nast named her editor in chief in 1914.

Chase's marriage, which had faltered some years earlier, ended in divorce about this time, and she resumed a relationship with an earlier suitor, an English engineer named Richard Newton. Chase married Newton in 1921 but kept her first husband's name professionally; the couple remained together until Newton's death in 1950.

During nearly four decades at the helm of *Vogue*, Chase made it the leading magazine of its kind in the world and established herself as the doyenne of fashion. Her stature was recognized as early as 1935, when the government of France awarded her the Legion of Honor for her promotion of French fashion. Always a strong ally of the fashion industry, she worked closely with designers, merchants, and advertisers to bring the best of contemporary clothing design to *Vogue*'s upper-class readership.

Combining an innate sense of chic with strong business acumen, Chase was quick to devise and employ innovations that would attract readers and increase revenue. During World War I, when Paris fashion houses were temporarily closed, she encouraged new creations by New York clothing designers and staged a series of fashion shows, the first in the United States, which were duly reported in *Vogue*. After the war she resumed close ties with the French fashion industry, preeminent in the world, while continuing to publicize the work of American designers. Skillfully tying advertising to fashion news, she expanded *Vogue*'s readership and its revenues by listing high-end stores throughout the country where clothes featured in the magazine could be purchased.

Vogue avoided contemporary social issues and politics, although it was avowedly antisuffragist in the years before the passage of the Nineteenth Amendment in 1920, stating editorially that women could perform "important public work" without having the right to vote. During the Great Depression, Chase tacitly acknowledged the straitened circumstances of many of *Vogue*'s readers by publishing an annual issue focusing on "More Taste Than Money," a phrase that she coined. During World War II Chase served as an adviser to the U.S. government on the design of uniforms for members of the newly created women's armed forces units.

Although fashion was always preeminent in the pages of *Vogue*, Chase also included articles on contemporary art and design. She published essays and fiction by sophisticated contemporary writers, including Dorothy Parker, Robert Benchley, and Robert Sherwood. She also trained a generation of fashion and society reporters and editors, many of whom went on to positions of importance at rival publications.

A tiny woman of seemingly limitless energy, Chase remained editor in chief of *Vogue* until 1952, when she stepped aside to become chair of the board. Two years later she published an autobiography, *Always in Vogue*, written with her daughter. While on holiday with her daughter and son-in-law, she died in Sarasota, Florida.

• In addition to her autobiography, biographical information on Chase is in *Current Biography* (1940); *Past Imperfect* (1942), a memoir by her daughter, Ilka Chase; "France Awards the High Priestess of Fashion a Ribbon," *Newsweek*, 24 Aug. 1935, pp. 25–26; "Stylocrats," *Time*, 18 Aug. 1947, p. 47; "Fifty-nine Years in Fashion," *Life*, 8 Nov. 1954, pp. 123–24, 127; and articles in the *New York Times*, 27 Sept. 1940 and 13 Mar. 1957. Obituary notices are in the *New York Times* and the *New York Herald Tribune*, both 21 Mar. 1957.

ANN T. KEENE

CHASE, Hal (13 Feb. 1883–18 May 1947), professional baseball player, was born Harold Homer Chase in Los Gatos, California, the son of Edgar Chase, a logger and timber cutter originally from Maine, and Mary (maiden name unknown). Chase dropped out of Los Gatos High School in his sophomore year to play baseball with the amateur teams that flourished in the Santa Clara Valley, then was invited to play baseball and run track for the Brothers of Santa Clara University. Although a high school dropout, he was awarded an athletic scholarship. He later boasted that he rarely attended classes.

His first big break came in 1903, when he was signed by the Los Angeles Angels of the Pacific Coast League while playing with the Victoria, British Columbia, team of the Southwest Washington League. He was already a solid hitter with a strong, accurate throwing arm.

He played in every one of the team's 173 games in 1904, and his outstanding work drew the attention of the New York Highlanders (soon to change their name to the Yankees).

Chase, a handsome, red-haired six-footer, proved to be a good drawing card from the start on a talent-thin, sixth-place ball club. He raised his batting average seventy-four points, to .323, in his second season and was among the American League's top batsmen. He tied a fielding mark for first basemen that year by accepting twenty-two chances in one game.

Chase liked to play far in back of the first-base bag. When an opposing batsman laid down a bunt in his direction, he would charge the ball, catch the runner going from first to second, then race to his position just in time to complete a double play.

By 1906 Chase was earning $6,000 a year, the largest salary paid to a New York player up to that time. But in 1908 Chase deserted the ball club in order to play for Stockton in the "outlaw" California League after quarreling with Yankees manager Norman "Kid" Elberfeld, who had insinuated that Chase was not putting forth his best efforts. It was not the last time these charges would be leveled against him.

Yankees president and co-owner Frank Farrell allowed his contentious infielder to return to the ball club a year later, hoping that a new manager, George Stallings, might be able to "encourage" Chase to behave. New York's many attractions were an irresistible lure for Chase. He regularly held court with an admiring entourage of chorus girls, pool sharks, card sharps, and Bowery ruffians. His after-hours gluttony cost him two wives and his relationship with his only child, Hal, Jr., but his soirees did not appear to diminish his diamond prowess. (Chase married Nellie Heffernan in 1908; sometime after their son was born, they were divorced. The year that he married a second time, to Anna Cherrug, is unknown; nor can the date of their divorce be determined.)

George Stallings was no more capable of controlling Chase than his predecessor had been. As the 1910 season wound down, Stallings complained to Farrell that Chase had "laid down" on the team during a road trip to Detroit. Citing an undetermined illness, Chase left the ball club again, purportedly to play "outlaw ball" in California. Owner Farrell decided to ask League president Ban Johnson to arbitrate the matter. Curiously, he absolved Chase and upbraided Stallings instead. Johnson hated Stallings and merely used this incident as an excuse to embarrass and annoy a foe. Farrell then fired Stallings and appointed Chase as Yankees player-manager in 1910.

The second-place Yankees of 1910 dropped to sixth place in 1911 under Chase's stewardship, and after this lackluster season he resigned to concentrate on his ball playing. During the 1913 campaign Yankees manager Frank Chance stormed into the press box one day to complain to Heywood Broun of the *New York Tribune* that Chase was "throwing games." Frank Farrell traded Chase to the Chicago White Sox on 31 May, two days after the accusation was publicly aired.

Hal Chase gave no intimation to Chicago management of any salary dissatisfaction on his part—he told White Sox owner Charles Comiskey he was considering early retirement in order to pursue a private business venture in Philadelphia. But all the while Chase was secretly negotiating with the Federal League for a higher salary. He served notice on 15 June 1914 that he would exercise the "ten-day" clause in his contract, terminating his employment. By terms of the National Agreement, technically he could not play for any other team in "organized baseball." He joined the Buffalo ball club of the newly formed Federal League, an "outlaw" interloper that was challenging the hegemony of the American and National Leagues.

After the Federal League folded in 1915, Chase was bypassed by the American League teams as punishment for betraying Comiskey. His diamond skills were still formidable, however, and the Cincinnati Reds selected him. He led the National League in hitting that year with a .339 average.

Chase refined his skills as a master "fixer" in Cincinnati by inducing teammates to place bets for and against the ball clubs the Reds were to play. Manager Christy Matthewson suspended Chase without pay on 9 August 1918 for "indifferent play," a codeword for throwing games.

Baseball observers believed that the league at last had the goods on Chase. A hearing was held on 30 January 1919 before National League president John Heydler. However, Christy Matthewson was in France with the American Expeditionary Forces and could not testify. New York Giants manager John McGraw had agreed to testify against Chase, but on the stand he described him as a "man above reproach." McGraw's eyebrow-raising comments were never adequately explained. But they seemed to satisfy Heydler, who cleared Chase of all charges.

Still confident that this sure-handed first baseman could contribute to his ball club, McGraw signed Chase to a 1919 contract. Then, in a strange turn of events, McGraw hired Christy Matthewson, Chase's accuser, to coach the Giants.

There was considerable acrimony in the Giants dugout that season. Chase was benched in August for spotty play by manager McGraw. The following month McGraw removed him, along with infielder Heinie Zimmerman, from the starting lineup without explanation. Neither Chase nor Zimmerman would ever play major league baseball again.

The exiled Chase moved back to California, where he became part owner of the San Jose team of the Mission League. Later he tried to bribe a Pacific Coast League pitcher into throwing a game in Los Angeles. Chase was barred from the Mission League when the Black Sox scandal broke on 29 September 1920—baseball's darkest hour—and was named in a subsequent indictment by a Cook County grand jury in Chicago. He was arrested in San Jose but never extradited. Hal Chase's role in the "fix" was acknowledged by "Sleepy" Bill Burns, star witness for the prosecution, who was present at meetings between the eight corrupted ballplayers and the gamblers.

Thereafter, Hal Chase drifted into limbo. He landed in the obscure Copper League, which was comprised of pick-up teams in back-water Arizona mining towns. Chase played ball in the 1920s alongside former Black Sox players Buck Weaver and Claude Williams. On other occasions he supplemented his income by hustling local pool players, selling automobiles, and working as a rancher in Porterville, California.

He spent his last years in the Williams, California, ranch he had purchased for his sister's family during his ballplaying days. He died in Colusa, California.

To his contemporaries in the game of baseball, Hal Chase was known as "the Prince." He was an enormously gifted athlete whose agility and catlike reflexes established him as the top fielding American League first baseman of the "Dead Ball Era" (1900–1920). A "Fancy Dan" first baseman and contact hitter, Chase's sterling accomplishments included an impressive .291 career batting average. Four times Chase hit better than .300 in a season. Yet these achievements were largely negated by his having been branded by historians as the most corrupt player ever to appear on a big league diamond.

• There are many articles about Chase in the clipping file at the Baseball Hall of Fame Library, Cooperstown, N.Y. He is also prominently mentioned in numerous baseball anthologies, but there is no full-length biography. Gib Bodet, based on conversations with Chase's only son and some independent research, completed an overly sympathetic unpublished monograph in 1991, "The Life and Times of Prince Hal Chase." For a more balanced account see Robert C. Hoie, "The Hal Chase Case," in the Society of American Baseball Research, *Baseball Historical Review* (1981), pp. 34–41.

An interview with Hal Chase, Jr., appears in Richard Scheinin, "Error Apparent: The Crooks of Summer," San Jose *Mercury News*, 27 Feb. 1993, pp. 1D, 10D, 11D. Earlier accounts of his life and times can be found in Ira L. Smith, *Baseball's Famous First Basemen* (1957); Lee Allen, "How They Knew Chase Was Guilty," *Baseball Digest*, May 1961, pp. 25–32; John A. Heydler, "A Defense of the Hal Chase Affair," *Baseball Magazine*, Dec. 1920, pp. 327–29; and Hal Chase, "Doing the Comeback Stunt," *Baseball Magazine*, Oct. 1917, pp. 559–61.

For a scholarly consideration of the relationship between professional gamblers, sports figures, and politicians up through the Black Sox scandal, see Richard Lindberg, "The Evolution of an Evil Business," *Chicago History*, July 1993, pp. 38–53. Harold Seymour presents a lucid account of baseball gambling and Hal Chase's role in the events leading up to and including the Black Sox scandal in: *Baseball: The Golden Age* (1971). His account is superior to Eliot Asinof's quasinovel *Eight Men Out* (1963) in scholarship and historical interpretation. For Chase's baseball statistics, refer to Macmillan's *Baseball Encyclopedia*, 8th ed. (1990), and John Thorn and Peter Palmer, eds., *Total Baseball*, 2d ed. (1991). An obituary is in the *New York Times*, 19 May 1947.

RICHARD C. LINDBERG

CHASE, Ilka (8 Apr. 1905?–15 Feb. 1978), actress and author, was born in New York City, the daughter of Francis Dane Chase, a hotel manager, and Edna Alloway Woolman, editor of *Vogue* magazine. She was given her unusual first name in honor of a Hungarian friend of her mother. Chase, whose parents divorced when she was a child, was educated at a succession of boarding schools, including convent schools in Manhattan and Suffern, New York, run by the Sisters of the Holy Child, and Mrs. Dow's School, Briarcliff Manor, New York. Most summers were spent at her grandmother's estate at Brookhaven, Long Island. At age sixteen Chase was sent to finishing school in Groslay, France, and later attended a convent school at Neuilly, outside Paris. In 1923 she returned to New York to make her society debut at the Cosmopolitan Club.

Interested in a theatrical career since early childhood, Chase had acted in many school productions. In the spring of 1924 she joined the Stuart Walker stock company in Cincinnati, Ohio, and that summer made her professional acting debut as an Italian immigrant in Edward Sheldon and Dorothy Donnelly's *The Proud Princess*. In October 1924 Chase acted on Broadway for the first time when she played a housemaid in *The Red Falcon*, starring Carlotta Monterey. She then toured the West Coast with a company run by actor/manager Henry Miller and spent the summer of 1926 with a Rochester, New York, stock company directed by George Cukor, who became a close friend of Chase. While in Rochester, Chase met and married actor Louis Calhern. The couple, who had no children, stayed together for less than a year and were divorced in New York in early 1927.

In 1929 Chase moved to Hollywood to pursue a career in films. Tall, dark, and slender but lacking classic beauty, she had small "character" parts in numerous films, including *Paris Bound* (1929), with Fredric March; *South Sea Rose* (1929), with Lenore Ulric and Charles Bickford; *Why Leave Home?* (1929), with Dixie Lee and Sue Carol; *On Your Back* (1930), with H. B. Warner; *Let's Go Places* (1930), with Lola Lane and Walter Catlett; *The Floradora Girl* (1930), with Marion Davies; *Fast and Loose* (1930), with Miriam Hopkins and Carole Lombard; *Once a Sinner* (1931), with Joel McCrea; and *The Gay Diplomat* (1931), with Genevieve Tobin.

In January 1932 Chase returned to Broadway to play Grace Macomber in Philip Barry's *The Animal Kingdom*, a role that she repeated in the film version made later in the year. For the remainder of her acting career Chase divided her time equally between the theater and films. She made her strongest mark on stage as the malicious Sylvia Fowler in Clare Boothe Luce's *The Women*. The popular comedy opened at the Ethel Barrymore Theatre in December 1936 with an all-female cast, including Margalo Gillmore and Ruth Hammond. Chase stayed with the play for all but the last three weeks of its nearly two-year run. Most notable among Chase's other stage appearances are her roles in *Forsaking All Others* (1933), a comedy with Tallulah Bankhead; *Days without End* (1934), an unsuccessful drama by Eugene O'Neill; and *Co-Respondent Unknown* (1936), a sex farce with James Rennie and Peggy Conklin. She also appeared in two musicals—*Revenge with Music* (1934), with Libby Holman, and *Keep off the Grass* (1940), with Jimmy Durante and Ray Bolger.

Chase's best known film is the popular romantic drama *Now, Voyager* (1942), in which she played the sister-in-law of leading lady Bette Davis. Chase also appeared in *No Time for Love* (1943), with Claudette Colbert and Fred MacMurray; *Miss Tatlock's Millions* (1948), with John Lund and Monty Woolley; *Johnny Dark* (1954), with Tony Curtis; *It Should Happen to You* (1954), with Judy Holliday and Jack Lemmon; *The Big Knife* (1955), with Jack Palance and Shelley Winters; and *Ocean's Eleven* (1960), with Frank Sinatra and Dean Martin.

In July 1935 Chase married William Murray, an advertising executive; they had no children. Murray's influence with radio networks helped the witty and sophisticated Chase get her own program, "Luncheon at the Waldorf," a Saturday afternoon, half-hour talk show aimed at educated, well-to-do housewives. "Luncheon at the Waldorf," which was broadcast from the Empire Room of the Waldorf-Astoria Hotel, ran during 1940 and 1941 on the NBC-blue network. Chase used her many contacts in the theatrical and literary worlds, the fashion industry, and high society to land guests such as journalist Dorothy Thompson and interior decorator Elsie de Wolfe. In 1942 a revamped version of the program, called "Penthouse Party," aired in an evening time slot. From 1945 to 1949 Chase was a frequent panelist on the Mutual network's "Leave It to the Girls," a discussion program in which celebrity guests fielded questions from listeners on social and romantic matters.

Capitalizing on the fame gained from her radio program, Chase wrote a bestselling autobiography, *Past Imperfect* (1942), and a further memoir, *Free Admission* (1948). She moved into fiction with the novel *In Bed We Cry* (1943), which she adapted unsuccessfully for the stage in 1944 (she also starred in the production). Chase's later fictional works are *I Love Miss Tillie Bean* (1946), *New York 22* (1951), *The Island Players* (1956), *Three Men on the Left Hand* (1960), *The Sounds of Home* (1971), and *Dear Intruder* (1976). Chase's fiction is considered by critics as formulaic and shallow but an accurate reflection of the language and attitudes of mid-twentieth-century New Yorkers. Most of her heroines are worldly career women who end up with the man of their dreams. Chase also wrote nonfiction books on travel and social advice. These include *The Carthaginian Rose* (1961), *Elephants Arrive at Half-Past Five* (1963), *Second Spring and Two Potatoes* (1965), *Fresh from the Laundry* (1967), *The Varied Airs of Spring* (1969), *Around the World and Other Places* (1970), *Worlds Apart* (1972), and *The Care and Feeding of Friends* (1973). She collaborated on her mother's memoir, *Always in Vogue* (1954).

Chase acted on television in the legal drama series "The Trials of O'Brien" (1965–1966), starring Peter Falk, and played the Wicked Stepmother in Rodgers and Hammerstein's musical adaptation of *Cinderella* (1957), starring Julie Andrews. She was also a panelist on three quiz shows— "Celebrity Time" (1949–1950), "Masquerade Party" (1952–1957), and "Keep Talking" (1958–1959). With Durward Kirby she cohosted the interview show "Glamour-Go-Round" (1950).

Chase was active in World War II fundraising activities for the American Theatre Wing and served on the council of Actors Equity. Divorced from Murray in 1945, the following year she married Dr. Norton S. Brown, with whom she had no children. Chase died in Mexico City after suffering internal hemorrhaging at her summer home in Cuernevaca, Mexico.

• In addition to her two autobiographical works, other primary sources include clippings files, scrapbooks, and other material on Chase's career, which are held in the Billy Rose Theatre Collection at the New York Public Library for the Perfoming Arts, Lincoln Center. See also "Ilka Chase's Conversation Proves Real Iron Fist in Velvet Glove," *New York World-Telegram*, 23 Mar. 1942. An obituary is in the *New York Times*, 16 Feb. 1978.

MARY C. KALFATOVIC

CHASE, Lucia (24 Mar. 1897–9 Jan. 1986), ballet dancer and dance company director, was born in Waterbury, Connecticut, the daughter of Irving Hall Chase and Elizabeth Hosmer Kellogg. Her family was locally prominent, its wealth based in the Waterbury Clock Company. Following her education at Bryn Mawr College, Chase chose a theatrical and singing career, taking lessons from the noted director Rouben Mamoulian. Her gradually acquired, very broad ballet formation was undertaken with Mikhail Mordkin, who taught for many years in New York. Mordkin believed that great *acting* was an essential component of great dancing, and he gave Chase a foundation that enabled her, over three decades, to impart depth and conviction to a wide variety of starring and subordinate roles, both serious and comic. As Chase noted, Mordkin "did everything from the actor's point of view."

In 1926 Chase married Thomas Ewing, Jr., the owner of a carpet company. He died in 1933 but left her and their two sons financially secure. Encouraged by Mordkin, Chase then intensified her ballet studies, and in 1937, when Mordkin's company resumed activities, she was ready for the title role in *Giselle* and that of Lise in *La Fille Mal Gardée* (with Mordkin himself playing the part of "The Mother"), as well as roles in *The Goldfish, Trepak*, and other works Mordkin choreographed in the traditional style.

It was in large part owing to the moral and financial support of Chase that after two years of existence the Mordkin Ballet metamorphosed into what was named Ballet Theatre. Richard Pleasant worked closely with Chase in launching the venture, and most of the dancers and many of the assets of the Mordkin Ballet were incorporated into Ballet Theatre's opening season, which began in January 1940. The broad repertory was envisaged as including three wings—the classical (supervised initially by Michel Fokine, later mostly by Anton Dolin), the English (supervised by Antony Tudor), and the American (supervised by Eugene Loring and others). From the beginning there was a versatile freshness and American quality to most of the repertoire, except for the Fokine ballets, which shone under the unique supervision of the choreographer.

After the first year Pleasant resigned, and gradually Chase became the company's most prominent and energetic voice. In 1945 her status was fully recognized as she and the outstanding American stage designer and painter Oliver Smith were appointed codirectors, posts they held for three and a half decades. Chase thereby became both the de facto and de jure leader of one of the world's great performing organizations. In 1986 Anna Kisselgoff wrote, "American Ballet Theatre would not be here today if it had not been for Lucia Chase" (*New York Times*, 19 Jan. 1986). Not only was she the heart and soul, the essence, of American Ballet Theatre, she was often its core, for she provided or secured the basic wherewithal to pay the large, faithful company—including dancers, musicians, and staff—though sometimes only after a period of inactivity needed to regroup and finance a costly (even extravagant) operation. Her resilient, patient flexibility and her buoyant vision were indispensable qualities. Except when dealing with ballet matters, however, Chase was a very private person, maintaining homes in Waterbury and Narragansett, Rhode Island, and devoted to family rather than public life. But her extended family always included her dancers, for whom she had both affection and respect.

Because American Ballet Theatre was Lucia Chase and Lucia Chase was American Ballet Theatre, it is appropriate to chronicle Chase's life and career by reviewing the first four decades of the company. Ballet Theatre's opening programs presented ballets representing the basic ideals that were to guide the company: *Les Sylphides*, the pure, classical ballet "blanc," produced by its choreographer Fokine himself; *The Great American Goof*, Loring's comic ballet; and Tudor's soulful *Dark Elegies*. (Over the years one of the most steadfast elements in Chase's work was her production of most of Tudor's ballets, including *Dim Lustre* and *Romeo and Juliet*.) From the first, the company had an outstanding contingent of great ballet artists, such as Anton Dolin, Hugh Laing, William Dollar, and Nora Kaye, later to be joined by stars of the Ballets Russes and from abroad—Léonide Massine, Alicia Markova, André Eglevsky, and Igor Youskevitch—as well as by leading dancers developed within the company: Alicia Alonso, Rosella Hightower, and Melissa Hayden.

In the 1940s Chase produced Tudor's masterpiece *Pillar of Fire*; Jerome Robbins's romps *Fancy Free* and *Interplay*; Balanchine's *Waltz Academy*, *Themes and Variations*, and, most importantly, his revival of *Apollo*; revivals of Fokine's *Petrouchka*, *Bluebeard*, *Russian Soldier*, and *Carnaval*; Massine's *Aleko*; and Loring's

Billy the Kid, a landmark in American ballet inherited from Lincoln Kirstein's Ballet Caravan company. Another American choreographer presented by Chase's company was Agnes de Mille, whose *Fall River Legend* was a balletic treatment of a legendary American theme. This continual mix of a diverse repertoire and a wide choice of dancers gave the enduring company a broad appeal.

During the 1950s Chase brought forward a number of young choreographers' new work, enriching the repertoire with Herbert Ross's ironic and grim, Goya-influenced *Los Caprichos*, the Jean Cocteau and Jean Babilée *L'Amour et Son Amour*, and William Dollar's bittersweet *The Duel*, among many others.

The 1960s saw the change of the company's name from Ballet Theatre to American Ballet Theatre in recognition of its many successful overseas tours. Artistically, there was the first of ABT's full-length classics, the English choreographer David Blair's production of *Swan Lake*, which Oliver Smith designed. During this decade Eliot Feld developed from a dancer of promise to a fresh and original choreographer whose works for ABT included *Early Songs*, *At Midnight*, *Harbinger*, and *Intermezzo*.

In the 1970s Chase produced Tudor's enduring *The Leaves Are Fading*; a number of works by Glen Tetley, notably *Sphinx*; Mikhail Baryshnikov's *Don Quixote*; and Twyla Tharp's *Push Come to Shove*. When Chase retired in 1980, Baryshnikov succeeded her and Smith as ABT director.

This subjective selection of two dozen ballets from more than 100 produced demonstrates the breadth of Chase's taste and her energetic ability to forge a generous repertory over a very long time, using both her faithful dancers and more transient ones in ways that were almost always challenging. Though Chase was an excellent judge of casting, certain commentators have criticized various instances in which she cast herself. However, greater artists were not always available, and Chase, thoroughly coached in the roles, proved a resourceful team player and a responsible artist who contributed vitally, in terms of both characterization and execution, to a number of ballets, particularly those choreographed by Folkine and Tudor.

Chase performed regularly with the company throughout the 1940s, and her range of roles was broad, including classics such as Cerrito in Keith Lester's *Pas de Quatre*, Giselle in the Mordkin version, and Prelude in *Les Sylphides* (alongside Dolin, the nonpareil from Diaghilev days). In the modern field, in performances of Tudor's *Pillar of Fire*, Chase projected a cool, antipodal calmness, which was quite different from the deep love inherent in the role the choreographer created for himself and far from the exploding passion of Nora Kaye and Hugh Laing in the principal roles. The controlled elements were every bit as strong and valid as the seemingly unbridled ones. These characteristics made Chase a principal dancer as well as a principal administrator.

The growth of ballet in the United States has not been the result of one person's vision or activity, any more than the creation of ballet in France depended only on the genius of Lully or Beauchamp. But Chase played an indispensable role as one of American dance's most courageous and imaginative angels. "Without her," Robbins said, "the development of dance in America would be unimaginably poorer."

Lucia Chase received many honors, among them the *Dance Magazine* Award (1957), the Capezio Award (1968), and the Presidential Medal of Freedom (1980). She died in New York City.

• Letters from Chase may be found in the Agnes de Mille Papers in the Dance Collection, New York Public Library for the Performing Arts, Lincoln Center. The *New York Times* published a useful article by Anna Kisselgoff on 19 Jan. 1986. See also the memorials published in *Dance Magazine*, Mar. 1986, p. 50, and *Ballet Review* 18, no. 1 (1990): 54–66. An obituary is in the *New York Times*, 10 Jan. 1986.

BAIRD HASTINGS

CHASE, Mary Coyle (25 Feb. 1907–20 Oct. 1981), playwright, was born in West Denver, Colorado, the daughter of Frank Coyle, a salesman for a flour mill, and Mary McDonough. From her maternal uncles, Irish immigrants, Chase learned whimsical folklore, including the story of the pooka, the mischievous creature from Celtic legend who became the title character of her most famous play, *Harvey* (1944). From her mother, she recalled having learned the sympathy for the underdog or nonconformist that is also characteristic of her work. When Mrs. Coyle chased away some boys who were throwing snowballs at an infirm elderly lady, she told her daughter, "Never be unkind or indifferent to a person others say is crazy. Often they have a deep wisdom. We pay them a great respect in the old country, and we call them fairy people, and, it could be, they are sometimes" (Reef, p. 109).

Young Mary needed her mother's unconventional counsel, for she herself suffered from her ethnic neighborhood's fear of not measuring up to the standards of the dominant culture. When the name of one of her brothers appeared in the newspaper because a policeman had shot and wounded him for shaking a gum machine, mothers would not let their children play with Mary. Despite the social opprobrium, she continued to careen about the neighborhood herself and vengefully take aim at windows with handy rocks.

The problems of ethnicity were compounded for Mary by issues of gender, particularly expectations about women's dress and appearance. Mary was embarrassed by her homemade clothes, some of which retained the flour logo, "Pride of the Rockies." She was a bright and avidly curious girl who devoured Dickens at age eight and read Greek as a teenager. She attended the University of Colorado at Boulder for two years as a classics major but did not graduate. She later recalled that her time there was overshadowed by her failure to win a bid from a sorority and so "fit in" because of her lack of proper clothes. This sensitivity to adolescent fear of ridicule and to children's need for approval later surfaced in some of her plays, such as *Bernardine*

(1952), and in her children's books such as *Loretta Mason Potts* (1958).

When she started work at the *Denver News* in 1925, Chase solved her own problem by entering a milieu, journalism, in which a woman had to be unconventional and very dedicated to succeed. She would not leave a murder trial before the verdict was rendered, despite a telephone call from her father informing her that the family house was burning down. Although she also covered the usual "sob stories" and society notes relegated to women reporters, she gained a reputation for fearlessness by performing stunts such as taking truth serum, which did not work, and dressing as a man in order to sneak in and cover the dynamiting that would join the two halves of the Moffat Tunnel. Her penchant for another kind of stunt, the practical jokes later so vital to the comedy of her plays, cost Chase her job in 1931 when she telephoned her editor and impersonated an irate Irish woman protesting the quality of the food in the newspaper's charity basket.

Fortunately, she had another occupation to fall back on, that of housewife. In 1928 she had married newspaperman Robert Lamont Chase, who would later become editor of the *Rocky Mountain News*. Although they had three sons, unpaid bills, and frequent guests, Chase did not confine herself to homemaking. She founded a chapter of the American Newspaper Guild, wrote a weekly radio program for the Teamsters' Union, lobbied for an oleomargarine company, and held various jobs at depression-related government agencies. True to her iconoclastic spirit, she agitated for the rights of Hispanics in Denver and even walked a picket line, dressed to the nines.

As if all this activity were not enough for her relentless energies, Chase began to write plays. Her first was a Works Progress Administration play, *Me Third*, produced in Denver in 1937. Retitled *Now I've Done It*, this novice effort enjoyed the mixed distinction of a Broadway failure in 1937, despite a seven-week run. Undaunted, Chase continued to write plays: *Too Much Business* (1938); *Sorority House* (1939), which was later made into a movie; and *A Slip of a Girl* (1941).

Chase's most successful play came through a process of intense artistic fusion. She saw a neighbor who had lost her son in the war in the Pacific and wished that she could write something that might cheer her and others like her. She remembered her mother's advice about the wisdom of outcasts and her uncles' stories about the pooka. She started to work with doll-sized figures on her miniature stage and wrote *Harvey* (1944). It was produced on Broadway by Antoinette Perry and starred Frank Fay and Josephine Hull.

Harvey's enduring popularity stems not only from the title character, the iconoclastic pooka, but from a range of characters representing humanity's responses to the imagination, play, and spontaneity. The legal and psychiatric establishments weigh in against these disruptive intangibles and wish to institutionalize Elwood P. Dowd, Harvey's eccentric companion. Dowd himself speaks firmly for the imagination, saying, "I wrestled with reality for forty years, and I am happy to state that I finally won out over it." The audience, though, in many ways identifies with Elwood's sister Veta, who is torn between sympathy for her brother's whimsical charm and the demands of society, particularly the need to marry off her relentlessly conventional daughter Myrtle Mae. Chase and Veta lead the audience to a happy denouement in favor of nonconformity and fantasy, as Veta demands of the judge, "And what's wrong with Harvey? If Elwood and Myrtle Mae and I want to live with Harvey it's nothing to you. You don't even have to come around. It's our business."

Critical response to *Harvey* was mixed, with denigrators charging the play with promoting escapism and inebriation, and supporters such as critic Walter Kerr asserting that Harvey, the 6½′ rabbit, "was the human imagination, honoring itself, enjoying itself" (p. 171). The public also spoke resoundingly in *Harvey*'s favor: the Broadway production ran for 1,775 performances, and Chase won the Pulitzer Prize for the play. Chase wrote the screenplay for the 1952 movie with James Stewart, who also starred in a Broadway revival with Helen Hayes in 1972. Art Carney and Marion Lorne were the stars of a 1958 television version.

Harvey's great success was initially a mixed blessing for Chase. Although the Chases could now pay their debts, move to a large house in a fashionable Denver neighborhood, and take in Mary's elderly father, celebrity took its toll on Chase herself, creatively and personally. A play she wrote before *Harvey*, *The Next Half Hour*, failed on Broadway in 1945, and Chase went into a three-year imaginative slump. She was besieged with requests for money, interviews, and social appearances and even once found strangers staring at her when she awakened from a nap in her living room. A highly successful woman writer was also regarded as something of an anomaly. A *Cosmopolitan* article by Eleanor Harris notes that Chase had "the voluptuous figure of a real woman" and "doesn't look remotely like the public's conception of a woman writer" (p. 98). Chase conceded to the need for a defensive, somewhat frivolous persona, that of "the attractive Denver newspaperwoman" who had not written for money but who had gotten lucky (Reef, p. 108).

Good sense ultimately prevailed, however, since, as Chase commented, "Work is the solution; it stays with you when all else is gone" (Harris, p. 102). Her next works introduced Chase to a new field of success, as a writer about and for children and adolescents. *Bernardine* concerns the fantasy female ideal of adolescent boys like Chase's own sons. A play for children, *Mrs. McThing*, about a mother and son replaced by monstrous stick figures, became a Broadway success in 1952, starring Helen Hayes and Brandon De Wilde. Also in this vein were two children's novels. The title character of *Loretta Mason Potts* is a little girl who feels displaced in her mother's affections by her younger siblings and decides to live with another family while slipping into the charming yet sinister world of the Countess, from which she is rescued by her mother. *The Wicked Pigeon Ladies in the Garden* (1968) also addresses the fears and fantasies of an alienated young girl who must learn to value her home and parents despite their imperfections.

As these works for children suggest, Chase was regarding the generation gap from both sides in her later plays: *Lolita* (1954), *Midgie Purvis* (1961), *The Prize Play* (1961), *The Dog Sitters* (1963), *Mickey* (1969), and *Cocktails with Mimi* (1974). She identifies with the bright, mischievous children insatiably seeking attention, but she also sympathizes with the mothers who are now expected to relinquish play and imagination in order to take their places as staid members of society. Chase realizes how hard the maternal balancing act is: somehow the mothers must renew their imaginations in order to rediscover themselves and relate to their children while at the same time offering the children the protection and guidance of responsible adults.

Chase died in her lifelong home city of Denver. Her works place her firmly within the American literary tradition of individualistic opposition to a constricting society, but with particular sensitivity to the problems of nonconformity for girls and women of all ages. Her work, while humorous, is characterized by an underlying sadness that the wisdom of outcasts was so little appreciated and so often squelched, since, as Veta declares in *Harvey*, "It's our dreams that keep us going."

• Some of Chase's papers are in the University of Oregon Library, the Denver Public Library, and the University of Denver Library. Information about her life, career, and opinions can be found in her *New York Times* obituary, 23 Oct. 1981, and in two articles based on interviews with Chase: Wallis Reef, "She Didn't Write It for Money—She Says," *Saturday Evening Post*, 1 Sept. 1945, pp. 108–10, and Eleanor Harris, "Mary Chase: Success Almost Ruined Her," *Cosmopolitan*, Feb. 1954, pp. 98–104. For assessments of her work, see W. David Siever, *Freud on Broadway* (1955), and Walter Kerr, *God on the Gymnasium Floor* (1971).

VERONICA MAKOWSKY

CHASE, Mary Ellen (24 Feb. 1887–28 July 1973), writer and educator, was born in Blue Hill, Maine, the daughter of Edward Everett Chase, a lawyer, and Edith Lord, a teacher of Latin. Religion, education, and reading were basic to the Chase family's way of life, as described by Chase herself in three autobiographical volumes: *A Goodly Heritage* (1932), *A Goodly Fellowship* (1939), and *The White Gate* (1954). These books constitute a valuable record of life as lived by privileged families in a coastal New England town, where the influence of Puritanism, with its emphasis on religion and learning, was still strong.

After graduation at age seventeen from Blue Hill Academy, where her favorite studies were Greek and Latin, Chase entered the University of Maine. After two years there she followed her father's advice that she drop out for a year and broaden her experience by teaching in rural schools in the neighborhood of Blue Hill. "Living around" in the families of her pupils, as the custom was, she learned much that would later be useful in her writing. In 1909 she received her A.B. from the University of Maine and took a position as teacher of English in the progressive, coeducational Hillside Home School in Spring Green, Wisconsin. Three years later she taught for two years at the more traditional Miss Moffat's School for Girls in Chicago. During the summer of 1913 she studied German in Berlin and traveled in the Harz Mountains.

In 1914, the year of her father's death, she was diagnosed with tuberculosis and, on her doctor's advice, moved to Bozeman, Montana, to recuperate in its cold, dry air. She remained there three years, resting, reading, teaching in high school, and writing fiction for children. In 1917, her health restored, she entered the graduate school of the University of Minnesota, from which she received her Ph.D. in English literature in 1922. Her doctoral dissertation, *Thomas Hardy from Serial to Novel*, was published in 1927. Remaining in Minneapolis, she taught for four years in the university's English department as an assistant professor. During these years she published a sentimental novel, *Mary Christmas* (1926), and placed short stories in *Harper's Monthly Magazine*, *Scribner's Magazine*, and the *Atlantic Monthly*. In 1926 she was appointed to an associate professorship in English at Smith College in Northampton, Massachusetts, and three years later she was promoted to full professor. In Northampton she shared a house with her friend Eleanor Shipley Duckett, an Englishwoman who was a professor of ancient languages and literatures at the college. The two frequently visited England together, sometimes for prolonged sojourns. Chase's fondness for England is apparent in her book of essays *This England* (1936) and in her short novel *Dawn in Lyonesse* (1938).

Chase considered herself primarily a teacher and secondarily a writer. Her classes at Smith College were extremely popular, partly because her teaching was enlivened by a dramatic flair that she also brought to her frequent public lectures. One of her courses was on the Bible as literature. As a result of a strict upbringing in the Congregational church (she later became an Episcopalian), she had long been familiar with the Bible, but later she studied it in depth, relying mainly on her own efforts as a literary scholar. Especially useful was her knowledge of Greek and Latin and, even more so, her ability to read Hebrew, which she had acquired under the tutorship of Edith Margaret Chrystal, a specialist in Oriental languages and theology at Cambridge University. Chase published four books on the Bible for the general public, beginning with *The Bible and the Common Reader* (1944).

Chase's literary reputation rests largely on three novels reflecting the cultural and maritime traditions of the Maine coast: *Mary Peters* (1934), *Silas Crockett* (1935), and *The Edge of Darkness* (1957). In an article, "My Novels about Maine" (*Colby Library Quarterly*, Mar. 1962), Chase wrote that of all her books these novels meant the most to her, because in them she was celebrating "an inheritance of imperishable values [that] imposes a debt which cannot possibly either be underestimated or ever fully discharged." Her paternal grandfather had captained sailing ships in worldwide trade, frequently accompanied by his wife, who later fascinated her grandchildren with accounts of life at sea and in foreign lands. From her, Chase wrote, the children acquired a "sense of a great and various world beyond our own small harbor and our own Maine hills." To her grandmother's reminiscences Chase owed much of the content of her Maine novels, as well as her impulse to write them.

The three novels record three stages in the decline of the way of life and the seafaring character of the region. The action of *Mary Peters* takes place during the heyday of the sailing ship. *Silas Crockett* traces the gradual loss of status and fortune of four generations of Crocketts as steam replaced sails in transoceanic shipping. The Silas Crockett of the first generation is master of a sailing ship in the China trade. His son, after some experience sailing with his father, dies by accident as a crewman on a fishing schooner. His son captains a coastwise steamer first and then a ferryboat. Finally, Silas's great-grandson, also named Silas, ends as a gutter of herring in a canning factory. Of the three Maine novels, Chase considered *Silas Crockett* the most important, but she was fondest of the third, *The Edge of Darkness*, a realistic presentation of squalor and moral degradation in a once-prosperous town.

These novels were widely read and admired, appealing as they did to a taste at the time for fiction reflecting life in a specific region. Critics such as Theodore Morrison, Allan Nevins, Percy H. Boynton, and Robert Tristram Coffin praised them for their prose style, their realism, and their historical accuracy. These attributes are present in other of Chase's novels, notably *Windswept* (1941) and *The Lovely Ambition* (1960), which are set in Maine but are only incidentally regional. Their chief concern is with their characters' search for spiritual stability and meaning. *Windswept*, written as World War II approached, went through fifteen printings from 1941 through 1952. Robert Hillyer, writing in *Atlantic Monthly* (Dec. 1941), considered it Chase's best novel. By this time Chase had achieved an international reputation, many of her books having been translated into the major languages of Europe and Asia.

Chase retired from Smith College in 1955 but continued to live in Northampton, where she died. She never married. After her death her reputation underwent some diminishment. Many of her books, including some of her most distinguished volumes, went out of print, and critics and literary scholars ceased to pay attention to her work. Nevertheless, her books continued to be read, and her legacy as an author, a scholar, and a teacher remains secure.

• Chase's manuscripts and other papers are in the libraries of Smith College, Colby College, and the University of Maine, Orono. Perry D. Westbrook, *Mary Ellen Chase* (1965), is a biographical and critical study of Chases's life and writings through 1965. Evelyn H. Chase (Chase's sister-in-law), *Feminist Convert: A Portrait of Mary Ellen Chase* (1988), contains much interesting biographical material. The March 1962 issue of the *Colby Library Quarterly* is devoted in its entirety to articles by and about Chase. It also contains an extensive bibliography of Chase's writings. Obituaries are in the *Springfield (Mass.) Union*, 29 July 1973, and the *New York Times*, 30 July 1973.

PERRY D. WESTBROOK

CHASE, Philander (14 Dec. 1775–20 Sept. 1852), Episcopal bishop, was born in Cornish, New Hampshire, the son of farmer and town founder Dudley Chase and Allace Corbett. During his student days at Dartmouth College, at a time of religious ferment, Chase was stirred by the Book of Common Prayer and convinced by the arguments put forth in the tract *Essay on the Church* by the eighteenth-century Anglican theologian William Jones of Nayland. Chase rejected his boyhood Congregationalism and joined the Protestant Episcopal church. Graduating college in 1795, he married Mary Fay of Stockbridge, Vermont, in 1796. Following a religious calling, he prepared for the ministry by reading with American clergy rather than studying in an English seminary, an Anglican custom that ended with the separation of the Protestant Episcopal church after the American Revolution and the development of Episcopal seminaries in the United States. Chase was ordained a deacon in 1798 and a priest in 1799 at St. Paul's, New York City.

First an itinerant preacher in western New York State, Chase then served congregations in Poughkeepsie and Fishkill, New York. In New Orleans in 1805 he organized Christ Church, the first Episcopal parish in Louisiana. Six years later he returned to New England and, until 1817, was rector of Christ Church, Hartford. All this was preparation for his major life work, bringing the Episcopal church to the Middle West. He arrived in Ohio in 1818 and soon organized parishes at several locations, including Zanesville and Columbus. Chase was consecrated as the first bishop of Ohio in 1819, aware that this newly organized diocese had meager resources. Out of necessity he operated a sawmill and administered local educational institutions, serving first as principal of the Academy in Worthington and later as president of Cincinnati College; he also farmed his land in Worthington, ran his own printing press, and took charge of the town post office. His household merged with the schools and colleges he established, and his family often functioned as his staff. For periods of time Chase left his family in charge of the schools and farm enterprises while he traveled in the United States and in England in search of funds to sustain his work. Chase took great delight in his victories, but he resented the system that obliged clergy to test their endurance in order to keep their families from starving. He blamed the wealthy and established Episcopalians in the eastern cities for the situation: "Let those who live in luxury in our Eastern cities answer. Let them read the story of the *Rich* man and Lazarus, and see what will become of them, in the day of the visitation" ("Bishop's Report," in *Journal of the Proceedings of the Convention of the Diocese of Illinois* [21 June 1852], p. 8.) After twenty-two years of marriage, Mary Chase died in 1818 of tuberculosis. She had borne six children, two of whom had died in infancy. The following year he married Sophia May Ingraham, and they had three children.

Chase accepted the missionary challenge in part because it offered space and freedom to establish the church according to his theological convictions. Although he found it difficult to secure enough clergy for Ohio from seminaries in the East, he was captivated by the possibilities of training clergy right in the Middle West under his direct supervision. He proposed a seminary for Ohio in 1823 and, finding almost no local support, announced his first trip to raise funds in England. American churchmen—especially Bishop John Henry Hobart of New York—had competing plans for fundraising in England and unsuccessfully opposed Chase's activities abroad. Chase founded Kenyon College and the Gambier Theological Seminary in 1824 with donations from Lords Gambier, Bexley, Kenyon, and Lady Rosse. The seminary began in Bishop Chase's house, but soon collegiate Gothic buildings dotted the campus. Kenyon College began to overshadow the seminary, and the faculty publicly criticized Chase's autocratic manner. In 1831 the Ohio convention ruled that Chase could not be president of the college and seminary and bishop of the diocese. Unwilling to share authority, Chase resigned from both the presidency and the episcopate. He first settled his family on a forty-acre tract of forest land near Millersburg, Ohio, and then to a farm at Gilead, Michigan.

Chase's retirement ended in 1835 when he was elected the first bishop of Illinois. He purchased land near Peoria for a family farm and a new seminary, Jubilee College. The college, whose day-to-day administration was directed by the Reverend Samuel Chase, Chase's nephew, never received wide support and closed its doors in the 1860s; all attempts to revive it were unsuccessful. As Bishop of Illinois, Chase received negligible support from the independent-minded clergy and laity of the fast-growing Chicago churches; his episcopate was rooted in a rural and small-town preindustrial America, and he worked hard to settle churches in such agricultural communities. By the 1850s, the strength of the Episcopal church in Illinois was found in those emerging centers of commerce and industry fired by entrepreneurial capitalism. The up-and-coming booster vestrymen of Chicago resisted the bishop's authority and challenged Chase's traditional vision of society and church.

Tensions in Bishop Chase's episcopate reflected the growing pains of his denomination. Cultural as well as theological differences between clergy and laity were influenced by those in the Oxford movement in England and other ecclesiological reformers who were eager to introduce liturgical and ritual changes and by those church leaders who remained faithful to both Protestant and evangelical traditions. As the two traditions battled, distinctive regional differences were produced. Lacking long-established churches and vestries with deep-rooted ties to either tradition, the Middle West was a seedbed for Catholic developments in liturgy and theology during the 1830s as an American revival of Catholic or high church practices and English Oxford movement ideas swept the country. Chase was an old-fashioned churchman who opposed any deviation from the Book of Common Prayer service. As presiding bishop (1843–1852), he vigorously fought Catholic ritual and became spokesman for the evangelical party. Partisan battles in the church intensified under Chase's leadership in the House of Bishops and after passage of the 1844 canon for the trial of bishops. Chase feared any trends that might lead to doctrines and rituals identified with the Church of Rome. He also disliked techniques that had been adopted from the popular evangelical culture, which attracted some clergy in the evangelical party of his church, and he avoided interdenominational Protestant associations as thoroughly as he rejected changes brought about by the Oxford movement and the high church party at home. He remained deeply convinced of the primitive and apostolic foundation of the church he had chosen as a young adult. Ultimately, the evangelical party became his home, as their battle cry, "No priest, no Altar, no Sacrifice," best addressed his deeply rooted conservatism (Chorley, p. 73).

As the frontier bishop in Ohio and Illinois, Chase was a transitional figure whose efforts ensured that the diverse religious landscape of this new section of the nation included churches with strong ties to the historic traditions he valued. At the same time, he forged innovative strategies for his evangelism and helped define the role of the bishop in the new nation. He died in Jubilee, Illinois.

• Two important collections of Chase papers are found at the Illinois State Historical Society Library, Springfield, and in the Bishop Philander Chase Papers, Episcopal Diocese of Chicago Archives. *Chase's Reminiscences: An Autobiography* (2 vols., 1848) is an important source. Broadsides, pamphlets, and tracts written by Philander Chase and his nephew and close associate, Samuel Chase, are available in the Graff, Ayer, and Case collections at The Newberry Library, Chicago. Information on Chase's activities in Ohio (1819–1830) and Illinois (1835–1852) can be found in the published proceedings of the diocesan conventions and in the published proceedings of the General Convention of the Protestant Episcopal Church (1843–1852). Also useful are the Dudley Chase Papers in the archives at Kenyon College, Gambier, Ohio. The following published works are relevant: Laura Chase Smith, *The Life of Philander Chase* (1903), and Francis Joseph Hall, *A History of the Diocese of Chicago: Including a History of the Undivided Diocese of Illinois from Its Organization in 1835* (192?). Edward Clowes Chorley, *Men and Movements in the American Episcopal Church* (1948), is an important source for the denominational partisan battles, although Chase's churchmanship is painted too monochromatically, and the subtleties of his positions are not identified. Biographical sketches can be found in Hermon Griswold Batterson, *A Sketch-Book of the American Episcopate, during One Hundred Years, 1783–1883* (1884), and William Stevens Perry, *The Bishops of the American Church, Past and Present: Sketches, Biographical and Bibliographical . . .* (1897).

RIMA LUNIN SCHULTZ

CHASE, Pliny Earle (18 Aug. 1820–17 Dec. 1886), educator, natural philosopher, and physicist, was born in Worcester, Massachusetts, the son of Anthony Chase, an insurance company president and county treasurer, and Lydia Earle. A lifelong Quaker, Chase attended Worcester Latin School and the Friends' School in Providence, Rhode Island. In 1835 he entered Harvard University, where he excelled in mathematics and physics. It was in 1837, while at Harvard, that Chase made some of the first recorded observations on shooting stars. After his graduation with an A.B. in 1839, he took a series of teaching jobs. From 1839 to 1840 he served as principal of district schools in Worcester and Leicester, Massachusetts. From 1840 to 1843 he taught in Providence and Philadelphia at Quaker preparatory schools, and he worked as a private tutor. Also in 1843 he married Elizabeth Brown Oliver of Lynn, Massachusetts. Together they had six children. In 1844 he published a well-received textbook, *Elements of Arithmetic*. That same year he received his A.M. from Harvard.

He returned in 1845 to Philadelphia, where he conducted a private school for girls for the next three years. In 1848 he published *The Common School Arithmetic*, and in 1850, in conjunction with Horace Mann, he published *Mann & Chase's Arithmetic, Practically Applied*. Chase's textbooks garnered him recognition in and around Boston as a pedagogical innovator. Of Chase's textbooks, Harvard president Thomas Hill once remarked, "'*Chase*' and '*Chase & Mann*', as we called them, were worth all other arithmetics that I ever saw put together."

Chase's burgeoning teaching career was cut short by health difficulties. In 1848 he was afflicted by severe hemorrhaging of the lungs, a condition that recurred with diminishing frequency over the following ten years. When physicians advised him to pursue a career that allowed more time for outdoor exercise and fresh air, Chase took a position with North, Harrison, & Company, a large manufacturing concern with a foundry in Delaware and showrooms in Philadelphia. In 1851 he was elected a member of the Franklin Institute. Also in 1851 he became a partner in the foundry company, and he eventually became head of the firm under the new name Chase, Sharpe, and Thompson. Over the next fifteen years of his tenure there, the company often suffered heavy losses, despite a large international wholesale trade, as Chase's attention was split between his broad intellectual interests and the day-to-day affairs of running the business. In 1858 he delivered his first paper, on analogous roots in Sanskrit and English, before a meeting of the American Philosophical Society, an organization that he joined in 1863. He remained extremely active in the society for the rest of his life, delivering more than 130 papers on philology, astronomy, physics, meteorology, philosophy, and psychology. Sometime prior to 1860 he resumed teaching, giving classes in a renowned Philadelphia school for young ladies run by C. D. Cleveland. In 1861 he assumed ownership of the school. Finally, despite the upturn in the foundry business brought about by the Civil War, he sold his stake in the company in 1866. In the same year he gave up the finishing school, convinced that the Civil War had interfered with the running of private schools.

Chase published eleven papers on philology and linguistics in the *Transactions and Proceedings of the American Philosophical Society* between 1858 and 1865. With the help of dictionaries he sought out resemblances between the roots of Indo-European and Indo-European languages. His innovation was to apply probability calculations to argue that such resemblances were unlikely to be due to mere coincidence. Though his linguistic theories and methods were dismissed by eminent philologists of the day, Chase nonetheless enjoyed the lifelong reputation among his colleagues of being an able student of languages.

Chase's physical researches encompassed a wide range of phenomena at all sizes and scales and was firmly rooted in his belief in the power of analogies between molecular and cosmical laws. He wrote many short papers deriving estimates of the distance and mass of the sun from such phenomena as soap bubbles and the combustion of coal. He held to the general postulate that "all physical phenomena are due to an Omnipresent Power, acting in ways which may be represented by harmonic or cyclical undulations in an elastic medium." It was a belief widely held by nineteenth-century physicists that the universe was full of an elastic medium known as the aether, which mediated physical interactions between remote bodies. In his empirical investigations into the tides, rainfall, gravitation, solar heat, terrestrial magnetism, and planetary astronomy, Chase analyzed tables of observations, showing that these data could be expressed by harmonic equations. Among his contemporaries, he prompted comparisons to German astronomer Johannes Kepler.

Between 1863 and 1868 he investigated lunar and solar influences on daily and monthly fluctuations in barometric and oceanic tides, suggested formal analogies between laws of molecular action and those of attraction and rotation, and worked out numerical relations between gravity and magnetism. For the latter research he was awarded the Magellanic medal by the American Philosophical Society in 1864.

From 1868 to 1872 Chase was largely occupied with meteorological investigations and advanced evidence for lunar influences on rainfall, reporting the discovery of periodic patterns in records of rainfall in Philadelphia as well as several other cities in North America and Europe. During this period he also demonstrated the significance of anticyclonic storms to weather patterns. In 1871 Chase was appointed professor of natural science at Haverford College, where he taught for the rest of his life. From 1871 to 1874 Chase's research principally concerned understanding the positions of bodies in the solar system in terms of the harmonic relations between their distances.

Chase was elected to the American Association for the Advancement of Science in 1874. At about this time he began to synthesize his research results into a theory of cosmical development. He became chair of the Department of Philosophy and Logic at Haverford in 1875, and in 1878 he turned his research focus to quantifying various aspects of the nebular hypothesis of planetary formation. In 1884 he was appointed lecturer on psychology and logic at Bryn Mawr College for Women, but he never did lecture there because in the winter of 1885 he came down with a case of pneumonia from which he never fully recovered. Nonetheless, he was acting president of Haverford College in 1886, briefly replacing his brother, Thomas Chase, who was traveling in Europe.

Chase puzzled many of his colleagues in physics, even those who admired him. While his contributions to mathematical education and meteorology were of lasting value, his physical researches enjoyed a mixed reaction. His exposition of his own theories often fell short of mathematical demonstration, containing elements of intuition and speculative hypotheses, yet many of his conclusions agreed with those arrived at independently by others. On this, in 1872, Chase remarked, "My own faith in the significance of such coincidences, and in their suggestive value as indications of an instructive, intelligent as well as intelligible, purpose in nature, inclines me to the acceptance of speculations, based on thermodynamic, spectroscopic, and analogous theories, even before all their premises have been recognized as either axiomatic or rigidly demonstrable."

Chase died in Haverford, Pennsylvania, while presiding over the college's annual commencement.

• A collection of Chase's papers is held by the American Philosophical Society in Philadelphia. A list of his papers published by the society is given in volume 19 of the *Proceedings of the American Philosophical Society*. The index to the *Journal of the Franklin Institute* contains a list of his papers published there. For memoirs and obituaries, see Philip C. Garrett, "Memoir of Pliny Earle Chase," *Proceedings of the American Philosophical Society* 24 (1887): 287–95, which provides a complete overview of Chase's life; Samuel S. Greene, "Pliny Earle Chase," *American Antiquarian Society Proceedings* 4 (1887), which elaborates on Chase's personality and deep commitment to the Society of Friends; and "Pliny Earle Chase," *Journal of the Franklin Institute* 124 (1887): 229–31. An additional obituary is in the *Worcester Daily Spy*, 9 Feb. 1887.

JOHN HUSS

CHASE, Salmon Portland (13 Jan. 1808–7 May 1873), statesman, antislavery leader, and chief justice of the U.S. Supreme Court, was born in Cornish, New Hampshire, the son of Ithamar Chase, a glassmaker and tavernkeeper, and Janette Ralston. When Chase was nine years old, his father died. To ease the financial burden on his mother, Chase, the eighth of eleven children, moved to Ohio and lived with his uncle Philander Chase, an Episcopal bishop who instilled in him a sense of self-discipline and a "profound" awareness of his "religious obligations." In 1824 he entered Dartmouth, where he became deeply involved in the revival movement then sweeping the college. The revival experience reinforced his religious commitments and generated within him an intense and lasting struggle between his faith and his already quite active ambition, which would torment him throughout his life.

After graduating in 1826, Chase moved to Washington, D.C., where he started a school for the children of the community's privileged and studied law under the tutelage of Attorney General William Wirt. Overwhelmed by the heady atmosphere of the nation's capital, Chase temporarily subordinated his religious commitments to the goal of developing a "golden reputation." However, three years after arriving in Washington, Chase concluded that he could best achieve this goal in the West and so moved to Cincinnati in search of "Fame's proud temple." Within a few years he had achieved a reasonable standing as an attorney, numbering among his clients the Cincinnati branch of the Bank of the United States and authoring an important three-volume edition of the *Statutes of Ohio* (1833–1835).

In the spring of 1834 Chase married Catherine Jane Garniss, who died only a year and a half later after giving birth. This would not be Chase's only personal loss. Eliza Ann Smith, whom he married in 1839, died in 1845, and Sarah Bella Dunlop, whom he married in 1846, died in 1852. In addition, four of Chase's six children died when they were still very young. As difficult as each of these tragedies was to endure, none had a more profound impact on him than the death of his first wife. Devastated, he was convinced that, had he been more firmly committed to his faith and less distracted by a desire for "worldly advancement," he would not have left town on a business trip but would have stayed by her side, able to suggest alternate medical treatments that could have saved her life. Reawakened to the demands of the religious beliefs originally instilled in him during his childhood stay with his uncle and revival experience, Chase determined to direct his growing ambition toward causes more consistent with the teachings of his faith.

Initially this renewed commitment led to his involvement in the American Sunday School Union, but by 1837 Chase was becoming seriously interested in the slavery issue. In that year he defended in court the freedom of Matilda, a slave whose master had taken her into Ohio. Advancing an argument that he formulated with antislavery leader James G. Birney and that he would use repeatedly, Chase insisted the Constitution left slavery solely dependent on local law for its enforcement. The Founding Fathers, he maintained, had sought to "denationalize" slavery and withhold from it the support of the federal government. Hence, outside the jurisdiction of a slave state, no law could keep any individual enslaved. All slaves who came into free territory, including Matilda, reverted to their natural states of freedom. In 1842 Chase applied this same argument to the Van Zandt case, and in later years he used it in numerous other cases involving both escaped slaves and those who aided them. So committed did he become to the legal defense of runaways that he was known as the "attorney general for fugitive slaves."

Proceeding from the assumption that the Constitution was fundamentally an antislavery document, Chase resolved to organize a political force that would realize the founders' original intent by establishing an "absolute and unconditional divorce of the Government from slavery." In 1841 he joined the Liberty party but rejected its morally uncompromising, abolitionist stance. Instead, he insisted that the party develop a pragmatic program that emphasized specific actions the federal government could take to weaken slavery by denying it support. Through the numerous state and national party platforms and addresses he authored, Chase pressed for what would soon become standard antislavery demands such as an end to slavery in the District of Columbia, the banning of slavery from the West, and the prohibition of the interstate slave trade. By the late 1840s the Liberty party, under Chase's leadership, had developed into a significant political presence in many northern states.

The year 1848 was critical for Chase. Northern anxiety over the expansion of slavery intensified dramatically, giving the political antislavery movement an opportunity to attract a large following. At last Chase could combine his need to promote moral reform with his drive for personal prominence. The triumph of the Free Soil party would advance both objectives, and Chase labored tirelessly to bring the new party into being. In June 1848 he gathered opponents to the extension of slavery from each of the major parties along with the members of his own Liberty party in an Ohio Free Territory Convention. Building on this achievement, he helped organize the National Free Soil Convention in Buffalo and drafted its platform.

The broad-based antislavery coalition Chase had worked for was now in place, and he would be one of its first beneficiaries. Holding a balance of power in the new Ohio legislature, Free Soil representatives gained Democratic support and, early in 1849, elected Chase to the U.S. Senate. To secure Democratic votes, Chase and his allies agreed to grant the Democrats some patronage requests but not before first insisting that the reluctant Democrats join with them in repealing the state's restrictive Black Laws.

Chase's opponents accused him of being as "ambitious as Julius Caesar" in his pursuit of the Senate seat. This same charge would be made time and again as Chase's political career progressed. His vast ambition was indeed at work here as it would be in the future. He had struggled intensely for the honor that he attained, and his repeated denials of concern for his own gain only contributed to his image as a fiercely ambitious, deceitful manipulator. Yet it must be remembered that Chase insisted on obtaining repeal of the Black Laws before demanding that he be rewarded with a seat in the Senate; nor should it be forgotten that he worked tirelessly in the early days of the antislavery movement with little hope of national recognition and with great risk to his hard-earned local reputation. Given the religious commitments that defined his every action, Chase could never have sought personal advantage without first considering the cause of reform, and he could never have acted except from a belief that his own success would aid that cause. His protestations of a lack of ambition originated as much from a need to absolve himself of the sin of worldly pursuit as from a desire to deceive.

As senator, Chase asserted that the democracy held the key to an antislavery triumph, and he had advanced this view throughout the 1840s and the Democratic support he had received in the state legislature only confirmed him in this belief. In Washington, he aligned himself with the Democrats on economic issues. In Ohio he continued to press for a lasting Democratic–Free Soil alliance. On sectional issues, however, he was true to his antislavery principles. He rejected the Compromise of 1850, declaring it to be "sentiment for the north—substance for the south," and in 1854 he led the antiextensionist opposition in Congress to Stephen Douglas's Kansas-Nebraska Bill. His speech "Appeal of the Independent Democrats" focused the North's anger over what Chase claimed was an attempt to "permanently subjugate the whole country to the yoke of a slaveholding despotism. . . . The cause of human freedom," he declared, "is the cause of God."

In Ohio Chase worked feverishly to transform the popular reaction against the Kansas-Nebraska Act into a new political coalition. His initial attempt to fuse the antiextensionist forces with the Democrats failed, but he succeeded in organizing a new political alliance that brought together elements from all the major parties and won a smashing victory in the 1854 state elections. Treading carefully and demonstrating great toleration for a diversity of views, Chase then withstood a temporary nativist surge and managed to pull together Know Nothings, Protestant Germans, and antiextensionist Whigs, Democrats, and Free Soilers behind his successful 1855 bid for the state's governorship on the Republican ticket.

Chase's triumph inspired adherents of the new political movement throughout the North, and while characteristically insisting that he loved the "cause better than any personal triumph," Chase, looking ahead, had to admit that "it would be mere folly to deny" that a Republican presidential nomination in 1856 would be "gratifying." Chase's insatiable ambition was again warring with his sense of duty as he contemplated the first of four attempts to reach the nation's highest office. He played a key role in organizing the national Republican movement in 1856, but divisions within the Ohio delegation, his image as an antislavery radical, concern that he was dangerously ambitious, and his disappointingly weak national organization combined to destroy his hopes for the nomination.

In 1857 Chase gained reelection. Although his victory was by a significantly reduced majority, it nevertheless helped him remain an influential national figure. His activities as governor on behalf of fugitive slaves and for a free Kansas heightened his political prestige and made him a leading candidate for his party's 1860 presidential nomination. Chase clearly wanted to be the Republican standard bearer, but his hopes were dashed for the same reasons they had been four years earlier.

The Ohio legislature elected Chase to the Senate early in 1860, and in 1861 the governor of Ohio chose him as a delegate to the Washington Peace Conference. There he opposed any accord that would take effect before the inauguration of Abraham Lincoln and specifically attacked the Crittenden Compromise as too favorable to the South. Appointed by Lincoln as secretary of the Treasury, Chase, after some hesitation, urged the president to resupply Fort Sumter. By then he was ready to accept the coming conflict. Sadly he concluded, "The truth is that God seems to be punishing [us] for our sins—among the greatest I believe [is] that of complicity with slavery."

As secretary of the Treasury, Chase's role in the Union's struggle for survival was critical. He had been focused during his entire political career on the slavery issue, and now he would have to master the complexities of financing a war of unprecedented scale. Staffing the mushrooming Treasury bureaucracy was burden enough, but finding the funds to prosecute the war would be his greatest challenge. When Chase took office, the government was already in debt with few obvious means of rapidly increasing its revenues. Assuming the war would be over quickly, Chase at first relied heavily on borrowing to meet the Treasury's needs. His insistence on receiving bank loans in specie angered many bankers, but they acquiesced, meeting the short-term financial requirements of the government.

By the close of 1861 it was clear that the war would not be as short as most northerners had thought and that the financial demands on the government would be far greater than originally predicted. To satisfy these expanding requirements, in early 1862 Chase obtained congressional approval for the circulation of paper money as legal tender. This was a difficult decision for a hard money advocate like Chase, but he reluctantly concluded that it was justified as a "war necessity" if accompanied by a program of increased taxes and additional loans. To assist him in marketing the new bonds authorized by Congress, he chose Philadelphia financier and family friend Jay Cooke. Although he was meticulous in his personal dealings with the wealthy banker, Chase's financial ties to Cooke inevitably raised questions about the secretary's professional ethics. While Cooke did an effective job, Chase decided that additional measures were necessary to deal with the continuing national emergency. Early in 1863 he gained congressional assent to an act rationalizing the country's currency by establishing a national banking system. For the Democratically inclined Chase, this was yet another great departure. The exigencies of the conflict had forced a transformation in his economic philosophy. Acting from entirely new assumptions, Chase had wrought a revolution in the country's financial structure.

Finances were not Chase's only concern during his tenure in the Lincoln cabinet. While Simon Cameron remained secretary of war, Chase assisted in the administration of military affairs, particularly in the western theater. In addition, it was his job to regulate trade between the Union and the Confederacy, a complex and demanding assignment. Perhaps the most significant of his duties was responsibility for confiscated and abandoned property, which placed him in charge of the South Carolina Sea Islands slave community. He immediately took advantage of his position to initiate and direct the Port Royal Experiment, giving former slaves the opportunity to work for the first time as free laborers.

Chase also fought more directly for the rights of the slaves. He moved faster than did Lincoln toward emancipation, and when the president finally did agree to a proclamation, Chase pushed for one that would be more inclusive and free of any reference to colonization or compensation. He also had an impact on the final text of the proclamation. Ever conscious of the religious vision that had brought him into politics, Chase had urged the insertion of "In God We Trust" on the new legal tender. Now he persuaded the president to conclude his Emancipation Proclamation by invoking the "gracious favor of Almighty God." Following the issuance of the proclamation, Chase continued his efforts on behalf of the newly freed slaves. He was a strong advocate of their use as soldiers, of their access to land, and as he had been since the 1840s, of their right to vote.

Chase's ties to the Lincoln administration weakened over time. In part this resulted from honest differences with the president over both style and substance. It should not be surprising that the somber, focused secretary would feel ill at ease with the folksy president. "The truth is," Chase once explained, "I have never been able to make a joke out of this war." The secretary objected also to Lincoln's failure to consult with his cabinet and coordinate its actions, but mainly he was distressed by what he saw as the president's lack of aggressiveness in the pursuit of a military victory.

Chase's ever-active ambition contributed to his discontent with the administration. The same ambition that had propelled him to his position in the cabinet left him feeling stifled at his failure to advance further. Unable to resist the chance to enhance his power, at the close of 1862 he joined with a group of Republican senators in an attempt to remove William Seward from the cabinet and strengthen both himself and the radical orientation of the administration. In dramatic fashion the president outmaneuvered Chase, revealing his duplicity and publicly humiliating him. Nevertheless, still driven by the promise of greater fame, Chase made himself available for the 1864 Republican presidential nomination. A growing number of Republicans, frustrated with the conduct of the war, favored his candidacy, and the secretary was not above encouraging them. However, early in 1864 their efforts to replace Lincoln became too aggressive, and when, with Chase's approval, they distributed the "Pomeroy Circular" advocating Chase's nomination, a backlash ruined his prospects and further weakened his position in the administration.

In the end it was a dispute over patronage that led to the severing of Chase's ties with the Lincoln government. In each of a series of patronage disputes during his tenure at the Treasury Department, Chase was angered by Lincoln's removal or rejection of a Chase appointee. A number of times Chase went so far as to tender his resignation in protest, but each time the president rejected the offer. In June 1864, secure at last in his renomination, the president shocked Chase by accepting another such offer.

Within six months, however, Lincoln appointed Chase chief justice of the U.S. Supreme Court, a position he had long coveted. The country was in the process of redefining its federal system, and Chase would have the opportunity to influence the outcome. Uninhibited by his position on the bench, he often reiterated his long-held support for universal male suffrage and made clear his opposition to military government in the South. In his 1866 *Ex Parte Milligan* decision, he opposed the imposition of military rule where military operations did not exist. The following year he stood with the Court's minority in supporting the test oath requirements of Reconstruction governments in the South, and in 1869, speaking for the majority in *Texas v. White*, he endorsed the theoretical basis of Congressional Reconstruction by ruling that the Union was inviolable, therefore, the Confederate states had never actually seceded. By attempting secession they had simply forfeited some of their rights.

Chase's most celebrated involvement in Reconstruction was his role as presiding officer in the Senate impeachment trial of Andrew Johnson. Angering Senate radicals who hoped to turn the event into a political contest, Chase ruled that the trial had to be conducted as a formal judicial proceeding. He had disapproved of Johnson's failure to back universal male suffrage but had also distanced himself from the radicals' endorsement of military rule in the South. His insistence that courtroom practices be followed further alienated his Republican colleagues and produced a sympathetic reaction from some Democrats.

The trial ended in the spring of 1868, just as the political parties were selecting presidential nominees for the fall canvass. With Ulysses S. Grant assured of the Republican nomination, only the Democrats remained open to Chase. Never able to abandon his dream of the presidency, Chase allowed a number of Democrats to push for his selection. His support for universal amnesty and an end to military rule in the South was popular with Democrats across the nation, but his principled commitment to black male suffrage proved to be his undoing. Although he was ready to modify his stand, his persistent identification with a position anathema to most Democrats along with his record as founder of the Republican party doomed what always had been an unlikely nomination.

Chase had the opportunity to deal with a number of crucial constitutional issues during his last years on the Court. In *Hepburn v. Griswold* (1870) he confronted once again the currency issue that had troubled him so during the Civil War. He had supported legal tender then only in order to deal with the fiscal emergency that was confronting the country. In 1870 he held with the majority that paper money was unconstitutional, since it violated the spirit of the contract clause of the Constitution as well as the due process clause of the Fifth Amendment. With this difficult and controversial decision, Chase returned to his hard money roots and gained favor with his new Democratic friends. His final act as chief justice was to join in dissent in the important 1873 *Slaughterhouse Cases*. Near death, he spoke out one last time for the rights of the less powerful, arguing that the equal protection clause of the Fourteenth Amendment gave the federal government authority to protect individuals from unjust state action. He died in New York City.

The image of Chase as fundamentally devoted to reform is not without its dissenters. Both contemporaries and historians have emphasized instead his intense ambition and propensity to engage in political maneuver. There can be no question that from his youth Chase possessed an inordinate drive for personal advancement. But it is equally clear that throughout his extraordinary career he remained true to the goals of reform to which he had so passionately dedicated himself as a young man. It was the forceful fusion of his ideals and his ambition that gave Chase his power and his greatness. Few careers trace the nation's bitter strife or illuminate its torturous journey through Civil War as clearly as does Chase's.

• Numerous collections of Chase's papers are scattered throughout the country. The most important ones are located at the Library of Congress, the Historical Society of Pennsylvania, and the Cincinnati Historical Society. A 43-reel microfilm edition of selections from these and many other collections has been produced by University Publications of America, *The Salmon P. Chase Papers*. Portions of Chase's papers are available in published form. Most useful is a series initiated by Kent State University Press. The first three volumes, edited by John Niven, are *The Salmon P. Chase Papers, Volume I: Journals, 1829–1872* (1993); *The Salmon P. Chase Papers, Volume II: Correspondence, 1823–1857* (1994); and *The Salmon P. Chase Papers, Volume III: Correspondence, 1858–March, 1863* (1996). Other important editions of Chase's papers are Edward G. Bourne et al., eds., "Diary and Correspondence of Salmon P. Chase," *Annual Report of the American Historical Association for the Year 1902* 2 (1903); David Donald, ed., *Inside Lincoln's Cabinet: The Civil War Diaries of Salmon P. Chase* (1954); J. W. Schuckers, *The Life and Public Service of Salmon Portland Chase* (1874); and Robert B. Warden, *An Account of the Private Life and Public Services of Salmon Portland Chase* (1874).

The most important book-length biographies are Albert Bushnel Hart, *Salmon Portland Chase* (1899); the more recent Frederick J. Blue, *Salmon P. Chase: A Life in Politics* (1987); and Niven, *Salmon P. Chase: A Biography* (1995). Several books contain useful perspectives on various aspects of Chase's career. Eric Foner, *Free Soil, Free Labor, Free Men* (1970), offers a valuable analysis of Chase's belief in the antislavery nature of the Constitution as well as an examination of his role in the formation of the Republican party. William E.

Gienapp, *The Origins of the Republican Party, 1852–1856* (1987), presents a contrasting perspective on Chase's role in Republican politics as well as a largely critical view of his character. Stephen E. Maizlish, *The Triumph of Sectionalism: The Transformation of Ohio Politics, 1844–1856* (1983), explores Chase's Ohio career in detail. His performance as secretary of the Treasury is treated at length in Bray Hammond, *Sovereignty and an Empty Purse* (1970). Of the many excellent studies of specific issues in Chase's life, the three most significant are Peter Walker's personality study, "Salmon Chase: Abolition, Union, and 'The Great Moral Revolution,'" in his *Moral Choices* (1978); Gienapp, "Salmon P. Chase, Nativism and the Formation of the Republican Party in Ohio," *Ohio History* 93 (Winter–Spring 1984): 5–39; and Louis Gerteis, "Salmon P. Chase, Radicalism and the Politics of Emancipation, 1861–1864," *Journal of American History* 60, no. 1 (June 1973): 42–62.

STEPHEN E. MAIZLISH

CHASE, Samuel (17 Apr. 1741–19 June 1811), associate justice of the Supreme Court, was born in Somerset County, Maryland, the son of Thomas Chase, an Episcopal rector at St. Paul's in Baltimore, and Martha (or Matilda) Walker. He was instructed primarily in the classics by his father. Chase began the study of law in the offices of Hammond & Hall in 1759 in Annapolis, Maryland, and was admitted to the bar in 1761. The next year he married Anne Baldwin; they had seven children (three of whom died in infancy) before her death in the late 1770s.

A militant supporter of colonial rights in the 1760s, Chase served in the Maryland legislature from 1764 to 1788 and became known as the "Maryland Demosthenes." Because of his "intense convictions and energetic eloquence," he was sent to the Continental Congress in 1774 as a delegate from Maryland. In 1776, when Maryland instructed its delegates to the Continental Congress to vote against independence, Chase launched a successful campaign to persuade the Maryland assembly to reverse its position. In the next two days he rode one hundred miles and arrived in Philadelphia just in time to sign the Declaration of Independence.

While in the Continental Congress between 1774 and 1778, he played an active role on thirty committees, participating in almost all congressional action. In 1776 he was appointed, along with Benjamin Franklin, Charles Carroll, and John Carroll, to win the support of Canada for the Revolution. The mission was unsuccessful. Chase's career in Congress came to a sudden end in 1778 when Alexander Hamilton denounced him for using privileged information to speculate in the flour market.

Chase returned to Baltimore, where he continued to invest in mercantile and land ventures, practice law, and restore his political reputation. In 1783 he was sent by the governor of Maryland to England to recover funds owed to the state by the Bank of England. although he was unsuccessful in his financial mission, Chase did meet the great and near-great English political leaders such as Edmund Burke, with whom he spent a fortnight. In 1784 he married Hannah Kilty "Kitty" Giles of Kennbury Berks, England; they had two daughters.

Opposed to the Constitution of 1787, Chase was one of eleven members of the Maryland ratifying convention who voted against its adoption. His chief criticism of the document was that it would lead to a government of the few controlled by rich merchants. This view is particularly surprising in light of his later antidemocratic speeches as a judge. He wrote an article, under the pen name "caution," expressing his opposition. Once the Constitution was ratified, Chase was appointed to a committee to draw up a Bill of Rights to be added to the document. Given his future conflicts in the areas of free press and the trial by jury, it is ironic that they were among the rights proposed by the committee.

In 1788 Chase was out of office and bankrupt. Having always lived beyond his means, he went into debt buying large amounts of land. At this time he gained a position as a judge in the criminal court of Baltimore County. In 1791 he became chief judge of the general court of Maryland, thus beginning his turbulent career on the bench. In 1794 a Baltimore grand jury issued a presentment against Chase, charging that he had abused his authority by censuring a sheriff and by not summoning a proper jury. At the same time he was accused of holding more than one judicial appointment. Nothing came of these charges, but they were symptomatic of the controversy he generated.

The reasons for Chase's conversion to the Federalist party have remained obscure. Perhaps his introduction to English conservatism during his stay in Great Britain in 1780s, along with what he perceived to be the excesses of democracy touched off by the French Revolution in 1790s, and the development of the Jeffersonian Republicanism, explain his political transformation. By 1795 he had switched from an avid Antifederalist to a partisan Federalist and a believer in the necessity of a strong central government.

In 1795 Chase resigned as chief judge of the Maryland General Court to accept President George Washington's appointment to the U.S. Supreme Court. Chase has often been depicted as simply a contentious Federalist who had the misfortune of becoming the only Supreme Court justice to have been impeached. However, a study of his opinions reveals that he was also one of the outstanding political and legal theorists of the period.

Hylton v. United States (1796), *Ware v. Hylton* (1796), and *Calder v. Bull* (1798) are striking opinions that helped to lay the foundation for judicial review and "substantive due process." In *Hylton v. United States* the question was whether a tax placed on carriages by Congress was a "direct tax" and therefore subject to the principle of apportionment among the states. Chase's opinion in this case upheld the act of Congress and defined direct taxes as either a poll tax or a land tax. *Ware v. Hylton* involved a conflict between a Virginia state law and a federal treaty. Chase declared, "A treaty cannot be the supreme law of the land, if any act of a state legislature can stand in its way." *Calder v. Bull* concerned the meaning of the ex post facto clause of the Constitution. The Court explained that the clause applies only to criminal, not civil, cases. More importantly, Chase suggested that there were higher natural or fundamental laws that were not specifically spelled out in the Constitution but that placed limits on legislative actions.

By expressing this concept of inherent limitations on legislative powers, Chase paved the way for the doctrine of what would later be called "substantive due process," that is, the interpretation of the due process clause guarantees of the Fifth and Fourteeth Amendments to acknowledge rights that are not specifically stated in the Constitution but that exist in the concept of natural law. In *Calder v. Bull* Chase declared that "An Act of the legislature (for I cannot call it a law), contrary to the great first principles of the social compact, cannot be considered a rightful exercise of legislative authority." These opinions prepared the way for the *Marbury v. Madison* (1803) decision, in which Chief Justice John Marshall declared an act of Congress unconstitutional.

Paradoxically, Chase's decisions provided the judicial infrastructure not only for the "broad construction" of the Constitution, but also for the "strict construction" of that document. In one of his circuit court decisions, *United States v. Worral* (1798), Chase made it clear that he rejected the theory of "federal common law." According to this view, when a federal constitutional or statutory law does not provide the answer to a particular issue presented in a case, a federal judge may decide either that the state law should be applied or that the judge should invent a new rule of federal common law. Although most contemporary federal judges opposed Chase's decision, eventually his position was upheld by the Supreme Court in the early nineteenth century.

Between 1800 and 1804 Chase became known as one of the most vitriolic and hostile critics of the Jeffersonian Republicans in the federal judiciary. Increasingly concerned by the Republicans' attacks on the administration of John Adams, Chase presided over several criminal trials and proceedings in which he used his position as a judge to silence what he believed to be destructive and dangerous attacks on the government. Two of the most sensational of these lawsuits involved John Fries's treason trial and James Callender's sedition trial.

Fries was a militia officer who in 1800 had led a group of angry Pennsylvanians in rebellion against federal tax collectors. Fries was arrested, tried, and convicted of treason. But his conviction was overturned when it was discovered that one of the jurors was biased before he heard the evidence. Later that year Chase presided over a new trial. William Lewis and Alexander Dallas, leading members of the Philadelphia bar and avid Republicans, represented Fries. They planned to concede the facts of the case but to argue that the facts did not fall under the legal definition of treason. Once the jury was impaneled, Chase destroyed their strategy by confining the defense to the facts of the case. Lewis and Dallas denounced the ruling and withdrew from the case. Left without counsel, Fries was again convicted and sentenced to death; he was later pardoned by Adams.

By shrewdly manipulating Chase, Dallas and Lewis made it appear that Chase drove them from the case, leaving Fries defenseless before a ruthless and prejudiced Federalist judge who was trying to preserve the operation of an aristocratic judicial system. At his impeachment the prosecution contended that by restricting the arguments of Fries's lawyers, Chase was unconstitutionally depriving Fries of assistance of counsel.

Chase's aggressive and partisan attitude erupted again in the 1800 sedition trial of James Callender, a scurrilous and sensation-seeking newspaper editor. The trial was held in Virginia, where the leading members of the Virginia bar were openly critical of the Sedition Act. Three prominent Virginia lawyers rallied to Callender's defense. Chase did not hide his contempt for Callender; he conducted the trial in the prejudicial manner for which he had become famous. He forced hostile jurors to serve, and he required the defense lawyers to submit all questions they planned to ask their key witness, John Taylor of Caroline, to him. Chase then refused to allow Taylor to testify. He badgered and insulted the defense counsel so often they withdrew from the trial. Lacking legal counsel, Callender was convicted and Chase sentenced him to the maximum penalty, a fine of $200 and nine months in prison. By the end of Callender's trial Chase had a well-deserved reputation among the Republicans as a "hanging judge."

The event that touched off his impeachment was a political harangue Chase made to a Maryland grand jury on 2 May 1803. Chase condemned the repeal of the Judiciary Act of 1801, which abolished the offices of sixteen circuit judges, and the recent change in the Maryland constitution that had established universal suffrage. He warned that these changes brought about by the Republicans would destroy all protection for both property rights and personal liberty and would thus drive the country into a mobocracy.

On 5 January 1804 John Randolph, a radical Republican who was fanatically devoted to the principle of states' rights, rose in the House of Representatives and demanded an investigation of Chase. By 26 March seven articles of impeachment were placed before the House that made a number of specific charges of misconduct against Chase. Among the allegations was that, at the circuit court in Baltimore in May 1803, Chase did "pervert his official right and duty to address the grand jury," by delivering "an intemperate and inflammatory political harangue." Meanwhile Chase was busy lining up some of the most distinguished Federalist lawyers in the county to defend him. Robert Goodloe Harper became his chief counsel, and he put together a defense team that included James A. Bayard, Joseph Hopkinson, Philip Barton Key, Charles Lee, Luther Martin, and Philip Wickham.

The political nature of the trial was apparent to all participants. Moreover, the question of Chase's innocence or guilt hinged on how the Senate would define "high crimes and misdemeanors," as stated in the Constitution. A broad definition of this term, advocated by Chase's strongest detractors, would include any actions that could be viewed as bad conduct, including excessive partisanship and the use of intemperate language on the bench. A narrow definition would include only criminal actions subject to formal indictment.

Taking place in the Senate in 1805, the trial was long, bitter, and dramatic. Vice President Aaron Burr, who at the time was under indictment for the murder of Alexander Hamilton, presided. Chase's lawyers showed that the charges against him were motivated primarily by political considerations and that a conviction would undermine the independence of the judiciary. Because of a split in the Republican party between the moderates and radicals over the definition of "high crimes and misdemeanors," the prosecution failed to muster the two-thirds majority of the Senate necessary to gain a conviction.

Chase's acquittal meant that John Marshall and his court were safe from future attacks of this kind. It also demonstrated to Jefferson and future presidents that impeachment was a clumsy and inefficient way to handle politically hostile judges. On the other hand, members of the judiciary learned that it was dangerous for judges to use the bench to express political opinions that were contrary to prevailing democratic beliefs. After this confrontation, John Marshall attempted to establish the Supreme Court as an institution that was considered "above politics" and concerned only with legal-juridical questions. Chase, meanwhile, remained on the Court until his death; however, he never again played as prominent a role in Court matters, generally deferring to Marshall.

Chase was a mass of contradictions. His passionate, impetuous temperament entangled him in a lifetime of controversy that was capped with his impeachment as a Supreme Court justice, while his persuasive and remarkable opinions earned him a prominent place in the intellectual history of the early Supreme Court. Despite his irascible and partisan nature, the profound and rich political and legal content of his decisions established Chase as one of the seminal thinkers of the early Court, and perhaps the most notable jurist to sit on the Court before John Marshall. He died in Baltimore.

• Collections of Chase's papers are in the Maryland Historical Society, the New-York Historical Society, and the New York Public Library. His Supreme Court decisions are located in *U.S. Reports* from 2 *Dallas* to 6 *Cranch*; his impeachment trial is covered in 62nd Cong., 2d sess., S. Doc. 876. James Haw et al., *Stormy Patriot: The Life of Samuel Chase* (1980), is a full biography on Chase. Biographical sketches are in Leon Friedman and Fred L. Israel, eds., *The Justices of the United States Supreme Court, 1789–1969: Their Lives and Major Opinions*, vol. 1 (1969); and in Clare Cushman, ed., *The Supreme Court Justices: Illustrated Biographies, 1789–1993* (1993). For a recent assessment of his shift from Antifederalist to Federalist, see Stephen Presser, "The Original Misunderstanding: The English, the Americans, and the Dialectic of Federalist Constitutional Jurisprudence," *Northwestern University Law Review* 84 (1989): 106–85. For a discussion of the role of the development of the judiciary in the early republic and an evaluation of his impeachment trial, see Richard E. Ellis, *The Jeffersonian Crisis: Courts and Politics in the Young Republic* (1973).

MARGARET HORSNELL

CHASE, Stuart (8 Mar. 1888–16 Nov. 1985), social theorist and writer, was born in Somersworth, New Hampshire, the son of Harvey Stuart Chase, a public accountant, and Aaronette Rowe. Chase was born into a family that had lived in New England since the seventeenth century. He attended Massachusetts Institute of Technology in 1907–1908 and then completed his college education at Harvard University. Upon graduating cum laude in 1910, he became a certified public accountant and entered his father's accounting firm in Boston. In 1914 he married Margaret Hatfield; they had two children. The marriage ended in divorce in 1929. One year later, he married Marian Tyler.

Spurred by his interest in social issues and an extraordinary circle of former classmates, including journalists Walter Lippman and John Reed, and poet T. S. Eliot, Chase left accounting and took a position with the Food Administration of the Federal Trade Commission in Washington, D.C., in 1917. There he conducted several investigations of waste and corruption, including one of the meat-packing industry with novelist Upton Sinclair. Chase's critical reports played a part in his being dismissed by the commission at the insistence of Republicans in Congress in 1922.

In 1921, hoping to bring more scientific efficiency and engineering precision into government, Chase joined, along with the economic philosopher Thorstein Veblen, the "Technical Alliance," later known as the "Technocracy" movement. He also worked with the Labor Bureau, a research organization providing technical service for labor unions and cooperatives. In 1924 he joined with social scientist Lewis Mumford and others to start the first regional planning association. In 1925 Chase published his first nonfiction success, *The Tragedy of Waste*, which attracted attention for its criticism of the flaws of the American industrial system.

Two years later, with the assistance of Frederick J. Schlink, Chase wrote *Your Money's Worth* (1927), a story of "Alice in Wonderland, the consumer as Alice, modern salesmanship as Wonderland." *Your Money's Worth* pleaded for the purchasing of consumer goods according to specifications, standards, and tests. It analyzed the ways Americans decided what they desired or needed, and asked how often goods delivered what their advertisers had promised. It discussed how products, though manufactured with thousands of specifications, were being sold through normal channels or advertising that relied more on fantasy and fiction than on detail. "It is a maxim among advertising agents that when you know the truth about anything, the real inner truth—it is very hard to write the surface stuff which sells it," Chase wrote. Shortly after its publication, *Your Money's Worth* became a Book-of-the-Month Club bestseller. *Your Money's Worth* generated popular excitement about consumer problems and methods of consumer protection, and led to the creation of the first independent consumer product-testing organizations.

Over the next two decades Chase produced more than a dozen bestselling books. In 1929 he published *Men and Machines* and *Prosperity: Fact or Myth?*, works that explored the impact of machines and industry on the national economy, culture, and living patterns. Together with the artist Diego Rivera, he traveled to Mexico and published *Mexico: A Study of Two Cultures* (1931), measuring the cultural and economic distance machines had taken Americans from the preindustrial era. In 1932 he wrote *A New Deal*, which advocated more rigorous planning in the United States, greater government spending, and thorough regulation of private business. After its publication, Chase received credit for coining a new slogan and shaping important elements of Franklin D. Roosevelt's first presidential campaign agenda.

As the Roosevelt administration developed its legislative and social philosophy, Chase became one of its foremost public interpreters, analysts, and in most instances, supporters. Although his work was oriented toward central planning, even conservatives were impressed with the way Chase undressed the most complicated economic problems and conversed about them in enjoyable, colloquial prose. One of Chase's longtime critics wrote that while his logic "wobbles, his sentences march. His thought is incurably superficial, but his gusto and relish, his flair for effective phrases, his power to dramatize his subject, are unfailing."

In 1936 Chase's *Rich Land, Poor Land*, a plea for attention to the subject of the conservation of natural resources, appeared. In 1938 he wrote one of the first popular books about the potential power of the new science of linguistics, *The Tyranny of Words*. Opposed to warfare, Chase supported the isolationists before the outbreak of World War II. In *The New Western Front* (1939), he argued that the United States should keep out of European and Far Eastern conflicts. During the war, he prepared a multivolume series outlining his vision for a postwar world. Afterward, he turned his attention to the social sciences, to labor, and eventually to the environment. His *The Proper Study of Mankind* (1948) was a staple introduction to the social sciences at hundreds of college campuses for several decades. In 1961 he joined a group of prominent intellectuals who went to the Soviet Union to promote understanding between the two superpowers. His last book, *Bombs, Babies and Bulldozers*, appeared in 1982. He died in Redding, Connecticut.

Chase, as much as any writer of his generation, placed the most important social thinking of the day in front of the public. *A New Deal* had a notable influence on the Roosevelt program and brought Chase into Roosevelt's "brain trust." In addition, his views as an economist, his uncompromising support for government intervention in the economy, and his ability to explain social theory in layman's terms made Chase central to the world of ideas for half a century.

• A collection of Chase's personal papers is in the Library of Congress. Among his most influential works that have not already been mentioned are, in economics, *Idle Money, Idle Men* (1940); *Where's the Money Coming From?* (1943); *Tomorrow's Trade* (1945); and *The Economy of Abundance* (1934); and, on various aspects of communication, *The Power of Words* (1954); *Guides to Straight Thinking* (1956); and *Roads to Agreement* (1951). His other books include *A Honeymoon Experiment*, with first wife Margaret Chase (1916); *The Nemesis of American Business* (1931); *Government in Business* (1935); *A Primer of Economics* (1941); *The Road We Are Traveling* (1942); *Goals for America* (1942); *Democracy under Pressure* (1945); *Men at Work* (1945); *For This We Fought* (1946); *Some Things Worth Knowing* (1958); *Live and Let Live* (1960); *American Credos* (1962); *Money to Grow On* (1964); *The Most Probable World* (1968); *Danger—Men Talking: A Background Book on Semantics and Communication* (1969). Sources on Chase include Norman Silber, *Test and Protest* (1983), and "About the Author," *Guides to Straight Thinking* (1956). An obituary is in the *New York Times*, 17 Nov. 1985.

NORMAN SILBER

CHASE, William Calvin (22 Feb. 1854–3 Jan. 1921), African-American journalist, was born in Washington, D.C., the son of William H. Chase, a blacksmith, and Lucinda Seaton. He attended schools in Washington and, at the age of ten, upon the death of his father, went to work selling newspapers and, later, doing odd jobs around newspaper offices. Completing the preparatory department at Howard University, he took a position in the government printing office. He was later appointed by Frederick Douglass to a position in the office of the recorder of deeds, a post Douglass held, then moved on to become a clerk in the War Department. In 1886 he married Arabella V. McCabe; they became parents of two children.

Despite his government appointments, Chase early in his life showed a primary interest in journalism. Even as he held his government posts, he wrote for and even served as editor of newspapers serving Washington's black community. In 1882, by means that cannot be determined, he founded a newspaper of his own, the *Washington Bee*. Although he later took law courses at Howard, gaining admission to the bar in 1889 and beginning a practice he never abandoned, the *Bee* became his life's work. He died at his desk.

Of the many African-American newspapers established in the nineteenth century, the *Bee* was among the longest lived, published continuously from its founding until early 1922, about a year after Chase's death. Although it never achieved the national prominence of some other papers, Washington's black community was quite influential during the years Chase was active, and he used the *Bee* to make himself a major force in that community's life.

Like many African-American editors of the time, Chase created in the *Bee* a newspaper that was combative, Republican, and deeply involved in the racial questions of its day. He was especially concerned about discrimination in the nation's capital, which increased notably during the first two decades of the *Bee*'s existence. After the turn of the century, he published articles that exposed discrimination in federal employment, a growing problem during the Theodore Roosevelt and Taft administrations. Later, he made the *Bee* a major voice in protesting the Wilson administration's onslaught, after 1913, against African-American federal workers.

Chase also became a notable figure in African-American politics. Throughout his career, he was a champion of racial solidarity and self-help, politically, economically, and socially. Indeed, despite an unceasing militance in opposition to discriminatory laws and practices, he argued against agitation for integrated education, citing, chiefly, the positive role autonomous schools could play for African-American teachers and students alike, especially in encouraging racial pride. "Mixed schools," he wrote in 1883, "will do more to impress our children that they must forever be flunkies and servants than anything else."

At the same time, he often tended to take a somewhat erratic course in dealing with other prominent black leaders. From the beginning, he engaged in running battles, usually quite personalized but focusing particularly on questions of political partisanship, with such emerging, influential African-American leaders as T. Thomas Fortune, himself editor of a newspaper in New York. He also entered into erratic alliances with the various major organizations, from Fortune's Afro-American Council in the late nineteenth century to the subsequent National Association for the Advancement of Colored People—an organization he sometimes praised but also sometimes vilified as the "National Association for the Advancement of Certain People," mainly because of personal tensions with its major figures.

From 1895 until 1915 both Chase and the *Bee* figured in the politics surrounding Booker T. Washington's leadership, the central defining issue of the age. Financial considerations were not entirely absent from Chase's role. Until about 1905 Chase was generally opposed to Washington, despite his own tendency to favor strategies based on self-help and racial solidarity, strategies at the heart of Washington's program. He generally sided with those who focused on Washington's accommodationism, condemning Washington's apparent willingness to compromise on issues of political and social rights to gain economic improvement. After that time, Washington, always aware of the influence of the African-American press, began to provide Chase with financial support for the publication of the *Bee*. Chase, while remaining militant on issues of racial justice, responded by making the newspaper one of Washington's most consistent supporters.

Despite his activities in national affairs, and despite the real crises he confronted as an African American in Jim Crow America, Chase achieved his greatest influence through his role in an area of controversy that was almost entirely local, leadership of the District of Columbia's schools for black children. It was not a minor issue. These schools provided a major source of employment for Washington's educated African-American community and served as the institutional focus for that community as well. Even before becoming editor of the *Bee*, Chase had attacked what he saw as corruption and favoritism on the part of school officials, and he continued to do so throughout his career.

After about 1910 Chase gradually emerged as the chief spokesman for members of the District's African-American community dissatisfied with the management of the schools. Attacking the leadership of Roscoe Conkling Bruce, assistant superintendent for black schools and one-time protégé of Booker Washington, Chase made what he continued to see as corruption in the schools a central theme in the pages of the *Bee*. He also became the moving spirit in a "Parents' League" formed to exert pressure on the District's board of education to bring about, particularly, Bruce's ouster. Through his efforts, Chase did much to produce a 1920 congressional investigation of the schools and of Bruce's administration, resulting in the assistant superintendent's departure, at the urging of the board, a few months later.

Fully living up to the motto he himself gave the *Bee*, "Honey for friends, stings for enemies," Chase was a significant voice in turn-of-the-century African-American life.

• The literature on Chase is far from voluminous. Most important are a sketch in William Simmons, *Men of Mark* (1887), and a dissertation by Hal S. Chase, "'Honey for Friends, Stings for Enemies'" (Univ. of Pennsylvania, 1973). William Calvin Chase also figures in such standard works as August Meier, *Negro Thought in America* (1963), and Louis Harlan, *Booker T. Washington* (1972; repr. 1983).

DICKSON D. BRUCE, JR.

CHASE, William Merritt (1 Nov. 1849–25 Oct. 1916), artist and teacher, was born in Nineveh, Indiana, the son of David Hester Chase, a merchant, and Sarah Swaim. At age twelve Chase moved with his family to Indianapolis, where he attended public schools and worked in his father's shoe store. Chase showed little interest in commerce but demonstrated considerable artistic talent. Around 1866 he began to study with local painters Barton S. Hays and Jacob Cox. Bored with the shoe store and Indianapolis, Chase joined the U.S. Navy as an apprentice in 1867. He quickly realized that he had made a mistake and successfully sought a discharge within a few months. Cox and Hays then convinced David Chase to send his son to New York City to study at the National Academy of Design.

From 1869 until 1870 Chase studied at the National Academy of Design. Between sessions he rejoined his family, first in Indianapolis and then in St. Louis, where they moved after his father's business failed. Now without financial support from his family, Chase opened a studio in St. Louis, where he won the attention of local art collectors and businessmen and eked out a meager existence painting highly detailed still lifes and portraits. When a group of business leaders offered to underwrite his further education in Europe, he leaped at the opportunity.

From 1872 until 1877 Chase studied at the Royal Academy in Munich. Along with fellow students Frank Duveneck, Frederick Dielman, Walter Shirlaw, and other young Americans, he learned the "Munich manner," a style derived from the works of Frans Hals and Diego Velázquez. Karl von Piloty, Wilhelm Diez, and Alexander von Wagner instructed the students in a bravura approach that employed fluid brushwork and the rich tones of the Renaissance and emphasized large paintings of historical subjects.

Chase rejected the subject matter preferred by his mentors but absorbed their dictates regarding the bravura manner. His talents were recognized by his teachers, and Chase won several awards at the academy. When he submitted works to annual exhibits of the National Academy of Design in 1875 and 1877 and to the Centennial Exposition in Philadelphia in 1876, his paintings received critical acclaim. In 1877 Chase left Munich with Duveneck and fellow student John Twachtman to spend a year painting in Venice. There he continued to find inspiration in works of the Renaissance but began to alter his palette, experimenting both with the manipulation of light and with brighter colors. While in Venice he submitted works to the Society of American Artists in New York, a newly formed organization that was revolting against the moribund academic style of the National Academy of Design. The society brought Chase together with other younger painters who would dominate American art well into the twentieth century.

In 1878 Chase returned to New York City as an instructor at the Art Students League, a school formed by dissidents from the student body of the National Academy of Design. He stressed pure painting, applying oil with heavily laden brushes directly on canvas without using pencil or chalk drawings as a guide. Chase's students became devoted followers, and he provided strong encouragement for them, especially promoting the careers of women artists such as Dora Wheeler, Rosina Emmet, and Lydia Field Emmet. He also was elected president of the Society of American Artists in 1880 and again in 1885; he would hold that office until 1895. As a member of the Art Club, American Water Color Society, and Tile Club and as an organizer of the annual exhibits of groups such as the Painters in Pastel, Chase became a recognized leader of the New York art world.

In the 1880s and early 1890s Chase continued to abandon what he now characterized as the "brown sauce" of Munich, adopting the colors of the impressionists as well as some of their theories about light. His portraits, landscapes, and genre scenes won praise from critics and juries and brought a parade of guests to his elaborate Tenth Street studio. This space, filled with art objects, oriental bric-a-brac, and heavy furniture, became the center of a genteel bohemianism. Guests were greeted by an impeccably dressed Chase and served by an African-American servant attired in a Turkish costume. The flamboyant Chase was often the subject of newspaper stories, magazine articles, and art journal accounts that emphasized not only his paintings but also his bohemian lifestyle.

With colleagues from the Art Students League and the Society of American Artists, Chase returned to Europe each spring to view the art exhibitions in London and Paris, and then traveled to Spain, Holland, or Italy to paint. The impact of impressionism, and especially the art of Alfred Stevens, appealed to Chase, but Hals and Velázquez remained the inspiration for his formal portrait painting in terms of colors used, poses, and concern for careful modeling of the face and hands. Chase, together with Robert Blum, his friend and confidant, experimented with pastels, and Chase produced landscapes and portraits in high keys. He married Alice Brémond Gerson, the subject of many of his works, in 1886. They had eight children. His trips to Europe curtailed because of family obligations, Chase found inspiration in the parks of Brooklyn and Manhattan and at Shinnecock, Long Island.

Chase bought a home at Shinnecock in 1891 and offered a summer art school at the site. Over the next decade hundreds of students, including Rockwell Kent, Charles Sheeler, Howard Chandler Christy, Annie T. Lang, Joseph Stella, Charles W. Hawthorne, and Katherine Budd, studied there under the demanding direction of Chase and his assistants. Some students came from the Art Students League or from the Brooklyn Art School, where Chase also taught, but young artists from across the country also attended. Chase painted at Shinnecock as well, producing landscapes of light and color populated by his wife or children. Chase's colorful lifestyle and his enormous body of work drew attention to the school.

William and Alice Chase occupied a series of beautifully decorated homes in New York City filled with European and American paintings. They entertained the Spanish dancer Carmencita, the art patroness Isabella Stewart Gardner, prominent writers, journalists, musicians, and fellow artists as well as his students. In 1896 Chase accepted a teaching position at the Pennsylvania Academy of the Fine Arts, commuting to Philadelphia several days each week, and was also a guest instructor at the Art Institute in Chicago. He formed his own school in New York City in 1896, the Chase School of Art (later renamed the New York School of Art).

During the next two decades, Chase's students included Georgia O'Keeffe, Charles Demuth, Marsden Hartley, and Edward Hopper. He exposed his pupils to the works of both European and American painters, and even when they abandoned his style of impressionism for postimpressionism, precisionism, cubism, and futurism, he took pride in their work. Nearly every summer from 1903 to 1913 Chase took groups of students to Italy, Spain, Holland, England, or Belgium, where he conducted classes, escorted them to art museums, and exposed them to art currents that he often found repugnant. The 1913 International Exhibition of Modern Art (the Armory Show) represented all that was wrong in "modernism," declared Chase. He contended that the postimpressionists did not treat subject matter with respect, employed poor techniques, and moved beyond reality in their works.

From the 1880s until his death Chase served as a consultant to art museum directors, as a jurist at major exhibitions such as the annual Carnegie International Exposition, and as a mentor to other artists. He purchased paintings from his students, found places for their work in exhibitions, and promoted their careers. He exhibited his own work in the United States and in Europe, winning medals and prizes. He painted portraits of the rich and wellborn, but some of his best works were those of his wife and his children. He also produced still lifes and landscapes that gained widespread notice. A Fellow of the National Academy of Design and a member of the Ten (a group of American impressionists), Chase was recognized as a distinguished artist and teacher, yet the artist who had seemed revolutionary in 1878 had become a conservative defender of the art establishment by the time of World War I.

When Chase died in New York City, fellow artists, former students, and critics lauded his contributions to American art. His style of painting, largely unfashionable and unnoticed during the next forty-five years, regained popular and critical acclaim in the 1960s. Exhibitions of American impressionism, scholarly studies of that style, and sales at art galleries served to place him in a small pantheon of artists who had created what was characterized as an "American style." As an artist, Chase contributed to the emergence of impressionism in the United States with his Shinnecock landscapes and paintings of park scenes in New York City and Brooklyn. As a teacher, he influenced hundreds of students with his emphasis on technique and quality in art. As a professional leader, Chase helped to create an atmosphere that brought attention to the significant changes taking place in art. Chase's career spanned four decades during which he played a critical role in shaping American art.

• The major collections of Chase manuscripts are at the Parrish Art Museum in Southampton, New York, and at the Archives of American Art in Washington, D.C. The latter has many collections containing scattered letters to and from Chase. A full listing of fugitive manuscripts, Chase's own writings, and other primary sources can be found in Keith L. Bryant, Jr., *William Merritt Chase: A Genteel Bohemian* (1991). An earlier biography by a former student is Katharine Metcalf Roof, *The Life and Art of William Merritt Chase* (1917). For an analysis of Chase's art, see Ronald G. Pisano, *A Leading Spirit in American Art: William Merritt Chase, 1849–1916* (1983) and *William Merritt Chase* (1979). An overall assessment can be found in William H. Gerdts, *American Impressionism* (1984). An obituary is in the *New York Times*, 26 Oct. 1916.

KEITH L. BRYANT, JR.

CHATEAUBRIAND, François-René de (4 Sept. 1768–4 July 1848), writer and statesman, was born in Saint-Malo, Brittany, the son of René-Auguste Chateaubriand and Apolline de Bedée. Chateaubriand's well-educated mother came from a noble family in nearby Plancoët. His father, a descendant of illustrious ancestors, not only had restored the family fortune by serving as a gentleman corsair but in 1761 had also bought both the castle of Combourg and the title of vicomte de Combourg. The cold, turreted castle and its beautiful natural surroundings would leave a lasting impression on the boy, the youngest of six surviving children.

When the vicomte died in 1786, Chateaubriand's brother inherited the fortune and title and helped François-René obtain a lieutenant's rank in the army. Rejecting both sides in the French Revolution, the young nobleman sailed from Saint-Malo for America on 8 June 1791, and, after a pleasant interlude on the French island of Saint Pierre near Newfoundland, landed in Baltimore on 10 July. From there he hurried on to Philadelphia carrying a letter of introduction to President George Washington from the marquis de la Rouërie, who, as Colonel Armand, had fought with the Americans at Brandywine and Yorktown. Although in his *Travels in America*, published thirty-five years later, Chateaubriand described an interview with the American leader, we know from Washington's correspondence that the two never met. The young traveler did, however, go on to New York, perhaps to Boston, then up the Hudson and on to Niagara, where he broke his arm and remained for some time; but he did not, as he claimed, go down the Ohio and Mississippi, on to Florida, and back north overland. There are two reasons for being certain of that fact. First, since he began his return voyage to France from Philadelphia on 10 November, he had only four months in America, far too little time for such a journey; and second, as scholars such as Joseph Bédier and Gilbert Chinard have shown, in the *Travels* all of the material about the Ohio, the Mississippi, and the Southeast is taken from William Bartram, Jonathan Carver, François Charlevoix, Gilbert Imlay, and other well-known travelers Chateaubriand read before publishing his own account in 1827.

Back in France, Chateaubriand in 1793 married Céleste Buisson de la Vigne, whose fortune turned out to be less than was needed for his debts and with whom he was unable to live for years, first because he joined the royalist émigré forces and was wounded at Thionville and second because, aided by his brother, he fled to England, where he remained from 1793 to 1800. During those years his brother and his sister-in-law were among many royalists executed in France, the death of his mother led to his becoming an ardent Roman Catholic, and he underwent extreme poverty while supporting himself as teacher and translator. He was, however, continuously writing a huge manuscript that would become the basis for much of his later work, and in 1797, using a London printer, he published his first book, *Essai historique, politique, et moral sur les révolutions*.

Returning to France he brought out a novelette, immediately popular, called *Atala* and in 1802 published his first major work, the *Genius of Christianity*, which included *Atala* and *René*, another novelette, both written in colorful, eloquent style. In the first of these two, the old Indian Chactas tells René, the young Frenchman, the story of his tragic love for Atala, a Christian Indian who committed suicide in order to carry out her mother's vow of virginity for her. Just as *Atala* is a highly romantic tale that offers imaginative pictures of North American flora and fauna to match the idealized portraits of savages, so *René* is a melancholy, sentimental tale that the Werther-like hero tells in turn to Chactas and which, with its pathetic fallacy, its thoughts of suicide and hints at incest, and its lonely, alienated protagonist, gave the early nineteenth century a *mal de René*. The bulk of *Genius of Christianity*, however, is a defense of the theory that "of all religions that have ever existed, the Christian religion is the most poetic, the most humane, the most favorable to liberty, to the arts, and to letters." This theory, as well as the complex nature of the *Genius*, is suggested by the titles of its three books and its many chapters, among them "The Existence of God Proved by the Marvels of Nature," "Poetry in Its Relationship to Man," "On Gothic Churches," and "The Picturesque Effect of Ruins." The enormous success of Chateaubriand's book was due in part to its appearance almost simultaneously with the famous concordat by which Napoleon restored Catholicism as the semiofficial state religion.

Chateaubriand's political life began shortly after his first publications, when in 1803 he was named secretary to the French embassy in Rome and then ambassador to Valais, an independent republic in Switzerland. When Napoleon captured the duke d'Enghien and executed him as an object lesson to the Bourbons, the now famous writer resigned and in 1806–1807 traveled Egypt and the Holy Land, a journey that resulted in two books, one an epic called *The Martyrs* (1809), the other his travel journal (1811). On his return from the East, the now bitter anti-Bonapartist edited a journal, the *Mercure*, which Napoleon shut down. And when Chateaubriand was elected to the French Academy in 1811, Napoleon censored his acceptance speech. With the emperor's exile in 1814, however, Chateaubriand was made a peer of France, with the title of vicomte, and served not only as minister to Berlin (1821) and ambassador to England (1822), but also as foreign minister during the Spanish War of 1823–1824 and as ambassador to Rome in 1828. Always independent and excessively proud, he often opposed government policies as a matter of principle, as when in 1816 his published opinions on the duties of constitutional monarchy cost him his position as a minister of state and, because of his lack of money, forced him to sell his home near Paris.

Although all their married life Chateaubriand and his wife maintained a friendly relationship, they had no children, and she remained at home whenever he traveled. On the other hand, he was beloved by many women and was often romantically, if platonically, involved with them, as with Charlotte Ives in his first English period and Pauline de Beaumont, who while sick with a lingering illness visited him in Rome and died there. The most lasting of these liaisons was that with the great beauty Madame Récamier, in whose famous salon Chateaubriand reigned for the last two decades of his life. In fact, during those years she aided him in publishing his *Complete Works* and as he composed his *Memoirs from beyond the Grave*, a remarkable historical, autobiographical, poetic, and fictional account of his life and times. During that period, in 1827, he brought out *The Natchez*, *The Last of the Abencerages*, and *Travels in North America*, all heavily dependent on the manuscript he had written while in England in the 1790s. In 1836 his translation of Milton's *Paradise Lost* appeared and in 1844 his much-admired biography of the Trappist reformer Rancé. Chateaubriand's last ten years were spent with his wife in a ground-floor apartment on the rue de Bac in Paris. There he continued to dictate, to attract admirers, and to pay daily visits to Madame Récamier, who lived a short walk away, and there he died.

Chateaubriand's reputation both as statesman and as a man of letters had, much like that of Edgar Allan Poe in America, suffered in less romantic eras. Nevertheless, for nearly three decades he was not only a powerful and popular figure in the French government, but a man of honor who spoke unhesitantly for what he considered the worthy cause. And during those same three decades he was the most admired literary figure in France, giving way only slowly in that respect to Victor Hugo, who as an adolescent publishing his first volume of poems hoped "to be Chateaubriand or nothing."

• Of the three editions of Chateaubriand's *Oeuvres complètes*, the best may be the Garnier edition (12 vols., n.d.). For letters, the most nearly complete edition is the *Correspondence générale de Chateaubriand* (5 vols., 1912). Nearly every important work by Chateaubriand has at least one edition in French, for example, *Voyages en Amérique* (2 vols., 1964) and *Mémoires d'outre-tombe* (4 vols., 1948). Among the dozens of books written about Chateaubriand, there are, in French, Gilbert Chinard, *L'Exotisme américain dans l'oeuvre de Chateaubriand* (1918); Maurice Levaillant, *Chateaubriand* (1936), *Le Véritable Chateaubriand* (1951), and *Chateaubriand: prince des sauvages* (1960); André Maurois, *René, ou la vie de Chateaubriand* (1938), and the English translation, *Chateaubriand: Poet, Statesman, Lover* (1938); and Pierre Moreau, *Chateaubriand, l'homme et l'oeuvre* (1956). For English translations and studies, see *Atala and René* (1952; 1963); selections from the *Mémoires* (1961); *Travels in America*, ed. and trans. Richard Switzer (1969); Joan Evans, *Chateaubriand* (1939); Thomas C. Walker, *Chateaubriand's Natural Scenery* (1946); and Richard Switzer, ed., *Chateaubriand Today* (1970) and *Chateaubriand* (1971).

PERCY G. ADAMS

CHATMON, Armenter. *See* Carter, Bo.

CHAUNCEY, Isaac (20 Feb. 1772–27 Jan. 1840), naval officer, was born in Black Rock, Connecticut, the son of Wolcott Chauncey and Ann Brown, occupations unknown. Chauncey entered the merchant marine early in life and at nineteen secured his own command. He was commissioned a navy lieutenant on 11 June 1799 and ordered to superintend construction of the frigate *President* in New York. Chauncey subsequently joined the ship's complement and cruised the West Indies under Captain Thomas Truxtun throughout the Quasi-War with France. In 1802 he transferred to the frigate *New York* as part of Commodore Richard V. Morris's Mediterranean Squadron. On 10 August 1803 that vessel was rocked by an accidental explosion, and Chauncey distinguished himself by smothering a fire threatening the ship's magazine. Command of the frigate *John Adams* was conferred on him in 1804, and in this capacity he fought against the Barbary pirates. Chauncey was present on board the frigate *Constitution* during the August 1804 bombardment of Tripoli and there received commendation from Commodore Richard Preble. Returning home, he was promoted to captain on 24 April 1806.

The peacetime establishment offered few opportunities for advancement, so in 1806 Chauncey received a furlough to pursue commercial activities. He sailed to China commanding John Jacob Astor's trading vessel *Beaver* until confronted by the British warship HMS *Lion* off Whampoa. When the captain demanded that Chauncey muster his crew for examination and possible impressment, he staunchly refused, even after an armed party subdued his vessel. Chauncey promptly informed the captain that by his action the *Beaver* was technically a prize and demanded international adjudication. The British commander relented, and Chauncey returned to the United States unmolested. In 1807 Chauncey was directed to take charge of the New York navy yard, and he remained there until the advent of renewed conflict with Great Britain. On 31 August 1812 navy secretary Paul Hamilton appointed him commanding officer of all naval forces on strategic Lakes Ontario and Erie. Control of Lake Ontario, in particular, was deemed critical to U.S. military success.

In early October Chauncey arrived at the frontier port of Sackets Harbor, New York, which became his base and headquarters. Until then American naval assets on Lake Ontario had consisted of the schooner *Oneida*, which was badly outnumbered by vessels of the Canadian Provincial Marine. Chauncey, however, expedited the transfer of 140 carpenters, 700 sailors, and 100 pieces of heavy ordnance from New York and commenced an intricate program of naval construction. He was assisted by the talented shipwright Henry Eckford, who launched his first vessel, the corvette *Madison*, in only forty-five days. Concurrently, Chauncey created the nucleus of a naval squadron by purchasing and outfitting six civilian schooners. On 8 November 1812 he raided the British naval base at Kingston, Ontario, disabled the Canadian flagship *Royal George*, and captured several merchant vessels. Chauncey also dispatched Lieutenant Jesse D. Elliott to Erie, Pennsylvania, with orders to initiate a similar building program there. The year 1812 ended with the Americans enjoying undisputed control of Lake Ontario. It had been an impressive debut for Chauncey, who received the honorary title of commodore.

In the spring of 1813 an unprecedented naval arms race commenced on the Great Lakes. Elements of the Royal Navy had arrived at Kingston under captain Sir James Lucas Yeo, who laid the keels of several warships. Chauncey, meanwhile, received orders to assist the army of General Henry Dearborn in reducing British strong points along the lake shore. On 27 April 1813 he successfully conducted the first amphibious operation of U.S. history by capturing the provincial capital of York (Toronto). This was followed up by the 27 May reduction of Fort George, Upper Canada, another substantial American victory. Yeo, however, took advantage of Chauncey's absence from Sackets Harbor and on 29 May nearly captured it. The Americans spent several weeks repairing damage to Eckford's latest warship, *General Pike*, before Chauncey could resume operations. The opposing fleets collided off Burlington Bay on 28 September 1813 whereupon Chauncey pummeled Yeo but failed to destroy him. The loss of several schooners to storms curtailed further American efforts, and Chauncey restricted himself to assisting the movement of the army of General James Wilkinson to the St. Lawrence River. Yeo, though roughly handled, was still positioned to contest control of the lake.

Chauncey's construction program crested in the spring of 1814 with the addition of several powerful warships. With superb planning, he and Eckford had two frigates, *Superior* and *Mohawk*, nearly completed and two large brigs, *Jones* and *Jefferson*, on the stays. Yeo countered with two large frigates of his own and also began building an enormous battleship, HMS *St. Lawrence*, with 102 guns. Chauncey's reputation, however, had become complicated by a contretemps with General Jacob J. Brown. Brown had launched his Niagara invasion in July 1814 with an understanding from the government that Chauncey would support his movements. The commodore, unfortunately, received no such order from either President James Madison or navy secretary William Jones and was reluctant to leave Sackets Harbor exposed to another attack. He subsequently refused to sail to Niagara, and Brown's attack foundered. When Chauncey fell ill for two weeks in August, Stephen Decatur was ordered north from New London to replace him. He sailed before Decatur's arrival, however, and blockaded Kingston for several weeks. When HMS *St. Lawrence* sailed in early October, Chauncey relinquished the lake to Yeo and began building two vessels of similar girth: *Chippewa*, with 130 guns, and *New Orleans*, with 110 guns. They were the largest warships of their class in the world and were nearly completed when word of peace arrived in January 1815.

After the war, Chauncey was ordered to command the navy yard in Portsmouth, New Hampshire, and there supervised construction of the ship-of-the-line *Independence*. This vessel became his flagship when in June 1816 he replaced Decatur as commander of the Mediterranean Squadron. While on station, Chauncey assisted Consul William Shaler during his negotiations with Algiers, and a peace treaty was reaffirmed. Chauncey was succeeded by Commodore John Stewart in 1818, returned to the United States, and from 1821 to 1824 served on the Board of Navy Commissioners in Washington, D.C. His old command at the New York navy yard was reactivated for him between 1825 and 1832, and the following year he again functioned as navy commissioner. Chauncey succeeded an ailing John Rodgers as president of the board in 1837 and remained in this capacity until his death in Washington, D.C.

Historians are divided over Chauncey's abilities, especially during the War of 1812. A splendid sailor, he was also the most capable naval administrator of his day. The building campaign at Sackets Harbor was conducted on the very periphery of civilization yet was characterized by remarkable speed and efficiency. By war's end Chauncey commanded a major naval force. The British, enjoying far fewer resources, were hard-pressed to keep apace of him and were prevented from shipping badly needed supplies to other theaters such as Lake Erie and Lake Champlain.

Chauncey's immense bureaucratic skill must be weighed against certain tactical deficiencies. Personally fearless, he nevertheless refrained from combat unless conditions of battle virtually assured him of victory. This hesitation played directly into British hands: as long as Yeo kept his fleet intact, he could thwart American control of Lake Ontario. Perhaps a more serious shortcoming was Chauncey's attitude toward combined operations. Like many contemporaries, he engaged in keen interservice rivalry. His spirit of cooperation with the army, initially friendly, deteriorated sharply after the nearly successful attack on his base at Sackets Harbor. Chauncey's apprehensions were not totally unjustified, but his flat refusal to assist Brown at Niagara doomed American aspirations there to bloody stalemate. Having created for himself a splendid naval resource, Chauncey was reluctant to employ it daringly or decisively.

Chauncey was married (date unknown) to Catharine Sickles of New York and had three children. Two of them, John S. Chauncey and Charles W. Chauncey, became naval officers.

• Chauncey's official correspondence is in RG 45, Captains' Letters, National Archives. Large collections also exist at the Clements Library, University of Michigan, and the New-York Historical Society. Scattered material may also be found in the Charles T. Harbeck Papers, Huntington Library, San Marino, Calif.; the Franklin D. Roosevelt Library, Hyde Park, N.Y.; the Lilly Library, Indiana University; and the Historical Society of Pennsylvania. Printed sources include Dudley W. Knox, ed., *Documents Related to the Wars with the Barbary Powers* (6 vols., 1939–1944); William S. Dudley, ed., *The Naval War of 1812* (2 vols., 1985–1990); and Ernest A. Cruikshank, ed., *Documents Relating to the Invasion of the Niagara Peninsula* (1920). There are no reliable biographies, but informative sketches are in John H. Brown, *American Naval Heroes* (1899); Fletcher Pratt, *Preble's Boys* (1950); and Christopher McKee, *A Gentlemanly and Honorable Profession* (1991). For insights about his naval operations consult Dudley, "Commodore Isaac Chauncey and U.S. Joint Operations on Lake Ontario, 1813–1814," in *New Interpretations of Naval History*, ed. William B. Cogar (1989), pp. 139–55, and Frederick C. Drake, *The War for the Inland Seas* (1996). Analysis of his building activities is in Kevin J. Krisman, "The *Jefferson*: The History and Archaeology of an American Brig from the War of 1812" (Ph.D. diss., Univ. of Pennsylvania, 1989), and Patrick A. Wilder, *The Battle of Sackett's Harbour* (1994).

JOHN C. FREDRIKSEN

CHAUNCY, Charles (1592–19 Feb. 1672), Puritan minister and president of Harvard College, was born in Yardley-Bury, Hertfordshire, England, the son of George Chauncy, a member of the lesser gentry, and Agnes Welch Humberstone. In 1605 Chauncy was sent to the Westminster School, which narrowly escaped the notorious Gunpowder Plot of that year. He entered Trinity College, Cambridge, in 1610, received the B.A. in 1614, a master's degree in 1617, and in 1624 was awarded a second bachelor's degree in divinity. After taking his first degree, Chauncy became a fellow of the college and eventually served as lecturer in Hebrew and Greek.

Revered as a scholar, Chauncy's preaching skills were highly praised as well. In 1627 he became vicar of Ware in Hertfordshire, a lucrative position in the patronage of Trinity College. As a minister with strong Puritan feelings, Chauncy vehemently opposed Common Prayer worship as unscriptural and objected to the profanation of the Sabbath encouraged by James I's *Book of Sports* (1618). In 1630 and again in 1634 he was brought before His Majesty's Commissioners for Causes Ecclesiastical for refusing to wear the Anglican surplice or recite the litany during services and for attempting to convince his parishioners that the Church of England encouraged idolatry. On the second occasion he was imprisoned for several months. Although he submitted to the authorities and recanted his beliefs, Chauncy's conscience bothered him and he retracted his submission before departing for New England.

As one of the most learned English divines to migrate to America, Chauncy was warmly welcomed by the Plymouth colonists on his arrival in 1638. But his habit of defending his personal interpretation of Scripture as an absolute guide to Christian practice, regardless of the opinions of his contemporaries, caused trouble for him in America as it had in England. In Plymouth, Chauncy insisted that total immersion was the only lawful form of baptism and demanded that the Lord's Supper be celebrated in the evening. His New England antagonists were like-minded Puritans and not Anglican persecutors, but Chauncy would still not accept their reasoning that "sprinkling" was an equally lawful form of baptism and that the time of day was immaterial to the celebration of communion. Unable to resolve the dispute, Chauncy left Plymouth for the nearby town of Scituate where he found support for his baptismal views.

Chauncy remained in Scituate until 1654, but competition among religious factions within the town made it difficult for him to earn a living. The number of his supporters was small, and so too was his salary. In 1630 he had married Catherine Eyre, who emigrated with him and bore their eight children. Faced with the struggle of supporting his family, Chauncy accepted a call to return to his old parish in Ware now that Puritans ruled in England. On his way back through Boston, however, Chauncy was approached with an offer to become the new president of Harvard College. His reputation as a scholar made him the obvious choice to succeed Henry Dunster, who had recently been forced to resign because he had renounced the practice of infant baptism altogether. Among New England's orthodox leaders, Baptist beliefs were associated with religious anarchy; consequently, the Harvard overseers were cautious in approaching Chauncy and insisted that he "forbeare to disseminate or publish any Tenets concerning the necessity of immersion in Baptisme." Chauncy accepted the offer and was installed as Harvard's second president in November 1654.

Chauncy trained some of the leading clergymen of New England's next generation, including Samuel Willard and Solomon Stoddard, as well as the judge and diarist Samuel Sewall, and two leading poets of early New England, Edward Taylor and Benjamin Tompson. As president, Chauncy was no innovator; he maintained the curriculum instituted by his predecessors and focused his energy on the students' religious education. He professed an interest in natural sciences, but some of the texts used by the college failed to keep pace with changes in seventeenth-century thought on the laws of nature. During his presidency the college faced fiscal difficulties from which Chauncy's personal fortunes suffered as well. At times the number of students included only a precious few who paid their tuition and expenses.

The relative decline of the college in the 1660s was exacerbated by changes in New England's religious culture. In 1662, a synod of churches approved the Half-Way Covenant, which amended baptismal practices for the sake of more inclusive membership. Its supporters, like the Cambridge minister Jonathan Mitchell, believed the change was necessary for New England's churches to encompass the entire population rather than a dwindling remnant of the original settlers, and they believed that the clergy's role should be to convert the indifferent population to a godly way of life. Chauncy, whose Puritan beliefs were rooted in his English background, where godliness required a withdrawal from society rather than an effort to embrace it, never grasped the need for the Half-Way Covenant within Puritanism's new American circumstances, and his *Antisynodalia Scripta Americana* (1662) denounced the proposed changes. A leading voice among the opponents of the Half-Way Covenant, he triggered a controversy that spread from the churches into colonial politics.

The effect of Chauncy's opposition to the Half-Way Covenant, combined with fellow Harvard corporation member Mitchell's strong support for it, made Harvard's mission within New England religious culture difficult to define and contributed to the overall sense of decline and drift at the college during Chauncy's presidency, which ended with his death in Cambridge, Massachusetts. It was not until nearly the turn of the eighteenth century, when American-born and Harvard-trained scholars like Increase Mather, Samuel Willard, and John Leverett assumed the college leadership, that Harvard regained a sense of direction and began to grow and adapt to the changing world. Chauncy's career was profoundly shaped by his remarkable education at Trinity College, Cambridge, and by the trials of being an English Puritan in the age of Laudian persecution. In migrating to America he helped to establish high standards of learning and scholarship in the colonial world, but he had more difficulty in adapting his combative and exclusive approach to godly life to the new form of Puritan society taking shape in New England.

• Chauncy's publications, in addition to those mentioned above, include *The Retraction of Charles Chauncy* (1641), *God's Mercy Shown to His People* (1655), and *The Plain Doctrine of the Justification of a Sinner* (1659). The text of the "Articles Objected by His Majesty's Commissioners for Causes Ecclesiastical against Charles Chauncey, Clerk . . . " is reprinted in John Demos, ed., *Remarkable Providences, 1600–1760* (1972). The most complete biographical information on Chauncy, including a list and description of his publications, can be found in William Chauncey Fowler, *Memorials of the Chaunceys* (1858). The best assessment of his Harvard presidency is in Samuel Eliot Morison, *Harvard College in the Seventeenth Century* (1936). On Chauncy's career in Plymouth and Scituate, see William Bradford, *Of Plymouth Plantation, 1620–1647* (1952). An interesting contemporary biographical sketch is in Cotton Mather, *Magnalia Christi Americana*, vol. 1 (1853), pp. 463–76. Insights into Chauncy's close relationship with his students and his affinity for a fellow English emigrant who shared his somewhat exclusivist Puritan beliefs can be seen in Francis Murphy, ed., *The Diary of Edward Taylor* (1964).

MARK A. PETERSON

CHAUNCY, Charles (1 Jan. 1705–10 Feb. 1787), Congregationalist clergyman, was born in Boston, Massachusetts, the son of Charles Chauncy, a merchant, and Sarah Walley. The elder Charles died when his son was six, and although Chauncy's mother remarried, little is known of Chauncy's early life. After preparing at the Boston Latin School, Chauncy entered Harvard at age twelve, receiving his B.A. in 1721 and his M.A. three years later. Chauncy's college days apparently were typical; records indicate that he was fined for playing cards before his graduation.

After candidating for several pastoral posts and being offered a position as assistant at Boston's New Brick Church, Chauncy in 1727 became the assistant to Thomas Foxcroft at Boston's First or Old Brick Church. There he remained until his death, becoming the senior pastor on Foxcroft's death in 1769. During

Chauncy's tenure at Old Brick, the congregation identified itself with the more liberal strains of eighteenth-century New England Puritanism, finally in 1731 adopting the Half-Way Covenant that relaxed standards for church membership, dropping public testimony of conversion as a prerequisite to membership that same year, and offering baptism to all adults beginning in 1736.

Chauncy's enduring impact on religious life stems from his strident opposition to the evangelical style prominent during the Great Awakening of the 1740s, the proto-Unitarian and universalist tendencies in several treatises he wrote shortly after the Awakening but refrained from publishing until just before his death, his opposition to proposals to settle an Anglican bishop in the colonies in the 1760s, and his support for American independence during the era of the American Revolution. Many of his positions have led most later interpreters to view Chauncy as a liberal who jettisoned much Puritan ideology; others, however, have seen Chauncy as one who sought to preserve what he thought integral to New England's distinctive religious life and adapt Puritan thought to changing times.

In the controversy surrounding the Great Awakening, Chauncy's primary opponent was Jonathan Edwards (1703–1758), then pastor at Northampton, Massachusetts, where revival impulses first emerged in New England. Edwards and others endorsing the evangelical style of the Awakening regarded vital religion as primarily a matter of the affections and believed individuals could be moved to affirm the work of God in their lives through the stirring of the affections. Hence they also encouraged itinerant evangelists such as George Whitefield, whose powerful oratory could move large crowds, to proclaim the message of salvation wherever they could gain a hearing.

Chauncy's concern with Awakening religion was twofold. While he, too, regarded authentic religion as involving human sensibilities, he felt Edwards and his associates reduced religion to emotional excess, minimized the role of reason in accepting the truth of the gospel, and caused those who had not undergone a cataclysmic conversion to doubt the authenticity of their religious experiences. Jonathan Mayhew, Chauncy's friend and pastor of Boston's West Church, argued even more strongly in his own writings that reason played a central role in religious experience. Chauncy's other major complaint concerned the impact of itinerants on the ministry of settled clergy with their own congregations. For Chauncy, itinerants undermined the ministry of the settled clergy, particularly by fostering fears that ministers were themselves unconverted, and thereby challenged traditional patterns of religious authority.

Chauncy's early criticism came in *Enthusiasm Described and Caution'd Against* (1742), a tract published in Scotland that same year under the title *A Letter from a Gentleman in Boston to Mr. George Wishart, One of the Ministers of Edinburgh, concerning the State of Religion in New-England* (which led the University of Edinburgh to confer on him a D.D. degree), and the anonymous *The Late Religious Commotions in New-England Considered* (1743). Chauncy reportedly traveled more than 300 miles to gather firsthand information for his major critique of the revivals, *Seasonable Thoughts on the State of Religion in New-England* (1743), a counter to Jonathan Edwards's *Some Thoughts on the State of Religion in New-England* (1742). Chauncy also engaged in a paper war with George Whitefield on the merits of the Awakening. Whatever the effects of the Awakening in revitalizing New England religious life, it left a lasting division between those who espoused evangelicalism and those who were wary of its presumed excesses.

The issues raised by the evangelical revivals, particularly the emphasis on the necessity of an emotional experience of conversion with its theological base in the Calvinist notion that God elected only a few to salvation, caused Chauncy to rethink his theological position once the controversy ebbed. By the mid-1750s, Chauncy had drafted a manuscript to which he gave the code name the "pudding" in an effort to keep its contents secret. He did share it with a few close friends, but he felt the time was not ripe for public release because his arguments were too explosive. Chauncy waited until 1784 to publish *The Mystery Hid from Ages and Generations* and had the work printed in London rather than Boston. Nevertheless, the views it contained are indicative of the theological stance that undergirded Chauncy's thinking from the 1750s on.

Even before the "pudding" appeared, Chauncy released other works whose titles echo the major thrust of the "pudding." *Salvation for All Men*, extracts from other writings on universal salvation, appeared anonymously in 1782, though Chauncy's hand in the manuscript was widely known. The following year, while *The Mystery Hid from Ages and Generations* was in press, Chauncy issued *Divine Glory Brought to View in the Final Salvation of All Men*. Its title was a direct play on that of a work by Joseph Eckley, *Divine Glory, Brought to View in the Condemnation of the Ungodly* (1782), which attacked the universalism advanced in *Salvation for All Men*. Then in 1784 there also appeared *The Benevolence of the Deity*. Common themes run through all these works and Chauncy's final major treatise, *Five Dissertations on the Scriptural Account of the Fall; and Its Consequences*. (1785).

Chauncy argued that the primary characteristic of God was goodness or benevolence. Such goodness, he reasoned, meant that God intended for all creation to experience happiness. Ultimate happiness could not come if even unrepentant humanity were consigned to eternal damnation. Hence God must will the final salvation of all, though mortals might not understand precisely how such universal salvation would transpire. On the surface, Chauncy's position undercut the orthodox notion that those not elected to salvation will receive final condemnation and thus helped weaken the dominance of Calvinism in New England theology. Chauncy regarded his position as an authentic rendering of the gospel message, one that had been a "mystery hid from ages and generations." In his mind, he was conserving what he believed to be the real testimony of Christianity. In the early nineteenth century his views would be taken up by the nascent Unitarian movement, and later generations of Unitarians would continue to regard Chauncy as one of their ideological forerunners.

In the 1760s, after Britain had extended its North American colonial empire to include Canada, many New Englanders feared that the Church of England would attempt to settle a bishop in the colonies. Puritans from the seventeenth century on abhorred episcopal polity, in part because in Britain bishops exercised both civil and religious functions and had used their power to repress Puritan dissenters. Chauncy entered the fray with several pieces, arguing that episcopacy as it existed in the Church of England was unscriptural and therefore unwarranted. Some of his antiepiscopal works came in an exchange with Thomas Bradbury Chandler, a Church of England cleric in New Jersey, who insisted that a colonial bishop would have only religious authority. His most sustained attack was *A Compleat View of Episcopacy, as Exhibited from the Fathers of the Christian Church, until the Close of the Second Century* (1771), a work that revealed Chauncy's detailed knowledge of patristics. The move to establish a colonial episcopal see came to naught, eclipsed by the political turmoil that issued in the American Revolution.

When hostilities erupted, the elderly Chauncy aligned himself with the patriot cause, again gaining notoriety for his outspokenness. Documentation of his proindependence stance survives primarily in correspondence, especially with English dissenter Richard Price. After the British closed Boston's port to trade in 1774, a town committee commissioned Chauncy to write a tract outlining the patriot position. In *A Letter to a Friend, Giving a Concise, but Just, Representation of the Hardships and Sufferings the Town of Boston Is Exposed To*, Chauncy equated British policy with slavery, for the demise of economic liberty to him spelled the end of political liberty, and he called for active resistance. Since "forcing from us our rights and privileges as English subjects, is the grand point in view," Chauncy wrote, "we shall naturally be urged on to contrive expedients to prevent, if possible, our being in this way, brought into bondage." His patriot support was so well known that he had to flee from Boston during the British occupation.

Chauncy was not only a man of controversy. He took seriously the larger responsibilities of the Puritan cleric and throughout his career served on church councils, preached the requisite election and ordination sermons, and worked with town committees to improve schools and to provide adequately for the poor. In his own day he was known as much for his charitable work as for his acerbic involvement in ecclesiastical disputes. When Chauncy died in Boston, his peers remembered him for his deep personal piety as well as for his plain, reasoned preaching style and stern sense of discipline.

Chauncy outlived three wives. In February 1727 he was married to Elizabeth Hirst, with whom he had one son and two daughters. After her death in 1737, he was married in 1739 to Elizabeth Phillips Townsend, a widow, who died in 1757. Mrs. Townsend's daughter, Rebecca, lived with the Chauncys until her marriage. In January 1760 he was married to Mary Stoddard, a woman of financial means, who died in 1783.

• Chauncy ordered his personal papers destroyed at his death. Numerous letters and papers relating to Chauncy are found in collections at the Massachusetts Historical Society and in the Ezra Stiles Papers, Yale University. A complete list of Chauncy's published writings is in the biography by Charles H. Lippy, *Seasonable Revolutionary: The Mind of Charles Chauncy* (1981). Another biography is Edward M. Griffin, *Old Brick: Charles Chauncy of Boston, 1705–1787* (1980). See also John Corrigan, *The Hidden Balance: Religion and the Social Theories of Charles Chauncy and Jonathan Mayhew* (1987).

CHARLES H. LIPPY

CHAUVENET, William (24 May 1820–13 Dec. 1870), mathematician and educator, was born in Milford, Pennsylvania, the son of William Marc Chauvenet, a farmer and later a businessman, and Mary Kerr. Chauvenet was educated in a private school in Philadelphia by Dr. Samuel Jones, and his academic record was so impressive that Jones persuaded the elder Chauvenet that his son should attend Yale University rather than become a merchant. The young Chauvenet showed a market aptitude for mathematics, and upon learning that Yale required a knowledge of both Latin and Greek he mastered these languages in one year. He entered Yale in 1836, and at the end of his first year there he took the first prize for Latin composition. His studies at Yale included both the classics and mathematics, and he received his A.B. with high honors in 1840.

Returning to Philadelphia, Chauvenet worked as an assistant to Alexander D. Bache at Girard College on observations of the terrestrial magnetic field; and later at the observatory of Philadelphia High School he became involved in astronomy with Sears C. Walker. In 1841 Chauvenet was appointed professor of mathematics in the U.S. Navy and gave shipboard instruction to midshipmen on the USS *Mississippi*. He found this to be unsatisfactory and in 1842 transferred to the Naval Asylum school in Philadelphia, where he instituted an eight-month course of instruction. Also in 1842 Chauvenet married Catherine Hemple of Philadelphia; they had four sons and one daughter.

Finding an eight-month study program inadequate, Chauvenet proposed a four-year course of study and began lobbying for the creation of a separate naval school devoted solely to academic studies. In 1845 he moved to Fort Severn in Annapolis, Maryland, where a two-year program of instruction was initiated in a new naval school. Chauvenet is regarded as one of the founders of the U.S. Naval Academy at Annapolis, which was formally established with a four-year course of study in 1851. At the Naval Academy Chauvenet was department head and professor of mathematics and astronomy from 1845 to 1853, and professor of astronomy, navigation, and surveying from 1853 to 1859. In 1855, after declining the offer of a professorship in mathematics at Yale, he accepted a similar position at Washington University in St. Louis, Missouri. Upon the death of Joseph Hoyt in 1862, Chauvenet became the second chancellor of Washington University.

Chauvenet's mathematical work was essentially of an elementary character, focusing on his duties as a teacher of naval personnel. At the Naval Academy he frequently taught four to six hours daily, and under such circumstances the quality and quantity of his work was truly remarkable. He wrote only fourteen papers, but his reputation lies in his exemplary textbooks, which were much needed at the times in which they appeared. The first of these, *Binomial Theorem and Logarithms for the Use of Midshipmen at the Naval School in Philadelphia* (1843), was very detailed. This was followed by *A Treatise on Plane and Spherical Trigonometry* (1850), which his contemporaries regarded as the most complete account of the subject written in the English language. Going through many editions, it offered a masterful treatment of the material and many applications to problems of interest in astronomy, geodesy, and navigation. Perhaps even more influential was his two-volume *A Manual of Spherical and Practical Astronomy* (1863); the first volume was subtitled *Spherical Astronomy*, while the second was subtitled *Theory and Use of Astronomical Instruments, Method of Least Squares*. His final book, *A Treatise on Elementary Geometry* (1870), was intended to replace the various inferior and abridged translations of Adrien-Marie Legendre's *Éléments de Géométrie*, which had been in widespread use for more than forty years. Chauvenet's books were noted for their clarity and simplicity both for use in the classroom and for self-study. While they contained little in the way of original discoveries, their improved methodology and fresh new presentations were real pedagogical contributions.

In 1869, on account of ill health, Chauvenet retired from his position as Washington University chancellor. He left St. Louis and ultimately settled in Minnesota. He died in St. Paul, Minnesota.

During his brief lifetime Chauvenet was a leader in American mathematical and educational circles, and he was much admired for both his scholarship and his reputation as a teacher. His lasting fame lies in his crucial role in the founding of the Naval Academy and in his assuring that its curriculum in mathematics and navigation was set out on a proper academic basis. Chauvenet was an original member of the American Association for the Advancement of Science, served as its general secretary in 1859, and was elected its president for 1870. He was one of the incorporators of the National Academy of Sciences, and from 1868 until his death he was vice president of that organization. In 1925 the Mathematical Association of America founded the Chauvenet Prize for Mathematical Exposition, to be awarded every five years, and at the Naval Academy an academic building was named Chauvenet Hall.

• Chauvenet's role in the foundation of the U.S. Naval Academy is briefly discussed in various histories of the academy, including Jack Sweetman, *The U.S. Naval Academy—An Illustrated History* (1979). A more detailed account was given in G. W. Littlehales, "William Chauvenet and the United States Naval Academy," *Proceedings of the U.S. Naval Institute* 31 (Sept. 1905): 605–12. An obituary, which includes a list of publications, is in the National Academy of Sciences, *Biographical Memoirs* 1 (1877): 227–44.

JOSEPH D. ZUND

CHÁVEZ, Carlos (13 June 1899–2 Aug. 1978), influential Mexican composer/conductor, author, and educator, of Spanish and some Indian descent, was born Carlos Antonio de Padua Chávez y Ramírez in Mexico City, the seventh son of Augustin Chávez, an inventor, and Juvencia Ramírez, a teacher. His mother supported the children after her husband's death in 1902. Chávez began his musical studies at an early age and studied piano, first with his elder brother Manuel, then with Asunción Parra, and later with composer and pianist Manuel M. Ponce (1910–1914) and pianist and teacher Pedro Luis Ogazón (1915–1920). Chávez credited Ogazón with introducing him to the best classical and Romantic music and with developing his musical taste and technical formation. He received little formal training in composition, concentrating instead on the piano, analysis of musical scores, and orchestration. Chávez's maternal grandfather was Indian, and from the time Chávez was five or six his family frequently vacationed in the ancient city-state of Tlaxcala, the home of a tribe that opposed the Aztecs. He later visited such diverse Indian centers as Puebla, Jalisco, Nayarit, and Michoacan in pursuit of Indian culture, which proved a significant influence on his early works.

The period of the Mexican Revolution, beginning with the overthrow of Díaz in 1910, coincided with Chávez's development as a composer. Mexico's growing nationalism was a reaction against the long Díaz dictatorship, in which Indian and mestizo lands had been confiscated and the middle class oppressed. Chávez's interest in indigenous culture, concurrent with this rise of Mexican nationalism, facilitated his exposure to the inner circle of Mexican cultural politics. A concert of his works was performed in 1921, and the same year Vasconcelos, the vigorous minister of education and government patron of the arts, commissioned Chávez to compose *El fuego nuevo* (*The New Fire*), a ballet on Aztec subject matter. The production fell through, but Chávez became an accepted member of the Mexican cultural elite.

Chávez married Otilia Ortiz in 1922; they had three children. After their wedding, the couple immediately left for Europe; they visited Berlin for five months and made short stops in Vienna and Paris. The European trip was followed by two longer visits to the United States (1923–1924 and 1926–1928). Chávez lived in New York during the second visit and established what would become long-standing connections with composers, publishers, and performers, including Aaron Copland, Henry Cowell, and Edgard Varèse. Varèse, in particular, helped involve him in the International Composers' Guild and later in the Pan American Association of Composers, organizations that sponsored performances of works by living composers. Chávez gained further prominence at home by writing a regular series of articles on contemporary music and art for the Mexico City newspaper *El universal*, beginning in 1924 and continuing during his travels.

In the summer of 1928 Chávez accepted the directorship of the Mexico Symphony Orchestra, the first permanent professional symphony orchestra in Mexico. Under his direction for the next twenty years, the orchestra became known for its promotion of new works by Mexican and internationally recognized composers. Chávez held the equally important directorship of the National Conservatory of Music in Mexico City from December 1928 until March 1933, and again for the 1934 season. The Chávez family lived in Mexico City until 1933, when they moved permanently to suburban Lomas de Chapultepec. Chávez also served as chief of the Department of Fine Arts in the Mexican Secretariat of Education from March 1933 to May 1934 but resigned because of political changes.

Chávez founded the National Institute of Fine Arts at the request of the president of Mexico in 1947 and served as its director until 1952. He helped revise the National Conservatory music curriculum to incorporate twelve-tone technique and new scales, and with the support of the conservatory and the Mexico Symphony he strove to establish significant musical performance and study in rural areas. He also founded advanced academies for research of music history and bibliography, new music, and folk and popular music. Chávez's versatility, organizational skills, and multidimensional musical skills allowed him to become a driving force in the growth of Mexican music in the second quarter of the twentieth century. For his diverse contributions Chávez received many formal honors from Mexico, the United States, and other countries, including the Mexican National Prize of Arts and Sciences, honorary memberships in the American Academy of Arts and Sciences and the National Institute of Arts and Letters, the French Légion d'honneur, the Star of Italian Solidarity, the Swedish Order of the Pole Star, and the Belgian Order of the Crown.

Chávez's works reveal the influences of Romanticism, particularly the music of Robert Schumann, Mexican folk music, and pre-Hispanic Aztec myth and ritual. Notable Aztec-influenced works include the ballet *Los cuatro soles* (1925) and *Xochipili* (1940) for winds and percussion. His scoring for the latter includes traditional Indian drums, bone and wooden rasps, and trombone to imitate the ancient shell trumpet. Chávez quotes popular Mexican dances in *Caballos de vapor* (*Horse-Power Ballet Suite*, 1926–1932). He draws upon Indian themes of the Yaqui, Seri, and Huichole tribes in *Sinfonía India* (Symphony no. 2, 1936). Politically motivated works from the mid-thirties include *Llamadas* (*Sinfonía proletaria*, 1934) for mixed chorus and orchestra and *Obertura republicana* (1935) for orchestra.

Chávez's seven symphonies were composed between 1933 and 1960. The first, the *Sinfonía de Antigona* (1933), is based on incidental music he composed for Jean Cocteau's modifications of Sophocles. From the Third Symphony (1951–1954) on, the symphonies lack programmatic connections (though the Fourth Symphony [1953] is subtitled "Romantic"). Chávez's popular *Toccata* (1942) for percussion is scored for Indian drums and Latin percussion but does not otherwise have a particularly Mexican flavor. His four *Soli* (1933–1966) feature wind soloists with a variety of supporting ensembles and embody a fresh personal idiom of continuous variation that avoids conventional methods of repetition. Chávez died in the Coyoacan suburb of Mexico City.

Chávez's many strengths as a composer include his versatility with small and large musical media, his rhythmic vitality and contrapuntal flair, his sparkling orchestrations, and his unique angular melodic style. These justify his place as one of the foremost Latin-American composers of the twentieth century.

• Some of Chávez's personal papers are in the Mexican National Archive; manuscripts can be found at the Performing Arts Library at Lincoln Center and in the Library of Congress. Important large-scale compositions by Chávez not mentioned in the text include *Antígona* (incidental music for Cocteau's setting of Sophocles's play, 1932), which inspired *Sinfonía de Antigona* (Symphony no. 1, 1933); Piano Concerto (1938–1940); Concerto for Four Horns and Orchestra (1938; rev. 1964); *La hija de Cólquide* (1943), a ballet on the Greek story of Medea (for Martha Graham); Violin Concerto (1948–1950); *The Visitors* (an opera in three acts, libretto by Chester Kallman, 1953); *Elatio* for orchestra (1967); *Discovery* for orchestra (1969); *Clio*, a symphonic ode (1969); *El sol* for mixed chorus and orchestra or band (corrido mexicano, 1934); and *Prometheus Bound* (cantata on English translation of Aeschylus for vocal soloists, mixed chorus, and orchestra, 1956). Among his chamber ensemble works are *Sextet* (1919); Sonatina for violin and piano (1924); Sonatina for cello and piano (1924); *Energía* for mixed ensemble of nine instruments (1925); Sonata for Four Horns (1929–1930); *Three Spirals* for violin and piano (1934); four string quartets (1919–1944); and *Tambuco* for six pieces of percussion (1964). Notable solo works include six piano sonatas (1917–1961); *Three Pieces* for guitar (1923); Sonatina for piano (1924); *Foxtrot* for piano (1925); *10 Preludes* for piano (1937); *Upingos* for solo oboe (1957); *Invencion* for piano (1958); and *Mañanas mexicanas* for piano (1967). Chávez's two books were sparked by trips to the United States. *Toward a New Music: Music and Electricity* (1937), was the outcome of a 1932 research visit. Chávez held the Charles Eliot Norton Chair of Poetics at Harvard in 1958–1959 and he published some of his lectures in *Musical Thought* (1961), his most important literary creation. Articles by Chávez include "The Two Persons," *Musical Quarterly* 15 (1929): 153–59; "The Function of the Concert," *Modern Music* 15 (Jan–Feb 1938): 71–75; and "The Music of Mexico" (1933), published in *American Composers on American Music*, ed. Henry Cowell (1962). The major biography is Roberto García Morillo, *Carlos Chávez: Vida y Obra* (1960). Roberto Halffter, *Carlos Chávez: Catalogo Completo de sus Obras* (1971), is a complete listing of his works to 1969, and Robert L. Parker, *Carlos Chávez, Mexico's Modern Day Orpheus* (1983), contains a chronology, biography, discussion of fifty works, bibliography, catalog of works, and discography. See also Paul Rosenfeld, "Carlos Chávez," *Modern Music* 9 (1932): 153–59; Herbert Weinstock, "Carlos Chávez," *Musical Quarterly* 22 (1936): 435–45; Nicholas Slonimsky, *Music of Latin America* (1945); Henry Cowell, "Chávez," in *The Book of Modern Composers*, 2d ed., ed. David Ewen (1950); and Aaron Copland, "Composers from Mexico," in his *The New Music: 1900–1960* (1968). An obituary is in the *New York Times*, 4 Aug. 1978.

ROBERT ROLLIN

CHÁVEZ, César Estrada (31 Mar. 1927–23 Apr. 1993), labor leader and social activist, was born in North Gila Valley, near Yuma, Arizona, the son of Librado Chávez and Juana Estrada. In 1888 two-year-old Librado, his siblings, and his mother immigrated to the Arizona territory to join his father, who had fled the harshness of life at Hacienda del Carmen in Porfirian, Mexico. Juana Estrada, also a native of Chihuahua, married Librado in 1924, and soon after the couple purchased a small grocery/garage/pool hall not far from his parents' 160-acre ranch and raised six children. After losing their property during the depression, the family soon joined the migrant harvest circuit.

Dramatic changes in the family's social and economic position from his youth in predepression Arizona to the migrant worker experience in California of the late 1930s were seared into César Chávez's consciousness. Regular attendance at Laguna School outside Yuma, mixed with farm chores shared with siblings, was replaced by half-days and repeated absences in some thirty schools in California's fertile valleys. The rhythm of migrant life determined the family's residences and access to education.

Most winters were spent in the Imperial Valley just over the California-Arizona border, bunching carrots and picking mustard greens and peas. After that there was work in cabbage, lettuce, and broccoli, followed by cantaloupes and watermelons in spring. In late May the Chávez family traveled to Oxnard for beans, to Beaumont for cherries, or to Moorepark and San Jose for apricots. During early summer they turned their hands to picking lima beans, corn, and chili peppers or to topping sugar beets in the Sacramento Valley. In August, grapes, prunes, cucumbers, and tomatoes needed tending in the Fresno area. From October through Christmas the cotton harvest occupied them in the San Joaquin Valley. The annual routine began anew with their return to their Brawley base in the Imperial Valley. His mother's Mexican Catholicism sustained the family during difficult times of little or no work and impelled them to share with others in times of good harvest. Faced with his elderly parents' decline and his father's injury in an auto accident, Chávez ended his formal education with graduation from eighth grade at age fifteen in 1942. Not long after, he joined the U.S. Navy for a two-year stint, mustering out soon after the war ended.

Like many returning Mexican-American veterans, Chávez married. In 1948 he wed Brawley-born Helen Fabela, whose farm worker family had settled in Delano, California. Reflecting the high postwar birth rate, the couple had eight children between 1949 and 1959. With a growing family to support, Chávez returned to the migrant life, traveling up and down the state with his parents, his young bride, and their children. The Chávezes might have continued with this annual migration had it not been for another postwar trend among the newly politicized ethnic and racial communities during the 1950s: founding and joining organizations dedicated to challenging injustice and prejudice exacerbated by wartime social tensions. Groups sprang up throughout the southwestern and midwestern cities with high concentrations of Mexican-heritage populations.

In California one of the many associations that responded to the renewed interest in neighborhood activism and political and civil rights was the Community Service Organization (CSO). Established in Los Angeles in 1947 with the combined financial support and backing of the Chicago-based Industrial Areas Foundation, a project of social activist Saul Alinsky, and the Civic Unity League, founded by Ignacio Lopez, outspoken editor of the southern California weekly *El Espectador*, the CSO backed the candidacy of Edward Roybal for the Los Angeles city council. The group devoted its efforts to voter registration campaigns, citizenship drives, educational improvements, better municipal services, and curbing police brutality.

With its successes in Los Angeles, the CSO looked to other parts of California and Arizona to establish new chapters and build membership. Organizing campaigns were launched in urban centers and agricultural towns such as San Jose and Stockton. In San Jose, CSO organizer Fred Ross recruited an initially reluctant César Chávez, who was living with his family in the Mexican-American barrio Sal Si Puedes ("Get out if you can"). Beginning as a volunteer and then as a paid organizer, Chávez eventually rose to director of the group in 1958. Helen Chávez frequently moved her family to central valley towns he targeted for membership drives and sent out postcard reminders of meetings. From these experiences Chávez learned organizing skills and established networks with other Mexican-American community activists, such as Dolores Huerta and Gilbert Padilla.

In the late 1950s and early 1960s Chávez turned his attention from voter registration campaigns and urban issues to the plight of the men, women, and children who labored in the fields. When the CSO policy board rejected his proposal for organizing agricultural workers, he resigned from the organization in 1962.

With Dolores Huerta and other CSO contacts, Chávez formed the Farm Workers Association the same year. For several years the two recruited members. Huerta based her operation in Stockton, where she received valuable help from her mother and relatives. Chávez centered his efforts in Delano, aided by his brother Richard and supported by his wife, Helen, who worked in the fields and raised their family.

In 1965 the Agricultural Workers Organizing Committee (AWOC), a largely Filipino union led by Larry Itliong and financed by the American Federation of Labor–Congress of Industrial Organizations, approached Chávez and Huerta to honor their strike against Delano grape growers. The membership of the renamed National Farm Workers Association (NFWA) voted to respect the walkout, thus inaugurating "la huelga," the well-known Delano grape strike.

From 1965 to 1970 the United Farm Workers Organizing Committee, or UFWOC (as the merged AWOC and NFWA became known in 1966), battled the California wine grape and, later, table grape producers. Frustrated with the futility of picketing miles of fields and facing the local power of corporate agriculture, the UFWOC resorted to civil rights era tactics of massive protest marches, civil disobedience, boycotts, and hunger strikes by Chávez, sustained by a philosophy of nonviolence borrowed from Martin Luther King, Jr., and Mahatma Gandhi. Fitting this civil rights activism with appeals to unity based on Mexican Catholicism, liberation theology, and a sense of cultural pride, Chávez won contracts with wine growers vulnerable because of highly visible labels. The UFWOC then trained its resources against table grape growers.

Under the charismatic leadership of Chávez, striking farm worker families united with diverse groups of community activists, labor unions, Mexican-American organizations, student demonstrators, religious supporters, consumer groups, average housewives, antiwar protesters, sympathetic politicians, and African-American allies to build an international boycott to force concessions from agribusiness. After five years Chávez's farm workers union finally negotiated the historic grape contracts with a majority of California grape producers in Delano in 1970.

The years from 1970 to 1975 were difficult for Chávez and the United Farm Workers (UFW), as the union was renamed in 1973. In the same year of its triumphs in the grape vineyards, it confronted a lettuce strike in the Salinas area and rival Teamster contracts with vegetable producers. In addition, complicated three-year contract renewals with grape growers loomed on the horizon. Faced with immense resistance from corporate agriculture, Chávez reinforced the boycott, undertook national speaking tours, and organized major protests and picketing across the country. In California, violence broke out. Kern County jails were filled because of massive arrests in 1973. In addition to labor troubles with Gallo wines, the union became involved with another protracted boycott of lettuce, grapes, wines, and other products.

Buoyed by the election in 1974 of union supporter Governor Jerry Brown, Chávez and his political allies in the Democratic party turned to Sacramento, seeking a solution to the constant turmoil in the fields. This coalition devised a legislative compromise between corporate agriculture and the union: the Agricultural Labor Relations Act established the Agricultural Labor Relations Board (ALRB). For the first time in California's history, farm workers engaged in government-supervised collective bargaining.

With the ALRB in place in 1975, Chávez's farm workers seemed on the verge of embarking on a new era of agricultural labor relations. The UFW did, in fact, win the majority of elections. But strife in the fields was not over, as Teamster organizers mounted campaigns and growers mobilized their political power in Sacramento to end funding for the ALRB. Proposition 14, backed by Chávez and the UFW, to make the ALRB a permanent part of the California constitution, failed in 1976. The 1980 victory of pro-agribusiness former California governor Ronald Reagan over presidential incumbent Democrat Jimmy Carter indicated a national shift toward the right and away from labor issues. The election of Republican governor George Deukmejian, an ally of agribusiness, confirmed a change in political direction in California. In addition, the UFW encountered internal dissent against the authoritarian leadership of Chávez. Disagreements resulted in the departure of key longtime members of the leadership team. Union membership, which had peaked in the 1970s at 100,000, began to drift downward.

Chávez and the farm workers fought back in the 1980s with new tactics. Experimenting with technological approaches to political organizing, the UFW invested in direct mail and computer-generated mailing lists. Criticism that Chávez was departing from his earlier vision and abandoning field organizing mounted. The decline in UFW activity, which also characterized the labor movement in general during the Reagan era, caused observers to conclude that the farm workers' cause had lost its power and that its leader had lost his moral authority.

César Chávez died in his sleep in San Luis, Arizona, not far from his birthplace, where he had gone to testify in a legal suit against growers. Malnutrition as a youngster, years of debilitating fasts, and the heavy burden of leadership had exacted their toll on the modest and dignified Chávez. After years of decline, the influence of the leader seemed to rise again as a great outpouring of grief over his unexpected passing overtook farm workers and the many middle-class supporters who had participated in or honored union boycotts. A funeral mass attended by mourners estimated at 50,000 and witnessed by millions more on major national and international broadcasting networks seemed to breathe new life into the farm workers' cause.

In his sixty-six years César Chávez succeeded on many levels. His greatest concern was improving the conditions of men, women, and children who worked in the fields—a life he had shared. Whether or not one agreed with his views, as a result of his commitment a nation became aware of the plight of Mexican-heritage field workers. Not only were wages raised but work conditions improved, including the provision of water and toilets in the fields, the regulation of pesticides, and the institution of grievance procedures. Workers under union contract received health and pension benefits. Chávez also inspired the Chicano civil rights movement of the 1960s. Politicized by *la causa*, the farm workers' cause, *el movimiento* mobilized farm worker families, middle-class Latino organizations, Mexican-American high school and college students, and activist Chicanas to demand their rights and embrace a new sense of cultural pride. Through his message of nonviolence, fairness, and respect, Chávez also reached beyond the Mexican-American community, the second largest minority in the United States, to involve middle-class Anglos and other races in a cross-class and cross-race alliance for social justice. Recognizing the significance of Chávez as a leader of the Mexican-American community and as a national advocate for peaceful social change, President William Clinton presented the nation's highest civilian honor, the Medal of Freedom, posthumously to his widow, Helen Chávez, in 1994.

• Chávez's papers are deposited at the Archives of Labor and Urban Affairs, Wayne State University, Detroit, Mich. Chávez did not publish a memoir; however, an oral history with him and other union activists forms the basis of Jacques Levy, *César Chávez: Autobiography of La Causa* (1975). Other contemporary works on Chávez during the years his movement was getting started include John Gregory Dunne, *Delano: The Story of the California Grape Strike* (1966); Peter Matthiessen, *Sal Si Puedes: César Chávez and the New American Revolution* (1969); Ronald B. Taylor, *Chávez and the Farm Workers* (1975); and Joan London and Henry Anderson, *So Shall Ye Reap* (1970). Academic literature on Chávez and the farm workers did not appear until the 1980s. Linda C. Majka and Theo J. Majka, *Farm Workers, Agribusiness, and the State* (1982), is an important early effort. See also J. Craig Jenkins, *The Politics of Insurgency: The Farm Worker Movement in the 1960s* (1985). With the opening of the UFW archives to the public in the mid-1980s, more scholarly works are in the offing. See Margaret Eleanor Rose, "Women in the United Farm Workers: A Study of Chicana and Mexicana Participation in a Labor Union, 1950 to 1980" (Ph.D. diss., UCLA, 1988) and "Gender and Civic Activism in Mexican American Barrios in California: The Community Service Organization, 1947–1962," in *Not June Cleaver: Women and Gender in Postwar America, 1945–1960*, ed. Joanne Meyerowitz (1994). Obituaries are in the *New York Times* and the *Los Angeles Times*, 24 Apr. 1993.

MARGARET ROSE

CHAVEZ, Dennis (8 Apr. 1888–18 Nov. 1962), U.S. senator, was born Dionisio Chavez in Los Chavez, New Mexico, the son of David Chavez, a farmer and justice of the peace, and Paz Sanchez. When Dennis was seven the family moved to Albuquerque, New Mexico, in search of employment and educational opportunities. Economic hardship forced young Dennis to discontinue his schooling in 1901. In the following years he helped support his family by taking a job delivering groceries.

Chavez began working for the Albuquerque Engineering Department in 1906. His interest in New Mexico Democratic politics was apparent when in 1908, at the age of twenty, he gave his first political speech for Democratic congressional candidate Octaviano Larrazolo. Two years later Chavez became actively involved in the campaign of gubernatorial candidate William McDonald. McDonald won the 1911 election, and just days after the victory, Chavez married Imelda Espinosa. The couple had three children.

Chavez decided to enter political life for himself, and in 1916 he unsuccessfully ran for the clerkship of Bernalillo County. In return for his campaign assistance, Senator Andrieus A. Jones in 1917 rewarded Chavez with a Senate clerkship and an opportunity to attend Georgetown University Law School. Chavez took advantage of the opportunity and received his law degree in June 1920. He then returned to Albuquerque to establish a criminal law practice. As a local attorney, Chavez continued to be active in state Democratic politics. He won election to the New Mexico House of Representatives in 1922 and the U.S. House of Representatives in 1930, receiving much of his support from the large Hispanic electorate of that state.

During his two-term tenure in the House of Representatives, Chavez introduced the Pueblo Lands Bill, which created a commission to sort out non-Indian claims to Pueblo Indian lands in New Mexico. He also sponsored legislation for public land grants for educational facilities in New Mexico. After Franklin Roosevelt's inauguration, Chavez became an ardent New Dealer and a key sponsor of the Farm Credit Administration.

Chavez made his bid for a U.S. Senate seat in 1934, challenging incumbent senator Bronson M. Cutting. Chavez lost the election, which was marred by charges of fraud. He challenged the results, and Cutting, returning to Washington, D.C., after a trip to New Mexico in relation to the allegations, died when his airplane crashed. Governor Clyde Tingley appointed Chavez to replace the late senator, and voters later confirmed the appointment in November 1936. Chavez spent the remainder of his career in the Senate, facing a close contest for reelection only once, in 1952.

In the Senate, Chavez served on a number of important committees, including the powerful Appropriations Committee and its Defense Subcommittee, Education and Labor, Indian Affairs, Irrigation and Reclamation, Territories and Insular Affairs, and Public Works. In the first year after his election, he supported President Roosevelt's plan to pack the U.S. Supreme Court with justices sympathetic to the New Deal. Chavez also became involved in a battle against Commissioner of Indian Affairs John Collier over the commissioner's plan to reduce livestock on the Navajo Indian reservation. Chavez, who believed strongly in assimilation, also rejected Collier's intention of reinforcing a separate identity for Native Americans.

In overseas relations, Chavez was a bit hesitant in accepting a broader U.S. role in the growing European conflict. He first voted against the 1941 Lend-Lease Act but for the measure on a second vote. He also voted against extending the length of service of reservists and the arming of merchant ships. However, he cosponsored the Chavez-McAdoo Bill, creating a radio station to broadcast anti-Fascist and anti-Nazi propaganda to Latin America. Because of his interest in Puerto Rican affairs, Chavez became known as "Puerto Rico's Senator." In 1942 he gained approval of an investigation into the situation in Puerto Rico, which found that unemployment and food shortages on the island were caused by the war and overpopulation. Chavez recommended continuing Works Progress Administration projects on the island and suggested that English be taught in the schools as the primary language, again illustrating his belief in integration and assimilation.

Chavez received widespread attention in 1944, when he introduced a bill to create a permanent and more powerful Fair Employment Practices Commission. The commission had earlier been established on a temporary basis to encourage nondiscriminatory hiring practices, but its jurisdiction had been limited to the federal government and defense industries. Unfortunately for Chavez, a bloc of southern senators eventually succeeded in filibustering the bill after a four-year struggle. Although he failed to pass the bill, Chavez succeeded in inspiring like-minded politicians and in laying groundwork for the future civil rights legislation of the 1960s. He was also highly rated by organized labor.

Chavez found the 1950s to be difficult years. He decried the McCarthy era as "a period when we quietly shackled men's minds." As chair of the Defense Appropriations Subcommittee, Chavez opposed the Dwight D. Eisenhower administration's reduced defense budgets. He supported the 1957 Civil Rights Act and helped pass a 1959 public housing bill over a presidential veto.

When Chavez died in Washington, D.C., Vice President Lyndon Johnson remembered him as a man "who recognized that there must be champions for the least among us." During his long political career Chavez succeeded in obtaining extensive funds for his state through his position on the Appropriations Committee and as chair of the Subcommittee on Defense Appropriations. He secured funding for the establishment of defense and research facilities in New Mexico, such as Holloman Airforce Base and the White Sands Missile Range, that have continued to serve as cornerstones of the state's economy. For many years Chavez was the only Hispanic member of the Senate. He encouraged greater Hispanic involvement in politics, both indirectly as a role model for future leaders and directly through his numerous political protégés.

• Chavez's papers are collected at the University of New Mexico's Zimmerman Library in Albuquerque and include a short biographical profile. For a brief discussion of Chavez's early years and a comparison with the career of New Mexico senator Joseph M. Montoya, see Maurilio Vigil and Roy Lujan, "Parallels in the Career of Two Hispanic U.S. Senators," *Journal of Ethnic Studies* 13 (Winter 1986): 1–20. A helpful and fairly lengthy obituary is in the *New York Times*, 19 Nov. 1962.

SCOTT C. ZEMAN

CHAVIS, John (1763–13 June 1838), Presbyterian minister and teacher, was born in Granville County, North Carolina; the names of his parents are unknown. He grew up as a free black near Mecklenberg, Virginia. By his own account, Chavis was born free and was a revolutionary war army veteran. Details of his military service and the events of his life immediately following the war are not known, but he began his studies for the Presbyterian ministry in 1792 at the age of twenty-nine. According to an apocryphal account, one planter had a wager with another that it was impossible to educate a black man. In order to settle their dispute, they sent Chavis to the College of New Jersey (now Princeton University). More than likely, Chavis's religious fervor and potential for scholarship attracted the attention of Presbyterian leaders in Virginia, who believed a black clergyman might do a better job of evangelizing slaves and free blacks than white ministers.

During his three years at the College of New Jersey, Chavis studied under the private tutelage of the college president, John Witherspoon, who often instructed one or two black students and several Native Americans as well. Chavis's studies in New Jersey ended when Witherspoon died in 1794. The next year he resumed studies at Liberty Hall Academy (now Washington & Lee University) in Lexington, Virginia, also a Presbyterian school. Chavis completed his studies there in 1799, and when it licensed him to preach in early 1800, the Lexington Presbytery expressed hopes that he would serve the blacks of the community.

After leaving the Lexington Presbytery in 1801 Chavis served the Hanover, Virginia, Presbytery before going to work under the supervision of the Synod of Virginia in 1804. Ultimately, he also preached in Maryland and North Carolina. At the beginning of each new assignment, Presbyterian leaders admonished Chavis to focus his efforts on the evangelization of slaves and free blacks, but his preaching attracted large numbers of whites and hardly any blacks. In 1883 one white North Carolinian remembered Chavis as a "venerable old Negro preacher," who was "respected as a man . . . familiar with the proprieties of social life, yet modest and unassuming, and sober in language and customs." Southern white admirers seemed to look beyond his race, while slaves and free blacks were unable to identify with one of their own who sounded and behaved like a white man.

By 1807 Chavis had opened a small school and devoted almost all of his attention to that endeavor. During the school's first year of operation he taught both white and black children together, but some white parents objected. The next year he advertised daytime classes for white students and evening classes for blacks. At different times, Chavis operated his school in Chatham, Wake, Orange, and Granville counties of North Carolina, and it attracted prominent white students, including the sons of the state's chief justice Leonard Henderson; James Horner, who later founded the Horner School in Oxford, North Carolina; Charles Manly, who later served as the state's governor; Willie P. Mangum, a prominent Whig senator; and Abram Rencher, who became governor of New Mexico.

Chavis charged low tuition rates, which kept his school full while providing ample money for his own support and that of his wife. By March 1828 he was able to boast that the enrollment had reached sixteen. The small, orderly school ran for about thirty years before political developments forced it to close. The 1831 insurrection of Nat Turner created a climate of fear and distrust among white southerners that resulted in severe restrictions on the black population. The North Carolina legislature passed a law that prevented blacks from preaching or teaching, thus creating economic hardships for Chavis.

By 1832 the 69-year-old Chavis turned to the Orange, North Carolina, Presbytery for support. After careful study, the Presbytery resolved to take up a collection for his support. The sums forwarded to Chavis were never sufficient, and there is evidence that he found his situation extremely embarrassing. In 1833 he hoped to earn money for himself by publishing an essay entitled "The Extent of the Atonement," but he needed the Presbytery to pay publication costs. Many other religious leaders had already written on the subject, and the Presbytery decided that such an essay would not be interesting enough to sell. Chavis continued to depend on them for charity throughout the remainder of his life. From October 1834 to April 1835 the Presbytery expended $81.95 for his support, but the sum was not always as generous. In the fall of 1835, when the Orange Presbytery divided, the new Roanoke Presbytery assumed Chavis's support. In 1837 it resolved to pay him $50 annually.

John Chavis retained a close personal relationship with his former student, Senator Willie P. Mangum, and advised him to reject the demands of the abolitionists during the mid-1830s. His position on slavery was cautious because he feared for the plight of masses of black people who would face homelessness and uncertain futures. Chavis did not want them to be more miserable than they already were. His position seems startling, but no one was anymore aware of the difficulties of living free than this impoverished man, who constantly depended on the charity of whites for support.

John Chavis died in North Carolina sometime between the April and October 1838 meetings of the Presbytery. At the October meeting, they resolved to continue support for his widow.

• The Papers of Willie P. Mangum, in the Manuscript Collection of the University of North Carolina Library, contains letters that Chavis wrote to Mangum. For additional information on the life and career of Chavis, see Sidney Kaplan and Emma Nogrady Kaplan, *The Black Presence in the Era of Revolution*, rev. ed. (1989); Ira Berlin, *Slaves Without Masters: The Free Negro in the Antebellum South* (1974); Benjamin Quarles, *The Negro in the American Revolution* (1961); John Hope Franklin, *The Free Negro in North Carolina, 1790–1860* (1943); Benjamin Brawley, *Negro Builders and Heroes* (1937); G. C. Shaw, *John Chavis, 1763–1838* (1931); and Carter G. Woodson, *Negro Makers of History* (1928).

Important articles include Gossie Harold Hudson, "John Chavis, 1763–1838: A Social-Psychological Study," *Journal of Negro History* 64 (Spring 1979): 142–54; Margaret Burr Des Champs, "John Chavis as a Preacher to Whites," *North Carolina Historical Review* 32 (Apr. 1955): 165–72; W. Sherman Savage, "The Influence of John Chavis and Lunsford Lane on the History of North Carolina, *Journal of Negro History* 25 (Jan. 1940): 14–24; Edgar W. Knight, "Notes on John Chavis," *North Carolina Historical Review* 7 (July 1930): 326–45; and Stephen Weeks, "John Chavis: Antebellum Negro Preacher and Teacher," *Southern Workman* (Feb. 1914): 101–06.

THEODORE C. DELANEY

CHAYEFSKY, Paddy (29 Jan. 1923–1 Aug. 1981), writer for stage, screen, and television, was born Sidney Chayefsky in the Bronx, New York, the son of Harry Chayefsky, at the time an executive with a dairy, and Gussie Stuchevsky. After school at DeWitt Clinton High School and City College of New York, where he graduated in 1943, Chayefsky was drafted into the army and shipped to Germany. A notoriously sloppy and lazy soldier, Chayefsky earned his nickname, Paddy, when he tried to get out of kitchen duty to attend Catholic mass. After he was injured by a land mine he was shipped to a London hospital, where he and a composer friend wrote a musical, *No T.O. for Love* (1945), which was produced successfully in London and Paris by the Special Services. The author and director Garson Kanin saw the show and had Chayefsky assigned to work with him on a documentary, *The True Glory* (1945). After the war, Chayefsky returned to the United States and tried to make a living as a playwright while supporting himself by working in his uncle's printing shop and through playwriting grants, some small acting parts, magazine fiction, and radio scripts. In one of these lean years, 1949, Chayefsky married Susan Sackler; they had one son. Undaunted by rejections of some stage and film scripts, Chayefsky finally carved his niche as a television writer, first by writing for two weekly series, "Danger" and "Manhunt" (both 1952). His series work attracted the attention of David Susskind, the producer of the "Philco Television Playhouse" (1953–1955), an hour-long Sunday night drama series. Chayefsky wrote eleven dramas for the series, only one of which was an adaptation.

Unlike other television writers, many of whom were more interested in quantity than quality, Chayefsky was a perfectionist who insisted on control of his material, participation in rehearsals, and, eventually, producing his own shows. While this attitude (more common in writers for the stage than in those for film or television, where the writer is hardly at the top of the pecking order) caused friction, it also gave Chayefsky a name recognition and prestige unusual for television and screen writers.

Chayefsky's teleplays are the dramatic equivalent of the short story. Chayefsky understood well the limitations of his medium. He had an excellent ear for the language of simple New York working-class men and women. He was interested in the lives of people who saw themselves as ordinary. *Marty* (1953), perhaps his greatest success, dramatizes the falling in love and blossoming of a homely Bronx butcher who has hitherto lived with his mother and spent Saturday nights with his male buddies.

Chayefsky was also able to adapt his scripts so that they could be successful in three media. The teleplays *Marty* (1954) and *Bachelor Party* (1957) became successful films. *Marty* won the 1955 Academy Award for Best Picture. The teleplay *Middle of the Night* (1956) was expanded into a successful Broadway play that was a triumph for its star, Edward G. Robinson. In 1959 it was made into a film with Fredric March and Kim Novak. From his television work Chayefsky was able to claim the prestige and fame hitherto accorded only stage writers like Tennessee Williams, Arthur Miller, and William Inge.

The film version of *Marty* came at a time when prestigious, black-and-white serious films, America's version of foreign "art" films, were one of the film industry's responses to the inroads made by television. There is some irony to the fact that people would leave their homes to see something they had already seen on television, but *Marty*'s success, and Hollywood's subsequent awarding the film its top prize, said much about the new, uneasy marriage between television and film. What was particularly interesting about Chayefsky's participation in the film version of *Marty* was the extraordinary amount of artistic control he was given. His contract stipulated that he would be present for rehearsals and shooting and that he would execute any needed rewrites. Hollywood seldom, if ever, gave its writers such authority. In 1957 Chayefsky began his own producing organization, Carnegie Productions, so that he could more fully control his material.

The 1950s were Chayefsky's salad days. His television plays and their film and stage adaptations brought him success and prestige. However, television moved to Hollywood, and the days of the live New York–based drama ended by the mid-1950s, and with them Chayefsky's primacy on the small screen. Except for a television adaptation of his stage play *Gideon* in 1971, Chayefsky's career as a television writer ended in 1955. Chayefsky was a creature of New York. Even his most successful films were set and filmed there. It is interesting to note that his first film not based on a teleplay was a dark vision of Hollywood stardom, *The Goddess* (1958).

In the late 1950s and 1960s, Chayefsky focused his energies on the stage. *The Tenth Man* (1959), a romantic, secularized updating of Ansky's Yiddish classic *The Dybbuk*, was a hit in the 1959–1960 Broadway season. The quasi-Shavian Biblical drama *Gideon* followed in 1961. His attempt at a Brechtian history play, *The Passion of Josef D.*, failed on Broadway in 1964. His last produced play, the satire *The Latent Heterosexual*, was a success in regional theaters and in England but was never produced in New York.

As Chayefsky had defined a kind of television drama that had its heyday in America in the 1950s, for the 1970s he created a hyperarticulate genre of dark satiric film in *The Hospital* (1971) and *Network* (1976). Both films are unusually wordy and articulate, but both were enormous successes. They show the cynicism and dehumanization of two major American institutions, the health industry and television. In a medium that was more and more youth oriented, *Network* and *The Hospital* center on the moral and spiritual awakening of disillusioned middle-aged men. Chayefsky took his name off the screen credits for the film adaptation of his novel *Altered States* (novel, 1978; film, 1979) when the director, Ken Russell, had actors spout Chayefsky's dialogue at breakneck speed and, often, minimum intelligibility. In a Chayefsky film, the words are everything. *Altered States* was Chayefsky's first foray into science fiction. It was also his only published novel.

Paddy Chayefsky's major work came in the early years of television when it was still New York–based and live serious drama was both popular and prestigious for the fledgling industry. In the mid-1950s Chayefsky proved himself the master of realistic drama for the stage as well as the small and large screen. By the time he died of cancer in New York, still lionized as the representative of a lost era of literacy and quality in writing for television and film, he was considered by many to be the best television writer and the best screenwriter of his, and perhaps any, generation.

• Chayefsky's work has been published in a three-volume collection: *Plays, Screenplays I*, and *Screenplays II* (1994). Two full-length studies of Chayefsky's life and work are John M. Clum, *Paddy Chayefsky* (1976), and Shaun Considine, *Mad As Hell: The Life and Work of Paddy Chayefsky* (1994). Both contain extensive bibliographies. Helpful comprehensive essays are Francie C. Brown, "Paddy Chayefsky," in *Dictionary of Literary Biography*, vol. 7: *Twentieth Century American Dramatists* (1981); and Sam Frank, "Paddy Chayefsky," in *Dictionary of Literary Biography*, vol. 44: *American Screenwriters* (1986). A comprehensive bibliography of writings on Chayefsky can be found in Philip C. Kolin, ed., *American Playwrights since 1945: A Guide to Scholarship, Criticism, and Performance* (1988). An eloquent obituary, written by Herbert Mitgang, was published in the *New York Times*, 5 Aug. 1981.

JOHN M. CLUM

CHEATHAM, Benjamin Franklin (20 Oct. 1820–4 Sept. 1886), soldier, was born at "Westover," a plantation near Nashville, Tennessee, the son of Leonard Pope Cheatham, a lawyer and planter, and Elizabeth Robertson. Frank, as he was called, was tutored at home, then attended a boys' school in Nashville, and later spent two years at a college in Kentucky (1837–1839). For about the next two years, Cheatham worked at a dry goods store in Philadelphia, Pennsylvania. He then returned to work on his family's plantation and to help his father in his job as postmaster at Nashville.

In the early 1840s Cheatham joined a local militia company and was made captain of it when the Mexican War started. Joining the First Tennessee Regiment, Cheatham's regiment fought in the battle of Monterrey, 21–23 September 1846, and he received a slight wound. The regiment later joined Winfield Scott's army for the Veracruz campaign then was discharged at the termination of its service in May and returned to Nashville. Cheatham raised the Third Tennessee Regiment and became its colonel. This unit reached Veracruz in November 1847, saw brief garrison duty at Mexico City, and was mustered out at Memphis on 24 July 1848.

Cheatham traveled to California after the war and from 1849 to 1853 operated a store and hotel in Stockton. He then resumed planting in Tennessee and was appointed a major general in the state militia in 1853, holding command of the Second Division when the Civil War began. Cheatham served as Democratic party candidate for mayor of Nashville in the fall of 1857 but lost the election. Between 1855 and 1859 he acted as a sales agent for a company that made farm implements. He also raised race horses and in 1860 became owner of the Nashville Race Track.

Governor Isham Harris appointed Cheatham a brigadier general in the Provisional Army of Tennessee on 9 May 1861, and Confederate president Jefferson Davis appointed him to the same rank on 9 July. In the latter month, Cheatham joined General Leonidas Polk (1806–1864) and assumed command of Polk's Second Division at Columbus, Kentucky. On 7 November 1861, at the battle of Belmont, Missouri, Cheatham led a bayonet charge that helped rout the Union force. He received promotion to the rank of major general on 10 March 1862.

Shortly before this promotion, Polk's troops evacuated Columbus and moved to join General Albert Sidney Johnston's army at Corinth, Mississippi. At the battle of Shiloh, Cheatham led one of his brigades in an attack on the Hornet's Nest on the morning of 6 April and lost three horses. He received a slight wound in the shoulder at an unknown point during the two-day battle. Cheatham's Tennesseans accompanied General Braxton Bragg's army on its invasion of Kentucky in the early fall of 1862. On 8 October, during the battle of Perryville, his division struck the left flank of the Union army and routed much of one corps.

Cheatham's division fought next in the battle of Stones River, Tennessee. Their attack against the Union right on 31 December 1862 was uncoordinated, most accounts stating that Cheatham was drunk and incapable of directing his division. His biographer cites conflicting reports on the degree of Cheatham's intoxication and concludes, "His troops were poorly served by their divisional commander for the early part of the battle and suffered needless casualties until Cheatham managed to rally them for a concerted movement" (Losson, p. 91). His relations with Bragg became strained after the battle, especially when the latter's official report criticized Cheatham for not attacking promptly.

At the battle of Chickamauga, Georgia, 19–20 September 1863, Cheatham performed well. His men repulsed enemy attacks on the first day of fighting and helped put pressure on the Union left flank the next day. Bragg reorganized the army in November and took away from Cheatham most of his Tennessee troops. The division fought in the battle of Lookout Mountain on 24 November, but Cheatham was absent on leave. He returned in time to participate in the battle of Missionary Ridge on 25 November, where the division held its position until ordered to retreat that night.

General Joseph E. Johnston replaced Bragg and reorganized the Army of Tennessee in early 1864, returning to Cheatham's division the Tennessee troops taken from him by Bragg. Cheatham's men were not heavily engaged in the Atlanta campaign until the battle of Kennesaw Mountain on 27 June, when they successfully repulsed several heavy assaults. The promotion of General John Bell Hood to replace Johnston on 18 July resulted in Cheatham receiving temporary command of Hood's corps. Cheatham performed poorly at the battle of Peachtree Creek on 20 July, but he led the corps again two days later in the battle of Atlanta. Replaced by General Stephen D. Lee on 27 July, Cheatham returned to his division. When General Alexander P. Stewart was wounded on 28 July, Cheatham took over Stewart's corps for several weeks. He was on sick leave and missed the battle of Jonesboro.

In late September, after General William J. Hardee's transfer from the army, Cheatham was promoted to command Hardee's corps, and he led his troops in the invasion of Tennessee in November. Again Cheatham was embroiled in controversy, when he allowed the Union army of General John M. Schofield to march past him at Spring Hill on the night of 29 November, although responsibility for this debacle belongs equally to Hood, Cheatham, and one of Cheatham's division commanders, General John Calvin Brown. Cheatham's corps suffered heavy casualties in the battle of Franklin the next day. The corps held the army's right flank at the battle of Nashville on 15 December, facing only diversionary attacks. The following day Cheatham shifted his men to the left flank, where they bore the brunt of the Union assault and were routed.

Cheatham took the remnants of his corps to join Joseph Johnston in North Carolina in January 1865. Delayed at Salisbury by problems with the railroad, Cheatham missed the battle of Bentonville. Johnston reorganized his army in April, and Cheatham took over a division under a new corps commanded by Hardee. Cheatham signed his parole on 1 May at Greensboro following the surrender of the army on 26 April.

After the surrender Cheatham returned to Nashville. He married Anna Bell Robertson in 1866 and moved to a farm in Coffee County that his in-laws had owned; the couple had five children. Cheatham ran unsuccessfully for the U.S. Congress in 1872. He served as superintendent of state prisons from 1875 to 1879. President Grover Cleveland appointed him postmaster at Nashville in October 1885. He died at his brother Felix's home in Nashville.

Cheatham was very popular with his men during the war because of the concern he showed for their needs and well-being. No one ever questioned his bravery or boldness in action, but his love of alcohol sometimes impaired his performance on the battlefield. He did well leading a brigade or a division but did not have the capacity for corps command.

• Cheatham's papers are in the Southern Historical Society Collection, University of North Carolina, Chapel Hill; the Archives of the University of the South, Sewanee, Tenn.; and the Tennessee State Library and Archives in Nashville. The only biography of Cheatham to date is Christopher Thomas Losson, *Tennessee's Forgotten Warriors: Frank Cheatham and His Confederate Division* (1989), which is a revision of Losson, "Command Disorder: Benjamin Franklin Cheatham and the Army of Tennessee, 1862–1865" (master's thesis, Univ. of Mississippi, 1978). Timothy D. Johnson, "Benjamin Franklin Cheatham: The Making of a Confederate General" (master's thesis, Univ. of Alabama, 1982), treats Cheatham's Civil War career. Eulogistic tributes by his contemporaries are James Davis Porter, "A Sketch of the Life and Services of Gen. B. F. Cheatham," *Southern Bivouac* 2 (1883–1884): 145–50, and "B. F. Cheatham, Major General C.S.A.: A Tribute to His Memory by Bishop C. T. Quintard," *Southern Historical Society Papers* 16 (1888): 349–54. The most extensive obituary is in the Nashville *Daily American*, 5–7 Sept. 1886.

ARTHUR W. BERGERON, JR.

CHEATHAM, Henry Plummer (27 Dec. 1857–29 Nov. 1935), congressman and public official, was born near Henderson, Granville (now Vance) County, North Carolina, the son of a house slave about whom little is known. He attended local public schools and worked on farms during the 1860s and 1870s before graduating with honors from Shaw University in 1882. He became principal of the Plymouth Normal School for Negroes, a state-supported institution, and held this position from 1882 until 1884. He returned to Henderson and, after the retirement of the white Republican incumbent, won election as Vance County registrar of deeds, serving in this capacity from 1885 to 1888. During this time he also studied law, though he never established a practice.

Cheatham's career in national politics began in 1888. Unable to agree on a single candidate, delegates to the Republican convention for the Second Congressional District, the so-called "Black Second," nominated both Cheatham and George A. Mebane, another African American, for the U.S. House of Representatives. After Mebane's subsequent withdrawal, Cheatham had the edge over his Democratic opponent, Furnifold M. Simmons, because the district's African Americans and Republicans still voted in great numbers. Cheatham enjoyed a reputation as being responsible and courteous, but during the campaign he warned black constituents that local Democrats wanted to reestablish slavery. He narrowly won the election with 16,704 votes to Simmons's 16,051.

Cheatham took his seat in the Fifty-first Congress, which was controlled by Republicans. A member of the Education Committee, he introduced a bill for federal aid to education that received a favorable report but never reached the floor for debate. Supporting the interests of Carolina tobacco farmers, he endorsed the protectionist McKinley Tariff of 1890 and served on a House-Senate conference committee considering the proposal. Cheatham also favored the Federal Elections Bill, introduced by Henry Cabot Lodge of Massachusetts, to safeguard the voting rights of African Americans, especially in southern states. Preferring personal contact in the committee room to delivering speeches, Cheatham did not speak in behalf of the measure on the floor but did address the House Republican caucus on the subject. The Lodge bill passed the House but died in the Senate.

As a first-term congressman desiring reelection, Cheatham took special interest in federal patronage in his district, securing more than eighty appointments for his constituents. These were chiefly postal jobs, but he also helped to fill internal revenue, customs, and judicial positions in eastern North Carolina and secured appointment of African Americans as census enumerators and clerks in the nation's capital. His hard work did not really pay off, however. Not all his appointees performed ably, and some were arrested for fraud and embezzlement. His parceling out of patronage alienated both whites, who complained of black domination, and certain African Americans, who believed he had not secured enough of the spoils for his own people.

By 1890 agricultural depression in the South had caused a decline in the proportion of black voters in Cheatham's district as African Americans sought opportunity elsewhere. It also increased demands from farmers for government aid. Accordingly Cheatham, addressing a primarily white audience in Wilson during the campaign, discussed neither the Federal Elections Bill nor the tariff but devoted himself mainly to depressed agricultural conditions. He also defended his patronage record in a manner calculated to avoid offending whites or exciting blacks, but at the same time he condemned steel magnate Andrew Carnegie for importing laborers while neglecting to hire African Americans. His successful appeal to white farmers helped to offset the black exodus from his district, allowing Cheatham, who had relocated to Littleton because of reapportionment, to defeat his last-minute Democratic challenger, James M. Mewborne, with 16,943 votes to 15,713.

Cheatham's victory in 1890, the year of a Democratic landslide in House contests, earned for him the distinction of being the only African American elected to the Fifty-second Congress. With Democrats in control, however, his influence diminished considerably. Nevertheless, Cheatham remained active. He persuaded a New Jersey Republican to propose an amendment to an appropriation bill to provide money for a black progress exhibit at the World's Columbian Exposition. Cheatham also introduced a bill, killed in committee, that proposed appropriating $100,000 "for the purpose of collecting, preparing, and publishing facts and statistics pertaining to the moral, industrial, and intellectual development and progress of the colored people of African descent residing in the United States." The fate of such endeavors led Cheatham to conclude that "whenever the colored people of this country ask for anything, something unfortunate intervenes to hinder their getting what they ask."

Cheatham won renomination by acclamation in 1892 and at that year's Republican National Convention seconded President Benjamin Harrison's renomination in a brief speech. But the congressman's political base had been weakened by the general assembly's revisions of the state election law, which reduced the African-American vote, and by the redrawing of political boundaries, which, in effect, destroyed the "Black Second," a citadel of Republican strength. As a result, Cheatham lost the race to Democrat Frederick A. Woodard, a Wilson lawyer and banker who drew the color line during the campaign and captured 13,925 votes to Cheatham's 11,812. Fraudulent election practices and the black discontent over patronage issues also hurt Cheatham, as did the presence of a Populist candidate who split the non-Democratic vote. The Raleigh *Signal*, a Republican newspaper, praised the defeated congressman as a "faithful public servant who has done all that he could for the whole state" and who "reflected great credit on his race, the Republican party and himself."

Cheatham tried for a political comeback in 1894. After a prolonged and bitter battle for the Republican congressional nomination, he lost the hotly contested general election to Woodard by a vote of 9,413 to 14,721. As before, a Populist took a portion of the non-Democratic vote. Cheatham sought the congressional nomination again in 1896 but lost to his more militant brother-in-law, George H. White, a lawyer and former state legislator, who defeated Woodard in the general election. Cheatham never again sought elective office but continued his political activity. President William McKinley in 1897 appointed him registrar of deeds for the District of Columbia, a position he held until 1901, when he returned to Littleton. There he farmed and helped found a local hospital.

In 1907 Cheatham relocated to Oxford, North Carolina, and became superintendent of the North Carolina Orphanage for Negroes, which he had been instrumental in establishing in 1882. He held this post for the next twenty-eight years. Cheatham transformed the orphanage by means of more effective administration and the construction of seven brick buildings with modern designs and facilities. He functioned as a benevolent father figure, disciplining the children and assigning each tasks to perform in the cottages and on the farm operated by the orphanage. "No success without labor" was the creed by which Cheatham managed his orphanage and training school.

Cheatham was married twice and had three children with Louise Cherry and three with Laura Joyner. He died in Oxford. Cheatham was one of North Carolina's most distinguished African-American citizens. An educated, discreet, and diplomatic man, he impressed even white Democrat Josephus Daniels, who remarked that he had regarded Cheatham highly as a man who had gained the confidence of both races.

• Cheatham left no personal papers. The Matt W. Ransom Papers, Cyrus Thompson Papers, and Marion Butler Papers in the Southern Historical Collection, University of North Carolina at Chapel Hill; and the Elias Carr Papers at East Carolina University in Greenville have some letters relating to Cheatham's career. His speeches and votes are in the *Congressional Record* (1889–1893). Some detailed information about Cheatham is in Frenise A. Logan, *The Negro in North Carolina, 1876–1894* (1964); Eric Anderson, *Race and Politics in North Carolina, 1872–1901: The Black Second* (1981); and *Contested Election Case of "Cheatham v. Woodard"* (1896). See also Maurine Christopher, *Black Americans in Congress* (1976); Samuel D. Smith, *The Negro in Congress, 1870–1901* (1940); and George W. Reid, "A Biography of George Henry White, 1852–1918" (Ph.D. diss., Howard Univ., 1974). An obituary is in the *Oxford Public Ledger*, 3 Dec. 1935.

LEONARD SCHLUP

CHECKLEY, John (1680–15 Feb. 1754), Anglican clergyman and pamphleteer, was born in Boston, Massachusetts, the son of English parents, whose names are not known. Educated at the Boston Latin School under the tutelage of Ezekiel Cheever, he later studied at Oxford, though he appears never to have matriculated; he did, however, learn Latin, Greek, and Hebrew. Evidently a person of some means, he traveled extensively throughout Europe, collecting paintings, books, and manuscripts. He remained in Europe for some fifteen years but returned to Boston by 1710. In 1713 he married Rebecca Miller, daughter of Samuel Miller, a prosperous innkeeper of Milton, Massachusetts. Two of their children survived to adulthood. Checkley opened in 1717 a small store in Boston, eventually named the "Crown and Blue-Gate," where he sold books, medicines, and other merchandise. He was a central figure among a group that included Thomas Walter, John Read, Mather Byles, and Joseph Green, and he became a layman at the Episcopalian King's Chapel.

Checkley was also very much involved in the founding of the *New-England Courant*. The founders included James Franklin; his younger brother and apprentice, Benjamin Franklin, also author of the "Silence Dogood" letters; George Steward; John Gibbons; the Reverend Henry Harris, an assistant rector at King's Chapel; and the young printer and contributor, Thomas Fleet. All were of British origin and educated men, some of Anglican background and persuasion, with awareness of literary trends in London, not to mention familiarity with political and religious issues. Another of this group was the physician James Douglass, whose criticism of inoculation to combat smallpox created a controversy in Boston as well as the occasion for the first appearance of the newspaper in August 1721.

Checkley authored the inaugural essay in the first number of *Courant*. His affiliation with the *Courant* proved, however, to be brief. In response to Checkley's opening criticism of the Matherite clergy, the Reverend Thomas Walter of Roxbury contributed a broadside, "The Little-Compton Scourge; or, The Anti-Courant," an attack on Checkley's views of predestination as well as a rejoinder to his criticism of the clergy. James Franklin, the printer and publisher, printed Walter's views in the second number of the *Courant*. Checkley's response, in the third number, was a vitriolic personal attack that induced Franklin to issue an apology and to say that he encouraged contributions only when they contained no "malicious reflections." Checkley never again contributed to the *Courant*.

Checkley knew the theological literature of the period, and he developed an unwavering belief in the Apostolic origin of the episcopacy. He was also a partisan of the interests of the Church of England in the North American colonies. His publication in Boston of the Reverend Charles Leslie's treatise, *The Religion of Jesus Christ the Only True Religion; or, A Short and Easie Method with the Deists . . .* (1719), attracted the attention of the Boston magistrates. One of his purposes in publishing this work appeared to be his hope of proving the existence of bishops in the days of the apostles. Checkley's unstated but clear purpose was to apply the analogy to contemporary New England by noting that Anglicans had bishops, whereas Congregationalists did not. That same year, Checkley published, but did not attach his name to, another volume, *Choice Dialogues between a Godly Minister and an Honest Clergyman Concerning Election and Predestination*, in which he assailed the foundations of the Congregational church. In December 1719 a law was passed empowering magistrates to tender oaths of allegiance to anyone suspected of disaffection to the king or government. Almost immediately Checkley was required to affirm the oaths, and in annoyance he refused to sign them. He refused a second time and was fined £6 and costs.

In 1722 he went to England for eight months, evidently in search of Holy Orders, but did not succeed, ironically but very possibly because of his refusal to sign the oaths in Boston. A few months later he published his *Modest Proof of the Order and Government Settled by Christ and His Apostles* (1723), which received immediate and wide attention for its argument on behalf of a diocesan episcopacy and stimulated a pamphlet war. The publication was followed soon after by *A Defence of . . . A Modest Proof*. Checkley also published *A Discourse Shewing Who is a True Pastor of the Church of Christ* in London in that same year, and he republished Leslie's *Short and Easy Method with the Deists*, to which he added "A Discourse Concerning Episcopacy in Defense of Christianity and the Church of England," arguing that the sacraments were invalid without an appropriately ordained bishop presiding in a diocese and that those who offered such sacraments without having been ordained by a bishop were guilty of sacrilege. Moreover, Checkley deftly asserted that episcopacy was a necessary link to royalty, thereby bringing politics into this volatile brew.

Having now attacked the ecclesiastical, political, and theological foundations of Congregationalism, Checkley found himself prosecuted by the Massachusetts General Court and fined £50 but only after a spirited defense by fellow Anglican John Read. This trial, however, was among the very last in New England to prevent publication of theological and ecclesiastical views by means of legal sanction. At about this same time, Checkley was also involved in the founding of the Boston Episcopal Charitable Society, which has had a long and distinguished record of social work in Boston. Checkley evidently founded a circulating library around that same time, but it was destroyed by fire in 1747. Checkley traveled once more to England, in 1727, in search of Holy Orders and once more was disappointed. He returned to Boston and resumed his bookselling and apothecary business, though he seems also to have branched out to real estate and the export of goods to London, while doubtless also importing goods for sale in his store. In 1728 he wrote to the bishop of London an account of the hardships suffered by Anglicans in Massachusetts, complaining especially of the unjust system of taxation that forced Episcopalians to support the Congregational order. In 1730 he published the argument that he had made at his trial for seditious libel some six years earlier. He also remained active in King's Chapel and led the opposition to the effort of the assistant minister, the Reverend Henry Harris, to become rector.

In 1738, on his third attempt, Checkley received Holy Orders and was posted by the Society for the Propagation of the Gospel to Providence, Rhode Island, where he became rector of King's Church. He served as minister there for more than ten years, performing his ministerial duties throughout the region, especially for Native Americans, with tireless energy. He died in Providence after having been incapacitated by illness for more than two years.

Checkley's importance as a partisan of the high church movement in colonial North America cannot be overestimated, nor can his role in checking Puritan hegemony and promoting the growth of other churches be overlooked.

• The principal source of information on Checkley remains Edmund F. Slafter, *John Checkley; or, The Evolution of Religious Tolerance in Massachusetts Bay* (2 vols., 1897), while Isaiah Thomas, *The History of Printing in America*, repr. ed. (1970), also contains useful information. A more recent publication that emphasizes the controversial thought and confrontational tactics, and no less Checkley's critically important role in the development of Anglicanism in colonial North America, is John Frederick Woolverton, *Colonial Anglicanism in North America* (1984), while Charles E. Clark, *The Public Prints: The Newspaper in Anglo-American Culture, 1665–1740* (1994), sheds light on Checkley's brief involvement in the founding of the *New-England Courant*.

WILLIAM L. JOYCE

CHEESEEKAU (1760?–1 Oct. 1792), Shawnee war chief of the Kispoko division, whose Anglicized name was Sting, was born possibly on the Tallapoosa River, Alabama, the son of Pukeshinwa, a Kispoko war chief, and his wife Methoataaskee. He was also known as Pepquannakek (Gunshot), Popoquan (Gun), and

Shawnee Warrior. About the time of his birth the family moved north from the Creek country to join other Shawnees on the Scioto River, in present-day Ohio, where the younger children, including the famous Tecumseh and Tenskwatawa, were probably born. After the death of Pukeshinwa at the battle of Point Pleasant (10 Oct. 1774), when the Shawnees under Cornstalk were defeated by Virginians, Cheeseekau increasingly shouldered the responsibility for his younger brothers and became a mentor of Tecumseh. Cheeseekau rose to prominence as a hunter and warrior during the revolutionary war, when the Shawnees joined the British-Indian alliance and tried to destroy the new American settlements in Kentucky. By the time warfare between Shawnees and the United States resumed in 1786, he was known as one of the tribe's most daring and militant warriors.

In the face of American expansion across the Ohio, many Shawnees were attracted by invitations from the Spanish government to quit the North and settle on their territory about Cape Girardeau in what is now Missouri. In 1788 Cheeseekau assembled a party to emigrate, reached Missouri the following year, but evidently found it unsuitable, probably because an American colony under George Morgan (1743–1810) was settling the same area offered the Indians. Cheeseekau led his party to join Dragging Canoe's Lower Cherokees (Chickamaugas) on the lower Tennessee River, settling at the town of Running Water on Lookout Mountain. The thirty or so Shawnee warriors under Cheeseekau assisted the Chickamaugas to resist the growth of American settlements on the Holston, French Broad, and Cumberland rivers; to impede traffic on the Tennessee River; and to solicit support from other Indian peoples and Spain. They earned a reputation for extreme anti-Americanism, and Cheeseekau himself became known to whites as "the Shawnee warrior."

On 22 March 1790 Cheeseekau led a joint Shawnee-Cherokee attack on Major John Doughty's detachment as it ascended the Tennessee on a peace mission to the southern tribes, defeating the Americans and driving them back downstream. He continued to oppose any negotiations with the United States, and one Cherokee leader, Fool Charles, who treated with the Americans was physically beaten by the Shawnees. Cheeseekau's activities reached a peak in 1792. On 26–27 June his men overran and burned Zeigler's Station, north of the Cumberland, in what was called "the boldest stroke ever made by Indians in this quarter." Probably encouraged by this victory, the Chickamaugas planned an all-out assault upon the frontiers and appealed for help both to Spain and to the Shawnees in the North, who were fomenting resistance to the United States in Ohio. It appears that Cheeseekau was initially selected to lead a Cherokee delegation to Mobile and Pensacola, in search of arms and ammunition from the Spaniards, but ultimately the Chickamauga war leader, John Watts, headed the mission.

Upon the return of Watts with encouraging word of Spanish support, the Chickamaugas held a council at Willstown, Alabama, at the beginning of September, and Cheeseekau was one of those who vehemently argued for an attack upon the American settlements. When the Indians agreed to the campaign, Cheeseekau led the Shawnee contingent in a Cherokee-Creek invasion of the Cumberland under the command of Watts. On 30 September the Indians approached Buchanan's Station, an outpost of Nashville, and Cheeseekau persuaded the Indians to attack it directly, at night, instead of waiting for the morning. The assault was unsuccessful, however, and Cheeseekau was fatally wounded, apparently in the first fire about midnight. He was carried off but died soon after in the presence of Tecumseh. The repulse at Buchanan's Station blunted the Indian offensive in Tennessee, and Tecumseh appears to have led most of his brother's party home to Ohio during the ensuing winter.

Cheeseekau's career symbolizes the growing intertribal solidarity among many Indians in the years following the American Revolution. His party among the Chickamaugas had a counterpart in those Cherokees who, at the same time, were domiciled with the Ohio Shawnees, and his activities illustrate the wider efforts of the Shawnees to develop a pantribal confederacy. The activities of Tecumseh were, to some extent, his legacy. Cheeseekau had at least one wife and at least one daughter. Americans spoke of his ferocity, but Stephen Ruddell, who lived with the Shawnees, said that he instilled into Tecumseh "correct, manly & honorable principles. . . . He taught him to look with contempt upon every thing that was mean."

• Among several primary sources the most important are the narrative of Stephen Ruddell, January 1822, Draper Manuscripts, State Historical Society of Wisconsin, Madison, series YY, vol. 2, pp. 120–32; *American State Papers, Indian Affairs*, vol. 1 (1832); and Colton Storm, ed., "Up the Tennessee in 1790," *East Tennessee Historical Society Publications* 17 (1945): 119–32.

The secondary material relating to Cheeseekau is incomplete and confused. Benjamin Drake, *Life of Tecumseh* (1841), fails to identify Cheeseekau with Shawnee Warrior. John P. Brown, *Old Frontiers* (1938), has both names but erroneously believed they referred to different individuals. Albert V. Goodpasture, "The Shawnees Warrior," *Tennessee Historical Magazine* 4 (1918): 177–84, failed to make the connection with Cheeseekau and inaccurately credited Shawnee Warrior with leading the Cherokee attack on Lieutenant William Snoddy's force on Caney Fork River, an incident he also misdated. Lyman C. Draper was the first historian to link Cheeseekau and Shawnee Warrior, but his work was unpublished, and the identification was printed by Glenn Tucker, *Tecumseh: Vision of Glory* (1956), who, however, added errors of his own. See also James P. Pate, "The Chickamauga" (Ph.D. diss., Mississippi State Univ., 1969).

JOHN SUGDEN

CHEEVER, George Barrell (17 Apr. 1807–1 Oct. 1890), clergyman and reformer, was born in Hallowell, Maine, the son of Nathaniel Cheever II, a printer and bookseller, and Charlotte Barrell. He was one of five children in a prosperous family. His father died when he was twelve, and he became extremely close to his mother, whose ardent Congregational faith significantly shaped his career. He entered Bowdoin College in 1821 and was a classmate of Franklin Pierce, Nathaniel Hawthorne, Henry W. Longfellow, and Calvin Stowe. He graduated Phi Beta Kappa, was an avid member of the "praying circle," and frowned upon the worldly and impious affairs of such classmates as Hawthorne, who belonged to the "Eat, Drink, and Be Merry Club."

Throughout college Cheever was torn between Unitarian and Congregational beliefs and considered abandoning the ministry to become a schoolteacher. However, owing largely to his mother's urging, he declined an appointment as the preceptor of Hallowell Academy to enroll at Andover Theological Seminary, which inculcated the orthodox views of Congregationalism. Initially Cheever was unhappy at Andover; he refused to sign the matriculation pledge that required all students to declare their "earnest" and "definite" intent to enter the "ministry of the gospel," and he remained skeptical about the doctrine of God as a tripartite Trinity. Unitarians, who emphasized the "oneness" of God rather than a distinct separation between the Father, Son, and Holy Spirit, were a source of considerable theological controversy, and Cheever contemplated matriculating to Harvard College, the center of Unitarian teaching. Nevertheless, he overcame his hesitations regarding Congregationalism and following a public confession of faith he graduated from Andover in 1830. He spent three years as a substitute minister and in 1833 was appointed the pastor of the Howard Street Congregational Church in Salem, Massachusetts. That same year, after grappling for so long with Unitarianism, he commenced a vigorous attack on it and never again strayed from Christian orthodoxy.

Cheever joined the temperance reform movement in 1833; two years later he attained national prominence with his enormously popular temperance tract, *Enquire at Amos Giles' Distillery*. The essay, cast in the form of a dream, was a thinly disguised portrayal of John Stone, a well-liked Unitarian deacon in Salem who owned a distillery. Cheever's neighbors were outraged by his slander: he received a public horsewhipping, was sued and convicted for libel, and was sentenced to thirty days in jail. He immediately became a cause célèbre among the nation's temperance reformers and abolitionists (who also opposed the use of alcohol) and a popular reform hero.

Cheever expanded his reform efforts in 1834 by joining the antislavery crusade; he became a member of the Salem Anti-Slavery Society and attacked the Congregational church for trying to exclude abolitionist ministers from the pulpit. But he kept his distance from such fervent abolitionists as William Lloyd Garrison and other radicals of the American Anti-Slavery Society who relentlessly attacked the sin of slavery and championed full equal rights for blacks. In 1836, with his health impaired from overwork, he resigned his pastorate, abandoned his reform efforts, and toured Europe, Asia, and Africa for three years.

In 1839 Cheever was appointed pastor of the Allen Street Presbyterian Church in New York City, and although he was well liked among his parishioners he considered the general state of religion in the city to be "altogether periodical." The "Spirit of God," he lamented, was too often hidden. He concluded that the cause of impiety stemmed primarily from the influx of Catholic immigrants and the rise of Catholicism, which he saw as an enemy of the Gospel and of the Protestant tenet of "justification by faith." He became a prominent spokesman for the burgeoning nativist movement, and in numerous speeches and sermons he denounced "Romanism" and "Popery" as anti-Christian and a form of "hierarchical despotism." His most popular lectures during the 1840s, however, were a series of picturesque commentaries on the life of John Bunyan, which he gave during the winter of 1843–1844. In 1845 he married Elizabeth Hoppin Wetmore, the daughter of a wealthy merchant; they had no children. The following year he assumed the pastorate of the Church of the Puritans in New York City, one of the country's wealthiest and most fashionable parishes. His denunciations against Catholicism, Sunday commerce, and hard liquor pleased his middle-class congregants, and his reform messages reached a much wider audience through his frequent contributions to the *Independent* and the *Evangelist*, two of the country's leading religious weeklies. By 1846 Cheever was one of the most popular and influential preachers in the country.

Cheever resumed his attack on slavery in 1850 following a fourteen-year hiatus. The numerous concessions to slaveholders that resulted in the Compromise of 1850 outraged his moral, political, and religious sensibilities. However, from 1850 to 1857 he considered himself a "respectable" antislavery advocate, meaning that he vigorously opposed the extension of slavery but remained largely silent over immediate and unqualified abolition. His position stemmed in part from his desire to avoid being viewed as a "fanatic" and ostracizing his congregation; but following the Dred Scott decision of 1857, in which the Supreme Court denied both the right of slaves to become citizens and the right of Congress to exclude the extension of slavery, Cheever emerged as one of the nation's most radical white abolitionist ministers.

Beginning in 1857 Cheever embraced all moral actions designed to bring about a swift end to slavery. He condemned the Supreme Court for the Dred Scott decision, lambasted Congress for perpetuating the evil, and attacked anyone who refused to embrace immediate abolitionism. He was one of the very few white ministers who defended John Brown's 1859 siege of the federal arsenal at Harpers Ferry, Virginia (now West Virginia) in a failed effort to incite a massive slave revolt and start a revolution. His two most enduring and influential reform works, *God against Slavery* (1857) and *The Guilt of Slavery and the Crime of Slave-Holding, Demonstrated from the Hebrew and Greek Scriptures* (1860), argued that the Bible categorically denounced slavery. "The conflict is not between

North and South," he wrote in *The Guilt of Slavery*, "but between the South and God, and woe to him that striveth with his Maker." His newfound radicalism alienated him from former friends and a large portion of his wealthy and conservative congregation. Outraged parishioners almost succeeded in ousting him from his pulpit, and church attendance declined precipitously. He continued, though, to cling tenaciously to his ministry and refused to compromise his moral stance.

During the Civil War Cheever was one of Lincoln's most vocal critics for not acting decisively to end slavery immediately and establish full equal rights: "Our government seems blasted with the spirit of indecision and delay," he railed in 1863. Although he alienated conservatives and moderates, such radicals as Garrison, Gerrit Smith, William Goodell, and Parker Pillsbury praised his courageous efforts. At the end of the war, Charles Sumner referred to him as "one of the *iron posts* in the balustrade by which *we ascend*!"

Cheever retired from his pastorate in 1867 but remained a prolific writer committed to the cause of equal rights. He was among the relatively few abolitionists after the war who continued the assault on all forms of racial discrimination as "violations of God's laws." Not until 1886, at the age of seventy-nine, did he curtail his radical reform efforts. After forty-one years of an extremely intimate marriage, the death of his wife distressed him immensely, and he devoted his remaining years to writing her memorial. Cheever died in Englewood, New Jersey.

• The extensive Cheever papers are housed at the American Antiquarian Society in Worcester, Mass. His most widely read works include *God's Hand in America* (1841); *The Hierarchical Despotism* (1844); *Lectures on the Pilgrim's Progress* (1844); *A Defense of Capital Punishment* (1846); *God's Vouchers for His Written Word . . .* (1881); and *Faith, Doubt, and Evidence* (1888). The only biography on Cheever is the comprehensive but outdated Robert M. York, "George B. Cheever: Religious and Social Reformer, 1807–1890," *University of Maine Bulletin*, 57, no. 12 (Apr. 1955): 3–239. For a more recent discussion of Cheever within the context of the ministry see John R. McKivigan, *The War against Proslavery Religion: Abolitionism and the Northern Churches, 1830–1865* (1984). Obituaries include H. T. Cheever, ed., *Memorial Address* (1892); and *Memorabilia of Geo. B. Cheever* (1891). See also the *Congregational Yearbook* (1891).

JOHN STAUFFER

CHEEVER, John (27 May 1912–18 June 1982), novelist and short-story writer, was born John William Cheever in Quincy, Massachusetts, the son of Frederick Lincoln Cheever, a shoe salesman, and Mary Liley, a gift shop operator. John Cheever was descended from New England seafarers, but his father was an unsuccessful businessman whose wife's decision to open a gift shop to support the family undermined the father's pride and left the son feeling neglected. In this family background are the roots of several of Cheever's main themes as a writer: the power and the restrictiveness of the New England heritage, the fragility of masculine self-esteem, women's need for outlets for their energies, and the tensions in intimate relationships between men and women.

Cheever attended Thayer Academy in South Braintree, Massachusetts, from which he was expelled at age seventeen for smoking and lack of application. This crisis led to his first publication, a short story, "Expelled," which was accepted by Malcolm Cowley for the 1 October 1930 issue of the *New Republic*, a coup described by Cheever's biographer Scott Donaldson as "one of the most unusual across-the-transom acceptances in magazine history." The story, despite the youth of the author and his barely resisted temptation to attack the school, has a sophistication of content and structure that attracted the editor's attention. Its language has a Hemingway-like economy, and its characters are drawn with remarkable complexity, especially given the story's brevity.

The year following his expulsion, he traveled in Europe with his older brother Fred, with whom he shared a closeness derived in part from the marital tensions of their parents. Following their return, the brothers shared an apartment in Boston, and Fred supported the young author while he wrote stories. In 1934 John moved to New York City and continued to write, supporting himself in meager fashion writing synopses of novels for MGM. Here he met Mary Winternitz, daughter of the dean of the Yale Medical School, and they were married in 1941. They had three children. His daughter's biography, *Home before Dark* (1984), and excerpts from Cheever's journals and letters published since his death reveal that the Cheever marriage was contentious and unhappy after the early years and that his relationship with his children was attentive but complicated by his problems with alcohol, sexual identity, and financial security.

Cheever served in the U.S. Army during World War II and then returned to a life as a full-time writer, except for brief stints as a scriptwriter for television and a teacher of creative writing. From 1954 to 1956 he taught at Barnard College, a position that gave him particular pleasure in that he had not himself attended college. By all accounts he was a success in the classroom and was in demand as an instructor in writing programs at the University of Iowa and Boston University. He also taught creative writing at Sing Sing prison, an experience that provided him with a vivid sense of the prison setting he later used in the novel *Falconer* (1977).

Cheever's earliest stories, most of which appeared first in magazines, were published in 1943 by Random House in a volume titled *The Way Some People Live*. Although most of these stories are more sketches than fully developed narratives, the volume contains at least one story that is a precursor to the fiction for which Cheever would become famous. "The Brothers" deals with an extraordinarily close relationship between two brothers, which they come to recognize as overly exclusive when a woman enters their lives. Complex fraternal relationships appear in many of Cheever's later works, including the Wapshot novels and *Falconer*.

Cheever's second collection, *The Enormous Radio and Other Stories* (1953), shows considerable development in thematic complexity and narrative technique. All fourteen stories first appeared in the *New Yorker*, and several are among his best-known short fiction. Many combine realistic details of urban life with plots involving the human passions and dilemmas more typical of the romance tradition, a narrative approach that was to mark Cheever's fiction throughout his career. Another trademark technique appearing in these stories is the use of supernatural elements and interventions. The title story, for example, measures the disintegration of the relationship of a young New York couple by detailing their reactions to conversations of other tenants in their apartment building, which they can mysteriously overhear by turning on their new radio. The stories were well received by reviewers, many of whom were impressed by the combination of realistic settings and fablelike plots, and they established Cheever as a major writer of short fiction.

Cheever next turned to novel writing, publishing *The Wapshot Chronicle* in 1957. Some parts of the novel had originally appeared as short stories, and this fact, coupled with Cheever's already established reputation in the short-story form, fostered debate on his relative strengths in the two narrative forms. The novel introduces the Wapshot family—father, mother, two brothers, and a domineering maiden aunt—and the fictional New England village of St. Botolphs. As a narrative, the novel is somewhat episodic, more impressive for its memorable characters and comic scenes than for a large sense of purpose. In it Cheever explores most of his major themes, including the family conflict resulting from the father's business failure and the mother's decision to work outside the home, the particular closeness of brothers, the complexity of male-female relationships, and a certain ambivalence about the New England heritage. Despite some critical disagreement about the strength of its narrative achievement, the novel won the National Book Award for fiction in 1958.

This work was followed by the publication of two short-story collections. *The Housebreaker of Shady Hill and Other Stories* (1958) has a unity that, as in works such as Ernest Hemingway's *In Our Time* or Sherwood Anderson's *Winesburg, Ohio*, transcends the individual stories. All the stories are set in the fictional suburb of Shady Hill; some characters appear in several stories; and the themes of love and loss, closeness and distance, hope and despair, are explored with a unifying seriousness. The stories balance the details of everyday life with apparently supernatural interventions in a synthesis that leads the reader beneath the polished surfaces of the characters' lives to the motives and meanings at the core. One of the best stories, "The Country Husband," involves Francis Weed, a happily married suburbanite whose life is turned upside down when his airplane crash-lands, and he discovers that he lives in a world in which it is impolite and unwelcome to tell about his experience. During his consequent loss of satisfaction with his life, he insults his neighbors and falls in love with a teenage babysitter. He is restored to the community when a psychiatrist prescribes woodworking, a hobby in which natural materials are shaped for human use, a metaphor for Weed's need to feel placed in his society. Only Jupiter the dog is allowed to run free at the end, and the reader is informed that this is only until he is poisoned by a neighbor whose garden he regularly tramples. The thematic depth and lyrical style in these stories would not be surpassed in Cheever's career.

In 1961 he published another collection of stories, *Some People, Places, and Things That Will Not Appear in My Next Novel*. More uneven than the Shady Hill volume, the collection includes stories about expatriates looking for fulfillment away from America as well as stories that continue to examine American mores. Perhaps the story that most reveals the tone of this volume is "The Death of Justina," in which the protagonist, an advertising copywriter, is unable to arrange for the burial of his great-aunt who has died in his home because the zoning laws of his suburb make no provision for unexpected death. More than Cheever's earlier stories, these explore the growing disillusionment of many Americans of the period, and they are more critical of the surfaces of American life. In interviews Cheever expressed his sense of the fifties as a decade that went terribly wrong, and these stories began to explore his sense of uneasiness and dismay.

Cheever's next book, *The Wapshot Scandal* (1964), a sequel to his first novel, is very different from the *Chronicle* in focus and tone. The essentially comic adventures of Moses and Coverly Wapshot in the first novel have given way to alcoholism, marital discord, and sexual confusion. Most of the novel is set in cities, suburbs, and even a missile base, rather than in the tranquil village of St. Botolphs. Moses, the older and favored son, sinks into alcoholism after discovering his wife's infidelity. Coverly, perhaps because he maintains a stronger connection to his past, seems to accept the complications of the present with more success. The novel is perhaps most interesting for giving more than usual attention to the plight of a woman, Moses's wife, who cannot find a moral center to her comfortable life and who ends up banished (or liberated) as an expatriate in Italy.

Also in 1964, Cheever published a short-story collection, *The Brigadier and the Golf Widow*, and his fictional achievements were recognized with a cover story in *Time*, Cheever's first real national attention. Like *The Wapshot Scandal*, the stories are darker in theme and tone than most earlier Cheever stories. The title story depicts the Cold War paranoia that led Americans who could afford it to build bomb shelters in their backyards. The husband and wife in the story spend their evenings negotiating over which of their relatives will be permitted to join them in their shelter. The marriage ends when the wife discovers that the husband has given a precious key to the shelter to his mistress. The collection also contains the well-known story "The Swimmer," which in 1966 was made into a movie starring Burt Lancaster.

Bullet Park, published in 1969, is considered by many to be Cheever's best novel. It continues to convey a sense of the troubled aspects of American life in the 1960s, concerning itself with matters such as drug addiction, mental illness, alienation, and violence. However, it also conveys a deep appreciation of marital and parental love and overtly rejects the negative attitudes toward suburbia that pervaded social criticism of the decade. As was typical of most of Cheever's best fiction, the novel stands with one foot in the tradition of the realistic novel of manners, detailing suburban life with its commuter trains, chain saws, and cocktail parties, and the other in the American romance tradition, presenting the essential conflict in values between two main characters by naming them Hammer and Nailles. The novel is tightly structured, especially compared to the episodic narrative form of the Wapshot novels, and it makes use of an omniscient narrator whose heavily interventionist voice makes the blend of romance and realism work. In the world of Shady Hill the crises were resolved, and the characters returned to their former lives. In Bullet Park the characters survive their crises, but they do not come through unscathed by their initiation into pain, helplessness, and irrationality.

The relatively "dark" books of the sixties were followed by *The World of Apples* in 1973. This book was a change of pace for Cheever; in it he found a basis for hope and joy again. One of its reviewers, Larry Woiwode, said that the book makes it seem "as though Cheever were growing progressively young." Although the stories are well crafted and provide a pleasant reading experience, as a collection, *The World of Apples* has been less valued critically than the earlier volumes. In retrospect, the stories in this collection seem to be reestablishing a basis for Cheever to celebrate life. Most of the characters are brought in touch with bedrock values that they come to perceive as underpinning the external appearances of their lives, and most are transfigured by the experience.

Many readers of Cheever were surprised by his next work, the novel *Falconer*, published in 1977. The novel is set in a prison where Ezekiel Farragut, the main character, is incarcerated for fratricide. His wife visits only to taunt him. He is a drug addict who, in the course of the novel, falls in love with another man. Farragut is finally "saved," which in the novel means being allowed to escape, in an unabashedly religious resurrection scene. In the light of revelations about Cheever's private life that emerged after his death—revelations about his alcoholism, his marital unhappiness, and his homosexual liaisons—the themes and situations of the novel seem less startling than they did when it was first published, and there are obvious continuities with earlier fiction, including the dark side of fraternal and marital relationships. The novel was very well received, and Cheever found himself on the cover of *Newsweek* and as a guest on "The Dick Cavett Show."

Falconer's success probably led to the decision of Alfred A. Knopf, Cheever's publisher, to bring out a volume of Cheever's short stories. Cheever agreed to make a selection, and *The Collected Stories of John Cheever* appeared in 1978, again to great critical acclaim and efforts to place Cheever in an appropriately elevated position in American literary history.

One final work, *Oh What a Paradise It Seems*, appeared in 1982. This short novel is probably the most mystifying of Cheever's works. It seems to celebrate physical love, the beauty of chance encounters, social responsibility, and family life. But it also deals with violent death, toxic pollution, and insane interventions in daily life, such as the poisoning of food in supermarkets. For all its celebrative tone, the undercurrent of American life is again portrayed as dark and violent and capable of destroying its positive aspects, such as pristine skating ponds and uncomplicated love.

John Cheever had recovered from heart problems first suffered in 1973 and had been successfully treated for alcoholism in 1975 when, in 1980, he was diagnosed with cancer. He was able to remain at home and to continue to write until his death. In 1984 his daughter Susan published *Home before Dark*, a memoir of her father, in which she breaks the news of his troubled sexuality and difficulties with addiction. After his death, the family permitted the publication of selections from Cheever's journals, and his son Ben has edited his father's letters for publication. These very personal documents reveal his less-than-perfect relationships with his wife and children, his battles with alcoholism, his infidelities, and his bisexuality as well as his thoughts and feelings about his career.

By the end of his life, Cheever saw his literary reputation solidly established. He was frequently compared with his contemporaries and friends Saul Bellow and John Updike, both writers of major achievement in both the novel and short-story forms. Beneath its realistic texture and its delineation of manners, Cheever's fiction is essentially romantic and even moralistic. His descriptions of the cultural behavior of his times provide us with insight into the decades of the forties, fifties, sixties, and seventies, but his main interest is always in the individual and the impact of the culture on individual lives. Underlying his comic tone, his toleration of human foibles, and his preference for affirmative endings is a firm sense of right and wrong, of the life-enhancing and life-destroying possibilities in human choices and actions. His closest literary ancestors are probably Henry James and F. Scott Fitzgerald. Like James, Cheever focuses on the connections between the individual and society and reveals the inner nature of his characters by outward gestures. Like Fitzgerald, he is known for a lyric style and a successful combination of romantic motivation with realistic settings and topics.

In a conversation with fellow author John Hersey in 1978, Cheever expressed the view that style in literature could be used either to enlarge or to diminish the subject and that he had come to feel that the writer's responsibility was to enlarge. Cheever's growing popularity during his life and since his death is due, in large part, to the fact that his work gives us an expanded sense of our possibilities as Americans and as human beings.

• There is no archival collection of Cheever's papers; his correspondence is located in numerous libraries. Susan Cheever has published a second memoir of her father and the Cheever family, *Treetops: A Family Memoir* (1991). His son Benjamin Cheever edited a collection of Cheever's letters, *The Letters of John Cheever* (1988), and a selection from his journals was edited by Robert Gottlieb, *The Journals of John Cheever* (1991). John D. Weaver published *Glad Tidings, a Friendship in Letters: The Correspondence of John Cheever and John D. Weaver, 1945–1982* (1993).

The first full-length biography of Cheever, Scott Donaldson, *John Cheever: A Biography*, was published in 1988. The first critical studies of Cheever were Samuel Coale, *John Cheever* (1977), and Lynne Waldeland, *John Cheever* (1979). Collections of critical essays are R. G. Collins, ed., *Critical Essays on John Cheever* (1982), and Francis J. Bosha, ed., *The Critical Response to John Cheever* (1994). Patrick Meanor, *John Cheever Revisited*, appeared in 1995. Additional full-length studies include George W. Hunt's thematic study, *John Cheever: The Hobgoblin Company of Love* (1983), and James O'Hara, *John Cheever: A Study of the Short Fiction* (1989). An obituary is in the *Boston Globe*, 22 June 1982.

LYNNE M. WALDELAND

CHEN, Joyce (14 Sept. 1917–23 Aug. 1994), restaurateur, author, and chef, was born Liao Jia-ai in Beijing, China, the daughter of Liao Xin-shi, a railroad administrator and city executive; her mother's family name was Wu. As a high-ranking Chinese official, Chen's father was able to employ several servants, but both parents encouraged Chen to learn to do things for herself. She often recalled her mother warning, "You had better learn how to cook . . . so you don't [ever] have to eat raw rice" (*Chicago Sun-Times*, 11 Feb. 1982). The youngest of nine children, Chen learned an appreciation of good food from her parents, who entertained often in their home, and she learned to cook by watching her mother, the family chef, and her governess. When Chen was sixteen, her family moved to Shanghai, her father's hometown. Politically active as a teen, Chen was aware of dramatic changes taking place in China in the 1940s, and long after she immigrated to the United States, she recalled with emotion the hunger and meager living conditions among China's poor. In 1943 Chen married Thomas Chen (Chen Dazhong), who was a dealer and importer of leather goods and later of Chinese antiques.

In 1949 Chen, her husband, and their two small children left China to escape the Communist revolution. Following the advice of a cousin who had lived in the United States, the Chens moved to the university community of Cambridge, Massachusetts, where their third child was born. In Cambridge, the Chens regularly invited Chinese students from Harvard University, the Massachusetts Institute of Technology, and Boston University to traditional home-style dinners. It "made them feel at home," she recalled, "and they made me feel the same in this new country." The popularity of her dishes with neighbors and friends encouraged her to become more adventurous. When her daughter's school had a bake sale, she prepared the traditional American cookies and two dozen egg rolls. The egg rolls were a sensation, selling out in just five minutes. Opening a restaurant that would make "American customers happy and Chinese customers proud" became her goal (*Joyce Chen Cookbook*, pp. 2–3).

In 1958 Chen and her husband opened in Cambridge the Joyce Chen Restaurant, one of the first in the United States that served northern-style Chinese food. At the time, most Americans identified Chinese cooking with chow mein and chop suey—dishes that were basically American, rather than Chinese, in origin. Chen introduced and popularized the cuisine more typical of Beijing and Shanghai, which was a style of cooking that was relatively unknown in the United States and included such regional delicacies as mandarin pancakes, steamed buns, and pan-fried dumplings. One of Chen's first customers stormed out of the restaurant furious that she did not serve French bread and other staples of 1950s-style "Chinese" fare. Undeterred, Chen devised a new strategy to introduce suspicious customers to unfamiliar foods. She set up a buffet with all the standard Western foods such as turkey and roast beef but also added authentic Chinese dishes such as moo shu pork to encourage the development of a more sophisticated palate among her clientele. She renamed Chinese dumplings (or pot stickers) "Peking ravioli" to appeal to her customers' established tastes. Gradually she replaced the Western foods with Chinese dishes, and the restaurant thrived. Within ten years, she had opened a second restaurant in Cambridge, and her establishments regularly boasted such celebrity customers as Danny Kaye, Julia Child, and John Kenneth Galbraith.

In 1960 Chen began teaching cooking classes at the Cambridge and Boston Adult Education Center. In 1962 she published the *Joyce Chen Cookbook*, a volume that combined recipes with lessons on technique as well as Chinese history and customs. Her attention to nutrition earned her cookbook a laudatory preface from Paul Dudley White, the physician to former President Dwight D. Eisenhower. The book quickly became the standard in Chinese cooking. Its success led in 1966 to the creation of the "Joyce Chen Cooks" television show, filmed in Boston and aired on as many as one hundred Public Broadcasting System stations in the United States and Canada. The first Asian American in the United States to have her own show, Chen, at WGBH, had the same producer as Julia Child, another contemporary paragon of cooking on television.

Believing that food and culture went hand in hand, Chen envisioned her efforts as something much broader than mere instructions on preparing food. In her view, the book, the show, and her restaurant were also tools to teach others about Chinese culture, a project in which she took great pride and satisfaction. The restaurant, for example, established special culinary events, at which the meal was accompanied by lectures on the heritage of the dishes. In contrast to the custom of most Chinese restaurant managers who maintained separate menus for Chinese and American customers, Chen offered only one.

Many of Chen's chefs came from China, and at a time when quotas made emigration from China an exceedingly difficult prospect, Chen herself helped many of them obtain permission to enter the United States. Chen's husband, whom she divorced in 1966, and a number of her former employees went on to open their own restaurants in the Cambridge area. But because of her enthusiasm for cooking and her generosity, Chen never objected to training potential competitors. In the early 1970s, she offered the use of her kitchen for a job-training project teaching new chefs.

In the 1970s Chen also became an entrepreneur in the food service industry and a well-known figure in international affairs. In 1972 she returned to China to discover that her brother Liao Jia-reng, who had been killed in Shanghai in 1927, had since become a popular Communist hero. Chen was granted freedom to travel unescorted and an invitation to serve as an adviser to the Chinese Board of Trade. By the early 1970s Chen's businesses had prospered. An astute businesswoman, she later created Joyce Chen Products, a business that sold Chinese utensils and equipment, and Joyce Chen Specialty Foods, which marketed Chen's own stir-fry sauces for home use. Her products company invented the "Peking pan," a flat-bottomed wok designed for use on American electric ranges, now a staple of home cooking equipment. In 1983 Boston mayor Kevin White appointed Chen the city's ambassador to China. The following year, when President Ronald Reagan hosted a dinner for Chinese Premier Zhau Zi-ying, Chen attended and led the party in delivering a traditional Chinese toast. In 1996 *Nation's Restaurant News* named Chen as one of the fifty most influential people in the history of the food service industry.

In the 1970s and 1980s Chen became more concerned about nutrition and healthy cooking and adapted her traditional recipes accordingly. At the request of instructors at Harvard Medical School, she incorporated into her menu dishes for customers with heart problems or special dietary restrictions. Her cookbook replaced lard, the traditional Chinese cooking fat, with vegetable oil, lowered salt and fat contents, and made monosodium glutamate optional.

An extraordinarily successful businesswoman and unique cultural envoy, Chen not only introduced a generation of Americans to authentic Chinese cooking but also used Chinese cuisine to educate a generation of Americans about her culture. In Julia Child's words, "Joyce Chen really brought Chinese food to people's attention. She gave people an appreciation of Chinese food—and it was GOOD." Chen's productive and energetic life was tragically cut short by the onset of multi-infarct dementia and Alzheimer's disease in the mid-1980s. After an extended illness, she died in Lexington, Massachusetts.

• A short autobiographical sketch of Chen is in the preface to her *Joyce Chen Cookbook* (1962; 2d ed., 1982). A more extensive biography and a family history are in the preface and text of a cookbook by Chen's daughter, *Helen Chen's Chinese Home Cooking* (1994). Profiles in *Fine Dining*, Summer 1979, and the *Chicago Sun-Times*, 11 Feb. 1982, offer insight into Chen's thoughts on cooking and Chinese culture. A profile in the *Nation's Restaurant News*, Feb. 1996, which accompanies Chen's nomination to the journal's Hall of Fame, places her business innovations and contributions in historical context. Other useful sources on Chen include articles in *Time*, 29 Jan. 1973; the *Independent Journal*, 12 May 1982; the *Washington Post*, 30 Oct. 1983; the *Middlesex News*, 16 Jan. 1984; and the *Seattle Post-Intelligencer*, 5 May 1982. Obituaries are in the *New York Times*, 26 Aug. 1994, and *Newsweek*, 5 Sept. 1994.

MICHELLE BRATTAIN

CHENEY, Benjamin Pierce (12 Aug. 1815–23 July 1895), transportation executive, was born in Hillsborough, New Hampshire, the son of Jesse Cheney, a blacksmith, and Alice Steele. Born into an impoverished family, he attended local common schools until the age of ten and then went to work in his father's shop. After nearly two years working with his father, he relocated to Francistown, New Hampshire, where he took a job in a tavern and later worked in a local store.

At the age of sixteen Cheney entered the field in which he would make his mark—transportation—as a stagecoach driver. Initially responsible for a run between Nashua and Exeter, New Hampshire, he soon switched to a route than ran between Keene and Nashua. He spent six years on that route, where he averaged fifty miles a day in transit. One of his passengers was Daniel Webster, with whom he began a lifelong friendship. Skilled in his work, Cheney earned a reputation for both efficiency and honesty, and he was soon entrusted with the transportation of large sums of cash to and from Boston banks. When several local stage lines consolidated operations in Boston in 1836, Cheney relocated to that city, where he served for the next six years as a general agent for the lines (whose business extended throughout northern New England into Canada) from his office at No. 11 Elm Street. Although compensated handsomely for his work, Cheney wanted his own firm. Accordingly, he formed Cheney & Company's Express between Boston and Montreal (in partnership with Nathaniel White and William Walker) in 1842. Express companies were a relatively new entry into the transportation field—the first American firm had been formed in 1839—which specialized in safely transporting money and other valuables.

Cheney's firm began operating at a time when travel conditions were still primitive at best. Cheney & Company shipped freight initially by railroad from Boston to Concord, New Hampshire (which was the furthest extension of the Boston & Lowell Railroad at that time), and then by four-horse team to Montpelier, Vermont, and then by stagecoach messenger to Burlington, Vermont, and finally by boat to Montreal.

Despite the unwieldiness of its operation, the new company prospered. By 1852 the firm was sufficiently established to buy out a rival, Fisk and Rice's Express, which had competed with Cheney & Company for business in Burlington. Other consolidations followed—keeping up with an industry-wide trend—and the expanded firm eventually became the United States & Canada Express Company. Although the business was occasionally hazardous (an accident during a return trip from Canada by rail in 1854 cost Cheney his right arm), Cheney's hard work and solid grasp of details paid off in a lucrative operation. He took time in 1865 to marry Elizabeth Clapp; the couple had five children.

The United States & Canada Express Company eventually gained control of most of the northern New England freighting business, and its profits provided Cheney with the basis of his considerable personal fortune. In 1879 he merged the firm with the American Express Company, becoming the treasurer and a director as well as one of the largest stockholders of the new firm. Cheney held these posts until his retirement, and in his later years he began to look beyond New England for potential investments. He was an early promoter of the Northern Pacific Railroad and later became an enthusiastic supporter of the Atchison, Topeka & Santa Fe Railroad. Well acquainted with the leaders of Wells, Fargo & Company, he became a member of that firm's board of directors and also joined the board of the Overland Mail Company (an affiliated firm) in March 1860. Well respected for his expertise in the industry, Cheney and two other directors (representing both Wells Fargo and Overland Mail) conducted a cross-country inspection tour in the spring of 1863.

Closer to home, Cheney also held interests in the Vermont Central Railroad and was both a founder and director of the Market National Bank of Boston and the American Loan & Trust Company. Long interested in local history, he was an active member of the New England Historic and Genealogy Society for many years. Dartmouth College benefited from his philanthropy, receiving $50,000 toward the establishment of an academy in Washington Territory. In 1886 Cheney donated a bronze statue of Daniel Webster to the state of New Hampshire (later placed in the State House Park in Concord) and expressed satisfaction in commemorating "a son of New Hampshire, who as a patriot was unexcelled and as an orator and statesman was without a peer." A longtime resident of an elegant estate, "Elm Bank," near Wellesley, Massachusetts, Cheney died there.

Largely forgotten today, Cheney deserves to be remembered for his role in the development of the U.S. express industry. His greatest legacy was his contribution to the creation of today's American Express Company.

• While the bulk of Cheney's papers is apparently lost, portions of his correspondence survive in the William F. Dalrymple Papers at the State Historical Society of Wisconsin and in the Connecticut and Passumpsic River Railroad collection at the Dartmouth College library. Secondary literature on Cheney is scarce; the best source remains William Robert Cochran, *History of the Town of Antrim, New Hampshire . . .* (1880). Although it ignores Cheney's contributions to the firm's development, Alden Hatch, *American Express: A Century of Service* (1950), provides a thorough if laudatory account of the firm's history. An obituary is in the *Boston Evening Transcript*, 23 July 1895.

EDWARD L. LACH, JR.

CHENEY, Charles Edward (20 Feb. 1836–15 Nov. 1916), Episcopal clergyman and bishop of the Reformed Episcopal church, was born in Canandaigua, New York, the son of E. Warren Cheney, a physician, and Altie Wheeler Chipman. After graduating from Hobart College in 1857, having decided to enter the priesthood of the Episcopal church, Cheney attended Virginia Theological Seminary at Alexandria, Virginia, graduating in 1859. He was ordained a deacon in the Episcopal church by Bishop William Heathcote Delancey on 21 November 1858 and was ordained priest by Delancey on 4 March 1860. In between Cheney served as assistant rector of St. Luke's Church, Rochester, New York, and then minister-in-charge of St. Paul's Church, Havana, New York. He left New York in the spring of 1860 to become rector of the newly organized parish of Christ Church, Chicago, conducting his first service there a week after his ordination to the priesthood. Cheney married Clara Emma Griswold only a few weeks after arriving in Chicago. Clara Griswold Cheney was an indispensable partner to Cheney in editing church and denominational publications until her death in 1911.

Cheney's manner was that of an upstate New York Episcopal aristocrat, with his ramrod-stiff back (in contrast to his diminutive stature) and an enormous pair of powder-puff side-whiskers (subtly attracting attention away from the baldness that crept over him in his twenties). But his religious convictions were fervently evangelical. Like his preceptors at Virginia Seminary, he was impatient with those who only "admire the beautiful moral precepts of the New Testament" and who "never will be led to make them the guiding principle of your life." And he had no use for "any essential doctrine which does not find its basis and ultimate authority in the Bible." That limitation excluded any notions of church order that made claims to apostolic succession in its ministry or that denied the validity of ministries in nonepiscopal Protestant denominations. In particular, his evangelical principles excluded any "high" view of the efficacy of baptism. Although Cheney accepted the responsibility laid upon him by the Episcopal prayer book to baptize infants and then declare "this child now regenerate," he had done so in the customary evangelical fashion of attaching several mental reservations to the words he was uttering. And yet Cheney loved the Episcopal church and all that he believed it stood for. By 1869 Cheney had built up Christ Church, not only into a new stone church building worth more than $100,000 but into a congregation with 300 communicants and a "congregation numbering 600 or 700 ordinarily" on Sunday mornings.

Cheney's loyalty to the Episcopal church was sorely tried during the 1860s by the aggressive internal growth of Anglo-Catholicism, especially since the "high church" Anglo-Catholics repudiated Protestant doctrine, denied the validity of nonepiscopal ministries, and attributed heightened significance to the sacraments. When the sympathies of Henry John Whitehouse, the bishop of Illinois, shifted toward Anglo-Catholicism, Cheney found himself involved in conflicts that forced him to question his loyalty to the church. His conscience was troubled in particular by the prayer book's requirement to pronounce baptized infants regenerate because he believed it engendered "the notion that the sacrament of baptism was a magical charm possessed of inherent saving power." And so, in the late 1860s Cheney decided to drop the use of this controversial vocabulary from his administrations of baptism.

Cheney's action provoked an immediate response from Bishop Whitehouse in April 1869. Whitehouse already had been angered by questions Cheney had raised concerning the handling of diocesan finances and by Cheney's identification with evangelical protests against Anglo-Catholicism. When Cheney refused to yield to Whitehouse's demand that the baptismal liturgy be administered precisely as printed in the prayer book, Whitehouse issued a citation to Cheney to await trial for violating the canons of the Episcopal church.

The court that was convened to try Cheney included Bishop Whitehouse as judge and five Illinois clergymen as assessors. Cheney, who had the support of Christ Church, was represented by a team of lawyers headed by Melville Weston Fuller. When the trial opened on 21 July 1869, the assessors overruled all the objections raised by Cheney's counsel; this led Fuller, the next day, to obtain an injunction from the Superior Court of Chicago, based on an appeal to the secular courts claiming that Cheney's civil rights had been imperiled by the proceedings of the ecclesiastical court. Not until early 1871 was the injunction lifted. Whitehouse proceeded to reopen the trial, but without one of the original assessors, and on 7 February 1871 found Cheney guilty of the original violations. Cheney insisted that the reassembled court was canonically defective, but Whitehouse nevertheless found him "contumacious" and deposed him from the priesthood on 2 June 1871.

Christ Church rallied behind Cheney, retaining him as rector and defying Whitehouse's attempts to reclaim the church's property for the diocese of Illinois. Then, on 15 November 1873, Bishop George David Cummins of Kentucky announced his withdrawal from the Episcopal church to organize a new evangelical Episcopalian denomination, the Reformed Episcopal church. Cheney attended the organizational meeting held in New York City on 2 December 1873 and was unanimously elected a missionary bishop for the Reformed Episcopal church. He was consecrated by Cummins in Christ Church on 14 December 1873. In September 1875, when the Reformed Episcopalians were reorganized on a diocesan (or synodical) basis, Cheney was elected bishop of Chicago. Although he continued to serve as rector of Christ Church, he also sat on numerous Reformed Episcopal committees and boards and served as presiding bishop of the Reformed Episcopal church from 1876 until 1877 and again from 1887 until 1889.

Cheney's career as a bishop in the Reformed Episcopal church was almost as unhappy as his priesthood in the Episcopal church. After Cummins's premature death in 1876, the Reformed Episcopal church was racked by a power struggle between radical evangelicals who wanted more stringent reforms of Episcopal practice (especially concerning the use of vestments) and moderates like Cheney, who wanted to preserve a number of more traditional Episcopal practices. Eventually, in 1897 the Fourteenth General Council of the Reformed Episcopal church moved to ban the use of all vestments in worship except for the black gown. Cheney denounced the ban as a violation of "all Christian liberty" and resigned all of his church offices, retaining only his Chicago episcopate and Christ Church. He died in Chicago.

Few of his parishioners who left recollections of Cheney's ministry describe him as a power in the pulpit, but he was valued as a "faithful" and even "lovable" pastor. Because Cheney was the conveyer to the Reformed Episcopalians of the traditional episcopal orders received from Bishop Cummins, the question of the validity of the Reformed Episcopal church's episcopal orders has usually hung on whether Cheney, as a deposed priest, was an eligible recipient of consecration as a bishop. The prevailing opinion has been to agree with Cheney's original contention that Bishop Whitehouse's 1871 ecclesiastical court was canonically defective, making Cheney's subsequent deposition illegal, and to assert therefore that Cheney's consecration and the subsequent Reformed Episcopal consecrations performed by him are irregular but valid. Additionally, Cheney's appeal to a secular court for an injunction against ecclesiastical proceedings occupies an important place in church-state jurisprudence, especially in the context of efforts in the early 1870s to pass a national civil rights law (based on the Fourteenth Amendment) that would extend federal civil rights jurisdiction to church cases.

• Cheney's sermon manuscripts and parish register are housed in the Kuehner Memorial Library of the Philadelphia Theological Seminary. Two collections of his sermons were published in his lifetime, *Sermons* (1880) and *A Neglected Power and Other Sermons* (1916). Cheney also published a lengthy defense of Reformed Episcopal principles in *What Do Reformed Episcopalians Believe? Eight Sermons Preached in Christ Church, Chicago* (1888) and in his *Personal Reminiscences of the Founding of the Reformed Episcopal Church* (1913). Several of Cheney's historical papers were privately published by the Chicago Literary Club, including *A King of France Unnamed in History* (1902), *The Second Norman Conquest of England* (1907), *The Barefoot Maid at the Fountain*

Inn (1912), and *A Belated Plantagenet* (1914). On the issues surrounding Cheney's trial and the organization of the Reformed Episcopal church, see *The Trial of the Rev. Charles Edward Cheney* (1869), a collection of news clips; Alexandrine Cummins, *Memoir of George David Cummins, D.D., First Bishop of the Reformed Episcopal Church* (1878); E. Clowes Chorley, *Men and Movements in the American Episcopal Church* (1946); and Allen C. Guelzo, *For the Union of Evangelical Christendom: The Irony of the Reformed Episcopalians* (1993). Rodney Howat Longmire, "Charles Edward Cheney, Bishop of the Reformed Episcopal Church" (S.T.M. thesis, Lutheran Theological Seminary, 1965), includes a concise biographical treatment of Cheney.

ALLEN C. GUELZO

CHENEY, Ednah Dow Littlehale (27 June 1824–19 Nov. 1904), social reformer and author, was born in Boston, Massachusetts, the daughter of Sargent Smith Littlehale, a partner in a successful grocery business, and Ednah Parker Dow. By Cheney's own admission she was precocious and undisciplined as a young girl, attending several private schools without distinguishing herself at any of them. Her religious upbringing was unorthodox if not unusual for the times. She described her father as a Universalist, liberal in both politics and religion. An early supporter of woman suffrage, her father was, however, a firm "Unionist" who found the fiery, abolitionist sermons of Theodore Parker dangerous. Still, Ednah became a disciple and friend of the iconoclastic Unitarian preacher after she was hired as a nurse and tutor for his daughter. She was among a core of more than 200 leading Bostonians who attended the Twenty-eighth Congregational Society and looked to Parker—the greatest of the Transcendentalist ministers—for spiritual direction.

In 1853 she married an artist, Seth Wells Cheney, and accompanied him to Europe. A daughter, Margaret Swan, was born to the couple in 1855. Tragically, Ednah Cheney was widowed less than a year later and never remarried.

Involvement in philanthropic and reform associations began early. In 1851 Cheney helped found the Boston School of Design, a coeducational training institution for careers in art and drafting. Following the death of her husband, she worked to establish the New England Hospital for Women and Children to provide medical education and surgical experience for women wishing to enter the profession. She served first as secretary and then as president of that organization until 1902. Although she supported the push for full political and economic rights of women, Cheney believed that such gains would be useless without the necessary educational and vocational experience to enjoy them. Through the New England Women's Club founded in 1868, she fought for a variety of women's causes, including dress reform and educational equality. She helped establish the Massachusetts Women's School Suffrage Association for school board elections and the Horticultural School for Women in Boston and was an active member of the American Association for the Advancement of Women. Perhaps her most rewarding work, however, was on behalf of the "freedmen." As the secretary of the Teachers' Commission of the Freedman's Bureau, she traveled widely throughout the South. Her first book, *The Handbook for American Citizens* (1866), was designed for use in the newly established schools and included the text of the Constitution and a brief survey of U.S. history. Looking back over a "century of emancipation," she saw the promise of a democratic civilization in the abolition of slavery. "I believe that it is by the union of these races," she wrote, "that American citizenship will become welded into a higher country and a nobler manhood" (*Reminiscences* [1902], p. 166).

Cheney's most lasting literary contribution came as a chronicler of the New England Renaissance. She was the most important woman of the "later Transcendentalists"—the second generation of intellectuals and reformers in the Emersonian tradition. As early as 1840 she fell under the spell of Ralph Waldo Emerson, eventually counting Margaret Fuller, Elizabeth Palmer Peabody, and James Freeman Clark among her many friends in the literary and religious circles of greater Boston. Her *Louisa May Alcott: Her Life, Letters and Journals* (1889) was the first biography of the celebrated author and includes important selections of Alcott's now lost diary on life at the Fruitlands commune—the ill-fated social experiment of the quixotic Transcendentalist patriarch Amos Bronson Alcott. A prolific essayist, Cheney published important discourses on Emerson, Goethe, and the history of American art. Many of these themes were first explored as summer lectures at the Concord School of Philosophy where Cheney taught regularly starting in 1878. Although most of her fictional writing was unremarkable, she also gained some notoriety as an author of juvenile literature with the appearance of *Faithful to the Light* (1871) and several subsequent novels.

Like other New England reformers and intellectuals of the postbellum period, Ednah Cheney's activism reflected a sincere, liberal religious piety. Never ordained, Cheney confessed that she was "very much inclined to preaching," speaking often in southern black congregations as well as liberal societies in the North. For over three decades she was actively involved in the free religion movement, which opposed the credalism of New England Calvinism in favor of the authority of the individual conscience. Religion was understood as a positive "social force" when it proclaimed a progressive gospel of human progress and reason. "Religion wedded to science," she declared, "must give us bread for all, shelter for all, health, freedom, education for all" (in *Proceedings of the Free Religious Association* [1870]: 43). Cheney believed what her mentor Theodore Parker had preached, that religion emancipated from tradition and working for social betterment would help to usher in the kingdom of God.

Unlike her friend Louisa May Alcott, Cheney was not an author of great originality or imagination. Her biographies were generally sympathetic and impressionistic interpretations that lacked the critical edge of modern scholarship. Nevertheless, her long career as a leader in social reform was remarkable, and her writings provide articulate expressions of the cultural values and assumptions of mid-Victorian America. Following her death in Boston, Cheney was remembered by her longtime friend and fellow activist Julia Ward Howe as a woman of "luminous intellect" with "unusual powers of judgment and of sympathy" (*Julia Ward Howe, 1819–1910*, p. 394). In her autobiography written two years earlier, she mused that nearly her entire life had been "contained within the nineteenth century" (*Reminiscences*, p. 161). Indeed, few others were more representative of the social and religious impulses of those times than Ednah Cheney.

• Any biographical treatment of Ednah Cheney must include her familial eulogies, *Memoir of Seth Wells Cheney* (1881) and *Memoir of Margaret Swan Cheney* (1889). Consult also *Municipal Suffrage for Women* (1889), an American Woman Suffrage Association pamphlet, and *Records of the New England Freedman's Aid Society, 1862–1876*. For her "reminiscences" of contemporaries, see "Remembrances of Mr. Alcott's Conversations," *Open Court* 2 (Aug. 1888): 1131–33, 1142–44; "Emerson and Boston," in *The Genius and Character of Emerson*, ed. Franklin B. Sanborn (1885); "Theodore Parker the Pastor," *West Roxbury Magazine* (1900): 52–56; and "Lucretia Mott," in *Prophets of Liberalism* (1900). Published lectures from the Concord School include *The Life and Genius of Goethe*, ed. with Franklin B. Sanborn (1886); and *Gleanings in the Fields of Art* (1881). Her novels for children are *Sally Williams* (1874), *Child of the Tide* (1875), *Jenny of the Lighthouse* (1877), *Nora's Return* (1890), and *Stories of the Olden Time* (1890).

Ann Douglas, "Introduction to the Chelsea House Edition," in *Louisa May Alcott* (1980), offers a perceptive analysis of Cheney as biographer of a Victorian icon. Remembrances by contemporaries include Julia Ward Howe, *Reminiscences, 1819–1899* (1900); Franklin B. Sanborn, *Recollections of Seventy Years* (1909); and *The Journals of Bronson Alcott*, ed. Odell Shepard (1938). On Cheney's religious involvements, see William R. Hutchison, *The Transcendentalist Ministers* (1859); Anne C. Rose, *Transcendentalism as a Social Movement, 1830–1850* (1981); and Stow Persons, *Free Religion: An American Faith* (1947). Obituaries are in the *Boston Herald*, 20 Nov. 1904, and the *Boston Evening Transcript*, 19 Nov. 1904.

LAWRENCE W. SNYDER

CHENNAULT, Claire Lee (6 Sept. 1893–27 July 1958), military officer and airline executive, was born in Commerce, Texas, the son of John Stonewall Jackson Chennault, a small-scale cotton grower, and Jessie Lee. Chennault grew up on a small farm in Franklin Parish in northeastern Louisiana. His mother died when he was eight years old. Two years later, his father married Lottie Barnes, a local schoolteacher. Educated in the nearby town of Gilbert, he entered Louisiana State University in 1909. Shortly thereafter, his stepmother, who had persuaded him to continue his education, died. "I was alone again," he later wrote, "and really never found another companion whom I could so completely admire, respect, and love."

Chennault left LSU at the end of the second semester and enrolled in the teacher's training program at State Normal School at Natchitoches. Completing his course of study in July 1910, he began teaching in the fall in a one-room country school in Athens, Louisiana. In 1911 he married Nell Thompson, a fellow teacher; over the next seventeen years, they had eight children.

Unable to support his family on the salary of a rural teacher, Chennault searched for opportunity elsewhere. He held a number of jobs before finding work with the Goodyear tire factory in Akron, Ohio, in 1916. With a long-standing interest in a military career, Chennault eagerly joined the army shortly after the United States entered World War I in April 1917. Sent to Fort Benjamin Harrison, Indiana, for officer training, he received his commission on 27 November 1917 and was assigned to ground duties with the air service. Initially rejected for flying training, Chennault persisted until he was accepted in the fall of 1918. He won his wings at Kelly Field, Texas, on 6 April 1919. One year later he was discharged from the service.

Chennault tried cotton farming in Franklin Parish during the summer of 1920 but quickly realized that a military career held more promise. He applied for and was granted a commission in the regular army in September 1920. Over the next decade he served in a variety of assignments.

In 1930–1931 Chennault attended the Air Corps Tactical School at Langley Field in Virginia. After Chennault's graduation in 1931 it moved to Maxwell Field, Montgomery, Alabama, and Chennault remained with the school as pursuit instructor. In an air corps textbook and a series of articles in a service journal ("The Role of Defensive Pursuit"), he argued that an effective warning system and aerial teamwork would make possible the reliable interception and destruction of bombers. At a time when the air corps was emphasizing the invulnerability of its strategic bomber force, Chennault's views found little favor with his superiors. In February 1937 a retirement board recommended his separation from the service on medical grounds; he suffered from deafness and chronic bronchitis. The frustrated airman accepted the board's decision and retired at his permanent rank of captain on 30 April 1937.

Although Chennault's views about pursuit aviation had little impact in the United States, they attracted the attention of officials in other nations who wished to develop a modern air force. In May 1937 Chennault sailed for China, having earlier negotiated a two-year contract to serve as the government's adviser on pursuit aviation, responsible for selecting equipment, training, and organizing an aircraft warning system.

Chennault barely had time to survey the air force when full-scale war between China and Japan broke out in the summer of 1937. After the fledgling Chinese Air Force proved no match for the powerful Japanese air arm, Chennault took on the task of rebuilding the air force and opened a training school in Kunming in western China.

With the Japanese Air Force dominating the skies over China, the Nationalist government in 1941 recruited a volunteer group of American airmen to protect the supply route from Burma into China. Secretly sanctioned by President Franklin D. Roosevelt, the American Volunteer Group (AVG) marked the beginning of a covert U.S. aerial capability that would continue in the decades ahead.

Chennault took command of the AVG in the summer of 1941. Trained in the aerial combat techniques that he had developed during four years of war with Japan, the group was ready for action shortly after the Japanese attacked Pearl Harbor on 7 December 1941. The Flying Tigers, as they came to be called in the press, compiled an impressive record. While other American fighter squadrons, especially in the Philippines, fared poorly against the Japanese, Chennault's pilots claimed some 300 enemy planes destroyed at a cost of twelve aircraft and four pilots lost during seven months of aerial action. Thanks in large part to the quality of their leadership, the AVG provided one of the few bright spots during the early dark days of the war, and Chennault became a national hero.

Ordered into regular service in the U.S. Army Air Forces in April 1942, Chennault assumed command of the China Air Task Force, which replaced the AVG. In March 1943, after being promoted to major general, he took charge of the newly created Fourteenth Air Force. A controversial figure during the war years, Chennault frequently clashed with the theater commander, General Joseph Stilwell, over the priority that should be given to aviation. Despite the many problems with his superiors, Chennault's leadership of the Fourteenth Air Force produced outstanding results. Operating at the distant end of a long supply line in a low-priority theater, Chennault's airmen used their limited resources to advantage, claiming 2,600 enemy aircraft destroyed and 2.2 million tons of shipping sunk or damaged. Despite this record, Chennault was denied a promotion to lieutenant general and commander of all air forces in the theater; his superiors, General Hap Arnold and General George C. Marshall, saw him as too closely tied to the Chinese. With Roosevelt's death in April 1944, the overall commanders no longer felt constrained by the president's support of Chennault and could withhold from him greater authority. Bitterly disappointed, Chennault requested retirement in July 1945 and returned to the United States in August.

Chennault returned to China in January 1946 to explore opportunities for commercial aviation in the war-torn country. Working with his partner, Whiting Willauer, Chennault used his close contacts with Chinese officials to obtain a contract to carry relief supplies from the coast of China into the interior. Chennault became president of CNRRA Air Transport, which began operations on 31 January 1947.

Estranged from his wife for several years, Chennault obtained a divorce in 1946. In December of that year he married Anna Chan, a Chinese reporter with the China News Agency during the latter years of the war who had covered the Fourteenth Air Force. The union, a happy one by all accounts, produced two daughters.

In 1948 Chennault and Willauer formed Civil Air Transport (CAT), a wholly commercial airline, to replace the relief operation. CAT soon became involved in China's growing civil war. It frequently served as a paramilitary adjunct to the Nationalist government, carrying arms, munitions, and troops. In 1949, as the position of Chiang Kai-shek's regime deteriorated, CAT also began contract flying for the Central Intelligence Agency (CIA), which hoped to establish anti-Communist resistance groups in western China.

In April 1950, after CAT had left the mainland for Taiwan with the remnants of the Nationalist regime, the CIA secretly purchased the airline. Chennault, an outspoken anti-Communist who always hoped to form and lead an international volunteer group to fight against Communist regimes throughout the world, provided the leadership for the CIA's first air proprietary. Under his guidance CAT airdropped agents and supplies into China, supported anti-Communist forces in Burma, and provided the pilots to fly resupply missions for the French at Dienbienphu in 1954. Later CAT evolved into Air America, which would play a prominent role in CIA operations in Southeast Asia during the Vietnam War.

In 1955 the CIA, concerned with financial losses, imposed tighter controls on its air proprietary. Relegated to the figurehead position of chairman of the board, Chennault divided his time between homes in Taipei and Monroe, Louisiana. He died in New Orleans two days after the White House announced his promotion to lieutenant general. It had come ten years too late, he told his wife.

In a career full of controversy, Chennault advocated his beliefs—whether on the value of pursuit aviation, the role of air power in China during World War II, or the proper course of the American government in the postwar struggle against communism—with a fierce determination that few could match. Motivated less by the desire for money or power than the belief that his views were correct, he often suffered a frustration that left him bitter with resentment. Although Chennault rarely found favor with his superiors, his ability to inspire subordinates placed him in the front rank of American combat commanders during World War II. Later he was instrumental in developing the CIA's covert air operations.

• The major collection of Chennault papers is at the Hoover Institution, Stanford University. Additional material is at the U.S. Air Force Historical Research Agency, Maxwell Air Force Base, Ala. Chennault's memoirs, *Way of a Fighter* (1949), reveal his acerbic character but contain a number of factual errors. By far the best biography of the controversial airman is Martha Byrd, *Chennault: Giving Wings to the Tiger* (1987). Daniel Ford, *Flying Tigers: Claire Chennault and the American Volunteer Group* (1991), covers the AVG, while William M. Leary, *Perilous Missions: Civil Air Transport and CIA Covert Operations in Asia* (1984), details Chennault's postwar career. An obituary is in the *New York Times*, 28 July 1958.

WILLIAM M. LEARY

CHERNISS, Harold Fredrik (11 Mar. 1904–18 June 1987), classicist and educator, was born in St. Joseph, Missouri, the son of David Benjamin, a health inspector, and Theresa Hart. In 1921 Cherniss entered the University of California at Los Angeles and transferred to the Berkeley campus after one semester. In 1925 he graduated from the University of California at Berkeley with an A.B. and highest honors in Greek and political science. He remained at Berkeley for his graduate studies and, in 1929, received his Ph.D. in Greek, Latin, and Sanskrit. Among his mentors at Berkeley was Roger Miller Jones, who inspired Cherniss's passion for Greek philosophy, and for Plutarch in particular. While a graduate student, Cherniss also studied at the University of Chicago, in the summer of 1926; the University of Göttingen, in 1927; and the University of Berlin, in 1928. He would later publish his doctoral dissertation, "The Platonism of Gregory of Nyssa" (1930). In 1929 he married Ruth Meyer of White Plains, New York. They had two daughters.

Cherniss first taught as an instructor of classics at Cornell University, from 1930 to 1933. He then became an associate of Greek at Johns Hopkins University, until 1936, when he was made an associate professor. From 1936 to 1940 he was assistant editor and, from 1940 to 1942 editor, of the *American Journal of Philology*. In 1942 he volunteered for the U.S. Army, where he served in intelligence, primarily in the European theater, and advanced from the rank of private to that of captain.

Between 1935 and 1945 Cherniss published three works that would significantly affect the direction of scholarship of early Greek philosophy. In the first of these, *Aristotle's Criticism of Presocratic Philosophy* (1935), Cherniss addressed the daunting problem of how one properly reconstructs the teachings of the presocratic philosophers (generally, those from Thales to Socrates). Since their original works survive only in sparse fragments, scholars are forced to rely on commentaries by later writers, Aristotle's in particular. By a meticulous and thorough examination of all of Aristotle's writings, Cherniss showed that Aristotle purposely revised the teachings of his predecessors such that they cannot be reliably reversed to reconstruct a history of presocratic philosophy. Similarly, in his study *Aristotle's Criticism of Plato and the Academy* (1944), Cherniss applied his characteristic attention to detail to investigate how and why Aristotle adopted his interpretations of Plato's and Plato's students' writings. Cherniss's account debunks, among other scholarly trends, the tendency to attribute Aristotle's frequently dubious testimony on Plato's doctrines to secret oral teachings given by Plato.

In *The Riddle of the Early Academy* (1945), a series of tightly argued lectures delivered by Cherniss at Berkeley and published while he was abroad, he dealt further with Aristotle's criticism of Plato and his academy and the related question of what Plato after all must have done there. Scholars, he argued, have too often inferred the nature of Plato's private teachings from meager textual evidence and an unwarranted contemporary model of the academy. According to Cherniss, however, Plato would not have tried to impose his doctrines upon his students, "for he knew that true knowledge must come from within the soul itself and that nothing learned under compulsion remains fixed in the mind." Here and in other works, Cherniss also criticized what he saw as an emerging trend among literary critics, the increasingly common appeal to the identity, biography, and personality of an author to explain his or her work. One effect of Cherniss's research has been to check academic indulgence in this regard and to steer the path of research on the ancients away from historical reconstruction and toward the arguments of the texts themselves.

After leaving the army in 1946, Cherniss became a professor of Greek at the University of California at Berkeley. In 1948 he joined the School of Historical Studies at the Institute for Advanced Study in Princeton, New Jersey, until his retirement on 11 March 1974, when he assumed the role of professor emeritus. Though most of the books for which he is known were written in the first decade or so of his career, his later accomplishments were impressive and important contributions to the scholarly literature. Cherniss published more than a dozen articles, a two-volume annotated bibliography, *Plato (1950–1957)* (1960, 1961), and scores of book reviews. His book reviews, written over the course of nearly half a century, have been described as models of the art and further examples of his magnificent scholarship. Speaking of one review in particular, Gregory Vlastos remarked, "it is much more than a point by point refutation. . . . What it offers on the detailed topics that come into the review is unsurpassed in sureness and penetration of judgement in treatments of the same topics in any book or essay known to me on the history of Greek mathematics."

In 1976 Cherniss also published essays on and an English translation of Plutarch's *Moralia* in two volumes, as part of the Loeb Classical Library collection. Within these volumes are *The Platonic and Stoic Essays of Plutarch*, for which Cherniss was awarded the Charles J. Goodwin Award of Merit from the American Philological Association. He worked from then on to write a second volume to his work *Aristotle's Criticism of Plato and the Academy*, but he was unable to complete it before his death. He died in Princeton, New Jersey.

• Forty-one of Cherniss's articles and book reviews, along with a bibliography, have been collected by Leonardo Tarán in *Harold Cherniss: Selected Papers* (1977). Cherniss's dissertation, "The Platonism of Gregory of Nyssa," was revised and published in 1971. A short biographical article by Tarán appears in *Gnomon-Kritische Zeitschrift für die gesamte klassische Altertumswissenschaft*, vol. 60, n. 7 (1988), pp. 665–66. An obituary is in the *New York Times*, 12 July 1987.

DOMOKOS HAJDO

CHERRINGTON, Ernest Hurst (24 Nov. 1877–13 Mar. 1950), temperance reformer and Methodist layman, was born in Hamden, Ohio, the son of George Cherrington, a Methodist clergyman, and Elizabeth

Ophelia Paine. After attending the preparatory department of Ohio Wesleyan University (1893–1897), Cherrington taught school in Ross County, Ohio, and edited the *Kingston* (Ohio) *Tribune* (1900–1901). In 1903 he married Betty Clifford Denny; they had two children.

Cherrington began his career in temperance reform by speaking occasionally for the Ohio Anti-Saloon League but was soon given a full-time position in charge of the league's Canton district (1902). He entered the prohibition movement during a slack period for the reform, after the Prohibition party had discredited itself by splitting in 1896 but before a new strategy had won the support of American prohibitionists. The anti-saloon approach was untested, and its workers were paid poorly and were subjected to constant criticism from party prohibitionists. While in Canton Cherrington attracted the attention of Purley A. Baker, state superintendent of the Ohio Anti-Saloon League, and was made Baker's assistant. When Baker was named national superintendent of the Anti-Saloon League of America (ASLA), he appointed Cherrington to head the league's flimsy organization in Washington State (1905). Using methods pioneered in Ohio—establishing a newspaper, enrolling sympathetic Protestant churches, diligent fundraising, and canvassing political candidates—Cherrington "gave structure and power to an organization which would soon be strong enough to manipulate the state legislature" (Clark, p. 84). He capped four successful years in Washington by leading a victorious campaign for a state local-option law, giving cities and counties the right to determine if they would be dry or wet.

Cherrington was then recalled to the Midwest to become assistant editor of the surging ASLA's new national newspaper, the *American Issue*. By 1910 Cherrington had become editor of the *American Issue* as well as director of all publication activity for the national league. In the latter capacity he organized the American Issue Press, a publishing company that poured forth vast amounts of temperance propaganda from its printing plant in Westerville, Ohio, during the 1910s. In addition to the national newspaper, one of Cherrington's key publications was the annual *Anti-Saloon League Yearbook* (1908–1932), which disseminated voluminous data on all aspects of the liquor issue, including famous but sometimes misleading maps of the United States and each state showing graphically in white-versus-black contrast the progress of restrictive measures against the liquor traffic. The *Yearbook* displayed Cherrington's characteristically Progressive belief that the presentation of facts would convince Americans to rid their land of the curse of liquor. The image of a constantly advancing movement created by Cherrington's propaganda contributed significantly both to the ASLA's ability to hold the leadership of the prohibitionist forces and to the ultimate triumph of its cause. Providing monetary support for the burgeoning publishing enterprise involved Cherrington in fundraising, and he soon became a key financial official of the national league. By the eve of national prohibition, the national and state leagues together were enjoying annual revenues of nearly $2.5 million. Cherrington also assisted the prohibition drive by organizing and overseeing its national speakers' bureau. During the crucial campaign for the Eighteenth Amendment, Cherrington, now secretary of the ASLA's national executive committee in addition to his other responsibilities, occupied a key position among the dry leadership.

As the campaign neared fruition in 1919, Cherrington launched two significant initiatives. First, he persuaded the leadership of the ASLA to sponsor formation of the World League Against Alcoholism, justified both by the desire to spread the blessings of prohibition to societies around the world and by the need to protect prohibition in the United States. In pushing the ASLA toward international prohibitionism, Cherrington opposed the organization's general counsel, Wayne B. Wheeler, who urged instead concentration on maintaining the prohibitory regime at home through vigorous enforcement of the Volstead Act, the federal statute that implemented the Eighteenth Amendment to the Constitution. The rift between the two strategies became more public when Cherrington published a plan for reorganization of the league that called for prohibitionist resources to be employed in a renewed campaign of education. Factional conflict, exacerbated by shrinking financial support following passage of the Eighteenth Amendment, crippled the ASLA for the next eight years until Wheeler's death, which, together with the manifest difficulties of enforcement, cleared the way for adoption of Cherrington's strategic prescription. Factional maneuvering also prevented Cherrington's election to the league's national superintendency following Baker's resignation in 1924. By 1927, however, prohibitionists had too little time remaining for an educational campaign. The onset of the Great Depression led Americans to see prohibition in a new light, and passage of the Twenty-first Amendment in 1933 repealed the Eighteenth, sweeping away prohibitionists' great legislative achievement while destroying what little political power they still had.

After repeal, Cherrington remained active in both temperance reform and the Methodist Episcopal church, in which he had long played a leading lay role. Particularly noteworthy were his contributions to the movement for Methodist unification and his long association with the Federal Council of Churches. He retired in 1948 and died in Worthington, Ohio.

Cherrington's internationalism and his emphasis on education rather than law enforcement have led historians to see him as the most cosmopolitan and intellectual dry leader during the Anti-Saloon League era. Yet for Cherrington education was always instrumental to the triumph of his cause, and he never wavered from his conviction that in prohibition lay the best solution to the liquor problem. He was able to discuss such matters reasonably precisely because of his sublime faith that discussion would inevitably culminate in others' coming to adopt his point of view. He embraced internationalism with the same confidence that ultimately the world would acknowledge the virtues of the American way as defined by the Anti-Saloon League. Although the world never accepted prohibition and his fellow Americans rejected it, both the propaganda Cherrington produced and the prohibition amendment he was unable to maintain had an enduring impact on the American perception of alcohol.

• Cherrington's voluminous papers are held at the Ohio Historical Society and are available in a microfilm edition, which also contains the *American Issue*. His books are *History of the Anti-Saloon League* (1913), *The Evolution of Prohibition in the U.S.A.* (1920), and *America and the World Liquor Problem* (1922). In the absence of a biography of Cherrington, the best treatment is in K. Austin Kerr, *Organized for Prohibition* (1985). Cherrington's career in Washington State is discussed in Norman H. Clark, *The Dry Years* (1965; rev. ed. 1988). See also the biographical article in Cherrington's *Standard Encyclopedia of the Alcohol Problem*, vol. 2 (1924–1930), pp. 565–66, which includes a photograph.

JACK S. BLOCKER, JR.

CHESBRO, Jack (5 June 1874–6 Nov. 1931), baseball pitcher, was born John Dwight Chesbro in North Adams, Massachusetts, the son of Chad Chesbro. His mother's name is unknown. He developed his baseball skills on the sandlots in the western part of the state. In 1894 Chesbro and several of his friends accepted employment at the state mental hospital in Middletown, New York, where they played for the hospital baseball team. It was at this time that his easygoing personality earned him the nickname "Happy Jack."

Following a year's employment at the hospital, Chesbro signed his first professional contract with the Albany club of the New York State League. When first the team and then the league collapsed, the young pitcher finished the year performing for Springfield, Massachusetts, in the Eastern League. In 1896 Chesbro played with Roanoke in the Virginia League, but again his team folded, and he completed the season pitching semiprofessional baseball in Cooperstown, New York. Still searching for a stable baseball franchise, the right-handed pitcher next found employment with the Richmond club of the Atlantic League. Chesbro labored for the Richmond franchise from 1897 to 1899, when his contract was purchased by the Pittsburgh Pirates of the National League. At age twenty-five, the chunky pitcher, who stood 5′9″ and weighed 180 pounds, was in the major leagues.

In 1901 the Pirates gained their first National League championship, with Chesbro contributing 21 victories and only 10 defeats, earning the top winning percentage in the league. The Pirates repeated as National League champions in 1902, while Chesbro improved his mark to 28 victories against six losses.

Seeking more money, in 1903 Chesbro left the Pirates for the New York Highlanders (later to become the Yankees) who were in their maiden American League season. Chesbro won 21 games and lost 15 for the Highlanders, who finished in fourth place. However, in 1904 Chesbro enjoyed perhaps the finest season of any pitcher in the twentieth century. In light of baseball trends regarding the extensive use of relief pitchers, it seems likely that Chesbro's 1904 numbers will continue to stand the test of time. Chesbro won 41 games against 12 losses in a season in which he started 51 games, completing 48 and leading the American League with 454.2 innings pitched and 239 strikeouts. Despite these achievements, the season ended on a sour note in the next to last game of the year when the Highlanders lost the pennant to the Boston Red Sox after Chesbro uncorked a wild pitch to let the winning run score. Unfortunately, Chesbro suffered a great deal of anguish when Highlander fans focused on the wild pitch rather than the 41 victories.

Chesbro never regained his 1904 form, although in 1905 and 1906 he won 19 and 24 games, respectively. An ankle injury in 1907 dropped Chesbro to only 10 victories, while in 1908 the Highlanders finished last and Chesbro compiled a losing record of 14 victories and 20 defeats. He tried to make a comeback in the 1909 season but was released by the Highlanders. He was briefly picked up by the Red Sox but was ineffective and retired. Attempting to account for his abrupt decline, Chesbro blamed the strain of throwing the now-outlawed spitball. In 1905, however, the right-hander had lauded the pitch, maintaining that it was the "most effective ball that possibly could be used," as a little moisture could make the ball drop from several inches to a foot. While the spitball may have placed stress on Chesbro's arm, it is worth noting that he hurled more than 1,400 innings between 1903 and 1906. The Highlanders had overworked their ace pitcher.

Chesbro returned to Massachusetts and along with his wife, Mabel Shuttleworth, managed a chicken farm in Conway. He also managed a sawmill and a lumberyard. He served as baseball coach at Amherst College in 1911, and in 1912 he attempted an unsuccessful comeback with the Highlanders. Chesbro continued to farm until his death from a heart attack in Conway. He was elected to the Baseball Hall of Fame in 1946.

• A file on Chesbro is at the National Baseball Hall of Fame in Cooperstown, N.Y. For biographical information, see Lee Allen and Thomas Meany, *Kings of the Diamond* (1965); Martin Appel and Burt Goldblatt, *Baseball's Best: The Hall of Fame Gallery* (1980); and Ira L. Smith, *Baseball's Famous Pitchers* (1954). For baseball in the late nineteenth and early twentieth centuries, see Charles Alexander, *Our Game: An American Baseball History* (1991); Warren Goldstein, *Playing for Keeps* (1989); Ben Rader, *Baseball: A History of America's Game* (1992); Lawrence S. Ritter, *The Glory of Their Times* (1966); Harold Seymour, *Baseball: The Early Years* (1960); and David Q. Voigt, *American Baseball* (3 vols., 1966–1983). Obituaries are in the *New York Times*, 7 Nov. 1931, and the *Chicago Tribune*, 9 Nov. 1931.

RON BRILEY

CHESEBROUGH, Caroline (30 Mar. 1825–16 Feb. 1873), novelist and short-story writer, was born in Canandaigua, New York, the daughter of Nicholas

Goddard Chesebrough, a merchant and postmaster, and Betsy Kimball. Chesebrough was educated at the Canandaigua Seminary.

Chesebrough wrote sentimental fiction for adults and children. Using the pseudonym Caroline Chesebro', she began her career by publishing short works in magazines in 1848. Among the publications in which Chesebrough's sketches and stories subsequently appeared were *Graham's*, the *Knickerbocker*, *Putnam's*, *Harper's*, and the *Atlantic Monthly*.

Chesebrough's first book was *Dream-land by Daylight* (1851), a collection of sketches and tales. More conventional than her later work, these stories feature the orphaned girls, long-suffering women, and beautiful deaths characteristic of sentimental fiction. In "Shades and Sunbeams," the opening tale, the sisters Margaret and Ellen, deserted by their father, separated from one another, and buffeted by fortune, are finally reunited shortly before Margaret's youthful death. In "Aurora Borealis," another story in the collection, Chesebrough adopts a supernatural motif; after hardworking little Alice dies, the child's spirit appears in visions to each of her family members, counseling them against bad choices and offering them moral support.

Despite the conventionality of these early tales, they manifest Chesebrough's keen sympathy for social pariahs. "The Human Verb," for example, deals with a woman wrongly accused of impropriety by a judge and subsequently driven to suicide by the incarceration and death of her brother.

Between 1851 and 1856, Chesebrough was highly prolific. In 1852, her first novel, *Isa, a Pilgrimage*, appeared; it was followed by *The Children of Light* (1853), *The Little Cross-Bearers* (1854), *Susan, the Fisherman's Daughter; or, Getting Along* (1855), *The Beautiful Gate, and Other Stories* (1855), *Victoria* (1856), and *Philly and Kit* (1856). Of these, *Susan, the Fisherman's Daughter*, is the most ambitious. In plot and number of characters, its scope is epic, though unlike the traditional epic it recounts the stories of women seeking to work out their own destinies in a society that severely limits female roles.

Chesebrough's complex plotting in *Susan* interweaves the lives of four female protagonists; the fortunes of Susan, the title character, are representative. The daughter of a poor but virtuous fisherman, Susan is befriended by a series of men whose idea of improving her lot in life is to mold her into their personal vision of the ideal woman. Leighton, a scholar, seizes upon the girl as a fit subject for him to educate in his own heartless metaphysics. Wealthy Mr. Baldwin introduces her into the company of his cultivated children.

The plans that the idealistic social worker Mr. Falcon have for Susan reveal the selfish motivations of these supposed benefactors. Falcon, seconded by Leighton and Mr. Baldwin, wants Susan to marry the mentally disturbed young Clarence Baldwin, over whom she has a soothing influence. Even though the girl finds this proposal repugnant, she does not shirk from the self-sacrifice and is saved from the marriage only by Clarence's death.

In 1856 Chesebrough moved out of her family's home. After an eight-year hiatus in publication, she brought out her novel *Peter Carradine; or, The Martindale Pastoral* (1863). Because of its complex characterization, this novel is generally considered her best. As in *Susan*, Chesebrough divides the role of protagonist among several young women. Typical of the sentimental novel, much of the plot revolves around the matrimonial choices of these women characters. Sally Green, who defies her parents by secretly marrying a cad, ends in misfortune. Mercy Fuller, in contrast, is the true sentimental heroine; a highly virtuous woman, she leads Peter Carradine, the vigorous male protagonist, from coldness to love.

In addition to *Peter Carradine*, Chesebrough published four books between 1863 and 1865—*The Sparrow's Fall* (1863), *Amy Carr* (1864), *The Fisherman of Gamp's Island* (1865), and *The Glen Cabin* (1865). Chesebrough's last completed novel, *The Foe in the Household*, appeared in 1871.

A denominational novel, *The Foe in the Household* deals with domestic and doctrinal conflicts between and within the households of a benevolent Mennonite bishop and a conniving Methodist camp preacher. Although the novel revolves around standard sentimental motifs, its women characters possess a rebelliousness and strength atypical of most sentimental heroines. After the widowed Delia Trost, whose secret first marriage to a non-Mennonite would have resulted in her excommunication had it been revealed, weds a Mennonite clergyman, she demonstrates her continuing independence by speaking in favor of people censured by the community. Delia's youthful transgression is too great to be countenanced in a sentimental heroine (even an unconventional Chesebrough heroine), and she predictably dies at the novel's end. Delia's daughter, however, is rewarded with marriage to a local industrialist, even though she is even more independent and outspoken than her mother.

In addition to working as a novelist, Chesebrough taught at Packer Collegiate Institute, a girls' school in Brooklyn, New York, from 1865 until 1873. According to her students, Chesebrough was an inspiring and challenging teacher. Chesebrough died in Piermont, New York, where she shared a home with a brother and sister. She is buried in the family cemetery in Canandaigua.

Both during her lifetime and subsequently, popular success eluded Chesebrough. Her work was, however, respected in certain literary circles. In a preface to *Dream-land by Daylight*, E. F. Eliot, a friend of Edgar Allan Poe's, praised Chesebrough's writings for an "exquisite perception of natural beauty . . . combined with a sense of its relation to the moral emotions" (p. viii). Chesebrough's obituary in the *New-York Tribune* (19 Feb. 1873) commended the sympathy that her novels extend to wayward or doubting people. By the end of the nineteenth century, Chesebrough's work had fallen into neglect. The independent-mindedness of Chesebrough's heroines gained the novelist favor with some feminist critics in the 1970s. Nonetheless, because her writing lacks the descriptive vividness of regional culture that characterizes the best sentimental novels, her texts were still out of print as of the 1990s and seem likely to remain so.

• Chesebrough's papers are scattered; manuscript materials are archived at the New-York Historical Society and the New York Public Library. In addition to nineteenth-century imprints, Chesebrough's major novels are available on microfilm in the Wright American Fiction series. Critical study of Chesebrough's work is scant. The most complete modern assessment of Chesebrough appears in Nina Baym's *Woman's Fiction* (1978). More disparaging of Chesebrough and sentimental culture—but, given the paucity of work on Chesebrough, nonetheless useful—are H. R. Brown, *The Sentimental Novel in America, 1789–1860* (1940); Helen W. Papashvily, *All the Happy Endings* (1956); and Ann Douglas, *The Feminization of American Culture* (1977). Biographical information is similarly lacking; the fullest accounts of Chesebrough's life appear in Marjorie Jane Hunt, "The Short Stories of Caroline Chesebro'" (M.A. thesis, George Washington Univ., 1970); Lina Mainiero, ed., *American Women Writers* (1979); Lucy M. Freibert and Barbara A. White, eds., *Hidden Hands: An Anthology of American Women Writers, 1790–1870* (1985); and Elizabeth Ammons et al., eds., *The Oxford Companion to Women's Writing in the United States* (1995).

TESS LLOYD

CHESNUT, James, Jr. (18 Jan. 1815–1 Feb. 1885), U.S. senator, was born in Mulberry, near Camden, South Carolina, the son of James Chesnut, Sr., and Mary Cox. A son of one of South Carolina's wealthiest planters, Chesnut attended Princeton College from 1831 to 1835. Graduating with honors, he was selected to give an "honorary oration" at his graduation ceremony. Though offered a position as aide to Governor Pierce Mason Butler, Chesnut, at the insistence of his autocratic father, declined, choosing instead to read law under nationally known Charleston lawyer James Louis Petigru. Chesnut opened his own practice in Camden in 1838. The following year, his elder brother's death made him heir apparent to the family plantations, which he eventually inherited. In 1840 he married Mary Boykin Miller. The union produced no children. It was, however, the most important aspect of Chesnut's later fame. Mary Boykin Chesnut was to become—deservedly—the most celebrated diarist of the American Civil War. Her keen perception of personalities and situations and her skillful use of language to convey them make her "diary" (actually a memoir of the war years written after the war in diary form) an invaluable source of information on life in the upper strata of Confederate society. Her fame and that of her diary have shed more light on her husband than he otherwise would have received.

In 1840 James Chesnut was elected to the state legislature, where he served until 1846 and from 1849 to 1851 before being elected to the state senate in 1852. Over the next decade he served six years in that house as well, being elected its president in 1856. Though considered a moderate within South Carolina politics, because he opposed the state's more radical politicians, who had supported the nullification of federal law in the early 1830s and who were foremost in agitating for secession, Chesnut did attend the essentially secessionist Nashville Convention in 1850. No major issues during the 1840s and 1850s forced him to take a definitive position in the South Carolina legislature. His attendance at the Nashville Convention indicates that he favored secession at that time only if it could be carried out in cooperation with several other southern states. In South Carolina that was considered a moderate position. In 1858 he was elected to the U.S. Senate in what was then viewed as a victory for the moderate faction within South Carolina.

Two years later Abraham Lincoln was elected president of the United States. Though Chesnut had not previously declared a position on the issue of secession—then loudly threatened by many in the South as a fitting reaction should Lincoln win the election—he promptly resigned his seat in the Senate even before South Carolina seceded and returned to South Carolina to use his political influence for that cause. He attended the secession convention and actually helped draft the state's ordinance of secession. This done, he was elected to the Confederacy's Provisional Congress, where he sat on the Committee on Naval Affairs and the Committee on Territories. Though not on the committee to write the provisional constitution, he was on the committee to write the permanent constitution. The most striking position he took while in the Provisional Congress was to advocate the reopening of the African slave trade, banned in the United States for more than half a century before the Civil War. The measure was not adopted.

Once the first session of the Provisional Congress was over in the spring of 1861, Chesnut joined the staff of Brigadier General P. G. T. Beauregard as an aide-de-camp with the rank of colonel. In this capacity he was the ranking member of the three-man delegation that, on 11 and 12 April 1861, carried out the final, unsuccessful negotiations with Union major Robert Anderson aimed at securing the surrender to Confederate forces of Fort Sumter, in Charleston Harbor. It was Chesnut who, at 3:20 A.M., 12 April 1861, deemed Anderson's final reply unsatisfactory and, therefore, decided that Confederate batteries should open fire one hour from that time. After Sumter, Chesnut continued on Beauregard's staff, following the general when he was transferred to Virginia and serving with him during the first battle of Manassas (Bull Run). Prior to the battle, during early July 1861, Chesnut was the staff officer selected by Beauregard to carry to Confederate president Jefferson Davis an unrealistic proposal for offensive action that later became an issue of dispute between the president and the general. Later that year Chesnut transferred to the staff of Davis.

In 1862 the South Carolina legislature named Chesnut a member of the five-man executive council that would virtually run the state. His particular duty on the council was that of organizing the state's militia.

When in October of that year a vacancy on Davis's staff offered him the opportunity to return to that duty, Chesnut resigned from the council and returned to Richmond. In October 1863 Davis sent Chesnut on a fact-finding mission to the distressed Army of Tennessee, and on the strength of Chesnut's report, the Confederate president determined to make his second western trip of the war to visit the army. In April 1864 Chesnut was sent to South Carolina again, this time with a commission as a Confederate brigadier general and an assignment to bring out the last of the state's manpower—by conscription or persuasion—to combat the approaching Union army of William T. Sherman. He led a brigade into Georgia in an attempt to cooperate in the defense of Savannah, but after its fall he was returned to administrative duties.

After the war Chesnut was impoverished. Though his father's death in 1866 finally gave him the inheritance, by this time it amounted to no more than the land itself, deeply encumbered with debt. Years of what Mary Chesnut called "scraping and saving" followed. By 1868 James Chesnut was once again active in South Carolina politics, working diligently to bring an end to the Reconstruction government in the state. Making a number of speeches urging South Carolina voters to elect Democrats, he played an energetic role in the electoral campaign of 1876, resulting in the election of Wade Hampton (1818–1902) as governor and the restoration of Democratic party rule. He was disappointed, however, in receiving no political appointment in return. In 1878 his right to vote was restored, but in 1882 he was again disappointed when President Chester A. Arthur did not offer him a position on the new Federal Tariff Commission. He died at his home near Camden.

• Many of Chesnut's papers are in the Williams, Manning, Chesnut collection, South Caroliniana Library, Columbia, S.C. The best sources of information about him are works by and/or about his wife: Ben Ames Williams, ed., *A Diary from Dixie* (1905); C. Vann Woodward, ed., *Mary Chesnut's Civil War* (1981); and Woodward and Elisabeth Muhlenfeld, eds., *The Private Mary Chesnut* (1984). Additional information can be found in Charles E. Cauthen, *South Carolina Goes to War* (1950).

STEVEN E. WOODWORTH

CHESNUT, Mary Boykin Miller (31 Mar. 1823–22 Nov. 1886), diarist and memoirist, was born at "Mount Pleasant," a plantation near Statesburg, South Carolina, the daughter of Stephen Decatur Miller, a lawyer and a politician, and Mary Boykin. At an early age she moved with her parents to "Plane Hill," a plantation nearer Statesburg. Her father, who had served in the House of Representatives in 1817–1819, helped found the States Rights party in South Carolina in 1824. He was elected governor in 1828 and a U.S. senator in 1830. He resigned in 1833 and resumed the practice of law, partly because of the greater influence in state and federal politics of John C. Calhoun, an advocate of nullification. Mary, who had been taught at home and enjoyed reading, in 1835 entered Madame Talvande's expensive French School for Young Ladies in Charleston, South Carolina. While there she studied history, literature, rhetoric, and science, and she learned to read and speak French and read German. She also met James Chesnut, Jr., a graduate of Princeton's class of 1835, the uncle of one of Mary's schoolmates, and Mary's future husband. Her father suddenly took her away to Mississippi in 1836. He and the rest of the family were already settled there, he owned three unprofitable plantations and hundreds of slaves, and he was perhaps concerned that Chesnut was too interested in his accomplished daughter—which he assuredly was.

Mary's time in Mississippi was filled with all the excitement of life on the southwestern frontier—visits to New Orleans, Mississippi River steamboat races, Choctaw Indians and wilder Native Americans, even packs of wolves, and numerous young would-be suitors. After only a year in Mississippi, Mary was transferred for safety back to the Talvande school, and her mother and her siblings also soon returned to Charleston. She and Chesnut, who was by 1837 a practicing attorney in Camden, South Carolina, often saw each other and fell in love. Her father died in Mississippi in 1838, and his widow called Mary back to Mississippi to help settle the debt-plagued estate. This accomplished, mother and daughter returned to Charleston, where Mary in 1839 promised to marry Chesnut. First, however, he took his ailing older brother John Chesnut to France for medical treatment, which proved unsuccessful. John's death back home in 1839 burdened James Chesnut with family responsibilities, including substantial management of his parents' plantations, one of which was "Mulberry," three miles south of Camden. Married in 1840, James and Mary Chesnut first lived at Mulberry with his parents and two unmarried sisters. His father, a retired colonel, remained a Unionist until his death in 1866.

Mary Chesnut's life from 1840 was in large part in the shadow of her husband's career. She may have somewhat regretted marrying when only seventeen and thus missing the excitement of being a sought-after "southern belle." Energetic James Chesnut was a member of the lower house of the General Assembly of South Carolina (1840–1846, 1850–1852), a member of the state senate (1852–1858), and—eloquently advocating the popular cause of secession—a member of the U.S. Senate beginning in 1858. Once there, he defended slavery as the best means for the South to promote what in a speech in Congress he called "commerce, civilization, and Christianity." During their first five years of marriage, Mary and her husband lived mostly at Mulberry, a part of his time spent on duty at Columbia. They traveled to London in 1845 and to New Jersey, New York, and Philadelphia in 1847 and 1848 to visit relatives on both sides and also so that Mary—in poor health and chronically depressed—could consult physicians. The Chesnuts built and moved into their own house, naming it "Frogvale," in Camden in 1848.

In 1850, when her husband was officially opposing the Wilmot Proviso prohibiting slavery in land acquired from Mexico, she expressed her opposition to slavery in a letter to him. She also wrote numerous letters to her mother in Alabama and to her siblings. In 1854 the Chesnuts built and moved into a bigger house, called "Kamchatka," in fashionable north Camden. Mary, who was sadly childless, took delight in the children of her sister Catherine "Kate" Miller Williams and Kate's husband David. For all of 1857 she cared for the first three of Kate's children while the parents were in Europe. Two more were born, and Mary called all five of them her "little sweet Williams." In 1858 senator-elect James Chesnut sold Kamchatka; the couple distributed their slaves and moved to Washington, D.C. Mary was her husband's part-time secretary, helped him balance his moral reservations about slavery against his states' rights stance, and became a gracious, literary-minded hostess. During the summer months of 1859 and 1860 she visited relatives scattered from Alabama to New Jersey.

When war seemed inevitable, James Chesnut resigned from the Senate in November 1860. He returned home, helped draft secession papers, and, as an aide to Confederate general Pierre Gustave Toutant Beauregard, delivered that man's evacuation terms to Fort Sumter. He was Beauregard's aide again at the first battle at Manassas, was a member of the executive council of South Carolina until 1862, and was a colonel on Confederate president Jefferson Davis's staff until 1864. As a brigadier general he commanded reserves in South Carolina until the end of the war. During these years Mary followed her husband to his various posts, sometimes at the expense of her health or equanimity; often she was quartered with him in unsavory hotels and boardinghouses, sometimes so ill with depression, headaches, and stomach pains that she was prescribed opium and morphine for relief. Still, she accompanied him to or later joined him at Montgomery, Alabama, the first Confederate capital; Charleston, where she witnessed the siege of Fort Sumter; and Richmond, Virginia, where she welcomed Davis and other high-ranking Confederate officers into her home and where she became an intimate friend of Davis's wife Varina. Finally, she became a terrified refugee in North Carolina, avoiding General William Tecumseh Sherman's advancing armies. At war's end, she and her husband made their way back to Mulberry, which had been damaged by Union soldiers.

Mary Chesnut's wartime experiences were varied and intense, often tragic in nature. Nevertheless, the excitement of war provided a stimulant to a childless southern matron who before the war was frustrated and depressed. Her husband was too cool-headed, aristocratic, and self-sacrificial to suit her energetic and unfulfilled nature. If he had asked, he could have obtained an important commission in the Confederate army and achieved glory, or he could have successfully requested a diplomatic appointment in London or in Paris. Doing neither, he remained self-effacing and largely unappreciated. For her part, she plunged into what wartime activities were available to her through his assignments, accepted all challenges—personal, familial, social, and political—with a fierce commitment, and began keeping the finest diary by any southern woman during the four-year conflict between the states.

Mary Chesnut started her diary in February 1861, kept at it sporadically for a total of perhaps twelve "volumes," of which seven are extant. The first five volumes run through 8 December 1861; the sixth, January to February 1865; the seventh, 7 May to 26 July 1865. Evidence permits the conclusion that she recorded nothing between August 1862 and October 1863, perhaps because of arduous hospital duty. After the war, the Chesnuts had monumental problems. James Chesnut's mother had died in 1864; his father, blind and partially deaf, died in 1866. James Chesnut inherited land, debts, and former slaves still dependent on the Chesnuts. The only cash he and Mary had for a long time came from their sale of butter and eggs.

James Chesnut was back in politics by 1868, and Mary was left to manage business matters. Gradually, their fortunes improved. In 1873 they built a big house, "Sarsfield," in Camden. James was frustrated in the late 1870s and early 1880s when he failed to be elected or appointed to any position in the improving political climate of South Carolina. In 1881 Mary began rewriting her wartime diaries and continued doing so until 1884. She reordered and sometimes expanded incidents, composed new ones, deleted especially critical passages, and cut down unpleasant references to family matters—notably to her father-in-law's mulatto slave babies. Deleting frequent bits of self-praise, she sketched herself as a great reader. She hated slavery, calling it a "black incubus" and referring to herself as a would-be abolitionist; yet she was offended by and unsympathetic to "dirty" and "savage" slaves. She also simultaneously loathed dictatorial southern patriarchs and admired chivalric southern males.

In February 1885 Mary's husband died, and her mother died five days later. The legal consequence of her husband's death was the bequeathment of property, which he had controlled, to a male Chesnut heir. As his widow, Mary inherited a little money but many debts. She retained Sarsfield and an annual income of little more than a hundred dollars, which she augmented by modest sales of butter and eggs from a small dairy farm she managed. In her spare time she tried without success to assemble her husband's papers for a biographical memorial. There is no evidence that she returned to the rewriting of her war diaries. Having suffered for some years from a heart condition, she died at Sarsfield.

The Chesnut diaries have had a curious history. Excerpts were selected, edited, and published by Isabella Martin and Myrta Lockett Avary as *A Diary from Dixie, as Written by Mary Boykin Chesnut . . .* (1905). In the process, Martin mislaid parts of Chesnut's work. Ben Ames Williams, the novelist who patterned Cinda Dewain, the central character of his *House Divided* (1947), on Mary Chesnut, edited her *A Diary from*

Dixie in 1949. C. Vann Woodward in 1981 published his carefully annotated *Mary Chesnut's Civil War*, which combines diaries and retrospective memoirs, and he and Elisabeth Muhlenfeld edited the original diaries as *The Private Mary Chesnut: The Unpublished Civil War Diaries* in 1984. Only recently has it been possible to make a final judgment, which is that Chesnut has given the world one of the most vivid and significant portraits of an era. Her woman's perspective on the Old South's social, political, patriarchal, ideological, and physical efforts to survive, together with numerous implications accounting for its failure to do so, provides essential reading for anyone interested in Confederate history. On 18 March 1861 Chesnut penned her most frequently quoted lines, which begin: "I wonder if it be a sin to think slavery a curse to any land. [Northern abolitionist Charles] Sumner said not one word of this hated institution which is not true. Men and women are punished when their masters and mistresses are brutes and not when they do wrong. . . . God forgive us, but ours is a *monstrous* system and wrong and iniquity. Perhaps the rest of the world is as bad—this *only* I see." These lines reveal much concerning their complex and fascinating author.

• The extant manuscripts of Chesnut's diary are in the Atlanta Society Collections, Georgia. Much of her correspondence and many other papers are in the South Caroliniana Library at the University of South Carolina. Elisabeth Muhlenfeld, *Mary Boykin Chesnut: A Biography* (1981), and Mary A. DeCredico, *Mary Boykin Chesnut: A Confederate Woman's Life* (1996), are detailed accounts of her life. Earlier critical treatments of Chesnut are in Edmund Wilson, *Patriotic Gore: Studies in the Literature of the American Civil War* (1962); Daniel Aaron, *The Unwritten War: American Writers and the Civil War* (1973); and Ben Irvin Wiley, *Confederate Women* (1975). Tim Hamling, "Legendary Americans: Mary Chesnut," *Ideals* 49 (Aug. 1995): 22–23, is a succinct profile. Pertinent background material is in Douglas Southall Freeman, *The South to Posterity* (1939; rev. ed., 1983); Charles E. Cauthen, *South Carolina Goes to War, 1860–1865* (1950); James B. Meriwether, ed., *South Carolina Women Writers* (1979); Elizabeth Fox-Genovese, *Within the Plantation Household: Black and White Women in the Old South* (1988); and Drew Gilpin Faust, *Mothers of Invention: Women of the Slaveholding South in the American Civil War* (1996).

ROBERT L. GALE

CHESNUTT, Charles Waddell (20 June 1858–15 Nov. 1932), writer, was born in Cleveland, Ohio, the son of Andrew Jackson Chesnutt, a horse car driver, and Ann Maria Sampson. His parents were free African Americans who had left Fayetteville, North Carolina, in 1856 to escape the oppressiveness of life in a slave state and its sparse opportunity. They were married in Cleveland in 1857. During the Civil War, Chesnutt's father served four years as a teamster in the Union army, but the family returned to Fayetteville in 1866 because A. J. Chesnutt's father, Waddell Cade (a local white farm owner—the name Chesnutt came from A. J.'s mother, Ann), helped his son establish a grocery store there. Young Charles helped in the store and over the years heard many things there about southern life and folkways that he recorded or remembered and that later became part of or informed his writings. Charles attended the Howard School, which existed through the efforts of local black citizens and the Freedmen's Bureau; but after his father lost his store and moved to a nearby farm, Charles was forced at age fourteen to change his role in the school from that of eager pupil to pupil-teacher in order to help with family finances. He continued to read widely in various fields, especially in literature, thereby further educating himself.

Chesnutt began teaching in Charlotte, North Carolina, in 1872 and in the summers in other North and South Carolina communities. In the fall of 1877 he returned to Fayetteville to work in the new state normal school there. The following summer he married one of the school's teachers, Susan U. Perry, and the first of their four children was born the following spring. Though Chesnutt became principal of the normal school at age twenty-two and continued to study varied subjects regularly, he felt restricted in opportunities and intellectually isolated in the post–Civil War South. In 1883 he used his self-taught ability to take shorthand at 200 words per minute to escape, first to New York for a few months and then to Cleveland, where he was joined by his family in April 1884. He lived there the rest of his life.

In Cleveland, Chesnutt worked as an office clerk and court reporter, passed the Ohio bar exam in 1887 (with the highest grade in his group), and established a prosperous legal stenography firm, eventually after several moves acquiring a fourteen-room home. More importantly, he worked at becoming a writer. He had been moving in that direction for some time, and in 1872 a local weekly Negro newspaper had published his condemnation of the reading of dime novels. The growth of his interest in literature and his ambition to become a writer are reflected in numerous entries in his journals during the 1870s and 1880s, especially as he became more and more aware of what had been written and was being written about the South and black people, subjects about which he felt confident of his own better knowledge and understanding. His journal entry for 29 May 1880 spoke of a purpose for his intended writing that would improve the South and all of its people. It included the declaration, "I think I must write a book." However, before he would accomplish that goal there were to be years of sketches, tales, and stories, beginning in 1885 published in various periodicals, including eventually such widely known magazines as *Family Fiction*, *Puck*, *The Overland Monthly*, *The Crisis*, *The Southern Workman*, *The Century*, *The Outlook*, *Youth's Companion*, and various newspapers in some of the nation's larger cities.

Chesnutt's most important breakthrough came with the publication of his tale "The Goophered Grapevine" in the *Atlantic Monthly* for August 1887. Although the editors did not then know the author's race, this was the first piece of short fiction published by an African American in a magazine with such prestige as to easily put the work before the majority of American readers. Chesnutt would publish short fiction and articles (both usually concerning racial matters) for much of the rest of his life, but very much tapering off after the early part of the twentieth century.

"The Goophered Grapevine" was the first of three of his stories in the *Atlantic Monthly* that focused on conjuring as an important aspect of black folklife. This is revealed in post–Civil War tales about earlier times in the Fayetteville area told by Uncle Julius, a shrewd and likable character who uses the stories to his own advantage and along the way also reveals much about what slavery meant in the daily concerns of its victims, of which he had been one. These three tales and four other Uncle Julius tales became Chesnutt's first book, *The Conjure Woman*, published by Houghton Mifflin (1899). In these stories Chesnutt broadened the range of racial realism in American literature, and all of his five volumes of fiction would deal with various facets of racial problems, with strong focusing on the experiences and points of view of his African-American characters, though his concerns were always for both blacks and whites in American society and particularly in the South.

The stories of his second book of fiction, *The Wife of His Youth and Other Stories of the Color Line*, also published by Houghton Mifflin (1899), are in most ways quite different from the conjure stories and illustrate the variety of Chesnutt's skill and art. They are more contemporary and less rural and folk oriented, with more focus (sometimes ironically) on middle-class African Americans, especially those with light skin color. About half of these stories are set in North Carolina, and about half in Ohio. As its title suggests, this book intended to demonstrate the complex difficulties and sensitivities of those who (like Chesnutt himself) were of obvious racially mixed blood in societies both north and south, in which they aspired to rise even in the face of uncertainties about how that would be viewed. Chesnutt had very light skin and few Negroid features. He wrote about respect and injustice from personal concern and experience. These stories are sometimes tragic and sometimes comic, as he tried to write from a balanced and whole view of racial phenomena he had observed at close hand. Various reviews called attention to Chesnutt's presentation of African-American characters in other than stereotypes and his making them of real interest and concern as individual human beings. Notable among such reviews was high praise from William Dean Howells in the *Atlantic Monthly* for May 1900, which took note of both of Chesnutt's volumes of fiction and of his biography of Frederick Douglass (1899) in the Beacon Biographies Series. Howells also identified Chesnutt with various well-known contemporary writers of realistic fiction whom Howells championed.

On 30 September 1899 Chesnutt had closed his stenography business in order to pursue writing full time. In the autumn of 1900 Houghton Mifflin brought out *The House behind the Cedars*, the first of three novels Chesnutt would publish. It is a fuller and more straightforward exploration of some of the miscegenation themes that had been found in his second volume of stories. The primary setting of the novel is the Fayetteville area, and it focuses on the emotional and practical (and sometimes tragic) difficulties of relatively white African Americans who chose to pass as white in the post–Civil War South. Although Chesnutt himself chose not to pass even though he could have, he knew those who had done so and understood and sympathized with their motives. Another novel, *The Marrow of Tradition*, followed from Houghton Mifflin in October 1901. This work, with his largest cast and most complicated plot, also is set in North Carolina. It is based on the riot that occurred in Wilmington in 1898 when white supremacists took over the city government with accompanying violence against blacks. In addition to having concerns with racial justice, as had his first novel this book also has some focus on the aspirations of African Americans who choose to participate in the more highly respected professions. However, this work is even more interracial, its principal characters are white, and there is more direct criticism of the white population. While Howells praised the straightforwardness of the novel's moral concerns, he was disturbed by its bitterness. It did not sell well enough for Chesnutt to continue his attempt to succeed as a full-time author, and he reopened his stenography business before the year was over.

While disappointment and the need to gain financial stability slowed Chesnutt's literary aspirations, he did publish one more novel. Another North Carolinian, Walter Hines Page, while an editor at Houghton Mifflin had praised Chesnutt's accuracy of local color and had assisted his progress. Now Page persuaded Chesnutt to leave Houghton Mifflin, even though his relations with that firm had been good; and in September 1905 (the year in which Thomas Dixon's racially negative novel *The Clansman* was a bestseller) Page's firm (Doubleday, Page & Company) brought out *The Colonel's Dream*. Its protagonist, a former Confederate officer, returns to his southeastern North Carolina hometown and proposes a plan to bring it out of the economic hardships caused by the Civil War and its aftermath. He is willing to invest his own resources, but the plan is rejected because of greed and racial prejudice in the community. Reflecting Chesnutt's continuing loving concern for the area where he had spent his formative years, this book is dedicated to "the great number of those who are seeking, in whatever manner or degree . . . to bring the forces of enlightenment to bear upon the vexed problems which harass the South."

However, the various-faceted message for the South (and the country as a whole) that pervades Chesnutt's fiction and nonfiction, particularly concerning economic and social justice in relation to race, was not being accepted by those for whom it was most intended. He now turned his efforts more to other aspects of his life, among them his family, his business, and his involvement in several cultural organizations in Cleveland. One of these was the prestigious bibliophilic Rowfant Club, which refused membership to this nationally respected author three times before finally admitting him in 1910. His satiric "Baxter's Procrustes" (*Atlantic Monthly*, June 1904) is based on that club, and many think it is his best-written story. His career as a writer resulted in his publishing between 1885 and 1931 sixty-one pieces of short fiction (including those in the two volumes); one biography; thirty-one speeches, articles, and essays; seven poems; and three novels. Also, he left unpublished a sizable correspondence, one play, six novels, fifty-three essays and speeches, eighteen short stories (most of which have now been published by Render), three journals, and one notebook.

Chesnutt's published fiction, particularly his five books, was his most important accomplishment both artistically and in his attempts to improve social (particularly racial) relations. However, in addition to his fiction, his early work as an educator, his stenographic work in Cleveland, and his other writings, he also was active in various other pursuits that gave him pleasure, visibility, influence, reputation, and opportunity. In Cleveland he was valued as a public speaker, a public citizen, and a writer. He put his concerns, his knowledge of the law, and his respected reputation and personality to good use in speaking out on political and legal matters locally and nationally, particularly when they concerned the rights of African Americans. Early in his career as a writer he had made the acquaintance of George Washington Cable and through this association had joined in the efforts of the Open-Letter Club, a project of several persons interested in and knowledgeable about the South to provide accurate information about that region and racial matters. (Also, over the years Cable offered Chesnutt literary encouragement and advice.) Chesnutt was an active member of the National Association for the Advancement of Colored People (NAACP) in Cleveland and nationally, and there was mutual respect between him and both Booker T. Washington and W. E. B. Du Bois. Though these two leaders took somewhat different approaches to the problems of African Americans and how best to solve them, Chesnutt saw merit in some aspects of the positions of both men and said so publicly, but also spoke up when he disagreed with them. He was a member of the General Committee of the NAACP and of Washington's Committee of Twelve for the Advancement of the Interests of the Negro Race. He addressed immediate socioeconomic problems and in various ways tried to promote awareness of and concern over the racial situation in America (particularly in the South—William Andrews has referred to his three novels as a New South trilogy). Chesnutt felt that the racial situation was undermining American democracy and that solutions to it would require sensitive understanding, ethical and moral conscience, and courage. In both his fiction and nonfiction his view of the proper future for African Americans was for gradual assimilation of them into the mainstream of American life through education and hard work. His three daughters and his one son all graduated from well-known colleges, and he lived to see them established in their chosen endeavors and moving into that mainstream, as he had in his way before them. For example, his daughter Helen became a nationally respected teacher of Latin in the Cleveland school system, and his son became a dentist.

Though the major part of Chesnutt's literary career ended with the publication of *The Colonel's Dream* in 1905, respect for him as a pioneering writer continued. Among the recognition given him was an invitation to attend Mark Twain's seventieth birthday party at Delmonico's in New York in 1905 and membership in the National Arts Club in 1917. In 1913 Wilberforce University gave him an honorary degree, and in 1928 he was awarded the NAACP's prestigious Spingarn Medal for his "pioneer work as a literary artist depicting the life and struggle of Americans of Negro descent, and for his long and useful career as scholar, worker and freeman of one of America's greatest cities." That same year *The Conjure Woman* was republished by Houghton Mifflin in a special edition with a foreword by the literary critic and leader in racial concerns Joel Spingarn. In 1926 the committee to choose the first recipient of the newly established Harmon Foundation Award for the work of an African-American writer during the preceding year recommended that the chronological stipulation be waived and the first award be given to Chesnutt to acknowledge his pioneering work and his continuing example to other African-American writers. This was not allowed, and unfortunately Chesnutt never knew of this acknowledgment of high esteem from a distinguished panel of his literary peers both black and white.

Chesnutt was the first important African-American writer whose primary genre was fiction and the first African-American writer to be published primarily by major publishers and major periodicals. Writing and publishing during times that were not very socially, politically, or legally favorable to African Americans in general, Chesnutt wrote fiction to provide entertainment and to call attention to racism and social injustice, especially for middle-class light-skinned blacks and working-class blacks in small towns and the rural South. He believed that the sources of as well as the solutions to their problems were in the South, so he wrote about the South and in ways that he intended to be more accurate, realistic, and better than those of others using similar subject matter. He purposefully dealt with topics regarding racial problems, such as miscegenation, which he felt other southern writers were avoiding or mistreating. In doing this he used various literary devices, including accurate dialect and details of local color and black life, satire, humor, irony, pathos, and even first-person point of view for nonblack characters. However, while he wrote with unblinking truth and obvious strong social purpose, he also wrote without rancor and with attention to and faithful portrayal of both sides of problems, creating a variety of memorable characters. He understood and presented many aspects of the South's problems and their effects on all parts of the southern community, with the hope that this would assist better understanding and solutions. He especially hoped to counter the too often derogatory and stereotypical portrayal of black characters and to make readers more aware of the positive and often complex humanity and variety of African Americans, the mistreatment of minorities and their need for greater social justice, and the fallibility of human nature. He was best at writing short fiction, but his novels, articles, and speeches also helped create the personal and literary reputation and respect he enjoyed during his lifetime.

Sylvia Render has pointed out that Chesnutt promoted American ideals in popular American forms and in accord with accepted contemporary literary standards, and was published by very reputable firms. However, after his death his works were generally underread and undervalued until attention to them revived in the 1960s. In his Spingarn Medal acceptance Chesnutt said, "I didn't write my stories as Negro propaganda—propaganda is apt to be deadly to art—but I used the better types [of Negroes], confident that the truth would prove the most valuable propaganda." A few months later he wrote to James Weldon Johnson, "I wrote the truth as I saw it, with no special catering to anybody's prejudices." He died in Cleveland.

• The most important sources for unpublished Chesnutt writings and related materials are the Chesnutt collection of the Cravath Library at Fisk University and the Chesnutt papers at the Library of the Western Reserve Historical Society, Cleveland. Richard H. Brodhead edited *The Journals of Charles W. Chesnutt* (1993) and a volume of all of Chesnutt's conjure stories, *The Conjure Woman and Other Conjure Tales* (1993). Sylvia Lyons Render published most of Chesnutt's previously unpublished or uncollected short fiction in *The Short Fiction of Charles W Chesnutt* (1974), with a long helpful introduction, and in the 1981 revised edition a bibliography of published and unpublished works by Chesnutt. She also is the author of *Charles W. Chesnutt* in the Twayne United States Authors Series, which though published in 1980 was essentially completed much earlier. Curtis W. Ellison and E. W. Metcalf, Jr., in 1977 published *Charles W. Chesnutt: A Reference Guide*, which provides easy access to secondary materials. Especially important is William L. Andrews, *The Literary Career of Charles W. Chesnutt* (1980), with a bibliography of Chesnutt's works. More general studies, each with its own distinctiveness, are Helen M. Chesnutt (his daughter), *Charles Waddell Chesnutt: Pioneer of the Color Line* (1952); J. Noel Heermance, *Charles W. Chesnutt: America's First Great Black Novelist* (1974); and Frances Richardson Keller, *An American Crusade: The Life of Charles Waddell Chesnutt* (1978), with a good bit of detail and family background.

JULIAN MASON

CHESSMAN, Caryl Whittier (27 May 1921–2 May 1960), criminal and writer, was born in St. Joseph, Michigan, the son of Serl Whittier Chessman, whose occupations were varied and who spent some time on welfare, and Hallie Cottle. Because of his mother's precarious health, Chessman and his parents moved to southern California a few months after his birth. Chessman was a sickly child, suffering from attacks of pneumonia, asthma, and encephalitis. (Psychiatrists suggest that his bout with encephalitis may have precipitated his psychopathic tendencies.) A serious car accident in Los Angeles in 1929 left his aunt dead, his mother paralyzed from the waist down, and Chessman with a broken nose and jaw. Overwhelming medical bills forced the family onto welfare, and he obtained a paper route to help out.

While delivering papers he committed his first crime, stealing food from a porch. At Glendale High School he fell in with other students who committed minor burglaries, forgeries, and car thefts. In 1937 he was caught stealing from a store's cash register and was taken to the Glendale police station, where he escaped through an opened window. Later that year Chessman was arrested for stealing a car and sent to a forestry camp. After running away from this camp twice, he was committed to the Preston State Industrial School in September 1937. When he was released unconditionally from there in April 1938, he returned immediately to a career of crime, holding up houses of prostitution. On the morning of his seventeenth birthday, Chessman was arrested and recommitted to Preston for car theft and forgery. Released in 1939, he was only free for two weeks before receiving a ten-day sentence in the Los Angeles County Jail for stealing a gasoline cap. At age eighteen Chessman married a former high school classmate, but the marriage was annulled a few months later.

Seemingly unable to resist crime's lure, Chessman again stole a car and received six months in a road camp. Paroled on 30 June 1940, he began to work for his father, who ran a venetian-blind business from the family home. That summer Chessman and a girlfriend eloped to Las Vegas; their marriage lasted seven years. Chessman next helped organize a gang of boy bandits who robbed cars daily for two weeks. After a police car surprised the gang robbing a Hollywood gas station, Chessman was convicted of four counts of first-degree burglary and sentenced to multiple five-to-life terms in San Quentin.

As a prisoner Chessman quickly won privileges and responsibilities for himself. He taught school, worked in the warden's office, starred on the prison debating team, and wrote scripts for a weekly radio program. In 1943 as a reward for good behavior he was transferred to a minimum-security prison at Chino, where he conceived a plot to assassinate Adolf Hitler. He escaped from Chino and was on his way to Germany via Mexico when he was rearrested and returned to San Quentin in January 1944. In 1947 Chessman appeared before the Adult Authority and was granted an eleven-year parole, effective the fall of that year, the same year he and his wife were divorced. Forty-six days after his release, he was arrested for felony charges, including armed robbery and kidnapping with intent to rob. The public prosecutor accused him of being the "Red Light Bandit," who—impersonating the police with a flashing light—had terrorized people parking in lovers' lanes, a charge Chessman repeatedly denied. Four months after his arrest, the jury found Chessman (who insisted on acting as his own lawyer) guilty of three counts of kidnapping for the purpose of robbery (in addition to fourteen other felonies). Because he had purportedly moved women from one car to another before sexually assaulting them, Chessman was given the death penalty under California's "Little Lindbergh Law." This law applied to kidnapping cases in which robbery was the motive.

During the eleven years that Chessman spent in San Quentin on Death Row, he became a prolific writer and a law student to orchestrate his own appeals against his sentence. His first book, *Cell 2455, Death Row* (1954), which was translated into twelve languages, sold over half a million copies and was made into a movie in 1955. Forbidden to write for publication after the storm this book raised, Chessman smuggled subsequent manuscripts out of his cell through underground prison channels. These books were *Trial by Ordeal* (1955), *The Face of Justice* (1957), and *The Kid Was a Killer* (1960), an autobiographical novel. Written in an unsophisticated but energetic style, Chessman's first three books deal with his life in prison and his difficulties preparing his own appeals. In the introduction to *Trial by Ordeal* he states, "You're thirty-three years old; sixteen of those years have been lived outside the law or inside the walls of some institution. Behind you are reform schools, jails, prison, prison escape, gun fights, a long and sometimes violent record of crime. Behind you, too, are more than six years of a living death and a living hell in San Quentin Prison's forbidding Death Row" (p. 4).

Most of Chessman's legal appeals, prepared with the help of lawyers Rosalie Asher and George T. Davis, centered around the transcript of Chessman's original trial (the court reporter died during the trial and the replacement had difficulty reading the original notes) and the prejudices of Deputy District Attorney J. Miller Leavy and Judge Charles W. Fricke. Also in 1951 the Little Lindbergh Law had been amended to eliminate the death penalty. Those who considered Chessman's death sentence unwarranted included faculty members at the University of California, Belgium's Queen Mother, and the Vatican. Some supporters of Chessman's appeals believed he was guilty but thought his crimes did not merit the death penalty. He received eight stays of execution and took his case to the U.S. Supreme Court seventeen times. A last-minute, sixty-day reprieve was granted by California governor Edmund G. Brown and was supported by the State Department because of fears that an execution would provoke riots during a planned visit to Uruguay by President Dwight Eisenhower in March. Despite his notable and numerous supporters and his own relentless activity, Caryl Chessman was executed in the gas chamber at San Quentin. He is remembered for his vigorous appeals against his death sentence and for his honest, emotional accounts of life on Death Row.

• In addition to Chessman's own four works, see William M. Kunstler, *Beyond a Reasonable Doubt? The Original Trial of Caryl Chessman* (1961), which focuses on Chessman's legal dilemmas, and Milton Machlin and William R. Woodfield, *Ninth Life* (1961), a journalistic biography. Bernice Freeman Davis, a reporter who befriended Chessman during his stay on Death Row, includes a section on him in her book *The Desperate and the Damned* (1961) describing his writing and his life in prison. A further account of Chessman's prison years can be found in Clinton T. Duffy, *88 Men and 2 Women* (1962). A thorough review of the legal implications of Chessman's case is in the *Minnesota Law Review* 44 (Apr. 1960): 941–97. Andrew O. Largo, *Caryl Whittier Chessman, 1921–1960: Essay and Critical Bibliography* (1971), has an exhaustive list of sources on both Chessman and the case. An obituary is in the *New York Times*, 3 May 1960.

SUSAN E. GUNTER

CHESTER, Colby Mitchell, Jr. (23 July 1877–26 Sept. 1965), lawyer and business executive, was born in Annapolis, Maryland, the son of Colby Mitchell Chester, a lieutenant commander (later a rear admiral) in the U.S. Navy, and Melancia Antoinette Tremaine. He attended Yale University, where he was awarded a Ph.B. from the Sheffield Scientific School in 1897 and a B.A. in 1898. Chester then enrolled at New York Law School, where he received an LL.B. in 1900. That same year he was admitted to the New York bar but delayed the practice of law to join his father, then commander of the battleship USS *Kentucky*, on a cruise to the Philippines.

Upon his return in 1901, Chester briefly practiced with the law firm of Carter, Hughes & Dwight, and then with Ritch, Woodford, Bovee & Butcher. He left in 1902 to establish the firm of Ely, Billings & Chester with two former classmates. In April 1904 Chester married Jessie Campbell Moore, whose father was a partner in Manning, Maxwell, and Moore, Inc., a Bridgeport, Connecticut, railroad and industrial supply company. The couple had three children.

Chester joined his father-in-law's company and served as treasurer from 1904 to 1911, when he left to practice corporation law in the New York firm of Dawes, Abbott & Chester. During this period he also served as first lieutenant in the New York National Guard. When the United States entered World War I in 1917, Chester volunteered and was commissioned a major in the infantry. Although he desired combat duty, he was assigned instead to Camp Meade, Maryland; Camp McArthur, Texas; and Camp Mills, South Carolina, before joining the Inspector General's Office in Washington, D.C. While he awaited an overseas assignment, the armistice was signed; he was discharged on 27 December 1918.

Chester was soon contacted by his friend Marjorie Merriweather Post, owner of the Postum Cereal Company, who wanted his help managing the company. Postum was then a small, successful company in Battle Creek, Michigan, with sales of $18 million and four products: POSTUM cereal beverage, GRAPE-NUTS cereal, POST TOASTIES cereal, and INSTANT POSTUM cereal beverage. Post felt the company needed the more efficient and effective management Chester could contribute. On 9 April 1919 Chester began his career at Postum as assistant treasurer. In 1922 the company was listed on the New York Stock Exchange, moved its headquarters to New York, and elected Chester treasurer and member of the board of directors. He then served as vice president before becoming president in 1924.

Chester felt that as a public corporation, Postum had a responsibility to grow and increase earnings. he also believed that the packaged convenience foods then becoming popular would play a major role in the future of the industry. Although no large-scale consolidation of companies with dissimilar products had yet occurred in the food industry, Chester initiated a program of mergers with existing companies to add products that would diversify the Postum line, promote efficiency within the chaotic food distribution system, and take advantage of economies of scale. The companies merged into Postum from 1925 to 1929 were leaders in their fields, with established brands and high-quality, popular, noncompeting products that would complement the more seasonal Postum cereals. These included JELL-O gelatin, MINUTE Tapioca, BAKER's chocolate, Franklin Baker coconut, LOG CABIN syrup, LA FRANCE laundry products, CALUMET baking powder, MAXWELL HOUSE coffee, and CERTO fruit pectin. Clarence Birdseye's Frosted Foods was purchased in 1929, and the name General Foods Corporation was then adopted to convey the expanded scope of the business. By the end of 1929, General Foods had sales of more than $128 million and offered more than eighty products.

With more resources available for research and development, Chester was able to play a leading role in developing a revolutionary new industry—frozen foods. He believed that conveniently packaged frozen foods would one day be distributed nationally, bringing otherwise perishable and seasonal foods to consumers throughout the year. According to C. W. W. Cook, former chairman and CEO of General Foods, Chester showed unusual vision and courage by investing millions of dollars to develop processes, products, and markets for frozen foods, especially since he knew the line was unlikely to become profitable during his tenure as president.

Chester continued as president until 1935, when he became chairman of the board of directors. He retired from this office in 1943 to take the new position of chairman of the executive committee, which was created so that the company could retain his leadership through World War II. In 1946 Chester ended his active involvement in the company's management, although he continued as honorary chairman of the board until becoming director emeritus in 1958.

Claire, as Chester was called, was repeatedly described as honest, ethical, judicious, modest, sincere, warm, idealistic, and farsighted. His leadership style and philosophy reflected these qualities and emphasized responsibility to employees, consumers, stockholders, the business community, and the country. At General Foods this leadership resulted in progressive personnel policies, goodwill, and an excellent reputation. And his influence in the National Association of Manufacturers as director (1935), president (1936), and chairman (1937) reformed a militantly anti–New Deal organization into a more cooperative advocate of industry that focused on public relations.

Chester's business interests included membership on the boards of Manning, Maxwell, and Moore, Inc. (chairman); Zonite Products Corporation (chairman); Lehigh Valley Railroad (executive committee chairman); New Jersey, Indiana & Illinois Railroad; 20th Century–Fox Film Corporation; Chase Manhattan Bank; and Manufacturers Hanover Trust Company.

In addition, Chester was a spokesman or fundraiser for many civic, philanthropic, and educational concerns. He was a member of the Yale University Development Committee; the St. John's College Advisory Board; the Deafness Research Foundation; the Citizen's Committee for the Hoover Report; the National Institute of Social Sciences, where he served as president from 1942 to 1945; the National Fund for Medical Education; the Republican party, for which he served as national finance chairman; Boy's Clubs of America, serving in the capacity of director; and numerous societies. His work for the American Red Cross from 1941 to 1952 included chairmanships of the New York chapter and the National War Fund in 1945.

Providing a model for business leadership with his integrity and enlightened philosophy, Chester led Postum through a period of growth and expansion that created one of the largest food companies in the country and established the frozen food industry. He died in Greenwich, Connecticut.

• Many speeches and articles by Chester, as well as information pertaining to his career at General Foods, are held at the Kraft Foods, Inc., Archives in Morton Grove, Ill. A number of these speeches have been published in *Vital Speeches of the Day* and other periodicals. Chester outlined his management philosophy and its application at General Foods in "Management's Responsibilities in Industrial Relations," a speech given before the Personnel Conference of the American Management Association in 1939 and reprinted in the *American Management Association Personnel Series*, no. 36 (1939): 3–14. Contemporary newspaper and magazine articles provide biographical information and coverage of his business activities and speeches. See W. F. L. Tuttle, "The Corporate Personality of General Foods," *Groceries*, Nov. 1931, for a sketch of General Foods, its management, and its personality; Daniel R. Maue, "'Never Recovered from a Round-Robin,'" *System*, Feb. 1931, for Chester's background, character, and style; "Let Them Eat Cake," *Fortune*, Oct. 1934, pp. 68–75, 122, 124, 126, 129–32, 135, 137, for a profile and history of General Foods and of Chester; C. M. Chester, Jr., as told to C. W. Steffler, "Frozen Foods Make Debut," *Forbes*, 1 Nov. 1930, pp. 13–14, for Chester's views about frozen foods; and *Time*, 13 Dec. 1937, pp. 59–60, 62, 64, 66, for an analysis of Chester's leadership of the National Association of Manufacturers.

ALISSA M. BERMAN

CHESTER, George Randolph (1869–26 Feb. 1924), author, was born probably in Hamilton County, Ohio, although Chester himself once stated he was born in Richmond, Indiana. When questioned about this discrepancy in *Cosmopolitan* (May 1911), Chester coolly replied, "I really don't care. Do you prefer any particular city?" Chester preferred to sidestep any questions concerning his birth and early childhood. His attitude prompted critics to speculate that his early life was less than happy. Consequently, Chester's parentage is unknown. The information Chester did provide tells of his leaving home at a very early age to make his way in the world. He worked a wide variety of jobs, including as an engine operator in a planning mill; a pen-and-ink artist in Davenport, Iowa; a cook and a waiter in a restaurant; a plumber; a paper-hanger; a ribbon salesman; a chain dragger for a civil engineer; a bill clerk; and a designer in a chair factory. In 1895 he married Elizabeth Bethermel of Connersville, Indiana. They had two sons.

Just before the turn of the century, Chester began work as a writer for the *Detroit News*. He was no ordinary reporter; often the stories he wrote were highly exaggerated to dramatize his "eyewitness" accounts. Unfortunately, this meant Chester sometimes left out crucial details—such as the victim's name—but his stories were nonetheless riveting. In 1901 Chester took a job with the *Cincinnati Enquirer*, where he was soon promoted to Sunday editor. As Sunday editor he was able to let his creative instincts blossom. Because Chester was responsible for producing five to eighteen columns a week of original copy, he conveniently filled them with his own imaginative stories. The first of these stories, "Strikebreaker," was later published in *McClure's Magazine* (Sept. 1905). Chester's tales were eventually syndicated, appearing in twenty-five newspapers. Tasting early success, Chester left his job at the *Cincinnati Enquirer* to devote himself wholly to writing short fiction.

Perhaps the most popular of Chester's characters was J. R. Wallingford. This character, a stout, suave, yet sly high financier, first appeared in the opening episode of *Get-Rich-Quick Wallingford: A Cheerful Account of the Rise and Fall of an American Business Buccaneer* (1908). Wallingford reappeared in several other books written by Chester, including *Young Wallingford* (1910), *Wallingford and Blackie Daw* (1913), and *Wallingford in His Prime* (1913). Readers delighted in Wallingford's adeptness at swindling affluent businessmen, all the while maintaining a sublime and benevolent countenance.

Chester was extremely thorough in detailing not only Wallingford but the many lesser characters in his novels as well. Many critics have noted the striking satirical resemblance between Chester's fictitious characters and the nouveaux riches of the late 1800s. Chester's other short stories and novels, including *The Cash Intrigue* series (1909), *The Making of Bobby Burnit* (1909), and *Five Thousand an Hour* (1912), largely carried on in the same vein as the *Wallingford* books and stories. Chester routinely concluded his stories cryptically, always leaving open the possibility of another plot turn in the future.

In 1910, shortly after the Wallingford series had been published, Chester authored a writer's handbook, *The Art of Short Story Writing*, in which he stated that the "business story" was the most popular genre of his times: "The romance of millions and how they were made or stolen . . . [is one of] the things which interest the live public of today." In the same volume he also wrote his credo: "Talk literature little; and work at it much; earn money, and spend it." When earning for Chester reached its peak, he and his first wife were divorced. In 1911 Chester married Lillian De Rimo of Cincinnati, Ohio, in Paris amid rumors that his divorce was not yet final. They had no children.

Chester's subsequent novels, *The Ball of Fire* (1914), *Cordelia Blossom* (1914), *The Son of Wallingford* (1921), and *On the Lot and Off* (1924), and several plays were written in conjunction with his second wife. It is unclear to what extent Lillian Chester contributed to her husband's later books, but critics noticed a definitive change in style, most notably the inclusion of sympathetic female characters. In his earlier books Chester frequently portrayed the female characters as traitors to their sex because they exhibited such "unfeminine" traits as aggressiveness and recklessness.

In the early 1920s Chester and his wife began writing screenplays in Hollywood. Only two of these, however, were successful: *Black Beauty* (1921) and *The Son of Wallingford* (1921; based on the popular series). In 1921 Chester returned to what had made him famous: writing stories of intrigue for magazines. Inspired by his Hollywood experience, Chester developed a new series, "The Adventures of Izzy Iskovitch," for the *Saturday Evening Post*. The final episode of the series was published posthumously in May 1924. Although Chester worked extremely hard (as witnessed by his sheer productivity in such a short time) to achieve an early level of financial success, he rarely took a vacation or a day off. He died in New York City.

The pertinence of Chester's stories and characters to the flurry of turn-of-the-century America led to their enormous popularity. Beginning first as a reporter of real-life human events, Chester soon saw the creative potential of narrating these events in rich detail while also creating a forum in which to comment on the excesses of the time.

• Other books by George Randolph Chester include *The Early Bird: A Businessman's Love Story* (1910); *The Jingo* (1912); *A Tale of Red Roses* (1914); *Blue Pete's Escape* (1914); *The Enemy*, with Lillian Chester (1915); and *The Wonderful Adventures of Prince Toofat* (1922). For more on Chester, see Herbert Corey, "The Author of Wallingford," *Cosmopolitan*, May 1911, and an editorial in the *Saturday Evening Post*, 10 May 1924. Obituaries are in the New York newspapers of 27 Feb. 1924, and more detailed articles are in the *Cincinnati Enquirer*, 27 Feb., 2, 15 Mar. 1924.

CATHERINE GOLDBERG

CHESTER, Thomas Morris (11 May 1834–30 Sept. 1892), lawyer and Civil War correspondent, was born in Harrisburg, Pennsylvania, the son of George Chester and Jane Maria (maiden name unknown), restaurateurs. When, as a young man of eighteen, Chester decided to emigrate to Liberia, he wrote Martin H. Freeman, his former teacher at the Avery Institute in Pittsburgh, that his passion for liberty could no longer "submit to the insolent indignities and contemptuous conduct to which it has almost become natural for the colored people dishonorably to submit themselves." It was a bold assertion of independence for one who had come of age in a household long associated with the anticolonization sentiments of radical abolitionism. But the country's willingness to appease southern interests, symbolized by the passage of the Fugitive Slave Law in 1850, persuaded Chester, sometime before his 1853 graduation, to emigrate.

Anxious to recruit the son of such a prominent black family, leaders of the Pennsylvania Colonization Society led Chester to believe that he could complete his education in Monrovia. But the colony could not meet his needs, and within a year Chester was back in the United States where, with the support of the New York Colonization Society, he attended Thetford Academy in Vermont from 1854 to 1856. Following graduation Chester returned to Monrovia, where he became active in politics and published and edited the short-lived *Star of Liberia*, which appeared intermittently between 1859 and 1861. He also taught school at the new settlement of Robertsport and in Monrovia. During this period he made frequent trips back to the United States, under the auspices of the Colonization Society, to promote emigration to Liberia.

Continued troubles with political rivals in Monrovia persuaded Chester in 1861 to return to the United States where he continued to work for the cause of colonization. Abraham Lincoln's Emancipation Proclamation prompted him to delay his return to Liberia in early 1863. Chester headed the recruitment drive in central Pennsylvania for the two black Massachusetts regiments but ceased his activities when it became clear that blacks would not be appointed officers. Before resigning the civilian appointment, however, Chester became the first black to be given a captaincy in the Pennsylvania state militia when he raised a company to help defend the state capital against Confederate forces in the weeks before Gettysburg.

In 1864 Chester was employed by John Russell Young, editor of the Philadelphia *Press*, as a war correspondent attached to the Army of the James. He was the first and only African American to report on the war for a major daily newspaper. Chester's dispatches provide the most sustained accounts of black troop activity around Petersburg and Richmond in the last year of the war. He reported on the contributions of black troops to the war effort, sent moving accounts of the death and carnage of battle, and, with a rakish sense of humor, provided glimpses into camp life. Chester was one of the first reporters to enter Richmond, and with some bravado and a touch of irony he wrote his next dispatch seated in the chair of the Speaker of the Confederate House of Representatives. Chester remained in Richmond until June 1865, reporting on efforts to rebuild the city and on the activities of the African-American community.

In 1866 Chester was commissioned by the Garnet League, the Harrisburg chapter of the Pennsylvania Equal Rights League, to undertake a fund-raising tour of Britain and the continent. Even before his assignment with the *Press* Chester had been thinking of studying law in England and in 1863 had briefly visited London, where he made invaluable contacts in abolitionist circles. The tour was a rousing personal success although it is unclear exactly how much money he raised. During his visit to Russia, Chester was introduced to the royal court by Cassius M. Clay, U.S. minister to St. Petersburg. Chester was invited to join the annual review of the imperial guard and to dine with the royal family.

At the conclusion of his mission Chester applied and was admitted to Middle Temple, London, where he studied law from 1867 to 1870. In April 1870 he became the first African American to be called to the English bar. A few weeks later Chester argued his first case in the hallowed halls of the Old Bailey, defending a shoemaker charged with murder. Although all the evidence pointed to the defendent's guilt, Chester's skillful cross-examination saved his client from the gallows. The accused was sentenced instead to ten-year's penal servitude.

A few months after his return to the United States in mid-1870, Chester decided to settle in New Orleans, having been impressed with the level of black political power in the city. By the time of his arrival in 1871, the Republican party was immobilized by factionalism and violence. On 1 January 1872, in the streets of New Orleans, Chester was shot (but not seriously wounded) by members of one of the political factions.

In 1873 Chester was admitted to the Louisiana bar, the first black man to be admitted according to contemporary news accounts, and he played a prominent role in many of the civil rights suits brought by blacks under the state's new antidiscrimination laws. In May 1873 he was commissioned a brigadier general in the Louisiana state militia by Governor William Kellogg. The militias had been formed by Republican administrations to fill the void left by departing federal troops. Two years later Kellogg appointed Chester superintendent of public education for the First Division, which included areas around New Orleans. The following year Chester was moved to head the Fifth Division with offices in Delta, Madison Parish. Chester retained both the rank of brigadier general and the position of superintendent until the return to power of the Democrats in 1876.

With the aid of powerful friends in Pennsylvania, particularly members of the Cameron family, Chester was appointed U.S. commissioner for New Orleans in 1878, a position he held for almost two years. In December 1882 he was sent, as an assistant to the U.S. attorney for the Eastern District of Texas, on a special mission to investigate political violence in the area. But disputes with Washington over payments for expenses led to the termination of his appointment before he had completed his investigation.

Chester married Florence Johnson, twenty-one years his junior, in 1879. Little else is known of his life except that in 1884 he was named president of the North Carolina "Wilmington, Wrightsville and Onslow Railroad," a company established by African Americans to build a rail system connecting the towns to important markets in Virginia. The plans never materialized, and Chester returned to his law practices in Louisiana and Pennsylvania. Chester died at his mother's home in Harrisburg of an apparent heart attack.

Chester was fiercely independent, driven by what he called "self respect and pride of race." As he told many audiences at home and abroad, he was descended from a long line of independent black men and women who had openly defied all forms of racial restrictions. In Liberia his work as editor and teacher contributed to the social and political life of Robertsport and Monrovia. In the United States he sought to push the country toward realizing the dream of full equality for all its people.

• Letters from and about Chester are in the American Colonization Society papers at the Library of Congress; in the Simon Cameron papers, Historical Society of Dauphin County, Pa.; in the Massachusetts Historical Society; in the archives of the Society of the Middle Temple, London; in Records of the General Agent (record group 60) at the National Archives; and in the Jacob C. White papers at the Moorland-Spingarn Library, Howard University. See also Rayford W. Logan and Michael R. Winston, eds., *Dictionary of American Negro Biography* (1982), and R. J. M. Blackett, *Thomas Morris Chester: Black Civil War Correspondent* (1989).

R. J. M. Blackett

CHEVERUS, John Louis Anne Magdalen Lefebvre de (28 Jan. 1768–19 July 1836), Catholic prelate, was born in Mayenne, France, the son of Jean-Vincent-Marie Lefebvre de Cheverus, a civil judge in Mayenne, and Anne-Charlotte Lemarchand des Noyers. Cheverus received his early education at a local college in Mayenne. Then, in 1781, he was sent to the Collège Louis-le-Grand, the so-called seminary of the Revolution, in Paris. After graduating from Louis-le-Grand, Cheverus entered the Saint Magloire Seminary in Paris, and on 18 December 1790, after finishing his seminary education, he was ordained to the Catholic priesthood. The very next day the French government ordered all priests to take an oath to uphold the civil constitution of the clergy, which Cheverus refused to do. As a nonjuring priest, he served parishes in Mayenne in the early part of 1791. By June of that year, however, political opposition to nonjuring clergy had begun in Mayenne, and when Cheverus refused to read a pastoral letter of his newly elected juring bishop on 17 July, subsequently putting that refusal into writing, he sealed his fate in France. In June of 1792 he was imprisoned for a few days in Mayenne and then released to his uncle's care.

Sometime between June and September of 1792 Cheverus left Mayenne for Paris where he hid out to escape being detected. In May the French government ordered all nonjurors to be exiled, and by the end of the year Cheverus had fled to England for safety. In 1793 he taught French and mathematics in a boarding school run by a Protestant minister in Wallingford in Berkshire. A year later he built a church in Tottenham, about six miles from London, and was pastor there until the middle of 1796 when he received an invitation from Father Francis Matignon, a fellow French émigré, to join him in Boston, where there was great need for Catholic priests. In response to that invitation, Cheverus offered his services to Bishop John Carroll of Baltimore and was assigned to the New England area.

In October 1796 Cheverus arrived in Boston, and for the next twenty-seven years he served the Catholic community in the New England area. During his early years he was a missionary to American Indians, Irish Catholic immigrants, and French Canadians in Maine. At the same time, he was an assistant to Francis Matignon, pastoring the Irish and French Catholics in Boston. Between 1799 and 1803 he helped to establish Boston's Holy Cross Church, and during 1805 he was instrumental in bringing Elizabeth Seton of New York into the Catholic church.

With a typical Gallican sense of the church, Cheverus believed that immigrant Catholics in the United States should adapt themselves to American ways and be conspicuous only by their virtue and zeal for the common good. Although some of his Boston parishioners were members of an elite foreign mercantile and governing class, most were poor Irish workers who were capable of making little impact upon the society. Cheverus also helped to found and support the Boston Athenaeum Society, served on several other learned societies, and was regularly involved in public service projects in the city. The Unitarian pastor William Ellery Channing considered him both a friend and a benefactor to the city.

Respected by both his parishioners and the Protestant leadership in Boston, Cheverus was Bishop Carroll's logical choice in 1808 to become the first Catholic bishop of Boston. Because of difficult communications with Rome and the impediments of travel, Cheverus was not consecrated bishop until 1 November 1810. At that time, although the newly erected diocese of Boston extended from Boston to Maine and had perhaps no more than 2,000 Catholics, there were only three priests to serve the entire diocese.

Cheverus served as bishop of Boston from 1810 to 1823. During these years he saw the Catholic population of the diocese grow to approximately 3,850 and the number of priests to five. He also supervised the establishment of five new churches and invited the Ursuline nuns to build a convent in Boston for the emerging immigrant Catholic church. Perhaps his greatest legacy to Boston, however, was his irenic spirit of cooperation and his ability to gain respect for himself and his religious tradition. He was both learned and metropolitan and was considered a man of culture as well as a deeply pious Christian whose primary pastoral emphasis was the love of God and neighbor.

Although Cheverus respected American ways and institutions, he was in head and heart a French monarchist who believed it his duty to be devoted to God, country, and king—in that order. In 1823, therefore, when the king of France, Louis XVIII, invited him to return to his native country to accept a vacant episcopal see, he did not refuse. Despite the regrets and pleadings of Boston Protestants as well as Catholics, Cheverus left the United States in September 1823 to assume the episcopacy of Montauban, the chief city in Département de Tarn-et-Garonne.

By July 1826 Cheverus was named archbishop of Bordeaux and made a peer of the realm. One year later he was admitted to the Chamber of Peers, and on 1 February 1836 he became a cardinal of the Catholic church. In France as in the United States he was known for the good relations he created with Protestants and for his ability to communicate with his people. Shortly after he became a cardinal, Cheverus died in Bordeaux.

• Cheverus's personal correspondence and pastoral letters are located in the archives of the archdioceses of Boston, Baltimore, and Bordeaux, and in the diocese of Montauban. The most comprehensive and well-documented biography in English is Annabelle Melville, *Jean Lefebvre de Cheverus, 1768–1836* (1958). Information on his contributions to the diocese of Boston can also be found in Robert H. Lord et al., *History of the Archdiocese of Boston in the Various Stages of Its Development, 1604–1943* (3 vols., 1944). Obituaries are in the *New York Commercial Advertiser*, 8 Sept. 1836; and the *Boston Evening Transcript* and *Boston Daily Advertiser*, both 9 Sept. 1836.

PATRICK W. CAREY

CHEVES, Langdon (17 Sept. 1776–26 June 1857), lawyer, congressman, and financier, was born in Bull Town Fort, South Carolina, the son of Alexander Chivas (or Chivis) of Buchan, Aberdeenshire, Scotland, and Mary Langdon. It is not known when or why he changed the spelling of his last name. Alexander Chivas had migrated to America in 1762 and established himself as a frontier trader. A Loyalist supporter, he lost his livelihood during the Revolution and moved to the low country. Cheves's mother, daughter of supporters of the colonial rebellion, died in 1779, and Langdon's aunt, Mrs. Thomas Cheves, cared for young Langdon. He attended Andrew Weed's school, and in 1785 his father took him to Charleston. He continued his formal schooling briefly but then pursued vigorous independent study. He apprenticed in a shipping merchant's office, gaining experience in business and finance by keeping the firm's accounts. He read for the law with Judge William Marshall and was admitted to the bar in 1797. Successful as a Charleston lawyer, he moved into the political arena. His first elected office was as warden of his city ward in 1802; he then served from 1802 to 1809 in the state legislature and became attorney general in 1809. He won national office in 1810 when he ran for Congress on the Republican ticket. In 1806 he married Mary Elizabeth Dulles; they had fourteen children. In addition to the law and politics, Cheves enjoyed success in designing and building houses and in farming.

During his congressional tenure, Cheves joined South Carolina's distinguished congressmen, John C. Calhoun, William Lowndes, and D. R. Williams, in supporting the War of 1812 as one of the "War Mess" group. He also served on the Committee on Naval Affairs and as chair of the Ways and Means Committee and the Select Committee on Naval Establishment. His colleagues recognized his competence and elected him to replace Henry Clay as Speaker of the House in the Thirteenth Congress when Clay joined the delegation to formulate the Treaty of Ghent. During the debate over Treasury secretary Alexander Dallas's bill to recharter the Bank of the United States, Cheves spoke forcefully against reestablishing the institution, which he would nevertheless later head. In 1815 Cheves decided against reelection and returned to Charleston to practice law, refusing further national service even though he was offered the post of secretary of the treasury to succeed Albert Gallatin. He preferred life in South Carolina, and from 1816 to 1819 he served as justice of the court of appeals of his home state.

In January 1819 Cheves began perhaps his most important national role as the shaper of American banking. Supported by President James Monroe and mercantile stockholders, he reluctantly agreed to serve as president of the troubled Second Bank of the United States (BUS). After being elected a director of the bank in January 1819, he accepted its presidency on 6 March 1819. By so doing, he apparently sacrificed an opportunity to serve as an associate justice of the U.S. Supreme Court, an occupation he preferred over banking. His sense of responsibility, combined with the urging of his friends and associates, convinced him that the nation needed his honesty and integrity to stabilize the economy and restore confidence in the BUS. Despite his high expectations, Cheves's four years as president of the bank caused him great distress. His task was monumental: the nation suffered in the economic downturn after the War of 1812, and the bank was a convenient scapegoat for all the nation's financial woes. In fact, the bank was on the verge of failure.

Cheves instituted conservative policies, reining in the southern and western offices and insisting that each branch office balance its own accounts and cease issuing paper to be redeemed at other branches, particularly at those in the East. No longer could the branch offices depend on the total assets of the BUS to guarantee local paper. Cheves further insisted that state and local banks meet their loan commitments to the BUS through regular payments in specie or reliable notes. Hostile bankers and creditors, accustomed to renewing their notes rather than paying balances due, complained bitterly; they joined a growing chorus of disillusioned citizens who blamed the BUS for the nation's economic woes. In Cincinnati, Gorham Worth, motivated partly by Cheves's action to replace him as cashier, characterized Cheves as a man "hated, as Hell ought to be, by some, and worship'd, as the Devil is, by Others." One Charlestonian cautioned him in 1819, "you may press your rigid systems to extremes. . . . some directors who acted with you at first, do so no longer, and . . . disinterested men begin to question the wisdom and advantage of your administration." Many stockholders lost confidence in his decisions, particularly when he withheld dividend payments. Others, who sought funds for speculation and investments, opposed his tight restrictions on money. Despite the alarms, his steadfast friends sent positive news. Robert Y. Hayne, traveling in the West, assured Cheves that he had "the public confidence" even though many despised the bank. Longtime associate South Carolinian H. W. DeSaussure consoled Cheves: "I fear you have found the place a bed of thorns. But when the offices are purified, & the business of the Country resumes . . . it will be comparatively a pleasant post."

Cheves worked to mitigate the anger that produced anti-bank toasts such as that at an 1822 St. Patrick's Day dinner in Cincinnati: "The United States Bank—The sink of corruption, the engine of illegitimate power; that bane of society a monied aristocracy, may our country soon be delivered from its pestiferous influence." To change the BUS's direction and improve its image, Cheves attacked mismanagement and corruption: he hired new branch directories and new employees and initiated investigations at the branches. Cheves's reputation for integrity and his common sense stood him in good stead. The BUS, a complex national institution with far-flung branch offices, constituted a national corporation of unprecedented scope. Cheves, without useful models on which to pattern his policies, is generally credited with achieving his major goals: to restore a sound currency and maintain the nation's credit. Although Cheves rued "the waste of 3 or four years of the prime of my life," when he came to retire as BUS president, he felt satisfied that he had "saved the Bank from ruin" and done everything "to restore the rottenness of the Institution to Soundness."

When Nicholas Biddle replaced him as BUS president in December 1823, Cheves was appointed chief commissioner of claims under the Treaty of Ghent, and when its business was completed, he moved to Philadelphia to practice law. In 1829 he returned to South Carolina and refused all offers of elected office. He sought a private life out of the limelight, in part because his strong opposition to nullification proved unpopular with many state leaders. He returned to public life in 1850 to participate in the Nashville Convention. In his eloquent address, he advocated united resistance against the North but opposed separate state action as unwise and impractical. He returned to farming in his later years and lived quietly in financial ease with his family in the home he designed near Savannah. He died at his daughter's home in Columbia, South Carolina, and is buried in Magnolia Cemetery, Charleston.

• The papers of Langdon Cheves are available at James Madison University Library and on microfiche; they consist of family and official papers. The Bank of the United States portion includes several hundred letters exchanged between Cheves and bankers and stockholders throughout the country. The Kirby papers, available at the Cincinnati (Ohio) Historical Society Library, contain letters and documents on the BUS and Cheves. Nicholas Biddle, Cheves's flamboyant successor as president of the BUS, overshadows Cheves in most banking studies; historians usually mention Cheves's competence and honesty only briefly. More detailed studies of Cheves's banking career include Louisa P. Haskell, "Langdon Cheves and the United States Bank: A Study from Neglected Sources," *Annual Report of the American Historical Association* 1 (1896): 363–71, and chaps. 2–4 of Marion A. Brown, "The Interrelationship of State and National Policy: The Second Bank of the United States and Ohio, 1803–1860" (Ph.D. diss., Univ. of Cincinnati, 1989). John B. O'Neall, *Biographical Sketches of the Bench and Bar of South Carolina*, vol. 1 (1859), pp. 133–39, includes material on Cheves. Controversy over Cheves appears in Governor Benjamin Perry's "Reminiscences of Public Men—Langdon Cheves," *Nineteenth Century* (Aug. 1869), and a positive response by Mrs. D. J. McCord appears in the same title (Apr. 1870). Cheves's obituary is in the *New York Daily Times*, 1 July 1857, and in the *Charleston Mercury* and Charleston *Courier*, both 27 July 1857.

MARION A. BROWN

CHEVROLET, Louis (25 Dec. 1878–6 June 1941), mechanic, race car driver, and engine designer, was born in La Chaux-de-Fonds, Switzerland, the son of Joseph Felicien Chevrolet, a clockmaker, and Angelina Marie (maiden name unknown). Louis Chevrolet's family moved to Beaune, France, when he was six years old. From his father Louis acquired basic mechanical skills and an appreciation for the importance of precision in machine parts manufacture. While still teenagers, Louis and his two brothers, Arthur and Gaston, established a bicycle making shop. They used the brand name "Frontenac" for their bicycles, a name Louis later applied to automobiles he manufactured.

The Frontenac bicycle-making business was not a great success, and in 1898 Louis Chevrolet found employment as a mechanic at the Mors Auto Company. His employer sent him to work in a new dealership in Montreal, Canada, in 1900. Before the year was out, Chevrolet had moved to Brooklyn, New York, where he worked as a mechanic at another French car dealership.

In the first decade of the twentieth century, automobile racing was fantastically popular on both sides of the Atlantic. Car companies sought to establish their products by winning road, track, hill-climbing, and endurance races. In 1905, at Sheepshead Bay, New York, Chevrolet got his chance to break into this new motor sport as a substitute driver for Fiat. He won the race, defeating the sport's leading driver, Barney Oldfield. In this and two other victories over Oldfield in 1905, Chevrolet displayed reckless daring that won the enthusiastic approval of the racing press. That same year, he married Suzanne Treyvoux, one of his many racing fans. They would have two children.

By 1907, when William C. Durant, president of the Buick Motor Car Company, set up an audition on the company's track in Flint, Michigan, Chevrolet was widely regarded as the best race car driver in the world. His fearless driving style impressed Durant, who offered him a place on Buick's racing team at a time when the company's cars consistently beat their American competition. Between 1906 and 1910 the Buick team of "Bullet Bob" Burman, Louis Strang, and Louis Chevrolet compiled the best record of any American race car manufacturer. And Chevrolet, with his passion for high performance, also acquired a more sophisticated understanding of automobile engineering. In 1909 he opened a garage in Detroit, where he began to design and test four- and six-cylinder automobile engines.

In 1910 a bankers' consortium reorganized General Motors Corporation, which had included the Buick Company since 1908. Durant was forced to relinquish managerial control over all GMC operations. Subsequently, Buick announced a drastic reduction in the company's racing program, and Durant approached Louis Chevrolet with a proposal to put Chevrolet's six-cylinder engine into a car that could be mass produced. Chevrolet agreed to design the car, and the Chevrolet Motor Company was established in Detroit and Flint. In 1912 Louis Chevrolet's Detroit garage was expanded into a factory that produced 2,999 large, high performance six-cylinder touring cars. However, the car did not sell well. At the same time, Durant prepared a factory he owned in Flint to produce another touring car powered by Chevrolet's four-cylinder engine.

In 1913 Durant consolidated Chevrolet Motor Company manufacturing operations in Flint. After that year, Chevrolet played no role in the management of the company that bore his name. He remained primarily interested in automobile racing and race car development, and he and brothers, Arthur and Gaston, continued to enter and win automobile races. They also spent increasing amounts of time testing engines at the Indianapolis Speedway.

By 1916 the Chevrolet Motor Company had introduced a series of increasingly less expensive four-cylinder models in an effort to produce a car that could compete with Ford's phenomenally successful Model T. In response, Louis Chevrolet broke completely with Durant over the decision to switch from high-performance, high-priced cars to the low-price mass market. By 1915 Louis Chevrolet had sold all his shares of Chevrolet stock. Thus, he did not profit when Durant regained control of General Motors in 1916 by offering five shares of Chevrolet's booming stock for single shares of General Motors.

In 1916 Louis and Arthur Chevrolet established the Frontenac Motor Company. Their company had difficulty making a profit selling its limited production of racers, but as drivers, Louis, Arthur, and younger brother Gaston Chevrolet remained in the forefront of American automobile racing. In 1919 the Chevrolet brothers accepted an offer made by the Monroe Motor Company to jointly produce a line of Monroe-Frontenac racing cars in Indianapolis. In 1920 Gaston drove a Chevrolet-designed racer using a new straight eight-cylinder engine to victory in the Indianapolis 500. Later that year Gaston was killed when he crashed at the Los Angeles Speedway. However, their brother's death did not discourage Louis and Arthur Chevrolet. In 1921 another Chevrolet-designed Monroe-Frontenac racer won the Indianapolis 500.

The back-to-back triumphs at Indianapolis convinced the Stutz Motor Company to put $1 million into Louis Chevrolet's plan to produce a commercial sports car using the straight eight engine, but the sports car's sales were poor. In 1926 Louis and Arthur Chevrolet avoided the bankruptcy that resulted from the ill-fated sports car venture by producing an eight-valve push-rod cylinder head that greatly enhanced the engine performance of Ford's Model T. Perhaps as many as 10,000 of these Frontenac heads were sold, mostly to enthusiasts who raced their souped up "Fronty Fords."

In 1928 airplane manufacturer Glenn Martin helped the Chevrolet brothers establish the Chevrolet Aircraft Corporation after they successfully demonstrated a lightweight engine dubbed the Chevrolair 333.

Although Martin's company eventually used a version of the engine, the Chevrolair 333 was a business failure for Louis Chevrolet. By 1933 he had been forced to liquidate all of his investments. He had moved to Detroit searching for gainful employment. Perhaps ironically, Louis Chevrolet was hired as a mechanic by the Chevrolet Division of General Motors in Detroit. In 1938 his career in the automobile industry was ended by the first of a series of paralyzing strokes. After he died in Detroit, Chevrolet was buried next to his brother Gaston at the Holy Cross Cemetery near the Indianapolis Speedway.

• Louis Chevrolet's papers have not been preserved, but records of his racing career are kept at the Speedway Museum in Indianapolis. His contribution to motor sports is noted in Griffith Borgeson, *The Golden Age of the American Racing Car* (1966). For information on the early history of General Motors see Alfred Dupont Chandler, *Strategy and Structure: Chapters in the History of the Industrial Enterprise* (1962). An obituary is in the *New York Times*, 7 June 1941.

RONALD EDSFORTH

CHEW, Benjamin (29 Nov. 1722–20 Jan. 1810), lawyer and judge, was born at West River, Anne Arundel County, Maryland, the son of Samuel Chew, a physician who became chief justice of the lower counties of Pennsylvania (present-day Delaware), and Mary Galloway. In 1732 increasing pressure for religious conformity in once-tolerant Maryland led Chew's father, a Quaker, to seek the more congenial atmosphere of Philadelphia. There Chew received a classical education and from 1736 or 1737 to 1741 studied law under Andrew Hamilton, a leading colonial lawyer best known for his defense of New York printer John Peter Zenger against charges of seditious libel. After Hamilton died Chew continued his law studies with his father, who had moved to another Quaker community, Dover, in the lower counties. The elder Chew, a supporter of the Penn family, had been appointed Prothonotary (court clerk) of Kent County in 1739 and chief justice of the lower counties in 1741. In 1743 Benjamin was admitted to study law at the Middle Temple, London, where he gained both the sophisticated professional skills and the personal connections with the Penns on which his career was to be based.

Returning to Dover after his father's death in 1744, Chew began the practice of law. With Pennsylvania and the lower counties under a single proprietary governor and council, Chew's activities increasingly spanned both colonies. In September 1746 he was admitted to the bar of the Pennsylvania Supreme Court. In 1747 Chew married his cousin Mary Galloway, with whom he had five children, four of whom lived to adulthood. In October 1750 he was elected a Kent County representative to the separate assembly of the lower counties, serving as Speaker from 1753 to 1757. His abilities and connections soon led to his appearance on a wider stage. In 1750 he was appointed to the commission established under a decree of the English Court of Chancery to settle the boundary between Maryland and Pennsylvania. Eventually, in a final report that he drafted in 1768, the boundary was established as the line still known by the names of its surveyors, Mason and Dixon. In 1754, as secretary to a Pennsylvania delegation that included Benjamin Franklin, he attended the Albany Congress, which adopted the farsighted but ultimately unsuccessful colonial Plan of Union, of which Franklin was a principal author.

Chew moved in 1754 to Philadelphia, where he developed an extensive private practice and was soon recognized as a leader of the bar. In Philadelphia, Chew, like the contemporary generation of Penns, abandoned the Quaker faith to join the Church of England. In 1755 he was appointed attorney general and a member of the council for both colonies, while continuing to serve as Speaker of the assembly in the lower counties. In the same year he was appointed recorder of the city of Philadelphia, an office in which he exercised the petty criminal jurisdiction of the mayor's court. After his first wife died in 1755, Chew married Elizabeth Oswald in 1757; they had eight children.

Chew represented the interests of the Penns, both as private lawyer and as political leader of the council. As a council leader he was arrayed against the popularly elected assembly under the leadership of Franklin and Joseph Galloway, his first cousin and contemporary at the bar, in its continuing struggle to wrest control of the provincial government from the proprietors. In the difficult decade that preceded the Revolution, Chew, working closely with Governor John Penn, had a major role in dealing with conflict arising from the land claims of Indians and settlers under overlapping grants from Pennsylvania and other colonies. He also was a leader in articulating the united opposition of the province to the Stamp Act and subsequent British revenue measures without significant internal dissension and violence.

In 1765 Chew was appointed register general for Pennsylvania and the lower counties. In that office he was responsible for probating wills in Philadelphia County and appointing deputy registers for the other counties. When Chew resigned as attorney general in 1769, he became less active at the bar but continued to serve as recorder and register general. In 1774 Governor Penn appointed Chew chief justice, a position that he held until the summer of 1776 when the revolutionary Provincial Convention suspended the operations of the proprietary government. Chew had resigned as recorder before his appointment to the supreme court but continued to serve as register general at the request of the revolutionary government until the office was eliminated in March 1777.

The tides of revolution also affected Chew's personal life. In 1774 he had been a gracious host to the members of the Continental Congress, including his old acquaintance, George Washington, and John Adams. Chew, however, did not support the Declaration of Independence, advocating resistance and reform rather than separation from Britain. In August 1777, as the armies of Washington and British general Sir William Howe jockeyed for position around Philadelphia where the Continental Congress sat, Chew, former governor Penn, and about thirty other former proprietary or Crown officers were arrested by order of the Pennsylvania Executive Council on the recommendation of the congress. Chew and Penn were paroled to Union Iron Works, a substantial property in Hunterdon County, New Jersey, of which Chew's wife's uncle was a part owner. Delicate negotiations with the congress and the Pennsylvania Council finally led to their release and return to Philadelphia in July 1778, shortly after the departure of British forces from the city. Meanwhile, in October 1777, "Cliveden," Chew's country home, had been the scene of a fierce and critical engagement in the battle of Germantown. Chew was forced to sell the badly damaged property in 1779, though he was able to repurchase it in 1797.

Unlike Joseph Galloway, who led Pennsylvania's delegation to the First Congress but became a leading Loyalist when his moderate views were rejected, Chew made his peace with the revolutionaries. Nevertheless, for nearly fifteen years as a silent Federalist, he played no significant role in a state governed by the constitution of 1776 adopted under the leadership of Franklin and other radicals whom he had so long opposed. He declined to reenter private law practice but continued to be an active and respected member of the community, serving on the city's common council. General Washington lived in Chew's house during the winter of 1781–1782 and, while in Philadelphia for the Constitutional Convention in 1787, attended the dinner celebrating the marriage of Chew's daughter Peggy to one of his former officers.

With the adoption in 1790 of a more conservative state constitution, Federalists actively sought Chew's services. In 1791 Governor Thomas Mifflin appointed him president of a reconstituted high court of errors and appeals, which had jurisdiction to review decisions of the supreme court and the county registers of probate. Chew's appointment evidently reflected the need to assure impartiality on a court on which sat the justices of the supreme court and the presiding judges of the five circuit courts of common pleas. Though he ceased active participation in 1804 for reasons of health, he remained president nominally until the legislature abolished the court in 1806.

Chew, who had always complained of ill health, was virtually incapacitated in his last years. He died at his home in Philadelphia. His remarkable transition from the world of the Penns to the brave new world of the early federal republic is a tribute not only to his longevity but to his intellectual abilities and the moderation and reasonableness of his political positions. According to an obituary, as lawyer and judge Chew "was distinguished by the accuracy and extent of his forensic knowledge, quickness of perception, strength and closeness of argument, and soundness of judgment." Later generations benefited from those qualities through the handful of his arguments and judicial opinions that survived in the published reports of Pennsylvania's colonial and early state courts. Chew was also a man of great dignity and courtliness, skilled in the social graces demanded by his personal and public circumstances. A contemporary called him "a man of consummate worth, rather than of real greatness," one of whom a stranger "would have been ready to exclaim, 'This is one of the ancient and well bred nobles of the land.'"

• The Chew Family Papers are in the Historical Society of Pennsylvania. Benjamin Chew's compilation, *Laws of the Government of New-Castle, Kent and Sussex, upon Delaware*, was published in 1752. Brief reports of eight cases in the Pennsylvania Supreme Court in which he appeared as counsel or attorney general between 1760 and 1773, and one on which he sat as recorder in 1772, appear in Alexander J. Dallas, *Reports of Cases Ruled and Adjudged in the Courts of Pennsylvania before and since the Revolution*, ed. Thomas I. Wharton (1790; rev. ed. 1830), vol. 1, pp. 3–19, 110, and vol. 2, p. 240; six cases on which he sat as chief justice between 1774 and 1776, including three with opinions or rulings by him, are reported in vol. 1, pp. 20–29. Eight cases on which he sat as president of the high court of errors and appeals between 1792 and 1804, including several with full opinions, are reported in Dallas, vol. 2, p. 286, and vol. 4, p. 95. Also see Alexander Addison, *Reports of Cases in the County Courts of the Fifth Circuit and the High Court of Errors and Appeals* (1800), pp. 59, 114–19, 327; and Horace Binney, *Reports of Cases Adjudged in the Supreme Court of Pennsylvania*, vol. 2 (1810), p. 525. The principal published source on Chew is Burton A. Konkle, *Benjamin Chew, 1722–1810* (1932), in which are reprinted an obituary (*United States Gazette*, 22 Jan. 1810) and an appreciation (*Port Folio*, Feb. 1811). As to Cliveden, also known as "Chew House," owned by the Chew family from 1797 until acquired by the National Trust for Historic Preservation in 1972, see Mark M. Boatner, *Landmarks of the American Revolution* (1973), pp. 406–8.

L. KINVIN WROTH

CHEW, Ng Poon (28 Apr. 1866–13 Mar. 1931), clergyman and lecturer, was born in Guangdong Province, China, the son of Ng Yip and Wong Shee. His Chinese name was Wu P'ang-tsao. He was raised by his grandmother in a poor Chinese village. Hoping that he would become a Taoist priest, his grandmother sent him to a Taoist shrine, but the most significant event in the development of his personal dreams came about in 1879, when one of his uncles returned to China after spending eight years in California. The stories his uncle told, plus the inspiration provided by the sight of 800 Mexican dollars that his uncle had brought home, motivated Chew, like so many members of his generation in China, to go to the United States.

Chew went to San Francisco in 1881. After spending time with a relative in the city, he worked as a houseboy on a ranch outside San Jose, California. He learned English by attending school at the local Chinese Presbyterian mission at night. Around this time he began to use Chew, rather than Ng, as his surname. Converted to Christianity in 1882, Chew studied at Occidental College before entering San Francisco Theological Seminary, from which he graduated in 1892. In that same year he was ordained, and he married Tso Chun Fah of San Francisco; the couple had five children.

Chew served as assistant pastor in San Francisco (1892–1894) and worked for the Presbyterian Board of Foreign Missions in southern California (1894–1899). He resigned from the ministry in 1899 and determined to do something more active for his people, the Chinese Americans. He had arrived in California one year before the passage of the Chinese Exclusion Act (1882), which specifically forbade the importation of Chinese laborers. One result of this act was that the Chinese community in California went through a long period of internal and external crisis. Chew persuaded friends to join him in founding the *Hua Mei Hsin Pao* (Chinese-American weekly) in San Francisco in 1899. In the following year, he changed the name of the paper to the *Chung Sai Yat Po* (China west daily), which would run until 1951. Between 1905 and 1911 the paper (which was the only Chinese daily newspaper in the United States) gave more than two-thirds of its editorials to discussions of politics, reforms, and revolution within China itself. In 1904 Chew was instrumental in saving exiled Chinese leader Sun Yat-sen from deportation from San Francisco; Chew rescued Sun Yat-sen and gave him the means to proceed from the United States to London.

Chew devoted the last third of his life to making Chinese matters and the Chinese Americans more visible and more acceptable to their native-born American counterparts. He lectured extensively on the Chautauqua and Lyceum circuits and crossed the North American continent at least eighty times in his travels, working for better understanding between Americans and the Chinese-American community. In 1901 he went on the first of what would become many cross-country tours on behalf of the Chinese-American community; he addressed the U.S. House of Representatives and met personally with President Theodore Roosevelt. He also served as adviser to the Chinese consulate-general of San Francisco (1906–1913) and was vice consul in that city from 1913 until his death. He became a Mason and was the first Chinese American in California to become a Shriner.

One of the most active and influential Chinese Americans of his time, Chew was of the "new generation" of Chinese Americans that managed to voice its opposition to the prejudice that Chinese Americans encountered, even if that generation was not able to reverse the effects of the prejudice. Chew spoke out strongly against the Chinese exclusion acts, but he did not live to see their repeal in 1943. Nonetheless, he and his friends had laid the groundwork for much of the improvement that came after his death. Along with other Chinese Americans of his generation, such as Senator Hiram Fong of Hawaii, Chew managed to leave matters for his fellow Chinese Americans in a better state than that in which he found them when he arrived in the United States in 1881.

• There is little information available on Chew. Good sources include E. A. Wicher, *The Presbyterian Church in California, 1849–1927* (1927); Jack Chen, *The Chinese of America* (1980); and numerous articles and editorials in the daily newspaper that Chew founded. Obituaries are in the *San Francisco Examiner*, 14 Mar. 1931, and *Chung Sai Yat Po*, 14, 17 Mar. 1931.

SAMUEL WILLARD CROMPTON

CHEYNEY, Edward Potts (17 Jan. 1861–1 Feb. 1947), historian, was born in Wallingford, Pennsylvania, the son of Waldron J. Cheyney, a businessman in the chemical and mining industries, and Fannie Potts. He graduated with a B.A. from the University of Pennsylvania in 1883 and, after travel in Europe, entered the university's Wharton School of Finance, from which in 1884 he received a bachelor's degree in finance. He apparently never received a doctorate. In 1884 Cheyney began fifty years of teaching at the University of Pennsylvania as an instructor in history, Latin, and mathematics. He became assistant professor of history in 1890 and professor in 1897. He married Gertrude Levis Squires in 1886; they had three children.

Cheyney's first historical publications were in the field of American history, but he turned to English history in 1895 with *Social Changes in England in the Sixteenth Century as Reflected in Contemporary Literature*. With his colleagues, James Harvey Robinson and Dana C. Munro, Cheyney in the 1890s edited a series of source materials in European history for use in graduate seminars. He also produced textbooks for undergraduates: *An Introduction to the Industrial and Social History of England* (1901), *A Short History of England* (1904), and *Readings in English History* (1908). Cheyney joined the American Historical Association in 1890 and with his election to the AHA's executive council in 1901 became one of its most influential members.

A believer in "scientific" history, Cheyney expressed his conception of scientific history nowhere more forcibly than in his 1923 presidential address to the AHA, "Law in History." He saw in history an inevitable progression of events and outlined six historical "laws" of continuity, interdependence, impermanence and mutability, democracy, necessity for free consent, and moral progress in comparison to which the work of individuals seemed relatively insignificant.

To Cheyney the most significant historical development was the simultaneous growth of nationalism and individual freedom. To this fundamental conviction, he added an interest in the connection between history and contemporary events that was characteristic of the "New History," an interpretative school sympathetic to social science that encouraged scholars to consider all dimensions of human activity rather than just the history of politics and institutions. In *An Introduction to the Industrial and Social History of England* (1901), he acknowledged that "socialism" had come to occupy a prominent place in British political thought, defining the term as simply the willingness to consider the general good ahead of individual preference. Socialism as an attempt to create the ideal society free from competition he consigned to the realm of philosophical speculation rather than history.

In *A Short History of England* (1904) and in succeeding books, Cheyney made his central theme the development of England as a nation. Also in 1904, he produced *European Background of American History, 1300–1600*, the first volume in the *American Nation* series, edited by Albert B. Hart. In a project designed to establish American history as worthy of study on its own terms, Cheyney struck a somewhat dissonant note by insisting throughout that America was largely an extension of Europe, and more specifically, of England. Cheyney's most substantial contribution to scholarship, *A History of England: From the Defeat of the Armada to the Death of Elizabeth with an Account of English Institutions during the Later Sixteenth and Early Seventeenth Centuries* (2 vols.; 1914, 1926), added much detail to the discussion of a period that had previously been neglected but was not a profound work of historical interpretation. In 1929 he was appointed Henry Charles Lea Professor of History.

Cheyney broadened his range when, two years after retiring from teaching in 1934, he published *The Dawn of a New Era 1250–1453* (1936), discussing the economic and religious history of Europe in greater depth than had hitherto been done. Just before this, Cheyney had once more approached the subject of social reform in *Modern English Reform: From Individualism to Socialism* (1931), the origin of which were lectures he had delivered at the Lowell Institute in 1928. He portrayed the history of nineteenth- and early twentieth-century England as the gradual and inevitable democratization of the political process by powerful forces outside political parties. There remained, in his view, the threat of a communist uprising, but this was minor compared to what he saw as the continuous history of progressive reform.

Cheyney's retirement was marked by the presentation of his portrait, which was hung in the university library, and by a commemorative volume, *Portrait of a Historian* (1935), edited by his colleague, William E. Lingelbach. In this volume, John Franklin Jameson, his close associate for many years in the AHA and on the editorial board of the *American Historical Review* reminded a new generation of Cheyney's many contributions to the association as chair of the committee on the Justin Winsor Prize from 1899 to 1908 and chair of the committee on the bibliography of modern British history from 1909 to 1933. Cheyney was chair of the *American Historical Review* editorial board for most of his period of service from 1912 to 1920, and when the leadership of the AHA and the management of the *American Historical Review* came under attack between 1913 and 1915, largely by southern and western historians who found eastern control of the historical profession undemocratic and intellectually stifling, Cheyney drafted a historical account of the journal and defended the board's conduct at the 1915 annual meeting of the AHA. Probably influenced by his mother's Quaker ancestry, Cheyney stood apart from most professional historians in opposing America's entry into World War I. Cheyney reciprocated the esteem his historical colleagues and the University of Pennsylvania displayed toward him when he published a history of the university in 1940.

From his retirement in 1934 until 1940, Cheyney served as curator of the Henry Charles Lea Library at the University of Pennsylvania. In 1938 the Social Science Research Council asked Cheyney to direct a study of the freedom of inquiry. The project resulted in a series of essays edited by him and published in the *Annals of the American Academy of Political and Social Science* in November 1938. Cheyney died in Chester, Pennsylvania.

• Cheyney's papers are in the University of Pennsylvania archives. There is also extensive Cheyney correspondence in the John Franklin Jameson Papers and in the records of the American Historical Association, both of which are in the Library of Congress. For biographical information, see William E. Lingelbach, ed., *Portrait of a Historian* (1935), which includes Cheyney's "Last Will and Testament (Academic)," an affectionate and candid statement about the university to which he had devoted his entire career. See also Roy Nichols's autobiography, *A Historian's Progress* (1968); Elizabeth Donnan and Leo Stock, eds., *An Historian's World: Selections from the Correspondence of John Franklin Jameson* (1956); and Joshua L. Chamberlain, ed., *University of Pennsylvania Illustrated, 1740–1900* (1902). Obituaries are in the *New York Times*, 2 Feb. 1947, and the *American Historical Review* 52 (Apr. 1947): 647–48.

MOREY ROTHBERG

CHICKERING, Jonas (5 Apr. 1798–8 Dec. 1853), piano manufacturer, was born in Mason Village, New Hampshire, the son of Abner Chickering, a blacksmith, and Eunice Dakin. Not long after his birth, the family moved to New Ipswich, New Hampshire, where as a youth he attended the village school and worked on the family farm and in his father's blacksmith shop. He showed natural musical ability at an early age and taught himself to play the fife and clarinet and to read music at sight. Chickering also had a mechanical bent of mind and apprenticed himself to a cabinetmaker, John Gould, at age seventeen. As a youth of nineteen he reportedly repaired the only piano in town, a delicate instrument that at one time had belonged to Princess Amelia, the daughter of King George III.

In 1818 Chickering went to Boston, where he worked first for the cabinetmaker James Barker and then from 1819 to 1823 for John Osborne, a leading piano maker in Boston. In Osborne's workshop there was no division of labor, and Chickering mastered all the details of piano making. In 1823 he went into partnership with James Stewart on Tremont Street, producing about twelve square pianos a year under the name Stewart & Chickering. Their first piano, a square with a compass of five octaves and four notes, was sold to James Bingham for $275. That same year Chickering married Elizabeth Harraden; they had four children. After Stewart returned to Europe in 1827, Chickering worked alone until he formed a partnership with John MacKay in 1830. MacKay, a retired sea captain and wealthy businessman, had a keen appreciation of Chickering's work. By providing the young piano manufacturer with the necessary capital to set up a factory, he allowed Chickering to concentrate once again on the technical problems of improving the piano. MacKay aggressively promoted and sold Chickering pianos throughout the United States and returned from his voyages to South America with mahogany and rosewood for the firm. When MacKay was lost at sea in 1841, Chickering bought out the heirs and carried on alone until his own sons entered the business in 1852.

The challenge to Chickering and other piano makers in the early nineteenth century was to create a stronger frame for the piano that would withstand the ever-increasing tension on the strings and the extremes of the American climate. The six-octave wood-framed piano, which Chickering set out to improve, was constantly out of tune as a result of the weather and coal-fueled furnaces. Chickering worked on this problem for ten years with "patient industry" and "untiring zeal." He decided that the strain of tension on the strings must be met by a material capable of sustaining it. He chose iron, although most piano makers frowned on the introduction of metal to strengthen the frame, thinking it would be detrimental to the tone quality. In 1837 Chickering took out a patent for a one-piece cast-iron frame for a square piano, improving on Alpheus Babcock's 1825 invention. The iron frame allowed Chickering to use heavier strings, which gave the piano greater volume and resonance. In 1843 he patented a cast-iron frame for a grand piano, his most significant innovation. The Chickering pianos won highest honors at the Crystal Palace Exhibition in London in 1851. With the advent of concert halls in the United States, Chickering pianos were much in demand. In 1850 Jenny Lind toured America with a Chickering piano, as did Louis Moreau Gottschalk, America's first piano virtuoso, in 1852. By the early 1850s Chickering had become the most important piano manufacturer in the country, producing more than one thousand pianos each year.

In 1852, however, a fire destroyed the Chickering factory at 334 Washington Street. Undaunted, Chickering laid the groundwork for a new five-story establishment at 791 Tremont Street. The new factory had a 120-horsepower steam engine and was said to have been the largest building in the United States with the exception of the Capitol in Washington, D.C. Chickering died in Boston of a stroke before the new factory was completed. After his death his three sons, whom he had made partners in 1852 and whom he had trained well in the business, went on to achieve new honors for the company. In 1867 Chickering and Steinway pianos both won first prize at the celebrated International Paris Exposition, and C. Frank Chickering was decorated with the Imperial Cross of the Legion of Honor by Emperor Napoleon III for his "distinguished service to music." The "American system," as it was called, of piano construction, with the one-piece cast-iron frame and overstringing, revolutionized piano making and was soon adopted by all European makers. When presented with a Chickering grand piano after the Paris Exposition, composer Franz Liszt is said to have exclaimed, "It is imperial! I never thought a piano could have these qualities!" Toward the end of the century, Von Bülow, De Pachman, Joseffy, and other great artists endorsed the piano and gave brilliant performances in New York's Chickering Hall, which the Chickering brothers had built in 1875. After the death of George H. Chickering in 1896, the firm was bought by the American Piano Company in 1908. From 1905 to 1911 Arnold Dolmetch formed his own division in the Chickering factory, where he produced harpsichords, clavichords, viols, and lutes. In 1927 the operations were moved from Boston to East Rochester, New York, where in 1932 it became part of the Aeolean American Corporation. In 1985 the Wurlitzer company acquired the firm.

Chickering's greatest contribution to the modern piano was the one-piece cast-iron frame for grand piano patented in 1843. Music historian Arthur Loesser has written, "The Paris awards [of 1867] were a resounding vindication of the American principles of piano construction—of the one-piece frame first practically applied by Chickering, and the later developments of stringing and scaling worked out by Steinway" (Loesser, p. 513). Chickering, a genial man, shy and unassuming by nature, lived to see his firm become one of the two most important piano businesses in America in the nineteenth century. In a tribute to Chickering, given at an 1895 trade dinner of the Piano Manufacturers' Association in New York, William Steinway stated, "Too much honor cannot be given to Jonas Chickering, the father of American piano making."

• The Chickering archives are located at the Smithsonian Institution. The most complete account of Chickering's life is in Richard G. Parker, *A Tribute to the Life and Character of Jonas Chickering by One Who Knew Him Well* (1854). See also Helen Hollis, "Jonas Chickering, the Father of American Piano-forte Making," *Antiques* 8 (1973): 227–30. Alfred Dolge, *Pianos & Their Makers* (1911; repr. 1972), provides excellent biographical sketches of Chickering and his three sons, all of whom were Dolge's contemporaries. For a history of the Chickering firm see Chickering & Sons, *Achievement—An Ascending Scale, Being the Short History of the House of Chickering and Sons* (1920), Daniel Spillane, *History of the American Pianoforte* (1890; repr. 1969); Chickering & Sons, *The Commemoration of the Founding of the House of Chickering & Sons upon the Eightieth Anniversary of the Event, 1823–1903* (1904); and Nancy A. Smith, "Pianoforte Manufacturing in Nineteenth-Century Boston," *Old Time New England* 8 (1978): 37–47, a publication of the Society for the Preservation of New England Antiquities. See also Cyril Ehrlich, *The Piano: A History* (1973), and Rosamond Harding, *The Piano: Its History Traced to the Great Exhibit in 1851* (1973), for the technical development of the piano in Europe and America, and Arthur Loesser, *Men, Women and Pianos* (1954; repr. 1974), for a brilliant social history of the piano and its place in society. An obituary is in the *Boston Herald*, 9 Dec. 1853.

MARGARET MORELAND STATHOS

CHILD, Charles Manning (2 Feb. 1869–19 Dec. 1954), experimental zoologist, was born in Ypsilanti, Michigan, the son of Charles Chauncey Child and Mary Elizabeth Manning, farmers. He was delivered by his maternal grandfather, who practiced medicine in Ypsilanti. When Child was three weeks old, his mother took him home to the family farm in Higganum, Connecticut. Child was educated at Wesleyan University in Middletown, Connecticut, and received a Ph.B. in 1890 and an M.S. in biology in 1892. After dabbling in experimental psychology at the University of Leipzig in Germany, he switched to zoology and earned a Ph.D. from that institution in 1894.

Child spent the following year doing independent research at the Naples Zoological Station (NZS) and in 1895 began teaching at the University of Chicago, where he remained until his retirement in 1937. In 1916 he was made a full professor, and from 1934 until his retirement he served as chairman of the zoology department. He spent his summers doing research at NZS, the Marine Biological Laboratory at Woods Hole, Massachusetts, and at various marine stations up and down the Pacific Coast. In 1930 he was a visiting professor at Duke University, and in 1930–1931 he was a Rockefeller Foundation Visiting Professor at Tohoku Imperial University, Sendai, Japan. From 1937 until his death, he was a guest lecturer at Stanford University.

As a young scholar, Child was intrigued by the workings of the nervous systems of invertebrates. He later became interested in embryology, particularly the process of cleavage, the first few cell divisions in a fertilized egg. This work led him to study regeneration in the lower invertebrates such as coelenterates and planarians (hydras and flatworms). In 1911, in an effort to explain why these axiate organisms almost always regenerated a head from the anterior region and a tail from the posterior region, he propounded the gradient theory, his most important contribution to the field of zoology. After observing that regeneration and embryonic development are closely related, Child postulated that these physiological processes are governed by antero-posterior dominance. In both situations, an apical dominant region, or anterior, is formed first, followed by other parts, which form in relation to it. Child believed that those cells closer to an organism's anterior function at a higher metabolic rate than do cells closer to its posterior, and that this metabolic rate, which is gradated so that it decreases in direct proportion to the distance from the anterior, determines cell differentiation during regeneration and development.

Child's gradient theory was first published in *Die physiologische Isolation von Teilen des Organismus als Auslösungsfaktor der Bildung neuer Lebewesen und der Restitution* (1911). Child suggested that, because anterior domination declines with distance, the size of an organism is limited by what he called physiological isolation. In organisms that cannot regenerate, physiological isolation leads to atrophy, degeneration, absorption, or death; however, in organisms that can regenerate, physiological isolation results in asexual reproduction. The gradient theory was further developed in *Individuality in Organisms* (1915), wherein he argued that every organism's size, form, structural pattern, and correlation of cellular activities develop as they do because the most metabolically active region dominates the growth and development of all other regions. Child employed the gradient theory as a means of understanding aging, the development of the nervous system, and behavior and published his ideas on these subjects in *Senescence and Rejuvenescence* (1915), *The Origin and Development of the Nervous System from a Physiological Viewpoint* (1921), and *Physiological Foundations of Behavior* (1924), respectively. In 1941 he published *Patterns and Problems of Development*, a summary of his conclusions regarding the gradient theory.

The chief criticism of Child's theory at the time of its propagation was that it was based on experiments with simple animals, and therefore did little to explain development in nonaxiate organisms. The theory was later criticized on the grounds that it did not explain regeneration in axiate organisms either. Many physiologists have since come to the opinion that planarian regeneration is governed by special cells called neoblasts; these cells contain large amounts of ribonucleic acid, which serves as a catalyst during cell division, and are present in great numbers during regeneration. Despite these criticisms and later developments, the gradient theory offered one of the first explanations of cellular organization.

Although Child had no difficulty getting his ideas published in respected journals of science, he came to believe that a publication geared toward research in morphogenesis, particularly concerning the nature of the unity and order of the organism, would stimulate research in this field. In 1928, under the auspices of the University of Chicago, he founded the journal *Physiological Zoology* and served as its editor for two years. By the late 1950s, the journal became an important forum for researchers in experimental zoology.

Child received a number of honors during his lifetime. In 1919 he served as president of the American Society of Zoologists. He was a fellow of the American Association for the Advancement of Science and in 1929 served as vice president of the association's zoology section. He was elected to the National Academy of Sciences in 1935. He was a foreign member of the Linnaean Society of London, an honorary member of the Société Royale Zoologique de Belgique, and a member of a number of American scientific organizations.

In 1899 Child married Lydia Van Meter; the couple had one daughter. In 1937 he retired to Palo Alto, California, where he lectured occasionally at Stanford, continued his experiments with embryos, and indulged his passion for the outdoors by hiking the Sierra Nevada Mountains. He died in Palo Alto.

Child's career was devoted to understanding how an organism composed of many cells that are both integrated and independent organizes its own development in terms of size, shape, and correlation of activities. Although that question remains to be answered satisfactorily, much of what physiologists know about the answer is derived from Child's research. Because his research was published in more than 230 articles in thirty-nine different journals on three continents between 1892 and 1954, he was widely regarded as one of the most important contributors to zoological theory and interpretation of his time.

• A few manuscripts pertaining to Child can be found in various collections in the archives of the Stanford University Library, but the bulk of his papers did not survive. Libbie H. Hyman, "Charles Manning Child, 1869–1954," National Academy of Sciences, *Biographical Memoirs* 30 (1957): 73–103, presents a good discussion of the developments and significance of Child's career, as well as a complete bibliography of his work. An obituary is in the *New York Times*, 21 Dec. 1954.

CHARLES W. CAREY, JR.

CHILD, David Lee (8 July 1794–18 Sept. 1874), abolitionist, was born in West Boylston, Massachusetts, the son of Zachariah Child and Lydia Bigelow, farmers. Child graduated from Harvard College in 1817 and became submaster of the Boston Latin School the next year. In 1820 he went to Lisbon, Portugal, to serve as secretary of the American legation. In 1823 he joined the Spanish army and fought to defend that country's democratic constitution against promonarchical French invaders "in consequence of my love of liberty and my abhorrence of fraud, cruelty, and despotism."

Child returned to Massachusetts in 1824 to study law and was admitted to the Suffolk County bar in 1828. That same year he was elected to the state legislature and became editor of the *Massachusetts Journal*. The paper supported President John Quincy Adams in his losing bid for a second term. Also in 1828 Child married Lydia Maria Francis, a prominent Boston author. His earnings as a lawyer were modest, in large part because he refused to turn away clients who were unable to pay, and he gave away much of what he did collect to needy individuals and worthy causes. The resulting bare-bones lifestyle probably provided the inspiration for his wife's bestselling work, *The Frugal Housewife* (1829).

Shortly after his marriage Child became interested in the abolition movement. Freeing the slaves appealed to the romantic streak in him in a way that the dry practice of law never could. In 1832 he, William Lloyd Garrison, and fourteen other men founded the New England Anti-Slavery Society. As a trustee of Noyes Academy in Canaan, New Hampshire, he played an important role in opening that school to black students. A proponent of gradual rather than immediate emancipation, Child wrote a series of impassioned letters to Edward S. Abdy, the English philanthropist, thereby attracting the attention of abolitionists in Great Britain. In 1833 he published his first antislavery tract, *The Despotism of Freedom*. Two years later he accepted an invitation from Benjamin Lundy, the Quaker antislavery colonizer, to help establish a free-labor colony for emancipated blacks in Tamaulipas, Mexico. The plan collapsed when the Texas revolutionary government successfully laid claim to the 172,000 acres that Lundy had received permission from the Mexican provincial governor to settle.

In 1835 Child was elected vice president of the Massachusetts Anti-Slavery Society and nominated by his fellow abolitionists to run for the U.S. Senate. Instead of running, in 1836 Child embarked on a quixotic venture to ease the plight of slaves on Caribbean sugar plantations, where the living conditions were perhaps the most brutal in the Western Hemisphere. Child set out to prove that sugar could be produced less expensively from sugar beets raised by free northern laborers than from slave-grown southern sugarcane, which could curtail the demand for slaves on the plantations. After spending most of that year in Belgium studying sugar beets, he bought 100 acres in Northampton, Massachusetts. With the assistance of Edward Church, his partner, and Maximin Isnard, the French vice consul at Boston and one of the early developers of the beet-sugar industry in France, Child began operating the first beet-sugar farm and factory in the United States. In 1839 their efforts won a silver medal at the Massachusetts State Exposition for raw and refined sugar, and in 1840 Child published *Culture of the Beet, and Manufacture of Beet-Sugar*.

In 1841 Child and his wife were invited to coedit the *National Anti-Slavery Standard*, a weekly newspaper based in New York City. Hoping optimistically that his beet-sugar project was on the verge of succeeding, he opted to remain on the farm and write an occasional editorial while Lydia moved to New York to assume the bulk of the editor's responsibilities. Unfortunately, the beet-sugar venture was doomed from the start. Even with government backing, European beet-sugar producers were never able to compete successfully with cane sugar until after the emancipation of West Indian slaves, and Child's project was grossly undercapitalized. In its best year the factory produced a mere 1,300 pounds of sugar, and in 1841 the insolvent venture closed, leaving Child to make a go of it on his own.

The combined strain of living alone, laboring unceasingly, and staving off bankruptcy dampened Child's enthusiasm for beet-sugar production, but his commitment to abolition never flagged. In 1843 he published a pamphlet, *The Texas Revolution*, and moved to New York to join his wife as coeditor of the *Standard*. The next year, amid charges of mismanagement of the paper and a dispute over Child's unabashed support of the Whig party, he stepped down as coeditor and moved to Washington, D.C., to report on the national scene for the *Standard*. While in Washington, he published another antislavery pamphlet, *The Taking of Naboth's Vineyard*. In 1846 he returned to Northampton to live alone amidst the detritus of his failed dream.

Shortly thereafter Lydia Child gave up the editorship of the *Standard* and rejoined her husband on the farm in Northampton, where she continued her literary career and he dabbled at law and farming. In 1852 the couple moved to Wayland, Massachusetts, to a farm that Lydia's father gave to her in the form of a trust to keep it from falling into the hands of Child's creditors. Child continued to farm and practice law, and his commitment to abolition remained strong. He contributed as generously as he could to the cause of black freedom, and in 1861 he published the pamphlet *Rights and Duties of the United States Relative to Slavery under the Laws of War*. Following the publication of this tract, Child withdrew completely from public life. When he became too old to practice law, he concentrated on farming, and once a year he invited all the neighborhood children to his farm to feast on the fruit he had raised. He died, childless, in Wayland.

• Child's papers are located in the Anti-Slavery Collection, Department of Rare Books and Manuscripts, Boston Public Library; the Child papers, Massachusetts Historical Society; and the David Lee Child Papers, Department of Rare Books, Cornell University Library. He is featured prominently in the pages of Deborah Pickman Clifford, *Crusader for Freedom: A Life of Lydia Maria Child* (1992), and Carolyn L. Karcher, *The First Woman in the Republic: A Cultural Biography of Lydia Maria Child* (1994). Child's importance as an abolitionist is assessed in John F. Hume, *The Abolitionists* (1905); Jane H. Pease and William H. Pease, *Bound with Them in Chains: A Biographical Story of the Antislavery Movement* (1972); and Donald M. Jacobs, ed., *Courage and Conscience: Black and White Abolitionists in Boston* (1993). His contributions to the beet-sugar industry in the United States are assessed in F. S. Harris, *The Sugar-Beet in America* (1926), and a publication of the U.S. Beet Sugar Association, *The Beet Sugar Story* (1959). An obituary is in the *New York Times*, 28 Sept. 1874.

CHARLES W. CAREY, JR.

CHILD, Francis James (1 Feb. 1825–11 Sept. 1896), philologist and editor, was born in Boston, Massachusetts, the son of Joseph Child, a sailmaker, and Mary James. After attending the Boston Latin School, he matriculated at Harvard College; he ranked first in his class and was elected class orator. Following his graduation in 1846, he became a tutor in mathematics at his alma mater and then, in 1848, in history and political economy. Also in 1848 he published his edition of *Four Old Plays*. At this time he began his lifelong friendship with the poet James Russell Lowell. In 1849 he traveled to Europe, where he studied at the universities of Göttingen and Berlin. He returned to Harvard in 1851 and succeeded Edward Tyrrel Channing as the fourth Boylston professor of rhetoric and oratory, shifting "the emphasis of his professorship from the 'pernicious doctrines' of rhetoric and oratory to literary criticism and balladry" (Ried, p. 275). In 1854 he received a Ph.D. from the University of Göttingen despite not having written a dissertation. In 1860 Child married Elizabeth Ellery Sedgwick; they had four children.

As a result of his work on *Four Old Plays*, in the 1850s Child accepted the general editorship of a series of books titled the British Poets, published in Boston by Little, Brown. For the series Child himself edited the volumes on Edmund Spenser, Thomas More, and Thomas Hood, as well as *English and Scottish Ballads* (8 vols., 1857–1858). Child considered his lengthy introduction to the Spenser edition (*Poetical Works of Edmund Spenser* [5 vols., 1855]) "more complete and more correct than any former biography" of the poet. The edition itself was "the best edition [of Spenser] in existence" at the time of Child's death (Kittredge, p. 740). The ballad collection formed the basis for much of Child's subsequent scholarly activity and for his ultimate importance and reputation. A number of Child's publications appeared in the 1860s. He provided the Italian lyrics to the humorous operetta *Il pesceballo* (1862); wrote *Observations on the Language of Chaucer* (1863) and *Observations on the Language of Gower's "Confessio Amantis"* (1873); edited *Poems of Religious Sorrow, Comfort, Counsel and Aspiration* (1863); and compiled *War-songs for Freemen* (1862). Of these, his work on Chaucer and Gower is most significant, examining in a detailed manner the poets' language, pronunciation, and versification. In 1876 Child became chair of English at Harvard, thus establishing one of the first English departments in the United States.

Child devoted most of his scholarly life to identifying and analyzing ballads, in which he first became interested while living in Germany in the late 1840s and early 1850s and which he had first written about in the 1850s. As Paul E. Ried noted, Child had set for himself a monumental task requiring "the collection and authentication of every version of every English ballad and every Scottish ballad in existence." To authenticate a single ballad, Child sometimes had to read scores of books in twelve different languages. Published in ten parts, *English and Scottish Popular Ballads* (5 vols., 1883–1898) is an enlargement of his original work and his greatest contribution to scholarship. In the earlier edition, Child had worked from printed texts; in the later, from manuscripts. Child was among the first scholars to apply the comparative method to folklore, which became the foundation for serious research in that area of scholarship. In the end, Child included more than 300 ballads, most in multiple versions, including fifteen of "Lord Randal," for example, but he died before he was able to write an introduction to his work. The extent of his achievement has, nevertheless, continued to be appreciated. According to Steven Swann Jones, "Rarely has an entire field, especially one as complex and extensive as the ballad, been defined quite so single-handedly by one individual."

Child died in Boston shortly after having completed his fiftieth year of teaching at Harvard, apparently without having ever missed meeting a single scheduled class.

• Child's papers are in the Widener Library at Harvard University. Other primary materials on Child include *A Scholar's Letter to a Young Lady: Passages from the Later Correspondence of Francis James Child* (1920), *Letters on Scottish Ballads, from Professor Francis J. Child to W. W. Aberdeen* (1930), and *The Scholar-Friends: Letters of Francis James Child and James Russell Lowell*, ed. M. A. De Wolfe Howe and George William Cottrell (1952). The most significant articles on Child are George Lyman Kittredge, "Professor Child," *Atlantic Monthly*, Dec. 1896, pp. 737–42; Paul E. Ried, "Francis J. Child: The Fourth Boylston Professor of Rhetoric and Oratory," *Quarterly Journal of Speech* 55 (Oct. 1969): 268–75; and Steven Swann Jones's article on Child in the *Dictionary of Literary Biography* (1988). Also of interest is M. A. De Wolfe Howe, "'Il Pesceballo': The Fishball Operetta of Francis James Child," *New England Quarterly* 23 (June 1950): 187–99, and J. McMurtry, *English Language, English Literature: The Creation of an Academic Discipline* (1985), pp. 65–110.

BENJAMIN FRANKLIN V

CHILD, Lydia Maria Francis (11 Feb. 1802–20 Oct. 1880), author and abolitionist, was born in Medford, Massachusetts, the daughter of David Convers Francis, a baker, and Susannah Rand. Although her father's business success allowed her older brother and intellectual mentor, Convers, to be educated at Harvard College and Harvard Divinity School, Lydia (who went by her middle name) received her education in a dame school and a local seminary. After the death of her mother in 1814, she was sent to live with her sister, Mary Francis Preston, in Norridgewock, Maine Territory. She remained with her sister until 1820 and during this period studied at a local academy preparing to become a teacher. Convers, continuing to oversee his younger sister's intellectual development, introduced her to the works of Homer, Ben Johnson, John Milton, and Sir Walter Scott.

In 1821 Lydia returned to Massachusetts and took up residence with Convers, now a minister of the Unitarian church in Watertown. Located near Boston, Watertown later became a hotbed of Transcendentalist thought. In Convers's home she came into contact with such intellectuals as Ralph Waldo Emerson, Theodore Parker, and John Greenleaf Whittier. In addition, she befriended Margaret Fuller of nearby Cambridge, with whom she shared an interest in belletrist Madame de Staël. Although she was busy teaching in a girls school she had opened, Lydia found time during these years to produce the first of four novels.

Hobomok, a Tale of the Times (1824), set in seventeenth-century Massachusetts, recounted the trials and tribulations of Mary Conant. Forbidden by her tyrannical father to marry her Episcopalian lover, Mary rebels and instead marries Hobomok, a Pequod, with whom she has a child. Although the tale ends with Conant reunited with her white lover, the story contains the nascent arguments for religious and racial toleration that would later characterize her writings. Some critics found the subject matter of *Hobomok* rather scandalous, but the reading public had no such reservations. At the tender age of twenty-two, Lydia had launched what seemed to be a promising writing career.

Following up on the warm reception given *Hobomok*, Lydia's second novel, *The Rebels; or, Boston before the Revolution*, was published in 1825. This novel, which details the events leading up to the Boston Tea Party, was more favorably received by the literary establishment, and by 1826 Lydia felt confident enough in her abilities to begin publishing the bimonthly *Juvenile Miscellany*, the first periodical published solely for children within the United States. Filled with educational literature as well as stories and poetry that Lydia herself wrote, the *Juvenile Miscellany* was both a fulfilling and profitable venture for the next eight years. In 1828 Lydia Francis married David Lee Child. A graduate of Harvard College, Child epitomized the educational breadth and depth that his wife had been denied because of her sex. He had practiced law in Boston as well as served in the state legislature and had edited the political organ the *Massachusetts Whig Journal*. David broadened Lydia's horizons by introducing her to an array of social reforms such as Indian rights and abolitionism. It was through her husband that Child was first exposed to the ideas of the radical abolitionist William Lloyd Garrison. While her diverting prose and light poetry made her famous, her unstinting support of abolitionism ultimately made her infamous. Because her husband was a dubious breadwinner at best, Child supported them with her writing. She published *The Frugal Housewife* (1829) and *The Mother's Book* and *The Little Girl's Own Book* (1831) in quick succession. This prescriptive literature for women earned her a favorable international reputation. At the height of her popularity she published *An Appeal in Favor of That Class of Americans Called Africans* (1833), which called for immediate emancipation (without compensation to owners) and racial equality as well as argued against colonization in Africa. Although Wendell Phillips, William Ellery Channing, and Charles Sumner credited *An Appeal* with shaping their own antislavery views, Child was almost immediately ostracized by a public that formerly had adored her. The *Juvenile Miscellany* was forced to shut down the following year because of so many canceled subscriptions. Despite the emotional and financial hardship caused by her antislavery views, Child refused to be silenced.

The childless couple's financial difficulties were further exacerbated by David's decision to raise sugar beets as an alternative to slave-produced sugarcane. His experiment was a dismal failure, and in 1841, in an effort both to aid the abolitionist cause and support their household, Lydia accepted the editorship of the *National Anti-Slavery Standard*, the New York newspaper for the American Anti-Slavery Society. She left the paper only two years later, however, because she was unwilling to countenance violence and vitriol as acceptable weapons for battling the evil of slavery. David accepted the editorship of the *Standard* in 1843, but he too had trouble pleasing the fractured society and was forced to resign in 1844. After legally separating her finances from those of her husband, Child turned to journalism to support herself. She wrote prodigiously for both newspapers and periodicals, and with the publication of *Letters from New York* (1843–1845) regained some of her former popularity. During these years she also championed greater equality between the sexes, but her unfavorable experience with the American Anti-Slavery Society made her loathe to join outright either the suffrage or woman's rights movements.

Following an estrangement of nearly a decade, the Childs had permanently reconciled by 1852, when they moved to Wayland, Massachusetts, to live in the home that Child would eventually inherit from her father. Despite their isolation in remote Wayland, the couple continued to participate in current events. Their unprepossessing home sheltered runaway slaves, and after their good friend Charles Sumner was caned insensible by Congressman Preston Brooks because of Sumner's "Crime against Kansas" speech, Child retaliated by writing the poem "The Kansas Emigrants." In 1859 she was drawn further into public events by her sympathy for John Brown and his raid on Harpers Ferry. Although she did not condone his violent means, Child admired the courage with which he battled slavery. Thus, upon hearing that Brown had been wounded in the attack, she contacted Governor Henry Wise of Virginia and offered her services at Brown's sickbed.

Although Brown gently declined her aid, when news of Child's offer became public she was denounced by the proslavery camp as a troublemaker. In particular, Mrs. James Mason, wife of the author of the Fugitive Slave Act, wrote a letter to Wise condemning Child for offering comfort to a murderer. Mrs. Mason had tried to win sympathy for her position by discussing the aid given by southern ladies to slave women in childbirth, but Child turned the tables on her by responding that, whereas northern women also assisted in childbirth, "after we have helped the mothers, *we do not sell the babies*" (*Letters of Lydia Maria Child*, p. 135). The Child–Wise–Mason correspondence was packaged as a pamphlet, and soon 300,000 copies blanketed the North. Child continued to demand equal treatment for blacks, and so in 1861 she willingly edited former slave Harriet Jacobs's novel *Incidents in the Life of a Slave Girl*. She followed this in 1865 with *The Freedmen's Book*, a collection of short poems, biographical sketches, and essays created with the hope of inculcating pride in newly freed blacks. *Aspirations of the World: A Chain of Opals*, the final anthology of her work, was published in 1878, two years before her death in Wayland.

Although best known for her antislavery writings, Child evinced an interest in all areas of social reform. Throughout her long career she commented on such issues as Indian rights, equal rights for women, educational reform, and religious toleration. She sacrificed a burgeoning national career in the 1830s by remaining true to her own conscience and becoming one of the first Americans to speak out against the institution of slavery.

• A large collection of Child's papers can be found at Cornell University; others are located at the Boston Public Library, the Massachusetts Historical Society, the American Antiquarian Society, the Schlesinger Library of Radcliffe, the Houghton Library at Harvard, and the New York Public Library. *The Collected Correspondence of Lydia Maria Child*, ed. Milton Meltzer et al. (1980), contains most of Child's papers and is available on microfiche. Meltzer et al. have also produced a published version of her papers and letters, *Lydia Maria Child, Selected Papers* (1982). Child's other works include *The History of the Condition of Women in Various Ages and Nations* (1835), *Philothea, a Romance* (1836), and *The Progress of Religious Ideas through Successive Ages* (1855). Full-length studies include Helene G. Baer, *The Heart Is Like Heaven: The Life of Lydia Maria Child* (1964), and Milton Meltzer, *Tongue of Flame: The Life of Lydia Maria Child* (1965). She is also discussed in Seth Curtis Beach, *Daughters of the Puritans* (1905); Susan Phinney Conrad, *Perish the Thought: Intellectual Women in Romantic America, 1830–1860* (1976); and Margaret Farrand Thorp, *Six Persuasive Women* (1919).

CATHERINE TEETS-PARZYNSKI

CHILD, Richard Washburn (5 Aug. 1881–31 Jan. 1935), author and diplomat, was born in Worcester, Massachusetts, the son of Horace Walter Child, a prosperous shoe manufacturer, and Susan Sawyer Messinger. He attended Harvard University, receiving an A.B. in 1903 and an LL.B. in 1906. He did legal work for a Boston engineering firm before opening in 1915 a law office in New York that specialized in organizing businesses. In 1933 he created the law partnership of Child, Handel and Axman in New York.

Drawn to the charismatic personality of former president Theodore Roosevelt, Child worked to create the Progressive Republican League, the predecessor on the state level to the national Progressive party, in Massachusetts in 1911. Covering for *Collier's* magazine the defeat of Roosevelt at the Republican National Convention of 1912 disillusioned him with the political status quo, and he developed a critique of American democracy, believing that political parties eschewed issues and too often beguiled voters with simplistic slogans, which resulted in too much meaningless talk and not enough constructive legislation. Like so many young Progressives of his generation, Child turned his attention to the Great War as a reform crusade, first as a correspondent in Europe and Russia and, once the United States formally entered the conflict, doing publicity and finance work for the Treasury Department. During the last months of the war, he expressed misgivings over possible American participation in the coming peace conference. In 1919, as editor of *Collier's* and the magazine's correspondent at the Paris Peace Conference, Child attacked President Woodrow Wilson for espousing American participation in a strong League of Nations, since it had the potential to drag the country into European quarrels needlessly, to threaten the Monroe Doctrine, and to stir up conflicting nationalist sentiments among American ethnic groups.

Child supported General Leonard Wood for the Republican presidential nomination in 1920 as the man best suited to carry out the legacy of Roosevelt. When Warren G. Harding received the party's nod, Child wrote speeches and served as an adviser to the nominee, helping to craft Harding's deliberately confusing fence straddle on the league that contributed to the Republican victory. On 26 May 1921 President Harding named Child ambassador to Italy, a post he held until his resignation on 11 February 1924.

Harding's secretary of state, Charles Evans Hughes, had enough confidence in Ambassador Child to name him as an unofficial observer to the April–May 1922 Genoa Conference, convened to address Europe's political and economic problems. The conference accomplished nothing, and the experience only reinforced Child's growing isolationism. In spite of his contempt for Old World diplomacy (or perhaps because of it), Child became the chief observer to the more important Lausanne Conference, held in the winter of 1922–1923, which was to deal with revisions in the Allied peace treaty with a revitalized Turkey. He predicted to his parents that "this conference will be a welter of intrigue" (Child papers, 15 Nov. 1922), and the American diplomat played an active role in the diplomatic maneuvering. Frustrated by the lack of specific instructions from Washington but knowing that Hughes wanted an Open Door policy of equal economic opportunity for all nations implemented in the Near East, Child read a statement supporting the Open Door in Turkey during a conference debate over the fate of Western Thrace. The unexpected declaration led several American newspapers to denounce the Harding administration for being overly eager to procure economic advantages while eschewing concomitant political responsibilities in the world. Still, Turkey, Great Britain, and France all endorsed the Child statement, thus securing the American objective, at least on paper. Child also tried to act as an intermediary between the Allies and Turks. When the conference finally broke down, the ambassador came away believing that the leaders of Western Europe were essentially weak men.

If Child had misgivings about American democracy and Allied statesmanship, he greatly admired Benito Mussolini, praising him to the State Department following the March on Rome (28 Oct. 1922) and, subsequently, comparing him favorably with Theodore Roosevelt. Child proved to be a tireless publicist for Italian-style fascism, which he likened to a well-run American corporation. He defended censorship of the press in Italy as a positive good and denied that the Fascists murdered their political opponents. To further polish *Il Duce*'s image, Child collaborated with him on an autobiography in 1928, with Mussolini's brother Araldo doing most of the actual writing and Child the revising. Its bombast was such that Mussolini wisely chose not to have it published in Italian.

Following his stint as ambassador, Child served on the National Crime Commission in 1925, writing *Battling the Criminal* (1925) to arouse popular concern. That year he also published a memoir of his work for the State Department, *A Diplomat Looks at Europe*. In addition to turning out numerous articles for the Hearst newspapers and the *Saturday Evening Post*, he was president of the Arbitration Society of America and assisted Secretary of Commerce Herbert Hoover in organizing Mississippi flood relief in 1927. Although he was a lifelong Republican, Child campaigned for Franklin D. Roosevelt in 1932 and was rewarded with an appointment as adviser to Secretary of State Cordell Hull at the London Economic Conference (June–July 1933). He became a roving ambassador, charged with investigating economic conditions in Europe.

Child married four times, with the first three unions ending in divorce. He married Elizabeth Scott Mallett in 1904 (no children); Maude Louisa Parker in 1916 (two children); Eva Sanderson in 1927 (no children); and Dorothy Gallagher Everson in 1931 (one child). He died in New York City of pneumonia.

Child was a gifted promoter of causes. Before World War I he influenced millions of people with his writings that suggested New Nationalist Progressive solutions to social problems, emphasizing the importance of big government and strong leaders presiding over large-scale corporations with the aid of a vigorous citizenry. In the 1920s he quickened American interest in foreign affairs and helped to rationalize a pragmatic isolationism of continued world economic interests with minimal political involvement. His lionization of Mussolini and Italian fascism in the *Saturday Evening Post* and in his books was sincere and effective. If he was naive about the evil side of *Il Duce*, it was a delusion he shared with many people across the political spectrum.

Child was best known during his lifetime for the many articles and short stories he wrote for popular magazines, especially the *Saturday Evening Post* and *Collier's*, and for the novels and extended essays that often originated as short pieces. His writing struck a popular chord because of his breezy colloquial style, sympathetic treatment of popular concerns of the day, and shrewd observations of the human condition.

• Child's small collection of papers, consisting mostly of personal letters, is in the Manuscript Division of the Library of Congress. In addition to his crime book, diplomatic memoir, and Mussolini's autobiography mentioned above, Child's major publications include *Jim Hands* (1910), *The Man in the Shadow* (1911), *The Blue Wall* (1912), *Potential Russia* (1916), *Bodbank* (1916), *The Vanishing Men* (1919), *The Velvet Black* (1921), *The Hands of Nara* (1922), *The Writing on the Wall: Who Shall Govern Us Next?* (1929), and *The Pitcher of Romance* (1930). A full-length silent film, *The Mad Whirl* (1924), was based on Child's short story, "Here's How," which was published in his *Fresh Waters and Other Stories* (1924). Child's second wife wrote a memoir of her life as a diplomatic wife, Maude Parker Child, *The Social Side of Diplomatic Life* (1925). On his diplomatic career, see U.S. Department of State, *Papers Relating to the Foreign Relations of the United States, 1922–23* (1938); Steven Wagler Bianco, "Richard Washburn Child: Italian-American Relations, 1921–1924" (master's thesis, Univ. of Iowa, 1970); and Daniel E. Fausz, "Richard Washburn Child: America's Spokesman on Europe and Fascism, 1915–1935" (master's thesis, Vanderbilt Univ., 1985). His obituary is in the *New York Times*, 1 Feb. 1935.

PETER H. BUCKINGHAM

CHILD, Robert (1613–1654), physician and Remonstrant against Puritan rule in Massachusetts, was born in Kent, England, the son of John Child, a gentleman farmer (mother's name unknown). He attended Corpus Christi College, Cambridge, receiving his B.A. in 1632 and his M.A. in 1635. He then studied medicine in Europe, first at the University of Leyden and then the University of Padua, from which he received his M.D. on 13 August 1638.

After graduation, Child traveled extensively in Europe and also went briefly to New England. Wherever he went, he made detailed notes about the plants and agriculture. Child also became good friends with John Winthrop, Jr., a friendship that survived the turmoils of Child's second visit to Massachusetts in the mid-1640s. Child, having letters of introduction on his first visit to the colonies, was well received by the leaders in Boston. Following his initial visit, Child acquired land in Saco, Maine, and invested in an iron works proposed by the younger Winthrop. This latter project eventually failed, with Child losing £450. However, in the early 1640s, Child believed that New England held great promise for success and profit. Returning home in 1641, he planned to go back to New England as early as 1643; he finally sailed in late summer 1645. However, except for the finalization of his Maine land patent, his name does not appear in the Massachusetts records until May 1646, when he presented his famous Remonstrance to the General Court.

The "Remonstrance and humble Petition" of Robert Child and six others was presented to the General Court on 19 May 1646. The Remonstrance offered a gloomy description of the condition of the colony, stating that many lived in poverty under the control of a tyrannical government. It called for reforms to make life better for all citizens. First, the petitioners requested that the laws of England be enforced so that the rights of the people could be protected. Second, they urged that all Englishmen in the colony be given the rights of freemen, primarily the right to vote and participate in government, regardless of whether they belonged to the official Congregational church. Finally, the Remonstrance urged that all members of the Church of England be accepted for church membership or be allowed to form their own congregation "according to the best reformations of England and Scotland," or, in other words, on the Presbyterian model. Child was a strong Presbyterian and believed in that system, in which associations of ministers ran the churches, rather than Massachusetts's existing Congregational order. The petitioners concluded the Remonstrance with a threat to appeal to Parliament if their requests were denied.

The General Court finally considered the Remonstrance on 7 October 1646. It appointed a committee to answer the petitioners and, believing that they intended to appeal no matter what the committee did, selected Edward Winslow to go to England to handle this case. Winslow was also instructed to deal with the case brought up by Samuel Groton when the Massachusetts government seized his land and banished him from the colony. In November, the General Court responded to the petition, charging the Remonstrants with defamation of the government, slander of the churches, and weakening of the laws by encouraging sedition. All were found guilty. Child was fined £50, but he refused to pay. He prepared to sail to England to present his case in person. However, he was detained the night before he planned to leave the colony for failure to pay the £50 fine. At that time, he possessed additional documents requesting that liberty of conscience be established in Massachusetts and questioning the legality of the colony's charter. These seditious papers resulted in Child's arrest, along with most of the other Remonstrants. Child was not put in jail but remained in Boston after posting a bond of £800. When the Court of Assistants met in March 1647, it referred the case to the General Court. Child went to prison rather than post an additional bond. When the trial finally took place in June 1647, the petitioners were found guilty of conspiracy against the government. Child was fined £200 and threatened with imprisonment if the fine was not paid.

Child left Massachusetts sometime after mid-1647, still planning to appeal the case in England. However, the case was already lost, for the colony's representative, Winslow, had convinced the Commissioners for Plantations to uphold the colony's charter and the authority it gave the existing Puritan government. Prior to Child's return to England, Winslow and Child's brother, Major John Child, had exchanged salvos over the Remonstrance. John Child defended the Remonstrance in *New-England's Jonas* (1647), while Winslow summarized the colony's case in *New England's Salamander Discovered* (1647). By April 1648 Robert Child gave up the fight, realizing that victory was impossible.

Although Child never returned to New England, he continued his friendship and correspondence with Winthrop. Their letters contained discussions of many subjects, including husbandry, chemistry, possible industrial endeavors, and alchemy. Child also engaged in a variety of scientific experiments and considered establishing a medical practice in Kent. In 1651, at the request of his friend Samuel Hartlib, Child wrote "A Large Letter Concerning the Defects and Remedies of English Husbandry." In many ways this essay is a summary of all the information he gathered during his earlier travels in Europe. The essay provided good evidence of "Child's powers as an observer and a practical man of science." Child went to Ireland in 1651 or 1652, where he served as an agricultural expert for Colonel Arthur Hill, a commissioner of revenue for Ulster whose duties included putting new farmers on sequestered lands. Child died of unknown causes in Ireland sometime between February and May 1654. He was never married.

Child is primarily remembered as a major participant in an attempt to circumvent the Puritan government of Massachusetts. Although this is not a legacy to be ignored, Child was involved in many other areas. During his lifetime, his interests included medicine, industrial development, and agriculture. His friendship with Winthrop produced numerous letters discussing a variety of practical matters as well as various political issues, and Child's discussion of European agriculture based on his travels was one of the best such essays written during the seventeenth century.

• Primary sources related to Robert Child and the Remonstrance include Major John Child, *New England's Jonas*, ed. W. T. R. Marvin (1869); Edward Winslow, "New England's Salamander Discovered," Massachusetts Historical Society, *Collections*, 3d ser., 2 (1830): 110–45; "Letters of Robert Child to John Winthrop, Jr.," Massachusetts Historical Society, *Collections*, 5th ser., 1 (1871): 148–64; and J. K. Hosmer, ed., *Winthrop's Journal* (1908). The major discussion of Robert Child's life is found in George L. Kittredge, "Dr. Robert Child the Remonstrant," Colonial Society of Massachusetts, *Publications*, 21 (1920): 1–146.

CAROL SUE HUMPHREY

CHILDERS, Lulu Vere (28 Feb. 1870–6 Mar. 1946), founder and director of the School of Music at Howard University and singer, was born in Dryridge, Kentucky, the daughter of former slaves Alexander Childers and Eliza Butler. She studied voice at the Oberlin Conservatory of Music and in 1896 was awarded a diploma that was replaced by a bachelor's degree in 1906 when the conservatory began granting degrees. The Oberlin Conservatory chapter of Pi Kappa Lambda, a national honor society, elected her a member in 1927. She studied voice further with Sydney Lloyd Wrightson at the Washington Conservatory of Music, with William Shakespeare, and with Oscar Devries at Chicago Musical College.

As a singer Childers enjoyed modest distinction. During her college years and shortly afterward, she performed in the Midwest with the Eckstein-Norton Music Company, a quartet of singers and their accompanist teamed with concert pianist Harriet A. Gibbs. The group contributed their earnings to the development of a music conservatory at Eckstein-Norton University, an industrial school in Cane Springs, Kentucky. She rarely gave solo recitals, preferring solo parts in oratorios and other larger works. A review in the *Washington Bee* (2 June 1906) described her voice as "wonderfully sweet and sympathetic, a very pleasing contralto possessing a wide range, reaching the lower as well as the higher register with comparative ease."

Childers went to Howard University in 1905 as an instructor in methods and vocal music and the director of the choir, following tenures as a public school teacher in Ulrichsville, Ohio (c. 1896–1898), as the director of music at Wiley University in Marshall, Texas (1898–1900), and as the director of the music department and choral director at Knoxville College (1900–1905). She faced a challenge at Howard University, where it was quite unusual for a woman to be assigned the responsibility for heading a department and directing a choral organization. In a short time, however, she developed the university choir, which had been in existence since 1874, to a new level of competence and presented Mendelssohn's *Elijah*. With Childers as a soloist, along with Harry T. Burleigh, Charlotte W. Murray, Sidney Woodward, and Pearl Barnes, the performance garnered positive reviews and drew favorable attention to the music program at Howard. Childers also won community support through her position as director of the choir at Plymouth Congregational Church. At the same time, she built Howard's music program to the point that the board of trustees, in the catalog of 1912, could state: "The work of the Music Department . . . has grown in standard, excellence, and success, until the time has come when it should take some definite name under which it can realize many of the great possibilities which lie before it. It will, therefore, be designated, hereafter, . . . as the Conservatory of Music of Howard University." Following a period of sustained growth, the conservatory became the School of Music in 1918.

Regular performances by the university choir of works such as Handel's *Messiah* (1912), Gabriel Pierne's *The Children's Crusade* (1915), and Samuel Coleridge-Taylor's *Hiawatha* (1919) were major events in the Washington community, as were the weekly vespers services offered to the public in Howard's Andrew Rankin Chapel. The Howard University orchestra, band, and women's and men's glee clubs flourished and made appearances in other cities. During Childers's tenure, the university presented Gilbert and Sullivan's operetta *The Mikado* (1923), which Childers herself directed, and the operas *Il Trovatore* (1939), *Faust* (1940), and *I Pagliacci* (1942). Operatic productions were unusual for an undergraduate college, especially since, except for some soloists and members of the National Symphony Orchestra who joined the university symphony, the performers consisted entirely of faculty and students. Reviewing the production of *Faust*, Glenn D. Gunn, music critic of the *Times-Herald*, wrote, "The choruses were brilliant, the ballet picturesque, the orchestra competent" (21 May 1939).

One additional activity that began under Childers and continued into later years was an annual recital series that brought outstanding musicians to the Washington community. The recitals drew large audiences and provided rare occasions in the rigidly segregated city of Washington, D.C., when black and white patrons sat together. One recital scheduled for the 1938–1939 concert series led to an event that was reported in newspapers worldwide. Marian Anderson, contralto, was contracted to appear in the series, and university officials, aware of Anderson's standing as an artist, sought a larger auditorium. After she was refused the use of facilities by the board of education and also by the Daughters of the American Revolution because of her race, she accepted the offer of Harold Ickes, secretary of the interior, to perform at the Lincoln Memorial, where she appeared on Easter Sunday 1939 before an audience of 75,000.

Childers's greatest contribution was the establishment of the Howard University School of Music in Washington, D.C. When she went to Howard, instruction in music was limited to precollege courses in piano and voice culture provided by one teacher. At her retirement Childers left in place a full-fledged School of Music, the largest and most comprehensive school of music in a historically black university and comparable in its offerings to many larger schools. In the process of transforming the music unit at Howard University into a degree granting program, she was a pioneer, for music had not achieved its present national status as a worthy member of the collegiate body. She trained many successful singers, one of whom, soprano Lillian Evanti, was the first African American to sing opera in Europe with an established company. Childers was described by her students and peers as "noble and regal in bearing," "meticulous to a fault," and "generous with her time and money."

Childers retired in 1940. She never married and died at her home in Howell, Michigan. Howard University awarded her an honorary doctor of music degree (1942) and named the classroom portion of the fine arts complex in her honor (1956). Lois Mailou Jones, Howard University professor and artist of international fame, painted a portrait of Childers, which was hung in the building in 1964.

• References to Childers are found in Doris Evans McGinty, "Black Women in the Music of Washington, D.C., 1900–20," in *New Perspectives on Music: Essays in Honor of Eileen Southern*, ed. Josephine Wright and Samuel Floyd (1992). Reminiscences of and tributes to Childers are contained in *Semi-Centennial of the School of Music, College of Fine Arts, Howard University, 1914–1964* (1964), a pamphlet issued by the School of Music, Howard University. An account of Childers's life is found in McGinty's article in *Dictionary of Ameri-*

can Negro Biography, ed. Rayford W. Logan and Michael R. Winston (1982). For discussions of the development of music at Howard University, including information about Lulu Childers, see Walter Dyson, *Howard University: The Capstone of Negro Education* (1941), and Logan, *Howard University: The First Hundred Years, 1867–1967* (1969).

DORIS EVANS MCGINTY

CHILDRESS, Alvin (c. 1907–19 Apr. 1986), actor on stage, screen, television, and radio, was born in Meridian, Mississippi, where his father was a dentist and his mother a schoolteacher. He attended Rust College in Holly Springs, Mississippi, where he received a B.A. in 1931. Though Childress had intended to become a doctor when he entered college, he moved to New York City only months after graduation to begin an acting career. He performed on Broadway in stylized "Negro" roles in such plays as *Savage Rhythm* (1932), *Brown Sugar* (1937), and *Two on an Island* (1940). He also appeared in a number of New York–produced "all-black" films, including *Dixie Love* (1933), *Hell's Alley* (1938), and *Keep Punching* (1939).

Childress spent a good deal of his career affiliated with off-Broadway acting companies. He joined the Federal Theater Project, appearing in three of its 1937 New York productions at the Lafayette Theater: *Sweet Land*, *The Case of Philip Laurence*, and *Haiti*. A long association with the American Negro Theater brought him featured stage roles, including Reverend Alfred Davidson in *Rain* (1941), Captain Tom in *Natural Man* (1941), and Noah in *Anna Lucasta* (1944). He also performed in many of the troupe's radio dramas, which were broadcast regionally on a New York radio station. He became a teacher of both stage and radio acting techniques for the company.

Childress is best remembered, however, for his role in the CBS television series *Amos 'n Andy*, which aired from 1951 to 1953. Adapted from the popular radio program, in which African-American roles had been played by white performers affecting exaggerated accents, *Amos 'n Andy* came to television with an all-black cast. Childress, who had auditioned for all the male roles, was cast as Amos Jones, the soft-spoken, down-to-earth taxi driver who served as the show's narrator. Fearing that he was too light-skinned to be a credible "Negro" character, the producers insisted he play the role in blackface makeup. Amos was a pillar of the community, a dedicated family man and co-owner of a taxicab company in Harlem. However, he was the sole positive role model in a cast of characters who were otherwise portrayed as underhanded con-men, shiftless slackers, and shrewish women. Civil rights organizations, notably the National Association for the Advancement of Colored People waged a campaign against the presentation of these demeaning stereotypes. When Blatz Beer withdrew sponsorship at the end of 1952–1953 season, CBS dropped the series from its prime-time schedule.

Childress, however, defended *Amos 'n Andy*, telling an interviewer that he "didn't feel it harmed the Negro at all," pointing out that "the series had many episodes that showed the Negro with professions and businesses like attorneys, store owners, and so on, which they never had in TV or movies before." Along with other members of the cast, he predicted that canceling the show would have the overall negative effect of eliminating opportunities for black performers, ensuring that American television would develop as a "lily white" dramatic venue. This proved to be the case for almost two decades.

With *Amos 'n Andy* out of production, Childress moved to Los Angeles to attempt a film career but managed to appear in only two Hollywood features: the screen adaptation of *Anna Lucasta* (United Artists, 1959) and *The Man in the Net* (United Artists, 1959). His fortunes in decline, the veteran actor was forced to take a job as a parking lot attendant. Giving up on his hopes of remaining an actor, he took a civil-service examination and became a social worker for the county of Los Angeles.

In 1971 Childress was coaxed by producer Richard Alan Simmons into accepting a minor role in *Banyon*, a made-for-television movie. During the 1970s there was a renaissance of situation comedy programs starring African-American performers, many produced by Norman Lear's Tandem Productions. Lear helped revive Childress's show business career, offering him guest roles on three top-rated sitcoms: *Sanford and Son* (1972), *Good Times* (1974), and *The Jeffersons* (1976). These led to other television appearances as well as film opportunities. Childress performed character roles in such major studio releases as *The Day of the Locust* (1975), *The Bingo Long All-Stars and Motor Kings* (1976), and *The Main Event* (1979).

The actor developed a series of debilitating illnesses in the 1980s, including Parkinson's Disease, diabetes, and pneumonia. He died in Inglewood, California. He was survived by his wife Sophie.

• An excellent source of information on Childress is Melvin Patrick Ely, *The Adventures of Amos 'n Andy: A Social History of an American Phenomenon* (1991), which draws on extensive interviews with Childress and documents made available by Childress. See also Bart Andrews and Arghus Juilliard, *Holy Mackerel! The Story of Amos and Andy* (1986). Henry T. Sampson, *Blacks in Black and White: A Source Book on Black Films* (1977); *Notable Names in the American Theatre* (1976); Tim Brooks, *The Complete Directory to Prime Time TV Stars* (1987); and David Inman, *The TV Encyclopedia* (1991). An obituary is in *Variety*, 30 Apr. 1986.

DAVID MARC

CHILDS, George William (12 May 1829–3 Feb. 1894), publisher, biographer, and philanthropist, was born in Baltimore, Maryland. The names of his parents are not known. In *Recollections* (1890), his autobiography, Childs shrouds his family origins in mystery, making no reference to his parents or early childhood, beginning instead with an explanation of how he had had from a young age "a rather remarkable aptitude for business." At twelve he worked a summer job as an errand boy in a Baltimore bookstore for two dollars a week. He reflects in *Recollections* that this first job taught him valuable lessons about the "wholesome habit of doing things directly and in order."

At age thirteen Childs entered the U.S. Navy and was stationed in Norfolk, Virginia. Because he did not like navy life, he returned to Baltimore after fifteen months and attended school for a year. At age fourteen, with no family or money, he moved to Philadelphia, where he worked as a clerk and errand boy in the bookstore of Peter Thomson. In the evenings he accompanied Thomson to book auctions, where he "became familiar with the titles and prices of valuable books" (*Recollections*, p. 11) and came into contact with important publishers, such as the Harpers, Lippincotts, and Putnams. By age eighteen Childs had saved enough money to open a business in the old *Public Ledger* building. He does not indicate in *Recollections* what kind of business he operated, but he was successful enough by 1850 to join the publishing firm of R. E. Peterson. In 1854 the company changed its name to Childs and Peterson. Among the successful publications of this house were Elisha Kane's *Arctic Explorations* (1856), which yielded Kane $70,000 in royalties, and Samuel Austin Allibone's *Critical Dictionary of English Literature and British and American Authors* (1858), the first volume of which was dedicated to Childs. In 1860 Childs bought out Peterson, and three years later he left the book publishing business. Sometime during these years Childs married his partner's daughter, Emma Bouvier Peterson; they had no children.

On 3 December 1864, with the silent backing of his closest friend, Anthony J. Drexel, Childs purchased the *Public Ledger* for an estimated $150,000, or slightly more than the paper's annual loss. Within a week he doubled the price of the paper to two cents and raised advertising rates "to a profitable figure," resulting in a sharp decrease in circulation. But Childs and his chief editor, William V. McKean, were able to win back the readership by elevating the paper's tone, maintaining a high level of accuracy and morality, and refusing to print scandal or sensation. Childs instructed his editors to delay publication of a story until they were absolutely sure about the facts, preferring to print a story "correctly the following day." The paper also provided extra space for financial and business news.

On 20 June 1867 Childs opened the new *Public Ledger* building at the corner of 6th and Chestnut. The following month his workers thanked him "for having built a palace for them to work in." He was popular with his employees, and his consideration for them was extraordinary. He paid good wages, hired women for the same wages as men, instituted a pension plan, provided life insurance so that families would not be left destitute, and gave paid vacations and Christmas bonuses. In addition, he presented a cemetery to the Philadelphia typographical society and, with Drexel, established in Colorado Springs, Colorado, a home for printers whose health had failed.

What made Childs happiest about his publishing business was that it allowed him to meet many famous people, and much of his autobiography describes encounters with prominent Europeans and Americans. At "Wootton," his home in the then brand-new suburb of Bryn Mawr, he and his wife hosted many famous people. Those meriting attention in *Recollections* include Washington Irving; Nathaniel Hawthorne; Charles Dickens; Generals Ulysses S. Grant, William T. Sherman, George Meade, and Philip Sheridan; the duke and duchess of Buckingham; and Dom Pedro II, emperor of Brazil, for whom Childs hosted a 600-guest reception in 1876. Two chapters of *Recollections* deal with Grant, whom he met after the victory at Vicksburg in 1863 and with whom he maintained a close friendship until Grant's death in 1885. At that time Childs published *Recollections of General Grant*.

Childs amassed a large and valuable library that included a handwritten 1703 Cotton Mather sermon; the 1841 seventeen-page manuscript of Edgar Allan Poe's "Murders in the Rue Morgue"; two volumes inscribed to Dickens; the original manuscript of *Our Mutual Friend*; and the desk on which Lord Byron wrote *Don Juan*, as well as a variety of poems, letters, and manuscripts by William Godwin, James Fenimore Cooper, Jonathan Swift, Samuel Coleridge, and John Keats. His prized possession was a large folio containing portraits and signed letters of every president from George Washington to Benjamin Harrison, which included eight letters from various presidents to Childs himself. He donated much of his collection to the Drexel Institute (now Drexel University) when it opened in 1892.

Throughout the 1880s Childs generously gave considerable time and money to many important civic projects in Philadelphia, which included the founding of the Zoological Garden, the Pennsylvania Museum, the School of Industrial Arts, and America's first suburban development in Wayne. In 1887, when President Grover Cleveland appointed him a member of the U.S. Military Academy board of visitors, Childs donated a portrait of Grant and commissioned portraits of Sheridan and Sherman, all three of which were hung in Grant Hall. In addition, Childs gave money for several monuments in Great Britain, including a memorial window at Westminster Abbey honoring poets George Herbert and William Cowper (1877), a memorial drinking fountain to the people of Stratford commemorating Queen Victoria's Jubilee (1887), a window honoring John Milton to St. Margaret's, Westminster (1888), and the reredos to the Church of St. Thomas in Winchester in memory of Bishops Lancelot Andrewes and Thomas Ken. Childs died in Philadelphia.

Called the most notable citizen of Philadelphia since Benjamin Franklin, Childs was recognized as a true journalist. In the words of former New York governor John T. Hoffman, Childs was one who understood "the difference between the liberty of the press and the license of the press." But he received the most praise for being an open-handed philanthropist. Indeed, Childs wanted most to be remembered for his generosity: "If asked what, as the result of my experience, is the greatest pleasure in life, I should say doing good to others. Being generous grows on one just as being mean does." The Drexel family received the *Public Ledger*, with George William Childs Drexel assuming the editorship. Drexel sold the paper in 1903.

• Childs's papers are housed at Drexel University. Useful biographical information about Childs is in James Parton, *George W. Childs: A Biographical Sketch* (1870); J. W. Forney, *Anecdotes of Public Men* (1873; repr. 1970); and Frederic Hudson, *Journalism in the U.S. from 1690–1872* (1872; repr. 1968). Childs is also discussed in E. Digby Baltzell, *Philadelphia Gentlemen: The Making of a National Upper Class* (1958). See also Nicholas B. Wainwright, "*The Philadelphia Inquirer*, Oldest Daily Paper in the United States," supplement to the *Philadelphia Inquirer*, 16 Sept. 1962. Notices regarding Childs's death and legacy are in the *New York Times*, 3 and 4 Feb. 1894, and the *Athenaeum*, 10 Feb. and 17 Mar. 1894, as well as in newspapers worldwide.

DAVID BOOCKER

CHILDS, Richard Spencer (24 May 1882–26 Sept. 1978), business executive and political reformer, was born in Manchester, Connecticut, the son of William Hamlin Childs and Nellie White Spencer. His father founded the Bon Ami Company and, together with his other business ventures, became one of the wealthiest men in Brooklyn, New York, where the family moved in 1892. Richard Childs attended Yale University from 1900 to 1904 and earned a B.A. In 1904 he joined the advertising agency of Alfred William Erickson; eventually becoming a junior partner, he remained with the firm until 1918. He married Grace Pauline Hatch in 1912. They had four children (their firstborn died a day after birth). From 1919 to 1920 Childs was manager of the Bon Ami Company, and from 1921 to 1928 he was head of the drug specialties division of the A. E. Chew Company, a New York exporter. Childs worked for the American Cyanamid Company from 1928 to 1947 and headed its Lederle Laboratories division from 1935 to 1944.

Childs's interest in making democracy work better in city, county, and state government became, however, to use his phrase, "the controlling factor in my life." The reformer in him had first surfaced when in 1903 he accompanied his father to the polls in Brooklyn to vote for Mayor Seth Low, who was seeking reelection as the Citizens Union–Fusion candidate. Childs was stumped by a ballot that contained a long list of mostly obscure people running for obscure offices. After voting blindly for the word "Republican" in each of fifteen contests he knew nothing about, he decided that it was not practically possible for voters generally to make informed choices among a large number of candidates. Meanwhile, he joined good government groups: the National Municipal League (NML, now the National Civic League) and the City Club of New York in 1908 and the Citizens Union of New York in 1909. Later he became president of the City Club of New York (1926–1938) and chair of the Citizens Union of New York (1941–1950).

Childs came to understand that the political party or "machine" favored the long ballot, because by nominating satisfactory candidates for the major offices, political leaders could divert the voters' attention away from the minor candidates. The latter were often less qualified but were nominated because of their usefulness to party leaders. As Childs reasoned, with only a few candidates running for election at one time, each citing clear-cut issues and competing for important posts, voters could adequately scrutinize these highly visible offices for themselves without needing to depend on party labels and "ticket makers," the political leaders who are, often, choosing candidates for minor elective offices. In 1908 Childs wrote an essay embodying this thought, "The Doctrine of the Short Ballot," and sent it to James Bryce and several other scholars. The reply he received from Bryce particularly encouraged him. Bryce, then British ambassador to the United States, wrote, "Your pamphlet seems to me to contain a great deal that is both true and opportune and I hope you will continue to write along these lines."

Childs wanted strictly technical and administrative offices and those of minor importance made appointive. A luminous appointing officer—the mayor or governor—could be held accountable for the character of his administration, because responsibility was concentrated—a corollary to his "short ballot principle." He also believed in a unicameral state legislature, for fewer legislators with more power would make each more important and interesting and, consequently, would draw voters' attention to them. In his view, the short ballot would make democracy more real, because popular control of representative government would be easier.

In 1909–1910, with Woodrow Wilson's participation, Childs developed the National Short Ballot Organization (NSBO) to advance the short ballot doctrine. Subsidized by his father, who contributed $10,000 a year for ten years, Childs ran the organization, over which Wilson, then president of Princeton University, presided. With more than 10,000 members in the NSBO by 1912, the short ballot movement spread, winning wide support from governors, political science professors, and publishers. When the NSBO was consolidated with the NML in 1921, Childs shifted his energies to the league, serving as its president from 1927 to 1931.

Childs's second major Progressive Era reform was the council-manager plan of municipal government, based on his theory of the new controlled-executive plan, which he conceived in 1912. It embodied the short ballot idea, for only the council—a single group of officials—was elected. So that all elected officials were equally important, the "mayor," or the council member elected with the largest number of votes, was not to be separately elected by the people. Childs preferred the mayor to be chosen by the council. Powers were completely unified in the council. A single executive—the city manager, as Childs called him—was appointed and served at the pleasure of the council. Policy and administration were not separated, for the council had collective and ultimate responsibility. As stated in the NML's *A Model City Charter and Municipal Home Rule* (1916), Childs's city manager was to "show himself to be a leader, formulating policies and urging their adoption by the council." Some one hundred cities adopted the city manager plan by 1919, the end of the Progressive Era. Indirectly, Childs had launched a new profession: city management.

In 1947 Childs became a full-time volunteer at the NML, where he worked for the next thirty years. Still speaking out for the short ballot and the council-manager plan, he also promoted other reforms. He stimulated activities among state medical and bar associations to support legislative and constitutional reforms to replace elective county coroners, usually laymen, with appointive medical examiners trained in forensic pathology. He encouraged reapportionment of rural-dominated state legislatures to more accurately reflect population distribution. He pleaded for the appointment of local and state judges, arguing that their election gave political significance to their offices, to which, he pointed out, voters paid scant attention. Because he wanted national political conventions accurately to reflect the electorate's views concerning the choice of presidential nominees, he proposed changes in the methods by which delegates to these conventions were selected.

In 1970 Childs expressed his philosophy of life in a letter with these words, "A sense of purpose is one of the essentials of happiness along with a sense of progress, a sense of being esteemed, freedom from pain and freedom from anxiety." This attitude toward life was exemplified the same year in a statement defining the role of the Citizens Union of New York, the reform organization he was active in for more than six decades. He wrote, "We are reformers; i.e., innovators, pioneers, ground-breakers. We should usually be ahead of our constituency. We endorse hopeless causes and work to carry them into wide support." John E. Bebout, a former assistant director of the NML, said of Childs, "For three-quarters of a century, he bore the badge of reform proudly and joyfully. . . . One man, one 'happy reformer' has had an immense impact on the way our public interest is conducted" (Bebout, pp. 5, 8).

Childs died in Ottawa, Canada. He was a principal figure in the local reform movement for a good part of the twentieth century. Long ballots have not disappeared in local elections, but their use has steadily declined. In 1994 approximately 2,700 municipalities and some counties had adopted the council-manager plan. Some large cities and counties have an important ingredient of the council-manager plan: a chief administrator. Notably successful was Childs's effort to professionalize postmortem medical examinations. The popularity of council-manager government indicates the continuing importance and relevance of structural reform.

• Butler Library at Columbia University holds Childs's papers. Transcripts of two interviews with Childs are included in the Oral History Collection of Columbia University. Childs wrote three books: *Short Ballot Principles* (1911), *Civic Victories* (1952), and *The First 50 Years of the Council-Manager Plan of Municipal Government* (1965). The *Short Ballot Bulletin* appeared under his editorship from 1911 to 1920. Childs published numerous articles on political reform. A selected bibliography is in Alva W. Stewart, "Richard S. Childs: His Contribution to American Local and State Government in the 20th Century," Council of Planning Librarians, Exchange Bibliography 1273, May 1977, pp. 8–12. Two major pieces by Childs that define him are "The Short Ballot," *Outlook* 92 (17 July 1909): 635–39; and "The Theory of the New Controlled-Executive Plan," *National Municipal Review* 2 (Jan. 1913): 76–81. For a critical study of the council-manager plan, see John Porter East, *Council-Manager Government: The Political Thought of Its Founder, Richard S. Childs* (1965). Among many articles about Childs are Richard Stillman, "Richard Childs: A Republican Businessman as an Evangelist for Municipal Reform," *Midwest Review of Public Administration* 7, no. 1 (Jan. 1973): 4–10; and John E. Bebout, "Richard S. Childs, Happy Reformer," *National Civic Review* 68, no. 1 (Jan. 1979): 5, 8. An obituary is in the *Brooklyn Heights Press*, 5 Oct. 1978.

BERNARD HIRSCHHORN

CHILDS, Thomas (17 July 1796–8 Oct. 1853), army officer, was born in Pittsfield, Massachusetts, the son of Timothy Childs, a physician, and Rachael Easton. On 6 April 1813 Childs enrolled at the U.S. Military Academy, West Point, and graduated there as a third lieutenant of artillery on 11 March 1814. Two months later he rose to second lieutenant and was immediately pressed into service along the Niagara frontier. Childs fought in the 25 July 1814 battle of Lundy's Lane and also the ensuing defense of Fort Erie, Upper Canada. He distinguished himself during the 14 August 1814 repulse of British forces and won favorable mention in General Edmund P. Gaines's official dispatch. A month later he commanded a detachment during General Jacob J. Brown's sortie and was rewarded with a captured brass quadrant sight by order of President James Madison. Childs remained in the service after the war and in 1819 married Ann Eliza Coryton of Alexandria, Virginia. They had nine children. Because promotion in the postwar army was extremely slow, he did not obtain his captaincy until 1 October 1826.

From 1836 to 1842, Childs fought with distinction in Florida's Second Seminole War. He planned and executed the successful attack on Fort Drane, 21 August 1836, which restored communication with several isolated posts. Childs also became an early exponent of riverine warfare. In June 1841 he led an expedition to Haulover, covering 250 miles by boat and an additional 50 on foot, and in a surprise attack captured thirty-four Indians. Among his subordinates on this occasion was a young William Tecumseh Sherman. For his services against the Seminoles, Childs received two brevet promotions; to major in 1836 and to lieutenant colonel in 1841. His health declined, however, in consequence of diseases contracted in this tropical clime.

Having departed Florida, Childs's military career entered its final and most accomplished phase. From 1843 to 1847 he commanded an artillery battalion during the occupation of Texas. As part of Zachary Taylor's little army, Childs acquitted himself well at the battles of Palo Alto and Resaca de la Palma, acquiring a third promotion to brevet colonel. During the siege of Monterrey, he led a detachment that perilously scaled 800-foot cliffs and stormed Loma de Independencia, which towered above the Bishop's palace. Childs subsequently joined Winfield Scott's invasion of Mexico and fought well at the victories of Veracruz and Cerro Gordo. In this last encounter, he was accorded the honor of accepting the surrender of enemy forces.

On 16 February 1847 Childs advanced to the rank of major of the line and assumed command of the First Artillery Regiment. It was in this capacity that he performed his most celebrated task, the defense of Puebla. On 13 April 1847 General Scott appointed him military governor of that city, which sat astride American lines of communication. When Scott moved against Mexico City, Puebla was besieged by 8,000 men under General Antonio López de Santa Anna. Childs, possessing only 400 effectives and 1,200 invalids, successfully withstood repeated attacks for twenty-eight days. When Santa Anna was finally obliged to withdraw, Childs secured his fourth and final brevet promotion to brigadier general.

Upon termination of the Mexican conflict in 1848, Childs transferred north and spent three years commanding the garrisons of Fort McHenry and Pensacola. He then took charge of military operations in East Florida with headquarters at Fort Brooke (Tampa) where, unable to withstand a bout of yellow fever, he died.

Childs exemplified the growing influence of West Point professionalism in the U.S. Army and was quite possibly the most effective regimental officer of his day. Recklessly brave, he was also a meticulous planner who oversaw every detail of the operations entrusted to him. In thirty-nine years of active service, Childs campaigned from Canada to the swampy Everglades of Florida and sunbaked valleys of Mexico with successful results. Such was his reputation that General Scott, upon hearing of his death, ordered all officers of the First Artillery to wear black crepes for thirty days. Childs is commemorated by present-day Lake Childs, Florida.

• Childs's 1848 letterbook is at the Southern Historical Collection, Wilson Library, University of North Carolina. The Berkshire Athenaeum, Pittsfield, also maintains a small file on him. Printed correspondence regarding his Seminole War activity is in "General Childs, U.S. Army," *Historical Magazine* 22 (Nov.–Dec. 1873): 299–304, 371–74; 23 (Mar. 1874): 169–71; and 24 (Apr. 1875): 280–84. Mexican War information appears in Richard B. Winders, "Puebla's Forgotten Heroes," *Military History of the West* 24 (1994): 1–23. Background information may be gleaned from Elias Child, *Genealogy of the Child, Childs and Childe Families* (1881); and George W. Cullum, *Biographical Register of Officers and Graduates of the U.S. Military Academy* (1891). Insight about an unusual family legacy may be found in John C. Fredriksen, "Colonel Childs and His Quadrant," *Military Collector and Historian* 39 (Fall 1987): 122–24. Finally, an excellent overview of the army in which Childs served is William B. Skelton, *An American Profession of Arms* (1992).

JOHN C. FREDRIKSEN

CHINN, May Edward (15 Apr. 1896–1 Dec. 1980), physician and cancer researcher, was born in Great Barrington, Massachusetts, the daughter of William Lafayette Chinn, a former slave who had escaped to the North from a Virginia plantation and had unsteady employment as a result of race discrimination, and Lulu Ann Evans, a domestic worker. Occasionally William Chinn worked at odd jobs and as a porter. Raised in New York City, May Chinn was educated in the city's public schools and at the Bordentown Manual Training and Industrial School (N.J.), and she attended Morris High School in New York. A severe bout with osteomyelitis of the jaw plagued her as a child and required extensive medical treatment. Her family's poverty forced her to drop out of high school in the eleventh grade for a factory job. A year later she scored high enough on the entrance examination for Teachers' College at Columbia University to be admitted to the class of 1921 without a high school diploma.

Chinn's early ambition was to be a musician. Despite the family's poor economic situation, her parents financed piano lessons that gave her some professional opportunity in music as a young adult. For several years in the early 1920s she was a piano-accompanist for the famed singer Paul Robeson. Initially music education was her major at Columbia. She was the only African American and female in her music classes, and ridicule from one professor caused her to abandon music for study in the sciences. The switch to science, combined with her childhood experience of being treated for osteomyelitis, led to her decision to become a medical doctor. After graduating from Columbia University with a B.S. degree in 1921, she was admitted to the Bellevue Hospital Medical College (now New York University Medical College) and in 1926 became its first African-American woman graduate. In 1926 she was one of the first three African Americans to be accepted as interns at New York City's public Harlem Hospital. (The other two were men.)

Upon completion of her internship Chinn faced the "color" barrier confronted by all African-American physicians; she could not gain admitting privileges for her patients at any hospital in New York City. She opened an office in a brownstone on Edgecombe Avenue in Harlem next to the Edgecombe Sanitarium, a private hospital owned and operated by a group of black physicians. In return for living and office space, she answered all-night emergency calls at the sanitarium. During the 1930s she studied dermatology and gynecology at the Post-Graduate Hospital Medical School in New York, and in 1933 she received an M.S. degree in public health from Columbia University.

Chinn's interest in cancer research was elicited by the clinical experience of seeing so many patients in advanced stages of the disease, and this led to the development of a "fanatical preoccupation" in understanding and treating cancer. No hospital in New York City would allow her to do cancer work because of her race, but she was unofficially allowed to work with resident physicians at Memorial Hospital and was instructed in how to perform biopsies. Between 1928 and 1933 she studied cytological methods for the diagnosis of cancer under George Papanicolaou, developer of the Pap Smear. African-American physicians in Harlem, having learned of her connection at Memorial and her training and clinical experience there, began to send her specimens for biopsies. In 1944 she was appointed to the staff of the Strang Clinic affiliated with Memorial and New York Infirmary Hospital. While working at the Strang Clinic over the next twenty-nine years, she helped to devise ways to detect cancer in the asymptomatic patient. Her evaluation of patients' family histories to detect cancer in the early stages was recognized as a significant approach to cancer understanding and treatment at the time.

Over the course of her 52-year career Chinn became a legend in Harlem. She was one of a handful of African-American women in medicine in the mid-1920s through the 1930s and 1940s who pioneered in overcoming barriers of race and gender in medical school, in post-graduate training, and in gaining hospital appointments. In addition to her family medical practice and cancer work, Chinn was a clinician and medical adviser in New York State Department of Health–supported day care centers in New York City (1960–1977), a staff member of the New York Infirmary for Women and Children (1945–1956), physician assigned to escort fifty severely handicapped persons of the St. Jeanne Valois Guild of New York City to Paris, Lourdes, and Rome, where she had a special audience with Pope John III (1961), and a medical consultant to 100 refugees from southern Africa who were attending colleges throughout the United States (1978). After her retirement from private practice in 1977, Chinn continued to work in three Harlem day care centers sponsored by the state department of health.

Chinn's cancer research and clinical practice was recognized by her election as a member of the New York Academy of Sciences in 1954, and in 1957 she received a citation from the New York City Cancer Committee of the American Cancer Society. She was elected to the Society of Surgical Oncology in 1958, became a Fellow of the American Geriatrics Society in 1959, and was elected to medical membership of the American Society of Cytology in 1972 and as a Life Member of the American Academy of Family Physicians in 1977. In 1975 she was a founder of the Susan Smith McKinney Steward Medical Society, named for the first African-American woman licensed to practice medicine in the state of New York. Chinn received a Teachers' College Distinguished Alumnus Award from Columbia University in May 1980 and an honorary doctor of science degree from New York University in June 1980. She died while attending a reception in Avery Hall at Columbia University.

• Chinn's papers are housed in the Schomburg Center for Research in Black Culture, New York City. Her interview for the Black Women's Oral History Project, Schlesinger Library, Radcliffe College, Cambridge, Mass., was published in *The Black Women's Oral History Project*, ed. Ruth Edmonds Hill (1991). Feature articles on Chinn include Nadine Brozan, "For a Doctor at 84, a Day to Remember," *New York Times*, 17 May 1980, and George Davis, "A Healing Hand in Harlem," *New York Times Magazine*, 22 Apr. 1979. An obituary is in the *New York Times*, 3 Dec. 1980.

ROBERT C. HAYDEN

CHIPMAN, Nathaniel (15 Nov. 1752–15 Feb. 1843), jurist, U.S. senator, and conservative political leader, was born in Salisbury, Connecticut, the son of Samuel Chipman, a blacksmith and farmer, and Hannah Austin. Chipman entered Yale University in 1773. He joined the Continental army as an ensign during his senior year, in spring 1777, receiving his degree in absentia. Chipman was promoted to lieutenant during the winter at Valley Forge and was present at the battle of Monmouth in June 1778. In October Chipman resigned his commission to study law, complaining that an officer's salary was insufficient to "support the character of a gentleman" (Chipman, p. 32). One of the first graduates of Tapping Reeve's famous law school in Litchfield, Connecticut, Chipman was admitted to the Connecticut bar in 1779. The same year he moved to the new frontier state of Vermont, writing a friend excitedly that "there is not an attorney in the state, . . . think what a figure I shall make, when I become the oracle of law to the state of Vermont" (Chipman, p. 29).

Chipman joined his father in Tinmouth, Vermont, where he met Sarah Hill, whom he married in 1781 and with whom he had seven children. Initially, many of his neighbors were less than enthusiastic with Chipman's aristocratic style. But the new state's governor, Thomas Chittenden, was an old neighbor and friend of Chipman's father and appointed Chipman to a number of positions, including state's attorney for Rutland County (1781–1785). Elected to the Vermont Assembly in 1784, Chipman became leader of the minority loyal opposition that favored Vermont's independence from New York but opposed what was seen as the dangerously radical policies of the Chittenden-Allen faction. The overriding desire for statehood ameliorated conflict between these two factions through the 1780s, and Chipman played an active role in a government he otherwise opposed. In 1784 he served on a special legislative committee charged with the revision of the state's statute law on condition that he be allowed to keep for his own use the law library that the state had confiscated from a New York lawyer. As the only person with legal training in the state at this time, Chipman enjoyed a virtual monopoly on legal knowledge in Vermont. He was elected in 1786 by the legislature as the first lawyer to serve on the state supreme court.

Throughout his career Chipman resigned from influential positions to make more money in private law practice, yet returned time and again to public service.

After only a year on the Vermont Supreme Court, Chipman resigned to concentrate on building up his personal finances through his law practice and investments in lands and trade. In 1789 the legislature elected Chipman chief justice of the supreme court, one of the commissioners to settle the boundary dispute with New York, and a representative to Congress to arrange Vermont's admission to the Union. He played a key role at the Vermont convention that approved the Constitution in 1791 but resigned as chief justice shortly afterward when George Washington appointed him to the U.S. District Court for Vermont. In 1793 Chipman resigned that position to return to his more lucrative private law practice.

In 1796 the legislature again elected Chipman chief justice, luring him back with an appointment to a special committee revising the statutes of the state, a committee he dominated. In 1797 Chipman resigned from the supreme court for the third time, having been elected to the U.S. Senate. A Federalist ally of Alexander Hamilton, Chipman disdained the Jeffersonians, most particularly his bête noire, Matthew Lyon, one of Vermont's congressional representatives. A leading advocate of the Alien and Sedition Acts, Chipman rejoiced at Lyon's arrest for his supposedly scurrilous attacks on President John Adams. But, much to Chipman's disgust, Lyon became a popular hero and was reelected to Congress while serving time in jail. The political tides had turned toward Jeffersonian Republicanism. At the end of Chipman's term in 1803, his name was not even mentioned in the Vermont legislature as a candidate.

Chipman again represented Tinmouth in the Vermont Assembly from 1806 to 1809 and in 1811. In 1813 he was elected to Vermont's unique Council of Censors, an elected body selected by the voters of Vermont every seven years that judged the constitutionality of Vermont's laws. Later that year he was once more elected chief justice of the Vermont Supreme Court but was removed from office in the Democratic sweep of 1815. The next year he was appointed professor of law at Middlebury College. Though he held the professorship for the rest of his life, Chipman taught actively for only a year. In 1817 he retired from the practice of law because of deafness and, with one exception, left public life; in 1836 Chipman served for a third time on a special committee to revise the statutes of the state.

Few people dominated the legal development of a new state so completely as did Chipman. After the Revolution, a Burkean regard for precedent dominated Chipman's legal thought. But he also insisted that American precedent and American case law, not Blackstone and British law practice, should have authority in American courtrooms. In 1793 he made one of the first efforts to create a body of published American case law, producing *Reports and Dissertations*, a collection of key decisions by Vermont's supreme court. The same year he wrote *Sketches of the Principles of Government*, rejecting Enlightenment ideas of natural law and arguing that reason and the sanctity of property must form the cornerstone of law in the United States. Convinced that violent popular passions produced violent governments, Chipman sought to establish an independent, nonelective judiciary as a constitutional bulwark against the base appetites of the majority. He also called for a bicameral legislature in Vermont. In both reformist efforts, Chipman consistently failed; but he remained an unswerving supporter of the Constitution and the Union. He opposed the Virginia and Kentucky Resolutions, the Hartford Convention of 1814, and John C. Calhoun's call for nullification in the early 1830s. Chipman died at his home in Tinmouth.

• Chipman's personal papers did not survive the nineteenth century, though a great many are published in the only biography of Chipman, written by his brother, Daniel Chipman, *Life of the Hon. Nathaniel Chipman* (1846). In addition to his works already mentioned, Chipman was the author of *The Constitutionalist* (1814) and his *Sketches of the Principles of Government* was revised in 1833 as *Principles of Government*. On Chipman's political opinions, see Samuel B. Hand and P. Jeffrey Potash, "Nathaniel Chipman," in *A More Perfect Union*, ed. Michael Sherman (1991), and Roy J. Honeywell, "Nathaniel Chipman: Political Philosopher and Jurist," *New England Quarterly* 5 (1932): 555–84. On his battle with Lyon, see Aleine Austin, *Matthew Lyon* (1981).

MICHAEL A. BELLESILES

CHISHOLM, Henry (22 Apr. 1822–9 May 1881), pioneer in the Great Lakes iron and steel industry, was born in Lochgelly, Scotland, near Edinburgh, the son of Charles Stuart Chisholm, a mining contractor; his mother's name is not known. Two years after his father's untimely death in 1832, Chisholm ended his education and apprenticed in carpentry. At seventeen he left for Glasgow to pursue his trade, then moved on to Montreal in 1842 with his new wife, Jean Allen of Dunfermline, but little else. He did well as a building contractor in that growing port city and developed further business contacts in the lower Great Lakes region. In 1850 he contracted to build a pier and breakwater for the Cleveland and Pittsburgh Railroad's terminus in Cleveland and settled there permanently. Over the next several years Chisholm amassed considerable capital as a contractor for local railroads, and with the advent of Great Lakes iron ore traffic he spotted a new field of opportunity. In 1857 he invested $25,000 in partnership with David and John Jones, Welsh-born Pennsylvania ironmasters whose new iron-rail mill needed capital. After several expansions and reorganizations, this partnership became the business for which Chisholm remains best known, the Cleveland Rolling Mill Company. As the enterprise expanded Chisholm brought in several important new partners, notably his brother William, who left the merchant marine to join the partnership, and the brothers Andros B. and Amasa Stone, budding railroad and financial magnates with wide business connections and growing capital resources.

Henry Chisholm emerged as the central figure in the complex of firms centering on Cleveland Rolling

Mill, which, despite its name, soon branched out from its origins in re-rolling soft iron rails to become a primary iron and steel producer. Quick to appreciate the advantages of Bessemer steel for rails, Chisholm installed the first operating converters west of Pittsburgh in 1868, probably relying on the Stone brothers' expanding railroad interests as a market. Like Andrew Carnegie, whose career and concerns paralleled his remarkably, Chisholm had a business style that was notable for innovation and integration of operations, but he was far less systematic or single-minded. Chisholm had a positive abhorrence for selling raw iron or steel to unrelated manufacturers and insisted that Cleveland Rolling Mill and its associated companies had to develop marketable finished products. He also abhorred waste and by ignoring received practices in his tradition-bound industry was able to make finished goods out of the considerable amounts of Bessemer scrap left over from rolling rails, a significant industry first. Chisholm preceded Carnegie in re-using scrap, and he also directed the first successful rolling of rod and wire stock from Bessemer steel, using scrap in his existing iron mills. In 1871 William Chisholm produced the first Bessemer-steel screws, another significant innovation. But Chisholm's seat-of-the-pants innovations were probably more directed at efficiently using equipment and materials already in hand than at rationalizing the production process in the way that Carnegie later became known. When shown a new, highly efficient continuous rod mill designed by his superintendent, William Garrett, Chisholm resisted investing in it until a drastic tariff reduction on rod stock forced him to approve the idea shortly before his death.

Unlike Carnegie, and much more typical of his day, Chisholm seems to have aimed primarily at assuring a supply of raw materials and access to markets rather than at the ruthless cost reduction that underlay the centralized management of Carnegie Steel. Chisholm achieved his aims by building a network of associates and companies that controlled ownership of different aspects of the production process and specialized in certain products. Chisholm himself oversaw Cleveland Rolling Mill and probably coordinated the Cleveland-area producers in which he and his family had financial interests. In addition to Cleveland Rolling Mill, associated producer firms included the Union Steel Screw Company, the American Sheet & Boiler Plate Company, the Cleveland Power Shovel Company, and H. P. Nail Company. Through such nets, he and a group of associates, including his brother William, the Stones, Fayette Brown, and others, controlled the Lake Superior ore that Chisholm's companies relied on, the shipping that brought it to his furnaces and mills, and the firms that produced such finished goods as boiler plate, steam shovels, steel screws, wire nails, and other rod and wire products. A similar complex in Chicago, set up shortly after the Civil War and overseen by Chisholm's son William, paralleled the Cleveland facilities and relied on the same ore and shipping. The resulting industrial enterprise, one of the largest of its day, was a complex network of interlocking partnerships that traded among one another and controlled ore beds, transportation, and production and shipment of finished goods as well as raw steel, and were major employers in Cleveland and the upper Great Lakes. But the Chisholm network, based as it was on interlocking ownership of coordinating firms, never matched Carnegie's organizational innovations or the internal efficiency that Carnegie Steel was to achieve.

Chisholm, relying on a work force largely from the British Isles, actively managed his companies as a benevolent paternalist, an approach that seems to have suited his workers. An early death, however, spared him the violent confrontations that his son William did much to instigate with an increasingly unskilled immigrant, Eastern European labor force. Chisholm died in Cleveland at age fifty-nine, possibly following a stroke, leaving his widow and five grown children.

• A retrospective series of short articles about Chisholm appeared in the *Cleveland Plain Dealer* on 26 and 31 Mar. and 11 Apr. 1942, and aspects of his life and career are discussed in William Garrett, "Landmarks in the Rolling Mill History of the United States," *Iron Trade Review*, 14 Nov. 1901, pp. 1–7; J. H. Kennedy, *A History of the City of Cleveland* (1896); Emilius Randall and Daniel Ryan, *History of Ohio: Rise and Progress of an American State* (1912); James Ford Rhodes, "The Coal and Iron Industry of Cleveland," *Magazine of Western History* 2 (1885): 337–45; William G. Rose, *Cleveland: The Making of a City* (1950); "A Group of Cleveland Manufacturers," *Magazine of Western History* 3 (1885–1886): 174–77; and "William Chisholm," *Magazine of Western History* 4 (1886): 247–50.

MARC L. HARRIS

CHISHOLM, Hugh Joseph (2 May 1847–8 July 1912), capitalist, was born in Chippawa, Ontario, Canada, the son of Alexander Chisholm and Mary Margaret Phelan. His father died when he was thirteen, causing him to go to work for the Grand Trunk Railroad as a newsboy on the passenger train that ran between Toronto and Detroit. Three years later, having completed the night school course at a Toronto business college, he and a brother acquired the rights to sell newspapers aboard all Grand Trunk trains running between Chicago, Illinois, and Halifax, Nova Scotia, as well as on board most of the steamboats that plied the St. Lawrence River. In 1867 the two brothers established Chisholm Brothers, a publishing company that produced the first railroad and tourist guides and souvenir brochures. In 1872 Chisholm exchanged his interest in the partnership's Canadian operations for his brother's rights to its New England business and moved to Portland, Maine.

That same year Chisholm became a citizen of the United States, married Henrietta Mason (with whom he was to have one child), opened a publishing company in Portland, and established the Somerset Fibre Company in Fairfield, Maine, which specialized in producing hardened fibre ware from wood pulp. Having developed an appreciation for the substantial profits then being made in the manufacture of paper for printed material, Chisholm organized in 1881 the Umbagog Pulp Company, a wood-pulp mill, at Livermore Falls on the Androscoggin River. Six years later he also established at Livermore Falls the Otis Falls Pulp Company, a paper manufacturing concern, and served as its treasurer, general manager, and principal owner. The community that grew up around these operations became known as Chisholm.

Meanwhile, Chisholm became increasingly interested in the possibility of building a similar but much larger complex further upstream in the middle of the Maine wilderness, where he could take greater advantage of the Androscoggin's hydraulic power. In 1882 he began exploring the region around Penacook Falls (later known as Rumford Falls), where the Androscoggin drops 200 feet in less than a mile, thus making it an excellent location for a hydroelectric power plant. In 1883 he and his business partners began acquiring property near the falls, and in 1890 he organized the Rumford Falls Power Company and helped to plan and locate the dam and other appurtenances for converting water power to electricity. That same year he rehabilitated a local narrow-gauge railroad, renamed the Portland and Rumford Falls Railway, by which he connected Rumford Falls to the outside world via the Grand Trunk and Maine Central railroads, and established near the power plant the Rumford Falls Paper Company. Over the next eight years he also established a real estate agency, a lumber company, and the Rumford Falls and Rangely Lakes Railroad. Between 1899 and 1901 the paper company was converted to a wood-pulp operation whose production was dedicated to the nearby and much larger Oxford Paper Company, a fully integrated paper manufacturing operation that was organized by Chisholm to specialize in the production of fine book paper. In 1900 he contracted with the United States government to provide all postcards sold through the U.S. postal system. His firm belief in paternalism and "company welfare," ideas that were prevalent among paper-mill owners of the day, resulted in the creation of a model mill town at Rumford Falls; he had brick cottages and parks built for the workers, established a mechanics' institute that doubled as a social club, and provided for the intellectual stimulation of his workers by setting up an educational institution.

In 1898 Chisholm served as one of the principal architects for the creation of the International Paper Company, a merger of twenty pulp and paper mills located throughout New England and upstate New York, whose combined production of newsprint comprised about 60 percent of the total output in the United States. That same year the company's first president resigned and the second one died, whereupon Chisholm assumed the presidency and moved to New York City. Under his leadership International Paper became the largest pulp and paper manufacturing organization in the world. In 1907 he resigned this position to become chairman of the board. He left International Paper in 1909 and became president of the Oxford Paper Company in 1910. He died in New York City.

Chisholm was responsible for the development in the United States of the first integrated paper manufacturing operation, whereby one company controlled the production process from the cutting of the trees to the shipping of the finished product. More than any other single individual, he was also responsible for introducing modern organizational and management techniques to the paper industry in the United States.

• A biography is Hugh J. Chisholm [Jr.], *A Man and the Paper Industry: Hugh J. Chisholm (1847–1912)* (1952). Obituaries are in the *New York Times*, 9 July 1912, and *Paper*, 10 July 1912.

CHARLES W. CAREY, JR.

CHISHOLM, Jesse (1805–4 Apr. 1868), trader and frontier diplomat, was born probably in or near present-day Blount County, Tennessee, the son of Ignatius Chisholm, an adventurer of Scottish descent, and a part Cherokee woman, Martha Rogers, the daughter of Cherokee leader Charles Rogers. Jesse was most likely the first child of the union.

By at least 1816, Ignatius Chisholm joined the movement out of Tennessee that had started as early as 1809, when the Cherokees were cajoled into giving up their lands in Tennessee in exchange for new lands in Arkansas. Settling along the Spadra River in Arkansas, Jesse Chisholm grew to adulthood hunting and exploring the western land, which he found already occupied. The Osage, a resident tribe on the Arkansas, deeply resented the eastern intruders, and from 1810 until 1817 Chief Clermont's Osage warriors routinely attacked and killed isolated Cherokee families. In retaliation, Chisholm's grandfather and father and a party of Cherokee warriors brutally destroyed Clermont's Osage village near present-day Claremore, Oklahoma, in the fall of 1817. For years afterward, the Chisholm family enjoyed high political status among both the Western Cherokees, later called the Old Settlers, and the U.S. Army.

In September 1826 Chisholm scouted for a group of army officers through what is now central Oklahoma and southern Kansas on a gold-hunting expedition. Other visits introduced Chisholm to the customs and languages of the Comanches and Kiowas and gave him an intimate familiarity of the geography along the southwestern part of the Great Plains.

Re-joining the band led by their distant relative Oolootka (John Jolly), Ignatius and Jesse Chisholm settled at Three Forks village, near Cantonment Gibson in Indian Territory. Ignatius Chisholm's young widowed aunt, Diana (or Tiana) Rogers Gentry, came west with them. In May 1829 the disgraced Tennessee governor, Sam Houston, arrived at Three Forks, and Chief Jolly welcomed him as a Cherokee brother. After a few months, Houston (who was still married to his first wife) married Diana in a Cherokee ceremony. For the following two years, the future Texas hero pursued several financial schemes. His and Diana's store, the Wigwam Neosho, became a success and may have influenced Jesse Chisholm to become a trader. Houston went to Texas in 1833, perhaps on a mission for Andrew Jackson, leaving his Cherokee wife behind. She and the Chisholm family took over the trading post.

That summer, Jesse Chisholm purchased two wagons and went to Colonel Auguste Pierre Chouteau's trading post located south of the future site of Norman, Oklahoma. For the rest of the year he traded with various tribes up the Canadian River and at Council Grove, west of the site of Oklahoma City. A year later Chisholm showed up at James Edwards's store, which was located near the present site of Holdenville, Oklahoma. Edwards, who was not an Indian, operated on Indian land because he had married a Creek woman. Edwards and Chisholm became friends. Because of Chisholm's linguistic skills and his understanding of the geography of the Plains, Edwards offered the younger man a business partnership. In 1836 Chisholm married Edwards's daughter, Elizabeth; the couple had two children.

All of the scattered bands of Cherokees living in the United States were thrown into turmoil in 1838, when the U.S. government forced them to give up their homes. For one long season thirteen thousand people streamed west under an army guard; four thousand died and were buried along the Trail of Tears before the bitter survivors reached Indian Territory. Cherokee bands that had not seen each other for generations were forcibly reunited. That fall, after the last of the Eastern bands had arrived, Chisholm found himself involved in a desperate civil war among the various factions. One night, radical members of an Eastern Cherokee clan attacked the leaders of the Ridge Party, whose willingness to cooperate with the federal government was seen as having led to the Trail of Tears. The assassins, believed by some to be followers of Chisholm's uncle John Rogers, Jr., murdered three powerful spokesmen: Major Ridge, his eldest son, John Ridge, and Elias Boudinot died practically in the same instant. Because the radicals disliked Old Settlers nearly as much as the Ridge party, Chisholm was able to act as peacemaker and go-between among the factions, but it took the federal government to eventually end the internecine conflict.

In 1843 Chisholm's now recognized talent as peacemaker was called upon by Sam Houston, who, during a second term as Texas president, faced the prospect of Comanche bands waging war on Texas settlements. For the three previous years Comanches had ruthlessly embarked on a wave of terror against outlying and even coastal Texas settlements in retaliation for the murder of thirty-five Comanche women, warriors, and chiefs during a peace-conference in San Antonio in March 1840. Although they had come under a flag of truce, the Indians were surrounded by a troop of heavily armed Texas soldiers, who, in an event called the Council House Massacre, killed all the warriors and some women. Chisholm took on the dangerous mission of seeking out the remote Comanche bands and trying to persuade them to come in and sign a peace agreement. Seven years of great effort concluded with a treaty at San Saba Mission, signed by representatives of the Peneteka Comanches and signed and witnessed by Chisholm on 10 December 1850.

In 1845 leaders of the Cherokee Nation sent word to Chisholm that Sequoyah, the revered spiritual leader and intellectual who had created the Cherokee alphabet, was missing and presumed dead. Chisholm interrupted what he was doing for Houston and traveled to Mexico. After a long search, Chisholm found that Sequoyah's body had been buried in San Fernando.

After the San Saba Treaty was signed, Chisholm escorted fifty Indian chiefs to the East as their interpreter and guide. While in Washington, D.C., the group attended sessions inside the U.S. Capitol and met with the Senate in a series of treaty talks. Chisholm met President James K. Polk and toured the capital as a celebrity. When he arrived back in Indian Territory, Chisholm found that his wife had died, and he promptly married Sahahkee McQueen, a Cherokee woman; they had four children. In addition to his natural children, Chisholm adopted several former Indian captives.

In 1850 Jesse purchased the old buildings of Colonel Chouteau's trading post on the Canadian River. Plains tribes preferred this post because it bordered open country. Eight years later Chisholm moved his operations farther west, building a trading post on the North Canadian River not far from the future site of Fort Reno. This location, Chisholm's Old Ranch, connected with the older meeting ground at Council Grove. It became the western-most store and a favorite winter camping ground for the Comanches and Kiowas. By 1859 Chisholm was trading goods to the Comanches far out onto the Llano Estacado.

When the Civil War began, many tribes split into factions supporting opposing sides. Chisholm found his trading more valuable than before, as Indian Territory became a buffer between Union Kansas and Confederate Texas. Within a year of the war's outbreak, Chisholm had pioneered a route north from his ranch along the North Canadian River to a creek near the site of Wichita, Kansas. From there he visited several Union army posts and sold them much-needed supplies, thousands of buffalo robes to individual soldiers and hundreds of beef cattle to the army's commissary over the course of the war. Free to travel anywhere, Chisholm assumed a critical role as liaison between the Confederate and Union authorities. By the end of the war, Chisholm had developed a working knowledge of fourteen Indian languages and earned universal trust between North and South as well as the West. An indication of his stature was the meeting he held with several Plains tribes at Cottonwood Grove on the Washita River in 1865. At the gathered assembly, Chisholm persuaded the Indians to agree to a compact called the "Confederate Indian Tribes." Primarily intended to pacify Union authorities, the pact declared Indian neutrality in the Civil War.

Besides his success as a trader, Chisholm's diplomatic accomplishments also were impressive. For four dark years he maneuvered inside a four-way tangle of opposing interests: From the north, Kansas Jawhawkers roamed the countryside. From across the Red River, Texas deserters and horse thieves robbed and killed. The Confederate Choctaw Light Horse police and other quasi-military Indian organizations confiscated "enemy" farms and hanged fugitives at will. And, from the west, fierce Comanche and Kiowa warriors threatened all comers. Incredibly, Chisholm was never injured by anyone. His admirers say that he never carried a gun or dealt in whiskey—if so, a fact truly unique among American frontiersmen.

In 1866 Joseph G. McCoy, a visionary livestock feeder and shipper from Springfield, Illinois, persuaded the Union Pacific Railroad to build track into Kansas. When the rails terminated at Abilene, McCoy built a huge cow pen, a hotel, and several businesses designed to cater to the needs of Texas cattlemen. That fall McCoy advertised high prices for longhorn cattle that reached Abilene. The next year, a flood of Texas cattle crossed the Red River. Not too far north of the Red River the cattlemen discovered Chisholm's wagon tracks, which led them on a short route to Kansas. Chisholm's trail covered only the upper half of Oklahoma. It began near Chouteau's old post, crossed the Canadian River above the site of Tuttle, crossed the prairie, and followed the North Canadian and Cimmaron rivers into Kansas. By end of the decade, more than 100,000 head of cattle each year followed the path to Kansas. Most cattle drivers of the time were ignorant of Chisholm's legacy and among themselves referred to the route as "The Trail," "McCoy's Trail" or the "Abilene Trail." From the beginning, however, eastern cattle buyers and railroad officials publicized the route as "Chisholm's Trail," and by 1875 the name was universally accepted. Even today the trail's namesake is often confused with John Simpson Chisum, a Texas cattle king.

In his last days, Chisholm took a few wagons to a salt works thirty miles north of Reno and camped near a combined village of Comanches and Kiowas. After a long day of trading, Chisholm and the Indians feasted on bear meat cooked in a copper kettle. That night Chisholm took violently ill and died before dawn. Members of his trading party buried the old man on the bank of Left Hand Creek. In an act of reverence, Comanche chief Ten Bears placed his own presidential medal on Jesse's chest.

• A manuscript by Jim Cloud, "Chisholm's Old Ranch," is in the Western History Collection, University of Oklahoma. Also see Ray Asplin, "The History of Council Grove," *Chronicles of Oklahoma* 45 (Winter 1967–1968). The first published material on Chisholm was T. U. Taylor, *Jesse Chisholm* (1939). Mary Randolph Wilson Kelsey has a rich if slightly confused entry on Chisholm's family in her *James George Thompson, 1803–1879, Cherokee Trader* (1988). Stan Hoig, *Jesse Chisholm: Ambassador of the Plains* (1991), is a fully researched work.

VERNON R. MADDUX

CHISOLM, Alexander Robert (19 Nov. 1834–10 Mar. 1910), soldier and financier, was born in Beaufort, South Carolina, the son of Edward Newfville Chisolm and Mary Elizabeth Hazzard, planters. Orphaned at an early age, he was sent to New York City to be raised by an aunt. In 1852 he quit his studies at Columbia College to return to "Chisolm's Island," his family's ancestral estate sixty miles south of Charleston. Until the outbreak of the Civil War Chisolm administered the coastal plantation, which covered 4,000 acres and employed more than 200 slaves.

Following South Carolina's secession, Chisolm offered his services to Governor Francis Pickens, who in March 1861 appointed him a lieutenant colonel of state forces. Chisolm's familiarity with the water approaches to Charleston, where state troops were confronting the U.S. garrison at Fort Sumter, made him valuable to Brigadier General Pierre G. T. Beauregard, the local commander, who appointed him a volunteer aide-de-camp. Before the bombardment of 12–13 April, Beauregard five times sent Chisolm to Fort Sumter to ascertain the intentions of its commander, Major Robert Anderson, and to call for Anderson's surrender. On the thirteenth, with Sumter in flames, Chisolm again went to the fort to offer assistance in putting out the fire and to confirm Anderson's recently announced capitulation. Beauregard later praised his "indefatigable and valuable assistance night and day" during the Charleston crisis, especially his willingness to row back and forth to the fort at the risk of being fired upon by U.S. or South Carolina guns.

After Beauregard and his staff were transferred to Virginia, Chisolm played a multifaceted role in the campaign of First Manassas. Dispatched to the Shenandoah Valley on 17 July, Chisolm, now a first lieutenant in Confederate service, helped guide General Joseph E. Johnston's army to a juncture with Beauregard before a Union invasion force could strike the latter along Bull Run. During the climactic battle on the twenty-first, Chisolm carried messages from Beauregard to all parts of the field, including one that brought Brigadier General Thomas Jonathan "Stonewall" Jackson's Virginia brigade into action at a critical point. Later in the fight Chisolm single-handedly rallied a demoralized Virginia regiment, then led a cavalry force in harassing retreating Yankees near Cub Run bridge. The commander of the cavalry noted that Chisolm "distinguished himself by his gallant coolness and bravery."

By early 1862 Lieutenant Chisolm had proven himself one of Beauregard's most enterprising troubleshooters. A fellow staff officer described him as "seldom at a loss for resources in an emergency." That February he accompanied Beauregard (now a full general) to the western theater. There he carried orders to commanders in Tennessee and Alabama, chiefly to secure reinforcements for Beauregard's Army of Mississippi. At Shiloh, 6–7 April, he transmitted every order Beauregard issued and helped guide the Confederate withdrawal. That summer he was transferred to

Charleston, headquarters of Beauregard's new command, the Department of South Carolina and Georgia.

Throughout 1863 Chisolm observed the series of defeats Beauregard inflicted on Union troops attempting to capture the coastal port. During the siege he was also involved in testing and operating a number of "David"-type torpedo boats, with which Beauregard hoped to sink enemy vessels. In early 1864 Beauregard sent his aide to northern Florida, where he helped resist Union incursions in the Jacksonville area.

By May 1864 Chisolm was back in Virginia serving Beauregard, who was commanding the Department of North Carolina and Southern Virginia, in the defense of Petersburg and Richmond. At Drewry's Bluff on the sixteenth, Chisolm helped position a division of Beauregard's command in a preemptive strike against Major General Benjamin F. Butler's Army of the James. When the strike sent the Federals reeling south, Chisolm helped turn a captured cannon against the fugitives.

In the fall of 1864 Chisolm, now a captain, was at Beauregard's side in Alabama and Mississippi. When William T. Sherman's armies rampaged across Georgia in November and December heading for Savannah, Chisolm acted as Beauregard's liaison with Lieutenant General William J. Hardee, commanding the Savannah defenses. Chisolm suggested methods of constructing a pontoon bridge over the Savannah River, by which Hardee's 10,000 troops evacuated the city hours before it fell on 21 December. In the war's final weeks Chisolm followed Beauregard to North Carolina, where General Johnston was making a futile effort to stop Sherman's juggernaut. When Johnston's army lay down its arms at Greensboro, Chisolm signed the parole of its troops.

Returning to his war-ravaged estate, Chisolm regained prosperity through a cotton and shipping firm he helped establish in Charleston. In 1869 he relinquished his partnership in that venture to return to New York City, where he founded a brokerage firm. He was also an early member of the New York Consolidated Stock and Petroleum Exchange, a competitor to the New York Stock Exchange. Chisolm twice applied for membership in the older exchange but was rejected both times. In 1875 he married Helen Margaret Schieffelin Graham; they had one son.

In 1877 Chisolm and Thomas Jordan, formerly chief of staff to General Beauregard, cofounded a weekly trade paper, the *Mining Record*. The influential periodical later expanded to include news of many financial markets. Chisolm disposed of his interest in what had become known as the *Financial and Mining Record* in 1890, when he was accused of a conflict of interest stemming from his refusal to resign his seat on the exchange. By then he had contributed to *Century* magazine three articles about his war service, which in 1887–1888 were included in the four-volume compilation *Battles and Leaders of the Civil War*. He died in New York City.

As a Confederate staff officer, Chisolm was a model of efficiency, resourcefulness, and versatility. His ability to discharge weighty responsibilities—supervising troop dispositions, acting as liaison between General Beauregard and other field commanders—suggests that he deserved higher rank than the first lieutenant's commission he held at war's end. Beauregard several times sought his promotion, only to be thwarted by laws limiting the rank of aides-de-camp. Chisolm gained greater authority in postwar life. After fleeing the economic pressures that Reconstruction imposed on his native South Carolina, he spent two decades as a major figure in the financial and commercial circles of the North. The expatriate capitalist lost much of his influence, however, after failing to gain a seat on the New York Stock Exchange and being forced to sell his interest in the *Financial and Mining Record*.

• Many of Chisolm's personal papers are among the Bee-Chisolm Family Papers in the South Carolina Historical Society, Charleston, as well as in two collections at Duke University Library, the Augustin L. Taveau Papers and the Confederate Papers Collection. His articles include "Notes on the Surrender of Fort Sumter" and "The Shiloh Battle-Order and the Withdrawal Sunday Evening," in *Battles and Leaders of the Civil War*, vol. 1, ed. Robert U. Johnson and Clarence C. Buel (1884–1887), and "The Failure to Capture Hardee," in *Battles and Leaders of the Civil War*, vol. 4, ed. Johnson and Buel (1884–1887). The definitive source on his family is William Garnett Chisolm, *Chisolm Genealogy* (1914). For Chisolm's service on Beauregard's staff see Alfred Roman, *The Military Operations of General Beauregard* (2 vols., 1884), and T. Harry Williams, *P. G. T. Beauregard, Napoleon in Gray* (1954). Sources on Chisolm's postwar financial career include the various annual reports of the Consolidated Stock and Petroleum Exchange and S. A. Nelson, *The Consolidated Stock Exchange of New York* (1907). A brief obituary is in the *New York Times*, 11 Mar. 1910.

EDWARD G. LONGACRE

CHISOLM, Julian John (16 Apr. 1830–1 Nov. 1903), physician, was born in Charleston, South Carolina, the son of Robert Trail Chisolm, a planter, and Harriet Emily Schutt. He was also known as John Julian Chisolm.

Prior to his formal training in medicine, Chisolm spent three years in the office of Elias Horlbeck, a prominent practitioner in Charleston. Following the award of his M.D. in 1850 from the Medical College of the State of South Carolina, Chisolm continued his studies in Paris, with emphasis on eye surgery. He returned to Europe in 1859 to visit hospitals in London and Paris. With the outbreak of war between Italy and Austria, he traveled to Milan to observe the treatment of the wounded from the battles at Magenta and Solferino.

After his first trip to Europe, Chisolm practiced medicine in Charleston and, with Francis T. Miles, organized the Charleston Preparatory Medical School. In 1857 he founded the Hospital for Negroes; in 1858 he became the professor of surgery at his alma mater. For the care of his growing number of surgical patients, he opened a private, sixty-bed surgical hospital in Charleston in 1860.

Shortly after the outbreak of the Civil War in 1861, Chisolm published the first edition of *Manual of Military Surgery for the Use of Surgeons in the Confederate States Army*, drawing heavily on his experience as an observer in military and civilian hospitals in Europe. Demand for this manual led to a second edition in 1862 and a third in 1864.

Judah P. Benjamin, the Confederate secretary of war, appointed Chisolm to the rank of surgeon in the Provisional Army on 20 September 1861 and ordered him to report to the South Carolina Hospital in Manchester, Virginia, near Richmond. As its chief, he applied his knowledge of military hospitals to set up one of the first general hospitals in the Confederacy. In November 1861 he was ordered to Charleston to establish a medical purveyor's office for receiving and distributing medicines and surgical instruments to Confederate military physicians in the field and in hospitals. The purveyor's office was moved to Columbia, South Carolina, in 1862. Here Chisolm was allowed by Samuel Preston Moore, the Confederate surgeon general, to establish one of the first Confederate medical laboratories for manufacturing pharmaceuticals from indigenous plants as replacements for drugs made scarce by the Union naval blockade. The laboratory also tested drugs for purity.

In addition, Chisolm was in demand to perform the more complicated surgical operations on wounded soldiers in the Columbia hospitals. Toward the end of the war, the movement of William Tecumseh Sherman's Union army forced Chisolm to move his purveyor's office first to Chester and then to Newberry, both in South Carolina; at the latter site, he turned over his supplies to the Union army in April 1865. Letters that he wrote as medical purveyor indicate that he was an able, energetic administrator with little tolerance for inefficiency or fraud. He was also a thoughtful person, finding time to share his medical expertise with civilians. An article he wrote for the *Confederate States Medical and Surgical Journal* described a way to reduce complications of traumatic wounds. In the latter part of the war, his invention of an anesthesia inhaler to conserve scarce chloroform demonstrated his creativity. Although it saw limited use during the war, the "Chisolm inhaler" was sold by a New York surgical instrument manufacturer for more than thirty years after its invention.

Following the war, despite offers of several other positions, Chisolm returned to Charleston, where he was elected dean of the Medical College of the State of South Carolina and began the task of reorganizing the faculty. In 1866 he returned again to Europe, this time concentrating on learning more about the diagnosis and treatment of diseases of the eye and ear. Finding postwar conditions in Charleston too professionally restrictive, in 1868 Chisolm moved to Baltimore, where he confined his practice to the treatment of eye and ear disorders. A few months after his arrival, a special chair was created for him at the University of Maryland, and he was soon elected dean of the medical faculty. He founded the Baltimore Eye and Ear Hospital in 1871. Two years later, the University of Maryland offered him one of the first full professorships in eye and ear surgery, which he accepted. To care for the less fortunate, he founded the Presbyterian Charity Eye, Ear and Throat Hospital in Baltimore in 1877.

Chisolm made many contributions to medicine and surgery in his teaching, his more than 100 professional publications, his invention, and his founding of institutions. Besides his Civil War and ophthalmic writings, he is especially noted for his advocacy of early ambulation of patients after cataract surgery, for being one of the first ophthalmologists to perform surgery for cataract on an outpatient basis, and for his early practice of antisepsis in eye surgery. He was a leader in the development of ophthalmology as a surgical specialty during the nineteenth century, as was evidenced by his publications on the diagnosis and treatment of eye disorders and his selection as the chairman of the Section of Eye, Ear, Nose and Throat of the American Medical Association in 1884.

Chisolm had two children with his first wife and cousin, Mary Edings Chisolm, whom he married in 1852 and who died in 1888. His second marriage, to M. Elizabeth Steele in 1894, resulted in another child. In September 1894 Chisolm suffered a stroke from which he only partially recovered. He died in Petersburg, Virginia.

• For information on Chisolm see "Biographical Sketch of Julian J. Chisolm, M.D.," *Virginia Medical Monthly* 5, no. 10 (1879): 782–90; J. J. Carroll, *Julian John Chisolm, M.D., 1830–1903, Published by Members of His Family and Former Associates upon the 100th Anniversary of His Birth* (1930); Charles Snyder, "Our Ophthalmic Heritage: Julian John Chisolm," *Archives of Ophthalmology* 67 (1962): 168–70; Roger Sherman, "Julian John Chisolm, M.D., Confederate Surgeon," *American Surgeon* 52, no. 1 (1986): 1–8; and W. C. Worthington, "Confederates, Chloroform, and Cataracts: Julian John Chisolm (1830–1903)," *Southern Medical Journal* 79, no. 6 (1986): 748–52. An obituary is in the *Journal of the American Medical Association* (14 Nov. 1903): xli.

F. TERRY HAMBRECHT

CHISUM, John Simpson (14 Aug. 1824–22 Dec. 1884), cattleman, was born in Hardeman County, Tennessee, the son of Claiborne C. Chisum and Lucinda Chisum, farmers. Claiborne Chisum, who reportedly altered the spelling of his surname (from Chisholm) about 1815, moved his family to Red River County, Texas, in 1837.

Educational opportunities in frontier Texas were limited, and John S. Chisum went to work while young. When Lamar County, Texas, was created in 1840, he acquired a tract of land and promoted the town site of Paris. After it won the county seat election in 1846, he successfully bid to erect its first courthouse, a log structure. In 1853 he was elected Lamar County clerk, a position he resigned in 1854 to enter the cattle business with S. K. Fowler, who financed the establishment of a ranch in Denton County. Stocking their range with $2 calves from South Texas, over time they built a large herd that supplied slaughter beeves at $40 a head to Confederate buyers in Louisiana during the Civil War. The partners then invested the acquired paper script of questionable value in more livestock.

After Chisum and Fowler ended their association in 1864, Chisum, anticipating a postwar influx of farmers, disposed of his North Texas holdings and relocated in more remote West Texas, settling along the Concho River near San Angelo. The underpopulated area offered much open range for his livestock, an estimated 10,000 head. There he branded his animals with a rustler-proof "rail" (a single streak from shoulder to thigh) and earmarked them with easily recognizable deep slits that caused the lobe to dangle limply, or "jingle," giving rise to the popular name for his spread—the Jinglebob.

In 1866 Chisum sold 600 steers to Texas ranchers Oliver Loving and Charles Goodnight, who had just blazed a cattle trail to Fort Sumner, New Mexico, over which to supply the military garrison and dependent Mescalero Apaches at the White Mountain Reservation. Although Loving was killed on the trail in an Indian attack the next year, Goodnight continued drives to New Mexico for the next several years, filling a government contract in part with Jinglebob steers. After 1868 Chisum sent his own herds to Fort Sumner, mostly driven by his brother, Pittser, who soon convinced John that the territory offered far better grass and much more water than West Texas.

Between 1870 and 1872 John Chisum sold his Texas property and moved his animals to open-range grasslands about thirty-five miles south of Fort Sumner, establishing his headquarters along the Pecos River at a large cottonwood grove called Bosque Grande. He soon secured a contract to supply the White Mountain Reservation and nearby Fort Stanton, and, despite occasional losses to rustlers and renegade Indians, by 1877 he was the territory's (if not the nation's) most substantial cattle rancher. His 100,000 animals grazed the whole length of the Pecos River from Fort Sumner southward to the Texas line, 150 miles away. He sold Jinglebob cattle at Forts Sumner and Stanton, New Mexico; Tascosa, Texas; and Dodge City, Kansas, his paths to these places becoming popularly known as Chisum's trails. This unfortunate homophonous duplication of the historic Chisholm Trail further east obscured Chisum's significance and contributions.

By 1878 Chisum was convinced that his chief competitor in supplying beef to reservations, L. G. Murphy, who also operated a bank and trading post at nearby Lincoln, New Mexico, was increasing his herds at Chisum's expense by rustling Jinglebob calves before they could be branded and marked. Their rivalry heated appreciably when Alexander McSwain, a business associate of Chisum, opened a rival store in Lincoln and when Chisum founded a bank there purposely to compete with Murphy. Then, when English rancher John H. Tunstall, also a Chisum associate, was shot and killed because of a separate business dispute with Murphy, the celebrated Lincoln County War commenced, in which William H. Bonney (alias Billy the Kid) came to infamy. Chisum's role in that bloody range war—either as behind-the-scene instigator of violence or innocent victim of lawlessness—continues to be debated by scholars and aficionados of the old West; in any case, it ended after territorial governor Lew Wallace offered amnesty to all but the worst perpetrators of violence, such as Bonney.

Chisum reportedly lost 10,000 head of cattle in the war, and, in debt and declining health, in 1879 he sold most of his remaining livestock to Robert D. Hunter and Albert G. Evans, prominent midwestern cattle brokers, and the rest to his brother, Pittser, who began ranching along the Canadian River, north of Fort Sumner. During his final years, John Chisum raised saddle horses near Roswell, in the process pioneering large-scale irrigation of such crops as alfalfa, oats, and apples.

Chisum never married. When he died of throat cancer at Eureka Springs, Arkansas, his estate was valued at about $500,000. He was buried in the family plot at Paris, Texas.

• The best, most scholarly study of Chisum is Harwood P. Hinton, "John Simpson Chisum, 1877–84" (M.A. thesis, Columbia Univ., 1955), which was serialized in the *New Mexico Historical Review* 31 (1956): 177–205, 310–37; and 32 (1957): 53–65. Mary Whatley Clarke, *John Simpson Chisum: Jinglebob King of the Pecos* (1984), is far less reliable. Clarence S. Adams and Tom E. Brown, Sr., *Three Ranches West: A True Story of John S. Chisum, the Cowman Who Opened the West for the Cattle Trade* (1972), despite its title, is historical fiction based on the rancher's life; however, it does contain a valuable bibliography. Roy Willoughby, "The Range Cattle Industry in New Mexico" (M.A. thesis, Univ. of New Mexico, 1933), has much information on Chisum and his contemporaries. See also short sketches of Chisum contained in James Cox, *Historical and Biographical Record of the Cattle Industry and the Cattlemen of Texas and Adjacent Territory* (2 vols., 1894); George A. Wallis, *Cattle Kings of the Staked Plains* (1957); and Walter Prescott Webb and H. Bailey Carroll, eds., *The Handbook of Texas* (2 vols., 1952).

JIMMY M. SKAGGS

CHITTENDEN, Hiram Martin (25 Oct. 1858–9 Oct. 1917), historian and civil engineer, was born in Cattaraugas County, New York, the son of William Chittenden and Mary Wheeler, farmers. Chittenden was appointed to the U.S. Military Academy, but he spent two terms at Cornell University in 1879–1880 to broaden his education before entering West Point in the spring of 1880. He graduated from the military academy in 1884, ranked third in a class of thirty-seven cadets, a position that earned him an assignment in the Corps of Engineers. After marrying Nettie Parker later that year (a union that produced three children), Chittenden spent the next three years in postgraduate study at the Engineer School of Application in New York City. Then, after a year of mapping and surveying for the Department of the Platte, he was transferred to river and harbor work on the Missouri and Ohio rivers, where he remained until 1896.

The only bright spot in this last assignment was summer work in 1891–1893 building roads in Yellowstone National Park, a service that also produced Chittenden's first book, *The Yellowstone National Park: Historical and Descriptive* (1895). While on duty in Yellowstone he joined with others, such as Theodore Roosevelt, in opposition to the building of a railroad through the park. His contribution to this cause was to publish articles in *Harper's Weekly* and *Forest and Stream*.

Chittenden first gained a national reputation as a pioneer advocate of federal aid to irrigation in the American West. In 1896 Congress authorized a survey of reservoir sites in Wyoming and Colorado and an investigation of the function of reservoirs in general. Assigned to conduct this investigation, Chittenden made three trips into the arid West, organized his data, and completed his report (*Preliminary Examination of Reservoir Sites in Wyoming and Colorado*) in November 1897, all within fifteen months. Chittenden's recommendations were that reservoirs were feasible means for regulating stream flow and for irrigation and—more important—should be constructed by the federal government. During the next five years the report gained increasing attention and support from individuals and organizations, including George Maxwell of the National Irrigation Association, the conservationist Gifford Pinchot, and Frederick Newell, chief hydrographer of the U.S. Geological Survey, and was a powerful force ("the strongest single influence," in the words of one U.S. senator) in the passage of the Newlands Act of 1902 that first authorized federal construction of irrigation dams. After service (at home) during the Spanish-American War, Chittenden returned to rivers and harbors work (which he believed was a waste of time and taxpayers' money) on the Missouri River until 1906, leavened by special assignments. The first of these tasks was to chair in 1904 a commission to investigate conditions in Yosemite Park. The most important results of this survey helped to convince Congress to acquire the Yosemite Valley from California to add to the surrounding highlands already in the park, to keep a railroad out of the park, and to reduce its area to eliminate timber and mining interests within it.

During these years Chittenden spent many of his winter evenings and weekends working on a study of the fur trade of the trans-Mississippi West: "I didn't care enough about the Missouri River to waste any unnecessary energy thereon, for I felt as certain then as I do now that it would be all labor lost. I, therefore, had no compunction in directing as much of my time as I could to work which I believed would be of a great deal more use to my countrymen." *The American Fur Trade of the Far West* was published in 1902. Beginning with a brief overview of the origins of the fur trade in eastern North America, it provided a detailed description and analysis of the major fur-trading companies operating west of the Mississippi River (except for the omission of those in the Southwest). The work was a great pioneering venture in scholarship, for there was nothing that had paved the way except for Washington Irving's *Astoria* (1836) and *Captain Bonneville* (1837).

Chittenden, a conscientious historian, went to the sources to ground his massive work. He located in private hands the papers of the great St. Louis fur-trading families of the Chouteaus and Sublettes. He interviewed, consulted newspapers, visited document repositories in St. Louis and throughout the West, and corresponded with experienced historians. *The American Fur Trade* remains the standard overview and has never been imitated. It has the faults and virtues of its age but nevertheless has remained the authority. Chittenden's writing style is clear although the topical organization of the book is confusing in places. He was sparing in the use of footnotes and somewhat imprecise about the value of his bibliographical sources. In addition to the Southwest, Chittenden neglected or deemphasized the domestic and international political ramifications of the trade and the economic side of the fur business. He also made several errors of fact, such as his crediting the discovery of South Pass to Etienne Provost in 1823 rather than to the returning Astorians in 1813. In spite of these flaws, the work's enduring power confirms its author's evaluation: "This work I put down as emphatically a thing well done and this view is confirmed as time goes on."

Chittenden's two other large historical works, both of which he edited, lack the superb quality and influence of *The American Fur Trade*. *History of Early Steamboat Navigation on the Missouri River* (1903) was constructed around the colorful memoirs of Joseph La Barge, a retired river pilot whom Chittenden had met in St. Louis. It included documentation and remained the standard in the field until 1962. *Life, Letters, and Travels of Father Pierre-Jean de Smet, S.J., 1801–1873* (1905), written and edited with Alfred T. Richardson, a businessman and newspaper editor from Nebraska, was a four-volume work that contained a brief (144-page) biography of the Jesuit missionary that introduced the letters section. Unfortunately, the collection contains only about 30 percent of de Smet's correspondence and was edited in a careless manner.

In historiographical terms, Chittenden was a transitional figure. Methodologically, in his reliance on sources, his use of footnotes, and his attempt to be objective in his scholarship, he represented the newer scientific study of history. More important, he used Darwinian evolution to explain matters such as Great Britain's victory in the Boer War, U.S. acquisition of the Philippines, and the displacement of the Native Americans. Essentially, however, Chittenden's historical work was in the traditional romantic vein that glorified primitive heroic individuals such as Jim Bridger, colorful institutions such as the disappearing steamboat, and historic sites such as the Oregon Trail.

Chittenden had a second tour of duty in Yellowstone Park (1899–1906), served as the Corps of Engineers' district engineer in Seattle (1906–1910), and, after retirement from the army in 1910, served as chairman of the first board of port commissioners in

Seattle (1911–1915), in which position he protected the interest of the public against developers. Chittenden also became embroiled in a controversy concerning the new conservation movement of the Theodore Roosevelt years. One of the arguments for forest conservation was that they regulated stream flow. Basing his position on his experiences in Yellowstone Park and others' studies of the problem, Chittenden attempted to refute this view in an article published in the *Proceedings* of the American Society of Civil Engineers in 1908. His article was highly publicized (and even attacked by President Roosevelt), but it did not stop the passage of the Weeks bill to create an Appalachian National Forest, a measure its supporters defended by stating that the government reserves would play a part in controlling floods.

Chittenden died in Seattle of locomotor ataxia. His significance lies primarily in his historical work. However, his efforts to preserve Yellowstone and Yosemite also created an enduring legacy. The roads in Yellowstone Park follow—with one exception—the roads that he constructed. Finally, his investigation of reservoir sites was enormously influential in bringing the national government into the irrigation business, helping to transform the economic life of the American West.

• The bulk of Chittenden's personal papers are located at the Washington State Historical Society, with an additional few pieces located at the University of Washington library. Another major deposit is his official correspondence with the Office of the Chief of Engineers contained in the Records of the Chief of Engineers in the National Archives. Several of Chittenden's unpublished writings are in *H. M. Chittenden: A Western Epic*, ed. Bruce Le Roy (1961). Chittenden is also the author of *War or Peace: A Present Duty and a Future Hope* (1911). A biography of Chittenden is Gordon B. Dodds, *Hiram Martin Chittenden: His Public Career* (1973). Obituaries are in the *New York Times* and the *Seattle Post-Intelligencer*, both 10 Oct. 1917.

GORDON B. DODDS

CHITTENDEN, Martin (12 Mar. 1769–5 Sept. 1840), governor of Vermont, was born in Salisbury, Connecticut, the son of Thomas Chittenden, the first governor of Vermont, and Elizabeth Meigs. Chittenden moved with his family to Williston, Vermont, in the early 1770s after his father purchased a land grant from his friend and political ally, Ethan Allen. His father's involvement in Vermont politics had considerable impact on Chittenden; he grew up at the center of Vermont's political life as the region first struggled to achieve independence from New York's and New Hampshire's land claims and then negotiated its role with the rebelling American colonies in their bid for independence from the British Empire.

Chittenden attended Mares School and Dartmouth College, graduating in 1789. He then moved to Jericho, Vermont, where he pursued agricultural and mercantile interests and a political career. In 1796 he married Anna Bentley; they had twelve children. Chittenden held many public offices, including justice of the peace (1789); representative from Jericho to the Vermont General Assembly (1790–1798); aide-de-camp to Lieutenant Governor Olcott (1790); clerk of the Chittenden County Court (1790–1793); delegate to the Bennington Convention to ratify the federal Constitution (1791); captain of Jericho's First Militia (1793); judge for Chittenden County (1793–1795); lieutenant colonel of the First Regiment, Seventh Division of the Vermont militia (1794); and chief justice (1796–1813). This tradition of public service continued after he moved to Williston in 1798, where he served both as that town's representative to the Vermont General Assembly (1798–1800) and as a brigadier general (and later a major general) of the Vermont militia (1799–1803), while retaining his position as chief justice.

Chittenden entered national politics with his election to the U.S. House of Representatives, where he served four terms (1803–1813). As a staunch Federalist, he vehemently opposed Jefferson's 1807 embargo of French and English trade and proposed legislation in Congress calling for its repeal; the legislation did not pass.

In 1811 Chittenden sought election as the governor of Vermont, running against his brother-in-law, Jonas Galusha. This election was the first of five gubernatorial contests that pitted these two men against one another. Galusha won in 1811 and 1812, but in the 1813 election neither candidate secured a majority, and the issue was decided by the general assembly, which granted the office to Chittenden by the narrow margin of one vote.

During his two years as governor (1813–1814), Vermont was rocked by the political battles between Jeffersonians and Federalists, which had reached their peak during the War of 1812. Chittenden played an active role in these political contests, condemning the war as detrimental to the interests of Vermont. In 1813 he refused to allow the Vermont militia to serve on the western side of Lake Champlain (which lay within New York's border) and recalled the militia stationed near Plattsburgh, New York. In a proclamation issued to justify this action, he wrote that "the military strength and resources of this State must be reserved for its own defence and protection exclusively excepting in cases provided for by the Constitution of the U. States; and then under orders only from the Commander-in-Chief." Although Vermont's militia officers failed to comply with his order and remained in New York, Chittenden's stance in this matter sparked questions in the Congress as to his patriotism. Several members of Congress advocated prosecuting Chittenden in federal court, but no action was taken.

After being reelected to the governorship in 1814, Chittenden proposed to the Vermont General Assembly that it send delegates to the Hartford Convention, where Federalist representatives from the New England states had gathered to discuss and propose amendments to the federal Constitution in order to better protect their rights within the national government. Although the general assembly decided not to send delegates to the convention, Chittenden's secretary of state, William J. Hall, attended unofficially.

In 1815 Chittenden lost the governor's seat to his brother-in-law, who secured a majority of the popular vote. Chittenden was the last Federalist governor of Vermont. After his defeat he retired to his farm in Williston, where he devoted himself to agricultural pursuits and served briefly as a judge of probate for Chittenden County (1821–1823). Chittenden died in Williston.

As a member of one of Vermont's leading families and as a political figure in his own right, Chittenden was at the center of many of the political upheavals of Vermont's early history, including the settlement of the land grants, the state's entry into the Union in 1791, and the partisan conflict between Jeffersonians and Federalists that led to Federalism's ultimate decline after 1815.

• Many of Chittenden's proclamations as governor were published. During his term in the U.S. Congress, he signed his name to a public condemnation of the War of 1812, *An Address of Members of the House of Representatives of the Congress of the United States to Their Constituents, on the Subject of the War with Great Britain* (1812), and his own legislation against the embargo was published as *Mr. Chittenden's Motion for a Repeal of the Embargo Laws* (1808). One study exists of the Chittenden family: Alvan Talcott, *Chittenden Family: William Chittenden of Guilford, Connecticut and His Descendants* (1882). Chittenden's life and career are addressed briefly in local histories of Chittenden County, including W. S. Ryan, ed., *History of Chittenden County* (1886); C. H. Hayden, ed., *History of Jericho* (1916); and F. Kennon Moody and Floyd D. Putnam, *The Williston Story* (1961). *Proceedings of the Vermont Historical Society* and that organization's journal, *Vermont History*, mention Chittenden periodically, primarily in reference to Federalism and the War of 1812. John J. Duffy, "Broadside Illustrations of the Jeffersonian-Federalist Conflict in Vermont, 1809–1816," *Vermont History* 49, no. 4 (Fall 1981): 209–22, provides background information on the political turbulence of early nineteenth-century Vermont. *The Records of the Governor and Council of the State of Vermont*, Vols. 3–8 (1787), present details of Chittenden's term in office as well as a short biographical sketch.

ELIZABETH DUBRULLE

CHITTENDEN, Russell Henry (8 Feb. 1856–26 Dec. 1943), nutritional biochemist, was born in Westbrook, Connecticut, the son of Horace Horatio Chittenden, an employee of a small manufacturing firm, and Emily Eliza Doane. A rather retiring child, Chittenden grew up in New Haven in a simple home, attending a small private school, a public school, and for college preparation, French's School in Westbrook. His family had difficulty paying tuition, so French engaged him to clean the classrooms and teach the lower classes in Latin, mathematics, and geography. French also arranged for him to attend the Sheffield Scientific School at Yale, where George J. Brush arranged for Chittenden to become a laboratory assistant to pay his laboratory fees and tuition. In 1875 Chittenden obtained his Bachelor of Philosophy degree. For graduation, original investigative work and a thesis were required. At a professor's suggestion Chittenden investigated the composition of the edible muscle of *Pecten irradians*, the scallop, and found their sweet taste when cooked was associated with glycogen and glycols; he published his results in the *American Journal of Science*. Chittenden married Gertrude Baldwin in 1877; they had two daughters and one son.

To get more training in physiological chemistry Chittenden went to Strasbourg in Alsace to work in the laboratory of Felix Hoppe-Seyler, but the rigid professor's laboratory and the atmosphere of the German-occupied city discouraged him. He moved to the Heidelberg laboratory of Willy Kühne, who had read his paper on scallops and gave Chittenden a position in his laboratory. Kühne soon offered him another position as his assistant for lecture demonstrations. Besides attending Kühne's lectures in physiology and Robert Wilhelm Eberhard Bunsen's in chemistry, Chittenden carried out three separate projects. Two were histochemical studies of the sarcolemma of the frog's sartorius muscle and the epithelium of the eye, and the third concerned the formation of hypoxanthine from albumin. Kuhne took special interest in the able American and not only guided him academically but also introduced him to many prominent European scientists and encouraged him to visit many German laboratories.

On his return to Yale Chittenden resumed teaching, and in 1880 he received the first Ph.D. in physiological chemistry awarded in the United States. His thesis summarized his work on glycogen and glycol in scallops and the oxidation of glycogen with bromine and silver oxide. In 1882 Chittenden was appointed professor in the Sheffield School, and within two years he was elected permanent secretary of the school's board. By 1886 the laboratory of physiological chemistry occupied most of the second floor of Sheffield Hall; in 1889 it was moved to the nearby former residence of Joseph Sheffield, benefactor of the school. At first physiological chemistry occupied the entire first floor, but it soon grew to occupy the entire building. Chittenden taught a year course of lectures, demonstrations, and laboratories. He encouraged his brighter students to remain for more courses and original work; by 1900 eleven candidates had fulfilled the requirements for the Ph.D. One was Lafayette Mendel, who became Chittenden's successor, and another was Yandel Henderson, who became a professor of physiology at Yale.

Chittenden realized the importance of chemistry in understanding the functions of the body and encouraged its expansion in the medical school as well as independently. His success in establishing physiological chemistry at Yale resulted in Columbia's asking him to begin a course there. Unwilling to cut his ties with Yale, Chittenden sent W. J. Gies and A. N. Richard to New York to set up the laboratory and act as instructors, while he lectured there once a week.

In 1898 Chittenden was elected director of the Sheffield School, a position he held until his retirement in 1922. Under Chittenden the Sheffield School expanded and developed into the foremost institution for biological teaching in the United States. When Yale wanted to consolidate the Sheffield School with the medical school, Chittenden vigorously resisted the merger. He felt that physiological chemistry should be an independent discipline and that the Sheffield School should teach this subject to biological, agricultural, and medical students. A year after Chittenden retired, however, the Sheffield School was merged with the medical school.

Chittenden's most significant scientific contributions fall into two categories. One was the action of enzymes on ingested food. Chittenden began this work with studies of the splitting action of diastase on starch. In 1882 he returned to Heidelburg to work with Kühne on the mechanism by which ingested protein was made available to the animal by enzymes.

Little had been known about the composition of albuminoids (proteins) until after 1850, when the new method of fractional precipitation with neutral salts was introduced. It then became evident that there were numerous albuminoid substances. It was later discovered that soluble ferments from biological and plant juices acted on albuminoids, breaking them down into smaller units termed albumoses. Kühne and Chittenden were drawn to studies of the digestion of albuminoids by Georg Meissner's discovery that pepsin digested protein incompletely.

In a series of carefully conducted experiments, Chittenden and Kühne established that protein digestion was a gradual process which produced a complex mixture that could not be resolved by the available methods. They reported that pepsin split albumin into fractions, the first of which they called syntonin. Further treatment with the enzyme cleaved syntonin into protoalbumose (soluble in water) and heteroalbumose (soluble only in salt solutions). These primary albumoses were degraded by a third enzyme treatment to deuteroalbumoses. Tryptic digestion of albumin, in contrast, yielded equal amounts of hemipetones, further digested into the amino acids leucine and tyrosine, and antipeptones, which were resistant to enzyme attack. Kühne and Chittenden's work on the hydrolytic products of enzyme digestion of proteins, although largely ignored later because of the introduction of better methods of hydrolysis and identification, prepared the way for brilliant work on amino acids and nutrition by Lafayette Mendel.

Chittenden's second area of interest was initiated by studies of the toxicology of arsenic, which led to the development of sensitive methods for detection, important in forensic medicine. This work later developed into a study of the toxicity of other metals as well as an investigation of the toxic effect of alcohol on the human body. When Chittenden became a member of the referee board of the Secretary of Agriculture, these investigations were extended to food preservatives and additives.

Chittenden became involved in evaluating whether Horace Fletcher's system of slow and deliberate eating was in fact beneficial to health. In his carefully planned study Chittenden found no evidence to support Fletcher's idea, but the study awakened his interest in determining human food requirements. He demonstrated that a man could maintain perfect health with a total intake of 2,500 to 2,600 calories per day, containing fifty grams of protein. During World War I Chittenden served on numerous committees involved in providing food to the people of war-torn Europe.

Chittenden served as editor for several journals and was on the original editorial boards of the *Journal of Experimental Medicine* and the *American Journal of Physiology*. He was a founder of the *Society of Biological Chemistry* and became its first president in 1906. After he retired he spent much of his time writing articles, including some on the history of the Society of Biological Chemistry and of the Sheffield Scientific School.

Chittenden was a reserved man but a lifelong friend to his intimates. He was kind and devoted to the Sheffield school and its students. He died in New Haven.

• Chittenden's papers are in the Archives of Yale University, along with his manuscripts "History of the Sheffield Scientific School," "History of Physiological Chemistry in the United States," a monograph written for his children and entitled "Sixty Years of Service in Science," and "The First Twenty-Five Years of Physiological Chemistry in the United States." A detailed biography is Hubert Bradford Vickery, "Russell Henry Chittenden, 1856–1943," National Academy of Sciences, *Biographical Memoirs* 24 (1944): 56–104. The experiments of Kühne and Chittenden are described in Joseph Fruton, *Molecules and Life: Historical Essays on the Interplay of Chemistry and Biology* (1972). On Chittenden's administration of the Sheffield School, see Robert E. Kohler, *From Medicinal Chemistry to Biochemistry* (1982).

DAVID Y. COOPER

CHITTENDEN, Thomas (6 Jan. 1730–25 Aug. 1797), Vermont governor, was born at East Guilford, Connecticut, the son of Ebenezer Chittenden and Mary Johnson, farmers. As a youth he received only a rudimentary education that left him barely able to read and write. Noted for his strength and athletic prowess, Chittenden worked on his father's farm until he was 18, when he gave up agriculture to become a sailor aboard a West Indies merchant vessel. Unfortunately for Chittenden, the French captured his ship and marooned its crew on a Caribbean island; it took him several difficult months to make his way back to Connecticut. Abandoning his maritime ambitions, in 1749 he married Elizabeth Meigs of East Guilford, with whom he had ten children. Soon after their marriage the young couple moved to the western Connecticut frontier town of Salisbury. There Chittenden farmed and rose to prominence over the next quarter century, holding various local offices, serving as colonel of militia 1756–1760, and representing Salisbury in the Connecticut legislature from 1765 to 1772.

In the early 1770s, despite his position and influence in Litchfield County, Chittenden relocated to the northwestern New England frontier, an area claimed by New York but known as the New Hampshire

Grants by the New England speculators and settlers who had invested in New Hampshire titles to lands west of the Connecticut River. He bought a substantial tract in the town of Williston from the Onion River Land Company of Ethan Allen and Ira Allen in May 1773 and a year later moved to the banks of the Winooski River. Forced off his farm in the spring of 1776 when the American retreat from Canada left the Champlain Valley open to British invasion, Chittenden moved his family south to safety and turned his attention to the heated Yankee versus Yorker dispute over the political future of the Grants. Casting his lot with the anti–New York faction of the Allen brothers and the Green Mountain Boys, he participated in a series of sparsely attended conventions that culminated in the January 1777 creation of the state of New Connecticut. Older and more politically experienced than most of his backwoods colleagues, though still barely literate, by the time the fledgling state assumed the name Vermont five months later Chittenden was the acknowledged choice to head its new government. The July 1777 convention that met at Windsor to draft a state constitution named him president of the Council of Safety, a twelve-man body authorized to govern until elections could be held. When the first elected state officers were sworn in the following March, Chittenden became governor of Vermont, a post he held for eighteen of the next nineteen years.

As governor of independent Vermont, Chittenden headed what became known as the Arlington Junto, a western Vermont faction composed of Ethan and Ira Allen, Jonas Fay and Joseph Fay, and a handful of others who met frequently at the governor's wartime home to defend the state against a formidable roster of internal and external foes. While the war kept Congress, New York, New Hampshire, and other potential American enemies from overwhelming Vermont, Chittenden and his allies used a variety of strategies to keep their government's Vermont opponents divided and ineffective. The confiscation and sale of loyalist estates raised state revenues without imposing unpopular taxes and served as a convenient vehicle for banishing troublemakers regardless of their position on the war. The creation of new townships out of the state's large supply of ungranted lands brought in both funds and settlers friendly to the Chittenden regime. By taking land in lieu of salary and expenses, Chittenden amassed a real estate portfolio of some 40,000 acres, second only to Ira Allen's holdings among Vermont land speculators.

Beginning in 1781, Chittenden and a few other Vermont leaders engaged in secret negotiations with Frederick Haldimand, British governor-general of Canada, about the prospect of returning Vermont to the Empire as a separate province. The Vermont conspirators justified these negotiations to their American critics as a patriotic ruse that kept the British army in Canada from ravaging the unprotected northern American frontier. Few American observers believed this explanation, but Cornwallis's surrender at Yorktown in the fall of 1781 forestalled Haldimand's plans to force Vermont's leaders to make a choice between Crown and Congress, and the Revolution ended with the embattled Green Mountain republic maintaining its separate existence.

After the war, Chittenden held his place atop the Vermont government even as the state's other first-generation leaders, most notably the Allen brothers, gave way to new, more sophisticated challengers. Through most of the 1780s, Vermonters extolled their governor as the champion of the common man and the spirit of backwoods justice over the letter of the law on such issues as legal-tender laws and the property rights of settlers evicted from their farms for inadequacies in their land titles. As the political battles of competing factions intensified and nascent party structures emerged in Vermont, Chittenden remained above the fray and seemed immune to challenges to his authority. The lone break in his tenure as governor came in 1789 when the scandal surrounding his role in granting the town of Woodbridge to close friend Ira Allen several years earlier cost him a majority at the polls. The legislature selected Moses Robinson, a strong advocate of Vermont's admission into the federal union, to replace him. Chittenden had favored keeping Vermont politically independent and forging close commercial ties with Canada, but his return to power in 1790 came too late to reverse the march toward statehood that had accelerated sharply under Robinson. Chittenden accepted the inevitable by presiding over the January 1791 convention at Bennington that ratified the U.S. Constitution and set the groundwork for Vermont to become the fourteenth American state two months later.

Chittenden's last years as governor were a time of growth and prosperity for Vermont. The state's population increased rapidly with thousands of settlers moving north from southern New England in search of cheap, fertile land and abundant economic opportunity. Chittenden's popularity peaked during these boom years for his state; for many Vermonters, as the fact and folklore of the pioneer era blended into historical legend, he became the living symbol of revolutionary fortitude and republican virtue. When his health declined, in July 1797 he announced his decision not to seek reelection; he died in office before a successor could be chosen. His death occurred at Williston, Vermont. "His many and useful services to his country, to the state of Vermont, and the vicinity wherein he dwelt, will be long remembered by a grateful public," one Green Mountain newspaper declared shortly after Chittenden's death, "and entitle him to be named with the Washingtons, the Hancocks, and Adamses of his day."

• The largest collection of Thomas Chittenden manuscripts is at the Vermont State Archives; most of these papers appear in John A. Williams, ed., *The Public Papers of Thomas Chittenden* (1969). The Vermont Historical Society and the University of Vermont Library have small but noteworthy Chittenden collections. E. P. Walton, ed., *Records of the Governor and Council of the State of Vermont*, vols. 1–4 (1873–1880), contains transcripts of many Chittenden documents. There is no substantial biography of Chittenden; despite its title, Daniel Chipman's *A Memoir of Thomas Chittenden, First Governor Vermont* (1849) contains only a few pages on his career. The most detailed published sketches are "Biography of Thomas Chittenden, Esq. First Governor of Vermont," *The Literary and Philosophical Repertory* 2 (1815): 207–28; Odella Fay Wright, comp., *A History of the Town of Williston* (1913), pp. 7–23; Marshall True, "Why Are There No Biographers of Thomas Chittenden?" in *Lake Champlain: Reflections on Our Past*, ed. Jennie E. Versteeg (1987), pp. 210–15; David Read, "Thomas Chittenden, His Life and Times," in *The Vermont Historical Gazetteer* 1, ed. Abby M. Hemenway (1867–1891), pp. 905–29; and *Exercises at the Dedication of the Monument, Erected by the State to Thomas Chittenden, First Governor of Vermont, at Williston, Vt., August 19, 1896* (1896), pp. 24–53. Briefer sketches include Jacob G. Ullery, comp., *Men of Vermont* (1894), pp. 39–43; Prentiss C. Dodge, comp., *Encyclopedia Vermont Biography* (1912), pp. 27–28; Hiram Carleton, ed., *Genealogical and Family History of the State of Vermont*, vol. 1 (1903), pp. 1–4; Alvan Talcott, comp., *Chittenden Family: William Chittenden of Guilford, Conn. and His Descendants* (1882), pp. 33–35; and Ignatius Thomson, *The Patriot's Monitor for Vermont* (1810), pp. 199–201. For useful background on early Vermont politics, see Hiland Hall, *The History of Vermont, from Its Discovery to Its Admission into the Union in 1791* (1867); Chilton Williamson, *Vermont in Quandary: 1763–1825* (1949); Michael A. Sherman, ed., *A More Perfect Union: Vermont Becomes a State* (1991); and Michael A. Bellesiles, *Frontier Revolutionaries: Ethan Allen and the Struggle for Independence on the Early American Frontier* (1993).

J. KEVIN GRAFFAGNINO

CHIVERS, Thomas Holley (18 Oct. 1809–18 Dec. 1858), poet, was born in Washington, Georgia, the son of Colonel Robert Chivers, a prosperous mill owner and cotton farmer, and a Miss Digby (first name unknown). The oldest of seven children, Chivers developed mystical beliefs as a child after his favorite sister claimed to "converse with the angel of the Lord" on her deathbed, and he later wrote frequently about death and his own paradisiacal visions. In 1827 Chivers married his first cousin Frances Elizabeth Chivers, but for reasons still unknown his pregnant wife left him the next year. Blaming this breakup on the slanders of "a cursed fiend," Frances's widowed aunt, Chivers remained bitter about his failed marriage to the end of his life; in his will he left Frances and his daughter, whom he had never been allowed to meet, just one dollar each. To avoid the local scandal, Chivers enrolled in medical school at Transylvania University in Lexington, Kentucky, graduating with distinction in 1830. He practiced medicine briefly and then, from 1831 to 1833, traveled extensively on the western frontier, visiting then-distant outposts like Cincinnati and St. Louis. He was especially impressed by his trip to the Cherokee Nation; some of his subsequent poetry displays a sympathetic but romanticized fascination with Native-American culture and myth.

During his time at medical school, Chivers wrote poems that detailed his broken marriage, subsequently collecting these pieces into his first book, *The Path of Sorrow; or, The Lament of Youth* (1832). While the self-righteous tone of these lyrics confirms the judgment of critic C. H. Watts that Chivers was "distressingly egotistical," the verse contains experiments in diction and meter that, while mostly unsuccessful, nonetheless chart the direction for Chivers's later poetic innovations. In 1833 Chivers wrote a pamphlet, *The Constitution of Man*, of which no copy has survived, but its argument about the innate divinity of human nature can be reconstructed from an extensive, unsympathetic review in the *Western Monthly Magazine* (July 1833). In 1834 Chivers published a verse drama, *Conrad and Eudora; or, The Death of Alonzo*, the first of many treatments of the famous "Kentucky Tragedy" murder case, in which Jereboam O. Beauchamp, defending his wife's questionable honor, murdered Solicitor General Solomon P. Sharp. After a year of leisurely travel in the North, Chivers returned in 1835 to Georgia, but because his father generously guaranteed him a substantial income, the poet soon resumed his wanderings, living for short periods in such cities as Philadelphia, New York, and Boston. Despite his northern travels, Chivers remained a southern slaveholder in outlook and practice, believing that slavery was ordained by God and that abolitionism attacked the rights of property owners. In 1835 Chivers began sending poems to magazines for publication. His work was negatively reviewed by Edgar Allan Poe in the *Southern Literary Messenger* (Mar. 1835). Undaunted, two years later Chivers published his third book, a collection of fifty lyrics entitled *Nacoochee; or, The Beautiful Star, with Other Poems*.

Having only recently obtained a divorce from his first wife after extensive litigation, Chivers married Harriette Hunt, a young woman from Springfield, Massachusetts, in 1837. In spite of his happy marriage, the next few years were personally and artistically difficult. Chivers's beloved mother, with whom he claimed an almost telepathic sympathy, died in 1838. In the same year he rewrote *Conrad and Eudora* as "Leoni; or, the Orphan of Venice," but his hopes for a production of the play were never realized. The birth in 1839 of the first child of his second marriage, Allegra Florence, and the delivery of a son in 1840 fulfilled the promise of his vision eight years earlier of two childlike angels descending to earth; two more children were born over the next three years. However, Allegra's death in 1842 after a brief illness left Chivers distressed that his medical knowledge could not save his favorite child. His father also died in 1842, and the deaths of his and Harriette's other three children followed in 1843. (Chivers later fathered three more children, at least two of whom survived him.) Devastated by his familial tragedy, Chivers poured out his grief in *The Lost Pleiad and Other Poems* (1845), a collection of elegiac, short lyrics.

In 1840 Chivers had begun corresponding with Poe, who subsequently printed some of Chivers's poems in *Graham's Magazine*. In a brief article for *Graham's*, Poe wrote that Chivers "was one of the best and one of the worst poets in America" (Dec. 1841). According to Poe, Chivers's best quality was his melodic verse, while his worst traits were his ungrammatical sentences and his "mad" metaphors. Poe later apologized to Chivers for his comments. When by chance they met for the first time on a New York street in 1845, the teetotaling Chivers was shocked by Poe's drunkenness and soon after offered to take care of Poe financially if he would move to Georgia, an option Poe never seriously entertained. Chivers felt he could discuss his poetic ideas with Poe as a friend and an equal. For his part, Poe seems to have appreciated Chivers's poetry, quoting it approvingly in some of his lectures, and he once wrote to Chivers that, "Except yourself I have never met the man for whom I felt that intimate *sympathy* (of intellect as well as soul) which is the sole basis of friendship." Nonetheless, Poe's letters seem opportunistic: they often request financial assistance, which Chivers (perhaps fearing that it would be spent unwisely) was hesitant to provide.

In 1848 Chivers completed *Search after Truth; or, A New Revelation of the Psycho-Physiological Nature of Man*. This antimaterialist tract was influenced by Andrew Jackson Davis, a prominent spiritualist, in whose journal, *The Univercoelum, or, Spiritual Philosopher*, Chivers published fourteen poems and three essays. Following Poe's death in 1849, Chivers worked on his "New Life of Edgar A. Poe" (unpublished until 1952), which celebrated Poe's genius while admitting his weaknesses. In the early 1850s Chivers began to contribute poetry to the *Georgia Citizen*, a weekly journal published in Macon; *Leoni*, his revision of *Conrad and Eudora*, was published there in 1851.

Chivers's next collection of poetry, *Eonchs of Ruby* (1851), precipitated the plagiarism controversy for which he has been most often remembered. *Eonchs* contained an homage to Poe, "The Vigil in Aiden," as well as other poems that reviewers suggested imitated Poe's style. Angered that he should be characterized as Poe's disciple, Chivers publicly and privately defended his own originality in increasingly strident letters, culminating in a series of editorials in the *Waverley Magazine* (1853), submitted under the pseudonyms "Fiat Justitia" and "Felix Forresti," in which he argued that Poe, though a great poet, was himself a plagiarist. Chivers claimed, for instance, that "The Raven," published in 1845, was based on his own "To Allegra Florence in Heaven," a poem Chivers insisted Poe had read in manuscript in 1843. Other writers moved quickly to defend Poe's reputation in the pages of the same journal, and the ensuing epistolary battle ended only after the exasperated *Waverley* editor refused to publish any more of the vitriolic exchange. Recent scholars of both Chivers and Poe generally agree that at least some of Chivers's claims are justified and conclude that each man was influenced by the other (see esp. Lombard, Watt). In his own time, however, Chivers himself was judged the plagiarist, and his limited reputation was damaged to the extent that only the *Georgia Citizen* would any longer accept his submissions.

In addition to becoming a belligerent combatant in a literary feud, Chivers published three books in 1853. *Memoralia; or, Phials of Amber Full of the Tears of Love* was a reissue of *Eonchs* with the addition of some new poems. *Virginalia; or, Songs of My Summer Nights* contained some of Chivers's most effective experiments with diction, meter, rhyme, and refrain ("Apollo," "Lily Adair," "Pas d'Extase") and also some of his most obvious failures ("Rosalie Lee"). *Atlanta: The True Blessed Isle of Poesy; A Paul Epic—In Three Lustra* (1853), a metaphysical verse romance, once again presented Chivers's ideas about heaven and mortal existence. Chivers returned to Georgia in 1855 and did not again travel in the North. Asked to write a Fourth of July poem in 1856 by the citizens of his hometown, he responded with a patriotic pamphlet, *Birth-Day Song of Liberty*. Although professionally inactive, he was offered a professorship of physiology and pathology in Savannah, which he declined. Shortly before his death in Decatur, Georgia, he published *The Sons of Usna: A Tragi-Apotheosis in Five Acts* (1858), a play based on the Irish myth of Deidre.

Much of Chivers's poetry is pedestrian and clichéd, and most of his poems deal with a limited range of subjects, like love, death, and heavenly visions. Nonetheless, his experiments with diction, meter, and line anticipate modern verse by treating the sound of poetry as a way to communicate meaning. Some of his poems, in fact, leave denotation behind to imitate the sound they depict. For instance, the close of "Chinese Serenade for the Ut-Kam and Tong-Koo" mimics the sound of a gong: "Bo-an-owng, ba-ang, bing! / Bee-ee-eeing, ba-ang, bong!" Chivers's musical rhymes and refrains often create incantatory, aurally entrancing rhythms, while his few experiments with a free-verse line directly anticipate Walt Whitman, as in the opening lines of "The Roll of Fame" (1854):

> In the Autumn of the world, when the honey of the
> Summer still lay on the flowers of the years,
> I stood on the evergreen banks of the beautiful River
> of Time. . . .

His poetry has not been completely neglected: Swinburne, Dante Gabriel Rossetti, Kipling, and Vachel Lindsay were influenced by Chivers's musical lyrics. An unremarkable poet in many ways, Chivers's significance lies in his creativity with poetic sound.

• The Perkins Library at Duke University holds important Chivers manuscripts. Chivers's letters are collected in *The Correspondence of Thomas Holley Chivers*, ed. Emma Lester Chase and Lois Ferry Parks (1957). *Chivers' Life of Poe*, unpublished in his lifetime, is edited by Richard Beale Davis (1952). Charles Henry Watts, *Thomas Holley Chivers: His Literary Career and His Poetry* (1956), is the standard biographical and interpretive source and contains a dated but extensive bibliography. Charles M. Lombard, *Thomas Holley Chivers* (1979), includes fresh observations on Chivers's debt to Swedenborg and on his use of Georgian folk materials, including African-American dialect and rhythms. S. Foster Damon, *Thomas Holley Chivers, Friend of Poe* (1930), though often digressive, remains a useful biography. A chapter on the poet in Edd Winfield Parks, *Ante-Bellum Southern Literary Critics* (1962), provides the most thorough examination of Chivers's mystical theory of literature. Chivers's dramatic interpretations of the "Kentucky Tragedy" are analyzed in Richard

Beale Davis, "Thomas Holley Chivers and the Kentucky Tragedy," *Texas Studies in Language and Literature* 1 (Summer 1959): 281–88, and in William Goldhurst "The New Revenge Tragedy: Comparative Treatments of the Beauchamp Case," *Southern Literary Journal* 22 (Fall 1989): 117–27.

JEFFREY D. GROVES

CHOATE, Joseph Hodges (24 Jan. 1832–14 May 1917), lawyer and diplomat, was born in Salem, Massachusetts, the son of George Choate, a physician, and Margaret Manning. He was the salutatorian of the Harvard class of 1852 and graduated from Harvard Law School in 1854. He was admitted to the Massachusetts bar in 1855, and in 1857, after admission to the New York bar, became a partner in the firm of Evarts, Southmayd, and Choate. In October 1861 he married Caroline Dutcher Sterling; they had six children.

Choate won many difficult and celebrated cases, one of the most celebrated being the Fitz-John Porter case. General Porter was relieved of command and court-martialed on charges of disobedience and treasonous inactivity by General John Pope after the second battle of Manassas. He was convicted in January 1863, dismissed, and forever disqualified to hold any office under the United States. Porter pressed for an appeal of the judgment, and in 1878 President Rutherford B. Hayes appointed an advisory board to reexamine the case. Choate, working pro bono, used evidence not available during the war and convinced the board to overturn the judgment, completely vindicating Porter. Congress restored his rank (but did not reimburse him for back pay) in 1886. Choate regarded this as his most challenging and important legal victory.

A notable case that Choate lost was *Mugler v. Kansas*, an 1887 challenge to a state prohibition law. A beer manufacturer was fined, jailed, and had his business confiscated for selling alcohol without a license. Choate argued that a state could not prohibit personal consumption or sale of alcohol outside the state and that the act deprived Mugler of property without due process of law, in violation of the Fourteenth Amendment. Although the U.S. Supreme Court upheld the statute, it announced that it would scrutinize the substance of state legislation, pointing the way to the years ahead in which the Court would often act as champion of laissez-faire economic policy.

Choate is probably most remembered for his argument against the federal income tax in the two cases of *Pollock v. Farmer's Loan and Trust Co.*, which he won before the Supreme Court at the height of its defense of property rights. In 1894 Congress passed an income tax, of 2 percent on personal income over $4,000, to make up for revenue lost in the reduction of the tariff and to shift the burden of taxation from consumers to producers. An income tax had been collected during the Civil War, repealed in 1872, and reinstated as constitutional by the Supreme Court in the case of *Springer v. United States* (1881). The revival of the income tax was part of the populist agenda, made more urgent by the economic depression of 1893. President Grover Cleveland reluctantly allowed the act to become a law without his signature.

In perhaps the most closely followed case between the Civil War and the New Deal, Choate led a legal team, including William D. Guthrie and George F. Edmunds, in a challenge to the income tax. They made three arguments against the act. First, a tax on the income from land was effectively a tax on the land itself—a direct tax—and thus required to be apportioned among the states on the basis of population, according to Article I, section 9 of the Constitution. Second, a tax on income from other property was either a direct tax and likewise unconstitutional or, if not a direct tax, unconstitutional for want of uniformity, in its $4,000 exemption, under Article I, section 8, of the Constitution. Third, Congress could not tax the income from state and municipal bond interest.

Precedent as well as popular opinion was clearly against the challengers of the act, but Choate turned his rhetorical skills from the technical questions to the broader ones of social philosophy and policy. In the midst of the greatest economic depression in the nation's history, with the memory of labor conflict and all manifestations of the late nineteenth-century "social question" in mind, Choate appealed to the Court as guardians of minority rights against majoritarian tyranny. Assuming that "this Court was created for the purpose of maintaining the Constitution against unlawful conduct on the part of Congress," he attacked the principles behind the income tax as "communistic, socialistic—what shall I call them—populistic, as any ever have been addressed to any political assembly in the world." He warned the Court that it must stop the advance of class warfare before it was too late, that the Court "cannot hereafter exercise any check if you now say that Congress is untrammeled and uncontrollable." He implored the Court to come to the defense of property rights, which was "the very keystone upon which all civilized government rests."

A majority of the Court decided that taxes of income from land were direct taxes and that Congress could not tax the income from state and municipal bonds. However, the Court was evenly divided on the most important questions raised, whether the tax on personal property was a direct tax or void as an indirect tax for lack of uniformity and whether the parts of the statute already struck down invalidated the entire act. Thus the Court agreed to a rehearing, when the ninth Justice, Howell Jackson, would be present.

In the second decision, in 1895, a narrow 5–4 majority settled these outstanding issues in the challengers' favor. Justice Melville Fuller now held that there was no difference between taxes on real and personal property, although this distinction had figured significantly in the Court's prior decision to strike down the land taxes. The entire income tax was held unconstitutional in that taxation of income from property (but not labor) must be apportioned among the states according to population. Such an apportionment was practically impossible, since states of the same population, but vastly different per capita incomes, would be assessed the same amount of tax.

Pollock is generally regarded as the most notorious example of judicial aggrandizement in the service of wealth. Although there were good grounds on which to object to the income tax as policy and even on the basis of natural justice, there was little to support such objections in American constitutional law. Choate may have engaged in antipopulist demagoguery, though there were emotions on both sides. (Justice Brown's dissenting opinion prophesied that the decision would reduce the country to a "sordid despotism of wealth.") In 1909 Congress passed an amendment to reverse the decision, which was ratified as the Sixteenth Amendment in 1913.

Choate served as president of the New York State constitutional convention in 1894. He was also active in Republican party politics and New York civic affairs. He spent his life battling Tammany Hall Democrats in New York and ran an unsuccessful campaign against Thomas Platt for the U.S. Senate in 1897 to challenge boss rule in his own party. In 1899 President William McKinley appointed him U.S. ambassador to Great Britain. He was instrumental in working out the remaining differences between the two states and cementing Anglo-American friendship in the years before World War I. During his years at the Court of St. James's, Choate arranged for the United States and Great Britain to settle the Alaska-Canada boundary dispute by arbitration; won Britain's consent to abrogate the Clayton-Bulwer Treaty, allowing the United States to proceed with the Panama Canal unilaterally; and secured Britain's implied assent to the Open Door policy in China.

Choate's ambassadorship ended in May 1905. Two years later he headed the American delegation to the Second Hague Conference, where his legal background served in the elaboration of conventions of international law. His last efforts in public affairs were spent encouraging American preparedness for entry into World War I. He died in New York City.

Choate was a founder and trustee of the American Museum of Natural History and was involved in various civic concerns, including the Metropolitan Museum of Art, New York Hospital, the New York State Charities Association, and the Carnegie Endowment for International Peace. Equating the rule of law with the rule of lawyers, he believed firmly in classical liberal principles and in a nationalism tempered by federalism, with the federal judiciary acting as ultimate umpire of the system.

• Choate wrote an autobiography of his early years, *Boyhood and Youth* (1917). A bibliography of his works is in Frederick C. Hicks, ed., *Arguments and Addresses of Joseph Hodges Choate* (1926). An early biography is Edward S. Martin, *Life of Joseph H. Choate* (2 vols., 1920). The Fitz-John Porter case is the subject of Otto Eisenschiml, *The Celebrated Case of Fitz-John Porter* (1950). For the setting of the income tax cases, see Arnold Paul, *Conservative Crisis and the Rule of Law: Attitudes of Bar and Bench, 1887–1895* (1960), and Alfred H. Kelly et al., *The American Constitution: Its Origins and Development*, 7th. ed. (2 vols., 1992). The cases themselves are reported in 157 U.S. 429 and 158 U.S. 601 (1895). Bradford Perkins, *The Great Rapprochement: England and the United States, 1895–1914* (1968), provides diplomatic background.

PAUL MORENO

CHOATE, Rufus (1 Oct. 1799–13 July 1859), lawyer and politician, was born in Essex County, Massachusetts, the son of David Choate, a teacher and farmer, and Miriam Foster. Choate was educated at Dartmouth College, from which he graduated as valedictorian in 1819. Perhaps inspired by Daniel Webster's role in the Dartmouth College Case, which took place during his time in college, Choate decided to go into the law. After a few months at the Dane Law School at Harvard, he apprenticed in the office of U.S. Attorney General William Wirt in Washington. In 1823 he returned to Massachusetts to begin his legal career and by 1825 was sufficiently well established to marry Helen Olcott, the daughter of a prominent entrepreneur. They had seven children, four of whom lived to maturity. In 1834 Choate moved to Boston where he rapidly became one of the leaders of the bar and a popular public orator and lecturer on legal and historical topics such as "The Position and Function of the American Bar as an Element of Conservatism in the State" (1845), "The Importance of Illustrating New England History by a Series of Romances like the Waverly Novels" (1833), and "The Power of a State Developed by Mental Culture" (1844). He turned down offers of judicial office and also of a professorship at the Dane Law School, but he did serve for a year (1853–1854) as attorney general of Massachusetts. Choate had a large and heterogeneous practice. Many of his cases involved litigation over railroad or other business disputes produced by a burgeoning industrial economy; others were spectacular murder or divorce trials. He became renowned as a courtroom pleader with a remarkable command of the jury. His legal reputation rested on this eloquence and mastery rather than on the intrinsic importance of the cases he was involved with. Noted for his wit, nervous energy, copious flow of long, convoluted sentences, use of glowing imagery, and ability to "tear a passion to tatters" in the courtroom, Choate also fascinated his contemporaries with his exotic, even bizarre, appearance. He was lean, six-feet tall, with a shock of dark hair, piercing eyes, and a prematurely wrinkled face. A profoundly private person, he found his greatest pleasure and solace, neither in his work nor in his personal relationships, but in the books, particularly the classics, that he read constantly throughout his life.

Choate served briefly in the Massachusetts legislature from 1825 to 1827 and in the U.S. House of Representatives from 1830 to 1832. He was active in organizing the new Whig party in Massachusetts in 1834 and represented the party in the U.S. Senate from 1841 to 1845. Although he was temperamentally unsuited for the life of an active politician, he spoke ably in defense of the Whig policy on the tariff and against the annexation of Texas. His most solid achievement in the Senate was the role he played in the debates that led to the dedication of the new Smithsonian Institution to the "increase of knowledge" rather than to the more utilitarian ends of popular education. Choate however, failed, in his effort to make the heart of the new institution a great scholarly library. His struggle with Joseph Henry, the first secretary of the Smithsonian, marked the beginning of a rift between "humanist" scholars and scientists as they struggled for public support in a culture that was hostile to anything that might be construed as intellectual elitism.

Outside of Congress Choate became one of the most effective public spokesmen for the Whig party. He not only defended its specific policies but articulated a fairly consistent philosophy of the relationship between men and the state and of the conditions for social cohesion and order in the modern world. Politically Choate was a devoted adherent of Daniel Webster, whom he idolized as the model of the disinterested and patriotic statesman. Philosophically he was a disciple of Edmund Burke and attempted to apply Burke's conservative ideas about the state and nation to the turbulent democracy of antebellum America. Like all modern conservatives, he feared the disintegrating power of individualism. He saw this potential as particularly dangerous in America, where there were so few restraints on the imperious individual will and so little reverence for traditions and institutions, which in older nations served to bind individuals into a community. According to Choate, the recent origins of the American Republic made it all too easy to regard the state as no more than a contract, as ephemeral as "an encampment of tents on the great prairie, pitched at sun-down, and struck to the sharp crack of the rifle next morning," without authority or the ability to command either awe or affection. In Burkean language Choate asserted the importance of the state as the embodiment of that organic chain of generations that is the bedrock of civilization, "a structure, stately and eternal, in which the generations may come, one after another, to the great gift of this social life."

In a democratic society the health and stability of the state depended upon the ability of the people to practice some form of republican virtue, which Choate identified both with self-restraint and the ability to feel oneself part of a wider whole. Americans, he was convinced, needed to develop an imaginative identification, an emotional attachment, to the state and the nation that was more than a utilitarian recognition of its practical advantages. His was one of the many voices calling for the development of a distinctive national literature—and in particular for the creation of novels on American historical themes—as one of the more effective ways to make people feel the authoritative claims of their country upon their loyalty. The law would also play a major role in this cohesive process. Choate took a very exalted and almost religious view of the law as the distilled wisdom of many generations that constrained by its weight the willful desires of present generations. He urged his fellow lawyers to see themselves essentially as an arm of the state, whose conservative duty it was to uphold law as a necessary brake on liberty and particularly to oppose the "eternal" principles of the law to the temporary popular majorities of the day.

Choate's conservatism and fear of social disintegration allied him with the Cotton rather than the Conscience Whigs on the question of slavery. Like his idol Webster, he saw the Union as the epitome of the cohesion of the state and thus the greatest of goods whose defense took precedence over all other minor goods. He forcefully defended Webster's role in the Compromise of 1850 and in one of the great speeches of his career, his 1853 eulogy on Webster's death, insisted that conscience in public affairs must be "instructed by political teaching." His last years were spent in increasingly bitter opposition to what he called the short-sighted philanthropy that put the interests of abolition above the wider interests of the whole nation and to the new Republican party, which he denounced as a sectional faction. Like other Cotton Whigs he offered no solution to the problem of slavery except the healing process of time and the suppression of agitation. His last important political act was to declare his public support for the Democratic candidate, James Buchanan, in the presidential election of 1856, as the only hope of keeping the nation together. By the late 1850s Choate's health was failing, and in July 1859 he embarked on a voyage to Europe in the hope of recovery. He died en route in Halifax, Nova Scotia.

Choate was one of the most famous lawyers of antebellum Massachusetts and a renowned orator in that "Golden Age" of American oratory. The rise of strong antislavery feeling in Massachusetts, however, clouded Choate's reputation somewhat among his contemporaries, as it had Webster's. His failure to grapple seriously with the problem of slavery was a fatal flaw in an otherwise rather attractive conservatism but was typical of the stance of others in his party. He utterly failed to understand the degree of moral outrage over slavery that had welled up in New England and underestimated the potency of the concept of individual rights, which his notorious dismissal of the Declaration of Independence as no more than "glittering and sounding generalities" revealed. After his death he was remembered as a fascinating character rather than as an important historical figure. He has been revived by modern historians as a figure worth studying because he articulated with great verve a quite influential strain of conservative political thinking in Jacksonian America and because he touched on problems of social cohesion and political obligation of lasting importance in the modern state.

• The major collections of papers by or relating to Choate are the Rufus Choate and Samuel Gilman Brown collections in Houghton Library, Harvard University, and the Choate collection in the Archives of Dartmouth College. Choate's most important speeches are printed in Samuel Gilman Brown, *The Works of Rufus Choate, with a Memoir of His Life* (2 vols., 1862). The memoir was also published separately as *The Life of Rufus Choate* (1870). Choate's law student, Edward G.

Parker, produced the lively *Reminiscences of Rufus Choate, the Great American Advocate* (1860). His life was also recalled by E. P. Whipple, *Recollections of Eminent Men* (1886), and John B. Cogswell, "Memoir of Rufus Choate," *Memorial Biographies of the New England Genealogical Society*, vol. 3 (1883), pp. 383–486. Joseph Neilson, *Memories of Rufus Choate* (1884), contains a number of letters from people who knew him. More modern biographies are Claude M. Fuess, *Rufus Choate: The Wizard of the Law* (1928), and Jean V. Matthews, *Rufus Choate: The Law and Civic Virtue* (1980). There is an excellent discussion of Choate in Daniel Walker Howe, *The Political Culture of the American Whigs* (1979), pp. 225–37.

JEAN V. MATTHEWS

CHOATES, Harry (26 Dec. 1922–17 July 1951), Cajun musician, was born in Rayne, Louisiana. He grew up in Port Arthur, Texas, where he received no formal education, steeped himself in the local honky-tonk scene, and learned to play fiddle on a borrowed instrument that he purportedly never returned. He also played the guitar, steel guitar, and accordion.

Starting in the late 1930s, Choates played in a series of bands, including those led by Leroy "Happy Fats" LeBlanc, Julius "Papa Cairo" Lamperez, and Leo Soileau. Known for his skill as a fiddler, he never stayed with one band for long but thoroughly mastered the style of the Cajun string bands in the 1930s, a subgenre of Cajun music combining the western swing and honky tonk from country music with some of the Cajun French language and song repertoire. Choates may have learned his much-imitated version of "Jolie Blonde" from Leo Soileau while playing with Soileau and his Aces, who also recorded a version for Bluebird in 1935 as "La Valse de Gueydan" with vocal stylings similar to Choates's more famous version. Amédé Breaux is usually given credit for first recording the song with his 1928 "Ma Blonde Est Partie" for Columbia. The Hackberry Ramblers contributed their own "Jolie Blonde" on a 1936 Bluebird recording.

Cajun string bands from the mid-1930s such as the Hackberry Ramblers, Soileau's groups, and Choates's own group, the Melody Boys, represent a period of influx of American popular musical styles and practices into Cajun music. Many changes took place: the bass and drum set were introduced; amplification appeared, allowing the fiddle to be on equal terms with the (louder) accordion; the steel guitar emerged as a melody instrument as the accordion disappeared; and many songs were sung in English.

Although not a fluent Cajun French speaker, Choates learned to sing convincingly in that language as well as in English, and he distinguished himself as an instrumentalist on the pivotally important violin. He first recorded as a fiddler with Happy Fats and the Rayne-Bo Ramblers in 1940, before wartime shellac rationing and a musicians' union ban on recording imposed a slowdown on the recording industry. Alcoholism, a problem for Choates since age twelve, cut short his army service during World War II.

Choates married Helen Daenen from Orange, Texas, in 1945; they had two children. After the war, seeking a record to help him promote his live performances, he made his definitive recording of "Jole Blon" (*jolie blonde*, or "pretty blond girl") for Bill Quinn's young Gold Star label in Houston, Texas. Choates's arrangement, with its regular eight-bar phrases and slightly contrasting instrumental section in the form, has become the most well-known version of that song. Initial sales of the disc were aided by airplay on a Houston radio station.

It is impossible to say if this waltz would have attained its unofficial status as "the Louisiana national anthem" without Choates's recording of it, or if Choates himself would be so well remembered today had he not made it, but together man and song made history. The song remains today one of the most durable standards of the Louisiana French song repertoire and an icon of regional culture, adopted by Cajun and black Creole musicians alike.

Choates subsequently recorded many more sides for Gold Star in both French and English in the late 1940s, toured from southwestern Louisiana to Austin, Texas, and appeared on live television in San Antonio on a country-western program. By 1950 he had become "the most popular Cajun musician of his day" (Ancelet and Morgan, p. 26).

Choates and his wife divorced in 1950 as his drinking problems continued; the following year he was jailed in Austin, Texas, for failing to make support payments to his family. He died in his third day of custody, and police never gave an explanation of his death to his family, nor is there any record of a follow-up investigation. Conjectures concerning which was fatal, alcoholism or police brutality, seem unlikely to be resolved. His body was transported to and buried in Port Arthur, Texas, with fundraising assistance from local radio announcer and western swing program host Gordon Baxter.

• Of the biographical sources on Choates, Tim Knight's liner notes to *Harry Choates, Fiddle King of Cajun Swing* (Arhoolie CD 380) are the most comprehensive account, and the recording itself is the most widely available compilation. *J'ai Été Au Bal* (Arhoolie CD 331) contains his seminal version of "Jole Blon." John Broven, *South to Louisiana* (1983), has some additional biographical information. Barry Jean Ancelet and Elemore Morgan, Jr., *The Makers of Cajun Music* (1984), situates Choates's career in the historical context of the Cajun westward migration into Texas. Bill C. Malone, *Country Music, U.S.A.* (1985), mentions country artist Moon Mullican's satirical recording of "Jolie Blonde" and discusses Choates as part of the history of honky-tonk country music of the period. A version of "Jolie Blonde" similar to Choates's is transcribed in Raymond François, *Yé Yaille, Chère!* (1990).

MARK F. DEWITT

CHOPIN, Kate O'Flaherty (8 Feb. 1850–22 Aug. 1904), novelist and short-story writer, was born in St. Louis, Missouri, the daughter of Thomas O'Flaherty, a merchant, and Eliza Faris. Thomas was an Irish immigrant who became wealthy in the burgeoning Mississippi River trade. Eliza was, on her mother's side, from a prominent St. Louis Creole family. Both parents were devout Catholics, and Kate received her schooling at the Sacred Heart Academy in St. Louis. After the death of Thomas O'Flaherty in 1855, Eliza never remarried, and Kate was raised in a multigenerational household of independent women.

On 9 June 1870 Kate O'Flaherty married Aurelian Roselius Oscar Chopin, the son of a Louisiana French-Creole family. The couple settled in New Orleans, where Oscar became involved in the cotton trade. Initially, his business was successful, but after suffering financial setbacks, in 1879 he moved the family to Cloutierville, a small town in Natchitoches Parish in northwest Louisiana. Managing small plantation properties and operating a general store, Oscar suffered additional financial losses, and in 1882 he fell ill with a recurrent fever, dying in December of that year. Widowed at thirty-two, Kate Chopin was left with the heavy responsibility of six children and thousands of dollars of debt. She took control of Oscar's businesses, sold some of the property, and within two years settled her husband's financial affairs. In 1884 she moved back to St. Louis.

Chopin's immersion in domestic and business affairs left her with little inclination to write during her Louisiana years. Yet during this period she was gathering impressions of the mixture of Creole, Cajun, and African-American cultures that later found their way into her fiction—impressions of the streets of New Orleans, the Creole resort on Grand Isle, and the small-town loves and hates of Cloutierville. Chopin's own increasingly free spirit—she engaged in unconventional activities such as smoking cigarettes and walking about the city alone—also colored her fictional portraits of women.

Resettled in St. Louis, Chopin's life soon underwent another shattering change when her mother died in June 1885. Both as a personal outlet and to supplement her family's income, Chopin began to write stories and poems. In 1889 she published a poem and two stories. By April 1890 she had completed her first novel, *At Fault*, a somewhat autobiographical story of a young Creole widow, set in both Louisiana and St. Louis. Impatient after the novel's rejection by *Belford's Monthly*, in September Chopin had it printed and distributed at her own expense. Although critical response was mixed, the appearance of this novel gained her the increased attention among the literary community that she desired. She also wrote a second novel in 1890, "Young Dr. Gosse," which was rejected by multiple publishers and which she eventually destroyed.

The following year Chopin produced sixteen short stories, a play, an essay, and a few translations from French. Although her short fiction was being published locally, she wanted her work to appear in nationally known eastern magazines. She made this breakthrough first with a series of children's stories, which began to appear in 1891 in *Youth's Companion* and *Harper's Young People*, followed by stories for adults: "At the 'Cadian Ball" in *Two Tales* (1892) and "A Visit to Avoyelles" and "Désirée's Baby" in *Vogue* (1893). Most of her writings from this period were well received, although the subject matter of a few offended would-be publishers. She quickly learned that the stories most apt to be accepted were her Louisiana local-color tales.

Chopin's annus mirabilis was 1894. In January the prestigious *Century* magazine finally published a story it had accepted three years earlier, "A No-Account Creole"; in September the *Atlantic* published a story, and the December issue of the *Century* included another. But the most important event of 1894 for Chopin was the release in March, by Houghton, Mifflin and Company, of her first collection of short stories, *Bayou Folk*. This volume met with immediate critical acclaim, and Chopin was catapulted from virtual anonymity to celebrity. She was frustrated, however, by what she perceived to be the shallowness of most of the reviews. She confided to her 1894 diary that the worthwhile ones "might be counted upon the fingers of one hand." Most saw her only as a local-colorist, praising her achievement with words such as "charming" and "quaint."

During the 1890s, as Chopin's fiction became increasingly well known, she herself moved into the center of the intellectual, literary, and social life of St. Louis. The Thursday evening gatherings at her home on middle-class Morgan Street became something of a salon, whose music, wit, and intellectual conversation particularly attracted avant-garde literati and journalists.

Originally, Chopin patterned her art after the genteel realism of William Dean Howells, but by the early 1890s her model was shifting to the bolder realism of Guy de Maupassant. Her fiction especially reflects Maupassant's influence after she began translating his tales, between 1894 and 1898. In November 1897 the Chicago firm Way & Williams published a second collection of Chopin's stories, *A Night in Acadie*. The stories in this volume, like those in *Bayou Folk*, are set in Louisiana, but they further push the boundaries of the local-color genre. The new stories depict various kinds of awakenings in its women characters, some of whom are more passionate than Chopin's earlier heroines and bolder in their insistence on freedom from traditional limitations. Critical response to this volume was generally favorable, if not as enthusiastic as that to *Bayou Folk*.

Shortly before the release of *A Night in Acadie*, in June 1897 Chopin began writing another novel, working during the next half-year on a manuscript that she called "A Solitary Soul" but that would eventually be published as *The Awakening*. In 1898 Way & Williams accepted this novel as well as a third collection of stories titled "A Vocation and a Voice." Awaiting the publication of the novel, in July 1898 Chopin wrote her most daring story of sexual passion, "The Storm."

In November 1898 Herbert S. Stone & Company acquired Chopin's story collection and novel and in April 1899 released *The Awakening*. The novel tells the story of Edna Pontellier, wife of a well-to-do Creole businessman and mother of two young sons. Edna experiences a sexual awakening that in turn leads her to seek emancipation from her society's restrictive roles for women—to seek, in short, to possess and govern her own life. In this novel Chopin fuses the awakening of Edna's passions with the sensuous setting on Grand Isle: "The voice of the sea is seductive; never ceasing, whispering, clamoring, murmuring. . . . The voice of the sea speaks to the soul. The touch of the sea is sensuous, enfolding the body in its soft, close embrace" and "the very passions themselves were aroused within her soul, swaying it, lashing it, as the waves daily beat upon her splendid body."

Despite favorable prepublication reviews and personal letters praising the novel, general critical response to *The Awakening* was harsh, at times scathing, both in St. Louis and nationally. Reviews tended to praise Chopin's artistry but deplore her subject matter. What reviewers found most disturbing was not Edna's infidelity itself, but her animal-like sensuality and the objectivity, even sympathy, with which the author treats her. The *St. Louis Globe-Democrat*, for example, declared the book unhealthy and "morbid," speculating that "the author herself would probably like nothing better than to 'tear it to pieces' . . . if only some other person had written it" (13 May 1899), and the *Providence Sunday Journal* dubbed it "gilded dirt" (4 June 1899).

Contemporaries of Chopin claimed that St. Louis libraries even banned the novel, although Emily Toth provides evidence refuting this story. In any case, the harsh reviews demoralized Chopin, as did the devastating news that Stone had decided not to publish the new short-story collection. Over the next two years, her creative output diminished, virtually ending by mid-1902. She was also troubled by financial difficulties and saddened by the deaths of family members and friends, and by 1903 Chopin herself was ailing, perhaps from diabetes or emphysema. Nevertheless, she was excited by the April 1904 opening of the St. Louis World's Fair, which she visited almost daily. One especially hot August day, Chopin returned from the fair exhausted and by midnight was suffering from severe head pain. Two days later she died, evidently from a cerebral hemorrhage.

After Chopin's death, her work was largely ignored for more than fifty years. By the late 1960s, however, a revival of interest in her fiction was emerging, which continued to develop over the next two decades. Her works are widely taught at universities and have been the subject of considerable critical attention. *The Awakening* has been translated into several languages. Chopin is now seen as a pioneer of both American realism and feminist consciousness. To a degree that was ahead of her time, she rejected both conservative and liberal didacticism and discarded traditional assumptions in an attempt to depict honestly and empathetically the inner life of women.

• The primary collection of Chopin's papers and manuscripts is at the Missouri Historical Society in St. Louis. *The Complete Works of Kate Chopin*, ed. Per Seyersted (1969), is the standard edition of her writings, supplemented by Emily Toth's edition of *A Vocation and A Voice: Stories by Kate Chopin* (1990). Two scholarly biographies are Seyersted, *Kate Chopin: A Critical Biography* (1969), and Toth, *Kate Chopin* (1990). Especially helpful to students of *The Awakening* are Margo Culley, ed., *The Awakening: An Authoritative Text, Biographical and Historical Contexts, Criticism*, 2d ed. (1994), and Bernard Koloski, ed., *Approaches to Teaching Chopin's "The Awakening"* (1988). Both of these collections and the biographies contain bibliographies of the several books and countless articles devoted to Chopin.

GAY BARTON

CHOTINER, Murray (4 Oct. 1909–30 Jan. 1974), attorney and Republican political consultant, was born in Pittsburgh, Pennsylvania, the son of Albert H. Chotiner, a small business entrepreneur, and Sarah Chass. In 1921 his family moved to California, where his father began development of a chain of theaters. Four years later Chotiner graduated from Los Angeles High School, where he starred in debate. He attended the University of California, Southern Branch (now University of California, Los Angeles), for one year, again participating on the debate team and in student government, then left in 1926 to attend Southwestern Law School. He received his LL.B. in 1929, the youngest graduate in the school's history to that date. Before taking and passing the California bar in 1931, Chotiner worked at Security First National Bank. In 1932 he married Phyllis Sylvia Levenson. They had one child before divorcing in 1955.

From the beginning of his career as a criminal lawyer in Newport Beach, Beverly Hills, and Los Angeles, Chotiner was a Republican party activist. By 1944 he had risen from precinct worker in the unsuccessful reelection campaign of President Herbert Hoover in 1932 to president of the statewide California Republican Assembly. Along the way, he ran unsuccessfully for the state assembly in 1938 and served as vice chair of the Los Angeles Republican Central Committee. Chotiner's major contributions in politics, however, were more as tactician than as party official. His career as a strategist and organizer began with his service as southern California manager for Earl Warren's 1942 gubernatorial campaign. In 1946 he served as campaign manager for Senator William F. Knowland's reelection campaign, and in the same year he branched out as an independent consultant, helping, among others, young Richard M. Nixon in his campaign against Democratic congressman Jerry Voorhis. Chotiner, paid a $500 retainer by a conservative businessmen's group (the "Committee of 100"), devised the strategy of branding Voorhis a Communist sympathizer by comparing his voting record to those of a number of extremely liberal Democrats in Congress. After defeating Voorhis, Nixon relied on Chotiner for political advice for the rest of his political career.

In the late 1940s Chotiner established one of the first important political public relations firms, Murray M. Chotiner and Associates (he had invented the middle initial *M* while a high school student). A skillful technician, he prepared himself by taking a course in the design of billboards and mastering details, including which colors and type of glue worked best on bumper stickers. Chotiner's sometimes ruthless tactical skills were, however, more significant in his success than these technical arts. His most notorious such contribution was as manager for Nixon's 1950 Senate campaign against incumbent Democrat Helen Gahagan Douglas. Perfecting the 1946 strategy that had worked against Voorhis, Chotiner came up with the idea of distributing, on a pink-colored sheet, a comparison of Douglas's voting record with that of the American Labor party's Vito Marcantonio. This portrayal of Douglas as "the pink lady," soft on communism, helped produce a landslide victory for Nixon, vaulting him to the forefront of rising stars in the national Republican party.

Having attended every Republican National Convention since 1936, Chotiner went to the 1952 convention as a member of the California delegation pledged to favorite son governor Warren. Known to his fellow delegates as Nixon's closest political associate, Chotiner played a key role in derailing Warren's chances for the vice presidential nomination by conducting and publicizing the results of an opinion poll that suggested the governor's potential weaknesses as a national candidate. After Nixon ultimately gained the vice presidential nomination on the ticket with Dwight D. Eisenhower, he made Chotiner his national campaign manager. When a slush-fund charge threatened to knock Nixon off the ticket in mid-campaign, Chotiner surreptitiously intercepted his candidate's hastily penned offer to resign and helped to orchestrate Nixon's nationally televised "Checkers speech," which defused the crisis and kept Nixon on the ticket.

Chotiner's association with Nixon continued during the latter's first vice presidential term. Chotiner oversaw, for example, Nixon's nationwide speaking tour during the 1954 congressional campaigns. But that relationship ended in 1956 as a result of charges brought by the Senate committee, chaired by John McClellan, investigating racketeering activities. Allegations that Chotiner had used his influence in the White House on behalf of unsavory clients, though never proved, destroyed for a time his usefulness to Nixon. That year Chotiner married Ruth Arnold; they had no children and divorced in 1963. For the next decade, during which he resumed his Los Angeles law practice, Chotiner played no visible role in Nixon's various campaigns, surfacing only briefly during the 1962 California gubernatorial campaign to urge Nixon not to attack the John Birch Society's Robert Welch. In 1965 he married Amalia Mueller; they had no children and divorced in 1971. In 1968 Chotiner reemerged as a key Nixon political operative, serving as an assistant to campaign manager John Mitchell, with responsibilities as national liaison to fourteen state party organizations. After winning the presidency, Nixon wanted to appoint Chotiner as chairman of the Republican National Committee, but strong opposition from then-chairman Ray Bliss and others—largely because of Chotiner's reputation for questionably aggressive political tactics—caused Nixon to withdraw the proposal. Instead Nixon appointed Chotiner general counsel in the Office of the Special Representative for Trade Negotiations. By 1970, however, Chotiner was back at Nixon's side as special counsel, in which capacity he helped Vice President Spiro Agnew devise and carry out a sustained, brutal verbal assault against "radiclib" Democratic senators during the 1970 congressional elections. In 1971 he married Nancy Michel; they had no children.

Ironically, given Chotiner's reputation as the "dark presence" in the Nixon entourage, he had left White House service before the Watergate episode and the revelations of 1972–1973 that ultimately brought political ruin upon his longtime chief. Repelled by what he considered the arrogance of the younger men who had emerged around Nixon, such as H. R. Haldeman and John Ehrlichman, Chotiner retreated to a Washington, D.C., law practice in 1971. His only apparent connection to the "dirty tricks" related to Watergate was his hiring of two special agents to pose as reporters and provide daily reports on the 1972 Democratic presidential campaign of George McGovern. Chotiner died in Washington, D.C., from complications resulting from injuries sustained in an automobile accident.

• Chotiner did not publish memoirs, nor did he produce other significant writings. Brief mention of his personal background and coverage of his political activities appears in most major biographies of Richard M. Nixon; the best coverage is in Roger Morris, *Richard M. Nixon: The Rise of an American Politician* (1990). Also informative is William L. Roper, "Nixon's Man to See," *Nation*, 2 July 1955, pp. 4–7. Detailed obituaries are in the *Los Angeles Times* and the *New York Times*, both 31 Jan. 1974.

GARY W. REICHARD

CHOTZINOFF, Samuel (4 July 1889–9 Feb. 1964), music critic, author, and pianist, was born Shmul Chotzinoff in Vitebsk, Russia, the son of Moyshe Bear, a retail merchant, and Rachel Traskenoff. A promising piano student from the age of ten, Samuel emigrated with his parents to the United States at age seventeen, where he continued his piano studies with Oscar Shack at Columbia University. He left Columbia in 1911 without receiving a diploma (although he would receive an honorary doctorate from the university in 1947).

In 1909 Chotzinoff began what would prove to be a highly successful career as an accompanist. He was "discovered" by accident by the New York drama critics as a result of a botched piano performance during a Broadway play. The play, a moderate box-office success titled *The Concert*, starred Leo Dietrichstein in the role of a struggling pianist. To cover for the nonmusical actor, the producers hired Chotzinoff to play behind the scenes the notes that Dietrichstein would appear to be playing onstage, using a specially rigged concert grand whose keys made no sound when depressed. When Chotzinoff's sudden illness made it necessary for a substitute to play the behind-the-scenes music, Dietrichstein's timing was thrown off, causing him to keep "playing" well after the backstage piano had fallen silent. The ruse was thereby exposed, and almost overnight Chotzinoff found himself renowned.

Violinist Efrem Zimbalist was the first to take advantage of Chotzinoff's newfound celebrity. A Russian emigrant exactly Chotzinoff's age, Zimbalist retained Chotzinoff as his accompanist from 1910 through 1917. Two years later another young violinist, Jascha Heifetz, retained Chotzinoff's talents and eventually became his brother-in-law when Chotzinoff married Heifetz's sister Pauline in 1925. Several years later the Heifetz-Chotzinoff relationship was momentarily strained when Chotzinoff, by then the music critic for the *New York World*, heavily criticized Heifetz's playing of the Beethoven "Kreutzer" Sonata. "He was sore as the devil," Chotzinoff told friends afterward, "but I told Jascha that I can only review his concerts as his critic and not as his brother-in-law."

Chotzinoff's tenure as a music critic began at the *World* in 1925, where he succeeded Deems Taylor upon the latter's recommendation, and continued at the *New York Post* from 1934 until 1941. His reputation as a critic, coupled with his inner-circle status as Heifetz's brother-in-law, led to a series of close friendships with many of the musical celebrities of that era. It was one of those friendships that prompted David Sarnoff, the founder and chairman of the board of the Radio Corporation of America, to commission Chotzinoff to persuade the renowned conductor Arturo Toscanini, then living in semiretirement in Italy, to return to New York to conduct a new symphony orchestra on the National Broadcasting Company radio network.

Although few gave Chotzinoff any chance of persuading the great conductor to overcome his dislike of radio (Toscanini had nothing but contempt for the limited dynamic ranges of radio broadcasts and phonograph recordings), Chotzinoff eventually prevailed and in the process managed to introduce the legendary maestro to a vast new audience in the Americas. The success of that venture led Sarnoff to retain Chotzinoff's services as a music consultant to the NBC network, of which he became general music director in 1948. Three years later, in the wake of the explosive growth of television as a new entertainment medium, Chotzinoff spearheaded a series of televised operas for NBC. One of the first of these televised productions was the 1951 world premiere of Gian Carlo Menotti's *Amahl and the Night Visitors*, which Chotzinoff had commissioned as NBC musical director.

Chotzinoff retired from his NBC post in 1955, when he reached the then-mandatory retirement age of sixty-five. He continued his writing career, turning out a well-received biography of Beethoven and a book of reminiscences about his friend Toscanini. Chotzinoff was working on his memoirs when he died in New York City.

• The memoirs of Samuel Chotzinoff were published posthumously under the title *Days at the Morn* (1964). His other books include *Eroica* (1955), a biography of Beethoven; a book of reminiscences titled *A Lost Paradise* (1955); and another posthumously published autobiographical work, *A Little Night Music* (1964). By far his best-known book also proved to be his most controversial: *Toscanini: An Intimate Portrait* (1956), which was published while the legendary maestro was still living. In it Chotzinoff revealed intimate details of Toscanini's raging temper, arbitrary treatments of friends, and contemptuous assessments of contemporary composers and conductors. B. H. Haggin, whose career as a critic partly overlapped Chotzinoff's, condemned him in a subsequent book, *Conversations with Toscanini* (1959), for having violated "the privacy that Toscanini had expected a friend to preserve."

JAMES A. DRAKE

CHOUTEAU, Auguste Pierre (9 May 1786–25 Dec. 1838), fur trader and Indian diplomat, was born in St. Louis, Missouri, the son of Jean Pierre Chouteau, a fur trader and one of the founders of St. Louis, and Pelagie Kiersereau. He attended the United States Military Academy at West Point from 17 July 1804 until 20 June 1806 and became an ensign in the Second United States Infantry. After serving briefly as aide to General James Wilkinson, he resigned from the military on 13 January 1807.

In June 1807 Chouteau accompanied the expedition commanded by Nathaniel Pryor that attempted to return the Mandan chief, Sheheke, to his people on the Missouri River in what is now North Dakota. Sheheke had accepted the invitation of the Lewis and Clark Expedition to travel to the East, and Chouteau saw his return as an opportunity to trade with the Mandans. The expedition met near disaster, however, in September 1807 when it reached a village of the Arikaras on the Missouri, south of the Mandans. The Arikaras were at war with the Mandans and would not let the chief pass. A battle ensued, several of Chouteau's men were killed, and the expedition turned back. In 1809, as a member of the St. Louis Missouri Fur Company, Chouteau accompanied another expedition to the mouth of the Knife River as the Mandan chief was again escorted homeward.

During the War of 1812, Chouteau served as a captain in the Missouri Territorial Militia, but in 1815 he returned to trading in partnership with Julius DeMun. The two outfitted an expedition to the headwaters of the Arkansas River, left St. Louis in September 1815, and reached the Rocky Mountains by December. Moving south into Spanish territory, they made contact with authorities in Taos and Santa Fe and were arrested on 1 June 1817. The Spanish held Chouteau and DeMun in jail for forty-eight days and then confiscated their furs and other property estimated at more than $30,000 in value.

Returning to Missouri by the end of 1817, Chouteau soon entered the family business of trading with the Osage Indians. In 1802 Chouteau's father had established a trading post for that purpose on the east side of the Grand (Neosho) River near present-day Salina, Oklahoma. After the manager of the post was killed in 1821, Chouteau moved there to take charge in person. Two years later, he bought the trading house of Brand

and Barbour on the Verdigris River near its mouth on the Arkansas and within a short time became the leading merchant in what was known as the Three Forks, the area in which the Grand and Verdigris joined the Arkansas River. Chouteau bought trade goods from St. Louis, traded them for furs brought by Indians to the Three Forks, and shipped the furs to New Orleans. In 1824 he sold 38,000 pounds of furs in the Crescent City. As the fur trade played out because of the depletion of the animal population, Chouteau depended increasingly on supplying the Indians in return for their annuities from the government. He earned such a reputation for equitable transactions that Sam Houston, who lived in the Three Forks area from 1829 to 1832, recommended him for appointment as an agent to the Osages.

Chouteau enjoyed the life of a frontier aristocrat at his residence on the Grand River, a large two-story log house with a piazza. Washington Irving visited Chouteau in 1832 and recorded his arrival as follows: "Old negro runs to open gate—mouth from ear to ear—Group of Indians round trees in court yard roasting venison—Horses tether[ed] near—negroes run to shake hand and take horses. . . . Horses, dogs of all kinds—hens flying and cackling, wild turkeys, tamed geese. Piazza with buffalo skin thrown over railing" (M. James, *The Raven* [1929], p. 89). Chouteau had married his cousin Sophie Labbadie in St. Louis in August 1814 and had a family of six children there, but at his home on the Grand he also had an Osage wife named Rosalie who bore him several children. Irving noted that a supper of venison, roast beef, bread, cakes, and coffee was served by the "half breed sister of Mr. Chouteau's concubine" (James, *Raven*, p. 90).

During the mid-1830s "Colonel" A. P. Chouteau, as he was generally called to distinguish him from his uncle Auguste Chouteau of St. Louis, expanded his trading house business in what is now Oklahoma and became an Indian diplomat. He planned a chain of posts reaching from the Three Forks to the Plains Indians country and built at Camp Holmes on the Canadian River in present-day Hughes County in 1835, at present-day Lexington on the Canadian River in 1837, and near present-day Fort Sill in 1837. In 1834 Chouteau accompanied an expedition commanded by Colonel Henry Leavenworth (who became ill and was replaced by Colonel Henry Dodge) to meet chiefs of the Wichita, Comanche, and Kiowa tribes at the Wichita Village on the North Fork of the Red River in present-day Kiowa County. The following year, due in part to Chouteau's influence, the Comanches and Wichitas signed treaties with the United States. In 1837 Chouteau received an appointment from the War Department to visit the Kiowas and Apaches of the western plains, and he convinced both to send delegations to Fort Gibson and sign a treaty there. G. Montfort Stokes, U.S. agent to the Cherokees, considered Chouteau better acquainted with Indian tribes and manners than any man west of the Mississippi River.

Chouteau died at his residence on the Grand River and was buried with military honors at Fort Gibson. In spite of his success as a fur trader and his important services as an Indian diplomat, he was deeply in debt at the time of his death, and creditors soon seized much of his property.

• Joseph B. Thoburn and Muriel H. Wright, *Oklahoma: A History of the State and Its People* (4 vols., 1929), is very helpful on Chouteau's entire career. His trading post business is detailed in Wayne Morris, "Auguste Pierre Chouteau: Merchant Prince at the Three Forks of the Arkansas," *Chronicles of Oklahoma* 48 (Summer 1970): 155–63. Information on his expeditions with the Mandan chief is in Donald Jackson, ed., *Letters of the Lewis and Clark Expedition with Related Documents, 1783–1854* (2 vols., 1962). A detailed account of his misadventure with the Spanish in New Mexico is found in *Annals of Congress*, 15th Cong., 1st sess. (1818), vol. 2, pp. 1960–66. For the story of Chouteau's father, see William E. Foley and C. David Rice, *The First Chouteaus: River Barons of Early St. Louis* (1983).

RANDOLPH B. CAMPBELL

CHOUTEAU, Jean Pierre (10 Oct. 1758–10 July 1849), fur trader and Indian agent, was born in New Orleans, Louisiana, the son of Pierre LaClede and Marie Therese Chouteau. In accordance with French law, Jean Pierre Chouteau used his mother's surname. Pierre, as he was most widely known, moved to St. Louis with his mother in 1764. Little is known of his education, formal or informal. Taking advantage of St. Louis's position as the gateway to American, French, and Spanish commercial activities among the Native Americans in the trans-Mississippi West, Pierre and his half brother Auguste Chouteau became deeply involved in the Indian fur trade there.

In 1794 the Chouteaus obtained a charter from the regional Spanish government that gave them exclusive rights to trade a variety of supplies with the Osage Indians in what is today Missouri. Pierre Chouteau lived among the Osage at Fort Carondelet in western Missouri. The brothers held the charter until 1802, when the Spanish awarded the contract to Manuel Lisa, a recent arrival to St. Louis. When the Americans assumed control over the region as a result of the Louisiana Purchase in 1803, all Spanish contracts were nullified. At this time Pierre Chouteau reestablished his relations with the Osage Indians and was officially designated by President Thomas Jefferson as Indian agent for that tribe. Chouteau was so influential among the Osage that he persuaded 3,000 members of the tribe to migrate with him to Salina, a western trading jurisdiction of his in Present-day northeastern Oklahoma.

Pierre Chouteau's most ambitious trading venture began in 1809 when he and eight others organized the St. Louis Missouri Fur Company (commonly referred to as the Missouri Fur Company). The list of investors included such notables as his half brother Auguste, Lisa, and explorers Meriwether Lewis and William Clark. The investors had intended to trade with the Native Americans of the Pacific Northwest, a region that was then dominated by the British North West Company operating from Canada. In addition to their roles as private entrepreneurs in pursuit of profit, the investors also served as paradiplomats in the American effort to win the allegiance of the Native Americans from the British traders. In 1809 Lewis, the territorial governor, awarded the Missouri Fur Company and Pierre Chouteau, as its agent, a contract to return to his village a Mandan chief, Shahaka, who had been persuaded to visit Washington, D.C.

Owing to its lack of capital, men, and supplies, the Missouri Fur Company did not prosper, however, and was dissolved in 1814. Chouteau continued to trade with a variety of local Indian tribes on a smaller scale in the region of Missouri and Oklahoma until 1820, when he retired to an estate he established on the outskirts of St. Louis.

Pierre Chouteau married Pelagie Kiersereau in 1783. Although it is unknown what happened to his first wife, in 1794 he married Brigitte Saucier, with whom he had eight children. His eldest son, Auguste Pierre, attended the U.S. Military Academy at West Point, and his second son, Pierre, Jr., went on to a distinguished career with the American Fur Company and later was the founder of the Baltimore and Ohio Railroad.

Chouteau remained active in his old age, serving as host to visiting dignitaries such as the famous French military figure the marquis de Lafayette, who was his guest in 1825. He died at his St. Louis estate. Pierre Chouteau, notable today chiefly for having been a successful Indian trader and western fur trader, also became one of the most prominent citizens of a city that through its history has boasted many nationally and internationally prominent residents.

• References to Jean Pierre Chouteau can be found in the Chouteau Family Papers and the Pierre Chouteau Collection at the Missouri Historical Society–Jefferson Memorial, St. Louis. Also see Thomas James, *Three Years among the Indians and Mexicans*, ed. Walter B. Douglas (1916), and Frederick Billon, *Annals of St. Louis in Its Territorial Days from 1804 to 1821* (1888).

JEROME O. STEFFEN

CHOUTEAU, Pierre, Jr. (19 Jan. 1789–6 Sept. 1865), merchant and financier, was born in St. Louis, Missouri, the son of Jean Pierre Chouteau, a trader and Indian agent, and Pelagie Kiersereau. He was familiarly known as Cadet, meaning second son. The Chouteaus were the most prominent family in St. Louis, the original founders of the town, and the very heart of its business and social life. Pierre Chouteau, Jr., gained only a rudimentary academic education in this frontier town, learning to speak and read English in addition to his native French. More important, he apprenticed in the fur trade from the age of fifteen on, learning the business that was the economic foundation of St. Louis and the best chance for profits on the early western frontier.

Chouteau served first as a clerk in his uncle Auguste Chouteau's office before branching out on his own, in 1807, to trade with the Osage Indians. From 1810 to 1812 he supervised his family's interest in the Dubuque, Iowa, lead mines. In 1813 he went into partnership with his brother-in-law, Bartholomew Berthold, selling hardware, groceries, and dry goods from a store housed in St. Louis's first brick building. The Chouteaus typically consolidated their economic power by making alliances within the family. In similar vein, also in 1813, Chouteau married his first cousin, Emilie Gratiot; they would raise five children.

The partnership of Berthold and Chouteau quickly expanded into the fur business, sending traders to the Otoes and Pawnees in 1814 and backing, with considerable financial loss, an 1819 expedition to the Rocky Mountains led by the veteran trader Manuel Lisa. The fur trade was an intensely contested business, and Berthold and Chouteau found themselves challenged at every turn. But by the early 1820s they were powerfully placed in the trade on the lower reaches of the Missouri River serving the various bands of the Dakotas, the Poncas, Omahas, Otoes, Pawnees, and Osages. To the north the Columbia Fur Company, led by the dynamic Scot Kenneth McKenzie, was the dominant force.

Berthold and Chouteau's principal early competition came from the firm led by Jean P. Cabanné, who was also a relative. This competition was eliminated when Cabanné was incorporated into Berthold and Chouteau in 1823. But more powerful opponents quickly appeared in an ever-widening fur trade. In 1824 Missouri entrepreneur William H. Ashley devised a practical system for bringing beaver pelts from the Rocky Mountains using the Platte overland route. A more immediate challenge came from John Jacob Astor and the American Fur Company, which opened a Western Department in St. Louis in 1822. That same year, Berthold and Chouteau, along with their new partner Bernard Pratte, entered into an agreement with the American Fur Company to provide them with bison robes and deerskins in return for provisions and trade goods. This arrangement proved to be highly profitable, and the stage was set for Chouteau's rise to prominence in the fur business.

On 20 December 1826 Berthold, Chouteau, and Pratte, by then known as B. Pratte and Co., signed another agreement with Astor designating them the sole western agent of the American Fur Company. The American Fur Company would provide the trade goods and cover the transportation and insurance costs; B. Pratte and Co. would provide the furs. Chouteau became director of the Western Department with control over the trading posts and most of the fur trade on the Missouri below the mouth of the Big Sioux River. In a similar agreement, made in 1827, the Columbia Fur Company became the Upper Missouri Outfit of the American Fur Company with jurisdiction above the Big Sioux River.

In 1829 Chouteau reluctantly—for it was a risky business—entered the competition for Rocky Mountain beaver pelts. Each year for the next ten years Chouteau sent expeditions to the mountains. As he had anticipated, this endeavor brought only financial loss, but he felt obliged to persevere in order to challenge rivals who in turn were competing for the more reliable robe trade of the Great Plains.

One major achievement during these years was Chouteau's sponsorship of steamboat navigation on the upper Missouri. On 17 June 1832 the first steamboat made it to Fort Union at the mouth of the Yellowstone River, so revolutionizing the scale and speed of transportation on the Missouri. Chouteau was on board and he was widely praised for his promotion of this innovation.

In 1834 the ailing John Jacob Astor sold the Western Department, including the Upper Missouri Outfit, to B. Pratte and Co. The company was now called Pratte, Chouteau and Co. (Berthold having died in 1831), and after Bernard Pratte's death in 1836 the company was again reorganized, this time under the name Pierre Chouteau Jr. and Co. It was popularly known, however, as the American Fur Company. From this time on until it was sold in 1865, and despite attempts by rivals to intervene, Chouteau's company dominated the Missouri fur trade.

Chouteau parlayed his profits and influence from the fur business into many other endeavors. Early in his career, in 1820, he was elected delegate to the constitutional convention of Missouri as an advocate for the continuance of slavery. He was also a major supplier of treaty goods to the Indians, and he exerted considerable influence on the details of treaties. After 1843 he became involved in the Missouri iron business, in both mining and production sectors. And in 1851 he was one of the original incorporators of the Ohio and Mississippi Railroad. Through hard work, shrewd (some would say unscrupulous) dealings, and carefully cultivated connections, Chouteau became one of the leading financiers in the United States.

Chouteau yielded operational control of his fur trade empire to his son Charles in 1849. His health, never good, deteriorated rapidly. In 1859 he became blind, and in 1862 Emilie died. Three years later he died and was buried alongside his wife in St. Louis. He left behind an estate worth several million dollars.

• The papers of Pierre Chouteau, Jr., are housed in the Missouri Historical Society, St. Louis. The best single source is Janet Le Compte, "Pierre Chouteau, Junior," in *The Mountain Men and the Fur Trade of the Far West*, vol. 9, ed. Le Roy R. Hafen (1972). Chouteau is also a central figure in David J. Wishart, *The Fur Trade of the American West, 1807–1840* (1992), and John E. Sunder, *The Fur Trade on the Upper Missouri, 1840–1865* (1965). The Chouteau family in general is the subject of William E. Foley and C. David Rice, *The First Chouteaus: River Barons of Early St. Louis* (1983).

DAVID J. WISHART

CHOUTEAU, René Auguste (7? Sept. 1749–24 Feb. 1829), pioneer in the western fur trade and explorer, was born in New Orleans, Louisiana, where he was baptized on 9 September, 1749, the son of René Auguste Chouteau and Marie Thérèse Bourgeois. His father was a French immigrant who operated a tavern in New Orleans. The marriage of his parents broke up shortly after his birth, and his father returned to France. His teenage mother proved herself resourceful and eventually went to live with a prominent fur trader, Pierre Laclède, in 1757. In view of Catholic church policies she did not obtain a divorce from her first husband. Laclède had come to New Orleans from France in 1755, and in subsequent years he and Marie Thérèse had four children. Laclède was extremely fond also of Chouteau and remained very close to him throughout his life. When in 1762 French officials awarded Laclède a monopoly of the fur trade in the Missouri region, he took his young stepson along as his assistant in an exploring party on the Mississippi River to establish a new trading post. Even at an early age Chouteau revealed great business acumen and common sense.

As they made their way into the wilderness the political situation changed significantly. Under the Treaty of Paris concluded by France and England in 1763, the French ceded the territory east of the Mississippi River to Great Britain. That was another inducement for Laclède to be close to his business ventures, and he moved his family from New Orleans to the Illinois country late in 1763. Within a month he had established the first of several forts on the west bank of the Mississippi River, thus laying the foundations for the future site of St. Louis. In February 1764 Laclède put Chouteau in charge of thirty men to build a new village at the site. Laclède sought to honor the reigning king, Louis XV, by naming the settlement after his patron saint, Louis IX.

Chouteau and Laclède continued their close association while they built one of the major fur trading ventures in the Mississippi Valley. By the time Laclède died on 20 June 1778, Chouteau was a major figure in the firm and had directed many innovative policies. He was especially adept at developing good relations with Indian tribes, particularly the Osages in what is now Missouri. Between 1794 and 1802 he monopolized that trade and became one of the wealthiest individuals in the region. Meanwhile, he had married Marie Thérèse Carré in 1786, and the union led to seven children.

When the United States acquired Louisiana in 1803, Chouteau revealed himself to be very adaptable, and he took an active role in the organization of the new territory. The new governor appointed him as a justice on the first territorial court, and he served as a colonel in the St. Louis militia. When St. Louis was incorporated as a town in 1809, Chouteau became chairman of the board of trustees. His diplomatic skills with Indian tribes gave him considerable political influence, and in 1815 he accepted an appointment as a U.S. Indian commissioner. In that capacity he conducted extensive negotiations with the Sioux, Iowa, Sauk, and Fox tribes. Throughout this period he continued to expand his fur trading business, which by 1820 had grown to be one of the largest in the United States. He himself was one of the wealthiest individuals west of the Mississippi River. Although his operations were extensive, he spent most of his time in St. Louis, from which he supervised his far-flung business operations.

As in many business firms during the nineteenth century, family ties were extremely important in the Chouteau enterprises. He worked very closely with his half-brothers. One of his most trusted associates was Jean Pierre Chouteau, who extended the fur trade into Oklahoma where in 1796 he established the first permanent white settlement, in Salina. In 1809 he founded his own firm, the St. Louis Missouri Fur Trade Company. René Chouteau died in St. Louis. Jean Pierre Chouteau's two sons, Auguste Pierre Chouteau and Pierre Chouteau, also were active in the fur trade but soon branched out into railroads, mining, banking, and rolling mills. By the time of the Civil War the Chouteaus were one of the richest families in the West.

Chouteau is significant as a pioneer business entrepreneur and explorer in the eighteenth- and nineteenth-century American West. During his life he transcended French, British, and American ownership of the Mississippi Valley to build a great business dynasty. He was instrumental in the development of St. Louis as a major business entrepôt through his contacts with Native Americans, Eastern merchants, and European importers. As a major business executive, he also reflected a strong sense of civic duty and responsibility, as evidenced by his public service and his role as first citizen of St. Louis during the early years of its growth.

• The Chouteau manuscripts are in the Missouri Historical Society, St. Louis. See also John Francis McDermott, "Laclède and the Chouteaus: Fantasies and Fact," unpublished manuscript in the John Francis McDermott Mississippi Valley Research Collection, Lovejoy Library, Southern Illinois University at Edwardsville. The best secondary work is William E. Foley and C. David Rice, *The First Chouteaus: River Barons of Early St. Louis* (1983). The definitive genealogy is Mary B. Cunningham and Jeanne C. Blythe, *The Founding Family of St. Louis* (1977). Also useful are John Francis McDermott, ed., *The Early Histories of St. Louis* (1952) and *The French in the Mississippi Valley* (1965), and J. Thomas Scharf, *History of St. Louis City and County, from Its Earliest Periods to the Present Day* (1883).

GERALD D. NASH

CHOVET, Abraham (25 May 1704–24 Mar. 1790), anatomist and surgeon, was born in London, England, the son of David Chovet, a well-to-do wine merchant of Swiss Huguenot origin. His mother's name is unknown. Chovet was apprenticed to Peter Gougoux Lamarque, a "foreign brother" of the Company of Barber-Surgeons of London. After the expiration of his seven-year indenture in 1727, Chovet went to France, where he attended the lectures and dissections of J. B. Winslow in Paris and learned to make anatomical preparations of wax. There is no record that he received the degree of doctor of medicine at this time, but he may have received that degree in 1759. His name appears in the "List of Promotions" in the *Gentleman's Magazine* of that year, with the designation "a Dr of physick," as though that was the "promotion" he received. In any case, Chovet was frequently thereafter called "physician" or "doctor of physic," and he signed and dated the title page of one of his books as "Abra: Chovet, M.D. Jamaica—1762" (Samuel Auguste André David Tissot, *Avis au People sur sa Santé* [1763], College of Physicians of Philadelphia). He married in England (wife's name unknown) and had one child.

Returning to England with a number of natural and artificial anatomical preparations, Chovet offered a course of lectures to laymen and medical students. For their guidance he prepared a *Syllabus, or Index, of All the Parts That Enter the Composition of the Human Body* (1732), which was a topical outline of the subject and of the contents of the twelve lectures of the course. The next year he sought, unsuccessfully, the support or approval of the Royal Society of London for making improved models, in which the arteries and veins should be made of glass, "with a red liquor in imitation of Blood to circulate thro' them." Chovet was admitted a foreign brother of the Company of Barber-Surgeons in 1734, and that same year he was appointed demonstrator in anatomy in the company. In 1735 he was reappointed demonstrator and also was made a liveryman (full member) of the company. He resigned the teaching post in 1736, and after 1740 his name no longer appeared on the roll of the company.

Little is known of Chovet's life in the ensuing thirty years. Apparently for a time he traveled around England lecturing on anatomy. There is a record of his demonstrations in Manchester and Bury in Lancashire in 1742. George W. Norris (*Early History of Medicine in Philadelphia* [1886]) said that he went to Barbados in 1744. He was in Antigua in 1747, when he signed a petition there on behalf of a Protestant school in Ireland. In 1759 he was in Jamaica, where he lived until about 1771, when, fleeing a slave uprising, he moved to Philadelphia, where he remained until his death.

In Philadelphia, Chovet organized a course of lectures on anatomy. His inaugural lecture, delivered on 30 November 1774, was attended by the governor, the trustees and faculty of the College of Philadelphia, the clergy, physicians, medical students, and "a considerable number of the most respectable inhabitants of this city" (*Pennsylvania Gazette*, 30 Nov. 1774). The course made use of his anatomical collection and was repeated for at least the next three years. So successful and well attended were they that Chovet completed an amphitheater to his house in January 1778 in which to deliver his lectures.

Chovet's anatomical collection attracted the attention of visitors to the city. John Adams made a detailed list of its contents in 1774 and described it as "most admirable" and "more exquisite" than the collection at the Pennsylvania Hospital. The marquis de Chastellux in 1780 pronounced it superior to the collection at Bologna. George Washington was taken there during the Constitutional Convention in 1787 but offered no comment. In addition to anatomical specimens, Chovet owned "a notable and rare collection of books."

Chovet's medical practice, according to Benjamin Rush, was old-fashioned, following the tenets of Hermann Boerhaave, professor of institutes of medicine at the University of Leiden, with scant attention to recent discoveries and new theories, such as those of William Cullen of Edinburgh. Moreover, unlike other physicians in the city, Chovet did not keep a shop but gave his patients prescriptions to take to a local pharmacist. During the American Revolution his sentiments were Tory. Though he remained on friendly personal terms with some rebels, like Christopher Marshall, whose library he saved during the British occupation of Philadelphia, and gave his parole to the new state on 1 May 1777, he delighted to discomfit the Whigs with witty and sarcastic sallies. Despite a habit of spicing conversation with profanity, he was amusing and entertaining and scurried about from one tea table to another during the war, retelling reports, rumors, and jokes to cheer his Loyalist hostesses. None of this bothered his patients, who were said to be principally rich Quakers like Henry Drinker, or Tories like Mrs. Joseph Galloway. But all these were reasons why he was not popular with his professional colleagues. It may be significant that though he was one of the original twelve senior fellows of the College of Physicians in 1787, his name appears last in the manuscript minutes, almost as if his nomination was an afterthought.

By 1785 Chovet, now past eighty years old, no longer lectured regularly. His wife died that year, and he thought of disposing of his collection. "Some public spirited gentlemen of the Town of Boston" considered buying it for the new medical school of Harvard College, but Chovet's price of 1,200 guineas was too steep, and the gentlemen would not "higgle" over it. After Chovet's death the collection was opened to public view for a time and then was offered to the Pennsylvania Hospital, whose managers purchased it in 1793, paying Chovet's daughter an annuity of £30. His library was sold at auction in 1794.

As cataloged by the hospital in 1794, the collection contained eight wax representations of the human body and its interior parts, forty-four wet preparations of different parts (such as lungs, liver, kidney, heart, intestines), and sixty-three dried preparations—115 pieces in all. Hailed as a notable addition to the scientific resources of the city, the collection was used by the professors of anatomy and physiology of the University of Pennsylvania for a quarter of a century. In 1824 the hospital gave it to the university, where it was displayed and studied at the Wistar Institute until 1888, when a fire destroyed the building and most of its contents.

Chovet and his collection enjoyed a reputation beyond their place and time. Rees's *Cyclopaedia* mentioned both appreciatively in 1810, a French surgeon in 1827 inquired about the collection, and Heber Chase's *The Medical Student's Guide*, a handbook prepared for medical students in 1849, named Chovet as one of five persons "whose names deserve the most enduring celebrity" in Philadelphia. No less than for his anatomical museum Chovet was remembered as "a real eccentric." For many years Philadelphia physicians and antiquarians were delighted to quote examples of his wit and humor, both sometimes sharp, such as his assertion that "that physician was an impostor, who did not live until he was eighty." He died in Philadelphia.

• William Shaw Miller, "Abraham Chovet: An Early Teacher of Anatomy in Philadelphia," *Anatomical Record* 5 (1911): 147–71, slightly extended in *Annals of Medical History* 8 (1926): 375–93, is the principal account of Chovet. Among important contemporary or near-contemporary sources are "An Account of the Late Dr. Abraham Chovet," *Columbian Magazine* 3 (1790): 138–39; marquis de Chastellux, *Travels in North America in the Years 1780, 1781 and 1782*, ed. Howard C. Rice, Jr., vol. 1 (1963), pp. 146–47; Benjamin Rush, *Autobiography*, ed. George W. Corner (1948), pp. 81–82; James L. Whitehead, ed., "Autobiography of Peter Stephen Du Ponceau," *Pennsylvania Magazine of History and Biography* 63 (1939): 323–29; and John F. Watson, *Annals of Philadelphia, and Pennsylvania in the Olden Time*, vol. 2 (1881), pp. 380–81. Other information must be gleaned from various contemporary sources—newspapers, diaries (e.g., Elizabeth Drinker, Grace Growdon Galloway, Ezra Stiles), and journals of travel (e.g., Baron Ludwig Von Closen, Baron Cromot DuBourg, Johann David Schoepf). Evidence of Chovet's lectures in Manchester, Bury, and other Lancashire towns in 1742 is from W. Brockbank and F. Kenworthy, eds., *The Diary of Richard Kay, 1716–1751, of Baldingston, Near Bury: A Lancashire Doctor* (1968), p. 52. The purchase of Chovet's specimens by the Pennsylvania Hospital is recorded in the managers' minutes. The collection is listed in *A Catalogue of the Books Belonging to the Medical Library of the Pennsylvania Hospital* (1790). Some pieces from the collection apparently survived the Wistar Institute fire; a few are in that institution and others are in private possession.

WHITFIELD J. BELL, JR.

CHOYNSKI, Joseph Bartlett (8 Nov. 1868–25 Jan. 1943), boxer, was born in San Francisco, California, the son of Isadore Choynski, a Jewish writer and book store owner, and Harriet Ashin. Although both of Choynski's parents were intellectuals, and writers such as Mark Twain and Bret Harte were frequent houseguests, Joe was a rebellious youth who dropped out of high school. He preferred physical activity and took jobs that built his strength, working as an apprentice blacksmith and in a candy factory, where his job was to roll 300-pound barrels of sugar to wherever needed. He joined the Golden Gate Athletic Club and became an outstanding amateur boxer.

Choynski was 5′11″ tall and weighed between 160 and 170 pounds. In those times, boxers of that size were classified as heavyweights, and it was inevitable that Choynski would become the rival of his fellow San Franciscan and future heavyweight champion James J. Corbett. Choynski became a professional in 1888 and his first major battle was with Corbett in a famous fight on a barge near Benicia, in the bay. Choynski wore driving gloves and Corbett donned five-ounce boxing gloves to protect his hands. The result was a thrilling battle in which both men suffered great punishment, Corbett winning by a clean knockout in the twenty-seventh round.

In 1890 Choynski became the first noted American boxer to fight in Australia. There he won two fights but was twice stopped by the heavier Joe Goddard, with Choynski having to quit both fights because of exhaustion after knocking his opponent down many times. The trip was very profitable financially, however, and Choynski returned to the United States with $28,000 in his pocket. Under the management of Charles E. "Parson" Davies, Choynski ran up a string of successes including a knockout of the well-known black heavyweight George Godfrey at Coney Island. In 1893 Choynski toured the country with another black heavyweight, the famous Peter Jackson, with whom he gave sparring exhibitions.

In 1894 Choynski fought another future heavyweight champion, Bob Fitzsimmons, in Boston. Choynski floored Fitzsimmons with a left hook in the third round, whereupon the bell was rung prematurely to end the round. Fitzsimmons recovered and had Choynski on the verge of a knockout in the fifth round when the fight was halted by the police and declared a draw.

In 1896 Choynski knocked out Jim Hall and fought inconclusive short battles with Kid McCoy and Tom Sharkey. He then fought the Irish heavyweight champion Peter Maher at New York City, at first giving Maher a bad beating, but losing by a surprise knockout in the sixth round. In 1897, in San Francisco, Choynski fought still another future heavyweight champion, Jim Jeffries, to a twenty-round draw. The much larger Jeffries later admitted that he received the hardest blow of his career, one that broke his nose and wedged his lips between his teeth.

Choynski was a robust man, very strong for his size, which was an important factor in his ability to cope with opponents who were many pounds heavier. He was a powerful puncher, often setting a faster pace than his opponents could match, and a skillful boxer, almost able to equal Corbett's left jab, speedy footwork, and ability to dodge blows. He was ruggedly handsome, friendly, and often called "Chrysanthemum Joe" because of his large mop of blonde hair.

In his later years in the ring, Choynski had many victories, including another knockout of Jim Hall, a trouncing of Goddard in a no-decision contest in Philadelphia, a knockout of Maher in 1903 and, most notably, a three-round knockout of future heavyweight champion Jack Johnson in Galveston, Texas, in 1901. It was illegal for a white man and a black man to fight in Texas at that time, and the police arrived soon after the knockout and arrested both Choynski and Johnson. They were held in the same jail cell for twenty-eight days before being pardoned by the governor. During this time they were permitted to spar, and Choynski taught the less experienced Johnson many of the skills that afterward made him a champion.

Choynski suffered an unfair defeat at New York's Broadway Athletic Club in 1900, in which he was evidently the victim of collusion between his opponent, former middleweight champion Kid McCoy, and the referee. The bell was rung prematurely in the second round, which saved McCoy from being counted out, and McCoy was again on the verge of a knockout when the bell rang to end the third round. Choynski was walking to his corner when McCoy struck him from behind and knocked him out. No foul was called, and Choynski was ruled the loser when unable to answer the bell for the fourth round. Choynski suffered another disastrous beating in 1900 when he was held to a contract to fight welterweight champion Joe Walcott, even though Choynski was suffering at the time from badly damaged ribs. Walcott, a foot shorter and many pounds lighter than Choynski, gave him a terrific beating, ending the fight in seven rounds.

Near the end of his career, Choynski fought and lost (either officially or unofficially) to both future heavyweight title claimant Marvin Hart and the famous Philadelphia Jack O'Brien. Choynski's last fight was on 24 November 1904 when he was adjudged by newspaper reporters to be the loser in six rounds to Jack Williams in Philadelphia.

Choynski had married Louise Anderson Miller of Cincinnati, Ohio, in 1895. They had a happy marriage but no children. After his retirement, he sold sporting goods in a department store for a time and then was the boxing instructor at the Pittsburgh, Pennsylvania, Athletic Club from 1912 to 1922. He briefly studied chiropractic in San Francisco and then moved to Chicago and sold insurance. His last fifteen years were spent in Cincinnati, where he gave private boxing lessons until his health failed, and he died there after a long illness.

Choynski is considered to be the greatest Jewish heavyweight of all time. Although never a world champion, he fought many champions and beat several of them, in a career of about eighty fights. Together with the better-known Corbett, he was instrumental in replacing the crude slugging of bare-knuckle fighting with the skills of modern boxing. Like Corbett, he was well spoken and gentlemanly and helped lift his sport toward respectability.

• The best source of information on Choynski is a biographical chapter by Ken Blady in *The Jewish Boxers' Hall of Fame* (1988). A long article on his career, "Choynski Passes On" is in *The Ring*, April 1943, pp. 20–23, 39. His record appears in the 1977 edition of *The Ring Record Book*. Good accounts of his barge fight with Corbett are in Corbett's autobiography, *The Roar of the Crowd* (1925), and Rex Lardner, *The Legendary Champions* (1972). His fight with Jeffries is described in J. W. McConaughy, *Big Jim Jeffries* (1910). The *Philadelphia Item* provides good accounts of his fights with Walcott, McCoy, and many others. See also William Kramer and Norton Stern, "San Francisco's Fighting Jews," *California History* 53 (1947), and Steven Riess, "A Fighting Chance: The Jewish American Boxing Experience," *American Jewish History* 79 (1985): 223–54. An interesting obituary is in the *New York Herald Tribune*, 26 Jan. 1943.

LUCKETT V. DAVIS

CHRISTENSEN, Harold (25 Dec. 1904–20 Feb. 1989), ballet dancer and teacher, was born Harold Farr Christensen in Brigham City, Utah, the son of Christian Bjerregaard Christensen, a musician and teacher of social dances, and Mary Isabell Farr. As a youth in Brigham City and Ogden, Utah, Christensen was instructed in the social dances of the day by his father and by his uncle Moses Christensen, who was president of the American National Association, Masters of Dancing in 1916–1917. After one year at West Point (1924–1925), Harold returned to the family dancing school in Ogden, then under the direction of his older brother Willam. Harold trained in ballet under Willam, and in 1927 he took over the school so that Willam and a third brother, Lew, could tour in vaudeville with a ballet act.

Harold Christensen's career developed within the context of dance as a family business. In 1929–1930 he taught in the Seattle studio of his uncle Frederic Christensen and then moved to New York to improve his ballet technique under the Italian master Stefano Mascagno. In 1932 Harold joined Lew in the Christensen Brothers and Company vaudeville act, replacing Willam. With partners Ruby Asquith and Josephine McKendrick, the brothers toured on the Radio-Keith-Orpheum circuit, playing vaudeville's most prestigious theaters, including the Palace and the Hippodrome.

In 1934 Harold and Lew and their partners left vaudeville to perform in the Broadway musical *The Great Waltz*. That same year they began taking classes at the School of American Ballet, where they studied with George Balanchine and Pierre Vladimirov. The foursome was taken into Balanchine's American Ballet Ensemble as it became the resident dance company of the Metropolitan Opera (1935), and Harold danced in the corps de ballet for two years (the 1935–1936 season and the 1936–1937 season).

Like his more famous brother Lew, Harold was a founding member of Ballet Caravan, an experimental company backed by Lincoln Kirstein (who had brought Balanchine to the United States) to provide opportunities for young American choreographers. (The Caravan toured during the opera's off season.) Harold chose not to choreograph; instead, he served as stage manager, in addition to dancing. In Lew Christensen's 1938 *Filling Station*, Harold created the comic role of the befuddled motorist.

In early 1940 Harold went to San Francisco to teach for Willam at the San Francisco Opera Ballet (SFOB) School, while Willam toured with the Opera Ballet. Later that year Harold married his former vaudeville partner, Asquith, who also joined the faculty of the SFOB School and performed leading roles with the company; they had three children. In Willam Christensen's 1940 *Swan Lake*—the first complete production of that work staged by an American—Harold filled the role of Rothbart and led the Czardas in act 3.

In 1942 Harold and Willam made a clear division of responsibilities in the small family-run ballet organization in San Francisco: Willam remained artistic director of the company, and Harold assumed responsibility for the school. As director of the San Francisco Ballet (SFB) School for thirty-three years, Harold trained generations of dancers for the company (which was directed by Willam from the time it became independent from the opera in 1942 until 1951 and by Lew from 1951 until 1984).

Strict in his manner and military in his bearing, Harold was nicknamed "the General" by his students, in view of his year at West Point. Christensen excelled as a teacher of beginning and intermediate students, instilling in young bodies the essentials of line and placement. Influenced by his training at the School of American Ballet, he guided SFB School policy in the direction of Balanchine's style even before his brother Lew, who was more generally recognized as a Balanchine dancer, assumed directorship of the San Francisco Ballet. Harold maintained a heavy teaching schedule and worked tirelessly to promote the SFB School as a means of supporting his brothers' company. "He worked six days a week for most of those years," recalled his wife after his death. "Even our two weeks' vacation was cut to one because of the need to prepare for the summer session. 'Don't tell anybody it's Washington's Birthday,' he used to say. 'They have to be here for rehearsals'" (*San Francisco Chronicle*, 21 Feb. 1989).

As director of the SFB School, Harold played a crucial role in the Christensen ballet enterprise in San Francisco. Income from the school subsidized the company at a time when both were family-run, for-profit concerns. In the days before federal funding, tax-exempt status, and corporate grants, Christensen's attention to detail, fiscal conservatism, and administrative sense brought needed stability to both the company and the school. Also, to help mount seasons with the limited number of dancers available, Christensen returned to the stage at age forty-six to recreate the role of the motorist in the 1951 revival of *Filling Station*.

In 1959 the high standards of training maintained at the San Francisco Ballet School attracted a major Ford Foundation grant, under which would-be professional dancers west of the Mississippi River would be given scholarships to the school; those east of the Mississippi were given similar scholarships to the School of American Ballet. To find the most qualified students to receive Ford scholarship money, Harold traveled throughout the western United States and personally auditioned hundreds of students annually until his retirement in 1975. He died in San Anselmo, California. Among the dancers who studied at the SFB School and went on to other companies are Jocelyn Vollmar, Suki Schorer, Frank Ohman, Conrad Ludlow, Cynthia Gregory, Terry Orr, and Onna White.

With his brothers Willam and Lew, Harold Christensen is recognized as a pioneer of ballet in the western United States. Because of Harold and Lew Christensen's high standards and their receipt of Ford Foundation grants for individual scholarships, the San Francisco Ballet School played a significant role in the decentralization of ballet training in mid-twentieth-century American ballet. In 1973 the Christensen brothers shared the prestigious Dance Magazine Award with Rudolf Nureyev, and in 1984 the Christensens received the Capezio Award.

• The chief repository of materials documenting the career of Harold Christensen is the San Francisco Performing Arts Library and Museum, which houses the Christensen-Caccialanza Collection as well as archival materials relating to the history of the San Francisco Ballet and its school. For a brief overview of the brothers' careers, see Olga Maynard, "The Christensens: An American Dance Dynasty," *Dance Magazine*, June 1973, pp. 44–56. An obituary is in the *San Francisco Chronicle*, 21 Feb. 1989.

DEBRA HICKENLOOPER SOWELL

CHRISTENSEN, Lew (6 May 1909–9 Oct. 1984), ballet dancer, choreographer, and company director, was born Lewellyn Farr Christensen in Brigham City, Utah, the son of Christian Bjerregaard Christensen, a musician and teacher of social dances, and Mary Isabell Farr. Lew Christensen was raised in a family that emphasized developing one's talents in music and dance. One uncle, Moses Christensen, was active in the American National Association, Masters of Dancing and served as that organization's president in 1916–1917. Lew studied the cello under his father and began ballet training under another uncle, Lars Peter Christensen, who forwarded the talented nephew to the Italian maestro Stefano Mascagno in New York.

Christensen began his performing career with his older brother, Willam Farr Christensen, touring in vaudeville with a ballet act (1927–1934). In this popular context, the Christensens presented balletic tours de force in a fast-paced style geared to appeal to mass audiences. Billed variously over the years as Le Crist Revue, the Berkoffs, the Mascagno Four, and the Christensen Brothers and Company, the act always highlighted Lew's matinee idol good looks, his speed, and his prodigious ability to turn multiple pirouettes. Starting in small-time vaudeville theaters, the act was picked up by the Radio-Keith-Orpheum circuit and eventually played vaudeville's most prestigious houses, including the Hippodrome and the Palace.

In 1934 Lew and another brother, Harold, and their partners exchanged vaudeville for Broadway, dancing in the lavish musical *The Great Waltz*. They began to take class with George Balanchine at the recently founded School of American Ballet, where Lew also came under the influence of Lincoln Kirstein, the Harvard-educated patron who had brought Balanchine to the United States to promote ballet as an American art form. Christensen joined Balanchine's American Ballet Ensemble in 1935 as it became the resident dance company at the Metropolitan Opera. He consolidated his reputation as a *danseur noble* in the title roles of Balanchine's *Orpheus and Eurydice* (1936) and *Apollo* (1937). As the first of Balanchine's American Apollos, Christensen set a new standard for future performances of this staple of the Balanchine canon; his interpretation was described by Kirstein as "more golden baroque, more the Apollo Belvedere than [the first Apollo] Serge Lifar's dark, electric, archaic animalism of nine years before. But at last here was an American dancer with his own individual classical attitude, using his six feet of height with a suave and monumental elegance which was wholly athletic, frank, musical, and joyful, and wholly unlike the smaller-scaled grace of the Russian prototype" (*Ballet: Bias and Belief* [1973], p. 196).

Between opera seasons, Christensen and a group of dancers from Balanchine's company toured in Kirstein's Ballet Caravan, an experimental company dedicated to producing new ballets on American themes. While functioning as Ballet Caravan's ballet master, Christensen created *Filling Station* (1938), a roadside fable starring himself as Mac, the station attendant, and *Charade* (1939), a witty takeoff on a turn-of-the-century coming-out party.

Between Ballet Caravan tours, Christensen went to Hollywood to dance Balanchine's choreography in the filmed version of *On Your Toes* (1939) and *I Was an Adventuress* (1940). He was ballet master for the summer season of the St. Louis Municipal Opera in 1940 and that fall appeared as guest artist with the San Francisco Opera Ballet, under the direction of his brother Willam. Lew danced the role of Prince Siegfried in his brother's *Swan Lake*, a landmark production because it was the first full-length version of that ballet staged by an American choreographer. In 1941 Lew choreographed a Broadway play, Philip Barry's *Liberty Jones*, and then returned to Kirstein's circle as ballet master and leading dancer of the re-formed American Ballet Caravan for its 1941 South American good will tour on the eve of U.S. entry into World War II. Just before that tour, Christensen married another leading Balanchine dancer, Gisella Caccialanza, a former protégée of the famed Italian pedagogue Enrico Cecchetti; they had one child. Following the tour and the final disbanding of the Caravan, Christensen performed with Eugene Loring's Dance Players while waiting to be drafted. For Loring's company, he choreographed *Jinx* (1942), a sinister ballet about an accident-prone clown in a superstitious circus troupe. Christensen was inducted into the army in November 1942 and served in the European theater.

Christensen returned from Europe in July 1946 and joined Kirstein and Balanchine's latest venture, Ballet Society. Attempting a comeback after the four-year hiatus in his career, he regained sufficient technique to perform leading and secondary roles in more Balanchine repertory, including *The Four Temperaments* (1948), in which Christensen partnered Elise Reiman in the "Second Theme." But combat had taken a heavy toll on his physique, and as his fortieth birthday approached, he embarked on a new phase of his career: teaching and choreographing in San Francisco, where his brother Willam was director of the San Francisco Ballet (now independent of the opera). The strong family ties that affected Christensen's early training influenced this career choice. From 1949 to 1951 Willam and Lew shared leadership of the San Francisco company, while Lew returned to New York intermittently to help Balanchine mount the early seasons of the newly christened New York City Ballet.

In 1951 Willam returned to Utah, leaving San Francisco Ballet to Lew, who was also named NYCB administrative director in 1952. For two years Christensen administered both companies and implemented an exchange policy by which the companies shared repertory and, occasionally, leading dancers. This relationship between New York City Ballet and San Francisco Ballet made Christensen an early and important exponent of Balanchinian neoclassicism in the American West as well as a key figure in the dissemination of Balanchine's choreography. The exchange program also prompted one of Christensen's most enduring ballets, *Con Amore* (1953), a tongue-in-cheek examination of lovers' foibles, which was mounted by both companies.

From the mid-1950s until the end of his life, Christensen focused solely on the San Francisco company, choreographing over sixty ballets and divertissements (including dance scenes for the San Francisco Opera through the early 1960s). Under his leadership the company made its first East Coast appearances (Jacob's Pillow, 1956) and its first international tours (1957–1959). In 1959, in acknowledgment of the superior training that dancers received in Christensen's company and its school, the Ford Foundation selected the SFB School to be one of two recipients for scholarship money to support the training of professional dancers; the other recipient was Balanchine's School of American Ballet. In 1963, when the Ford Foundation announced its groundbreaking $8 million program to fund seven American ballet companies, Christensen's SFB received the largest amount after New York City Ballet.

In the dance community Christensen's reputation was based solidly on his success as a Balanchine performer during the 1930s and 1940s. Many of his works reflected his tutelage in Balanchinian neoclassicism: *Encounter* (1936), *Vivaldi Concerto* (1949), *Masque of Beauty and the Shepherd* (1954), *Sinfonia* (1959), *Divertissement d'Auber* (1959), *Symphony in D* (1967), and *Vivaldi Concerto Grosso* (1981). But as the sole artistic director and chief choreographer of SFB from 1951 to 1973, Christensen was forced to create in a variety of styles, to provide balanced programming for his company's seasons. Thus abstract or non-narrative works were supplemented by tales and romances: *The Nutcracker* (1954), *The Dryad* (1954), *Lady of Shalott* (1958), *Beauty and the Beast* (1958), *Fantasma* (1963), and *Don Juan* (1973); comedic or playful works that betrayed his native wit: *Caprice* (1959), *Original Sin* (1961), *Il Distratto* (1967), *Stravinsky Pas de Deux* (1976), and *Scarlatti Portfolio* (1979); and essays on American themes: *American Scene* (1952), *Emperor Norton* (1957), and *Life: A Pop Art Ballet* (1965).

As a choreographer Christensen enjoyed mixed treatment at the hands of the press. A series of collaborations with commercial artist Tony Duquette in the late 1950s and early 1960s led to charges that SFB repertory relied too heavily on elaborately costumed story ballets. Also, some critics were quick to label Christensen's work derivative of Balanchine, even in ballets that showed little resemblance to the master's oeuvre. But dance critic Arlene Croce, reviewing SFB in 1978, concluded that although his ballets were sometimes eccentric or uneven, Christensen's was "a choreographic mind of no small distinction. The Christensen ballets hold a provocative secret. They ought to be better known than they are" (*Going to the Dance* [1982], p. 135). In 1979 Christensen won a bronze medal for choreography at the first International Ballet Competition in Jacksonville, Mississippi, for the virtuoso "hoop solo" from *Scarlatti Portfolio*. By the time of his death, in Burlingame, California, *Filling Station* had been staged by six companies; *Con Amore*, by nine.

With characteristic modesty and detachment, Christensen downplayed the success of his long career in dance. Late in life he declared, "I'm not trying to save the art of ballet or the world. Ballet is just a craft I know" (*Dance Magazine*, Dec. 1981, p. 69). But the American dance community showed its respect by presenting Lew, along with his brothers Willam and Harold, two of its most prestigious honors: the Dance Magazine Award in 1973 and the Capezio Award in 1984. Another measure of Christensen's importance to the history of ballet in the United States is found in the writings of Lincoln Kirstein, a lifelong friend and supporter of Christensen's work. Reflecting on his attempts to establish a company of American ballet dancers, Kirstein wrote, "It was how Lew danced on stage and behaved off that signified to me a future, and within it a potential for American male dancers" (*Thirty Years: The New York City Ballet* [1978], p. 301). Kirstein went on to admit that he viewed male dancers in New York City Ballet as part of an "apostolic succession in our history which I date from Lew Christensen through Jacques d'Amboise" (p. 303).

• The chief repository of materials documenting the career of Lew Christensen is the San Francisco Performing Arts Library and Museum, which houses the Christensen-Caccialanza Collection as well as archival materials relating to the history of the San Francisco Ballet. For an overview of the Christensen brothers' family background and intertwined careers, see Olga Maynard, "The Christensens: An American Dance Dynasty," *Dance Magazine*, June 1973, pp. 44–56. Cobbett Steinberg, "Lew Christensen: An American Original," *Encore: The Archives for the Performing Arts Quarterly* 1 (Summer 1984), contains a useful annotated chronology of Lew's career; the same author's *San Francisco Ballet: The First Fifty Years* (1983) also contains valuable information on the Christensens. An obituary is in the *New York Times*, 10 Oct. 1984.

DEBRA HICKENLOOPER SOWELL

CHRISTIAN, Charlie (29 July 1916–2 Mar. 1942), musician, was born Charles Christian in Dallas, Texas; his father was a blues guitarist and singer, his mother a pianist (their names are unknown). The family moved to Oklahoma City when Christian was five, and he grew up there amid the diverse musical styles of the Southwest. Itinerant blues guitarists and singers played everywhere, and the young Christian also would have heard Texas blues bands, ethnic dance music, cowboy songs, rural banjo pickers, and white and black fiddle players, both in person and on radios and jukeboxes. Oklahoma City was home to Walter Page's Blue Devils, and Christian heard Lester

Young during Prez's two tours with the group; most of the mid- and southwestern jazz bands also played there. The early western swing bands, finally, often had electric guitarists who pioneered the improvised single-note lines that typified Christian's jazz playing. Although he did not play in either the school's concert band or its symphony orchestra (they had no place for guitar), he did receive formal training in harmony. The writer Ralph Ellison, a childhood neighbor and friend, remembered that the guitarist's group played light classics as well as the blues.

Christian played trumpet as a child, but he switched to guitar at age twelve and played in the family string band (his four brothers were musicians). He also occasionally played piano and bass during the early 1930s. He was familiar with the electric guitar by 1937, at the latest, probably introduced to it by Eddie Durham, who was touring with the Count Basie band. Christian played professionally with a variety of territory bands, and by 1939 he enjoyed a growing reputation throughout the Southwest. The pianist Mary Lou Williams told critic and record producer John Hammond (1910–1987) about him, and Hammond arranged an audition with Benny Goodman, who was already considering adding an electric guitarist to his small group. Christian walked into the audition dressed in a purple shirt, bright green suit, and pointed yellow shoes—an affront to the bandleader's sartorial conservatism. But Hammond sneaked Christian onto the bandstand when Goodman was on a break, and Christian greatly impressed the leader with his playing. He joined Goodman in August 1939. Within two months he was featured on Goodman recordings like "Flying Home," "Rose Room," and "Seven Come Eleven," making an immediate impact on the jazz world.

Part of the appeal, of course, was the newness of the instrument and its sound. People were used to the sparer sound of an acoustic guitar, and Christian produced a beautiful bell-like tone with percussive qualities. With the electric guitar's amplification, other instruments could no longer drown out the instrument. From his first appearance on record, moreover, the genius of Christian's musical conception was clear. His solos consisted of long, uncluttered lines of eighth notes with a strong blues feeling. He played with a firm tone, flawless time, and a powerful sense of swing and drive. His playing always seems both logical and effortless, so "right" that it never fails to excite and interest. Like his contemporary, Lester Young, Christian was rooted in the blues tradition and sought to tell a story in his music. Like Young's, Christian's linear style also pointed toward later be-bop innovations. Indeed, bop players made some of Christian's favorite melodic figures their own.

Christian reached a temporary plateau in his development around 1940, but in 1941 he made a series of wonderfully relaxed and swinging chamber jazz recordings with the Edmond Hall Celeste Quartet, marked by unique double voicings and intricate rhythmic interplay with the young bassist Israel Crosby. He also spent much of the last year of his life playing regularly, often all night, at Minton's Playhouse on 118th Street in New York City with musical innovators like Kenny Clarke and Thelonious Monk. His work during these sessions reveals that he was the most musically advanced and original of all these players, moving toward the language of bop, as he stretched out his lines and intensified his already propulsive sense of swing.

By early 1942 Christian's was among the most important voices in all of jazz. But he collapsed with tuberculosis in mid-1941, and he spent the last months of his life in the Seaview Sanitarium on Staten Island, where he died.

Christian is a critical figure in the history of American music. His recordings are almost uniformly classic performances, and critics regard his solos as among the most creative in jazz for their eloquence and simplicity. His popularization of the electric guitar, finally, left a legacy that would later spread to the blues, rhythm and blues, and rock and roll. Only twenty-five years old at his death, Christian changed the face of American popular music.

• There is still no definitive biography of Christian. Gunther Schuller, *The Swing Era: The Development of Jazz, 1930–1945* (1989), pp. 562–78, provides the best critical analysis of his music and influence. James Lincoln Collier, *The Making of Jazz: A Comprehensive History* (1978), pp. 342–46, and Frank Tirro, *Jazz: A History*, 2d ed. (1993), pp. 255–58, offer concise, accurate overviews of Christian's life and music. Ira Gitler, *Swing to Bop* (1985), pp. 40–43, contains comments by several musicians on Christian and his music. Also see Nat Shapiro and Nat Hentoff, *The Jazz Makers* (1957).

RONALD P. DUFOUR

CHRISTIAN, Henry Asbury (17 Feb. 1876–24 Aug. 1951), physician, was born in Lynchburg, Virginia, the son of Camillus Christian, a banker, and Mary Elizabeth Davis. Christian graduated from Randolph Macon College in 1895 with a B.A. and an M.A., after which he entered the Johns Hopkins Medical School and received an M.D. in 1900. In 1903 he received an A.M. in pathology from Harvard College and became an assistant to the pathologist Frank B. Mallory at the Boston City Hospital. In the years between 1903 and 1905, he taught pathology at the Harvard Medical School. Christian's interest in internal medicine began in 1905, when Harvard appointed him instructor. In 1907 he advanced to assistant professor of the theory and practice of physic. From 1908 to 1912 Christian served as dean of the Harvard Medical School. He became the chief of medicine at the Carney Hospital in 1907. One year later, he succeeded Reginald H. Fitz as the Hershey Professor of the Theory and Practice of Physic at the Harvard Medical School. He held this professorship for thirty-one years.

Christian joined the staff of the Peter Bent Brigham Hospital in Boston when it opened in 1910. In the early days of the hospital, a joint arrangement between the Harvard Medical School and the hospital made it possible for the senior staff to receive some pay for their instruction of the medical students. Reginald Fitz, who installed the clinical teaching program at the Brigham, appointed Christian to supervise the students while they served their month-long clinical clerkship on the hospital's wards. In this position, Christian demanded detailed recording of each patient's illness and progress and also introduced a close collaboration between the ward activities and the clinical laboratories. He accomplished this by setting up small laboratories adjacent to the wards and insisting that much of the laboratory work be done by the house officers and students. Christian's method of teaching clinical clerks was derived from his teacher at the Johns Hopkins Hospital, William Osler, who had taught him the importance of observing, recording, tabulating, communicating, and performing most of the laboratory work on their patients.

Through the influence of Christian and colleague Harvey Cushing, the Peter Bent Brigham Hospital developed into a leader in research and teaching in the era from 1930 to 1950. While Hershey Professor, Christian also established close affiliations between the Harvard Medical School and the Boston Children's Hospital, the Infants Hospital, and the Free Hospital for Women. These affiliations, which have expanded and continued, strengthened the pediatrics department at Harvard Medical School.

As a clinical investigator, Christian made significant contributions to the study of renal disease by investigating the mechanisms of the development of renal failure and the action of diuretics. This work was important because of the frequency of renal failure resulting from streptococcal infections that could not be controlled because there were no antibiotics for treatment. Christian's investigation of cardiac function was unique because he studied the heart as a pump rather than listened to the sounds caused by the closing of valves and the rushing of blood through the heart chambers. He was interested in how cardiac muscle accelerated the flow of blood.

From 1918 to 1921 Christian served as a major in the Medical Reserve Corps of the U.S. Army. When World War I ended, he remained chairman of the National Research Council's Division of Medical Sciences. He married Elizabeth Sears Seabury in 1921; they had no children.

Medical organizations greatly interested Christian. He was particularly involved in the activities and policies of the Association of American Physicians, the American Association of Pathologists and Bacteriologists, and the sections on pathology and physiology of the American Medical Association. Through his interest in promoting clinical investigation, he was a charter member of the American Society for Clinical Investigation and served as its secretary in 1906 and later as its president in 1919. Christian was also instrumental in founding the Federation for Clinical Research, which at times was jocularly referred to as the "YMCA," or the "Young Mens *Christian* Association." Christian was a member of numerous distinguished societies, including the American Academy of Arts and Sciences, and was an honorary fellow of the Royal College of Physicians in London. In 1935 he was elected president of the Association of American Physicians, and in 1947 he was awarded the Distinguished Service Medal of the American Medical Association.

Christian devoted a great deal of time in his later years to writing. He edited for Oxford University Press *The Oxford Medicine* (1928, 1940) and *Oxford Monographs on Diagnosis and Treatment* (1928), and he was the author of the revised edition of Osler's *The Principles and Practice of Medicine: Designed for the Use of Practitioners and Students of Medicine* (1938).

During World War II, because of the shortage of teachers, Christian consented to return to help teach the students at the Harvard Medical School. From 1942 to 1946 he served as visiting physician to the Beth Israel Hospital. In 1943 he served as a professor of clinical medicine at Tufts College Medical School. Christian died from a coronary occlusion in Whitefield, New Hampshire.

• Christian's papers are in the rare book section of the Countway Library of Medicine, Harvard University. Herman L. Blumgart, "Henry Asbury Christian, 1876–1951," *Harvard Medical Alumni Bulletin* 26 (Jan. 1952): 64–66. Obituaries are in the *New York Times*, 26 Aug. 1951, and the *New England Journal of Medicine* 245 (6 Dec. 1951): 912–913.

DAVID Y. COOPER

CHRISTIANCY, Isaac Peckham (12 Mar. 1812–8 Sept. 1890), lawyer, judge, and senator, was born in Johnstown, Fulton County, New York, the son of Thomas Christiancy, a blacksmith, edge tool maker, and farmer, and Zilpha Peckham. When Isaac was twelve, his father was injured, leaving Isaac responsible for helping to support his family by tending their small farm. At age eighteen Christiancy began to teach school while attending academies at Johnstown, Kingsborough, and Ovid, New York. In 1834 he undertook legal studies with the help of John Maynard. Via an Erie Canal packet boat and a Great Lakes steamer, he journeyed to Monroe County, Michigan, in May 1836. There he soon entered the law office of Robert McClelland and served as an assistant clerk in the U.S. Land Office. In 1838 he was admitted to the bar, and he continued in the land office until it moved to Detroit in 1841. A shortage of funds saved him from partaking in the era's wild land speculation that resulted in financial ruin for others seemingly more fortunate. In 1839 he married Elizabeth McClusky. They had a large family: seven children survived childhood while two died in infancy.

In addition to maintaining a private practice, Christiancy served as Monroe County prosecuting attorney from 1841 to 1846. His legal career prepared him for a political one, at first in the Democratic party, but what he perceived to be that party's proslavery predilections led him to join Michigan's growing antislavery forces. In 1848 he attended the Buffalo convention that organized the Free Soil party, pledged to halt slavery's expansion into the western territories. In 1849 he was elected to the state senate to represent Michigan's

Third District (Monroe, Lenawee, Hillsdale, and Branch counties). In 1852 he ran as the Free Soil candidate for governor, winning 5,850 votes (or 7 percent of the total) but losing to his former legal associate McClelland, who ran successfully as the Democratic nominee.

Besides his subsequent judicial career in Michigan, Christiancy's most significant role was in helping to organize the Republican party. As a leading member of the Free Soil party, he was in a position to ease the transition to the new antislavery party. In July 1854 he joined in the call for the meeting of those protesting the Kansas-Nebraska Act in Jackson, Michigan, that helped to establish the Republican party. As chair of the Free Soil (or Free Democratic) Committee, he withdrew that party's state ticket, thus clearing the way for fusion with former Whigs and Democrats in a Republican party that unified northern opposition to slavery's expansion while toning down abolitionist ideology. In addition to editing the Monroe *Commercial*, a Republican newspaper, he served as a delegate to the party's 1856 national convention in Philadelphia, sitting on the Resolutions Committee.

Although in 1857 Christiancy garnered some support for selection to the U.S. Senate, he instead won election as an associate justice to the newly formed Michigan Supreme Court. Reelected in 1865 and 1873, he helped guide the court through its formative years, serving as its chief justice in 1872, and he won praise for the quality of his judicial statesmanship. During the Civil War he served for a short time on the staffs of George Custer and A. A. Humphreys.

Christiancy, like many antebellum reformers, later regretted that postwar economic developments created unsettling social divisions. He especially lamented how corporate growth spawned two seemingly opposing classes, "the employers and the employed." The growing power of special corporate interests had worried Christiancy before the war, but slavery had seemingly overshadowed this threat. Yet as a jurist he maintained a moderate reputation while avoiding partisan politics. In January 1875 he was elected to the U.S. Senate by a coalition of Democrats and Republicans eager to replace the controversial Radical, Zachariah Chandler. Characteristically, Christiancy evidenced a legalist outlook in the Senate in approaching such issues as Reconstruction politics in Louisiana and the impeachment of Secretary of War William Belknap. Christiancy served primarily as a moderate Republican, and his Senate career proved to be short and undistinguished.

The death of Christiancy's first wife in December 1874 resulted in an unfortunate second marriage in 1876 to Lilly Lugerbeel. The now elderly Christiancy may have been the victim of a scheme by a young woman eager to exploit the apparent wealth and gullibility of the U.S. senator. Christiancy carelessly expressed affections for the woman, a clerk in a department store, who insisted on marriage. To avoid a scandal, Christiancy honored his "proposal," only to be told by his new wife of twenty-four hours that she did not love him. The embarrassing situation forced Christiancy to resign from the Senate in 1879. He was thereupon appointed as U.S. minister to Peru, where he served until 1881. Shaken and dejected on his return, he sued for divorce and retired to Lansing, Michigan. He practiced law and dabbled in local history until his death in Lansing.

• Christiancy's antebellum opinions are primarily in the manuscript collections of fellow Mich. politicians, such as Austin Blair, Burton Historical Collections, Detroit Public Library. Christiancy wrote "Recollections of the Early History of the City and County of Monroe," *Michigan Pioneer and Historical Collections* 6 (1884): 361–73. Details of his life are in A. D. P. Van Buren, "Memoir of Judge Isaac Peckham Christiancy," *Michigan Pioneer and Historical Collections* 18 (1892): 333–40; Talcott E. Wing, ed., *History of Monroe County, Michigan* (1890); *Michigan Biographies*, vol. 1 (1924); and *Early History of Michigan, with Biographies of State Officers, Members of Congress, Judges and Legislators* (1888). *Michigan Reports of Supreme Court Decisions*, vols. 5–31, contains his state supreme court contributions. For his role in Michigan politics see Floyd B. Streeter, *Political Parties in Michigan, 1837–1860* (1918); Ronald P. Formisano, *The Birth of Mass Political Parties, 1827–1861* (1971); and Harriette M. Dilla, *The Politics of Michigan, 1865–1878* (1912). An obituary is in the *Detroit Tribune*, 9 Sept. 1890.

VERNON L. VOLPE

CHRISTIANSEN, Jack (20 Dec. 1928–29 June 1986), football player and coach, was born John LeRoy Christiansen in Sublette, Kansas, the son of Leroy Christiansen and Catherine (maiden name unknown). Following a grain elevator accident in 1930 that killed his father, Christiansen briefly lived with his paternal grandparents in Wray, Colorado. During the Great Depression, fearing they could not provide for the education of Jack and his sister, who was two years older, Christiansen's grandparents arranged for the youngsters to enter the Odd Fellows Orphanage in Canon City, Colorado. Christiansen attended the local schools in Canon City from the third grade on. Six-feet-one and spindly as he reached his teens, Christiansen excelled in football and track in high school, but an accidental gunshot wound to his left arm during his senior year threatened to preclude football thereafter. In 1947 he enrolled at Colorado A & M (now Colorado State University). There he initially confined his participation in sports to track, where he ran the 100-yard dash in 9.8 seconds, tying a school record in the event. He also ran the 220- and 440-yard dashes and was a member of the relay team that won the Skyline Conference title his senior year; for three consecutive years he held the conference's 440 title. His love for football, however, caused Christiansen to disregard his physician's advice to avoid contact sports. He made the powerful Colorado A & M football squad as a reserve defensive back his sophomore year but soon became a starting safety. He also returned punts and saw some action at halfback. Carrying the ball mainly on sweeps and reverses, he set a single-game school rushing record that endured for almost twenty years. In the spring of 1951 Christiansen married Doris

Erickson, who was studying for a master's degree in physical education at Colorado A & M. The couple would have four children.

The Detroit Lions selected Christiansen in the sixth round of the 1951 National Football League (NFL) draft and used him at first on kick returns. As a rookie he set an NFL record by returning four punts for touchdowns. Christiansen said he set the record because opposing teams preferred to kick him rather than to star Lions running back Doak Walker, who also returned punts. A string of injuries led Detroit to use Christiansen on offense early in the 1952 season, but subsequently the Lions made a trade that created a spot for Christiansen at defensive left safety. In both 1952 and 1953 the Lions won NFL championships with Christiansen playing a key role. Despite Christiansen's youth, the defensive backfield of Christiansen and Yale Lary at the safeties and Jim David and Carl Karilavac at the cornerback positions became known as "Chris' Crew." The quartet played together through the 1957 season when the Lions won another NFL title, defeating the powerful Cleveland Browns as they had done on two previous occasions. Christiansen made All-Pro for six consecutive seasons and amassed 46 career interceptions, an achievement made more impressive by the fact that opposing quarterbacks soon learned to avoid passing in his area. Christiansen rated a 103-yard kickoff return in the 1956 Pro Bowl game as his top individual thrill. Although he believed he could have played a few more seasons, ligament damage to an ankle persuaded Christiansen to retire following the 1958 campaign. He then joined the San Francisco 49ers as an assistant coach in 1959, and during the 1963 season he became the team's head coach. His record with the 49ers was 26–38–3, and only once during his five years at the helm did the 49ers have a winning season.

Wanting to remain in the Bay Area to provide stability for his family, Christiansen joined Stanford University as an assistant in 1969. He became head coach in 1972 and remained at Stanford through 1976. In 1973, Christiansen's second season at the helm, Stanford won seven games but thereafter slipped to records of 5–4–2, 6–4–1, and 6–5. Alumni dissatisfaction grew, in part because Christiansen's predecessor had led Stanford to consecutive Rose Bowl triumphs, and Stanford decided to buy out the remaining two years of his contract just prior to the final game of the 1976 season. Christiansen remained coach long enough to defeat arch-rival California. "In a display of storybook emotion," wrote a *New York Times* correspondent of the game, "the Stanford players carried Christiansen on their shoulders on the field before the game, and carried him off again after winning, 27–24, with a touchdown in the last couple of minutes." Stanford hired Bill Walsh to replace him. Christiansen then returned to the NFL for seven seasons, holding down assistant coaching positions with Kansas City, Seattle, and Atlanta. In 1967 he was selected to the Colorado Sports Hall of Fame and in 1970 to the Pro Football Hall of Fame. He died in Stanford, California, where he maintained his permanent home.

• Material on Christiansen is available at the Media Relations Office, Department of Athletics, Physical Education, and Recreation, Stanford University; and at the Pro Football Hall of Fame, Canton, Ohio. Brief entries on Christiansen are in Murray Olderman, *The Defenders* (1973), and Denis J. Harrington, *The Pro Football Hall of Fame* (1991). Also useful are Stan Groshandler, "Chris' Crew," *Football Digest* 3 (Nov. 1973): 54–57, and Jack Newcombe, "You've Got to Be Good and Mean," *Sport* 20 (Dec. 1955): 21, 62–65. An obituary is in the *New York Times*, 1 July 1986.

LLOYD J. GRAYBAR

CHRISTMAN, Elisabeth (2 Sept. 1881?–26 Apr. 1975), labor organizer and reformer, was born in Germany, the daughter of Henry Christman, a laborer and musician, and Barbara Guth. Probably in 1884 she immigrated to Chicago with her parents. At the age of thirteen Elisabeth left the German Lutheran school she attended to work at the Eisendrath Glove Company.

The value of unionization soon played a prominent role in Christman's life. At Eisendrath's she worked ten hours a day, six days a week, paid for the electricity that powered her sewing machine, and bought her own needles and machine oil. In 1898 when a co-worker led a strike against the company, Christman followed. After ten days, the company met the workers' demands for higher pay, a union shop, and electric power supplied at the company's expense.

Following a second strike in 1902, Christman helped organize the glove workers into a women's local of the newly formed International Glove Workers Union of America (IGWUA). From 1905 to 1911 she served as shop steward, from 1912 to 1917 as president, and at one time chair of the grievance committee. From 1913 to 1931 she was secretary-treasurer of the IGWUA, only one of two women at the time holding high office in an international union. She served as vice president of the IGWUA from 1931 to 1937.

Christman joined the Women's Trade Union League (WTUL) in 1904. WTUL membership included union and nonunion men and women who allied with unions and middle- and upper-class women who endorsed labor organization and better conditions for women workers. Christman served on the WTUL Chicago branch executive board from 1910 to 1929 and became affiliated with the Bryn Mawr Summer School for training women in labor leadership. Between 1914 and 1926 she served on the joint administrative committee of the school and on the executive committee of the American Labor Education Service.

Christman went where she was needed to support strikers and to help settle labor grievances. After the arrest in Chicago of thirteen women during a 1915 canvas glove makers strike over unequal pay, Christman stepped in to successfully mediate for eight hundred striking workers many of whom could not speak English. In the 1920s her negotiating skills averted a strike by workers of the Philadelphia Waist and Dressmakers Union, and her efforts brought many southern women workers into trade unions. Her involvement with the WTUL and women's labor issues soon consumed her time, and although at one time Christman was engaged she never married.

Seeking to ensure good working standards and conditions for women who took industrial jobs, Christman cointroduced in 1916 a resolution before the American Federation of Labor (AFL) convention to create the Women in Industry Service (WIS). Although not established by the AFL, with the outbreak of World War I the agency was officially instituted under the U.S. government. When WIS became an agency, Christman became chief field representative during the war for women workers, joining only thirty-seven other women to be officially named to a wartime defense position under the National War Labor Board. In this capacity Christman traveled throughout the country to factories, settling grievances before they got out of hand. She talked to both workers and foremen, trying to convince them of the need to increase standards of health and safety and to pay a minimum and equal wage.

In 1919 Christman was appointed to the WTUL's national executive board, and by 1921 she was elected secretary-treasurer of the league, a position she kept for nearly thirty years. The league headquarters moved from Chicago to Washington, D.C., in 1930, and there Christman became an integral part of a nationwide network of women organizers and workers. In 1921 she also took on the duties of editing the league's influential publication, *Life and Labor* (renamed the *Life and Labor Bulletin* in 1922).

In 1923 Christman protested the U.S. Supreme Court's ruling in *Adkins v. Children's Hospital*, which declared minimum-wage laws for women unconstitutional. Although a valiant fighter for women's rights, she argued against the Equal Rights Amendment, maintaining that it would not guarantee women equality in the workplace. At the 1933 AFL convention she urged delegates to organize the five million working women into unions. She presented a resolution suggesting that a board of men and women introduce unions to industries that resisted organized labor. The resolution was adopted in part a year later.

In 1934 Christman was the first woman named to the Code Authority of the National Recovery Administration during the New Deal. She examined the conditions and wages of women workers and testified at congressional hearings that concerned the hiring of women. She also served on an advisory board of the National Industrial Recovery Act of 1933, an agency establishing production quotas, prices, and resources for each industry.

During World War II Secretary of Labor Frances Perkins asked for Christman's services when an increased need for women workers loosened protective labor laws. In 1942 Christman became a special agent of the Women's Bureau concerned with issues of equal pay. Called "a convincing and forceful woman," Christman pressured the unions and companies like General Motors to agree to equal pay by emphasizing that soldiers needed to be assured that the wage structure would remain intact on their return from the war.

Shortly before the end of World War II Christman returned to her duties at a financially troubled WTUL. She attempted to keep the organization afloat through fundraising and many times did not pay her own salary. She stayed with the WTUL until it went broke in 1950. In her final report for the WTUL, Christman asserted that the organization had achieved some success and had "ploughed the hard fields and planted them with the seeds of accomplishment." In 1950 she became the legislative representative for the Amalgamated Clothing Workers' of America.

Although Christman officially retired in 1952, she continued paying union dues and giving advice to women on organizing and settling labor disputes. She died in Delphi, Indiana. Throughout her long life Christman promoted women's unionization, equal pay, and protection, and she was respected for her indefatigable dedication to the rights of the woman worker. Described as "the most loyal" woman in the labor movement, she sought neither fame nor notoriety but worked diligently toward a better working environment for women.

• Elisabeth Christman left no papers. The WTUL papers are at the Library of Congress and the Schlesinger Library at Radcliffe College. Other sources include the Mary Anderson Papers at the Schlesinger Library; the Margaret Dreier Robins Papers at the University of Florida; the Agnes Nestor Papers and Chicago-branch WTUL papers at the Chicago Historical Society; and interviews with Lillian Herstein by Dr. Elizabeth Balanoff on 26 Oct. 1970, 6 Nov. 1970, and 18 Feb. 1971 at Roosevelt University. Writings by Christman include "Conventions—A Complement to Workers Education," *American Federationist* 36 (Aug. 1929): 921–25; "Women's Trade Union League of America," *Labor Information Bulletin* 7 (Sept. 1940): 10–12; and "Work at Adequate Wages," *Survey Midmonthly* 76 (1940): 48. Biographical and union details are in Gladys Boone, *The Women's Trade Union Leagues in Great Britain and the United States of America* (1942); Eleanor Ellis Perkins, "Elizabeth [*sic*] Christman: 'Co-Worker,'" *Christian Science Monitor*, 19 Jan. 1946; Mary Anderson, *Woman at Work: The Autobiography of Mary Anderson as Told to Mary N. Winslow* (1951); Agnes Nestor, *Woman's Labor Leader* (1954); Rose Schneiderman, *All for One* (1967); James J. Kenneally, *Women and American Trade Unions* (1978); Philip S. Foner, *Women and the American Labor Movement* (1980); Barbara Mayer Wertheimer, *We Were There: The Story of Working Women in America* (1977); and Diane Kirkby, *Alice Henry: The Power of Pen and Voice, the Life of an Australian-American Labor Reformer* (1991). Obituaries are in the *Chicago Tribune*, 17 Apr. 1975, and the *Washington Post*, 29 Apr. 1975.

MARILYN ELIZABETH PERRY

CHRISTY, Edwin Pearce (1 Nov. 1814–21 May 1862), blackface minstrel and manager, was born in New York City, the son of Robert Christy and Ruth Wheaton. Nothing is known about his education. It is reported that he was once an office boy to a New York lawyer, a hotel clerk, and a traveling shoe salesman. In the early 1830s he became a comic blackface singer with the Purdy and Welch Circus in New Orleans, claiming to have been inspired by the singing and dancing of slaves in that city's Congo Square.

Actually, blackface song-and-dance specialties such as Thomas Dartmouth Rice's were common inter-acts on the American stage by the 1820s, and the growing vogue of blackface "minstrel" performance centered in Pennsylvania and New York, to which Christy returned. In Rochester, New York, Christy, adept on banjo and tambourine, formed an act with singer-instrumentalists Dick Sliter and John Daniels and "jig dancer" John Perkins. By 1835 Christy had settled in Buffalo, New York, where apparently in 1835 he married Harriet Harrington, a widowed saloonkeeper. They had two sons (both later minstrels), and Christy adopted Harriet's son George, who in 1839 joined Christy and Thomas Vaughn in a singing act.

In 1842 Christy formed the Virginia Minstrels. (It typifies the era that another blackface troupe specializing in sentimental ballads founded by Dan Emmett—the author of "Dixie"—bore the same name.) Vaughn and George (Harrington) Christy were joined by Lansing Durand. Led by the senior Christy, they toured the Midwest and South. In 1844, adding Enom Dickerson, Earl Pierce, and Zeke Backus, they became the Christy Minstrels.

Although the honor of performing the first "minstrel show" as a full evening onstage is contested by scholars (it surely happened sometime between 1842 and 1844), by 1846 it was clear that Christy had created American minstrelsy's classic form by joining broad comedy to song and dance in a three-part sequence. "Christy's Far Famed and Original Band of Ethiopian Minstrels" opened at Palmo's Opera House in New York City on 27 April 1846, replacing a sentimental-singing troupe called the Ethiopian Serenaders that had left for England in the hope of repeating "Jim Crow" Rice's success there. Moving to Mechanics Hall on Broadway in 1847, Christy's troupe ran (there and on tour) for more than 2,700 performances.

Christy became the first "interlocutor" (the word itself a spoof of highfalutin language). After a band walked onstage playing, Christy followed in tuxedo but not in blackface. He introduced himself and one by one his blackfaced, swallowtail-coated or gaudily calico-shirted, great-collared, striped-trousered troupe. Having arranged them in a standing semicircle, Christy boomed, "Gentlemen, be seated!"

Following this number, Christy (and all subsequent interlocutors) presided over a program of rapid-fire cross-talk—jokes, malapropisms, puns, songs—starring the semicircle's "endmen"—the grotesquely large-grinning Tambo and Bones, so named for the instruments they played. The interlocutor acted dense, repeating the comics' riddling queries solemnly, giving the audience time to make its own guesses just before the endman's cackling punch line. The intermediate "olio," or variety show, featured acrobatics, dance duets, comb-playing, "stump speeches" (parodying the era's "speechifying" oratory), and George's female impersonations. The finale was a prototypical musical comedy, upon whose nominal story line and innovative language ("hunky dory" came from one) were hung a series of dialogues, songs, and dances. Researcher Gary Engle believes these "can be considered the essence of the minstrel art—short farces, Shakespearean burlesques [a poignant "Nigger's Seben Ages of Man"], theatrical lampoons of contemporary fads [the apocalyptic Millerites]." Christy held it all together.

Christy's shows became, in Robert Toll's words, "a mandatory stop for rural visitors" to New York. Dan Wilmeth calls them the first American stage entertainment to "avoid the elitist reputation of legitimate drama and commit itself to the new common-man audience," an audience insecure in an era of etiquette books but lured by circuses and fireworks, lectures on mesmerism and phrenology, and innovations such as the telegraph (a favorite Christy song-sketch was "The Rail Road Trabeller," a brief history of American transportation and communication). The minstrel clown has been called "America's fool," a spirit of highbrow-deflating anarchy. The white audience could laugh at "Negro" characters (even Mark Twain believed blacks were accurately portrayed) and "work out their feelings about race and slavery," while enjoying this "peculiar" music and dance.

Christy called himself the "Originator of Ethiopian Minstrelsy and the first to harmonize Negro Melodies," though the latter were usually written by whites. Because the young composer Stephen Foster at first did not fancy an "Ethiopian" environment for his songs, in 1847 Christy began buying them from Foster and calling them his own. In 1851 (with Foster's permission) he published "Old Folks at Home," though Foster got the royalties. In 1852 Foster chose to give himself credit, but Christy continued to introduce the songs. (In the 1939 motion picture biography of Foster, *Swanee River*, Christy is played by Al Jolson.)

Christy's Plantation Melodies went through five annual editions. Like the shows these songs enforced stereotypical views of a carefree life lived by ungrammatical, good-hearted slaves. In keeping with a perilous age, there were many songs to the newly dead. Christy's own composition, "Snow Drop Ann," is a love song to a "charming colored dove" whose chorus is "De hawk fly high, de bird fly low / Sweet snowdrop Ann, I lub you! / It's no odds how de wind does blow / This darkey's heart is always true." His most enduringly popular song was "Buffalo Gals" (1848).

Christy became a wealthy owner of circuses and "opera houses"; in 1853 alone he earned nearly $48,000. After an 1854 tour to San Francisco he retired and disbanded the troupe, but the demand continued. George Christy and Wood's Minstrels eventually rewrote *Uncle Tom's Cabin* as the play *Happy Uncle Tom.* Still other "Christys" arose and Edwin Christy won an 1855 New York Supreme Court ruling that entertainment was like any other trade; since Christy had given no license for the use of his name, he retained its exclusive use. In 1857 a licensed troupe called J. W.

Raynor and Earl Pierce's Christy Minstrels opened in London. They were so successful that for the rest of the century "Christys" literally became a British synonym for "minstrels." (In the 1960s a white American folksinging troupe continued this tradition, calling itself "The New Christy Minstrels.")

According to annalist T. Allston Brown, "Mr. Christy was a man of violent temper. . . . [He was] entirely self-willed and had too little regard for the feeling of others." As the Civil War approached, Christy sensed ruin. Apparently divorced and remarried to a Mary (maiden name unknown) and said to be suffering severe personal problems, Christy jumped from a window of his New York City home; he lingered twelve days before dying.

Though undeniably racist, Edwin Pearce Christy's minstrel show, an emblem of its times, has been called America's only contribution to the stage genre. Even if that is not true, the minstrel show was essential to the development of the stage musical, in the eyes of the world a distinctly American invention.

• The five editions of Edwin P. Christy, *Christy's Plantation Melodies*, were published in Philadelphia between 1851 and 1856 and in London approximately a decade later. Christy's life and the minstrel show in general are glimpsed in articles such as Dan B. Wilmeth, "Stage Entertainment" in the *Handbook of American Popular Culture*, ed. Thomas M. Inge, vol. 1 (1978). See also James Weldon Johnson, *The Book of American Negro Spirituals* (1925); Carl Wittke, *Tambo and Bones* (1930); Robert Toll, *On with the Show* (1972) and *Blacking Up* (1986); Gary Engle, *This Grotesque Essence: Plays from the American Minstrel Stage* (1978); William T. Leonard, *Masquerade in Black* (1986); and Eric Lott, *Love and Theft: Blackface Minstrelsy and the American Working Class* (1993). A major source of material on minstrelsy is the Buffalo and Erie County Public Library, Buffalo, N.Y.

JAMES ROSS MOORE

CHRISTY, George N. Harrington (6 Nov. 1827–12 May 1868), blackface minstrel star, was born in Palmyra, New York, the son of Harriet Harrington, a tavern-keeper; nothing is known about Christy's natural father. When in about 1842 his widowed mother married Edwin Pearce Christy, a performer, blackface comic minstrel singer, and theater manager, George took his stepfather's surname. Even as a child Christy was involved in the theater, appearing first in 1842 in Buffalo, New York, where he performed as a jig dancer. His venues included circuses, small theaters, and taverns; entertainers often appeared in blackface at such places. Later in 1842 Christy joined with his stepfather and Tom Vaughan, a banjoist, to form a loosely connected troupe of blackface performers. The three men made up the core of "E. P. Christy's Minstrels," organized in late 1843 in emulation of Dan Emmett and the Virginia Minstrels, the first minstrel show troupe. Like other such companies, Christy's Minstrels performed skits, jokes, songs, and instrumental numbers in ensemble, and thus provided entertainment for a whole evening's program. On 15 February 1847 Christy's Minstrels began a six-year run at Mechanics Hall in New York City and proceeded to solidify their reputation as the most popular and influential minstrel show of the day.

During the antebellum period George Christy reigned as the genre's best comic. He was the headlining member of the Christy's Minstrels until a dispute with his stepfather in October 1853 prompted him to go his own way. He joined forces with fellow blackface performer Henry Wood to establish the Wood and Christy's Minstrels. Their partnership lasted until 1 May 1858. Christy's skill and powerful theatrical personality, along with the company's mastery of farcical comedies, led the Wood and Christy's Minstrels to the top of the blackface business during this period. After 1858 Christy seldom stayed with one troupe for any extended time; rather, he moved annually from company to company, always as the featured minstrel. He performed throughout much of the United States, including the South and the West.

Christy was an unusually versatile performer during a period in which theatrical specialization had become the rule. He was, by all accounts, an excellent dancer as well as an outstanding comic. In the typical minstrel show line, he took the role of Mr. Bones, one of the two "endmen," and was thus responsible (with Mr. Tambo) for the bulk of the show's humor. Fellow actor H. P. Grattan said that Christy was "justly celebrated as the very best 'end man and bones' ever seen in a nigger [*sic*] troupe" (Nathan, pp. 144–45). Christy was also renowned for his "wench" roles, which he claimed to have introduced to minstrelsy. Such roles continued a long and honored tradition of cross-dressed playacting. Christy's "wench" roles were novel in that the ersatz female was also ersatz black, thus opening new and more complicated possibilities for class-, race-, and gender-based humor. Christy became particularly famous for his depiction of "Miss Lucy Long."

Christy also authored several important collections of minstrel show routines, jokes, and songs. Among the best known are *Christy and White's Ethiopian Melodies* (1854), *George Christy and Wood's Melodies* (1854), *Christy's Panorama Songster* (1860), *George Christy's Essence of Old Kentucky* (1862), and *Christy's Bones and Banjo Melodist* (1865).

Little is known about Christy's personal life. It is unclear whether or not he ever married. A romance novel published some seventeen years after his death played on the legend of Christy's life, which "abounded with romantic incidents" (Pastor, p. 6), suggesting that he was quite a ladies' man. More than one source, including the *New York Times* obituary (15 May 1868) notes that Christy earned a great amount of money in minstrelsy but spent it "as fast as it was made." Christy, in common with many of his fellow blackface actors, was not unsympathetic to the southern perspective on slavery. His burlesque of *Uncle Tom's Cabin* (which he called *Happy Uncle Tom*) became quite famous, and Christy assured an audience in Charleston in late 1860 that he and his minstrels did not support the northern cause. He died in New York City at his mother's home.

• No extensive collection of Christy's papers exists. The Stephen Foster Collection at the University of Pittsburgh and the University of Chicago both have thin manuscript holdings. The paucity of primary sources seems to have impeded a full and reliable rendering of Christy's life. Edward LeRoy Rice, *Monarchs of Minstrelsy* (1911), contains the fullest biography, but it is a scant page and includes some inaccurate information. Hans Nathan, *Dan Emmett and the Rise of Early Negro Minstrelsy* (1962), is useful on the early years of the genre. Robert Toll, *Blacking Up: The Minstrel Show in Nineteenth-Century America* (1974), holds some fresh, original research. Anthony "Tony" Pastor's fanciful *George Christy, or, The Fortunes of a Minstrel* (1885), is intriguing for its biographical implications.

DALE COCKRELL

CHRISTY, Howard Chandler (10 Jan. 1873–3 Mar. 1952), artist, was born in Morgan County, Ohio, the son of Francis Marion Christy and Mary Chandler, farmers. Christy revealed a precocious ability to draw. At age ten he earned $10 by painting a black and white bull against a blue sky for a local butcher's shop sign. At thirteen he sketched the log schoolhouse in Orange, Ohio, where James A. Garfield, later the twentieth president, had taught. David Ross Locke (aka "Petroleum B. Nasby"), editor of the *Toledo Blade*, bought and published the picture and offered Christy a job. Instead, after limited schooling in Duncan, Ohio, he moved in 1890 to New York City. For money to do so, he painted landscapes on seashells and also created Christmas cards, which sold poorly until he quit lettering "Xmus" on them. His family helped finance lessons for him at the Art Students League and then at the National Academy of Design, where he was tutored for two years by William Merritt Chase, the popular portrait painter, whose displeasure at Christy's decision to become an illustrator and not a portraitist caused him to stop speaking to Christy for three years. During this period he lived in considerable poverty.

In 1895 Christy sold some illustrations to *Scribner's Magazine* and *Leslie's Weekly*. In 1898 he married Maybelle Gertrude Thompson, one of his several attractive models; the couple had one child. Paid by *Scribner's* and *Leslie's* in 1898, Christy became an art correspondent with the Second U.S. Regulars during the Spanish-American War. He wrote "An Artist at El Pozo" (*Scribner's*, Sept. 1898) about combat action observed at Santiago, Cuba, and sketched many scenes, including some involving Colonel Theodore Roosevelt and his Rough Riders. Reproductions of Christy's picturesque pastels were assembled in his *Men of the Army and Navy: Characteristic Types of Our Fighting Men* (1899). His work received a boost when he illustrated "The Lion and the Unicorn," a short story by Richard Harding Davis (*Scribner's*, Aug. 1899). In 1899 he also published pastel sketches of theatrical personalities Maude Adams, Joseph Jefferson, and Ellen Terry. These were the first of a long series of rich, famous, and influential Christy sitters.

In 1901 Christy began to provide illustrations for books by such popular writers as Henry Wadsworth Longfellow, Thomas Nelson Page, James Whitcomb Riley, and Mary Roberts Rinehart. His pictures for Riley's *An Old Sweetheart of Mine* (1902) so pleased author and public alike that he illustrated nine more publications by Riley. *The Complete Works of James Whitcomb Riley* (6 vols., 1913) reprinted numerous Christy illustrations. In colors and black and white, the pictures seemed so integral to the texts that ten of Riley's reissued titles were called "Christy-Riley" books. Christy's painting of a soldier's dream girl was the genesis of his famous "Christy girl," capitalizing on the popularity of portraits both serious and lighthearted of young ladies by John Singer Sargent and Charles Dana Gibson. The Christy girl had deep-set eyes, a saucy nose, pouty mouth, and firm jawline and often was accompanied by a stalwart, attentive male escort. The best examples are in *The American Girl as Seen and Portrayed by Howard Chandler Christy* (1906), *The Christy Girl* (1906, with illustrations accompanying thirty-five love lyrics by various poets), and *Liberty Belles* (1912). Posing for some of his later Christy girl efforts was model Nancy May Palmer, whom he married in 1919 following his divorce that year from Maybelle. Nancy also posed for his World War I posters titled *Americans All* and *Fight or Buy Bonds!*

From 1920 or so Christy concentrated almost exclusively on portrait painting, which proved highly profitable. His subjects included Alben W. Barkley, Calvin Coolidge, Grace Coolidge, Warren Harding, Amelia Earhart, Mary Baker Eddy, John Nance Garner, Will H. Hays, Charles Evans Hughes, Benito Mussolini, Edward Vernon Rickenbacker, Will Rogers, John Philip Sousa, Lawrence Tibbett, and Crown Prince Umberto of Italy. Unlike Sargent, who subtly included telltale signs of personality in his portraits, Christy typically combined lively accuracy in depicting his subjects' features and flattering suggestions of their hygienic, suave self-confidence.

Christy's most ambitious work was *Signing of the Constitution* (1940), which involved three years of research and six months of painting. It is a 20′ × 30′ oil depicting thirty-seven signers and one secretary and now hangs in the Rotunda of the U.S. Capitol. The most impressive features of the work are George Washington standing at an elevated desk, Benjamin Franklin seated, and the flags, three draped windows, and a glittering chandelier; less admirable aesthetically are too many relaxed faces gazing at the viewer as though posing for a group photograph. Details are careful but excessive, and a lack of subordination of some parts makes for a flatness displeasing to modern critics.

In his last years, Christy resided and maintained a studio in the Café des Artistes on Sixty-seventh Street in New York City. While living there, he painted a Park Lane Hotel mural, which featured nudes described as so "snappy" by contemporaries that they augmented the hotel owners' income. Christy heard that artists living in or frequenting the Café des Artistes were invited to paint nudes at one panel each but were squabbling. So he offered to paint every panel himself and did so (1934, 1941–1943). In addition to fifty or so attractively clean, healthy, frisky females, Christy included a boy, a man, and a few animals. Since the "murals" were actually painted on canvas, some were detached and went to a club in Texas, while another later graced the Christy Room of the Sherry-Netherlands Hotel in New York City. Christy's *My Old Kentucky Home* (1940) depicts Stephen Collins Foster playing the piano and evoking images from several of his best-known songs. The painting was dedicated on the Fourth of July at the headquarters of the Honorable Order of Kentucky Colonels in Bardstown, Kentucky.

Christy transmitted his easy, sumptuous style of painting to students in classes he occasionally taught at the Artists' and Artisans' Institute, the Art Students League, the Chase School, and the Cooper Union. He was untroubled by advances in the international art community. For this reason later critics have unfortunately ignored his work, which has energy, verve, and versatility, if also perhaps too many sentimentally posed figures. Amid his several honors, the one most revealing is a special medal presented to him in 1941 by the Society for Sanity in Art. Christy died at his residence in the Artistes Hotel.

• A few papers relating to Christy are in the Samuel W. Marvin Correspondence in the University of Virginia library, Charlottesville, and in the Homer Adams Holt Papers in the West Virginia Department of Archives and History Collections, Charleston. The following contain material concerning Christy: S. J. Woolf, "Creator of the Christy Girl," *New York Times Magazine*, 18 Jan. 1948; Arthur William Brown, "Howard Chandler Christy: A Tribute to a Great American on His 80th Birthday," *American Artist* 16 (Jan. 1952): 50–51, 68; William Gerdts, *The Great American Nude: A History in Art* (1974); Lyn Wall Smith and Nancy Dustin Wall Moure, *Index to Reproductions of Paintings Appearing in More Than 400 Books, Mostly Published since 1960* (1977); and Walt Reed and Roger Reed, *The Illustrator in America, 1880–1980: A Century of Illustration* (1984). Frank Luther Mott, *A History of American Magazines, 1930–1968* (5 vols., 1930–1968), calls Christy one of the best illustrators of fiction and of covers for *Collier's*, *Delineator*, *Hearst's Magazine*, *Home Magazine*, *Leslie's Weekly*, *McClure's Magazine*, and *Scribner's Magazine*. Anthony J. Russo and Dorothy R. Russo, *A Bibliography of James Whitcomb Riley* (1944), identifies the books Christy illustrated; Peter Revell, *James Whitcomb Riley* (1970), says Christy's figures in Riley's books have "a distinctly middle-class, comfortably settled air." Donald H. Dyal, *Historical Dictionary of the Spanish American War* (1996), describes Christy's war work. An obituary is in the *New York Times*, 4 Mar. 1952.

ROBERT L. GALE

CHRISTY, June (20 Nov. 1925–21 June 1990), jazz singer, was born Shirley Luster in Springfield, Illinois. She moved to Decatur, Illinois, as a young child and at age thirteen began singing the popular songs of the day with a local band. After graduating from high school she settled in Chicago, where she secured work as the "girl" singer with local society bands. Uncomfortable with both the style and repertoire of such bands, Luster signed on in 1938 with a dance unit led by Boyd Raeburn. Having begun to adopt the jazz style, Raeburn's band received more lucrative engagements and Luster's reputation soared in Chicago and the surrounding area. At the peak of the band's local renown, she contracted scarlet fever and had to take a leave of absence.

After her recovery, Luster worked with Benny Strong's band at Chicago clubs. It was at the Three Deuces that singer Anita O'Day claimed to have seen Luster perform, amazed by the similarity in their voices and style. When O'Day decided to leave Stan Kenton's band in 1945, she reportedly recommended Luster, who began a six-year association with the ensemble. The three female singers most closely associated with Kenton—O'Day, Luster, and Chris Connor—did indeed share a breathy, vibratoless tone associated with the cool jazz of the West Coast, a whimsical sense of rhythm that played around the front and back of the beat, and an almost melancholy reading of ballads. These qualities would be identified with Luster until the end of her career, though she would develop a style more distinct from O'Day's. Critics occasionally faulted her intonation.

Shortly after Luster joined the Kenton band, the group was booked for a dance in Corpus Christi, Texas, and en route to the engagement someone in the band suggested that Luster—who by that time was singing as "Sharon Leslie"—change her name to the more musical "Christi" or "Christy." She added "June" and from 1945 on worked as June Christy. Her first Capitol recording with Kenton under that name, "Tampico" (based on "And Her Tears Flowed Like Wine" recorded earlier by O'Day), sold a million copies.

The year 1946 was a momentous one for Christy. She married Bob Cooper, a tenor saxophonist and arranger with Kenton whose tenure with the band almost exactly coincided with her own. She was named best female vocalist in the *Metronome* jazz poll and best female vocalist with a big band by *Down Beat*, a title she was to win again in 1947, 1948, and 1950. Also in 1946 Christy issued an album with Nat King Cole titled "Nat Meets June," and toward the end of the year she appeared with the Kenton band in a number of short films.

After scoring such hits as "It's Been a Long, Long Time" and "Shoo Fly Pie and Apple Pan Dowdy," Christy left the Kenton band in 1951 and went on to establish a solo career. She returned to the band on several occasions for reunion concerts and sang with it on a tour of Europe in 1953 and of the United States in 1959. She and Kenton recorded a very successful album of vocal and piano duets in 1955 that included songs such as "Prelude to a Kiss" and "Angel Eyes." Though she also worked with other big bands, including one led by her husband in 1956 and another led by Ted Heath in 1957–1958, she made most of her appearances with a trio under her own direction.

Of Christy's post-Kenton recordings, nine albums and several solo sides were recorded with Pete Rugolo. One of the most successful of these efforts was their 1953 recording of "Something Cool," a saloon song released initially by Capitol as a single. Its success prompted a ten-inch LP in 1954 and a twelve-inch LP with four additional songs in 1955. By the fall of 1956 the album had sold a hefty 93,000 copies. Christy released "Something Cool" in stereo format in the early 1960s. By that time she had refined her extended song arrangements into short cantatas. The stereo version of "Something Cool" had a form of A A B A C D D E A A, with letters other than "A" denoting a new musical section within the arrangement. She also gave increasing attention to scatting, even recording prewritten scat lines on "How High the Moon."

By 1965 Christy had cut her last recordings for Capitol and in the remainder of her career made only a few recordings for other labels. She had largely retired from performing by the end of the decade but made some appearances with the Kenton band in the 1970s. June Christy died in Los Angeles, survived by her husband and a daughter. Though plagued by alcoholism, she had achieved considerable success as an artist. Her "wistful, foggy alto," recalled the *New York Times*, "epitomized 'cool' jazz singing in the 1940's and 50's."

• For discussions of Christy by her contemporaries, see R. J. Gleason, "I'd Like to Do 'Recitals,' Says June," *Down Beat* 16, no. 5 (1949): 3; "Too Easy to Get Lost in Record Biz Jungle: June," *Down Beat* 21, no. 8 (1954): 7; and J. Tynan, "The Misty Miss Christy," *Down Beat* 23, no. 2 (1956): 13. William F. Lee, *Stan Kenton: Artistry in Rhythm* (1980), treats her work with Kenton. For more on her solo recordings, see W. Friedwald, *Jazz Singing—America's Great Voices from Bessie Smith to Bebop and Beyond* (1990). An obituary is in the *New York Times*, 24 June 1990.

HORACE CLARENCE BOYER

CHRYSLER, Walter Percy (2 Apr. 1875–18 Aug. 1940), automobile manufacturer, was born in Wamego, Kansas, the son of Henry Chrysler, a railroad engineer, and Anna Maria Breyman. Chrysler's life was bound up with the creation of modern America's transportation system. He grew up in Ellis, Kansas, a railroad shop town, at a time when the townspeople still worried about Native American raiders. As a boy, Chrysler developed an abiding fascination with machines while watching the mechanics in the local railroad repair shops and occasionally accompanying his father in the engineer's cab of a Union Pacific locomotive. He developed an aggressive, quick-tempered personality playing with other working-class boys in the railroad yards and streets of Ellis. For most of his life, Chrysler remained outspoken and excitable, but he was also intelligent, hard working, and capable of intense concentration. These qualities enabled him to rise through the ranks of the railroad industry and then become one of the founders of America's automobile industry.

Chrysler completed high school in Ellis in 1892. His father offered to send him to college, but he wanted to work with machines. When his father refused to sponsor him as an apprentice, he took a dollar-a-day job as a sweeper in the local Union Pacific shop. Six months later, in 1893, his father relented, and he began a four-year term as a mechanic's apprentice. Chrysler was ambitious and, in his own words, "mad with curiosity" about machines. He frequently worked through the night, learning practical mechanics as he repaired the Union Pacific's locomotives. He also studied engineering, taking correspondence courses offered by the Salt Lake City Business School. When he finished his apprenticeship in 1897, Chrysler had developed mechanical skills that were in great demand. He was a restless young man with little patience for incompetent or authoritarian foremen. As a result, he moved frequently as a journeyman mechanic. By 1900 he had held, and lost or quit, at least six different jobs at railroad shops in Kansas, Colorado, Wyoming, and Utah.

In June 1901, after a year of working in the roundhouse of the Denver & Rio Grande Western Railroad in Salt Lake City, Chrysler married his childhood sweetheart, Della V. Forker, the daughter of an Ellis shopkeeper. Chrysler was soon promoted to roundhouse foreman, and the couple had the first of their four children. Della provided Walter with a secure private life that made it easier for him to take risks in the business world. Although his job changes frequently disrupted family routines and friendships, his marriage endured until his wife's death in 1938.

Chrysler began his rapid ascent through the ranks of railroad management in 1902 when he became general foreman at the Colorado & Southern Railroad shops in Trinidad, Colorado. The salary was $140 a month. Chrysler could have worked his way up the Colorado & Southern corporate ladder, but he still craved fresh technical challenges. In 1903, when a friend offered him the opportunity to oversee construction of a new roundhouse for the Fort Worth & Denver City Railroad, he moved his family to Childress, Texas, where he was made master mechanic at a salary of $160 a month. In 1905 Chrysler moved again to become supervisor in the sprawling Chicago Great Western Railroad shops in Oelwein, Iowa. This position with a major trunk line allowed Chrysler to master the full range of American railroad technology. When he was only thirty-three years old, Chrysler was named superintendent of motive power for the entire Chicago Great Western line at a monthly salary of $350.

Although now a secure member of the middle class, Chrysler remained ambitious and somewhat resentful of other railroad executives who made more money without seeming to exercise more authority than he did. In December 1910 these resentments exploded during an argument with the president of the Chicago Great Western, and Chrysler quit. Although he had to take a pay cut, he quickly found a new position as superintendent at the Allegheny works of the American Locomotive Company. Chrysler flourished in this new manufacturing job. He had responsibility for both the design of locomotives and the design of production processes. His reputation grew as he turned an unprofitable plant into a moneymaker. By 1912 his title was works manager, and his salary was $8,000 a year.

That year James Storrow of the recently reorganized General Motors Corporation (GM) asked Chrysler to take over management of the world's second largest automobile plant, the Buick Motor Company in Flint, Michigan. Chrysler had been fascinated by cars ever since 1908 when he had borrowed $5,000 to purchase a Locomobile at the Chicago automobile show. To learn all he could about the new automotive technology, Chrysler completely disassembled the new car in his garage in Oelwein before putting it on the road. He eagerly accepted Storrow's offer even though it meant another move for his family and a $2,000 salary reduction.

Chrysler quickly won the full confidence of Buick president Charles W. Nash and was given complete freedom to reorganize the company's production. During the next three years, he more than doubled Buick's output while reducing the plant's payroll by one-fourth. Chrysler introduced comprehensive piecework schedules and rigorous cost accounting methods to get control of loosely managed operations, and then he systematically redesigned production processes beginning with the paint shop. He conducted daily morning inspection tours in the vast plant looking for ways to improve efficiency. Altogether, he directed innovations—including the invention of special purpose machines and assembly line methods—that amounted to true mass production. However his achievements at Buick have been generally overlooked by historians fixated on the story of Henry Ford and the Model T.

In 1915, after working for three years without a raise, Chrysler demanded and got a salary increase from $6,000 to $25,000 a year. This enabled him to begin purchasing GM stock. In the spring of 1916 William C. Durant regained control of General Motors, forcing Nash and Storrow out of the organization. The two men tried to convince Chrysler to join them in establishing a new car company in Racine, Wisconsin, but Durant offered him $500,000 a year to stay on as president of Buick and GM vice president in charge of automotive production. It was an offer Chrysler could not refuse. By drawing most of his salary in GM stock Chrysler was able to quickly accumulate a significant fortune. But he was unable to work for long with the brilliant but erratic Durant. In 1919, when Durant pushed ahead with acquisitions and construction projects that he opposed as unnecessary and too expensive, Chrysler resigned and announced he was retiring from the industry.

His retirement lasted less than a year. In 1920–1921 many automobile companies were failing as a national recession cut deeply into sales, and bankers pressured them to pay back loans taken out to finance wartime expansion. Chrysler was besieged with offers from financially troubled companies. In 1920 he agreed to try to rescue Willys-Overland, the third largest automobile and truck manufacturer in the United States, for a salary of $1 million a year. He became the company's executive vice president and was given full authority to cut costs and streamline production. Although Chrysler was able to shed Willys's unprofitable aircraft and harvester operations, a combination of steeply declining automobile sales and a huge debt burden doomed his efforts. The company was liquidated in 1921, but not before Chrysler had recruited a team of Willys engineers, Fred Zeder, Owen Skelton, and Carl Breer, to design a radically new high-performance, moderately priced automobile.

Even before he had left Willys-Overland, Chrysler had become the chairman of Maxwell Motors' reorganization and management committee. In 1923 Chrysler was named president of the newly reorganized Maxwell Motor Company. He brought his design team of Zeder, Skelton, and Breer to Maxwell where they continued to develop a car they called "the Chrysler." Their new Chrysler Six automobile was unveiled in New York City in January 1924 before it actually went into production. The Chrysler car was low slung, with a short wheelbase, high-compression engine, and four-wheel hydraulic brakes. It was an immediate sensation. Using positive publicity to great advantage, Chrysler obtained banker support for the capital improvements needed to mass produce the Chrysler Six. The moderately priced car sold extremely well, and the company turned a $4 million profit in 1925. That year Chrysler discontinued the Maxwell car line and renamed the company Chrysler Corporation.

By 1928 the Chrysler Corporation had earned $46 million in profits and was the country's third largest automobile manufacturer. Chrysler and his general manager K. T. Kellar, a former master mechanic at Buick, wanted to expand into the low-priced market dominated by Ford and GM's Chevrolet. To do so they needed to acquire basic parts production facilities including a large foundry and various forge shops, which would cost at least $75 million to construct. To avoid the delay and uncertainties involved in such a massive project, Chrysler acquired the Dodge Motor Company from the banking house of Dillon, Read, and Company for $170 million in Chrysler Corporation stock. The purchase enabled Chrysler Corporation to sell the popular Dodge car while doubling the number of dealers selling its other models. The Dodge acquisition also lowered the cost of basic components, thus preparing the way for the Plymouth, Chrysler Corporation's 1928 entry in the low-price automobile market.

As the 1920s came to a close, Chrysler launched one last great project, the construction of the 77-story Chrysler Building in New York City. Inspired by his admiration for the Eiffel Tower and by a desire to invest his personal fortune in something solid, the Chrysler Building was for a short time after its completion in 1930 the tallest structure in New York City. Chrysler's oldest son, Walter Chrysler, Jr., was made the first president of the Chrysler Building Corporation.

During the Great Depression, Chrysler directed his automobile company's retrenchment program. By the winter of 1932–1933 Chrysler plants were operating at less than 40 percent of capacity, but Chrysler continued to fully support his research and development staff. As the national economy began to recover in 1933, Chrysler introduced aerodynamic body styling and a "floating ride" that combined redesigned seat placement and improved suspension to greatly enhance passenger comfort. Strong car sales enabled the corporation to pay off its debts and surge ahead of Ford to become America's second largest automobile maker in the mid-1930s.

Chrysler turned over the presidency of his company to K. T. Kellar in July 1935, but he remained chairman of its board of directors. In the late 1930s he suffered from arterial sclerosis. His wife's death seems to have hastened his decline. He died after suffering a stroke at his estate in Great Neck, Long Island.

Chrysler played a major role in America's second, automobile-centered, industrial revolution. He was personally responsible for bringing technological and managerial knowledge that had accumulated in the railroad industry into the automobile industry. Building on that knowledge, he developed modern mass production methods at Buick that paralleled more famous developments at the Ford Motor Company. Chrysler was also a moving force behind the redesign of the American automobile in the 1920s. The streamlined high-performance cars for which the United States became famous in the mid-twentieth century were all descendants of the 1924 Chrysler Six. Like a Horatio Alger hero, Chrysler demonstrated that it was indeed possible to rise from obscurity to the top of the social and economic pyramid in the United States during the early twentieth century.

• Walter Chrysler's autobiography, *Life of an American Workman* (1937; repr. 1950), written in collaboration with Boyden Sparkes, remains the essential source of information on his life. Michael Moritz and Barrett Seaman, *Going For Broke: The Chrysler Story* (1981), and Robert B. Reich and John Donahue, *New Deals: The Chrysler Revival and the American System* (1985), contains chapters on Chrysler's career.

RONALD EDSFORTH

CHRYSLER, Walter Percy, Jr. (27 May 1909–17 Sept. 1988), art collector and benefactor, was born in Oelwein, Iowa, the son of Walter P. Chrysler (1875–1940), founder of the corporation that bears his name, and Della Viola Forker. "Collecting has always been in my blood," Chrysler said. He was brought up amid his family's art collection, was taken to many art museums and galleries, and his wealth facilitated acquiring what was to become his passion. While attending Hotchkiss School, he used his father's birthday gift to purchase his first work of art, a Renoir watercolor, which included a small nude figure. His dormitory master was horrified, and, as Chrysler later recalled, "busted it over his knee and threw it in the trashcan" (*Chicago Tribune*, 19 Sept. 1988). While attending Dartmouth College in the early 1930s, Chrysler set up a publishing venture and established an arts magazine in collaboration with another student, Nelson Rockefeller, the future governor of New York and vice president of the United States. The Grand Tour of Europe followed his college years. Not only did he meet such artists in Paris as Braque, Leger, Matisse, and Picasso, but he went on to purchase some of their works, early evidence of his admirable prescience. These acquisitions formed the foundation of his modern art collection, to which he then added American paintings, including works by Thomas Hart Benton (1889–1975), Charles Ephraim Burchfield, and John Marin.

During the 1930s Chrysler devoted much of his time to the Museum of Modern Art in New York City. He supervised its collection of Surrealist and Dada works, a number of which he had donated (along with other important pieces). He chaired its library committee. And he freely lent his art work to exhibitions elsewhere.

Accompanying this activity, Chrysler entered the automobile business, as expected. In 1934 he headed the Airtemp Division of the Chrysler Corporation, then became a director of the corporation, and in 1935 also took on the post of president of the Chrysler Building. He retired from active business in 1956.

In 1940 he renewed his association with Nelson Rockefeller, assisting him in Washington while Rockefeller was coordinator of Inter-American Affairs. During World War II, he served as a naval officer, ultimately resigning that post in December 1944. During this period, Chrysler met Jean Esther Outland, and they were married on 13 January 1945. He had earlier married Margeret Price Sykes; it was a short-lived union that ended in divorce in 1939. Neither marriage produced any children.

After the war Chrysler continued his interest in art, often buying "against fashion." When one of his exhibitions, concentrating on Picasso, opened at the Virginia Museum of Fine Arts in 1941, a local newspaper observed, "Modern art struck Richmond like a bomb." His second Richmond show, held a decade later, concentrated on seventeenth-century Dutch and Flemish painters, a more conventional presentation.

In 1958, two years after Chrysler retired from business, he decided to house a portion of his collection in Provincetown, Massachusetts, but the limited space and facilities there ultimately led him to search for a new home. In 1970 he accepted an offer from Norfolk, Virginia, which, as he explained, had bid the "mostest firstest." Within a brief time the Chrysler Museum acquired a positive rating, "a testimony to one man's lifetime passion for acquisition and art" (*Wall Street Journal*, 1 Apr. 1976).

Chrysler purchased a large house near his museum, the better to maintain his personal involvement. He was its director until 1976 and chaired its board of trustees until 1974. During these years he continued to augment the museum's holdings with paintings, graphic art, books, artifacts, and glass. His interest in glass may have stemmed from the early 1930s when he would visit the Long Island estate of the elderly Louis Comfort Tiffany; the furniture Chrysler purchased for the museum concentrated on the same period as Tiffany's Art Nouveau glass.

Chrysler also devoted attention to the major collection of books, documents, and rare recordings that he later donated to the Virginia Opera Association. Jean Chrysler shared her husband's attraction to books and helped develop the Norfolk museum's extensive holdings. Theater and the movies were not omitted from Chrysler's attention; he produced or backed several Broadway shows and films. His eclecticism also embraced the collection of decorative objects, stamps, and toys as well as involvement in horse racing and other sports.

Chrysler relied primarily on his own judgment in amassing his collections (and in pruning them through sale and trade). This approach may have achieved fine results but occasionally led to difficulties. When he presented six Picasso canvases for inclusion in the artist's eightieth birthday celebration in New York in 1961, Picasso examined photographs of these works and wrote "faux" across two of them. The next year, the authenticity of a number of Chrysler's other acquisitions was questioned when they were displayed at the National Gallery of Canada in Ottawa. The dealers who had sold Chrysler these paintings insisted they they had not guaranteed their authenticity but merely indicated their attribution! When the Chrysler Museum opened in Norfolk, the paintings in question had been weeded out.

Throughout his career, Chrysler was both a benefactor and a leader in building a superior collection of art. "I collect with my heart and with my mind," he insisted (*Look*, 6 Mar. 1956). Overconfidence occasionally resulted in dubious acquisitions. One observer noted, "It was horribly difficult to tell him anything" (*Life*, 2 Nov. 1967). But art remained his life, and the Chrysler Museum was the pinnacle of his ambition. Socializing meant little to him. His knowledge of art was honed by constant exposure to it, by reading, and through contacts with dealers and curators. Chrysler died in Norfolk, Virginia.

The overall evaluation of Walter P. Chrysler, Jr., remains positive. Thomas C. Colt, director of the Portland (Oreg.) Art Museum, described Chrysler as both "dynamic and adventuresome" and "one of America's great collectors and connoisseurs." John Russell, art critic of the *New York Times*, characterized him as "the most underrated art collector of the past 50 years and more" ("Time Rescues a Collector's Reputation," 11 Aug. 1991).

• The Smithsonian Institution Archives of American Art in New York include pertinent material from the Thomas Clyde Colt Papers as well as an interview conducted by Dorothy Seckler on 5 Sept. 1964. My own interview with Ronald A. Kuchta, director of the Everson Museum of Art in Syracuse, N.Y., provided valuable information for this article. Kuchta was curator of the Chrysler Museum from 1961 to 1968. Of interest is Walter P. Chrysler, Jr., "What Motivates a Person to Be a Collector of Art," *American Artist*, Nov. 1980, pp. 12, 92. For details on Chrysler's early life, see the *New York Times*, 10 Sept. 1930; *Life*, 27 Jan. 1941; John Lerch, "Walter P. Chrysler, Jr.'s Collection of Twentieth Century Masterpieces," *Country Life*, May 1938, pp. 44–46, 94–98; and Stuart Greenspan, "Driven to Collect," *House and Garden*, pp. 32 ff.

On the Chrysler Art Museum in Provincetown, see the *New Yorker*, 26 July 1958, pp. 18–19, and Rosemary Blackmon, "Cape Cod Notes . . . ," *Vogue*, 1 Aug. 1952, pp. 40–47. For additional information on the Norfolk Museum, see Malcolm N. Carter, "The Chrysler Museum: Clouded by Controversy," *Art News*, Feb. 1976, pp. 56–62, and Benjamin Forgey, "The Chrysler Museum, Suddenly Splendid," *Washington Post*, 26 Feb. 1989. On the controversial art show, see William A. Gill, *The Collector's* Puzzling Path," *Life*, 2 Nov. 1962, pp. 80–84, and *The New Statesman*, 14 Dec. 1962, pp. 865–66.

An obituary is in the *New York Times*, 19 Sept. 1988. Data on his actual and unexecuted wills is in the *Washington Post*, 24, 26 Feb. 1989.

MURRAY M. HOROWITZ

CHURCH, Alonzo (9 Apr. 1793–18 May 1862), schoolmaster, college teacher, and college president, was born in Brattleboro, Vermont, the son of Reuben Church and Elizabeth Whipple. He attended Middlebury College and was graduated in 1816. He then left Vermont for Georgia and first resided in Putnam County, where he was a schoolmaster. In 1817 he married Sarah J. Trippe while in Putnam County; they had eight children. His religious fervor as an educator earned him the attention of powerful Presbyterians at the University of Georgia, and he became a professor of mathematics at the university in 1819. A year later he was ordained in the Presbyterian Church. The combination of teacher-preacher was not uncommon among university faculty of this era.

Though little is known about Church's career as a faculty member, he was successful enough that in 1829 he was selected to succeed Moses Waddel as president of the university. Church served in that office until 1859. The first decade of Church's presidency was marked by modest growth and relative fiscal prosperity, though the state's contribution remained limited. Beginning in the 1820s, the formally nondenominational university experienced opposition from denominational colleges set up by Methodists, Baptists, and Presbyterians. There was some denominational opposition to Church's selection, since Baptists and others objected to Presbyterian control of the institution (both Church and his predecessor were Presbyterians). Political opposition in the state legislature also complicated Church's tenure. Under his leadership, however, the university was able to maintain itself in the face of increasingly strident criticism.

Educationally, Church was mainly a traditionalist, a believer in the classical curriculum. During his presidency, however, the university took a few halting steps away from a totally prescribed course of study that embraced only classical learning. The freshman and sophomore year studies firmly emphasized the classics, but mathematics, French, history, botany, and literary study were also taught. The junior and senior year courses de-emphasized the classics without eliminating them, adding studies in mathematics, the sciences, and political economy. Calculus was introduced into the curriculum in the 1830s, along with additional modern languages, chemistry, astronomy, and physics. In 1831 a botanical garden was started that proved to be quite popular, though at times it also threatened to drain university finances. Classical learning, however, remained the major priority for the university and its president.

Church was a stickler for detail and punctuality. These attributes earned him mixed reviews from both faculty and students. He was quick to impose restrictions on outspoken members of the student body whose drinking and intermittent rebelliousness threatened the image of the university. He instituted censorship of student commencement speeches and debate topics to prevent negative political reaction to the university from the state legislature.

Poorer economic conditions, diminished state support, curricular challenges, and new faculty members with different ideas all combined to make the last two decades of Church's stewardship of the university a substantially more difficult period. Though he was willing to add nonclassical studies to the curriculum, Church resisted a reorganization of the university, which was intended to bring more directly applied studies, such as agriculture and teacher education, to a place of prominence. A series of faculty resignations began in the late 1840s and continued into the next decade, and student enrollment began to fall in this period. Faculty who were beginning to see themselves as professional academics felt little affinity for Church's desire to have them concentrate on student discipline. In 1855 the resignation of John LeConte, a prominent scientist on the faculty who left to take a position at a medical college in New York, provoked a storm of controversy. Church defended his policies, explaining that mobility among the professors was not unusual and that LeConte was leaving for a lighter teaching load. Students were not persuaded by this explanation, and they expressed displeasure with LeConte's departure, perhaps knowing that at least part of his motivation for leaving was dissatisfaction with Church's custodialism and fear for the institution's future. This concern eventually spread to the board of trustees, and the situation intensified when LeConte published a rebuttal to the president's defense.

Church survived the battle, threatening to resign and actually announcing his resignation in 1856. He managed to garner enough support to persuade the trustees to ask him to stay on. Over the next few years, however, Church was faced with enrollment fluctuations, continuing rancor amongst the faculty, and a plan to enlarge and diversify the institution that was much like the earlier one he had defeated. Controversy finally took its toll on Church, and he resigned in November 1859. He retired to a nearby farm, where he died.

Church's lengthy tenure as president of the University of Georgia was marked by both accomplishment and failure. He presided over a campus that grew in number of buildings and faculty and in reputation. His failures with regard to faculty and student relations, however, along with a basically narrow view of the curriculum, made his presidency difficult.

• Primary source material relevant to Church's presidency is in the University Archives at the University of Georgia Library. On relations with students, see E. Merton Coulter, *College Life in the Old South* (1928). For administrative matters, see Robert P. Brooks, *The University of Georgia under Sixteen Administrations* (1956). The fullest account of Church and his presidency is in Thomas G. Dyer, *The University of Georgia: A Bicentennial History, 1785–1985* (1985).

WAYNE J. URBAN

CHURCH, Alonzo (14 June 1903–11 Aug. 1995), mathematician and philosopher, was born in Washington, D.C., the son of Samuel Robbins Church, a judge, and Mildred Hannah Letterman Parker. Church attended Princeton University, receiving an A.B. in 1924 and a Ph.D. in mathematics in 1927. While at Princeton, Church married Mary Julia Kuczinski, a practical nurse, in 1926; they had three children.

Church began his academic teaching career in 1929 at Princeton, following a two-year National Research Fellowship. He remained at Princeton until 1967, eventually becoming a full professor of mathematics and philosophy. His first decade there was especially productive. Church founded the *Journal of Symbolic Logic* in 1936 and served it in an editorial capacity until 1979, helping to establish it as the premier journal in the field. Also in 1936, he published two landmark papers in mathematical logic, resulting in what have come to be known as "Church's Theorem" and "Church's Thesis." Both flow from work on the decidability problem, i.e., the problem of whether there is an effective, algorithmic method for a formal system (such as arithmetic or predicate logic) which determines, or decides, in a finite number of mechanical steps whether a particular statement is provable within that formal system. In 1931 Kurt Gödel had published his famed incompleteness proof, in which he showed that any consistent formal system capable of expressing the truths of arithmetic would contain true statements that were unprovable within that system, and, as such, the system would be incomplete. While a decision procedure for sentential logic (or propositional calculus) had been developed, namely, truth-tables, none had been demonstrated for predicate logic. Church's Theorem showed that no such procedure for predicate logic is possible.

Church's Thesis reflects on the very notion of effectiveness. This notion of effectiveness (or, in Church's terminology, effective calculability) was held to be imprecise, though intuitive. Church proposed the thesis that effectiveness is identical with, and so replaceable by, the more rigorous notion of recursion. Mathematical functions are said to be recursive if they can be defined by mathematical induction. At the same time, Church's student, Alan Turing, proposed a notion of computable functions as ones for which the values could be determined by computing machines (what have come to be called Turing machines). These computable functions turn out to be the same as recursive functions. Because of this equivalence among computability, recursiveness, and effective calculability (what Church called λ-definability), Church's thesis was seen as a benchmark in modern theories of computation and in the development of digital computing capabilities.

During the 1940s and beyond, Church's focus gradually shifted from technical mathematical concerns to formal semantic theory and issues in the philosophy of language. One area of focus was the theory of types, which was formulated by Bertrand Russell to overcome logical paradoxes that beset the foundations of mathematics and set theory. For example, Russell articulated the set of all sets that do not contain themselves as elements, which produced the result that this set both did and did not contain itself as an element. The theory of types was proffered to resolve such paradoxes, based on the assumption that different types, or levels, of meaningful statements could be enunciated, where $type_0$ might be about objects in the world and $type_1$ would be about objects in $type_0$. The problem was in the "grammatical" rules that allowed such a set to be formulated in the first place. The simplified theory of types, which Church advocated, modified these formation rules by requiring that every variable be assigned a number that signified its type and any statement of the form "*x* is a member of *y*" would be meaningful if and only if *x*'s type-number is one less than *y*'s type-number.

A second area of focus for Church in connection with semantics and the philosophy of language was intensional semantics. Following the work of the German logician Gottlob Frege, Church distinguished the extension, or denotation, of a term and the intention, or sense, of a term. Many philosophers contended that extensional semantics promised to be a fruitful field of study but that intensional semantics did not because of both formal and informal difficulties associated with intensions. Much of Church's later work was devoted to formulating a logic of intensional semantics that would overcome those difficulties. This work spanned more than four decades, from an early paper in 1951, "A Formulation of the Logic of Sense and Denotation" (in *Structure, Method, and Meaning*, ed. Paul Henle et al., pp. 3–24), to his last publication, in 1995, during his lifetime, "A Theory of the Meaning of Names" (in *The Heritage of Kazimierz Ajdukiewicz*, ed. Vito Sinisi, pp. 69–74).

After retiring from Princeton in 1967, Church went to the University of California at Los Angeles, where he continued to teach and publish as a professor of philosophy and mathematics. In 1978 he was elected a member of the National Academy of Sciences. He retired in 1990 and two years later moved to Hudson, Ohio, where he lived until his death there.

An unwavering commitment to rigor and precision united all of Church's work, ranging from his early Thesis and Theorem to later semantic analysis, as exemplified in "The Need for Abstract Entities in Semantic Analysis" (*American Academy of Arts and Sciences Proceedings* 80 [1951]: 100–112): "The difference of a formalized language from a natural language lies not in any matter of principle, but in the degree of completeness that has been attained in the laying down of explicit syntactical and semantical rules, and the extent to which vagueness and uncertainties have been removed from them" (p. 111). This commitment was passed on to his students, many of whom, such as Alan Turing, Stephen Kleene, and Raymond Smullyan, went on to lead the next generation of logicians.

• Church's Thesis appeared in "An Unsolvable Problem in Elementary Number Theory," *American Journal of Mathematics* 58 (1936): 345–53; and Church's Theorem appeared in "A Note on the Entscheidungsproblem," *Journal of Symbolic Logic* 1 (1936): 40–41, 101–2. Several of Church's other influential papers, including "The Need for Abstract Entities in Semantic Analysis" and "Intensional Isomorphism and Identity of Belief" (*Philosophical Studies* 5 [1954]: 65–73), are frequently anthologized. His books include *The Calculi of Lambda-Conversion* (1941) and the *Introduction to Mathematical Logic, Volume 1* (1956). For a more general audience, he contributed numerous entries to the 1972 edition of the *Encyclopedia Brittanica*. The two-volume edition of Church's *Collected Writings*, ed. Tyler Burge and Herbert Enderton (1997), contains a complete bibliography of Church's published writings. Obituaries are in the *New York Times*, 5 Sept. 1995; *Modern Logic* 5 (Oct. 1995): 408–10; and *The Bulletin of Symbolic Logic* 1 (Dec. 1995): 486–88.

DAVID B. BOERSEMA

CHURCH, Benjamin (1639–17 Jan. 1718), soldier, was born in Plymouth, Massachusetts, the son of Richard Church, a carpenter, and Elizabeth Warren. He married Alice Southworth in 1667; the couple had eight children. Early in life Church followed his father's trade, and he first appeared in public records as a trial juror in Plymouth, 25 October 1668. Two years later he was listed as a freeman of "Duxburrow" (Duxbury, Plymouth Colony), where he also sat on trial juries and served as constable. In 1674 he acquired land in Saconet (later Little Compton, R.I.) from the Plymouth General Court and claimed to be "the first English Man that built upon that Neck, which was full of Indians." Church described himself as "a Person of uncommon Activity and Industry," though little is known of his personal life at the time. He gained the favor of the local Indians and, by his own estimation, even won their "great esteem." He became acquainted with Awashonks, the "Squaw Sachem" of the Sakonnet Indians, and their friendship led to Church's early involvement in King Philip's War. In June 1675, shortly before hostilities commenced, Church received information of the impending assault from Awashonks and Weetamoo, the "Queen of Pocasset," and he passed this report on to Plymouth officials. His subsequent military exploits in the conflict were chronicled in his *Entertaining Passages Relating to King Philip's War* (1716).

Commissioned a captain by the Plymouth General Court, Church was one of the few New England writers or public figures of the period who consistently advised and presented a secular approach to the war. He criticized those who anticipated "the fancy of a Mighty Conquest" and warned that if the colonists hoped to defeat the natives, "they must make a business of the War, as the Enemy did." Critical of what he viewed as a timid and ineffective policy of concentrating troops in fortified garrisons, Church instead advised sending companies out to actively pursue the native bands. In addition, Church was one of the few colonial leaders who openly admitted appreciating the natives' martial skills, and of all the colonial field commanders, he made by far the most extensive and effective use of Indian troops. He recognized that they were superior to colonial militia troops, and he led units that included both captured enemies and Christianized natives from the Praying Towns. Promising captives that "if any would behave themselves well, he would do well by them, and they should be his men," Church also pointed out that good service under him represented a way for the natives to "prove themselves" and dispel the malicious attitude that many colonists held against them. Further, Church warned that the practice of selling Indian captives into slavery, widely employed as an official government policy during the conflict, would prove counterproductive to the war effort. Church valued his relationship with local natives, even those who had followed Philip (Metacom), and feared "the loss of the good Will and Respect of some that before were his good Friends" that might result from transporting captured prisoners.

Entertaining Passages was primarily a self-serving narrative of Church's role in and view of the war, emphasizing his own accomplishments and contributions. Church was quick to point out, in retrospect, that if colonial officials had heeded his advice the war would have ended sooner. After receiving a wound in the Great Swamp Fight (19 Dec. 1675) against the Narragansett Indians in Rhode Island, Church complained that officials ignored his counsel to occupy the enemy fort, the result of which, he was confident, would have been to force the natives "either to surrender themselves . . . or to have perished by Hunger and the severity of the season," as well as to have minimized English losses experienced on the return march. Church also felt that his services and those of his soldiers were not appreciated or rewarded adequately; when at the end of the conflict the General Court of Plymouth unanimously voted him "their Thanks," he added pointedly, "which was all that Capt. Church had for his aforesaid Service." His company tracked down and killed Philip; their final service in the war was to round up straggling bands of the enemy. One of the last Indians captured was supposedly named Conscience, and Church included this account as a fitting—and perhaps allegorical—ending of his narrative. "Conscience, said the Captain, smiling, then the war is over; for that was what [the colonists] were searching for, it being much wanted." This ending reflects the difference between *Entertaining Passages* and other contemporary histories of the war. Not only did Church's work lack the pious, introspective point of view that characterized most of the accounts, but it also served unselfconsciously to promote the reputation of the author. Still, the account presented the unique perspective of someone intimately involved in the conflict.

After the war, Church continued to be active in land dealings in Bristol, Saconet, Pocasset, Little Compton, and Freetown. During the 1680s he held various public offices, including magistrate for Saconet and Pocasset, and magistrate, selectman, and deputy to the General Court for Bristol. He was also an original member of the First Congregational Church of Bristol in 1687. The following decade saw the renewal of hostilities in New England, with the outbreak of King William's War and Queen Anne's War. Church was commissioned on 6 September 1689 as major and commander in chief of Plymouth forces for the first eastern expedition, which took place later that fall, against the Abenakis and other Maine tribes. He was commissioned and served in four subsequent expeditions to Maine between 1690 and 1704, reaching the rank of colonel by the latter date. He last appeared in the town records of Bristol as moderator of the town meeting 23 March 1696; by 18 January 1700 he was listed in the Bristol County Deed Book as "late of Bristol—now of Tiverton," indicating his move to Fall River, where he had purchased a lot in 1694. His final public service posts were for the town of Little Compton, where he returned by 1705; in addition to his duties as magistrate, he was chosen as the town's representative to the General Court in 1706 and 1710 and as moderator of the town meeting on 18 March 1713. Church died after a fall from his horse near Little Compton, where he was buried in the graveyard of the Congregational Church. He stands out not only for his military accomplishments but also for his unique perspective on the period.

• Various editions of Church's *Entertaining Passages Relating to King Philip's War*, published by his son Thomas Church, have been produced. The work was first published in Boston in 1716. The 1829 edition, edited by Samuel G. Drake, was copied from the rare 1772 reprint of the original. The 1865 edition, edited by Henry M. Dexter, includes an introductory memoir that provides a detailed biographical sketch of the colonel. References to Church appear frequently in the Plymouth Colony Records, Bristol County Deeds, Bristol Town Records, and Little Compton Town Records. Information can also be found in the Proprietors' Records of Saconet and Bristol County Probate Records.

MICHAEL J. PUGLISI

CHURCH, Benjamin (24 Aug. 1734–Jan. 1778?), physician, poet, and traitor, was born in Newport, Rhode Island, the son of Benjamin Church, a vendue master, and Hannah Dyer. By 1740 the family had moved to Boston, and in 1750 young Benjamin entered Harvard College. It was at Harvard that Church first developed his writing skills, sharpening his talents through biting satires on his classmates and the professors. After graduating in 1754, Church studied medicine and for several months in 1757 served as surgeon aboard the Massachusetts snow-of-war, the *Prince of Wales*. Leaving the service he went to London, where he continued his medical studies and married Sarah Hill. When he returned to Boston in 1759, Church began an active local practice and won particular notice for his use of smallpox inoculation.

Beginning in 1768 Church became actively involved in town politics and was especially well known as a member of the Committee of Correspondence. Following the Boston Massacre in 1770, Church performed the autopsy on Crispus Attucks, one of the victims. He was also active in the fraternity of Freemasons and in 1772 became master of the Rising Sun Lodge. Meanwhile his literary talents, notably his patriotic poetry, were reinforcing his liberal political views. On the anniversary of the Boston Massacre in 1773, Church was chosen as the town orator and delivered a fiery speech in opposition to continued British rule, declaiming that "Loyalty stands on tiptoe at the shocking recollection, while justice, virtue, honor, patriotism became suppliants for immoderate vengeance."

Although Church was elected as one of Boston's delegates to the Provincial Congress in 1774, some Whigs, notably Paul Revere, began to suspect that Church was behind tactical information leaks to the British authorities. Following the battles at Lexington and Concord in April 1775, Church disregarded friendly advice and returned to British-held Boston. He claimed that British soldiers took him prisoner and brought him before General Thomas Gage. It was later learned, however, that Church voluntarily made the visit, and it is now known that he was one of Gage's informers by this time. Later, rumors held that Church was writing simultaneously for the Tory press, but, if so, it was in a disguised and ineffectual manner quite unlike his well-known style promoting the colonists' views.

To all outward appearances, Church continued his work for the American cause, and in May 1775 the Massachusetts Provincial Congress entrusted him to convey a letter to the Continental Congress in Philadelphia. The provincial congress requested advice on the establishment of a civil government in Massachusetts, and Church was to confer with the Continental Congress "respecting such other matters as may be necessary to the defence of this colony, and particularly the state of the army therein."

On 25 July 1775 Congress appointed Church as the first director of the Continental army hospital at Cambridge. His administration quickly proved contentious, and an official inquiry into his conduct was called. The regimental surgeons cleared him of the charges of neglect, but Church sought to resign his commission on 20 September. He remained on being assured of General George Washington's "Unwillingness to part with a good Officer." However, on 29 September Church was arrested when an incriminating coded letter was intercepted at Newport, Rhode Island. The letter, entrusted to Church's mistress for delivery, informed (although not very accurately) Major Maurice Cane of the British regulars of colonial troop strengths and allocations. On 4 October Church was brought before a council of war at Cambridge with Washington presiding. There Church maintained his patriotism, claiming that his letter was simply a ploy to confuse the British, "calculated to impress the Enemy with a strong Idea of our Strength & Situation in order to prevent an Attack." The military tribunal was unconvinced and found him guilty of having "carried on a criminal Correspondence with the Enemy." Because the Articles for the Government of the Army provided "very inadequate punishment" for the crime, a committee from the Continental Congress referred the matter to the Massachusetts House of Representatives, of which Church was still a member. The house "utterly expelled" Church from the legislature and ordered him "apprehended and secured." On 6 November Congress resolved to place Church in close confinement until a further determination could be made. At first jailed in Norwich, Connecticut, Church was returned to Massachusetts in June 1776 and placed under house arrest until a mob attacked the house, after which he was confined more securely in the Boston jail. In June 1777 a proposal by British general William Howe to exchange Church for a Dr. James McHenry (1753–1816) of Philadelphia, a captured patriot, was rejected both by Congress and popular furor in Boston. Finally, on 9 January 1778, the Massachusetts legislature directed the sheriff of Suffolk County to place Church aboard the sloop *Welcome*, bound for the island of Martinique, first searching "his Person & Baggage to prevent his carrying any Letters or other papers that may be to the detriment of the American States." Shortly after sailing, the ship disappeared in a violent coastal storm leaving no survivors.

Before September 1775, Church's strong poetry and speeches combined with his political activity had secured him a place among the patriotic leadership of the Revolution in Massachusetts. However, his attempt to assist both sides in anticipation of the outcome of the Revolution ended in failure. The extent of Church's treasonous activity, beyond the single intercepted letter, is unknown, as are the possible benefits of his act to the British military leadership. However, the psychological blow was enormous. He was abhorred by former friends and colleagues, who were particularly bitter about being betrayed by one of their own, and that remains the abiding judgment of Benjamin Church.

• The best general sketch of Church's life is given by Clifford K. Shipton, comp., *Sibley's Harvard Graduates*, vol. 13 (1965). His literary career is well covered in Jeffrey B. Walker, *The Devil Undone: The Life and Poetry of Benjamin Church, 1734–1778* (1982), which includes a complete edition of Church's poetry. Still the best study of Church as a traitor is Allen French, *General Gage's Informers* (1932; repr. 1968), which finally proved the case based on then newly discovered manuscripts.

EDWARD W. HANSON

CHURCH, Frank (25 July 1924–7 Apr. 1984), Idaho senator, was born in Boise, Idaho, the son of Frank Forrester Church, a sporting goods store owner, and Laura Bilderback. A high school debater and student body president, he won an American Legion oratorical scholarship to Stanford University, graduating in 1947. The same year he married his boyhood sweetheart, Bethine Clark, daughter of former Idaho governor Chase Clark. After graduation from Stanford Law School in 1950, Church returned to Boise to practice law and raise two young sons. He became active in Democratic party politics as chairman of the Young Democrats of Idaho, losing a bid for the Republican-dominated Idaho legislature in 1952.

In the 1956 U.S. Senate race, Church won a surprise victory over the favored Republican incumbent. He and Bethine stumped the state together, and throughout his public career she was his closest political ally. At the age of thirty-two, Church was the youngest senator and the fifth youngest ever elected. He earned respect early in his first Senate term for his key role in the passage of the 1957 Civil Rights Act. He was rewarded for his efforts by Majority Leader Lyndon Johnson with an appointment to the Foreign Relations Committee in 1959, becoming chair in 1979. He gained national television exposure in 1958 as a member of Senator John McClellan's Select Committee on Improper Activities in the Labor or Management Field, better known as the "Rackets" committee. In 1959 Church proposed a feasibility study for the Sawtooth National Park, initiating a series of national wilderness protection bills that became career benchmarks. A promising young Democratic "comer," Church was invited to deliver the keynote address to the 1960 Democratic National Convention. His rousing speech condemned slow economic growth and called for increased military spending.

Church was reelected by 24,500 votes in 1962, the first Democrat from the conservative Republican state of Idaho ever to serve two consecutive Senate terms. After a five-week fact-finding tour of the Far East late in 1962, Church began to question U.S. military involvement in Vietnam. In 1963 he introduced a Senate resolution opposing aid to the Ngo Dinh Diem regime in South Vietnam, becoming only the fourth senator (joining Wayne Morse, George McGovern, and Ernest Gruening) to publicly break with President Johnson over this issue. His antiwar stance typified his political style: "a sense of outrage against practices—whether in business, labor, or government—he believed to be morally wrong" (Church, *Father and Son*, p. 51). His second-term accomplishments included leadership in passage of the 1963 Nuclear Test Ban Treaty, the 1964 Civil Rights Act, the 1964 Endangered Wilderness Act, and the 1967 National Wild and Scenic Rivers System and service as the congressional delegate to the United Nations in 1966. Church was one of the first senators to make voluntary financial disclosures beginning in 1964, a provision later mandated in the 1973 Campaign Reform Bill.

Church won a third Senate term in 1968 by a 60 percent margin. As chair of the Subcommittee on Western Hemisphere Affairs he encouraged U.S. policy makers to allow self-determination for Latin American nations. To curb what he perceived to be an unconstitutional expansion of the war in Southeast Asia, he proposed using the congressional purse power. He teamed with Senator John Sherman Cooper (R.-Ky.) to add the Cooper-Church amendment to the 1969 military appropriations bill in order to bar U.S. ground troops from Laos and Thailand. Church called this a "reassertion of Congressional prerogative." After President Richard Nixon revealed the "secret" invasion of Cambodia early in 1970, a second Cooper-Church amendment prohibited the future deployment of American troops or advisers to Cambodia without congressional consent. In 1972 Church and Clifford Case (R.-N.J.) amended the appropriations bill to end all funding for the war in Indochina subject to agreement for release of all prisoners of war (POWs). A second Case-Church amendment passed in 1973 ended funding for the bombing of Cambodia. The Cooper-Church and Case-Church amendments served as groundwork for the passage of the important 1973 War Powers Act, which limited presidential authority to wage undeclared war. This act was passed by Congress over the veto of President Nixon.

Church's third-term record included sponsorship of the 1972 Social Security Act with its cost-of-living (COLA) adjustment, the 1969 National Environmental Policy Act, the 1972 Sawtooth National Recreation Area Bill, and co-sponsorship of the law allowing the eighteen-year-old vote. In 1974 he led the Senate fight to reject a pay raise for Congress and criticized the Nixon pardon. From 1973 to 1976 he took an important assignment as chair of the Foreign Relations Subcommittee on Multinational Corporations. Finding evidence of complicity and bribery between U.S. oil companies and Middle East nations and of International Telephone and Telegraph (ITT) plans to undermine elections in Chile, his public position was clear: "We must never accede to the rationale, in foreign policy or in business, that we must become as corrupt as those we come up against."

Church was reelected a fourth time in 1974 with a 36,000-vote margin, becoming the ranking Democrat on Interior and Insular Affairs. He sponsored and passed the Hells Canyon National Recreation Area Act in 1975. As chair of the Senate Select Committee on Intelligence (1975–1976), a position he called a "political minefield," he investigated alleged abuses of the Central Intelligence Agency (CIA) and the Federal Bureau of Investigation (FBI). The "Church committee" found shocking evidence of illegal government operations: assassination plots against foreign leaders, harassment of political dissidents, and surveillance of such "radicals" as Martin Luther King, Jr., and Adlai Stevenson (1900–1965). Church was outraged: "If we're going to lay claim to being a civilized country, we must make certain in the future that no agency of our government can be licensed to murder. The President of the United States cannot become a glorified godfather." Many of the one hundred Church committee recommendations were subsequently implemented, including the requirement that the president personally authorize covert activities and inform the appropriate congressional committee of such orders.

Because of his Intelligence Committee responsibilities, Church got a late start in his bid for the 1976 presidential nomination, and he withdrew after winning presidential primaries in Nebraska, Idaho, Oregon, and Montana. He visited Cuba in 1977 on a goodwill mission for President Jimmy Carter. He demanded the withdrawal of Soviet combat troops from Cuba before allowing Senate ratification of the 1979 SALT II treaty. The same year he led the floor debate for ratification of the Panama Canal Treaty, which restored control of the canal to Panama. In 1980 his Central Idaho Wilderness Act passed, which included the 2.2-million-acre River of No Return Wilderness Area.

The 1980 senatorial race in Idaho was made bitter by a National Conservative Political Action Committee media blitz charging that Church "gave away Panama." Church lost by 4,262 votes, less than 1 percent, in a surprise defeat to Congressman Steve Symms. After leaving the Senate, Church practiced international law, traveled, and lectured on international affairs until his death in Bethesda, Maryland, from a recurrence of pancreatic cancer first diagnosed when he was twenty-three.

• The Frank Church Papers, including over 400 films and videotapes, are cataloged in the Boise State University Library. See Ralph Hansen and Deborah Roberts, *The Frank Church Papers: A Summary Guide* (1988). For a flavor of Church's own writing and thinking, see his last major published work, "It's Time We Learned to Live with Third World Revolutions," *Washington Post*, 26 Mar. 1984. Although a scholarly biography has not yet been written, Frank Forrester Church, *Father and Son: A Personal Biography of Senator Frank Church of Idaho* (1985), contains valuable insights. For an analysis of Church's position on Vietnam, see Gustaf J. Brock, "The Doves Have Won: Senator Frank Church and the Vietnam War" (M.A. thesis, Washington Univ., 1989), and Mary Jane Hogan, "Frank Church Visits Southeast Asia," *SHAFR Newsletter*, Dec. 1991, pp. 1–13. The Church committee report, *Select Committee Report of Alleged Assassination Plots Involving Foreign Leaders* (1975), is fascinating reading, as is a staffer's description of the committee process in Loch K. Johnson, *A Season of Inquiry* (1985). See also F. A. O. Schwartz, Jr., "Recalling Major Lessons of the Church Committee," *New York Times*, 30 July 1987. For an analysis of the impact of Idaho politics on Church's career, read Ron Hatzenbuehler and Bert Marley, "Why Church Lost: A Preliminary Analysis of the Church-Symms Election of 1980," *Pacific Historical Review* 56 (Feb. 1987): 99–111. An obituary is in the *New York Times*, 8 Apr. 1984.

MARY JANE HOGAN

CHURCH, Frederic Edwin (4 May 1826–7 Apr. 1900), landscape painter, was born in Hartford, Connecticut, the son of Joseph Church, a businessman, and Eliza Janes; he was descended from Richard Church, one of the founders of Hartford. Church was interested in painting at an early age, but his father initially discouraged his interest, hoping his son would pursue a career as a physician. Nevertheless, when he was sixteen Church studied briefly in Hartford with two local artists, and by the spring of 1844 his interest in landscape was already apparent, for he was painting nature scenes. In June 1844 he went to Catskill, New York, to study with Thomas Cole, who was at the height of his fame as America's leading landscape painter. Cole had not previously accepted pupils but was persuaded to take Church by Hartford collector and patron Daniel Wadsworth, a friend of Joseph Church. Church's status as Cole's pupil was an important ingredient in his early success, for it brought him to the attention of leading critics and patrons.

Remaining in Catskill until the spring of 1846, Church watched Cole paint some of his finest works, ranging from pure landscapes to complex imaginary allegories. Cole probably offered only limited technical instruction to Church—Cole observed that Church already had "the finest eye for drawing in the world" (Louis L. Noble, *The Life and Works of Thomas Cole* [1853], ed. Elliot S. Vessel [1964], p. 272)—but he did convey certain deeply held ideas about landscape painting. Chief among these was that the artist had a moral duty to do more than simply imitate the physical reality of the external world and should attempt through his or her works to address profound issues concerning humankind and the human condition. Cole considered his own imaginary works, such as the five-canvas *Course of Empire* (1836, New-York Historical Society) and the four-part *Voyage of Life* (1840, Munson-Williams-Proctor Institute, Utica, N.Y.; second version 1842, National Gallery of Art), his most important vehicles for conveying such content. Church painted several major works in this vein, and although he eventually abandoned the overtly allegorical style favored by Cole, he never wavered from his commitment to creating meaningful and instructive images.

Church began exhibiting pictures in New York at the National Academy of Design's annual exhibition in 1845. His first important success, *Hooker and Company Journeying through the Wilderness from Plymouth to Hartford, in 1636* (1846, Wadsworth Atheneum, Hartford, Conn.), is a historical landscape that celebrates the founding of his home town and his own ancestry. Somewhat contrived in composition, with figures arranged on a stagelike foreground, the painting owes much to Cole's example. However, it also provides ample evidence of Church's own inclinations, for details of foliage, branches, and rocks are handled with extraordinary precision, and the radiant, all-encompassing light indicates how carefully he had studied natural phenomena. *Hooker and Company* became Church's first important sale, for it was purchased by the Wadsworth Gallery (now Atheneum) in Hartford in the fall of 1846.

Church settled in New York in 1847 and established a yearly routine of sketching in oil and pencil during summer trips in New York state and New England and painting finished pictures in his studio during the fall and winter. He thus regularly contributed works to the spring exhibition at the National Academy. Also in 1847, Church established a profitable association with the American Art-Union, which not only exhibited his pictures but also purchased many of them for distribution by lottery to its members. Most of Church's works from the late 1840s are straightforward American landscapes, such as *Scene on the Catskill Creek, New York* (1847, Washington County Museum of Fine Arts, Hagerstown, Md.). These paintings are characterized by a crisp realism that found acceptance among patrons and connoisseurs under the influence of English author John Ruskin's "truth to nature" aesthetics. During this time Church also regularly exhibited imaginary and allegorical works reminiscent of Cole, such as *The River of the Water of Life* (1848, unlocated) and *The Plague of Darkness* (1849, unlocated). In recognition of his increasing prominence as a painter, Church was elected an associate of the National Academy in 1848.

In 1849 Church reached a new level of artistic maturity with paintings such as the highly dramatic *Above the Clouds at Sunrise* (Gulf States Paper Corporation, Tuscaloosa, Ala.) and his first masterpiece, *West Rock, New Haven* (New Britain Museum of American Art, New Britain, Conn.). According to the *Bulletin of the American Art-Union* (Apr. 1849), *West Rock* proved that Church had "taken his place, at a single leap, among the great masters of landscape." Depicting the well-known geological monument in the distance and men haying in the pastoral foreground, *West Rock* exudes painstaking realism. This truthfulness, along with the theme of the harvest and the bounties of the New World being reaped by its virtuous citizens, accounts for much of the work's appeal. But *West Rock* also held deeper meaning for Church's contemporaries, for the site was associated with an event from Connecticut's early colonial history that was seen as having prefigured the later American quest for independence. Church's painting, then, celebrates the peace and prosperity of the present but suggests that they are possible only because of the struggles of the past. In this way, he made a straightforward landscape resonate with the kind of deeper meaning that Cole believed to be essential. Owing largely to the success of *West Rock*, Church was made a full member of the National Academy in 1849 at the age of twenty-three, the youngest artist ever so honored.

In the summer of 1850 Church made his first trip to Maine, beginning a lifelong association with the state. A number of fine marine and coastal paintings, including *Beacon, off Mount Desert Island* (1851, private collection), resulted from his visits. Also around 1850 he read German naturalist Alexander von Humboldt's *Cosmos*, paying particular attention to the chapter on landscape painting and its relationship to modern science. Influenced by Humboldt's concept of "heroic" landscapes that could portray the essential characteristics of distinct zones of the earth, Church began painting synthetic compositions, such as *New England Scenery* (1851, George Walter Vincent Smith Art Museum, Springfield, Mass.). These works fuse panoramic scope with intricate, scientifically correct detail, and although their didactic emphasis recalls Cole's moralizing landscapes, their strongly nationalistic tone and promise of revelation through scientific knowledge made them especially appealing to Church's contemporaries.

Humboldt's description of the tropics of South America as a subject worthy of a great painter fired Church's imagination, and he made the first of two trips there in the spring of 1853. Traveling with his friend and colleague Cyrus Field, Church sought out many spectacular sites and made careful pencil studies and oil sketches of plants, animals, river scenes, mountains, and volcanoes. When he returned to New York in the fall of 1853, he did not immediately translate these studies into finished works but instead continued to paint North American pastoral landscapes, such as *A Country Home* (1854, Seattle Art Museum). By the fall of 1854 Church was ready to grapple with his exotic new subject matter; his first finished tropical landscapes, including *Tamaca Palms* (1854, Corcoran Gallery of Art, Washington, D.C.) and *La Magdalena* (1854, National Academy), appeared at the National Academy in the spring of 1855, where they caused a sensation. Even more successful was the four-by-six-foot *Andes of Ecuador* (1855, Reynolda House Museum of American Art, Winston-Salem, N.C.), his largest canvas to date and his first to depict a vast expanse of scenery from a high vantage point, which implies that the viewer is literally hovering in the air or perched on greatly elevated eminence. *The Andes of Ecuador* heralded a new power in Church's art and a vision of the world more closely attuned to dramatic scenery and vast, overwhelming prospects. Virtually every year over the next decade Church produced a grand landscape, usually large in scale and often shown alone, rather than in a regular exhibition. In the process, he created one of the most remarkable series of landscapes produced by any artist of the era.

The first of Church's so-called "Great Pictures" and the one that brought him widespread fame in the United States and abroad was the 3½-by-7½-foot *Niagara* (1857, Corcoran Gallery). Shown as a one-picture, paid-admission exhibition in a New York commercial art gallery and reproduced as a popular chromolithograph, *Niagara* almost instantly became one of the best-known paintings in the United States. Many other artists before Church had attempted to portray America's most famous natural wonder, but none equaled Church in capturing its majesty. He made detailed drawings and sketches of the falls from a variety of vantage points and, once back in his studio, used them as sources for the final canvas. So great was his determination to capture the genuine color and appearance of the water that he was said to have worked only when the sky was clear and the sun was shining brightly. Church completed the painting in the brief span of two months. Showing the great sweep of Horseshoe Falls from the Canadian side, *Niagara* has no actual foreground; the viewer is seemingly suspended just above the water, greatly increasing the sense of drama. So successful was the painting in recreating the actual look and feel of the falls that even Ruskin, who saw it in London while it was on loan in Britain, professed amazement.

Following the triumph of *Niagara*, Church returned in the spring of 1857 to South America to gather material for a new series of tropical landscapes. The first to appear, *Heart of the Andes* (1859, Metropolitan Museum of Art), is the most complex work of his career. Displayed in a darkened room with carefully controlled lighting and surrounded by molding designed to resemble an elaborate window frame, *Heart of the Andes* overwhelmed crowds with its intricately painted foreground of tropical plants and its breathtaking vistas along several vanishing points to a mountainous distance. Like *Niagara*, *Heart of the Andes* was exhibited throughout the United States and England for paid admission, receiving widespread critical and popular acclaim.

During the late 1850s and early 1860s Church was at the height of his powers, painting large-scale exhibition pieces, such as *Twilight in the Wilderness* (1860, Cleveland Museum of Art), a view of a pristine forest with a resplendent sunset overhead; *The Icebergs* (1861, Dallas Museum of Art), a northern counterpart to *Heart of the Andes*; and *Cotopaxi* (1862, Detroit Institute of Arts), considered the best of his many views of the famous South American volcano. Church's activities and his public prominence were, of necessity, somewhat diminished by the upheaval of the Civil War, but he continued to paint major works in the years immediately following the war's end. Paintings such as *Rainy Season in the Tropics* (1866, Fine Arts Museums of San Francisco), *Niagara Falls, from the American Side* (1867, National Gallery of Scotland, Edinburgh), and *The Vale of Saint Thomas, Jamaica* (1867, Wadsworth Atheneum) retain much of the dramatic power of his earlier efforts, but they reveal an increasing emphasis on visionary effects of light and atmosphere that recall the paintings of the great English master of landscape J. M. W. Turner. Through such means, Church softened some of the insistent detail that had been a hallmark of his style, probably in response to the changing tastes of postbellum America, which increasingly came to consider overly detailed realism old-fashioned. At a time when young painters such as James A. M. Whistler, Winslow Homer, and Thomas Eakins were becoming known for their figure paintings, landscapes by men such as Church quickly fell from favor. In 1860 Church married Isabel Mortimer Carnes; they had six children, two of whom died in infancy.

Beginning in the 1860s Church spent more and more time removed from the New York art world, concentrating his efforts on his family and on the construction of an elaborate home, which he called "Olana," built on a hill overlooking the Hudson River just across from Catskill. He continued to travel and made an extensive visit to Europe and the Near East in 1867–1868. Although a number of important paintings based on his experiences in the Old World resulted from his trip, only a few, such as *Jerusalem from the Mount of Olives* (1870, Nelson-Atkins Museum, Kansas City, Mo.), approach the power of his earlier works. He also returned often to South American subject matter, but his tropical paintings became less convincing as his memory of the landscape dimmed. His last successful full-scale work was *Morning in the Tropics* (1877, National Gallery of Art), which depicts a tropical river at dawn. Lush and verdant and painted from a viewpoint that suggests that the viewer can actually step into its space rather than hover above, *Morning in the Tropics* has a poetic, introspective quality unlike any of Church's earlier works.

Although Church produced relatively few finished works of note after 1880, he continued to paint oil sketches while living at Olana. Often focusing on the changing patterns of light and weather in the sky, these oil sketches are among his most brilliantly painted and remarkable achievements. Known only to friends and associates and not publicly exhibited in his lifetime, Church's oil sketches reveal that his powers as a painter diminished little, if at all, during his last years. The sketches are now housed at Olana and the Cooper-Hewitt Museum in New York.

Church died in New York City in the home of his longtime friend and patron William H. Osborn. A memorial exhibition of his works was held at the Metropolitan Museum of Art that same year. During the early years of the twentieth century his reputation faded, and interest in him and his works revived gradually only after about 1945. By the 1960s Church was once again considered one of the most important American painters of the mid-nineteenth century, and his most significant works began to enter public collections. He was the subject of a major monographic exhibition at the National Gallery of Art in 1989–1990. Although generally considered a member of the Hudson River School, Church stands apart from most of his contemporaries because of the variety of his subject matter and, most especially, because of his highly intellectual approach to painting and his commitment to conveying meaning through his works. Indeed, during the period between 1855 and 1865 he painted what are arguably the most important landscapes created by any American artist.

• Church's home, Olana, near Hudson, N.Y., houses the most important collection of papers, documents, and works of art pertaining to his career. It is maintained by the New York State Department of Parks and Recreation and is open to the public. Gerald L. Carr, *Frederic Edwin Church: Catalogue Raisonné of Work of Art at Olana State Historic Site* (1994), provides thorough documentation of the collection as well as a great deal of information about the painter. The Cooper-Hewitt Museum in New York owns several hundred drawings and oil sketches. David Huntington, *The Landscapes of Frederic Church: Vision of an American Era* (1966), the first modern study of the artist's life and work, remains a fundamental source. Several publications by Franklin Kelly, most notably *Frederic Edwin Church and the National Land-*

scape (1988), an examination of his North American landscapes, and *Frederic Edwin Church* (1989), the catalog of the monographic exhibition held at the National Gallery of Art in 1989–1990, offer additional documentation. Notable studies on particular aspects of his career include Theodore E. Stebbins, *Close Observation: Selected Oil Sketches by Frederic E. Church* (1978); Carr, *Frederic Edwin Church: "The Icebergs"* (1980); Elaine Evans Dee, *To Embrace the Universe: Drawings by Frederic Edwin Church* (1984); Katherine E. Manthorne, *Creation and Renewal: Views of Cotopaxi by Frederic Edwin Church* (1985); and Kevin J. Avery, *Church's Great Picture "The Heart of the Andes"* (1993).

FRANKLIN KELLY

CHURCH, John Adams (5 Apr. 1843–12 Feb. 1917), mining engineer, was born in Rochester, New York, the son of Pharcellus Church, a Baptist clergyman, and Chara Emily Conant, the sister of an eminent Hebraist. Maintaining an interest in his family's early history, Church published a book on *The Descendants of Richard Church of Plymouth, Mass.* in 1913. Graduating from the Columbia University School of Mines in 1867 with an E.M., he was a member of the school's first class. He then traveled in Europe for several years, visiting metallurgical establishments and taking a practical course at Clausthal, the site of famous lead and silver mines in the Harz Mountains. On returning to the United States, he published *Notes on a Metallurgical Journey* (1873). He taught mineralogy at Columbia for one semester in 1872–1873. Between 1872 and 1874 he served as assistant editor for the *Engineering and Mining Journal*, for which he abstracted and wrote commentary on contemporary developments.

In 1877 Church served as a mining observer for the U.S. Geographical Surveys West of the One Hundredth Meridian, commonly known as the Wheeler Survey after Lieutenant George M. Wheeler of the Corps of Engineers. Investigating the mines of the Comstock Lode at Virginia City, Nevada, Church proposed that kaolinization, the chemical reaction that turned rock into clay minerals, provided the heat source for the Comstock mines, which were the hottest in the world. He published this theory in two short installments in the annual reports of the Wheeler Survey and in a longer form in a paper in the *Transactions of the American Institute of Mining Engineers* (7 [1878]: 45–76). An 1879 book, published the same year he received his Ph.D., *The Comstock Lode, Its Formation and History*, represents the results of his Columbia doctoral work. Church's theory provoked wide discussion, especially by G. F. Becker of the new U.S. Geological Survey in the next volume of the *Transactions* and then in Geological Survey Monograph 3, published in 1882. From 1878 to 1881 Church served as a professor of mining and metallurgy at Ohio State University. In 1880 he became superintendent of Arizona's Tombstone Milling and Mining Company. At Tombstone he solved a problem with slags from the blast furnaces by replacing iron fluxes with manganese. These new fluxes became the standard in lead-silver mills.

Church married Jessie A. Peel of Los Angeles in 1884; they had one child. In 1886 she accompanied him to China, where he spent four years working for Viceroy Li Hung Chang. Church opened silver mines 150 miles north of the Great Wall and introduced modern methods and machinery but was hampered by primitive conditions and native superstitions. Church creatively solved flux problems again, using crushed magnetite. A supposed dragon protecting local coal supplies forced import of distant coal. Herbert Hoover's autobiography, recounting Hoover's own engineering work in China from 1899 to 1902, underscores the difficulties faced by Western engineers in China at the turn of the century.

Returning to the United States in 1890, Church set up a consulting practice. He was active in professional circles, publishing papers and commentaries and serving as a vice president of the American Institute of Mining Engineers in 1907 and 1908. He collaborated with Robert Peele on the *Mining Engineers' Handbook* (1918), which went to a third edition in 1945, and he provided one of the "hefty responses from the luminaries of the day" to Franz Posepny's book on ore deposits, which had been republished in 1901 by the American Institute of Mining Engineers. Church continued his consulting work until his death in New York City.

Church was a member of the first generation of American mining engineers to be trained in a formal school of mines. This training prepared him for a career in government service, academics, and industrial and consulting work. His work in silver-lead mining and milling, building on his early study in Europe and his observations in the Comstock Lode, made him a technical leader of his generation. As early as 1871, in an article in *North American Review*, he stressed the need for scientific training of mining engineers. With education, he claimed, "The enormous losses which are to-day experienced, even in the best conducted works, and the absurdities which are perpetuated in the name of mining, will pass away with the ignorance that causes them."

• There is no known repository of Church's papers. Church's shorter published mining papers appear in the *Transactions of the American Institute of Mining Engineers*, the *Engineering and Mining Journal*, and the *American Journal of Science*. Other works appear in popular periodicals, such as two long discussions of military campaigns in Cuba and Puerto Rico during the Spanish-American War in *Review of Reviews* 18 (1898): 168, 282. Obituaries are in the *New York Herald*, 13 Feb. 1917; the *New York Tribune*, 14 Feb. 1917; and the *Engineering and Mining Journal*, 10 Mar. 1917.

PETER L. GUTH

CHURCH, Robert Reed (18 June 1839–29 Aug. 1912), one of the first wealthy African Americans of the post-Emancipation era, was born in either Memphis, Tennessee, or Holly Springs, Mississippi, the son of a light-skinned house servant from Virginia, Emmeline, and her white, Virginia-born master, Charles B. Church. Robert would later say that his African heritage was slight. While giving testimony before a congressional committee holding hearings in response to the 1866 Memphis race riot, Church stated, "My father is a white man; my mother is as white as I am. Captain Church is my father; he used to have a packet line. My father owned my mother." Robert benefited from a paternity that went unacknowledged: "my father always gave me everything I wanted, although he does not openly recognize me." Captain Church owned steamships during the 1850s, making regular trips between Memphis and New Orleans, and he taught his son how to run the business. Beginning as a dishwasher, Robert progressed to cook and finally to steward, purchasing groceries wholesale, keeping accounts, and managing the provision of food, drink, and gambling on his father's boat.

The father instilled pride and a sense of honor in his son. "He taught me to defend myself," Robert recalled, "and urged me never to be a coward. 'If anybody strikes you, hit him back, and I'll stand by you.'" This advice was taken to heart by the violent-tempered Robert, who, as an adult, would pull his pistol on a railroad conductor, a policeman, a sheriff, and a snowball throwing crowd. Whenever Church felt threatened or discriminated against, he defended himself passionately. He was wounded at least three times, including once during the 1866 Memphis race riot when he was shot in the back of the head for defending his saloon from an Irish policeman who looted his whisky and $290 from his cash box.

When the Federal navy closed the Mississippi to Confederate shipping in 1862, Church struck out on his own in Memphis. Having learned to manage liquor and gambling on the riverboats, he naturally turned to the saloon business and by the close of the Civil War had opened his own bar. In the years that followed, he traded up to a saloon and billiard hall.

Church continued a cordial relationship with his father, visiting him every Sunday. And he married for the second time. An early slave marriage that took place in 1857 at the New Orleans end of the river boat run, with Margaret Pico, had produced one child, a daughter, whose education he financed; that marriage ended in separation. In Memphis, near the time of the Emancipation Proclamation of 1 January 1863, he married a literate lady's maid, Louisa "Lou" Ayrers, whose master provided a trousseau purchased in New York and a wedding reception. Their first child, Mary, was born in September of that year. In later years she was educated at a preparatory school run by Antioch College in Ohio, earned degrees from Oberlin College, and became the social activist known as Mary Church Terrell, author of *A Colored Woman in a White World* (1940). When Church and his second wife divorced, probably in 1870, Lou was given custody of Mary and her younger brother. After the divorce, Lou established a prosperous hairdressing shop for white ladies that she later moved to New York City. In 1885 Church married a college-educated school principal, Anna Wright, with whom he had two more children. One of them, Robert Church, Jr., became a national black Republican patronage adviser to Republican presidents during the 1920s. The senior Robert Church gave little time to politics. He did let friends nominate him for city government in 1882 and 1886 but was soundly trounced by more popular black candidates and never engaged in politics again, except when he served as a delegate to the Republican Presidential Convention of 1900.

Church saw the yellow fever epidemics of 1878 and 1879 as opportunities for investment in city real estate. After first moving his family to northern safety, out of the plague-infested city, he returned to purchase land and houses at distress sales, where panic-stricken Memphians sold property previously worth thousands of dollars for a few hundred. With his savings invested in bargain-priced real estate, Church emerged as a great landowner, who was said to have collected $6,000 a month from rents on property all across Memphis. His properties included undeveloped land, residential housing, and commercial buildings, some of them in the red light district.

Myth and exaggeration invariably spring up in tales of high achievement. Many accounts say that Church bought the first $1,000 bond to restore the ruined credit of the defaulted 1885 city government, even though city records do not report his name among the first bond buyers. And virtually all popular accounts say Church became the first black millionaire, although his real wealth seems not to have exceeded $700,000. The truth is that Church did invest in Memphis bonds, and he was certainly rich.

Church represented the black capitalism that Booker T. Washington advocated. Industry, thrift, and shrewd investment had led to a family fortune that enriched the black community. At the end of the century, when African Americans were excluded from the segregated public parks, Church built a park, playground, concert hall, and auditorium for blacks on Beale Street. Admission fees were generally charged, but free times opened the gates to all, and Thanksgiving dinners were annually served for the poor at Church Park. The wealth that Church made in real estate also helped to finance the first black-owned bank in Memphis. Solvent Savings Bank opened on Beale Street in 1906 with Church as president, sharing power with eighteen other black capitalists and community leaders. It remained sound at his death, but it eventually went bankrupt. Church died in Memphis.

Church never attended school, wrote a letter, or made a public speech, but he gained the respect and admiration of his community. "Church's life reads like a page torn from fiction," his obituary declared. And two of his five children became nationally prominent through their own efforts, which was no small accomplishment.

• Few relevant letters exist in the Robert R. Church Family Papers at Memphis State University Library. Other sources are the Mary Church Terrell memoir cited above; U.S. Congress, *Report on Memphis Riots and Massacres,* 39th Cong., 1st sess., 1866. H. Rept. 101, pp. 226–27; G. P. Hamilton,

The Bright Side of Memphis (1908), pp. 91–92, 98–100; and Annette E. Church and Roberta Church, *The Robert R. Churches of Memphis* (1974). The estate controversy (his daughter from his slave marriage sued for her share of the estate and won) is covered in the Memphis *Commercial Appeal,* 16 Nov. 1928. An obituary is in the *Commercial Appeal,* 30 Aug. 1912.

DAVID M. TUCKER

CHURCH, Robert Reed, Jr. (26 Oct. 1885–17 Apr. 1952), politician and businessman, was born in Memphis, Tennessee, the son of Robert Reed Church, Sr., a banker and businessman, and Anna Sue Wright, a school principal. The wealth and prestige of his father afforded young Church opportunities not available to most African-American children of his day. After attending a parochial school in Memphis and Oberlin Academy in Oberlin, Ohio, Church studied at Morgan Park Military Academy in Chicago, Illinois, and then enrolled in the Packard School of Business in New York City. He completed the business course and worked on Wall Street for several years before returning to Memphis in 1909 to help his father in the management of the Solvent Savings Bank and Trust Company and other family enterprises. In 1911 he married Sara Paroda Johnson, a schoolteacher; they had one child.

Church's rise to political power began in 1911, when, as a leader in the Colored Citizens Association of Memphis, he agreed to support Edward H. Crump, the successful Reform candidate for mayor, in exchange for pledges to build public parks and paved streets for blacks. The following year Church won a seat on the Tennessee delegation to the Republican National Convention and supported the renomination of President William Howard Taft. After the death of his father in 1912, Church and his sister, Annette Elaine Church, inherited rental property valued at more than a million dollars. Church was elected president of the bank in 1912 but resigned the following year to devote more time to politics and his real estate interests. Believing that members of his race could best achieve their goals through the ballot, he founded the Lincoln League in 1916 to encourage blacks to register to vote. He also used his personal funds to organize voting schools and to pay poll taxes. The league failed to elect its black candidate for Congress in 1916, but its ticket outpolled the regular Republican slate by a margin of 4 to 1.

In 1917 Church helped to establish the Memphis branch of the National Association for the Advancement of Colored People (NAACP), the organization's first chapter in Tennessee. Elected to the national board of directors two years later, he represented branches of the NAACP in fourteen southern states. As racial antagonism intensified at the end of the First World War, Church advised the mayor of Memphis that blacks would not instigate trouble in the city but would defend themselves if attacked. In 1920 white Republicans sought to curb Church's power by refusing him entry to the county convention in Memphis. Although Church and his supporters sent a delegation to the national convention and lost a seating contest before the Credentials Committee, he enhanced his standing with national Republican leaders by announcing that he would return to Tennessee and fight for recognition in the party. In the presidential election of 1920, Church's Black and Tan faction supplied the margin of votes that carried the Republican party to victory in Memphis and the state of Tennessee.

Church reached the height of his influence in the early 1920s. He maintained an office in Memphis on Beale Street, where the poor came for financial aid, politicians came for advice, and job seekers came for recommendations. Characterized as "a famed manipulator behind the scenes, a leading voice in the famed smoke-filled rooms in Republican high councils" (*Press-Scimitar*, 18 Apr. 1952), he influenced appointments of postmasters, judges, and other federal officials in Tennessee and neighboring southern states. Knowing that racial conditions in the South ruled out the acceptance of black appointees, he sought to recommend whites who would serve all citizens fairly and justly. Although tendered two presidential appointments, Church declined them because he wanted to maintain his political independence. In local elections he generally supported the candidates of the Memphis political boss Crump, a white Democrat. Crump seldom engaged in race baiting or harassed blacks, and federal officials obligated to Church rarely interfered with Crump. In the 1920s and 1930s the city government of Memphis spent over $10 million on public improvements, school buildings, libraries, and health services for blacks. The federal government also completed two housing projects for blacks during the same period.

After winning a bitter seating contest at the Republican National Convention in 1928, Church later served on the committee to notify Herbert Hoover of his presidential nomination. Although never an admirer of Hoover, Church advised black voters to support the party ticket: "The Republican party offers us little. The Democratic party offers us nothing. . . . I choose the Republican party" (*Chicago Defender*, 3 Nov. 1928). The following year he voiced displeasure with President Hoover's racial policies by refusing to serve on his national advisory committee. "Mr. President," he wrote to Hoover on 6 November 1929, "the Negro having stood the scorn of time can stand the indifference and neglect of even so good a man as you are."

With the election of a Democratic president in 1932, Church's influence rapidly declined. During the depression the city government raised assessments on his property, and his rental income did not cover his tax bill. In 1938 he moved to Philadelphia to work in the political organization of the Pennsylvania Republican leader Joseph Pew. While maintaining his voting registration in Memphis, he later lived in Chicago and Washington, D.C. In 1941 the city of Memphis, which had claimed most of his property for nonpayment of taxes, sold his home at a tax sale. At the invitation of black labor leader A. Philip Randolph, Church accepted membership on a national board that lobbied for a permanent Fair Employment Practices Committee (FEPC). In 1944 he organized and then chaired the Republican American Committee, a group of 200 blacks who pressured Republicans in Congress to support the enactment of the FEPC and other civil rights legislation.

With the prospect of electing a Republican president and making a political comeback, Church returned to Memphis in the spring of 1952 to seek a seat on the Tennessee delegation to the Republican National Convention as a strong supporter of General Dwight D. Eisenhower for the presidential nomination. Church suffered a fatal heart attack in his Memphis hotel room during a telephone conversation with a friend about Republican politics.

At a time when lynch mobs posed a threat to blacks in the segregated South, Church boldly crusaded for civil rights and relied on the ballot box to secure public benefits for members of his race. "Born to wealth and acquiring more by astute management, Bob Church could have divorced himself from the problems of his people," the *Pittsburgh Courier* declared on 3 May 1952. "Instead, he unselfishly threw himself in the Negro's struggle and used his money, time and influence to further the interests of his people in their struggle for full citizenship in our Republic."

• The Robert R. Church Family Papers are in the Mississippi Valley Collection at the University of Memphis Library. A detailed description of the Church Family Papers is Pamela Palmer, ed., *The Robert R. Church Family of Memphis* (1979). A file of newspaper clippings on Church is in the Memphis Public Library. A biography is Annette E. Church and Roberta Church, *The Robert R. Churches of Memphis* (1974). See also George Washington Lee, *Beale Street Where the Blues Began* (1934), on his early political career from the perspective of a black associate; and Shields McIlwaine, *Memphis Down in Dixie* (1948), on his political career from the perspective of a white observer. See Lester C. Lamon, *Black Tennesseans, 1900–1930* (1977) and *Blacks in Tennessee, 1791–1970* (1981), for historical assessments. Obituaries are in the Memphis *Commercial Appeal* and the Memphis *Press-Scimitar*, 18 Apr. 1952.

THOMAS N. BOSCHERT

CHURCH, Thomas Dolliver (27 Apr. 1902–30 Aug. 1978), landscape architect, was born in Boston, Massachusetts, the son of Albert Church, an inventor, and Wilda Wilson. He grew up in the ranching landscape of the Ojai Valley, California. Following high school in Berkeley, in 1918 Church entered the University of California at Berkeley as a law student but changed his major in 1919 after taking an elective course in the history of landscape architecture, graduating in 1922 with an A.B. in landscape architecture. After receiving an M.S. in city planning and landscape architecture from Harvard University in 1926, Church was awarded the Sheldon Travelling Fellowship, which enabled him to study historic gardens in Italy for several months and to travel in Spain, France, and England.

Between 1927 and 1930 Church taught landscape architecture at Ohio State University and at the University of California at Berkeley. In 1929 he married Elizabeth Roberts; they would have two daughters. That same year he opened his own office in Pasatiempo and moved in 1932 to San Francisco, where he practiced until his retirement in 1977. Church's practice centered on designing private gardens for rich and upper-middle-class clients such as Dewey Donnell and Charles deBretteville.

From the 1950s on, Church was involved in the landscape design of a number of prestigious projects, including the General Motors Technical Center in Detroit (1956), the Stanford Medical Center (1956), and the headquarters of *Sunset* magazine in Menlo Park, California (1962), working most frequently with architects William Wurster and Gardner Dailey. He also served as the consulting landscape architect on several university campus master plans, including the University of California at Berkeley, Stanford University, and the University of California at Santa Cruz. From 1971 to 1975 Church participated in the planning of the main entrance section of Longwood Gardens in Kennett Square, Pennsylvania.

Church's work was widely published in professional journals and in such popular magazines as *House Beautiful* and *Sunset*. His book *Gardens Are for People: How to Plan for Outdoor Living* (1955; rev. ed., 1983) further reinforced his reputation, which rested upon the adroit skill he displayed in designing gardens that were appropriate for the California region in their livability and economical use of materials. His style is characterized by a confident use of flowing curved forms, with abstractly designed ground planes of wood decking and concrete or brick paving. Diagonal sight lines are created by trellises, walls, and screens of such materials as asbestos, cement, and wood. His simple palette of plants emphasizes textures and form, and trees are often treated like pieces of living sculpture, their limbs carefully pruned to reveal abstract forms. Church aimed to create settings of "visual endlessness" and harmonious restfulness.

While Church's abstract designs are superficially similar to those of other modernist Californian designers, he was an eclectic artist not bound by the social agenda of modernism, or its commitment to breaking free of historicist allusions and its insistence on the use of machine-made materials. His work reveals a synthesis of diverse sources, such as the Cubist paintings of Picasso and Jean Arp, the overlapping planes of which are similar to the forms of his garden designs, as well as the architect Alvar Aalto and historic precedents, including Mediterranean garden traditions and nineteenth-century French park design. Despite his eclecticism, Church's approach to design was fundamentally humane, since he always showed a deep concern for creating gardens that met his clients' needs. His sensitive and essentially humanist concern for meeting his clients' needs, rather than any aesthetic ambivalence, accounts for his oscillation, from the late fifties on, between designs in which historicist precedent is evident and those that are based on fluid abstractions, for which he is best known.

Church's importance as a landscape architect lies in the pioneering role that he played in the early development of modernism and in the quality of his garden designs. Executed with meticulous craftsmanship, his designs are artful and timeless; they synthesize with effortless ease a broad diversity of stylistic sources into memorable expressions of place and of the personality of the owner. He died at his home in San Francisco.

• Church's papers, consisting of his office records, largely photographs and drawings, will be given to the Documents Collection, College of Environmental Design, University of California, Berkeley, upon the death of his widow. His principal publications, other than those mentioned in the text, include *Your Private World: A Study of Intimate Gardens* (1969). The most complete assessment of his work is Pam-Anela Messenger, "Thomas Church: His Role in American Architecture," *Landscape Architecture* 67, no. 2 (1977): 128–39, 170. For an analysis of his early work, see David C. Streatfield, "Thomas Church and the California Garden 1929–1950," in *Festschrift: A collection of essays on architectural history* (1978), pp. 68–75. Suzanne L. Reiss, *Thomas D. Church, Architect, Interviews*, 2 vols. (1978), contains biographical data and invaluable insights in a series of interviews with individuals who worked with Church in a variety of capacities. See also Michael Laurie, "Thomas Church, California Gardens, and Public Landscapes," in *Modern Landscape Architecture: A Critical Review*, ed. Marc Treib (1993).

DAVID C. STREATFIELD

CHURCHILL, Edward Delos (25 Dec. 1895–28 Aug. 1972), surgeon, was born in Chenoa, Illinois, the son of Ebenezer Delos Churchill, a grain merchant, and Maria Farnsworth. Churchill's parents and both brothers graduated from college. The family, staunchly Presbyterian, felt a special responsibility to make the most of its given talents. In 1912 Churchill entered Northwestern University, where he majored in biology. His teacher and lifelong friend Sidney Kornhauser had earned his doctorate at Harvard University and Cold Spring Harbor and encouraged Churchill to do the same. Churchill spent an extra year at Northwestern to earn a master's degree in biology, which qualified him to enter the second-year class of Harvard Medical School. In 1920 he won a two-year appointment as a surgical house officer at the Massachusetts General Hospital, followed by another two years as resident surgeon. Years later, after developing his own residency program, he expressed warm affection for the older surgeons who took part in his training, but of the apprenticeship system he lamented, "What a wastage of the vigorous and creative years of youth."

Following his residency, in addition to assisting older surgeons, Churchill found a position in the laboratory of Cecil Drinker, professor of physiology in the Harvard School of Public Health. Drinker reinforced Churchill's interest in thoracic surgery, while introducing him to the ways of academic advancement. In 1926 Churchill was granted a Moseley Fellowship, an opportunity to spend a year visiting the master surgeons of Britain and the Continent and studying with August Krogh and his wife in Copenhagen, Denmark. At the year's end he married Mary Lowell Barton of Boston; they had four children. In autumn 1927 he returned to a full-time surgical appointment at the Massachusetts General, where he was given a small laboratory for physiologic research. Churchill promptly became involved with bronchiectasis and tuberculosis, then came the break which gave him national visibility—the first successful pericardiectomy for constrictive pericarditis in this country, in July 1928. In the fall of that year, he accepted a surgical appointment at the Boston City Hospital, but after a year of failure to convince its senior surgeons of the importance of research, he returned to the Massachusetts General with promise of adequate research support. Within six months his chief, E. P. Richardson, suffered a devastating stroke. In 1931 Churchill was appointed to succeed him as John Homans Professor of Surgery and chief of the West Surgical Service.

The medical school and the hospital faced a major change in 1933 when James B. Conant succeeded A. Lawrence Lowell as president of Harvard. Conant, a biochemist, believed the teaching hospitals with their increasing emphasis on basic as well as clinical research were draining strength away from the university toward the periphery. Churchill's able defense of surgical research and the educational role of the teaching hospital can be found in his autobiographical treatise, *To Work in the Vineyard of Surgery* (1958).

Churchill took his place quickly among the leaders of thoracic surgery. His report of an extraordinary series of successful resections for bronchiectasis was followed a few years later by segmental resection and, with Belsey, the concept of the bronchopulmonary segment as the surgical unit of the lung. An early advocate of resection for pulmonary tuberculosis, he recommended, under appropriate indications, lobectomy (removal of the lung's component lobes) in lieu of pneumonectomy (total resection of the lung) for cancer of the lung. With his colleague Richard Sweet, he took up the challenge of esophageal resection for carcinoma, and with Oliver Cope, the operative treatment of hyperparathyroidism. For reasons not entirely clear he gave only lukewarm laboratory support to Jack Gibbons's experiments with extracorporeal circulation; indeed throughout his career he was surprisingly cool to the explosive growth of cardiac surgery. By strongly supporting Henry Beecher's appointment at Harvard as professor of anesthesia, he contributed greatly to the academic acceptance of that discipline.

In 1940 Churchill implemented his "rectangular" system of resident training as opposed to the competitive "pyramidal" Halsted system. The Churchill plan, which introduced a new dimension into university surgical residencies, involved selecting a given number of senior medical students for their five years of surgical training required by the American Board of Surgery. Although not a member of that board, Churchill was a close friend and adviser to Evarts Graham, its first chairman. Years later he took little part in the formation of the Board of Thoracic Surgery, fearing that specialty boards too often were preoccupied with technical proficiency as opposed to basic considerations of physiology and logical planning.

Kept in reserve by the U.S. Army during World War II, Churchill was chairman of the National Research Council's Committee on the Management of Chest Wounds. In March 1943 he went overseas as colonel and surgical consultant to the North African–Mediterranean Theater of Operations. He served overseas for nearly three years, arguably the apotheosis of his career. After the war he wrote, "Military surgery is not to be regarded as a crude departure from acceptable surgical standards . . . but as a development of the science of surgery to carry out a specialized and highly significant mission." Churchill emphasized the logical staging of care of the wounded man in a military theater of operations, such as the mobile surgical hospital. At war's end he was given the Distinguished Service Medal and the Excelsior Surgical Society was founded in his honor.

On his return to Harvard and Massachusetts General, Churchill's services were preempted by the Hoover Commission for Reorganization of the Executive Branch of the Government in Washington, D.C. Among the civilian honors that followed were presidencies of the American Surgical Association (1946) and the American Association for Thoracic Surgery (1949). At home, his attention was directed to the development of the surgical resident program and restructuring the surgical staff of the hospital. In the fall of 1953 he had a significant cerebro-vascular episode, which limited his clinical practice but allowed him to remain active in departmental matters and the development of young surgeons. He retired to emeritus status in 1961 and rarely returned to the hospital, though his advisory influence remained strong. Shortly before his death in Strafford, Vermont, *Surgeon to Soldiers* (1972), his war diary, appeared, which he described as "World War II as seen in a rear-view mirror."

• Churchill's collected papers and publications have been archived and are available in the Rare Books Division of the Countway Library in Boston. Churchill's autobiographical *To Work in the Vineyard of Surgery* (1958), is technically the reminiscences of J. Collins Warren with extensive footnotes and comments by Churchill. A wide-ranging bibliography of Churchill with a brief curriculum vitae appears in a Festschrift for Churchill in *Annals of Surgery* (Nov. 1963). In 1991 the Countway published *Wanderjahr, the Education of a Surgeon, Edward D. Churchill,* the diary of his fellowship year, edited and annotated from his unpublished memoirs by John Gordon Scannell. Of particular interest is his address to the American Surgical Association, "Science and Humanism in Surgery," which appears in *Annals of Surgery* 126 (1947). His contributions to surgical residency training were presented at length to the New England Surgical Society in 1973 (J. G. Scannell, *Let Us Now Praise Famous Men, American Journal of Surgery* 127 [1973]: 365–70).

JOHN GORDON SCANNELL

CHURCHILL, Frank Edwin (20 Oct. 1901–14 May 1942), composer, was born in Rumford, Maine. His parents' names are unknown. When he was four his family moved to southern California, where he remained all his life. Churchill was a born musician, largely self-taught. While studying for a medical career at the University of California at Los Angeles, he spent hours at the piano. He dropped out of college to take a job playing honky-tonk piano in Tijuana. Following that he played in a theater orchestra accompanying silent films. His skill landed him a job as a staff pianist at KNX radio in Los Angeles from 1924 to 1929. In December 1930 Churchill accepted an offer to join the stable of composers at the Walt Disney Studios, where he wrote music for the first time. By then Churchill had given up thoughts of becoming a doctor and turned to a career of composing music.

Sound pictures created a lot of excitement among motion picture producers in the early 1930s, and Walt Disney was no exception. He put together the talents of his animators and composers in a series of animated short films known as the Silly Symphonies. Frank Churchill wrote the music for sixty-five of those cartoons, including the most famous of all, *The Three Little Pigs*. Churchill wrote the song "Who's Afraid of the Big Bad Wolf?" in five minutes. He claimed it came easily to him because of a childhood experience that had made a lasting impression on him. He had grown up on a ranch in San Luis Obispo, California, and liked to visit the pigs, sit on the fence, and play the harmonica for them. One day a wolf made a raid on the ranch, and young Frank witnessed the death of one of the three pigs in the pen. Ironically, he was asked years later to write a song about fictitious characters facing a similar threat. The song sold 39,000 copies in New York City in the first three days after its publication in 1933. Many suggested the song's popularity was due to the fears of the times, the American depression, and the rise of Hitler in Europe. The lyrics were reportedly a group effort by members of the Disney staff, including Ted Sears of the story department, and Vance "Pinto" Colvig, who did character voices (he was best known for his voice of the cartoon character Goofy). Churchill continued writing songs and instrumental music for the Silly Symphonies during the 1930s, including "Old King Cole" (1933), "Lullaby Land" (1933, with Leigh Harline), "The Tortoise and the Hare" (1935), "Who Killed Cock Robin" (1935), and "Three Orphan Kittens" (1935).

On 21 December 1937 *Snow White and the Seven Dwarfs* premiered at the Carthay Circle Theater in Los Angeles to an enthusiastic audience that stood and cheered at the end. Running eighty-three minutes, it was the first full-length animated feature. The songs for the film were written by Frank Churchill, with lyrics by Larry Morey, and include "Heigh-Ho," "Whistle While You Work," "With a Smile and a Song," "I'm Wishing," "One Song," and "Some Day My Prince Will Come." Churchill wrote twenty-five songs for the film, but only eight were used. Bob Thomas, in his book *Walt Disney: An American Original* (1976), writes about Disney's taste in music:

Early attempts at *Snow White* songs did not please him. He complained that they followed the pattern of Hollywood's musicals, which introduced songs and dances at regular intervals without regard to the progression of the story. "We should set a new pattern, a new way to use music," he argued. "Weave it into the story so somebody just doesn't burst into song." (p. 136)

Snow White and the Seven Dwarfs set a precedent for animated musicals, and "Heigh-Ho" and "Whistle While You Work" were favorites on the radio for years to come.

The first live-action film produced by Disney in 1941, *The Reluctant Dragon*, featured four Churchill songs. Then came *Dumbo* in the same year, with songs by Churchill ("Casey, Jr." and "Baby Mine") and Oliver Wallace ("When I See an Elephant Fly"). The lyricist for both songwriters was Ned Washington. Churchill and Wallace received the Academy Award that year for Best Scoring of a Musical Picture.

Bambi (1942) was Churchill's final project for the Disney studio. He wrote all of the songs, again with lyricist Morey, as well as many of the instrumental themes. He received an Oscar nomination for "Love Is a Song," which opens the film and sets the mood for the serious and tender story to follow.

Described by his colleagues, Churchill was tall and thin, quiet and reserved; his hands were those of a musician, with long, slender fingers. He had the demeanor of a serious-minded surgeon. He loved cats, horse racing, and golf and was an avid reader. Frank Churchill was with the Disney studio for twelve years and gave the world many enduring songs and singable melodies. Despondent over his failing health, he took his own life, killing himself with a shotgun on his ranch near Newhall, California, three months before *Bambi* was released. He was survived by his widow.

• Biographical materials about Churchill and selected sheet music are housed in the archives of the Walt Disney Studio, Burbank, Calif. A limited amount of biographical information exists in files at the library of the Academy of Motion Picture Arts and Sciences, Los Angeles. *The Music of Disney: A Legacy in Song* (1992) includes a book with information on Churchill and photos as well as three compact disc recordings with seven of Churchill's songs from the animated films. An obituary is in *Variety*, 20 May 1942.

LINDA DANLY

CHURCHILL, Thomas James (10 Mar. 1824–14 May 1905), soldier and politician, was born near Louisville in Jefferson County, Kentucky, the son of Samuel Churchill and Abby Oldham, farmers. After graduating from St. Mary's College in Bardstown in 1844, Churchill attended Transylvania University and studied law. He joined the First Kentucky Mounted Riflemen Regiment as a lieutenant at the beginning of the Mexican War. Enemy cavalrymen captured Churchill in January 1847, and he remained a prisoner in the city of Mexico until the war had almost ended. Churchill purchased a plantation near Little Rock, Arkansas, in 1848 and began raising cotton. In 1849 he married Ann Sevier; they had four children. He received an appointment as postmaster at Little Rock in 1857.

When the Civil War began, Churchill attempted unsuccessfully to recruit a cavalry regiment in the vicinity of Fort Smith to serve the Confederate Army. He soon raised the First Arkansas Mounted Riflemen and was elected its colonel in June 1861. The regiment joined General Ben McCulloch's army and fought in the battle of Wilson's Creek, Missouri. Churchill lost two horses in the battle and impressed his superiors with his gallantry. He performed well again in the battle of Elkhorn Tavern, Arkansas. On 6 March 1862 Churchill was promoted to brigadier general. He assumed command of a brigade in Major General Earl Van Dorn's Army of the West and accompanied that command to Corinth, Mississippi.

Churchill's brigade joined the army of Major General Edmund Kirby Smith in East Tennessee after the Confederates evacuated Corinth in May 1862. Churchill assumed command of one of Kirby Smith's divisions during the invasion of Kentucky that fall. In the battle of Richmond, Churchill led an attack that broke the Union right flank and drove it back, but despite this performance he received orders on 10 December to report for duty in the Trans-Mississippi Department. When Churchill reached Little Rock, Lieutenant General Theophilus H. Holmes assigned him to command troops stationed at Fort Hindman, located at Arkansas Post on the Arkansas River. Union land and naval forces under Major General John A. McClernand and Admiral David D. Porter moved against the fort in January 1863. Of the approximately 6,000 men in the garrison, Churchill estimated that only 3,000 of them were actually available to fight. He asked Holmes for some reinforcements and more weapons but was told "to hold out until help arrived or all dead." Federal troops overran part of the Confederate lines on 11 January, and some of Churchill's troops raised unauthorized white flags, forcing him to surrender the remainder of the garrison.

For three months, Churchill remained a prisoner of war at Camp Chase, Ohio. He was assigned to the Army of Tennessee after his exchange and assumed command of a brigade in Major General Patrick R. Cleburne's division. Churchill suffered the stigma of the loss of Arkansas Post and was replaced in brigade command in August 1863. In December he received orders to return to the Trans-Mississippi Department. There he was assigned to head a brigade of Texas cavalrymen, but they resented his conduct at Arkansas Post and would not serve under him. Churchill then took over a brigade of Arkansas infantrymen in Major General Sterling Price's District of Arkansas.

The Union invasion of the Red River valley in Louisiana in March 1864 resulted in Lieutenant General Kirby Smith, now commanding the Trans-Mississippi Department, ordering reinforcements to Major General Richard Taylor's army in northwestern Louisiana. Price divided his infantry brigades into two divisions, and Churchill assumed command of one of them. As senior brigadier, he acted as temporary commander of both divisions sent to relieve Taylor. Churchill's men arrived at Mansfield too late to participate in the battle fought there on 8 April. Since his troops had not been bloodied in that engagement, Taylor assigned them the important task of trying to outflank Major General Nathaniel P. Banks's Union army at Pleasant Hill the next day. Churchill's attack did not hit the enemy flank and was repulsed with heavy losses.

Kirby Smith ordered Churchill's divisions back to Arkansas on 14 April to oppose Union troops under Major General Frederick Steele in what became known as the Camden Campaign. His men attacked the Federals in the battle of Jenkins's Ferry on 30 April and drove them back, though the Confederates suffered significant casualties. Churchill held temporary command of the District of Arkansas in the fall of 1864 while Price conducted a raid into Missouri. On 18 March 1865 Churchill was promoted to major general. He went to Texas about the time of the surrender of the Trans-Mississippi Department and received his parole there in June. (A parole was a signed document in which a prisoner of war promised to fulfill the stated conditions so that he might be released to go home.)

Churchill returned to Arkansas after the war. He was elected lieutenant governor in 1866 but was prevented by federal authorities from assuming office. The end of Reconstruction and the return of the Democrats to power in that state marked the beginning of his political career. He was elected state treasurer in 1874 and reelected twice to that post. Arkansas voters elected Churchill as governor on 6 September 1880, and he assumed that office on 13 January 1881. Although Churchill oversaw some positive programs, including the construction of a school for teachers, the creation of a state board of health, and the adoption of regulations for the practice of surgery and medicine, his term as governor was overshadowed by a scandal dating to his days as treasurer. An audit revealed a deficit in the treasury, and the state's attorney general filed suit against him to recover the missing funds. Eventually Churchill had to repay more than $23,000. In 1881 his use of state militia troops to quell unrest in Perry County after the breakdown of civil authority also hurt him politically. He returned to his plantation at the end of his term and remained out of politics. Churchill died at the home of a daughter in Little Rock.

• A biography of Churchill has yet to be published. Biographical sketches of him appear in a number of standard sources, including Clement A. Evans, ed., *Confederate Military History*, vol. 10 (1899). The best summary of his term as governor appears in F. Clark Elkins, "Thomas James Churchill," in *The Governors of Arkansas*, ed. Timothy P. Donovan and Willard B. Gatewood, Jr. (1981). Obituaries are in the Little Rock *Arkansas Democrat* and the Little Rock *Arkansas Gazette*, both 16 May 1905.

ARTHUR W. BERGERON, JR.

CHURCHILL, Winston (10 Nov. 1871–12 Mar. 1947), novelist and politician, was born in St. Louis, Missouri, the son of Emma Bell Blaine and Edward S. Churchill. His mother died shortly after his birth. Left in the care of his maternal grandmother until her death two years later, he was a short time thereafter taken in and raised by his mother's half sister, Louisa Blaine Gazzam, and her husband, James Braiding Gazzam, who lived in genteel poverty. Two manuscripts written later in his life (Jonathan and Gideon mss., Baker Library) demonstrate the influence of Churchill's upbringing on both his personal life and his novels. The absolute standards that the Gazzams instilled in him left him with lifelong feelings of guilt and inadequacy.

After Churchill graduated with honors from a St. Louis academy in 1888, his uncle secured for him a job in a paper warehouse. He detested the business world, however, and when a position opened up for his district at the U.S. Naval Academy, he directly approached his local congressman and received an appointment in 1890. While at Annapolis he compiled a good academic record and participated in a number of sports. He also began to write stories, and upon graduation he resigned his commission and secured editorial positions first at the *Army and Navy Journal*, then at *Cosmopolitan Magazine*.

But Churchill was more eager to be a writer than a magazine employee. The transition was made possible by his marriage in 1895 to Mabel Harlakenden Hall, the daughter of a successful St. Louis businessman; they had three children. Because Mabel Churchill's father had left her a modest income, they agreed that Churchill should devote full time to his own writing. Much to the disapproval of both families, he quit his position and began work on a novel.

Churchill met George P. Brett of the Macmillan Company in 1886, beginning a close working relationship that lasted nearly a quarter-century. The first result of their collaboration was *The Celebrity* (1898), which achieved most of its publicity because it was widely believed to be a parody of the popular writer Richard Harding Davis.

The novel was a successful first effort, but Churchill's mind had already turned to the American past. In the next six years he published three historical novels, each a bestseller, putting him in the forefront of American authors. *Richard Carvel* (1899) tells the story of the American Revolution, especially the war in the South; *The Crisis* (1901) depicts the story of the Civil War as it was played out in St. Louis; *The Crossing* (1904) portrays the westward movement. The critical reaction to these historical novels was almost as enthusiastic as the response of the reading public. As both contemporary critics and later commentators have pointed out, Churchill's ability to portray actual historical characters surpassed his talent at developing purely fictional characters—most of whom are wooden paragons of virtue or the epitome of evil. Churchill did prodigious research for these novels, and he was much more upset by suggestions that he had made mistakes in historical details than by the strictly literary criticisms. "I have no patience with literary cant," he wrote. "The lawyer prepares his brief to secure a verdict; so must the author. . . . I make a business of writing. Action and atmosphere, bone and blood are the things I try to put into books" (*Boston Globe*, 8 Jan. 1903). Rather than being narrowly nationalistic, Churchill's historical novels celebrated the greatness of the Anglo-Saxon.

During these years there was much confusion, particularly on the part of his British readers, between the new novelist and the rising British politician (and would-be novelist) of the same name. The two men took an almost instant dislike toward one another, although they carried forward a delicately balanced relationship from that point on (see letters, Baker Library).

The royalties from *Richard Carvel* enabled the Churchills to build an imposing house high on a hill overlooking the Connecticut River near Cornish, New Hampshire. "Harlakenden House" became a center for much of the social life of what was referred to as the Cornish Colony—a collection of writers, artists, architects, and intellectuals who had settled in the area.

President Theodore Roosevelt (1858–1919) was an enthusiastic admirer of Churchill's novels, and the two men had a close relationship almost from the beginning of Roosevelt's presidency. Churchill's growing admiration for Roosevelt was instrumental in turning the novelist's interests away from the past to the problems of contemporary society. Clearly, Roosevelt's emphasis on presidential leadership fit in well with the leadership principle that was an important element in Churchill's writings.

In 1902 Churchill was elected as a Republican to the New Hampshire legislature, where he served two terms. By 1906 he was so disgusted by the corruption he witnessed in Concord and the ability of the Boston and Maine Railroad to run the state in its own interests that he was persuaded to run for the Republican nomination for governor. Although most of the locals still identified him as an outsider, he received wide support from across the country and was nearly nominated. The defeat did not surprise or discourage him; instead, he helped unite the progressive elements in the state, producing considerable reform legislation and the election of Robert Bass as governor in 1910. Churchill's political activities and writings attracted nationwide attention over the next ten years, but his only other run for political office was for governor on the Progressive party ticket in 1912—a futile act that he undertook out of loyalty to Roosevelt. Still there can be no doubt that Churchill's writings, his extensive expenditure of time and energy at forming a real reform party in New Hampshire and the nation was a force in whatever success the insurgent movement achieved.

Despite the time that Churchill devoted to practical politics during these years, he did not abandon his primary career. Various explanations have been offered for why a man who had achieved fame and fortune as a historical novelist should switch to the uncertain field of problem novels. The best answer is that after about 1902 he decided to tell the reading public not what it wanted to hear, but what he thought it should hear. The transition was not as sudden as it might seem; many readers and critics considered *Coniston* (1906) a continuation of his study of the past. Based on the career of the successful New Hampshire political boss Ruel Durkee, the novel shows how Jethro Bass (Churchill's best fictional portrait) successfully wins control of his state from the true leaders (the old aristocrats) through manipulation of the spoils system, which Churchill associated with the triumph of the Jacksonian movement. At the conclusion of the novel, Jethro surrenders his political control to the railroads.

Mr. Crewe's Career (1908) continues the story of politics in New Hampshire. Churchill's portrait of the title character is largely a self-parody, and Humphrey Crewe is neither the hero nor the center of interest in the novel. Writing about the book years later, Churchill said that it "was more or less autobiographical. I like to think that I was making fun, perhaps more or less unconsciously of myself." The novel is basically a portrait of the domination of the state by the railroads and—through the real hero, Austen Vane—of the rescue of the state and the nation by an unstoppable reform movement. His next novel, *A Modern Chronicle* (1910), marks another step in Churchill's evolution from historical romancer to social philosopher. Its surface subject is divorce, but the theme is really the individual's search for self-integration and moral roots in an industrial society devoted to business and competition. It is the most artistic of Churchill's novels.

Until about 1910 Churchill believed that the evils of contemporary society were the product of business domination of politics and that the way to cure the evils was through political reform. Thereafter he gradually came to believe that political and economic reforms were insufficient. What was needed was a religion that would rise above dogma and unite people. Churchill began to devote most of his time to preaching the new faith. Not an original thinker, he encountered, absorbed, and popularized the new ideas of his age in many fields with the zeal of the convert. He had slipped off the mantle of entertainer and donned that of social critic and social prophet. The transition had been coming for some time; in *The Inside of the Cup* (1913) it was completed. Churchill used the novel's plot as a vehicle to put forth the theology of the Social Gospel as expressed by its leading theologian, Walter Rauschenbusch, who wrote glowingly of the book to both Churchill and Brett. The core of this new religion, which Churchill expounded in speeches across the country, was an unlimited faith in God combined with self-reliance. The world would be transformed, the kingdom of god on earth would be brought about, by the reborn individuals who would lead others to the truth. Although Churchill was describing himself as a socialist by this time, his was the religious socialism of the Social Gospel, not that of Karl Marx or even of his self-appointed teacher, Upton Sinclair. He was reading widely in socialist literature, but, as is clear in *A*

Far Country (1915), he continued to emphasize the reborn individual.

Churchill's last published novel, *The Dwelling Place of Light*, appeared in 1917. The setting is that of a bitter strike, but the theme of the path to self-realization is essentially the same. The tone of the novel, however, is much more somber than anything Churchill had written previously; for the first time, his heroine dies within the pages of the novel. Although the possibility of general salvation is still present, it is far more remote than in any of his earlier works. The novel was the bridge between his earlier optimism and his later withdrawal—a fact temporarily obscured by the revival of his millennialist ideas during America's participation in World War I.

During the early war years, Churchill was in Washington, D.C., researching his next novel. While there he wrote a series of propaganda articles for the navy. At the same time, encouraged by Franklin D. Roosevelt, who was then undersecretary of the navy, he investigated Secretary of Navy Josephus Daniels and presented his highly critical conclusions to President Woodrow Wilson. Following an invitation by the British government to visit the war front, Churchill returned to write *A Traveller in War-Time with an Essay on the American Contribution and the Democratic Idea* (1918). The final essay in this volume symbolizes the most hopeful aspects of the Progressive mind. Churchill felt that the transcendent issue of the war and the times was industrial democracy. The book presents an optimistic view of the future, but it also indicts American society and the capitalistic system. Churchill's three-act play, *Dr. Jonathan* (1919), dramatized his belief that "the issue of the war is industrial democracy, without which political democracy is a farce."

From 1918 until about 1921 Churchill underwent a series of mystical experiences that dramatically altered his life. At this time he was also suffering from a transient encephalitis that apparently heightened the intensity of his religious experiences. While still working on a novel and beset by financial difficulties, he decided that his new faith could not be expressed in a novel. He submitted his manuscript, minus the narrative (which turned it into a form of non-Freudian psychology), to Brett, who had automatically accepted everything that Churchill had written for more than two decades; the publisher could not accept what Churchill called the "Skychology" manuscript.

Although Churchill repudiated the ideas expressed in his social novels in favor of his new religious vision, he never stopped writing, and he certainly did not live in the isolation that most scholars have suggested was his life during the 1920s and 1930s. He took up painting under the guidance of Maxfield Parrish, traveled widely, and wrote hundreds of letters to people who were interested in his philosophy of "noncontention." Even though the family's income was slim, he steadfastly refused lucrative offers from Hollywood.

The product of two decades of thought and writing, *The Uncharted Way* appeared in 1940, just as Churchill's namesake in Great Britain had come center stage. But after 1939 the public was not much interested in a philosophy of noncontention. Reviewers devoted their attention to the fact that there was an American Winston Churchill who had once been famous. Churchill's new religion bore little resemblance to traditional Christianity, except for a reliance on his unusual interpretations of the writings of the Hebrew prophets, Jesus, and Paul.

Immediately after the publication of *The Uncharted Way*, Churchill turned his hand to a new formulation of his ideas in an attempt to demonstrate that the fundamental ideas of the Hebrew prophets were identical with those of the classical Greek philosophers. At the age of seventy-five he was still looking for the elusive truth he had so often felt within his grasp. He died quietly of a heart attack in Winter Park, Florida, and was buried beside his wife on the hillside overlooking the Connecticut River that they both had loved.

• Nearly all of Churchill's vast correspondence, manuscripts, receipts, and a variety of other papers are in the extensive Churchill collection in Baker Library, Dartmouth College. A complete listing of all of Churchill's publications and virtually all of the writings about him is in Eric Steinbaugh, *Winston Churchill: A Reference Guide* (1985). The most complete biography is Robert W. Schneider, *Novelist to a Generation: The Life and Thought of Winston Churchill* (1976). Warren I. Titus, *Winston Churchill* (1963), is also useful.

ROBERT W. SCHNEIDER

CHURCHMAN, William Henry (23 Nov. 1818–18 May 1882), educator of the blind, was born in Baltimore, Maryland, the son of Quakers Micajah Churchman and Eliza (maiden name unknown). At the age of fifteen his eyesight began to fail, which was attributed to strain from reading and "overstudy" of languages and mathematics. At age eighteen he entered the newly founded Pennsylvania Institution for the Blind as an advanced pupil who had the equivalent of a common-school education but needed specialized training in the skills relevant to the blind, especially writing and reading raised print. A model pupil of the institution, he graduated three years later and spent a year as a teacher there before taking an appointment in 1840 as a teacher of mathematics and music at the Ohio Institution for the Blind in Columbus.

One of the first blind people to become a teacher of the blind, Churchman epitomized the goal of the founders of schools for the blind: he became a living example of the intelligence and ability that, it was hoped, all blind people could display. His talents as a teacher and as a showpiece prompted the Tennessee Institution for the Blind in 1844 to appoint him principal, a post he held until 1847. During this era Churchman often arranged exhibitions of his blind students (and himself) before state legislatures and other civic-minded bodies; one such exhibition before the Indiana legislature in 1844 resulted in that state's first appropriation of funds for the education of its blind children at other states' institutions. The legislature did not think there were sufficient numbers of blind children in Indiana to justify the establishment of an institution for their education until Churchman, in the summer of 1846, undertook to canvass the state, correcting the 1840 census, which had drastically undercounted the blind population, and demonstrating to the general public that education of the blind was feasible and desirable. His efforts persuaded the state legislature to establish the Indiana Institution for the Education of the Blind in Indianapolis in 1847, and Churchman accepted the position of "acting superintendent." His position was labeled temporary because the trustees of the institution doubted that a blind person could, by himself, hold a position of such responsibility; his position became permanent in 1851.

Churchman supervised all aspects of the Indiana Institution from the beginning, including the design of its buildings to provide maximum ventilation. Legend has it that as Churchman went through the halls and rooms he detected imperfectly mixed mortar and unsatisfactory bracings in the woodwork with the top of his cane. He also advertised the school widely, garnering support from the public and recruiting his pupils personally.

Churchman's curriculum focused particular attention on preparing the blind to become self-supporting. His innovations solved some of the problems that plagued existing institutions for the blind and garnered him national and international recognition. Instead of paying instructors to teach blind students manual manufacturing skills, Churchman gave his instructors the free use of the workshops and of the pupils' labor; the instructor bought his own raw materials and sold the finished goods for his own profit. Appealing to the instructor's "enlightened self-interest" guaranteed the quality of instruction and saved the institution the expense and anxiety of managing the industrial training, leaving its resources free to develop the intellectual curriculum. The pupils, according to Churchman, learned that their labor was their duty, a means of payment for their education; just as they were not paid to do math problems, Churchman argued, so they should not be paid to learn to make salable goods. He also advocated that funds be set aside for each graduating pupil, which would provide them with sufficient capital to start their own businesses.

Churchman was also an acknowledged leader in publicizing statistics about the causes of blindness and a pioneer in the campaign for the prevention of blindness. His success in the education of the blind was instrumental in getting the Indiana Institution included under the administration of the Department of State Public Instruction rather than under the aegis of the Board of Charity. By 1868, Churchman's institution was acknowledged as the first to be designated a school rather than an asylum.

Despite his successes, Churchman was dismissed from the superintendency of the Indiana Institution, probably in 1853, as that position was designated as a political appointment. He became the superintendent of the Wisconsin Institution for the Blind in Janesville, where he remained until 1861, when, perhaps because sighted men were drawn away by the Civil War, he was asked to return to the Indiana Institution, and he again became the superintendent. He held this position until his retirement in 1879, in spite of the efforts of the New York Institution for the Blind to woo him away with the promise of a doubled salary.

The New York Institution's eagerness to hire Churchman was testimony to his achievement of national stature. He was instrumental in organizing the first professional association of educators of the blind. By his instigation, the second convention of workers with the blind was held in Indianapolis in 1871, and from this convention the American Association of Instructors of the Blind was formed, with Churchman as its vice president. Elected its president in 1876, he served until 1879.

Churchman was married to Mary Marshall, but it is not known when the marriage occurred or whether he and his wife had children. After retiring from professional life, he spent his last three years with his half brother, F. M. Churchman, at whose home southeast of Indianapolis he died.

William Henry Churchman was one of the first disabled citizens of the United States to rise to prominence and one of the pioneers of the field of special education. He served as a living example of the capabilities and achievements of the blind and of the handicapped in general. An inspiring teacher, he taught his blind students, and the sighted public, the need for the state to provide all citizens with an education that would enable them to be self-supporting and self-respecting.

• Churchman's own statements about his ideas for the education of the blind can be found in the annual reports of the Tennessee, Indiana, and Wisconsin Institutions for the Blind, especially the *Indiana Annual Reports* for 1862 and 1867. The *Proceedings of the American Association of Instructors of the Blind* (1853, 1871–) also contain many statements by, and references to, Churchman; the 1878 volume contains an address he gave as president, and the 1882 volume contains an obituary. Personal anecdotes about Churchman, and a history of the Indiana institution, can be found in George S. Cottman, "William Henry Churchman and the School for the Blind," *Indiana Magazine of History* 10 (Mar. 1914): 77–82, and Ida Helen McCarty, "Indiana's Blind," *Indiana Magazine of History* 19 (Sept. 1923): 291–98.

MARY KLAGES

CHUTE, Beatrice Joy (3 Jan. 1913–6 Sept. 1987), novelist and short story writer, was born in Hazelwood, Minnesota, the daughter of William Young Chute, a real estate agent, and Englishwoman Edith Mary Pickburn. Joy Chute, as she preferred to be called, grew up in Hazelwood, about eight miles outside of Minneapolis, and was graduated from West High School in Minneapolis in 1929. She once observed that she and her older sisters, M.G. and Marchette, who also became writers, had the good fortune of sharing a tutor who, in their private grammar school, emphasized English composition and encouraged them to write. Like the Brontës, Chute and her sisters played endless writing games as children. Chute took extension work at the University of Minnesota, did secretarial work for her father for ten years, and later worked for the Property Owners' Association and the Minneapolis Better Housing Committee.

When her father died in 1939, Chute and her sisters spent a year in California and then settled in New York City with their mother. Chute published her first work, a juvenile short story, in 1931. She wrote for *Boys Life* and the English publication *Boys Own Paper* and later contributed juvenile short stories to many magazines. One writer commented that during her career Chute had written "literally hundreds" of sports stories for boys. Her first book, *Blocking Back* (1938), was also for juvenile readers. It was followed by *Shattuck Cadet* (1940), *Camp Hero* (1942), *Shift to the Right* (1944), and *Teen-Age Sports Parade* (1949). Chute had a knack for writing realistic tales about camp life and sports.

When Chute published her first adult book, *The Fields Are White* (1950), a *New York Times* reviewer commented that Chute may not have been the first to say that life begins at forty, but she was probably the first to make it sound easy. Other adult novels and stories followed, including *The End of Loving* (1953), *Greenwillow* (1956), *Journey to Christmas* (1958), *The Moon and the Thorn* (1961), *Mr. Bodley's Oak* (1965), *One Touch of Nature, and Other Stories* (1965), *The Story of a Small Life* (1971), *Katie, an Impertinent Fairy Tale* (1978), and *The Good Woman* (1986). Perhaps her best-known work was *Greenwillow*, a story set in a mythical country that resembles Ireland. The work depicts the Reverend Birdsong's influence on the village, the flowering of young love, and the people's commitment to the land. The story was adapted for a Broadway musical with music and lyrics by Frank Loesser.

Once, in a personal note, Chute remarked that she found writing an especially difficult, demanding, and interesting profession. She said that most of her material came "from observation, experience and imagination," and she lamented that her "craft demands an almost unlimited willingness to rewrite."

Chute, who never married, doted on her niece and nephew and on all children. In the 1950s she spent two afternoons a week at the Police Athletic League, which provided recreation for underprivileged children. She also volunteered at the McMahon Memorial Center for temporarily homeless children from Spanish Harlem. Through the Foster Parents' Plan for War Children she helped support one Polish, one Italian, two Chinese, and two Korean children.

In 1964 Chute became an adjunct professor of English and creative writing at Barnard College, where she taught until her death. She also served as director of Books across the Sea, a division of the English Speaking Union promoting American books abroad, and from 1959 to 1961 was president of the U.S. chapter of PEN (Poets, Playwrights, Editors, Essayists and Novelists). Chute died in New York City.

• Chute's life is examined in Anna Rothe, ed., *Current Biography 1950* (1951). She is also treated in James M. Ethridge and Barbara Kapola, eds., *Contemporary Authors* (1967), and *Something about the Author*, vol. 2 (1971). An obituary is in the *New York Times*, 15 Sept. 1987, and the *Chicago Tribune*, 16 Sept. 1987.

MARY A. GARDNER

CIANCABILLA, Giuseppe (21 Aug. 1871–16 Sept. 1904), anarchist and journalist, was born in Rome, Italy, the son of Alessandro Ciancabilla, a lumber merchant, and Appollonia Corinaldini. Raised in modest circumstances, but studious and intelligent, Ciancabilla pursued classical studies in secondary school, and in his late teens he began to write poems and articles for various publications.

The 1890s were a time of great social tumult in Italy. The discontent of peasants and workers was manifesting in such uprisings as the Fasci Sicliani and the Moti di Maggio in Milan, and the government was responding with harsh repressive measures, directed particularly at the leaders of the growing socialist and anarchist movements. In this agitated political climate, Ciancabilla espoused socialism and quickly became influential within the Federazione Socialista Romana and a contributor to the anticlerical *L'Asino*. Swept up by enthusiasm for the Hellenic cause during the 1897 war between Greece and Turkey, Ciancabilla joined a brigade of Italian volunteers led by the anarchist Amilcare Cipriani. A participant in several battles, Ciancabilla also wrote dispatches for the socialist organ *Avanti!* Compelling examples of Ciancabilla's vigorous, vivid prose, these articles were widely reprinted. After returning to Rome, he resumed his socialist activism and served as a correspondent for *Avanti!* In this capacity he conducted a sympathetic interview with Errico Malatesta, the leading Italian anarchist, then clandestinely staying in Italy. Shortly thereafter Ciancabilla, with his companion, Ersilia Cavedagni Grandi, herself a fiery anarchist, left surreptitiously for Switzerland. (Although they never married, the couple announced in the radical press that they were joined in a "free union," and they remained together until Ciancabilla's death.)

In mid-October 1897 Ciancabilla sent a declaration to Malatesta's L'Agitazione of Ancona announcing his conversion to anarchism. Alienated from what he saw as the corrupt and cowardly nature of democratic socialism, Ciancabilla declared that "my aspirations eternally rebellious and intolerant of any yoke have at last found their fulfillment" (Rosada, p. 32). The couple traveled briefly to Brussels, then to Paris, where Ciancabilla's contacts with the anarchist group Les Temps Nouveau influenced his thinking toward libertarianism. Forced to leave France, he edited the short-lived *L'Agitatore* in Neuchâtel; following his apologia of Luigi Luccheni, the assassin of Empress Elizabeth of Austria, he was expelled from Switzerland. Hounded by the police in London, Ciancabilla, under a pseudonym and in disguise, sailed for the United States late in 1898.

In Paterson, New Jersey, where many Italians, among them anarchists, worked in the silk mills, Ciancabilla immediately assumed the editorship of *La Questione Sociale*, which had been established in 1895. His acerbic polemics against organizational anarchism as authoritarian sparked controversies with Malatesta's followers. In August 1899 Malatesta himself arrived to assume the editorship of *La Questione Sociale*.

On 16 September 1899 Ciancabilla founded *L'Aurora*, which he devoted to unrestrained advocacy of antiorganizational anarchism. He called for the abolition of church, state, and private property and the demolition of bourgeois society by any and all means. Not a pure individualist, since he believed in the spontaneous revolt of the workers, he nonetheless rejected all authority that infringed on the freedom of the individual. Ciancabilla also espoused the individual act, the *attentat*. Among those who knew Ciancabilla in Paterson was Gaetano Bresci, who would kill King Umberto I of Italy in 1900. Ciancabilla's unsentimental revolutionary passion was perhaps best expressed in his poem "Primo Maggio" (*Fiori di Maggio* [1900]), which laments "the sickening sweet rhetoric of love and brotherhood" that "has penetrated into our soul with lying hope" and calls instead for "the hour of justice, of the great victory, / when from the vivid blood sprouts the new history, / to cancel the infamy and the shame of servitude."

The polemics between Ciancabilla and the Malatestians intensified, taking the form of vile personal invective and resulting in physical violence. Perhaps for this reason, in 1900 Ciancabilla moved himself, Ersilia, and *L'Aurora* first to Yohanghany, Pennsylvania, and then to Spring Valley, a mining town in Illinois, where a goodly number of Italian, French, and Belgian comrades lived. He extolled the shooting of President William McKinley by the anarchist Leon Czolgosz in September 1901 (as he had that of the Italian king by Bresci); speculating on the motives of the assassin, he cited the grievances of workers exploited, starved, and beaten by "the capitalist imperialist friends of McKinley" (Vecoli, "Free Country"). When such rhetoric attracted the attention of Americans, Ciancabilla was threatened with tar and feathering, if not worse, by an enraged mob. After serving several months in jail, he resurfaced, in February 1902, in Chicago, where he published *La Protesta Umana* in a magazine format. Defiant as always, Ciancabilla wrote: "Especially now we should show we are alive when everyone wishes that we were dead" (letter, 14 Sept. 1902). Unabashed he continued his ferocious attacks on bourgeois capitalism, the American Federation of Labor (AFL), the state, the church, social democrats, and organizational anarchists.

In a letter to Jacques Gross dated 25 April 1902, Ciancabilla expressed his views on the condition of the anarchist movement:

> These heterodox opinions which I defended in our movement with the ardor of my temperament have brought unto me the fervent hatred on the part of our organizers, their excommunications, and their low and filthy slander. . . . The more I live and learn to know the anarchists, the more the individuals disgust me: that is everywhere, in Italy as in France, in England and in America; always the same shabby thoughts, the same narrow and sectarian spirit; the same tendency toward the cloister, to the chapel. But this makes me love the great and radiant idea which one day will free us from all this filth.

In the same letter Ciancabilla revealed another side of his personality. Despite his "poor, wandering life," he derived happiness from his "sweet, and strong and wise companion" (Ersilia), to whom he attributed the "spirit and vivacity in the fight that makes me enthusiastic without tiring me!"

Having few comrades in Chicago, Ciancabilla and Ersilia compiled and produced *La Protesta Umana* entirely by themselves. He became so proficient in the printer's trade that he typeset articles directly as he composed them. Meanwhile, the couple lived with Russian comrades: Abe Isaak, a Mennonite turned anarchist, who with his wife, Mary, and son Abe, Jr., published the anarchist journal *Free Society*; and the Jewish Edelstadt family, who were related to David Edelstadt, a Yiddish anarchist poet and journalist. Ciancabilla and Ersilia found the Windy City infertile ground, however, and in March 1903 they moved to San Francisco, where Germinal, an anarchist group of Spaniards, French, and Italians provided support for *La Protesta Umana*, which occasionally published supplements in French and Spanish. Although he was confronted by a continuous deficit, Ciancabilla managed to publish *La Protesta Umana* as a weekly for another eighteen months. In 1904, after a long bout with tuberculosis, he died at the German Hospital in San Francisco. He was only thirty-three. Luigi Galleani succeeded him as the dominant personality among antiorganizational anarchists.

Of a passionate, uncompromising temperament, Ciancabilla was characterized by his biographer as "a romantic knight of a past epoch" (Fedeli, p. 7). He was also the most intellectual of the Italian radicals in the United States. Others were more powerful orators, and more popular leaders, but none could match the power of his pen. A "merciless polemicist," he was also an eloquent poet and astute critic of the world around him. Although he did not write a major theoretical work, he enriched the literature of Italian anarchism with translations of Peter Kropotkin's *La conquista del pane* (The conquest of bread, 1899) and Jean Grave's *La societa' al domani della rivoluzione* (Society the day following the revolution, 1900). These and other writings circulated widely in Italy, despite sequestrations by the police, and exerted a strong influence on Italian anarchism. Italian historians credit Ciancabilla with having introduced the individualist tradition of Anglo-American anarchism into Italy. Ciancabilla's legacy to Italian-American anarchism was to introduce a powerful libertarian strain into the movement.

• A few, but interesting, Ciancabilla letters can be found in the Jacques Gross and Max Nettlau archives of the International Institute of Social History, Amsterdam, which also holds files of the publications edited by Ciancabilla; the Italian police files on Ciancabilla and Ersilia Cavedagni Grandi are particularly informative. Collected writings of Ciancabilla have been published in *Gli Anarchici, chi sono cosa vogliono* (1921) and *Verso la morte* (1949). Ugo Fedeli, *Giuseppe Ciancabilla* (1965), is largely composed of extracts from his writings. The most complete account is by Anna Rosada in *Il movimento operaio italiano: Dizionario biografico, 1853–1943*, ed. Franco Andreucci and Tommaso Detti, vol. 2 (1976). A contemporary appreciation is *Primo Maggio: impressioni e ricordi di Giuseppe Ciancabilla* (1906). For context, Paul Avrich, *Sacco and Vanzetti: The Anarchist Background* (1991), is valuable, but see also Rudolph J. Vecoli, "'Free Country': The American Republic Viewed by the Italian Left, 1880–1920," in *In the Shadow of the Statue of Liberty: Immigrants, Workers, and Citizens in the American Republic, 1880–1920*, ed. Marianne Debouzy (1988), and "*Primo Maggio* in the United States: An Invented Tradition of the Italian Anarchists," in *May Day Celebration*, ed. Andrea Panaccione (1988; English ed., 1992). For Ciancabilla's influence on Italian anarchism see Enzo Santarelli, *Il socialismo anarchico in Italia* (1973), and Pier Carlo Masini, *Storia degli anarchici italiani* (1974).

RUDOLPH J. VECOLI

CIARDI, John (24 June 1916–30 Mar. 1986), poet-translator, was born in Boston, Massachusetts, the son of Carminantonio Ciardi, an insurance premium collector, and Concetta Di Benedictis. Ciardi was delivered by a midwife at his parents' home in Boston's Little Italy. Three years later his father died in an automobile accident, and his mother moved her family seven miles away to Medford, where the poet grew up across the street from the Mystic River. After high school, he went to Bates College in Maine for a year and a half before transferring to Tufts College in Medford for financial reasons. He majored in English and learned poetry from John Holmes, himself an accomplished poet-teacher, who became a surrogate father for Ciardi. He graduated with honors in 1938 and went to the University of Michigan to study poetry with Roy Cowden. There he won the Avery Hopwood Poetry Award in 1939, the same year he received an M.A. in English.

Ciardi taught English at the University of Kansas City for two years before enlisting in the U.S. Army Air Corps in 1942. As a gunner on board a B-29, Ciardi was stationed on Saipan and flew some sixteen missions over Japan in 1944–1945; he was discharged in 1945 with the Air Medal and Oak Leaf Cluster at the rank of technical sergeant. After the war, he returned to the University of Kansas City for the spring term in 1946; during this time he met and by the summer married Myra Judith Hostetter, a journalism instructor. In September he began teaching at Harvard, where he remained until 1953, when he moved to Rutgers to set up a creative writing program. In 1955 Ciardi was named director of the Bread Loaf Writers' Conference, and the next year he was named poetry editor of the *Saturday Review*. In 1961 he resigned his professorship, which he called "planned poverty," in order to earn a better living for his family, which had by then grown by the addition of three children. He was determined to earn his living lecturing, at which he had made a national reputation, and writing, for which he was equally applauded. He hosted a television program called "Accent" on the CBS network in 1961–1962. After leaving the Bread Loaf directorship in 1972 and his position as columnist at *SR* in 1977, Ciardi began studying word histories and started a weekly radio program on the subject called "A Word in Your Ear," which was broadcast to more than 200 stations on the National Public Radio network from 1977 until his death. He died three months short of his seventieth birthday at his home in Metuchen, New Jersey.

Including three volumes that were published posthumously, Ciardi left behind twenty books of poems, the first appearing in 1940 and the last in 1993. He put together his *Selected Poems* in 1984, and a much more comprehensive edition, *The Collected Poems of John Ciardi*, edited by Edward Cifelli, was published in 1997. Including three other posthumously published books, Ciardi produced sixteen volumes of children's poetry, one of which, *Blabberhead, Bobble-Bud & Spade*, is a collection of selected poems. Ciardi's tour de force translation of Dante's *Divine Comedy* began appearing in 1954 with the publication of *The Inferno*; *The Purgatorio* followed in 1961 and *The Paradiso* in 1970. The complete work was published in 1977 in a trade edition by W. W. Norton. Notable among Ciardi's remaining publications are his 1950 anthology, *Mid-Century American Poets*, and his 1959 textbook, *How Does a Poem Mean?* His three volumes of word histories are *A Browser's Dictionary* (1980), *A Second Browser's Dictionary* (1983), and *Good Words to You* (1987).

Ciardi rarely addressed literary highbrows, who in turn generally considered him beneath their attention. Early in his career, he tried to educate the intelligent reader of what he called "general culture" to the difficult "modern" poetry being written at mid-century. His lectures to this wide middlebrow audience were extremely popular both for content and Ciardi's characteristic delivery—with his deep voice, easy manner, and an exceptional ability to quote long poems from memory. Audiences left his lectures with a new understanding of what modern poets were trying to do—and how they were trying to do it. Ciardi had been raised in an era when poetry mattered enough to the public at large to be published in daily newspapers that also carried poetry review columns as a regular feature. The country had a high regard and deep respect for the poet. But in the 1950s and 1960s, as Ciardi came to realize that there were fewer and fewer readers of general culture, he ceased writing for such an ideal reader and wrote only for himself and other poets, trying to capture the human significance of everyday matters in what he called "the unimportant poem."

At his best, Ciardi has a strong masculine voice, even in love poems, and he is an especially good narrative poet, as his 1971 autobiography, *Lives of X*, demonstrates. The poems about his family, which he called "tribal poems," are also excellent, both for their psychological probings into identity and the various patterns he chose to express them in. In an interview conducted shortly before his death and broadcast at the University of Missouri-Kansas City as part of a John Ciardi memorial, Ciardi remarked on the various styles he employed: "My impulse has always been to try to phrase the poem to sound like the subject matter. That is . . . , I try to make every poem fit itself rather than all subject matter fit a predetermined style" ("*New Letters* on the Air," May 1986). Richard Wilbur, in an obituary essay on Ciardi in *Proceedings of the American Academy* (1986), may have written the finest three sentences yet produced in Ciardi criticism:

> At any time, as in the later poem "Minus One," it was in his power to be formally dazzling. But the characteristic Ciardi poem is not a full-dress performance: it is technically muted and relaxed; colloquial; ruminative; it has the movement of developing thought; it pauses to toy with its own words; it gets carried away by memory or example; it ends with an offhand air. Often such poems begin with a trivial occasion and proceed, in the key of comedy, toward what proves after all to be a serious theme. (pp. 62–63)

• The bulk of the Ciardi papers are divided between Wayne State University and the Library of Congress, although letters and manuscripts have turned up in various libraries throughout the country. William White, *John Ciardi: A Bibliography* (1959), is excellent, but nothing similar has been done covering the poet's last twenty-six years. Some of the more important books of Ciardi's poetry that have come out since 1960 are *Person to Person* (1964), *The Little That Is All* (1974), *The Birds of Pompeii* (1985), and *Echoes* (1989). See also *The Collected Poems of John Ciardi*, ed. Edward M. Cifelli (1997). Ciardi's children's verse began appearing in 1959 with *The Reason for the Pelican* and included several books that earned him the 1982 award of the National Council of Teachers of English for lifetime contributions to the field. Among them are *The Man Who Sang the Sillies* and *I Met a Man* (1961), *You Know Who* (1964), *The Monster Den* (1966), *Someone Could Win a Polar Bear* (1970), and *Fast and Slow* (1975). Among his other books are two collections of essays that had originally appeared in *Saturday Review: Dialogue with an Audience* (1963) and *Manner of Speaking* (1972).

A scholarly biography is Cifelli, *John Ciardi: A Biography* (1997). Also of biographical interest is *The Selected Letters of John Ciardi*, ed. Cifelli (1991); *Saipan: The War Diary of John Ciardi* (1988); and David H. Bain, *Whose Woods These Are: A History of the Bread Loaf Writers' Conference* (1993). Of critical interest are Edward Krickel, *John Ciardi* (1980), and Vince Clemente, ed., *John Ciardi: Measure of the Man* (1987). See also Miller Williams, "Nothing Is Really Hard But to Be Real," in *The Achievement of John Ciardi* (1969), for a discussion of Ciardi's voice; Cifelli, "The Size of John Ciardi's Song," *CEA Critic* (Nov. 1973): 21–27, for comments on the Ciardi poetics at work; John Frederick Nims, "John Ciardi: The Many Lives of Poetry," *Poetry* (Aug. 1986): 283–99, for a summary of Ciardi's themes and techniques; and Richard Wilbur, "John Ciardi, 1916–1986," *Proceedings of the American Academy*, 2d ser., 37 (1986): 58–63, for an obituary statement that summarizes Ciardi both biographically and critically.

EDWARD M. CIFELLI

CICOTTE, Eddie (19 June 1884–5 May 1969), baseball player, was born Edward Victor Cicotte in Detroit, Michigan, the son of Ambrose Cicotte, a railroad foreman, and Archangel (maiden name unknown). He claimed Cadillac, the French founder of Detroit, as his great-great grandfather. Cicotte attended St. Ann's Catholic School in Detroit for eight years.

Cicotte began his baseball career as a teenager in the mining towns of northern Michigan and was signed by a Detroit Tiger scout who saw him pitch for Sault Sainte Marie. In 1905 Cicotte played for Augusta, Georgia, of the South Atlantic League. That same year he married Rose Ellen Freer in Macon, Georgia; they were to have three children. In late August, Cicotte was called up to the Tigers along with teammates Ty Cobb and Nap Rucker.

In 1906 Detroit sent Cicotte to Indianapolis, where he developed the knuckleball, a pitch that Jimmy Cannon once described as a "curveball that didn't give a damn." He later learned the spitball from its developer, Elmer Stricklett, who learned it from its inventor, Frank Corridor. Armed with his new weaponry, Cicotte worked his way back to the majors, joining the Boston Red Sox in 1908. He remained in Boston until July 1912 when he was sold to the Chicago White Sox. At 5′9″ and 175 pounds, Cicotte established himself as an excellent control pitcher and had "more pitches than a carnival barker." In addition to the knuckleball and spitball, he threw what was variously called the shine ball, the emery ball, or the "mystery pitch," for which Cicotte would alter the surface of the ball by shining it with an emery board. When thrown cross-seamed, the ball could break either way.

In 1917 Cicotte had his best season, leading the White Sox to a World Series championship. He led the American League in wins with 28, in earned run average with 1.53, and in innings pitched with 346⅔. He also had seven shutouts, struck out 150, and walked 70, while giving up only 246 hits. Any pitcher whose hits and walks combined are fewer than innings pitched has had a superb season. In the World Series he was 1–1, as the White Sox defeated the New York Giants four games to two.

When the White Sox won another pennant in 1919, Cicotte led the American League in wins with 29, in innings pitched with 306⅔, and in complete games with 30. He had an ERA of 1.82 and five shutouts, striking out 110 while walking only 49 and giving up 256 hits. In the World Series Cicotte was 1–2, with an ERA of 2.91. The White Sox were defeated by the Cincinnati Reds five games to three in a best of nine series that would become infamous for the Black Sox scandal.

In 1917 White Sox owner Charles Comiskey allegedly promised Cicotte a $10,000 bonus if he won 30 games; and when Cicotte approached 30 wins, Comiskey ordered him benched. The White Sox had the lowest meal money in the league and wore dirty uniforms because Comiskey had complained about the size of the laundry bill. At the same time Comiskey treated the press lavishly, plying them with food and drink. White Sox player salaries generally were also the lowest in the league, except for Eddie Collins's, whose $15,000 contract came with him in a trade from Philadelphia. Cicotte made only $5,000 in 1919. These factors undoubtedly contributed to the decision by eight White Sox players to fix the 1919 World Series in return for a payoff from gamblers.

The fix was orchestrated by Arnold Rothstein, a key figure in the New York criminal world of gambling, extortion, and prostitution. Cicotte's teammate Chick Gandil was identified as the ringleader who brought Cicotte and others into the scheme, although by some accounts Cicotte was an early and key co-conspirator. After months of widespread rumors, the fix was exposed in late September 1920, with the White Sox in a tight pennant race. A gambler by the name of Bill Maharg, known formerly as major league pitcher Bill Graham, charged in an interview in a Philadelphia newspaper that the White Sox had fixed the first two games of the 1919 World Series. The following day Cicotte and teammate Joe Jackson admitted to a Chicago prosecutor and grand jury that they had taken part in the conspiracy. Cicotte admitted to throwing two games and to being paid $10,000 before the first game of the Series. He reputedly signaled the gamblers that the fix was on by hitting Maurice Rath in the back on the second pitch of the first game. Cicotte lost that game, started and lost game four, and then won game seven.

Cicotte unwittingly waived his immunity rights, talked to prosecutors and the grand jury, and signed a confession without benefit of counsel. He told the grand jury that he participated in the conspiracy in order to pay off the mortgage on his farm and secure the future of his family. The papers quoted him as saying he did it "for the wife and kiddies," a line that was used repeatedly to mock him.

Cicotte and six other players were indicted, and the trial took place in February 1921. By then evidence had vanished and confessions signed by Jackson and Cicotte had disappeared, probably at the behest of Rothstein and Comiskey. In the end the jury issued a verdict of not guilty. Afterward, federal judge Kenesaw Mountain Landis, the new commissioner of major league baseball, issued an order banning the seven, along with infielder Fred McMullin, from baseball for life.

The scandal became emblematic of disillusionment in the post–World War I years. If the World Series could be fixed, then surely nothing was above reproach, a notion immortalized by F. Scott Fitzgerald in *The Great Gatsby*.

After his banishment, Cicotte played semiprofessional baseball for a few years under an assumed name. He then was employed by the Ford Motor Company in Detroit as a plant guard. After his retirement from Ford in 1944, he moved to five acres outside Detroit, where he raised strawberries and lived near his children and grandchildren. His son Eddie, Jr., had a brief professional baseball career, and his grandnephew Al Cicotte, whom he coached, had a short career in the majors as a pitcher.

In his thirteen-year major league career Eddie Cicotte won 208 games and lost 149. He is ranked among the top 300 players of the twentieth century, and the top 100 pitchers, by baseball historians John Thorn and Peter Palmer. If Cicotte's career had not ended with the Black Sox scandal, he would likely have been elected to the National Baseball Hall of Fame. He died in Detroit.

• Both the National Baseball Library in Cooperstown, N.Y., and the offices of the *Sporting News* in St. Louis, Mo., maintain clipping files on Cicotte. For his pitching statistics, see John Thorn et al., eds., *Total Baseball*, 4th ed. (1995). Two major works on the Black Sox scandal contain information on Cicotte: Eliot Asinof, *Eight Men Out* (1963), and Victor Luhr, *The Great Baseball Mystery* (1977). In *The Hustler's Handbook* (1965), chap. 11, Bill Veeck provides interesting insights into the scandal and Cicotte's role in it. Arnold "Chick" Gandil's account of the scandal with comments on Cicotte appeared in *Sports Illustrated*, 17 Sept. 1956. Lewis Thompson and Charles Boswell, "Say It Ain't So, Joe," *American Heritage* 11, no. 4 (June 1960): 22–27, is also of interest. Information on Cicotte's parents and his education is in a letter from Virginia Cicotte, Eddie's daughter, to baseball historian David Voigt, as of the mid-1990s in Mr. Voigt's possession. Obituaries are in the *New York Times*, 9 May 1969, and the *Sporting News*, 24 May 1969.

RICHARD C. CREPEAU

CILLEY, Joseph (c. 1734–25 Aug. 1799), soldier and politician, was born at "Ledge Farm" in Nottingham, New Hampshire, the son of Joseph Cilley and Alice (or Elsie) Rawlins (or Rollins), farmers. During his youth Cilley worked alongside his father, learning how to farm. A self-taught lawyer, he also was a businessman. In 1756 he married Sarah Longfellow; they had ten children and established a farm, "The Square," near Nottingham.

Before the Revolution, Cilley sat in the New Hampshire Provincial Congress. As the news of the Intolerable Acts filtered into New Hampshire, he decided to act. On 15 December 1774 he was a member of a patriot group that broke into Fort William and Mary (later Fort Constitution) near Portsmouth and hauled away British cannons, muskets, and other ammunition stores. Their action was timely, as British vessels entered the harbor of Portsmouth shortly thereafter.

When the revolutionary war broke out, Cilley enlisted for duty, and his regiment participated in the siege of Boston. On 20 May 1775 he accepted a commission as major of the Second New Hampshire Infantry under General Enoch Poor. After the evacuation of Boston, he headed south with General John Sullivan's brigade to New York and then to the St. Lawrence to help relieve American troops under General John Thomas. Cilley joined in the retreat of the Canadian expedition. Upon his return to New York, he narrowly avoided capture in the battle of Long Island. He participated in the retreat from New York, fighting alongside his men in the battles of Trenton and Princeton.

In recognition of his bravery and steadfast loyalty to the patriot cause, Cilley was commissioned major of the Eighth Continental Infantry on 1 January 1776. Ten months later he was appointed lieutenant colonel of the First New Hampshire Infantry, which was created at the end of 1776 after the Continental army was reorganized for long-term service. He succeeded the disenchanted John Stark as colonel of the regiment and held the post for the next four years. In July 1777 Cilley and his men fought at Fort Ticonderoga, where they struggled valiantly before being forced to make a hasty retreat. Two months later, under his leadership, the First New Hampshire joined Benedict Arnold's forces at the battle of Saratoga. His regiment distinguished itself for the capture of British military stores at Bemis Heights. The First New Hampshire then regrouped during the cold wintry months at Valley Forge.

With the War for American Independence showing no signs of abating, Cilley and his regiment persevered. During the summer of 1778 he and his men participated in the battle of Monmouth. A year later Cilley received orders to join the campaign in western New York against the Iroquois. In so doing, he renewed his acquaintance with his old commander, General Sullivan. Cilley's own state of New Hampshire rewarded his outstanding military service, passing a unanimous resolution noting "that the worthy Colonel Joseph Cilley be presented with a pair of pistols as a token of this State's good intention toward merit in a brave office."

In January 1781 Cilley retired from the Continental army after George Washington issued a general order reducing New Hampshire's three regiments to two and returned to his private business affairs, which his wife and eldest son had been managing efficiently during his absence. Shortly after his retirement from the army, Cilley was appointed justice of the peace and of the quorum for Rockingham County.

Cilley's military career, however, was far from over. By 1783 he was once again offering help in reorganizing his state's militia. For his efforts with the militia, he was first appointed brigadier general, and in 1786 he was promoted to major general, a post he held until the close of 1792. During the first year of his term as major general, he helped repel a protest movement in New Hampshire that was similar to the outbreak of hostilities in Massachusetts known as Shays's Rebellion. Several hundred farmers had gathered in Exeter to intimidate the legislature into issuing paper money, but Cilley's 2,000 militiamen suppressed the movement.

In his later years, Cilley opted to run for elected office. Although his initial candidacies for state elector and for state senator failed in the late 1780s, his enthusiasm for public office propelled him to try again, and in 1790 he emerged victorious. He served a one-year term in the state senate that year and in the state house of representatives in 1792. He also was a member of the Governor's Council from 1797 to 1798. In the various disputes between Alexander Hamilton and Thomas Jefferson, Cilley sided with the latter. He agreed with many of the principles espoused by Jeffersonian Republicans, such as small government with necessary checks on executive power, rotation in office, and wide representation by the people. A friend of the marquis de Lafayette, Cilley sided with the Revolutionists during the French Revolution.

Cilley died in Nottingham, New Hampshire. A report noted, "He bore his pains with great fortitude, and died with a calm and composed mind." Had he lived, he would have been gratified by the revolution of 1800, in which Thomas Jefferson and his fellow Republicans ousted the rival Federalists from power. According to Lafayette in a letter that he wrote from White Plains in July 1778, Cilley and four other colonels who had served at the battle of Monmouth were "among the most distinguish'd officers of any army in the world." Cilley had a long history of activism in the cause of American independence. Once the war was over, he was actively involved in state politics.

• Cilley's Regimental Book is in the New Hampshire State Archives in Concord. The Returns of the First New Hampshire Regiment, 1778–1780, are located at the New Hampshire Historical Society in Concord. Muster rolls and payrolls of the First New Hampshire for the period 1777 to 1780 are in the Maryland, Journal B, No. 1 and No. 2 Collection at the Library of Congress. A 1778 letter signed from the marquis de Lafayette to Henry Laurens that mentions Cilley by name is at the South Carolina Historical Society in Charleston. A biography of Cilley reflecting the author's interest in genealogy is John Scales, *Life of General Joseph Cilley* (1921). Additional information about Cilley is in two articles by Scales for *Granite State Magazine*: "General Joseph Cilley: His Career after He Left Command of the First Regiment," Nov. 1911, pp. 89–95, and "General Joseph Cilley: His Ancestors," July/Sept.–Oct./Dec. 1900, pp. 177–84. Although dated, valuable material on Cilley's birthplace is in E. C. Cogswell, *History of Nottingham, Deerfield, and Northwood* (1878). While the literature on the American Revolution is vast, important studies on the war experience that mention Cilley's involvement include John R. Elting, *The Battles of Saratoga* (1977); Rupert Furneaux, *The Battle of Saratoga* (1971); and Howard H. Peckham, *The Toll of Independence: Engagements and Battle Casualties of the American Revolution* (1974). Books on the history of New Hampshire that mention Cilley include Paul W. Wilderson, *Governor John Wentworth and the American Revolution: The English Connection* (1994), and Lynn Warren Turner, *The Ninth State: New Hampshire's Formative Years* (1983).

ELIZABETH T. VAN BEEK

CISNEROS, Eleanora de. *See* De Cisneros, Eleanora.

CIST, Jacob (13 Mar. 1782–30 Dec. 1825), anthracite coal pioneer, naturalist, and inventor, was born in Philadelphia, Pennsylvania, the son of Charles Cist, a journalist and publisher, and Mary Weiss. The eldest son of a large, prominent family, Cist proved responsible, practical, and curious from a young age. After completing elementary school in Philadelphia, he studied for three years at the Moravian Academy (Nazareth Hall) in Nazareth, Pennsylvania, where he exhibited particular interests in geography, manufacture, and illustration. Cist became proficient at sketching in ink and in oils, landscapes and factories being among his prominent themes. He also showed a knack for writing, publishing short pieces of prose and verse in magazines and newspapers.

At age fifteen Cist returned to Philadelphia and began working for his father, who was formally trained in medicine and owned a publishing house. Cist's father was also a partner in an anthracite mining concern. Cist learned something about both business and the natural sciences from his father. During his three years in his father's Philadelphia printing establishment, it was the official government printer for John Adams's administration. When his father opened a new printing house in Washington, D.C., in 1800, Cist moved there and became manager. In 1800 the nation's capital moved from Philadelphia to Washington, and Cist added a clerkship in the U.S. Post Office Department to his publishing work. When Jefferson became president in 1801 the family printing business closed, but Cist managed to retain his clerkship while overseeing his father's business affairs in Washington. In 1803 he patented his first invention, an artist's paint-mixing mill.

With his father's death in 1805 Cist inherited shares in the Lehigh Coal Mine Company, which he found to be so poorly managed that he nearly sold the stock. In 1807 he resigned his clerkship and returned to Pennsylvania, where he married Sarah Hollenback of Wilkes-Barre, the daughter of Matthias Hollenback, a wealthy merchant and land baron. They had five daughters. His father-in-law offered Cist a partnership in the family business. He accepted the offer, moved to Wilkes-Barre, and in 1808 was appointed the borough's first postmaster, an office he held for the rest of his life. In that same year he patented a mineral black made from anthracite coal to be used in printer's ink and leather lacquer.

Cist spent two years learning the mercantile trade from his father-in-law—driving cattle, purchasing goods, and transporting cargo down the Susquehanna River. He soon assumed responsibility for all facets of the business, including the management of extensive real-estate holdings, among them 48,500 acres of anthracite coal land. Thus, at a time when wood, bituminous (soft) coal, and charcoal were the most commonly used fuels and anthracite use was limited, Cist was investigating the prospects for developing extractive and manufacturing industries involving anthracite coal. Those prospects improved greatly when the War of 1812 precipitated a fuel crisis in Philadelphia. A British blockade of the Chesapeake and Delaware bays in 1813 prevented the shipment of Virginia bituminous coal to Philadelphia, tripling the price of coal. The inflated prices sparked interest among some Philadelphia merchants and artisans in obtaining anthracite coal from the Lehigh and Wyoming valleys. In 1813 Cist and his partners obtained a lease on Lehigh Coal Mine Company land near Mauch Chunk, Pennsylvania, and began mining, shipping tons of anthracite coal by wagon and barge to Philadelphia. Cist spared no effort in increasing the demand for anthracite. Because anthracite was difficult to ignite in existing stoves, he invented and patented an anthracite heating stove in 1814. He spoke to tradesmen about the advantages of anthracite: it generated more heat and less soot, smoke, and smell than bituminous coal. He drew sketches detailing potential modifications to existing forges, nail and glass furnaces, kilns, and stills to permit the use of anthracite. Still, demand for anthracite fluctuated according to the price of bituminous coal, which dropped again when Madison declared peace in 1815; at that time Cist and his partners ceased operation.

Cist, however, was dogged in his advocacy of anthracite. In 1815 he published the results of his marketing campaign as a pamphlet on the necessity of introducing anthracite coal into general use, with testimonials from blacksmiths, brewers, distillers, gunsmiths, and bankers. It was distributed primarily to artisans and was reprinted in the *Wilkes-Barre Gleaner*. When not occupied with his duties as postmaster and merchant, Cist spent much of his time "geologizing" throughout northeastern Pennsylvania, mapping geologic formations and describing the local strata; he became commonly regarded as a local scientific expert as well as business leader. Cist helped found the Luzerne County Agricultural Society in 1810, taking particular interest in increasing the local availability of higher quality fruit trees. His paper advocating the superiority of New York gypsum as a fertilizer was read before the Pennsylvania Agricultural Society in 1813. In 1816 he served as Luzerne County treasurer. In the same year he founded the Wilkes-Barre Bridge Company. When Wilkes-Barre's first bank opened in 1817, Cist became a charter member and first cashier.

Cist came to the attention of the wider scientific community in 1821, when he responded to French geologist Alexandre Brongniart's request in the *American Journal of Science and the Arts* for information on American coal deposits and plant fossils. Cist sent the journal coal and fossil samples to be forwarded to Brongniart, and in 1822 the journal published the results of Cist's research on anthracite, along with a map and excerpts from his pamphlet. Brongniart appended the species name *cistii* to several specimens and acknowledged Cist in a letter to the journal. Cist became known as the leading local expert on Pennsylvania anthracite. The journal's editor, Yale professor of mineralogy Benjamin Silliman, cited Cist in his research papers, maintained a correspondence with him, and published other articles by Cist, including one on entomology with a plate of Cist's insect drawings (1824). Cist spent years preparing hundreds of drawings of insects for a work on American entomology, never completed and since lost.

Although Cist was largely unsuccessful in developing large industrial and domestic markets for anthracite in Philadelphia, he played a significant part in laying the groundwork for future anthracite extraction and use, not only by publicizing its advantages but also through his role in companies devoted to the development of Pennsylvania's bridges and canals. His contributions to science were modest but timely, coming when geologists were engaged in correlating stratigraphic successions on different continents and establishing the extent of exploitable mineral resources. Cist died in Wilkes-Barre, apparently as the result of gout and a liver infection.

• Cist's letters, manuscripts, maps, and drawings are held at the Wyoming Historical and Geological Society, Wilkes-Barre, Pa., and at the Academy of Natural Sciences of Philadelphia. His scientific articles appear in the *American Journal of Science and the Arts*, vols. 4, 8, and 9. A succinct chronology of Cist's life is in Oscar Jewell Harvey and Ernest Gray Smith, *A History of Wilkes-Barre and Wyoming Valley*, vol. 4 (1929). An important biographical source is H. Benjamin Powell, *Philadelphia's First Fuel Crisis: Jacob Cist and the Developing Market for Pennsylvania Anthracite* (1978), and references cited therein.

JOHN HUSS

CLAFLIN, Horace Brigham (18 Dec. 1811–14 Nov. 1885), merchant and businessman, was born in Milford, Massachusetts, the son of John Claflin, a country storekeeper, farmer, and justice of the peace, and Lydia Mellen. Horace Claflin was educated at common school and at Milford Academy, and at an early age he clerked in his father's store. One of his first teachers later recalled that even at a young age Claflin told him that his only ambition was to "spend his life in trade." He was, according to accounts of his peers, "a born merchant."

In 1831 Claflin, along with his brother and brother-in-law, took over his father's general store in Milford. The next year, the brothers opened a dry goods store in Worcester, Massachusetts. In 1833 the Claflin brothers split the stores, Horace getting the newer store in Worcester. By 1839 Claflin's store was doing $200,000 per year in business. In 1836 Claflin married Agnes Sanger; they moved on 1 July 1843 to New York City. There he entered a partnership with William F. Bulkley, a longtime New York dry goods merchant. Claflin contributed $30,000 in capital, and in ten years the firm did an annual business of $1 million and served customers from every state and territory. In 1850 the partners built a new store at 57 Broadway, and a year later, in July 1851, Bulkley retired. Claflin admitted as a partner William H. Mellen, who had begun as a clerk for Claflin, and the business became known as Claflin, Mellen & Co. In 1853 Claflin built another new building, called the Trinity Building, at 111 Broadway. By 1860 the firm's business amounted to more than $13 million a year.

Like all New York merchants, Claflin did the greatest share of his business on credit. The Civil War caught Claflin with one half of the firm's accounts receivable in the Confederacy. Forced to suspend business, Claflin asked his creditors to reduce their claims 30 percent and to extend his time to pay. Fortunately, the booming demand occasioned by the war made it possible for Claflin to pay his discounted debts early and in full. Commentators of the time ascribe the firm's survival to Claflin's reputation for integrity and his standing in the city's commercial community. In 1864 Mellen retired and the firm became known as H. B. Claflin & Co. The war proved very profitable for business, and Claflin emerged from the conflict with sales amounting to $72 million and with the reputation of being the largest dry goods house in the world.

The panic of 1873 again threatened Claflin's business. Although the business held millions of dollars of good commercial paper, the banks, fearing for their own survival, refused to discount commercial paper. Claflin again found himself forced to suspend business and to ask his creditors for more time. Realizing that their future depended on Claflin's survival, the creditors granted the extension. And again, by offering large stocks of goods at reduced prices for cash, Claflin paid off his obligations early.

H. B. Claflin & Co. not only grew, it innovated. Claflin pioneered in bringing the dry goods jobber and the manufacturer closer together, becoming the consignee of the great Northeast manufactories. Claflin understood the great gain to labor through subdivision, and his business organization provided a model for other merchants. He shared the profits of his business with his employees, which by the 1880s numbered over 1,000. Claflin worked on very close margins—only 3 percent or 4 percent—and depended on high volume and rapid turnover for profits. "I prefer not to make large profits," he was once quoted as saying.

In 1875 Claflin was sued by the U.S. government for the recovery of $1.5 million in tariff duties on imported silk that the government claimed had been fraudulently undervalued. Several other New York silk importers settled quietly to avoid the bad publicity, but Claflin defiantly fought the matter in court and won. Indeed, some of those involved in the federal prosecution were, in turn, indicted for attempting to blackmail Claflin.

Contemporaries considered Claflin's personal manner as having "an utter absence of ostentation," noting that "he was as simple in his tastes and habits as the mechanic or the day laborer." Nevertheless, he was one of the most prominent men of his times. He served on the board of directors of many corporations and philanthropic organizations, including the Central National Bank and Continental Insurance Co. (both of which he helped organize), Home Life Insurance Co., New York Life Insurance Co., and the Union Ferry Co. The Brooklyn Society for Prevention of Cruelty to Children was organized in Claflin's house in Brooklyn in 1880. He was one of the first vice presidents of the American Society for the Prevention of Cruelty to Animals, and he also served as vice president of the Brooklyn Association for Improving the Condition of the Poor. He is quoted as saying, "We must try to give pleasure to poor people, not to the rich; they do not need our attention." Claflin was a longtime trustee of the Plymouth Church in Brooklyn, and a longtime friend of the pastor Henry Ward Beecher.

Claflin was a pioneer in the development of large, nationwide wholesaling. The large dry goods business that he founded and built was instrumental in making New York City the most important dry goods market in the United States. Claflin died at his home in Brooklyn. His son John Claflin succeeded him in heading the dry goods business.

• After Claflin's death, his family and friends published a 161-page memorial book simply titled *Horace B. Claflin* (1885). This book contains several short biographical sketches of Claflin and also contains excerpts from newspaper obituaries from across the nation. *The National Cyclopedia of American Biography* (1907) and *Appleton's Cyclopedia of American Biography* (1893) contain lengthy and interesting entries on Claflin. There is also C. H. Wright, *Genealogy of the Claflin Family* (1903). An obituary is in the *Brooklyn Daily Eagle*, 16 Nov. 1885.

JAMES D. NORRIS

CLAFLIN, Tennessee Celeste (26 Oct. 1845–18 Jan. 1923), radical feminist, was born in Homer, Ohio, the daughter of Reuben Buckman Claflin, a backcountry horse trader and sometime grist mill operator, and Roxanna Hummel, daughter of a Pennsylvania tavern keeper. The youngest of ten children, Tennessee experienced a bizarre, unsettled childhood. In early youth, while staying with relatives in Pennsylvania, she showed a knack for fortune telling, which her parents promptly put to use in a traveling family medicine show laced with spiritualist remedies. By age thirteen she rivaled her older sister Victoria Claflin Woodhull as the family's wonder child, gifted in magnetic healing, clairvoyance, and the promotion of a bottled cancer cure. Frequent scandal, including charges of manslaughter, blackmail, and adultery against young Tennessee, kept the Claflins on the move across Ohio, Illinois, and Missouri. In Chicago in 1866 she secretly married a gambler named John Bartels, but he disappeared from her life in less than a year.

Meanwhile in St. Louis, sister Victoria married Colonel James Harvey Blood, a thoughtful spiritualist and free-love advocate who brought some reform-minded ballast to the Claflin family mood. He introduced the sisters to a strong mix of mystic socialism, philosophical anarchism, and faith in both reincarnation and greenback currency. Under his influence, and guided also by a vision of Demosthenes who spoke to Victoria one day in Pittsburgh, the entire family moved to New York City in 1868. Tennessee soon improved the family's fortunes by serving the needs of the aging, recently widowed rail tycoon Cornelius Vanderbilt with her magnetic healing. She declined the marriage offer these ministrations inspired but gladly accepted Vanderbilt's stock market tips. With his support Tennessee (who now changed her name to Tennie C.) and Victoria (who used the last name of her first husband, Dr. Canning Woodhull) embarked in the winter and spring of 1870 on a brief but spectacular career as Wall Street brokers. Their invasion of this male sphere startled the press but won applause from Whitelaw Reid, the young managing editor of the *New York Tribune*. Reid's surviving correspondence from January to April 1870 includes several steamy thank-you notes from the sisters for his friendly editorials. In the spring of 1870 they launched their own newspaper, *Woodhull & Claflin's Weekly*, a radical sheet promoting free love, world government, Karl Marx's *Communist Manifesto*, and Victoria Woodhull's decision to run for president.

From this point on, Claflin loyally supported every move in her sister's sensational political career, deferring to Woodhull's impulses and emulating them in her own less publicized ventures. More earthy and lighthearted than Woodhull, she resembled more than her sister the caricature limned of them—the fictional Audacia Dangyereyes—in Harriet Beecher Stowe's serialized novel, *My Wife and I* (1872). Claflin pursued a more gregarious personal life than did her sister but nonetheless found time to accompany Woodhull in her forays into the woman suffrage movement. She delivered her own first political speech, in German, to New York's German-American Progressive Society in August 1871 and used the occasion to announce her candidacy for a seat in Congress. Nothing came of that, but she published a book under her name, *Constitutional Equality, a Right of Woman* (1871), helped organize Section 12 of Marx's International Workingmen's Association, and carried the red banner of the Paris Commune in a commemoration march up Fifth Avenue. The following summer she took honorary command of two of the city's black regiments, the Veteran Guards and the Spencer Grays, and promised in the press to design a unisex military uniform for herself.

The sisters' newspaper notoriety caught up with them in November 1872 when they published in a special issue of their *Weekly* an exposé of Rev. Henry Ward Beecher's adulterous relationship with Elizabeth Tilton, thus helping to ignite the most celebrated scandal of the decade. This landed Woodhull and Claflin in New York City's Ludlow Street jail for four weeks on a charge of passing obscenity through the mails. Though they were ultimately acquitted, this episode proved to be the peak of their American careers. Thereafter they resorted increasingly to the lecture circuit to make ends meet, with Claflin handling tour arrangements for her more famous sister.

When Cornelius Vanderbilt died in 1877 and his survivors contested his will on grounds that his spiritualist tendencies proved his incompetence, Claflin and Woodhull suddenly left the country for England amid rumors that their exile had been subsidized by Vanderbilt's most-favored heir to squelch their testimony about the commodore. To ensure that their shocking reputations and money problems were now behind them, the sisters set about improving their genealogy, revising their past, and exploring English social possibilities. When Victoria married a London banker in 1883, Tennessee (the name she reassumed in England) matched the move by marrying a prosperous dry goods merchant named Francis Cook, a widower with spiritualist leanings, in October 1885.

When Cook was made a baronet a year later, she became Lady Cook, marchioness of Montserrat, complete with a castle in Portugal. As she put it in 1890 during one of her frequent visits to the United States, "Now we are rich and up in the world."

Cook died in 1901, leaving Tennessee in ample wealth, free to pursue the life of garden parties and philanthropy for homeless girls, a world removed from the lurid adventures of her youth. Attractive and cheerful to the end, she died in London. Woodhull outlived her by four years. The sisters' reputation for innovation, impudence, and prophecy along the fighting edge of women's rights survived them to flourish once again during the feminist surge in the 1960s.

• In the absence of personal papers or memoirs, details of Claflin's life must be extracted mainly from biographical studies of her sister. Of these the most thorough remains Emanie Sachs, *"The Terrible Siren": Victoria Woodhull (1838–1927)* (1928). Johanna Johnston, *Mrs. Satan: The Incredible Saga of Victoria C. Woodhull* (1967), is alert to Claflin family relations. A comprehensive bibliography is in Madeleine B. Stern, *We the Women* (1963). Page Smith, *Daughters of the Promised Land: Women in American History* (1970), and Christopher Lasch, *The World of Nations: Reflections on American History, Politics, and Culture* (1973), offer brief interpretations. Claflin's first political speech is printed in the *New York Times*, 12 Aug. 1871. Obituaries are in the *New York Times* and the *Times* (London), 20 Jan. 1923.

GEOFFREY BLODGETT

CLAGETT, Wyseman (Aug. 1721–4 Dec. 1784), New Hampshire lawyer, judge, and revolutionary war leader, was born in Bristol, England, the son of Martha (maiden name unknown) and Wiseman (also spelled Wyseman) Clagett, an attorney of Barnard's Inn, who inherited the manor of Broad Oakes, Wimbish, Essex, which was sold for the benefit of its creditors in 1749. The younger Clagett received a classical education, studied at the Inns of Court, and was admitted an attorney of the King's Bench. In 1748, after being commissioned a notary public, he removed to the British colony of Antigua in the West Indies. There he served as a notary and secretary of the colony and enjoyed the patronage of John Weeks, a wealthy planter, who in 1750 left him an annuity of £50 sterling for life.

By October 1757 Clagett had moved to Portsmouth, New Hampshire, a port heavily involved in trade with Antigua. In that month he was admitted as an attorney of the New Hampshire Superior Court. He quickly found a place in society and joined St. John's Masonic Lodge in April 1758. In 1759 he married Lettice Mitchell, the daughter of Sarah Taylor and Dr. George Mitchell of Portsmouth; her father had been deputy surveyor of the King's Woods and a master of the lodge. At the time of her marriage, she was painted by Joseph Blackburn, a leading colonial portraitist.

In Portsmouth, Clagett represented private clients in civil litigation and legislative matters and was involved in civic affairs. As notary, he played an important role in the recording of losses inflicted by war and weather on Portsmouth shipping. He provided legal and notarial services to Benning Wentworth and his nephew John Wentworth, successive royal governors of New Hampshire and surveyors general of the woods. Clagett achieved his greatest renown, however, as an active justice of the peace. The rigor with which he fulfilled that function caused the phrase "I will Clagett you!" to become synonymous with "I will prosecute you." This reputation and his connections with the Wentworths undoubtedly led to his appointment as King's attorney for the province in 1765. In that capacity he prosecuted major criminal cases, including the unusual indictment of Ruth Blay for the capital offense of concealing the death of her bastard child. Clagett expressed to the jury his abhorrence at the severity of the penalty, but she was convicted and, despite three reprieves granted by Governor John Wentworth, was hanged in December 1768.

Clagett's politics at this period reflected the relative inertness of prerevolutionary New Hampshire. He served on a Portsmouth committee to draft legislative instructions protesting the Stamp Act in 1765 and administered the oath by which Portsmouth's stamp distributor publicly renounced his commission. These activities did not bring Clagett into immediate disfavor with the Wentworths, who sought to maintain a precarious balance between English and colonial interests. In November 1768, however, as the Townshend Act duties of 1767 increased tensions, he incurred John Wentworth's displeasure for agreeing to a "trifling" bail in the case of a mob ringleader. Perhaps spurred by this episode and Wentworth's views of the Blay case, Clagett went to England with his wife and young children in June 1769 to seek a new professional situation among family and friends. While there, he became associated with supporters of the colonial cause.

Despite English opportunities, Clagett returned to New Hampshire in 1771 at his wife's insistence. In 1772 he moved his family and his law practice to Litchfield, in newly established Hillsborough County, and that same year was appointed a justice of the peace and of the quorum, entitling him to sit on the county court of general sessions of the peace. By the spring of 1775 he had joined the revolutionary war movement, representing Litchfield and the adjoining town of Nottingham West (now Hudson) in both the last house of representatives summoned by Governor Wentworth and the revolutionary Third Provincial Congress. In subsequent provincial congresses, he served on critical committees to correspond with other colonies and to draft the plan that became New Hampshire's first constitution.

Pursuant to that plan, the Fifth Provincial Congress in January 1776 declared New Hampshire's independence and adopted a brief "Form of Government" under which it became the house of representatives. The house chose Clagett to serve on the council. He was secretary to a committee appointed to draw up a declaration of New Hampshire's independence in June 1776 and was a relatively inactive member of the all-important committee of safety from July to December

1776. In 1777 and 1780 he represented Merrimack and Bedford. As a representative of Litchfield, he was chosen for the council again in 1781, and two years later he represented the town in the house again. Clagett also served as attorney general from 1776 to 1777, sat as a justice of the Hillsborough Court of General Sessions in 1777, was appointed a special justice of the superior court in 1778, and served as New Hampshire's first and only solicitor general from 1781 until the abolition of the office under the more elaborate and more representative constitution recommended by a convention and ratified by the towns in 1783.

Clagett was imposing and striking in appearance and manner, with a pronounced facial tic described by one observer as "appalling to the beholder, and indicative of anything but placidity and mildness." He was known for his wit as well as for the elegance of the Latin and English verse in which he often expressed it. Mercurial in nature, he could be "Sanguine and despondent, by sudden changes of his mind, for which no reason could be assigned." He could be "rough and boisterous in his manners, [which] were rendered still more offensive by a profanity as reckless and extravagant as can well be conceived"; he nevertheless "possessed real kindness of heart" (Atherton, pp. 27–28, 35–36). Anecdotal evidence suggests that Clagett's eccentricity kept him from winning recognition as a lawyer and political leader of the first rank. Yet his professional abilities were greatly admired, and, as one of the few lawyers in the revolutionary war movement, he played an important role in the framing and administration of New Hampshire's first independent government.

Clagett's personality also made him a difficult husband and father, tyrannical to his wife and neglectful of their eight children. Despite these disadvantages, his son Clifton became a lawyer who served three terms in Congress and had a brief and stormy career on the New Hampshire Superior Court. In his late years, Clagett lived in reduced financial circumstances, whether as a result of his devotion to public service during the Revolution or his own improvidence. As one writer put it, he could be seen riding on "an indifferent poney" in the worn finery of an earlier day, in which "he exhibited a striking picture of dilapidated importance" (Atherton, p. 37). He died and was buried in Litchfield, leaving a very modest estate.

• Clagett's notarial register (1759–1766), his notarial seal, and an undated manuscript, "Soliloquy, or Dying Words of Pious Liberty Tree," are in the Massachusetts Historical Society. Court records in the New Hampshire State Archives, Concord, and the offices of the clerks of court for Rockingham and Hillsborough counties document his law practice. For other documentation, see Nathaniel Bouton et al., eds., *Documents and Records Relating to New Hampshire*, vols. 6–9, 13, 18 (1867–1941); Journal of the Committee of Safety, *Laws of New Hampshire* 4 (1916): 615, 687–88; and Wentworth letterbooks transcript, New Hampshire Archives. Examples of his literary style and illustrative anecdotes are found in a detailed and credible biographical sketch by Charles H. Atherton, "Memoir of Wyseman Clagett," in the New Hampshire Historical Society publication, *Collections* 3 (1832): 24–39; see also Nathaniel Adams, *Annals of Portsmouth* (1825), pp. 216, 224, 278–81, and Charles W. Brewster, *Rambles about Portsmouth*, 1st ser. (1859): 234–38. These three sketches are the basis of an unflattering caricature of Clagett in Kenneth Roberts's novel, *Northwest Passage* (1937). For his English roots, see Brice M. Clagett, "Notes," *New England Historical & General Register* 141 (1987): 95, and other sources cited there. For the Masonic connections, see Gerald D. Foss, *Three Centuries of Free Masonry in New Hampshire* (1972), pp. 16–20, 24–28, 405. For the Blackburn portrait, now in the Brooklyn Museum, see John H. Morgan, "Notes on Blackburn and His Portrait of Lettice Mitchell," *Brooklyn Musical Quarterly* 6, no. 1 (1919): 21–33. For Clagett's notarial activities, see William G. Saltonstall, *Ports of Piscataqua* (1941), pp. 39–40, 42–43.

L. Kinvin Wroth

CLAGHORN, George (6 July 1748–3 Feb. 1824), army officer and shipwright, was born in Chilmark, Massachusetts, the son of Shubael Claghorn, a soldier, and Experience Hawes. He was a great-grandson of James Claghorn of Scotland, who was captured at the battle of Dunbar and deported to the colonies by Cromwell. His father was a veteran of the Louisburg expedition of 1745. Claghorn himself eventually settled in New Bedford and in 1769 married Deborah Brownell of Dartmouth. They had eight children.

Claghorn embraced the patriot cause and in 1776 was commissioned first lieutenant in Captain Manasseh Kempton's Dartmouth company. By 1779 he had risen to captain in Colonel Hawthorne's regiment and the following year transferred to Colonel Abel Mitchell's regiment. His final rank was that of major, while serving with Colonel William Turner's regiment in 1781. Claghorn subsequently served as colonel of the Second Regiment, Second Brigade, Fifth Division, Massachusetts militia for many years after the war. He retained the honorary title of colonel long after his military service had ended.

After the Revolution, Claghorn returned to New Bedford and commenced a career in shipbuilding. He promptly became one of the most celebrated shipwrights of his day. One of Claghorn's first designs was the 175-ton whaler *Rebecca*, launched at New Bedford in March 1785. This vessel was reputedly the first American ship to round Cape Horn into the Pacific and return. In October 1793 Claghorn constructed an even larger ship, the *Barclay*, of 270 tons. The following year Congress, in response to Algerian depredations against American shipping, authorized creation of a national navy. The navy was to consist of six frigates, four of forty-four guns and two of thirty-six guns, to be constructed at six ports along the Atlantic coast. The naval architect chosen to design the fleet was Philadelphia Quaker Joshua Humphreys, whose designs were much larger and stouter than contemporary warships. The frigate *Constitution* was to be constructed at Hartt's navy yard in Boston, and Claghorn, in recognition of his skill with large ships, was selected to build it.

Claghorn relocated his family to Boston, but work on the *Constitution* proceeded by fits and starts. The keel was laid and the frigate was nearing completion when the government reached an accord with the Algerians in 1795. Work was suspended for several months until mounting difficulties with France induced Congress to resume funding. The launch date for the *Constitution* was set for 20 September 1797, but Claghorn went to great lengths warning the public to keep their distance in the event of an accident. Unfortunately, the *Constitution* stuck on its ways and defied all attempts to move it. A second attempt two days later met with similar results, and Claghorn resolved to wait until the next sufficient tide. The *Constitution* successfully entered its destined element on 21 October 1797 amidst festive celebrations. No blame was ever attached to Claghorn for the embarrassing delays, but he nonetheless moved back to New Bedford. His subsequent construction efforts are unknown. Around 1804 he moved again, to a farm in Seekonk, Rhode Island, where he resided for nearly twenty years until his death there.

Claghorn was a significant shipbuilder of the early national period. However, he is best remembered for having constructed the most famous warship of American history. The *Constitution* was a carefully crafted masterpiece that fully realized the potential of Humphrey's innovative designs. For this reason alone, Claghorn's place in the pantheon of American naval tradition is secure.

• Scattered material by Claghorn is at the Massachusetts Historical Society, the New-York Historical Society, the Historical Society of Pennsylvania, and the Clements Library, University of Michigan. Biographical data is found in William M. Emery, *Colonel George Claghorn* (1931), and William C. Claghorn, *The Barony of Cleghorne* (1931). Insights into his skill as a builder can be found in John S. Barrows, "The Beginnings and Launching of the U.S. Frigate Constitution," Bostonian Society, *Proceedings* (1925): 23–37, Howard I. Chapelle, *The History of the American Sailing Navy* (1949), and William M. Fowler, "America's Super Frigates," *Mariner's Mirror* 59 (1973): 49–56. Finally, for greater historical perspective, consult John M. Murphey, *American Ships and Shipbuilders* (1860), and Marshall Smelser, *The Congress Founds the Navy, 1787–1798* (1959).

JOHN C. FREDRIKSEN

CLAGUE, Ewan (27 Dec. 1896–12 Apr. 1987), economist and civil servant, was born in Prescott, Washington, the son of John Clague and Eleanor Christian Cooper, farmers and immigrants from the Isle of Man, Great Britain. Clague attended the University of Washington, earning an A.B. in economics in 1917. After two years in the U.S. Army, 1917–1919, he returned to the University of Washington, where he earned an A.M. in economics in 1921. He went on to study for his doctorate in economics at what was then perhaps the nation's leading institution of higher education in the fields of labor economics and industrial relations, the University of Wisconsin.

At the university in Madison, first Richard Ely and then John R. Commons and Selig Perlman trained an unmatched cadre of labor economists. Clague attended Wisconsin in the heyday of Commons and Perlman, a period during which the two economists mentored students who staffed the new state and federal administrative agencies charged with regulating industries and furthering social welfare.

While completing his graduate studies, Clague served in the U.S. Bureau of Labor Statistics from 1926 to 1928 and as a research assistant in the Business Research Bureau of the Metropolitan Life Insurance Company in 1928–1929, receiving his Ph.D. in economics in 1929. Clague then spent the year 1930 as a member of the Institute of Human Relations at Yale University, and from there went to the Pennsylvania School of Social Work in Philadelphia, where he remained from 1931 to 1936. In 1923 he married Dorothy Vermilyea Whipple, a pediatrician, with whom he had four children, three of whom lived to adulthood.

In 1936, when Franklin D. Roosevelt's New Deal established a new federal administrative agency to implement the Social Security law enacted the previous year, Clague was invited to serve as the Social Security Board's first assistant chief of the Bureau of Research and Statistics, a position he held for only a year before being promoted to director, a post he held from 1937 to 1940. He rose from there to become director of the Bureau of Employment Security, responsible for compiling, collating, and publicizing data concerning employment stability, a job he held until 1946.

From his initial appointment to the Social Security Board until his retirement from government service in 1965, Clague remained a career federal civil servant. He was among the Wisconsin-trained economists and civil servants responsible for creating the modern social security system, especially its old-age benefits and unemployment insurance features, which became the keystone of the entire U.S. social welfare system. In 1946 he transferred to the Department of Labor, where he served as the commissioner of labor statistics until he retired, except for the year 1954–1955, when he acted as a special assistant to Secretary of Labor James P. Mitchell.

The consummate career civil servant, Clague served Democratic and Republican administrations faithfully and won the respect of both parties for his painstakingly accurate statistical reports on employment levels, real wage rates, and standards of living. Under his aegis, the Bureau of Labor Statistics' regularly announced Consumer Price Index (CPI) became the statistical bible used by union-management negotiators in establishing wage increases and by federal administrators in setting social security and other welfare payment levels. For his performance as a civil servant the National Civil Service League in 1958 named Clague as one of the top ten federal career men.

After his retirement, Clague served as a counselor to the secretary of labor (1966–1968), as a senior associate of the economic consulting firm of Leo Kramer, Inc. (1968–1977), and as a member of the U.S. national committee on UNESCO. During the first decade of his retirement he also taught labor statistics and lectured at universities such as UCLA, Pennsylvania, Michigan State, and Drexel. Clague also found time to write or cowrite a series of books, among which the most notable were *The Bureau of Labor Statistics* (1968), *The All-Volunteer Army: An Analysis of Demand and Supply* (1971), *The Aging Worker and the Union* (1971), and *Manpower Policies and Programs: A Review* (1976). He died in a nursing home in Bethesda, Maryland.

Clague should best be remembered as one of the outstanding members of the first generation of federal civil servants who created the modern American administrative and welfare state. Together with his teachers and peers at the University of Wisconsin Clague brought the use of academic experts to make and administer public policy, what was known as the "Wisconsin idea," to the nation's capital.

• No readily available collection of Clague papers exists. The official records of the Social Security Administration and the Department of Labor in the National Archives, Washington, D.C., and also the library of the Department of Labor are filled with material concerning Clague's contributions as a civil servant. His contributions to the social security system can best be followed in Charles McKinley and Robert W. Frase, *Launching Social Security* (1970). One of the best introductions to the social security system during Clague's tenure is Arthur J. Altmeyer, *The Formative Years of Social Security* (1966). For a history of the Department of Labor that cites Clague's contributions and also covers his tenure with the agency, see Jonathan Grossman, *The Department of Labor* (1973). An obituary in the *New York Times*, 15 Apr. 1987, offers a succinct summary of his life.

MELVYN DUBOFSKY

CLAIBORNE, William (1600–1677), American Indian trader and political leader in Virginia, was baptized at Crayford, County Kent, England, on 10 August 1600, the son of Thomas Claiborne, a former mayor of King's Lynn, County Norfolk, and Sarah James, the daughter of a London brewer. Making the Chesapeake his home after 1621, Claiborne served as a Virginia councillor (1624–1637, 1643–1661), secretary of state (1626–1634, 1652–1661), treasurer (1642–1660), parliamentary commissioner (1651–1660), deputy governor (1652–1660), and the first major general of militia (1644–1646).

Claiborne began a significant and eventful colonial career in 1621, receiving appointment as the surveyor of Virginia right out of Pembroke College, Cambridge. He arrived in Jamestown in October of that year, accompanying several other notables from Kent, including the new governor Sir Francis Wyatt, Wyatt's uncle George Sandys, and his cousin Henry Fleet. Only five months later, the colony of Virginia barely survived the sudden and devastating Powhatan uprising of 22 March 1622. In the aftermath of that tragedy, the sponsoring Virginia Company of London proved impotent and bankrupt, allowing local leaders like Wyatt, Sandys, Claiborne, and a handful of others to monopolize political, economic, judicial, and diplomatic authority in the vacuum of power.

As surveyor, Claiborne laid out "New Towne" in 1624, a Jamestown suburb for the colonial elite, and patented 900 acres of prime lands for himself by 1626. He quickly became one of Virginia's ten largest tobacco exporters and eventually owned another 12,000 acres throughout the colony.

Claiborne's greatest significance, however, was as a pioneering fur trader and the most prominent proponent of Virginia's commercial and territorial domination of the Chesapeake Bay. Using his influence as surveyor, councillor, and secretary of state to secure monopoly trading rights and set Indian policies in the late 1620s and early 1630s, Claiborne established strong personal ties with the powerful, beaver-rich Susquehannock tribe living near present-day Columbia, Pennsylvania. The potential for fur trade profits was so great that Claiborne and the Susquehannocks created an inspired and enduring interest group comprised of investors from the Virginia Council of State, such as William Tucker; influential London merchants headed by Maurice Thomson; and royal officials like Sir William Alexander, earl of Sterling. Armed with a royal trading license and substantial funding, Claiborne in August 1631 established his headquarters on Kent Island in the northern Chesapeake. The settlement was Virginia's most distant and became the capital of an English mercantile empire designed to monopolize the lucrative beaver trade of North America.

Although Claiborne's early returns from the beaver trade were encouraging enough to suggest an alternative means of livelihood in the colonial Chesapeake to tobacco and slavery, competition, controversy, and armed conflict quickly doomed his Kent Island enterprise. In June 1632 King Charles I granted a proprietary charter to Cecil Calvert, second baron of Baltimore, who two years later founded the colony of Maryland, which encompassed Kent Island and some one hundred Virginia settlers within its boundaries. For the next quarter-century, Claiborne and the Calverts, Virginia and Maryland, and their respective supporters in England, were bitter, bloody rivals for control of the northern Chesapeake and its profitable furs.

After negotiations and litigation failed to end the stalemate, Claiborne's fellow Virginia councillors ousted the royal governor, Sir John Harvey, in April 1635, charging him with treason against their interests. About this time (1635) Claiborne married Elizabeth Boteler (or Butler); they had six children. The Maryland militia invaded Kent Island in February 1638, confiscating property valued at £10,000 sterling and condemning the absentee Claiborne to death as a rebel. The Susquehannocks strongly objected to such treatment of their old trading partner, whom they "exceedingly seemed to love," and they coupled their refusal to trade furs to the Marylanders with a devastating decade-long war against the colony.

For five years after the fall of Kent Island Claiborne was absent from the Chesapeake, attempting to colonize another private island (Roatan) off the coast of

Honduras as a member of the Providence Island Company. He returned to Virginia in 1643 after the Spanish expelled his colonists in the Caribbean, and for the remainder of that decade his Puritan friends and parliamentary supporters from the Providence Island venture helped him politically isolate and militarily harass Maryland. In March 1652 Claiborne and other business partners of Maurice Thomson successfully invaded both Virginia and Maryland at the head of a strong parliamentary fleet under orders from the republican Commonwealth of England.

Claiborne had in effect nullified Lord Baltimore's authority in Maryland and reunified "greater Virginia" under the control of his commercial and political associates on both sides of the Atlantic. Between 1652 and 1657 he served as secretary of state of both provinces under the governorship of the Virginia Puritan merchant-planter Richard Bennett. When in July 1652 Claiborne's Susquehannock allies signed a peace treaty with sympathetic negotiators, Claiborne regained his beloved Kent Island and possessed more power over Chesapeake affairs than any Englishman before or since. His domination was short-lived, however, for the political fortunes of key London allies declined during the protectorate of Oliver Cromwell, and by 1658 Maryland was restored to independence under Calvert control. The Susquehannocks were engaged in deadly struggles with Iroquois rivals, and it was apparent that the tidewater beaver trade in Chesapeake Bay could never be revived.

Claiborne retired from political affairs after 1660 to manage his 5,000-acre estate, "Romancoke," in New Kent County. Ever restless for profitable adventure and fair treatment, he was still petitioning royal officials for the return of his "Island of Kent in Maryland" when he died sometime after March 1677. Claiborne was survived by four sons, three of whom were prominent planters and militia colonels in New Kent County and the other a large land owner in Jamaica.

According to historian Robert Brenner, "William Claiborne may have been the most consistently influential politician in Virginia throughout the whole of the pre-Restoration period." He was the last of the early merchant-planter oligarchs, and no Virginia colonist ever held a greater variety of important offices simultaneously or enjoyed such a lengthy political career. He was a farsighted commercial imperialist who anticipated the prominent role that fur trades and London policymakers would play in colonial affairs after 1660. Above all, Claiborne was the prototypical acculturated frontiersman, who first recognized the significance of local Indians in determining the physical survival and financial success of the English. Like many politicians then and later, he derived personal profit from every public duty he performed, most particularly raiding, and trading with, American Indians. Claiborne's unprecedented half-century friendship with the Susquehannocks was important for the development of both Chesapeake colonies, and his military campaigns against the hostile Pamunkeys in the 1620s and 1640s earned him higher rank and more extensive personal rewards than any other Virginian in the early seventeenth century.

• The key published documents for understanding the career of William Claiborne are in William Hand Browne et al., eds., *Archives of Maryland* (73 vols., 1883–), esp. vols. 1–5; Clayton Colman Hall, ed., *Narratives of Early Maryland, 1633–1684* (1910); H. R. McIlwaine, ed., *Minutes of the Council and General Court of Colonial Virginia*, 2d ed. (1979); "Claiborne vs Clobery et als. in the High Court of Admiralty," *Maryland Historical Magazine* 27–28 (1932–1933); and Susan Myra Kingsbury, ed., *Records of the Virginia Company of London* (4 vols., 1906–1935).

The best secondary sources on Claiborne include Nathaniel C. Hale, *Virginia Venturer: A Historical Biography of William Claiborne, 1600–1677* (1951); Raphael Semmes, *Captains and Mariners of Early Maryland* (1937); Erich Isaac, "Kent Island," *Maryland Historical Magazine* 52 (1957); Virginia M. Meyer and John Frederick Dorman, eds., *Adventurers of Purse and Person: Virginia, 1607–1624/25*, 3d ed. (1987), pp. 184–91; Robert Brenner, *Merchants and Revolution: Commercial Change, Political Conflict, and London's Overseas Traders, 1550–1653* (1993), pp. 120–24, 157–58, 167, 183–88; J. Frederick Fausz, "Merging and Emerging Worlds: Anglo-Indian Interest Groups and the Development of the Seventeenth-Century Chesapeake," in *Colonial Chesapeake Society*, ed. Lois Green Carr et al. (1988); and Fausz, "'To Draw Thither the Trade of Beavers': The Strategic Significance of the English Fur Trade in the Chesapeake, 1629–1660," in *Le Castor Fait Tout: Selected Papers of the Fifth North American Fur Trade Conference, 1985*, ed. Bruce G. Trigger et al. (1987), pp. 42–71.

J. FREDERICK FAUSZ

CLAIBORNE, William Charles Coles (1775–23 Nov. 1817), frontier politician, was born in Sussex County, Virginia, the son of William Claiborne, a small landowner, and Mary Leigh. He attended Richmond Academy and studied briefly at the College of William and Mary until financial difficulties ended his formal instruction at age fifteen. John Beckley, a fellow Virginian who was clerk of the U.S. House of Representatives, hired Claiborne as an assistant in his office. In this capacity Claiborne met the leading statesmen of the period, including his mentor and later benefactor, Thomas Jefferson.

Claiborne decided to study law when North Carolina congressman John Sevier recognized the young clerk's talent and offered encouragement. He returned to Virginia for studies and, upon passing the bar, moved to the frontier in 1794 to practice criminal law in Sullivan County, Tennessee. Representing his county in the 1796 statehood convention, Claiborne helped to draft the original Tennessee constitution. When Sevier became governor of Tennessee, he appointed Claiborne, then only twenty-one years old, to serve as a judge on the state supreme court. In August 1797 Tennessee voters chose Claiborne to complete Andrew Jackson's unexpired congressional term and reelected him in subsequent elections, though he remained under the legal constitutional age to hold the office.

Claiborne chaired the congressional committee that supervised the Mississippi Territory, and in that capacity he investigated allegations of political impropriety leveled against Governor Winthrop Sargent. On 25 July 1801 President Jefferson replaced Sargent as governor of the Mississippi Territory with Claiborne. He brought his new wife, Elizabeth "Eliza" W. Lewis of Nashville, with him, and they arrived at Natchez on 23 November. (The couple had one child, and Eliza died in 1804.) Despite the intense rivalry of vying factions, Governor Claiborne maintained a moderate course resulting in substantial progress for the territory and its inhabitants. Creation of new counties, settlement of land claims, and reforms in public health, education, and internal security were provincial successes in Claiborne's tenure. Additionally, continuing negotiations with regional Indian tribes and with Spanish Louisiana trained the young governor in larger national policy issues.

Upon the purchase of Louisiana in 1803, Jefferson sent Claiborne and General James Wilkinson to New Orleans as his commissioners to effect the orderly transfer from French to American authority. Jefferson's appointment of Claiborne as governor of the Territory of Orleans was implicit in this arrangement, and Claiborne remained at New Orleans to begin the challenge of making the recently purchased territory truly American. Conversant in neither French nor Spanish, unfamiliar with local customs and practices, and Protestant in a Roman Catholic region, Claiborne faced many cultural obstacles in governing this new territory. Creoles remained suspicious of the governor and leery of Americanization. His subsequent alliances with Creole families in his second marriage, in 1806 to Clarissa Duralde, with whom he had one child before she died in 1809, and third marriage, in 1809 to Sophronia "Suzette" Bosque, with whom he had two children, helped bridge this.

Claiborne was an enigmatic leader. Contemporaries sometimes mistook his prudence for indecision when facing difficulties, but he shunned rashness, frequently seeking instruction and approval from peers and superiors. During crises, most notably the Burr Conspiracy (1805–1807) and the battle of New Orleans (1815), Claiborne seemed weak in consigning extraordinary powers upon Generals James Wilkinson and Andrew Jackson. Though his leadership and policies generated vociferous criticism, Claiborne was an honorable man who assumed responsibility for his actions. He even fought a duel in 1807, when Daniel Clark charged that Claiborne demonstrated incompetence by abdicating responsibilities during the Burr affair.

Criticism notwithstanding, Claiborne enjoyed certain accomplishments as a territorial governor. In 1810 he secured the Baton Rouge district as the United States annexed the West Florida parishes, joining them to the Territory of Orleans. In January 1811 he directed the effective military suppression of the German Coast slave insurrection, an uprising that threatened New Orleans. In 1812 Louisiana became the eighteenth state, with Claiborne its first elected governor.

The War of 1812 presented Louisiana with dual threats of internal unrest in plantation districts and external invasion by the British, but Claiborne remained confident. Despite low militia enlistments and few Creoles joining the Forty-fourth Infantry, newly created for coastal defense, Claiborne overestimated Louisiana's potential troop strength in official communications with General Jackson. When Jackson arrived in December 1814, he declared martial law and initiated active procedures for defending New Orleans from impending attack. Unlike Jackson's scornful assessment, Claiborne's faith in the valiant efforts of Louisiana militia and fervent civilian patriotism vindicated his earlier confidence in the loyalty of Louisiana's citizens.

In 1817 they rewarded Claiborne by electing him to the U.S. Senate, completing the cycle of his political journey, but he died in New Orleans before taking office. A competent emissary of Jeffersonian Republicanism, Claiborne effectively administered demanding frontier regions and prepared diverse communities for statehood.

• For additional information on Claiborne, see Nathaniel Herbert Claiborne, *Notes on the War in the South; with Biographical Sketches of the Lives of Montgomery, Jackson, Sevier, and the Late Gov. Claiborne, and Others* (1819); W. C. C. Claiborne, *The Official Letter Books of W. C. C. Claiborne* (6 vols., 1917); and Joseph T. Hatfield, *William Claiborne: Jeffersonian Centurion in the American Southwest* (1976).

JUNIUS P. RODRIGUEZ

CLAIRE, Ina (15 Oct. 1892–21 Feb. 1985), actress, was born Ina Fagan in Washington, D.C., the daughter of theatrical parents Joseph Fagan and Cora B. Claire. After her father's accidental death when Ford's Theatre in Washington collapsed, Claire left Holy Cross Academy in the eighth grade and with her mother (who was also an actress) played the Orpheum, Keith, and Proctor vaudeville circuits. Lauded in later life for her technique, Claire credited the discipline of three daily performances. She made her first New York appearance in 1909, impersonating Scotsman Harry Lauder. Two years later, at age nineteen, she appeared as Prudence, the independent woman-in-distress in the New York production of London's Gaiety hit *The Quaker Girl*, laying claim to musical comedy—and as it turned out, literary—fame. F. Scott Fitzgerald often recalled her impact on his fifteen-year-old soul. He "felt a melancholy love" for her and another actress, Gertrude Bryan, and subsequently they "blurred into one lovely entity, THE GIRL. She was my second symbol of New York . . . THE GIRL for romance." Aaron Latham has found Claire/THE GIRL in several Fitzgerald stories; in 1934, the author still hoped to cast her in a film (never made) of his novel *Tender Is the Night*.

Richard Rodgers was nine when his grandfather took him to the Park Theatre to see *The Quaker Girl*. Rodgers, who became noted for his romantic show melodies, recalled, "I found out what it was like to fall in love with a real live actress. But beautiful and beautifully equipped though she was, I was too young and too innocent." Others remarked her tipped-up nose and yielding chin, her beauty and humor, her verve and panache.

In 1913 Claire appeared at London's Adelphi Theatre as Una Trance, sharing honors with American expatriate Joseph Coyne in the Gaiety show *The Girl from Utah*. Theatrical historian Kurt Ganzl called the "little ingenue George Edwardes had imported from America" a "real hit on all counts," and Noel Coward, then fourteen, remembered her performance for the rest of his life. In her next London show Claire blacked up to sing a "coon song," a sentimental ballad derived from minstrelsy. She then returned to New York, where in her second *Ziegfeld Follies* (1916) she sang Jerome Kern's songs and introduced Louis Hirsch's greatest hit, "Hello, Frisco." According to historian Gerald Bordman, playwright Guy Bolton then persuaded impresario David Belasco that Claire should try straight comedy.

The results were *Polly with a Past* and *The Gold Diggers*, with combined runs of three years. In one she played a maid-adventuress who made up wildly entertaining stories about her past, in the other the archetypal money-chasing chorus girl. After *Bluebeard's Eighth Wife* in 1921, Kern and Anne Caldwell hoped to lure her back to musical comedy, but instead in 1922 she chose *The Awful Truth*. From then on, she was Broadway's favorite light sophisticate, her delicate, droll banter filled with mockery and irony. By 1924 her portrait was in the "first ladies" gallery at the Empire Theatre.

The effervescent Claire was also a "member" of the Algonquin (Hotel) Round Table. In *Wit's End*, James R. Gaines records her story about throwing author John V. A. Weaver to the ground as part of his initiation: "From the floor, Weaver said, 'Listen, Mom, put on your glasses and let's fight fair.' At that, Claire laughed and declared, 'He's in, he's in. He'll do just fine.'"

Though the Algonquin wits won fame for their criticism, they were also "a production play factory," and their associate actresses—Claire, Helen Hayes, Peggy Wood, Lynne Fontanne, Tallulah Bankhead, and Margalo Gilmore—regularly starred in these interwar year plays, which marked the peak of American light comedy. After a definitive performance as the thieving heroine of the Frederick Lonsdale manor-house comedy import *The Last of Mrs. Cheyney* in 1925–1926, Claire scored major triumphs in plays by Samuel N. Behrman, *Biography* (1932), *The End of Summer* (1936), and *The Talley Method* (1941).

Her earlier excursion into films had been unsatisfactory (typical was her Jeanne d'Arc in the amateurish *National Red Cross Pageant* (1917), but in 1926 Claire returned to Hollywood. Hazel-eyed and blonde, often on the best-dressed list, she was a regular member of the international sophisticate society characterized by Coward. Her life was relatively private until her 1929 marriage to John Gilbert, idol of the silent screen, then in the midst of his unsuccessful attempt to make the transition to sound (her 1919 marriage to newspaperman James Whittaker had ended in 1925). Their transatlantic quarrels made news, and they divorced in 1931. One of her best film roles came in 1930 as the Ethel Barrymore character in George S. Kaufman and Edna Ferber's *The Royal Family*, but, saying Hollywood plots "were really for children," she returned to Broadway and appeared in only one more film, the 1943 morale-booster *Stage Door Canteen*.

She now appeared in the Behrman plays, first as portrait painter Marion Froude in *Biography*, which began its career in London. In 1932 she toured in Robert Sherwood's *Reunion in Vienna*. She continued in similar vein through 1946, when Brooks Atkinson said of her revival of George Kelly's *The Fatal Weakness*: "There is nothing funnier in New York than the opening scene when Miss Claire, wound up with excitement, tries to talk over the telephone, read a letter, give orders to her maid and greet her sister simultaneously" (*New York Times*, 20 Nov. 1946).

Claire again left the stage for seven years, living at first on San Francisco's Nob Hill and subsequently in California's Sonoma Valley with lawyer and financier William R. Wallace, Jr., whom she had married in 1939. Her marriages left no children. Her swan song in 1954, as Lady Elizabeth Mulhammer, dabbler in spiritual cults, in the New York production of T. S. Eliot's *The Confidential Clerk* brought forth Walter Kerr's characterization: "She is like a dazzling line-drawing from the most fashionable magazine of the Twenties." John Mason Brown called her a "chic Lady Bracknell . . . the comic spirit incarnate."

In 1967 Coward wrote of her, "She is quite remarkably and quite genuinely as vital as ever. She talks away without drawing breath and her eyes twinkle and she looks at most in her forties." Wallace died in 1975, and Claire became a regular source for theatrical biographers and historians. She died in San Francisco, California.

One of her interviewers said Claire judged herself "difficult and shy at first in rehearsals, needing to see how the whole play worked before understanding her character." In her 1990 autobiography, Helen Hayes suggested that "technique" in Claire's (and her) sense had finally become *derriere-garde*. Of her art, Claire once said, "There is not a minute that a comedienne can rest." Brown agreed: "When there is no comedy, she . . . creates it by the machine gun rapidity of her speech, by the contagious smile which keeps dancing in her eyes, by the mere twinkle of her personality."

• Theater programs and clippings of Claire are found in archives such as the New York Public Library for the Performing Arts, Lincoln Center, and the Theatre Museum, London. A biography of Claire has yet to be published, but she is prominently mentioned in many books of theatrical biography and memoirs, as well as in books about F. Scott Fitzgerald, such as James R. Mellow's *Invented Lives* (1984) and Aaron Latham's *Crazy Sundays* (1971), and many of Noel Coward's autobiographical writings, including *The Noel Coward Diaries* (1982). A useful introduction to her Algonquin Round Table years is James Gaines, *Wit's End* (1977).

Her photographs appear in sources such as Cleveland Amory and Frederic Bradlee, *Vanity Fair* (1960). An obituary is in the *New York Times*, 22 Feb. 1985.

JAMES ROSS MOORE

CLAMPITT, Amy Kathleen (15 June 1920–10 Sept. 1994), poet and editor, was born in New Providence, Iowa, the daughter of Roy Justin Clampitt and Lutie Pauline Felt, farmers. As a child, Clampitt did not want to become a writer, but instead she wanted to become a painter. But, as a result of her grandfather's influence, Clampitt read avidly and majored in English at Grinnell College in Iowa. She graduated in 1941. That same year Clampitt was awarded a fellowship to Columbia University, but she was disappointed by academic work and left without finishing her degree. Rather than return to Iowa, Clampitt stayed in New York City as a secretary for Oxford University Press. She subsequently served as promotion director for college textbooks until 1951.

Clampitt postponed her literary career because poetry was not considered a serious profession in the 1940s. At that time she remarked, "Poets were looked upon as figures of fun . . . a kind of threat, really, to the way other people lived" (Hosmer, p. 82). This prejudice hindered Clampitt for thirty years. Only after two trips to England, service as a reference librarian at the National Audubon Society between 1952 and 1959, a brief return to Iowa, and then a job as a freelance editor in New York in the 1960s did Clampitt finally decide to become a writer. Being a research librarian and editor helped her acquire a knowledge of nature and confidence as a writer; however, Clampitt's trips to England most influenced her development as a poet. Clampitt could not help but be impressed by England's history; it was after she "went into Christ Church and *smelled* it, that [she] believed in the presence of the past" (interview with Laura Fairchild; emphasis Clampitt's). Initially, however, she focused her creative energies toward novels instead of poetry, but her attempts in that literary genre were rejected by publishers.

Clampitt was fifty-four when she issued a collection of poems titled *Multitudes, Multitudes* (1974) at her own expense. The nonconfessional mode of Clampitt's poetry attracted the attention of Howard Moss, the poetry editor of the *New Yorker*. He declared, "Right away I knew that she was the real thing." From then on her poems appeared regularly in the *New Yorker*, *Atlantic Monthly*, *Kenyon Review*, *Prairie Schooner*, and *Yale Review*. From 1977 until 1982 she was an editor at E.P. Dutton.

Clampitt's literary coup was her anthology *The Kingfisher*, nominated for a National Book Critics Circle Award in 1983. The poems are linked by Clampitt's "all process and no arrival" argument, which hinges on a person's need to enforce order and stasis amid the continual flux of history and nature. For example, the much-anthologized "Beach Glass" compares the ocean, which constantly turns debris over, to the mind, which places each event in order. In the poem, debris and events both receive an equal amount of attention and are equally vulnerable to forces of change. Although critics struggled with Clampitt's erudite language and sophisticated syntax, response to *The Kingfisher* was overwhelmingly positive. Edmund White called it "one of the most brilliant debuts in recent American literary history." Helen Vendler, writing in the *New York Review of Books*, described the poems as being capable of triumph "over the resistance of language, the reason why poetry lasts." Likewise, Paul Olson stated that *The Kingfisher* is a book of "tough stuff, full of dirt and doctrine."

Critics also warmly praised Clampitt's second anthology, *What the Light Was Like* (1985), which is more autobiographical and structurally tighter than *The Kingfisher*. Although she seldom strays from the principal argument of "all process and no arrival," the poems deal with unexplainable events, including the deaths of her family and friends. In effect, the poems work out a process by which to grieve, finding momentary relief from grief in the poetic form of an elegy. True to Clampitt's philosophy, the structural movement in this book is cyclical rather than linear, and the cycle "Voyages" (*A Homage to John Keats*, 1984) is the "eye" of this poetic storm. As a general rule in *What the Light Was Like* Clampitt offers no answers to the questions she asks, except for the consolation that she finds in the motion of becoming.

In *Archaic Figure* (1987) Clampitt explores the various landscapes by which the feminine experience has sustained itself. Clampitt juxtaposes places such as ancient Greece, Berlin, and the American Midwest and scarcely bearable emotional states, such as depression, devastation, exile, and alienation. Using headaches as its thematic device, *Archaic Figure* winds its way among prominent women writers linked by a consciousness of pain: Dorothy Wordsworth, Margaret Fuller, George Eliot, Virginia Woolf. *Archaic Figure* received the customary praise for a Clampitt anthology, but critical responses were divided between those who thought the theme of headaches was a "self-indulgence" (i.e, Frank J. Lepkowski), and those who thought the poem "An Anatomy of Migraine" was the nerve or "center" of the book (i.e, Mark Rudman).

Using pioneers as its thematic device, Clampitt's 1990 collection of poems, *Westward*, examines how landscapes transform individuals much as the individuals transform the landscape. This book features poems about kudzu, subway singers, Clampitt's father, her dying cousin—a switchboard operator, John Milton, John Donne, and Samuel Taylor Coleridge. The customary Clampitt argument—"all that we know, that we're made of, is motion"—underpins these diverse topics. Yet these poems reflect a softening of the typical Clampitt characteristics, which include complex forms, sophisticated diction, and intertangled allusions. Critics responded accordingly. Martha Duffy stated that "these poems speak directly to the reader, as if the writer had discarded the scrim of erudition."

Clampitt's last book, *A Silence Opens* (1994), is appropriately titled for a book containing poems in which people are silenced by oppressive landscapes: Pocahontas, a drowning victim, the youth at Tiananmen Square, Dante. Each poem is a lesson in how to listen and respond to silence. As Barbara Hoffert stated, "Here is poetry not as a commendation of being but simply as being itself." Shortly after *A Silence Opens* was published, Clampitt died in Lenox, Massachusetts.

Fortunately, Clampitt enjoyed accolades for her poetic genius during her lifetime. She was awarded a Guggenheim Fellowship in 1982, an American Academy and Institute of Arts and Letters Award (1984), and, in 1990, a Lila Wallace–Reader's Digest Writer's Award. Finally, in 1992 she was awarded a John D. and Catherine T. MacArthur Fellowship. Before her death she spent several years teaching poetry at the University of Wisconsin, at the College of William and Mary (1984–1985), and at Amherst College (1986–1987).

Clampitt was a self-proclaimed nomad her entire life. Even so, her poems argue that the American landscape is still capable of providing stasis in the postmodern world. Images, characters, or places that stand alone in their starkness are tied to numerous literary and historical allusions. They are never independent in their isolation, but rather are interdependent in the continual motion of becoming. In effect, Clampitt's poems offer her readers "a sort of foothold" in the postmodern world.

• Other works by Clampitt include *The Isthmus* (1981), an anthology written while attending a workshop sponsored by Publishers for Employment; *The Summer Solstice* (1983), a limited edition printed by Sarabande Press on handmade paper; and *Predecessors, Et Cetera* (1991), a collection of essays. Important interviews include Laura Fairchild's interview in *American Poetry Review*, July–Aug. 1987. A more recent interview by Robert Hosmer, Jr., can be found in the *Paris Review* 35 (1993): 77–109. Obituaries are in the *Chicago Tribune*, 18 Sept. 1994; the *Los Angeles Times*, 13 Sept. 1994; the *New York Times*, 12 Sept. 1994; *The Times* (London), 20 Sept. 1994; and the *Washington Post*, 13 Sept. 1994.

TAMARA HORN

CLAPP, Asahel (5 Oct. 1792–17 Dec. 1862), physician, botanist, and geologist, was born in Hubbardston, Massachusetts, the son of Reuben Clapp and Hepzibah Gates, farmers. When Clapp was a small child, his family moved to Montgomery, Franklin County, Vermont, near the Canadian border. Later, after acquiring sufficient learning for the purpose, he moved to Shelton, Vermont, to teach school. At about eighteen years of age and desiring to learn medicine, he moved to St. Albans, Vermont, and apprenticed himself to Dr. Benjamin Chandler. The completion date of his training and his whereabouts thereafter are unknown until he arrived in New Albany, Indiana, early in 1817.

Upon his arrival in this tiny community, Clapp became its first physician and soon joined the family of the town's founders by his marriage to Lucinda Scribner in 1819; they had one child. After the death of his first wife (probably in childbirth), he married, in January 1822, the young widow of another of the founders and the mother of one child, Elizabeth Edmonds Scribner. The couple had a son and daughter together.

Clapp kept a daily journal from 1819 until his death, containing brief firsthand accounts of his medical practice, patients, treatments, results, and consultations. The journal gives evidence that he pioneered autopsies as a part of his medical practice as early as 1820. In it he recounts matter-of-factly the morbidity and mortality of epidemics of "fever" (malaria), measles, pneumonia, and cholera.

Although he had never regularly attended medical school lectures, Clapp made it a part of his travel plans to attend the public introductory lectures presented by the medical faculty preceding the regular lectures of the school year. He attended introductory lectures at medical colleges in Louisville, Kentucky; Cincinnati, Ohio; Philadelphia, Pennsylvania; and New York City for nearly a decade. His importance as a practitioner, preceptor of medical apprentices and leader in the professional community (local and state) was chronicled in succinct entries in his journal.

Quite early in his practice, Clapp supplied other practitioners with drugs. Responding to the growing needs of families and physicians in the more remote areas around his community, he and a kinsman, Dr. William Augustine Scribner, established a separate drug business and store, which soon included a general line of merchandise.

Clapp organized the New Albany Medical Society in 1842 and was a founding member and twice president of the Indiana State Medical Society (1820 and 1850). He also founded the New Albany Lyceum as a forum for learning and exchanging new ideas. Physicians and scientists from Louisville, Cincinnati, and the East frequently contributed to its regular programs.

In 1833, while seeking medical care for a serious eye infection in various medical centers in the United States, Clapp was introduced to the medical and scientific communities of Cincinnati, Philadelphia, New York, New Haven, and Boston.

As New Albany lay at the junction of a variety of ecosystems, Clapp gradually became a serious student and eventually an authority on indigenous botany and the new science of geology. By first delineating the layers of limestone at the falls of the Ohio River near his home, and collecting, describing, and exchanging specimens of fossil corals and other invertebrates, Clapp fostered the interest of colleagues, students, and laymen in this new discipline. Focusing on small fossil invertebrates required Clapp to purchase a microscope and develop skill in its use. By supplementing his extensive experience in the field with publications (texts and periodicals) and information from his correspondents, he developed considerable expertise in taxonomic and medical botany over several decades. He was elected a corresponding member of the Academy of Natural Sciences of Philadelphia in 1837. By midcentury, he was appointed chairman of the Committee on Medical Botany of the American Medical Association, and he published a lengthy report, "A Synopsis; or Systematic Catalogue of the Indigenous and Naturalized, Flowering and Filicoid Medicinal Plants of the United States" (*Transactions of the American Medical Association* 5 [1852]: 689–906).

Clapp's lifetime pursuit resulted in his acquiring an extensive library of medical and scientific texts and periodicals. He corresponded and exchanged specimens of dried flowering plants, mineral samples, and fossil invertebrates with colleagues in the United States and England. He and his wife hosted numerous visitors, including physicians, ministers of the gospel, military officers, scientists, and members of various U.S. exploring expeditions to the far West. In his journal entries Clapp recorded daily weather data: ambient temperatures, barometric pressure, precipitation, storms, droughts, and river water levels. These records provide the earliest such precise information on the climate at the region of the Falls. Clapp died in New Albany, Indiana.

Although he was a lifelong medical practitioner, whose self-discipline kept him, his colleagues, and students apprised of discoveries that could be adopted in practice, Clapp's contributions to the developing sciences of geology and botany became his claim to a modest fame.

• Clapp's personal, professional, and educational experiences are briefly recorded in his daily *Journals* (1819–1862), photostatic copies of which are in the collections of the Indiana Division of the Indiana State Library, Indianapolis, Ind. His correspondence has survived only in the collected letters of some of his correspondents. The greatest number of letters are in the Library of the Academy of Natural Sciences, Philadelphia; the Papers of S. G. Morton at the American Philosophical Society, Philadelphia; the Torrey Collection at the Herbarium, Columbia University, New York; J. J. Crooks Collection, New York Botanical Gardens, New York; and the C. W. Short Papers, Southern Historical Collection, University of North Carolina, Chapel Hill. See also J. L. Chandler, "Obituary Notice of Dr. Asahel Clapp, of Indiana," *Boston Medical and Surgical Journal* 68 (12 Feb. 1863): 44–45; K. M. Rabb, "Dr. Asahel Clapp," *Indianapolis Sunday Star*, 30 Aug. 1931; and M. Homoya, "Indiana's First Resident Botanist: The Contributions of Dr. Asahel Clapp," *Outdoor Indiana* 56 (Mar. 1991): 8–13. A newspaper obituary is in the *New Albany Daily Ledger*, 17 Dec. 1862.

EUGENE H. CONNER

CLAPP, Charles Horace (5 June 1883–9 May 1935), geologist, was born in Boston, Massachusetts, the son of Peleg Ford Clapp and Mary Lincoln Manson, occupations unknown. His parents died when he was young, but a sister oversaw his education, and he graduated in 1905 from the Massachusetts Institute of Technology (then Boston Technology) with a B.S. After two years as assistant state geologist and instructor of geology and mining in North Dakota, he returned to MIT and completed his Ph.D. in 1910, with a dissertation on the igneous rocks of Essex County, Massachusetts. In 1911 Clapp married Mary Brennan of Devil's Lake, North Dakota; they had eight children.

While still a graduate student, Clapp began field survey work with the Canada Geological Survey, which he left in 1913 to become professor and head of the Department of Geology at the University of Arizona. While there he took on a post as assistant geologist with the U.S. Geological Survey, with which he worked until 1925.

It was in the state of Montana that Clapp's professional and administrative career bloomed. Hired initially in 1916 as head of the geology department with the Montana School of Mines in Butte, he became acting president of the school in 1918 and president the following year. During World War I Clapp emerged as a respected community leader and aggressive school president, active in campaigning for the War Chest and in getting federal appropriations to build up the school. As the war ended, he worked with a Butte mining engineer, Arthur V. Corry, to lobby successfully for a state bureau of mines and metallurgy. The primary mission of the newly created bureau was to undertake a state geological survey and to promote the economic development of mineral resources in Montana. Clapp was named director of the new bureau.

As bureau director, Clapp led by example, initiating a thorough stratigraphic mapping, field description, photographic record, and economic assessment of Montana geology. Furthermore, he promoted a strong conservationist ethic in a state where greed and haste had long been the rule. In the first bulletin issued by the bureau, he wrote: "Conservation is now taken by most practical men to mean: 'Utilization, with a maximum efficiency and a minimum waste.' This definition applies particularly to conservation in the mining industry, for, unlike agricultural products, which are annually replenished, the product of the mines consists of only one crop, which must meet the future, as well as the present needs." Clapp's support for progressive conservation principles led to some conflicts, especially with the Montana Mining Association. Despite these clashes, Clapp prevailed in establishing economic planning and conservation of resources as the norm in Montana.

While in Butte, Clapp acquired a strong regional reputation for promoting professional and economic development. In 1921 he left his two positions in Butte to become president of the State University of Montana at Missoula, where he remained until his death. Clapp hoped to redirect the predominantly liberal arts orientation of the state university toward more practical goals. He experienced some success in this direction, mainly by hiring and supporting Charles Deiss, who founded a first-rate geology department at Missoula. Clapp did not neglect the liberal arts mission of the university, however, and actively promoted studies in traditional disciplines such as music and religion.

Because of chronic underfunding of the state university system, Clapp faced enormous administrative problems. Funds were insufficient to hire needed faculty; low salaries made hiring and retaining competent faculty difficult; and the physical plant was always too small for the number of students enrolled. Despite such hurdles, Clapp succeeded in raising private funding to expand the campus and to undertake some new construction, gradually instituted higher academic standards, and persuaded the faculty to take a series of salary cuts. Throughout his term as president, he continued to do fieldwork and publish articles. As a colleague remarked, "Dr. Clapp almost literally worked himself to death." He died of natural causes in Missoula.

Clapp was a competent geologist and a superb administrator. He was a member of the American Association for the Advancement of Science, the Geological Society of America, and the Institute of Mining and Metallurgical Engineers. His many publications helped provide a foundation for the planned economic development of Montana's resources. His efforts in directing two state schools and the bureau of mines helped establish Montana's reputation for high-quality education in geological science and mining technology. His strategy for success consisted of encouraging the state to invest short-term mineral profits in educational and planning infrastructure. In this way, he was a solid proponent of what the social historian David F. Noble has termed "America by design."

• Clapp's mission statement for the bureau he helped create is published as "The Montana State Bureau of Mines and Metallurgy," *University of Montana Bulletin, Bureau of Mines and Metallurgy*, no. 1 (May 1919). Clapp's reports on some of his more significant survey work include two in the *Canada Department of Mines, Geological Survey*, "Geology of the Victoria and Saanich Map-Areas, Vancouver Island," memoir 36 (1913), and "Geology of the Nanaimo Map-Area," memoir 51 (1914); "Geology of a Portion of the Rocky Mountains of Northwestern Montana," *Montana Bureau of Mines and Geology*, memoir 4 (1932); and, with C. F. Deiss, "Correlation of Montana Algonkian Formations," *Bulletin of the Geological Society of America* 42 (1931): 673–96. A brief biographical account of Clapp and a bibliography of his works were published by Charles Deiss in the *Proceedings of the Geological Society of America for 1935* (1936). Clapp's administrative career is described in Terrence McGlynn, *Montana Tech, 1893–1984* (1984), and Harold Guy Merriam, *The University of Montana: A History* (1970). See also the obituary in the Butte newspaper, the *Montana Standard*, 10 May 1935.

PAT MUNDAY

CLAPP, Cornelia Maria (17 Mar. 1849–31 Dec. 1934), zoologist, educator, and biologist, was born in Montague, Massachusetts, the daughter of Richard C. Clapp, a teacher and farmer, and Eunice Amelia Slate. Her parents ensured that she had an excellent education in the public and private schools of her home town, which had been home to several generations of her ancestors. A lifelong learner, Clapp summarized her eclectic academic career: "I was all bent on one thing, then another . . . first an entomologist, then a conchologist and then a fish woman."

In 1868 Clapp enrolled at Mount Holyoke Seminary in South Hadley, Massachusetts, from which she graduated three years later. She taught Latin at Potter Hall, a Pennsylvania boys' school, then in 1872 was asked to be on the faculty at Mount Holyoke. At the time, she admitted later, "To my consternation, I didn't know what I was to teach!" Clapp was an instructor first in mathematics, then in natural history, before that field was renamed zoology. She also directed gymnastics classes.

Clapp conducted experiments with her former science teacher, Lydia Shattuck. They collected pond water and prepared microscopic slides to view amoebas, of which they had previously only read descriptions in books. Clapp and Shattuck also observed other flora and fauna in the water drops.

In 1874 Shattuck invited Clapp to accompany her to noted naturalist Louis Agassiz's Anderson School on Penikese Island near Buzzards Bay, Massachusetts. Agassiz encouraged female scientists to aspire for advanced education and research opportunities. His motto "study nature, not books" profoundly affected Clapp. "I had an opening of doors at Penikese. I looked and saw a thousand new doors," she explained in a 1921 interview. "Everybody was talking. Discussions in every corner. I felt my mind going in every direction" (Clapp papers). The Anderson School spurred Clapp to concentrate on biology as a career.

Resuming lectures in zoology at Mount Holyoke, Clapp transformed her teaching methods, deciding to study science by focusing on animals and plants first-hand rather than using textbooks. Her enthusiastic personality enhanced her original presentations. She stressed fundamental principles and facts while encouraging her students to be curious and perceptive. She introduced her class to embryology by renting a hen and displaying chicks from one day old to fully developed. Another time, she sent crabs scurrying into the classroom. "Whatever she goes into," former student Sarah French remarked, "she goes into it head over heels." One student, Louise Baird Wallace, was advised to sign up for Clapp's class because Clapp had a tank of live frogs. "I came; I saw; she conquered," Wallace reminisced. "Her bounding vitality and thirst for knowledge were contagious" (*Mount Holyoke Alumnae Quarterly* 19 [1935]: 1–9).

As an instructor, Clapp inspired several generations of women biologists and enriched them with basic research techniques. Embracing observation as a primary research tool, she took her students on excursions to some "splendid place for bugs," snakes, clams, or other creatures. According to another student, Hattie Savage, they devoted days to "petting the dear, dirty ugly things" and "then cutting them to pieces."

Clapp participated in several walking trips to collect specimens in the White Mountains, the American South, and Europe. The Mount Holyoke trustees provided $100 in the summer of 1878 for the support of her work. In 1882 she studied chick embryology with William T. Sedgwick at the Massachusetts Institute of Technology, and in the next year she researched earthworms at Williams College with Edmund Beecher Wilson.

The Marine Biological Laboratory at Woods Hole, Massachusetts, was a professional epiphany for Clapp. Arriving in 1888 while carpenters were completing buildings and before equipment had been delivered, Clapp was one of the laboratory's first students. Director Charles Otis Whitman assigned her the laboratory's first personal research problem, an examination of the toadfish, which became known as "Dr. Clapp's fish." Her research, analyzing the direction of cleavage of toadfish eggs, was crucial for the advancement of marine biology and embryology.

In the 1880s, as doctoral degrees became a requirement for faculty positions at many universities, Clapp decided to acquire advanced education. She earned a Ph.B. and a Ph.D. from Syracuse University in 1888 and 1889 to fulfill Mount Holyoke's teaching requirements but sought more rigorous research instruction. She took a three-year leave (1893–1896) from Mount Holyoke, which had become a college in 1888, and studied with Whitman at the University of Chicago. Clapp completed a doctorate in biology in 1896 with the dissertation "The Lateral Line System of Batrachus Tau."

Every summer Clapp researched at Woods Hole, seeking more sophisticated results with regard to the effect of egg cleavage on an embryonic axis. "The atmosphere of that laboratory was an inspiration, the days were peaceful and quiet," she remarked in "Some Recollections." "There were no lectures nor anything else to distract the attention from the work at hand." She challenged colleague Wilhelm Roux's conclusions, rejecting his simplistic theories and offering the hypothesis that the first egg cleavage did not determine the embryonic axis. Clapp presented her results in neurological seminars at Woods Hole and published them in 1891 in the *Journal of Morphology*.

Clapp supported Woods Hole until her death. She was the first woman elected to the laboratory's board of trustees and also served as librarian and corporation member when Woods Hole affiliated with the Carnegie Institution to upgrade its facilities. She was well liked by her colleagues, one of whom described her as "an energetic woman with practical short hair and a willingness to wade in after an enticing specimen" (Maienschein, p. 179). Clapp Road at Woods Hole was dedicated in her honor.

Named a professor at Mount Holyoke College in 1904, Clapp developed zoological facilities there, including a laboratory, dissecting room, and "aqua vivarium." She initiated a Biological Club to encourage students' individual work. The Mount Holyoke trustees granted funds to reserve a room at Woods Hole specifically for Mount Holyoke research students. Her creativity in the classroom and the laboratory and her "virile scholarship" earned Clapp professional recognition despite gender biases of that era. "I have always had an idea that if you want to do a thing," she once declared, "there is no particular reason why you shouldn't do it" (Clapp interview, Mount Holyoke archives).

A member of the Society of American Zoologists and Association of American Anatomists, Clapp was selected a fellow of the American Association for the Advancement of Science and starred in the first five editions of *American Men of Science*, which included the nation's most important zoologists. In 1906 her former students, friends, and colleagues endowed the Cornelia M. Clapp Fellowship at Mount Holyoke to support a distinguished professor of zoology.

Clapp, who never married, retired in 1916, moving to Mount Dora, Florida, where she was active in civic and suffrage matters. She continued to spend summers at Woods Hole. In 1921 Mount Holyoke christened its new biology laboratory Clapp Hall. After almost forty summers at Woods Hole, Clapp was the last surviving member of the Penikese school when she died in Mount Dora.

• The Cornelia M. Clapp Papers are at the Mount Holyoke College Library. Clapp's "Relation of the Axis of the Embryo to the First Cleavage Plane," is reprinted in *Defining Biology: Lectures from the 1890s*, ed. Jane Maienschein (1986). See also Clapp, "Some Recollections of the First Summer at Woods Hole, 1888," *Collecting Net* 2 (1927): 2–10.

Articles on Clapp in the *Mount Holyoke Alumnae Quarterly* include much of vol. 19 (May 1935), and Emma Perry Carr, "One Hundred Years of Science at Mount Holyoke College," vol. 20 (1936): 135–38.

See also Arthur C. Cole, *A Hundred Years of Mount Holyoke College: The Evolution of an Educational Ideal* (1940); Frank R. Lillie, *The Woods Hole Marine Biological Laboratory* (1944); and Margaret W. Rossiter, *Women Scientists in America: Struggles and Strategies to 1940* (1982). An obituary is in the *New York Times*, 2 Jan. 1935.

ELIZABETH D. SCHAFER

CLAPP, Elsie Ripley (16 Nov. 1879–28 July 1965), progressive educator and community school leader, was born in Brooklyn, New York, the daughter of William Clapp and Sarah Ripley. Her well-off family, then living in New York City's fashionable Washington Square, sent her to Vassar College, 1899–1903. She transferred to Barnard College, Columbia University, where she received the B.A. degree in English in 1908. She also earned the M.A. degree in philosophy from Columbia University in 1909. She enrolled in a philosophy of education course under John Dewey at Teachers College, Columbia University, in 1907 and was his teaching assistant during 1909–1913 and 1925–1929. The long and close contact with Dewey confirmed her leanings as a child-centered progressive educator. She held teaching and administrative posts at Ashley Hall, Charleston, South Carolina, 1913–1914; Brooklyn Heights Seminary, New York, 1914–1921; Milton Academy, Milton, Massachusetts, 1921–1922; City and Country School, New York, New York, 1922–1924; and the Junior School of Rosemary Hall, Greenwich, Connecticut, 1924–1925. In these elite private schools she practiced her child-centered philosophy but had little opportunity to apply Dewey's community school concept that a school should also be community-centered, consciously interacting with community residents, activities, and problems and involving students in community uplift and development.

The 1930s economic depression provided the background for the first of Clapp's two community school experiments. During 1929–1934 she was principal of the Rogers Clark Ballard Memorial School, a rural school in Jefferson County, near Louisville, Kentucky. For learning experiences, she and her teachers used community resources and people, along with books, field trips, plays, and special days like May Day. Children in the nine-grade school were organized in yearlong individual and group projects. They studied about farm and village life, Kentucky Indians, white settlers, and subsequent state history; held school country fairs; and examined school and community health, social, and other needs. Community residents were encouraged to attend games, films, and other events, helping to make the school a center for community recreation. Math, science, social studies, and other subjects were woven into school and community projects in a variety of ways.

By the early 1930s Clapp was a leader in the Progressive Education Association (1919–1957), headed its Committee on School and Community Relations, and was adviser to various government agencies. Her second community school experience occurred at a New Deal subsistence homestead site, Arthurdale, West Virginia, during 1934–1936. First Lady Eleanor Roosevelt was shocked by reports of the near starvation of jobless coal miners' families at Scotts Run, West Virginia. Roosevelt visited there unrecognized 18–19 August 1933, reporting on the appalling conditions to President Franklin D. Roosevelt. He directed the Interior Department to use "subsistence homestead" funds in the National Industrial Recovery Act to buy part of the Richard M. Arthur farm, whose taxes were in arrears. Arthurdale, fifteen miles southeast of Morgantown, became the resettlement community for nearby displaced coal miner families. It was the first of some fifty homestead communities in the United States during the New Deal period.

Clapp was asked to visit Arthurdale and to report on its school needs. She consulted with local school officials and with local relief workers. Her past community school experience was brought to Eleanor Roosevelt's attention and the two women met in February 1934 and agreed on the need for a community school at Arthurdale. In the summer of 1934 Clapp was appointed director of the Arthurdale School and moved there with several of her Ballard School teachers. The Arthurdale School opened in September 1934 with 21 teachers and 580 children in a community of 200 selected jobless families. For two years, until her departure in 1936, she made the Arthurdale School a model of its kind.

Classes were organized into interest groups rather than by formal grades. The nursery school, a source of community pride, served as a child care center. Eleanor Roosevelt, using money earned by her speeches and writings, paid Clapp's salary and other school expenses. Philanthropist Bernard Baruch contributed generously to the nursery school, which was not eligible for state funds.

Arthurdale, then a beehive of construction, was a natural place to involve schoolchildren with community activities. First graders saw buckwheat threshed, potatoes disked, and homes being built. When homesteaders acquired cows, children studied butter and cheese making. A log cabin was restored and used by fourth graders for a study of pioneer life. Children painted, sang folk songs, and wrote and produced plays. There were square dances, sports, and an annual summer music festival. Parents liked the school, although some felt that the 3 R's were being neglected.

When funds could not be found to support the Arthurdale community school as a private school, its control and finance had to be transferred to the state and county. Homesteaders wanted Clapp to remain, but she felt she should leave. Officials connected with the project, homesteaders, and longtime area residents praised the community school as the best thing about Arthurdale.

Critics faulted Arthurdale for cost overruns and alleged mismanagement. An attempt was made to provide quick housing before Christmas 1933, but the prefabricated cottages that were ordered were not suitable for winter use and did not fit the prepared foundations. Eleanor Roosevelt hired a New York architect to recut, rebuild, and winterize them, and costs soared. Interior Secretary Harold Ickes wrote in his diary, "We have been spending money down there like drunken sailors." To create jobs, a factory was planned in 1935 to make post office furniture and mailboxes; however, an Indiana company making the same products strongly objected. The congressman from the Indiana district blocked U.S. Post Office appropriations for the factory. In a 4 August 1934 *Saturday Evening Post* article, a critic called Arthurdale wasteful; others called it communistic. By 1938 national sentiment for reform waned, and Congress cut subsistence homestead funds in 1939. In 1942 Congress directed that government property in the homesteads be sold.

Clapp was editor of *Progressive Education*, the journal of the Progressive Education Association, from October 1937 through May 1939. Her articles and two books, describing in detail her Kentucky and West Virginia community school experiences, are considered original contributions at a time when community schools were favored by some progressive educators. She wrote *The Use of Resources in Education* (1952). In an earlier book, *Community Schools in Action* (1939), reminiscent of her mentor, Dewey, she described a community school as meeting "the urgent needs of people. [It is] a place used freely and informally for all the needs of living and learning. It is, in effect, the place where learning and living converge." Clapp lived in retirement in Exeter, New Hampshire, where she died. She never married.

• The Center for Dewey Studies, Southern Illinois University, Carbondale, has the "Elsie Ripley Clapp Papers 1910–1943." Clapp's articles include "Plays in a Kentucky County School," *Progressive Education* 8, no. 1 (Jan. 1931): 34–39; "A Rural Community School in Kentucky," *Progressive Education* 10, no. 3 (Mar. 1933): 123–28; "The Teacher in Social Education," *Progressive Education* 10, no. 5 (May 1933): 283–87; and "Schools Socially Functioning," *Progressive Education* 15, no. 2 (Feb. 1938); 89–90.

The Arthurdale School is described in College of Education, West Virginia University, *Report of the Survey of Arthurdale School* (1940); Thomas H. Coode and Dennis E. Fabbri, "The New Deal's Arthurdale Project in West Virginia," *West Virginia History* 36, no. 4 (July 1975): 291–308; Richard S. Little and Margaret Little, *Arthurdale—Its History, Its Lessons for Today* (1976); Franklin Parker, "The Progressive Educator: Elsie Ripley Clapp," in *The Fiftieth Anniversary of the Homesteading of Arthurdale, W. Va.*, ed. Jettie and Charles Eble (1984); and Bob Robinson, "Great Social Experiment in Arthurdale Inconclusive," *Dominion-Post* (Morgantown, W. Va.), 7 June 1981. Criticism of Arthurdale is in Harold L. Ickes, *The Secret Diaries of Harold L. Ickes: Vol. I: The First Thousand Days, 1933–1936* (1953), and Wesley Stout, "The New Homesteaders," *Saturday Evening Post*, 4 Aug. 1934, pp. 5–7, 61–65.

Eleanor Roosevelt described Arthurdale in *This I Remember* (1949) and *Eleanor Roosevelt's My Day*, ed. Rochelle Chadakoff (1989). Eleanor Roosevelt's involvement in Arthurdale is described in Bruce G. Beezer, "Arthurdale: An Experiment in Community Education," *West Virginia History* 26, no. 1 (Oct. 1974): 17–36; Tamara K. Hareven, "Arthurdale: A Venture in Utopia," in *Eleanor Roosevelt: An American Conscience* (1975); Joseph P. Lash, "Mrs. Roosevelt's 'Baby'—Arthurdale," in *Eleanor and Franklin* (1971); Lash, *Eleanor Roosevelt: A Friend's Memoir* (1964); and Graham White and John Maze, *Harold Ickes of the New Deal: His Private Life and Public Career* (1985).

Clapp's first community school work at the Junior School of Rosemary Hall is mentioned in Harold Rugg and Ann Shumaker, *The Child-Centered School: An Appraisal of the New Education* (1928). Her Ky. and W.Va. community schools are mentioned in Rugg, *Foundations for American Education* (1947), and Rugg and B. Marian Brooks, *The Teacher in School and Society: An Introduction to Education* (1950). Doctoral dissertations on her Arthurdale community school are Stephen Edward Haid, "Arthurdale: An Experiment in Community Planning, 1933–1947" (Ph.D. diss., West Virginia Univ., 1975); and Martin L. Berman, "Arthurdale, Nambé, and the Developing Community School Model: A Comparative Study" (Ph.D. diss., Univ. of New Mexico, 1979). Obituaries are in the *Exeter News-Letter* (Exeter, N.H.), 12 Aug. 1965, and the *New York Times*, 31 July 1965.

FRANKLIN PARKER

CLAPP, George Hubbard (14 Dec. 1858–31 Mar. 1949), businessman and numismatist, was born in Allegheny, Pennsylvania (later absorbed into the north side of Pittsburgh), the son of DeWitt Clinton Clapp, a steel company official, and Delia Dennig Hubbard. He graduated from the University of Pittsburgh in 1877 with a bachelor of philosophy degree and was named the "first scholar" in the Scientific Department. Around 1882 he married Anne W. Love; they would have two children. Clapp worked as an engineer at the Penn Cotton Mill and then at Park Brothers' Black Diamond Steel Works, where he met Captain Alfred Ephraim Hunt. Hunt and Clapp established the chemical department of the recently founded Pittsburgh Testing Laboratory; they took PTL over entirely in 1887. In 1888, when Clapp returned from a European vacation, Hunt greeted him with the words, "Well, you don't know it, but you are in the aluminum business" (Carr, p. 16).

In July 1888 Hunt had formed a company in Pittsburgh to acquire and exploit the Charles Martin Hall patents for making aluminum by electrolysis. After 1907 this company was known as the Aluminum Company of America, or Alcoa. Clapp became treasurer and secretary of the new company. In 1892 he resigned as treasurer in favor of Andrew W. Mellon. Thus credit for the creation of Alcoa can be allocated as follows: Hall invented the process; Clapp and Hunt came up with the venture capital ($20,000), which made the process commercially viable; and the Mellons provided the working capital from 1891 onward. Clapp never sold any of his stock, except on one occasion in 1891, when he parted with twenty-eight shares so that Arthur Vining Davis, later president of Alcoa, could have a stake.

From 1891 onward Clapp was in an enviable position: he had a job at PTL that provided him with a good income and a passive investment (Alcoa), which was growing at a rapid rate and would soon make him a very wealthy man. He spent more and more time on two intellectual pursuits: conchology and numismatics.

Clapp was introduced to shell collecting around 1869 by his grandfather. Clapp joined the Conchological Society of Great Britain and the Malacological Society of London. He assembled a collection of 120,000 mollusk shells, which he donated to the Carnegie Museum in Pittsburgh. He also wrote a study of the shells found on the western shores of Lake Erie, which was published by the Carnegie Museum in 1916. He commented in a letter to Edward T. Newell of September 1937:

> A package, just in, takes me back to the "love of my youth," conchology. It is a few shells from K[entuck]y., and contains one that is the *rarest of the rare*, a *sinistral* shell, young but alive, so I *must* try to raise it. In over fifty years of collecting I never found one, this one I cannot name until it grows up, hence my excitement.

Clapp began collecting coins as an adolescent in the 1870s by going through the receipts of a toll bridge across the Allegheny River. In June 1878 he was one of the founders of the Western Pennsylvania Numismatic Society. After 1880 he remained a member but stopped collecting, because he "was working and money was very scarce" (letter to Sydney P. Noe, 14 May 1944). In March 1921 his brother, Charles Edwin Clapp, Sr., gave him some large cents to get him started again. Large cents are copper cents, minted by the United States between 1793 and 1857, twenty-eight millimeters in diameter and over 10 grams in weight; they were replaced by the smaller-size cent starting in

1856. Clapp acquired his brother's collection of large cents in a series of transactions between 1921 and 1924. His brother, who was a vice president of the Crucible Steel Company, sold his cent collection in order to buy a partnership for his son, Charles Edwin Clapp, Jr., in a Wall Street brokerage firm. The younger Clapp was an alcoholic, and his bankruptcy after the stock market crash of 1929 led Charles senior to sell his other coins, including one of the great collections of pine tree shillings, which was sold to Massachusetts banker Carl Würtzbach. George Clapp bought most of the other prefederal coins.

Howard R. Newcomb's die study of the cents of 1801–1803 published in 1925 inspired Clapp to embark on die studies of his own. Most coins are struck from pairs of dies. In primitive mints, such as the Philadelphia mint in its early years, the varieties can be distinguished by careful study. Clapp admired Newcomb greatly, saying, "In his line,—the Large Cents,—he can well be classed with the late Edward T. Newell in his line of Greece and Rome" (letter to Homer K. Downing, repr. in *Penny-Wise* 15 [15 May 1981]: 137). In 1931 Clapp published a die study of 1798 and 1799 in the same format as Newcomb; in 1934 he published a study of the varieties of 1804–1814; Newcomb and Clapp then collaborated on a study of the varieties of 1795, 1796, 1797, and 1800, which appeared in 1947. Clapp was always open to new scientific methods, and in 1945 he helped pioneer the spectrographic analysis of coins' metallic content.

In 1937 Clapp deeded his first line collection of large cents to the American Numismatic Society. He gave his second line collection of large cents to the Carnegie Museum of Pittsburgh. He also gave the museum an important collection of prefederal American coins. From 1907 until his death in Sewickley, Pennsylvania, Clapp was president of the Board of Trustees of the University of Pittsburgh and as such was instrumental in moving the university from the north side of Pittsburgh to Oakland. Clapp was also a trustee of the Carnegie Institute of Technology, from 22 September 1896, and from 1898 until his death he was a member of the museum committee of the institute, serving as chairman from 1909 to 1945. Also a member of the American Chemical Society, he received the society's Pittsburgh award in 1939.

• Documents on Clapp's life are dispersed. Alcoa kept very good archives in Pittsburgh, partly in response to numerous antitrust suits. The Carnegie Museum of Natural History has newspaper clippings and other documents about Clapp. The American Numismatic Society in New York City has numerous letters from Clapp, mostly to Sydney Philip Noe; the correspondence covers the last dozen years of Clapp's life (1937–1949), and his personality comes through vividly. Clapp published numerous short notes in numismatic periodicals, invariably about die varieties: "New Varieties of 1796 Cents," *Numismatist* 47 (Jan. 1934): 18; "Varieties of the Lafayette Dollar," *Coin Collector's Journal* 1 (Nov. 1934): 180–81; "United States Cents of 1796," *Coin Collector's Journal* 2 (Apr. 1935): 13; and "Notes on Some Varieties of the U.S. Cents of 1793–4," *Coin Collector's Journal* 2 (Feb. 1936): 244. Two interesting letters of Clapp were published in *Penny-Wise* 15 (15 May 1981): 136–40; a third letter was published in *Penny-Wise* 23 (15 May 1989): 192.

A good short account of Clapp's life is provided by "Resolution Adopted in Memoriam George Hubbard Clapp by the Board of Trustees University of Pittsburgh at the Annual Meeting June 14, 1949." His obituary in the *New York Times*, 1 Apr. 1949, probably prepared by a family member, also is informative. On his role at Alcoa, see Charles C. Carr, *Alcoa: An American Enterprise* (1952), and George David Smith, *From Monopoly to Competition: The Transformations of Alcoa 1888–1986* (1988). Another good history, which complements Smith, is Margaret B. W. Graham and Bettye H. Pruitt, *R&D for Industry: A Century of Technical Innovation at Alcoa* (1990). All three histories provide a good guide through the Alcoa archives.

JOHN M. KLEEBERG

CLAPP, Margaret Antoinette (11 Apr. 1910–3 May 1974), educator and diplomat, was born in East Orange, New Jersey, the daughter of Alfred Chapin, an insurance broker, and Anna Roth. Educated in public schools, she received an A.B. with honors from Wellesley College in 1930, having served as student government president her senior year. Moving back to New Jersey, she commuted to New York City where she attended graduate school part time and taught English literature first at the Todhunter School (1930–1939) and then following its merger, at the Dalton School (1939–1942). She received an A.M. from Columbia University in 1937.

In 1942–1943 Clapp taught in the evening at the City College of New York (CCNY) while working days as a researcher for the British Broadcasting System. She also worked as a researcher for the American Red Cross in 1945. She accepted a yearlong appointment (1945–1946) at the New Jersey College for Women (now Douglass College) and also taught at Columbia as an instructor (1946) before accepting a position as a government researcher in Washington, D.C. Clapp was back in New York by September 1946 when she again taught evenings at CCNY.

In 1946 Clapp received her Ph.D. in American history from Columbia, having worked under Allan Nevins. In 1947 a revised version of her dissertation was published as *Forgotten First Citizen: John Bigelow*. Brooklyn College appointed her an assistant professor of history on the strength of this publication. Clapp told friends, "I've been sold to the Dodgers." Somewhat unexpectedly, her book won the Pulitzer Prize for biography in May 1948, as a result of which she received national attention as well as the notice of the presidential search committee of her alma mater. Recognizing that the prospects for most women to have academic careers was still limited, Clapp "took a gamble" and accepted a call from Wellesley to become its eighth president the following year.

Clapp labored through long hours, a habit learned during her student days, when she came to understand that "to have anything, one has to choose among many possible uses of . . . time." Her "brisk" leadership pace helped consolidate the financial and academic success of Wellesley. She increased the college's endowment threefold and made larger amounts available for financial aid; she also constructed three new dormitories, an arts center, and a new library wing. Clapp paid particular attention to faculty life issues, increasing salaries by 150 percent, building a faculty club, and instituting a liberal leave policy for junior faculty.

As one of only a handful of female college presidents, in this era, Clapp challenged some accepted ideas about domesticity and women's roles. She proposed that especially able young women enter college at age sixteen, and that older women set up voluntary day care and domestic services to free younger, working mothers to have careers. Recognizing that organized feminism had abated, Clapp was moderate in her tone and often preferred to let Wellesley's excellence and her own work speak for themselves.

Circumspection characterized Clapp's professional life, as evidenced by the restraint she showed in dealing with the unwelcome attentions of visiting instructor and poet May Sarton, whose pursuit of Clapp began about 1963 and persisted for years. Although Sarton's appointment was not renewed, perhaps in part because of her interest in Clapp, Clapp's refusal to respond to most of Sarton's behavior appears to confirm her poise and self-discipline.

In 1966 Clapp retired to engage in new interests and to give the college a chance for "fresh vision and new leadership" under a new president. Having become convinced that "people should move outside their own cultures at some time in their lives," she accepted the principalship (presidency) of Lady Doak, a women's college in South India. Not given the authority she had hoped for, she resigned the following year and became a consultant for the Danforth Foundation in India. In 1968 she accepted an appointment as cultural attaché to India for the U.S. Information Agency (USIA). In just two years her competence earned her appointment as minister councilor of public affairs, where she was the first woman to hold this position, heading the largest educational and cultural program within the USIA. Although U.S.-India relations were strained at this time, Clapp managed to navigate the diplomatic waters safely and expand programs in India. Staffing cutbacks led to her resignation in 1971; she retired to Tyringham, Massachusetts, with her sister. There she developed cancer and died.

Clapp's legacy as an administrator and quiet pathfinder for women is most apparent at Wellesley, where the library was renamed for her to honor her achievements and service in "building excellence" throughout the college. Her career illustrates both the challenges women scholars faced during and after the depression, and the opportunities created for women by World War II and later by the changing social and political realities of the 1960s and 1970s. As a scholar and an independent, working woman, Clapp met with success in this transitional period in American life when women's roles outside the home were beginning to expand but were still not validated, and when the internal, isolationist focus of so much of American culture was giving way to an understanding of the United States as a world power with international obligations. Clapp's life demonstrated the potential for ability, faith in oneself, and work to prevail despite ingrained cultural assumptions about the limits of what a woman could—or ought—to do.

• Clapp's papers are in the Wellesley College Archives, and include correspondence, speeches, clippings, a 1972 oral interview, and material on her post-Wellesley work with Lady Doak and the Danforth Foundation. In addition to *Forgotten First Citizen*, Clapp contributed a chapter, "The Social and Cultural Scene," to *The Greater City: New York 1898–1948* ed. Allan Nevins and John Krout (1948), a cultural and social history of New York City. She also edited *The Modern University* (1950), a collection of essays, and contributed the chapter "Contemporary Universities: Some Problems and Trends." A useful profile published at the time she won the Pulitzer Prize appears in *Current Biography 1948*. Material on her presidency at Wellesley appears in Jean Glasscock, ed., *Wellesley College, 1875–1975: A Century of Women* (1975). The Sarton episode is documented in Margot Peters, *May Sarton: A Biography* (1997). A retrospective of Clapp's presidency was published in the *Wellesley Alumnae Magazine*, July 1966. Her obituary is in the *New York Times*, 4 May 1974.

CYNTHIA BROWN

CLAPPE, Louise Amelia Knapp Smith (28 July 1819–9 Feb. 1906), writer, was born in Elizabeth, New Jersey, the daughter of Moses Smith, a schoolteacher, and Lois Lee. Her father died in 1832, her mother in 1837; subsequently she was raised in Amherst, Massachusetts, by a guardian, attorney Osmyn Baker. She attended the Female Seminary in Charlestown, Massachusetts, in 1838 and the Amherst Academy from 1839 to 1840. In 1839, while traveling by stagecoach in Vermont, Clappe met Alexander Hill Everett, a diplomat, orator, editor of the *North American Review*, and a man twice her age. The two kept up an extended (and, on his part, romantic) correspondence until 1847, when Everett died. She married Fayette Clapp, a doctor, in 1848 or 1849. (Despite the spelling of her husband's name, documentary evidence indicates that Louise herself preferred a final "e" in Clappe, just as she preferred Louise to Louisa, the original spelling of her first name.)

The couple sailed to California in 1849 and eventually moved from San Francisco to the northern gold mines. They lived in two rough mining camps—Rich Bar and Indian Bar—on the north fork of the Feather River. From these camps Clappe wrote twenty-three letters to her sister Mary Jane, or "Molly," in Massachusetts, in 1851–1852 under the *nom de plume* "Dame Shirley." The Shirley Letters, as they were later called, were first published serially in the *Pioneer*, a San Francisco literary periodical, in 1854–1855. The letters' wealth of historical detail and their compassionate but unflinching view of multiethnic life in the mines make them what novelist and historian Wallace Stegner has called the "finest of all Gold Rush books."

Clappe was sometimes startled by the rough living conditions she encountered in the mines, including racial tension, vigilante violence, and an outdoor autopsy. But she was exhilarated by the cultural heterogeneity of the camps and found that, despite their failings, "the miners, as a class, possess many truly admirable characteristics." Her sympathy for their lonely lives kept her from too severely criticizing their raucous misconduct. When she saw a parade of "most intensely drunk" Chilean miners, for instance, she told her sister:

> [I suppose] I ought to have been shocked and horrified—to have shed salt tears, and have uttered melancholy Jeremiads over their miserable degradation. But the world is so full of platitudes, my dear, that I think you will easily forgive me for not boring you with a temperance lecture, and will good-naturedly let me have my laugh, and not think me *very* wicked after all.

In her final letter she writes, without irony, that despite the dangers and deprivations of her experiences in the mines, "I *like* this wild and barbarous life; I leave it with regret. . . . I look kindly to this existence, which to you seems so sordid and mean. Here, at least, I have been contented."

Despite the contentment she says she felt in the camps, the Clapps' marriage foundered when they left the mines in November 1852. Fayette Clapp left Louise shortly thereafter; they were officially divorced on 4 April 1857. Clappe taught in the San Francisco public school system from 1854 to 1878. She lived the remainder of her life, with recurrent ill health, in the general area of New York City. She died at Overlook Farm, near Morristown, New Jersey, a home for elderly people run by two nieces of Bret Harte, an author who borrowed incidents from Clappe's writing for his own Gold Rush fiction but who never acknowledged the debt.

The Shirley Letters were not published in book form until 1922; since then they have been eagerly studied by social historians searching for details about the California Gold Rush. The literate buoyancy of the letters, however, makes their appeal more than strictly historical. Through the rhetorical persona of "Dame Shirley," Clappe demonstrates a lively mastery of epistolary conventions and an ability, in Lawrence Clark Powell's words, to transform her personality into "iridescent prose." Clappe's frontier "epistles" to her distant sister in "the States" stand out, amid the voluminous body of Gold Rush literature, as a distinctive combination of social portraiture and imaginative art.

• Clappe's original letters from the mines have never been found, but all of her manuscript papers are in the California State Library in Sacramento. Thomas C. Russell's publication of *The Shirley Letters* in 1922 includes the only known biographical sketch of Clappe by a contemporary (Mary Viola Tingley Lawrence, one of Clappe's pupils). Carl I. Wheat edited the letters for the Grabhorn Press in 1933 and for Alfred A. Knopf in 1949. The most thorough historical research is in Rodman Wilson Paul, "In Search of 'Dame Shirley,'" *Pacific Historical Review* 33 (May 1964): 127–46. Literary assessments of her work can be found in Franklin Walker, *San Francisco's Literary Frontier* (1939); Lawrence Clark Powell, *California Classics* (1971); Stephen Fender, *Plotting the Golden West: American Literature and the Rhetoric of the California Trail* (1981); and Michael Kowalewski, "Imagining the California Gold Rush: The Visual and Verbal Legacy," *California History* 71 (Spring 1992): 61–73.

MICHAEL KOWALEWSKI

CLAPPER, Raymond Lewis (30 May 1892–1 Feb. 1944), journalist and radio commentator, was born near La Cygne, Kansas, the son of John William Clapper and Julia Crowe, farmers. Shortly after his birth Clapper's family moved to Kansas City, Kansas, where his father worked in packinghouse factories. His parents, hardworking but poor, showed little interest in books, politics, or the world outside their strict, religious home life, which was supplemented only by regular attendance at the Baptist church. Through grade school Clapper avidly read newspapers, including the *Kansas City Star*, keeping an extensive clipping file, which he shared with fellow students. After grade school he went to work for a local print shop as a printer's devil, ultimately working his way to journeyman printer status. The shop's owners shared books with him and nurtured the young man's appreciation of the arts and politics. His hero was Kansas editor William Allen White, and he dreamed of owning a newspaper. After three years Clapper entered high school at age seventeen, juggling his class work with his printing duties. At Presbyterian church socials he met sixteen-year-old Olive Vincent Ewing, the daughter of a local grocer. Within two years, in March 1913, they left school and eloped; their marriage produced two children.

In the fall of 1913 Clapper and his wife enrolled at the University of Kansas. He studied journalism, becoming editor of the school paper and campus correspondent for the *Kansas City Star*, while she took classes in social work. After the spring semester ended in 1916, they left without graduating and moved to Kansas City, Missouri, where Clapper joined the staff of the *Star*. His reporting quickly caught the attention of the United Press (UP), a news service owned by the Scripps-Howard chain, which hired him that same year and sent him to Chicago. He set his sights on being a political reporter in Washington, and after stints for UP in Milwaukee, St. Paul, and New York, the wire service moved him in 1923 to Washington.

Clapper scooped his fellow journalists at the 1920 Republican National Convention when he was tipped off that Warren G. Harding would be the party's nominee. In 1925 he reported on the controversial Scopes trial, and in 1930 he traveled to London to cover an international naval conference. Generally, though, he covered the White House and Congress, becoming manager of the UP Washington bureau in 1929. Outraged at the corruption he saw, Clapper methodically compiled evidence for a book, *Racketeering in Washington* (1933). That same year he joined the *Washington Post* as a reporter, and in 1934 he began his daily column, "Between You and Me." In December 1934 he moved his column to the Scripps-Howard chain, which syndicated it to 176 papers with ten million readers. He liked writing a column, he said, because "in a straight news story you have to leave out so much background, so much meat." He wanted "to feature it [the news] so that people will see and understand what really goes on in the government." He also wrote for magazines, was a news anchor and commentator for the Mutual radio network, and frequently traveled the lecture circuit.

Clapper built a reputation as a conscientious and fair reporter and commentator, never registering to vote so he would owe allegiance to neither political party. "To be fearless and objective. In our business those are the trademarks of quality," Clapper wrote. His hallmark, though, was an ability to interpret complicated political events for the average reader in the hinterlands. When the *Saturday Evening Post* ran a profile of Clapper in November 1943, the magazine called him "The Average Man's Columnist."

Clapper admired President Franklin D. Roosevelt and most New Deal programs, but he never let this affect his reporting. When he disagreed with Roosevelt, as he did when the president ran for a third term, Clapper showed no hesitancy to voice criticisms. When war began in Europe, Clapper drew on travels in England, France, Germany, Austria, and Russia to argue that the United States should help Europe fend off Nazism. This stance earned him the disdain of isolationists and death threats. But even when wrongly accused from the floor of the House of being a British agent, Clapper never backed down. In 1939 his colleagues elected him president of the Gridiron Club.

After the attack at Pearl Harbor on 7 December 1941, Clapper expanded his reporting to include battle coverage. He reported on the invasion of Italy and traveled with the U.S. Navy in the South Pacific. While reporting on the invasion of the Marshall Islands, Clapper was killed when a Navy fighter-bomber he was in left formation to give him another view of a bombed airfield and collided in the air with another plane. Writing of his death, the *New York Times* noted that Clapper produced "what were generally accepted as among the most objective, tolerant and understanding views on national and foreign affairs." In an editorial the *Times* wrote that the circumstances of Clapper's death did not surprise his fellow journalists: "He was no armchair reporter. He got around. He went and saw. He tracked news to its source. . . . he had no axe to grind, no dogma to sell. It was the truth that he sought." The navy honored Clapper by naming a ship after him, and his friends in journalism established an annual award to recognize a Washington reporter whose work embodies Clapper's own most notable professional qualities: fairness, painstaking reporting, and sound craftsmanship.

Clapper was a journalism journeyman. Although his columns were not especially profound, they were noteworthy for his sometimes eloquent defenses of democracy and individual freedoms; for his attacks on racism, government wrongheadedness, and corruption; and for political analysis so clear it could be understood by average readers. He is rarely mentioned in media history books or journalists memoirs, except when the author quotes from Clapper's work to make a particular point. Like hundreds of other journalists, Clapper plodded through his career, diligently providing Americans carefully researched, thorough, and unbiased reports about their government.

• Clapper's papers are in the Library of Congress. *Watching the World* (1944; repr. 1976), a compilation of Clapper's work, includes a biographical sketch by his wife, photographs, and an introduction by contemporary journalist Ernie Pyle. Other information on him is in Charles Fisher, *The Columnists* (1944), and Leo C. Rosten, *The Washington Correspondents* (1937). Obituaries and memorial articles include "Clapper Is Killed in Pacific Crash," *New York Times*, 4 Feb. 1944; "Ship to Bear Clapper's Name," *New York Times*, 18 Feb. 1944; and Thomas L. Stokes and Dick Fitzpatrick, "A Reporter—First, Last, and Always," *Quill*, Mar.–Apr. 1944.

JAMES L. AUCOIN

CLARE, Ada. *See* McElheney, Jane.

CLARK, Abraham (15 Feb. 1726–15 Sept. 1794), surveyor, politician, and signer of the Declaration of Independence, was born in Elizabethtown (now Elizabeth), New Jersey, the son of Thomas Clark, a farmer, town alderman, and county judge, and Hannah Winans. Although he was referred to as "the poor man's counsellor," as far as is known he had no formal education or legal training, having turned as a young man to surveying and writing land conveyances because a "frail" constitution made him unfit for active farming. He did transact a good deal of legal business, including drawing up deeds, mortgages, and other papers. He married Sarah Hatfield (or Hetfield), probably in 1749. They had ten children, six or seven of whom survived childhood.

Clark first held office while New Jersey was a royal colony, serving as clerk of the assembly from 1752 to 1766 and as sheriff for Elizabethtown and Essex County from 1766. When England and the colonists disagreed over parliamentary policies, Clark became a Whig. In 1774 he was chosen as a member of the New Jersey Committee of Safety and in 1775 as a representative to the new Provincial Congress. In June 1776, when New Jersey replaced all of its representatives to the Continental Congress with a group clearly committed to joining a confederacy for "defence," Clark's support of independence earned him a place in the delegation that went on to sign the Declaration of Independence. He continued to serve in the Congress from 1776 to 1789, with the exception of those years when he was ineligible because of term limits imposed by the Articles of Confederation or because he was a member of the New Jersey legislature.

In this period Benjamin Rush characterized Clark as "a sensible but cynical man" who wanted "more to please the people than promote their real and permanent interests." Despite finding fault, he concluded that Clark was "warmly attached to the liberties and independence of his country" (Gerlach, p. 486, n. 59). In her biography of Clark, Ruth Bogin concludes that he was a "radical republican" who hated "tyranny" and consistently sought to provide a measure of equality that would ensure a foundation of independent yeoman citizens for the new republic. As a member of Congress he opposed special privileges and remuneration for Continental army officers, arguing that all soldiers (officers and enlisted men, Continental or militia forces) should be treated similarly. He also objected to the policies of Robert Morris, which would favor investors and speculators, and wanted to protect the sovereignty of the states. Toward the end of the war he fought against half pay for life for officers and against a standing army. At the same time Clark advocated increasing the powers of the central government when doing so would protect New Jersey from its larger and landed neighbors New York and Pennsylvania.

In New Jersey politics during the 1780s, Clark favored legislation that would protect debtors through paper money and bankruptcy laws and provide cheaper legal services. As a result he has been called the "generalissimo of the papermoney forces" and "a bitter foe of the legal profession"(McCormick, pp. 198, 181). Clark wrote a series of articles signed "Willing to Learn" in the newspaper *Political Intelligencer* (14 Dec. 1785–26 Apr. 1786) and a pamphlet, *The True Policy of New-Jersey, Defined* (1786), in which he argued for paper money issued as loans to help the state's husbandmen and mechanics who "alone" had changed New Jersey "from a howling wilderness to pleasant fields, gardens, towns and cities." He characterized the lawyers who opposed this plan as "true to their client" and "their God . . . MONEY." His efforts led to the passage of a paper money bill despite the opposition of Governor William Livingston, William Paterson, and John Witherspoon.

In the mid-1780s Clark was also involved in New Jersey's efforts to pay directly the Continental debts held by state residents and then count this against the state's quota due the central government. When Congress ruled against permitting this, Clark was behind the legislature's March 1786 resolution not to meet national requisitions until policies were changed—a maneuver that helped reinforce the sense of crisis in national affairs. When a conference was called to meet in Annapolis, the New Jersey legislature sent William Churchill Houston, James Schureman, and Clark with power to discuss regulation of trade "and other important matters," a broader authorization than that given other states' representatives. Delegates from only five states attended, so Clark suggested calling another meeting.

The New Jersey legislature named Clark as a delegate to the Philadelphia convention, a position he declined, apparently because he was a current member of Congress. Because he missed the convention and was silent during the ratification debate, Clark was later accused of being an anti-Federalist, which he denied. A more accurate description is that he was "lukewarm toward the Constitution" (McCormick, pp. 276–77) but did not campaign against it. Clark noted in 1789 that, while he thought "some parts" were "too hard upon the liberties of the people," providing for too "consolidated" and "too expensive" a government, he supported ratification along with amendments to protect individual liberties because it would help solve the economic problems of New Jersey and was generally in the state's interest (Bogin, pp. 134–36). In endorsing the Constitution despite its imperfections, Clark reflected the position of his state.

Charges that Clark was an anti-Federalist surfaced in the bitterly waged 1789 election campaign, in which he was a candidate from the eastern section of the state for representative to Congress. In an election famous for "skullduggery" and which became the first disputed election Congress had to settle under the Constitution, Clark was among those defeated by a slate from the western part of the state. When election was held for the members of the Second Congress in 1791, however, Clark won. Reelected in 1793, he served until his death. As a member of Congress Clark aligned himself with the nascent Jeffersonian Republican party. He supported debtor interests, opposed using the military to enforce the excise laws, favored a small national army, opposed pay raises for military officers, and wanted to use economic pressure to obtain a commercial treaty from England while also forcing the surrender of the western posts. His positions were generally consistent with those he had taken in the 1770s and 1780s.

Clark died suddenly in Elizabethtown a few hours after suffering a stroke while observing the construction of a local bridge. Over the course of his long political career he had supported independence, served in the legislatures of both state and nation, and advocated a stronger central government while working for what he saw as the best interests of farmers, artisans, and soldiers.

• Clark left no personal papers. Most of his legislative speeches were short, and he was not interested in publishing them at the time. Some of his letters are in Carl E. Prince et al., eds., *The Papers of William Livingston* (1979–1988), and Edmund C. Burnett, ed., *Letters of Members of the Continental Congress* (8 vols., 1921–1936). Genealogical studies are Ann Clark Hart, *Abraham Clark, Signer of the Declaration of Independence* (1923) and "The Family of Abraham Clark," *Genealogical Magazine of New Jersey* 7 (1932): 89–102. Ruth Bogin, *Abraham Clark and the Quest for Equality in the Revolutionary Era, 1774–1794* (1982), examines his ideas and career. Additional information on his political role is in Larry R. Gerlach, *Prologue to Independence: New Jersey in the Coming of the American Revolution* (1976); Richard P. McCormick, *Experiment in Independence: New Jersey in the Critical Period, 1781–1789* (1950); and Mary R. Murrin, *To Save this State from Ruin: New Jersey and the Creation of the United States Constitution, 1776–1789* (1987).

MAXINE N. LURIE

CLARK, Alvan (8 Mar. 1804–19 Aug. 1887), artist and telescope maker, was born in Ashfield, Massachusetts, the son of Alvan Clark and Mary Bassett, farmers. He attended a local grammar school and worked briefly for a wagonmaker. In 1826 Clark married Maria Pease, and the couple had four children. Clark spent the next decade engraving cylinders used to print textiles, before opening a portrait studio in Boston in 1836.

In 1844 Clark's son George melted a piece of an old dinner bell and made a 5-inch mirror that revealed the satellites of Jupiter. The project led the elder Clark to tackle telescope construction. His ability to locate the slight errors in the 15-inch objective lens at Harvard gave him the confidence and determination to enter the telescope business. The first recorded sale of a Clark telescope—a 5-inch achromatic refractor—came in 1848. Around 1850 Clark founded Alvan Clark & Sons with his sons George and Alvan Graham Clark in Cambridgeport, Massachusetts. There was only one other commercial telescope maker in the United States (Henry Fitz), and a popular interest in astronomy and a growing market for telescopes flourished. Around 1860 Clark closed his portrait studio to devote himself to telescope production.

Clark and his son Alvan were superb opticians, and they figured and tested most of the large objective lenses produced in the factory. George was the mechanic of the firm, responsible for the telescope mounts, spectroscopes, photometers, and photographic instruments. In the 1870s he made the apparatus that Simon Newcomb used to measure the speed of light. By 1855 the Clarks had produced a dozen objective lenses for telescopes, ranging from 4 to 7½ inches aperture. By 1860 the firm had produced a 12-inch objective that showed Mimas, the innermost satellite of Saturn. In 1860 the Clarks received an order from the University of Mississippi for an 18½-inch lens, 3½ inches larger than the instruments at Harvard and in Pulkowa, Russia. This was the first of five times that the Clarks surpassed the world record for lens size. In 1873 the firm finished a 26-inch lens for the U.S. Naval Observatory; twelve years later a similar telescope was erected at the University of Virginia. The Clarks were also well regarded abroad, and in 1883 they produced a 30-inch lens for the Russian Observatory in Pulkowa. In 1887 the Clarks' 36-inch lens for the Lick Observatory was sent to California. The 40-inch objective that was mounted at the Yerkes Observatory in 1897 was the largest lens used to date.

In addition to making telescopes, Clark took an active interest in the scientific fruit of their use. He made his first astronomical discovery in 1851—an apparently unknown eighth-magnitude double star in Canis Minor. When William R. Dawes, a well-known English double star seeker, heard of the find, he commented that Clark's "eye, as well as his telescope must possess extraordinary power of definition" (Dawes, p. 257). Alvan Graham found more than a dozen interesting binaries. The most important, which he spotted while testing the 18½-inch telescope in January 1862, was the companion of Sirius, a star whose existence astronomer Friedrich W. Bessel had predicted in 1844. Alvan Graham's discovery earned him the Lalande Prize of the Paris Academy of Sciences in 1862.

Alvan Graham went on three solar eclipse expeditions: to Shelbyville, Kentucky, with the U.S: Coast Survey party (1869); to Jerez, Spain, again with the Coast Survey (1870); and to Creston, Wyoming, with a party organized by the U.S. Naval Observatory (1878). In 1870, using a simple single-prism spectroscope, he charted the spectrum of the aurora borealis.

Clark joined the American Association for the Advancement of Science in 1850, and at the 1856 meeting he read a paper describing a double eyepiece micrometer able to measure celestial distances too great to be brought within the field of view of a single eyepiece. He received a gold medal from Czar Alexander III of Russia in 1885, and in 1867 he was awarded the Rumford Medal of the American Academy of Arts and Sciences for his ability to figure nearly perfect lenses and for his method of local correction. George joined the American Academy of Arts and Sciences in 1878, as did Alvan Graham in 1881. Alvan Graham was also a member of the American Association for the Advancement of Science and the Société Astronomique de France.

In 1840 Clark, who was a renowned marksman, obtained a patent (No. 1,565) for a false-loading muzzle, consisting of a hollow piece of metal that fits onto the end of the muzzle of a muzzle-loading rifle and protects the muzzle during loading. In 1851 he obtained a patent (No. 8,509) for, according to the patent application, a "simple and substantial eye-piece wherein ready access may be easily had to the glasses or lenses in order either to cleanse or repair them, as the case may require." Alvan Graham obtained a patent (No. 399,499) for a four-element, multipurpose photographic lens in 1889. Bausch & Lomb manufactured the rapid, rectilinear "Double Gauss" lenses, advertising them as "an epoch in the construction of Photographic Objectives."

As business grew, Alvan Clark & Sons hired about a half-dozen assistants, most of them European immigrants. Carl Axel Robert Lundin, a Swedish optician and mechanic, worked with the Clarks from 1874 until his death forty-one years later. In recognition of his work with telescopes, Lundin received a medal from the 1876 Centennial Exhibition, a diploma from the 1893 World's Columbian Exposition, fellowship in the American Association for the Advancement of Science, charter membership in the American Astronomical Society, and membership in the Swedish Society at Harvard University. Clark died in Cambridgeport, Massachusetts.

Alvan Clark & Sons figured importantly in the great expansion of astronomical facilities that occurred in the second half of the nineteenth century. Almost every American observatory built during this period and some observatories abroad housed an equatorial refracting telescope made, at least in part, by the Clarks. Their optical work was recognized as unexcelled anywhere in the world and was the first significant American contribution to astronomical instrument making.

• The only manuscript sources are scattered letters from the Clarks, which survive in the archives of the institutions that bought their telescopes. For additional biographical information, see William R. Dawes, "New Double Stars Discovered by Mr. Alvan Clark," *Monthly Notices of the Royal Astronomical Society* 17 (1857): 257–59, and Deborah Jean Warner, *Alvan Clark & Sons: Artists in Optics*, 2d ed. (1995).

DEBORAH JEAN WARNER

CLARK, Alvan Graham (10 July 1832–9 June 1897), telescope maker, was born in Fall River, Massachusetts, the son of Alvan Clark and Maria Pease. At the age of sixteen, after a good education, Clark went to work in a machine shop. A few years later he joined his father and brother and spent the rest of his career with Alvan Clark & Sons, the productive and renowned telescope makers of Cambridgeport, Massachusetts. He and Mary Willard, whom he married in 1865, had four children.

Like his father, Clark's forte was optics, and he figured or tested most of the large lenses produced in the Clark factory. After his father's death in 1887, Clark took responsibility for important objectives such as the 20-inch for the Denver Observatory, the 24-inch for the Lowell Observatory, the 24-inch Bruce photographic doublet for the Harvard College Observatory, the 36-inch visual achromatic objective lens and its photographic corrector installed at the Lick Observatory in 1887, and the 40-inch installed at the Yerkes Observatory in 1897. The 36-inch and 40-inch instruments were the largest refracting telescopes at the time they were built, and the 40-inch has never been surpassed. Actual work on many of these instruments, however, was entrusted to C. A. R. Lundin, a Swedish optician who had been with the Clarks since 1874 and who would take over the operation of the firm after Alvan Graham Clark's death.

Unlike most nineteenth-century American firms, Alvan Clark & Sons did not advertise their wares or show them off at local or international exhibitions. Others did the work for them. The Clark's large telescopes were amply described in the national press, their smaller ones often received local coverage, and their factory was featured on the cover of *Scientific American* in 1887. An English astronomer who visited the United States in 1876 wrote that "America is fortunate in possessing in Alvan Clark the greatest living master of the art of constructing large object-glasses of good definition." In 1885 a satisfied Clark customer declared the refracting telescope to be "the noblest instrument that man has yet constructed" and suggested that it was as "sublime and elevating" to contemplate the telescope and the men who made it as it was to contemplate the universe itself. An article in the 1890s described the Clark's work as "a source of pride to every American"; at a time when industry was rapidly industrializing, the Clarks continued to engage in "honest work, in which brain and hand wrought together," and they always put quality ahead of quantity. Another remarked that Alvan Graham Clark "carried lens making to the highest state of perfection the world has ever seen, so that a so called mechanical occupation was transferred to the realm of high art."

In January 1862, while testing the 18½-inch telescope that would eventually be mounted in the Dearborn Observatory in Chicago, Clark spotted the companion of Sirius, a star whose existence had been predicted in 1844 but that had never before been seen. In honor of this discovery, Clark received the Lalande Prize of the Paris Academy of Sciences in 1862. Clark found more than a dozen other interesting binaries in subsequent years, but he left the determination of their separations and position angles to others.

Clark went on three solar eclipse expeditions: to Shelbyville, Kentucky, in 1869, as a member of the United States Coast Survey party; to Jerez, Spain, in 1870, again as a member of a Coast Survey party; and to Creston, Wyoming, in 1878, with a party organized by the U.S. Naval Observatory. In 1870, using a simple single-prism spectroscope, Clark charted the spectrum of the aurora borealis.

In 1893, at the first meeting of the Congress of Astronomy and Astrophysics, Clark speculated on telescopes of the future. He was then working on the 40-inch telescope for the Yerkes Observatory and was confident that refractors (that is, telescopes that used lenses to gather and focus light) would continue to prove superior to reflectors (that is, telescopes with large mirrors). Moreover, there is "practically no limit" to their size. As it happened, however, Clark's prediction was wrong, and research astronomers were soon to prefer reflectors to refractors.

In 1889 Clark obtained a patent (No. 399,499) for a four-element, multipurpose photographic lens. Bausch & Lomb manufactured these rapid rectilinear, "double Gauss" type lenses, and advertisements touted them as "an epoch in the construction of Photographic Objectives." They did not, however, remain on the market for any length of time.

Clark was a member of the American Association for the Advancement of Science (1879), the American Academy of Arts and Sciences (1881), and the Société Astronomique de France (1894). He died in Cambridgeport.

• There are no known repositories of Clark's papers. Clark's major published works are "Possibilities of the Telescope," *Astronomy and Astro-Physics* 12 (1893): 319–20, and "Great Telescopes of the Future," *Astronomy and Astro-Physics* 12 (1893): 673–78. His work is discussed in the context of the family business in Deborah Jean Warner, *Alvan Clark & Sons: Artists in Optics* (1968). For a contemporary view on his discovery, see S. W. Burnham, "Double-Stars Discovered by Mr. Alvan G. Clark," *American Journal of Science* 17 (1879): 283–89. An obituary was written by Oliver C. Wendell, "Alvan Graham Clark," American Academy of Arts and Sciences, *Proceedings* 33 (1897): 520–24, and another is in the *Cambridge Chronicle*, 12 June 1897.

DEBORAH JEAN WARNER

CLARK, Bennett Champ (8 Jan. 1890–13 July 1954), senator and federal judge, was born Joel Bennett Clark in Bowling Green, Missouri, the son of James Beauchamp "Champ" Clark, a congressman, and Genevieve Bennett. As the son of a long-time Democratic congressman from Missouri and Speaker of the House of Representatives, young Clark was reared largely in the political environment of Washington, D.C. He graduated Phi Beta Kappa from the University of Missouri in 1913 and received a law degree from George Washington University in 1914. From 1913 to 1917 he served as parliamentarian in the House of Representatives and even wrote a manual on parliamentary procedures.

In 1917 he volunteered for the army, served in the American Expeditionary Force in Europe, and rose from the rank of captain to colonel by the time he left military service after the end of World War I. He was one of seventeen charter members of the American Legion, serving one year as national commander. After leaving the army, he practiced law in St. Louis.

Clark was over six feet tall and weighed more than 200 pounds. He was bright, had real political courage, and became an exceptionally able public speaker. He enjoyed good food, good drink, and good conversation. In 1922 he married Miriam Marsh of Iowa; the couple had three children, all sons. After her death in 1943, he married Violet Heming in 1945.

Clark's book, *John Quincy Adams: "Old Man Eloquent,"* was published in 1932. In that same year he won election to the U.S. Senate as a Democrat from Missouri. He was reelected in 1938. Senator Clark supported earlier liberal Democratic positions including antitrust policies and trade reciprocity, and he was committed to freedom of speech. Nonetheless, he was not really a New Dealer and voted against many of President Franklin D. Roosevelt's proposals, including the Agricultural Adjustment and National Recovery acts, veterans legislation, and court packing. As the Jeffersonian Democrat that he was, Clark objected to big government, big bureaucracy, big military, and large government indebtedness.

The two-thirds rule for nominations in Democratic national conventions had prevented his father from winning the Democratic presidential nomination in 1912. Consequently, Bennett Clark played a major role in doing away with that rule at the 1936 Democratic National Convention.

Like his father and his home state, Clark opposed American involvement in European wars and alliances. And along with North Dakota's Gerald P. Nye, from 1934 to 1936 Clark was an active member of the Senate special committee investigating the munitions industry. Clark wholly supported the committee's recommendations, including its proposal for government ownership of the munitions industries. He worked shoulder to shoulder with Nye and other leading noninterventionists in urging adoption of neutrality legislation designed to prevent American economic involvement in foreign wars and to limit the president's discretionary powers in applying neutrality restrictions. Like Nye he would have preferred more severe economic restrictions and more mandatory controls on the president than the Neutrality acts of 1935, 1936, and 1937 provided, but he worked for adoption and application of those as the best they could get.

Like most noninterventionists, Clark was not a pacifist. He favored building and maintaining sufficient military and naval forces to defend the United States in the Western Hemisphere. Nonetheless, he objected to what he saw as excessive military and naval appropriations urged in President Roosevelt's second term. He thought those preparations were not essential for national defense and were designed to wage war abroad.

After World War II erupted in Europe in 1939, Clark opposed Roosevelt's efforts to repeal the neutrality laws and to extend aid to the victims of aggression. Clark contended that the United States could not be half in war and half out. He feared that Roosevelt's steps-short-of-war to aid victims of Axis aggression were really steps-to-war, and he fought them with commanding vigor.

In 1941 both Senator and Miriam Clark were active in the America First Committee, the leading "isolationist" or noninterventionist pressure group appealing for mass support before the Japanese attack on Pearl Harbor. Miriam Clark was chair of the Washington, D.C., chapter of America First and became a member of the America First national committee. Senator Clark traveled all over the United States addressing America First rallies.

After the Japanese attack on Pearl Harbor on 7 December 1941, Clark ceased his noninterventionist activities, joined his fellow senators in voting for war against the Axis states, and supported the war effort. Nearly all who had opposed American entry into the war before Pearl Harbor, however, were portrayed as "isolationists," and their loyalty was suspect. Like most other noninterventionists in elective office at the time, Clark was rejected the next time he faced the voters, in 1944, in spite of the wide margins of his primary and general-election victories in 1932 and 1938.

With the death of Roosevelt in 1945, however, Clark's fellow Democrat from Missouri, Harry S. Truman, became president and appointed Clark an associate justice of the U.S. District Court of Appeals in the District of Columbia. He held that position until his death in Gloucester, Massachusetts.

• Clark's papers (along with his father's) are deposited in the Joint Collection of the University of Missouri Western Historical Manuscript Collection and the State Historical Society of Missouri, University of Missouri, Columbia. A large collection, it is open for research. The records of the Senate special committee investigating the munitions industry as well as the thirty-nine bound volumes of its hearings and documents and the seven volumes of its reports are in the National Archives, Washington, D.C. The papers of the Senate Foreign Relations Committee on which Clark served also are in the National Archives. A full scholarly biography of Clark has yet to be published. Among the theses written on his public career see Nancy L. King, "'Willing to Pay the Price for Peace': Senator Bennett Champ Clark and American Foreign Relations" (master's thesis, Univ. of Maryland-College Park, 1975). For a brief contemporary biographical account see Jack Alexander, "Missouri Dark Mule," *Saturday Evening Post*, 8 Oct. 1938, pp. 5–7, 32–37.

WAYNE S. COLE

CLARK, Bobby (16 June 1888–12 Feb. 1960), clown, was born Robert Edwin Clark in a church rectory (his grandfather was the church sexton) in Springfield, Ohio, the son of Victor Brown Clark, a railroad conductor, and Alice Marilla Sneed. His father died when Bobby was six. As a young boy Clark sang in the church choir and played the bugle. His fascination with outlandish costumes, which became one of his theatrical trademarks, was apparent at an early age. When he was in the fourth grade Bobby met Paul McCullough, four years his senior, and a close friendship was formed that lasted over thirty-five years. The two boys soon put together a bugling and tumbling act that they performed at the local YMCA. Clark and McCullough's act was received so favorably by the residents of the area that, at the ages of seventeen and twenty-one, respectively, they decided to embark upon a career in show business. They began to place advertisements in various theatrical publications. The response was favorable and Clark and McCullough, as they now called themselves, were hired by a minstrel troupe as tumblers, buglers, and handymen, with a combined weekly salary of twenty-five dollars. They were on their way.

As members of the minstrel troupe, Clark and McCullough were called upon to blow their bugles, perform some acrobatic stunts, and sing a few songs. After twelve weeks of travel and no pay, they were left stranded in a small town in Delaware. A second minstrel tour left them stranded in Florida with a joint treasury of eighteen cents. They managed to get to Atlanta, where they played their minstrel routine, enabling them to earn enough money to return to Springfield. They refined their tumbling act and were soon hired by the Hagenbeck-Wallace Circus. It was here that Clark decided that their future lay in comedy, and from that association evolved the Clark and McCullough act that so amused circus audiences for many years.

In 1906 the two youthful performers joined the Ringling Brothers Circus, where they polished up their act considerably. Their sole objective now was to make the audience laugh. In the process, McCullough became the foil and Clark the catalyst. During their six years of circus life, Clark honed his comedic skills by developing some of the routines that were to characterize his later work in vaudeville and musical comedy. These included improvising his own comedy skits, designing his bizarre costumes, and most importantly, adopting his famous painted-on glasses. Audiences were soon laughing as much at Clark's antics as they were at McCullough's acrobatic spills.

By 1912 Clark and McCullough were ready to move up the theatrical ladder to vaudeville. For some time Clark had been frustrated by the limitations the circus format had imposed on their act. Circus clowns are by and large mute, and their acts contain no dialogue. Clark, probably more than McCullough, sought a medium that would enable both of them to speak. Vaudeville was the popular medium of the time, and in December 1912 Clark and McCullough made their vaudeville debut in New Brunswick, New Jersey. Their act was mainly physical and initially the same one they had perfected in the circus; but as time went on, they substituted dialogue for some of their broader actions on stage. Their costumes were symbolic of their act. Clark wore oversized spectacles painted on with burnt cork, a battered top hat, tight-fitting pants, a faded top coat, and a pair of well-worn boots, and puffed on a huge cigar. McCullough sported an ancient moth-eaten fur coat, a straw hat, string tie, checkered suit, white shoes, and a silly hairline mustache, and carried a college pennant. Before long the two had become well-known performers on the B. F. Keith Vaudeville Circuit. After five years in vaudeville the team moved on to burlesque, where they enjoyed a successful stint as a part of the Columbia Burlesque Wheel.

In 1922 the musical comedy stage beckoned, and Clark and McCullough enjoyed their first foreign engagement in the London production of *Chuckles of 1922*, which was little more than a burlesque show. Irving Berlin, who had seen the *Chuckles* show, was impressed and signed Clark and McCullough to appear in his *Music Box Revue*, which opened in October of the same year. It was this show that marked the emergence of Clark and McCullough as a major comedy team. They appeared in another *Music Box Revue* and finally achieved stardom on Broadway in *The Ramblers* in 1926. The next few years were devoted to making sound movie shorts, but in 1930 Clark and McCullough returned to Broadway to star in George Gershwin and Ira Gershwin's *Strike Up the Band*, the most notable production they ever appeared in as a team. Other Broadway shows and short films followed, but by the time the team appeared in *Earl Carroll's Vanities* in 1936, McCullough was showing signs of severe depression. A brief stay in a sanitarium did not help. All the years of playing second fiddle to Bobby Clark's clowning had taken their toll, as did McCullough's realization that his half of the act was no longer necessary to Clark's success. At the end of the *Vanities* run McCullough committed suicide. Bobby Clark was devastated and went into seclusion for several months.

In the fall of 1936 Clark resumed his career, this time as a solo comic, and scored a huge success when he appeared opposite Fanny Brice in the second edition of that year's *Ziegfeld Follies*. There followed a number of successful musical comedies, including *Star and Garter*, *Mexican Hayride*, and *As the Girls Go*. Clark's last stage appearance was in the road company of *Damn Yankees* during the season of 1956–1957. He died in New York City.

Bobby Clark's comedy was unique in many ways, yet aspects of his comedic style resembled those of other comedians of his time. His loping walk was similar to that of Groucho Marx, his outlandish costumes appeared to resemble those of Ed Wynn, and he chased girls around just as Harpo Marx did. But the painted-on glasses were Clark's own creation, and they became his real trademark. No one cavorted or sang his way around a stage with the speed of Bobby Clark. Critics loved his work, and he was often referred to as the funniest man of his time—a fitting tribute to one of the last of the knockabout comedians.

• The best account of Clark's life and career is in the chapter on Clark in Stanley Green's excellent *The Great Clowns of Broadway* (1984). There is also useful material in Joe Laurie, Jr., *Vaudeville: From the Honky Tonks to the Palace* (1953), and Gerald Bordman, *American Musical Comedy: From Adonis to Dreamgirls* (1982). There are brief but pithy references to Clark in Ethan Mordden, *Broadway Babies: The People Who Made the American Musical* (1983), and in John E. DiMeglio, *Vaudeville, U.S.A.* (1973). John Lahr in his affectionate biography of his father, *Notes on a Cowardly Lion* (1969), relates some of Bert Lahr's delightful reminiscences of Clark. David Ewen writes of Clark's roles in many shows in his *New Complete Book of the American Theater* (1970). Charles and Louise Samuels, *Once upon a Stage: The Merry World of Vaudeville* (1974), have a sketch of both Clark and McCullough but must be read with caution.

CHARLES W. STEIN

CLARK, Catherine Taft (31 Dec. 1906–2 May 1986), business executive, was born in Whitewater, Wisconsin, the daughter of Warren G. Taft, a machinist, and Louise West. Taft attended public schools in Whitewater, but as her father died when she was a child, she was unable to attend college. Instead, at nineteen she took a job as secretary to the local college president, where she claimed to learn as much as a formally enrolled student. From there, Milwaukee was her next stop; she worked at Schuster's, a major department store, where she gained experience in retailing and marketing.

In 1931 Catherine Taft married a banker from Beloit, Russell J. Clark, and the couple settled in Oconomowoc, a town near Milwaukee. Russell Clark, an investment banker experienced in matters of finance, was a perfect complement to Catherine Clark, a woman of formidable business acumen. In 1934 she left Schuster's to devote herself to homemaking and raising her two children, only to return to the business world as soon as they came of school age.

In 1943 Clark discovered a rich, whole-wheat bread at Alfred Marsh's bakery in the neighboring town of Delafield. With a small amount of borrowed capital, she and her husband bought the bakery and acquired Marsh's oven, dough mixer, a delivery truck, and the recipe. They then started their own bakery in a small store on Main Street in Oconomowoc. Shortages during the war years slowed the growth of the business, but by 1946 she was baking and selling to some dozen gourmet groceries in the Milwaukee area. Clark was convinced that if people tasted her bread they would like it. To promote it, she enlisted a group of friends to distribute samples door-to-door in Madison, Waukesha, and Wauwatosa.

The bread was renamed Brownberry, a name taken from the brown wheat berries, freshly ground for the bread. This old-fashioned, hearty bread was made only from natural ingredients without preservatives. For a commercial bakery this was a very new idea in the 1940s.

As Clark put it herself, "I guess I always had a yen to make lots of money." The bread was priced higher than other breads, but the quality and flavor of the bread immediately won customers. The bakery doubled in production every year for the first five years, and Clark purchased more ovens, more mixers, a bread-wrapping machine, and more trucks. By 1954 she had plowed back $400,000 in earnings for a new plant in Oconomowoc, and in 1959, when the Clark family moved to San Francisco, she expanded her operation by purchasing other bakeries in California and Ohio. At the same time, her interest in the Oconomowoc bakery was unremitting, as she spent 70 percent of her time overseeing its operation.

The *Wall Street Journal* recognized this innovative entrepreneur in 1960 when it included her (the only woman among fourteen men) in its publication, "The New Millionaires and How They Made Their Fortunes." By 1960 Brownberry Ovens was making fifteen products, including six types of bread and pastries. Clark traveled to Europe a number of times to learn the secrets of other types of baked goods.

By the late 1960s, business had so expanded that Clark considered the possibility of a merger or sale but waited for the right offer. In 1972 Brownberry Ovens merged with the Peavey Company of Minneapolis. At the time of the merger, sales were $5.5 million per year, and the net after-tax profit for 1972 was $311,264. Even after the merger, Clark continued her personal involvement in the Wisconsin operation as chair of the Brownberry board of directors, commuting from San Francisco to oversee the Oconomowoc bakery. Through subsequent mergers the plant was acquired by Best Foods.

Retired from management after 1979, Clark was still an active woman. At age seventy she became a syndicated columnist, writing a monthly article on the process of home-baking bread. Her concern was that the art of home bread baking might be lost, and she hoped that the "heavenly taste sensation of butter melting on thick slabs of fragrant homemade bread warm from the oven" would be recaptured by young homemakers.

Clark served as a member of the Wisconsin governor's committee on industry in the early 1960s. In 1972 she was cited as one of two of Wisconsin's business executives of the year. In 1979 she received the Horatio Alger Award in recognition of "having overcome unusual early disadvantages to achieve outstanding success in life."

While Clark was extremely proud of the accomplishments of women in business, she was solidly in touch with women's reality. In 1976, in response to a reporter's question as to whether it was easier for a woman to get to the top today, she replied, "It is not easy to climb up; not even for men. There is a lot of political maneuvering. For a woman to get equal pay, she has to be smarter and she has to work harder." Clark was an individualist and attributed her success to the maxim with which most women of her generation would agree, saying, "The best way to get men to do a good job working under a woman is to make them think that her suggestions are really theirs."

As a pioneer in the use of natural ingredients for her baked goods, Catherine Clark was ahead of her time, but she also was a woman of wide accomplishments and even wider interests. In both Oconomowoc (including nearby Milwaukee) and San Francisco she was active in civic and cultural affairs. She found the time to play the flute, bicycle the streets of Oconomowoc, work a berry and vegetable garden, develop a California winery, restore an old San Francisco firehouse, bring up two children, and spend Christmases in Vienna while building a fortune and supporting cultural institutions in both communities. She died in San Francisco.

• Newspaper and magazine accounts of Clark's life are in the Oconomowoc Public Library. A scrapbook of Clark's accomplishments is held at the Oconomowoc Historical Society. Information for this article was also gleaned from informal interviews with Winnifred Eschweiler of Hartland, Wisconsin, and Ruth W. Behling of Oconomowoc.

ELIZABETH HITZ

CLARK, Champ (7 Mar. 1850–2 Mar. 1921), Speaker of the House of Representatives, was born James Beauchamp Clark in Lawrenceburg, Anderson County, Kentucky, the son of John Hampton Clark, a traveling dentist and buggy maker, and Althea Jane Beauchamp. Although he received only a rudimentary education, Clark began teaching school himself at the age of fifteen. From 1867 to 1870 he attended Kentucky University (now Transylvania University), from which he was expelled for shooting at a fellow student. In 1872 entered Bethany College in West Virginia and graduated in 1873 after a single year of study. The prizes he received at commencement earned him the presidency of Marshall College in West Virginia for a year. He then completed the course of study at the Cincinnati Law School in 1875. While in law school, he shortened his name to "Champ," which would fit better in a newspaper headline. In 1881 he married Genevieve Bennett; they had four children, one of whom was Bennett Champ Clark, a U.S. senator.

In 1875 Clark moved to Missouri—first to Moberly, then Renick, and then the town of Louisiana—where he taught school from 1875 to 1876 and practiced law from 1876 to 1890. He became active in Democratic politics, serving as a presidential elector in 1880 and as prosecuting attorney for Pike County for four years at the end of the decade. In 1888 he won election to the Missouri legislature, where he wrote the state's Australian ballot law and antitrust legislation. From that springboard, he sought election in 1890 to the U.S. House of Representatives from Missouri's Ninth District. His effort to unseat the incumbent, Richard Norton, failed, but he won the Democratic nomination two years later. Clark gained national attention when he addressed an audience at New York's Tammany Hall on 4 July 1893. The Democratic party in Missouri, he said, "is true as the needle to the pole, can't be seduced, can't be bought, can't be bullied" (Morrison, "America's Ring-Tailed Roarer," p. 61). In an era that esteemed effective oratory, this triumph made Clark a sought-after lecturer on the Chautauqua speaking circuit for the next twenty years.

Clark served one term in Congress, where he supported the free coinage of silver, an income tax, lower tariffs, and the direct election of senators. Defeated in the Republican national landslide of 1894, he was reelected in 1896 and served continuously until 1920. The district that had been known as the "Bloody Ninth" became the "peaceful Ninth" during those years (Morrison, "Political Biography," p. 97). He served on the House Ways and Means Committee and the Foreign Affairs Committee in the Democratic minority that lasted until 1911. He supported the war with Spain in 1898 but criticized the William McKinley administration's annexation of Hawaii and the Philippine Islands.

As his oratorical reputation for defending the Democrats grew, Clark became a rising figure in the House minority. He was a candidate for the party leadership in 1903 but lost to John Sharp Williams of Mississippi. He then became a loyal ally of Williams. In 1904 Clark served as permanent chairman of the Democratic National Convention, an assignment that also helped his chances of becoming minority leader.

When Williams was elected to the Senate in 1907, he gave Clark advance notice of his candidacy. The Missourian rounded up support from his colleagues and received the unanimous endorsement of the caucus in early 1908. By the time Clark assumed a leadership role for the Democrats, the presidency of Theodore Roosevelt and intraparty differences over the protective tariff had made the Republicans more divided and faction-ridden than at any previous time during Clark's tenure in Congress. The dictatorial rule of Speaker Joseph G. Cannon added to Republican factionalism during the first year of the presidency of William Howard Taft.

Clark and his party endeavored to capitalize on the mounting disarray of the GOP in the House during the special session that began in the spring of 1909. His initial attempt at working with the Republican opponents of Cannon, known as "Insurgents," collapsed when Democratic defections prevented a reduction in the Speaker's power. In the battle over the Payne-Aldrich Tariff, Clark kept his party together and intensified internal Republican divisions about protective tariff legislation. When the House convened in its regular session in the fall of 1909, Clark led the fight to curb the power of Cannon that ended in victory in the spring of 1910. Throughout the rest of the year, Clark kept the House minority as a unit to amend the measures that Taft and the Republicans offered in a more progressive direction.

In the election of 1910, Clark and his party benefited from the tension between Taft and Roosevelt, the legacy of "Cannonism," and the internal bickering of the progressive and conservative Republicans. The Democrats used the issue of inflation as a way to counter GOP support for the protective tariff. When the votes were counted, the Democrats had gained control of the House of Representatives for the first time since 1894. Clark became Speaker in March 1911, when another special session convened to take up a trade agreement with Canada. His skillful parliamentary leadership had brought the Democrats back to power. One progressive reporter at the time called him "a man of commanding presence, a ready, forceful and often witty speaker" who had "been steadily gathering strength and leadership in his party" (Sarasohn, p. 61).

As Speaker in the 1911 sessions of Congress, Clark continued to hold the Democrats together and to make issues regarding tariff reduction and antitrust policy that shaped the party's agenda for the 1912 presidential election. He found that the fight against Cannon had reduced the Speaker's power, and he served not as the sole leader of his party but as a kind of coequal with the majority leader and the powerful chairmen of committees. By then Clark was being mentioned as a possible candidate himself. He had the support of western Democrats who had long followed William Jennings Bryan, he won the endorsement of William Randolph Hearst and his newspapers, and his record as Speaker had been better than observers had expected. His backers depicted him "as a rock of safety" (Gould, p. 153).

Clark's main challenger for the nomination in 1912 was the new Democratic governor of New Jersey, Woodrow Wilson, who had surged to the front of the nomination race in 1911 because of his fresh face and progressive record. With the Republicans split between Taft and Roosevelt, the Democratic nomination became more of a prize in early 1912. As that happened, the mainstream of the Democratic party looked to Clark as a safe alternative to the unknown Wilson. The largest obstacle to Clark's candidacy was the perception that he was a political lightweight. One element in that judgment was the campaign song "You Gotta Quit Kickin' My Dawg Around." Another was the Speaker's propensity for indiscreet statements. During the debate over trade reciprocity with Canada, Clark observed that he hoped to annex "every foot of the British North American possessions, no matter how far north they may extend" (Gould, p. 163). Clark also faced Bryan's reluctance to see the Speaker obtain the Democratic nomination. Clark and Bryan had long been at odds over the leadership of the Democratic party, and Bryan feared that the Speaker would sell out to the conservative wing of the party.

During the first half of 1912 Clark became the Democratic frontrunner. In April and May he outpaced Wilson and arrived at the national convention in Baltimore with nearly 500 delegates committed or leaning toward him, but he was still short of the two-thirds needed for the nomination. In the political jockeying before the convention opened, Clark made a crucial mistake. When party conservatives selected Alton B. Parker, the nominee in 1904, as the temporary chairman, Bryan wired all the candidates, urging them to block Parker. Wilson agreed, but Clark did not, which made Wilson seem a progressive champion. Later, because Clark had the backing of the conservative New York delegation, Bryan dramatically changed his delegate vote from Clark to Wilson on the fourteenth ballot. Wilson won on the forty-sixth ballot. Clark never forgave Bryan for denying him the Democratic nomination and probably the presidency in 1912. In his defeat, the Speaker attached less weight to the deals the Wilson forces had made with party bosses in Illinois and Indiana.

Clark cooperated during the enactment of Wilson's New Freedom program in his first term, although he broke with the president over the issue of the Panama Canal tolls in 1914. When the United States entered World War I, however, Clark opposed the war and the draft. He joined with other agrarian Democrats in standing against the administration's war policies. The Speaker's position contributed to the disunity of his party on Capitol Hill that led to the Republican resurgence in 1918. Clark lost his Speakership when the Republicans regained control of the House in 1919. He was defeated in the Republican landslide of 1920 and died a few months later in Washington, D.C. His two-volume memoirs, published the year before his death, did little to enhance his historical standing.

Clark's reputation has never escaped the foolishness of his 1912 campaign song and the criticisms of reporters who favored Wilson for president. Modern scholars regard him as an effective party leader who revitalized the House Democrats through the use of the Democratic caucus and increased power for the committees. Clark is one of the underrated Speakers in the history of Congress and an important figure in the evolution of the modern Democratic party during the era of Wilson.

• Clark's papers were long believed to have been destroyed, but a substantial collection of family and political papers is now at the Western Historical Manuscripts Collection at the University of Missouri, Columbia. Other Clark letters are in the papers of William Jennings Bryan and Woodrow Wilson at the Library of Congress. Clark's own writings include his autobiography, *My Quarter Century in American Politics* (2 vols., 1920), and numerous articles for contemporary periodicals, such as "The Political Situation in the United States," *Forum* 43 (June 1910): 634–37; "The Duty of the Democrats," *Independent* 72 (25 Jan. 1912): 176–79; and "Democracy Is Safe," *Forum* 58 (Nov. 1917): 517–25. For assessments of Clark in his own time, see Ray Stannard Baker, "What about the Democratic Party?" *American Magazine* 70 (June 1910): 147–60; and Alfred H. Lewis, "The Honorable Champ," *Cosmopolitan* 51 (Nov. 1911): 760–65. Geoffrey F. Morrison, "A Political Biography of Champ Clark" (Ph.D. diss., St. Louis Univ., 1971), is available from University Microfilms. Morrison also published "Champ Clark and the Rules Revolution of 1910," *Capitol Studies* 2 (Winter 1974): 43–56, and "America's Ring-Tailed Roarer: Speaker of the House Champ Clark," *Gateway Heritage* 10 (Spring 1990): 57–63. *The Papers of Woodrow Wilson*, ed. Arthur S. Link et al., vols. 23–29 (1977–1993), shed light on many aspects of Clark's relations with Wilson. Lewis L. Gould, *Reform and Regulation: American Politics from Roosevelt to Wilson* (1986; repr. 1996), and David Sarasohn, *The Party of Reform: Demo-*

crats in the Progressive Era (1989), consider Clark as a party leader. An excellent obituary is in the *New York Times*, 3 Mar. 1921.

LEWIS L. GOULD

CLARK, Charles (24 May 1811–17 Dec. 1877), governor of Mississippi and Confederate general, was born the son of James Clark and Charlotte Alter, farmers. The third of ten children in a Methodist family that had moved from Maryland to Ohio, Clark graduated from Augusta College in Kentucky in 1831. He then accompanied an uncle to Mississippi, read law and then practiced law and taught school in Natchez. In 1835 he moved to Fayette in Jefferson County upon his marriage to Ann Eliza Darden, who was to bear him a son and three daughters. Espousing the pro-banking and internal improvements policies of Clay Whiggery, he served in the Mississippi House of Representatives from 1838 to 1844. During the Mexican War he raised a volunteer company and served as colonel of the Second Mississippi Infantry.

By the 1850s Clark had established himself as a successful and wealthy trial lawyer. His legal fees were often paid in land, and he pyramided them into a large plantation in Bolivar County. In 1851 he moved to "Doro," his new plantation, and by 1860 he owned 3,000 acres and fifty-three slaves. A Unionist during the secession crisis of 1850–1851, he became increasingly radical in his politics as he amassed his fortune in slave property and represented the large planting interests of Bolivar County in the legislature from 1856 to 1861. After his defeat as a Whig candidate for Congress in 1857, he switched to the Democratic party. A delegate to the Democratic national conventions in Charleston and Baltimore, he backed John C. Breckinridge for the presidency in 1860 on a southern plank of congressional protection for slavery in the territories.

Although defeated in his bid as an immediate secessionist in the election for the Mississippi secession convention, Clark was to play a leading role in the Confederate history of Mississippi. He was appointed Jefferson F. Davis's replacement as major general of Mississippi state troops and on 22 May 1861 accepted a commission as a brigadier general in the Confederate army. He commanded a division under Albert Sidney Johnston at Shiloh, where he was wounded in the shoulder. He later took part in Breckinridge's, assault on the Union lines at Baton Rouge. Here, in August 1862, a bullet shattered his right thigh, crippling him for the rest of his life. He was taken prisoner and paroled in late 1862.

In October 1863, Clark was elected as Mississippi's second and last Confederate governor. Despite a fiery inaugural speech exhorting his fellow Mississippians never to yield, Clark lacked the financial and political resources to shore up the crumbling war effort. Vicksburg and its surrounding plantation districts and Jackson, the state capital, had already been lost to Union forces, and the state government had to relocate to Macon. Clark's efforts to reorganize state forces for defensive purposes were hamstrung by a bankrupt treasury and the breakdown of political control throughout much of the state. His relations with the Confederate government in Richmond quickly became entangled in a controversy over Confederate policies of impressing slaves and suspending the writ of habeas corpus. By late 1864 Clark was a caretaker for a state government whose authority had collapsed, and on 22 May 1865 he formally surrendered the state to Union forces.

Taken prisoner at the war's end, Clark was held at Fort Pulaski, near Savannah, until he was paroled upon taking an oath of allegiance in September 1865. Clark resumed his law practice but took little part in Mississippi's Reconstruction politics. The new Democratic administration appointed him chancellor of his judicial district in 1876, and shortly thereafter Clark died at his Bolivar plantation.

• Clark's papers are at the Mississippi Department of Archives and History in the Charles Clark Papers and Correspondence collection. There is no biography, but sketches of his life can be found in *Biographical and Historical Memoirs of Mississippi* (1891), and Robert Lowry and William H. McCardle, *A History of Mississippi* (1891). Florence W. Sillers, *History of Bolivar County, Mississippi* (1948), and Annie E. Jacobs, "The Master of Doro Plantation: An Epic of the Old South," typescript in the Mississippi Department of Archives and History, provide additional material. Clark's record as Confederate governor is covered in John K. Bettersworth, *Mississippi in the Confederacy* (1961), and W. Buck Yearns, ed., *The Confederate Governors* (1985).

WILLIAM L. BARNEY

CLARK, Charles Edward (19 Dec. 1889–13 Dec. 1963), lawyer, law professor, dean of Yale Law School, and federal appellate judge, was born in Woodbridge, Connecticut, the son of Samuel Clark, a successful dairy farmer, and Pauline Marquand. Clark kept farmer's hours, believed in the redeeming virtue of hard work and candor, and accepted the conventional personal and family mores of New England Calvinism. His political opinions would change from New England Republicanism to New Deal Democracy, but his personal values remained a constant, rooted in many generations of Connecticut yeomanry.

Clark graduated first in his class at Yale College (1911) and Yale Law School (1913). He would always value academic achievement. A math whiz, he believed that mathematics was the best preparation for law, a faith that underlay his classic empirical studies of the disposition of lawsuits. In 1915 he married Dorothy Gregory, moved from New Haven to the neighboring town of Hamden, and reared two children.

Clark practiced law from 1913 to 1919 in New Haven, specializing in estates and real estate, found time to coauthor a classic treatise on Connecticut probate law and to begin his study of covenants (agreements) that bound successive owners of land to the original terms of the sale. Unfulfilled by the practices of law, looking for intellectual challenge, and deeply devoted to Yale, he accepted a post at Yale Law School in 1919 and never cut those ties.

At Yale, Clark played a crucial role in the two events that shaped modern American legal thought and activity: the emergence of the jurisprudence of "legal realism" and the so-called "litigation explosion." Clark was one of the first and most consistent legal realists. The realists attacked the notion that law was a science of formal rules and called instead for a study of how cases were actually handled in real courts. What to other realists was a romantic quest was to Clark a sensible and lifelong commitment to the empirical study of the outcome of law and law enforcement. A prolific researcher and writer in the cause of legal realism, he was also its chief sponsor as dean of Yale Law School, using it as what Myres S. McDougal, a colleague, called "a litmus test" to measure candidates for faculty posts. When Clark resigned his deanship to assume a federal appellate seat in 1939, legal realism at Yale never fully recovered.

Clark used social science tools, including early computers, to pinpoint flaws in federal, state, and local legal systems. His findings challenged the most sacred shibboleth of trial practice—the value of the jury. Clark's study of legal procedure in Connecticut revealed that in the vast majority of civil cases, jury verdicts were very similar to bench decisions, juries cost more than they were worth, and jury verdicts were appealed—with more cost and delay—twice as often as judges' findings. In the course of his comments on the jury process, Clark reported that the courts of Connecticut were not the common law bastions that less empirical commentators believed but were quasi-administrative agencies handling debt collection and management of divorce decrees. That view of courts has become conventional wisdom.

Clark was also the chief draftsman of the Federal Rules of Civil Procedure (1935–1938)—the rules that still govern trial practice in federal courts. The new rules profoundly changed the way in which lawsuits were conducted by increasing the scope of pretrial discovery and the authority of trial judges to manage litigation in pretrial conferences. These far-reaching changes led to more open courts and a veritable flood of litigation.

In the midst of the Great Depression crisis, there was no more glaring failure of law than the delay, confusion, and denial of justice occasioned by arcane and antiquated procedural technicalities. The obvious answer was massive refashioning of the rules of pleading a lawsuit in federal court. For Clark, this was an opportunity for application of realist principles—reform of procedure by merging outdated common law pleading with the simpler methods of making a claim in equity. Although the ideal of procedural reform had been introduced by corporate lawyers at the American Bar Association to protect the interests of their clients, Clark saw simplified procedure as an aid to any plaintiff or defendant who wanted a case heard and determined on its merits, not as a weapon for the well-financed corporate bar.

In the spring of 1933, Clark found an ally—Connecticut's Homer Cummings, Franklin Delano Roosevelt's new attorney general. Cummings, prodded by Clark, convinced the first New Deal Congress to pass the Enabling Act of 1934, permitting the Supreme Court to revise pleading in the lower federal courts. Clark, chosen as the draftsman of the new rules, led a blue-ribbon collection of law professors and lawyers through two years of labor in the direction of more equitable, open, and flexible rules of procedure. Clark's mark was on the whole and in 1954 New Jersey Chief Justice Arthur T. Vanderbilt called Clark "the maestro of all things procedural."

Clark was offered a post on the D.C. circuit in 1937. He wanted very much to be a federal appellate court judge and strongly supported Roosevelt and the New Deal, including the plan to reorganize the Supreme Court in 1937, but he declined the judgeship offered that summer because he believed that his work at Yale was not yet done. In 1939, at the urging of his former Yale colleague and good friend William O. Douglas, newly appointed to the U.S. Supreme Court, and Clark's many other friends and former students and colleagues in Washington, FDR asked him to serve on the Second Circuit Court of Appeals. Clark accepted, in large measure because he believed the second circuit was the finest bench in the land. On it sat two of the greatest jurists of their day, Augustus N. Hand and Learned Hand. The circuit covered New York, Connecticut, Vermont, and Puerto Rico. Clark got one of the Connecticut seats and served until his death twenty-four years later.

From the bench he continued to participate in the empirical work of legal realism and took an active part in the various conferences of judges on his circuit. He chaired the statistics committee of the National Judicial Conference, pleading for efficiency in administration of courts' dockets. On the bench as at Yale he insisted that energetic administration of the law materially aided justice, and he lobbied for the passage of state procedural reform acts.

On the court Clark was an indefatigable worker and a much-respected judicial craftsman, but some of his dissents became legendary. Privately he conceded that the court had become so conservative that he felt his dissents meant more than his concurrences. In long-standing dialogues with Jerome Frank, another Yale realist on the court, and with the two Hands, Clark fashioned a jurisprudence of realism. His correspondence with the other judges demonstrated his dogged faith in the importance of facts rather than an obstinate adherence to outmoded doctrines and his belief that only informed judicial discretion could level the playing field for the parties.

Clark was an even stronger supporter of First Amendment principles. He sat on the panel of the second circuit that heard the appeals of contempt proceedings against alleged Communists for refusing to testify before the Congress, as, for example, in the 1947 *U.S. v. Josephson* case. Dissenting from his brethren on these panels, Clark criticized the Smith

Act of 1940—under which the Communists had been prosecuted—for violating guarantees of free speech essential to a democracy. Clark also spoke publicly against the mind-deadening scare tactics of the McCarthyites; he quietly but persistently marshaled the liberal legal community against the "red scare." Clark died after a full day of work in his office in New Haven, a short walk from his beloved Yale Law School.

• The Clark papers are housed at Sterling Memorial Library, Yale University. Clark was the author of six legal casebooks on pleading and procedure and real covenants; eleven reports, including *A Study of the Business of the Federal Courts* (1934) and *A Study of Law Administration in Connecticut* (1937); 157 articles, some of which were widely reprinted; twenty-five comments; and thirty-six published addresses and lectures. Clark wrote thousands of opinions while he sat on the Second Circuit Federal Court of Appeals; a bibliography of these opinions, compiled by Solomon C. Smith, reference librarian at Yale Law School, was published as number 16 of the Yale Law Library Publications (Oct. 1968). For additional information on Clark, see Peninah Petruck, ed., *Judge Charles Edward Clark* (1991); the encomia gathered in *Yale Law Journal* 73 (Nov. 1963): 1–13; and the introduction to Charles Alan Wright and Harry M. Reasoner, eds., *Procedure—The Handmaiden of Justice* (1965).

PETER CHARLES HOFFER

CLARK, Charles Heber (11 July 1841–10 Aug. 1915), journalist and humorist, known by the pseudonym "Max Adeler," was born in Berlin, Maryland, the son of Annabella McCullough and William James Clark. Two years after Clark's birth, his father, an itinerant Episcopal clergyman, moved his family to Churchtown, Pennsylvania, where his abolitionist sympathies were more acceptable to his congregation. In 1856 financial problems forced the family to live apart, and at age fifteen Clark found himself in Philadelphia, where he took a series of low-paying jobs. He served the Union cause as a member of the Blue Reserves for about one month in 1862 and slightly longer in the summer of 1863.

Clark's career in journalism began in June 1865, when the *Philadelphia Inquirer* hired him as a reporter. He had found his niche, and about two months later he became one of the paper's editors, writing both editorials and book reviews. In 1867 he accepted an editorial position with the Philadelphia *Daily Evening Bulletin.* In addition to writing editorials and music and drama criticism, Clark contributed humorous sketches, which were widely reprinted, many first under the pseudonym "John Quill" and then as "Max Adeler" (the name of a character in a storybook that Clark had enjoyed as a boy). It was the Max Adeler persona, an unwittingly comic journalist, that made Clark famous. His humor, like that of some of his contemporaries, often depends upon a kind of exaggeration derived from the tall tale tradition and the literary burlesque.

In 1871 Clark married Clara Lukens, the daughter of a wealthy Quaker, who in 1875 helped Clark purchase a share of the *Philadelphia Evening Bulletin* (as it had been renamed in 1870) and in 1876 bought the young couple a large house in the village of Conshohocken, near Philadelphia, where Clark lived the rest of his life. The Clarks had five children.

By 1882 Clark had published six books. *The Noble Pile* (1869), a pamphlet burlesque of the dedication proceedings for the *Sunday Transcript* building, was followed by five Max Adeler titles. Of these, the most successful was *Out of the Hurly-Burly* (1874), a blend of grotesque humor and sentimentality focusing on the trials and tribulations of small-town life. The American talent for invention, a frequent object of Clark's humor, here takes the form of a combination stepladder, ironing board, and settee with a will of its own. The book (thanks in part to the skill of one of its illustrators, Arthur B. Frost, who also illustrated Clark's next two books) sold about one million copies during Clark's lifetime.

One of Clark's stories, "Professor Baffin's Adventures," first published in a British Christmas annual (1880) and republished as the title story in *The Fortunate Island and Other Stories* (1882), seems to have inspired Mark Twain's *A Connecticut Yankee in King Arthur's Court* (1889). Clark's story describes the experiences of an American professor and his daughter who, after a shipwreck, wash up on an island that had broken off and drifted away from England during Arthurian times.

In 1882 Clark sold his share of the *Bulletin* and purchased a trade journal, the *Textile Record of America*, which he published and edited for twenty years. During this period he all but abandoned the writing of fiction, which he considered frivolous, and focused primarily on economic affairs, using editorials, speeches, pamphlets, and, on two occasions, testimony before congressional committees to promote the protective tariff and, later, bimetallism (the return to both a gold and silver standard for American currency). He also helped organize the Manufacturers' Club of Philadelphia, whose journal he edited from 1887 to 1896.

A devout churchgoer, Clark taught Sunday school for nearly forty years, switching from the Episcopal church to the Presbyterian in 1895 in protest over what he regarded as excessive ritualism. One of his Sunday school pupils, J. Elwood Lee, made Clark president of the company Lee founded in 1888 for manufacturing surgical instruments. The company flourished, and when it merged with Johnson & Johnson in 1905, Clark became a director. His financial gains from this venture enabled Clark to sell the *Textile Record* in 1903 and retire from regular journalism.

Clark returned to the committed writing of fiction and after 1900 published three novels under his own name. Of these the most interesting is *The Quakeress* (1905), a story of a young Quaker woman (modeled on Clara Lukens Clark) during the Civil War who falls in love with a charming but unprincipled southerner. Clark's reputation rests, however, on his earlier, humorous works.

After the death of his first wife in 1895, Clark married Elizabeth Killé Clark in 1897. He died in Eagles Mere, Pennsylvania.

• Some Clark papers, including a typescript of his autobiography (written 1905–1912), are in private hands. The autobiography, edited by David Ketterer, was published as *Charles Heber Clark, a Family Memoir* (1995). The Franklin Inn Club Papers, held by the Pennsylvania Historical Society, Philadelphia, include a file on Clark and three Clark typescripts in boxes that deal with entertainment for the club. The Temple University library has a file on Clark containing clippings from the Philadelphia *Daily Evening Bulletin.*

Additional Clark titles include *Elbow Room* (1876), *Her Second Husband* (a play; 1877), *Random Shots* (1878), *Transformations* (1883), *Captain Bluitt: A Tale of Old Turley* (1901), *Things Generally* (a collection of items not assembled by Clark from his 1875–1877 humorous column in *Street and Smith's New York Weekly*; 1902), *In Happy Hollow* (1903), and *By the Bend of the River* (a retrospective collection; 1914).

Aside from Clark's autobiography, the best source of information is David Philip Dussere, "A Critical Biography of Charles Heber Clark ('Max Adeler'): American Journalist and Humorist" (Ph.D. diss., Univ. of Arkansas, 1974), which includes a full bibliography of primary and secondary sources. See also Frederic L. Clark, "Charles Heber Clark," *Bulletin* [Historical Society of Montgomery County, Pa.] 3 (Apr. 1943): 333–47. On the Quill/Adeler/Twain connections see David Ketterer, "'Professor Baffin's Adventures' by Max Adeler: The Inspiration for *A Connecticut Yankee in King Arthur's Court*?" *Mark Twain Journal* 24, no. 1 (1986): 24–34 (revised and included in *A Family Memoir*), and "'The Fortunate Island' by Max Adeler: Its Publication History and *A Connecticut Yankee*," *Mark Twain Journal* 29, no. 2 (1991): 28–32; and Horst H. Kruse, "Mark Twain's *A Connecticut Yankee:* Reconsiderations and Revisions," *American Literature* 62, no. 3 (1990): 464–83, and "Literary Old Offenders: Mark Twain, John Quill, Max Adeler, and Their Plagiarism Duels," *Mark Twain Journal* 29, no. 2 (1991): 10–27. A reprinting of Clark's "The Women's Millennium" (the first and most significant of his Quill sketches), edited with an introduction by Ketterer, appears in *Science-Fiction Studies* 15, no. 1 (1988): 82–87.

DAVID KETTERER

CLARK, Daniel (1766–13 Aug. 1813), merchant, diplomat, and territorial delegate, was born in Sligo, Ireland. Although his parents' names are unknown, his family's wealth and connections were sufficient to provide him with an education at Eton and other English schools. Declining fortunes in Ireland prompted the Clarks in 1785 or 1786 to emigrate to America, where they settled in Germantown, outside of Philadelphia.

Clark's uncle Colonel Daniel Clark, a wealthy merchant and planter in Spanish Louisiana, offered his nephew a position as clerk in his New Orleans counting house, where Clark began working in December 1786. Through his engaging personality and extraordinarily keen business sense, the young Irishman rapidly earned a partnership in the firm, assumed a respected place in the upper levels of French society, and gained the friendship of the Spanish governor, Don Estaban Miró, who gave him a place in his secretary's office. Clark secured similar official and personal connections with successive Spanish governors and their intendants. Official reports containing important information from the Cabildo and the commandancies crossed his desk, and he used that information to economic and political advantage.

As dependence on American trade increased and the opportunities multiplied, Clark in 1793 formed a lucrative partnership with Daniel Coxe of Philadelphia, collected commissions from other American-based counting houses, and bought and sold cargoes. He sliced through the maze of Spanish commercial regulations at dockside to assure low duties and the rapid movement of cargoes to the marketplace. Successfully circumventing Spanish regulations, he directed the flow of specie to American merchants and earned the appellation "merchant prince" of New Orleans.

Clark's diplomatic career began in 1798, when the Mississippi Territory was organized. Andrew Ellicott, the American boundary commissioner in Natchez, asked Clark to serve as the temporary American vice consul in New Orleans pending the arrival of a regular consul. Governor Manuel de Gayoso agreed to his appointment, and Clark, who did not become an American citizen until late in 1798, came to represent American interests. He quickly gained trade concessions that allowed American vessels to carry goods to and from New Orleans on the same terms as Spanish ships and permitted exporters to ship goods from New Orleans to American territory on the Mississippi without payment of any duty. Spanish officials rejected the two regular consuls from Washington, and Clark retained his position as temporary consul until Thomas Jefferson secured his appointment in 1801. As consul he became a central figure in the transfers of Louisiana.

Clark's reports to Jefferson, James Madison, and Congress from 1801 to 1803 proved the best source of information on Spanish policy and plans, economic conditions, and the attitudes of the people in the colony. Beginning in December 1802 he informed Jefferson and Madison of the various Spanish and American schemes that focused on the future of the new western states as well as the rumors concerning Louisiana's transfer to France. Earlier, in June 1802, he reported, too, that Spain intended to close New Orleans to American trade. Such action would be disastrous to westerners and to Clark's own expanding business interests. Clark had inherited his uncle's estate and acquired large property holdings on the Ouachita, in West Florida, and in New Orleans, where he had established a ropewalk. He was senior partner in the new company of Chew and Relf, and he had acquired ships with which he planned to export cotton to England. In the summer of 1802 he visited London and Liverpool to arrange credit for this new enterprise and took the opportunity to visit Paris to learn more of the impending transfer of Louisiana from Spain to France.

Clark was alarmed when French officials scoffed at the possibility of trade agreements with the Americans. Equally disturbing news greeted him on his return to New Orleans—the Spanish had closed the port to American trade in October 1802. He hastened to Natchez to speak to William Charles Coles Claiborne, governor of the Mississippi Territory. He advocated immediate military action to seize New Orleans before the French arrived in force. News of the American purchase in April 1803 brought relief that quickly gave way to concern about Spanish hostility. Clark's influence among the Gallic leadership and the formidable armed force he organized to resist any attempt to interfere ensured that the transfer proceeded without incident.

During the uncertainties surrounding the transfers, Clark formed a disparaging opinion of Claiborne's leadership qualities, and he resented Claiborne's appointment as governor of the new territory. Clark had the trust and confidence of the Gallic population and some of the new American residents, who resented the governor's dictatorial powers, and he became the focus around which the Gallic opposition rallied. When he refused service on the governor's council in 1804, the French leadership followed his lead, refused appointment, and embarrassed the governor. Clark's influence and popularity gained signatures on the Louisiana Remonstrance that commanded the attention of Congress. The grievances chronicled Claiborne's inadequacies, condemned his extensive powers, criticized common law innovations, censured the embargo on slave importations, demanded early statehood, and led to the establishment of an elective legislature.

The new territorial government degenerated with a series of disputes between the Gallics and the Anglo-Americans, made worse by Claiborne's persistent vetoes. The legislature, in revolt against Claiborne, elected Clark as territorial delegate to Congress in 1806. Clark spent his single term in Congress associated with the Federalists, trying to have Claiborne removed, and attempting to advance his own career. His taunts led Claiborne to issue a challenge to a duel, which Clark accommodated. The governor suffered a painful wound, and Clark received applause.

The nemesis to Clark's promising political career proved to be his alleged association with Aaron Burr and, more specifically, his condemnation of General James Wilkinson, who had been compromised by his association with Burr. In cooperation with John Randolph, Clark provided the congressional committee investigating Wilkinson with evidence of the general's treachery. Following Jefferson's lead, the press vilified Clark and glorified the general. Not even the publication of Clark's book *Proofs of the Corruption of Gen. James Wilkinson* (1809), could restore his popularity. Clark retired from public life and attended to his ever expanding business interests. Early in 1813 he moved to one of his plantations in New Orleans, where he died.

Clark never married, but he did establish a relationship with Marie Zulime Carriere Des Granges. They had two daughters. Litigation over his extensive estate dragged through the courts from 1834 to 1890.

• No collection of Clark papers is extant. His diplomatic dispatches are in the Archives of the State Department in Washington, D.C., Foreign Relations, 1789–1803. The most significant of these documents were published as "Documents: Despatches from the United States Consulate in New Orleans, 1801–1803," *American Historical Review* 32 (1927). For Clark's speeches and positions in Congress see *Annals of the Congress of the United States, 1789–1824*, 10th Cong. (1834–1856). Nolan B. Harmon, Jr., *The Famous Case of Myra Clark Gaines* (1946), contains an excellent biographical sketch of Clark and a detailed description of litigation inaugurated by his daughter. John S. Kendall, "The Strange Case of Myra Clark Gaines," *Louisiana Historical Quarterly* 20 (1937), gives an especially astute analysis of Clark's character as well as the complexities of his daughter's litigation. Dunbar Rowland, ed., *The Official Letter Books of W. C. C. Claiborne, 1801–1816* (1917), and William B. Hatcher, *Edward Livingston, Jeffersonian Republican and Jacksonian Democrat* (1940), provide an account of Clark's opposition to Claiborne. For an account of Clark's mercantile connections with Philadelphia see C. Richard Arena, "Philadelphia–Spanish New Orleans Trade in the 1790s," *Louisiana History* 2 (1961).

CAROLYN E. DE LATTE

CLARK, Daniel (24 Oct. 1809–2 Jan. 1891), politician and jurist, was born in Stratham, New Hampshire, the son of Benjamin Clark, a farmer and blacksmith, and Elizabeth Wiggin. He began his education at the district school near his farm home, but preferring books to farm labor, Daniel went to Hampton Academy intermittently, which qualified him to enter Dartmouth College. Because his family had limited means, Clark had to pay for his advanced education by teaching during vacations from his own studies. After graduating from college in 1834 with the highest honors of his class, he studied law in Exeter, New Hampshire, first with George Sullivan and then with James Bell. He was admitted to the bar in 1837.

Although Clark began his law practice in Epping, New Hampshire, he sensed that Manchester was becoming a business and industrial center and moved there in 1839. Indeed, Manchester was the "principal source of energy in the state" (Morison and Morison, p. 157). Its Amoskeag Manufacturing Company, begun in 1831, grew to be predominant in the textile industry. In that growing city, Clark built up a large law practice. As he advanced as a lawyer and became prominent in political affairs, he embarked on a lifetime of public service. He was city solicitor, a member of the school board, a member of the first board of trustees of the public library, and chief engineer of the fire department. For the five years 1842, 1843, 1846, 1854, and 1855 he represented his city as a Whig in the New Hampshire House of Representatives.

In 1840 Clark married Hannah W. Robbins. They apparently had no children, and she died in 1844. Two years later Clark married Ann(e) W. Salter, with whom he had two sons.

Shortly after Clark settled in Manchester, the state engaged him to lead the prosecution of Jonas L. Parker in a murder case. Clark's adversaries on the defense team included New Hampshire lawyer and future U.S. president Franklin Pierce. While Clark did not win this case, he did gain much attention and respect for his ability in conducting the prosecution.

As Clark achieved political prominence in New Hampshire, his Whig party was disintegrating, and he worked to organize the Republican party. He was an uncompromising opponent of slavery and, during the campaign of 1854–1855, spoke in every part of the state against the Kansas-Nebraska Bill. Clark influenced New Hampshire opinion on this controversial legislation, which opened the door to slavery in the Kansas Territory and had the effect of repealing the Missouri Compromise of 1820. A meeting of state Republicans chose Clark as one of six delegates at large (other delegates were chosen by district) to the 1856 Republican National Convention in Philadelphia, which nominated John C. Frémont as the first Republican presidential candidate. As a presidential elector that year, Clark cast his vote for Frémont.

In 1855 Clark was nominated for the U.S. Senate, but the venerable Bell, with whom he had studied law, was elected. When Senator Bell died in 1857, the Republican caucus of the New Hampshire legislature needed only one ballot to nominate Clark, who was then elected to complete the remaining four years of Bell's term. Clark entered the Thirty-fifth Congress on 27 June 1857. He was reelected in 1860, and his strong voice of support for the Union was heard frequently in Washington, D.C., during the Civil War.

Senator Clark gained recognition through his service on several committees, as chair of the Committee on Claims (Thirty-seventh through Thirty-ninth Congresses), and as president pro tempore of the Senate (Thirty-eighth Congress). The latter position put him in the line of presidential succession, after the vice president. He was also acknowledged as an accomplished debater, on a par with Senate notables such as Charles Sumner. But some who sought reconciliation with the South criticized him for his uncompromising opposition to slavery, secession, and northern sympathizers. Clark made his thoughts clear, as during the Kansas-Nebraska debates, when he stated, "We have had enough of bowing down, and the people in my region have got sick of it." When those southern senators whose states had seceded from the Union left their seats in the chamber, Clark offered the resolution suspending them on 11 July 1861.

Clark vigorously supported the Abraham Lincoln administration throughout the Civil War, not only from the Senate but in his home state. When Lincoln asked for 75,000 volunteers after the firing on Fort Sumter, Clark spoke at a Manchester benefit for the men who answered the president's call, and when Manchester men returned home after the war, he spoke in their honor. Even though he was a strong candidate owing to the prominence he had earned in the Senate, Clark was defeated for reelection in 1866. One of four candidates, he lost on the fourth ballot, when the legislature chose Aaron H. Cragin, a Republican from Lebanon, as his successor. The defeat may have been in part because of his "lacking the elements of personal popularity," but the New Hampshire tradition of "rotation in office" was certainly also a factor (Lyford, p. 194).

Clark's Senate term did not expire until 3 March 1867, but he resigned his seat on 27 July 1866 to accept an appointment from President Andrew Johnson as U.S. district judge for New Hampshire. Secretary of the Navy Gideon Welles wrote in his diary that he told the president he "regretted the appointment of Clark." Welles felt that, in the struggle between the Congress and the president over Reconstruction policy, Clark had too often been in opposition to Johnson on constitutional points. The president replied to Welles that he thought some good might come from the appointment of Clark.

Clark's years on the bench earned him a reputation as an excellent jurist, an able administrator of the courts, and a judge who was sought after to preside in other federal courts on the New England circuit. He continued to give scholarly speeches at public occasions and to hold positions with Manchester's cultural and business organizations. In 1866 he was a delegate to the "Loyalists' Convention" in Philadelphia, when southerners who had opposed secession and the Confederacy met with border state and northern congressmen to promote the role of Congress in reconstructing the Union. As president of the New Hampshire Constitutional Convention of 1876, he enhanced the sessions with his commanding presence and impressive speech.

At age seventy, Clark, in excellent health, refused retirement with a salary for life. Generally reserved and formal in his relationships, he took his obligations seriously and was regarded respectfully as a judge and a statesman. He continued to serve his community as a trustee of the Manchester Savings Bank and the city library and, when he died, was the oldest director of the Amoskeag Company. He remained on the bench until his death in Manchester.

• Collections of Clark papers are at the New Hampshire State Library, the New Hampshire Historical Society Library, and Dartmouth College. Charles H. Bell, *The Bench and Bar of New Hampshire* (1894), includes a summary of Clark's life and career and indicates the respect of his colleagues. Maurice D. Clark, *Manchester: A Brief Record of Its Past and a Picture of Its Present* (1875), is important for a perspective on Clark's role in that fast-growing industrial city. Elizabeth Forbes Morison and Elting E. Morison, *New Hampshire: A Bicentennial History* (1976), gives a sketch of Manchester's importance in Clark's day. James O. Lyford, *Life of Edward H. Rollins: A Political Biography* (1906), provides essential details of the New Hampshire political background. For Senator Clark's early remarks on the Kansas question see the *Congressional Globe*, 35th Cong., 1st sess., 1858, app., p. 107. To follow his part in debates see also subsequent issues of the *Globe* (1858–1865). Gideon Welles, *Diary of Gideon Welles, Secretary of the Navy under Lincoln and Johnson*, vol. 2, 1864–1866 (1911), contains Welles's remarks about Clark's appointment as New Hampshire judge. An obituary is in the *New York Times*, 3 Jan. 1891.

SYLVIA B. LARSON

CLARK, Dutch (11 Oct. 1906–5 Aug. 1978), professional football player, was born Earl Harry Clark in Fowler, Colorado, the son of Harry Clark, a farmer and railroad worker, and Mary Etta Lackey. His nickname was derived from "Little Dutch," an older brother having been called "Big Dutch" because of a speech problem. When his family moved to Pueblo, Colorado, Clark quit attending public schools and began working as a "call boy" in a railyard, "rousting" brakemen and engineers from their rooming houses early in the morning. After two years he returned to school, attending Pueblo Central High School, where he was an outstanding football, basketball, and baseball player. Noted particularly for his broken-field running, he led his high school football team to the final game of the state playoffs for two years in a row. He also played center on the basketball team that lost in the championship game of the National Interscholastic Tournament.

Attracting the attention of many college and university coaches, Clark accepted an offer to play at Northwestern University. Upon arriving at Northwestern, he became homesick and found that people "kept talking to me, yakking at me. They wouldn't leave me alone." After one week he returned home and soon entered Colorado College. There he became a triple-threat player, running as left halfback (tailback) and also calling plays for the single-wing attack. In Clark's junior year, Alan Gould of the Associated Press selected Clark on his All-American team, passing over many better known players in the East and thus creating a stir in the football world. In 1930 Clark married Dorothy Schrader; they had two sons.

When he graduated in 1931, Clark had several prospects in professional football. He chose to accept a contract at $140 a game—during this time many players were making about $100 a game—with the Portsmouth (Ohio) Spartans of the National Football League (NFL). Clark signed with Portsmouth at a time when small-town franchises such as the Spartans were disappearing from the league. The Spartans, originally an independent semiprofessional team, had entered the league in 1930.

Clean-cut in appearance and behavior, Clark was one of many collegians coming into the NFL in the 1930s who enhanced the image of the league, which previously had been scorned by university coaches and administrators. Standing six feet tall and weighing 183 pounds, Clark brought his great agility to a good football team. Joining him in the backfield was Glenn Presnell, a remarkable runner, passer, and kicker. Several outstanding players anchored a strong line. In Clark's first year the Spartans finished second in the league; because the Green Bay Packers refused to play the Spartans in a tentatively scheduled game, the Spartans were denied the opportunity to tie for the NFL championship. The following year Clark led the league in points scored, and the Spartans met the Chicago Bears in a playoff game at the Chicago Stadium for the championship. But Clark did not play in the game, which the Spartans lost, because he had a contract to coach basketball at Colorado College, and the president would not permit him to miss the first game of the basketball season.

Clark was not happy in Portsmouth. The Spartans' management was slow in meeting its payroll and sometimes ran out of money. Despite Clark's dissatisfaction, he may have been instrumental in persuading teammates to continue to play during one of the financial crises. A local reporter, though acknowledging that Clark was a remarkable player, portrayed him as an aloof man who, unlike his teammates, did not become a part of the community. He also did not endear himself to fans when he declared that he preferred basketball to football.

Clark left professional football in 1933, taking the position of athletic director and head coach of football, basketball, and baseball at the Colorado School of Mines. In 1934 a group organized by George Richards, the wealthy owner of a Detroit radio station, purchased the Spartans, moved the franchise to Detroit, and renamed it the Lions. George "Potsy" Clark, the Lions' head coach and Dutch Clark's coach in Portsmouth, persuaded Clark to return to the team. He became at once the Lions' premier runner, pacing all the other backs on the team and in the league in various statistical categories. Along with Presnell, he led the Lions to the NFL championship in 1935. As the single-wing tailback for the Lions, Clark called the offensive signals. His generalship was no more evident than in the title game against the New York Giants, when he ran forty yards for a touchdown.

Potsy Clark constantly battled Richards, who finally fired him in 1936; Dutch Clark then accepted the position of player-coach of the Lions. The team finished second, with records of seven wins and four losses two years in a row under his guidance. All the while Clark, too, quarreled with Richards. Deciding that his playing days were over, Clark left the Lions to become coach of the Cleveland Rams in 1939. He was with the Rams for two years, his record being 11 wins, 20 losses, and 2 ties. After World War II he served briefly as coach of the Seattle Bombers and then returned to the Rams, who had moved to Los Angeles, as an assistant coach. In 1950 he became athletic director and football coach at the University of Detroit. After his wife died in 1952 and a son reached his senior year in college, Clark left the athletic world, and in 1954 he became a sales representative for a tool company in Detroit. He recalled later that he really did not like coaching: "I was a lousy coach—I just couldn't tell a kid to do something 50 times when I had always been able to pick up things the first time." He also disliked the speaking engagements that were required of him as coach. No longer coaching, he was free, he said, to bet on the horses. Eventually Clark moved back to Colorado and lived there the remainder of his life.

An excellent dropkicker and passer, Clark nonetheless was at his best as a runner. With rather thin lower legs and well-muscled thighs, he was agile and strong. Though nearly blind in his left eye, he had good vision of the field in front of him. Those who saw him play marveled at his running. He was "like a rabbit in the brush," said Potsy Clark, "the hardest man in football to tackle." Professional Football Hall of Famer Bronko Nagurski called him "the most elusive back I have seen or played against." Mel Hein of the Giants viewed him as the "greatest triple threat back of his era . . . if not the greatest all-around back of all time." Of himself Dutch Clark said that "I was made of Indian rubber . . . I could run all day."

The records Clark established as a player were outstanding. He led the league in scoring in three years, averaged 4.8 yards a carry from 1932 through 1937, scored 23 touchdowns in those years, passed for 42 additional touchdowns, and kicked 15 field goals and 72 extra points. He was a fierce competitor who seemed to excel at crucial moments. In his seven-year career he was an all-league selection six times. In 1963 he was elected as a charter member to the Professional Football Hall of Fame.

Clark died in Canon City, Colorado. Surviving him were his sons and his second wife, Ruth (maiden name unknown).

• The best account of Clark, both in and out of football, is his autobiographical essay "Dutch Clark," in Myron Cope, *The Game That Was: The Early Days of Pro Football*, rev. ed. (1974), pp. 67–76. See also George Allen and Ben Olan, *Pro Football's 100 Greatest Players* (1982), pp. 84–86; Arthur Daley, *Pro Football's Hall of Fame* (1963), pp. 140–50; and Alexander M. Weyand, *Football Immortals* (1962), pp. 149–54. Especially useful for reading about Clark's days in Portsmouth are C. Robert Barnett, *The Spartans and the Tanks* (1983); Barnett, "The Spartans Live On (in Detroit)," *Coffin Corner* 2, no. 10 (Oct. 1980): 6ff; Carl M. Becker, "The 'Tom Thumb' Game: Bears vs. Spartans, 1932," *Journal of Sport History* 22, no. 3 (Fall 1995): 216–27. Contemporary comments on Clark as a player and personality appear in several articles in the *Portsmouth Daily Times*, including "Dutch Clark Likes Wildwest Stories; Wants to Quit Pro Game," 11 Dec. 1932; "Dutch Clark Unable to Play in Bears Game," 13 Dec. 1932; "No Chance for Clark to Play," 15 Dec. 1932; and "700 Persons Attend Football Mass Rally," 10 Dec. 1931. Following Clark's death, articles on his life appeared in his hometown newspapers: "Football Hero 'Dutch' Clark Died," *Canon City Daily Record*, 7 Aug. 1978, and "Gridiron Legend Clark Dead at 71," *Pueblo Star-Journal*, 6 Aug. 1978. An interesting obituary is in the *New York Times*, 6 Aug. 1978.

CARL M. BECKER

CLARK, Edward (19 Dec. 1811–14 Oct. 1882), lawyer and business leader, was born in Athens, Greene County, New York, the son of Nathan Clark, a successful pottery manufacturer, and Julia Nichols. Clark began schooling with a tutor and then attended an academy at Hudson, New York. At age twelve he went to Lenox Academy, run by John Hotchkin, reputedly reading every book in the school's 500-volume library; at age sixteen he went to Williams College, graduating in 1831.

Clark began reading law that fall with Ambrose L. Jordan in Hudson. After three years, he established his own office, and was admitted to the New York bar in 1834. In 1835 he married Jordan's eldest daughter, Caroline; and in May 1837 went into partnership with Jordan. A year later Jordan and Clark moved their legal practice to New York City, where they developed a large, lucrative practice. Ambrose eventually rose to be state attorney general. Clark, whom an associate described as "quiet and undemonstrative," although successful, accomplished nothing of note during this period. But in 1848 poorly educated, uncouth, sometime-actor and mechanical genius Isaac Merritt Singer came to Ambrose & Clark for help; Clark's first task was to recover for Singer clear title to a machine that he had invented to carve wood. Thereafter, Clark found himself increasingly involved with Singer's legal tangles. Singer, unable to pay Clark's legal fees, instead paid Clark with a one-third interest in his patents.

In 1850 Singer recognized how to redesign a Lerow & Blodgett sewing machine, thereby producing the first machine incorporating all ten elements critical for any successful sewing machine. In September 1850 Singer formed a partnership that included Clark to build an improved machine (it was awarded a patent on 12 Aug. 1851); by early 1851, after buying out two partners, Clark and Singer were equal owners. On 1 January 1852 their partnership became I. M. Singer & Co. Clark, leaving his law practice behind, took responsibility for legal, financial, and marketing matters; Singer handled manufacturing and was principally involved with new designs of stitching mechanisms, an effort that soon led to twenty-two additional patents.

The company immediately found itself in a bitter legal batter with Elias Howe, who had patented his sewing machine in 1846; in 1854 a Boston court upheld Howe's claims, forcing the industry to pay Howe exorbitant fees of $25 a machine. Though Howe won initially, the three leading manufacturers—Singer, Wheeler & Wilson, and Grover & Baker—each held important patents that went beyond Howe's coverage; soon an internecine patent war developed, threatening all manufacturers and Howe's fees (Howe did not manufacture machines). On 24 October 1856, largely through Clark's efforts, Howe and the three principal manufacturers agreed to pool their patents and charge a $15 fee for each machine under license. With some modifications, the pool continued until 8 May 1877, when the last patent in the pool expired.

Clark, beginning with little capital, first tried to develop Singer sales by selling territorial rights. This proved disappointing. In 1856 Clark began repurchasing these rights, eventually bringing all sales under direct company control through branch offices. To improve selling, he also tried to make commission agents work on an exclusive contract. This proved unworkable, so Clark, also beginning in 1856 with the New York sales office, began drawing agents from the ranks of mechanics who had worked in the company factory on Mott Street in New York City, thus creating a full-time sales force that was knowledgeable about the product. This approach took on increasing importance with the 1856 introduction of the "Turtle Back" model designed for home use. Clark recognized that development of home sales relied critically on support services—demonstration, instruction, supplies, attachments, repairs, and credit. Clark recognized typical households could not afford the full price of a new machine, so he introduced installment buying through a "hire-purchase" contract. With just $5 down, $5 a month, a family could own a Singer. In combining these elements, Clark also laid the foundation for the most sophisticated and successful marketing organization in the world.

The stark contrast in personalities and lifestyles between Clark and Singer apparently created increasing tension in the partnership; on Saturday, 6 June 1863, in a meeting with Singer, Clark apparently forced the dissolution of the partnership and the creation of a new company, the Singer Manufacturing Company. Eighty percent of the shares went to Singer and Clark, the remainder to four employees, who, with Singer and Clark, composed the board of directors and—because neither Clark nor Singer could serve as president while either lived—became the new company's officers. As a result, 26-year-old Inslee Hopper became president. Singer soon moved to England, playing no future role in the company. Clark remained actively involved in company management—although he did take the time to travel extensively in Europe and wintered one year in Italy—and assumed the presidency at age sixty-five after Singer's death the previous year.

During Hopper's presidency, Clark clearly played a leading role in pushing for the company's rapid development. He had in the 1850s pushed European sales with little sucess. By 1865, however, at his urging Singer Manufacturing had two general agents established in Europe, in London and Hamburg. On 8 May 1867, Clark asked the board to create a committee to investigate "the subject of opening a workshop in Europe" (quoted in Davies, p. 44). A week later, with a favorable report, the company initiated the steps that soon led to its first overseas manufacturing facility, becoming one of the first American multinational companies. In 1882 Singer opened a huge factory in Glasgow, Scotland, to serve its burgeoning European sales. Domestically, when the patent pool ended Clark ordered prices cut 50 percent to "strike terror into the minds" of competitors (quoted in Davies, p. 58). Singer Manufacturing, long the leading firm, soon dominated the industry worldwide, capturing as much as 90 percent of the total market over the next thirty years.

In 1877 Clark began the process that completed his considerable contributions to American management and market techniques. Recognizing that Singer Manufacturing had failed to identify and utilize fully its best approaches to marketing or developed systematic and comprehensive reporting systems, Clark called a special meeting to identify such practices and systems, intending to then make them the company standard. In November 1878 he sent out a printed letter to all domestic and foreign agents, laying out the recommended structure; refined over the next decade, it became the core framework for what was perhaps that day's most successful marketing organization.

In 1854 Clark had purchased a home, "Apple Hill," in his wife's hometown, Cooperstown, New York. He and his family first spent summers there; in 1869 he tore down the old house and built a mansion of cut stone that was named "Fernleigh"; it became his permanent home. Clark also commissioned construction of the landmark Dakota apartment building at Seventy-second Street and Central Park West in New York City and made substantial gifts to his alma mater, Williams College. Clark died of typhoid at Fernleigh in 1882, survived by only one of his three sons.

• There are extensive original materials detailing Clark's career, particularly his work at Singer Manufacturing. The largest collections of papers relating to Clark is in the Singer collections at the State Historical Society of Wisconsin. There are also approximately sixteen cubic feet of papers preserved in three manuscript collections at the New York Historical Association's Farmers' Museum in Cooperstown, N.Y. Finally, the Greene County Historical Society in Coxsackie, N.Y., has a small set of letters from Clark to his father and brother dated 1840–1846; they are among the Fox-Clark papers. The only extensive published account of Clark's career at Singer Manufacturing is in Robert B. Davies, *Peacefully Working to Conquer the World: Singer Sewing Machines in Foreign Markets, 1854–1920* (1976).

FRED CARSTENSEN

CLARK, Emily Tapscott (8 Sept. 1892–2 July 1953), editor and writer, was born in Richmond, Virginia, the daughter of the Reverend William Meade Clark, rector of St. George's Church in Fredericksburg, Virginia, and Nancy Tapscott. The Clark family moved to Richmond in 1896 when the scholarly Mr. Clark became rector of St. James's Episcopal Church and editor of the *Southern Churchman*. Emily Clark graduated in 1909 from the Virginia Randolph Ellett school in Richmond and passed the entrance exam for Bryn Mawr but decided not to attend college. In 1920 she was writing a column for the book page in the *Richmond Evening Journal* when that newspaper ceased publication. The loss of the book page prompted her plan to publish a literary magazine.

Without capital and with only local book-review experience, Clark and three other Richmonders—Hunter Stagg, Margaret Waller Freeman (later the second Mrs. James Branch Cabell), and Mary Dallas Street—founded *The Reviewer* in 1921. Only Clark and Stagg stayed with the magazine for its full run of forty-four months. Isabel Paterson wrote prophetically about the magazine in the *New York Tribune*, "We shan't be surprised if future historians reckon the beginning of a great Southern literary renaissance from the date of the founding of *The Reviewer*." Writing in 1947, the critics Frederick J. Hoffman, Charles Allen, and Carolyn Ulrich classified *The Reviewer* as one of the three best of the southern little magazines.

The Reviewer appeared in thirty-one issues, published in Richmond between 1921 and 1924, then moved to Chapel Hill, North Carolina, under the editorship of Paul Green for one more year. It began as a semimonthly journal, then became a monthly, and then a quarterly. The personality, sensibility, and energy of Emily Clark created and shaped *The Reviewer*. Although Clark's family had no money, they were connected to many of the first families of Virginia. Clark interested James Branch Cabell in the magazine, and he edited the first three issues of the second volume. Through Cabell she met Joseph Hergesheimer; Hergesheimer in turn introduced her to H. L. Mencken and Carl Van Vechten. Clark referred to these four men as the "godfathers" of the journal, and each contributed articles and also helped her attract work from such well-known writers as Gertrude Stein, John Galsworthy, Amy Lowell, and Ronald Firbank. Clark's published letters to Joseph Hergesheimer in *Ingénue among the Lions* (1965, ed. Gerald Langford) reveal a somewhat coy, demanding, pretentious, flirtatious, snobbish, and gossipy personality. Yet the letters also reveal an ambitious and persistent woman determined to use her connections to secure important contributions for the journal.

Clark explained in 1931, "We had no [editorial] policy beyond a fixed standard of good writing, and a determination to make articulate the new Southern consciousness then becoming apparent." The journal was eclectic, established writers appearing alongside unknown ones, and Clark frequently published the work of local contributors because of their support of the journal. She used the work of many southern writers but also featured the work of writers from other parts of the country and from abroad.

Established Virginian writers like Cabell, Ellen Glasgow, and Mary Johnston published pieces in *The Reviewer*. Perhaps the most interesting contributors, however, were young writers, not well known at the time, such as Allen Tate, Paul Green, Lynn Riggs (author of *Green Grow the Lilacs*, adapted for the stage as *Oklahoma!*), Margery Latimer (later Mrs. Jean Toomer), and Sara Haardt (later Mrs. H. L. Mencken). Two writers first published in *The Reviewer* were Frances Newman, author of the avant-garde novel *The Hard-Boiled Virgin* (1926), and Julia Peterkin, winner of the Pulitzer Prize for her 1928 novel *Scarlet Sister Mary*.

Clark gave up editing *The Reviewer* in 1924 to marry a wealthy Philadelphian, 68-year-old Edwin Swift Balch, a distinguished explorer, scientist, and philanthropist. Balch supported *The Reviewer* with a $3,000 contribution and then proposed to Clark, who moved to Philadelphia upon her marriage. When her husband died three years later, she was left a wealthy woman.

Under her maiden name Clark published two books, *Stuffed Peacocks* in 1927 and *Innocence Abroad* in 1931. *Peacocks* consisted of satirical sketches, several of them thinly disguised treatments of Richmonders. "Lustre Wear," for example, satirized Henry Anderson, an international lawyer and one-time fiancé of Ellen Glasgow. *Innocence* tells the lively story of Clark's experience editing *The Reviewer* and includes sketches of literary figures of the time. Clark also published pieces in such magazines as *Virginia Quarterly Review*, *American Mercury*, and *Smart Set*.

For the rest of her life Clark lived in Philadelphia, keeping an apartment in New York City for a number of years. She reviewed books for newspapers, maintained her literary connections, and conducted a literary salon. A patron of the arts, she left two-thirds of her estate to the University of Virginia to stimulate the appreciation and creation of American literature. Her significance as a literary figure rests on *The Reviewer*, a modest but important contribution to the little-magazine movement, and on her two books, which chronicle a chapter in the literary life of Richmond in the 1920s.

She died in Philadelphia and is buried in Hollywood Cemetery in Richmond.

• Clark's papers (including manuscripts and letters to her) have not been found. Her letters are in collections at the New York Public Library, the University of Virginia, the University of Texas, and Yale University. Dorothy M. Scura writes on *The Reviewer* in *American Literary Magazines*, ed. Edward Chielens (1992). Maurice Duke lists and annotates the contents of *The Reviewer* in *Resources for American Literary Study* 1 (Spring 1971): 58–103. Elizabeth Scott discusses *The Reviewer* in *Virginia Cavalcade* 27 (Winter 1978): 128–43. Edgar MacDonald places *The Reviewer* in the Richmond context in *The History of Southern Literature*, ed. Louis D. Rubin, Jr., et al. (1985). Frederick J. Hoffman, Charles Allen, and Carolyn Ulrich analyze *The Reviewer* in *The Little Magazine: A History and a Bibliography* (1947). Obituaries appear in the *New York Times*, 4 July 1953, and the *Richmond Times Dispatch*, 3 July 1953.

DOROTHY M. SCURA

CLARK, Francis E. (12 Sept. 1851–26 May 1927), Congregational minister and founder of the Christian Endeavor Society, was born Francis Edward Symmes in Alymer, Quebec, Canada, the son of Charles Carey Symmes, a businessman, and Lydia Clark. His father died of cholera in 1854, and shortly thereafter his mother also died, leaving Francis orphaned at the age of eight. He was legally adopted by his uncle, the Reverend Edward W. Clark of Auburndale, Massachusetts, and took the Clark name. He attended Kimball Union Academy in Meriden, New Hampshire, and then enrolled at Dartmouth College in Hanover, New Hampshire, where he excelled in both writing and oratory and edited the college newspaper. He was also actively involved in the weekly prayer meetings conducted at the college and was a member of the school's Theological and Missionary Society. In 1873 Clark graduated from Dartmouth and enrolled at Andover Theological Seminary in preparation for a ministerial career in the Congregational church. In 1876 he married Harriet Abbott, whom he had met while doing missionary work in Andover; they had four children.

Upon graduation from Andover, Clark became minister of the Williston Memorial Congregational Church in Portland, Maine. Under Clark's leadership, the small congregation experienced rapid growth. At Williston Clark first began ministering to young people. In 1881 he started a weekly youth meeting devoted to prayer and the study of the Bible. He named his new youth group the Williston Young People's Society of Christian Endeavor. The goal of this society was "to promote an earnest Christian life among its members, to increase their mutual acquaintance, and to make them more useful in the service of God." Later that year Clark described his new youth meetings in an article published in the *Congregationalist*, "How One Church Cares for Its Young People." Shortly after publication, other area churches began adopting Clark's Christian Endeavor idea. There was such a demand from local churches for information concerning these new societies that Clark wrote a two-page brochure explaining how churches could start societies of their own. The brochure was distributed to delegates at the first annual Christian Endeavor conference in 1882. That same year Clark wrote *The Children and the Church*, a book-length description of the principles of the society. By 1883 the Christian Endeavor Society included fifty-six local chapters and just under 3,000 members.

In 1883 Clark became minister at the Phillips Congregational Church in Boston where his new youth organization received more exposure. Two years later he opened a national office in the city. He also began publishing and editing the *Golden Rule* (later the *Christian Endeavor* World), which became the official organ of the society. In 1887 he resigned from his position at Phillips Church to become president of the United Society of Christian Endeavor, a post he would hold for the next thirty-eight years. As president, Clark supervised more than 250 local chapters and almost 15,000 members.

The Christian Endeavor Society became one of America's first evangelical youth ministries. Under the motto For Christ and the Church, it upheld traditional doctrines such as the atonement of Christ, authority of the Bible, and the necessity of holy living. The society also stressed cooperation among Christian denominations. Clark was forced to defend the movement against accusations from denominational leaders who feared the interdenominational approach of the Christian Endeavor Society would turn young people away from the established churches. He asserted that his youth society was designed to support, not undermine, the local congregation. Clark and the society also took decisive stands on several issues, championing temperance and prohibition. In his writings and speeches, Clark emphasized the importance of patriotism, citizenship, and family values.

The Christian Endeavor Society developed a worldwide ministry under Clark's leadership, sponsoring numerous missionaries around the world. A tireless promoter of the society, Clark traveled around the world four times. In 1895 he helped organize the World's Christian Endeavor Union to represent the ever-growing international flavor of the organization. By the time of his death, the World's Christian Endeavor Union included members in more than forty nations.

Clark died in Newton, Massachusetts. Throughout his career, he authored more than thirty books and numerous tracts and pamphlets promoting the ministry of the Christian Endeavor Society, and the organization he founded was still in existence more than seventy years after his death.

• Clark's autobiography, *Christian Endeavor in All Lands*, was published in 1906. The best sources of information on Clark's career and ministry are the official Christian Endeavor periodicals, the *Golden Rule* and its successor, *Christian Endeavor World*. Most of the works addressing his ministry were written by friends and coworkers in the Christian Endeavor Society. They include W. Knight Chaplin, *Francis E. Clark: Founder of the Christian Endeavor Society* (1920), and W. Shaw, *The Evolution of an Endeavorer* (1924). An obituary is in the *New York Times*, 27 May 1927.

JOHN FEA

CLARK, Frederic Horace (?1860–27 Jan. 1917), pianist and inventor, and **Anna Steiniger** (19 Apr. 1848–Dec. 1891?), pianist, were born, respectively, in Liebeshain, Illinois, and Magdeburg or Potsdam, Prussia. Clark (whose literary pseudonym was Leopold St. Damian) claimed in *Liszts Offenbarung* (Liszt's revelation [1907]) that he was born in Liebeshain, but the town, supposedly near Chicago, is not to be found on any historical map. Little is known about their parents except that Clark's father was apparently a member of the governing board of the Northwestern Railways, Steiniger's father was a captain in the Prussian army and an instructor at (later also in charge of) the Royal Artillery School, and her mother was the daughter of a Lutheran preacher.

In 1876 Clark escaped from his parents to Europe and literally walked through most of it to the south of Italy to meet his idol, pianist Franz Liszt. Upon Liszt's recommendation, Clark in 1877 entered the Leipzig Conservatory, where he studied piano with Dr. Oscar Paul. Clark is believed to have earned a diploma in 1880. He returned to the United States on one or two occasions for at least two years, working as an organist and performing. Subsequently, again in Germany, Clark studied privately with some well-known German teachers, primarily with Ludwig Deppe in Berlin. Soon after meeting Deppe's assistant, young German pianist Anna Steiniger, Clark proposed to her, and they were married in 1882. The couple had three children.

Steiniger began to play in public at the age of ten. Early on she vowed to refute the Prussian assertion that "musicians are generally no more intelligent than 'cows.'" Around 1871 Steiniger met Deppe, with whom she studied for twelve years. She eventually became his assistant and a prime exponent of his pedagogical method, which was based on conscious arm-weight manipulation and an emphasized participation of the upper arm, shoulder, and back. Well known in Europe, Steiniger often accompanied some of the best female singers on the Continent.

In 1885 Clark and Steiniger moved to Boston and established a piano school, but they failed to arouse significant interest. In addition to performing in several concerts with the Boston Symphony Orchestra, Steiniger played five seasons of recitals dedicated to solo and chamber music. Evidence suggests that around 1885 or 1886 she participated in the first complete performance of Beethoven's sonatas for violin and piano with a Mr. Crysdale, the concertmaster of the BSO. Steiniger also claimed to be "the greatest Beethoven-pianist from Germany ever to come to live in Boston." She was an independent thinker and a shrewd and insightful observer. Her often bitter and sarcastic comments on both European and American societies and their attitudes toward women, as demonstrated in her semiautobiography *Iphigenia, Baroness of Styne* (1896), reveal her commitment to fight for the rights of female musicians working in a field traditionally dominated by men.

Following Steiniger's death, Clark apparently moved to Chicago and then to Valparaiso, Indiana. By 1900 he was remarried, to a former American student of his (name unknown); they had three children. In 1903 at the latest Clark was again in Germany, presumably alone. This was the most productive period of his life. Always under extreme hardship and poverty, he spent his last four years in Zurich, where he died.

According to Rudolf Breithaupt's *Handbuch der modernen Methodik und Spielpraxis* (3d ed, 1912), Clark was the first scholar to discuss and graphically illustrate the rolling movement of the arm and wrist, as demonstrated in his *Lehre des einheitlichen Kunstmittels beim Klavierspiel* (The doctrine of unified art of piano playing [1885]). He was therefore a pioneer in the physiological approach to piano playing. Clark criticized other contemporary piano methods for focusing on only a part (finger, hand, or forearm) of the tone-building process and thereby encouraging isolated movements. Clark did not, however, criticize Liszt's playing, and he seems to have been among the first to understand fully the change in piano technique introduced by Liszt. Liszt rejected the traditional still-hand placement and avoided using fixed positions and percussive finger action, instead using all available physical resources and channeling them into flowing gestures.

Drawing on the work of Liszt and German physicist Hermann Helmholtz, Clark treated the pianist's body as a unit. He conceived the idea of a chain of motion transfer, in which the rotating momentum of impulses from the shoulder blades is transferred to smaller and smaller levers. The physiological facts on which Clark based his method have been corroborated by Otto Ortmann in his book *The Physiological Mechanics of Piano Technique* (1929). Ortmann's photographs of hand movements are almost identical to the diagrams in Clark's book. Some other students of Deppe (such as Elisabeth Caland) as well as acquaintances of Clark (such as Dr. Friedrich Adolf Steinhausen) borrowed extensively from Clark's work, without adequately citing him as the source.

During his ten solitary years in Berlin Clark developed his "Cherubim-doctrine," an intricate and highly speculative philosophic system in which religious (Christian) hierarchy and doctrine become a model for the coordination (*harmonie*) between mental and physical parameters of artistic performance, thus mirroring the human harmony with the universe and with the Creator.

Clark's design for his *Harmonie-Piano* reflects both his work in the physiology of piano technique and his "Cherubim-Doctrine." Developed by 1913, the piano bears the Royal German Patent Number 225,367. It consists of two parallel keyboards, elevated to shoulder level, angled at a 45° inclination. The pianist stood between the keyboards with outstretched arms, thus establishing an axis from fingertips to the solar plexus through the arms, shoulders, and spine. Invoking the ancient Greek principle of the golden mean, Clark claimed that this posture blended all extensors and flexors into one unbroken vortex-like motion. He also inserted springs under the keys to preserve the original key resistance at the new inclination. The caps of the keys were slightly concave to allow the fingers to cling to them. In this position the thumb plays more with its flat side and is closer to and more even with the other fingers. Several pairs of pedals enabled the pianist to continue playing while moving between the keyboards.

Clark's other innovations include an edition entitled *The Artists Unified; or, Poetic Edition of Classical Works of Modern Instrumental Music* (1891). Using a special graphic design he outlined the rhythmic and motivic flow in music, delineating the accumulation of rhythmic tension in larger phrases, as well as in their subordinate units. Clark's Impromptu op. 4, no. 3 (1884), written for his own method of playing and printed in his graphic layout, appears to have been the first musical illustration of poet Henry Wadsworth Longfellow's epic *Hiawatha*.

Clark published a series of articles in the journal *Music*, in which he presents a pseudointellectual analysis of six Beethoven piano sonatas: these studies are among the first attempts to reconstruct the original creative process. Although some of Clark's conclusions are highly speculative and exaggerated, the essays demonstrate a subtle imagination and a profound knowledge of form, structure, and music history.

Clark's writings reveal a person of intense intellect, almost fanatical beliefs, and relentless drive. He sometimes bent historical truth, insisting that many of his thoughts and ideas came directly from Liszt and Johannes Brahms, a claim that cannot be verified. Clark even stated that Brahms was the first to experiment with early models of the *Harmonie-Piano*. In the memory of his contemporaries, however, Clark remained an honest, direct, naive, and childlike person, full of intense emotions and somewhat detached from everyday life.

Clark provided a significant link between the age of instinctive performance and the age of scientific approaches to piano technique, study, and interpretation. Unfortunately, his eccentric character and an obsession with religion later in his life made many of his writings convoluted and nearly incomprehensible. Consequently, he was labeled a charlatan and, after having been ignored throughout much of his lifetime, was quickly forgotten after his death.

• Clark's written works and the music he published are as elusive as are his biographical data, as most of his works were self-published. The publishing firm Clayton F. Summy, which published several of his compositions, has no record of Clark or his works. For a comprehensive biography of Clark, see Robert Andres, "Frederic Horace Clark: A Forgotten Innovator" (M.M. thesis, Univ. of Kansas, 1992). Also informative are Andres, "'Cherubim-Doctrine,' *Harmonie-Piano*, and Other Innovations of Frederic Horace Clark" (D.M.A. diss., Univ. of Kansas, 1993), which includes a detailed analysis of Clark's theosophical doctrine and his practical contributions to piano technique; Bettina Walker, *My Musical Experiences* (1892), which contains a firsthand description of Clark and Steiniger; Bertrand Ott, *Lisztian Keyboard Energy* (1992), including a technical analysis of Clark's observations of Liszt's playing and information about Clark's verifiable encounters with Liszt; and John Storer Cobb, *Anna Steiniger, a Biographical Sketch: In Which Is Contained a Suggestion of the Clark-Steiniger System of Piano-forte Playing* (1886).

ROBERT ANDRES

CLARK, George Rogers (19 Nov. 1752–13 Feb. 1818), revolutionary war general and "conqueror of the Northwest," was born in Albemarle County, Virginia, the son of John Clark and Ann Rogers, planters. The Clarks were descended from Scottish immigrants who came to Virginia early in the eighteenth century; George Rogers Clark's flaming red hair was a mark of his Celtic ancestry. Four of his brothers were officers in the revolutionary army, and his youngest brother, William Clark, forged a trail across the continent with his Albemarle friend and neighbor, Meriwether Lewis.

In 1772, at the age of twenty, George Rogers Clark left home, having borrowed money from his father to purchase surveying instruments and a geometry book. He journeyed to Pittsburgh and from there took a flatboat down the Ohio River. He staked a claim to some fine bottomland "about forty miles below Wheeling" (in present-day West Virginia) and began clearing land for a farm. He almost immediately got caught up in the Indian fighting known as Dunmore's War. In the spring of 1775 he packed his rifle and surveying kit and ventured to the new settlements in Kentucky in order to, as he told the first Kentuckian he encountered, "lend you a helping hand if necessary." Clark knew it was only a matter of time before the Kentucky settlements attracted the attention of the Ohio tribes. When news of the outbreak of the Revolution reached Kentucky, a popular meeting, styling itself "a Respectable Body of Prime Riflemen," declared its loyalty to the American cause and sent Clark east to Williamsburg to obtain political recognition and gunpowder. He got both from Governor Patrick Henry, a champion of the frontier, though he himself had never strayed west of the Blue Ridge Mountains. Transporting the gunpowder to Pittsburgh and then through hostile Indian country down the Ohio River took Clark the better part of a year, but when the Indian assault came in 1777 Kentucky was armed.

Tribes north of the Ohio—Shawnee, Wyandot, and Miami—objected to the settlement of Kentucky because it was their favorite hunting ground. Supplied by British officials in Detroit, they laid siege to Kentucky's palisaded villages throughout the summer and fall of 1777. By then Governor Henry had made Clark a major of militia and put him in charge of Kentucky's defense. Although he lacked military training, Clark instinctively knew that offense was sometimes the best defense. A raid on British outposts in the West might interrupt the flow of supplies and discourage the volatile Indians. There were two such outposts south of Detroit, both of them former French fur-trading settlements—Kaskaskia on the Mississippi River south of St. Louis and Vincennes on the Wabash River. Clark's scouts informed him that Kaskaskia was without British defenders. His plan to divide his meager resources and lead an expedition across 450 miles of wilderness with no supply posts, bases, or allies bordered on the absurd, but therein lay its chance of success. No one, neither the British, the French, nor the Indians, expected a foray from beleaguered Kentucky; surprise was Clark's main weapon.

In the autumn of 1777 he journeyed back to Williamsburg and sold his scheme to Governor Henry, who promoted him to lieutenant colonel and gave him £1200 for expenses. In Pittsburgh he recruited 150 riflemen without telling them their mission and camped them on an island at the falls of the Ohio so they could not desert.

On 26 June 1778 Clark started down the Ohio River with about 175 men. Leaving their flatboats at the ruins of Fort Massac, an old French outpost at the mouth of the Tennessee River, Clark and his men plunged into the wilderness. To continue by river, especially on the much-traveled Mississippi, was to invite discovery. Hiking single file, Indian fashion, the company made the 125 miles across southern Illinois in six days. The surprise was complete; the French commandant was asleep in bed when Clark tapped him on the shoulder to inform him that he had been taken prisoner. Clark quickly won over the French inhabitants of the town when he informed them that he had come as a friend, not an enemy, and promised to respect their property and religion. Learning from French traders that there were no British in Vincennes, he sent Captain Leonard Helm with a platoon to occupy that outpost on the Wabash. The Indians were still a potential problem, but British power south of Detroit had been eliminated.

At Detroit, Henry Hamilton, the lieutenant governor of Canada, had plans of his own that summer. Satisfied that his Indian allies could continue to harass Kentucky, he planned to send his regular troops against Pittsburgh. When he learned of Clark's exploit, he simply changed targets. With a handful of regulars, some Canadian militia, and Indians, he swept down the Wabash in the fall of 1778 and seized Vincennes, taking Helm prisoner. Hamilton then sent his regulars back to Detroit, discharged the Indians, and settled in for the winter in the company of the genial Kentuckian, Captain Helm.

In Kaskaskia Clark was facing one of the wettest winters on record. He learned of the fall of Vincennes on 29 January 1779. Within five days he recruited French militia to supplement his band of Kentuckians and set out across Illinois with a force of 170 men. The terrain they had to cross—hardwood forests and thick bluestem prairie broken by marshy wetlands—was forbidding even in the summer. The heavy winter rains, which filled marshes and turned creeks into torrents, made it all but impossible. There was not even a trail to follow, since normal traffic went by river, and at the end of the line the swollen Wabash surrounded Vincennes like a gigantic moat. The sight of this inland sea, Clark later wrote, "would have been enough to have stopped any set of men that was not in the same temper that we was."

Undaunted, Clark set his men to building rafts, which ferried the company across to the east side of the river. A few hundred yards from Vincennes they captured a French villager who was hunting ducks in the marshes. From him they learned that the village and its British garrison were in wintry somnolence. Clark sent the villager to alert the other French residents to stay in their houses lest they be treated as enemies. (He was aided by Kentuckians' reputation among the French as ferocious barbarians.) On the night of 25 February he posted his men at the peepholes of the fort, turning the stockade into a prison for the British. When the shooting started, British soldiers came running out of the blockhouse in the middle of the fort, only to be cut down by Kentucky rifles. After a short fight Hamilton was induced to surrender, and the Northwest was once again in American hands. Clark sent Hamilton, known among Kentuckians as "the hair buyer" because of the bounty he placed on scalps, east to Virginia to stand trial for war crimes.

Clark's recapture of Vincennes disrupted British plans and confused the Indians. It also boosted western morale and unleashed a new flood of immigrants down the Ohio. When a new British-Indian assault was launched on Kentucky in 1780, Virginia's western province was better prepared than ever. The Indians conducted sporadic raids throughout the rest of the war, but Kentucky's survival was assured. Equally important, because of the American presence in Kaskaskia and Vincennes at the end of the war, Benjamin Franklin, in peace negotiations with the British, could claim boundaries for the new republic that stretched west to the Mississippi River and north to the Great Lakes.

In the spring of 1781 Clark journeyed east to Richmond (Virginia's new capital) to secure authorization for an attack on Detroit. Governor Thomas Jefferson was very interested, but their discussions were interrupted when a British amphibious force commanded by the traitor Benedict Arnold suddenly appeared in the Chesapeake. Arnold raided Richmond, sending the governor scampering ignominiously to safety, and burned some of the public buildings. Among the items put to the torch were the financial vouchers for Clark's Illinois campaigns. Clark was already in financial difficulties as a result of his public service; Arnold's action unwittingly condemned him to a lifetime of poverty.

Virginia had financed Clark's Illinois campaigns by allowing him to borrow money from a New Orleans merchant, who Virginia planned to repay with flour, which the merchant could sell for Spanish gold. However, Virginia never shipped the flour, in part because the Kentucky settlements could barely feed themselves, and Clark's source of money dried up. To complete the Vincennes campaign, he borrowed money from merchants in Kaskaskia and St. Louis, pledging as security his property in Kentucky. He expected to be reimbursed by the state, but the vouchers for his expenses were burned in the Richmond fire. In 1787 the U.S. Congress, having been given the Northwest, offered to reimburse Virginia for its expenses in conquering the territory. At the governor's request Clark prepared new records of his expenses, but they mysteriously disappeared in Richmond (they were discovered in the attic of the state capitol in 1913).

Hounded by his creditors, Clark turned his Kentucky property over to his brothers and moved across the river to Clarksville, where he built a small house on the only parcel of land that he could call his own. He never married. His only companions were a few books and the whiskey bottle. In 1812 a stroke left him partially paralyzed, and six years later another one killed him.

• John Bakeless, who has written biographies of a number of revolutionary heroes, has the most detailed and colorful account of Clark: *Background to Glory: The Life of George Rogers Clark* (1957). Lowell H. Harrison, *George Rogers Clark and the War in the West* (1976), is more recent, somewhat more scholarly in tone, and less detailed. A delightfully written account of Clark's Illinois campaigns can be found in Dale Van Every, *A Company of Heroes: The American Frontier, 1775–1783* (1962), the second in a splendidly written trilogy on the early frontier.

NORMAN K. RISJORD

CLARK, Grenville (5 Nov. 1882–13 Jan. 1967), attorney and world government advocate, was born in New York City, the son of Louis Crawford Clark, a wealthy banker, and Marian de Forest Cannon. He attended Pomfret School and then entered Harvard College, where he joined the exclusive Porcellian Club and graduated Phi Beta Kappa in 1903. Three years later, after earning a Harvard law degree, he joined the distinguished New York City law firm of Carter, Ledyard and Milburn, becoming friends with a young fellow clerk, Franklin D. Roosevelt. In 1909 Clark set up his own firm, establishing a partnership with two Harvard classmates, Elihu Root, Jr., the son of the secretary of state, and Francis W. Bird. That same year Clark married Fanny Dwight; they had five children, three of whom survived childhood.

Through Bird, Clark became interested in Republican politics, and when Progressive Republicans followed Theodore Roosevelt out of the party in 1912, Clark took an active role in their third-party effort. Two years later, when World War I broke out in Europe, he became convinced that America would be drawn into the hostilities. The U.S. Army had already begun running military training camps in Plattsburgh, New York, for college student volunteers. In 1915 Clark and a group of friends proposed that an extra session be added for young civic leaders. That August the "businessman's Plattsburgh" drew an enrollment that, as one historian observes, "sounded like 'Who's Who' and 'The Social Register' combined." Clark then helped organize a group of Plattsburgh alumni, the Military Training Camps Association, which sponsored similar programs in fourteen locations across the country. The association, with Clark as secretary, became an influential lobby for military preparedness, while the camps provided initial training for an estimated 80 percent of the combat officers who later served in the war. Once America entered the hostilities, the association screened all officer candidates until the army established its own system. Clark then moved to the adjutant general's office, where, rising from major to lieutenant colonel, he supervised the recruitment and training of 130,000 technicians.

Clark returned to his law firm after the war and continued to practice there intermittently until his retirement in 1948. He operated in the most elite Wall Street legal circles, and although his success owed something to his impressive social connections, he was also widely admired for his dedication and hard work. An opposing attorney observed: "He prepares like a scientist and hangs on like a leech." In the public sphere, Clark organized the National Economy League to oppose increases in veterans' pensions in 1931 (though he later said that the effort had been misguided), and he helped President Franklin Roosevelt draft the National Economy Act of 1933. Clark wrote the president: "I like many things you are doing and spend a fair amount of my time saying so." Nevertheless, when Roosevelt launched his "court-packing plan" in 1937, Clark organized a national committee of 250 lawyers to help defeat the proposal. During the late 1930s his concern over a series of new loyalty laws led him to organize and chair a national committee of the American Bar Association to champion the Bill of Rights. The committee initiated a number of successful free-speech cases, and its quarterly, *Bill of Rights Review*, which Clark coedited, won wide respect during the three years of its publication.

As World War II loomed in Europe, Clark published *A Federation of Free Peoples* (1939), advocating world government to resolve international disputes. But by May 1940 Clark had concluded that America must prepare for war. In a speech to the Plattsburgh alumni that month, he called for a national Selective Service Act. Through his Washington contacts—including his Harvard classmate, Supreme Court justice Felix Frankfurter—Clark learned that many politicians (including the president) thought the draft too unpopular to sponsor in an election year and that the isolationist secretary of war, Harry Woodring, opposed it. Working behind the scenes, Clark and Frankfurter helped speed Woodring's departure and then persuaded Roosevelt to appoint Henry L. Stimson, a respected Republican and a supporter of the draft, to his post. Clark worked to have a draft bill introduced in Congress and persuaded Roosevelt not to oppose it. The law passed by one vote in September 1940. Clark soon joined Stimson's staff and served throughout the war; among other tasks, he helped compose Roosevelt's war message on 8 December 1941. He also advocated, unsuccessfully, for a national service law that would organize the civilian workforce as the army organized the military.

With victory in sight, Clark left Washington in July 1944 and turned to the topic that would preoccupy him for the rest of his life: the effort to secure the international rule of law. In October 1945 he convened forty distinguished citizens near his country home in Dublin, New Hampshire; their Dublin Declaration called for the formation of a world federal government. Working with Harvard law professor Louis B. Sohn, Clark published a series of books and articles on the topic, culminating in their *World Peace through World Law* (1958). This book proposed creating an international system of administration, courts, revenue, and police that would promote total disarmament and provide "an effective system of *enforceable* law." It was translated into more than a dozen languages, and although it had little immediate impact on global politics, it continues to hold an important place in the literature of world government. In addition, Clark established a World Law Fund, served as vice president of the United World Federalists, sponsored a Soviet-American conference in 1960, monitored America's arms negotiations through his personal acquaintances in government, and tirelessly lobbied political leaders around the world on the need for disarmament and international law. Clark believed that the United Nations must be reorganized or supplemented to provide for compulsory participation in world government, arms inspection, and some constraints on national sovereignty. He also continued his concern for civil rights, speaking out for academic freedom throughout the Cold War and providing bail for Freedom Riders in 1961. Clark's wife died in 1965; not long thereafter he married Mary Brush. They had no children. He died in Dublin.

Clark spent few of his years in government service, yet for half a century he helped to shape U.S. policy-making. If his most ambitious goal—world federation—remained unrealized, he nevertheless used his wide contacts and formidable energy to keep three cardinal principles on the public agenda: the sanctity of the Bill of Rights, the importance of military strength in time of war, and the need to replace war with law as a way of resolving global conflicts.

• Clark's papers are at Dartmouth College (Hanover). Correspondence with him appears in the papers of Robert Bass Perkins and Douglas Arant, both at Dartmouth; Henry Lee Shattuck, Massachusetts Historical Society Library (Boston); Institute for World Order, Rutgers University (New Brunswick); and, at Harvard Law School Library (Cambridge), Felix Frankfurter, Mark De Wolfe Howe, Arthur Eugene Sullivan, Charles Culp Burlingham, Richard Hinkley Field, and Louis Bruno Sohn. Norman Cousins and J. Garry Clifford, eds., *Memoirs of a Man* (1975), is a collection of essays about his life. Gerald T. Dunne, *Grenville Clark: Public Citizen* (1986), provides a full-length biography. See also Samuel R. Spencer, Jr., "Clark and the Selective Training Service Act of 1940" (Ph.D. diss., Harvard Univ., 1947); Irving Dilliard, "Grenville Clark: Public Citizen," *American Scholar* 33 (Winter 1963–64): 97–104; Walter Millis, *Road to War: America 1914–1917* (1935); Kai Bird, *The Chairman: John J. McCloy, the Making of the American Establishment* (1992); and Henry L. Stimson and McGeorge Bundy, *On Active Service in Peace and War* (1947, 1948). An obituary is in the *New York Times*, 13 Jan. 1967.

SANDRA OPDYCKE

CLARK, Henry James (22 June 1826–1 July 1873), zoologist and microscopist, was born in Easton, Massachusetts, the son of Henry Porter Clark, a Swedenborgian clergyman, and Abigail Jackson Orton. During his youth, the family moved to Brooklyn, New York, where Clark was educated. After receiving an A.B. in 1848 from New York University, he taught for two years in White Plains, New York. Attracted first to the study of botany, in 1850 he went to Cambridge, Massachusetts, to study with the renowned Harvard botanist Asa Gray. (During this time he taught for one term at an academy in Westfield, Mass.) However, once Clark arrived at Harvard, he came under the influence of Louis Agassiz, and his interests were redirected to zoological studies.

By 1853 Clark was helping in the museum that Agassiz had begun to develop, unpacking and arranging fish. In 1854 he earned an S.B. from the Lawrence Scientific School of Harvard University and in that same year became an assistant to Agassiz. Although Clark's mature work was in zoology, the first published notice of his research was in botany (1856). It recorded an occasion at which Agassiz and Gray discussed Clark's work on anomalies in the growth rings of climbing dogwood (*Proceedings of the American Academy of Arts and Sciences* 3:335). His botanical interests likewise informed his subsequent studies in the histology and morphology of animals that encompassed some of the most elementary forms as well as his concern with fundamental questions of the nature and origin of life (including spontaneous generation). In 1854 he married Mary Young Holbrook; the couple had eight children.

Clark was hired by Agassiz in 1855 to assist with his major research and publishing project, *Contributions to the Natural History of the United States*, and this relationship continued until 1863. The first two volumes appeared in 1857 and volume 3 and volume 4 in 1860 and 1862, respectively. While working for Agassiz, Clark had available a richness of specimens and equipment, and he became an accomplished microscopist while demonstrating notable skill as an illustrator. He also encountered Agassiz's precarious financial situation and conflict that affected Clark as well as other Agassiz subordinates, resulting from differing concepts of the roles of the senior scientist and his students and assistants. In 1859 Clark was made assistant curator in Agassiz's Museum of Comparative Zoology, and from 1860 to 1865 he was assistant professor of zoology in the Lawrence Scientific School. The university had no funds to support the professorship, and Clark was paid by Agassiz. In 1861 Clark lectured on histology in the museum.

By 1863 Clark had been involved with Agassiz for a decade and believed that he had not been adequately recognized or credited for the work he had done. Early in that year, their relationship was broken over issues involving back pay owed to Clark and a work on the Lucernaria (a group of medusae) that Clark had in preparation but had not revealed to Agassiz. The conflict became an open one when Agassiz refused to have the question of Clark's involvement in the *Contributions* reviewed by capable judges. Clark issued a printed three-page statement, *A Claim for Scientific Property*, in July 1863. Distributing it in the United States and Europe, he asserted in the statement that significant parts of volumes 2, 3, and 4 of the *Contributions* were prepared by him but not adequately credited to him by Agassiz. Clark pointed out that the microscopical parts especially were his not only in detail but contained his thoughts and interpretations. For example, he claimed credit for the work on turtle embryology in volume 2, "the theory of the development, the anatomy and histology of Coryne mirabilis" (a hydroid) in volume 4, and other specific parts. Agassiz refused to acknowledge the critique, and Clark was effectively barred from teaching or conducting research in the museum, though he held his professorship until his term expired in 1865.

It is perhaps some gauge of Clark's community support in the period of this controversy that he was able to present a series of twelve Lowell Institute lectures in Boston in February and March 1864. They were published in revised form as *Mind in Nature; or, The Origin of Life, and the Mode of Development of Animals* (1865). The book was accompanied by more than 200 illustrations, most of them by Clark. Although popular lectures, the book also included a great deal of original work and was both detailed and philosophical. He argued for five large and standing major divisions of animals while looking to the operation of natural laws of the Creator for variation within those groups. The work reflected Agassiz's influence. Clark's contemporary biographer called it "perhaps the most remarkable general zoological work as yet produced in this country" (Packard, p. 323).

In 1866 Clark presented a paper to the Boston Society of Natural History in which he addressed the question of the relation of sponges to flagellate Infusoria (protozoa) and presented his confirmation of sponges as animal rather than vegetable. This research has been considered his most significant microscopical study, although not all of his conclusions were accepted.

Also in 1866, Clark was appointed professor of botany, zoology, and geology in the Pennsylvania State University. He remained in that position until 1869 when he became professor of natural history at the University of Kentucky. Neither of these appointments allowed him sufficient time for research, and in

1872 he was made professor of veterinary science at the University of Massachusetts. During his short connection with that institution (as its first trained zoologist) he began a museum in comparative and pathological anatomy and taught human anatomy and physiology, comparative anatomy and zoology, and comparative physiology. Clark died at Amherst, Massachusetts of tuberculosis of the abdominal glands.

Clark became a fellow of the American Academy of Arts and Sciences in 1856 and was a member of the Boston Society of Natural History beginning in 1857. In 1872 he was elected to the National Academy of Sciences. He was noted for his thoroughness and devotion to his research. Clark's work on Lucernariae was published posthumously by the Smithsonian Institution in 1878.

• Clark's papers in the library of the Museum of Comparative Zoology at Harvard include his diaries, manuscripts, drawings, and several letters. The university archives has documents relating to his association with Harvard and the controversy with Agassiz. Other significant works by Clark include "On the Spongiae Ciliatae as Infusoria Flagellata; or, Observations on the Structure, Animality, and Relationship of Leucosolenia botryoides, Bowerbank," *Memoirs of the Boston Society of Natural History* 1, pt. 3 (1868): 305–40 and plates; and *Lucernariae and Their Allies, a Memoir on the Anatomy and Physiology of Haliclystus auricula, and Other Lucernarians, with a Discussion of Their Relations to Other Acalephae, to Beroids, and Polypi* (Smithsonian Contributions to Knowledge, no. 242) (1878). Biographies appear in the *Proceedings of the American Academy of Arts and Sciences* 9 (1874): 328–30, and A. S. Packard, Jr., *Biographical Memoirs of the National Academy of Sciences* 1 (1877): 317–28; the latter includes a bibliography of Clark's works. His relationship with Agassiz is traced in Edward Lurie, *Louis Agassiz: A Life in Science* (1960), and Mary P. Winsor, *Reading the Shape of Nature: Comparative Zoology at the Agassiz Museum* (1991).

CLARK A. ELLIOTT

CLARK, John (28 Feb. 1766–12 Oct. 1832), governor of Georgia, was born in Edgecombe County, North Carolina, the son of Elijah Clarke and Hanna Arrington, farmers. He enjoyed only brief formal education. He was not yet in his teens when his family settled in the Georgia back country above Augusta. The American Revolution broke out soon after they arrived, and Clark's father became one of the Whig leaders. Though still a boy, John Clark, who at some point dropped the "e" from his name, joined his father's unit and fought with it at the battle of Kettle Creek and other engagements during the last years of the war. By the end of the conflict he had risen to the rank of captain. Clark continued in the military service of the state and was involved in the fighting between Georgians and the Creek Indians that followed American independence. By 1796 Clark had reached the rank of major general in the Georgia militia. He also farmed, speculated in land, and held political office.

In 1792 Clark married Nancy Williamson, a member of a prominent upcountry family, and they had four children. This union, along with his military record, increased his status among settlers in the western part of the state, and in 1801 the citizens of Wilkes County elected him to the general assembly. There he became an opponent of James Jackson, who was Georgia's rising political star. Clark and Jackson split over the Yazoo controversy that arose when speculators bribed legislators to gain control of vast tracts of land for a few cents an acre. Clark was less critical of the speculators than Jackson, perhaps because both he and his father had been tied to them. The division inspired by Yazoo was also seen in the bitter rivalry between Clark, who became spokesman for the North Carolina immigrants who settled in Georgia's Broad River valley, and William H. Crawford, who spoke for Virginians who settled in the same area. The conflict between these two men became heated and personal, and in 1806 they fought a duel, in which Crawford was wounded. The next year Clark issued another challenge, which Crawford rejected, and the furious Clark expressed his anger by publicly horsewhipping a Crawford ally, Judge Charles Tait.

Rivalries quieted down when Crawford was elected to the U.S. Senate in 1807, but by the end of the War of 1812, Georgia politics had heated up again. In 1819 Clark ran for governor as the champion of frontier farmer interests against George M. Troup, the spokesman for the coastal aristocracy and rising piedmont planter class, a rivalry that echoed the economic, social, and geographic divisions that had plagued colonial and revolutionary politics in Georgia. The legislature elected Clark by thirteen votes, a margin that was cut to two votes when he was reelected in 1821. In office he advocated a system of free public schools, prison reform, and democratic political reforms. Though he was unable to enact most of the measures he proposed, Clark was able to push through a constitutional amendment to make the office of governor popularly elected. Ironically, in the election that followed in 1825 he lost to Troup by some 700 votes out of the roughly 40,000 ballots that were cast. This was Clark's last political outing. In 1827 he moved to Florida, and soon afterward President Andrew Jackson appointed him a federal Indian agent. He died at St. Andrew's Bay.

Clark's career reveals the power of personality and ambition in early Georgia politics. His stand on national issues, when he had one, was generally in accord with the Jeffersonian Republicans in his state. However, when local issues were being debated, he could and did differ with other Georgians of that party. These differences, with their overtones of class conflict, were magnified by family feuds, personal vendettas, and rivalries that went back to Georgians' North Carolina and Virginia origins. Historians look upon Clark as representative of this sort of factionalism and one of the last of a breed of political figures whose roots were sunk deep in Georgia's colonial and revolutionary past.

• Ulrich B. Phillips, *Georgia and State Rights* (1902), remains the standard treatment of the period, although George R. Lamplugh, *Politics on the Periphery: Factions and Parties in*

Georgia, 1776–1806 (1986), is a useful update and expansion of Phillips's work. Also covering the period and Clark's role in it are F. N. Boney, "The Politics of Expansion and Secession, 1820–1861," in *A History of Georgia*, ed. Kenneth Coleman (1977); and Jack Nelson Averitt, "The Democratic Party in Georgia, 1824–1837" (Ph.D. diss., Univ. of North Carolina, 1957). See also C. Peter Magrath, *Yazoo: Law and Politics in the New Republic; Case of "Fletcher vs. Peck"* (1966).

HARVEY H. JACKSON

CLARK, John Bates (26 Jan. 1847–21 Mar. 1938), economist, was born in Providence, Rhode Island, the son of John Hezekiah Clark, a merchant of modest prosperity, and Charlotte Huntington. In his early youth his family moved to Minneapolis. Clark returned east in 1865 to attend Brown University and later Amherst College. In 1868 his father's failing health required him to interrupt his studies to take over the family business (farm machinery) in Minnesota. Following his father's death, the business was sold and Clark returned to Amherst, from which he graduated in 1872.

After seriously considering entry into the Congregational ministry, the profession of many of his New England ancestors, Clark joined the growing band of American students in Germany who were preparing for academic careers. Clark sought a preparation in economics, having studied the subject with Amherst president Julius Seelye and the standard textbook of Amasa Walker. Clark spent 1874 and 1877 in Heidelberg and six months of 1876 at Zurich.

Clark's European experience had a profound impact on him. While he has left no detailed account of his time there, he always acknowledged Karl Knies of Heidelberg as his most influential teacher. Although Knies was a leading member of the German historical school, which was transplanted to the United States in the much less dogmatic form of "institutional economics," he was more open to formal economic analysis than most of his German colleagues; indeed, his seminar attracted the notable Austrian theorists Eugen von Böhm-Bawerk and Friedrich von Wieser.

On returning to the United States, Clark in 1876 became professor of economy and history at Carleton College in Northfield, Minnesota. Soon after arriving, he was, for two years, largely incapacitated by a debilitating illness that seems permanently to have lowered his energy level. (The Clark family memorials are reticent about the nature of the illness; Alvin Johnson, who was Clark's colleague at Columbia University, believed that it was typhoid.) Clark nevertheless had a long life and excellent work habits. Even in poor health, he always strove to write a page or two a day. In 1875 he married Myra Smith, one of the early graduates of Vassar College; they had four children.

Clark first gained recognition as the author of a series of articles in the *New Englander*, which in 1886 were published as *The Philosophy of Wealth*. In this, the work of a young, Victorian Germanophile, Clark portrayed commerce (at least in the United States) as little better than theft, and elevated moral sentiments abound. While the book has always been something of an embarrassment to Clark's admirers, it showed flashes of theoretical insight that were developed in his later works, such as an original statement of the principle of diminishing marginal utility ("effective utility" in Clark's terminology), which radically altered the way economists view the world. Although the moral fervor of the essays in *Philosophy* is muted in Clark's later work, his son John Maurice Clark, a distinguished economist in his own right, observed that Clark's work remained "permeated by a social-ethical system that is not always well integrated with the technical economic analysis."

At a meeting in 1885 in Saratoga, New York, of the American Historical Association, Clark joined with political economists Richard Ely and Henry Carter Adams to issue the "call" that led to the formation of the American Economic Association. The invitation was especially directed to the young German-trained economists who were dissatisfied with the low level of American teaching and research in economics. The new association's avowed purposes were to encourage German-type historical and empirical research and to provide a sympathetic hearing for the critics of the doctrine of laissez-faire, which was generally expounded, often quite crudely, in American classrooms. While no necessary connection between the methodology of the German historical school and suspicion of laissez-faire existed, in Bismarck's Germany these two ingredients were almost always found together.

By virtue of his interest in economic theory and his unfailing good manners, Clark was the least combative personality of the three founders of the new association. In the United States the debate over the best methodology for economics never reached the bitterness of the *methodenstreit* between the historical school and the theorists that blighted the growth of economics in Germany before World War I. (Mainly because the historical school won, the refugee scholars from Hitler's Europe who did so much for American economics were largely German theorists.) Clark shared with Francis Amasa Walker, son of Amasa Walker and the first president of the American Economic Association, the main credit for bringing about this fortunate outcome. Within ten years after its founding, almost all economists in the United States, both "Germans" and adherents of the "old", that is, classical political economy of John Stuart Mill and David Ricardo, had joined the association.

In 1888 Clark published *Capital and Its Earnings*, which many scholars view as the foundation of the modern theory of capital and interest. In it Clark made clear for the first time the connections among capital, income, and the interest rate. He identified capital as the stock of productive power, income as the flow of services yielded by capital, and the interest rate as the ratio of income to the value of the capital stock. According to Clark, individual capital goods can be created, used, and scrapped; capital as "an endlessly reincarnating fund of productive power" endures. Interest can be paid because, over time, "capital is productive." That is, income can be increased by sacrificing consumption in order to build additional capital goods.

In the 1890s Clark turned his attention to the problem of how income would be distributed among the cooperating factors of production in a static state, one in which technology and consumer tastes do not change. In these investigations he was hampered by a limited mathematical training that did not include calculus. Nevertheless, his mathematical intuition was sound. Using "words and pictures" he was able to correct the notion, derived from Ricardo and the classical economists, that land rent was somehow unique—a surplus that remained to landlords after competition had determined the share of production that went to capitalists and workers. To derive rent as a surplus, earlier economists had treated land as the fixed factor of production. Clark devised a set of diagrams to show that, in a two-factor model, what is viewed as rent and what is viewed as a payment for use of a factor is a matter of geometrical taste. When the fixed and variable factors are interchanged on the diagram, what was rent becomes factor payment and vice versa. Although other economists, most notably Philip Wicksteed of Britain and Knut Wicksell of Sweden, provided more rigorous proofs of this theorem, Clark's demonstration reached the widest audience and is still incorporated in many economic textbooks, such as Paul Samuelson's *Principles of Economics*.

After completing his work on capital and distribution theory, Clark turned his attention to what he called "dynamics"—changes in prices and costs that cause departures from the static state—but did not achieve comparable success. Still, his last major work, *The Essentials of Economic Theory, as Applied to Modern Problems of Industry and Public Policy* (1907), contains many wise observations on the economic consequences of population growth, technological change, and the rise of large firms. In an earlier paper, "The Theory of Economic Progress" (*Publications of the American Economic Association* [1896]), Clark had made clear his conviction that, notwithstanding the usefulness of the static state as an analytical tool, the closer any real-world situation approximated it, the worse the human condition. Technological change, with its often unsettling effects, he argued, is the all-important engine of economic progress.

Before his views on dynamics could be developed further, Clark in 1911 became director of the history and economic section of the newly organized Carnegie Endowment for International Peace in New York City. While with the Carnegie Endowment, Clark helped to launch the studies that became the *Social and Economic History of the World War* (1935), which still remains the most ambitious research project in the social sciences ever undertaken by a private foundation. The director of the project, Clark's friend and Columbia colleague, historian James Shotwell, however, could devise no organizing principle and exercised poor quality control. While the published studies of the project ultimately numbered more than 100, they have been little used by historians of the Great War.

Clark's concern for world peace continued after he left the Carnegie foundation in 1923. His last book, *A Tender of Peace: The Terms on Which Civilized Nations Can, If They Will, Avoid Warfare*, appeared in 1935.

Clark was an active participant in the policy debates of his era, especially in the debate on the "trust question" that raged in the thirty years before World War I. The sudden appearance of the large industrial corporation after the Civil War had compelled economists to consider its economic and political consequences. Forced to confront and reappraise two of the strongest intellectual influences of his youth, Clark had to balance the belief of his German teachers that increasing corporate growth was inevitable and no bad thing if superintended by the state against the view of the English classical economists that all markets were naturally competitive when left alone by the state. As late as 1890 the eminent English economist Alfred Marshall warned against assuming that firms of the size of the Standard Oil Company were the wave of the future. He correctly pointed out that no other large firm of the time had achieved anything like the success of Standard and many that had sought rapid growth had ended in bankruptcy.

Clark's views leaned toward conventional laissez-faire in *The Control of Trusts: An Argument in Favor of Curbing the Power of Monopoly by a Natural Method* (1901). His "natural method" was little more than market competition purged of unfair tactics plus government regulation of railroad rates to prevent the type of preferential rebates that Standard Oil had often secured. In a 1912 revision of the book, written with his son John Maurice, the subtitle was dropped and the natural method was replaced with a list of more specific recommendations for controlling trusts, which were a blueprint for an antitrust policy—restrictions on mergers, exclusive dealing, interlocking company directors, and unfair competition. Both Clarks welcomed the Clayton Act and the Federal Trade Commission Act that followed in 1914.

Modern economic analysis has laid bare the contradictions in Clark's work on the trusts by showing that antitrust policy rests more on populist ideology than on any demonstration that the restrictions imposed on business behavior will increase economic welfare. Clark, in fact, never embraced the doctrinaire hostility to the large firm that characterizes the fervent supporters of antitrust. He stressed that "competition among the few" often sufficed to preclude the emergence of monopoly profits because of the price discipline enforced by potential competition (the possibility that high profits would draw new firms into the industry). He doubted that price fixing agreements among rival firms could be effectively enforced.

Clark taught at Carleton College (1877–1881), Smith College (1882–1895), Amherst College, and from 1895 to 1923 at Columbia. Many of his students went on to distinguished careers in academia and government and remembered him with affection even though his reticence and loosely organized courses prevented him from becoming a powerful presence in the classroom. Clark's influence was mainly exerted through his writings and conversation—and through his economist son.

As the first economist in the United States to deserve and gain an international reputation, Clark received many honors and awards in his lifetime. From 1893 to 1895 he served as the third president of the American Economic Association. He is widely considered, along with Irving Fisher, to be one of America's preeminent economists. He died in New York City.

• Clark's papers are in the special collections library of Columbia University and in its Columbiana collection. A nearly complete bibliography of his published works is in *A Bibliography of the Faculty of Political Science, Columbia University, 1880–1930* (1931), and in *Economic Essays Contributed in Honor of John Bates Clark*, ed. J. H. Hollander (1927). The privately printed *John Bates Clark: A Memorial Volume Prepared by His Children* (1938), contains much interesting biographical information. Clark's role in the launching of the American Economic Association is traced in A. W. Coats, "The First Two Decades of the American Economic Association," *American Economic Review* 50, no. 4 (1960): 555–74, and in Joseph Dorfman, *The Economic Mind in American Civilization*, vols. 2 and 3 (1949). The influence of religion in Clark's work is treated in John R. Everett, *Religion in Economics: A Study of John Bates Clark, Richard Ely and Simon Patten* (1946), and Dorothy Ross, *The Origins of American Social Science* (1991). The development of Clark's views on monopoly, the modern corporation, and antitrust is considered in H. B. Thorelli, *The Federal Antitrust Policy: Origination of an American Tradition* (1954), and B. J. Klebamer, "Trusts and Competition: A Note on John Bates Clark and John Maurice Clark," *Social Research* 29 (1962): 473–79. A critical exposition of Clark's economic theory is George Stigler, *Production and Distribution Theories: The Formative Period* (1941). A mathematical formulation of Clark's treatment of capital and interest is Paul Samuelson, "Parable and Realism in Capital Theory: The Surrogate Production Function," *Review of Economic Studies* 29 (1963): 193–96. An obituary is in the *Economic Journal*, Sept. 1938.

DONALD DEWEY

CLARK, John Maurice (30 Nov. 1884–27 June 1963), economist, was born in Northampton, Massachusetts, the son of John Bates Clark and Myra Almeda Smith. Clark's father, himself a noted economist, won regard as a distinguished scholar for his contributions to economic theory and had a profound personal and professional influence on his son. J. M. Clark received his undergraduate degree from Amherst College in 1905 and his Ph.D. in economics from Columbia University in 1910. His thesis had been supervised by his father, with whom he coauthored an expanded revision of J. B. Clark's *The Control of Trusts*, published in 1912. After holding positions at Colorado College (1908–1910), Amherst College (1910–1915), and the University of Chicago (1915–1926), he taught at Columbia University from 1926 to 1957 and was named to the John Bates Clark Professorship of Political Economy, established in honor of his father, in 1951. He married Winifred Fiske Miller in 1921; they had two children.

In addition to being an influential writer in several areas of economics, Clark was active in policy deliberations related to antitrust and to public works during the depression of the 1930s; he served in a number of private and governmental organizations concerned with public policy matters. Professional recognition and honors included his election in 1935 as president of the American Economic Association, of which his father had been the third president (1894–1895), and his 1952 receipt of the AEA's second Francis A. Walker Medal. The AEA's highest award, the medal was given every five years between 1947 and 1977 for a "contribution of the highest distinction to economics"; the award citation noted the variety of Clark's contributions, along with his concern for ethical matters and interdisciplinary approaches. He also served as an honorary president of the International Economic Association.

Clark's most influential contributions to economic theory are presented in his *Studies in the Economics of Overhead Costs* (1923), which had significant implications for microeconomic theory, the design of public policy toward business, and employment policy. To Clark, overhead costs were those that "do not vary with output" or "are not traced to units of output." While such costs had to be covered by business in the long run, they did not need to be covered in the short run. Clark drew on this concept to explain behavior in various sectors where the primary issue was the increased or full utilization of equipment and labor. His treatment of labor as an overhead cost, with its implications for social policies regarding employment and reducing the fluctuations of the business cycle, was unusual for the time. Clark argued that the nature of overhead costs led to the development of monopoly power and price discrimination, as well as to generating social costs and influencing changes in the business cycle. He further contended that overhead costs meant that perfect competition could not exist and that more attention needed to be paid to the dynamic rather than the static characteristics of the economy. The book continues to be cited for its discussions of internal and external economies of scale and their effects on industrial structure and for the distinctions made between true economies of scale, conceived as having social benefits, by lowering costs and prices when output increases, and advantages of size, which yield only private benefits. These ideas, novel at the time, played a key role in the emergence of the theories of monopolistic and imperfect competition in the 1930s.

Several of the ideas in *Studies in the Economics of Overhead Costs* were extended in an influential article published in the *American Economic Review* (30 [June 1940]: 241–56) titled "Toward a Concept of Workable Competition," the basis of Clark's 1961 book, *Competition as a Dynamic Process*. Both the article and the book are important in the study of industrial organization and antitrust policy. Distinguishing "workable" and "effective" competition from "pure" and "perfect" competition, Clark emphasized the dynamic nature of markets, with considerations of entry and of exit and the full range of alternatives open to consumers and producers. This work triggered further theoretical analysis and detailed empirical studies by others and is often credited with having helped to modernize the study of industrial organization.

Although Clark's most enduring achievements were in microeconomics, he also made several significant contributions to the emerging macroeconomic theory and policy debates of the 1920s and 1930s. His article in the *Journal of Political Economy* (25 [Mar. 1917]: 217–35), "Business Acceleration and the Law of Demand: A Technical Factor in Economic Cycles," is regarded as a fundamental contribution to business cycle theory. Clark's concept of the accelerator, relating changes in investment to the changing rate of growth of output, was a featured characteristic in many subsequent models of business fluctuations in the years after the Keynesian revolution. In 1934 he published, with the National Bureau of Economic Research, *Strategic Factors in Business Cycles*, in which he examined the empirical and theoretical literature on business cycles, presenting several new ideas and anticipating concepts such as "multipliers." His concern with economic stabilization and contracyclical economic policy led him to discuss their problems and effects in *Economics of Planning Public Works*, written for the National Planning Board in 1935. In addition to working with several government agencies both during and after the depression, he was a member of the United Nations' "Group of Experts," charged with recommending appropriate macroeconomic policies to its members. Clark wrote a separate, but concurring, statement to the group's report in 1949, pointing to the prospective inflationary problems of wage-price policy, an issue he was to return to in the U.S. context.

Several of Clark's other important publications are less easy to categorize. *Social Control of Business* (1926) presented arguments on the need for controls over business by government and various institutions of society, using legislation and other means in the interests of achieving economic welfare. His argument emphasized the interdependence of the modern economy and the complexity of laws dealing with economic forces, claiming, in effect, that the age of extreme individualism had come to an end. The broad definition of social control, with the interests of all parties influencing behavior in the market and in society, raised many issues that Clark returned to in his discussion of a "society of responsible individuals in responsible groups" in *Alternative to Serfdom* (1948). That book, based on a 1947 series of lectures at the University of Michigan, was meant as a response to Friedrich A. Hayek's *The Road to Serfdom* (1944), particularly in presenting a more positive role for the state, but it has not had the survival power of the Hayek volume. *The Costs of the World War to the American People* (1931), prepared for the Carnegie Endowment for International Peace, while somewhat neglected, is an interesting theoretical and empirical study, one of the more important volumes of the endowment's many publications. It followed his earlier interests in the economics of war, as seen in *Readings in the Economics of War* (1918), which he coedited with Walton H. Hamilton and Harold G. Moulton.

Despite the wide range of Clark's contributions, the number of important students and colleagues he fostered, and all the acclaim he received during his lifetime, he was subsequently not regarded as a dominant figure in the development of economics. This reflects two characteristics of the discipline at the end of the twentieth century: on the one hand, a neglect of the teachings of earlier economists and, on the other, the tendency to examine the core of Clark's writings about economics in narrow, highly technical terms. This type of critique, however, fails to do justice to the wide range of Clark's interests and his concern with the ethical aspects of economics and economic welfare. His willingness, and capacity, to extend his theoretical insights and empirical studies into the realm of practical policy remains a model for the development of the discipline and its practitioners.

• The John Maurice Clark Papers are at Columbia University. Many of Clark's journal articles and essays were republished in *Preface to Social Economics: Essays on Economic Theory and Social Problems* (1936) and *Economic Institutions and Human Welfare* (1957). A useful, albeit brief, intellectual biography is C. Addison Hickman, *J. M. Clark* (1975); it also contains an extensive bibliography. A useful discussion of Clark's economic writings and their impact is in Joseph Dorfman, *The Economic Mind in American Civilization*, vols. 4–5: *1918–1933* (1959). A more recent work on Clark is Laurence Shute, *John Maurice Clark: A Social Economics for the Twenty-first Century* (1997). An obituary is in the *New York Times*, 28 June 1963.

STANLEY L. ENGERMAN

CLARK, Joshua Reuben, Jr. (1 Sept. 1871–6 Oct. 1961), diplomat and church leader, was born near Grantsville, Utah, the eldest of the ten children of Joshua Reuben Clark, Sr., and Mary Louisa Woolley, Mormon farmers. Although the family was poor, Clark showed great promise early on and was encouraged to pursue an education. He graduated from the University of Utah in 1898 and went on to Columbia University Law School in 1903. While there he came to the attention of both James Brown Scott and John Bassett Moore, pioneers in the international law movement. Upon graduation (1906), he followed Scott to the State Department, where the latter had been appointed solicitor. Clark became assistant solicitor.

Owing to the fact that Scott was away much of the time, Clark basically ran the solicitor's office. He became friends with Francis Mairs Huntington Wilson, an assistant secretary of state, and the two later wielded great influence in the department. In fact, after the appointment of Philander C. Knox as secretary of state in 1909 (and Clark's promotion to solicitor the following year), Clark and Huntington Wilson, in Knox's virtual absence from the day-to-day operations of his department, were more or less in charge. Together they engineered the U.S. intervention into Nicaragua's Bluefields revolt against Jose Santos de Zelaya, the country's dictatorial ruler. Clark eventually came to regret this action as well as the whole idea of U.S. military intervention.

Even more fateful was Clark's involvement with U.S.–Mexican relations. When the Mexican Revolution broke out in 1910, the U.S. State Department faced a series of dilemmas with respect to military intervention. Large numbers of U.S. citizens were living in northern Mexico, and intervention would endanger their lives. On the other hand, various revolutionary groups found it in their interest to provoke just such an intervention. Clark responded to the situation with dogged legalism and an iron-willed self-restraint. In the end, his policy paid off.

With the election of Woodrow Wilson in 1912, Clark left the State Department to practice international law. He served on several claims commissions and maintained law offices in both Washington and New York. He played an important behind-the-scenes role in the battle of isolationists against the League of Nations. At the same time, he took part in the Washington Conference on the Limitations of Armaments of 1921, acting as legal counsel to Charles Evans Hughes.

In 1927, Clark was drawn back into the vortex of U.S.–Mexican affairs. The Mexican Revolution had resulted in laws curtailing the rights of U.S. oil companies south of the border. By now an old hand with such difficulties, Clark was invited to accompany the new ambassador, Dwight Morrow, to Mexico City. Together Clark and Morrow spent nearly two years struggling with the oil controversy while the two countries edged toward confrontation. The combination of Clark's legalism and Morrow's pragmatism eventually won the day. Instead of bluster, the United States appealed to Mexican law itself, winning support on both sides of the border and averting catastrophe.

In 1928, Clark was appointed undersecretary of state. During his ten months at this post he conducted research on the Monroe Doctrine and concluded that the Roosevelt Corollary (which was often used to justify U.S. intervention in Latin America) was neither historically nor legally justifiable. His argument, embodied in the *Clark Memorandum*, released in 1930, marked a turning point in Latin American diplomacy.

When Dwight Morrow returned to the United States in 1930 to run for the Senate, Herbert Hoover (1874–1964) appointed Clark to take his place. Although Clark was neither wealthy—a prime requisite for ambassadorships at the time—nor a career diplomat, he once again accepted the assignment, and in November 1930 he took charge of the country's most sensitive and volatile diplomatic post. He continued Morrow's evenhanded policy and appealed, when he had to, over the heads of puppet presidents to the military *jefe* in charge. Fortune graced him with a relatively quiet tenure. He retired from public life in 1933.

Despite his public career, Clark remained an essentially private person. He married Luacine Annetta Savage of Salt Lake City in 1898, and they raised four children. Clark always aspired to be a gentleman farmer; he was happy to retire from the diplomatic world and settle down at his Grantsville ranch. However, leaders of the Mormon church tapped him to be second counselor to church president Heber J. Grant, becoming first counselor in 1934. Clark remained one of the church's ruling triumvirate for almost thirty years.

There was a curious duality in Clark's nature. On the one hand, he strongly believed in the legal settlement of international disputes. On the other hand, he came to have grave doubts about international law itself and the World Court in particular. Toward the end of his life, he became an outspoken opponent of nuclear weapons and U.S. involvement abroad. The world, as he saw it, was hell-bent for destruction, and only a pure and aloof United States could save it. He died in Salt Lake City.

• The papers of J. Reuben Clark, Jr., are found in special collections at the Brigham Young University Library. Unfortunately they remain closed to the public at large. There is a biography of Clark's public career by Frank W. Fox, *J. Reuben Clark: The Public Years* (1980), and of his religious career by D. Michael Quinn, *J. Reuben Clark: The Church Years* (1983). David H. Yarn has edited several volumes of Clark's papers, many of them dealing with religious themes, including *J. Reuben Clark: Selected Papers on Religion, Education, and Youth* (1984), and *J. Reuben Clark: Selected Papers on International Affairs* (1987).

FRANK W. FOX

CLARK, Lewis Gaylord (5 Oct. 1808–3 Nov. 1873), editor of *The Knickerbocker Magazine*, was born in Otisco, New York, the twin brother of Willis Gaylord Clark, a journalist and poet. The twins were talented, but not wealthy; locally educated, they were encouraged to seek literary employment by their maternal uncle, Willis Gaylord, editor of the *Genessee Farmer and Albany Cultivator*.

At the age of twenty-four, Lewis Gaylord Clark moved to New York City, where he invested his savings and his hopes in *The Knickerbocker Magazine*, founded in 1833 by Samuel Langtree, a physician, and first edited by Charles Fenno Hoffman, then by Timothy Flint. In 1834 Clark married Ella Maria Curtis, with whom he eventually parented five children.

In an effort to make the *Knickerbocker* the most distinguished literary periodical in the country, Clark solicited contributions from such established writers as Henry Wadsworth Longfellow, James Fenimore Cooper, William Cullen Bryant, and Washington Irving, after whose humorous fictional character, Diedrich Knickerbocker, the magazine took its name. To keep his magazine solvent in a market just learning to value American authors and still without international copyright legislation, Clark worked vigorously to cultivate and pay contributors, stimulate public taste, and represent prosperous, conservative New York.

One of his innovations was a monthly section of reportage and letterlike gossip. Clark's "The Editor's Table," filled with accounts of dinner parties and celebrity visits, was widely copied by other periodicals of the day. He and his brother, who was now earning a reputation as a poet and as editor of the *Philadelphia Daily Inquirer*, produced reviews and informal prose for the *Knickerbocker*. In their day, Willis was considered the more gifted of the brothers; his column of informal prose, called *Ollapodiana* (after Dr. Ollapod in George Colman's play, *The Poor Gentleman*, who, in turn, was named for the Spanish *olla podrida*, a dish of meat and vegetables), which he sent faithfully to his brother for the *Knickerbocker*, was one of its most valued features.

However, Lewis Clark had chosen the more promising of the two cities; New York had replaced Boston as a literary capital. Clark mocked the Transcendentalism of Ralph Waldo Emerson and Henry David Thoreau and regarded James Russell Lowell and other New England abolitionists as fanatics. Although he claimed to take an apolitical stance, Clark and his supporters were identified with the Whig party, anti-Jacksonian advocates of northern business interests such as protective tariffs. He often published sentimental or predictable verse, but in his articles he showed more adventurous taste, including essays on native American cultures, Icelandic legends, and European history. In January 1839, Clark noted that the magazine had presented serious essays on sixty subjects.

Clark's own writing, subordinated to the needs of his magazine was often occasional, yet he made substantial contributions in the short essay, the witty anecdote, and the sustained parody. He produced an "Editorial Narrative-History of the Knickerbocker Magazine" in 1850 that offers a portrait of the antebellum intellectual and social life of New York. His series of parodies of American newspapers, entitled *"The Bunkumville Flagstaff and Independent Echo,"* satirizes reviews and advertisements and remains a significant contribution to American humor. In 1852 Clark published an anthology, *Knick-Knacks from an Editor's Table*, reprinting pieces from his column.

When *The Knickerbocker Magazine* failed financially in 1861, Clark's loyal contributors collaborated on a volume of their own work, called *The Knickerbocker Gallery* (1855), published for the benefit of the editor who had served his magazine so devotedly. After a stint in the New York Custom House, Clark retired to a small cottage on the Hudson, at Piermont, near Nyack, where he is buried.

• In addition to *Knick-Knacks from an Editor's Table*, Clark edited *The Literary Remains of the Late Willis Gaylord Clark, Including the Ollapodiana Papers, The Spirit of Life, and a Selection from his Various Prose and Poetical Writings* (1844); *The Knickerbocker Sketch-Book: A Library of Select Literature* (1845); *The Lover's Gift; and Friendship's Token* (1848) and *The Life, Eulogy and Great Orations of Daniel Webster* (1855). The best biographical source is *The Letters of Willis Gaylord Clark and Lewis Gaylord Clark*, ed. Leslie W. Dunlap (1940). Lewis and Willis Gaylord Clark are represented briefly in the anthology *Minor Knickerbockers*, ed. Kendall B. Taft (1947). See also Perry Miller, *The Raven and the Whale: The War of Words and Wits in the Era of Poe and Melville* (1956); Frank Luther Mott, *A History of American Magazines, 1791–1850* (1930); Benjamin T. Spencer, "A National Literature, 1837–1855," *American Literature* 8 (1936): 125–59. An obituary by Thomas Bangs Thorpe is in *Harper's New Monthly Magazine*, Mar. 1874, pp. 587–92.

BETTE S. WEIDMAN

CLARK, Marguerite (22 Feb. 1883–25 Sept. 1940), actress, was born Helen Marguerite Clark in Avondale, Ohio, a suburb of Cincinnati, the daughter of Augustus James Clark, a haberdasher, and Helen Elizabeth Golden. Clark attended local public schools and an Ursuline convent at St. Martin, Ohio, where she showed an early talent for singing and acting. After the death of her mother in 1893 and her father in 1896, Clark's older (by twelve years) sister Cora became her guardian.

At the request of her sister, Clark abandoned formal education in favor of a potentially lucrative theatrical career (with her sister serving as her personal manager). Sixteen-year-old Clark made her professional debut in 1899 as a supernumerary with Baltimore's Strakosch Opera Company. Moving to New York, she played small parts in several musical productions, including *The Wild Rose* (1902), with Eddie Foy. In this production she was seen by prominent actor De Wolf Hopper, who cast the petite, dark-haired actress as Polly in the musical comedy *Mr. Pickwick* (1903). She worked again with Hopper in *Happyland* (1905) and *The Pied Piper* (1908).

In January 1910 Clark made her first appearance in a lead role in the unsuccessful musical *The King of Cadonia*. Later in the year she starred in the dramatic play *The Wishing Ring* by Owen Davis and the popular comedy *Baby Mine* by Margaret Mayo. Producer Winthrop Ames cast Clark in *The Affairs of Anatol* (1912), costarring John Barrymore, *Snow White and the Seven Dwarfs* (1912), *Are You a Crook?* (1913), and *Prunella; or, Love in a Dutch Garden* (1913). "Miss Clark presented an ideal child's figure and acts the early scenes with delightful naïveté. In the line of refined ingenues she has no rival on the American stage," said the *New York Dramatic Mirror* (29 Oct. 1913) of Clark's performance in *Prunella*. While appearing in a revival of *Merely Mary Ann* in 1914 Clark was offered a movie contract by Adolph Zukor, head of the Famous Players Motion Picture Company. Cora Clark, who continued as her sister's manager throughout her career, thought movies were a fad, but she advised Clark to accept Zukor's lucrative three-year, $1,000-per-week offer. Clark never acted on stage again.

Clark's first movie was the well-received *Wildflower* (1914), directed by Allan Dwan, in which she played a naïve young girl who elopes with a dissolute young man. Zukor promoted Clark as "strictly a picture star," and publicity for the film did not mention Clark's stage career. Her second screen effort, *The Crucible* (1914), a drama of a girl unjustly committed to a reformatory, was also a success. Scenes in the film were shot at New York's Bedford Institute (the majority of Clark's thirty-nine films were made in New York). Clark soon became a major box-office draw, her popularity exceeded only by that of Charles Chaplin, Douglas Fairbanks, and Mary Pickford. For *The Goose Girl* (1915), Clark's services were loaned to producer Jesse Lasky. It was the first instance of a top contract player being loaned to a rival film studio. Among Clark's other films are *The Pretty Sister of Jose* (1915), based on a Frances Hodgson Burnett story; *The Prince and the Pauper* (1915), in which Clark played both title characters; and *Prunella* (1918), directed by Maurice Tourneur, a film version of her stage success. Clark's portrayal of *Snow White* (1916), another film version of one of her stage vehicles, later served as Walt Disney's model for his cartoon character. Clark also starred in a trio of "Bab" comedies—*Bab's Diary* (1917) and *Bab's Burglar* (1917), both co-starring Richard Barthelmess, and *Bab's Matinee Idol* (1917)—based on *Saturday Evening Post* short stories about an impulsive schoolgirl by Mary Roberts Rinehart.

Short and slender, with luminous dark eyes, Clark was often compared to Pickford, who was also a Famous Players star. There was some rivalry between the two performers (a rivalry more strongly felt by their managers—Clark's sister and Pickford's mother—than by the actresses themselves). Clark's screen image was more roguish and impudent than Pickford's but equally winsome and innocent. In private life, Clark was a practical, serious person with few artistic aspirations. She followed her forceful sister Cora's advice without protest and was somewhat blasé about her career. "Marguerite was not lazy, but it was Cora who provided the vast energy and backbreaking work which went into the creation of a star in those days" (Zukor, p. 114).

While on a war bond promotion tour during World War I, Clark met Lieutenant Harry Palmerston Williams, the scion of a Louisiana sugar and lumber fortune and an aviation enthusiast. They were married in Greenwich, Connecticut, in August 1918. The couple had no children. Clark continued to make films, including *Uncle Tom's Cabin* (1918), in which she played both Little Eva and Topsy, and the comedy *Come Out of the Kitchen* (1919), based on an Alice Duer Miller play, but her popularity was fading. Her final screen appearance was an uncharacteristically sophisticated role in the marital farce *Scrambled Wives* (1921). Clark produced the film herself, in conjunction with First National Pictures. It was her only screen effort not done under her contract with Famous Players, which by the end of Clark's career had merged into Paramount Pictures.

After completing *Scrambled Wives*, Clark retired to Williams's estate at Patterson, Louisiana. She was active in charitable activities and served for a time on Louisiana's motion picture censorship board. After her husband's death in an airplane accident in 1936, she lived with her sister Cora on New York's Central Park West. Clark died in New York City of pneumonia contracted while she was being treated for a cerebral hemorrhage she had suffered five days earlier.

• A valuable source of information on Clark is Curtis Nunn, *Marguerite Clark: America's Darling of Broadway and Silent Screen* (1981), written by a retired history professor and long-time Clark admirer. See also DeWitt Bodeen's detailed article "Marguerite Clark Was a Bit More Sophisticated than Pickford But Not So Hard-working" in *Films in Review*, Dec. 1964, pp. 611–25, and Alan Dale, "Sensible, Sensible Marguerite Clark," *Green Book Magazine*, July 1916, pp. 161–66, an interview with the actress that discusses her career and personality. Clark is mentioned in the autobiographies of Samuel Goldwyn, *Behind the Screen* (1923), and Adolph Zukor, *The Public Is Never Wrong* (1953). Obituaries are in the *New York Times*, 26 Sept. 1940, and *Variety*, 2 Oct. 1940.

MARY C. KALFATOVIC

CLARK, Mark Wayne (1 May 1896–17 Apr. 1984), general and college president, was born in Watertown, New York, the son of Charles C. Clark, a U.S. Army colonel, and Rebecca Ezekiels, the daughter of a Jewish immigrant. Clark's father led the typical peripatetic life of an army officer, serving in Puerto Rico, the Philippines, and China prior to World War I. An army officer's pay was adequate to raise a family, so the Clarks lived well, if modestly. As was often the case with army officers, Charles Clark pushed his son to follow in his footsteps, and Mark entered West Point in June 1913. At West Point Clark met and struck a lifelong friendship with Dwight D. Eisenhower, who was two years ahead of him. Well liked by his fellow cadets, Clark graduated in April 1917 near the bottom of his class due to problems with math; he was commissioned into the U.S. Army.

Clark took over an infantry company and arrived in France on 1 May 1918. Quickly advancing to battalion commander in the Eleventh Infantry Division, Captain Clark was wounded during frontline action in the Vosges Mountains in mid-June and worked as a staff officer in supply for the duration of the war. In France he first met his later mentor George C. Marshall.

Like so many of the U.S. Army's drastically reduced officer corps, Clark spent the 1920s in various uneventful postings around the country and gained a reputation with his superiors as an "exceptionally capable officer." In 1921 Clark traveled around the country recruiting young men for the U.S. Army by promoting "Americanism" in the popular "Chautauqua programs." In this job he learned the nature of public relations. In 1924 Clark attended the Infantry School's Advanced Officers Course at Fort Benning, Georgia. In May 1924 he married Maurine Doran; they had two children. As the threat of war grew in the 1930s, the U.S. Army began to groom experienced officers like Clark for top leadership positions. In 1933 he attended the prestigious Command and General Staff College at Fort Leavenworth, Kansas, and in 1936 the elite Army War College.

In the late 1930s Clark built a reputation as an effective trainer of troops. In 1937 he was posted to the

Third Infantry Division in Fort Lewis, Washington, where he came into close contact with Brigadier General Marshall, who was stationed at Vancouver Barracks, Washington. Clark regularly consulted with Marshall on his maneuver plans. When Marshall was promoted to deputy chief of staff, he encouraged Clark to keep consulting him on designing realistic field exercises. In January 1940 Clark directed the first amphibious operation involving some 14,000 men from both the army and the navy. Eisenhower, who had just arrived from the Philippines, played chief umpire for the army units and was as impressed as Marshall with Clark's execution of the sophisticated maneuvers. These innovative amphibious maneuvers drew the attention of his superiors.

Clark was instrumental in bringing "Ike" Eisenhower back from his isolation in the Philippines and in securing his appointment at Fort Lewis, further cementing their friendship. Clark also brought Ike to the attention of Marshall, the new army chief of staff. Eisenhower would later remark that Clark was "more responsible than anybody in this country for giving me my opportunity," and Clark would say the same of Eisenhower. When the United States entered World War II, these "Marshall men" quickly rose to the top.

In 1942, acting on Clark's suggestion, Marshall selected Eisenhower to head the new European theater of operations. In this position Eisenhower shaped the crucial World War II working relationship with the British. Marshall wanted younger men with solid experience in training troops and chose Clark as Eisenhower's deputy. Clark came to command the U.S. II Corps in England. The team of Eisenhower and Clark, together with the British, planned Operation Torch, the 8 November 1942 invasion of North Africa. Clark's daring submarine reconnaissance mission to the North African coast, and his controversial handling of the armistice negotiations with the Vichy representative Admiral Jean-Louis Darlan, brought him both accolades and vilification as well as a promotion to lieutenant general.

Calling him "the best trainer, organizer, and planner I have ever met," Eisenhower selected Clark to command the Fifth U.S. Army in the Salerno amphibious landing of 9 September 1943. After the capture of Naples on 1 October, campaigning in Italy turned into a bloody slugging match with the dug-in Germans. With his daredevil inspection tours into the frontlines, Clark won the respect of his troops.

During the winter of 1944, Clark's military reputation suffered permanently from three fateful decisions: the Rapido fiasco, the failed "end run" at Anzio, and the bombing of Monte Cassino. The Germans repulsed the two-pronged Allied attack against the Gustav line across the Rapido River and bottled up the American troops who had landed on the small beachhead at Anzio (Operation Shingle). The assault of the Thirty-sixth Division across the Rapido cost the lives of 1,700 men and prompted a rare congressional inquiry into World War II operations in 1946. What should have been investigated was Clark's controversial decision to bomb Monte Cassino. The total flattening of the venerable old Benedictine abbey turned out to be a show of American air power in which no vital German positions were destroyed.

In May 1944 the Allies finally cracked the German defenses. A race ensued between Lieutenant General Sir Oliver Leese's British Eighth Army and Clark's American Fifth Army for the glory of capturing Rome. Clark desperately wanted to take Rome before the beginning of the Allied invasion of Normandy (Operation Overlord) scheduled for 5 June. The American Fifth Army took Rome on 5 June, and Clark, ever mindful of publicity, dashed into the Eternal City to have his picture taken. Such deft maneuvering for photo opportunities vis-à-vis his allies built Clark's reputation as a "publicity hound" and an "Anglophobe." The Allied landing in Normandy on 6 June, however, quickly eclipsed the liberation of Rome. With the two-pronged invasion of France in Normandy and on the Mediterranean coast in August (Operation Anvil), the Italian campaign became a secondary theater of operation (the "forgotten front"), and the strength of Clark's Fifth Army steadily decreased with the reassignment of forces and equipment to Anvil.

In November 1944 President Franklin D. Roosevelt and the Combined Chiefs of Staff promoted Clark to commander of the Fifteenth Army Group, which put him in charge of all Allied forces in Italy representing sixteen different nations. Under Clark's command the combined Fifth and Eighth armies finally cracked the dogged German resistance at the Gothic line and crossed the Po River in the winter of 1944 and the spring of 1945. Clark and the Allies took the German surrender in Italy on 2 May.

After Victory in Europe (V-E) Day, Clark moved into the center of the early Cold War. His Fifteenth Army Group almost initiated combat when Josip Tito's Yugoslav partisans tried to seize territories along the Italian and Austrian borders (Venezia Giulia, Trieste, and Carinthia). Clark took command of U.S. forces in occupied Austria on 6 July. Clark brought the Soviet depredations in Austria to the attention of the Truman administration. His forceful actions in resisting Soviet political and economic pressures, in helping the displaced persons, in feeding the local population by securing minimum survival rations, and in rebuilding the Austrian economy with massive American aid delighted the Austrians. As in Italy, however, his showmanship and lust for publicity antagonized the British. "He is [a] Clarkophile first, last and all the time," commented a British diplomat.

In January through April 1947, his final months in Austria, Clark's diplomatic skills and patience—never his strongest suit—were tested. As deputy to the foreign ministers in the London and Moscow meetings, Clark acted as a principal negotiator in the difficult initial rounds of writing an Austrian peace treaty ("state treaty"). Clark left Austria in May 1947. *Time* magazine summed up well Clark's role in the early years of the postwar Austrian occupation: "Mark Clark had done more than any man to help give Austria the means and the courage for independence" (24 June 1946).

After his return to the United States, Clark took over the command of the Sixth Army at the Presidio in San Francisco in June 1947 and became chief of Army Field Forces in October 1949. On 12 May 1952 President Harry Truman appointed him commander in chief of the United Nations forces in Korea. Like in Italy during World War II, Clark once again saw himself confronted with bogged-down forces; as in the latter stages of the Italian campaign, he once again bitterly complained about a lack of personnel and matériel. To regain the advantage for the UN forces, he stepped up the bombing war in North Korea. After tortuous armistice negotiations, mainly deadlocked over prisoner of war repatriation, Clark signed the Korean armistice on 27 July 1953. This made him "the first United States Army commander in history to sign an armistice without victory," as he ruefully noted in his memoirs. Clark, who had become relentlessly anti-Communist as a result of his Austrian experience, felt that an increase of resources and the dropping of the atomic bomb could have dealt the Communist "breed of bandits" a decisive defeat.

Clark often struck a similar theme as president of The Citadel (1 Mar. 1954–1 July 1965), where he ended a distinguished, long, and active career. The cold warrior Clark accepted this last mission to preach his fierce anti-Communism to the cadets. Like Senator Joseph R. McCarthy, Clark saw "hidden enemies" subverting the U.S. government, and like many in the South he branded the civil rights movement's demands for integration a "Communist plot."

Clark retired in 1965. His wife died in 1966, and a year later he married Mary Applegate. In December 1969 President Richard Nixon appointed Clark to the American Battle Monuments Commission, and a few months later his colleagues elected him their chairman. Like other retired generals, Clark was hawkish throughout the Indochina war and praised President Nixon for bombing North Vietnam. Clark died in Charleston, South Carolina.

Notwithstanding Korea, where he came in late trying to save an impossible situation, the apex of Clark's career came in Europe during and after World War II. Martin Blumenson's judgment seems sound that Clark, Eisenhower, George Patton, and Omar Bradley made up "the essential quartet of American leaders who achieved victory in Europe" (*Mark Clark*, p. 1). Along with Lucius Clay and Douglas MacArthur, the American proconsuls in the German and Japanese occupations, Clark in Austria was instrumental in helping to build the postwar American anti-Communist "empire." Clark's strengths were loyalty to his superiors when given difficult commands and a strong sense of duty in adversity. As Allied commander in Italy and American proconsul in postwar Austria, it was Clark's destiny to play the first fiddle in secondary theaters. Had he been appointed successor to General Clay as high commissioner in Germany in 1949 (he was a candidate), he might have gone on to higher levels of military and political office like his friend Eisenhower and his mentor Marshall.

• Clark's personal papers, including an extensive diary, are in The Citadel Archives-Museum, Charleston, S.C. His official wartime, Austrian, and Korean correspondence is in the Defense Department and State Department files at the National Archives. Oral histories with Clark are deposited at the U.S. Army History Institute, Carlisle Barracks, Pa., and Columbia University's Butler Library. Clark wrote two volumes of memoirs, *Calculated Risk* (1950) and *From the Danube to the Yalu* (1954). Martin Blumenson's biography, *Mark Clark* (1984), is long on World War II and short on postwar Austria and Korea. For his relationship with Eisenhower, see Daniel D. Holt, "An Unlikely Partnership and Service: Dwight Eisenhower, Mark Clark, and the Philippines," *Kansas History* 13 (Autumn 1990): 149–65. For his role in Italy during World War II, see Carlo D'Este, *World War II in the Mediterranean* (1990). The U.S. Army official histories are Blumenson, *Salerno to Cassino* (1969), and Ernest F. Fisher, Jr., *Cassino to the Alps*. A cameo biographical sketch is in D. Clayton James, *A Time for Giants* (1987). For Monte Cassino, see Ronald Schaffer, *Wings of Judgment: American Bombing in World War II* (1985); for the Rapido, see Lee Carraway Smith, *A River Swift and Deadly* (1989); and for background on the complications with Tito, see Roberto G. Rabel, *Between East and West: Trieste, the United States, and the Cold War, 1941–1954* (1988). For Clark's central role in the reconstruction of Austria, see Günter Bischof, "Between Responsibility and Rehabilitation: Austria in International Politics, 1940–1950" (2 vols., Ph.D. diss., Harvard Univ., 1989); Bischof, "Mark Clark und die Aprilkrise 1946," *Zeitgeschichte* 13 (Apr. 1986): 229–51; and the cover story "An American Abroad," *Time*, 24 June 1946. For background on Korea, see Burton I. Kaufman, *The Korean War* (1986); and for the Korean armistice negotiations, see Rosemary Foot, *A Substitute for Victory: The Politics of Peacemaking at the Korean Armistice Talks* (1990). An obituary is in the *New York Times*, 17 Apr. 1984.

GÜNTER BISCHOF

CLARK, Myron Holley (23 Oct. 1806–23 Aug. 1892), New York governor, was born in Naples township, Ontario County, New York, the son of Joseph Clark and Mary Sutton, farmers. He attended district schools, was apprenticed to a cabinetmaker, and began clerking in a store at eighteen. At twenty-one he moved to the county seat, Canandaigua, where he also clerked for two years. Clark then returned to set up his own hardware business with partners in Naples. He was successful in business and in 1830 married Zilpha Watkins, with whom he had five children.

Clark was active in his rural community, rising to the rank of lieutenant colonel in the largely ceremonial militia and participating in local politics as a Whig. He served as county sheriff, 1837–1839, moving his business permanently to Canandaigua at that time.

Clark was also active in the temperance movement, attracted, like many rural New Yorkers of evangelical Protestant and New England origin, by its claims that restricting alcohol could dramatically reduce crime, poverty, disease, and violence within families and communities. Like the majority of temperance advocates also, he believed laws, not just appeals to drinkers to abstain, were needed to control alcohol's evil effects. Clark was regarded locally as a fanatic on the subject, and he used the issue to win the office of president of Canandaigua in 1850 and 1851.

As the temperance issue became entwined with hostility toward the flood of new immigrants from Ireland and Germany, who routinely consumed alcohol, local Whigs elected Clark in 1851 to the state senate. In 1852 he introduced a bill to "suppress drinking houses and tippling shops," which was ignored. The following year, however, he presented a bill closely resembling Maine's successful Maine Law of 1851, which forbade the manufacture and sale of alcoholic beverages. Patient, shrewd in his tactics, and a persuasive speaker on the issue, Clark guided the measure through the senate only to see it fail in the assembly. Reelected to the senate in the fall of 1853 and made chair of a select committee on the liquor traffic, he reintroduced the bill in 1854, taking advantage of Democratic divisions to guide it to passage in both houses. Democratic governor Horatio Seymour, however, vetoed the measure as oppressive, unequal in its impact (by depriving those who made or sold alcohol of their living), and a violation of the state's bill of rights.

Galvanized temperance reformers wanted to make Clark governor. To well-established Whig leaders like Thurlow Weed, however, Clark was a relatively inexperienced outsider whose pet issue could easily divide Whigs as well as Democrats. Nevertheless, knowing that Clark would back the reelection of Weed's longtime ally Senator William H. Seward in the state legislature, that Clark was at least the second choice of many Whigs, and that no better candidates could be had, Weed helped Clark to the nomination for governor in 1854. The platform ignored temperance to concentrate on Whig opposition to the recently passed Kansas-Nebraska Act, which threatened to spread slavery into Kansas.

The election of 1854 proved one of the most complicated in New York history. Clark won additional nominations from conventions representing temperance organizations, Free (antislavery) Democrats, and opponents of the Kansas-Nebraska Act and was called the "Fusion" candidate. In later years he claimed to have been New York's first Republican governor, but the name was carefully avoided during the election. Although Clark, who belonged to a Know Nothing (anti-immigrant) lodge in Canandaigua, also hoped for support from that group, an American (Know Nothing) party convention declared his council irregular and nominated its own candidate for governor. The divided Democrats fielded two candidates as well. Clark won by a mere 309 votes in the four-way race, winning 33 percent of the total vote. Political observers were amazed at the strength of the liquor and immigration issues and their ability to alter partisan voting patterns. Clark drew support principally from Whigs, but so did his Know Nothing opponent.

As governor, Clark followed Weed's advice to delay patronage appointments until after Seward's reelection. When, however, he took advice from temperance friends as well as Weed in making appointments, relations between the two cooled. Clark signed a new Maine-style prohibition law in 1855, which drew widespread protests, open defiance, even threats of armed resistance. In 1856 the state court of appeals declared the law unconstitutional. A revised law passed the assembly but died in the senate, reflecting growing ambivalence among antiliquor politicians about their ability to secure prohibition through laws.

Although Clark took popular positions in favor of expanded public education and against stock gambling and speculation in railroads, his leadership was suspect. He quarreled with the legislature in 1856 over calling a special session, and, although he desired renomination, leaders of the newly formed Republican party feared losing votes by endorsing such a strong symbol of temperance.

Clark returned to his business interests in Canandaigua. In 1862 he received a patronage appointment from Abraham Lincoln's administration as collector of the new internal revenue tax. Clark retained his faith in prohibition. He was a candidate for governor in 1870 on a temperance ticket and ran again in 1874 representing the Prohibition party. In neither case did he campaign actively, and he received few votes. He died in Canandaigua. Clark's rapid rise to the state's highest political office reflected the hope that easy answers could be found to New York's complex social problems in the mid-nineteenth century.

• Papers from Clark's governorship are in the New York State Library, Albany. Occasional letters may also be found in the papers of correspondents, including those of Thurlow Weed, University of Rochester. Hendrik Booraem V, *The Formation of the Republican Party in New York* (1983), provides a context for his political career, as does William E. Gienapp, *The Origins of the Republican Party, 1852–1856* (1987). See also Charles F. Milliken, *History of Ontario County, N.Y., and Its People* (1911), and John A. Krout, "The Maine Law in New York Politics," *New York History* 17 (1936): 260–72. An obituary is in the *New York Times*, 24 Aug. 1892.

PHYLLIS F. FIELD

CLARK, Peter Humphries (1829–21 June 1925), educator, politician, and civil rights leader, was born in Cincinnati, Ohio, the son of Michael Clark, a barber, and his wife (name unknown). Clark was the product of a complex, mixed racial ancestry that provided the basis for a lifelong struggle to find a place for himself in both the white and African-American worlds. The oral tradition of Peter Clark's family contends that Michael Clark was the son of explorer William Clark, a Kentucky slaveowner who had children by his mulatto slave Betty. Major Clark is said to have freed Betty and their children and settled them in Cincinnati. There she married and started another family with John Isom Gaines, an affluent black man who owned a steamboat provisioning business. Quite light-complexioned and able to claim descent through a prominent white family, Peter Clark also had darker relatives to remind him of his African ancestry.

Clark's straddling of the color line was evident throughout his life. For years, for example, he belonged at the same time to local churches affiliated with the African Methodist Episcopal, white Unitarian, and Congregationalist denominations. That he felt completely comfortable in neither the white nor the black world contributed to the instability in his racial thought. At one time or another, and occasionally simultaneously, Clark advocated integrationist, separatist, and emigrationist strategies for African-American advancement. Though perhaps less driven by complex personal backgrounds, other black leaders of the time also expressed contradictory responses to the problem they shared with Clark: finding an opening for blacks in a society at once democratic and thoroughly permeated by racism.

Clark had an extremely difficult time making a life for himself in antebellum Cincinnati's social climate of prejudice and discrimination. He had the best education available to an African American under the circumstances, graduating in 1846 from a segregated, private high school supported by white philanthropy. For years, however, he could not find dignified work consistent with his education and self-respect. He attempted an apprenticeship as a typemaker but quit because racial proscription blocked access to the status of craftsman. Then, though he felt cutting hair was undignified, he took over his father's barbershop, only to give that up when white customers demanded he not serve blacks. At this point, in 1848 or 1849, feeling that life in America offered no future for a black man, Clark began to consider emigration to West Africa. John McMiken, a wealthy white colonizationist from Cincinnati, arranged to send Clark and a party of 100 blacks to a settlement on the Liberia–Sierra Leone border. Clark got no further than New Orleans. When he saw the filthy, unseaworthy schooner McMiken had commissioned for the journey, Clark returned to Cincinnati.

During this time Clark also had been working, without pay, as a teacher in the segregated schools of Cincinnati, so when the opportunity for paid teaching employment arose in 1852, he seized it. It was around this time that he finally gave up the idea of emigrating. In 1857 he rose from teacher to principal of a black elementary school, and in 1866 he became principal of the segregated high school. In addition to filling administrative and classroom duties, for many years he worked after school, without pay, training blacks for the teaching profession.

The movement for school desegregation among Ohio African Americans presented Clark with a formidable dilemma. In speeches and interviews in the black press, he acknowledged that desegregation would mean better schools for blacks. Yet he knew that black teachers would not be hired to teach white children, and this would mean a loss to the race of one of its few sources of dignified, intellectual, and well-paying employment. Furthermore, he did not believe that white teachers, even if unprejudiced, could be role models for black youth. For opposing desegregation, which most Cincinnati blacks favored, Clark fell out of favor in his own community. This, along with charges that he had bribed a witness in a political corruption case to save political allies from going to jail, led to his firing in 1886. He then worked briefly selling textbooks before becoming principal at the segregated State Normal and Industrial School at Huntsville, Alabama, but Clark soon left there because, it was reported, he could not accept the harsh southern racial order. In 1888 he moved to somewhat more congenial St. Louis, where he taught in the black public schools until retiring in 1908.

Black education provided Clark's most stable institutional base as a race leader, but simultaneously he was deeply involved in politics as a campaign speaker, editor of ephemeral campaign newspapers, occasional candidate, and sometime recipient of patronage. He was a master of political oratory, known throughout the northern states for his emotional expositions of the evils of racism. Clark's political affiliations, however, shifted too often and unpredictably for him to emerge as a political boss. Finding Republicans unwilling to advance the political and legal promises of Congressional Reconstruction or to provide patronage jobs that would help free blacks from the constraints of a racist job market, and realizing that party circles were full of racial prejudice, Clark quickly grew disillusioned. In 1872 he began to search for alternatives. Clark became a Liberal Republican, then went back to being a Republican, then declared himself an independent, and then became affiliated with the Marxian socialist Workingmen's party during the period of heightened class conflict in 1877–1878. He next returned to calling himself a Republican, only to announce in 1882 that he was a Democrat. In his political meandering, Clark found few reliable white allies. Furthermore, he gained few significant personal rewards. He briefly served as a pensions agent under President Ulysses S. Grant and was appointed the first black trustee of Ohio State University by Democratic governor George Hoadly in 1884.

It is not clear that Clark really wished to wield political power. Though he was ambitious for himself and his friends and frequently spoke of politics in practical terms as a struggle for jobs and money, there is little evidence that he wished to gain influence through personal control of such political assets as nominations and patronage. Whether he spoke of jobs or group empowerment in explaining his shifting political allegiances, Clark's goal in electoral politics was ultimately to achieve black inclusion in the American mainstream.

The last third of Clark's life was spent in an obscurity that is surprising considering the notoriety of his middle years. Having exhausted so many affiliations and strategies in the 1870s and 1880s, thereafter he seemed not to know where to turn for answers. After settling in St. Louis, Clark retreated from public life and rarely spoke out on racial issues. In the last decades of his life, he appears to have devoted himself entirely to teaching and to his family. Clark had married Frances Williams in 1854. They had three children: Herbert, who appears to have lived a precarious existence dependent on political jobs; Ernestine, the first black woman graduate of Cincinnati Normal School, who became a schoolteacher; and Consuelo, a graduate of Boston University Medical School, who was one of the first African-American women doctors. Clark died in St. Louis.

Prominent in black public life from the 1850s through the 1880s, Clark is acclaimed for the dynamic but controversial leadership he brought both to the development of Cincinnati's segregated black public school system and to the creation of postenfranchisement northern black political strategy. The legacy of his active, middle years, however, is uncertain. Clark helped widen the debate about black political strategy, and his ambivalence about desegregation prefigures a twentieth-century African-American view. Yet the instability of his views and affiliations undermined his influence, both in his own time and much later, when his life was briefly rediscovered during the black revolution of the mid-twentieth century. Clark's educational work made more durable, practical contributions: the teachers he trained worked in segregated school systems throughout the Ohio Valley until well into the twentieth century.

• The elusive nature of Clark's public career, the obscurity of his last years, and the lack of a collection of his personal papers account for his minimal scholarly treatment and the absence of a biography. Clark's only published work, *The Black Brigade of Cincinnati: Being a Report of Its Labors and a Muster-Roll of Its Members, Together with Various Orders, Speeches, and Etc., Relating to It* (1864), chronicles the labors of Cincinnati African Americans who were impressed into Union army service. Two brief biographical sketches have been the source for most of the work on Clark: see William J. Simmons, *Men of Mark: Eminent, Progressive, and Rising* (1887), pp. 374–83, and Dovie King Clark, "Peter Humphries Clark," *Negro History Bulletin* 5 (1942): 176. See also David A. Gerber, "Peter Humphries Clark: The Dialogue of Hope and Despair," in *Black Leaders of the Nineteenth Century*, ed. Leon Litwack and August Meier (1988). Lawrence Grossman, "In His Veins Coursed No Bootlicking Blood: The Career of Peter H. Clark," *Ohio History* 83 (Winter 1977): 79–95, is also useful. For a discussion of Clark's affiliation with a radical socialist political group, see Herbert G. Gutman, "Peter H. Clark: Pioneer Negro Socialist, 1877," *Journal of Negro Education* 34 (Fall 1965): 413–18, which includes the text of Clark's speech before Cincinnati railroad workers during the 1877 strike. An obituary is in the St. Louis *Argus*, 26 June 1925.

DAVID A. GERBER

CLARK, Septima Poinsette (3 May 1898–15 Dec. 1987), educator and civil rights activist, was born in Charleston, South Carolina, the daughter of Peter Porcher Poinsette, a caterer who was a former slave, and Victoria Warren Anderson, who took in laundry to supplement the family income. Septima's mother, who had been raised in black-governed Haiti, instilled in her daughter a determination to succeed in spite of white racism.

Clark was trained as a teacher at Charleston's Avery Normal Institute. After graduating in 1916 she received the licentiate of instruction and began her teaching career. Because African Americans were not allowed to teach in the public schools of Charleston, Clark accepted a position on Johns Island at the Promise Land School. Although she remained there until 1919, Clark immediately encountered the inequities in salaries between black and white teachers. While on Johns Island Clark also began a career in adult education, teaching islanders to read their Bibles and the various handbooks of organizations to which they belonged. She also became a member of the National Association for the Advancement of Colored People (NAACP).

Returning to Charleston to teach at Avery, Clark participated in the local movement to integrate South Carolina's public school faculties. Clark and others collected between 10,000 and 20,000 signatures on NAACP-circulated petitions, contributing to a campaign that resulted in a 1920 state law that allowed blacks to teach in Charleston's black public schools. The following year blacks also became eligible to become public school principals.

In 1920 Septima Poinsette married Nerie Clark, a navy cook. They had two children, one of whom died before her first birthday. By 1925 Clark was a widow, and she never remarried. Clark returned to Johns Island to teach again at Promise Land, from 1927 to 1929, and then she moved to Columbia, South Carolina, where she would remain until 1946. With her surviving son living with his paternal grandparents in North Carolina, Clark began teaching at the Booker T. Washington School. She also earned college credits at New York's Columbia University, where she took courses in math, astronomy, and curriculum building; in 1937 she went to Atlanta University to study social science research methods applicable to rural settings (her instructors included W. E. B. Du Bois). In 1942 Clark earned a baccalaureate degree in English and elementary education from Benedict College in Columbia. She received a master's degree from Virginia's Hampton Institute in 1946.

In Columbia, Clark attended her first interracial meetings and became active in civic groups and clubs throughout the capital city, including the black branch of the Young Women's Christian Association, the Palmetto Education Association, and the NAACP. In Columbia, too, working with Wil Lou Gray, the director of the South Carolina Adult Education Program, her career in citizenship education began. In 1935 Gray was asked to start a program at Camp Jackson that would teach black soldiers to read; many of them were functionally illiterate. The program was designed to help these soldiers with daily survival tasks—from reading bus schedules to signing pay slips and counting change. It became a prototype for the citizenship education schools Clark would establish in the 1950s.

In 1947 Clark returned to Charleston to care for her ailing mother.

In 1954 South Carolina, by law, barred teachers from belonging to the NAACP, seeing it as a subversive organization because of its role in the forefront of the civil rights movement. Clark, unlike many of her colleagues, refused to withdraw her membership. As a result she lost not only her job but her retirement benefits as well. This, however, proved to be fortuitous. Two years earlier Clark had learned of the work of a nontraditional, interracial institution in Monteagle, Tennessee, called the Highlander Folk School. There adult students and grassroots community leaders, through workshops and seminars, discussed and designed strategies for combating southern problems such as "segregation, discrimination, racism, and ignorance."

From 1953 to 1957 Highlander focused workshops on public school desegregation and leadership training for civil rights activists on the grassroots level. Clark attended her first Highlander workshop in 1954 and one year later conducted a workshop herself and became a fieldworker to recruit students. By 1956 she was Highlander's director of workshops and later became its director of education. In the summer of 1955 Rosa Parks attended one of Clark's workshops and then, after returning to Montgomery, Alabama, refused to give up her seat on a city bus. The action, which was not spontaneous but planned, inaugurated the modern civil rights protest movement. Parks said that she always was in "awe" of Clark and greatly impressed by her "great courage and dignity and wisdom," which she hoped would "rub off" on her.

At Highlander until 1961, Clark developed a citizenship education program, which taught African Americans to read and write to pass voter registration literacy tests and to participate in the political process in the South. The program also taught black people daily survival skills. Highlander's program became a model for other such programs throughout the South, including the Night School for Adults on Johns Island. In 1961 Clark moved to Atlanta, and her model citizenship education program became part of Martin Luther King, Jr.'s Southern Christian Leadership Conference (SCLC). Clark became supervisor of teacher training and a member of the SCLC's executive staff, though often a beleaguered one because she was not only a woman but one who held firm beliefs and spoke her mind. As a result, she met bemusement and resentment from some male colleagues in the organization.

Clark trained community leaders, particularly of rural areas. They were taught techniques for teaching their neighbors to compute, read, and write, skills essential to the full citizenship to which they aspired. Among those affiliated with the citizenship education program, in various capacities, were activists Fannie Lou Hamer and Hosea Williams and future U.S. ambassador to the United Nations, Andrew Young. Clark noted that the program "formed the grassroots basis of new statewide political organizations in South Carolina, Georgia, and Mississippi."

Clark's training programs and citizenship education schools equated literacy, among other things, with political liberation. Clark correctly noted that prior to the 1960s major civil rights organizations like the NAACP and SCLC did not focus on voter registration but rather on public accommodations and the desegregation of public education. Between 1957 and 1961 the citizenship school concept began to catch on. Inspired by the citizenship school idea, in 1962 SCLC, along with the Congress of Racial Equality (CORE), the NAACP, the Student Non-Violent Coordinating Committee (SNCC), and the National Urban League, formed the Voter Education Project, which trained more than 10,000 teachers for citizenship schools. The training occurred in time for the passage of the 1965 Voting Rights Act, which rendered unconstitutional arbitrary voter registration requirements, including literacy testing for blacks.

When she retired from SCLC in 1970, Clark received the Martin Luther King, Jr., Award "for great service to Humanity"; in 1976 she was given the Race Relations Award from the National Education Association and in 1979 the Living Legacy Award from President Jimmy Carter. She was presented with the Order of the Palmetto, South Carolina's highest civilian award, in 1982. She died on Johns Island.

Septima Clark was a grassroots regional leader and educator who presented another tactical direction to the civil rights movement that complemented King's "mass protest" strategy and the NAACP's litigation. Clark, the Highlander school, and ultimately the SCLC believed that the centerpiece of the "New Southern Agenda" was effective use of the ballot, which meant not only voter registration but also citizenship education and community organization and development.

• There is a collection of Septima P. Clark Papers at the Robert Scott Small Library at the College of Charleston, S.C. She wrote an autobiography, *Echo in My Soul* (1962), and contributed to Cynthia Stokes Brown, ed., *Ready from Within: Septima Clark and the Civil Rights Movement* (1986). She also wrote several articles explaining the citizenship education concept, including "Citizenship and Gospel," *Journal of Black Studies* 10, no. 4 (June 1980): 461–66, and "Literacy and Liberation," *Freedomways* (First Quarter, Winter 1964): 113–24. Brown also wrote an excellent biographical sketch about Clark for *Notable Black American Women*, ed. Jessie Carney Smith (1991). See also Grace Jordan McFadden's biographical sketch in *Black Women in America: An Historical Encyclopedia*, ed. Darlene Clark Hine, vol. 1 (1993). An important volume is Vicki L. Crawford et al., eds., *Women in the Civil Rights Movement: Trailblazers and Torchbearers, 1941–1965* (1990). C. Alvin Hughes has written an informative article on the Highlander Folk School, "A New Agenda for the South: The Role and Influence of the Highlander Folk School, 1953–1961," *Phylon* 46, no. 3 (Sept. 1985): 242–50. Brian Lanker, *I Dream a World: Portraits of Black*

Women Who Changed America (1989), includes a photograph of Clark. An obituary is in the *New York Times*, 17 Dec. 1987.

NANCY ELIZABETH FITCH

CLARK, Sonny (21 July 1931–13 Jan. 1963), jazz pianist, was born Conrad Yeatis (or Yetis) Clark in Herminie, Pennsylvania. His parents' names are unknown. Clark began to play the piano at age four. In 1943 his family moved to Pittsburgh, where, while continuing to study piano, he also played the vibraphone and bass in a high school band.

Following his mother's death, Clark traveled to Los Angeles in 1951 with his older brother, who was a professional pianist. Clark was briefly associated with most of the leading jazz musicians in the area, including saxophonists Wardell Gray, Stan Getz, Dexter Gordon, Art Pepper, and Zoot Sims, trumpeter Art Farmer, drummer Shelly Manne, guitarist Barney Kessel, and singer Anita O'Day. Early in 1953 he made his first recordings as a sideman with vibraphonist Teddy Charles and then with Pepper. He joined bassist Oscar Pettiford's trio and traveled to San Francisco, where Clark also worked briefly with tenor saxophonist Vido Musso and led his own trio at the Down Beat Club.

While in San Francisco, Clark met clarinetist Buddy DeFranco. He recorded with an ad hoc big band accompanying DeFranco in Los Angeles in September, and around this time he replaced Kenny Drew in DeFranco's quartet. They toured Europe in January and February 1954 as part of writer Leonard Feather's "Jazz Club, USA" package. Clark made numerous recordings with the clarinetist, who said, "Sonny was a sweet little guy. He was just a nice, bright person. Great humor." By touring with DeFranco, Clark began to acquire a reputation beyond the Los Angeles area.

Early in 1956 Clark was once again based in the Los Angeles area, where he joined bassist Howard Rumsey's Lighthouse All Stars, recorded baritone saxophonist's Serge Chaloff's album *Blue Serge*, and participated in recordings by alto saxophonist Sonny Criss and trombonist Frank Rosolino. In February 1957 he became a member of singer Dinah Washington's accompanying trio, thereby gaining an opportunity to return to New York in April. At the club Birdland he led a trio with bassist Sam Jones and drummer Art Taylor; later, around 1959, he performed at the Bohemia Club with tenor saxophonist Johnny Griffin, bassist Wilbur Ware, and drummer Philly Joe Jones. Recordings from this period include albums with tenor saxophonists Sonny Rollins (*The Sound of Sonny*), Hank Mobley (*Hank Mobley Sextet*), Johnny Griffin, and Clifford Jordan (all 1957); and his own albums *Dial "S" for Sonny*, *Sonny Clark Trio*, *Sonny's Crib* (also 1957), and *Cool Struttin'* (1958).

Clark was largely inactive from 1959 into 1961, owing to a heroin addiction that had plagued him from a young age. Fellow jazz pianist and drug addict Hampton Hawes described this period: "Sonny and I earned ourselves a righteous moniker: the Gold Dust Twins. . . . We were strung as bad as you can get, way out on the edge and starting to burn people. The only reason we weren't in the park with the muggers was that we were musicians" (Hawes and Asher, p. 106). His occasional recordings included the album *Sonny Clark Trio* (1960).

Clark was continually ill during the last two years of his life. Little is known of his nightclub work during this period apart from appearances in 1961 at the White Whale in Greenwich Village. Nonetheless, he made significant recordings, most notably *Leapin' and Lopin'* (1961), which is probably his finest album as a leader. He also served as a sideman for albums with alto saxophonist Jackie McLean, guitarist Grant Green, and tenor saxophonists Ike Quebec and Dexter Gordon, including Gordon's *Go!* (1962). In late October 1962 Clark was hospitalized with a leg infection. He was released and performed at Junior's club on 11 and 12 January, but the following day, after a drug overdose, he suffered a fatal heart attack in New York City.

Although Clark composed a number of themes, few have entered the standard jazz repertoire. He is best remembered as a hard-bop pianist who amalgamated the principal styles of pianists Bud Powell and Horace Silver, capturing the characteristic clarity and headlong rush of Powell's ever-changing single-note lines but also showing a strong affinity for Silver's willingness to repeat ideas and for his characteristically tuneful and relaxed use of swing riffs and piano blues formulas.

• A biography, including remembrances from fellow musicians and a bibliography, is Ib Skovgaard and Ebbe Traberg, *Some Clark Bars: Sonny Clark, a Discography* (1984). Other surveys are by Michael James, "Sonny Clark," *Jazz Monthly* 9 (May 1963): 3–9; Jean Dumas-Delage, "L'itinéraire d'un pur," *Jazz magazine*, no. 108 (July 1964): 28–30; Johnny Simmen, "Sonny Clark," *Coda*, no. 162 (Aug. 1978): 16–17; and David Rosenthal, "Wynton Kelly, Elmo Hope, Sonny Clark: Three Neglected Jazz Piano Greats of the 1950s," *Keyboard* 9 (June 1983): 56, 58–61. See also Ira Gitler, pamphlet notes to *The Complete Verve Recordings of the Buddy DeFranco Quartet/Quintet with Sonny Clark* (1986). Hampton Hawes and Don Asher, *Raise Up Off Me: A Portrait of Hampton Hawes* (1974; repr. 1979). Obituaries are in *Jazz* 2 (Feb. 1963): 15; *Down Beat*, 28 Feb. 1963, p. 13; and *Jazz magazine*, no. 92 (Mar. 1963): 18–19.

BARRY KERNFELD

CLARK, Thomas March (4 July 1812–7 Sept. 1903), Episcopal bishop, was born in Newburyport, Massachusetts, the son of Thomas March Clark, a shipper, and his second wife, Rebecca Wheelwright. Both the Clark and Wheelwright families were committed Presbyterians, and Clark was raised "in the straitest fold of the Presbyterian Church" (*Reminiscences*, p. 7), which included the recitation of the shorter Westminster Catechism every Sunday. At age fourteen he entered Amherst College but neglected his studies and dropped out. He entered Yale College in 1828, graduating in 1831. For the next two years he was head of the high school in Lowell, Massachusetts. Then, deciding to become a minister in the Presbyterian church, he entered Princeton Theological Seminary (1833–1835), where he studied under Charles Hodge and Archibald Alexander.

At Princeton Clark was taught the "rigid doctrines" of high Calvinism, that is, the total depravity of man, unconditional election, a limited atonement, irresistible grace, and the perseverance of the saints, doctrines against which he later rebelled. He was licensed to preach and for several months in 1835 supplied the pulpit of Old South Church in Boston. Gradually, however, he became dissatisfied with "the shackles of a harsh and complicated creed" and Puritan worship, which he considered barren and wearisome. "[M]y entrance into the Episcopal Church was precipitated by consciousness of my unfitness to express in extemporaneous prayer the sentiments of an intelligent congregation whose Christian experience had in a great many cases been matured before I was born" (*Reminiscences*, p. 33). The beauty and order of the Book of Common Prayer attracted Clark to the Episcopal church. He was ordained deacon on 3 February 1836 at Grace Church, Boston, and priest on 6 November 1836, again at Grace Church by Alexander Viets Griswold, the evangelical bishop of the Eastern Diocese. At the time of Clark's ordination the Episcopal church was very small, comprising fewer than 600 parishes and 763 clergy, but in the decade from 1830 to 1840 it would grow considerably.

On 18 November 1836 Clark became rector of Grace Church, Temple Place, Boston, and served there until 1843. In 1838 he married Caroline Howard, with whom he would have two children. In 1843 he was called to St. Andrew's Church, Philadelphia, the "Paradise of Ministers," where "the clergy were an influential element of society, and it was the custom of the people to go to church regularly" (*Reminiscences*, p. 77). He remained in Philadelphia until 1846, when he became assistant minister at Trinity Church, Boston, where Manton Eastburn, fourth bishop of Massachusetts, was rector. Clark found it difficult being an assistant after ten years as the rector of two significant parishes, so in 1850 he accepted the call to be rector of Christ Church, Hartford, Connecticut. He appreciated the atmosphere of the diocese of Connecticut because "it runs to no extremes, leaning neither to Geneva nor Rome, unmoved by the doctrine of the one or the blandishments of the other. The Low Church party can hardly be said to exist in Connecticut and there is no large diocese in the Church where there is today a less amount of rampant and excessive ritualism" (*Reminiscences*, p. 108).

Clark has been called the founder of the Broad Church Movement in the Episcopal church. This party avoided the extremes of both the Low Church party, which viewed the Episcopal church as a part of American Protestantism with few distinctive characteristics, and the Ritualists or Anglo-Catholics, who stressed practices and beliefs that appeared to be Roman Catholic, such as the adoration of the sacrament and the real presence of Christ in the Eucharist. The Broad Church party was broadminded, nonpartisan, open to new discoveries of truth (such as evolution), tolerant of others, and committed to Christian unity. It stressed the teachings of the Apostles' and Nicene creeds as the essential elements of Christianity. At the same time Clark was a thorough evangelical committed to the incarnation, the atonement, and the divinity of Jesus Christ. Broad Church adherents were also called Liberal Evangelicals.

While Clark was at Hartford, he was elected, much to his surprise, the fifth bishop of Rhode Island and was ordained and consecrated at Grace Church, Providence, on 6 December 1854. He served as rector of Grace Church from 1854 to 1866. Clark served as bishop for forty-nine years, one of the longest episcopates in the Episcopal church. Under his leadership the diocese grew and harmony prevailed.

While bishop of Rhode Island, Clark wrote two books of significance. *Primary Truths of Religion* (1869) was an explication of the fundamental principles of Christianity, and his *Reminiscences* (1895) provided insightful reflections on sixty years of the Episcopal church, especially the first Lambeth Conference (1867) and the decline of party strife. On 7 February 1899 John Williams, presiding bishop of the Episcopal church died; because Clark was the senior bishop by consecration, he became the twelfth presiding bishop, a post he held until his death. Clark was a patient leader, an effective bishop, a popular preacher, and a reconciling presence in the Episcopal church. He died in Providence.

• Clark's papers and sermons are in the Archives of the Episcopal Church in Austin, Tex. Two other books by Clark are *Lectures on the Formation of Character* (1852) and *The Dew of Youth and Other Lectures to Young Men and Young Women on Early Discipline and Culture* (1874). His sermon on "Immortality" was published in *Christian Truth and Modern Opinion: Seven Sermons Preached in New York by Clergymen of the Protestant Episcopal Church* (1874). The most complete study is Mary Clark Sturtevant, *Thomas March Clark: Fifth Bishop of Rhode Island: A Memoir*, ed. Lata Griswold (1927), which relies heavily on *Reminiscences*. Henry Codman Potter, a contemporary, discusses Clark briefly in *Reminiscences of Bishops and Archbishops* (1906).

DONALD S. ARMENTROUT

CLARK, Tom Campbell (23 Sept. 1899–13 June 1977), attorney general of the United States and U.S. Supreme Court justice, was born in Dallas, Texas, the son of William Henry Clark, an attorney, and Virginia "Jennie" Falls. His parents, who had moved to Dallas from Mississippi, were from aristocratic southern families, and both of Tom's grandfathers had been officers in the Confederate army. His father, besides being active in Democratic party politics, was a talented and capable lawyer. Unfortunately, William Clark also suffered from alcoholism, and by the time Tom reached school age, William's drinking problem had devastated a once thriving legal practice and the family's finances. Tom had to deliver newspapers and work in a drugstore to help out. He nevertheless managed to become one of the first Eagle Scouts in the United States at age fourteen and to participate in oratory and debate at Bryan Street High School, from which he graduated in 1917.

Inspired by the patriotic fervor then sweeping the country, William sent Tom to the Virginia Military Institute (VMI) to become an officer. Because of the family's financial problems, Tom had to drop out of VMI after one year. He then returned to Texas and enlisted in the National Guard, serving as a sergeant in the 153d Infantry Division until the armistice ended World War I five months later.

In January 1919 Clark returned to college at the University of Texas. He paid his own way by doing a variety of odd jobs that ranged from washing dishes to grading papers for a professor. Although originally blackballed by fraternities because he was sharing an apartment with a Jew, Clark eventually joined Delta Tau Delta and became the president of its Texas chapter during his senior year. He also served as business manager of the university's yearbook and its student newspaper. Clark earned a bachelor of arts from Texas in 1921 and an LL.B. from the university's law school in 1922.

After graduation Clark joined his brother Bill Clark at their father's Dallas law firm. Because William Clark's drinking problem was well known, the firm did not do well. Despite shaky financial prospects, in 1924 Tom Clark married Mary Jane Ramsey. They had three children, two of whom lived into adulthood.

In 1927 the struggling Clark accepted an offer from the new Dallas County district attorney, Bill McCraw, who was a friend of Clark's brother, to become the assistant district attorney in charge of civil litigation. While working for McCraw, Clark was allowed to continue doing private legal work on the side, and as a result of the contacts he made through the district attorney's office, his practice flourished. In 1930 a Dallas court appointed him a master in chancery, giving him the job of taking evidence in the case of Columbus Marion "Dad" Joiner, a Texas oil industry pioneer who had brought in a big strike but lacked the money to pay those who had financed him and was on the verge of bankruptcy. In two years Clark earned $20,000 from the Joiner case. It also brought him into contact with rising oil tycoons, such as H. L. Hunt, Clint Murchison, and Sid Richardson, and through them Clark became involved in a good deal of profitable oil litigation.

In 1932 Clark resigned from the district attorney's office and later that year formed a profitable partnership with his former boss McCraw. In 1934 McCraw ran successfully for attorney general of Texas, with Clark serving as his campaign manager. Despite McCraw's departure for Austin, the firm, to which Clark added two other lawyers, continued to prosper, garnering a $12,000 per year retainer from the Texas Petroleum Council in 1935. Suspicious that Clark was making so much money because of his ties to McCraw, a subcommittee of the Texas Senate twice investigated the Dallas attorney.

By 1937 Clark had become so successful that he had to take a considerable pay cut to accept a position with the U.S. Department of Justice. He went to Washington believing that Senator Tom Connally, a family friend, had arranged for him a job as an assistant attorney general, only to learn the promised appointment was really as an assistant *to* the attorney general, a position of lesser rank and salary. Although disappointed, Clark decided not to return to Dallas. His first Justice Department assignment, in the Bureau of War Risk Litigation, involved traveling around the country cleaning up claims left over from World War I. Clark's work impressed his superiors, and in 1938 they transferred him to the Antitrust Division. He served as chief of its Wage and Hours Unit and later headed the division's New Orleans field office and supervised its operations on the West Coast. Following the Pearl Harbor attack, Clark was designated the civilian relocation coordinator, a job that involved handling the legal aspects of the relocation and internment of Japanese Americans. Although supportive of this program at the time, Clark later characterized his involvement in it as one of the two biggest mistakes of his life.

In late 1942 Clark returned to Washington to take charge of the Antitrust Division's War Frauds Unit, an organization that prosecuted profiteers and swindlers preying on the nation's burgeoning military procurement program. In his new job he worked closely with Senator Harry Truman of Missouri, who chaired a Senate committee investigating waste and corruption in defense industries. Clark's work in the War Frauds Unit impressed not only Truman but also Attorney General Francis Biddle, who in 1943 promoted him to assistant attorney general. At first Clark headed the Antitrust Division, but when Biddle reorganized the Justice Department in late 1943 and early 1944, transferring many of Antitrust's functions (including war frauds prosecutions) to the Criminal Division, he put Clark in charge of that unit. While running the Criminal Division, Clark prosecuted German spies before a military tribunal and argued and won his first case in the Supreme Court.

Clark also kept in touch with Truman. At the 1944 Democratic National Convention he promoted the Missourian for the vice presidential nomination. In 1945 Truman became president, and Biddle, with whom he was at odds politically, soon resigned. Encouraged by Senator Connally and Speaker of the House Sam Rayburn, the president made Clark Biddle's successor.

As attorney general, Clark remained interested in antitrust, initiating 160 new enforcement actions and personally arguing *United States v. Paramount Pictures* (1948) in the Supreme Court. He made two other successful appearances before the high tribunal, persuading it to uphold both a contempt judgment against John L. Lewis and the United Mine Workers Union and federal jurisdiction over oil-rich lands off the California coast. Clark also promoted the adoption of the Administrative Procedures Act of 1946, set up the Attorney General's Committee on Juvenile Delinquency, and organized a National Conference on Citizenship.

In addition, Clark fostered civil rights for African Americans. He pressured the Federal Bureau of Investigation (FBI) to investigate lynchings and called for the enactment of federal legislation to punish the perpetrators. Probably his most important innovation was having the Justice Department file an amicus curiae brief, which helped persuade the Supreme Court to declare judicial enforcement of racially restrictive covenants in deeds unconstitutional in *Shelley v. Kraemer* (1948). A sharp break with past departmental policy, this brief was the first of many Justice would file during the next few decades in important civil rights cases in which the federal government was not itself a party.

Clark was one of the principal architects of the Truman administration's domestic anti-Communist policies. A leading advocate of the loyalty program for federal employees that the president established in 1947, he secured an expansion of his department's investigative authority that included authorization for the FBI to make increased use of wiretaps. Under Clark's leadership Justice drafted the first Attorney General's List of dangerous political organizations. He also personally authorized a 1948 prosecution of the top leaders of the American Communist party under the Smith Act, despite a dearth of evidence against the defendants.

When on 28 July 1949 Truman nominated Clark to replace the recently deceased libertarian Frank Murphy on the Supreme Court, liberals and radicals protested vehemently. They accused Clark of being not only a redbaiting extremist but also insensitive to the rights of criminal defendants. He also faced allegations of hostility to African Americans and labor, Republican complaints about his handling of vote frauds in Truman's Kansas City political base, and criticism of his legal abilities. Clark received strong support from leaders of the bar, however, and the Senate confirmed him overwhelmingly, 73 to 8.

His critics' concerns about Clark's commitment to civil liberties proved well founded. During his first four years on the bench, he consistently supported anti-Communist loyalty-security measures, rejecting libertarian claims in civil liberties cases 66 percent of the time. After Earl Warren replaced Fred Vinson as chief justice in 1953, the Court began to move in a more liberal direction. So did Clark, but only briefly. When liberal majorities handed down decisions in 1957 that permitted defense attorneys to access some FBI files, severely restricting the utility of the Smith Act as an instrument for prosecuting the Communist party and overturning contempt convictions of individuals who had refused to cooperate with federal and state legislative investigations of subversive activities, he dissented vigorously. Cowed by hostile reaction in Congress to the Court's rulings, other justices joined Clark on the conservative side of such issues. He spoke for the majority in *Uphaus v. Wyman* (1959), holding that a state's need to unearth subversive activities outweighed any invasion of privacy its investigation might entail, and in another case upholding the dismissal of a public employee for invoking the Fifth Amendment before a congressional committee. Liberal appointments in 1962 again made Clark part of the minority on internal security issues, however, consigning him to perpetual dissent in such cases.

The same was not true of civil rights cases. Clark consistently supported the majority's efforts to enhance the rights of African Americans. In *Burton v. Wilmington Parking Authority* (1961) he wrote an innovative opinion holding that a private restaurant that rented space from a municipal agency must comply with the Equal Protection Clause of the Fourteenth Amendment. Clark also spoke for the Court in *Heart of Atlanta Motel v. United States* (1964) and *Katzenbach v. McClung* (1964), decisions upholding the public accommodations provisions of the Civil Rights Act of 1964 and their application to a restaurant serving a purely local clientele as valid exercises of the power of Congress to regulate interstate commerce. In addition, he wrote opinions overturning criminal trespass convictions against sit-in demonstrators and invalidating transfer policies designed to forestall school integration.

Clark endorsed most of the Warren Court's pathbreaking decisions subjecting the apportionment of state legislatures to control by the federal judiciary and supported its controversial efforts to end religious exercises in public schools. When the Court's 1962 ruling, in *Engel v. Vitale*, that school prayer violated the First Amendment evoked public outcry and alarm, Clark publicly criticized the press's treatment of the decision as misinformed. A good Presbyterian, he sought with his majority opinion in *Abington School District v. Schempp* (1963), holding Bible reading in public schools unconstitutional, to reassure Americans that the Court was not hostile to religion. Eschewing sophisticated legal analysis, Clark addressed the concerns of ordinary citizens about its rulings.

Most of Clark's majority opinions attracted far less public attention than *Schempp*. They dealt with such mundane matters as antitrust, taxation, interstate commerce, immigration, and labor law. Nearly 20 percent involved criminal procedure. In this area Clark, a former prosecutor who identified with law enforcement, was often out of step with the Warren Court's liberal majority. For example, he dissented from the Court's landmark decision in *Miranda v. Arizona* (1966), holding that police must inform suspects of their rights before attempting to interrogate them. But it was Clark who wrote the majority opinion in *Mapp v. Ohio* (1961), requiring state courts to join the federal judiciary in excluding evidence seized in violation of the Fourth Amendment. He also spoke for the Court when it reversed convictions of defendants whose right to a fair trial had been violated by excessive pretrial publicity or the presence of television cameras in the courtroom.

Like *Mapp*, those opinions were products of Clark's determination to promote the fair and effective administration of justice. He believed that the growth of popular disaffection with the courts during the 1960s was caused largely by a "breakdown of judicial procedures" and that the way to halt this collapse was to enhance the efficiency of the judicial system. Thus, despite his law and order mentality, he supported the decriminalization of victimless crimes, because these were clogging the courts, impairing their capacity to provide prompt justice. In 1957 Clark became chair of the Section of Judicial Administration of the American Bar Association (ABA). He revitalized that moribund body and played a leading role in establishing the Joint Committee for the Effective Administration of Justice, which between 1961 and 1964 coordinated the efforts of the ABA and other groups interested in improving judicial administration. Clark also helped found the National College of State Trial Judges and chaired its board of directors.

For a decade, while serving as a Supreme Court justice, Clark flew around the country giving speeches, chairing meetings, and otherwise crusading for the reform of the administration of justice. Perhaps fortunately for Clark's health, in 1967 President Lyndon Johnson appointed Clark's son Ramsey attorney general. Because the Justice Department so often represented one of the parties before the Supreme Court, Tom Clark believed that for him to continue to sit would compromise the fairness of the Court's work. He resigned on 12 June 1967.

What followed was a very active retirement. Clark traveled around the country, serving as a trial judge and sitting on every single U.S. Circuit Court of Appeals. In addition, he pressed on with his crusade to improve the administration of justice. Besides giving speeches and writing articles, he chaired an ABA special committee on evaluation of disciplinary enforcement and served as the first director of the Federal Judicial Center, which Congress established in 1968. He died at Ramsey Clark's New York City home almost exactly ten years after his retirement from the Supreme Court. Although not remembered as a great justice, Clark built a reputation as one of the outstanding leaders in the national campaign to improve the administration of justice.

• Clark's papers have been divided. The portion relating to his pre-Court career is housed at the Harry S. Truman Presidential Library in Independence, Mo., while his Supreme Court papers and correspondence and other material pertaining to his involvement in efforts to reform the administration of justice are in the Tarlton Law Library of the University of Texas School of Law in Austin, Tex. Don Larrimer, *Biobibliography of Justice Tom C. Clark*, Tarlton Legal Bibliography Series no. 27 (1985), contains a list of Clark's writings. The best overview of his career is Michal R. Belknap, "Tom Campbell Clark," in *The Supreme Court Justices: A Biographical Dictionary*, ed. Melvin I. Urofsky (1994). John P. Frank, *The Warren Court*, chap. 5 (1964), and Richard Kirkendall, "Tom C. Clark," in *The Justices of the Supreme Court: Their Lives and Major Opinions*, ed. Leon Friedman and Fred L. Israel, vol. 4 (1969; 3d ed., 1997), are more detailed, but unfortunately the former was written while Clark was still on the Court and the latter nearly a decade before his death. Mimi Clark Gronlund, "Tom Clark: The Formative Years" (master's thesis, George Mason Univ., 1984), provides informative detail concerning the justice's early life; while Mary Purser Beeman, "New Deal Justice: Tom Clark and the Warren Court, 1953–1967" (Ph.D. diss., Univ. of Texas at Austin, 1993), examines his judicial career. The numerous articles that explore Clark's commitment to reforming the administration of justice include Frank, "Justice Tom Clark and Judicial Administration," *Texas Law Review* 46 (1967): 5–56; James A. Gazell, "Justice Tom C. Clark as Judicial Reformer," *Houston Law Review* 15 (1978): 307–29; and Dennis D. Dorin, "Tom C. Clark: The Justice as Administrator," *Judicature* 61 (Dec.–Jan. 1978): 271–77. For valuable insights into Clark's jurisprudence see Marc Srere, "Note: Justice Tom C. Clark's Unconditional Approach to Individual Rights in the Courtroom," *Texas Law Review* 64 (1985): 421–42; Thomas M. Mengler, "Public Relations in the Supreme Court: Justice Tom Clark's Opinion in the School Prayer Case," *Constitutional Commentary* 6 (1989): 331–49; and Paul R. Baier, "Justice Clark, the Voice of the Past, and the Exclusionary Rule," *Texas Law Review* 64 (1985): 415–19. A good obituary is in the *New York Times*, 14 June 1977.

MICHAL R. BELKNAP

CLARK, Walter McKenzie (19 Aug. 1846–19 May 1924), chief justice of the North Carolina Supreme Court, was born in Halifax County, North Carolina, the son of David Clark II, a wealthy planter and brigadier general in the North Carolina militia during the Civil War, and Anna Maria Thorne. His ancestors were educated, talented, and economically successful. Clark was largely raised at "Ventosa," his father's plantation, where his childhood was financially secure and devoted to learning. While most eastern North Carolina children tilled fields, Clark read books. A teacher described him, at age eleven, as "very studious and, what is rather remarkable in a boy of his age, seems to be so from the love of study." At age fifteen Clark entered the Confederate army. He attained the rank of major and fought in many battles, including Antietam, which involved another future jurist of note, Oliver Wendell Holmes, Jr. While in later life Clark urged southerners to forget the "lost cause," his fascination with the Civil War never faded. As an adult he compiled a five-volume history of the regiments and battalions from North Carolina.

In February 1863 Clark resigned his commission to complete his education at the University of North Carolina and then commenced reading law under Judge William H. Battle. Judge Battle's well-stocked mind and *Blackstone's Commentaries* provided the staples of Clark's formal legal education. After completing his studies under Battle and returning to the Confederate army for the duration of the war, Clark was still too young to practice law. Pursuing further studies with a New York City law firm, he completed the law course at the Columbian (now George Washington University) Law School in Washington, D.C., in 1866. Clark practiced law briefly in his native county of Halifax. In late 1873 he moved to Raleigh, the state capital, where he was employed as director and general counsel for North Carolina of two railroads. In 1874 he married Susan Washington Graham, daughter of William A.

Graham, former North Carolina governor, U.S. senator, secretary of the navy, and Whig candidate for vice president. They had seven children and passed the remainder of their lives in Raleigh.

In 1885 Clark, a Jeffersonian Democrat whose watchword was "the public welfare is the supreme law," became a superior court judge. The appointment was well received. One correspondent wrote, "[O]ne more honest & impartial Judge has been added to the list, one who knows the law . . . and will administer it, without fear or favor." Another wrote, "No man had the endorsement of the profession more unanimously than yourself and . . . no man was ever more entitled to it." Clark managed his trial courts with an efficiency unusual for his day. In 1889 Governor Daniel Gould Fowle appointed Clark an associate justice of the supreme court. Clark won successive elections and served on the court thirty-five years—the longest tenure to date. He was chief justice from 1903 to 1924.

As citizen and jurist, Clark championed legal reforms that benefited women. He viewed suffrage for women as "a logical development of the movement which has elevated women to the rights of human beings." His writings on the subject influenced the suffrage movement nationally. They were viewed as crucial, for example, in securing ratification of the suffrage amendment in Indiana. This suffragettism evolved naturally from his career-long effort as a jurist to liberate women from a common law that had categorized them with infants, lunatics, and convicts. Clark also contributed significantly to the abolition of common-law doctrines that were unfavorable to children and to the adoption of legal policies protecting them. Children in the workplace particularly benefited from his reforms. When his court adopted the parent-child immunity doctrine, which prohibits a child from recovering damages from its parent, Clark dissented vigorously (*Small v. Morrison*, 185 1923). Over fifty years later, state legislators who supported a partial abrogation of the doctrine referred in floor debate to the arguments articulated in Clark's dissent. In 1914 the North Carolina congressional delegation urged President Woodrow Wilson to appoint Clark to the U.S. Supreme Court. Instead, Wilson appointed John H. Clarke of Ohio, prompting the Columbia Law School faculty to later observe that the president had appointed the wrong Clark.

Clark never confined himself to his judicial duties. He managed his ancestral family plantation and another that his father had given him, and he concerned himself with numerous subjects and endeavors. He was a product of the "progressive era" and was associated with many significant proponents of "progressive" thought and action; his correspondence includes communications with, for example, Louis Brandeis, Samuel Gompers, Gifford Pinchot, Theodore Roosevelt, Upton Sinclair, and Woodrow Wilson. His "progressive" positions, in addition to those favoring women and children, included advocacy of direct election of federal judges and abolition of life tenure, opposition to business monopolies and combines, support for labor—especially for reforms to promote job safety and a workers' compensation system—and advocacy of humane treatment for prisoners and public support for their families.

Clark was a prolific writer on law, government, history, and agriculture. One editor wrote to him that "We welcome anything from your pen." Clark compiled a sixteen-volume set of the *State Records of North Carolina* and edited and annotated the reprints of the *North Carolina Reports*. A longtime trustee of Trinity College (predecessor of Duke University), Clark associated extensively with academia. He declined college presidencies and law school deanships, however, to remain on the bench. Several of Clark's proposals for legal reforms to eliminate discrimination against women and children were adopted long after his death. His legal and political opinions thus have influenced public policy beyond his time, illustrating the assertion that "[l]ike ancient English forms of procedure, American judges can rule us from their graves." Clark died in Raleigh. A hemlock shades the simple marker that adorns his grave in Raleigh's Oakwood Cemetery.

• The Walter Clark Papers are located in the North Carolina State Archives in Raleigh. See also Aubrey Lee Brooks and Hugh Talmage Lefler, *The Papers of Walter Clark* (2 vols., 1948, 1950). Accounts of his career are found in Aubrey Lee Brooks, *Walter Clark: Fighing Judge* (1944), and Willis P. Whichard, "A Place for Walter Clark in the American Judicial Tradition," 63 *North Carolina Law Review* 287 (1985).

WILLIS P. WHICHARD

CLARK, Walter Van Tilburg (3 Aug. 1909–10 Nov. 1971), novelist and teacher, was born in East Orland, Maine, the son of Walter Ernest Clark, a teacher and university president, and Euphemia Abrams. Clark once suggested that landscape creates character, implying that landscape not only forms the person but also the writer. He was speaking of the American West, which was essential to his own writing, giving him theme and setting for all of his best works. But the irony is that, Clark was not a native westerner. He was born in the East, and instead of spending his childhood on a ranch, he was reared as the eldest child of intellectuals. His father was head of the department of economics at City College of New York and was selected president of the University of Nevada in 1917; and his mother was a talented amateur musician. Being an outsider and an intellectual made Clark even more aware not only of landscape, but also of people's relations to one another and to the natural world.

The West of Clark's works was the West of his late childhood, the mountain and desert of the eastern slopes of the Sierra Nevada. Clark attended Reno schools and the University of Nevada, where he earned a B.A. in English in 1931 and an M.A. in 1932, with a creative thesis retelling the Tristram legend. The interest in tragic myth became a hallmark of Clark's writing; though the rest of his works used his western background, they addressed all humanity, not just westerners.

In 1932 he returned to the East to earn another M.A. (1934) from the University of Vermont, this time with a critical thesis on the poetry of Robinson Jeffers, whose dark poetry had an abiding influence on Clark's own work. He had already published a collection of verse, *Ten Women in Gale's House and Shorter Poems* (1932). He would later disparage this poetry, reflecting a continuing concern with the value of his work, which later incapacitated him as a writer. Although he continued to write poetry, he published little of it; all of his publications after 1935 were in prose.

In 1933 Clark married Barbara Frances Morse—like himself, an easterner—whom he met in Nevada; they had two children. In 1936 he began teaching English and coaching basketball, tennis, and dramatics at an experimental school in Cazenovia, New York. He continued to write, completing *The Ox-bow Incident*, the story of the lynching of innocent men by a mob driven by their own moral and physical cowardice as well as by racism. Published by Random House in 1940, the novel expressed Clark's moral values directly: he believed in justice, courage, and freedom and that all people have a responsibility to defend them.

Good reviews of the novel established Clark's name; Clifton Fadiman proclaimed it "sort of what you might call a masterpiece." When the novel was made into a movie in 1943, the *New York Times* reviewer said that "for sheer, stark drama . . . [it] is currently hard to beat." Still, although the novel sold well and his short stories were regularly published, Clark continued teaching, in 1945 accepting a job at the high school in Rye, New York. That year he also published *The City of Trembling Leaves*, a semiautobiographical novel that had been through several versions. Perhaps because it was so different from *The Ox-bow Incident* and struck some readers as derivative of Thomas Wolfe, the new novel disappointed most critics. The work possesses, however, a complex and intricate structure and is not simply another story about a sensitive young man. Despite the novel's cool reception, Clark achieved some success when his story "The Wind and the Snow of Winter" won the O. Henry Award in that year.

In 1946, worn down by overwork, Clark returned permanently to the West, first to Taos, New Mexico, and then to a ranch in Washoe Valley, Nevada, where he wrote *The Track of the Cat* (1949), the last of his three published novels. This long, carefully composed novel about the hunt for an apparently dangerous mountain lion picks up some of the same moral and tragic themes as *Ox-bow* but presents them in a much richer symbolic context, making it probably Clark's finest work. Read favorably by most reviewers, the book was briefly a bestseller. In 1949 Clark moved to Virginia City, Nevada, his "favorite town," where he remained until 1954 and to which he would return in his last years. Even though that stark and beautiful landscape could not help him overcome his increasing inability to complete projects, it was emotionally satisfying, for he was in "the country . . . which I loved most," his "beloved mountains and deserts and old mining towns." In 1950 he published *The Watchful Gods and Other Stories*. Clark's short stories, which were generally successful (several of them, especially "The Portable Phonograph," were anthologized extensively in the 1950s), as well as *The Track of the Cat*, perhaps most clearly express another of his major themes: the necessity for human beings to respect the natural world and not exploit it. The title story tells how a young boy, in killing a rabbit, becomes aware that he has violated life.

The Watchful Gods was his final book. Clark continued to write but published little, took part in various writers' conferences and programs, and, from necessity as well as interest, taught, in 1952 accepting a part-time position at the University of Nevada. In 1953 Clark resigned his position in protest against the university president's attempt to control the speech of faculty members who disagreed with him. The resignation was a sign of Clark's continuing commitment to justice. In a fine irony, Clark received an honorary D. Litt. from the University of Nevada in 1969.

From 1954 to 1956 Clark taught at the University of Montana, leaving there for San Francisco State College, where he would remain until 1962, the last three years directing the creative writing program. He was generally recognized as an important American, not just western, writer; Wallace Stegner wrote in 1973 that Clark's books "are on the permanent shelf." Nevertheless, his "silence" continued: although he worked at perhaps four novels, including an epic of the West as well as other projects, he was dissatisfied with all of them. In 1962 he returned to Reno, where he first began a biography of and then turned to editing the papers of Alfred Doten, a Nevada pioneer. The biography remained unfinished, but Doten's journals were published in 1973, after Clark's death. In 1969 Clark's wife died, and his own health deteriorated. He died two years later in Reno.

• Clark's papers are in the Special Collections Department at the University of Nevada Library, Reno, Nev. An excellent bibliography of his published works up to 1965, including uncollected stories, is in Richard Etulain, "Walter Van Tilburg Clark: A Bibliography," *South Dakota Review* 3 (Autumn 1965): 73–77. Biographical matters as well as Clark's comments on his work are given in *Contemporary Authors* (9–12R, 1974); further autobiographical remarks and a biographical sketch by his son Robert are in *Walter Van Tilburg Clark: Critiques*, ed. Charlton Laird (1983). Short biographies are included in Max Westbrook, *Walter Van Tilburg Clark* (1969), and L. L. Lee, *Walter Van Tilburg Clark* (1973). An obituary is in the *New York Times*, 12 Nov. 1971.

L. L. LEE

CLARK, William (1 Aug. 1770–1 Sept. 1838), explorer, Indian agent, and governor of Missouri Territory, was born in Caroline County, Virginia, the son of John Clark III, a planter, and Ann Rogers. Although he was informally educated, Clark acquired the refinement and intellectual development usually reserved for those who had been exposed to formal study. His family noted of him that at a young age he demonstrated leadership skills as well as an intellectual curiosity about the natural phenomena of his native Virginia.

In 1785 the Clark family moved to Kentucky, where they established a residence, "Mulberry Hill," near Louisville. At this time Clark began a military career during which he played a significant part in the unfolding conflict between Native Americans of the Ohio Valley and American settlers who streamed into the region after the War of Independence. Initially his role was offensive. For example, in 1789 Clark joined a local militia led by Colonel John Hardin that engaged and destroyed a group of Wea Indians on the Wabash River who had been giving trouble to local settlers. Clark's military role thereafter was confined to defending settlements south of the Ohio River until 1791, when he served as an acting lieutenant under General Charles Scott, whose forces, as in earlier campaigns, marched north of the Ohio River to destroy hostile Indian forces. It was as a lieutenant in the army of General Anthony Wayne, however, that Clark made his most noteworthy contribution to the Indian campaigns of the Ohio Valley.

In addition to undertaking various engineering assignments (such as fort construction), his most distinguished contribution was in the area of intelligence and diplomacy. Between 1793 and 1795 Clark was used extensively to keep track of Spanish forces near American territory. His diplomatic skill was especially evident in 1795, when General Wayne sent Clark on a diplomatic mission to a Spanish fort that had been built on the Mississippi River south of St. Louis in violation of the treaty of San Lorenzo. After meeting with the Spanish commandant, Clark determined that the fort did not pose a significant threat to the United States and thus did not insist that it be dismantled. At the same time, Clark collected valuable intelligence data on Spanish military forces and armament, including a sketch of Fort Chickasaw.

In 1796 Clark resigned from the military to begin a career as a mercantile capitalist supplying goods to the city of Louisville. His career plans were interrupted, however, when Meriwether Lewis, a military colleague from the Wayne campaign, asked him to help command an expedition to explore the far Northwest under the sponsorship of the federal government. The Lewis and Clark Expedition, as it came to be known, left St. Louis in May 1804, arriving in present-day North Dakota by that November. After wintering there with the Mandan Indians, the expedition, in the spring of 1805 moved on to the Great Falls of the Missouri River in present-day Montana before crossing the Continental Divide. By Christmas the explorers had reached their destination and settled into winter quarters at Fort Clatsop on the Pacific coast. The expedition left the Pacific Northwest in the spring of 1806 and safely arrived back in St. Louis on 23 September of that year.

When Lewis and Clark began their transcontinental journey the stakes were high. The United States was then in a race with England to find an all-water route to the Pacific for quicker access to exotic trade goods in the Far East. A second, and equally important, objective of the expedition was to make detailed scientific observations of the region. The far Northwest represented a natural laboratory as yet unspoiled by the modern world. Thus it was important to study the flora and fauna, the climate and geography, and the peoples of the region because, according to President Thomas Jefferson, doing so would lead to a better understanding of higher truths that would contribute to "extending and strengthening the authority & justice among the people."

Clark was the principal cartographer on the mission and is also credited with having made significant ethnographic contributions. The objective and detached way in which Clark described the native inhabitants, as reflected in the Lewis and Clark journals, is striking for the early nineteenth century. For example, on the sexual mores of the Chinooks, Clark observed that they "appear to view sensuality as a necessary evil, and do not appear to abhor it as a crime in the unmarried state." Clark also is responsible for having named a number of flora and fauna.

After the expedition, President Jefferson continued to enlist Clark as a scientific observer. In 1807, for example, Clark was dispatched to Big Bones Lick, Kentucky, where he excavated the fossils of Pleistocene mammals. Clark's long-time interest in natural history is evident in his contributions to the natural history museum at the University of Virginia and in the private museum of considerable size that he kept in St. Louis. At Clark's death, members of the Academy of Natural Science wore black armbands in his honor.

Clark was also a significant figure in early nineteenth-century American Indian policy as well as in the military and political affairs of the frontier. In 1808 Jefferson appointed Clark Indian agent for the Louisiana Territory and brigadier general of that territory's militia. In 1809 Clark became an investor in the Missouri Fur Company, whose main interest was trade with the Indians of the far Northwest, an area then dominated by British traders. Clark's career as a mercantile capitalist was brief; it abruptly ended when the Missouri Fur Company was dissolved at the beginning of the War of 1812.

In 1813 Missouri was established as a separate territory, and Clark was appointed territorial governor. As governor, brigadier general, and inspector general of the territorial militia and superintendent of Indian affairs, Clark was concerned primarily with defending the West against Indian attacks urged on by the British. Clark's fears of such attacks persisted because even after the Treaty of Ghent officially ended the War of 1812 on 25 December 1814, skirmishes with Native-American British allies continued, into the spring of 1815. Clark's concerns were also prompted in part by what he saw as the effectiveness of British trading policies in contrast to the ineffectiveness of American trading policies. In Clark's view, the British were successful in trading with the Native Americans because their policies were consistent and because the British took "the most rigorous Measures against . . . improper conduct toward the Indians." On the other hand, Clark believed that the United States did little to prevent shoddy trading practices, including the abusive use of liquor as a trade item. Clark stubbornly clung to the belief that the U.S. government needed to own and operate a trading company that was large enough to win the allegiance of Native Americans.

Clark's views on Indian relations were not shared by most settlers who came to Missouri after the War of 1812. The agricultural interests of these new settlers led them to follow a much more aggressive policy toward Indians, and thus they were not sympathetic to the continued efforts of Clark and others to assimilate the Indian people. Because of his views, Clark, despite his illustrious career, was soundly defeated in the first statehood gubernatorial election in 1820. In 1822 Clark was appointed superintendent of Indian affairs in St. Louis. In 1824–1825 he acted as surveyor general for Illinois, Missouri, and Arkansas, and in 1828 he laid out the town of Paducah, Kentucky.

Clark had married Julia Hancock in 1808, and they had five children. A year after Julia Clark's death in 1820, Clark married again, this time to Harriet Radford, a cousin of his deceased wife. Clark's second marriage produced two children before Harriet Clark died on Christmas Day 1831. Clark spent his last years in the vicinity of St Louis, where he died at the home of his eldest son.

• Clark's papers are at the Missouri Historical Society in St. Louis; the Draper Collection at the Wisconsin Historical Society, Madison; and the Kansas State Historical Society, Topeka. The only published biography of William Clark to date is Jerome O. Steffen, *William Clark: Jeffersonian Man on the Frontier* (1978). For an earlier study of both Lewis and Clark see John Bakeless, *Lewis and Clark: Partners in Discovery* (1947). See also Harlow Lindley, "William Clark—Indian Agent," *Mississippi Valley Historical Association Proceedings* 2 (1908–1909): 64–65, and Reuben Gold Thwaites, "William Clark, Soldier, Explorer, Statesman," *Missouri Historical Society Collections* 2 (1906): 1–24. Also see James Ronda, *Lewis and Clark among the Indians* (1984). The Lewis and Clark Expedition has received far more extensive study. For the most recent edition of the Lewis and Clark journals, see Gary Moulton, ed., *The Journals of the Lewis and Clark Expedition* (1983–). Also of interest is Paul Cutright, *Lewis and Clark: Pioneering Naturalists* (1969).

JEROME O. STEFFEN

CLARK, William Andrews (8 Jan. 1839–2 Mar. 1925), businessman and politician, was born in Connellsville, Pennsylvania, the son of John Clark, a farmer and Presbyterian elder, and Mary Andrews. In 1856 Clark moved to Van Buren County, Iowa. He taught school in Iowa and briefly in Missouri. He also attended Iowa Wesleyan College for two years as a law student, although the precise years of his attendance and whether he graduated are unknown. Most likely his college years fell between 1859 and 1862.

The chaos of the Civil War and the discovery of gold in Colorado sent the determined Clark west after college. He began his mining career in Gilpin County, Colorado. The year 1863 found him mining successfully near Bannack City, Montana Territory, earning about $2,000 in gold in a year's work. Using his mining stake, he turned to freighting and merchandising with remarkable success. Clark delivered ox-drawn cargoes of freight from Salt Lake City to Virginia City, Montana, and other mining camps, and he transported large consignments of goods from the Pacific Northwest to stores he established at Helena, Montana, and Elk City, Idaho. In 1867 he secured the government contract to carry the mail between Missoula, Montana, and Walla Walla, Washington Territory. His merchandising trips included excursions to the East, where in 1869 he married his hometown sweetheart Katherine L. "Kate" Stauffer. They had six children.

On his return to the West, he and his partners established the First National Bank of Deer Lodge in 1872 in Deer Lodge, Montana. By buying gold dust for resale to eastern banks, Clark built his bank into one of the more stable financial institutions in the country. Soon he turned to the financially struggling mining industry in Butte, Montana, investing heavily in four mines, the Original, Colusa, Mountain Chief, and Gambetta. To learn more about his new business, he went to New York City to study metallurgy and assaying at Columbia University's School of Mines (1872–1873).

Back in Montana, he made a rich silver strike at the Travona mine in 1874 by applying his new knowledge. He also opened a branch bank in Butte, and in 1879 Clark joined Nathaniel P. Hill (a former chemist who had solved the puzzle of reducing Colorado's complex silver ores) and other associates in creating the Colorado and Montana Smelting Company, later known as the Colorado Smelting and Mining Company. The firm built a large concentrating and smelting facility near Butte to process the complex silver and base ores, such as copper, which was the first smelter built in Butte for that purpose. As the mining region became more of a copper producer, Clark developed the huge Butte Reduction Works, initially capable of processing 200 tons of ore per day. He profited handsomely by feeding ore to his plant from mines he owned either with others or by himself, including the very productive Elm Orlu property. To complement his mining holdings, he branched out into related Montana industries, acquiring water systems, electrical plants, railroads, and vast tracts of timber.

In 1888 Clark bought the rich United Verde copper mine and smelter at Jerome, Arizona, and later developed the company towns of Jerome and Clarkdale, which he ruled autocratically, suppressing organized labor and being hard nosed in dealing with employees over higher wages and a shorter working day. At the peak of production, the Verde yielded $10 million annually in copper and silver. According to the historian Michael Malone, Clark was a millionaire by the mid-1880s, and at the turn of the century he was worth about $50 million. However, Clark was not entirely fulfilled by his great fortune. By the late 1880s, he kept his family in Europe and New York for most of the year and became a self-conscious Francophile.

Clark eventually turned ambitiously to politics, hoping to win a seat in the U.S. Senate to prove his worth as a gentleman of high social standing. In so doing, he followed a ruthless path that would prove to be his greatest mistake. Although respected for his part in securing Montana's statehood, his desire to go to Washington tarnished his hard-won reputation as a self-made man and led to the infamous "Clark-Daly feud." Marcus Daly was the founder of the giant Anaconda Copper Company in Butte. The causes of their mutual animosity are uncertain, but their intense rivalry and personal hostility are well documented.

In 1888 Clark, a Democrat, ran unsuccessfully for the office of territorial delegate to the U.S. Congress before Montana became a state. His defeat largely was due to the unscrupulous tactics of Daly, who, although a Democrat, faced federal prosecution for fraudulent acquisition and logging practices and wanted a Republican to defend his interests with the federal Republican administration. Clark also had been the subject of protracted federal timber trespass suits, but he never forgave Daly for thwarting his political ambition. The feud continued when Montana became a state in 1889. In that year and again in 1893, Clark failed to secure a seat in the so-called Millionaires' Club of the U.S. Senate. In 1899 Clark's money overcame Daly's opposition, but his victory was short-lived. Various legislators raised accusations of bribery allegedly exceeding $450,000. Daly and Senator Thomas H. Carter of Montana pressed an investigation of the election before a Senate committee, which resolved that Senator Clark's election be declared void on account of bribery. On 15 May 1900, before the full Senate could act on the committee's findings, Clark resigned his position, claiming that he had only tried to keep his state free of the abusive power of Daly and the mighty Anaconda Company.

Unwilling to abandon his quest, Clark seized the opportunity created when the dreaded Standard Oil Company absorbed Daly's Anaconda into the giant Amalgamated Copper Company in 1899. By playing on popular fears of eastern domination by the huge trust, and by joining forces with Montana's third copper king, F. Augustus Heinze, Clark was elected in 1901. Like many other monied men who sought high political office for social status rather than public service, Clark was an undistinguished legislator. Although he insisted on being called "Senator" for the rest of his life, he did not seek reelection in 1906 and departed from Congress in 1907.

In his later years, Clark devoted considerable time and expense to building an elaborate art collection, which comprised assorted sculptures and antiques, mediocre paintings, and some very valuable works by Rembrandt, Van Dyck, Titian, Thomas Gainsborough, William Hogarth, and others of equal note. He eventually donated it to the Corcoran Gallery of Art in Washington, D.C. Although a tough practical businessman, Clark was also a man of intellectual curiosity.

Clark's other passion was building the socially obligatory mansion of successful business elites. The result was a 131-room monstrosity on Fifth Avenue in New York City, completed in 1906, which was so garish and costly that it was widely ridiculed by Clark's contemporaries.

Clark's personal life provided little compensation for his public humiliation. His wife died in 1893. In 1904 he announced that three years before he had secretly married Anna La Chapelle, a Butte woman forty years his junior whose education he had been financing in France. They had two children, but the marriage was another source of scandal. As Mark Twain said of him in a 1907 profile, "To my mind he is the most disgusting creature that the republic has produced since [Boss] Tweed's time."

Clark died in New York City, where he had tried vainly to impress the eastern social establishment. He may be regarded as an unrestrained frontier capitalist who owed his success to hard work, good timing, and a willingness to take risks. When asked to offer advice for achievement in business, he emphasized—without a trace of irony—personal character, stating on one occasion that "the most essential elements of success in life are—a purpose, increasing industry, temperate habits, scrupulous regard for one's own word, and a faithful performance of every promise." Although best remembered for his political feud with Daly, by 1900 he was the greatest independent mine owner in the world. More important, Clark personified the amoral business tactics, political corruption, and excessive display of America's Gilded Age.

• There are apparently no existing manuscript personal or business papers of William A. Clark. However, the papers of Martin Maginnis, Samuel T. Hauser, and others in the Montana Historical Society Archives contain significant material on Clark. The Society of Montana Pioneers published Clark's pamphlet, *Montana's Distinguished Pioneer, W. A. Clark, Gives Historical Reminiscences* (1924). By far the most reliable broad biographical analysis of Clark's career and lifestyle is Michael P. Malone, "Midas of the West: The Incredible Career of William Andrews Clark," *Montana: The Magazine of Western History* 33 (1983): 1–17. Malone's excellent *The Battle for Butte: Mining and Politics on the Northern Frontier, 1864–1906* (1981) portrays Clark as less of a villain than earlier accounts. Additional sources include an extensively critical assessment by William D. Mangam, *The Clarks of Montana* (1939); a standard work by C. B. Glasscock, *The War of the Copper Kings* (1935); and [unattributed], *Progressive Men of the State of Montana* (1902), pp. 1104–7. For Clark's politics, see especially Forrest L. Foor, "The Senatorial Aspirations of William A. Clark, 1898–1901: A Study in Montana Politics" (Ph.D. diss., Univ. of Calif., Berkeley, 1941), and K. Ross Toole, "The Genesis of the Clark-Daly Feud," *Montana Magazine of History* 1 (1951): 21–33. Another useful source is Mark Twain, "Senator Clark of Montana," in *Mark Twain in Eruption*, ed. Bernard De Voto (repr. 1968). The extent to which Clark's behavior was comparable to that of other notable western mining elites can be found in Richard H. Peterson, *Bonanza Rich: Lifestyles of the Western Mining Entrepre-*

neurs (1991). Obituaries are in the *New York Times*, 3, 7, 15 Mar. 1925; *Butte Miner*, 3, 7 Mar. 1925; and *Anaconda Standard*, 3 Mar. 1925.

RICHARD H. PETERSON

CLARK, William Bullock (15 Dec. 1860–27 July 1917), professor of geology and administrator of scientific organizations, was born in Brattleboro, Vermont, the son of Barna Atherton Clark, a merchant, and Helen Bullock. Clark graduated from Brattleboro high school in 1879 and entered Amherst College the following year. After receiving his bachelor's degree in 1884, he traveled to Europe with two of his professors and settled in Munich for graduate studies in paleontology, receiving a Ph.D. in 1887. Two years earlier, a Department of Geology had been organized at Johns Hopkins University in Baltimore, and the founder of that department, George H. Williams, was able to convince the university administration he needed more assistance.

Clark first came to Baltimore in 1887 as curator of the geological museum at $600 per year, but that fall he was advanced to instructor and taught courses in the fields of paleontology and stratigraphy; Williams's specialty was petrology. The following year Clark received a part-time appointment with the U.S. Geological Survey (USGS) in Washington, D.C., and maintained that association until his death. In 1891 Clark published USGS *Bulletin* 83, "Eocene," one of a series of major summaries of the various geologic time segments prepared for the International Congress of Geologists meeting in Washington, D.C. In later years he did extensive fossil collecting on the Atlantic and Gulf Coastal Plain and in paleontology is best known for his studies of fossil echinoderms, particularly the echinoids on which two monographs were published in the USGS *Professional Paper* series. Besides his paleontological contributions, Clark had an extensive and varied bibliography in several different fields of sedimentary geology.

The federal appointment was ancillary, for throughout his life Clark was associated with Johns Hopkins University. When Williams died unexpectedly during the summer of 1894, Clark was advanced to full professor and was immediately faced with the problems associated with hosting the annual meeting of the Geological Society of America held in Baltimore that December. He successfully organized that gathering, an indication of his administrative skill.

Unexpectedly thrust into the position of head of the Department of Geology, Clark continued to hold that post for the next twenty-three years. During that time, the department became one of the finest graduate schools of geology, with a broad-based faculty considerably expanded over the more narrow limits that existed under Williams's tenure. Clark arranged for many specialists from the USGS to give lectures or courses within the department. Graduate students were expected to be well rounded, even if the emphasis in research by most was on paleontology and stratigraphy, the fields of most concern to Clark.

Once Clark was established at the university, he could start a family. In 1892 he married Ellen Strong of Boston; they had four children.

Along with his paleontology, Clark was also interested in climatology. At his urging, in 1892 the Maryland legislature instituted a State Weather Service of which he was director until his death; this agency was soon judged the finest in the country in studies of climate. Four years later, the Maryland Geological and Economic Survey became a state agency, with Clark as state geologist, a duty he performed along with his academic role. The survey resulted indirectly from a summary of the geology and geography of Maryland that Williams and Clark had helped prepare for the Chicago World's Columbian Exposition of 1893.

Under Clark's leadership as state geologist, in addition to annual reports of investigations and studies of the geology of selected counties, nine major volumes about the stratigraphy and fossils of various portions of the geologic column in the state were produced; a tenth was in press when he died. These green-bound volumes remain invaluable monographic sources for data on the rocks and fossils of the East and Gulf Coast regions. Clark contributed to several of the series, including those on "Cretaceous," "Eocene," and "Pliocene."

In 1898 a Highway Division was instituted under the Maryland Survey. Its aim was to investigate road construction, classify road-building materials, and study the distribution of such material within the state. This work was a model for other states and continued until 1910, when a separate state agency undertook highway investigations, with Clark as state road commissioner. In 1900 Clark was Maryland commissioner on a resurvey of the Mason-Dixon line, the boundary between Maryland and Pennsylvania. During the Maryland Survey's early years, its employees also studied the forests within the state, and this effort led in 1906 to a State Board of Forestry, with Clark as executive officer. He was also a prime force in the Conservation Commission of Maryland.

Both his students and his professional colleagues commented on Clark's pleasing personality and ability to get along with people. With all his academic and administrative duties, Clark was also active in Baltimore life. After the fire of 1904 destroyed part of the city, he helped plan the rebuilding of docks and parks; for years he headed one of the charity organizations.

In 1908 Clark was elected to the National Academy of Sciences and in addition was appointed to a committee to cooperate with the National Conservation Commission. This coordination was one of the strands leading to the North American Conservation Conference held in 1908 at the White House.

Shortly after the National Research Council was formed in 1916, as a result of the concern of the National Academy of Sciences about the lack of preparedness in America in the face of the conflict in Europe, Clark was appointed a member. He began organization of an extensive survey of the Atlantic seaboard and Gulf states to locate raw materials for road construction and fortifications. Overseeing this survey entailed both numerous conferences and considerable travel in a short time, and the strain probably contributed to his death, which occurred at West Haven, Maine.

• Two biographical sketches of Clark are J. M. Clarke, "Memorial of William Bullock Clark," *Bulletin of the Geological Society of America* 29 (1918): 21–28, which contains a portrait and bibliography, and E. B. Matthews, "William Bullock Clark PhD., LLD., State Geologist 1896–1917," *Maryland Geological Survey* 10 (1918): 31–37. There are at least two other memorials: Clarke, "Biographical Memoir of William Bullock Clark 1860–1917," National Academy of Sciences, *Biographical Memoirs* 9 (1919): 1–18, and B. K. Emerson, "William Bullock Clark (1850–1917)," *Proceedings of the American Academy of Arts and Sciences* 54 (1919): 412–15. Two works that discuss the principal organizations with which Clark was associated are F. J. Pettijohn, *A Century of Geology 1885–1985 at the Johns Hopkins University* (1988), and J. P. Reger, "Maryland," in *The State Geological Surveys: A History*, ed. A. A. Sokolow (1988), which was published by the Association of American State Geologists.

ELLIS L. YOCHELSON

CLARK, William Mansfield (17 Aug. 1884–19 Jan. 1964), physical chemist, was born in Tivoli, New York, the son of James Starr Clark, an Episcopal clergyman, and Caroline Scovill Hopson. During his secondary education at the Hotchkiss School in Lakeville, Connecticut, Clark excelled in mathematics and English, debated, and was the class poet on his graduation in 1903. He then studied at Williams College, where he became interested in chemistry and gained recognition for reading a more advanced text by the chemist Ira Remsen in preference to the standard, elementary text. At his graduation in 1907, he was invited to stay one more year at Williams as Professor Leverett Mears's assistant and do advanced study, which led to an M.A. in 1908. He went on to do graduate work in chemistry at Johns Hopkins University, where Remsen was then president as well as professor of chemistry. Clark's doctoral research with Harmon Morse on osmotic pressure of cane sugar solutions earned him a Ph.D. in 1910. That same year he married Rose Williard Goddard; they had two daughters.

During his collegiate summers, Clark worked at the U.S. Fish Commission in Woods Hole, Massachusetts, as assistant to the head of chemical research, Carl Alsberg, who interested Clark in biochemistry. D. D. Van Slyke, Alsberg's successor in 1909, became seriously ill on his way to Woods Hole, leaving Clark alone in the laboratory, so he decided to prepare solutions that Van Slyke would need. When Clark tried to standardize an ammonia solution with a variety of indicators, he obtained inconsistent results. This puzzling finding was a source of his studies of acidity and indicators, which began during his employment in the Dairy Division of the U.S. Department of Agriculture from 1910 to 1920.

There, in research on the amount of acid in dairy products, Clark began to use the hydrogen electrode to determine the acidity of solutions. At that time, alkali was added to cow's milk for the feeding of infants because cow's milk was thought to be too acidic. Clark's paper in *Journal of Medical Research* (31 [1915]: 431) showed that bovine and human milk have nearly the same hydrogen ion concentration. In that paper, he introduced the terms "pH" and "buffer." His studies on the use of indicators and the hydrogen electrode led to a set of papers in the *Journal of Bacteriology* on methods for determining acidity. The demand for copies was so great that Clark revised and extended those papers into his classic monograph, *The Determination of Hydrogen Ions* (1920), one of the most influential books for twentieth-century chemical and biochemical research. The second and third editions appeared in 1923 and 1928.

In 1920 Clark became professor of chemistry in the U.S. Hygienic Laboratory, the precursor of the National Institutes of Health, and began to study oxidation-reduction. This research resulted in a series of Public Health Reports; a review, "Reversible Oxidation-Reduction in Organic Systems" (*Chemical Reviews* 2 [1926]: 127–78); and a 340-page compilation of methods and results published as Hygienic Laboratory Bulletin No. 151 (1928). After his retirement, he wrote *Oxidation-Reduction Potentials of Organic Systems* (1960).

In 1927 Clark was appointed De Lamar Professor of Physiological Chemistry at Johns Hopkins University in spite of his protestations that he did not know "the difference between the thymus and the thyroid glands and less of their functions." At Johns Hopkins he campaigned for rigor and emphasis on physical chemical principles in the teaching of biochemistry to medical students. His own contribution was an influential and respected book, *Topics in Physical Chemistry* (1948). His research at Johns Hopkins was mainly studies of oxidation-reduction of biochemically important metalloporphyrins.

Clark was appointed to the editorial board of the *Journal of Biological Chemistry* in 1933 and served for eighteen years, advocating high standards of writing as well as high standards for research. His presidential address to the American Society of Bacteriologists in 1933 discussed the future of scientific publishing (*Journal of Bacteriology* 27 [1934]: 1–18). He made an important contribution in World War I by discovering a method of producing pure casein, essential for airplane construction and previously imported. During World War II he was chairman of the Division of Chemistry and Chemical Technology of the National Research Council and therefore in charge of chemical research related to the war effort.

Clark's research on both acidity and oxidation-reduction provided the foundation for much subsequent chemical and biochemical research, including Peter Mitchell's Nobel Prize–winning research on the chemiosmotic hypothesis, which began to appear shortly before Clark's death. Clark was elected to the National Academy of Sciences in 1928 and the American Philosophical Society in 1939. He was president of the Society of American Bacteriologists (1933) and the

American Society of Biological Chemists (1933–1934). He gave many honorary lectures, including, in 1952, the Remsen Memorial Lecture at Johns Hopkins, which commemorates the chemist whose text introduced Clark to the field.

Clark's main avocations were reading, golf, and gardening. He bought a summer home in Lakeville, Connecticut, and produced an impressive garden. He was a quiet man with "an unusual capacity for friendship," according to biographer Hubert Bradford Vickery. Clark died in Baltimore, Maryland.

• Clark's autobiographical notes, in *Annual Review of Biochemistry* 31 (1962): 1–24, are valuable and thought-provoking. Clark's writing was noteworthy for his use of quotations; his autobiographical notes begin with, "When I find a bit of leisure, I trifle with my papers. This is one of the lesser frailties" (Horace, *Satires* I, iv). Hubert Bradford Vickery's "William Mansfield Clark," National Academy of Sciences, *Biographical Memoirs* 39 (1967): 1–36, concludes with a chronological list of Clark's publications.

PAUL HAAKE

CLARK, William Thomas (29 June 1831–12 Oct. 1905), soldier and politician, was born in Norwalk, Connecticut, the son of Levi Clark and Fanny (maiden name unknown). Little is known of his family except that they were poor, and he was forced to leave the common schools of Norwalk at the age of thirteen. Afterward he did odd jobs, taught school, and studied law. In 1854 he moved to New York City, where he was admitted to the bar in 1855. In 1856 he married Laura Clark (no relation) from Hartford, Connecticut.

Following his marriage, Clark moved to Davenport, Iowa, and became a law partner of Judge John F. Dillon, a well-known Republican. In 1861 Clark helped to raise the Thirteenth Iowa Infantry Regiment at Davenport and was commissioned first lieutenant and adjutant of that unit. Promoted to captain and assistant adjutant general in March 1862, he remained a staff officer throughout the Civil War, serving with the Army of the Tennessee and fighting in many western battles, including Shiloh, Corinth, Jackson, and Vicksburg. He was James B. McPherson's adjutant general at Atlanta and was brevetted brigadier general for his service there on 22 July 1864. Following the war, Clark was promoted to brigadier general on 31 May and was brevetted major general on 24 November 1865. In June 1865 he had joined the staff of Major General Godfrey Weitzel at Brownsville, Texas. He helped negotiate Weitzel's failed attempt to bribe General Tomas Mejia to surrender the city of Matamoros to Mexican Liberal forces.

Clark resigned from the army in 1865 and settled at Galveston, where he was cashier of one of the first national banks established in Texas. In 1867 he became involved in the newly formed Texas Republican party, siding with the Edmund J. Davis, or Radical, faction of the party after 1868. In 1869 he was elected to Congress from the Third District, which included the cities of Galveston and Houston and some of the richest plantation counties in the state. During the election he enjoyed support from black voters in the Union League and from city businessmen, and in Congress he introduced legislation designed to appeal to both of these groups. He unsuccessfully advocated the sale of the state's public lands to the United States in order to create a fund to support railroad construction and black education, while he successfully secured federal appropriations for the construction of jetties in the port of Galveston. Clark's political position was always perilous, however. In 1871 a Radical faction within his own party challenged his renomination, charging that he had done little for blacks. With the help of Governor Edmund J. Davis he was renominated, but he then encountered a strong Democratic challenge from De Witt C. Giddings, who offered businessmen a more conservative brand of leader. Initial results showed Giddings the victor, but the state election board certified Clark, after hearing charges of Democratic fraud in the election. Giddings challenged Clark's election in Congress, and on 13 May 1872 Giddings was seated in place of Clark.

Clark returned to Texas, where the Grant administration named him postmaster at Galveston. He held this office for two years in the face of efforts by his old ally, Governor Davis, to have him removed. Davis believed that Clark had made a deal with the Democrats, allowing Giddings to take the seat in Congress in return for Giddings's backing of Clark for the postmastership, one of the richest patronage positions in Texas. Clark was finally removed in 1874 and, like many other carpetbagger officeholders of Reconstruction, spent most of the rest of his life in federal jobs around the country. From 1876 until 1880 he lived in Washington, D.C., holding several minor government offices. From 1880 to 1883 he was employed as chief clerk of the Internal Revenue Department. He moved to Fargo, North Dakota, in 1883 and worked as an attorney and newspaper man. He settled in Denver in 1890 and then in 1898 returned to Washington, D.C., where he worked as a special inspector for the Internal Revenue Service. He held the latter post until the time of his death in New York City.

• Some of Clark's correspondence during Reconstruction is found in the James P. Newcomb Papers, University of Texas Archives, Austin, and the Governor's Papers (Edmund J. Davis), Texas State Archives, Austin. For information on Clark's career during Reconstruction, see Carl H. Moneyhon, *Republicanism in Reconstruction Texas* (1980). A lengthy obituary is in the *New York Tribune*, 13 Oct. 1905.

CARL H. MONEYHON

CLARKE, Corson Walton (1814–22 Sept. 1867), actor, was born in Elizabethtown, New Jersey. One of his first appearances was in 1837 in New York at the Franklin Theatre in a production of *Othello*, for which he used the stage name "Walton." He played in various melodramas at the National and Park theaters in 1838. By 1839 he was a member of a distinguished company under J. W. Wallack at the National, and by 1840 he was using his proper name, billed most often as "Mr. C. W. Clarke." Clarke was best known for his work in melodrama and tragedy but also acted in a wide variety of plays from Shakespearean dramas to contemporary comedies, potboilers, burlesques, and farces. Like many rising actors of his day, he often performed in as many as four plays in one day, learning two to four new roles per week. Like other leading actors of his time Clarke also had fifty or more roles ready in repertoire at any given time.

In the 1840s Clarke worked mostly at the Park Theatre, where he became a "great favorite," the Bowery Theatre, and Burton's Theatre; in the 1850s he worked at Barnum's American Museum, where he became director of amusements in 1852. It was largely under his influence and direction that Barnum's "lecture room" grew into a prominent, legitimate theater. While there he staged a number of melodramatic extravaganzas, including *Uncle Tom's Cabin*. Clarke left Barnum's in 1857, only to rejoin the museum two years later. "It will be seen," wrote George C. D. Odell, "that Barnum had greatly strengthened the company by the engagement of the former Museum favorites, Clarke and Emily Mestayer. His company would, to say the least, compare favourably with that at either Bowery . . . " (vol. 7, p. 255).

Throughout the 1840s and 1850s Clarke was very popular and consistently drew good houses. His benefit performances not only outdrew others in the same company but often attracted an array of stars who volunteered to perform with him. He played starring roles alongside many of the leading lights of his time, including Edward Eddy, J. R. Scott, Edwin Forrest, Mrs. Shaw (Shaw-Hamblin), W. E. Burton, Fanny Wallack, J. B. Booth, Jr., Josephine Russell, Henry Placide, Caroline Chapman, and Emily Mestayer. Clarke also worked with the most prominent managers: J. W. Wallack, Sr., J. W. Wallack, Jr. , W. E. Burton, and T. S. Hamblin, among many others. In 1850 he starred as Edward Middleton in W. H. Smith's *The Drunkard; or, The Fallen Saved*, a moral temperance tale of a man who loses everything through drink and is restored to the world, and to his family, through religion. This production, probably directed by Clarke, was so successful, despite the competition of other prominent actors and producers who were doing the play, that it ran for more than 150 performances (the first play ever to run more than 100 continuous performances), sticking Clarke with the tag "Drunkard Clarke."

Nevertheless, he continued to perform repeatedly in a broad spectrum of drama, including *King Lear*, *Macbeth*, *Romeo and Juliet*, *Wild Oats*, *The Rivals*, *The School for Scandal*, *She Stoops to Conquer*, *George Barnwell*, and countless melodramas in which he was apparently a reliable star. Most prominent and frequent among them, besides *The Drunkard* and *Uncle Tom's Cabin*, were *The Vicar of Wakefield*, *The Corsican Brothers*, *Damon and Pythias*, *Don Caesar de Bazan*, *Eustache Baudin*, *Charlotte Temple*, *Perfection*, *The Stranger*, *Money*, *London Assurance*, *The Last Nail*, *Luke the Labourer*, *The Lady of Lyons*, *The Hunchback*, *The Serious Family*, *Rake's Progress*, *All That Glitters Is Not Gold*, *Faint Heart Never Won Fair Lady*, and *Thérèse*, in which he might have made his last appearance in September 1866. He died suddenly in New York City, reportedly of a heart attack.

Clarke was a prominent and popular presence on the New York stage, both as a star and in support of the brightest theatrical personalities of his day. His repertoire, as both actor and director, covered a huge number and variety of plays, from Shakespeare to contemporary melodrama. His appeal and versatility kept him constantly before the theatergoing public during the 1840s and 1850s.

• There is very little information readily available on Clarke's life. His career can be ferreted out of George C. D. Odell, *Annals of the New York Stage*, vols. 4–8 (1928–1936). Richard Moody, *Dramas from the American Theatre, 1762–1909* (1966), is helpful with details about *The Drunkard*. Other useful information on surrounding theaters and personalities can be found in the *Oxford Companion to the American Theatre*, vol. 4 (1984), pp. 148, 212, 697, 698, and in George D. Ford, *These Were the Actors* (1955). Among older works, T. Allston Brown, *History of the American Stage* (3 vols., 1903, 1964), is very interesting because it is organized by venue and, within that, chronology. It has snippets of information on the lives of a few actors, but they are very few and idiosyncratically selected, and the volumes are difficult to use because the index includes no names of persons. J. N. Ireland, *Records of the New York Stage from 1750 to 1860* (1866; repr. 1966), also affords detailed cast lists and occasional details about the lives of actors and producers, but it is quite incomplete and has little on Clarke. Obituaries are in the *New York Times*, 23 Sept. 1867, and the *New York Clipper*, 28 Sept. 1867.

DANIEL LARNER

CLARKE, Edith (10 Feb. 1883–29 Oct. 1959), electrical engineer, was born near Ellicott City, Maryland, the daughter of John Ridgely Clarke, a lawyer and gentleman farmer, and Susan Dorsey Owings. Orphaned at age twelve, Clarke was raised by an older sister. In 1904 Clarke decided to use her inheritance to obtain an education and enrolled at Vassar College, where she studied mathematics and astronomy and received an A.B. in 1908.

After graduating, Clarke taught math and physics at a private secondary school in San Francisco for a year, then taught mathematics at Marshall College in Huntington, West Virginia, for two years. In 1911, having recovered from a serious illness and having become disillusioned with the teaching profession, she determined to do something with her life that she truly enjoyed and enrolled at the University of Wisconsin to study civil engineering. However, after a thoroughly enjoyable summer of work in New York City as a "computer" for American Telephone and Telegraph Company, in 1912 she left school to assume a full-time position with AT&T in that capacity. Females with training in math and science found it impossible at the time to gain employment as engineers; instead, engineering firms assigned them to perform the many tedious and time-consuming calculations that design and research demanded. Until 1915 Clarke worked as the computer for a research engineer who specialized in the mathematical theory of transmission lines and electric circuits, and she took great pleasure in manipulating hyperbolic functions, equivalent circuits, and graphical analysis. From 1915 to 1918 she supervised the computers in AT&T's Transmission and Protection Engineering Department by day while studying radio at Hunter College and electrical engineering at Columbia University by night. In 1918, having determined once again to become an engineer, she enrolled at the Massachusetts Institute of Technology and in 1919 became the first woman to earn an M.S. in electrical engineering from that prestigious school.

Despite this achievement, Clarke was unable to obtain a position as an engineer. She settled for a position with General Electric Company (GE) in Schenectady, New York, in the Turbine Engineering Department as a trainer and supervisor of computers calculating mechanical stresses in high-speed turbine rotors. In her spare time, she invented a graphical calculator, which could be used to solve equations involving current, voltage, impedance, and admittance in power transmission lines. The rather simple device—two calibrated radial arms attached to a base chart, all of which was mounted on a piece of cardboard—took into account distributed resistance, inductance, and capacitance while providing a graphical solution of line equations involving hyperbolic functions in less than a tenth of the time previously required. Her application for a patent on the "Clarke calculator" was filed in 1921 and approved four years later.

The filing of the patent marked the end of Clarke's fascination with computing; frustrated in her attempt to be taken seriously as an engineer, in 1921 she accepted a one-year appointment to teach physics at the Constantinople Women's College in Turkey. Her absence during the next year apparently convinced GE's management of her worth to the company, and in 1922 she returned to GE, not as a computer, but as a full-fledged engineer in the Central Station Engineering Department. In 1925 she invented a voltage regulator for long-distance power transmission lines that prevented an excessive drop in terminal voltage, thereby making it possible for such lines to transmit more current by maximizing voltage. She received a patent for the device in 1927. In 1930 she oversaw an engineering group studying power system stability. In 1933 she transferred to the Analytical Division, where she analyzed electrical apparatuses and systems.

Shortly after becoming an engineer, Clarke realized that, unlike herself, most of her colleagues did not possess a firm grasp of mathematical principles. Because she could see that transmission lines were getting longer and that power systems were becoming interconnected and therefore more complex, she set out to demonstrate the problem-solving capabilities of higher mathematics. "Steady-State Stability in Transmission Systems–Calculation by Means of Equivalent Circuits or Circle Diagrams" (1926), the first paper presented before the American Institute of Electrical Engineers (AIEE) by a woman, showed how to calculate the maximum power that a line could carry without instability by using hyperbolic functions. "Simultaneous Faults on Three-Phase Systems" (*Transactions of the AIEE* 50 [1931]: 919–39) showed how to solve virtually any problem involving a multiphase transmission system by using symmetrical components. "Three-Phase Multiple-Conductor Circuits" (*Transactions of the AIEE* 51 [1932]: 809–21) and "Stability Limitations of Long-Distance A-C Power Transmission Systems" (*Electrical Engineering* 60 [1941]: 1051–59), the latter coauthored with Selden B. Crary, won prizes from the AIEE for their application of higher mathematics to electrical engineering. In 1943 she published the first volume of *Circuit Analysis of A-C Power Systems*. This volume was a compilation of notes and lectures given to new members of her department and was written "to help the power transmission engineer solve some of his problems." A second volume, written with the textbook needs of college seniors and graduate students in electrical engineering in mind, was used as a standard text in graduate courses for many years. Clarke retired from GE to her native Maryland in 1945 but came out of retirement in 1947 to teach electrical engineering at the University of Texas. In 1948 she became the first female fellow of the AIEE. She won the Society of Women Engineers Achievement Award in 1954. She served on the AIEE Power Transmission and Distribution Committee from 1925 to 1927 and the AIEE Code of Principles of Professional Conduct Committee from 1950 to 1953. Clarke, who never married, retired from the University of Texas in 1956 and died in Olney, Maryland.

Clarke was the first professionally employed female electrical engineer in the United States as well as one of the first female engineers in any discipline in this country. Her eighteen technical papers greatly simplified transmission line and power system analysis by the use of applied mathematics. Clarke's ability to succeed in a male-dominated profession served as an inspiration to other women who aspired to a career in science and technology and helped break down the barriers that had precluded women from pursuing such careers.

• Clarke's papers are located in the Edith Clarke File, General Electric Company, Schenectady, N.Y. James E. Brittain, "From Computer to Electrical Engineer: The Remarkable Career of Edith Clarke," *IEEE Transactions on Education* E-28, no. 4 (Nov. 1985): 184–89, presents an excellent account of the technical aspects of Clarke's achievements. Alice C. Goff, *Women Can Be Engineers* (1946), pp. 50–65, concentrates more on Clarke's human side. Obituaries are in *Electrical Engineering* 79 (Jan. 1960): 108, and the *New York Times*, 4 Nov. 1959.

CHARLES W. CAREY, JR.

CLARKE, Edward Hammond (2 Feb. 1820–30 Nov. 1877), physician, was born in Norton, Massachusetts, the son of Pitt Clarke, a Congregationalist minister, and Mary Jane Stimson, a poet. Clarke received an A.B. from Harvard University in 1841, graduating at the head of his class. He then entered the University of Pennsylvania Medical School, but pulmonary illness kept him from receiving his M.D. until 1846.

After graduation, Clarke traveled to Europe to gain special knowledge of the diseases of the ear. He returned to Boston, where he established his medical practice and, in 1846, helped reorganize the Boston Society for Medical Observation, which had been defunct for eight years. Around 1850 he assisted in the founding of Boylston Medical School in Boston as a rival to Harvard; however, the state legislature never granted this institution the privilege of conferring degrees. On 14 October 1852 Clarke married Sarah Loring; they had two daughters.

Clarke was appointed professor of materia medica at Harvard University in 1855, a position he held until his resignation in 1872. There he focused his lectures on therapeutics. He compared the effects of drugs on animals and humans, studied the efficacy and harm of varying drug dosages and duration of treatment, and the ways in which light, heat, and the power of the imagination could affect the action of drugs. In addition to several materia medica entries in the *New American Cyclopedia*, Clarke's primary contribution to this field of study, coauthored with Robert Amory, was *Physiological and Therapeutical Action of Bromides of Potassium and Ammonium* (1872).

Clarke developed what contemporaries claimed was the largest private practice in Boston. He "knew, as very few practitioners really know, what remedies could and could not do,—but especially what they *could* do in the way of alleviating suffering or shortening disease" (Holmes, in *Visions*, p. xix). After resigning his professorship in 1872, Clarke was immediately appointed to Harvard University's Board of Overseers. He also accepted the mayor of Boston's appointment as a park commissioner. Despite a long-standing, debilitating illness, this new position allowed him more time for writing.

The work of Clarke's that received the most public attention was *Sex in Education* (1872). At the time, much controversy existed over admitting women into colleges and medical schools. Clarke argued that the "delicate and extensive [reproductive] mechanism" which is "peculiar to the female" became functionally active at precisely the same time a woman became eligible for higher education. Clarke warned women that if they pursued academic study, their "reproductive machinery" would not become fully "manufactured" because the "force" needed for this functional development would be diverted to the brain. He cited many cases of women graduates from college and professional schools who were "excellent scholars, but with underdeveloped ovaries." Boys, according to Clarke, had been slowly maturing reproductively since birth and thus could pursue intellectual matters because they did not need to expend nearly as much energy at that "critical stage" on their developing "reproductive machinery." It was not that women did not have the mental capacity to compete equally with men in education, or that there was anything improper in medicine for women to study; rather, they were restricted from pursuing higher education by their own natural reproductive biology. His solution was to develop a "special and appropriate education" for women that would allow "a just and harmonious development of every part."

Sex in Education was an immediate bestseller, with seventeen editions appearing between 1873 and 1886. Clarke's obituary in the *Boston Daily Advertiser* claimed that this work "was like a trumpet-call to battle, and started a contest which is not over yet." Critics, including Julia Ward Howe, Eliza Bisbee Duffey, George Fisk, Anna Manning Comfort, and Anna Callander Brackett, published book-length replies within a year; the physicians Mary Putnam Jacobi, Emily Pope, Emma Call, and C. Augusta Pope, as well as Louis Marvel, each critically addressed Clarke's work later. Clarke's follow-up, *The Building of a Brain* (1874), was "widely read, but [it] provoked less sharp antagonism" (Holmes, in *Visions*, p. xx).

Clarke's final work, *Visions: A Study of False Sight (Pseudopia)* (1878), was written and dictated "to occupy his mind and turn it away in some measure from dwelling only on the tortures" of his painfully diseased body; it offered scientific explanations of visions that people had claimed to experience during their dying moments. He compiled many cases from his own medical practice and those of his contemporaries, as well as drawing on the illusions and visions discussed in literature. Clarke died in Boston, and *Visions* was posthumously published in 1878, having been edited with an introduction by his colleague, Oliver Wendell Holmes.

As a professor, Clarke gained renown for interesting, model lectures in therapeutics. In his own extensive Boston private practice, he gained much success for applying this knowledge of therapeutics, especially in the treatment of nervous disorders.

• Additional significant works by Clarke are *Observations on the Nature and Treatment of Polypus of the Ear* (1867) and his contributions to *A Century of American Medicine, 1776–1876* (1876). Memorial accounts include "The Death of Dr. Clarke," *Boston Medical and Surgical Journal* 97 (1877): 657–59, and Oliver Wendell Holmes, "Introduction and Memorial Sketch," in Clarke's *Visions* (1878), pp. vi–xxii. Mary Roth Walsh provides a full account of the response to *Sex in Education* in *Doctors Wanted: No Women Need Apply* (1977), especially pp. 119–35.

PHILIP K. WILSON

CLARKE, Elijah (1742?–15 Jan. 1799), Georgia patriot, was born in Edgecombe County, South Carolina. It seems likely, though not certain, that he was the son of Elijah Clarke of Anson County, North Carolina, and that he was of Scotch-Irish descent; his mother is unknown. He married Hannah Harrington around 1763; the couple had at least one child. Very little is known of his life until 1773, when he and his wife moved to the area of Georgia that became known as Wilkes County. Clarke soon became an ardent patriot in the crisis years that led to the American Revolution.

Clarke became a captain in the Georgia militia and rose to the rank of lieutenant colonel by 1778. During the year that followed his promotion, British forces reconquered nearly the entire state of Georgia and reinstated a royal governor. In this state of affairs, it was the patriot resistance movement—led by Clarke, John Dooly, and John Twiggs—that kept the state of Georgia from falling entirely under British control. Clarke emerged as a bold and ruthless leader of the resistance movement and laid the foundations for his later status as a folk hero of Georgia.

On 14 February 1779 Clarke led the left flank of the American force that overwhelmed Tory soldiers at Kettle Creek, near present-day Washington, Georgia. As a partisan fighter, Clarke had few equals. He went on to fight the British and Tories at Musgrove's Mill, South Carolina (Aug. 1780), and in a number of other small but important engagements. In mid-September 1780 Clarke attempted to lay siege to the Tory-held fort at Augusta, Georgia. Compelled to raise the siege because of the approach of Tory reinforcements, Clarke led hundreds of patriots and camp followers north through Cherokee lands to safety in present-day Tennessee. Clarke returned to besiege Augusta again in 1781, but the final Tory surrender on 5 June 1781 was made to Colonel Henry Lee and General Andrew Pickens, who had arrived to take command late in the action. Clarke may have been disappointed in this result, but the end of the revolutionary war confirmed both his hero status and his wealth—under the policy of confiscation and amercement of Tory property, Clarke was granted the plantation estate of a prominent Loyalist, Thomas Waters.

Clarke remained in the forefront of Georgia affairs. He represented Wilkes County in the Georgia General Assembly (1781–1790), and he was elected brigadier general in 1786 and then major general in 1792 of the Wilkes County militia. He was named to the board of Indian affairs for the state and both fought against the Creek Indians and also helped to negotiate a treaty with them (1785). Clarke and his fellow negotiator General John Twiggs were upset when their treaty was overridden by a federal treaty with the Creek Indians in 1790.

During the last decade of his life Clarke made a number of moves that strayed over the line from zealous patriotism toward becoming more of a free agent and perhaps even toward rebellion. He resigned his commission as major general in February 1794 and held meetings in Wilkes County to discuss a possible invasion of Spanish East Florida on behalf of the French. In communication with the French representative to the United States, Charles Genet, Clarke was apparently offered money and a major generalship in the French army in return for an invasion of the Spanish-held territory. Although this possibility ended with the recall of Genet, Clarke went on to lead an action that can only be described as a swashbuckling expedition. He led men of Wilkes County across the Oconee River into Creek territory and set up a town and some forts. A constitution of the "Trans-Oconee Republic" was written, and Clarke was named as the provisional political leader.

In July 1794 Georgia governor George Matthews issued a proclamation against Clarke; the latter surrendered himself to a tribunal in Wilkes County that swiftly acquitted the former hero of any wrongdoing. Clarke returned briefly to his new settlement, but the appearance of both federal and Georgia state troops across the river compelled him to give up his designs for state building. By 28 September 1794 the forts and the settlement had been burned, and Clarke's men had withdrawn from the area. Clarke had failed in the most ambitious effort of his career.

Although he was later involved in another plan against Spanish East Florida, Clarke had made his ultimate effort by 1794. His last years were spent in a slow decline toward impoverishment; he had lost money in his adventures and was able to preserve only the Waters plantation from his creditors. He died in Richmond County, Georgia, and his remains were later taken to the Elijah Clarke State Park near Lincolntown, Georgia. His son John Clarke later served as governor of Georgia (1819–1823).

Clarke was a true patriot of the state of Georgia rather than of the United States as a whole. A fervent revolutionary and a bold partisan, he rivaled Francis Marion and Thomas Sumter in his fighting abilities during the Revolution. By dint of his military leadership he became a genuine and powerful hero to the people of Georgia, and by the early 1790s many of them were ready to follow him into extraordinary and extralegal adventures. In his efforts to serve the armies of revolutionary France and his desire to create a new state, Clarke prefigured the activities of Aaron Burr in 1805. Clarke's Indian fighting and his appeal to the average backwoodsman of Georgia most resemble the vigor and heroic qualities of a later southern leader, Andrew Jackson. Although he was hampered by his provincial outlook and ruthless temperament, Clarke was clearly an important leader of the American Revolution and the early republic. It is not too much to say that his intrepid spirit and reckless desire for expansion more closely resembled the attitudes of the people of the American frontier during this period than did the more august presence of the commander in chief, George Washington.

• There are almost no primary sources available. Clarke's life and career have been discussed in Richard K. Murdock, "Elijah Clarke and Anglo-American Designs on East Florida," *Georgia Historical Quarterly* 35 (1951): 174–90, and Edwin Bridges, "To Establish a Separate and Independent Government," *Furman Review* 5 (1974): 11–17. Older but still valuable sources are William Bacon Stevens, *A History of Georgia*, vol. 2 (1859), E. Merton Coulter, *Georgia: A Short*

History (1947), Kenneth Coleman, *The American Revolution in Georgia 1763–1789* (1958), and Louise Frederick Hays, *Hero of Hornet's Nest* (1946).

SAMUEL WILLARD CROMPTON

CLARKE, Frank Wigglesworth (19 Mar. 1847–23 May 1931), chemist, was born in Boston, Massachusetts, the son of Henry W. Clarke, a hardware merchant, and Abby Fisher. Clarke's mother died within a fortnight of his birth, leaving the infant in the care of his widowed father and a circle of relatives. Clarke traveled frequently, but not far, during his youth, spending time in the homes of grandparents in Uxbridge and Boston and eventually following his remarried father through a series of homes in Woburn, Worcester, and Watertown. Clarke changed schools as frequently as addresses but nevertheless developed a strong interest in mineralogy and chemistry. Like many children of his age and situation, Clarke took pleasure in collecting and chemical experiments; unlike most, he pursued these interests by choosing to pursue a scientific rather than classical course of study in college. Entering the small Lawrence Scientific School of Harvard University in 1865, Clarke worked closely with the noted analytical chemist Wolcott Gibbs. After taking his B.S. in the customary two years, Clarke stayed on for a year of postgraduate research in mineral analysis under Gibbs's direction. While completing his first scientific paper, he also acquired experience as a teacher by lecturing on chemistry at the Boston Dental College. In 1869 Clarke served a six-month stint as research assistant to James M. Crafts of Cornell University and then returned to Boston, where he resumed his duties at the Boston Dental College, taught in private schools, and composed articles for local newspapers and magazines.

Clarke's uncertain prospects for a career in science received a powerful boost when, in 1873, he caught the attention of Joseph Henry, secretary of the Smithsonian Institution. The immediate cause was a large manuscript that Clarke had sent Henry summarizing the best current values for the specific gravities, boiling points, and melting points of solids and liquids. Clarke, excited by the success of Mendeleev and other Europeans in finding periodicities in the properties of the chemical elements, believed that other patterns might emerge from tables properly arranged. Henry shared his interest and made Clarke's volume the first in a series of publications on the constants of nature. Henry also helped the young Clarke obtain his first regular teaching position, a professorship at Howard University. In 1874, a year after assuming his post at Howard, Clarke accepted an invitation to join the faculty at the University of Cincinnati as professor of chemistry and physics. During the next nine years, Clarke undertook systematic work on the recalculation of atomic weights, pursued a variety of projects in analytical chemistry, composed a textbook of chemistry, compiled new tables of physical constants, and became known as a critic of the traditional college curriculum through his contributions to popular magazines.

In 1883 Clarke was appointed chief chemist of the U.S. Geological Survey (USGS), a post he held until his retirement in 1924. Clarke devoted much of his time at the survey to supervisory duties and the more-or-less routine analysis of minerals, but he also maintained his interest in the compilation and analysis of chemical and physical data. This passion found expression in *The Data of Geochemistry*, a critical summary of much of what was known of the composition of the earth's crust. Published as a *Bulletin* of the USGS in 1908, Clarke's book went through four subsequent editions and became not only a standard source of information on the minerals of the earth's surface but also an important stimulus for new work on their chemical reactions. Clarke's estimates of the abundance of elements in the crust remained authoritative into the 1950s.

Although best known for his meticulous compilations of physical and chemical data, Clarke never considered such work an end in itself. As a young man, he was powerfully impressed by Darwin's theory of evolution, particularly by the implication that diverse life forms are descended from some one or a small number of ancestors, and by the young science of thermodynamics, which suggested that energy, although manifest in many forms, is essentially unitary. Clarke considered his studies of atomic weights and his investigations of the properties of minerals as prolegomenon to a future unification of matter theory. In his essays for a popular audience, Clarke was a vigorous advocate of the idea that chemical atoms were the products of an evolutionary process—a process still under way in nebulae and stars. Some one or a small number of "true" elements might, he suggested, be the source of the many elements known to chemists. Shared ancestry would, he thought, explain the familylike resemblances to be found in the periodic table. Likewise, in his writings on geochemistry, he devoted special care to the origins of igneous rocks. These he considered to be descended from locally homogeneous magmas through a differentiation akin, in some respects, to the evolutionary process by which living species are descended from common ancestors. Through these writings, Clarke both expressed and helped propagate the evolutionary worldview that became such a marked characteristic of scientific thought in the decades around 1900.

Clarke served as honorary curator of minerals of the United States National Museum from 1883 until 1924. His standing as a leading authority on atomic weights was acknowledged by the American Chemical Society, which in 1892 charged him with preparing a table of atomic weights for use in the United States. Clarke later served as chairman of the International Committee on Atomic Weights. He was a member of the National Academy of Sciences, a chevalier of the Legion of Honor, and, in 1901, was elected president of the American Chemical Society.

Clarke had married Mary P. Olmsted of Cambridge, Massachusetts, in 1874. Together they had three children, all daughters. Clarke died in Chevy Chase, Maryland.

• A modest collection of Clarke's papers is at the Smithsonian Institution Archives; most deal with his work on the constants of nature. Clarke's diaries are held by the Library of Congress. Obituaries include Charles E. Munroe, "Frank Wigglesworth Clarke," *Proceedings of the American Chemical Society* (1935): 21–30, and L. M. Dennis, "Frank Wigglesworth Clarke, 1847–1931," National Academy of Sciences, *Biographical Memoirs* 15 (1932): 139–65, which includes a bibliography of Clarke's publications.

JOHN W. SERVOS

CLARKE, Fred Clifford (3 Oct. 1872–14 Aug. 1960), baseball player and manager, was born in Winterset, Iowa, the son of William D. Clarke and Lucy Cutler, farmers. His brother was the major league outfielder Joshua Clarke. He attended Dickenson, Iowa, public schools and played left field for the Des Moines Stars and Mascots in the Newsboys League and in 1891 for the Carroll, Iowa, semipro club. His professional baseball career began in 1892 with Hastings of the Nebraska State League, continued in 1893 with St. Joseph, Missouri, of the Western Association and Montgomery, Alabama, of the Southern League, and in 1894 with Savannah of the Southern League.

Clarke's performance at Savannah impressed Barney Dreyfuss, owner of the Louisville Colonels. The 5′10″ Clarke, who batted left-handed and threw right-handed, signed with that National League club for a $100 guarantee and $175 a month in 1894. He shares the major league record for most hits in a first game with four singles and a triple in his June debut against Philadelphia. His major league career was spent with the same team, playing first in Louisville from 1894 to 1899, and from 1900 to 1915 in Pittsburgh, where Dreyfuss had shifted the franchise when the National League abolished its 12-club experiment and contracted to eight teams.

Clarke's batting ability, daring baserunning, and dynamic playing style resembled Ty Cobb's. During his major league career he batted .315 with 2,708 hits and 506 stolen bases in 2,245 games. Although weighing only 165 pounds, he possessed line-drive power with 359 doubles, 223 triples, 67 home runs, and 1,015 runs batted in. Clarke hit safely in 31 straight games in 1895 and batted above .300 in 10 of his first 13 seasons, finishing second to Willie Keller with a career-high .406 in 1897. One of the era's fastest runners, he used his elbows as much as his legs on the basepaths. Clarke tried to jar the ball loose from infielders on close plays at the bases, a style that led to many altercations. Defensively, Clarke's fielding percentage ranked first among National League left fielders for nine seasons, and he handled more than 5,000 chances during his career. He twice tied existing major league records for left fielders, making four assists in a 1910 game and 10 putouts in a game the following season.

In 1897 Dreyfuss appointed Clarke, then only 24, as Louisville manager, making him one of the youngest managers in major league history. Although it did not fare well at first, Clarke's club improved dramatically when it merged with Pittsburgh in 1900. His energetic, inspirational managerial style readily won over the other players, and his teams combined superb physical conditioning with an intense desire to win. Clarke managed Louisville from 1897 to 1899 and Pittsburgh from 1900 to 1915, recording 1,602 career victories and a .576 won-lost percentage. Shortstop Honus Wagner, outfielder Ginger Beaumont, and pitchers Deacon Phillippe, Jesse Tannehill, Sam Leever, Jack Chesbro, Vic Willis, and Albert Leifield made the Pirates an outstanding club. Clarke, who was paid $3,600 annually to manage Pittsburgh, ranked with John McGraw of the New York Giants and Frank Chance of the Chicago Cubs as the best National League managers of his era. Under Clarke, Pittsburgh won National League pennants from 1901 to 1903 and in 1909, and his teams finished second five times. Clarke helped the Pirates take the 1903 pennant by hitting .351, but his club lost the first twentieth-century World Series in eight games to the Boston Red Sox. In 1909 he sparked the Pirates to a club-record 110 wins and their first World Series title, slugging two home runs against the Detroit Tigers. The 1909 Pirates have rarely been surpassed in season victories.

In 1925 Clarke returned to the Pirates to coach for the world championship club, and he served as vice president and assistant manager in 1926. He later presided over nonprofessional baseball leagues and made a fortune operating the Little Pirate Ranch near Winfield, Kansas, where he raised wheat and livestock. In 1945 the Veterans Committee elected him to the National Baseball Hall of Fame.

Clarke, who married Annette Gray in October 1898 and had two daughters, died at Winfield, Kansas. A crowd favorite, he remains among the Pirates' all-time leaders in career batting average, hits, triples, and stolen bases. His Pittsburgh clubs won nearly 60 percent of their games, ranking him among the franchise's most successful managers.

• No known collections of Clarke's papers exist. The National Baseball Library at Cooperstown, N.Y., has material on his career. For Clarke's role as a player-manager, see Frederick G. Lieb, *The Pittsburgh Pirates* (1948). Clarke's statistical accomplishments are detailed in *The Baseball Encyclopedia*, 8th ed. (1990). Obituaries appear in the *New York Times* and the *Winfield Daily Courier*, 15 Aug. 1960. (Some of the personal information about Clarke in this entry was supplied by Mrs. Neal Sullivan, his daughter.)

DAVID L. PORTER

CLARKE, George (1676–12 Jan. 1760), lieutenant governor and acting governor of New York, was born in Swainswick, Somersetshire, England, the son of George Clarke, a government official. His mother's name is unknown. Although acquiring no more than a common school education, he did service with an attorney and then for about two years practiced law in

Dublin, Ireland. His career as an attorney ended as a result of his assault on a merchant. Clarke's uncle, William Blathwayt, a member of Parliament and the Board of Trade, in his role as auditor general of the plantations, in 1702 arranged Clarke's appointment as his deputy in New York. Clarke, arriving in New York on 23 July 1703, launched a 42-year career as a public official in the colony. During a brief visit to England in 1705, Clarke married Anne Hyde, the daughter of Edward Hyde, governor of North Carolina and a relative of Queen Anne, and Catherine Rigby. The couple had ten children.

After the death of Matthew Clarkson in 1703, Clarke was named secretary of the province, a post he held until becoming lieutenant governor in 1736. On 20 February 1705 Clarke was appointed clerk of the council of New York, and from 1716 to 1736 he was a member of that body. Clarke also served as a judge on the court of appeals. Regarded as a cohort of the "court party" (those who held on to office as distinct from the "outs" or "popular party"), Clarke was a close confidant of governors John Montgomerie (1728–1731) and William Cosby (1732–1736). He retained strong ties with influential Englishmen, most notably Horace Walpole. Clarke was relatively detached from New York's social elite; until 1738 he resided on a hundred-acre estate on Long Island (present site of North Hempstead). In 1718 Clarke served as a commissioner in the adjustment of the New York–Connecticut boundary.

Elected president of the New York Council in 1736, Clarke served as acting governor after Cosby's death on 10 March 1736. A commission naming Clarke lieutenant governor (dated 30 July 1736) arrived in New York on 30 October 1736. Clarke very much wanted to be governor, but in June 1737 John West, baron De La Warr, received that appointment. Clarke offered to purchase the governorship from De La Warr, but the offer was refused. De La Warr, however, never went to New York, and Clarke exercised the full powers of the governorship.

Clarke adroitly neutralized the powerful Lewis Morris faction in the legislature by patronizing them, thus causing the group to lose its popular favor as a reform, antiadministration party. Clarke continued to balance political factions, but toward the end of his administration faced strong opposition, mostly over the issue of control of government expenditures, from the political following behind Chief Justice James DeLancey.

Intrusion by the assembly on executive authority in New York reached its height under Clarke's administration. He permitted the legislature to initiate specific designation of appropriations, thus giving the legislators greater control over public policy. Clarke also signed measures for extension of paper money issues, limitation of the life of a revenue act to one year, and the triennial election of assemblymen. Clarke had no success in prodding New Yorkers to diversify their economy (by placing less reliance on wheat) or to develop manufacturing.

Clarke received little assistance from the legislature in attempting to prepare New York's frontier defenses against the French. He succeeded, however, in retaining the Seneca Indians' friendship, and the Indians prohibited construction of French trading posts on their lands. Clarke wanted legislative aid for settling immigrants on the frontier; this, however, was refused.

Clarke's humaneness was tested during the "Great Negro Plot" of 1741, a slave insurrection scare prompted by a series of fires. He did little to stay the hysteria or to check the initial wave of executions but used his influence to mitigate punishment by permitting seventy-two accused persons to be transported out of the colony.

Clarke was New York's preeminent land speculator in his time. In all he acquired 102,467 acres (twenty-two different tracts) in the Mohawk Valley. He evaded the 2,000-acre limit per person by using trustees (proxies). Lands were released to him once the patents were granted. As lieutenant governor, Clarke, together with his son Edward, who had succeeded him as secretary of the province, controlled the granting process.

With the arrival of George Clinton as the colony's new executive in 1743, Clarke's role as acting governor ceased. On his return to England, Clarke was captured by a French privateer and held prisoner before being released by the French. He obtained from Parliament an indemnity for losses incurred during his captivity and for the destruction of his home in New York City in the fires of 1741. In England, Clarke purchased a handsome estate, "Hyde," in the county of Chester, from the wealth that he had obtained in America. He died at Hyde and was buried in Chester Cathedral.

Clarke had no regrets in leaving New York. He had achieved his purpose in going to the New World by making a fortune. While a public servant in New York he could afford to rise above the political fray because the public positions that he held, except as acting governor, were royal appointments with no time limits on tenure. Though not very successful in upholding the royal prerogative while acting governor, Clarke, nevertheless, quieted political factionalism in the colony. William Smith, a contemporary, gave Clarke a fitting tribute: "He was sensible, artful, active, cautious; had a perfect command of his temper, and was in his address spacious and civil."

• Official correspondence of Clarke to the Board of Trade and other English officials is found in E. B. O'Callaghan, ed., *Documents Relative to the Colonial History of the State of New York*, vol. 6 (1855). See also O'Callaghan, ed., *Letters of Isaac Bobin Esq., Private Secretary of Hon. George Clarke, Secretary of the Province of New York, 1718–1730* (1872). *The Letters and Papers of Cadwallader Colden*, in New-York Historical Society, *Collections* 50–56 (1918–1923) and 67–68 (1937), contain Clarke correspondence; a "history" of Clarke's administration as acting governor is located in vol. 68, pp. 283–355. Two important analyses of Clarke as governor are in William Smith, *The History of the Province of New-York*, vol. 2 (1829; repr. 1972), pp. 24–59, and Stanley N. Katz,

Newcastle's New York: Anglo-American Politics, 1732–1753 (1968). For Clarke and the alleged slave conspiracy of 1741, see Thomas J. Davis, *A Rumor of Revolt: The "Great Negro Plot" in Colonial New York* (1985). Edith Fox, *Land Speculation in the Mohawk Country* (1949), examines in depth Clarke's land speculations; the author had access to family papers belonging to George Hyde Clarke of Hyde Hall, Ostego County, N.Y. O'Callaghan, ed., *Voyage of George Clarke, Esq., to America* (1867), has a biographical sketch, Clark's will, and a genealogy of Clarke's offspring.

HARRY M. WARD

CLARKE, Grace Giddings Julian (11 Sept. 1865–18 June 1938), suffragist and reformer, was born in Centerville, Indiana, the daughter of George Washington Julian, a Republican congressman from Indiana, and Laura Giddings, the daughter of Ohio Republican congressman Joshua R. Giddings. After spending her early years in Washington, D.C., Grace and her family left Washington in the spring of 1871 at the end of her father's congressional term, residing first in Centerville, Indiana, until settling permanently in Irvington, a suburb of Indianapolis, in 1873. There she attended local schools and completed her education at Butler University, earning a bachelor's degree in 1884 and a master's degree in philosophy in 1885.

Through her parents she met prominent politicians and reformers, particularly those working for woman suffrage. Her father had introduced a constitutional amendment for the enfranchisement of women to Congress in 1868 and during her youth served several terms as president of the American Woman Suffrage Association. May Wright Thompson Sewall, a friend of her mother's and a leading Indiana suffragist and club woman, subsequently became a critical ally.

When her mother died in 1884, she became her father's assistant and the next year moved with him to the New Mexico Territory, where he served as surveyor general. In 1887 she married her father's secretary, attorney Charles Burns Clarke. In 1889 the three returned to the Julian family's Irvington mansion, where they lived the remainder of their lives.

In the late 1880s Clarke became involved in the club movement in Indianapolis, attending the 1892 biennial convention of the General Federation of Women's Clubs (GFWC) and founding, the same year, the Irvington Woman's Club. In 1900 she was instrumental in organizing a state affiliate to the GFWC, which in 1906 absorbed the older Indiana Union of Literary Clubs, whose members included men as well as women. From 1909 to 1911 she served as president of the Indiana Federation of Clubs; in 1912 she joined the board of the GFWC, serving as chair of its Press Committee until 1916.

By 1899 Clarke had begun to work with the National American Woman Suffrage Association in conjunction with her club activities. Always concerned with voting rights for women, Clarke organized the Woman's School League in 1909 to secure the election of women to local school boards. After it successfully campaigned on behalf of female candidates, she steered its conversion into the Woman's Franchise League of Indiana in 1911, recruiting membership from local club women and organizations. At the national meeting of the GFWC in 1912 she pushed, unsuccessfully, for organizational endorsement of woman suffrage, a position she pressed until it was finally adopted by the federation in 1914. President Woodrow Wilson appointed her in 1916 as head of the women's division of the Federal Employment Bureau of Indianapolis. In 1917 she brought together diverse constituencies, including the Indiana Federation of Clubs, the Woman's Christian Temperance Union of Indiana, the Indiana Mothers Congress, the Woman's Franchise League of Indiana, the Association of Collegiate Alumnae, and the Indiana Consumers League, to found the Legislative Council of Indiana Women in order "to originate and promote legislation in the interest of women and children."

While she continued to support woman suffrage, after 1917 her interests increasingly turned toward world peace and disarmament. She attended the founding convention of the League to Enforce Peace in 1918. During the 1920 presidential campaign the Democratic party sponsored her speeches throughout Indiana on behalf of James M. Cox and the League of Nations. Disillusioned when the League to Enforce Peace stood by Warren G. Harding's proposal to scrap the League of Nations, she turned her efforts first to the Indianapolis World Court Committee and later to the Indiana Council on International Relations, serving on its advisory committee from 1926 to 1932.

Active in literary pursuits throughout these years, Clarke wrote a weekly column on club work and women's issues for the *Indianapolis Star* (1911–1929). Having assisted her father in the publication of *Later Speeches on Political Questions with Select Controversial Papers* (1889), she was astutely conscious of his significant historical role and carefully provided for the transfer of his papers to the Library of Congress. She published several historical sketches and completed her biography, *George W. Julian,* in 1923. From 1931 to 1933 she sat on the City Plan Commission of Indianapolis. In her last years illness and hearing problems limited her activities. She died at her Irvington home.

Grace Giddings Julian Clarke was part of a transitional generation in which the earlier, radical women's rights agitation matured into the genteel late nineteenth-century woman suffrage movement. Her successful recruitment of club women into suffrage support combined with her knowledge of practical politics enabled real advances for women within the context of Progressivism, including representation on school boards and other government offices, limited suffrage, and a greater voice in international affairs. Her later interests in pacifism and internationalism underscore her continued broad-minded commitments to humanitarian issues.

• The Indiana State Library holds a sizable collection of the papers of Grace Giddings Julian Clarke, including materials she received from May Wright Sewall on the beginnings of suffrage work in Indianapolis. Ida Husted Harper, ed., *The History of Woman Suffrage,* vol. 6 (1922), provides further insights into her career. Obituaries are in the *Indianapolis Star,* 19 June 1938, and the *Indianapolis News,* 20 June 1938.

CAROL LASSER

CLARKE, Hans Thacher (27 Dec. 1887–21 Oct. 1972), biochemist, was born in Harrow, England, the son of Joseph Thacher Clarke, an archaeologist, and Agnes von Helferich. In 1886 inventor George Eastman named Clarke's father, who had developed an interest in photography, the first representative for Eastman Kodak in Europe. In 1905 Clarke entered University College in London, from which he received a bachelor's degree in chemistry in 1908. After serving there as a lecturer in chemistry, he obtained in 1911 a two-year scholarship for study in Europe and worked with the protein and carbohydrate chemist, Emil Fischer, at the University of Berlin. He received a doctorate from the University of London in 1914. In Berlin he met Frieda Planck, niece of the physicist Max Planck. She became Clarke's wife in 1914; they had four children.

Upon the invitation of Eastman, Hans Clarke came to the United States in 1914 as research chemist for Kodak in Rochester, New York. There he developed the Kodak line of fine chemicals, which the company had previously imported from Germany, until the war in Europe had cut off the supply. He devised preparations of essential organic chemicals, not only for Kodak but also to meet the teaching and research needs of American universities. In 1918 he became director of the Division of Organic Chemicals and, in that capacity, supplied over 2,000 organic substances to educational and research institutions.

Clarke had few publications of original research while in Rochester, but found an outlet for his endeavors in synthesis in the annual volumes of *Organic Syntheses*. Launched by noted University of Illinois chemist Roger Adams in 1921 with Clarke as a cofounder and an associate editor for its first eleven years, the series was important for the development of organic chemistry in the United States. The volumes contained tested methods of synthesis and provided a record of the appearance of new procedures, reagents, and instruments. Clarke had twenty-six of his own syntheses published, and he also served as checker for many of the preparations submitted to the series.

After fourteen years with Kodak, Clarke left Rochester but remained a consultant to the company until 1970. In 1928 Clarke became professor of biochemistry and chairman of the biochemistry department at Columbia University's College of Physicians and Surgeons (CPS). In the 1920s biochemistry departments were part of medical or agricultural schools, biochemistry being regarded as an applied science and of lower status than the major divisions of chemistry. CPS, one of the oldest biochemistry departments in the nation, had deteriorated by 1928 and become ingrown and narrowly focused. A superb organizer, Clarke quickly reinvigorated it. By 1940 the department was the largest and most influential producer of American biochemists. Shortly after his arrival Clarke secured a $100,000 grant, enabling him to hire ten new faculty members. He enlarged the library holdings and built new laboratories. He assembled both a strong faculty and talented graduate students. Many of his ninety-four Ph.D. students became leaders in biochemistry, distinguishing themselves as heads of departments and research institutes, National Academy of Science members, and Nobel Prize winners (Konrad Bloch in 1964 and William Stein in 1972). Clarke's admission policy was unique. Not overly concerned with college grades, he required a long interview and often admitted students on the basis of potential, insight, and creativity. He also enriched the department by inviting European refugees from fascism to join the research staff.

Clarke was a skilled writer and editor. He served on the editorial board of the *Journal of Biological Chemistry* from 1930 to 1951 and was editor of several important treatises. He published only a small number of research papers, most of which concerned biologically active substances containing sulfur. His most significant contribution was the determination in 1935 of the structure and the synthesis of the sulfur-containing part of the vitamin thiamine, which American Robert R. Williams had isolated in 1933.

More important than his own studies was the research group that Clarke formed at CPS. In 1933 he invited Rudolf Schoenheimer, a German refugee and major figure in metabolism research, to join the CPS staff. He brought together Schoenheimer and Columbia's physical chemist, Harold Urey, to discuss the application of Urey's 1932 discovery of deuterium to the study of metabolism. Urey provided Schoenheimer with both the hydrogen isotope and the assistance of a new Ph.D. in physical chemistry, David Rittenberg. Schoenheimer and Rittenberg developed a research program using deuterium-labeled compounds as tracers to determine the metabolic pathways of lipids. Clarke wrote the proposals for the large grants needed to fund the research as it expanded into protein and carbohydrate metabolism, using new isotopes of carbon and nitrogen provided by Urey. The outcome was a revolution in the understanding of what happens in living cells. Clarke was the editor of the two treatises that presented the knowledge acquired by tracer research: *The Dynamic State of Body Constituents* (1942) and *The Use of Isotopes in Biology and Medicine* (1948).

During World War II, Clarke was special assistant to Vannevar Bush, director of the Office of Scientific Research and Development, for the international penicillin project and was coeditor of *The Chemistry of Penicillin* (1949), the report of the investigations into the nature of penicillin and its wartime preparation. Among his many honors was election to the National Academy of Sciences in 1942 and the presidency of the American Society of Biological Chemists in 1947. CPS had a mandatory retirement age of sixty-eight, and in 1956 Clarke became a guest lecturer and researcher at Yale University. In 1964, when Yale needed his laboratory space, he moved to the Children's Cancer Research Foundation in Boston.

From 1929 Clarke had a country estate in Scotland, Connecticut, and devoted himself there to his family and to his secondary career in music as a clarinetist and violist. Frieda Clarke was an accomplished violinist, and the couple performed regularly with chamber groups in Rochester and New York. The clarinet was his favorite instrument. His knowledge of its literature was extensive, and he performed both classic and contemporary compositions. After Frieda's death in 1960, he married Flora de Peyer in 1963. He and his second wife had no children. He died in Boston. At a memorial service in New York, his musician friends played his favorite music.

Clarke influenced American biochemistry primarily as an editor, educator, and administrator. As an editor of the *Journal of Biological Chemistry*, he helped make the journal into the primary vehicle for the publication of original biochemical research, and he transformed the biochemistry department of CPS into a major institution for both biochemical research and the training of outstanding doctoral students. He thereby had a major role in the transformation of American biochemistry into a fundamental discipline for solving biological problems.

• Clarke's personal and professional papers are in the American Philosophical Society Library, Philadelphia, Pa. For an insightful personal essay on his profession, see his "Impressions of an Organic Chemist in Biochemistry," *Annual Review of Biochemistry* 27 (1958): 1–14. Hubert B. Vickery's comprehensive biography in National Academy of Sciences, *Biographical Memoirs* 46 (1975): 3–20, contains a bibliography of Clarke's works. David Shemin has a concise essay in *American Philosophical Society Yearbook* (1974): 134–37. Robert E. Kohler considers the development of American biochemistry departments in *From Medical Chemistry to Biochemistry* (1982), which includes a valuable study of biochemistry at CPS. For an excellent treatment of the innovative tracer research program and Clarke's role in it, see Kohler's "Rudolf Schoenheimer, Isotopic Tracers, and Biochemistry in the 1930s," *Historical Studies in the Physical Sciences* 8 (1977): 254–98. An obituary is in the *New York Times*, 22 Oct. 1972.

ALBERT B. COSTA

CLARKE, James Freeman (4 Apr. 1810–8 June 1888), Unitarian minister, was born in Hanover, New Hampshire, the son of Samuel C. Clarke, a physician, druggist, and businessman, and Rebecca Parker Hull. Clarke was named for his step-grandfather James Freeman, an early leader of the Unitarian movement in America and minister of King's Chapel, Boston. Shortly after Clarke's birth, the family moved to Newton, Massachusetts; he lived primarily in the Freeman household thereafter, and Freeman played a large role in his early education. Clarke continued his education at Harvard College (A.B., 1829) and graduated from Harvard Divinity School in 1833, after which he began his career as a Unitarian minister in Louisville, Kentucky, where he stayed until 1840.

Clarke felt culturally isolated in Louisville and missed the intellectual stimulation of Cambridge friends such as Frederic Henry Hedge and Margaret Fuller. He shared with them an enthusiasm for German literature and philosophy and a receptiveness to the philosophical idealism preached by Ralph Waldo Emerson that came to be known in New England as transcendentalism. In Louisville, Clarke established the *Western Messenger* (1833–1836), a periodical that promoted liberal religious ideas in the West and supported Emerson's controversial views, making it the first periodical of the Transcendentalist movement.

In 1839 Clarke married Anna Huidekoper, the daughter of a wealthy and influential Unitarian layman Harm Jan Huidekoper, a contributor to the *Western Messenger*. The Clarkes, who would have four children, moved to Boston in 1840 where Clarke founded the Church of the Disciples in 1841, intending to put into practice his ideas about church reform. The church was supported by voluntary contributions from the congregation rather than from pew sales and rentals and also included greater participation by the congregation in the worship service and in other social and organizational functions. On the important question of creed, Clarke advocated only a loose requirement of faith in Jesus, as liberally interpreted by the individual church member, as the sole doctrinal requirement for the church. Clarke launched the church successfully, attracting a small nucleus of members committed to his new efforts and preaching to somewhat larger congregations who supported both the novelty of the church and the earnestness of his preaching and pastoral activities.

Clarke maintained his position as an ally of the Transcendentalists and progressive reformers among the Boston Unitarians during the turbulent 1840s, as signified best by his controversial decision to exchange pulpits with the increasingly radical Theodore Parker, although many other Unitarian ministers refused to do so. Like Parker and Hedge, but in contrast to Emerson, he remained firmly committed to the church and to his ministerial vocation, believing that the church provided a necessary institutional base for the pursuit of cultural reform and the preservation of important spiritual values.

The demands of his ministry were increased by Clarke's literary activities, including a brief stint as editor of the *Christian World* (1847–1848), and a continuing involvement in denominational affairs and social reform efforts. The strain of these activities, augmented by the blow of his first child's death from scarlet fever in 1849, brought on a crisis in Clarke's health; he recuperated temporarily after a trip to Europe later in 1849 but suffered a severe attack of typhoid fever in early 1850. In order to recuperate fully, Clarke retreated with his family to the Huidekoper estate in Meadville, Pennsylvania, where they remained until they returned to Boston in the fall of 1853. The financial backing of Anna Clarke's family made this retreat possible and had also given Clarke a measure of financial freedom throughout the 1840s, allowing him to pursue his ministerial work with fewer restraints than he might otherwise have had.

Clarke resumed his pastorate at the Church of the Disciples in 1854, beginning one of the most active and influential periods of his life. He had done a significant amount of writing during his stay in Meadville, and as his works were published in the next decades, his public stature grew. He assumed a more prominent role in Unitarian denominational affairs, serving as secretary of the American Unitarian Association from 1859 to 1861.

Although the controversy among the Unitarians over Emersonian Transcendentalism gradually evaporated in the 1840s, the denomination was split by a new controversy after the Civil War. The efforts of Henry Whitney Bellows to organize the National Conference of Unitarian Churches, which Clarke supported, were resisted by a number of ministers who regarded Bellows's attempts to build unity and institutional solidarity in the denomination as a potential threat to doctrinal freedom. They opposed the wording of the National Conference constitution as too restrictive and eventually formed the Free Religious Association. Clarke, who retained a measure of respect from the Free Religionists, worked toward accommodations that would keep them within the National Conference but remained committed to a liberally defined Christian denomination. He emerged with Hedge as a defender of a broad church position, which attempted to augment Unitarian organizational stability and denominational expansion while accommodating a wide range of theological views and political positions.

Clarke's position as a theological and ecclesiastical mediator among Unitarians is suggested by his "Five Points" of Unitarian belief, a representative summation of late nineteenth-century American liberal theology published in his *Vexed Questions in Theology* (1886). Revising the five points of Calvinism, Clarke posited a new religious outlook based on "the fatherhood of God, . . . the brotherhood of man, . . . the leadership of Jesus, . . . salvation by character, . . . and the progress of mankind onward and upward forever." Although Clarke's points are grounded in the history of Christian doctrine and clearly show Unitarianism's continuing connection with its roots in Protestant theology, they are notable for an implicit denial of supernatural qualities to Jesus and an omission of the importance of his atonement. They instead reflect Clarke's emphasis on character, energy, and optimism.

Clarke also argued for a deeper understanding of world religions, and his two-volume work *Ten Great Religions* (1871, 1883) was an important example of a widening interest in comparative religions among the liberal religious community and showed a broad sympathy for them. Clarke argued that a comparative study of world religions would both reveal the distinctions among them and contribute to an understanding of their cultural roots, but he was also convinced that all non-Christian religions were in some way partial or "one-sided." Christianity, as Clarke saw it, held a progressive or evolutionary potential, as shown by its long history of change, and thus "alone, of all human religions, seems to possess the power of keeping abreast with the advancing civilization of the world." Clarke envisioned an evolving universal religion that would express what he regarded as the unity and progressive quality of humanity.

Clarke's contribution to the development of American religious liberalism in the nineteenth century arose from his skills as a synthesizer within a denomination in almost continual controversy. He was committed to ecclesiastical reform but firm in his recognition of the necessity of the church. He was inclined toward a spiritual and noncreedal theology and sympathetic with the bolder and more progressive thinkers among the Unitarians, but he remained steadily unwilling to abandon the Christian origins of New England Unitarianism. In this role as progressive mediator, he helped to lay the groundwork for the intellectual reconciliation that the Unitarians experienced in the 1890s. Clarke died in Boston after several years of gradually declining health, remaining active as a minister until near the very end of his life.

• Clarke's major manuscript collections are in the Andover-Harvard Theological Library of Harvard Divinity School, the Harvard University Library, and the Massachusetts Historical Society. An early compilation of Clarke's autobiographical writings and correspondence is *James Freeman Clarke: Autobiography, Diary, and Correspondence*, ed. Edward Everett Hale (1891). Of particular importance among Clarke's writings not mentioned in the text are his contributions to *Memoirs of Margaret Fuller Ossoli*, ed. James Freeman Clarke et al. (1852); *Common-Sense in Religion* (1874); *Self-Culture: Physical, Intellectual, Moral, and Spiritual* (1880); and *Anti-Slavery Days* (1884). A useful survey is Leonard Neufeldt, "James Freeman Clarke," in *The Transcendentalists: A Review of Research and Criticism*, ed. Joel Myerson (1984). The most comprehensive biographical study is Arthur S. Bolster, Jr., *James Freeman Clarke: Disciple to Advancing Truth* (1954). Clarke's experience in Louisville and his editorship of the *Western Messenger* are assessed in Charles E. Blackburn, "James Freeman Clarke: An Interpretation of the Western Years (1833–1840)" (Ph.D. diss., Yale Univ., 1952); and Robert D. Habich, *Transcendentalism and the Western Messenger: A History of the Magazine and Its Contributors, 1835–1841* (1985). Clarke's role in American Unitarian history is discussed in Conrad Wright, ed., *A Stream of Light: A Sesquicentennial History of American Unitarianism* (1975). For his contribution to the study of comparative religion see Arthur Versluis, *American Transcendentalism and Asian Religions* (1993).

DAVID M. ROBINSON

CLARKE, James Paul (19 Aug. 1854–1 Oct. 1916), Arkansas governor and U.S. senator, was born in Yazoo County, Mississippi, the son of Walter Clarke and Ellen White. His father's death in 1861 left his mother to raise him alone. Clarke attended the University of Virginia where he earned a law degree in 1878. In 1879 he moved to Helena, Arkansas, where he developed a lucrative law practice. He married Sallie Moore Wooten in 1883; they had three children.

Clarke entered politics in 1887 as a member of the state house of representatives. Two years later he became a state senator, serving in the 1891 session as president and ex officio lieutenant governor. He served a term as state attorney general, and the Democratic party nominated him in 1894 for governor. Facing challenges from the nominees of the Republicans and the agrarian-oriented Populists, Clarke, from the black belt, delta region, claimed to be the farmer's true friend. In his last speech of the campaign, Clarke stated that "the people of the South looked to the Democratic party to preserve the white standards of civilization." Arkansans overwhelmingly elected Clarke.

As governor, Clarke advocated many reforms, most of which failed passage in the Arkansas legislature. That body refused his call for a constitutional convention, turned down his efforts to shift taxation from landowners to business enterprises, and rejected a bill to create a state railroad commission. This latter action so infuriated the tempestuous governor that he hunted down his main legislative opponent, spit in his face, and pulled a pistol on him at a Little Rock hotel. Bystanders halted the melee. Despite his lack of success with the General Assembly, Governor Clarke's administration and that of his successor indicated a gradual weakening of the conservative control of the post-Reconstruction Democratic party in the face of the Populist challenge.

Clarke attempted to oust U.S. Senator James K. Jones in the 1896 election, but he lacked adequate statewide support. After defeat, Clarke damaged his progressive credentials by serving as a member of the board of directors and lobbyist for the Springfield, Little Rock, Gulf Railroad. He won a state land grant for that company in 1897.

Clarke moved to Little Rock in 1897 and again challenged Senator Jones in 1902. In this contest, Clarke enjoyed decisive support from Governor Jeff Davis (1862–1913), a rabble-rousing opponent of the conservative wing of the Democratic party. Davis, running for reelection, expanded his support in the delta by backing Clarke. Davis already had strong support from his own region, the Ozark hill country. A week before the primary ended, Davis wired his supporters: "Save Clarke, all hell can't beat me." Clarke began his term in the U.S. Senate on 4 March 1903.

As senator, Clarke proved to be quite independent. He voted for the Panama Canal treaty against his party's wishes. He backed the Hepburn Act, direct election of U.S. senators, the Clayton Antitrust Act, and setting up a children's bureau in the Labor Department. He also supported attempts to give independence to the Philippines. Despite his maverick tendencies, his party selected him as Senate president pro tempore in 1913 and 1915, the first Arkansan so honored. He voted for workmen's compensation for railroad employees, tariff reduction, and currency reform. One scholar named Clarke as one of the few southern senators who had a "La Follette–style radicalism." He never related well, however, to the administration of Woodrow Wilson. He was one of seven Democrats who blocked the president's 1915 bill to create a federal corporation to purchase merchant vessels to carry American goods during the First World War. He opposed the Adamson Act of 1916, which mandated an eight-hour day for railroad workers. He voted against these bills on constitutional grounds, believing that the federal government had no power to perform these duties. By these actions, Clarke demonstrated both his independence and the limitations of his progressivism. The Arkansas senator never broke entirely with President Wilson, and he supported his reelection. Clarke died in Little Rock, just a month before the 1916 election.

Clarke was the first nonconservative Democratic governor in Arkansas after Reconstruction. He won election to the U.S. Senate by aligning himself with the radical faction of the state Democratic party. His congressional career was generally progressive, yet he could be a political independent with a conservative streak. As with most southern progressives of his era, he either supported or did not oppose the disenfranchisement and segregation of the black minority.

• There is no major collection of papers for James P. Clarke. Important material can be found in the Little Rock *Arkansas Gazette* and the Little Rock *Arkansas Democrat*. Collections of the papers of Presidents Theodore Roosevelt, William Howard Taft, and Woodrow Wilson help place Senator Clarke in national politics. Arkansas collections that contain information about Clarke are the papers of Arkansas politicians Thomas Chipman McRae, George Washington Hays, Charles Hillman Brough, and Joseph Taylor Robinson at the University of Arkansas at Fayetteville.

For secondary sources on Clarke's career, see Richard L. Niswonger, "James Paul Clarke," in *The Governors of Arkansas: Essays in Political Biography,* ed. Timothy P. Donovan and Willard B. Gatewood (1981). For a fuller perspective, consult Joe T. Segraves, "Arkansas Politics, 1874–1918" (Ph.D. diss., Univ. of Kentucky, 1973), and Niswonger, *Arkansas Democratic Politics, 1896–1920* (1990). For his role in the 1896 election, see Niswonger, "Arkansas and the Election of 1896," *Arkansas Historical Quarterly* 34 (Spring 1975): 41–78. Concerning Clarke's relationship with Governor Jeff Davis, see Raymond Arsenault, *The Wild Ass of the Ozarks: Jeff Davis and the Social Bases of Southern Politics* (1984). On Clarke as a progressive, see Anne Firor Scott, "A Progressive Wind from the South, 1906–1913," *Journal of Southern History* 29 (Feb. 1963): 53–70. On the southern progressives and their failures regarding race, see Jack T. Kirby, *Darkness at the Dawning: Race and Reform in the Progressive South* (1972). A full obituary is in the Little Rock *Arkansas Gazette,* 3 Oct. 1916.

JAMES M. WOODS

CLARKE, John (8 Oct. 1609–20 Apr. 1676), Baptist preacher and colonial agent, was born in Westhorpe, Suffolk, the son of Thomas Clarke, a man of unknown occupation and middling rank, and Rose Keridge. John Clarke had some college education (possibly at Cambridge) and some medical training (possibly at Leyden). He studied Hebrew. While still in England he married Elizabeth Harges, daughter of John Harges, lord of the manor of Wreslingworth, Bedfordshire. They had no children.

John Clarke became a fervent Puritan and went to Boston in 1637 along with his wife, two brothers, and one sister. He quickly took the side of Anne Hutchinson in the Antinomian controversy and left Massachusetts with her and then joined the part of her following that founded Newport, Rhode Island, in 1639. There he obtained a large grant of land and gradually built up his holdings. After the brief pastorate of Robert Lenthall, Clarke became the preacher of the town church and carried it forward after it split; the other branch went in a direction he firmly opposed, toward a religion based on direct inspiration from the Holy Spirit. The two sides agreed, however, on the principle of religious freedom. Clarke in Newport was just as emphatic on this point as was Roger Williams in Providence, and rather more effective in his day.

Clarke, possibly by 1644, decided that infant baptism was unscriptural; the rite should be for adult believers only. He went on to conclude that it should be by total immersion. As a result of these beliefs, his church became the second Baptist church in America by 1648. With his firm encouragement, it favored a wide participation in discussions of religion and opposed the ministerial dominance that was advancing elsewhere in New England. In 1650 Clarke began to act as a missionary and in the course of his endeavors was jailed and fined in Massachusetts in 1651. Clarke's book, *Ill Newes from New-England; or, A Narrative of New-Englands Persecution. Wherein Is declared That While Old England Is Becoming New, New-England Is Become Old* (1652), told his version of his experiences in Massachusetts in 1651, gave his views on where the Massachusetts churches were going wrong, and argued for religious freedom.

Immediately after his release from jail, the colonial government of Rhode Island asked him to serve as its agent in London. He and his wife moved back to England, where he enthusiastically joined in the Baptist and Fifth Monarchist parts of the sectarian upsurge during the Protectorate. He was jailed twice and fined once for Fifth Monarchist agitations.

When news of the Restoration reached Newport, his colony decided to petition for a royal charter. Though the officials toyed with other plans, in 1661 they asked Clarke to serve as agent but did little to finance his work. After a bitter controversy with John Winthrop, Jr., (1606–1676) over the location of the Connecticut border, he won a charter in 1663. It allowed religious liberty in sweeping terms, a feature that was especially dear to him; allowed colonial self-government on a pattern like the one worked out in Massachusetts; set boundaries in terms that led to over eighty years of controversy; and defined the rights of Rhode Island colonials in the British Empire. Among other things, it allowed Rhode Island inhabitants to travel freely within the king's dominions and thereby overruled the banishment on pain of death that Massachusetts had decreed for Anne Hutchinson, Roger Williams, and others.

Clarke returned to Newport in 1664, resumed preaching at the Baptist church, and filled a variety of positions in secular government. His public service was limited by a long controversy over payment of his expenses as agent (never fully funded) and by the beginning of factional polarization in about 1671 that put him out of office. His church, which had undergone a schism in his absence, underwent another soon after his return concerning the day of the week—seventh or first—to be observed as the sabbath; a few years later it faced a major heresy case. His own preference for a church with minimal canons of orthodoxy was frustrated step by step.

The institutions he had done so much to shape did not remain as he had wished, and in other ways his autumn years were not a time of harvest. Elizabeth Clarke died in 1670 or shortly earlier. John married Jane Fletcher in 1671, who died a year later after the birth of their daughter, who survived a little longer. Then in 1673 he married Sarah Davis, widow of Nicholas Davis, who brought with her at least five children, evidently to the pleasure of their step-father.

John Clarke's death in Newport was scarcely noticed amid the great excitements of King Philip's War. By his will he left his property in the hands of trustees. After Sarah Clarke's death, the trustees and their successors were to manage the bulk of the estate to earn income for charitable expenditures. The trust exists today and may well be the oldest such entity in the United States.

• Some Clarke papers exist in the Winthrop papers at the Massachusetts Historical Society in Boston, the Newport Historical Society, the library of Colgate University in Hamilton, N.Y., and a few other places. The family Bible is at the Rhode Island Historical Society in Providence. Clarke's report on the pseudopregnancy of Anne Hutchinson in 1638, as given (perhaps inaccurately) in John Winthrop's journal, is conveniently printed in Emory Battis, *Saints and Sectaries: Anne Hutchinson and the Antinomian Controversy in the Massachusetts Bay Colony* (1962). His defense of predestination is in the records of the First Baptist Church, Newport Historical Society. The most valuable study of Clarke's life is James H. Christian, "John Clarke: Baptist Statesman" (Ph.D. diss., Eastern Baptist Theological Seminary, 1950). See also Wilbur Nelson, *The Hero of Aquidneck: A Life of Dr. John Clarke* (1938); Robert J. Wilson III, *A Lively Experiment: The Extraordinary Career of Dr. John Clarke of Newport, Rhode Island, 1609–1676* (1983); and the occasionally useful Thomas W. Bicknell, *The Story of Dr. John Clarke, The Founder of The First Free Commonwealth of the World on the Basis of "Full Liberty in Religious Concernments"* (1915).

SYDNEY V. JAMES

CLARKE, John Hessin (18 Sept. 1857–22 Mar. 1945), U.S. Supreme Court justice, was born in New Lisbon, Ohio, the son of John Clarke, a lawyer and judge, and Melissa Hessin. Young John grew up as a member of the local elite, with his father active in local Democratic politics. Following graduation from New Lisbon High School in 1873, John enrolled at Western Reserve College. There he took a broad range of courses and, influenced by reading the work of Walter Bagehot, undertook the study of law. He graduated Phi Beta Kappa in 1877 and passed the Ohio bar examination cum laude in 1878.

After two years of practicing law in New Lisbon, Clarke moved to nearby Youngstown to become part-owner of a weekly Democratic newspaper, the *Youngstown Vindicator*. He continued to practice law while becoming active in local politics. In 1882 he sold his interest in the newspaper and interrupted his political activity in order to concentrate fully on the law. He turned to corporate law and honed his skill as a trial attorney. Although a liberal Democrat, Clarke was continually employed by wealthy, conservative clients. Late in life, he spoke about some of his wealthier clients, "Perhaps they preferred to have me with rather than against them in the courts." Clarke sought to raise the cultural level of the Youngstown community by giving public lectures on literature and leading the local public library movement. He soon moved to larger issues, speaking out statewide against the free coinage of silver, even though his own party supported it. He accepted a partnership at a prominent Cleveland law firm specializing in railroad and corporate law.

In 1904 Clarke was the Democratic candidate for the U.S. Senate but lost to incumbent Mark Hanna as the state of Ohio voted overwhelmingly Republican. Clarke had run on a progressive platform denouncing trusts, tariffs, colonialism, and imperialism and advocating the use of initiatives and referendums. His policies were called "populistic, socialistic and anarchistic" by Hanna and worried conservatives in the Ohio Democratic party. By 1914 progressivism had taken hold in Ohio and in the country as a whole with the election two years before of Woodrow Wilson as president. Many of the policies Clarke had advocated a decade earlier had become law. With the adoption of the Seventeenth Amendment to the U.S. Constitution, calling for the direct popular election of U.S. senators, Clarke declared his candidacy for the Democratic party's nomination for an Ohio Senate seat. He faced Ohio's attorney general, Timothy Hogan, and soon found that his candidacy was not popular with voters and many key members of the state Democratic party. As a result, Clarke was quite willing to withdraw from the race when President Wilson nominated him for a federal judgeship.

Clarke, aged fifty-seven, in 1914 took his place on the bench of the Federal District Court for the Northern District of Ohio. After sixteen years of Republican appointments, Wilson sought to fill as many federal judgeships as possible with progressive Democrats, hoping to groom them for possible Supreme Court nomination. By 1916 Clarke had been on the bench two years and performed as Wilson had hoped. Following the retirement of Charles Evans Hughes, Clarke was rewarded with a nomination to the high court. Unlike Wilson's previous nominee, Louis Brandeis, Clarke's nomination sailed through the Senate without controversy, and he was unanimously confirmed on 24 July 1916.

Clarke joined the Court under Chief Justice Edward D. White and found two sympathetic liberal colleagues in Brandeis and Oliver Wendell Holmes. Following Clarke's first majority opinion as a justice, Holmes remarked to the new member that it was clear, convincing, and charmingly written. Clarke's relations with Justice James McReynolds, the former attorney general who had recommended Clarke for his initial federal judgeship, were strained. The conservative McReynolds felt betrayed by Clarke, who often sided with Brandeis in contentious cases.

Clarke's main contributions to the Supreme Court came in the areas of patent and antitrust law. In *United States v. Reading Co.* (1920) he wrote for a Court majority declaring that Reading Railroad's ownership of a New Jersey railway, coal mining, and carrying company was an illegal monopoly constituting "a menace to and undue restraint upon interstate commerce." This important precedent was used to enforce the Sherman Antitrust Act during the presidency of Franklin D. Roosevelt. In *Abrams v. United States* (1919) Clarke wrote the majority opinion upholding the conviction of six Russian-born aliens under the Espionage Act of 1918. The Bolshevik partisans had distributed more than 15,000 leaflets in New York City condemning President Wilson's intervention against the Russian revolution and calling for resistance by the American working class. Clarke saw the leaflets as a direct attempt to undermine the U.S. war effort. In dissent, Holmes, joined by Brandeis, challenged Clarke's contention, wondering how "the surreptitious publishing of a silly leaflet by an unknown man" could create an immediate danger to the government. Clarke, though a consistent supporter of civil liberties, including free speech, never regretted his opinion in *Abrams*, saying that wartime considerations had to take precedence. Perhaps Clarke's two most important dissents occurred in *Hammer v. Dagenhart* (1918) and *Bailey v. Drexel Furniture Co.* (1922), in which he supported the use of the Constitution's commerce clause and the taxing power by Congress to justify enacting legislation on child labor standards.

Justice Clarke felt that the Supreme Court was a tedious and restraining institution. He lamented the fact that he had to spend countless hours scrutinizing the minutiae of relatively unimportant cases and was unable to speak out on the issues of the day. Within a year's time, in 1921–1922, both his sisters died of heart failure, he had seen Chief Justice White deteriorate while still on the bench, and he recognized that his own hearing was beginning to fail. As he neared his sixty-fifth birthday, he would soon be eligible for retirement benefits, but, feeling that a wealthy individual had no reason to accept a government pension, he decided to resign on 18 September 1922, saying that he wished to read books and travel. He wrote to his successor, George Sutherland, that he could expect "a dog's life" as a Supreme Court justice. Woodrow Wilson said that he was "sorry—deeply sorry" that Clarke was departing. "Like thousands of other liberals throughout the country, I have been counting on the influence of you and Justice Brandeis to restrain the Court in some measure from the extreme reactionary course which it seems inclined to follow," Wilson said (letter from Wilson to Clarke, 5 Sept. 1922). Justices Holmes, William R. Day, and Willis Van Devanter said that they would miss him terribly, and the other justices expressed their respect and affections, except for McReynolds, who refused even to sign the formal letter sent by the whole Court.

In his resignation letter Clarke had also mentioned that he wished to "serve some public causes." Much was made by the press of this aside, and when asked about it in a subsequent interview Clarke said that he would like to concentrate on facilitating America's entrance into the League of Nations. In response he received an overwhelming number of invitations for speaking engagements, and he soon found himself the leading advocate of the revived League movement, which had fallen from the agenda since Wilson had left office. He worked tirelessly, setting up a nonpartisan organization, but he found obstacles at every turn from within the Democratic party, from Wilson himself, and from presidents Warren Harding and Calvin Coolidge. The organization turned its sights to other issues, such as U.S. membership in the World Court. Clarke formally left the movement in the fall of 1927. He continued to give speeches on world peace, and in 1937 he gave a nationwide radio address in support of President Franklin D. Roosevelt's attempt to expand the number of Supreme Court justices. He died at his home in San Diego, California, just as deliberations began on the formation of the United Nations.

John Hessin Clarke gave voice to such progressive liberal causes as trust-busting, labor standards, and world peace that were high on the agenda of early twentieth-century America. His campaigns for the Senate, tenure as a Supreme Court justice, and years as an elder statesman for liberal policies exemplify his lifelong spirit and commitment to public causes.

• Clarke's papers are at the Western Reserve University Library, Cleveland, Ohio. The definitive biography is Hoyt Landon Warner, *The Life of Mr. Justice Clarke: A Testament to the Power of Liberal Dissent in America* (1959) , which contains an extensive bibliography. For an account of Clarke's judicial philosophy, see David M. Levitan, "The Jurisprudence of Mr. Justice Clarke," *Miami Law Quarterly* 7 (Dec. 1952): 44–72. The following cases can be found in *United States Reports*: *United States v. Reading Co.*, 253 U.S. 26; *Abrams v. United States*, 250 U.S. 616; *Hammer v. Dagenhart*, 247 U.S. 251; and *Bailey v. Drexel Furniture Co.*, 259 U.S. 20. A eulogy by Clarke, "Woodrow Wilson, the World Court, and the League of Nations," delivered at the memorial service following Wilson's death, can be found as an extension of the remarks by Carter Glass in the *Congressional Record* 74 (27 Jan. 1931): 3268–72. An obituary is in the *San Diego Union*, 23 Mar. 1945.

ARTEMUS E. WARD

CLARKE, John Mason (15 Apr. 1857–29 May 1925), paleontologist, was born in Canandaigua, New York, the son of Noah Turner Clarke, a principal of Canandaigua Academy, and Laura Mason Merrill. Encouraged by his father, whose teaching included the sciences, Clarke began when he was young to collect fossil specimens of Devonian age invertebrates in an area where they were common; he later said that "the shale cliffs along the shore and the ravines of the lake teemed with fossils."

Educated at his father's academy, Clarke then attended Amherst College (A.B., 1877), where his interest in geology was further enhanced by the professor of geology, Benjamin K. Emerson. After graduating in 1877, Clarke taught for a year at Canandaigua Academy and then returned to Amherst College as assistant to Emerson. In 1881 Clarke became an instructor in geology and zoology at Smith College. In 1883–1884 he studied in Göttingen, Germany, and after his return found that he no longer had a position at Smith, having been fired for "heterodoxy." For a year he taught at Massachusetts Agricultural School in Amherst, and in 1886 he petitioned to become an assistant to James Hall, state paleontologist and the director of the state museum at Albany, New York. Clarke was accepted, and he spent the remainder of his professional life with the State Museum and Education Department of New York. From 1894 he was also professor of geology and mineralogy at Rensselaer Polytechnic Institute in Troy, New York. After Hall's death in 1898 Clarke was appointed state paleontologist.

Clarke married Emma Juel Sill; they had one child. The date of their marriage and how it ended are unknown. In 1895 he married Fannie V. Bosler; they had no children.

Clarke's geologic work focused primarily on invertebrate fossils of the Devonian period (395 to 345 million years ago) and the stratigraphy of the rocks in which they are found. Nowhere more than in New York State, he said, "is the full and variant succession of Devonic events so well recorded or at least so clearly and simply presented." In his studies, which also covered other periods of the ancient Paleozoic era, he painstakingly described brachiopods, trilobites, sponges, and eurypterids in the context of their geologic sequence. He named many new genera and species. Some of the significant geological publications that appeared before Hall's death under the names of Hall and Clarke were largely the work of Clarke.

In order to determine the geologic boundary between the Silurian and the Devonian periods, Clarke and Charles Schuchert, a paleontologist with the U.S. Geological Survey, traveled in 1900 to several regions of eastern Canada, including the Gaspé peninsula of Quebec Province. There they worked out the geologic sequence, which Clarke summarized in what Schuchert described as Clarke's "master work" ("Early Devonic History of New York and Eastern North America," *New York State Museum Memoir* 9, pt. 1 [1908] and pt. 2 [1909]). Clarke became intrigued with the Gaspé area and spent summers there for nearly twenty years. He wrote *The Heart of Gaspé* (1913) and *L'île Percée* (1923) about the geology, scenic beauty, bird life, history, and local customs of that region.

In 1904 Clarke's title became state geologist and paleontologist of New York and director of the State Museum and of the Science Division of the Education Department, University of the State of New York. Within a short time, his staff was greatly enlarged. Under his urging and direction, the department became a significant facility, occupying a new building by 1913. On its second floor was the museum, which displayed collections gathered from within the state of invertebrate fossils, illustrated restorations of early geological creatures, and other striking exhibits ranging in theme from toadstools to habitat groups of Indians, especially the Iroquois. Clarke obtained private funding as well as state monies for the museum exhibits. Although he envisioned an even larger state museum in Albany and from 1916 worked toward its fulfillment, his hopes were dashed in 1922 when the state legislature chose instead to fund an exhibit as a memorial to Theodore Roosevelt at the American Museum of Natural History in New York City.

Always devoted to his native state, beginning in 1913 Clarke encouraged the establishment of at least six state parks to protect areas of geological scenery that he considered of high educational value. Beginning in 1901, he had tablets placed at sites of significance in the history of New York geology. He worked to establish an international agreement with Great Britain to maintain the integrity of Niagara Falls from possible abuse by power companies. He encouraged publications on the birds and the wildflowers of New York.

Clarke was elected to the National Academy of Sciences in 1909. He was president of the Paleontological Society in 1909 and of the Geological Society of America in 1916. He was honored with the Hayden Medal of the Philadelphia Academy of Natural Sciences in 1908, a gold medal from the Permanent Wild Life Protection Fund in 1920, and the Thompson Gold Medal of the National Academy of Sciences in 1925. He died in Albany, New York.

Clarke's bibliography of more than 450 titles includes biographies of several of his colleagues, including a long one on James Hall (1921). His colleagues considered his work comprehensive, exhaustive, and basic in the field of invertebrate paleontology.

• Some of Clarke's professional papers are in the New York State Archives, and some of his personal papers are in the Albany Institute of History and Art. Clarke's most significant geological publications appeared in bulletins of the New York State Museum. Some of his other important works are, with James Hall, "Descriptions of Trilobites and Other Crustacea of the Oriskany, Upper Heiderberg, Hamilton, Portage, Chemung, and Catskill Groups," *Paleontology of New York* 7 (1888); with Hall, "An Introduction to the Study of the Genera of Paleozoic Brachiopoda," *Paleontology of New York* 8, pt. 1 (1892) and pt. 2 (1894); and, with Rudolf Ruedemann, "The Eurypterida of New York," *New York State Museum Memoir* 14 (2 vols., 1912). Biographies are by Charles Schuchert, *Bulletin of the Geological Society of America*, 37 (1926): 49–93, and *Biological Memoirs of the National Academy of Sciences* 12 (1927): 181–244, both with bibliographies; and Charles Keyes, *Pan-American Geologist* 44, no. 1 (1925): 1–16.

ELIZABETH NOBLE SHOR

CLARKE, Joseph Ignatius Constantine (31 July 1846–27 Feb. 1925), journalist, poet, and playwright, was born in Kingstown, near Dublin, Ireland, the son of William Clarke, a barrister, and Ellen Quinn. After the 1858 death of his father, Joseph Clarke moved with his family to London, where he began work as an apprentice in the reading room of the Queen's Printers. In addition to the education he received as a boy in a series of Irish Catholic Schools, Clarke was privately tutored in French and Latin. He secured a civil service sinecure when he was sixteen.

Three years later patriotism led to Clarke's involvement in the Fenian movement, an Irish revolutionary organization founded in New York in 1858 for the purpose of establishing an independent Irish republic. During the day he worked as a clerk in the Home Office; by night he was an activist in one of the many Irish Republican Brotherhood centers in London. Linked to the December 1867 Clerkenwell explosion, which was intended to promote the release of two imprisoned American officers, and pursued by authorities, Clarke escaped to Paris in February 1868 and sailed for New York in April. Met by his brother Charles, he was soon employed by the weekly *Irish Republic* as a journalist.

Clarke's political writings attracted the attention of the Republican party, which led him to participate in the successful campaigns of presidential candidate Ulysses S. Grant and vice presidential candidate Schuyler Colfax. Clarke began writing for the Democratic *New York Herald* after the election. He wrote about his travels and did one of the earliest interviews in daily journalism with the Mormon leader Brigham Young. Clarke also directed several different departments at the *Herald*, including the drama, music, and literary departments. In 1873 he married Mary Agnes Cahill, with whom he had two sons.

From 1883 to 1895 Clarke served as managing editor of Albert Pulitzer's *New York Morning Journal*, in which he launched a crusade to commemorate the quadricentennial of the discovery of the New World by Christopher Columbus. Three years later Clarke became the editor of the literary weekly *Criterion*, a position he held until 1900. In 1903 he returned to the *Herald* as Sunday editor for three years. He resigned from the *Herald* to work as publicity director for the Standard Oil Company; he held that position until 1913.

Although Clarke's interests in the theater and opera had their beginnings during his days at the Queen's Printers, his career as a playwright did not blossom until 1896, when he collaborated with American playwright Charles Klein on *Heartsease*, a play written for Henry Miller's first starring role. In his posthumous autobiography, *My Life and Memories* (1925), Clarke writes, "It was at first a modern play, but for the second year I rewrote it in three weeks as an eighteenth-century costume play at the behest of Charles Frohman who had taken it over under the idea that the public just then wanted color." His next play, *For Bonnie Prince Charlie* (1897), was tailored for the talents of the husband and wife team Robert Taber and Julia Marlowe. In 1898 *The First Violin*, a dramatization of the Jessie Fothergill novel for actor Richard Mansfield, met with adverse criticism from reviewers. Even so, Gerald Bordman claims that "this sort of soppy romance appealed to a sizeable audience. Although wartime excitement was keeping many playgoers away from the theatre and hurting ticket sales, *The First Violin* did good business during its prebooked, month-long visit, so Mansfield kept it in his repertory for a while" (*American Theatre*, p. 424). *Her Majesty, the Girl Queen of Nordenmark* (1900), a dramatization of the novel by Elizabeth Knight Tompkins, starred Grace George. A religious theme and elaborate spectacle dominated *The Prince of India* (1906), Clarke's rendition of the Lew Wallace novel, much of which was written in both blank and rhymed verse. Starring William Farnum, the play enjoyed a two-month run as part of a transcontinental tour.

Clarke's literary reputation lies primarily in his poetry and journalistic writings rather than in his dramatic works in spite of his failed attempts, along with other serious-minded New York idealists, to promote a movement for the endowment of an arts theater, influenced in part, by William Butler Yeats's trip to the United States in 1903 and 1904. His best known poem, "The Fighting Race" (1898), immortalized the Irish dead of the battleship *Maine*. Clarke used his 1914 trip to the Orient as the basis of *Japan at First Hand* (1918). The American Irish Historical Society, which he had served as president from 1913 to 1923, honored Clarke with a dinner at the Hotel Astor in 1924; it was his last public appearance. He died in New York City.

Perhaps Clarke's life and career are best summed up by Rupert Hughes, the *Criterion* writer and arts critic, in his introduction to Clarke's memoirs:

> There was almost nothing that did not interest Mr. Clarke cordially: his life abounded in sympathy, poetry, gayety, keen wit, an everlasting love of stories, to hear, to tell, and to greet with laughter. He had as little cyncism as it was possible for a man to have who also had such enormous acquaintance with life through his daily handling of news.

• In addition to Joseph Ignatius C. Clarke, *My Life and Memories* (1925), see also E. J. McGuire, "Memorial of Jos. I. C. Clarke," *Journal of the American Irish Historical Society* 24 (1925): 227–40. Margaret G. Mayorga, *A Short History of the American Drama* (1932), Gerald Bordman, *American Theatre: A Chronicle of Comedy and Drama, 1869–1914* (1994), and articles in *Theatre Magazine*, Aug. 1902, Jan. and Feb. 1903, and Sept. 1905, are brief but helpful sources. Obituaries and related articles are in the *New York Times*, 28 Feb. and 6 Mar. 1925, and *Variety*, 4 Mar. 1925.

LOUIS A. RACHOW

CLARKE, Kenny (?9 Jan. 1914–26 Jan. 1985), jazz drummer and bandleader, was born Kenneth Clarke Spearman in Pittsburgh, Pennsylvania, the son of Charles Spearman and Martha Grace Scott. His birth date is almost always given as 9 January, but writer Ursula Broschke Davis maintains that the actual date is 2 January. His mother played piano, and at a young age he learned to play both this instrument and, in church, pump organ. Biographers concur that his boyhood was miserable, and he hid the experience behind rosy and contradictory memories. His father abandoned the family. When he was around five years old, his mother died. Her companion, a Baptist preacher, placed him in the Coleman Industrial Home for Negro Boys in Pittsburgh, where he tried a few brass instruments before taking up drums. At about age eleven or twelve he resumed living with his stepfather. He attended several elementary schools and Herron Hill Junior High School before dropping out at age fifteen to become a professional musician. After an argument with his stepfather, he was placed in a foster home.

Upon turning sixteen years old, Spearman lived on his own, initially working day jobs while getting established in music. He was a local professional by age seventeen, drumming and occasionally playing piano. At one point he toured in a band that included trumpeter Roy Eldridge, and he briefly joined the Jeter-Pillars orchestra in St. Louis before spending three years with Leroy Bradley's orchestra at the Cotton Club in Cincinnati.

Moving to New York City late in 1935, Spearman dropped his surname, thereafter working as Kenny Clarke. He doubled as a vibraphonist in a trio with his half-brother Frank Spearman, a bassist who also took Clarke as a surname to capitalize on his brother's new-found fame. Clarke played alongside guitarist Freddie Greene in tenor saxophonist Lonnie Simmons's band at the Black Cat in Greenwich Village. Still doubling on vibraphone, he joined Edgar Hayes's band in April 1937, touring Europe from December 1937 to April 1938 and briefly working alongside trumpeter Dizzy Gillespie. At some point he joined pianist Claude Hopkins's band; the chronology is uncertain.

Clarke became a member of Teddy Hill's big band, again including Gillespie. Hill puzzled over the drummer's abandonment of a steady four-beat rhythm on the bass drum in favor of irregular accents and reportedly asked, "What is this klook-mop stuff you're playing?" Hence his nickname, Klook. Dissatisfied, Hill fired Clarke, who then performed with reed player Sidney Bechet at the Long Cabin in Fonda, New York (c. Dec. 1939–Jan. 1940); they recorded together in February. Later that year he accompanied singers Mildred Bailey and Billie Holiday on record, joined Eldridge's band, and served as the house drummer at the Apollo Theater in Harlem.

Clarke spent the summer of 1941 in Louis Armstrong's big band. He also toured with Ella Fitzgerald, who was leading the memorial Chick Webb band, and recorded in a small band accompanying Fitzgerald in

October 1941. In this same year Hill, who had disbanded and taken a job managing Minton's Playhouse in Harlem, hired Clarke to lead the house band that included trumpeter Joe Guy, pianist Thelonious Monk, and bassist Nick Fenton. Hill encouraged sitting in: guitarist Charlie Christian and Gillespie were regulars there, and many other renowned musicians appeared. In this setting, Clarke collaborated with Monk in writing "Fly Right," which became a bebop standard under a new title, "Epistrophy." More generally, the sessions became famous for demonstrations of virtuosity—unexpected harmonies, fast tempos, unusual keys—that discouraged those whose style did not fit in well. These experimental sounds were crucial to the development of bebop.

At Kelly's Stable in New York, Clarke led his own Kansas City Six, including Monk and tenor saxophonist Ike Quebec, and then played alongside Gillespie in alto saxophonist Benny Carter's septet from 10 December 1941 to 4 February 1942. He joined Henry "Red" Allen's band for performances in Chicago and Boston. In mid-1943 Clarke was drafted into the army. One year later, while stationed in Alabama, he married singer Carmen McRae. Absent without leave for 107 days, he was captured and shipped overseas in September 1944. He played trombone and sang in Europe until his discharge in April 1946. Out of New York for three years, Clarke missed the full flowering of the bebop style, and Max Roach, not Clarke, became its foremost exponent on drums.

During his army service, Clarke was once again known as Spearman. Shortly after his discharge he became a Muslim and took the name Liaquat Ali Salaam. He replaced Roach in Gillespie's big band, and from May to September 1946 he made a series of classic bop recordings, including "Oop Bop Sh'Bam" and "One Bass Hit (part 1)" with Gillespie's sextet. During this period Clarke also participated in a session with saxophonist Sonny Stitt; recorded "Epistrophy" and other titles with his own 52nd Street Boys, which included trumpeter Fats Navarro and pianist Bud Powell; and joined a recording session under Navarro's leadership.

After recording with Gillespie again in August 1947, he joined Gillespie's big band in December, touring Europe from January to March 1948. Clarke considered this the finest musical experience of his life; unfortunately his drumming was not well captured on Gillespie's recordings. Clarke stayed in Paris, performing, teaching, recording, and helping Nicole Barclay to organize the forthcoming Paris Jazz Festival. Returning to New York in August, he joined Tadd Dameron's band at the Royal Roost and recorded with Dameron and numeous bebop all stars between August 1948 and April 1949. Early in 1949 he played with bassist Oscar Pettiford's big band and trio, and he recorded the second of trumpeter Miles Davis's "Birth of the Cool" sessions. Around this time, or perhaps a bit later, Clarke became a heroin addict. He remained on narcotics at least into the 1960s, but unlike many of his colleagues, Clarke was somehow a discreet user. Many people did not know that he was addicted, and he did not exhibit stereotypical characteristics such as irresponsibility or exploitation of friendships.

Late in 1948 Clarke and McRae separated permanently. They had no children and divorced in 1956. He returned to Paris for the festival in May 1949 as a member of another all-star bop ensemble, and in Zurich he gave a concert with saxophonist Charlie Parker and Davis. Again he stayed in Europe, touring Belgium with pianist Bernard Peiffer and making Paris his home base. He worked there with bassist Pierre Michelot and later toured to Tunis in a group that included saxophonist James Moody and singer Annie Ross. Clarke also toured Europe with Moody and Michelot under saxophonist Coleman Hawkins's leadership. Reunited with Bechet, he recorded "Klook's Blues" and "American Rhythm" in October 1949.

Clarke had a child from an affair with Ross. In 1951 they brought their son to Pittsburgh to be raised by Clarke's brother Chuck. Clarke toured with singer Billy Eckstine and in August 1951 recorded with both Parker's quintet and vibraphonist Milt Jackson's quartet. With pianist John Lewis replacing Horace Silver and bassist Percy Heath replacing Ray Brown, Jackson's quartet became the long-lived Modern Jazz Quartet. Clarke performed with this quartet at the first Newport Jazz Festival (with Silver in 1954) and recorded the albums *MJO* (1952) and *Django* (1953–1955), which exemplify his mastery of wire brushes on the drum set. But Clarke quarreled with Lewis over the quartet's artistic direction and leadership, and he quit the group around March 1955, saying, "I wouldn't be able to play the drums my way again after four or five years of playing eighteenth-century drawing-room jazz" (Hennessey, p. 100).

Clarke recorded prolifically during these years. In 1954 he contributed to numerous classic hard bop recordings under Davis's leadership, including "Solar," "Walkin'," "Airegin," "Oleo," and "Bags' Groove." He served as a talent scout and resident drummer for Savoy Records, to which he brought Silver, Saxophonists Pepper Adams and Cannonball Adderley, and trumpeter Donald Byrd, among others. He joined Pettiford's group at the Café Bohemia in mid-1955 and continued with Pettiford and pianist Phineas Newborn at Basin Street West in March 1956.

At this point Clarke, exhausted from continuous studio and nightclub work, moved to Paris in search of a more relaxed life. Apart from a few brief periods, he spent the remainder of his life in Europe. He continued to record prolifically. After working in Jacques Hélian's orchestra, he held long engagements in Paris at the Club St. Germain (1957–1958; 1963; early 1970s) and the Blue Note (1959–1962; 1964–1966), with regular breaks for concerts and tours throughout Europe. Among his longstanding associates were pianists Martial Solal, Bud Powell, René Urtreger, and Raymond Fol; organists Lou Bennett and Eddy Louiss; electric guitarists Jimmy Gourley and René Thomas; and bassists Michelot, Michel Guadry, and Jimmy Woode. Organized variously into three- and four-piece rhythm sections, Clarke and these associates accompanied such soloists as saxophonists Lester Young, Stan Getz, Dexter Gordon, Johnny Griffin, and Sonny Stitt; trumpeter Gillespie; and trombonist J. J. Johnson. The spirit of these years was later captured in the movie *'Round Midnight* (1986). In 1962 Clarke settled in Montreuil-sous-Bois, east of Paris, and married Daisy Dina Wallbach; they had a son. Clarke was never able to take French citizenship. Instead he renewed his residency status as an immigrant every three years.

With arranger Francy Boland as co-leader, Clarke recorded *The Golden Eight* in 1961. This led to the formation of the Clarke-Boland Big Band. Widely recognized as Europe's finest jazz big band, the group began touring in 1966 and remained active to 1972. From 1967 Clarke taught at the St. Germain-en-Laye Conservatoire (to 1972) and at the Kenny Clarke Drum School at the Selmer musical instrument company in Paris.

He returned to the United States to receive a Duke Ellington Fellowship from Yale University (1972), to participate in a reunion of Gilliespie's band in Chicago (1976), to receive awards from the cities of Pittsburgh and New York, and to teach at the University of Pittsburgh (1979). He performed at jazz festivals throughout Europe to 1983. Having already suffered a heart attack in 1975, he died in Montreuil-sous-Bois.

Clarke is widely remembered as calm, kind, dignified, self-effacing, quiet, and a complete professional. A generous teacher, he was infinitely patient, even with amateur musicians. He was only known to lose his composure when accompanying those few leading jazz musicians who could not keep a steady beat. His biographer Mike Hennessey, keen to establish the drummer's significance, uncritically accepts imprecise, exaggerated, and sometimes impossible claims. For example, he states that Clarke developed a new style of rhythm section playing with Simmons in 1936 after hearing bassist Jimmy Blanton's recordings with Duke Ellington, but these discs were made in 1940. It is impossible to know just what Clarke did because of undocumented events; the rapid interchange of ideas; the concurrent contributions of Sid Catlett, Jo Jones, Shadow Wilson, and other drummers; Clarke's own unsubstantiated claims; and his absence from the scene during army service while Max Roach made his mark in bebop. Nonetheless, no one questions his stature as one of the greatest and most innovative jazz drummers. Music educator Theodore Dennis Brown documents Clarke's achievements on the tracks with Bechet in 1940 and from amateur recordings made live at Minton's in 1941: as components of an overriding sense of musicality that distinguished his playing, Clarke made such innovations as clicking the hi-hat cymbal closed on the "backbeat" (beats two and four of the measure); accenting in an improvisatory manner (and staying out of the bass player's way) by "dropping bombs" (irregular accents) on the bass drum rather than marking every beat with that drum; keeping a steady flowing sound on the ride cymbal; and articulating phrases in fragmented and assymetrical ways, in response to the improvising soloist.

• A tape and transcript of Clarke's oral history, taken by Helen Oakley Dance in 1977, are held at the Institute of Jazz Studies, Newark, N.J. The central biographical source is Mike Hennessey, *Klook: The Story of Kenny Clarke* (1990), which also includes a detailed catalog of recordings based on that published by Michael Haggerty with Matthew Annenberg, *A Flower for Kenny* (1985). Other published surveys and interviews include George Hoefer, "Klook," *Down Beat*, 28 March 1963, pp. 22–23; John Shaw, "Kenny Clarke," *Jazz Journal* 22 (Oct. 1969): 4–5; Bill Quinn, "Kenny Clarke: Rhythm Revolutionary," *Jazz Times* (Nov. 1980): 12–14; Haggerty, "Conversation with Kenneth ('Kenny') Spearman Clarke: Under Paris Skies," *Black Perspective in Music* 13 (1985): 195–221; and Ursula Broschke Davis, *Paris without Regret* (1986). See also John Chilton, *Sidney Bechet: The Wizard of Jazz* (1987). For musical analysis, see Theodore Dennis Brown, "A History and Analysis of Jazz Drumming to 1942" (Ph.D. diss., Univ. of Michigan, 1976); and Thomas Owens, *Bebop: The Music and Its Players* (1995). An obituary is in the *New York Times*, 27 Jan. 1985.

BARRY KERNFELD

CLARKE, Lewis G. (1815–1897), author and antislavery lecturer, was born into slavery on the plantation of his maternal grandfather, Samuel Campbell, in Madison County, Kentucky, the son of Campbell's mixed-race slave daughter Letitia and her white, Scottish-immigrant husband, Daniel Clarke, a soldier in the American Revolution. Lewis Clarke's middle name is variously recorded as either George or Garrand. Clarke's family history, which he traced back to the founding of the nation, inspired his quest for freedom and his subsequent dedication to the abolition cause in the North.

Clarke's first six years were spent with his parents and nine siblings and were the only family life and childhood he experienced. Betsey Campbell Banton, one of Samuel Campbell's daughters and Clarke's maternal aunt, whom he likened to a "female Nero," claimed Clarke by right of dowry, taking him from his parents to her home in Lexington, Kentucky. Clarke saw his family only three times in the next ten years, a period that began what he called his "pilgrimage of suffering."

Subjected to beatings and mental cruelty, and undernourished for nearly ten years, Clarke divided long days between serving the Banton family and spinning flax and hemp on a foot-wheel machine. From the age of ten, his chronic health problems were exacerbated by unremitting labor and Betsey Banton's policy of meting out adequate food based on the measure of Clarke's production at the spinning wheel. Bouts of illness and exhaustion when he was unable to meet the imposed standard were occasioned by starvation and confinement in a drafty attic room. Sometime around 1831 the Bantons' years of bickering and violence ended in divorce. Their misfortune, however, was to Clarke's advantage. Betsey Banton "mortgaged" Clarke to Tom Kennedy to work in the tobacco fields, but as Clarke later recalled, even the brutality of an overseer, constant hunger, and heat exhaustion were preferable to servitude in the Banton home.

The death of Samuel Campbell in 1831 ruined any hope Clarke had of being reunited with his family. The patriarch's death precipitated a property struggle among Campbell's white descendants, leaving, against his promise of their freedom, his African-American descendants to the vicissitudes of life in bondage. Clarke's family was dispersed at the auction block, each of his siblings and his mother sold to a different bidder. At Kennedy's death, Clarke, then about twenty, was transferred to Kennedy's son. Clarke then hired his time for twelve dollars a month, a system that permitted him to contract for his own labor and provide for his own keep, while remitting the net of his wages to Kennedy. Splitting rails, loading coal into furnaces, and peddling grass seed across the state line with a modicum of supervision provided Clarke with his first taste of freedom and selfhood. Five years later, in 1840, the younger Kennedy died suddenly, and his executors auctioned off the estate. Because Clarke's "title" was entailed to multiple mortgages, it remained in probate for more than a year, permitting him to continue hiring his time.

Rumors soon mounted that Clarke was to be sent to Louisiana and sold into the lucrative slave market of the Deep South. To avoid this fate, Clarke and a companion attempted to escape bondage with Clarke disguised as a white master accompanied by a slave attendant. The ruse might have been successful, but they were forced to turn back, lacking confidence and confused by signposts they could not read.

Two weeks later, in August 1841, Clarke made his second bid for freedom. Under the guise of his independent employment, he traveled fifty miles to Lexington, where he made a clandestine visit to his youngest brother, Cyrus. It was probably on this occasion that the seed was planted for Clarke's return for Cyrus the following year. From Lexington he headed due north toward the Ohio River; the next day he was in Aberdeen, across the Ohio River. Within a week he arrived in Cincinnati, where he found shelter among friends of the Underground Railroad. Not until November did he manage to locate his brother Milton (whose escape preceded Clarke's by a year), then living in Oberlin, Ohio. Greeted at his arrival in Oberlin by Milton and Ohio abolitionists, Clarke enjoyed a sense of family and community unknown to him since his earliest childhood. Engaged in the abolitionist cause, he became a speaker on a lecture circuit that took him throughout the North over the next twenty years.

Clarke risked capture by returning to Kentucky in July 1842 to rescue his brother Cyrus. Cyrus's unstable mental health, induced by terror and exacerbated by the increase in slave patrols and the fear of vigilante reprisal if caught, made the return journey particularly harrowing. Finally free, Cyrus comprised the third member of the celebrated fugitive slave brother trio, who turned their energies and talents toward aggressive campaigns both against slavery and for the elevation of their race.

Illiterate for the first few years after his escape from slavery, Clarke dictated the account of his life in slavery to his amanuensis-editor Joseph C. Lovejoy in 1845. One year later Clarke's lightly amended narrative was republished together with the narrative of Milton Clarke, leaving to posterity the fundamental record of their family: *Narratives of the Sufferings of Lewis and Milton Clarke, Sons of a Soldier of the Revolution, during a Captivity of More Than Twenty Years among the Slaveholders of Kentucky, One of the So Called Christian States of North America. Dictated by Themselves*. The Clarkes' combined autobiographies immediately enjoyed critical praise and popular sales.

In the preface to Clarke's narrative, Lovejoy testified to his eloquence as a public speaker and his ability to move audiences with a "wave of deep feeling." No doubt this ability to tap into the current of nineteenth-century sentimentalism and to convey through the story of his life the atrocities of slavery brought Clarke to the attention of Harriet Beecher Stowe. Impressed by the narrative of Clarke's escape from Kentucky and the heroism exhibited in his return to the South for Cyrus, Stowe engaged Clarke for a series of interviews at her home. These meetings, she claimed several years later in *The Key to "Uncle Tom's Cabin"* (1854), not only provided her with factual material for her controversial novel, but Clarke's personal, often Byronic attributes, leagued with those of Frederick Douglass, provided the character model upon which she based the courageous and defiant fugitive slave George Harris.

Around the time the Fugitive Slave Law of 1850 was passed, initiating the second and largest movement of blacks into Canada, Clarke left Ohio for Canada West, settling in Sandwich, where he invested in farmland and entered politics. Unlike renowned fugitives William Wells Brown or Douglass, who primarily confined their abolitionist activities to the United States, Clarke was more interested in promoting Canada West as the center for black settlement and antislavery resistance. His efforts to encourage black migration to Canada aimed at counteracting by force of representation what many perceived as the inevitable U.S. annexation of Canada. As an incentive to that end, he helped organize the Agricultural, Mechanical, and Educational Association of Canada West, a committee designed to educate and acculturate newly immigrant fugitives from slavery. Clarke became one of the association's trustees and general traveling agent shortly after its charter on 1 March 1859.

Canadian census records show Clarke married and in residence in Windsor, Ontario, in 1861. He remained ambivalent about colonization for most of his life; his desire for a separate African-American state in Canada, the Caribbean, South America, or even Kansas was mitigated by his concern that immigration undermined black community and history, prolonging the dissipating effects of slavery. After the death of his wife, about whom little is known, Clarke sold his Canadian lands in 1874 and moved back to Oberlin, accompanied by his children. In the late 1870s or early 1880s he returned to Lexington, Kentucky, where he advocated agricultural labor and lived the remainder of his life. At Clarke's death the governor of Kentucky ordered his body laid in state in the Civic Auditorium, where thousands paid tribute to his life and work, the first such honor accorded an African American in that state's history. His body was returned to Oberlin for burial, and his grave is marked by a headstone that memorializes him as "the original George Harris of Harriet Beecher Stowe's Book, Uncle Tom's Cabin."

• The most complete and sophisticated assessment of the slave narrative tradition, including Clarke's place in it, is William L. Andrews, *To Tell a Free Story: The First Century of Afro-American Autobiography, 1760–1865* (1988). For a collection of miscellaneous primary documents, including Clarke's jointly written "Report of the Committee on Emigration of Amherstburg Convention" (17 June 1853), see C. Peter Ripley, ed., *The Black Abolitionist Papers, vol. 2: Canada, 1830–1865* (1986). For brief reports about Clarke's work contemporary with his life, see *Signal of Liberty*, 9 Jan. 1843; *Emancipator*, 11 May 1843; *Liberator*, 26 Aug. 1859; Chet Lampson, *The Jefferson Gazette* (1896); and "A Chat with George Harris," in *Oberlin Jubilee Volume* (1883). For twentieth-century studies about the political and social milieu in which Clarke worked and lived, without direct reference to Clarke, see William H. Pease and Jane H. Pease, *Black Utopia* (1963); Benjamin Quarles, *Black Abolitionists* (1969); and Jason H. Silverman, *Unwelcome Guests: Canada West's Response to American Fugitive Slaves, 1800–1865* (1985). For facts about and interpretations of Clarke's life and work, see Jean Vacheenas and Betty Volk, "Born in Bondage: History of a Slave Family," *Negro History Bulletin* 36 (1973): 101–6.

GREGORY S. JACKSON